FIREARMS TRAFFICKING

A Guide for Criminal Investigators

First Edition

D1716388

FIREARMS TRAFFICKING

A Guide for Criminal Investigators

First Edition

Dale Armstrong

2018

First Published in 2018 by Prudens Group Consulting LLC
225 Main Street - P.O. Box 270
Saco, ME. 04072
prudensgroup@yahoo.com

Available through Lulu.com, Amazon.com, and fine book stores everywhere.

International Standard Book Identification - ISBN-13: 978-0-692-15880-7
Library of Congress Card Number; 2018908598

LIMIT OF LIABILITY/DISCLAIMER OF WARRANTY

TRADEMARK NOTICE

COVER PHOTOGRAPH CREDIT: © Can Stock Photo Inc. / pklick360

Library of Congress Cataloging-in-Publication Data

Armstrong, Dale.
Firearms trafficking: a guide for criminal investigators / Dale Armstrong. —1st ed.
Includes bibliographical references and index.
ISBN-13: 978-0-692-15880-7
1. Firearms trafficking investigation—United States.
2. Firearms trafficking prevention—United States.

Dedication

This book is dedicated to my family who endured the stresses and hardships associated my 30-year career in federal law enforcement which, ironically, gave me the knowledge and real-world experiences to produce this book.

Table of Contents

ABOUT THE AUTHOR XVII

ACKNOWLEDGEMENTS XIX

WHAT PEOPLE ARE SAYING ABOUT THIS BOOK… XXI

PREFACE XXIII

    WHERE IS THE COMMON GROUND? XXIII

INTRODUCTION 1

    GUN CRIME IS LIKE AN INDUSTRIAL FIRE 3

CHAPTER 1 - HISTORICAL CONTEXT OF THE FEDERAL FIREARMS LAWS ... 5

    THE 2ND AMENDMENT AND THE U.S. SUPREME COURT 5

        Figure 1.1 Seal of the U.S. Supreme Court 5

    FEDERAL FIREARMS LAWS THROUGH THE YEARS 6

        The Non-Mailable Firearms Act of 1927 6

        The National Firearms Act of 1934 6

        Figure 1.2 G-Man Elliot Ness 7

        The Federal Firearms Act of 1938 7

        The Gun Control Act of 1968 7

        Figure 1.3 The Saturday Night Special 8

        The Commerce in Firearms and Ammunition Regulations of 1975 8

        The Arms Export Control Act of 1976 8

        The Comprehensive Crime Control Act of 1984 8

        The Law Enforcement Officers Protection Act of 1986 8

        The Firearms Owners Protection Act of 1986 8

        Figure 1.4 Carlos Lehder Rivas of the Medellin Cartel 9

        The Undetectable Firearms Act of 1988 9

        Figure 1.5 ATF Form 4473 Completed by John Hinckley Jr. to Purchase Handgun 9

        The Crime Control Act of 1990 9

        The Brady Handgun Violence Prevention Act of 1994 9

        Figure 1.6 Semi-Automatic Assault Rifle 10

        The Violent Crime Control and Law Enforcement Act of 1994 10

        The Lautenberg Amendment of 1996 10

    THE CHANGING FACE OF CRIME GUNS 10

        1920s and 1930s 10

        1940s and 1950s 11

        1960s and 1970s 11

        Figure 1.7 Raven Arms Pistol 11

        1970s and 1980s 11

1980s and 1990s...12
Figure 1.8 Author in 1987 with Bales of Narcotics in the Mid-Florida Keys.........12
1990s and 2000s..12
Figure 1.9 President Reagan at the Brandenburg Gate in 1987............................13
Figure 1.10 Inexpensive Military Firepower "From Russia With Love"™..............13
2010s:..13
Figure 1.11 Bump Slide Stock...14

CHAPTER 2 - TERMINOLOGY RELATED TO FIREARMS TRAFFICKING INVESTIGATION **15**
Figure 2.1 Ammunition...16
Figure 2.2 Clip..18
Figure 2.3 Magazine 27
Figure 2.4 Glock Switch 34

CHAPTER 3 - BASIC FIREARMS SAFETY AND NOMENCLATURE **37**
FIREARMS SAFETY 101...37
PERFORMING A MACHINE GUN FUNCTIONALITY FIELD TEST....................38
DETERMINING BARREL LENGTH AND OVERALL LENGTH OF
A RIFLE OR SHOTGUN..39
Figure 3.1 Determination of Barrel Length..39
Figure 3.2 Determination of Overall Firearm Length 40
OTHER RESOURCES 40
Figure 3.3 Basic Firearms Nomenclature..41

CHAPTER 4 - APPLICABLE LAWS & LEGAL INFORMATION...........**43**
Figure 4.1 U.S. District Court Pattern Jury Instructions – Presumption of
Innocence and Proof Beyond a Reasonable Doubt...43
Figure 4.2 U.S. District Court Pattern Jury Instructions – On or About
and Knowingly..45
ACTUAL AND CONSTRUCTIVE POSSESSION 45
INTERSTATE NEXUS: THE MOVEMENT OF FIREARMS IN,
OR AFFECTING, INTERSTATE OR FOREIGN COMMERCE............................46
RELEVANT CONDUCT 49
EXTRADITION 49
LURE..50
TABLE 4.1 Overview of Federal Firearm Laws..51
STRAW PURCHASES OF FIREARMS 62
Figure 4.3 The Barnacle Allegory: Scraping Barnacles vs. Catching the Big Fish 63
CURIO AND RELIC PROVISIONS...64
LAWFUL INTERSTATE TRANSPORTATION OF FIREARMS 66

ALIENS, ILLEGAL ALIENS, NON-IMMIGRANT ALIENS, AND
PERMANENT RESIDENT ALIENS 66

   Alien 66
   Illegal Alien 66
   Nonimmigrant Alien 66
   Permanent Resident Alien 67

INTERNATIONAL TRAFFIC IN ARMS REGULATIONS (ITAR)
AND FIREARMS IMPORTS 68

   Exportation 68
   Importation 69

OTHER RESOURCES 72

TABLE 4.2 Overview of State Laws 73

**CHAPTER 5 - FORFEITURE OF FIREARMS AND THE ILLEGAL
PROCEEDS OF FIREARMS TRAFFICKING** **75**

TYPES OF FORFEITURE AND THE FORFEITURE OF FIREARMS 76

   Summary Forfeiture 76
   Administrative Forfeiture 76
   Judicial Forfeiture 76
   Consent to Forfeiture 77
   Options for Disposition of Crime Guns in the Absence of Forfeiture 77

FORFEITING THE PROCEEDS OF ILLEGAL FIREARMS TRAFFICKING 77

   Asset Tracking 77
   Money Flow Analysis 78
   Forfeiture Statutes. 78
   Crimes Listed as Specified Unlawful Activity 78
   Other Assets; Money Judgements and Substitute Assets 79
   Figure 5.1 Dirty Money 80

TRADITIONAL AND TRADE BASED MONEY LAUNDERING SCHEMES 80

   Figure 5.2 The Money Laundering Cycle 82
   Trade Based Money Laundering 82
   Cryptocurrency Conversion 83

OTHER RESOURCES 85

**CHAPTER 6 - CRIME GUN INTELLIGENCE CENTERS & TRAFFICKING
LEAD RESOURCES** **87**

   Figure 6.1 Commodity to Crime Gun 88

ATF CRIME GUN INTELLIGENCE CENTER, NIBIN, AND CRIME GUN
TRACING 89

   Figure 6.2 An Intelligence Led Approach to Reducing Armed Crime 89
   National Integrated Ballistic Information Network (NIBIN) 90
   ATF National Tracing Center 91
   Figure 6.3 Firearms Tracing and Identification 92

Demand Letter Programs...93
ATF Multiple Sales Information 94
ATF Stolen Firearms Database 94
Firearm Recovery Notification Program 94
ATF Out-of-Business Records Repository 95
Access 2000...95
ATF NTC FFL "Monitor" and "No Contact" Services 95
ATF Firearms and Explosives Licensing Center......................................95
ATF Firearms and Explosives Imports Branch..95
ATF FTS First Look Reports...96
Partial Serial Number Trace Capabilities 96
ATF Obliterated Serial Number Program 97
Figure 6.4 Methods of Serial Number Obliteration...............................98
ATF Firearms and Ammunition Technology Division 98
ATF National Firearms Act (NFA) Registration and Transfer Record.......99
ATF Industry Operations (IO) Office Files...99
LeadsOnline 99
Acoustic Ballistic Detection Data 99
Treasury Enforcement Communications System (TECS) 99
National Instant Criminal Background Check System (NICS) 100

REGIONAL CRIME GUN PROCESSING PROTOCOLS 101

Figure 6.5 Crime Guns are Informants – Let Them Tell You What They Know......104

CRIME GUN INTELLIGENCE PRODUCTION STANDARDS
AND RELIABILITY RATING PROCESS 105

Standard of Reasonable Indication 105
Reliability of Information 105

OFFICER DEVELOPMENT OF LOCAL GUN-CRIME ARRESTS FOR
FEDERAL COURT AND CRIME GUN LEAD EXPLOITATION...........105

Figure 6.6 Federal Adoption Checklist: Steps for State or
Local Officers to Take Following a Gun Crime Arrest 106

FEDERAL AGENCY INVESTIGATION OF ADOPTED-REFERRED LOCAL
GUN-CRIME ARRESTS AS PART OF A COMPREHENSIVE STRATEGY..........110

Figure 6.7 Federal Adoption Checklist: Steps for Federal Agents to Consider
During Adoption of a State/Local Gun Crime Arrest 111

GENERAL RESOURCES FOR TRAFFICKING INVESTIGATIVE LEAD
DEVELOPMENT..113

HUMINT via Cooperating FFLs..113
OSINT via Online Classified Gun Sales Sites...113
National Crime Information Center (NCIC) Recovered Gun File............113
State/Local Firearms Databases and Systems...113
State/Local Pawn Shop Details...113
Department of Homeland Security Export Enforcement Coordination Center........114
U.S. Commerce Department...114
El Paso Intelligence Center..114
National Gang Intelligence Center 114
National Gang Targeting, Enforcement and Coordination Center............115

Regional Information Sharing Systems..115
Sentry..115

CHAPTER 7 - FIREARMS TRAFFICKING INDICATORS......................**117**

INDICATORS IN AGGREGATE CRIME GUN TRACE DATA 117

INDICATORS IN FEDERAL FIREARMS LICENSEE RECORDS.........118

CASE STUDY: CALI BOUND 121
Figure 7.1 Firearms, Plastic Explosives, and an Unmanned Remote-Controlled
Plane bound for the Cali Cartel in 1989...121

INDICATORS OF FIREARMS PARTS KITS AND GHOST
GUN TRAFFICKING...122

INDICATORS IN PURCHASER BEHAVIOR 123

INDICATORS IN RECOVERED CRIME GUNS....................................124

INDICATORS AT SECONDARY SOURCE MARKETS SUCH AS
GUN SHOWS AND FLEA MARKETS..124

INDICATORS IN INTERNATIONAL POLITICAL AND CIVIL UNREST...........126

**CHAPTER 8 - COOPERATIVE COMPLIANCE, DETERRENCE,
AND PREVENTION**...**129**

PREVENTION AND DETERRENCE TECHNIQUES TO REDUCE THE
FIREARMS SUPPLY AVAILABLE TO THE CRIMINAL ELEMENT.....................130
Enlist Industry Assistance...130
"Don't Lie for the Other Guy"..131
Focused FFL Inspections and Training..................................131
Secondary Source Markets..132
Local Ordinance Compliance..132

FFL SAFETY, SECURITY, DISASTER RESPONSE AND EMERGENCY
PREPAREDNESS..133
Structural Security 133
Inventory Security...136
Personnel Security...137
Safe Business Practices...137
Customer Safety and Security..139
Disaster Response and Emergency Preparedness.................140

**CHAPTER 9 - COMMON INVESTIGATIVE TECHNIQUES AND SKILLS
APPLICABLE IN FIREARMS TRAFFICKING INVESTIGATION**..................**143**

DECONFLICTION...143

EXPLOITATION OF ELECTRONIC COMMUNICATION DEVICES
AND TECHNICAL SURVEILLANCE METHODS..................................144
Legal Process Hierarchy..144
Electronic Communications Terminology...............................145

Language to Create Re-Usable Court Order 147
Figure 9.1 Re-Usable Court Order Language 147
Standard and Roving Court Ordered Title III Electronic Interception 151
Figure 9.2 U.S. Attorney's Office; Checklist for Title III Affidavit Requirements 152

CONFIDENTIAL INFORMANT SUITABILITY, USE, AND CONTROL 155

COOPERATING DEFENDANTS 158

Proffer Agreement 158
Cooperation Agreement & Immunity 158
"5k Letter" and Motion for Sentence Reduction 159

UNPLANNED ENFORCEMENT ACTIONS 159

CHAPTER 10 - INVESTIGATING FIREARMS TRAFFICKING SCHEMES 162

THE TEN PRIMARY TYPES OF FIREARMS TRAFFICKING
INVESTIGATIONS 162

TYPE 1: PRELIMINARY FIREARMS TRAFFICKING LEAD AND
STRAW PURCHASE INVESTIGATION 163

PHASE I: PRE-INTERVIEW STEPS 164
Figure 10.1 ROI EXAMPLE: RECEIPT OF INFORMATION AND
PRELIMINARY INVESTIGATION ROI 165
Figure 10.2 STANDARD FFL INTERVIEW QUESTIONS 167
Figure 10.3 ROI EXAMPLE: FFL INTERVIEW 169
PHASE II: INTERVIEW STEPS 170
Figure 10.4 STANDARD INTERVIEW QUESTIONS AND
ADVISORIES FOR FIREARMS PURCHASER 172
Figure 10.5 ROI EXAMPLE: FIREARMS PURCHASER INTERVIEW 177
PHASE III: DETERMINING THE BEST COURSE OF ACTION 178
NO Criminal Violations and NO Criminal Intent 179
CASE STUDY: SHORT TIME TO CRIME LEAD AND
'STATE OF MIND' COMPLICATIONS 179
Criminal Violations WITHOUT Criminal Intent 180
Figure 10.6 WARNING NOTICE OF UNLICENSED FIREARMS
DEALING IN VIOLATION OF FEDERAL LAW 181
Figure 10.7 WARNING NOTICE OF STRAW PURCHASING IN
VIOLATION OF FEDERAL LAW 182
Criminal Violations WITH Criminal Intent 183
How Not to Run a Firearms Trafficking Investigation 183
Determining what to do with the FFL 186
NO Regulatory or Criminal Violations and NO Criminal Intent 186
Regulatory or Criminal Violations WITHOUT Criminal Intent 186
Criminal Violations WITH Criminal Intent 186

TYPE 2: UNLICENSED FIREARMS DEALING INVESTIGATION 187

CASE STUDY: OPERATION BEANTOWN BANGERS 191
CASE STUDY: OPERATION MONEY BACK GUARANTEE 193

TYPE 3: FEDERAL FIREARMS LICENSEE INVESTIGATION AND
APPLICATION OF A KLEIN CONSPIRACY 194

USE OF THE KLEIN CONSPIRACY AGAINST CORRUPT FFLS 198
CASE STUDY: OPERATION NEW YORK SHUTTLE 200
CASE STUDY: OPERATION TRAIL OF GUNS 202

TYPE 4: SECONDARY SOURCE MARKET INITIATIVE 203

Goals of a Secondary Source Market Operation 203
Initiative Staffing and Positioning 203
CASE STUDY: OPERATION CASH AND CARRY 205

TYPE 5: FEDERAL FIREARMS LICENSEE THEFT INVESTIGATION 206

PHASE I: DEFINING AND PROTECTING THE CRIME SCENE 206
PHASE II: INITIAL INTERVIEWS AND AREA CANVAS 207
PHASE III: CRIME SCENE PROCESSING 209
PHASE IV: FOLLOW-UP INVESTIGATION 213

TYPE 6: INTERSTATE CARRIER THFT IVESTIGATION 217

TYPE 7: FIREARMS IMPORT TRAFFICKING AND
FRAUD INVESTIGATION 221

Constructed Sales and Fraud 222
VRA Treaty Fraud 222
Embargoed Country Import Fraud 222
Armor Piercing Ammunition Import Fraud 222
External Safety Installation Fraud 223
Unsuccessful Trace Data Indicators 223
Prevention, Deterrence, and Detection 223
Investigation of Detected Violations 225
CASE STUDY: OPERATION SALT MINE SURPLUS 227
Figure 10.8 More than 600 Illegally Imported Tokarev Pistols Seized by ATF
in West Palm Beach, FL in 2006, and on Their Way to the Smelter in 2007 228
Figure 10.9 Firearms on a Display Table in Ukraine Salt Mine 228
Figure 10.10 Ukrainian Military Officers Negotiating an Arms Deal at
Lunch with U.S. Firearm Importers 229

TYPE 8: FIREARMS EXPORT TRAFFICKING AND
SMUGGLING INVESTIGATION 229

Figure 10.11 Standard Questions for Ammunition Salesperson 235
Figure 10.12 Standard Questions for Purchaser of Ammunition 237
Figure 10.13 Questions for Debriefing a Suspect, CI, or Cooperating
Defendant on Fireams Trafficking 240
Consular Notification 243
Alien Smuggling and Terrorism 244
General Information on the Legal Process of Importing and Exporting Firearms ... 244
CASE STUDY: OPERATION MONTREAL PIPELINE 245
CASE STUDY: OPERATION YUKON JACK 246

TYPE 9: FIREARM CASTINGS, FLATS, PARTS KITS, AND
GHOST GUN INVESTIGATION 247

Figure 10.14 Firearm & Non-Firearm Castings 247
Figure 10.15 Firearm Flat 247

Figure 10.16 Firearm Parts Kit Commonly Encountered in Firearms
Export Trafficking...248
Figure 10.17 Author in 2018 with 4,500 Firearm Castings and "80% Receivers"......249
Figure 10.18 Ghost Gun Receiver Jigs, Metal Shaping, and Metal
Milling Equipment..250
Imported NFA Firearm Parts Kits 252
Figure 10.19 ATF Approved Destruction Illustration for Creation of
Importable Firearm Parts Kit...253
Figure 10.20 Author with Seizure of Trafficked Sten Machineguns
Made from Imported Parts Kits..257

TYPE 10: INTERNET-BASED FIREARMS TRAFFICKING
INVESTIGATION 257

Regions of the Web and Types of Firearms Markets.......................................258
PHASE I: SCOPING, PLANNING, INVESTIGATIVE OPERATIONS 260
The Don'ts of Internet Investigation 261
PHASE II: IDENTIFYING OTHER CUSTOMERS AND PLANNING
ARRESTS AND RECOVERIES..265
PHASE III: SHUTDOWN THE SOURCE 268
Figure 10.21 ATF Warning Banner on Forfeited Website...............................270
CASE STUDY: OPERATION LETHAL WEAPON IV....................................270
Figure 10.22 Sealed Metal Part Containing CZ Scorpion Machinegun
from Argentina...271
Figure 10.23 Silencer from Argentina 272
Figure 10.24 Briefcase Machinegun in Patterson, New Jersey 273
CASE STUDY: OPERATION THE WORLD IS NOT ENOUGH....................274
Figure 10.25 HK MP5 Machinegun from Germany 274
CASE STUDY: OPERATION INCOMING FIRE...276

CHAPTER 11 - GANG INVESTIGATION FOCUSED ON ARMED
VIOLENCE & CRIME GUN SOURCES 279

PHASE I: IDENTIFY THE GANG..280

PHASE II: INTELLIGENCE COLLECTION...281

Case and Information Management 281
Preliminary Meetings...282
Preliminary Data..283
Deconfliction 283
Intelligence Analyst (IA) Research...284

PHASE III: INVESTIGATION...284

TABLE 11.1 Investigative Techniques: Risk of Compromise Vs.
Reward of Information..285
HISTORICAL–OVERT TECHNIQUE..286
CASE STUDY: SEVERING CHARGES CAN BE BENEFICIAL –
KRAMER ET AL...288
Figure 11.2 Ben Kramer's Fort Apache Marina Business Card.......................288
Systematically Investigate All Armed Violent Gang Crimes, Past and Present..........289
Exploitation of Recovered Digital Communication and Storage Devices...........290
Interviews and Proffers of Witnesses, Victims, Suspects, and
Cooperating Defendants 290

Victim and Witness Rights...291
Financial Analysis and Asset Identification...291
PRO-ACTIVE COVERT TECHNIQUE...291
UC and CI Approaches..292
Wall-Off Arrests and Car Stops..292
Department of Corrections Calls and Records..293
Automated License Plate Readers..293
Video Surveillance and Facial Recognition...294
Global Positioning System (GPS) Tracking Devices 294
Electronic Communication Records and Data Analysis.....................................294
Standard or Roving Court Ordered Title III Electronic Interception 296

FEDERAL VIOLATIONS APPLICABLE IN ARMED VIOLENT GANG
INVESTIGATIONS...297

CASE STUDY: OPERATION BLOOD RED 305

CASE STUDY: OPERATION BLACK DIAMOND......................................304
Figure 11.3 Gang Indicia and Firearms Recovered in Maine 304

OTHER RESOURCES...307

CHAPTER 12 - INTERNATIONAL LAW ENFORCEMENT 309

Figure 12.1 Author in Sarajevo, Bosnia in 1997 on Investigative Assignment...........309
Figure 12.2 Firearms Trafficking to Mexico ,1977 311

INVESTIGATIVE AND DETERRENT SUPPORT RESOURCES...........312

U.S. Department of State Blue Lantern Program..312
U.S. Department of State, Directorate of Defense Trade Controls 313
ATF International Firearms Tracing Program...313
U.S. DHS, Homeland Security Investigations 314
The International Criminal Police Organization©. INTERPOL 314
INTERPOL Notices 315
INTERPOL BALLISTIC INFORMATION NETWORK (IBIN). 315
World Customs Organization...316
Europol...316
North Atlantic Treaty Organization (NATO®) Trust Funds 317

UNIFORM PROTOCOLS AND PROCEDURES 317

International Protocols and Cooperative Initiatives 318
Regional Protocols and Cooperative Initiatives...320

TRAINING RESOURCES..321

International Law Enforcement Academies (ILEA)...321
Figure 12.3 Author/Instructor with Class at ILEA Budapest, Hungary 321
ATF's International Training Program (ITP)...322
U.S. DOJ International Criminal Investigative Training Assistance
Program (ICITAP) and Overseas Prosecutorial Development and
Training (OPDAT)..322
U.S. Agency for International Development (USAID) 325
INTERPOL 325
CASE STUDY: OPERATOIN SPHINX 326

Figure 12.4 Return of 3000 Year Old Egyptian Funerary Mask.............................326
Figure 12.5 Stinger Missiles in West Palm Beach Warehouse............................327
Figure 12.6 Check for $91,000 in Laundered Money Proceeds............................327
Figure 12.7 Undercover ATF Agent Walking to Meet Money Launderer.................328
Figure 12.8 Alleged Pakistani ISI Agents...330
CASE STUDY: OPERATION ABOVE THE LAW..............................331

APPENDIX A - ACRONYMS 333

APPENDIX B - REGIONAL CRIME GUN PROTOCOLS 337

1996 INTERSTATE FIREARMS TRAFFICKING COMPACT 337
1997 YOUTH CRIME GUN INTERDICTION INITIATIVE (YCGII) MOU..............339
2004 – 2006 PALM BEACH COUNTY GUN CRIME PROTOCOLS, REVISED 342
2012 IACP RESOLUTION: REGIONAL CRIME GUN PROCESSING PROTOCOLS.......347
NEW JERSEY PUBLIC LAW 2013 CHAPTER 162; TITLE 52 OF REVISED STATUTES.....349

APPENDIX C - ATF FORMS 353

ATF FORM 4473 – FIREARMS TRANSACTION RECORD 353
ATF FORM 6 – APPLICATION & PERMIT FOR IMPORTATION OF FIREARMS 359
ATF FORM 3310.11 – FFL FIREARMS INVENTORY THEFT/LOSS REPORT 365
ATF PUBLICATION 5300.11 – BEST PRACTICES: TRANSFERS OF FIREARMS BY
PRIVATE SELLERS 367
ATF PUBLICATION 3313.8 – PERSONAL FIREARMS RECORD 369

APPENDIX D - SAMPLE LETTERS, AFFIDAVITS, AND COURT ORDERS........371

CONSENT TO FORFEITURE OR DESTRUCTION OF PROPERTY
AND WAIVER OF NOTICE 371
PRESERVATION LETTER 373
AUTHORIZATION AND CONSENT TO SEARCH CELL PHONE & DISCLOSE
CELL-SITE AND CELL PHONE USAGE INFORMATION 375
AUTHORIZATION AND CONSENT TO ASSUME ONLINE IDENTITY................376
AUTHORIZATION AND CONSENT TO RELEASE RECORDS......................377
SEARCH WARRANT FOR CELL SITE SIMULATOR TO ID A PHONE 378
SEARCH WARRANT FOR CELL SITE SIMULATOR TO LOCATE A PHONE...........386
SEARCH WARRANT FOR CELL PHONE LOCATION LAT-LONG-GPS HISTORY........393
COURT ORDER FOR TOWER DUMP 400
COURT ORDER FOR PEN ON CELL PHONE 410
COURT ORDER FOR PEN ON CELL PHONE 418
COURT ORDER FOR PEN ON DEVICE IP 431
APPLICATION FOR INTERNET T-III – ELECTRONIC COMMUNICATIONS INTERCEPT........441
KLEIN CONSPIRACY INDICTMENT EXAMPLE...............................467
FINANCIAL ASSETS SEIZURE WARRANT BASED ON FIREARMS TRAFFICKING.......477

APPENDIX E - LICENSED FIREARM IMPORTER
MARKING ABBREVIATIONS 513

INDEX 517

BIBLIOGRAPHY 523

END NOTES.. 535

About the Author

Dale Armstrong has over thirty years of experience investigating violent crime and firearms trafficking. Mr. Armstrong began his law enforcement career in 1986 as a special agent with the U.S. Customs Service in the Florida Keys, where he conducted narcotics investigations, operated a high-speed interceptor vessel, and seized thousands of pounds of narcotics. Mr. Armstrong joined the Bureau of Alcohol, Tobacco, Firearms, and Explosives in 1987 as a special agent in Fort Lauderdale, Florida, assigned to investigate violent gang crime and firearms trafficking as well as criminal arsons and bombings. Mr. Armstrong served as an ATF manager for more than two decades, with assignments as a Resident Agent in Charge in Ashland, Kentucky, in West Palm Beach, Florida, and Portland, Maine, and was assigned as Program Manager of the Violent Crimes and Firearms Trafficking Programs in Washington, D.C. Mr. Armstrong served as the Assistant Special Agent in Charge of ATF's Boston Field Division from 2013 to 2015, where he managed more than one hundred special agents and task force officers throughout the New England region. Mr. Armstrong was a member of ATF's supervisory staff, coordinating his agency's role in the response to, and investigation of, the Boston Marathon Bombings in 2013.

Mr. Armstrong's additional experience includes serving as a member of the Miami Special Response Tactical Team, and as the Assistant Team Leader of the Louisville Special Response Tactical Team. He served as Acting Assistant Special Agent in Charge in Louisville, Kentucky and in San Juan, Puerto Rico. Mr. Armstrong served as an instructor at the ATF Special Response Team training facility at Fort McClellan, Alabama, at the ATF National Academy at the Federal Law Enforcement Training Center in Glynco, Georgia, at the International Law Enforcement Academy in Budapest, Hungary, at the ATF Firearms Trafficking Course and Complex Investigations Course, and at the Maine Basic Law Enforcement Training Program in Vassalboro, Maine. Mr. Armstrong's investigations resulted in U.S. Supreme Court case law (*Smith v. United States*, 508 U.S. 223 (1993)), and were covered on episodes of Dateline NBC. Mr. Armstrong helped pioneer ATF's efforts to combat internet-based illegal firearms trafficking and authored and produced a number of ATF's national policies, as well as ATF's *Guide to Investigating Illegal Firearms Trafficking* (ATF Publication 3317.1) in 1997, the ATF *Safety & Security Information for Federal Firearms Licensees* (ATF Publication 3317.2) in 1997, and the *Firearms Trafficking Investigation Guide* in 2009

In recognition of accomplishments throughout his career, Mr. Armstrong was the recipient of more than two dozen *Sustained Superior Performance Awards* and *Special Act Awards*, the 2008 ATF *Supervisor of the Year Award*, the *Secretary's Certificate Award* from Treasury Secretary Rubin in 1997, a *Vice Presidential National Performance Review "Hammer" Award* presented by Vice President Gore in 1997, and was a runner-up finalist in the Harvard University/Ford Foundation *Innovations in American Government Award* in 1997 for his work on the creation of a firearms trafficking enforcement initiative.

Mr. Armstrong served on a number of committees, including the Federal Executive Association of Southern Maine, where he was President during 2012 and 2013, the Maine Project Safe Neighborhoods Executive Committee, the Maine Chiefs of Police Association, the Palm Beach County Criminal Justice Commission, the Palm Beach County Chiefs of Police Association and Law Enforcement Planning Council, the Palm Beach County Weed and Seed Executive Committee, and the Palm Beach County Pandemic Flu Planning Committee. Mr. Armstrong is a Certified Protection Professional (CPP) through the American Society of Industrial Security (ASIS), a recognized expert witness in federal court on the movement of firearms in interstate and foreign commerce, and a Certified Federal Law Enforcement Instructor.

Mr. Armstrong earned a bachelor's degree from Westfield State College in 1985 and was inducted into their Criminal Justice Alumni Hall of Fame in 2016.

Mr. Armstrong currently serves as an adjunct faculty member of the Criminal Justice Department at Southern Maine Community College and is owner and President of Prudens Group Consulting, LLC.

Acknowledgements

I extend my sincere thanks to the many dedicated special agents, inspiring managers, skilled federal prosecutors, insightful academics, and dedicated policy makers who I have had the pleasure of working with and learning from over the span of thirty years—from the crime-fighting crucible days in South Florida in the 1980s, through the transformative studies and policy days in Washington, D.C. in the 1990s, to the investigation innovations in the 2000s in West Palm Beach, Boston, and the cyber-world. It was quite a ride, and I wouldn't change a thing. I am very grateful to have actually been paid to perform such exciting and personally gratifying work.

A special thanks to my uncle, retired ATF special agent Doug Wenner, who inspired me to become a federal agent and helped me navigate the rigorous hiring process. Special thanks to Stephen Barborini, my ATF academy roommate, partner in fighting crime, one of the best ATF agents to ever carry the badge, and someone who still fights the good fight now as Detective at the Palm Beach County Sheriff's Office. Special thanks to the old ATF Fort Lauderdale crew: special agents Edgar Domenech, Lazaro Gomila, Gerald Droze, Gary Wallace, Larry O'Dea, N. Kelly Newsom, Adam Price, Mike Molinari, Mike Fitzpatrick, Pam Bradley, Bobby Hurley, Bob Manske, and George Henderson—the crew who worked with me in South Florida in the early years of my career when we tackled interstate and international firearms traffickers supplying guns to gangs from Miami to New York, cartels in Colombia, and posses in Jamaica. Special thanks to "Jersey Boys" Dominic Polifrone and Joe Greco, who were true innovators in trafficking investigation (Project LISA & Pattern Crimes) when they were not taking down Icemen.

Special thanks to my DEA friends Joe Kilmer, Tom Feeney, and Tom Hill, with whom I worked the gun-side of some big cases that took down outlaw motorcycle gangs, cartel members, and some of the original Miami Thunderboat Row smugglers.

Special thanks to my Louisville Division friends Bill Curley, George Teston, Todd Willard, Betty Kearns, and the Charleston crew: we made it back from Copperhead Road. Special thanks to the ATF Firearms Division crew: Joe Vince, Jerry Nunziato, Ron Schuman, Lew Raden, Jim Allison, Joe Bisbee, Carlos Sanchez, Willie Brownlee, Tristan Moreland, Sony Fields, Louie Quinonez, Larry Ford, Terry Austin, former Senior Treasury Department Advisor Susan Ginsburg, Professor David Kennedy, Dr. Anthony Braga, and Dr. Glenn Pierce—who all worked tirelessly to help create the Youth Crime Gun Interdiction Initiative, Project LEAD, and who developed significant advancements in the understanding of firearms trafficking indicators, patterns, schemes, and investigative techniques. Special thanks to strategic thinker Pete Gagliardi, the Baron of Ballistics, who has always been at the forefront of combatting armed crime.

Special thanks to the accomplished Assistant United States Attorneys who took on tough firearms trafficking prosecutions: Bruce Reinhart (now Federal Magistrate), Janice LeClanche, John MacMillan, Barbara Ward, Barbara Petras, Dave Mellinger (Smith v. U.S., 508 U.S. 223 (1993)), Darcie McElwee-Leighton, Craig Wolfe, Margaret Grohban, Todd Lowell, and Maine U.S. Attorney Paula Silsby. Special thanks to some great ATF attorneys; Barry Orlow, Joe Allen, Stephen Rubenstein, Teresa Ficaretta, and Jack Patterson.

Special thanks to the ATF West Palm Beach crew who worked on large-scale firearms import fraud and internet trafficking cases: special agents Jeff Kunz, Dan Dooley, Mike Barbercheck,

Vince Holmes, Troy Stratton, Seth Berger, Janice Castillo, George Krapppmann, Ray Garcia, Hugh O'Connor, Dan Woolbert, Kelly Brady, and long-term undercover Dick Stoltz. Special thanks to the ATF Portland, Maine crew, who always made firearms trafficking investigation a priority: Doug Kirk, PJ McNeil, Malcolm VanAlstyne, Mike Grasso, Brent McSweyn, John Morris, Steve Hickey, Chris Durkin, and Mike Layton. Special thanks to the ATF Boston Division agents who work tirelessly on interstate gun traffickers and armed violent gangs; John Mercer, Jack Kelter, John Hayes, BJ White, Kellie Senecal, Brian Oppedisano, Jim Ferguson, Ross Marchetti, Brian Person, Anthony Dipaolo, Brian Meehan, Scott Riordan, Dan Prather, and Mike Zeppieri

Special thanks to current and former senior ATF executives who have fought the good fight with me: Malcolm Brady, James Brown, Bob Creighton, Godfather Alex D'Atri, Mike Bouchard, Joe Anarumo, Dan Kumor, Ken Croke, John Bradley, Carlos Canino (Hoot!), Regina Lombardo, Tom Brandon, Hugo Barrera, Julie Torres, Eric Harden, Chris Pelletier, Jamie Higgins, Marvin Richardson, and Patti Galupo. Special thanks to the agents who dedicated years to furthering training on firearms trafficking investigations: Mark Kraft, Randy Beach, Ben Hayes, and Martha Brognard.

Special thanks to former Palm Beach County Criminal Justice Commission Director Diana Cunningham, Krissy Carlson (now at ATF), Palm Beach County Sheriff Rick Bradshaw, former Palm Beach County State Prosecutor Barry Krischer, Laurie Van Duesen, and other Palm Beach County law enforcement leaders who joined me in implementing the Palm Beach County Gun Crime Protocols which became a national law enforcement best practice and the IACP Resolution, "Regional Crime Gun Processing Protocols".

Thanks to ATF for a great 30 years and for providing permission to use some of the forms, pictures, and information in this text. I would do another 30 all over again without hesitation if it were not for that mandatory retirement age.

There are many others who deserve my thanks—I hope you know who you are.

What People Are Saying About this Book...

"Thefts and illegal diversions of firearms from legitimate commerce represent important sources of guns to violent criminals. In Firearms Trafficking: A Guide for Criminal Investigators, Dale Armstrong provides an incredibly detailed assessment of the varied pathways through which violent criminals acquire firearms. I particularly appreciate the attention devoted to contemporary gun enforcement challenges such as the production of ghost guns, the use of crypto-currency in money laundering schemes, and the illicit sale of firearms through the internet. With the keen eye of a seasoned investigator, Armstrong then identifies the vulnerabilities of firearms traffickers to smart enforcement and careful regulation rooted in the strategic analysis of intelligence and gun data resources. His insights are equally useful to policy makers interested in improving the capacity of law enforcement to shut supply lines of illegal guns and to investigators seeking practical opportunities to detect and apprehend gun traffickers. This book should be mandatory reading for anyone interested in reducing serious violence by keeping guns out of the wrong hands." ----- *Anthony A. Braga, Ph.D., Distinguished Professor and Director, School of Criminology and Criminal Justice, Northeastern University*

"FIREARMS TRAFFICKING is a must have for every police chief, every violent crime investigator, every federal agent who deals with armed criminals. It is simply the one-stop-shopping guide for all the best options in crime-gun enforcement. From the "Saturday Night Special" to the weapons of transnational crime groups, it lays out the best practices, the laws, the cases, and the stories behind them. At a time when America's cities are still struggling with gun crime, this is a must read." ---- *Bill Bratton, Former Police Commissioner of New York, Boston and former Chief of the Los Angeles Police Department*

"Gun violence caused by illegally obtained, carried, and used firearms causes incalculable harm. It can be addressed by criminal investigations carried out under existing law to a degree far greater than is generally understood. Dale Armstrong understands, and has written a master class in how to do so – the product of a life fighting gun trafficking and gun crime, on the streets and in the courts. "Firearms Trafficking" is a signal event in the struggle for public safety in the United States." --- *David Kennedy, Director of the National Network for Safe Communities, John Jay College of Criminal Justice*

"Dale Armstrong has written the bible of gun trafficking. The book is the practical text for learning the art of putting together a firearms trafficking case, the laws, the pitfalls, and how to leverage partnerships for the best results. This book is more than a how to; It is also a history of the crime gun's development as a driver of violence in the United States. Armstrong takes us from the days of bootleggers with Tommy Guns in Chicago, to the ways deranged assassins obtained pistols, to the vast arsenals of drug cartel bosses like Carlos Lehder. Its part text book, part law book, part history book and part action/adventure story of real cases involving notorious bad guys. There is no other book like it". ---- *John Miller, Deputy Commissioner, Intelligence & Counterterrorism, New York Police Department*

"Armstrong's book on Firearms Trafficking is unrivaled in both scope and substance. This tome covers firearms trafficking both domestically and internationally. The history of gun laws in the United States, replete with interesting anecdotes, is succinctly reviewed. The evolution of gun laws, and a comparative analysis of federal and state laws, that are masterfully outlined and a must-read for criminal justice professionals and students, make for fascinating reading. The inclusion of glossaries and federal forms are a valuable resource.

Based on his training, education and experience, Armstrong is at his best when outlining the pitfalls of federal/state firearms investigations. He acknowledges, and warns against, the competition between law enforcement units and concludes that their inability to share information thwarts efforts to solve crime. His experience led to the promulgation of firearm trafficking indicators that are in use today; the comprehensive list is included.

The writer is unflinching in his analysis of armed violent gangs and their ability to ruin neighborhoods and communities. He was involved in large scale drug and gun operations conducted by nefarious and violent gangs. It makes for chilling reading realizing that this is not some tale fashioned by an author in the comfort of their own home; he was in the thick of things and the pictures and case studies provide guidance for law enforcement. The chapter on case studies could be a stand-alone workbook for those in the criminal justice field. These case studies are powerfully instructive and delineate the effective investigatory techniques that were used.

Lastly, cognizant of the global world in which we live, the author concludes with a chapter on international firearms trafficking. It is a commanding, but cautionary tale about the movement of large caches of weapons around the globe and the techniques arms dealers use to make that happen; the prevailing theme is about cooperation between international law enforcement agencies. Like his other chapters, and what makes this book mandatory reading, is that the author, in virtually every chapter provides the resources that law enforcement should know and utilize.

This book should be required reading for law enforcement professionals, and if used as a textbook in universities will provide students with a comprehensive overview of the world of firearms trafficking and the knowledge needed to combat this scourge." ----- *Alice Perry, J.D., Ph.D., Associate Professor, Criminal Justice Department, Westfield State University*

Preface

It is said that from every end comes a new beginning. That is where I find myself, following a 30-year career as a federal agent and having spent much of that time combatting armed violent crime and firearms traffickers. Much was accomplished during those years, and I'd like to think my efforts contributed in some small way to the more than 50% decline in violent crime and gun crime from its peak in 1991 to the present. Much remains to be done. There is still plenty of armed violent crime in America, and there are still persons who are willing to traffic firearms to violent criminals, gang members, and terrorists. Gun violence is depleting this country of cultural and economic resources and eroding the basic quality of life for those who find themselves in high crime areas. I don't want my accumulated knowledge and experience in taking down firearms traffickers to be lost. I want to pass it on, and have that knowledge remain in the good fight. So, from the end of my federal law enforcement career comes a new beginning, as I write this book to provide current and future criminal investigators with a tool to use in the ongoing fight to prevent armed crime, arrest armed violent offenders, and halt firearms trafficking.

The only commodity referenced in the Bill of Rights is firearms. Firearms have a long history in America. Firearms are romanticized and firearms are demonized. Firearms serve a very different function depending on who is holding them. In the right hands firearms are tools for recreation, survival, or self-defense; in the wrong hands they can become deadly tools of violent victimization. Firearms serve different purposes depending on where you live. In rural areas they are often used for sport, recreation, collecting and trading, and hunting; in urban areas they are often used for security, self-defense, and as a means to an end for both legal and illegal actions. Solutions to gun crime are colorized by Blue State versus Red State stances and too often too many are convinced only they know the solutions. Clearly there are fierce opinions on both sides of the debate for and against gun laws and honestly, no one side has a monopoly on the correct solutions. This guide will not take sides in that debate. This guide will provide information to criminal investigators on how to enforce existing firearms laws. The vigorous enforcement of existing firearms laws through investigation and arrests as well as interdiction and deterrence seem to be something that voices on both sides of the debate agree on.

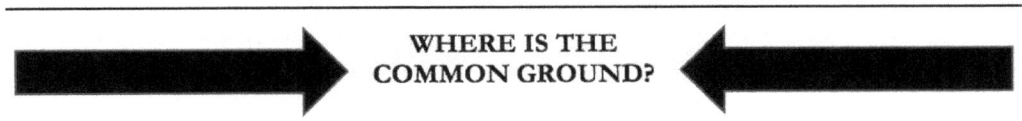

WHERE IS THE
COMMON GROUND?

"The government owes its citizens its most vigorous efforts to **enforce penalties against those who violate our existing laws.** The NRA has members proudly serving in law enforcement agencies at every level. Rank and file law enforcement want to arrest bad people – not harass law-abiding gun owners and retailers." - *Wayne Lapierre, Executive Vice President and Chief Executive Officer of the National Rifle Association in a March 14, 2011 letter to President Obama.*

"You can always have more laws, but if you don't **enforce the ones on the books**, there's no reason to go and have additional laws..." - *Michael Bloomberg, then Mayor of New York City and Co-founder of Mayors Against Illegal Guns in a January 24, 2011 interview with Katie Couric, CBS News.*

FIGURE P.1

The vast majority of crime guns recovered in the U.S. are born of a legal industry, unlike many forms of contraband such as narcotics. This guide will help investigators identify and apprehend those who traffic firearms from the legal market to the black market, changing firearms from "Commodity to Crime Gun" and, in the process, denigrating and endangering the Second Amendment right of all law-abiding citizens.

Introduction

Let's start with a definition.

Firearms Trafficking–The unlawful diversion of firearms done for the purpose of profit, power, or prestige, in furtherance of other criminal acts or terrorism. [ii]

The primary goal of every firearms trafficking investigation is to <u>protect public safety</u> by stopping the source of crime guns. Three strategies to achieve that goal by reducing firearms trafficking and improving cooperative compliance are:

1. Community Outreach and Industry Education
2. Prevention and Deterrence
3. Investigation, Arrest, and Prosecution

Most good criminal investigators can investigate any violation of law by breaking down the law into its elements of proof and then determining if evidence exists to prove each element. While that holds true for the investigation of firearms trafficking violations, these complex investigations also require a knowledge of rulings, regulations, and important case law to ensure the proper application of the law and a successful investigation. There is no Federal "Firearms Trafficking Law". Instead, there is a collection of laws that may apply to specific actions in different types of firearms trafficking schemes, and many of those laws require the investigator to prove knowledge, intent, and willfulness to violate the law. Proving violations of these laws is difficult, and there are substantial "gray areas" in which persons can legally operate. Because of this, and the additional facts that firearms are a lawful commodity, and law-abiding individuals do have a constitutional right to possess firearms, criminal investigators must use tact and discretion when conducting interviews. This is serious business, and it has to be done correctly to protect the public and to prevent interference with the lawful commerce of firearms. Firearms trafficking investigations are a delicate dance between protecting people's life, liberty, and pursuit of happiness (Declaration of Independence)[iii], free of gun violence, versus people's right to bear arms (Second Amendment to the U.S. Constitution)[iv] and be secure in their persons, houses, papers, and effects (4th Amendment to the U.S. Constitution)[v]. As with any dance, if you are not properly trained and practiced you will not look good doing it, and you may get asked to leave the floor. Violating someone's Constitutional rights is a sure-fire way to end up the subject of a civil suit, a work place disciplinary action, criminal charges, or a congressional hearing–and maybe all four.

Any firearms ownership information gathered during an investigation must be treated as sensitive private information, and no investigator should take it upon themselves to create their own ownership database, or they may run afoul of a variety of laws. While the National Firearms Act of 1934[vi] does allow for the registration of machine guns, silencers, destructive devices, or "any other weapons" in the National Firearms Registration and Transfer Record, this does NOT include handguns, rifles, and shotguns. To ensure that the federal government does not have, or start, a registration of handguns, rifles, or shotguns, Title 18 of U.S.C. § 926(a)(3) of the Firearm Owners Protection Act of 1986[vii] states: *"No such rule or regulation prescribed after the date of the enactment of the Firearms Owners' Protection Act may require that records required to be maintained under this chapter or any portion of the contents of such records, be recorded at or transferred to a facility owned, managed, or controlled by the United States or any State or any political subdivision thereof,* **nor that any system of registration of firearms, firearms owners, or firearms transactions or dispositions be established.** *Nothing*

in this section expands or restricts the Secretary's authority to inquire into the disposition of any firearm in the course of a criminal investigation."

A good firearm trafficking investigator will also need thick skin. You will be stuck between two opposing political factions, one of which will vilify you for not doing enough and one which will vilify you for doing too much. You will simultaneously be labeled an industry shill and a jack-booted thug. They will say inflammatory things about you to rile up angst among their supporters and drive fund raising. The work you do is important, but it is a political football. The late great Glenn Fry sang about dealing with all the influences on a criminal trade in his 1984 hit, "Smugglers Blues"©: *"Perhaps you'd understand it better standing in my shoes... It's the politics of contraband, it's the smugglers blues"*.

Aside from cosmetic features, the technology of firearms has not changed much over the past 70 years. Firearms are a mature commodity. They do what they were designed to do quite well. With proper maintenance, a firearm like the AK-47, invented more than 70 years ago, will last indefinitely. The number of privately owned guns in the U.S. is at an all-time high[viii], estimated at well over 300 million, with that number increasing each year by about 10 million[ix]. That is just under one firearm for every person. Of course, firearm ownership is not spread out evenly. According to a study published in the "Injury Prevention" journal, one-third of adults in the U.S. report owning a firearm[x]. Those who fear the government would try to take all those guns, and those who want the government to take all those guns should keep those numbers in mind. It would neither be physically possible nor constitutional. Guns are here to stay—legally, culturally, and by the numbers. The daunting task for firearms trafficking investigators is to prevent those firearms from ending up in the hands of criminals. Effective firearms trafficking investigation *does* prevent armed crime. And, for every dollar invested in efforts to combat illegal firearms trafficking, society saves hundreds of thousands of dollars in prevented costs associated with victims of armed crime. Historically, law enforcement has focused on solving armed crime once it happens, but that means there is already a victim. That is reacting to armed crime rather than proactively preventing armed crime by limiting the ability of criminals to access and misuse firearms. When it comes to gun crime, there needs to be as much focus on prevention as there is on solution.

While the investigation of firearms trafficking has been a law enforcement priority since gun crime became a problem in the U.S., the ability to identify firearms traffickers grew by leaps and bounds in the 1990s, due to research that identified firearms trafficking indicators, and technology that advanced the ability to data mine vast quantities of information in order to focus limited resources where they could achieve the biggest impact. Those advances and efficiencies were largely the result of ATF efforts to become more intelligence led and to comply with the newly enacted Government Performance and Results Act of 1993. Today's firearms trafficking investigations are driven by crime gun intelligence developed by fusion centers such as ATF's Crime Gun Intelligence Centers, which represents the gold standard for crime gun intelligence and analysis as well as armed violent crime and firearms trafficking lead development.

Although it is impossible to include everything necessary to conduct complex illegal firearms trafficking investigations in every type of firearms trafficking scheme, this guide does its best to cover the topic comprehensively. This guide provides a brief history of the federal firearms laws, and includes chapters on terminology, firearms safety and nomenclature, intelligence analysis and lead development techniques, current firearms laws, forfeiture and financial investigations, interdiction, and deterrence and investigative techniques. It also provides real-life case examples illustrating the successful application of investigative techniques, strategies that target firearms traffickers, gang investigations with a focus on armed violent crime and crime gun sources, and international law enforcement agencies.

GUN CRIME IS LIKE AN INDUSTRIAL FIRE

Image Credits: www.commons.wikimedia.org

At the scene of any large industrial fire, the majority of fire-fighters will attack the fire by spraying foam and water for suppression and containment. However, to have any chance at putting out that fire, there needs to be a specialist who knows how to turn the valves and shut off the flow of flammable chemicals to the fire. The same holds true for armed crime. Most law enforcement officials are working to suppress and contain armed violent crime; however, there is a vital need for specialists who can turn the valves that shut off the flow of firearms to violent criminals and extinguish the armed crime inferno. That is the role of the firearms trafficking investigator.

FIGURE I.1

This guide serves four primary purposes:

1. To assist criminal investigators in the U.S. and abroad with developing a thorough understanding of firearms trafficking terminology, the laws applicable to firearms trafficking and forfeiture, development of crime gun intelligence, firearms trafficking indicators, and the ability to successfully investigate a wide variety of firearms trafficking schemes and armed gang violence.
2. To assist law enforcement instructors and criminal justice educators tasked with teaching current and future criminal investigators the art of gun crime and firearms trafficking investigation. Competent and relevant training is crucial to identifying, investigating, apprehending, and successfully prosecuting firearms traffickers while not interfering with the lawful commerce of firearms.
3. To assist law enforcement leaders in developing comprehensive strategies that enhance trafficking lead development and address the full gun crime spectrum, from *Trafficker to Trigger-Puller©*, allowing for the focusing of limited resources on those who are the source of firearms to violent criminals, gangs, and terrorists.

4. To inform researchers and policy makers on the nuanced and complex real-world process of detecting and investigating a wide variety of firearms trafficking schemes using existing firearms laws. This text discusses the many ways that firearms go from *Commodity to Crime Gun©*.

Those who profit from illegally arming violent criminals and perpetuating the cycle of violence, victimization, and suffering are a special breed of bad guy. This guide will help criminal investigators set their sights on stopping armed violent crime by stopping those who fuel it.

Chapter 1
Historical Context of the Federal Firearms Laws

"The right to bear arms; A well-regulated Militia, being necessary to the security of a free State, the right of the people to keep and bear arms, shall not be infringed."[xi]
The 2nd Amendment to the U.S. Constitution, written by James Madison and ratified in December of 1791

There are many opinions about the actual meaning of the 2nd Amendment. We all know about opinions – they vary, and every one's got one. When it comes to the 2nd Amendment, the only opinion that matters is that of the Supreme Court of the United States (SCOTUS), and they have several rulings on the topic.

THE 2ND AMENDMENT AND THE U.S. SUPREME COURT

In 1875 U.S. v. Cruikshank[xii] was one of the first SCOTUS firearm rulings. Members of the KKK were being sued for not allowing black citizens the right to assembly and to bear arms. Part of the SCOTUS ruling said that the right of each individual to bear arms was not granted under the Constitution. Ten years later, the Presser v. Illinois[xiii] ruling said that the 2nd Amendment only limited the federal government from prohibiting gun ownership, not the States. In 1894, SCOTUS heard the Miller v. Texas[xiv] argument of Franklin Miller, who said he should be able to carry a concealed firearm for protection, and that the State of Texas had no right to stop him. SCOTUS did not agree with Mr. Miller and ruled that the 2nd Amendment does not apply to State laws such as the Texas law restricting the carrying of dangerous weapons. In these three cases collectively, SCOTUS made clear before 1900 that the 2nd Amendment does not prohibit States from setting their own rules on gun ownership.

Figure 1.1 *Seal of the U.S. Supreme Court*

IMAGE CREDIT: *www.supremecourt.gov.*

Then in 1939 SCOTUS heard the case of U.S. v. Miller.[xv] In that case Jack Miller, no relation to Franklin Miller from Texas, had been arrested for carrying an unregistered sawed-off shotgun across state lines in violation of the National Firearms Act of 1934. Mr. Miller said this Federal law violated his 2nd Amendment right. SCOTUS did not agree, stating that "in the absence of any evidence tending to show that possession or use of a 'shotgun having a barrel of less than eighteen inches in length' at this time has some reasonable relationship to the preservation or efficiency of a well-regulated militia, we cannot say that the Second Amendment guarantees the right to keep and bear such an instrument." With this ruling SCOTUS made it clear that the Federal government could establish rules for firearms ownership.

The next SCOTUS ruling on the 2nd Amendment would not come for 69 years. That case was District of Columbia v. Heller in 2008[xvi]. In that case Mr. Heller, a special police officer in Washington, DC, argued that the DC ban on all handguns violated his 2nd Amendment right. SCOTUS agreed, and ruled that despite State laws, individuals who were not part of a militia did have the right to bear arms. SCOTUS held, "The Second Amendment protects an individual right to possess a firearm unconnected with service in a militia, and to use that arm for traditionally lawful purposes, such as self-defense within the home." It appears that the DC handgun ban went beyond rules for owning handguns and was a complete ban on owning handguns. Just two years later SCOTUS would rule again on the issue in McDonald v. City of Chicago[xvii]. Chicago had a city-wide handgun ban and Mr. McDonald challenged this. In a similar 5 to 4 ruling, SCOTUS affirmed its decision in the Heller case, saying the 2nd Amendment "applies equally to the federal government and the States." Bottom line – regulation yes, bans no.

FEDERAL FIREARMS LAWS THROUGH THE YEARS

All Federal firearms laws are a direct result of a crime trend or incident that made a significant impression on the country and generated the political will for Congress and the President to pass laws. The first Federal firearms law came 136 years after ratification of the 2nd Amendment. Others followed. An overview of those laws and the precipitating events follow.

The Non-Mailable Firearms Act of 1927 (Title 18 U.S.C. § 1715)[xviii]. In 1918, General Thompson invented the Thompson submachine gun with the intention of making a fortune selling it to the U.S Military. Unfortunately for him, World War I ended in 1918, so the demand for submachine guns waned. What was just around the corner, however, was Prohibition, which passed with the Volstead Act in 1919. The decade of the "Roaring Twenties" began, and proved the theory that for every action, there is an equal and opposite reaction. This huge undertaking to get rid of booze led to a flood of booze and crime. The continued demand for alcohol spawned a black market run by organized criminal mobs and syndicates led by gangsters like Al Capone who became infamous celebrities. Public corruption bootleggers, gang-slayings, and moonshiners filled the headlines. Gangsters wanted firepower to fight for turf, and they could get it by sending $170 to the Thompson machinegun company, who would send them their submachine guns through the mail. The public eventually had enough of the crime that easy criminal access to submachine guns exacerbated, and the Non-Mailable Firearms Act of 1927 made it illegal to ship handguns and other concealable firearms through the U.S. mail.

The National Firearms Act (NFA) of 1934 (Title 26 U.S.C. § 5861)[xix]. The Non-Mailable firearms act did little to slow the machinegun crime wave. America was having its first drive-by shootings, with gangsters shooting out the windows of cars speeding down city streets. Al Capone's henchman, Machinegun Jack, was shooting up Chicago. In1929, he was responsible for the St. Valentine's Day massacre, in which Bugs Moran and six others were lined up and shot dead with Thompson machine guns. Baby Face Nelson was shooting up Kansas City. Dillinger was cutting a swath through the Midwest, committing bank robberies and murders with his Thompson submachine gun. Machine Gun Kelly was doing the same in the Memphis area and Bonnie and Clyde were on their own murderous machine gun crime spree with their Browning Automatic Rifles (BAR) stolen from an armory. Elliott Ness and the Untouchables were having success, but gun violence was still a problem. The public had had enough. President Roosevelt and the Congress announced that "the greatest threat to the personal liberties of citizens was firearms violence," as they passed the NFA into law to curb the lawlessness and the rise of gangster culture during prohibition. President Franklin D. Roosevelt hoped this act would eliminate machine guns from America's streets. Machine guns, short-barreled rifles (SBR) and shotguns, silencers, as well as "any other weapons" (AOW) such as cane and pen guns were required to be registered, and a tax was required to be paid on each gun each time it was sold. The tax was and still is $200;

Figure 1.2 *G-Man Elliot Ness*

IMAGE CREDIT: www.atf.gov

however, in 1934 that was the equivalent of $2500 today. America was in the middle of the Great Depression and there were not many who had that kind of money.

The Federal Firearms Act (FFA) of 1938[xx]. The interstate crime sprees of bank robbers like Dillinger and Bonnie and Clyde helped drive this law. It required anyone shipping firearms through interstate or foreign commerce to get a Federal Firearms License (FFL) to be in the business. The Licensees were required to keep records of the persons they acquired firearms from and sold firearms to. The Licensees would also be prohibited from selling firearms to certain persons, such those under indictment and persons convicted of crimes of violence.

The Gun Control Act (GCA) of 1968 (Title 18, U.S.C. §§ 922, 924, & 926)[xxi]. Gun crime appeared to be under control in the 1940s and 1950s, and things were quiet. John Kennedy, then a young U.S. Senator from Massachusetts, saw an emerging problem with the easy importation of foreign surplus military weapons and supported a bill to stop this[xxii]. The bill was defeated. In the U.S., gun laws follow incidents, and there had not yet been one involving this issue. Then in November 1963 in Dallas, Texas, President Kennedy was shot dead by Lee Harvey Oswald using an Italian Carcano imported surplus military rifle. President Johnson called it "mail order death". A short time later, Senator Dodd of Connecticut offered up a draft of what would become the Gun Control Act of 1968. Vigorous debate on the bill dragged on until 1966, when Americas first mass-shooting caught on film took place at the University of Texas in Austin, when a man who had just killed his wife and mother climbed the Texas Tower and with a high-powered rifle killed 13 people and wounded 22 others. Two more years of debate on the gun control bill ensued, and then Martin Luther King was assassinated by James Earl Ray in April 1968, followed by the assassination of Robert Kennedy by Sirhan Sirhan in June 1968. The Gun Control Act was passed in October 1968. The GCA replaced the Federal Firearms Act of 1938, expanded licensing and recordkeeping requirements for gun dealers, expanded the list of those who could not possess firearms beyond those under indictment to include all convicted felons, drug users, the adjudicated mentally ill, illegal aliens, and those who had, renounced their citizenship. All firearms would have to have a unique serial number as would any firearms approved for importation. The ATF Form 4473, the Firearms Transfer Transaction Record, was created to determine the eligibility of the possessor to own a firearm. It was determined this form would stay with the FFL and not go to the government for a registration. The GCA also outlawed the mail order sale of all rifles and shotguns and required FFLs to make a report to law enforcement when 2 or more handguns were purchased by someone within 5 business days.

ROSCOE VEST POCKET .22—$12.95 Brand new 6-shot German revolver that sells in the $28 - $30 range. A tight accurate well-made piece. 3" Bbl., 5" overall. Fires popular American made .22 short ammo. Side gate loading. Has a fine steel rifled barrel with blade front sight. Excellent for target or plinking. 10-day money-back guar. $12.95. For C.O.D. send $7.50 deposit. Leather holster $2.25. Send check, cash or M.O. to: SEAPORT TRADERS, INC., Dept. PS-8, 409 E. 12th St., Los Angeles 15, Calif.

(Advertisement)

Figure 1.3 *The Saturday Night Special*

IMAGE CREDIT: *Seaport Traders Inc.., Advertisement*

The Commerce in Firearms and Ammunition Regulations (Title 27 C.F.R. § 178) of 1975 re; Multiple Handgun Sale Reporting[xxiii]. In the 1970s cheap and small revolvers were hitting the streets and were being trafficked in interstate commerce from source areas to market areas in violation of Federal law. There was no effective way to monitor this trafficking activity. In July of 1975 a key Amendment to the Code of Federal Regulations (CFR) was made that required all FFLs to report to ATF the sale or other disposition of two or more pistols or revolvers at one time or during any five consecutive business days to an unlicensed person. This provision only applied to handguns. This was done to monitor and deter illegal interstate commerce in pistols and revolvers by unlicensed persons.

The Arms Export Control Act (AECA) of 1976 (Title 22 U.S.C. § 2751[xxiv]**).** In the early 1970s, political instability in many countries around the globe, the proliferation of military weapons, and an upsurge in terrorism led to passage of the Arms Export Control Act (AECA), which established controls over the import and export of defense articles (including firearms) and defense services.

The Comprehensive Crime Control Act of 1984[xxv]**.** The 1980s saw its fair share of mass shootings and armed violent crime by recidivist felons and armed career criminals (ACCs). In 1984 James Hubert walked into a San Ysidro, California McDonalds fast food restaurant with an Uzi, killed 21 persons and wounded 19 others, before being killed by police. The Comprehensive Crime Control Act, signed into law by President Reagan, provided for a minimum mandatory jail sentence of 15 years to life for a felon with 3 or more convictions for drug trafficking or violent crime who was caught in possession of a firearm or ammunition (Title 18, U.S.C. § 924(e)).

The Law Enforcement Officers Protection Act of 1986[xxvi]**.** The 1980s also brought a growing concern about "cop killer" bullets. The Law Enforcement Officers Protection Act, passed in 1986, made it illegal for anyone to manufacture or import armor-piercing ammunition.

The Firearms Owners Protection Act (FOPA) of 1986 (also known as the McClure-Volker Act)[xxvii]**.** In response to what was seen as unnecessary overreach by some provisions of the GCA of 1968, the Firearms Owners Protection Act was signed into law in 1986 by President Reagan. The act loosened restrictions on gun sales by reopening interstate sales of long guns on a limited basis; it legalized shipments of ammunition through the U.S. Mail; it removed the requirement for recordkeeping on sales of ammunition; and it provided for safe passage of persons traveling with firearms stored unloaded in the trunk of their car while passing through U.S. states other than their own (Title 18 U.S.C. § 926(A)). In the 1980s, the Cocaine Cowboy and Colombian Cartel violence in South Florida were in full swing. Crack cocaine turf wars were driving new levels of gun crime in U.S. cities. As a result, through an add-on to the FOPA known as the Hughes Amendment, the FOPA banned the sale of machine guns manufactured after the date of its enactment to civilians, restricting sales of these weapons to the military and law enforcement. The act also created significant minimum mandatory sentences for the use of a firearms during and in relation to federal crimes of violence or drug trafficking crimes (Title 18 U.S.C. § 924(c)).

Figure 1.4 Carlos Lehder Rivas of the Medellin Cartel
IMAGE CREDIT: USMS

The Undetectable Firearms Act of 1988xxviii. The threat of terrorism was rising in the 1980s and the technology to manufacture undetectable polymer firearms had arrived. President Reagan signed into law the "act to amend Title 18, United States Code, to prohibit certain firearms especially useful to terrorists". The act made it illegal to manufacture, transfer, or possess any firearm that, after removal of the grips, stock, and magazines, is not detectable by a walk-through metal detection unit or does not generate an accurate image in standard airport imaging technology. Any firearm or major component must have 3.7 ounces (105 g) of steel to be detectable. Title 18 U.S.C. § 922(p) of the GCA of 1968.

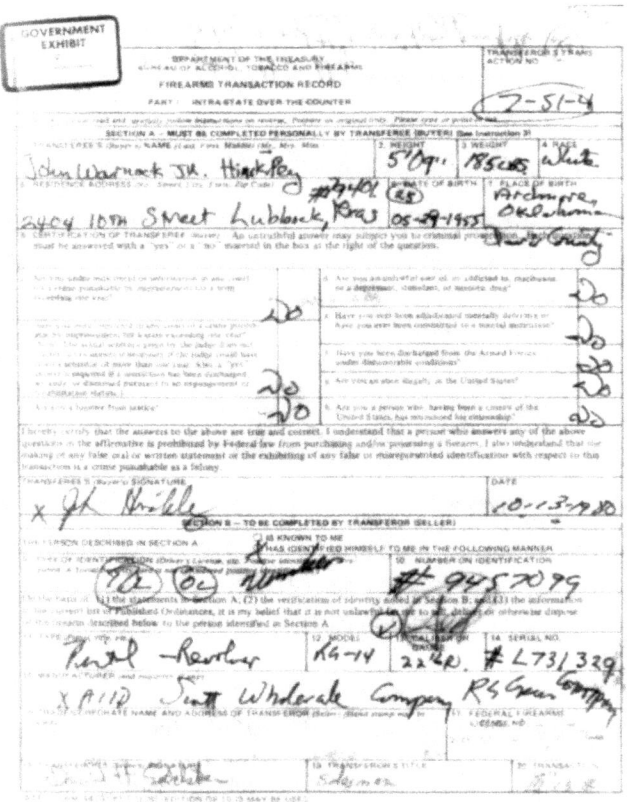

Figure 1.5 ATF Form 4473 Completed by John Hinckley Jr. to Purchase the Handgun He Used to Shoot President Reagan and Others
IMAGE CREDIT: ATF

The Crime Control Act (CCA) of 1990xxix. Armed crime continued to rise in the late 1980s, and there were growing concerns about gun crime around schools, and about the assembly of imported semi-automatic rifle and shotgun parts. The Crime Control Act that was signed into law by President George H.W. Bush set forth many actions, such as the Federal Victim/Witness provisions. Some of the provisions in this act also established Gun Free School Zones and outlawed the assembly of semi-automatic rifles or shotguns made from illegally imported parts.

The Brady Handgun Violence Prevention Act of 1994xxx. In 1986 America watched on TV as John Hinckley Jr. opened fire on Ronald Reagan in Washington, D.C., as the President was walking a short distance to the Presidential limousine. Shot in the melee were President Reagan, Secret Service agents, and White House Press Secretary James Brady. John Hinckley Jr., who had been previously adjudicated as mentally ill and was not allowed to possess a firearm, had purchased the firearm from an FFL in

Texas by simply lying on the ATF Form 4473 Transfer Transaction Record when asked if he was previously adjudicated as mentally ill. Purchasing a firearm was based on the honor system. James and Sarah Brady initiated a campaign to require background checks before anyone could purchase a firearm from a licensed firearms dealer. The answers that people put on the ATF Form 4473 Firearms Transfer Transaction Record would be verified with a records check. Eight years after the shooting, the Brady Bill was signed into law by President Clinton.

The Violent Crime Control and Law Enforcement Act of 1994[xxxi]. In response to armed crime with serious firepower that was becoming too common in the late 1980s and early 1990s, the Violent Crime Control and Law Enforcement Act was signed into law by President Clinton. It is commonly referred to as the "Assault Weapon Ban", and it targeted large capacity magazines and what were defined as assault weapons: firearms with 5 specific features, including pistol grip, large capacity detachable magazines, collapsible stocks, flash suppressors, and bayonet mounts. In 2004 the law sunset and was not renewed.

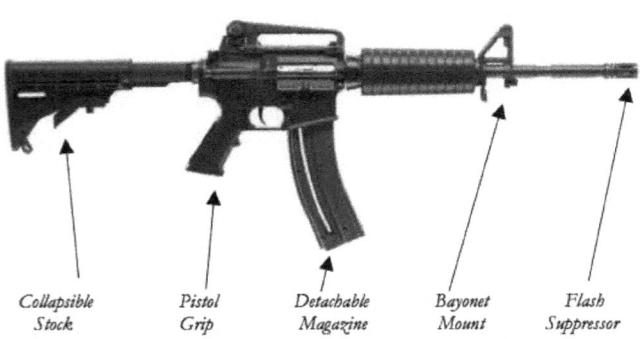

Collapsible Stock   Pistol Grip   Detachable Magazine   Bayonet Mount   Flash Suppressor

Any Semi-Automatic Rifle With 2 or More of These 5 Named Features

***Figure 1.6** Semi-Automatic Assault Rifle*

IMAGE CREDIT: Author

The Lautenberg Amendment of 1996 (Title 18 U.S.C. § 922(g)(8) and 922(g)(9)[xxxii]. Shortly after passage of the Violence Against Women's Act (VAWA) of 1994, and in response to data from studies that increased the awareness of the volume of domestic violence and the consequences of the proximity of a firearm in domestic situations, the Lautenberg Amendment, named for its sponsor, Senator Lautenberg (D-NJ), was signed into law by President Clinton. The law made it a felony for anyone with a prior misdemeanor conviction for domestic violence or for anyone under a court-issued domestic violence restraining order to be in possession of firearms or ammunition. The law is referred to as an amendment as it amends Title 18 U.S.C. § 922(g) of the GCA of 1968.

THE CHANGING FACE OF CRIME GUNS

Criminals' crime gun preferences change. Some of those changes are based on price, some are based on availability, some are based on geo-political events, some are based on changes in the law, and other changes are based on the influence of pop culture. The following provides an overview of some of these crime gun preference changes, and the factors that drove them.

1920s and 1930s:
The Guns: The crime guns of choice, were the Thompson submachine gun and the Browning Automatic Rifle (BAR).
Why? This was the gangster era. As is often the case when any commodity the public wants is criminalized by a government, prohibition did not end the demand for alcohol, it just shifted control of the alcohol market from one that was taxed and regulated for safety by the government to one that was unregulated and all the profit went to gangsters. Prohibition created a lucrative black market that criminals found to be worth fighting over. Machine guns were widely available,

readily accessible, and provided the firepower that gangsters wanted to control their turf and that bank robbers wanted to take down banks and shake police chases. The Thomson and the BAR were the preferred weapon of choice by the like of Baby Face Nelson, Bonnie and Clyde, Dillinger, Al Capone, Lucky Luciano, Bugs Moran, Pretty Boy Floyd, and Machinegun Kelly.

What Changed? Passage of the Non-Mailable Firearms Act, the National Firearms Act, and the Federal Firearms Act tightened the gun market. The end of prohibition wiped out the lucrative black market that had been run, and fought over, by gangsters. Armed crime rates dropped.

1940s and 1950s:

This was a period of relative calm in America, with steady economic growth. It saw some of the lowest crime rates of the 20th Century. There were no significant gun crime trends.

1960s and 1970s:

The Guns: The Saturday Night Special was a cheap and concealable .22 or .38 caliber revolver and became the street gun of choice. In 1975 Lynyrd Skynyrd's™ hit song "Saturday Night Special"© on their album "Nuthin Fancy"© sang of the tragic consequences of that tiny firearm when it was in the wrong place at the wrong time. High-powered imported surplus military rifles were also becoming popular like the Italian Carcano rifle purchased by Lee Harvey Oswald.

Why? This was the beginning of significant law enforcement resources focused on drug enforcement. The war on drugs was declared, the black market for drugs in this new prohibition was growing, and significant cultural changes were under way. Drug dealers wanted concealable firearms and the little revolvers were widely available, inexpensive, and people were trafficking them from source areas. Radical groups of the era such as the Symbionese Liberation Army (SLA), Black Liberation Army (BLA), Fuerzas Armadas de Liberación Nacional (FALN), and Weather Underground took full advantage of the availability of surplus military rifles.

What Changed? The Gun Control Act of 1968 clamped down on imports of surplus military rifles and set up increased records requirements for persons selling and buying firearms. The Multiple Sales Handgun Report of 1975 helped ATF investigators root out interstate trafficking of handguns like the Saturday Night Special.

1970s and 1980s:

The Guns: Criminals began to transition away from the cheap revolvers and toward semi-automatic pistols. First on the scene were the "Ring of Fire" guns. These were manufactured by Davis Industries™, Jennings Firearms™, Bryco Arms™, Lorcin Engineering Co™, Raven Arms™, Phoenix Arms™, Arcadia Machine & Tool™ (AMT), and Jimenez™, Sundance™. Many of these companies were associated with each other and operated in the Southern California and Southern Arizona regions, in a geographic ring; thus the moniker, "Ring of Fire".

Figure 1.7 *Raven Arms Pistol*

IMAGE CREDITT: *Authors Collection*

Why? The firearms were small caliber concealable semi-automatic pistols. The criminals liked semi-automatics with the capacity to reload quickly with a new magazine. This was an improvement over the cheap revolvers. Assault weapons had not really shown up yet. The primary tactical rifle on the market was the Ruger Mini-14.

What Changed? The guns were of poor quality, prone to jams, had poor range and poor lethality. Your opponent might be able to keep fighting or even get away after being shot by one of these small caliber pistols. The manufacturers started to go out of business. Crime was still increasing in the U.S., and a new breed of drug gang wanted more firepower. It was coming.

1980s and 1990s:

The Guns: This was the era of the rise of the machine pistol such as the Intra-tech™ Tech 9, Military Arms Corp™ (MAC)-10, Ingram™, Cobray™, and Uzi™. These were semi-automatic pistols of a higher quality than the "Ring of Fire" guns and came with 30-round magazines. They were also easy to convert to fire as machine guns.

Why? Miami's Cocaine Cowboys wanted firepower. The Jamaican Shower Posse, Medellin and Cali Cartels, FARC (Fuerzas Armadas Revolucionarias de Colombia), Nicaraguan Sandanistas and Contras, Peruvian Shining Path Guerillas, Jamaat al Muslimeen in Trinidad and Tobago, and Irish Republican Army (IRA) all wanted firepower and they were coming to the U.S. to get it. They wanted firepower for their operations in the U.S., and they began large-scale smuggling of these firearms back to South America to be used in jungle wars against their governments and competing cartels. Terrorists were looking for undetectable plastic guns they could get into secure locations. This was also the beginning of the influence of popular culture on criminals' crime gun preferences. It started to become all about "image", and certain guns pro-

Figure 1.8 *Author in 1987 with Bales of Narcotics in the Mid-Florida Keys*

IMAGE CREDIT: Author

vided an intimidation factor as well as a fashionable gangster "swagger" factor. Stick-Up Street Culture had arrived. In the 1980s, "Miami Vice" was a hit television show that glamorized the South Florida fast life, making firearms a fashion statement. In 1983, the movie "Scarface" showed the lead character, played by Al Pacino, using a plethora of firearms popularized at the time, including the Colt AR-15. High speed boat loads of cocaine and cash were routinely intercepted and cocaine was being cooked as the first wave of crack hit the streets.

What Changed? In 1988 the manufacture, transfer or possession of undetectable firearms was banned in federal law signed by President Reagan. A 1989 Executive Order was issued banning the importation of assault weapons. The U.S. made Colt AR-15 and Ruger Mini-14 started to become more prevalent, and both fired a high powered .223 caliber rifle round. These rifles had more magazine capacity, greater lethality and knock down power, and greater range than the machine pistols that fired handgun rounds. Street gangs engaged in turf wars wanted more firepower for drive-by shootings. Cartels and Narco-Terrorists wanted more firepower for battles against their government. Geo-political events would usher in the next change.

1990s and 2000s:

The Guns: First came Chinese-made AK-47 rifles, SKS rifles and Norinco pistols, then the former Soviet Bloc (Warsaw Pact; Romanian, Yugoslavian) made AK-47 rifle variants and pistols such as the Tokarev, Makarov, and CZ.

"Mr. Gorbachev, Tear Down This Wall!"

Speech by President Reagan in West Berlin at the Brandenburg Gate on June 12, 1987 calling for the leader of the Soviet Union to remove the wall between East and West Berlin. The wall fell on November 9, 1989 and along with it the Soviet Union. A great achievement for world peace but the door was also opened for cold war weapons to hit the U.S. streets.

Figure 1.9 *President Reagan at the Brandenburg Gate, 1987*

IMAGE CREDIT: *Reagan Library*

Why? These are military grade firearms with military grade imported ammunition at rock bottom prices. A firearm of that quality could not be made for the price it was being sold. The people selling these firearms in the former Soviet bloc countries assumed control of these stockpiles after the fall of communism. They had no manufacturing costs. These weapons were pure profit, so they could afford to sell them at a low price and in bulk. When in the wrong hands, these inexpensive firearms hit the street as a triple threat: military grade quality and reliability; high-capacity magazines and tactical accoutrements; and large-caliber ammunition with long range and penetration power.

What Changed? These weapons are still prevalent among criminals today, but their import numbers were affected by a 1998 import ban on non-sporting rifles from China. Additionally, a Voluntary Restraint Agreement (VRA) restricted the import of Soviet Block sourced firearms under certain circumstances and slowed their import slightly. However, some U.S. based companies began manufacturing their own AK47 rifle variants. These firearms have become icons for drug dealers and gang members. The Romanian and Yugoslavian AK-47 rifle as well as the Tokarev, the Makarov, and the CZ pistol are part of a more ominous new face of crime guns.

Figure 1.10 *Inexpensive Military Firepower "From Russia With Love"©: Tokarevs, Makarovs, CZs, and AKs*
IMAGE CREDIT: *Author*

2010s:

The Guns: Ghost guns, unfinished receivers, 80% receivers, firearm castings, firearm flats, firearm parts kits, printed guns, and used guns from secondary source markets provide a variety of options for obtaining untraceable guns. They are homemade, reliable, and untraceable. Also popular are assault pistols, which are AR-15 and AK-47 firearms manufactured with no shoulder stock and a barrel shorter than 16 inches, so they are considered pistols. Normally, a barrel length less than 16 inches on a rifle would require the firearm to be registered as an SBR in the NFA; however, since it was manufactured without a shoulder stock, it was not designed with the intent to fire from the shoulder, and therefore it is a pistol and not a rifle under the legal definition. These weapons fall into a category of legal firearm modifications that some refer to as "lawful but awful". Accoutrements made to go with these pistols include forearm "stabilizers"[xxxiii]. Items are also available to make them fire like a machine gun but without converting the firearm to a machine gun as defined in Federal law, thus not violating any law – until 2018. These items are referred to as multi-burst trigger activators, and include Gatling gun type rotators, trigger feath-

ering devices, binary trigger systems, and stock attachments such as the Bump Slide Stock™, which are all quite effective. Following the mass-shooting on October 1, 2017 in Las Vegas, Nevada, where the shooter, using bump-fire assisted rifles, fired more than 1100 rounds from the 32nd floor of Mandalay Bay down into a concert crowd killing 58 people and injuring 851more, the ATF was directed to revisit their initial ruling. The ATFs review is on-going following a period of public comment collection however a final ruling has not been made as of the writing of this book.

Figure 1.11 *Bump Slide Stock*

IMAGE CREDIT: *Author*

Why? For a criminal, an assault weapon is great, but a highly concealable and untraceable assault weapon is better than great. Some refer to these as "lawful but awful". It has the same quadruple threat: military quality, high-capacity magazines, large-caliber ammunition with penetration power, and long range – but even beyond that, it has conceal-ability, no paper trail, and it presents a desired image.

What Changed? Nothing has changed yet; but, like the weather, if you wait long enough it will. Deregulated silencers and SBRs were recently under consideration, but at present they are not moving forward in legislation. Homemade printed guns are now a thing.

Polymer and metal printers are operational and the plans for most commercially made firearms are available on the internet. There is no way to remove all those firearm plans from the internet and it is unclear if trying to force their removal would be legal. On July 10, 2018 the U.S. Department of Justice settled the case of *Defense Distributed v. United States Department of State* (838 F.3d 451 (5th Cir. 2016)) making the sale and transfer of printable firearm plans protected free speech under the first amendment to the U.S. Constitution.[xxxiv] However, as of the writing of this book other Federal courts have stayed this decision and it is uncertain how this will end. Defense Distributed™, also known as LMT Defense™, produces the Ghost Gunner™ box and the Liberator™ polymer handgun. Homemade plastic gun polymers are getting better, and soon a 100% polymer firearm may be capable of firing more than a couple of rounds without deforming or exploding. A fully polymer firearm would be a violation of the undetectable firearms act of 1988.

There is no legal prohibition against the manufacture of home-printed metal guns, however their quality compared to a traditionally manufactured firearm is currently inferior. For a point of comparison, remember that when the first craft beer breweries started they were inferior to commercially manufactured beer however in short order those craft beers became very good. They turned the beer market in the U.S. upside down and have had a significant impact on the market share of the large brewers. Does the same type of market transformation lay ahead for the firearms industry?

Chapter 2
Terminology Related to Firearms Trafficking Investigation

A powerful agent is the right word. Whenever we come upon one of those intensely right words in a book or a newspaper the resulting effect is physical as well as spiritual, and electrically prompt.
By Mark Twain from an Essay on William Dean Howells in 1906.

The first step in understanding a subject involves defining it. A definition is the statement of the meaning of a term. What follows are definitions of firearms trafficking terminology. Some of these terms are defined in the law, some are street slang, some are law enforcement jargon, other terms were developed through research on recovered crime gun data (e.g., time-to-crime), and others are government functions and databases. Criminal investigators need to have a working knowledge of these terms and definitions in order to effectively investigate firearms trafficking and communicate with other firearms trafficking investigators in a common language. Normally a section of terms appears in a glossary at the end of the book; however, this textbook is designed so that each chapter serves as a sequential building block of knowledge, leading up to Chapters 10 and 11, in which the textbook covers the conduct of actual firearms trafficking and armed violent gang investigations.

Access 2000 (A2K)[xxxv] - A series of automated database systems that allows the electronic records of FFLs to be searched by serial number only. A2K is maintained by ATF and provided free of charge to Firearms Industry Members. The data remains the property of the FFL. The system gives FFLs the voluntary ability to provide ATF access to serial number requests in online searches to improve the ability to trace recovered crime guns on a 24/7 basis, and reduces the resources FFLs need to dedicate to responding to trace requests.

Acoustic Gun Shot Detection System[xxxvi] - An alert system that uses an array of microphones in a geographic area, a processing unit, and a user-interface to immediately detect and convey the location of gunfire. These systems are used by law enforcement, security, and the military to identify the occurrence and location of gunfire. For law enforcement, this allows for rapid response without relying on the chance that someone will report the shots fired. These systems can be used outdoors, in urban or rural areas, or inside buildings. Different manufacturers of such systems include ShotSpotter® and Raytheon® Boomerang. Other terms for these systems include gunfire locators, acoustic ballistics detection systems, and gunshot detection systems.

Acquisition & Disposition Record - The documentation that all FFLs are required to maintain, consisting of the receipt (date and source) and disposition (date and transferee) of all firearms, as well as a complete description of the firearm(s). Acquisition and Disposition Records may be hard copy or electronic. (Title 27 C.F.R. § 478.125)

Agent Provocateur - A person who intentionally entices another person to commit an illegal or rash act, or falsely implicates their participation in such an act. An Agent Provocateur (French for one who incites or provokes)[xxxvii] may be acting out of their own sense of duty or may be employed by law enforcement or another entity. With respect to firearms trafficking, every country has different laws concerning what law enforcement techniques are allowed during an investigation, and criminal investigators must take care not to violate those laws when dealing with citizens in a foreign country or they may break that country's laws by acting as an agent provocateur. Investigators should coordinate with their agency's foreign attachés or legates (legal attaché) to ensure that their actions fall within this category.

Ammunition - Ammunition or cartridge cases, primers, bullets, or propellant powder designed for use in any firearm. (Title 18 U.S.C. § 921(a)(17)(a))

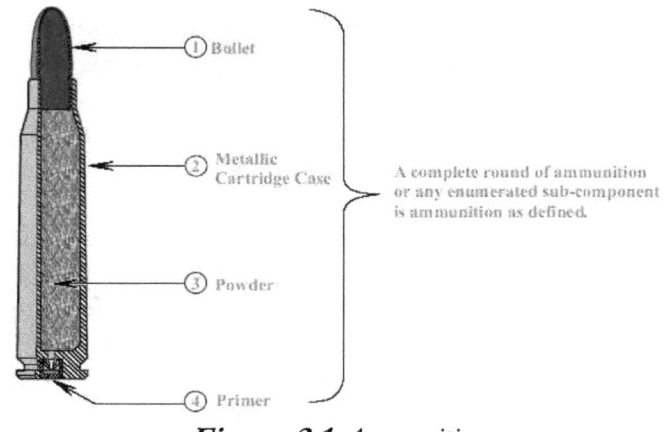

Figure 2.1 *Ammunition*
IMAGE CREDIT: *www.ATF.gov*

Antique Firearm - Any firearm manufactured in or before 1898 (including any firearm with a matchlock, flintlock, percussion cap, or similar type of ignition system); and any replica of any firearm if such replica is not designed or redesigned for using rim-fire or conventional center-fire fixed ammunition or uses rim-fire or conventional center-fire fixed ammunition which is no longer manufactured in the United States and which is not readily available through the ordinary channels of commercial trade. (NOTE: Antique firearms are not considered firearms under federal law and are not subject to the provisions of the GCA.) (Title 18 U.S.C. § 921(A)(16))

Ant Trade - A term used to describe numerous shipments of small numbers of weapons that, over time, result in the accumulation of large numbers of illicit weapons by unauthorized end users.[xxxviii]

Armor Piercing Ammunition - A projectile or projectile core which may be used in a handgun and which is constructed entirely (excluding the presence of traces of other substances) from one or a combination of tungsten alloys, steel, iron, brass, bronze, beryllium copper, or depleted uranium; or a full jacketed projectile larger than .22 caliber designed and intended for use in a handgun and whose jacket has a weight of more than 25 percent of the total weight of the projectile. (Title 18 U.S.C. § 921(g)(17)(B))

ATF Form 3310.4: Report of Multiple Sale or Other Disposition of Pistols and Revolvers - The form that all FFLs are required to complete and submit to ATF whenever they transfer more than one handgun within a 5-business-day period to the same individual. Form 3310.4 contains full identifying information concerning the purchaser, firearms, date of transfer, and FFL.

FFLs are required by federal law to forward this form to ATF and to the designated chief law enforcement official in that area. (Title 18 U.S.C. § 923(g)(3))

ATF Form 4473: Firearms Transaction Record - The form that all FFLs must complete and maintain to document the transfer of firearm(s) to an unlicensed individual. Form 4473 is completed by both the purchaser and the FFL, and contains full identifying information concerning the purchaser, firearm, date of transfer, and FFL number. The primary purpose of the form is to determine the eligibility of the purchaser to legally acquire and possess firearms[xxxix]. (See image in Appendix C.)

ATF Form 6: Application and Permit for Importation of Firearms, Ammunition and Implements of War - The form used to apply for a permit, effective for a fixed period of time, giving the holder permission to import firearms, ammunition, and implements of war. This form is required to import any items listed on the United States Munitions List. (See Appendix C.)

Auto-loading (or self-loading) - An auto-loading (or self-loading) firearm that uses energy created by the firing of a cartridge to operate the firearm. The auto-loading mechanism extracts each fired case from the chamber, ejects the spent case from the firearm, loads a new cartridge in the chamber, and prepares the firearm to be fired, but does not fire the firearm.

Block Gun - A slang term used to refer to a gun shared by gang members. The gun is usually left concealed in a common space (out on the block), such as under a piece of lumber in a yard or in a drop ceiling, where any gang member can access it if needed; however, no one risks having it in their possession for longer than necessary. This is also referred to as a community gun. A recovered block gun should be traced and processed for the presence of DNA and latent fingerprints to establish prior possession.

Blue on Blue - Also referred to as police on police, this is a dangerous situation in which two law enforcement groups unknowingly engage each other upon showing up at the same enforcement action, not expecting the other to be present. The resulting conflict can result in injury or death to law enforcement, informants, suspects, and/or innocent bystanders. This situation may occur when one or both of the law enforcement groups has failed to deconflict their enforcement action.

Body-On-It - A slang term used by criminals to refer to a gun that has been used in a shooting. In a firearm trafficking investigation, a suspect may ask for guns without any bodies on them to be sure they will not be linked to crimes they did not commit if they are apprehended with the firearm at a later date.

Bolt Action - An action manually operated by a bolt mechanism. The bolt mechanism is used to load a cartridge into the chamber area, extract each fired shell case from the chamber, and eject the spent shell case from the firearm. This action must be repeated prior to each firing.

Buffer Tube Brace - A tube that protrudes from the rear of a large pistol in the location where a stock would attach if the firearm were manufactured to fire from the shoulder. The buffer tube can accept the installation of a stabilizing device, also known as a forearm stabilizer, stabilizer brace, or stabilizer blade that facilitates one handed firing.

Burner Gun - This is a firearm that has been used in too many crimes to risk having in one's possession. Some criminals will simply dump the gun in a lake, river, or ocean. Other criminals will sell a burner gun to traffickers taking guns to others countries in Central or South America. They make their money, and the gun is removed from the country unable to come back on them.

Bump Fire - Bump firing is the act of using the recoil of a semi-automatic firearm to fire individual shots in rapid succession, which simulates the rate of a fully automatic firearm. This is achieved by the attachment of various devices such as a bump slide stock or other mechanism. (See the definition of "Multi-burst Trigger Activator" for more information.)

Buy-Bust - A law enforcement term referring to an enforcement operation that consists of an undercover agent or confidential informant making a buy of evidence from a suspect which is then immediately followed with the suspect's arrest.

Buy-Walk - A law enforcement term referring to an enforcement operation that consists of an undercover agent making a buy of evidence from a suspect, after which the suspect is allowed to leave without being arrested at that time. This term can be confused with the term "walk of evidence," which is often a prohibited practice.

Bureau of Alcohol, Tobacco, Firearms and Explosives (ATF) - An agency within the U.S. Department of Justice that enforces the federal laws concerning firearms and explosives, arson, tobacco, and alcohol. The agency has a long history under different agency names, including the Bureau of Prohibition, in the days of Elliott Ness. In more recent times the agency's primary focus has been on preventing violent crime by investigating violent armed criminals and armed criminal organizations as well as those who traffic firearms to these criminals.

Caliber - The diameter of the projectile/bullet portion of ammunition, or the diameter of the barrel of the firearm it is intended to be expelled from. It is measured to the hundredth or thousandth of an inch. In the U.S., caliber may be expressed in numerals representing the distance between opposing lands, or grooves. In Europe, caliber may be expressed in millimeters.

Cartridge Head-stamp Identification Catalogue (CHIC) - A database maintained by ATF that catalogues the head-stamp markings of ammunition to aid in the identification of manufacturers and to aid in proving interstate movement of the ammunition for purposes of a criminal investigation.

Clip - A device used to store multiple rounds of ammunition together as a unit, ready for insertion into the magazine or cylinder of a firearm. A clip speeds up the process of loading and reloading the firearm, as several rounds can be loaded at once, rather than one round being loaded at a time. Several types of clips exist. Slang terms include stripper-clip and slide-strip.

Figure 2.2 *Clip*

IMAGE CREDIT: Author

Cold War Weapon - A slang term used to describe any number of handguns and rifles imported into the United States from former Warsaw Pact Countries and the former Soviet Union. This includes AK-47 rifles as well as Makarov, Tokarev, and CZ pistols.

Community Oriented Policing (COP)[xl] - A philosophy that promotes organizational strategies that support the systematic use of partnerships and problem-solving techniques between the police and the community. These strategies proactively address the immediate conditions that give rise to public safety issues such as crime, armed violence, social disorder, and fear of crime. A common COP strategy in use today is SARA[xli] – Scanning, Analysis, Response, and Assessment.

Confidential Informant (CI) - A person who is a source of information for law enforcement. This person is afforded anonymity, and may engage in criminal activity under the control and direction of a law enforcement official. After vetting a potential CI for motives and background, if approved and selected for use, a written contract typically is entered into with the CI, establishing rules of operation and potential remuneration for their services. Some agencies rank CI's by sensitivity or duration of use. CI's are usually reviewed and re-approved periodically. Some agencies will not have CI's testify or be exposed, while other agencies allow for this and establish this in the CI contract.

Concealed Carry - A term used to describe the authorization of a person to carry a concealed firearm on their person, usually after securing a permit from the state or locality in which they reside. In 2017, 42 states allowed concealed carry with a permit, while 8 states allowed concealed carry without a permit.

Constitutional Carry - A term used to describe the authorization of a person to carry a concealed firearm or open carry firearm without any permitting requirement as long as the person is not otherwise prohibited from possessing firearms and ammunition. Also known as permit-less carry, in 2017 this was allowed in 7 states: Alaska, Arizona, Idaho, Kansas, Maine, Vermont, West Virginia, and Wyoming.

Constructed Sale - A term for the creation of a fraudulent sale history between the cost of a firearm at point of import or manufacture and the first retail sale. The Firearm and Ammunition Excise Tax (FAET) is calculated on the gross profit between those two costs. Under-reporting that profit via a constructed sale agreement between two parties is an illegal business practice and a criminal fraud. This is also referred to as a fraudulently structured sale.

Constructive Possession - The concept that a person is considered to be in possession of an object (such as a firearm) even if they don't have actual physical possession on their person if they have had knowledge of the object as well as the ability to exercise authority, dominion, or control over the object. Constructive possession does not require physical possession or legal ownership.

Controlled Buy - A law enforcement term referring to a technique in which a confidential informant, acting under the direction and control of law enforcement, makes a purchase of evidence from a suspect.

Controlled Delivery - A law enforcement term referring to a technique in which intercepted firearms or narcotics constituting a violation of the law are delivered under the surveillance and control of law enforcement for the purpose of documenting their receipt by a suspect. A controlled delivery is usually followed by the suspect's arrest, particularly when firearms are the commodity.

Cooperating Witness (CW) - A source of information who may or may not be afforded anonymity, and who is usually cooperating under a written legal agreement with terms; sometimes the terms include consideration in a pending criminal case against the CW.

Cosmoline™ - A generic name used to describe rust-inhibiting grease used by the military to preserve firearms and parts. A trafficker may refer to surplus military firearms as "packed and wrapped in cosmoline".

Crime Gun - Any firearm that is illegally possessed, used in a crime, or suspected to have been used in a crime. This may include firearms found abandoned if it is suspected that these were used in a crime or were illegally possessed[xlii]. (NOTE: The ATF National Tracing Center only traces crime guns for law enforcement.)

Crime Gun Intelligence (CGI) - Intelligence produced through the analysis of all available information relating to firearms used in violent crime, and that provides timely actionable leads to the identification of shooters and the sources of their firearms for investigation and prosecution.

Crime Gun Intelligence Center (CGIC) - Led by ATF, and located in most major metropolitan areas, these are fusion-style inter-agency collaborations focused on rapid collection, management, and analysis of crime gun ballistics, trace and other forensics evidence, as well as human intelligence (HUMINT) produced in real time, for the purposes of identifying and apprehending shooters and the illegal traffickers who supply them with firearms; disrupting armed criminal activity; and preventing future armed violent crime.

Curios and Relics - Firearms that are of special interest to collectors by reason of some quality other than sporting use, or which have been recognized as curios or relics. (Title 27 C.F.R. § 478.11) To be deemed a curio or relic by ATF, a firearm must fall within one of the following categories:
➢ Firearms which were manufactured at least 50 years prior to the current date, not including replicas; or,
➢ Firearms which are certified by the curator of a municipal, state, or federal museum which exhibits firearms to be curios or relics of museum interest, and any other firearms which derive a substantial part of their monetary value from the fact that they are novel, rare, bizarre, or because of their association with some historical figure, period, or event. Proof of qualification of a particular firearm under this category may be established by evidence of present value and evidence that like firearms are not available except as collector's items, or that the value of like firearms available in ordinary commercial channels is substantially less. (NOTE: Curios or relics are still firearms subject to the provisions of the GCA; however, curio or relic firearms may be transferred in interstate commerce to licensed collectors or other licensees.)

DEA Internet Connectivity Endeavor (DICE)[xliii] - A database focused on consolidation and coordination by using an automated deconfliction system to help make connections between disparate bits of information, such as telephone numbers, e-mail addresses, bank account numbers, physical addresses, and license plate numbers. DICE allows federal, state and local agencies to load their own information and deconflict it among themselves and also to determine if any other agencies have interest in the same or similar information.

Deconfliction - The process of coordination and information sharing among law enforcement agencies to maximize officer safety, the effectiveness of investigations, and the efficient use of resources, through the utilization of a system or process that informs agencies when they are investigating or have a shared interest in a given person, location, crime, or operational enforcement event. Deconfliction is **critical** in firearms trafficking investigations. Deconfliction prevents Blue on Blue scenarios in which two or more law enforcement agencies unknowingly confront each other in an enforcement operation. Numerous deconfliction systems are available to law enforcement and include: HIDTA NINJAS (High Intensity Drug Trafficking Areas Narcotics Joint Agency System), DICE, RissNet (Regional Information Sharing System Network) and various agency case management systems.

Defense Articles - Any item designated in the United States Munitions List, and any technical data regarding these items, including technical data recorded or stored in models, mockups, or other items that reveal technical data directly relating to items designated in Title 22 C.F.R. § 121.1 (U.S. Munitions List) or Title 27 C.F.R. § 447.21 (U.S. Munitions Import List). Defense articles also include forgings, castings, and other unfinished products, such as extrusions and machined bodies, that have reached a stage in manufacturing where they are clearly identifiable by mechanical properties, material composition, geometry, or function as defense articles.

Demilitarized (DEMIL) - A term used to describe the process of destroying a firearm or other type of weapon in order to eliminate its functional capabilities to the point where it may no longer be re-assembled for use as originally intended. This is also referred to as deactivation. DEMIL methods range from removal and destruction of critical features to total destruction by cutting, crushing, shredding, melting, burning, or other methods.

Deactivated War Trophy (DEWAT) - A term used to describe a firearm secured as a war trophy that has been rendered non-functioning in accordance with specific standards.

Double Action - A type of firing action whereby a single squeeze of the trigger both cocks and fires the weapon. Both pistols and revolvers may use this action. Some pistols shift from double action on the first shot to single action for each ensuing shot, as the action of the slide following firing cocks the hammer.

Drop-In Auto Sear - This device, also known as an "AR15 Auto Sear" or "Auto Sear II," is a small combination of parts designed and intended for use in quickly and easily converting AR15 variant rifles to automatically shoot more than one shot without manual reloading, by a single function of the trigger. As a result, ATF has classified the auto sear as a machine gun as defined by Title 26 U.S.C. § 5845(b).

Engaged in the Business - A person devoting time, attention, and labor to buying, selling, manufacturing, importing, repairing, or pawn brokering firearms as a regular course of trade or business with the "principal objective of livelihood and profit" through that labor. This does not include occasional sales and/or purchases of firearms for enhancement and/or disposition of a personal collection or for hobby. (Title 18 U.S.C. § 921(a)(21)(A) and Title 27 C.F.R. § 478.11)

El Paso Intelligence Center (EPIC) [xliv] - EPIC offers tactical, operational, and strategic intelligence support to federal, state, local, tribal, and international law enforcement organizations. The center provides access to information, with the opportunity to collaborate daily through exchanges with LE analysts and operators, as well as routine engagement with our federal, state, local, tribal, and international partners. EPIC also provides access to cutting-edge technology as well as deconfliction services. EPIC is a multi-agency fusion center maintained by DEA.

eTrace - A system that allows for the secure submission of recovered crime gun trace requests to ATF, and enables the user to receive trace results and perform analyses of the data, all via the Internet. eTrace is the most efficient way for domestic and international law enforcement to submit trace requests, receive data, and analyze their aggregate crime gun data[xlv].

Extradition - A state or nation making a request to another state or nation to turn over an individual for purposes of arrest, criminal trial, and/or punishment. The approval of such requests is based on existing law in the involved states and on treaties between the nations involved. Requests for extradition usually result in an extradition hearing in the state or nation where the suspect is located, and during such hearings the judge or magistrate will determine the identity of the person, the validity of the charges, and the legality of the proposed extradition based on existing laws or treaties. Article IV, Section 2, Clause 2 of the US Constitution[xlvi] provides for the following: A person charged in any state with treason, felony, or other crime, who shall flee from justice, and be found in another state, shall on demand of the executive authority of the state from which he fled, be delivered up, to be removed to the state having jurisdiction of the crime. Extradition frequently comes into play in firearms trafficking investigations, as suspects often operate across state lines and across national borders.

Federal Firearms Licensee (FFL) - Any person, partnership, or business entity holding a valid license issued by ATF under the authority of Title 18 U.S.C. Chapter 44 that allows them, or their employees, to "engage in the business" of dealing, manufacturing, importing, or repairing firearms. The term also includes those persons who are pawnbrokers dealing in firearms. By law, all FFLs must keep records of their firearms transactions. (Title 18 U.S.C. 921§ (a)(11)(B) and Title 27 C.F.R. § 478.11)

Financial Crime Enforcement Network (FinCEN)[xlvii] - FinCEN safeguards the financial system from illicit use, combats money laundering, and promotes national security through the collection, analysis, and dissemination of financial intelligence and strategic use of financial authorities. FinCEN carries out its mission by receiving and maintaining data on certain financial transactions, primarily those involving suspicious activity or large amounts of cash, and providing access to that information to approved users.

Firearm - Any weapon (including a starter gun) which will or is designed to, or may readily be converted to, expel a projectile by the action of an explosive; in addition, the frame or receiver of any such weapon, any firearm muffler or silencer, and any destructive device. The term does not include antique firearms. (Title 18 U.S.C. §921(a)(3))

Firearms and Explosives Excise Tax (FAET)[xlviii] - FAET is one of the manufacturers' excise taxes imposed under Chapter 32 of the Internal Revenue Code. The tax is imposed on the manufacture, production, importation, and sale of firearms, shells or cartridges. FAET was first imposed in 1919 and is currently enforced and collected by the United States Tax and Trade Bureau (TTB), a former division of ATF that remained in the Department of the Treasury when ATF was transferred to the Department of Justice in 2003. The Pitmann-Robertson Act of 1937 mandated that all revenue from FAET and related excise taxes be earmarked for hunting-related activities. The United States Fish and Wildlife Commission places this revenue in a trust fund that is administered on behalf of the states. (Title 26 U.S.C. § 4181(a); Title 27 C.F.R. § 53.61(a))

Firearm Castings - These are commonly blocks of metal in the shape of firearm receivers. They are considered receiver blanks and sometimes will be referred to as 80% receivers. They need milling, drilling, and finishing to become a functional firearm component subject to the GCA and NFA within the U.S. Types of firearms manufactured from castings include AR-15 and M-4 variant style rifles as well as numerous types of semi-automatic pistols.

Firearms Dealer - Any person (licensed or unlicensed) "engaged in the business" of dealing, manufacturing, importing, repairing, or pawn brokering firearms is a Firearms Dealer by definition. Title 18 U.S.C. 921 § (a)(11)(B) and Title 27 C.F.R. § 478.11)

Firearms Diversion - The movement of a firearm(s) out of lawful commerce and into the illegal marketplace, through an illegal method or for an illegal purpose. This definition includes international, interstate, and intrastate firearms trafficking; stolen firearms cases; illegal NFA weapon transfers; straw purchases; unlicensed transactions; and unrecorded or intentionally mis-recorded sales by a licensed manufacturer, retailer, or wholesaler/distributor. (NOTE: While all acts of trafficking are diversion, not all acts of diversion rise to the level of trafficking. If a convicted felon convinces a family member to straw purchase a single gun for him, it is an act of diversion that merits law enforcement attention, but it does not rise to the level of firearms trafficking as defined. By contrast, if several individuals repetitively straw purchase guns for criminal associates or supply a street gang with firearms, it would clearly constitute trafficking. Both examples would constitute violations of federal law[xlix].)

Firearm Flats - These are commonly flat pieces of metal with drilled holes and cut out blocks that, when the sides are folded up, becomes a lower firearm receiver that will accept and hold all of the internal components of the firearm. They are considered receiver blanks and sometimes will be referred to as 80% receivers. The types of firearms manufactured from flats are AK-47 variant style rifles and MAC-10 style pistols.

Firearm Parts Kit - Parts kits that are most often smuggled out of the country commonly consist of external and internal components of a firearm, minus the lower receiver which constitutes the actual firearm. These parts kits are not firearms under the GCA or NFA but they have everything needed to make a firearm once a lower receiver is obtained. Firearms castings and flats are used to make the lower receiver. Flats, castings, and firearm parts kits are easy to obtain in the U.S. since they are not actual firearms and therefore there are no records or questions asked to purchase these items. They are then illegally smuggled to cartels and gangs in Mexico as well as other Central and South American Countries where they are fully assembled into untraceable firearms. Although these are U.S. sourced firearms, they have no valid traceable markings and will never be attributed to being U.S. sourced through ATF trace data. Firearms parts kits that are most commonly being imported into the U.S. are comprised of the cut-up components of machine guns and other un-importable firearms. These firearms usually have some collectible, historical, or display trophy value (e.g., Sten Submachine guns) however it is illegal to import these fully functional firearms into the U.S. One solution to this is to cut up the firearm into non-functional parts which can then imported into the U.S. where persons may use the parts to re-assemble non-functional firearms or machine guns for display purposes only.

Firearms Trace - The tracking of a recovered crime gun's history, from its source (manufacturer/importer) through the chain of distribution (wholesaler/retailer), to the first non-licensed purchaser of the firearm. Firearms trace requests may be submitted to the ATF National Tracing Center on an ATF Form 3312.1, Crime Gun Information Request Form, via mail or fax, or electronically via eTrace for any law enforcement agency that has this system. (See eTrace for additional information[l].)

Firearms Trafficking - Unlawful firearms diversion done for the purpose of profit, power, or prestige, in furtherance of other criminal acts or terrorism[li]. Several slang terms exist for firearms trafficking, including "gun running", "contraband capitalism", and "merchants of death".

Firearms Trafficking Corridor - A route of transportation that is frequently used by firearms traffickers to transport/move firearms from a source area to a market area. This may include interstate highways, railways or air routes, as well as the U.S. mail and other common carriers such as UPS, DHL, and FedEx[lii]. Slang terms used to describe a firearm trafficking corridor is "Iron Pipeline" and "Full-Metal Freeway". For example, I-95 runs from source areas such as Florida, Georgia, and South Carolina north to market areas such as Baltimore, Philadelphia, Newark, and New York City. I-95 is a known interstate highway trafficking corridor. An example of an air route firearms trafficking corridor runs from Orlando, Florida to San Juan, Puerto Rico. Numerous firearms are purchased in Florida and placed in the US Mail or in the checked bags on an airline and flown to San Juan, PR where they are illegally sold on the street.

Firearms Trafficking Gateway - A border crossing point, port of entry, airport, bus terminal, or train station that firearm traffickers frequently pass through when transporting firearms from a source area to a market area[liii]. For example, a border crossing on the southwest border that has a high incidence or firearms and firearms parts kits smuggling via a variety of concealment methods.

Firearms Trafficking Indicator - An event(s) that cues an investigator to take preliminary investigative steps to determine all the facts surrounding that event and determine if a full criminal investigation is warranted. This may include a person associated with multiple firearms traces, short time to crime traces, numerous multiple sales, or numerous reports of firearms thefts. The presence of one or more indicators alone does not prove that firearm trafficking is taking place but indicators are leads that should be further examined.

Flash Suppressor - A device attached to the muzzle of a rifle that, during firing, reduces its visible flash by dispersing the burning gases that exit the muzzle.

Flea Market - A one-time or recurring event having a primary purpose of providing a public exhibition, forum, or marketplace for general merchandise, secondhand articles, antiques, and other miscellaneous commercial goods other than firearms but whose merchandise may include firearms, ammunition, and firearms accessories. A flea market is not a gun show.
(Title 27 C.F.R.§ 478.100(b) (2005))

Full-Metal Freeway - A slang term for a firearm trafficking corridor, often used to describe highways due to the movement of firearms on the highway from southern source areas to northern market areas. (See firearms trafficking corridor for more information.)

Fully-Automatic Firearm - A firearm that fires more than one round, automatically reloading and firing continuously with one depression of the trigger. (See machinegun for more information.)

Gun Show - An event or function sponsored by any national, state, or local organization devoted to the collection, competitive use, or other sporting use of firearms, or an organization or association that sponsors functions devoted to the collection, competitive use, or other sporting use of firearms in the community. A flea market is not a gun show. (Title 27 C.F.R.§ 478.100(b) (2005))

Gun Show Loophole - A term used by to describe the means by which private firearms sellers manage to transfer firearms to other persons without having to identify the purchaser or conduct a background check. Only FFLs are required to record all transactions and conduct background checks through the National Instant Criminal Background Check System.

Ghost Gun - A slang term used to refer to a firearm manufactured outside the chain of the licensed firearms industry, making the firearm untraceable—a ghost. Ghost guns are also associated with the terms "unfinished receivers" and "80% receivers". Ghost guns can be milled out using ghost gun "boxes" that are loaded by CAD (computer-aided drafting) plans for certain firearms like an AR-15. Other ghost guns come pre-formed with a special jig designed to hold the unfinished receiver, allowing the purchaser the ability to drill all the necessary holes to make the receiver functional as a firearm. Many ghost guns have no markings of any kind, while others have the appearance of brand name guns with serial numbers; however, the numbers are not real and are not traceable as the guns were not made by the real manufacturers and logged into their records. These are counterfeit knock-offs. There are numerous websites that sell ghost gun boxes, CAD plans for firearms, and other kits with jigs, for anyone to manufacture their own untraceable firearms in the style of virtually every known commercially manufactured firearm.

Handgun - A firearm which has a short stock and is designed to be held and fired by the use of a single hand, and any combination of parts from which a handgun can be assembled. (Title 18 U.S.C. § 921 (a)(29)(A) and (B)).

Incomplete Receiver - This is a term used to describe forgings, castings, or machined bodies which have been partially milled or modified and are classified as firearms but are not fully machined or modified to the point of functionality as firearms receivers.

Inspection Warrant – A document permitting the conduct an FFL inspection in those instances in which a special agent has less than probable cause but more than mere suspicion to believe that evidence of a violation of 18 U.S.C. Chapter 44 exists on the premises of an FFL. It may also be used when a licensee will not permit an authorized warrantless inspection. An inspection warrant is obtained under ATF's statutory authority contained in the Gun Control Act (Title 18 U.S.C. § 923(g)).

Intelligence Led Policing[liv] **(ILP)** - Intelligence-led policing is a business model and managerial philosophy where data analysis and crime intelligence are pivotal to an objective, decision-making framework that facilitates crime and problem reduction, disruption and prevention through both strategic management and effective enforcement strategies that target prolific and serious offenders.

International Association of Chiefs of Police™ (IACP) [lv] - Founded in 1893, the association comprised of law enforcement executives works to advance the science and art of police services; to develop and disseminate improved administrative, technical and operational practices and promote their use in police work; to foster police cooperation and the exchange of information and experience among police administrators throughout the world; to bring about recruitment and training in the police profession of qualified persons; and to encourage adherence of all police officers to high professional standards of performance and conduct.

International Firearms Tracing Program[lvi] - An ATF program that handles requests from foreign law enforcement agencies; contacts foreign dealers in order to obtain firearm disposition information; and promotes comprehensive firearms tracing through training, firearm vault reviews, and the expansion of eTrace among ATF's foreign law enforcement partners in conjunction with the US Department of State, and INTERPOL.

International Criminal Police Organization® (INTERPOL)[lvii] - An international organization that facilitates police enforcement actions, investigations, and intelligence activities between law enforcement agencies in different countries.

Illicit Arms Records and Tracing Management System (iARMS) - The iARMS system, operated by INTERPOL, facilitates information exchange and investigative cooperation among law enforcement agencies in relation to the international movement of illicit firearms, as well as licit firearms that have been involved in the commission of a crime.

Interstate Nexus - An element of proof in many Title 18 criminal firearm violations which involves establishing that a recovered crime gun previously moved in or affecting interstate or foreign commerce (Title 18 U.S.C. § 921 (a)(2)).

Iron Pipeline - A slang term for a firearm trafficking corridor, often used to describe Interstate-95 due to the movement of firearms up the highway from southern source areas to northern market areas. (See firearms trafficking corridor for more information.)

Lawful but Awful - A slang term used to refer to any ATF rulings that make certain types of firearms or firearms parts lawful, even though many in law enforcement may find them to be awful. The bump slide and other multi-burst trigger activators, when first ruled legal by ATF, were considered lawful but awful firearm parts. Currently there are AR15 and AK47 pistols with forearm braces as well as tactical shotgun pistols which some place into the category of lawful but awful.

LEAD[lviii] - ATF's automated firearms trafficking information system that provides investigative leads to investigators by analyzing crime gun trace data, suspect gun information, stolen firearms information, and multiple sales information to identify recurring trends and patterns that may indicate firearms trafficking. LEAD is not an acronym and simply refers to an investigative lead. LEAD is available in ATF's eTrace.

LeadsOnline - A commercial database that has access to large volumes of pawn records, including the pawn of firearms. Firearms tracing traces a firearm to the first retail sale. Once a firearm is sold privately or pawned, the ATF Firearms trace may or may not be able to document that movement in the secondary source market. LeadsOnline may contain information on a firearms movement in the secondary source market.

Lend Lease Gun - A lend lease gun is a firearm that was part of the lend lease act of 1941. That act was the principal means for allowing the lending of U.S. military aid and supplies to foreign nations who were allies during World War II. In exchange for the U.S. lending military aid and supplies to these foreign nations, that country would guarantee a land lease to the U.S. for the placement of a military base. Millions of firearms were provided to foreign nations under this program, including Smith and Wesson Victory Revolvers, Savage Enfield 303 Rifles, M1Garand Rifles, and 1911A1 .45 caliber pistols, Browning Automatic Rifles, and Thompson Submachine

Guns. Regulations related to the act are meant to shield U.S. small-arms makers from foreign competition by prohibiting the re-import of these U.S. made military firearms unless they are being sold to the U.S. government, a law enforcement agency, or if the weapons are 50 or more years old and qualify as a Curios and Relics.

Lever Action - A breech-loading action using a lever mechanism to pull back the bolt to expose the breech or chamber area. Manually operating the lever mechanism opens the breech and extracts, then ejects each fired shell case from the chamber. In certain firearms, the lever mechanism also chambers a loaded cartridge in preparation for the next shot.

Lie and Buy - A slang term for a firearm purchase transaction where the purchaser lies in response to questions on the ATF Form 4473 in order to be able to secure a firearm from the FFL. The purchaser may lie about their status as someone prohibited from possessing a firearm or they may lie about their address or the true intended recipient of the firearm. The lie is most often about a material fact relative to the person's lawful ability to purchase and possess the firearm. The lie successfully enables the purchaser to make the gun buy.

Lie and Try - A slang term for an attempted firearm purchase transaction where the purchaser lies in response to questions on the ATF Form 4473 while attempting to secure a firearm from the FFL, only to be denied the purchase by the FFL or because they fail the criminal background check. The purchaser may lie about their status as someone prohibited from possessing a firearm or they may lie about their address or the true intended recipient of the firearm. The lie is most often about a material fact relative to the person's lawful ability to purchase and possess the firearm. The lie is unsuccessful and the purchaser fails in their try.

Lightning Link - This device, also known as an "Auto Dis-connector" or "Auto Connector" is a small L-shaped piece of slotted metal manufactured by SWD of Atlanta, GA and is designed and intended for use in quickly and easily converting AR15 variant rifles to shoot automatically more than one shot, without manual reloading, by a single function of the trigger. As a result, ATF has classified the auto sear as a machine gun as defined by Title 26 U.S.C. § 5845(b).

Lure - A law enforcement tactic where a person is enticed or invited to appear at a location for the purpose of apprehending them. Prior approval from DOJ is required if the lure involves causing a foreign citizen to travel to the U.S. for the purpose of their arrest, and several conditions must exist to secure DOJ approval. (More information is available in Chapter 5, Applicable Laws and Legal Information.)

Magazine - An ammunition storage and feeding device within or attached to a repeating firearm. Magazines may be integral to the firearm (fixed) or removable (detachable). The magazine functions by moving the cartridges stored in the magazine into a position where they may be loaded into the chamber by the action of the firearm.

Figure 2.3 *Magazine*
IMAGE CREDIT: *Author*

Malum in Se - A Latin phrase meaning "wrong or evil in itself," and referring to conduct assessed as sinful or inherently wrong by nature, independent of regulations governing the conduct, such as murder or robbery.

Malum Prohibitum - A Latin phrase referring to conduct that constitutes an unlawful act only by virtue of statute, such as regulatory violations.

Market Area [lix] - An area where firearms acquired in a source area are unlawfully marketed and/or transferred to the criminal element/prohibited persons/juveniles. Factors that foster a market area include lack of FFLs/flea markets/gun shows in an area and strict or thorough state/local gun laws that limit firearms possession and availability. (NOTE: A market area's source may be in the same city/county/state or it may be in a different city/county/state.)

Machine Gun - Any weapon which shoots, is designed to shoot, or can be readily restored to shoot automatically more than one shot, without manual reloading, by a single function of the trigger as well as the frame or receiver of any such weapon, any part designed and intended solely and exclusively, or combination of parts designed and intended for use in converting a weapon into a machinegun, and any combination of parts from which a machinegun can be assembled if such parts are in the possession of or under the control of the person. Slang terms used to describe machineguns include "Chopper" (chops people down), "Gat" (Gatlin Gun), and "Sandman" (puts people to sleep). (Title 26 U.S.C. § 5845(b); Title 18 U.S.C. § 921(a) (23); Title 27 C.F.R. § 478.11, 479.11)

Money Laundering - The investment or transfer of money from unlawful activities or sources into legitimate channels so that its original source cannot be traced. Firearms trafficking is a specified unlawful activity (SUA) for purposes of money laundering statutes. (Title 18 U.S.C. § 1956(c)(7))

Multi-Burst Trigger Activator - A device that affixes to a firearm trigger guard area, frame or receiver, or stock area and allows a semi-automatic firearm to fire at a rate approaching that of fully automatic firearms. All of the devices enhance the rate of speed at which the trigger is pulled. The trigger is still pulled once for each bullet fired therefore not violating the definition of a machinegun in federal law. Devices that attach to the trigger area include brand names such as "The GAT™" and "Hell-Fire™". Devices that attach to the stock area include brand names such as "Bump Slide™" and "Bump Stock". Devices that attach to the frame or receiver include binary trigger systems that cause a bullet to fire with a trigger pull and fire another bullet with the trigger release creating a simulated two-round burst. A slang term used to describe this category of device is "Full-Auto Viagra". In 2010 ATF issued a ruling that these devices did not constitute an illegal machine gun; however, in 2018 the Trump Administration directed ATF to revisit this ruling and that process is underway.

Mutual Legal Assistance Treaty (MLAT) - An agreement between two or more nations for the purpose of gathering and exchanging information in an effort to investigate criminal violations and enforce criminal laws. Most modern nations have developed mechanisms for requesting and obtaining evidence for criminal investigations and prosecutions.

Narcotics and Dangerous Drugs Information System (NADDIS) [lx] - A data pointer index and collection system operated by DEA that contains all DEA investigative reports and records on individuals. NADDIS is a system by which intelligence analysts, investigators and others in law enforcement retrieve reports from the DEA's Investigative Filing and Reporting System.

National Crime Information Center (NCIC) Gun File [lxi] - This file is 1 of 21 files in the NCIC system, and contains data on stolen, lost, and firearms recovered (seized, purchased, recovered, abandoned, retained) by any law enforcement agency. This information includes the date and location of recovery and the recovering agency. Recovered guns can be stolen guns or guns that have not been reported stolen. Entry of recovered firearms into this file is voluntary. Recovered stolen firearms remain in the file until the agency reporting the theft removes the file. Non-stolen firearm recovery entries are automatically purged 3 years after entry. NCIC is maintained by the Federal Bureau of Investigation (FBI).

National Firearms Registration and Transfer Record (NFRTR) - A registry maintained by ATF that includes the name, address, personal identification information, photograph, and fingerprints of individuals who possess NFRTR weapons. The system also contains all identifying information concerning the NFRTR weapon owned/transferred by the individual. NFRTR weapons include machine guns, silencers, pen guns, short-barreled rifles, and shotguns, as well as destructive devices (Title 26 U.S.C. § 5841). The NFRTR is maintained by ATF. ATF special agents and investigators may request a record search to obtain a certification as to the registration status of a weapon or the existence of registered weapons by calling the NFRTR Branch. Because the registration relates to tax information, disclosure of the information is strictly limited by the provisions of Title 26 U.S.C. § 6103.

National Instant Criminal Background Check System (NICS)[lxii] - A national records system, operated by the FBI, that checks the background of every unlicensed person during the process of acquiring a firearm from an FFL, for the purpose of preventing prohibited persons from acquiring firearms illegally. NICS is maintained by the FBI. (Title 18 U.S.C. § 922(t); Title 28 C.F.R. Part 25)

National Integrated Ballistics Identification Network (NIBIN) [lxiii] - An interstate automated ballistic imaging network in operation in the U.S., maintained by ATF and available to most major population centers with a crime laboratory. The NIBIN system maintains images of spent bullet casings and projectiles recovered at crime scenes as well as test-fired casings and projectiles from recovered crime guns, and compares the images for matches. The system automates ballistics evaluations and provides actionable investigative leads in a timely manner. NIBIN is the network that links the Integrated Ballistics Identification System™ (IBIS) systems produced by Forensic Technology Inc.™ (FTI) and used in major cities.

National Tracing Center (NTC)[lxiv] - Maintained by ATF, this is the only facility/operation in the world that traces the history of recovered crime guns for any international, federal, state, or local law enforcement agency. In addition to crime gun trace data the NTC stores information concerning the multiple sale of firearms, suspect guns, stolen firearms, and firearms with obliterated serial numbers. It is the only repository for all FFL out-of-business records.

New-In-The-Box - A slang term used by firearms traffickers or purchasers to describe firearms that are unused, clean, and relatively new, and unlikely to have a body on it. A slang phrase used to describe good condition military firearms is "packed and wrapped in Cosmoline".

NFA Gun Trust - A trust established for the purpose of purchasing NFA firearms (machine guns, silencers, short barreled rifles/shotguns, destructive devices, and any other weapons) and having them registered in the name of the trust rather than a person. Multiple persons can be members of the trust and possess/use the NFA weapon(s). The NFA Gun Trust was previously referred to as a "loophole" by some. However, in January 2016 the U.S. Attorney General signed ATF Final Rule 41F requiring that a Chief Law Enforcement Official sign the application forms and that all members of the NFA Trust be listed as responsible persons and be subject to criminal background checks.

Notice of Unlicensed Firearms Dealing Violation - A form letter served by a criminal investigator on an individual knowingly or unknowingly engaged in the business of dealing in firearms without a license. Service of this notice satisfies the "knowingly/willfully" element of proof in an unlicensed firearm dealing investigation for an individual who continues to engage in unlicensed firearms dealing practices after being served notice. Notice letters help bring unknowing dealers into cooperative compliance and provide a stronger criminal case against those who continue to violate the law after being warned and informed as to how to comply. (See example in Figure 10.6.)

Notice of Straw Purchase Violation - A form letter served by a criminal investigator on an individual knowingly or unknowingly engaged in straw purchases of firearms. Service of this notice satisfies the "knowingly/willfully" element of proof required in a straw purchase investigation. Notice letters help bring straw purchasers into cooperative compliance with the law and provide for a stronger criminal case against those who continue to violate the law after being warned and informed as to how to comply. See example in Figure 10.7.

Open Carry - A term used to describe the authorization of a person to openly carry a firearm on their person in public. This is also known as plain sight carry. In 2017, this was allowed without a permit in 25 states; it is allowed without a permit in certain areas of 7 other states; and it is allowed with a permit in 16 other states.

Out of Business Records Center (OOB) [lxv]- An ATF repository that warehouses all the records of FFLs who have gone out of business. FFLs are required by law to provide their records to ATF upon going out of business. The records are placed on microfilm, catalogued, and stored for later use to complete crime gun trace requests. It is against federal law for ATF to place this information in a computer database.

Pocket Litter - A law enforcement term used to refer to material that accumulates in an individual's pockets, including scraps of paper containing names, phone numbers, and other notes, identity cards, business cards, transportation tickets, personal photographs, receipts for firearms purchases, money order stubs, drug wrappers with residue, thumb drives, and similar material. When a person is arrested, this information is taken into custody by law enforcement where is can be analyzed and exploited for potentially important intelligence and leads.

Point of Contact (POC)[lxvi] - A state or local law enforcement agency that has chosen to serve as an intermediary between an FFL and the federal databases checked by NICS. A POC performs a records/background check on every unlicensed person during the process of acquiring a firearm from an FFL, for the purpose of preventing prohibited persons from acquiring firearms illegally.

Principal Objective of Livelihood and Profit - The intent of the sale or disposition of firearms is predominantly one of obtaining livelihood and pecuniary gain, as opposed to other intents, such as liquidating a personal firearm collection. (See Title 18 U.S.C. § 921(a) (22)) (More information is available in Chapter 5, Applicable Laws and Legal Information.)

Probable Cause Warrant - A type of warrant that may be obtained for the premises of an FFL when a special agent has probable cause to believe that evidence of a violation of law exists on those premises. This type of warrant may be used to secure records. A probable cause warrant may be obtained pursuant to Rule 41 of the Federal Rules of Criminal procedure.

Prohibited Person - Someone who is falls into 1 of 9 categories of persons prohibited by federal law from purchasing or possessing a firearm or ammunition, including: previously convicted felons; persons unlawfully using or addicted to drugs; persons who have been adjudicated as mentally ill or committed to a mental institution by a court against their will; persons dishonorably discharged from the armed services; illegal aliens and non-immigrant aliens; persons under court issued restraining order for stalking, harassing, or threatening an intimate partner or child of that partner; and persons with domestic violence related misdemeanor convictions. (See Title 18 U.S.C. § 922(g).)

Pump Action - An action manually operated by means of a forearm slide. The sliding forearm or mechanism is mechanically linked to the breech block. Manually operating the sliding forearm or mechanism in a back-and-forth action opens and closes the breech, cocks the firearm, and loads a cartridge into the chamber. This back-and-forth action is also used to extract and eject each shell case from the chamber area and must be repeated prior to each firing.

Reasonable Cause Warrant (for an FFL) - May be obtained to conduct an FFL inspection when a special agent has less than probable cause but more than mere suspicion to believe that evidence of a violation of Title 18 U.S.C. Chapter 44 exists on the premises of an FFL. It may also be used when a licensee will not permit an authorized warrantless inspection.

Receiver - This is a term used to describe a functional firearm frame or receiver. A functional frame or receiver is classified as a firearm.

Receiver Blank - This is a term used to describe forgings, castings, or machined bodies such as AR15 receiver castings, AK47 receiver flats, or unfinished polymer pistol receiver. These items are not classified as firearms. The firearms industry, firearms hobbyists and enthusiasts, as well the trafficking sub-culture often refer to receiver blanks as "80% receivers".

Reverse - A law enforcement term referring to a tactic where law enforcement, acting in an undercover capacity, is supplying an illegal item to a suspect which will, at some point, be followed by their arrest. This sensitive tactic, also known as a sting, requires significant supervisory oversight to ensure that entrapment is not an issue. Usually the suspect is arrested following the transfer of the item, especially if that item is a firearm, as the firearm should not be allowed to leave the area of the transfer controlled by law enforcement.

Rifle - A weapon designed or redesigned, made or remade, which is intended to be fired from the shoulder and is designed or redesigned and made or remade to use the energy of an explosive to fire only a single projectile through a rifled bore for each single pull of the trigger. (Title 18 U.S.C. § 921 (a)(7))

Ring-of-Fire - A term that refers to a group of firearms manufacturers that were located in a geographic ring in southern California and includes brand names such as Davis Industries, Jennings Firearms, Bryco Arms, Lorcin Engineering Co, Raven Arms, Phoenix Arms, Arcadia

Machine & Tool (AMT), Jimenez, and Sundance. The firearms produced were inexpensive small-caliber concealable semi-automatic pistols.

Rip - A law enforcement term referring to a tactic in which law enforcement intercepts an item which is either contraband or proceeds of an illegal act and the take the item into law enforcement custody without alerting the suspect that law enforcement has taken the item. The suspect will assume they have been "ripped-off", the investigation continues, and the suspect will be arrested at a later date. Illegally shipped firearms may be ripped before the end user suspect obtains them so that an investigation can continue without allowing firearms to enter the public domain in the hands of the suspect. There must be probable cause to support a legal forfeiture of any item to be "ripped".

Ruse - A law enforcement term referring to a tactic in which law enforcement uses a planned action to deceive a suspect in order to gain tactical or investigative surprise or advantage. A ruse is often used to lure a wanted person to a location where it will be safer to apprehend them.

Secondary Source Market [lxvii]- A source of firearms that may be legal or illegal. Secondary sources often include gun shows, flea markets, pawnshops, internet sale and auction sites, and unlicensed/private sales and transfers. Secondary source firearms are more difficult to trace due to multiple unrecorded transfers or breaks in the transaction history paper trail of the firearm.

Semi-Automatic Firearm - Any repeating rifle which utilizes a portion of the energy of a firing cartridge to extract the fired cartridge case and chamber the next round, and which requires a separate pull of the trigger to fire each cartridge. (Title 18 U.S.C. § 921 (a) (28))

Serial Number - A unique number conspicuously affixed to the frame or receiver of each firearm manufactured or imported into the US, as required by the GCA of 1968. Firearms traffickers may sometime obliterate the serial number in an attempt to defeat the ability to trace the firearm.

Short-Barreled Rifle - A rifle having a barrel or barrels of less than 16 inches in length or an overall length of less than 26 inches. Also known as a sawed-off rifle or SBR. (Title 18 U.S.C. § 921 (a)(8))

Short-Barreled Shotgun - A shotgun having a barrel or barrels of less than 18 inches in length or an overall length of less than 26 inches. Also known as a sawed-off shotgun. (Title 18 U.S.C. § 921 (a)(6))

Shotgun - A weapon designed or redesigned, made or remade, and intended to be fired from the shoulder and designed or redesigned and made or remade to use the energy of an explosive to fire through a smooth bore either a number of ball shot or a single projectile for each single pull of the trigger. (Title 18 U.S.C. § 921 (a)(5))

Silencer - Any device for silencing, muffling, or diminishing the report of a portable firearm, including any combination of parts, designed or redesigned, and intended for use in assembling or fabricating a firearm silencer or firearm muffler, and any part intended only for use in such assembly or fabrication. (Title 18 U.S.C. § 921 (a) (24)) Also known as muffler and suppressor.

Single Action - A type of firing action that requires the firearm to be manually cocked before firing. This action is associated with some revolvers where the hammer must be manually cocked for each shot. The term also applies to some semiautomatic pistols where the recoil action of the firearm re-cocks the hammer after each discharge.

Source Area [lxviii]- An area where firearms traffickers have easy access to large numbers of firearms they can readily acquire and transport to other locations for unlawful resale and transfer to criminals, prohibited persons, and juveniles. Factors that foster a source area include an abundance of FFLs, flea markets, and gun shows in the area, relaxed or nonexistent state and local gun laws, and proximity to urban centers or other locations where guns are sought commodities.

Source of Information - A person who provides information to law enforcement but who is not involved in criminal activity themselves. They may or may not want anonymity; however, they do not rise to the level of a confidential informant and will not be taking actions at the direction of law enforcement.

Stabilizer Brace - A stabilizing brace, also known as a forearm stabilizer or stabilizing blade is a device that attaches to the buffer tube protruding from the rear of a pistol and braces against the forearm of the user to facilitate one-handed firing.

Sting - A law enforcement term referring to a tactic in which law enforcement is posing in an undercover capacity as a victim or a criminal for the purpose of engaging others involved in criminal activity to make an approach to the undercover and engage in a criminal act. This is a sensitive tactic that requires significant supervisory oversight to prevent entrapment issues.

Storefront - A law enforcement term referring to a tactic involving a long-term sting operation in which law enforcement is posing in an undercover capacity as a store that also conducts illegal activity (e.g., purchases stolen goods, firearms, narcotics). This is a sensitive tactic that requires significant supervisory oversight to ensure proper planning is involved in locating the storefront, maintaining and administering the storefront to prevent any safety or entrapment issues, and to ensure the storefront does not generate additional crime in the area, such as an increase in burglaries and thefts.

Stolen Firearms Database - A database maintained by ATF's NTC containing information relating to ALL firearms thefts from FFLs as well as thefts of firearms from interstate carriers and the military. Under Title 18 U.S.C. § 923(g)(6), FFLs must report any theft or loss of firearms from their inventory or from an interstate shipment to ATF within 48 hours after the theft or loss is discovered.

Straw Purchase - The acquisition of a firearm(s) from a federally licensed firearms dealer by an individual (the "straw"), done for the purpose of concealing the identity of the true intended receiver of the firearm(s).

Sub-Machinegun - A machine gun that fires pistol ammunition. (See Machine Gun for full definition.)

Suspect Gun [lxix]- An unrecovered firearm(s) that is suspected to have been illegally trafficked or diverted. For example, multiple sales reports and FFL records indicate that an individual has purchased 25 firearms, 15 of which have been recovered in crimes, traced, and entered into

LEAD; however, 10 of the 25 have not been recovered. Therefore, they are entered into the Firearms Recovery Notification Program as it is suspected that these remaining firearms have also been illegally trafficked.

Suspect Person [lxx]- An individual that is under active criminal investigation and is suspected to be illegally possessing, using, or trafficking firearms.

Switch - This device, also known as an "Glock Switch" is a small metal device that, without any tools, can be affixed in seconds to a handgun to convert the handgun to fire as a machine gun. There are switches available for numerous types of semi-automatic pistols, including Glock and Berretta. Because they convert handguns to shoot automatically more than one shot, without manual reloading, by a single function of the trigger, ATF has classified the auto-sear as a machine gun as defined by Title 26 U.S.C. § 5845(b).

Figure 2.4 Glock Switch

IMAGE CREDIT: www.atf.gov

Transnational Organized Crime (TOC) - A term used to describe organized crime coordinated across national borders, involving groups or networks of individuals working in more than one country to plan and execute illegal business ventures. In order to achieve their goals, these criminal groups use systematic violence and corruption.

Time-to-Crime[lxxi] - The number of days between the acquisition of a firearm from a retail market and the first known use of that firearm in a crime. The date of the first known use may not be the same day the firearm is recovered by law enforcement. Prior use of a firearm in a crime may be determined through forensic exams such as a ballistic hit in NIBIN, a confession, or a witness statement.

Time-to-Recovery[lxxii] - The number of days between the acquisition of a firearm from a retail market and law enforcement's recovery of that firearm. A short time to crime usually means the firearm will be easier to trace; however, it is not necessarily an indicator of firearms trafficking. When several short time-to-crime traces involve the same individual or FFL, or when a short time-to-crime trace is coupled with multiple sales information, this may be an indication of illegal trafficking activity.

Time to Sale [lxxiii]- The number of days between a retail FFL's receipt of a firearm and the sale or transfer of that firearm. A short time to sale, particularly when a number of inexpensive or identical handguns are involved, may indicate the federally licensed firearms dealer is specifically ordering the firearms at the request of an illegal trafficker or is directly involved with illegal trafficking.

Treasury Enforcement Communications System (TECS)[lxxiv] - A system now maintained by the Department of Homeland Security, TECS is a computerized information system designed to identify individuals and businesses suspected of or involved in violation of federal law. TECS is also a communications system permitting message transmittal between Treasury law enforcement offices and other national, state, and local law enforcement agencies. TECS provides access to the FBI's National Crime Information Center (NCIC) and the National Law Enforcement Telecommunication Systems (NLETS), and has the capability of communicating directly with state and local enforcement agencies. NLETS provides direct access to state motor vehicle departments.

Trip - A law enforcement term referring to a situation in which an undercover officer and/or confidential informant leaves a controlled location and travels with or at the request of the suspect(s) to another location. Tripping is usually discouraged or even prohibited due to an increase in safety risks posed by new and unknown locations that have not yet been scouted or secured by a surveillance and react team.

Undercover (UC) - A law enforcement term referring to a tactic in which a law enforcement official poses as someone other than a law enforcement official in order to engage suspects of a criminal investigation and gather evidence of criminal violations. Undercover operations carry significant safety risks and must only be performed by authorized law enforcement officers who are properly supervised, from the level of identity backstopping for the undercover persona, to the tactical considerations for safely monitoring an undercover operation and rescuing the undercover with a react team at a moment's notice.

U.S. Munitions List (USML) - A list of articles, services, and related technology designated as defense and space-related by the U.S. Federal Government. This designation is pursuant to sections 38 and 47(7) of the Arms Export Control Act (Title 22 U.S.C. §§ 2778 and 2794(7)). These articles fall under the export and temporary import jurisdiction of the Department of State. There are 21 categories on the USML, and the first 3 deal with firearms and ammunition (Title 22 C.F.R. § 121.1).

U.S. Munitions Import List (USMIL) - A list of articles, services, and related technology designated as defense and space-related by the U.S. Federal Government. This designation is pursuant to sections of the AECA. These articles fall under the permanent import jurisdiction of the several federal agencies. There are 21 categories on the USMIL, and the first 3 deal with firearms and ammunition (Title 27 C.F.R. § 447).

Vertical Prosecution - The assignment of one prosecutor to handle a case from intake to prosecution and through the appeals process. This is a law enforcement best practice for complex firearms trafficking or armed violent gang cases.

Walk - A law enforcement term referring to a tactic in which law enforcement officials allow a person or item to leave an area that is under the control of law enforcement. This may mean allowing a suspect to leave an area after an undercover purchase of narcotics from the suspect. This may also mean allowing a suspect to leave an area after they purchased an item from a law enforcement official or confidential informant acting at the direction of a law enforcement official. The act of walking certain items is sensitive and may be prohibited, depending on the type of item. No law enforcement agency should walk a firearm as this would endanger public safety. (NOTE: Allowing a suspect to leave with an item while under full surveillance and with a bona fide plan to arrest the suspect and regain control of the item, with no break in surveillance, is not considered a walk because law enforcement has not let the item be removed from surveillance, and plans to recover the item.)

Wall-Off – A law enforcement technique used to protect a larger investigation from compromise by conducting a planned arrest of an investigative target using probable cause or evidence collected and developed independently from the larger investigation. Often times a car stop by a local police office will be used to accomplish this. A car stop by a local police officer for this purpose is referred to as a wall-stop.

Witness Device – A term used to describe those electronic devices that witness and record the images or sound/conversation of criminal activity. The world is not full of witness devices and there are often more electronic witness devices that observe crime than real life witnesses.

Chapter 3
Basic Firearms Safety and Nomenclature

This is my rifle. There are many like it, but this one is mine. My rifle is my best friend. It is my life. I must master it as I must master my life. Without me, my rifle is useless. Without my rifle, I am useless. I must fire my rifle true. I must shoot straighter than my enemy who is trying to kill me. I must shoot him before he shoots me. I will....
Excerpt from the Rifleman's Creed, written in 1941 by United States Marine Corp
Major General William H. Rupertus.

Firearms trafficking investigators are absolutely going to be recovering, handling, and identifying firearms. It is imperative that all investigators have a thorough understanding of firearms handling and safety measures as well as a basic understanding of firearms nomenclature.

FIREARMS SAFETY 101

The following firearms safety protocols are something every investigator must commit to memory and follow when they are processing a recovered firearm.

✓ Treat EVERY firearm as if it is loaded.

✓ If you are unfamiliar with a firearm, do not attempt to clear it yourself. Ask for help from someone who is familiar with the firearm.

✓ ALWAYS keep your finger off the trigger and outside the trigger guard.

✓ ALWAYS keep the muzzle pointed in a safe direction throughout the entire clearing process. Use a firearm clearing containment device whenever available. Place the firearm muzzle in the device so that any unintentional discharge will be contained.

✓ Remove the magazine or source of ammunition before manipulating the firearm in any way. Magazine releases are found in different locations on different firearms. Remember that even with the magazine removed there may be a round of ammunition in the chamber that can still fire.

✓ Pull back the slide, open the breech to eject any remaining round, and then visually and physically inspect the chamber to ensure that the firearm is completely unloaded.

✓ If the firearm will be maintained as evidence, locate and activate the safety. For firearms with a safety, lock the bolt or slide it back into the rear position, and place a zip tie or other form of block or strap through the weapon so the breech cannot close forward fully[lxxv].

PERFORMING A MACHINE GUN FUNCTIONALITY FIELD TEST

The machine gun functionality field test is easy to learn and perform, and is extremely useful knowledge for an investigator to have during any firearms trafficking investigation that may involve the illegal manufacture or trafficking of machine guns. In addition, it is useful to teach this test to undercover agents or confidential informants, so that in the event that they are making a purchase of a suspect machine gun, they can test the firearm during the undercover purchase to prevent being duped by the suspect into buying an ordinary firearm.

A machine gun will fire automatically when the bolt is cycled, and while the trigger is held to the rear following a single trigger pull. A machine gun will stop firing automatically when the shooter releases the trigger. Some machine guns will continue to fire until the magazine is completely empty even if the trigger is released. This is usually the result of a malfunction or wear on internal parts. This type of machinegun is referred to as a "run-away".

There are a number of variations in the way machine guns function. Some firearms will not function unless a magazine is seated, so the investigator should insert an empty magazine during the functionality field test. Some firearms will fire from an open bolt (when the bolt is locked back with the chamber open), while others will fire with a closed bolt. However, this will not affect the functionality field test. The machine gun functionality field test is highly accurate and can be used to establish probable cause that the examined firearm is or is not a machine gun. However, in rare instances, some firearms may field test fully automatic but may not be capable of actually firing fully automatic, while other firearms may test semi-automatically but may still meet the definition of a machine gun under Federal law, due to their design or the presence of a machine gun receiver and internal components. Machine gun functionality field testing provides the investigator with a probable indicator of a firearm's capability; however, for a conclusive finding for presentation in a court of law, the investigator should submit the firearm to a firearms laboratory that can make a definitive ruling and determine how to classify the firearm under the law. The ATF Firearms Technology Division in Martinsburg, West Virginia is the definitive expert in the classification of all types of firearms, silencers, and destructive devices under both the GCA and NFA.

To perform a machine gun functionality field test, an investigator will need to manually cycle the action of an unloaded firearm while holding the trigger in a depressed position to the rear. The following are the steps of a machine gun functionality field test;

✓ Ensure the firearm is unloaded.
✓ With the bolt or slide forward, pull the trigger to the rear and hold it in this depressed position while completing the next step.
✓ Pull the bolt or slide completely to the rear and then release it (the bolt or slide should go forward to a closed position).
✓ Release the trigger and then pull the trigger a second time.
✓ If the firing pin mechanism can be heard audibly falling when the trigger is pulled the second time, then the field test indicates the firearm is semiautomatic. The noise will sound like a metallic click. The click indicates that the firing pin mechanism locked back during the cycling of the action, and therefore would have only fired a round during the first action.
✓ If the firing pin mechanism cannot be heard audibly falling when the trigger is pulled the second time, then the field test indicates the firearm is fully automatic. The absence of a click indicates that the firing pin mechanism remained forward during the cycling of the action,

which would have fired a round with each cycling.

- ✓ For firearms with a safety or a selector switch, place the switch in each of the available positions and repeat the functionality field test. The firing pin mechanism should not function with the safety or selector switch in the "SAFE" position. If it does, the firearm may be capable of fully-automatic fire, or someone may have manipulated the internal components in an attempt to make the firearm function as a machine gun.
- ✓ For investigators who determine they want to actually fire a machinegun at a range to field test its functionality, the following precautions should be considered.
- ✓ Non-commercially manufactured machine guns can malfunction, resulting in injury or death. Consider allowing firearms experts in a proper examination facility to determine the functionality of the firearm.
- ✓ A run-away machine gun will fire all the rounds in a magazine before it stops firing. To safely determine if a machine gun will fire as a machine gun, meaning more than one round with a single function of the trigger, the investigator need only load 2 rounds in the magazine. If both rounds fire with one trigger pull, the investigator may next load 3 or 4 rounds to see if those fire with one trigger pull, or if the firearm stops firing when the trigger is released. If an investigator loads and inserts a 30-round magazine and pulls the trigger on a run-away machine gun, they are likely to experience a dangerous rapid muzzle rise and loss of control of the firearm, as well as where the rounds fired go, creating the potential for injury or death.

DETERMINING BARREL LENGTH AND OVERALL LENGTH OF A RIFLE OR SHOTGUN

The ability to determine the barrel length and overall length of a firearm is useful in any firearms-related investigation; however, it is particularly useful when trying to determine if a shotgun has a barrel length of less than 18 inches and an overall length of less than 24 inches, or if a rifle has a barrel length of less than 16 inches or an overall length of less than 24 inches. Firearms with barrel and/or overall lengths under these standards must be registered with ATF in the NFA as a short-barreled rifle (SBR) or shotgun. Possession of an unregistered SBR, such as a sawed-off-shotgun, is a felony under the NFA.
\
The following procedures should be used to accurately and correctly determine the barrel length of a rifle or shotgun:

- ✓ Ensure that it is unloaded.) Close the breech, cylinder, or bolt.
- ✓ Insert a straight rod down the muzzle end of the barrel until contact is made with the face of the bolt face or breech face.

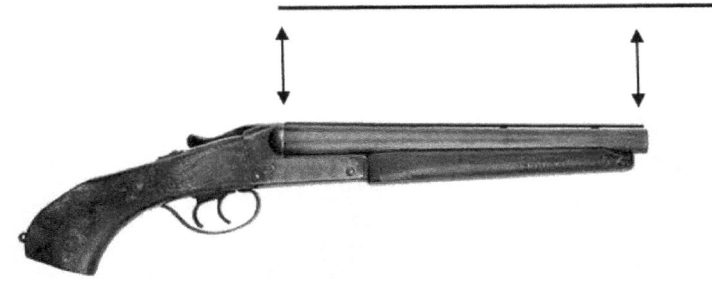

Figure 3.1 Determination of Barrel Length; *Measure the Rod after Removal from Barrel*

Image Credit; Author

- ✓ Mark the rod at the muzzle end (furthest point) to denote the true barrel length.

✓ Withdraw the rod and measure the distance marked off on the rod.
✓ Removable barrel extensions, poly chokes, and flash suppressors are not considered part of the measured barrel length; however, permanently affixed attachments are considered part of the barrel and should be included in the measurement.

The following procedures should be used to accurately and correctly determine the overall length of a rifle or shotgun:

✓ Examine the firearm and ensure that it is unloaded.
✓ For break-open type firearms, close the action.
✓ Lay the firearm on its side on a table with the butt of the stock aligned with one side of the table and the barrel of the weapon in line with (parallel) the other edge of the table.

✓ The overall length of the firearm can then be determined by measuring the distance of the table edge from the beginning (where the butt of the firearm is) to the point where the end of the barrel(s) is located. See Figure 3.

CORRECT MEASUREMENT

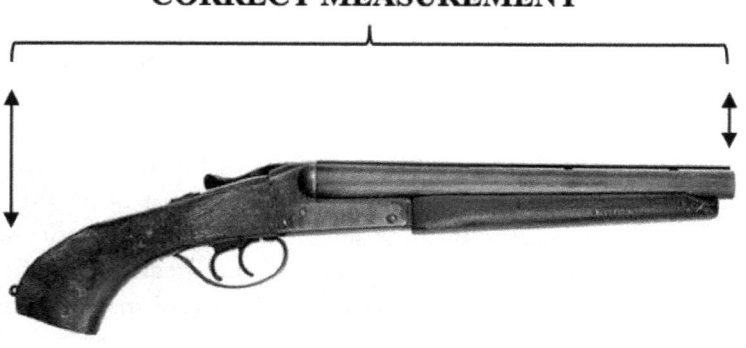

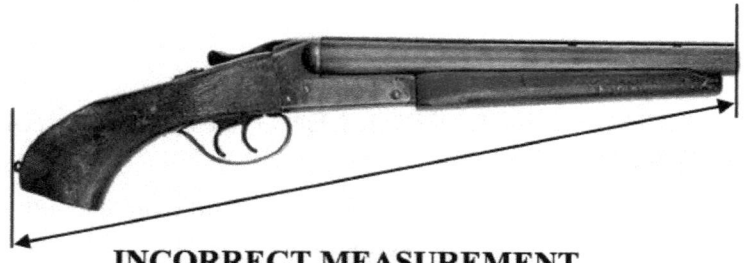

INCORRECT MEASUREMENT

Figure 3.1 *Determination of Overall Firearm Length*

Image Credit; Author

OTHER RESOURCES

Additional firearms nomenclature terminology appears in Chapter 2. Additional resources for information on firearms nomenclature include the following publications;

Blue Book Value of Guns 37th Edition. By Fjestad (2016, April), published by Blue Book Publications, Inc.

Firearms Identification & Tracing Procedures (ATF Publication 6320.1, Rev. Ed. 2008, May). By U.S. Department of Justice, Bureau of Alcohol, Tobacco, Firearms and Explosives.

ATF Guidebook; Importation & Verification of Firearms, Ammunition, and Implements of War (Rev. Ed. 2012). By U.S. Department of Justice, Bureau of Alcohol, Tobacco, Firearms and Explosives. (Rev. Ed 2015). Washington, D.C. Retrievable from: *https://www.atf.gov/firearms /firearms-guides-importation-verification-firearms-ammunition-firearms-verification-overview*

PISTOL

A weapon originally designed, made, and intended to fire a projectile (bullet) from one or more barrels when held in one hand, and having; a chamber(s) as an integral part(s) of, or permanently aligned with, the bore(s); and a short stock designed to be gripped by one hand at an angle to and extending below the line of the bore(s).

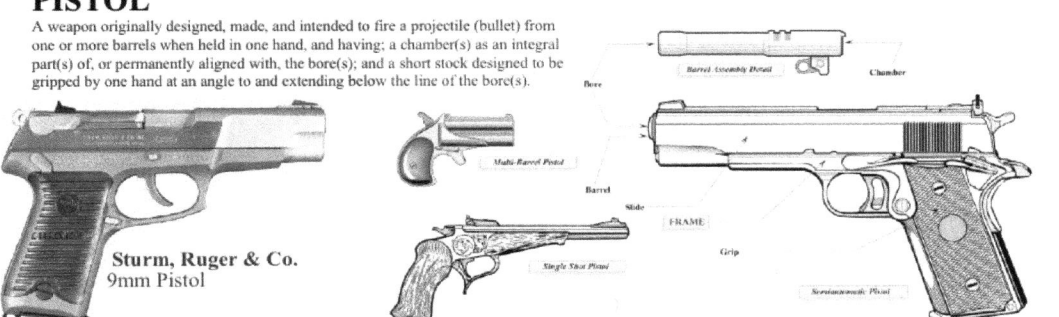

Sturm, Ruger & Co.
9mm Pistol

REVOLVER

A projectile weapon, of the pistol type, having a breechloading chambered cylinder so arranged that the cocking of the hammer or movement of the trigger rotates it and brings the next cartridge in line with the barrel for firing.

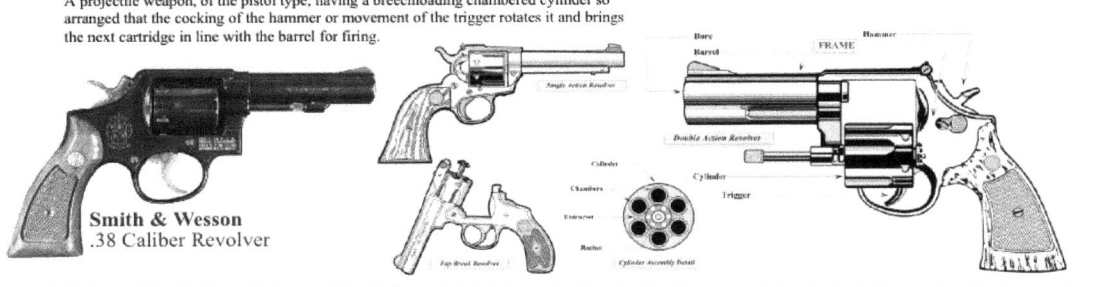

Smith & Wesson
.38 Caliber Revolver

SHOTGUN

A weapon designed or redesigned, made or remade, and intended to be fired from the shoulder, and designed or redesigned and made or remade to use the energy of the explosive in a fixed shotgun shell to fire through a smooth bore either a number of ball shot or a single projectile for each pull of the trigger.

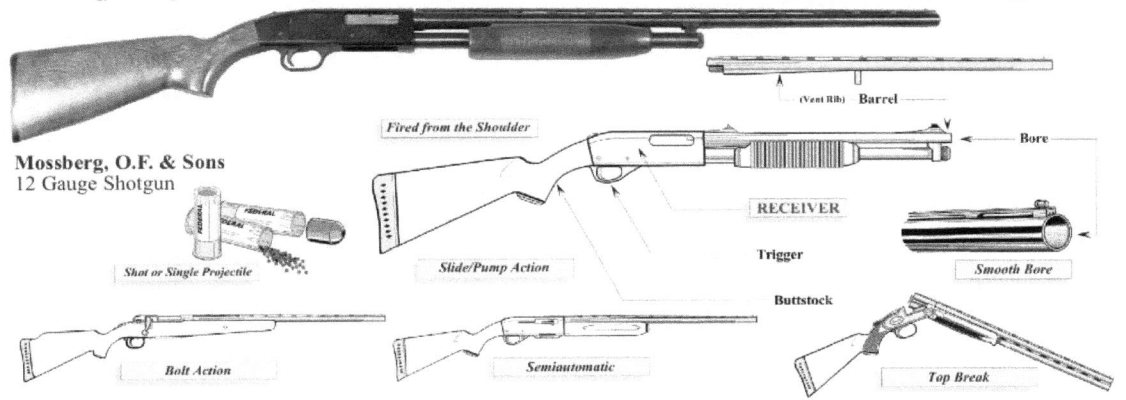

Mossberg, O.F. & Sons
12 Gauge Shotgun

RIFLE

A weapon designed or redesigned, made or remade, and intended to be fired from the shoulder, and designed or redesigned and made or remade to use the energy of the explosive in a fixed metallic cartridge to fire only a single projectile through a rifled bore for each single pull of the trigger.

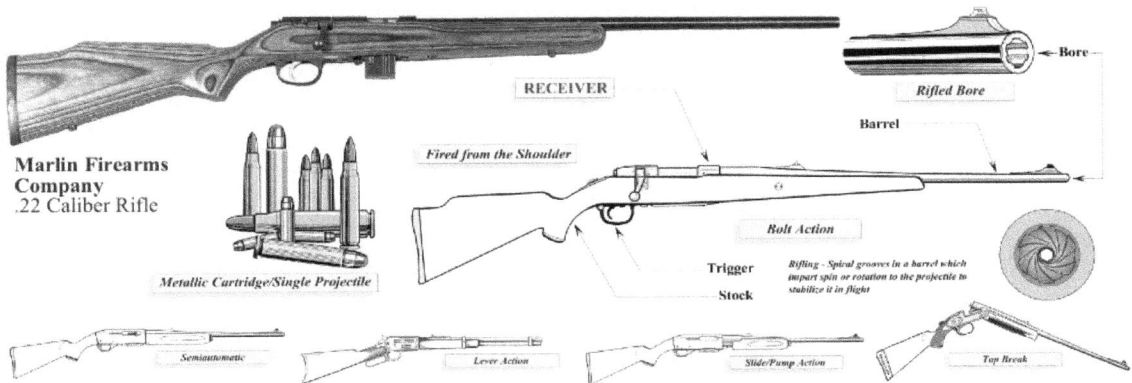

Marlin Firearms
Company
.22 Caliber Rifle

Figure 3.3 *Basic Firearms Nomenclature* lxxvi
Image Source; ATF

41

Chapter 4
Applicable Laws &
Legal Information

"The safety of the people shall be the highest law."
Marcus Tullius Cicero, Roman Politician and Lawyer in 63 BC

The federal firearms laws of the United States have most frequently been formed in reaction to events that spurred public outcry. These laws are forged in the crucible of heated debate by legislators with strong opposing opinions. Federal firearms laws attempt to walk the line between protecting citizens' rights to life, liberty and the pursuit of happiness endowed by their Creator and referred to as "unalienable rights" in the *Declaration of Independence,* and the right to bear arms as established under the *Second Amendment* of the *U.S. Constitution.* Some people want the government to create a safe environment free of gun violence while others want the right to use firearms to protect themselves from gun violence. The laws produced at the federal level have sought to protect all of these rights and as a result, contain a number of "grey areas." For an investigator to have any success in proving violations of those laws they will need to know the nuances of the federal firearms laws, court case law, and certain terminology. Discussed first are a set of fundamental principles that are common across the federal firearms laws.

PRESUMPTION OF INNOCENCE AND PROOF BEYOND A REASONABLE DOUBT

The standard of proof required to sustain a conviction for a violation of any federal firearm law almost goes without saying. It is: all persons are initially presumed innocent, and establishment of proof beyond a reasonable doubt is required to establish and sustain a criminal conviction. This standard is thoroughly explained in the U.S. District Court Pattern Jury Instructions (Figure 4.1), as this is the guidance that a U.S. District Court Judge explicitly provides to a jury when instructing them on how to determine guilt or innocence during deliberations following a trial.

U.S. DISTRICT COURT PATTERN JURY INSTRUCTIONS – PRESUMPTION OF INNOCENCE AND PROOF BEYOND A REASONABLE DOUBT

It is a cardinal principle of our system of justice that every person accused of a crime is presumed to be innocent unless and until his or her guilt is established beyond a reasonable doubt. The presumption is not a mere formality. It is a matter of the most important substance.

The presumption of innocence alone may be sufficient to raise a reasonable doubt and to require the acquittal of a defendant. The defendant before you has the benefit of that presumption throughout the trial, and you are not to convict them of a particular charge unless you are persuaded of his or her guilt of that charge beyond a reasonable doubt.

The presumption of innocence until proven guilty means that the burden of proof is always on the government to satisfy you that the defendant is guilty of the crime with which he or she is charged beyond a reasonable doubt. The law does not require that the government prove guilt beyond all possible doubt; proof beyond a reasonable doubt is sufficient to convict. Proof beyond a reasonable doubt means proof which is so convincing that you would not hesitate to rely and act on it in making the most important decisions in your own lives. The burden of proof never shifts to the defendant. It is always the government's burden to prove each of the elements of the crime[s] charged beyond a reasonable doubt by the evidence and the reasonable inferences to be drawn from that evidence. The defendant has the right to rely upon the failure or inability of the government to establish beyond a reasonable doubt any essential element of a crime charged against him or her.

If, after fair and impartial consideration of all the evidence, you have a reasonable doubt as to the defendant's guilt of a particular crime, it is your duty to acquit him or her of that crime. On the other hand, if, after fair and impartial consideration of all the evidence, you are satisfied beyond a reasonable doubt of the defendant's guilt of a particular crime, you should vote to convict him or her.

Figure 4.1

ON OR ABOUT, KNOWINGLY, DELIBERATE IGNORANCE, AND WILLFULLY

While not explicitly stated in each of the statues in the GCA, virtually all of the statutes require the investigator to prove that the defendant(s) "knowingly" and "willfully" committed the alleged violations "on or about" a certain date. These factors regarding the suspect's "state of mind" are commonly referred to as "general intent". General intent means that the person is aware of the nature of their conduct, and it is those circumstances incident to their conduct that make the conduct criminal. An investigator must have a thorough understanding of these terms, and keen awareness of the types of evidence indicating their presence, in order to prove a violation of most of the federal firearms laws under the GCA.

There is no way a suspect's state of mind can be proved directly, because no one can read another person's mind and tell what that person is thinking. However, a suspect's state of mind can be proved indirectly from the surrounding circumstances documented during the investigation. This may include what the defendant said, what the defendant did, how the defendant acted, and any other facts or circumstances in evidence that are relevant to establishing the defendant's likely state of mind.

The investigator may also determine a suspect's state of mind by considering whether it is reasonable to conclude that the actions a suspect knowingly did, or did not do, were likely to produce certain results. For example, it may be reasonable to conclude a that suspect knowingly intended to violate the law by providing false information to an FFL when they certified that they were purchasing firearms only for themselves on the ATF Form 4473 if they purchased ten of the same type of firearm and sold them less than a month after their purchase.

The term "willfully" is not usually covered in pattern jury instructions, as it means something different depending on the elements of proof for each violation of law being investigated. In general, the word "willfully" means that the act was committed voluntarily and purposely, with the specific intent to do something the law forbids; that is, with bad purpose, either to disobey or disregard the law. There is no requirement that the government show evil intent on the part of a defendant in order to prove that the act was done.

"On or about" and "knowingly" are best explained through U.S. District Court Pattern Jury Instructions as this is the guidance that a U.S. District Court Judge provides directly to a jury when explaining what these terms mean when they are determining guilt or innocence during deliberations following a trial.

U.S. DISTRICT COURT PATTERN JURY INSTRUCTIONS – ON OR ABOUT AND KNOWINGLY

You will note that the indictment charges that the offense was committed *"on or about"* a certain date. The Government does not have to prove with certainty the exact date of the alleged offense(s). It is sufficient if the Government proves beyond a reasonable doubt that the offense was committed on a date reasonably near the date alleged.

The word *"knowingly"*, as that term has been used from time to time in these instructions, means that the act was done voluntarily with knowledge of the situation and not because of mistake, accident, or other innocent reason. BUT, the violator is not required to have any intent to break any law, nor does that person have to know that there is any law that forbids the conduct in question. Knowledge of the criminal statute governing the conduct is not required. You may also find that the defendant acted knowingly if you determine deliberate ignorance by finding beyond a reasonable doubt that the defendant:

1. was aware of a high probability that [*e.g.*, firearms were in the defendant's automobile], and
2. deliberately ignored the truth or avoided learning the truth.

You may not find such knowledge, however, if you find that the defendant actually believed that [*e.g.* no firearms were in the defendant's automobile], or if you find that the defendant was simply careless.

Figure 4.2

ACTUAL AND CONSTRUCTIVE POSSESSION

Establishing possession is required in many federal firearms violation investigations. Under federal law there are two kinds of possession: actual and constructive. A person who knowingly has direct physical control over a firearm at a given time is established to be in actual possession of it. If a person is carrying a firearm on their person, they are in actual possession of the firearm. A person who, although not in actual possession, knowingly has both the power and the intention, at a given time, to exercise dominion or control over a firearm, either directly or through another person or persons, is then in constructive possession of it. If a person is in a vehicle and they know a firearm is in the glove box, trunk, under a seat, in a concealed compartment, or being held by another person in the car, and they have the ability to access the firearm(s) at any point in time, they are in constructive possession of the firearm. Knowledge of the firearm and access

to the firearm equal constructive possession. Possession of any kind does not require ownership, and possession may be sole or joint. If one person alone has actual or constructive possession of a firearm, possession is sole. If two or more persons share actual or constructive possession of a firearm, possession is joint.

INTERSTATE NEXUS: THE MOVEMENT OF FIREARMS IN, OR AFFECTING, INTERSTATE OF FOREIGN COMMERCE

One of the most common justifications for enacting a federal law is for Congress to exercise its power to regulate commerce between the states and with foreign nations. As a result, most federal criminal violations and virtually all federal firearms violations will require the investigator to establish that the firearm or ammunition has some nexus to interstate or foreign commerce.

Title 18 U.S.C. § 921(a)(2) defines "interstate or foreign commerce" to include commerce between any place in a state and any place outside of that state, or within any possession of the United States (not including the Canal Zone) or the District of Columbia, but such term does not include commerce between places within the same state, but through any place outside of that state. The term "state" includes the District of Columbia, the Commonwealth of Puerto Rico, and the possessions of the United States.

The investigator will not have to show that the suspect personally transported or caused the transportation of a firearm or ammunition in interstate or foreign commerce unless that is a specific element of the law being investigated. In most instances the investigator will be required to establish that the firearm or ammunition has, at some point between the time it is manufactured to the time it is possessed by the suspect, traveled in interstate or foreign commerce.

An investigator does not have to prove exactly where firearms or ammunition were manufactured; but rather, that they were not manufactured in the state where the violation is being charged. Presenting evidence or testimony that they were not manufactured in that state establishes that they traveled in interstate or foreign commerce in order to be present in that state. There are two primary methods to establish that a firearm previously moved in, or affected, interstate or foreign commerce.

✓ **Records and Testimony of FFLs:** An investigator should first request a trace of the recovered crime gun. Successful trace results will show the history of the firearm, from the manufacturer or importer, through the wholesaler, to the first retail sale. The investigator can then determine which person in the trace chain (manufacturer, wholesaler, retailer) they will use to establish the movement of the firearm in interstate or foreign commerce and request an AUSA issue a subpoena for that person's appearance in court and the production of records related to the firearm. For example, a representative from Smith and Wesson may be subpoenaed to produce records and testimony showing that a recovered Smith and Wesson was manufactured in the State of Massachusetts, or a representative from Century Arms International may be subpoenaed to produce records and testimony to show that a certain firearm bearing their importer marking was imported into the U.S. from Germany by their company. Proving interstate nexus by bringing representatives from the firearms industry to court is rare, and with as many crime guns that are recovered in the U.S. each year, it would be logistically and financially difficult for most manufacturers to employ enough representatives to testify.

✓ **Testimony of an Investigator:** Testimony of an investigator is the primary method to establish that a firearm or ammunition previously traveled in, or affected, interstate or foreign commerce. The U.S. District Court will accept the testimony of an investigator to establish that a firearm or ammunition traveled in, or affected, interstate or foreign commerce if the investigator can be qualified as an expert in interstate nexus or, based on the investigator's training and experience, if they have had any specialized training in interstate nexus and can testify as to what conclusions they would draw from their training and experience regarding whether a particular firearm or ammunition previously traveled in, or affected, interstate or foreign commerce.

Establishing interstate nexus should not be taken lightly. This is not as simple as looking at the markings on a firearm which indicate the city and state of import or city and state of manufacture. Any investigator or prosecutor who introduces proof of interstate nexus to a grand jury, in a sworn affidavit, or in courtroom testimony, based exclusively on the city and state markings on the recovered firearm does so at the peril of their own credibility by presenting erroneous information.

Under Title 27 C.F.R. § 178.92(i) the Director of ATF may authorize alternate means of identification by the licensed manufacturer or importer should they request this. In other words, the city and state of manufacture for certain gun manufactures become synonymous with their name and it becomes part of their brand. For example, Smith and Wesson® is synonymous with Springfield, Massachusetts, while Ruger® and Colt® are synonymous with Connecticut. Certain manufacturers may decide that for reasons such as production costs, it may be more beneficial for them to manufacturer some of their firearms in a different location. That manufacturer may not want to disassociate these firearms from the city and state their brand is associated with, so they apply to the Director of ATF to be allowed to stamp these firearms with the city and state of their location brand when in fact these firearms are manufactured in a different city and state. The manufacturer will know from a model number or serial number that these firearms were made in the other location for purposes of accurately responding to crime gun trace requests from ATF. This is proprietary business information maintained in ATF records and reference libraries. The alternate means of identification scenario is far more common than most investigators and prosecutors probably realize.

Within ATF there are special agents trained as certified experts on establishing interstate nexus. These agents attend a dedicated course on interstate nexus training, are provided with an extensive library of firearms reference materials, have access to all firearms trace data, have access to the ATF Firearms Technology Division firearms experts who make all technical rulings in the firearms industry, have access to the ATF multi-thousand technical firearms reference library, and have access to all of the records for "alternate means of identification" authorized by the Director of ATF to any manufacturer. When it comes to establishing interstate nexus for ammunition, these agents have access to ATF's CHIC, an extensive electronic image catalogue of ammunition head-stamp markings past and present. In addition, these special agents attend additional advanced trainings on interstate nexus throughout their career that includes tours of numerous firearms manufacturers and importer facilities within the U.S. as well as tours of European firearms manufacturers and proof houses. ATF interstate nexus experts are the gold standard for any prosecutor who wants to establish that a firearm has traveled in interstate or foreign commerce without any potential for unintentionally presenting erroneous information or having a defense attorney raise reasonable doubt regarding the origin and interstate nexus of the firearms in a case.

For investigators outside of ATF trying to establish interstate nexus they will need to research the firearm using firearm reference manuals, such as the Blue Book of Gun Values, in conjunction with firearm trace results and FFL records.

Any investigator attempting to establish interstate nexus through their own testimony should be well versed in the history of the specific firearm(s) involved in the case as well as general firearms types and nomenclature, including the definition of a firearm, firearms terminology, as well as licensing and markings requirements under the GCA and the C.F.R. During testimony the defense may be allowed to conduct a "voir dire" (preliminary) examination of the investigator to determine their background and qualifications before they are allowed to present their opinion testimony in court. Following the voir dire, the defense will be allowed to directly question the investigator about their knowledge of federal firearms laws and the history of the firearm(s) in question. While it is impossible to predict the questions a defense attorney may ask about federal firearms law, at a minimum the investigator must know these points.

✓ Prior to 1968 serial numbers were not required on .22 caliber rifles and on shotguns. In addition, serial numbers could be duplicated by manufacturers, and serial numbers could appear anywhere on the firearm.

✓ Under federal law, the definition of "firearm" does not include any type of air-powered pistol such as a BB gun, nor does it include any firearm manufactured prior to 1898, or any unmodified replica of a firearm manufactured prior to 1898. Firearms manufactured prior to 1898 are considered antiques and are often black powder firearms with antique ignition systems such as flint or match lock ignitions.

✓ Under Title 18 U.S.C. § 921 (a)(3) a firearm is defined as (A) any weapon (including a starter gun) which will or is designed to or may readily be converted to expel a projectile by the action of an explosive; (B) the frame or receiver of any such weapon; (C) any firearm muffler or firearm silencer; or (D) any destructive device. The definition of "firearm" does not include antique firearms.

✓ Under Title 27 C.F.R. § 478.11 a firearm frame or receiver is that part of a firearm which provides housing for the hammer, bolt or breechblock, and firing mechanism, and which is usually threaded at its forward portion to receive the barrel.

✓ Since 1968, Title 27 C.F.R. § 178.92 has required that all firearms manufactured in the U.S must be marked with a serial number on the frame or receiver, and that the firearm must also include markings indicating the name of the manufacturer, city and state of manufacture, model (if assigned), and the caliber or gauge must conspicuously appear on the frame, receiver, barrel, or slide of the firearm.

✓ Since 1968, Title 27 C.F.R. § 178.92 has required that all firearms imported into the U.S must be marked with a serial number on the frame or receiver, and that the firearm must also include markings indicating the name of the importer, city and state of import, country of origin, model (if assigned), and the caliber or gauge must conspicuously appear on the frame, receiver, barrel, or slide of the firearm. All firearms importers are assigned a 3-letter abbreviation by ATF which they may mark their firearms with in lieu of their full name. ATF maintains a reference library of these importer markings, and a copy appears in Appendix E. Firearms imported into the U.S. must display a serial number using standard English language letters and numerals. If the firearm has a serial number with Cyrillic, Arabic, Chinese, or other non-English characters, the importer must stamp the firearm with a new and unique serial number prior to the completion of the importation. Imported firearms often have patent numbers, model numbers, part numbers, proof house numbers, and other markings that can be confused with the correct serial number; therefore, the investigator must be well versed in firearms identification when analyzing the markings on an imported firearm in order to ensure that the firearm is properly traced and identified for establishing interstate or foreign nexus.

Investigators should contact their local ATF office for assistance if they are having trouble establishing interstate or foreign commerce on a recovered crime gun.

RELEVANT CONDUCT

Relevant conduct is uncharged conduct that constitutes a criminal act related to the underlying offense of which a defendant is convicted. Relevant conduct is activity that may not result in an indictable offense but may be used to increase a defendant's possible sentencing range under the Federal Sentencing Guidelines. Relevant conduct is admissible in the Pre-Sentence Investigation (PSI) report prepared by the U.S. Probation Office and presented to the judge for use in determining sentencing. Information and evidence documenting relevant conduct is provided by investigators and the AUSA to the probation officer preparing the PSI. In general, firearms trafficking convictions do not result in what many would call a significant term imprisonment. Establishing the defendant's relevant conduct for inclusion can potentially increase a defendant's sentence. Relevant conduct that can increase a defendant's sentence includes evidence of drug trafficking or violent crime involvement by the defendant. Relevant conduct may include recorded conversation between an undercover agent and a firearms trafficker where the trafficker indicates that they used firearms to protect themselves during firearms or drug trafficking, or that they sell firearms to other people they know will use the gun in crimes, so they obliterate the serial number. This is relevant conduct, as it shows the firearms trafficker is willfully using or supplying firearms to other violent criminals. They may be an unlawful user of drugs, which is a violation of Title 18 U.S.C. 922(g)(3). This violation is not often charged but might be used as relevant conduct.

Relevant conduct is legal, but is viewed as controversial by some. The defendant may receive an increased sentence based on information for which they were not indicted, tried, or convicted of. As such, investigators should only recommend relevant conduct for inclusion in the PSI that they believe to be significant and incontrovertible.

EXTRADITION

Extradition frequently comes into play in firearms trafficking investigations, as suspects often operate across state lines and national borders. A defendant indicted in one state but arrested in another will have the opportunity for an extradition hearing before being transferred to the state where the indictment and arrest warrant were issued. The same holds true for a person indicted in the U.S but arrested in a foreign country.

Extradition is the term describing the formal process whereby a state or nation makes a request to another state or nation to turn over an individual for purposes of arrest, criminal trial, and/or punishment. The approval of an extradition request is based on existing law in the involved states and on treaties between involved nations. Requests for extradition usually result in an extradition hearing in the state or nation where the suspect is located, and during such hearings the judge or magistrate will determine the identity of the person, the validity of the charges, and the legality of an extradition based on existing laws or treaties. Article IV, Section 2, Clause 2 of the U.S. Constitution provides for the following: A person charged in any state with treason, felony, or other crime, who shall flee from justice, and be found in another state, shall on demand of the executive

authority of the state from which he fled, be delivered for removal to the state having jurisdiction of the crime.[lxxvii]

International extradition is the formal process by which a person found in one country is surrendered to another country for trial or punishment. The process is regulated by treaty and conducted between the U.S. Federal Government and the government of a foreign country. The process of international extradition differs considerably from domestic interstate extradition, commonly referred to as interstate extradition, mandated by the Constitution, Art. 4, Sec. 2.

Under Title 18 U.S.C. § 3184, a request for extradition may be granted only pursuant to a treaty. Some countries will grant extradition without a treaty; however, every such country requires an offer of reciprocity by the U.S. if extradition is allowed in the absence of a treaty. Under Title 18 U.S.C. §§ 3181 and 3184, the U.S. may pursue extradition of persons other than U.S. citizens, even where there is no treaty, if the person(s) have committed crimes of violence against U.S. citizens in foreign countries. A list of countries with which the U.S. has extradition treaties with can be found in the Federal Criminal Code and Rules following Title 18 U.S.C. § 3181. As this list is subject to change, investigators should consult with the DOJ Criminal Division, Office of International Affairs (OIA), to verify the accuracy of the information. Investigators will need to coordinate extensively with an AUSA in order to secure the approval of an extradition. Investigators should always coordinate through the AUSA, and never initiate unapproved direct contact with a foreign official in the country where extradition will be sought.

LURE

A lure involves using a subterfuge to entice a criminal defendant to leave a foreign country so that he or she can be arrested in the United States, in international waters or airspace, or in a third country for subsequent extradition, expulsion, or deportation to the United States. Lures can be complicated schemes, or they can be as simple as inviting a fugitive by telephone to a party in the United States. During the conduct of international firearms trafficking investigations, an investigator may determine that it would be more advantageous to pursue proper approvals to lure a suspect to a location where they can be arrested, rather than pursuing extradition.

Some countries will not extradite a person to the U.S. if the person's presence in that country was obtained through the use of a lure or other ruse. In addition, some countries may view a lure of a person from its territory as an infringement on its sovereignty. Unapproved lures could result in the investigator being considered an agent provocateur in that foreign country and the investigator could in fact be in violation of the laws of the foreign country. Consequently, investigators should never initiate a lure without first securing the approval of an AUSA. That AUSA will research the lure proposal and consult with the DOJ OIA before approving the undertaking of a lure to the U.S. or a third country.[lxxviii]

TABLE 4.1 Overview of Federal Firearm Laws

Trafficking Crimes Related to the Disposition, Movement and Possession of Firearms Under the Gun Control Act of 1968

Title 18 U.S.C. §	Makes it illegal for	To	Mental Element(s)	Potential Penalty	Other
922(a)(1)(A) Dealing in Firearms without a License	Any person	Engage in the business of dealing in firearms without a license.	Willful and Knowing	Up to 5 years in prison and/or fine	Dealing includes being "engaged in the business" with the "principle objective of profit and livelihood". Title 18 USC § 921(a)(21); Engaged in the business as applied to a **dealer** in **firearms**, as defined in section 921(a)(11)(A), a person who devotes time, attention, and labor to dealing in **firearms** as a regular course of trade or business with the principal objective of livelihood and profit through the repetitive purchase and resale of **firearms**, but such term shall not include a person who makes occasional sales, exchanges, or purchases of **firearms** for the enhancement of a personal collection or for a hobby, or who sells all or part of his personal collection of **firearms**; Title 18 USC § 921(a)(22); The term "**with the principal objective of livelihood and profit**" means that the intent underlying the sale or disposition of firearms is predominantly one of obtaining livelihood and pecuniary gain, as opposed to other intents, such as improving or liquidating a personal firearms collection: *Provided*, That proof of profit shall not be required as to a **person** who engages in the regular and repetitive purchase and disposition of **firearms** for criminal purposes or **terrorism**. These are restrictive definitions that make this violation challenging to prove.
922(a)(2) Interstate Shipment of Firearms	FFL	Ship firearms interstate except to another FFL.	Willful and Knowing	Up to 5 years in prison and/or fine	There are exceptions for returns and replacements from an FFL to individuals and shipments to a law enforcement officer, military member and certain other persons for official use. See 18 U. S. C. §1715.
922(a)(3) Interstate Transportation	non-FFL	Transport or receive firearm obtained in another state into his state of residency.	Willful and Knowingly	Up to 5 years in prison and/or fine	The term, "state of residence", is a defined term at 27 C.F.R. § 478.11
922(a)(4) Interstate Shipment of NFA Firearms form an FFL to non-FFL	non- FFL	Transport a destructive device, machinegun, short- barreled shotgun, or short-barreled rifle in interstate or foreign commerce.	Willful and Knowing	Up to 5 years in prison and/or fine	The Attorney General may authorize exceptions consistent with public safety and necessity.

Title 18 U.S.C. §	Makes it illegal for	To	Mental Element(s)	Potential Penalty	Other
922(a)(5) Interstate Transfer of a Firearms	non- FFL	Deliver firearm to unlicensed person whose residence is in a state different from transferor's.	Willful and Knowing or having reasonable cause to believe transferee resides in another state[4]	Up to 5 years in prison and/or fine	"Deliver" includes transfer, sale, trading, giving, and transporting. There are exceptions for transfer pursuant to a bequest or intestate succession or temporary loan/rental for lawful sporting purpose.
922(a)(9) Receipt of a Firearm by Someone who does not Reside in any State	non- FFL	Receive a firearm if the person does not reside in any state.	Willful and Knowing	Up to 5 years in prison and/or fine	There is an exception for "lawful sporting purposes."
922(b)(1) FFL Selling a Firearm to an Underage Person	FFL	Sell or deliver any firearm or ammunition to any person who the FFL knows or has reason to know is less than 18 years of age or a handgun or handgun ammunition to any person who the FFL knows or has reasonable cause to believe is less than 21 years of age.	Willful and Knowing or having reasonable cause to believe the transferee is underage	Up to 5 years in prison and/or fine	
922(b)(2) FFL Selling a Firearm in Violation of State or Local Laws	FFL	Sell or deliver any firearm to a non-FFL where the transfer would violate a state or local law or ordinance at the place of transfer.	Willful and Knowing or having reasonable cause to believe that the transferee resides in another state	Up to 5 years in prison and/or fine	There is an exception for an FFL who knows or has reasonable cause to believe that the purchase or possession would not be in violation of state law of published ordinance. Delivery under this circumstance would not be willful.
922(b)(3) FFL Selling a Firearm to a non- resident of FFL's State	FFL	Sell or deliver any firearm to a non-FFL residing in a state other than the FFL's	Willful and Knowing or having reasonable cause to believe that the transferee resides in another state	Up to 5 years in prison and/or fine	Exception: Sale of a long gun if the transferee meets in person with the FFL and the transfer of the firearm complies with the laws of both states, or the transfer is a temporary loan or rental of a firearm for lawful sporting purposes. (Formerly known as the "contiguous state rule," since at one time, such sales could only be made to residents of states contiguous to the FFL's.)

Title 18 U.S.C. §	Makes it illegal for	To	Mental Element(s)	Potential Penalty	Other
922(d) Selling a Firearm to a Prohibited Person.	Any person	Sell or dispose of a firearm or ammunition to a prohibited person; <ul><li>Convicted Felon</li><li>Fugitive from Justice</li><li>Unlawful use of Drugs</li><li>Adjudicated Mentally Ill</li><li>Illegal Alien</li><li>Dishonorable Discharge</li><li>Renounced US Citizenship</li><li>Under Court Issued Domestic Restraining Order</li><li>Convicted Domestic Abuser</li></ul>	Transferor must know or have reasonable cause to believe the transferee is a prohibited person.	Up to 10 years in prison and/or fine	This law may be applicable in firearms trafficking investigations where traffickers who are gang members provide firearms to other gang members who they know have served time in prison or are unlawful users of drugs. Relevant definitions are found at § 921(a).
922(e) Delivering a Firearm to a Common Carrier for Interstate Shipment Without notifying the Carrier	Any person	Deliver a firearm or ammunition to a common carrier for transport to a non-FFL in interstate or foreign commerce without providing written notice to the carrier.	Willful and Knowing	Up to 5 years in prison and/or fine	This law would be applicable in firearms trafficking investigations where persons transport the firearms illegally on an airline, bus, or train. Common carriers include airlines, trains, bus lines, or shipping services such as FedEx or UPS.
922(g) Possession of a Firearm by a Prohibited Person	Any prohibited person	Possess or receive a firearm or ammunition <ul><li>Convicted Felon</li><li>Fugitive from Justice</li><li>Unlawful use of Drugs</li><li>Adjudicated Mentally Ill</li><li>Illegal Alien</li><li>Dishonorable Discharge</li><li>Renounced US Citizenship</li><li>Under Court Issued Domestic Restraining Order</li><li>Convicted Domestic Abuser</li></ul>	Know they are in possession of a firearm and they fit a prohibited class but need not know they are prohibited.	Up to 10 years in prison and/or fine	Often times an illegal firearm possession violation is easier to prove than an actual trafficking violation. See § 921(a) for definitions of each category of prohibited person; there are also relevant definitions at 27 C.F.R. § 478.11 Possession includes constructive possession where a person exercises care, custody, control, or dominion over the firearm. The "Armed Career Criminal" sentencing enhancement at 18 U.S.C. § 924 (e) subjects a § 922 (g) convict to a minimum 15 years imprisonment if he/she has had at least 3 prior convictions for state or federal crimes of violence or serious drug trafficking offenses committed on separate occasions.
922(i) Interstate Transportation or Shipment of Stolen Firearms	Any person	Transport or ship a stolen firearm or ammunition in or affecting interstate or foreign commerce	Know or have reasonable cause to believe the firearm was stolen	Up to 10 years in prison and/or fine	This law may be applicable to firearms trafficking investigations involving the theft of firearms from private individuals or from FFLs and the perpetrator traveled to another state to traffic the firearms.

Title 18 U.S.C. §	Makes it illegal for	To	Mental Element(s)	Potential Penalty	Other
922(j) Possession of a Stolen Firearm	Any person	Receive, possess, conceal, store, barter, sell, or dispose of a stolen firearm or ammunition	Know or have reasonable cause to believe the firearm was stolen	Up to 10 years in prison and/or fine	This law may be applicable to firearms trafficking investigations involving the theft of firearms from private individuals or from FFLs.
922(k) Receiving, Shipping, or Transporting a Firearm with an Obliterated Serial Number *or* Possession of a Such a Firearm that was Previously Shipped in Interstate of Foreign Commerce	Any person	Transport, ship, or receive in interstate or foreign commerce a firearm with the serial number obliterated or altered, or to possess such a firearm that has been so transported or shipped.	Willful and Knowing	Up to 5 years in prison and/or fine	This law may be applicable in firearms trafficking investigations where the trafficker is removing the serial numbers of the firearms in an effort to evade detection.
922(l) Importation of a Foreign Firearm	Any person	Except as provided by §925(d), to import or bring firearms or ammunition into the United Sates, or to possess such firearms or ammunition, or to receive such firearms or ammunition.	Knowing as to the importation; Willful as to possession or receipt	Up to 5 years in prison and/or fine	This law may be applicable in firearms trafficking investigations involving firearms being imported into the U.S. illegally. This is often the case where persons order firearms on the internet from sources that are based in other countries.
922(n) Indicted Person Receiving/Shipping/Transporting a Firearm	Any person under indictment or information	Ship, Transport, or receive a firearm or ammunition in interstate of foreign commerce.	Willful and Knowing	Up to 5 years in prison and/or fine	"Any Person Under Indictment" is defined as under indictment for a crime that would render someone prohibited under Title 18. This does not apply to the possession of firearms the person owned or possessed prior to the indictment.
922(o) Possession or Transfer of a Machinegun	Any person	Transfer or possess a machinegun.	Knowingly possess a firearm and that the firearm operates as a machinegun	Up to 10 years in prison and/or fine	The term "Machinegun," is defined in 18 U.S.C. § 921(a)(23) This subsection does not apply to transfer or possession under the authority of the United States, state or local government or agencies. This law does not apply to the lawful transfer or possession of a machinegun that was lawfully possessed prior to the effective date of this subsection (May 19, 1986).
922(t) Brady Check Requirements	FFL	Fail to complete "Brady" background check on a firearms purchaser.	Knowing	Up to 1 year in prison and/or fine	See exceptions in § 922(t)(3)

Title 18 U.S.C. §	Makes it illegal for	To	Mental Element(s)	Potential Penalty	Other
922(u) Theft of a Firearm from an FFL's Inventory	Any person	Steal or unlawfully take away from the person or premises of an FFL any "inventory" firearm.	Knowing	Up to 10 years in prison and/or fine	This statute covers theft, burglary and robbery, as well as lesser criminal interference with ownership and possessory rights in states whose codes have such provisions.
922(x)(1) Selling a Handgun or Handgun Ammunition to a Juvenile	Any person	Sell, deliver, or otherwise transfer a handgun or handgun ammunition to a juvenile (less than 18 years old).	Knowing transfer to a person the transferor knows or has reasonable cause to believe is a juvenile	Up to 1 year in prison, but if the person knew or had reasonable cause to know that the handgun would be used in an act of violence, 10 years, and/or fine	"Juvenile" is defined in § 924(a)(6)(A)(ii) See exceptions in § 922(x)(3).
922(x)(2) Possession of a Handgun or Handgun Ammunition by a Juvenile	A juvenile	Possess a handgun or handgun ammunition.	Knowing	Up to 1 year in prison, *but* probation and no incarceration if the juvenile has no previous convictions or juvenile adjudications.	"Juvenile" is defined in § 924(a)(6)(A)(ii) See exceptions in § 922(3).
923(a) Dealing Firearms from a Location Other than the Licensed Premises	FFL	Conduct business at a non-licensed location	Willful and Knowing	Up to 5 years in prison and/or fine	As mentioned above (*see* § 922(a)(1)(A), we recommend this as a possible charging alternative to § 922(a)(1)(a) where what the FFL has done is to engage in the business at an unlicensed location.
924(b) Ship, Transport or Receive Firearm with Intent to Commit a Felony	Any person	Ship, transport, or receive a firearm in interstate or foreign commerce with the intent to commit a felony with the firearm or knowing or having reasonable cause to know that a felony will be committed with the firearm.	Knowing transportation with specific intent or with knowledge or reasonable cause to believe the firearm will be used to commit a crime.	Up to 10 years in prison and/or fine	

Title 18 U.S.C. §	Makes it illegal for	To	Mental Element(s)	Potential Penalty	Other
924(c) Use or Carry Firearm to Commit a federal Crime of Violence or Drug Trafficking Crime	Any person	To use or carry a firearm during and in relation to a federal crime of violence or a drug trafficking crime.	Willful and Knowing	Minimum of 5 years in prison to life and/or fine, depending on the firearm used and whether it is the persons first conviction. The death penalty is applicable if the offense resulted in murder.	Penalties are mandatory and mandatorily consecutive. "Drug trafficking crime" is defined in § 924(c)(2). "Crime of violence" is defined in § 924(c)(3). "Use" means active use, such as threatening with the firearm, shooting it, or trading the firearm for drugs. "Carry" means that the defendant must have physically moved the firearm from one place to another, and that it must have been easily accessible for use during the underlying crime. Conspiracy to commit § 924(c) is a violation covered by 18 U.S.C. § 924(o), the penalty for which is 20 years to life.
924(k) Smuggling a Firearm into the United States to Commit or Promote Specified Crimes	Any person	Smuggle or knowingly bring a firearm into the U.S. or attempt to do so with the intent to engage in or promote specified illegal conduct to include a drug trafficking crime or crime of violence.	Willful and Knowing with specific intent to engage in or promote certain illegal conduct.	Up to 10 years in prison and/or fine	"Drug trafficking crime" is defined in § 924(c)(2). "Crime of violence" is defined in § 924(c)(3).
924(n) Traveling Interstate to Promote Illegal Firearms Trafficking	Any person	Travel from any state or foreign country into a state and acquire or attempt to acquire a firearm in such a state	Willful and Knowing with specific intent to engage in § 922(a)(1)(A) (i.e., dealing in firearms without a license)	Up to 10 years in prison and/or fine	This law is applicable in interstate firearms trafficking rings where persons travel from one state to another to obtain firearms and then return to traffic those firearms. This situation often involves multiple defendants as part of a conspiracy.

Trafficking Crimes Related to Records and False Statements					
Title 18 U.S.C. §	Makes it illegal for	To	Mental Element(s)	Potential Penalty	Other
922(a)(6) Providing False or Fictitious Information When Buying Firearms from an FFL	non-FFL	Make a false statement or display a false document to an FFL in attempt to acquire a firearm or ammunition and that statement was intended or was likely to deceive the FFL with respect to any fact material to the lawfulness of the sale.[5]	Willful and Knowing the false statement is intended or likely to deceive the dealer with respect to any fact material to the lawfulness of the sale.	Up to 10 years in prison and/or fine	This law is applicable in firearms trafficking investigations involving straw purchases where the "straws" are providing false information about the intended recipient of the firearm. This law cannot be charged where the false statement was not intended to deceive the FFL or where the FFL was a party to or cause of, the crime.
922(b)(5) FFL Failing to Keep Required Records	FFL	Dispose of a firearm without making entries in records required to be kept under § 923.	Willful and Knowing	Up to 5 years in prison and/or fine	Proving willful and knowingly in an FFL investigation requires the investigator to know the FFLs state of mind and this is a significant challenge.
922(m) FFL Omitting Information from or Falsifying Records	FFL	Making false entry in, or failing to make appropriate entry in, or failing to properly maintain records required under §923 or regulations.	Knowing	Up to 1 year in prison and/or fine	
924 (a)(1)(A) False statements in required records or in applying for a license or for relief of disability	Any person	Knowingly make a false statement or representation with respect to information required to be kept on FFL's records or in applying for any license, exemption or relief from disability under the GCA.	Knowing	Up to 5 years in prison and/or fine	This law has a lower threshold to prove than § 922(a)(6) as it does not require willfulness nor an intent or likelihood that the statement have been likely to deceive the FFL.
1001 False Statements	Any person	Make or use a false material statement in a Government-related matter.	Willful and Knowing the false statement was made for a bad purpose	Up to 5 years in prison and/or fine	This is the general Federal False Statement Statute. Where a false statement falls into one of the specific GCA violations, that charge should be used. The general false statements charge is useful where a subject lies to investigators during an interview. The general false statement charge is also useful when a false statement is entered on the ATF Form 4473 that does not relate to a material fact to the lawful possession of the firearm by the purchaser.

		Trafficking Crimes Related to International Borders			
Title & U.S.C. §	**Makes it illegal for**	**To**	**Mental Element(s)**	**Potential Penalty**	**Other**
Title 22 U.S.C. § 2778 Arms Export Control Act (AECA)	Any person	Willfully violate any provision of 22 U.S.C. § 2778 or any rule or regulation issued thereunder, or who willfully in a registration or license application or required report, makes any untrue statement of a material fact or omits to state a material fact required to be stated therein or necessary to make the statements therein not misleading.	Willful and Knowing	Up to 10 years in prison and/or fine	The implementing regulations of the AECA related to importations are found at Title 27, C.F.R. § 447. The Munitions Import List is found at 27 C.F.R. § 447.21. a) Importing articles on the U.S. Munitions Import List without a permit; b) Engaging in the business of importing Munitions Import List without registering under this part; or c) Otherwise violating any provisions of this part. 27 C.F.R. § 447.62 prohibits willful false statements or concealments of fact on registration or permit applications.
Title 18, U.S.C. § 542 Entry of goods by means of false statement	Any person	Enters or attempts to enter any imported merchandise into the U.S. by means of false or fraudulent document or statement	Willful and Knowing	Up to 2 years in prison and/or fine	18 U.S.C. Chapter 27 (18 U.S.C. §§ 542, 545 and 554) are primarily enforced by U.S. Immigrations and Customs Enforcement Agency (ICE).
Title 18, U.S.C. § 545 Smuggling goods into the U.S.	Any person	With intent to defraud the U.S., smuggles or attempts to smuggle merchandise which should have been invoiced, or fraudulently imports into the U.S. any merchandise contrary to law, or receives, conceals, buys, sells or in any manner facilitates the transportation, concealment or sale of such merchandise after importation, knowing it to have been imported contrary to law.	Willful and Knowing	Up to 20 years in prison and/or fine	18 U.S.C. § 545 provides that a defendant's possession of such goods, unless explained to the satisfaction of the jury, is evidence sufficient to authorize conviction under this section. The term "U.S." does not include the Virgin Islands, American Samoa, Wake Island, Midway Islands, Kingman Reef, Johnston Island or Guam.
Title 18, U.S.C. § 554 Smuggling goods out of the U.S.	Any person	Fraudulently and knowingly exports or attempt to export from the U.S. any merchandise contrary to any U.S. law or regulation, or receives, conceals, buys, sells or in any manner facilitates the transportation, concealment or sale of such merchandise, prior to exportation, knowing the merchandise to be intended for exportation contrary to U.S. law or regulation.	Willful and Knowing	Up to 10 years in prison and/or fine	Applicable regulations related to unlawful exportations may be found in International Traffic in Arms Regulations, Title 22, C.F.R. Part 127.

Trafficking Crimes Related to the National Firearms Act of 1934					
Title 26 U.S.C. §	Makes it illegal for	To	Mental Element(s)	Potential Penalty	Other
5861(a)(1) Dealing in NFA Weapons	Any person	To engage in the business as a manufacturer or importer of, or dealer in NFA firearms without having paid the special occupational tax required by 26 U.S.C. § 5801 for his business or having registered as required by 26 U.S.C. § 5802	Knowingly: In order to obtain a conviction under the NFA, the government must prove the defendant knew the features or characteristics of the weapon that brought it under the NFA. *Staples v. United States*, 114 S.Ct. 1793 (1994). This applies to each of the NFA violations that follow.	Up to 10 years in prison and/or fine	The NFA defines firearms at 26 U.S.C. § 5845(a) to include: (1) shotguns having a barrel or barrels less than 18 inches in length; (2) weapons made from a shotgun if such weapon as modified has an overall length of less than 26 inches or a barrel or barrels of less than 18 inches in length; (3) a rifle having barrel of less than 16 inches in length; (4) a weapon made from a rifle if such weapon as modified has an overall length of less than 26 inches or barrel or barrels of less than 16 inches in length; (5) any other weapon as defined in 26 U.S.C. §5845(e); (6) machineguns as defined in 26 U.S.C. §5845(b); (7) silencers as defined in 18 U.S.C. §921(a)(24); and destructive devices as defined in 26 U.S.C. §5845(f). NFA violations may be useful in a variety of firearms trafficking scheme investigations where illegal machineguns, silencers, machinegun conversion parts, short barreled rifles or shotguns, or destructive devices are being trafficked. Sentencing guidelines for NFA violations is higher than for many GCA violations. This applies to each of the NFA violations that follow.
5861(b)		To receive or possess a firearm transferred to him in violation of this Chapter		Up to 10 years in prison and/or fine	.
5861(c)		To receive or possess a firearm made in violation of this Chapter		Up to 10 years in prison and/or fine	
5861(d)		To receive or possess a firearm which is not registered to him in the National Firearms Registration and Transfer Record		Up to 10 years in prison and/or fine	
5861(e)		To transfer a firearm in violation of this Chapter		Up to 10 years in prison and/or fine	
5861(f)		To make a firearm in violation of this Chapter		Up to 10 years in prison and/or fine	

Title 26 U.S.C. §	Makes it illegal for	To	Mental Element(s)	Potential Penalty	Other
5861(g)		To obliterate, remove, change or alter the serial number or other identification of a firearm required by this Chapter		Up to 10 years in prison and/or fine	
5861(h)		To receive or possess a firearm having the serial number or other identification required this Chapter obliterated, removed, changed or altered		Up to 10 years in prison and/or fine	
5861(i)		To receive or possess a firearm which is not identified by serial number as required by this Chapter		Up to 10 years in prison and/or fine	
5861(j)		To transport, deliver, or receive any firearm in interstate commerce which has not been registered as required by this Chapter		Up to 10 years in prison and/or fine	
5861(k)		To receive or possess a firearm which has been imported or brought into the U.S. in violation of this Chapter		Up to 10 years in prison and/or fine	
5861(l)		To make, or cause the making of, a false entry on any application, return, or record required by this Chapter, knowing such entry to be false		Up to 10 years in prison and/or fine	

General Crimes That May be Applicable in Firearms Trafficking Investigations					
Title 18 U.S.C. Section	Makes it illegal for	To	Mental Element(s)	Potential Penalty	Other
2 Aiding and Abetting	Any person	Aid, abet, counsel, command, or solicit a criminal act.	Willful and Knowing with the intent to assist in the commission of a crime	Same as for the underlying crime	This law may be applicable in a variety of firearms trafficking schemes and is an easier case to make than conspiracy because proof of an agreement is not required, HOWEVER, the underlying crime must have been accomplished and not merely planned.
3 Accessory after the fact	Any person	Receive, relieve, comfort or assist an offender in order to hinder or prevent apprehension, trial or punishment of the person.	Willful and Knowing that person has committed an offense against the U.S.	One-half the term of imprisonment for the principal violator	This law may be applicable to straw purchasers who provide firearms to someone they know is trafficking the firearms.
4 Misprision of a Felony	Any person	Know of and fail to report a felony.	Willful and Knowing there was an actual commission of a federal felony	Up to 3 years in prison and/or fine	This law may be applicable to straw purchasers who provide firearms to someone they know is trafficking the firearms.
371 Conspiracy	Any person	Agree with at least one other person to violate the law, with one person committing at least one overt act in furtherance of the agreement.	True agreement with the intent to accomplish the objective(s) of the conspiracy	Up to 5 years in prison if the underlying crime is a felony and/or fine	This law may be charged when straw purchase rings have conspired together to traffic firearms. In addition, when investigating a corrupt FFL, one consideration is use of a "Klein Conspiracy" as a theory of charging. It can be charged where there is a conspiracy to defraud the U.S. of money or property or interfere with or obstruct lawful government functions by dishonest means. *See Dennis v. United States*, 384 U.S. 855, 861 (1966). If the government can show two or more defendants engaged in a course of conduct to obstruct, impede or evade ATF's enforcement of the federal firearms laws through failure to make required records with "off- paper" sales, falsification of required records, or other unlawful activities this type of theory can be effective. This will allow for a felony charge where individual FFL records keeping violations are often charged as a misdemeanor. See Chapter 7 for additional information on the application of the Klein Conspiracy in firearms trafficking investigations.

Title 26 U.S.C. §	Makes it illegal for	To	Mental Element(s)	Potential Penalty	Other
1341 Mail Fraud	Any person	Use the mail to perpetrate or advance a scheme to defraud.	Willful and Knowing use of the mail with specific intent to perpetrate or advance a scheme to defraud	Up to 5 years in prison; 30 years if the scheme involves a financial institution, and/or fine	This law may apply to any person who reports firearms they trafficked as stolen and who also file an insurance claim for their fraudulent loss.
1715 Non-Mailable Articles	Any person	Mail a pistol, revolver, or other firearm capable of being concealed on the person.	Knowingly deposits such article	Up to 2 years in prison and/or fine	This law may be applicable to persons trafficking firearms on the internet or in classified advertisements who are shipping handguns to the purchasers through the mail.
1956(a)(1) Money Laundering	Any person	"Launder" the proceeds of specified crimes by purchasing firearms.	Willful and Knowing with specific intent to promote the crime or to violate the IRC	Up to 20 years in prison and/or fine	Firearms trafficking is an SUA for money laundering. Illegal proceeds gained through firearms trafficking are forfeitable.
2117 Burglary	Any person	Burglarize a place or conveyance containing interstate or foreign shipments.	Willful and Knowing breaking or entering with intent to commit a larceny therein	Up to 10 years in prison and/or fine	This law may be applicable during the investigation of thefts of firearms from an FFL or interstate carrier. For thefts of firearms from an FFL the investigator should use 18 USC 922(u).
1951 Interference with commerce by threats or violence	Any person	Whoever in any way or degree obstructs, delays or affects commerce or the movement of any article in commerce, by robbery or extortion or attempts conspires to do so, or commits or threatens physical violence to any person or property in furtherance of a plan to violate this section.	Willful and Knowing acts	Up to 20 years in prison and/or fine	This law may be applicable during the investigation of thefts of firearms from an FFL or interstate carrier.

STRAW PURCHASES OF FIREARMS

Under Title 18 U.S.C. § 922(a)(6), it is unlawful "for any person in connection with the acquisition or attempted acquisition of a firearm or ammunition from a licensed importer, licensed manufacturer, licensed dealer, or licensed collector, knowingly to make any false or fictitious oral or written statement or to furnish or exhibit any false, fictitious, or misrepresented identification intended or likely to deceive with respect to any fact material to the lawfulness of the sale or other disposition of such firearm or ammunition..." A person who completes an ATF Form 4473 during the purchase of a firearm certifies that they are purchasing the firearm for themselves. If in fact they are purchasing it for someone else this is a violation of the above listed statue and referred to as a Straw Purchase or Lie and Buy. The purchaser is putting themselves up as a "straw" to conceal the true identity of the person who is the intended recipient of the firearm.

Straw purchasers who do this for firearms traffickers may do so for remuneration in the form of cash or narcotics. Other straw purchasers may be purchasing a firearm for someone they know is prohibited by law from possessing firearms because they fall into one of the categories of prohibited persons listed Title 18 U.S.C. §§ 922(g) or 922(n). A prohibited person would not pass the NICS background check if they attempted to purchase the firearm themselves. A straw purchaser may also be purchasing a handgun for someone who is a resident of a state other than that in which the firearm is being purchased.

The Barnacle Allegory: Scraping Barnacles vs. Catching the Big Fish

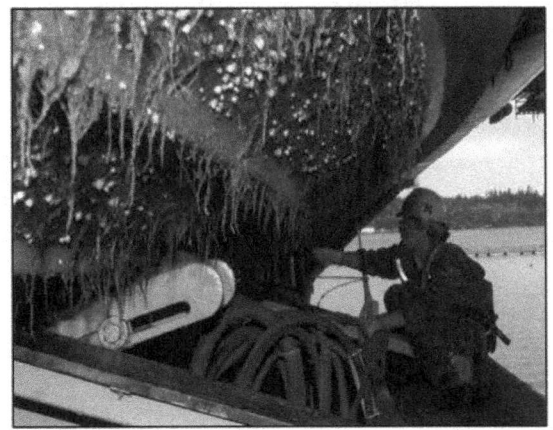

IMAGE CREDIT: U.S. Navy Photo by Mass Communication Seaman Apprentice Christopher Frost/Released

IMAGE CREDIT: Ernest Hemingway Collection John F. Kennedy Presidential Library and Museum, Boston

An ATF special agent was on the stand during the trial of a defendant who was charged with 18 USC 922(a)(6), straw purchasing by providing false information to an FFL during acquisition of a firearm. The straw purchaser had only purchased 3 or 4 firearms in total. The defense attorney tried to make light of the case by using the usual arguments and calling the case a paperwork violation, and that his client was simply charged with making an error in his answers on the form. He then he asked the agent if he would agree that the defendant was not a big fish in the world of criminal traffickers. The agent responded, "No, he is not a big fish. He is a barnacle." Asked to explain during the AUSA re-direct questioning, the agent said that straw purchasers are barnacles. A couple of barnacles on the bottom of your boat are not a problem, but hundreds of barnacles on the bottom of a boat are a major problem for the operation and performance of the boat, and can affect safety. No one likes to scrape barnacles: it's unpopular and requires lots of work. Everyone would rather be out catching the big fish, but these are few and far between. The reality is, there are lots of barnacles out there, they pop up one after the other, and someone has to scrape them. Every now and then you can catch the big fish, but scraping barnacles is a full-time job that never stops.

Figure 4.3

The straw purchaser violates federal law by making false material statements to the FFL on ATF Form 4473. Facts which have been found to be material to the lawfulness of the sale or other disposition of a firearm are: the true name and identity of the actual purchaser; the true status of the purchaser under Title 18 U.S.C. §§ 922(g) or 922(n); the true place of residency, including street address of the actual purchaser; and the date of birth of the actual purchaser. See Appendix C to review an ATF Form 4473, Firearms Transfer Transaction Record.

If the false statement to the licensee is not material to the lawfulness of the sale or disposition of the firearm, a more appropriate charge would be violation of Title 18 U.S.C. § 924(a)(1)(A). That statute prohibits knowingly making any false statement or representation with respect to the information the FFL is required to keep in their records. Since an FFL is required to maintain ATF Form 4473s in their records, a false statement with respect to any information required on the ATF Form 4473 violates Title 18 U.S.C. § 924(a)(1)(A). In addition, any false statement on an ATF Form 4473 may constitute a violation of Title 18 U.S.C. § 1001.

Most courts have found that it is immaterial that the actual purchaser and straw purchaser are residents of the state in which the licensee's business premise is located, that they are not prohibited from receiving or possessing firearms, and that they could have lawfully purchased firearms from the licensee. See United States v. Polk, 118 F.3d 286 (5th Cir. 1997).

Persons legitimately purchasing a firearm as a gift for another person are not considered to be in violation of Title 18 U.S.C. §§ 922(a)(6) or 924(a)(1)(A) when they indicate they are the actual buyer on the ATF Form 4473. The person executing the Form 4473 in that situation is considered to be the true purchaser. Gift certificates for firearms also are permissible. The person redeeming the gift certificate would be the actual purchaser of the firearm and would be properly reflected as such in the dealer's records.

Criminal defense attorneys may try to portray straw purchase cases as technical violations or argue that the straw purchaser is just a small-time violator. The problem with this portrayal is the fact that the bulk of domestically trafficked firearms in the U.S. start with straw purchasers. Straw purchasers are quite often the first step in a chain of events that puts a gun in the hands of a criminal who goes on to commit an armed crime of violence against another innocent victim.

CURIO AND RELIC PROVISIONS

During the course of a firearms trafficking investigation an investigator may come across firearms being sold by someone they believed to be an FFL who is selling firearms without requiring purchasers to complete an ATF Form 4473 or a NICS background check. Before investigators move forward with pursing criminal violations they need to ensure they are not dealing with Curio and Relic (C&R) firearms and someone who is actually a licensed C&R collector. Under Title 27 C.F.R. § 478.11, firearms classified as C&R are of special interest to collectors by reason of some quality other than is associated with firearms intended for sporting use or as offensive or defensive weapons. To be recognized as a C&R, a firearm must fall within one of the following categories:

- ✓ Firearms which were manufactured at least 50 years prior to the current date, but not including replicas thereof;
- ✓ Firearms which are certified by the curator of a municipal, state, or federal museum which exhibits firearms to be C&Rs of museum interest; and
- ✓ Any other firearms which derive a substantial part of their monetary value from the fact that they are novel, rare, bizarre, or because of their association with some historical figure, period, or event. Proof of qualification of a particular firearm under this category may be established by evidence of present value and evidence that like firearms are not available except as collector's items, or that the value of like firearms available in ordinary commercial channels is substantially less.[lxxix]

Firearms classified by ATF as C&Rs are still firearms subject to the provisions of the GCA; however, an individual may secure a license from ATF to be a collector of C&R firearms and that C&R license affords the licensee certain exemptions from the GCA to collect these firearms. C&R firearms may be transferred in interstate commerce between licensed collectors or other GCA licensees. Investigators dealing with the holder of a C&R license should be aware that the special provisions and GCA exemptions afforded to the holder of a C&R license apply solely to transactions involving designated C&R firearms, not all firearms. A C&R license holder has the same status under the GCA as a non-licensee except for any transactions in C&R firearms. The C&R license is a collector's license, not a license that authorizes the holder to engage in the business of dealing in firearms. An FFL must be obtained from ATF prior to engaging in the business of dealing in any firearms, including firearms classified as C&R. Unlike the applicant for an FFL, an applicant for a C&R license is not required to submit a photograph or fingerprints with their application. A C&R license enables a collector to obtain C&R firearms in interstate commerce, including handguns classified as C&R without executing an ATF Form 4473, undergoing a NICS background check, or being subject to a waiting period. Licensed C&R collectors are required to keep a bound Acquisition and Disposition Log to record the acquisition and disposition of C&R firearms. However, whenever a C&R licensee disposes of a C&R firearm, the purchaser is exempt from executing an ATF Form 4473 and the NICS background check requirement. Nonetheless, it is a violation of the GCA for a C&R licensee to knowingly transfer a firearm to any person prohibited under the GCA from receiving or possessing a firearm. Without a NICS background check, the C&R licensee may have a difficult time determining whether the buyer is prohibited.

C&R licensees are not required to forward their records to ATF when they go out of business, unlike any person who is a federally licensed firearms retailer, wholesaler, manufacturer, or importer.

ATF maintains the approved list of all C&R firearms. This list includes a variety of firearms, some of which do appear in various lists of most frequently traced crime guns.

A firearm is automatically classified as a C&R 50-year after the date of manufacture, assuming it is as originally configured. This rule applies to foreign-made military handguns as well as foreign-made military assault rifles that would otherwise be non-importable into the United States. However, under the C&R classification, these firearms may be importable. There is no requirement for a firearm to be officially listed in ATF's C&R list as long the firearm meets the "50-year" test.

Firearms classified as a C&R because they may have been rare a number of years ago do not lose their C&R status if changes in world politics and import laws have caused these firearms to become plentiful. Once a firearm is classified as a C&R, it retains that classification even if it becomes readily available. Examples include the Yugoslavian and Albanian SKS semiautomatic rifles, CZ 52 and CZ 82 pistols, as well as the Makarov pistols. These well-built foreign made military grade firearms were once rare but are now in abundant supply and may be acquired at a relatively low cost.

For detailed information on C&Rs as well as a comprehensive listing of firearms currently considered C&Rs, investigators should refer to the most recent ATF Publication 5300.11, Firearms Curios and Relics List.

LAWFUL INTERSTATE TRANSPORTATION OF FIREARMS

Title 18 U.S.C. § 926(A) allows any person who may lawfully possess a firearm in one to state to transport that firearm to another state where they may lawfully possess that firearm IF, during that transportation the firearm is unloaded and neither the firearm nor ammunition being transported is readily or directly accessible to the passenger compartment, or, in the case of vehicles without a compartment separate from the driver's compartment, in a locked container other than the glove box or console. For purposes of this statutory exemption, the travel must be an uninterrupted transit. That means no stopping in a state where the possessor would not be able to possess the firearm. This law is particularly useful to know for state or local investigators investigating state or local level trafficking law based on the discovery of firearms in the trunk of a car during a traffic stop on an interstate freeway. That out-of-state resident may be exempt from the state or local law if they were transporting a firearm in accordance with Title 18 U.S.C. § 926(A).

ALIENS, ILLEGAL ALIENS, NON-IMMIGRANT ALIENS, AND PERMANENT RESIDENT ALIENS

The conduct of firearm trafficking investigations will often require a working knowledge of the terms alien, illegal alien, nonimmigrant alien, and permanent resident alien with a green card in order to know whether an alien's possession of firearms or ammunition is lawful or whether an alien's statements on an ATF Form 4473 or statement to an investigator is truthful and accurate.

Alien - An alien is anyone who is not a U.S. citizen or national.

Illegal Alien - An illegal alien as defined by Title 27 C.F.R § 478.11 is anyone who is unlawfully in the U.S. who is not a valid immigrant, nonimmigrant, or has parole status. An illegal alien is any alien:

➢ who unlawfully entered the U.S. without inspection and authorization by an authorized immigration officer and who has not been paroled into the U.S. under Title 8 C.F.R § 212(d)(5) of the Immigration and Nationality Act (INA).
➢ who is a nonimmigrant and whose authorized period of stay has expired or who has violated the terms of the nonimmigrant category in which he or she was admitted.
➢ who is under INA Title 8 C.F.R § 212(d)(5)) whose authorized period of parole has expired or whose parole status has been terminated; or
➢ who is under an order of deportation, exclusion, or removal, or under an order to depart the U.S. voluntarily, whether or not he or she has left the U.S.

An illegal alien is prohibited from shipping, transporting, receiving, or possessing a firearm or ammunition under Title 18 U.S.C. § 922(g)(5)(A).

Nonimmigrant Alien - A nonimmigrant alien is an alien in the U.S. in a nonimmigrant classification status as defined by INA Title 8 C.F.R § 101(a) (15) and Title 8 U.S.C. 1101(a) (15). In general, "nonimmigrant aliens" are tourists, students, business travelers, and temporary workers who enter the U.S. for fixed periods of time; they are lawfully admitted aliens who are not lawful permanent residents. If a nonimmigrant alien overstays their period approved for being present in the U.S. or if they otherwise void the terms that allow them to be present in the U.S. as a nonimmigrant alien, they lose this classification and become an illegal alien.

A nonimmigrant alien is prohibited from shipping, transporting, receiving, or possessing a firearm or ammunition under Title 18 U.S.C. § 922(g)(5)(B) unless the alien falls within one of the exceptions provided in Title 18 U.S.C. § 922(y)(2), such as: a valid hunting license or permit, admitted for lawful hunting or sporting purposes, certain official representatives of a foreign government, or a foreign law enforcement officer of a friendly foreign government entering the U.S. on official law enforcement business. A nonimmigrant alien may also apply to ATF for a waiver from the prohibition on shipping, transporting, receiving, or possessing a firearms or ammunition.

A nonimmigrant alien who possesses a valid hunting license from a state within the U.S. or falls within any of the other exceptions or exemptions that allow nonimmigrant aliens to possess firearms may purchase or rent firearms to hunt or to use at a shooting range. A valid, unexpired hunting license or permit from any state within the U.S. satisfies the hunting license exception to the nonimmigrant alien prohibition. The hunting license or permit does not have to be from the state where the nonimmigrant alien is purchasing the firearm.

A nonimmigrant alien without residency in any state may not purchase and take possession of a firearm. A nonimmigrant alien may only purchase a firearm through a licensee where the licensee arranges to have the firearm directly exported. A nonimmigrant alien who falls within an exception may, however, purchase and take possession of ammunition.

A nonimmigrant alien who has established residency in a state may purchase and take possession of a firearm from an unlicensed person, provided the buyer and seller are residents of the same state, and no other state or local law prohibits the transaction. A nonimmigrant alien with residency in a state may purchase a firearm from a licensee, provided the sale complies with all applicable laws and regulations.

Permanent Resident Alien - A permanent resident alien is someone who possesses a "green card" and is not in nonimmigrant status. A permanent resident alien may ship, transport, receive, or possess a firearm or ammunition in the same way that a U.S. citizen may.

All permanent resident aliens and authorized nonimmigrant aliens need an alien registration number (also known as an A-number) or admission number to purchase a firearm from an FFL. An FFL cannot complete the sale without an A-number. This is the case even if the nonimmigrant alien has a state permit that ATF has determined qualifies as a "NICS alternative" and therefore does not need to have a NICS background check.

An alien registration number is a unique 7, 8, or 9-digit number assigned to a noncitizen by the Department of Homeland Security (DHS) upon the creation of a file.

An admission number is the number on a CBP Form I–94 or CBP Form I–94W, the arrival/departure form Customs and Border Protection (CBP) gives most nonimmigrant aliens when they arrive in the U.S. While most nonimmigrant aliens will automatically receive an admission number when they enter the U.S., Canadians will not. However, if a Canadian asks a CBP official for an admission number when they enter the U.S., they will be given an admission number.

INTERNATIONAL TRAFFIC IN ARMS REGULATIONS (ITAR) AND FIREARMS IMPORTS

The Arms Export Control Act (AECA) was passed into law in 1976 during the Cold War as a means for the U.S. to establish control over the import and export of defense articles and their subsequent re-distribution. Title 22 U.S.C. § 2778(a)(1) states that in furtherance of world peace and the security and foreign policy of the U.S., the President is authorized to control the import and the export of defense articles and defense services and to provide foreign policy guidance to persons of the U.S. involved in the export and import of such articles and services. The President is authorized to designate those items which shall be considered as defense articles and defense services for the purposes of this section and to promulgate regulations for the import and export of such articles and services. The items so designated shall constitute the U.S. Munitions List. (USML)

Exportation - The U.S. Department of State (DOS), Directorate of Defense Trade Controls (DDTC) is responsible for oversight of the export and temporary import of defense articles and services governed by Title 22 U.S.C. § 2778 of the AECA. The International Traffic in Arms Regulations (ITAR) implements the export provisions of the AECA through regulations contained in Title 22 C.F.R. §§ 120-130. The import provisions of the AECA are implemented through regulations contained in Title 27 C.F.R. § 447. The regulations contained in the ITAR are updated annually.

The U.S. Department of Commerce, Bureau of Industry and Security, Export Counseling Division regulates the exportation of sporting shotguns, shotgun parts, sporting shotgun ammunition, firearm-type accessories and certain parts (e.g. sights, scopes, and mounts).

Title 22 C.F.R. § 121.1 contains the USML. The List contains 21 categories of controlled defense articles and munitions. Most items related to firearms trafficking will be found in Category I - Firearms, Close Assault Weapons and Combat Shotguns

A defense article means any item or technical data designated in the USML. There is additional policy contained in Title 22 C.F.R. §120.3 that lists the designation of additional items to the USML. These additional items include forgings, castings, and other unfinished products, such as extrusions and machined bodies, that have reached a stage in manufacturing where they are clearly identifiable by mechanical properties, material composition, geometry, or function as defense articles listed on the USML.

To possess or attempt to possess any defense article with intent to export or transfer such defense article in violation of Title 22 U.S.C. §§ 2778 and 2779, or any regulation, license, approval, or order issued thereunder. No person may knowingly or willfully attempt, solicit, cause, or aid, abet, counsel, demand, induce, procure, or permit the commission of any act prohibited by, or the omission of any act required by Title 22 U.S.C. §§ 2778 and 2779, or any regulation, license, approval, or order issued thereunder.

It is also unlawful to use or attempt to use any export or temporary import control document containing a false statement or misrepresenting or omitting a material fact for the purpose of exporting, transferring, re-exporting, retransferring, obtaining, or furnishing any defense article, technical data, or defense service. Any false statement, misrepresentation, or omission of material fact in an export or temporary import control document will be considered as made in a matter within the jurisdiction of a department or agency of the United States for the purposes of Title 18 U.S.C. § 1001, Title 22 U.S.C. §§ 2778 and 2779.[lxxx]

Importation - ATF is responsible for approving the importation of firearms. Title 27 C.F.R. § 447.21 contains the U.S. Munitions Import List (USMIL). The List contains 21 categories of controlled defense articles and munitions. Most items related to firearms trafficking will be found in Category I - Firearms, Close Assault Weapons and Combat Shotguns.

A defense article means any item or technical data designated in the USMIL. There is additional policy contained in Title 27, C.F.R. § 447.22 that lists the designation of additional items to the USMIL. These additional items include articles on the USMIL that are in a partially completed state, such as forgings, castings, extrusions, and machined bodies, which have reached a stage in manufacture where they are clearly identifiable as defense articles. If the end-item is an article on the USMIL, (including components, accessories, attachments and parts) then the particular forging, casting, extrusion, machined body, etc., is considered a defense article subject to the controls of this part, except for such items as are in normal commercial use. This regulation is very pertinent to firearms trafficking investigation trends, as castings of firearms frames and receivers, such as AR-15s, as well as firearms parts, have become a popular commodity that is frequently trafficked into the U.S illegally.

Title 27 C.F.R. § 447.62 prohibits anyone from willfully:
a. importing articles on the U.S. Munitions Import List without a permit;
b. engaging in the business of importing Munitions Import List without registering under this part; or
c. otherwise violating any provisions of this part.

Title 27 C.F.R. § 447.62 prohibits willful false statements or concealments of fact on registration or permit applications.[lxxxi]

Persons who engage in the importation of defense articles in violation of the above regulations are in criminal violation of Title 22 U.S.C. §§ 2778 and 2779.

The legal process that FFL importers must adhere to when importing firearms or ammunition into the U.S. is as follows:

✓ The FFL importer submits an ATF Form 6, Application and Permit for Importation of Firearms, to ATF for review. See Appendix C to review ATF Form 6 and 6A. Following review and approval, the ATF Form 6 permit is returned to applicant along with two blank ATF Forms 6A.

✓ In addition to the ATF Forms 6 and 6A already required to obtain the release of firearms, firearm parts, or ammunition, the FFL importer must also present to CBP officials a copy of the export license authorizing the export of the articles from the country of export. If the exporting country does not require the issuance of an export license, the FFL importer instead must present a certification, signed under penalties of perjury, attesting to that effect.

✓ CBP may conduct a physical examination of the articles to ensure the articles imported match the articles described and approved for importation on the Form 6 and completed Form 6A.

✓ CBP then completes Section II of the first Form 6A if they are satisfied that the shipment of firearms, ammunition or implements of war are authorized by ATF. The CBP official then returns the Form 6 to the FFL importer who sends a Form 6A, with Section II completed, to the ATF Firearms and Explosives Imports Branch (FEIB)

✓ Within 15 days after the articles have been released by CBP, including release from a Customs Bonded Warehouse (CBW) or Free Trade Zone (FTZ), the importer MUST complete the marking requirements of Title 27 C.F.R § 478.92 and/or § 479.102 and the record keeping requirements of Title 27 C.F.R § 478.122. This includes marking each firearm with importer markings, the addition of a unique serial number for firearms that do not have one or has an unacceptable serial (e.g., uses Cyrillic, Chinese, or Arabic Characters), and any required physical modifications necessary for the firearm to be imported legally (e.g., addition of a safety to handguns).

✓ Within that same 15 days, Title 27 C.F.R. § 478.112 requires that each FFL importer of firearms must complete Section III of the second ATF Form 6A and forward it directly to the ATF FEIB. An original signature must be placed in block 19 of the form.

✓ FFL importers are also required to maintain permanent records of the importation of firearms, including Forms 6 or 6A, in accordance with Title 27 C.F.R. § 478.129(d).

According to CBP and ATF, more than 5 million firearms were imported into the U.S. in 2017, with a value of close to $2 billion[lxxxii]. Those firearms enter the U.S. through more than 300 CBP ports of entry in the United States, Puerto Rico, and the U.S. Virgin Islands. In accordance with Title 27 C.F.R. § 53.61(a), the Firearms and Ammunition Excise Tax (FAET) is 10% of the sale price of pistols and revolvers and 11% of the sale price of other firearms and ammunition, so in addition to protecting public safety, scrutiny of firearms and ammunition importations is also important to collecting significant sums of tax revenue due to the federal government.

In addition to CBP operated ports of entry, firearms and ammunition may be placed in a CBW. A CBW is a building or other secured area in which imported dutiable merchandise may be stored, manipulated, or undergo manufacturing operations without payment of duty for up to 5 years from the date of importation. Authority for establishing bonded warehouses is set forth in Title 19, U.S.C., § 1555. The regulations covered the operation of bonded warehouses is found at Title 19 C.F.R § 19.

When firearms or ammunition are placed in a CBW, the proprietor of the CBW assumes liability for the items under a warehouse bond. This liability is generally cancelled when the merchandise is exported, withdrawn for consumption in the U.S. following payment of duty, destroyed under CBP supervision, or withdrawn for supplies to a vessel or aircraft.

There are eleven different classes of CBWs authorized under Title 19 C.F.R. § 19.1:

1. Premises that may be owned or leased by the Government, when the exigencies of the service as determined by the port director so require and are used for the storage of merchandise undergoing examination by CBP, under seizure, or pending final release from CBP custody. Merchandise will be stored in such premises only at CBP direction and will be held under "general order".

2. Importer's private warehouse used exclusively for the storage of merchandise belonging to or consigned to the proprietor. A class 4 or 5 warehouse may be bonded exclusively for the storage of goods imported by the proprietor, in which case it shall be known as a private bonded warehouse.

3. Public bonded warehouse used exclusively for the storage of imported merchandise.

4. Bonded yards or sheds used for the storage of heavy and bulky imported merchandise, including: stables, feeding pens, corrals, other similar buildings or limited enclosures for the storage of imported animals; and tanks for storage of imported liquid merchandise in bulk.

5. Bonded bins or parts of buildings or elevators used for the storage of grain.

6. Bonded warehouses established for the manufacture in bond, solely for exportation of articles made in whole or in part of imported materials or of materials subject to internal revenue tax; and for the manufacture for domestic consumption or exportation of cigars made in whole of tobacco imported from one country.

7. Bonded warehouses established for smelting and refining imported metal-bearing materials for exportation or domestic consumption.

8. Bonded warehouses established for the cleaning, sorting, repacking, or otherwise changing the condition of, but not the manufacturing of, imported merchandise, under CBP supervision, and at the expense of the proprietor.

9. Bonded warehouses, known as "duty-free stores," used for selling conditionally duty-free merchandise for use outside the Customs territory. Merchandise in this class must be owned or sold by the proprietor and delivered from the warehouse to an airport or other exit point for exportation by, or on behalf of, individuals departing from the Customs territory or foreign destinations. These stores may also sell other than duty-free merchandise.

10. Bonded warehouses for international travel merchandise, goods sold conditionally duty-free aboard aircraft and not at a duty-free store. This is based on amendments to Title 19 U.S.C. § 555(c), approved 11/00. Regulations governing this type of warehouse are being written.

11. Bonded warehouses established for the storage of General Order (G.O.) merchandise. G.O. is any merchandise not claimed or entered for 15 days after arrival in the U.S. (or final U.S. destination for in-bond shipments).

There are a variety of restrictions on the type of firearms and ammunition that may be legally imported, as well as the country of origin of the firearm or ammunition. In May 1994 the U.S. instituted a firearms imports embargo against China. Sporting shotguns, however, are exempt from the embargo. In 1998 the U.S. and Russia entered into a Voluntary Restraint Agreement (VRA) which prohibits firearms imports, with some enumerated exceptions, from Georgia, Kazakhstan, Kyrgyzstan, Moldova, Russian Federation, Turkmenistan, Ukraine, Uzbekistan. Exceptions to the VRA may include firearms from those countries that were outside those proscribed countries for the preceding five years prior to import into the U.S.

The U.S State Department maintains a list of proscribed countries from which firearms imports are prohibited. Those countries include Afghanistan, Belarus, Burma, China Cuba, Democratic

Republic of Congo, Haiti, Iran, Iraq, Libya, Mongolia, North Korea, Rwanda, Somalia Sudan, Syria, Angola, and Vietnam. Exceptions to the prohibition may include firearms imported under wavier from the U.S. State Department as well as surplus military Curio and Relic firearms that were manufactured in these countries prior to becoming proscribed or embargoed and had been outside those proscribed countries for the preceding five years prior to import into the U.S.

Restrictions also exist on armor piercing ammunition in Title 27 C.F.R. § 478.37. It is illegal to manufacture or import into the U.S any armor piercing ammunition for transfer to anyone other than a federal or state government agency. That ammunition must be manufactured with at least 50% of the projectile tip colored black and the surface of each package must use contrasting color to depict the words "ARMOR PIERCING" in block letter at least 1/4-inch in height and "FOR GOVERNMENTAL ENTITIES OR EXPORTATION ONLY" in block letter at least 1/8-inch height as well as the caliber or gauge of the ammunition.

OTHER RESOURCES

Resources containing extensive information concerning the importation of firearms include the following publications;

ATF Guidebook; Importation & Verification of Firearms, Ammunition, and Implements of War (2017, March, 28). By U.S. Department of Justice, Bureau of Alcohol, Tobacco, Firearms and Explosives. Washington, D.C.

Importing into the US – A Guide for Commercial Importers, CBP Publication No. 0000-0504. (Rev. March 2014). By U.S. Department of Homeland Security, Customs and Border Protection. Washington, D.C.

Federal Firearms Regulation Reference Guide (ATF Publication 5300.4). (Rev. Ed 2014). By U.S. Department of Justice, Bureau of Alcohol, Tobacco, Firearms and Explosives. Washington, D.C.

TABLE 4.2 Overview of State Laws

State	State Requirements for Private Citizens				State Requirements for Federal Firearms FFLs					State Laws Related to Firearms Trafficking				
	Permit Required to Purchase Firearms **	Concealed Carry ***	Must Report Stolen Firearm	Firearm Registration ****	State License Required	Residential Dealers Prohibited	Background Checks on Employees	Security Measures Required	Theft or Loss Reporting	Straw Purchase & False Statement Laws	Firearms Trafficking Laws	Background Checks on ALL Firearm Sales	Crime Gun Tracing Required	Gun Show Regulations
AL	*--	S	--	--	Yes	--	--	--	--	Yes	--	--	--	Yes
AK	--	C	--	--	--	--	--	--	--	--	--	--	--	--
AR	--	C	--		--	--	--	--	--	--	--	--	--	--
AZ	--	C	--	--	--	--	--	--	--	--	--	--	--	--
CA	Yes	M	Yes	Yes-AW	Yes	--	--	Yes	Yes	Yes	Yes	Yes	--	Yes
CO	--	S	Yes		--	--	--	--	--	Yes	Yes	Yes	--	Yes
CT	Yes	S	--	Yes-AW	Yes	--	Yes	Yes	--	--	--	Yes	Yes	Yes
DE	--	M	Yes	--	Yes	--	Yes	--	--	--	--	Yes	--	--
DC	Yes	S	Yes	Yes	Yes	--	--	Yes	--	--	--	Yes	--	--
FL	--	S	--	--	--	--	--	--	--	--	--	--	--	--
GA	--	S	--	--	--	--	--	--	--	Yes	--	--	--	--
HI	Yes	M	--	Yes	Yes	--	--	--	--	--	--	--	--	--
IA	Yes-H	S	--	--	--	--	--	--	--	--	--	--	--	--
ID	--	C	--	--	--	--	--	--	--	--	--	--	--	--
IL	Yes	S	Yes		--	--	--	--	--	Yes	--	--	Yes	Yes
IN	--	S	--	--	Yes	--	--	--	--	--	--	--	--	--
KS	--	C	--	--	--	--	--	--	--	--	--	--	--	--
KY	--	S	--	--	--	--	--	--	--	Yes	--	--	--	--
LA	--	S	--	--	--	--	--	--	--	Yes	--	--	--	--
ME	--	C	--	--	--	--	--	--	--	--	--	--	--	Yes
MD	Yes-H	M	Yes	Yes-AW	Yes	--	--	--	--	Yes	Yes	Yes	--	Yes
MA	Yes	M	Yes	--	Yes	Yes	--	Yes	Yes	Yes	--	--	--	--
MI	--	S	Yes	--	--	--	--	--	--	--	--	--	--	--
MN	Yes-H	S	--	--	--	--	--	Yes	--	Yes	Yes	--	--	--
MO	--	C	--	--	--	--	--	--	--	Yes	--	--	--	--
MS	--	C	--	--	--	--	--	--	--	Yes	--	--	--	--
MT	--	S	--	--	--	--	--	--	--	--	--	--	--	--
NE	Yes-H	S	--	--	--	--	--	--	--	--	--	--	--	--
NH	--	C	--	--	Yes	--	--	--	--	--	--	--	--	--
NJ	Yes	M	Yes	Yes-AW	Yes	--	Yes	Yes	Yes	Yes	Yes	--	Yes	--
NY	Yes-H	M	Yes	Yes-H-AW	Yes	--	--	--	--	Yes	--	Yes	Yes	Yes
NC	Yes-H	S	--	--	--	--	--	--	--	--	--	--	--	--
ND	--	C	--	--	--	--	--	--	--	Yes	--	--	--	--
NM	--	S	--	--	--	--	--	--	--	--	--	--	--	--
NV	--	S	--	--	--	--	--	--	--	--	--	Yes	--	--
OH	--	S	Yes	--	--	--	--	--	--	--	--	--	--	--
OK	--	S	--	--	--	--	--	--	--	Yes	--	--	--	Yes
OR	--	S	--	--	--	--	--	--	--	Yes	--	Yes	--	Yes
PA	--	S	--	--	Yes	--	--	Yes	--	Yes	Yes	Yes	Yes	--
RI	Yes-H	M	Yes	--	Yes	--	--	Yes	--	Yes	Yes	Yes	--	--
SC	--	S	--	--	--	--	--	--	--	--	--	--	--	--
SD	--	S	--	--	--	--	--	--	--	--	--	--	--	--
TN	--	S	--	--	--	--	--	--	--	--	--	--	--	Yes
TX	--	S	--	--	--	--	--	--	--	--	--	--	--	--
UT	--	S	--	--	--	--	--	--	--	Yes	--	--	--	--

State	State Requirements for Private Citizens				State Requirements for Federal Firearms FFLs					State Laws Related to Firearms Trafficking				
	Permit Required to Purchase Firearms **	Concealed Carry ***	Must Report Stolen Firearm	Firearm Registration ****	State License Required	Residential Dealers Prohibited	Background Checks on Employees	Security Measures Required	Theft or Loss Reporting	Straw Purchase & False Statement Laws	Firearms Trafficking Laws	Background Checks on ALL Firearm Sales	Crime Gun Tracing Required	Gun Show Regulations
VA	--	S	--	--	--	--	Yes	--	--	Yes	--	--	Yes	Yes
VT	--	C	--	--	--	--	--	--	--	--	--	--	--	--
WA	--	S	--	--	Yes	--	Yes	--	--	--	--	Yes	--	--
WV	--	C	--	--	--	--	--	Yes	--	Yes	--	--	--	--
WI	--	S	--	--	Yes	--	--	--	--	--	--	--	--	--
WY	--	C	--	--	--	--	--	--	--	--	--	--	--	--

* - - = No
**YES-H = The state only requires a permit to purchase a handgun.
***For Purposes of this Chart there are 3 concealed carry types; S = The state SHALL issue a permit to any applicant who may legally possess firearm. M = The state MAY issue a permit if they chose. C = The state has Constitutional Carry which allows anyone to carry a concealed firearm as long as it is legal for them to possess the firearm
****For purposes of this Chart there are 3 registration types; Yes = All firearms. Yes-H = Handguns Only, Yes-AW = Assault Weapons Only

Chapter 5
Forfeiture of Firearms and the Illegal Proceeds of Firearms Trafficking

"The first and most important rule of gun-running is, never get shot with your own merchandise. The second rule of gun-running is always ensure you have a fool-proof way of getting paid, preferably in advance, preferably to an offshore account."
Yuri Orlov (played by Nicholas Cage) in the 2005 film, LORD OF WAR,
written and directed by Andrew Niccol

Asset forfeiture has been described as "the divestiture without compensation of property used in a manner contrary to the laws of the sovereign." [lxxxiii] The government confiscates property because it has been made, imported, transferred, possessed, or used in violation of the law. The principle objective of any forfeiture action should be law enforcement oriented. When used, forfeiture is either punitive or remedial. Punitive purposes of forfeiture are to punish the criminal, deter illegal activity, remove the tools of the criminal trade, and disrupt the organization. Remedial purposes of forfeiture are to protect the community and return assets to victims.[lxxxiv]

The types of assets that are subject to seizure and forfeiture by the government are property that is contraband, proceeds of crime, property that facilitates crime, and the property of a criminal enterprise. Most recovered crime guns are handguns, rifles, and shotguns which are legal commodities that were either illegally possessed or illegally used in a crime. Firearms illegally possessed or used in a crime are property that facilitates crime. The firearm itself is not illegal contraband in the same way that narcotics or counterfeit currency are illegal contraband. The term "illegal firearm" is a misnomer frequently used to describe a firearm that was illegally possessed or used, but the firearm in and of itself is not illegal. Under federal law the only firearms that are truly contraband are machine guns, silencers, sawed-off shotguns, and other specified devices that are not registered with ATF in accordance with the NFA. There is also derivative contraband, which is property that is legal to possess but has been used in some manner to support a crime. Examples of this include drug scales or paraphernalia. In the case of contraband machine guns, this may include machinery used to manufacture the machine guns or vehicles used in their transport.

For an investigator to lawfully and permanently seize a crime gun, and never return the firearm to the owner or the owner's designated third party, the firearm must be forfeited so that the government gains legal title. Taking a firearm from someone and not returning it without properly forfeiting the firearm may be a violation of the 4th and 14th Amendments to the U.S Constitution that protect persons from unreasonable search and seizure, as well as the deprivation

of property without due process of law.[lxxxv] For any property to be forfeited there must be a specific statute that authorizes forfeiture of the property or asset, and there must be sufficient evidence to establish that the property or asset is subject to forfeiture as defined in the statute. The forfeiture process must include notice, to the person from whom it is seized, of the government's intent to seize the firearm, and they must be afforded an opportunity to challenge the forfeiture.

TYPES OF FORFEITURE AND THE FORFEITURE OF FIREARMS

Summary Forfeiture. With this non-judicial forfeiture, there is a law that has established that a certain type of property has no lawful or legitimate purpose and is therefore deemed contraband. Examples include narcotics, counterfeit currency, and unregistered machine guns or silencers. These forfeitures generally require no legal process, as no one can have a right in that which is contraband.

Administrative Forfeiture. With this non-judicial forfeiture, agencies with the proper duly authorized statutory authority may pursue administrative forfeiture of recovered crime guns. The seizing investigator must show probable cause that the firearm being seized was illegally possessed or used in a crime. The person from whom the firearm is seized is noticed of their right to contest the forfeiture, and the seizure of the firearm is advertised, so that anyone else who may have claim to the firearm may see that it was seized. If anyone contests the forfeiture, the administrative forfeiture will cease, and the government must pursue judicial forfeiture. It should be noted that any attempt to contest a forfeiture and file claim to the firearm can be used as evidence in a criminal case. In other words, if a prohibited person, such as a convicted felon, files claim to a firearm being forfeited from them, this statement may potentially be used against as an admission of ownership and possession. If they do not contest the forfeiture, the government will win legal title over the firearm and a Final Declaration of Forfeiture will be issued. ATF has administrative forfeiture authority for firearms and ammunition under the CGA, Title 18 U.S.C. § 924(d)) when it can be shown that a firearm or ammunition was used in any knowing violation of most of the subsections of Title 18 U.S.C. § 922. In addition, ATF has administrative forfeiture through the NFA, Title 26 U.S.C. § 5872 for any firearm involved in any violation of Title 26 U.S.C. §§ 5801-5861, and any vehicles used to transport NFA firearms. Timelines for how quickly administrative forfeiture must be initiated from the moment of seizure of the firearms by law enforcement, how quickly notice of forfeiture must be made, and how long public notice of the forfeiture must be posted are proscribed by the Civil Asset Forfeiture Reform Act (CAFRA) of 2000. Real estate may not be seized through administrative forfeiture, and the value of any property that is allowed to be seized for administrative forfeiture may not exceed $500,000. If the property to be forfeited exceeds that value, it must be judicially forfeited.

Judicial Forfeiture. Investigators and prosecutors may use the federal court system to pursue judicial forfeiture. Judicial forfeiture involves a criminal or civil indictment listing the specific property to be forfeited. All persons that may have claim to the property are noticed, and they may challenge the forfeiture in federal court. There are 2 types of judicial forfeiture:

➤ **Criminal Forfeiture.** Criminal forfeiture is an "in-personam" action; that is, an action against the property owner, and one which must be pursued as part of a criminal prosecution of the property owner. The forfeiture is treated as part of the defendant's criminal case. The criminal indictment will briefly describe what crimes these items were alleged to have been used in that make them subject to forfeiture. The defendant will be noticed of the planned forfeiture, and they may challenge the forfeiture in federal court along with the criminal charges they face. The defendant may plead or be found guilty of the charges and that the items are subject to forfeiture. If this occurs, the judge will finalize and declare the items forfeited during sentencing.

> **Civil Forfeiture.** Civil forfeiture is an "in-rem" action; that is, an action against the property itself without regard to the guilt or innocence of the property owner. The owner may not be charged with a crime, but the property is charged with having been used in a crime and subject to forfeiture. The title of the court action may read "U.S. vs. 15 Firearms and 230 Rounds of Ammunition". The indictment will briefly describe what crimes these items were alleged to have been used in that make them subject to forfeiture. The owner of the property will be noticed of the planned forfeiture and may challenge the forfeiture in federal court. It is rare that civil forfeiture is used to forfeit firearms and ammunition, and it is recommended as the forfeiture option of last resort.

Consent to Forfeiture. With this non-judicial forfeiture, a person of interest, suspect, or defendant can authorize their consent to the forfeiture and destruction of firearms or ammunition that they are willing to voluntarily turn over to the investigator. The authorization of their consent should be done in writing using a form that has the consentee sign and expressly abandon any rights to file a claim for the firearm at a later date or petition for remission and mitigation of the forfeiture, and expressly waive all constitutional, legal and equitable claims arising out of and/or defenses to forfeiture of the property in any proceeding, including any claim of innocent ownership and any claim or defense under the Eighth Amendment, and including any claim that such forfeiture constitutes an Excessive Fine. Departments should have a standard consent to forfeiture form drawn up to use for this purpose that is reviewed and approved by Counsel. An example of a Consent to Forfeiture or Destruction of Property and Waiver of Notice appears in Appendix D.

Options for Disposition of Crime Guns in the Absence of Forfeiture. In the absence of proper forfeiture authority or other manner of securing legal title over a recovered crime gun, a law enforcement agency may find that they do not have any legal standing to keep or destroy the firearm. If an investigator finds themselves in that situation, they are still not required to return a firearm to someone who is legally prohibited from having the firearm; however, they may have to provide the firearm to that person's designee who may legally possess the firearm. A prohibited person may direct the firearm be provided to an FFL who will sell the firearm and provide the person with the proceeds of the sale. A prohibited person may direct the firearm be provided to a museum, relative, friend, or any other person or entity that is not prohibited from possessing a firearm.

FORFEITING THE PROCEEDS OF ILLEGAL FIREARMS TRAFFICKING

Money is the prime reason criminals engage in almost any type of illegal activity, and firearms traffickers are no different. Money-laundering becomes necessary to deal with the profit generated by their crime, and it is the method by which criminals disguise the illegal origins of their gains and protect their assets purchased with those gains, to avoid the suspicion of law enforcement agencies and prevent leaving a trail of incriminating evidence. The two most widely used investigative techniques for pursuing forfeiture of illegal assets are asset tracking and money flow analysis.

Asset Tracking. A process in which an investigator focuses on the trafficker and, through investigation, tracks and locates their hidden assets and then moves to forfeit those assets. This type of forfeiture investigation is most common in a firearm trafficking investigation.

Money Flow Analysis. A process in which an investigator analyzes aggregate data and suspicious money flow indicators, such as Banking Anti-Money Laundering (AML) Cash Transaction Reports (CTR) and Suspicious Activity Reports (SAR), to identify the flow of illegal proceeds, and then works back to determine who is involved with the money, what crime is being committed, and how to charge the violator and forfeit the illegal assets. Use of the money flow analysis process to detect money laundering is akin to data mining aggregate crime gun data in ATF's LEAD to detect firearms trafficking.

Forfeiture Statutes. While there is a wide array of federal forfeiture statues, the following are a few of the forfeiture statutes that are most frequently associated with firearms trafficking investigations.

Narcotics Offenses. The following two statutes allow for forfeiture of the proceeds of the crimes as well as any property used to commit the narcotics offenses:
➤ Title 21 U.S.C. § 853 authorizes criminal forfeiture
➤ Title 21 U.S.C. § 881 authorizes civil forfeiture

Racketeering and Organized Crime. The RICO statute, Title 18 U.S.C. § 1963, allows the forfeiture of any property acquired or maintained through the racketeering activity as described in the statute.

Terrorism. The terrorism statutes provide wide-ranging authority for forfeiture. These two statutes allow the government to forfeit all assets, foreign or domestic, of any individual, entity, or organization engaged in planning or perpetrating any act of domestic or international terrorism against the United States, its citizens and residents, or their property.
➤ Title 18 U.S.C. § 981(a)(1)(G), (H) authorizes civil forfeiture
➤ Title 28 U.S.C. § 2461(c) authorizes criminal forfeiture

Money Laundering, Mail and Wire Fraud, and Other Financial Crimes. These two statutes authorize forfeiture for money laundering, mail and wire fraud, tax evasion including failure to pay Firearms and Ammunition Excise Tax (FAET), as well as many other crimes:
➤ Title 18 U.S.C. § 981 authorizes civil forfeiture
➤ Title 18 U.S.C. § 982 authorizes criminal forfeiture

The type of crime will determine what is subject to forfeiture. In money laundering cases, the statutes allow the forfeiture of all property involved in the money laundering offense. In mail and wire fraud cases, the statutes only allow for the forfeiture of the proceeds of the crime.

Structuring and Other Currency Violations. These two statutes authorize civil and criminal forfeiture for cases involving structuring (illegally breaking up transactions to avoid reporting requirements) and other currency violations, such as bulk cash smuggling. They allow the forfeiture of all property involved in and any property traceable to the structuring activity.
➤ Title 31 U.S.C. § 5317(c) authorizes criminal and civil forfeiture for structuring and currency violations
➤ Title 31 U.S.C. § 5332 authorizes criminal and civil forfeiture for bulk cash smuggling

Crimes Listed as Specified Unlawful Activity. A Specified Unlawful Activity (SUA) is a specific set of crimes defined in Title 18 U.S.C. § 1956(c)(7). These crimes include a variety of state and federal crimes, including fraud, obscenity, kidnapping, homicide, drug offenses, and firearms trafficking. The following two forfeiture statutes allow the forfeiture of the proceeds of any SUA.

➤ Title 18 U.S.C. § 981(a)(1)(C) authorizes civil forfeiture
➤ Title 28 U.S.C. § 2461(c) authorizes criminal forfeiture of anything that could be forfeited through civil forfeiture

The following firearms trafficking-related offenses are SUAs for purposes of money laundering:

➤ **Title 18 U.S.C. §922(l)**. The knowing importation or possession of any firearm or ammunition imported into the U.S. in violation of the GCA.

➤ **Title 18 U.S.C. § 924(n)**. Anyone who intentionally travels from any state or foreign country into any other state of the U.S. and acquires or attempts to acquire a firearm that other state in furtherance of conduct constituting a violation of Title 18 U.S.C. § 922(a)(1)(A) – dealing in firearms without a license.

➤ **Title 26 U.S.C. § 7201** of the Internal Revenue Code (IRC). Any person who willfully attempts in any manner to evade or defeat any tax imposed. This includes evading or defeating payment of the NFA tax for the making or transferring of NFA firearms as well as Firearms and Ammunition Excise Tax (FAET) due on firearms or ammunition imported into the U.S.

➤ **Title 26 U.S.C. § 7206**. Anyone who willfully makes false statements, executes false documents, removes or conceals goods and property, or destroys records in order to evade or defeat a tax due. This includes evading or defeating payment of the NFA tax for the making or transferring of NFA firearms as well as Firearms and Ammunition Excise Tax (FAET) due on firearms or ammunition imported into the U.S.

➤ **Title 26 U.S.C. § 4216(b)**. Constructive Sale Price – anyone who conducts a sales transaction that is not at arms-length for the purpose of causing the first retail sale to be less than fair market value in order to evade the amount of taxes due. This includes evading or defeating payment of the NFA tax for the making or transferring of NFA firearms as well as Firearms and Ammunition Excise Tax (FAET) due on firearms or ammunition imported into the U.S.

➤ **Title 22 U.S.C. § 2778**. The Arms Export Control Act

An example of a seizure warrant designed to forfeit illegal proceeds and assets derived from the illegal proceeds of firearms trafficking appears as the last exhibit in Appendix D.

Other Assets; Money Judgments and Substitute Assets. In investigations in which the illegal proceeds of a criminal enterprise such as firearms trafficking have been spent or cannot be located for forfeiture, the investigator should consider other forfeiture options available to them.

✓ **Money Judgments**. When a defendant no longer holds the proceeds involved in the offense, the investigator may seek a money judgment through the criminal judicial forfeiture process to secure a preliminary order of forfeiture for the value of the proceeds not recovered. This is tantamount to a lien against any assets the defendant may have or earn in the future. Money judgments are in effect until the full amount is collected or the death of the defendant. Because a money judgment is not specific to an asset, no notice of forfeiture is required until an asset is identified and seized.

✓ **Substitute Assets**. If the government is unable to locate assets forfeited in a preliminary order of forfeiture, the government may seek to forfeit substitute assets not directly forfeitable in relation to the underlying crime, up to the value of the missing assets. Substitute assets do not need to be traceable to the offence. The government may amend an existing order of forfeiture to include subsequently identified assets belonging to the defendant. Third party interests in any asset must be identified and protected. Substitute asset provisions apply in

narcotics cases as well as any fraud and economic crimes related to Title 18 U.S.C. § 982(b)(1) and Title 28 U.S.C. § 2461(c). Conditions for which a judge may enter an order for substitute assets includes any asset that by an act or omission of the defendant:
➢ cannot be located following due diligence efforts;
➢ has been transferred, sold, or otherwise provided to a third party;
➢ has been placed beyond the jurisdiction of the court;
➢ has been substantially diminished in value; and/or
➢ has been co-mingled with other property which cannot be divided without difficulty.

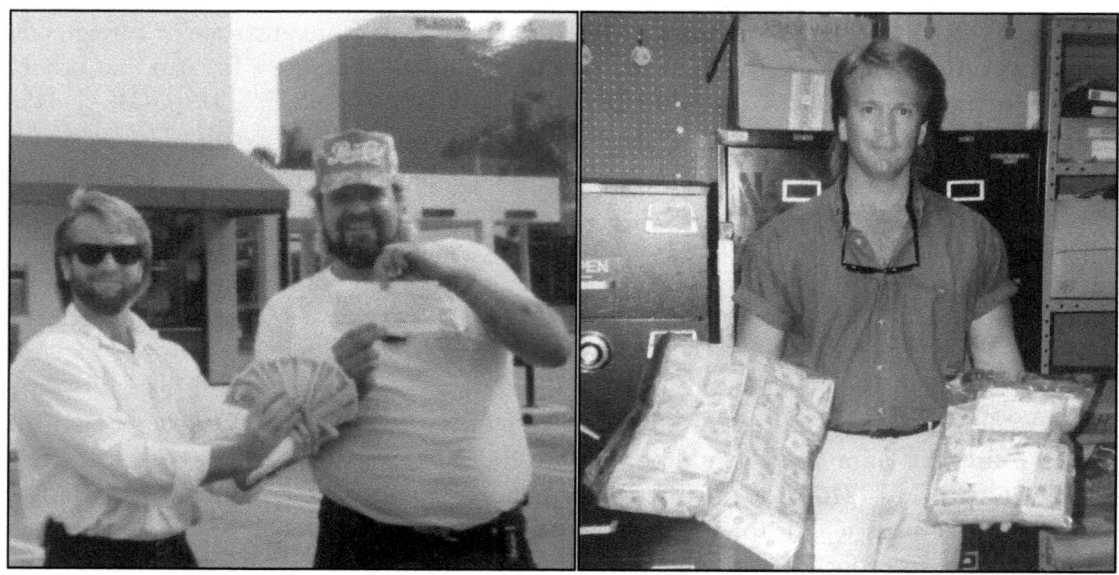

FIGURE 5.1 *Dirty Money – The Author in 1991 with a Member of the South Florida Outlaws*
Motorcycle Organization and Other Forfeited Proceeds
Source: Author's Collection

TRADITIONAL AND TRADE BASED MONEY LAUNDERING SCHEMES

The three stages of money laundering are:
1. Placement – the placing of illicit proceeds into the financial system.
2. Layering – the criminal attempts to separate the proceeds from the crime through a series of transactions; and
3. Integration – the point at which the illicit funds re-enter the economy disguised as legitimate funds. [lxxxvi]

Firearms traffickers may attempt to launder their illegal proceeds using one of the following money laundering schemes.

Structuring or "smurfing". This involves breaking down cash deposits into amounts below the CTR reporting threshold of $10,000 and using couriers, also known as "surfs", to make the deposits in several banks or to buy cashier's checks in small denominations from multiple banks. This accomplishes placement and, if done multiple times, can accomplish layering and placement.

Wire and Electronic Funds Transfers. This is a method through which the trafficker uses banks to transfer control of money to other institutions. Multi-institution transfers remain a primary tool for launderers at all stages of the laundering process, but particularly in layering operations. Funds can be transferred through several different banks in several jurisdictions, in order to blur the trail to the source of the funds. Additionally, transfers can be made from a large number of bank accounts, into which deposits have been made by "smurfing" to a principal collecting account, often located abroad in an offshore financial center where the funds will later be retrieved for placement.

Legitimate Business Ownership. Dirty money can be added to the cash revenues of a legitimate business enterprise, particularly those that are already cash intensive, such as restaurants, bars, car washes, or convenience stores. The extra money is simply added to the till. The cost for this laundering method is the tax paid through sales and income tax. With companies whose transactions are better documented, invoices can be manipulated to simulate legitimacy. A used car dealership, for example, may offer a customer a discount for paying cash, then report the original sale price on the invoice, thus "explaining" the existence of the extra illicit cash. A corrupt FFL may use their gun store to create invoices for the sale of ammunition or firearm accessories that do not exist, thus explaining the existence of the extra illicit cash they may be making from illegal trafficking on the side. Ammunition is a high cost item and no records of its receipt or sale are required, so extra cash is relatively easy to launder.

"Shell" Corporations. These exist on paper but transact either no business or minimal business. A related concept, used mostly in the U.S., is the special purpose vehicle. These are set up, usually offshore, complete with bank accounts in which money can reside during the layering phase. The shell corporation has many potential uses. One example is to buy real estate or other assets, then sell them for a nominal sum to one's own shell corporation, which can then pass the funds on to an innocent third party for the original purchase price.

Real Estate Transactions. These can cloak illicit sources of funds or serve as legitimate front businesses, particularly if they are cash intensive. Properties may be bought and sold under false names or by shell corporations and can readily serve as collateral in further layering transactions. Traffickers may purchase homes by convincing persons to accept a written contract at a value far less than the cash the trafficker will pay the seller. The seller gets undocumented cash profit while the trafficker can re-sell the house at market value and launder the value between the market value sale price and the false low-ball purchase price.

Credit Card Advance Payments. A credit card holder may make a large payment with illegal funds to the issuing bank, resulting in a credit with a negative balance due back to the card holder. The bank then pays out the balance with a check, which can be deposited into a personal account as apparently clean money. In recent years, increased bank scrutiny of these transactions has discouraged this money-laundering technique.

Currency Exchange Bureaus. In general, these are not as heavily regulated as banks, so they are sometimes used for laundering. Two main laundering techniques are used. The first is to change large amounts of criminal proceeds in local currency into low-bulk foreign currency ($5s and $10s into $100s) for physical smuggling out of that country, and the second is electronic funds transfers to offshore centers.

"Offshore" financing. The subject might claim a fictitious offshore transaction – such as a loan or investment – as the source of his funds, or actually move money offshore and then invest or "loan" the money back to himself. This scheme is difficult to prove, because records are beyond subpoena power; however, it occurs rather infrequently in routine fraud cases.[lxxxvii]

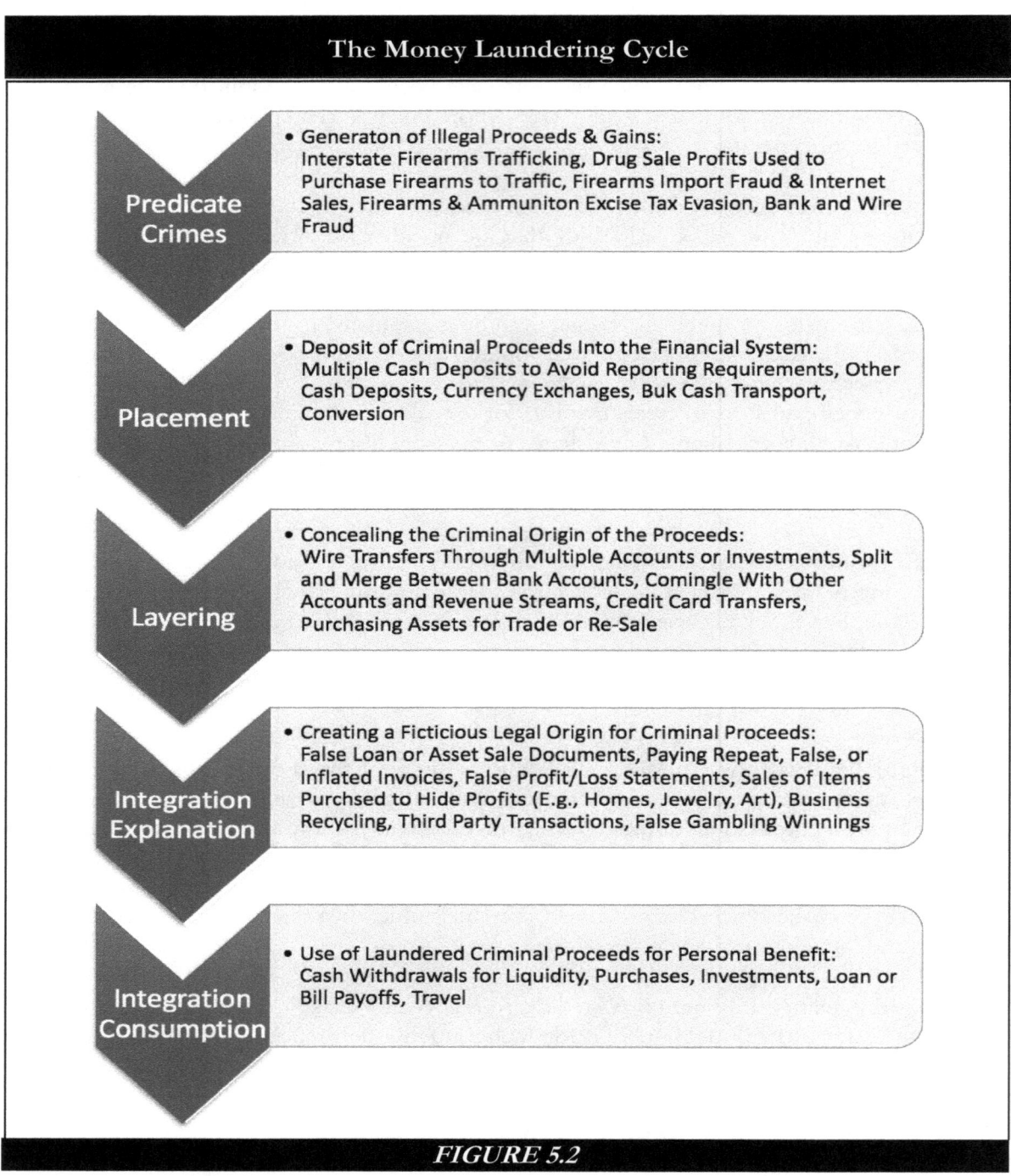

The Money Laundering Cycle

Predicate Crimes
- Generaton of Illegal Proceeds & Gains: Interstate Firearms Trafficking, Drug Sale Profits Used to Purchase Firearms to Traffic, Firearms Import Fraud & Internet Sales, Firearms & Ammuniton Excise Tax Evasion, Bank and Wire Fraud

Placement
- Deposit of Criminal Proceeds Into the Financial System: Multiple Cash Deposits to Avoid Reporting Requirements, Other Cash Deposits, Currency Exchanges, Buk Cash Transport, Conversion

Layering
- Concealing the Criminal Origin of the Proceeds: Wire Transfers Through Multiple Accounts or Investments, Split and Merge Between Bank Accounts, Comingle With Other Accounts and Revenue Streams, Credit Card Transfers, Purchasing Assets for Trade or Re-Sale

Integration Explanation
- Creating a Ficticious Legal Origin for Criminal Proceeds: False Loan or Asset Sale Documents, Paying Repeat, False, or Inflated Invoices, False Profit/Loss Statements, Sales of Items Purchsed to Hide Profits (E.g., Homes, Jewelry, Art), Business Recycling, Third Party Transactions, False Gambling Winnings

Integration Consumption
- Use of Laundered Criminal Proceeds for Personal Benefit: Cash Withdrawals for Liquidity, Purchases, Investments, Loan or Bill Payoffs, Travel

FIGURE 5.2

Trade Based Money Laundering (TBML). The Financial Action Task Force (FATF), an inter-governmental body that sets global anti-money-laundering standards, defines TBML as the process of disguising the proceeds of crime and moving value through the use of transactions in an attempt to legitimize their illicit origins. TBML value transfer techniques often involve the creation of false documents for the goods being purchased and transferred. While governments world-wide have undertaken extensive AML-BSA measures to detect and prevent traditional money laundering schemes, there are currently no such comprehensive reporting and tracking systems in place to detect and prevent TBML. In a 2014 article entitled "Trade and Money Laundering, Uncontained", The Economist labeled trade the weakest link in the fight against money laundering.[lxxxviii] TBML is the fastest growing type of money laundering at the international level. TBML schemes may include the following processes.

- ✓ **Under and Over Value Invoice Fraud.** Transnational Organized Crime groups can transfer the value of illegal proceeds from one country to another by overvaluing exports on an invoice or undervaluing imports on an invoice to shell corporations or business fronts they operate at each end of the trade. If a group uses $1 million in illegal proceeds to purchase a commodity in the U.S. and sells it to a company owned by the group company in a foreign country at an undervalued price of $500K, the group will have laundered $500K when they sell those commodities at fair market value in the foreign country. This scheme also results in a reduction of fees, duties, tariffs, and taxes that may be due.

- ✓ **Price Manipulation and Misrepresentation.** Certain types of commodities are more advantageous for a TBML scheme than others. Precious metals and jewelry are popular because they carry an accepted store of value worldwide, provide anonymity, are easily changed in form, and hold possibilities of double invoicing, false shipments, counterfeit replicas, and other fraudulent practices. Fine art and other valuable items such as rare coins or stamps are attractive for laundering purposes because false (inflated) certificates of sale can be produced. These objects are easily moved internationally or resold at market value to integrate the funds. In the domestic gun trafficking market traffickers from locations with cheap narcotics will travel to rural areas where they will sell the drugs, and then pour the money from drug sales into gun purchases. The guns purchased will then be brought back to the drug market area and sold on the street there where the trafficker makes a second illegal profit. Converting drug profits into guns that are subsequently trafficked in interstate or foreign commerce may be an act in furtherance of an SUA.

- ✓ **Informal Value Transfer Systems.** These include "hawalas", an Arabic word for a particular international underground banking system. Handed cash in country A, a hawaladar can turn it into cash (or sometimes gold or other precious metals and gems) in country B. The hawala includes the complete service from placement to integration. Similar services are provided under other names in other parts of the world.

- ✓ **Cryptocurrency Conversion.** There are more than 20 types of cryptocurrency in use today. Bitcoin™, Ether™, Litecoin™, and Monero™ are among the more widely used brands. Cryptocurrencies are popular to some for the extreme transaction privacy these afford for the fact that they are decentralized and unregulated. They operate outside established centralized international banking norms. To date, no government has been able to regulate and control a cryptocurrency, and it is theorized that the only way to do so would be to shut down the internet. For criminals, this level of privacy is attractive, and outweighs the risks of price fluctuations and occasional thefts through hacking. Cash is converted to cryptocurrency and can then be transferred around the globe digitally without detection or the filing of bank reports such as SARs or CTRs. Cryptocurrency depends on blockchain technology to protect privacy and to validate the authenticity of each crypto-coin. Blockchain is a digital ledger in which transactions made in cryptocurrency are recorded chronologically and publicly. The blockchain is like a spreadsheet shared and duplicated thousands of times across a network of computers. Rather than a centralized tracking system, blockchain is a shared and continuously reconciled database existing on millions of computers simultaneously, which makes it extremely difficult to hack or counterfeit. Blockchain is not controlled by a single entity, and therefore has no single point of potential failure[lxxxix]. Cryptocurrencies such as Bitcoin generally work as follows.

➢ First someone must establish a "wallet". There are "cold storage wallets" and "hot wallets". Cold storage wallets are detached from the internet and are more secure. Cold storage wallets may include secure storage devices or a "paper wallet," which is a combination of a secure device and printed copies of security keys. A hot wallet is a wallet software loaded on a device capable of internet connectivity such as a mobile phone or computer. An example of a wallet provider is Coinbase™. Hot wallets are more susceptible to theft; however, they provide ready access to cryptocurrency. Many users store large amounts of cryptocurrency in cold storage wallets and smaller amounts in hot wallets.[xc] Investigators should keep the two types of wallets in mind when they are determining where a suspect may be storing their cryptocurrency.

➢ Once an individual has a wallet they may purchase the cryptocurrency which is placed in their wallet.

➢ A cryptocurrency transaction is a transfer of value between wallets that gets included in the block chain. Wallets keep a secret piece of data called a private key or seed, which is used to sign transactions, providing a mathematical proof that the transactions have come from the owner of the wallet.[xci]

➢ Services such as Coinbase™ or Circle™ can allow a bitcoin user to sell bitcoin to their bank accounts. This effectively converts bitcoin into regular currency however once conversion is done through a standard bank, the conversion transaction would become subject to reporting requirements such as SARs and CTRs. Criminal users of cryptocurrency would more probably seek out un-regulated cryptocurrency ATMs to cash out their cryptocurrency.

➢ Cryptocurrency can also be converted to cash using various exchange services. The seller will need to determine the currency they wish to convert the crypto-currency to (e.g., dollars, pounds, euros, other types of cryptocurrency, etc.).

➢ Holding cryptocurrency can result in value fluctuation from day to day, whereas conversion to cash, bank deposits, or commodities such as precious metals will lock the value in once the user has converted out of the cryptocurrency.

➢ For criminals, the preferred method of operation would be to hold their proceeds in the form of cryptocurrency, and use cryptocurrency to conduct any legal or illegal purchase or transaction they need to make. This keeps their funds out of the centralized banking system, and the encrypted digital value has transfer capability anywhere on the globe to anyone else with a cryptocurrency wallet.

➢ When conducting a search warrant for cryptocurrency investigators should look for the device or storage drive the cryptocurrency is stored on as well as a ledger and passwords. There is no helpdesk, software support, or password change options for cryptocurrency so the possessor is likely to have this information written down somewhere or stored in their phone. If they were to lose the password, the crypto currency becomes inaccessible. A ledger will contain transaction histories and key information and will track incoming and outgoing cryptocurrency in the same way as a checkbook ledger.

➢ Monero™ is currently the only known cryptocurrency with "total security" where there is no transaction history associated with the cryptocurrency. Other cryptocurrencies may be moving to this model.

➢ There currently is no known software available to hack cryptocurrency passwords. If investigators seize a device containing cryptocurrency, they have the following options for accessing the cryptocurrency for purposes of cashing it out for forfeiture;
  o Secure the password from the owner to access the cryptocurrency.

- o Consider working with a prosecutor to secure court order to force the owner to turn over the password. Should they refuse they may have to sit in jail until they comply with the court order.
- o Negotiate obtaining the password from the owner/defendant as part of a plea agreement.
- o Forfeit the device and keep it even if the investigator is not able to access the cryptocurrency. This accomplishes one of the primary purposes of forfeiture which is to deny criminals access to their illegal gains and proceeds. The device can be placed in cold storage and someday the technology may become available to get into the device. This is similar to the development of DNA testing over the past 40 years. Initially law enforcement collected DNA samples in the 1980s and 1990s however a system to effectively match the DNA to others did not exist. Nationwide investigators still gathered and maintained DNA samples and kept them in evidence vaults. Then, the day came where DNA testing was highly developed and a system was created to link DNA samples. Those old samples were entered into the new system and cases were solved all over the nation as DNA matches were made. Eventually the same will happen with cryptocurrency – the technology will catch up and enable the investigator to access the cryptocurrency on the device. An industry of modern-day treasure hunters has already formed and these folks are working hard to crack cryptocurrency passwords to access locked accounts. People who own cryptocurrency pass away and without a password their estate is left with no option but to use someone to try and hack into the account if they want to recover the funds. Eventually these motivated treasure hunters will develop technology and software to defeat various cryptocurrency password will become available.

OTHER RESOURCES

This chapter is a short primer on forfeiture, focused primarily on the forfeiture or firearms, and with an overview of the forfeiture of illegal firearms trafficking proceeds. For detailed information on the conduct of financial investigations, financial interview questions, and template language for affidavits and subpoenas, investigators may find the following books useful.

Financial Investigations Guide, by the U.S. Department of Justice, Asset Forfeiture and Money Laundering Section, retrievable from:
https://www.justice.gov/sites/default/files/criminal-afmls/legacy/2011/05/12/fin-invguide.pdf

Money Laundering: A Guide for Criminal Investigators, by John Madinger, published 2011 by CRC Press, ISBN 9781439869

Chapter 6
Crime Gun Intelligence Centers & Trafficking Lead Resources

"It is a capital mistake to theorize before one has data. Insensibly one begins to twist facts to suit theories, instead of theories to suit facts."

Sherlock Holmes, in The Adventures of Sherlock Homes:
A Scandal in Bohemia, by Arthur Conan Doyle, 1891

The Introduction to this book notes that three primary methods to impact firearms trafficking and improve cooperative compliance are:
1. Community Outreach and Industry Education
2. Prevention and Deterrence
3. Investigation, Arrest, and Prosecution

Underpinning each of these methods is the proper and timely collection and analysis of data to produce intelligence and actionable leads that can focus limited resources where they can have the most effective impact. Firearms trafficking investigations are often information-intensive, as the investigator must identify suspects who often use fictitious identities and addresses and who work with multiple co-conspirators to prevent the detection of their unlawful activities. When conducting these investigations, investigators should take full advantage of the unique information systems and unique investigative techniques that can assist their investigative or interdiction efforts.

The following section covers the importance of working with a fusion-style intelligence center like an ATF Crime Gun Intelligence Center (CGIC), knowing the available sources of information for proper deconfliction and investigation of firearms trafficking, comprehensive crime gun processing protocols, and strategic development of local gun crime arrests into federal cases and firearms trafficking leads.

ATF CGICs provide intelligence that is effective at targeting the entire spectrum of gun crime from the *Trafficker to Trigger Puller*© and is converted from *Commodity to Crime Gun*©.

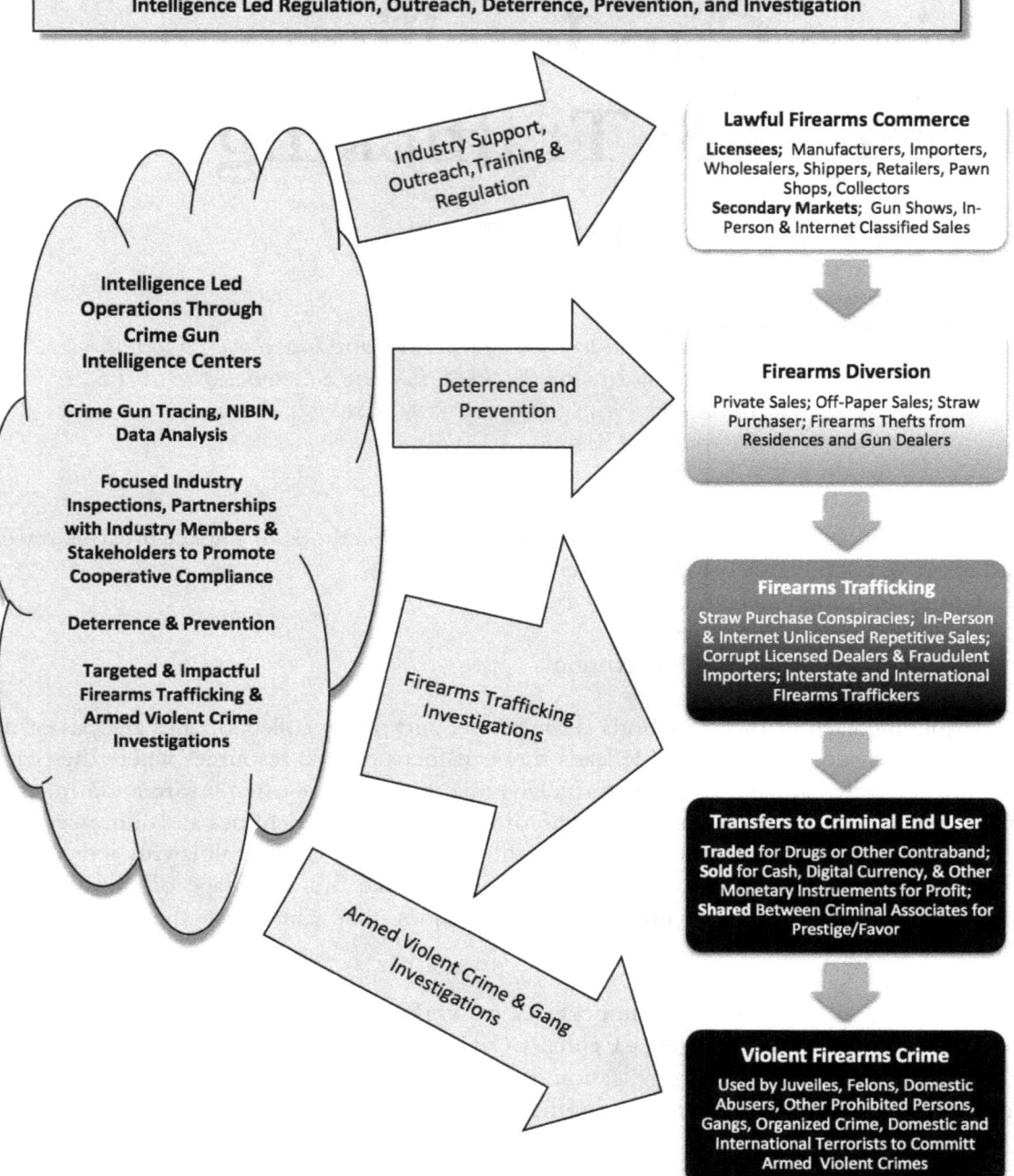

Figure 6.1 ©

ATF CRIME GUN INTELLIGENCE CENTER, NIBIN, AND CRIME GUN TRACING

ATFs first Crime Gun Intelligence Centers (CGIC) were formed in 1996. Over the past decade the concept has been refined and fully integrated with ATF-unique databases and technology, such as NIBIN, to become highly effective crime gun intelligence fusion centers. During the past 4 years ATF has formed CGICs in many major metropolitan areas. CGICs afford state and local law enforcement partners with access to unique crime gun intelligence, technology, and databases that are critical to intelligence-led policing (ILP) and targeted operational efforts to reduce armed violent crime and halt crime gun sources.

CGIC partners can collaborate on data analysis designed to produce actionable intelligence that impacts on armed violent crime in their specific area. The unique assets available at the CGIC allow members to work on the entire spectrum of gun crime from the trafficker to the triggerman. Today's CGIC concept was designed by ATF to be scalable and exportable to any size city that is willing to undertake the effort.

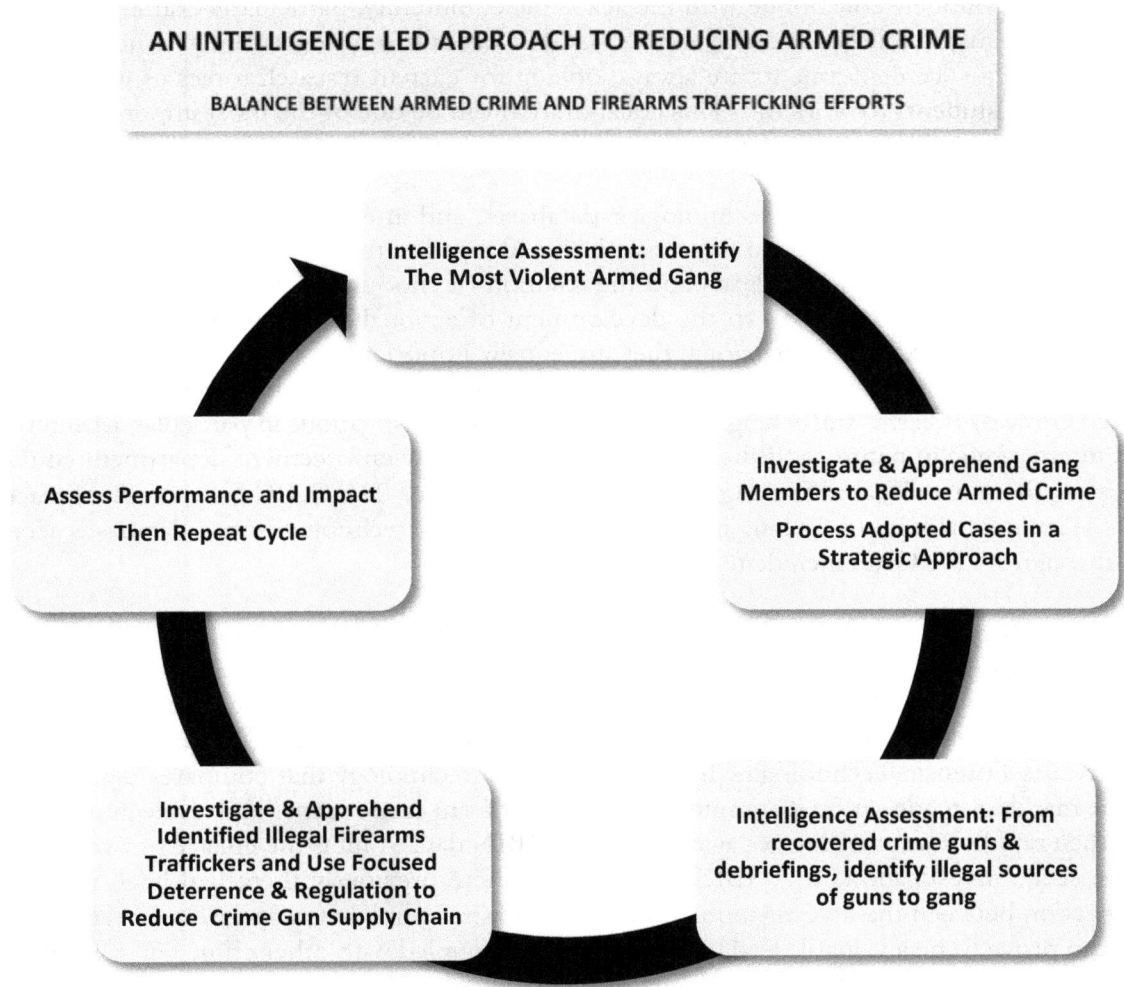

Figure 6.2

To produce successful outcomes, CGICs require intensive ongoing collaboration among the ATF, other federal agencies, local police departments, local crime laboratories, probation and parole units, area violent crime units, state and federal prosecutors, intelligence analysts, community groups. CGICs also require an ongoing evaluation component. This type of collaboration focuses on the rapid collection, processing, and analysis of recovered crime gun and ballistics information in real time to produce actionable Crime Gun Intelligence (CGI).

Actionable CGI consists of the sum of all available information relating to firearms that are used in violent crime, the analysis of which is designed to: provide relevant leads; identify shooters and their sources of firearms in support of investigation and prosecution; disrupt criminal activity; and prevent future violence. Actionable CGI is one successful outcome of a CGIC. CGIC outcomes at the strategic level take place when this intelligence assists leaders in effectively allocating limited resources so that they can achieve the most impact, and when the intelligence provides decision-makers with the most accurate crime gun intelligence available for use in crafting community-wide or regional strategies.

CGICs also routinely collaborate with the academic community, particularly criminal justice departments at major colleges and universities. CGICs benefit from research that is no or low cost and criminal justice departments are always looking for current research topics as well as topics for graduate students to work on. This collaboration can be one of the most important in terms of evolving the CGIC to meet new crime trends.

There are a number of unique technologies, databases, and intelligence assets available through an ATF CGIC that are specific to firearms crime, and together these create a synergistic effect on the development of actionable leads and the solution of shooting and trafficking crimes. Not only are these resources critical to the development of actionable intelligence for armed crime and firearms trafficking investigations, they are equally important to the CGIC's ability to serve as a point of deconfliction for any federal, state or local law enforcement agency investigating armed crime or firearms trafficking. Firearms trafficking investigations in particular are interstate and international in nature, and therefore more than one law enforcement department could be targeting the same illegal trafficking activity at the same time. The CGIC is an excellent place to deconflict any firearms trafficking investigation. The unique technologies and databases accessible through ATF CGICs include the following:

National Integrated Ballistic Information Network. NIBIN technology drives the core mission of CGICs. NIBIN is an automated ballistic imaging network that aids law enforcement investigations by linking shooting crimes and crime gun recoveries to produce valuable leads that can solve shootings. The Integrated Ballistic Identification Systems (IBIS®), produced by Ultra Electronics Forensic Technologies Inc.®, is the actual technology that compares digital images of the markings made on fired ammunition recovered from crime scenes and crime gun test fires, and then rapidly compares images against earlier NIBIN data. A hit is the linkage of two different crime scene investigations by NIBIN participants where previously there had been no known connection between the investigations. This hit establishes a link between cases or investigations and can prove to be a valuable lead, particularly when coupled with other crime gun related intelligence. By searching in an automated environment either locally, regionally, or nationally, NIBIN partners are able to discover links among firearms-related violent crimes more quickly, including links that would never have been identified absent the technology. The CGIC serves as a clearinghouse for these leads.

Four critical steps that the CGIC partners need to implement for NIBIN to achieve maximum effectiveness include:

➤ Immediate comprehensive collection of all ballistics evidence and submission to NIBIN
➤ Rapid entry and comparison of all ballistics evidence in NIBIN
➤ Thorough follow-up on any NIBIN hits from comprehensive intelligence work-ups through focused investigation
➤ Feedback on the NIBIN hit and intelligence referral effectiveness and value

A common obstacle encountered during the implementation of these four critical steps may include pushback from laboratory units regarding the request for rapid turnaround times for ballistics submission to NIBIN. This is a core need and a myriad of solutions exist to allow the lab to achieve expedited turnaround times. Management must make this a priority in order for this to work. A study conducted by Rutgers University of NIBIN in the State of New Jersey revealed that in instances where there are two shooting events linked by ballistics through NIBIN, 50% of the time, a third shooting event utilizing the same firearm will occur within 90 days. This revelation truly underscores the need for rapid turn-around time[xcii].

Another common obstacle encountered is inter-department competition. When NIBIN starts producing leads and group meetings are held to review targeting and determine who has intelligence, confidential sources, pending charges, or other information of use against the targets, this information must be shared and used toward the higher goal of apprehending shooters in the community. Too often within a Department there is significant competition between gang units, drug units, detective units, major crime units, and street crime units to the extent that they do not share intelligence or targeting information. Management must make this a priority in order for this to work, and incentivize sharing while implementing consequences for not sharing critical information.

ATF National Tracing Center. The NTC is the only crime gun tracing facility in the U.S. The NTC's mission is to conduct firearms tracing to provide investigative leads for federal, state, local and foreign law enforcement agencies. The NTC processes more than 400,000 crime gun trace requests each year. The NTC provides critical information to law enforcement agencies by helping domestic and international law enforcement agencies solve firearms crimes by detecting firearms trafficking and tracking the intrastate, interstate, and international movement of crime guns. More than 6,800 law enforcement agencies, including agencies in 43 foreign countries, are current users of eTrace, a web-based bi-lingual firearms tracing system used to assist in the tracing of U.S.-sourced firearms.[xciii]

A crime gun trace begins when a law enforcement agency discovers a firearm at a crime scene and requests a trace through the NTC. Tracing is a systematic process, using FFL records, of tracking the movement of a firearm from its manufacture or from its introduction into U.S. commerce by an importer, through the distribution chain, i.e., wholesaler/retailer, to identify an unlicensed purchaser. "Urgent" firearms trace requests are usually completed in less than 24 hours. Trace requests classified as "Routine" are completed within five days on average. Crime gun tracing is a manual process performed by hundreds of persons located at ATF's NTC. There is no computerized database of handgun and long gun owners – that would be considered a registration and that is prohibited under federal law in Title 18, U.S.C. § 926(a)(3) of the FOPA.

Crime gun tracing serves two primary functions. First, tracing enables law enforcement officials to reconstruct the history of a recovered crime gun, which may lead to the identification of witnesses, the discovery of other persons involved in the crime, or apprehension of a suspect(s). In

fact, for any law enforcement officer charging someone with a firearms possession violation, it would be difficult to take the stand in a criminal trial and face questions from a defense attorney if they are charging someone with possession but never traced the firearm to discover and investigate its ownership history and records.

Second, when tracing is done comprehensively with every recovered crime gun in a community, the analysis of the aggregate data, coupled with all the other information contained in the eTrace system, can identify patterns of firearms trafficking for investigation, and FFLs with high rates of crime gun traces for inspection. Comprehensive tracing can lead to opportunities for the development of strategies to intervene in the supply side of illegal markets that fuel a community's armed violence.

Firearms may be traced by submitting a Trace Request form to the ATF NTC. See Figure 6.3 for an example of an ATF Trace Form and the process for proper completion of the form.

The most effective method of firearms tracing is through ATF's eTrace, which allows law enforcement agencies to transmit crime gun trace requests, monitor the progress of their trace request, and receive crime gun incident related data results through a secure web-based platform. The system also allows users to query aggregate firearm trace related data for trends, patterns, and leads in their city in a real-time environment. eTrace customers can also retrieve, print and download completed trace results.

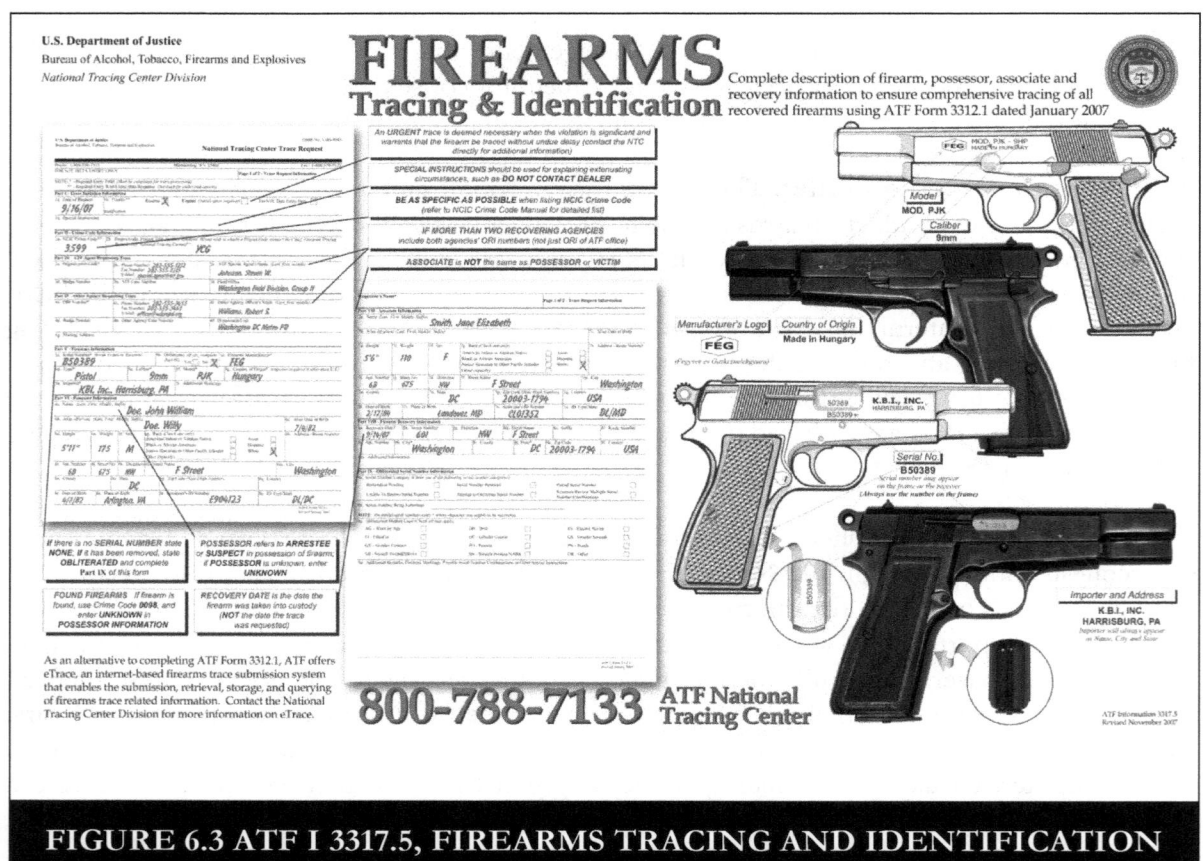

FIGURE 6.3 ATF I 3317.5, FIREARMS TRACING AND IDENTIFICATION

Source: ATF

eTrace allows users immediate access to query firearm trace related data stored in the ATF Firearms Tracing System (FTS) database, through an online search utility. The eTrace application provides the capability to initiate a search for traces on virtually any data field or combination of data elements that appear in a crime gun trace. For example, users can search by a firearm's serial number, an individual's name, the type of crime, the date of recovery, and numerous other identifiers.

Registered users can also generate various statistical reports from aggregate trace data regarding the number of traces submitted over time, the top firearms traced, and the average time-to-crime rates. The LEAD Report's online query tool provides ATF users with the ability to access a combination of five simple queries and two profile reports. The LEAD Report's simple query and profile report functions will limit results to multiple sales, FFL thefts and completed trace requests only. The "Search for Trace Requests" query option available in the eTrace main menu allows users to access all firearm trace request data regardless of the current status as well as all multiple sales, FFL thefts, interstate thefts, and suspect gun transactions.

The eTrace application is available to all qualified federal, state, local and international law enforcement agencies. ATF users and CGIC members have access to all trace data in the FTS database. Non-ATF users' access is limited to the traces submitted by their agency. Any law enforcement department can establish an eTrace account by applying online at: https://etrace.atf.gov/etrace/.

Numerous firearms intelligence data bases interface through eTrace and produce a synergistic effect for generating firearms trafficking leads. This intelligence is available in some form to eTrace users and in unlimited form to all CGIC members.[xciv] Those firearms intelligence data bases include the following:

✓ **Demand Letter Programs.** The NTC is responsible for issuing various demand letters, which ensures that it collects FFL data vital to the success of the firearms tracing process. It determines which FFLs qualify, prepares and mails the Demand Letters, receives FFL demand letter responses, enters the data into the Firearms Tracing System, and coordinates demand letter activities with the Office of Field Operation's refusals of letters and failures to respond, responds to questions, and prepares reports regarding the status of the demand letters.[xcv]
  ➤ **Demand Letter 1** is issued to FFLs who do not comply with their statutory responsibility to respond within 24 hours to firearm trace requests. FFLs who receive Demand Letter 1 are required to send to ATF their acquisition and disposition records for the past three years and continue to send the records on a monthly basis until told otherwise. The information submitted allows ATF to trace firearms properly and timely if the FFL continues to be uncooperative with requests.
  ➤ **Demand Letter 2** is sent to FFLs who have had ten or more guns traced to them within the previous calendar year with a "time-to-crime" of three years or less. The affected FFLs are required to submit limited information regarding "used" guns they acquired the previous year, including the manufacturer/importer, model, caliber or gauge, and serial number, along with the acquisition date. No names of owners are submitted. The FFL is required to submit this information quarterly, and until informed otherwise. The used gun information received as a result of Demand Letter 2 enables ATF to trace any used guns sold by the FFLs under demand. Without this information, ATF would not be able to link the secondary market firearm to the dealer.

> ➤ **Demand Letter 3** is issued monthly to assist ATF in its efforts in investigating and combating the illegal movement of firearms along and across the Southwest border of the U.S. ATF is requiring licensed dealers and pawnbrokers in Arizona, California, New Mexico and Texas to submit record information concerning multiple sales of certain rifles defined as semi-automatic rifles capable of accepting a detachable magazine and with a caliber greater than .22 (including .223/5.56 caliber).

✓ **ATF Multiple Sales Information.** When a private individual purchases two or more handguns in a 5-business day period from an FFL, under 18 U.S.C. § 923(g)(3) the FFL is required to report this information to ATF. The report includes identifying information concerning the purchaser, firearms, date of transfer, and FFL. Multiple sales reporting was implemented by Congress in 1972 with the specific intent to aid law enforcement in the identification of interstate firearms trafficking. This information is maintained in the eTrace system.

The NTC uses multiple sales information to produce the Daily Multiple Sales Reports. ATF users and some CGIC members can request that the NTC place them on the daily multiple sales report e-mail list. Those on the list receive a daily report of all multiple sales transactions entered into the FTS during the preceding day. Each entry also lists any other multiple sales reports and traces that match to the purchaser by last name and date of birth. This can be a useful tool for identifying currently active traffickers within days of gun purchases being made.

✓ **ATF Stolen Firearms Database.** This database contains information relating to ALL firearms thefts from FFLs as well as information relating to thefts of firearms from interstate carriers. Under Title 18 U.S.C. § 923(g)(6), FFLs must report any theft or loss of firearms to ATF within 48 hours after the theft or loss is discovered. ATF enters identifying information on firearms stolen from FFLs and interstate carriers into NCIC and into eTrace. The system can be queried for all information concerning FFL thefts, including: descriptions of firearms reported stolen, lost, or missing by an FFL; FFL and interstate carrier theft trends; similarities in theft modus operandi; FFL theft-reporting patterns indicative of illegal diversion and fraudulent theft reporting; and firearms theft recovery location information. This system is useful when investigating firearms traffickers committing FFL/interstate carrier thefts or when investigating an FFL for illegal diversion and fraudulent theft-reporting to cover up that illegal diversion. Copies of the original FFL and Interstate Theft/Loss Reports, signed by the FFL or other originator, are preserved.

✓ **Firearm Recovery Notification Program (FRNP)[xcvi].** Formerly known as the ATF Suspect Gun Program, the FRNP is an improved version of its predecessor operated by ATF's NTC that monitors crime gun traces for recoveries of firearms identified as suspected of being illegally trafficked and under active investigation, but which have not yet been recovered. Information regarding guns suspected to have been trafficked is submitted by special agents and investigators during their investigations. Should a suspect gun be recovered and traced, the FRNP[xcvii] will contact the investigator who entered the firearm as a suspect gun and provide him/her with the contact telephone number of the individual who recovered and traced the firearm. The investigator may then contact the trace requester and obtain information surrounding the use of the firearm in a crime and recovery The FRNP serves as a pointer system and, as such, also serves a useful deconfliction purpose. Additionally, persons currently under active criminal investigation who are suspected of illegally using or trafficking in firearms but who have not yet been discovered in possession of, or associated with, a firearm may be entered in the FRNP, and should a firearm be recovered and traced, the FRNP will alert the investigator who entered the person in the FRNP and provide him/her with the contact telephone number of the individual who recovered and traced the firearm. The investigator is then able to contact the trace requester and obtain information surrounding the relationship of the recovered firearm to the individual who was entered in the Suspect Name File. Examples of FRNP uses include:

> An individual is under investigation for unlicensed firearms dealing. That individual may be entered into the FRNP Suspect Name File, and if a firearm is recovered, traced, and associated with the suspect, the FRNP notifies the investigator.

> A violent criminal or gang offender is under investigation for illegal firearms possession. That individual may be entered in the FRNP Suspect Name File, and if a firearm is recovered, traced, and associated with the suspect, the FRNP notifies the investigator.

✓ **ATF Out-of-Business Records Repository (OOB).** Any FFL that goes out of business is required to forward their records to the ATF OOB Repository. The Repository microfilms and catalogues these records for use in completing crime gun trace requests. These records are vital to successfully completing crime gun trace requests. The benefit of OOB is an expedited trace result on firearms that would otherwise be untraceable with the out-of-business FFL.

✓ **Access 2000 (A2K).** This system was developed as a cooperative partnership between ATF and the licensed firearms industry in an effort to reduce the time FFLs spend responding to crime gun trace requests. This system consists of a series of automated database systems provided to licensed Firearms Industry Members free of charge. The system gives FFLs the autonomy to provide ATF access to conduct serial number requests in online searches, which reduces the need for FFLs to manually provide this information while also improving response time and success rates for crime gun traces. The data remains the property of the FFL, and ATF can only access data relative to specific crime guns being traced. The benefit of A2K is an expedited trace result.

✓ **ATF NTC FFL "Monitor" and "No Contact" Services.** During the course of an investigation into suspected violations of law by an FFL, an investigator may want to utilize the FFL "Monitor" or "No Contact" services. Through the FFL "Monitor" service, an investigator will be notified by the NTC of all firearms traced back to a specified FFL. Through the FFL "No Contact" service, an investigator may request that the NTC not contact a specified FFL for firearms trace information. Both of these services have advantages to offer an investigator conducting an FFL investigation.

✓ **ATF Firearms and Explosives Licensing Center (FELC).** The ATF FELC receives and processes applications from persons seeking a Federal Firearms or Explosives license. All of the information on the application is entered and maintained in the Firearms Licensing System (FLS). This system includes information regarding all active licenses, active license addresses, responsible persons associated with the license, d.b.a. (doing business as) names, corporate names, licensee telephone numbers, FFL photographs, and fingerprints.

✓ **ATF Firearms and Explosives Imports Branch (FEIB).** The ATF FEIB is responsible for fulfilling ATF statutory responsibilities relative to the import provisions of the Gun Control Act of 1968, the National Firearms Act, and the Arms Export Control Act of 1976,

including: processing all ATF Form 6 applications to import firearms, ammunition, and implements of war into the United States; processing all applications to register under the Arms Export Control Act as an importer of U.S. Munitions List articles, including the collection and deposit of registration fees; and issuing International Import Certificates to effect the release of U.S. Munitions Import List articles intended to be imported into the U.S. Information from the FEIB is vital in international firearms trafficking investigations.

In addition to the crime gun intelligence available through eTrace, additional data available to CGIC members for use in the development of firearms trafficking leads and combatting armed crime in their community includes the following:

✓ **ATF FTS First Look Reports**. Using all the data elements coalesced within eTrace, the NTC produces the "First Look" reports on a weekly basis for authorized recipients. The reports contain the results of 15 queries of the FTS records related to crime guns traces and multiple sale records from the previous week. The "First Look" queries use combinations of basic firearm trafficking indicators as their criteria and provide the investigator with information on activity currently taking place and that cannot be generated through Online LEAD. The following parameters are used to generate these "First Look" queries.

➤ Multiple sale records processed in the past week by NTC in which the purchaser (based on the last name, first three letters of first name, DOB, and state of residence) also appears on one or more previous firearm traces.

➤ Crime gun traces processed in the past week by the NTC in which the recovered firearm was purchased in a multiple sale.

➤ Crime gun traces where firearms recovered on different dates were purchased on the same date at the same FFL. This is useful for one-gun-a-month states.

➤ Crime gun traces processed in the past week by the NTC with a time-to-crime of less than 12 months. This is considered a fast time-to-crime.

➤ More than one Multiple Sale Record at the same FFL on the same day.

➤ Crime gun traces in which the purchaser and possessor was under 26 years of age and the time-to-crime was less than 12 months.

➤ Crime gun traces in which the firearm was either recovered outside the U.S. or was traced by a foreign police agency.

➤ Crime gun traces in which either the purchaser or possessor were born outside the United States.

➤ Multiple sales in which the purchaser was born outside the United States.

➤ Crime gun traces processed by the NTC in the past week in which the first three letters of the purchaser's last name, date of birth, gender, and State of residence all appear in a prior crime gun trace or Multiple Sale Record.

➤ Multiple Sale Records of five or more firearms processed by the NTC.

➤ Crime gun traces that were successfully traced back to a Multiple Sales purchase in a State other than the recovery State.

➤ FFL thefts reported to the NTC in the past week.

➤ Stolen firearm recoveries from FFL thefts processed by the NTC in the past week.

✓ **Partial Serial Number Trace Capabilities**. Firearms having the serial number removed or obliterated or with only a partial serial number remaining may be traceable. Investigators should attempt to trace any recovered firearm involved in an ATF investigation where a partial serial number has been raised. The NTC may be able to provide the requester with a narrow list of potential serial numbers. These "candidates" can then be traced and the results provided to the requester to determine which, if any, firearm may be the one in question.

✓ **ATF Obliterated Serial Number Program (OSNP).** The OSNP is available to research and analyze crime gun trace requests involving obliterated, altered, or removed serial numbers in order to successfully trace such firearms and provide investigative leads to the field. The OSNP will assist with any case involving a firearm for which the importer's or manufacturer's serial number has been removed, defaced, or altered. Many firearms manufactured or imported prior to the Gun Control Act of 1968 have no serialization. These can be reviewed and researched by the OSNP. Once a firearm's partial serial number is communicated to the OSNP and traced, the program can provide an investigator with a series of possible trace results, one of which should be the correct firearm. The investigator can sort through the options to find the right one. This could be a significant firearm trafficking lead, as firearms traffickers are known to obliterate serial numbers so they can't be traced to the purchaser.

The OSNP has established a list of standardized obliteration terms to describe the majority of types of obliteration encountered. Properly communicating the type of obliteration to the OSNP is critical, as they maintain a system to track this information and may be able to advise the investigator of other traces in the area where the same obliteration method was used. The obliteration terms are as follows:

➤ **Grinder Concave (GRV)** - A type of obliteration process that results in a concave grinder impression in the area of the receiver where the serial number should be. This is consistent with obliteration caused by a bench grinder or a hand-held drill-grinding wheel.

➤ **Grinder Coarse Surface (GRC)** - A type of obliteration process that results in a coarsely sanded surface in the area where the serial number should be that is on an even plane with the surrounding unaffected areas of the firearm.

➤ **Grinder Smooth Surface (GRS)** - A type of obliteration process that results in a smooth surface in the old serial number area that is on an even plane with the surrounding unaffected areas of the firearm.

➤ **Scratched Pointed Hand Tool (SCN)** - A type of obliteration process that uses a pointed hand tool, such as an awl or nail, to scratch/disfigure the serial number until it is unreadable.

➤ **Scratched Broad Tipped Hand Tool (SCB)** - A type of obliteration process that uses a broad pointed hand tool, such as a standard blade screwdriver or chisel, to scratch/disfigure the serial number until it is unreadable.

➤ **Drill (DRI)** - A type of obliteration process that uses a drill to bore out the serial number. This process may create a through-and-through hole in the frame or receiver, or the drill may only bore down enough to obliterate the serial number. Marks left by a drill bit on different firearms can be compared for similarities, such as drill bit size, number of holes, and characteristics of the base of drill holes (e.g., round base or triangle base).

➤ **Electric Scribe (ELS)** - A type of obliteration process that uses an electric scribe to scratch/disfigure the serial number by making several passes over the area, or pressing the scribe into each character in the serial number until it is unreadable.

➤ **Punch (PUN)** - A type of obliteration process that uses a tool to make a series of punch marks/holes, randomly or in pattern, over and around the serial number until it is unreadable. Punch marks/holes on different firearms can be compared for similarities, such as mark/hole size, number of marks/holes, and characteristics of the tool.

➤ **Peened (PND)** - A type of obliteration process in which a hammer or similar blunt object is used to pound the area containing the serial number until it is unreadable.

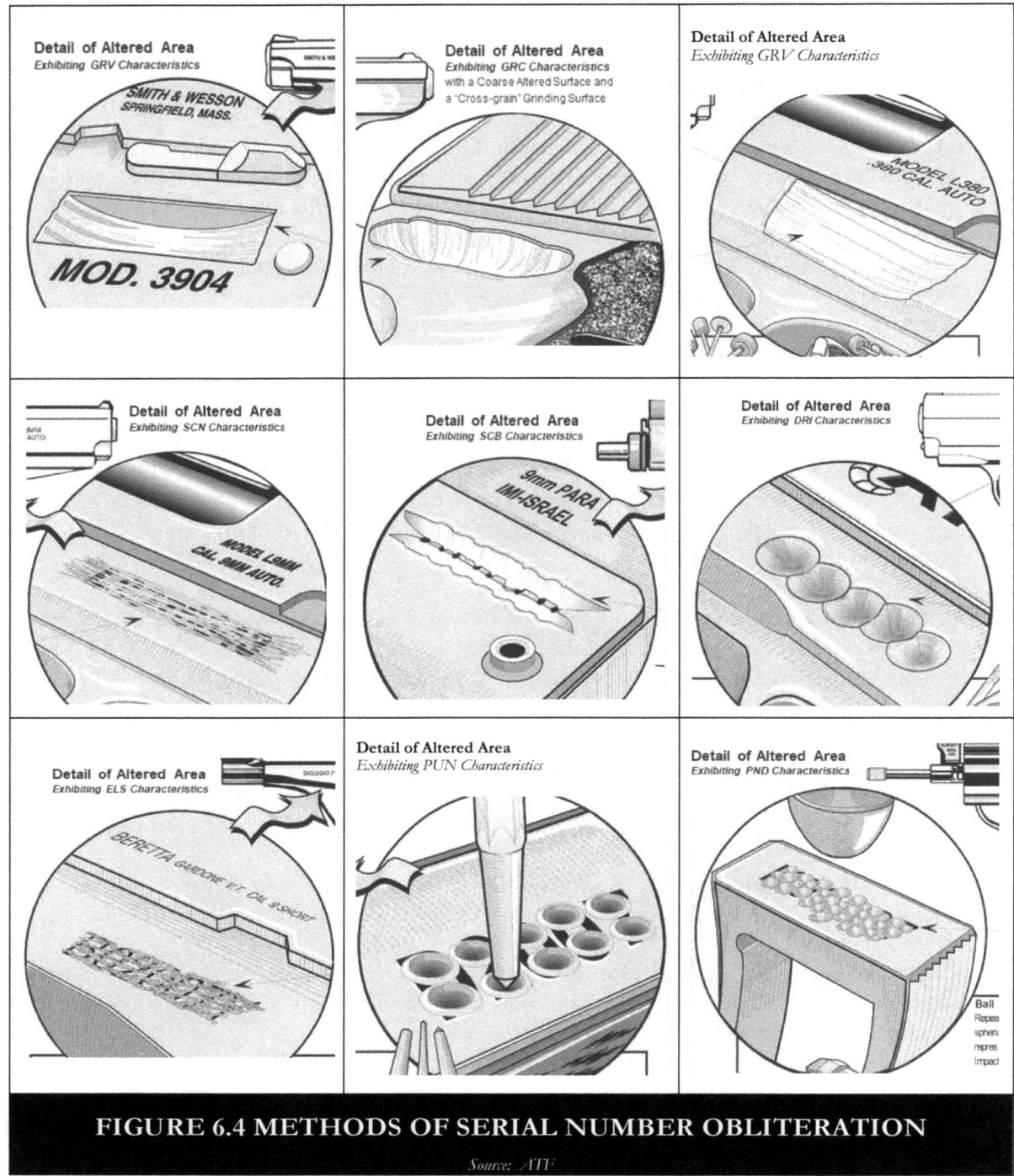

FIGURE 6.4 METHODS OF SERIAL NUMBER OBLITERATION

Source: ATF

✓ **ATF Firearms and Ammunition Technology Division (FATD)[xcviii].** The ATF FATD provides expert technical support on firearms and ammunition to the Bureau, the firearms and ammunition industry, the general public, and other federal, state, local and foreign law enforcement agencies. The division is the federal technical authority relating to firearms and ammunition and their classification under federal laws and regulations. The FATD maintains an extensive firearms reference collection, as well as firearms technical reference files and a library. FATD is responsible for the technical evaluation of firearms to determine if they meet the requirements for importation into the United States. FATD also provides expert firearms testimony to the US Attorneys, State Prosecutor Offices, District Attorney's offices, and military courts regarding the identification and origin of firearms, how they are regulated under federal law, and other matters relating to firearms and the firearms industry. FATD is divided into two branches: the Firearms Technology Industry Services Branch (FTISB) and the Firearms Technology Criminal Branch (FTCB) that are responsible for all matters involving the technical aspects of firearms, providing overall guidance on the classification, identification, function and evaluation of weapons affecting the Bureau's criminal and regulatory enforcement mission. FATD branches serve as the primary point of contact for other law enforcement agencies requiring assistance in matters involving the technical aspect of firearms.

✓ **ATF National Firearms Act (NFA) Registration and Transfer Record (NFRTR).** The NFRTR is the registry of all NFA weapons. Authorized investigators may use the NFRTR to check or cross-reference ownership names, addresses, or weapons descriptions related to all registered NFRTR weapons. The NFRTR maintains the fingerprints and photographs of all those with registered firearms. The NFRTR system can be searched by name, city, state, or firearm type, make, or serial number. Because the registration contains tax information, disclosure of this information is strictly limited by the provisions of 26 U.S.C. § 6103.

✓ **ATF Industry Operations (IO) Office Files**. Authorized investigators may coordinate with IO investigators to utilize information in IO office files, including complete histories of individual FFLs, types or prior violations cited (if any), types of firearms in inventory, specific business practices, suppliers/wholesalers frequently used, photographs and other identifying information from the license, and descriptions of security systems/video monitors that may be in use.

✓ **LeadsOnline.** This is a commercial database that contains access to pawn records, including the pawn of firearms. These pawned firearms re-enter the market as used guns. Since a crime gun trace only takes the firearm to the first retail sale, once a firearm is sold privately or pawned the ATF Firearms trace may or may not be able to document that movement in the secondary source market. LeadsOnline may contain information on a firearms movement in the secondary source market that can be used to further the trace. LeadsOnline is part of ATFs Secondary Market Program (SMP).

✓ **Acoustic Ballistic Detection Data**. The ShotSpotter® system exists in a number of major metropolitan areas. The system gathers data on actual shots being fired such as the time, date and location. ATF CGICs has several years of historical acoustic ballistic detection data for lead exploitation and strategic planning. This information is useful for ongoing shooting investigations, particularly when mapped with other firearms intelligence. The aggregate data for each city is also useful for strategic planning and deployment of resources. For example, ShotSpotter's 2017 National Gun Fire Index Key Finding 4[xcix] maps the hours of the day when most shootings take place. In other reports findings also document a much higher prevalence of shootings during summer months and on weekends.[c]

✓ **Treasury Enforcement Communications System (TECS).** This system is managed by DHS, Customs and Border Protection (CBP). TECS is linked to NLETS and NCIC; however, it also contains a wealth of its own information and can be searched via Soundex system to find similar-sounding names. Authorized users can use TECS to search for, or enter, lookouts on persons and property which can result in a hit when the person under a lookout leaves or enters the U.S. This is particularly useful in international firearms trafficking investigations. TECS also contains all historical border crossing information for all persons leaving or entering the U.S.

TECS contains the following banking and financial information:
➤ Currency Transaction Reports (CTR), Form 4789
➤ Reports of International Transportation of Currency or Monetary Instruments (CMIR), Customs Form 4790
➤ Reports of Foreign Bank and Financial Accounts (FBAR), Treasury Form 90-22.1
➤ Currency Transaction Reports by Casinos, Form 8362
➤ Suspicious Activity Reports (SARs), Form TDF 90-22.47

TECS contains the following information concerning aircraft and vessels:
➤ Private Aircraft Enforcement System (PAES) which identifies tail numbers, owner and pilot of aircraft, as well as aircraft and passenger arrival
➤ Vessel and aircraft sightings
➤ Land Border primary and secondary operations concerning motor vehicles and their passengers entering the United States

TECS also contains investigative and case management information for current and former agencies of the U.S Treasury Department, including ATF, IRS, USSS, and FINCEN.

✓ **National Instant Criminal Background Check System (NICS)**. The National Instant Criminal Background Check System (NICS) is used to conduct background checks on all persons purchasing firearms from FFLs. The FBI is responsible for administering the NICS and ATF is responsible for enforcing the Brady law. ATF's two primary responsibilities with regard to the Brady law implementation are regulating and inspecting FFLs to ensure that they comply with the Brady law, and investigating criminal violations of the Brady law committed by FFLs or individuals. In addition to producing referrals on prohibited person who attempt to acquire firearms, the ATF NICS system also provides useful intelligence for firearms trafficking and gang investigations.

➤ **Mapping of Denial Information** - ATF has the capability to plot the locations of the FFLs and in many cases the addresses of the denied purchasers in denied firearms transactions. Mapping the location of attempted firearms purchasers against a targeted gang may reveal persons who reside with or very near to a targeted gang member and who may then be approached for suitability as confidential informants, as the attempt to purchase a firearm was a felony.

➤ **Not Referred Weekly Report** - Each week the CGICs receive a report containing the names and identifying information on persons who were denied in an attempt to purchase a firearm, but whose criminal histories did not rise to the level of a formal investigative referral. This report can be cross-referenced against the targets of ongoing gang and criminal organizations investigations and persons who are matches may be approached for suitability as confidential informants, as the attempt to purchase a firearm was a felony.

➤ **At Risk FFL Queries** - ATF systematically reviews denials by FFL association and has developed a method for identifying "at risk" dealers by determining their denial-to-transaction ratio. An FFL with a higher number of denials is an FFL who has more frequent encounters with the criminal element. ATF Industry Operations will be made aware of these FFLs so that during an inspection they can look for the presence of any issues that might arise from such a situation. During an inspection the IOI should look in the FFL's Acquisition and Disposition log for any firearms listed on ATF F 4473 that resulted in a NICS denial and then determine if the firearm was sold within the following days to a person with the same last name, address, or other linking information. This may be straw purchase activity where the denied person sent a spouse, friend, or relative back to the FFL to purchase the firearm.

REGIONAL CRIME GUN PROCESSING PROTOCOLS

CGICs are collaborative fusions centers that are dependent on the proper and timely collection and processing of crime guns and ballistics evidence in order to generate actionable CGI. Regional Crime Gun Processing Protocols are the standard operating procedures to ensure the proper timely collection and processing of crime guns and ballistics evidence gets done.

The protocols are a set of predefined actions consistently undertaken by law enforcement and forensic personnel which are designed to generate rapid actionable intelligence from crime gun and ballistics evidence recovered during criminal enforcement or investigative operations within the geographic region where armed criminals are operating and moving between multiple law enforcement jurisdictions.

The first objective of a Regional Crime Gun Processing Protocol is to ensure that all possible information and evidence is efficiently and effectively extracted from EVERY crime gun taken into custody and every piece of ballistics evidence left behind at a crime scene. This objective results in the creation of both tactical and strategic intelligence for law enforcement to act upon.

The second objective is to ensure that CGI is generated, disseminated, and used by the law enforcement agencies within the region that require the information. Where there is a CGIC, the CGI is developed and referred out from the CGIC. However, the CGIC governing boards must recognize the limitations of a CGIC. It is recommended that CGIC governing boards never restrict any law enforcement parties from developing trafficking leads and conducting trafficking investigations that are not generated by the CGIC. This will hurt morale, squander the vast experience or numerous investigators who are capable of performing these functions, and only serve to diminish the number of cases and impact on firearms trafficking. Additionally, persons at the CGCI may not have local knowledge of persons of interest or small hot spots of crime that a local office knows. If all CGI referrals must come from a CGIC, then the CGIC may not refer out smalls bits of information that would mean something to a local field office, but not rise to the level of a referral at the CGIC. What is recommended is that all leads developed, and all cases initiated, are deconflicted and coordinated through the CGIC for case enhancement and tracking. CGIC boards must be cognizant of this, as there is a tendency to sometimes try and pigeonhole everything into a CGIC, thus reducing the potential impact on firearms trafficking and armed violent crime.

Criminals operate without regard for jurisdictional boundaries. A criminal may be involved with a shooting incident in one town leaving behind shell casings, and then be found in another jurisdiction in possession of the firearm during a routine traffic stop. The firearm gets placed in the evidence room in one town while the other town is still looking for that gun that was used in their shooting incident. A Regional Gun Crime Processing Protocol is designed to prevent the crime

gun sitting in one department's evidence room from never being discovered by the town with the shooting. By following the protocol, both departments will have submitted their evidence to NIBIN, and the system will advise both agencies of the hit. The first department will be able to recover the crime gun used in their shooting from the second department and they will have a suspect to interview for their shooting. NIBIN is to ballistics evidence what AFIS (Automated Fingerprint Identification System) is to fingerprint evidence.

Today's Regional Crime Gun Processing Protocols often include the following core requirements for processing recovered crime guns and ballistics evidence.
➢ All recovered crime guns will be traced through eTrace.
➢ All recovered crime guns must be queried in NCIC to determine if they are stolen.
➢ All recovered crime guns will be processed for trace evidence to include DNA and latent fingerprints for comparison to known samples or to CODIS (Combined DNA Index System) or AFIS (Automated Fingerprint Identification System).
➢ All recovered crime guns will be test fired, and the casing from that test fire will be entered into NIBIN.
➢ All ballistics evidence recovered at crime scenes must be processed for trace evidence to include DNA and latent fingerprints for comparison to known samples or to CODIS or AFIS.
➢ All ballistics evidence recovered at crime scenes must be entered into NIBIN.
➢ All suspects arrested with a crime gun must be read their Miranda Rights and asked a minimum set of questions designed to elicit crime gun source information.
➢ All suspects arrested with a crime gun should be asked for their consent to allow a DNA swab to be taken, and their refusal to provide one should be documented.
➢ All persons with a suspect arrested in possession of a crime gun must be interviewed to lock in their statement and prevent the creation of a false alibi at a later date.

Regional Crime Gun Protocols are effective because the common denominator in all armed crimes are the firearms and ballistics evidence which contain evidence and can tell a story. Crime guns are informants, and when correctly handled they will tell you everything they know about where they came from and who committed the crime. Just as criminals operate with disregard to jurisdictional boundaries, so does the gun crime evidence, once a protocol causes it to be processed comprehensively throughout a region. By exploiting the information from crime guns and ballistics evidence acquired across multiple jurisdictions in a region, more evidence gets processed, more shootings get linked, and more suspects get identified and arrested. By using these protocols to identify and apprehend shooters more quickly, they are taken off the street sooner, allowing less time for them to shoot and kill again. Over time, consistently-applied protocols will be institutionalized by law enforcement in the region and become a sustainable solution. [ci]

By way of background, the regional crime gun processing protocol concept began in the mid-1990s and, initially, was a set of agreements to comprehensively trace all crime guns and investigate firearms trafficking. Since then the agreements have evolved into a comprehensive set of protocols for the rapid collection and processing of all crime gun evidence and data, and the production of actionable CGI. Some of these regional crime gun protocols are codified in law.

A brief evolutionary history of regional crime gun processing protocols includes the following:
➢ 1996 Interstate Firearms Trafficking Compact of 14 East Coast States & District of Columbia
➢ 1997 ATF Youth Crime Gun Interdiction Initiative (YCGII) Memorandum of Understanding
➢ 2004 Palm Beach County Gun Crime Protocols

- ➢ 2012 IACP Resolution: Regional Crime Gun Processing Protocols
- ➢ 2013 New Jersey Public Law 2013 Chapter 162; Title 52 of Revised Statutes

Regional Crime Gun Protocols are living documents, and should be modified as needed to keep up with new technologies and stay ahead of emerging crime trends. All signatory agencies to the protocols should have input in revisions. The Palm Beach County Gun Crime Protocols were first developed in 2004, with a revised version adopted in 2006 following a comprehensive 13 critical tasks training sponsored by the Palm Beach Criminal Justice Commission in conjunction with Forensic Technologies Inc®. Since 2006 additional revisions have been adopted by the signatories to the Palm Beach County Gun Crime Protocols as well as detailed standard operating procedures for carrying out the requirements.

Regions interested in initiating a Crime Gun Protocol in their area should contact their local ATF Office. Additional information on all that goes into creating a regional crime gun protocol may be found in *13 Critical Tasks, An Inside Out Approach to Solving More Gun Crime,* written by Pete Gagliardi of Triple Barrel Strategies LLC, in conjunction with Forensic Technology Inc.

In order to successfully determine what is needed to implement a Regional Crime Gun Protocol, a regional board comprised of the proper stakeholders or executive level leaders need to initiate an assessment of what is known in Business as the *Golden Triangle: people, processes, and technology.* All individuals involved have to be properly trained, incentivized, and resourced for a Crime Gun Protocol to actually take effect and work. Putting the Regional Crime Gun Protocol down on paper and getting everyone to agree to it is the easy part, and is just a preliminary step.

Appendix B contains a number of the above-listed crime gun processing protocols for review. They may be customized and fit to the needs of any area experiencing armed crime that is looking for ways to improve their ability to investigate and impact that armed crime.

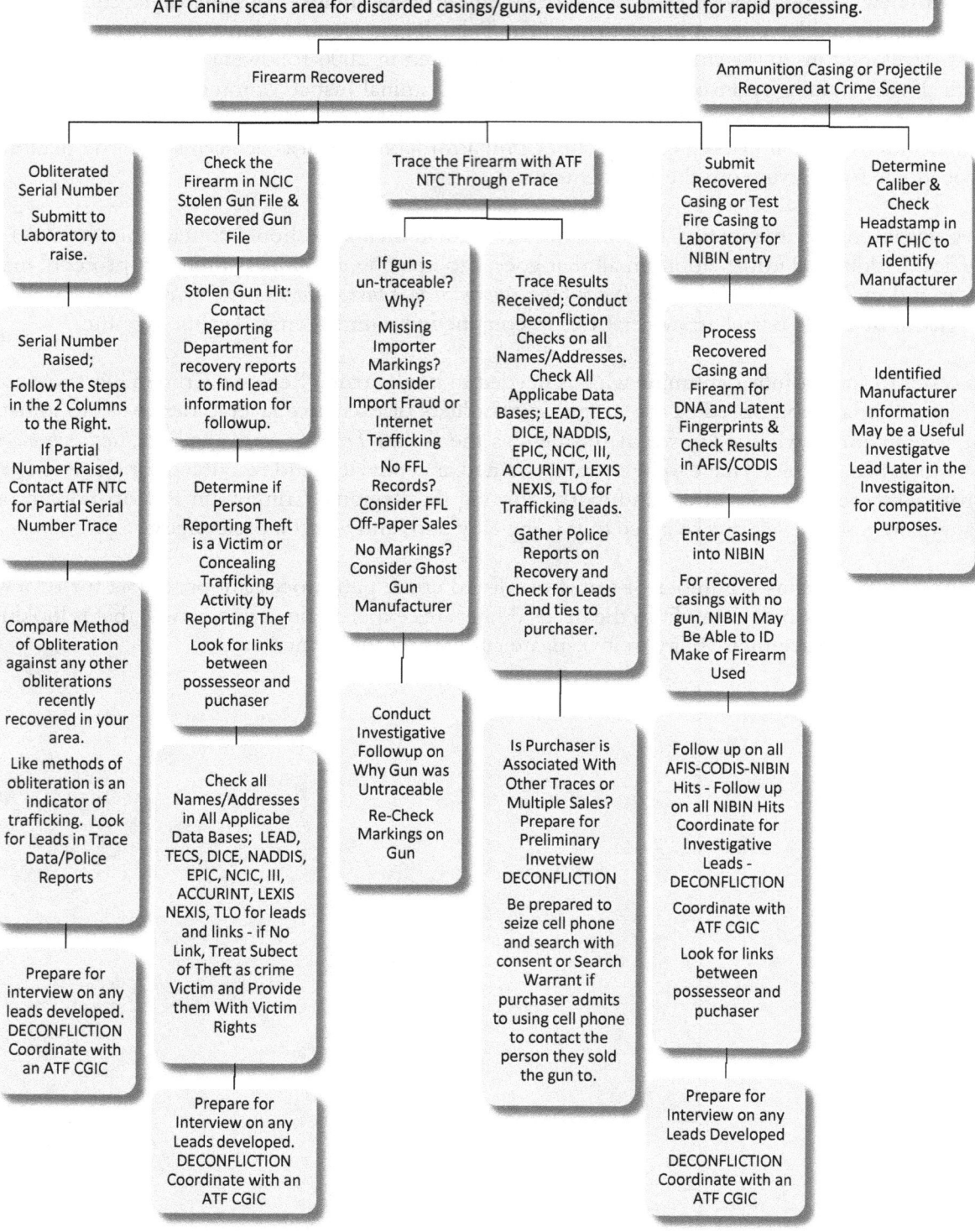

CRIME GUNS ARE INFORMANTS! LET THEM TELL YOU WHAT THEY KNOW

Firearm/Shooting Incident called in via 911 or Ballistic Accoustic Detection System & Regional Crime Gun Protocols are Followed; Officer responds, identifes witnesses-victims, takes statements, collects evidence, ATF Canine scans area for discarded casings/guns, evidence submitted for rapid processing.

Firearm Recovered

Ammunition Casing or Projectile Recovered at Crime Scene

Obliterated Serial Number

Submitt to Laboratory to raise.

Serial Number Raised;

Follow the Steps in the 2 Columns to the Right.

If Partial Number Raised, Contact ATF NTC for Partial Serial Number Trace

Compare Method of Obliteration against any other obliterations recently recovered in your area.

Like methods of obliteration is an indicator of trafficking. Look for Leads in Trace Data/Police Reports

Prepare for interview on any leads developed. DECONFLICTION Coordinate with an ATF CGIC

Check the Firearm in NCIC Stolen Gun File & Recovered Gun File

Stolen Gun Hit: Contact Reporting Department for recovery reports to find lead information for followup.

Determine if Person Reporting Theft is a Victim or Concealing Trafficking Activity by Reporting Thef

Look for links between possesseor and puchaser

Check all Names/Addresses in All Applicable Data Bases; LEAD, TECS, DICE, NADDIS, EPIC, NCIC, III, ACCURINT, LEXIS NEXIS, TLO for leads and links - if No Link, Treat Subect of Theft as crime Victim and Provide them With Victim Rights

Prepare for Interview on any Leads developed. DECONFLICTION Coordinate with an ATF CGIC

Trace the Firearm with ATF NTC Through eTrace

If gun is un-traceable? Why?

Missing Importer Markings? Consider Import Fraud or Internet Trafficking

No FFL Records? Consider FFL Off-Paper Sales

No Markings? Consider Ghost Gun Manufacturer

Conduct Investigative Followup on Why Gun was Untraceable

Re-Check Markings on Gun

Trace Results Received; Conduct Deconfliction Checks on all Names/Addresses. Check All Applicabe Data Bases; LEAD, TECS, DICE, NADDIS, EPIC, NCIC, III, ACCURINT, LEXIS NEXIS, TLO for Trafficking Leads.

Gather Police Reports on Recovery and Check for Leads and ties to purchaser.

Is Purchaser is Associated With Other Traces or Multiple Sales? Prepare for Preliminary Invetview DECONFLICTION

Be prepared to seize cell phone and search with consent or Search Warrant if purchaser admits to using cell phone to contact the person they sold the gun to.

Submit Recovered Casing or Test Fire Casing to Laboratory for NIBIN entry

Process Recovered Casing and Firearm for DNA and Latent Fingerprints & Check Results in AFIS/CODIS

Enter Casings into NIBIN

For recovered casings with no gun, NIBIN May Be Able to ID Make of Firearm Used

Follow up on all AFIS-CODIS-NIBIN Hits - Follow up on all NIBIN Hits Coordinate for Investigative Leads - DECONFLICTION

Coordinate with ATF CGIC

Look for links between possesseor and puchaser

Prepare for Interview on any Leads Developed

DECONFLICTION Coordinate with an ATF CGIC

Determine Caliber & Check Headstamp in ATF CHIC to identify Manufacturer

Identified Manufacturer Information May be a Useful Investigatve Lead Later in the Investigaiton. for compatitive purposes.

Figure 6.5 ©

CRIME GUN INTELLIGENCE PRODUCTION STANDARDS AND RELIABILITY RATING PROCESS

In addition to crime gun processing protocols, CGICs should have intelligence production and rating standards. Intelligence should be collected and developed if it relates to criminal violations of the law. Intelligence should not be collected and developed if it simply relates to non-criminal associations, hobbies, or activities. CGICs should consider implementing the following standards:

✓ **Standard of Reasonable Indication**. The standard of "reasonable indication" is substantially lower than probable cause, but more than mere suspicion. In determining whether there is reasonable indication of a federal criminal violation, an investigator may take into account any facts or circumstances that a prudent investigator would consider. The standard does require specific facts indicating a past, present, or future violation. There must be an objective factual basis for initiating an investigation based on the intelligence; a mere hunch is insufficient. Firearms trafficking indicators are an example of reasonable indication.

✓ **Reliability of Information**. CGI referrals should come with a reliability rating regarding the specific facts or circumstances being referred for review and possible use in the initiation of a criminal investigation. This reliability rating system is particularly important in situations where specific facts indicative of a past, current, or impending criminal violation are reported anonymously. For example, while the allegation may contain great specificity constituting a reasonable indication, the anonymity of the source places the reliability of the information in the unknown category. The three ratings are described below and these ratings should appear at the bottom of CGI referrals.
  ➢ **Extremely Reliable** - Characterized as information from a previously proven reliable source, information obtained through first hand observation or surveillance, information from official records, information from official government databases, information documented during official government activities, and/or information that agrees with other information on an individual or group. Most CGI referrals relating to data from eTrace and other authorized databases or ATF IOI FFL inspections would fall into this category.
  ➢ **Reliable** - Characterized as information provided by an upstanding citizen who has no personal agenda for providing the information, information from a previously proven reliable source but the information has not been corroborated and/or information that agrees somewhat with other information on an individual or group.
  ➢ **Unknown** - Characterized as information from a source whose reliability is unknown and/or information from an unreliable source that, considering other known facts, is possibly true.

OFFICER DEVELOPMENT OF LOCAL GUN-CRIME ARRESTS FOR FEDERAL COURT AND CRIME GUN LEAD EXPLOITATION

There are a number of situations in which the arrest of an armed subject by a state or local policy officer or deputy sheriff may be better suited for prosecution in federal court rather than State court. These cases are referred to by many names: Federal Adoptions, Exile cases, and Project Safe Neighborhoods (PSN) cases. The suspect arrested may be a gang member in an ongoing federal investigation, a person who resides in a strategically targeted hotspot of armed violent crime, or a multi-convicted felon and the sentencing exposure for their possession of a firearm is greater in federal court. For their part, when a state or local officer makes their initial arrest and is considering referring the case for federal prosecution, they should undertake the steps delineated in Figure 6.6 to prepare the case for a successful federal prosecution.

FEDERAL ADOPTION CHECKLIST: STEPS FOR STATE OR LOCAL OFFICERS TO TAKE FOLLOWING A GUN CRIME ARREST

ACTIONS RE. THE RECOVERED CRIME GUN(S)

✓ **Treat the crime gun like an informant.** Get all the information possible from that crime gun. A crime gun by itself can provide a wealth of information about its owner or possessor, its trafficking history, and links to other shooting crimes.

✓ **Trace.** Always submit the crime gun for tracing through an eTrace account or any protocols already established by their department. Individual trace results could be vital to the case and aggregate trace data helps identify illegal firearm traffickers.

✓ **NCIC.** Ensure that the crime gun is checked through NCIC for possible information regarding its status as reported lost or stolen. If it is stolen, print the NCIC hit and keep it in your records. Once the stolen firearm is removed from NCIC the record will no longer exist, and the paper copy may be needed for future reference.

✓ **Photographs and Trace Evidence.** All crime guns can be a source of important trace evidence. Photograph the crime gun in place and submit it along with any magazines and ammunition for examination by a laboratory for the existence of latent fingerprints and DNA trace evidence.

✓ **NIBIN.** Submit the crime gun for test-firing by a crime lab. If a Department allows its officers to test-fire recovered crime gun, officers should only do so if they know the firearm is safe. Any test-fire casings should be submitted to NIBIN.

ACTIONS RE. THE DEFENDANT(S)

✓ **Fingerprint Defendant.** The officer should try to personally fingerprint the defendant, making an extra card for submission to ATF if you believe you will be seeking federal prosecution. This can be done by placing just one thumbprint on the corner of a report. The purpose of this is to have a fingerprint examination link the print from the person being arrested to fingerprints that correspond to a prior felony conviction, proving that the person is a convicted felon. The defendant will be fingerprinted at the jail but this corrections officer fingerprints people all day long, and will not be able to remember that particular person in order to state in court that the person sitting at the defense table is the same person they fingerprinted six months ago. The arresting officer will remember, however.

✓ **Post-Miranda Statement.** Advise the defendant, preferably in writing, of their Miranda Rights, and obtain an expressed waiver. The officer should then attempt to obtain a written or taped statement from the defendant regarding the defendant's possession of the firearm(s), how they obtained the firearm, and their prior felony conviction information or other prohibited status, such as being a fugitive, an illegal alien, or an unlawful drug user. Document all statements by the defendant, whether formal or spontaneous, relating to the firearm(s) and/or criminal record in the police report. If the interview is custodial it should be audio and video recorded in accordance with department policy. The following are questions the officer should ask:

- ✓ What is the specific crime and what was their role in it?
- ✓ If the case is drug related, how did they use and store the gun, and what was its relation to the drug business. Was it for protection from rip-off's? Did customers see the gun?
- ✓ If they won't admit to possessing the gun, ask them about any loose ammunition. Convicted felons and other prohibited persons can't possess ammunition under federal law (Title 18 U.S.C. § 922(g)), but may admit to possessing ONLY the ammunition in an attempt to appear cooperative yet still distancing themselves from the gun.
- ✓ Ask them about their prior arrest record, and specifically ask them about prior felony convictions, outstanding fugitive warrants, court issued domestic violence restraining orders, misdemeanor domestic violence convictions, or alien status.
- ✓ Ask them about drug use past and present. Defendants often won't admit to drug trafficking or to possession of large amounts of drugs, but they may speak freely of past and current drug use. You may ask them about current drug use to determine if they will need treatment or face withdrawal problems in jail. Federal law prohibits gun possession by an unlawful user of controlled substances (Title 18 U.S.C. § 922(g)(3)). The drug use must be contemporaneous to the possession.
- ✓ Ask them about any accomplices and their roles.
- ✓ Ask them about crime gun source information:
  - ➤ When and where did you get the gun?
  - ➤ Was anyone else with you when you stole the gun? OR
  - ➤ Did you know the gun was stolen? OR
  - ➤ How much did you pay for the gun?
  - ➤ Do you have other guns?
  - ➤ If the serial number is obliterated: Did you remove the serial number? If not, who did?
  - ➤ If gun is a sawed-off: Did you cut down this barrel? If not, who did?
  - ➤ If the gun is a silencer or machinegun: Did you make it? If not, who did, or where did you get it?
  - ➤ If we gave you money to buy a gun, where would you go to buy one right now?
  - ➤ Does your source have other guns for sale, and who else has bought from the source?
  - ➤ How do you contact this person and when was the last time you spoke to them? NOTE: If they admit to speaking with this person on their cell phone or via email, these admissions may be used to get a search warrant for evidence of those calls on the cell phone or emails from the email provider.
  - ➤ What name do you call them?
  - ➤ Do they work with anyone else?
  - ➤ Where do they live and where do you meet them?
  - ➤ Is your source violent and is the source armed?
  - ➤ Can you introduce someone to your source so they can buy a gun?
- ✓ Ask them about gang membership and affiliations.

✓ Does the suspect(s) have information about other violent crimes, gangs, firearms trafficking?

✓ If yes, go through those crimes and gang members and identify as much as they are willing to say. Keep interviewing the defendant as long as they are willing to speak. This may be the only chance you have to speak to them.

✓ Always ask the suspect(s) for consent to provide a DNA swab and document any refusal to provide one.

✓ Does the suspect(s) have potential as a cooperating defendant?

ACTIONS RE: WITNESSES OR ACCOMPLICE(S)

✓ **Witness and Accomplice Interviews.** If there are other persons present with the defendant when they are arrested (e.g., other persons in a vehicle during a car stop), the officer should interview these people too, and document their statements to prevent them from creating a false alibi at a later date. Provide them with a Witness Rights Card where required by law. Prior to the interview, call in a criminal history check to determine if they too may be prohibited from possessing a firearm. If the witness/accomplice appears to be providing a false alibi on the firearm, consider asking the following questions:

✓ When and where did you get the gun?

✓ How much did you pay for the gun?

✓ What is the make, model, and caliber of the gun?

✓ Is the gun currently loaded?

✓ Where is the magazine (or cylinder) release, and where is the safety on the gun?

✓ What type of ammunition do you buy and what is loaded in the gun right now?

✓ How much did you pay for a box of that ammunition?

✓ When was the last time you cleaned the gun and is the gun clean now?

✓ When was the last time you shot the gun? Where do you go shooting? If a gun range, which one?

✓ Who else knows this is your gun?

✓ Where do you store the gun at home?

✓ Do you have a concealed weapons permit?

✓ Do you own any other guns?

These are reasonable questions to ask a person who owns a firearm. Most gun owners would be able to answer each of these questions. However, someone falsely claiming ownership and/or creating a false alibi will have trouble answering these questions.

ACTIONS RE. DOCUMENTATION & ESTABLISHING FEDERAL CONTACT

Following the interviews and clearing the scene the officer should proceed with the following steps:

✓ **Reporting.** Prepare a detailed narrative report regarding the arrest and the surrounding circumstances, including a complete description of the firearm, vehicle information, witness/accomplice information, and a listing all officers present at the arrest.

✓ **Recordings.** If the arrest began with or involved a 911 call, obtain and preserve a copy of that recorded 911 call. If the arrest began with or involved a video-recorded traffic stop, obtain and preserve a copy of that video recording.

✓ **Call a Federal Agency.** Call your local federal agent and discuss the merits of bringing the case for federal prosecution because this is a member of a targeted gang, a known recidivist offender in a targeted hot spot enforcement operation, or an armed career criminal with 3 or more felony convictions for crimes of violence or drug trafficking, and when the federal sentencing exposure is much greater than state sentencing exposure.

✓ **Charging Strategy.** If federal prosecution is going to be pursued, the defendant should initially be booked on violations other than state firearm violations, as a quick guilty plea to a firearms-related charge in state court could preclude later federal prosecution. While the defendant could be prosecuted for the same crime in federal court, a DOJ petite policy waiver would be required, and a number of factors must be present for that to take place.

Figure 6.6 ©

Some of the more common federal charges that apply to local arrests of persons for possession of a firearm or committing an armed crime include:

✓ **Title 18 U.S.C. § 922(g).** It shall be unlawful for any person to receive or possess a firearm or ammunition who is: 1) a convicted felon; 2) a fugitive from justice; 3) an unlawful user of or is addicted to controlled substances; 4) adjudicated mentally ill or previously involuntarily committed to a mental institution; 5) dishonorably discharged from U.S. Military; 6) an alien illegally in the U.S.; 7) documented to have renounced US citizenship; 8) under a court issued domestic violence restraining order; 9) convicted of a misdemeanor crime of domestic violence. A conviction may result in a prison sentence of up to 10 years.

✓ **Title 18 U.S.C. § 924(e). This is the** Armed Career Criminal Act. It shall be unlawful for any person with three or more prior felony convictions for violent crimes or drug trafficking crimes to receive or possess a firearm that has moved in or is affecting commerce. Federal criminal case law has established that for purposes of this statute, prior crimes of violence may include: aggravated assault/battery; assault/battery on a law enforcement officer; carjacking; robbery, burglary of an occupied dwelling; rape/sexual battery; murder/manslaughter; kidnapping; arson/bombing; treason; and other crimes involving the use or threatened use of violence. A prior drug trafficking conviction must be for a crime in which conviction could have resulted in a prison sentence of 10 years or more. Any person convicted of the Armed Career Criminal Act will receive a minimum mandatory prison sentence of at least 15 years, up to life.

✓ **Title 18 U.S.C. § 924(c).** Using, carrying, or possessing a firearm during, or in furtherance of, a drug trafficking crime or federal crime of violence. Any person convicted of this crime faces a prison sentence of: 5 years if a firearm is used/possessed during the offense; 7 years if a firearm is brandished; 10 years if a firearm is discharged during the offense; 10 years if the firearms is a sawed-off rifle or shotgun; 10 years if the firearm is an assault weapon; 30 years if the firearm is a machinegun, silencer, or destructive device; and an additional 25-year consecutive sentence for each additional act. All sentences are minimum mandatory and must run consecutive to sentences for other charges in the case. This charge is applicable to armed pharmacy robberies, standard armed drug trafficking, trading guns for drugs, armed home invasions where drugs were the target, other armed business robberies, shootings between gangs over drugs, armed kidnapping, and other crimes of violence.

✓ **Title 18 U.S.C. § 924(h).** Any person who transfers a firearm to another person knowing that firearm will be used to commit a federal crime of violence or drug trafficking crime may be imprisoned for up to 10 years.

✓ **Title 18 U.S.C. § 924(j).** Any person who, during the commission of an offense under Title 18 U.S.C. § 924(c), causes the death of a person through use of a firearm may be imprisoned for up to life in prison, or put to death.

✓ **Title 18 U.S.C. § 924(o).** Any person who conspires to commit an offense under Title 18 U.S.C. § 924(c) may be imprisoned for up to 20 years.

✓ **Title 18 U.S.C. § 3559(c).** This is the Federal Three Strikes Law: the commission of a serious violent felony by someone having two prior convictions for violent felonies or serious drug offenses. The Three Strikes Law results in a sentence of life in prison.

FEDERAL AGENCY INVESTIGATION OF ADOPTED-REFERRED LOCAL GUN-CRIME ARRESTS AS PART OF A COMPREHENSIVE STRATEGY

ATF is a federal agency that accepts local firearms and armed crime arrests for further investigation and workup into a case presentable in federal court under certain circumstances. Based on this authors personal experience and according to current ATF Acting Director Thomas Brandon, "there is no better partner than ATF" when it comes to investigating State and local armed crime arrests and presenting them for federal prosecution as part of a comprehensive armed crime reduction strategy.

Once the arresting officer follows the previously described steps to develop their local gun crime arrest and it is determined that the adoption of the case into federal court is warranted as the defendant is a "worst of the worst" multi-convicted felon or armed career criminal[cii], a member of a targeted gang, a known violator in a strategically targeted armed crime hot-spot, or other initiative, the case will be further investigated by a federal agent. The arresting officer will remain part of that investigation as a partner.

As part of that investigation, the ATF special agent will ensure all crime gun evidence and ballistics evidence is properly developed and utilized with other data to generate any possible CGI and actionable leads. The special agent who accepts the case for a workup for federal prosecution will undertake many of the steps listed in Figure 6.7.

FEDERAL ADOPTION CHECKLIST: STEPS FOR FEDERAL AGENTS TO CONSIDER DURING ADOPTION OF A STATE/LOCAL GUN CRIME ARREST

✓ **Deconfliction.** Conduct deconfliction checks by running the defendant's name, phone number, address, and other identifiers in case management systems, TECs, DICE, and other systems to determine if they are the target of any other investigation. If they are, the agent will coordinate with that Department appropriately.

✓ **Gather Reports.** Gather all police reports, notes, video and audio recordings (to include recorded interviews, 911 calls, and cruiser or body-cam video/audio recordings), lab reports, and any documents created that relate to the case.

✓ **Determine Violations and Elements of Proof.** Determine the appropriate federal firearms charge, and then ensure all required elements of proof for the federal violation are documented.

✓ **Intelligence Workups.** Perform or request intelligence work-ups on the defendant through various CGIC data bases, TECS and FINCEN checks where appropriate, and OSINT development of their online presence and social media footprint.

✓ **Establish Interstate or Foreign Commerce Nexus.** Retrieve firearms for examination and establish proof of the firearm or ammunition's prior movement in and affecting interstate or foreign commerce.

✓ **Firearm Functionality.** Perform a functionality exam on the crime gun(s).

✓ **Pocket Litter.** Review material recovered from the defendant's person when arrested and examine for evidence. Deconflict and query names, phone numbers, addresses.

✓ **Restoration of Rights Check.** Determine if the defendant has had his or her rights to possess a firearm restored through a pardon or clemency at the state or federal level.

✓ **NCIC.** Check the firearm in NCIC to determine if it is stolen. If yes, follow up on that lead and obtain related police reports.

✓ **Crime Gun Trace.** Submit a crime gun trace request to the ATF NTC, follow up on the results with interviews, and ensure all crime gun source leads are investigated.

✓ **Federal Firearms Licensee (FFL) Records.** If the trace results reveal an FFL where an ATF Form 4473 reflecting the purchase of the firearm exists, secure the ATF Form 4473 from the FFL following the protocols and FFL questions outlined in Chapter 10, Figure 10.2 (Interview Questions for Federal Firearms Licensees). Treat the ATF Form 4473 as evidence and, where appropriate, submit it to a crime laboratory for handwriting analysis or latent print examination through the use of a ninhydrin treatment.

✓ **Latent Trace Evidence Exams.** Submit the firearm for testing for DNA and latent fingerprints and send known fingerprints and any DNA swabs taking at the arrest to the lab for comparison.

✓ **NIBIN Entry.** Coordinate the submission of the crime gun for entry into NIBIN and perform investigative follow-up if the firearm is linked to other shooting crimes.

✓ **Electronic Communication Device Evidence.** If there was as a cell phone with the defendant when they were initially arrested, and if probable cause exists, secure a search warrant to download the phone and examine its contents.

✓ **Jail Intelligence.** If the defendant is in custody on state or local charges, obtain copies of the suspect's phone calls, mail log, commissary deposit log, and visitor log to determine what they have said while in jail on this case.

✓ **Crime Scene Observation.** If the arrest of the defendant by local police took place in a public location, go to that location at the same time of day or night and observe and document the surroundings, background noise level, and lighting conditions. Look for any nearby occupied structure where witnesses to the original crime may be present. Look for nearby businesses that may have on-premise video security recording equipment and get consent or use a subpoena to secure the video for examination.

✓ **Vehicle Examination.** If the arrest involved a vehicle that is accessible, observe and search the vehicle for evidence. If the vehicle is stolen, ask the vehicle's owner to look in the vehicle and determine if there is anything in the vehicle that is not theirs. This may yield additional trace evidence that could have important trace evidence such as DNA or latent fingerprints.

✓ **Electronic Communication Records.** If the defendant has been arrested for a crime of violence, secure a court order for historical cell tower geo-location data for the defendant's cell number, and attempt to use the geo-location information to place them at the scene of the crime. See Appendix D for a template affidavit.

✓ **Evidence & Forfeiture.** Process any evidence subject to administrative or judicial forfeiture, such as the firearm and ammunition, a vehicle that transported an illegal NFA weapon, or the illegal proceeds of firearms or drug trafficking. Firearms and ammunition need to be administratively or judicially forfeited as they are not inherently contraband subject to summary forfeiture like narcotics. The government must complete forfeiture to gain legal title to the items so they may be disposed of at the end of the case rather than returned to a third party designated by the defendant. See Chapter 5 for guidance on the administrative or judicial forfeiture of firearms and ammunition.

✓ **NFA Checks.** Determine the registration status of any National Firearms Act weapon (e.g., machine guns, silencers, etc.).

✓ **Cooperator Potential.** Determine if the arrest of the armed violent offender can lead to their potential cooperation or be incorporated into a larger criminal gang investigation.

✓ **Recommend Prosecution.** Compile the investigative documentation for presentation to the U.S. Attorney's Office.

✓ **Judicial Follow-through.** Work with the assigned AUSA to secure an indictment and arrest warrant, appear at initial appearance and bond hearings, produce discoverable materials for the defense, appear at suppression hearings, trial, or plea agreements hearings, provide information for the pre-sentence investigation and appear at the sentencing, assist the AUSA with any appeals, and dispose of the evidence properly at the end of the case.

Figure 6.7 ©

GENERAL RESOURCES FOR TRAFFICKING INVESTIGATIVE LEAD DEVELOPMENT

There are a variety of general sources of information that can generate trafficking leads or provide information useful in an ongoing investigation.

✓ **HUMINT via Cooperating FFLs**. FFLs are the people who chose to get a license and adhere to the records keeping requirements, regulations, and laws, and whose business and livelihood is adversely impacted by those who sell firearms without a license, keeping no records, paying no sales tax, and asking no questions of customers. FFLs often know who these people are because they encounter them at gun shows and other firearms related forums. FFLs are often a good source of information on persons who are dealing in firearms without a license. In addition, a cooperative FFL can alert investigators when his shop has been frequented by straw purchasers, and the FFL can assist by calling them back to the store for a gun sale monitored by investigators for an arrest. Cooperative FFLs may allow to act as employees and conduct or observe firearms transactions with a suspect trafficker or straw purchaser. The FFL may assist in the timing of firearms pickups by the trafficker to ensure special agents can conduct surveillance of the deal and arrest the subject, or the FFL may be willing to introduce the investigator in an undercover capacity to a trafficker as an "off paper" source of firearms.

✓ **OSINT via Online Classified Gun Sales Sites.** There are numerous domestic online classified firearms sales sites on the internet. Gunbroker.com, Grabbagun.com, Gunbuyer.com, Guns.com, and Armslist.com are just a few. All are forums where people buy and sell firearms. All have search capabilities and, with practice, an investigator can figure out how to sort historical sales information by a user's handle, thus seeing the volume and type of firearms being sold. This type of OSINT can be exploited for locating unlicensed firearms dealers on the internet as well as persons who would meet an out of state resident to sell handguns to.

✓ **National Crime Information Center (NCIC) Recovered Gun File**. This system allows an investigator to check for the recovery of stolen guns by other law enforcement agencies that are involved in that investigator's firearms theft investigation, or "suspect guns" recovered by other law enforcement agencies that are involved in that investigator's trafficking investigation. Law enforcement agencies that enter firearms into the Recovered Gun File might not request a trace on the firearm. Without a trace request, ATF's eTrace system will not receive a hit; however, running a firearm through the recovered gun file might reveal that an investigation's "suspect" or stolen guns have, in fact, been recovered by law enforcement officials somewhere in the country.

✓ **State/Local Firearms Databases and Systems**. Some states and local areas maintain firearms registrations or other types of databases (e.g., California Automated Firearms System, Illinois Firearm Owners Identification, and Michigan Handgun Safety Inspection) containing firearms related information. The information contained in these systems may be useful to an ongoing firearm trafficking investigation, and special agents should be familiar with their area systems and make contact with special agents in areas of the country that may be linked to the investigation, to determine what systems exist there that could be of use.

✓ **State/Local Pawn Shop Details**. Most states and local municipalities have detectives assigned specifically to monitor pawn shops' acquisition and sales of all property, including

firearms. Investigators should consider meeting with area pawn shop detectives to enhance ongoing investigations or identify indicators of firearms trafficking and other intelligence the pawn shop detectives may possess.

✓ **Export Enforcement Coordination Center (E2C2)**. Established by executive order within the Department of Homeland Security (DHS) and located in Vienna, VA, the E2C2 became operational in 2012. This interagency center, with over 20 partner departments and agencies, coordinates export enforcement information sharing and deconflicts enforcement activities. E2C2 may be of use to firearms trafficking investigators examining the movement of firearms in commerce out of the US. E2C2 can provide investigators with critical deconfliction and investigative pointer information. Since its inception, E2C2 has processed thousands of de-confliction requests from across the export enforcement, licensing, and intelligence communities, with many of them receiving positive hits in a partner agency's system. Deconfliction alerts investigators from different agencies that their investigations are overlapping, enabling them to pool information and work together. You may find additional information regarding E2C2 at the following link; *https://2016.export.gov/e2c2/index.asp*.

✓ **DHS U.S. Customs and Border Protection (CBP) National Targeting Center (NTC)**. CBP NTC is located in Reston, Virginia, and provides tactical targeting and analytical research in support of customs and anti-terrorism efforts 24 hours a day. These tactical targets develop from a combination of border crossing data and raw information that detect and prevent terrorists (and implements of terror) from crossing the U.S. border. Investigators in the field can receive quick and coordinated intelligence analysis in ongoing criminal investigations through the CBP NTC and their round-the-clock analytical tools.

✓ **U.S. Commerce Department**. The Commerce Department's Bureau of Industry and Security maintains records on all legal shotgun exports from the United States. They also function as a source of information on international business regulations and trade patterns.

✓ **El Paso Intelligence Center (EPIC)**. EPIC's primary mission is to provide a complete and accurate intelligence picture of worldwide drug movement to federal law enforcement entities, with an emphasis on the movement of drugs, weapons, and illegal aliens into the United States. It analyzes raw data and provides tactical and operational intelligence to agencies involved in the anti-drug effort. EPIC also provides strategic assessments of drug movement and concealment techniques. In addition, EPIC is mandated to support state and local law enforcement entities with drug intelligence. All fifty states, Puerto Rico, and the Virgin Islands have signed agreements with EPIC. ATF maintains a Gun Desk at EPIC to assist in disrupting the unlawful diversion of firearms to criminals from both legitimate and illegitimate sources; to identify, investigate, and stop firearm traffickers, particularly those who supply firearms to narcotics organizations, young criminals, and gangs; and to expand the use of technology to trace crime guns, process data, develop leads, and share critical information. This is of particular use for investigators conducting firearms trafficking investigations involving Mexico. See https://www.epic.gov.

✓ **National Gang Intelligence Center (NGIC)**. The NGIC, established by Congress in 2005 in Title 34 U.S.C. § 41507, is a multi-agency effort that integrates the gang intelligence assets of federal, state, local, and tribal law enforcement entities to serve as a centralized intelligence resource for gang information and analytical support. The mission of the NGIC is to support law enforcement agencies through timely and accurate information sharing as well as the strategic and tactical analysis of law enforcement focusing on the growth, migration, criminal activity, and association of gangs that pose a significant threat to communities throughout the United States.

✓ **National Gang Targeting, Enforcement and Coordination Center (GangTECC).** GangTECC is a multi-agency center created by the U.S. Attorney General in 2006 to help disrupt and dismantle the most significant and violent gangs in the United States. The Director is from the U.S. DOJ Criminal Division. The investigators staffing GangTECC are from the FBI, ATF, DEA, the USMS, BOP, and ICE. They work in close collaboration with the Gang Squad prosecutors of the U.S. DOJs Criminal Division and with analysts and others at the NGIC. GangTECC is intended as "one stop shopping" via phone and e-mail for local, state, tribal, and federal investigators and prosecutors engaged in significant anti-gang efforts. To that end, GangTECC assists the initiation of gang-related investigations; it aids in the coordination and effectiveness of gang-related initiatives, investigations, and prosecutions; it develops an enhanced understanding of the national gang problem and proposes strategies to neutralize the most violent and significant threats.

✓ **Regional Information Sharing Systems (RISS).** RISS is a national program of regionally oriented services designed to enhance the ability of local, state, federal, and tribal criminal justice agencies to identify, target, and remove criminal conspiracies and activities spanning jurisdictional, state, and sometimes international boundaries. RISS facilitates rapid exchange and sharing of information among the agencies pertaining to known suspected criminals or criminal activity, and enhances coordination and communication among agencies in pursuit of criminal conspiracies determined to be inter-jurisdictional in nature. RISS offers services, tools, and resources to aid law enforcement and criminal justice entities in areas of: information sharing, analysis, telecommunications, equipment loans, confidential funds, training, and technical assistance. See https://www.riss.net.

✓ **Sentry.** This is a real-time online database maintained by the Federal Bureau of Prisons. It contains information on all federal prisoners incarcerated since 1981. The information includes physical description, inmate profile, inmate location or release location, numerical identifiers, personal history data, security designation, past and present institution assignments, custody classification, and sentencing information.[ciii]

Chapter 7
Firearms Trafficking Indicators

"There are over 550 million firearms in worldwide circulation. That's one firearm for every twelve people on the planet. The only question is: How do we arm the other eleven?"

Yuri Orlov (played by Nicholas Cage) in the 2005 film, LORD OF WAR,
written and directed by Andrew Niccol

Firearms trafficking indicators are events that signal to an investigator to take a closer look at the events. The presence of one or more of the indicators discussed in this chapter is not proof of a crime or probable cause that firearms trafficking is taking place, but indicators are leads that should be further examined. This is not a "future crimes" unit, but, comprehensively collected and properly researched, data can produce indicators that can be powerful predictors of ongoing or future trafficking activity. These indicators allow investigators to focus limited resources where they may achieve the most impact against firearms traffickers. After learning of one or more indicators, an investigator should conduct a preliminary investigation of the factors surrounding the indicators, evaluate the totality of the circumstances, and determine if a full investigation of potential firearms trafficking criminal violations is warranted.

Firearms trafficking indicator leads are generated by a variety of sources. They may come from the analysis of crime gun trace data by analysts, HUMINT, ATF's Online LEAD and eTrace, or an ATF CGIC. They may come from examination of a recovered crime gun, from observed firearm purchaser behavior, from records that FFLs must file with law enforcement, such as Multiple Sales Forms and Pawn Records, or from the examination of FFL records in their store by ATF Industry Operations Investigators (IOIs) and Special Agents (SAs), other federal agents, or local police officials. Those inspecting the records of FFLs in their store should have a lawful reason and the authority to do so. Some of the indicators may seem obvious to the point of absurdity, and you may wonder why anyone would be so obvious in their behavior. Just remember, you are (probably) not a criminal and you are thinking logically. The fact that someone is committing a crime involving firearms is a good indicator they are not using effective logic skills and are not approaching risk management in quite the same way that most of us do. General indicators of potential firearms trafficking may include the following:

INDICATORS IN AGGREGATE CRIME GUN TRACE DATA

✓ Crime Gun Trace data showing a crime gun recovery in one state that was part of a multiple purchase of handguns from an FFL in another state, or crime gun traces in another state that trace back to multiple purchasers in another state, all of whom purchased the firearms from

the same FFL. Multiple purchasers of firearms in one state that are being traced in another state is a strong indicator of a straw purchasing ring.

✓ Multiple short time-to-crime gun traces associated with an individual or FFL may indicate an active firearms trafficker. It is usually easier to trace a crime gun and locate the illegal trafficker for firearm(s) that have a short time-to-crime. A time-to-crime or time-to-recovery of less than 3 years is considered short, and worthy of further examination.

✓ Analysis of the background of a crime gun possessor shows a personal link to the purchaser of that crime gun. This might include a past common residence, a past common employment or school location, a listed place of birth that is the same, an arrest where both were present, and/or a common drug arrest or gang arrest history.

✓ Multiple recent crime gun traces associated with a common purchaser, a common address, or a common FFL. For an FFL this may be the product of high sales volume. The investigator should look at the ratio of crime gun traces to sales volume during a defined time.

✓ Incidents in which handguns are recovered from a juvenile may be an indicator of firearms diversion or trafficking because, with few exceptions, juveniles cannot obtain handguns lawfully.

✓ For crime gun trace requests where the ATF NTC results advise that the firearm could not be traced because the firearm is foreign-made and the trace requestor did not list the importer information, the investigator should re-check that firearm to find the firearm's importer markings. If it is determined that a foreign-made firearm recovered in the US did not have any importer markings, this may be an indicator this firearm was illegally imported into the US via an illegal purchase from a website source, or it may indicate the presence of import fraud. Import fraud involves firearms that were lawfully approved for importation into the US; however, after their arrival, the FFL failed to place the importer markings on the firearm prior to selling it in the US. This is an untraceable firearm. The investigator should check with the ATF NTC to determine if there are numerous incomplete crime gun traces in their area due to lack of importer markings. If there are, the possessors of those recovered crime guns should be interviewed to attempt to determine the source[civ].

INDICATORS IN FEDERAL FIREARMS LICENSEE RECORDS

✓ Multiple short time-to-sale rates for an FFL. This may indicate that firearms being recovered in crimes were specifically ordered for or by a person or persons. A trafficker may be locating firearms from private sellers in the secondary market on the internet and having those firearms shipped to a designated FFL from whom they pick them up. This would allow the online seller to comply with the law; however, the trafficker could still traffic the firearm(s) and feel comfortable that since the firearm passed through private transactions, a trace will not find its way to them.

✓ Frequent reports of firearms thefts or losses by an FFL, regardless of when or if those firearms are recovered, may be a sign of firearms trafficking by a corrupt FFL who is selling firearms to people "off-paper", with no record, and covering this in their records by reporting the firearms lost or stolen.

✓ Frequent purchases of fewer than two handguns in a 5-business day period from one FFL or multiple FFLs in an area by the same individual may indicate that an individual is actively trying to prevent detection by avoiding the multiple sales reporting requirement on FFLs who must advise ATF when they sell 2 or more handguns in 5 business days to the same person.

✓ An ATF Form 4473 on which the purchaser lists a distant city as their place of birth and the city where that firearm is ultimately recovered as a crime gun is the same city listed as the purchaser's place of birth. This may indicate that the purchaser still travels to that city or has connections to others in that city that resulted in the trafficking of firearms to that location.

✓ FFLs who often cannot account for firearms they received or often do not have information needed to complete firearms trace requests. This may indicate an FFL who either improperly maintains records or is diverting firearms off paper. In this event, the investigator should contact the wholesaler(s) or other source of the firearm which the FFL cannot account for, and determine how many other firearms the FFL has received from that source. The FFL's records should then be checked for the presence of these firearms. Additionally, this indicator may be a sign that the FFL in the trace chain who reports transferring a firearm to the FFL who can produce no record is actually the FFL who is illegally diverting firearms. In some instances, an FFL who is illegally diverting firearms may provide fictitious information to the NTC when questioned as to the disposition of a firearm. That fictitious information from the FFL in question may involve reporting to the NTC that they transferred the firearms to another FFL (usually a large wholesaler is identified) when in fact the firearm was illegally diverted.

✓ FFLs who have no records to reflect the receipt of firearms found at their store/in their inventory. These "off the books" firearms may be discovered during a visit or a routine inspection of an FFL, and they may be an indicator of unlawful diversion activity by the FFL. In the event that "off the books" firearms are found, the source of the firearm should be determined. Checks to see if the firearm(s) are stolen should be performed. Once the source is determined, efforts should be made to determine if other firearms have been obtained by the FFL from this source for which the FFL has no record. This information will assist in determining if the FFL is unlawfully diverting firearms "off the books" without the required paperwork. The FFL could be operating as an off-the-books pawn shop for local criminals or they could be selling off-paper firearms they secured through secondary source markets.

✓ Multiple purchases of the same model firearm or inexpensive firearms. Firearms traffickers will often order multiple inexpensive firearms of the same model. This activity is indicative of a firearms trafficker, not a firearms collector, if the firearms being ordered have no collector's value.

✓ Multiple purchases by a single individual at one or more FFLs, over weeks or months, of firearms commonly recovered as crime guns in that area or region. Collectors generally do not collect inexpensive handguns of the same model, make, and caliber. Inexpensive semi-automatic pistols, assault-style rifles, and pistol grip shotguns are more commonly involved in firearms trafficking.

✓ Multiple purchases over a short period of time by individuals who live in the same neighborhood or apartment complex, particularly when the firearms are of the same make and model or the purchases are from the same FFL. This may indicate that these individuals are working together in a trafficking or straw purchase conspiracy.

✓ Multiple purchases of firearms by persons who have no known or visible means of income or for whom the cost of the purchases appear to exceed any reasonable financial means may be an indication of someone being paid to make straw purchases.

✓ Multiple purchases of firearms by females (typically under 25 years old) or who are buying large caliber handguns or assault rifles may be an indicator of straw purchases for someone else, particularly if investigation and research indicates that the purchaser is living with someone who has a prior felony conviction, a domestic violence conviction, or a history of drug arrests.

✓ Multiple purchases or firearms, or crime gun traces that come back to purchasers with a recent drug arrest history. Firearms traffickers often target drug addicts for use as straw purchasers by paying the drug addict just enough for them to get high if they are willing to go in a gun store and purchase firearms for the trafficker.

✓ Multiple one-handgun purchases by different individuals from an FFL over a short period of time, particularly when the firearms are of the same make and model may indicate that multiple individuals are engaged in straw purchasing firearms and attempting to circumvent the multiple purchase reporting requirements.

✓ Multiple purchases of firearms by someone displaying a recently-issued government identification (e.g., a driver's license) may be indicative of an individual who just obtained fraudulent identification. This person may be using a false name, and may live in a different state or country. They may be trying to show an in-state address in order to buy handguns for an FFL.

✓ An ATF Form 4473, Firearms Transaction Record (records maintained by the FFL that reflect firearms sale information), on which the front and back of the form are completed with the same handwriting. Federal statute requires completion of Section A of the form by the purchaser and the remainder of the form by the licensee. If two separate handwriting styles do not appear on an ATF Form 4473, this may indicate illegal activity.

✓ An ATF Form 4473 on which different color inks or different handwriting styles are present on the form, particularly if the description of multiple firearms shown as purchased on the form are written in different handwriting styles or colors. This may indicate the FFL, or an employee, has added firearms to a previously completed transaction form and the added firearms were actually transferred in an off-paper sale to someone else. This indicator may also manifest when a crime gun trace is followed through to the purchaser, and the purchaser advises the investigator that even though the firearm is listed on the form they signed, they did not purchase that firearm.

✓ An ATF Form 4473 on which the purchaser answers "yes" or leaves unanswered any question in the section that asks the purchaser if he/she is a person prohibited from possessing firearms. This may indicate an oversight on the FFL's part, and the individual believes they may be prohibited or they are not the intended recipient of the firearm. An FFL should not sell a firearm when there is no answer or an answer of yes to any of the questions designed to determine a person's eligibility to possess a firearm.

✓ FFLs whose records indicate that they transfer large numbers of firearms to themselves for a private collection, especially if those firearms are inexpensive handguns, multiple handguns of the same make and model, or other types of firearms not normally viewed as collectable or useful for sporting/hunting purposes. FFLs are allowed to transfer firearms to themselves through their records; however, certain types of transfers may indicate an FFL who is engaged in unlawful diversion of these firearms through off-book private sales.

✓ Retail FFLs whose records reflect the transfer of large numbers of firearms to other FFLs, especially if those firearms are inexpensive handguns. This may indicate unlawful diversion of firearms. Most retail FFLs sell the majority of their inventory to retail customers. An FFL engaged in unlawful diversion of firearms may try to mask this activity by fraudulently listing other FFLs as the recipients of firearms, when, in fact, the firearms were diverted elsewhere. Follow-up should be performed with the listed recipient FFL to ensure that they did, in fact, receive all those firearms and are actually in business.

CASE STUDY: CALI BOUND

United States v. Candiotti, et al - District of South Florida - 729 F. Supp. 840 (1990)

In 1989 ATF agents in the West Palm Beach Field Office noticed that a South Florida retail FFL listed the transfer of twenty-five AR-15 rifles and twelve MAC-11 pistols to another FFL. This seemed out of place for a retail FFL and, through investigation, ATF determined the other listed FFL was out of business and never received those firearms. Additional investigation revealed that the first FFL was working with a security company to provide security at properties in Columbia owned by Cali Cartel members, and

FIGURE 7.1 *Firearms, Plastic Explosives, and an Unmanned Remote-Controlled Plane bound for the Cali Cartel in 1989 and Intercepted by ATF & USCS in West Palm Beach, FL*
Source: ATF S/A Steve Barborini

that Israeli military personnel were training the security teams.[cv] Working with U.S. Customs Service agents (USCS), the ATF agents were able to determine that firearms were being shipped to Columbia, and that there were plans to ship more firearms, as well as Tovex plastic explosives and an unmanned remote-control plane that could carry a 35-pound payload[cvi]. It appeared that

the Cali Cartel members wanted both defensive security at their properties and offensive capabilities to deal with competitors. Their plan was to kill Pablo Escobar, head of the rival Medellin Cartel, by flying the unmanned remote-controlled plane with a payload of plastic explosives into his mountain top Ranchero. Multiple people, to include a former police officer, were arrested and convicted of numerous violations of the federal firearms laws and Pablo Escobar never sent a thank you note to the agents for intercepting all that firepower which was bound for sicarios. This was more than 20 years before the use of unmanned aerial drones to kill people entered the lexicon of the American public. This case directly resulted from detection of a firearm trafficking indicator.

✓ The discovery, during an FFL inspection, that an FFL is failing to keep proper records of firearms dispositions or failing to submit an ATF Form 3310.4 Handgun Multiple Sale notice to ATF and local law enforcement when a multiple sale of handguns is made. This may indicate that an FFL is intentionally hiding illegal activity by others, or is directly engaged in illegal firearms trafficking activity.

✓ Most FFLs are law-abiding, compliant in their recordkeeping, and responsive in a very matter-of-fact manner when contacted by an investigator for information or during records examinations. FFLs who try to lead or take an active role in directing an investigator during the examination of the FFL's records, or who try to tell the investigator how to interpret transfers when they are not being asked for input, or who are persistent in trying to find out what specific records the investigator is looking at may be indicative of an FFL who is trying to prevent the investigator from detecting problematic issues in the records.

✓ For leads related to the international trafficking investigations, an ATF Form 4473 on which the firearm purchaser lists a foreign country as the place of birth and also displays a recently-issued government identification. This may be indicative of an individual who just entered the country, obtained identification, and intends to purchase firearms and quickly leave the country with the acquired firearms.

✓ Investigators need to understand how their state or local laws on firearms or FFLs may influence the manner in which those individuals attempt to conceal illicit activity. For example, in Massachusetts certain firearms classified as assault rifles are illegal under state law and cannot legally be transferred; however, the frame of such firearms can be transferred. Investigators in Massachusetts may want to look further into FFL records when they see a large number of ATF Form 4473s on which the FFL has written "FRAME" on the form, indicating that the sale involved only the frame of an assault weapon.

INDICATORS OF FIREARMS PARTS KITS AND GHOST GUN TRAFFICKING

✓ The recovery of foreign-made firearms, particularly machine guns, that have no importer markings and appear to have welded seams in several locations across the receiver. This may be an indication that a person has purchased a firearms parts kit, which is a collection of imported parts of a former firearm that has been torch cut into 3 pieces and made inoperable for the purpose of import approval, and then welded it back together to form a functional firearm.

✓ Firearms parts kits are untraceable, as they are foreign made and will have no importer markings on them from which the trace would start. The prevalence of this activity in an area may show up in the unsuccessful trace data as a trace that could not be completed because the requestor did not provide importer markings.

✓ The recovery of firearms that appear to be well-known commercially manufactured makes and models (e.g., Colt AR-15, Glock 17), but which have no markings at all. This may be an indication that a person purchased an incomplete receiver and used a Ghost Gun Box or Jig to mill out or drill out pieces of the incomplete receiver, thus turning it into a fully functional firearm. The prevalence of this activity in an area may show up in the unsuccessful trace data as a trace that could not be completed because the requestor did not provide proper markings information.

✓ The recovery of firearms that appear to be well-known commercially manufactured makes and models (e.g., Colt AR-15, Glock 17), and have all markings and a serial number, but for which the trace comes back to an individual who still possesses the gun they purchased. This may be an indication of a duplicate serial number that a person received when they purchased an incomplete but marked receiver and used a Ghost Gun Box or Jig to mill out or drill out pieces of the incomplete receiver, thus turning it into a fully functional firearm. The prevalence of trace results with duplicate firearm serial numbers may be indicative of Ghost Guns.

INDICATORS IN PURCHASER BEHAVIOR

✓ In high international trafficking source areas (e.g., Florida and the Southwest Border Region), investigators should look for the presence of rental cars or taxicabs in the parking lots of FFLs whose businesses are located near an airport or seaport. International traffickers sometimes fly to the U.S, rent a car or hail a taxi, travel to an FFL with false identification or a straw purchase, unlawfully acquire firearms, pack them into a box that they drop for shipment at a UPS or FEDEX location, and then return to the airport for the return flight out of the country. This is most common in major cities and where the intended destination requires air travel rather than driving across a border.

✓ In high international trafficking source areas (e.g., Florida and the Southwest Border Region), investigators should check on those FFLs selling firearms parts kits to determine which customers are buying bulk firearms parts kits.

✓ Tips received from an FFL who reports that persons came into their store to look at firearms and only one person looked at the firearms and asked questions before they left the store; then, later that day or the next day, the other people who were with the individual asking the questions came back in to purchase the firearms. This may be an indicator that a trafficker was determining which firearms they would direct their straws to purchase, and the trafficker wanted to know prices so he could provide the proper amount of cash to the straw purchasers. FFLs should not allow a firearms sale if they suspect it is a straw purchase; however, sometimes FFLs will make the sale and then call law enforcement. If the FFL calls prior to the trafficker returning, law enforcement has an opportunity to be present when the trafficker and straws come back, if the FFL is willing to cooperate with law enforcement. Law enforcement should never tell an FFL to make a sale if they do not intend to be present to stop the firearms from being trafficked. Law enforcement should advise the FFL that they should not sell a firearm if they suspect that the transaction will be a straw purchase.

INDICATORS IN RECOVERED CRIME GUNS

✓ The recovery of multiple firearms with obliterated serial numbers may indicate that an active firearms trafficker engaged in efforts to prevent detection. Efforts should be made to document the type of serial number removal method (e.g., filing, grinding, drilling, the size of the drill bit used, and the number of holes made during each removal) to determine if the firearms are coming from the same potential trafficker. Traffickers usually use the same obliteration method, and multiple firearms displaying that obliteration method points to one trafficker. In order to identify the trafficker, efforts should be made to fully debrief each person found with one of the firearms for information on the source. Every effort should be made to have a forensic laboratory attempt to raise the serial number or locate the hidden micro serial number that many handguns have, and which are not commonly obliterated. Being able to trace just one of these firearms often leads to the trafficker and their source firearm possessor. The investigator should also contact the ATF National Tracing Center (NTC), as the NTC can trace firearms with partial serials to give the investigator several possible firearms to follow up on. The ATF NTC may also have information on other firearms with similar obliteration methods.

✓ Long gun trafficking is often harder to initially detect from traditional sources of information such as Multiple Sales Reporting by an FFL. FFLs are not required to submit Multiple Sales Reports on long guns to ATF or the chief law enforcement officer in the area because, with few exceptions, the Multiple Sales Reporting requirement only applies to handguns. As a result, in many parts of the country, an individual could buy hundreds of assault rifles or tactical shotguns from just one FFL in fewer than 5 business days and the FFL would not be required to notify ATF or the chief law enforcement officer. If that same individual purchased just two handguns from that FFL in a 5-business day period, the FFL would be required to notify ATF and the chief law enforcement officer in the area. Long gun trafficking indicators may be developed in the following ways:

➤ Investigators could determine the most frequently recovered and traced long guns in their area, and when that type of a firearm is traced to an FFL in their area, they may want to check in that FFL's records to see if that long gun was part of a larger multiple purchase of long guns or part of multiple purchases of long guns over a span of time. If it was, this may be an indicator of long gun trafficking.

➤ Investigators could determine which FFLs in their areas have the highest volume of long gun traces, and then check in those FFLs' records for the multiple purchase of long guns by persons. If multiple purchases are detected, this may be an indicator of long gun trafficking. The same purchaser behaviors apply to long guns being trafficked as for handguns being trafficked. Traffickers usually purchase less expensive non-collectable semi-automatic rifles and shotguns, frequently with tactical features rather than bolt action rifles or traditional hunting long guns.

➤ ATF IOIs or local police officials in some locations have regulatory authority, and may proactively search FFL records for the presence of long gun multiple purchases as they conduct their normal inspection of the FFLs records.

INDICATORS AT SECONDARY SOURCE MARKETS SUCH AS GUN SHOWS AND FLEA MARKETS

A gun show is a temporary venue in which individuals come together and devote time to the collection, competitive use, or sporting use of firearms. Gun shows and flea markets sometimes become a secondary source market venue for firearms traffickers. Potential indicators of firearms trafficking at gun shows or flea markets include:

✓ Firearms transactions occurring in the parking lots of gun shows, FFL businesses, or flea markets instead of inside the venue where the sale might be witnessed by others. This may be an indicator of an illegal transaction.

✓ Individuals selling firearms inside the venue who have posted signs at their table proclaiming "No Paperwork Required," "Private Collection Sale," "Private Dealer," "No Sales Tax," or "No Brady Checks Required." While persons are allowed to make private firearms sales, persons who devote time and attention to the repetitive sale of firearms that are not from a personal collection and who do so with the principal objective of gaining some form of livelihood from those sales are crossing the line into illegal unlicensed firearms dealing.

✓ Unlicensed firearm vendors with multiple tables displaying a changing inventory of firearms from show to show. These are indicators of someone who devotes time, attention, and labor to the acquisition (inventory re-stocking) and sale of firearms for profit. An unlicensed firearms dealer who is traveling great distances and incurring travel expenses for fuel, lodging, and table acquisition may be trying to earn a profit to cover these operating expenses. This may be an indicator of illegal unlicensed firearms dealing.

✓ An unlicensed firearms dealer who is taking orders from gun show customers to get them certain firearms that the dealer does not already have in his collection. This may be an indicator of illegal unlicensed firearms dealing as they are taking orders as well as re-stocking, and not just disposing of their collection.

✓ Unlicensed dealers who routinely set up their vendor tables near the entrance of a gun show venue so that they may have first opportunity to purchase firearms from individuals entering the show with a firearm to sell. This may be an indicator of illegal unlicensed firearms dealing as they may be re-stocking for additional sales and not just disposing of their collection.

✓ Firearms acquired at the shows by an unlicensed dealer and that are displayed for sale later that same day or that same weekend by the same unlicensed dealer—particularly at a higher price. This may be an indicator of illegal unlicensed firearms dealing.

✓ Individuals frequently seen acquiring and selling firearms at area gun shows and flea markets who have no posted license to sell firearms (licensed dealers must post a copy of their FFL), and who have a substantial inventory primarily consisting of modern-day or inexpensive firearms new in their boxes. This may be an indicator of illegal unlicensed firearms dealing.

✓ Individuals selling firearms at area gun shows and flea markets who have no posted license and who have the ability to accept credit card payment for firearms purchases. This may be an indicator of illegal unlicensed firearms dealing.

✓ Conversation with an unlicensed firearms dealer in which they talk about their profit margin while bargaining on a price, or observation of an unlicensed dealer's ledger indicating purchase price, sale price, and profit may be an indicator of illegal unlicensed firearms dealing.

INDICATORS IN INTERNATIONAL POLITICAL AND CIVIL UNREST

✓ Political and civil unrest as well as high levels of organized crime can be indicators for trafficking patterns. In the 1980s, when Columbia was experiencing high levels of violence due to powerful drug cartels, areas of the U.S. where large numbers of Columbians had relocated their residence recorded significant spikes in purchases of multiple firearms in under 5 days. by persons who listed their place of birth as Columbia. These firearms frequently made their way to Columbia and were used in armed violent acts. In November, 1985, the M19 terrorist group took over the Columbian Palace of Justice and held the 25 Supreme Court Justices hostage. When the siege ended, half of the Supreme Court Justices had been killed. A number of the firearms recovered from the M19 group in that incident were long guns such as AR-15s that had been purchased in South Florida less than a year earlier. In the early 1990's, ATF agents in South Florida seized a cache of firearms headed to the National Liberation Army, a Colombian guerilla group. It is estimated that 600 assault rifles were purchased by straws and then concealed in machine parts and were intended to be smuggled into Colombia[cvii].

✓ Political and civil unrest in Northern Ireland was a serious problem for decades, and purchases of firearms by persons who listed their place of birth as Ireland often spiked in areas of the U.S. where large numbers of Irish natives had relocated their residence to. During the 1980s and early 1990s in South Florida, ATF arrested multiple individuals involved in trafficking firearms to the Provisional Irish Republican Army (IRA)[cviii]. These cases frequently started with firearms recovered in Ireland and England and traced to persons purchasing those firearms in South Florida in transactions involving multiple purchases of handguns.

✓ Political unrest and terrorism in Trinidad and Tobago during the 1980s and 1990s occasionally took place as the Jamaat Al Muslimeen, a radical Muslim terrorist group, tried to take over the country and establish a Muslim Nation in the Caribbean[cix]. In 1990 the group took over the parliament building and two dozen persons were killed in the violence. Following several days of siege, 34 members of the group surrendered, and most of the long guns used in the coup attempt had been purchased in South Florida just months earlier. Long guns are not part of the multiple sales reporting requirements for FFLs so when the straw purchaser in this case purchased hundred or long guns, the FFL did not have to alert ATF or local law enforcement. ATF perfected a criminal case against Louis Haneef[cx], the purchaser of those firearms, and went on to interrupt additional trafficking schemes in the years to follow based on the exploitation of multiple handgun purchase information and HUMINT.

✓ Political and civil unrest in Haiti was a serious problem in the 1980s and early 1990s, as attempts at violent regime change were more than just a rare occurrence. Multiple purchases of handguns by persons who listed their place of birth as Haiti often spiked in areas of the U.S. where large numbers of Haitians had relocated their residence to. These spikes often directly coincided with pending elections or civil unrest. ATF agents in South Florida frequently interrupted trafficking schemes to Haiti based on the exploitation of this multiple handgun purchase information.

✓ Political and civil unrest in Jamaica was a serious problem in the 1980s and early 1990s, as Jamaican posses jockeyed for power and control of drug trade routes to the U.S. The Shower Posse, led by Vivian Blake and Jim Brown, used straw purchasers to secure firearms throughout South Florida in the 1980s. Blake was indicted on 37 counts of racketeering and conspiracy by a Fort Lauderdale Federal Grand Jury in 1998, in a case that linked him to 8 murders, 4 attempted murders, the smuggling of 1,000 tons of cocaine into the U.S., and firearms smuggling[cxi]. ATF agents in South Florida frequently interrupted trafficking schemes to Jamaica based on the exploitation of this multiple handgun purchase information.

Where will firearms purchase data indicate the next international problem may be lurking? Firearms multiple purchase data and ATF IOI information on long gun purchase data may hold the answer. Investigators need to have an awareness of historical and current international hotspots so they can recognize the indicators and warning signs that may appear before them in the data.

Most notable is the armed violence currently occurring in Mexico due to battles among powerful drug cartels, which are playing out in much the same way they did in Columbia decades earlier. Firearm and firearm parts trafficking to Mexico is an enormous problem, and multiple handgun and long gun purchase information is one key component in the identification of traffickers of firearms to Mexico.

When will the Jamaat Al Muslimeen make their next attempt to acquire firearms for the purpose of a coup attempt in Trinidad and Tobago to install a Muslim government? The vigilant monitoring of firearms trafficking data for indicators of trafficking may reveal this.

Venezuela is experiencing economic collapse and any population in crisis is going to seek out firearms for survival. In the void of a collapsed government, the military does not always emerge in control and sometimes it is a group that has been able to amass enough firearms that takes control. The vigilant monitoring of firearms trafficking data for indicators of trafficking may reveal the emergence of such a group.

An area known as the "Triple Frontier" in South America, at the border intersection of Argentina, Brazil and Paraguay, is one of South America's longest-standing and busiest contraband and smuggling centers. Anything from drugs and firearms to pirated software are available at the Triple Frontier[cxii]. This area is also a long-standing and large radical Muslim stronghold. Will multiple firearms purchase data predict an emerging event born of this region? The vigilant monitoring of firearms trafficking data for indicators of trafficking may reveal this.

Chapter 8
Cooperative Compliance, Deterrence, and Prevention

One of the primary goals in any firearms trafficking enforcement strategy, initiative, or individual investigation is to protect public safety by stopping any additional illegal firearms trafficking from occurring. This can be achieved through an investigation leading to arrest or through the use of interviews and warnings as well as community outreach and education that lead to deterrence, prevention, and cooperative compliance with the law. Some people need to be arrested, but many do not. The importance of an effective deterrence and prevention strategy cannot be overstated.

Federal firearms laws have shades of grey, and there will always be a percentage of persons who appear to be trafficking firearms in violation of the law but who lack knowledge of the law and willful criminal intent. The firearms from these persons may still end up with others who use them in crimes; however, oftentimes the most effective method to end this source of firearms is through interviews and education that result in cooperative compliance with the law. When dealing with firearms trafficking, investigation leading to arrest and incarceration is the long and expensive way to end a source of trafficked firearms, and should be reserved for those who have knowledge of the law and willful criminal intent. The cost-benefit analysis between successful cooperative compliance versus investigation and incarceration is overwhelmingly in favor of cooperative compliance. Public service announcements and training, as well as deterrence and prevention interviews and warning letter service that results in cooperative compliance are far less expensive to society than an investigation, litigation, and trial; and incarceration can cost of tens of thousands of dollars per inmate per year. In addition, there is potential loss of income tax revenue while that person is incarcerated, potential outflow of social service expenses to assist a family left behind if the income provider is gone, and the felony conviction disability that attaches to the defendant limits their future earning potential. If deterrence and prevention can work to stop a source of crime guns and achieve cooperative compliance, it should always be considered as the first option.

PREVENTION AND DETERRENCE TECHNIQUES TO REDUCE THE FIREARMS SUPPLY AVAILABLE TO THE CRIMINAL ELEMENT

Enlist Industry Assistance. In high-availability areas near the U.S. border, or other areas known to be sources of illegal firearms exportation, enlist the cooperation of FFLs to explain to their non-U.S. citizen customers the legal requirements for declaring firearm exports from the U.S. by means of any common carrier they may board for travel (e.g., airline, bus line, etc.). This can be facilitated by providing FFLs with pre-approved advisories outlining the federal firearms laws as they apply to firearms exports and nonresident purchases. The FFL may agree to voluntarily post the advisory in a conspicuous location, or the FFL may choose to provide a copy of the notice to those individuals to whom the FFL feels the advisory may apply. This can serve as a deterrent against both intentional and unintentional international firearms trafficking, and can assist investigators later in proving the "knowingly and willfully" element of various federal firearms laws should a criminal case be initiated.

In 2001, with passage of the Patriot Act, rules were established for the banking industry that required them to "Know Your Customer" (KYC). The KYC rules are designed to enlist the banking industry in preventing and identifying money launders.

Since the passage of GCA in 1968, FFLs have had certain laws and regulations to abide by which require a level of KYC as well. FFLs must ensure that customers are properly identified prior to the sale or purchase of a firearm. All purchasers are required to furnish a valid government-issued picture identification card to verify their identity and their current residential address.

FFLs should confirm that the person standing before them and answering the questions on the ATF Form 4473 is the same person appearing on the ID photograph. As a suggestion (not required by law or regulation), an FFL may want to keep a photocopy of the purchaser's ID and attach it to the ATF Form 4473.

Additionally, resident aliens must prove continuous residency in a state for at least 90 days prior to the transfer of a firearm.

FFLs are also required to refuse a sale if they suspect that straw purchasing or another illegal act is being committed. To assist FFLs in their ability to detect and prevent straw purchasing and illegal acts, it may be useful for an investigator to provide FFLs with information on common firearms trafficking indicators to be aware of in their area. These include the following:

✓ someone who appears to be purchasing a firearm that another person with them advised them to get, and/or for which another person provided the purchaser with money to conduct the purchase;

✓ someone who does not haggle over or question the price of the firearm: cost is not an issue; they just want to acquire the firearm, and are paying in cash of the same denomination (e.g., $800 in $10 bills) or are using a pre-paid credit card;

✓ someone who attempts to conceal the fact that they entered the store with another person or have been having conversations with another person;

✓ someone who wants to buy a large number of the same model firearm, or similar firearms (e.g., 15 of the same type of small handgun or "assault style" rifle);

✓ someone who returns after a first purchase of firearms to order and purchase more of the same type of firearm;

- ✓ someone who lacks the physical stature to handle the firearm being purchased and appears to have no working knowledge of firearms: they do not appear to know how to hold the firearm, they do not know what caliber ammunition the firearm takes, they do not know how to operate the firearm and do not ask for directions, they do not speak knowledgably about operating a firearm, etc.;
- ✓ someone who attempts to structure their purchases to avoid multiple handgun purchase reporting requirements;
- ✓ someone who appears to intentionally avoid entering into conversation or is evasive in answering any questions posed to them; or
- ✓ someone who arrives in a vehicle with out-of-state license plates and other persons remain in the vehicle while the purchaser enters the store.

"Don't Lie for the Other Guy". ATF and the National Shooting Sports Foundation (NSSF), a trade association for the firearms industry, partnered in designing an educational program to assist firearm retailers in the detection and deterrence of straw purchases. The goal of the "Don't Lie for the Other Guy" program is to reduce firearm straw purchases at the retail level and to educate would-be straw purchasers on the penalties of knowingly participating in an illegal firearm purchase. Videos, public service announcements, and training materials are available for investigators and FFLs at www.dontlie.org.

Focused FFL Inspections and Training. State or local agencies may find, through crime gun trace analysis, that an FFL in their area is a problematic source of crime guns, and they may request an ATF examination of the business. ATF Industry Operations Investigators (IOIs) are authorized to conduct an annual inspection of an FFL to ensure that all records are being kept properly, that the inventory on hand matches the records, that background checks are being conducted appropriately, and that all persons operating at the business are vetted responsible persons. ATF inspections of FFLs that have been identified as high-volume sources of crime guns can foster increased compliance with laws and regulations, and increased attention to detail in maintaining accurate records, all of which can serve as effective deterrents to any unlawful activity that may be occurring. However, ATF inspections should not be used as a means to search an FFL's records and obtain evidence of wrongdoing if there is already an ongoing criminal investigation. In that situation a search warrant supported by probable cause and signed by a judge should be secured.

The four different types of FFL inspections conducted by IOIs are as follows:

- ✓ **Application Inspections.** These are used to verify that an applicant for a federal firearms license is eligible for a license and agrees to follow federal laws related to buying and selling firearms. These inspections may be conducted either over the telephone or in person; however, an in-person inspection is the preferred method. The IOI interviews the individual applying for the license and, during the in-person inspections, the IOI also interviews store employees and other responsible persons.

- ✓ **Compliance Inspections.** These are used to investigate whether an FFL is complying with federal firearms laws, including ensuring that Forms 4473, Firearms Transaction Record, and A&D books are accurately maintained. These records are vital for documenting that only non-prohibited persons purchased firearms, and for enabling law enforcement to trace recovered crime guns. There is no computerized database of firearms owners in the U.S., and FFL records are the primary source of crime gun trace information. Except in very limited circumstances, the Firearms Owners Protection Act of 1986 (Chapter 44, Title 18 U.S.C.) prohibits ATF by law from inspecting an FFL more than once a year. This limitation does not apply to the service of a search warrant during a criminal investigation.

✓ **Renewal Inspections**. These are used to verify the accuracy of renewal application information and to determine whether an FFL's license should be renewed based on the FFL's history of compliance with record-keeping requirements, regulations, and laws.

✓ **Limited Purpose Inspections**. These are narrow-scope inspections conducted for a specific purpose. They may include situations in which an IOI visits a store to review and approve an FFL's new inventory software, or to answer specific questions which the FFL has requested of ATF and which require an IOI review the matter in person, or to search Forms 4473 for the purchase of a particular firearm used in a crime.

ATF uses information from their CGICs to focus their limited number of IOIs on those inspections where they may have the most impact on detecting and deterring faulty record-keeping or full-blown criminal violations. To put the need for focused inspections in perspective, in 2017 there are about 620 ATF IOIs responsible for oversight of over 139,000 FFLs, which include importers, manufacturers, gun-smiths, wholesalers, retailers, pawn brokers, and C&R collectors[cxiii]. Of this total, just over 50,000 are the wholesale and retail dealers. To put a fine point on perspective related to the number of FFLs, by comparison, in 2017 there were just over 14,000 McDonald's restaurants, 25,000 grocery stores, 60,000 pharmacies, 32,000 coffee shops, and 10,000 7-11 Stores.[cxiv] All of these businesses combined add up to just a little more than the total number of FFLs for which 620 ATF IOIs have oversight responsibility.

In addition to FFL inspections, investigators can request that ATF IOIs provide a training seminar to area FFLs on topics that may be germane to crime gun problems being experienced in the area, with the goal of enlisting FFLs to assist in preventing the problem.

Secondary Source Markets. In areas where gun shows or flea markets are identified as a source of illicit secondary market sales through unlicensed dealing or "off-paper" sales, investigators may find it useful to meet with the gun show/flea market promoters or managers to establish open lines of communication, foster a cooperative atmosphere, and provide better understanding of federal and state firearms laws as they apply to firearms sales and transfers taking place at gun shows or flea markets. Investigators should cite examples of how firearms sourced from their gun show or flea market have been used in crimes, or how that might have been possible. It is important to respect the lawful commerce of firearms while also advising the promoter or manager that you are interested in protecting the community from gun violence as well as the rights of law-abiding gun show or flea market attendees. Investigators may request that ATF IOIs approach the event operator to suggest placing an informational booth at the event to hand out educational materials and be available to answer questions.

Local Ordinance Compliance. Investigators with state or local departments should always know all the FFLs that are in their area of jurisdiction. FFL address listings are public information, and any law enforcement agency may request this information from ATF. This information may be useful to local law enforcement agencies during their development of critical incident response plans for dealing with large-scale disasters or civil unrest situations in their cities. During such times, investigators will want to work with the FFLs in their area, and to have plans in place to prevent their firearms inventories from being stolen and subsequently trafficked. This information may be useful for those state or local agencies that have local ordinances that apply to businesses, such as zoning or pawn shop regulations, and the state or local agency needs to know where these businesses are located. This information may be useful for establishing a friendly rapport with FFLs. FFLs are persons who chose to abide by the law and become licensed to sell firearms. Their businesses can be adversely impacted by those operating outside the law and, as a result, FFLs can be of assistance in identifying straw purchasers who are in their store to acquire merchandise for unlicensed dealers operating in the area.

FFL SAFETY, SECURITY, DISASTER RESPONSE AND EMERGENCY PREPAREDNESS

The importance of assisting FFLs in hardening their stores against all types of theft to keep firearms from ending up trafficked on the streets cannot be overstated. In 2017, the number of reported robberies of FFLs increased 227% since 2013, and burglaries of FFLs increased 71%. Additionally, the quantity of firearms stolen increased as thefts become more frequent. In 2013, 3,355 firearms were stolen in burglaries, compared with 7,841 in 2017, with steady increases each year in between. The trend is slightly different for robberies, which tend to give thieves less time to gather up firearms: that number increased from 96 in 2013 to 370 in 2016, then fell to 288 in 2017.[cxv]

As part of any crime gun supply reduction strategy, federal, state and local law enforcement should assist FFLs in conducting a safety and security assessment of their store to help prevent them from becoming a crime victim and having their inventory fall into the hands of firearms traffickers. There is a wealth of information that can be provided to FFLs to help them improve personnel security, physical security, inventory and records control, and disaster response plans.

Traffickers and other violent criminals target FFLs firearm inventories using the entire spectrum of theft, from shoplifting and employee pilferage through interstate shipment theft, burglary, robbery, and smash and grabs. Each year thousands of FFLs become the victims of crime. FFLs may be injured or killed, and tens of thousands of firearms are stolen from their inventories and trafficked on the streets. Experience has shown that in some instances thieves spend a considerable amount of time evaluating a business to detect vulnerabilities in security, employee behaviors, business practices such as how shipments are received, and police response times.

It can be a challenge for any FFL to balance a comprehensive security program with the need to offer an inviting and non-threatening business environment. Investigators should visit FFLs and provide them with information on theft trends in the area, and offer them a security assessment. Investigators should encourage FFLs to conduct an annual risk assessment of their store security and business practices to determine what improvements are needed and possible to implement. After all, they are selling firearms and ammunition, not Q-Tips® and Kleenex®.

The primary areas for risk assessment should include Structural Security, Inventory Security, Personnel Security, Safe Business Practices, Customer Safety and Security, and Disaster Response and Emergency Preparedness.

Structural Security. Structural security is a combination of the physical characteristics of a business facility and its location. A thorough evaluation of structural security should be done on a regular basis. Do actual or perceived structural security weaknesses make the business an attractive target to criminals? The following are structural security assessment recommendations.

✓ **Evaluate the business location.** Have property crimes been increasing in the area? Is this business in a remote area where crime is unlikely to be witnessed and where the police response time may be slow? Has this store already been a victim of theft/loss? If yes, criminals have already had success at this store, and they may be back if they don't see any security improvements.

✓ **Evaluate locks and key control.** Can any door or window be opened from the outside without keys? Do any former employees have access to keys? Are keys stored or kept near the container or door for which they are used? Have any business keys been lost or stolen? If the answer is yes to any of these questions it is time to replace, re-key, improve locks, and improve procedures for storing and tracking keys. A key assignment and control log should be instituted.

✓ **Evaluate windows, doors, and door frames.** Can any of these be opened or broken through from the outside with minimal force? Is it time to reinforce or replace windows and/or doors? Would it be useful to install security glass, burglar bars, or roll-down security gates on windows, doors, and vents? Barriers such as concrete-filled posts or large cement planters may deter thieves from using a vehicle to smash through the building to gain access. Consider replacing any exterior hollow core doors with solid metal or sheet metal faced solid wood doors. Also consider installing steel doorframes and long throw dead bolts, and welding or preening any hinge pins to prevent their easy removal.

✓ **Evaluate other unsecured openings.** Does the business have air conditioning units in open windows or a hole in an exterior wall? These units are easily removed, and it is not uncommon for theft entries to be made this way. Are chimneys and other vents blocked or narrowed sufficiently to prevent entry?

✓ **Evaluate the walls and ceilings of the business and any adjoining business.** Criminals will sometimes ignore doors and windows and cut through adjoining walls or the ceiling to gain access. In some cases, the wall next to the doorway is easier to break thorough than a secured door. Poorly protected adjoining businesses also provide an easy entry point for criminals who choose to go through unreinforced walls. This form of entry may have a second unintended consequence as it may avoid triggering the alarm system on doors and windows. One method to thwart this is by having motion sensor and detection capabilities with the alarm system. Another method to thwart this is to reinforce the walls and ceiling with 9-gauge expanded steel mesh panels in the walls of the business or just around a room where firearms are stored during non-business hours.

✓ **Evaluate exterior lighting and surrounding structures, shrubs, and trees.** Is the business and surrounding area well-lit at night? Are there areas in which criminals can conceal themselves to monitor the business and where they could enter and leave the building concealed by bushes or under cover of darkness? Are there structures or objects such as trash cans or dumpsters next to the building that may provide cover or easy access to the roof or windows?

✓ **Evaluate the front windows and entrance.** Can employees see persons approaching the store or vehicles parked outside? Can passersby see into the store to be able to detect a robbery or burglary in progress?

✓ **Evaluate the need for an alarm system.** Request an evaluation of the business and recommendations for alarm system security. A simple system is far less expensive than the cost of serious injury to an employee or customer or the loss and replacement of inventory. Some states require an alarm system on specific types of businesses such as firearms dealers. Is the business in compliance with state and local law regarding the alarm system and other security requirements?

✓ **Evaluate any existing alarm system.** Is the system sufficient for the nature and size of the business? Are all points of entry monitored? Is there a panic button connected to the local police department in case of an emergency? Is there a tamper alarm? Is there cellular backup to protect during power failures or if power and phone lines are cut? Is the system tested on a regular basis? Who is on the alarm company call list, and is the point of contact information correct and current? Have members of the business met with local law enforcement to agree on protocols when the alarm is tripped? Have there been issues with apparent false alarms? If so, is the problem in the system, or might a criminal be studying the alarm response procedure?

✓ **Protect and routinely change alarm codes.** Is the number of persons at the business who know the alarm code controlled and documented? Are alarm codes unrelated to easily recognizable names and number sequences? Are alarm codes changed on a regular basis and whenever there is employee turnover? Are alarm codes written down and left in the business premise where they are easily accessible to thieves or unauthorized employees?

✓ **Evaluate the need for a video monitor system or upgrade.** Having video cameras can have a significant deterrent effect on crime. They can also be instrumental in solving thefts. Do existing cameras face in a direction that will capture people's faces and features? Do cameras monitor the interior and exterior of the business? Are cameras recording at all times? Is the video recorded to internet storage rather than maintained in on-site equipment that criminals can take or destroy? Is the recording system outdated and unreliable, and in need of upgrading? Upgrades to security systems may produce savings on insurance costs.

✓ **Evaluate the installation of a remotely activated electronic security entrance.** Would there be value for the business in being able to visually screen customers before they gain access to the store, in order to enter to prevent access by suspicious or threatening persons? Businesses in or near high crime areas and those who have already been victims of crime may want to give this some serious consideration. The existence of an electronic security entrance often means criminals need someone in the business to let them exit the building, thus acting as a deterrent for the criminal to cause an incapacitating injury to the store employee.

✓ **Evaluate the store layout.** Are unsecured firearms displayed within reach of customers? Does the business have blind spots in which customers can access inventory undetected? Are display cases kept locked unless an employee is displaying a firearm or other item from that case? Are there times when employees have their backs to customers, such as to access a computer or a register, and could that equipment be moved to prevent this? Do any business activities require that employees enter the rear of the store or storage locations, leaving customers unattended?

✓ **Evaluate after-hours security practices.** Are firearms and ammunition secured? If thieves break into the store, are firearms readily accessible or are secondary measures in place, such as the use of hardened locking cables on the firearms or the removal of firearms from display areas for placement in a gun vault? Are display cases constructed of shatterproof glass, with locks on access points?

✓ **Evaluate the type of information provided by an answering message.** Avoid using a telephone answering message to announce weekends and other times when the business owner will be out of town. When the message says the business is closed and the owner is attending a certain gun show, the underlying message is that the business may be unprotected.

✓ **Inventory Security.** Inventory security is the process by which business merchandise and equipment is accounted for from the date it is acquired to the date it is disposed. At the core of inventory security is the practice of complete and consistent documentation. For firearms inventory accountability, accurately completed ATF Form 4473 Forms and an up-to-date and accurately completed Acquisition and Disposition (A&D) Record are required by law. The following additional steps are recommended practices to help an FFL protect their inventory:

➤ **Maintain accurate records and conduct periodic physical inventories and reconciliations.** Without reliable records, it is impossible to determine if firearms have been transferred or are still in inventory. If this cannot be established and a crime occurs, the licensee will not be able to provide ATF and local law enforcement authorities with an accurate list of stolen firearms, and this could prevent solving the crime and recovering the stolen items. Without reliable records, an FFL may not even become aware that firearms are missing from inventory, and that a crime has occurred that will result in an unexplainable financial loss. Complete physical inventory counts that are reconciled to the A&D inventory log enable an FFL to know which firearms have been transferred legally and which firearms are missing and must be reported to ATF as lost or stolen. The frequency of inventories may be dictated by the sales and inventory volume of the business, but at a minimum, an annual floor-to-ceiling inventory is recommended.

➤ **Accurately record your physical inventory in your records.** Remove firearms from their shipping containers after receipt, and physically view the firearm when recording the acquisition. An accurate inventory must include a physical comparison of firearms with the acquisition description. Occasionally firearms are shipped that do not match firearms listed in shipping manifests. Occasionally the markings on firearms boxes can bear markings that are different from those on the actual firearm. Do not rely on packaging, manifests, or labeling to record firearms acquisition information.

➤ **Require two-party inventories where possible.** If possible, never allow one person to have singular oversight of any part of the business, including sales transactions, handling monies, and particularly the inventory process. Many internal thefts stem from situations in which a single person is in control of the physical firearms inventory and records. In addition to incorporating a second party in a regular review of the acquisition and disposition records, physical inventories should be conducted by at least two persons whenever possible.

➤ **Protect inventory records.** Thefts of firearms often include the theft of records. Some criminals are aware that the records may be the only way to determine which firearms were stolen. Records should be secured after hours in a location separate from the firearms inventory.

➤ **Keep timely acquisition and disposition records.** Federal regulations generally require that acquisitions be recorded in the A&D log by the close of the next business day, and that dispositions be recorded in the A&D within 7 days. While not required by regulation, it is advisable that firearms dispositions be recorded in the A&D log at the time the firearms transaction occurs, so that in the event of a theft the records are current and the loss of inventory can be quickly determined.

➤ **Physically examine each shipment of firearms received at the time of receipt.** Federal law requires that common and contract carriers who deliver firearms in interstate commerce obtain written acknowledgement of receipt from the actual recipient. Before an FFL signs for a shipment they should conduct a rudimentary examination of the shipment. Determine, at a minimum, that the number of firearms indicated on the carrier's documents is the number of firearms received. A best practice would be to open each package to verify that the shipment matches the order exactly. Physically check each firearms box received in a new shipment, particularly on a large shipment, to ensure that boxes are not empty. Interstate theft of firearms sometimes occurs when an FFL is receiving a large shipment of multiple firearms and the thief steals firearms from boxes in the center of the shipment. If each box is not checked upon receipt, it may be days or months before the theft is discovered, and this delayed discovery can hamper the investigation.

➤ **Keep display cases locked at all times.** This is a standard practice in the jewelry and electronics trade, another industry that is prone to shoplifting and internal theft. It is recommended that FFLs follow this practice as well.

Personnel Security. The same care that is given to the safe handling and storage of firearms should be given to the selection of employees who the FFL authorizes to do that work. It is neither lawful nor in the FFL's best interests to hire persons to handle firearms and ammunition without having them subjected to a proper background check to ensure they have no issues in their background that would prevent them from legally possessing firearms or ammunition. The importance of hiring conscientious and trustworthy persons is underscored by the high level of responsibility placed upon persons who are in a position to transfer firearms.

✓ **Institute an applicant and employee screening process.** FFLs should conduct background checks on all applicants and periodic checks on all employees. Applicants should also be required to provide references, and these references should be contacted and interviewed. Consider asking the reference for the name of another reference who was not provided by the applicant. Require that each applicant produce a valid government-issued identification card. If it appears that an applicant or employee may not be eligible to possess or transfer firearms, the local police or local ATF office may be able to provide guidance to the FFL.

Safe Business Practices. Safe business practices are often the least expensive and most immediately beneficial steps an FFL can take to limit the risks of becoming a crime victim.

✓ **Implement a structured training program.** A structured and standardized training program for new employees and for existing employees' continuing education on new regulations and rulings is highly encouraged as an effective safe business practice. Ensuring that employees understand federal firearms laws and regulations, safety and security procedures, business protocols for records completion, and inventory control will protect the employees, the customers, and the business.

✓ **Familiarize employees with firearms laws.** Employees should understand and be able to explain applicable firearms laws to customers who have questions. Employees should understand how to make a lawful transfer and how to recognize an unlawful transaction, such as a straw purchase. The National Shooting Sports Foundation (NSSF), in partnership with ATF, created video and brochure training materials entitled "Don't Lie for the Other Guy" that provide instruction to FFLs on how to recognize straw purchases. These materials are available from the NSSF and the local ATF Office.

✓ **Show only one firearm at a time to a customer.** If the customer requests to handle another firearm, secure the first firearm before displaying another. If the firearms are kept in a locking display case or other security device, ensure that only one firearm is unlocked or unsecured at a time.

✓ **Disable display firearms.** Use trigger locks or plastic ties to ensure that the firearms cannot be loaded or fired while being examined. Customers should never be allowed to load firearms or handle ammunition while handling a firearm.

✓ **Do not leave a customer unattended when they are handling a firearm.** If an employee must leave a customer who is handling a firearm, control of that firearm has been relinquished to the customer. A best practice is for the employee to return the firearm to its storage location before leaving the customer unattended.

✓ **Keep ammunition stored separately from the firearms and out of the reach of customers.** This practice can aid in the prevention of ammunition shoplifting and ensure that firearms remain unloaded while on display.

✓ **Do not meet with customers who request after hours or off-site meetings.** This is particularly important if a customer asks that firearms be brought to the meeting for viewing. An FFL should report this type of request to their local ATF office or police department.

✓ **Wipe down all countertops and door handles each night.** A clean surface makes it easier to capture and preserve fingerprints and DNA as well as other trace evidence. Fingerprints and DNA can make the difference between an unsolved crime and capturing the criminals.

✓ **Do not leave counter and safe keys in the cash register at night.** Many burglaries have been made worse by ready access to keys left in the cash register. The cash register is logically one of the first targets in a burglary.

✓ **Ship firearms via shippers that have strong tracking protocols and require signatures at the point of deliver.** The shipping carrier should be asked how each point of transfer will be documented. Detailed documentation makes it easier to track a lost, damaged, or stolen shipment. Carriers that require each package handler to scan the package provide a traceable chain of custody that acts as a deterrent to interstate theft by carrier employees. It also creates a tracking history that allows investigators to contact anyone who handled a stolen firearm while it was in transit.

✓ **Provide safety and security training for employees.** Ensure that employees know what to do if a crime is committed or discovered. Prepare a specific procedure for them to follow. Post important telephone numbers and keep procedures where they can be readily utilized. Explain the importance of protecting keys, combinations, codes, alarm system features, and any other security plans or procedures you have. Advise your employees not to reveal this information to non-employees, including family members.

✓ **Record the description of suspicious persons and their vehicles.** If an individual, or individuals, raise your suspicions or specifically ask you to assist them in subverting the law, record their identification, their physical description and the vehicle description and license plate if you can safely do this. Criminals frequently visit the stores they intend to victimize before the crime, in an effort to assess their target. Many crimes have been solved through physical and vehicle descriptions recorded by employees and witnesses who grew suspicious of a person or a customer's actions, questions, or activity.

✓ **Strictly control firearms at gun shows.** Prepare an inventory of all firearms removed from the store for display or sale at a gun show, and store the list separately. It is not recommended that an FFL bring their A&D log with them to the gun show if they will be returning to their business premises in time to record all transactions as required by law.

Customer Safety and Security. Purchasers of firearms assume a level of responsibility for protecting themselves and the public from the consequences of the theft or loss of their firearms. FFLs have an opportunity to model appropriate firearms handling as well as to provide information and products that can help purchasers with this responsibility. This may include the following:

✓ **Insist on complete firearms safety.** By demonstrating safe firearms handling, including clearing and unloading procedures, customers have the opportunity to learn and repeat these firearms safety procedures after they leave the store. This is the highest form of customer service. FFLs could provide information to purchasers on how to properly transfer their new firearm should they decide they no longer want it.

✓ **Recommend safe storage methods.** Federal law requires that firearm safety or locking devices be available for purchase and provided to anyone purchasing a firearm. It is recommended that you advertise these to your customers for storing their firearms. Advise customers to take their firearms directly home rather than leaving the firearms in their vehicle while taking care of other errands. Remind your customers that firearms should always be unloaded when being stored.

✓ **Recommend firearms safety courses.** FFLs should recommend firearms safety courses to their customers who may or may not be required to take such courses in order to obtain a concealed weapon permit in their state. The National Rifle Association (NRA) offers a variety of courses for adults and children. Training has been shown to decrease firearms accidents. NRA firearm safety programs are conducted by more than 93,000 NRA Certified Instructors nationwide. For customers who have children at home, they should be informed that children can learn firearm safety in NRA programs offered through civic groups such as the Boy Scouts, Jaycees, and the American Legion, and in schools. Since 1988 the NRA's Eddie Eagle Gun Safe[cxvi] program has provided instruction to millions of children pre-K through 3rd grade. The main point of the instruction is that if the child sees a gun when no adult is present, they should: "STOP! Don't Touch. Leave the Area. Tell an Adult."

✓ **Personal Firearms Record.** Provide customers with a free copy of ATF Publication 3312.8, Personal Firearms Record. This pamphlet was developed to provide firearms owners an easy and complete way to maintain a record of their firearm purchases and descriptions. This is the customer's own record that they can store in a secure, private location. In the event of theft or loss, the purchaser can retrieve this document and provide an accurate description of the firearm(s) to law enforcement for investigation and potential recovery, and the purchaser can communicate this information to their insurance carrier if they are filing a claim.

Disaster Response and Emergency Preparedness. Every business should have a disaster response and emergency preparedness plan. FFLs should have a plan in place to safeguard their business records and firearms inventory from loss or theft in the event of a natural disaster or civil unrest. FFLs should have a plan in place for the recovery and temporary relocation and securing of their firearms inventory in order to protect the public from the risk posed by having their firearms and ammunition fall into wrong hands. The following suggestions may be useful in assisting FFLs in creating a disaster response and emergency preparedness plan.

✓ **Digital Records.** Create and maintain an up to date set of records that includes: insurance policies; supplier and business contact lists; computer records file backups; and a second set of business records. These should be in a location where you can retrieve them in the event of an emergency. Ideally a digital copy of all the records will be created and uploaded to an internet storage location where it will always be readily retrievable to facilitate the re-creation of inventory records and a return to business operations.

✓ **Phone Tree.** Create a list of employee phone numbers and establish a plan under which, in the event of a disaster, they have a phone number to call to report that they are OK. This process is commonly referred to as a phone tree which people call up the list and the final designated person receives calls that can account for everyone and their condition or needs.

✓ **Relocation.** Secure your inventory in place using your standard security protocols or implement the use of safes or cable locks that can secure and protect inventory. Plan for a secondary location where the inventory could be relocated to and secured if necessary.

✓ **Lock-Down.** When advanced warning of a threat is available (e.g., Forecasted Hurricane) the FFL should perform a full inventory of their firearms before closing and take the A&D log with them to maintain until the threat has passed.

✓ **All-Hazards Plan.** Any disaster response and emergency preparedness plan should be an "All-Hazards" plan with contingency planning for all manner of threats to the business, including weather events, flooding, fire, earthquakes, and civil unrest and looting. Know what the potential hazards in your area could be. Plans should define the most appropriate protective action for each hazard to ensure the safety of employees and customers, to alert emergency responders, and to identify how employees will communicate with each other following the emergency.

✓ **Hazard Placard Posting.** Talk to your local fire, police and emergency medical services to determine their response time to your business, their knowledge of your business and its hazards, and their capabilities to stabilize an emergency at your facility. Ensure that you have the proper placards posted indicating the storage of ammunition, so that in the event of a fire, first responders will know the hazards they may face with ammunition detonating in the fire.

✓ **Emergency Medical Facility.** Know where the nearest medical facility to the business is located.

✓ **Contingency Operation.** FFLs should include in their plans a contingency to establish business operations in another location should their business premises be destroyed or rendered temporarily uninhabitable. In such circumstances ATF would be authorized to grant variances to relocated business operations.

Chapter 9
Common Investigative Techniques and Skills Applicable in Firearms Trafficking Investigation

"You know my method. It is founded upon the observation of trifles."
Sherlock Holmes in The Boscombe Valley Mystery by Arthur Conan Doyle in 1891

There are several areas of investigative techniques and skills that an investigator will find useful in all manner of firearms trafficking investigation. This chapter will provide a basic primer on best practices associated with those techniques and skills. Investigators should always look to subject matter experts, their department training and policies, and their prosecutor for further guidance on when and where to employ these techniques and skills.

DECONFLICTION

Firearms trafficking almost always crosses over city, state, or national boundaries and therefore falls into the jurisdiction of multiple law enforcement agencies, all of whom could be investigating the crime at the same time. Deconfliction is a critical first step in processing any and all firearms trafficking leads of any kind. Investigators MUST deconflict the information received in any lead (e.g., name, address or phone number) against the various agencies and databases that could be pertinent. In the arena of firearms trafficking, deconfliction should start with a call to an ATF Field Office or CGIC. These centers will have the ability to advise the investigator if their information is the subject of any investigation by ATF currently or in the past, and if there are any hits in any of ATF's unique firearms intelligence databases. ATF systems useful in deconfliction include the agency's current case management system known as NForce, the agency's future case management systems known as Spartan, eTrace, LEAD, FELC, GangNET, and NICS. Investigators should also deconflict investigative information through DEA's DICE system, HSI's TECs system, El Paso Intelligence Center's (EPIC) EPIC-10 check, HIDTA NINJAS, and Riss-Net. Other deconfliction checks should also include checks in NCIC, Accurint Lexus Nexus or TLO, and FinCEN. Deconfliction checks and an intelligence workup can and should overlap. If the investigator gets a hit during deconfliction, they should deconflict and coordinate their efforts with the other agency before proceeding any further. Failing to deconflict a lead can lead to interference in another agency's investigation, and potentially create a life-threatening situation in a variety of ways, particularly in ongoing surveillances or if undercover officers or confidential informants become involved, or in what is known as a blue on blue situation where two or more law enforcement agencies show up at the same enforcement action where neither agency is anticipating that the other will be there. Deconfliction is an ongoing process throughout an investigation, and not just something done at the beginning of a case. Each new name, address, phone number, email address, website, and other important identifiers should be run through an established deconfliction process.

EXPLOITATION OF ELECTRONIC COMMUNICATION DEVICES AND TECHNICAL SURVEILLANCE METHODS

The effective exploitation of electronic communication devices and the use of technical surveillance are arguably some of today's most important skills for an investigator to master. A great investigator has always been someone who is a skilled communicator and interviewer, has great instincts and can think on their feet, is curious and thinks analytically, has great observational skills, and works well with a team; but today, a great investigator must also possess the technical knowledge to employ modern technical surveillance techniques and exploit electronic communication devices to further an investigation. A significant amount of time and training must be devoted to keeping current with these technologies for an agency or department and its investigators to be fully successful. For every new technology that aids law enforcement in their investigation, there is a new technology, app, or countermeasure developed and made available to the criminal element, enabling them to jump ahead of law enforcement. This technology arms race is underway and is not going to stop. Law enforcement agencies must be prepared to invest in on-going in-service training on the employment of new technology in investigations or risk being marginalized and rendered ineffective.

Today's electronic communication devices contain critical information—they are "witness devices" that document the pattern of life and criminality of the user. The applicability of employing technical surveillance techniques and exploiting electronic communication devices cuts across every type of firearms trafficking investigation as well as armed crime and gang investigations. Case law with respect to all technical surveillance methods is evolving as rapidly as the technology itself, so investigators must consult with the assigned case AUSA to determine the legality of the planned use of any technical surveillance techniques or electronic communication device exploitation. Not only does the approval level to secure these methods change at the national level based on new case law, but there can be differences within each of the 94 Federal Judicial Districts and 12 Regional Circuits.

Legal Process Hierarchy. The current legal process hierarchy of approval levels and the corresponding data available with each level is as follows:

✓ **Preservation Letter.** This will compel a service provider to maintain all manner of records, data, and communications for up to 90 days, at which time and investigator may use a subpoena, court order, or search warrant to obtain them.

✓ **Subpoena.** This will compel a provider to turn over transactional records such as subscriber information that includes name, number, and billing records. etc. Grand jury subpoenas may be issued by a federal grand jury for a criminal investigator to serve or a criminal investigator may make use of an administrative subpoena issued by a federal agency that has been granted with specific legal authority to issue such subpoenas.

✓ **Court Order.** This will compel a provider to turn over information related to numbers dialed from or to a phone, as well as historical cell phone location information. A wire or oral court order is used for a T-III live conversation intercept of conversation or email.

✓ **Search Warrant.** This will compel a provider to turn over live cell phone identification and location information, as well as the content of stored communications (e.g., e-mail, voice mail, text messages, etc.) that were held by the provider based on their receipt of a preservation letter.

Electronic Communications Terminology. Before getting into the specific techniques, the following are acronyms and definitions that investigators should become familiar with:

✓ **Burner Phone.** An inexpensive cell phone purchased with pre-paid minutes and no contract that is considered disposable after temporary use with the intent of concealing the purchaser or user's identity. While burner phones are fairly effective at providing a user anonymity, burner phones are still trackable through cell tower triangulation. In addition, burner phones purchased in the U.S. must be activated by calling a number designated by the company issuing the phone. If an investigator knows the company, they may be able to get information indicating where the phone was sold. If it is less than 60 days from the date of purchase, the store may have security video of the purchaser and this may be helpful in identifying the person using the burner phone.

✓ **Cell Site or Tower.** A cell site is the location where the wireless antenna and network communications equipment is placed. A cell site consists of a transmitter/receiver, antenna tower, transmission radios, and radio controllers. A cell site is operated by a Wireless Service Provider (WSP).

✓ **Integrated Circuit Card ID (ICCID).** This number uniquely identifies each SIM card internationally and is functionally the SIM card's serial number. A full ICCID is 19 or 20 characters.

✓ **International Mobile Equipment Identifier (IMEI).** This is a unique 15-digit number that serves as the serial number of electronic communication devices. The IMEI usually appears on the label located on the back of the device. The IMEI is automatically transmitted by the phone when the network asks for it. The last 6 digits of an IMEI is the actual serial number.

✓ **Internet Protocol Address (IP).** This is a unique numerical label assigned to each device connected to a network that uses internet protocol for communication. An IP address serves two principal functions: host or network interface identification and location addressing.

✓ **Internet Service Provider (ISP).** This is a company that provides customers with the ability to access and use the internet. The company may offer the ability to transmit and receive data using one of several technologies, including dial-up, DSL, cable modem, wireless, or dedicated high-speed interconnects.

✓ **Mobile Equipment Identifier (MEID).** This is the unique identification number embedded in a wireless phone by the manufacturer. It is used on CDMA devices in the United States. Each time a call is placed, the MEID is automatically transmitted to the base station so the wireless carrier's mobile switching office can check the call's validity.

✓ **Mobile Identification Number (MIN), Mobile Subscriber ID (MSID), Mobile Subscriber International SDN (MSISDN) Number.** The MIN, also referred to as the MSID, is a number that uniquely identifies a mobile device subscriber. In the U.S., the MIN is derived from the 10-digit decimal telephone number assigned to a handset. Unlike an IMEI or MEID, the MIN is not an attribute of the physical device but is a number stored in the provider's data base. An MSISDN is a number used to identify a mobile phone number internationally. MSISDN is defined by the E.164 numbering plan. This number includes a country code and a National Destination Code which identifies the subscriber's operator.

✓ **Subscriber Identity Module (SIM) Card.** Cell phones require a small microchip, approximately the size of a small postage stamp, known as a SIM Card, in order to operate. The SIM Card is internal to the cell phone and stores the cell phone's configuration data and information about the phone itself, such as which calling plan the subscriber is using. When the subscriber removes the SIM Card, it can be re-inserted into another phone that is configured to accept the SIM card and used as normal. Each SIM Card is activated by use of a unique numerical identifier; once activated, the identifier is locked down and the card is permanently locked in to the activating network.

✓ **Short Message Service (SMS).** This is a method of communication that sends text between electronic communication devices. The "short" part refers to the maximum size of the text messages, which is160 characters but can be expanded to 918 characters (letters, numbers, or symbols in the Latin alphabet). SMS is a store-and-forward service, meaning that when you send a text message to a phone, the message does not go directly to the recipient's cell phone. The advantage of this method is that your recipient's cell phone doesn't have to be active or in range for you to send them a message. The message is stored until the cell phone is turned on or moves into range, at which point the message is delivered. The message will usually remain stored on the phone's SIM card until it is deleted.

✓ **Multimedia Messaging Service (MMS).** This is a standard way to send messages; it is very similar to SMS, however MMS includes multi-media content such as pictures or video. Providers may refer to such a message as a PXT, a picture message, or a multimedia message.

✓ **Voice Over Internet Protocol (VoIP).** This is an IP telephony term for a set of facilities used to manage the delivery of voice information over the Internet. VoIP involves sending voice information in digital form in discrete packets rather than by using the traditional circuit-committed protocols of the public switched telephone network. The advantage of VoIP and internet telephony is that it avoids the tolls charged by ordinary telephone service. VoIP providers include Magic Jack, Vonage, and Skype.

Electronic Communication Device Records and Data Analysis. Collection and analysis of electronic communication records will be vital in most firearms trafficking investigations. Many of these devices are being referred to as "witness devices" due to the volume and nature of data they collect. They are a virtual witness. Cell phone records may be obtained with a subpoena, court order, or search warrant depending on the type of records being sought, and the case agent should consult with their AUSA to determine which is required in their Judicial District. In addition, the U.S. DOJ Computer Crimes and Intellectual Property Section (CCIPS) provides investigators with information and resources on obtaining evidence such as location information, Electronic Communications Privacy Act (ECPA) Title 18 U.S.C. § 2701-2712 information, issues such as securing consent, encryption, forensics, privacy/protection act information, search protocols, and templates for court orders and search warrants that are compliant with the most recent technology and court decisions. When requesting any electronic communication device information, the investigator should also take these steps:

✓ **Permission Level and Case Law.** Consult with the assigned case AUSA to determine the proper permission levels required for use in their Judicial District. Case law regarding the use of these techniques is evolving. Requests that may require a court order today may require a search warrant in the future, and this could vary between Judicial Districts.

✓ **Language to Create Re-Usable Court Order.** For agencies with no administrative subpoena power, the investigator should include language that will allow the court order to be re-used to identify the subscriber information on any persons contacted by the target device or that contact the target device. This will eliminate the need for multiple grand jury subpoenas and significantly expedite identification of targets for intelligence workups and investigation. Figure 9.1 contains an example of the churning language that would be used as a paragraph within the affidavit for the court order.

LANGUGE FOR RE-USABLE COURT ORDER

IT IS FURTHER ORDERED, pursuant to Title 18 U.S.C. § 2703(d), that Virgin Mobile USA LLC; Sprint Spectrum LLP; T-Mobile USA, Inc.; Celco Partnership d/b/a Verizon Wireless; Cingular Wireless; and AT&T Wireless and AT&T Mobility; and/or any other wireless or hardline telecommunications company (collectively, the "Service Providers") shall furnish agents of [AGENCY] with the following information for a period beginning up to thirty (30) days prior to the date of the request and running through the duration of the Court's Order, for the telephone numbers dialing or being dialed from the Target Telephone and for the Target Telephone:
  (a) Subscriber's name;
  (b) Subscriber's address;
  (c) Subscriber's local and long-distance telephone connection records, or records of session times and durations, including cell site activations;
  (d) Length of service (including start date) and types of service utilized;
  (e) Telephone or instrument number (including ESN, IMSI, UFMI and/or SIM numbers) or other subscriber number of identity, including any temporarily assigned network address; and
  (f) Means and source of payment for such service (including any credit card or bank account number).

NOTE: See Appendix D for examples of applications containing this language.

FIGURE 9.1

✓ **Non-Disclosure.** Include a non-disclosure clause in the court order to prevent a service provider from alerting the subscriber.

✓ **Sealing.** Include justification to have the court order sealed until arrests are made in the investigation.

Investigators should gather cell phone data for analysis to determine pattern of life activity such as the regular criminal activities of traffickers as well as to document and map associations between sources of firearms and customers. The following types of electronic communication device data and analysis are available:

✓ **Tower Dump.** This is a form of historical cell-site data that reveals all the cellular phones that utilized a particular tower at a chosen point in time. Because hundreds of phones can contact a particular tower even in a short time frame, a tower dump from a single tower at a single point of time generally will not be particularly helpful. Rather, this type of information is typically most helpful when you can cross-reference tower dumps from multiple towers and/or timeframes in order to identify phones of potential interest by virtue of the fact that they appear on each of the tower dump lists. Tower dumps are useful in determining what phones were active at a very specific point in time and in a certain location.

✓ **Historical Cell Tower Geo-Location Data.** Historical cell tower geo-location data is what is known as "course-grain" data. While this data is fairly accurate, it is not as accurate as cell phone GPS data which is known as "fine grain" data. Call detail records for cell phones can establish the exact dates, times, and general locations of cell phones relative to the longitude and latitude of geographically-fixed cell towers when cell phones are used to initiate, receive, or terminate a voice call or send or receive text messages. Investigators should secure a court order for historical cell tower geo-location data for firearm traffickers to assist in establishing where they are getting firearms from and where they are trafficking them to. Geo-locating cell phones associated with defendants, accomplices, and witnesses can establish cell phone movement patterns, interstate travel, and proximity to meetings with other co-conspirators or sources of crime guns.

✓ **Latitude-longitude Data.** Also known as E911 or GPS data, this is useful to determine the precise location information about the wireless device itself. This is "fine grain" information. The device can be tracked via GPS technology built into the wireless device or by triangulating on the device's signal using data from several of the provider's cell towers. Not all providers are capable of providing latitude-longitude data and those that do often have this data stored in a way that requires a number of steps to generate the data for the requestor. In addition, investigators should have intelligence analysts map the geo-location data against data collected for the same time period from any acoustic ballistic detection systems in the area to determine if gang members can be placed at any gunshot detection sites.

✓ **Cell Site Simulator Technology (CSST).** CSST is also known as IMSI Catcher, digital analyzer, Stingray, and Triggerfish. The CSST has a passive mode and an active mode. In the passive mode, a CSST uses its digital analyzer to identify legitimate cell sites and map out their coverage areas. In the active mode, the CSST uses its cell site simulator to mimic a wireless carrier cell tower in order to force all nearby mobile phones and other cellular data devices to connect to it. Cell phones attach to the strongest nearby cell tower and the CSST sends out a power signal to attract all cell phones in the area. Depending on the type of CSST, it may be able to gather identifying information about the device, such as the IMSI, metadata about who a suspect is dialing and the duration of the call, data usage and websites visited, and the content of SMS text messages and voice calls. The use of CSST requires establishment of probable cause, and there are DOJ policies and guidelines for the expedient deletion of all non-target cell phone signals gathered by the CSST. The investigator must secure a court order to use a CSST, which is considered a type of Pen register. See Appendix D to review an example of language used in an affidavit for this type of court order. A CSST may be useful in situations where all methods to identify a suspect's cell phone number have failed, investigators should consider the use of CSST that will, over time and surveillance of the target while on the move, identify their cell number through a process of elimination. On June 22, 2018 the U.S. Supreme Court held in Carpenter v. U.S. that a search warrant is required when the government seeks to track a person's movements in real time.

✓ **Pen Register, Dialed Number Recorder (DNR) or Trap and Trace.** Investigators should use these technical surveillance methods to track in real time the various types of communications among members of a firearms trafficking ring, their sources, and their customers. The application process, use, and reporting process for these methods are contained in Title 18 U.S.C. §§ 3121 through 3127. The Pen register and DNR record or decode dialing (out-going phone calls), routing, addressing, or signaling information transmitted by the targeted phone number. The Trap and Trace records or decodes dialing (in-coming phone calls), routing, addressing, or signaling information transmitted from others to the targeted phone number. These technical surveillance techniques may only be used after the investigator secures a court order.

✓ **Automated License Plate Readers (ALPR).** ALPRs are computer-connected high speed camera systems that may be mounted in a vehicle or on a fixed location such as a street light or overpass. ALPRs automatically capture all license plate numbers that come into view, along with the location, date, and time. The image of the license plate may also include an image of the vehicle and sometimes its driver and passengers. The image of the license plate may be automatically run in a database to identify the person to whom the license plate is registered. ALPRs can be used proactively to identify persons coming and going from a gun show who have a history of being the source of firearms to convicted felons. The ALPR may be used to run the criminal history of those leaving show and entering a main public roadway. ALPR can be loaded with particular license plates to look out for when trying to locate a fugitive or suspect on the move. ALPR stored data may be queried to potentially identify all vehicles driving by the scene of an FFL burglary or robbery shortly before and after the incident in an effort to identify the shooter(s) or witnesses. Consult with the case AUSA to determine the proper permission required to use ALPRs and maintain certain ALPR data within your judicial district.

✓ **Video Surveillance and Facial Recognition.** This includes the use of pole cameras, drop car cameras, and exploitation of existing business surveillance cameras in the area where a firearms trafficker or straw purchasers operate, in and around a gun store, or where they may supply a gang. When placed and installed correctly by trained technical operations officers, these surreptitious devices can gather a wealth of intelligence and video evidence completely undetected. Law enforcement may use surreptitious video recording devices without the need to secure a court order as long as they are not recording audio and are only recording activities taking place in an area within view of the general public (U.S. v. Jackson, 213 F.3d 1269). The continuous covert recording of activity which persons are conducting in an area

where they have a reasonable expectation of privacy require a court order. Investigators may also want to determine if the city in which the gang operates maintains a video monitoring system or ALPR system throughout the city that could be used to enhance surveillance abilities or used exclusively as surveillance. Some cities have automated their jail booking photographs into a facial recognition system, and agencies may run photographs against the system to potentially identify unknown suspects. At least 39 states use facial recognition with their Department of Motor Vehicle photograph files[cxvii]. The FBI's Next Generation Identification (NGI) database has as many as 52 million police mugshots[cxviii] in its system, which is accessible to law enforcement and the FBI's Facial Analysis, Comparison, and Evaluation (FACE) services division can access numerous other photographic databases. In 2019 DHS plans to deploy the Homeland Advanced Recognition Technology (HART) database which will reportedly include at least seven biometric identifiers, including face and voice data, tattoos, DNA, scars, and other "physical descriptors" on as many as 500 million people, and they plan to have Iris data available by 2021[cxix]. Consult with the case AUSA to determine the proper permission required to use any of these techniques within your judicial district.

✓ **Global Positioning System (GPS) Tracking Devices.** The use of GPS trackers, also known as "bird dogs", or a vehicle's own built in geo-location software such as On-Star® may be useful in documenting the activities of firearms traffickers as they travel to meet a source or make sales. See Appendix D to review an example of language used in an affidavit for this type of court order. GPS devices, with or without their own power source, can only be used after securing a court order. Securing the records for a highway toll transponder (e.g., E-ZPass®, SunPass®, or FasTrak™) may be obtained with a subpoena or court order. Securing cellphone GPS data may also accomplish identifying a suspect's movements as well as establishing pattern of life activities that could yield other co-conspirators' firearms source locations. Consult with the case AUSA to determine the proper permission required to use any of these techniques within your judicial district. In most instances the placement of a "real-time" tracker will require a search warrant. In addition, special care must be exercised when installing a GPS tracker, and the action should include sufficient operational planning. For example:

➤ **Practice placing the GPS tracker on a like make and model vehicle before placing the device on the suspect vehicle.** Look up the vehicle in the local classified ads and find a car lot where it is for sale. Go there and look underneath that vehicle and practice placing the device. You need an area of steel that will hold the magnetic backing and preferably in location not easily seen by the operator or even a mechanic who might be under the vehicle changing oil. Once the investigator knows the exact location of placement they will be able to move much more quickly when placing the device on the actual suspect vehicle.

➤ **Surveil the suspect first and determine where the optimal location will be to place the tracker on the vehicle.** Will it be at the subject's residence, on a street while they are parked at work, or while they are parked in a grocery store parking lot? Wherever it will be, ideally the vehicle will not be in the suspect's line of sight. If investigators plan to conduct placement on the suspect's vehicle on the street in front of the suspect's house, they should consider placing vehicles on the street one at a time to fill the spot in front of the suspect's residence and force the suspect to park farther down the street and out of direct line of sight from their residence.

✓ **Standard and Roving Court Ordered Title III Electronic Interception.** As a last resort, after the means to further investigate the high-level targets of the gang are exhausted, and after demonstrating that a necessity to further the investigation exists, investigators may want to consider employment of a T-III wire intercept. The definitions, criminal acts justifying use of a T-III intercept, application process, use, and reporting process for this technical surveillance method are contained in Title 18 U.S.C. §§ 2510, 2516, 2517, 2518 and 2519. Use of a T-III intercept is a highly sensitive technical surveillance technique that often requires a significant amount of resources to staff properly, and therefore a full review of the need to use this technique should be undertaken by law enforcement agency management in coordination with the assigned AUSA.

➢ Court Ordered T-III intercepts may be used to record the conversations of people during telephone communications, using emails, using text messages and other electronic communication means. Court ordered T-III intercepts may be placed in fixed locations where targets meet to have in-person conversations. Court ordered T-III intercepts may be "roving", targeting a person rather than a specific phone or location. In some instances, gun traffickers or gang members may use "burner" phones, which are inexpensive prepaid cell phones that are disposable which they can switch frequently. If a target is known to use burner phones and change phones frequently, the investigator may want to use a "roving" T-III rather than trying to apply for a new T-III intercept each time a new phone is used. Securing a court ordered T-III intercept should not be an investigative goal; it is an investigative technique of last resort that may or may not be useful during your specific investigation to achieve the established goal of stopping the firearms trafficker, their sources, and their customers.

➢ Each law enforcement agency will have detailed policy and procedures for planning, funding, securing, installing, operating, and reporting on the installation of a court ordered T-III interception. In addition to following those procedures, investigators will also need to coordinate with their designated AUSA to gain their support and ensure they will agree to pursue a court ordered T-III interception. The DOJ Criminal Division, Office of Enforcement Operations (OEO) requires specific language be included in all T-III affidavits that are targeting violent organizations or organizations believed to possess and traffic in firearms, to ensure that all investigators and prosecutors are aware of standard risk mitigation guidelines.

To ensure that investigators and AUSAs know when application of a T-III interception is possible and how to properly draft the application, a roadmap for this process is contained in the U.S. Attorneys Manual as the T-III Procedures Checklist which appears as Figure 9.1. This checklist ensure that all means have been attempted or considered and exhausted without gathering enough information about the primary targets and violations and therefore the necessity exists for the use of a T-III interception to further the investigation. Prior to the deployment of an approved T-III interception investigators and prosecutors will engage in minimization briefings where they will establish and learn procedures to minimize listening to any conversations not related to criminal activity or any protected/privileged conversations such as those with an attorney. In the event the investigation leads to the gathering of protected or privileged conversations or material a "taint-team" will be established to gather and hold that information away from the gang investigators and prosecutors so as not to taint the investigation or expose them to information they should not know or have access to.

U.S ATTORNEY'S OFFICE; CHECKLIST FOR TITLE III AFFIDAVIT REQUIREMENTS

1. **Agent Qualifications**: brief description of law enforcement background of affiant—
   [ ] training
   [ ] prior T-III experience
   [ ] relevant job experience
   [ ] if local, deputization as task force officer, qualified under 18 U.S.C. § 2510(7)
   [ ] federal law enforcement agency affiliation, qualified under 18 U.S.C. § 2510(7)

2. **Identification of Target Phone**: detailed description of the device that you seek to intercept, including at minimum—
   [ ] telephone number
   [ ] service provider
   [ ] subscriber name and address
   [ ] electronic serial number (ESN) or international mobile subscriber identity (IMSI) or International Mobile Equipment Identity (IMEI) or mobile equipment identity (MEID)
   [ ] direct connect identity (UFMI) number, if applicable
   [ ] user(s) of target phone

3. **Target Subjects**: list by full name and/or moniker all persons for whom you have established probable cause of involvement in the conspiracy, even if you do not believe that you will intercept them over the target phone. *Target interceptees* can also be listed separately—those target subjects who are expected to be intercepted.

4. **Predicate Offenses**: list offenses committed by target subjects. To conduct wire or oral intercept: must show probable cause to believe violation of at least one offense under 18 U.S.C. § 2516(1). To conduct electronic intercept: must show probable cause to believe violation of any federal felony. Primary narcotics offenses are 21 U.S.C. §§ 841, 843, and 846. Primary money laundering offenses are 18 U.S.C. §§ 1956 and 1957. Include non-predicate offenses if applicable.

5. **Goals of Investigation**: describe the reasons for tapping target phone and the information expected to be obtained.

6. **Prior Applications**: list all prior electronic surveillance involving either named target subjects or target phone, including
   [ ] date of each prior application, whether approved or denied by a court
   [ ] authorizing court, including state and foreign if known
   [ ] which target or interceptee was named or overheard during the tap
   [ ] type of communication intercepted [wire/oral/electronic]

7. **Target Subjects**: list by full name and/or moniker all persons for whom you have established probable cause of involvement in the conspiracy, even if you do not believe that you will intercept them over the target phone. *Target interceptees* can also be listed separately—those target subjects who are expected to be intercepted.

8. **Predicate Offenses**: list offenses committed by target subjects. To conduct wire or oral intercept: must show probable cause to believe violation of at least one offense under 18 U.S.C. § 2516(1). To conduct electronic intercept: must show probable cause to believe violation of any federal felony. Primary narcotics offenses are 21 U.S.C. §§ 841, 843, and 846. Primary money laundering offenses are 18 U.S.C. §§ 1956 and 1957. Include non-predicate offenses if applicable.

9. **Goals of Investigation**: describe the reasons for tapping target phone and the information expected to be obtained.

10. **Prior Applications**: list all prior electronic surveillance involving either named target subjects or target phone, including
    [ ] date of each prior application, whether approved or denied by a court
    [ ] authorizing court, including state and foreign if known
    [ ] which target or interceptee was named or overheard during the tap
    [ ] type of communication intercepted [wire/oral/electronic]
    [ ] telephone number of phone tapped, if available
    [ ] date range of prior wiretap
    [ ] whether electronic surveillance is still ongoing or when ended

    These may be obtained via an electronic surveillance records (ELSUR) check conducted by investigating agency of DEA, FBI, and ICE indices. Include prior state and foreign wiretaps known to the affiant. Note whether prior interceptions are part of, or related to, your investigation. The check has to be current within 45 days of DOJ authorization of the wiretap.

11. **Probable Cause**: evidence establishing that this phone is being used to further the offenses. *Focus on actual use of target phone to facilitate and commit crimes*.
    [ ] **Background**—brief summary of criminal organization, including structure, timing of investigation, roles of target subjects, and goals of investigation.
    [ ] **Confidential Sources**—identify each CS and state separately for each CS:
    [ ] CS's basis of knowledge
    [ ] why CS is believed to be reliable
    [ ] how CS has been corroborated
    [ ] all favorable and unfavorable facts bearing on credibility, including CS's motivation for cooperating

12. <u>Minimization plan</u>: state how wiretap will be minimized, tailoring to any specific facts of investigation (e.g., potential interception of privileged conversations, such as attorney-client, husband-wife, doctor-patient, priest-penitent). Ask for after-the-fact minimization of coded or foreign language communications. Tailor the minimization plan for the type of intercept, i.e., wire, electronic, etc.

13. <u>Jurisdiction</u>: Demonstrate the connection to the district where the order is to be issued.
    [ ] location of phone or
    [ ] location of signal diversion or
    [ ] location of first overhearing (place of minimization)

14. <u>Differences/Issues for Extensions/Renewals</u>:
    [ ] leave in previous target subjects, add all new ones identified during wiretap so far
    [ ] incorporate prior affidavit(s) by reference, greatly condense background
    [ ] for OEO purposes, probable cause can consist of three or four recent incriminating calls
    [ ] the most recent incriminating call should be within 7 days prior to approval by the AAG. See Footnote 2.
    [ ] pen/toll analysis section is <u>not needed</u>, unless wiretap has been down for more than 21 days
    [ ] update necessity, with examples of recent surveillance, interviews, arrests, etc.

15. <u>Differences/Issues for Text Messages—wire versus electronic</u>:
    [ ] must have separate probable cause to believe subject has used and will use text messaging feature to facilitate the predicate crimes
    [ ] must have separate pen/toll analysis section for text messages, or explanation for lack of records with which to make an analysis
    [ ] must have separate statement of how text messages will be minimized—after-the-fact
    [ ] if actual incriminating text message is not possible to obtain, can use subject's reference to use of text messaging accompanied by toll/pen data showing text message(s) to/from other phones used by co-conspirators.

Footnote 1: For example, CS meets with low-level distributor Target A and discusses purchase of two kilos of cocaine. Target A tells CS that he needs to call "his man" [supplier] to see if cocaine is available. CS does not know who supplies cocaine to Target A. Target A tells CS that he will meet with CS later to inform him if cocaine is available. Minutes later, phone records verify that Target A's phone is used to call a phone [the target phone] used by cocaine supplier [Target B]. An hour later, Target A meets with CS and tells him that the two kilos will be ready the next morning. Assuming that other elements are satisfied, CS's meeting with Target A, coupled with the immediate use of Target A's phone to call target phone, establishes PC to believe that target phone is being used to facilitate drug offenses.

Footnote 2: If a call within 7 days prior to AAG approval is not possible, the affidavit should explain why (i.e., the target was out of the country but expected to return, the target sporadically but reliably used the phone).

COMMON TITLE III APPLICATION PACKET DEFICIENCIES

1. The application packet contains internal inconsistencies, e.g., between the affidavit, the proposed order, and the application; the target lists do not match.
2. The supporting affidavit contains stale toll/pen records, or such records are missing altogether. Toll/pen records must be no more than 10 days old.
3. The necessity and exhaustion sections of the affidavit contain boilerplate language with no reference to the specific case at issue.
4. The supporting affidavit does not sufficiently establish the qualifications of confidential informants referenced therein or does not sufficiently address why the confidential informant is in a position to know that which the affidavit alleges he or she knows.
5. The application and supporting affidavit fails to establish separate probable cause and minimization procedures for electronic communications (e.g., text messages, faxes and the like) as opposed to wire communications. Probable cause for wire communications is not sufficient to obtain intercepts of electronic communications.
6. The supporting affidavit for an extension or "spinoff" request does not contain sufficiently detailed factual support, i.e., it fails to quote the underlying intercept and/or to provide characterizations of inexplicit statements or coded language.
7. The supporting affidavit is over-inclusive, containing irrelevant or peripheral facts unrelated to the target facility or probable cause.
8. The extension request is submitted immediately before the underlying authority expires; requests for extensions should be submitted as soon as possible after the AUSA determines that an extension will be required.

FIGURE 9.2 [cxx]

CONFIDENTIAL INFORMANT SUITABILITY, USE, AND CONTROL

There are times where firearms trafficking and armed violent gang investigations can rely heavily on a confidential informant. Confidential informants can be valuable to any investigation when properly vetted and controlled. When not properly vetted and controlled they can bring ruin to innocent persons, an investigation, an investigator, and even an agency. As such, it is critical that any department or agency involved in these types of investigations have formal established policy to ensure the following:

✓ Potential CIs are vetted for initial suitability based on set standards designed to ensure the potential CI has no background issues that would preclude their effectiveness to testify in court.

✓ CIs are registered and sign a contract or agreement listing their responsibilities, restrictions, and what they can expect from the contracting agency in terms of confidentiality, remuneration, and protection from threats.

✓ CIs are reviewed periodically for continued suitability.

✓ CIs are deactivated when no longer needed or in use, and there are provisions to remove a

155

CI for cause that will ensure the CI is not used again by other agencies.[cxxi]

In addition to formal policies on vetting, suitability reviews, and deactivation, investigators should be trained on the proper control and use of CI's. The Four-C's of CI's are Control, Confidentiality, Corroboration, Considerations:

✓ **Control and Direction**. CI's should be provided specific direction on what they should and should not do. Do not strategize the investigation with CI's or divulge investigative information they are not aware of. CI's are an "Investigative Tool" to be closely controlled, and they should never control the investigator or the investigation. If they are not the right tool for the job, have them introduce a UC and cut them out of the case.

✓ **Confidentiality and Respect.** CIs need to be treated with respect and afforded the confidentiality they deserve. Investigators should not refer to them as Rats or Snitches, because not only is this demeaning, it can be compromising when overheard.

✓ **Corroboration and Caution**. CIs are engaged in illegal activities or deceptive behavior, and that behavior can go both ways. Independent corroboration should be a standard investigative practice. Be especially cautious of CIs who are cooperating in consideration for a reduction in charges or sentencing. Their information needs to always be independently corroborated. If they are cooperating against a former friend, understand that this is probably highly distasteful to them and they probably hold anger at the investigator for that situation. They may much rather find a way to compromise the investigator than their friend.

✓ **Considerations.** Investigators should, at a minimum, ensure that the following issues have been considered before using the CI operationally:

➢ Does the CI have ongoing issues with drug use, any past history of truthfulness issues, any prior arrests for offenses related to false statements, any arrests for crimes of moral turpitude such as involving criminal acts considered highly reprehensible in society (e.g., child sex crime offenses)? If yes, their value as a CI may be very limited, as it will be difficult to place them on the stand and have a jury find them to be credible.

➢ Ensure that the CI knows they are never to meet with any suspects without your approval or control.

➢ Ensure that the CI knows that all meetings and conversations with any suspect must be recorded if at all possible, and that the investigator must be immediately notified of any unrecorded meeting or conversation. The investigator must immediately document any unrecorded meeting, explain why this took place, debrief a CI, and memorialize what happened in a report of investigation.

➢ Ensure that the CI understands "Pre-Disposition" and "Entrapment", and that they know they may never plant an idea in the suspect's mind to commit a crime.

➢ Ensure that the CI has not made promises, created an inducement or incentive, or pressured any suspect(s) to commit any crimes those persons were not inclined to commit.

✓ **Dealing with a CI's Personal Problems.** Do not make the CI's problems the investigators problems. The CI's assistance is a "business" agreement and there should have been a formal CI contract or agreement signed when they were initially approved. Investigators must use their best judgment around CIs and when a CI is getting off-track, always refer them back to the original CI contract or agreement they signed. Always document all interactions with a

CI, never meet a CI of the opposite gender alone, and never socialize with a CI; they are not your buddy.

✓ **Payments to CI's.** Document all payments made to Cis, whether it is reward money, daily subsistence, or travel/operating expenses. Never make promises for any reward amounts prior to an operation. Execute receipts with CIs only when payments are made and have a witness sign the receipt as well. Never pay CIs any additional funds from personal monies.

✓ **CI Confidentiality, Threats, and Relocation Issues.** During discussion of the initial contract or agreement, discuss fully the meaning of confidentiality and the potential for them to need to testify in court, that they should never tell anyone they are acting as a CI, what will happen if they come under a threat, and that while relocation is an option in certain circumstances, if, how, and where that will occur is scenario-based and will be discussed further if the need arises.

✓ **CI Periodic Reviews.** During regular intervals the investigator should conduct a formal review of the CI that includes their role in any active or pending cases, information they may have on new violations, their willingness to deploy to a strategically targeted area in a new investigation, amounts of money paid for rewards or subsistence, and any new criminal history they may have collected. If the CI has failed to advise the control investigator of new arrests or new drug problems, this should be considered as possible grounds for dismissal.

✓ **Enforcement Operations Utilizing a CI.** The following are basic best practices when utilizing a CI during any kind of enforcement operation:

➤ Do not allow the CI to plan the operation times or meeting locations with the suspect unless it is done at the direction of the investigator.
➤ Develop and utilize plans for contacting the CI during operations, such as mobile telephone calls or text messages, the use of issued burner phones; establish verbal and visual codes to convey certain situations, such as a rip or other emergency where the CI needs help.
➤ Ensure that the CI understands they are not to take any unplanned trips with the suspect(s) away from the location.
➤ Do not allow the CI to manipulate any electronic surveillance and recording or transmitting equipment. The investigator turns the equipment on and off.
➤ Investigators will maintain visual surveillance of the location at all times prior to, during, and after an enforcement operation such as a controlled purchase of evidence
➤ Always physically search the CI's person and their vehicle prior to and after each operation where they meet a suspect(s), and document this in an ROI.
➤ Ensure that the CI understands not to "Front" any buy money to a suspect unless that was previously approved and planned. That is an invitation to be ripped off. Ensure that the CI knows that in the event of a rip, they should give up the money and do whatever is needed to get out safely or give the pre-determined verbal and visual signal for a rescue.
➤ Directly after the operation where a controlled purchase has been made, debrief the CI and document their statement in an ROI.
➤ After the controlled purchase, consider having the CI make a recorded telephone call to the suspect to confirm the "Buy" by thanking the suspect for a good deal or jacking them up if it was a bad deal.
➤ Do not allow the CI to attend any pre-operation or post-operation briefings

➤ Do not allow the CI to know any investigative methods and means such as the "Take-Down" or "Bust" signals.

➤ Ensure the Surveillance team and any other Agents/Officers assisting in the operation know the CIs appearance and attire.

➤ Be aware of a CI recording your conversations without your consent in "One-Party" consent states. In "Two-Party" states, recording without the investigator's permission is a crime and their service as a CI is terminated.

✓ **Other Considerations.** Any agency considering the approval or authorization of proactively using a CI or UC in an operation should weigh the risks and benefits of the operation, giving careful consideration to the following factors:

➤ The risk of personal injury to individuals, property damage, financial loss to persons or businesses, damage to reputation, or other harm to persons;

➤ The risk of civil liability or other loss to the government;

➤ The risk of invasion of privacy or interference with privileged or confidential relationships;

➤ The risk that individuals engaged in undercover operations may find themselves in a situation where they are pressed to become involved in illegal conduct;

➤ The suitability of government participation in the type of activity that is expected to occur during the operation.[cxxii]

➤ The CI's level of knowledge with the commodities to be purchased.

➤ The UC's prior training, properly backstopped UC identity and cover story, and level of knowledge with the commodities to be purchased.

➤ The UC's contact with a defendant, except via passive listening, is not allowed after formal charges in an indictment have been brought against them or arrest via criminal complaint takes place (Hoffa v. U.S., 87 S. Ct. 408).

COOPERATING DEFENDANTS

There are times when firearms trafficking and armed violent gang investigations can rely heavily on cooperating defendants. At the federal level, investigators will work with the assigned AUSA to determine the viability of a defendant's ability to cooperate and what type of cooperation agreement would best suit the situation. Cooperating defendants need to enter into a cooperation with the government. The preferred methods of formalized agreements between the cooperating defendant and the government are:

✓ **Proffer Agreement.** A written agreement with the government establishing a debriefing in which the defendant must disclose their full role in a crime, and this statement can't be used against them as evidence. However, if other evidence allows investigators to document that the cooperator's role in the crime is different than their account, they may be charged.

✓ **Cooperation Agreement & Immunity.** This is a type of plea agreement in which the defendant agrees to plead guilty at a later date, after the cooperation is complete and the government feels the cooperator has met the terms of the agreement. The level of immunity granted may be none, limited, or full, and this is usually dependent on the cooperator's role in the crime and the type of crime.

✓ **"5k Letter" and Motion for Sentence Reduction**. Once indicted for a violation involving a minimum mandatory sentencing provision, the only way for a cooperating defendant to avoid that mandatory minimum sentence is to have the AUSA complete a 5K Letter and Motion for Sentence Reduction and file it with the judge. This letter will include the details of all cooperation and the usefulness of that cooperation and is only filed after all cooperation is completed so that the cooperator has incentive to be fully forthcoming and so the cooperator gets credit for all their cooperation.

All cooperating defendant agreements must, at a minimum, includes the following requirements:

✓ the cooperator must always tell the truth and they will be charged with any false statements or material omissions;

✓ the cooperator must fully disclose their entire role in all crimes as well as their past criminal history;

✓ the cooperator must meet with the government whenever they are called for a de-briefing or testimony;

✓ the cooperator will not commit any more crimes.

UNPLANNED ENFORCEMENT ACTIONS

Firearms trafficking investigations and armed violent gang investigations inherently involve fluid situations where, regardless of the level of prior operational and contingency planning, there is always the potential for an unplanned enforcement action in order to protect public safety by preventing the trafficking of firearms or the commission of a violent crime.

These situations may arise based on observations while on a surveillance, based on urgent information received from a CI or heard on an electronic interception, based on members of the public straying into an ongoing operation, based on police responding to an incident in the middle of a surveillance or other enforcement action, or even based on an investigator being at a gun store or gun show when a robbery or other violent crime takes place.

While it is impossible to think of all the scenarios that would cause an investigator to take an unplanned enforcement action, it's a fact that violent encounters come at unpredictable times and often unfold quickly. Investigators should train continually to be mentally and physically prepared, for their own safety, the safety of fellow law enforcement officers partners, and the safety of the public.

Violent encounters always have the potential of generating a sympathetic nervous system (SNS) activation for the investigator, members of the public, and responding law enforcement officers. This SNS activation can result in motor skill deterioration, auditory exclusion, tunnel vision, and/or impaired cognitive functioning. The ability of an investigator to control their heart rate is a key to avoiding or recovering more quickly from an SNS activation. However, the most important aspect of preparing to win a violent confrontation in an unplanned enforcement action is for an investigator to develop confidence in their firearm skills, tactics, and defensive tactics, because when the time to perform arrives, the time to prepare has passed.[cxxiii]

Investigators should consider the following when they find themselves facing, or contemplating the need to undertake an unplanned enforcement:

✓ **Assess the situation.** At first glance, the situation observed may seem clear-cut; however, when there is time, conduct a 360-degree scan of the area, looking specifically for additional suspects and other law enforcement officers. Remember that there may be other plainclothes or off-duty law enforcement officers in the area. This scan will help to break tunnel vision should you begin to experience an SNS activation.

✓ **Determine if it is necessary for you to take action.** Has the situation turned into an arrest situation? Is there a violent crime in progress? Is a suspect fleeing a violent crime?

  ➤ If there is an active shooter, or if someone's life is in imminent risk of death or serious harm, then you are probably going to take action. While you are not legally required to take action, any good investigator will feel a moral and ethical obligation to act. The Law Enforcement Officer "Good Samaritan Act," found at Title 28 U.S.C. § 2671, states that a federal law enforcement officer (LEO) is construed to be within his or her "scope of employment" (on or off duty) to take reasonable action, including the use of force, to protect an individual in their presence from a crime of violence, to provide immediate assistance to an individual who has suffered or who is threatened with bodily harm, or to prevent the escape of any individual the Federal LEO reasonably believes has committed a crime of violence.

  ➤ If there are uniformed officers on the scene when the investigator arrives at an evolving event, the investigator should hesitate to get involved until such officers appear to be free to be approached for introductions. If the situation escalates to the point where the investigator needs to assist, they should verbally and visually announce their identify by displaying their badge. The investigator's firearm should not be visible at that point, and they should wait for the uniformed officer(s) to indicate that they are able to assist before the investigator enters fray or displays their firearm.

✓ **Formulate a plan of action.** The fact that violent encounters are dynamic and ever-changing does not diminish the importance of formulating a plan if time allows. If immediate action is not necessary, consider contacting local law enforcement to get a marked unit to assist in taking action. When requesting marked local law enforcement units, the investigator will need to clearly explain who they are, what they are observing, provide a description of their clothing and/or vehicle, and that the investigator will be assisting the uniformed officer(s) in taking action upon their arrival. If the investigator feels that immediate action is necessary, they should attempt to take action at a time and place that is to their advantage and the suspect's disadvantage. The investigator should attempt to exploit their appearance as just another member of the public to move to a position of advantage and cover. Additionally, the investigator should attempt to take action at a time when the suspect is separated from other people or when they are distracted.

✓ **If you decide it is necessary to take action, as soon as it is tactically prudent, verbally identify yourself as "Police" loudly and repeatedly throughout the incident.** You are not legally required to give a verbal warning prior to taking action, and announcing you are law enforcement may not be tactically sound until after you begin to take action. Even though you may not be in uniform and fit the stereotypical appearance of a law enforcement officer, you know who you are, and while you expect others to heed your commands, remember that members of the public will not know you are law enforcement unless you announce it. Additionally, in stressful situations, members of the public can fall prey to auditory exclusion and tunnel vision due to an SNS activation the same as yours, so you must announce loudly and repeatedly, "Police" periodically throughout the incident.

✓ **As soon as tactically prudent, visually identify yourself as law enforcement with a badge around your neck, your pocket credentials, or other overt display of your law enforcement identity.** It may take you a moment to retrieve and don any type of visual identification. If you have a firearm in your hands, it will require you to achieve a one-handed grip as well so only do so when it will not put you or others at further risk. Consider holstering your firearm as soon as tactically sound to help avoid being misidentified by responding officers.

✓ **Determine if it is necessary to go "hands on" to control the suspect or if you can wait for the arrival of responding officers to assist.** At some point, all suspects need to be physically controlled and restrained. Consider holding a suspect at gunpoint and giving verbal commands rather than immediately going hands on. Ensure that you are carrying some type of restraints if you plan to go hands on.

✓ **Call 911 and inform local law enforcement of the situation.** You should expect that others will be calling 911 and providing information about this incident which may be incomplete or inaccurate. If possible, contact 911 and notify them that you are either a plainclothes or off-duty law enforcement officer involved in an incident.

✓ **Responding uniformed officers win any challenge to you.** Upon seeing responding officers, verbally identify yourself as "Police" and follow their commands immediately and completely. Despite the fact that you know you are law enforcement, responding officers may not be as confident based upon your potential non-standard law enforcement appearance.

✓ **Requesting Marked Units Perform a Traffic Stop.** Should an investigator determine that there is an immediate need to intercept firearms that they believe are about to be trafficked, and they decide to try and do this in a manner that will not make the suspect think they are targeted, the investigator may call a marked unit to perform a traffic stop. As long as the unit waits until there is an actual traffic infraction that allows them to pull the subject over and see firearms in plain view or via consent search, the firearms can be seized and forfeited based on the investigator's known probable cause. Police may stop a motorist for a traffic infraction regardless of the officer's motive being to assist the investigator recover firearms (Arkansas v. Sullivan, 121 S Ct. 1876). Should it be determined that the only way to get into the vehicle is to have a canine check for the odor of drugs, that is permissible if the vehicle is in a public area (U.S. v. Place, 103 S Ct. 2637).

Chapter 10
Investigating Firearms Trafficking Schemes

"You get rich by giving the poorest people on the planet the means to continue killing each other."
Agent Valentine (played by Ethan Hawke) to Yuri Orlov (played by Nicholas Cage)
in the 2005 film, LORD OF WAR, written and directed by Andrew Niccol.

The investigative checklists that appear in this chapter are intended to provide the investigator with reference guides for the development of investigative leads, investigative steps to follow, and techniques to consider during the course of the ten primary types of firearms trafficking investigations.

The level of success an investigator has in conducting any of the ten primary types of firearms trafficking investigations will be in large part determined by how well the investigator knows and employs the foundational skills and firearms trafficking knowledge presented in Chapters 1 through 9.

THE TEN PRIMARY TYPES OF FIREARMS TRAFFICKING INVESTIGATIONS;

➢ TYPE 1: Preliminary Firearms Trafficking Lead and Straw Purchase Investigation
➢ TYPE 2: Unlicensed Firearms Dealing Investigation
➢ TYPE 3: Federal Firearms Licensee Investigation and Application of the Klein Conspiracy
➢ TYPE 4: Secondary Source Market Initiative
➢ TYPE 5: Federal Firearms Licensee Theft Investigation
➢ TYPE 6: Interstate Carrier Theft Investigation
➢ TYPE 7: Firearms Import Trafficking and Fraud Investigation
➢ TYPE 8: Firearms Export Trafficking and Smuggling Investigation
➢ TYPE 9: Firearm Castings, Flats, Parts Kits and Ghost Gun Investigation
➢ TYPE 10: Internet Based Firearms Trafficking Investigation

These investigative checklists, while comprehensive, are not all-inclusive and should not be viewed as the only possible steps to take during a particular type of firearms trafficking investigation. Each investigation will have a unique set of facts, and investigators need to be curious and imaginative in the manner in which they employ various investigative techniques.

Many of the ten types of firearms trafficking investigation sections in this chapter will be followed by a case example that the author personally participated in or supervised. These are intended to demonstrate the application of the techniques discussed. U.S. District Court case numbers have been provided for each case study so that an investigator or prosecutor may research these cases through PACER (Public Access to Court Electronic Records) and obtain copies of the actual indictments, search warrant affidavits, T-III Orders, and other information that may be useful as go-byes, templates, or general information to their own investigations. For the most part, the names of defendants do not appear in the narratives and are irrelevant to their illustrative purpose.

While this text is intended to impart a solid working knowledge on the conduct of these types of investigations, there is no substitute for hands-on experience, so get out there and make these cases. There is a wide variety of firearms trafficking types, and only by working on all of the types can law enforcement make an impact on the supply side of armed crime.

TYPE 1: PRELIMINARY FIREARMS TRAFFICKING LEAD AND STRAW PURCHASE INVESTIGATION

Firearms trafficking enforcement as a law enforcement priority varies from agency to agency. The priority is higher for those agencies with direct jurisdiction over firearms trafficking investigations, such as ATF, or with state or local agencies in areas with a high rates of gun crime. Regardless of the priority level, pursuing firearms trafficking investigations will always start with leads. While there are a variety of ways to detect firearms trafficking schemes, as discussed in Chapters 6 and 7, the majority of firearms trafficking leads are generated through the results of a crime gun trace, the review of eTrace or HUMINT, or an ATF CGIC lead referral.

Firearms trafficking leads require solid investigation and can lead to complex investigations which prevent armed crime by stopping the further flow of firearms to the criminal element. Oftentimes a criminal trafficking scheme is not readily apparent when initially processing a potential firearm trafficking lead, and only through effective intelligence gathering, interviews, and investigation will a clear picture of the full scope of criminality begin to appear. Special agents must use tact and discretion when conducting all firearms trafficking lead interviews. Firearms are a lawful commodity, and there are many types of licensed and unlicensed private transfers of firearms that are lawful. Not all leads will be determined to involve criminal activity, and the investigator must exercise good judgment so that they do not interfere with the lawful commerce of firearms. Oftentimes when following up on a firearms trafficking lead the investigator will interview law abiding gun owners who possessed the firearm at some point, before it left their possession and went on to others who trafficked the firearms and used the firearms in a crime of violence. Not all persons who possessed a firearm that was later used in a crime are firearms traffickers, and investigators must remain keenly aware of this.

At some point during the preliminary investigation of a firearms trafficking lead the investigator will need to determine what potential crimes were committed, what are the necessary elements for proving those crimes, if there is criminal intent (which oftentimes has to be willfully and knowingly in violation of the law), and which method will be most effective at preventing further firearms trafficking. To ensure that this is done effectively and uniformly, departments and agencies should establish basic protocols to be used in dealing with each lead generated from a crime gun trace. The outline of a basic protocol for processing a firearm trafficking lead includes the following three phases.

PHASE I: PRE-INTERVIEW STEPS

✓ **Deconfliction.** Conduct a full deconfliction of all names, addresses, phone numbers, and other information as these are encountered. Firearms trafficking routinely crosses the jurisdiction of multiple local, state, and federal agencies, and deconfliction is critical to preventing a blue on blue situation, or needless interference in on-going investigations, and general investigative effectiveness. See Chapter 9 for a description of a complete deconfliction process.

✓ **Intelligence Workups.** Before conducting an interview, the investigator should conduct a full intelligence workup that should include criminal history checks as well as Accurint and other commercial data base indices on all persons, addresses, and phone numbers, so the investigator can review the full background. The workup should also involve a request to an ATF CGIC for potential multiple firearm sales information and other crime gun traces that might be associated with the case. Oftentimes an investigator will have just one chance to speak to someone before they stop speaking, so the investigator must be as prepared as possible for the interview. For example, it may be important to know that the person you intend to interview has a history of recent drug arrests that may make them exploitable by drug traffickers as a straw purchaser. The person may have a past arrest, a driver's license history, or a residential history in another state close to where the firearm was recovered in a crime; such history may indicate that the person still has ties back to that community and is funneling guns there. Look for common addresses or other links to information associated with any crime gun trace information. Conduct NCIC checks on the firearm in NCIC to see if the purchaser or another person in the crime gun trace chain has a history of reporting firearms stolen which could indicate a method being used to cover up firearms that were actually illegally trafficked. A full open source social media workup should be performed. The pictures and information that people openly place on their social media platforms often prove valuable to that first interview, and allow the investigator to challenge false statements or to probe deeper when the purchaser is not being fully forthcoming.

✓ **Records Collection and Police Contacts.** If the lead involves a crime gun trace, contact the department requesting the trace and obtain a copy of the police report associated with the crime gun recovery. Conduct deconfliction checks and intelligence workups on each new person and address named in the police report who are associated with the firearm. Contact the local police department where the purchaser resides and see what intelligence is available about that subject and that address.

✓ **Create an Opening Report of Investigation (ROI).** Investigators should take the time to properly memorialize the information gathered and steps taken in a preliminary report. Most agencies now have automated reporting systems and this information becomes part of the aggregate data that can be queried in the future. Document the type of lead being investigated and where it came from. Was it generated from ATF's eTrace or a regional CGIC, or receipt of information from a confidential source, or receipt of information from another law enforcement agency? FIGURE 10.1 is an example of an ROI based on a lead developed from a crime gun trace. A similar ROI should be written if the lead is based on a multiple handgun purchase or other type of firearms trafficking lead referral from a CGIC. If the lead involves intelligence developed or received from a confidential source, the ROI should include an "Intelligence Assessment" paragraph at the bottom of the ROI to indicate that there is a "Reasonable Indication" that the information could be useful to a criminal investigation and the intelligence should be rated as either extremely reliable, reliable, or of unknown reliability. An example of an intelligence assessment statement may read as follows: The anonymous information provided by this confidential source is considered reliable as the source has provided accurate information in the past and, in this instance, the information is corroborated by independent information that has been gathered by this Investigator. There is a reasonable indication this information may be useful to a criminal investigation, and it is therefore being documented.

ROI EXAMPLE: RECEIPT OF INFORMATION AND PRELIMINARY INVESTIGATION ROI

RECEIPT OF INFORMATION: PRELIMINARY INVESTIGATION
On December 15, 2018, Special Agent Richard Roe received information indicating that a Glock semi-automatic pistol, Model 23, 9mm, serial number 123XYZ, recovered in an illegal possessory crime by the Big City Police Department (BPD) on November 21, 2018 was traced to a retail purchase in Kingston, ME on May 13, 2017.

NARRATIVE
1. On November 21, 2018, investigators from BPD recovered a firearm (Glock semi-automatic pistol, Model 23, 9mm, serial number 123XYZ) from the possession of James CRAZE (w/m, DOB 7/30/1980, SSN 000-00-000, FBI # 5551212) who illegally possessed the firearm at his residence at 666 Apple Lane, in Big City, MA.
2. The ATF National Tracing Center determined that Sam JONES (w/m, DOB 2/26/1980, SSN 000-00-000, address 1212 Mocking Bird Lane, Rockfish, ME) purchased the firearm on May 13, 2017 from Federal Firearms Licensee (FFL) The Trading Post, 15 Main Street, Kingston, ME.
3. Deconfliction queries of N-Force, TECS, and DICE produced no additional cases or leads on James CRAZE or Sam JONES.
4. Queries of eTrace revealed Sam JONES is not associated with any other firearms traces of multiple handgun purchases. Queries of the ANR-NICs database were negative for JONES.
5. NCIC queries reflect that none of the firearms have been reported stolen.
6. The FBI criminal history printout for James CRAZE indicates a history of narcotics possession and sale arrests as well as a felony conviction for armed robbery. A review of the BPD incident report relating to the arrest of CRAZE and recovery of the firearm indicates that CRAZE is a member of the Bad Boyz street gang. A copy of a booking photograph for CRAZE was attached to the report.
7. The FBI criminal history printout for Sam JONES indicates 2 prior arrests for drug possession and public intoxication.
8. Accurint records indicate that Sam JONES currently resides at the address listed on the ATF Forms 4473 associated with his firearm purchases; however, JONES had a prior address in 2009 of 601 Apple Lane in Big City, MA which is less than ½ mile from the residence of firearms possessor James CRAZE.

ATTACHMENTS: ATF Trace Form re. Trace Number T20141234567
BPD Police Report Number 14-1234567
Accurint, NCIC, and CCH printouts

FIGURE 10.1

✓ **Interview the Federal Firearm Licensee (FFL).** The first interview should be with the FFL who sold the firearm, unless there is any reason to believe the FFL is involved with the purchaser and may alert the purchaser before the investigator can interview them. In that case, the investigator may want to coordinate with another investigator and conduct both interviews simultaneously.

The purpose of trying to interview the FFL before the purchaser is to gain insight into what the FFL can remember, if anything, about the sale, and to secure a photocopy of the ATF Form 4473 Firearms Transfer Transaction to use during the purchaser interview. FFLs are only required to turn over an original ATF Form 4473 to ATF special agents upon request. Other law enforcement investigators may need a subpoena, a search warrant, or a court order if they want to secure the original ATF F 4473. Prior to taking the original ATF F 4473 the investigator should allow the FFL to make a copy to keep in their records. The investigator should provide the FFL with a receipt for the original ATF Form 4473, and the record must be returned to the FFL when the investigator no longer needs the original form. The original record belongs to the FFL's business. Investigators should always advise the FFL that their presence is specific to an investigation of someone other than the FFL, and has nothing to do with ATF's FFL inspection process.

There is a set of basic FFL interview questions that every investigator should ask during the FFL interview, as well as a basic standard for writing the ROI of that interview. A more detailed list of questions may need to be created by the special agent prior to conducting the interview, based on the specifics of the firearms trafficking lead received. Those basic questions and the FFL ROI appear as FIGURE 10.2 and FIGURE 10.3 in this chapter. A responsible FFL interview gathers additional information regarding the purchaser, gathers documentary evidence, and documents the process the FFL followed during the sale to ensure that it was completed as required by federal law and regulation, and did not involve errors that could jeopardize any potential violations by the purchaser. For example, the purchaser may indicate on the ATF Form 4473 that they were purchasing the firearm for another person, or that they have a drug problem, and the FFL misses those written answers and makes the sale, or tells the purchaser to fill out the ATF Form 4473 and just answer no to those questions. Those are errors in a proper firearms sale and could jeopardize charges against the purchaser relating to false statements on the ATF Form 4473. When the FFL provides improper guidance, such as "just answer no to all the questions", this can set up an entrapment by estoppel defense. Entrapment by estoppel is an exception to the maxim that ignorance of the law is no defense.[cxxiv] Standard entrapment refers to situations where the government official encourages and induces the defendant to engage in criminal conduct where the defendant was not already predisposed to commit the crime, while entrapment by estoppel refers to the official's representation that the conduct in question is in fact legal, and the defendant's reliance on that representation.[cxxv] In the case of a firearms purchaser, the FFL, being a licensed agent of the government, advises the purchaser to just answer no to those questions on the ATF Form 4473, even though false statements on the form are a felony. In U.S. v. Tallmadge, the courts held that "Congress has not only granted certain persons the exclusive right to engage in the business of selling firearms, it has also given them the affirmative duty of inquiring of a prospective buyer whether he has a criminal record that would make it unlawful for him to purchase a firearm (18 U.S.C. § 922(d) (1)). In addition, the Treasury Department requires licensees to inform buyers concerning the restrictions imposed by Congress on the purchase of firearms. Clearly, the United States Government has made licensed firearms dealers federal agents in connection with the gathering and dispensing of information on the purchase of firearms."[cxxvi]

STANDARD FFL INTERVIEW QUESTIONS

The following questions should be asked when an investigator intends to secure a copy or original ATF Form 4473 from an FLL. During the interview, it is important to be professional: start with a proper introduction and display of credentials, advise the FFL of your purpose, and inform them that this is not part of their one-time annual inspection. Then ask the following:

✓ Did you hold a valid Federal Firearms License on the date the purchaser completed the ATF Form 4473?

✓ How long have you been a licensed Federal Firearms dealer?

✓ What is the name of the salesperson who observed the completion of this ATF Form 4473? *(Always try to interview the actual sales person)*

✓ Do you always ask for a driver's license or other form of valid government issued photo ID when a customer wants to buy a gun?

✓ Do you compare the photo on the ID to the person presenting the ID to make sure they are the same person?

✓ Do you keep a photocopy of the ID that was presented by the purchaser? *(If yes, secure copy)*

✓ Do you have the purchaser read and complete in their own handwriting section A of the ATF Form 4473 to include the answers to questions 11A through 11L, questions 12, 13, 14, 15 if a non-US citizen, and the certification statement above the signature and date blocks (blocks 16, 17)?

✓ Are you always available to assist a purchaser if he/she has any questions?

✓ What was the price the purchaser paid for this firearm(s)?

✓ Did the purchaser pay with cash, check or credit card? *(if credit card, secure information)*

✓ Do you remember this sale and this person? *(If yes, ask questions A Thru J below)*

   A. Do you remember if this purchaser had any questions when completing the ATF Form 4473, and, if they did, what your response was to the question(s)? (e.g., they were not sure if they were a felon or if they had a domestic abuse conviction, or they mentioned they might want to sell the gun later).

   B. Do you remember if this purchaser was alone or with somebody when they came into the store?

   C. If they were with someone, please describe why you think this, what this person looked like, and their actions or statements during the transaction?

   D. Do you remember if this purchaser made any comments after they were told they passed (or failed to pass) the background records check?

   E. Did the purchaser leave a cell phone number to be called back if the purchase involved a delayed purchase?

   F. Would you be able to identify a picture of this purchaser from a photo-lineup? *NOTE: If yes, display a case law compliant photo-lineup, array, or loose photo stack, and have FFL initial and date the picture they identify as the purchaser. Before displaying the photos, provide the following guidance:*

      I am going to show you several individual photographs. I want you to look at each photograph and let me know if you recognize anyone, and if so, from where. You may or may not recognize anyone in the photographs. Remember to look at the facial features, such as the eyes, nose or mouth, because other features such as hair can change. Remember that the photos may be older or newer. Lastly, if you do recognize someone, let me know how positive you are of the identification.

G. Do you remember what this person used for transportation to arrive at the store? *(description of vehicle/license plate if possible)*

H. Did it appear that anyone was waiting for them outside in a vehicle? *(if yes, get description)*

I. Has this person made prior purchases of firearms that you remember or that the records reflect? *(If yes, obtain copies of those ATF Form 4473s and interview salesperson who handled those transactions)*

J. Is there anything else you can remember about this purchase that I have not asked about?

✓ Does the store have a video monitoring system that would have recorded the transaction? (If yes, secure a copy)

✓ Are there any other store employees who might have observed the sale or remember the purchaser and transaction? (If yes, ask the appropriate questions from the list above)

✓ Has the purchaser been back to the store any other times, and do they have any current sales pending?

✓ Would you be willing to call the purchaser back and allow investigators to be in the store behind the counter when they come in so investigators can overhear or handle the transaction? NOTE: If the FFL allows this, make sure that any statements made orally or in writing by the purchaser are made to the dealer and not to a UC investigator. To charge a straw purchaser with making false statements to an FFL, they have to make those statements to the FFL, not a UC investigator.

✓ Please do not let the purchaser know that we have been to the store or have asked any questions.

FIGURE 10.2

If the FFL describes other persons who were with the purchaser and who appeared to be selecting the firearms or providing the money for the purchase, remind the FFL of their obligation to prevent suspected straw purchases and report such incidents to ATF.

If the actual salesperson who handled the sale of the firearm is no longer working at the FFL and cannot be located, the investigator should conduct an interview with the FFL, asking them to describe the steps on how they handle each firearms sale, to document that this is a standard business practice that would have been used with this purchaser as well.

If the investigation is preliminary, a copy of the 4473 may be obtained for use in interviewing the purchaser with the original being secured at a later date should a case develop. The investigator should treat any original ATF Form 4473 as evidence. Depending on the needs of the investigation, there is the potential for a forensic science laboratory to develop latent fingerprints and palm prints on the form using a ninhydrin treatment; DNA may be recovered from the form; and handwriting analysis may be performed on the form.

The results of the FFL interview should be memorialized in an ROI. An example of an FFL interview ROI appears in FIGURE 10.3.

ROI EXAMPLE: FFL INTERVIEW

INTERVIEW

Report of interview with Joe Firepower on December 19, 2018 at 3:00 PM, at Federal Firearms Licensee (FFL) The Trading Post, 15 Main Street, Kingston, ME, by special agent Roe, Bureau of Alcohol, Tobacco, Firearms, and Explosives, Portland, ME Field Office.

NARRATIVE

1. On December 17, 2018, S/A Richard Roe went to FFL The Trading Post, 15 Main Street, Kingston, ME and interviewed Mr. Joe Firepower. S/A Roe identified himself as an ATF special agent to Mr. Firepower. During the interview Mr. Firepower stated he is a clerk for The Trading Post, has been for 10 years, and dealt with Sam JONES on May 13, 2017 during the acquisition of a Glock, Model 23, 9mm semi-automatic pistol, serial number 123XYZ, for $560 in cash. During the interview, Mr. Firepower advised that Mr. JONES, as is standard with all firearms purchases at The Trading Post, was required to read and complete the ATF Form 4473 as well as answer all the questions on the ATF Form 4473 in his own handwriting and affix his signature to the form. Mr. Firepower further advised that he was available to answer any questions or concerns that would have come up during completion of the form by JONES, but JONES had no questions during the forms completion. Mr. Firepower stated that he does remember the purchase of the firearm by JONES; however, he does not believe he would be able to identify JONES from a photo array. Mr. Firepower advised that he does not remember seeing anyone else who appeared to be with JONES during the transaction, but that he may have missed seeing others who were with JONES. In addition, Mr. Firepower advised that, as is standard with all firearms transactions, he required JONES to produce a valid driver's license, and that Mr. Firepower compared the photograph and information on the presented license to JONES and the form to make sure that they were one in the same person. Mr. Firepower stated that they have a video surveillance of purchases in the store, and at S/A Roe's request he provided a copy of the recording for that transaction on a CD to S/A Roe. S/A Roe reviewed the video on the Trading Post system and was able to observe an individual who appeared to be James CRAZE standing one aisle away from JONES during the purchase. At the request of S/A Roe, Mr. Firepower reviewed their computerized records for December 19, 2018. S/A Roe retained as evidence the ATF Form 4473 Firearms Transaction Record dated May 13, 2017 bearing transferor transaction number 1703 and the signature of JONES, as well as a CD containing a video recording of the transaction. A receipt for the ATF Form 4473 along with a copy of the Form 4473 was provided to Joe Firepower at FFL The Trading Post to maintain in his records. Mr. Firepower was advised that this was not part of an annual inspection of his FFL business.

ATTACHMENTS: Photocopy of Original ATF Form 4473 dated May 13, 2017
CD Video Surveillance System Recording

FIGURE 10.3

✓ **Determine Potential Federal Violations.** There is no firearms trafficking statute in federal law. There is a collection of laws that may apply depending on the actions of the firearms purchaser and what they are thinking at the time of the firearm purchase. The investigator should review information gathered during deconfliction, the intelligence workup, and the FFL interview, and determine the potential violations that may exist, as well as the elements

of proof involved with those charges. Knowing this is critical to structuring the purchaser interview. Common violations of federal law that apply in these types of firearms trafficking investigations include:

➢ **18 U.S.C. § 922(a)(1)(A):** Known as "dealing in firearms without a license", this is a knowingly/willfully violation, so the suspect must know that the law exists and consciously violate it. The investigator must establish that the purchaser has a principle objective of livelihood and profit from selling firearms without a license, and not simply occasional sales or to enhance or dispose of a private firearm collection.

➢ **18 U.S.C. § 922(a)(6):** Known as "lie and buy", this involves a purchaser providing false information to an FFL during the acquisition of a firearm. The investigator must show that the false statement is relative to a material fact regarding the lawful possession of the firearm. The investigator must show willfulness and an intent by the purchaser that the false statement was likely to deceive the FFL.

➢ **18 U.S.C. § 1001:** Known as lying to a federal agent, this involves a purchaser making a false statement to a federal agent during an interview or a false statement to an FFL on the ATF Form 4473 during a firearm purchase that does not have to involve a material fact regarding lawful possession of the firearm. This charge may be applicable to a purchaser who makes false statements on material facts to agents during an interview. For example, the purchaser writes on the ATF Form 4473 that they live at one address within a state when they really lived at a different address in that same state. This false statement is not a material fact related to lawful possession of the firearm, but it is a false statement.

➢ **18 U.S.C. § 924(a)(1)(A):** This involves making false statements to an FFL on matters they are required to keep in their records. This includes false statements on an ATF Form 4473 as well as false statements that cause the FFL to place false information in their acquisition and disposition log. This charge, which carries a maximum 5 years prison term rather than the more common maximum 10-year prison term, does not require the investigator to show willful intent.

PHASE II: INTERVIEW STEPS

The importance of preparing for the interview of the firearm cannot be overstated. After an investigator has reviewed all the intelligence materials gathered, interviewed the FFL, collected a copy of the ATF Form 4473, determined the potential violations and their elements of proof, and thought about the interview questions as well as the potential obstacles to overcome during the interview, they are ready to conduct an interview with the first known retail purchaser of the firearm.

✓ **In-Person.** The interview should always be conducted in person and in most situations it will be done at the person's place of residence or work. Observing body language and demeanor during the interview is important, and these non-verbal cues would be missed in an interview over the telephone or in an email. If the investigator cannot travel to the person, they should enlist the support of another investigator to complete the interview in person. This could be done through a local ATF CGIC or a detective in another department.

✓ **Coordination**. If the interview is in the jurisdiction of another law enforcement agency, the investigator should advise that agency that they will be in the area conducting an interview. The investigator should consider informing the local ATF office of the investigator's intent to conduct a firearm trafficking-related interview, as they may be able to send a person to accompany the investigator. It may prove useful for the investigator to have someone at the interview who has a local knowledge perspective and who could be called in the future for assistance in the investigation, or to be asked to initiate another investigation.

✓ **Safety Considerations**. The investigator should contact their office to advise where they are just prior to approaching the location where they will attempt to contact and interview the purchaser, and advise they will follow up with a telephone call when the investigator is clear of the interview. The interview should involve two investigators whenever possible, and this is preferable when the subject to be interviewed is of a different gender than the interviewer.

✓ **Checklist of Materials to Have at the Interview.** The investigator special should consider bringing the following materials with them to the interview:

  ➢ A Copy of ATF Form 4473(s) for potential display during the interview.
  ➢ If the lead involves a crime gun trace, try to obtain a photograph (e.g., booking photograph or driver's license photograph) of the crime gun possessor associated with the trace for possible display during the interview.
  ➢ Warnings Letters for Unlicensed Dealing and Straw Purchase for potential issuance during the interview. See Figures 10.6 and 10.7 of this chapter.
  ➢ ATF Publication 3312.8, Personal Firearms Record and ATF Publication 5300.21, Best Practices, Transfer of Firearms by Private Sellers for potential issuance during the interview. See Appendix C for this form.
  ➢ Any witness rights forms required for use by your department that you may issue during the interview if it becomes apparent that this person will be a witness.
  ➢ Any affidavit forms that your department uses to take written statements from a witness in the event that the person is willing to complete a written sworn affidavit.
  ➢ A consent to search form in the event that the investigator determines the subject's residence needs to be searched and they will consent to this, or in the event that the investigator plans to seize their cell phone as evidence and they will consent to its search. If the subject admits to purchasing the firearm for someone else and to using their cell phone to communicate with that person, their cell phone contains evidence of a crime and, in consultation with the AUSA, the phone may be subject to seizure. See Appendix D for examples of forms to secure consent to search a cell phone, access an email or other online account, or consent to assume someone's online identity.
  ➢ A handwriting exemplar collection form in the event that there is a need to collect a handwriting exemplar from the person for subsequent comparison.
  ➢ Any forms used by your department to document a confidential informant for use in the event that the person is interested in serving as a confidential informant in the investigation.
  ➢ An electronic recording device for use in the event that the purchaser agrees to make a recorded statement or in the event that the investigator determines they want to surreptitiously record the interview in accordance the laws of the jurisdiction and policies of their department. It is advisable that the investigator record these interviews. If the investigator plans to record the interview surreptitiously, they should start the recording upon arrival at the location, include a standard introductory statement that includes the

date, time, location, purpose of the interview, and conclude the recording following the interview and departure from the location with a standard closing statement noting the date and time the recording is concluded. All surreptitious one-party consensual recordings should be performed in accordance with federal or state law and in accordance with the investigator's internal agency policy. All recordings should be treated as evidence.

✓ **Prepared Questions**. Each interview will need to be crafted to the specific situation; however, there are a number of questions common to most firearms trafficking related purchaser interviews that should be asked. See FIGURE 10.4 of this chapter for a list of questions.

➢ Start the interview with a proper introduction and display of credentials; then advise the purchaser you are there to speak to them about what they did with a firearm they previously purchased. If there are other firearms they purchased you may want to wait until you ask the questions about the first firearm before you ask about other firearms purchased.

➢ In addition to the interview, as you approach the residence, note vehicle license plates and descriptions at the location and try to identify any other persons at the location.

➢ Start the interview with general background questions. It is helpful to begin with casual conversation (i.e. weather, compliments on the yard or a vehicle, etc.), to have the person get used to speaking with you and answering questions, before easing into more direct questions about the firearm purchase. During these questions the investigator should probe residency status to determine if the person is an actual resident of the state and actually resides at the address they listed on the ATF Form 4473.

➢ At the conclusion of the interview, should the investigator suspect the purchaser was or is engaged in straw purchasing or dealing in firearms without a license, they should serve a written warning on the purchaser prior to departing the location. The service of these warning letters accomplishes several purposes, including: having a deterrent effect, causing cooperative compliance with the law, and/or documenting the subject's future willful and knowingly intent, should they continue conducting illegal activities.

➢ The investigator should memorialize the details of the interview in an ROI. An example of a firearm purchaser interview ROI appears in FIGURE 10.5.

STANDARD INTERVIEW QUESTIONS AND ADVISORIES FOR FIREARMS PURCHASER

GENERAL INFORMATION AND RESIDENCY QUESTIONS
✓ Are they available to speak and is anyone else in the home at the time?
✓ How long have they lived there?
✓ Who else lives with them and how long have they lived there?
✓ Is this where they consider their residence?
✓ Do they have a residence in another state?
✓ Where else have they lived in the past 5 years?
✓ What do they do for a living?

Following the general questions, begin to focus questions on the firearms purchase with general questions about that transaction.

GENERAL PURCHASE QUESTIONS
- ✓ Is the address on the ATF Form 4473 where they live currently and on the date of the firearm purchase?
- ✓ Why did they choose that gun store to purchase a firearm from?
- ✓ Did anyone go with them to the gun store when they purchased the firearm? If yes, who was this person and how do they know them? (*get contact information for later interview*)
- ✓ Did this person go in the store when the firearm was purchased and did they look at firearms while there?
- ✓ How did they get to the gun store to make the purchase?
- ✓ Did they read and complete section A of the ATF Form 4473 to include the answers to questions 11A through 11L and the certification statement above the signature and date blocks (blocks 16, 17)? (Show the purchaser a copy of the ATF Form 4473)
- ✓ Did they ask the salesperson any questions while conducting the purchase?
- ✓ Do they remember the salesperson they dealt with? (If yes, ask them to describe)
- ✓ Did the salesperson provide them with any information during the purchase?
- ✓ How much did they pay to purchase the firearm(s)?
- ✓ How did they purchase the firearm(s) (cash, check, credit card, PayPal for online purchase)?
- ✓ Where did they get the funds to purchase the firearm?
- ✓ Did they purchase any other firearms from this gun store at any time?
- ✓ If yes – how did they pay for those purchases?
- ✓ Did they purchase any firearms from any other gun store or person in the past?

After these general purchase questions, if the investigator suspects this to be a straw purchase, the investigator should begin to ask questions that further probe that possibility. These questions are more specific to the firearm, ammunition, magazines, and shooting that only a person who actually purchased the firearm for their own use would know. A straw purchaser is buying the firearm on behalf of someone else who is the intended possessor and the straw purchaser often does not spend any time shooting or learning the nomenclature characteristics of the firearm(s) being purchased.

GENERAL STRAW PURCHASE QUESTIONS
- ✓ What made them purchase that firearm?
- ✓ Do they remember what caliber that firearm was?
- ✓ How many rounds does that firearm hold when fully loaded?
- ✓ What was the finish on that firearm?
- ✓ How does the trigger pull on that firearm?
- ✓ How many magazines came with that firearm?
- ✓ Did they shoot the firearm they purchased? If yes, when and where?
- ✓ Where did they purchase or get the ammunition for the gun?
- ✓ Prior to that, when and where was the last time they went shooting?
- ✓ Was anyone with them when they went shooting? (*Identify this person for later interview*)
- ✓ If the purchaser has trouble answering questions on shooting or nomenclature of the firearm the investigator should advise the subject that;
  - ➤ Investigators don't often ask questions to which they don't already know the answer and that you are there to get the truth and clear the matter up.

> ➤ The firearm(s) was already recovered in a crime, and that person is cooperating with law enforcement.
>
> ➤ Where applicable, advise them that this is a federal investigation, and that if they do not want to answer questions now, they may be provided with a subpoena to appear before a federal grand jury and answer the same questions from an Assistant United State Attorney (AUSA) while under oath.
>
> ➤ Advise them that this matter will not be going away until all the questions are answered

Persons with substance abuse problems are often exploited by drug dealers to become straw purchasers. These straw purchasers are getting high and getting by. They are willing to buy guns and ignore the consequences if it means they can make a few dollars to get their next fix. If the purchaser has a drug arrest history or appears to have a drug addiction problem, the investigator should also ask questions designed to probe that possibility, and document additional federal law violations. It will be important to determine if they were a user of controlled substances contemporaneous to completing the ATF Form 4473 and possessing the firearm or ammunition.

GENERAL STRAW PURCHASE QUESTIONS FOR PURCHASERS WITH SUBSTANCE ABUSE HISTORY

✓ I know that you have recent arrests for controlled substance possession. Do you have a drug addiction or are you a recreational user?

✓ What kind of drugs are they using, how long have they been using, and were they using when they purchased the firearm(s)?

If their drug use was ongoing and contemporaneous to the purchase and possession of the firearm, show the purchaser a copy of the ATF Form 4473 they completed and signed and show them the question that asks if they are an unlawful user of, or addicted to, controlled substances. Ask why they answered no to that question. Remind them that false statements on the ATF Form 4473 are a felony and that possession of a firearm by someone using controlled substances is a felony under Title 18 USC Section 922(g)(3).

If they appear to have no visible means of income to support the expenditure of funds to purchase the firearm(s) the investigator should point that out and ask: Did they purchase the firearm for someone else in exchange for drugs or in exchange for cash so they could purchase drugs.

✓ Are they seeking treatment or under treatment for an ongoing drug addiction?

✓ Do they feel they were exploited by their drug dealer into purchasing the firearm(s) for them?

✓ How do they normally get in contact with their dealer and how often does the dealer ask them to purchase firearms?

✓ Would they be willing to cooperate with law enforcement during the investigation?

✓ Would they be willing to give consent to search their cellphone?

This can be done by having the purchaser sign a consent to search form and providing their password to open the phone so it may be downloaded for intelligence exploitation and corroborative evidence of what the purchaser has already told the investigator. If the purchaser states they use the phone to contact their dealer by text or phone calls but will not voluntarily turn over the phone, the investigator may be able to seize the phone as evidence on the spot based on the statements that the phone was used for communications during an illegal act. The phone may be secured, and the investigator would need to obtain a search warrant to download the phone and examine the information. For a person who rises to the level of a suspect, gaining access to their cell phone through consent or search warrant will be important to securing information vital to furthering the investigation. The cell phone data will reveal who they have been speaking with, when, and what was said in text messages. Cell phone data can reveal their travels, as well as the potential for images of illegal activity. Exploitation of communication devices is critical at all phases of a firearms trafficking investigation.

Following the straw purchase and drug user questioning the investigator should ask a number of additional question to probe the methods used in the trafficking scheme and why the purchaser no longer has the firearm(s).

GENERAL QUESTIONS REGARDING WHY THE PURCHASER NO LONGER HAS THE FIREARM(S)

- ✓ Do they still have the firearm(s)?
- ✓ If they still have the firearms, what are their plans for the firearm(s)?
- ✓ If they don't have the firearm(s):
  - ➢ Who did they sell the firearm(s) to?
  - ➢ When did they sell the firearm(s)?
  - ➢ Where did the sale take place? *Determine later if the location was a public area such as a parking lot that was within 1000 feet of a school zone.*
  - ➢ How much did they sell the firearm(s) for?
  - ➢ Did they ask the buyer any questions?
  - ➢ Did they record the identity of the purchaser or look at their identification?
  - ➢ Do they remember the car the buyer was driving and do they remember the license plate or the state the license plate was from?
  - ➢ Do they remember if other persons were with the purchaser and what they looked like?
  - ➢ How often do they buy and sell firearms and how do they make it known to prospective purchasers that they have firearms for sale?
  - ➢ Did the purchaser contact them on their cell phone, by text message, or by email?

The investigator should obtain the phone or email information so that subpoenas for records of those services may be obtained. If the seller used their phone to call or text the purchaser, then the investigator should consider retaining the phone as evidence for subsequent download in accordance with local laws and their agencies policies. The purchaser can give you consent to search and download the phone, and this may help them get the phone back quickly, as a search warrant will not be required. The image on the phone may increase the investigator's understanding of the scope of trafficking as well as provide other incriminating evidence, such as: locations the purchaser traveled to that may correspond to trafficking routes and meeting places, incriminating emails and text messages, or phone numbers associated with persons involved in the firearms trafficking scheme.

If the purchaser recalls who they sold the firearm to then ask the purchaser:
- ✓ What type of information can they provide to identify the purchaser?
- ✓ Do they recall where the person was from and what transportation they used?
- ✓ Could they identify the person in a photo array?
- ✓ Were there other persons with the purchaser?

If the purchaser states the firearm was stolen:

✓ Ask if they reported the firearm stolen, when, and where? *(if yes, secure a copy of the police report for leads)*

If they did not report the firearm stolen, advise them they need to report it stolen and that as an investigator you are obligated to ensure that the firearm theft report is filed. Advise the purchaser that there is no other option, and they need to be reminded that filing a false police report is a felony, as is making false statements to a federal agent (if applicable). If the purchaser continues to insist that the gun was stolen, make sure a theft report is filed with local police, and advise the purchaser that the firearm has been recovered in a crime and that it may be returned to them after it is no longer needed as evidence.

If the purchaser appears deceptive and/or refuses to identify who they sold the firearm to, the investigator should state:

✓ Investigators don't often ask questions to which they don't already know the answer and that you are there to get the truth and clear the matter up.

✓ The firearm(s) was already recovered in a crime, and that person is cooperating with law enforcement.

✓ Where applicable, advise them that this is a federal investigation, and that if they do not want to answer questions now, they may be provided with a subpoena to appear before a federal grand jury and answer the same questions from an Assistant United State Attorney (AUSA) while under oath.

✓ Advise them that this matter will not be going away until all the questions are answered.

If the investigator suspects this person to be dealing in firearms without a license violation, the investigator should begin to ask questions that further probe that possibility. These questions are more specific to the elements of proof required in a dealing in firearms without a license violation which include the principle objective of livelihood and profit, knowingly and willful violation of the law, as well as selling firearms and acquiring additional firearms to sell.

GENERAL QUESTIONS RELATED TO DEALING IN FIREARMS WITHOUT A LICENSE:

✓ How much did they sell the firearm for? *(this information is important for comparison to the purchase price to document a principle objective of livelihood and profit)*

✓ How often do they buy and sell firearms?

✓ Where do they sell the firearms? *(e.g., gun show or flea market, online auction site, classified ads)*

✓ Where do they get their firearms? (e.g., online purchases, pawn shops, street sales, gun shows or flea markets, classified ads)

✓ Do they have a firearm collection? If yes, what kinds of firearms do they collect, how many do they have, and how often do they sell firearms from the collection?

✓ How much do they make selling firearms in general?

✓ Do they pay sales tax to the state?

✓ Do they declare the income on their income tax return to the Internal Revenue Service (IRS) or the state?

✓ Do they know they may need a license from ATF to engage in the business of dealing in firearms?

FIGURE 10.4 ©

ROI EXAMPLE: FIREARMS PURCHASER INTERVIEW

DESCRIPTION OF ACTIVITY

INTERVIEW

Report of interview with Sam JONES (w/m, DOB 2/26/1980, SSN 000-00-000, cell phone 207-333-4444) on December 29, 2018 at 6:15 PM, at his residence of 1313 Mockingbird Lane, Rockfish, ME by S/A Richard Roe and S/A John Doe, Bureau of Alcohol, Tobacco, Firearms, and Explosives, Portland, ME Field Office.

NARRATIVE

1. On December 29, 2018, S/A Roe accompanied by S/A Doe went to the residence address of Sam JONES, as identified by JONES on an ATF Form 4473, which is 1313 Mockingbird Lane, Rockland, ME. The purpose of the interview was to determine the disposition of a Glock, Model 23, 9mm semi-automatic pistol, serial number 123XYZ, purchased by JONES for $560 in cash from FFL the Trading Post in Kittery, ME on May 13, 2017.

2. Upon arrival at the location S/A Roe noted the location to be a small mobile home on a wooded lot with one vehicle in the driveway identified as a 1999 Toyota Tacoma Pickup, Brown, with ME License Plate 098765. S/A Roe could see an EZPass Highway Toll Transponder affixed on the inside of the vehicles windshield.

3. S/A Roe accompanied by S/A Doe knocked on the door to the residence and were greeted by an individual who identified himself as Sam JONES and who physically matched the ME driver's license photograph of JONES that S/A Roe had in his possession. S/A Roe advised JONES that he was there to speak to him about the Glock he purchased from The Trading Post in Kingston, ME back in May of 2017. JONES agreed to speak with S/A Roe and provided the following information during in response to initial questioning: JONES advised that he has lived at the Rockfish home for 3 years, he pays a monthly rent of $400, and he lives there alone. JONES said he is originally from MA but had not lived there for a number of years and now considers himself a Mainer. JONES stated that he used to work lobstering on the Miss Downeaster but he injured himself and is now collecting disability. JONES stated that the pickup in the driveway was his and he had owned it for 5 years. JONES decided he needed a handgun for self-protection and saw a sale flyer for the Trading Post so he drove there and purchased the firearm. Jones said that he went by himself to the gun store. JONES said that he remembers filling out the form, he had no questions for the sales associate, he paid $560 in cash with money. JONES said that the firearm was stolen from his mobile home during a burglary about 6 months ago, but he did not file a police report because he did not like the local police department.

4. S/A Roe advised JONES that he was there to find out how this gun was recovered in a crime in Boston and he advised JONES that he usually knows the answers to most of the questions he asks and does that to see if he can trust the person he is speaking with. S/A ROE advised JONES that if in fact the gun was stolen that S/A Roe would bring the police out and a report would be filed. S/A ROE reminded JONES that false statements to a federal agent and filing a false police report were felonies. In response, JONES stated that the gun was stolen and that was what happened.

5. S/A Roe then advised JONES that the firearm was recovered from an individual by the name of James CRAZE who is a gang member in Big City, MA, that JONES used to live on the same street as CRAZE, and that video surveillance from the Trading Post seems to show that CRAZE was in the store when JONES bought the handgun. JONES stated that he used to know CRAZE but has not seen him in years. S/A Roe then asked JONES how he could afford $560 for the firearm is he is on disability. Jones did not respond. S/A Roe then asked JONES how many times his EZPass Toll Transponder records, and state that his cell phone records would show he either spoke with or visited CRAZE in Boston. S/A Roe told JONES that his recent drug arrests indicated that maybe JONES had a drug problem and that CRAZE was giving him drugs and paying him to purchase firearms. S/A Roe advised JONES that this matter was not going to go away and he may want to consider that CRAZE is talking to law enforcement investigators in Big City, MA. JONES responded with the following:

    JONES stated that he did know CRAZE and he did meet him at The Trading Post in Kingston, ME on the day of the gun purchase. JONES admitted that he purchased the firearm using money supplied by CRAZE, gave CRAZE the gun in the parking lot, and that CRAZE gave him a small amount of heroin.

    JONES admitted that he had done this in the past with guns he purchased in classified ads and that the Glock was the first time he purchased a firearm from a gun store, but CRAZE wanted a Glock. JONES admitted he knew CRAZE had been to jail before for his arrests. JONES admitted that during other purchases CRAZE had other people with him from MA who he did not know. At this point JONES said that he did not want to say any more and he needed time to think.

6. S/A Roe provided JONES with a WARNING NOTICE OF UNLICENSED FIREARMS DEALING IN VIOLATION OF FEDERAL LAW and a WARNING NOTICE OF STRAW PURCHASE, and advised him that these were warnings advising him to stop these activities. JONES declined to sign the warning notices; however, he took possession of them and this was witnessed by S/A Doe. S/A Roe advised JONES that this matter would be further investigated and that he might be recommended for prosecution to the US Attorney's Office at some point. S/A Roe advised JONES that if he remembered any more about his activities related to firearms sales with others and wanted to talk or cooperate further to please call S/A Roe as soon as possible. S/A Roe provided JONES with a slip of paper containing S/A Roe's cell phone number.

ATTACHMENTS:
WARNING NOTICE OF UNLICENSED FIREARMS DEALING IN FIREARMS
WARNING NOTICE OF STRAW PURCHASE

FIGURE 10.5

PHASE III: DETERMINING THE BEST COURSE OF ACTION

At this point in the preliminary investigation the investigator needs to examine the information they have collected and make a determination as to how to proceed with the FFL and the firearm purchaser. There are several options on how to proceed based on the information collected and whether or not this information indicates there were criminal violations and criminal intent to commit those violations. The range of options for dealing with the firearms purchaser involve the following situation-based responses:

✓ **NO Criminal Violations and NO Criminal Intent but Potential for Future Criminal Violations**. When it is determined that no criminal violations and no criminal intent are present but that the potential exists for future violations if the person continues their activities – or that the person appears to lack a general knowledge of the law, then the special agent shall:

➤ Verbally provide the purchaser with general information about the applicable federal laws. Thank them for being a responsible gun owner. Memorialize the interview in an ROI only if your agency requires this.

➤ Provide the purchaser with copies of ATF Publication 3312.8, Personal Firearms Record and ATF Publication 5300.21, Best Practices, Transfer of Firearms by Private Sellers.

CASE STUDY: SHORT TIME TO CRIME LEAD AND 'STATE OF MIND' COMPLICATIONS
United States v. Morrill – District of Maine – 2:12-cr-00149-JDL

In June of 2012 the ATF Portland, Maine Field Office initiated an investigation based on a request for assistance from ATF New York to complete the urgent trace of a crime gun that was used to shoot at two New York Police Department Officers. The shooter had escaped but dropped the firearm while fleeing officers. Completing the end-to-end trace could provide a valuable lead for solving who shot at those officers. The initial crime gun trace result indicated the firearm had been purchased just 30 days earlier at an FFL in Maine, which is an extremely short time to crime indicator. A time of under 3 years is considered a short time to crime – this was just 30 days.

All proper deconfliction and intelligence workups were completed and then the first retail purchaser was quickly located and interviewed by ATF agents. The subject admitted purchasing the firearm and then after deciding it was not quite what he wanted, decided to list it for sale through a local classified add magazine. The seller, a security guard in Portland, ME, admitted he sold the firearm in the parking garage where he worked to two people in a car, one of whom he had identified by name. The seller had not asked for any identification but had asked for the purchaser's name during the time of sale and was able to recall it. The seller stated that one person completed the purchase while the other person in the car said the gun was for them. The purchaser used money from the second person to make the purchase and then gave them the gun. Through additional intelligence workups ATF agents were able to more fully identify a suspect based on the name provided by the seller. A parking garage security video captured the entire firearm exchange between the first seller, the purchaser, and the second person in the car on video, and ATF agents secured that as evidence. The image on the video was the same person that ATF agents had identified as a suspect. This person as well as the second person in the car were located and interviewed. The second person in the car had just relocated to Maine from New York City. The second person in the car admitted to ATF special agents that he was the one actually getting the gun for himself but changed his mind and that days later he sold the firearm to someone else who he does not know. ATF agents were able to locate and secure a video recording from a nearby bank that showed the second person in the car withdrawing funds from an ATM that were then used a short time later to purchase the firearm in the garage. Agents believe the third person, whom they could not identify, was the person who eventually brought the firearm to New York where it was used to shoot at New York City Police Officers.

The original seller who purchased the firearm from an FFL did not violate any laws. When he purchased the firearm at the FFL he intended to keep the firearm for himself, so he did not provide false information to the FFL during the acquisition of the firearm. When he changed his mind later and decided to sell the firearm he was legally able to do so. He sold the firearm in a parking lot and was not required to ask any questions of the purchasers. The original seller was not repetitively buying and selling firearms so he was also not an unlicensed firearms dealer.

The first person in the car who purchased the firearm even though it was for the second person in the car committed no trafficking-related violations. As a private citizen he was able to purchase the firearm from the unlicensed seller and turn right around and give it to someone else. He would not have been able to do that if the seller was an FFL. The first person in the car was arrested by ATF agents after they were able to determine he was a convicted felon and should not have been in possession of a firearm at all, but had he not been prohibited from possessing firearms the transfers were legal.

The second person in the car did not violate any laws. He was able to take the firearm from his friend who had just purchased it from the private seller using the second person's money. It was also not a violation that he decided the next day that he did not want the firearm and sold it to someone else he just met whose name he never asked. Some may think it is strange or suspect it to be illegal that anyone would so casually transfer guns in this way but they do and it is legal in the manner described here.

None of these three individuals violated any laws with respect to the sale and transfer of a firearm. This is how a firearm went from being purchased from an FFL in Maine through the hands of at least 4 people to being used to shoot at two New York Police Department Officers in just 30 days. This situation illustrates the challenges that investigators will encounter with the "state of mind" elements of proof related to many federal firearm violations. This is why investigators must understand the nuances of the federal firearms laws to successfully navigate a firearm trafficking investigation.

Criminal Violations WITHOUT Criminal Intent – If the investigator determines, at any point during the preliminary investigation, that the purchaser committed criminal violations without any criminal intent, the investigator should consider taking the following steps:

✓ During the interview with the purchaser, the investigator should determine whether to serve a Warning Letter for Straw Purchasing or Unlicensed Dealing in Firearms, or whether to verbally advise the person of the information contained in the warning letters. Warning letter templates for Straw Purchasing and Unlicensed Dealing in Firearms are found in FIGURE 10.6 and FIGURE 10.7. The investigator shall make this determination based on the situation at hand and in the interests of ensuring they do not interfere with the lawful commerce in firearms. In either situation, the written or verbal warning will be documented in an ROI and shared with the appropriate regional ATF CGIC.

✓ Provide the purchaser with copies of ATF Publication 3312.8, Personal Firearms Record and ATF Publication 5300.21, Best Practices, Transfer of Firearms by Private Sellers.

AGENCY LETTERHEAD
DATE

TO: Name and Address of Suspect

WARNING NOTICE OF UNLICENSED FIREARMS DEALING IN VIOLATION OF FEDERAL LAW

Recently, your participation in the purchase, sale and/or other transfer of firearms has come to the attention of the (Law Enforcement Agency Name). We seek the cooperative efforts of the general public to comply with the law and that is why we are contacting you on this matter.

Your firearms activity appears to bring you within the definition of a dealer in firearms as that term is defined by the Gun Control Act. A dealer in firearms is defined as "a person who devotes time, attention, and labor to dealing in firearms as a regular course of trade or business with the principal objective of livelihood and profit through the repetitive purchase and resale of firearms. *See* 18 U.S.C. § 921(a)(21)(C). A person convicted of unlawfully engaging in the business of dealing in firearms without a license in violation of 18 U.S.C. § 922(a)(1)(A) is subject to imprisonment for not more than 5 years and/or a fine of up to $250,000.

This letter serves to officially warn you to cease and desist engaging in the business of dealing in firearms until you have sought and obtained a Federal Firearms License. A Federal Firearms License would authorize the purchase and resale of firearms from a licensed business premise. Continued activity without the required license could result in a recommendation for criminal prosecution.

This Warning Notice does not constitute a bar to the United States, or any state or municipality, from prosecuting you for any criminal offense related to any unlawful firearm transaction that has already taken place.

Should you wish to apply for a Federal Firearms License, you may obtain copies of the ATF Form 7, Application for Firearms License, at www.ATF.gov at the following link: https://www.atf.gov/firearms/instructions-form-77cr-application-federal-firearms-license

Should you have any questions or require additional information about this matter, please contact your local ATF office or this agency at XXX-XXX-XXXX.

WARNING NOTICE SERVED BY:

Investigator: _____ **Date:** _____

Location: _____

ACKNOWLEDGEMENT OF RECEIPT OF THIS WARNING NOTICE:

Recipient's Signature: _____ **Date:**_____

FIGURE 10.6

AGENCY LETTERHEAD
DATE

TO: Name and Address of Suspect

WARNING NOTICE OF STRAW PURCHASING IN VIOLATION OF FEDERAL LAW

Information received by (name of agency) indicates that you may have acquired one or more firearms from a federally licensed firearms dealer for, or on behalf of, another person. This letter officially notifies you that federal law prohibits you from providing false information to a Federal Firearms Licensee regarding the person who is the actual transferee-buyer of the firearm(s).

Specifically, federal law at Title 18, United States Code, Sections 922(a)(6) and 924(a)(1)(A), provides that it is unlawful for any person to make a false statement on a Firearms Transaction Record, ATF Form 4473, when acquiring a firearm from a Federal Firearms Licensee. For example, it is unlawful to knowingly provide a false or incorrect name, address, place of birth, or other information on ATF Form 4473. It is also unlawful to misrepresent that you are the actual transferee-buyer of a firearm when you are acquiring the firearm for someone else. **You are <u>not</u> the actual transferee-buyer of a firearm if you are acquiring the firearm for, or on behalf of, any other person**, unless the firearm is a *bona fide* gift, or is being retrieved after repair. Any person convicted of making a false statement to a Federal Firearms Licensee when acquiring a firearm may be imprisoned for up to ten (10) years for violating Section 922(a)(6), or five (5) years for violating Section 924(a)(1)(A). Such person may also be fined up to $250,000.

We seek the cooperative efforts of the general public to comply with the law, and that is why we are contacting you on this matter. This letter serves to officially warn you to cease and desist engaging in the straw purchase of firearms for other persons. Continued straw purchases of firearms could result in a recommendation for criminal prosecution.

This Warning Notice does not constitute a bar to the United States, or any state or municipality, prosecuting you for any criminal offense related to any unlawful firearm transaction that has already taken place.

Should you have any questions or require additional information about this matter, please contact your local ATF office or this agency at XXX-XXX-XXXX.

WARNING NOTICE SERVED BY:

Investigator: _____   **Date:** _____

Location: _____

ACKNOWLEDGEMENT OF RECEIPT OF THIS WARNING NOTICE:

Recipient's Signature: _____   **Date:** _____

FIGURE 10.7

✓ **Confidential Source.** In any of the aforementioned purchaser scenarios the investigator should try to ascertain if the purchaser may be someone who is interested in cooperating with law enforcement by providing information on other persons trafficking in firearms or committing other crimes. They may also want to cooperate with law enforcement by proactively placing phones calls or conducting meetings as directed in furtherance of a criminal investigation. Investigators should always be alert for this opportunity and be prepared to document someone as a confidential source.

Criminal Violations WITH Criminal Intent – If the investigator determines, at any point during the preliminary investigation, that the purchaser committed criminal violations with criminal intent, the investigator has a number of investigative options to consider.

First and foremost, in the interests of public safety, the investigator must prevent the additional transfer of firearms from the straw to a trafficker or violent criminal. These people are trafficking guns, not Q-Tips™. Firearms trafficking investigators must be highly sensitive to the risk of crime gun leakage while the investigation is ongoing.

✓ **How NOT to Run a Firearms Trafficking Investigation** - It goes without saying that grabbing news headlines by touting a case that involves 100, 500, or 3000 guns is not a good thing if you watched all those guns get trafficked or orchestrated each gun order over months or years. ATF's Fast and Furious investigation involved flawed logic and did not follow ATF's training or policy regarding the conduct of firearm trafficking investigations. Likewise, if a police agency in a northeast market area state makes a 500-gun trafficking case but all those guns were ordered by a UC or CI and were purchased over months, that too could pose public safety problems for the following reasons:
  ➢ Having a UC or CI advise someone to go off to a source area (usually another state) and to acquire firearms for the UC or CI to buy is sending a trafficker off to commit crimes in another state that is not controlled or surveilled by case investigators, and that puts the general public at risk. The trafficker is probably going to traffic drugs to those states and then they, or some straw purchasers they find, are going into gun stores and putting false information into the FFLs records. Felonies are being committed, and risk to the public is being created. Compounding this issue is when that criminal activity is detected by investigators in the other state and the case investigators ask those investigators to stand down, take no action, and let the subjects leave with the guns.
  ➢ That trafficker is driving across towns and states with guns in the car on their return trip, and this creates risk for the unsuspecting law enforcement officer who might pull this car over for a traffic stop. The officer has no idea that car is carrying guns that a UC or CI in another state placed an order for, but the trafficker knows they have guns in the car.
  ➢ If this trafficking scheme plays out over the course of months, how would an investigator know if they are the only one this trafficker is selling guns to? The trafficker is making great money from the investigators who are buying all those guns and the trafficker is probably reinvesting and buying more guns to sell on the street. Those are crime guns going to the street. Moreover, most of these purchases are not going undetected in the source areas, and these cases usually only move forward when the officer and prosecutor in the investigation ask investigators in the source state to not interfere. That is a sure sign that this is a constructed trafficking case and not an actual trafficking case.
  ➢ When all those purchased guns are traced, that data skews where that city's real crime gun trafficking problems are coming from. Those were orchestrated purchases, and the actual firearms trafficking source in the city may be masked by this data.

There are, unfortunately, 100, 500, and 3000-gun firearms trafficking cases out there where the trafficker has been able to go undetected and traffic that many firearms before an investigator detects and apprehends them. However, they are truly few and far between, as domestic trafficking goes, unless the case is predicated predominantly on high numbers of undercover purchases.

Investigators should be spending their time focusing on those who are known to be responsible for trafficking crime guns into their city, and not arresting persons for whom the only guns known to be trafficked are those the investigators ordered and purchased. All the time spent on those cases takes time away from going after the actual sources of crime guns in a city. It is easy for a CI to find desperate people in a crime-ruled and impoverished area who are willing to drive a few hours to purchase guns if someone is going to pay them over and over again. Investigators must guard against this. Unless the target is already associated with recovered crime guns in the area through HUMINT or trace data, that could be a case of investigating a constructed target of opportunity rather than following actionable intelligence-created opportunities to investigate the right target.

The bottom line is an investigator should never let trafficked guns walk unless there is a fully vetted and supported operational plan to keep them under constant surveillance until they can be safely seized.

In situations where a straw purchaser obtains firearms and there was not time for the investigator to have a pre-approved operational plan, if sufficient probable cause exists to seize and forfeit the firearms, the investigator should consider several options to recover the firearms, while at the same time allowing the investigation to continue to fully identify and dismantle any other members of a larger trafficking organization. These options are referred to as unplanned enforcement actions and must be done on the fly using all of the training, knowledge and experience that the investigators know in order to safely execute and protect public safety.

✓ **Traffic Stop.** Have a participating state or local marked law enforcement vehicle pull over the straw purchaser pulled over in a traffic stop meant to culminate in the discovery and retention of the firearms. The traffic stop would be routine and based on a traffic violation, but the officer would go on to locate and recover the firearms based on probable cause existing in the case. This prevents the transfer of the firearms from occurring and may in turn produce new investigative leads. Should the occupants of the vehicle be new or unknown participants in the trafficking ring, they may be fully identified, which in turn will yield additional information for follow-up investigation. Any recovered firearms should be exploited for leads by tracing the firearm(s), entering them into NIBIN, and processing them for latent fingerprints and DNA. Any new names, addresses, or phone numbers gained in this process should be fully deconflicted.

✓ **Shipping Rip.** If the firearms are being shipped via a common carrier (UPS, DHL, FedEx, etc.), or are being checked through luggage on an airline flight or other carrier, the delivery of the firearms without notification to a common carrier is a violation of Title 18 U.S.C. 922(e), and the firearms may be seized by investigators with a search warrant. This prevents the transfer of the firearms from occurring, and may in turn produce new investigative leads. The investigation may then continue with the traffickers believing the shipment of firearms was stolen in transit. Any recovered firearms should be exploited for leads by tracing the firearm(s), entering them into NIBIN, and processing them for latent fingerprints and DNA. Any new names, addresses, or phone numbers gained in this process should be fully deconflicted.

✓ **USPS Search Warrant.** If the firearms are being shipped via the U.S. mail, investigators should coordinate with the U.S. Postal Inspectors who will assist in the interception and recovery of the firearms with a search warrant. This would prevent transfer of the weapons from fully occurring and may produce new investigative leads. The investigation could then continue with the traffickers believing the shipment of firearms was stolen in transit. Any recovered firearms should be exploited for leads by tracing the firearm(s), entering them into NIBIN, and processing them for latent fingerprints and DNA. Any new names, addresses, or phone numbers gained in this process should be fully deconflicted.

If the investigator has the cooperation of the FFL, and the FFL has a way to contact the straw purchaser, the following steps should be considered:

✓ **Domestic Lure.** Have the FFL call the straw purchaser to advise them that their firearms are ready for pickup, and have an undercover agent pose as a salesperson in the store to document the transaction and any incriminating statements. A team outside can then arrest the straw purchaser and seize the firearms in a manner and location deemed reasonable through pre-operational planning. OR

✓ **Delay to Gather Data and Evidence.** Have the FFL call the straw purchaser and advise them that there has been a delay in the firearm sale approval, but that it should come through soon and he would call back when it did. This will provide time for the investigator to secure court orders for the historical cell data of the straw purchaser to try and identify the traffickers. The investigator may also want to consider pursuing a court order for a DNR or Trap and Trace on the straw purchaser's phone in an attempt to identify the traffickers. The investigator should use language in the application that allows the court order to be used as a means to secure subscriber information from service providers as well.

Whether the investigator chooses to arrest the straw purchasers with the firearms or just seize the firearms and make no effort to conceal the investigation, it is preferable if a prearranged operational plan exists. However, if this is an exigent situation, then an unplanned enforcement action may be necessary to prevent the firearms from getting away. Once the arrest or contact for seizure of firearms is made, the following options should be considered:

✓ **Controlled Delivery.** Determine if the straw purchaser will agree to participate in a controlled delivery of the firearms to the firearms trafficker. If yes, they should be documented as a CI.

✓ **Interview.** Interview the straw purchaser to identify who they were purchasing for, how many times they have done this, how much they are paid per gun purchase, whether there are other straw purchasers involved, how many FFLs they purchase from, whether any FFLs were involved with allowing the straw purchase, and how they communicate with the firearms trafficker, other straws, and any FFL. If they advise that they communicate to the others on their cell phone or by email, you should confirm with your AUSA that it will be allowed for you to seize the phone as evidence and then get a consent to search or search warrant for its contents.

✓ **Warning Letter Service.** During any interview with the straw purchaser, the investigator should serve a Warning Letter for Straw Purchasing or Unlicensed Dealing in Firearms. Templates for these warning letters appear in FIGURE 10.6 and FIGURE 10.7 in this chapter. A

copy of the letter should be left with the straw purchaser, and the investigator should keep the original signed letter for their file. The investigator should document service of the warning letter in their agency's case management system for retrieval in the future by other investigators. The investigator should consider providing a copy of this letter to the regional ATF CGIC, so that it may be accessible to numerous agencies combatting firearms trafficking.

✓ **ATF FRNP.** The investigator should coordinate with ATF to enter any purchased and unrecovered firearms in the Firearms Recovery Notification Program maintained by the ATF NTC. This system will provide an alert to the investigator in the event that any of these other firearm(s) are recovered in crimes and traced. This will be a source for additional leads during the investigation.

✓ **Prosecution or Deterrence.** The goal of this type of investigation will be to recommend prosecution. However, if it turns out that charges cannot be perfected, it is possible that the interview and service of the warning letter will be enough to deter the purchaser from continuing their activities. If that is the case the investigator has succeeded in stopping this source of crime guns through appropriate and reasonable deterrence measures. The service of a warning letter satisfies the willful and knowingly elements of many of the federal laws related to firearms trafficking and if the purchaser continues to buy and sell firearms without a license or conduct straw purchases, the prior service of the warning letter will enhance that new criminal case and improve both prosecutorial and jury appeal.

Determining what to do with the FFL. The range of options for the FFL involves situation-based responses.

✓ **NO Regulatory or Criminal Violations and NO Criminal Intent.** Investigators should anticipate that this will most frequently be the situation. During the processing of a firearms trafficking lead the majority of FFL interviews will result in no reason to believe the FFL is involved in committing any regulatory or criminal violations with criminal intent. When it is determined that no regulatory or criminal violations are present then nothing more needs to be done with the FFL.

✓ **Regulatory or Criminal Violations WITHOUT Criminal Intent** – During the processing of a firearms trafficking lead the investigator may determine during the FFL interview that regulatory or criminal violations without any criminal intent have taken place. This may include the discovery of improper recordkeeping, errors or omissions in records, failure to follow required procedures such as conducting background records checks, or an admission during the interview to allowing a firearm purchase to take place that should have been recognized as a straw purchase. In these instances, the investigator should verbally counsel the FFL regarding the infractions and advise them that these issues will be reported to an ATF IOI for whatever action they deem appropriate.

✓ **Criminal Violations WITH Criminal Intent** – While not common, during the processing of a firearms trafficking lead, the investigator may determine that the FFL is involved in criminal violations with criminal intent either as an individual or in a conspiracy with others. In these instances, the investigator should immediately contact their local ATF office to coordinate an investigation. FFLs are regulated by ATF and the agents are well versed in how federal law and regulations apply to FFLs. The goal of this type of investigation will be to recommend federal prosecution of the FFL to the U.S. Attorney's Office. However, if it turns out that charges cannot be perfected, the information documented in the investigation should be provided to ATF IO for use in holding the FFL accountable through regulatory proceedings which may results in punishment up to and including the revocation of the FFL's license. More detailed information regarding the investigation of an FFL follows in this chapter.

The objectives of a firearms trafficking strategy are to deny criminals access to firearms and reduce armed violent crime levels by reducing the availability of illicit secondary market firearms. In some instances, the objectives of this type of strategy are attained through criminal investigations and enforcement activities; however, in other instances a combination of criminal enforcement and prevention-deterrence efforts or solely prevention-deterrence efforts may be more appropriate for attaining the strategy's objectives. In instances where the subject of an investigation may be in violation of the federal or state firearms laws but has not demonstrated criminal intent or met established prosecutorial threshold levels, and in those instances or geographic areas where prosecution of firearms traffickers lacks jury appeal, prevention efforts geared toward impacting firearms trafficking and achieving the strategy's goals should be pursued.

TYPE 2: UNLICENSED FIREARMS DEALING INVESTIGATION

There are numerous methods to develop leads on potential unlicensed firearms dealers. For each of those methods, the investigator should keep in mind the lead development resources discussed in Chapter 6 and the indicators of firearms trafficking discussed Chapter 7. Those methods include:

➢ Receipt of a researched lead generated by an ATF CGIC
➢ Receipt of HUMINT from an FFL or unhappy customer that someone is selling firearms without a license.
➢ Receipt of information from an active CI.
➢ Observations made at a local gun show, flea market, or area classified advertisement that shows the same person or phone listing consistently selling different types of firearms.
➢ Using the predefined reports in ATF's LEAD, review of the ATF NTCs daily multiple sale email or first look email, firearms trace analysis, or firearms trafficking studies.

Once an unlicensed dealing suspect is identified, an investigator should consider the following steps:

✓ **Deconfliction.** Conduct a full deconfliction of all names, addresses, phone numbers, and other information as they are encountered. Firearms trafficking routinely crosses the jurisdiction of multiple local, state, and federal agencies, and deconfliction is critical to preventing a blue on blue situation, needless interference in on-going investigations, and general investigative effectiveness. See Chapter 9 for a description of a complete deconfliction process.

✓ **ATF Firearms Licensing Search.** Investigators should determine if the suspect is actually licensed to deal in firearms with ATF or was previously licensed to deal in firearms with ATF. Oftentimes persons selling firearms in classified advertisements or via online auction sites may appear to be dealing without a license because they do not put any information about their FFL in the sales information. It is important to know this from the start. If it turns out the suspect was previously licensed, it is important to know whether the suspect's license was revoked by ATF or whether the individual intentionally gave up his license. In the later scenario, the person may have acquired a license solely to obtain large quantities of firearms for illegal resale or for other illicit purposes. In either case, it is important to obtain complete copies of the suspect's licensing history; this will help the investigator establish the "willful" element that is present in many federal firearms statutes. Moreover, if the individual was at one time licensed as an FFL, the investigator will have an easier time establishing the *knowingly-and-willfully* element in a charge for dealing in firearms without a license (18 U.S.C. §922(a)(1)(A)).

✓ **ATF FRNP.** Enter all firearms suspected to have been purchased by the unlicensed dealer to be re-sold into the FRNP so that, should these be recovered and traced, the investigator will be notified and can pursue that investigative lead.

✓ **Links Between Purchaser and Possessor.** As firearms known to have been purchased by the suspected unlicensed dealer are recovered, look for links between the purchaser and the possessor. Attempt to conduct an interview with the possessor to determine how they acquired the firearm. If they acquired the firearm from the suspected unlicensed dealer, find out how much they paid for the firearm to later compare to the suspect's original purchase price in order to help establish a principle objective of livelihood and profit.

✓ **Electronic Communications Device Analysis.** Cell records analysis may be useful in determining who the unlicensed dealer's source is, as well as their customers. If the unlicensed dealer is prolific, investigators may want to pursue a court-ordered PEN. Investigators should make sure to use language in the application for the court order that will allow the initial court order to be used in subsequent requests to identify subscriber information.

✓ **Enlisting FFLs.** If unlicensed dealing is occurring at a gun show or flea market, consider enlisting actual FFLs as sources of information or assistance. Unlicensed dealers infringe on an FFL's lawful livelihood, and FFLs will often help investigators identify unlicensed dealers.

✓ **Collecting Security Recordings.** If unlicensed dealing is occurring at a gun show or flea market, check for security cameras and consider obtaining copies of recordings that may document the extent of an individual's unlicensed sales activities. Also consider contacting the gun show promoter for copies of documents denoting fees paid by the suspect to maintain a table at the show. The investigator needs to decide when to do this in the investigation, as attempts to secure fee documents or video evidence from venue security cameras prior to the perfection of a criminal could compromise the investigation. Investigators should always provide the promoter with a subpoena to secure any records or recordings.

✓ **Surveillance.** Consider surveillances to document the extent of unlicensed sales and to identify individuals purchasing firearms from the unlicensed dealer for later interviews and investigative follow-up.

✓ **Full Intelligence Workup.** A full intelligence workup should be performed on the unlicensed dealer, including financial workup include checks for SARs in FinCEN and CTRs in TECs. A full online profile workup should be performed to determine what OSINT is available where the unlicensed dealer is talking about their dealing online in their own words or where the unlicensed dealer is posting and selling firearms in online classified advertisements and gun board sites.

✓ **Shipping Records.** Consider securing subpoena records from area interstate carriers (e.g., UPS, DHL, U.S. Postal Service) for all packages sent or received from the unlicensed dealer's address, to try and identify the source of firearms or the potential shipment of firearms.

✓ **Mail Cover.** Consider the use of a mail cover at the unlicensed dealer's residence to document real-time packages being received by the unlicensed dealer that may reveal sources.

✓ **Evidence Purchases.** Consider making purchases of firearms from the unlicensed dealer using an undercover (UC) investigator or confidential informant (CI). All CIs should be properly vetted, documented and approved. All UCs should have proper prior training and a properly backstopped UC identity. The UC or CI should be knowledgeable of firearms and well-practiced in what they should ask to elicit conversation from the unlicensed dealer on topics such as:

➤ Why are no paper or records checks required? Tell them you appreciate it because you were denied at a dealer once before and you don't need those problems. This would show a propensity to sell to persons with a criminal history.

➤ Can they can take orders for specific guns? This is re-stocking, and shows that this is not just the one-time disposition of a firearms collection. This shows they are engaged in the business.

➤ How long have they been selling guns? A long history could help establish that they are engaged in the business.

➤ Can someone make decent money selling guns? This could help show a principle objective of livelihood and profit.

➤ Where will they be selling next? Do they sell online? This could help establish that they are engaged in the business.

➤ Dicker over the price of guns and ask them what they think a fair markup on their guns is. They may tell the UC or CI that they need to get a certain price as they have to make a living. This could help show a principle objective of livelihood and profit.

➤ Dealing in firearms without a license is a knowingly and willful crime. The UC or CI should make efforts to document that the subject knows they should have a license to sell firearms. The UC or CI may ask the unlicensed dealer what the FFLs think about his competition or if they are worried about ATF learning about this conversation.

➤ When purchasing guns, it is recommended that at least 3 purchases be made, preferably on separate dates and at different locations or venues. The UC or CI should also get conversation with the unlicensed dealer that they are not charging any sales tax. This could help show a principle objective of livelihood and profit, establish "engaged in the business," and document state sales tax issues, as well as lead to issues related to whether or not they are declaring profits as income on their income taxes.

➤ If the investigator is going to attempt to show that the unlicensed dealer is willing to sell handguns to out-of-state residents or convicted felons, the law requires that the investigator use actual felons or out-of-state residents and not just persons who say they are. This means using a CI with a prior felony conviction or a UC investigator from another state. This will lead to additional federal charges or can be used as "relevant conduct" in a sentencing phase.

➤ Once the investigator has a feel for how predisposed the unlicensed dealer may be to other criminal activity, the investigator may have the UC or CI ask the unlicensed dealer if they have access to machine guns or silencers, or if they would be willing to trade guns for narcotics.

➤ Electronically record all UC and CI contact and purchases from the unlicensed dealer. At a minimum, the recording should be audio, and video is preferred if the investigator has access to the appropriate surreptitious recording equipment. The investigator should ensure that their prosecutor is aware of the one-party consensual recording and the fact that the proper authority to do so exists.

✓ **Crime Gun Intelligence.** Firearms purchased from an unlicensed dealer could yield a trove of information important to the investigation.
   ➤ **NCIC Checks.** Check the firearm in NCIC to make sure it is not stolen. If it is, that is a significant lead to follow up on. The UC or CI may want to visit the unlicensed dealer a week or two later and tell them the police took the gun during a traffic stop and said it was stolen and then ask why that is and what they can do to make it right.
   ➤ **Crime Gun Tracing.** Firearms purchased should be traced immediately; however, the investigator should ask that the ATF NTC only trace to the retail FFL and not contact that retail FFL for the purchaser information. The investigator can then go to the FFL and look through the records to find the purchaser rather than asking the FFL to identify the purchaser, as that could compromise the investigation. If the purchaser is the unlicensed dealer, at some point it will be important to determine the price paid for the firearm, in order to show that it was less than the price the UC or CI paid.
   ➤ **NIBIN.** Firearms purchased should be submitted to a lab for test-firing and the submission of the test fires to NIBIN to determine if the firearm was used in a prior shooting.
   ➤ **NCIC Recovered Gun File.** While at the FFL, the investigator should look through the records for other firearms purchased by the unlicensed dealer that may be documented in the dealer's records. If the whereabouts of additional firearms purchased by the unlicensed dealer are unknown, trace the firearm and check the firearm through the NCIC recovered gun file to determine if the firearm has already been recovered elsewhere. If so, pursue those investigative leads. If the firearms have not yet been recovered, enter the firearms into ATFs FRNP to be notified when they are recovered.

Once an unlicensed dealer is arrested or the covert phase of the investigation concludes, the investigator should consider the following steps:

✓ **Documenting Profit.** Go to any FFLs identified as sources of firearms for the unlicensed trafficker and determine prices paid for firearms in comparison to the prices the unlicensed dealer sold those firearms for. This step will help establish that the unlicensed dealer has a principle objective of livelihood and profit. Depending on the amount of proceeds documented, investigators may want to explore money laundering violations as well as asset identification for forfeiture purposes.

✓ **Search Warrants.** If a search warrant is served at the home of an unlicensed dealer, it is important to remember that not all firearms may be subject to seizure and forfeiture. Only those firearms that are known to be possessed for the purpose of re-sale should be seized and forfeited. This could be based on prior or current statements or advertisements posted by the defendant about the firearms they have for sale; this could be based on the appearance of price tags on firearms in the home; or this could be based on finding the firearms stored in a portable locker that investigators have seen the defendant use to transport guns to guns shows. The investigator needs to be able to articulate why the firearms are suspected to be evidence of dealing in firearms without a license. Possession of a collection of firearms is not a crime, and is not evidence of dealing in firearms without a license.

✓ **Electronic Communication Device Exploitation.** If the suspect communicated about un-licensed firearms sales with customers, the UC, or a CI during the investigation, those communication devices such as cell phone or computers should be listed as items that may be seized for evidence during the search warrant. Those devices should be imaged and ana-lyzed for additional evidence.

✓ **Interview.** At the culmination of a dealing in firearms without a license case, the investigator will likely have the opportunity to interview the unlicensed dealer. If this is a post arrest and post Miranda warnings interview, it will be custodial, and the interview should be video and audio recorded. If this is a pre-arrest interview, the investigator should try and interview the suspect at the agency office in a formal interview room where audio and video recording capabilities exist. The investigator should be fully prepared to discuss all firearms purchased by the suspect, their disposition, purchase and sale prices, profit margin, and other acts show-ing they were engaged in the business of dealing in firearms for the principle objective of livelihood and profit. They may deny that they were violating the law, but the investigator needs to remain focused on getting the suspect to answer questions about where all the fire-arms they purchased went to.

CASE STUDY: OPERATION BEANTOWN BANGERS
US v. GOODWIN – DISTRICT OF MAINE - 2:10-cr-00122-DBH

In October of 2009 the ATF Portland, Maine Field Office initiated an investigation after a review of the NTC daily multiple sales email revealed multiple purchases of numerous handguns by an individual that appeared suspicious and merited further scrutiny.

Deconfliction and a full intelligence workup was performed. The ATF agent began to investigate the purchaser as well as the sole FFL who the purchaser was buying all the handguns from. As this investigation was beginning, a deconfliction coordination by the FBI through ATF in Boston indicated that the FBI had surveilled several Latin King gang members from Boston to Maine where they purchased 4 handguns the same individual that ATF Portland was investigating for potential firearms trafficking violations.

ATF agents entered all of the known handgun purchased by the suspect into the ATF FRNP so the agent would be notified of any firearms recovered and traced by law enforcement. The sus-pect was run in the ATF FELC and NFRTR and did not have a license to sell firearms or possess NFA firearms.

Subpoenas were issued for cell phone records and their analysis revealed that the suspect had contact with a Massachusetts telephone number 260 times between August and December of 2009. That phone number was associated with a multi-convicted felon in Boston who was the target of an ATF Boston investigation for being the source of firearms with obliterated serial numbers to gang members who had used them in a number of crimes, including a homicide. Further intelligence workup on the subject in Boston revealed he had a fake Maine driver's li-cense," and had been denied during the NIC's check while attempting to purchase firearms from an FFL in Maine in August 2009. The system had worked, so he moved to find private sellers who were not required to conduct background checks or keep any records.

The ATF agents in Maine sought to determine why felons and gang members in Massachusetts knew to contact someone in Maine for firearms. That search found the suspect's phone number in a local Maine classified advertisement where he listed firearms for sale. The suspect's ad was right next to a Project Safe Neighborhoods full-page Public Service Announcement advising private sellers and buyers of firearms regarding the categories of prohibited persons and of the fact that persons could not purchase handguns in a state where they were not a resident.

Once the classified ad for the suspect was found, ATF UC agents from Massachusetts were directed to contact the suspect in Maine and arrange to purchase handguns. In early 2010 the ATF UCs met with the suspect on 2 occasions purchasing 10 handguns. During those meetings the UCs made it clear they were from Massachusetts and were glad they did not need to go through a background check. The suspect went on to state that he knew how hard it was for people to get guns in Massachusetts and that they should obliterate the serial numbers, but if they did not and he was ever asked who he sold the guns to he would tell law enforcement he could not remember. During one transaction the suspect had his young daughter in the back seat of his car during the deal.

After a UC purchase on March 3, 2010, the suspect was detained and given an opportunity to cooperate, knowing that he would be charged and arrested at a later date. The suspect confessed to his trafficking activities and agreed to cooperate. The suspect provided consent to search his home, where a number of other firearms were seized. The suspect identified the Boston target from a photo lineup as the person he had sold more than 100 firearms to. The suspect admitted that the FFL he purchased the handguns from knew what he was doing. The suspect purchased guns all over the internet, and had them shipped to the FFL, where he would get them for a fee to the FFL.

On March 4, 2010, in a deal set up by the cooperating suspect, the Boston target and another multi-convicted felon and gang member drove from Boston to Maine to meet their trafficker. ATF Boston agents surveilled the Boston targets on the drive up to Maine. ATF Portland agents were arranged around the deal location. The Maine suspect sold several firearms to the 2 Boston suspects, who were then quickly arrested by ATF agents.[cxxvii]

Both Boston targets were convicted felons and gang members. The second Boston target was a career criminal with 3 or more prior violent felony convictions. This suspect had just been released from a prison stay for an armed robbery conviction. The owner of the vehicle that the suspects arrived in was a third gang member and an armed career criminal out of Boston who had stayed home that day.

A separate investigation of the FFL was initiated, and UC agents were able to purchase a firearm from the FFL off-paper on the first cold approach. The FFL would later surrender his license. The FFL was not prosecuted, as he had a terminal illness and passed shortly thereafter.

In July of 2010 the Maine defendant pled guilty to selling handguns to an out-of-state resident and was sentenced to 3 months in federal prison.

In June of 2010 the first Boston defendant pled guilty to being a convicted felon in possession of firearms and was sentenced to 52 months in federal prison.

In 2010 the second Boston defendant was convicted of being an armed career criminal in possession of firearms and sentenced to 15 years in federal prison.

CASE STUDY: OPERATION MONEY BACK GUARANTEE

United States v. Beavers, et al. – District of Maine - 2:09-cr-00081-DBH

In October 2008 ATF Portland, Maine Field Office special agents and Lewiston, ME officers were receiving information from different HUMINT sources that two individuals were selling guns on the street out of the trunk of their car to anyone with money to purchase them.

At the same time, during the review of multiple handgun sales data and NTF First Look data, two individuals started showing up as frequent purchasers of handguns. The sources were able to provide law enforcement with contact information for the two individuals selling firearms. Intelligence workups revealed that the two individuals selling firearms were the same two individuals appearing in the multiple handgun sales data. Deconfliction checks indicated no other law enforcement officials were working on the two individuals. Intelligence workups had identified the individuals and where they live as well as where they were getting some of their firearms and how much they were paying for them. Checks with the ATF FELC indicated neither individual was licensed with ATF to sell firearms.

A UC ATF Task Force Officer (TFO) made contact with the individuals and began to purchase firearms from them. The unlicensed dealers said anyone unhappy with their guns could return them for a money back guarantee. This is a good indicator they considered themselves to be engaged in a business. The prices paid to by the UC to purchase the items were compared against what records showed they paid for the firearms and it was clear they were engaged in the business of dealing in firearms without a license for the principle objective of livelihood and profit. Over the course of the next two meetings, the UC purchased handguns and sawed-off shotguns, some of which the two individuals had removed the serial numbers from. The firearms were sent to the lab in an attempt to raise the serial numbers with no success. All were checked for latent trace evidence and test fired for entry into NIBIN. Those firearms with serial numbers were traced and checked in NCIC to determine if these were stolen. The two individuals believed the UC to be affiliated with a motorcycle gang from Massachusetts who was in Maine to start a new chapter. The UC told the two individuals he had a friend in Massachusetts who was a sergeant at arms for the club who was looking to purchase firearms to gear up for a turf war with another club in the area. The two unlicensed gun dealers were glad to sell firearms to these out-of-state motorcycle gang members and a final UC deal was set up to purchase more firearms and arrest the two firearms traffickers.

In December 2008 the two unlicensed dealers sold two UCs from Massachusetts a MAC-12 pistol, a sawed-off shotgun with an obliterated serial number, and an SKS rifle. Before the deal concluded, the two unlicensed dealers also solicited the two UCs to contact their clubhouse in New York to ask if they would take care of a problem for a few thousand dollars. One of the unlicensed dealers wanted the club to take care of his sister-in-law in Albany, NY who was currently divorcing his brother. They wanted the motorcycle gang members to put a gun to her head and to beat her into signing divorce papers waiving her child custody rights. The UCs told the unlicensed dealers they would think about it and then ATF special agents and Lewiston Policy Department Officers moved in and arrested both individuals.

Intelligence workups were performed immediately following the arrests to identify the sister-in-law in Albany, NY to let her know what her brother in law had planned for her.

The U.S. Attorney's Office in Maine secured a federal grand jury indictment charging both individuals with multiple counts of possession and transfer of unregistered NFA short-barreled shotguns (Title 26 U.S.C. § 5861), possession and transfer of firearms, having previously traveled in or affecting interstate or foreign commerce, which have no serial numbers (Title 18 U.S.C. § 922(k)), false statements to an FFL during the acquisition of firearms Title (18 U.S.C. § 922(a)(6)), and dealing in firearms without a license (Title 18 U.S.C. § 922(a)(1)(A)).

Following the arrests, ATF special agents processed the newly purchased firearms, to include checks in the ATF NFRTR to confirm the short-barreled shotguns were not legally registered. The ATF special agents gathered the ATF Form 4473s completed by the defendants when they purchased the firearms from an FFL. During special agent interviews of the FFLs it was determined the two unlicensed dealers had purchased other firearms from the FFL. Those firearms were entered into ATF's FRNP so that agents would be notified if the firearms were recovered and traced by law enforcement.

While out on bond, one of the defendants fled to Mexico but was eventually apprehended and returned to the U.S. after several months. Important note to other traffickers – prisons in Mexico are not especially welcoming to American gun traffickers. Both defendants eventually pled guilty to all charges. In 2009 the first defendant was sentenced to 48 months in prison followed by 36 months of supervised release. In 2010 the second defendant was sentenced to 66 months in prison followed by 36 months of supervised release.

TYPE 3: FEDERAL FIREARMS LICENSEE INVESTIGATION AN APPLICATION OF A KLEIN CONSPIRACY

There are numerous methods to develop leads on potential unlicensed firearms dealers. Investigators should keep in mind the lead development resources discussed in Chapter 6 and the indicators of firearms trafficking discussed Chapter 7. Those methods include:
➢ Receipt of a researched lead generated by an ATF CGIC.
➢ Receipt of HUMINT from a disgruntled FFL employee or unhappy customer.
➢ Receipt of information from an active CI.
➢ Using the predefined reports in ATF's LEAD, review of the ATF NTC's daily multiple sale email or first look email, firearms trace analysis, or firearms trafficking studies.
➢ Detection of one or more firearms trafficking indicators as described in Chapter 7.
➢ Observations made of the FFLs sales practices at a local gun show.

Once it is determined that an FFL may be involved in criminal activity an investigator should consider the following steps:

✓ **Deconfliction.** Conduct a full deconfliction of all names, addresses, phone numbers, and other information as it is encountered. Firearms trafficking routinely crosses the jurisdiction of multiple local, state, and federal agencies and deconfliction is critical to preventing a blue on blue situation, needless interference in on-going investigations, and general investigative effectiveness. See Chapter 9 for a description of a complete deconfliction process. In the case of an FFL, any investigator should contact ATF to coordinate the investigation, as FFLs are regulated by ATF and ATF records inevitably will be part of the investigation.

✓ **FFL Monitor and No Contact Service from the ATF NTC.** From the outset of the investigation, the investigator needs to determine if they want the FFL contacted by the ATF NTC to conduct traces of recovered crime guns during the investigation. It is highly recommended that the investigator use the ATF NTC FFL "Monitor" and "No Contact" Services. Through the FFL "Monitor" service, an investigator will be notified by the NTC of all firearms traced back to a specified FFL; however, with the No Contact provision, the trace will be stopped before the NTC calls the FFL to determine who they sold the firearm to. This affords the investigator a steady flow of intelligence without compromising the case.

✓ **FFLs Sources of Firearms.** Determine the full extent of an FFL's illegal diversion of firearms by first identifying all the FFL's firearms sources (wholesalers/distributors) for later comparative analysis to the transactions the FFL actually records. The FFL's sources can be identified in the following ways:
  ➤ Request a check of the ATF IO file FFL to locate any sources of firearms that were documented in previous inspections, as well as any other violations that may have been cited.
  ➤ Serve subpoenas on interstate carriers (e.g., UPS, DHL, U.S. Postal Service) that may deliver to the FFL to obtain shipment records identifying wholesalers, distributors, or others that have shipped packages to the FFL's address.
  ➤ Check any crime gun traces that are attributed to the FFL in eTrace to determine sources of firearms for the FFL.

✓ **Full Intelligence Workup.** A full intelligence workup should be performed on the FFL, including a financial workup and checks for SARs in FinCEN and CTRs in TECs. A full online profile workup should be performed to determine what OSINT is available where the FFL is talking about their illegal dealing to others.

✓ **False Theft/Loss Reports.** If it is suspected that the FFL is illegally diverting firearms and then reporting those firearms as lost or stolen, the investigator should consider the following:
  ➤ Contact the ATF Stolen Firearms Program to obtain copies of all FFL theft/loss reports (ATF F 3310.11, *FFL Theft/Loss Report*). If the false reports can be substantiated, the false statements on the ATF form constitute a violation of Title 18 U.S.C. § 1001. Check with ATF for the existence of any recordings of the initial verbal theft reports made via telephone by the FFL.
  ➤ Check with local law enforcement for any stolen property reports filed by the FFL, as well as any investigative records prepared by the law enforcement agency and any 911 recordings that may have been made when the FFL first reported the firearms theft.
  ➤ Apply for a court order for historical cell data or cell GPS data for the FFL and their employees' cell phones to determine their location at the time of any reported burglary.
  ➤ Conduct an ISO (Insurance Services Office) Claims Search online to determine if the FFL has a past history of filing insurance claims for other types of losses at their home or other businesses or that have been denied for suspicion of fraud.
  ➤ Subpoena from the FFL's insurance carrier any insurance claims filed by the FFL, as well as the original envelopes used to mail those documents or fax transmittal sheets used to send in the claims. Also check to see if the insurance carrier recorded any telephonic conversations with the FFL relating to the claims. Should it be proven that the FFL falsely reported a theft or loss, these documents and recordings will be useful in documenting the elements of the violations, showing profit motive, proving wire and mail

fraud violations, and documenting assets gained through illegal activity that would be subject to forfeiture.

➤ Once theft reports are obtained, ensure that all stolen firearms from previously reported thefts are in NCIC and check to determine if any have been recovered. Recoveries of these firearms may be found through checks of Project LEAD or the NCIC recovered gun file.

➤ If recoveries are found, obtain recovery reports and conduct investigative follow-up to determine the relationship of the possessor and recovery date/location to the FFL location and date of loss. Also determine if multiple stolen firearms are being recovered in close proximity to one another or over a widely dispersed pattern.

✓ **Surveillance.** If an FFL is identified as having a high level of crime guns traces with short time-to-crimes, an investigator may consider a prolonged surveillance of the FFL's place of business. This prolonged surveillance will assist in determining the business patterns of the FFL and may assist in determining whether it is the FFL who is engaged in illicit activities, whether it is the FFL's clientele engaged in illicit activities, or both. The surveillance may assist also assist in identifying the firearms traffickers or straw purchasers.

✓ **Evidence Purchases.** Consider making purchases of firearms from the FFL using a CI or UC. Both should be knowledgeable and conversational about firearms, and well-practiced in the type of conversation to have with the FFL to get an idea of what kinds of violations they may be committing and willing to commit for the UC or CI. Ideally, the investigator would have already been briefed by a cooperating defendant straw purchaser as to what the FFL is doing and how to approach them. If the FFL is selling firearms off-paper to out-of-state residents or convicted felons, or to straw purchasers on their behalf, the investigators need to remember that they need to have an actual out-of-state resident or convicted felon involved in the deal for this to be a violation. An investigator from out-of-state can be brought in, or a CI with a prior felony conviction could be used. The UC or CI straw purchaser should make it clear that they are purchasing the firearm(s) for this person who is standing nearby and should try to pay for the firearms using cash taken from this other person in front of the FFL. The UC or CI straw should have this other prohibited person be the one to pick out which gun to buy. They may want to bring up that their friend has had trouble with the background check in the past, or that they don't like paying the extra sales tax in the state they live in. The UC or CI should try to determine if the other employees in the gun store are aware of the transaction and are participating in these methods.

✓ **Electronic Surveillance.** Electronically record all undercover or informant contacts and purchases from the FFL. At a minimum this should be an audio recording, but video is preferred.

✓ **Crime Gun Intelligence.** Firearms purchased from an unlicensed dealer could yield a trove of information important to the investigation.
    ➤ **NCIC Checks.** Check the firearm in NCIC to make sure it is not stolen. If it is, that is a significant lead to follow up on. If any firearms are stolen, follow up on stolen firearms information (e.g., link between FFL and theft, other potential defendants). When used guns are purchased, the UC or CI may want to visit the FFL a week or two later and tell them the police took the gun during a traffic stop and said it was stolen and then ask why that is and what they can do to make it right.
    ➤ **Crime Gun Tracing.** Firearms purchased should be traced immediately, but the investigator should ask that the ATF NTC only trace to the retail FFL and not contact that retail

FFL for the purchaser information. The trace information will assist in identifying the wholesales the FFL uses for supply.

> **NIBIN.** Firearms purchased should be submitted to a lab for test-firing and the submission of the test fires to NIBIN to determine if the firearm was used in a prior shooting.

✓ **Illegal NFA Weapons.** If any of the purchased firearms are machine guns, silencers, or other illegal NFA weapons, the investigator should work this investigation jointly with ATF, in order to have access to NFA weapon registration information. The transfer of unregistered NFA firearms is a serious violation. All suspected machine guns, silencers, or other illegal NFA weapons should be sent to the ATF FATD, where they can be examined and classified by experts as to their status as a machine gun or silencer as defined under the law.

✓ **Obliterated Serial Numbers.** If the purchased firearms have obliterated serial numbers, they should be submitted to a laboratory to attempt to raise the serial numbers and then traced through the ATF NTC if whole or partial serial numbers are recovered.

✓ **Gun Show Involvement**. If the FFL's illegal activity is occurring at a gun show or flea market, determine whether the venue utilizes security cameras and makes recordings of venue activities. If so, consider obtaining copies of those recordings to see if any of the FFL's illicit activities have been recorded. However, note that attempts to secure video evidence from venue security cameras prior to the perfection of a criminal case could negatively impact the investigation by prematurely notifying the promoters of the gun show or the FFL under investigation. Investigators should first consider conducting independent surveillance to document the extent of the FFL's activities, identify others who may be involved with assisting the FFL in unlawful sales, document any off-premise sales of firearms, document violations of the Brady law or any state waiting periods, and identify the individuals purchasing firearms from the FFL who should be interviewed at a later time. Identify any individuals assisting the FFL and conduct full deconfliction checks and intelligence workups on them.

✓ **Electronic Communications Device Records Analysis.** Cell records analysis may be useful in determining who the unlicensed dealer's source is as well as their customers. If the unlicensed dealer is prolific, investigators may want to pursue a court ordered PEN. Investigators should make sure to use language in the application for the court order that will allow the initial court order to be used in subsequent requests to identify subscriber information.

✓ **Search Warrants.** If a search warrant is served at the business of an FFL it is important to remember that not all firearms in the inventory may be subject to seizure and forfeiture. Only those firearms directly tied to the violations should be seized and forfeited. Usually, an FFL search warrant focuses on recovering the records as they will contain false statement or omissions involving the violations that were investigated. Firearms that are not listed in the A and D Log or other records are "off-paper" firearms and may be subject to seizure.

✓ **Electronic Communication Device Exploitation.** If the FFL communicated during any illegal firearms sales with customers, the UC, or a CI during the investigation, those communication devices such as cell phones or computers should be listed as items that may be seized for evidence during the search warrant. Those devices should be imaged and analyzed for additional evidence.

✓ **Interview.** At the culmination of an FFL case, the investigator will likely have the opportunity to interview the unlicensed dealer. If this is a post arrest and post Miranda warnings interview,

it will be custodial, and the interview should be video and audio recorded. If this is a pre-arrest interview, the investigator should try and interview the suspect at the agency office in a formal interview room where audio and video recording capabilities exist. The investigator should be fully prepared to discuss all aspects of the violations with the FFL.

USE OF THE KLEIN CONSPIRACY AGAINST CORRUPT FFLS

Where the FFL and one or more persons are acting together to commit any type of firearms trafficking activity, the investigator should consider recommending a violation of the Klein Conspiracy to the AUSA for prosecution. The federal conspiracy charge is as follows:

Title 18 U.S.C. § 371: If two or more persons conspire either to commit any offense against the United States, **OR** to defraud the United States, or any agency thereof in any manner or for any purpose, and one or more of such persons do any act to affect the object of the conspiracy, each shall be fined not more than $10,000 or imprisoned not more than 5 years, or both.

Title 18, U.S.C. § 371 actually defines two different offenses:

(1) Conspiracy to violate another law of the United States (Traditional Conspiracy), OR
(2) Conspiracy to defraud the United States (Klein Conspiracy).

In choosing to pursue a Klein Conspiracy, investigators should remember that the maximum potential jail sentence for a conviction for conspiracy is 5 years, whereas many federal firearms violations have a maximum penalty of up to 10 years in prison. The practical reality, however, is that many stand-alone FFL violations are misdemeanor recordkeeping violations or a felony where the non-binding sentencing guideline range is frequently less than 5 years.

The first part of the conspiracy law is where 2 or more persons, neither being the government, conspire to commit another offense that is prohibited by a substantive criminal statute. In FFL investigations, this conduct could include agreements to commit any number of federal firearms violations, from lying on the ATF F 4473 (Title 18 U.S.C. § 922(a)(6)) to providing firearms to a convicted felon (Title 18 U.S.C. § 922(d)). When it can be shown that two or more persons conspired to commit an identifiable substantive offense, a conspiracy case is a straightforward way to charge the FFL, firearms traffickers, and their associates.

The second part of the conspiracy law is where person may also violate section 371 by conspiring or agreeing to "defraud" the United States. This type of fraud involves the cheating, impairing, obstructing, or defeating lawful government functions by deceit. Lawful government functions include collecting taxes and collecting records allowed as part of a regulatory purpose.

This theory has long been successfully used in tax prosecutions, where the government alleges that a defendant conspired to defraud the United States by "impeding, impairing, obstructing, and defeating the lawful functions of the IRS in the ascertainment, computation assessment, and collection of revenue" (United States v. Klein, 247 F.2d 908, 915 (2d Cir. 1957)). The investigator must show not just that they failed to do something, but there also must be proof that the intent was to impede or obstruct the lawful functioning of a government agency. In the firearms trafficking context, there would have to be evidence that the defendant's intent was to obstruct, impede, or evade ATF's enforcement of the federal firearms laws.

Use of the Klein conspiracy as a charging vehicle allows the prosecution to present the totality of the defendant's illegal conduct in a unified prosecution theory that focuses on the defendant's unlawful intent to profit by evading federal firearms regulations.[cxxviii] A Klein conspiracy can be predicated on any deceptive conduct, including recordkeeping offenses, prohibited transactions, or conduct that is not itself a specific violation of the GCA. Conduct that may be the factual basis for a Klein conspiracy includes omissions from records when selling firearms "off the books", making false entries in required records, creating and maintaining false ATF Forms 4473, submitting false information in an FFL application, filing false theft reports, submitting false or incomplete records to the ATF NTC during a crime gun trace, making false entries or omissions in the acquisition and disposition log, knowingly failing to file multiple handgun purchase forms, or making other false statements to ATF personnel. Many of these individual charges would fall under the following charges:

➢ Title 18 U.S.C. § 922(a)(6): The false or fictitious statement with regard to any fact material to lawfulness of sale of firearm.
➢ Title 18 U.S.C. § 922(b)(5): An FFL failing to note in his records the name, age, and place of residence of firearm purchaser.
➢ Title 18 U.S.C. § 922(m): An FFL making a false entry in their records.
➢ Title 18 U.S.C. § 922(t): Requirement to conduct a background check on purchasers.
➢ Title 18 U.S.C. § 923(g)(1)(A): An FFL failing to maintain records as required by regulation.
➢ Title 18 U.S.C. § 924(a)(1)(A): Knowing and willful false statements in dealer records.

A number of the above charges, when applied to an FFL, are misdemeanors. Charging and proving any of the above crimes at trial becomes a technical discussion of ATF recordkeeping requirements. By charging a Klein conspiracy, the conduct at the root of the various recordkeeping violations still comes into evidence, which can strengthen the overall case, and is presented within a larger context of obstructing ATF, and not within the narrow confines of the various requirements of the recordkeeping laws and regulations.[cxxix]

Although each of the above violations, alone, may lack jury appeal because they appear to be non-threatening or technical recordkeeping violations, in the aggregate, they can present a powerful case that the FFL was flaunting federal law for profit and preventing ATF from access to information to which it is entitled by law.

Using a broadly-defined Klein conspiracy instead of individual substantive firearms offenses expands the amount of evidence that should be admissible at trial. For example, conduct that otherwise might be excluded under Federal Rule of Evidence 404(b) as "other act" evidence can be converted into acts in furtherance of the conspiracy. Because impeding the federal regulatory scheme is the purpose of the conspiracy, the government is able to introduce evidence of the good reasons for the regulations (e.g., keeping guns away from convicted felons, facilitating traces of recovered crime guns), and how the defendant's conduct interfered with these purposes. Similarly, since profit is almost always the motive for the FFL to commit these offenses, the prosecution should be able to introduce evidence of the defendant's overall financial dealings. Evidence of the defendant's greed tends to make the underlying conduct look less like technical regulatory violations.

✓ **Options When Prosecution is Declined.** If the investigation culminates with a recommendation for prosecution, however prosecution is declined, investigators should refer all case information to ATF's IO. The ATF IOIs will review the evidence to determine whether administrative actions can be taken against the FFL up to and including revocation of their license to sell firearms.

✓ **FFL Investigation Nuances.** There are a number of nuances in federal law afforded to FFLs that investigators should remain aware of throughout the investigation:

➤ FFLs may only be subjected to an inspection of their business and records once in any one-year time period.

➤ ATF cannot use their annual inspection as a means to collect evidence on the FFL during a criminal investigation. That requires a search warrant.

➤ The FFL's records belong to the FFL, and a non-ATF investigator may need a subpoena to obtain them.

➤ A number of the individual recordkeeping violations with respect to gun sales are misdemeanors, not felonies.

➤ Following a felony conviction, an FFL does not automatically lose their license or the right to possess and sell firearms. FFLs can maintain their license and firearms possession right through all of their appeals process.

CASE STUDY: OPERATION NEW YORK SHUTTLE

United States v. Collette, et al. – District of Maine - 2:08-cr-00112-GZS

In December of 2005 ATF Portland, Maine Field Office special agents initiated an investigation after a review of crime gun trace data indicated several firearms recovered in Queens, NY had been purchased within the past two years from an FFL in Freeport, ME.

A total of 5 different purchasers were identified. Deconfliction queries indicated that no other law enforcement agency was investigating the subjects. Intelligence workups indicated that the persons may have common associations in the Freeport, ME area, and some had prior arrests for drug possession but no convictions. The 5 purchasers were interviewed, none had the firearms they had purchased, most were uncooperative, but some were forthcoming about the purchases of firearms. Interviews revealed that a gang member from Queens who was only known as D-Block would pay them in cash or drugs to purchase firearms for him. He would then take the guns back to Queens, NY and sell them. Intelligence workups resulted in identifying D-Block, and he was a multi-convicted felon. The interviews also determined that D-Block had cultivated the FFL to allow the straw purchases to take place, and that D-Block would actually come into the store, pick out the firearms and pay for them, then the straw purchasers would fill out the ATF Form 4473, after which the firearms were provided to D-Block.

To corroborate the reported accounts of straw purchasing facilitated by the FFL, two ATF UC agents posing as a couple where the woman was a Maine resident and her boyfriend was a New Hampshire resident entered the store for the purpose of conducting a straw purchase. The UC agents engaged the FFL in conversation, and were able to have the FFL agree to allow the girlfriend to purchase handguns, knowing that the handguns were actually for her boyfriend, who picked out the firearms, paid for them, and was a resident of New Hampshire. Purchases were made on more than one occasion while the investigation of the other straw purchasers and D-Block was underway.

Once D-Block became aware that the straw purchasers were being interviewed, he created false bills of sale showing that the straw purchasers sold the guns to other persons, and told some of the straws to give those to ATF special agents. It should be noted that the overt interviews and law enforcement scrutiny of the straw purchasers early in the investigation was intended to have a deterrent effect, to end the gun purchases, and to prevent additional firearms from being trafficked while the investigation progressed and criminal charges were perfected. This was successful.

Following the UC portion at the start of the investigation, a search warrant was served at the FFL business premise for the purpose of recovering the original ATF Form 4473s that reflected all the straw purchases, as well as the A & D log that reflected false entries by the FFL. Additionally, it was discovered that the FFL had failed to file reports of multiple handguns sales for some of the straw purchases. This reporting omission helped to conceal the firearms trafficking activity from ATF.

A federal grand jury investigation ensued, and some of the straw purchasers were proffered and provided testimony. The investigation culminated in the arrest of 5 straw purchasers, the FFL, and D-Block, the trafficking ring organizer for various firearms trafficking and possession violations as well as drug trafficking violations. All were charged in a Klein Conspiracy for intentionally conspiring to defraud the U.S. government of information it was entitled to lawfully collect with respect to firearms recordkeeping. All caused false information to be placed on ATF Form 4473s and the A & D log as to the true recipient of the firearms, who was an out-of-state resident and multi-convicted felon. In addition, the FFL failed to file multiple handgun sales forms lawfully required under federal law. In a twist, one of the straw purchasers was also charged with providing false information to the grand jury and distributing over 50 grams of crack cocaine brought from New York to Maine by D-Block. The ring trafficked more than 25 handguns, all of which were placed in ATF's FRNP so that agents would be notified of their recovery by law enforcement. During the investigation, 8 of the firearms purchased prior to the initiation of an investigation had already been recovered and traced in incidents in Queens, NY, including drug trafficking, residential burglary, possession of firearms with obliterated serial numbers, criminal weapon possession, reckless endangerment, obstruction, resisting arrest, concealed weapon violations, and a self-inflicted gunshot wound.

All of the straw purchasers pled guilty to making false statements on the ATF Form 4473 (18 U.S.C. § 922(a)(6)) and cooperated with the government. They received sentences ranging from 36 months of probation to 120 months in federal prison. The FFL pled guilty to conspiracy to intentionally defraud the U.S. Government of records and information it is required to keep (Klein Conspiracy), illegal sale of handguns to out-of-state residents, and false statements to government agents, as well as surrendering their license, and providing cooperation to the government. The FFL was sentenced to two months in federal prison followed by a period of supervised release.

D-Block was indicted for conspiracy to distribute and possess with intent to distribute cocaine base in excess of 50 grams (Title 21 U.S.C. § 841), conspiracy to intentionally defraud the U.S. government of records and information it is required to keep (Klein Conspiracy – Title 18 U.S.C. § 371), multiple counts of aiding and abetting false statements in a firearm transaction (Title 18 U.S.C. § 922(a)(6)), dealing in firearms without a license (Title 18 U.S.C. § 922(a)(1)(A)), and multiple counts of possession of a firearm by a prohibited person (Title 18 U.S.C. § 922(g)).

D-Block was not interested in cooperating with the government or the plea agreement offered. Following a trial in Portland, ME in 2009, D-Block was convicted on all charges. The Klein Conspiracy allows the AUSA to present the entire scope of the trafficking scheme to include bringing officers from NYC to testify on the crimes committed in Queens, NY with crime guns supplied by D-Block. A U.S. District Court Judge sentenced D-Block to 25 years in federal prison followed by 120 months of supervised release.[cxxx] At his sentencing D-Block stated he should have known ATF stood for "Avoid The Felony". See Appendix D for an example of a Klein Conspiracy indictment.

CASE STUDY: OPERATION TRAIL OF GUNS

United States v. McLeod, et al. – District of South Florida – 9:00-cr-08013-PCH

In 1999 the ATF West Palm Beach Field Office initiated an investigation of an area FFL after analysis of crime gun trace data and NICs data indicated issues that warranted investigation. Analysis performed on crime gun trace data and NICs denial data from 1995 to 1999 indicated that this FFL showed up in the top 3 FFLs for crime gun traces and the most NICs denials. The agents were looking into why a store that had the most NICs denial where criminal did not get the gun also had high numbers of crime gun traces where guns purchased from the FFL were recovered in crimes.

Full deconfliction and intelligence workups were performed. HUMINT sources were developed, and agents learned from more than one source that at this FFL, if someone was denied a firearm purchase for failing the NICs background check, store employees would coach the person to go get a friend who could pass the NICs background check and purchase the gun.

ATF UC agents with proper backstopped identities were brought in to work with CIs who were actual convicted felons to determine if this process existed at the store. The CI entered the FFL's store, completed the ATF Form 4473, and was denied on the NICs background check due to their felony conviction. The CI was told to find a friend who could pass the background check. Later, the CI returned with the ATF UC who was instructed to complete the ATF Form 4473. The UC passed the NICs background check and purchased the firearm. All transactions were electronically recorded by the ATF UC.

Purchases were made on more than one occasion, and after one purchase a store employee asked the CI to come in the back where the store employee displayed a MAC-10 9mm pistol with silencer, fired it into a pile of tires to demonstrate how effective the silencer was, and asked if the CI was interested in purchasing the item. The CI said yes, and paid for the firearms while the ATF UC agent was directed to complete the ATF Form 4473, and no mention of the silencer was made. The silencer had no serial numbers and was not registered in the ATF NFRTR.

In January of 2000, federal search and arrest warrants were served at the store to recover records and arrest the FFL and a store employee. The two were indicted for possession and transfer of an unregistered silencer (Title 26 U.S.C. § 5861), aiding and abetting straw purchases (Title 18 U.S.C. §§ 2 and 922(a)(6)), providing firearms to someone they knew to be a convicted felon (Title 18 U.S.C. § 922(d)(1)), and conspiring to defraud the U.S Government of records it is lawfully entitled to have (Title 18 U.S.C. § 371 – Klein Conspiracy). In this instance, the store employee and owner conspired to place false information on the ATF Form 4473 and in the A

& D Log by selling firearms to persons knowing they were for prohibited persons. The FFL also failed to file required multiple handgun purchase forms.

Both defendants pled guilty, and in August of 2001 the owner was sentenced to 30 months in federal prison followed by 36 months supervised release and a $60,000 fine, while the store employee was sentenced to 14 months in federal prison. Firearms sold illegally by the FFL traveled far and wide and continued to be recovered in crimes after this case. Some of the firearms recovered from the Arizona home of mobster Sammy the Bull Grava no in 2001 during a narcotics search warrant were directly traced back to this FFL.[cxxxi]

TYPE 4: SECONDARY SOURCE MARKET INITIATIVE

Secondary source markets are a lawful and legitimate part of firearms commerce that afford collectors, licensees, hunters, target shooters, and novices an opportunity to buy, trade, and sell firearms. Secondary source markets can include both paper and online classified advertisements, flea markets, and gun shows. Secondary source markets are frequented by licensed as well as unlicensed firearms dealers. Unlicensed sellers conduct firearms sales without keeping records, asking questions, or conducting background checks. The opportunity to purchase firearms with no questions asked is a draw for gang members and prohibited persons, such as convicted felons who would not be able to pass a background check because it is illegal for them to acquire or possess firearms under Title 18 U.S.C. § 922(g).

Goals of a Secondary Source Market Operation. When a secondary source market is determined by investigators to be a source of crime guns for criminals and gang members, efforts should be undertaken to halt this illegal activity. The goals of this type of initiative will be to:
➢ Identify and apprehend prohibited persons acquiring firearms or ammunition.
➢ Identify and apprehend straw purchasers and the firearms traffickers they are working for.
➢ Successfully complete the first 2 goals without causing any interference with the lawful commerce in firearms by law abiding citizens attending the event.

Enforcing the law and halting illegal firearms traffickers helps preserve and safeguard the secondary market as a lawful source of firearms for the law-abiding gun owner and helps the lawful FFL by removing illegal traffickers who cut into the FFL's business and livelihood.

Initiative Staffing and Positioning. Investigators should coordinate the initiative with local police (e.g., gang or violent crime unit along with marked patrol units). The initiative will benefit from having members of the local law enforcement community present who have a working knowledge of local criminals and gang members on sight, and who have marked patrol units available in the event a traffic stop is needed.

Investigators should be assigned to three primary positions or locations:
➢ unmarked observers and spotters inside the venue.
➢ unmarked observers and spotters outside the venue in the parking lot area.
➢ unmarked patrol units and agents in designated staging areas away from the venue but on a major direct route of travel to the venue.

The following are procedures for how investigators may want to stage their operation:

➤ The inside spotters will watch for known prohibited persons and person- using straws to make purchases from FFLs or making direct purchases from unlicensed dealers.

➤ The inside spotters should focus their interest on known gang members and prohibited persons making purchases of the known top traced crime guns known to that area. If the most frequently traced crime guns are inexpensive pistols or AK47 or AR15 variants, then set up near those dealers selling those types of firearms.

➤ The inside spotters should try to surreptitiously document the trafficking-related activity with photographs and then call out descriptions or text the photographs of the suspects to outside units who can surveil those persons as they leave the venue and head for their cars with firearms or ammunition.

While the inside spotters are conducting surveillance, outside units should also be vigilant in the parking lot for signs of illegal trafficking such as parking lots firearms sales. Sales made outside the venue in parking lots is a strong indicator of unlicensed firearms dealing and potentially the sale of an illegal NFA firearm that could not be displayed inside the venue.

Out-of-state or out-of-country license plates in the parking lot are an indicator of someone who may be unlawfully acquiring firearms in the U.S. and not in their country or state of residence. At gun shows in states along the Northern border, license plates on vehicles from Canada merit watching to see if the owner comes back to their car and loads in firearms. Investigators should coordinate with HSI or CBP to place a lookout on the vehicle so it can be checked for undeclared firearms or ammunition when returning to Canada. The same holds true for vehicles on the southern border.

When contacted by the inside units with information on purchasers that merit attention, the outside units will observe and document whether the firearms and ammunition are placed in the vehicle trunk or in the passenger compartment, identify the car and license plate, and call in records checks to see determine if any convicted felons, fugitives, or stolen vehicles are involved.

Investigators may want to consider using an ALPR placed near the venue's exit who could automatically read license plates, run histories, and report on stolen vehicle statuses, as well as criminal histories of owners. ALPRs are controversial and investigators must use care to follow their department's policy regarding the deletion of all collected data. It is recommended that investigators only keep records and information on persons/vehicles/addresses that are suspected to be prohibited from possessing firearms or otherwise engaged in an unlawful activity that will be investigated. All other data should be deleted. Do not maintain records or information on persons simply because they attended a gun show, as this is a lawful activity that should not be recorded and maintained by any government entity.

➤ Parking lot observer units will report to marked units and investigators staged nearby when a known felon or fugitive is in a vehicle with a firearm, when a stolen vehicle is discovered, or when another violation of law is believed to be present in the vehicle.

➤ The marked units will perform traffic stops away from the venue where safe and legally possible, and then, based on the events of the traffic stop and developed probable cause, make arrests, secure consent to search or search warrants, and seize firearms. The investigator will then conduct follow-up investigation on illegal possession or trafficking cases.

➤ Actionable intelligence developed by spotters inside the venue on unlicensed dealer activity may be followed up later in a separate investigation following the steps covered in the unlicensed dealer investigation section of this chapter.

It is imperative that these initiatives be conducted in a manner that does not interfere with the lawful commerce of firearms and with attention to public safety. During the initiative, all actions inside the venue and in the parking lot should be done discretely, and law enforcement should not be marked with any indicia. All efforts should be taken to have any required enforcement actions take place away from the venue.

CASE STUDY: OPERATION CASH AND CARRY

United States v. Frazier - District of South Florida – 9:98-cr-08060-DTKH

In December of 1997 the ATF West Palm Beach Field Office initiated an investigation after receiving information from a CI that an individual was selling firearms at gun shows all over the state of Florida without any paperwork or questions asked, and he was hurting the business of the FFLs at those gun shows. The CI further advised that the individual sell to anyone, including convicted felons.

A full deconfliction and intelligence workup was performed and it was determined that the suspect previously was an FFL, so he clearly knew the law with respect to being engaged in the business of dealing in firearms for the principle objective of livelihood and profit, and that he should not be selling firearms to prohibited persons.

The CI was sent to the next gun show to approach the suspect, gather conversation, and purchase a firearm. The CI was a previously convicted felon, and made this clearly known to the suspect who then sold him a Colt AR-15 rifle that had been modified to a pistol platform. During the conversation, the suspect advised the CI that he did have some machine guns available, as well as marijuana if he wanted any.

At the next gun show the CI introduced a UC ATF agent to the suspect. The UC ATF agent negotiated a deal to purchase machine guns and marijuana. During the conversation, the suspect told the UC ATF that he used to be an FFL, but that it was easier and he could make a lot more money selling guns without all the paperwork.

A final meeting was set up with the suspect, and the UC purchased 5 firearms, 2 of which were machine guns, from the suspect. The suspect was then arrested and found to be armed with a pistol and to have a bag of marijuana on his person.

The entire investigation was conducted at gun shows, and at no time did any of the investigative activities become known to other patrons or interfere with the lawful commerce in firearms at the gun show. The arrest removed a source of firearms to criminals, and illegal competition to the FFLs at the gun shows who were following the law. The arrest also sent a message to other traffickers exploiting gun shows that ATF would be there to enforce the law and protect the business interests of law abiding FFLs.

The suspect pled guilty to unlawful possession and transfer of machine guns and in November of 1998 was sentenced to 30 months in federal prison followed by 36 months of supervised release.

TYPE 5: FEDERAL FIREARMS LICENSEE THEFT INVESTIGATION

FFL Theft Investigation. These investigations may involve burglaries, robberies, or smash and grabs crimes and since these robberies involve situations where the criminals and the store employees are usually both armed, they can result in shootings and homicide. In most instances the investigation will involve a joint effort between the state or local law enforcement agency and ATF as both have a jurisdictional interest in the crime. FFL theft investigations usually start with a call to 911 to the local police or with the FFL filing ATF Form 3310.11, Federal Firearms Licensee Firearms Inventory Theft/Loss Report with ATF.

An FFL investigation consists of a multipart operation[cxxxii]:

PHASE I: Defining and protecting the crime scene.
PHASE II: Initial interviews of victims and witnesses and canvassing of the area.
PHASE III: Crime scene processing, detection and collection of trace and physical evidence.
PHASE IV: Follow-up investigation to include in-depth interviews, modus operandi examination, suspect development, and consideration or all options.

PHASE I: DEFINING AND PROTECTING THE CRIME SCENE

➤ The first investigators on the scene should proceed with caution and sweep the store checking for suspects or victims.
➤ Once the store is secure, define the crime scene. Is it just the interior of the store or does it involve exterior entrances, the roof and exterior walls, and the parking lot. Make a determination and segregate the area with crime scene tape to control access to the area.
➤ For crime scene areas exposed to the elements, determine if temporary shelter should be brought in to protect evidence.
➤ If there are blood and body fluids present, make sure all investigators are aware to use universal precautions.

The importance of protecting the crime scene from disturbance cannot be overemphasized. Oftentimes much of the evidence required to prove that a crime occurred in a specific manner and by a particular person will be found at the crime scene. If this evidence is compromised, improperly tampered with, or destroyed, the likelihood of successfully concluding a case can be greatly diminished.

Crime scene protection can pose challenges, and the investigator will need to work with the store owner to assure them everything will be done to solve the crime and turn the store back over to them to resume business as quickly as possible. Understandably, establishments will be concerned with resuming normal business operations, as this is their livelihood. Make sure the FFL and their employees are provided with victim witness rights information.

It is imperative that a crime scene be completely sealed and held as long as necessary whenever any of the following crimes occur:

➢ A homicide, serious injury, or hostage situation occurs during the theft.
➢ The criminal commits another crime, such as rape, during the theft.
➢ The criminal is at the scene for an extended period.
➢ A substantial number of firearms are taken.

Often the store owner wants to get back to business as quickly as possible. When it is not necessary to seal off the entire building, the exact locations where the criminal was present should be determined, and these areas protected. After these areas are secured, the owner can reopen for business in other parts of the store. The investigator must be careful and avoid premature judgments about where the criminal was in the building. Make certain that the victim and witnesses point out the specific areas and those areas are secured.

The perpetrators of an FFL burglary, robbery, or smash and grab sometimes injure themselves during the commission of the crime. It may be helpful to canvass area hospitals to determine if anyone came in for treatment of serious cuts or broken bones during the period of time after the suspected crime occurred.

PHASE II: INITIAL INTERVIEWS AND AREA CANVAS

✓ **Robbery/Smash and Grab.** Robbery, including smash and grabs, is usually a crime committed by strangers to the FFL and is accompanied by the threat of violence. It is usually completed quickly and dynamically and can pose challenges for the witnesses and victims to memorize the exact appearance of the perpetrator(s). Immediate questioning of victims and witnesses is essential.

✓ **Burglary.** Burglary is usually a crime committed at hours of the day when very few witnesses will be around. Nonetheless, efforts must be made to locate any potential witnesses for questioning, as this may produce valuable investigative leads.

✓ **Each victim and witness should be separated and individually interviewed.** Individual interviews are of great importance as it is imperative that witnesses do not influence each other's recollection of descriptions and events. Independent observations are what the investigator is seeking, and variations in the accounts of witnesses are to be expected. No two persons perceive and describe a situation in exactly the same way, especially when the situation is stressful and life-threatening. In fact, when the stories are identical, the investigator should also consider the possibility of a false reporting and the options that go with this scenario such as a staged crime for insurance fraud or to cover firearms trafficking.
  ➢ When conducting the initial interview, the investigator must seek more than a physical description of the perpetrators. The witness should be asked if they recall any particular actions, mannerisms, speech impediments, accents/dialects, or physical peculiarities of the suspects. Keep in mind that virtually every person has at least one unique physical characteristic. Questions such as "What was the most unusual feature of the robber's appearance?" or "What was the most striking thing about the suspect's appearance?" can generate useful information and may elicit information not previously mentioned or considered.

➤ Interview all the store personnel thoroughly. Gather all the information you can concerning the criminals, their modus operandi, their speech patterns or slang used, how they acted, how long the criminals were in the store, and in what areas of the store the criminals were. Then determine how many firearms they believe were stolen, and gather an accurate and complete description of each firearm, including manufacturer, model, type, caliber, importer, and serial number.

✓ **ATF IOIs Can Assist in Determining the Description of those Firearms Stolen.** If a large number of firearms are taken, offer to the victim that ATF will bring in IOIs to go through the records and conduct a full reconciliation to determine what should be there and what is not there. This can be very helpful to the victims, as it is one less thing they need to deal with, and it is very helpful to the investigators to get a complete and accurate accounting of the firearms stolen.

✓ **Enter Stolen Firearms into ATF Stolen Firearms Database and NCIC.** As soon as a complete and accurate list of the firearms stolen is compiled, it is imperative that this information get reported on to ATF on the ATF Form 3310.11, Federal Firearms Licensee Firearms Inventory Theft/Loss Report. In accordance with Title 18 U.S.C. § 923(g)(6), FFLs are required to file this report with ATF within 48 hours of the theft. ATF will enter the firearms into the ATF Stolen Firearms Database and NCIC so that ATF and the investigators will be notified as any of the stolen firearms are recovered later.

✓ **Surrounding Area Preliminary Canvass and Interviews.** The investigator should canvass surrounding businesses and homes for potential witnesses who may have seen or heard something that may produce leads as to the time of crime, number and description of perpetrators, dialects used, method of entry or escape, and sound of vehicle(s). Also, consider asking questions concerning the neighborhood, such as types and frequency of crimes in the area, gangs, other known criminals in the area, and any unusual loitering in the area by subjects who may have been evaluating/casing the business. If witnesses are located, they should each be interviewed separately, as previously stated under the robbery section. A canvass should be conducted the day of the theft and the day after the theft during the time the theft occurred to try and encounter those witnesses who pass by the area on a schedule.

✓ **Surrounding area video systems.** Investigators should canvass the area within a few blocks to determine if any homes or businesses have video monitor systems that may have captured images at the gun store, or of vehicles or pedestrians on streets leading near the gun store to see if images captured the perpetrator's approach or departure.

✓ **Police Traffic Stop Checks.** Ask the local department to produce a run of any traffic or parking tickets issued in the immediate area of the gun store within a short period before and after the crime to determine if there are any viable leads in this information.

✓ **False 911 Calls for Service.** Ask the local department if they had any unusual or anonymous calls for 911 service at the same time as the robbery. This may be a diversionary call by the robbers.

PHASE III: CRIME SCENE PROCESSING

Processing the crime scene will be critically important to the investigation and, where available, this should be performed by trained crime scene investigator (CSI) technicians with input from investigators who have knowledge of the crime based on interviews. If this crime took place in a remote area where no CSIs are available, the investigators should use their training, knowledge, and expertise to process the scene. The following reference materials are a useful guide containing specifics on proper evidence recovery, preservation, and packaging.

> ➤ **Crime Scene and Evidence Collection Handbook** (ATF Publication 7110.2). By the U.S. Department of Justice, Bureau of Alcohol, Tobacco, Firearms and Explosives. (Rev. Ed. 2004, September). Washington, DC.
> ➤ **Special Agents' Guide to ATF Laboratory Services** (ATF Publication 7110.1). By the U.S. Department of Justice, Bureau of Alcohol, Tobacco, Firearms and Explosives. (Rev. Ed. 2012, June). Washington, DC.

Robbery. The success of a robbery investigation depends on the investigator's ability to recognize, collect, and evaluate available information and physical evidence. Robbery is a crime that is typically committed within a few minutes. The robber will enter a store, wait for the best opportunity to strike, brandish a weapon, and steal the firearms. Even an inexperienced robber develops rudimentary plans about their intended actions before, during, and after committing a robbery. The detailed plans of professionals may include information about police activity in the area, business practices of the target, and alternative escape routes. Because robberies usually occur rapidly and involve some planning to avoid the police, police intervention is not a common occurrence. Arriving after the robbery has taken place, investigators have only one method of solving the crime: by conducting a thorough investigation that leads to the identity and apprehension of the guilty party. A critical task in the investigative procedure is the discovery of possible trace and physical evidence that may place a suspect at the crime scene.

- ✓ **Alarm and Video Systems.** Look for the presence of an alarm system. If an alarm system is present, determine the type, (e.g., linked to private company, and linked directly to police department or alarm/siren only). If the alarm was tripped and the system is linked to a private company or police department, contact those locations and gather available information as to the time of alarm, was a panic button sounded, and the response time to the scene after receiving alarm signal. Is a video system part of the store security and if yes, obtain and review copies of the captured images?

- ✓ **Types and Location of Evidence.** As soon as possible after the potential evidence or possible presence has been identified, the crime scene should be processed. Physical evidence may take many forms, including tire tracks and paint transfers; however, the most commonly encountered types of evidence at robbery scenes are fingerprints, DNA, fired cartridges, and binding material. At the scene, the investigator can usually narrow the search for evidence by having the victim and witnesses point out the criminal's movements during the crime. By retracing the actions of the robber, the investigator can determine the likely places where the evidence can be found. Areas identified as possibly containing physical evidence should be secured immediately.

- ✓ **Search the Route or Departure.** Following the criminal's presumed route of flight may also yield evidence. Almost routinely, offenders will discard clothing or disguises along the escape route. Gloves, masks, hats, or covering clothing may be found openly discarded or placed in dumpsters or trash cans along the route of travel. Firearms, money, jewelry, or other articles taken from the store, or a weapon used during the robbery, may also be discarded. During flight, the robber may also lose personal items (such as a wallet containing identification) that may be useful in their identification. This author can attest that more than once they have found the perpetrators driver's license lying on the ground at or nearby the scene of a gun store theft. Search all possible routes of departure, look in alleys, abandoned buildings, in dumpsters, in storm drains, ditches, and underneath parked cars.

✓ **Trace Evidence.** Latent fingerprints and DNA are extremely valuable evidence, and it is necessary to conduct a thorough search of all surfaces around the crime scene that potentially retained prints and DNA. The counters, gun display cases, cash registers, money trays, and other furniture touched by the robbers should be processed for latent prints and DNA. Although doors typically contain only fingerprint smears, they should still be processed. Occasionally, the robber may handle papers, checks, or currency during the course of the crime. Any articles or documents handled by the robber should be processed by the crime laboratory. Not to be overlooked are obvious locations for fingerprints and DNA. For example, the robber may have posed as a customer and handled several items in the store prior to committing the robbery. These items may not have been taken during the robbery. In many gun stores, firearms are kept in glass display cases where the robber(s) may have left fingerprints or DNA.

✓ **NIBIN.** When shots are fired, the shell cartridges found at the crime scene may be valuable items of evidence linking this shooting to other shooting crimes. Investigators must submit the cartridges to NIBIN for input. In shooting incidents where no crime gun is recovered, NIBIN can be used to examine the projectile or casing and identify the type of firearm from which the projectile and/or casing were expended. For example, an FFL robbery results in a homicide. The projectile, believed to be 9mm, is recovered from the victim, but no firearm is recovered. NIBIN examination confirms that the projectile is 9mm and can also advise the investigator of the type of 9mm pistol used (e.g., Glock or Sig Sauer). Identifiable fingerprints sometimes can be developed from the spent cartridges of an automatic weapon because imprints may be left when the shell is forced into the spring-loaded magazine.

✓ **Comparative Analysis Materials.** Material that was used to bind or gag a victim is important evidence and must be preserved. This includes strips of adhesive tape, wire, clothesline, cord, a necktie, shoelaces, cloth, or any material used to immobilize the victim that may contain fingerprints, hairs, or DNA from the perpetrator. In addition, these items can be used for comparative analysis with any similar material found in the suspect's possession or residence at a later time. The specific type of material used, the knots made, and the manner in which the victim was bound can all help to establish a part of the robber's modus operandi.

✓ **Modus Operandi.** Specific information concerning the robbery and modus operandi should be documented and forwarded to ATF for entry into the stolen firearms database and for comparison against the modus operandi of other FFL robberies locally and nationally. This may yield information that could link the suspect(s) to other FFL robberies in a specific area or across jurisdictions.

✓ **Victim Injury Evidence.** In the case of injured or deceased victims, photographs should be taken of their injuries. If the victim is not seriously hurt, his/her scratches or bruises may heal by the time of any trial, and recorded evidence of their existence must be available. If the victim is more seriously injured, doctors' statements and hospital reports are important documentation of injuries sustained during a crime. When the victim is deceased, the body should not be moved until all pertinent information has been recorded, including its relative position in the crime scene. Photographs should show details of the wounds and blood patterns. If the victim was shot, high velocity blood spray (a fine mist, rather than drops) may indicate the direction the victim was facing when shot, and the direction from which the bullet came. After the measurements are taken and the diagrams drawn, the body should be examined for evidence of bullets, gun powder stippling marks, starring of the edges of the flesh around a gunshot wound, hairs, fibers, and paint or glass chips. Starring patterns or stippling marks can assist in indicating the distance between the shooter and the victim. Submit all recovered projectiles and casings recovered to NIBIN, where available, for ballistic examination and comparison.

Burglary. When investigating the scene of a burglary/breaking and entering offense, consider how the crime was perpetrated and collect evidence accordingly.

- ✓ **Tool Marks.** Consider how the perpetrators entered the premises. Check the doors and windows. If entry was made by prying a door or cutting a hole in a roof or wall, look for and collect tool marks left on surfaces for later comparison to tools of the perpetrators. If the door or doorknob has a smooth surface, look for and collect latent fingerprints.

- ✓ **Trace and Physical Evidence.** Consider what surfaces in the room might have been touched by the perpetrator. Fingerprints might appear on a table, under a window where entry took place, on a metal filing cabinet, on a glass display case, or on any object that might have been held by the perpetrator. Many FFLs have glass display cases to house their firearms. These are excellent surfaces for the recovery of latent fingerprints.

- ✓ **Out of Place Articles.** Collect articles that might be considered out of place. For example, collect any used matches or cigarette butts lying on the floor. Look for articles of clothing such as gloves, hats, handkerchiefs, or masks. Articles of clothing may have trace body fluids, hairs, or other types of fibers that can later be compared to identified suspects. Also look for wallets, pieces of paper, credit card receipts or other receipts and notes that may contain identifying information or handwriting exemplars, or handkerchiefs or clothing in unusual places or near where the offense occurred.

- ✓ **Alarm Systems.** Look for the presence of alarm systems. If an alarm system is present, determine the type, (e.g., linked to a private company, linked directly to the police department, or an alarm/siren only). If the system is linked to a private company or the police department, contact those locations and gather available information, such as the time the alarm was set, time the alarm was tripped, method the alarm was tripped—motion inside or door/window break, frequency of alarm use, whether the alarm was deactivated, and whether the alarm was disabled. Obtain information from the owner/manager as to who has access to alarm codes. If the alarm system, telephone, or electrical lines at the business were cut or disabled, document the method used, and consider tool mark presence for later comparative analysis. Also, note this activity as a modus operandi for comparison to other FFL or business thefts in the area.

Smash and Grabs. Most smash and grabs occur when the store is unoccupied, and most criminals utilize a stolen vehicle to break through a window or wall of the store. Smash and grabs that

occur during regular store hours are usually done to defeat store security measures such as electronic door buzzers that allow the store owner to deny access to, or exit from, a store. Smash and grabs occurring during regular store hours are another form of robbery, and the investigator should follow the robbery checklists appearing in this section as well as the smash and grab checklist that follows.

✓ **Modus Operandi.** The method and time of a smash and grab is often a tell-tale modus operandi of the criminal(s) and particular note should be made of this. Did the criminal use a vehicle? Was the vehicle stolen? When did the criminal commit the smash and grab? Did the criminal use a large object found near the scene to smash through a window?

✓ **Non-Vehicle Smash and Grab.** If the item used to commit the smash and grab was not a vehicle, determine what it is and whether it has any latent evidentiary value (e.g., would it bear latent fingerprints or body fluids such as blood). If evidence is available, collect and conduct the appropriate follow-up investigation. Such evidence may be useful in later comparative analysis to items in the suspect's residence or environment.

✓ **Vehicle Smash and Grab.** If the item used to commit the smash and grab was a vehicle, but the vehicle was driven off by the criminals after the theft, consider what possible evidence could have been left at the scene. Broken vehicle glass, chrome fragments, decorative metal or plastic trims, or paint smears or chips that may have been dislodged on impact; mud, dirt, or plant matter uncommon to the area that may have fallen off the vehicle; and tire impressions or skid marks. For tire marking, take exact measurements of the marking dimensions and photograph all marks, as these may all be valuable leads and evidence for later comparison analysis against suspect vehicles. Glass, trim, and paint chips may be used to identify the exact make, model, year, and color of the suspect vehicle. Consider from the scene the type of damage the vehicle may have sustained for use in developing a description of the vehicle to search for. Take exact measurements (height/width) of those parts of the building that may have gouged, scraped, or dented the vehicle. Also consider what types of paint, fabric, fibers, or blood (if the vehicle struck a store occupant) may have been transferred onto the vehicle that you will be searching for.

➢ If the vehicle used to commit the smash and grab is left at the scene, or if a suspect smash-and-grab vehicle is found abandoned elsewhere, consider what personal articles, papers, fingerprints, hair, blood, fibers, and DNA can be collected to establish the identity of the criminals or that can be used for later comparative analysis to the criminals and their surroundings. Also consider "super gluing" the entire vehicle under a tent to preserve all latent fingerprints.

➢ If the suspected vehicle used to commit the smash and grab is located in the possession of a suspect, but not enough evidence exists to arrest the suspect and seize the vehicle, consider obtaining a search warrant for the vehicle to collect evidence. With the search warrant, document damage for comparative analysis and look for evidence such as glass particles or parts of the building from where the smash and grab occurred. Also consider "super glue fuming" the entire vehicle under a tent to preserve all latent fingerprints should the suspect deny ownership of the vehicle and ownership records do not indicate the suspect as the vehicle's owner.

➢ Conduct vehicle identification number and license plate NCIC checks to determine ownership and theft status of the vehicle. If the vehicle is not stolen, conduct the appropriate follow-up investigation with the determined owner. If the vehicle is stolen, follow up with a stolen vehicle investigation. Determine where the vehicle was stolen and check this information against the known residences or places of employment or frequenting of any suspects. Determine if other smash and grabs have occurred in the area using stolen vehicles, and compare the source locations of those stolen vehicles against the information in the current investigation.

PHASE IV: FOLLOW-UP INVESTIGATION

When the initial police response and preliminary investigation fails to result in the apprehension of suspects, a detailed follow-up investigation must be conducted to obtain and analyze additional information that can assist in leading to the development of suspects, recovery of the stolen firearms, and an eventual arrest in the case.

✓ **Electronic Communications Device Analysis.** Investigators should conduct a tower dump for the exact time of the theft to gather information on all the cell phones that were in the location of the gun store and pinging the tower at the same time as the crime. Use this data to compare to the cell phone numbers of suspects and gun store employees. If this was a burglary at 3AM, it would be unusual for a gun store employee's phone to be pinging at the store at the same time. Investigators should get a court order for cell phone historical data as well as cell phone call logs of all suspects as they are identified, so that their information can be analyzed. This information can also assist in geo-locating suspect's phones at specific times. Investigators should make sure to use language in the application for the court order that will allow the initial court order to be used in subsequent requests to identify subscriber information. See Appendix D for examples.

✓ **Re-Interviewing Victims and Witnesses.** Re-interviewing the victim and/or witnesses is a basic task of the follow-up investigation. The unhurried, in-depth questioning may clarify old information or uncover new facts. The follow-up interview also serves to test the validity of earlier statements made by the witnesses. The interviewing investigator should assist, but not influence, the witness to recall observations. The investigator should cautiously question the witness to stimulate their memory and, when appropriate, employ visual aids. For example, to help identify the type of vehicle that the criminal may have used, the investigator can show photographs of various vehicles similar to the type initially described by the witness. If the witness and/or victim saw the criminal(s) and there are suspects, the investigator may want to utilize photographic stacks, lineups, or arrays that contain a photograph of any potential suspects.

✓ **Identifying Reluctant Eyewitnesses.** Possible eyewitnesses to a robbery or burglary who may be reluctant to come forward should be located and interviewed. These persons may deny that they saw the offense because of the desire "not to be involved." Others may not cooperate because they fear or hold an antagonistic position law enforcement. An investigator must find a way to gain this person's trust to obtain the necessary information. The investigator may use cell tower dump information to locate these people or conduct a traffic canvas by handing out leaflets asking for information to traffic passersby at the same time of day of the theft. If the burglary happened at 3AM, conduct a canvass of all cars passing by at 3AM and hand out leaflets asking for information. A delivery driver may take that route each night at that time and may be able to provide the description of a vehicle or person in the area the night of the theft. Even cooperative witnesses may present challenges to an investigator. It is usually difficult for victims and witnesses to describe with a high degree of accuracy the physical characteristics or actions of a robber. This apparent lack of recall is not necessarily

an attempt to conceal the truth. A number of emotional and physiological factors affect a person's ability to observe, retain, and remember the events of a shocking or violent experience.

✓ **Surrounding Area Secondary Canvass and Interviews.** A secondary neighborhood canvass should be conducted in the immediate vicinity of the robbery/burglary and along the criminal's probable route of flight. The key elements of a canvass are questioning persons who may have information about the crime and searching for discarded evidence. In conducting canvass interviews, the investigator should immediately state the purpose of their questions. This will put citizens at ease that may otherwise be apprehensive about "official" questioning. The investigator should also emphasize the potential importance of all information, regardless of how trivial it may seem to the citizen. Some witnesses do not volunteer information simply because they are not aware of its significance. Initially, the investigator should seek general information, such as a description of any unusual occurrence witnessed by the citizen. Once the general inquiry is completed, the investigator may describe the suspect and getaway vehicle and ask whether the citizen saw either. As the initial canvass will likely occur at a time other than when the robbery occurred, it is possible that some witnesses who regularly pass by the location to and from work or school will not be contacted at that time. Therefore, the scene should be visited periodically.

✓ **Public Requests for Help and Rewards for Information.** The investigator can seek information from the public by releasing a video image or composite drawing of a suspect or vehicle, or an unusual firearm that was stolen to the media and asking for information to help solve the crime and identify the suspects. A tips line can be placed in the release to afford anonymity to the caller. Reward money can be offered for information leading to the successful arrest and prosecution of the suspects.

✓ **Evaluating Modus Operandi.** Because robberies, burglaries, and smash and grabs are often recidivistic crimes, a study of the modus operandi is of great importance. In the absence of physical evidence, the techniques used and the mannerisms of the suspects are often the most valuable clues to their identity. The following information pertains to modus operandi.

  ➤ **Modus Operandi Factors.** When attempting to identify the criminal through modus operandi, the investigator needs to evaluate pertinent data that places the emphasis on the criminal. This includes the type of robbery/burglary; the location of the robbery/burglary; the time of day of the robbery/ burglary; the proximity to police department shift changes; the use of diversionary calls for service; the use of stolen cars taken from a particular area; the method of entry; the proximity to highway routes of escape; the number of members in the criminal group; the age, sex, and other identifiers specific to the perpetrators.

  ➤ **Criminal Planning and Preparation:** The criminal's thought process in deciding to rob/burglarize a specific business and the manner in which the criminal commits the crime are of considerable interest to the investigator. Target selection alone sometimes offers clues to the suspect's identity and displays a pattern that can be considered a modus operandi. The robbery of a gun store usually entails some planning. A quickly planned robbery may involve a robber entering a gun store, evaluating the store's vulnerability while pretending to browse, and then making a decision about committing the robbery. In a more thoroughly planned robbery, the robber considers not only the victim of the robbery, but such factors as the number of accomplices that will be needed, the weapons to use, the number of persons likely to be present during the robbery, and the escape route. A fast entry and an apparent knowledge of routine or personnel, or both, or timing to coincide with an unusual amount of inventory on hand are indications of thorough planning.

> **Language Characteristics:** It is important for the investigator to determine the exact words spoken by the robbers. The voice tone, accent, dialect, slurring, impediments, stuttering, and slang are important factors in modus operandi evaluation. The robber's characteristic orders, threats, phrases, story, speech effects, and accents should be determined. The criminal's manner of speech is an important part of the modus operandi in the crime of robbery. The opening and closing comments of the robbery are highly characteristic. As part of their planning, the criminal has usually determined a set of orders that they will give the victim, such as, "This is a stickup, do as I say and no one gets hurt. Now, everyone to the back of the store and keep your hands up." Some criminals will repeat this statement without modification at each crime. Some criminals will interject the same aggressive phrases or explicative over and over to intimidate the victims and they may use this same speech at other crimes. At times, robbers may refer to each other by given names or nicknames during a holdup. The investigator should specifically ask a witness if the robber mentioned any names.

> **Perpetrator Behavior and Mannerisms.** The manner in which the criminal conducted him or herself while committing the crime can identify characteristics unique to that perpetrator. For example, the attitude of the suspect during the robbery should be ascertained. Determine if the suspect was seen as nervous, intoxicated, under the influence of narcotics, or belligerent. The means used to rob the victim (e.g., displaying a gun or a note) and the treatment of the victim by the criminal should also be detailed. How severe was the use of violence? Were restraints used? Was the victim locked up? Was a gag or blindfold used? Did they apologize for what they were doing and provide some kind of justification? If an assault occurred, the type of injury should be noted, and if the victim was beaten, this information should be considered with regard to identifying the known modus operandi. Other peculiarities, such as locking victims in closets, having them take their clothes off, or cutting telephone wires can help connect several robberies and identify suspects. Often burglars will perform some sort of desecration of the victim's establishment. This may involve defecating or urinating in the business or using the telephone to make phone calls, all of which can leave DNA behind. In any case, this type of activity is important modus operandi information and provides valuable comparative evidence. Additionally, an investigator should always check the telephone records of a burglarized business for the suspected time period of the burglary. The burglar may have called a friend or called home, and this type of lead could help solve a burglary rapidly.

✓ **Firearm Related Leads:** The type of firearms, ammunition, or firearm paraphernalia taken during the theft (e.g., only handguns or only assault weapons) should also be evaluated. Periodically, the investigator should check the ATF stolen firearms database, the NCIC recovered gun database, and ATF's LEAD to determine if the firearms stolen have been recovered anywhere, and the investigator has inadvertently not been notified by the systems. If recoveries have occurred, conduct the appropriate follow-up investigation to determine how the firearms arrived at their recovery point.

✓ **Shooting but No Firearm.** In thefts during which a shooting incident took place, no firearm was recovered, but NIBIN was able to identify the make, model and caliber of the firearm from a casing left at the scene, the investigator should periodically check with ATF's NTC or the local law enforcement agency for like gun-type recoveries. The criminal committing the FFL theft may sell, lose, otherwise dispose of the firearm, or be apprehended in another crime

with the firearm, and the firearm may be sitting in a law enforcement agency's evidence room. The investigator can also request a list of all like-gun traces in a specific area and recover those firearms for ballistic comparison to the projectiles and/or casings in custody.

✓ **Focusing on Suspects.** Solving an FFL theft is difficult for many reasons. Eyewitness accounts of robberies are not always accurate or reliable because the confrontation between robbers and witnesses is highly emotional and of short duration. In many cases, very little physical evidence is found at the scene. Consequently, what traces of evidence are found usually become crucial factors in focusing and concluding an investigation. Because the motive for robbery of a gun store is self-evident—to obtain firearms and money—determining why the crime was committed does not usually lead to the development of suspects. Above all, the investigator must be thorough and patient. Both eyewitness accounts and physical evidence should be used to reconstruct the crime and establish a timeline of events. No physical evidence should be overlooked or discounted. Many times, the value of evidence cannot be determined during the initial stages of an investigation but becomes evident, and crucial, as the investigative process continues to turn up additional information. To justify concluding a general inquiry and focusing an investigation on a specific suspect or group of suspects, the investigator must develop information that points to their possible guilt.

➤ **General Suspect Considerations.** Although primary consideration is given to the evidence and information collected, the investigator should not underestimate the importance of the personal characteristics, personality, attitudes, and habits of the suspect. Consider the total suspect. Does the suspect have the skills and knowledge needed to commit the robbery? Did the suspect have the means, opportunity, and capability? Does the suspect have any previous arrests or convictions for similar offenses where the modus operandi compares with the case under investigation? Is there any evidence or alibi that would place the suspect elsewhere at the time of the crime?

➤ **Deconfliction.** Conduct a full deconfliction of all names, addresses, phone numbers, and other information as they are encountered. Firearms theft and trafficking investigations routinely involve the jurisdiction of multiple local, state, and federal agencies and deconfliction is critical to preventing a blue on blue situation, needless interference in on-going investigations, and general investigative effectiveness. See Chapter 9 for a description of a complete deconfliction process. In the case of an FFL, any investigator should contact ATF to coordinate the investigation as FFLs are regulated by ATF and inevitably ATF records will be part of the investigation. Consider placing any suspects in ATF's FRNP suspect name file so the investigator will be alerted if any firearms or data comes into LEAD that is associated with the suspects name.

➤ **Cooperator.** Should one suspect in a multiple suspect investigation flip, the investigator should consider all the standard options to progress the investigation. The cooperating suspect may be either enlisted as a CI or the case AUSA may want them to secure an attorney and enter into a formal proffer or other type of cooperation agreement. Once the cooperator is able to provide assistance, they may be used to make recorded calls to other suspects to gather incriminating evidence, help locate and recover the stolen firearms, provide historical information on the other suspects and prior crimes, consent to the search of their phone for copies of communications with other suspects, conduct monitored and recorded meetings with the other suspects to purchase different types of evidence, and provide testimony before a grand jury about the crime.

➤ **Considering All Options.** Prior thefts may provide information as to potential suspects, or may indicate that fraudulent reporting of thefts is occurring for the purpose of insurance fraud. Accordingly, you should check the ATF Stolen Firearms Database, local police department records, and FFL insurance carrier and ISO records for prior thefts. If FFL fraudulent theft reporting is suspected, contact the ATF Stolen Firearms Programs to obtain copies of any ATF Forms 310.11, FFL Theft/Loss Report previously filed by the FFL. Oftentimes, these reports will be completed in the FFL's own handwriting, and false reports on those forms are a felony under Title 18 U.S.C. § 1001. Also check for the existence of recordings of the initial verbal theft report via telephone. Refer to the FFL Investigation section of this chapter for more information on this topic.

➢ **The Interview.** Once a suspect is identified or arrested, potentially the most important part of the investigation will be the defendant interview. If multiple suspects exist, each must be interviewed separately. If the suspects are not in custody, the interviews should be conducted simultaneously by multiple investigators to preclude coordination between the suspects. An investigator must have a working knowledge of all the facts, and use good interviewing techniques to make the interview effective. The defendant's interview can make or break a case, and the investigator will more than likely only have one chance to conduct an interview with the defendant. A fully successful investigation is one in which all suspects are arrested and successfully prosecuted, and all the firearms are recovered or accounted for and returned to the theft victims.

TYPE 6: INTERSTATE CARRIER THFT INVESTIGATION

Firearms are a valuable commodity, and are routinely targeted for theft and pilferage while they are being shipped in interstate or foreign commerce. These firearms are then trafficked and resold for profit and frequently find their way to the criminal element where they are used in a crime. The theft of any commodity having a value of over $100 is a federal felony under Title 18 U.S.C. § 659. However, a number of other federal firearms violations are involved when the commodity stolen is a firearm(s). Firearms moving between licensed manufacturers, wholesalers, and retailers get from point A to point B via interstate carrier shipments. These may be bulk shipments via a trucking, airline, or marine shipping carrier, or these may be smaller shipments via FedEx, UPS, DHL, or the USPS. This is a form of theft of firearms from an FFL, since these firearms are usually in transit from one FFL to another, and they belong to an FFL. Preventative and investigative techniques include the following;

✓ **Prevention and Deterrence.** Most thefts of firearms from interstate carriers are crimes of opportunity where someone has the ability to take a package containing firearms without being detected as opposed to truck hijackings or warehouse robberies where there may be victims and witnesses. If investigators have jurisdiction over an area that has frequent thefts of firearms from interstate carriers, maybe due to proximity to the shipping location of a major gun manufacturer, the investigator should remember that it is easier to prevent theft than solve a theft, and a deterrence and education program to assist a local carrier may be of value. Areas to assess would include:
  ➢ Access control for the building, warehouse, and shipping containers.
  ➢ Structural security to include any weaknesses in doors, windows, roof, or walls, the presence of a video system, lock and key control logs, and lighting considerations.
  ➢ Personnel security to include proper screenings to prevent infiltration of the labor force by criminals.
  ➢ Inventory security to include package scanning on each change or hands to have a digital

chain of custody, technical monitoring such as end to end real time embedded GPS tracking of packages, and requesting that gun manufacturers wrap their boxes in ways that do not display large commercial gun logos that attract the wrong kind of attention.

✓ **Enter Stolen Firearms into ATF Stolen Firearms Database and NCIC.** The first order of business following detection of a theft of firearms from an interstate carrier shipment is to ascertain how many firearms were stolen and their complete descriptions. As soon as a complete and accurate list of the firearms stolen is compiled, it is imperative that this information get reported to ATF on the ATF Form 3310.11, Federal Firearms Licensee Firearms Inventory Theft/Loss Report. In accordance with Title 18 U.S.C. § 923(g)(6) FFLs who have losses due to interstate theft are required to file this report with ATF within 48 hours of detecting the theft. ATF will enter the firearms into the ATF Stolen Firearms Database and NCIC so that ATF and investigators will be notified as any of the stolen firearms are recovered later.

✓ **ATF IOIs Can Assist in Determining the Description of those Firearms Stolen.** If a large number of firearms is taken, offer to the victim that ATF will bring in IOIs to go through the records and conduct a full reconciliation to determine what should be there and what is not there. This can be very helpful to the victims, as it is one less thing they need to deal with, and it is very helpful to the investigators to get a complete and accurate accounting of the firearms stolen.

✓ **CargoNet™.** Any investigator tasked with investigating a theft of firearms from an interstate carrier should call ATF for assistance. In addition, an investigator should consider joining CargoNet. This online service is free to law enforcement and, through CargoNet's alliance with the National Insurance Crime Bureau (NICB), law enforcement can use CargoNet to:
  ➤ upload cargo thefts individually or in batches using a system-to-system feed
  ➤ search the database for people, cargo, or vehicles
  ➤ analyze cargo theft trends
  ➤ carry out analysis to link common elements of multiple items, people, or events
  ➤ interact with other agencies and task forces

✓ **Video Systems and Interviews**. The investigator should contact the interstate carrier's security department and determine what kinds of video recordings and other records are maintained that may provide investigative leads. The investigator should expeditiously contact persons who may have been in a position to observe or participate in the theft. With respect to witnesses, these people may have never come forward and may deny that they saw the offense because of a desire "not to be involved" or their familiarity with the perpetrator. Others may not cooperate because they fear or have an antagonistic feeling toward law enforcement. An investigator must find a way to gain this person's trust to obtain the necessary information.

✓ **Interview.** The investigator will want to determine who the known person to handle the package was, and then conduct a full deconfliction and intelligence workup on that person, analyzing any prior criminal history for theft arrests, recent drug arrests indicating an addiction problem, or other noteworthy factors in their past or current associations. Once that information is gathered the investigator should conduct the interview. You should ask them how they think the firearm(s) were stolen and if they know of anyone who may have done it. If the person appears to be deceptive, the investigator may want to offer them a polygraph examination to rule them out.

✓ **Crime Scene Processing:** If there is an identified crime scene, such as a burglarized tractor trailer, processing the crime scene will be critically important to the investigation and, where available, this should be performed by trained crime scene investigator (CSI) technicians to gather all latent fingerprints, DNA, or other trace evidence, such as tool marks to cut a lock or pry open a door.

✓ **Modus Operandi.** Because theft is often a recidivist crime, a study of the modus operandi is of great importance. In the absence of physical evidence, the techniques used and mannerisms of the criminals are often the most valuable clues to their identity. Consider the types of firearms, ammunition, or firearms paraphernalia taken during the theft (e.g., only handguns or only assault weapons). Specific information concerning the theft and modus operandi should be documented and forwarded to ATF for entry into the stolen firearms database and for comparison against the modus operandi of other interstate thefts locally and nationally. This may yield information that could link the suspect(s) to other interstate thefts in a specific area or across jurisdictions.

✓ **Interstate Carrier Records.** Check the local police department records, CargoNet records, and interstate carriers' insurance carrier records for prior thefts involving the same shipping origin or destination points. Prior thefts may provide information as to potential suspects. If prior theft reports are obtained, ensure that all stolen firearms from those thefts are in NCIC, and check to determine if any have been recovered.

✓ **Firearms Recovery Leads.** During the investigation, recoveries of these firearms may be found through periodic checks of the ATF Stolen Firearms Database or of the NCIC recovered gun file. If recoveries are found, obtain recovery reports and conduct an investigative follow-up to determine any potential relationship between the possessor, the recovery date, the recovery location of the interstate carrier, and the date of loss. Also determine if multiple stolen firearms are being recovered in close proximity to one another or over a widely dispersed pattern.

✓ **Interstate Carrier Employee Theft Types.** There are instances where the theft is committed by an employee of the interstate carrier and not an outsider. The following are the types of methods of theft an investigator should look for if interstate carrier employee theft is being considered.

  ➢ **Carry Outs**: An employee picks up a package containing firearms, conceals it in some manner, and walks out of the warehouse with it or secrets it in a location (e.g., above a drop ceiling in a warehouse restroom) for later retrieval.

  ➢ **Throw Outs**: An employee picks up a package containing firearms and throws it in a dumpster or over a compound fence, retrieving the firearms at a later time.

  ➢ **Over Labeling**: After a package has been scanned and entered into the system an employee "over labels"; that is, places a shipping label bearing the employee's address or other address such as a mail drop OVER the true shipping label on a package containing firearms. This will cause the package to go to the location designated by the employee rather than the originally designated destination.

  ➢ **Large Shipment - Select Package Pilferage**: An employee sees a large gun shipment containing multiple firearms boxes, removes one or more firearms from a few of the packages in the center of the shipment, and then leaves the building with them. Often an FFL may not check inside every box on a large shipment of firearms. As a result, this theft may go undetected for days or months. Further, if detected many months later, the

FFL may believe this is a theft by their employee, or a loss due to an inventory error of some kind, rather than associating it with an interstate theft many days or months earlier.

Standard Investigative Techniques. Straight-forward investigative techniques are useful in interstate carrier theft investigations occurring via throw outs, carry outs, or over labeling. The investigator should consider surveillance, employee interviews, carrier records examination, and follow-up investigation on any firearm recoveries.

Examine carrier records and systems that are available, as the carrier may have electronic tracking systems that can retrieve information concerning the destination of packages, if you can identify the origination point. These systems may also be queried for packages that have been sent to specific suspect addresses. Identify all addresses that over labeled packages may have been forwarded to, as well as any residents of those locations, and look for a link/relationship to the suspected employee.

✓ **Coordination with Carrier Security.** Work with the carrier's security coordinator to look for evidence such as discarded packages or packages of firearms yet to be picked up by the criminal that may be located in the trash dumpsters or other facility locations.

✓ **Deconfliction.** As suspects are developed, conduct a full deconfliction of all names, addresses, phone numbers, and other information as these are encountered. Firearms theft and trafficking investigations routinely involve the jurisdiction of multiple local, state, and federal agencies, and deconfliction is critical to preventing a blue on blue situation, needless interference in on-going investigations, and general investigative effectiveness. See Chapter 9 for a description of a complete deconfliction process. Consider placing any suspects in ATF's FRNP suspect name file so the investigator will be alerted if any firearms or data comes into LEAD that is associated with the suspects name.

✓ **Full Intelligence Workup.** A full intelligence workup should be performed on all suspects. A full online profile workup should be performed to determine what OSINT is available where the suspect may be talking about their new guns or showing off firearms in pictures that may be the stolen firearms.

✓ **Trash Pulls.** Obtaining discarded trash from a suspect's residence may also yield such evidence. Discarded package material at a suspect's residence is strong evidence in an investigation implicating the suspect in the theft; moreover, the packaging material may bear the suspect's latent fingerprints.

✓ **Trace and Physical Evidence.** For any packaging or other materials found with search warrants, searches with carrier security, or trash pulls, the materials should be submitted to a laboratory and examined for the presence of latent fingerprints and DNA for later comparison to know samples from suspects.

✓ **Electronic Communications Device Analysis.** Investigators should get a court order for cell phone historical data as well as cell phone call logs of all suspects as they are identified so that their information can be analyzed. Review the geo-location record of all suspects' cell phones to identify other potential suspects, drop sites for firearms, and possible mailbox drop sites. Investigators should make sure to use language in the application for the court order that will allow the initial court order to be used in subsequent requests to identify subscriber information. See Appendix D for examples.

✓ **Cooperator.** Should one suspect in a multiple suspect investigation flip, the investigator should consider all the standard options to progress the investigation. The cooperating suspect may be either enlisted as a CI or the case AUSA may want them to secure an attorney and enter into a formal proffer or other type of cooperation agreement. Once the cooperator is able to provide assistance, they may be used to make recorded calls to other suspects to gather incriminating evidence, help locate and recover stolen firearms, provide historical information on other suspects and prior crimes, conduct monitored and recorded meetings with other suspects to purchase evidence, and provide testimony before a grand jury about the crime.

✓ **The Interview.** Once a suspect is identified or arrested, potentially the most important part of the investigation will be the defendant interview. If multiple suspects exist, each must be interviewed separately. If the suspects are not in custody, the interviews should be conducted simultaneously by multiple investigators to preclude coordination between the suspects. An investigator must have a working knowledge of all the facts and use good interviewing techniques to make the interview effective. The defendant's interview can make or break a case, and the investigator will more than likely only have one chance to conduct an interview with the defendant. A fully successful investigation is one in which all suspects are arrested and successfully prosecuted, and all the firearms are recovered or accounted for and returned to the theft victims.

TYPE 7: FIREARMS IMPORT TRAFFICKING AND FRAUD INVESTIGATION

Firearms import fraud leads to the illegal importation of thousands of firearms into the U.S each year, the loss of FAET revenue, and the distribution of untraceable firearms into the domestic marketplace.

For firearms, firearms parts, castings, and flats to be lawfully imported into the U.S. they must be brought in by a licensed importer that has secured approval for the importation from ATF via an ATF Form 6, Application and Permit for Importation of Firearms.

Once an ATF Form 6 is approved the importer has up to 1 year to complete the import and may also decide not to complete the import. If the importation is completed, the importer must submit an ATF Form 6A to the ATF FEIB listing all the firearms that were imported.

In general, firearms must be suitable for sporting purposes or be a Curios and Relic to be approved for importation into the U.S. All handguns must also meet certain prerequisites involving size and safety in order to have a "qualifying score" on an ATF Form 4590, which is a "Factoring Criteria for Weapons." Foreign-made military handguns and long guns in their original configuration may not be imported unless they are curios and relics.

Other limiting importation factors include the 1998 VRA Treaty signed between the U.S. and the Russian Federation to limit the importation of firearms and ammunition into the U.S. from Russia. In that agreement there is a list of firearms that are exempt and can be imported under Title 22 C.F.R. § 447.52(b)(1)(i)(ii).

In addition to the limitations placed on Russian made firearms under the VRA, the State Department has placed other limitations and embargos on firearms manufactured in and originating from other countries which you must be aware of when investigating an illegal importation case. These limitations are delineated in 22 CFR §§ 447.52 (Import Restrictions Applicable to Certain Countries) and 447.57.

Firearms import fraud often involves the illegal importation of firearms into the United States via a scheme to make the importation appear to be legal and often to avoid the payment of excise taxes or costs associated with properly marking imported firearms. Agents may be alerted to potential firearms import fraud in a variety of ways.

✓ **Constructed Sales and Fraud.** Investigators should review the amount of Firearms and Ammunition Excise Tax (FAET) being paid on the importation of firearms and ammunition for certain imports by certain importers in their area. If the amounts appear significantly low compared to the volume of firearms and ammunition being imported investigators should examine the relationship between the importer and the first retail dealer to whom the imports were sold. The Excise Tax on firearms imports is 10% for handguns and 11% for long guns based on the profit between the importer's cost and the first retail sale price. If an importer brings in a handgun that cost them $100 and their first sale is for $200, then a 10% excise tax is due on the $100 profit. An illegal constructed sale practice occurs when the importer and first retail dealer are in an arrangement to fraudulently avoid this tax by claiming that the first sale only netted a tiny profit which greatly reduces the FAET due, and then the second retail sale reflects the true value of the firearms. If an importer constructs a sale to indicate they only made $10 on each handgun sold on the first retail sale rather than $210, they reduce the FAET owed from $21 on the $210 down to $1 on the $10 claimed. Importations often come in large lots so the reduction in FAET of $20 per imported firearm on the importation or 5000 firearms is $100,000 not paid in FAET to the Department of the U.S. Treasury.

✓ **VRA Treaty Fraud.** Investigators should review the records of firearms manufactured in the former Soviet Union or Warsaw Pact Nations that are imported into the U.S. Under the VRA treaty these firearms are not importable into the. U.S unless they have been in a non-embargoed country for 5 or more years. Because of this, firearms in locations such as the Ukraine are not importable into the U.S. and have a lower value. Importers can purchase the firearms for less, then create false documents to show they were actually in another non-embargoed country for 5 years to make them legally importable in the U.S. Document authentication efforts through agency attachés or Interpol may be possible in determining the validity of such documents.

✓ **Embargoed Country Import Fraud.** Non-sporting firearms from China, such as SKS rifles, may not be imported into the U.S., and as a result they have a low price on the world market due to lack of demand. A corrupt importer may purchase these firearms at a greatly reduced price, move them to a non-embargoed country where they will have the Chinese marking removed, and will add other allowable markings making these firearms appear to be legally importable into the U.S. If an investigator suspects this is going on, this may be detectable by submitting one of the firearms for laboratory analysis to find the prior markings.

✓ **Armor Piercing Ammunition Import Fraud.** Armor piercing ammunition may not be imported into the U.S., and as a result this type of ammunition has a low price on the world market due to lack of demand. A corrupt importer may purchase this ammunition at a greatly reduced price, repackage it in packaging that makes no reference to armor piercing, ensure that the ammunition projectiles do not have the required black tips, and then import this into the U.S. as non-armor piercing ammunition. This is more common for .762 caliber ammunition and other military grade ammunition from foreign source countries. Examination of several bullets randomly picked from the cases within the shipment would prove useful. The SME examiner would use a bullet puller to separate the projectile from the casing. They would then use a magnet to see if there is enough steel in the projective to be picked up by a magnet. If the magnet picks up the bullet, this is an indication of a steel armor piercing core. Next, the investigator would use a small bolt cutter to cut the projectile in half and visually examine the interior for the steel core. Finally, the SME examiner would send a bullet to ATF's FATD for classification as armor piercing or non-armor piercing. Armor piercing ammunition cannot be imported in to the U.S. and would be forfeitable.

✓ **External Safety Installation Fraud.** Recovered foreign-made handguns that do not have a positive manually operated external safety as required by the ATF Factoring Criteria may be an indication of an importation fraud. Many foreign military handguns, such as the Soviet bloc firearms, do not have external safeties. Importers are required to install external safeties on these handguns before they can be approved by ATF for importation. However, once the firearm is in the U.S., a private citizen purchasing the firearm does not violate federal law by removing the safety.

✓ **Unsuccessful Trace Data Indicators.** Investigators should review the "unsuccessful trace data" in their area and determine the volume of traces that were not successful due to "no importer markings". Investigators may want to conduct follow-up on those firearms to see if they really don't have importer markings. If they do not, there may be import fraud occurring. Title 27 CFR § 478.112 (d)(2) allows an importer 15-days from the time of import into the U.S. to make the required markings and modifications. These may be firearms that were imported and then re-sold before the importer markings were placed on them or before a Cyrillic serial number was replaced with a U.S numerical serial number. For an importer who brings in thousands of firearms, the requirement to place markings on all those firearms within 15 days of their import is a cost. If the importer can get those out of a bonded warehouse before the markings are placed on them, the importer will save that cost and be able to sell firearms that are untraceable back to them.

The above examples may indicate that an unscrupulous importer secured an approved ATF Form 6 to import firearms and, rather than bear the cost of installing required external safety's or inscribing proper serial number and importer markings, the importer managed to simply sell the firearms without doing so. Individuals found to possess such firearms should be interviewed in an attempt to identify the illegal source. One individual possessing one such firearm may not rise to the level of a case that would merit prosecution. However, finding an importer engaged in import fraud involving hundreds or thousands of firearms would merit significant attention.

Prevention, Deterrence, and Detection. To prevent, deter, and detect import fraud at the point of entry, prior to having any improperly or illegally imported firearms enter commerce in the U.S. firearms marketplace, ATF and CBP at the national level, or local ATF and CBP investigators may partner together to examine certain types of firearms or ammunition imports for indicators of fraud Instituting a prevention, deterrence, and detection initiative will also help foster a level of cooperative compliance from the industry. When everyone knows no one is looking, some will take advantage of that; however, once it is known that attention is being paid, the risk of being caught returns, and people comply with the law. A well-planned program of prevention, deterrence, and detection protects the public from illegally imported firearms and does not interfere with the lawful commerce in firearms.

The following is a basic overview of the current process for importing firearms, certain firearm parts, and ammunition:

✓ An FFL submits an ATF eForm 6 or paper version Form 6 (ATF F 5330.3A), Application and Permit for Importation of Firearms, Ammunition, and Implements of War to ATF's FEIB for consideration and authorization.

✓ ATF's FEIB reviews the application to ensure that the items to be imported can be imported into the United States (i.e., firearms are not from embargoed countries or VRA-affected controlled countries, and plans to add U.S. serial numbers and external safeties are delineated).

✓ ATF's FEIB determines the items as described on the ATF Form 6 may be imported and they issue a Permit Number that is affixed in the upper left-hand block of the ATF Form 6 and returned to the importer. In making this decision, ATF's FEIB usually does not inspect an actual sample or digital image of the items to be imported. The decision is based on the honor system that the importer will only import what they described on the ATF Form 6.

✓ Once the ATF Form 6 is approved by ATF's FEIB, the FFL Importer has 2 years to conduct the importation, and at no time is the FFL required to contract ATF to advise where and when the importation will take place. ATF has no way of knowing where or when the importation will take place or if the importation will take place at all. ATF is only notified of the import after is completed if the FFL Importer files the ATF Form 6A listing the items that have been imported.

✓ DHS-CBP is the agency that encounters the firearm or ammunition importation as it enters the U.S. CBP does not routinely notify ATF for assistance with examining when they encounter these importations. In some instances, CBP personnel will see the approved ATF Form 6 and assume that the items have already been scrutinized by ATF since there is an ATF approved the Form 6, and therefore further inspection of the importation is not warranted.

The following is a basic overview of a process to close the gap in enforcement and ensure that only those items approved for importation by ATF are actually allowed to be imported by CBP:

✓ ATF and CBP partner to determine import scrutiny parameters. This may involve imports of certain kinds of firearms or ammunition (e.g., AK47 variants or .762 caliber ammunition), certain amounts of firearms (e.g., shipments of over 50 firearms or 1000 rounds of ammunition), firearms or ammunition from certain countries, or firearms where additional features or the addition of a U.S. serial number are required for importation and release from a bonded warehouse.

✓ ATF begins to notify CBP of approved importations that meet established parameters and provides CBP with copies of the approved ATF Form 6.

✓ CBP places a watch for this information in their Automated Targeting System (ATS) at their National Targeting Center (CBP-NTC), so that when the import does arrive in the U.S., the ATS would advise any CBP inspector coming across the importation to call the designated ATF Point of Contact (POC) to arrange for Firearms SME assistance in the inspection of the items to ensure that what is being imported matches what was approved for importation on the ATF Form 6. ATF SMEs may be agents, members of ATF's FATD, IOIs, or special contractors who have an in-depth knowledge of the firearms import provisions and firearms nomenclature. ATF SMEs and CBP personnel would look for the following:

- ➤ Conduct a comparative analysis of the items being imported to the description of items approved for import on the ATF Form 6.
- ➤ Examine firearm receivers to ensure that the caliber and country of origin markings on the receiver match those that were approved on the ATF Form 6.
- ➤ Examine firearm receivers for signs of the removal of prior markings that may indicate removal of marking indicating the receivers were made in an embargoed country.
- ➤ Examine certain types of ammunition for the presence of undeclared armor piercing ammunition.
- ➤ Consider follow-up verification through overseas attachés to determine the authenticity of a letter certifying any VRA affected firearms were actually in a non-embargoed country for 5 or more years prior to import.
- ➤ For other items on the enhanced scrutiny list, CBP would notify ATF when those items clear the border zone or a bonded warehouse and are allowed to move into the U.S. This would afford ATF the opportunity to visit that FFL importer to ensure importer markings, proper U.S serial numbers, or after-market safeties have been added to the firearms within 15 days of import (Title 27 C.F.R. § 478.112(d)(2)) and before they move into commerce. This would also allow ATF to monitor first retail sale activity to determine if constructed sales are being used to fraudulently undervalue the imported items and illegally reduce or avoid paying FAET.
- ➤ Any items identified during the inspection as being imported illegally would be seized and forfeited by CBP, since the items have still not cleared CBP and have not officially entered into the U.S. Illegally imported items can be administratively forfeited by CBP under:
  - ○ Title 18 U.S.C. § 545 – Smuggling goods into the U.S. and,
  - ○ Title 26 U.S.C. § 2778 - Import Provisions of the Arms Export Control
- ➤ CBP would provide ATF with 1 sample of each type of illegally imported item to be maintained as evidence for further investigation. Illegally imported items can be administratively forfeited by ATF as the items were imported in violation of Title 18 U.S.C. § 922(1) – Illegal importation of firearms (See also Title 27 C.F.R. § 478 Subpart G- Importation and Title 27 C.F.R. § 447 Subpart E – Permits)

Investigation of Detected Violations. Post-seizure criminal investigation would be conducted jointly between ATF and HSI special agents in accordance with their existing June 2009 MOU. The following are some basic steps for that subsequent investigation:

- ✓ **Deconfliction.** As suspects are developed, conduct a full deconfliction of all names, addresses, phone numbers, and other information as these are encountered. Firearms theft and trafficking investigations routinely involve the jurisdiction of multiple local, state, and federal agencies, and deconfliction is critical to preventing a blue on blue situation, needless interference in on-going investigations, and general investigative effectiveness. See Chapter 9 for a description of a complete deconfliction process.

- ✓ **Full Intelligence Workup.** A full intelligence workup should be performed on all suspects. A full online profile workup should be performed to determine what OSINT is available where the suspect may be talking about their new guns or showing off firearms in pictures that may be the stolen firearms.

- ✓ **Prior Importations Examination.** Contact ATF's FEIB to secure copies of previously approved ATF Form 6's for this importer to determine if there are prior shipments that should be scrutinized for past undetected violations.

✓ **ATF FRNP.** Consider placing any suspects in ATF's FRNP suspect name file so the investigator will be alerted if any firearms or data comes into LEAD that is associated with the suspect's name. Consider placing certain previously imported firearms into the FRNP so the investigator will be alerted when these firearms are recovered so they may be examined.

✓ **NCIC Recovered Gun File.** Query any previously imported firearms being scrutinized in the NCIC recovered gun file to determine if these have been previously recovered in crimes and are available for examination.

✓ **Authenticating VRA Certification Letters.** For VRA affected firearms, work with overseas attachés and Interpol or use MLATs to try and authenticate any certification indicating that these firearms were in a non-embargoed country for 5 years or more prior to importation to the U.S. A false letter attached to an ATF Form 6, and any false statements on an ATF Form 6 with respect to the firearm type or true country of origin would be a violation of Title 18 U.S.C. 1001.

✓ **Bribery of Foreign Officials.** Determine why any foreign official might participate in arranging for a false VRA certification letter, why one importer seems to have a stranglehold on all the available firearms in one particular country, or why any other suspicious activity that may need approval from a foreign official may be taking place. It is illegal for a U.S. citizen or business to bribe a foreign official under the Foreign Corrupt Practices Act (FCPA) of 1977, Title 15 U.S.C. § 78.

✓ **Border Crossings and Financial Issues.** Determine when suspects from the U.S. may have traveled to foreign countries to meet with officials by checking TECs for border crossings. As part of a financial workup, check TECs for CTRs, Reports of International Transportation of CMIR (Customs Form 4790), Reports of FBAR (Treasury Form 90-22.1), and FinCEN for SARs as well.

✓ **ATF FATD.** Send all suspected illegally imported firearms and ammunition to ATF's FATD for classification and to establish that these are in a configuration that violates the law.

✓ **Electronic Communications Device Analysis.** Investigators should get a court order for cell phone historical data as well as cell phone call logs of all suspects as they are identified so that their information can be analyzed. Review the call records to determine what officials the suspects have been communicating with and the historical geo-location data to observe travels. See Appendix D for examples.

✓ **Cooperator.** Should one suspect in a multiple suspect investigation flip, the investigator should consider all the standard options to progress the investigation. The cooperating suspect may be either enlisted as a CI or the case AUSA may want them to secure an attorney and enter into a formal proffer or other type of cooperation agreement. Once the cooperator is able to provide assistance, they may be used to make recorded calls to other suspects to gather incriminating evidence, help locate and recover the stolen firearms, provide historical information on the other suspects and prior crimes, conduct monitored and recorded meetings with the other suspects to purchase different types of evidence, and provide testimony before a grand jury about the crime.

✓ **Controlled Delivery.** In the case of any type of import fraud, a cooperator may be able to help investigators track an incoming illegal import for seizure and forfeiture following a controlled delivery to other suspects.

✓ **The Interview.** Once a suspect is identified or arrested, potentially the most important part of the investigation will be the defendant interview. If multiple suspects exist, each must be interviewed separately. If the suspects are not in custody, the interviews should be conducted simultaneously by multiple investigators to preclude coordination between the suspects. An investigator must have a working knowledge of all the facts and use good interviewing techniques to make the interview effective. The defendant's interview can make or break a case, and the investigator will more than likely only have one chance to conduct an interview with the defendant.

✓ **Violations.** The various charges that apply to import fraud as described above include, but are not limited to:
  ➢ Title 18 U.S.C. § 1001: False statements and representations (on the ATF Form 6).
  ➢ Title 18 U.S.C. § 545: Smuggling into the U.S.
  ➢ Title 26 U.S.C. §§ 6651(a)(1) and (2): Failure to file a required return or failure to pay any tax due as part of FAET.
  ➢ Title 18 U.S.C. §922(l): Illegal importation of firearms (an SUA for money laundering).
  ➢ Title 18 U.S.C. § 1956: Money laundering.
  ➢ Title 18 U.S.C. §923(i): Licensing violation for failure to place all required identification data on an imported firearm.
  ➢ Title 18 U.S.C. § 371: Klein Conspiracy.
  ➢ Title 18 U.S.C. §922(a)(1)(A): Importation of firearms without an importer's license.

CASE STUDY: OPERATION SALT MINE SURPLUS

United States v. Baltz – Southern District of Florida - 9:05-cr-80209-DMM

In April of 2005 ATF West Palm Beach, Florida Field Office special agents initiated an investigation of an FFL importer and FFL retailer following a referral of information from an ATF IOI indicating that during an inspection of the FFL importer there appeared to be a number of firearms with no records and with improper markings.

ATF special agents arrived at the FFL importer's place of business that same day and found 625 Russian-made Tokarev semi-automatic pistols with no importer markings or proper U.S. serial numbers. The firearms were seized for forfeiture as they had been illegally imported in violation of Title 18 U.S.C. § 922(l). Investigation revealed that the importer had imported 1000 Tokarev pistols with an approved ATF Form 6; however, on the form, the importer indicated that they would add the U.S. serial numbers and an external safety as required by law for importation. The importer was able to import the firearms and clear CBP. However, he did not make the proper markings or add the external safety within 15 days of importation as required by law. In fact, the FFL importer had sold 375 of the Tokarev pistols at the West Palm Beach Gun Show that prior weekend, and all the firearms had no importer markings or U.S. serial numbers, so these are untraceable guns.

Figure 10.8 More than 600 Illegally Imported Tokarev Pistols Seized by ATF in West Palm Beach, FL in 2006, and on Their Way to the Smelter in 2007

Source: Authors Collection

Investigation also revealed that proper documentation showing these Russian-made Tokarev pistols were in a non-embargoed Russian affiliated country for at least 5 years was not available. The firearms had been imported in violation of the 1996 Voluntary Restraint Agreement (VRA) treaty. As the investigation progressed, it was determined that the importer FFL had paid an individual to get a retail FFL and go into the business to serve as a straw retail FFL that the importer would make the first retail sale of all imported firearms to. The sale would be for a very minimal profit so that the FAET tax would be calculated on this fraudulently undervalued profit rather than fair market value. This is an illegal practice known as a "constructed sale". ATF special agents interviewed the straw retail FFL and was able to gain that person's cooperation in the investigation.

Figure 10.9 Firearms on a Display Table in Ukraine Salt Mine

Source: Authors Collection

This cooperator stated that a shipment of 55 German Lugers was just about to take place, and the agents put a plan in place to conduct a controlled delivery of the firearms that would document the entire fraud from start to finish and culminate in seizure of the firearms and the arrest of the FFL importer. At this point the cooperator, under the direction of ATF agents, made recorded phone calls to the FFL importer to document how the fraudulent importation would take place, how much the profit of the fraudulent first retail sale would be and how much should be charged for fair market value during the actual second retail sale in which they would make their profit. In July 2005 a shipment of 55 German Luger pistols was imported into the U.S., cleared CBP, and was transferred to the FFL importer's home. A federal search warrant was served to recover the firearms on that day. Also recovered were various original import documents that should have been stored at the business location and German Waffen tool marking stamps that the FFL would use to stamp on the Lugers to fraudulently increase their value by claiming they had rare proof marks. During the search warrant, an in-depth interview with the FFL importer was conducted, during which the FFL importer made numerous false statements to ATF special agents.

In December 2005 ATF special agents arrested the FFL importer based on a federal grand jury indictment for the illegal importation of firearms (18 U.S.C. § 922(l)), obstruction of justice (18 U.S.C. § 1503), failure to pay proper FAET based on constructed sales (Title 26 U.S.C. § 4216(b)), and false statements to agents (18 U.S.C. § 1001). The importer FFL was subsequently held in pre-trial detention, pled guilty to illegal importation and excise tax violations, and agreed to forfeit more than $59,000 in currency and a vehicle.

During the investigation, ATF special agents learned the following regarding sources of firearms for illegal importation. The FFL importer had frequently traveled to the Ukraine to purchase large lots of firearms for importation into the U.S. These firearms were former Soviet Union military surplus stored in the Ukraine Salt Mines because of their ideal temperature and humidity levels. Following the fall of the Soviet Union, these firearms became a profitable asset owned by the Ukraine[cxxxiii]. The FFL importer arrested in this case is not the only U.S. based importer who has been to the Ukraine to bid on batches of firearms. The FFL importer arrested in this case would purchase firearms that would be transshipped to Germany where a company would be paid to create a false document showing that the firearms had been in Germany for 5 years when in fact they had just arrived. The firearms would then be imported into the U.S. based on these fraudulent documents. The firearms available for purchase in the Ukraine Salt Mines included AK-47 variants, Tokarev and Makarov pistols, PPSH41 machine guns, German Lugers and P-38 pistols, CZ Scorpions, as well as numerous types of high capacity magazines.[cxxxiv]

Figure 10.10 *Ukrainian Military Officers Negotiating an Arms Deal at Lunch with U.S. Firearm Importers*

Source: Authors Collection

In May 2006 the FFL importer was sentenced to 30 months in federal prison followed by 36 months supervised release.

TYPE 8: FIREARMS EXPORT TRAFFICKING AND SMUGGLING INVESTIGATION

The illegal export and trafficking of U.S. sourced firearms and firearms parts to violent gangs, cartels, transnational organized crime, and terrorists has a destabilizing effect on emerging democracies, fuels intolerable levels of violence, and drains limited resources. Significant numbers of U.S. sourced crime guns are recovered and traced in Mexico, Guatemala, Brazil, Colombia, Jamaica, and Haiti, to name a few. An investigator looking into firearms export trafficking and

smuggling should be coordinating with both ATF and his, as both of these agencies have jurisdiction and important information and resources available to assist in these types of investigations.

Firearms export trafficking and smuggling investigations will routinely focus on crime guns sourced through straw purchase rings, secondary source markets, unlicensed dealer sources, as well as large-scale unlicensed manufacturing of trafficked/smuggled firearms parts, flats, and castings trafficking. These investigations may also focus on land, sea, or air smuggling routes and involve coordination with CBP and foreign law enforcement officials to intercept shipments and prevent the international trafficking of firearms. Combatting illegal firearms export trafficking and smuggling starts with leads. Leads come in a variety of forms:

✓ **Indicators.** Review Chapter 7, Firearm Trafficking Indicators, and in specific the indicators based on crime gun trace data, FFL records, purchaser behaviors, firearm parts kits, and ghost guns, and gun show, flea markets, and secondary source markets. ATF has much of the firearms trafficking indicator information.

✓ **Border Intercepts.** CBP routinely intercepts all manner of incoming and outgoing smuggling at border crossings. Leads of seized shipments of firearms are very important for investigators. These provide opportunities for interviews with the possessors, crime gun tracing to determine origin points, as well as other persons and FFLs to interview, leads on the vehicle used to transport the shipment, and leads on the modus operandi of the smuggling attempt (e.g., type of concealment method used, identification of a body shop that makes a particular type of hide, etc.). CBP and HSI have the border intercept intelligence information.

✓ **ATF CGIC Referral.** ATF CGICs are fusion centers for CGI, and they routinely analyze aggregate crime gun data and create actionable intelligence referrals regarding all types of illegal firearms trafficking, including firearms export trafficking. Investigators should review Chapter 6 for an itemization of the various databases members of an ATF CGIC have access to for lead development.

✓ **HUMINT.** Sources of information from CIs or cooperating defendants can be excellent sources of leads to initiate a firearms export trafficking investigation.

Once a lead is received, there are numerous different firearms export trafficking schemes, and the investigative techniques used will be case specific. Investigators may want to consider the following investigative techniques.

✓ **Deconfliction.** As suspects are developed, conduct a full deconfliction of all names, addresses, phone numbers, and other information as these are encountered. Firearms theft and trafficking investigations routinely involve the jurisdiction of multiple local, state, and federal agencies, and deconfliction is critical to preventing a blue on blue situation, needless interference in on-going investigations, and general investigative effectiveness. See Chapter 9 for a description of a complete deconfliction process.

✓ **Full Intelligence Workup.** A full intelligence workup should be performed on all suspects. A full online profile workup should be performed to determine what OSINT is available where the suspect may be talking about their activities or showing off firearms in pictures that may be the stolen firearms.

✓ **Border Crossings and Financial Issues.** Determine when suspects from the U.S. may have traveled to foreign countries to by checking TECs for border crossings. As part of a financial workup, check TECS for CTRs, Reports of International Transportation of CMIR (Customs Form 4790), Reports of FBAR (Treasury Form 90-22.1), and FinCEN for SARs as well.

✓ **ATF FRNP.** Consider placing any suspects in ATF's FRNP suspect name file so the investigator will be alerted if any firearms or data comes into LEAD that is associated with the suspects name. Consider placing certain previously imported firearms into the FRNP so the investigator will be alerted when these firearms are recovered so they may be examined.

✓ **ATFs LEAD.** Query all suspects and addresses in ATF's LEAD system to determine if these have been previously involved with recovered crime guns.

✓ **NCIC Recovered Gun File.** Query any purchased firearms in the NCIC recovered gun file to determine if these have been previously recovered in crimes and if yes, conduct follow-up to gather incident reports and interview the possessor concerning how they acquired the firearm.

✓ **Crime Gun Intelligence.** Firearms intercepted during attempts to illegally export, or firearms recovered in a foreign country could yield a trove of information important to the investigation.
  ➢ **NCIC Checks.** Check recovered firearms in NCIC to determine if these are stolen. If they are, that is a significant lead to follow up on.
  ➢ **Crime Gun Tracing.** Ensure that recovered firearms are traced immediately; however, the investigator may want to ask that the ATF NTC only trace to the retail FFL and not contact that retail FFL for the purchaser information if they suspect the FFL is involved in the trafficking. The investigator can then go to the FFL and look through the records to find the purchaser rather than asking the FFL to identify the purchaser, as that could compromise the investigation.
  ➢ **NIBIN.** All recovered firearms purchased should be submitted to a lab for test-firing and the submission of the test fires to NIBIN to determine if the firearm was used in a prior shooting.

✓ **ATF FATD.** Send any seized firearms parts kits, castings, and flats and ammunition to ATF's FATD for classification under the law and to establish if these are finished enough to constitute a firearm, or are just parts and castings that are not firearms but still are illegal to export without proper approvals.

✓ **Obliterated Serial Numbers.** If any recovered firearms have obliterated serial numbers they should be submitted to a laboratory to attempt to raise the serial numbers and then traced through the ATF NTC if whole or partial serial numbers are recovered. A successfully raised serial number often leads to trace results in which numerous firearms were purchased from an FFL and the purchaser made no attempt to conceal their identity or connection to the trafficker since they assumed that without the serial number the firearm was untraceable.

✓ **Gun Show Involvement**. If the firearms being purchased for illegal export are coming from a gun show or flea market, determine whether the venue utilizes security cameras and makes recordings of venue activities. If so, consider obtaining copies of those recordings to see if any of the firearm purchase activities by the suspects have been recorded. If a gun show is a significant source of trafficked firearms, investigators may want to consider conducting a Secondary Source Market Initiative at the location.

✓ **Electronic Communications Device Analysis.** Investigators should get a court order for cell phone historical data as well as cell phone call logs of all suspects as they are identified so that their information can be analyzed. Review the call records to determine which suspects are communicating and what are suspects are involved, along with historical geo-location data to observe travels. As suspects are identified, investigators may want to secure a court order for a PEN or DNR on phones, email or other communication methods being used by the suspect. See Appendix D for examples.

✓ **Lookouts.** If the firearms are being driven across land borders, ensure that a "lookout" or "stop and search" request on the suspects has been entered in TECS and the CBP-NTC ANS so that the suspect can be stopped at the border and properly searched.

✓ **Common Carrier Smuggling.** If the firearms are being smuggled out of the U.S. by being placed in luggage on a bus, airline, or passenger ship, check with local carriers and determine if reservations exist for the identified suspects. This will provide special agents with the opportunity to surveil the unlawful export attempt and intercept the firearms. If the suspect is not disclosing that their luggage or packages contain firearms, this may serve as the basis for additional federal charges. In addition, have the carrier check their records to identify any previous trips by the suspect. This may also provide you with the opportunity to obtain terminal video surveillance from the dates on which the suspect travelled, determine travel frequency for scheduling independent surveillance, and provide suspect dates to search for firearms purchase records at source dealers. In this type of case, in the event that firearms are discovered in luggage used by the suspect, investigators may want to coordinate with TSA, CBP, or other security personnel to only seize (or "rip") the firearms while allowing the suspect to leave. This will prevent the firearms from being illegally exported, and potentially allow the investigation to continue. The investigator should use this technique if there are other suspects in the organization yet to be identified or if the investigation must continue to fully dismantle the unlawful organization. The suspect who is "ripped" will probably assume that the firearms were discovered and stolen by baggage handlers somewhere in the process. Document the extent of the ITAR violations and the illegal profits realized by the organization for potential asset forfeiture.

✓ **Traffickers Using Airlines.** Some firearms export traffickers, such as those from the Caribbean or South America, will use quick airline trips to obtain and illegally export firearms. They may fly into the U.S, meet with pre-arranged straw purchasers, hail a taxi to take them to the FFL, make their purchases, take a taxi to a shipping location and ship the firearms out using FedEx, UPS, or other common delivery service. They will then take a taxi back to the airport and fly out. If this is the case and investigators have the assistance of the FFL, it may be possible for the investigator to have the FFL hail a taxi or Uber™ that arrives is actually an UC vehicle with a UC agent driving. The UC could then take the suspect to the shipping location and take them to the airport, while other agents intercept the package. The UC may also be able to gain incriminating conversation during the ride. The suspect could be allowed to leave the country for a later arrest, or arrested at some point in the UC vehicle journey. All UC conversation must be recorded.

Primary Consideration. Public safety is always the primary consideration in firearms trafficking investigations, and the bottom line is that an investigator should never let trafficked guns walk unless there is a fully vetted and supported operational plan to keep them under constant surveillance until they can be safely seized.

In situations where a straw purchaser obtains firearms and there was not time for the investigator to have a pre-approved operational plan, if sufficient probable cause exists to seize and forfeit the firearms, the investigator should consider several options to recover the firearms, while at the same time allowing the investigation to continue to fully identify and dismantle any other members of a larger trafficking organization. These options are referred to as unplanned enforcement actions and must be done on the fly using all of the training, knowledge, and experience that the investigators know, in order to safely execute and protect public safety:

✓ **Traffic Stop.** Have a participating state or local marked law enforcement vehicle pull over the straw purchaser in a traffic stop meant to culminate in the discovery and retention of the firearms. The traffic stop would be routine and based on a traffic violation, but the officer would go on to locate and recover the firearms based on probable cause existing in the case. This prevents the transfer of the firearms from occurring and may in turn produce new investigative leads. Should the occupants of the vehicle be new or unknown participants in the trafficking ring, they may be fully identified, which in turn will yield additional information for follow-up investigation. Any recovered firearms should be exploited for leads by tracing the firearm(s), entering them into NIBIN, and processing them for latent fingerprints and DNA. Any new names, addresses, or phone numbers gained in this process should be fully deconflicted.

✓ **Shipping Rip.** If the firearms are being shipped via a common carrier or delivery service provider (UPS, DHL, FedEx, etc.), or are being checked through luggage on an airline flight or other carrier, the delivery of the firearms without notification to a common carrier is a violation of Title 18 U.S.C. 922(e) and the firearms may be seized by investigators with a search warrant. This prevents the transfer of the firearms from occurring and may in turn produce new investigative leads. The investigation may then continue with the traffickers believing the shipment of firearms was stolen in transit. Any recovered firearms should be exploited for leads by tracing the firearm(s), entering them into NIBIN, and processing them for latent fingerprints and DNA. Any new names, addresses, or phone numbers gained in this process should be fully deconflicted.

✓ **FFL Assistance.** If the investigator has the cooperation of the FFL and the FFL has a way to contact the straw purchaser, the following steps should be considered:
  ➢ **Domestic Lure.** Have the FFL call the straw purchaser to advise them that their firearms are ready for pickup, and have an undercover agent pose as a salesperson in the store to document the transaction and any incriminating statements. A team outside can then arrest the straw purchaser and seize the firearms in a manner and location deemed reasonable through pre-operational planning. OR
  ➢ **Delay to Gather Data and Evidence.** Have the FFL call the straw purchaser and advise them that there has been a delay in the firearm sale approval but that it should come through soon and he would call back when it did. This will provide time for the investigator to secure court orders for the historical cell data of the straw purchaser to try and identify the traffickers. The investigator may also want to consider pursuing a court order for a DNR or Trap and Trace on the straw purchaser's phone in an attempt to identify the traffickers. The investigator should use language in the application that allows the court order to be used as a means to secure subscriber information from service providers as well.

> ➤ **FFL Guidance.** At no time should the investigator tell the FFL that they should or should not make a sale, unless it is a controlled sale as described above that will result in a seizure. For other FFL transactions the investigator should tell the FFL to follow the rules and regulations that they always follow.

✓ **Cooperator.** Should one suspect in a multiple suspect investigation flip, the investigator should consider all the standard options to progress the investigation. The cooperating suspect may be either enlisted as a CI or the case AUSA may want them to secure an attorney and enter into a formal proffer or other type of cooperation agreement. Once the cooperator is able to provide assistance, they may be used to make recorded calls to other suspects to gather incriminating evidence, help locate and recover the firearms being trafficked, provide historical information on the other suspects and prior crimes, conduct monitored and recorded meetings with the other suspects to purchase different types of evidence, and provide testimony before a grand jury about the crime.

✓ **Controlled Delivery.** A cooperator may be able to help investigators deliver a shipment of firearms or firearms parts to a trafficker who can be subsequently arrested or followed to the border and arrested.

✓ **The Interview.** Once a suspect is identified or arrested, potentially the most important part of the investigation will be the defendant interview. If multiple suspects exist, each must be interviewed separately. If the suspects are not in custody, the interviews should be conducted simultaneously by multiple investigators to preclude coordination between the suspects. An investigator must have a working knowledge of all the facts and use good interviewing techniques to make the interview effective. The defendant's interview can make or break a case, and the investigator will more than likely only have one chance to conduct an interview with the defendant. Sample interview questions for FFLs who are the source of firearms smuggled out of the country, purchasers of firearms and ammunition being smuggled out of the country, and persons to be debriefed on firearms trafficking follow.

Sample Interview Questions: Securing an ATF Form 4473
For investigators who plan to secure an ATF Form 4473 from an FFL they should remember the following:

✓ FFLs may turn over ATF Form 4473s to ATF special agents, but other law enforcement officials may be required to produce a subpoena for the record. Investigators should coordinate this with ATF.

✓ FFLs are licensed with ATF, and the government only has the ability to inspect an FFL once in any one-year period. Any investigator securing records form an FFL should ensure that they understand that it is part of a separate investigation, and not part of their annual inspection.

✓ An original ATF Form 4473 belongs to the FFL until they go out of business, at which point they are required by law to turn their records over to ATF. Investigators should ensure that FFLs have a photocopy of any record being taken, that they are provided with a receipt for the record being taken, and that the investigator returns the original record to the FFL after it is no longer needed for evidence.

✓ Figure 10.2 contains a list of comprehensive FFL interview questions to be used any time an investigator is securing an ATF Form 4473 as evidence. These questions are designed to lock all required information into place and rule out the use of certain criminal defenses such as entrapment by estoppel.

Sample Interview Questions: Ammunition Sales
The manufacture of ammunition is regulated under federal law; however, the transfer and sale of ammunition was deregulated with the passage of the FOPA of 1986. Federal law does prohibit the same 9 categories of persons who are prohibited from possessing firearms from possessing ammunition under Title 18 U.S.C. § 922(g). However, because no questions are asked and no records checks are performed on purchasers of ammunition, sometimes a prohibited person or trafficker will use a straw-man to purchase firearms but will purchase ammunition themselves. Investigators should always ask FFLs if they happen to keep any business records on ammunition sales just in case as these could provide valuable leads on a trafficker or help prove an unlawful purchase and possession of ammunition violation on a prohibited person such as a convicted felon or illegal alien.

The following questions are designed to gather all pertinent sales and identity information from a retail ammunition dealer. Interviews with the retailer, who may or may not be an FFL, should always be conducted in a professional manner, and they should be thanked for their cooperation at the conclusion of the interview. In the case of FFLs, they should be made aware that the interview is part of a specific criminal investigation on another individual and is not part of their annual inspection.

STANDARD QUESTIONS FOR AMMUNITION SALESPERSON

The following questions should be asked when an investigator intends to secure a copy or original ATF Form 4473 from an FFL.
- ✓ What is the name of the salesperson who handled this ammunition sale?
- ✓ *(Always try to interview the actual sale person)*
- ✓ Do you ever ask for a driver's license or other form of valid government-issued photo ID when a customer wants to buy ammunition?
- ✓ Do you compare the photo on the ID to the person presenting the ID to make sure they are the same person?
- ✓ Do you keep a photocopy of the ID that was presented by the purchaser?
- ✓ *(If yes, secure a copy)*
- ✓ Are you always available to assist a purchaser if he/she has any questions?
- ✓ What was the price the purchaser paid for this ammunition?
- ✓ Did the purchaser pay with cash, check or credit card? *(if credit card, secure information)*
- ✓ Do you remember this sale and this person? *(If yes, ask questions A thru I below)*
  - A. Do you remember if this purchaser had any questions when making the purchase? (e.g., Did they ask questions that made them seem unfamiliar with the ammunition? Did they ask if they need to go through a records check or fill out paperwork?)
  - B. Do you remember if this purchaser was alone or with somebody when they came into the store?
  - C. If they were with someone, please describe why you think this, what this person looks like, and their actions or statements during the transaction?
  - D. Did the purchaser leave a cell phone number?
  - K. Would you be able to identify a picture of this purchaser from a photo-lineup? *NOTE: If yes, display a case law compliant photo-lineup, array, or loose photo stack, and have FFL*

235

initial and date the picture they identify as the purchaser. Before displaying the photos, provide the following guidance:

I am going to show you several individual photographs. I want you to look at each photograph and let me know if you recognize anyone, and if so, from where. You may or may not recognize anyone in the photographs. Remember to look at the facial features, such as the eyes, nose or mouth, because other features such as hair can change. Remember that the photos may be older or newer. Lastly, if you do recognize someone, let me know how positive you are of the identification.

    E. Do you remember what this person used for transportation to arrive at the store? *(description of vehicle/ license plate if possible)*

    F. Did it appear anyone was waiting for them outside in a vehicle? *(if yes, get description)*

    G. Has this person made prior purchases of ammunition, firearms, or firearms gear that you remember or that the records reflect? *(If yes, obtain copies of those ATF Form 4473s and interview salesperson who handled those transactions)*

    H. Is there anything else you can remember about this purchase that I have not asked about?

✓ Does the store have a video monitoring system in the store that would have recorded the transaction? *(If yes, secure a copy)*

✓ Are there any other store employees who might have observed the sale or remember the purchaser and transaction? *(If yes, ask the appropriate questions from the list above)*

✓ Has the purchaser been back to the store any other times and do they have any current sales pending for any items?

✓ Would you be willing to call the purchaser back and tell them you have a deal on a new shipment of ammunition and allow investigators to be in the store behind the counter when they come in so investigators can over hear or handle the transaction?

✓ Please do not let the purchaser know that we have been to the store or have asked any questions.

FIGURE 10.11 ©

Sample Interview Questions: Ammunition Purchaser

Do not start the interview by asking if they purchased the ammunition. Start the interview with that as an accepted fact, and push the focus of the interview to a more serious crime. The purchaser will likely admit purchasing the ammunition if they do not think that is your focus but deny using the ammunition to further a more serious crime. For example:

✓ Show the purchaser supporting documentation for the ammunition purchase in question, and tell them that you are not interested in what they did with the ammunition; instead, you need to know if they have a gun. Most persons will distance themselves from the gun possession, claim they did not buy and do not own a gun, but that they bought the ammunition for a friend who has a gun. This is still a confession to the purchase of ammunition and its illegal possession if they are a prohibited person. If they still have the ammunition, they may be willing to prove this by showing it to you, at which time it should be seized for evidence if they are prohibited or if there is probable cause they are trafficking ammunition to a foreign country. OR –

✓ Tell the purchaser you are investigating a shooting that involved ammunition of the type they recently purchased and that you need to know what they did with that ammunition. They will quickly deny any involvement in the shooting and likely admit to the ammunition purchase and tell you exactly what they did with it or show you that they still have it. If they still have the ammunition, you should seize it.

In a trafficking investigation, gear questions on determining the purchaser's knowledge of the ammunition. If they purchased the ammunition to traffic, they may not be able to answer basic questions that an ordinary gun owner could answer. Review the standard questions for an ammunition purchaser in Figure 10.12.

STANDARD QUESTIONS FOR PURCHASER OF AMMUNITION

- ✓ Are they available to speak and is anyone else in the home at the time?
- ✓ How long have they lived there?
- ✓ Who else lives with them and how long have they lived there?
- ✓ Is this where they consider their residence?
- ✓ Do they have a residence in another state?
- ✓ Where else have they lived in the past 5 years?
- ✓ What do they do for a living?

Following the general questions, begin to focus questions on the firearms purchase with general questions about that transaction.

GENERAL PURCHASE QUESTIONS:
- ✓ Why did they choose that store to purchase ammunition from?
- ✓ Did anyone go with them to the gun store when they purchased the ammunition?
- ✓ If yes, who was this person and how do they know them? *(get contact information for later interview)*
- ✓ Did this person go in the store when the ammunition was purchased and did they look at firearms while there?
- ✓ How did they get to the store to make the purchase?
- ✓ Did they ask the salesperson any questions while conducting the purchase?
- ✓ Do they remember the salesperson they dealt with? (If yes, ask them to describe)
- ✓ Did the salesperson provide them with any information during the purchase?
- ✓ How much did they pay to purchase the ammunition?
- ✓ How did they purchase the ammunition (cash, check, credit card, PayPal if online)?
- ✓ Where did they get the funds to purchase the ammunition ?
- ✓ Did they purchase any firearms from this gun store at any time?
- ✓ If yes – how did they pay for those purchases?
- ✓ Did they purchase any firearms or ammunition from any other gun stores or persons?
- ✓ What made them purchase that ammunition?
- ✓ Do they remember what caliber the ammunition was?
- ✓ If they purchased for their firearm, how many rounds does that firearm hold when fully loaded?
- ✓ How many magazines came with that firearm?
- ✓ When and where was the last time they went shooting?
- ✓ Was anyone with them when they went shooting? *(Identify this person for later interview)*

Persons with substance abuse problems are often exploited by drug dealers to become straw purchasers. If the purchaser has a drug arrest history or appears to have a drug addiction problem, the investigator should also ask questions designed to probe that possibility and document additional federal law violations. It will be important to determine if they were a user of controlled substances contemporaneous to purchasing the ammunition.

✓ I know that you have recent arrests for controlled substance possession. Do you have a drug addiction or are you a recreational user?

✓ What kind of drugs are they using, how long have they been using, and were they using when they purchased the ammunition?

✓ If they appear to have no visible means of income to support the expenditure of funds to purchase the ammunition the investigator should point that out and ask: Did they purchase the ammunition for someone else in exchange for drugs or in exchange for cash so they could purchase drugs.

✓ Are they seeking treatment or under treatment for an on-going drug addiction?

✓ Do they feel they were exploited by their drug dealer into purchasing the firearm(s) for them?

✓ How do they normally get in contact with their dealer, how often does the dealer ask them to purchase ammunition, and do they ever ask to purchase firearms?

✓ Would they be willing to cooperate with law enforcement during the investigation?

✓ Would they be willing to give consent to search their cellphone?

This can be done by having the purchaser sign a consent to search form and providing their password to open the phone so it may be downloaded for intelligence exploitation and corroborative evidence of what the purchaser has already told the investigator. If the purchaser states they use the phone to contact their dealer by text or phone calls but will not voluntarily turn over the phone, the investigator may be able to seize the phone as evidence on the spot based on the statements that the phone was used for communications during an illegal act. The phone may be secured and the investigator would need to secure a search warrant to download the phone and examine the information. For a person who rises to the level of a suspect, gaining access to their cell phone through consent or search warrant will be important to securing information vital to furthering the investigation. The cell phone data will reveal who they have been speaking with, when, and what was said in text messages. Cell phone data can reveal their travels as well as the potential for images of illegal activity. Exploitation of communication devices is critical at all phases of a firearms trafficking investigation.

Following the drug user questioning the investigator should ask a number of additional questions to probe the methods used in the trafficking scheme and why the purchaser no longer has the ammunition.

✓ Do they still have the ammunition?

✓ If they still have the ammunition, what are their plans for the ammunition?

✓ If they don't have the ammunition:

✓ Who did they sell the ammunition to?

✓ When did they sell the ammunition?

✓ Where did the sale take place?

✓ How much did they sell the ammunition for?

✓ Did they ask the buyer any questions?

✓ Did they record the identity of the purchaser or look at their identification?

✓ Do they remember the car the buyer was driving and do they remember the license plate or the state the license plate was from?

- ✓ Do they remember if other persons were with the purchaser and what they looked like?
- ✓ Did the purchaser contact them on their cell phone, by text message, or by email?
- ✓ How often do they buy and sell ammunition and how do they make it known to prospective purchasers that they have other ammunition or firearms for sale?

The investigator should obtain the phone or email information so that subpoenas for records of those services may be obtained. If the seller used their phone to call or text the purchaser then the investigator should consider retaining the phone as evidence for subsequent download in accordance with local laws and their agencies policies. The purchaser can give you consent to search and download the phone and this may help them get the phone back quickly as a search warrant will not be required. The image on the phone may increase the investigator's understanding of the scope of trafficking as well as provide other incriminating evidence such as locations the purchaser traveled to that may correspond to trafficking routes and meeting places, incriminating emails and text messages, or phone numbers associated with persons involved in the firearms trafficking scheme.

If the purchaser recalls who sold the ammunition to them, ask the purchaser:
- ✓ What type of information can they provide to identify the purchaser?
- ✓ Do they recall where the person was from and what transportation they used?
- ✓ Could they identify the person in a photo array?
- ✓ Were there other persons with the purchaser?

If the purchaser appears deceptive and/or refuses to identify who they sold the ammunition to, the investigator should state:
- ✓ Investigators don't often ask questions to which they don't already know the answer and that you are there to get the truth and clear the matter up.
- ✓ The ammunition was already recovered in a crime and that person is cooperating with law enforcement.
- ✓ Where applicable, advise them that this is a federal investigation, and that if they do not want to answer questions now, they may be provided with a subpoena to appear before a federal grand jury and answer the same questions from an AUSA while under oath.
- ✓ Advise them that this matter will not be going away until all the questions are answered.

FIGURE 10.12 ©

Sample Interview Questions re. Debriefing a Suspect, CI, or Cooperating Defendant Regarding International Trafficking Information

While conducting a debriefing with a suspect, CI, or cooperating defendant, the investigator should ask direct questions that gather information establishing the elements of the violation being investigated, and should also design questions to substantiate or corroborate any claims about violations by others, in order to rate the reliability of the intelligence and be able to quickly determine the presence of actionable intelligence.

QUESTIONS FOR DEBRIEFING A SUSPECT, CI, OR COOPERATING DEFENDANT ON FIREAMS TRAFFICKING

✓ Do you know anybody who is involved with taking, shipping, or having others smuggle any of the following items to *[Name of Foreign Country]*?

➤ Firearms, high capacity magazines, or ammunition?

➤ Firearms parts, flats, castings, high capacity?

➤ Milling machines, drill presses, lathes, hydraulic presses, or other firearms manufacturing equipment?

➤ Low explosives such as black powder, gun powder, pyrodex, flash powder or the compounds to manufacture them?

➤ High explosives such as commercial explosives, exploding target binary compounds, stolen military explosives such as C4, homemade explosives such as TATP or the chemicals to manufacture them?

➤ Military or homemade grenades or the parts to manufacture them?

➤ Grenade launchers, LAWS rockets (MANPADS: Man Portable Air Defense Systems), Stinger or Toe missiles, or similar devices?

➤ Bulk amounts of camouflage BDU uniforms, caps, boots, or any police or military clothing?

➤ Bulk amounts of tactical gear, web belts, cartridge belts, ammo pouches, holsters, gun cases or other police or military gear?

➤ Tactical or bulletproof vests?

➤ Night vision equipment, binoculars, or similar equipment?

✓ Are you involved with taking, shipping, or having others smuggle any of the following items to *[Name of Foreign Country]*?

✓ If yes, explain in detail to whom, when, how often, any accomplices, etc. Provide as much identifying information about each person as possible (e.g., Names, street names, physical description, addresses, phone numbers, emails, vehicles used).

✓ What would be the best way to catch a gun trafficker or gun load transporter in the act?

✓ Are you familiar with any gangs, cartels, criminal organizations, or criminals in *[Name of Foreign Country]* that are getting guns from the U.S.?

✓ If so, who are you familiar with and which organizations are you familiar with?

✓ How are these people or criminal organizations getting guns, ammunition, grenades, explosives, etc.?

✓ How do you know this?

✓ How can we catch people acquiring guns, ammunition, grenades, and explosives for these criminal organizations?

✓ How do you know this information?

Acquisition and Payment

✓ Who do you know that traffics guns to *[Name of Foreign Country]*?

✓ Have you ever been asked to purchase guns or ammunition for anyone?

✓ Who do you know that recruits people to buy guns or ammunition for them?

✓ Where did they find their recruits? (labor pool stands, bars, parks, schools, gun shows, etc.)

✓ Do the recruits know each other?

✓ Where does that person get the guns (gun stores, pawn shops, gun shows, online, classified advertisements, the streets, friends, etc.)?

✓ Where does that person get their money from to make the purchases and pay the recruits?

✓ Does that person seem knowledgeable about guns?

✓ Does that person buy the guns directly or do they pay someone else to buy the guns for them?

✓ How are the guns paid for (in cash, drugs, pre-paid credit cards, Electronic Benefit Transfer (EBT) cards, other trade, etc....)?

✓ Is a commission paid for each gun purchased or gun purchase form? How much?

✓ Provide as much identifying information about each person as possible (e.g., names, street names, physical descriptions, addresses, phone numbers, emails, vehicles used).

✓ Is the gun dealer or sales clerk involved? Why do you think this?

✓ What kinds of IDs are people using to purchase guns from licensed dealers?

✓ If these IDs are fraudulent, how and where are they being made, where are they being acquired, who is supplying them, and who arranges to get them for people?

✓ In the event of illegal aliens using false IDs, are they using IDs that show them to be U.S. citizens? (If so, this would be a violation of Title 18 U.S.C. § 911, a felony offense.)

✓ Is a restaurant, bar, automotive repair shop, metal work shop, or other business or location used to acquire or pay for guns, ammunition, explosives, etc.?

✓ Is a bank, other money exchange business, Western Union, or other money transfer business used to pay for the guns or to wire money to buy guns?

✓ How do you (or the trafficker) know what type of guns to get? Are you provided a list, or does the actual buyer place the order directly with the dealer?

✓ Which guns are the most in demand?

Gun Shows

✓ Are gun shows being used as a source to acquire guns?

✓ Which ones? Why are they used? Are there certain gun dealers used? If so, explain.

✓ Do the purchases take place at the show? Are the firearms delivered at the gun show, in the parking lot, or does delivery take place somewhere else?

✓ Do you know anyone who recruits buyers to get guns or ammunition at gun shows?

✓ Have you ever bought a gun for anyone at a gun show? Has anyone ever asked you to buy them a gun or ammunition at a gun show?

✓ Do you know anybody who goes to gun shows and specializes in buying assault rifles, 9mm pistols, or any other particular gun?

Transportation and Border Crossings

✓ Who in the organization actually takes or ships the guns to *[Name of Foreign Country]*?

✓ How are the guns being taken to *[Name of Foreign Country]*? Private passenger vehicle, bus, train, shipping container, shipped by FedEx or other delivery service, boat, freighter, cruise line, private airplane, commercial airline, underground tunnel, etc.?

✓ How often is a gun load sent to *[Name of Foreign Country]*?

✓ Are they using specially-equipped vehicles or vehicles with secret compartments to transport firearms and ammunition into Mexico?

✓ Are there shipping or transportation companies being used (air, sea, ground)?

✓ Where are the guns being introduced into *[Name of Foreign Country]*? What is the name of the border town or crossing, seaport, airport or air strip or actual physical address?

✓ Do you know of any corrupt police or customs officials involved in the U.S. or *[Name of Foreign Country]* that helps get the loads across the border?

✓ Are the same border crossings used each time? If not, how are border crossings selected?

✓ What are the preferred times to cross the border and why?

✓ Are any of the vehicles, shipping or transport companies, also used to run drugs, money, or precursor chemicals to *[Name of Foreign Country]*?

Load Vehicles

✓ Do you know how many guns can be loaded into a vehicle without risking detection?

✓ Do you know how much ammunition can be safely concealed in a vehicle per load without risking detection?

✓ Do you know of the hiding places (natural voids) within a vehicle that are used to hide guns, ammunition, grenades, or explosives?

✓ Are you familiar with any special techniques to make hidden compartments?

✓ What vehicles are selected for use as load vehicles and why (mini-van, truck, rental car, etc.)?

➢ How and where are load vehicles bought? From individuals? Used car lots? Are car dealers used to acquire load vehicles? Explain the process.

➢ Are automotive body shops used to hide the guns and/or to make hidden compartments? Which body shops?

✓ Are rental cars used? *If Yes:*

➢ Are they rental cars or rental trucks?

➢ Where are they secured (country and company)?

➢ Who secures them and how do they secure them?

✓ Are stolen vehicles being used? *If Yes:*

➢ Are they coming from the U.S. or *[Name of Foreign Country]*?

➢ Who is stealing them?

➢ Where do they dispose of them?

✓ Are commercial shippers (truck lines) being used?

✓ Are persons using common carriers such as bus lines, trains, or commercial air travel?

✓ Are persons shipping guns in the mail (FedEx, etc.)?

✓ If yes, who? Are they using drop boxes? Where?

Firearm Manufacturing or Alterations

✓ Is anyone obliterating the serial numbers off the guns? *If Yes*

✓ Who is doing it and where are they doing this? In the US or *[Name of Foreign Country]*?

✓ How are they doing it? (See Figure 6.4 for Methods of Serial Number Obliteration)

✓ Is anyone converting the firearms to machine guns? *If Yes:*

✓ What types of guns are being converted? Rifles or handguns? Ghost Guns?

✓ Who is doing it, where are they doing it (U.S. or *[Name of Foreign Country]*), and how much extra do they charge for this?

✓ How are they doing it and where are those parts coming from?

✓ Is anyone supplying silencers? *If Yes:*

✓ What types of firearms are the silencers attached to?
✓ What are the silencers being made from?
✓ Who is doing it, where are they doing it (U.S. or *[Name of Foreign Country]*), and how much extra do they charge for this?
✓ How are they doing it (order or parts assembly) and where are those parts coming from?

Explosives
✓ Is anyone making purchases of black powder or other explosive material?
✓ Are they doing it in quantities under 50 pounds to make sure there is no record?
✓ Who is doing this? Where are they doing this?
✓ What is it being used for?
✓ Is anyone purchasing the components to make bombs (galvanized pipe, hollow grenade husks at gun shows, etc.)?

FIGURE 10.13

Consular Notification

In the event a foreign national is detained or arrested, the investigator should determine what country the foreign national is from. The investigator should then determine if that country is on the list of mandatory consular notification. The U.S. Department of State provides a pocket guide for law enforcement with a list of the countries that require mandatory consular notification if one of their citizens is arrested or detained. That pocket guide may be retrieved from: https://travel.state.gov/content/dam/travel/CNAtrainingresources/ CNA%20Pocket%20Card_BW.pdf

The U.S. State Department recommends the following statement be read to any foreign national who is arrested or detained in the U.S. from a non-mandatory notification country[cxxxv]:

> *As a non-U.S. citizen who is being arrested or detained, you may request that we notify your country's consular officers here in the United States of your situation. You may also communicate with your consular officers. A consular officer may be able to help you obtain legal representation and may contact your family and visit you in detention, among other things. If you want us to notify your consular officers, you can request this notification now, or at any time in the future. Do you want us to notify your consular officers at this time?*

The U.S. State Department requires that the following statement must be read to any foreign national who is arrested or detained in the U.S. from a mandatory notification country:

> *Because of your nationality, we are required to notify your country's consular officers here in the United States that you have been arrested or detained. We will do this as soon as possible. In addition, you may communicate with your consular officers. You are not required to accept their assistance, but your consular officers may be able to help you obtain legal representation and may contact your family and visit you in detention, among other things. Please sign to show that you have received this information.* [cxxxvi]

For additional information on this topic, investigators may contact the U.S. Department of State at Telephone: 202-485-7703 or email: consnot@state.gov.

Consular notifications are an important aspect of arresting or detaining foreign nationals, and the way in which a country perceives the U.S. to honor the consular notification process may translate into how U.S. citizens arrested or detained abroad in these countries are treated.

Alien Smuggling and Terrorism

In the event that information is uncovered concerning illegal aliens or activity that constitutes smuggling, the investigator should contact U.S. Immigration and Customs Enforcement (ICE).

In the event that information is uncovered relative to terrorist activities or groups, the investigator should contact the nearest FBI office or Joint Terrorism Task Force (JTTF).

If firearms, firearms parts and kits, or ammunition are being supplied to terrorists or terrorist organizations this may constitute a violation of Title 18 18 U.S.C. § 2339B, Providing Material Support to Terrorist Organizations, which carries a penalty of up to 15 years in prison.

General Information on the Legal Process of Importing and Exporting Firearms

For information regarding the legal requirements and proper procedures for importing firearms by licensed and non-licensed persons, investigators should refer to Chapter 4 of this text or the most recent edition of the *ATF Guidebook: Importation & Verification of Firearms, Ammunition, and Implements of War.*

For information on the purchase and possession of firearms and ammunition by illegal aliens, resident aliens, and non-immigrant aliens in the U.S. investigators should refer to Chapter 4, or ATF Publication 5300.18, *Non-Immigrant Aliens Purchasing Firearms and Ammunition in the United States.*

The legal exportation of firearms other than sporting shotguns is regulated by the U.S. Department of State, Directorate of Defense Trade Controls. Those who want information about obtaining an export license as well as detailed handgun and rifle exportation information should contact:

> Department of State
> Directorate of Defense Trade Controls PM/DTC SA-1, Room 1200
> Washington, DC 20037
> Telephone: 202-663-1282   Website: www.pmddtc.state.gov

The U.S. Department of Commerce (DOC) oversees the legal exportation of sporting shotguns with barrels between 18 and 28 inches in length. The DOC requires a general license to export these items. There is no fee for a general license. For information on this matter, contact:

> Outreach and Education Services Division
> Office of Exporter Services - Bureau of Industry and Security - Department of Commerce
> 1401 Constitution Avenue, NW. - Room 1009 - C
> Washington, DC 20230
> Telephone: 202-482-4811 Web site: www.bis.doc.gov

CASE STUDY: OPERATION MONTREAL PIPELINE
United States v. Gertsch – District of Maine – 1:11-cr-00161-JAW

In April of 2011 ATF Portland, Maine Field Office special agents initiated an investigation after a review of multiple handgun sales information indicated a purchase of handguns associated with an address in an area known to the agents to be problematic. This purchase was fairly innocuous however the reviewer of the multiple handgun sales information had local knowledge of the address and knew this purchase needed scrutiny. This is a perfect example of why the use of a CGIC should NEVER preclude investigators in other locations from also analyzing and reviewing data for trafficking indicators. If that had been done here, the regional CGIC would not have referred this innocuous 2 handgun purchase to the ATF Portland Field Office. CGICs are great at developing crime gun leads but local knowledge is vital and it should never be expected that a CGIC in another State or City will be able to identify every lead in a location somewhere else. The more eyes analyzing the data the better – as long as there is deconfliction before action.

Deconfliction checks indicated no other law enforcement agencies were investigating the purchaser. Intelligence workups revealed that the purchaser had recently secured a Maine ID card and apparently did not actually live at the address, but had only stayed there for a day or two. The purchaser was already gone the day after the multiple purchase of handguns. Intelligence workups showed the purchaser had listed multiple addresses in the past in the U.S., including Michigan, New York, and Texas, but was actually a Canadian-born member of the Mohawk Nation[cxxxvii]. Under the Jay Treaty of 1794 (example of the use of junior high school History class information later in life), he is allowed to freely cross the border between the U.S. and Canada. The intelligence workup also showed that the subject and his brother had other U.S. IDs issued in Michigan, Texas, and New York, and held pilot licenses and could fly freely between the U.S. and Canada.

During an interview with the FFL and examination of the ATF Form 4473, the ATF special agent discovered that the FFL had written the subject's cell phone number on the back of the form. Subpoenas for cell phone call data and cell tower information were used to secure data for analysis. The analysis revealed that the subject had only been in Maine for a short period of time, and the only calls made were to several FFLs, several private citizens selling firearms in local classified advertisements, hotels, taxis, the Greyhound™ bus line, and pizza delivery services. Cell tower information revealed that the subject entered the state of Maine coming straight up I-95 from Boston, MA to Augusta, ME. The purchaser drove around Augusta for several days purchasing firearms from FFLs and private citizens, and then went straight down I-95 back to Boston at the end of January 2011. ATF special agents immediately contacted DHS-HSI, and had them place a border lookout into TECs in case the subject tried to re-enter Canada with the firearms. A subpoena for records to Greyhound indicated that the subject had entered and exited Portland, Maine for Boston via Greyhound, and then purchased a ticket on Greyhound from Boston to Montreal, Canada. He was rolling down 295 out of Portland, Maine - as Jackson Browne sang in his 1978 hit "Nothing but Time"©.

A court order for a PEN on the purchaser's cellphone was secured; however, the phone had been disconnected shortly after the subject departed Maine and it appeared to have been a burner phone just for this trafficking run. All known purchased firearms were entered into ATF FRNP so agents would be notified if they were recovered by law enforcement and traced.

All FFLs were interviewed, and the ATF Form 4473s were recovered as evidence. All private sellers the purchaser called were identified and interviewed, and additional firearms the purchaser

obtained were identified through this process. Investigation into the prior addresses listed by the purchaser in Texas, New York, and Michigan indicated firearms traces associated with some of those addresses. ATF agents in Maine enlisted the assistance of ATF attaché's in Canada in the investigation. The attaché's worked with Canadian law enforcement officials and were able to determine that the purchaser lived on a Native Reserve in Quebec, Canada, and that the purchaser and his family were suspected by local police in the area to be firearms traffickers[cxxxviii].

The U.S. Attorney's Office in Bangor, Maine secured a federal indictment for multiple counts of providing false information to an FFL during the acquisition of firearms (Title 18 U.S.C. § 922(a)(6)). ATF special agents then coordinated with ATF attaché's and HSI agents in Portland, ME to locate the purchaser in Canada and ensure that all proper notices and lookouts were in place to apprehend the subject should he attempt to re-enter the U.S. In October 2011, based on a formal extradition request, Canadian law enforcement officials arrested the purchaser and, following an extradition hearing, he was brought to Maine to face federal charges. In January 2013, following a guilty plea, the purchaser was sentenced to 16 months in federal prison followed by 36 months supervised release.

CASE STUDY: OPERATION YUKON JACK

United States v. Hatton – District of Maine – 1:10-cr-00079-JAW

In June of 2006 the ATF Portland Maine Field Office opened an investigation after an inspection of an FFL revealed that they were unable to account for 76 firearms that should be in their inventory. Deconfliction and intelligence workups were performed, and the missing firearms were placed in the ATF FRNP so that investigators would be notified if the firearms were recovered by law enforcement and traced. Shortly after the investigation was opened, crime guns recovered in Canada were traced and the case agent was notified that some of the missing guns had already been smuggled to Canada and used in crimes. One of the firearms had been used in a drug rip-off in an Ottawa Hotel Room that ended in a shooting with 2 persons dead. The firearm was recovered from a construction site days later. The serial number had been obliterated, but an internal serial number had not, so the firearm could be traced and a ballistics examination matched the firearm to the shooting.

In Maine, information from HUMINT sources indicated that several employees at the FFL were engaged in facilitating straw purchases. ATF tested this by sending UC agents into the store where they were able to conduct straw purchases on several occasions with different employees. During the investigation various straw purchasers were identified and interviewed. The investigation was conducted with ICE and the Royal Canadian Mounted Police (RCMP). Later in the investigation UC RCMP officers were also used to conduct straw purchases at the FFL to show they could purchase firearms "off-paper" to bring back to Canada. The investigation led to the identification of a 5-person trafficking ring that had trafficked more than 80 firearms to Canada. Those 5 persons were arrested and cooperated, leading to additional defendants, the service of a search warrant for records, and the arrest of 4 employees of the FFL.

By the end of Operation Yukon Jack™ (the Black Sheep of Canadian Liqueurs) a total of 9 persons were recommended for federal prosecution, 2 of whom were Canadian citizens and all of whom felt snake-bit (another gratuitous Yukon Jack™ reference). The Canadian citizens were not prosecuted in the U.S., but were arrested and jailed in Canada. The other 7 defendants all pled guilty in the U.S to straw purchase conspiracy charges and received sentences ranging from probation to 18 months in federal prison.[cxxxix]

TYPE 9: FIREARM CASTINGS, FLATS, PARTS KITS, AND GHOST GUN INVESTIGATION

Firearm castings, flats, and parts kits are not classified as firearms, and the domestic transfer of those items within the U.S. are not regulated by the GCA or NFA.[cxl] However, they are regulated for import into or export out of the U.S. under Title 22 U.S.C. § 2778 of the AECA, as they are listed items on the USML. The same holds true for ghost gun parts; however, once a ghost gun is manufactured it is classified as a firearm under the GCA or NFA, and is subject to the import and export provisions of the AECA. Let's start with some terminology:

✓ **Firearms Castings.** These are commonly blocks of metal in the shape of firearm receivers. They are considered receiver blanks and sometimes will be referred to as 80% receivers. They need milling, drilling, and finishing to become a functional firearm component subject to the GCA and NFA within the U.S. Types of firearms manufactured from castings include AR-15 / M-4 variants.

✓ **Firearms Flats.** These are commonly flat pieces of metal with drilled holes and cut out blocks so that, when the sides are folded up, they become lower firearm receivers that will accept and hold all of the internal components of the firearm. They are considered receiver blanks and sometimes will be referred to as 80% receivers. The types of firearms manufactured from flats are AK-47 variant style rifles and MAC-10 style pistols.

✓ **Firearms Parts Kits**. A firearms parts kit commonly consists of the external and internal components of a firearm minus the lower receiver which constitutes the actual firearm. Firearm parts kits are frequently used in unlicensed firearms manufacturing as well as illegal exportation. These parts kits are not classified as firearms under the GCA or NFA, but they have everything needed to make a firearm once a lower receiver is obtained. Firearms castings and flats are used to make the lower receivers. Flats, castings, and firearm parts kits are easy to obtain

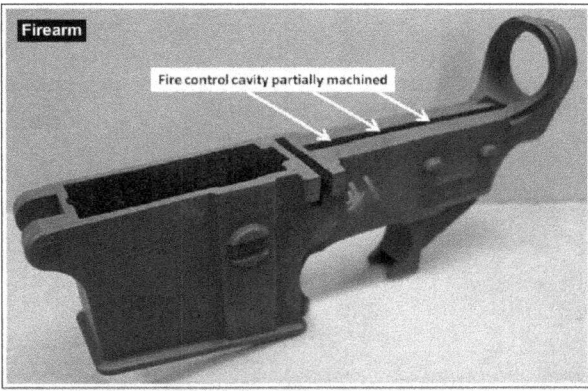
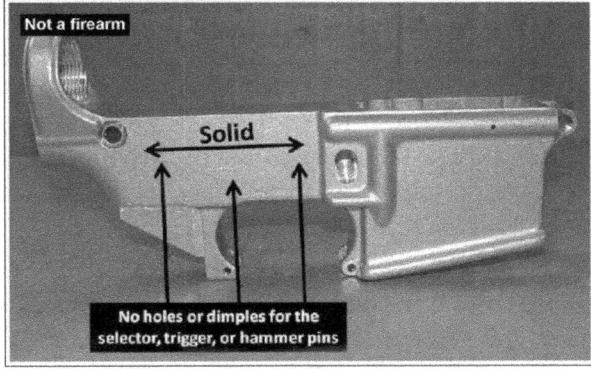

Figure 10.14 *Firearm & Non-Firearm Castings*

Source: ATF

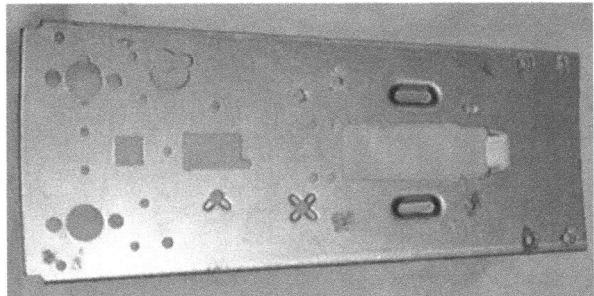

Figure 10.15 *Firearm Flat*

Source: ATF

in the U.S. through gun shows as well as many internet supply sites, and since they are not actual firearms and there are no records required or questions asked when purchasing these items. They are then illegally smuggled out of the U.S. to cartels and gangs in Mexico, other Central and South American countries, and the Caribbean, where they are fully assembled into untraceable firearms. Although these are U.S. sourced firearms, they have no valid traceable markings and will never be attributed to being U.S. sourced through ATF trace data.

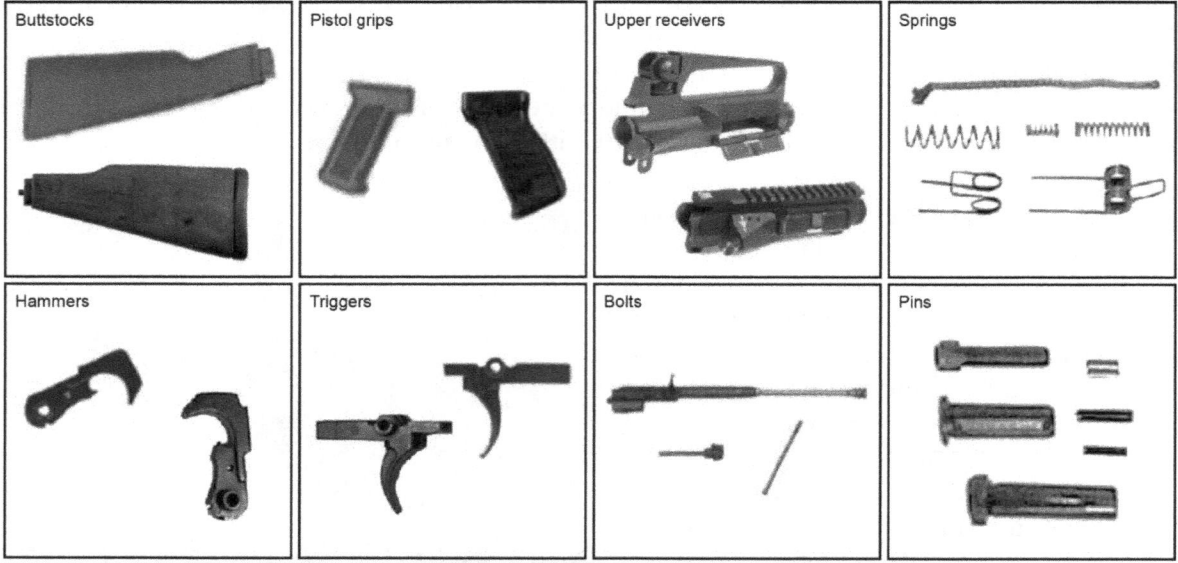

Figure 10.16 *Firearm Parts Kit Commonly Encountered in Firearms Export Trafficking*

Source: ATF

✓ **Ghost Gun.** This is a slang term used to refer to a firearm manufactured outside the chain of the licensed firearms industry making the firearm untraceable – a ghost. Ghost guns may have no markings on them at all or they may appear to be legitimate guns from well-known manufacturers, and having serial numbers. However, the serial numbers are not real and are not traceable, since the guns were not made actually made by the real manufacturers and logged in their records.

✓ **Incomplete Receiver.** This is a term used to describe forgings, castings, or machined bodies which have been partially milled or modified and are classified as firearms but are not fully machined or modified to the point of functionality as firearm receivers.

✓ **Receiver.** This is a term used to describe a functional firearm frame or receiver. A functional frame or receiver is classified as a firearm.

✓ **Receiver Blank.** This is a term used to describe forgings, castings, or machined bodies such as AR15 receiver castings, AK47 receiver flats, or unfinished polymer pistol receivers. These items are not classified as firearms.

Unlicensed persons are not required by federal law to place serial numbers on firearms they manufacture if they do not intend to sell the firearms at the time of manufacture. Further, according to ATF, if they later decide to sell the firearm, they don't have to place markings on it if their activity does not rise to the level of dealing which would require a license. This is an untraceable firearm – a ghost gun. If the person making and selling these firearms crosses the line and becomes engaged in the business of manufacturing and dealing in firearms without a license for the principle objective of livelihood and profit, then they are in violation of Title 18 U.S.C. § 922(a)(1)(A) and the firearms would also be required to have serial numbers.

Ghost guns present a number of challenges for law enforcement. First and foremost, establishing that the firearm moved in or affected interstate or foreign commerce will be difficult with a firearm that has no markings or fictitious markings. Ghost guns with fictitious or duplicative markings can produce false leads in trace results or erroneously appear untraceable in a way that indicates that a manufacturer or retailer may have issues with their recordkeeping.

For a private citizen, possession of a ghost gun can inadvertently result in their arrest by local law enforcement for possession of a firearm with altered or removed serial numbers when in fact this is not true. However, it will take time and money to untangle such an arrest.

A private citizen diminishes their ability to *have* a stolen firearm recovered and returned to them if the firearm has no markings, as law enforcement won't be able to place a stolen firearm description in NCIC or check the NCIC recovered gun file.

The bottom line is that the increasing production and distribution of unmarked or improperly marked ghost guns into commerce in the U.S. and abroad presents challenges to law enforcement, risks to possessors and FFLs, and undermines society's sys-

Figure 10.17 *Author in 2018 with 4,500 Firearm Castings and "80% Receivers" for M1911 Pistols and AR15 Rifles from Korea - Seized by ATF Springfield, MA Office for Import Fraud Violations*
Photograph by; Terence Adamo

tem of recordkeeping and criminal background checks established by federal, state, and local laws which are designed to prevent firearms from being acquired by prohibited persons and to ensure that crime guns can be traced by law enforcement to solve crimes.

A rapidly growing trend is the manufacture of polymer pistols such as a Glocks. When the polymer receiver blank is purchased, it comes with a jig that the receiver blank is placed in, and guides the user to drill and cut out the proper areas to finished the blank into an actual firearm receiver. This process is relatively inexpensive and requires very little expertise.

A longer-standing trend is the manufacture of AR15 and AK47 rifles from flats, forgings, and castings.

To mill out an AR15 blank the manufacturer will need at least a drill press and milling equipment. Optimally, the manufacturer would have a Computer Numerical Control (CNC) machine. This machine mills out the chosen firearm receiver blank using computer guided milling which is guided the chosen firearm design loaded in the Computer Aided Design software (CAD). CAD schematics for numerous firearms can be purchased online and once loaded into the CNC, the

milling is automatic and requires very little human intervention. This equipment can be very expensive, with CNC machines running in the tens of thousands of dollars and small bench top machines costing upwards of $1500.

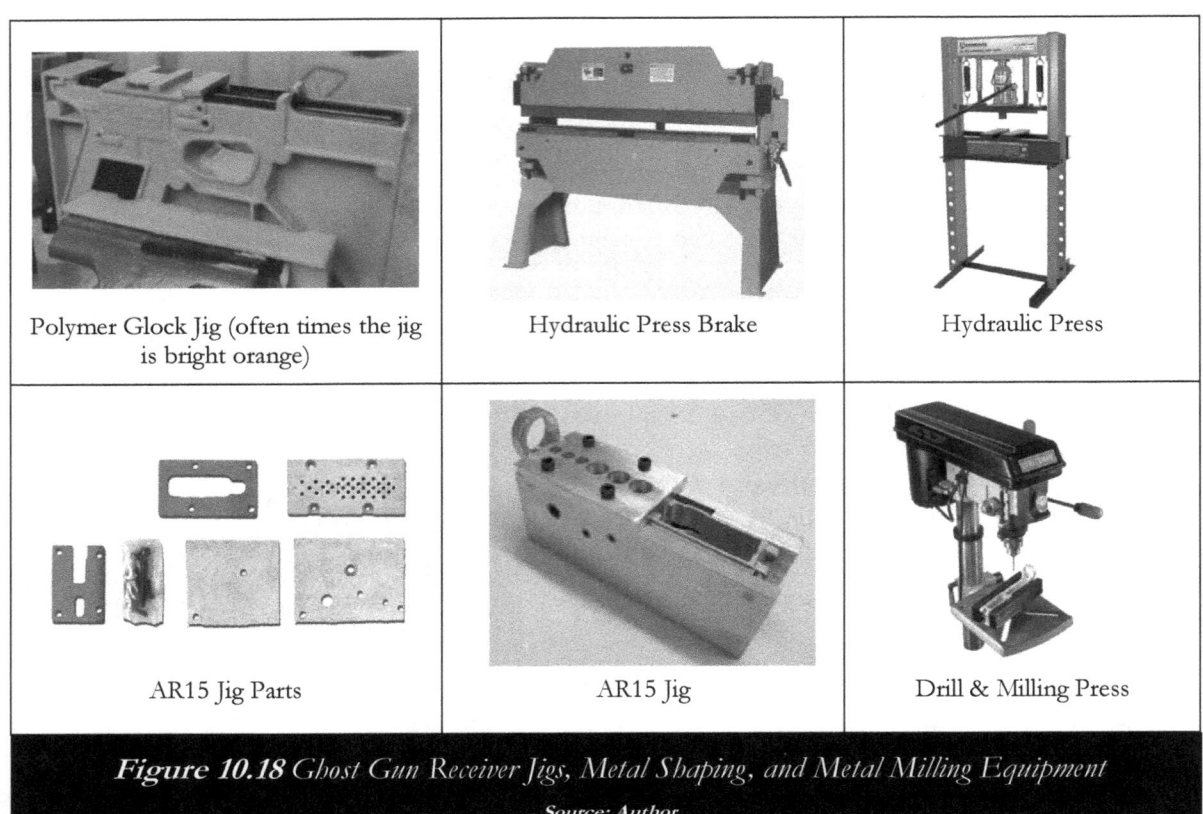

Polymer Glock Jig (often times the jig is bright orange)	Hydraulic Press Brake	Hydraulic Press
AR15 Jig Parts	AR15 Jig	Drill & Milling Press

Figure 10.18 Ghost Gun Receiver Jigs, Metal Shaping, and Metal Milling Equipment
Source: Author

For bending AK47 flats into a receiver, a metal brake or hydraulic press with a custom molding fixture is required. A hydraulic press brake is a machine that bends flat metal into angles. There are commercial brakes and homemade brakes available. A hydraulic press is a hydraulic tool mounted in a stand that allows a person to put tons of pressure on a flat and force it into shape around a fixture. In general, the equipment needed to manufacturing AK flats into firearm receivers is less expensive and less complicated than the equipment needed for AR15 manufacturing, but the equipment is still not cheap. Figure 10.17 illustrates the types of equipment that an investigator may encounter during an unlicensed firearms manufacturing or dealing investigation.

There are hobbyists out there who are operating with this equipment with no FFL and are in compliance with the law. There are also persons who throw "AR Parties" or "AK Parties" where they provide the equipment and people can bring their castings and flats and use the equipment to manufacture their firearms for a party admission fee, and this too is compliant with the law. This is in the same vein as making ceramic coffee mugs at a craft shop that has an expensive kiln for you to use.

However, understandably, it is reasonable to question why some would spend thousands of dollars on equipment just to make one or two firearms for themselves. The purchase of thousands of dollars in drilling, milling, and bending equipment may be an indicator of someone who is consistently manufacturing these types of firearms, and re-sale would seem a logical step to re-coup costs. Obvious candidates for further investigation may include;

✓ Unlicensed persons with criminal histories or ties to cartels or gang.

✓ Unlicensed persons with SARs, CTRs, Reports of International Transportation of CMIR (Customs Form 4790), and Reports of FBAR (Treasury Form 90-22.1) in FinCEN and TECs with patterns indicating that this financial activity is tied to the manufacturing and sales.

✓ Unlicensed persons in TECs with regular border crossings to countries that are known destinations for US sourced firearms and firearms parts.

Once a person is identified for further investigation, the following are some basic steps to determine the scope of their operation:

✓ **Surveillance.** Investigators or the use of surreptitious video monitoring can determine the level of activity at a location and identify shipments, potential customers, and other activity. This may lead to the discovery of firearms being sold and shipped.

✓ **Records.** Area shippers can be subpoenaed for a list of all packages delivered to the location. This will assist in determining their sources of flats or castings and may help establish volume and a pattern of unlicensed manufacturing and trafficking. The same shippers can be subpoenaed for records of packages shipped from that address to determine who they may be shipping firearms to. If this is discovered, the investigator must move quickly to prove their violations, secure arrest and search warrants, and prevent additional shipments. For illegal exploitation shipments, the investigator should coordinate with HSI. For shipments in the U.S. mail, the investigator should coordinate with U.S. Postal Inspectors.

✓ **Internet Intelligence - OSINT.** A full social media workup should be performed, and once any conversation by the source is found discussing the manufacture or sale of these items, the investigator should serve a preservation letter on the account, followed 30 days later by a search warrant to obtain the email conversation.

✓ **Establishing the Interstate of Foreign Commerce Nexus Element of Proof.** For firearm parts kit and ghost gun investigations there are ample violations when those firearms are being illegally imported or exported from the U.S. The challenge for an investigator will be establishing a nexus to interstate or foreign commerce in a case involving someone illegally possessing, manufacturing, or dealing in ghost guns without a license.

✓ **Prohibited Persons.** It is illegal for convicted felons and other categories of prohibited persons to possess firearms or ammunition (Title 18 U.S.C. § 922(g)) if it can be established that the firearm previously moved in or affected interstate or foreign commerce. For a ghost gun with no markings, there is no way to establish this by researching the recovered firearm. The only way to establish this would be to prove that the defendant moved the firearm itself in interstate or foreign commerce. This would be done through a confession, or potentially through cell phone or other GPS record analysis showing that the defendant crossed state lines when it can be shown that the firearm was with them. If a nexus to interstate or foreign commerce cannot be established, then no federal violation exists and consideration would need to be given to a state violation.

✓ **Unlicensed Manufacturing or Dealing.** Persons who devote time and attention to manufacturing or dealing in firearms, with the principle objective of livelihood or profit must have a license issued by ATF if the firearms manufactured or dealt had previously moved in or affected interstate commerce (Title 18 U.S.C. § 922(a)(1)(A)). To establish this in a dealing or manufacturing case, an investigator may be able to purchase firearms from the suspect in a manner that crosses state lines; or, an investigator may be able to document that the suspect is illegally exporting the firearms. The investigator can establish this through UC or CI conversation and evidence purchases. Another possible way to document this is to conduct a mail cover, and subpoena shipping records for packages received at the suspect's location. The investigator may then search those records for firearms parts purchases by the suspect and determine if the supplier(s) of those parts are out-of-state or in a foreign country.

✓ **Lookouts.** If there is an indication that this person may be illegally shipping the parts or firearms, or physically transporting these items across a border, place the subject and his address in TECs with a lookout so that CBP can give proper search attention to this person when they or their packages are encountered at a border crossing.

✓ **Gun Shows**. Conduct observation at area gun shows to determine if this person is selling any manufactured firearms in the local area.

✓ **Advertising.** Search online gun boards and chat rooms for signs of this person advertising firearms for sale.

✓ **UC or CI Approach**. If there is an indication that this person is selling to random persons rather than specific clients, a UC or CI purchase of firearms will assist in establishing the manufacturing and dealing without a license violation.

✓ **Financial Analysis and Forfeiture.** If there are criminal violations, there may be asset forfeiture potential for the proceeds of these crimes. The investigator should run checks of TECS and FinCEN for SARs, CTRs, Reports of International Transportation of CMIR (Customs Form 4790), and Reports of FBAR (Treasury Form 90-22.1), and conduct a full financial workup to determine the asset flow, what assets are forfeitable, what valued assets such as vehicles served as conveyances of illegal items, and if money laundering can be detected. These crimes will often involve electronic wires and mailings, so this may lead to mail and wire fraud violations. In addition to assets, machinery and equipment used to facilitate the violations are subject to forfeiture. CNC machines can be worth as much as $20,000 each, and forfeiture may be useful. Experts in properly powering down, storing, and appraising CNC machines should be consulted and used during such an operation.

Imported NFA Firearm Parts Kits

NFA firearm parts kits are more commonly associated with being imported into the U.S., and are comprised of the cut-up components of machine guns and other un-importable firearms. These firearms usually have some collectible, historical, or display trophy value (e.g., Sten Submachine guns) however it is illegal to import these fully functional firearms into the U.S. One solution to this is to cut up the firearm into non-functional parts which can then imported into the U.S. where persons may use some the parts to re-assemble a non-functional firearm or machine gun for display purposes only.

For machine guns to be properly destroyed and considered not readily restorable for purposes of importation into the U.S., the receivers must be severed with a cutting torch in at least three critical areas across the receiver. Those areas must be cut in a manner that removes at least 1/4 inch of material at each cut location. Each type of firearm will have specified locations where the 3 cuts must be made. ATF's FATD makes the rulings that establish where those cuts must be to fully render the machine gun receivers as nothing more than chunks of metal that cannot be readily restored to function.

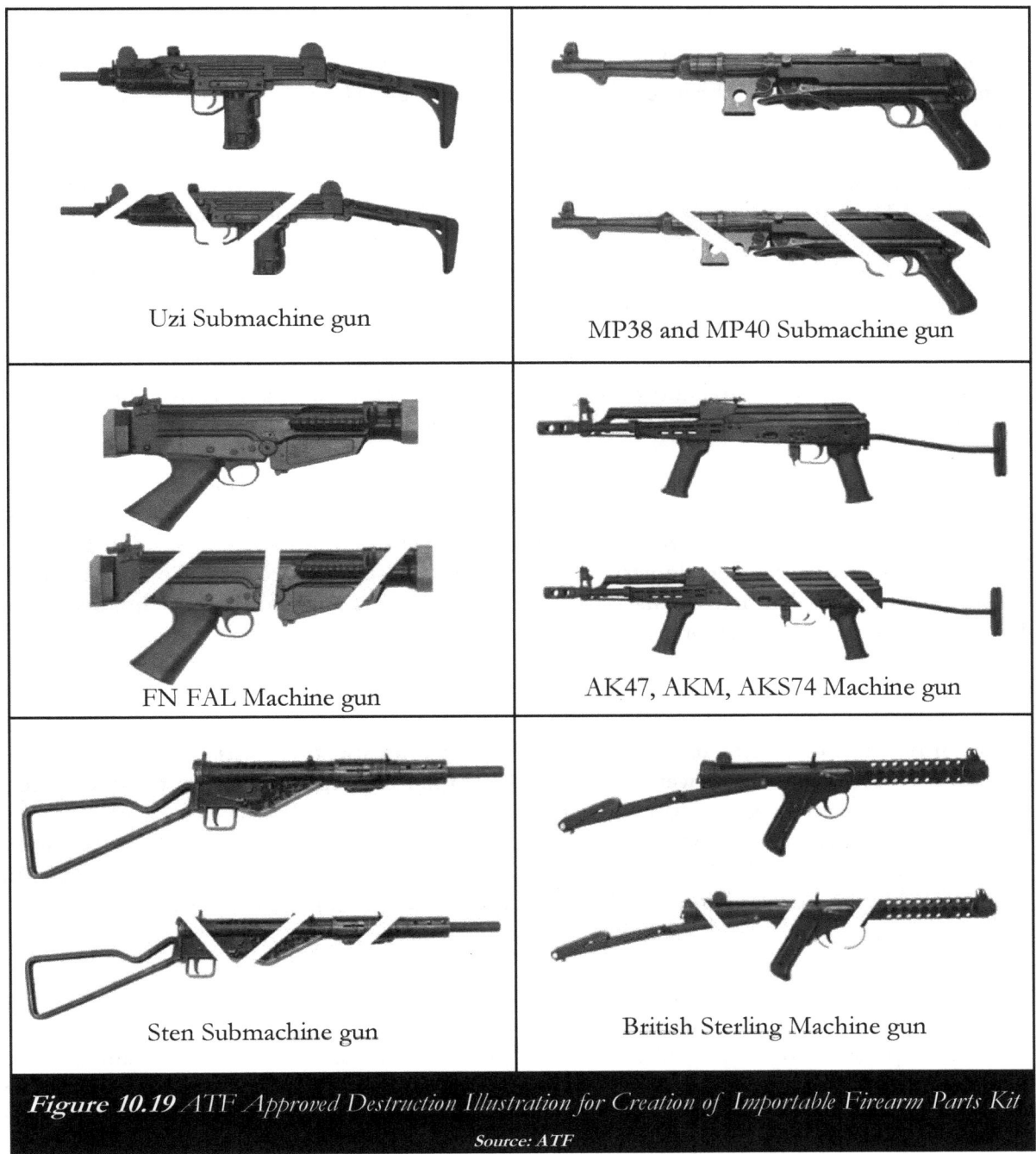

Uzi Submachine gun

MP38 and MP40 Submachine gun

FN FAL Machine gun

AK47, AKM, AKS74 Machine gun

Sten Submachine gun

British Sterling Machine gun

***Figure 10.19** ATF Approved Destruction Illustration for Creation of Importable Firearm Parts Kit*

Source: ATF

Figure 10.19 depicts the specified locations for ATF-approved torch cuts of machine gun frames for several types of firearms. Alternate methods of destruction may be used if critical areas of the

receiver are completely destroyed and rendered non-restorable. However, all requests for alternate destruction methods must be submitted to ATF's FATD for approval.

For detailed information regarding the legal requirements and proper procedures for importing firearms by licensed and non-licensed persons, agents should refer to the *ATF Guidebook: Importation & Verification of Firearms, Ammunition, and Implements of War* (Rev. Ed 2015) that is available on line at: https://www.atf.gov/firearms/docs/guide/atf-guidebook-importation-verification-firearms-ammunition-and-implements-war/download.

The importation of firearm parts kits is regulated under the GCA, NFA, and AECA. In general, an import license must be obtained from the U.S. DOS, DDTC and an approved ATF Form 6 must be secured from ATF prior to importation.

The importation of properly cut-up firearms as parts kits is legal as long as they have an ATF-approved ATF Form 6 and they are cut to the specific standards established by ATF's FATD.

Problems arise when these machine gun receivers are not destroyed to ATF-specified standards, which are designed to prevent the firearm from ever becoming readily restorable to a functional firearm. When these machine guns are not properly destroyed the design features of the receiver may still be intact, and the receiver could be "readily restorable" to machine gun configuration, which would make it illegal to import and illegal to possess in the U.S., particularly if the purchaser assembles the parts back to a fully functional machine gun.

Investigators should recognize a potential firearm parts kits violation when they recover a firearm, usually a foreign made rifle, that has weld marks across the receiver, no importer markings, and functions as a machine gun. Investigators are most likely to encounter a re-assembled firearm after it is recovered somewhere domestically in the U.S. Investigators are most likely to encounter a collection of parts that may not have been properly cut up at a port of entry or bonded warehouse, in an importer's inventory, or through online sales. Any investigator encountering such a firearm should consider the following investigative steps and background information on firearms parts kits:

✓ **Examination of Recovered Firearm.** Examine the firearm for seams or welds where the frame or receiver sections were welded into a complete machine gun. Contact the nearest ATF Field Office to request assistance from the ATF's FATD who can examine the firearm, render an expert opinion on how the firearm was assembled, and classify the firearm as an illegal firearm or machine gun under federal law. Oftentimes ATF's FATD will be able to render a preliminary opinion based on a quality set of overall photographs of the recovered firearm.

✓ **Deconfliction.** Conduct a full deconfliction of all names, addresses, phone numbers, and other information as it is encountered. Firearms trafficking routinely crosses the jurisdiction of multiple local, state, and federal agencies and deconfliction is critical to preventing a blue on blue situation, needless interference in on-going investigations, and general investigative effectiveness. See Chapter 9 for a description of a complete deconfliction process. In the case of an FFL, any investigator should contact ATF to coordinate the investigation as FFLs are regulated by ATF, and inevitably ATF records will be part of the investigation.

✓ **Interview Possessor.** Interview the possessor regarding how they acquired the firearm, from whom they acquired the firearm, what configuration it was in when they got it, and whether they know anyone else who may have these firearms or firearm parts. Usually firearms parts kits are brought in via bulk importations, and if there is one, there are likely to be many more.

✓ **Find the Source.** It is important to try and get to the source early to prevent these items from spreading out in to the general public. The agent should try to track the parts kits back to the source of importation, to conduct a thorough investigation of the importer focused on the proliferation of a bulk importation of potentially illegal parts kits. Arranging a product recall may become necessary if the firearms are not property destroyed and they were distributed.

✓ **Contact ATF FEIB and Examine ATF Form 6.** All imported firearm parts kits, although not functional firearms, may not be imported into the U.S. unless the importer secures and submits an ATF Form 6-Application for Firearm Import to ATF describing the parts and how they were cut, and that application is subsequently approved by ATF. To be approved for importation, the applicant must state "Firearms de-activated to ATF Specifications - See attached parts list" on the ATF Form 6. This means the importer is confirming to ATF that firearms have been cut to ATF's FATD specifications and are not readily restorable to be a firearm or machine gun. The approval process can be an honor system in which ATF makes a ruling on the ATF Form 6 Application for Importation based on what the importer writes on the application. Occasionally samples of a cut-up firearm are submitted to ATF for examination along with the ATF Form 6. They have up to one year to make the importation and never need to tell ATF when or where that importation will take place. CBP will encounter the firearm parts kits when they are finally imported, accompanied by the approved ATF Form 6. They may look at the parts and see if they match the description listed on the ATF Form 6 if they have a level of knowledge in this are that would allow them to do so. In most instances, because these are just parts, they are cleared for entry. The investigator should contact the ATF's FEIB to obtain copies of any ATF Form 6 that was submitted and approved or denied, and use the description of what was to be imported to compare against what was actually imported.

✓ **Parts that Require No Approvals.** It should be noted that some minor firearm components such as stocks, grips, screws, and firing pins, do not require an approved Form 6. Title 22 C.F.R. §447.21(c)(2) specifically excludes "minor components and parts..., except barrels, cylinders, receivers (frames), or complete breech mechanisms when the total value does not exceed $100 wholesale in any single transaction."

✓ **Proper Destruction Methods.** The accepted method for cutting a firearm is three torch cuts through the frame or receiver, in specified locations established by ATF's FATD, with each cut displacing at least 1/4 inch of metal and with enough internal components and receiver removed that it can pass an ATF's FATD approval after an evaluation. If an alternate method of destruction has been approved by ATF FATD, a description of that alternate method should accompany the approved ATF Form 6. An alternate method of destruction may be accomplished by saw cutting, or a plasma cutter. These make very clean cuts, but the restriction on the amount of receiver that can be left attached is more limiting than the torch cut method. Alternate methods are submitted to ATF's FATD whose written approval must be obtained before the import request is approved. When an investigator encounters alternate methods of destruction, they should request a copy of the ATF Form 6 and attachment from ATF Imports Branch to ensure they know what was required and whether or not it was done.

✓ **ATF FATD Assistance and Classification.** If an investigator recovers a firearm parts kit and is unsure if the parts kit was properly cut and destroyed, they should take photographs and contact their local ATF office for assistance in having the ATF's FATD examine the photographs and render an expert opinion and classification. If this recovery takes place during a CBP inspection, it is recommended that CBP hold the shipment until confirmation is received from ATF's FATD that the parts are properly cut and may be imported legally.

✓ **Interview Importer.** Once a determination indicates the parts are not properly cut and not eligible for lawful importation, CBP or ATF may consider forfeiting the parts as a violation of Title 18 U.S.C. § 922(l) or 18 U.S.C. § 545. At that time an interview should be conducted with the importer to determine their level of knowledge and intent regarding the attempted importation of these illegal firearms and firearms parts. There may be false statements on the ATF Form 6 which would constitute violation of Title 18 U.S.C. § 1001.

✓ **Deconfliction.** Once a determination indicates that the parts are not properly cut and not eligible for lawful importation, a full deconfliction of all individual and business names associated with the importer as well as their contact information should be conducted to determine if other law enforcement agencies have the importer under investigation currently or have had them under investigation in the past.

✓ **Potential Violations.** If criminal intent is established during the investigation, then potential federal violations for illegally importing firearm parts kits includes, but is not limited to: Title 18 U.S.C. § 922(l) - improper importation of a firearm, which is also an SUA for money laundering; Title 18 U.S.C. § 922(o) and Title 26 U.S.C. § 5861 - unlawful possession of a machine gun; Title 18 U.S.C. § 922(a)(1)(A) – unlicensed manufacturing or dealing in firearms; Title 18 U.S.C. § 545 - smuggling violations; Title 22 U.S.C. § 2778, the AECA; Title 18 U.S.C. § 923(i) - licensing violations by licensed importer or manufacture for failure to mark firearms with a serial number and importer information; and Title 26 U.S.C. § 7201 involving the failure to pay FAET importation.

✓ **Financial Analysis.** If there is criminal intent to commit a fraud, there may be asset forfeiture potential for the proceeds of this import as well as prior improper imports. The investigator should run checks of TECS and FinCEN for SARs, CTRs, Reports of International Transportation of CMIR (Customs Form 4790), and Reports of FBAR (Treasury Form 90-22.1), and conduct a full financial workup to determine the asset flow, what assets are forfeitable, what valued assets such as vehicles served as conveyances of illegal items, and if money laundering can be detected. Importation will often involve electronic wires and mailings, so this may lead to mail and wire fraud violations.

✓ **Valued Asset Forfeiture.** If the investigator finds indications or the movement and laundering of illegal trafficking proceeds through the review of financial databases, they should use FinCEN services to secure credit history information to identify bank accounts and credit cards. Once these are identified, the investigator can use subpoenas to secure the records and begin to examine these to document the amounts of illegal proceeds for forfeiture.

✓ **Firearm Parts Recall and Forfeiture.** If the investigator determines that all or some of the illegal firearm parts kits were already distributed into the U.S., an effort should be undertaken to determine where and to whom those kits were provided. A plan should be devised for issuing a recall notice on these firearms parts kits or actually deploying investigators to those lo-

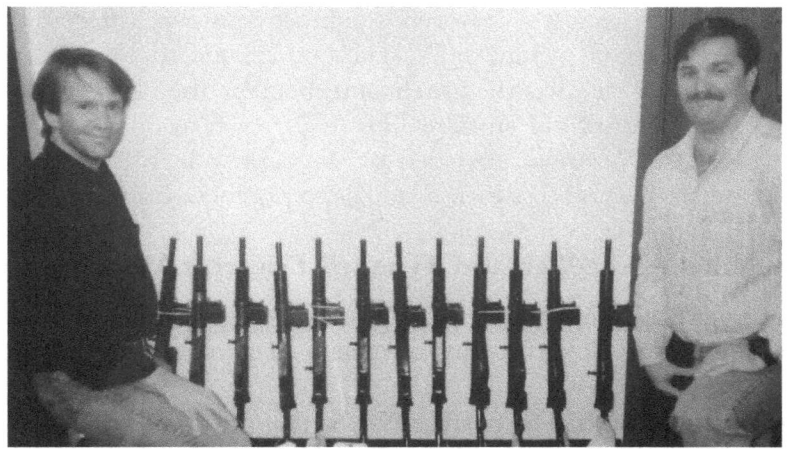

Figure 10.20 Author with Seizure of Trafficked Sten Machineguns Made from Imported Parts Kits in1993
Source: Author's Collection

cations to recover the improper parts kits. If during the recall any of the firearm parts kits are found to have been completely assembled to a functional machine gun or possessed by a prohibited person, a criminal investigation of those violations should be initiated.

TYPE 10: INTERNET-BASED FIREARMS TRAFFICKING INVESTIGATION

Internet-based firearms trafficking is a growing concern that will continue to become more problematic in the future as computer technology continues to evolve producing higher levels of anonymity and becoming consistently more intuitive, affordable, and accessible. Based on anecdotal information, firearms trafficking by means of the internet likely exceeds the combined amount of illegally trafficked firearms sold at flea markets and gun shows.

The benefits that internet sources of firearms offer afford traffickers, violent lone wolves, gang members, cartels, transnational criminal organizations, and terrorists are many:

➢ The purchaser and seller can be anonymous or identify themselves with fictitious names, and anonymity often attracts criminal violators.
➢ The purchaser can use pay systems to ensure that they receive their product before final transfer of funds.
➢ The purchaser and seller never have to physically meet anyone, which reduces the biggest risk for a purchaser to be arrested or ripped-off.
➢ The purchaser can have bulk items shipped to a mail drop where they can watch and wait until they feel it is safe to take possession of the shipment, and then never use the drop again.

A 2017 Rand Corp study entitled *Behind the Curtain: The illicit trade of firearms, explosives, and ammunition on the dark web,* reported the following key findings.

➢ The US appears to be the most common source country for arms that are for sale on the dark web. Almost 60% of the firearms listings are associated with products that originate from the US. However, Europe represents the largest market for arms trade on the dark web, generating revenues that are around five times higher than the U.S.

➢ Firearms listings (42%) were the most common listings on the dark web, followed by arms-related digital products (27%) and others, including ammunition (22%).

➢ The dark web has the potential to become the platform of choice for individuals (e.g. lone-wolf terrorists) or small groups (e.g. gangs) to obtain weapons and ammunition behind the anonymity curtain provided by the dark web. In addition, the dark web could be used by vulnerable and fixated individuals to purchase firearms.[cxli]

Regions of the Web and Types of Firearms Markets

Internet-based firearms trafficking is taking place as all levels of the internet. The activity includes both legal and illegal firearms trafficking. The regions of the internet activity include:

➢ **Surface Web.** The Surface Web is that portion of the www that is catalogued, readily accessible to the general public, and searchable with standard search engines such as Google™ and Bing™. The surface web is where most of the general public routinely operates, and it is exactly as described, just the visible surface of the www.

➢ **Deep Web.** Below the Surface Web is a vast deep web that has not been indexed by search engines, and consists of classified advertisements, forums, blogs, chat rooms, and many invite-only groups. To find an uncatalogued site on the deep web you need to know the web address of the site you are looking for.

➢ **Dark Web.** The Dark Web is a small portion of the deep web that contains intentionally concealed sites and information that requires specific software to find and use. The Dark Web affords a high level of anonymity. Some legitimate uses of the Dark Web include Media Outlets that use the dark web to receive anonymous information from sources through software such as The Onion Router (TOR™), the Invisible Internet Project (I2P™), and Securedrop™. Other legal uses include social services and domestic violence victims who need to communicate without being cyber-stalked. However, anonymity attracts the criminal element, and illicit uses of the Dark web include child pornography as well as narcotics, firearms, and human trafficking.[cxlii]

TOR is a commonly used free software that is used for anonymous online communication as well as deep and dark web surfing and shopping. The TOR routes the user's communications through multiple layers of routers to mask the user's true IP. Oftentimes the only way to identify someone on the Dark Web is to work to establish a user's "digital footprint" on the Surface Web, then identify the user through their surface web activity.[cxliii] To do this the TOR user has to make a mistake that reveals a tidbit of information that can link them to their surface web activity.

It is very easy for purchasers to locate and order firearms, machine guns, silencers, firearms parts, firearms flats and castings, and ammunition. Detection of firearms trafficking may be done through observation and analysis of online postings; however, the most effective method is via UC contact by a sworn law enforcement official trained in the methods of UC. At all times the focus must be on detecting and investigating criminal activity and must not focus on associations or cause interference with the legal commerce in firearms. The primary categories of firearms suppliers, legal and illegal, operating on the www include:

✓ **Major Retailers.** Major retailers advertise on the internet and require a customer to go to a specific store operated by the retailer to make the firearm purchase. Examples of major retailers in this category include Cabela's® or Bass Pro-Outlets®.

✓ **Online Retailers.** Online retailers transfer purchased firearms to an FFL in the state where the purchaser resides so that the purchaser may lawfully take possession of the firearm. Online retailers are non-chain FFLs who can enhance their sales and customer base by selling online and shipping firearms sold to the purchaser's designated FFL in their state of residence.

✓ **Online Auction and Marketplace Sites.** Online auction and marketplace sites conduct transactions in a variety of ways. Some enable users to search for firearms by major city or zip code, which can assist in person-to-person transactions once a desired firearm is found by a purchaser. Examples of online auction and market place sites include sites dedicated just to firearms sales and sites dedicated to sales or all types of items. Sites just for firearms often allow searches by gun type regardless of location and then, when done legally, the private seller would ship the firearm to an FFL the purchaser designates in the state in which the purchaser resides. Such online auction and marketplaces include GunsAmerica.com™, Gunbroker.com™, Armslist.com™, Grabagun.com™, Guninternational.com™, and Gunbuyer.com™. An investigator may find domestic unlicensed firearms traffickers on these sites, and should establish a UC account and learn how to research the sale volume and patterns of sellers to detect unlicensed dealers. There are sites that sell just about anything in addition to guns, and these sites include Craigslist™, eBay™, and Alibaba™. While many of these sites have implemented "no firearms sales" policies over the years, it is possible to still find firearms parts and silencers labeled as something else. There will not be standard guns sales on these sites but the more nuanced parts kits, flats, castings, and illegal NFA weapons being listed by other names. The screening mechanisms can fail to identify these items but certain users know how to find them. Examples would include the sale of silencers labeled as "solvent traps" or for use with paint ball guns when in fact they are silencers. Other examples include illegal parts that can convert firearms to fire as machine guns; however, the term firearm and machine gun are never listed.

✓ **Online Classifieds.** Online classified advertisements allow purchasers to conduct searches of major cities, regions of states, or by a specified distance such as a 20-mile radius of the purchaser's zip code. This can assist in person-to-person transactions once a desired firearm is found by a purchaser and tends to involve more unlicensed firearms dealers than FFLs. Online classified advertisements may or may not involve a site totally dedicated to the sale of firearms and firearms supplies. In the Northeast, Maine's "Uncle Henrys™ - Everything Under the Sun," is a popular paper, and runs online classified advertisement that provides a forum for users to sell just about everything, including firearms. At the national level, "Shotgun News" is a popular paper that runs online classified advertisement that provides a forum strictly for firearms and firearms accoutrements. An investigator may find domestic unlicensed firearms traffickers on these sites, and should establish a UC account and learn how to research the sale volume and patterns of sellers to detect unlicensed dealers. Once a suspect is identified, conduct a full deconfliction and intelligence workup to ensure that the person is not licensed or already under investigation, and then begin a UC approach to include evidence buys and recorded emails.

✓ **Online Forums.** Online forums and social-media networks enable users to advertise firearms for sale in addition to sharing firearms knowledge. When firearms are sold via these forums, the transfer can occur person-to-person or door-to-door, meaning the firearm is shipped or mailed. Such sites include the National Gun Forum™, the Firearms Forum™, and Firearms Talk™. An investigator may use their UC identity to review or initiate UC conversation in these forums, as persons using these sites often have knowledge of online sources of firearms to refer others to.

✓ **Dark Web Sites.** The dark websites facilitate sales between sellers and buyers who truly seek to remain anonymous and to operate outside laws and regulations. Buyers and sellers use special online tools to complete the entire transaction and protect the identity of both parties. Sellers ship the firearms, often disassembled or concealed in other items, and in packages that are mislabeled as something other than firearms or firearm parts. There is level of risk for getting ripped-off on the dark web, buying a fraudulent item, or, if the seller can identify the intended purchaser of an illegal item, the purchaser could become the target of blackmail. The two common types of transactions on the dark web are:

➢ **Crypto Markets.** These sites bring together multiple sellers, known as 'vendors', managed by marketplace administrators in return for a commission on sales. Crypto markets provide third-party services that afford a degree of payment protection to customers, such as secure escrow in which payment is released to vendors only after customers have received and are satisfied with their purchases, as well as a process for third-party dispute adjudication. One of the more notorious crypto markets was Silk Road.

➢ **Vendor Shops.** These sites, also known as 'single-vendor markets', are set up by a vendor to make sales for that vendor alone. These vendors sell directly to customers. Customers may trade off third party protection for a better price.

Once the online part of the transaction is finalized, the products purchased are normally shipped by post using special shipping techniques to minimize the risk of detection. This often includes breaking down firearms into parts or secreting them into other items and then shipping them in separate parcels marked as products other than firearms or firearm parts.

An investigator with good technical knowledge of firearms is absolutely necessary to find sites and other internet sources of illegal firearms. Sites often appear legitimate at first, but key parts and terms can reveal what the seller may really have available. The primary form of support the investigator will need is an intelligence analyst who can link data from various sources together, and who can put together referral packages on each identified purchaser. These investigations can be labor-intensive; however, they are well worth the time if the investigator can shut down a site that may be responsible for trafficking thousands of illegal and untraceable firearms to gangs, cartels, terrorists, and violent lone wolves.

The volume of trafficking detected in each case, as well as the types of violations and techniques to investigate those violations, will vary greatly, just as they do in traditional firearms trafficking cases. Investigators may find large volume unlicensed firearms dealers on a site like Guns America.com by noticing unlicensed persons with hundreds of "hits" (sales) over time. Investigators may find sellers shipping handguns direct to purchasers in other states. Investigators may also find persons selling illegal NFA weapons or operating from a foreign country and willing to ship firearms direct to U.S. purchasers without complying with any importation requirements. The investigator will need to find and identify suspicious internet trafficking activity.

There are three primary phases in any internet trafficking investigation. Those goals, as well as suggested steps and techniques for achieving those goals, are discussed in this section.

PHASE I: SCOPING, PLANNING, INVESTIGATIVE OPERATIONS

Fully identify the illegal source of firearms, the level of criminal intent of the source, the types of commodities for sale, and the methods of payment and shipment used by the source. Then establish a plan to stop the source of firearms. This may be accomplished using the following techniques:

✓ **Clean Computer.** Obtain a clean, agency authorized, undercover computer and hard drive. It is recommended that the investigator use a separate hard drive for each investigation and that drive will be considered the original evidence.

✓ **UC Persona.** Open an undercover email account using an agency authorized and back-stopped undercover identity. Preferably the identity will include an online history, but if it does not the investigator needs to spend time logging into and setting up UC accounts at online firearms auction sites and forums so that a real life online user history is formed. Undercover email accounts can easily be established for free using Hotmail™, Gmail™, or other similar service providers. You can also further hide the identity of your computer by using any one of a number of online anonymizer services, such as www.anonymizer.com. Any investigator opening an online undercover identity, undercover website, or opening other undercover accounts should log those undercover identities with their agency to include user names and passwords.

✓ **The Don'ts of Internet Investigation.** Investigators should never do any of the following:
   ➢ Conduct online undercover investigation or intelligence activity using personal equipment or a personal website, email address, social network, or service account.
   ➢ Conduct online undercover investigation or intelligence activity using an official government computer, as this will have an IP that shows the government as the owner, and tech savvy criminals know how to open IP headers.
   ➢ Create an online persona or account using the name, identify information, photo, business logo, etc., of an actual person or company without their expressed written permission.
   ➢ Assume the existing online persona or account of someone without their expressed written permission. See Appendix D for a template Authorization to Assume Online Identity form.
   ➢ Initiate actual UC contact and conversation with a suspect unless you are a sworn law enforcement officer.
   ➢ Use approved UC online identities or accounts for personal or inappropriate purposes.
   ➢ Interfere with the lawful commerce of firearms online.

✓ **Initiate Contact, Open, and Identify IP.** Once the investigator has identified a potential source, initiate an undercover email, and attempt to get a return email from the source that will contain their IP. IP stands for Internet Protocol, which is a unique numerical address that all computing devices and smartphones use to identify itself and communicate with other devices in the IP network. Any device connected to the IP network must have a unique IP address within the network. An IP address is analogous to a street address or telephone number in that it is used to uniquely identify an entity. The location of IP headers depends on the internet service provider (e.g., Gmail or Hotmail). Instructions for how to open an IP header can be found at each service provider's website.

Once the investigator receives a return email, open the IP header in the email. Once the source email IP header is opened, look for the IP number. Once the investigator identifies the IP numerical address, they will need to go to ARIN Whois (whois.arin.net) to identify the service provider this IP is registered to. ARIN is the American Registry of Internet Numbers. The WHOIS service gives contact and registration information for IP addresses, autonomous system numbers (ASN), organizations or customers associated with these resources, and related points of contact. It does not include information on domain names or military networks.[cxliv] The following specific information is available through WHOIS lookup and search functions:

- ➢ WHOIS search feature for IP addresses: Find domain name owner from IP Address, search origin of IPs.
- ➢ ARIN search: Find out who is behind that IP address, conduct a reverse IP check, look up IP address owner, and complete an IP address search.
- ➢ WHOIS IP address lookup: Research IP addresses, IP lookup, Shows ISP network blocks.
- ➢ WHOIS lookup for IP addresses: IP address tracer, Search IP address owner, IP address reverse lookup, IP address location, find out who owns an IP address.

To find out registration information about a domain name, the investigator should go to www.internic.net which is the Internet Network Information Center (InterNIC) operated by the National Science Foundation. They are responsible for the registration of all IP addresses ending in .com, .org, .net, .gov, and .edu.

Once the investigator has information on the service provider regarding who the IP or domain name is registered to, that business will get a subpoena to disclose the information related to the person to whom that device is registered. This may or may not be the identity of your source, depending upon their level or technological proficiency to hide their true IP. This will only work for domestic service providers, as a U.S. subpoena carries no authority in a foreign country. If the IP is in a foreign country, the investigator may want to work with the AUSA to pursue an MLAT to have the foreign country secure this information.

The investigator can sometimes get the source to identify themselves and their address through undercover email conversation; however, should still follow the above steps to corroborate what is revealed in the email conversation.

- ✓ **Deconfliction.** Conduct a full deconfliction of all emails, websites, names, addresses, phone numbers, and other information as it is encountered throughout the investigation. Internet based firearms trafficking can be seen by investigators anywhere in the country and any agency could be working on the source at any time. Deconfliction is critical to preventing a blue on blue situation, needless interference in on-going investigations, and general investigative effectiveness. See Chapter 9 for a description of a complete deconfliction process.

- ✓ **Full Intelligence Workup.** A full intelligence workup should be performed on the source once they are identified, including financial checks for SARs in FinCEN and CTRs in TECs. A full online profile workup should be performed to determine what OSINT is available where the unlicensed dealer is talking about their dealing online in their own words or where the unlicensed dealer is posting and selling firearms in online classified advertisement and gun board sites. This will be particularly useful to help identify anyone who may be anonymously trafficking on the Dark Web.

- ✓ **Forfeiture.** If the investigator finds indications or the movement and laundering of illegal trafficking proceeds through the review of financial databases, they should use FinCEN services to secure credit history information to identify bank accounts and credit cards. Once these are identified, the investigator can use subpoenas to secure the records and begin to examine these to document the amounts of illegal proceeds for forfeiture.

- ✓ **Website History Determination.** Investigators should utilize the Wayback Machine™ (www.archive.org/web/web.php) to identify the history of the source website and determine how many years the site has operated and what has been for sale. The Wayback Machine is the archive service of the internet. Using the Wayback Machine investigators may capture and save digital images of each iteration of the website.

✓ **Website Metadata Examination.** The investigator should have computer forensics specialists download a copy of the website and examine the source code running in the background. One tactic that illegal firearms traffickers use is to place words in the data that are not visible on the page. These words will be tied to items for sale that the proprietor does not want to publicly advertise but that they search engines to hit on. A site can run "silencer" or "machine gun" in the background metadata and this will give the site hits for anyone searching with those words - even though they don't actually appear in any visible way on the site.

✓ **Email Preservation Letter.** The investigator should serve a preservation letter on the email service provider so they begin to store all the email traffic for later retrieval via a search warrant. The results will allow the investigator to read all the emails sent and received by the source and their other customers. This can be done every 30 to 90 days. See Appendix D for an example of a Preservation Letter.

✓ **Determine Payment and Shipping Methods as well as Venue.** Conduct UC email conversation with the source that can determine their level of criminal intent, the types of illegal firearms for sale, the payment methods they accept (e.g., Western Union™, PayPal™, money order, bitcoin™, credit card), and shipping methods they use (e.g., FedEx™, UPS™, U.S. Postal Service). The investigator will also want to establish venue and jurisdiction over the source and their violations, and this can be done via the online emails and evidence purchases. Venue can also be established where the source's internet service provider is located. For foreign-based websites, venue can be established through undercover email and evidence purchases. If the website is domestically based and the location is identified, it is recommended that the investigator coordinate with law enforcement officials and the local ATF office in that area, so they can corroborate evidence and statements through observation and assist in any search warrant service.

✓ **UC Purchases of Evidence and Price Identification.** Using the UC persona, place an undercover order for an item (illegal firearm) and have it shipped to a UC address. Over the course of the investigation, at least one of each type of product available for sale on the site as possible. It is important to know the cost of each items being sold. Later in the investigation, after securing payment records and email records of other customers, the investigator will see how much money other purchasers sent to the site and from there the investigator may be able to determine what that purchaser paid for based on the amount. For example, if a silencer is $650 and a purchaser wired $1,950 to the site, this may indicate the purchase of three silencers.

✓ **Foreign Based Websites.** Once the investigator identifies the types of firearms being sold, if the Web site is foreign based, contact the ATF National Tracing Center and try to secure data on unsuccessful traces on that type of firearm because the importer markings were not provided during the trace request. It may be that those foreign-manufactured firearms actually did not bear an importer mark because they were illegally imported via a Web site order. These may be leads. In fact, the recovery of foreign-made firearms bearing no importer markings may be an indicator of illegal importation.

✓ **Trace Evidence.** Upon receipt of any purchased item, photograph the package, packaging materials, and contents upon its arrival. Look for hairs or other trace evidence in the package

and swab for DNA before processing for latent fingerprints. Any developed trace evidence may be useful for comparison against known samples from the suspect(s) at a later date. If the package has a return address that is handwritten, save this for later handwriting comparison against known exemplars from the suspect. Note what the illegal source identified the contents of the package to be (e.g., truck parts, toys, computer parts, etc.…).

✓ **NCIC Checks.** Check the firearm in NCIC to determine if it is stolen. If it is, that is a significant lead to follow up on. If any firearms are stolen, follow up on stolen firearms information (e.g., link between FFL and theft, other potential defendants).

✓ **Crime Gun Tracing.** Firearms purchased should be traced immediately; however, the investigator should ask that the ATF NTC only trace to the retail FFL and not contact that retail FFL for the purchaser information. The trace information will assist in identifying the wholesaler the FFL uses for supply. This only applies to domestic sources of firearms.

✓ **Obliterated Serial Numbers.** If the purchased firearms have obliterated serial numbers they should be submitted to a laboratory to attempt to raise the serial numbers and then traced through the ATF NTC if whole or partial serial numbers are recovered.

✓ **NIBIN.** Firearms purchased should be submitted to a lab for test-firing and the submission of the test fires to NIBIN to determine if the firearm was used in a prior shooting. NIBIN is used in countries all over the world, and an investigator may request a special search in the country of origin.

✓ **ATF FATD.** Depending on the type of weapon purchased, it may require examination and classification by the ATFs FATD to determine if it is an illegal NFA weapon. This might be accomplished preliminarily by emailing quality digital photographs of the items to the ATF's FATD.

✓ **Extradition Treaty and Foreign Gun Laws.** If ordering from a website source in a foreign country, determine whether that country has an extradition treaty with the U.S., and whether firearms trafficking is an extraditable offense under the treaty. The investigator should also attempt to review that country's gun laws and attempt to order an item that is a violation of both U.S. law and that country's law, as this may be helpful in extradition efforts. Some countries do not allow law enforcement to conduct undercover operations at all, while others do not allow the use of electronic surveillance, so your evidence may be of no use to officials in a foreign country in those instances. Understanding the foreign source country's laws will often explain why the suspect sells certain items in a certain way, and why they ship things in a certain way. For example, in Germany the barrel is the firearm and the receiver is not whereas in the U.S. it is just the opposite. When purchasing firearms from a source in Germany, you may get guns with no barrels as the seller tries to comply with German law. In Argentina it is legal to possess Glock switches and silencers but not machineguns and this will impact how a trafficker operates. In Brazil the civilian ownership of firearms is illegal and AR15 or AK47 rifles that sell for $1000 in the U.S. can be sold for as much as $15,000 on the street in Brazil, providing a strong incentive for gun smuggling to that country.

✓ **Law Enforcement Cooperation.** On a foreign based trafficking source, the investigator should ensure that they have involved both ATF and HSI. Both agencies have jurisdiction, and different capabilities to bring to bear. The agencies are compelled to work together on international trafficking cases in accordance with a 2009 MOU.

✓ **TECS and CBP NTC Lookouts.** If there is an indication that this person may be illegally shipping the firearms into or out of the U.S., place the subject and their address in TECs with a lookout so that CBP or ICE can give proper search attention to their packages as they are encountered entering or exiting the U.S. Not only will this help prevent any firearms from getting trafficked to others while the investigator is working to establish violations, it will produce leads for the case, as the lookout will include a notification to the investigator. **NOTE:** Any items seized and forfeited will cause notice to be sent to the person listed on the package. The investigator can ask that the CBP or ICE agent postpone making notification during a sensitive phase in the investigation. The investigator may also want to give consideration to organizing a controlled delivery of the package to the intended recipient culminating with their arrest and interview.

PHASE II: IDENTIFYING OTHER CUSTOMERS AND PLANNING ARRESTS AND RECOVERIES

Fully identify the trafficking source and their scope of trafficking by identifying their customers who ordered and received illegal firearms and then establishing plans to retrieve the firearms, arrest recipients, and prevent the use of these firearms in future crimes. This may be accomplished using the techniques discussed below.

✓ **Email Search Warrant.** Secure and serve a search warrant to obtain email traffic maintained by the internet service provider who was previously served with a preservation letter. **NOTE:** To keep this step from being revealed to the source, only ask for emails the source has sent and emails the source has received AND READ. Do not ask for unread emails. Unopened emails copied by the service provider in response to a search warrant request may show up as opened following that process. The source will be able to see that their prior unread emails have now been opened. The investigator can serve another preservation letter and go back with another search warrant for those emails at a later date.

✓ **Processing Customer Emails.** Once the investigator receives the email information they will need to read and scan for pertinent emails as well as organize and analyze the information. They will need to open the IP header for each email and follow the previously described process to identify the person's having email conversation with the source. These emails may contain name and shipping information that identify other customers, but this should be corroborated through IP identification.

✓ **Create Customer Files.** Once the investigator begins to identify customers who have purchased illegal firearms or caused an illegal importation of firearms, they need to start a file on each person. The first information to go in this file will be all the pertinent emails which may hold discussion about the illegal items they have purchased and received.

✓ **Shipping Records.** Subpoena each shipper the source is known to use (e.g., FedEx, UPS, DHL). Ask for all packages sent to and sent from the shipping location of the firearms source. Request that the information be provided on a disk in Excel format so that it may be easily sorted and analyzed. Begin to match the shipping records to the emails indicating purchases. This will be the second piece of information for the customer file. This information will show that the customer received the package from the source after they ordered an illegal

firearm by email. If U.S. mail was used, contact the U.S. Postal Service Inspectors (USPS) and request their assistance in the investigation. The USPS can query the source name and address in their system and identify every person who ever received a signature-required delivery from the site. In addition, they can determine the date, the time, the location where the package was received, and the name of the person who signed for the package, and produce an electronic copy of the signature, and identify the USPS employee who delivered the package.

✓ **Payment Records.** Subpoena each payment service provider the shipper accepted payment through (e.g., Western Union, PayPal, Credit Cards, Bank Wire Transfers). The investigator should have documented the payment accounts of the source as they were making payments for evidence being purchased. Request that the information be provided on a disk in Excel format so that it may be easily sorted and analyzed. Begin to match the payment records to the emails indicating purchases. This will be the third piece of information for the customer file. This information will show that the customer paid for items later received in the package from the source after they ordered the illegal firearm by email. The investigator should now be able to begin to determine what each customer purchased and received. This information will either be in the email or revealed based on how much money the customer paid compared to the known prices of items for sale.

✓ **Crime Gun Intelligence Development.** For each customer identified, conduct full intelligence workups on them and add that information to the customer file. The investigator will want to determine if these purchasers are prohibited from having firearms, or are gang members, cartel associates, on the terrorist watch list, or apparently firearms traffickers also. The following database checks should be conducted.
  ➤ **eTrace.** To determine any other firearms history associated with crime gun recoveries, multiple handgun purchases, or stolen firearms.
  ➤ **NCIC and Accurint.** To determine criminal history and other firearms possession prohibiting factors.
  ➤ **TECS.** To determine any border crossings or Reports of International Transportation of CMIR (Customs Form 4790).
  ➤ **FinCEN.** To determine if there are SARs, Reports of FBAR (Treasury Form 90-22.1), other Financial reports, and to run a financial history.
  ➤ **ATF FELC.** To determine if the person is or was an FFL.
  ➤ **ATF FEIB.** To determine if the person actually completed an ATF Form 6 application to import the item or has submitted ATF Form 6 in the past which can help to establish that the purchaser knows the legal process to import firearms into the U.S.
  ➤ **ATF NFRTR.** To determine if this person possesses any registered NFA weapons which helps establish that they know the requirements of the NFA
  ➤ **Local Police Department and Databases.** To determine what intelligence may exist on the purchaser at their local police department.
  ➤ **Gang Databases and JTTF Checks.** To determine the status of the purchaser in regard to their ties to this type of activity.

✓ **Source Identification.** Before the source can be indicted they must be identified. Is the person the UC has been dealing with a real person or are they a fictitious identify or a boiler room operation where 20 people are posing as the same person. There are several options for this part of the investigation:

- ➤ **Lure.** The investigator may seek DOJ approval to lure the foreign national trafficker to the U.S. or to a country that has extradition provisions with the U.S. (e.g., Bahamas) to discuss a deal, at which point they can be fully identified and potentially arrested. This is a sensitive investigative procedure and must have prior DOJ approval.

- ➤ **Foreign Travel.** If a lure is not approved or the source will not travel to the U.S., the investigator may seek approval to set up a meeting in the source's foreign country to identify the source. This may lead to a second meeting the in U.S. in which the subject is willing to travel to the U.S., where they will be arrested or, this meeting can be turned over the authorities in the foreign country who will take action against the source.

- ➤ **HUMINT.** Determine if your agency has any international CIs or sources of information that that have the ability to physically identify the source or their location. Through U.S. attachés, determine if law enforcement in the foreign country has any way to confirm the identity of the source and if they will do so based on an informal request or if they require an MLAT.

- ➤ **OSINT.** Research of open source material may lead to documents, photographs, and other information indicating that the source of firearms is an actual person. This should be one piece of the identity confirmation and not relied on exclusively, since someone could be using their identity. OSINT may only confirm that the identity of such a person exists.

- ➤ **Electronic Communications Device Analysis - PEN.** At this point in the investigation, it may be useful to secure a court order for PEN on the email, IP, or domain name of the source. This will yield additional significant information on the source of firearms with the potential for identification of the illegal trafficker, as well as information on additional customers. Investigators should make sure to use language in the application for the court that will allow the initial court order to be used in subsequent requests to identify subscriber information.

- ➤ **Internet T-III.** If all attempts to identify the illegal internet trafficked have failed, an internet T-III may be an option. If the investigator can show that they have exhausted all possible means to identify and apprehend the source, they may qualify for approval of a T-III electronic interception of the email traffic in real time. A traditional T-III on a phone is manpower-intensive; however, an email T-III is not. Email traffic does not need to be monitored 24 hours a day; it only needs to be downloaded once daily for review and minimization. This eliminates the need for shift staffing and overtime to cover a 24-hour monitoring process. Further, emails are the written word, so no transcriptions and the associated costs are involved. A T-III can only be performed if the source is located in the U.S. or if a foreign-based source is using a U.S.-based internet service provider. Email conversations will be placed in the customer files as they are matched. A plan to prevent the observed real-time trafficking of firearms will need to be put in place. That will include attempting to rapidly identify any purchaser, tracking their package, intercepting their package, and either holding the package until a later round-up or conducting a controlled delivery. The investigator should not allow guns to walk. See Appendix D for a template of an internet T-III application and affidavit.

- ➤ **MLATS for Foreign Based Internet Service Providers.** Only U.S. based internet service providers are subject to subpoenas, court orders, and search warrants issued by U.S. Courts. Fortunately, foreign firearms traffickers frequently end up using U.S. internet service providers, particularly if they are looking to appeal to U.S. based customers. However, should an investigator encounter a firearms trafficker using an internet service provider in a foreign country, they may still be able to serve search warrants for evidence

on email and other internet service providers through the use of an MLAT. The investigator and AUSA should consider this and explore the merits of pursuing an MLAT to have law enforcement in a foreign country assist in the investigation.

✓ **Organize Case Takedown.** Once the investigator is able to identify the source to the extent that they can secure an indictment, they should move forward with plans to take the case down and conduct a roundup of persons in the U.S. who previously received firearms from the source. The following steps may be useful in that process.

➢ **Prepare Intelligence Referrals on Customers.** Prepare the customer files into referral packages on each person who received illegal firearms from the source. Rate the referrals based on urgency. Referrals on persons who have been identified as prohibited from possessing firearms, gang members, or associated with terrorism are the top priorities.

➢ **Identify Local Assistance.** The investigator will need to find other investigators nearby who can assist. This is why, from the start, it is prudent to have ATF and HSI involved in the investigation. They have offices throughout the U.S., and their offices can handle these referrals. The referral packages should be sent out with a date sometime in the future (usually 30 days later) when all investigators will conduct an enforcement action. The recipient of the package will conduct additional surveillance of the location and local intelligence checks and then determine if they will handle this as a "knock and talk", a search warrant service, or a search and arrest warrant service. The goal is to recover as many of the illegal trafficked firearms as possible. The recipient of the referral will take statements from each possessor if possible, gather evidence, and pursue their own possession cases against the customer in their area. However, the evidence will also be used in the overarching case against the firearms trafficking source.

✓ **Enforcement Roundup.** On the designated date and time, all investigators who received a referral package will conduct their enforcement action. This simultaneous action will preclude warnings being sent out on the internet to customers so they can get rid of evidence or have time to prepare to resist investigators. The results of each enforcement action will be reported back to the case agent(s).

PHASE III: SHUTDOWN THE SOURCE

The final goal is to present the evidence to a grand jury and secure an indictment, arrest, extradition where needed, and successful prosecution of the source, as well as seizure and forfeiture of the website.

✓ **Hard Drive Evidence.** After conclusion of all UC email conversations, make 3 duplicates of the hard drives. The original hard drive becomes evidence, one hard drive is a working copy, and 2 hard drives go to the AUSA who can provide 1 copy to the defense at the time of any discovery production.

✓ **Extradition.** In conjunction with the AUSA, research the extradition treaty the U.S. may have with the firearms trafficker's country. If it there is an extradition treaty that allows the trafficker to be indicted and extradited to the U.S., then the proceed with securing an indictment and the AUSA will seek approval from DOJ to request extradition. If extradition is approved, a provisional warrant will be issued that officials in the foreign country can serve. Once arrested, the subject then has the right to an extradition hearing in which the U.S. must prove that the person arrested is the same person wanted in the U.S. for the alleged violations.

If the hearing is successful the subject will be extradited to the United States to face charges.

✓ **MLATS.** In addition to an extradition package, the investigator and AUSA should consider an MLAT requesting copies of foreign business records, foreign tax returns, foreign court records, police reports, etc., that are seized from the defendant or otherwise publicly available in that country. For each item, complete a separate MLAT request rather than one MLAT listing all the items. Responses to MLATs do not come until they are fully completed. By filing individual MLATs, the foreign country will be able to respond as each item is completed rather than responding only after the last item is collected.

✓ **Options to Extradition.** If extradition is not possible, the investigator should work through their agency or Interpol to establish contacts with law enforcement in the foreign country that could investigate the subject for violations there that could lead to shutting down the source. Part of that coordination should involve asking law enforcement in the foreign country for copies of computer or paper records seized that may document persons in the U.S. who received firearms from the source. In addition, the investigator should still work with the AUSA to secure an indictment and have the source entered into NCIC as a wanted person. This will allow them to be arrested should they travel to the U.S. or, potentially, a country with an extradition treaty with the U.S. The investigator should consider working with Interpol to secure a Red Notice that will let all countries know this person is wanted by the U.S.

✓ **International Intelligence Sharing.** Investigators should work through their agency to share information and intelligence on international firearms traffickers, particularly those operating on the internet and hiding behind gaps in laws between nations. INTERPOL maintains a system of notices to alert member countries to imminent firearm-related threats.

   ➤ An Orange Notice can be issued to warn police, public entities, and other international organizations about potential threats posed by disguised firearms which they may not detect under normal circumstances.

   ➤ A Purple Notice can be issued to share information about specific firearms, their parts and related objects, as well as modus operandi for firearm-related crime including firearm trafficking.[cxlv]

✓ **Website Forfeiture.** Any website domain name ending in .com, .org, and .net that was knowingly used to facilitate the illegal trafficking of firearms is subject to forfeiture. The forfeiture of a website serves several purposes[cxlvi]:

   ➤ Following the forfeiture of the website a Government Warning Banner provides a deterrent effect by allowing others to see very publicly that internet criminal activity does not go unnoticed and that persons and businesses are held accountable.

   ➤ Following the forfeiture of the website a Government Warning Banner placed at the site provides information to persons letting them know what the site was doing illegally, and how to contact the investigator if a person has information about the illegal activities or purchased items they wish to turn in. Forfeiture of websites is possible because VeriSign, which controls the .net and .com names, and the Public Interest Registry, which runs .org, are U.S. based organizations. After domain names are seized, they are processed for forfeiture to the U.S. Guidance and a checklist for investigators to use in preparing to seize and forfeit a domain name may be obtained from the Internet Corporation for Assigned Numbers and Names (ICANN). ICANN was created in 1997 by President Clinton and placed in the U.S. Department of Commerce. In 2016 ICANN became a private global non-profit that manages the internet's domain name system.

In 2017 the ATF Denver Field Division seized and forfeited a website that was charged with selling unregistered illegal silencers by calling them "solvent traps". Figure 10.19 shows the ATF warning banner that was placed on the website after it was forfeited.

Pursuant to a seizure warrant issued by the United States District Court for the District of Utah, the Bureau of Alcohol, Tobacco, Firearms and Explosives (ATF) has seized the website www.darksidedefense.com.

The seizure warrant was issued based on the Court's finding of probable cause that the website facilitated the unlawful sale of items marketed as "solvent traps." ATF has determined that these "solvent traps" are, in fact, silencers. Silencers are firearms that are subject to the licensing and registration provisions of the National Firearms Act (NFA). Title 26, United States Code, Sections 5801-5872.

It is a violation of the NFA to manufacture, receive, transport, or deliver a silencer that has not been registered in the National Firearms Registration and Transfer Record. Title 26, United States Code, Section 5861.

If you purchased a "solvent trap" from Darkside Defense, please contact ATF at 1-800-ATF-GUNS (800-283-4867).

FIGURE 10.21 ATF Warning Banner on Forfeited Website

Source: ATF

CASE STUDY: OPERATION LETHAL WEAPON IV

United States v. Deisernia – Southern District of Florida – 9:03-cr-80102-KAM

In November of 2002 special agents at the ATF West Palm Beach Field Office had just completed a search warrant through which they recovered several high-quality Brugger and Thomet silencers. During an interview with the defendant, he admitted he had purchased the items from a website and they were shipped directly to him. The defendant identified the website as fullautoglock.net. and stated that the website sold a variety of items, including silencers, Glock and Berretta switches to convert handguns to fire fully automatic, and numerous types of machine guns.

ATF agents established an investigation and secured a UC computer and hard drive as well as an agent with a fully backstopped UC identity and credit card. Deconfliction and intelligence workups were performed on the website, the email prompt and other identifying information, and no other agencies appeared to be working on the target.

The investigation progressed quickly through a series of undercover emails and the purchase of silencers, Glock switches, and machine guns. Agents noted that silencers and Glock switches arrived in cardboard packages, but the machine guns came disassembled and welded inside a metal device that was labeled as a truck part.

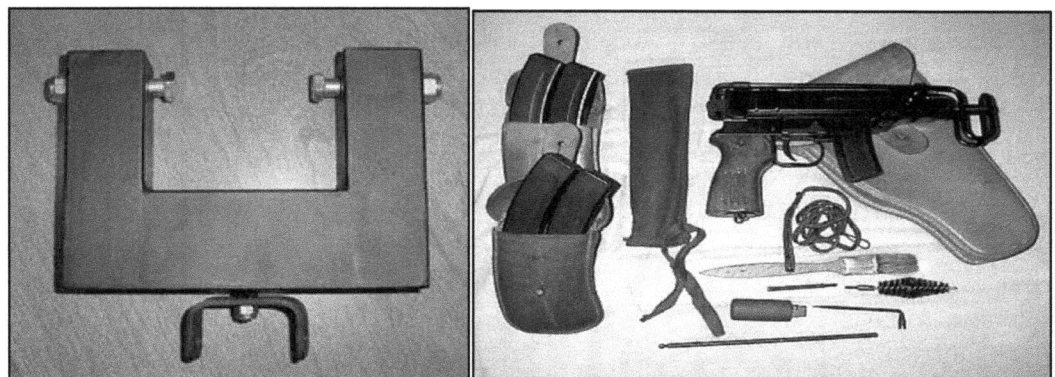

Figure 10.22 Sealed Metal Part Containing CZ Scorpion Machinegun from Argentina

Source: ATF S/A Steve Barborini

The website was operating through MSN Hotmail, a U.S. based internet service provider; however, the trafficker was located in Buenos Aires, Argentina. Later in the investigation it was determined that it was legal to have silencers and Glock switches in Argentina, but machine guns were illegal; this explained the difference in packaging used by the trafficker. With each item ordered on the internet, funds were wired via Western Union to the source, and the items would show up in the mail in brown packages just days later.

At this point, agents served preservation letters followed by search warrants on the internet service provider for the various email addresses being used by the trafficker, and served subpoenas on the shipping company and Western Union. The emails showed communications between each purchaser and the trafficker. The Western Union records showed how much money each purchaser wired to the trafficker's account, and the shipping records showed the package each customer then received from the trafficker. Between examination of emails and examination of the wire transfers, agents were able to determine what the U.S. customers had received, since agent knew the prices of each item for sale on the website. For example, if a Glock switch cost $300 and a customer wired $900 and the only way to spend exactly $900 on the site meant purchasing 3 Glock switches, a picture of the illegal purchases emerged.

ATF agents requested that U.S. Postal Inspectors secure postal records and the identities of persons living at each address receiving a package, to assist in corroborating that the person residing at the address was the same person placing the order, just in case someone else used the address to receive a package they would retrieve from the front door.

The aggregate of the email, shipping, and wire transfer records began to accurately portray what U.S. customers were illegal purchasing and importing firearms from the site. Agents continued to work on identifying those customers while at the same time trying to more fully identify the source in order to shut it down as soon as possible to prevent additional trafficking.

Because the trafficker was using a U.S. based internet service provider, a court order for an internet T-III intercept was secured for the primary email address used for sales by the trafficker. Had the internet service provider been in Argentina, a T-III would not have been possible. In 2002 this was the first internet T-III intercept conducted by ATF. The T-III allowed agents to fully identify the scope and size of the trafficking. In the 30-day wire period, 6573 emails were intercepted. The 6573 emails had to be scanned in a minimization process to determine those emails pertinent to violations of the law. Unlike a traditional T-III intercept of telephone conversations, an internet T-III does not need to be monitored 24 hours a day and emails are in writing so no transcriptions must be produced. The emails were downloaded and reviewed once a day. A plan was in place to prevent any identifiable firearms sales from reaching their destination during the T-III. This would include rapid identification of IP addresses to identify purchasers as well as coordinated package intercepts and possible controlled deliveries.

As the T-III progressed, illegal NFA purchasers were identified in the U.S. and in 6 foreign countries, including Greece, Canada, Haiti, South Africa, Norway, and Sweden. The goal was to recover as many illegal firearms in the U.S. as possible before they could be used in crimes and create victims, while also shutting down the site so no additional NFA weapons would illegally enter the country.

Figure 10.23 *Silencer from Argentina*
Source: ATF S/A Steve Barborini

Referrals on these purchases were sent out all over the U.S. to ATF offices with actions required that would range from the service of search and arrest warrants, to controlled deliveries of packages, to knock and talks with suspects. The referrals were sorted in three category levels and sent all across the country to be prepared for a nationwide roundup on a planned date.

Permission was secured from the federal judge issuing the court order to use intercepted information in referrals to foreign law enforcement on packages sent to their countries. Two international referrals were sent during this time. The first international referral was sent to Canada, and Canadian Customs was able to intercept a package containing a disassembled machine gun bound for an individual who was a convicted felon known to be a large-scale drug trafficker and a Hells Angels supplier. Canadian officials conducted a controlled delivery that resulted in the subject's arrest, and the recovery of a large amount of narcotics. A second international referral was provided to the State Department; the referral related to a package of 15 full-auto Glock switches being shipped to Haiti. The intended recipient of the package was in LEAD making multiple purchases of Glock handguns in Broward County, FL the year before. The State Department advised that there was a potential coup plot involved.

Due to the volume of planned domestic U.S. referrals, a test referral was sent out first. That referral was sent to the ATF San Francisco Division and resulted in the service of a search warrant on an FFL who had purchased a number of Glock switches from the trafficker. Several illegal NFA Glock switches were recovered, the FFL was arrested and cooperated, leading to others to whom he had already sold some of the Glock switches to.

In May of 2003 a nationwide roundup took place resulting in the seizure of 24 machine guns, 16 silencers, 6 pipe bombs, 7 converted Glock handguns, 9 Glock switches, 3 short-barreled rifles, and thousands of rounds of ammunition, as well as numerous T-I firearms. These items were seized from convicted felons, gang members, a skinhead who also had a pipe bomb in his living room, and an individual with a house full of guns and pipe bombs and a list of people at work he was going to kill. In addition, the leader of a Mosque in Patterson, NJ purchased a number of illegal machine guns and was the subject of a search and arrest was conducted by ATF with the FBI JTTF. The subject of that arrest warrant pled guilty.

Shortly after the nationwide takedown the website shutdown. Email traffic was picked up by the T-III that indicated that purchasers advised the source that ATF had conducted search and arrest warrants. That was the intended and expected outcome.

Figure 10.24 Briefcase Machinegun Ordered in Patterson, NJ – The Deer will never see him coming.
Source: ATF S/A Steve Barborini

During 2003 efforts continued to definitively identify the person in Argentina who was the trafficker so that they could be indicted. ATF agents knew an email address, physical address, and two names for the trafficker, but before an indictment could be secured the person sending emails would have to somehow be physically identified. By chance, ATF had an international source who was consulted and actually knew the subject in Buenos Aires, had been to his home, and was able to corroborate information and positively identify a photograph of the subject.

In June of 2003 the subject in Buenos Aires, Argentina was indicted on an 11-count indictment for unlicensed importation of NFA firearms (Title 18 U.S.C. § 922 (a)(4)), unlawful importation of firearms (Title 18 U.S.C. § 922(l)), unlawful transfer of machine guns (Title 18 U.S.C. § 922(o)), aiding and abetting (Title 18 U.S.C. § 2), and smuggling (Title 18 U.S.C. § 545).

The U.S. DOJ sought extradition and a provisional warrant was issued. The subject was arrested in September 2004 in Buenos Aires. In May of 2005 Argentine authorities ruled that although the subject committed acts for which extradition to the US would be allowed, he also committed violations of Argentine law for which he would be prosecuted; therefore, extradition would be denied. The subject was then sentenced to a significant jail sentence in Argentina and his federal arrest warrant in the U.S. remains in place should he ever travel once released.

Evidence gathered from the Wayback Machine (the internet archive) indicated that the website had been operating for at least 2 years and probably for as many as 5 years: the trafficker indicated in emails that he had been operating for 5 years. The level of activity seen during the investigation indicated that the subject trafficked as many as 150 illegal NFA firearms a month with worldwide distribution, and trafficked as many as 3000 illegal NFA firearms over the course of 5 years. This case stopped the source and, with records collected during search warrants on the day of the roundup, identified other large-scale internet traffickers for investigation.

CASE STUDY: OPERATION THE WORLD IS NOT ENOUGH

Roland Spiegel, et al. – Criminal Prosecution in Germany

In March of 2004 the ATF West Palm Beach Field Office initiated an investigation into international internet-based firearms trafficking by MODELLBAUSPIEGEL@AOL.COM. This site had been identified as supplying firearms and machine gun during a prior investigation of an internet trafficking site in Argentina.

Deconfliction and intelligence workups were performed on the website and email address. During the initial days of the investigation a name for the person operating the website was determined, and it was also determined that the website sold firearm parts, including machine gun receivers, deactivated firearms, and firearms converted to air guns. The site was found to be operating from Germany and using a foreign based internet service provider.

A clean UC computer and hard drive were secured, and a UC agent with a backstopped identify and UC credit card took on the investigation. During several UC email communications, additional email addresses used by the trafficker were identified as well as the various shipping methods used and payment methods ac-

Figure 10.25 *HK MP5 Machinegun from Germany*
Source: ATF S/A Steve Barborini

cepted by the trafficker. The trafficker also discussed what was legal, what was not legal, and how to make shipments into the U.S. in a manner to avoid detection. The UC agent made several purchases from the website, including several machine guns and pistol receivers. Payment methods included wire transfers to a bank account in Germany and Pay pal. It was noted that all firearms arrived without barrels. Research of the law in Germany indicted that barrels and bolts are considered the firearm in Germany, not the receiver. In the U.S. the receiver is the firearm and the barrel and bolt are just a part.

The packages containing the firearms were received by the UC at the undercover address in West Palm Beach, FL. The packages were labeled as containing "diecast chassis for models". Later the trafficker wrote an email stating that the cover label "works as usual". The FedEx packages and packaging material were preserved for latent print development and handwriting comparison potential. Latent prints were developed.

Subpoenas were issued for records of all packages delivered by FedEx that came from the trafficker's address in Germany. Subpoenas were issued to Pay Pal for all payments made to the account belonging to the trafficker in Germany. Analysis of those records showed that over the course of 3 years the trafficker received 485 separate payments from 155 people in the U.S. totaling more than $200,000. PayPal was just one of several means of payment accepted by the trafficker; however, the other methods were outside the U.S. The available records were exploited to produce referrals to other ATF offices to recover illegal weapons purchased by U.S. customers. The investigation then shifted focus to identifying the source for indictment and arrest. During December of 2004 the trafficker indicted that he would be traveling to the "Shot Show" in Las

Vegas, NV to meet with the UC on larger deals. ATF moved forward to secure approval from DOJ to conduct a lure, with the intent of identifying the suspect and arresting him. As that request was moving forward, the trafficker advised that his Russian wife could not get a Visa to travel to the U.S., so he would not be coming; he suggested that the UC come to the IWA Gun Show in Nuremburg, Germany in March 2005.

It was determined that travel to Germany would be necessary in order to physically identify the trafficker. In February of 2005 the ATF secured DOJ undercover review committee approval to travel to Germany for this purpose.

Between the approval of travel to Germany and the departure for the IWA Gun Show, the trafficker advised the UC that he had items for sale that did not appear on the website, including a fully functional Colt M203 Grenade Launcher, and that he could get grenades to go with it. The ATF UC purchased the Grenade Launcher, but told the trafficker he did not need grenades. The grenade launcher arrived in two separate unmarked packages at the UC address in West Palm Beach, FL.

Goals and logistical plans were established for the trip to Germany. The goals were:
➢ Conduct a UC meeting with the trafficker and physically identify them.
➢ Attempt to covertly gather fingerprint and handwriting exemplars for comparison to FedEx packages received in the U.S.
➢ Attempt to identify additional accomplices and sources of firearms for the trafficker.
➢ Coordinate with German law enforcement officials to determine if their laws were violated by the trafficker and to introduce German UC agents for follow-up.

In March 2005 the ATF West Palm Beach Field Office supervisor, two agents, and an ICE agent traveled to Germany where they met with official at the Kriminalhauptkommisar of the Bundereskriminalamt (BKA German National Police) and Hessisches Landeskriminalamt (LKA Hessisches State Police). It was determined that BKA would monitor the case and that LKA UC agents would be introduced to the trafficker by ATF UC agents. LKA was able to identify the trafficker as someone who had been previously convicted for weapons trafficking in Europe. LKA was able to provide the trafficker's fingerprints to ATF; these were later matched to latent fingerprints on multiple packages received in the U.S.

Initial plans were to meet the trafficker at the IWA Gun Show in Nuremburg; however, plans were later changed to meet the trafficker at his home so he could display some of his inventory. The ATF and LKA UCs agreed to meet the trafficker at the Hanau, Germany train station and then had diner at a nearby restaurant. Following the diner, at the trafficker's invitation, they proceeded to the trafficker's home in Grosskrotzenburg, Germany for a private meeting. Once at the residence the UCs were brought to the gun room in the trafficker's basement. The UCs were wearing transmitters and were quietly reporting what they were observing to the cover teams. The UCs advised that the basement contained dozens of machine guns, machine gun receivers, handguns, Glock Switches, belt-fed machine guns, and laser engravers. Plans were made for much larger shipments of machine guns into the U.S., and the LKA UC was going to be the local point of contact for those future transactions. The trafficker advised that he could supply 300 M-14 machine guns, 400 HK MP5 machine guns, and 6 HK 21 belt fed machine guns, and that the barrels and bolts would be shipped in separate packages. The trafficker advised that he had access to an additional 1000 HK MP5 machine guns after that, as well as unlimited numbers of Glock Switches, AK-47 receivers, and Norinco 1911 pistols. The LKA UC also arranged for a future purchase of a large number of handguns, as this would be a clear violation of the law in Germany. While handling some of the machine guns in the basement, the ATF UC noted they all had German Government Issue proof marks which was unusual.

On April 13, 2005 the LKA UC advised the ATF West Palm Beach Field Office agents that they had just purchased a large number of handguns and ammunition from the trafficker and had set other meetings to purchase at least 50 more HK MP5 machine guns in an attempt to learn the trafficker's source and allow for time to conduct an electronic interception of the trafficker's phones. During the phone conversations the LKA was able to determine that the trafficker's source was a former prosecutor who had actually prosecuted the trafficker in the past. LKA set up one final deal, and on May 25, 2005 they arrested the trafficker after he delivered 70 handguns and an HK MP5 machine gun. This was followed by a search warrant at the trafficker's home where an additional 300 firearms, laser engravers, gun barrel turning equipment, numerous gun parts, and computers were seized.

The trafficker cooperated and the details of the trafficking scheme unfolded. The trafficker had struck up a partnership with his former prosecutor after telling him how much money they could make together if they could access firearms marked for disposal. The former prosecutor knew people at the German Weapons Registration Division who were responsible for tracking registered German firearms as well as destroying government firearms that were being replaced with new ones. The German law enforcement firearms sent for destruction were not being destroyed. They were falsely certified as destroyed, removed from the registry, and then sent to the former prosecutor, who provided them to the trafficker to sell over the internet in other countries.

Following the trafficker's cooperation, 1100 firearms were seized from a warehouse, along with part to assemble an additional 650 machine guns, all of which had been previously reported as destroyed. The former prosecutor was arrested, and LKA served a search warrant at the German Weapons Registration Division where they seized additional firearms and documents showing the conspiracy to declare firearms destroyed that were actually being sold.

In the U.S., several persons who illegally purchased firearms from the trafficker were arrested and those firearms were seized. The trafficking website was successfully shut down, ending this enormous source of illegal and untraceable weapons to violent criminals, gangs, and transnational organized crime around the globe.

CASE STUDY: OPERATION INCOMING FIRE

Stephen Qiao, et al. – District of Maine - Magistrate No's. 2:12-mj-155-JHR and 2:12-mj-231-JHR - Criminal Prosecution in China

---

In March of 2012 the ATF Portland, Maine Field Office initiated an investigation after intelligence searches of internet firearms sales determined that a source was selling firearm receivers online through Alibaba.com.

Deconfliction and intelligence workups were completed and indicated that Chengdu Hongguang (CDHG) Machine-Building Co, Ltd, a manufacturing factory located in the Chengdu Hongguang Region of China, was advertising and selling AR-15 rifle lower and upper receivers.

As with all internet cases, the seller would be tested to determine if they were selling firearms in violation of importation laws. The goals of the internet investigation were to shut down the illegal source of firearms to the U.S., identify any U.S. based purchasers and recover the purchased firearms, and make arrests where necessary.

A clean UC computer and hard drive were secured and a UC agent with a backstopped identify and UC credit card took on the investigation. During several UC communications, orders were placed that resulted in purchases of firearms receivers for AR-15s, AR-10s, and M-16s, as well as silencers and Glock switches. All were shipped directly from China to the UC address in Portland, Maine. None were imported using an approved ATF Form 6 or declared to CBP. Attempts were made to identify other U.S. firearms purchasers by obtaining all shipping records and wire transfer records related to CDHG. While this had worked in prior internet investigations, this time a large manufacturing company was involved that was shipping many types of items around the world. The records revealed thousands of shipments and wire transfers with no way to determine which were related to firearms as opposed to the legal commodities CDHG manufactured. Attempts to identify other U.S. purchasers by securing emails sent to CDHG was difficult as they did not use a U.S. based internet service provider. As one point it that appeared they were using a service provider in Australia and an MLAT was provided to Australian authorities to secure emails; however, they only found a server at the location thought to be a service provider. CDHG communications were routed through numerous proxy servers, making access to electronic communications records difficult. Some shipping records had package comments describing the contents in the same fashion as the UC purchased items, so those were reviewed. Investigation revealed some U.S. purchasers who illegally imported Glock switches, firearm receivers, and silencers. Referrals on these individuals were sent out, and a number of the items were recovered; however, some individuals, including one who had purchased more than 200 firearm receivers, had already re-sold the items.

The standard techniques for identifying the trafficker and U.S. customers were not as effective in this investigation so at this point, the focus became shutting down the flow of illegally imported and unregistered NFA firearms to U.S. customers. ATF special agents coordinated with DHS-HSI and their attaché in Beijing, China. Officials at the China Customs - Anti-Smuggling Bureau, International Enforcement Cooperation Office became involved in the investigation. Officials in China began to monitor the sales and emails of CDHG on the internet and after 2 weeks requested that ATF place an order for sixty AR-10 and M-16 firearm receivers website along with Glock Switches and Silencers which they would intercept. In December the ATF UC placed the order and alerted DHS-HSI, who in turn alerted Chinese Officials. On December 24, 2013 the ATF UC received an email advising the order was being shipped. On December 25, 2013 Chinese Officials intercepted the package, arrested 5 persons in China, and shut down the illegal firearms factory. This eliminated the illegal source of firearms to U.S. customers.

In January 2015 two of the defendants were convicted in court in Chengdu Province, China, of illegally manufacturing and exporting firearms. Their conviction led to a sentence of life in prison in China for the main defendant and 14 years in prison in China for the other defendant. The status of the other 3 defendants is unknown.

Current trends indicate that a large volume of internationally sourced firearms and firearm parts transferred to the U.S. via internet sales are coming from the Philippines, South Korea, China, and other parts of Southeast Asia. The cases are out there.

This concludes Chapter 10, which was predicated on the application of everything presented in the first nine chapters. I leave the reader with the following thoughts and ask that you heed them by using the knowledge you have gained to shut down the illegal suppliers of firearms to violent criminals, gangs, cartels, transnational organized crime, and terrorists.

The great aim of education is not knowledge but action.
Herbert Spencer, English Philosopher, 1820-1903

Experience is the teacher of all things.
Julius Caesar, Roman Politician 100-44BC

Chapter 11
Gang Investigation Focused on Armed Violence & Crime Gun Sources

"I am just a businessman, giving the people what they want.
All I do is satisfy a public demand."
Alphonse Capone, 1930

Armed violent gang crime remains a serious problem across the U.S. in big and small cities. Gang-related crimes are, by their very nature, more difficult to prosecute than other sorts of crimes, due to interconnected relationships and complex dynamics between rival gangs. Today's perpetrator may be tomorrow's victim. Witnesses and juries may be intimidated by actual or implied threats of violence from a gang-involved defendant.[cxlvii]

Combatting armed violent gangs is an arduous process; however, when done correctly the positive impact that removing an armed violent gang from a community produces is immeasurable in terms of reducing violent victimization, and increasing a community's sense of security and well-being.

The investigation of armed violent gangs and criminal enterprises will involve sensitive investigative issues and techniques as well as the expenditure of large amounts of resources related to the purchase of evidence, the use of fully backstopped undercover operatives and confidential informants, various electronic monitoring techniques, transcription of audio recordings, law enforcement overtime, leased surveillance vehicles, and travel. These types of investigations call for enhanced risk management and oversight to ensure that public safety is always the primary consideration, and that sound investigative decisions are made and followed. Public safety trumps case longevity, and sometimes a case must be shut down early to protect that primary goal. Additional management oversight is also necessary to ensure that proper fiscal choices are being made and implemented.

The primary goal of an armed violent gang investigation is to protect public safety by stopping the gang's armed crimes, incarcerating the entire hierarchy of the gang so that it is difficult for them to reconstitute, and removing their assets. This chapter focuses exclusively on investigating armed violent gangs and their sources of firearms, and incarcerating chronic violent predators in a community. This is but one important component of any larger gang reduction strategy that often includes community outreach as well as gang prevention, interdiction, and suppression.

At the strategic level, the process begins with an intelligence assessment utilizing a crime gun intelligence fusion center like an ATF CGIC. The intelligence assessment will identify those gangs and criminal enterprises in a designated area that are responsible for a disproportionate amount of armed violent crime. A proper CGIC intelligence assessment designed to identify the most violent armed gang in an area sometimes yields surprising results, and the gang brought into focus may not be the most visible, well known, or prolific drug trafficking gang in the area. Trust the data. Surprising results should be welcomed as an important revelation brought about by proper analysis, and not viewed with suspicion because it does not align with an existing widely-held view. Member agencies in the CGIC must ensure that any regional gun crime protocols are being followed, in order to ensure the timely development of Crime Gun Intelligence throughout the investigation.

At the operational level, the ensuing investigation of the identified armed violent gang or criminal enterprise should focus on federal violations involving the criminal misuse of firearms, and on the criminal enterprise-related crimes. It will be important for managers to keep investigators focused on solving those armed crimes that have occurred and proving how those crimes were committed by the gang in furtherance of the criminal enterprise. A gang investigation lacking in focus and management oversight sometimes defaults to a street level drug investigation in which investigators conduct multiple drug buys from individual gang members but never focus on the overarching criminal conspiracy or prior shooting crimes. That type of unfocused case may result in a large number of gang member arrests, but for individual cases with minimal sentencing potential. It's a "sugar high" case that has an initial rush of energy and media attention followed by a crash and a reconstituted gang shortly thereafter. An armed violent criminal gang investigation should use a wide variety of investigative techniques to gather evidence that will document all elements of proof for the federal violations being investigated. No single technique, such as narcotics purchases by confidential informants or undercover personnel, should be relied on exclusively to perfect the investigation.

The following is a "Gang Investigation 101" outline of the of the three phases of an armed violent gang investigation.

PHASE I: IDENTIFY THE GANG

The investigator must utilize all available intelligence assets to identify the gang for further assessment and investigation. This process should take into consideration the following CGIC and other resources:

✓ Analysis of Uniform Crime Report (UCR) coupled with GEOINT hot spot crime mapping that should incorporate armed crime occurrence locations, analysis of NIBIN hits, and an analysis of gunshot acoustic detection system (e.g., Shot Spotter® or Raytheon Boomerang®) historical data. It is particularly important to analyze multiple NIBIN hits in an area to see what gang ties there may be to those crimes. The point of an armed violent gang investigation is to focus on the gang that is involved in the region's shooting crimes.

✓ Debriefings of Confidential Informants (CI), cooperating defendants, and other sources of human intelligence (HUMINT).

✓ Meetings with local departments (e.g., Gang Unit, Intelligence Unit, Detective Bureaus) in those identified areas of high armed violent crime and gang activity to assist in identifying specific gang members, their current and past criminal activity, their hierarchy, their modus operandi, and their area of operation. At the same time, the investigator should explore the department's ability to dedicate resources to participate in a focused joint long-term investigation of the armed violent gang. Discuss the use of supplemental funding available for investigative expenses and state or local overtime costs through DOJ Organized Crime Drug Enforcement Task Force (OCDETF), High Intensity Drug Trafficking Area (HIDTA), or Joint Law Enforcement Operations (JLEO). It will be important for the investigation to consist of a team of local, state and federal law enforcement agencies.

Upon conclusion of the assessment process and identification of an armed violent gang(s) or criminal enterprise for investigation, the investigator and their supervisor should meet with their local U.S. Attorney's Office (USAO) to discuss the gang, and the rationale for targeting the gang, and to secure their support for the investigation and the dedicated assignment of an AUSA for vertical prosecution in a long-term, multi-defendant, and complex investigation against a specific armed violent gang, to achieve a positive community impact.

At the conclusion of Phase I, the investigator has identified the gang through an intelligence-led approach, formed a team of local, state and federal law enforcement agencies, gained supervisory buy-in, and arranged for the assignment of a dedicated prosecutor.

PHASE II: INTELLIGENCE COLLECTION

During this phase the focus will be on gathering detailed intelligence and information on the gang's crimes, including current and past criminal activity of the gang and each known gang member, as well as the gang's hierarchy, modus operandi, and area of operation. In this phase investigators should develop a roadmap for how to investigate and target the gang's leadership and other impact players as well as the known or suspected armed crimes they have engaged in, and continue to engage in. As with any trip, the roadmap may have to change during the course of the investigation. Part of that roadmap will be the identification of the specific criminal violations involved so that investigators have a clear understanding of the elements of proof that will need to be documented. During this phase investigators should also begin to identify and target potential cooperators, including informants, unwitting sources, and witnesses who will help to prove your case, inclusive of past and present crimes, the criminal enterprise, and associations. Intelligence collection can be accomplished through the following procedures.

Case and Information Management. From the start of this process, assume that the investigation will be large, and initiate proper case management from the start. While collecting information for the case, investigators should err on the side of caution and collect everything.

✓ Enter all collected police reports from prior arrests and contacts with gang members into a case management system capable of automatically deconflicting names, addresses, phone numbers, and aliases appearing in all reports loaded into the system, in order to identify possible links and new leads. This database needs to be searchable. Where available, HIDTA offers the Case Explorer system for this purpose.

✓ Create regular "to do lists" and use lead sheets to assign tasks and track their completion.

✓ Make sure all investigative participants practice disciplined and timely evidence handling and processing procedures.

✓ Make sure all investigative participants practice disciplined and timely event-based report writing.

✓ Investigators must understand the difference between evidence and intelligence. Categorize intelligence by reliability level and sources. Single source intelligence may be inaccurate or incomplete. Multiple source intelligence is always preferred. Scrutinize, verify, and corroborate all intelligence. Only verified and corroborated intelligence should be used as the basis of an operational decision or action.

✓ Investigators should be mindful of opportunities to turn intelligence into evidence; for example, to turn hearsay into direct testimony.

✓ Investigators should be mindful of situations in which evidence contradicts intelligence, and they should side with evidence.

✓ Investigators should also be practical and compassionate, and realize there will be times when evidence must be used as intelligence in order to protect a victim, a witness, or a CI.

Preliminary Meetings. Meet with local departments, gang units, and other law enforcement assets that work in the area where the identified gang or criminal enterprise exists, in order to collect all known information on gang members.

✓ In areas with a CGIC, meetings involving the appropriate units from each department participating in the CGIC are a critical first step. The group must work together and comprehensively share their intelligence in order to identify:
  ➢ the most problematic member of the identified gang to focus on, and
  ➢ the specific past armed violent crimes that can be identified for investigation as predicates in a Federal Racketeering Influenced Corrupt Organization (RICO) or Violent Crimes in Aid of Racketeering (VCAR) case.

✓ Begin to lay out a strategy to investigate those specific crimes:
  ➢ develop lists of witnesses and victims to interview,
  ➢ identify the gang members suspected of perpetrating those crimes, and
  ➢ identify gang members who may be the most likely to cooperate if arrested.

✓ Create files on each identified target and potential predicate crime.

✓ Focus on any and all NIBIN hits, as these are shooting investigations that start with a significant ballistics lead.

✓ Gather reports on all past contacts and arrests for every gang member. Make note of past arrests where more than one gang member was present during each police contact or arrest, and have an Intelligence Analyst map these associations. It is vital to establish evidence of associations and an enterprise in most federal gang charges; therefore, documentation of gang members being arrested together is important to establishing these associations and potentially others.

Preliminary Data. In addition to being useful for establishing evidence of association and existence of a criminal enterprise, investigators should be familiar with the following potential uses of preliminary data:

✓ Federal Rules of Evidence, Rule 404b[cxlviii] allows for the introduction of "other crimes, wrongs, or acts", often referred to as "prior bad acts", in court. The rule prohibits the introduction of other crimes, wrongs, or acts to prove the character of a person in order to show that they are more likely to commit the current crime charged; however, the rule does allow the introduction of "prior bad acts" as evidence for limited purposes associated with a relevant issue, such as motive, opportunity, intent, preparation, plan, knowledge, identity, or absence of mistake or accident. This may include prior arrests as these relate to unlawful firearms possession, narcotics possession and trafficking, or other violent crimes, including assault and murder, all of which may be admissible in federal court under the umbrella of the enterprise or conspiracy. The assigned AUSA will determine what prior bad acts may qualify as 404b evidence; thus, they should be made aware of all existing data.

✓ Relevant conduct is uncharged conduct that constitutes a criminal act related to the underlying offense of which a defendant is convicted. Relevant conduct is activity that may not result in an indictable offense but may be used to increase a defendant's possible sentencing range under the Federal Sentencing Guidelines. Relevant conduct is admissible in the PSI report prepared by the U.S. Probation Office and is presented to the judge for use in determining sentencing.

✓ Identify existing evidence in police custody that may be of use in the planned investigation. This may be firearms, narcotics, trace evidence to include DNA and fingerprints, cell phone records, "pocket litter" containing phone numbers or gang member names, photographs, actual cell phones or other digital communication or digital storage devices that could be exploited for contacts, photographs, and communications.

✓ Gather available information on hierarchy/structure of the gang and have an IA create a hierarchy flowchart.

✓ Gather additional criminal enterprise evidence from materials gathered during prior arrests or search warrants.

✓ Documentation of gang graffiti and the location of that graffiti in a neighborhood that delineates a gang's declaration of dominion and control over a territory, established boundaries, and zones of gang operation. Map gang crimes to show their presence inside those established boundaries.

✓ Documentation of gang members with common gang tattoos or articles of affiliation that match the documented graffiti.

✓ Photographs recovered of gang members posing with each other showing gang signs or symbols; posing with firearms, narcotics, or cash; or committing other crimes.

Deconfliction. Deconfliction is vital in any professional law enforcement investigation and should include the following steps when conducting a gang investigation:

✓ Query each name, phone number and address identified in ATF's case management system, TECs, and DICE, and conduct EPIC-10 queries in order to identify any other past or current and on-going investigations of the gang or individual members. If any past cases are discovered, contact that agency to gather that intelligence and information. If any current cases are discovered, contact that agency and determine if your efforts can be performed jointly with that case or whether your case should be pursued separately.

✓ All investigative and enforcement actions throughout the investigation must be deconflicted. Every planned search warrant, arrest warrant, undercover meetings, and each new person identified in the investigation must be deconflicted to prevent a blue on blue scenario. Numerous deconfliction systems are available to law enforcement, including HIDTA NINJAS, DICE, and RissNet.

Intelligence Analyst (IA) Research. Investigators should task their IAs to conduct the following research and analysis:

✓ Gather OSINT material by conducting a full social media exploitation with each of the identified gang members/suspects. Locate social media pages and document photos that may contain images of narcotics use and possession as well as packaged for distribution, cash, firearms use or possession by prohibited persons, and associations among members. These photographs may prove valuable to establishing associations, possession of evidence relative to prohibited items and crimes, and actions related to an ongoing enterprise. The importance of this technique cannot be understated. A full gang-focused OSINT workup should include searches of online publications, blogs, discussion groups and chat rooms, cell phone video content available on YouTube® and citizen media sites, and other social media such as Facebook®, Myspace®, Twitter®, and Instagram®. These searches should be of known gang members, girlfriends, associates, relatives, and anyone else who "tags" a target gang member in their social media feed.

✓ Past Police Contact Link Analysis. Gather police reports, field contact/identification stop reports, and traffic stop reports for all of the suspects, and document which gang members were present at each arrest, for mapping in a link analysis chart.

Crime Gun Tracing and Firearms Trafficking Intelligence. Run all gang members, their associates, girlfriend/boyfriend/spouses, and their known addresses through eTrace to identify any associated crime gun traces, multiple sales, or unrecovered firearms associated with those names and addresses. When investigating leads related to crime gun tracing and firearms trafficking intelligence and information, investigators should follow the preliminary firearms trafficking investigation protocols that appear in Chapter 10.

At the conclusion of Phase II, the investigative law enforcement agency partners should meet with the dedicated AUSA to provide them with a full briefing on the gang and its hierarchy, the gang crimes to be investigated as predicate offenses for RICO or VICAR, their current modus operandi, area of operation, and the investigative plan.

PHASE III: INVESTIGATION

The investigation phase of gang investigation may use a historical and overt investigative approach, a pro-active and covert investigative approach, or both. Gang investigations can be successful using pro-active covert approach or a historical overt approach; however, a combination of both provides investigators with more options and more opportunities to succeed.

Public safety and the type of crimes identified for investigation will be the determining factor in which approach to use first. If this gang is highly volatile and dangerous to the public on a routine basis then an overt approach may be beneficial in providing a slight deterrent effect. If the gang knows there is an active investigation they may curtail the blatant violence. In other instances covert investigation allows investigators to gather more evidence in a shorter period of time, leading to more immediate arrests. Each gang investigation's needs will be different.

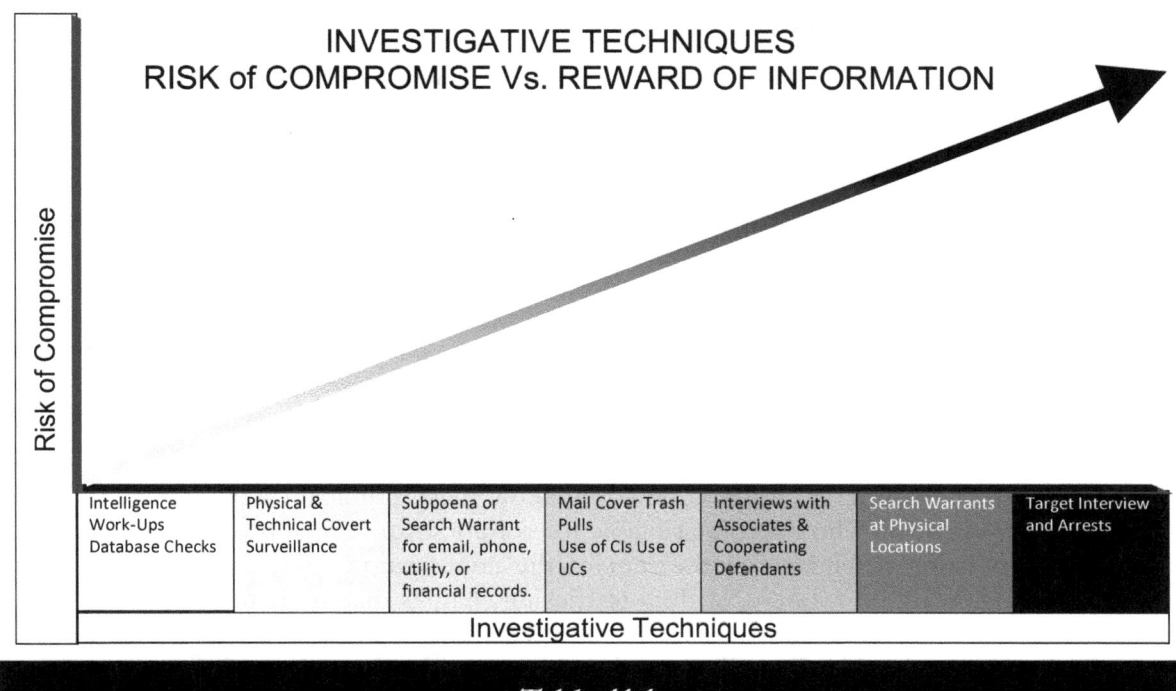

Table 11.1

High priority leads can be found at the intersection of Geography, Events, Time, and Solvability factors (GETS)[cxlix]. As the investigator moves through the investigative phase they should always be cognizant of the elements of proof for all violations being investigated, and understand how different evidence will tell them different things. Different types of intelligence "hits" reveal different facts.

✓ **NIBIN**. A NIBIN hit will link a recovered crime gun to shooting scenes and tell investigators the "What, When, and Where" of a shooting crime.

✓ **eTrace**. An eTrace hit may link a crime gun possessor or shooter to the gun, and the gun to the potential trafficker, telling investigators the "Who, When and Where" of a violent crime or trafficking crime.

✓ **Trace DNA or Latent Fingerprints**. A trace DNA or latent fingerprint hit links a crime gun possessor, shooter, or trafficker to the gun, and these positive results may tell the investigator the "Who," and maybe the Who Else," of a shooting or possessory crime.

✓ **Historical Cell Tower Data Mapping Hit.** A cell phone location hit, which is the intersection of the shooter's and the victim's cell phone locations, often tells the investigator the "Where" of a shooting crime. That moment in time when the shooter's and the victim's paths crossed can sometimes be documented through mapping the cell site historical data of both cell phones.

This chapter will first discuss Historical-Overt investigative techniques; however, this does not mean that the Historical-Overt investigation must be performed before the Proactive-Covert investigation.

HISTORICAL–OVERT TECHNIQUE

The historical and overt investigation utilizes law enforcement techniques such as interviews and targeted prosecutions which gang members will see and learn about. It will be no secret that they are being targeted for investigation by law enforcement. These are techniques to use if the investigation is at a stage where investigators are not concerned that gang members know they are being investigated. This approach can cause changes in the gang's modus operandi, and can have a deterrent effect on some gang activity, but this won't last. Gangs have to continue their illicit activities to make money, hold power in a community, and control territory.

The following are historical and overt investigative techniques that investigators should consider for applicability in their armed violent gang investigation.

Targeted Cases for Adoption into Federal Court. The investigative team should meet with the local District Attorney's Office to determine how many criminal cases are pending against targeted gang members who might be suitable for adoption for federal prosecution, as an aid in creating cooperating defendants at the start of the investigation. Illegal firearms possession, armed trafficking, armed robbery, or drug trafficking charges that are pending at the local level are often suitable for prosecution in federal court. When reviewing cases for adoption into federal court, investigators should follow the procedures discussed in Chapter 6 regarding the processing and development of local cases for federal court and lead exploitation.

Criminal Act Investigation. Identify past violent crimes and predicate acts that may be unsolved or pending in state court that could be more fully investigated to identify additional participants or evidence that the crime was committed in furtherance of the enterprise. Various investigative techniques, such as subpoenas to compel federal grand jury testimony, should be considered. In addition, the following are useful for purposes of documenting a criminal enterprise:

✓ The specific geographic locations of the crimes document turf. Note if this area of crime matches to areas marked off by gang graffiti. This indicates the gang's declaration of their right to commit and control crime in this area.

✓ Document the use or threatened use of violence by gang members against potential witnesses or victims, particularly if the gang member initiating the threat is doing so to intimidate witnesses and victims.

✓ Document all crime committed by the gang against rival gangs as well as all crime that follows a set of the gang's "rules" or "charter documents".

✓ Document all crimes by a gang member on behalf of another gang member or in order to improve his own ranking in the gang.

✓ Document all money movement between gang members, particularly the upward movement of criminal proceeds from lower members to higher members.

✓ Document through photographs, phone records, and witness statements any instances of gang members or associates being used to warn others when police are present. Identify who was making the warnings and who was being warned.

✓ Identify and document the ranking gang members, leaders, and organizers. This may be done through interviews and proffers or it may be done through the use of confidential informants (CIs) and undercover investigators (UCs) who gather this information through conversation or observation. For example, investigators may direct a CI to try to approach and speak with the suspected leader of the gang, to see if other gang members stop the CI during the approach as part of a security and screening of people trying to get to the leader. This may help confirm the hierarchy of the gang.

✓ Identify gang members who may be overtly charged with criminal violations that are separate from the larger conspiracy, to try and develop cooperating defendants and create an air of suspicion and mistrust among gang members. Gang members may become suspicious of those recently arrested for fear that they may be cooperating, whether it is true or not. This can be disruptive to gang operations. Frequently a firearm possession charge under Title 18 U.S.C. § 922(g) may be available, depending upon the prohibited person status of individual gang members. At this phase of the investigation the investigator should already have intelligence workups on each gang member, and know which are prohibited persons for purposes of possessing firearms or ammunition.

A charge that is often readily available is Title 18 U.S.C. § 922(g)(3): the possession of a firearm or ammunition by someone who is an unlawful user of, or addicted to, any controlled substance. A person who uses a controlled substance and has lost the power of self-control with reference to the use of controlled substance, and any person who is a current user of a controlled substance in a manner other than as prescribed by a licensed physician. Such use is not limited to the use of drugs on a particular day, or within a matter of days or weeks before, but rather that the unlawful use has occurred recently enough to indicate that the individual is actively engaged in such conduct. A person may be an unlawful current user of a controlled substance even though the substance is not being used at the precise time the person seeks to acquire a firearm or receives or possesses a firearm. An inference of current use may be drawn from evidence of a recent use or possession of a controlled substance, or a pattern of use or possession that reasonably covers the present time, e.g.: a conviction for use or possession of a controlled substance within the past year; multiple arrests for such offenses within the past 5 years if the most recent arrest occurred within the past year; or persons found through a drug test to use a controlled substance unlawfully, provided that the test was administered within the past year.[d] To successfully charge someone with a violation of Title 18 U.S.C. § 922(g)(3), the investigator should establish that the use of illegal drugs is contemporaneous to the possession of the firearm or ammunition. Oftentimes a suspect apprehended with a firearm and packaged narcotics will state that the narcotics are for personal use, as a deflection from the more serious armed trafficking charge. That is an admission to Title 18 U.S.C. § 922(g)(3).

✓ Occasionally it is an advantageous prosecutorial strategy to allow basic possessory firearms charges to be severed from the larger case and tried separately. The defense usually sees the separation of charges as a benefit to their clients, as breaking cases into smaller parts can lessen the impact that a single jury would feel if presented with the totality of all the charges in one case together. This can be advantageous to the prosecution, as the defense may reveal some of their defense strategies during the first trial on possessory gun charges.

CASE STUDY: SEVERING CHARGES CAN BE BENEFICIAL

KRAMER ET AL.

United States v. Kramer, et al. – Southern District of Florida – 1:87-cr-00879-JIC

The tactic of severing gun possessory charges from the larger conspiracy case to determine defense strategies was in full swing in April of 1989 in the case of U.S. v. Benjamin Barry Kramer (943 F. 2n 1543). Kramer was the world champion of offshore powerboat racing, and owned Fort Apache Marina on the notorious "Thunder Boat Road" in Miami, FL, the heart of go-fast ocean racer manufacturing in the 1980s, as well as high stakes drug smuggling. Agents from DEA had shown that between 1982 and 1987 Kramer had smuggled almost 600,000 pounds of marijuana into the U.S. and laundered as much as $10 million in cash with his partner, race car driver Randy Lanier. Kramer's racing team member, actor James Caan, had no role in the operation. Kramer, a previously convicted felon, was apprehended with firearms at one point dur-

FIGURE 11.1 *Ben Kramer's Fort Apache Marina Business Card*

Source: Author

ing the investigation, and this author investigated the federal gun charges with the DEA. The government agreed to a defense motion to sever the gun charges from the main case, as this would be an opportunity to try those charges first and learn some of the defense strategies before the larger drug case was tried. Kramer was looking at multiple life sentences on the drug charges in the DEA's case in South Florida, as well as cases in Illinois and New York. On April 18, 1989, this author was sitting in U.S. District Court in Miami waiting for Kramer to be brought to court to start hearings on the federal gun charges. He never showed, however, because on that morning he had someone fly a helicopter into the South Florida Metropolitan Correctional Center (MCC) to help him escape. Kramer had paid this person to learn how to fly a helicopter for this purpose, but the pilot probably could have used a few more lessons. As Kramer hung onto one of the helicopter skids, the pilot could not adjust for the lopsided weight and crashed into the concertina wire loops on top of perimeter fence. Kramer would recover, only to be sentenced to life in prison in the Colorado Supermax. The strategy to allow the defense motion to sever the gun charges was helpful in learning defense tactics leading up to the primary prosecution for narcotics.

Kramer was not the first person to try a helicopter escape from MCC. In 1986, Gary Betzner, who later testified about alleged guns-for-drugs schemes to arm the Contra rebels in Nicaragua, hired a pilot to fly a helicopter into that same prison. Unbeknownst to Betzner, he had been dealing with undercover agents, and the helicopter that picked him up carried agents who arrested him when he ran to it. Kramer was the last to try a helicopter escape, however, because after this helicopter escape attempt MCC and the other federal correctional centers around the U.S. installed wire grids over the prison yards to discourage this activity.

Systematically Investigate All Armed Violent Gang Crimes, Past and Present. Start by researching all recovered crime guns associated with any crimes or suspected crimes by the gang, and ensure that all firearms have been immediately entered into NIBIN and traced. Follow-up on all trace results for leads for potential firearms trafficking or diversion violations. Follow the standard CGI development processes and firearms trafficking investigation protocols covered in Chapters 6 and 8. Triage the unsolved armed violent crimes by organizing them using a priority-based targeting system. The following are common shooting crime triage and targeting preferences initially developed by ATF in Chicago and now in use by some ATF CGICs:

✓ **Last is First**. Organize the crimes by date of occurrence, and give precedence to the investigation on the most recent crime and then work backwards. The last (most recent) crime goes first.

✓ **Worst is the First**. Identify the crime scene that is the most violent crime, and give it precedence in the investigation to solve it.

✓ **Shortest Time Between Occurrence of Shooting and NIBIN Correlation**. Identify the crime with the shortest time between the shooting occurrence date and the date that the firearm is later recovered: a lead/hit is actually generated through NIBIN correlation.

✓ **Recovered Firearms**. Identify the scene most closely linked to the most violent crime scene that has recovered firearms to work with. This expands available lead exploitation potential by allowing the investigator the chance to identify latent fingerprint or DNA trace evidence on the firearms or, through a crime gun trace or other CGIC data source, to identify the firearm purchaser.

✓ **Multiple Firearms, Investigations and Scenes**. Identify the scene most closely linked to the most violent crime scene that has the most links to other scenes or the most firearms and cartridge cases associated to a scene.[cli]

Investigation of NIBIN hits that link recovered crime guns and ammunition casings recovered at shooting crimes that gang members are suspected to have committed will often cross jurisdictional areas and will involve the need to have multiple agencies or departments join the investigation. When a NIBIN hit is received, the investigator should start by collecting all police reports related to NIBIN-linked shootings and thoroughly examine these crimes, and coordinate with the area CGIC for full intelligence deconfliction and analysis. Investigators may then need to coordinate with multiple departments who have shootings linked through NIBIN to gang members or specific predicate acts being investigated. Investigators will need to exercise tact and

diplomacy to enlist each new department and convince them to merge their shooting crime into the larger gang case rather than leave it as a stand-alone act handled by the department.

Exploitation of Recovered Digital Communication and Storage Devices. Arguably one of the most important investigative steps in any investigation today is the proper examination and exploitation of cell phones, smart phones, computers, highway toll transponders, other forms of digital communication devices and digital storage devices, and "witness devices" such as Amazon™ Echo, and Alexa or Google™ Home. There may already be cell phones or computers belonging to targeted gang members that are sitting in a local police department's evidence room based on a prior arrest. Investigators should check for these items, determine their potential usefulness to the investigation, and follow proper legal process to gain physical access to the device, and authorization to examine its contents. Searching and examining the contents of any device requires a search warrant. As these items are recovered investigators must take steps to properly preserve them for evidence (e.g., ensuring that the charge does not run out prior to downloading, ensuing that media is placed in a protective Faraday storage bag) and having someone with the proper training and equipment to download information contained on the device with exploitation technology such as Cellebrite®. It is critical that investigators contact their digital media collection specialists for guidance and assistance. The remote wiping or locking of seized electronic devices by suspects is on the rise, and protecting the seized device from receiving any signal is the only way to prevent this from happening.

Establishing Community Rapport. As investigators go into the community and begin to interview suspects, witnesses, and victims, they should also focus on establishing relationships and community rapport that may later yield important tips or information. Investigators will have a high hurdle to overcome, as armed gangs intimidate the members of their community into staying quiet for fear of the consequences. Community members need to develop a trust of the investigators before any meaningful cooperation can begin. Properly notify victims and witnesses of their rights in accordance with the Federal Victim and Witness Protection Act of 1982. Create a plan to protect cooperating witnesses and victims, and educate witnesses on the protection that is available. This is vital to ensuring that victims and witnesses feel comfortable coming forward and providing their full cooperation.

Interviews and Proffers of Witnesses, Victims, Suspects, and Cooperating Defendants. Interviews and proffers will be important to the investigation. Developing a cooperating defendant who can be the "historian", the person who can relate the history that ties all the evidence and criminal acts together, can be a critical part of the investigation. Remember, you want a historian who sings, not a storyteller who composes. Offer everyone arrested the opportunity to cooperate. More cooperators equals more intelligence, and the ability to corroborate more events with multiple different sources. More cooperators mean fewer trials and therefore the ability to use limited resources to focus on impacting violent crime. An offer of compromise is not a promise of leniency. It will be important to fact check and independently corroborate what the historian tells you to make sure they are being completely accurate and truthful. Before going into an interview of proffer, investigators should be fully prepared with all the questions they need to cover, but also be ready to be flexible, in order to cover unanticipated topics that may come up. The investigator and assigned AUSA need to be vigilant during these interviews and proffers, in order to identify those persons who should be brought before a federal grand jury to provide testimony or be compelled to testify. Cooperating defendants need to enter into a cooperation agreement with the government. The preferred methods of formalized agreements, as discussed in Chapter 9, between the cooperating defendant and the government include the following:

➢ Proffer Agreement
➢ Cooperation Agreement & Immunity
➢ "5k Letter" and Motion for Sentence Reduction

All cooperating defendant agreements must, at a minimum, include the following requirements:

➢ The cooperator must always tell the truth and they will be charged with any false statements or material omissions.
➢ The cooperator must fully disclose their entire role in all crimes as well as their past criminal history.
➢ The cooperator must meet with the government whenever they are called for a de-briefing or testimony.
➢ The cooperator will not commit any more crimes.

Victim and Witness Rights. Investigators must understand that, in many instances, today's gang member could be tomorrow's shooting victim. Any crime victim is a victim and based on the fact set they may be entitled to notification of their rights. Many states have established victim and witness rights. At the federal level, the Victims of Crime Act was enacted in 1984 and updated in 2004 with the Crime Victim Rights Act, Title 18 U.S.C. § 3771, which is part of the Justice for All Act of 2004. Investigators should ensure that all victims and witnesses are provided with information on their federal rights and that they are aware of resources available to keep them from harm. Ensuring that victims and witnesses feel safe is not only the right thing to do and a public safety priority, but it is paramount to securing their full cooperation. Once the word gets out that the investigators mean what they say and will protect victims and witnesses from gang retaliation, the level of cooperation and the number of witnesses will grow.

Financial Analysis and Asset Identification. Identifying assets related to the proceeds of criminal activity is an important part of any gang investigation. Identifying the flow of assets can assist in establishing gang member hierarchy, the assets themselves are often forfeitable, and their movement can lead to additional criminal charges such as money laundering and various frauds. At the outset of a gang investigation investigators should engage their SME Financial Investigators (FI) for purposes of asset identification. SME-FIs should be tasked with the identification, seizure, and forfeiture of assets relied upon by criminals and their associates to further their criminal activities. In addition, SME-FIs should provide specific guidance to the investigators on the review, organization, and analysis of financial documents, vehicle and property records, anti-money laundering bank reports, and other information that has been obtained in the course of their investigations. SME-FIs should also assist investigators in the identification and charging of financial crimes, including money laundering violations (Title 18 U.S.C. §§ 1956, 1957), along with their elements of proof and SUAs. See Chapter 5 for additional guidance on the forfeiture of crime guns and illegal proceeds.

PRO-ACTIVE COVERT TECHNIQUE

The pro-active and covert investigation utilizes law enforcement techniques such as undercover approaches, use of confidential informants, and a variety of electronic tracking and interception techniques designed to go undetected by gang members. These are techniques to use if the investigation is at a stage where investigators do not want gang members to know they are being investigated. This approach is designed to prevent any changes in the gang's modus operandi.

The following are pro-active and covert investigative techniques that investigators should consider for applicability in their armed violent gang investigation.

UC and CI Approaches. Through CIs alone, or in conjunction with a UC investigator, the investigative team should explore how to approach members of the gang to make purchases of firearms and/or narcotics through a logical and methodical targeting process. All CIs should be properly vetted, documented, and approved. All UCs should have proper prior training, a properly backstopped UC identity, and a knowledge of the type of product they intend to discuss or purchase.

If investigators are targeting the most violent armed gang in the area they should expect that at some point in this process the UC or CI will be ripped-off. Proper operational planning will allow the UC or CI to react appropriately and defuse the situation: to leave the buy money and get out. Proper operational planning will allow for a react team to rescue the UC or CI if needed; however, the preferred outcome will be to allow the UC or CI to safely extricate themselves from the situation, identify those who robbed them, and use this armed robbery as a predicate act in the larger case. Having armed investigators rush into an armed robbery prematurely can cause greater risk to the UC or CI, the react team, and the general public, and can compromise the investigation.

In addition to the standard in-person street purchase techniques, the case agent should also consider the potential for cold approaches on social media sites or the use of cooperating witnesses or CIs who are already set as a "friend" with a suspect in a social media environment, as a means of accessing protected sections of the suspect's social media page where more important photographs may exist.

The use of CIs and/or UCs to conduct narcotic purchases from gang members will be important to the investigation, but this should not be viewed as the primary or sole investigative technique used to target an armed violent gang. Investigators must target the gang's criminal enterprise and violent crimes as well as their associations, and full enterprise must be investigated for the case to be effective. Exclusive use of narcotics purchases to target an armed violent gang is 1980s law enforcement, and is simply an ineffective and inefficient approach for today's investigations. A properly focused armed gang investigation is focused on a gang that law enforcement has targeted based on proper research and intelligence development, not an investigation of opportunity simply because someone has a CI who can make a drug buy from someone. Investigators need to control CIs and direct them to an identified and targeted violent gang rather than going after targets the CI discovers and brings to the investigator.

Wall-Off Arrests and Car Stops. Identify gang members who may be advantageous to arrest for purposes of garnering their cooperation in a covert process known as a wall-off arrest. If the targeted gang member is engaged in illegal activity, assign the task of independently developing a case to arrest them, or find independent probable cause for a search warrant or car stop that will result in gathering evidence leading to their arrest. This process will wall-off this arrest from the larger gang conspiracy investigation and protect that case from being compromised. Information from the larger investigation indicating when the target may be holding illegal narcotics or firearms can be used; however, the probable cause to conduct a car stop and discover these items must be developed separately by the officer who will make the traffic stop. For example, the officer may find the target committing a traffic violation which can lead to their stop. Then, through observation, conversation, and/or the use of a drug dog they may develop probable cause to make an arrest and search the vehicle, or just search the vehicle, and then find the narcotics or firearms. This type of arrest could be handled as a stand-alone case walled-off from the larger gang conspiracy investigation.

Department of Corrections Calls and Records. Investigators should identify those gang members currently incarcerated, particularly those recently jailed and held for pending cases, and secure a subpoena for copies of the following:

✓ **Recorded Jail/Prison Telephone Calls** - Obtain copies of recorded conversation and review these to determine what criminal activities they may still be involved with, who they may be directing, and what requests they are making of other gang members. Inmates have no expectation of privacy for conversations they hold with other persons over a corrections facility telephone. Most corrections facilities have signs posted above each telephone advising inmates of this.

✓ **Call Logs** – Determine who has been placed on the approved telephone call list for the inmate.

✓ **Visitor Logs** – Determine what other gang members are visiting them, when, and why.

✓ **Received and Outgoing Mail Logs** – Determine what other gang members they are communicating with.

✓ **Written Correspondence** - Gather any copied written correspondence between suspects, defendants, and victims who may substantiate the criminal enterprise, associations, or other crimes.

✓ **Commissary Deposit Logs** – Determine what other gang members are making deposits into the commissary.

✓ **Additional Crimes and Associations** – Determine if the jail has any incidents in which the inmate was involved in assaults that were gang related, or if any contraband (cell phones, narcotics, weapons) has been intercepted or removed from the inmate.

Examine these records for evidence of associations and the criminal enterprise, particularly the recorded jail calls, in which gang members may still try to control gang activities through phone communication.

Automated License Plate Readers. ALPRs may be mounted in a vehicle or on a fixed location such as a street light or overpass near a drug trafficking house or other criminal activity operated by the gang, to identify individuals who might be turned into witnesses, as well as to identify and document gang members and their sources of illicit supplies coming and going from the location. Should there be a nearby shooting, the stored data may be queried to identify all vehicles driving by the scene shortly before and after the shooting, in an effort to identify the shooter(s) and/or witnesses. This technical surveillance technique usually does not require a court order or any other level of judicial permission; however, case law with respect to all technical surveillance methods is evolving, so investigators should consult with the assigned case AUSA to determine the legality of the planned use and the proper permission levels required to use ALPRs within that judicial district.

Video Surveillance and Facial Recognition. The use of pole cameras, drop car cameras, and existing business surveillance cameras in the area where the gang operates and commits their crimes and narcotics trafficking activities in public areas may be useful in establishing associations, methods of operation, territory control, and actions, as part of the criminal enterprise. When placed and installed correctly by trained technical operations officers, these surreptitious devices can gather a wealth of intelligence and video evidence completely undetected. Law enforcement may use surreptitious video recording devices without the need to secure a court order as long as they are not recording audio and are only recording activities taking place in an area within view of the general public. The continuous covert recording or activity which persons are conducting in an area where they have a reasonable expectation of privacy require a court order. Investigators may also want to determine if the city in which the gang operates maintains a video monitoring system or ALPR system throughout the city that could be used to enhance surveillance abilities or used exclusively as surveillance. Some cities have automated their jail booking photographs into a facial recognition system, and agencies may run photographs against the system to identify unknown suspects. These technical surveillance techniques usually do not require a court order or any other level of judicial permission; however, case law with respect to all technical surveillance methods is evolving, so investigators should consult with the assigned case AUSA to determine the legality of the planned use and the proper permission levels required to use Video Surveillance and Facial Recognition systems within that judicial district.

Global Positioning System (GPS) Tracking Devices. The use of GPS trackers, also known as "bird dogs", or a vehicle's own built in geo-location software such as On-Star® may be useful in documenting the activities of gang members and documenting their location in relation to violent crimes being investigated. See Appendix D to review an example of language used in an affidavit for this type of court order. GPS devices, with or without their own power source, can only be used after securing a court order. Securing the records for a highway toll transponder (e.g., E-ZPass®, SunPass®, or FasTrak™) may be obtained with a subpoena or court order. Securing cellphone GPS data may also accomplish identifying a suspect's movements as well as establishing a pattern of life activities that could lead to the identification of other co-conspirator and drug or firearms source locations. Case law with respect to all technical surveillance methods is evolving, so investigators should consult with the assigned case AUSA to determine the legality of the planned use and the proper permission levels required to use ALPRs within that judicial district.

Electronic Communication Records and Data Analysis. Collection and analysis of electronic communication records will be vital in any gang investigation. This includes electronic devices as well as the various forms of communication conducted on those devices, including email, SMS text messaging, IP, domain names, and VOIP. These records may be obtained with a subpoena, court order, or search warrant depending upon the type of records being sought. See Chapter 9 for more information on these types of technical surveillance methods, and Appendix D for sample application affidavits and court orders. The following types of collection are useful in a gang investigation.

✓ **Tower Dump:** This is a form of historical cell-site data that reveals all the cellular phones that utilized a particular tower at a given point in time. Because hundreds of phones can contact a particular tower even in a short time frame, a tower dump from a single tower at a single point of time generally will not be particularly helpful. Rather, this type of information is typically most helpful when a crime occurred at the intersection of two tower zones and you can cross-reference tower dumps from multiple towers and set small timeframe parameters in order to identify phones of potential interest by virtue of the fact that they appear on each of the tower dump lists. Tower dumps are useful in determining the cell phones there were at or near a shooting crime or robbery. Once those phones are known, investigators can then identify the subscribers to those cell phones and examine those persons to see if they are viable suspects in the crime.

✓ **Historical Cell Tower Geo-Location Data:** This "course-grain" information can be gathered by placing a cell phone at the scene of a crime and querying the data specific to that phone rather than all phones associated with a specific tower. This information may place gang members suspected in violent crimes at a known crime scene. Call detail records for cell phones can establish the exact dates, times, and general locations of cell phones relative to the longitude and latitude of geographically-fixed cell towers when cell phones are used to initiate, receive, or terminate a voice call or send or receive text messages. Geo-locating cell phones associated with defendants, accomplices, witnesses, or victims and can establish cell phone movement patterns and proximity to crime scenes or other relevant locations. "Crime occurs where the offender's space overlaps with the victim's space".[clii] Geo-mapping a suspect's historical cell tower data over a crime victims historical cell tower data can show you where the two paths crossed at the same moment in time, which may be the location of the crime.

✓ **Latitude-longitude Cell Data**: Also known as GPS data, this "fine-grain" data is similar to historical cell tower geo-location data, but is far more accurate in placing the location of a device. For solving an armed violent crime this fine grain data should be relied upon first over the course grain cell tower data that is based on triangulation. In addition, investigators may find it useful to map the geo-location data against data collected for the same time period from any acoustic ballistic detection systems in the area to determine if gang members can be placed at any gunshot detection sites.

✓ **Pen Register, Dialed Number Recorder (DNR) or Trap and Trace:** Investigators should use these technical surveillance methods to track in real time the various types of communications between members of a criminal enterprise or gang, their customers, and even when gang members contact witnesses and victims. A Pen may be secured for a cell phone, an IP, an email, a domain name, a mobile broadband account and text messages, or a VOIP. These records can establish communications between gang member shortly before or after criminal acts, which may be useful in establishing the conspiracy.

✓ **Cell Site Simulator Technology:** A CSST may be useful in situations where all methods to identify a suspect's cell phone number have failed, investigators should consider the use of CSST that will, over time and surveillance of the target while on the move, identify their cell number through a process of elimination. CSSTs may also be used to identify drug purchasers at a drug sales location. In addition, a CSST may be used to locate a particular cell phone in real time, in order to locate a gang member for arrest.

When requesting any of the above electronic communication device information, the investigator should also attend to the following:

✓ Consult with their assigned case AUSA to determine the proper permission levels required for use in their Judicial District. Case law regarding the use of these techniques is evolving.

✓ Requests that may require a court order today may require a search warrant eventually. On June 22, 2018 in Carpenter v. U.S. 585 U.S. (2018), SCOTUS ruled that a search warrant is required to obtain any electronic data information related to location[cliii]. This would include historical cell tower geo-location data, latitude-longitude data, and CSSTs.

✓ Include a non-disclosure clause in the court order to prevent a service provider from alerting the subscriber.

✓ Include justification to have the court order sealed until arrests are made in the investigation.

✓ For agencies with no administrative subpoena power, the investigator should include language that will allow the court order to be re-used to identify the subscriber information on any persons contacted by the target device or that contact the target device. This will eliminate the need for multiple grand jury subpoenas and significantly expedite identification of targets for intelligence workups and investigation. See Appendix D for examples of affidavits containing this language.

Standard or Roving Court Ordered Title III Electronic Interception. As a last resort, after the means to further investigate the high-level targets of the gang are exhausted, and after demonstrating that a necessity to further the investigation exists, investigators may want to consider employment of a T-III wire intercept. The definitions, criminal acts justifying use of a T-III intercept, application process, use, and reporting process for this technical surveillance method are contained in Title 18 U.S.C. §§ 2510, 2516, 2517, 2518 and 2519. Use of a T-III intercept is a highly sensitive technical surveillance technique that often requires a significant amount of resources to properly staff, and therefore a full review of the need to use this technique should be undertaken by law enforcement agency management in coordination with the assigned AUSA.

Court Ordered T-III intercepts may be used to record the conversations of people during telephone communications, using emails, using text messages and other electronic communication means. Court ordered T-III intercepts may be placed in fixed locations where targets meet to have in-person conversations. Court ordered T-III intercepts may be "roving," which target a person rather than a specific phone or location. In some instances, gang members may use "burner" phones which are inexpensive prepaid cell phones that are disposable, and which they can switch frequently. If a target is known to change phones frequently, the investigator may want to use a "roving" T-III rather than trying to apply for a new T-III intercept each time a new phone is used.

Securing a court ordered T-III intercept should not be an investigative goal; it is an investigative technique of last resort that may or may not be useful during your specific investigation to achieve the established goal of stopping armed violent crime by dismantling a gang.

Any law enforcement agency utilizing a T-III intercept will need a formal policy and detailed procedures for planning, funding, securing, installing, operating, and reporting on the installation of a court ordered T-III interception. In addition to following those procedures investigators will need to coordinate with their designated AUSA to gain their support and ensure that they will agree to pursue a court ordered T-III interception. The DOJ Criminal Division Office of Enforcement Operations (OEO) requires specific language be included in all T-III affidavits that are targeting violent organizations or organizations believed to possess and traffic in firearms, to ensure that all investigators and prosecutors are aware of standard risk mitigation guidelines.

To ensure that investigators and AUSAs know when application of a T-III interception is possible and how to properly draft the application, a road map for this process is contained in the U.S. Attorneys Manual, T-III Procedures Checklist. See Figure 9.1.

FEDERAL VIOLATIONS APPLICABLE IN ARMED VIOLENT GANG INVESTIGATIONS

Once an armed violent gang or criminal enterprise is identified for targeting and investigation, it is important that investigators understand the variety of federal charges that may apply to past and ongoing criminal activity by the gang, and investigate those activities with an understanding of the elements of proof required to establish these violations. Keep in mind that in a gang investigation many of the applicable federal violations will be part of a criminal conspiracy and Pinkerton liability will apply. Pinkerton liability holds that each member of the criminal enterprise conspiracy is responsible for the actions of the other members performed during the conspiracy. For example, if one member commits murder with a firearm as part of the gang's criminal enterprise all members of the enterprise conspiracy share liability for the crime and may be charged under the "umbrella" of the criminal enterprise conspiracy.

The following federal criminal charges, above and beyond standard firearms possessory or trafficking violations, may be applicable during an investigation designed to dismantle and eliminate an armed violent gang or criminal enterprise.

Title 18 U.S.C. § 1951: Interference with Commerce by Robbery or Extortion (Hobbs Act). Whoever in any way or degree obstructs, delays, or affects commerce or the movement of any article or commodity in commerce, by robbery or extortion, or attempts or conspires so to do, or commits or threatens physical violence to any person or property in furtherance of a plan or purpose to do anything in violation of this section shall be fined under this title or imprisoned not more than twenty years, or both.
Elements
1. The defendant obtained, or attempted to obtain, property from another without that person's consent. The property may be contraband, such as illegal drugs.
2. The defendant did so by wrongful use of actual or threatened force, violence, or fear.
3. As a result of the defendant's actions, interstate commerce, or an item moving in interstate commerce, was actually or potentially delayed, obstructed, or affected in any way or degree.

Title 18 U.S.C. § 1959: Violent Crime in Aid of Racketeering. Whoever for the purpose of gaining entrance to or maintaining or increasing position in an enterprise engaged in racketeering crimes, murders, kidnaps, maims, assaults with a dangerous weapon, commits assault resulting in serious bodily injury upon, or threatens to commit a crime of violence shall be imprisoned up to twenty years or for life, or death if the crime resulted in a death.
Elements
1. The existence of an "enterprise" as defined in Title 18 U.S.C. § 1959(b)(2).
2. The charged enterprise engaged in, or its activities affected, interstate or foreign commerce

3. The charged enterprise engaged in "racketeering activity" as defined in Title 18 U.S.C. §§ 1959(b)(1), 1961(1).

4. The defendant committed one of the following crimes—or conspired or attempted to commit one of these crimes—which crime violated state or federal law: murder, kidnaping, maiming, assault with a dangerous weapon, assault resulting in serious bodily injury, threatening to commit a crime of violence.

5. The crime of violence was committed either: 1) as consideration for the receipt of, or as consideration for a promise or agreement to pay, anything of pecuniary value from the charged enterprise, or 2) for the purpose of gaining entrance to or maintaining or increasing position in the charged enterprise.[cliv]

Title 18 U.S.C. § 1962: Racketeer Influenced and Corrupt Organizations Act. The RICO Act was passed by Congress with the declared purpose of seeking to eradicate organized crime. The RICO act makes it unlawful for any person who has received any income derived directly or indirectly from a pattern of racketeering activity, or through collection of an unlawful debt in which such person has participated as a principal to use or invest, directly or indirectly, any part of such income, or the proceeds of such income, in acquisition of any interest in, or the establishment or operation of, any enterprise which is engaged in, or the activities of which affect, interstate or foreign commerce. Any person found guilty of RICO shall be imprisoned up to twenty years or for life, or death if the crime resulted in a death.

Elements

1. An enterprise existed. An "enterprise" includes any individual, partnership, corporation, association, or other legal entity, and any union or group of individuals associated in fact although not a legal entity.

2. The enterprise affected interstate commerce.

3. The defendant was associated with or employed by the enterprise.

4. The defendant engaged in a pattern of racketeering activity. A "pattern of racketeering activity" requires at least two acts of racketeering activity committed within ten years of each other. The government must show that the racketeering predicates are related, and that they amount to or pose a threat of continued criminal activity. Racketeering predicates are related if they have the same or similar purposes, results, participants, victims, or methods of commission, or otherwise are interrelated by distinguishing characteristics and are not isolated events. And,

5. The defendant conducted or participated in the conduct of the enterprise through that pattern of racketeering activity through the commission of at least two acts of racketeering activity as set forth in the indictment.

RICO acts include state and federal offenses related to the following:
18 U.S.C. § 924c: Armed Crimes of Violence
18 U.S.C. § 36: Drive By-Shooting
18 U.S.C. § 1958: Solicitation to Commit Murder
18 U.S.C. § 2119: Carjacking
18 U.S.C. § 2118: Robbery of a Pharmacy
18 U.S.C. § 1951: Robbery-Hobbs Act
18 U.S.C. § 1201: Kidnapping
18 U.S.C. § 1203a: Hostage Taking
18 U.S.C. § 844i: Arson
21 U.S.C. § 841: Drug Trafficking

Other predicate acts for RICO include mail and wire fraud, gambling, bribery, and money laundering.

Title 18 U.S.C. § 3: Accessory After the Fact. Whoever, knowing that an offense against the United States has been committed, receives, relieves, comforts or assists the offender in order to hinder or prevent his apprehension, trial or punishment, is an accessory after the fact. The maximum sentence and fine are set at half those of the underlying crime and 15 years if the underlying crime in punishable by life imprisonment or death.

Elements
1. The crime of _____ had been committed by _____.
2. The defendant knew that this crime had been committed and that _____ had committed it.
3. The defendant thereafter intentionally received, relieved, comforted, or assisted _____ in order to hinder and prevent that person's apprehension, trial, or punishment for the crime of _____.
4. The essential elements of the underlying crime must be given to the jury.
5. The crime of _____ has ___ essential elements which are:

Title 18 U.S.C. § 1512(d)(2): Tampering with a witness, victim, or informant by harassment.
Elements
1. The defendant intentionally harassed another person.
2. The harassment hindered, delayed, prevented, or dissuaded any person reporting to a law enforcement officer or judge of the United States
3. The commission or possible commission of—
   a. a federal offense,
   b. violation of a condition of probation,
   c. violation of a condition of supervised release,
   d. violation of a condition of parole, or a
   e. violation of a condition of release pending judicial proceedings.

Title 18 U.S.C. § 1513(a)(1)(A): Obstructing justice by retaliating against a witness, victim, or an informant.
Elements
1. The defendant killed or attempted to kill another person with the intent to retaliate against any person for:
   a. the attendance of a witness or party at, or
   b. any testimony given at, or
   c. any record, document, or other object produced by a witness at an official proceeding.

Title 18 U.S.C. § 922(h): The Bodyguard Statute. Any person who while employed by someone who is prohibited under 922(g), uses or possesses a firearm during that employment may be imprisoned for up to 10 years.
Elements
1. The defendant possessed, shipped, transported, or received a firearm or ammunition.
2. The defendant did so in or affecting interstate or foreign commerce or the firearm or ammunition had traveled in interstate or foreign commerce at some point during its existence.
3. The defendant did so in the course of being employed for a person prohibited under Title 18 U.S.C. § 922(g).

4. The defendant did so knowingly; that is, the defendant must know that the person for whom the defendant was employed was a prohibited person and that the item was a firearm or ammunition, and that possession must be voluntary and intentional.

Title 21 U.S.C. § 841(a)(1): Manufacturing, Distributing, Dispensing or Possessing with Intent to Manufacture, Distribute or Dispense Controlled Substances.
Elements
1. The defendant knowingly or intentionally possessed [controlled substance].
2. The defendant possessed the substance with the intent to distribute it.
3. The weight of the [controlled substance] defendant possessed was at least [name amount]

Title 21 U.S.C. § 843(b): Use of Communication Facility in Causing or Facilitating the Commission of Felonies Under the Controlled Substances Act or the Controlled Substances Import and Export Act.
Elements
1. The defendant knowingly used a communication device, e.g., telephone, email, etc.
2. During use of the communication device the defendant acted with the intent to commit, cause or facilitate the commission of a drug trafficking crime. (Use of phones or email to arrange drug trafficking deals.)

Title 21 U.S.C. § 848: Continuing Criminal Enterprise. Any person who engages in a continuing criminal enterprise shall be sentenced to a term of imprisonment which may not be less than 20 years and which may be up to life imprisonment, to a fine not to exceed the greater of that authorized in accordance with the provisions of title 18 or $2,000,000 if the defendant is an individual or $5,000,000 if the defendant is other than an individual, and to the forfeiture prescribed in section 853 of this title; except that if any person engages in such activity after one or more prior convictions of him under this section have become final, he shall be sentenced to a term of imprisonment which may not be less than 30 years and which may be up to life imprisonment, to a fine not to exceed the greater of twice the amount authorized in accordance with the provisions of title 18 or $4,000,000 if the defendant is an individual or $10,000,000 if the defendant is other than an individual, and to the forfeiture prescribed in section 853 of this title.
Elements
1. The defendant's conduct must constitute a felony violation of federal narcotics law.
2. The conduct must take place as part of a continuing series of such violations (five or more drug transactions).
3. The defendant must undertake the activity in concert with five or more persons.
4. The defendant must act as the organizer, supervisor, or manager of the criminal enterprise.
5. The defendant must obtain substantial income or resources from this enterprise.

The following federal criminal sentencing enhancement provisions may be applicable during an investigation designed to dismantle and eliminate an armed violent gang or criminal enterprise;

Title 18 U.S.C. § 521: Criminal Street Gangs. The Federal "Criminal Street Gangs" Statute was enacted as part of the Violent Crime Control and Law Enforcement Act of 1994 and is not a substantive offense but serves as a penalty enhancement of up to 10 years. The high level of knowledge and intent requirements to successfully apply this sentencing enhancement makes its application very difficult. The Statute is as follows:

(a) Definitions.

    (1) "conviction" includes a finding, under state or federal law, that a person has committed an act of juvenile delinquency involving a violent or controlled substances felony.

    (2) "criminal street gang" means an ongoing group, club, organization, or association of 5 or more persons—

        (i) that has as 1 of its primary purposes the commission of 1 or more of the criminal offenses described in subsection (c);

        (ii) the members of which engage, or have engaged within the past 5 years, in a continuing series of offenses described in subsection (c); and

        (iii) the activities of which affect interstate or foreign commerce.

    (3) "state" means a state of the United States, the District of Columbia, and any commonwealth, territory, or possession of the United States.

(b) Penalty. The sentence of a person convicted of an offense described in subsection (c) shall be increased by up to 10 years if the offense is committed under the circumstances described in subsection (d).

(c) Offenses. The offenses described in this section are—

    (1) a federal felony involving a controlled substance (as defined in section 102 of the Controlled Substances Act (Title 21 U.S.C. § 802)) for which the maximum penalty is not less than 5 years;

    (2) a federal felony crime of violence that has as an element the use or attempted use of physical force against the person of another; and

    (3) a conspiracy to commit an offense described in paragraph (1) or (2).

(d) Circumstances. The circumstances described in this section are that the offense described in subsection (c) was committed by a person who—

    (1) participates in a criminal street gang with knowledge that its members engage in or have engaged in a continuing series of offenses described in subsection (c);

    (2) intends to promote or further the felonious activities of the criminal street gang or maintain or increase his or her position in the gang; and

    (3) has been convicted within the past 5 years for—

        (i) an offense described in subsection (c);

        (ii) a state offense—

            (A) involving a controlled substance (as defined in section 102 of the Controlled Substances Act (Title 21 U.S.C. § 802)) for which the maximum penalty is not less than 5 years' imprisonment; or

            (B) that is a felony crime of violence that has as an element the use or attempted use of physical force against the person of another;

            (C) any federal or state felony offense that by its nature involves a substantial risk that physical force against the person of another may be used in the course of committing the offense; or

            (D) a conspiracy to commit an offense described in subparagraph (a), (b), or (c).

Sample Enhanced Penalty Information re; Title 18 U.S.C. § 521

The United States Attorney for the _____ District of _____ charges:

Between on or about *(DATE)* , and on or about *(DATE)* , the *(GANG NAME)* was a criminal street gang, as that term is defined in Title 18 U.S.C. § 521(a), that is an ongoing group, club, organization, and association of five or more persons that (i) had as one of its primary purposes the commission of one or more of the criminal offenses described in Title 18 U.S.C. § 521(c), (ii) the members of which were engaging in, and had engaged within the past five years, in a continuing series of offenses described in Title 18 U.S.C. § 521(c), and (iii) the activities of which affect interstate and foreign commerce.

The offense charged in [COUNT__] of the Indictment filed in the above captioned matter on [DATE], that is Title 21 U.S.C. § 846, is an offense described in Title 18 U.S.C. § 521(c).

At all times relevant to [COUNT__] of the Indictment filed in this matter, the defendants *(NAME)*, *(NAME)*, each of whom committed the offense charged in [COUNT__] of the Indictment filed in this matter, were persons who:

participated in the *(GANG NAME)* with knowledge that its members were engaging in and had engaged in a continuing series of offenses described in Title 21 U.S.C. § 521(c), that is the offenses charged in [COUNT __ as Racketeering Acts 1 and 2, and COUNTS __ through __, and COUNTS __ and __] of the Indictment filed in this matter, intended to promote and further the felonious activities of the *(GANG NAME)*, and maintain and increase his position therein, and at the time of the offense charged in [COUNT__] of the Indictment filed in this case, had been convicted within the past five years of an offense specified in Title 18 U.S.C. § 521(d)(3), as more particularly described in Paragraphs __ through __ of this Enhanced Penalty Information.

On or about [DATE], defendant *(NAME)* was convicted in [New Jersey Superior] Court of aggravated assault, in violation of [CITE STATUTE], a felony crime of violence having as an element the use or attempted use of physical force against another. Thereafter;

On or about [DATE], defendant *(NAME)* was convicted in [CITE COURT NAME] Court of conspiracy to distribute heroin, in violation of [CITE STATUTE], a drug crime for which the maximum penalty was not less than five years' imprisonment.

On or about [DATE], defendant *(NAME)* was convicted in [CITE COURT NAME] Court of possession with intent to distribute cocaine, in violation of [CITE STATUTE], a drug crime for which the maximum penalty was not less than five years' imprisonment.

On or about [DATE], defendant *(NAME)* was convicted in [CITE COURT NAME] Court of possession of cocaine and possession with intent to distribute cocaine, in violation of [CITE STATUTE], each a drug crime for which the maximum penalty was not less than five years' imprisonment.

On or about [DATE], defendant (NAME) was convicted in [CITE COURT NAME] Court of distribution of heroin within 1,000 feet of a school, in violation of [CITE STATUTE], a drug crime for which the maximum penalty was not less than five years' imprisonment.

On or about [DATE], defendant (NAME) was convicted in [CITE COURT NAME] Court of possession with intent to distribute a controlled dangerous substance, in violation of [CITE STATUTE], a drug crime for which the maximum penalty was not less than five years' imprisonment.

On or about [DATE], the defendant (NAME) was convicted in [CITE COURT] Court of possession with intent to distribute cocaine, in violation of [CITE STATUTE], a drug crime for which the maximum penalty was not less than five years' imprisonment.

Accordingly, at sentencing the United States shall seek increased punishment of each of the above defendants, as such punishment is authorized under Title 18 U.S.C. § 521.

FIGURE 11.2 [clv]

Title 18 U.S.C. § 924(c): Using, carrying, or possessing a firearm during, or in furtherance of, a drug trafficking crime or federal crime of violence.
<u>Sentence</u>: 5 years if a firearm is used or possessed during the crime; 7 years if a firearm is brandished during the crime; 10 years is firearm is discharged during the crime; 10 years if the firearm is a sawed-off rifle or shotgun; 10 years if the firearm is an assault weapon; 30 years if the firearm is machine gun, silencer, or destructive device; and 25 years consecutive for each additional act. All sentences are minimum mandatory and must run consecutive to sentences for other charges.
<u>Elements</u>
1. The defendant committed the elements of a crime of violence or drug trafficking crime prosecutable in federal court; and
2. The defendant knowingly used, carried or possessed a firearm.
3. The use or carrying of the firearm was during and in relation to, or the possession of the firearm was in furtherance of, the defendant's drug trafficking crime or crime of violence.
   Note: In a conspiracy, where a defendant is not the principal, the defendant must have had advance knowledge that an accomplice would use or carry a gun during the relevant drug crime or crime of violence, and could have withdrawn from the crime after it became apparent that a confederate was carrying a gun. In addition, "use" includes a scenario where a defendant trades a firearm for drugs.

The following are Federal Crimes of Violence and Drug Trafficking Crimes that may include Discharge of a Firearm.

Title 18 U.S.C. § 924c: Armed Crimes of Violence
Title 18 U.S.C. § 36: Drive-By Shooting
Title 18 U.S.C. § 1958: Solicitation of Murder
Title 18 U.S.C. § 2119: Carjacking
Title 18 U.S.C. § 211: Robbery of a Pharmacy
Title 18 U.S.C. § 1951: Robbery-Hobbs Act
Title 18 U.S.C. § 1201: Kidnapping

Title 18 U.S.C. § 1203(a): Hostage Taking
Title 18 U.S.C. § 844i: Arson
Title 21 U.S.C. § 841: Drug Trafficking

Title 18 U.S.C. § 924(h): Any person who transfers a firearm to another person knowing that firearm will be used to commit a federal crime of violence or drug trafficking crime may be imprisoned for up to 10 years.
<u>Elements</u>
1. The defendant knowingly transferred a firearm; and
2. The defendant knew that the firearm would be used in a crime of violence or drug trafficking crime.

A "crime of violence" is defined in Title 18 U.S.C. § 924(c)(3), and a "drug trafficking crime" is defined in Title 18 U.S.C. § 924(c)(2). These predicate crimes should not be state offenses.

Title 18 U.S.C. § 924(j): Any person who, during the commission of an offense under Title 18 U.S.C. § 924(c), causes the death of a person through use of a firearm may be imprisoned for up to life in prison, or put to death.
<u>Elements</u>
1. The defendant possessed, carried, used, or brandished a firearm.
2. The defendant did so during and in relation to a crime of violence or a drug trafficking crime, or in furtherance of a crime of violence or a drug trafficking crime which may be prosecuted in federal court [the court should instruct the jury as to all the essential elements of the underlying crime].
3. The defendant caused the death of a person through the use of the firearm.

Title 18 U.S.C. § 924(o): Any person who conspires to commit an offense under Title 18 U.S.C. § 924(c) may be imprisoned for up to 20 years.
<u>Elements</u>
1. Two of more defendants conspired to commit the elements of a crime of violence or drug trafficking crime prosecutable in federal court; and
2. Two or more defendants knowingly used, carried or possessed a firearm.
3. The use or carrying of the firearm was during and in relation to, or the possession of the firearm was in furtherance of, the defendant's conspiracy to commit a crime of violence or drug trafficking crime.

This statute is frequently used during home invasion gang investigations.

Gang investigations will often involve instances of the destruction of evidence by suspects and defendants as well as tampering, intimidation, and retaliation against victims, witness and informants. The following federal crimes will apply to evidence and witness tampering related violations.

Title 18 U.S.C. § 3: Accessory after the fact.
Title 18 U.S.C. § 1512(d)(2): Tampering with a witness.
Title 18 U.S.C. § 1513(a)(1)(A): Obstructing justice by retaliating against a witness, victim, or informant.

CASE STUDY: OPERATION BLOOD RED

**United States v. Benton, et al - District of Connecticut – 3:15-cr-00174-JCH and
United States v. Benton, et al – District of Maine – 1:15-cr-00040-JAW**

In January 2014 the ATF New Haven, CT Field Office and the New Haven Police Department initiated an investigation of an armed violent street gang identified as Red Side Guerilla Brims ("RSGB"), a subset of the Bloods street gang.

The initiation of the investigation followed extensive intelligence research and the modification of law enforcement protocols to ensure that all gang intelligence information and crime gun intelligence information was shared with the key investigative team. Protocols were established to ensure that the comprehensive and timely use of NIBIN was in place. A list of unsolved shootings as well as violent active RSGB members was identified. The intelligence indicated that RSGB was heavily engaged in narcotics trafficking and related acts of violence, including murder, attempted murder, assaults, and armed robberies.

Additional intelligence exploitation efforts took advantage of jail phone call recordings for RSGB in custody, the movement of pending state charges into federal court to develop cooperating defendants, and the service of search warrants to review cell phones already in police custody from recent RSGB arrests. Crime gun intelligence was developed by tracing and submitting to NIBIN all firearms already in custody that had been recovered from RSGB in other crimes.

Surveillance targeted RSGB for traffic stops when it was known they were carrying drugs and guns, and additional pressure was added to these persons to cooperate. The recovered crime guns were exploited for CGI. All of this intelligence and investigative work paid off, and NIBIN started linking shootings and homicides to crime guns being recovered. Crime gun tracing revealed 2 trafficking rings within the RSGB. One group was securing firearms from South Carolina and trafficking them to New Haven, while the second group was actively securing firearms in Bangor, ME. Deconfliction of targets as they were developed tied the Bangor, ME trafficking group to an ongoing investigation by ATF Portland, ME agents of an FFL and straw purchasers operating in Bangor, ME. The ATF Portland office had already made UC purchases of straw-purchased firearms from an employee of the FFL, followed by the service of a federal search on the FFL to recover the records and copies of the FFL's video recordings of these transactions. The ATF New Haven investigation identified additional straw purchasers. One cooperator stated that the RSGB trafficked crack cocaine and heroin up to Bangor, and then bought guns with the profits, which they trafficked back to New Haven. The cooperator estimated that they trafficked 4 guns a week over the course of 2 years.

The development of cooperators became important to the investigation, and key interviews and proffers detailed the organization's operations, which helped identify further suspects and solve shootings. Following this comprehensive investigative strategy, investigators were able to attribute the following crimes to the gang: 10 homicides, 29 non-fatal shootings or unlawful discharges of a firearm, numerous armed robberies, and firearms and narcotics trafficking between multiple states. The investigation culminated in the federal indictment of 32 RSGB members and associates between the states of Connecticut and Maine. Six members of the organization were also charged with a 34-count federal RICO and VICAR indictment in relation to five homicides and several violent shooting acts. Additional homicides were charged in state court.

Over the course of several months in 2016, all 32 RSGB defendants pled guilty to their federal charges and received multi-decade long prison sentences[clvi]. At the Bangor sentencing of one gang member to 25 years in prison and five years of supervised release, the U.S. District Court judge said, "The message to those people like members of the Red Side Guerilla Brims is this: Stay away from Bangor."[clvii]

This investigation addressed the full spectrum of gun crime from the source through the firearms trafficking chain to the violent criminals who used them to terrorize a community. This case followed the intelligence led model by focusing on the solution of armed crimes and utilized both covert and overt techniques. During the investigation a number of other state and local law enforcement agencies in the New Haven area and the Bangor area joined in the investigation and played key roles. The impact of the case in New Haven is apparent in the Uniform Crime Report statistics for the City. In 2011 the city had 34 homicides and was listed as the second most violent small city in the country. In 2016 the number of homicides was 13, and violent crime in other categories was down as well.[clviii]

CASE STUDY: OPERATION BLACK DIAMOND

United States v. Rosga, et al – Eastern District of Virginia – 3:2010-cr-00170

In October of 2009 a member of the Hells Angels Motorcycle Gang was shot several times in the driveway of the gangs clubhouse in Caanan, Maine. Knowing that gang shootings like this are usually committed by rival gangs and that if not addressed, start a cycle of violent retaliation, the ATF Portland Maine Field Office initiated an investigation of the incident. ATF partnered with the Maine State Police homicide detectives and began investigating where the evidence was taking

them. During deconfliction checks the by the ATF case agent in Portland he found that there was a large investigation of the Outlaws Motorcycle Organization by ATF agents in Richmond, VA. In the ATF Virginia investigation, which was initiated in 2008, several ATF long term undercover agents had been "patched" into the Mongols Motorcycle Gang. They were then recruited by the rival Outlaws Motorcycle Gang to join their club and eventually "patched" over to the Outlaws. Their investigation was focused on the armed crimes being committed by the Outlaws. During their long-term undercover they established contact with the Outlaws in Maine and were able to document conversations with members that proved the Outlaws committed the shooting of the member of the Hells Angels and that the shooting was directed by others in the Outlaws. This violent armed crime committed in furtherance of the gang, coupled with other armed and violent crimes documented by the undercover ATF agents throughout the eastern half of the U.S. led to significant RICO, VICAR, and

FIGURE 11.3 *Gang Indicia and Firearms Recovered in Maine*
IMAGE CREDIT: Author

GCA case against the Outlaws. In June 2010 ATF and its law enforcement partners served more than 50 federal arrest warrants and 42 Federal search warrants in 10 States. The arrests included some entire Outlaw Chapters as well as Chapter Presidents, Enforcers, and the National President of the Outlaws. The search warrants resulted in the seizure and forfeiture of more than 70 firearms, narcotics, currency and properties. Most of the arrests took place without incident however during an arrest of one member of the Outlaws in Old Orchard Beach, Maine he opened fire on the approaching ATF Special Response Team who returned fire resulting in his death[clix] (*https://www.youtube.com/watch?v=CVAR-juyi7E*). In a testament to the strength of the case, every defendant in the case pled guilty or was convicted by jury trial and many have received lengthy jail sentences. This case followed the intelligence led model by focusing on the solution of armed crimes with an additional eye toward preventing an escalation of armed gang violence. The case primarily utilized covert techniques and incorporated some overt techniques after the wave of arrest and search warrants.

OTHER RESOURCES

This chapter discussed investigative methods for targeting an armed violent gang or criminal organization. The larger issue of sustaining a reduction in gang violence within a community over the long term requires a far more diverse set of tactics, polices, strategies, and partners. Law enforcement cannot arrest their way out of a gang violence problem, as the root causes are far beyond a law enforcement solution. The following common elements are often associated with the sustained reduction of gang problems:

➢ Community leaders must recognize that gangs are present in the community, and that suppression strategies must be complemented by prevention and intervention strategies.
➢ Community leaders must reach a consensus on the nature of the problem and the critical points for intervention.
➢ The combined leadership of the justice system and community-based organizations must focus on the mobilization of political and community resources to address gang problems.
➢ Leaders must create a mechanism or structure to coordinate community-wide efforts.
➢ A team comprising representatives from law enforcement officers, prosecutors, judges, probation officers, corrections officers, school personnel, community-based organizations, grassroots agencies, and other groups must prepare a set of policies and practices for the design and mobilization of community efforts and with the buy-in and support of community members.[clx]

Written in 1996 by U.S. DOJ Office of Juvenile Justice and Delinquency Programs, "The National Juvenile Justice Action Plan" provided a comprehensive plan for communities to holistically address gang violence, and this plan remains relevant today. Additional in-depth information regarding RICO, VICAR, gang prosecutions, criminal indictment templates, jury instruction examples, and sentencing provisions may be found in the following resources available to the public through the DOJ website.

Criminal RICO – A Manual for Federal Prosecutors, Sixth Revised Edition, by U.S. Department of Justice, Organized Crime and Racketeering Section, (May 2016) Washington, DC.

Violent Crimes in Aid of Racketeering – A Manual for Federal Prosecutors, by U.S. Department of Justice, Organized Crime and Racketeering Section, (Dec. 2006) Washington, DC.

Gang Prosecution Manual, by U.S Department of Justice, Office of Juvenile Justice and Delinquency Programs and Institute for Intergovernmental Research, (July 2009), Washington, DC.

U.S Attorneys Manual - Criminal Resource Manual, by U.S. Department of Justice, Offices of the United States Attorneys, Washington, DC.

Chapter 12
International Law
Enforcement

"When bad men combine, the good must associate; else they will fall,
one by one..."
Written by Edmund Burke, Anglo-Irish Statesman in 1770.

More than 210,000 intentional homicides were committed with firearms globally in 2016 according to the Small Arms Survey report, "Global Violent Deaths 2017". That same study revealed that the highest rates of firearms-inflicted lethal violence took place in countries located in Central America and the Caribbean.[clxi]

Many of the firearms used to create this global carnage are illegally trafficked to the violent end users. International firearms trafficking is accomplished through a myriad of sources and supply routes. Transnational Organized Criminals (TOCs) are probably the most significant source of trafficked small arms and light weapons (SALW) that international law enforcement encounters in crimes within their countries. TOCs are one of the most dangerous problems facing the world in the 21st century. They undermine open and free societies and pose a serious obstacle to economic development by distorting competition in world markets, taking advantage of failed states or contested spaces, and in some instances by establishing partnerships of convenience with terrorists, destabilizing militias, paramilitary groups, and warlords. The reach of TOCs can secretly control some countries, undermine their security and stability, and potentially affect world peace.

Figure 12.1 *Author in Sarajevo, Bosnia in 1997 on*
Special Investigative Assignment

IMAGE CREDIT: Author

TOCs such as the Russian and Balkan mafias, the Latin drug cartels, the Asian Triads, and the West African syndicates are engaged in illicit enterprises that include the transshipment of SALW, drugs, various types of contraband, counterfeit medicines, and currency, as well as human trafficking, laundered money, financial fraud, embargoed commodities, and cybercrime.

Behind the supply of illegal goods and services is often a web of TOCs. Although a TOC may specialize in one aspect of criminal behavior, they are often involved in related crimes. An arms trafficker may be paid in diamonds or precious metals, drugs, or commodities and natural resources (e.g., oil), which are in turn sold and the proceeds laundered and possibly channeled legitimately into the international financial system. These commodities, such as oil or blood diamonds, may come from embargoed sources. These criminal transactions are interwoven purposefully to make it almost impossible to separate one from the other. TOCs have tremendous financial resources and spare no expense to corrupt government and law enforcement officials. They also have extensive worldwide networks to support their operations and are inherently nimble, adapting quickly to change, because they are unencumbered by adherence to laws or regulations.[clxii]

The rise of TOCs also coincides with the misuse of technologies to commit cyber-hacking to steal trade secrets or other assets, to conduct ransom-ware attacks and extortion, and to commit large-scale identity fraud, and trafficking in SALW, drugs, and human beings. Cybercrime is particularly complex because the nature of cyberspace is borderless, and the internet allows for an increased range of clients, speed, and ease of conducting transactions, along with lower associated costs and risk of detection. The investigation of internet-based firearms trafficking is discussed in Chapter 9.

Following the September 11, 2001 attacks on the U.S., federal law enforcement agencies ramped up international efforts against terrorists and those who might supply terrorists with arms. In 1997 and 1998, DEA successfully arrested Syrian born arms trafficker Monzer Al Kassar and Russian born arms trafficker Viktor Bout[clxiii] in similar sting operations in foreign locations where they agreed to sell weapons to the Columbian FARC to target American law enforcement. Both were arrested and convicted in the U.S. of a variety of federal violations. Al Kassar had a history of supplying arms in Iran-Contra, Croatia, Bosnia, and Somalia, and had ties to the Achille Lauro hijacking[clxiv]. Viktor Bout had a history of supplying arms to Bosnia, Charles Taylor and the Revolutionary United Front in Sierra Leone, and other African civil wars.

In 2000, Italian authorities arrested Ukrainian born Leonid Efimovich Minin[clxv], who also had a history of supplying arms to Charles Taylor and Revolutionary United Front in Sierra Leone.

These are the upper echelon of international arms traffickers, and while they supplied countless arms to any nefarious group who could pay the price, there are also times when they supplied arms to groups on behalf of sponsor countries' intelligence agencies. There are others like them in operation today, but they are few and far between. Today, the internet trafficking of firearms, castings, and parts kits are what small groups of terrorist and cartels tend to gravitate to. While technology may change the manner in which SALW are trafficking internationally, the news headlines indicate that SALW is a longstanding historical problem in every country, and all law enforcement needs to work together in order to impact this issue.

Between 2006 and 2012, the Canadian Border Services Agency seized over 65,000 illegal weapons along the border, with U.S. firearms making up approximately one third of all illegal weapons seized at the border. Security experts believe that most guns entering Canada are able to pass through the border with ease.[clxvi]

Mexican drug cartels pay "straw purchasers" in the U.S. up to $500 per gun for buying arms from legitimate gun stores. The straw purchases are U.S. citizens who have a clean record and can pass the criminal background checks. They purchase guns from retail stores and immediately hand over the firearms to drug cartel members.[clxvii]

An investigation by the Toronto Star reported on how guns are purchased in the U.S and trafficked into Canada. The report described a common scenario, in which a gun would first be purchased in the U.S. for $150. The gun would then be smuggled across the border and sold in the city of Windsor for $800 to $1,000 to a trafficker. The trafficker would then move the gun farther north into the city of Toronto, where that gun is sold for at least $2,000. Pistols in Toronto are also available for rent for $600 per night, according to the Toronto Star. Up to 70 percent of all crimes involving guns in Canada involve firearms purchased in the United States and smuggled into the country.[clxviii]

In 2011, authorities in China broke up 69 arms trafficking rings that were operating within the country. Nineteen cases involved the smuggling of fully assembled guns, while the remaining cases involved ammunition and gun parts. Many arms traffickers in China use the Internet to move their product. In a three-month campaign, Chinese law enforcement monitored webpages, blogs, and online forums in an investigation that eventually led to the seizure of 2,000 firearms and 32,000 bullets.[clxix]

In 2007 the U.S. and Mexican governments entered into the Merida Initiative, in which they agreed to a regional security framework guided by the principle of shared responsibility. Among its domestic obligations, the U.S. committed to intensify its efforts to combat the illegal trafficking of weapons and ammunition to Mexico and elsewhere in the Americas.[clxx] Thirty years earlier, in 1977, the U.S government was holding hearings on the issue of firearms trafficking to Mexico.

"Black market trafficking usually takes place on a regional or local level; publicly available data suggests that the multi-ton, intercontinental shipments organized by the 'merchants of death' account for only a small fraction of illicit transfers. Among the most important forms of illicit traff

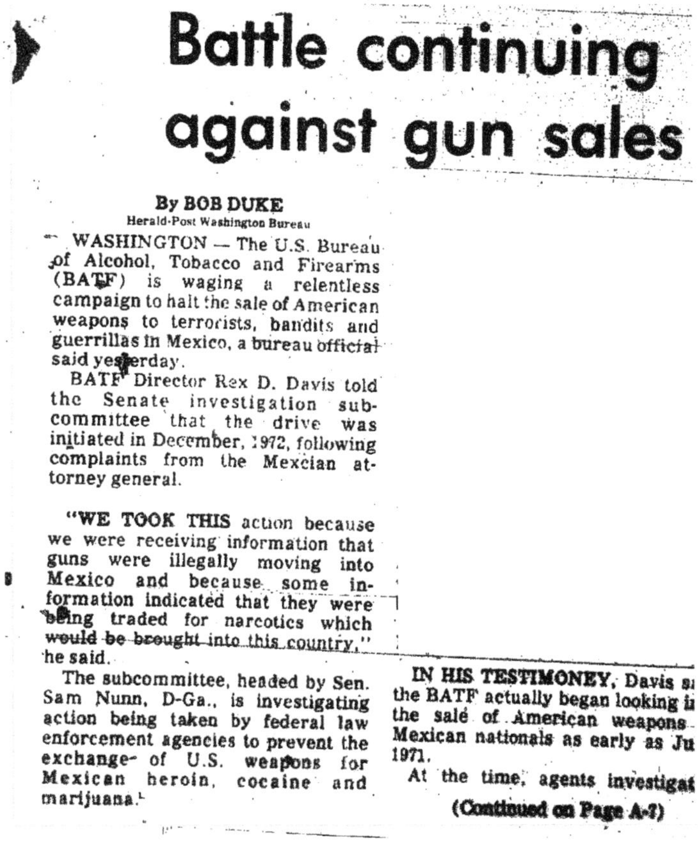

Battle continuing against gun sales

By BOB DUKE
Herald-Post Washington Bureau

WASHINGTON — The U.S. Bureau of Alcohol, Tobacco and Firearms (BATF) is waging a relentless campaign to halt the sale of American weapons to terrorists, bandits and guerrillas in Mexico, a bureau official said yesterday.

BATF Director Rex D. Davis told the Senate investigation subcommittee that the drive was initiated in December, 1972, following complaints from the Mexican attorney general.

"WE TOOK THIS action because we were receiving information that guns were illegally moving into Mexico and because some information indicated that they were being traded for narcotics which would be brought into this country," he said.

The subcommittee, headed by Sen. Sam Nunn, D-Ga., is investigating action being taken by federal law enforcement agencies to prevent the exchange of U.S. weapons for Mexican heroin, cocaine and marijuana.

IN HIS TESTIMONY, Davis s the BATF actually began looking ii the sale of American weapons Mexican nationals as early as Ju 1971.

At the time, agents investigat

(Continued on Page A-7)

Figure 12.2 Firearms Trafficking to Mexico, 1977

IMAGE CREDIT: Herald-Post Washington

bers of weapons that, over time, result in the accumulation of large numbers of illicit weapons by unauthorized end users."[clxxi]

In a statement to the United Nations Security Council on April 25, 2012, United Nations Secretary-General Ban Ki-moon noted, "There are no quick solutions to illicit flows, there is only a sustained process that requires the commitment of all"[clxxii] This chapter will provide an overview of investigative support resources, uniform protocols and procedures, and training resources available to international law enforcement officials in their sustained and committed fight against illegal arms trafficking.

INVESTIGATIVE AND DETERRENT SUPPORT RESOURCES

U.S. Department of State Blue Lantern Program. Blue Lantern was established in 1990 and monitors the end-use of defense articles (inclusive of firearms), technical data, services, and brokering activities exported through commercial channels and subject to Department of State licenses or other approvals under the AECA and ITAR. This end-use monitoring is required by U.S. law and includes pre-license, post-license, and post-shipment checks to verify the bona fides of foreign consignees and end-users, confirm the legitimacy of proposed transactions, and provide reasonable assurance that:

1) the recipient is complying with the requirements imposed by the US Government with respect to use, transfers, and security of defense articles and defense services; and

2) that such articles and services are being used for the purposes for which they are provided.

The Blue Lantern program is managed by the Regional Affairs and Analysis Division (RAA) Office of Defense Trade Controls Policy (DTCP), Directorate of Defense Trade Controls (DDTC), Bureau of Political-Military Affairs (PM) at the U.S. Department of State. Generally, checks are conducted by Department of State personnel working from U.S. embassies and consulates worldwide, with the goal of preventing fraud and the illegal diversion of weapons from legal channels and end-users. The U.S Department of Defense operates a similar program known as Golden Sentry.

Indicators that the trigger increased scrutiny from the Blue Lantern program include;

➤ an unfamiliar end-user
➤ incomplete or suspect supporting documentation
➤ scanty or derogatory background information or end-use description
➤ reticence or evasiveness by a U.S. applicant or purchasing agent
➤ payment in cash or at above-market rates
➤ end-user's unfamiliarity with the product or its use
➤ end-user declines customary associated services (installation, warranty, spares, repair)
➤ excessive or inconsistent with needs or inventory of end-user
➤ items that are in demand by embargoed countries such as Iran
➤ especially sensitive items (e.g., night vision, unmanned aerial systems, missile-related, high-caliber weapons)
➤ unfamiliar intermediary
➤ unusual routing, including trans-shipment through multiple countries or companies
➤ countries, cities, or ports of concern; free trade zones (FTZ)
➤ vague or suspicious delivery locations (e.g., P.O. boxes) or shipping/packaging instructions
➤ designation of freight forwarders as foreign consignees or end-users
➤ foreign intermediate consignees (trading companies, freight forwarders, export companies) with no apparent connection to the end-user[clxxiii]

U.S. Department of State, Directorate of Defense Trade Controls. The DOS-DDTC is responsible for oversight of the export and temporary import of defense articles and services governed by Title 22 U.S.C. § 2778 of the AECA. The U.S. ITAR implements the export provisions of the AECA through regulations contained in Title 22 C.F.R. §§ 120-130. The import provisions of the AECA are implemented through regulations contained in Title 27 C.F.R. § 447. The regulations contained in the ITAR are updated annually. The DOS-DDTC is a valuable source of information for international law enforcement agencies investigating the trafficking of U.S. sourced firearms.

In addition to DOS-DDTC, the U.S. Department of Commerce, Bureau of Industry and Security, Export Counseling Division regulates the exportation of sporting shotguns, shotgun parts, sporting shotgun ammunition, firearm-type accessories and certain parts (e.g. sights, scopes, and mounts).

Title 22 C.F.R. § 121.1 contains the USML. The list contains 21 categories of controlled defense articles and munitions. Most items related to firearms trafficking will be found in Category I— Firearms, Close Assault Weapons and Combat Shotguns

A defense article means any item or technical data designated in the USML. There is additional policy contained in Title 22 C.F.R. §120.3 that lists the designation of items additional to the USML. These additional items include forgings, castings, and other unfinished products, such as extrusions and machined bodies that have reached a stage in manufacturing where they are clearly identifiable as defense articles on the USML by mechanical properties, material composition, geometry, or function. This regulation is very pertinent to firearms trafficking investigation trends, as castings of firearms frames and receivers, such as AR-15s, have become a popular commodity that is frequently trafficked out of the U.S. illegally.

ATF International Firearms Tracing Program. ATF's International Firearms Tracing Program processes crime gun trace requests from foreign law enforcement agencies through contacts established with foreign dealers in order to obtain firearm disposition information. This program also promotes comprehensive crime gun tracing through training, firearms evidence vault reviews, and the expansion of access and use of eTrace for international law enforcement, the U.S. Department of State, and INTERPOL©. International law enforcement agencies may access these services through U.S. Embassy and Consulate Regional Security Offices or through direct contact with ATF Attachés. ATF Attachés serve as ATF representatives in the host country and may assist directly or indirectly with international investigations, technical firearms queries, and requests for crime gun tracing and firearms trafficking training. The following is a list of ATF's foreign offices where Attachés are stationed:
  ➢ ATF Canada Offices: Ottawa, Ontario (U.S. Embassy), Vancouver, British Columbia (U.S. Consulate), Toronto, Ontario (U.S. Consulate)
  ➢ ATF Colombia Offices: Bogotá, Colombia (U.S. Embassy)
  ➢ ATF El Salvador Office: San Salvador (U.S. Embassy)
  ➢ ATF Europe Offices: Lyon, France (Interpol), Hague, Netherlands (Europol)
  ➢ ATF Mexico Office: Mexico City, Mexico (U.S. Embassy), Monterrey (U.S. Consulate), Ciudad Juarez (U.S. Consulate), Tijuana (U.S. Consulate)
  ➢ ATF Iraq Office: Baghdad, Iraq (U.S. Embassy)
  ➢ ATF Caribbean Office: Miami (ATF Miami Field Division)

U.S. DHS, Homeland Security Investigations (HSI). HSI investigates international smuggling operations and enforces the U.S. export laws. This includes illegal firearms and ammunition smuggling activities that fuel violence both domestically and abroad.

HSI works with law enforcement partners to target the illegal movement of U.S. origin firearms and ammunition, with the ultimate goal of preventing the procurement of these items by drug cartels, terrorists, human rights violators, foreign adversaries, and other transnational criminal organizations and individuals who utilize these weapons to facilitate criminal acts of violence. HSI's investigative strategy includes the identification and prosecution of criminal networks and individuals responsible for the acquisition and movement of firearms and other dangerous weapons from the United States, as well as the seizure and forfeiture of money and valuable property derived from or used to facilitate this criminal activity. HSI has attachés in many U.S. embassies around the globe who are accessible to provide assistance and to coordinate with international law enforcement.

The International Criminal Police Organization©. INTERPOL, founded in 1914 and headquartered in Lyon, France, is the world's largest international police organization, with 192 member countries. INTERPOL assists law enforcement around the globe by providing access to the tools and services they need in order to be effective. INTERPOL provides training, intelligence, and investigative support to facilitate cooperative international law enforcement functions. INTERPOL combats global terrorism, cybercrime, organized and emerging crime; it investigates fugitives and crimes against children, and provides major event security support.

✓ **Firearms Tracing: U.S. Sourced Firearms.** INTERPOL has assets to facilitate the tracing of firearms and ammunition. An ATF representative is assigned to INTERPOL in Lyon, France, who can assist in the tracing of any U.S. sourced crime guns around the globe. U.S. sourced firearms are those manufactured in the U.S. or which were at one point in their life cycle imported into the U.S., and which bear U.S. firearms importer markings. The ATF representative can provide information and guidance on the proper identification of firearms for purposes of initiating a trace request.

✓ **Firearms Tracing: Tracing International Sourced Firearms.** INTERPOL operates the Illicit Arms Records and tracing Management System (iARMS™), which is a system that facilitates information exchange and investigative cooperation between law enforcement agencies in relation to the international movement of illicit firearms, as well as licit firearms that have been involved in the commission of a crime. Law enforcement worldwide can record firearms in the iARMS system and search seized weapons to check if they have been reported as lost, stolen, trafficked or smuggled. This can help identify potential links between crimes in different parts of the world, as well as possible firearms trafficking or smuggling routes. iARMS is an integral part of the international strategy and operational framework to combat both illicit trade in SALW and terrorism.[clxxiv]

✓ **Firearms Identification: INTERPOL Firearms Reference Table (IFRT).** This interactive online tool allows users to automatically import the unique identifiers of a firearm to conduct a search or make a trace request via a direct connection to iARMS. IFRT utilizes a standardized methodology to identify and describe firearms, enabling investigators to obtain or verify the details of a firearm—including the make, model, caliber and serial number. This information is regularly updated in consultation with firearm experts. The IFRT contains:

➢ more than 250,000 firearm references

- more than 57, 000 firearm images
- extensive information on firearm markings, including trademarks, logos and insignias
- thousands of useful definitions and terms for firearm parts, accessories, functions and processes
- company histories
- acronyms
- manufacturers' codes

The proper identification and description of a specific firearm is a fundamental aspect of a firearm-related crime investigation, and significantly increases the chances of acquiring firearm ownership history through an international trace request.[clxxv]

✓ **INTERPOL Notices.** INTERPOL maintains a system of notices to alert member countries to imminent firearms-related threats.
- An Orange Notice can be issued to warn police, public entities, and other international organizations about potential threats posed by disguised firearms which they may not detect under normal circumstances.
- A Purple Notice can be issued to share information about specific firearms, their parts, and related objects, as well as the modus operandi for firearm-related crime, including firearm trafficking.[clxxvi]

✓ **Ballistics Comparison to Solve Shooting Crimes: INTERPOL Ballistic Information Network (IBIN).** IBIN was established in 2009 and is the only large-scale international ballistic data sharing network in the world. IBIN supports the global networking of Integrated Ballistics Identification Systems®(IBIS) and provides a global platform for the centralized collection, storage and cross-comparison of ballistic data. IBIS is the technology used throughout the U.S. and is linked through the NIBIN network[clxxvii].

The sharing of ballistics information is critical to the solution of shooting crimes. Each weapon has a unique marking, similar to a fingerprint, that is left on a bullet or shell casing as it is fired, and which can be traced back to that weapon. In the same manner as fingerprint data, ballistics data can be shared among countries to link crimes and criminals across international borders. Sharing ballistics data can assist law enforcement agencies in finding connections between separate crimes that might otherwise remain undetected.

More than 60 counties use IBIS technology worldwide, and currently 19 countries are linked through IBIN, with more to follow. The 19 countries operational on IBIN include Barbados, Belize, Chile, Denmark, Ecuador, Guatemala, Hong Kong (China), Ireland, Jamaica, Former Yugoslav Republic of Macedonia, Lesotho, Mexico, Namibia, Netherlands, Norway, Portugal, Spain, Sweden, and the United Kingdom, plus Greece's IBIS data (from summer 1997 through summer 2012).

INTERPOL member countries that possess IBIS® technology and equipment can connect directly to IBIN free of charge as long as they possess have a valid Service Level Agreement (maintenance service) with the IBIS technology supplier Ultra Electronics Forensic Technology Inc., and have been invited to join IBIN by INTERPOL.

Additional information about IBIN may be found at the following location: http://www.interpol.int/Crime-areas/Firearms/INTERPOL-Ballistic-Information-Network-IBIN

World Customs Organization ©. The WCO, located in Brussels, Belgium, established in 1952 and formally known by international convention as the Customs Co-operation Council (CCC), has provided leadership in expanding the avenues of international trade and security. The WCO's successes include work in areas covering the development of global standards, the simplification and harmonization of customs procedures, trade supply chain security, the facilitation of international trade, the enhancement of customs enforcement and compliance activities, anti-counterfeiting and piracy initiatives, public-private partnerships, integrity promotion, and sustainable global customs capacity-building activities. The WCO is the only international body dedicated exclusively to international customs and border control matters.[clxxviii] CBP is the lead agency representative for the U.S. at the WCO. There are 177 members in the WCO. The WCO provides members with the following investigative and intelligence tools to secure their borders and intercept illegal firearms trafficking.

✓ **Regional Intelligence Liaison Offices (RILOs).** As information and intelligence exchange is one of the pillars of the WCO Enforcement Strategy, the organization set up a global network of RILOs. The RILO is a regional center for collecting, analyzing, and supplementing data, as well as disseminating information on trends, modus operandi, routes, and significant cases of fraud. The network currently comprises 11 offices situated around the world.

✓ **Customs Enforcement Network (CEN).** To enable WCO members to combat transnational organized crime more effectively, the organization developed a global system for gathering data and information for intelligence purposes, known as CEN. It is not only a database; it is also a dedicated website and an encrypted communication tool, providing the ability to share and disseminate information and intelligence on customs offences in a timely, reliable, and secure manner with direct access 24/7, and offering:
➢ a database of (non-nominal) customs seizures and offences, comprising data required for the analysis of illicit traffic in the various areas of customs competence
➢ alerts, as well as information of use to customs services
➢ a "Concealment Picture Database" to illustrate exceptional concealment methods and to exchange x-ray pictures
➢ a communication network facilitating cooperation and communication among customs services and CEN users at the international level.
The CEN uses technologies to perform reliable, secure, and inexpensive operations. It is internet-based with effective database protection, only permitting access to authorized users.[clxxix]

✓ **ENVIRONET.** As WCO members recognize that environment protection is a global priority, the organization launched ENVIRONET, a real-time communication tool for information exchange and cooperation in the area of environmental border protection among customs services, competent national agencies, international organizations and their regional networks, as well as other enforcement authorities with similar responsibilities. As one of the Customs Enforcement Network Communication (CENcomm) applications, ENVIRONET is internet-based and accessible only to a closed user group, with information transmitted via the tool encrypted and secured.

Europol. Headquartered in The Hague, Netherlands, Europol is the European Union's (EU) law enforcement agency, with 28 EU members. The EU works to protect the citizens of the EU through operational focus on illicit drugs, human trafficking, illegal immigration, cybercrime, intellectual property crime, cigarette smuggling, euro counterfeiting, VAT (Value Added Tax) fraud, money laundering, organized crime and outlaw motorcycle gangs, and terrorism. Illicit weapons trafficking is the common thread that runs through all of these illicit activities.[clxxx]

North Atlantic Treaty Organization (NATO®) Trust Funds. Founded in 1949 by 12 countries, NATO now has 29 member countries. Individual NATO member states and partners set up Trust Funds to provide resources to help partner countries implement practical projects in the areas of demilitarization, defense transformation, or capacity building. Any partner country with an individual program of partnership and cooperation with NATO may request assistance. A specific Trust Fund can then be established to allow other countries to provide financial support on a voluntary basis or to make in-kind contributions such as equipment or expertise.

Trust Funds were first developed in the framework of NATO's Partnership for Peace (PfP) program, which promotes bilateral cooperation with non-member countries in Europe, the South Caucasus, and Central Asia. However, over the years, the use of NATO/PfP Trust Funds have been opened to all NATO's partners, including countries on the southern Mediterranean rim and in the broader Middle East region as well as partners from farther across the globe. Some partners are beneficiaries of trust funds, and others contribute as donors.

The original aim of NATO/PfP Trust Funds was to provide the Alliance with a practical mechanism to assist partners with the safe destruction of stockpiled anti-personnel landmines so they could meet Ottawa Convention prohibitions of the use, stockpiling, production and transfer of anti-personnel mines and their destruction.

Initial success in the safe destruction of anti-personnel landmines in the Ukraine and the Balkans led to an extension of the use of Trust Funds to include projects to destroy conventional munitions, such as SALW. These include a 12-year project in the Ukraine which is the largest demilitarization project of its kind in the world. The destruction of surplus stockpiles of arms and munitions reduces the threat to individual partner countries as well as the wider region. It also ensures that such materials are put beyond the reach of terrorists and criminals. As of February 2017, Trust Funds have assisted in the destruction of over 626,000 SALW and 162,000,000 rounds of ammunition.[clxxxi]

UNIFORM PROTOCOLS AND PROCEDURES

Just as domestic firearms traffickers often operate by exploiting the differences among state laws in the U.S., international traffickers often operate by exploiting the differences among the laws of different countries. For example, in the U.S. the frame or receiver of a firearms constitutes the firearm that is regulated and has marking requirements whereas a barrel or stock is just a part and no markings or records of their movement are required; however, in Germany, the barrel of a firearm constitutes the firearm and is regulated and has marking requirements whereas a frame or receiver is just a part. In the U.S. a firearm silencer must be registered to the owner through ATF; however, in Argentina silencers are unregulated.

Gap analysis is the process of identifying those differences and determining methods to close them or prevent their exploitation. Law enforcement activities seek to prevent the exploitation of these differences. Laws and protocols seek to close the gap. Regional protocols for firearms trafficking and universal crime gun processing procedures are very effective for combatting firearms trafficking and armed crime. Examples of U.S. domestic regional crime gun protocols appear in Appendix B. International crime gun protocols can promote uniformity in crime gun processing and investigation, and can have a positive impact on reducing firearms trafficking and armed violent crime within countries and across international borders. Following are a number of international and regional protocol and cooperation agreement models available for countries to emulate or join.

International Protocols and Cooperative Initiatives

✓ **INTERPOL. Firearms Recovery Protocol** provides investigators with specific guidance on the processing of recovered crime guns to maximize intelligence and lead exploitation. For more information see:
https://www.interpol.int/Crime-areas/Firearms-trafficking/Publications-and-resources

✓ **INTERPOL. Resolution on the Optimized Use of Firearms Tools and Initiatives—** adopted by the INTERPOL General Assembly at its 80th Session in Hanoi (2011). For more information see:
https://www.interpol.int/Crime-areas/Firearms-trafficking/Cooperation-instruments-and-initiatives

✓ **INTERPOL. Resolution on the Manufacture, Use and Control of f\Firearms—** adopted by the INTERPOL General Assembly at its 66th Session in New Delhi (1997). For more information see:
https://www.interpol.int/Crime-areas/Firearms-trafficking/Cooperation-instruments-and-initiatives

✓ **UN. Protocol Against the Illicit Manufacturing of and Trafficking in Firearms, Their Parts and Components and Ammunition, supplementing the United Nations Convention against Transnational Organized Crime**—adopted by UN General Assembly resolution 55/255 (2001) and entering into force on 3 July 2005. For more information see:
http://www.unodc.org/pdf/crime/a_res_55/255e.pdf

The UN Firearms Protocol was adopted by Resolution 55/255 in May of 2001, entered into force in July 2005, and is the only legally binding instrument on small arms at the global level. The U.S. is not a signatory to the UN Firearms Protocol, and the protocol is not binding on a non-signatory nation. The UN Firearms Protocol supplements the United Nations Convention against Transnational Organized Crime and represents the commitment of the international community to counter TOCs.

The UN Firearms Protocol provides a framework for members to control and regulate licit arms and arms flows, to prevent their diversion into the illegal circuit, and to facilitate the investigation and prosecution of related offences without hampering legitimate transfers. This is similar to processes in the U.S. that seek to prevent illegal firearms trafficking while protecting the rights of persons engaged in the lawful commerce of firearms.

Primary goals of the UN Firearms Protocol are to promote and strengthen international co-operation and cohesive mechanisms to prevent, combat, and eradicate illicit manufacturing of and trafficking in firearms, their parts, and components and ammunition. Any federal signing on to the UN Firearms Protocol makes a commitment to adopt and implement a series of crime-control measures that aim at: a) establishing as a criminal offence the illicit manufacturing of and trafficking in firearms in line with the Protocol's requirements and definitions; b) adopting effective control and security measures, including the disposal of firearms, in order to prevent their theft and diversion into the illicit circuit; c) establishing a system of government authorizations or licensing intended to ensure legitimate manufacturing of, and trafficking in firearms; and d) ensuring adequate marking, recording, and tracing of firearms, and effective international cooperation for this purpose.

The UN Firearms Protocol defines tracing as the systemic tracking of firearms and, where possible, their parts, components and ammunition, from manufacturer to purchaser, for the purpose of assisting federal parties in detecting, investigating, and analyzing illicit manufacturing and illicit trafficking. This is very similar to the process of crime gun tracing by the ATF NTC in the U.S. Internationally recovered crime guns may be traced through the ATF NTC.

The UN Firearms Protocol defines a firearm as any portable barreled weapon that expels, is designed to expel, or may be readily converted to expel a shot, bullet, or projectile by means of an explosive, excluding antique firearms or their replicas. Antique firearms and their replicas shall be defined in accordance with domestic law. In no case, however, shall antique firearms include firearms manufactured after 1899. This is very similar to the definition of a firearm in the U.S. under 18 U.S.C. § 921(a)(3).

✓ **UN. Convention Against Transnational Organized Crime**—adopted by the UN General Assembly resolution 55/25 (2000). For more information see:
http://www.unodc.org/unodc /en/organized-crime/intro/UNTOC.html

✓ **UN. International Instrument to Enable States to Identify and Trace, in a Timely and Reliable Manner, Illicit Small arms and Light Weapons**—adopted by a UN General Assembly resolution on 8 December 2005 (see paragraph 35). For more information see:
http://www.poa-iss.org/InternationalTracing /ITI_English.pdf

✓ **UN. Program of Action (PoA) to Prevent, Combat and Eradicate the Illicit Trade in Small Arms and Light Weapons in All Its Aspects**—adopted unanimously by UN Member federals at the July 2001 (see part II paragraph 37 and part III paragraph 9). For more information see:
http://www.poa-iss.org/poa/poahtml.aspx

✓ **UN. Security Council Resolution 1373**— (2001), adopted unanimously by The UN Security Council in 2001, the Resolution adopts a wide-ranging, comprehensive set of steps and strategies to combat international terrorism, including measures to eliminate the supply of weapons to terrorists. (see article 2a and article 3a). For more information see:
https://www.unodc.org/pdf/crime/terrorism /res_1373_english.pdf

✓ **World Customs Organization. Recommendation Concerning the Protocol Against the Illicit Manufacturing of and Trafficking in Firearms, their Parts and Components and Ammunition, Supplementing the United Nations Convention against Transnational Organized Crime**—(29 June 2002). For more information see:
http://www.wcoomd.org/-/media/wco/public/global/pdf/about-us/legalinstruments/recommendations/enforcement /firearms20recommendation20200220en.pdf?la=en

Regional Protocols and Cooperative Initiatives

✓ **Association of Southeast Asian Nations (ASEAN). Joint Communiqué of the 28th ASEAN Chiefs of Police Conference**—Brunei Darussalam, 25-29 May 2008 (see article 8.3). For more information see:
http://asean.org/?static_post=joint-communique-of-the-28th-asean-chiefs-of-police-conference-brunei-darussalam-25-29-may-2008

✓ **ASEAN. Manila Declaration on the Prevention and Control of Transnational Crime**—1998. For more information see:
http://asean.org/?static_post=manila-declaration-on-the-prevention-and-control-of-transnational-crime-1998-introduction

✓ **European Union (EU). European Convention on the Control of the Acquisition and Possession of Firearms by Individuals**. For more information see:
http://asean.org/?static_post=manila-declaration-on-the-prevention-and-control-of-transnational-crime-1998-introduction (article 9.2).

✓ **EU.** Political consensus reached on the text of the Regulation implementing Article 10 of the United Nations' Firearms Protocol and establishing export authorization and import and transit measures for firearms, their parts and components, and ammunition (Media Release, 29 June 2011) Organization for Security and Co-operation in Europe.
For more information see:
http://europa.eu/rapid/press-release_MEMO-11-470_en.htm?locale=en

✓ **Organization for Security and Co-Operation in Europe (OSCE).** OSCE Document on Small Arms and Light Weapons adopted at the 308th Plenary Meeting of the OSCE Forum for Security Co-operation, 24 November 2000. For more information see:
https://www.osce.org/fsc/20783

✓ **OSCE.** Best Practice Guide on Marking, Record-keeping and Traceability of Small Arms and Light Weapons (September 2003). Proposes solutions with respect to marking, record-keeping, legislation and criminal penalties, exchange of information, and international cooperation. For more information see:
https://www.osce.org/fsc/13630

✓ **Organization of American States (OAS).** Inter-American Convention against the illicit manufacturing of and trafficking in firearms, ammunition, explosives and other related materials (CIFTA), adopted on 14 November 1997 and entered into force in July 1998. The Convention aims to help eradicate the illicit transnational arms market that fuels the violence associated with drug trafficking, terrorism and international organized crime (see preamble). For more information see:
http://www.oas.org/en/sla/dil/inter_american_treaties_A-63_illicit_manufacturing_trafficking_firearms_ammunition_explosives.asp

✓ **Southern African Development Community.** Protocol on the Control of Firearms, Ammunition and Other Related Materials in the Southern African Development Community (SADC) Region. For more information see:
https://www.sadc.int/documents-publications/show/796

✓ **Wassenaar Arrangement (WA) on Export Controls for Conventional Arms and Dual-Use Goods and Technologies.** The Wassenaar Arrangement was established to foster regional and international security and stability by promoting transparency and greater responsibility in transfers of conventional arms and dual-use goods and technologies, thus preventing destabilizing accumulations. Participating states seek, through their national policies, to ensure that transfers of these items do not contribute to the development or enhancement of military capabilities which undermine these goals, and are not diverted to support such capabilities. The aim is also to prevent the acquisition of these items by terrorists.

Participating federals apply export controls to all items set forth in the List of Dual-Use Goods and Technologies and the Munitions List, with the objective of preventing unauthorized transfers or re-transfers of those items.

The participating federals of the Wassenaar Arrangement are: Argentina, Australia, Austria, Belgium, Bulgaria, Canada, Croatia, Czech Republic, Denmark, Estonia, Finland, France, Germany, Greece, Hungary, India, Ireland, Italy, Japan, Latvia, Lithuania, Luxembourg, Malta, Mexico, Netherlands, New Zealand, Norway, Poland, Portugal, Republic of Korea, Romania, Russian Federation, Slovakia, Slovenia, South Africa, Spain, Sweden, Switzerland, Turkey, Ukraine, United Kingdom and United States. For more information see: https://www.wassenaar.org

TRAINING RESOURCES

International Law Enforcement Academies (ILEA). The U.S. Department of State, Bureau of International Narcotics and Law Enforcement Affairs, Criminal Justice Programs Division operates ILEAs in Bangkok, Budapest, Gaborone, Roswell, and San Salvador, where they serve four regions: Europe, Africa, South America and Asia.

The first ILEA was created in Budapest following then-President Clinton's speech at the United Nations General Assembly during the UN's 50th Anniversary in 1995. He called for the establishment of a network of ILEAs throughout the world to combat international drug trafficking, criminality, and terrorism through strengthened international cooperation. The U.S. and participating nations established ILEAs depending on regional needs.

Figure 12.3 *Author/Instructor with Class at ILEA Budapest, Hungary in 1998*

IMAGE CREDIT: *Author*

The ILEAs serve a broad range of foreign policy and law enforcement purposes for the U.S. and for the world. In addition to helping protect American citizens and businesses through strengthened international cooperation against crime, the ILEAs' mission is to buttress democratic governance through the rule of law; to enhance the functioning of free markets through improved legislation and law enforcement; and to increase social, political, and economic stability by combating narcotics trafficking and crime.[clxxxii]

ILEAs provide training on small arms trafficking investigations, complex financial investigations, computer crime investigation, crime scene investigations, anti-gangs training, and combatting domestic and transnational terrorism.

ATF's International Training Program (ITP). ATF's ITP routinely supports requests for training by various host nations on topics including firearms trafficking, comprehensive firearms tracing and the use of eTrace, as well as arson and explosives investigation. Training can be provided at academies in the U.S. that participants travel to, or training can be provided in a host country. ATF's ITP also coordinates with the U.S. Department of State to provide subject matter experts for instruction at all of the ILEAs.

U.S. DOJ International Criminal Investigative Training Assistance Program (ICITAP) and Office of Overseas Prosecutorial Development, Assistance, and Training (OPDAT). ICITAP and OPDAT are engaged in the work of international criminal justice development, capacity building, and reform. ICITAP was established by the U.S. Congress in 1986 to provide training to police forces in Latin America and the Caribbean on how to conduct criminal investigations. Since that time, globalization has generated enormous and unforeseen opportunities for the growth of crime, and ICITAP's mission has evolved with this change to become a full-service criminal justice development agency in the overseas rule of law development and assistance mission.

OPDAT was created in 1991 in response to the growing threat of transnational crime. Through OPDAT's programs, partnerships are developed with foreign justice systems that, in turn, build capacity to achieve national security and justice sector outcomes.

Given the globalization of crime, the U.S. has moved to extend its first line of defense abroad, in order to better protect its citizens, as well as those of partner nations. A key strategy of ICITAP/OPDAT is to help build foreign police and prosecutorial agencies that are committed to the rule of law. Where there is rule of law, citizens can have an expectation of safety, fairness, due process, and accountability. Rule of law development also helps foster capable and strong partners in the fight against transnational crime, firearms trafficking, corruption, and terrorism; in so doing, it helps halt criminality before it reaches the U.S. The safety and future prosperity of the U.S and that of partner countries depends on the strengthening of the rule of law overseas.

ICITAP and OPDAT are committed to fostering the rule of law through development and assistance. ICITAP focuses on police, forensics, corrections, and border security development, and OPDAT works with partner countries to develop and strengthen fair, just, and accountable justice sector institutions, particularly prosecutorial and judicial bodies. ICITAP and OPDAT also work together to ensure that proper connections are made and assistance is coordinated in the reform of the host country's criminal justice system.

ICITAP and OPDAT's programs are authorized and funded through interagency agreements with the U.S. Department of State, the U.S. Agency for International Development (USAID), and the Department of Defense.

ICITAP. ICITAP's mission is to work with foreign governments to develop effective, professional, and transparent law enforcement capacity that protects human rights, combats corruption, and reduces the threat of transnational crime and terrorism, in support of U.S. foreign policy and national security objectives. ICITAP works in three general types of environments, each requiring a unique approach: 1) emerging democracies and developing countries; 2) countries combating terrorism; and 3) countries undergoing stabilization and reconstruction or international peacekeeping (ICITAP has participated in the majority of U.S. and international peacekeeping operations, including those in Bosnia and Herzegovina, East Timor, El Salvador, Guatemala, Haiti, Iraq, Kosovo, and Panama).

ICITAP currently operates in about forty countries worldwide. As an international law enforcement development organization, ICITAP's activities go beyond training and equipping foreign police forces. ICITAP works to achieve sustainable, institutional development in its overseas programs, rather than individual skills enhancement. ICITAP fosters sustainable development by designing all training and development programs in cooperation with host country institutions. ICITAP also tailors assistance programs to the unique requirements of the host country, taking into account the country's resources and readiness for reform, and best practices. ICITAP's development methods encompass the following.
1) *Fostering Long-Term Institutional Reform*—placing senior law enforcement advisors to reside in-country to provide long-term rule of law assistance. This assistance centers on fundamental institutional reform, establishment of training academies, and standing up of anti-corruption, and other vetted investigative and police units.
2) *Providing Expert Advice*—engaging subject matter experts to provide specialized training in the host country.
3) *Serving as Mentors*—working side-by-side to offer expert guidance to host country counterparts.

This exposes foreign law enforcement not only to new techniques and technologies, but also to international standards for policing, evidence management and analysis, prosecution, and management of prisons and inmates.

The general subject areas in which ICITAP provides training and technical assistance include both institutional development and law enforcement capacity building areas: Institutional Development; Organizational Development; Academy and Instructor Development; Information Systems; Law Enforcement Capacity Building; Basic Police Services; Specialized Law Enforcement and Tactical Skills; Criminal Investigations; Marine and Border Security; Policing in a Democracy; Terrorism and Transnational Crime; International Post Conflict Law Enforcement Responders; Public Integrity and Anticorruption; Forensics; Criminal Justice Coordination; and Corrections.

In 2016, ICITAP facilitated more than 3,600 distinct training events to more than 330,000 participants. ICITAP draws upon subject matter experts from numerous federal, state, and local law enforcement agencies as well as expert contract personnel. By involving federal agents as partners in ICITAP's programs, ICITAP opens up opportunities for the exchange of information and best practices between U.S. law enforcement and host nation counterparts.

OPDAT. Through its programs, OPDAT strengthens host nations' institutions by promoting the rule of law; assisting in code reform; facilitating transition to the accusatory system; promoting case-based mentoring to prosecutors and investigative agents; and training judges and their personnel. These efforts have led to more effective investigations and prosecutions and have improved the judicial efficiency in host nations.

OPDAT builds strong international partners who can work with the U.S. to fight crime before it spreads from country to country. OPDAT has Resident Legal Advisors (RLAs) and Intermittent Legal Advisors (ILAs) posted in countries around the world, providing expert assistance to foreign counterparts to help develop justice systems that can effectively combat TOCs, corruption, and terrorism consistent with international standards and in furtherance of U.S. national security.

OPDAT's programs support the U.S. Government's National Security Strategy as well as the law enforcement and justice policy goals. This involves assisting foreign counterparts in developing and implementing capabilities to address and combat: terrorism; foreign terrorist fighters; terrorism financing; money laundering and economic crimes; organized crime; corruption; cybercrime; intellectual property crimes; trafficking in persons; trafficking in narcotics; firearms trafficking; and other transnational criminal activities.

OPDAT accomplishes these goals by long-term, multi-year engagement through Resident Legal Advisors (RLAs) and Intermittent Legal Advisors (ILAs). These advisors provide expert advice to foreign governments on legal frameworks; conduct capacity building and case-based mentoring for prosecutors, investigators, and judges; and assist their counterparts with institutional development and reform. Drawing on the full expertise of federal law enforcement agencies when engaging with international partners, OPDAT is able to respond quickly and effectively to a wide range of new and emerging threats, while maintaining its ongoing work with host countries.[clxxxiii] ICITAP and OPDAT are invaluable resources for international law enforcement to seek out for training opportunities.

Regardless of whether firearms trafficking is being conducted by a few people or a TOC, the physical movement of most illegal trafficked firearms can be categorized into two methods: Commercial Services and Non-Commercial Methods.

Commercial services involve firearms secreted in cargo containers, in the mail or other shipping services, and often concealed in, or mixed with, other metal objects and parts that can disguise the firearm(s) from detection technology. For example, in the Caribbean, firearms are often secreted within panels and compartments of vehicles being transported between countries for resale. Utilization of commercial services is used for the trafficking of large and small amounts of firearms and is used to create distance between the trafficker and the commodity during transit. Large amounts of firearms can be broken up into smaller shipments to reduce the risk of the entire shipment being detected and seized. A strategy designed around mass cargo examination is impractical from a resource perspective and due to the potential adverse effect such a tactic could have on lawful commerce.

Non-commercial methods involve traditional smuggling methods to traverse borders and successfully traffic firearms into a market country. No matter how extensive a country's border and marine patrol resources are, no border can be fully secured from determined smugglers. Countries experiencing high levels of firearms violence should explore the deployment of national protocols that establish high level rules and regulations, such as the UN Firearms Protocol discussed in this chapter, or the Palm Beach County Gun Comprehensive Crime Gun Protocols, the IACP Regional Crime Gun Processing Protocols, or New Jersey Public Law 2013 Chapter 162, Title 52—all of which appear in Appendix B.

Countries should utilize resources and best practices available to them through the WCO to effectively interdict commercial and non-commercial illegal firearms trafficking. Studying the data on recovered crime guns can help identify trends and patterns used by firearms traffickers, which allows law enforcement to focus limited resources where they will have the largest impact. Countries should take advantage of firearms trafficking training programs offered through ATF, the ILEAs, and ICITAP-OPDAT.

Most importantly, countries need to specifically dedicate law enforcement resources to detecting, deterring, investigating, and arresting firearms traffickers. There need to be uniform strategies in place for reacting to an incident involving the recovery of firearms and fully processing those weapons, as well as how to develop and move on actionable intelligence regarding the modus operandi of traffickers and where firearms are trafficked and stored. Effectively addressing firearms trafficking is resource and intelligence intensive, and it places law enforcement in a proactive prevention posture, rather than a reactive posture in which dealing with armed crime means waiting for the next armed crime victim to be created and following up with an investigation.

U.S. Agency for International Development (USAID). USAID's mission is to promote and demonstrate democratic values abroad, and advance a free, peaceful, and prosperous world. USAID's objective is to support partners in becoming self-reliant and capable of leading their own development journeys. Progress toward this is measured by reducing the reach of conflict, preventing the spread of pandemic disease, and counteracting the drivers of violence[clxxxiv], instability, transnational crime, and other security threats.[clxxxv]

USAID provides resources for international law enforcement and prosecutors to target armed criminal gangs[clxxxvi] as well as firearms traffickers[clxxxvii] throughout the world[clxxxviii], with a strong focus in developing nations.

INTERPOL™. A variety of trainings, conferences, and symposiums on firearms trafficking and armed crime issues are available around the globe each year through INTERPOL. Through a tailored curriculum, INTERPOL works with member nations to provide the tools necessary to respond effectively to the challenges of transnational firearm-related crime and firearms trafficking. Training courses and reference materials can enhance the skills of investigators to combat firearms trafficking and raise their awareness of the tools available to assist them in their efforts.

The INTERPOL Firearm Forensics Symposium (IFFS) is designed for individuals who investigate firearms-related crimes, heads of police agencies, and those who shape policy aimed at combating firearm crime.

CASE STUDY: OPERATOIN SPHINX

United States v. Mohsen, et al. – Southern District of Florida - 9:01-cr-08087-DLG

In December of 1998 the ATF West Palm Beach Field Office initiated an investigation based on information from a CI that he had met individuals looking for arms to supply abroad.

The CI advised that an Egyptian international diamond broker who had ties to international arms traffickers was looking for new sources of supply. Deconfliction and full intelligence workups were performed that corroborated the CI's information regarding the Egyptian being an international diamond broker.

A meeting between the CI, the Egyptian and an ATF UC was set up to hear what the Egyptian had in mind. At the first meeting in Mizner Park in Boca Raton, FL, the Egyptian said he was looking for military weapons such as missiles. He said he had connections in Pakistan who would be funneling these items to Osama Bin Laden (OBL). This was 3 years prior to the 9/11 attack; however, OBL was already an infamous and wanted terrorist for the U.S. Embassy bombings in Kenya and Tanzania. The Egyptian was told that these arms were available for a price, and that it would take some time before final logistics of the deal could be discussed.[clxxxix]

Whether the information was true or not, at that point, with a clear nexus to terrorism, the FBI and the U.S. Customs Service (USCS) were alerted and asked to participate in the investigation. In subsequent UC meetings with the Egyptian he advised that his organization consisted of persons who could launder money, secure false travel papers, and put him in touch with high level people around the world who needed arms. He also told his new partners, the ATF CI and UC, that they would need to be able to travel internationally to meet some of his customers, but without a travel trail tied to their names. The Egyptian brought in one of his associates who specialized in providing fraudulent passports, and the ATF UC purchased three passports: one fraudulent Venezuelan passport and two fraudulent U.S. passports. The sale of these was a violation of Title 18 U.S.C. § 1543.

At a meeting a short time later, the Egyptian advised that he had some potential customers who would fly in from Egypt to meet with them. In a show of good faith, he provided the ATF CI and UC with 2 Egyptian Funerary Masks that he said were stolen from Egypt and were very valuable. These were accepted by the ATF UC. They were confirmed by the laboratory to be authentic and more than 3000 years old. This was a violation of the Antiquities Act, Title 6 U.S.C. §§ 431 to 433.

Figure 12.4 *Author Returning a 3000-year old Stolen Egyptian Funerary Mask to Egyptian Ambassador Fahmy and Minister of State for Antiquities Affairs Director Zahi Hawass at the Egyptian Embassy in Washington, DC*
IMAGE CREDIT: ATF, Annette Starks

The Funerary Masks were repatriated to the Egyptian Embassy at the conclusion of the investigation.[cxc]

At this juncture of the investigation an intelligence apparatus was deconflicting and conducting intelligence workups on each new name, address, phone number, and travel itinerary. ATF had arranged for a specialized long-term UC agent to join the investigation as the primary arms supplier. He was fully trained and fully backstopped. In preparation for this role he was sent to a Department of Defense Stinger Missile training where he learned how to operate the missile and became familiar with its nomenclature, pricing, places of manufacture, and reasonable cover stories as to how he could have come to possess stolen or diverted missiles. ATF purchased a number of inert Stinger missiles for UC props, as well as dozens of Stinger and TOE missile crates.

Figure 12.5 Author with Stinger Missiles in a West Palm Beach Warehouse in 2000
IMAGE CREDIT: Author

According to the arrangements made by the Egyptian, an additional four Egyptian citizens traveled from Egypt to South Florida in 1999 to view Stinger and TOE missiles in an undercover warehouse in West Palm Beach, Florida and discuss deals for their purchase. The four were videotaped in possession of the weapons and audio taped with regard to their intent to illegally export the arms and broker them to other individuals, which constituted a conspiracy to violate Title 26 U.S.C. § 5861 and the Arms Export Control Act. These individuals were wealthy lawyers and former high-ranking Egyptian military officers.

While this deal was being arranged, the ATF UC advised the Egyptian that they had completed an arms sale and needed to clean up the proceeds. The Egyptian said he would get his guy on it. He advised that his guy was a well-known Wall Street Investment Banker, former Goldman Sachs guy who had an office in the World Trade Center. Intelligence workups confirmed that this individual was a very high-profile Wall Street figure and former head of an international section of the Duetsche Bank. A meeting was set up, and the ATF CI and UC met with the money launderer in his 91st-floor World Trade Center office. They got to know each other and discussed the need for discretion, as this money was from the sale of arms to people who would not want

to be exposed. They then got down to business, and the money launderer accepted $100,000 in cash, which he said he would launder through multiple off-shore accounts and return back to the ATF UC, less a 10% fee. The money launderer was told that if this first deal went smoothly, they would be back with the rest of their recent profits for him to launder.[cxci]

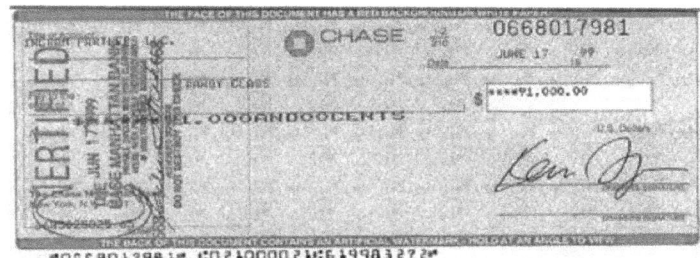

Figure 12.6 Check for $91,000 in Laundered Money Proceeds
IMAGE CREDIT: Author

At a subsequent meeting in South Florida the money launderer provided the ATF UC agent with a check for $90,000 in laundered proceeds and accepted another $250,000 in cash to be laundered. The money launderer showed up to the deal in a late model yellow Ferrari and later took the money in this vehicle to his yacht, all while under surveillance.

Figure 12.7 Surveillance Photograph Undercover ATF Agent Walking to Meet Money Launderer Who Just Pulled Up in Ferrari
IMAGE CREDIT: ATF S/A Steve Barborini

The investigation had many moving parts and required constant supervision, risk management, and significant CI control. The CI was a force of nature with a prolific gift of gab and he was constantly coming up with side deals through the Egyptian.

At one point the Egyptian introduced the ATF CI to an associate of the Gambino Crime family who was brokering loads of hijacked merchandise. In July 1999, the CI traveled to New York City and met with the Gambino representative and reviewed a load of stolen crystal. The FBI confirmed that the load had been stolen. The CI said he was interested and was then also offered a load of stolen Minolta copies that had a value of over $1,000,000. The CI was directed to introduce a UC FBI agent to the Gambino associate and get back to the arms case. This re-focused the CI and took him out of the equation of a case that would result in a take-down later in the year.

Back in Boca Raton, the four Egyptians were losing interest in the arms deal, allegedly having found a different source on the world market. This was the beginning of a cavalcade of negotiations with a litany of representatives from the world's hotspots. First the Egyptian entered into conversations with close associates of President Kabila of the Democratic Republic of the Congo. That nation was engaged in a civil war, needed weapons, and were cash-strapped, but had plenty of blood diamonds. A tentative deal was struck for a load of arms in exchange for blood diamonds, to be paid at a meeting in Vienna. Approvals for the UC to travel to Vienna were being secured when Libyan Prime Minister Muammar Gaddafi stepped in and negotiated a peace settlement to end the civil war. They no longer needed arms. Next up, the Egyptian began negotiating with persons in Hungary who expressed a desire for the arms on behalf of persons in Serbia. This was 1999, and that was the year the Serbian conflict ended, so that deal fell through, as the end of that war was already in sight. Down but not out, the Egyptian then began negotiating with a contact he had with rebels in Chechnya. Chechen rebels were fighting with Russia and needed arms, but later in 1999 the Russians moved in and squashed the revolt, and the Egyptian's contact stopped taking calls. Peace and the end to conflict was great for the world; not so great for illegal arms traffickers.

Later in 1999, the Egyptian said his original contacts in Pakistan were ready to meet and deal. The ATF CI, the UC, the Egyptian and two Pakistanis who flew in from Lahore met for lunch at the Tribeca Grill in New York City (arranged by MOSHEN). The meeting went well, and the two Pakistanis stated that they were looking for Stinger missiles, parts for F-16s, and heavy water.

This meeting was surveilled by ATF, FBI, and USCS agents from West Palm Beach, as well as members of the JTTF of New York. The Pakistanis mentioned ties with OBL during this meeting and stated that some of the arms would be funneled to him in Afghanistan. During the meeting they expressed disdain for America, and one of the men said they would have no problem killing everyone in the restaurant. Intelligence assets confirmed that one of the Pakistanis at this meeting worked for Pakistan's ISI.[cxcii]

A second meeting was established, and in August 1999 the two Pakistanis traveled to South Florida where they met with ATF UC agents and examined 12 Stinger missiles, several M-16 machine guns, and plastic explosives at an undercover warehouse in West Palm Beach. The ATF UCs advised that the weapons were diverted and there would of course be no paperwork or declaration of the items; when exported, they would need to be smuggled out. The Pakistanis were very interested in purchasing the items and also to establish future purchases. They stated that the government of Pakistan had set up a secret military budget account to purchase weaponry like this. At this point a Pakistani living in Patterson, NJ was introduced to the ATF UC as the primary U.S. point of contact (POC) for the Pakistanis. For the next year the deal was on again and off again, as the ISI agents waited for their government budget funds to be available. They were advising the U.S.-based Pakistani of the status of the budget, and U.S. intelligence assets corroborated that the statements about the Pakistani budget process were accurate.

During November 2000 the two Pakistanis summoned their U.S. POC to London, England to finalize arrangements. When the Pakistani POC returned he advised that the first deal would be for 75 Stinger missiles at $30,000 each, for a total deal of $2.25 million. This deal would be followed by others, for a total of 500 Singer missiles. The Pakistani POC told the ATF UC that his partners wanted them to set up two bank accounts, and both their names would be on both accounts, so that both parties would have to agree in order for any money to be withdrawn. One last condition that the Pakistanis wanted in the deal was for the ATF UC to be able to accept an additional amount of wired money that they should launder and then return to the Pakistani POC. This money would be used for future deals and operations in the U.S. to make things easier than having to deal with international wire transfers. They wanted to minimize the risk of wire transfers by getting all their operational money into the U.S. at one time. The ATF UC advised that the group had someone capable of doing this. The Pakistani POC then advised that the wire transfer would be for $32 million.

Approvals were secured for the ATF UC to establish two joint bank accounts with the Pakistani POC, and in December of 2000 the Pakistani POC flew from Patterson, New Jersey to Fort Lauderdale, Florida, where the two accounts were opened at a bank in Boca Raton, FL. The logistics of the deal were established. The Pakistani POC would view the missiles in a Conex container which would then be filled with other commodities to conceal them. The Pakistani POC would then direct his partners to initiate the wire transfer. Once the funds were in the account, they would watch the Conex container be loaded onto a ship, and then the Pakistani POC would sign bank papers for the movement of the money to the UC for payment and for transfer to launder.

On the day of the deal the ATF UC was advised that the funds would move from Pakistan to Dubai, United Arab Emirates, and then a cooperative bank official in Dubai would cover the tracks and wire the funds to the bank in Boca Raton, FL. The ATF UC received a faxed business contract from the bank official on bank stationary which showed that there was to be a $32 million wire transfer for the purchase of computer equipment. The bank documents also showed the account from which the funds would be transferred and confirmed that $32 million was in the account.

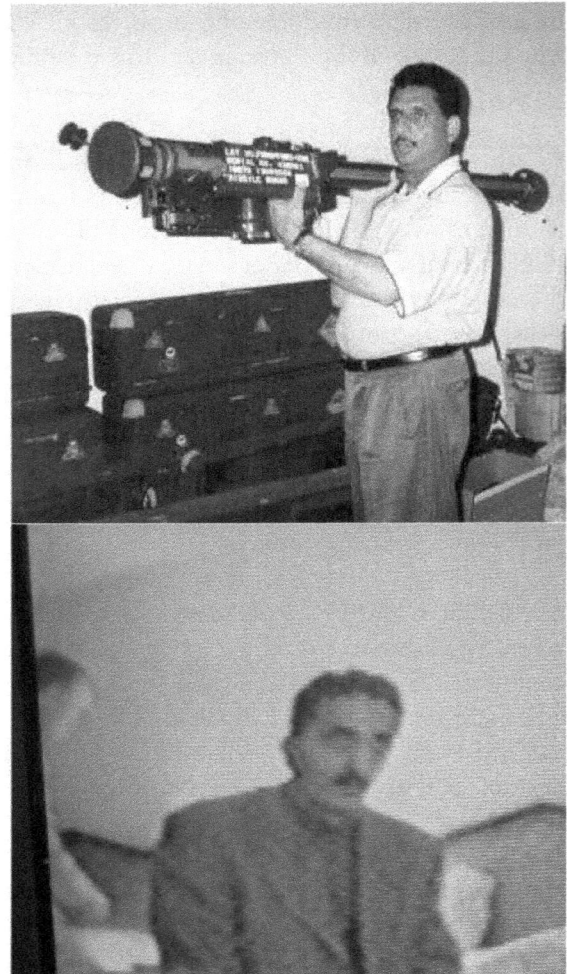

***Figure 12.8** Alleged Pakistani ISI Agents in a Warehouse in West Palm Beach, FL and a Hotel Room in Palm Beach Gardens, FL Negotiating a Stinger Missile Deal in 2000*
IMAGE CREDIT: Author

As the deal began, the ATF UC and the Pakistani viewed the Stinger missiles, and the Pakistani POC directed the wire to take place. The bank in Boca Raton showed that the wire transfer was pending, but the funds would not fully come through. The funds were held up at the incoming wire transfer hub. The Pakistani partners were being careful and were using a tactic known as an "error screen" to ensure that the deal would progress and that they would not be ripped off. The transfer coming through kept leaving one digit off the full routing numbers, so the money appeared to be coming through but the transaction could never be completed until the routing numbers were corrected. This went back and forth, until the Pakistani POC became frustrated. The deal was called off, and the ATF UC told the Pakistani POC that he should call when his partners were serious.

While waiting to be ready to attempt the deal again, the Pakistani POC wanted to know if the ATF UC had a way to secure "heavy water" from nuclear plants and nuclear triggers. The Pakistani POC advised that if they were able to obtain this material his partners would be very interested and could have Dr. Qadeer, a scientist, confirm the authenticity of the material. It was determined that the Pakistani POC was referring to Dr. Abdul Qadeer Khan, also known as A.Q. Khan, who was in charge of Pakistan's atomic bomb program at that time.[cxciii] This portion of the investigation did not evolve, and was handled as an intelligence matter. In 2004 Dr. Kahn was charged by Pakistan with the proliferation of nuclear technology to Iran, Libya, and North Korea. Dr. Kahn confessed to these charges and was confined in Pakistan for some time before being released.[cxciv]

In June of 2001 the Pakistani POC contacted the ATF UC to say they were ready to do the deal. At this juncture, plans were made to arrest the defendants present in the U.S. Two separate deals were established to bring all of the Egyptians associates to Florida, where they would be arrested for the on-going conspiracy.

The first deal would be with the money launderer and his new partner from Connecticut who agreed to launder $2.1 million in proceeds from what they believed was an illegal arms deal. The second deal would be with the Egyptian and the Pakistani POC to discuss the logistics of the pending arms deal that was back on again, and to launder an additional $1 million.

On the morning of June 12, 2001, the money launderer and his new partner showed up in their private jet at the Ft Lauderdale executive airport. They met with the ATF UC agents, advised that they would require a 25% fee this time, as they were flying the cash to England for laundering. They then took 2 large suitcases they believed were filled with $2.1 million in cash, and were arrested.

On the afternoon of June 12, 2001, the ATF UC met the Egyptian and the Pakistani POC, and took them to the West Palm Beach UC warehouse to discuss the arms deal and take possession of $1 million in cash in duffle bags. Following the meeting they were arrested. At the same time, agents arrested the passport source at his residence in Jersey City, New Jersey.[cxcv]

All were indicted for charges ranging from conspiracy to violate the Arms Export Control Act, to conspiracy to possess unregistered destructive devices, passport violations, and money laundering violations. All of the defendants pled guilty, and the Ferrari and $180,000 in proceeds were forfeited.[cxcvi]

All of the defendants were arrested 3 months prior to the 9/11 attacks and, in a twist of irony, the money launderer was out on bond confined to his New Jersey home rather than in his office at the World Trade Center that day.[cxcvii]

CASE STUDY: OPERATION ABOVE THE LAW

United States v. Skaritka – Southern District of Florida – 9:2002-cr-80177-DTKH-1

In August 2002 the ATF West Palm Beach Field Office received information from the FBI Legate at the U.S. Embassy in Prague, Czech Republic, that the Prague authorities had intercepted a package bound for the U.S. that contained a machinegun. The package had been mailed by an individual at a Prague Hotel to a Nico Toscani in Hypoluxo, Florida. Prague authorities turned over the package to the U.S. Embassy in Prague for follow-up by U.S officials after they were unable to locate the person who initiated shipment of the package. The FBI in Prague contacted the ATF West Palm Beach Field Office and arrangements were made to bring the package to the U.S. for a controlled delivery attempt and investigation.

Upon receipt of the package an ATF firearms expert identified the firearm receiver as a CZ, Model # 25 sub-machinegun. Deconfliction checks indicated no other investigations associated with the address in Hypoluxo, FL or Toscani. ATF NFA checks indicated that no machineguns were registered to the Hypoluxo address or to Toscani. Records checks indicated Toscani did reside at the Hypoluxo, FL address however it appeared that this was not his true name and that he and his brother were illegal alien overstays from the Czech Republic. ATF contacted CBP to have border lookouts placed on the individuals and to have CBP join in the investigation.

Surveillance revealed that the brothers worked very little. In September 2002 ATF contacted the U.S. Postal Inspectors to assist in conducting a controlled delivery of the package to TOSCANI. ATF agents removed the firing pin from the machinegun and placed it back in the package along with a transmitter that would activate once the package was opened and send a signal to the agents. ATF agents then secured an anticipatory federal search warrant that would allow agents to enter the residence and recover the firearm as soon as the package was opened. More than a month had passed since the package was shipped in Prague so agents devised a plan to make the

shipping delay appear acceptable. During August 2002 Prague experienced massive flooding so agents water stained the package to make it appear that it had been caught up in that event. Just prior to the controlled delivery a number of agents and police officers were placed in the area to prevent the package from getting out of a secure perimeter area. In addition, an ATF helicopter pilot was hovering in a stationary surveillance approximately 1 mile from the location. Following controlled delivery of the package the ATF pilot, using a special zoom lens, was able to observe and videotape Toscani walk onto his back balcony with the package, open it, and take out the machinegun. ATF agents then initiated the search warrant and as they entered the residence they found Toscani sitting with the receiver in his lap. Toscani stated "I was just about to call ATF! - I think someone mailed me a machinegun." During a search of the residence several magazines specifically for a CZ sub machinegun were found in Toscani's bedroom closet, as well as an upper receiver and other parts to complete the assembly of additional CZ machineguns. Other firearms as well as an illegal short-barreled Uzi and prescription narcotics were discovered and seized for evidence. Toscani was interviewed and confessed to ordering the machinegun. Toscani also stated he was a former employee of Intratec Firearms in Miami, FL. Toscani made several false statements during the interview regarding his alien status and later was charged with Title 18 U.S.C. 1001 violations for those false statements in addition to machinegun violations and possession of firearms by an illegal alien.

The investigation revealed Toscani had entered the U.S. legally after being given political asylum several years earlier under his birth name. He then legally changed his name to Nico TOSCANI, which was the name of his favorite movie character played by Stephen Segal character in the movie "Above The Law."

On June 19, 2003 in US District Court in West Palm Beach, FL, Nico TOSCANI was sentenced to 41 months in prison followed by 36 months of supervised release following his conviction for machinegun and false statement violations in a jury trial. The jury did not believe that Toscani was above the law.

This chapter opened with the following quote: *"When bad men combine, the good must associate; else they will fall, one by one...".* This chapter will conclude with that quote, because nothing could be truer in today's world.

Appendix A
Acronyms

The following list contains acronyms that the user may encounter throughout this Guidebook and whose full name is important for investigators to know for its relevance to firearms trafficking investigations. Acronyms do not always consist of the first letter of each word in a name. The acronym for the Bureau of Alcohol, Tobacco, Firearms and Explosives is simply ATF. The agency is often referred to as BATF, BATFE, and ATFE and these are incorrect. When the agency was formed in 1972 the acronym established in law was ATF. When the agency transitioned from the Department of U.S. Treasury to the U.S. Justice Department in 2003 and became the Bureau of Alcohol, Tobacco, Firearms and Explosives the ATF acronym remained, established in law.

ACC – Armed Career Criminal
AECA – Arms Export Control Act
AFIS – Automated Fingerprint Information System
AK-47 – Avtomat Kalashnikov Model 1947
ALPR – Automated License Plate Reader
AML – Anti-Money Laundering
AOW – Any Other Weapon (NFA)
AR-15 – Armalite Rifle Model 15
ASEAN – Association of Southeast Asian Nations
ASIS – American Society of Industrial Security
ATF – Bureau of Alcohol, Tobacco, Firearms, and Explosives
ATT – Arms Trade Treaty (UN)
AUSA – Assistant United States Attorney
A&D – Acquisition and Disposition Log
BAR – Browning Automatic Rifle
BSA – Bank Secrecy Act
C&R – Curio and Relic
CAD – Computer Aided Design Software
CAFRA – Civil Asset Forfeiture Reform Act of 2000
CBP – Customs and Border Protection
CBW – Customs Bonded Warehouse
CCA – Crime Control Act of 1990
CCIP – Computer Crime and Intellectual Property Section (DOJ)
CGIC – Crime Gun Intelligence Center

CEN – Customs Enforcement Network(WCO)
CFR – Code of Federal Regulations
CHIC – Cartridge Head-stamp Identification Catalogue (ATF)
CHIPS – Clearing House Interbank Payments System
CI – Confidential Informant
CIMR – Currency or Monetary Instruments Report
CLEO – Chief Law Enforcement Official
CNC – Computer Numerical Code Machine
CODIS – Combined DNA Index System
COP – Community Oriented Policing
COPS – Office of Community Oriented Policing Services (DOJ)
CS – Confidential Source
CSST – Cell Site Simulator Technology
CTR – Cash Transaction Record
CW – Cooperating Witness
DDTC – Directorate of Defense Trade Controls
DEA – Drug Enforcement Administration
DEMIL – Demilitarization
DEWAT – Deactivated War Trophy
DHS – Department of Homeland Security
DICE – DEA Internet Collection Endeavor
DOC – Department of Commerce

DOD – Department of Defense
DOJ – Department of Justice
DOJ-OIA - Department of Justice Office of International Affairs
DOS – Department of State
DTO – Drug Trafficking Organization
EPIC – El Paso Intelligence Center
ESI – Electronic Storage Information
EU – European Union
FAET – Firearms and Ammunition Excise Tax
FATD – Firearms and Ammunition Technology Division (ATF)
FATF – Financial Action Task Force
FCPA – Foreign Corrupt Practices Act
FEDWIRE - Federal Reserve Wire Network
FBI – Federal Bureau of Investigation
FEIB –Firearms & Explosives Imports Branch (ATF)
FFA – Federal Firearms Act of 1938
FFL – Federal Firearms Licensee
FELC – Firearms & Explosives Licensing Center
FIFO – First In, First Out
FinCEN – Financial Crimes Enforcement Network
FLETC – Federal Law Enforcement Training Center
FOPA – Firearms Owners Protection Act of 1986
FRNP - Firearms Recovery Notification Program (ATF)
FTI – Forensic Technologies Inc.
FTS – Firearms Tracing System (ATF)
GETS – Geography, Events, Time, Solvability factors
GCA – Gun Control Act of 1968
GIS – Geographic Information System
GPRA – Government Performance and \ Results Act of 1993
HIDTA – High Intensity Drug Trafficking Area
HSI – Homeland Security Investigations
HTTPS – Hyper Text Transfer Protocol Secure
IACP – International Association of Chiefs of Police
iARMS – Illicit Arms Records and Tracing Management System (INTERPOL)

IBIN – INTERPOL Ballistics Identification System
IBIS – Integrated Ballistics Identification System
ICE – Immigration and Customs Enforcement
ICITAP - International Criminal Investigative Training Assistance Program
IFRT – INTERPOL Firearms Reference Table
III – Interstate Identification System
IOI – Industry Operations Investigator
ILEA – International Law Enforcement Academy
ILP – Intelligence Led Policing
INA – Immigration and Nationality Act
INTERPOL – International Criminal Police Organization
IP – Internet Protocol
IRS – Internal Revenue Service
ISP – Internet Service Provider
ITAR – International Traffic in Arms Regulations
JTTF – Joint Terrorism Task Force (FBI)
KYC – Know Your Customer
LEOPA – Law Enforcement Officers Protection Act of 1986
MANPADS – Man-Portable Air Defense System
MLAT – Mutual Legal Assistance Treaty
MOA – Memorandum of Agreement
MOD – Merchants of Death
MOU – Memorandum of Understanding
NADDIS – Narcotics and Dangerous Drugs Information System (DEA)
NCIC – National Crime Information Center
NFA – National Firearms Act of 1934
NFRTR- National Firearms Registration and Transfer Record (NFA)
NIBIN – National Integrated Ballistics Identification Network
NICS – National Instant Criminal Background Check System
NINJAS – Narcotics Joint Agency System (HIDTA) NLETS – National Law Enforcement Telecommunications System
NORINCO – China North Industries Corporation

NRA – National Rifle Association

NSSF – National Shooting Sports Foundation

NTC – National Tracing Center (ATF)

OAS – Organization of American States

OCDETF – Organized Crime Drug \ Enforcement Task Force

ODTC – Office of Defense Trade Controls

OOB – Out-Of-Business Records Center

OPDAT - Overseas Prosecutorial Development, Assistance, and Training

OSCE - Organization for Security and Co-Operation in Europe

POC – Point of Contact State (NICS)

PSN – Project Safe Neighborhoods

RAC – Resident Agent in Charge

RICO – Racketeer Influenced Corrupt Organization

RILO – Regional Intelligence Liaison Officer (WCO)

RISSNET – Regional Information Sharing System Network

ROCIC – Regional Organized Crime Information Center

SA – Special Agent, GS1811, Criminal Investigator

SAC – Special Agent in Charge

SADC – Southern African Development Community

SALW – Small Arms & Light Weapons

SAR – Suspicious Activity Report

SARA – Scanning, Analysis, Response, Assessment

SBR – Short Barreled Rifle

SCOTUS – Supreme Court of the United States

SMG – Sub-Machine Gun

SMP – Secondary Market Program

SUA – Specified Unlawful Act

SWIFT – Society for Worldwide Interbank Financial Telecommunication

TBML – Trade Based Money Laundering

TECS – Treasury Enforcement Communications System

TI – Title I GCA Firearm

TII – Title II NFA Firearm

TIII – Electronic Wire Interception

TOC – Transnational Organized Crime

TOR – The Onion Router

TTB – Tax and Trade Bureau

UC – Undercover

UCR – Uniform Crime Report (FBI)

UN – United Nations

UNDOC – United Nations Office on Drugs & Crime

UPS – United Parcel Service

USAO – United States Attorney's Office

USC – United States Code

USCG – United States Coast Guard

USITC – United States International Trade Commission

USML – United States Munitions List

USMIL – United States Munitions Import List

USMS – United States Marshalls Service

USPS – United States Postal Service

USSS – United States Secret Service

VAWA – Violence Against Women Act

VCAR – Violent Crime in Aid of Racketeering

WA – Wassenaar Arrangement

WCO – World Customs Organization

Appendix B
Regional Crime Gun Protocols

Interstate Firearms Trafficking Compact - 14 East Coast States & District of Columbia; 1996

**MEMORANDUM OF UNDERSTANDING
TO COMBAT THE ILLEGAL DISTRIBUTION OF FIREARMS**

This agreement is entered into by the Governors of the signatory states and the Director of the Bureau of Alcohol, Tobacco, and Firearms. The parties hereto agree that it is to their mutual benefit to cooperate in eliminating the illegal trafficking of firearms and in the investigation and prosecution of cases involving criminal misuse of firearms.

BACKGROUND

As the number of violent crimes committed with firearms continues to rise nationwide, government officials must develop and implement new law enforcement strategies to combat this dangerous trend.

Despite the diligent efforts of law enforcement, firearms continue to be available to those who engage in criminal activity. Some licensed firearms dealers are engaged in unlawful distribution of firearms. Many other firearms are purchased with fraudulent identification or through straw purchases, where a seemingly legitimate purchaser turns firearms over to the ultimate (and illegal) possessor. Each party to this agreement recognizes that only through the development of an interstate cooperative effort can this difficult problem be brought to an identifiable resolution.

PURPOSE

This memorandum will formalize relationships between the participating agencies with regards to policy and procedures, utilization of resources, planning and training, in order to maximize inter-agency cooperation and coordination.

OBJECTIVES

- Each participating agency shall develop a comprehensive detailed strategy to thwart the illegal distribution and possession of firearms. -
- Establish procedures governing interagency cooperation.
- Provide for an effective communication system among the participating agencies.
- The primary focal point to facilitate effective communication will be the Bureau of Alcohol, Tobacco and Firearms, who shall act as the central recipient of all information relating to firearms used in crimes. In furtherance of this agreement, the Bureau of Alcohol, Tobacco and Firearms shall trace all firearms used in crimes and provide intelligible firearms trace data to all participating agencies.
- Identify and target illegally possessed firearms to their source, interdict illegal gun shipments, enforce existing firearms laws, and arrest and prosecute individuals involved in these offenses.
- Where applicable, conduct joint investigations.
- Increase investigative and prosecution effectiveness through specialized training.
- Each of the states and ATF will coordinate exchange of information to ensure that licenses are in compliance with both federal and state licensing requirements for firearms dealers.

It is the intent of the signatories that this multi-state agreement insure coordination, cooperation, and the mutual conduct of joint investigations. The result of this mutual cooperation and coordination will be the successful prosecution of illegal firearms traffickers in state and federal jurisdictions.

IN WITNESS WHEREOF, the parties have hereunto executed this Memorandum of Understanding.

William Donald Walker - Maryland

Gaston Caperton - West Virginia

Carroll A. Campbell, Jr., S.C.

Sharon Pratt Kelly, Mayor - DC

Bruce Sindlum - Rhode Island

Thomas Carper - Delaware

Daniel R. Black, ATF

Lawton Chiles - Florida

Christine Todd Whitman - N.J.

Lowell Weicker - CT

John R. McKernan, Jr. - ME

Mario Cuomo - New York

James B. Hunt - North Carolina

George Allen - Virginia

DEPARTMENT OF THE TREASURY
BUREAU OF ALCOHOL, TOBACCO AND FIREARMS

THE YOUTH CRIME GUN INTERDICTION INITIATIVE (YCGII) MEMORANDUM OF UNDERSTANDING

The parties signing this memorandum of understanding hereto agree that it is to their mutual benefit to cooperate in eliminating the illegal flow of firearms to youth through enforcement efforts involving the investigation and prosecution of illegal firearms traffickers and through study focusing on the illegal youth firearms market to determine the trends, patterns, and scope of that market and develop effective strategies to address the market.

BACKGROUND

The YCGII was developed by the Department of the Treasury (Enforcement) and the Bureau of Alcohol, Tobacco and Firearms (ATF) in partnership with the Department of Justices' Office of Community Oriented Policing Services (COPS) and the National Institute of Justice (NIJ). Need for the YCGII stems from the fact that firearms related youth homicides have nearly tripled since 1985. Through intervention in the illicit firearms markets, we will try to reduce or stop the upward spiral of youth on youth firearms related homicides.

To accomplish this, the YCGII will not be strictly limited to focusing on illegal traffickers of firearms to the Federally defined "juvenile." Rather, participating ATF field offices and police departments will focus on illegal firearms traffickers to youth, understood as including the Federally defined under 18 years of age, with flexibility to focus on illegal firearms traffickers who supply young people up to 24 years or older if circumstances warrant.

PURPOSE:

This memorandum will formalize relationships between the participating agencies with regard to policy and procedures, utilization of resources, and planning/training in order to maximize interagency cooperation and coordination,

OBJECTIVES:

The nationwide YCGII program has four basic inter-related objectives which will apply in each site:

1) working with U.S. Attorneys and State/local prosecutors to intensify ATF and local police efforts to investigate and incarcerate individuals who illegally traffic in firearms to young people and ensure those arrested are prosecuted in the appropriate venue, which shall be determined on a case by case basis.

2) to ensure local police departments trace all crime guns recovered, and in particular, those firearms taken from youth.

3) to combine the efforts of ATF special agents, local police and NIJ researchers to develop new methods of mapping illegal firearms trafficking patterns and practices, especially as this relates to the illegal trafficking of firearms to youth.

-2-

4) to provide more ATF support for State and local enforcement efforts aimed at intervening in the illegal local youth firearms market.

CONDITIONS AND PROCEDURES:

- ATF agrees to furnish an ATF owned laptop computer to the   Police Department.   Police Department agrees and acknowledges that this equipment shall remain the property of ATF and the U.S. Government, unless otherwise specified.

-            Police Department agrees to assume the cost of replacement or repair of ATF owned equipment, in the event of unauthorized movement, alteration, damage or destruction caused by its employees, contractors, or any other person under its control.

- ATF retains the right to remove ATF owned equipment upon (1) receipt of written notification of the termination of participation in the YCGII by the   Police Department; (2) termination of the YCGII program by ATF, or (3) the cancellation of this MOU by ATF. If the ATF owned equipment will be removed from the   Police Department, written notice of the removal will be provided by ATF not less than 10 business days to the actual removal of the equipment.

- ATF and   Police Department acknowledge their understanding that the operations described in this MOU are subject to audit by ATF; the U.S. Department of the Treasury, Office of Inspector General; the General Accounting Office; and other auditors designated by the U.S. Government. Such audits may include reviews of any and all records, documents, reports, accounts, invoices, receipts, or other evidence.

- The parties agree that premature disclosure of certain firearms trace information can reasonably be expected to interfere with pending or prospective law enforcement proceedings. This law enforcement sensitive information includes data that can link a traced firearm to: the location of a crime; the Federal firearms licensee; retail purchaser or possessor of a traced firearm; or to firearms trafficking patterns involving a traced firearm. It is agreed that the law enforcement sensitive firearms trace information generated pursuant to this Agreement shall not be disclosed to a third party without the consent of both parties of this Agreement.

CONCLUSION

It is the intent of the signatories that this agreement ensures coordination, cooperation and the mutual conduct of enforcement and research activities. The result of this mutual cooperation and coordination will be the successful prosecution of illegal firearms in State and Federal jurisdictions as well as the development of an accurate picture of the illegal youth firearms market and the development of new strategies to effectively interrupt this market and impact on the rate of juvenile related firearms violence. The research findings will be published at the conclusion of this initiative for the benefit of all law enforcement.

Parties to this agreement may terminate their participation at any time upon written notification of their intent to withdraw to all other parties in the agreement. At such time that other Federal government resources may become available, a new Memorandum of Understanding will be initiated.

In witness whereof, the parties have hereunto executed this Memorandum of Understanding.

Division Director

Bureau of ATF

Chief of Police

Police Department

Palm Beach County Gun Crime Protocols; 2004 and Revised 2006

U.S. Department of Justice

Bureau of Alcohol, Tobacco,
Firearms and Explosives

Miami Field Division

www.atf.gov

November 23, 2004

OPEN LETTER TO ALL PALM BEACH COUNTY CHIEFS OF POLICE

The purpose of this letter is to provide you with a status update on implementation of the Palm Beach County Crime Gun Protocols Memorandum of Understanding that each of you signed during the past year as part of a Law Enforcement Planning Council (LEPC) endeavor.

As you know, the goals of the crime gun protocols are; 1) to increase the solution rate of shooting crimes; 2) to increase the strength of each gun crime-related cases for prosecution purposes, 3) to help establish a comprehensive countywide approach to addressing gun crime, and 4) to ensure armed criminals get prosecuted in the venue (State or Federal) that exposes them to the maximum sentencing potential.

To assist in getting the protocol information to all of your officers, the LEPC agreed that training materials and information on the crime gun protocols should be distributed to each Departments training officer. This is now being done. Attached to this open letter are copies of the following documents that have been mailed to your training officer for distribution and further training in your department;

1) Open Notice to Training Officers
2) Copy of the Palm Beach County Crime Gun Protocols Memorandum of Understanding
3) ATF Publication 3310.10 - *Project Safe Neighborhoods: Making the Case* (enough copies for every officer in your Department)

The above materials are being forwarded to each training officer under cover of a notice from the Gun Safety Task Force that is a subgroup of the Palm Beach County Criminal Justice Commission.

Thanks for all your support in this endeavor. If you have any questions or require additional information regarding this matter, please contact me at 561-835-8878.

Dale L Armstrong
Resident Agent in Charge
West Palm Beach Field Office

Palm Beach County Gun Crime Protocols
Policy Recommendations

Purpose:

Firearm-related crime often crosses multiple jurisdictional areas and, therefore, the mutual sharing of certain types of firearm crime information is important in a coordinated approach to solving these crimes. A comprehensive approach to combating firearm-related crime involves identifying, investigating and arresting armed violent criminals as well as those persons who illegally supply firearms to the criminal element.

The comprehensive submission of all recovered crime guns, bullet projectiles, and ammunition casings to the Palm Beach County Sheriffs Office Crime Laboratory for entry into the National Integrated Ballistics Identification Network (NIBIN) will assist in solving shooting-related crimes and generating additional investigative leads. There is no cost to an agency for these services.

The complete processing of all recovered crime guns and arrestees produces stronger cases that can reduce an officer's court time when the case results in a plea agreement.

As such, the following techniques and procedures are outlined and are intended to be guidelines in the implementation of a multi-jurisdictional and comprehensive approach to combating firearm-related crimes. These guidelines are not intended to replace, supersede or otherwise preclude the application of the Florida Rules of Criminal Procedure and/or Florida Rules of Evidence in any court hearing. They do however supersede previous recommendations and agreements by agencies regarding this policy.

Policy Recommendations:

General:

- o It is recommended that agencies adopt a policy regarding the protocols to be utilized in investigating firearm related crimes and incidents.

- o It is recommended that all departmental issued firearms and/or firearms authorized for use by departmental personnel be test fired and two casings kept at the department in case of theft of the firearm.

- o A crime gun is any firearm that is illegally possessed, used in a crime, or suspected by law enforcement to have been used in a crime. This may include a firearm found abandoned if the recovering law enforcement agency has reason to believe the firearm may have been used in a crime or illegally possessed. A crime bullet is defined as any projectile from a crime gun.

- o All crime guns and crime bullets should be photographed at the crime scene without being disturbed before being collected or processed.

o All recovered crime guns, bullets, or ammunition casings or other potential ballistics evidence should be entered in the National Integrated Ballistics Identification Network (NIBIN).

o All recovered crime guns should be traced through the U.S Department of Justice, Bureau of Alcohol, Tobacco, Firearms and Explosives' (ATF) National Tracing Center to assist in Identifying illegal sources of crime guns. This may be accomplished by; Submitting an ATF Form 3312.1 (National Tracing Center Trace Request Form) via mail or fax to the ATF NTC at the toll free fax number listed at the top of the form – OR; Submitting the firearm to the Palm Beach County Sheriffs Office (PBSO) Crime Laboratory and requesting that they trace the firearm (PBSO has electronic trace capability).

o To perfect a strong prosecutable case and for developing crime gun intelligence, officers at the scene of a crime should ask a series of basic questions of the suspect(s) and/or witnesses to establish gun possession. By establishing statements from everyone the potential for false alibis at a later time is limited.

Procedures for Processing Crime Guns and Related Evidence:

o Depending on the situation, crime gun(s) and/or ammunition will be processed with sterile swabs for the collection of DNA evidence and/or treated with superglue fumes, or any other processing methods which would produce the best possible latent print evidence, to assist in preserving any existing latent fingerprints for identification. This may be accomplished by the Departments Crime Scene Unit or by submitting the crime gun(s) and ammunition to the PBSO Crime Laboratory. The recovering department will be responsible for the collection and submission of all DNA suspect/elimination standards to the PBSO Crime Lab. DNA analysis requests must be initiated by telephoning the PBSO DNA Evidence Coordinator

o The crime gun(s) will be test-fired and the expended bullet projectile and ammunition casing will be submitted to the PBSO Crime Laboratory for entry into NIBIN. The first test-fire from a recovered crime gun is the best evidence for entry into NIBIN therefore officers who recover firearms should not unnecessarily discharge the firearm prior to submission to the crime laboratory. The test fire may be performed by the recovering Department where that capability exists, or the firearm may be submitted to the PBSO Crime Laboratory for test-firing.

o When submitting a crime gun or ammunition components to the PBSO Crime Laboratory, the recovering department should complete a PBSO Property Report for all crime guns submitted to the PBSO Crime Laboratory so that laboratory officials have all pertinent information such as crime gun description, make, model, serial number, caliber, country of origin and importer, suspected possessor, and recovery date and location. Note: The submission request form to PBSO must indicate whether the crime gun is to be submitted for DNA, fingerprints, test firing and/or just entry into NIBIN. For example; If your department has already swabbed and fingerprinted the firearm, please note that PBSO only needs to test fire and enter into NIBIN.

o All bullet projectiles and/or ammunition casings recovered at all crime/shooting scenes should be submitted to the PBSO Crime Laboratory for entry into NIBIN. (Maintaining care custody and control of the "crime bullet" or casing is critical. Loss of the crime bullet or casing may lead to the suppression of the ballistic expert's testimony connecting the bullet to the defendant's firearm.)

o The crime gun information should be checked in NCIC for possible information regarding it's status as reported lost or stolen. If the crime gun appears to be stolen, print the NCIC hit record and maintain it in the file. Once the stolen firearm record is cleared/removed from NCIC the record will no longer exist and the paper copy must be maintained in a departmental file as this will be needed for the investigation and for future reference if and when a NIBIN, AFIS, or DNA hit is obtained.

Procedures for processing all crime gun related arrests:

o The arresting officer should ensure the defendant is fingerprinted. This will assist in defendant identification at a later date. Whenever possible, a thumb print should be obtained on a notice to appear form or field interview card/report, if circumstances dictate that a subject will not be transported to a booking facility.

o Advise the defendant of his or her Miranda Rights when required.

o Request that the defendant allow a DNA sample to be obtained. Refusal to cooperate should be noted in the arrest report.

o Attempt to obtain a written or taped statement from the defendant regarding the defendant's possession of the firearm(s), how they obtained the firearm, and any prior felony conviction information. Document all statements by the defendant, whether formal or spontaneous, relating to the firearm(s) and/or criminal record in the police report. Document all refusals by the defendant to provide information relating to the firearm(s).

o Attempt to obtain statements from any witnesses, associates, and accomplices (e.g., other passengers in a car stop) of the defendant regarding the facts and circumstances of the offense. This assists in establishing the defendant's firearm possession and precludes false alibis by accomplices claiming the firearm was theirs at some later date.

o Prepare a detailed narrative report regarding the arrest and surrounding circumstances, including a complete description of the firearm, (make, model, serial number, caliber, country of origin and importer,) vehicle information, witness/accomplice information, and a listing all officers present at the arrest. If the arrest began with or involved a 9-1-1 call(s), obtain and preserve a copy of that taped 9-1-1 call(s) and CAD report(s). If the arrest involved a video-taped traffic stop, obtain and preserve a copy of that tape. If the arrest involves a foot pursuit, fight or struggle that was recorded by the communications center, preserve a copy of the tape.

o Obtain a criminal history printout for the defendant and ascertain the number and types of prior felony convictions. Use the criminal history information coupled with the defendant's action for which you made the arrest to determine which law violations apply and which venue (Federal or State) provides for the maximum possible sentence.

INTERNATIONAL ASSOCIATION OF CHIEFS OF POLICE

RESOLUTION

Adopted at the 119th Annual Conference
San Diego, CA
October 3, 2012

Regional Crime Gun Processing Protocols
Submitted by the Firearms Committee
FC.028.a12

WHEREAS, a "Crime Gun" for the purposes of this resolution *includes any firearm used in crime or suspected to have been used in crime. This may include firearms abandoned or otherwise taken into law enforcement custody that are either suspected to have been used in a crime or whose proper disposition can be facilitated through a firearms trace;* and

WHEREAS, crime Gun Tracing and NCIC (National Crime Information Center) queries can help police identify and track purchasers, owners and possessors of firearms; and

WHEREAS, ballistics Evidence, bullets and cartridge cases discharged from a crime gun can be used to link a firearm to prior crimes and to link two or more crimes together; and

WHEREAS, forensic Evidence such as DNA, latent fingerprints, and other trace evidence like hairs and fibers can help police link Crime Guns and Ballistics Evidence to a criminal; and

WHEREAS, the armed criminals of today are mobile and evidence of their crimes is easily dispersed across police districts, cities, states and international borders as well; and

WHEREAS, a regional approach is necessary because a law enforcement officer's degree of success in solving a murder in one city can be dependent upon what an officer in the next town over does or does not do with the crime gun he or she seizes in a traffic stop; and

WHEREAS, scientific and information technology tools like eTrace for crime gun tracing, NCIC for stolen firearms reporting and recognition, NIBIN for ballistics evidence, CODIS for DNA, and AFIS for fingerprints, can help police develop and share information about the identity of armed criminals across wide geographic regions; and

WHEREAS, maximum benefits from these intelligence-led policing tools can be achieved through collaboratively defined crime gun processing protocols consistently applied by the law enforcement agencies operating within a region where armed criminals are likely to be crisscrossing multiple police jurisdictions; and

WHEREAS, regional crime gun and evidence processing protocols can provide law enforcement agencies with timely and actionable information to help identify and apprehend armed suspects quickly thereby denying them the opportunity to re-offend and to perfect stronger criminal cases against them; and

WHEREAS, more armed criminals convicted and Justice served helps to preserve the peace and protect the public; now, therefore, be it

RESOLVED, that the IACP views regionally applied crime gun and evidence processing protocols as a best practice for the investigation of firearm related crimes and encourages law enforcement officials, prosecuting attorneys and forensic experts to collaborate on the design of mutually agreeable protocols best suited for their region.

The protocols should address each of the following critical areas:

• The thorough investigation of each gun related crime including the safe and proper collection of all crime guns & related evidence.

• The performance of appropriate NCIC transactions (e.g. stolen, recovered).

• The timely and comprehensive tracing of all crime guns through ATF & eTrace.

• The timely processing of crime gun test fires and ballistics evidence through NIBIN.

• The timely lab submission and analysis of other forensic data from crime guns and related evidence (e.g. DNA, latent fingerprints, trace evidence).

• The generation, dissemination and investigative follow-up of the intelligence derived from the application of the regional protocols.

§§1,3 -
C.52:17B-9.18 &
52:17B-9.19
§4 - Note

P.L.2013, CHAPTER 162, *approved September 18, 2013*
Assembly, No. 3797 *(Third Reprint)*

1   An Act concerning ²[certain seized and recovered] the reporting of
2   information relating to certain² firearms ²[and] ‚² supplementing
3   ³Title 52 of the Revised Statutes,³ ²[Title 52 of the Revised
4   Statutes] and amending P.L.1966, c.37².
5
6   **Be It Enacted** *by the Senate and General Assembly of the State*
7   *of New Jersey:*
8
9   1. ²(New section)² The Legislature finds and declares that to
10   further provide for the public safety and the well being of the
11   citizens of this State, and to respond to growing dangers and threats
12   of gun violence, it is altogether fitting and proper for the law
13   enforcement departments and agencies of this State to fully
14   participate, through the utilization of electronic technology, in
15   interjurisdictional information and analysis sharing programs and
16   systems to deter and solve gun crimes.
17   To effectuate this objective, it shall be the policy of this State for
18   its various law enforcement agencies to utilize fully the federal
19   Criminal Justice Information System to transmit and receive
20   information relating to the seizure and recovery of firearms by law
21   enforcement, in particular the National Crime Information Center
22   System to determine whether a firearm has been reported stolen; the
23   Alcohol, Tobacco, Firearms, and Explosives E-Trace System to
24   establish the identity of a firearm's first purchaser, where that
25   firearm was purchased and when it was purchased; and the National
26   Integrated Ballistics Identification Network to ascertain whether a
27   particular firearm is related to any other criminal event or person.
28
29   ²[2. Whenever a law enforcement agency seizes or recovers any
30   firearm, the agency shall promptly enter the make, model, caliber,
31   and serial number of that firearm into the National Crime
32   Information Center 2000 System to determine whether that firearm
33   was reported stolen.]²

**EXPLANATION – Matter enclosed in bold-faced brackets [thus] in the above bill is
not enacted and is intended to be omitted in the law.**

Matter underlined thus is new matter.
Matter enclosed in superscript numerals has been adopted as follows:
¹Assembly ALP committee amendments adopted February 14, 2013.
²Senate SLP committee amendments adopted May 9, 2013.
³Assembly amendments adopted in accordance with Governor's
recommendations September 9, 2013.

1   [2]2. Section 3 of P.L.1966, c.37 (C.52:17B-5.3) is amended to
2   read as follows:
3   3. a. All local and county police authorities shall submit a
4   quarterly report to the Attorney General, on forms prescribed by the
5   Attorney General, which report shall contain the number and nature
6   of offenses committed within their respective jurisdictions, the
7   disposition of such matters, information relating to criminal street
8   gang activities within their respective jurisdictions, information
9   relating to any offense directed against a person or group, or their
10   property, by reason of their race, color, religion, gender, disability,
11   sexual orientation, gender identity or expression, national origin, or
12   ethnicity and such other information as the Attorney General may
13   require, respecting information relating to the cause and prevention
14   of crime, recidivism, the rehabilitation of criminals and the proper
15   administration of criminal justice.
16   b. A law enforcement officer who responds to an offense
17   involving criminal street gang activity shall complete a gang related
18   incident offense report on a form prescribed by the Superintendent
19   of State Police. All information contained in the gang related
20   incident offense report shall be forwarded to the Superintendent of
21   State Police for inclusion in the Uniform Crime Report.
22   c. A law enforcement officer who seizes or recovers a firearm
23   that was unlawfully possessed, used for an unlawful purpose,
24   recovered from a crime scene or is reasonably believed to have been
25   used in or associated with the commission of a crime, or is
26   otherwise acquired as an abandoned or discarded firearm shall
27   complete, within 24 hours of the entering of the required
28   information relating to that firearm into the New Jersey Trace
29   System and such other State and federal database systems as
30   prescribed by the superintendent, a seized or recovered firearms
31   incident report on a form prescribed by the superintendent. The
32   incident report shall be filed with the State Police in a manner and
33   time prescribed by the superintendent.[2]
34   (cf: P.L.2010, c.110, s.1)
35
36   [2][3. Whenever a law enforcement agency seizes or recovers a
37   firearm that was unlawfully possessed, used for an unlawful
38   purpose, recovered from the scene of a crime, is reasonably
39   believed to have been used or associated with the commission of a
40   crime, or is acquired by the agency as an abandoned or discarded
41   firearm, the agency shall, as soon as may be practicable, but in no
42   case more than 24 hours after the agency has taken possession of
43   the firearm, enter the appropriate information relating to that
44   firearm into the New Jersey Trace System which, as part of the
45   federal Criminal Justice Information System, makes information
46   relating to that firearm's first purchaser and where and when it was
47   purchased, available to all law enforcement agencies.][2]

1   **²[4.] 3.²** Whenever a law enforcement agency seizes or
2   recovers a firearm that was unlawfully possessed, used for any
3   unlawful purpose, recovered from the scene of a crime, is
4   reasonably believed to have been used or associated with the
5   commission of a crime, or is acquired by the agency as an
6   abandoned or discarded firearm, the agency shall arrange for every
7   such firearm that **²**, in accordance with protocols promulgated by
8   the Attorney General and superintendent,**²** is determined to **²**merit
9   and**²** be suitable for National Integrated Ballistics Identification
10   Network data entry and examination to be test-fired as soon as may
11   be practicable and the results of that test-firing be forthwith
12   submitted to the National Integrated Ballistics Identification
13   Network to determine whether the firearm is associated or related to
14   a crime, criminal event, or any individual associated or related to a
15   crime or criminal event or reasonably believed to be associated or
16   related to a crime or criminal event.
17   Whenever a law enforcement agency recovers any spent shell
18   casing at a crime scene or has reason to believe that the recovered
19   spent shell casing is related to or associated with the commission of
20   a crime or the unlawful discharge of a firearm, the agency shall, as
21   soon as may be practicable, submit the ballistics information to the
22   National Integrated Ballistics Identification Network.
23
24   **³[²['5.]** 4.²** The Superintendant of State Police shall make
25   available to the public quarterly reports summarizing firearms trace
26   data received from the Bureau of Alcohol, Tobacco, Firearms, and
27   Explosives. An initial report shall be issued summarizing data
28   received within the preceding 10 years. Quarterly reports shall be
29   issued summarizing data currently received. The reports shall
30   include particular and aggregate information on:
31   a. The state of origin of the recovered firearm;
32   b. The identity and city location of the firearm's source vendor;
33   c. The type of firearm recovered;
34   d. The manufacturer, make, and model of the recovered firearm;
35   e. The crime which was committed with the recovered firearm;
36   and
37   f. Any other information the superintendent deems
38   appropriate.**¹]³**
39
40   **¹[5.] ²[6.¹] ³[5.²] 4.³** This act shall take effect **²[**immediately**]**
41   on the first day of the fourth month following enactment, but the
42   Attorney General may take such anticipatory action in advance
43   thereof as shall be necessary for the implementation of this act**²**.

A3797 [3R]
4

1   ———————————

2

3   Requires collection and reporting of certain firearms

4   information.

Appendix C
ATF Forms

ATF FORM 4473 – Firearms Transaction Record

OMB No. 1140-0020
OMB No. 1140-0020

U.S. Department of Justice
Bureau of Alcohol, Tobacco, Firearms and Explosives

Firearms Transaction Record

	Transferor's/Seller's Transaction Serial Number *(If any)*
WARNING: You may not receive a firearm if prohibited by Federal or State law. The information you provide will be used to determine whether you are prohibited from receiving a firearm. Certain violations of the Gun Control Act, 18 U.S.C. 921 et. seq., are punishable by up to 10 years imprisonment and/or up to a $250,000 fine. Read the Notices, Instructions, and Definitions on this form. Prepare in original only at the licensed premises *("licensed premises" includes business temporarily conducted from a qualifying gun show or event in the same State in which the licensed premises is located)* unless the transaction qualifies under 18 U.S.C. 922(c). All entries must be handwritten in ink. **"PLEASE PRINT."**	

Section A - Must Be Completed Personally By Transferee/Buyer

1. Transferee's/Buyer's Full Name *(If legal name contains an initial only, record "IO" after the initial. If no middle initial or name, record "NMN".)*

Last Name *(Including suffix (e.g., Jr, Sr, II, III))* | First Name | Middle Name

2. Current State of Residence and Address (**U.S. Postal abbreviations are acceptable. Cannot be a post office box.**)

Number and Street Address | City | County | State | ZIP Code

3. Place of Birth U.S. City and State **-OR-** Foreign Country	4. Height Ft. ____ In. ____	5. Weight *(Lbs.)*	6. Sex ☐ Male ☐ Female	7. Birth Date Month	Day	Year

8. Social Security Number *(Optional, but will help prevent misidentification)* | 9. Unique Personal Identification Number *(UPIN)* if applicable *(See Instructions for Question 9.)*

10.a. Ethnicity	10.b. Race *(In addition to ethnicity, select one or more race in 10.b. Both 10.a. and 10.b. must be answered.)*
☐ Hispanic or Latino ☐ Not Hispanic or Latino	☐ American Indian or Alaska Native ☐ Black or African American ☐ White ☐ Asian ☐ Native Hawaiian or Other Pacific Islander

11. Answer the following questions by checking or marking *"yes"* or *"no"* in the boxes to the right of the questions.	Yes	No
a. Are you the actual transferee/buyer of the firearm(s) listed on this form? **Warning: You are not the actual transferee/buyer if you are acquiring the firearm(s) on behalf of another person. If you are not the actual transferee/buyer, the licensee cannot transfer the firearm(s) to you.** *Exception: If you are picking up a repaired firearm(s) for another person, you are not required to answer 11.a. and may proceed to question 11.b. (See Instructions for Question 11.a.)*	☐	☐
b. Are you under indictment or information in any court for a **felony**, or any other crime for which the judge could imprison you for more than one year? *(See Instructions for Question 11.b.)*	☐	☐
c. Have you ever been convicted in any court of a **felony**, or any other crime for which the judge could have imprisoned you for more than one year, even if you received a shorter sentence including probation? *(See Instructions for Question 11.c.)*	☐	☐
d. Are you a fugitive from justice? *(See Instructions for Question 11.d.)*	☐	☐
e. Are you an unlawful user of, or addicted to, marijuana or any depressant, stimulant, narcotic drug, or any other controlled substance? **Warning: The use or possession of marijuana remains unlawful under Federal law regardless of whether it has been legalized or decriminalized for medicinal or recreational purposes in the state where you reside.**	☐	☐
f. Have you ever been adjudicated as a mental defective **OR** have you ever been committed to a mental institution? *(See Instructions for Question 11.f.)*	☐	☐
g. Have you been discharged from the Armed Forces under **dishonorable** conditions?	☐	☐
h. Are you subject to a court order restraining you from harassing, stalking, or threatening your child or an intimate partner or child of such partner? *(See Instructions for Question 11.h.)*	☐	☐
i. Have you ever been **convicted** in any court of a misdemeanor crime of domestic violence? *(See Instructions for Question 11.i.)*	☐	☐

12.a. Country of Citizenship: *(Check/List more than one, if applicable. Nationals of the United States may check U.S.A.)*
☐ United States of America *(U.S.A.)*   ☐ Other Country/Countries *(Specify)*

		Yes	No
12.b. Have you ever renounced your United States citizenship?		☐	☐
12.c. Are you an alien **illegally** or **unlawfully** in the United States?		☐	☐
12.d.1. Are you an alien who has been admitted to the United States under a nonimmigrant visa? *(See Instructions for Question 12.d.)*		☐	☐
12.d.2. If "yes", do you fall within any of the exceptions stated in the instructions?	☐ N/A	☐	☐

13. If you are an alien, record your U.S.-Issued Alien or Admission number *(AR#, USCIS#, or I94#)*:

Previous Editions Are Obsolete

Transferee/Buyer Continue to Next Page
STAPLE IF PAGES BECOME SEPARATED

Page 1 of 6

ATF E-Form 4473 (5300.9)
Revised October 2016

353

I certify that my answers in Section A are true, correct, and complete. I have read and understand the Notices, Instructions, and Definitions on ATF Form 4473. I understand that answering "yes" to question 11.a. if I am not the actual transferee/buyer is a crime punishable as a felony under Federal law, and may also violate State and/or local law. I understand that a person who answers "yes" to any of the questions 11.b. through 11.i and/or 12.b. through 12.c. is prohibited from purchasing or receiving a firearm. I understand that a person who answers "yes" to question 12.d.1. is prohibited from receiving or possessing a firearm, unless the person answers "yes" to question 12.d.2. and provides the documentation required in 18.c. I also understand that making any false oral or written statement, or exhibiting any false or misrepresented identification with respect to this transaction, is a crime punishable as a felony under Federal law, and may also violate State and/or local law. I further understand that the repetitive purchase of firearms for the purpose of resale for livelihood and profit without a Federal firearms license is a violation of Federal law. *(See Instructions for Question 14.)*

14. Transferee's/Buyer's Signature	15. Certification Date

Section B - Must Be Completed By Transferor/Seller

16. Type of firearm(s) to be transferred *(check or mark all that apply):*	17. If transfer is at a qualifying gun show or event:
☐ Handgun ☐ Long Gun *(rifles or shotguns)* ☐ Other Firearm *(frame, receiver, etc. See Instructions for Question 16.)*	Name of Function: _____ City, State: _____

18.a. Identification *(e.g., Virginia Driver's license (VA DL) or other valid government-issued photo identification.)* *(See Instructions for Question 18.a.)*

Issuing Authority and Type of Identification	Number on Identification	Expiration Date of Identification *(if any)*		
		Month	Day	Year

18.b. Supplemental Government Issued Documentation *(if identification document does not show current residence address) (See Instructions for Question 18.b.)*

18.c. Exception to the Nonimmigrant Alien Prohibition: If the transferee/buyer answered "YES" to 12.d.2. the transferor/seller must record the type of documentation showing the exception to the prohibition and attach a copy to this ATF Form 4473. *(See Instructions for Question 18.c.)*

Questions 19, 20, or 21 Must Be Completed Prior To The Transfer Of The Firearm(s) *(See Instructions for Questions 19, 20 and 21.)*

19.a. Date the transferee's/buyer's identifying information in Section A was transmitted to NICS or the appropriate State agency:	19.b. The NICS or State transaction number *(if provided)* was:

Month	Day	Year

19.c. The response initially (first) provided by NICS or the appropriate State agency was:	19.d. The following response(s) was/were later received from NICS or the appropriate State agency:
☐ Proceed ☐ Delayed ☐ Denied *[The firearm(s) may be transferred on* ☐ Cancelled _____ *if State law permits (optional)]*	☐ Proceed _____ *(date)* ☐ Overturned ☐ Denied _____ *(date)* ☐ Cancelled _____ *(date)* ☐ No response was provided within 3 business days.

19.e. *(Complete if applicable.)* After the firearm was transferred, the following response was received from NICS or the appropriate State agency on:

_____ *(date).*   ☐ Proceed   ☐ Denied   ☐ Cancelled

19.f. The name and Brady identification number of the NICS examiner. *(Optional)*	19.g. Name of FFL Employee Completing NICS check. *(Optional)*
_____ *(name)* _____ *(number)*	

20. ☐ No NICS check was required because a background check was completed during the NFA approval process on the individual who will receive the NFA firearm(s), as reflected on the approved NFA application. *(See Instructions for Question 20.)*

21. ☐ No NICS check was required because the transferee/buyer has a valid permit from the State where the transfer is to take place, which qualifies as an exemption to NICS. *(See Instructions for Question 21.)*

Issuing State and Permit Type	Date of Issuance *(if any)*	Expiration Date *(if any)*	Permit Number *(if any)*

Section C - Must Be Completed Personally By Transferee/Buyer

If the transfer of the firearm(s) takes place on a different day from the date that the transferee/buyer signed Section A, the transferee/buyer must complete Section C immediately prior to the transfer of the firearm(s). *(See Instructions for Question 22 and 23.)*

I certify that my answers to the questions in Section A of this form are still true, correct, and complete.

22. Transferee's/Buyer's Signature	23. Recertification Date

Transferor/Seller Continue to Next Page
STAPLE IF PAGES BECOME SEPARATED
Page 2 of 6

ATF E-Form 4473 (5300.9)
Revised October 2016

354

24. Manufacturer and Importer *(If any) (If the manufacturer and importer are different, the FFL must include both.)*	25. Model *(If Designated)*	26. Serial Number	27. Type *(See Instructions for Question 27.)*	28. Caliber or Gauge
1.				
2.				
3.				
4.				

REMINDER - By the Close of Business Complete ATF Form 3310.4 For Multiple Purchases of Handguns Within 5 Consecutive Business Days

29. Total Number of Firearms Transferred *(Please handwrite by printing e.g., zero, one, two, three, etc.* **Do not use numerals.)**	30. Check if any part of this transaction is a pawn redemption. ☐ Line Number(s) From Question 24 Above:
31. For Use by Licensee *(See Instructions for Question 31.)*	32. Check if this transaction is to facilitate a private party transfer. ☐ *(See Instructions for Question 32.)*

33. Trade/corporate name and address of transferor/seller and Federal Firearm License Number *(Must contain at least first three and last five digits of FFL Number X-XX-XXXXX.) (Hand stamp may be used.)*

The Person Transferring The Firearm(s) Must Complete Questions 34-37.
For Denied/Cancelled Transactions, the Person Who Completed Section B Must Complete Questions 34-36.

I certify that: (1) I have read and understand the Notices, Instructions, and Definitions on this ATF Form 4473; (2) the information recorded in Sections B and D is true, correct, and complete; and (3) this entire transaction record has been completed at my licensed business premises ("licensed premises" includes business temporarily conducted from a qualifying gun show or event in the same State in which the licensed premises is located) unless this transaction has met the requirements of 18 U.S.C. 922(c). Unless this transaction has been denied or cancelled, I further certify on the basis of — (1) the transferee's/buyer's responses in Section A (and Section C, if applicable); (2) my verification of the identification recorded in question 18 (and my re-verification at the time of transfer, *if Section C was completed)*; and (3) State or local law applicable to the firearms business — it is my belief that it is not unlawful for me to sell, deliver, transport, or otherwise dispose of the firearm(s) listed on this form to the person identified in Section A.

34. Transferor's/Seller's Name *(Please print)*	35. Transferor's/Seller's Signature	36. Transferor's/Seller's Title	37. Date Transferred

NOTICES, INSTRUCTIONS, AND DEFINITIONS

Purpose of the Form: The information and certification on this form are designed so that a person licensed under 18 U.S.C. 923 may determine if he/she may lawfully sell or deliver a firearm to the person identified in Section A, and to alert the transferee/buyer of certain restrictions on the receipt and possession of firearms. The transferor/seller of a firearm must determine the lawfulness of the transaction and maintain proper records of the transaction. Consequently, the transferor/seller must be familiar with the provisions of 18 U.S.C. 921-931 and the regulations in 27 CFR Parts 478 and 479. In determining the lawfulness of the sale or delivery of a rifle or shotgun to a resident of another State, the transferor/seller is presumed to know the applicable State laws and published ordinances in both the transferor's/seller's State and the transferee's/buyer's State. *(See ATF Publication 5300.5, State Laws and Published Ordinances.)*

Generally, ATF Form 4473 must be completed at the licensed business premises when a firearm is transferred over-the-counter. Federal law, 18 U.S.C. 922(c), allows a licensed importer, manufacturer, or dealer to sell a firearm to a nonlicensee who does not appear in person at the licensee's business premises only if the transferee/buyer meets certain requirements. These requirements are set forth in section 922(c), 27 CFR 478.96(b), and ATF Procedure 2013-2.

After the transferor/seller has completed the firearms transaction, he/she must make the completed, original ATF Form 4473 *(which includes the Notices, General Instructions, and Definitions)*, and any supporting documents, part of his/her permanent records. Such Forms 4473 must be retained for at least 20 years and after that period may be submitted to ATF. Filing may be chronological *(by date of disposition)*, alphabetical *(by name of purchaser)*, or numerical *(by transaction serial number)*, as long as all of the transferor's/seller's completed Forms 4473 are filed in the same manner.

FORMS 4473 FOR DENIED/CANCELLED TRANSFERS MUST BE RETAINED: If the transfer of a firearm is denied/cancelled by NICS, or if for any other reason the transfer is not completed after a NICS check is initiated, the licensee must retain the ATF Form 4473 in his/her records for at least 5 years. Forms 4473 with respect to which a sale, delivery, or transfer did not take place shall be separately retained in alphabetical *(by name of transferee)* or chronological *(by date of transferee's certification)* order.

If the transferor/seller or the transferee/buyer discovers that an ATF Form 4473 is incomplete or improperly completed after the firearm has been transferred, and the transferor/seller or the transferee/buyer wishes to correct the omission(s) or error(s), photocopy the inaccurate form and make any necessary additions or revisions to the photocopy. The transferor/seller should only make changes to Sections B and D. The transferee/buyer should only make changes to Section A and C. Whoever made the changes should initial and date the changes. The corrected photocopy should be attached to the original Form 4473 and retained as part of the transferor's/seller's permanent records.

Exportation of Firearms: The State or Commerce Departments may require a firearms exporter to obtain a license prior to export. **Warning:** Any person who exports a firearm without proper authorization may be fined not more than $1,000,000 and/or imprisoned for not more than 20 years. See 22 U.S.C. 2778(c).

Section A

The transferee/buyer must personally complete Section A of this form and certify *(sign)* that the answers are true, correct, and complete. However, if the transferee/buyer is unable to read and/or write, the answers *(other than the signature)* may be completed by another person, excluding the transferor/seller. Two persons *(other than the transferor/seller)* must then sign as witnesses to the transferee's/buyer's answers and signature/certification in question 14.

ATF E-Form 4473 (5300.9)
Revised October 2016

When the transferee/buyer of a firearm is a corporation, company, association, partnership, or other such business entity, an officer authorized to act on behalf of the business must complete Section A of the form with his/her personal information, sign Section A, and attach a written statement, executed under penalties of perjury, stating: (A) the firearm is being acquired for the use of and will be the property of that business entity; and (B) the name and address of that business entity.

Question 1. If the transferee's/buyer's name in question 1 is illegible, the transferor/seller must print the transferee's/buyer's name above the name written by the transferee/buyer.

Question 2. Current Residence Address: A rural route (RR) may be accepted provided the transferee/buyer lives in a State or locality where it is considered a legal residence address. County and Parish are one and the same.

If the transferee/buyer is a member of the Armed Forces on active duty, his/her State of residence is the State in which his/her permanent duty station is located. If the service member is acquiring a firearm in a State where his/her permanent duty station is located, but resides in a different State, the transferee/buyer must list both his/her permanent duty station address and his/her residence address in response to question 2. If the transferee/buyer has two States of residence, the transferee/buyer should list his/her current residence address in response to question 2 *(e.g., if the transferee/buyer is purchasing a firearm while staying at his/her weekend home in State X, he/she should list the address in State X in response to question 2).*

Question 9. Unique Personal Identification Number (UPIN): For transferees/buyers approved to have information maintained about them in the FBI NICS Voluntary Appeal File, NICS will provide them with a UPIN, which the transferee/buyer should record in question 9. The licensee should provide the UPIN when conducting background checks through the NICS or the State POC.

Question 10.a. and 10.b. Federal regulations (27 CFR 478.124(c)(1)) require licensees to obtain the race of the transferee/buyer. This information helps the FBI and/or State POC make or rule out potential matches during the background check process and can assist with criminal investigations. Pursuant to Office of Management and Budget (OMB), effective January 1, 2003, all Federal agencies requiring collection of race and ethnicity information on administrative forms and records, were required to collect this information in a standard format. (See 62 FR 58782) The standard OMB format consists of two categories for data on ethnicity: "Hispanic or Latino," and "Not Hispanic or Latino" and five categories for data on race: American Indian or Alaska Native, Asian, Black or African American, Native Hawaiian or Other Pacific Islander, and White.

Ethnicity refers to a person's heritage. Persons of Cuban, Mexican, Puerto Rican, South or Central American, or other Spanish culture or origin, regardless of race, are considered Hispanic or Latino.

Race - one or more of the following responses must be selected: (1) American Indian or Alaska Native - A person having origins in any of the original peoples of North and South America (including Central America), and who maintains a tribal affiliation or community attachment; (2) Asian - A person having origins in any of the original peoples of the Far East, Southeast Asia, or the Indian subcontinent including, for example, Cambodia, China, India, Japan, Korea, Malaysia, Pakistan, the Philippine Islands, Thailand, and Vietnam; (3) Black or African American - A person having origins in any of the Black racial groups of Africa; (4) Native Hawaiian or Other Pacific Islander - A person having origins in any of the original peoples of Hawaii, Guam, Samoa, or other Pacific Islands; and (5) White - A person having origins in any of the original peoples of Europe, the Middle East, or North Africa. Any other race or ethnicity that does not fall within those indicated, please select the closest representation.

Question 11.a. Actual Transferee/Buyer: For purposes of this form, a person is the actual transferee/buyer if he/she is purchasing the firearm for him/herself or otherwise acquiring the firearm for him/herself. *(e.g., redeeming the firearm from pawn, retrieving it from consignment, firearm raffle winner).* A person is also the actual transferee/buyer if he/she is legitimately purchasing the firearm as a bona fide gift for a third party. A gift is not bona fide if another person offered or gave the person completing this form money, service(s), or item(s) of value to acquire the firearm for him/her, or if the other person is prohibited by law from receiving or possessing the firearm.

Actual TRANSFEREE/buyer examples: Mr. Smith asks Mr. Jones to purchase a firearm for Mr. Smith *(who may or may not be prohibited).* Mr. Smith gives Mr. Jones the money for the firearm. Mr. Jones is **NOT THE**

Page 4 of 6

ACTUAL TRANSFEREE/BUYER of the firearm and must answer **"NO"** to question 11.a. The licensee may not transfer the firearm to Mr. Jones. However, if Mr. Brown buys the firearm with his own money to give to Mr. Black as a gift *(with no service or tangible thing of value provided by Mr. Black),* Mr. Brown is the actual transferee/buyer of the firearm and should answer **"YES"** to question 11.a. However, the transferor/seller may not transfer a firearm to any person he/she knows or has reasonable cause to believe is prohibited under 18 U.S.C. 922(g), (n) or (x).
EXCEPTION: If a person is picking up a repaired firearm(s) for another person, he/she is not required to answer 11.a. and may proceed to question 11.b.

Question 11.b. - 12. Generally, 18 U.S.C. 922(g) prohibits the shipment, transportation, receipt, or possession in or affecting interstate commerce of a firearm by one who: has been convicted of a felony in any Federal, State or local court, or any other crime, punishable by imprisonment for a term exceeding one year *(this does not include State misdemeanors punishable by imprisonment of two years or less);* is a fugitive from justice; is an unlawful user of, or addicted to, marijuana or any depressant, stimulant, or narcotic drug, or any other controlled substance; has been adjudicated as a mental defective or has been committed to a mental institution; has been discharged from the Armed Forces under dishonorable conditions; is subject to certain restraining orders; convicted of a misdemeanor crime of domestic violence under Federal, State or Tribal law; has renounced his/her U.S. citizenship; is an alien illegally in the United States or an alien admitted to the United States under a nonimmigrant visa. Furthermore, section 922(n) prohibits the shipment, transportation, or receipt in or affecting interstate commerce of a firearm by one who is under indictment or information for a felony in any Federal, State or local court, or any other crime, punishable by imprisonment for a term exceeding one year. An information is a formal accusation of a crime verified by a prosecutor.

A member of the Armed Forces must answer "yes" to 11.b. or 11.c. if charged with an offense that was either referred to a General Court Martial, or at which the member was convicted. Discharged "under dishonorable conditions" means separation from the Armed Forces resulting from a dishonorable discharge or dismissal adjudged by a General Court-Martial. That term does not include any other discharge or separation from the Armed Forces.

EXCEPTION: A person who has been convicted of a felony, or any other crime, for which the judge could have imprisoned the person for more than one year, or who has been convicted of a misdemeanor crime of domestic violence, is not prohibited from purchasing, receiving, or possessing a firearm if: (1) under the law of the jurisdiction where the conviction occurred, the person has been pardoned, the conviction has been expunged or set aside, or the person has had their civil rights *(the right to vote, sit on a jury, and hold public office)* taken away and later restored, AND (2) the person is not prohibited by the law of the jurisdiction where the conviction occurred from receiving or possessing firearms. Persons subject to this exception, or who receive relief from disabilities under 18 U.S.C. 925(c), should answer "no" to the applicable question.

Question 11.d. Fugitive from Justice: Any person who has fled from any State to avoid prosecution for a felony or a misdemeanor; or any person who leaves the State to avoid giving testimony in any criminal proceeding. The term also includes any person who knows that misdemeanor or felony charges are pending against such person and who leaves the State of prosecution.

Question 11.f. Adjudicated as a Mental Defective: A determination by a court, board, commission, or other lawful authority that a person, as a result of marked subnormal intelligence, or mental illness, incompetency, condition, or disease: (1) is a danger to himself or to others; or (2) lacks the mental capacity to contract or manage his own affairs. This term shall include: (1) a finding of insanity by a court in a criminal case; and (2) those persons found incompetent to stand trial or found not guilty by reason of lack of mental responsibility.

Committed to a Mental Institution: A formal commitment of a person to a mental institution by a court, board, commission, or other lawful authority. The term includes a commitment to a mental institution involuntarily. The term includes commitment for mental defectiveness or mental illness. It also includes commitments for other reasons, such as for drug use. The term does not include a person in a mental institution for observation or a voluntary admission to a mental institution.

EXCEPTION: Under the NICS Improvement Amendments Act of 2007, a person who has been adjudicated as a mental defective or committed to a mental institution in a State proceeding is not prohibited by the adjudication or commitment if

ATF E-Form 4473 (5300.9)
Revised October 2016

the person has been granted relief by the adjudicating/committing State pursuant to a qualifying mental health relief from disabilities program. Also, a person who has been adjudicated as a mental defective or committed to a mental institution by a department or agency of Federal Government is not prohibited by the adjudication or commitment if either: (a) the person's adjudication or commitment was set-aside or expunged by the adjudicating/committing agency; (b) the person has been fully released or discharged from all mandatory treatment, supervision, or monitoring by the agency; (c) the person was found by the agency to no longer suffer from the mental health condition that served as the basis of the initial adjudication/ commitment; or (d) the adjudication or commitment, respectively, is based solely on a medical finding of disability, without an opportunity for a hearing by a court, board, commission, or other lawful authority, and the person has not been adjudicated as a mental defective consistent with section 922(g)(4) of title 18, United States Code; (e) the person was granted relief from the adjudicating/ committing agency pursuant to a qualified mental health relief from disabilities program. **Persons who fall within one of the above exceptions should answer "no" to question 11.f.** This exception to an adjudication or commitment by a Federal department or agency does **not** apply to any person who was adjudicated to be not guilty by reason of insanity, or based on lack of mental responsibility, or found incompetent to stand trial, in any criminal case or under the Uniform Code of Military Justice.

Question 11.h. Qualifying Restraining Orders: Under 18 U.S.C. 922, firearms may not be sold to or received by persons subject to a court order that: (A) was issued after a hearing which the person received actual notice of and had an opportunity to participate in; (B) restrains such person from harassing, stalking, or threatening an intimate partner or child of such intimate partner or person, or engaging in other conduct that would place an intimate partner in reasonable fear of bodily injury to the partner or child; and (C)(i) includes a finding that such person represents a credible threat to the physical safety of such intimate partner or child; or (ii) by its terms explicitly prohibits the use, attempted use, or threatened use of physical force against such intimate partner or child that would reasonably be expected to cause bodily injury. An "intimate partner" of a person is: the spouse or former spouse of the person, the parent of a child of the person, or an individual who cohabitates or has cohabitated with the person.

Question 11.i. Misdemeanor Crime of Domestic Violence: A Federal, State, local, or tribal offense that is a misdemeanor under Federal, State, or tribal law and has, as an element, the use or attempted use of physical force, or the threatened use of a deadly weapon, committed by a current or former spouse, parent, or guardian of the victim, by a person with whom the victim shares a child in common, by a person who is cohabiting with, or has cohabited with the victim as a spouse, parent, or guardian, or by a person similarly situated to a spouse, parent, or guardian of the victim. The term includes all misdemeanors that have as an element the use or attempted use of physical force or the threatened use of a deadly weapon *(e.g., assault and battery)*, if the offense is committed by one of the defined parties. *(See Exception to 11.b. - 12.)* A person who has been convicted of a misdemeanor crime of domestic violence also is not prohibited unless: (1) the person was represented by a lawyer or gave up the right to a lawyer; or (2) if the person was entitled to a jury, was tried by a jury, or gave up the right to a jury trial. Persons subject to this exception should answer **"no"** to 11.i.

Question 12.d. Immigration Status: An alien admitted to the United States under a nonimmigrant visa includes, among others, persons visiting the United States temporarily for business or pleasure, persons studying in the United States who maintain a residence abroad, and certain temporary foreign workers. These aliens must answer "yes" to this question and provide the additional documentation required under question 18.c. Permanent resident aliens and aliens legally admitted to the United States pursuant to either the Visa Waiver Program or to regulations otherwise exempting them from visa requirements may answer "no" to this question and are not required to submit the additional documentation under question 18.c.

Question 13. U.S.-issued Alien Number or Admission Number: U.S.-issued alien and admission numbers may be found on the following U.S. Department of Homeland Security documents: Legal Resident Card or Employment Authorization Card (AR# or USCIS#); Arrival/Departure Record, Form I94, or Form 797A (I94#). Additional information can be obtained from www.cbp.gov. If you are a U.S. citizen or U.S. national then this question should be left blank.

Question 14. Under 18 U.S.C. 922(a)(1), it is unlawful for a person to engage in the business of dealing in firearms without a license. A person is engaged in the business of dealing in firearms if he/she devotes time, attention, and labor to dealing in firearms as a regular course of trade or business with the principal

objective of livelihood and profit through the repetitive purchase and resale of firearms. A license is not required of a person who only makes occasional sales, exchanges, or purchases of firearms for the enhancement of a personal collection or for a hobby, or who sells all or part of his/her personal collection of firearms.

Section B

Question 16. Type of Firearm(s): "Other" refers to frames, receivers and other firearms that are neither handguns nor long guns (rifles or shotguns), such as firearms having a pistol grip that expel a shotgun shell, or National Firearms Act (NFA) firearms, including silencers.

If a frame or receiver can only be made into a long gun *(rifle or shotgun)*, it is still a frame or receiver not a handgun or long gun. However, frames and receivers are still "firearms" by definition, and subject to the same GCA limitations as any other firearms. See Section 921(a)(3)(B). Section 922(b)(1) makes it unlawful for a licensee to sell any firearm other than a shotgun or rifle to any person under the age of 21. Since a frame or receiver for a firearm, to include one that can only be made into a long gun, is a "firearm other than a shotgun or rifle," it cannot be transferred to anyone under the age of 21, nor can these firearms be transferred to anyone who is not a resident of the State where the transfer is to take place. Also, note that multiple sales forms are not required for frames or receivers of any firearms, or pistol grip shotguns, since they are not "pistols or revolvers" under Section 923(g)(3)(A).

Question 17. Qualifying Gun Show or Event: As defined in 27 CFR 478.100, a gun show or event is a function sponsored by any national, State, or local organization, devoted to the collection, competitive use, or other sporting use of firearms, or an organization or association that sponsors functions devoted to the collection, competitive use, or other sporting use of firearms in the community.

Question 18.a. Identification: Before a licensee may sell or deliver a firearm to a nonlicensee, the licensee must establish the identity, place of residence, and age of the transferee/buyer. The transferee/buyer **must** provide a valid government-issued photo identification document to the transferor/seller that contains the transferee's/buyer's name, residence address, and date of birth. A driver's license or an identification card issued by a State in place of a license is acceptable. Social Security cards are not acceptable because no address, date of birth, or photograph is shown on the cards. A combination of government-issued documents may be provided. See instructions for question 18.b. Supplemental Documentation.

If the transferee/buyer is a member of the Armed Forces on active duty acquiring a firearm in the State where his/her permanent duty station is located, but he/she has a driver's license from another State, the transferor/seller should list the transferee's/buyer's military identification card and official orders showing where his/her permanent duty station is located in response to question 18.a. Licensees may accept electronic PCS orders to establish residency.

Question 18.b. Supplemental Documentation: Licensees may accept a combination of valid government-issued documents to satisfy the identification document requirements of the law. The required valid government-issued photo identification document bearing the name, photograph, and date of birth of transferee/buyer may be supplemented by another valid, government-issued document showing the transferee's/buyer's residence address. This supplemental documentation should be recorded in question 18.b., with the issuing authority and type of identification presented. For example, if the transferee/buyer has two States of residence and is trying to buy a handgun in State X, he may provide a driver's license *(showing his name, date of birth, and photograph)* issued by State Y and another government-issued document *(such as a tax document)* from State X showing his residence address. A valid electronic document from a government website may be used as supplemental documentation provided it contains the transferee's/buyer's name and current residence address.

Question 18.c. Exceptions to the Nonimmigrant Alien Prohibition and Acceptable Documentation: An alien admitted to the United States under a nonimmigrant visa is not prohibited from purchasing, receiving, or possessing a firearm if the alien: (1) is in possession of a hunting license or permit lawfully issued by the Federal Government, a State or local government, or an Indian tribe federally recognized by the Bureau of Indian Affairs, which is valid and unexpired; (2) was admitted to the United States for lawful hunting or sporting purposes; (3) has received a waiver from the prohibition from the Attorney General of the United States; (4) is an official representative of a foreign government who is accredited to the United States Government or the Government's mission to an international organization having its

ATF E-Form 4473 (5300.9)
Revised October 2016

headquarters in the United States; (5) is an official representative of a foreign government who is en route to or from another country to which that alien is accredited; (6) is an official of a foreign government or a distinguished foreign visitor who has been so designated by the Department of State; or (7) is a foreign law enforcement officer of a friendly foreign government entering the United States on official law enforcement business.

Question 19. NICS BACKGROUND CHECKS: 18 U.S.C. 922(t) requires that prior to transferring any firearm to an unlicensed person, a licensed importer, manufacturer, or dealer must first contact the National Instant Criminal Background Check System (NICS). NICS will advise the licensee whether the system finds any information that the purchaser is prohibited by law from possessing or receiving a firearm. For purposes of this form, contacts to NICS include State agencies designated as points-of-contact ("or POCs") to conduct NICS checks for the Federal Government.

The licensee should NOT contact NICS and must stop the transaction if there is reasonable cause to believe that the transferee/buyer is prohibited from receiving or possessing a firearm, including if: the transferee/buyer answers "no" to question 11.a.; the transferee/buyer answers "yes" to any question in 11.b. - 11.i. or 12.b. - 12.c.; the transferee/buyer has answered "yes" to question 12.d.l., and answered "no" to question 12.d.2.; or the transferee/buyer cannot provide the documentation required by questions 18.a, b, or c. **WARNING:** Any person who transfers a firearm to any person he/she knows or has reasonable cause to believe is prohibited from receiving or possessing a firearm violates the law, even if the transferor/seller has complied with the Federal background check requirements.

At the time that NICS is contacted, the licensee must record in question 19.a. - 19.c.: the date of contact, the NICS *(or State)* transaction number, and the initial (first) response provided by NICS or the State. The licensee may record the date the firearms may be transferred to the transferee/buyer (also known as the Missing Disposition Information (MDI) date) in 19.c. that NICS provides for delayed transactions *(States may not provide this date)*. If the licensee receives any subsequent response(s) before transferring the firearm, the licensee must record in question 19.d. any response later provided by NICS or the State, or that no response was provided within 3 business days. If the transaction was denied and later overturned in addition to checking the "Proceed" and entering the date, the licensee must also check the "Overturned" box and, if provided, attach the overturn certificate issued by NICS or the State POC to the ATF Form 4473. If the licensee receives a response from NICS or the State after the firearm has been transferred, he/she must record this information in question 19.e. **Note:** States acting as points of contact for NICS checks may use terms other than *"proceed," "delayed," "cancelled,"* or *"denied."* In such cases, the licensee should check the box that corresponds to the State's response. Some States may not provide a transaction number for denials. However, if a firearm is transferred within the three business day period, a transaction number is required.

NICS responses: If NICS provides a *"proceed"* response, the transaction may proceed. If NICS provides a *"cancelled"* or *"denied"* response, the transferor/seller is prohibited from transferring the firearm to the transferee/buyer. If NICS provides a *"delayed"* response, the transferor/seller is prohibited from transferring the firearm unless 3 business days have elapsed and, before the transfer, NICS or the State has not advised the transferor/seller that the transferee's/buyer's receipt or possession of the firearm would be in violation of law. (See 27 CFR 478.102(a) for an example of how to calculate 3 business days.) If NICS provides a *"delayed"* response, NICS also will provide a Missing Disposition Information (MDI) date that calculates the 3 business days and reflects when the firearm(s) can be transferred under Federal law. States may not provide an MDI date. *State law may impose a waiting period on transferring firearms.*

Questions 20 and 21. NICS Exceptions: A NICS check is not required if the transfer qualifies for any of the exceptions in 27 CFR 478.102(d). Generally these include: (a) transfers of National Firearms Act firearms to an individual who has undergone a background check during the NFA approval process; (b) transfers where the transferee/buyer has presented the licensee with a permit or license that allows the transferee/buyer to possess, acquire, or carry a firearm, and the permit has been recognized by ATF as a valid alternative to the NICS check requirement; or (c) transfers certified by ATF as exempt because compliance with the NICS check requirements is impracticable. If the transfer qualifies for one of these exceptions, the licensee must obtain the documentation required by 27 CFR 478.131. A firearm must **not** be transferred to any transferee/buyer who fails to provide such documentation.

A NICS check must be conducted if an NFA firearm has been approved for transfer to a trust, or to a legal entity such as a corporation, and no background check was conducted as part of the NFA approval process on the individual who will receive the firearm. Individuals who have undergone a background check during the NFA application process are listed on the approved NFA transfer form.

Section C

Questions 22 and 23. Transfer on a Different Day and Recertification: If the transfer takes place on a different day from the date that the transferee/buyer signed Section A, the licensee must again check the photo identification of the transferee/buyer at the time of transfer.

Section D

Question 24-28. Firearm(s) Description: These blocks must be completed with the firearm(s) information. Firearms manufactured after 1968 by Federal firearms licensees should all be marked with a serial number. Should you acquire a firearm that is legally not marked with a serial number (i.e. pre-1968); you may answer question 26 with "NSN" (No Serial Number), "N/A" or "None."

If more than four firearms are involved in a transaction, the information required by Section D, questions 24-28, must be provided for the additional firearms on a separate sheet of paper, which must be attached to this ATF Form 4473.

Types of firearms include, but are not limited to: pistol, revolver, rifle, shotgun, receiver, frame and other firearms that are neither handguns nor long guns (rifles or shotguns), such as firearms having a pistol grip that expel a shotgun shell (pistol grip firearm) or NFA firearms (machinegun, silencer, short-barreled shotgun, short-barreled rifle, destructive device or "any other weapon").

Additional firearms purchases by the same transferee/buyer may not be added to the form after the transferor/seller has signed and dated it. A transferee/buyer who wishes to acquire additional firearms after the transferor/seller has signed and dated the form must complete a new ATF Form 4473 and undergo a new NICS check.

Question 31. This item is for the licensee's use in recording any information he/she finds necessary to conduct business.

Question 32. Check this box, or write "Private Party Transfer" in question 31, if the licensee is facilitating the sale or transfer of a firearm between private unlicensed individuals in accordance with ATF Procedure 2013-1. This will assist the licensee by documenting which transaction records correspond with private party transfers, and why there may be no corresponding A&D entries when the transfer did not proceed because it was denied, delayed, or cancelled.

Privacy Act Information

Solicitation of this information is authorized under 18 U.S.C. 923(g). Disclosure of this information by the transferee/buyer is mandatory for the transfer of a firearm. Disclosure of the individual's Social Security number is voluntary. The number may be used to verify the transferee's/buyer's identity.

For information about the routine uses of this form see System of Records Notice Justice/ATF-008, Regulatory Enforcement Records System (68 FR 163558, January 24, 2003).

Paperwork Reduction Act Notice

The information required on this form is in accordance with the Paperwork Reduction Act of 1995. The purpose of the information is to determine the eligibility of the transferee to receive and possess firearms under Federal law. The information is subject to inspection by ATF officers and is required by 18 U.S.C. 922 and 923.

The estimated average burden associated with this collection is 30 minutes per respondent or recordkeeper, depending on individual circumstances. Comments about the accuracy of this burden estimate and suggestions for reducing it should be directed to Reports Management Officer, IT Coordination Staff, Bureau of Alcohol, Tobacco, Firearms and Explosives, Washington, DC 20226.

An agency may not conduct or sponsor, and a person is not required to respond to, a collection of information unless it displays a currently valid OMB control number. Confidentiality is not assured.

ATF E-Form 4473 (5300.9)
Revised October 2016

ATF FORM 6 – Application & Permit for Importation of Firearms

U.S. Department of Justice
Bureau of Alcohol, Tobacco, Firearms and Explosives

OMB No. 1140-0005 (07/31/2013)

Application and Permit for Importation of Firearms, Ammunition and Implements of War

Not for use by Members of the United States Armed Forces.

For ATF Use Only	For Applicant's Optional Use	
Permit No. (Valid for 12 months from the date appearing in Item 19 below.) NPR No.	Internal Control/Reference #	E-mail Address *(Optional)*

Section I - Application *(Submit in triplicate) - For Applicant Use*

1. Federal Firearms License *(If Any)*		2. Telephone No. *(Including Extension No.)*	3. Country of Exportation
License No. *(x-xx-xxx-xx-xxxxx)*	Expiration Date		

4. Name and Address of Customs Broker *(Including Zip Code)*

Check here if permit is to be returned to Customs Broker. ☐

5. Applicant's Name and Address *(Including Zip Code)*

Check here if permit is to be returned to applicant. ☐

6. Name and Address of Foreign Seller, if any

7. Name and Address of Foreign Shipper

8. Description of Firearms and Ammunition *(For firearms, enter (SG)-Shotgun; (RI)-Rifle; (PI)-Pistol; (RE)-Revolver; (DD)-Destructive Device; (MG)-Machinegun)*

	Name and Address of Manufacturer	Type *(Frame, Receiver, SG, RI, PI, RE, DD, MG)*	Caliber Guage or Size	Quantity *(Each type)*	Unit Cost *(U.S. Currency)*	U.S. Munitions Import List Category	Model	Length of Barrel *(Inches)*	Overall Length *(Inches)*	Serial No.	New (N) or Used (U)
	a.	b.	c.	d.	e.	f.	g.	h.	i.	j.	k.
Firearms ☐ See Attachement											
Implements of War ☐ See Attachement							Description				
Ammunition ☐ See Attachement		*(Ball Wad-cutter, Shot, AP, Tracer)* *(Rounds)*									

9. Certification of Origin. The items sought for importation in block 8:
a. Do not contain parts or components produced by or for the U.S. **military** and do not contain parts or components manufactured with U.S. military technical data or assistance. ☐
b. Contain parts or components produced by or for the U.S. **military** or parts or components manufactured with U.S. military technical data or assistance. ☐
c. Contain parts or components produced by or for the U.S. **military** or components manufactured with U.S. technical data or assistance that were sold abroad pursuant to a Direct Commercial Sale licensed by the Department of State. ☐

10. Specific Purpose of Importation, Including Final Recipient, If Known *(Use additional sheets, if necessary)*

11. Are You Registered as an Importer Pursuant to The Arms Export Control Act of 1976 Yes ☐ No ☐	12. If "Yes," Give Importer's Registration No. and Expiration Date *(A-xx-xxx-xxxx)*

Under the penalties provided by law, I declare that I have examined this application, including the documents submitted in support of it, and, to the best of my knowledge and belief, it is true, correct, and complete.

13. Name of Applicant *(Printed)*	14. Signature of Applicant	15. Title	16. Date

Section II - For ATF Use Only *(Please make no entries in this section)*

17. The Application Has Been Examined and the Importation of the Firearms, Ammunition, and Implements of War Described Herein is:

Approved ☐ Partially Approved for the Reason Indicated Here or on Attached Letter ☐	Disapproved for the Reason Indicated Here or on Attached Letter ☐ Withdrawn By Applicant Without Action ☐	Returned Without Action for Additional Information ☐ No Permits Required ☐

18. Signature of the Director, Bureau of Alcohol, Tobacco, Firearms and Explosives	19. Date

ATF E-Form 6-Part I (5330.3A)
Revised August 2011

359

Instruction Sheet for ATF Form 6 Part I (5330.3A)
(Submit in triplicate) (Detach this instruction sheet before submitting your application)

Paperwork Reduction Act Notice

This request is in accordance with the Paperwork Reduction Act of 1995. The purpose of this information collection is to allow ATF to determine if the article(s) described on the application qualifies for importation by the importer, and to serve as the authorization for the importer. This information is mandatory (18 U.S.C. 925(d), 26 U.S.C. 5844, 22 U.S.C. 2778).

The estimated average burden associated with this collection of information is 30 minutes per respondent or recordkeeper, depending on individual circumstances. Comments concerning the accuracy of this burden estimate and suggestions for reducing this burden should be addressed to Reports Management Officer, Document Services, Bureau of Alcohol, Tobacco, Firearms and Explosives, Washington, DC 20226.

An agency may not conduct or sponsor, and a person is not required to respond to, a collection of information unless it displays a currently valid OMB control number. Confidentiality is not assured.

General Information

1. An approved ATF Form 6 - Part I (5330.3A) is required to import firearms, ammunition, and implements of war into the United States or any possession thereof, except for certain exempt importations prescribed in 27 CFR Parts 447, 478 and 479. A military member of the U.S. Armed Forces who is on active duty outside the U.S., or who has been on active duty outside the U.S. during the 60-day period immediately preceding the intended importation, should complete ATF Form 6 - Part II (5330.3B) to import sporting type firearms or ammunition for his personal use.

2. Any person engaged in the business of importing firearms or ammunition for resale must be licensed as an importer under the Gun Control Act of 1968 and, if he is importing firearms, ammunition, firearms parts or implements of war *(other than sporting shotguns, shotgun shells, or shotgun parts)* he must also be registered as an importer under the Arms Export Control Act of 1976. No permit to import such articles for resale will be issued until the importer is properly licensed and registered.

3. A Federal firearms licensee other than an importer, may make an occasional importation of sporting firearms or ammunition *(excluding surplus military)* for himself or an unlicensed person in the licensee's State, provided that the firearms and ammunition are intended for personal use of the person for whom imported and not for resale. ATF Form 6 - Part I (5330.3A) is used to obtain approval for such importation.

4. A permit is not required for a firearm or ammunition brought into the United States or any possession thereof by any person who can establish to the satisfaction of U.S. Customs and Border Protection (CBP) that such firearm or ammunition was previously taken out of the United States or any possession thereof by such person.

5. A permit is not required for the return of a repaired firearm, or replacement firearm of the same kind and type, to the person in the United States who sent the defective firearm out of the United States for repair.

6. If you are a nonimmigrant alien do not complete this form. A nonimmigrant alien entering the U.S. temporarily needs to submit an ATF Form 6NIA (5330.3D) (Application and Permit for Temporary Importation of Firearms and Ammunition by Nonimmigrant Aliens) to temporarily import his personally owned firearms.

7. An unlicensed person may obtain a permit to import sporting type ammunition (excluding tracer or incendiary) and firearm parts (other than frames, receivers or actions) without engaging the services of a Federal firearms licensee, provided that the importation is for his personal use and not for resale.

8. A nonresident U.S. citizen returning to the United States or a nonresident alien immigrating to the United States, from a permanent residence outside of the United States may complete and forward the enclosed ATF Form 6 Part I permit application without having to utilize the services of a federally licensed firearms dealer. The nonresident should include a statement, either on the application form or on an attached sheet, that the firearms are being imported for his personal use and not for resale and that he is a nonresident U.S. citizen returning to the United States, or is a nonresident alien

immigrating to the United States. The firearms must accompany the nonresident U.S. citizen on entry into the United States, since once he is in the United States, and has acquired residence in a State, he may not directly import a firearm. He must engage the services of a federally licensed firearms dealer in his State of residence to import the sporting firearms *(excluding NFA and surplus military)* for him. A nonresident alien must bring in their firearms within 90 days of arrival in the United States, which is when they obtain State residency. If the firearms are to be imported after 90 days of arrival, he must engage the services of a federally licensed firearms dealer in his State of residence to import the sporting firearms *(excluding NFA and surplus military)* for him.

9. Under Arms Export Control Act of 1976 regulations in 27 CFR 447.41(c), a permit is not required for the importation of:

   a. U.S. Munitions Import List articles from Canada not subject to 27 CFR Part 478 and 479, except articles enumerated in Categories I, II, III, IV, VI(e), VIII(a), XVI, and XX; and nuclear weapons, strategic delivery systems, and all specifically designed components, parts, accessories, attachments, and associated equipment thereof.

   b. Minor components and parts of Category I(a) firearms, except barrels, cylinders, receivers (frames) or complete breech mechanisms, when the total value does not exceed $100 wholesale in any single transaction.

Preparation

10. The applicant shall prepare this form in triplicate. Required signatures must be in ink on all copies. Other entries must be in ink or be typewritten.

11. The application should be submitted approximately 60 days prior to the intended importation. All copies shall be submitted to:

    > Director
    > Bureau of Alcohol, Tobacco, Firearms, and Explosives
    > 244 Needy Road
    > Martinsburg, WV 25405
    > Attention: Firearms and Explosives Imports Branch

12. Any questions concerning the application should be referred to the Imports Branch at the above address or telephone (304) 616-4550.

13. If a licensee is applying to import an article for subsequent transfer to a known final recipient *(e.g., an individual, commercial entity, or government agency)*, the licensee must complete items 1 through 16, and identify the final recipient by name and address in item 10.

14. Item 9, Certification of Origin: The purpose of this certification is to determine whether items sought for importation require retransfer authorization from the Department of State. Applicants should check block 9a if the articles sought for importation were produced for the civilian market and were not associated with the U.S. military. Applicants should check block 9b if the articles sought for importation contain parts or components produced by or for the U.S. military or manufactured with U.S. military technical data or assistance, and the articles were provided by the U.S. government to a foreign government through a grant or foreign military sales program. Applicants should check block 9c if the articles sought for importation contain parts or components produced by or for the U.S. military or manufactured with U.S. military technical data or assistance, and the articles were sold abroad pursuant to an export license issued by the Department of State authorizing a Direct Commercial Sale (DCS). **NOTE:** If block 9b is checked, a written retransfer authorization from the Department of State must be attached to the application or the applications will be denied. **NOTE:** If block 9c is checked, either a copy of the export license authorizing the DCS or a written retransfer authorization from the Department of State must be attached to the application or the application will be denied.

Approval

15. The Director will approve the application or advise the applicant of the reason for the disapproval. In some cases it may be necessary to request additional

(INSTRUCTIONS CONTINUED ON REVERSE)

ATF E-Form 6-Part I (5330.3A)
Revised August 2011

information or to have the firearm or ammunition sent to ATF for examination to determine the import status.

16. The permit is valid for 12 months from the date of approval. The approved application will serve as the permit to import the article(s) described on the form.

17. After approval, the Director will retain one copy and forward the original to the applicant or his designated agent, along with copies of ATF Form 6A, Release and Receipt of Imported Firearms, Ammunition and Implements of War.

Release From Customs

18. No amendments or alterations may be made to an approved permit, except by the Director.

19. An approved ATF Form 6 - Part I (5330.3A) which is unused, expired suspended or revoked shall be returned immediately to the Director, Bureau of ATF, 244 Needy Road Martinsburg, WV 25405
Attention: Firearms and Explosives Imports Branch.

20. The ATF Form 6A, in duplicate with Section I completed, the approved permit, and any other necessary documents, must be presented to CBP officials handling the importation to effect release of the articles. For the commercial import (*i.e., import for resale*) of firearms, firearms parts and components, and ammunition, the importer also must present to CBP, in order to effect release of the articles, either a corresponding export license issued by the exporting country or a statement, under penalty of perjury, that the exporting country does not issue export licenses.

21. The CBP officer, after determining that the importation is in order, will execute the certificate of release on ATF Form 6A.

22. The CBP officer will forward the ATF Form 6A to the address shown on the form and return the permit and any additional copies of ATF F 6A, to the applicant.

Prohibited Persons Under U.S. Law

23. The importer of a firearm should be familiar with provisions of law governing who may lawfully possess a firearm in the United States. Generally, 18 U.S.C. 922 prohibits the shipment, transportation, receipt, or possession in or affecting interstate commerce of a firearm by one who has been convicted of a crime punishable by imprisonment for a term exceeding one year; by one who is a fugitive from justice; by one who is an unlawful user of, or addicted to,

marijuana, or any depressant, stimulant, or narcotic drug, or any other controlled substance; by one who has been adjudicated mentally defective or has been committed to a mental institution; by one who has been discharged from the Armed Forces under dishonorable conditions; by one who has renounced his or her U.S. citizenship; by one who is an alien illegally in the United States or is a nonimmigrant alien; by one who is subject to certain restraining orders; or by one who has been convicted of a misdemeanor crime of domestic violence. Furthermore, section 922 prohibits the shipment, transportation, or receipt in or affecting interstate commerce of a firearm by one who is under indictment or information for a crime punishable by imprisonment for a term exceeding one year.

Forms

24. Federal firearms licensees must retain this form as part of their ATF required records permanently as prescribed by 27 CFR 478.129(d). Importers registered under the Arms Export Control Act who do not also hold a Federal firearms license must retain this form as part of their ATF required records for at least the 6-year period prescribed by 27 CFR 447.34(b).

Additional Forms are available from:

> ATF Distribution Center
> 1519 Cabin Branch Drive
> Landover, MD 20785-3816

Or by accessing the ATF website at http://www.atf.gov

Privacy Act Information

The following information is provided pursuant to Section 3 of the Privacy Act of 1974 (5 U.S.C. § 552a(e)(3)).

1. **Authority.** Disclosure of the information requested on ATF Form 6 Part I (5330.3A) is mandatory pursuant to 18 U.S.C. 925 and Section 38 of the Arms Export Control Act of 1976 (22 U.S.C. 2778, 26 U.S.C. 5844) to obtain a permit to import firearms, ammunition, and implements of war.

2. **Purpose.** To determine if the article(s) qualifies for importation by the applicant.

3. **Routine Uses.** The information will be used by ATF to make determinations set forth in paragraph 2. In addition, information may be disclosed to other Federal, State, foreign and local law enforcement and regulatory agency personnel to verify information on the application and to aid in the performance of their duties with respect to the enforcement and regulation of firearms and/or ammunition where such disclosure is not prohibited by law. The information may further be disclosed to the Justice Department if it appears that the furnishing of false information may constitute a violation of Federal law. Finally, the information may be disclosed to members of the public in order to verify the information on the application when such disclosure is not prohibited by law.

4. **Effects.** Failure to supply complete information will delay processing and may cause denial of the application.

ATF E-Form 6-Part I (5330.3A)
Revised August 2011

U.S. Department of Justice
Bureau of Alcohol, Tobacco, Firearms and Explosives

OMB No. 1140-0007 (07/31/2014)

Release and Receipt of Imported Firearms, Ammunition and Implements of War

(See Instructions on Back)

Section I - Importation Information *(Use a separate ATF Form 6A (5330.3C) to describe articles imported under each permit. Also, use a separate form for each shipment under the same permit.)*

1. Name and Address of Importer	2. Name and Address of Foreign Seller
	3. Name and Address of Foreign Shipper
4. Federal License No. and/or AECA No. *(If any)* ▶ Expiration Dates	5. Country Where Manufactured *(Required)*
6. Import Permit No. *(When importation authorized by permit)* *(Required)*	7. Telephone No.	8. Gross Value of Shipment *(In U.S. dollars)*

9. Shipment of Firearms, Ammunition and/or Implements of War *(For firearms, enter (SG)-Shotgun; (RI)-Rifle; (RE)-Revolver; (DD)-Destructive Device; (MG)- Machinegun; (SI) Silencer; Frame or Receiver)*

	Name of Manufacturer a	Number and Kind of Packages b	Type c	Caliber Gauge or Size d	Quantity *(Each type)* e	U.S. Munitions Import List Category f	Model g	Serial No. h
Firearms								
Implements of War								
Ammunition			*(Ball Incendiary, Wadcutter, Shot, AP, Tracer)*					

Section II - Certification of Release From U.S. Customs and Border Protection

10. Port of Entry	11. Customs Entry or ID No.	12. Type of Entry ☐ Consumption ☐ Warehouse ☐ Informal	13. Date Released

14. I certify that the above articles were authorized for importation by the Director, Bureau of Alcohol, Tobacco, Firearms and Explosives, and were released from the custody of the U.S. Customs and Border Protection or were authorized to be removed from a Customs bonded warehouse or foreign trade zone.
Import Permit Number:

15. Signature of Customs and Border Protection Official	16. Title	17. Date

Section III - Verification of Importation (completed by licensed and/or registered importers only)

18. I have examined the above shipment and found it to:

☐ Contain the firearms, ammunition and/or implements of war in the exact quantity and as described in Item 9 above, or

☐ Contain the following discrepancies:

I declare under the penalties provided by law, that this verification of importation is true, correct and complete to the best of my knowledge and belief and that each firearm is marked and can be identified as required by 27 CFR Part 478.

19. Signature of Importer	20. Title or Status *(Individual, member of firm; if officer of corporation, give title)*	21. Date

ATF Form 6A (5330.3C)
Revised August 2011

Instructions for Federally Licensed and/or Registered Importers.

1. ATF Form 6A (5330.3C) is required for every importation of firearm(s), ammunition, and/or implements of war, with certain exceptions listed in 27 CFR Parts 447 and 478.

2. **Section I.** Importation Information. To obtain release of firearm(s), ammunition, and/or implements of war from the custody of U.S. Customs and Border Protection, the importer must complete Section I of the form, in duplicate, and present one copy to U.S. Customs and Border Protection along with his import permit, ATF Form 6 Part I (5330.3A). If the import includes a large number of firearms for which the serial numbers are not known at the time of import, the serial numbers must be reported in Section III of the form *(see below)* within 15 days after import.

    If the import is for firearms, their parts or components, or ammunition, the importer also must present to U.S. Customs and Border Protection a copy of the export license authorizing the export of the article or articles from the exporting country. If the exporting country does not require issuance of an export license, the importer instead must present to U.S.Customs and Border Protection a certification, under penalty of perjury, to that effect.

3. **Section II.** Certification of Release from U.S. Customs and Border Protection. The U.S. Customs and Border Protection official should complete Section II of this form if he is satisfied that the shipment of firearm(s), ammunition, and/or implements of war was authorized by the Director, Bureau of Alcohol, Tobacco, Firearms and Explosives. The U.S. Customs and Border Protection official should return the import permit, ATF Form 6 - Part I (5330.3A) to the importer and mail ATF Form 6A, with Section II completed, to the address specified below.

4. **Section III.** Verification of Importation. Within 15 days after the article(s) has been released from U.S. Customs and Border Protection, the licensed and/or registered importer must complete Section III of the duplicate copy of ATF Form 6A and mail it to the address specified below.

    Title 27 CFR Part 478 requires that within 15 days after release from U.S. Customs and Border Protection, each firearm imported shall be identified by engraving or casting on it the following: (1) serial number, (2) model, (3) caliber or gauge, (4) name of manufacturer and country where manufactured, and (5) the name, city, and State of the importer. If firearms serial numbers were not known or reported at the time of import, the importer must report those serial numbers in an attachment to block 18. He also must post in his permanent records all required information regarding the importation (27 CFR 478.112).

Instructions for Federal Firearms Licensees other than Importers.

1. ATF Form 6A is required for every importation of firearm(s), ammunition, and/or implements of war, with certain exceptions listed in 27 CFR Parts 447 and 478.

2. **Section I.** Importation Information. To obtain release of firearm(s), ammunition, and/or implements of war from the custody of U.S. Customs and Border Protection, the licensee must complete Section I of the form and present it to U.S. Customs and Border Protection along with his import permit, ATF Form 6-Part I (5330.3A).

3. **Section II.** Certification of Release from U.S. Customs and Border Protection. The U.S. Customs and Border Protection official should complete Section II of this form if he is satisfied that the shipment of firearm(s), ammunition, and/or implements of war was authorized by the Director, Bureau of Alcohol, Tobacco, Firearms and Explosives. The U.S. Customs and Border Protection official should return the import permit, ATF Form 6 - Part I (5330.3A) to the licensee and mail ATF Form 6A, with Section II completed, to the address specified below.

Instructions for Members of the U.S. Armed Forces

1. ATF Form 6A is required for the importation of firearms, ammunition or implements of war authorized for importation on ATF Form 6 -Part II (5330.3B).

2. **Section I.** Importation Information. To obtain release of firearms or ammunition from the custody of U.S. Customs and Border Protection, the member of the United States Armed Forces must complete Section I of the form and present it to U.S. Customs and Border Protection along with his import permit, ATF Form 6-Part II (5330.3B).

3. **Section II.** Certification of Release from U.S. Customs and Border Protection. The U.S. Customs and Border Protection official should complete Section II of this form if he is satisfied that the shipment of firearms, ammunition or implements of war was authorized by the Director, Bureau of Alcohol, Tobacco, Firearms and Explosives. The U.S. Customs and Border Protection official should return the import permit, ATF Form 6-Part II (5330.3B) to the member of the Armed Forces and mail ATF Form 6A, with Section II completed, to the address specified below.

Instructions for Persons not Licensed by or Registered with ATF

1. ATF Form 6A is required for the importation of firearm(s), ammunition, and/or implements of war, with certain exceptions listed in 27 CFR Parts 447 and 478.

2. **Section I.** Importation Information. To obtain release of firearm(s), ammunition, and/or implements of war from the custody of U.S. Customs and Border Protection, the individual must complete Section I of the form and present it to U.S. Customs and Border Protection along with his import permit, ATF Form 6-Part I (5330.3A).

3. **Section II.** Certification of Release from U.S. Customs and Border Protection. The U.S. Customs and Border Protection official should complete Section II of this form if he is satisfied that the shipment of firearms, ammunition, and/or implements of war was authorized by the Director, Bureau of Alcohol, Tobacco, Firearms and Explosives. The U.S. Customs and Border Protection official should return the import permit, ATF Form 6-Part I (5330.3A) to the individual and mail ATF Form 6A, with Section II completed, to the address specified below.

Record Retention Requirement

Federal firearms licensees must retain this form as part of their ATF required records permanently as prescribed by 27 CFR 478.129(d). Importers registered under the Arms Export Control Act who do not also hold a Federal firearms license must retain this form as part of their ATF required records for at least the 6-year period prescribed by 27 CFR 447.34(b).

Privacy Act Information

The following information is provided pursuant to Section 3 of the Privacy Act of 1974 (5 U.S.C. Section 552a(e)(3)).

1. **Authority.** Solicitation of this information is made pursuant to the Gun Control Act of 1968 (18 U.S.C. Chapter 44), and Section 38 of the Arms Export Control Act of 1976 (22 U.S.C. Section 2778). Disclosure of this information by the applicant is mandatory for the release and receipt of imported firearms, ammunition, and implements of war.

2. **Purpose.** To determine that the importation of firearms, ammunition, and implements of war has taken place, to verify that the item(s) was (were) released to and received by the importer or his agent, and to verify that the items released were the items listed on the application for importation.

3. **Routine Uses.** The information will be used by ATF to make the determinations set forth in paragraph 2.In addition, the information may be disclosed to other Federal, State, foreign and local law enforcement and regulatory agency personnel to verify information on the application and to aid in the performance of their duties with respect to the regulation of firearms, ammunition, and implements of war. The information may further be disclosed to the Department of Justice if it appears that the furnishing of false information may constitute a violation of Federal law.

4. **Effects of not supplying the information requested.** Failure to supply complete information will delay processing and may cause denial of the application.

ATF Form 6A (5330.3C)
Revised August 2011

Paperwork Reduction Act Notice

This request is in accordance with the Paperwork Reduction Act of 1995. This information collection is mandatory pursuant to 18 U.S.C. 925, 26 U.S.C. 5844, and 22 U.S.C. 2778. The purpose of this information collection is to allow ATF to determine that the article(s) described on the form have been released by the U.S. Customs and Border Protection to the importer and to verify that the article(s) authorized to be imported were received by the importer.

The estimated average burden associated with this collection information is 24 minutes per respondent or recordkeeper, depending on individual circumstances. Comments concerning the accuracy of this burden estimate and suggestions for reducing this burden should be directed to the Reports Management Officer, Document Services, Bureau of Alcohol, Tobacco, Firearms and Explosives, Washington, DC 20226.

An agency may not conduct or sponsor, and a person is not required to respond to, a collection of information unless it displays a currently valid OMB control number.

Mailing Information

Chief, Firearms and Explosives Imports Branch
Bureau of Alcohol, Tobacco, Firearms and Explosives
244 Needy Road
Martinsburg, WV 25405

ATF Form 6A (5330.3C)
Revised August 2011

ATF FORM 3310.11 – FFL Firearms Inventory Theft/Loss Report

U.S. Department of Justice
Bureau of Alcohol, Tobacco, Firearms and Explosives

OMB No. 1140-0039 (08/31/2017)

Federal Firearms Licensee Firearms Inventory Theft/Loss Report

All entries must be in ink. Please read notices and instructions on reverse carefully before completing this form.

Section A - Federal Firearms Licensee Information

Federal Firearms License Number	Federal Firearms Licensee Telephone Number *(Include area code)*

Trade/Corporate Name

Street Address of Federal Firearms Licensee	City	State
	Zip Code	Telephone Number *(with area code)*

Full Name of Person Making Report

Street Address of Person Making Report	City	State
	Zip Code	Telephone Number *(with area code)*

Section B - Theft/Loss Information

	Date	Time	Description of Incident
Date of Theft/Loss Discovered			☐ Burglary ☐ Robbery
			☐ Larceny ☐ Missing Inventory
Police Notification			ATF Issued Incident Number
ATF Notification			

Name of Local Authority to Whom Reported (For burglary, larceny or robbery, include the police report number and officer/detective name).

Street Address of Local Authority	Theft Location if Different from FFL Premises

City	State	Zip Code	City	State	Zip Code

Name and Telephone Number of the ATF Representative Notified *(If this report is the result of an ATF compliance inspection, provide the name and telephone number of the ATF Inspector.)*

Brief Description of Incident *(e.g., How firearms were stolen, etc.)*:

Section C - Description of Firearms

Acquisition Date	Type	Manufacturer	Model	Caliber/ Gauge	Serial Number

Certification

I hereby certify that the information contained in this report is true and correct. I also understand that failure to report the theft or loss of a firearm from my inventory or collection within 48 hours of the discovery of the theft/loss is a violation of 18 U.S.C. § 923(g)(6) punishable as a felony.

Signature of Licensee	Date

ATF E-Form 3310.11
Revised June 2014

OMB No. 1140-0039 (08/31/2017)

Important Notice

Section 923 (g), Title 18 U.S.C., requires each Federal Firearms Licensee (FFL) to report the theft/loss of a firearm from the licensee's inventory or from the collection of a licensed collector, within 48 hours of discovery **to the Bureau of Alcohol, Tobacco, Firearms and Explosives (ATF)** by calling 1-888-930-9275 and **to local law enforcement authorities.**

FFLs who report a firearm as missing and later discover its whereabouts should advise ATF that the firearms have been located. Licensees reporting theft/loss of firearms registered under the National Firearms Act must provide written notification to the National Firearms Act Branch, pursuant to 27 C.F.R. § 179.141.

This form should not be used by common carriers for reporting the theft/loss of firearms. Thefts/losses from interstate shipments must continue to be reported on ATF Form 3310.6. Interstate Firearms Shipment Report of Theft/Loss.

Instructions To Federal Firearms Licensed Dealers

1. FFLs must report the theft/loss of firearms to the ATF Stolen Firearms Program Manager within 48 hours of discovery (toll free 888-930-9275). Please leave a message and your call will be answered within the same or next business day. You may email your reports to stolenfirearmsprogrammanager@atf.gov, or via fax to (304) 260-3676 or (304) 260-3671.

2. This form is to be used to provide written notification of firearms thefts/losses **in addition to** reporting firearms thefts/losses by telephone to the ATF Stolen Firearms Program Manager. You must document in Section B the date that you reported the information by telephone. If the call is after normal business hours, you will fax or email this report to the Stolen Firearms Program via the email or fax noted below. The ATF Issued Incident Number will be provided to you at a later time to record in your A & D book. IF this is for a burglary of 10 or more, you will be directly transferred to an appropriate party to handle the incident. During normal business hours, or on the following business day, the Stolen Firearms Program Manager will provide you with an ATF Incident Number to record in this report. You will then be directed to forward a copy of this report to the address set forth in item 5 below.

3. A separate form is required for each theft/loss report. This form must be prepared in ink, signed, and dated. Please use ATF Form 3310.11A, Federal Firearms Licensee Theft/Loss Report Continuation Sheet, when the number of lost/stolen firearms exceeds the space allowed in Section C.

4. The description of the lost or stolen firearms provided in Section B of this form should be identical to the information contained in the Record of Acquisition and Disposition required by 27 CFR Part 178 Subpart H.

5. Upon completion, a copy must be maintained at your premises as part of your permanent records. A copy forwarded to the Stolen Firearms Program. You may email your report to stolenfirearmsprogrammanager@atf.gov, or via fax to (304) 260-3676 or (304) 260-3671. In the event you do not have a fax machine available, remit original to the following address:

> **Bureau of ATF**
> **National Tracing Center**
> **Attn: Stolen Firearms Program Manager**
> **244 Needy Road**
> **Martinsburg, WV 25405**

6. FFLs must reflect the theft/loss as a disposition entry in the Record of Acquisition and Disposition required by 27 CFR Part 178, Subpart H. The disposition entry should indicate whether the incident is a theft or loss, the ATF Issued Incident Number, and the Incident Number provided by the local law enforcement agency.

7. Should any of the firearms be located, they should be re-entered into the Record of Acquisition and Disposition as an acquisition entry.

8. Additional forms may be obtained through the ATF Distribution Center, 13882 Redskin Drive, Herndon, VA 20171, (703) 870-7256.

Paperwork Reduction Act Notice

The information required on this form is in accordance with the Paperwork Reduction Act of 1995. The purpose of this information is to provide notification to ATF of the theft or loss of firearms from the inventory of a Federal firearms licensee and from the collection of a licensed collector. The information is subject to inspection by ATF offices. The information on this form is required by 18 U.S.C. 923(g)(6).

The estimate average burden associated with this collection is 24 minutes per respondent or recordkeeper, depending on individual circumstances. Comments concerning the accuracy of this burden estimate and suggestions for reducing this burden should be directed to Reports Management Officer, Document Services, Bureau of Alcohol, Tobacco, Firearms and Explosives, Washington DC 20226.

An agency may not conduct or sponsor, and a person is not required to respond to, a collection of information unless it displays a currently valid OMB control number.

ATF E-Form 3310.11
Revised June 2014

U.S. Department of Justice
Bureau of Alcohol, Tobacco, Firearms
and Explosives
99 New York Avenue, NE
Washington, DC 20226
www.atf.gov

U. S. Department of Justice
Bureau of Alcohol, Tobacco, Firearms and Explosives

ATF P 5300.21
January 2013

TRANSFERS OF FIREARMS BY PRIVATE SELLERS

☐ An unlicensed individual may transfer a firearm to another unlicensed individual residing in the same State, provided that he or she has no reason to believe the buyer is prohibited by law from possessing firearms.

For a list of categories prohibiting a person from possessing a firearm, please refer to 18 U.S.C. 922(g) and (n).

☐ An unlicensed individual is prohibited from directly transferring a firearm to a person residing in another State.

Regardless of the purpose of the transfer (e.g. gift, trade, loan, sale, ownership, etc.), this restriction applies to all types of firearms.

☐ An unlicensed individual may complete a transfer to an out-of-State person through the following procedure:

- The unlicensed individual transfers the firearm to a Federal Firearms Licensee (FFL) located in the State of the person receiving the firearm.
- The FFL will transfer the firearm to the unlicensed out-of-State person.
- The FFL will be responsible for lawfully transferring the firearm.

☐ An unlicensed individual may transfer firearms directly to FFLs operating in any State.

☐ Under Federal law, there is no recordkeeping requirement pertaining to the transfer of a firearm between two unlicensed individuals.

☐ There may exist State or local laws that pertain to the transfer, including registration requirements. Contact the appropriate State agency for information regarding such requirements.

TRANSACTION ALTERNATIVES FOR PRIVATE SELLERS
(*Please remember, these are not requirements, but may prove beneficial to both you and law enforcement)

☐ For private sellers wanting assurance that other private individuals are not prohibited from possessing firearms, we encourage you to consider the following options:

- Transfer the firearm to the private individual through an FFL. The FFL will be responsible for conducting a background check on the person acquiring the firearm. The FFL will complete the required paperwork,

OR

- If you decide not to utilize the services of an FFL, examine the purchaser's identification document to confirm that the person is a resident of your State.

☐ If you are purchasing a firearm, record the acquisition in a "Personal Firearms Record," ATF P 3312.8.

- Be sure to include all identifying information marked on the firearm, including the serial number.
- List all other personal firearms in that record.
- Secure the record in a location separate from where you store your firearms.
- In the event the firearm is lost or stolen, this procedure will assist you in reporting the necessary information.
- If authorities recover the firearm this procedure may assist you in demonstrating that you are the rightful owner of the firearm.

ATF Publication 3313.8 – Personal Firearms Record

U.S. Department of Justice

Bureau of Alcohol, Tobacco, Firearms and Explosives

National Tracing Center

Lost/Stolen Firearms Investigations

Each year, thousands of firearms are reported lost or stolen. The owners' ability to adequately identify these firearms is central to law enforcement's ability to investigate these crimes and losses. Insurance claims and reacquisition of recovered firearms will also hinge on the ability to correctly identify these firearms.

By completing this record and maintaining it in a safe location, separate from your firearms, you will be not only protecting your own property, you will be taking an important first step in the effort to prevent thefts and to keep firearms out of the hands of criminals.

This is a personal record only. The information will not be collected or maintained by ATF or any other Federal Government agency.

Personal Firearms Record

Keep this list separate from your firearms to assist police in the event your firearms are ever lost or stolen.

"A stolen gun threatens everyone."

P 3312.8 (Revised August 2013)

Personal Firearms Record

Immediately report any theft or loss of firearms to your local police.

Firearms Description and Origin								
Manufacturer/ Importer	Model	Serial Number	Type	Caliber/ Gauge	Date Acquired	Cost	Purchase Location (Name and Address)	Sold/Transferred to: (Name, Address & Date)

A complete description of each firearm is vitally important to law enforcement in the investigation and recovery of your firearms and to your ability to prove ownership.

Appendix D
Sample Letter, Affidavits, and Court Orders

[AGENCY – DEPARTMENT LETTERHEAD]

CONSENT TO FORFEITURE OR DESTRUCTION OF PROPERTY

AND WAIVER OF NOTICE

I, **[PRINTED NAME],** hereby voluntarily surrender and relinquish all rights, title, and interest in, and all claims to the below-described property in order that said property may be disposed of by **[AGENCY OR DEPARTMENT]** in accordance with law. I understand that the above-described property may be subject to administrative or judicial forfeiture under State or Federal law or may otherwise be disposed of in accordance with law, including destruction as abandoned property or contraband material. I hereby expressly consent to such action by **[AGENCY OR DEPARTMENT]** without further notice.

In the event that **[AGENCY OR DEPARTMENT]** seeks to forfeit the above-described property, I understand that **[AGENCY OR DEPARTMENT]** may be required to send notice of any forfeiture proceeding. I hereby consent to the forfeiture of the above-described items. Furthermore, I expressly waive any right to receive notice of any forfeiture proceeding, any right to challenge any forfeiture, and any right to later request remission or mitigation of forfeiture or otherwise seek the return of the above-described property under Federal law. I hereby expressly waive all constitutional, legal and equitable claims arising out of and/or defenses to forfeiture of the above-described property in any proceeding, including any claim of innocent ownership and any claim or defense under the Eighth Amendment, including any claim that such forfeiture constitutes an Excessive Fine.

I further agree to unconditionally release and hold harmless the **[AGENCY OR DEPARTMENT],** its officers, employees and agents from any and all claims, grievances, entitlements, demands, damages, causes of action or suits, whether in their official or individual capacity, of whatever kind and description, and wherever situated, that might now exist or hereafter arise by reason of, or growing out of, or affecting, directly or indirectly, the possession, seizure, custody, destruction, or other lawful disposition of the above-described property. I further agree to hold harmless and indemnify the **[AGENCY OR DEPARTMENT],** its officers, employees, and agents, to the extent of the value of the above-described property, against any claims possessed by any third party that may arise in any way from the possession, seizure, custody, destruction, or other lawful disposition of the above-described property in accordance with law.

CONSENT TO FORFEITURE OR DESTRUCTION OF PROPERTY
AND WAIVER OF NOTICE

Page 2 of 2

ITEM(s)DESCRIPTION:_____

_____

_____

_____

_____

_____

Signature of Consentee:_____   _____
Printed Name: Date

Address;

Witness Signature:_____   _____
Printed Name: Date

Title, Agency:

PRESERVATION LETTER

[AGENCY – DEPARTMENT LETTERHEAD]

[DATE]

[Internet Service Provider (ISP) Company]
[Address]

Re: Request for Preservation of Records

Dear **[ISP Company]:**

Pursuant to Title 18, United States Code Section 2703(f), this letter is a formal request for the preservation of all stored communications, records, and other evidence in your possession regarding the following email address pending further legal process: **[Insert email address or other account to be preserved]**, hereinafter, "the Account".

It is requested that you not disclose the existence of this request to the subscriber or any other person, other than as necessary to comply with this request. If compliance with this request might result in a permanent or temporary termination of service to the Account, or otherwise alert any user of the Account as to your actions to preserve the information described below, please contact me as soon as possible and before taking action.

It is requested that you preserve, for a period of 90 days, the information described below currently in your possession, including records stored on backup media, in a form that includes the complete record. This request applies only retrospectively. It does not in any way obligate you to capture and preserve new information that arises after the date of this request. This request applies to the following items, whether in electronic or other form, including information stored on backup media, if available:

1. The contents of any communication or file stored by or for the Account and any associated accounts, and any information associated with those communications or files, such as the source and destination email addresses or IP addresses.

2. All records and other information relating to the Account and any associated accounts including the following:

a. Subscriber names, user names, screen names, or other identities;

b. Mailing addresses, residential addresses, business addresses, email addresses, and other contact information;

c. Length of service (including start date) and types of service utilized;

d. Records of user activity for any connections made to or from the Account, including the date, time, length, and method of connections, data transfer volume, user name, and source and destination Internet Protocol address(es);

e. Telephone records, including local and long distance telephone connection records, caller identification records, cellular site and sector information, GPS data, and cellular network identifying information (such as the IMSI, MSISDN, IMEI, MEID, or ESN);

f. Telephone or instrument number or other subscriber number or identity, including temporarily assigned network address;

g. Means and source of payment for the Account (including any credit card or bank account numbers) and billing records;

h. Correspondence and other records of contact by any person or entity about the Account, such as "Help Desk" notes; and

i. Any other records or evidence relating to the Account.

Thank you for your time and attention. Should you have questions or require additional information regarding this request, please contact me at **[phone number].**

Sincerely,

[SIGNATURE]

[PRINTED NAME]

[TITLE]

AUTHORIZATION AND CONSENT TO SEARCH CELL PHONE & DISCLOSE CELL-SITE AND CELL PHONE USAGE INFORMATION

I, _____, have been asked to give my consent to authorize the search of my personal cell phone and the disclosure of all data relating to my use of my personal cell phone, bearing telephone number (___) ___ -____, including, but not limited to, disclosure of: account information, the numbers dialed, the time and duration of calls, Caller-ID information, the location of cell site/sector information (physical address) at call origination (for outbound calling) and call termination (for incoming calls), all of which is hereinafter referred to as "Phone Usage Information." This disclosure may be either of stored historical information or of ongoing information on a "real-time" basis.

I understand that I have a right to refuse to give my consent to a search and may demand that a search warrant be obtained prior to any search of the person or property described below. I understand that any contraband or evidence of a crime found during the search can be seized and used against me in any court of law or other proceeding. I understand that I may consult with an attorney before or during the search. I understand that I may withdraw my consent to this search at any time prior to the search's termination.

I have read the above statement of rights, understand these rights, and hereby authorize **[AGENCY OR DEPARTMENT]** to conduct a complete search of my personal cell phone and associated records.

I therefore confirm that the company providing service for this phone (hereinafter "the Provider") may at any time, upon request of an authorized representative of the **[AGENCY OR DEPARTMENT]**, release to the **[AGENCY OR DEPARTMENT]** all of the Phone Usage Information specified above, without the need for any further written or legal authorization. I also acknowledge that I will not hold the Provider liable for any damage or loss suffered by me as a result of the release of this information to the **[AGENCY OR DEPARTMENT]**.

Finally, I acknowledge that this written permission is given by me knowingly and voluntarily, and as a condition for my receipt of this phone.

Signature of Consentee:_____   _____
Printed Name: Date

Address;

Witness Signature:_____   _____
Printed Name: Date

Title, Agency:

[AGENCY – DEPARTMENT LETTERHEAD]

AUTHORIZATION AND CONSENT TO ASSUME ONLINE IDENTITY

I, _____, hereby voluntarily provide my consent authorizing **[AGENCY OR DEPARTMENT]** or other Federal, State or Local Task Force officers to assume my Internet online identity.　　My Internet screen name(s), nick name(s), and/or e-mail addresses are as follows;_____

_____

The password(s) is/are as follows :_____

_____

I understand that these law enforcement officers will changes the password(s) to this account so that I will no longer have access to these accounts.　My Internet online identity may be used by these law enforcement officers for any official purpose relating to an official investigation, including sending and receiving e-mail making direct communications on systems such as **[ISPs]** instant messaging, and any other electronic communications.　I understand that I may not disclose this agreement or otherwise advise anyone that this permission has been granted as this would compromise, impede, and potentially obstruct an ongoing investigation.

I have been advised of my right to refuse to allow the assumption of my identity.　No one has made any threats, promises, or inducement in connection with this decision and I give this consent freely and voluntarily.

Signature of Consentee:_____ _____

Printed Name:　　　　　　　　　　　　　　　　　　　　　　　　　　　Date

Address;

Witness Signature:_____ _____

Printed Name:　　　　　　　　　　　　　　　　　　　　　　　　　　　Date

Title, Agency:

AUTHORIZATION AND CONSENT TO RELEASE RECORDS

I, _____, am the primary account holder of one or more accounts with **[ISP]** bearing the screen names:

_____

_____

I hereby grant my consent authorizing **[AGENCY OR DEPARTMENT]** to receive, review, copy and otherwise utilize, as that person or organization deems appropriate, all records of any kind provided by **[ISP]** relative to my account(s), including any alternate screen names or subaccounts.

I hereby authorize **[ISP]** to provide to that person or organization the following records relative to my account(s), including any alternate screen names or subaccounts:

All of the records listed on this form [Or, check only specific records below:]

- Basic subscriber information *
- IP connection logs & ANI info
- Account histories
- Buddy lists
- **[ISP]** Address book

* including but not limited to name, address, phone numbers, screen names, records of session dates & times, start & end dates of service, account balance, credit card or bank account number

Pursuant to this Authorization and Consent, I hereby agree to hold harmless and do forever hold harmless **[ISP]** for the disclosure of such records and do forever waive, on my behalf and on behalf of all my heirs or assigns, any and all claims arising, in whole or in part, out of **[ISP]** 's disclosure of records relative to my account(s) pursuant to this Authorization and Consent.

I hereby indemnify **[ISP]** against any and all claims or causes of action arising, in whole or in part, out of **[ISP's]** disclosure of records relative to my account(s) pursuant to this Authorization and Consent.

Signature of Consentee:_____ _____

Printed Name: Date

Address;

Witness Signature:_____ _____

Printed Name: Date

Title, Agency:

<u>Search Warrant for Cell Site Simulator to ID a Phone</u>

IN THE UNITED STATES DISTRICT COURT
FOR **[JUDICIAL DISTRICT]**

<table>
<tr>
<td>
IN THE MATTER OF THE USE OF A
CELL-SITE SIMULATOR TO IDENTITY
THE CELLULAR DEVICE CARRIED BY
[NAME OF SUSPECT]
</td>
<td>
Case No. _____

<u>**Filed Under Seal**</u>
</td>
</tr>
</table>

AFFIDAVIT IN SUPPORT OF
AN APPLICATION FOR A SEARCH WARRANT

I, **[AGENT NAME]**, being first duly sworn, hereby depose and state as follows:

INTRODUCTION AND AGENT BACKGROUND

1.   I make this affidavit in support of an application for a search warrant under Federal Rule of Criminal Procedure 41 to authorize law enforcement to employ an electronic investigative technique further described in Attachment B, in order to identify the cellular device or devices carried by **[NAME AND/OR PHYSICAL DESCRIPTION OF THE SUSPECT]** (the "Target Cellular Device"), described in Attachment A.

2.   I am a Special Agent with the **[AGENCY]**, and have been since **[DATE]**. **[DESCRIBE TRAINING AND EXPERIENCE TO THE EXTENT IT SHOWS QUALIFICATION TO SPEAK ABOUT THIS INVESTIGATION, CELLULAR DEVICES, AND OTHER TECHNICAL MATTERS]**.

3.   The facts in this affidavit come from my personal observations, my training and experience, and information obtained from other agents and witnesses. This affidavit is intended to show merely that there is sufficient probable cause for the requested warrant and does not set forth all of my knowledge about this matter.

4.   This Court has authority to issue the requested warrant under Federal Rule of Criminal Procedure Rule 41(b)(1) & (2) because the Target Cellular Device is currently believed to be located inside this district because **[PROVIDE EVIDENCE SUGGESTING THAT TARGET CELLULAR DEVICE IS CURRENTLY LOCATED IN THIS DISTRICT, E.G. THE TARGET CELLULAR DEVICE'S OWNER IS KNOWN TO SPEND MOST OF HIS TIME IN THIS DISTRICT; THE TARGET CELLULAR DEVICE'S OWNER WAS SEEN IN THIS DISTRICT X DAYS AGO; ETC.]**. Pursuant to Rule 41(b)(2), law enforcement may use the technique described in Attachment B outside the district provided the device is within the district when the warrant is issued.

5.   **[USE THIS PARAGRAPH IF THE UNIQUE IDENTIFIERS ARE EVIDENCE OF A CRIME.]** Based on the facts set forth in this affidavit, there is probable cause to believe that violations of **[STATUTES]** have been committed, are being committed, and will be committed by **[SUSPECT]**. There is also probable cause to believe that the identity of the Target Cellular Device will constitute evidence of those criminal violations. In addition, in order to obtain additional evidence relating to the Target Cellular Device, its user, and the criminal violations under investigation, law enforcement must first identify the Target Cellular Device. There is probable cause to believe that the use of the investigative technique described by the warrant will result in officers learning that identifying information.

6. Because collecting the information authorized by this warrant may fall within the statutory definitions of a "pen register" or a "trap and trace device," *see* 18 U.S.C. § 3127(3) & (4), this warrant is designed to comply with the Pen Register Statute as well as Rule 41. See 18 U.S.C. §§ 3121-3127. This warrant therefore includes all the information required to be included in a pen register order. See 18 U.S.C. § 3123(b)(1).

PROBABLE CAUSE

7.   [GIVE FACTS ESTABLISHING PROBABLE CAUSE. AT A MINIMUM, IT IS NECESSARY TO ESTABLISH PROBABLE CAUSE TO BELIEVE THAT THE SUSPECT IS LIKELY TO BE CARRYING THE TARGET CELLULAR DEVICE, AND THAT RECORDS ABOUT THAT CELLULAR DEVICE'S USE WILL BE PERTINENT TO THE INVESTIGATION. IF THE TARGET CELLULAR DEVICE IS BEING CARRIED BY SOMEONE WHO IS ALSO A SUSPECT, WHICH IS NORMALLY THE CASE, THEN IT WILL ALSO BE NECESSARY TO IDENTIFY THE SUSPECT AND ESTABLISH A CONNECTION BETWEEN THE SUSPECT AND THE SUSPECTED CRIME. ALSO, EXPLAIN WHY THERE IS PROBABLE CAUSE TO COLLECT IDENTIFYING INFORMATION FOR THE NEXT THIRTY DAYS. IF YOU SPECIFY PARTICULAR LOCATIONS IN ATTACHMENT A FOR USE OF THIS TECHNIQUE, ESTABLISH PROBABLE CAUSE TO BELIEVE THAT THE TARGET CELLULAR DEVICE WILL BE PRESENT AT THOSE LOCATIONS.]

MANNER OF EXECUTION

8. In my training and experience, I have learned that cellular phones and other cellular devices communicate wirelessly across a network of cellular infrastructure, including towers that route and connect individual communications. When sending or receiving a communication, a cellular device broadcasts certain signals to the cellular tower that is routing its communication. These signals include a cellular device's unique identifiers.

9.   To facilitate execution of this warrant, law enforcement may use an investigative device that sends signals to nearby cellular devices, including the Target Cellular Device, and in reply, the nearby cellular devices will broadcast signals that include their unique identifiers. The

investigative device may function in some respects like a cellular tower, except that it will not be connected to the cellular network and cannot be used by a cell to communicate with others. Law enforcement will use this investigative device when they have reason to believe that **[NAME AND/OR PHYSICAL DESCRIPTION OF THE SUSPECT]** is present. Law enforcement will collect the identifiers emitted by cellular devices in the immediate vicinity of the Target Cellular Device when the subject is in multiple locations and/or multiple times at a common location and use this information to identify the Target Cellular Device, as only the Target Cellular Device's unique identifiers will be present in all or nearly all locations. Once investigators ascertain the identity of the Target Cellular Device, they will cease using the investigative technique. Because there is probable cause to determine the identity of the Target Cellular Device, there is probable cause to use the investigative technique described by the warrant to determine the identity of the Target Cellular Device.

10. The investigative device may interrupt cellular service of cellular devices within its immediate vicinity. Any service disruption will be brief and temporary, and all operations will attempt to limit the interference cellular devices. Once law enforcement has identified the Target Cellular Device, it will delete all information concerning non-targeted cellular devices. Absent further order of the court, law enforcement will make no investigative use of information concerning non-targeted cellular devices other than distinguishing the Target Cellular Device from all other devices.

AUTHORIZATION REQUEST

11. Based on the foregoing, I request that the Court issue the proposed search warrant, pursuant to Federal Rule of Criminal Procedure 41. The proposed warrant also will function as a pen register order under 18 U.S.C. § 3123.

12.   I further request, pursuant to 18 U.S.C. § 3103a(b) and Federal Rule of Criminal Procedure 41(f)(3), that the Court authorize the officer executing the warrant to delay notice until 30 days from the end of the period of authorized surveillance. This delay is justified because there is reasonable cause to believe that providing immediate notification of the warrant may have an adverse result, as defined in 18 U.S.C. § 2705. Providing immediate notice to the person carrying the Target Cellular Device would seriously jeopardize the ongoing investigation, as such a disclosure would give that person an opportunity to destroy evidence, change patterns of behavior, notify confederates, and flee from prosecution. *See* 18 U.S.C. § 3103a(b)(1).   There is reasonable necessity for the use of the technique described above, for the reasons set forth above. *See* 18 U.S.C. § 3103a(b)(2).

13.   I further request that the Court authorize execution of the warrant at any time of day or night, owing to the potential need to identify the Target Cellular Device outside of daytime hours.

14.   **[IF YOUR JUDICIAL DISTRICT DOES NOT HAVE STANDARD FORMS/PROCEDURES FOR FILING UNDER SEAL, YOU CAN INSERT THIS LANGUAGE IN THE AFFIDAVIT. THIS IS RECOMMENDED.]** I further request that the Court order that all papers in support of this application, including the affidavit and search warrant, be sealed until further order of the Court. These documents discuss an ongoing criminal investigation that is neither public nor known to all of the targets of the investigation. Accordingly, there is good cause to seal these documents because their premature disclosure may seriously jeopardize that investigation.**]**

15.   A search warrant may not be legally necessary to compel the investigative

technique described herein. Nevertheless, I hereby submit this warrant application out of an

abundance of caution.

Respectfully submitted,

_____

[AGENT NAME]
Special Agent
[AGENCY]

Subscribed and sworn to before me
on _____:

_____
UNITED STATES MAGISTRATE JUDGE

ATTACHMENT A

This warrant authorizes the use of the electronic investigative technique described in Attachment B when the officers to whom it is directed have reason to believe that **[NAME AND/OR PHYSICAL DESCRIPTION OF THE SUSPECT]** is present. **[INCLUDE THE FOLLOWING IF LOCATIONS WHERE THE TECHNIQUE WILL BE USED ARE READILY ASCERTAINABLE AT THE TIME OF DRAFTING.]**This technique may be used at the following locations: **[LIST THE LOCATIONS AT WHICH YOU INTEND TO USE THE CANVASSING TECHNIQUE. WHEN POSSIBLE, LIMIT THE LOCATIONS INCLUDED TO THE VICINITY OF PRECISELY DESCRIBED AREAS. FOR LOCATIONS THAT DO NOT HAVE AN IMMEDIATE, APPARENT CONNECTION TO THE SUSPECT, IT MAY BE HELPFUL TO INCLUDE A REFERENCE TO WHY YOU BELIEVE THE SUSPECT WILL BE PRESENT AT THE LOCATION. FOR EXAMPLE: THE SUSPECT'S HOME (HOME ADDRESS); THE SUSPECT'S PLACE OF EMPLOYMENT (WORK ADDRESS); THE SUSPECT'S DAILY COMMUTE BETWEEN HIS HOME AND PLACE OF EMPLOYMENT.]**

ATTACHMENT B

The "Target Cellular Device" is the cellular device or devices carried by **[NAME AND/OR PHYSICAL DESCRIPTION OF THE SUSPECT]**. Pursuant to an investigation of **[IDENTIFY OF SUBJECT OF INVESTIGATION, IF KNOWN]** for a violation of [offense], this warrant authorizes the officers to whom it is directed to identify the Target Cellular Device by collecting radio signals, including the unique identifiers, emitted by the Target Cellular Device and other cellular devices in its vicinity for a period of thirty days, during all times of day and night.

Absent further order of a court, law enforcement will make no affirmative investigative use of any identifiers collected from cellular devices other than the Target Cellular Device, except to identify the Target Cellular Device and distinguish it from the other cellular devices. Once investigators ascertain the identity of the Target Cellular Device, they will end the collection, and any information collected concerning cellular devices other than the Target Cellular Device will be deleted.

This warrant does not authorize the interception of any telephone calls, text messages, or other electronic communications, and this warrant prohibits the seizure of any tangible property. The Court finds reasonable necessity for the use of the technique authorized above. *See* 18 U.S.C. § 3103a(b)(2).

<u>Search Warrant for Cell Site Simulator to Locate a Phone</u>

IN THE UNITED STATES DISTRICT COURT
FOR **[JUDICIAL DISTRICT]**

IN THE MATTER OF THE USE OF A CELL-SITE SIMULATOR TO LOCATE THE CELLULAR DEVICE ASSIGNED CALL NUMBER **[(xxx) xxx-xxxx]**, **[WITH INTERNATIONAL MOBILE SUBSCRIBER IDENTITY / ELECTRONIC SERIAL NUMBER xxxxxxx]**	Case No. _____ **Filed Under Seal**

**AFFIDAVIT IN SUPPORT OF
AN APPLICATION FOR A SEARCH WARRANT**

I, **[AGENT NAME]**, being first duly sworn, hereby depose and state as follows:

INTRODUCTION AND AGENT BACKGROUND

1. I make this affidavit in support of an application for a search warrant under Federal Rule of Criminal Procedure 41 to authorize law enforcement to employ an electronic investigative technique, which is described in Attachment B, to determine the location of the cellular device assigned call number **[(xxx) xxx-xxxx]**, (the "Target Cellular Device"), which is described in Attachment A.

2. I am a **[SPECIAL AGENT]** with the **[AGENCY]**, and have been since **[DATE]**. **[DESCRIBE TRAINING AND EXPERIENCE TO THE EXTENT IT SHOWS QUALIFICATION TO SPEAK ABOUT THIS INVESTIGATION, CELLULAR DEVICES, AND OTHER TECHNICAL MATTERS]**.

3. The facts in this affidavit come from my personal observations, my training and experience, and information obtained from other agents and witnesses. This affidavit is intended to show merely that there is sufficient probable cause for the requested warrant and does not set forth all of my knowledge about this matter.

4. One purpose of applying for this warrant is to determine with precision the Target Cellular Device's location. However, there is reason to believe the Target Cellular Device is currently located somewhere within this district because **[PROVIDE EVIDENCE SUGGESTING THAT TARGET CELLULAR DEVICE IS CURRENTLY LOCATED IN THIS DISTRICT, E.G. THE TARGET CELLULAR DEVICE'S OWNER IS KNOWN TO SPEND MOST OF HIS TIME IN THIS DISTRICT; THE TELEPHONE NUMBER AREA CODE ASSOCIATED WITH THE TARGET CELLULAR DEVICE CORRESPONDS TO THIS DISTRICT; THE TARGET CELLULAR DEVICE'S OWNER WAS SEEN IN THIS DISTRICT X DAYS AGO; CELL-SITE DATA OBTAINED FOR THE TARGET CELLULAR DEVICE INDICATED THAT IT WAS NORMALLY TO BE FOUND IN THIS DISTRICT, OR FOUND IN THIS DISTRICT X DAYS AGO; ETC.].** Pursuant to Rule 41(b)(2), law enforcement may locate the Target Cellular Device outside the district provided the device is within the district when the warrant is issued.

5. **[USE THIS PARAGRAPH IF THE LOCATION INFORMATION IS EVIDENCE OF A CRIME.]** Based on the facts set forth in this affidavit, there is probable cause to believe that violations of **[STATUTES]** have been committed, are being committed, and will be committed by **[SUSPECTS OR UNKNOWN PERSONS].** There is also probable cause to believe that the location of the Target Cellular Device will constitute evidence of those criminal violations **[, including leading to the identification of individuals who are engaged in the commission of these offenses and identifying locations where the target engages in criminal activity].**

6. **[USE THIS PARAGRAPH IF THE LOCATION INFORMATION WILL HELP TO EFFECTUATE AN ARREST AND/OR LOCATE A FUGITIVE.]** Based on

the facts set forth in this affidavit, there is probable cause to believe that **[FUGITIVE]** has violated **[STATUTES]**. **[FUGITIVE]** was charged with these crimes on **[DATE]** and is the subject of an arrest warrant issued on **[DATE]**. **[IF APPROPRIATE:]** There is also probable cause to believe that **[FUGITIVE]** is aware of these charges and has fled. There is also probable cause to believe that the Target Cellular Device's location will assist law enforcement in arresting **[FUGITIVE]**, who is a "person to be arrested" within the meaning of Federal Rule of Criminal Procedure 41(c)(4).

7. Because collecting the information authorized by this warrant may fall within the statutory definitions of a "pen register" or a "trap and trace device," *see* 18 U.S.C. § 3127(3) & (4), this warrant is designed to comply with the Pen Register Statute as well as Rule 41. See 18 U.S.C. §§ 3121-3127. This warrant therefore includes all the information required to be included in a pen register order. See 18 U.S.C. § 3123(b)(1).

PROBABLE CAUSE

8. **[GIVE FACTS ESTABLISHING THE PROBABLE CAUSE DESCRIBED ABOVE. AMONG OTHER THINGS, THIS SECTION GENERALLY SHOULD (1) ESTABLISH A CONNECTION BETWEEN THE TARGET CELLULAR DEVICE AND THE SUSPECTED CRIME AND/OR TARGETED INDIVIDUAL, (2) IDENTIFY THE SUBSCRIBER NAME AND ADDRESS FOR THE TARGET CELLULAR DEVICE [THIS INFORMATION CAN BE OBTAINED WITH A SUBPOENA TO THE WIRELESS PROVIDER FOR THE CALL NUMBER], (3) IDENTIFY THE PRIMARY USER(S) OF THE TARGET CELLULAR DEVICE, IF KNOWN, AND (4) EXPLAIN WHY THERE IS PROBABLE CAUSE TO MONITOR THE CELLULAR DEVICE'S LOCATION FOR THE NEXT THIRTY DAYS (OR**

FOR SOME SHORTER PERIOD OF TIME, IF YOU AMEND THIS REQUEST TO COVER A PERIOD LESS THAN THIRTY DAYS).]

<u>**MANNER OF EXECUTION**</u>

9. In my training and experience, I have learned that cellular phones and other cellular devices communicate wirelessly across a network of cellular infrastructure, including towers that route and connect individual communications. When sending or receiving a communication, a cellular device broadcasts certain signals to the cellular tower that is routing its communication. These signals include a cellular device's unique identifiers.

10. To facilitate execution of this warrant, law enforcement may use an investigative device or devices capable of broadcasting signals that will be received by the Target Cellular Device or receiving signals from nearby cellular devices, including the Target Cellular Device. Such a device may function in some respects like a cellular tower, except that it will not be connected to the cellular network and cannot be used by a cell phone to communicate with others. The device may send a signal to the Target Cellular Device and thereby prompt it to send signals that include the unique identifier of the device. Law enforcement may monitor the signals broadcast by the Target Cellular Device and use that information to determine the Target Cellular Device's location, even if it is located inside a house, apartment, or other building.

11. The investigative device may interrupt cellular service of phones or other cellular devices within its immediate vicinity. Any service disruption to non-target devices will be brief and temporary, and all operations will attempt to limit the interference with such devices. In order to connect with the Target Cellular Device, the device may briefly exchange signals with all phones or other cellular devices in its vicinity. These signals may include cell phone identifiers. The device will not complete a connection with cellular devices determined not to be the Target Cellular Device, and law enforcement will limit collection of information from devices other than

the Target Cellular Device. To the extent that any information from a cellular device other than the Target Cellular Device is collected by the law enforcement device, law enforcement will delete that information, and law enforcement will make no investigative use of it absent further order of the court, other than distinguishing the Target Cellular Device from all other cellular devices.

AUTHORIZATION REQUEST

12. Based on the foregoing, I request that the Court issue the proposed search warrant, pursuant to Federal Rule of Criminal Procedure 41. The proposed warrant also will function as a pen register order under 18 U.S.C. § 3123.

13. I further request, pursuant to 18 U.S.C. § 3103a(b) and Federal Rule of Criminal Procedure 41(f)(3), that the Court authorize the officer executing the warrant to delay notice until 30 days from the end of the period of authorized surveillance. This delay is justified because there is reasonable cause to believe that providing immediate notification of the warrant may have an adverse result, as defined in 18 U.S.C. § 2705. Providing immediate notice to the subscriber or user of the Target Cellular Device would seriously jeopardize the ongoing investigation, as such a disclosure would give that person an opportunity to destroy evidence, change patterns of behavior, notify confederates, and [continue to] flee from prosecution. *See* 18 U.S.C. § 3103a(b)(1). There is reasonable necessity for the use of the technique described above, for the reasons set forth above. *See* 18 U.S.C. § 3103a(b)(2).

14. I further request that the Court authorize execution of the warrant at any time of day or night, owing to the potential need to locate the Target Cellular Device outside of daytime hours.

15. **[IF YOUR DISTRICT DOES NOT HAVE STANDARD FORMS/PROCEDURES FOR FILING UNDER SEAL, YOU CAN INSERT THIS LANGUAGE IN THE AFFIDAVIT. THIS IS RECOMMENDED.]** I further request that

the Court order that all papers in support of this application, including the affidavit and search warrant, be sealed until further order of the Court. These documents discuss an ongoing criminal investigation that is neither public nor known to all of the targets of the investigation. Accordingly, there is good cause to seal these documents because their premature disclosure may seriously jeopardize that investigation.

16. A search warrant may not be legally necessary to compel the investigative technique described herein. Nevertheless, I hereby submit this warrant application out of an abundance of caution.

Respectfully submitted,

_____
[AGENT NAME]
Special Agent
[AGENCY]

Subscribed and sworn to before me
On: _____

_____
UNITED STATES MAGISTRATE JUDGE

ATTACHMENT A

This warrant authorizes the use of the electronic investigative technique described in Attachment B to identify the location of the cellular device assigned phone number **(XXX) XXX-XXXX**, **[WITH INTERNATIONAL MOBILE SUBSCRIBER IDENTITY / ELECTRONIC SERIAL NUMBER XXXXXXX]**, whose wireless provider is **[WIRELESS PROVIDER]**, and whose listed subscriber is **[NAME/UNKNOWN]**.

ATTACHMENT B

Pursuant to an investigation of **[IDENTIFY OF SUBJECT OF THE INVESTIGATION, IF KNOWN]** for a violation of **[OFFENSE]**, this Warrant authorizes the officers to whom it is directed to determine the location of the cellular device identified in Attachment A by collecting and examining:

1. radio signals emitted by the target cellular device for the purpose of communicating with cellular infrastructure, including towers that route and connect individual communications; and

2. radio signals emitted by the target cellular device in response to radio signals sent to the cellular device by the officers;

for a period of thirty days, during all times of day and night. This warrant does not authorize the interception of any telephone calls, text messages, other electronic communications, and this warrant prohibits the seizure of any tangible property. The Court finds reasonable necessity for the use of the technique authorized above. *See* 18 U.S.C. § 3103a(b)(2).

Search Warrant for Cell Phone Location Lat-Long-GPS History

IN THE UNITED STATES DISTRICT COURT
FOR **[JUDICIAL DISTRICT]**

<table>
<tr>
<td>

IN THE MATTER OF THE SEARCH OF
THE CELLULAR TELEPHONE
ASSIGNED CALL NUMBER **[(xxx) xxx-xxx]**, **[WITH INTERNATIONAL
MOBILE SUBSCRIBER IDENTITY /
ELECTRONIC SERIAL NUMBER
xxxxxxx]**
</td>
<td>

Case No. _____

Filed Under Seal
</td>
</tr>
</table>

AFFIDAVIT IN SUPPORT OF
AN APPLICATION FOR A SEARCH WARRANT

I, **[AGENT NAME]**, being first duly sworn, hereby depose and state as follows:

INTRODUCTION AND AGENT BACKGROUND

1. I make this affidavit in support of an application for a search warrant under Federal Rule of Criminal Procedure 41 and 18 U.S.C. §§ 2703(c)(1)(A) for information about the location of the cellular telephone assigned call number **[(XXX) XXX-XXX]**, **[WITH INTERNATIONAL MOBILE SUBSCRIBER IDENTITY / ELECTRONIC SERIAL NUMBER XXXXXXX]** (the "Target Cell Phone"), whose service provider is **[WIRELESS PROVIDER]**, a wireless telephone service provider headquartered at **[PROVIDER ADDRESS]**. The Target Cell Phone is described herein and in Attachment A, and the location information to be seized is described herein and in Attachment B.

2. I am a Special Agent with the **[AGENCY]**, and have been since **[DATE]**. **[DESCRIBE TRAINING AND EXPERIENCE TO THE EXTENT IT SHOWS QUALIFICATION TO SPEAK ABOUT THIS INVESTIGATION, CELLULAR TELEPHONES, AND OTHER TECHNICAL MATTERS]**.

3. The facts in this affidavit come from my personal observations, my training and experience, and information obtained from other agents and witnesses. This affidavit is intended

to show merely that there is sufficient probable cause for the requested warrant and does not set forth all of my knowledge about this matter.

4. **[USE THIS PARAGRAPH IF THE LOCATION INFORMATION IS EVIDENCE OF A CRIME.]** Based on the facts set forth in this affidavit, there is probable cause to believe that violations of **[STATUTES]** have been committed, are being committed, and will be committed by **[SUSPECTS OR UNKNOWN PERSONS]**. There is also probable cause to believe that the location information described in Attachment B will constitute evidence of these criminal violations, and will lead to the identification of individuals who are engaged in the commission of these offenses.

5. **[USE THIS PARAGRAPH IF THE LOCATION INFORMATION WILL HELP TO EFFECTUATE AN ARREST AND/OR LOCATE A FUGITIVE.]** Based on the facts set forth in this affidavit, there is probable cause to believe that **[FUGITIVE]** has violated **[STATUTES]**. **[FUGITIVE]** was charged with these crimes on **[DATE]** and is the subject of an arrest warrant issued on **[DATE]**. **[IF APPROPRIATE:]** There is also probable cause to believe that **[FUGITIVE]** is aware of these charges and has fled. There is also probable cause to believe that the location information described in Attachment B will assist law enforcement in arresting **[FUGITIVE]**, who is a "person to be arrested" within the meaning of Federal Rule of Criminal Procedure 41(c)(4).

PROBABLE CAUSE

6. **[GIVE FACTS ESTABLISHING THE PROBABLE CAUSE DESCRIBED ABOVE. AMONG OTHER THINGS, THIS SECTION SHOULD (1) ESTABLISH A CONNECTION BETWEEN THE TARGET CELL PHONE AND THE SUSPECTED CRIME AND/OR TARGETED INDIVIDUAL, (2) IDENTIFY THE SUBSCRIBER NAME AND ADDRESS FOR THE TARGET CELL PHONE [THIS INFORMATION CAN BE OBTAINED WITH A SUBPOENA TO THE WIRELESS**

PROVIDER FOR THE CALL NUMBER], (3) IDENTIFY THE PRIMARY USER(S) OF THE TARGET CELL PHONE, IF KNOWN, AND (4) EXPLAIN WHY THERE IS PROBABLE CAUSE TO COLLECT LOCATION INFORMATION FOR THE NEXT 30 DAYS (OR FOR SOME SHORTER PERIOD OF TIME, IF YOU AMEND ATTACHMENT B TO COVER A PERIOD LESS THAN 30 DAYS).]**

7. In my training and experience, I have learned that **[WIRELESS PROVIDER]** is a company that provides cellular telephone access to the general public. I also know that providers of cellular telephone service have technical capabilities that allow them to collect and generate at least two kinds of information about the locations of the cellular telephones to which they provide service: (1) E-911 Phase II data, also known as GPS data or latitude-longitude data, and (2) cell-site data, also known as "tower/face information" or cell tower/sector records. E-911 Phase II data provides relatively precise location information about the cellular telephone itself, either via GPS tracking technology built into the phone or by triangulating on the device's signal using data from several of the provider's cell towers. Cell-site data identifies the "cell towers" (i.e., antenna towers covering specific geographic areas) that received a radio signal from the cellular telephone and, in some cases, the "sector" (i.e., faces of the towers) to which the telephone connected. These towers are often a half-mile or more apart, even in urban areas, and can be 10 or more miles apart in rural areas. Furthermore, the tower closest to a wireless device does not necessarily serve every call made to or from that device. Accordingly, cell-site data is typically less precise that E-911 Phase II data.

8. **[IF THE PROVIDER IS CAPABLE OF COLLECTING E-911 PHASE II DATA:]** Based on my training and experience, I know that **[WIRELESS PROVIDER]** can collect E-911 Phase II data about the location of the Target Cell Phone, including by initiating a signal to determine the location of the Target Cell Phone on **[WIRELESS PROVIDER]**'s network or with such other reference points as may be reasonably available.

9. Based on my training and experience, I know that **[WIRELESS PROVIDER]** can collect cell-site data about the Target Cell Phone.

AUTHORIZATION REQUEST

10. Based on the foregoing, I request that the Court issue the proposed search warrant, pursuant to Federal Rule of Criminal Procedure 41 and 18 U.S.C. § 2703(c).

11. I further request, pursuant to 18 U.S.C. § 3103a(b) and Federal Rule of Criminal Procedure 41(f)(3), that the Court authorize the officer executing the warrant to delay notice until 30 days after the collection authorized by the warrant has been completed. There is reasonable cause to believe that providing immediate notification of the warrant may have an adverse result, as defined in 18 U.S.C. § 2705. Providing immediate notice to the subscriber or user of the Target Cell Phone would seriously jeopardize the ongoing investigation, as such a disclosure would give that person an opportunity to destroy evidence, change patterns of behavior, notify confederates, and flee from prosecution. *See* 18 U.S.C. § 3103a(b)(1). As further specified in Attachment B, which is incorporated into the warrant, the proposed search warrant does not authorize the seizure of any tangible property. *See* 18 U.S.C. § 3103a(b)(2). Moreover, to the extent that the warrant authorizes the seizure of any wire or electronic communication (as defined in 18 U.S.C. § 2510) or any stored wire or electronic information, there is reasonable necessity for the seizure for the reasons set forth above. *See* 18 U.S.C. § 3103a(b)(2).

12. I further request that the Court direct **[WIRELESS PROVIDER]** to disclose to the government any information described in Attachment B that is within the possession, custody, or control of **[WIRELESS PROVIDER]**. I also request that the Court direct **[WIRELESS PROVIDER]** to furnish the government all information, facilities, and technical assistance necessary to accomplish the collection of the information described in Attachment B unobtrusively and with a minimum of interference with **[WIRELESS PROVIDER]**'s services, including by initiating a signal to determine the location of the Target Cell Phone on

[WIRELESS PROVIDER]'s network or with such other reference points as may be reasonably available, and at such intervals and times directed by the government. The government shall reasonably compensate **[WIRELESS PROVIDER]** for reasonable expenses incurred in furnishing such facilities or assistance.

13. I further request that the Court authorize execution of the warrant at any time of day or night, owing to the potential need to locate the Target Cell Phone outside of daytime hours.

14. **[IF YOUR DISTRICT DOES NOT HAVE STANDARD FORMS/PROCEDURES FOR FILING UNDER SEAL, YOU CAN INSERT THIS LANGUAGE IN THE AFFIDAVIT. THIS IS RECOMMENDED.]** I further request that the Court order that all papers in support of this application, including the affidavit and search warrant, be sealed until further order of the Court. These documents discuss an ongoing criminal investigation that is neither public nor known to all of the targets of the investigation. Accordingly, there is good cause to seal these documents because their premature disclosure may seriously jeopardize that investigation

Respectfully submitted,

_____
[AGENT NAME]
Special Agent
[AGENCY]

Subscribed and sworn to before me on_____, 201____

_____
UNITED STATES MAGISTRATE JUDGE

ATTACHMENT A

Property to Be Searched

1. The cellular telephone assigned call number **(XXX) XXX-XXXX, [WITH INTERNATIONAL MOBILE SUBSCRIBER IDENTITY / ELECTRONIC SERIAL NUMBER XXXXXXX]** (the "Target Cell Phone"), whose wireless service provider is **[WIRELESS PROVIDER]**, a company headquartered at **[ADDRESS]**.

Information about the location of the Target Cell Phone that is within the possession, custody, or control of **[WIRELESS PROVIDER] [IF NEEDED: INCLUDING INFORMATION ABOUT THE LOCATION OF THE CELLULAR TELEPHONE IF IT IS SUBSEQUENTLY CALL NUMBER]**.

ATTACHMENT B

Particular Things to be Seized

All information about the location of the Target Cell Phone described in Attachment A for a period of thirty days, during all times of day and night. "Information about the location of the Target Cell Phone" includes all available E-911 Phase II data, GPS data, latitude-longitude data, and other precise location information, as well as all data about which "cell towers" (i.e., antenna towers covering specific geographic areas) and "sectors" (i.e., faces of the towers) received a radio signal from the cellular telephone described in Attachment A.

To the extent that the information described in the previous paragraph (hereinafter, "Location Information") is within the possession, custody, or control of **[WIRELESS PROVIDER]**, **[WIRELESS PROVIDER]** is required to disclose the Location Information to the government. In addition, **[WIRELESS PROVIDER]** must furnish the government all information, facilities, and technical assistance necessary to accomplish the collection of the Location Information unobtrusively and with a minimum of interference with **[WIRELESS PROVIDER]**'s services, including by initiating a signal to determine the location of the Target Cell Phone on **[WIRELESS PROVIDER]**'s network or with such other reference points as may be reasonably available, and at such intervals and times directed by the government. The government shall compensate **[WIRELESS PROVIDER]** for reasonable expenses incurred in furnishing such facilities or assistance.

This warrant does not authorize the seizure of any tangible property. In approving this warrant, the Court finds reasonable necessity for the seizure of the Location Information. *See* 18 U.S.C. § 3103a(b)(2).

Court Order for Tower Dump

UNITED STATES DISTRICT COURT
[JUDICIAL DISTRICT]

IN RE APPLICATION OF THE) UNITED STATES OF AMERICA FOR) AN ORDER PURSUANT TO) 18 U.S.C. § 2703(d))	MISC. NO. _____ **Filed Under Seal**

APPLICATION OF THE UNITED STATES
FOR AN ORDER PURSUANT TO 18 U.S.C. § 2703(d)

The United States of America, moving by and through its undersigned counsel, respectfully submits under seal this *ex parte* application for an Order pursuant to 18 U.S.C. § 2703(d). The Order would require [**PROVIDERS**] ("the Service Providers") to disclose certain records and other information pertaining to the cellular telephone towers described in Part I of Attachment A. The records and other information to be disclosed are described in Part II of Attachment A to the proposed Order. In support of this application, the United States asserts:

LEGAL BACKGROUND

1.   The United States may use a court order issued under 18 U.S.C. § 2703(d) to require a provider of electronic communication service to disclose records or other information pertaining to a subscriber to or customer of such service, not including the contents of any communications. Cellular service providers are providers of an electronic communications service, as defined in 18 U.S.C. § 2510(15). Accordingly, the United States may use a court order issued under 18 U.S.C. § 2703(d) to require the Service Providers to disclose the items described in Part II of Attachment A, which are "record[s] or other information pertaining to a subscriber to or customer of such service." 18 U.S.C. § 2703(c)(1).

2.   This Court has jurisdiction to issue the proposed Order because it is "a court of competent jurisdiction," as defined in 18 U.S.C. § 2711. *See* 18 U.S.C. § 2703(d). Specifically, the

Court **[CHOOSE ONE OR MORE:]** is a district court of the United States that has jurisdiction over the offense being investigated. *See* 18 U.S.C. § 2711(3)(A)(i). **[AND/OR]** is in a district in which the Service Providers are located or in which the items described in Part II of Attachment A are stored. *See* 18 U.S.C. § 2711(3)(A)(ii). **[AND/OR]** is acting on a request for foreign assistance pursuant to 18 U.S.C. § 2711(3)(A)(iii).

3.   A court order under § 2703(d) "shall issue only if the governmental entity offers specific and articulable facts showing that there are reasonable grounds to believe that ... the records or other information sought, are relevant and material to an ongoing criminal investigation." 18 U.S.C. § 2703(d). Accordingly, the next section of this application sets forth specific and articulable facts showing that there are reasonable grounds to believe that the records and other information described in Attachment A are relevant and material to an ongoing criminal investigation.

FACTS ABOUT THE ONGOING CRIMINAL INVESTIGATION

4.   The United States is investigating **[CRIME DESCRIPTION]**. The investigation concerns possible violations of **[STATUTEs]**.

5.   **[***INSERT FACTUAL PARAGRAPH(S) HERE. THESE PARAGRAPHS SHOULD PROVIDE "SPECIFIC AND ARTICULABLE FACTS SHOWING THAT THERE ARE REASONABLE GROUNDS TO BELIEVE THAT" THE RECORDS DESCRIBED IN ATTACHMENT A ARE "RELEVANT AND MATERIAL" TO THE ONGOING CRIMINAL INVESTIGATION. A SHORT FACTUAL SUMMARY OF THE INVESTIGATION AND THE ROLE THAT THE RECORDS WILL SERVE IN ADVANCING THE INVESTIGATION SHOULD SATISFY THIS CRITERION, ALTHOUGH A MORE IN-DEPTH EXPLANATION MAY BE NECESSARY IN PARTICULARLY COMPLEX CASES.***]**

FACTS ABOUT CELL TOWERS IN GENERAL

6.   Many cellular service providers maintain antenna towers ("cell towers") that serve specific geographic areas. Each cell tower receives signals from wireless devices, such as cellular phones, in its general vicinity. These cell towers allow the wireless devices to transmit or receive communications, such as phone calls, text messages, and other data. The tower closest to a wireless device does not necessarily serve every call made to or from that device.

7.   In addition to a unique telephone number, each cell phone is identified by one or more unique identifiers. Depending on the cellular network and the device, the unique identifiers for a cell phone could include an Electronic Serial Number ("ESN"), a Mobile Electronic Identity Number ("MEIN"), a Mobile Identification Number ("MIN"), a Subscriber Identity Module ("SIM"), a Mobile Subscriber Integrated Services Digital Network Number ("MSISDN"), an International Mobile Subscriber Identifier ("IMSI"), or an International Mobile Equipment Identity ("IMEI").

8.   Cellular service providers routinely maintain historical cell-tower log information, including records identifying the wireless telephone calls and communications that used a particular tower. For each communication, these records may include the telephone call number and unique identifiers for the wireless device in the vicinity of the tower that made or received the communication ("the locally served wireless device"); the source and destination telephone numbers associated with the communication (including the number of the telephone that called or was called by the locally served wireless device); the date, time, and duration of the communication; the "sectors" (i.e., the faces of the towers) that received a radio signal from the locally served device; and the type of communication transmitted through the tower (such as phone call or text message).

9. Based on the above facts, there is reason to believe that the records described in Attachment A would identify which wireless devices were in [**THE RELEVANT LOCATIONS**]

at the time [**THE CRIME OCCURRED**]. This information, in turn, will assist law enforcement in determining which persons were present [**FOR THE RELEVANT EVENT**].

<u>REQUEST FOR ORDER</u>

10.   The facts set forth in the previous section show that there are reasonable grounds to believe that the records and other information described in Attachment A are relevant and material to an ongoing criminal investigation. [**REVISE THIS SENTENCE AS NEEDED:**] Specifically, these items will help the United States to identify and locate the individual(s) who are responsible for the events described above, and to determine the nature and scope of their activities. Accordingly, the United States requests that the Service Providers be directed to produce all items described in Part II of Attachment A to the proposed Order.

11.   [**USE THIS PARAGRAPH IF YOU WANT TO PRECLUDE THE PROVIDERS FROM NOTIFYING THE SUBSCRIBER OF THIS APPLICATION AND ORDER. THIS IS RECOMMENDED.**] The United States further requests that the Order require the Service Providers not to notify any person, including individuals whose wireless devices connected to the cellular telephone towers described in Part I of Attachment A, of the existence of the Order for [**PERIOD REQUESTED, NOT TO EXCEED ONE YEAR**]. *See* 18 U.S.C. § 2705(b). [**REVISE THESE SENTENCES AS NEEDED, ADDING ADDITIONAL FACTS, IF AVAILABLE:**] Such a requirement is justified because the Order relates to an ongoing criminal investigation that is neither public nor known to all of the targets of the investigation, and its disclosure may alert the targets to the ongoing investigation. Accordingly, there is reason to believe that notification of the existence of the Order will seriously jeopardize the investigation, including by <u><<list applicable harm(s), such as one or more of the following:</u> giving targets an opportunity to flee or continue flight from prosecution, destroy or tamper with evidence, change patterns of behavior, intimidate potential witnesses, or endanger the life or physical safety of an individual>>. *See* 18 U.S.C. § 2705(b)(2), (3), (5). Some of the

evidence in this investigation is stored electronically. If alerted to the investigation, the subjects under investigation could destroy that evidence, including information saved to their personal computers.

12. **[INCLUDE THIS PARAGRAPH IN THE APPLICATION IF ORDER SHOULD BE SEALED. THIS IS RECOMMENDED.]** The United States further requests that the Court order that this application and any resulting order be sealed until further order of the Court. As explained above, these documents discuss an ongoing criminal investigation that is neither public nor known to all of the targets of the investigation. Accordingly, there is good cause to seal these documents because their premature disclosure may seriously jeopardize that investigation.

Respectfully submitted,

[AUSA NAME AND INFORMAITON]

UNITED STATES DISTRICT COURT
[JUDICIAL DISTRICT]

) IN RE APPLICATION OF THE) UNITED STATES OF AMERICA FOR) AN ORDER PURSUANT TO) 18 U.S.C. § 2703(d)) _____)	MISC. NO. ____ **<u>Filed Under Seal</u>**

<u>ORDER</u>

The United States has submitted an application pursuant to 18 U.S.C. § 2703(c)-(d), requesting that the Court issue an Order requiring **[PROVIDERS]** ("the Service Providers") to disclose the records and other information described in Attachment A to this Order.

The Court finds that the United States has offered specific and articulable facts showing that there are reasonable grounds to believe that the records or other information sought are relevant and material to an ongoing criminal investigation.

[USE THIS SENTENCE IF YOU WANT TO PRECLUDE THE PROVIDERS FROM NOTIFYING THE SUBSCRIBER OF THE APPLICATION AND ORDER. THIS IS RECOMMENDED.] The Court also finds that there is reason to believe that notifying any other person, including individuals whose wireless devices connected to the cellular telephone towers described in Part I of Attachment A, of the existence of the application of the United States, or the existence of this Order, will seriously jeopardize the ongoing investigation, including by **[LIST APPLICABLE HARM(S), SUCH AS ONE OR MORE OF THE FOLLOWING: GIVING TARGETS AN OPPORTUNITY TO FLEE OR CONTINUE FLIGHT FROM PROSECUTION, DESTROY OR TAMPER WITH EVIDENCE, CHANGE PATTERNS OF BEHAVIOR, INTIMIDATE POTENTIAL WITNESSES, OR ENDANGER THE LIFE OR PHYSICAL SAFETY OF AN INDIVIDUAL]**

IT IS THEREFORE ORDERED, pursuant to 18 U.S.C. § 2703(d), that the Service Providers shall, within ten days of the date of this Order, disclose to the United States the records and other information described in Attachment A to this Order.

[USE THIS SENTENCE IF YOU WANT TO PRECLUDE THE PROVIDERS FROM NOTIFYING THE SUBSCRIBER OF THE APPLICATION AND ORDER. THIS IS RECOMMENDED.] IT IS FURTHER ORDERED that the Service Providers shall not disclose the existence of the application of the United States, or the existence of this Order, to any other person, for **[PERIOD REQUESTED, NOT TO EXCEED ONE YEAR]**, EXCEPT THAT **[ISP** may disclose this Order to an attorney for <<Provider>> for the purpose of receiving legal advice.

[INCLUDE THIS PARAGRAPH IF THE APPLICATION AND ORDER SHOULD BE SEALED. THIS IS RECOMMENDED.] IT IS FURTHER ORDERED that the application and this Order are sealed until otherwise ordered by the Court.

_____
United States Magistrate Judge

_____
Date

ATTACHMENT A

I.   The Cell Towers

This Order applies to certain records and information associated with the following cellular telephone towers ("cell towers") at the following dates and times:

<u>Cell Towers</u>   <u>Dates</u>   <u>Times (**[list time zone]**)</u>

[Cell Tower #1] OR [The cell   **[Date #1]**   **[Time #1A to Time #1B]**
towers that provided cellular
service to **[Street Address #1]**]

[Cell Tower #2] OR [The cell   **[Date #2]**   **[Time #2A to Time #2B]**
towers that provided cellular
service to **[Street Address #2]**]

II.   Records and Other Information to Be Disclosed

For each cell tower described in Part I of this Attachment, the Service Providers named in the Order are required to disclose to the United States all records and other information (not including the contents of communications) about all communications made using the cell tower during the corresponding timeframe(s) listed in Part I, including the records that identify:

    A.   the telephone call number and unique identifiers for each wireless device in the vicinity of the tower ("the locally served wireless device") that registered with the tower, including Electronic Serial Numbers ("ESN"), Mobile Electronic Identity Numbers ("MEIN"), Mobile Identification Numbers ("MIN"), Subscriber Identity Modules ("SIM"), Mobile Subscriber Integrated Services Digital Network Numbers ("MSISDN"), International Mobile Subscriber Identifiers ("IMSI"), and International Mobile Equipment Identities ("IMEI");

    B.   the source and destination telephone numbers associated with each communication (including the number of the locally served wireless device and the number of the telephone that called, or was called by, the locally served wireless device);

C.   the date, time, and duration of each communication;

D.   the "sectors" (i.e., the faces of the towers) that received a radio signal from each

locally served wireless device; and

E.   the type of communication transmitted through the tower (such as phone call or

text message).

These records should include records about communications that were initiated before or terminated after the specified time period, as long as part of the communication occurred during the relevant time period identified in Part I.

CERTIFICATE OF AUTHENTICITY OF DOMESTIC BUSINESS RECORDS PURSUANT TO FEDERAL RULE OF EVIDENCE 902(11)

I, _____, attest, under penalties of perjury under the laws of the United States of America pursuant to 28 U.S.C. § 1746, that the information contained in this declaration is true and correct. I am employed by [Provider], and my official title is _____. I am a custodian of records for [Provider]. I state that each of the records attached hereto is the original record or a true duplicate of the original record in the custody of [Provider], and that I am the custodian of the attached records consisting of _____ (pages/DVDs/terabytes). I further state that:

a. all records attached to this certificate were made at or near the time of the occurrence of the matter set forth, by, or from information transmitted by, a person with knowledge of those matters;

b. such records were kept in the ordinary course of a regularly conducted business activity of [Provider]; and

c. such records were made by [Provider] as a regular practice.

I further state that this certification is intended to satisfy Rule 902(11) of the Federal Rules of Evidence.

_____   _____
Date   Signature

Court Order for PEN on Cell Phone
UNITED STATES DISTRICT COURT
[JUDICIAL DISTRICT]

IN RE APPLICATION OF THE) UNITED STATES OF AMERICA FOR) AN ORDER PURSUANT TO) 18 U.S.C. § 2703(d)))	MISC. NO. ____ **Filed Under Seal**

APPLICATION OF THE UNITED STATES
FOR AN ORDER PURSUANT TO 18 U.S.C. § 2703(d)

The United States of America, moving by and through its undersigned counsel, respect-fully submits under seal this *ex parte* application for an Order pursuant to 18 U.S.C. § 2703(d). The proposed Order would require **[INTERNT SERIVCE PROVIDER COMPANY NAME (ISP)]** a cellular service provider, located in **[CITY, STATE]**, to disclose certain records and other information pertaining to the cellular telephone assigned call number **(xxx) xxx-xxxx, [WITH INTERNATIONAL MOBILE SUBSCRIBER IDENTITY, ELECTRONIC SERIAL NUMBER xxxxxx],** as described in Part I of Attachment A to the proposed Order. The records and other information to be disclosed are described in Part II of Attachment A. In support of this application, the United States asserts:

LEGAL BACKGROUND

13.   **[ISP]** is a provider of an electronic communications service, as defined in 18 U.S.C. § 2510(15). Accordingly, the United States may use a court order issued under § 2703(d) to require **[ISP]** to disclose the items described in Part II of Attachment A, as these records pertain to a subscriber of electronic communications service and are not the contents of commu-nications. *See* 18 U.S.C. § 2703(c)(1).

14.   This Court has jurisdiction to issue the proposed Order because it is "a court of competent jurisdiction," as defined in 18 U.S.C. § 2711(3). *See* 18 U.S.C. § 2703(d). Specifically,

the Court **[CHOOSE ONE OR MORE]**: is a district court of the United States that has jurisdiction over the offense being investigated. *See* 18 U.S.C. § 2711(3)(A)(i). **AND/OR** is in a district in which [ISP] is located or in which the items described in Part II of Attachment A are stored. *See* 18 U.S.C. § 2711(3)(A)(ii). **AND/OR** is acting on a request for foreign assistance pursuant to 18 U.S.C. § 2711(3)(A)(iii).]

15.   A court order under § 2703(d) "shall issue only if the governmental entity offers specific and articulable facts showing that there are reasonable grounds to believe that the contents of a wire or electronic communication, or the records or other information sought, are relevant and material to an ongoing criminal investigation." 18 U.S.C. § 2703(d). Accordingly, the next section of this application sets forth specific and articulable facts showing that there are reasonable grounds to believe that the records and other information described in Part II of Attachment A are relevant and material to an ongoing criminal investigation.

THE RELEVANT FACTS

16.   The United States is investigating **[CRIME DESCRIPTION]**. The investigation concerns possible violations of, inter alia, **[STATUTES]**.

17.   **[INSERT FACTUAL PARAGRAPH(S) THAT PROVIDE "SPECIFIC AND ARTICULABLE FACTS SHOWING THAT THERE ARE REASONABLE GROUNDS TO BELIEVE THAT" THE RECORDS DESCRIBED IN ATTACHMENT A ARE "RELEVANT AND MATERIAL" TO THE ONGOING CRIMINAL INVESTIGATION. A FACTUAL SUMMARY OF THE INVESTIGATION AND THE ROLE THAT THE RECORDS WILL SERVE IN ADVANCING THE INVESTIGATION SHOULD ALSO BE INCLUDED.]**

<u>REQUEST FOR ORDER</u>

18.   The facts set forth in the previous section show that there are reasonable grounds to believe that the records and other information described in Part II of Attachment A are relevant and material to an ongoing criminal investigation. **[REVISE THE FOLLOWING SENTENCE AS NEEDED:]** Specifically, these items will help the United States to identify and locate the individual(s) who are responsible for the events described above, and to determine the nature and scope of their activities. Accordingly, the United States requests that **[ISP]** be directed to produce all items described in Part II of Attachment A to the proposed Order.

19.   **[INSERT JUSTIFICAITON FOR NONDISCLOSURE HERE. REVISE THE FOLLOWING PARAGRAPH AS NEEDED:]** The United States further requests that the Order require **[ISP]** not to notify any person, including the subscribers or customers of the account(s) listed in Part I of Attachment A, of the existence of the Order for **[TIME PERIOD REQUESTED, NOT TO EXCEED 1 YEAR]**. *See* 18 U.S.C. § 2705(b). This Court has authority under 18 U.S.C. § 2705(b) to issue "an order commanding a provider of electronic communications service or remote computing service to whom a warrant, subpoena, or court order is directed, for such period as the court deems appropriate, not to notify any other person of the existence of the warrant, subpoena, or court order." In this case, such an order would be appropriate because **[INCLUDE SPECIFIC FACTS AS AVAILABLE AND EXPLAIN WHY NOTIFICATION OF THE EXISTENCE OF THE ORDER WILL RESULT IN ONE OR MORE OF THE ADVERSE CIRCUMSTANCES LISTED IN 18 U.S.C. § 2705(B), SUCH AS SERIOUSLY JEOPARDIZING THE INVESTIGATION, INCLUDING BY GIVING TARGETS AN OPPORTUNITY TO FLEE OR CONTINUE FLIGHT FROM PROSECUTION, DESTROY OR TAMPER WITH**

EVIDENCE, CHANGE PATTERNS OF BEHAVIOR, OR NOTIFY CONFEDERATES.] *See* 18 U.S.C. § 2705(b).

20. **[INCLUDE THIS PARAGRAPH IF THE APPLICATION AND ORDER SHOULD BE SEALED:]**The United States further requests that the Court order that this application and any resulting order be sealed until further order of the Court. As explained above, these documents discuss an ongoing criminal investigation that is neither public nor known to all of the targets of the investigation. Accordingly, there is good cause to seal these documents because their premature disclosure may seriously jeopardize that investigation.

Respectfully submitted,

[SIGNATURE]

UNITED STATES
ATTORNEY_____

[AUSA NAME AND INFORMAITON]

UNITED STATES DISTRICT COURT
[JUDICIAL DISTRICT]

IN RE APPLICATION OF THE   )
UNITED STATES OF AMERICA FOR)
AN ORDER PURSUANT TO   )
18 U.S.C. § 2703(d)   )
_____)

MISC. NO. _____

<u>Filed Under Seal</u>

<u>ORDER</u>

The United States has submitted an application pursuant to 18 U.S.C. § 2703(d), requesting that the Court issue an Order requiring **[ISP],** an electronic communications service provider and/or a remote computing service located in **[CITY, STATE]** to disclose the records and other information described in Attachment A to this Order.

The Court finds that the United States has offered specific and articulable facts showing that there are reasonable grounds to believe that the records or other information sought are relevant and material to an ongoing criminal investigation.

[USE THIS SENTENCE IF YOU WANT TO PRECLUDE THE PROVIDER FROM NOTIFYING THE SUBSCRIBER OF THE APPLICATION AND ORDER. THIS IS RECOMMENDED.] The Court determines that there is reason to believe that notification of the existence of this Order will **[INCLUDE APPROPRIATE ADVERSE CIRCUMSTANCE(S) SPECIFIED IN 18 U.S.C. § 2705(B), SUCH AS THE FOLLOWING.]** seriously jeopardize the ongoing investigation, including by giving targets an opportunity to flee or continue flight from prosecution, destroy or tamper with evidence, change patterns of behavior, or notify confederates. *See* 18 U.S.C. § 2705(b)(2), (3), (5).

IT IS THEREFORE ORDERED, pursuant to 18 U.S.C. § 2703(d), that [ISP]shall, within ten days of the date of this Order, disclose to the United States the records and other information described in Attachment A to this Order.

[USE THIS SENTENCE IF YOU WANT TO PRECLUDE THE PROVIDER FROM NOTIFYING THE SUBSCRIBER OF THE APPLICATION AND ORDER. THIS IS RECOMMENDED.] IT IS FURTHER ORDERED under 18 U.S.C. § 2705(b) that [ISP]shall not disclose the existence of the application of the United States, or the existence of this Order of the Court, to the subscribers of the account(s) listed in Attachment A, or to any other person, for **[PERIOD REQUESTED, NOT TO EXCEED ONE YEAR],** except that [ISP]may disclose this Order to an attorney for [ISP]for the purpose of receiving legal advice.

[INCLUDE THIS PARAGRAPH IF THE APPLICATION AND ORDER SHOULD BE SEALED. THIS IS RECOMMENDED.]IT IS FURTHER ORDERED that the application and this Order are sealed until otherwise ordered by the Court.

_____
United States Magistrate Judge

_____
Date

ATTACHMENT A

I.   The Account(s)

The Order applies to records and information associated with the cellular telephone as-signed call number **(XXX) XXX-XXXX,** [with International Mobile Subscriber Identity/Electronic Serial Number xxxxxxx] (the "Account").

II. Records and Other Information to Be Disclosed

[ISP]is required to disclose the following records and other information, if available, to the United States for each Account listed in Part I of this Attachment, for the time period **[DATE RANGE]**:

A. The following information about the customers or subscribers of the Account:

1.   Names (including subscriber names, user names, and screen names);

2.   Addresses (including mailing addresses, residential addresses, business addresses, and e-mail addresses);

3.   Local and long distance telephone connection records;

4.   Records of session times and durations, and the temporarily assigned network addresses (such as Internet Protocol ("IP") addresses) associated with those ses-sions;

5.   Length of service (including start date) and types of service utilized;

6.   Telephone or instrument numbers (including MAC addresses, Electronic Serial Numbers ("ESN"), Mobile Electronic Identity Numbers ("MEIN"), Mobile Equipment Identifier ("MEID"), Mobile Identification Numbers ("MIN"), Sub-scriber Identity Modules ("SIM"), Mobile Subscriber Integrated Services Digital Network Number ("MSISDN"), International Mobile Subscriber Identifiers ("IMSI"), or International Mobile Equipment Identities ("IMEI"));

7.   Other subscriber numbers or identities (including the registration Internet Proto-col ("IP") address); and

8.   Means and source of payment for such service (including any credit card or bank account number) and billing records.

B. All records and other information (not including the contents of communications) re-lating to wire and electronic communications sent from or received by the Account, including the date and time of the communication, the method of communication, and the source and destination of the communication (such as source and destination email addresses, IP addresses, and telephone numbers), and including information regarding the cell towers and sectors through which the communications were sent or received.

CERTIFICATE OF AUTHENTICITY OF DOMESTIC BUSINESS RECORDS PURSUANT TO FEDERAL RULE OF EVIDENCE 902(11)

I, _____, attest, under penalties of perjury under the laws of the United States of America pursuant to 28 U.S.C. § 1746, that the information contained in this declaration is true and correct. I am employed by **[ISP]**, and my official title is _____. I am a custodian of records for **[ISP]**. I state that each of the records attached hereto is the original record or a true duplicate of the original record in the custody of **[ISP],** and that I am the custodian of the attached records consisting of _____ (pages/CDs/kilobytes). I further state that:

a. all records attached to this certificate were made at or near the time of the occurrence of the matter set forth, by, or from information transmitted by, a person with knowledge of those matters;

b. such records were kept in the ordinary course of a regularly conducted business activity of **[ISP]**; and

c. such records were made by **[ISP]** as a regular practice.

I further state that this certification is intended to satisfy Rule 902(11) of the Federal Rules of Evidence.

_____   _____
Date   Signature

Court Order for PEN on Cell Phone

UNITED STATES DISTRICT COURT
FOR THE **[JUDICIAL DISTRICT]**

IN RE APPLICATION OF THE   )
UNITED STATES OF AMERICA FOR)   MISC. NO. _____
AN ORDER AUTHORIZING THE)
INSTALLATION AND USE OF PEN   )
REGISTERS AND TRAP AND   )
TRACE DEVICES   )
_____)   Filed Under Seal

APPLICATION

The United States of America, moving by and through **[AUSA NAME]**, its undersigned counsel, respectfully submits under seal this *ex parte* application for an order pursuant to 18 U.S.C §§ 3122 and 3123, authorizing the installation and use of pen registers and trap and trace devices ("pen-trap devices") to record, decode, and/or capture dialing, routing, addressing, and signaling information associated with each communication to or from the cell phone number described in Attachment A. In support of this application, the United States asserts:

1.   This is an application, made under 18 U.S.C. § 3122(a)(1), for an order under 18 U.S.C. § 3123 authorizing the installation and use of a pen register and a trap and trace device.

2.   Such an application must include three elements: (1) "the identity of the attorney for the Government or the State law enforcement or investigative officer making the application"; (2) "the identity of the law enforcement agency conducting the investigation"; and (3) "a certification by the applicant that the information likely to be obtained is relevant to an ongoing criminal investigation being conducted by that agency." 18 U.S.C. § 3122(b).

3.   The undersigned applicant is an "attorney for the government" as defined in Rule 1(b)(1) of the Federal Rules of Criminal Procedure.

4.   The law enforcement agency conducting the investigation is the **[AGENT, AGENCY]**.

5.   The applicant hereby certifies that the information likely to be obtained by the requested pen-trap devices is relevant to an ongoing criminal investigation being conducted by the **[AGENT, AGENCY]**.

6.   This Court is a "court of competent jurisdiction" under 18 U.S.C. § 3122(a)(2) because it "has jurisdiction over the offense being investigated," 18 U.S.C. § 3127(2)(A)(i).

ADDITIONAL INFORMATION

7.   Other than the three elements described above, federal law does not require that an application for an order authorizing the installation and use of a pen register and a trap and trace device specify any facts. The following additional information is provided to demonstrate that the order requested falls within this Court's authority to authorize the installation and use of a pen register or trap and trace device under 18 U.S.C. § 3123(a)(1).

8. A "pen register" is "a device or process which records or decodes dialing, routing, addressing, or signaling information transmitted by an instrument or facility from which a wire or electronic communication is transmitted." 18 U.S.C. § 3127(3). A "trap and trace device" is "a device or process which captures the incoming electronic or other impulses which identify the originating number or other dialing, routing, addressing, and signaling information reasonably likely to identify the source of a wire or electronic communication." 18 U.S.C. § 3127(4).

9. In the traditional telephone context, pen registers captured the destination phone numbers of outgoing calls, while trap and trace devices captured the phone numbers of incoming calls. Similar principles apply to other kinds of wire and electronic communications, as described below.

10. The Internet is a global network of computers and other devices. Devices directly connected to the Internet are identified by a unique number called an Internet Protocol, or "IP" address. This number is used to route information between devices. Generally, when one device requests information from a second device, the requesting device specifies its own IP address so

that the responding device knows where to send its response. An IP address is analogous to a telephone number and can be recorded by pen-trap devices, and it indicates the online identity of the communicating device without revealing the communication's content.

11. A network is two or more computers or other devices connected to each other that can exchange information with each other via some transmission method, such as by wires, cables, or radio waves. The equipment that connects a computer or other device to the network is commonly referred to as a network adapter. Most network adapters have a Media Access Control ("MAC") address assigned by the manufacturer of the adapter that is designed to be a unique identifying number. An adapter's unique MAC address allows for proper routing of communications on a local area network and may be used for other purposes, such as authentication of customers by some network service providers. Unlike a device's IP address that often changes each time a device connects to the Internet, a MAC address is fixed at the time of manufacture of the adapter. Because the address does not change and is intended to be unique, a MAC address can allow law enforcement to identify whether communications sent or received at different times are associated with the same adapter.

12. On the Internet, data transferred between devices is not sent as a continuous stream, but rather it is split into discrete packets. Generally, a single communication is sent as a series of packets. When the packets reach their destination, the receiving device reassembles them into the complete communication. Each packet has two parts: a header with routing and control information, and a payload, which generally contains user data. The header contains non-content information such as the packet's source and destination IP addresses and the packet's size.

13. In addition, different Internet applications are associated with different "port numbers," or numeric identifiers. The port number is transmitted along with any communication using that application. For example, port 80 typically is associated with communications involving the World Wide Web.

14. A cellular telephone, or cell phone, is a mobile device that transmits and receives wire and electronic communications. Individuals using cell phones contract with cellular service providers, who maintain antenna towers covering specific geographic areas. In order to transmit or receive calls and data, a cell phone must send a radio signal to an antenna tower that, in turn, is connected to a cellular service provider's network.

15. In addition to a unique telephone number, each cell phone has one or more unique identifiers embedded inside it. Depending upon the cellular network and the device, the embedded unique identifiers for a cell phone could take several different forms, including an Electronic Serial Number ("ESN"), a Mobile Electronic Identity Number ("MEIN"), a Mobile Identification Number ("MIN"), a Subscriber Identity Module ("SIM"), an International Mobile Subscriber Identifier ("IMSI"), a Mobile Subscriber Integrated Services Digital Network Number ("MSISDN"), or an International Mobile Station Equipment Identity ("IMEI"). When a cell phone connects to a cellular antenna or tower, it reveals its embedded unique identifiers to the cellular antenna or tower, and the cellular antenna or tower records those identifiers as a matter of course. The unique identifiers—as transmitted from a cell phone to a cellular antenna or tower—are like the telephone number of an incoming call. They can be recorded by pen-trap devices and indicate the identity of the cell phone device making the communication without revealing the communication's content.

16. In addition, a list of incoming and outgoing telephone numbers is generated when a cell phone is used to make or receive calls, or to send or receive text messages (which may include photographs, videos, and other data). These telephone numbers can be recorded by pen-trap devices and then used to identify the parties to a communication without revealing the communication's contents.

17. A cell phone can also be used to exchange text messages with email accounts. The email addresses associated with those text messages can be recorded by pen-trap devices and then used to identify parties to a communication without revealing the communication's contents.

18. Cellular phones can connect to the Internet via the cellular network. When connecting through the cellular network, Internet communications sent and received by the cellular phone each contain the same unique identifier that identifies cellular voice communications, such as an ESN, MEIN, MIN, SIM, IMSI, MSISDN, or IMEI. Internet communications from a cellular phone also contain the IP address associated with that cellular phone at the time of the communication. Each of these unique identifiers can be used to identify parties to a communication without revealing the communication's contents.

19. These telephone numbers can include "post-cut-through dialed digits," which are numbers dialed from the cell phone after the initial call set up is completed. For example, some post-cut-through dialed digits may be the actual telephone number called, such as when a subject places a calling card, credit card, or collect call by first dialing a long-distance carrier access number and then, after the initial call is "cut through," dialing the telephone number of the destination party. That final number sequence is necessary to route the call to the intended party and, therefore, identifies the place or party to which the call is being made. In the event that the pen-trap devices capture some post-cut-through dialed digits that could be considered call content, such as account numbers or passwords, despite the government's use of reasonably available technology to avoid the recording or decoding of such content, the United States will make no affirmative investigative use of such information.

THE RELEVANT FACTS

20. The United States government, including the **[AGENT, AGENCY]**, is investigating **[CRIME DESCRIPTION].** The investigation concerns possible violations by unknown individuals of, inter alia, **INSERT LAW(S) VIOLATED.**

21.   **OPTIONALLY INSERT FACTUAL PARAGRAPH(S) HERE IF YOUR JUDICIAL DISTRICT REQUIRES THEM. FOR EXAMPLE, SOME DISTRICTS WILL INCLUDE A FACT PARAGRAPH LIKE THIS ONE: "THE INVESTIGATION RELATES TO THE PURCHASE AND SALE OF STOLEN CREDIT CARDS AND OTHER UNAUTHORIZED ACCESS DEVICES, WHICH ARE THEN USED TO PERPETRATE MAIL AND WIRE FRAUD. INVESTIGATORS BELIEVE THAT MATTERS RELEVANT TO THE OFFENSES UNDER INVESTIGATION HAVE BEEN AND CONTINUE TO BE DISCUSSED USING VERIZON WIRELESS CELL PHONE NUMBER 222-333-4444. VERIZON WIRELESS IS AN ELECTRONIC COMMUNICATION SERVICE PROVIDER DOING BUSINESS IN BEDMINSTER, NJ. INVESTIGATORS BELIEVE THAT THE LISTED SUBSCRIBER FOR THIS NUMBER IS JOHN JONES, A TARGET OF THE INVESTIGATION, …"**

22. The conduct being investigated involves use of the cell phone number described in Attachment A. To further the investigation, investigators need to obtain the dialing, routing, addressing, and signaling information associated with communications sent to or from that cell phone number.

23. The pen-trap devices sought by this application will record, decode, and/or capture dialing, routing, addressing, and signaling information associated with each communication to or from the cell phone number described in Attachment A, including the date, time, and duration of the communication, and the following, without geographic limit:

- IP addresses associated with the cell phone device or devices used to send or receive electronic communications

- Any unique identifiers associated with the cell phone device or devices used to make and receive calls with cell phone number described in Attachment A, or to send or receive other electronic communications, including the ESN, MEIN, IMSI, IMEI, SIM, MSISDN, or MIN

- IP addresses of any websites or other servers to which the cell phone device or devices connected

- Source and destination telephone numbers and email addresses

- "Post-cut-through dialed digits," which are digits dialed after the initial call set up is completed, subject to the limitations of 18 U.S.C. § 3121(c)[1]

GOVERNMENT REQUESTS

24. For the reasons stated above, the United States requests that the Court enter an Order authorizing the installation and use of pen-trap devices to record, decode, and/or capture the dialing, routing, addressing, and signaling information described above for each communication to or from the cell phone number described in Attachment A, to include the date, time, and duration of the communication, without geographic limit. The United States does not request and does not seek to obtain the contents of any communications, as defined in 18 U.S.C. § 2510(8).

25. The United States further requests that the Court authorize the foregoing installation and use for a period of sixty days from the date of the Court's Order, pursuant to 18 U.S.C. § 3123(c)(1).

26. The United States further requests, pursuant to 18 U.S.C. §§ 3123(b)(2) and 3124(a)-(b), that the Court order **[ISP]** and any other person or entity providing wire or electronic communication service in the United States whose assistance may facilitate execution of this Order to furnish, upon service of the Order, information, facilities, and technical assistance necessary

---

[1] *In the event that the pen-trap devices capture some post-cut-through dialed digits that could be considered call content, such as account numbers or passwords, despite the government's use of reasonably available technology to avoid the recording or decoding of such content, the United States will make no affirmative investigative use of such information.*

to install the pen-trap devices, including installation and operation of the pen-trap devices unobtrusively and with minimum disruption of normal service. Any entity providing such assistance shall be reasonably compensated by the [**AGENT, AGENCY**], pursuant to 18 U.S.C. § 3124(c), for reasonable expenses incurred in providing facilities and assistance in furtherance of this Order.

27. The United States further requests that the Court order [**ISP**] and any other person or entity whose assistance may facilitate execution of this Order to notify the applicant and [**AGENT, AGENCY**] of any changes relating to the cell phone number described in Attachment A, and to provide prior notice to the applicant and the [**AGENT, AGENCY**] before terminating or changing service to the cell phone number.

28. The United States further requests that the Court order that the [**AGENT, AGENCY**] and the applicant have access to the information collected by the pen-trap devices as soon as practicable, twenty-four hours per day, or at such other times as may be acceptable to them, for the duration of the Order.

29. The United States further requests, pursuant to 18 U.S.C. § 3123(d)(2), that the Court order [**AGENT, AGENCY**] and any other person or entity whose assistance facilitates execution of this Order, and their agents and employees, not to disclose in any manner, directly or indirectly, by any action or inaction, the existence of this application and Order, the resulting pen-trap devices, or this investigation, unless and until authorized by this Court, except that [**ISP**] may disclose this Order to an attorney for [**ISP**] for the purpose of receiving legal advice.

30. The United States further requests that this application and any resulting Order be sealed until otherwise ordered by the Court, pursuant to 18 U.S.C. § 3123(d)(1).

31. The United States further requests that the Clerk of the Court provide the United States Attorney's Office with three certified copies of this application and Order, and provide copies of this Order to the [**AGENT, AGENCY**] and [**ISP**] upon request.

32. The foregoing is based on information provided to me in my official capacity by agents

of the **[AGENT, AGENCY]**

I declare under penalty of perjury that the foregoing is true and correct.

Executed on _____.

_____

[AUSA NAME AND INFORMATION]

UNITED STATES DISTRICT COURT
FOR THE [JUDICIAL DISTRICT]

```
                                  )
IN RE APPLICATION OF THE          )
UNITED STATES OF AMERICA FOR      )      MISC. NO. ____
AN ORDER AUTHORIZING THE          )
INSTALLATION AND USE OF PEN       )
REGISTERS AND TRAP AND            )
TRACE DEVICES                     )
                                  )      Filed Under Seal
```

ORDER

[AUSA NAME], on behalf of the United States, has submitted an application pursuant

to 18 U.S.C. §§ 3122 and 3123, requesting that the Court issue an Order authorizing the installa-

tion and use of pen registers and trap and trace devices ("pen-trap devices") on the cell phone

number described in Attachment A, which is incorporated into this Order by reference.

The Court finds that an attorney for the government has submitted the application and

has certified that the information likely to be obtained by such installation and use is relevant to

an ongoing criminal investigation being conducted by the **[AGENT, AGENCY]** of unknown

individuals in connection with possible violations of **INSERT LAW(S) VIOLATED.**

IT IS THEREFORE ORDERED, pursuant to 18 U.S.C. § 3123, that **[AGENT,**

AGENCY] may install and use pen-trap devices to record, decode, and/or capture dialing, rout-

ing, addressing, and signaling information associated with each communication to or from the

cell phone number described in Attachment A., including the date, time, and duration of the

communication, and the following, without geographic limit:

- IP addresses associated with the cell phone device or devices used to send or
  receive electronic communications
- Any unique identifiers associated with the cell phone device or devices used to
  make and receive calls with cell phone number described in Attachment A, or to

send or receive other electronic communications, including the ESN, MEIN, IMSI, IMEI, SIM, MSISDN, or MIN

- IP addresses of any websites or other servers to which the cell phone device or devices connected

- Source and destination telephone numbers and email addresses

- "Post-cut-through dialed digits," which are digits dialed after the initial call set up is completed, subject to the limitations of 18 U.S.C. § 3121(c)

IT IS FURTHER ORDERED, pursuant to 18 U.S.C. § 3123(c)(1), that the use and installation of the foregoing is authorized for sixty days from the date of this Order;

IT IS FURTHER ORDERED, pursuant to 18 U.S.C. §§ 3123(b)(2) and 3124(a)-(b), that **[ISP]** and any other person or entity providing wire or electronic communication service in the United States whose assistance may, pursuant to 18 U.S.C. § 3123(a), facilitate the execution of this Order shall, upon service of this Order, furnish information, facilities, and technical assistance necessary to install the pen-trap devices, including installation and operation of the pen-trap devices unobtrusively and with minimum disruption of normal service;

IT IS FURTHER ORDERED, pursuant to 18 U.S.C. § 2703(d), that **[ISP]** , Virgin Mobile USA LLC; Sprint Spectrum LLP; T-Mobile USA, Inc.; Celco Partnership d/b/a Verizon Wireless; Cingular Wireless; AT&T Wireless and AT&T Mobility; and SBC Communications/Southern New England Telephone Company; and/or any other wireless or hardline telecommunications company (collectively, the "Service Providers") shall furnish agents of the **[AGENCY OR DEPARTMENT]**with the following information for a period beginning up to thirty (30) days prior to the date of the request and running through the duration of the Court's Order, for the telephone numbers dialing or being dialed from the Target Telephone and for the Target Telephone:

(a) Subscriber's name;

(b) Subscriber's address;

(c) Subscriber's local and long distance telephone connection records, or records of session times and durations, including cell site activations;

(d) Length of service (including start date) and types of service utilized;

(e) Telephone or instrument number (including ESN, IMSI, UFMI and/or SIM numbers) or other subscriber number or identity, including any temporarily assigned network address; and

(f) Means and source of payment for such service (including any credit card or bank account number).

IT IS FURTHER ORDERED that the **[AGENT, AGENCY]** reasonably compensate **[ISP]** and any other person or entity whose assistance facilitates execution of this Order for reasonable expenses incurred in complying with this Order;

IT IS FURTHER ORDERED that **[ISP]** and any other person or entity whose assistance may facilitate execution of this Order notify the applicant and the **[AGENT, AGENCY]** of any changes relating to the cell phone number described in Attachment A, including changes to subscriber information, and to provide prior notice to the [**AGENT, AGENCY**] before terminating or changing service to the cell phone number;

IT IS FURTHER ORDERED that the **[AGENT, AGENCY]** and the applicant have access to the information collected by the pen-trap devices as soon as practicable, twenty-four hours per day, or at such other times as may be acceptable to the **[AGENT, AGENCY],** for the duration of the Order;

IT IS FURTHER ORDERED, pursuant to 18 U.S.C. § 3123(d)(2), that [ISP]and any other person or entity whose assistance facilitates execution of this Order, and their agents and employees, shall not disclose in any manner, directly or indirectly, by any action or inaction, the existence of the application and this Order, the pen-trap devices, or the investigation to any person, unless and until otherwise ordered by the Court, except that **[ISP]** may disclose this Order to an attorney for **[ISP]** for the purpose of receiving legal advice;

[***OPTIONAL. Most providers do not require hard copies.] IT IS FURTHER ORDERED that the Clerk of the Court shall provide the United States Attorney's Office with three certified copies of this application and Order, and shall provide copies of this Order to the **[AGENT, AGENCY]** and **[ISP]** upon request;

IT IS FURTHER ORDERED that the application and this Order are sealed until otherwise ordered by the Court, pursuant to 18 U.S.C. § 3123(d)(1).

_____
Date

_____
United States Magistrate Judge

ATTACHMENT A

[ISP]

Facility	Number or identifier	Owner, if known	Subject of investigation, if known
cell phone number	**[INFO. REQUESTED]**	not known	unknown individuals

Court Order for PEN on Device IP

UNITED STATES DISTRICT COURT
FOR THE **[JUDICIAL DISTRICT]**

IN RE APPLICATION OF THE) UNITED STATES OF AMERICA FOR) AN ORDER AUTHORIZING THE) INSTALLATION AND USE OF PEN) REGISTERS AND TRAP AND) TRACE DEVICES) _____)	MISC. NO. ____ Filed Under Seal

APPLICATION

The United States of America, moving by and through **[AUSA NAME],** its undersigned counsel, respectfully submits under seal this *ex parte* application for an order pursuant to 18 U.S.C §§ 3122 and 3123, authorizing the installation and use of pen registers and trap and trace devices ("pen-trap devices") to record, decode, and/or capture dialing, routing, addressing, and signaling information associated with each communication to or from the IP address described in Attachment A. In support of this application, the United States asserts:

1.   This is an application, made under 18 U.S.C. § 3122(a)(1), for an order under 18 U.S.C. § 3123 authorizing the installation and use of a pen register and a trap and trace device.

2.   Such an application must include three elements: (1) "the identity of the attorney for the Government or the State law enforcement or investigative officer making the application"; (2) "the identity of the law enforcement agency conducting the investigation"; and (3) "a certification by the applicant that the information likely to be obtained is relevant to an ongoing criminal investigation being conducted by that agency." 18 U.S.C. § 3122(b).

3.   The undersigned applicant is an "attorney for the government" as defined in Rule 1(b)(1) of the Federal Rules of Criminal Procedure.

4.   The law enforcement agency conducting the investigation is the **[AGENT, AGENCY].**

5.   The applicant hereby certifies that the information likely to be obtained by the requested pen-trap devices is relevant to an ongoing criminal investigation being conducted by the **[AGENT, AGENCY]**.

6.   This Court is a "court of competent jurisdiction" under 18 U.S.C. § 3122(a)(2) because it "has jurisdiction over the offense being investigated," 18 U.S.C. § 3127(2)(A)(i).

<u>ADDITIONAL INFORMATION</u>

7.   Other than the three elements described above, federal law does not require that an application for an order authorizing the installation and use of a pen register and a trap and trace device specify any facts. The following additional information is provided to demonstrate that the order requested falls within this Court's authority to authorize the installation and use of a pen register or trap and trace device under 18 U.S.C. § 3123(a)(1).

8. A "pen register" is "a device or process which records or decodes dialing, routing, addressing, or signaling information transmitted by an instrument or facility from which a wire or electronic communication is transmitted." 18 U.S.C. § 3127(3). A "trap and trace device" is "a device or process which captures the incoming electronic or other impulses which identify the originating number or other dialing, routing, addressing, and signaling information reasonably likely to identify the source of a wire or electronic communication." 18 U.S.C. § 3127(4).

9. In the traditional telephone context, pen registers captured the destination phone numbers of outgoing calls, while trap and trace devices captured the phone numbers of incoming calls. Similar principles apply to other kinds of wire and electronic communications, as described below.

10. The Internet is a global network of computers and other devices. Devices directly connected to the Internet are identified by a unique number called an Internet Protocol, or "IP" address. This number is used to route information between devices. Generally, when one device requests information from a second device, the requesting device specifies its own IP address so

that the responding device knows where to send its response. An IP address is analogous to a telephone number and can be recorded by pen-trap devices, and it indicates the online identity of the communicating device without revealing the communication's content.

11. A network is two or more computers or other devices connected to each other that can exchange information with each other via some transmission method, such as by wires, cables, or radio waves. The equipment that connects a computer or other device to the network is commonly referred to as a network adapter. Most network adapters have a Media Access Control ("MAC") address assigned by the manufacturer of the adapter that is designed to be a unique identifying number. An adapter's unique MAC address allows for proper routing of communications on a local area network and may be used for other purposes, such as authentication of customers by some network service providers. Unlike a device's IP address that often changes each time a device connects to the Internet, a MAC address is fixed at the time of manufacture of the adapter. Because the address does not change and is intended to be unique, a MAC address can allow law enforcement to identify whether communications sent or received at different times are associated with the same adapter.

12. On the Internet, data transferred between devices is not sent as a continuous stream, but rather it is split into discrete packets. Generally, a single communication is sent as a series of packets. When the packets reach their destination, the receiving device reassembles them into the complete communication. Each packet has two parts: a header with routing and control information, and a payload, which generally contains user data. The header contains non-content information such as the packet's source and destination IP addresses and the packet's size.

13. In addition, different Internet applications are associated with different "port numbers," or numeric identifiers. The port number is transmitted along with any communication using that application. For example, port 80 typically is associated with communications involving the World Wide Web.

<u>THE RELEVANT FACTS</u>

14. The United States government, including the **[AGENT, AGENCY],** is investigating **[CRIME DESCRIPTION]**. The investigation concerns possible violations by unknown individuals of, inter alia, **INSERT LAW(S) VIOLATED.**

15. **OPTIONALLY INSERT FACTUAL PARAGRAPH(S) HERE IF REQUIRED BY YOUR JUDICIAL DISTRICT. FOR EXAMPLE, SOME DISTRICTS WILL INCLUDE A FACT PARAGRAPH LIKE THIS ONE: "THE INVESTIGATION RELATES TO THE PURCHASE AND SALE OF STOLEN CREDIT CARDS AND OTHER UNAUTHORIZED ACCESS DEVICES, WHICH ARE THEN USED TO PERPETRATE MAIL AND WIRE FRAUD. INVESTIGATORS BELIEVE THAT MATTERS RELEVANT TO THE OFFENSES UNDER INVESTIGATION HAVE BEEN AND CONTINUE TO BE DISCUSSED USING VERIZON WIRELESS CELL PHONE NUMBER 222-333-4444. VERIZON WIRELESS IS AN ELECTRONIC COMMUNICATION SERVICE PROVIDER DOING BUSINESS IN BEDMINSTER, NJ. INVESTIGATORS BELIEVE THAT THE LISTED SUBSCRIBER FOR THIS NUMBER IS JOHN JONES, A TARGET OF THE INVESTIGATION, ..."**

16. The conduct being investigated involves use of the **[IP ADDRESS OR EMAIL OR DOMAIN NAME OR MOBILE BROADBAND OR VOIP]** described in Attachment A. To further the investigation, investigators need to obtain the dialing, routing, addressing, and signaling information associated with communications sent to or from that IP address.

17. **LANGUAGE FOR IP:** The pen-trap devices sought by this application will record, decode, and/or capture dialing, routing, addressing, and signaling information associated with each communication to or from the IP address described in Attachment A, including the date, time, and duration of the communication, and the following, without geographic limit:

- IP addresses

- MAC addresses

- Port numbers

- Packet headers

LANGUAGE FOR EMAIL:

The pen-trap devices sought by this application will record, decode, and/or capture dialing, routing, addressing, and signaling information associated with each communication to or from the email account(s) described in Attachment A, including the date, time, and duration of the communication, and the following, without geographic limit:

- IP addresses, including IP addresses associated with access to the account

- Headers of email messages, including the source and destination network addresses, as well as the routes of transmission and size of the messages, but not content located in headers, such as subject lines

- the number and size of any attachments

LANGUAGE FOR DOMAIN NAME:

The pen-trap devices sought by this application will record, decode, and/or capture dialing, routing, addressing, and signaling information associated with each communication to or from the domain name described in Attachment A, including the date, time, and duration of the communication, and the following, without geographic limit:

- IP addresses

GOVERNMENT REQUESTS

2. For the reasons stated above, the United States requests that the Court enter an Order authorizing the installation and use of pen-trap devices to record, decode, and/or capture the dialing, routing, addressing, and signaling information described above for each communication to or from the IP address described in Attachment A, to include the date, time, and duration of

the communication, without geographic limit. The United States does not request and does not seek to obtain the contents of any communications, as defined in 18 U.S.C. § 2510(8).

3. The United States further requests that the Court authorize the foregoing installation and use for a period of sixty days from the date of the Court's Order, pursuant to 18 U.S.C. § 3123(c)(1).

4. The United States further requests, pursuant to 18 U.S.C. §§ 3123(b)(2) and 3124(a)-(b), that the Court order **[ISP]** and any other person or entity providing wire or electronic communication service in the United States whose assistance may facilitate execution of this Order to furnish, upon service of the Order, information, facilities, and technical assistance necessary to install the pen-trap devices, including installation and operation of the pen-trap devices unobtrusively and with minimum disruption of normal service. Any entity providing such assistance shall be reasonably compensated by the **[AGENT, AGENCY]**, pursuant to 18 U.S.C. § 3124(c), for reasonable expenses incurred in providing facilities and assistance in furtherance of this Order.

5. The United States further requests that the Court order **[ISP]** and any other person or entity whose assistance may facilitate execution of this Order to notify the applicant and the **[AGENT, AGENCY]** of any changes relating to the IP address described in Attachment A, and to provide prior notice to the applicant and the **[AGENT, AGENCY]** before terminating or changing service to the IP address.

6. The United States further requests that the Court order that the **[AGENT, AGENCY]** and the applicant have access to the information collected by the pen-trap devices as soon as practicable, twenty-four hours per day, or at such other times as may be acceptable to them, for the duration of the Order.

7. The United States further requests, pursuant to 18 U.S.C. § 3123(d)(2), that the Court order **[ISP]** and any other person or entity whose assistance facilitates execution of this Order,

and their agents and employees, not to disclose in any manner, directly or indirectly, by any action or inaction, the existence of this application and Order, the resulting pen-trap devices, or this investigation, unless and until authorized by this Court, except that **[ISP]** may disclose this Order to an attorney for **[ISP]** for the purpose of receiving legal advice.

8. The United States further requests that this application and any resulting Order be sealed until otherwise ordered by the Court, pursuant to 18 U.S.C. § 3123(d)(1).

9. The United States further requests that the Clerk of the Court provide the United States Attorney's Office with three certified copies of this application and Order, and provide copies of this Order to the **[AGENT, AGENCY]** and **[ISP]** upon request.

10. The foregoing is based on information provided to me in my official capacity by agents of the **[AGENT, AGENCY]**.

I declare under penalty of perjury that the foregoing is true and correct.

Executed on _____.

_____
[AUSA NAME AND INFORMATION]

UNITED STATES DISTRICT COURT
FOR THE **[JUDICIAL DISTRICT]**

IN RE APPLICATION OF THE)	
UNITED STATES OF AMERICA FOR)	MISC. NO. _____
AN ORDER AUTHORIZING THE)	
INSTALLATION AND USE OF PEN)	
REGISTERS AND TRAP AND)	
TRACE DEVICES)	
_____)	Filed Under Seal

ORDER

[AUSA NAME], on behalf of the United States, has submitted an application pursuant to 18 U.S.C. §§ 3122 and 3123, requesting that the Court issue an Order authorizing the installation and use of pen registers and trap and trace devices ("pen-trap devices") on the IP address described in Attachment A, which is incorporated into this Order by reference.

The Court finds that an attorney for the government has submitted the application and has certified that the information likely to be obtained by such installation and use is relevant to an ongoing criminal investigation being conducted by the **[AGENT, AGENCY]** of unknown individuals in connection with possible violations of **INSERT LAW(S) VIOLATED.**

IT IS THEREFORE ORDERED, pursuant to 18 U.S.C. § 3123, that **[AGENT, AGENCY]** may install and use pen-trap devices to record, decode, and/or capture dialing, routing, addressing, and signaling information associated with each communication to or from the IP address described in Attachment A., including the date, time, and duration of the communication, and the following, without geographic limit:

- IP addresses
- MAC addresses
- Port numbers
- Packet headers

IT IS FURTHER ORDERED, pursuant to 18 U.S.C. § 3123(c)(1), that the use and installation of the foregoing is authorized for sixty days from the date of this Order;

IT IS FURTHER ORDERED, pursuant to 18 U.S.C. §§ 3123(b)(2) and 3124(a)-(b), that **[ISP]** and any other person or entity providing wire or electronic communication service in the United States whose assistance may, pursuant to 18 U.S.C. § 3123(a), facilitate the execution of this Order shall, upon service of this Order, furnish information, facilities, and technical assistance necessary to install the pen-trap devices, including installation and operation of the pen-trap devices unobtrusively and with minimum disruption of normal service;

IT IS FURTHER ORDERED that the **[AGENT, AGENCY]** reasonably compensate **[ISP]** and any other person or entity whose assistance facilitates execution of this Order for reasonable expenses incurred in complying with this Order;

IT IS FURTHER ORDERED that **[ISP]** and any other person or entity whose assistance may facilitate execution of this Order notify the applicant and the **[AGENT, AGENCY]** of any changes relating to the IP address described in Attachment A, including changes to subscriber information, and to provide prior notice to the **[AGENT, AGENCY]** before terminating or changing service to the IP address;

IT IS FURTHER ORDERED that the **[AGENT, AGENCY]** and the applicant have access to the information collected by the pen-trap devices as soon as practicable, twenty-four hours per day, or at such other times as may be acceptable to the **[AGENT, AGENCY],** for the duration of the Order;

IT IS FURTHER ORDERED, pursuant to 18 U.S.C. § 3123(d)(2), that **[ISP]** and any other person or entity whose assistance facilitates execution of this Order, and their agents and employees, shall not disclose in any manner, directly or indirectly, by any action or inaction, the existence of the application and this Order, the pen-trap devices, or the investigation to any person, unless and until otherwise ordered by the Court, except that **[ISP]** may disclose this Order to an attorney for **[ISP]** for the purpose of receiving legal advice;

[*****OPTIONAL. Most providers do not require hard copies.**] IT IS FURTHER ORDERED that the Clerk of the Court shall provide the United States Attorney's Office with three certified copies of this application and Order, and shall provide copies of this Order to the **[AGENT, AGENCY]** and **[ISP]**upon request;

IT IS FURTHER ORDERED that the application and this Order are sealed until otherwise ordered by the Court, pursuant to 18 U.S.C. § 3123(d)(1).

_____

Date

_____

United States Magistrate Judge

ATTACHMENT A

[ISP]

Facility	Number or identifier	Owner, if known	Subject of investigation, if known
IP address	**[INFO. REQUESTED]**	not known	unknown individuals

Application for Internet T-III – Electronic Communications Intercept

IN THE UNITED STATES DISTRICT COURT
FOR THE **[JUDICIAL DISTRICT]**

IN THE MATTER OF THE APPLICATION OF THE UNITED STATES OF AMERICA FOR AN ORDER AUTHORIZING THE INTERCEPTION OF ELECTRONIC COMMUNICATIONS	Case No. _____

APPLICATION FOR INTERCEPTION
OF ELECTRONIC COMMUNICATIONS

The United States of America, through its counsel of record, **[NAME]**, Assistant United States Attorney, and **[NAME]**, United States Attorney, hereby applies to the Court pursuant to Section 2518 of Title 18, United States Code, for an order authorizing the interception of electronic communications. In support of this application, counsel states the following:

1. Applicant is an investigative or law enforcement officer of the United States within the meaning of Section 2510(7) of Title 18, United States Code, that is, an attorney authorized by law to prosecute or participate in the prosecution of offenses enumerated in Section 2516 of Title 18, United States Code. Applicant is also an "attorney for the Government" as defined in Rule 54(c) of the Federal Rules of Criminal Procedure, and is authorized to make an application to a Federal Judge of competent jurisdiction for an order authorizing the interception of electronic communications.

2. This application is for an order pursuant to Section 2518 of Title 18, United States Code, authorizing the interception of electronic communications until the attainment of the authorized objectives or, in any event, the end of thirty (30) days from the earlier of the day on which the investigative or law enforcement officers first begin to conduct an interception under the Court's order or ten (10) days after the order is entered, of an individual known only as

[TARGET ALIAS], and others as yet unknown, to and from a computer server with Internet Protocol address [TARGET SERVER IP ADDRESS], concerning federal felony offenses as provided for by Section 2516(3) of Title 18, United States Code, that is, [LIST OF OFFENSES], that are being committed by the above-named person and others as yet unknown.

3.   Pursuant to Section 2516 of Title 18, United States Code, the Attorney General of the United States has specially designated the Assistant Attorney General, any Acting Assistant Attorney General, any Deputy Assistant Attorney General or any acting Deputy Assistant Attorney General of the Criminal Division to exercise the power conferred on the Attorney General by Section 2516 of Title 18, United States Code, to authorize this Application. Under the power designated to him by special designation of the Attorney General pursuant to Order Number 2943-2008, of January 22, 2008, an appropriate official of the Criminal Division, Deputy Assistant Attorney General [NAME], has authorized this Application. Attached to this Application are copies of the Attorney General's order of special designation and the Memorandum of Authorization approving this Application.

4.   I have discussed the circumstances of the above offenses with [AFFIANT TITLE, NAME] of the [AFFIANT AGENCY], who has participated in the conduct of this investigation, and have examined his affidavit, which is attached as Exhibit 1 to this application and is incorporated herein by reference. Based upon that affidavit, your applicant states upon information and belief that:

         a.   there is probable cause to believe that an individual known only **as [TARGET ALIAS]**, and others as yet unknown, have committed, are committing, and will continue to commit violations of at least the following statutes: [LIST OF OFFENSES].

         b.   there is probable cause to believe that particular electronic communications of the individual known only as *"[TARGET ALIAS]*," and others as yet unknown, concerning the above-described offenses will be obtained through the interception of electronic communications. These electronic communications will concern **[SUMMARIZE POSSIBLE CONTENTS AS THEY RELATE TO VIOLATIONS OF THE LAW]**. These communications are expected to constitute admissible evidence of the above-described offenses;

c. normal investigative procedures reasonably appear to be unlikely to succeed if tried, as described in further detail in the attached affidavit;

d. there is probable cause to believe that the computer server with Internet Protocol address **[TARGET SERVER IP ADDRESS]**, owned by **[COLLOCATION PROVIDER NAME AND BUSINESS ADDRESS]** and located at **[COLLOCATION PROVIDER NAME]**'s data center, **[COLLOCATION PROVIDER SERVER ROOM ADDRESS]**, is being used and will continue to be used in connection with the commission of the above-described offenses;

5. There have been no prior applications in connection with this investigation for the interception of the oral, wire, or electronic communications of any of the individuals, facilities, or premises specified in this application.

6. This Court has territorial jurisdiction to issue the requested order under 18 U.S.C. § 2518(3) because communications passing through the TARGET SERVER will first be read by agents of the **[AFFIANT AGENCY]** in the **[DISTRICT]**, regardless of where the communications originate from or are sent to, and regardless of the location of the TARGET SERVER. *See United States v. Luong*, 471 F.3d 1107, 1109 (9th Cir. 2006) (jurisdiction for a Wiretap Act order lies in district where intercepted communications will first be heard); *United States v.*

Ramirez, 112 F.3d 849, 852 (7th Cir. 1997) (same); *United States v. Denman,* 100 F.3d 399, 403 (5th Cir.1996) (same); *United States v. Rodriguez,* 968 F.2d 130, 136 (2d Cir.1992) (same).

WHEREFORE, your applicant believes that there is probable cause to believe that the individual known only as **"[TARGET ALIAS],"** and others as yet unknown, are engaged in the commission of at least the following statutes: **[LIST OF OFFENSES],** and that **"[TARGET ALIA**S]," and others as yet unknown, is using the computer server with Internet Protocol address **[TARGET SERVER IP ADDRESS]**, owned by **[COLLOCATION PROVIDER NAME AND BUSINESS ADDRESS]** and located at **[COLLOCATION PROVIDER NAME]**'s data center, **[COLLOCATION PROVIDER SERVER ROOM ADDRESS]**, in connection with the commission of the above-described offenses; and that electronic communications of **"[TARGET ALIAS]"** and others yet unknown will be intercepted through monitoring of electronic communications to or from the above-described electronic mail accounts.

Based on the allegations set forth in this application and the affidavit of **[AFFIANT NAME, TITLE]** of the **[AFFIANT AGENCY],** attached as Exhibit 1, the applicant requests this court to issue an order pursuant to the power conferred upon it by Section 2518 of Title 18, United States Code, authorizing the [AFFIANT AGENCY] to intercept electronic communications to and from the computer server with Internet Protocol address **[TARGET SERVER IP ADDRESS]**, until such communications are intercepted that reveal the manner in which **"[TARGET ALIAS],"** and others as yet unknown, participate in the specified offenses and reveal the identities of their conspirators, evidence of their knowledge, place of operation, and nature of the conspiracy, or for a period of thirty days measured from the earlier of the day on which the investigative or law enforcement officers first begin to conduct the interception or ten days from the date of the order.

IT IS REQUESTED FURTHER that such interception of electronic communications to and from the computer server with Internet Protocol address **[TARGET SERVER IP ADDRESS]** be authorized on a twenty-four (24) hour basis.

IT IS REQUESTED FURTHER that this Court issue an order pursuant to Section 2518(4) of Title 18, United States Code, directing **[COLLOCATION PROVIDER NAME]**, an electronic communications service provider as defined in Section 2510(15) of Title 18, United States Code, to furnish and continue to furnish the **[AFFIANT AGENCY]** with all information, facilities and technical assistance necessary to accomplish the interceptions unobtrusively and with a minimum of interference with the services that **[COLLOCATION PROVIDER NAME]** is affording the persons whose communications are to be intercepted, and to ensure an effective and secure installation of electronic devices capable of intercepting electronic communications to or from the computer server with Internet Protocol address **[TARGET SERVER IP ADDRESS]** at **[COLLOCATION PROVIDER NAME]**. **[COLLOCATION PROVIDER NAME]** shall be compensated by the **[AFFIANT AGENCY]** for reasonable expenses incurred in providing such facilities or assistance.

IT IS REQUESTED FURTHER, to avoid prejudice to this criminal investigation, that the Court order **[COLLOCATION PROVIDER NAME]**, and its agents and employees not to disclose or cause a disclosure of this Court's order or the request for information, facilities, and assistance by the **[AFFIANT AGENCY]** or the existence of the investigation to any person other than those of their agents and employees who require this information to accomplish the services requested. In particular, **[COLLOCATION PROVIDER NAME]** and its agents and employees should be ordered not to make such disclosure to any of its subscribers, or to any interceptee or participant in the intercepted communications.

IT IS REQUESTED FURTHER that this Court direct that its order be executed as soon as practicable after it is signed and that all monitoring of electronic communications shall be

445

conducted in such a way as to minimize the interception and disclosure of the communications intercepted to those communications relevant to the pending investigation, in accordance with the minimization requirements of Chapter 119 of Title 18, United States Code.

Intercepted electronic communications will be minimized after-the-fact and as soon as practicable after such interception pursuant to Section 2518(5) of Title 18, United States Code. The electronic communications will be reviewed and minimized as follows: All electronic communications sent from or received by the target user account will be intercepted in their entirety and electronically stored on magnetic media. Working copies of all of the electronic communications will then be made from the magnetic media. As soon as practicable, these electronic communications will be reviewed and minimized. Agents will review those working copies, and based on the identities of the parties to the electronic communication and the subject matter and content of the electronic communication, will determine whether the communication appears to be pertinent to the criminal offenses listed in the Court's order or pertinent to other criminal activity. As soon as an electronic communication is determined to be non-pertinent, reviewing of the electronic communication will cease and the communications will be designated as non-pertinent. Minimized electronic communications will be spot-monitored to determine if they have subsequently become criminal in nature.

The interception of electronic communications authorized by this Court's order must terminate upon attainment of the authorized objectives or, in any event, at the end of 30 days measured from the earlier of a) the day on which investigative or law enforcement officers first begin to conduct an interception or b) 10 days after the order is entered.

IT IS REQUESTED FURTHER that the Court order that either Assistant United States Attorney ("AUSA") **[AUSA NAME]**, or any other AUSA familiar with the facts of the case provide the Court with a report on or about the tenth, twentieth, and thirtieth days following the earlier of the day on which the investigative or law enforcement officers first begin to conduct the interceptions or ten days from the date of this order, showing what progress has been made toward achievement of the authorized objectives and the need for continued interception. If any of the aforementioned reports should become due on a weekend or holiday, it is requested further that such report become due on the next business day thereafter.

IT IS REQUESTED FURTHER that the Court direct that its orders, this application and the accompanying affidavit and proposed order, and all interim reports filed with the Court with regard to this matter be sealed until further order of this Court, except that copies of the order, in full or redacted form, may be served on the **[AFFIANT AGENCY]** and **[COLLOCATION PROVIDER NAME]** as necessary to effectuate the Court's order as set forth in the proposed order accompanying this application.

I declare under penalty of perjury that the foregoing is true and correct.

Executed on April 16, 2019.

Respectfully submitted,
[USA NAME]
United States Attorney

By: _____
[AUSA NAME]
Assistant United States Attorney

IN THE UNITED STATES DISTRICT COURT
FOR THE **[JUDICIAL DISTRICT]**

IN THE MATTER OF THE APPLICATION OF THE UNITED STATES OF AMERICA FOR AN ORDER AUTHORIZING THE INTERCEPTION OF ELECTRONIC COMMUNICATIONS	Case No. _____

AFFIDAVIT IN SUPPORT OF APPLICATION AUTHORIZING
THE INTERCEPTION OF ELECTRONIC COMMUNICATIONS

I, **[AFFIANT NAME]**, being duly sworn, depose and state:

AGENT QUALIFICATIONS

1.   I am a **[AFFIANT TITLE]** with the **[AFFIANT AGENCY]**. **[DESCRIBE RELEVANT TRAINING, PRIOR TIII EXPERIENCE, AND RELEVANT JOB EXPERIENCE.]**

2.   I am an investigative or law enforcement officer of the United States within the meaning of Section 2510(7) of Title 18, United States Code, and am empowered by law to conduct investigations and to make arrests for offenses enumerated in Section 2516 of Title 18, United States Code.

3.   The facts in this affidavit come from my personal observations, my training and experience, and information obtained from other agents and witnesses. This affidavit is intended to show merely that there is sufficient probable cause for the requested warrant and does not set forth all of my knowledge about this matter.

SUMMARY

4.   **[OPTIONAL: GIVE A ONE OR TWO-PARAGRAPH SUMMARY OF THE INVESTIGATION AND THE NEED FOR THE WIRETAP ORDER, USING**

PLAIN LANGUAGE, TO SERVE AS A ROADMAP FOR THE REST OF THE AFFIDAVIT.].

IDENTIFICATION OF TARGET SERVER

5.   The TARGET SERVER is a computer with Internet Protocol address **[TARGET SERVER IP ADDRESS],** owned by **[COLLOCATION PROVIDER NAME, BUSINESS ADDRESS]** and located at **[COLLOCATION PROVIDER NAME]**'s data center, **[COLLOCATION PROVIDER SERVER ROOM ADDRESS]** (hereinafter, the "TARGET SERVER"). *[COLLOCATION PROVIDER NAME]* is a collocation provider: a facility that runs a data center and charges customers for the service of keeping servers operating, powered, air conditioned, and provided with Internet access.

6.   According to the records of **[COLLOCATION PROVIDER NAME], [DESCRIBE EVERYTHING KNOWN ABOUT THE SERVER]**

IDENTIFICATION OF TARGET SUBJECTS

7.   According to the records of **[COLLOCATION PROVIDER NAME]**, the TARGET SERVER is leased to someone who identified himself to **[COLLOCATION PROVIDER NAME]** as **[TARGET ALIAS]**. I believe that **"[TARGET ALIAS]"** is an alias and not the true name of the person leasing the server. The identity of the person or persons committing the offenses described in this affidavit is not known.

8.   **[DESCRIBE PERSONS WHO YOU THINK MIGHT BE USING THE SERVER TO COMMUNICATE, INCLUDING VICTIMS, CUSTOMERS, CO-CONSPIRATORS, ETC.].**

9. As such, the parties to the intercepted communications will include unknown persons. The remainder of this Affidavit will refer to those persons as SUBJECTS.

PREDICATE OFFENSES

10. As explained below, there is probable cause to believe SUBJECTS are committing offenses involving at least the following statutes: **[LIST OF OFFENSES];** and there is probable cause to believe SUBJECTS will continue to commit the above-listed offenses. The remainder of this affidavit will refer to this list as the "OFFENSES."

11. Title 18, United States Code, Section 2516(3) permits the interception of electronic communications for any federal felony. The maximum term of imprisonment authorized for each of the OFFENSES is more than one year. Thus, each of the OFFENSES is classified as a felony under 18 U.S.C. § 3559(a).

GOALS OF INVESTIGATION

12. Intercepting electronic communications passing through the TARGET SERVER will further the goals of **[E.G.: IDENTIFYING VICTIMS, CUSTOMERS, CO-CONSPIRATORS, AND DETERMINING THE LOCATION OF OTHER EVIDENCE.]**

PRIOR APPLICATIONS

13. Your Affiant has been informed that on or about [DATE OF REVIEW], a review of electronic and wire surveillance indices maintained by the Drug Enforcement Administration (DEA), indices maintained by the Federal Bureau of Investigation, and indices maintained by the Bureau of Immigration and Customs Enforcement (ICE) was conducted. As a result of this inquiry, DEA, FBI, and ICE electronic and wire surveillance indices revealed no prior

applications for a court order authorizing or approving the interception of electronic, wire, or oral communications concerning "**[TARGET ALIAS]**," or the Internet Protocol address **[TARGET SERVER IP ADDRESS]** for which authorization is currently sought.

PROBABLE CAUSE

RELEVANT COMPUTER AND INTERNET TERMS

[LIST ANY RELEVANT COMPUTER AND INTERNET TERMINOLOGY AND DEFINITIONS FROM THE BELOW OPTIONS AND DELETE THOSE TERMS NOT RELEVANT TO THE APPLICATION]

14.   Bot. A bot is a computer that has been compromised by malicious software for use in completing malicious and/or illegal tasks via remote direction. Most users that have a computer acting as a bot are not aware that their computers have been compromised. Compromised computer is synonymous with bot, and either may be used based on context. A larger number of bots, called a bot network or botnet, are typically controlled by one computer called a command and control server. The owner of the command and control server can direct the botnet to initiate a denial of service attack, send spam, operate as proxies (blindly forwarding Internet data), host phishing sites, or participate in other cyber-crime.

15.   Domain name. A domain name is the familiar easy-to-remember name used to identify computers on the internet. (e.g. cybercrime.gov). Domain names correspond to one or more IP addresses. The Domain Name System (DNS) is a hierarchical naming system for computers connected to the Internet. It associates information with domain names. Most importantly, it translates domain names meaningful to humans into the numerical identifiers associated with networking equipment for the purpose of locating and addressing these devices

worldwide. An often used analogy to explain the Domain Name System is that it serves as the "phone book" for the Internet by translating human-friendly computer names into IP addresses.

16.   Internet. The Internet is a collection of computers and computer networks which are connected to one another via high-speed data links and telephone lines for the purpose of sharing information.   Connections between Internet computers exist across state and international borders and information sent between computers connected to the Internet may cross state and international borders, even if those computers are located in the same state.

17.   Instant Messaging. Instant messaging (IM) is a collection of technologies that create the possibility of real-time text-based communication between two or more participants via the Internet. Instant messaging allows for the immediate transmission of communications, including immediate receipt of acknowledgment or reply.

18.   Internet Service Provider ("ISP"). An ISP is a commercial service that provides Internet connections for its subscribers. In addition to providing access to the Internet via telephone or other telecommunications lines, ISPs may also provide Internet e-mail accounts and other services unique to each particular ISP. ISPs maintain records pertaining to the individuals or companies that have subscriber accounts with them. Those records could include identifying and billing information, account access information in the form of log files, e-mail transaction information, and other information.

19.   IP Address. The Internet Protocol address (IP address) is a unique numeric address used by computers on the Internet. An IP address looks like a series of four numbers, each in the range of 0-255, separated by periods. Every computer attached to the Internet computer must be assigned an IP address so that Internet traffic sent from and directed to that

computer may be directed properly from its source to its destination. Most Internet service providers control a range of IP addresses.

20. <u>Log Files</u>. Log files are computer files containing information regarding the activities of computer users, processes/programs running on the system and the activity of computer resources such as networks, modems, and printers. Log files can be used to identify activities that occurred on a specific computer. Installation (or install or setup) of a program is the act and the effect of putting the program in a computer system so that it can be executed.

21. <u>Malicious Code.</u> Malicious code is a term used to describe any software code in any part of a software system or script that is intended to cause undesired effects, security breaches or damage to a system. Malicious code describes a broad category of system security terms that includes attack scripts, viruses, worms, Trojan Horses, backdoors, and malicious active content. It is often installed on a victim computer system via the Internet through spam that contains attachments or through a web site where code is injected to automatically download onto a victim system when it is viewed through a web browser. When it is installed onto a victim computer system to perform malicious activity, it is often referred to as malware.

22. <u>Phishing</u>. "Phishing" is defined as "tricking people into providing their personal and financial information by pretending to be from a legitimate company, agency or organization." Internet "Phishing" is conducted by a criminal who creates an Internet web site which is either a clone of an original web site or else is a customized web site that utilizes counterfeit marks in an effort to appear as if it is a site which belongs to a company or organization being used as part of the scheme. After the creation of the web site, the perpetrator(s) hosts the web site on a computer for viewing by Internet users. The computer used by the criminal is easily traceable back to the criminal. Once the counterfeit web site is

running, the perpetrator uses a variety of techniques to make it appear authentic through the use of corporate logos and graphics which closely emulate the real web site or organization. A mass e-mail solicitation is then performed in an effort to direct potential victims to the cloned web site where at which they are requested to provide specific financial and personal information. Once obtained by the perpetrator(s), this financial information is then abused for their own financial gain. Due to the relative anonymity with which these criminals are able to conduct this activity, traditional investigative techniques are inadequate in successfully proving the necessary elements of the offense(s). Popular corporations whose web sites are cloned by Internet "phishers" include banks, brokerage firms, and online auction-related sites such as eBay or PayPal.

23. Proxy. A proxy is a network service for making indirect connections to other network services. A client computer connects to a proxy and instructs it to connect to another computer. The destination computer perceives an incoming connection from the proxy, not the client computer. Like many network services, proxies have legitimate uses, but they are often used by cyber criminals to conceal their identity and location.

24. Server. A server is a centralized computer that provides services for other computers connected to it via a network or the Internet. The computers that use the server's services are sometimes called "clients." When a user accesses email, Internet web pages, or accesses files stored on the network itself, those files are pulled electronically from the server, where they are stored, and are sent to the client's computer via the network or Internet. Notably, server computers can be physically located in any location; for example, it is not uncommon for a network's server to be located hundreds (or even thousands) of miles away from the client computers. In larger networks, it is common for servers to be dedicated to a single task. For example, a server that is configured so that its sole task is to support a World Wide Web site is

known simply as a "Web server." Similarly, a server that only stores and processes e-mail is known as a "mail server."

25.   Spam E-mail. Also known as bulk or junk e-mail, spam e-mail, or simply spam involves sending nearly identical messages to numerous recipients by e-mail. A common synonym for spam is unsolicited bulk e-mail.

BACKGROUND ON COLLOCATION COMPANIES SUCH AS [COLLOCATION PROVIDER NAME]

26.   Collocation companies, such as **[COLLOCATION PROVIDER NAME]**, maintain server computers connected to the Internet. Their customers use those computers to operate servers on the Internet that, in turn, provide services to client computers.

27.   Collocation companies' customers place files, software code, databases, and other data on the servers. To do this, customers connect from their own computers to the server computers across the Internet. This connection can occur in several ways. It is frequently possible for the customer to directly access the server computer through the Secure Shell ("SSH") or Telnet protocols. These protocols allow remote users to type commands to the server. The SSH protocol can also be used to copy files to the server. Customers can also upload files through a different protocol, known as File Transfer Protocol ("FTP"). Servers often maintain logs of SSH, Telnet, and FTP connections, showing the dates and times of the connections, the method of connecting, and the Internet Protocol addresses ("IP addresses") of the remote users' computers (IP addresses are used to identify computers connected to the Internet). Servers also commonly log the port number associated with the connection. Port numbers assist computers in determining how to interpret incoming and outgoing data. For example, SSH, Telnet, and FTP are generally assigned to different ports.

28.   In some cases, a subscriber or user will communicate directly with a collocation company about issues relating to a website or account, such as technical problems, billing inquiries, or complaints from other users. Collocation companies typically retain records about such communications, including records of contacts between the user and the company's support services, as well as records of any actions taken by the company or user as a result of the communications.

29.   **[ESTABLISH PROBABLE CAUSE HERE. DESCRIBE USE OF TARGET SERVER WITHIN 6 MONTHS OF APPLICATION FOR CRIMINAL PURPOSES. DESCRIBE THE RESULTS OF OTHER INVESTIGATIVE METHODS, SUCH AS PEN/TRAPS, ECPA PROCESS, AND CONFIDENTIAL INFORMANTS.]**

NECESSITY

30.   Based upon your Affiant's training and experience, and based upon all of the facts set forth herein, it is your Affiant's belief that the interception of communications is the only available technique with a reasonable likelihood of securing the evidence necessary to prove beyond a reasonable doubt that SUBJECTS are engaged in the above-described offenses.

31.   Numerous investigative techniques that are usually employed in an investigation of this type have been tried and have failed, reasonably appear to be unlikely to succeed if they are tried, or are too dangerous to employ: **[THE BELOW EXAMPLES ARE JUST BOILERPLATE LANGUAGE EXAMPLES. THIS SECTION SHOULD BE VERY SPECIFIC TO YOUR CASE. EXPLAIN WHY EACH TECHNIQUE WILL NOT WORK, HAS BEEN TRIED AND FAILED, OR IS TOO DANGEROUS. USE SPECIFIC RATHER THAN GENERIC EXAMPLES. BE SURE TO COVER ALL**

POTENTIALLY APPLICABLE TECHNIQUES, INCLUDING: PHYSICAL SURVEILLANCE; USE OF GRAND JURY; CONFIDENTIAL SOURCES; UNDERCOVER AGENTS; SEARCH WARRANTS/SEIZURES; INTERVIEWS; PEN REGISTER/TOLL RECORDS; TRASH SEARCHES; ARRESTS; FINANCIAL INVESTIGATIONS; OTHER ELECTRONIC SURVEILLANCE; MOBILE TRACKERS; POLE CAMERA]

       a.   <u>Physical surveillance, grand jury subpoena for testimony, subject interviews, trash searches, and arrests.</u> The true names and locations of SUBJECTS are not known; in fact, one goal of the investigation is to learn those facts. Consequently, any investigative technique that requires knowledge of a subject's location is currently impossible to employ in this case. This includes physical surveillance of SUBJECTS, subpoenaing their testimony before a grand jury, interviewing them, searching their trash, and arresting them.

       b.   <u>Grand jury subpoena for records.</u> The government has used grand jury subpoenas directed to online service providers. These subpoenas have provided registration information for online accounts. However, because the SUBJECTS are actively seeking to evade detection and capture, they have consistently used false names in registering for online accounts. Consequently, grand jury subpoenas for records appear to be unlikely to determine the identity and location of SUBJECTS.

       c.   <u>Confidential sources.</u> [Confidential sources are unavailable, because SUBJECTS communicate, if at all, through the Internet only.] [These sources are only able to contact SUBJECTS via computer and would not be able to obtain the information sought through electronic surveillance.] [Information provided by cooperating sources, even if all sources agreed to testify, would not, without the evidence available through the requested electronic surveillance, result in a successful prosecution of all the participants.] [These sources are only able to contact the named interceptees via computer and would not be able to obtain the information sought through the electronic surveillance, authorization for which is sought with this affidavit and application.]

d.   Undercover Agents. [I believe that undercover agents would be of limited value in this investigation as] [the primary means of communication, transfer of monies, and facilitation of criminal activity of SUBJECTS occur primarily via computers and the Internet.] [As with cooperating sources, investigators believe that Undercover Police Officers and/or Agents would not be able to fully identify all members of this ongoing conspiracy or define the roles of those conspirators sufficiently for prosecution or that would define the knowledge or intent harbored by each of the participants in the fraudulent activities.] [Information provided by Undercover Police Officers and/or Agents, as well as cooperating sources, even if all sources agreed to testify, would not, without the evidence available through the requested electronic surveillance, result in a successful prosecution of all the participants.]

e.   Search warrants. [A search warrant of the TARGET SERVER was executed on **[DATE],** pursuant to a warrant issued by this Court under 18 U.S.C. § 2703. The warrant allowed the search of the TARGET SERVER for, among other things, configuration files and the contents of any Jabber communications stored on the server. However, this did not yield the contents of communications sent through the TARGET SERVER, because the TARGET SERVER had not been configured to save that information.] [Search warrants, by their nature, can reveal at most what passed through the TARGET SERVER in the past; they cannot be performed quickly enough or often enough to yield useful information about the ongoing efforts of SUBJECTS.] [As explained more fully above, logs indicate that the contents of the TARGET SERVER is regularly deleted.] [Furthermore, it is not presently known with any certainty where all of the targets of this investigation reside, or where they receive, hide, transfer, and conceal the proceeds of their crime.]

f.   Pen registers and trap and trace devices. As noted above, pen registers and trap and trace devices have been used in this investigation. Acting under orders from this Court, the **[AFFIANT AGENCY]** has been monitoring non-content information sent to or from the TARGET SERVER since **[DATE]**. As described above, those pen registers and trap and trace devices have revealed information suggesting that [communications relevant to the OFFENSES are being sent to and from the TARGET SERVER. Pen registers, telephone toll records, and subscriber information, however, are inadequate investigative techniques under the circumstances of this case. Pen registers and trap and trace devices cannot prove what is actually being said.

MINIMIZATION PLAN

32.   All interceptions will be minimized in accordance with Chapter 119 of Title 18, United States Code. All electronic communications sent from or received by the target user account will be intercepted in their entirety and electronically stored on computer storage media. Working copies of all of the electronic communications will then be made from the storage media. As soon as practicable, these electronic communications will be reviewed and minimized. Agents will review those working copies, and based on the identities of the parties to the electronic communication and the subject matter and content of the electronic communication, will

determine whether the communication appears to be pertinent to the criminal offenses listed in the Court's order or pertinent to other criminal activity. As soon as an electronic communication is determined to be non-pertinent, reviewing of the electronic communication will cease and the communications will be designated as non-pertinent. Minimized electronic communications will be spot-monitored to determine if they have subsequently become criminal in nature.

33.   [As some of the electronic messages obtained in the execution of the search warrant on the TARGET SERVER was in a foreign language, which I believe was Spanish, some of the electronic communications intercepted may be in Spanish. At the time of this writing, we do not have an employee assigned to this investigation who can translate Spanish to English to facilitate the minimization process. Accordingly, each intercepted communication that appears to be in a foreign language, particularly in Spanish, will be sent to a translator for translation. Once translated, each communication will be returned to the investigators responsible for the minimization.]

34.   [Describe whether privileged communications (attorney-client, husband-wife, doctor-patient, or priest-penitent) are a possibility and how they will be dealt with].

JURISDICTION

35.   If the Court grants the order, communications passing through the TARGET SERVER will first be read by agents of the **[AFFIANT AGENCY]** in the **[JUDICIAL DISTRICT]**, regardless of where the communications originate from or are sent to, and regardless of the location of the TARGET SERVER.

LENGTH OF INTERCEPTION

36.   Your Affiant believes that the facts alleged herein establish that SUBJECTS and others yet unknown and unidentified are engaged in an ongoing criminal enterprise. Evidence sought will be intercepted on a continuing basis following the first receipt of the particular communications that are the object of this request. Your Affiant further believes that the information in this affidavit provides probable cause to believe that the TARGET SERVER is being used to facilitate in the specified OFFENSES, and that the proposed surveillance of the TARGET SERVER will disclose evidence of these offenses. Therefore, it is requested that the interception not be required to terminate when the communications described herein are first intercepted, but be allowed to continue until communications are intercepted which fully reveal the scope of the enterprise, including the identities of all participants, their places and methods of operations, and the various criminal activities in which they are engaged which are in furtherance of the enterprise, not to exceed 30 days measured from the earlier of the day on which investigative or law enforcement officers first begin to conduct interception under this Court's Order or 10 days after the Order is entered.

CONCLUSION

37.   The above establishes probable cause for belief that—

a. SUBJECTS (as described above the the "INDENTIFICATION OF TARGET SUBJECTS" section) are committing, have committed, and are about to commit OFFENSES (as described above in the "PREDICATE OFFENSES" section);

461

b. the interception of electronic communications passing through the TARGET SERVER will concern the OFFENSES (such as [SUMMARIZE POSSIBLE CONTENTS]) and will be obtained through the interception of such communications;

c. normal investigative procedures have been tried and have failed;

d. the TARGET SERVER is leased to and commonly used by SUBJECTS.

Respectfully submitted,

_____

[AFFIANT NAME]
[AFFIANT TITLE]
[AFFIANT AGENCY]

Sworn to before me on **DATE**

_____

HON. **[JUDGE NAME]**
UNITED STATES DISTRICT JUDGE
[DISTRICT]

IN THE UNITED STATES DISTRICT COURT
FOR THE **[JUDICIAL DISTRICT]**

IN THE MATTER OF THE
APPLICATION OF THE UNITED
STATES OF AMERICA FOR AN ORDER
AUTHORIZING THE INTERCEPTION
OF ELECTRONIC COMMUNICATIONS

Case No. _____

ORDER AUTHORIZING INTERCEPTION OF
ELECTRONIC COMMUNICATIONS

Application under oath having been made before me by **[AUSA NAME],** Assistant United States

Attorney, The **[JUDICIAL DISTRICT**], investigative or law enforcement officer of the United

States within the meaning of Section 2510(7) of Title 18, United States Code, for an order au-

thorizing the interception of electronic communications pursuant to Section 2518 of Title 18,

United States Code, and full consideration having been given to the matter set forth therein, the

Court finds:

a.   there is probable cause to believe that an individual known only as **[TARGET

ALIA**S], and others as yet unknown, have committed, are committing, and will continue to com-

mit federal felony offenses as provided for by Section 2516(3) of Title 18, United States Code,

that is, at least the following statutes: **[LIST OF OFFENSES];**

b.   there is probable cause to believe that particular electronic communications of

"[TARGET ALIAS]," and others as yet unknown, concerning the above-described offenses will

be obtained through the interception of electronic communications. These electronic communi-

cations will concern **[SUMMARIZE POSSIBLE CONTENTS].** These communications are

expected to constitute admissible evidence of the above-described offenses;

c.   it has been established that normal investigative procedures reasonably appear to

be unlikely to succeed if tried;

d.   there is probable cause to believe that the computer server with Internet Protocol

address **[TARGET SERVER IP ADDRESS],** owned by **[COLLOCATION PROVIDER**

NAME, BUSINESS ADDRESS] and located at **[COLLOCATION PROVIDER NAME]'s**

data center, **[COLLOCATION PROVIDER SERVER ROOM ADDRESS],** is being used

and will continue to be used in connection with the commission of the above-described offenses;

WHEREFORE, IT IS HEREBY ORDERED that Special Agents of the **[AFFIANT**

AGENCY] are authorized, pursuant to an application authorized by a duly designated official of

the Criminal Division, Deputy Assistant Attorney General **[NAME],** United States Department

of Justice, pursuant to the power delegated to that official by special designation of the Attorney

General and vested in the Attorney General by Section 2516 of Title 18, United States Code, to

intercept wire and electronic communications to and from the computer server with Internet

Protocol address **[TARGET SERVER IP ADDRESS],** said interception to include the con-

tents of every Internet Protocol packet sent to or originating from that server;

PROVIDED that such interceptions shall not terminate automatically after the first interception

that reveals the manner in which "**[TARGET ALIAS]**," and others as yet unknown conduct

their illegal activities, but may continue until all communications are intercepted which reveal fully

the manner in which the above-named persons and others as yet unknown are committing the

offenses described herein, and which reveal fully the identities of their confederates and their

places of operation, or for a period of 30 days measured from the earlier of the day on which

investigative or law enforcement officers first begin to conduct an interception under this order

or 10 days after this order is entered, whichever is earlier.

IT IS ORDERED FURTHER that such interceptions are allowed on a 24-hour basis.

IT IS ORDERED FURTHER, based upon the request of the applicant pursuant to Section

2518(4) of Title 18, United States Code, that **[COLLOCATION PROVIDER NAME],** an

electronic communication service provider as defined in Section 2510(15) of Title 18, United

States Code, shall furnish the **[AFFIANT AGENCY]** with all information, facilities and technical assistance necessary to accomplish the interceptions unobtrusively and with a minimum of interference with the services that **[COLLOCATION PROVIDER NAME]** is according the person(s) whose communications are to be intercepted, with **[COLLOCATION PROVIDER NAME]** to be compensated by the **[AFFIANT AGENCY]** for reasonable expenses incurred in providing such facilities or assistance.

IT IS ORDERED FURTHER that, to avoid prejudice to the Government's criminal investigation, **[COLLOCATION PROVIDER NAME]** and its agents and employees not disclose or cause a disclosure of the order or the request for information, facilities and assistance by the **[AFFIANT AGENCY],** or the existence of the investigation to any person other than those of its agents and employees who require this information to accomplish the services hereby ordered. **[COLLOCATION PROVIDER NAME]** and its agents and employees shall not make such disclosure to any subscriber, interceptee, or participant in the intercepted communications.

IT IS ORDERED FURTHER that this order shall be executed as soon as practicable. This Order must terminate upon attainment of the authorized objective or, in any event, at the end of 30 days measured from the earlier of the day on which the investigative or law enforcement officer first begins to conduct the interception or 10 days from the date of the Order.

Intercepted electronic communications will be minimized after-the-fact and as soon as practicable after such interception pursuant to Section 2518(5) of Title 18, United States Code. The electronic communications will be reviewed and minimized as follows: All electronic communications sent from or received by the target user account will be intercepted in their entirety and electronically stored on magnetic media. Working copies of all of the electronic communications will then be made from the magnetic media. As soon as practicable, these electronic communications will be reviewed and minimized. Agents will review those working copies, and based on the identities of the parties to the electronic communication and the subject matter and content of the electronic communication, will determine whether the communication appears to be pertinent to the criminal offenses listed in the Court's order or pertinent to other criminal activity. As soon as an electronic communication is determined to be non-pertinent, reviewing of the electronic communication will cease and the communications will be designated as non-pertinent. Minimized electronic communications will be spot-monitored to determine if they have subsequently become criminal in nature.

IT IS ORDERED FURTHER that Assistant United States Attorney **[AUSA NAME]**, or any other Assistant United States Attorney with knowledge of the facts of this case, shall provide this Court with a report on or about the tenth, twentieth, and thirtieth days following the earlier of the day on which the investigative or law enforcement officers first begin to conduct the interceptions or 10 days from the date of this order, whichever occurs first, showing what progress has been made toward achievement of the authorized objectives and the need for continued interception. If any of the above-ordered reports should become due on a weekend or holiday, IT IS ORDERED FURTHER that such report shall become due on the business day thereafter.

IT IS ORDERED FURTHER that this order, the application, affidavit and proposed order, and all interim reports filed with this Court with regard to this matter, shall be sealed until further order of this Court, except that copies of the orders, in full or redacted form, may be served on the **[AFFIANT AGENCY]** and on **[COLLOCATION PROVIDER NAME]** as necessary to effectuate this Order.

DATED   HON. **[JUDGE NAME]**
             UNITED STATES DISTRICT JUDGE
             THE **[DISTRICT]**

SCANNED

UNITED STATES DISTRICT COURT
DISTRICT OF MAINE

UNITED STATES OF AMERICA	)
	)
v.	)
	)
WADE COLLETT	)
DURRELL WILLIAMS	)
a/k/a "D-Block"	)
	)

Criminal No. 08-

(18 U.S.C. §§ 2, 371, 922(b)(3), 922(b)(5), 922(g)(1), 924(a)(1)(A), 924(a)(1)(D), 924(a)(2) & 1001(a)(2))

08-112-P-S

INDICTMENT

The Grand Jury charges that:

Introduction

At all times relevant to this Indictment:

1.   Defendant Wade **COLLETT**, doing business as Red Wheel Enterprises, was a dealer in firearms, licensed under the provisions of Chapter 44 of Title 18 of the United States Code. Red Wheel Enterprises was located in Freeport, Maine.

2.   The Bureau of Alcohol, Tobacco, Firearms and Explosives (ATF), was an agency within the United States Department of Justice. As part of its lawful functions, ATF was responsible for enforcing federal firearms laws and preventing illegal firearms trafficking. ATF issued licenses to firearms dealers and issued regulations governing the sale and distribution of firearms and ammunition.

3.   Federal law prohibited certain categories of individuals, such as fugitives from justice and individuals convicted of a crime punishable by a term of imprisonment exceeding one year, from possessing firearms in or affecting interstate commerce. For this reason, firearms dealers were required to obtain information about the identity of individuals who sought to purchase firearms. Dealers were required to have each individual seeking to purchase a firearm

complete an ATF Form 4473, or Firearms Transaction Record. The Form 4473 required the

purchaser to provide his or her name, address and other identifying information. The purchaser

was also required to present a valid government-issued photo identification to the dealer.

  4. The Form 4473 also required the purchaser to answer a series of questions to

determine whether the purchase was permitted under federal law. One of the questions stated,

"Are you the actual buyer of the firearm(s) listed on this form? **Warning: You are not the**

actual buyer if you are acquiring the firearm(s) on behalf of another person. If you are not

the actual buyer, the dealer cannot transfer the firearm(s) to you." Several other questions

asked the purchaser to provide information to be used to determine whether the purchaser was

prohibited under federal law from receiving a firearm.

  5. Once a purchaser completed the Form 4473, the dealer was required to submit the

purchaser's identifying information to a representative of the National Instant Criminal

Background Check System (NICS), who would inform the dealer whether the purchaser was

permitted to receive the firearm.

  6. Dealers were required to retain all completed Forms 4473 in their permanent

records. Dealers were also required to record each sale of a firearm in a bound log, noting,

among other information, the firearm's manufacturer, model and serial number; the transaction

date; and the name and address of the purchaser. Dealers were required to retain these logs in

their permanent records.

2

COUNT ONE
(Conspiracy to Commit Offense Against the United States and to Defraud the United States)

1.   The allegations of the Introduction to this Indictment are repeated and incorporated by reference.

2.   From at least December 18, 2005, the exact date being unknown, and continuing until about February 20, 2006, in the District of Maine, the defendants,

WADE COLLETT and
DURRELL WILLIAMS a/k/a "D-Block,"

unlawfully conspired with each other and with individuals known and unknown to the grand jury to:

a.   defraud the United States by deceitful and dishonest means by impeding and obstructing the lawful government functions of ATF in enforcing federal firearms laws and preventing illegal firearms trafficking;

b.   knowingly cause false representations to be made with respect to information required to be kept in the records of a federal firearms licensee, licensed under Chapter 44 of Title 18, United States Code, an offense against the United States in violation of Title 18, United States Code, Section 924(a)(1)(A).

Methods of the Conspiracy

3.   It was part of the conspiracy that **COLLETT** and **WILLIAMS** completed sales of firearms through individuals who falsely claimed to be the true purchasers of the firearms (the "Straw Purchasers"), disguising the identity of the true purchaser.

4.   It was further part of the conspiracy that **COLLETT** and **WILLIAMS** would create and cause to be created records retained by **COLLETT** as a licensed firearms dealer that

3

falsely represented the identities of the purchasers, concealing the identity of the true purchaser from ATF.

Overt Acts

5.   In furtherance of the conspiracy and to accomplish its unlawful objectives, the following overt acts, among others, were committed in the District of Maine:

a.   **WILLIAMS** recruited Straw Purchasers and directed them to Red Wheel Enterprises to pose as the true purchasers of the firearms listed in Counts Two through Six of this Indictment.

b.   **WILLIAMS** caused the Straw Purchasers to falsely represent on ATF Forms 4473 that they were the actual buyers of the firearms listed in Counts Two through Six, when in fact they were not the actual buyers.

c.   **COLLETT** aided and abetted the fraudulent purchases of the firearms listed in Counts Two Through Six by allowing the Straw Purchasers to complete the Forms 4473, signing the Forms 4473, submitting the Straw Purchasers' identifying information to NICS representatives, and completing the sales transactions.

d.   **COLLETT** made false representations regarding the identities of the true purchasers of the firearms listed in Counts Two through Six in his bound logs of firearms acquisitions and dispositions.

e.   The offenses described in Counts Two through Six of this Indictment are hereby incorporated by reference and alleged as overt acts in furtherance of the conspiracy.

In violation of Title 18, United States Code, Section 371.

4

COUNTS TWO AND THREE
(Aiding and Abetting False Statements in Firearm Transactions)

On about the following dates, in the District of Maine, the defendants,

WADE COLLETT and
DURRELL WILLIAMS a/k/a "D-Block,"

aided and abetted the making of false statements and representations with respect to information

required by the provisions of Chapter 44 of Title 18, United States Code, to be kept in the records

of **COLLETT**, d/b/a Red Wheel Enterprises, a federal firearms licensee, licensed under Chapter

44 of Title 18, United States Code. Specifically, **WILLIAMS** knowingly induced and procured

Straw Purchaser #1 to claim falsely on ATF Forms 4473 that she was the actual buyer of the

following firearms:

Count	Date	Firearms(s)
TWO	December 18, 2005	Cobra Enterprises, model CB 9, 9 millimeter pistol, serial number CT020874; and Cobra Enterprises, model CA32, .32 caliber pistol, serial number CP016015
THREE	January 12, 2006	Cobra Enterprises, model Patriot 45, .45 ACP caliber pistol, serial number M005263

In truth and in fact, and as **COLLETT** and **WILLIAMS** well knew, Straw Purchaser #1 was not

the actual buyer of the firearms. **COLLETT** aided and abetted the making of this false

representation by allowing Straw Purchaser #1 to execute the Form 4473, signing the Form 4473,

submitting Straw Purchaser #1's identifying information to a NICS representative, and

completing the sales transaction.

In violation of Title 18, United States Code, Sections 924(a)(1)(A) and 2.

5

COUNTS FOUR THROUGH SIX
(Aiding and Abetting False Statements in Firearm Transactions)

On about the following dates, in the District of Maine, the defendants,

WADE COLLETT and
DURRELL WILLIAMS a/k/a "D-Block,"

aided and abetted the making of a false statement and representation with respect to information

required by the provisions of Chapter 44 of Title 18, United States Code, to be kept in the records

of **COLLETT**, d/b/a Red Wheel Enterprises, a federal firearms licensee, licensed under Chapter

44 of Title 18, United States Code. Specifically, **WILLIAMS** knowingly induced and procured

Straw Purchaser #2 to claim falsely on an ATF Form 4473 that he was the actual buyer of the

following firearms:

Count	Date	Firearm(s)
FOUR	February 1, 2006	Hi-Point Firearms, model JCP, .40 caliber pistol, serial number X725362; and Hi-Point Firearms, model JHP, .45 caliber pistol, serial number X436837
FIVE	February 18, 2006	Hi-Point Firearms, model JHP, .45 caliber pistol, serial number X432643; and Cobra Enterprises, model Patriot, .45 caliber pistol, serial number M005264
SIX	February 20, 2006	Cobra Enterprises, model Patriot, 9 mm pistol, serial number 01447; and Cobra Enterprises, model FS 380, .380 caliber pistol, serial number FS010835

In truth and in fact, and as **COLLETT** and **WILLIAMS** well knew, Straw Purchaser #2 was not

the actual buyer of the firearm. **COLLETT** aided and abetted the making of this false

representation by allowing Straw Purchaser #2 to execute the Form 4473, signing the Form 4473,

submitting Straw Purchaser #2's identifying information to a NICS representative, and

completing the sales transaction.

6

In violation of Title 18, United States Code, Sections 924(a)(1)(A) and 2.

COUNTS SEVEN THROUGH ELEVEN
(Felon in Possession of Firearms)

On about the following dates, in the District of Maine, the defendant,

DURRELL WILLIAMS a/k/a "D-Block,"

having been convicted of a crime punishable by imprisonment exceeding one year, specifically,

Criminal Possession of a Controlled Substance in the 5th Degree in the Supreme Court of the

State of New York for Queens County, Case Number SCI-N10935-2004, judgment having been

entered January 18, 2005, knowingly possessed, in and affecting commerce, the following

firearms:

Count	Date	Firearm(s)
SEVEN	December 18, 2005	Cobra Enterprises, model CB 9, 9 millimeter pistol, serial number CT020874; and Cobra Enterprises, model CA32, .32 caliber pistol, serial number CP016015
EIGHT	January 12, 2006	Cobra Enterprises, model Patriot 45, .45 ACP caliber pistol, serial number M005263
NINE	February 1, 2006	Hi-Point Firearms, model JCP, .40 caliber pistol, serial number X725362; and Hi-Point Firearms, model JHP, .45 caliber pistol, serial number X436837
TEN	February 18, 2006	Hi-Point Firearms, model JHP, .45 caliber pistol, serial number X432643; and Cobra Enterprises, model Patriot, .45 caliber pistol, serial number M005264
ELEVEN	February 20, 2006	Cobra Enterprises, model Patriot, 9 mm pistol, serial number 01447; and Cobra Enterprises, model FS 380, .380 caliber pistol, serial number FS010835

In violation of Title 18, United States Code, Sections 922(g)(1) and 924(a)(2).

7

COUNTS TWELVE AND THIRTEEN
(Sale or Delivery of Firearms Without Recording Required Information)

On about the following dates, in the District of Maine, the defendant,

WADE COLLETT,

being a licensed dealer of firearms, licensed under Chapter 44 of Title 18, United States Code,

willfully sold and delivered the following firearms to an individual without noting in his records,

required to be kept pursuant to Title 18, United States Code, Section 923, the name, age, and

place of residence of such individual.

Count	Date	Firearm
TWELVE	December 7, 2006	Smith & Wesson, Model SW9VE, 9 mm pistol, serial number PBZ7651
THIRTEEN	December 14, 2006	Kel-Tec, Model P-32, .32 caliber pistol, serial number C9Z77

In violation of Title 18, United States Code, Sections 922(b)(5) and 924(a)(1)(D).

COUNT FOURTEEN
(Illegal Sale of Firearm to Out-of-State Resident)

On about December 14, 2006, in the District of Maine, the defendant,

WADE COLLETT,

being a licensed dealer of firearms, licensed under Chapter 44 of Title 18, United States Code,

willfully sold and delivered a firearm, specifically a Kel-Tec, Model P-32, .32 caliber pistol,

serial number C9Z77, to a person who **COLLETT** knew and had reasonable cause to believe did

not reside in the State of Maine.

In violation of Title 18, United States Code, Sections 922(b)(3) and 924(a)(1)(D).

8

COUNT FIFTEEN
(False Statement to Government Agency)

On about January 11, 2007, in the District of Maine, in a matter within the jurisdiction of the Bureau of Alcohol, Tobacco, Firearms and Explosives (ATF), an agency within the executive branch of the United States, the defendant,

WADE COLLETT,

knowingly and willfully made materially false, fictitious and fraudulent statements and representations. Specifically, in response to questions posted to him by an ATF Special Agent during an in-person interview, **COLLETT** falsely claimed that he had not seen three individuals whose photographs were shown to him. In truth and in fact, as **COLLETT** well knew, all three individuals had visited his gun shop on multiple occasions and had purchased several firearms from him directly. In making these false statements, **COLLETT** was attempting to obstruct and impede a pending official investigation being conducted by ATF.

In violation of Title 18, United States Code, Section 1001(a)(2).

COUNT SIXTEEN
(False Statement to Government Agency)

On about January 26, 2007, in the District of Maine, in a matter within the jurisdiction of the Bureau of Alcohol, Tobacco, Firearms and Explosives (ATF), an agency within the executive branch of the United States, the defendant,

WADE COLLETT,

knowingly and willfully made a materially false, fictitious and fraudulent statement and representation. In response to questions posted to him by an ATF Special Agent during a telephone interview, **COLLETT** provided false information about firearms transactions that

9

occurred in his gun shop on November 2, 2006 and November 15, 2006, involving an individual known to **COLLETT** as "James Holdings." **COLLETT** claimed that Holdings had been accompanied by an unknown black male on only one of the above dates, and that the unknown black male was not depicted in photographs previously shown to **COLLETT** by the ATF Special Agent. In truth and in fact, as **COLLETT** well knew, the black male had accompanied "Holdings" on both occasions, and was depicted in photographs shown to **COLLETT** on January 11, 2007. In making these false statements, **COLLETT** was attempting to obstruct and impede a pending official investigation being conducted by ATF.

In violation of Title 18, United States Code, Section 1001(a)(2).

A TRUE BILL,

—

SIGNATURE REDACTED
Original on File in Clerk's Office

Assistant U.S. Attorney

Date: 6/11/08

10

Financial Assets Seizure Warrant Based on Firearms Trafficking

AFFIDAVIT OF [SPECIALAGENT NAME] IN SUPPORT OF COMPLAINT FOR FORFEITURE IN REM AND SEIZURE WARRANTS

I, _____, Special Agent with the _____, declare as follows:

BACKGROUND, TRAINING, AND EXPERIENCE OF AFFIANT

I, am a Special Agent ("SA") with the [AGENCY]. I have been an [AGENCY] Special Agent since _____. I have received training in Federal firearms laws and regulations at the [AGENCY] National Academy and Federal Law Enforcement Criminal Investigator Training Program. I have investigated numerous cases involving federal firearms violations, involving unlawful sales, possession, manufacturing, and transportation of firearms. I have acquired knowledge and experience as to firearms and ammunition and the interstate nexus of firearms and ammunition, due to investigations, research, records, familiarity, conferring with other experts, training, teaching, and certifications. I have participated in a variety of different aspects of those investigations, including surveillance, undercover operations to conduct controlled purchases of firearms and/or controlled substances, and the execution of search and arrest warrants. I have been the affiant on affidavits for search warrants relating to firearms and gang-related offenses.

In preparation of this affidavit I have incorporated summarized financial data prepared by [FINANCIAL ANALYST], assigned to work at [AGENCY]. [FINANCIAL ANALYST] training, knowledge, and experience include _____. His career in law enforcement, his education, and his personal experiences, provided [FINANCIAL ANALYST] with knowledge and skills necessary to review and interpret bank records, loan records, real estate records, investment records, tax returns, business records, applications, rental agreements, and asset records. In support of this affidavit, [FINANCIAL ANALYST] reviewed and analyzed sales and expenditure spreadsheets provided by PayPal, Amazon, WePay, and Ecwid. From these spreadsheets, [FINANCIAL ANALYST] prepared supplemental spreadsheets depicting product sales categories and periodic revenue measures. [FINANCIAL ANALYST] also prepared spreadsheets depicting bank account activity, both in detail and summary form.

I know based on my training and experience, and conversations with [FINANCIAL ANALYST] that business owners keep in their place of business various records and documents related to their business operations. The records would be retained by the proprietor for several reasons: 1) to be used for the preparation of State and Federal tax reporting forms; 2) to be used to prepare business operational and financial documents; and 3) to be used to monitor and determine business revenue flows. I know based on my experience, and for the reasons above, that these records would be retained for several years.

The records related to the manufacture, sale and transfer of National Firearms Act (NFA) firearms (firearm silencer parts) may include, raw material (aluminum, stainless steel) purchase orders, raw material purchase receipts, product specifications, product lists, price lists, customer lists, customer records, accounts payable records, accounts receivable records, customer order forms, sales invoices, sales journals, product finishing agreements, prototypes, product demonstration models, and shipping records. I know based on my experience that records associated with the illicit manufacture and distribution of NFA firearms (firearm silencer parts) may include hand-written notes and email interaction between seller and buyer that pierce the vail of legitimacy and provide details regarding the actual intended use of the products as firearm silencer parts.

I know based on my training and experience that in a scheme involving the evasion of tax the process of determining the true and correct amount of tax requires an examination, and at times a reconstruction, of the perpetrators business and personal financial history for the period preceding, during, and following the duration of the scheme. The records needed to make this examination may include but are not limited to bank records, loan documents, documents associated with the acquisition of assets, credit statements, records that reflect the satisfaction of debts, records related to locations for the storage of valued assets, records that tend to establish the perpetrator's financial status before the scheme, for instance tax returns, and records that define the scope of the business enterprise.

Based upon my training and experience I know that persons with businesses such as this one maintain computers either at their homes and/or their business to handle the daily bookkeeping, product ordering, and contact information related to day to day operations. These business owners use computers to track sales and expenses, maintain bank information, e-mail order, and correspond with suppliers via computers. You affiant believes that computer, storage media and/or devices (to include cellular phones) can provide valuable information related to the true business activities occurring at [COMPANY NAME].

The facts in this Affidavit come from my personal observations, my training and experience, and information obtained from other agents and witnesses. This Affidavit is being submitted for the purpose of obtaining search/seizure warrants. I have set forth the facts that I believe are necessary to establish probable cause for the requested search/seizure warrant and not all of the information revealed by the investigation.

DESCRIPTION OF PROPERTY SUBJECT TO FORFEITURE

This declaration and affidavit is submitted in support of the government's application for the issuance of Verified Complaints for Forfeiture in Rem or seizure warrant against the following described assets:

1) Property – Real Estate - [ADDRESS and LEGAL DESCRIPTION]

2) Property – Vehicle – [YEAR, MAKE, MODEL, VIN, LICENSE]

3) Property – Financial Account – [The monies and contents of PayPal account number _____, with the Business Name [COMPANY], with email address [COMPANY.COM]

4) Property – Financial Account – [The monies and contents of Wells Fargo account number _____, with the Business Name [COMPANY], with email address [COMPANY.COM] in the amount of $_____.

5) Property – The monies and contents of COINBASE.com, in account name [DEFENDANT], Identification Number _____, of an amount up to $_____.

Based on the information set forth in this Affidavit, there is probable cause to believe that the above listed assets are property, real or personal, which were involved in transactions or attempted transactions in violation of 18 U.S.C. § 1956(a)(1)(B)(i); to wit: financial transactions or attempted transactions that were conducted knowing that the transactions were designed to conceal or disguise the nature, location, source, ownership, or control of the proceed of "specified unlawful activity" (SUA), defined in 18 U.S.C. § 1956(c)(7) (incorporating the definition of "specified unlawful activity" contained in 18 U.S.C. § 1961(1)), to wit: wire fraud in violation of 18 U.S.C. § 1343. The assets are therefore subject to civil forfeiture pursuant to 18 U.S.C. § 981(a)(1)(A) and 18 U.S.C. § 984(a)(1).

There is probable cause to believe that the assets are subject to civil forfeiture pursuant to 18 U.S. C. § 981(a)(1)(C) because the assets constitute real or personal property with are derived from proceeds traceable to any offense constituting a specified unlawful activity as defined in 18 U.S.C. § 1956(c)(7) (incorporating the definition of "specified unlawful activity" contained in 18 U.S.C. § 1961(1)), to wit: wire fraud in violation of 18 U.S.C. § 1343. The assets are therefore subject to civil forfeiture pursuant to 18 U.S.C. §§ 981(a)(1)(C) and 984(a)(1).

Theory of Investigation

The National Firearms Act (NFA), codified under Title 26, United States Code, Chapter 53, defines certain weapons by their function, design, configuration and/or dimensions. The weapons meeting those criteria fall under the provisions of the NFA and are considered NFA firearms. The NFA imposes taxes on the making and transfer of NFA firearms, as well as strict regulations regarding the manufacture, registration and sale of such weapons. A "firearm silencer" or "firearm muffler" is an NFA firearm, defined in the NFA. A firearm silencer is generally composed of an outer tube, internal baffles, a front end-cap, and a rear end-cap. The definition of a firearm silencer makes any combination of parts, designed or redesigned, and intended for use in assembling or fabricating a firearm silencer an NFA firearm.

Manufacturers of unregistered firearm silencers and firearm silencer parts seek to sell their products in a manner that both evades their payment of taxes and evades detection by law and regulatory agencies. The primary means for accomplishing that end is to create a façade that the unregistered firearm silencers and firearm silencer parts are something else; namely, a gun cleaning "solvent trap" or a "dry storage container."

Beginning _____ 2014, [DEFENDANT], as an individual, and later through his [COMPANY], sold many thousands of unregistered firearm silencers and firearm silencer parts, falsely representing throughout, that the products he marketed were intended to be components for solvent traps, or most often described as components of dry storage containers.

[DEFENDANT], a machinist by trade, and owner/operator of a metal parts internet order business, both individually and through his business [COMPANY], marketed and advertised his products nationwide via the internet, with services Google, eBay, Amazon, and his own website(s). [DEFENDANT], both individually and through [COMPANY], profited greatly from sales of those products consumers purchased through PayPal, Amazon, and credit card.

[DEFENDANT] devised a scheme to obtain money by defrauding the U.S. Government of "making" and "transfer" taxes due on his manufacturing and transferring of unregistered National Firearms Act (NFA) firearms; namely firearm silencers (or suppressors). [DEFENDANT] used the internet to advertise, solicit orders from, correspond with, and receive payments from customers nationwide who sought to purchase NFA firearms (silencers and their components) from his company's website and other internet forums that hosted his products.

The effects of [DEFENDANT]'s scheme is that he illegally sold firearm silencers and firearm silencer parts far below the amount legitimate purveyors of these items could sell them. Further, by operating outside the regulatory oversight of the firearms industry [DEFENDANT] dispensed thousands of firearm silencers and firearm silencer parts to thousands of individuals without adhering to any firearms industry regulations imposed to prevent unauthorized persons from obtaining/possessing NFA firearms.

Statutes

The Gun Control Act of 1968 (GCA), as codified under Title 18, United States Code, Section 921(a)(3)(C) defines a "firearm" to include; "...any firearm muffler or firearm silencer..."

The terms "firearm muffler" and "firearm silencer" are further defined under Title 18, United States Code Section 921(a)(24) to mean: "...any device for silencing, muffling, or diminishing the report of a portable firearm, including any combination of parts, designed or redesigned, and intended for use in assembling or fabricating a firearm silencer or firearm muffler, and any part intended only for use in such assembly or fabrication."

The impact of Section 921(a)(24) is that the components of a silencer are considered as "silencers" by themselves, thereby making the "parts of a silencer" firearms and subject to regulations.

The NFA, as codified under Title 26, United States Code, Chapter 53, Section 5845(a)(7) defines a "firearm" to include: "any silencer (as defined in section 921 of Title 18, United States Code)."

The provisions of the NFA requires certain firearms meeting the following specifications be registered in the National Firearms Registration and Transfer Record.

1. A shotgun having a barrel or barrels of less than 18 inches in length;

2. A weapon made from a shotgun if such weapon as modified has an overall length of less than 26-inches or a barrel or barrels of less than 18 inches in length;

3. A rifle having a barrel or barrels of less than 16 inches in length;

4. A weapon made from a rifle is such weapon as modified has an overall length of less than 26 inches or a barrel or barrels of less than 16 inches in length;

5. Any other weapon, as defined in subsection (e);

6. A machinegun

7. Any silencer

8. A destructive device

The NFA imposes certain taxes upon the manufacture and transfer of NFA firearms. Initially, upon first engaging in the business of manufacturing NFA firearms, and again annually by July 1 of each year, that manufacturer is required to pay an occupational tax of $1,000 ($500 per year if annual gross sales are less than $500,000), Title 26 U.S.C. § 5801(a).

Title 26 U.S.C § 5821 - imposes a "Making Tax" of $200 per each firearm made, levied upon the person making the firearm.

Title 26 U.S.C. § 5811 - imposes a "Transfer Tax" of $200 per each firearm transferred, levied upon the transferor

In conjunction with the above taxes, the provision of the NFA require the manufacturer of NFA firearms to register the following with the Secretary:

1) Written application, in duplicate, to make and register the firearms

2) Evidence of proof of payment of the Making Tax

3) Identification of the firearm to be made

4) Identification to include fingerprints and photograph

5) Approval from the Secretary to make and register the firearm

6) Proof of making or possession of firearm would not violate a law

The manufacturer of NFA firearms shall identify each firearm made by a serial number, which may not be readily removed, obliterated, or altered, the name of the manufacturer, and as delineated by the Secretary the name of the city and state of manufacture, Title 26 U.S.C. § 5842(a) & (b).

Title 26 U.S.C. § 5861(a) – makes it unlawful for any person who engages in the business of manufacturing firearms without having paid the special (occupational) tax required by section 5801 for his business or having registered as required by section 5802.

Title 26 U.S.C § 5861(c) – makes it unlawful for any person to receive or possess a firearm made in violation of the provision of Chapter 53.

Title 26 U.S.C. § 5861(d) – makes it unlawful for any person to receive or possess a firearm which is not registered to him in the National Firearms Registration and Transfer Record.

Title 26 U.S.C. § 5861(f) & (e) – makes it unlawful for any person to "make a firearm" or "transfer a firearm" in violation of the provisions of Chapter 53, respectively.

Title 26 U.S.C. § 5861(i) – makes it unlawful for any person to receive or possess a firearm which is not identified by a serial number as required by Chapter 53.

Title 26 U.S.C. § 5861(j) – makes it unlawful for any person to transport, deliver, or receive any firearm in interstate commerce which has not been registered as required by Chapter 53.

Title 18 U.S.C. § 1343 – makes it unlawful for whoever, having devised or intended to devise any scheme or artifice to defraud, or for obtaining money or property by means of false or fraudulent pretenses, representations, or promises, transmits or causes to be transmitted by means of wire, radio, or television communication in interstate or foreign commerce, any writings, signs, signals, pictures, or sounds for the purpose of executing such a scheme.

[DEFENDANT] used the internet to advertise, solicit orders from, correspond with, and receive payments from, customers who sought to purchase illicit NFA firearms (silencers and their components), through his use of his company's website and other internet forums that hosted his products. [DEFENDANT]'s use of the internet was an integral component of his scheme, and was done in violation of Title 18 USC § 1343; wire fraud.

Forfeiture Statutes

18 U.S.C § 981(a)(1)(A) – subjects to forfeiture any property, real or personal, involved in a transaction or attempted transaction in violation of Title 18 U.S.C. §§ 1956 and 1957 or any property traceable to such property.

18 U.S.C. § 981(a)(1)(C) – subjects to forfeiture any property, real or personal, which constitutes or is derived from proceeds traceable to any offense constituting a "specified unlawful activity" as defined in 18 U.S.C. § 1956(c)(7) (incorporating the definition of "specified unlawful activity" contained in 18 U.S.C. § 1961(1). Wire Fraud is "specified unlawful activity" defined in § 1961(1).

18 U.S.C. § 981(a)(2)(A) – in cases involving illegal goods, illegal services, unlawful activities...the term "proceeds" means property of any kind obtained directly or indirectly, as the result of the commission of the offense giving rise to forfeiture, and any property traceable thereto, and is not limited to net gains or profit realized from the offense.

18 U.S.C. § 984(a)(1) – in any forfeiture action in rem in which the subject property is cash, monetary instruments in bearer form, funds deposited in an account in a financial institution (as defined in section 20 of this chapter), or precious metals – it shall not be necessary for the Government to identify the specific property involved in the offense that is the basis for the forfeiture; and **(2)(b)** whereby, no action pursuant to this section to forfeit property not traceable directly to the offense that is the basis for the forfeiture may be commenced more than 1 year from the date of the offense.

Investigation

Based on my experience, the advice from senior [AGENCY] S/As, my viewing of websites that appear to cater to consumers of firearms related accessories, and my reading of [AGENCY] technical reports related to "silencers," I know sellers and manufacturers of unregistered "silencers" and "silencer parts" offer to sell their products as gun cleaning "solvent traps" and "dry storage containers." The impetus behind characterizing firearm silencers and associated parts as something other than what they are truly intended for, is twofold: 1) by selling silencers and silencer parts as something else, the perpetrator believes he/she can evade the various taxes imposed by the NFA; and 2) by claiming the firearm silencers or silencer parts are unrelated to firearms the perpetrator believes he/she can effectively evade detection from the regulatory agencies that are charged with oversight of the firearms industry.

The website "[COMPANY.COM]" depicts various items for sale from [COMPANY], with address _____. The items listed for sale include:

1) Propriety Company Name Tubes, Cups, Caps and Kits

2) Brand Name Auto Parts Cups, Caps & Kits

3) Brand Name Aluminum Flashlight Cups, Caps and Kits

4) Oil filter & thread adapters

The website includes the following disclaimer at the bottom of the page:

"It is the responsibility of dealers and private owners to know and fully understand all federal, state, and local firearms laws in their area. [COMPANY] will not be held liable for any misuse of its products."

The above disclaimer clarifies [DEFENDANT]'s knowledge and intent for the products he sold were for use with firearms. If [DEFENDANT] truly believed his products were for use as dry storage components he would not advance the notion that his customers should know laws pertaining to firearms. For example, Brand Name Flashlight Parts and Napa/Wix, three companies whose product lines [DEFENDANT]'s products are designed to function in conjunction with as firearm silencers, do not have on their websites a similar disclaimer.

On _____ 2017, the [AGENCY] laboratory prepared a Report of Technical Examination of various parts obtained from [COMPANY].

The parts from [COMPANY] included eight (8) aluminum cups. The report provides the following details; "These aluminum cups each have a dimple in the center. The dimple is an indexing point to show where a hole is to be drilled. The cups serve to function as silencer baffles-components of the interior of a silencer that slow the flow of propellant gases by facilitating gas expansion within the silencer body, thereby facilitating sound reduction. The aluminum cups lack any markings of identification." The report continues by detailing that a part does not need to be complete in its entirety, but only manufactured to a point where its intended purpose is recognizable for what it is. From their examination, the examiners determined the aluminum cups were recognizable as silencer baffles, specifically "Z"baffles, and thereby were each "silencers."

The Report of the Technical Examination of the parts obtained from [COMPANY] concluded that the parts "…constitutes a combination of parts intended for use in assembling or fabricating a firearm silencer, therefore each is a "firearm silencer" as defined in 18 U.S.C. § 921(a)(24)."

Wells Fargo records for account ending -____ shows that in 2017 [DEFENDANT] paid approximately $_____ to Google Services for advertising placement on the Google search engine. The amount of money [DEFENDANT] spent to advertise with Google Services represented approximately 7% of [DEFENDANTS] total sales in 2017. It was through this advertising that [DEFENDANT] made his initial attempts to conceal. Through this advertising [DEFENDANT] knowingly advanced the falsehood that his products were for use as dry storage containers, rather than for use as firearm silencers and firearm silencer parts. The disclaimer [DEFENDANT] placed on his website offers support for the reasonable belief that [DEFENDANT] knew his products were intended for use as firearms silencers.

Transaction Analysis

PayPal is an electronic commerce (e-commerce) company that facilitates payments between parties through online funds transfers. PayPal allows customers to establish an account on its website, which is connected to a user's credit card or checking account.

PayPal provided records for account number ending _____, with user name [DEFENDANT], with business name [COMPANY], at email address [COMPANY.COM and DEFENDANT@EMAIL.COM] for the period _____, 2016 through _____ 2018. The account history documents show that [DEFENDANT] opened this account on _____2007. The records provided by PayPal consisted of an "All Transaction" spreadsheet that depicts summary data of more than 59,000 transaction events that affected this account; approximately half of the transactions are [COMPANY] product sales consisting of both NFA firearms related products (cups, end-cap sets and tubes with end caps) and non-NFA related products; product returns, denied transactions, and purchases.

PayPal provided records for account number ending _____, with user name [DEFENDANT], with business name [COMPANY], at email address [COMPANY.COM], for the period _____2017 through _____2018. The account history documents show that [DEFENDANT] opened this account on _____ 2017. The records provided by PayPal consisted of an "All Transaction" spreadsheet that depicts summary data of more than 28,100 transaction events that affected this account; approximately half of the transactions are [COMPANY] product sales consisting of both NFA firearms related products (cups, end-cap sets and tubes with end caps) and non-NFA related products; product returns, denied transactions, and purchases.

Both spreadsheets included extracts depicting "Pay Received" transactions, which jointly comprised more than 39,000 lines of summary data associated with individual sales. The spreadsheets were further reviewed to identify those transactions involving the sale of multiple aluminum and/or stainless steel "Z" style cups; determined to be NFA firearms (unregistered silencer parts) in the [AGENCY] laboratory - Technical Report.

Analysis of PayPal account ending _____ revealed that prior to _____ 2015, [DEFENDANT] sold products that were not readily associated with firearm silencers, namely:

1) Solid Brass Fasteners

2) Transmission Fittings

3) Power Steering Fittings

4) Engine Exhaust Fittings

5) Hydraulic Brake Fittings

6) Fuel Line Fittings

Some of the products offered prior to _____ 2015 included a part called "solvent trap oil filter adapter." The spreadsheets reveal that [DEFENDANT] continued to sell the adapters and the above listed products after _____ 2015. On _____ 2015, [DEFENDANT] completed a sale of "(18) Brand Name Flashlight Solvent Preformed Aluminum Cups" to an individual in [CITY,STATE], for a net price of $_____. Based on the technical analysis of similar products, and the determination that these aluminum cups are firearm silencer parts, NFA firearms, _____2015 was the date used to determine the beginning of when [DEFENDANT] implemented his scheme.

On _____ 2018, the ATF National Firearms Registration and Transfer Record was queried by the names [DEFENDANT], [COMPANY] to determine if at any time [DEFENDANT] registered with the Secretary to manufacture NFA firearms, registered any NFA firearms, or recorded the transfer of any NFA firearm. The results of that query returned "no record" of [DEFENDANT] or any of his associated entities being registered in the National Firearms Registration and Transfer Record.

The [COMPANY] website advertises that they offer Brand Name Auto Parts Cups and Brand Name Flashlight Cups. The BRAND NAME AUTO PARTS Cups are sized to fit into a BRAND NAME AUTO PARTS 4003 or Wix 24003 brand fuel filter, whereas the Brand Name Flashlight Parts Cups are sized to fit into "C-cell" and "D-cell" battery sized flashlight tubes. The use of aluminum and/or stainless steel "Z" style stackable cups in a tubed frame for the purported purpose of creating a storage container does not make sense. For instance, the storage area within the tube would largely be displaced by the "Z" style cups, leaving only the limited space between the cups for storage. Secondly, accessing anything stored below the first compartment would result in spillage of anything stored in the cups above it. The PayPal spreadsheet shows that occasionally a customer would purchase a combination of several aluminum cups with often just one stainless steel cup. I am not aware of a legitimate reason to alter the material used within a storage tube, nor a reason that would justify the added expense, of replacing an aluminum cup with one made from stainless steel. Lastly, if the "Z" style cups sold by [COMPANY] were truly for dry storage tubes, then the machining efforts by [COMPANY] to place the indexing mark in each cup represents a step in the manufacturing process that is arbitrary, wasteful, costly, and without a reason founded in legitimacy.

Analysis of PayPal account ending _____ revealed that from _____ 2015 through _____ 2018, [DEFENDANT] completed approximately 3,000 transactions wherein he sold to an individual, a quantity consisting of more than two aluminum/stainless steel "Z" style cup. Based on the amount of tax affixed to the "making" of an NFA firearm, and the amount of tax affixed to the "transfer" of an NFA firearm, the transactions identified in account _____represent approximately $1,200,000 (3,000 x ($200 + $200)) in evaded tax.

Analysis of PayPal account number ending _____revealed similar sales activity to that of PayPal account ending _____. Though opened on _____2017, the sales activity from its opening through _____, 2018, showed that [DEFENDANT] completed approximately 2,660 transactions wherein he sold to an individual, a quantity consisting of more than two aluminum/stainless steel "Z" style cup. Based on the amount of tax affixed to the "making" of an NFA firearm, and the amount of tax affixed to the "transfer" of an NFA firearm, the transactions identified in account _____ represent approximately $1,064,000 (2,660 x ($200 + $200)) in evaded tax.

In addition to receiving payment for product sales through PayPal, [COMPANY] accepted payments via debit and credit cards from Visa, MasterCard, Discover and American Express. Two companies handled the processing of these payments, Ecwid and WePay. The transaction summary spreadsheet obtained from WePay did not include the description of the products sold; however, it contained entries that correlated with the periodic deposits into

[COMPANY]'s bank account. The WePay spreadsheet was merged with the transaction summary spreadsheet. The spreadsheet provided detailed descriptions of the products sold by [COMPANY]. The merged spreadsheet, that covered the period _____2016 through _____ 2017, displayed transaction summary information for more than 2,900 actions. Analysis of the merged spreadsheet revealed approximately 830 transactions whereby [COMPANY] completed a sales transaction wherein [COMPANY] sold to an individual, a quantity consisting of more than two aluminum/stainless steel "Z" style cup. Based on the amount of tax affixed to the "making" of an NFA firearm, and the amount of tax affixed to the "transfer" of an NFA firearm, the transactions identified from the records of WePay and Ecwid represent approximately $331,600 (829 x ($200 + $200)) in evaded tax.

Additionally, [COMPANY] accepted payments via Amazon. Analysis of the sales spreadsheet provided by Amazon (for the period _____2016 through _____2018) revealed approximately 5,819 transactions whereby [COMPANY] completed a sales transaction wherein [COMPANY] sold to an individual, a quantity consisting of more than two aluminum/stainless steel "Z" style cup. Based on the amount of tax affixed to the "making" of an NFA firearm, and the amount of tax affixed to the "transfer" of an NFA firearm, the transactions identified from the records from Amazon represent approximately $2,32,600 (5,819 x ($200 + $200)) in evaded tax.

Collectively, the sales records of [COMPANY] show that [DEFENDANT] evaded approximately $5,178,000 in tax associated with his unregistered manufacture and illicit transfer of NFA firearms (firearm silencer parts). Further, the combined sales records show that [DEFENDANT] sold approximately 12,945 sets of "Z" style aluminum/stainless steel cups. The sets counted for the above computation were typically in quantities of (8) cups and it is reasonable to infer that each set of cups were for use in one (1) silencer. Based on a conservative count of "Z" style cups sold by [COMPANY], it is reasonable to believe [DEFENDANT] sold NFA firearms (firearm silencer parts) for more than 13,000 unregistered silencers.

[REAL ESTATE – ADDRESS – LEGAL DESCRIPTION]

[ADDRESS] is the address for [COMPANY] and is the location wherein the various NFA Firearms (firearm silencer parts) are manufactured, stored, and shipped from.

[TITLE COMPANY] provided records that pertained to [DEFENDANT]'s purchase of [COMPANY REAL ESTATE]. The records show that [DEFENDANT] initiated the purchase of this property in ___2016. The records show the selling price of $300,000, with terms of the purchase calling for the seller to provide financing. The initial terms showed the seller would finance $200,000 of the purchase price. The escrow documents show the terms for financing the $200,000 included an annual interest rate of 6 percent, for 15-years, resulting in a monthly mortgage payment of $1,500.00. The escrow Combined Closing Statement, dated _____2016, shows that [DEFENDANT] paid $100,000 at closing as part of his purchase of the property. The records reflect that [DEFENDANT] paid $100,000, on _____ 2016, with a wire transfer from [BANK], account number _____.

[BANK], account number ending _____, is an account opened in _____ 2001, by [DEFENDANT]; an account he maintains sole signature authority. The monthly account statement that covers the period _____ 2016 through _____ 2016 shows that on _____

2016 the balance in the account was $10,500. Between _____ 2016 and _____ 2016, the following deposits were made to account ending _____.

DEPOSIT DATE   AMOUNT   SOURCE

_____ $ 100,000.00 PayPal

_____ $ 250.00 Amazon Marketplace

_____ $ 60,000.00 PayPal

_____ $ 20,000.00 PayPal

_____ $ 500.00 Amazon Marketplace

The above deposits, offset by cash withdrawals of approximately $52,000, and expenditures, resulted in the balance in account ending _____ prior to the wire transfer to [TITLE COMPANY] being $100,000. Based on the above, it is reasonable to assert that at least $92,750.00 ($100,000 -$6,500 -$250 -$500) of the closing payment to purchase the [COMPANY REAL ESTATE] property is directly traceable to funds originating from PayPal.

PayPal account ending _____ was the account from which the above deposits ($100,000.00, $60,000.00, and $20,000.00) originated. The PayPal spreadsheet provided descriptions of the various products sold; the net selling price of which aggregated the balance prior to the transfers.

Based on the product descriptions, the sales were grouped into three categories:

1) Those items whose description was consistent with that of the items determined to be NFA firearms (firearm silencer parts), for example:

495

a. Brand Name Cup and Plugs

b. Brand Name Auto Parts Cap Sets

c. Stainless and Aluminum Steel Cups

d. Brand Name Flashlight (C-cell) cap sets

e. Tubes, with end caps (caps were shown to be indexed for drilling)

2) Those items whose description was indicative of products designed to attach something

(i.e. oil filter, tube) to a firearm, for example;

a. 3/4x28 to 7/8x24 thread Adapter .308 to .223

b. (steel 13) 1/2-28 to 12/16-16 Adapter Oil Filter

c. 3PC Oil Filter Threaded Adapter 2/3-28 to 1/2-16 to 3/4 NPT

d. 1/2-16 Maglite D-cell Cap

e. Extra Long Barrel Thread Protector 3/4 x28 2/3" Ruger 1022 Adapter 9mm

f. Tubes, sold without caps or cups

3) Those items whose description did not readily appear to describe a product associated

with NFA products or firearms, for example:

a. Hydraulic Fittings

b. Brake Line Fittings

c. Engine Exhaust Fittings

d. Transmission Fittings

e. Fuel Line Fittings

f. Sales with no product description

Prior to the transfer of $100,000.00 to [BANK], PayPal records for account ending _____ shows the transfer was funded from an existing balance on _____2016, of $250,000. The balance of $250,000 was the result of the accumulation of funds derived from the sale of products from each of the above three groups. The PayPal account records revealed the account balance had been increasing since _____ 2014, when the balance was $800.00. The account balance reflected sales deposits, periodic withdrawals (equaling $103,600.00) and expenditures (approximately $45,461); yet, over-time the account balance progressively increased from $792.88 (never dropping below this amount) to $250,000. The build-up of the account balance, between _____ 2015 and _____ 2016, involved more than 14,900 transactions that resulted in the following net sales proceeds from each product category:

1) NFA firearms (firearm silencer parts) - $320,000

2) Associated with firearm modification - $42,000

3) Not readily associated with NFA or firearms - $22,000

Prior to the $60,000.00 transfer to [BANK], the PayPal records for account ending _____show an account balance of $190,000. That balance being comprised of the amount in the account remaining after the $100,000.00 transfer, plus the net increase from sales of additional products (about 490 transactions) between _____ 2016 and _____ 2016.

1) NFA firearms (firearm silencer parts) - $28,000

2) Associated with firearm modification - $1700

3) Not readily associated with firearms - $50

Lastly, prior to the $20,000.00 transfer to [BANK], the PayPal records for account ending _____ show an account balance of $103,000. That balance being comprised of the amount in the account remaining after the $60,000.00 transfer, plus the net increase from sales of additional products (about 75 transactions) between _____ 2016 and _____2016.

1) NFA firearms (firearm silencer parts) - $3000

2) Associated with firearm modification - $400

3) Not readily associated with firearms - $10

The funds transferred to [BANK] from PayPal account ending _____ ($100,000.00, $60,000.00, and $20,000.00), originated from the collective net sales, between _____ 2015 through _____ 2016, consisting of nearly 12,000 transactions, from the following three groups of products:

1) NFA firearms (firearm silencer parts) - $350,000

2) Not NFA yet associated with firearm modification - $60,000

3) Not readily associated with firearms - $20,000

Based on the high volume of sales, the relatively low dollar value of each sale (sales of the NFA firearms products averaged just less than $70.00 each); that the sale of all products occurred throughout the period; and, that the withdrawals and expenditures were not sufficient to draw the account to, or near zero; two strategies were used to determine the composition of the funds in PayPal account ending _____ – "Involved In a Money Laundering Transaction" and "Traceable To an SUA.".

Involved In a Money Laundering Transaction:

As shown above, the proceeds from the sale of NFA firearms were co-mingled with proceeds from the sale of potentially legitimate products in PayPal account ending _____. [DEFENDANT] purposefully co-mingled his sales revenues in the PayPal account to make the proceeds from his sale of unregistered NFA firearms undiscernible from deposits from any other source. The sale of each NFA firearm was conducted in furtherance of the overall scheme to defraud the government of tax dollars imposed by Title 26, Chapter 53, by use of wire transmission; thereby, establishing the proceeds of each NFA firearm sale as "specified unlawful activity." The co-mingling of his sales revenues was done in an attempt to hide the SUA, and to conceal its source and nature amongst plausibly legitimate earnings. This action is a method of money laundering and constitutes a violation of Title 18 U.S.C. § 1956(a)(1)(B)(i).

Title 18 U.S.C. § 981(a)(1)(A) subjects to forfeiture any property, or property traceable to such property, real or personal, that was involved in a transaction in violation of Title 18 U.S.C. § 1956. Once the proceeds from the sale of NFA firearms were deposited into PayPal account ending _____, the funds within that account, in their entirety, became "involved" in a transaction. Therefore, the balance in PayPal account ending _____, prior to each transfer to [BANK] ($100,000.00, $60,000.00, and $20,000.00) constituted forfeitable property. Each transfer constitutes a transaction with [BANK]; with the "involved" funds again co-mingled with existing funds in the [BANK] account; then, further traced to the wire transfer of $100,000 [DEFENDANT] used to close his purchase of [REAL ESTATE ADDRESS AND LEGAL DESCRIPTION]. Therefore, pursuant to Title 18 U.S.C. § 981(a)(1)(A), [REAL ESTATE

ADDRESS AND LEGAL DESCRIPTION], is forfeitable, as it represents real property derived from funds involved in a money laundering transaction.

Traceable To an SUA:

An alternative approach to determining the composition of the funds in PayPal account ending _____ involves tracing the funds by using a generally accepted accounting principle for valuing business inventory. The funds in PayPal account ending _____ were traced using the "First-In, First-Out" method - this method is also referred to as "FIFO," with the underlying principle being that funds first deposited into a bank account are also assumed to be, the first funds to leave the bank account.

The activity in PayPal account ending _____ involved thousands of on-average low dollar deposits, coupled with hundreds of withdrawals (transfers and expenditures). To facilitate a FIFO analysis of the activity in this account the monthly deposits for each of the three product categories were aggregated. The balance in the account on _____2015 was $800. The table below is a summary of the sales from _____2015 through _____ 2015:

MONTH	NFA Firearm	Associated Firearms	Other	Monthly Total	Running Total
Beg. Bal.					$
July	$25,000	$ 3,000	$ 5,000	$	$
August	$25,000	$ 3,000	$ 5,000	$	$
September	$16,000	$ 2,000	$ 2,000	$	$
October	$ 8,000	$ 3,000	$ 2,000	$	$
November	$12,000	$ 4,000	$ 1,000	$	$
December	$ 8,000	$ 6,000	$ 1,000	$	$
TOTAL	$94,000	$21,000	$16,000	$	

In keeping with a FIFO analysis, any funds, whether from the sale of NFA firearms or not, the funds earned in _____ 2015 would be applied toward any withdrawals from the account prior to those of any funds earned in _____ 2015. By similar logic, all funds earned in 2015 would be applied toward any withdrawals from the account prior to those of any funds earned in 2016. The PayPal records detail that prior to the _____ 2016 transfer of $100,000.00 to [BANK], approximately $190,000 had been withdrawn (either as a withdrawal $100,000 or expenditure $50,000) from PayPal account ending _____. The greater amount of funds withdrawn ($150,000), than those deposited in 2015, inclusive of the beginning balance ($120,000), establishes that all earnings in 2015 had been depleted from the account prior to _____ 2016. In 2015, the sale of NFA firearms (firearm silencer parts) comprised approximately 68 percent of the sales, with firearms associated products and other non-firearms products comprising approximately 16 percent each.

_____ 2016 sales would be offset by the excess of withdrawn funds $130,000 ($150,000 - $120,000), resulting in approximately $5,000 in total sales that month. The offset was applied to the product groups based upon their respective percent of sales for the month of _____ 2016 (NFA firearms 62%, Firearms associated 33%, and Other 5%).

The adjusted net sales in _____ 2016, plus the sales completed from _____ 2016 through _____ 2016, resulted in a PayPal account balance comprised of proceeds from the sale of the three product groups. The FIFO method was instrumental in addressing the deposits that occurred earlier in the period; however, having exhausted all withdrawn funds against sales, the determination of the composition of the remaining account balance used for the transfers is based upon product group percentage of sales for that period (_____2016 (less FIFO offset) through _____ 2016). The resulting product group percentages are: NFA firearms – 79.4 percent, Firearms associated – 18.7 percent, and Other products – 1.9 percent.

I applied the FIFO method to determine the composition of the balance in the [BANK] account -81582, prior to the wire transfer to [TITLE COMPANY]. The balance in the [BANK] account prior to the $100,000.00 deposit was $6,563.95. I reduced the pre-existing funds with withdrawals until the pre-existing funds were depleted. Subsequent withdrawals were applied against the $100,000.00 deposit until the date of the wire transfer, resulting in $50,000 (of the $100,000) in unapplied funds from PayPal. I then multiplied the deposits from PayPal by the grouped product sale percentages. The sum of the PayPal deposits, times the 2016 sales percentage associated with NFA firearms (($50,00060 + 60,000 + 20,000) X .794) showed that the balance in the [BANK] account, of $125,000, was comprised of approximately $100,000 in funds traceable to NFA firearm sales. By similar exercise, the balance was comprised of approximately $25,000 of funds traceable to firearms associated products, and approximately $2,300 of funds traceable to other products not readily associated with firearms.

Applying the FIFO method, in conjunction with the grouped product sales percentages, resulted in a determination that $79,000 of the wire transfer was traceable to NFA firearms sales. Alternatively, by multiplying the wire transfer amount traceable to the PayPal deposits ($92,000), by the NFA firearms sales percentage, resulted in approximately $72,000 of the wire transfer being traceable to NFA firearm sales.

Title 18 U.S.C. § 981(a)(1)(C) subjects to forfeiture any property, real or personal, which constitutes or is derived from proceeds traceable to a violation of 18 U.S.C. § 1343, wire fraud.

The funds from the sale of NFA firearms (firearm silencer parts), the proceeds of a scheme to defraud, by use of interstate wire transmissions, were deposited into PayPal account ending _____, were then traced to [BANK] account ending _____ were then traced to [TITLE COMPANY] for use in purchasing [REAL ESTATE ADDRESS AND LEGAL DESCRIPTION]; thereby rendering, [REAL ESTATE ADDRESS AND LEGAL DESCRIPTION], forfeitable as real property derived from proceeds traceable to a violation of 18 U.S.C. § 1343.

[VEHICLE YEAR, MAKE, MODEL, VIN]

[DEFENDANT] submitted paperwork to [STATE] DMV that showed on _____ 2017, he purchased a [VEHICLE DESCRIPTION] from an individual [NAME/ADDRESS]. On _____ 2017, [DEFENDANT] transferred this vehicle to [COMPANY]. [DEFENDANT] provided [STATE] Department of Vehicles (DMV) a Statement of Facts form with the statement, "I, [DEFENDANT] am transferring the [VEHICLE DESCRIPTIOIN] to my company, [COMPANY]." [DEFENDANT] disclosed on the Application for Transfer by New Owner form that the address for [COMPANY] is at [REAL ESTATE ADDRESS AND LEGAL DESCRIPTION].

[DEFENDANT] stated on the Application for Title or Registration form he submitted to the [STATE] DMV when he registered the [VEHICLE DESCRIPTION] in [STATE], on _____, 2017, that [DEFENDANT] purchased the vehicle for $5,500. Records from [BANK], for account number ending _____, in the name [COMPANY], show that on _____, 2017, [DEFENDANT] initiated an Out-of-State Counter Withdrawal request that resulted in the issuance of a cashier's check made payable to [NAME], in the amount of $19,500. A memo

503

on the face of the cashier's check indicates the check was for a "Car Purchase" and that the remitter of the check was [COMPANY].

Involved In a Money Laundering Transaction:

[BANK] account statements for account ending _____ show that the balance in the account prior to the issuance of the cashier's check payable to [NAME] was approximately $90,000. Analysis of the account shows that with the exception of three early deposits that totaled $4,000, and a few large hardware store refunds that totaled approximately $2,500, the deposits to this account originated primarily from WePay and PayPal account ending _____, totaling approximately $300,000 and $250,000, respectively.

By applying the FIFO method, when the cashier's check was issued to purchase the [VEHICLE DESCRIPTION], the entire balance in the [BANK] account ($90,000) was comprised only of funds from WePay and PayPal, deposited into the account between _____2017 to _____ 2017 (all prior deposits being applied to account debits). A FIFO analysis would further refine the dates of _____ 2017 through _____ 2017 as the dates for deposit of the funds that funded the cashier's check.

The transaction summary spreadsheet obtained from WePay did not include a description of the products sold; however, it contained entries that correlated with the periodic deposits into [BANK] account ending _____. The transaction summary spreadsheet provided detailed descriptions of the products sold by [COMPANY]. The two transaction summary spreadsheets were merged to correlate the products sold with the funds transferred to [BANK] account ending _____. The merged spreadsheet covered the period _____, 2016 through _____ 2017.

WePay account _____ showed a fluctuating balance in the days preceding the transfer of funds to [BANK]; the balance from which the funds were derived to purchase the [VEHICLE

DESCRIPTION]. On _____ 2017, the balance in the WePay account was $6,000. Between _____ 2017 and _____ 2017, the WePay account incurred four (4) withdrawals totaling $7,000; effectively, eliminating the pre-existing balance. Between _____ 2017 and _____ 2017 WePay account _____ received deposits from the sale of NFA firearms products of approximately $12,000 (97.4%), and the sale of firearms associated products of approximately $300 (2.6%).

The spreadsheet of PayPal account ending _____ depicted similar sales activity to that observed in the spreadsheet for PayPal account ending _____. As with the latter account, PayPal account ending _____ showed a sustained increasing balance in the months preceding the transfer of funds to [BANK]; the balance from which the funds were derived to purchase the [VEHICLE DESCRIPTION]. On _____ 2017, the balance in PayPal account ending _____ was $29,825.18. Between _____ 2017 and _____ 2017 PayPal account ending _____ incurred three (3) withdrawals totaling $31,000; effectively, eliminating the pre-existing balance. Between _____ 2017 and _____ 2017, PayPal account ending _____ received deposits from the sale of NFA firearms products of approximately $33,000 (92%), sale of firearms associated products of approximately $2,100 (6%), and other products of $600 (2%). The funds attributable to "Other Products" during this time-period was for products whose product description field was blank.

The proceeds from the sale of NFA firearms were co-mingled with proceeds from the sale of potentially legitimate products in the WePay account and PayPal account ending _____. [DEFENDANT] purposefully co-mingled his sales revenues in these accounts to make the proceeds from his sale of unregistered NFA firearms undiscernible from deposits from any other source. The sale of each NFA firearm was conducted in furtherance of an overall scheme to defraud the government of tax dollars imposed by Title 26, Chapter 53, by use of wire transmission; thereby, establishing the proceeds of each NFA firearm sale as "specified unlawful activity." The co-mingling of his sales revenues was done in an attempt to hide the SUA, and to conceal its source and nature amongst plausibly legitimate earnings. This action is a method of money laundering and constitutes a violation of Title 18 U.S.C. § 1956(a)(1)(B)(i).

Title 18 U.S.C. § 981(a)(1)(A) subjects to forfeiture any property, or property traceable to such property, real or personal, that was involved in a transaction in violation of Title 18 U.S.C. § 1956. Once the proceeds from the sale of NFA firearms were deposited into WePay account _____ and PayPal account ending _____, the funds within those accounts, in their entirety, became "involved" in a transaction. Therefore, the funds from WePay account _____ and PayPal account ending _____, prior to each transfer to [BANK] constituted forfeitable property. Each transfer constitutes a transaction with [BANK]; with the "involved" funds further traced to the cashier's check of $30,000 [DEFENDANT] used to purchase the [VEHICLE DESCRIPTIOIN]. Therefore, pursuant to Title 18 U.S.C. § 981(a)(1)(A), the [VEHICLE DESCRIPTION], is forfeitable, as it represents personal property derived from funds involved in a money laundering transaction.

Traceable To an SUA:

Between _____2017 and _____ 2017, PayPal account ending _____ showed three $10,000 withdrawals, which by FIFO application would eliminate the _____ 2017 balance of $30,000 from being part of the funds available to be transferred for the car purchase.

Based on a FIFO analysis, and by looking at the deposits into [BANK] account ending _____, between _____ 2017 and _____ 2017, the deposits that occurred on, and those occurring just after _____ 2017, would comprise the funds behind the cashier's check, in the amount $20,000.

Based on those deposits, funds originating from WePay comprised approximately 26.6 percent of the funds and those from PayPal comprised approximately 73.4 percent.

DATE	WEPAY	PAYPAL
6/8/2017		$ 10,000
7/8/2017	$ 1,400	
8/01/2017	$ 1,400	
8/21/2017	$ 1,400	
8/30/2017	$ 1,400	
9/01/2017	$ 1,400	
9/20/2017		$ 6,500 (Balance of $22,000)
TOTAL	$ 7,000	$ 16,000
PERCENTAGE	25%	73%

Based on an analysis of their respective sales transaction spreadsheets, approximately $5,800 ($5,800 X 98%) of the funds from WePay were traceable to [DEFENDANT]'s scheme (sale of NFA firearms); and approximately $15,000 ($16,500 X 92%) of the funds from PayPal were traceable to that scheme. Together, the funds from WePay and PayPal, that are traceable to [DEFENDANT]'s scheme, total approximately $22,000.

Pursuant to Title 18 U.S.C. § 981(a)(1)(C), the [VEHICLE DESCRIPTION] is forfeitable in that it constitutes proceeds, or is traceable to proceeds of a scheme to defraud, by wire communication, a violation of Title 18 U.S.C. § 1343.

PayPal Account Ending _____

Between _____ 2017 and _____ 2018, approximately $490,000 was deposited into PayPal account ending _____. The table below depicts the monthly deposits attributable to the three product groups.

Month/Year	NFA Firearms	Firearms Associated	Other
November 2017	$ 60,000	$ 4,000	$ 900
December 2017	$ 60,000	$ 4,000	$ 900
January 2018	$ 91,000	$ 4,000	$ 900
February 2018	$ 60,000	$ 4,000	$ 900

March 2018	$ 80,000	$ 7,000	$ 900
April 2018	$ 80,000	$ 7,000	$ 900
May 2018 (4 days)	$ 10,000	$ 1,000	$ 600
Total	$ 441,000	$ 31,000	$ 6,000
Percentage	90%	7%	1.5%

The funds from the sale of the three product groups were co-mingled in PayPal account _____. The funds were co-mingled in an attempt to disguise the money earned from the sale of unregistered NFA firearms (firearm silencer parts) with that earned from the sale of legal products. [DEFENDANT] knowingly manufactured and sold metal parts, designed for the use as firearm silencers, and implemented a scheme involving nationwide internet marketing practices (i.e. wire transmissions) to sell those products, a SUA. The activity of co-mingling SUA proceeds with other seemingly legitimate funds, for the purpose of disguising the source of the SUA proceeds, is a form of money laundering.

PayPal account ending _____ was the virtual container wherein the proceeds of [DEFENDANT]'s total sales were blended. The funds, undiscernible as to "good" or "bad" money, in its entirety, are funds involved in a money laundering transaction. The funds presently within PayPal account _____, constitute funds involved in a money laundering transaction and are all forfeitable pursuant to Title 18 U.S.C. §§ 981(a)(1)(A) and 984(a)(1).

For PayPal account ending _____, for the period _____ through _____ 2018, the table above displays the amount of proceeds [DEFENDANT] realized from the sale of items in each product group. [DEFENDANT]'s sale of unregistered NFA firearms (firearm silencer parts) comprised 90 percent of the total sales for that period. The proceeds from the sale of unregistered NFA firearms are funds traceable to [DEFENDANT]'s overall scheme to defraud and are thereby forfeitable. Pursuant to Title 18 U.S.C. §§ 981(a)(1)(C) and 984(a), an amount not exceeding $402,267.10 is forfeitable.

[BANK] Account ending _____

Between _____, 2017 and _____, 2018, approximately $490,000 was deposited into [BANK] account ending _____ as transfers originating from PayPal account _____.

The funds originating from PayPal account _____ were the co-mingled funds of SUA proceeds and the revenue from the sale of other products. The funds were co-mingled in an attempt to further disguise the SUA proceeds as having a legitimate source. The activity of co-mingling SUA proceeds with other seemingly legitimate funds, for the purpose of disguising the source of the SUA proceeds, is a form of money laundering. The funds presently within [BANK] account ending _____, constitute funds involved in a money laundering transaction and are all forfeitable pursuant to Title 18 U.S.C. §§ 981(a)(1)(A) and 984(a)(1).

The funds deposited into [BANK] account ending _____, for the period _____ 2017 through _____ 2018, originating from PayPal account _____, are a blend of the proceeds from the sale of all three product groups. The table above displays the amount of proceeds [DEFENDANT] realized from the sale of items in each product group for that period. [DEFENDANT]'s sale of unregistered NFA firearms (firearm silencer parts) comprised 90 percent of the total sales for that period; thereby, it is reasonable to infer that 90 percent of the funds transferred from PayPal account _____ are traceable to [DEFENDANT]'s scheme. The proceeds from the sale of unregistered NFA firearms are funds traceable to [DEFENDANT]'s overall scheme to defraud and are thereby forfeitable. Pursuant to Title 18 U.S.C. §§ 981(a)(1)(C) and 984(a), an amount not exceeding $441,000 ($490,000 X 90%) is forfeitable from [BANK] account ending _____.

CoinBase Account _____

Between _____2017 and _____2018, approximately $55,000 was deposited into PayPal account ending _____. Sales of the three product groups were: NFA firearms $20,000 (36%), firearms associated $30,000 (56.5%), and other $4,000 (7.5%).

The funds from the sale of the three product groups were co-mingled in PayPal account _____. The funds were co-mingled in an attempt to disguise the money earned from the sale of unregistered NFA firearms (firearm silencer parts) with that earned from the sale of legal products. [DEFENDANT] knowingly manufactured and sold metal parts, designed for the use as firearm silencers, and implemented a scheme involving nationwide internet marketing practices (i.e. wire transmissions) to sell those products, a SUA. The activity of co-mingling SUA proceeds with other seemingly legitimate funds, for the purpose of disguising the source of the SUA proceeds, is a form of money laundering.

PayPal account ending _____ was the virtual container wherein the proceeds of [DEFENDANT]'s total sales were blended. The funds, undiscernible as to whether they were derived from sales of NFA firearms or legitimate products, in their entirety, are funds involved in a money laundering transaction. Withdrawals from PayPal account _____, that became transfers to [BANK] account ending _____, were comprised of the blended sales proceeds. [BANK] account ending _____ is [DEFENDANT]'s personal savings account. Each transfer from PayPal account _____ into [BANK] account ending _____ resulted in a co-mingling of the PayPal funds with any other funds resident or deposited into [BANK] account ending _____. Between _____ 2017 and _____ 2018, approximately $60,000 was transferred from PayPal account _____ into [BANK] account ending _____.

Between _____2017 and _____2018, approximately $85,000 was transferred from [BANK] account ending _____ to CoinBase account _____ and constituted a transaction comprised of co-mingled funds. The funds presently within CoinBase account _____ constitute funds involved in a money laundering transaction and are forfeitable pursuant to Title 18 U.S.C. §§ 981(a)(1)(A) and 984(a)(1).

Appendix E
Licensed Firearm Importer
Marking Abbreviations;

IMPORTER ABBREVIATION	FULL IMPORTER NAME
AAI NKC MO	AMERICAN ARMS INC. NORTH KANSAS CITY, MO
AAL PHLA PA	ACTION ARMS LTD, PHILADELPHIA PA
ACC INT/INTRAC KNOX TN	INTRAC ARMS INC – IAI – ACC INT KNOXVILLE, TN
ADCO WOBURN MA	ADCO SALES, INC. WOBURN, MA
AE CO NYC AE CO NYC	AMERICAN EAGLE ARMS CORP. NEW YORK, NY
API PAHRUMP NV	ARMSCOR PRECISION INC. PAHRUMP, NV
API SAN MATEO CA	ARMSCORP PRECISION SQUIRES BINGHAM SAN MATEO, CA
APINTL PAHRUMP NV	ARMSCOR PRECISION INT'L PAHRUMP, NV
ARL ORD ARLINGTON VA	ARLINGTON ORDNANCE CO/BLUE SKY PROD ARLINGTON, VA
ARMAMENTOS WPB FL	ARMAMENTOS INC., WEST PALM BEACH, FL
ARMORY USA HOUSTON TX	ARSENAL USA, HOUSTON TX
ATI ROCH NY	ATI AMERICAN TACTICAL IMPORTS INC.
ATI ROCHESTER NY	ATI AMERICAN TACTICAL IMPORTS INC.
ATI SUMMERVILLE SC	ATI AMERICAN TACTICAL IMPORTS INC.
B WEST LA CA	B WEST IMPORTS INC.
B WEST TUC AZ	B WEST IMPORTS INC.
BACO INC MORGAN UT	BROWNING ARS COMPANY - BACO MORGAN UT
BCI USA	BETA/CROW INTERNATIONAL INC. DALLAS, TX
BENET ARMS SF CAL	BENET ARMS (GOLD RUSH ARMS)
BSA CO BSA	BIRMINGHAM SMALL ARMS SAN ANTONIO, TX
BSA HOUSTON MO	BSA IMPORTS LLC HOUSTON, MO
BTC S EL MONTE CA	BRIKLEE TRADING CO. SOUTH EL MONTE, CA
BTC SEM CA	BRIKLEE TRADING CO. SOUTH EL MONTE, CA
C&A BCH VA	CAMPCO INTERNATIONAL INC. VIRGINIA BEACH, VA
C&A VA BCH VA	CAMPCO INTERNATIONAL INC. VIRGINIA BEACH, VA
C&A VA BH VA	CAMPCO INTERNATIONAL INC. VIRGINIA BEACH, VA
CAI GEORGIA VT	CENTURY INTL ARMS INC. GEORGIA, VT
CAI ST A VT	CENTURY ARMS INC. ST ALBANS, VT
CAI ST ALB VT	CENTURY ARMS INC. ST ALBANS, VT
CASCO BLOWING ROCK NC	CASCO ARMS-ALPINE FIREARMS BLOWING ROCK, NC
CASSI INC COLO SPGS COLO	CASSI INC. COLORADO SPRINGS, CO
CCF RICHMOND VA	CAPITOL CITY FIREARMS, RICHMOND, VA
CDI SWAN VT	CLASSIC DISTRIBUTORS INC. SWANTON, VT
CHERRYS GSO NC	CHERRYS INC., GREENSBORO, NC
CII VERSAILLES KY	CLEARVIEW INVESTMENTS INC., VERSAILLES, KY
CJA SFLD MI	CJA EQUIPMENT INCORPORATED, SOUTHFIELD, MI
CMI MIAMI FL	CHARTERED MERCHANTS INC., MIAMI, FL
COLE DIST S'VILLE KY	COLE DISTRIBUTING, SCOTTSVILLE, KY
CP MONROVIA CAL	CHESHIRE & PEREZ DIST CO INC., MONROVIA, CA

IMPORTER ABBREVIATION	FULL IMPORTER NAME
CSI LA CA	CHINASPORTS INC. (CSI) ONTARIO, CA
CSI CA L A USA	CHINASPORTS INC. (CSI) ONTARIO, CA
CSI ONT CA	CHINASPORTS INC. (CSI) ONTARIO, CA
DIG VA BCH VA	DOMINION IMPORT GROUPS LTD. VIRGINIA BEACH, VA
DSA INC LK BARRINGTON IL	DSA INC., LAKE BARRINGTON, IL
DUNAV IT LYNNWOOD WA	DUNAV INTERNATIONAL TRADING LYNWOOD, WA
EAA COCOA FL	EUROPEAN AMERICAN ARMORY
EAA HIALEAH FL	EUROPEAN AMERICAN ARMORY
EAA ROCKLEDGE FL	EUROPEAN AMERICAN ARMORY
ECCSA PENNSAUKEN NJ	EAST COAST COMBAT SHOOTING PENNSUAKEN, NJ
EIG C MAIMI FL	EIG CUTLERY MIAMI, FL
EMF CO STUDIO CITY CAL	EMF COMPANY INC.
ERS INC TEWKSBURY MA	EARLS REPAIR SERVICE INC. TEWKSBURY, MA
EXEL GARDNER MA	EXEL ARMS OF AMERICA INC. GARDNER MA
FED ORD INC SO EL MONTE CA	FEDERAL ORDNANCE INC., S EL MONTE, CA
FIE MIAMI FL	FIREARMS IMPORT & EXPORT MIAMI, FL
FIREARM IMP. EXP. MIAMI FL	FIREARMS IMPORT & EXPORT MIAMI, FL
FIREARMS INT'L CORP.	FIREARMS INTERNATIONAL CORP.
FNMI COLUMBIA SC	FN MANUFACTURING INC., COLUMBIA, SC
FTC WOODLAND HILLLS, CA	FIREARM TECH CO. WOODLAN HILLS, CA
GAI MIA FL	GERMAN ARMS IMPORT CORP. MIAMI, FL
GARCIA CORP WASH DC	FIREARMS INT'L CORP., GARCIA CORP. WASHINGTON, DC
GBE HB CA	GOOSE BERRY ENTERPRISES
GBE LA CA	GOOSE BERRY ENTERPRISES
GBS HB CA	GOOSE BERRY ENTERPRISES
GFCC CO SAC CA	CORPORATION, SACRAMENTO, CA
GFCC CO SACCA	CORPORATION, SACRAMENTO, CA
GFCC CO SACCO	CORPORATION, SACRAMENTO, CA
GIA KNOX TN	GILBERT INTERNATIONAL ARMS, KNOXVILLE, TN
GLNIC LA CA	GLNIC CORP OF AMERICA, LOS ANGELES, CA
GP TRAD ST ALB VT	GP TRADING LTD., ST ABLANS, VT
GPC W HURLEY NY	GUN PARTS CORP., WEST HURLEY, NY
GRC MTNSBG WVA	GIBBS RIFLE COMPANY, MARTINSBURG, WV
GSAD MANH BEA CA	GOLDEN STATE ARMS DIST. - GSAD INC.
GSI T'VILLE AL	GUN SOUTH INC.
GSI TRUSSVILLE AL	GUN SOUTH INC.
GUN SOUTH INC	BIRMINGHAM, AL
GUN SOUTH INC	GUN SOUTH INC., TRUSSVILLE, AL
GZS BALDWIN IL	GLENN ZANDERS SPORTING GOODS CO. BALDWIN, IL
HERTER'S	HERTERS INC – R D LARSON SPORTS INC. WASECA, MN
HK CHANTILLY VA	HECKLER & KOCH INC.
HK INC ARL VA	HECKLER & KOCH INC.
HK INC STERLING VA	HECKLER & KOCH INC.
HKD ASHBURN VA	HECKLER & KOCH DEFENSE INC., ASHBURN, VA
HKI COLUMBUS GA	HECKLER & KOCH INC., COLUMBUS, GA
HKI TRUSSVILLE AL	HECKLER & KOCH INC., TRUSSVILLE, AL
HLTC NAPA, CA	HING LONG TRADING COMPANY, NAPA, CA
IAC ALEX VA	INTERARMS, ALEXANDRIA, VA
IAC BILLERICA MA	INTERSTATE ARMS CORP, BILLERICA, MA
IACO SAC CA	INTER AMERICAN IMP/EXP SACRAMENTO, CA
IAI HOU TX	ISRAEL ARMS INTERNATIONAL INC., HOUSTON, TX
IAI I KNOX TN	INTRAC ARMS INC – IAI – ACC INT KNOXVILLE, TN

IMPORTER ABBREVIATION	FULL IMPORTER NAME
IAIE SCRA CA	INTER AMERICAN IMP/EXP, SACRAMENTO, CA
IDE MCLEAN VA	IDE, MCLEAN, VA (SHUN TONG ENT. INC.)
IDE USA SFLD MICH	IDE USA, SOUTHFIELD, MI
INT DIST INC MIAMI FL	INTERNATIONAL DISTRIBUTORS INC. MIAMI, FL
INTERARMS ALEX VA	INTERARMS, ALEXANDRIA, VA
INTERSTATE ARMS BILLERICA MA	INTERSTATE ARMS CORP. BILLERICA, MA
INTRAC KNOX TN	INTRAC ARMS INTERNATIONAL KNOXVILLE, TN
J L GALEF NY	J. L. GALEF & SONS (EAGLE ARMS), NEW YORK, NY
JJCO	JOHN JOVINO CO INC., NEW YORK, NY
JJCO NY NY	JOHN JOVINO CO INC., NEW YORK, NY
JLD ENT FARM CT	JLD ENTERPRISES INC., FARMINGTON CT
JO ARM HOU TX	JO ARMS & AMMUNITION CO, HOUSTON, TX
JPE PAS CA	J'S PACIFIC ENTERPRISE INC.
JPE POMONA CA	J'S PACIFIC ENTERPRISE INC.
KANEMATSU GOSHO	KANEMATSU GOSHO, USA INC. ARLINGTON, HEIGHTS, IL
KASC GBORO NC	KASC INC., GREENSBORO, NC
KBI HBG PA	KBI INC., HARRISBURG PA
KBI INC HBG PA	KBI INC., HARRISBURG PA
KBI ING HBG PA	KBI INC., HARRISBURG PA
KFS ATL GA	KENGS FIREARMS SPECIALTY INC., ATLANTA, GA
KFS ATLANTA GA	KENGS FIREARMS SPECIALTY INC., ATLANTA, GA
KSI POMONA CA	K SPORTS IMPORTS INC., POMONA, CA
LA DISTR NEW YORK	L A DISTRIBUTORS, NEW YORK, NY
LAI ALBION NY	LIBERTY ARMS INTERNATIONAL, ALBION, NY
LAI VICTORIA TX	LIBERTY ARMS INTERNATIONAL LLC. VICTORIA, TX
LHD WBORO MA	LEW HORTON DIST CO INC., WESTBORO, MA
LIBERTY	LIBERTY ORGANIZATION INC., LA CRESCENTA CA
LSI RENO NV	LEGACY SPORTS INTERNATIONAL, RENO, NV
LSI ALEXANDRAI VIRGINIA	LEGACY SPORTS INTERNATIONAL ALEXANDRIA,VA
MADISON IMPORT CORP	MADISON IMPORT-ROSCO-GEROCO L.A., CA
MAGTECH MADISON CT	MAGTECH AMMUNITION INC., MADISON CT
MARATHON PROD INC., WETH CT	MARATHON PRODUCTS INC., WETHERSFIELD, CT
MMBI MYERSVILLE MD	MMB IMPORTS LLC., MYERSVILLE, MD
MMC HB CA	MITCHELL MANUFACTURING CORP.
MRI MPLS MN	MAGNUM RESEARCH INC. (MRI), MINNEAPOLIS MN
NA RDGFLD NJ	NAVY ARMS COMPANY, RIDGEFIELD, NJ
NA CO RIDGEFIELD NJ	NAVY ARMS COMPANY, RIDGEFIELD, NJ
NASI MIDLAND TX	NORTH AMERICAN SALES INT., MIDLAND, TX
NATMIL VB AR	NATMIL, VAN BUREN, AR
NHC CO SAC CA	NEW HELVETIA TRADE GROUP, SACRAMENTO, CA
NHM SAC CA	NEW HELVETIA TRADE GROUP, SACRAMENTO, CA
NHM CO SAC CA	NEW HELVETIA TRADE GROUP, SACRAMENTO, CA
NHM CO SACCO	NEW HELVETIA TRADE GROUP, SACRAMENTO, CA
ODIN LORTON VA	ODIN INTERNATIONAL LTD., ALEXANDRIA, VA
ONYX ARMS GTF MT EVANS	CREED MILES II (ONYX ARMS), GREAT FALLS, MT
OOW INC CHARDON OH	OHIO ORDNANCE WORKS, CHARDON, OH
PAC MODESTO CA	PACIFIC ARMAMENT CORP., MODESTO, CA
PARA ORDNANCE INC	PARA ORDNANCE, FT LAUDERDALE, FL
PARA USA INC.	PARA ORDNANCE, FT LAUDERDALE, FL
PARS INTL LOU KY	PARS INTERNATIONAL CORP. LOUISVILLE, KY
PCM WI NY	PCM IMPORTERS, YONKERS, NY
PIC DECATUR GA	PRECISE IMPORTS CORP SUFFERN, NY
PPC USA	PP CORPORATION (PINDELL PALM CORPORATION)

IMPORTER ABBREVIATION	FULL IMPORTER NAME
POLY USA ATL GA	POLY USA INC, ATLANTA, GA
PTK INTL ATL GA	PTK INTERNATIONAL INC., ATLANTA, GA
PW REDMO WA	PW ARMS INC, REDMOND, WA
R GUNS CARPENTERSVILLE IL	R GUNS/SPORTSWEREUS INC. CARPENTERSVILLE, IL
R OX NJ	RIFLES ANTIQUES RELICS EXPRESS LLC., OX, NJ
RAAC SCOTTSBURG IN	RUSSIAN AMERICAN ARMCORY CO., SCOTTSBURG, IN
RAI WOODLAND HILLS CA	ROYAL ARMS INTERNATIONAL WOODLAND HILLS, CA
RG IND MIAMI FL	RG INSTUSTRIES, MIAMI, FL
RGUNS C'VILLE IL	R GUNS/SPORTSWEREUS INC., CARPETNERSVILLE, IL
ROSCO ARMS CO	MADISON IMPORT – ROSCO - GEROCO L.A., CA
RSA ENT INC OCEAN NJ	RSA ENTERPRISES INC., OCEAN, NJ
RTB CORP MIAMI FL	RTB CORP. - RTB WEST GERMANY, MIAMI, FL
SAC LATTA SC	SOUTHERN AMMUNITION COMPANY INC. LATTA, SC
SACO ARL VA	SECURITY ARMS CO. INC., ARLINGTON, VA
SAI CUMMING GA	STEYR ARMS INC., CUMMING, GA
SAI TRUSSVILLE AL	STEYR ARMS INC., TRUSSVILLE, AL
SAMCO MIA FL	SAMCO GLOBAL ARMS INC., MIAMI, FL
SGAI MIAMI FL	SAMCO GLOBAL ARMS INC., MIAMI, FL
SI GENESEO IL	SPRINGFIELD INC. (SI), GENESEO, IL
SIG SAUER INC EXETER NH	SIG ARMS INC. SIG SAUER, EXETER NH
SILE NY	SILE DISTRIBUTORS INC. NEW YORK, NY
SMI USA WEST POINT MS	STEYER MANNLICHER USA INC. WEST POINT, MS
SS KRESEGE CO TROY MI	KMART CORP – S.S. KRESGE CO. TROY, MICHIGAN
SSI ONTARIO CA	SAFARI SUPPLY INC., ONTARIO, CA
SSME PLANT CTY FL	SSME DEUTSCHE WAFFEN INC., PLANT CITY, FL
STEYR SECAUCUS NJ	STEYR ARMS INC., TRUSSVILLE, AL
TGI KNOX TN	TENNESSEE GUN, KNOXVILLE, TN
TRISTAR NKC MO	TRISTART ARMS LLC., NORTH KANSAS CITY, MO
USSG COCOA FL	US SPORTING GOODS INC.
USSG ROCKLEDGE FL	US SPORTING GOODS INC.
VALOR	VALOR CORP OF FLORIDA, MIAMI, FL
VEGA SAC CA	IACO - INTER AMERICAN IMP/EXP SACRAMENTO, CA
VFI FOXBORO MA	VULCANS FORGE INC., FOXBORO, MA
WAC	WINFIELD ARMS CORP., LOS ANGELES, CA
WPA ANAHEIM, CA	WPA - SPORTING SUPPLIES INTL. INC. ANAHEIM, CA
ZDF SLC UT	ZDF IMPORT/EXPORT INC., SALT LAKE CITY, UT

Index

1

13 Critical Tasks, An Inside Out Approach to Solving More Gun Crime,, 103

2

2ND AMENDMENT, 5

4

4th Amendment, 1
4th and 14th Amendments, 75

5

5k Letter, xii, 159, 291

8

80% receivers, 13, 22, 23, 25, 31, 247

9

924(c), 9, 56, 109, 110, 303, 304
924(h), 110, 304
924(j), 110, 304
924(o), 56, 110, 304

A

A&D, 333
Abdul Qadeer Khan, 330
Access 2000, 15, 95
Accessory After the Fact, 299
ACCOMPLICE, 108
Acoustic Ballistic Detection, 99
Acoustic Gun Shot Detection System, 15
Acquisition & Disposition, 16
Administrative Forfeiture, 76
Adoption, x, 286
AFIS, 333
Agent Provocateur, 16
AK-47, 2, 12, 13, 18, 23, 333
Alien, 53, 66, 67
ALPR, 149, 150, 204, 294, 333
American Society of Industrial Security, xviii
AML, 333
Ammunition, 8, 16, 17, 19, 40, 55, 70, 72, 334, 489, 494, 496, 498
Ant Trade, 16
Antique Firearm, 16
AR-15, 12, 13, 23, 25, 333
ARIN, 261, 262

Armed Career Criminal, 53, 109, 110, 333, 488
Armor Piercing, 16, 72
Armor piercing ammunition, 222
Arms Export Control Act, 8, 35, 58, 68, 333, 487
Arms Export Control Act (AECA) of 1976, 8
Arms Trade Treaty, 333
ASEAN, 320, 333
Assault Weapon, 10
Asset Tracking, 77
ATF Form 4473, 7, 10, 17, 27, 44, 57, 62, 63, 64, 65, 66
ATF Form 6, 17, 69
AUSA, 46, 49, 50, 63, 333, 402, 411, 416, 424, 425, 429, 435, 436, 444, 445, 461, 464
Automated License Plate Reader, 333
Automated License Plate Readers, xv, 149, 293

B

Bank Secrecy Act, 333
Barnacle Allegory, 63
barrel length, 13, 39, 40
Bill of Rights, xxiii
Black Liberation Army, 11
Block Gun, 17
blockchain, 83, 487
Blue on Blue, 17, 21
Bodyguard Statute, 299
Body-On-It, 17
Boomerang, 15
Bosnia, xv, 310, 323
Bot, 449
Brady Handgun Violence Prevention Act of 1994, 9, 487
Browning Automatic Rifle, 10, 333
Buffer Tube Brace, 17
Bump Fire, 18
Bump Slide Stock, 14
Bureau of Alcohol, Tobacco, Firearms and Explosives, 18, 40, 72, 333, 494, 495, 496, 497, 499
Burner Gun, 18
Buy-Bust, 18
Buy-Walk, 18

C

C&R, 64, 65, 333
CAD, 25, 333
Cali Cartel, xi, 121
Canada, 204, 245, 246, 272, 310, 311, 313, 321, 489
Capone, 6, 279
Carcano rifle, 11
Carpenter v. U.S, 149, 296, 487
Cartels, xix, 12, 491
Cartridge Head-stamp Identification Catalogue, 18
castings, 21, 23, 25, 31, 68, 69, 221, 230, 231, 240, 247, 248, 249, 250, 251, 258, 259, 310, 313

517

CBP, 67, 69, 70, 71, 72, 99, 114, 204, 223, 224, 225, 227, 228, 230, 232, 252, 255, 256, 265, 277, 316, 333
CBP NTC, 114
CBW, 70, 333
CCIP, 333
Cell Site Simulator, 148, 295, 333, 376, 384
CGI, 20, 90, 101, 102, 105, 110
CGIC, 20, 87, 89, 90, 91, 93, 94, 96, 101, 111, 117, 143, 163, 164, 170, 180, 186, 187, 194, 230, 280, 282, 289, 333
Charles Taylor, 310
Chechnya, 328
CHIC, 18, 47, 333
China, 13, 71, 222, 276, 277, 278, 311, 315, 334
CI, xiii, xv, 19, 155, 156, 157, 158, 159, 183, 184, 185, 187, 189, 190, 191, 194, 196, 197, 202, 205, 216, 221, 226, 234, 240, 252, 280, 282, 287, 292, 326, 327, 328, 333
Civil Asset Forfeiture Reform, 333
Civil Forfeiture, 77
Clip, 18
CNC machines, 250, 252
Cocaine Cowboys, 12
CODIS, 333
Cold War Weapon, 18
Columbian Palace of Justice, 126
Commodity to Crime Gun, ix, xxiv, 4, 87
Community Oriented Policing, 18, 333
Comprehensive Crime Control Act of 1984, 8
Concealed Carry, 19, 73, 74
Confidential Informant
    CI, 19, 333
Consent to Forfeiture, 77
Constitutional Carry, 19, 74
Constructive Possession, 19
Consular Notification, xiii, 243, 244, 497, 498
Continuing Criminal Enterprise, 300
Controlled Buy, 19
cooperating defendant, 108, 158, 159, 196, 240, 290, 291
Cooperating Witness
    CW, 19, 333
Cooperation Agreement, xii, 158, 291
Cosmoline, 20, 29
Crime Control Act (CCA) of 1990, 9
Crime Gun Intelligence
    CGI, 2, 20, 333, 491, 492
Crime Gun Intelligence Center, 87
    CGIC, 20, 333, 491, 492
Criminal Forfeiture, 76
Criminal Street Gangs, 300
cryptocurrency, xxi, 83, 84, 85, 487
CSST, 333
CTR, 78, 80, 100, 333
Curios and Relics
    C&R, 20, 27, 65
Customs and Border Protection, 67, 494
Customs Bonded Warehouse, 70, 333
CZ pistol, 13
Czech Republic, 321, 331

D

Dark Web, 258, 260, 262
DEA Internet Connectivity Endeavor
    DICE, 20
Declaration of Independence, 1, 43, 488, 499

Deconfliction, xiv, 20, 111, 114, 143, 164, 165, 187, 191, 193, 194, 200, 216, 220, 225, 230, 245, 246, 254, 256, 262, 270, 274, 277, 283, 305, 326
Defense Articles, 21
Defense Distributed, 14
Defense Distributed v. United States Department of State, 14
Defense Trade Controls, xv, 68, 244, 312, 313, 335, 497
Demand Letter, ix, 93
Demilitarized, 21
Democratic Republic of the Congo, 328
Department of Commerce, 68, 244, 269, 313, 333
Department of State, xv, 26, 35, 68, 243, 244, 312, 313, 321, 322, 334, 488, 497, 498
DICE, 20, 21, 111, 143, 165, 284, 333
Dillinger, 6, 7, 11
DISASTER RESPONSE, xi, 133
District of Columbia v. Heller, 6, 489, 499
Domain name, 449
Drop-In Auto Sear, 21
Dubai, 329
Duetsche Bank, 327

E

E2C2, 114
Edmund Burke, 309
Egypt, 326, 327
El Paso Intelligence Center
    EPIC, 21, 334, 489
Electronic Communication, xv, 111, 112, 146, 191, 197, 294
EMERGENCY PREPAREDNESS, xi, 133
Engaged in the Business, 21
EPIC, 21, 114, 334
eTrace, 22, 23, 26, 91, 92, 93, 94, 96, 102, 105, 106, 113, 495
EU, 316, 320, 334
Export Counseling Division, 68
Exportation, 68
Extradition, 22, 49, 50, 246, 264, 267, 268, 269, 273, 488, 497
Extradition -, 22

F

Facial Recognition, xv, 149, 294, 490
FAET, 19, 22, 70, 78, 79, 221, 222, 225, 227, 228, 229, 256, 334, 489
FALN, 11
FARC, 12, 310
Federal Adoption Checklist, 106, 111
Federal Adoptions, 105
Federal Firearms Act (FFA) of 1938, 7
Financial Crime Enforcement Network
    FINCEN, 22, 488
FinCEN, 22, 143, 188, 195, 226, 231, 251, 252, 256, 262, 266, 334
firearm castings, 13
firearm flats, 13, 23
Firearm Parts Kit, 23
firearm parts kits, 23, 230, 247, 252, 254, 255, 256, 257
Firearm Recovery Notification Program, 94
Firearms and Explosives Imports Branch, 70, 95
Firearms and Explosives Licensing Center, 95
Firearms Dealer, 23

Firearms Diversion, 23
Firearms Owners Protection Act (FOPA) of 1986, 8
Firearms Trace, 23
Firearms Tracing System, 92, 93, 334
Firearms Trafficking Corridor, 24
Firearms Trafficking Gateway, 24
Firearms Trafficking Indicator, 24
First Look Reports, 96
Flash Suppressor, 24
flats, 23, 31, 221, 230, 231, 240, 247, 248, 249, 250, 251,
    258, 259
Fort Apache Marina, xiv, 288
FTS, 92, 93, 94, 96, 334
Full-Metal Freeway, 24
Fully-Automatic Firearm, 24
Funerary Masks, 326

G

gangs, 279
GangTECC, 115
GCA, 7, 8, 9, 10, 16, 20, 23, 32, 38, 44, 48, 57, 59, 65, 334,
    335
general intent, 44
GEOINT, 280
Ghost Gun, 25
Ghost guns, 13, 25, 248, 249
Glenn Fry, 2
Gun Control Act (GCA) of 1968, 7
gun show, 24, 25, 73, 74, 124, 125, 132, 136, 139, 149, 159,
    176, 187, 188, 194, 197, 204, 205, 230, 231, 241

H

hawala, 83
Hells Angels, 272, 306
HIDTA, 21, 143, 281, 284, 334
Hobbs Act, 297, 298, 303
HUMINT, x, 20, 113, 117, 126, 184, 187, 193, 194, 202,
    230, 246, 267, 280

I

IACP Resolution: Regional Crime Gun Processing
    Protocols, 102
iARMS, 26, 314, 334, 490
IBIN, xv, 315, 334, 490
IBIS, 29, 334
ICANN, 269, 492
ICE, 58, 115, 153, 244, 246, 265, 275, 334, 448
ICITAP, xv, 322, 323, 324, 325, 334, 496
IFRT, 314, 334, 490
ILEA, xv, 321, 334
Immunity, xii, 158, 291
Importation, 17, 40, 54, 69, 72, 494
Incomplete Receiver, 25
Inspection Warrant, 25
Instant Messaging, 450
Intelligence Led Policing, 25, 334, 492
intelligence production and rating standards, 105
International Criminal Police Organization
    INTERPOL, 26

Internet, 20, 22, 333, 334, 371, 374, 414, 417, 418, 420,
    430, 431, 440, 441, 442, 443, 447, 449, 450, 451, 452,
    453, 455, 456, 462, 489, 490, 492, 494, 495, 497, 498
INTERPOL, xv, 26, 269, 313, 314, 315, 318, 325, 334, 490
Interstate Nexus, 26, 46
interstate or foreign commerce, 7, 26, 46, 47, 49, 51, 53,
    54, 55
Inventory Security, xi, 133, 136
IP Address, 450
IRA, 12, 126
Irish Republican Army, 12, 126
Iron Pipeline, 24, 26
ISI, xvi, 329
ITAR, 68, 334
ITAR), 68

J

Jackson Browne, 245
Jail Intelligence, 112
Jamaat al Muslimeen, 12, 126, 127
Jay Treaty, 245
JLEO, 281
JTTF, 334
Judicial Forfeiture, 76

K

Kennedy, xix, 7, 63
Klein Conspiracy, 61, 162, 198, 201, 202, 227, 465
Know Your Customer, 130, 334
knowingly, 30, 44, 45, 56, 57, 58, 62, 64, 65, 68, 373

L

Latitude-longitude Cell Data, 295
Lautenberg Amendment of 1996, 10
Law Enforcement Officers Protection Act of 1986, 8
Lawful but Awful, 26
LAWFUL INTERSTATE TRANSPORTATION OF
    FIREARMS, 66
LEAD, 26, 34, 93, 96, 105, 113
LeadsOnline, 26, 99
Lend Lease Gun, 26
Leonid Efimovich Minin, 310
Lever Action, 27
Liberator, 14
Lie and Buy, 27, 62, 170
Lie and Try, 27
Lightning Link, 27
LORD OF WAR, 75, 117, 129
Lure, 27, 32, 50, 185, 233, 267
Lynyrd Skynyrd, 11

M

M19, 126
MACHINE GUN FUNCTIONALITY FIELD TEST, 38
Magazine, 27, 37, 487, 491
Makarov, 12, 13, 18, 65
Malum in Se, 27
Malum Prohibitum, 28

519

Mandalay Bay, 14
Marcus Tullius Cicero, 43
Mark Twain, 15
Market Area, 28
Martin Luther King, 7
McDonald v. City of Chicago, 6
Medellin Cartel, vii, 122
merchants of death, 24, 311
Merida Initiative, 311
Mexico, xv, 23, 93, 114, 127, 194, 229, 242, 248, 311, 313,
    315, 321, 490, 491
Miami Vice, 12
Military Arms Corp, 12
Miller v. Texas, 5, 491, 499
MLAT, 28, 262, 267, 268, 269, 277, 334
Money Flow Analysis, 78
Money Judgments, 79
Money Laundering, 28, 62, 78, 82, 85, 333, 335, 488,
    489, 491, 493, 494
Monzer Al Kassar, 310
Motion for Sentence Reduction, xii, 159, 291
Muammar Gaddafi, 328
Multi-Burst Trigger Activator, 28
Multiple Handgun Sale Reporting, 8
Multiple Sales Handgun Report, 11
Mutual Legal Assistance Treaty, 28, 334

N

NADDIS, 28, 334, 498
Narco-Terrorists, 12
Narcotics and Dangerous Drugs Information System
    NADDIS, 28
National Crime Information Center
    NCIC, 28, 35, 496
National Firearms Act
    NFA, 1, 5, 6, 11, 59, 334, 491, 499
National Instant Criminal Background Check
    System, 25, 29, 100, 496
National Liberation Army, 126
National Tracing Center, 20, 23, 29, 91, 335, 495, 496
NATO, xv, 317
NCIC, 28, 35, 94, 99, 102, 106, 111, 113, 334
NCIC recovered gun file, 190, 196, 219, 226, 231, 249
New Jersey Public Law, 103, 346
New-In-The-Box, 29
NFA, 6, 13, 23, 29, 38, 39, 51, 59, 333, 334, 335, 491, 499
NFA Gun Trust, 29
NFRTR, 29, 334
NGIC, 114, 115
NIBIN, ix, 29, 34, 89, 90, 91, 102, 106, 111, 184, 185,
    190, 193, 197, 210, 211, 215, 231, 233, 264, 280, 282,
    285, 289, 305, 315, 334, 496
NICS, 29, 30, 63, 64, 65, 67, 100, 101, 334, 335
Non-Mailable Firearms Act of 1927, 6
Northeastern University, xxi
Nothing but Time, 245
Notice of Unlicensed Firearms Dealing Violation, 30
NRA, 334, 492
NSSF, 131, 138, 334
NTC, 29, 33, 91, 92, 93, 94, 95, 96, 111, 114, 335, 496

O

OAS, 320, 335

Obliterated Serial Number Program, 97
Obstructing justice, 299, 304
OCDETF, 335
OCDETF), 281
on or about, 44, 45, 444, 448, 464
OOB, 30, 95, 335
OPDAT, xv, 322, 323, 324, 325, 335, 496
Open Carry, 30
Orange Notice, 269, 315
Organization for Security and Co-Operation in
    Europe, 320
Osama Bin Laden, 326
OSINT, x, 111, 113, 188, 195, 220, 225, 230, 251, 262,
    267, 284
Oswald, 7, 11
Outlaws, 80, 306
Out-of-Business Records Repository, 95
overall length, 32, 39, 40, 59

P

Pablo Escobar, 122
Pakistan, 326, 328, 329, 330, 490
Palm Beach County Gun Crime Protocols, xx, 102, 103,
    340
Partial Serial Number Trace Capabilities, 96
parts kits, 13, 23, 24
Pen, 149, 188, 197, 232, 245, 267, 295, 377, 386, 408, 416,
    425, 429, 436, 454, 455, 457
people, processes, and technology, 103
Personnel Security, xi, 133, 137
Phishing, 451
Pocket Litter, 30, 111, 283
Portland, xvii, xx, 169, 177, 179, 191, 192, 193, 200, 202,
    245, 246, 276, 277, 305, 306, 491
President Kabila, 328
presumption of innocence, 43, 44
prevention, deterrence, and detection, 223, 224
Principal Objective of Livelihood and Profit, 30
Proffer Agreement, xii, 158, 291
Prohibited Person, 31, 53
Project Safe Neighborhoods, xvii, 105, 335, 494
Proof beyond a reasonable doubt, 44
Pump Action, 31
Purple Notice, 269, 315

R

Racketeer Influenced and Corrupt Organizations Act, 298
Raytheon Boomerang, 280
Receiver, 31
Receiver Blank, 31, 248
receiver blanks, 22, 23, 31, 247
Red Side Guerilla Brims, 305, 306
Regional Crime Gun Processing Protocols, xx, 101, 102,
    344, 490
Relevant conduct, 49, 283
Reliability of Information, x, 105
Re-Usable Court Order, xi, xii, 147
Reverse, 31
Revolutionary United Front, 310
RICO, 78, 282, 284, 298, 299, 305, 307, 335, 497
Ring of Fire, 11, 12, 492
Rip, 32
RISS, 115

ROI, xii, 157, 164, 165, 166, 168, 169, 172, 177, 179, 180
Rule 404b, 283
run-away, 38, 39
Ruse, 32
Russia, viii, 71, 221, 328

S

SAFETY, 37, 403
SALW, 309, 310, 314, 317, 335
Sandanistas, 12
SAR, 78, 335
SARA, 19, 335, 487
Saturday Night Special, vii, 11
Scarface, 12
SCOTUS, 5, 6, 335
secondary source market, 26, 32, 99, 125, 203
secondary source markets, 13
Serial Number, 32, 54, 400, 414, 419
Sherlock Holmes, 87, 143
Shining Path Guerillas, 12
Short-Barreled Rifle, 32
Short-Barreled Shotgun, 32
Shot Spotter, 280
ShotSpotter, 15, 493
Shower Posse, 12, 126, 488
Silencer, 32
Single Action, 33
Smugglers Blues, 2
Source Area, 33
Southern Maine Community College, xviii
Soviet Union, 18, 222, 229
Specified Unlawful Act, 335
Specified Unlawful Activity, 78
Stabilizer Brace, 33
Standard of Reasonable Indication, x, 105
state of mind, 44, 57
Stick-Up Street Culture, 12
Sting, 33, 492
Stinger Missile, 327
Stolen Firearms Database, 33
Storefront, 33
straw, 23, 30, 33, 57, 61, 62, 63, 64, 101, 113, 118, 120, 123, 126, 130, 131, 133, 138, 149, 164, 168, 172, 173, 174, 175, 182, 183, 184, 185, 186, 196, 200, 201, 202, 203, 228, 230, 232, 233, 235, 238, 246, 247, 305, 310
Straw Purchase, 30, 33, 62, 73, 74
Straw Purchasing, 180, 185
Structuring, 78, 80
SUA, 28, 62, 335
Sub-Machinegun, 33
Substitute Assets, 79
Summary Forfeiture, 76
Suspect Person, 34
Switch, 34
Symbionese Liberation Army, 11

T

Tampering with a witness, 299, 304
Tax and Trade Bureau, 22, 335, 489

TECS, x, 34, 99, 100, 111, 165, 231, 232, 252, 256, 265, 266, 335
Thompson submachine gun, 6, 10
Thunder Boat Road, 288
T-III, 145, 151, 152, 163, 267, 271, 272, 273, 296, 297, 439, 497
Time to Sale, 34
Time-to-Crime, 34
Time-to-Recovery, 34
Title III, xii, xv, 151, 296
TOC, 34, 309, 324, 335
TOCs, 309, 310, 318, 324
Tokarev,, 12, 13, 18
TOR, 258, 335
Tower Dump, 148, 294, 398
trafficker to the trigger puller, 87
Trafficker to Trigger-Puller, 3
Transnational Organized Crime, 34, 335
    TOC, 34
Transnational Organized Criminals, 309
Treat the crime gun like an informant, 106
Trinidad and Tobago, 12, 126, 127, 488
Trip, 35
Triple Frontier, 127

U

U.S. Constitution, 1, 5, 49, 499
U.S. Munitions Import List
    USMIL, 21, 35, 58, 69
U.S. Munitions List
    USML, 21, 35, 68
U.S. SUPREME COURT, 5
    U.S. v. Cruikshank, 5
U.S. v. Miller, 5
Ukraine, xiii, 71, 222, 228, 229, 317, 321
UN, 318, 319, 321, 324, 333, 335, 493
United Nations, 311, 318, 319, 320, 321, 335, 493
unplanned enforcement action, 159, 185
unsuccessful trace data, 123, 223
USAID, xv, 322, 325, 494
USML, 35, 68, 335

V

VCAR, 335
Venezuela, 127
Vertical Prosecution, 35
VICAR, 284, 305, 307
Viktor Bout, 310, 492
Violent Crime Control and Law Enforcement Act of 1994, 10, 498
Violent Crime in Aid of, 335
Violent Crime in Aid of Racketeering, 297
Vivian Blake, 126
Volstead Act, 6
Voluntary Restraint Agreement, 13, 71
VRA, xiii, 71, 221, 222, 224, 225, 226, 228
VRA Treaty, xiii, 221, 222

W

Walk, 35
Wall-Off, xv, 36, 292
Warning Letter, 180, 185
Wassenaar Arrangement, 321, 335
Weather Underground, 11
Website Forfeiture, 269
West Palm Beach, xiii, xvii, xix, 121, 202, 205, 227, 228,
    270, 274, 275, 276, 326, 327, 329, 331, 488, 492
Westfield State, xviii, xxii
WHOIS, 261, 262

willfully, 30, 44, 45, 49, 58, 68, 69
Witness Device, 36
World Customs Organization, xv, 316, 319, 335, 494, 498
World Trade Center, 327, 331
worst of the worst, 110

Y

Youth Crime Gun Interdiction Initiative, xix, 102, 488
Yuri Orlov, 75, 117, 129, 162

Bibliography

97th Congress 2d Session, US Senate, Subcommittee on the Constitution of the Committee on the Judiciary (1982, February). *The Right to Keep and Bear Arms*. Washington, DC: US Government Printing Office.

Ackerman, R., "Intelligence Key to Counterdrug Efforts," *SIGNAL Magazine*, October 2010.

Arms Export Control Act of 1976, 94th Congress, enacted on June 30, 1976. https://www.gpo.gov /fdsys/pkg/STATUTE-90/pdf/STATUTE-90-Pg729.pdf

Aubin, B., *"Kanesatake Chief in Exile,"* The Canadian Encyclopedia. December 5, 2013. https://www.thecanadianencyclopedia.ca/en/m/article/kanesatake-chief-in-exile/. (accessed June 2, 2018).

Baum, E., *Police Work: What is the SARA Model?,* June 2015, https://www.newsmax.com/fastfeatures/police-work-sara-model/2015/06/15/id/648577/ (accessed on January 7, 2017).

Bitoin, *How Does Bitcoin Work?,* 2017, https://bitcoin.org/en/how-it-works. (accessed June 17, 2018).

Blockgeeks, *What is Blockchain Technology? A Step-by-Step Guide for Beginners,* 2016, https://blockgeeks.com/guides/what-is-blockchain-technology /. (accessed June 17, 2018).

Blockgeeks, *Paper Wallet Guide; How to Protect Your Cryptocurrency*. 2017, https://blockgeeks.com/guides/paper-wallet-guide/.(accessed June 17, 2018).

Bloomberg, Fortune.Com, *Gun Thefts in the U.S. Are Skyrocketing and Investigators Have No Idea Why*. January 19, 2018, http://fortune.com/2018/01/19/gun-thefts-atf-firearm-retailers/. (accessed April 29, 2018).

Brady Handgun Violence Prevention Act of 1994, 103rd Congress, enacted on February 28, 1994. https://www.govinfo.gov/content/pkg/HJOURNAL-1994/html/HJOURNAL-1994.html

Brantingham, P. L. & Brantingham, P. J. (1993). *Environmental, Routine, and Situation: Toward a pattern theory of crime*. *Advances in Criminological Theory 5*: 259-294, https://www.ncjrs.gov/App/Publications/abstract.aspx?ID=160010. (accessed June 20, 2018).

Bruser, D., and Poisson, J., *Star investigation: How one U.S. gun broker moved firearms across the border*. The Toronto Star, April 18, 2013, https://www.thestar.com/news/investigations /2013/04/18/star_investigation _how_one_us_gun_broker_moved_firearms_across_the_ border.html (accessed May 6, 2018)

Campbell, D., MacKinnon, I., The Guardian, *Lord of War Arms Trafficker Arrested,* March 6, 2008, https://www.theguardian.com/world/2008/mar/07/thailand.russia. (accessed May 28, 2018).

Canfield, C., *Outlaw killed by ATF was suspect in Maine Shooting*, June 16, 2010, Associated Press, http://archive.boston.com/news/local/maine/articles/2010/06/16/outlaw_killed_by_atf_was_suspect_in_maine_shooting/, (accessed on July).

Carpenter v. U.S. 585 U.S.___(2018).

CBC News, *Border agents want more resources to stop gun smuggling*, June 14, 2013, http://www.cbc.ca /news/canada/windsor/border-agents-want-more-resources-to-stop-gun-smuggling-1.1373581. (accessed May 6, 2018).

Chivers, C.J., *"Ill-Secured Soviet Arms Depots Tempting Rebels and Terrorists,"* The New York Times, July 18, 2005. https://www.nytimes.com/2005/07/16/world/europe/illsecured-soviet-arms-depots-tempting-rebels-and-terrorists.html (accessed March 10, 2018).

Christensen, D., *Broward-based Boss of Jamaica's Brutal Shower Posse Gang Dies*. Sun Sentinel, March 30, 2010, http://articles.sun-sentinel.com/2010-03-30/news/fl-jamaican-posse-leader-obit-20100330_1_shower-posse-vivian-blake-extradition. (accessed on May 28, 2018).

Code of Federal Regulations, Title 22: §§ 120-130.

Code of Federal Regulations, Title 27 § 178, T.D. ATF-16, 40 FR 19202, May 2, 1975

Code of Federal Regulations, Title 27: § 447.

Code of Federal Regulations, Title 27 § 478.11.

Cohen, D., *Guns Seized in Raid on Broward Home – Fugitive Planned to Sell Weapons to Boca Area Gangs*. February 27, 1992, The Palm Beach Post, West Palm Beach, FL.

Commission of Enquiry for Trinidad and Tobago, *Report of the Commission of Enquiry to enquire into the events surrounding the attempted coup which occurred in the Republic of Trinidad and Tobago on 27th July, 1990*. March 13, 2014, http://unctt.org/wp-content/uploads/2013/03/1990-COUP-Report.pdf. (accessed May 28, 2018).

Comprehensive Crime Control Act, 98th Congress, enacted on October 12, 1984. https://www.govtrack.us /congress/bills/98/hr5963

Crime Control Act of 1990, 101st Congress, enacted on November 29, 1990. https://www.gpo.gov /fdsys/pkg/STATUTE-104/pdf/STATUTE-104-Pg4789.pdf

Cryptome. *Treasury Enforcement Communications System*. http://cryptome.info/irs-ci/36426.html (accessed March 17, 2017).

Declaration of Independence (U.S., 1776).

Defense Unlimited v. U.S. Department of State 838 F.3d 451 (5th Cir. 2016)

Department of the U.S. Treasury, Financial Crimes Enforcement Network. https://www.fincen.gov (accessed on March 17, 2017).

Department of the U.S. Treasury, (2015). *National Money Laundering Risk Assessment*. Washington, DC.

Department of U.S. Treasury, Bureau of Alcohol, Tobacco, and Firearms. (2000, June). *Following the Gun; Enforcing Federal Firearms Laws Against Firearms Traffickers*. Washington, DC.

Department of U.S. Treasury, Bureau of Alcohol, Tobacco, and Firearms. (1997). *A Progress Report: Gun Dealer Licensing & Illegal Gun Trafficking*. Washington, DC.

Department of U.S. Treasury, Bureau of Alcohol, Tobacco, and Firearms. (1999, February). *Youth Crime Gun Interdiction Initiative Crime Gun Trace Analysis Reports; The Youth Firearms Market in 27 Communities*. Washington, DC.

Department of the U.S. Treasury. Bureau of Alcohol, Tobacco, and Firearms. *Protecting America; The Effectiveness of the Federal Armed Career Criminal Statute*. March 1992, https://www.ncjrs.gov /pdffiles1/Digitization/137208NCJRS.pdf. (accessed May 28, 2018).

Department of U.S. Treasury, Financial Crime Enforcement Network, *Money Laundering Prevention; A Money Services Business Guide*. https://www.fincen.gov/sites/default/files /shared/prevention_guide.pdf. (accessed May 6, 2018).

Department of the U.S. Treasury. Financial Crime Enforcement Network, *Money Laundering Prevention*. https://www.fincen.gov/sites/default/files/shared/preventionguide.pdf. (accessed January 6, 2018).

Department of U.S. Treasury. National Institute of Justice. (2007, January). *Investigations Involving the Internet and Computer Networks (NIJ210798).* Washington, DC.

Department of the U.S. Treasury. *National Money Laundering Risk Assessment.* 2015, https://www.treasury.gov /resource-center/terrorist-illicit-finance/Documents/National%20Money%20Laundering%20Risk %20Assessment%20–%2006-12-2015.pdf. (accessed June 20, 2018).

Department of the U.S. Treasury. Tax and Trade Bureau, *FAET Reference Guide Firearms and Ammunition Excise Tax.* https://www.ttb.gov/firearms/reference_guide.shtml (accessed March 26, 2017).

District of Columbia v. Heller, 554 U.S. 570 (2008).

Domestic Violence Offender Gun Ban of 1996, 104th Congress, enacted on September 30, 1996. https://www.gpo.gov/fdsys/pkg/PLAW-104publ208/html/PLAW-104publ208.htm

Eisner, L.B., Roeder, O., *America's Faulty Perception of Crime Rates* (New York: Brennan Center for Justice, New York University School of Law, 2015, https://www.brennancenter.org/blog/americas-faulty-perception-crime-rates.

El Paso Intelligence Center. https://www.epic.gov (accessed on March 17, 2017).

EUROPOL, *About Europol,* https://www.europol.europa.eu/about-europol. (accessed on April 21, 2018).

Ezell, E., *Handguns of the World: Military Revolvers and Self-Loaders 1870 to 1945.* May, 1992, New York: Barnes and Noble.

Federal Firearms Act of 1938, 75th Congress, enacted on June 30, 1938. http://legisworks.org /sal/52/stats/STATUTE-52-Pg1250.pdf

Federal Rules of Evidence, Article IV, Relevance and Its Limits, Rule 404. Character, Evidence; Crime or Other Acts, https://www.rulesofevidence.org/article-iv/rule-404/. (accessed June 2, 2018).

Feinstein, A. (2011, November). *The Shadow World: Inside the Global Arms Trade.* US: Farar, Straus, and Giroux.

Firearm Owners Protection Act of 1986, 99th Congress, enacted on May 19, 1986. https://www.gpo.gov /fdsys/pkg/STATUTE-100/pdf/STATUTE-100-Pg449.pdf.

Fjestad, S.P., (2016, April). *Blue Book Value of Guns 37th Edition.* Minneapolis, MN: Blue Book Publications, Inc.

Gagliardi, P., (2009) *Helping Police Link More Crimes, Guns, and Suspects Using Regional Processing Protocols,* Forensic Science Policy & Management: An International Journal, 1:1, 43-48, DOI: 10.1080 /19409040802629710.

Gagliardi, P., (2014). *13 Critical Tasks, An Inside Out Approach to Solving More Gun Crime.* Quebec, Canada: Forensic Technology Inc.

Garfield, L., *There are 50,000 More Gun Shops Than McDonalds in the US,* October 6, 2017, Business Insider. October 6, 2017, http://www.businessinsider.com/gun-dealers-stores-mcdonalds-las-vegas-shooting-2017-10. (accessed April 29, 2018).

Gato, P., Windrem, R., Telemundo and MSNBC, *Hezbollah Builds a Western Base.* May 9, 2007, http://www.nbcnews.com/id/17874369/ns/world_news-americas/t/hezbollah-builds-western-base/#.WwyoBC-ZPVo. (accessed May 28, 2018).

Gibson, W., Cummins, K., *The Gun State, Exports in Violence; Guns Sold in State Begin A Vicious Circle.* May 21, 1989, The Sun Sentinel, Fort Lauderdale, FL.

Governing.Com, *States Use Facial Recognition Technology to Address License Fraud*, July 15, 2015, http://www.govern-ing.com/topics/public-justice-safety/states-crack-down-on-drivers-license-fraud2.html. (accessed April 22, 2018).

Government Accountability Office, *ATF Did Not Always Comply with the Appropriations Act Restriction and Should Bet-ter Adhere to Its Policies*, GAO Report 16-552, Washington, DC, 2016, https://www.gao.gov/assets/680/678091.pdf. (accessed June 20, 2018).

Government Accountability Office, *Firearms Trafficking – Efforts to Combat Firearms Trafficking to Mexico Have Improved, but Some Collaboration Challenges Remain*, GAO-16-223. (Washington, D.C. 2016), accessed May 29, 2018, https://www.gao.gov/products/GAO-16-223.

Government Accountability Office, *Firearms Purchased from Federal Firearm Licensees Using Bogus Identification*, GAO-01-427NI. (Washington, D.C. 2016), accessed May 29, 2018, https://www.gao.gov/products/GAO-01-427NI.

Government Accountability Office, *Internet Firearms Sales, ATF Enforcement Efforts and Outcomes of GAO Covert Test-ing*, GAO-18-24. (Washington, D.C. 2017), accessed May 29, 2018, https://www.gao.gov/products/GAO-18-24.

Greenberg, R., Dateline NBC, *"The Godfather of Terror"*. 2008, https://www.theguardian.com /world/2008 /mar/07/thailand.russia. (accessed May 28, 2018).

Groban, M., Hicks, P., *Conspiracy and Firearms—Will Firearm Conspiracy Charges Add Value to Federal Prosecutions*, U.S. Department of Justice. U.S. Attorney's Bulletin, Vol. 61, No. 4, (July 2013).

Gun Control Act of 1968, 90th Congress, enacted on October 22, 1968. https://www.gpo.gov /fdsys/pkg/STATUTE-82/pdf/STATUTE-82-Pg1213-2.pdf

Harrison, J., *"Former Calais Hardware Store Manager Sentenced to Home Confinement,"* The Bangor Daily News, June 8, 2011, https://bangordailynews.com/2011/06/08/news/bangor/former-calais-hardware-store-manager-to-be-sentenced-on-gun-charge/. (accessed June 2, 2018).

International Association of Chiefs of Police, http://www.theiacp.org (accessed on March 30, 2017)

International Association of Chiefs of Police. (2012, October, 3). *A Resolution of the Firearms Committee at the 119th Annual Conference: Regional Crime Gun Processing Protocols*. Alexandria, VA: IACP.

INTERPOL, *INTERPOL Ballistics Identification Network (IBIN)*, https://www.interpol.int/Crime-areas/Firearms-trafficking/INTERPOL-Ballistic-Information-Network-IBIN. (accessed on June 19, 2018).

INTERPOL, *INTERPOL Firearms Reference Table (IFRT)*, https://www.interpol.int/Crime-areas/Firearmstraffick-ing/INTERPOL-Firearms-Reference-Table-IFRT. (accessed on June 19, 2018).

INTERPOL, *iARMS – Illicit Arms Records and Tracing Management System Brochure*, January2017), Lyon, France. https://www.interpol.int/...brochures/Illicit-arms-records-and-tracing-management-system. (accessed on June 19, 2018).

INTERPOL, *International Alert System*, https://www.interpol.int/Crime-areas/Firearms-trafficking/Firearms-traf-ficking. (accessed on June 19, 2018).

Hersh, S., *Why is Washington going easy on Pakistan's nuclear black marketers?*, March 8, 2004, The New Yorker, New York, New York; The New Yorker.

Isikoff, M., *U.S Agents Seize Drug-Related Arms Cache.* June 20, 1989, The Washington Post, https://www.washing-tonpost.com/archive/politics/1989/06/10/us-agents-seize-drug-related-arms-cache/2f46a0d5-fe63-463b-ad89-cbf0ca80e630/?utm_term=.baeac236e3f6. (accessed May 28, 2018).

Jeffreys, D., *How Bin Laden's Followers Tried to Buy Nuclear Material.* Daily Mail, September 17, 2001, London, UK: Daily Mail.

Kalesan, B., Villarreal, M.D., Keyes, K.M., et al. *Gun Ownership and Social Gun Culture.* The BMJ, Injury Prevention. June 2015.

King, D., *The Governments Creepy Obsession with Your Face*, June 18, 2018, The Week, http://theweek.com /articles/779196/governments-creepy-obsession-face. (accessed June 18, 2018).

Kovach, G., *Tomb Raiders, Beware! The curse of the mummies has a new way to strike.* Newsweek, September 2, 2002, New York, New York. https://www.highbeam.com/doc/1G1-90891915.html. (accessed on June 2, 2018).

LaFlamme, M., *"Maine guns for Mass. drugs: Bay State criminals find Pine Tree State a great place to buy guns, sell drugs,"* Sun Journal, March 14, 2010, http://www.sunjournal.com/maine-guns-mass-drugs-bay-state-criminals-find-pine-tree-state-great-place-buy-guns-sell-drugs/. (accessed June 20, 2018).

Law Enforcement Officers Protection Act of 1985, 99th Congress, enacted on August 28, 1986. https://www.gpo.gov/fdsys/granule/STATUTE-100/STATUTE-100-Pg920/content-detail.html

Madinger, J. (2006). *Money Laundering, A Guide for Criminal Investigators.* Boca Raton, FL: CRC Press, Taylor & Francis Group.

Marbin, C., *Agent: Military Brass Aided Drug Cartel,* The Palm Beach Post, June 13, 1989, https://www.newspapers.com/newspage/130667255/. (accessed June 8, 2018).

Max, A., The Associated Press, *Arms Dealer Bust Embargoes With Impunity.* June 11, 2006, http://www.washingtonpost.com /wp-dyn/content/article/2006/06/11/AR2006061100416.html. (accessed May 28, 2018).

Maxwel, T., *Acton Resident Admits to Selling Firearms to Felons.* The Portland Press Herald. July 28, 2010.

Maxwell, T., *"Maine gun trafficker gets three-month term,"* The Portland Press Herald. November 23, 2010.

McDonald v. Chicago, 561 U.S. 742 (2010).

McGreal, C., *The US Gun Smugglers Recruited by One of Mexico's Most Brutal Cartels.* The Guardian. December 8, 2011, https://www.theguardian.com/world/2011/dec/08/us-gun-smugglers-mexico-cartel. (accessed May 6, 2018).

Miller v. Texas, 153 U.S. 535 (1894).

Montero, D., *Guns "R" Us*, November 14, 2002, The Nation, https://www.thenation.com/article /guns-r-us/. (accessed May 28, 2018).

Naim, M., *Illicit: How Smugglers, Traffickers, and Copycats are Hijacking the Global Economy.* October 2006, New York: Anchor Books, a Division of Random House.

Nathans Spiro, L., *Wall St.'s Soldier of Fortune.* November 2001, New York: Talk Magazine.

National Firearms Act (NFA), 73rd Congress, enacted on June 26, 1934. http://legisworks.org /congress/73/publaw-474.pdf

National Resource and Technical Assistance Center for Improving Law Enforcement Investigations and The Police Foundation under U.S. Bureau of Justice Assistance Grant N. 2016-MU-BX-K005. (2017, August). *Denver Crime Gun Intelligence Center Process Guide.* Washington, DC.

National Rifle Association, Institute for Legislative Action. *Firearms Safety in America 2013.* January 17, 2013.

National Rifle Association. NRA Explore, *Eddie Eagle*, https://eddieeagle.nra.org (accessed June 11, 2018).

National Sheriffs Association, Justice Solutions, National Organization of Murdered Children, Inc., (2011, August). *Serving Survivors of Homicide Victims During Cold Case Investigations: A guide for Developing a Law Enforcement Protocol.* https://www.sheriffs.org/sites/default/files /guidefordevelopingalawenforcementprotocolaugust172011.pdf. (accessed on May 6, 2018).

Newhard, *J.M, Bootleggers and Gun Control*, The CATO JOURNAL, Fall 2015. https://object.cato.org/ sites/cato.org/files/serials/files/regulation/2015/9/regulation-v38n3-3.pdf

Non-Mailable Firearms Act, 90th Congress, enacted on October 22, 1968.

North Atlantic Treaty Organization, The Fund for Peace, *Together Reducing Unsafe Surplus Tools of War (TRUST)*, 2006, Brussels, Belgium.

Norman, B., New Times of Broward and Palm Beach, *Irish Sting.* July 19, 2001, http://www.browardpalmbeach.com/news/irish-sting-6323923. (accessed May 28, 2018).

Officer.Com. *Responding with Fight or Flight*, October 1, 2008, https://www.officer.com/home/article /10248579/responding-with-fight-or-flight. (accessed May 19, 2018).

Pacenti, J., *4 Arrested on Arms, Laundering, Charges – Attorney Calls Case Something Out of "James Bond" Novel".* June 15, 2001, The Palm Beach Post, West Palm Beach, FL.

Pacenti, J., *Taliban Showed Interest in Boca Snitch.* September 26, 2001, The Palm Beach Post, West Palm Beach, FL.

Paoli, G.P., Aldrige, J. Ryan, Nathan, Warnes, R. (2017.) *Behind the Curtain; The illicit trade of firearms, explosives, and ammunition on the dark web.* Rand Corp., https://www.rand.org/pubs /research_reports/RR2019.html. (accessed March 23, 2018).

Piscitello, D., *Guidance for Preparing Domain Name Orders, Seizures & Takedowns,* Internet Corporation for Assigned Numbers and Names (ICANN), https://www.icann.org/en/system /files/files/guidance-domain-seizures-07mar12-en.pdf. (accessed May 21, 2018).

PBS Frontline. *Hot Guns; Ring of Fire Families.* June 1997, WGBH-TV, Boston, MA.

Police Executive Research Forum, *The Crime Gun Intelligence Center Model: Case Studies of the Denver, Milwaukee, and Chicago Approaches to Investigating Gun Crime*, May 2017, http://www.policeforum.org/assets /crimegunintelligencecenter.pdf. (accessed June 20, 2018).

Presser v. Illinois, 116 U.S. 252 (1886).

PTI, *Chinese smugglers use internet for trafficking arms*, The Times of India. April 5, 2012, https://www.gadgetsnow.com /tech-news/Chinese-smugglers-use-internet-for-trafficking-arms/articleshow /12546664.cms. (accessed May 6, 2018).

Quigley, K., *"Illegal Gun Sales Land Two Men in Federal Prison; Weapon Traced to Mobster Sammy the Bull Gravano,"* The Palm Beach Post, August 2001.

Quraishi, A., *Musharaf pardons nuclear chief.* February 5, 2005, CNN, Atlanta, GA.

Ratcliffe, J., *Pocket Guide to Intelligence Led Policing.* June 2008, www.jratcliffe.net (accessed on March 17, 2017).

Reinhart, B., *Implementing a Firearms Trafficking Strategy—Prosecuting Corrupt Federal Firearms Licensees*, U. S. Department of Justice, U.S. Attorney's Bulletin, Vol. 50, No. 1, (January 2002).

Rozen, L. *Meet Viktor Bout; The Real-Life Lord of War.* September 13, 2007, www.motherjones.com. (accessed on March 30, 2017)

Scinto, R., *"New Haven Police Release 2016 Crime Statistics."* Patch.com, January 12, 2017, https://patch.com/connecticut/newhaven/new-haven-police-release-2016-crime-stats. (accessed June 2, 2018).

Shimer, D., *"Gang members indicted for murder."* Yale News, October 2, 2015, https://yaledailynews.com/blog/2015/10/02/gang-members-indicted-for-murder/. (accessed June 2, 2018).

ShotSpotter™, *2017 National Gun Fire Index*, http://www.shotspotter.com/2017NGI. (accessed May 28, 2018).

ShotSpotter™, *2017 National Gun Fire Index*, http://www.shotspotter.com/system/content-uploads/2013NGI-online.pdf. (accessed May 28, 2018).

Small Arms Survey and Swiss Agency for Development and Cooperation, *Global Violent Deaths 2017 – Time To Decide*, (2017, December), http://www.smallarmssurvey.org/fileadmin/docs/U-Reports/SAS-Report-GVD2017.pdf. (accessed on April 21, 2018).

Small Arms Survey and Swiss Agency for Development and Cooperation. *Illicit Trafficking*, December 2017, http://www.smallarmssurvey.org/weapons-and-markets/transfers/illicit-trafficking.html. (accessed on May 6, 2018).

Stokes, John, *3D printed guns are now legal…What's next?*, July 14, 2018, Techcrunch.com, https://techcrunch.com/2018/07/14/its-now-legal-to-distribute-schematics-for-3d-printed-guns-in-the-u-s-what-happens-next/, accessed on July 21, 2018).

Sweig, J., *A Strategy to Reduce Gun Trafficking and Violence in the Americas*. Council on Foreign Relations. July 29, 2013, https://www.cfr.org/report/strategy-reduce-gun-trafficking-and-violence-americas. (accessed May 6, 2018).

The Economist, *Trade and Money Laundering, Uncontained*, May 3, 2014, https://www.economist.com/international/2014/05/03/uncontained. New York, (accessed June 16, 2018).

United Nations, Office on Drugs and Crime. (October 2012). *Digest of Organized Crime*. New York: United Nations.

United Nations, Office on Drugs and Crime. (2015). *Study on Firearms*. New York; United Nations.

United Nations Security Council, *Security Council, Concerned at Threat Posed by Illicit Cross-Border Trafficking, Asks for Assessment of UN Efforts in Helping States Counter Challenges*, April 25, 2012, https://www.un.org/press/en/2012/sc10624.doc.htm. (accessed May 6, 2018).

United States Constitution, (U.S., 1776).

United States. v. Bruscantini, 761 F.2d 640, 642 (11th Cir. 1985).

United States v. Cruikshank, 92 U.S. 542 (1875).

United States v. Eight Rhodesian Statues, 449 F. Supp. 193, 195 (C.D. Cal. 1978).

United States v. Hedges, 912 F.2d 1397, 1405 (11th Cir. 1990).

United States v. Louis Haneef, et al., U.S. District Court, Southern District of Florida, Criminal Docket No. 90-6161-CR-PAINE.

United States v. Miller, 307 U.S. 174 (1939).

United States, Plaintiff-appellee, v. Walter David Tallmadge, Defendant-appellant, 829 F.2d 767 (9th Cir. 1987).

U.S. Agency for International Development. *EASTERN AND SOUTHERN CARIBBEAN CITIZEN SECURITY*, https://www.usaid.gov/barbados/citizen-security. (accessed on May 12, 2018).

U.S. Agency for International Development. *MISSION, VISION, AND VALUES*, https://www.usaid.gov/who-we-are/mission-vision-values. (accessed on May 12, 2018).

U.S. Agency for International Development. *Success Story – From Firearms to Open Arms*, https://www.usaid.gov/sites /default/files/success/files/ss_gt_arms.pdf. (accessed on May 12, 2018).

U.S. Agency for International Development. *USAID/GUATEMALA COUNTRY FACT SHEET*, November 2017, https://www.usaid.gov/sites/default/files/documents/1862/Guatemala-External-Fact-Sheet-November-2017.pdf. (accessed on May 12, 2018).

U.S. Agency for International Development. *Virginia Security Contractor to Pay $44,000 Over Allegations of Illegally Exporting Firearms Accessories*, February 24, 2016, https://oig.usaid.gov/node/1965. (accessed on May 12, 2018).

U.S. Attorney's Office, District of Connecticut, *"Joint Investigation Dismantles New Haven Street Gang; Members Charges with 6 Murders,"* October 1, 2015, https://www.justice.gov/usao-ct/pr/joint-investigation-dismantles-violent-new-haven-street-gang-members-charged-6-murders. (accessed June 2, 2018).

U.S. Department of Homeland Security, U.S. Customs and Border Protection, *World Customs Organization Overview*, https://www.cbp.gov/border-security/international-initiatives/wco. (accessed on April 21, 2018).

U.S. Department of Justice. (2001). *Project Safe Neighborhoods: America's Network Against Gun Violence Implementation Guide for PSN Partners*. Washington, DC.

U.S. Department of Justice. Bureau of Justice Statistics, *Community Policing*, https://www.bjs.gov/index.cfm?ty=tp&tid=81 (accessed March 27, 2017).

U.S Department of Justice, Bureau of Justice Assistance, Office of Justice Programs and Global Justice Information Sharing Initiative; U.S. Department of Homeland Security, (2011, October). *Law Enforcement Guidelines For First Amendment-Protected Events*, Washington, DC.

U.S. Department of Justice. Criminal Division, Asset Forfeiture and Money Laundering Section, *Asset Forfeiture Process Version 1.0*, 1, Washington, DC, 2015.

U.S Department of Justice, Global Privacy and Information Quality Working Group, (2012, April). *Privacy, Civil Rights, and Civil Liberties Policy Development Guide for State, Local, and Tribal Justice Entities*. Retrieved May 5, 2018 from https://it.ojp.gov/GIST/31/Privacy--Civil-Rights--and-Civil-Liberties-Policy-Development-Guide-for-State--Local--and-Tribal-Justice-Entities--Privacy-Guide

U.S. Department of Justice. Bureau of Alcohol, Tobacco, Firearms and Explosives. *Annual Firearms Manufacturing and Export Update 2015*. Washington, Rev. Ed 2015.

U.S. Department of Justice. Bureau of Alcohol, Tobacco, Firearms and Explosives. *ATF Guidebook; Importation & Verification of Firearms, Ammunition, and Implements of War*, 2015, https://www.atf.gov/firearms/docs/guide/atf-guidebook-importation-verification-firearms-ammunition-and-implements-war/download. (accessed June 20, 2018).

U.S. Department of Justice. Bureau of Alcohol, Tobacco, Firearms and Explosives. (2013, January). *Best Practices: Transfers of Firearms by Private Sellers (ATF Publication 5300.21)*. Washington, DC.

U.S. Department of Justice. Bureau of Alcohol, Tobacco, Firearms and Explosives. (Rev. Ed. 2004, September). *Crime Scene and Evidence Collection Handbook (ATF Publication 7110.2)*. Washington, DC.

U.S. Department of Justice. Bureau of Alcohol, Tobacco, Firearms and Explosives. (2016, January). *Do I Need a License to Buy and Sell Firearms? (ATF Publication 5310.2)*. Washington, DC.

U.S. Department of Justice. Bureau of Alcohol, Tobacco, Firearms and Explosives. (Rev. Ed 2009, December). *Disaster Preparedness for Federal Firearms Licensees – (ATF Publication 3317.7)*. Washington, DC.

U.S. Department of Justice. Bureau of Alcohol, Tobacco, Firearms and Explosives. *E-Trace; Internet Based Firearms Tracing and Analysis, ATF Publication 3312.9*. Washington, Rev. Ed. 2009.

U.S. Department of Justice. Bureau of Alcohol, Tobacco, Firearms and Explosives. *FATD,* https://www.atf.gov /firearms/firearms-and-ammunition-technology. (accessed March 28, 2017).

U.S. Department of Justice. Bureau of Alcohol, Tobacco, Firearms and Explosives. *Facilitating Private Sales: A Federal Firearms Licensee Guide.* Retrieved March 26, 2017 from https://www.atf.gov/file/110076/download.

U.S. Department of Justice. Bureau of Alcohol, Tobacco, Firearms and Explosives. (2010, August). *Federal Firearms Licensee Quick Reference and Best Practices Guide (ATF Publication 5300.15, Rev. Ed.).* Washington, DC.

U.S. Department of Justice. Bureau of Alcohol, Tobacco, Firearms and Explosives. (2014). *Federal Firearms Regulation Reference Guide (ATF Publication 5300.4, Rev. Ed).* Washington, DC.

U.S. Department of Justice. Bureau of Alcohol, Tobacco, Firearms and Explosives. *FIREARMS COMMERCE; US Annual Statistical Update 2017.* Washington, Rev. Ed 2017.

U.S. Department of Justice. Bureau of Alcohol, Tobacco, Firearms and Explosives. *Firearms Curios or Relics List, ATF Publication 5300.11,* Washington, DC, Rev. Ed. December 2007.

U.S. Department of Justice. Bureau of Alcohol, Tobacco, Firearms and Explosives. (2008, May). *Firearms Identification & Tracing Procedures (ATF Publication 6320.1, Rev. Ed.).* Washington, DC.

U.S. Department of Justice. Bureau of Alcohol, Tobacco, Firearms and Explosives. (2012, March). *Firearms Tracing Guide: Tracing Firearms to Reduce Violent Crime (ATF Publication 3312.13).* Washington, DC.

U.S Department of Justice. Bureau of Alcohol, Tobacco, Firearms and Explosives. *Firearms Trafficking Investigation Guide, ATF Publication 3317.1.* Washington, DC, 1997, Rev. Ed 2009.

U.S. Department of Justice. Bureau of Alcohol, Tobacco, Firearms and Explosives. *Guide to Firearm Types, ATF M 3317.1.* Washington, DC, April 2006.

U.S. Department of Justice. Bureau of Alcohol, Tobacco, Firearms and Explosives. *How to Conduct a Firearms Inventory,* Washington, DC, July 2016.

U.S. Department of Justice. Bureau of Alcohol, Tobacco, Firearms and Explosives. *Industry Operations Investigators: What do IOIs do?,* https://www.atf.gov/resource-center/industry-operations-investigators. (accessed April 29, 2018).

U.S. Department of Justice. Bureau of Alcohol, Tobacco, Firearms and Explosives. *International Affairs Division.* https://www.atf.gov/resource-center/fact-sheet/fact-sheet-international-affairs-division (accessed on March 28, 2017).

U.S. Department of Justice. Bureau of Alcohol, Tobacco, Firearms and Explosives. *Loss Prevention for Firearms Retailers, ATF Publication 5380.1.* Washington, DC, January 2016.

U.S. Department of Justice. Bureau of Alcohol, Tobacco, Firearms and Explosives. "OPEN LETTER ON THE REDESIGN OF "STABILIZING BRACES",* https://www.atf.gov /file/11816/download. (accessed March 15, 2017).

U.S. Department of Justice. Bureau of Alcohol, Tobacco, Firearms and Explosives. *National Tracing Center Division, ATF Publication 3312.9,* Washington, DC, December 2009.

U.S. Department of Justice. Bureau of Alcohol, Tobacco, Firearms and Explosives. *National Tracing Center Division - Information for Law Enforcement Agencies, ATF Publication 3312.11, Rev. Ed.,* Washington, DC, August 2005.

U.S. Department of Justice. Bureau of Alcohol, Tobacco, Firearms and Explosives. *National Tracing Center Division – eTrace Internet-Based Firearms Tracing and Analysis, ATF Publication 3312.9, Rev Ed.*, Washington, DC, December 2009.

U.S. Department of Justice. Bureau of Alcohol, Tobacco, Firearms and Explosives. *National Integrated Ballistics Identification Network.* https://www.atf.gov/firearms/national-integrated-ballistic-information-network-nibin (accessed March 17, 2017).

U.S. Department of Justice. Bureau of Alcohol, Tobacco, Firearms and Explosives. *NIBIN Reference Guide; Identify and Target Shooters and their Sources of Crime Guns.* Washington, DC, 2018.

U.S. Department of Justice. Bureau of Alcohol, Tobacco, Firearms and Explosives. *Nonimmigrant Aliens Purchasing Firearms and Ammunition in the United States, ATF Publication 5300.18, Rev Ed.,* Washington, DC, July 2002.

U.S. Department of Justice. Bureau of Alcohol, Tobacco, Firearms and Explosives. *National Tracing Center, Out of Business Records Center.* https://www.atf.gov/firearms/discontinue-being-federal-firearms-licensee-ffl (accessed March 17, 2017).

U.S. Department of Justice. Bureau of Alcohol, Tobacco, Firearms and Explosives. *NTC Fact Sheet,* https://www.atf.gov /resource-center/fact-sheet/fact-sheet-national-tracing-center. (accessed April 28, 2018).

U.S. Department of Justice. Bureau of Alcohol, Tobacco, Firearms and Explosives. *Personal Firearms Record, ATF Publication 3312.8, Rev Ed.,* Washington, DC, August 2013.

U.S. Department of Justice. Bureau of Alcohol, Tobacco, Firearms and Explosives. *Safety and Security Information for Federal Firearms Licensees, ATF Publication 3317.2, Rev Ed.,* Washington, DC, February 2010.

U.S. Department of Justice. Bureau of Alcohol, Tobacco, Firearms and Explosives. *Special Agents Guide to ATF Laboratory Services, ATF Publication 7110.1.* Washington, DC, Rev. Ed. June 2012.

U.S. Department of Justice. Bureau of Alcohol, Tobacco, Firearms and Explosives. *State Laws and Published Ordinances, ATF Publication 5300.5,* Washington, DC, Rev. Ed 2004

U.S. Department of Justice. Bureau of Justice Assistance – Police Executive Research Forum. *Combatting Interstate Firearms Trafficking – "Guns First",* Washington, DC, October 1996.

U.S. Department of Justice. Bureau of Prisons, *Privacy Impact for the SENTRY Inmate Management System,* July 2, 2012. https://www.bop.gov/foia/sentry.pdf. (accessed April 28, 2018).

U.S. Department of Justice. Federal Bureau of Investigation, *National Crime Information Center.* https://www.fbi.gov/services/cjis/ncic (accessed March 17, 2017).

U.S. Department of Justice. Federal Bureau of Investigation, *National Instant Criminal Background Check System.* https://www.fbi.gov/services/cjis/nics (accessed March 17, 2017).

U.S. Department of Justice. Federal Bureau of Investigation, *National Instant Criminal Background Check System, Point of Contact States.* https://www.fbi.gov/services/cjis/nics/about-nics (accessed March 17, 2017).

U.S. Department of Justice. *Guidelines Regarding the Use of Confidential Informants,* 2001, https://www.justice.gov /archives/ag/attorney-general-renos-confidential-informant-guidelines-january-8-2001. (accessed May 28, 2018).

U.S. Department of Justice. *Gun Violence Reduction: National Integrated Firearms Violence Reduction Strategy.* Washington, D.C., 2001.

U.S. Department of Justice. ICITAP/OPDAT Program Support, Request for Proposal, Solicitation DJJI-17-RFP-1037 2017, https://govtribe.com/project/icitapopdat-worldwide-support-services/activity. (accessed on May 12, 2018).

U.S Department of Justice, Office of Justice Programs, Bureau of Justice Assistance. (1997, November). *The BJA Firearms Trafficking Program; Demonstrating Effective Strategies to Control Violent NCJ 166818.* Washington, DC.

U.S Department of Justice, Office of Justice Programs, National Institute of Justice. (2007, January). *Investigations Involving the Internet and Computer Networks NCT 210798.* Washington, DC.

U.S Department of Justice, Office of Juvenile Justice and Delinquency Prevention. (1996). *Combatting Violence and Delinquency; The National Juvenile Justice Action Plan.* Washington, DC.

U.S Department of Justice, Office of Juvenile Justice and Delinquency Prevention, *The Action Plan* https://www.ojjdp.gov/action/sec3.htm, (accessed on April 29, 2018).

U.S Department of Justice. Office of Juvenile Justice and Delinquency Programs and Institute for Intergovernmental Research, *Gang Prosecution Manual,* July 2009, https://www.nationalgangcenter.gov /Content/Documents/Gang-Prosecution-Manual.pdf. (accessed June 2, 2018).

U.S. Department of Justice. Office of Inspector General, *Inspections of Firearms Dealers by the Bureau of Alcohol, Tobacco, Firearms and Explosives. Report Number I-2004-005,* July 2004. https://oig.justice.gov/ reports/ATF/e0405/ background.htm. (accessed April 29, 2018).

U.S. Department of Justice. Undercover and Sensitive Operations Unit, *Attorney General's Guidelines on FBI Undercover Operations,* https://www.justice.gov/archives/ag/undercover-and-sensitive-operations-unit-attorney-generals-guidelines-fbi-undercover-operations. (accessed May 28, 2018).

U.S. Department of Justice. Organized Crime and Racketeering Section, (2016, May). *Criminal RICO – A Manual for Federal Prosecutors, Sixth Revised Edition.* Washington, DC.

U.S. Department of Justice. Organized Crime and Racketeering Section, (December 2006). *Violent Crimes in Aid of Racketeering – A Manual for Federal Prosecutors.* Washington, DC.

U.S. Department of Justice. *U.S. Attorney's Office Manual, Checklist for T-III Application Requirements,* https://www.justice.gov/usam/criminal-resource-manual-92-title-iii-procedures-attachment-c. (accessed May 12, 2018).

U.S. Department of Justice. *U.S. Attorney's Office Manual, Extradition,* https://www.justice.gov /usam/usam-9-15000-international-extradition-and-related-matters#9-15.100. (accessed April 8, 2017).

U.S. Department of Justice. *U.S Attorneys Manual – RICO,* https://www.justice.gov/usam/usam-9-110000-organized-crime-and-racketeering. (accessed June 20, 2018).

U.S. Department of Justice. *U.S. Attorneys Manual - Sample Enhanced Penalty Information for 18 U.S.C. § 521,* https://www.justice.gov/usam/criminal-resource-manual-1458-sample-enhanced-penalty-information-18-usc-521. (accessed May 12, 2018).

U.S. Department of State, Bureau of International Narcotics and Law Enforcement Affairs, https://www.state.gov/j/inl/c/crime/c44636.htm. (accessed on April 19, 2018).

U.S. Department of State. Bureau of International Narcotics and Law Enforcement Affairs, Criminal Justice Programs Division, *International Law Enforcement Academies,* https://www.state.gov/j/inl/c/crime/ilea/index.htm (accessed on April 19, 2018).

U.S. Department of State. *Consular Notification and Access Pocket Card,* https://travel.state.gov/content/dam/travel/CNAtrainingresources/CNA%20Pocket% 20Card_BW.pdf. (accessed May 20, 2018).

U.S. Department of State. Office of Defense Trade Controls Policy, *Blue Lantern End-Use Monitoring Program,* https://www.bis.doc.gov/index.php/documents/pdfs/1588-end-user-verification-blue-lantern/file. (accessed on April 21, 2018).

U.S. Department of State. Office of the Legal Adviser and Bureau of Consular Affairs, *Consular Notification and Access; Instructions for Federal, State, and Local Law Enforcement and Other Officials Regarding Foreign Nationals in the United States and the Rights of Consular Officials to Assist Them (Fourth Edition)*, August 2016, https://travel.state.gov/content /dam/travel/CNAtrainingresources/CNA_Manual_4th_ Edition_September_2017.pdf. (accessed June 2, 2018).

U.S. Library of Congress, Congressional Research Service, *Internet Firearm and Ammunition Sales.* By Chu, V.S., R42687, (August, 28 2012).

U.S. Library of Congress, Congressional Research Service, *Congressional Authority to Regulate Firearms: A Legal Overview.* By Chu, V.S., R43033, (April 5, 2013).

Violent Crime Control and Law Enforcement Act of 1994, 103rd Congress, enacted on September 13, 1994. https://www.gpo.gov/fdsys/pkg/BILLS-103hr3355enr/pdf/BILLS-103hr3355enr.pdf

Walker, M., *5 Held in Gun-Smuggling Ring.* April, 29, 2991, The Sun Sentinel, Fort Lauderdale, FL.

Wayne, L., *From Riches to Relative Rags.* October 27, 2001, The New York Times. https://www.nytimes.com /2001/10/27/business/from-riches-to-relative-rags.html. (accessed June 2, 2018).

Whittell, G., *A five-star disaster for the world.* October 26, 2001, The UK Times, London, England.

Wikipedia contributors, "Agent provocateur," *Wikipedia, The Free Encyclopedia,* https://en.wikipedia.org/w/index.php?title=Agent_provocateur&oldid=837433909 (accessed March 17, 2017.)

Wikipedia contributors, "Gunfire locator," *Wikipedia, The Free Encyclopedia,* https://en.wikipedia.org/w/index.php?title=Gunfire_locator&oldid=846270583 (accessed March 27, 2017).

Wikipedia contributors, "NADDIS," *Wikipedia, The Free Encyclopedia,* https://en.wikipedia.org/w/index.php?title=NADDIS&oldid=799823327 (accessed March 17, 2017).

Wilson, C., *Final guilty plea in $32 million arms plot.* November 16, 2001, Associated Press, New York, New York.

World Customs Organization, CEN Suite Brochure, http://www.wcoomd.org/-/media/wco /public/global/ pdf/topics/enforcement-and-compliance/tools-and-instruments/cen/cen-brochure.pdf?db=web. (accessed on April 21, 2018).

Zag, Z., *"500 Cops Raid Mohawk Territories,"* Warrior Publications, June 15, 2012, https://warriorpublications.wordpress.com/2011/06/15/500-cops-raid-mohawk-territories/. (accessed June 2, 2018).

End Notes

[i] Eisner, L.B., Roeder, O., *America's Faulty Perception of Crime Rates* (New York: Brennan Center for Justice, New York University School of Law, 2015) https://www.brennancenter.org/blog/americas-faulty perception-crime-rates.

[ii] U.S Department of Justice. Bureau of Alcohol, Tobacco, Firearms and Explosives. *Firearms Trafficking Investigation Guide, ATF Publication 3317.1*. Washington, 1997, Rev. Ed 2009.

[iii] Declaration of Independence (U.S. 1776) para. 2.

[iv] U.S. Constitution, amend. 2.

[v] U.S. Constitution, amend. 4.

[vi] National Firearms Act, 73rd Congress, enacted on June 26, 1934

[vii] Firearm Owners Protection Act, 99th Congress, enacted on May 19, 1986

[viii] National Rifle Association, Institute for Legislative Action. *Firearms Safety in America*. January 17, 2013.

[ix] U.S. Department of Justice. Bureau of Alcohol, Tobacco, Firearms and Explosives. *Annual Firearms Manufacturing and Export Update 2015*. Washington, Rev. Ed 2015.

[x] Kalesan, B., Villarreal, M.D., Keyes, K.M., et al. *Gun Ownership and Social Gun Culture*. The BMJ, Injury Prevention. June 2015.

[xi] U.S. Constitution, amend. 2.

[xii] *United States v. Cruikshank*, 92 U.S. 542 (1875).

[xiii] *Presser v. Illinois*, 116 U.S. 252 (1886).

[xiv] *Miller v. Texas*, 153 U.S. 535 (1894).

[xv] *United States v. Miller*, 307 U.S. 174 (1939).

[xvi] *District of Columbia* v. Heller, 554 U.S. 570 (2008).

[xvii] *McDonald v. Chicago*, 561 U.S. 742 (2010).

[xviii] Non-Mailable Firearms Act, 90th Congress, enacted on October 22, 1968.

[xix] National Firearms Act (NFA), 73rd Congress, enacted on June 26, 1934. http://legisworks.org /congress/73/publaw-474.pdf

[xx] The Federal Firearms Act of 1938, 75th Congress, enacted on June 30, 1938. http://legisworks.org /sal/52/stats/STATUTE-52-Pg1250.pdf

[xxi] The Gun Control Act of 1968, 90th Congress, enacted on October 22, 1968. https://www.gpo.gov /fdsys/pkg/STATUTE-82/pdf/STATUTE-82-Pg1213-2.pdf

[xxii] Newhard, J.M, *Bootleggers and Gun Control*, The CATO JOURNAL, Fall 2015. https://object.cato.org/sites/cato.org/files/serials/files/regulation/2015/9/regulation-v38n3-3.pdf (accessed on August 17, 2018)

xxiii Code of Federal Regulations, Title 27 § 178, T.D. ATF-16, 40 FR 19202, May 2, 1975.

xxiv Arms Export Control Act of 1976, 94th Congress, enacted on June 30, 1976. https://www.gpo.gov/fdsys/pkg/STATUTE-90/pdf/STATUTE-90-Pg729.pdf

xxv The Comprehensive Crime Control Act, 98th Congress, enacted on October 12, 1984. https://www.govtrack.us /congress/bills/98/hr5963

xxvi The Law Enforcement Officers Protection Act of 1985, 99th Congress, enacted on August 28, 1986. https://www.gpo.gov/fdsys/granule/STATUTE-100/STATUTE-100-Pg920/content-detail.html

xxvii The Firearm Owners Protection Act of 1986, 99th Congress, enacted on May 19, 1986. https://www.gpo.gov /fdsys/pkg/STATUTE-100/pdf/STATUTE-100-Pg449.pdf.

xxviii The Undetectable Firearms Act of 1988, 100th Congress, enacted on November 10, 1988. https://www.gpo.gov/fdsys/pkg/STATUTE-102/pdf/STATUTE-102-Pg3816.pdf

xxix The Crime Control Act of 1990, 101st Congress, enacted on November 29, 1990. https://www.gpo.gov /fdsys/pkg/STATUTE-104/pdf/STATUTE-104-Pg4789.pdf.

xxx The Brady Handgun Violence Prevention Act of 1994, 103rd Congress, enacted on February 28, 1994. https://www.govinfo.gov/content/pkg/HJOURNAL-1994/html/HJOURNAL-1994.html

xxxi The Violent Crime Control and Law Enforcement Act of 1994, 103rd Congress, enacted on September 13, 1994. https://www.gpo.gov/fdsys/pkg/BILLS-103hr3355enr/pdf/BILLS-103hr3355enr.pdf

xxxii Domestic Violence Offender Gun Ban of 1996, 104th Congress, enacted on September 30, 1996. https://www.gpo.gov/fdsys/pkg/PLAW-104publ208/html/PLAW-104publ208.htm

xxxiii U.S. Department of Justice. Bureau of Alcohol, Tobacco, Firearms and Explosives, "OPEN LETTER ON THE REDESIGN OF "STABILIZING BRACES", https://www.atf.gov/file/11816/download. (accessed March 15, 2017).

xxxiv Stokes, J., *3D guns are now legal…What's Next?*, July 14, 2018, www.Techcrunch.com, https://techcrunch.com/2018/07/14/its-now-legal-to-distribute-schematics-for-3d-printed-guns-in-the-u-s-what-happens-next/ (accessed on July 21, 2018).

xxxv U.S. Government Accountability Office, ATF Did Not Always Comply with the Appropriations Act Restriction and Should Better Adhere to Its Policies, GAO Report 16-552 (Washington, DC, June 30, 2016).

xxxvi Wikipedia contributors, "Gunfire locator," *Wikipedia, The Free Encyclopedia,* https://en.wikipe-dia.org/w/index.php?title=Gunfire_locator&oldid=846270583 (accessed March 27, 2017).

xxxvii Wikipedia contributors, "Agent provocateur," *Wikipedia, The Free Encyclopedia,* https://en.wikipe-dia.org/w/index.php?title=Agent_provocateur&oldid=837433909 (accessed March 17, 2017.)

xxxviii Small Arms Survey and Swiss Agency for Development and Cooperation. *Illicit Trafficking, December 2017,* http://www.smallarmssurvey.org/weapons-and-markets/transfers/illicit-trafficking.html. (accessed on May 6, 2018).

xxxix U.S. Department of Justice. Bureau of Alcohol, Tobacco, Firearms and Explosives. *Firearms Trafficking Investigation Guide, ATF Publication 3317.1.* Washington, 1997, Rev. Ed 2009, Section III PP 8 to14.

xl U.S. Department of Justice. Bureau of Justice Statistics, *Community Policing,* https://www.bjs.gov/in-dex.cfm?ty=tp&tid=81 (accessed March 27, 2017).

xli Baum, E., *Police Work: What is the SARA Model?*, June 2015, https://www.newsmax.com/fastfeatures/police-work-sara-model/2015/06/15/id/648577/ (accessed on January 7, 2017).

xlii U.S. Department of Justice. Bureau of Alcohol, Tobacco, Firearms and Explosives. *Firearms Trafficking Investigation Guide, ATF Publication 3317.1*. Washington, 1997, Rev. Ed 2009, Section III PP 8 to14.

xliii Ackerman, R., "Intelligence Key to Counterdrug Efforts," *SIGNAL Magazine*, October 2010.

xliv El Paso Intelligence Center. https://www.epic.gov (accessed on March 17, 2017).

xlv U.S. Department of Justice. Bureau of Alcohol, Tobacco, Firearms and Explosives, *E-Trace; Internet Based Firearms Tracing and Analysis, ATF Publication 3312.9*. Washington, Rev. Ed. 2009, December.

xlvi U.S. Constitution, art. IV, sec. 2, cl. 2.

xlvii Department of the U.S. Treasury, Financial Crimes Enforcement Network. https://www.fincen.gov (accessed on March 17, 2017).

xlviii Department of the U.S. Treasury. Tax and Trade Bureau, *FAET Reference Guide Firearms and Ammunition Excise Tax*. https://www.ttb.gov/firearms/reference_guide.shtml (accessed March 26, 2017).

xlix U.S. Department of Justice. Bureau of Alcohol, Tobacco, Firearms and Explosives. *Firearms Trafficking Investigation Guide, ATF Publication 3317.1*. Washington, 1997, Rev. Ed 2009, Section III PP 8 to14.

l Ibid.

li Ibid.

lii Ibid.

liii Ibid.

liv Ratcliffe, J., *Pocket Guide to Intelligence Led Policing*. (June 2008) www.jratcliffe.net (accessed on March 17, 2017).

lv International Association of Chiefs of Police, http://www.theiacp.org (accessed on March 30, 2017)

lvi U.S. Department of Justice. Bureau of Alcohol, Tobacco, Firearms and Explosives. https://www.atf.gov/resource-center/fact-sheet/fact-sheet-international-affairs-division (accessed on March 28, 2017).

lvii INTERPOL, www.interpol.int. (accessed March 29, 2017).

lviii U.S. Department of Justice. Bureau of Alcohol, Tobacco, Firearms and Explosives. *Firearms Trafficking Investigation Guide, ATF Publication 3317.1*. Washington, 1997, Rev. Ed 2009, Section III PP 8 to14.

lix Ibid.

lx Wikipedia contributors, "NADDIS," *Wikipedia, The Free Encyclopedia*, https://en.wikipedia.org/w/index.php?title=NADDIS&oldid=799823327 (accessed March 17, 2017).

lxi U.S. Department of Justice. Federal Bureau of Investigation, *National Crime Information Center*. https://www.fbi.gov/services/cjis/ncic (accessed March 17, 2017).

lxii U.S. Department of Justice. Federal Bureau of Investigation, *National Instant Criminal Background Check System*. https://www.fbi.gov/services/cjis/nics (accessed March 17, 2017).

lxiii U.S. Department of Justice. Bureau of Alcohol, Tobacco, Firearms and Explosives, *National Integrated Ballistics Identification Network*. https://www.atf.gov/firearms/national-integrated-ballistic-information-network-nibin (accessed March 17, 2017).

lxiv U.S. Department of Justice. Bureau of Alcohol, Tobacco, Firearms and Explosives, *National Tracing Center*. https://www.atf.gov/firearms/national-tracing-center (accessed March 17, 2017).

lxv U.S. Department of Justice. Bureau of Alcohol, Tobacco, Firearms and Explosives, *National Tracing Center, Out of Business Records Center*. https://www.atf.gov/firearms/discontinue-being-federal-firearms-licensee-ffl (accessed March 17, 2017).

lxvi Federal Bureau of Investigation, *National Instant Criminal Background Check System, Point of Contact States*. https://www.fbi.gov/services/cjis/nics/about-nics (accessed March 17, 2017).

lxvii U.S. Department of Justice. Bureau of Alcohol, Tobacco, Firearms and Explosives. *Firearms Trafficking Investigation Guide, ATF Publication 3317.1*. Washington, 1997, Rev. Ed 2009, Section III PP 8 to14.

lxviii Ibid.

lxix Ibid.

lxx Ibid.

lxxi Ibid.

lxxii Ibid.

lxxiii Ibid.

lxxiv Cryptome. *Treasury Enforcement Communications System*. http://cryptome.info/irs-ci/36426.html (accessed March 17, 2017).

lxxv U.S. Department of Justice. Bureau of Alcohol, Tobacco, Firearms and Explosives. *Firearms Trafficking Investigation Guide, ATF Publication 3317.1*. Washington, 1997, Rev. Ed 2009, Section XIII PP 176 to187.

lxxvi U.S. Department of Justice. Bureau of Alcohol, Tobacco, Firearms and Explosives, *ATF Guidebook; Importation & Verification of Firearms, Ammunition, and Implements of War*, 2015, https://www.atf.gov/firearms/docs/guide/atf-guidebook-importation-verification-firearms-ammunition-and-implements-war/download. (accessed June 20, 2018).

lxxvii U.S. Department of Justice. *U. S. Attorney's Manual*, 2018, https://www.justice.gov/usam/usam-9-15000-international-extradition-and-related-matters#9-15.100. (accessed April 8, 2017).

lxxviii U.S. Department of Justice. *U. S. Attorney's Manual*, 2018, https://www.justice.gov/usam/usam-9-15000-international-extradition-and-related-matters#9-15.630. (accessed April 15, 2017).

lxxix U.S. Department of Justice. Bureau of Alcohol, Tobacco, Firearms and Explosives, *Firearms Curios or Relics List, ATF Publication 5300.11*, Washington, Rev. Ed. December 2007.

lxxx Code of Federal Regulations, Title 22: §§ 120-130.

lxxxi Code of Federal Regulations, Title 27: § 447.

lxxxii U.S. Department of Justice. Bureau of Alcohol, Tobacco, Firearms and Explosives. *FIREARMS COMMERCE; US Annual Statistical Update 2017*. Washington, Rev. Ed 2017.

lxxxiii *United States v. Eight Rhodesian Statues*, 449 F. Supp. 193, 195 (C.D. Cal. 1978).

lxxxiv U.S. Department of Justice. Criminal Division, Asset Forfeiture and Money Laundering Section, *Asset Forfeiture Process Version 1.0*, 1, Washington, DC, 2015.

lxxxv U.S. Constitution, amends. 4 and 14, sec. 1.

lxxxvi Department of the U.S. Treasury. Financial Crime Enforcement Network, *Money Laundering Prevention*. https://www.fincen.gov/sites/default/files/shared/preventionguide.pdf. (accessed on January 6, 2018).

lxxxvii Department of the U.S. Treasury. *National Money Laundering Risk Assessment*. 2015, https://www.treasury.gov/resource-center/terrorist-illicit-finance/Documents/National%20Money%20Laundering%20Risk%20Assessment%20–%202006-12-2015.pdf. (accessed June 20, 2018).

lxxxviii The Economist, *Trade and Money Laundering, Uncontained*, May 3, 2014, https://www.economist.com/international/2014/05/03/uncontained. New York, (accessed on June 16, 2018).

lxxxix Blockgeeks, *What is Blockchain Technology? A Step-by-Step Guide for Beginners*, 2016, https://blockgeeks.com/guides/what-is-blockchain-technology /. (accessed on June 17, 2018).

xc Blockgeeks, *Paper Wallet Guide; How to Protect Your Cryptocurrency*. 2017, https://blockgeeks.com/guides/paper-wallet-guide/.(accessed on June 17, 2018).

xci Bitcoin, *How Does Bitcoin Work?*, 2017, https://bitcoin.org/en/how-it-works. (accessed on June 17, 2018).

xcii Rutgers University, Masters of Business and Science Program 2018, NIBIN DATA ANALYSIS, https://mbs.rutgers.edu/mbs-externship-exchange/nj-state-police-office-forensic-sciences. (accessed on August 30, 2018)

xciii U.S. Department of Justice. Bureau of Alcohol, Tobacco, Firearms and Explosives. https://www.atf.gov /resource-center/fact-sheet/fact-sheet-national-tracing-center. (accessed on April 28, 2018).

xciv Ibid.

xcv U.S. Department of Justice. Office of Inspector General, *Inspections of Firearms Dealers by the Bureau of Alcohol, Tobacco, Firearms and Explosives, Report Number I-2004-005*, July 2004. https://oig.justice.gov/ reports/ATF/e0405/ background.htm. (accessed on April 29, 2018).

xcvi U.S. Department of Justice. Bureau of Alcohol, Tobacco, Firearms and Explosives. *Firearms Trafficking Investigation Guide, ATF Publication 3317.1*. Washington, 1997, Rev. Ed 2009.

xcvii U.S. Government Accountability Office, *ATF Did Not Always Comply with the Appropriations Act Restriction and Should Better Adhere to Its Policies*, GAO Report 16-552, Washington, DC, 2016, https://www.gao.gov /assets/680/678091.pdf. (accessed June 20, 2018).

xcviii U.S. Department of Justice. Bureau of Alcohol, Tobacco, Firearms and Explosives. https://www.atf.gov_/firearms/firearms-and-ammunition-technology. (accessed March 28, 2017).

xcix ShotSpotter™, *2017 National Gun Fire Index*, http://www.shotspotter.com/2017NGI. (accessed on May 28, 2018).

c ShotSpotter™, *2017 National Gun Fire Index*, http://www.shotspotter.com/system/content-uploads/2013NGI-online.pdf. (accessed on May 28, 2018).

ci Gagliardi, P., (2009) *Helping Police Link More Crimes, Guns, and Suspects Using Regional Processing Protocols*, Forensic Science Policy & Management: An International Journal, 1:1, 43-48, DOI: 10.1080 /19409040802629710.

cii Department of the U.S. Treasury. Bureau of Alcohol, Tobacco, and Firearms. *Protecting America; The Effectiveness of the Federal Armed Career Criminal Statute.* March 1992, https://www.ncjrs.gov/pdffiles1/ Digitization/ 137208NCJRS.pdf. (accessed May 28, 2018).

ciii U.S. Department of Justice. Bureau of Prisons, *Privacy Impact for the SENTRY Inmate Management System*, July 2, 2012. https://www.bop.gov/foia/sentry.pdf. (accessed on April 28, 2018).

civ U.S. Department of Justice. Bureau of Alcohol, Tobacco, Firearms and Explosives. *Firearms Trafficking Investigation Guide, ATF Publication 3317.1.* Washington, 1997, Rev. Ed 2009, Section V, PP 27 to 32.

cv Marbin, C., (1989, June, 13) The Palm Beach Post. *Agent: Military Brass Aided Drug Cartel.* June 13, 1989, https://www.newspapers.com/newspage/130667255/. (accessed June 8, 2018).

cvi Isikoff, M., The Washington Post, *U.S Agents Seize Drug-Related Arms Cache.* June 20, 1989, https://www.washingtonpost.com/archive/politics/1989/06/10/us-agents-seize-drug-related-arms-cache /2f46a0d5-fe63-463b-ad89-cbf0ca80e630/?utm_term=.baeac236e3f6. (accessed May 28, 2018).

cvii Montero, D., The Nation, *Guns "R" Us*, November 14, 2002, https://www.thenation.com/article/guns-r-us/. (accessed May 28, 2018).

cviii Norman, B., New Times of Broward and Palm Beach, *Irish Sting.* July 19, 2001, http://www.broward-palmbeach.com/news/irish-sting-6323923. (accessed May 28, 2018).

cix Commission of Enquiry for Trinidad and Tobago, *Report of the Commission of Enquiry to enquire into the events surrounding the attempted coup which occurred in the Republic of Trinidad and Tobago on 27th July, 1990.* March 13, 2014, http://unctt.org/wp-content/uploads/2013/03/1990-COUP-Report.pdf. (accessed May 28, 2018).

cx *United States v. Louis Haneef, et al.,* U.S. District Court, Southern District of Florida, Criminal Docket No. 90-6161-CR-PAINE.

cxi Christensen, D., Sun Sentinel, *Broward-based Boss of Jamaica's Brutal Shower Posse Gang Dies.* March 30, 2010, http://articles.sun-sentinel.com/2010-03-30/news/fl-jamaican-posse-leader-obit-20100330_1_shower-posse-vivian-blake-extradition. (accessed on May 28, 2018).

cxii Gato, P., Windrem, R., Telemundo and MSNBC, *Hezbollah Builds a Western Base.* May 9, 2007, http://www.nbcnews.com/id/17874369/ns/world_news-americas/t/hezbollah-builds-western-base/#.WwyoBC-ZPVo. (accessed May 28, 2018).

cxiii U.S. Department of Justice. Bureau of Alcohol, Tobacco, Firearms and Explosives, *Industry Operations Investigators: What do IOIs do?*, https://www.atf.gov/resource-center/industry-operations-investigators. (accessed April 29, 2018).

cxiv Garfield, L. (2017, October, 6) *There are 50,000 More Gun Shops Than McDonalds in the US.* Business Insider. October 6, 2017, http://www.businessinsider.com/gun-dealers-stores-mcdonalds-las-vegas-shooting-2017-10. (accessed April 29, 2018).

cxv Bloomberg, Fortune.Com, *Gun Thefts in the U.S. Are Skyrocketing and Investigators Have No Idea Why.* January 19, 2018, http://fortune.com/2018/01/19/gun-thefts-atf-firearm-retailers/. (accessed April 29, 2018).

cxvi National Rifle Association. NRA Explore, *Eddie Eagle,* https://eddieeagle.nra.org (accessed June 11, 2018).

cxvii Governing.Com, *States Use Facial Recognition Technology to Address License Fraud*, July 15, 2015, http://www.governing.com/topics/public-justice-safety/states-crack-down-on-drivers-license-fraud2.html. (accessed April 22, 2018).

cxviii King, Dan. The Week, *The Governments Creepy Obsession with Your Face*, June 18, 2018, http://theweek.com /articles/779196/governments-creepy-obsession-face. (accessed June 18, 2018).

cxix Ibid.

cxx U.S. Department of Justice. *U.S. Attorney's Office Manual, Checklist for T-III Application Requirements,* https://www.justice.gov/usam/criminal-resource-manual-92-title-iii-procedures-attachment-c. (accessed May 12, 2018)

cxxi U.S. Department of Justice. *Guidelines Regarding the Use of Confidential Informants,* 2001, https://www.justice.gov /archives/ag/attorney-general-renos-confidential-informant-guidelines-january-8-2001. (accessed May 28, 2018).

cxxii U.S. Department of Justice. Undercover and Sensitive Operations Unit, *Attorney General's Guidelines on FBI Undercover Operations,* https://www.justice.gov/archives/ag/undercover-and-sensitive-operations-unit-attorney-generals-guidelines-fbi-undercover-operations. (accessed May 28, 2018).

cxxiii Officer.Com. *Responding with Fight or Flight,* October 1, 2008, https://www.officer.com/home/article /10248579/responding-with-fight-or-flight. (accessed May 19, 2018).

cxxiv *United States. v. Bruscantini,* 761 F.2d 640, 642 (11th Cir. 1985).

cxxv *United States v. Hedges,* 912 F.2d 1397, 1405 (11th Cir. 1990).

cxxvi *United States, Plaintiff-appellee, v. Walter David Tallmadge,* Defendant-appellant, 829 F.2d 767 (9th Cir. 1987).

cxxvii Maxwell, T., *"Maine gun trafficker gets three-month term,"* The Portland Press Herald. November 23, 2010.

cxxviii Reinhart, B., *Implementing a Firearms Trafficking Strategy—Prosecuting Corrupt Federal Firearms Licensees,* U. S. Department of Justice, U.S. Attorney's Bulletin, Vol. 50, No. 1, (January 2002).

cxxix Groban, M., Hicks, P., *Conspiracy and Firearms—Will Firearm Conspiracy Charges Add Value to Federal Prosecutions,* U.S. Department of Justice, U.S. Attorney's Bulletin, Vol. 61, No. 4, (July 2013).

cxxx LaFlamme, M., *"Maine guns for Mass. drugs: Bay State criminals find Pine Tree State a great place to buy guns, sell drugs,"* Sun Journal, March 14, 2010, http://www.sunjournal.com/maine-guns-mass-drugs-bay-state-criminals-find-pine-tree-state-great-place-buy-guns-sell-drugs/. (accessed June 20, 2018).

cxxxi Quigley, K., *"Illegal Gun Sales Land Two Men in Federal Prison; Weapon Traced to Mobster Sammy the Bull Gravano,"* The Palm Beach Post, August 2001.

cxxxii U.S. Department of Justice. Bureau of Alcohol, Tobacco, Firearms and Explosives. *Firearms Trafficking Investigation Guide, ATF Publication 3317.1.* Washington, 1997, Rev. Ed 2009, Section X PP 90 to152.

cxxxiii Chivers, C.J., *"Ill-Secured Soviet Arms Depots Tempting Rebels and Terrorists,"* The New York Times, July 18, 2005. https://www.nytimes.com/2005/07/16/world/europe/illsecured-soviet-arms-depots-tempting-rebels-and-terrorists.html (accessed March 10, 2018).

cxxxiv North Atlantic Treaty Organization, The Fund for Peace, *Together Reducing Unsafe Surplus Tools of War (TRUST),* 2006, Brussels, Belgium.

cxxxv U.S. Department of State. Office of the Legal Adviser and Bureau of Consular Affairs, *Consular Notification and Access; Instructions for Federal, State, and Local Law Enforcement and Other Officials Regarding Foreign Nationals in the United States and the Rights of Consular Officials to Assist Them (Fourth Edition),* August 2016, https://travel.state.gov/content/dam/travel/CNAtraingresources/CNA_Manual_4th_Edition_September _2017.pdf. (accessed June 2, 2018).

cxxxvi U.S. Department of State. *Consular Notification and Access Pocket Card*, https://travel.state.gov/content/dam /travel/CNAtrainingresources/CNA%20Pocket%20Card_BW.pdf. (accessed May 20, 2018).

cxxxvii Zag, Z., *"500 Cops Raid Mohawk Territories,"* Warrior Publications, June 15, 2012, https://warriorpublications.wordpress.com/2011/06/15/500-cops-raid-mohawk-territories/. (accessed June 2, 2018).

cxxxviii Aubin, B., *"Kanesatake Chief in Exile,"* The Canadian Encyclopedia. December 5, 2013. https://www.thecanadianencyclopedia.ca/en/m/article/kanesatake-chief-in-exile/. (accessed June 2, 2018).

cxxxix Harrison, J., *"Former Calais Hardware Store Manager Sentenced to Home Confinement,"* The Bangor Daily News, June 8, 2011, https://bangordailynews.com/2011/06/08/news/bangor/former-calais-hardware-store-manager-to-be-sentenced-on-gun-charge/. (accessed June 2, 2018).

cxl Government Accountability Office, *Firearms Trafficking – Efforts to Combat Firearms Trafficking to Mexico Have Improved, but Some Collaboration Challenges Remain,* GAO-16-223. (Washington, D.C. 2016), accessed May 29, 2018, https://www.gao.gov/products/GAO-16-223.

cxli Paoli, G.P., Aldrige, J. Ryan, Nathan, Warnes, R. (2017.) *Behind the Curtain; The illicit trade of firearms, explosives, and ammunition on the dark web,* Rand Corp., https://www.rand.org/pubs/research_reports/RR2019.html. (accessed May 20, 2018).

cxlii U.S. Library of Congress, Congressional Research Service, *Internet Firearm and Ammunition Sales.* By Chu, V.S., R42687, (August, 28 2012).

cxliii Government Accountability Office, *Internet Firearms Sales, ATF Enforcement Efforts and Outcomes of GAO Covert Testing,* GAO-18-24. (Washington, D.C. 2017), accessed May 29, 2018, https://www.gao.gov/products/GAO-18-24.

cxliv Paoli, G.P., Aldrige, J. Ryan, Nathan, Warnes, R. (2017.) *Behind the Curtain; The illicit trade of firearms, explosives, and ammunition on the dark web.* Rand Corp., https://www.rand.org/pubs/research_reports/RR2019.html. (accessed May 20, 2018).

cxlv INTERPOL, *International Alert System,* https://www.interpol.int/Crime-areas/Firearms-trafficking/Firearms-trafficking. (accessed on June 19, 2018).

cxlvi Piscitello, D., *Guidance for Preparing Domain Name Orders, Seizures & Takedowns,* Internet Corporation for Assigned Numbers and Names (ICANN), https://www.icann.org/en/system/files/files/guidance-domain-seizures-07mar12-en.pdf. (accessed May 21, 2018).

cxlvii U.S Department of Justice. Office of Juvenile Justice and Delinquency Programs and Institute for Intergovernmental Research, *Gang Prosecution Manual,* July 2009, https://www.nationalgangcenter.gov /Content/Documents/Gang-Prosecution-Manual.pdf. (accessed June 2, 2018).

cxlviii Federal Rules of Evidence, Article IV, Relevance and Its Limits, Rule 404. Character, Evidence; Crime or Other Acts, https://www.rulesofevidence.org/article-iv/rule-404/. (accessed June 2, 2018).

cxlix U.S. Department of Justice. The National Crime Gun Intelligence Governing Board, *Crime Gun Intelligence – Disrupting the Shooting Cycle,* August 2018.

cl Code of Federal Regulations, Title 27 § 478.11.

cli Police Executive Research Forum, *The Crime Gun Intelligence Center Model: Case Studies of the Denver, Milwaukee, and Chicago Approaches to Investigating Gun Crime,* May 2017, http://www.policeforum.org/assets /crimegunintelligencecenter.pdf. (accessed June 20, 2018).

clii Brantingham, P. L. & Brantingham, P. J. (1993). *Environmental, Routine, and Situation: Toward a pattern theory of crime. Advances in Criminological Theory 5*: 259-294, https://www.ncjrs.gov/App/Publications /abstract.aspx?ID=160010. (accessed June 20, 2018).

cliii *Carpenter v. U.S.* 585 U.S.___(2018).

cliv U.S. Department of Justice, Offices of the United States Attorneys, *U.S Attorneys Manual - Criminal Resource Manual.* https://www.justice.gov/usam/usam-9-110000-organized-crime-and-racketeering. (accessed June 20, 2018).

clv U.S. Department of Justice. *U.S. Attorneys Manual - Sample Enhanced Penalty Information for 18 U.S.C. § 521,* https://www.justice.gov/usam/criminal-resource-manual-1458-sample-enhanced-penalty-information-18-usc-521. (accessed May 12, 2018).

clvi Shimer, D., *"Gang members indicted for murder."* Yale News, October 2, 2015, https://yaledailynews.com/blog /2015/10/02/gang-members-indicted-for-murder/. (accessed June 2, 2018).

clvii U.S. Attorney's Office, District of Connecticut, *"Joint Investigation Dismantles New Haven Street Gang; Members Charges with 6 Murders,"* October 1, 2015, https://www.justice.gov/usao-ct/pr/joint-investigation-dismantles-violent-new-haven-street-gang-members-charged-6-murders. (accessed June 2, 2018).

clviii Scinto, R., *"New Haven Police Release 2016 Crime Statistics."* Patch.com, January 12, 2017, https://patch.com/connecticut/newhaven/new-haven-police-release-2016-crime-stats. (accessed June 2, 2018).

clix Canfield, C., *Outlaw killed by ATF was suspect in Maine Shooting,* June 16, 2010, Associated Press, http://archive.boston.com/news/local/maine/articles/2010/06/16/outlaw_killed_by_atf_was_suspect_in_maine_shooting/, (accessed on July).

clx U.S Department of Justice, Office of Juvenile Justice and Delinquency Prevention, *The Action Plan* https://www.ojjdp.gov/action/sec3.htm, (accessed on April 29, 2018).

clxi Small Arms Survey and Swiss Agency for Development and Cooperation, *Global Violent Deaths 2017 – Time To Decide,*(2017, December), http://www.smallarmssurvey.org/fileadmin/docs/U-Reports/SAS-Report-GVD2017.pdf. (accessed on April 21, 2018).

clxii U.S. Department of State, Bureau of International Narcotics and Law Enforcement Affairs, https://www.state.gov/j/inl/c/crime/c44636.htm. (accessed on April 19, 2018).

clxiii Campbell, D., MacKinnon, I., The Guardian, *Lord of War Arms Trafficker Arrested,* March 6, 2008, https://www.theguardian.com/world/2008/mar/07/thailand.russia. (accessed May 28, 2018).

clxiv Greenberg, R., Dateline NBC, *"The Godfather of Terror".* 2008, https://www.theguardian.com/world/2008 /mar/07/thailand.russia. (accessed May 28, 2018).

clxv Max, A., The Associated Press, *Arms Dealer Bust Embargoes With Impunity.* June 11, 2006, http://www.washingtonpost.com /wp-dyn/content/article/2006/06/11/AR2006061100416.html. (accessed May 28, 2018).

clxvi CBC News, *Border agents want more resources to stop gun smuggling,* June 14, 2013, http://www.cbc.ca /news/canada/windsor/border-agents-want-more-resources-to-stop-gun-smuggling-1.1373581. (accessed May 6, 2018).

clxvii McGreal, C., *The US Gun Smugglers Recruited by One of Mexico's Most Brutal Cartels.* The Guardian. December 8, 2011, https://www.theguardian.com/world/2011/dec/08/us-gun-smugglers-mexico-cartel. (accessed May 6, 2018).

clxviii Bruser, D., and Poisson, J., *Star investigation: How one U.S. gun broker moved firearms across the border.* The Toronto Star, April 18, 2013, https://www.thestar.com/news/investigations /2013/04/18/star_investigation _how_one_us_gun_broker_moved_firearms_across_the_border.html (accessed May 6, 2018) clxix PTI, *Chinese smugglers use internet for trafficking arms*, The Times of India. April 5, 2012, https://www.gadgetsnow.com/tech-news/Chinese-smugglers-use-internet-for-trafficking-arms/articleshow/12546664.cms. (accessed May 6, 2018).

clxx Sweig, J., *A Strategy to Reduce Gun Trafficking and Violence in the Americas.* Council on Foreign Relations. July 29, 2013, https://www.cfr.org/report/strategy-reduce-gun-trafficking-and-violence-americas. (accessed May 6, 2018).

clxxi Small Arms Survey and Swiss Agency for Development and Cooperation, *Illicit Trafficking,* December 2017, http://www.smallarmssurvey.org/weapons-and-markets/transfers/illicit-trafficking.html. (accessed May 6, 2018).

clxxii United Nations Security Council, *Security Council, Concerned at Threat Posed by Illicit Cross-Border Trafficking, Asks for Assessment of UN Efforts in Helping States Counter Challenges,* April 25, 2012, https://www.un.org/press/en/2012/sc10624.doc.htm. (accessed May 6, 2018).

clxxiii U.S. Department of State. Office of Defense Trade Controls Policy, *Blue Lantern End-Use Monitoring Program,* https://www.bis.doc.gov/index.php/documents/pdfs/1588-end-user-verification-blue-lantern/file. (accessed on April 21, 2018).

clxxiv INTERPOL, *iARMS – Illicit Arms Records and Tracing Management System Brochure,* January2017), Lyon, France. https://www.interpol.int/...brochures/Illicit-arms-records-and-tracing-management-system. (accessed on June 19, 2018).

clxxv INTERPOL, *INTERPOL Firearms Reference Table (IFRT),* https://www.interpol.int/Crime-areas/Firearmstrafficking/INTERPOL-Firearms-Reference-Table-IFRT. (accessed on June 19, 2018).

clxxvi INTERPOL, *International Alert System,* https://www.interpol.int/Crime-areas/Firearms-trafficking/Firearms-trafficking. (accessed on June 19, 2018).

clxxvii INTERPOL, *INTERPOL Ballistics Identification Network (IBIN),* https://www.interpol.int/Crime-areas/Firearms-trafficking/INTERPOL-Ballistic-Information-Network-IBIN. (accessed on June 19, 2018).

clxxviii U.S. Department of Homeland Security, U.S. Customs and Border Protection, *World Customs Organization Overview,* https://www.cbp.gov/border-security/international-initiatives/wco. (accessed on April 21, 2018).

clxxix World Customs Organization, CEN Suite Brochure, http://www.wcoomd.org/-/media/wco /public/global/ pdf/topics/enforcement-and-compliance/tools-and-instruments/cen/cen-brochure.pdf?db=web. (accessed on April 21, 2018).

clxxx EUROPOL, *About Europol,* https://www.europol.europa.eu/about-europol. (accessed on April 21, 2018).

clxxxi North Atlantic Treaty Organization. *Trust Funds: Supporting Demilitarization and Defence Transformation Projects.* (June 2016) https://www.nato.int/cps/en/natohq/topics_50082.htm. (accessed on April 21, 2018).

clxxxii U.S. Department of State. Bureau of International Narcotics and Law Enforcement Affairs, Criminal Justice Programs Division, *International Law Enforcement Academies,* https://www.state.gov/j/inl/c/crime/ilea/index.htm (accessed on April 19, 2018).

clxxxiii U.S. Department of Justice. ICITAP/OPDAT Program Support, Request for Proposal, Solicitation DJJI-17-RFP-1037 2017, https://govtribe.com/project/icitapopdat-worldwide-support-services/activity. (accessed on May 12, 2018).

clxxxiv U.S. Agency for International Development. *Success Story – From Firearms to Open Arms,* https://www.usaid.gov/ sites /default/files/success/files/ss_gt_arms.pdf. (accessed on May 12, 2018).

clxxxv U.S. Agency for International Development. *MISSION, VISION, AND VALUES*, https://www.usaid.gov/ who-we-are/mission-vision-values. (accessed on May 12, 2018).

clxxxvi U.S. Agency for International Development. *USAID/GUATEMALA COUNTRY FACT SHEET*, November 2017, https://www.usaid.gov/sites/default/files/documents/1862/Guatemala-External-Fact-Sheet-November-2017.pdf. (accessed on May 12, 2018).

clxxxvii U.S. Agency for International Development. *Virginia Security Contractor to Pay $44,000 Over Allegations of Illegally Exporting Firearms Accessories*, February 24, 2016, https://oig.usaid.gov/node/1965. (accessed on May 12, 2018).

clxxxviii U.S. Agency for International Development. *EASTERN AND SOUTHERN CARIBBEAN CITIZEN SECURITY*, https://www.usaid.gov/barbados/citizen-security. (accessed on May 12, 2018).

clxxxix Pacenti, J., (2001, September, 26). *Taliban Showed Interest in Boca Snitch*. September 26, 2001, The Palm Beach Post, West Palm Beach, FL: Palm Beach Post.

cxc Kovach, G., (2002, September, 2). *Tomb Raiders, Beware! The curse of the mummies has a new way to strike*. Newsweek. New York, New York. https://www.highbeam.com/doc/1G1-90891915.html. (accessed on June 2, 2018).

cxci Nathans Spiro, L., (2001, November). *Wall St.'s Soldier of Fortune*. New York: Talk Magazine.

cxcii Whittell, G., (2001, October, 26). *A five-star disaster for the world*. London, England; The UK Times.

cxciii Hersh, S., (2004, March, 8). *Why is Washington going easy on Pakistan's nuclear black marketers?* New York, New York; The New Yorker.

cxciv Quraishi, A., (2004 February, 5). *Musharaf pardons nuclear chief*. Atlanta, GA: CNN

cxcv Pacenti, J., (2001, June, 15). *4 Arrested on Arms, Laundering, Charges – Attorney Calls Case Something Out of "James Bond" Novel*. West Palm Beach, FL: Palm Beach Post.

cxcvi Wilson, C., (2001, November, 16). *Final guilty plea in $32 million arms plot*. New York, New York; Associated Press.

cxcvii Wayne, L., (2001, October, 27). *From Riches to Relative Rags*. The New York Times. https://www.nytimes.com /2001/10/27/business/from-riches-to-relative-rags.html. (accessed June 2, 2018).

CPSIA information can be obtained
at www.ICGtesting.com
Printed in the USA
LVHW061455100723
751961LV00007B/521

9 780692 158807

Introductory and Intermediate Algebra

Sixth Edition

Introductory and Intermediate Algebra

Sixth
Edition

Margaret L. Lial
American River College

John Hornsby
University of New Orleans

Terry McGinnis

VP, Courseware Portfolio Management:	Chris Hoag
Director, Courseware Portfolio Management:	Michael Hirsch
Courseware Portfolio Manager:	Matthew Summers
Courseware Portfolio Assistant:	Shannon Bushee
Content Producer:	Sherry Berg
Managing Producer:	Karen Wernholm
Producer:	Shana Siegmund
Manager, Courseware Quality Assurance:	Mary Durnwald
Manager, Content Development:	Rebecca Williams
Product Marketing Manager:	Alicia Frankel
Product Marketing Assistant:	Hanna Lafferty
Field Marketing Managers:	Jennifer Crum, Lauren Schur
Senior Author Support/Technology Specialist:	Joe Vetere
Manager, Rights and Permissions:	Gina Cheselka
Manufacturing Buyer:	Carol Melville, LSC Communications
Associate Director of Design:	Blair Brown
Program Design Lead:	Barbara Atkinson
Text Design, Production Coordination, Composition, and Illustrations:	Cenveo® Publisher Services
Cover Design:	Studio Montage
Cover Image:	Don White/Alamy Stock Photo

Library of Congress Cataloging-in-Publication Data

Names: Lial, Margaret L. | Hornsby, John, 1949- | McGinnis, Terry.
Title: Introductory and intermediate algebra / Margaret Lial, John Hornsby, Terry McGinnis.
Description: 6th edition. | Boston : Pearson, [2018]
Identifiers: LCCN 2016003623 | ISBN 9780134493756 (pbk. : alk. paper)
Subjects: LCSH: Algebra—Textbooks.
Classification: LCC QA152.3 .L56 2018 | DDC 512.9—dc23
LC record available at http://lccn.loc.gov/2016003623

3

ISBN 13: 978-0-13-449375-6
ISBN 10: 0-13-449375-3

To Dotty, Puddles, and Gus. You loved us unconditionally.

E.J.H. and T.R.M.

Contents

Preface   x

CHAPTER R   Prealgebra Review   1

R.1   Fractions   1
R.2   Decimals and Percents   17
Study Skills   Using Your Math Text   28

CHAPTER 1   The Real Number System   29

1.1   Exponents, Order of Operations, and Inequality   30
Study Skills   Taking Lecture Notes   38
1.2   Variables, Expressions, and Equations   39
Study Skills   Reading Your Math Text   46
1.3   Real Numbers and the Number Line   47
Study Skills   Using Study Cards   56
1.4   Adding Real Numbers   57
1.5   Subtracting Real Numbers   64
Study Skills   Completing Your Homework   73
1.6   Multiplying and Dividing Real Numbers   74
Summary Exercises Performing Operations with Real Numbers   86
1.7   Properties of Real Numbers   88
1.8   Simplifying Expressions   98
Study Skills   Reviewing a Chapter   105

Summary 106 • Review Exercises 110 • Mixed Review Exercises 114 • Test 115

CHAPTER 2   Equations, Inequalities, and Applications   117

2.1   The Addition Property of Equality   118
Study Skills   Managing Your Time   125
2.2   The Multiplication Property of Equality   126
2.3   More on Solving Linear Equations   133
Study Skills   Using Study Cards Revisited   145
Summary Exercises Applying Methods for Solving Linear Equations   146

2.4   An Introduction to Applications of Linear Equations   147
2.5   Formulas and Additional Applications from Geometry   161
2.6   Ratio, Proportion, and Percent   174
Summary Exercises Applying Problem-Solving Techniques   185
2.7   Solving Linear Inequalities   186
Study Skills   Taking Math Tests   200

Summary 201 • Review Exercises 205 • Mixed Review Exercises 208 • Test 209 • Cumulative Review Exercises Chapters R–2 211

CHAPTER 3   Graphs of Linear Equations and Inequalities in Two Variables   213

3.1   Linear Equations and Rectangular Coordinates   214
Study Skills   Analyzing Your Test Results   227
3.2   Graphing Linear Equations in Two Variables   228
3.3   The Slope of a Line   242
3.4   Slope-Intercept Form of a Linear Equation   258
3.5   Point-Slope Form of a Linear Equation   270
Summary Exercises Applying Graphing and Equation-Writing Techniques for Lines   279
Study Skills   Preparing for Your Math Final Exam   281
3.6   Graphing Linear Inequalities in Two Variables   282

Summary 289 • Review Exercises 293 • Mixed Review Exercises 296 • Test 297 • Cumulative Review Exercises Chapters R–3 299

CHAPTER 4   Systems of Linear Equations and Inequalities   301

4.1   Solving Systems of Linear Equations by Graphing   302
4.2   Solving Systems of Linear Equations by Substitution   312
4.3   Solving Systems of Linear Equations by Elimination   320
Summary Exercises Applying Techniques for Solving Systems of Linear Equations   328

4.4 Applications of Linear Systems **330**

4.5 Solving Systems of Linear Inequalities **342**

Summary 347 • Review Exercises 350 • Mixed Review Exercises 352 • Test 353 • Cumulative Review Exercises Chapters R–4 355

CHAPTER 5 Exponents and Polynomials **357**

5.1 The Product Rule and Power Rules for Exponents **358**

5.2 Integer Exponents and the Quotient Rule **366**

Summary Exercises Applying the Rules for Exponents **375**

5.3 An Application of Exponents: Scientific Notation **377**

5.4 Adding and Subtracting Polynomials **385**

5.5 Multiplying Polynomials **395**

5.6 Special Products **402**

5.7 Dividing a Polynomial by a Monomial **409**

5.8 Dividing a Polynomial by a Polynomial **413**

Summary 420 • Review Exercises 423 • Mixed Review Exercises 426 • Test 427 • Cumulative Review Exercises Chapters R–5 429

CHAPTER 6 Factoring and Applications **431**

6.1 Greatest Common Factors; Factor by Grouping **432**

6.2 Factoring Trinomials **442**

6.3 Factoring Trinomials by Grouping **449**

6.4 Factoring Trinomials Using the FOIL Method **453**

6.5 Special Factoring Techniques **459**

6.6 A General Approach to Factoring **468**

6.7 Solving Quadratic Equations Using the Zero-Factor Property **473**

6.8 Applications of Quadratic Equations **482**

Summary 494 • Review Exercises 498 • Mixed Review Exercises 502 • Test 503 • Cumulative Review Exercises Chapters R–6 505

CHAPTER 7 Rational Expressions and Applications **507**

7.1 The Fundamental Property of Rational Expressions **508**

7.2 Multiplying and Dividing Rational Expressions **518**

7.3 Least Common Denominators **524**

7.4 Adding and Subtracting Rational Expressions **530**

7.5 Complex Fractions **540**

7.6 Solving Equations with Rational Expressions **550**

Summary Exercises Simplifying Rational Expressions vs. Solving Rational Equations **562**

7.7 Applications of Rational Expressions **564**

Summary 576 • Review Exercises 581 • Mixed Review Exercises 584 • Test 585 • Cumulative Review Exercises Chapters R–7 587

CHAPTER 8 Equations, Inequalities, Graphs, and Systems Revisited **589**

8.1 Review of Solving Linear Equations and Inequalities in One Variable **590**

8.2 Set Operations and Compound Inequalities **605**

8.3 Absolute Value Equations and Inequalities **614**

Summary Exercises Solving Linear and Absolute Value Equations and Inequalities **626**

8.4 Review of Graphing Linear Equations in Two Variables; Slope **628**

8.5 Review of Systems of Linear Equations in Two Variables **640**

8.6 Systems of Linear Equations in Three Variables; Applications **649**

Summary 662 • Review Exercises 668 • Mixed Review Exercises 672 • Test 673 • Cumulative Review Exercises Chapters R–8 675

CHAPTER 9 Relations and Functions **677**

9.1 Introduction to Relations and Functions **678**

9.2 Function Notation and Linear Functions **689**

9.3 Polynomial Functions, Operations, and Graphs **697**

9.4 Variation **706**

Summary 717 • Review Exercises 720 • Mixed Review Exercises 721 • Test 722 • Cumulative Review Exercises Chapters R–9 723

CHAPTER 10 Roots, Radicals, and Root Functions **725**

10.1 Radical Expressions and Graphs **726**

10.2 Rational Exponents **739**

10.3 Simplifying Radical Expressions **749**

10.4 Adding and Subtracting Radical Expressions **762**

10.5 Multiplying and Dividing Radical Expressions **767**

Summary Exercises *Performing Operations with Radicals and Rational Exponents* 777
10.6 Solving Equations with Radicals 779
10.7 Complex Numbers 788

Summary 797 • Review Exercises 801 • Mixed Review Exercises 804 • Test 805 • Cumulative Review Exercises Chapters R–10 807

CHAPTER 11 Quadratic Equations, Inequalities, and Functions 809
11.1 Solving Quadratic Equations by the Square Root Property 810
11.2 Solving Quadratic Equations by Completing the Square 817
11.3 Solving Quadratic Equations by the Quadratic Formula 825
11.4 Equations Quadratic in Form 833

Summary Exercises *Applying Methods for Solving Quadratic Equations* 844
11.5 Formulas and Further Applications 846
11.6 Graphs of Quadratic Functions 856
11.7 More about Parabolas and Their Applications 866
11.8 Polynomial and Rational Inequalities 878

Summary 889 • Review Exercises 893 • Mixed Review Exercises 896 • Test 897 • Cumulative Review Exercises Chapters R–11 899

CHAPTER 12 Inverse, Exponential, and Logarithmic Functions 901
12.1 Composition of Functions 902
12.2 Inverse Functions 907
12.3 Exponential Functions 916

12.4 Logarithmic Functions 924
12.5 Properties of Logarithms 932
12.6 Common and Natural Logarithms 940
12.7 Exponential and Logarithmic Equations and Their Applications 946

Summary 955 • Review Exercises 959 • Mixed Review Exercises 962 • Test 963 • Cumulative Review Exercises Chapters R–12 965

CHAPTER 13 Nonlinear Functions, Conic Sections, and Nonlinear Systems 967
13.1 Additional Graphs of Functions 968
13.2 Circles and Ellipses 975
13.3 Hyperbolas and Functions Defined by Radicals 985
13.4 Nonlinear Systems of Equations 993
13.5 Second-Degree Inequalities and Systems of Inequalities 1000

Summary 1006 • Review Exercises 1010 • Mixed Review Exercises 1012 • Test 1013 • Cumulative Review Exercises Chapters R–13 1015

Appendix A Review of Exponents, Polynomials, and Factoring (Transition from Introductory to Intermediate Algebra) 1017

Appendix B Synthetic Division 1025

Appendix C Solving Systems of Linear Equations by Matrix Methods 1031

Answers to Selected Exercises A-1

Photo Credits P-1

Index I-1

Preface

It is with great pleasure that we offer the sixth edition of *Introductory and Intermediate Algebra.* We have remained true to the original goal that has guided us over the years—to provide the best possible text and supplements package to help students succeed and instructors teach. This edition faithfully continues that process through enhanced explanations of concepts, new and updated examples and exercises, student-oriented features like Pointers, Cautions, Problem-Solving Hints, Margin Problems, and Study Skills, as well as an extensive package of helpful supplements and study aids.

This text is part of a series that also includes the following books:

- *Basic College Mathematics,* Tenth Edition, by Lial, Salzman, and Hestwood
- *Prealgebra,* Sixth Edition, by Lial and Hestwood
- *Introductory Algebra,* Eleventh Edition, by Lial, Hornsby, and McGinnis
- *Intermediate Algebra,* Eleventh Edition, by Lial, Hornsby, and McGinnis
- *Developmental Mathematics: Basic Mathematics and Algebra,* Fourth Edition, by Lial, Hornsby, McGinnis, Salzman, and Hestwood

WHAT'S NEW IN THIS EDITION

We are pleased to offer the following new textbook features and supplements.

▶ *Revised Exposition*   With each edition of the text, we continue to polish and improve discussions and presentations of topics to increase readability and student understanding. We believe this edition is the best yet in this regard.

▶ *More Figures and Diagrams*   For visual learners, we have made a concerted effort to add mathematical figures, diagrams, tables, and graphs whenever possible.

▶ *Enhanced Use of Pedagogical Color*   We have thoroughly reviewed all pedagogical color in discussions and examples and increased its use wherever doing so would enhance concept development, emphasize important steps, or highlight key information.

▶ *Improved Study Skills*   Most of these special activities now include a *Now Try This* section to increase student involvement. Each is designed independently to allow flexible use with individuals or small groups of students, or as a source of material for in-class discussions.

▶ *More What Went Wrong? Exercises*   We have increased the number of these popular CONCEPT CHECK exercises, which highlight common student errors.

▶ *More Relating Concepts Exercises*   We have increased the number of these flexible groups of exercises, located at the end of many exercise sets. Specially written to help students tie concepts together, as well as compare and contrast ideas, identify and describe patterns, and extend concepts to new situations, these sets of problems may be used with individual students or collaboratively with pairs or small groups. All of these exercise sets have been added to MyMathLab and tagged for easy location and assignment.

▶ *Dedicated Mixed Review Exercises*   Each chapter review has been expanded to include a one-page set of Mixed Review Exercises to help students further synthesize concepts.

▶ *Learning Catalytics*   This interactive student response tool uses students' own devices to engage them in the learning process. Learning Catalytics is accessible through MyMathLab and can be customized to an instructor's specific needs. Instructors can employ this tool to generate class discussion, promote peer-to-peer learning, and use real-time data to adjust instructional strategy. As an introduction to this exciting new tool, we have provided prerequisite skills questions at the beginning of each section to check students' preparedness for the new section. Learn more about Learning Catalytics in the Instructor Resources tab in MyMathLab.

▶ *Enhanced MyMathLab Resources* Exercise coverage has been refined with new videos and homework problems, including new Relating Concepts questions added throughout the course. See pages xiv and xv for more details.

▶ *Data Analytics* We analyzed aggregated student usage and performance data from MyMathLab for the previous edition of this text. The results of this analysis helped us improve the quality and quantity of exercises that matter the most to instructors and students.

CONTENT CHANGES

Specific content changes include the following:

▶ **Exercise sets** have been updated with a renewed focus on conceptual understanding, skill development, and review. New or revised figures are included wherever possible.

▶ **Real-world data** in the examples and exercises has been updated.

▶ **More "word equations"** are included in application examples to help students translate words into equations.

▶ **Expanded Chapter R** includes new figures and exposition on fractions, as well as new discussion, examples, and exercises on converting between fractions, decimals, and percents.

▶ **Expanded Mid-Chapter Summary Exercises** in Chapter 2 continue our emphasis on the difference between simplifying expressions and solving equations. The mid-chapter Summary Exercises in Chapters 4, 6, 7, and 11 include new examples that illustrate and distinguish between solution methods.

▶ **Separate sections on slope-intercept form and point-slope form** now appear in Chapter 3 and include enhanced discussion and new examples and exercises.

▶ **Reorganized Chapter 5** introduces the rules for exponents and application to scientific notation at the beginning of the chapter, followed by the sections on polynomials and their operations.

▶ **Expanded Chapter 7** on rational expressions introduces the material in more sections that now include additional examples and exercises. Emphasis is given to recognizing equivalent forms of rational expressions.

▶ **Chapter 8,** which revisits topics from the first half of the course, includes **new Section 8.4** that reviews graphing linear equations in two variables and slope.

▶ **New Chapter 9** now includes the material on functions, function notation, linear functions, and variation. **New Section 9.3** introduces polynomial functions, graphs, and operations. Each subsequent chapter in the text presents a new class of functions.

▶ **The following topics are among those that have been enhanced and/or expanded:**
  Operations with signed numbers (Sections 1.4–1.6)
  Order of operations involving absolute value expressions (Sections 1.5 and 1.6)
  Solving linear equations in one variable (Sections 2.1 and 2.2)
  Solving linear inequalities with fractions (Section 2.7)
  Graphing linear equations in two variables using intercepts (Section 3.2)
  Solving linear systems of equations using elimination (Section 4.3)
  Dividing a polynomial by a polynomial (Section 5.8)
  Discussion of sums of squares and factoring perfect square trinomials (Section 6.5)
  General factoring strategies (Section 6.6)
  Solving systems of linear equations in three variables (Section 8.6)

Multiplying radical expressions (Section 10.5)
Solving quadratic equations by completing the square (Section 11.2)
Solving quadratic inequalities (Section 11.8)
Finding and graphing inverse functions (Section 12.2)
Graphing systems of linear inequalities (Section 13.5)

HALLMARK FEATURES

We have enhanced the following popular features, each of which is designed to increase ease-of-use by students and/or instructors.

▶ *Emphasis on Problem-Solving* We introduce our six-step problem-solving method in Chapter 2 and integrate it throughout the text. The six steps, *Read, Assign a Variable, Write an Equation, Solve, State the Answer,* and *Check,* are emphasized in boldface type and repeated in examples and exercises to reinforce the problem-solving process for students. We also provide students with **Problem-Solving Hint** boxes that feature helpful problem-solving tips and strategies.

▶ *Helpful Learning Objectives* We begin each section with clearly stated, numbered objectives, and the included material is directly keyed to these objectives so that students and instructors know exactly what is covered in each section.

▶ *Popular Cautions and Notes* One of the most popular features of previous editions, we include information marked **⊘ CAUTION** and **Note** to warn students about common errors and emphasize important ideas throughout the exposition. The updated text design makes them easy to spot.

▶ *Comprehensive Examples* The new edition features a multitude of step-by-step, worked-out examples that include pedagogical color, helpful side comments, and special pointers. We give special attention to checking example solutions—more checks, designated using a special **CHECK** tag and ✓, are included than in past editions.

▶ *More Pointers* Because they were so well received by both students and instructors in the previous edition, we incorporate more pointers in examples and discussions throughout this edition of the text. They provide students with important on-the-spot reminders and warnings about common pitfalls.

▶ *Ample Margin Problems* Margin problems, with answers immediately available at the bottom of the page, are found in every section of the text. This key feature allows students to immediately practice the material covered in the examples in preparation for the exercise sets. Many include guided solutions.

▶ *Guided Solutions* Selected exercises in the margins and in the exercise sets, marked with a ⒼⓈ icon, show the first few solution steps. Many of these exercises can be found in the MyMathLab homework, providing guidance to students as they start learning a new concept or procedure.

▶ *Updated Figures, Photos, and Hand-Drawn Graphs* Today's students are more visually oriented than ever. As a result, we include appealing mathematical figures, diagrams, tables, and graphs, including a "hand-drawn" style of graphs, whenever possible. We have incorporated depictions of well-known mathematicians as well as photos to accompany applications in examples and exercises.

▶ *Relevant Real-Life Applications* We include many new or updated applications from fields such as business, pop culture, sports, technology, and the health sciences that show the relevance of algebra to daily life.

▶ *Extensive and Varied Exercise Sets*   The text contains a wealth of exercises to provide students with opportunities to practice, apply, connect, review, and extend the skills they are learning. Numerous illustrations, tables, graphs, and photos help students visualize the problems they are solving. Problem types include skill building and writing exercises, as well as applications, matching, true/false, multiple-choice, and fill-in-the-blank problems.

In the Annotated Instructor's Edition of the text, the writing exercises are marked with an icon 🖉 so that instructors may assign these problems at their discretion. Students can watch an instructor work through the complete solution for all exercises marked with a Play Button icon ▶ in MyMathLab.

▶ *Special Summary Exercises*   We include a set of these popular in-chapter exercises in many chapters. They provide students with the all-important ***mixed review problems*** they need to master topics and often include summaries of solution methods and/or additional examples.

▶ *Step-by-Step Solutions to Selected Exercises*   Exercise numbers enclosed in a blue square, such as **11.**, indicate that a worked-out solution for the problem is available in MyMathLab. These solutions are given for selected exercises that most commonly cause students difficulty.

Resources for Success

MyMathLab Online Course for Lial/Hornsby/McGinnis *Introductory and Intermediate Algebra*, 6th edition

The corresponding MyMathLab course tightly integrates the authors' approach, giving students a learning environment that encourages conceptual understanding and engagement.

NEW! Learning Catalytics

Integrated into MyMathLab, Learning Catalytics use students' mobile devices for an engagement, assessment, and classroom intelligence system that gives instructors real-time feedback on student learning. LC annotations for instructors in the text provide corresponding questions that they can use to engage their classrooms.

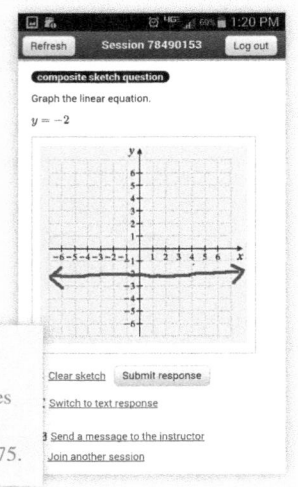

LC LEARNING CATALYTICS

1. Which digit in the number 40,163 is in the ones place?
2. Identify the place value of 8 in the number 9875.

5.5.14-GS   ≡ Question Help ⚙

Complete the division.

$2x - 6)\overline{12x^3 - 28x^2 - 8x - 48}$

To begin, set up the polynomials in a long division format if they aren't already written that way. Place them in descending order. Also, write in any missing terms, if necessary.

$2x - 6)\overline{12x^3 - 28x^2 - 8x - 48}$

What is the first step?

○ A. Divide the first term of the dividend by the first term of the divisor.
○ B. Divide the second term of the dividend by the second term of the divisor.
○ C. Divide the first term of the dividend by the second term of the divisor.
○ D. Multiply the first term of the dividend by the first term of the divisor.

Click to select your answer and then click Check Answer.   ②

10 parts remaining ▮▮▮   Clear All   Check Answer   ◄ ►

Expanded! Conceptual Exercises

In addition to MyMathLab's hallmark interactive exercises, the Lial team provides students with exercises that tie concepts together and help students problem-solve. Guided Solutions exercises, marked with a "GS" in the Assignment Manager, test student understanding of the problem-solving steps while guiding them through the solution process. Relating Concepts exercises in the text help students make connections and problem-solve at a higher level. These sets are assignable in MyMathLab, with expanded coverage.

NEW! Workspace Assignments

These new assignments allow students to naturally write out their work by hand, step-by-step, showing their mathematical reasoning as they receive instant feedback at each step. Each student's work is captured in the MyMathLab gradebook so instructors can easily pinpoint exactly where in the solution process students struggled.

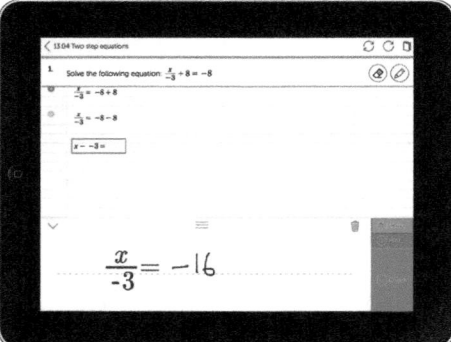

---

www.mymathlab.com

Resources for Success

Pearson

NEW! Adaptive Skill Builder

When students struggle on an exercise, Skill Builder assignments provide just-in-time, targeted support to help them build on the requisite skills needed to complete their assignment. As students progress, the Skill Builder assignments adapt to provide support exercises that are personalized to each student's activity and performance throughout the course.

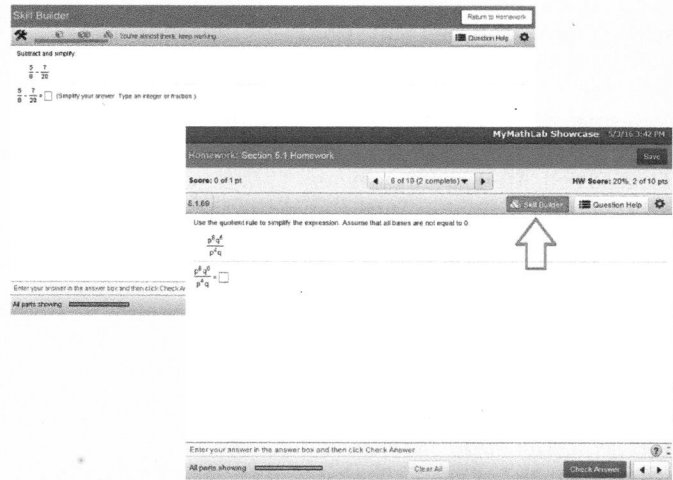

Instructor Resources

Annotated Instructor's Edition

ISBN 10: 0-13-444600-3 **ISBN 13:** 978-0-13-444600-4
The AIE provides annotations for instructors, including answers, Learning Catalytics suggestions, and vocabulary and teaching tips.

The following resources can be downloaded from www.pearsonhighered.com or in MyMathLab:

Instructor's Solutions Manual

This manual provides solutions to all exercises in the text.

Instructor's Resource Manual

This manual includes Mini-Lectures to provide new instructors with objectives, key examples, and teaching tips for every section of the text.

PowerPoints

These slides, which can be edited, present key concepts and definitions from the text.

TestGen

TestGen® (www.pearsoned.com/testgen) enables instructors to build, edit, print, and administer tests using a computerized bank of questions developed to cover all the objectives of the text.

Student Resources

Student Solutions Manual

ISBN 10: 0-13-444598-8 **ISBN 13:** 978-0-13-444598-4
This manual contains completely worked-out solutions for all the odd-numbered exercises in the text.

Lial Video Workbook

ISBN 10: 0-13-445686-6 **ISBN 13:** 978-0-13-445686-7
This workbook/note-taking guide helps students develop organized notes as they work along with the videos. The notebook includes

- Guided Examples to be used in conjunction with the Lial Section Lecture Videos and/or Objective-Level Video clips, plus corresponding Now Try This Exercises for each text objective.

- Extra practice exercises for every section of the text, with ample space for students to show their work.

- Learning objectives and key vocabulary terms for every text section, along with vocabulary practice problems.

www.mymathlab.com

ACKNOWLEDGMENTS

The comments, criticisms, and suggestions of users, nonusers, instructors, and students have positively shaped this text over the years, and we are most grateful for the many responses we have received. The feedback gathered for this revision of the text was particularly helpful, and we especially wish to thank the following individuals who provided invaluable suggestions for this and the previous editions:

Randall Allbritton, *Daytona State College*
Jannette Avery, *Monroe Community College*
Sarah E. Baxter, *Gloucester County College*
Linda Beattie, *Western New Mexico University*
Jean Bolyard, *Fairmont State College*
Tim C. Caldwell, *Meridian Community College*
Russell Campbell, *Fairmont State University*
Shawn Clift, *Eastern Kentucky University*
Bill Dunn, *Las Positas College*
Lucy Edwards, *Las Positas College*
Morris Elsen, *Cape Fear Community College*
J. Lloyd Harris, *Gulf Coast State College*
Terry Haynes, *Eastern Oklahoma State College*
Edith Hays, *Texas Woman's University*
Karen Heavin, *Morehead State University*
Christine Heinecke Lehmann, *Purdue University—North Central*
Elizabeth Heston, *Monroe Community College*
Sharon Jackson, *Brookhaven College*
Harriet Kiser, *Georgia Highlands College*
Valerie Lazzara, *Palm Beach State College*

Valerie H. Maley, *Cape Fear Community College*
Susan McClory, *San Jose State University*
Pam Miller, *Phoenix College*
Jeffrey Mills, *Ohio State University*
Linda J. Murphy, *Northern Essex Community College*
Celia Nippert, *Western Oklahoma State College*
Elizabeth Olgilvie, *Horry-Georgetown Technical College*
Enyinda Onunwor, *Stark State College*
Larry Pontaski, *Pueblo Community College*
Diann Robinson, *Ivy Tech State College—Lafayette*
Rachael Schettenhelm, *Southern Connecticut State University*
Jonathan Shands, *Cape Fear Community College*
Lee Ann Spahr, *Durham Technical Community College*
Carol Stewart, *Fairmont State University*
Fariheh Towfiq, *Palomar College*
Diane P. Veneziale, *Burlington County College*
Cora S. West, *Florida State College at Jacksonville*
Johanna Windmueller, *Seminole State College*
Gabriel Yimesghen, *Community College of Philadelphia*

Over the years, we have come to rely on an extensive team of experienced professionals. Our sincere thanks go to these dedicated individuals at Pearson Arts & Sciences, who worked hard to make this revision a success: Chris Hoag, Michael Hirsch, Sherry Berg, Shana Siegmund, Matt Summers, Alicia Frankel, and Ruth Berry.

We are especially pleased to welcome Callie Daniels to our team. She thoroughly reviewed all chapters and helped extensively with manuscript preparation. Special thanks to Shannon d'Hemecourt, who assisted once again with updating real data applications.

We are also grateful to Carol Merrigan and Marilyn Dwyer of Cenveo, Inc., for their excellent production work; Connie Day for her copyediting expertise; Cenveo for their photo research; and Lucie Haskins for producing another accurate, useful index. Jack Hornsby, Paul Lorczak, and Sarah Sponholz did a thorough, timely job accuracy checking page proofs and Jack Hornsby checked the index.

We particularly thank the many students and instructors who have used this text over the years. You are the reason we do what we do. It is our hope that we have positively impacted your mathematics journey. We would welcome any comments or suggestions you might have via email to math@pearson.com.

John Hornsby
Terry McGinnis

Prealgebra Review

R.1 Fractions

R.2 Decimals and Percents

Study Skills *Using Your Math Text*

R.1 | Fractions

The numbers used most often in everyday life are the **natural (counting) numbers,**

$$1, 2, 3, 4, \ldots,$$

The three dots, or *ellipsis points,* indicate that each list of numbers continues in the same way indefinitely.

the **whole numbers,**

$$0, 1, 2, 3, 4, \ldots,$$

and **fractions,** such as

$$\frac{1}{2}, \quad \frac{2}{3}, \quad \text{and} \quad \frac{11}{12}.$$

The parts of a fraction are named as follows.

$$\text{Fraction bar} \rightarrow \frac{3}{8} \begin{array}{l} \leftarrow \text{Numerator} \\ \leftarrow \text{Denominator} \end{array}$$

The fraction bar represents division $\left(\frac{a}{b} = a \div b\right)$*.*

OBJECTIVES

1 Identify prime numbers.

2 Write numbers in prime factored form.

3 Write fractions in lowest terms.

4 Convert between improper fractions and mixed numbers.

5 Multiply and divide fractions.

6 Add and subtract fractions.

7 Solve applied problems that involve fractions.

8 Interpret data in a circle graph.

Note

Fractions are a way to represent parts of a whole. In a fraction, the **numerator** gives the number of parts being represented. The **denominator** gives the total number of equal parts in the whole. See **Figure 1.**

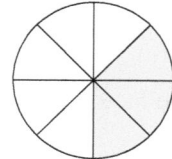

The shaded region represents $\frac{3}{8}$ of the circle.

Figure 1

A fraction is classified as being either a **proper fraction** or an **improper fraction.**

Proper fractions $\quad \dfrac{1}{5}, \dfrac{2}{7}, \dfrac{9}{10}, \dfrac{23}{25} \quad$ Numerator is **less than** denominator. Value is less than 1.

Improper fractions $\quad \dfrac{3}{2}, \dfrac{5}{5}, \dfrac{11}{7}, \dfrac{28}{4} \quad$ Numerator is **greater than or equal to** denominator. Value is greater than or equal to 1.

1

① Identify each number as *prime* or *composite*.

(a) 13

(b) 27

(c) 59

(d) 1806

② Write each number in prime factored form.

(a) 39

(b) 70

(c) 72

(d) 135

OBJECTIVE ① Identify prime numbers. In work with fractions, we will need to write numerators and denominators as *products*. A **product** is the answer to a multiplication problem. When 12 is written as the product 2×6, for example, 2 and 6 are **factors** of 12. Other factors of 12 are 1, 3, 4, and 12.

A natural number greater than 1 is **prime** if it has only itself and 1 as factors. "Factors" are understood here to mean natural number factors.

2, 3, 5, 7, 11, 13, 17, 19, 23, 29, 31, 37   First dozen prime numbers

A natural number greater than 1 that is not prime is a **composite number.**

4, 6, 8, 9, 10, 12, 14, 15, 16, 18, 20, 21   First dozen composite numbers

By agreement, the number 1 is neither prime nor composite.

EXAMPLE 1   Distinguishing between Prime and Composite Numbers

Identify each number as *prime* or *composite*.

(a) 33   Since 33 has factors of 3 and 11, as well as 1 and 33, it is composite.

(b) 43   There are no numbers other than 1 and 43 itself that divide *evenly* into 43, so the number 43 is prime.

(c) 9832   Since 9832 can be divided by 2, giving 2×4916, it is composite.

◀ **Work Problem ①** at the Side.

OBJECTIVE ② Write numbers in prime factored form. We *factor* a number by writing it as the product of two or more numbers.

Multiplication	Factoring	
$6 \cdot 3 = 18$	$18 = 6 \cdot 3$	Factoring is the reverse of multiplying two numbers to obtain the product.
↑ ↑ ↑	↑ ↑ ↑	
Factors Product	Product Factors	

Note

In algebra, a raised dot · is often used instead of the × symbol to indicate multiplication because × may be confused with the letter *x*.

A composite number written using factors that are all prime numbers is in **prime factored form.**

EXAMPLE 2   Writing Numbers in Prime Factored Form

Write each number in prime factored form.

(a) 35   We factor 35 using the prime factors 5 and 7 as $35 = 5 \cdot 7$.

(b) 24   We use a factor tree, as shown below. The prime factors are circled.

Divide by the least prime factor of 24, which is 2.	$24 = 2 \cdot 12$	
Divide 12 by 2 to find two factors of 12.	$24 = 2 \cdot 2 \cdot 6$	
Now factor 6 as $2 \cdot 3$.	$24 = \underbrace{2 \cdot 2 \cdot 2 \cdot 3}_{\text{All factors are prime.}}$	

◀ **Work Problem ②** at the Side.

Answers

1. **(a)** prime **(b)** composite **(c)** prime
   (d) composite

2. **(a)** $3 \cdot 13$ **(b)** $2 \cdot 5 \cdot 7$
   (c) $2 \cdot 2 \cdot 2 \cdot 3 \cdot 3$ **(d)** $3 \cdot 3 \cdot 3 \cdot 5$

Note

No matter which prime factor we start with when factoring, we will *always* obtain the same prime factorization. Verify that if we start with 3 instead of 2 in **Example 2(b)**, we obtain

$$24 = 3 \cdot 2 \cdot 2 \cdot 2.$$ The order of the factors is different, but the same prime factors result.

OBJECTIVE ❸ **Write fractions in lowest terms.** The following properties are useful when writing a fraction in *lowest terms*.

Properties of 1

Any nonzero number divided by itself is equal to 1. *Example:* $\frac{3}{3} = 1$

Any number multiplied by 1 remains the same. *Example:* $\frac{2}{5} \cdot 1 = \frac{2}{5}$

A fraction is in **lowest terms** when the numerator and denominator have no factors in common (other than 1).

Writing a Fraction in Lowest Terms

Step 1 Write the numerator and denominator in factored form.

Step 2 Replace each pair of factors common to the numerator and denominator with 1.

Step 3 Multiply the remaining factors in the numerator and in the denominator.

(This procedure is sometimes called **"simplifying the fraction."**)

EXAMPLE 3 **Writing Fractions in Lowest Terms**

Write each fraction in lowest terms.

(a) $\frac{10}{15} = \frac{2 \cdot 5}{3 \cdot 5} = \frac{2}{3} \cdot \frac{5}{5} = \frac{2}{3} \cdot 1 = \frac{2}{3}$ Use the first property of 1 to replace $\frac{5}{5}$ with 1.

(b) $\frac{15}{45}$ By inspection, the greatest common factor of 15 and 45 is **15**.

$$\frac{15}{45} = \frac{15}{3 \cdot 15} = \frac{1}{3 \cdot 1} = \frac{1}{3}$$ Remember to write 1 in the numerator.

If the greatest common factor is not obvious, factor the numerator and denominator into prime factors.

$$\frac{15}{45} = \frac{3 \cdot 5}{3 \cdot 3 \cdot 5} = \frac{1 \cdot 1}{3 \cdot 1 \cdot 1} = \frac{1}{3}$$ The same answer results.

(c) $\frac{150}{200} = \frac{3 \cdot 50}{4 \cdot 50} = \frac{3}{4} \cdot 1 = \frac{3}{4}$ 50 is the greatest common factor of 150 and 200.

Another strategy is to choose *any* common factor and work in stages.

$$\frac{150}{200} = \frac{15 \cdot 10}{20 \cdot 10} = \frac{3 \cdot 5 \cdot 10}{4 \cdot 5 \cdot 10} = \frac{3 \cdot 1 \cdot 1}{4 \cdot 1 \cdot 1} = \frac{3}{4}$$ The same answer results.

Work Problem ❸ at the Side. ▶

❸ Write each fraction in lowest terms.

(a) $\frac{8}{14}$

(b) $\frac{10}{70}$

(c) $\frac{72}{120}$

Answers

3. (a) $\frac{4}{7}$ (b) $\frac{1}{7}$ (c) $\frac{3}{5}$

4 Write $\frac{92}{5}$ as a mixed number.

5 Write $11\frac{2}{3}$ as an improper fraction.

Multiplying Fractions

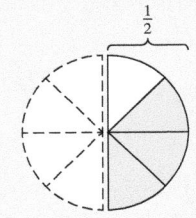

$\frac{3}{4}$ of $\frac{1}{2}$ is equivalent to $\frac{3}{4} \cdot \frac{1}{2}$, which equals $\frac{3}{8}$ of the circle.

Figure 2

Answers

4. $18\frac{2}{5}$

5. $\frac{35}{3}$

OBJECTIVE ▶ **4** **Convert between improper fractions and mixed numbers.** A **mixed number** is a single number that represents the sum of a natural number and a proper fraction.

$$\text{Mixed number} \rightarrow 5\frac{3}{4} = 5 + \frac{3}{4}$$

EXAMPLE 4   **Converting an Improper Fraction to a Mixed Number**

Write $\frac{59}{8}$ as a mixed number.

The fraction bar represents division. We divide the numerator of the improper fraction by the denominator.

$$\begin{array}{r} 7 \leftarrow \text{Quotient} \\ 8\overline{)59} \leftarrow \text{Numerator of fraction} \\ 56 \qquad\qquad \text{(dividend)} \\ \hline 3 \leftarrow \text{Remainder} \end{array}$$

Denominator of fraction (divisor) $\rightarrow$

$$\frac{59}{8} = 7\frac{3}{8}$$

◀ **Work Problem 4** at the Side.

EXAMPLE 5   **Converting a Mixed Number to an Improper Fraction**

Write $6\frac{4}{7}$ as an improper fraction.

We multiply the denominator of the fraction by the natural number and then add the numerator to obtain the numerator of the improper fraction.

$$7 \cdot 6 = 42 \quad \text{and} \quad 42 + 4 = 46$$

The denominator of the improper fraction is the same as the denominator in the mixed number, which is **7** here. Thus, $6\frac{4}{7} = \frac{46}{7}$.

◀ **Work Problem 5** at the Side.

OBJECTIVE ▶ **5** **Multiply and divide fractions.** See **Figure 2**.

Multiplying Fractions

To multiply two fractions, multiply the numerators to obtain the numerator of the product. Multiply the denominators to obtain the denominator of the product. *The product should be written in lowest terms.*

EXAMPLE 6   **Multiplying Fractions**

Find each product, and write it in lowest terms as needed.

(a) $\frac{3}{8} \cdot \frac{4}{9}$

$= \frac{3 \cdot 4}{8 \cdot 9}$ Multiply numerators. Multiply denominators.

$= \frac{3 \cdot 4}{2 \cdot 4 \cdot 3 \cdot 3}$ Factor the denominator.

$= \frac{1}{2 \cdot 3}$ $\frac{3}{3} = 1$ and $\frac{4}{4} = 1$; Remember to write 1 in the numerator.

$= \frac{1}{6}$ Write in lowest terms.

Continued on Next Page

(b)

$$2\frac{1}{3} \cdot 5\frac{1}{4}$$

$$= \frac{7}{3} \cdot \frac{21}{4}$$ Write each mixed number as an improper fraction.

$$= \frac{7 \cdot 21}{3 \cdot 4}$$ Multiply numerators. Multiply denominators.

$$= \frac{7 \cdot 3 \cdot 7}{3 \cdot 4}$$ Factor the numerator.

Think: $\frac{49}{4}$ means $49 \div 4$. $$= \frac{49}{4}, \quad \text{or} \quad 12\frac{1}{4}$$ Write in lowest terms and as a mixed number.

───────────────── **Work Problem ⑥ at the Side.** ▶

Two fractions are **reciprocals** of each other if their product is 1. See the table.

RECIPROCALS

Number	Reciprocal
$\frac{3}{4}$	$\frac{4}{3}$
$\frac{11}{7}$	$\frac{7}{11}$
$\frac{1}{5}$	5, or $\frac{5}{1}$
9, or $\frac{9}{1}$	$\frac{1}{9}$

Example: $\frac{3}{4} \cdot \frac{4}{3} = \frac{12}{12} = 1$

Because division is the inverse, or opposite, of multiplication, we use reciprocals to divide fractions.
    Figure 3 illustrates dividing fractions.

Dividing Fractions

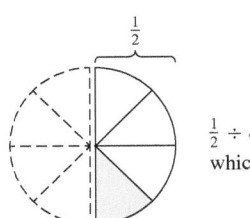

$\frac{1}{2} \div 4$ is equivalent to $\frac{1}{2} \cdot \frac{1}{4}$, which equals $\frac{1}{8}$ of the circle.

Figure 3

Dividing Fractions

To divide two fractions, multiply the first fraction by the reciprocal of the second. The result or **quotient** should be written in lowest terms.

As an example of why this procedure works, we know that

$$20 \div 10 = 2 \quad \text{and also that} \quad 20 \cdot \frac{1}{10} = 2.$$

⑥ Find each product, and write it in lowest terms as needed.

(a) $\frac{5}{6} \cdot \frac{3}{10}$

(b) $\frac{4}{7} \cdot \frac{5}{8}$

(c) $3\frac{1}{3} \cdot 1\frac{3}{4}$

Answers

6. (a) $\frac{1}{4}$ (b) $\frac{5}{14}$ (c) $\frac{35}{6}$, or $5\frac{5}{6}$

7 Find each quotient, and write it in lowest terms as needed.

(a) $\dfrac{2}{7} \div \dfrac{3}{10}$

(b) $\dfrac{3}{4} \div \dfrac{7}{16}$

(c) $\dfrac{4}{3} \div 6$

(d) $3\dfrac{1}{4} \div 1\dfrac{2}{5}$

EXAMPLE 7 **Dividing Fractions**

Find each quotient, and write it in lowest terms as needed.

(a) $\dfrac{3}{4} \div \dfrac{8}{5}$

$= \dfrac{3}{4} \cdot \dfrac{5}{8}$ Multiply by the reciprocal of the second fraction.

$= \dfrac{3 \cdot 5}{4 \cdot 8}$ Multiply numerators.
Multiply denominators.

$= \dfrac{15}{32}$ ◁ Make sure the quotient is in lowest terms.

(b) $\dfrac{3}{4} \div \dfrac{5}{8}$

$= \dfrac{3}{4} \cdot \dfrac{8}{5}$ Multiply by the reciprocal.

$= \dfrac{3 \cdot 4 \cdot 2}{4 \cdot 5}$ Multiply and factor.

$= \dfrac{6}{5},$ or $1\dfrac{1}{5}$

(c) $\dfrac{5}{8} \div 10$ ◁ Think of 10 as $\frac{10}{1}$ here.

$= \dfrac{5}{8} \cdot \dfrac{1}{10}$ Multiply by the reciprocal.

$= \dfrac{5 \cdot 1}{8 \cdot 2 \cdot 5}$ Multiply and factor.

$= \dfrac{1}{16}$ ◁ Remember to write 1 in the numerator.

(d) $1\dfrac{2}{3} \div 4\dfrac{1}{2}$

$= \dfrac{5}{3} \div \dfrac{9}{2}$ Write each mixed number as an improper fraction.

$= \dfrac{5}{3} \cdot \dfrac{2}{9}$ Multiply by the reciprocal of the second fraction.

$= \dfrac{10}{27}$ Multiply numerators and denominators.
The quotient is in lowest terms.

◀ **Work Problem 7 at the Side.**

OBJECTIVE 6 Add and subtract fractions. The result of adding two numbers is the **sum** of the numbers. **Figure 4** illustrates adding fractions.

Adding Fractions

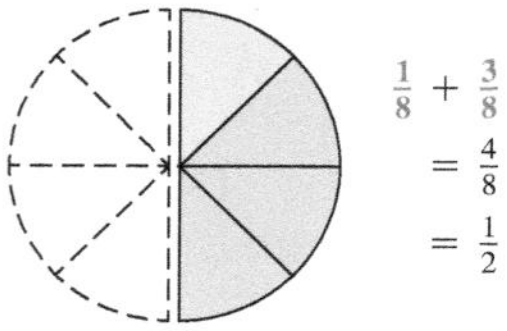

$\dfrac{1}{8} + \dfrac{3}{8}$

$= \dfrac{4}{8}$

$= \dfrac{1}{2}$

Figure 4

Adding Fractions

To find the sum of two fractions with the *same* denominator, add their numerators and *keep the same denominator.*

Answers

7. (a) $\dfrac{20}{21}$ (b) $\dfrac{12}{7}$, or $1\dfrac{5}{7}$ (c) $\dfrac{2}{9}$

(d) $\dfrac{65}{28}$, or $2\dfrac{9}{28}$

EXAMPLE 8 Adding Fractions (Same Denominator)

Find each sum, and write it in lowest terms as needed.

(a) $\dfrac{3}{7} + \dfrac{2}{7}$

$= \dfrac{3+2}{7}$ — Add numerators. Keep the same denominator.

$= \dfrac{5}{7}$ — The answer is in lowest terms.

(b) $\dfrac{2}{10} + \dfrac{3}{10}$

$= \dfrac{2+3}{10}$ — Add numerators. Keep the same denominator.

$= \dfrac{5}{10}$

$= \dfrac{1}{2}$ — Write in lowest terms.

──────── **Work Problem 8 at the Side.** ▶

If the fractions to be added do not have the same denominator, we must first rewrite them with a common denominator. For example, to rewrite $\frac{3}{4}$ as a fraction with a denominator of 12, think as follows.

$$\frac{3}{4} = \frac{?}{12}$$

We must find the number that can be multiplied by 4 to give 12. Because $4 \cdot 3 = 12$, by the second property of 1, we multiply the numerator and the denominator by 3.

$$\frac{3}{4} = \frac{3}{4} \cdot 1 = \frac{3}{4} \cdot \frac{3}{3} = \frac{3 \cdot 3}{4 \cdot 3} = \frac{9}{12}$$ ◁ $\frac{3}{4}$ is equivalent to $\frac{9}{12}$. See **Figure 5.**

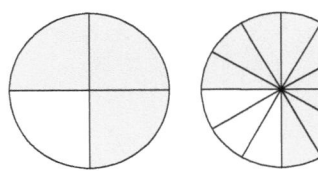

$\frac{3}{4}$ and $\frac{9}{12}$ are equivalent fractions.

Figure 5

Note

The process of writing an equivalent fraction is the reverse of writing a fraction in lowest terms.

Finding the Least Common Denominator (LCD)

To add or subtract fractions with different denominators, find the **least common denominator (LCD)** as follows.

Step 1 Write each denominator in prime factored form.

Step 2 The LCD is the product of every (different) factor that appears in any of the factored denominators. If a factor is repeated, use the greatest number of repeats as factors of the LCD.

Step 3 Write each fraction with the LCD as the denominator, using the second property of 1.

8 Find each sum, and write it in lowest terms as needed.

(a) $\dfrac{5}{11} + \dfrac{3}{11}$

(b) $\dfrac{5}{14} + \dfrac{3}{14}$

(c) $\dfrac{3}{5} + \dfrac{4}{5}$

Answers

8. (a) $\dfrac{8}{11}$ (b) $\dfrac{4}{7}$ (c) $\dfrac{7}{5}$, or $1\dfrac{2}{5}$

9 Find each sum, and write it in lowest terms as needed.

(a) $\dfrac{5}{12} + \dfrac{3}{8}$

(b) $\dfrac{7}{30} + \dfrac{2}{45}$

(c) $2\dfrac{1}{8} + 1\dfrac{2}{3}$

(d) $4\dfrac{5}{6} + 2\dfrac{1}{3}$

Answers

9. (a) $\dfrac{19}{24}$ (b) $\dfrac{5}{18}$ (c) $\dfrac{91}{24}$, or $3\dfrac{19}{24}$

(d) $\dfrac{43}{6}$, or $7\dfrac{1}{6}$

EXAMPLE 9   Adding Fractions (Different Denominators)

Find each sum, and write it in lowest terms as needed.

(a) $\dfrac{4}{15} + \dfrac{5}{9}$

Step 1   To find the LCD, write each denominator in prime factored form.

$$15 = 5 \cdot 3 \quad \text{and} \quad 9 = 3 \cdot 3$$

3 is a factor of both denominators.

Step 2 $\text{LCD} = 5 \cdot 3 \cdot 3 = 45$

In this example, the LCD needs one factor of 5 and two factors of 3 because the second denominator has two factors of 3.

Step 3   Now we can use the second property of 1 to write each fraction with 45 as the denominator.

$$\frac{4}{15} = \frac{4}{15} \cdot \frac{3}{3} = \frac{12}{45} \quad \text{and} \quad \frac{5}{9} = \frac{5}{9} \cdot \frac{5}{5} = \frac{25}{45}$$

At this stage, the fractions are *not* in lowest terms.

$$\frac{4}{15} + \frac{5}{9}$$

$$= \frac{12}{45} + \frac{25}{45} \qquad \text{Use the equivalent fractions with the common denominator.}$$

Make sure the sum is in lowest terms.

$$= \frac{37}{45} \qquad \text{Add numerators.}$$

Keep the same denominator.

(b) $3\dfrac{1}{2} + 2\dfrac{3}{4}$

Method 1 $3\dfrac{1}{2} + 2\dfrac{3}{4}$

$$= \frac{7}{2} + \frac{11}{4} \qquad \text{Write each mixed number as an improper fraction.}$$

Think: $\frac{7 \cdot 2}{2 \cdot 2} = \frac{14}{4}$

$$= \frac{14}{4} + \frac{11}{4} \qquad \text{Find a common denominator. The LCD is 4.}$$

$$= \frac{25}{4}, \quad \text{or} \quad 6\dfrac{1}{4} \qquad \text{Add. Write as a mixed number.}$$

Method 2 $3\dfrac{1}{2} = 3\dfrac{2}{4}$ Write $3\dfrac{1}{2}$ as $3\dfrac{2}{4}$. Then add vertically. Add the natural numbers and the fractions separately.

$+ 2\dfrac{3}{4} = 2\dfrac{3}{4}$

$$5\dfrac{5}{4} = 5 + 1\dfrac{1}{4} = 6\dfrac{1}{4}, \quad \text{or} \quad \frac{25}{4} \qquad \text{The same answer results.}$$

◀ **Work Problem 9 at the Side.**

The result of subtracting one number from another number is the **difference** of the numbers. **Figure 6** illustrates subtracting fractions.

Subtracting Fractions

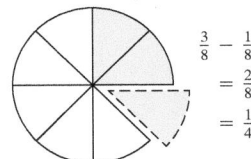

$$\frac{3}{8} - \frac{1}{8}$$
$$= \frac{2}{8}$$
$$= \frac{1}{4}$$

Figure 6

Subtracting Fractions

To find the difference of two fractions with the *same* denominator, subtract their numerators and **keep the same denominator.**

If the fractions have *different* denominators, write them with a common denominator first.

EXAMPLE 10 **Subtracting Fractions**

Find each difference, and write it in lowest terms as needed.

(a) $\dfrac{15}{8} - \dfrac{3}{8}$

$$= \frac{15 - 3}{8} \qquad \text{Subtract numerators.}$$
$$\qquad\qquad \text{Keep the same denominator.}$$

$$= \frac{12}{8}$$

$$= \frac{3}{2}, \quad \text{or} \quad 1\frac{1}{2} \qquad \begin{array}{l}\text{Write in lowest terms and}\\ \text{as a mixed number.}\end{array}$$

(b) $\dfrac{15}{16} - \dfrac{4}{9}$

$$= \frac{15}{16} \cdot \frac{9}{9} - \frac{4}{9} \cdot \frac{16}{16} \qquad \begin{array}{l}\text{Because 16 and 9 have no common}\\ \text{factors except 1, the LCD}\\ \text{is } 16 \cdot 9 = 144.\end{array}$$

$$= \frac{135}{144} - \frac{64}{144} \qquad \text{Write equivalent fractions.}$$

$$= \frac{71}{144} \qquad \begin{array}{l}\text{Subtract numerators.}\\ \text{Keep the common denominator.}\end{array}$$

(c) $\dfrac{7}{18} - \dfrac{4}{15}$

$$= \frac{7}{2 \cdot 3 \cdot 3} \cdot \frac{5}{5} - \frac{4}{3 \cdot 5} \cdot \frac{2 \cdot 3}{2 \cdot 3} \qquad \begin{array}{l}18 = 2 \cdot 3 \cdot 3 \text{ and } 15 = 3 \cdot 5, \text{ so}\\ \text{the LCD is } 2 \cdot 3 \cdot 3 \cdot 5 = 90.\end{array}$$

$$= \frac{35}{90} - \frac{24}{90} \qquad \text{Write equivalent fractions.}$$

$$= \frac{11}{90} \qquad \begin{array}{l}\text{Subtract. The answer is in}\\ \text{lowest terms.}\end{array}$$

Continued on Next Page

10 Find each difference, and write it in lowest terms as needed.

(a) $\dfrac{9}{11} - \dfrac{3}{11}$

(b) $\dfrac{5}{11} - \dfrac{2}{9}$

(c) $\dfrac{13}{15} - \dfrac{5}{6}$

(d) $2\dfrac{3}{8} - 1\dfrac{1}{2}$

(e) $10\dfrac{1}{4} - 2\dfrac{2}{3}$

(d) $4\dfrac{1}{2} - 1\dfrac{3}{4}$

Method 1 $4\dfrac{1}{2} - 1\dfrac{3}{4}$

$= \dfrac{9}{2} - \dfrac{7}{4}$ Write each mixed number as an improper fraction.

Think: $\dfrac{9 \cdot 2}{2 \cdot 2} = \dfrac{18}{4}$ $= \dfrac{18}{4} - \dfrac{7}{4}$ Find a common denominator. The LCD is 4.

$= \dfrac{11}{4}$, or $2\dfrac{3}{4}$ Subtract. Write as a mixed number.

Method 2 $4\dfrac{1}{2} = 4\dfrac{2}{4} = 3\dfrac{6}{4}$ The LCD is 4. $4\dfrac{2}{4} = 3 + 1 + \dfrac{2}{4} = 3 + \dfrac{4}{4} + \dfrac{2}{4} = 3\dfrac{6}{4}$

$- 1\dfrac{3}{4} = 1\dfrac{3}{4} = 1\dfrac{3}{4}$

$\overline{}$

$2\dfrac{3}{4}$, or $\dfrac{11}{4}$ The same answer results.

◀ **Work Problem 10 at the Side.**

OBJECTIVE ▶ 7 Solve applied problems that involve fractions.

EXAMPLE 11 Solving an Applied Problem with Fractions

The diagram in **Figure 7** appears with directions for a woodworking project. Find the height of the desk to the top of the writing surface.

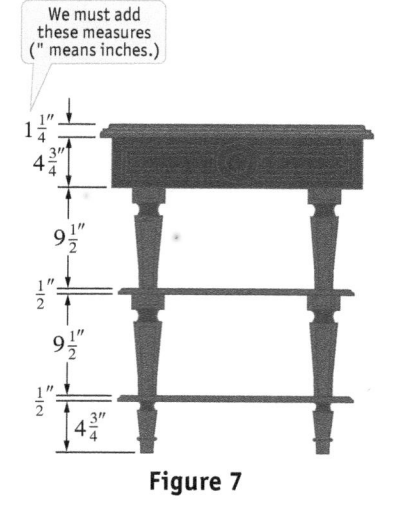

We must add these measures (" means inches.)

Figure 7

Think: $\dfrac{15}{4}$ means $15 \div 4$.

$1\dfrac{1}{4} \rightarrow 1\dfrac{1}{4}$ Add the section and writing surface heights to obtain the total height. The common denominator is 4.

$4\dfrac{3}{4} \rightarrow 4\dfrac{3}{4}$

$9\dfrac{1}{2} = 9\dfrac{2}{4}$

$\dfrac{1}{2} = \dfrac{2}{4}$

$9\dfrac{1}{2} = 9\dfrac{2}{4}$

$\dfrac{1}{2} = \dfrac{2}{4}$

$+ 4\dfrac{3}{4} \rightarrow 4\dfrac{3}{4}$

$\overline{}$

$27\dfrac{15}{4}$ Because $\dfrac{15}{4}$ is an improper fraction, this is not the final answer.

Because $\dfrac{15}{4} = 3\dfrac{3}{4}$, we have $27\dfrac{15}{4} = 27 + 3\dfrac{3}{4} = 30\dfrac{3}{4}$. The height is $30\dfrac{3}{4}$ in.

◀ **Work Problem 11 at the Side.**

---

11 Solve the problem.

To make a three-piece outfit from the same fabric, Jen needs $1\dfrac{1}{4}$ yd for the blouse, $1\dfrac{2}{3}$ yd for the skirt, and $2\dfrac{1}{2}$ yd for the jacket. How much fabric does she need?

Answers

10. (a) $\dfrac{6}{11}$ (b) $\dfrac{23}{99}$ (c) $\dfrac{1}{30}$ (d) $\dfrac{7}{8}$

(e) $7\dfrac{7}{12}$

11. $5\dfrac{5}{12}$ yd

EXAMPLE 12 Solving an Applied Problem with Fractions

An upholsterer needs $2\frac{1}{4}$ yd from a bolt of fabric to cover a chair. How many chairs can be covered with $23\frac{2}{3}$ yd of fabric?

To better understand the problem, we replace the fractions with whole numbers. Suppose each chair requires 2 yd, and we have 24 yd of fabric. Dividing 24 by 2 gives 12, the number of chairs that can be covered. To solve the original problem, we must divide $23\frac{2}{3}$ by $2\frac{1}{4}$.

$$23\frac{2}{3} \div 2\frac{1}{4}$$

$$= \frac{71}{3} \div \frac{9}{4} \qquad \text{Convert each mixed number to an improper fraction.}$$

$$= \frac{71}{3} \cdot \frac{4}{9} \qquad \text{Multiply by the reciprocal.}$$

$$= \frac{284}{27}, \quad \text{or} \quad 10\frac{14}{27} \qquad \begin{array}{l}\text{Multiply numerators.}\\ \text{Multiply denominators.}\\ \text{Write as a mixed number.}\end{array}$$

Thus, 10 chairs can be covered, with some fabric left over.

————————————————— Work Problem **12** at the Side. ▶

OBJECTIVE ▶ 8 Interpret data in a circle graph. In a **circle graph,** or **pie chart,** a circle is used to indicate the total of all the data categories represented. The circle is divided into *sectors,* or wedges, whose sizes show the relative magnitudes of the categories. The sum of all the fractional parts must be 1 (for 1 whole circle).

EXAMPLE 13 Using a Circle Graph to Interpret Information

In September 2015, there were about 3300 million (3.3 billion) Internet users worldwide. The circle graph in **Figure 8** shows the fractions of these users living in various regions of the world.

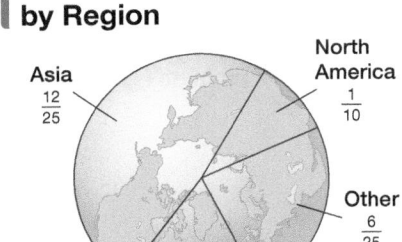

Worldwide Internet Users by Region

North America $\frac{1}{10}$

Asia $\frac{12}{25}$

Other $\frac{6}{25}$

Europe $\frac{9}{50}$

Data from www.internetworldstats.com

Figure 8

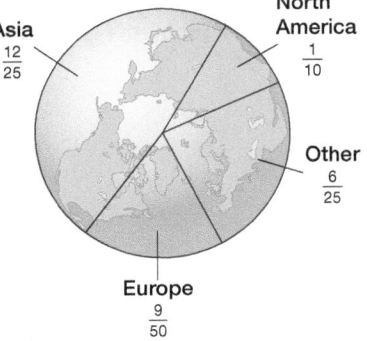

(a) Which region had the largest share of Internet users? What was that share?

In the circle graph, the sector for Asia is the largest, so Asia had the largest share of Internet users, $\frac{12}{25}$.

————————————————— **Continued on Next Page**

12 Solve the problem.

A gallon of paint covers 500 ft². (ft² means square feet.) To paint his house, Tram needs enough paint to cover 4200 ft². How many gallons of paint should he buy?

Answer

12. $8\frac{2}{5}$ gal are needed, so he should buy 9 gal.

13 Refer to the circle graph in **Figure 8.**

(a) Which region had the second-largest number of Internet users in September 2015?

(b) *Estimate* the number of Internet users in Asia.

(c) How many *actual* Internet users were there in Asia?

(b) *Estimate* the number of Internet users in Europe.

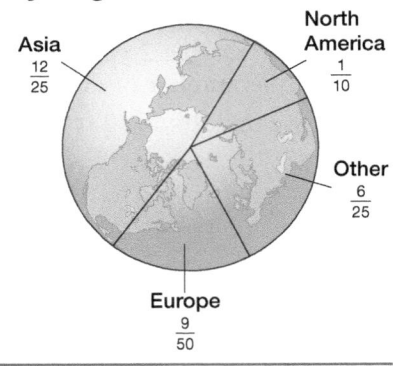

Worldwide Internet Users by Region

Data from www.internetworldstats.com

Figure 8 (repeated)

From the graph, a share of $\frac{9}{50}$ for Europe can be rounded to $\frac{10}{50}$, or $\frac{1}{5}$. The total number of Internet users, 3300 million, can be rounded to 3000 million (3 billion).

$$\frac{1}{5} \cdot 3000 = 600 \text{ million}$$ Multiply to estimate the number of Internet users in Europe.

(c) How many *actual* Internet users were there in Europe?

$$\frac{9}{50} \cdot 3300$$ Multiply the actual fraction from the graph for Europe by the number of Internet users.

$$= \frac{9}{50} \cdot \frac{3300}{1}$$ $a = \frac{a}{1}$ for all a.

$$= \frac{29,700}{50}$$ Multiply numerators.
Multiply denominators.

$$= 594$$ Divide.

Thus, 594 million, or 594,000,000 people in Europe used the Internet.

◀ **Work Problem 13 at the Side.**

Answers

13. (a) Other   (b) 1500 million
   (c) 1584 million

R.1 Exercises

FOR EXTRA HELP

Go to MyMathLab for worked-out, step-by-step solutions to exercises enclosed in a square ⬜ and video solutions to ▶ exercises.

CONCEPT CHECK *Decide whether each statement is* true *or* false. *If it is* false, *explain why.*

1. In the fraction $\frac{3}{7}$, 3 is the numerator and 7 is the denominator.

2. The mixed number equivalent of the improper fraction $\frac{41}{5}$ is $8\frac{1}{5}$.

3. The fraction $\frac{7}{7}$ is a proper fraction.

4. The number 1 is prime.

5. The fraction $\frac{17}{51}$ is in lowest terms.

6. The reciprocal of $\frac{8}{2}$ is $\frac{4}{1}$.

7. The product of 8 and 2 is 10.

8. The difference of 12 and 2 is 6.

Identify each number as prime *or* composite. ***See Example 1.***

9. 19

10. 61

11. 52

12. 99

13. 2468

14. 3125

15. 97

16. 83

Write each number in prime factored form. ***See Example 2.***

17. 30 ▶

18. 50

19. 57

20. 51

21. 124 ▶

22. 165

23. 252

24. 168

25. 500

26. 700

Write each fraction in lowest terms. ***See Example 3.***

27. $\frac{15}{18}$ ▶

28. $\frac{16}{20}$

29. $\frac{8}{16}$

30. $\frac{4}{12}$

31. $\frac{15}{50}$

32. $\frac{24}{64}$

33. $\frac{18}{90}$

34. $\frac{16}{64}$

35. $\frac{90}{150}$

36. $\frac{100}{140}$

Write each improper fraction as a mixed number. ***See Example 4.***

37. $\frac{77}{12}$

38. $\frac{101}{15}$

39. $\frac{83}{11}$

40. $\frac{67}{13}$

41. $\frac{12}{7}$

42. $\frac{16}{9}$

Write each mixed number as an improper fraction. **See Example 5.**

43. $2\frac{3}{5}$ **44.** $5\frac{6}{7}$ **45.** $10\frac{3}{8}$ **46.** $12\frac{2}{3}$ **47.** $10\frac{1}{5}$ **48.** $18\frac{1}{6}$

CONCEPT CHECK *Choose the letter of the correct response.*

49. For the fractions $\frac{p}{q}$ and $\frac{r}{s}$, which can serve as a common denominator?

     A. $q \cdot s$ **B.** $q + s$ **C.** $p \cdot r$ **D.** $p + r$

50. Which fraction is *not* equal to $\frac{5}{9}$?

     A. $\frac{15}{27}$ **B.** $\frac{30}{54}$ **C.** $\frac{40}{74}$ **D.** $\frac{55}{99}$

Find each product or quotient, and write it in lowest terms as needed.
See Examples 6 and 7.

51. $\frac{4}{5} \cdot \frac{6}{7}$ **52.** $\frac{5}{9} \cdot \frac{2}{7}$ **53.** $\frac{5}{12} \cdot \frac{3}{10}$ **54.** $\frac{3}{4} \cdot \frac{2}{15}$

55. $\frac{1}{10} \cdot \frac{12}{5}$ **56.** $\frac{1}{8} \cdot \frac{10}{7}$ **57.** $\frac{15}{4} \cdot \frac{8}{25}$ **58.** $\frac{21}{8} \cdot \frac{4}{7}$

59. $3\frac{1}{4} \cdot 1\frac{2}{3}$ **60.** $2\frac{2}{3} \cdot 1\frac{3}{5}$ **61.** $2\frac{3}{8} \cdot 3\frac{1}{5}$ **62.** $3\frac{3}{5} \cdot 7\frac{1}{6}$

63. $\frac{2}{5} \div \frac{7}{9}$ **64.** $\frac{2}{3} \div \frac{5}{7}$ **65.** $\frac{5}{4} \div \frac{3}{8}$ **66.** $\frac{7}{5} \div \frac{3}{10}$

67. $\frac{32}{5} \div \frac{8}{15}$ **68.** $\frac{24}{7} \div \frac{6}{21}$ **69.** $\frac{3}{4} \div 12$ **70.** $\frac{2}{5} \div 30$

71. $1\frac{3}{5} \div 2\frac{1}{3}$ **72.** $1\frac{1}{3} \div 2\frac{1}{2}$ **73.** $2\frac{5}{8} \div 1\frac{15}{32}$ **74.** $2\frac{3}{10} \div 1\frac{4}{5}$

Find each sum or difference, and write it in lowest terms as needed.
See Examples 8–10.

75. $\frac{7}{15} + \frac{4}{15}$ **76.** $\frac{2}{9} + \frac{5}{9}$ **77.** $\frac{7}{12} + \frac{1}{12}$ **78.** $\frac{3}{16} + \frac{5}{16}$

79. $\frac{5}{9} + \frac{1}{3}$ **80.** $\frac{4}{15} + \frac{1}{5}$ **81.** $\frac{3}{8} + \frac{5}{6}$ **82.** $\frac{5}{6} + \frac{2}{9}$

83. $3\frac{1}{8} + 2\frac{1}{4}$

84. $4\frac{2}{3} + 2\frac{1}{6}$

85. $\frac{7}{9} - \frac{2}{9}$

86. $\frac{8}{11} - \frac{3}{11}$

87. $\frac{13}{15} - \frac{3}{15}$

88. $\frac{11}{12} - \frac{3}{12}$

89. $\frac{7}{12} - \frac{1}{9}$

90. $\frac{11}{16} - \frac{1}{12}$

91. $6\frac{1}{4} - 5\frac{1}{3}$

92. $5\frac{1}{3} - 4\frac{1}{2}$

93. $\frac{5}{3} + \frac{1}{6} - \frac{1}{2}$

94. $\frac{7}{15} + \frac{1}{6} - \frac{1}{10}$

Solve each problem. ***See Examples 11 and 12.***

Use the chart to work Exercises 95 and 96.

95. How many cups of dry grits would be needed for eight microwave servings of Quaker Quick Grits?

96. How many teaspoons of salt would be needed for five stove-top servings? (*Hint:* 5 is halfway between 4 and 6.)

	Microwave	Stove Top		
Servings	**1**	**1**	**4**	**6**
Water or Milk	1 cup	1 cup	4 cups	6 cups
Grits	$\frac{1}{4}$ cup	$\frac{1}{2}$ cup	1 cup	$1\frac{1}{2}$ cups
Salt (optional)	Dash	Dash	$\frac{1}{4}$ tsp	$\frac{1}{2}$ tsp

Data from www.quakeroats.com

97. A piece of property has an irregular shape, with five sides as shown in the figure. Find the total distance around the piece of property. This distance is the **perimeter** of the figure.

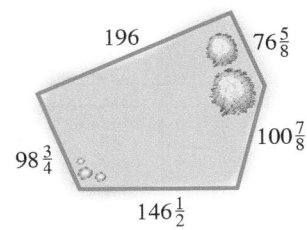

Measurements in feet

98. A triangle has sides of lengths $5\frac{1}{4}$ ft, $7\frac{1}{2}$ ft, and $10\frac{1}{8}$ ft. Find the perimeter of the triangle.
See Exercise 97.

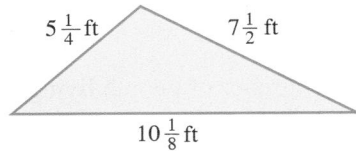

99. A hardware store sells a 40-piece socket wrench set. The measure of the largest socket is $\frac{3}{4}$ in., while the measure of the smallest socket is $\frac{3}{16}$ in. What is the difference between these measures?

100. Two sockets in a socket wrench set have measures of $\frac{9}{16}$ in. and $\frac{3}{8}$ in. What is the difference between these two measures?

101. Under existing standards, most of the holes in Swiss cheese must have diameters between $\frac{11}{16}$ and $\frac{13}{16}$ in. To accommodate new high-speed slicing machines, the U.S. Department of Agriculture wants to reduce the minimum size to $\frac{3}{8}$ in. How much smaller is $\frac{3}{8}$ in. than $\frac{11}{16}$ in.? (Data from U.S. Department of Agriculture.)

102. The Pride Golf Tee Company, the only U.S. manufacturer of wooden golf tees, has created the Professional Tee System. Two lengths of tees are the ProLength Max and the Shortee, as shown in the figure. How much longer is the ProLength Max than the Shortee? (Data from *The Gazette*.)

Shortee

$2\frac{1}{8}$ in.

ProLength Max

4 in.

103. A cake recipe calls for $1\frac{3}{4}$ cups of sugar. A caterer has $15\frac{1}{2}$ cups of sugar on hand. How many cakes can he make?

104. Kyla needs $1\frac{1}{8}$ yd of fabric to make a pillow. How many pillows can she make with $8\frac{3}{4}$ yd of fabric?

105. It takes $2\frac{3}{8}$ yd from a bolt of fabric to make a costume for a school play. How much fabric would be needed for seven costumes?

106. A cookie recipe calls for $2\frac{2}{3}$ cups of sugar. How much sugar would be needed to make four batches of cookies?

Approximately 40 million people living in the United States were born in other countries. The circle graph gives the fractional number from each region of birth for these people. Use the graph to work each problem. **See Example 13.**

107. Estimate the number of people living in the United States who were born in Asia.

108. Estimate the number of people living in the United States who were born in Latin America.

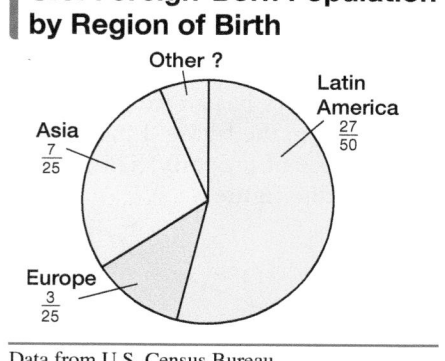

U.S. Foreign-Born Population by Region of Birth

Other ?

Latin America $\frac{27}{50}$

Asia $\frac{7}{25}$

Europe $\frac{3}{25}$

Data from U.S. Census Bureau.

109. How many people (in millions) were born in Europe?

110. How many people (in millions) were born in Latin America?

111. What fractional part of the foreign-born population was from other regions?

112. What fractional part of the foreign-born population was from Latin America or Asia?

R.2 | Decimals and Percents

Fractions are one way to represent parts of a whole. Another way is with a decimal fraction or **decimal,** a number written with a decimal point.

9.4,   14.001,   0.25   Decimal numbers

Each digit in a decimal number has a place value, as shown below.

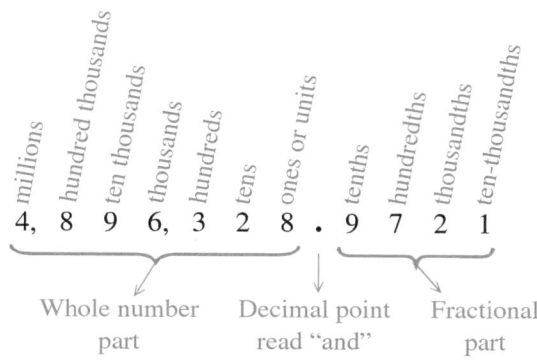

Whole number part — **Decimal point read "and"** — **Fractional part**

Each successive place value is ten times greater than the place value to its right and one-tenth as great as the place value to its left.

OBJECTIVE ▶ ❶ **Write decimals as fractions.** Place value is used to write a decimal number as a fraction.

Converting a Decimal to a Fraction

Read the decimal using the correct place value. Write it in fractional form just as it is read.

- The numerator will be the digits to the right of the decimal point.
- The denominator will be a power of 10—that is, 10 for tenths, 100 for hundredths, and so on.

EXAMPLE 1 | **Writing Decimals as Fractions**

Write each decimal as a fraction. (Do not write in lowest terms.)

(a) 0.95   We read 0.95 as "**ninety-five hundredths.**"

$$0.95 = \frac{95}{100} \leftarrow \text{For hundredths}$$

(b) 0.056   We read 0.056 as "**fifty-six thousandths.**"

$$0.056 = \frac{56}{1000}$$
↑
For thousandths

> Do not confuse **0.056** with **0.56,** read "fifty-six *hundredths,*" which is the fraction $\frac{56}{100}$.

--- **Continued on Next Page** ---

Continued on Next Page

OBJECTIVES

❶ Write decimals as fractions.
❷ Add and subtract decimals.
❸ Multiply and divide decimals.
❹ Write fractions as decimals.
❺ Write percents as decimals and decimals as percents.
❻ Write percents as fractions and fractions as percents.
❼ Solve applied problems that involve percents.

1 Write each decimal as a fraction. (Do not write in lowest terms.)

(a) 0.8

(b) 0.431

(c) 2.58

2 Add or subtract as indicated.

(a) $68.9 + 42.72 + 8.973$

(b) $351.8 - 2.706$

(c) $32 - 21.72$

(c) 4.2095   We read this decimal number, which is greater than 1, as "Four *and* two thousand ninety-five ten-thousandths."

$$4.2095 = 4\,\frac{2095}{10{,}000}$$ Write the decimal number as a mixed number.

$$= \frac{42{,}095}{10{,}000}$$ Write the mixed number as an improper fraction.

◄ **Work Problem 1** at the Side.

OBJECTIVE ▶ 2 Add and subtract decimals.

EXAMPLE 2 Adding and Subtracting Decimals

Add or subtract as indicated.

(a) $6.92 + 14.8 + 3.217$

Place the digits of the decimal numbers in columns by place value, so that tenths are in one column, hundredths in another column, and so on.

Be sure to line up decimal points.

```
    6.92      Decimal points are aligned.
   14.8
 + 3.217
  24.937
```

To avoid errors, attach zeros as placeholders so there are the same number of places to the right of each decimal point.

```
    6.92              6.920    Attach 0s.
   14.8    becomes   14.800
 + 3.217            + 3.217
                     24.937
```

6.92 is equivalent to 6.920.
14.8 is equivalent to 14.800.

(b) $47.6 - 32.509$

```
    47.6               47.600    Write the decimal numbers
 - 32.509   becomes  - 32.509    in columns, attaching 0s as
                       15.091    needed.
```

(c) $3 - 0.253$

```
    3.000    A whole number is assumed to have the
 - 0.253     decimal point at the right of the number.
   2.747     Write 3 as 3.000.
```

◄ **Work Problem 2** at the Side.

OBJECTIVE ▶ 3 Multiply and divide decimals. To multiply decimals, follow these steps.

Multiplying Decimals

Step 1 Ignore the decimal points and multiply as if the numbers were whole numbers.

Step 2 Add the number of **decimal places** (digits to the *right* of the decimal point) in each factor. Place the decimal point that many digits from the right in the product.

Answers

1. (a) $\frac{8}{10}$ (b) $\frac{431}{1000}$ (c) $\frac{258}{100}$

2. (a) 120.593 (b) 349.094 (c) 10.28

EXAMPLE 3 Multiplying Decimals

Multiply.

(a) 29.3×4.52

$$
\begin{array}{r}
29.3 \\
\times\ 4.52 \\
\hline
586 \\
1465\ \\
1172\ \ \\
\hline
132.436
\end{array}
$$

1 decimal place
2 decimal places
$1 + 2 = 3$
3 decimal places

(b) 31.42×65

$$
\begin{array}{r}
31.42 \\
\times\ \ 65 \\
\hline
15710 \\
18852\ \\
\hline
2042.30
\end{array}
$$

2 decimal places
0 decimal places
$2 + 0 = 2$
2 decimal places

The final 0 can be dropped and the product written 2042.3.

(c) 0.05×0.3

Here $5 \times 3 = 15$. Be careful placing the decimal point.

2 decimal places   1 decimal place
$$0.05 \quad \times \quad 0.3$$
$$= 0.015$$ — Do **not** write 0.150.

$2 + 1 = 3$ decimal places
Attach 0 as a placeholder in the tenths place.

——————— **Work Problem ③ at the Side.** ▶

To divide decimals, follow these steps.

Dividing Decimals

Step 1 Change the **divisor** (the number we are dividing *by*) into a whole number by moving the decimal point as many places as necessary to the right.

Step 2 Move the decimal point in the **dividend** (the number we are dividing *into*) to the right by the same number of places.

Step 3 Move the decimal point straight up, and then divide as with whole numbers to find the **quotient.**

EXAMPLE 4 Dividing Decimals

Divide.

(a) $233.45 \div 11.5$

Write the problem as follows. $11.5\overline{)233.45}$

$11.5\overline{)233.4\,5}$ To change the divisor 11.5 into a whole number, move *each* decimal point one place to the right.

To see why this works, write the division in fraction form and multiply by $\frac{10}{10}$. The result is the same as when we moved the decimal point one place to the right in the divisor and the dividend.

$$\frac{233.45}{11.5} \cdot \frac{10}{10} = \frac{2334.5}{115}$$ Multiplying by $\frac{10}{10}$ is equivalent to multiplying by 1.

——————— **Continued on Next Page**

③ Multiply.

(a) 9.32×1.4

(b) 2.13×51

(c) 0.06×0.004

$$\overset{5 \leftarrow \text{Quotient}}{\text{Divisor} \longrightarrow 25\overline{)125}}$$
↑ Dividend

Remember this terminology for the parts of a division problem.

Answers
3. (a) 13.048 (b) 108.63 (c) 0.00024

4 Divide.

(a) $451.47 \div 14.9$

(b) $5.476 \div 0.37$

(c) $7.334 \div 1.3$
(Round the quotient to two decimal places.)

Move the decimal point straight up, and divide as with whole numbers.

$$
\begin{array}{r}
20.3 \\
115\overline{)2334.5} \\
230 \\
\hline
345 \\
345 \\
\hline
0
\end{array}
$$

Move the decimal point straight up.

115 does not divide into 34, so we used 0 as a placeholder in the quotient.

(b) $8.949 \div 1.25$ (Round the quotient to two decimal places.)

$$1.25\overline{)8.949}$$

Move each decimal point two places to the right.

$$
\begin{array}{r}
7.159 \\
125\overline{)894.900} \\
875 \\
\hline
199 \\
125 \\
\hline
740 \\
625 \\
\hline
1150 \\
1125 \\
\hline
25
\end{array}
$$

Move the decimal point straight up, and divide as with whole numbers. Attach 0s as placeholders.

We carried out the division to three decimal places so that we could round to two decimal places, obtaining the quotient 7.16.

◀ **Work Problem 4 at the Side.**

Note

To round 7.159 in **Example 4(b)** to two decimal places (that is, to the nearest hundredth), we look at the digit to the *right* of the hundredths place. **If this digit is 5 or greater, we round up. If it is less than 5, we drop the digit(s) beyond the desired place.**

Hundredths place

7.15**9** 9, the digit to the right of the hundredths place, is 5 or greater.

≈ 7.16 Round 5 up to 6. $\approx$ means "is approximately equal to."

5 Multiply or divide as indicated.

(a) 294.72×10

(b) 19.5×1000

(c) $4.793 \div 100$

(d) $960.1 \div 10$

Multiplying or Dividing by Powers of 10 (Shortcuts)

• To **multiply** by a power of 10, **move the decimal point to the right** as many places as the number of zeros.

• To **divide** by a power of 10, **move the decimal point to the left** as many places as the number of zeros.

In both cases, insert 0s as placeholders if necessary.

EXAMPLE 5 Multiplying and Dividing by Powers of 10

Multiply or divide as indicated.

(a) 48.731×100

$= 48.73\ 1$ or 4873.1

Move the decimal point two places to the right because 100 has two 0s.

(b) $48.7 \div 1000$

$= 048.7$ or 0.0487

Move the decimal point three places to the left because 1000 has three 0s. Insert a 0 in front of the 4 to do this.

◀ **Work Problem 5 at the Side.**

OBJECTIVE ▸ 4 Write fractions as decimals.

Writing a Fraction as a Decimal

Because a fraction bar indicates division, write a fraction as a decimal by dividing the numerator by the denominator.

EXAMPLE 6 Writing Fractions as Decimals

Write each fraction as a decimal.

(a) $\dfrac{19}{8}$

$$8\overline{)19.000}$$ (2.375)

Divide 19 by 8. Add a decimal point and as many 0s as necessary.

$$\begin{array}{r} 16 \\ \hline 30 \\ 24 \\ \hline 60 \\ 56 \\ \hline 40 \\ 40 \\ \hline 0 \end{array}$$

$\dfrac{19}{8} = 2.375$ ← Terminating decimal

(b) $\dfrac{2}{3}$

$$3\overline{)2.0000\ldots}$$ (0.6666...)

$$\begin{array}{r} 18 \\ \hline 20 \\ 18 \\ \hline 20 \\ 18 \\ \hline 20 \\ 18 \\ \hline 2 \end{array}$$

$\dfrac{2}{3} = 0.6666\ldots$ ← Repeating decimal

• The remainder in the division in part (a) is 0, so this quotient is a **terminating decimal.**

• The remainder in the division in part (b) is never 0. Because a number, in this case 2, is always left after the subtraction, this quotient is a **repeating decimal.** A convenient notation for a repeating decimal is a bar over the digit (or digits) that repeats.

$$\dfrac{2}{3} = 0.6666\ldots, \quad \text{or} \quad 0.\overline{6}$$

We often round repeating decimals to as many places as needed.

$$\dfrac{2}{3} \approx 0.667 \quad \text{An approximation to the nearest thousandth}$$

Work Problem 6 at the Side. ▶

OBJECTIVE ▸ 5 Write percents as decimals and decimals as percents. The word **percent** means **"per 100."** Percent is written with the symbol **%**. *One percent means "one per one hundred," or "one one-hundredth."*

Percent, Fraction, and Decimal Equivalents

$$1\% = \frac{1}{100}, \quad \text{or} \quad 1\% = 0.01$$

EXAMPLE 7 Writing Percents as Decimals

Write each percent as a decimal.

(a) 73%   We use the fact that 1% = 0.01 and convert as follows.

$$73\% = 73 \cdot 1\% = 73 \cdot 0.01 = 0.73$$

Continued on Next Page

6 Write each fraction as a decimal. For repeating decimals, write the answer by first using bar notation and then rounding to the nearest thousandth.

(a) $\dfrac{2}{9}$

(b) $\dfrac{17}{20}$

(c) $\dfrac{1}{11}$

(d) $\dfrac{13}{5}$

Answers
6. (a) $0.\overline{2}, 0.222$ (b) 0.85
 (c) $0.\overline{09}, 0.091$ (d) 2.6

7 Write each percent as a decimal.

(a) 23%   (b) 310%

(c) $5\frac{1}{4}\%$ (d) 40%

(b) $125\% = 125 \cdot 1\% = 125 \cdot 0.01 = 1.25$ $1\% = 0.01$

A percent greater than 100 represents a number greater than 1.

(c) $3\frac{1}{2}\%$

First write the fractional part as a decimal.

$$3\frac{1}{2}\% = (3 + 0.5)\% = 3.5\%$$

Now write the percent in decimal form.

$$3.5\% = 3.5 \cdot 1\% = 3.5 \cdot 0.01 = 0.035$$ Be careful placing the decimal point.

◀ **Work Problem 7 at the Side.**

EXAMPLE 8   Writing Decimals as Percents

Write each decimal as a percent.

(a) 0.32

This conversion is the opposite of what we did in **Example 7** when we wrote percents as decimals. We use $1\% = 0.01$ in reverse.

$$0.32 = 32 \cdot 0.01 = 32 \cdot 1\% = 32\%   0.01 = 1\%$$

(b) $0.05 = 5 \cdot 0.01 = 5 \cdot 1\% = 5\%$ $0.01 = 1\%$

(c) $2.63 = 263 \cdot 0.01 = 263 \cdot 1\% = 263\%$ A number greater than 1 is more than 100%.

◀ **Work Problem 8 at the Side.**

---

8 Write each decimal as a percent.

(a) 0.71   (b) 1.32

(c) 0.06   (d) 0.685

Converting Percents and Decimals (Shortcuts)

- To convert a percent to a decimal, move the decimal point two places to the *left* and drop the % symbol.

- To convert a decimal to a percent, move the decimal point two places to the *right* and attach a % symbol.

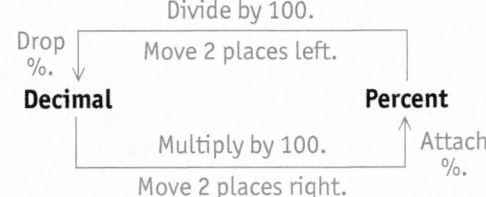

---

9 Convert each percent to a decimal and each decimal to a percent.

(a) 52%   (b) 2%

(c) 0.45   (d) 3.5

EXAMPLE 9   Converting Percents and Decimals by Moving the Decimal Point

Convert each percent to a decimal and each decimal to a percent.

(a) $45\% = 0.45$ (b) $250\% = 2.50$ (c) $9\% = 09\% = 0.09$

(d) $0.57 = 57\%$ (e) $1.5 = 1.50 = 150\%$ (f) $0.007 = 0.007 = 0.7\%$

◀ **Work Problem 9 at the Side.**

Answers

7. (a) 0.23 (b) 3.10, or 3.1 (c) 0.0525
   (d) 0.4
8. (a) 71% (b) 132% (c) 6% (d) 68.5%
9. (a) 0.52 (b) 0.02 (c) 45% (d) 350%

OBJECTIVE ▶ 6 Write percents as fractions and fractions as percents.

EXAMPLE 10 Writing Percents as Fractions

Write each percent as a fraction. Give answers in lowest terms as needed.

(a) 8%

We use the fact that $1\% = \frac{1}{100}$, and convert as follows.

$$8\% = 8 \cdot 1\% = 8 \cdot \frac{1}{100} = \frac{8}{100}$$

In lowest terms, $\qquad \frac{8}{100} = \frac{2 \cdot 4}{25 \cdot 4} = \frac{2}{25}.$

Thus, $8\% = \frac{2}{25}$.

(b) $175\% = 175 \cdot 1\% = 175 \cdot \frac{1}{100} = \frac{175}{100}$

In lowest terms, $\qquad \frac{175}{100} = \frac{7 \cdot 25}{4 \cdot 25} = \frac{7}{4},$ or $1\frac{3}{4}.$ ◁── A number greater than 1 is more than 100%.

(c) 13.5%

$= 13\frac{1}{2} \cdot 1\%$ Write 13.5 as a mixed number.

$= \frac{27}{2} \cdot \frac{1}{100}$ Write $13\frac{1}{2}$ as an improper fraction. Use the fact that $1\% = \frac{1}{100}$.

$= \frac{27}{200}$ Multiply the fractions.

─────── **Work Problem 10 at the Side. ▶**

We know that 100% of something is the whole thing. One way to convert a fraction to a percent is to multiply by 100%, which is equivalent to 1.

EXAMPLE 11 Writing Fractions as Percents

Write each fraction as a percent.

(a) $\frac{2}{5}$

$= \frac{2}{5} \cdot 100\%$ Multiply by 1 in the form 100%.

$= \frac{2}{5} \cdot \frac{100}{1}\%$ $a = \frac{a}{1}$

$= \frac{2 \cdot 5 \cdot 20}{5 \cdot 1}\%$ Multiply and factor.

$= \frac{2 \cdot 20}{1}\%$ Divide out the common factor.

$= 40\%$ Simplify.

(b) $\frac{1}{6}$

$= \frac{1}{6} \cdot 100\%$

$= \frac{1}{6} \cdot \frac{100}{1}\%$

$= \frac{1 \cdot 2 \cdot 50}{2 \cdot 3 \cdot 1}\%$

$= \frac{50}{3}\%$

$= 16\frac{2}{3}\%,$ or $16.\overline{6}\%$

─────── **Work Problem 11 at the Side. ▶**

10 Write each percent as a fraction. Give answers in lowest terms as needed.

(a) 20%

(b) 160%

(c) 1.5%

11 Write each fraction as a percent.

(a) $\frac{6}{25}$

(b) $\frac{2}{9}$

Answers

10. (a) $\frac{1}{5}$ (b) $\frac{8}{5}$, or $1\frac{3}{5}$ (c) $\frac{3}{200}$

11. (a) 24% (b) $22\frac{2}{9}\%$, or $22.\overline{2}\%$

12 Solve the problem.

A pair of jeans that regularly sells for $69 is on sale at 30% off. Find the amount of the discount and the sale price of the jeans.

OBJECTIVE ▶ **7** **Solve applied problems that involve percents.** The decimal form of a percent is generally used in calculations.

EXAMPLE 12 **Using Percent to Solve an Applied Problem**

A DVD with a regular price of $18 is on sale this week at 22% off. Find the amount of the discount and the sale price of the DVD.

The discount is 22% *of* 18. The word *of* here means multiply.

$$\begin{array}{ccc} 22\% & \text{of} & 18 \\ \downarrow & \downarrow & \downarrow \\ 0.22 & \cdot & 18 \end{array} \quad \text{Write 22\% as a decimal.}$$

$$= 3.96 \qquad \text{Multiply.}$$

The discount is $3.96. The sale price is found by subtracting.

$$\$18.00 - \$3.96 = \$14.04 \qquad \text{Original price} - \text{discount} = \text{sale price}$$

The sale price is $14.04.

◀ **Work Problem 12 at the Side.**

Answer

12. $20.70; $48.30

R.2 Exercises

FOR EXTRA HELP

Go to MyMathLab *for worked-out, step-by-step solutions to exercises enclosed in a square* ▢ *and video solutions to* ▶ *exercises.*

CONCEPT CHECK *Provide the correct response.*

1. For the decimal number 367.9412, name the digit that has each place value.

(a) tens   (b) tenths   (c) thousandths

(d) ones or units   (e) hundredths

2. For the decimal number 46.249, round to the place value indicated.

(a) hundredths   (b) tenths

(c) ones or units   (d) tens

3. Round each decimal to the nearest thousandth.

(a) $0.\overline{8}$ (b) $0.\overline{5}$

(c) 0.9762   (d) 0.8642

4. Find each product or quotient.

(a) 25.4×10 (b) 25.4×100

(c) $25.4 \div 100$ (d) $25.4 \div 1000$

Write each decimal as a fraction. (Do not write in lowest terms.) **See Example 1.**

5. 0.4   **6.** 0.6   **7.** 0.64   **8.** 0.82   **9.** 0.138

10. 0.104   **11.** 0.043   **12.** 0.087   **13.** 3.805   **14.** 5.166

Add or subtract as indicated. **See Example 2.**

15. $25.32 + 109.2 + 8.574$ **16.** $90.527 + 32.43 + 589.8$ **17.** $28.73 - 3.12$ **18.** $46.88 - 13.45$

19. $43.5 - 28.17$ **20.** $345.1 - 56.31$ **21.** $3.87 + 15 + 2.9$ **22.** $8.2 + 1.09 + 12$

23. $32.56 + 47.356 + 1.8$ **24.** $75.2 + 123.96 + 3.897$ **25.** ▶ $18 - 2.789$ **26.** $29 - 8.582$

Multiply or divide as indicated. **See Examples 3–5.**

27. 12.8×9.1 **28.** 34.04×0.56 **29.** 0.2×0.03 **30.** 0.07×0.004

31. ▶ $78.65 \div 11$ **32.** $73.36 \div 14$ **33.** $19.967 \div 9.74$ **34.** $44.4788 \div 5.27$

35. 57.116×100 **36.** 82.053×100 **37.** 0.094×1000 **38.** 0.025×1000

39. $1.62 \div 10$ **40.** $8.04 \div 10$ **41.** $24.03 \div 100$ **42.** $490.35 \div 100$

CONCEPT CHECK *Complete the table of fraction, decimal, and percent equivalents.*

	Fraction in Lowest Terms (or Whole Number)	Decimal	Percent
43.	$\frac{1}{100}$	0.01	
44.	$\frac{1}{50}$		2%
45.		0.05	5%
46.	$\frac{1}{10}$		
47.	$\frac{1}{8}$	0.125	
48.			20%
49.	$\frac{1}{4}$		
50.	$\frac{1}{3}$		
51.			50%
52.	$\frac{2}{3}$		$66\frac{2}{3}\%$, or $66.\overline{6}\%$
53.		0.75	
54.	1	1.0	

Write each fraction as a decimal. For repeating decimals, write the answer by first using bar notation and then rounding to the nearest thousandth. **See Example 6.**

55. $\frac{1}{8}$ **56.** $\frac{7}{8}$ **57.** $\frac{5}{4}$ **58.** $\frac{9}{5}$

59. $\frac{5}{9}$ **60.** $\frac{8}{9}$ **61.** $\frac{1}{6}$ **62.** $\frac{5}{6}$

Write each percent as a decimal. **See Examples 7 and 9(a)–(c).**

63. 54%   **64.** 39%   **65.** 7%   **66.** 4%   **67.** 90%

68. 10%   **69.** 117%   **70.** 189%   **71.** 2.4%   **72.** 3.1%

73. $6\frac{1}{4}\%$ **74.** $5\frac{1}{2}\%$ **75.** 0.8%   **76.** 0.5%

Write each decimal or whole number as a percent. **See Examples 8 and 9(d)–(f).**

77. 0.73   **78.** 0.83   **79.** 0.02   **80.** 0.08   **81.** 0.004   **82.** 0.005

83. 1.28   **84.** 2.35   **85.** 0.3   **86.** 0.6   **87.** 6   **88.** 10

Write each percent as a fraction. Give answers in lowest terms as needed.
See Example 10.

89. 51% **90.** 47% **91.** 15% **92.** 35% **93.** 2%

94. 8% **95.** 140% **96.** 180% **97.** 7.5% **98.** 2.5%

Write each fraction as a percent. See Example 11.

99. $\dfrac{4}{5}$ **100.** $\dfrac{3}{25}$ **101.** $\dfrac{7}{50}$ **102.** $\dfrac{9}{20}$ **103.** $\dfrac{2}{11}$

104. $\dfrac{4}{9}$ **105.** $\dfrac{9}{4}$ **106.** $\dfrac{8}{5}$ **107.** $\dfrac{13}{6}$ **108.** $\dfrac{31}{9}$

Solve each problem. See Example 12.

109. What is 50% of 320? **110.** What is 25% of 120? **111.** What is 6% of 80?

112. What is 5% of 70? **113.** What is 14% of 780? **114.** What is 26% of 480?

Solve each problem. See Example 12.

115. Elwyn's bill for dinner at a restaurant was $89. He wants to leave a 20% tip. How much should he leave for the tip? What is his total bill for dinner and tip?

116. Gary earns $15 per hour at his job. He recently received a 7% raise. How much per hour was his raise? What is his new hourly rate?

117. Find the discount on a leather recliner with a regular price of $795 if the recliner is on sale at 15% off. What is the sale price of the recliner?

118. A laptop computer with a regular price of $597 is on sale at 20% off. Find the amount of the discount and the sale price of the computer.

In a recent year, approximately 60 million people from other countries visited the United States. The circle graph shows the distribution of these international visitors by country or region. Use the graph to work each problem.

119. How many travelers visited the United States from Canada?

120. How many travelers visited the United States from Mexico?

121. What percent of travelers visited the United States from places other than Canada, Mexico, Europe, or Asia? (*Hint:* The sum of the parts of the graph must equal 1 whole, that is, 100%.)

122. Use the answer from **Exercise 121** to find how many travelers visited the United States from places other than Canada, Mexico, Europe, or Asia.

International Travelers to the United States

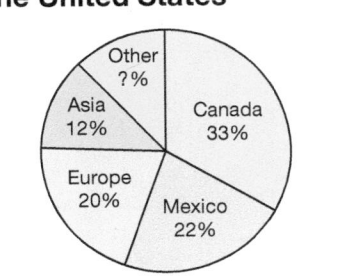

Other ?%
Asia 12%
Canada 33%
Europe 20%
Mexico 22%

Data from U.S. Department of Commerce.

Study Skills

USING YOUR MATH TEXT

---

30 Chapter 1 The Real Number System

1.1 Exponents, Order of Operations, and Inequality

OBJECTIVES

1. Use exponents.
2. Use the rules for order of operations.
3. Use more than one grouping symbol.
4. Know the meanings of $\neq$, $<$, $>$, $\leq$, and $\geq$.
5. Translate word statements to symbols.
6. Write statements that change the direction of inequality symbols.

OBJECTIVE 1 Use exponents. We can write a number as the product of its prime factors. For example,

81 can be written as $3 \cdot 3 \cdot 3 \cdot 3$. · indicates multiplication.

Here the factor 3 appears four times. In algebra, repeated factors are often written using an *exponent.*

$$\underbrace{3 \cdot 3 \cdot 3 \cdot 3}_{4 \text{ factors of } 3} = 3^4 \xleftarrow{} \text{Exponent}$$
$$\xleftarrow{} \text{Base}$$

In the **exponential expression** 3^4, the number 4 is the **exponent**, or **power**, and 3 is the **base**. An exponent tells how many times its base is used as a factor. We read 3^4 as "**3 to the fourth power,**" or "**3 to the fourth.**"

A number raised to the first power is simply that number.

$$6^1 = 6 \quad \text{and} \quad (2.5)^1 = 2.5 \quad \text{In general, } a^1 = a.$$

EXAMPLE 1 Evaluating Exponential Expressions

Find the value of each exponential expression.

(a) 5^2 means $5 \cdot 5$, which equals 25.
— 5 is used as a factor 2 times.
Read 5^2 as "5 to the second power" or, more commonly, "5 *squared.*"

(b) 6^3 means $6 \cdot 6 \cdot 6$, which equals 216.
— 6 is used as a factor 3 times.
Read 6^3 as "6 to the third power" or, more commonly, "6 *cubed.*"

(c) 2^5 means $2 \cdot 2 \cdot 2 \cdot 2 \cdot 2$, which equals 32.
2 is used as a factor 5 times.
Read 2^5 as "2 to the fifth power," or "2 to the fifth."
2^5 *does not equal* $2 \cdot 5$. Do not multiply the base and exponent.

(d) $\left(\frac{2}{3}\right)^3$ means $\frac{2}{3} \cdot \frac{2}{3} \cdot \frac{2}{3}$, which equals $\frac{8}{27}$. $\frac{2}{3}$ is used as a factor 3 times.

(e) $(0.3)^2$ means $0.3 \cdot 0.3$, which equals 0.09. 0.3 is used as a factor 2 times.

◄ Work Problem 1 at the Side.

1 Find the value of each exponential expression. Complete each blank as needed.

(a) 6^2 means ____ · ____.
which equals ____.

(b) 3^5

(c) $\left(\frac{3}{4}\right)^2$ means ____ · ____.
which equals ____.

(d) $\left(\frac{1}{2}\right)^4$

(e) $(0.4)^3$ means ____.
which equals ____.

Answers
1. (a) 6; 6; 36 (b) 243 (c) $\frac{3}{4}$; $\frac{3}{4}$; $\frac{9}{16}$
(d) $\frac{1}{16}$ (e) 0.4 · 0.4 · 0.4; 0.064

⚠ CAUTION
Squaring, or raising a number to the second power, is not the same as doubling the number. In Example 1(a),
5^2 means $5 \cdot 5$, *not* $5 \cdot 2$.
Thus $5^2 = 25$, *not* 10. Similarly, cubing, or raising a number to the third power, does *not* mean tripling the number. In **Example 1(b)**, $6^3 = 216$, *not* 18.

Your text is a valuable resource. You will learn more if you make full use of the features it offers.

Now Try This

General Features

Locate each feature, and complete any blanks.

▶ **Table of Contents**   This is located at the front of the text.
Find it and mark the chapters and sections you will cover, as noted on your course syllabus.

▶ **Answer Section**   *Tab this section at the back of the text.*
Refer to it frequently when doing homework. Answers to odd-numbered section exercises are provided. Answers to ALL Concept Check, writing, Relating Concepts, summary, chapter review, test, and cumulative review exercises are given.

▶ **List of Formulas**   Use this helpful list of geometric formulas, along with review information on triangles and angles, throughout the course.
Find this information at the back of the text.
The formula for the volume of a cube is _____.

Specific Features

Look through Chapter 2 and give the number of a page that includes an example of each of the following specific features.

▶ **Objectives**   The objectives are listed at the beginning of each section and again within the section as the corresponding material is presented. Once you finish a section, ask yourself if you have accomplished them. *See page _____.*

▶ **Margin Problems**   These exercises allow you to immediately practice the material covered in the examples and prepare you for the exercise set. Check your results using the answers at the bottom of the page. *See page _____.*

▶ **Pointers**   These small shaded balloons provide on-the-spot warnings and reminders, point out key steps, and give other helpful tips. *See page _____.*

▶ **Cautions**   These provide warnings about common errors that students often make or trouble spots to avoid. *See page _____.*

▶ **Notes**   These provide additional explanations or emphasize important ideas. *See page _____.*

▶ **Problem-Solving Hints**   These boxes give helpful tips or strategies to use when you work applications. *See page _____.*

The Real Number System

Positive and *negative numbers,* used to indicate temperatures above and below zero, elevations above and below sea level, and gains and losses in the stock market or on a football field, are examples of *real numbers,* the subject of this chapter.

1.1 Exponents, Order of Operations, and Inequality

Study Skills *Taking Lecture Notes*

1.2 Variables, Expressions, and Equations

Study Skills *Reading Your Math Text*

1.3 Real Numbers and the Number Line

Study Skills *Using Study Cards*

1.4 Adding Real Numbers

1.5 Subtracting Real Numbers

Study Skills *Completing Your Homework*

1.6 Multiplying and Dividing Real Numbers

Summary Exercises *Performing Operations with Real Numbers*

1.7 Properties of Real Numbers

1.8 Simplifying Expressions

Study Skills *Reviewing a Chapter*

1.1 Exponents, Order of Operations, and Inequality

OBJECTIVES

1. Use exponents.
2. Use the rules for order of operations.
3. Use more than one grouping symbol.
4. Know the meanings of ≠, <, >, ≤, and ≥.
5. Translate word statements to symbols.
6. Write statements that change the direction of inequality symbols.

OBJECTIVE ➤ 1 Use exponents. We can write a number as the product of its prime factors. For example,

81 can be written as 3 · 3 · 3 · 3. · indicates multiplication.

Here the factor 3 appears four times. In algebra, repeated factors are often written using an *exponent*.

$$\underbrace{3 \cdot 3 \cdot 3 \cdot 3}_{4 \text{ factors of } 3} = 3^{\overset{\leftarrow \text{ Exponent}}{4}}$$
Base

In the **exponential expression** 3^4, the number 4 is the **exponent,** or **power** and 3 is the **base.** An exponent tells how many times its base is used as a factor. We read 3^4 as **"3 to the fourth power,"** or **"3 to the fourth."**

A number raised to the first power is simply that number.

$$6^1 = 6 \quad \text{and} \quad (2.5)^1 = 2.5 \quad \text{In general, } a^1 = a.$$

1 Find the value of each exponential expression. Complete each blank as needed.

(GS) **(a)** 6^2 means ____ · ____,

which equals ____ .

(b) 3^5

(GS) **(c)** $\left(\dfrac{3}{4}\right)^2$ means ____ · ____,

which equals ____ .

(d) $\left(\dfrac{1}{2}\right)^4$

(GS) **(e)** $(0.4)^3$ means _____,

which equals ____ .

EXAMPLE 1 Evaluating Exponential Expressions

Find the value of each exponential expression.

(a) 5^2 means $\underbrace{5 \cdot 5,}$ which equals 25.
5 is used as a factor 2 times.

Read 5^2 as "5 *to the second power*" or, more commonly, "5 *squared*."

(b) 6^3 means $\underbrace{6 \cdot 6 \cdot 6,}$ which equals 216.
6 is used as a factor 3 times.

Read 6^3 as "6 *to the third power*" or, more commonly, "6 *cubed*."

(c) 2^5 means $2 \cdot 2 \cdot 2 \cdot 2 \cdot 2,$ which equals 32.
2 is used as a factor 5 times.

Read 2^5 as "2 *to the fifth power*," or "2 *to the fifth*."

2^5 ***does not equal*** $2 \cdot 5.$ ◄ Do ***not*** multiply the base and exponent.

(d) $\left(\dfrac{2}{3}\right)^3$ means $\dfrac{2}{3} \cdot \dfrac{2}{3} \cdot \dfrac{2}{3},$ which equals $\dfrac{8}{27}.$
$\frac{2}{3}$ is used as a factor 3 times.

(e) $(0.3)^2$ means $0.3 \cdot 0.3,$ which equals $0.09.$
0.3 is used as a factor 2 times.

◄ **Work Problem 1 at the Side**

⚠ CAUTION

Squaring, or raising a number to the second power, is not the same as doubling the number. In Example 1(a),

$$5^2 \quad \textbf{means} \quad 5 \cdot 5, \quad not \quad 5 \cdot 2.$$

Thus $5^2 = 25$, *not* 10. Similarly, cubing, or raising a number to the third power, does *not* mean tripling the number. In **Example 1(b)**, $6^3 = 216$, *not* 18.

Answers

1. **(a)** 6; 6; 36 **(b)** 243 **(c)** $\dfrac{3}{4}; \dfrac{3}{4}; \dfrac{9}{16}$

   (d) $\dfrac{1}{16}$ **(e)** 0.4 · 0.4 · 0.4; 0.064

OBJECTIVE ▶ **2** **Use the rules for order of operations.** When an expression involves more than one operation, we often use **grouping symbols,** such as parentheses ( ), to indicate the order in which the operations should be performed.

Consider the following expression.

$$5 + 2 \cdot 3$$

To show that the multiplication should be performed before the addition, we use parentheses to group $2 \cdot 3$.

$$5 + (2 \cdot 3) \quad \text{equals} \quad 5 + 6, \quad \text{which equals} \quad 11.$$

If addition is to be performed first, the parentheses should group $5 + 2$.

$$(5 + 2) \cdot 3 \quad \text{equals} \quad 7 \cdot 3, \quad \text{which equals} \quad 21.$$

Other grouping symbols are brackets [ ], braces { }, and fraction bars. (For example, in $\frac{8-2}{3}$, the expression $8 - 2$ is "grouped" in the numerator.)

To simplify an expression involving more than one operation, we use the following rules for **order of operations.** This order is used by most calculators and computers.

Order of Operations

If grouping symbols are present, work within them, innermost first (and above and below fraction bars separately), in the following order.

Step 1 Apply all **exponents.**

Step 2 Do any **multiplications** or **divisions** in order from left to right.

Step 3 Do any **additions** or **subtractions** in order from left to right.

If no grouping symbols are present, start with Step 1.

Note

Multiplication is understood in expressions with parentheses.

Examples: $3(7), \quad (6)2, \quad (5)(4), \quad 3(4 + 1)$

EXAMPLE 2 **Using the Rules for Order of Operations**

Find the value of each expression.

(a) $24 - 12 \div 3$ — Be careful. Divide first.
$= 24 - 4$ Divide.
$= 20$ Subtract.

(b) $9(6 + 11)$
$= 9(17)$ Work inside the parentheses.
$= 153$ Multiply.

(c) $6 \cdot 8 + 5 \cdot 2$
$= 48 + 10$ Multiply, working from left to right.
$= 58$ Add.

(d) $48 \div 2 \cdot 3$
$= 24 \cdot 3$ Divide.
$= 72$ Multiply.

Multiplications and divisions are done from left to right as they appear. Additions and subtractions are then done, again working from left to right.

Continued on Next Page

2 Label the order in which each
GS operation should be performed.
Then find the value of each
expression.

(a) $7 + 3 \cdot 8$

② ①

$= 7 +$ _____

$=$ _____

(b) $7 \cdot 3 - 2 \cdot 9$

○ ○ ○

$=$ _____ $-$ _____

$=$ _____

(c) $8 + 2(5 - 1)$

○ ○ ○

(d) $7 \cdot 6 - 3(8 + 1)$

○ ○ ○ ○

(e) $10 - 3^2 + 5$

○ ○ ○

3 Find the value of each expression.

(a) $9[(4 + 8) - 3]$

(b) $\dfrac{2(7 + 8) + 2}{3 \cdot 5 + 1}$

Answers

2. (a) 24; 31

   (b) ①, ③, ②; 21; 18; 3

   (c) ③, ②, ①; 16

   (d) ②, ④, ③, ①; 15

   (e) ②, ①, ③; 6

3. (a) 81   **(b)** 2

(e) $16 - 3(2 + 3)$ ⟵ Do *not* subtract $16 - 3$ first.

$= 16 - 3(5)$ Add inside the parentheses.

$= 16 - 15$ Multiply.

$= 1$ Subtract.

(f) $2(5 + 6) + 7 \cdot 3$

Start here. $= 2(11) + 7 \cdot 3$ Work inside the parentheses.

$= 22 + 21$ Multiply.

$= 43$ Add.

$2^3 = 2 \cdot 2 \cdot 2$, not $2 \cdot 3$

(g) $9 + 2^3 - 5$

$= 9 + 8 - 5$ Apply the exponent.

$= 12$ Add, and then subtract.

◀ **Work Problem 2 at the Side.**

OBJECTIVE ▶ **3 Use more than one grouping symbol.** In an expression like

$$2(8 + 3(6 + 5)),$$

we often use brackets, $[\ \ ]$, in place of the outer pair of parentheses.

EXAMPLE 3 Using Brackets and Fraction Bars as Grouping Symbols

Find the value of each expression.

Start here.

(a) $2[8 + 3(6 + 5)]$

$= 2[8 + 3(11)]$ Add inside the parentheses.

$= 2[8 + 33]$ Multiply inside the brackets.

$= 2[41]$ Add inside the brackets.

$= 82$ Multiply.

(b) $\dfrac{4(5 + 3) + 3}{3 \cdot 2 - 1}$ Simplify the numerator and denominator separately.

$= \dfrac{4(8) + 3}{3 \cdot 2 - 1}$ Work inside the parentheses.

$= \dfrac{32 + 3}{6 - 1}$ Multiply.

$= \dfrac{35}{5}$ Add and subtract.

$= 7$ Divide.

◀ **Work Problem 3 at the Side.**

Note

The expression $\frac{4(5+3)+3}{3\cdot2-1}$ in **Example 3(b)** can be written as a quotient.

$$[4(5+3)+3]\div[3\cdot2-1]$$

The fraction bar "groups" the numerator and denominator separately.

OBJECTIVE ▶ **4** **Know the meanings of** $\neq, <, >, \leq,$ **and** $\geq$. So far, we have used the equality symbol $=$. The symbols

$$\neq, \quad <, \quad >, \quad \leq, \quad \text{and} \quad \geq \quad \text{Inequality symbols}$$

are used to express an **inequality,** a statement that two expressions may not be equal. The equality symbol with a slash through it, $\neq$, means "is *not* equal to."

$$7 \neq 8 \quad \text{7 is not equal to 8.}$$

If two numbers are not equal, then one of the numbers must be less than the other. Reading from left to right, the symbol $<$ means "is less than."

$$7 < 8 \quad \text{7 is less than 8.}$$

Reading from left to right, the symbol $>$ means "is greater than."

$$8 > 2 \quad \text{8 is greater than 2.}$$

To keep the meanings of the symbols $<$ and $>$ clear, remember that the symbol always points to the lesser number.

$$\text{Lesser number} \rightarrow 8 < 15$$

$$15 > 8 \leftarrow \text{Lesser number}$$

Reading from left to right, the symbol $\leq$ means "is less than or equal to."

$$5 \leq 9 \quad \text{5 is less than or equal to 9.}$$

If either the $<$ part or the $=$ part is true, then the inequality $\leq$ is true. Thus, $5 \leq 9$ is true because $5 < 9$ is true. Also, $8 \leq 8$ is true because $8 = 8$ is true.

The symbol $\geq$ means "is greater than or equal to."

$$9 \geq 5 \quad \text{9 is greater than or equal to 5.}$$

EXAMPLE 4 **Using Inequality Symbols**

Determine whether each statement is *true* or *false*.

(a) $6 \neq 5 + 1$ This statement is false because $6 = 5 + 1$.

(b) $5 + 3 < 19$ The statement $5 + 3 < 19$ is true because $8 < 19$.

(c) $15 \leq 20 \cdot 2$ The statement $15 \leq 20 \cdot 2$ is true because $15 < 40$.

(d) $25 \geq 30$ Both $25 > 30$ and $25 = 30$ are false, so $25 \geq 30$ is false.

(e) $12 \geq 12$ Because $12 = 12$, this statement is true.

(f) $\frac{6}{15} \geq \frac{2}{3}$ Find a common denominator.

$\frac{6}{15} \geq \frac{10}{15}$ The statements $\frac{6}{15} > \frac{10}{15}$ and $\frac{6}{15} = \frac{10}{15}$ are false. Because at least one of them is false, $\frac{6}{15} \geq \frac{2}{3}$ is also false.

4 Determine whether each statement is *true* or *false*.

(a) $28 \neq 4 \cdot 7$

(b) $5 > 4 + 2$

(c) $25 \geq 10$

(d) $21 \leq 21$

(e) $9 \cdot 3 \geq 28$

(f) $\frac{4}{7} \leq \frac{5}{8}$

Answers

4. **(a)** false **(b)** false **(c)** true **(d)** true **(e)** false **(f)** true

Work Problem **4** at the Side. ▶

5 Write each word statement in symbols.

(a) Nine is equal to eleven minus two.

(b) Seventeen is less than thirty.

(c) Eight is not equal to ten.

(d) Fourteen is greater than twelve.

(e) Thirty is less than or equal to fifty.

(f) Two is greater than or equal to two.

6 Write each statement as another true statement with the inequality symbol reversed.

(a) $8 < 10$

(b) $3 > 1$

(c) $\dfrac{2}{3} \geq \dfrac{3}{5}$

(d) $0.5 \leq 1.2$

Answers

5. **(a)** $9 = 11 - 2$ **(b)** $17 < 30$
   (c) $8 \neq 10$ **(d)** $14 > 12$
   (e) $30 \leq 50$ **(f)** $2 \geq 2$
6. **(a)** $10 > 8$ **(b)** $1 < 3$
   (c) $\dfrac{3}{5} \leq \dfrac{2}{3}$ **(d)** $1.2 \geq 0.5$

OBJECTIVE ▶ 5 Translate word statements to symbols.

EXAMPLE 5 Translating from Words to Symbols

Write each word statement in symbols.

(a) Twelve **is equal to** ten **plus** two. $12 = 10 + 2$

(b) Nine **is less than** ten. $9 < 10$
    Compare this with "9 less than 10," which is written $10 - 9$.

(c) Fifteen **is not equal to** eighteen. $15 \neq 18$

(d) Seven **is greater than** four. $7 > 4$

(e) Thirteen **is less than or equal to** forty. $13 \leq 40$

(f) Six **is greater than or equal to** six. $6 \geq 6$

◀ **Work Problem 5 at the Side.**

OBJECTIVE ▶ 6 Write statements that change the direction of inequality symbols. Any statement with $<$ can be converted to one with $>$, and any statement with $>$ can be converted to one with $<$. *We do this by reversing both the order of the numbers and the direction of the symbol.*

$6 < 10$ becomes $10 > 6$.

EXAMPLE 6 Converting between Inequality Symbols

Write each statement as another true statement with the inequality symbol reversed.

(a) $5 > 2$ is equivalent to $2 < 5$.   **(b)** $\dfrac{1}{2} \leq \dfrac{3}{4}$ is equivalent to $\dfrac{3}{4} \geq \dfrac{1}{2}$.

◀ **Work Problem 6 at the Side.**

SUMMARY OF EQUALITY AND INEQUALITY SYMBOLS

Symbol	Meaning	Example
$=$	Is equal to	$0.5 = \frac{1}{2}$ means 0.5 is equal to $\frac{1}{2}$.
$\neq$	Is not equal to	$3 \neq 7$ means 3 is not equal to 7.
$<$	Is less than	$6 < 10$ means 6 is less than 10.
$>$	Is greater than	$15 > 14$ means 15 is greater than 14.
$\leq$	Is less than or equal to	$4 \leq 8$ means 4 is less than or equal to 8.
$\geq$	Is greater than or equal to	$1 \geq 0$ means 1 is greater than or equal to 0.

❗ CAUTION

Equality and inequality symbols are used to write mathematical *sentences.* Operation symbols ($+$, $-$, $\cdot$, and $\div$) are used to write mathematical *expressions* that represent a number. Compare the following.

Sentence: $4 < 10$ ← Gives the relationship between 4 and 10

Expression: $4 + 10$ ← Tells how to operate on 4 and 10 to get 14

1.1 Exercises

FOR EXTRA HELP

Go to MyMathLab for worked-out, step-by-step solutions to exercises enclosed in a square ▢ and video solutions to ▶ exercises.

CONCEPT CHECK *Decide whether each statement is* true *or* false. *If it is false, explain why.*

1. $3^2 = 6$

2. $1^3 = 3$

3. $3^1 = 1$

4. The expression 6^2 means that 2 is used as a factor 6 times.

Find the value of each exponential expression. ***See Example 1.***

5. 7^2 ▶

6. 4^2

7. 3^2

8. 8^2

9. 12^2

10. 14^2

11. 4^3

12. 5^3

13. 10^3 ▶

14. 11^3

15. 3^4

16. 6^4

17. 4^5

18. 3^5

19. ▶ $\left(\dfrac{2}{3}\right)^4$

20. $\left(\dfrac{3}{4}\right)^3$

21. $\left(\dfrac{1}{6}\right)^2$

22. $\left(\dfrac{1}{3}\right)^2$

23. ▶ $(0.04)^3$

24. $(0.05)^4$

Find the value of each expression. ***See Examples 2 and 3.***

25. GS ▶ $13 + 9 \cdot 5$
$= 13 +$ ___
$=$ ___

26. GS $11 + 7 \cdot 6$
$= 11 +$ ___
$=$ ___

27. GS $20 - 4 \cdot 3 + 5$
$= 20 -$ ___ $+ 5$
$=$ ___ $+ 5$
$=$ ___

28. GS $18 - 7 \cdot 2 + 6$
$= 18 -$ ___ $+ 6$
$=$ ___ $+ 6$
$=$ ___

29. GS $9 \cdot 5 - 13$

30. GS $7 \cdot 6 - 11$

31. GS $18 - 2 + 3$

32. GS $22 - 8 + 9$

33. $64 \div 4 \cdot 2$

34. $250 \div 5 \cdot 2$

35. $9 \cdot 4 - 8 \cdot 3$

36. $11 \cdot 4 + 10 \cdot 3$

37. $\dfrac{1}{4} \cdot \dfrac{2}{3} + \dfrac{2}{5} \cdot \dfrac{11}{3}$

38. $\dfrac{9}{4} \cdot \dfrac{2}{3} + \dfrac{4}{5} \cdot \dfrac{5}{3}$

39. $25.2 - 12.6 \div 4.2$

40. $12.4 - 9.3 \div 3.1$

41. $10 + 40 \div 5 \cdot 2$

42. $12 + 35 \div 7 \cdot 3$

43. $18 - 2(3 + 4)$

44. $30 - 3(4 + 2)$

45. $3(4 + 2) + 8 \cdot 3$

46. $9(1 + 7) + 2 \cdot 5$

47. $18 - 4^2 + 3$

48. $22 - 2^3 + 9$

49. $5[3 + 4(2^2)]$ **50.** $6[2 + 8(3^3)]$ **51.** $3^2[(11 + 3) - 4]$ **52.** $4^2[(13 + 4) - 8]$

53. $2 + 3[5 + 4(2)]$ **54.** $5 + 4[1 + 7(3)]$ **55.** $\dfrac{6(3^2 - 1) + 8}{3 \cdot 2 - 2}$

56. $\dfrac{2(8^2 - 4) + 8}{4 \cdot 3 - 10}$ **57.** $\dfrac{4(7 + 2) + 8(8 - 3)}{6(4 - 2) - 2^2}$ **58.** $\dfrac{6(5 + 1) - 9(1 + 1)}{5(8 - 4) - 2^3}$

CONCEPT CHECK *Insert one pair of parentheses in each expression so that the given value results when the operations are performed.*

59. $3 \cdot 6 + 4 \cdot 2$
     $= 60$

60. $2 \cdot 8 - 1 \cdot 3$
     $= 42$

61. $10 - 7 - 3$
     $= 6$

62. $15 - 10 - 2$
     $= 7$

63. $8 + 2^2$
     $= 100$

64. $4 + 2^2$
     $= 36$

Simplify each expression involving an operation as needed. Then determine whether the given statement is true *or* false. ***See Examples 2–4.***

65. $8 \geq 17$ **66.** $10 \geq 41$ **67.** $\dfrac{1}{2} \leq \dfrac{2}{4}$ **68.** $\dfrac{3}{9} \leq \dfrac{1}{3}$

69. $17 \leq 18 - 1$ **70.** $12 \geq 10 + 2$ **71.** $9 \cdot 3 - 11 \leq 16$

72. $6 \cdot 5 - 12 \leq 18$ **73.** $6 \cdot 8 + 6 \cdot 6 \geq 0$ **74.** $4 \cdot 20 - 16 \cdot 5 \geq 0$

75. $6[5 + 3(4 + 2)] \leq 70$ **76.** $6[2 + 3(2 + 5)] \leq 135$ **77.** $\dfrac{9(7 - 1) - 8 \cdot 2}{4(6 - 1)} > 3$

78. $\dfrac{2(5 + 3) + 2 \cdot 2}{2(4 - 1)} > 1$ **79.** $8 \leq 4^2 - 2^2$ **80.** $10^2 - 8^2 > 6^2$

Write each word statement in symbols. ***See Example 5.***

81. Fifteen is equal to five plus ten.

82. Twelve is equal to twenty minus eight.

83. Nine is greater than five minus four.

84. Ten is greater than six plus one.

85. Sixteen is not equal to nineteen.

86. Three is not equal to four.

87. Two is less than or equal to three.

88. Five is less than or equal to six.

Write each statement in words, and decide whether it is true *or* false. ***See Examples 4 and 5.***

89. $7 < 19$ **90.** $9 < 10$ **91.** $8 \geq 11$

92. $4 \leq 2$ **93.** $\dfrac{1}{3} \neq \dfrac{3}{10}$ **94.** $\dfrac{10}{7} \neq \dfrac{3}{2}$

Write each statement as another true statement with the inequality symbol reversed.
See Example 6.

95. $5 < 30$

96. $8 > 4$

97. $12 \geq 3$

98. $25 \leq 41$

99. $2.5 \geq 1.3$

100. $4.1 \leq 5.3$

101. $\dfrac{4}{5} > \dfrac{3}{4}$

102. $\dfrac{8}{3} < \dfrac{11}{4}$

One way to measure a person's cardiofitness is to calculate how many METs, or metabolic units, he or she can reach at peak exertion. One MET is the amount of energy used when sitting quietly. To calculate ideal METs, we can use the following expressions.

$14.7 - \text{age} \cdot 0.13$ For women

$14.7 - \text{age} \cdot 0.11$ For men

(Data from *New England Journal of Medicine*.)

103. A 40-yr-old woman wishes to calculate her ideal MET.

 (a) Write the expression, using her age.

 (b) Calculate her ideal MET. (*Hint:* Use the rules for order of operations.)

 (c) Researchers recommend that a person reach approximately 85% of his or her MET when exercising. Calculate 85% of the ideal MET from part (b). Then refer to the following table. What activity can the woman do that is approximately this value?

Activity	METs	Activity	METs
Golf (with cart)	2.5	Skiing (water or downhill)	6.8
Walking (3 mph)	3.3	Swimming	7.0
Mowing lawn (power)	4.5	Walking (5 mph)	8.0
Ballroom or square dancing	5.5	Jogging	10.2
Cycling	5.7	Skipping rope	12.0

Data from Harvard School of Public Health.

 (d) Repeat parts (a)–(c) for a 55-yr-old man.

104. Repeat parts (a)–(c) of **Exercise 103** for your age and gender.   For yourself 5 yr from now.

The table shows the number of pupils per teacher in U.S. public schools in selected states. Use the table to answer each question.

105. Which states had a number greater than 14.1?

106. Which states had a number that was at most 14.7?

107. Which states had a number not less than 14.1?

108. Which states had a number greater than 22.2?

State	Pupils per Teacher
Alaska	15.3
Texas	14.7
California	22.2
Wyoming	12.7
Maine	11.8
Idaho	18.4
Missouri	14.1

Data from National Center for Education Statistics.

Study Skills

TAKING LECTURE NOTES

Study the set of sample math notes given here.

- ▶ **Include the date and title** of the day's lecture topic.

- ▶ **Include definitions,** written here in parentheses—don't trust your memory.

- ▶ **Skip lines and write neatly** to make reading easier.

- ▶ **Emphasize direction words** (like *simplify*) with their explanations.

- ▶ **Mark important concepts with stars, underlining,** etc.

- ▶ **Use two columns,** which allows an example and its explanation to be close together.

- ▶ **Use brackets and arrows** to clearly show steps, related material, etc.

January 12   *Exponents*

Exponents used to show repeated multiplication.

$3 \cdot 3 \cdot 3 \cdot 3$ can be written 3^4 exponent (how many times it's multiplied)

base (the number being multiplied)

Read 3^2 as 3 to the 2nd power or 3 squared

3^3 as 3 to the 3rd power or 3 cubed

3^4 as 3 to the 4th power

etc.

Simplifying an expression with exponents

→ actually do the repeated multiplication

2^3 means $2 \cdot 2 \cdot 2$ and $2 \cdot 2 \cdot 2 = 8$

★ Careful! 5^2 means $5 \cdot 5$ NOT $5 \cdot 2$

so $5^2 = 5 \cdot 5 = 25$ BUT $5^2 \neq 10$

Example	Explanation
simplify $2^4 \cdot 3^2$	Exponents mean multiplication.
$2 \cdot 2 \cdot 2 \cdot 2 \cdot 3 \cdot 3$	Use 2 as a factor 4 times. Use 3 as a factor 2 times. $2 \cdot 2 \cdot 2 \cdot 2$ is 16 ⟩ $16 \cdot 9$ is 144 / $3 \cdot 3$ is 9
16 $\cdot$ 9	
144	Simplified result is 144 (no exponents left)

Now Try This

With a partner or in a small group, compare lecture notes. Then answer each question.

1 What are you doing to show main points in your notes (such as boxing, using stars, etc.)? _____

_____

2 In what ways do you set off explanations from worked problems and subpoints (such as indenting, using arrows, circling, etc.)? _____

_____

3 What new ideas did you learn by examining your classmates' notes? _____

_____

4 What new techniques will you try when taking notes in future lectures? _____

_____

1.2 | Variables, Expressions, and Equations

A **constant** is a fixed, unchanging number. A **variable** is a symbol, usually a letter, used to represent an unknown number.

$$5, \quad \frac{3}{4}, \quad 8\frac{1}{2}, \quad 10.8 \quad \text{Constants} \quad \bigg| \quad a, \quad x, \quad y, \quad z \quad \text{Variables}$$

An **algebraic expression** is a sequence of constants, variables, operation symbols, and/or grouping symbols, such as parentheses, square brackets, or fraction bars.

$$x + 5, \quad 2m - 9, \quad 8p^2 + 6(p - 2) \quad \text{Algebraic expressions}$$

2m means $2 \cdot m$, the product of 2 and m.

$6(p-2)$ means the product of 6 and $p-2$.

OBJECTIVE 1 Evaluate algebraic expressions, given values for the variables. To *evaluate* an expression is to find its *value*. An algebraic expression can have different numerical values for different values of the variables.

EXAMPLE 1 Evaluating Algebraic Expressions

Evaluate each expression for $x = 5$.

(a) $8 + x$
$= 8 + 5$ Let $x = 5$.
$= 13$ Add.

(b) $8x$ Multiplication is understood.
$= 8 \cdot x$
$= 8 \cdot 5$ Let $x = 5$.
$= 40$ Multiply.

(c) $2x - 9$
$= 2 \cdot x - 9$ $2x = 2 \cdot x$
$= 2 \cdot 5 - 9$ Let $x = 5$.
$= 10 - 9$ Multiply.
$= 1$ Subtract.

(d) $3x^2$
$= 3 \cdot x^2$ $5^2 = 5 \cdot 5$
$= 3 \cdot 5^2$ Let $x = 5$.
$= 3 \cdot 25$ Square 5.
$= 75$ Multiply.

Work Problem 1 at the Side. ▶

! CAUTION
$3x^2$ means $3 \cdot x^2$, **not** $3x \cdot 3x$. See **Example 1(d)**.

Unless parentheses are used, the exponent refers only to the variable or number just before it. We would need to use parentheses to write $3x \cdot 3x$ with exponents.

$$(3x)^2 \quad \text{means} \quad 3x \cdot 3x.$$

1 Evaluate each expression for $x = 3$.

GS **(a)** $x + 12$
$= \underline{\quad} + 12$
$= \underline{\quad}$

GS **(b)** $6x$
$= \underline{\quad} \cdot x$
$= 6 \cdot \underline{\quad}$
$= \underline{\quad}$

GS **(c)** $5x^2$
$= \underline{\quad} \cdot x^2$
$= 5 \cdot \underline{\quad}^2$
$= 5 \cdot \underline{\quad}$
$= \underline{\quad}$

(d) $16x - 10$

Answers
1. **(a)** 3; 15 **(b)** 6; 3; 18
(c) 5; 3; 9; 45 **(d)** 38

2 Evaluate each expression for $x = 6$ and $y = 9$.

(GS) **(a)** $4x + 7y$

$$= 4 \cdot \underline{\quad} + 7 \cdot \underline{\quad}$$

$$= \underline{\quad} + \underline{\quad}$$

$$= \underline{\quad}$$

(b) $\dfrac{4x - 2y}{x + 1}$

(c) $2x^2 + y^2$

EXAMPLE 2 **Evaluating Algebraic Expressions**

Evaluate each expression for $x = 5$ and $y = 3$.

(a) $2x + 5y$

> We could use parentheses and write 2(5) + 5(3).

$$= 2 \cdot 5 + 5 \cdot 3 \qquad \text{Let } x = 5 \text{ and } y = 3.$$

> Follow the rules for order of operations.

$$= 10 + 15 \qquad \text{Multiply.}$$

$$= 25 \qquad \text{Add.}$$

(b) $\dfrac{9x - 8y}{2x - y}$

$$= \dfrac{9 \cdot 5 - 8 \cdot 3}{2 \cdot 5 - 3} \qquad \text{Let } x = 5 \text{ and } y = 3.$$

$$= \dfrac{45 - 24}{10 - 3} \qquad \text{Multiply.}$$

$$= \dfrac{21}{7} \qquad \text{Subtract.}$$

$$= 3 \qquad \text{Divide.}$$

(c) $x^2 - 2y^2$

> $3^2 = 3 \cdot 3$

$$= 5^2 - 2 \cdot 3^2 \qquad \text{Let } x = 5 \text{ and } y = 3.$$

> $5^2 = 5 \cdot 5$

$$= 25 - 2 \cdot 9 \qquad \text{Apply the exponents.}$$

$$= 25 - 18 \qquad \text{Multiply.}$$

$$= 7 \qquad \text{Subtract.}$$

◀ **Work Problem** **2** **at the Side.**

OBJECTIVE **2** Translate word phrases to algebraic expressions.

EXAMPLE 3 **Using Variables to Write Word Phrases as Algebraic Expressions**

Write each word phrase as an algebraic expression, using x as the variable.

(a) The **sum** of a number and 9

$$x + 9, \quad \text{or} \quad 9 + x \qquad \text{“Sum” is the answer to an addition problem.}$$

(b) 7 **minus** a number

$$7 - x \qquad \text{“Minus” indicates subtraction.}$$

The expression $x - 7$ is incorrect. We cannot subtract in either order and obtain the same result.

(c) A number **subtracted from 12**

$$12 - x \qquad \boxed{\text{Be careful with order.}}$$

Compare this result with “12 subtracted from a number,” which is $x - 12$.

(d) The **product** of 11 and a number

$$11 \cdot x, \quad \text{or} \quad 11x$$

Answers

2. **(a)** 6; 9; 24; 63; 87 **(b)** $\dfrac{6}{7}$ **(c)** 153

Continued on Next Page

(e) 5 **divided by** a number

$$5 \div x, \quad \text{or} \quad \frac{5}{x}$$

$\frac{x}{5}$ is **not** correct here.

(f) The **product** of 2 and the **difference** of a number and 8

We are multiplying 2 times "something." This "something" is the difference of a number and 8, written $x - 8$. We use parentheses around this difference.

$$2 \cdot (x - 8), \quad \text{or} \quad 2(x - 8)$$

$8 - x$, which means the difference of 8 and a number, is **not** correct.

——————— **Work Problem 3 at the Side.** ▶

OBJECTIVE ▶ 3 Identify solutions of equations. An **equation** is a statement that two expressions are equal. *An equation always includes the equality symbol, = .*

$$x + 4 = 11, \qquad 2y = 16, \qquad 4p + 1 = 25 - p,$$
$$\frac{3}{4}x + \frac{1}{2} = 0, \qquad z^2 = 4, \qquad 4(m - 0.5) = 2m$$

⎫ Equations

To **solve an equation,** we must find all values of the variable that make the equation true. Such a value of the variable is a **solution** of the equation.

EXAMPLE 4 **Deciding Whether a Number Is a Solution of an Equation**

Decide whether each equation has the given number as a solution.

(a) $5p + 1 = 36$; 7

We could use parentheses and write 5(7) here.

$$5p + 1 = 36$$
$$5 \cdot 7 + 1 \overset{?}{=} 36 \qquad \text{Let } p = 7.$$
$$35 + 1 \overset{?}{=} 36 \qquad \text{Multiply.}$$

Be careful. Multiply first.

$$36 = 36 \checkmark \quad \text{True—the left side of the equation equals the right side.}$$

The number 7 is a solution of the equation.

(b) $9m - 6 = 32$; $\frac{14}{3}$

$$9m - 6 = 32$$
$$9 \cdot \frac{14}{3} - 6 \overset{?}{=} 32 \qquad \text{Let } m = \frac{14}{3}.$$
$$42 - 6 \overset{?}{=} 32 \qquad \text{Multiply.}$$
$$36 = 32 \qquad \text{False—the left side does } not \text{ equal the right side.}$$

The number $\frac{14}{3}$ is not a solution of the equation.

——————— **Work Problem 4 at the Side.** ▶

3 Write each word phrase as an algebraic expression, using x as the variable.

(a) The sum of 5 and a number

(b) A number minus 4

(c) A number subtracted from 48

(d) The product of 6 and a number

(e) A number divided by 7

(f) 9 multiplied by the sum of a number and 5

4 Decide whether each equation has the given number as a solution.

(a) $x - 1 = 3$; 2

(b) $2k + 3 = 15$; 7

(c) $7p - 11 = 5$; $\frac{16}{7}$

Answers

3. **(a)** $5 + x$ **(b)** $x - 4$ **(c)** $48 - x$
(d) $6x$ **(e)** $\frac{x}{7}$ **(f)** $9(x + 5)$

4. **(a)** no **(b)** no **(c)** yes

5 Write each word sentence as an equation. Use x as the variable.

(GS) **(a)** Three times the sum of a number and 13 is 19.

___ (___ + ___) = ___

(b) Five times a number subtracted from 21 is 15.

(c) Five less than six times a number is equal to nineteen.

(d) Fifteen divided by a number equals the number minus two.

6 Decide whether each of the following is an *equation* or an *expression*.

(a) $2x + 5y - 7$

(b) $\dfrac{3x - 1}{5}$

(c) $2x + 5 = 7$

(d) $\dfrac{x - 3}{2} = 4x$

OBJECTIVE ▶ 4 Translate sentences to equations.

EXAMPLE 5 Translating Sentences to Equations

Write each word sentence as an equation. Use x as the variable.

(a) Twice the sum of a number and four is six.

"Twice" means two times. The word *is* suggests equals.

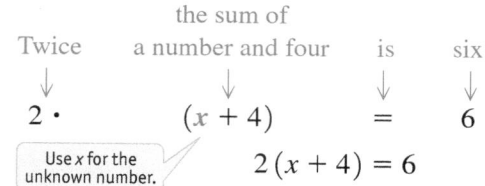

$$2(x + 4) = 6$$

(b) Nine more than five times a number is 49.

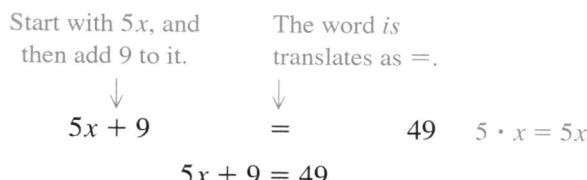

$$5x + 9 = 49$$

(c) Seven less than three times a number is equal to eleven.

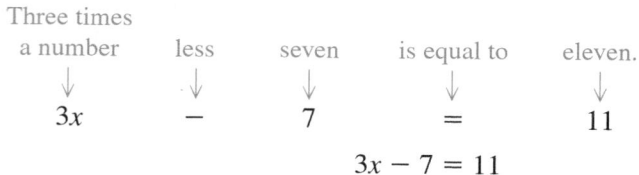

$$3x - 7 = 11$$

◀ Work Problem **5** at the Side.

OBJECTIVE ▶ 5 Distinguish between equations and expressions.

Distinguishing between an Equation and an Expression

An **equation** is a sentence—it has something on the left side, an = symbol, and something on the right side.

An **expression** is a phrase that represents a number.

$$\underbrace{4x + 5}_{\text{Left side}} = \underbrace{9}_{\text{Right side}}$$

Equation (to solve)

$$4x + 5$$

Expression (to simplify or evaluate)

EXAMPLE 6 Distinguishing between Equations and Expressions

Decide whether each of the following is an *equation* or an *expression*.

(a) $2x - 3 - 8$ Ask, "*Is there an equality symbol?*" The answer is no, so this is an *expression*.

(b) $2x - 3 = 8$ Because there is an equality symbol with something on either side of it, this is an *equation*.

(c) $5x^2 + 2y^2$ There is no equality symbol. This is an *expression*.

◀ Work Problem **6** at the Side.

Answers

5. (a) $3; x; 13; 19$ (b) $21 - 5x = 15$

   (c) $6x - 5 = 19$ (d) $\dfrac{15}{x} = x - 2$

6. (a) expression   (b) expression

   (c) equation   (d) equation

1.2 Exercises

FOR EXTRA HELP

Go to MyMathLab *for worked-out, step-by-step solutions to exercises enclosed in a square* ▢ *and video solutions to* ▶ *exercises.*

CONCEPT CHECK *Choose the letter(s) of the correct response.*

1. The expression $8x^2$ means _____ .

   A. $8 \cdot x \cdot 2$ **B.** $8 \cdot x \cdot x$ **C.** $8 + x^2$ **D.** $8x \cdot 8x$

2. For $x = 2$ and $y = 1$, the value of xy is _____ .

   A. $\dfrac{1}{2}$ **B.** 1 **C.** 2 **D.** 3

3. The sum of 15 and a number x is represented by _____ .

   A. $15 + x$ **B.** $15 - x$ **C.** $x - 15$ **D.** $15x$

4. Which of the following are expressions?

   A. $6x = 7$ **B.** $6x + 7$ **C.** $6x - 7$ **D.** $6x - 7 = 0$

CONCEPT CHECK *Complete each statement.*

5. For $x = 3$, the value of $x + 8$ is _____ .

6. For $x = 1$ and $y = 2$, the value of $5xy$ is _____ .

7. "The sum of 13 and x" is represented by the expression _____ . For $x = 3$, the value of this expression is _____ .

8. $2x + 6$ is an (*equation / expression*), while $2x + 6 = 8$ is an (*equation / expression*).

Evaluate each expression for (a) $x = 4$ and (b) $x = 6$. **See Example 1.**

9. $x + 7$ **10.** $x - 3$ **11.** $4x$ **12.** $6x$

13. $5x + 2$ **14.** $7x - 8$ **15.** $4x^2$ ▶   **16.** $5x^2$

17. $\dfrac{x + 1}{3}$ **18.** $\dfrac{x - 2}{5}$ **19.** $\dfrac{3x - 5}{2x}$ **20.** $\dfrac{4x - 1}{3x}$

21. $6.459x$ **22.** $3.275x$ **23.** $3x^2 + x$ **24.** $2x + x^2$

Evaluate each expression for **(a)** $x = 2$ *and* $y = 1$ *and* **(b)** $x = 1$ *and* $y = 5$.
See Example 2.

25. $13x - 2y$

26. $8x + 3y$

27. $8x + 3y + 5$

28. $4x + 2y + 7$

29. $3(x + 2y)$

30. $2(2x + y)$

31. $\dfrac{x}{2} + \dfrac{y}{3}$

32. $\dfrac{x}{5} + \dfrac{y}{4}$

33. $\dfrac{2x + 4y - 6}{5y + 2}$

34. $\dfrac{4x + 3y - 1}{2x + y}$

35. $2y^2 + 5x$

36. $6x^2 + 4y$

37. $\dfrac{3x + y^2}{2x + 3y}$

38. $\dfrac{x^2 + 1}{4x + 5y}$

39. $0.841x^2 + 0.32y^2$

40. $0.941x^2 + 0.2y^2$

Write each word phrase as an algebraic expression, using x as the variable.
See Example 3.

41. Twelve times a number

42. Fifteen times a number

43. Thirteen added to a number

44. Six added to a number

45. Two subtracted from a number

46. Eight subtracted from a number

47. The difference of twice a number and 6

48. The difference of 6 and three times a number

49. One-third of a number, subtracted from seven

50. One-fifth of a number, subtracted from fourteen

51. 12 divided by the sum of a number and 3

52. The difference of a number and 5, divided by 12

53. The product of 6 and four less than a number

54. The product of 9 and five more than a number

Decide whether each equation has the given number as a solution. *See Example 4.*

55. $x - 5 = 12$;   7

56. $x + 6 = 15$;   10

57. $5x + 2 = 7$;   1

58. $3x + 5 = 8$;   1

59. $6x + 4x + 9 = 11$; $\dfrac{1}{5}$

60. $2x + 3x + 8 = 20$; $\dfrac{12}{5}$

61. $2y + 3(y - 2) = 14;$ 3

62. $6x + 2(x + 3) = 14;$ 2

63. $2x^2 + 1 = 19;$ 3

64. $3r^2 - 2 = 46;$ 4

65. $\dfrac{z + 4}{2 - z} = \dfrac{13}{5};$ $\dfrac{1}{3}$

66. $\dfrac{x + 6}{x - 2} = \dfrac{37}{5};$ $\dfrac{13}{4}$

Write each word sentence as an equation. Use x as the variable. **See Example 5.**

67. The sum of a number and 8 is 18.

68. A number minus three equals 1.

69. Five more than twice a number is 5.

70. The product of a number and 3 is 6.

71. Sixteen minus three-fourths of a number is 13.

72. The sum of six-fifths of a number and 2 is 14.

73. Three times a number is equal to 8 more than twice the number.

74. Triple a number plus six equals five times the number.

75. A number divided by 3 equals four subtracted from the number.

76. Twelve divided by a number equals $\frac{1}{3}$ times the number.

Decide whether each of the following is an equation *or an* expression. **See Example 6.**

77. $3x + 2(x - 4)$

78. $5y - (3y + 6)$

79. $7t + 2(t + 1) = 4$

80. $9r + 3(r - 4) = 2$

81. $x + y = 9$

82. $x + y - 9$

83. $\dfrac{3x - 8}{2}$

84. $\dfrac{3x - 8}{2} = 11$

Relating Concepts (Exercises 85–88) For Individual or Group Work

*A **mathematical model** is an equation that describes the relationship between two quantities. For example, the life expectancy of Americans at birth can be approximated by the equation*

$$y = 0.180x - 283,$$

where x is a year between 1960 and 2010 and y is age in years. (Data from Centers for Disease Control and Prevention.)

Use this model to approximate life expectancy (to the nearest year) in each of the following years.

85. 1960

86. 1975

87. 1995

88. 2010

Study Skills

*T*ake time to read each section and its examples before doing your home-work.* You will learn more and be better prepared to work the exercises.

Approaches to Reading Your Math Text

Student A learns best by listening to his teacher explain things. He "gets it" when he sees the instructor work problems. He previews the section before the lecture, so he knows generally what to expect. **Student A carefully reads the section in his text AFTER he hears the classroom lecture on the topic.**

Student B learns best by reading on her own. She reads the section and works through the examples before coming to class. That way, she knows what the teacher is going to talk about and what questions she wants to ask. **Student B carefully reads the section in her text BEFORE she hears the classroom lecture on the topic.**

Which reading approach works better for you—that of Student A or that of Student B? _____

Tips for Reading Your Math Text

▶ **Turn off your cell phone and the TV.** You will be able to concentrate more fully on what you are reading.

▶ **Survey the material.** Glance over the assigned material to get an idea of the "big picture." Look at the list of objectives to see what you will be learning.

▶ **Read slowly.** Read only one section—or even part of a section—at a sitting, with paper and pencil in hand.

▶ **Pay special attention to important information given in colored boxes or set in boldface type.** Highlight any additional information you find helpful.

▶ **Study the examples carefully.** Pay particular attention to the blue side comments and any pointer balloons.

▶ **Do the margin problems in the workspace provided or on separate paper as you go.** These problems mirror the examples and prepare you for the exercise sets. Check your answers with those given at the bottom of the page.

▶ **Make study cards as you read.** Make cards for new vocabulary, rules, procedures, formulas, and sample problems.

▶ **Mark anything you don't understand.** *ASK QUESTIONS* in class—everyone will benefit. Follow up with your instructor, as needed.

Now Try This

Think through and answer each question.

1 Which two or three reading tips will you try this week? _____

_____

_____

2 Did the tips you selected improve your ability to read and understand the material? Explain. _____

_____

_____

_____

1.3 | Real Numbers and the Number Line

A **set** is a collection of objects. In mathematics, these objects are usually numbers. The objects that belong to a set are its **elements.** They are written between **braces** { }.

{1, 2, 3, 4, 5} ← The set containing the elements 1, 2, 3, 4, and 5

OBJECTIVE ▸ ❶ **Classify numbers and graph them on number lines.** The set of numbers used for counting is the *natural numbers*. The set of *whole numbers* includes 0 with the natural numbers.

Natural Numbers and Whole Numbers

{1, 2, 3, 4, 5, . . . } is the set of **natural numbers** (or **counting numbers**).

{0, 1, 2, 3, 4, 5, . . . } is the set of **whole numbers.**

We can represent numbers on a **number line** like the one in **Figure 1.**

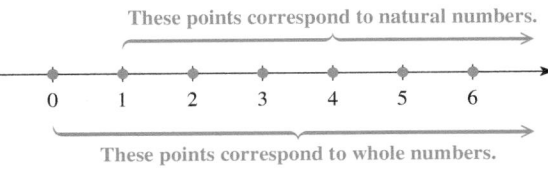

These points correspond to natural numbers.

These points correspond to whole numbers.

Figure 1

To draw a number line, choose any point on the line and label it 0. Then choose any point to the right of 0 and label it 1. Use the distance between 0 and 1 as the scale to locate, and then label, other points.

The natural numbers are located to the right of 0 on the number line. For each natural number, we can place a corresponding number to the left of 0, labeling the points $-1, -2, -3$, and so on, as shown in **Figure 2.** Each is the **opposite,** or **negative,** of a natural number. The natural numbers, their opposites, and 0 form the set of *integers.*

Integers

{ . . . , -3, -2, -1, 0, 1, 2, 3, . . . } is the set of **integers.**

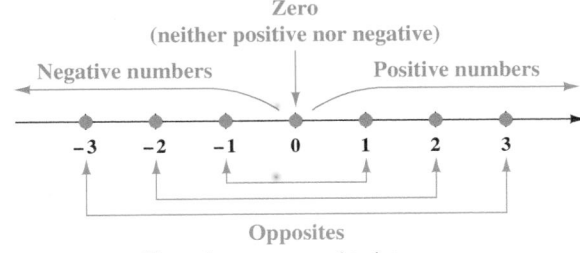

Zero
(neither positive nor negative)

Negative numbers   Positive numbers

Opposites
The points correspond to integers.

Figure 2

Positive numbers and *negative numbers* are **signed numbers.**

1 Use an integer to express the boldface italic number(s) in each statement.

(a) Erin discovers that she has spent $*53* more than she has in her checking account.

(b) The record high Fahrenheit temperature in the United States was *134*° in Death Valley, California, on July 10, 1913. (Data from *The World Almanac and Book of Facts*.)

(c) A football team gained *5* yd, then lost *10* yd on the next play.

EXAMPLE 1 **Using Negative Numbers**

Use an integer to express the boldface italic number in each statement.

(a) The lowest Fahrenheit temperature ever recorded in meteorological records was *129*° below zero at Vostok, Antarctica, on July 21, 1983. (Data from *The World Almanac and Book of Facts*.)

Use -129 because "below zero" indicates a negative number.

(b) The shore surrounding the Dead Sea is *1348* ft below sea level. (Data from *The World Almanac and Book of Facts*.)

Here "below sea level" indicates a negative number, -1348.

◄ **Work Problem** ❶ **at the Side.**

Fractions are *rational numbers*.

Rational Numbers

$\{x \mid x$ is a quotient of two integers, with denominator not $0\}$ is the set of **rational numbers.**

(Read the part in the braces as "*the set of all numbers x such that x is a quotient of two integers, with denominator not 0.*")

Note

The set symbolism used in the definition of rational numbers,

$$\{x \mid x \text{ has a certain property}\},$$

is **set-builder notation.** This notation is convenient to use when it is not possible to list all the elements of a set.

Because any number that can be written as the quotient of two integers (that is, as a fraction) is a rational number, *all integers, mixed numbers, terminating (or ending) decimals, and repeating decimals are rational.* The table gives examples.

RATIONAL NUMBERS

Rational Number	Equivalent Quotient of Two Integers
-5	$\frac{-5}{1}$ (means $-5 \div 1$)
$1\frac{3}{4}$	$\frac{7}{4}$ (means $7 \div 4$)
0.23 (terminating decimal)	$\frac{23}{100}$ (means $23 \div 100$)
0.3333..., or $0.\overline{3}$ (repeating decimal)	$\frac{1}{3}$ (means $1 \div 3$)
4.7	$\frac{47}{10}$ (means $47 \div 10$)

To **graph** a number, we place a dot on the number line at the point that corresponds to the number. The number is the **coordinate** of the point.

Answers

1. **(a)** -53 **(b)** 134 **(c)** $5, -10$

| EXAMPLE 2 | Graphing Rational Numbers |

Graph each rational number on a number line.

$$-\frac{3}{2}, \quad -\frac{2}{3}, \quad 0.5, \quad 1\frac{1}{3}, \quad \frac{23}{8}, \quad 3.25, \quad 4$$

To locate the improper fractions on a number line, write them as mixed numbers or decimals. The graph is shown in **Figure 3**.

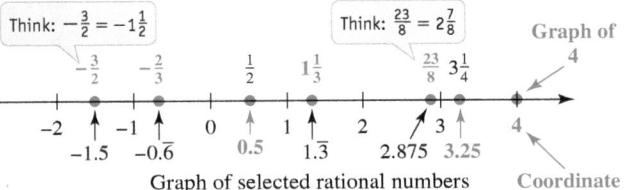

Graph of selected rational numbers

Figure 3

Think of the graph of a set of numbers as a picture of the set.

Work Problem ➋ at the Side. ▶

Not all numbers are rational. For example, the square root of 2, written $\sqrt{2}$, cannot be written as a quotient of two integers. Because of this, $\sqrt{2}$ is an *irrational number*. See **Figure 4**.

Irrational Numbers

$\{x \mid x$ is a nonrational number represented by a point on a number line$\}$ is the set of **irrational numbers.**

The decimal form of an irrational number neither terminates nor repeats.

Both rational and irrational numbers can be represented by points on a number line and together form the set of **real numbers.** See **Figure 5**.

Real Numbers

$\{x \mid x$ is a rational or an irrational number$\}$ is the set of **real numbers.**

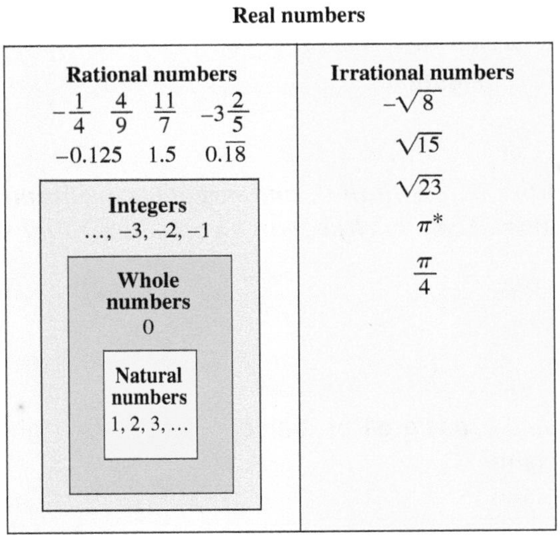

Real numbers

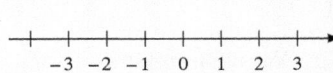
➋ Graph each rational number on a number line.

$$-3, \quad \frac{17}{8}, \quad -2.75, \quad 1\frac{1}{2}, \quad -\frac{3}{4}$$

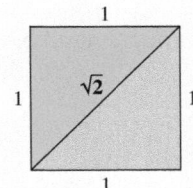

This square has diagonal of length $\sqrt{2}$. The number $\sqrt{2}$ is an irrational number.

Figure 4

Rational numbers	Irrational numbers
$-\frac{1}{4}$ $\frac{4}{9}$ $\frac{11}{7}$ $-3\frac{2}{5}$	$-\sqrt{8}$
-0.125 1.5 $0.\overline{18}$	$\sqrt{15}$
Integers ..., $-3, -2, -1$	$\sqrt{23}$
Whole numbers 0	π^*
Natural numbers $1, 2, 3, ...$	$\frac{\pi}{4}$

An example of a number that is not a real number is the square root of a negative number, such as $\sqrt{-5}$.

Figure 5

Answer

2.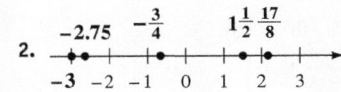

3 List the numbers in the following set that belong to each set of numbers.

$$\left\{ -7, \ -\frac{4}{5}, \ 0, \ \sqrt{3}, \ 2.7, \ 13 \right\}$$

(a) Whole numbers

(b) Integers

(c) Rational numbers

(d) Irrational numbers

EXAMPLE 3 Determining Whether a Number Belongs to a Set

List the numbers in the following set that belong to each set of numbers.

$$\left\{ -5, \ -\frac{2}{3}, \ 0, \ 0.\overline{6}, \ \sqrt{2}, \ \pi, \ 3\frac{1}{4}, \ 5, \ 5.8 \right\}$$

(a) Natural numbers: 5

(b) Whole numbers: 0 and 5
The whole numbers consist of the natural (counting) numbers and 0.

(c) Integers: $-5, 0,$ and 5

(d) Rational numbers: $-5, -\frac{2}{3}, 0, 0.\overline{6} \left(\text{or } \frac{2}{3} \right), 3\frac{1}{4} \left(\text{or } \frac{13}{4} \right), 5,$ and $5.8 \left(\text{or } \frac{58}{10} \right)$
Each of these numbers can be written as the quotient of two integers.

(e) Irrational numbers: $\sqrt{2}$ and π

(f) Real numbers: All the numbers in the set are real numbers.

◄ **Work Problem ③ at the Side.**

OBJECTIVE ▶ ② Tell which of two real numbers is less than the other. Given any two different positive numbers, we can determine which number is less than the other. Positive numbers decrease as the corresponding points on the number line go to the left. For example,

$$8 < 12 \text{ because 8 is to the left of 12 on the number line.}$$

This ordering is extended to all real numbers by definition.

Ordering of Real Numbers

For any two real numbers a and b, **a is less than b** if a lies to the left of b on a number line. See **Figure 6.**

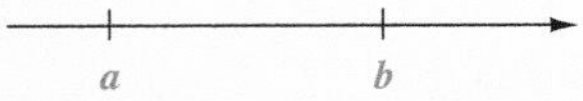

a lies to the left of b, or $a < b$.

Figure 6

Thus, any negative number is less than 0, and any negative number is less than any positive number. Also, 0 is less than any positive number.

The following also holds true.

Ordering of Real Numbers

For any two real numbers a and b, **a is greater than b** if a lies to the right of b on a number line. See **Figure 7.**

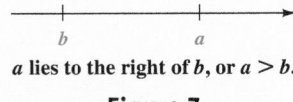

a lies to the right of b, or $a > b$.

Figure 7

Answers

3. (a) $0, 13$ (b) $-7, 0, 13$
   (c) $-7, -\frac{4}{5}, 0, 2.7, 13$ (d) $\sqrt{3}$

EXAMPLE 4	**Determining the Order of Real Numbers**

Is the statement $-3 < -1$ *true* or *false*?

Locate -3 and -1 on a number line. See **Figure 8.** Because -3 lies to the *left* of -1, -3 is less than -1. The statement $-3 < -1$ is true.

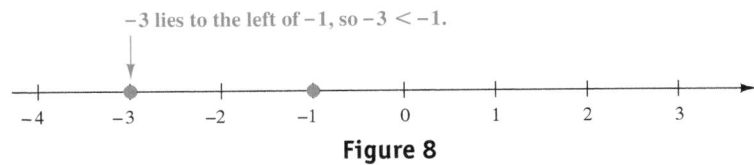

Figure 8

Also, the statement $-1 > -3$ is true because -1 lies to the *right* of -3 on the number line. See **Figure 8.**

———————— Work Problem ④ at the Side. ▶

OBJECTIVE ▶ ③ Find the additive inverse of a real number. For any real number x (except 0), there is exactly one number on a number line the same distance from 0 as x, but on the *opposite* side of 0. See **Figure 9.** Such pairs of numbers are *additive inverses,* or *opposites,* of each other.

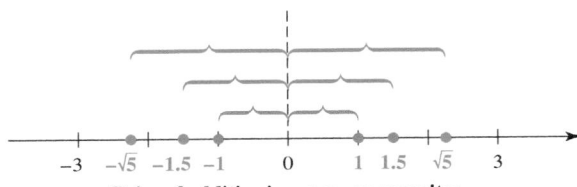

Pairs of additive inverses, or opposites

Figure 9

Additive Inverse

The **additive inverse** of a nonzero number x is the number that is the same distance from 0 on a number line as x, but on the *opposite* side of 0.

We indicate the additive inverse of a number by writing the symbol $-$ in front of the number. For example, the additive inverse of 7 is -7 (read "*negative* 7"). We could write the additive inverse of -4 as $-(-4)$, but we know that 4 is the opposite of -4. Because a number can have only one additive inverse, $-(-4)$ and 4 must represent the same number.

$$-(-4) = 4$$

Double Negative Rule

For any real number x, $-(-x) = x.$

The table in the margin gives examples of additive inverses.

Finding an Additive Inverse

The additive inverse of a nonzero number is found by changing the sign of the number.

A nonzero number and its additive inverse have opposite signs.

Work Problem ⑤ at the Side. ▶

---

④ Tell whether each statement is *true* or *false*.

ⓖ (a) $-2 < 4$

-2 is to the (*left / right*) of 4 on a number line, so the statement is (*true / false*).

ⓖ (b) $6 > -3$

6 is to the (*left / right*) of -3 on a number line, so the statement is (*true / false*).

(c) $-9 < -12$

(d) $-4 \geq -1$

(e) $-6 \leq 0$

ADDITIVE INVERSES

Number	Additive Inverse
-4	$-(-4)$, or 4
0	0
5	-5
$-\frac{2}{3}$	$\frac{2}{3}$
0.52	-0.52

Note that the number 0 is its own additive inverse.

⑤ Find the additive inverse of each number.

(a) 15   **(b)** -9

(c) -12 **(d)** $\frac{1}{2}$

(e) 0   **(f)** -0.1

Answers

4. **(a)** left; true **(b)** right; true **(c)** false
   (d) false **(e)** true
5. **(a)** -15 **(b)** 9 **(c)** 12
   (d) $-\frac{1}{2}$ **(e)** 0 **(f)** 0.1

6 Find each absolute value and simplify if needed.

(a) $\left|-9\right|$

(b) $\left|9\right|$

(c) $-\left|15\right|$

GS **(d)** $-\left|-9\right|$

$$= -\underline{\quad}$$

$$= \underline{\quad}$$

(e) $\left|9-4\right|$

GS **(f)** $-\left|32-2\right|$

$$= -\left|\underline{\quad}\right|$$

$$= \underline{\quad}$$

OBJECTIVE ▶ ④ Find the absolute value of a real number. Because additive inverses are the same distance from 0 on a number line, a number and its additive inverse have the same *absolute value.* The **absolute value** of a real number x, written $\left|x\right|$ and read *"the absolute value of x,"* can be defined as the distance between 0 and the number on a number line.

$\left|2\right| = 2$ The distance between 2 and 0 on a number line is 2 units.

$\left|-2\right| = 2$ The distance between -2 and 0 on a number line is also 2 units.

Distance is a physical measurement, which is never negative. ***Therefore, the absolute value of a number is never negative.***

Absolute Value

For any real number x,

$$\left|x\right| = \begin{cases} x & \text{if } x \geq 0 \\ -x & \text{if } x < 0. \end{cases}$$

By this definition, if x is a positive number or 0, then its absolute value is x itself.

$$\left|8\right| = 8 \quad \text{and} \quad \left|0\right| = 0$$

If x is a negative number, then its absolute value is the additive inverse of x.

$$\left|-8\right| = -(-8) = 8 \quad \text{The additive inverse of } -8 \text{ is 8.}$$

EXAMPLE 5   **Finding Absolute Value**

Find each absolute value and simplify if needed.

(a) $\left|0\right| = 0$ **(b)** $\left|5\right| = 5$ **(c)** $\left|-5\right| = -(-5) = 5$

(d) $-\left|5\right| = -(5) = -5$ **(e)** $-\left|-5\right| = -(5) = -5$

(f) $\left|8-2\right| = \left|6\right| = 6$ **(g)** $-\left|8-2\right| = -\left|6\right| = -6$

Absolute value bars are grouping symbols. In parts (f) and (g), we perform any operations inside the absolute value bars *before* finding the absolute value.

◀ **Work Problem ⑥ at the Side.**

Answers

6. (a) 9   (b) 9   (c) -15
   (d) 9; -9 (e) 5   (f) 30; -30

1.3 Exercises

FOR EXTRA HELP

Go to MyMathLab *for worked-out, step-by-step solutions to exercises enclosed in a square* and video solutions to ▶ *exercises.*

CONCEPT CHECK *Complete each statement.*

1. The number _____ is a whole number, but not a natural number.

2. The natural numbers, their additive inverses, and 0 form the set of _____ .

3. The additive inverse of every negative number is a (*negative / positive*) number.

4. If x and y are real numbers with $x > y$, then x lies to the (*left / right*) of y on a number line.

5. A rational number is the _____ of two integers, with the _____ not equal to 0.

6. Decimals that neither terminate nor repeat are _____ numbers.

Use an integer to express each boldface italic number representing a change. ***See Example 1.***

7. Between 2012 and 2013, the male population in the ▶ United States increased by ***1,212,795.*** (Data from U.S. Census Bureau.)

8. From 2010 to 2015, the mean SAT critical reading score for Ohio students increased by ***19.*** (Data from The College Board.)

9. From 2009 to 2014, newspaper circulation in the United States on Sundays went from 46,164 thousand to 42,751 thousand, a decrease of ***3413*** thousand papers. (Data from *Editor and Publisher International Yearbook.*)

10. In 1935, there were 15,295 banks in the United States. By 2015, the number was 6242, a decrease of ***9053*** banks. (Data from Federal Deposit Insurance Corporation.)

Graph each rational number on a number line. ***See Example 2.***

11. $0, 3, -5, -6$

12. $2, 6, -2, -1$

13. $-0.5, -6, -4, \dfrac{7}{4}, 4$

14. $-5, -\dfrac{7}{2}, -2, 0, 4.5$

15. $\dfrac{1}{4}, 2\dfrac{1}{2}, -3\dfrac{4}{5}, -4, -\dfrac{13}{8}$

16. $5\dfrac{1}{4}, \dfrac{41}{9}, -2\dfrac{1}{3}, 0, -3\dfrac{2}{5}$

List all numbers from each set that are the following. ***See Example 3.***

(a) *natural numbers*   **(b)** *whole numbers*   **(c)** *integers*

(d) *rational numbers*   **(e)** *irrational numbers*   **(f)** *real numbers*

17. $\left\{ -9, -\sqrt{7}, -1\dfrac{1}{4}, -\dfrac{3}{5}, 0, \sqrt{5}, 3, 5.9, 7 \right\}$

18. $\left\{ -5.3, -5, -\sqrt{3}, -1, -\dfrac{1}{9}, 0, 1.2, 4, \sqrt{12} \right\}$

19. $\left\{ \dfrac{7}{9}, -2.\overline{3}, \sqrt{3}, 0, -8\dfrac{3}{4}, 11, -6, \pi \right\}$

20. $\left\{ 1\dfrac{5}{8}, -0.\overline{4}, \sqrt{6}, 9, -12, 0, \sqrt{10}, 0.026 \right\}$

CONCEPT CHECK *Exercises 21–38 check understanding of the various sets of numbers.*

Give a number that satisfies the given condition.

21. An integer between 3.6 and 4.6

22. A rational number between 2.8 and 2.9

23. A whole number that is not positive and is less than 1

24. A whole number greater than 3.5

25. An irrational number that is between $\sqrt{12}$ and $\sqrt{14}$

26. A real number that is neither negative nor positive

Decide whether each statement is true *or* false.

27. Every natural number is positive.

28. Every whole number is positive.

29. Every integer is a rational number.

30. Every rational number is a real number.

31. Some numbers are both rational and irrational.

32. Every terminating decimal is a rational number.

Give three numbers between −6 *and* 6 *that satisfy each given condition.*

33. Positive real numbers but not integers

34. Real numbers but not positive numbers

35. Real numbers but not whole numbers

36. Rational numbers but not integers

37. Real numbers but not rational numbers

38. Rational numbers but not negative numbers

Select the lesser of the two given numbers. ***See Example 4.***

39. −11, −4

40. −9, −16

41. −21, 1

42. −57, 3

43. 0, −100

44. −215, 0

45. $-\dfrac{2}{3}, -\dfrac{1}{4}$

46. $-\dfrac{3}{8}, -\dfrac{9}{16}$

Decide whether each statement is true *or* false. ***See Example 4 and* Figures 6–8.**

47. $8 < -16$

48. $12 < -24$

49. $-5 < -2$

50. $-10 < -9$

51. $-4 > 0$

52. $-9 > 0$

53. $-11 > -10$

54. $-8 > -2$

For each number, find **(a)** *its additive inverse and* **(b)** *its absolute value. See* **Objectives 3 and 4.**

55. −2

56. −8

57. 6

58. 11

59. $-\dfrac{3}{4}$

60. $-\dfrac{1}{3}$

61. 4.95

62. 8.1

63. CONCEPT CHECK Match each expression in Column I with its value in Column II. Choices in Column II may be used once, more than once, or not at all.

I	II
(a) $\lvert -9 \rvert$	**A.** 9
(b) $-(-9)$	**B.** −9
(c) $-\lvert -9 \rvert$	**C.** Neither A nor B
(d) $-\lvert -(-9) \rvert$	**D.** Both A and B

64. CONCEPT CHECK Fill in each blank with the correct value.

The opposite of −5 is _____, while the absolute value of −5 is _____.

The additive inverse of −5 is _____, while the additive inverse of the absolute value of −5 is _____.

Find each absolute value and simplify if needed. **See Example 5.**

65. $\lvert -6 \rvert$

66. $\lvert -3 \rvert$

67. $-\lvert 12 \rvert$

68. $-\lvert 23 \rvert$

69. $-\left\lvert -\dfrac{2}{3} \right\rvert$

70. $-\left\lvert -\dfrac{4}{5} \right\rvert$

71. $\lvert 13 - 4 \rvert$

72. $\lvert 8 - 7 \rvert$

73. $-\lvert 6 - 3 \rvert$

74. $-\lvert 9 - 4 \rvert$

Decide whether each statement is true *or* false.

75. $\lvert -8 \rvert < 7$

76. $\lvert -6 \rvert \geq -\lvert 6 \rvert$

77. $4 \leq \lvert 4 \rvert$

78. $-\lvert -3 \rvert > 2$

79. $-4 \leq -(-5)$

80. $\lvert -6 \rvert < \lvert -9 \rvert$

81. $-\lvert 8 \rvert > \lvert -9 \rvert$

82. $-\lvert -5 \rvert \geq -\lvert -9 \rvert$

The table shows the percent change in the Consumer Price Index (CPI) for selected categories of goods and services from 2013 to 2014 and from 2014 to 2015. Use the table to answer each question.

83. Which category in which year represents the greatest percent decrease?

84. Which category in which year represents the greatest percent increase?

Category	Change from 2013 to 2014	Change from 2014 to 2015
Apparel	0.7	−1.9
Food	3.1	1.6
Energy	7.1	−17.1
Medical care	1.4	3.0
Transportation	−1.1	−7.9

Data from U.S. Bureau of Labor Statistics.

85. Which category in which year represents the least change?

86. Which category represents a decrease for both years?

Study Skills

USING STUDY CARDS

You may have used "flash cards" in other classes. In math, "study cards" can help you remember terms and definitions, procedures, and concepts. Use study cards to

▶ Help you understand and learn the material;

▶ Quickly review when you have a few minutes;

▶ Review before a quiz or test.

One of the advantages of study cards is that you learn the material while you are making them.

Vocabulary Cards

Put the word and a page reference on the front of the card. On the back, write the definition, an example, any related words, and a sample problem (if appropriate).

Front of Card

Integers   *p. 47*

Back of Card

Def: The natural numbers   {1, 2, 3, 4, ...}
their opposites   {-1, -2, -3, -4, ...}
and 0.   {0}

Integers   { ... , -3, -2, -1, 0, 1, 2, 3, ...}

⟶ *No fractions, decimals, roots*
⟶ *Related word: rational numbers*

Procedure ("Steps") Cards

Write the name of the procedure on the front of the card. Then write each step in words. On the back of the card, put an example showing each step.

Front of Card

Evaluating Absolute Value (simplifying)   p. 52

1. Work inside absolute value bars first (like working inside parentheses).
2. Find the absolute value (never negative).
3. A negative sign in front of the absolute value bar is NOT affected, so keep it!

Back of Card

Examples:

simplify $\left|\ 10 - 6\ \right|$ *Work inside: 10 − 6 = 4*
         $\left|\ 4\ \right| = 4$ *Absolute value of 4 is 4.*

simplify $-\left|\ -12\ \right|$ *Absolute value of −12 is 12.*
            -12 *Keep negative sign that was in front.*

Now Try This

Make a vocabulary card and a procedure card for material you are learning now.

1.4 Adding Real Numbers

OBJECTIVE ▶ **1** Add two numbers with the same sign. Recall that the answer to an addition problem is a **sum.** The numbers being added are the **addends.**

$$x + y = z \leftarrow \text{Sum}$$
$$\text{Addends}$$

EXAMPLE 1   Adding Numbers (Same Sign) on a Number Line

Use a number line to find each sum.

(a) $2 + 3$

   Step 1 Start at 0 and draw an arrow 2 units to the *right*. See **Figure 10.**

   Step 2 From the right end of that arrow, draw another arrow 3 units to the *right* to represent the addition of a *positive* number.

The number below the end of the second arrow is 5, so $2 + 3 = 5$.

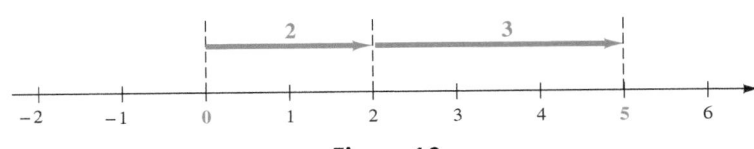

Figure 10

(b) $-2 + (-4)$

   (We write parentheses around -4 due to the $+$ and $-$ symbols next to each other.)

   Step 1 Start at 0 and draw an arrow 2 units to the *left*. See **Figure 11.**

   Step 2 From the left end of the first arrow, draw a second arrow 4 units to the *left* to represent the addition of a *negative* number.

The number below the end of the second arrow is -6, so $-2 + (-4) = -6$.

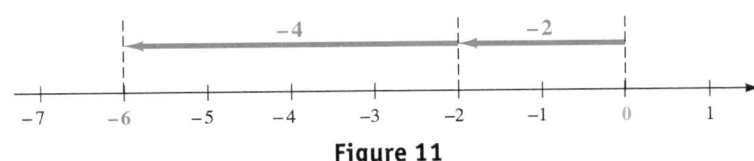

Figure 11

──────────── Work Problem **1** at the Side. ▶

In **Example 1(b),** the sum of the two negative numbers -2 and -4 is a negative number whose distance from 0 is the sum of the distance of -2 from 0 and the distance of -4 from 0. ***That is, the sum of two negative numbers is the opposite of the sum of their absolute values.***

Adding Signed Numbers (Same Sign)

To add two numbers with the *same* sign, add their absolute values. The sum has the same sign as the addends.

Examples: $2 + 4 = 6$ and $-2 + (-4) = -6$

OBJECTIVES

1 Add two numbers with the same sign.

2 Add two numbers with different signs.

3 Use the rules for order of operations when adding real numbers.

4 Translate words and phrases that indicate addition.

1 Use a number line to find each sum.

   (a) $1 + 4$

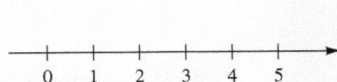

   (b) $-2 + (-5)$

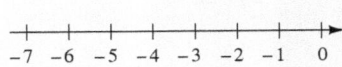

Answers

1. (a) $1 + 4 = 5$

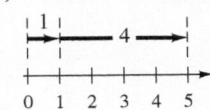

   (b) $-2 + (-5) = -7$

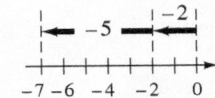

2 Find each sum.

(a) $-7 + (-3)$

(b) $-\dfrac{2}{5} + \left(-\dfrac{1}{2}\right)$

(c) $-1.27 + (-5.46)$

3 Use a number line to find each sum.

(a) $6 + (-3)$

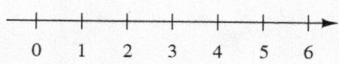

(b) $-5 + 1$

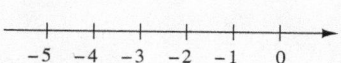

Answers

2. (a) -10 (b) $-\dfrac{9}{10}$ (c) -6.73

3. (a) $6 + (-3) = 3$

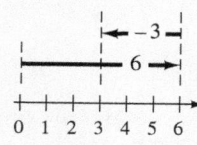

(b) $-5 + 1 = -4$

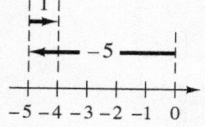

> **EXAMPLE 2** **Adding Two Negative Numbers**
>
> Find each sum.
>
> (a) $-9 + (-2)$ Both addends are negative.
>
> $\qquad = \underset{\uparrow}{-}(|-9| + |-2|)$ Add the absolute values of the addends.
>
> $\qquad\quad$ Sign of each addend
>
> $\qquad = -(9 + 2)$ Take the absolute values.
>
> $\qquad = -11$ The sum of two negative numbers is negative.
>
> (b) $\qquad -\dfrac{1}{4} + \left(-\dfrac{2}{3}\right)$ Both addends are negative.
>
> Think: $\left|-\dfrac{3}{12}\right| = \dfrac{3}{12}$ $\quad = -\dfrac{3}{12} + \left(-\dfrac{8}{12}\right)$ Write equivalent fractions using the LCD, 12.
> and $\left|-\dfrac{8}{12}\right| = \dfrac{8}{12}$
>
> $\qquad\qquad\quad = -\dfrac{11}{12}$ Add the absolute values of the addends. Use the common negative sign.
>
> (c) $-2.6 + (-4.7)$ Both addends are negative.
>
> $\qquad = -7.3$ Add the absolute values of the addends. Use the common negative sign.

—————— ◄ **Work Problem 2** at the Side.

OBJECTIVE ▸ **2** Add two numbers with different signs.

> **EXAMPLE 3** **Adding Numbers (Different Signs) on a Number Line**
>
> Use a number line to find the sum $-2 + 5$.
>
> **Step 1** Start at 0 and draw an arrow 2 units to the left. See **Figure 12.**
>
> **Step 2** From the left end of this arrow, draw a second arrow 5 units to the *right* to represent the addition of a *positive* number.
>
> The number below the end of the second arrow is 3, so $-2 + 5 = 3$.
>
>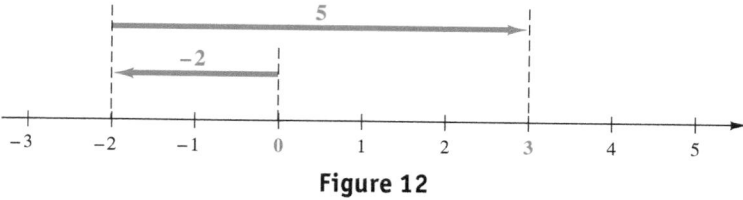
>
> **Figure 12**

—————— ◄ **Work Problem 3** at the Side.

Adding Signed Numbers (Different Signs)

To add two numbers with *different* signs, find their absolute values and subtract the lesser absolute value from the greater. The sum has the same sign as the addend with greater absolute value.

Examples: $-2 + 6 = 4$ and $2 + (-6) = -4$

EXAMPLE 4 Adding Signed Numbers (Different Signs)

Find each sum.

(a) $-12 + 5$

$$\begin{array}{cc} |-12| & |5| \\ \downarrow & \downarrow \end{array}$$

Find the absolute value of each addend, and subtract the lesser from the greater.

$= -(12 - 5)$

Use the sign of the addend with greater absolute value.

$= -7$

(b) $-8 + 12$

$= +(12 - 8)$

Find the absolute value of each addend, and subtract the lesser from the greater.

Use the sign of the addend with greater absolute value.

$= 4$

The $+$ symbol is understood.

(c) $\dfrac{5}{6} + \left(-1\dfrac{1}{3}\right)$

$= \dfrac{5}{6} + \left(-\dfrac{4}{3}\right)$ Write the mixed number as an improper fraction.

$= \dfrac{5}{6} + \left(-\dfrac{8}{6}\right)$ Find a common denominator.

$= -\left(\dfrac{8}{6} - \dfrac{5}{6}\right)$ $\left|\dfrac{5}{6}\right| = \dfrac{5}{6}$ and $\left|-\dfrac{8}{6}\right| = \dfrac{8}{6}$; Subtract the lesser absolute value from the greater.

Use a $-$ symbol because $\left|-\dfrac{8}{6}\right| > \left|\dfrac{5}{6}\right|$.

$= -\dfrac{3}{6}$ Subtract the fractions.

$= -\dfrac{1}{2}$ Write in lowest terms.

(d) $8.1 + (-4.6)$

$= +(8.1 - 4.6)$

$|8.1| > |-4.6|$

$= 3.5$

(e) $-16 + 16$

$= 0$

(f) $42 + (-42)$

$= 0$

In parts (e) and (f), the difference of the absolute values is 0. *In general, when additive inverses are added, the sum is 0.*

Work Problem **4** at the Side. ▶

OBJECTIVE 3 Use the rules for order of operations when adding real numbers.

EXAMPLE 5 Adding with Grouping Symbols

Find each sum.

Start here.

(a) $-3 + [4 + (-8)]$

$= -3 + [-4]$

$= -7$ We could write (-4).

(b) $8 + [(-2 + 6) + (-3)]$

$= 8 + [4 + (-3)]$

$= 8 + 1$

$= 9$

Continued on Next Page

4 Find each sum.

(a) $-8 + 2$

$= (+/-)(\underline{\quad} - \underline{\quad})$

$|-8| \quad |2|$

$= \underline{\quad}$

(b) $-15 + 4$

(c) $17 + (-10)$

(d) $\dfrac{3}{4} + \left(-1\dfrac{3}{8}\right)$

(e) $-9.5 + 3.8$

(f) $37 + (-37)$

Answers

4. (a) $-$; 8; 2; -6 **(b)** -11 **(c)** 7 **(d)** $-\dfrac{5}{8}$ **(e)** -5.7 **(f)** 0

5 Label the order in which each
GS operation should be performed.
Then find each sum.

(a) $2 + [7 + (-3)]$
   ② ①

$= 2 + \underline{\hspace{1cm}}$

$= \underline{\hspace{1cm}}$

(b) $6 + [(-2 + 5) + 7]$
   ○   ○   ○

(c) $-9 + [-4 + (-8 + 6)]$
   ○   ○   ○

(d) $|-8 + (-10)| + |7 + (-7)|$
       ○   ○   ○

6 Write a numerical expression for
each phrase, and simplify the
expression.

(a) 4 more than -12

(b) The sum of 6 and -7

(c) 7 increased by the sum of 8
   and -3

7 Solve the problem.
   A football team lost 8 yd on
first down, lost 5 yd on second
down, and then gained 7 yd on
third down. Find the total net
yardage for the plays.

(c) $|-9 + 3| + |7 + (-11)|$ — The absolute value bars serve as grouping symbols.

$= |-6| + |-4|$ Add inside the absolute value bars.

$= 6 + 4$ Find each absolute value.

$= 10$ Add.

◀ **Work Problem 5 at the Side.**

OBJECTIVE 4 Translate words and phrases that indicate addition. Problem solving requires translating words and phrases into symbols.

WORDS AND PHRASES THAT INDICATE ADDITION

Word or Phrase	Example	Numerical Expression and Simplification
Sum of	The *sum of* -3 and 4	$-3 + 4$, which equals 1
Added to	5 *added to* -8	$-8 + 5$, which equals -3
More than	12 *more than* -5	$(-5) + 12$, which equals 7
Increased by	-6 *increased by* 13	$-6 + 13$, which equals 7
Plus	3 *plus* 14	$3 + 14$, which equals 17

EXAMPLE 6   Translating Words and Phrases (Addition)

Write a numerical expression for each phrase, and simplify the expression.

(a) The **sum of** -8 and 4 and 6

$-8 + 4 + 6$ simplifies to $-4 + 6$,   which equals   2.

Add in order from left to right.

(b) 3 **more than** -5, **increased by** 12

$(-5 + 3) + 12$ simplifies to $-2 + 12$,   which equals   10.

Here we *simplified* each expression by performing the operations.

◀ **Work Problem 6 at the Side.**

EXAMPLE 7   Solving an Application Involving Addition

A football team **gained 3 yd** on first down, **lost 12 yd** on second down, and then **gained 13 yd** on third down. Find the total net yardage for the plays.

$3 + (-12) + 13$

$= [3 + (-12)] + 13$ Represent gains with positive numbers, losses

$= (-9) + 13$ with negative numbers.

$= 4$ Add from left to right.

The total net yardage on these plays was 4 yd.

◀ **Work Problem 7 at the Side.**

Answers

5. (a) 4; 6
   (b) ③, ①, ②; 16
   (c) ③, ②, ①; -15
   (d) ①, ③, ②; 18
6. (a) $-12 + 4$; -8 (b) $6 + (-7)$; -1
   (c) $7 + [8 + (-3)]$; 12
7. -6 yd

1.4 Exercises

FOR EXTRA HELP   Go to MyMathLab *for worked-out, step-by-step solutions to exercises enclosed in a square* and video solutions to ▶ *exercises.*

CONCEPT CHECK   *Complete each of the following.*

1. The sum of two negative numbers will always be a (*positive / negative*) number.
▶ Give a number-line illustration using the sum $-2 + (-3) = $ _____.

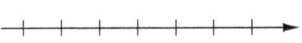

2. When adding a positive number and a negative number, where the negative
▶ number has the greater absolute value, the sum will be a (*positive / negative*)
   number. Give a number-line illustration using the sum $-4 + 2 = $ _____.

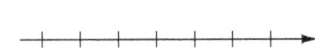

3. The sum of a number and its opposite will always be _____.

4. To simplify the expression $8 + [-2 + (-3 + 5)]$, begin by adding
   _____ and _____, according to the rules for order of operations.

Find each sum. **See Examples 1–5.**

5. $-7 + (-3)$

6. $-11 + (-4)$

7. $-10 + (-3)$

8. $-16 + (-7)$

9. $6 + (-4)$

10. $8 + (-5)$

11. $12 + (-15)$

12. $4 + (-8)$

13. $-16 + 7$

14. $-13 + 6$

15. $6 + (-6)$

16. $-11 + 11$

17. $-\frac{1}{3} + \left(-\frac{4}{15}\right)$

18. $-\frac{1}{4} + \left(-\frac{5}{12}\right)$

19. $-\frac{1}{6} + \frac{2}{3}$

20. $-\frac{6}{25} + \frac{19}{20}$

21. $\frac{9}{10} + \left(-1\frac{3}{8}\right)$

22. $\frac{5}{8} + \left(-1\frac{5}{12}\right)$

23. $2\frac{1}{2} + \left(-3\frac{1}{4}\right)$

24. $1\frac{3}{8} + \left(-2\frac{1}{4}\right)$

25. $-12.4 + (-3.5)$

26. $-21.3 + (-2.5)$

27. $7.8 + (-9.4)$

28. $14.7 + (-10.1)$

29. $10 + [-3 + (-2)]$

30. $13 + [-4 + (-5)]$

31. $5 + [14 + (-6)]$

32. $7 + [3 + (-14)]$

33. $-3 + [5 + (-2)]$

34. $-7 + [10 + (-3)]$

35. $-8 + [(-1 + 3) + (-2)]$

36. $-7 + [(-8 + 5) + 3]$

37. $-7.1 + [3.3 + (-4.9)]$

38. $-9.5 + [-6.8 + (-1.3)]$

39. $[-8 + (-3)] + [-7 + (-7)]$
   $= $ _____ $+ ($ _____ $)$
   $= $ _____

40. $[-5 + (-4)] + [9 + (-2)]$
   $= $ _____ $+ $ _____
   $= $ _____

41. $\left|-7+5\right|+\left|8+(-12)\right|$

42. $\left|-8+2\right|+\left|4+(-9)\right|$

43. $\left|-12+(-4)\right|+\left|-4+10\right|$

44. $\left|-10+(-2)\right|+\left|-8+17\right|$

45. $\left(-\dfrac{1}{2}+0.25\right)+\left(-\dfrac{3}{4}+0.75\right)$

46. $\left(-\dfrac{3}{2}+0.75\right)+\left(-\dfrac{1}{2}+2.25\right)$

Perform each operation, and then determine whether the statement is true *or* false.
Try to do all work mentally.

47. $-10+6+7=-3$

48. $-12+8+5=-1$

49. $\dfrac{7}{3}+\left(-\dfrac{1}{3}\right)+\left(-\dfrac{6}{3}\right)=0$

50. $-\dfrac{3}{2}+1+\dfrac{1}{2}=0$

51. $\left|-8+10\right|=-8+(-10)$

52. $\left|-4+6\right|=-4+(-6)$

53. $2\dfrac{1}{5}+\left(-\dfrac{6}{11}\right)=-\dfrac{6}{11}+2\dfrac{1}{5}$

54. $-1\dfrac{1}{2}+\dfrac{5}{8}=\dfrac{5}{8}+\left(-1\dfrac{1}{2}\right)$

55. $-7+\left[-5+(-3)\right]=\left[(-7)+(-5)\right]+3$

56. $6+\left[-2+(-5)\right]=\left[(-4)+(-2)\right]+5$

Write a numerical expression for each phrase, and simplify the expression.
See Example 6.

57. The sum of -5 and 12 and 6

58. The sum of -3 and 5 and -12

59. 14 added to the sum of -19 and -4

60. -2 added to the sum of -18 and 11

61. The sum of -4 and -10, increased by 12

62. The sum of -7 and -13, increased by 14

63. $\frac{2}{7}$ more than the sum of $\frac{5}{7}$ and $-\frac{9}{7}$

64. 0.85 more than the sum of -1.25 and -4.75

The table gives scores (above or below par—that is, above or below the score
"standard") for selected golfers during the 2015 PGA Tour Championship. Write a
signed number that represents the total score (above or below par) for the four rounds
for each golfer.

	Golfer	Round 1	Round 2	Round 3	Round 4	Total Score
65.	Dustin Johnson	-6	$+1$*	-4	-3	
66.	Billy Horschel	0	-4	-4	$+3$	
67.	Jason Dufner	-1	$+3$	-3	$+5$	
68.	Charles Howell III	-2	-2	$+5$	$+2$	

*Golf scoring commonly includes a + symbol with a score over par.
Data from www.pga.com

Solve each problem. See Example 7.

69. The surface, or rim, of a canyon is at altitude 0. On a hike down into the canyon, a party of hikers stops for a rest at 130 m below the surface. They then descend another 54 m. What is their new altitude? (Write the altitude as a signed number.)

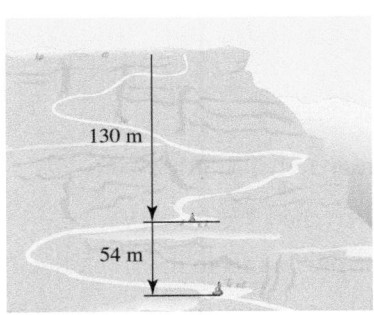

70. A pilot announces to the passengers that the current altitude of their plane is 34,000 ft. Because of some unexpected turbulence, the pilot is forced to descend 2100 ft. What is the new altitude of the plane? (Write the altitude as a signed number.)

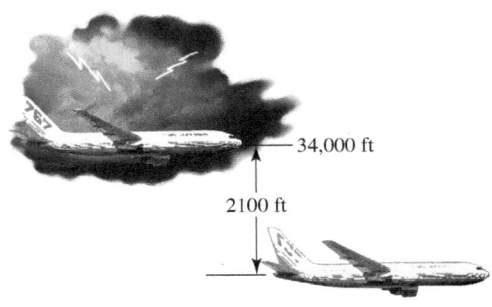

71. Based on 2020 population projections, New York will lose 5 seats in the U.S. House of Representatives, Pennsylvania will lose 4 seats, and Ohio will lose 3. Write a signed number that represents the total number of seats these three states are projected to lose. (Data from Population Reference Bureau.)

72. In 2020, Michigan is projected to lose 3 seats in the U.S. House of Representatives and Illinois 2. Projected to gain the most seats are California with 9, Texas with 5, Florida with 3, Georgia with 2, and Arizona with 2. Write a signed number that represents the algebraic sum of these changes. (Data from Population Reference Bureau.)

73. J. D. enjoys playing Triominoes every Wednesday night. Last Wednesday, on four successive turns, his scores were −19, 28, −5, and 13. What was his final score for the four turns?

74. Gail also enjoys playing Triominoes. On five successive turns, her scores were −13, 15, −12, 24, and 14. What was her total score for the five turns?

75. On three consecutive passes, a quarterback passed for a gain of 6 yd, was sacked for a loss of 12 yd, and passed for a gain of 43 yd. Find the total net yardage for the plays.

76. On a series of three consecutive running plays, a running back gained 4 yd, lost 3 yd, and lost 2 yd. Find his total net yardage for the plays.

77. The lowest temperature ever recorded in Arkansas was −29°F. The highest temperature ever recorded there was 149°F more than the lowest. What was this highest temperature? (Data from National Climatic Data Center.)

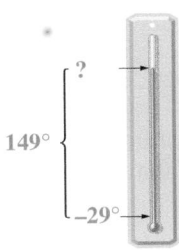

78. On January 23, 1943, the temperature rose 49°F in two minutes in Spearfish, South Dakota. If the starting temperature was −4°F, what was the temperature two minutes later? (Data from *Guinness World Records*.)

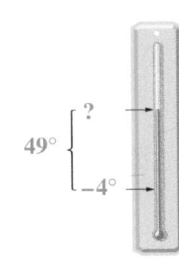

1.5 | Subtracting Real Numbers

OBJECTIVES

1. Subtract two numbers on a number line.
2. Use the definition of subtraction.
3. Use the rules for order of operations when subtracting real numbers.
4. Translate words and phrases that indicate subtraction.

1. Use a number line to find the difference $6 - 2$.

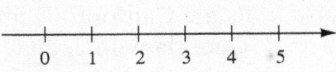

OBJECTIVE ▶ 1 **Subtract two numbers on a number line.** Recall that the answer to a subtraction problem is a **difference.** In the subtraction $x - y$, x is the **minuend** and y is the **subtrahend.**

$$x \quad - \quad y \quad = \quad z$$

Minuend Subtrahend Difference

EXAMPLE 1   **Subtracting Numbers on a Number Line**

Use a number line to find the difference $7 - 4$.

Step 1 Start at 0 and draw an arrow 7 units to the *right*. See **Figure 13**.

Step 2 From the right end of the first arrow, draw a second arrow 4 units to the *left* to represent the subtraction.

The number below the end of the second arrow is 3, so $7 - 4 = 3$.

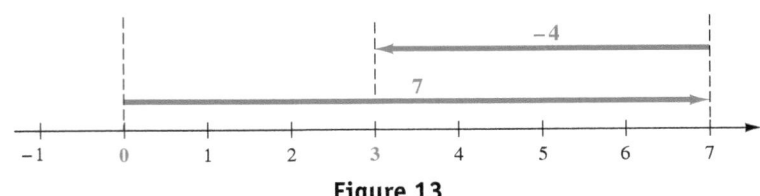

Figure 13

◀ **Work Problem** ❶ **at the Side**

OBJECTIVE ▶ 2 **Use the definition of subtraction.** The procedure used in **Example 1** to find $7 - 4$ is the *same* procedure for finding $7 + (-4)$.

$$7 - 4 \quad \text{is equal to} \quad 7 + (-4).$$

This shows that *subtracting* a positive number from a greater positive number is the same as *adding* the opposite of the lesser number to the greater.

Definition of Subtraction

For any real numbers x and y,

$$x - y \quad \text{is defined as} \quad x + (-y).$$

To subtract y from x, add the additive inverse (or opposite) of y to x. In words, change the subtrahend to its opposite and add.

Example: $4 - 9$
$$= 4 + (-9)$$
$$= -5$$

Answers

1. $6 - 2 = 4$

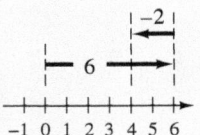

Subtracting Signed Numbers

Step 1 Change the subtraction symbol to an addition symbol, and change the sign of the subtrahend.

Step 2 Add the signed numbers.

EXAMPLE 2	**Subtracting Signed Numbers**

Find each difference.

(a) $12 - 3$

                ┌─ Change $-$ to $+$.

      $= 12 + (-3)$

No change ─┘   └─ Additive inverse of 3

        $= 9$ 12 has the greater absolute value, so the sum is positive.

(b) $5 - 7$

               ┌─ Change $-$ to $+$.

      $= 5 + (-7)$

No change ─┘   └─ Additive inverse of 7

        $= -2$ -7 has the greater absolute value, so the sum is negative.

(c) $-8 - 15$

               ┌─ Change $-$ to $+$.

      $= -8 + (-15)$

No change ─┘   └─ Additive inverse of 15

        $= -23$ The sum of two negative numbers is negative.

(d) $-3 - (-5)$

               ┌─ Change $-$ to $+$.

      $= -3 + 5$

No change ─┘   └─ Additive inverse of -5

        $= 2$ 5 has the greater absolute value, so the sum is positive.

(e) $\dfrac{3}{8} - \left(-\dfrac{4}{5}\right)$

    $= \dfrac{15}{40} - \left(-\dfrac{32}{40}\right)$ Write equivalent fractions using the LCD, 40.

    $= \dfrac{15}{40} + \dfrac{32}{40}$ Definition of subtraction

    $= \dfrac{47}{40}$ Add the fractions.

(f) $-8.75 - (-2.41)$

    $= -8.75 + 2.41$ Definition of subtraction

    $= -6.34$ Add the decimals.

─────────────────── **Work Problem ② at the Side.** ▶

② Find each difference.

(a) $6 - 10$

    $= 6 + (\_\_\_\_)$

    $= \_\_\_\_$

(b) $-2 - 4$

(c) $3 - (-5)$

    $= 3 + \_\_\_\_$

    $= \_\_\_\_$

(d) $-8 - (-12)$

(e) $\dfrac{5}{4} - \left(-\dfrac{3}{7}\right)$

(f) $7.5 - 9.2$

Answers

2. (a) $-10; -4$ (b) -6 (c) $5; 8$

    (d) 4 (e) $\dfrac{47}{28}$ (f) -1.7

3 Label the order in which each
GS operation should be performed.
Then perform the operations.

(a) $2 - [(-3) - (4 + 6)]$
  ◯   ◯   ◯

(b) $[(5 - 7) + 3] - 8$
   ◯   ◯   ◯

(c) $\left[-\dfrac{1}{6} - \left(-\dfrac{1}{3}\right)\right] - \dfrac{1}{4}$
       ◯   ◯

(d) $3|6 - 9| - |4 - 12|$
  ◯◯   ◯   ◯

Uses of the Symbol −

We use the symbol − for three purposes.

1. **It can represent subtraction,** as in $9 - 5 = 4$.

2. **It can represent negative numbers,** such as $-10, -2$, and -3.

3. **It can represent the additive inverse (or opposite) of a number,** as in "the additive inverse (or opposite) of 8 is -8."

We may see more than one use of − in the same expression, such as $-6 - (-9)$, where -9 is subtracted from -6. The meaning of the symbol depends on its position in the algebraic expression.

OBJECTIVE **3** **Use the rules for order of operations when subtracting real numbers.** As before, first perform any operations inside the grouping symbols.

EXAMPLE 3 Subtracting with Grouping Symbols

Perform each operation.

(a) $-6 - [2 - (8 + 3)]$ ← Work from the inside out.

$= -6 - [2 - 11]$ Add inside the parentheses.

$= -6 - [2 + (-11)]$ Definition of subtraction

$= -6 - (-9)$ Add inside the brackets.

$= -6 + 9$ Definition of subtraction

$= 3$ Add.

(b) $\dfrac{2}{3} - \left[\dfrac{1}{12} - \left(-\dfrac{1}{4}\right)\right]$

$= \dfrac{8}{12} - \left[\dfrac{1}{12} - \left(-\dfrac{3}{12}\right)\right]$ Write equivalent fractions using the LCD, 12.

$= \dfrac{8}{12} - \left[\dfrac{1}{12} + \dfrac{3}{12}\right]$ Work inside the brackets.

$= \dfrac{8}{12} - \dfrac{4}{12}$ Add inside the brackets.

$= \dfrac{4}{12}$ Subtract.

$= \dfrac{1}{3}$ Write in lowest terms.

(c) $|4 - 7| - 2|6 - 3|$ ← $2|6-3|$ means $2 \cdot |6-3|$.

$= |-3| - 2|3|$ Work within the absolute value bars.

$= 3 - 2 \cdot 3$ Find each absolute value.

Be careful. Multiply first.

$= 3 - 6$ Multiply.

$= -3$ Subtract.

◀ **Work Problem 3** at the Side.

Answers

3. (a) ③, ②, ①; 15
(b) ①, ②, ③; −7
(c) ①, ②; $-\dfrac{1}{12}$
(d) ③, ①, ④, ②; 1

OBJECTIVE ▶ 4 Translate words and phrases that indicate subtraction.

WORDS AND PHRASES THAT INDICATE SUBTRACTION

Word, Phrase, or Sentence	Example	Numerical Expression and Simplification
Difference of	The *difference of* −3 and −8	−3 − (−8) simplifies to −3 + 8, which equals 5
Subtracted from*	12 *subtracted from* 18	18 − 12, which equals 6
From ... , subtract	*From* 12, *subtract* 8.	12 − 8 simplifies to 12 + (−8), which equals 4
Less	6 *less* 5	6 − 5, which equals 1
Less than*	6 *less than* 5	5 − 6 simplifies to 5 + (−6), which equals −1
Decreased by	9 *decreased by* −4	9 − (−4) simplifies to 9 + 4, which equals 13
Minus	8 *minus* 5	8 − 5, which equals 3

*Be careful with order when translating.

> **❗ CAUTION**
>
> When subtracting two numbers, be careful to write them in the correct order, because, in general,
>
> $$x - y \neq y - x.$$ For example, $5 - 3 \neq 3 - 5$.
>
> *Think carefully before interpreting an expression involving subtraction.*

EXAMPLE 4 Translating Words and Phrases (Subtraction)

Write a numerical expression for each phrase, and simplify the expression.

(a) The **difference of** −8 and 5

When "difference of" is used, write the numbers in the order given.

$-8 - 5$ simplifies to $-8 + (-5)$,   which equals -13.

(b) 4 **subtracted from** the **sum of** 8 and −3

Here the operation of addition is also used, as indicated by the words *sum of*. First, add 8 and −3. Next, subtract 4 from this sum.

$[8 + (-3)] - 4$ simplifies to $5 - 4$,   which equals   1.

(c) 4 **less than** −6

Here 4 must be taken *from* −6, so write −6 first.

Be careful with order. ➔ $-6 - 4$ simplifies to $-6 + (-4)$,   which equals -10.

Notice that "4 less than −6" differs from "4 *is less than* −6." The statement "4 is less than −6" is symbolized $4 < -6$ (which is a false statement).

(d) 8, **decreased by** 5 **less than** 12

First, write "5 less than 12" as $12 - 5$. Next, subtract $12 - 5$ from 8.

$8 - (12 - 5)$ simplifies to $8 - 7$,   which equals   1.

— **Work Problem ④ at the Side.** ▶

4 Write a numerical expression for each phrase, and simplify the expression.

(a) The difference of −5 and −12

(b) −2 subtracted from the sum of 4 and −4

(c) 7 less than −2

(d) 9, decreased by 10 less than 7

Answers
4. **(a)** $-5 - (-12)$; 7
   (b) $[4 + (-4)] - (-2)$; 2
   (c) $-2 - 7$; −9
   (d) $9 - (7 - 10)$; 12

5 Solve the problem.

The highest elevation in Argentina is Mt. Aconcagua, which is 6960 m above sea level. The lowest point in Argentina is the Valdes Peninsula, 40 m below sea level. Find the difference between the highest and lowest elevations.

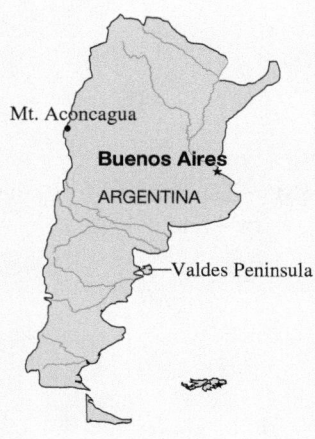

Mt. Aconcagua

Buenos Aires

ARGENTINA

Valdes Peninsula

EXAMPLE 5 **Solving an Application Involving Subtraction**

The record high temperature of 134°F in the United States was recorded at Death Valley, California, in 1913. The record low was −80°F, at Prospect Creek, Alaska, in 1971. See **Figure 14.** What is the difference between these highest and lowest temperatures? (Data from National Climatic Data Center.)

We must subtract the lowest temperature from the highest temperature.

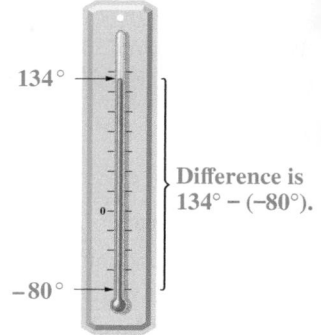

134°

Difference is 134° − (−80°).

0

−80°

Figure 14

Order of numbers matters in subtraction.

$$134 - (-80)$$
$$= 134 + 80 \qquad \text{Definition of subtraction}$$
$$= 214 \qquad \text{Add.}$$

The difference between the two temperatures is 214°F.

◀ **Work Problem 5 at the Side.**

Answer

5. 7000 m

1.5 Exercises

FOR EXTRA HELP *Go to* MyMathLab *for worked-out, step-by-step solutions to exercises enclosed in a square* ☐ *and video solutions to* ▶ *exercises.*

CONCEPT CHECK   *Fill in each blank with the correct response.*

1. By the definition of subtraction, in order to perform the subtraction $-6 - (-8)$, we add the opposite of _____ to _____ to obtain _____ .

2. To subtract y from x, add the _____ _____ , or _____ , of y to x.

3. By the rules for order of operations, to simplify $8 - [3 - (-4 - 5)]$, the first step is to subtract _____ from _____ .

4. "The difference of 7 and 12" translates as _____ , while "the difference of 12 and 7" translates as _____ .

Find each difference. **See Examples 1 and 2.**

5. $5 - 9$
▶

6. $6 - 11$

7. $4 - 7$

8. $8 - 13$

9. $-7 - 3$
GS $= -7 + (\underline{\hspace{1cm}})$
▶ $= \underline{\hspace{1cm}}$

10. $-12 - 5$
GS $= -12 + (\underline{\hspace{1cm}})$
  $= \underline{\hspace{1cm}}$

11. $-10 - 6$

12. $-13 - 16$

13. $7 - (-4)$
GS $= 7 + \underline{\hspace{1cm}}$
  $= \underline{\hspace{1cm}}$

14. $9 - (-6)$
GS $= 9 + \underline{\hspace{1cm}}$
  $= \underline{\hspace{1cm}}$

15. $6 - (-13)$
▶

16. $13 - (-3)$

17. $-7 - (-3)$
▶

18. $-8 - (-6)$

19. $-3 - (-12)$

20. $-7 - (-16)$

21. $\dfrac{1}{2} - \left(-\dfrac{1}{4}\right)$

22. $\dfrac{1}{3} - \left(-\dfrac{4}{3}\right)$

23. $-\dfrac{3}{4} - \dfrac{5}{8}$
▶

24. $-\dfrac{5}{6} - \dfrac{1}{2}$

25. $4.4 - (-9.2)$

26. $6.7 - (-12.6)$

27. $-7.4 - 4.5$

28. $-5.4 - 9.6$

Perform the indicated operations. **See Example 3.**

29. $(4 - 6) + 12$
▶

30. $(3 - 7) + 4$

31. $(8 - 1) - 12$

32. $(9 - 3) - 15$

33. $3 - (4 - 6)$

34. $6 - (7 - 14)$

35. $-3 - (6 - 9)$

36. $-4 - (5 - 12)$

37. $8 - (-3) - 9 + 6$

38. $12 - (-8) - 25 + 9$

39. $-9 - [1 - (4 + 2)]$

40. $-8 - [-5 - (9 - 2)]$

41. $[(-5 - 8) - 4] - 3$

42. $[(-9 + 1) - 11] - 4$

43. $|-5 - 6| + |9 + 2|$

44. $|-4 + 8| + |6 - 1|$

45. $|-8 - 2| - |-9 - 3|$

46. $|-4 - 2| - |-8 - 1|$

47. $|6 - 9| - 4|8 - 2|$

48. $|-2 - 5| - 3|9 - 3|$

49. $\frac{5}{8} - \left[\frac{1}{2} - \left(-\frac{3}{4}\right)\right]$

50. $\frac{9}{10} - \left[\frac{3}{10} - \left(-\frac{1}{8}\right)\right]$

51. $\left(-\frac{3}{8} - \frac{2}{3}\right) - \left(-\frac{9}{8} - 3\right)$

52. $\left(-\frac{3}{4} - \frac{5}{2}\right) - \left(-\frac{1}{8} - 1\right)$

53. $-5.2 - (8.4 - 10.8)$

54. $-9.6 - (3.5 - 12.6)$

55. $\left[(-3.1) - 4.5\right] - (0.8 - 2.1)$

56. $\left[(-7.8) - 9.3\right] - (0.6 - 3.5)$

57. $-12 - \left[(9 - 2) - (-6 - 3)\right]$

58. $-4 - \left[(6 - 9) - (-7 - 4)\right]$

59. $\left[-12.25 - (8.34 + 3.57)\right] - 17.88$

60. $\left[-34.99 + (6.59 - 12.25)\right] - 8.33$

CONCEPT CHECK *Suppose that x represents a positive number and y represents a negative number. Determine whether the given expression must represent a* positive *or* negative *number.*

61. $y - x$

62. $x - y$

63. $x + |y|$

64. $y - |x|$

65. $|x| + |y|$

66. $-(|x| + |y|)$

Write a numerical expression for each phrase, and simplify the expression.
See Example 4.

67. The difference of 4 and -8

68. The difference of 7 and -14

69. 8 less than -2

70. 9 less than -13

71. The sum of 9 and -4, decreased by 7

72. The sum of 12 and -7, decreased by 14

73. 12 less than the difference of 8 and -5

74. 19 less than the difference of 9 and -2

*Solve each problem. **See Example 5.***

75. The lowest temperature ever recorded in Illinois was $-36°$F on January 5, 1999. The lowest temperature ever recorded in Utah was on February 1, 1985, and was 33°F lower than Illinois's record low. What is the record low temperature in Utah? (Data from National Climatic Data Center.)

76. The lowest temperature ever recorded in South Carolina was $-19°$F. The lowest temperature ever recorded in Wisconsin was 36° lower than South Carolina's record low. What is the record low temperature in Wisconsin? (Data from National Climatic Data Center.)

77. The top of Mount Whitney, visible from Death Valley, has an altitude of 14,494 ft above sea level. The bottom of Death Valley is 282 ft below sea level. Using 0 as sea level, find the difference between these two elevations. (Data from *The World Almanac and Book of Facts*.)

78. The height of Mount Pumasillo in Peru is 20,492 ft. The depth of the Peru-Chile Trench in the Pacific Ocean is 26,457 ft below sea level. Find the difference between these two elevations. (Data from *The World Almanac and Book of Facts*.)

79. A chemist is running an experiment under precise conditions. At first, she runs it at $-174.6°F$. She then lowers the temperature by $2.3°F$. What is the new temperature for the experiment?

80. At 2:00 A.M., a plant worker found that a dial reading was 7.904. At 3:00 A.M., she found the reading to be -3.291. Find the difference between these two readings.

81. In August, Kari began with a checking account balance of $904.89. She made the following withdrawals and deposits.

Withdrawals	Deposits
$35.84	$85.00
$26.14	$120.76
$3.12	

Assuming no other transactions, what was her new account balance?

82. In September, Derek began with a checking account balance of $537.12. He made the following withdrawals and deposits.

Withdrawals	Deposits
$41.29	$80.59
$13.66	$276.13
$84.40	

Assuming no other transactions, what was his new account balance?

83. Kim owes $870.00 on her MasterCard account. She returns two items costing $35.90 and $150.00 and receives credit for these on the account. Next, she makes a purchase of $82.50, and then two more purchases of $10.00 each. She makes a payment of $500.00. She then incurs a finance charge of $37.23. How much does she still owe?

84. Charles owes $679.00 on his Visa account. He returns three items costing $36.89, $29.40, and $113.55 and receives credit for these on the account. Next, he makes purchases of $135.78 and $412.88, and two purchases of $20.00 each. He makes a payment of $400. He then incurs a finance charge of $24.57. How much does he still owe?

85. José enjoys diving in Lake Okoboji. He dives to 34 ft below the surface of the lake. His partner, Sean, dives to 40 ft below the surface, but then ascends 20 ft. What is the vertical distance between José and Sean?

86. Rhonda also enjoys diving. She dives to 12 ft below the surface of False River. Her sister, Sandy, dives to 20 ft below the surface, but then ascends 10 ft. What is the vertical distance between Rhonda and Sandy?

87. The federal budget had a surplus of $236 billion in 2000 and projected a deficit of $474 billion in 2016. Express the difference between these amounts as a positive number. (Data from U.S. Treasury Department.)

88. In 2008, undergraduate college students had an average (mean) credit card balance of $3173. The average balance decreased $2076 in 2011, then increased $366 in 2012, and then decreased $538 in 2013. What was the average credit card balance of undergraduate college students in 2013? (Data from Sallie Mae.)

Median sales prices for existing single-family homes in the United States for selected years are shown in the table. Complete the table, determining the change from one year to the next by subtraction.

	Year	Median Sales Price	Change from Previous Year
	2008	$198,100	——
89.	2009	$175,500	
90.	2010	$173,100	
91.	2011	$166,200	
92.	2012	$177,200	

Data from National Association of Realtors.

The two tables show the heights of some selected mountains and the depths of some selected trenches. Use the information given to answer each question.

Mountain	Height (in feet, as a positive number)
Foraker	17,400
Wilson	14,246
Pikes Peak	14,110

Trench	Depth (in feet, as a negative number)
Philippine	−32,995
Cayman	−24,721
Java	−23,376

Data from *The World Almanac and Book of Facts.*

93. What is the difference between the height of Mt. Foraker and the depth of the Philippine Trench?

94. What is the difference between the height of Pikes Peak and the depth of the Java Trench?

95. How much deeper is the Cayman Trench than the Java Trench?

96. How much deeper is the Philippine Trench than the Cayman Trench?

97. How much higher is Mt. Wilson than Pikes Peak?

98. If Mt. Wilson and Pikes Peak were stacked one on top of the other, how much higher would they be than Mt. Foraker?

Study Skills
COMPLETING YOUR HOMEWORK

You are ready to do your homework **AFTER** you have read the corresponding text section and worked through the examples and margin problems.

Homework Tips

▶ **Survey the exercise set.** Take a few minutes to glance over the problems that your instructor has assigned to get a general idea of the types of exercises you will be working. Skim directions, and note any references to section examples.

▶ **Work problems neatly.** Use pencil and write legibly, so others can read your work. Skip lines between steps. Clearly separate problems from each other.

▶ **Show all your work.** It is tempting to take shortcuts. Include ALL steps.

▶ **Check your work frequently to make sure you are on the right track.** It is hard to unlearn a mistake. For all odd-numbered problems and other selected exercises, answers are given in the back of the text.

▶ **If you have trouble with a problem, refer to the corresponding worked example in the section.** The exercise directions will often reference specific examples to review. Pay attention to every line of the worked example to see how to get from step to step.

▶ **If you are having trouble with an even-numbered problem, work the corresponding odd-numbered problem.** Check your answer in the back of the text, and apply the same steps to work the even-numbered problem.

▶ **Do some homework problems every day.** This is a good habit, even if your math class does not meet each day.

▶ **Mark any problems you don't understand.** Ask your instructor about them.

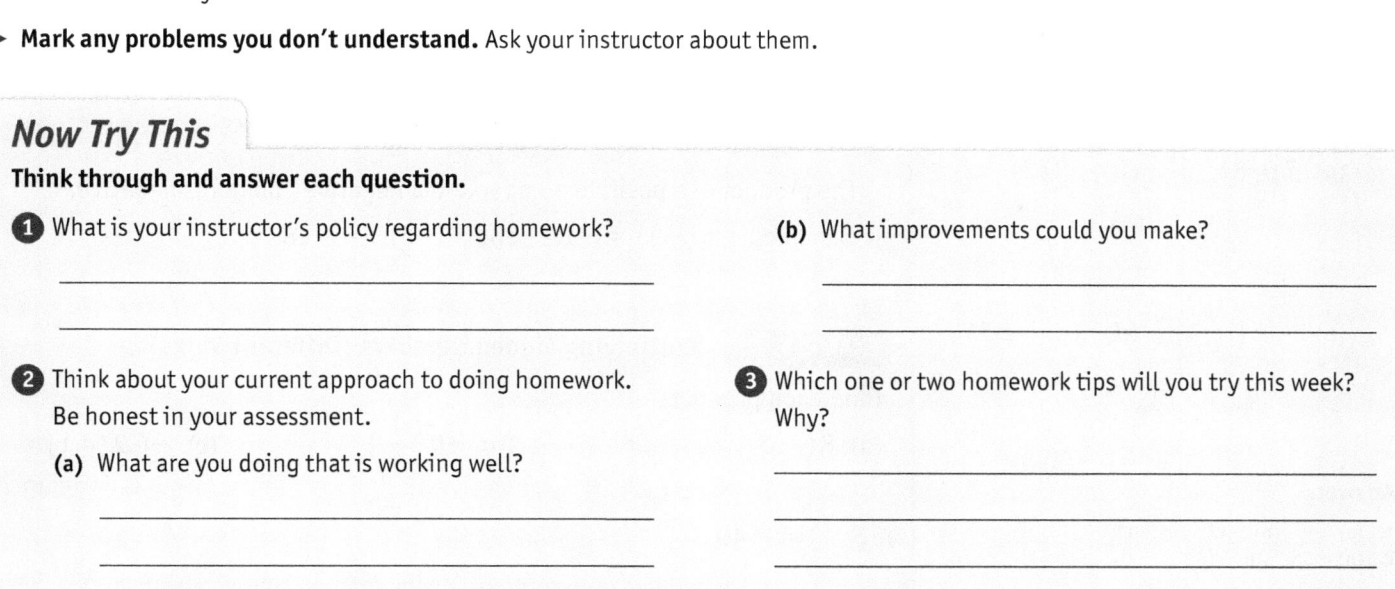

Now Try This

Think through and answer each question.

1 What is your instructor's policy regarding homework?

_____

_____

2 Think about your current approach to doing homework. Be honest in your assessment.

   (a) What are you doing that is working well?

   _____

   _____

(b) What improvements could you make?

_____

_____

3 Which one or two homework tips will you try this week? Why?

_____

_____

_____

1.6 Multiplying and Dividing Real Numbers

OBJECTIVES

1 Find the product of a positive number and a negative number.

2 Find the product of two negative numbers.

3 Use the reciprocal of a number to apply the definition of division.

4 Use the rules for order of operations when multiplying and dividing real numbers.

5 Evaluate expressions involving variables.

6 Translate words and phrases that indicate multiplication and division.

7 Translate simple sentences into equations.

The result of multiplication is a **product.** We know that the product of two positive numbers is positive. And we also know that the product of 0 and any positive number is 0, so we extend that property to all real numbers.

> **Multiplication Property of 0**
>
> For any real number x, the following hold.
> $$x \cdot 0 = 0 \quad \text{and} \quad 0 \cdot x = 0$$

OBJECTIVE ▶ **1** Find the product of a positive number and a negative number. Observe the following pattern.

$$3 \cdot 5 = 15$$
$$3 \cdot 4 = 12$$
$$3 \cdot 3 = 9$$
$$3 \cdot 2 = 6$$
$$3 \cdot 1 = 3$$
$$3 \cdot 0 = 0$$
$$3 \cdot (-1) = ?$$

The products decrease by 3.

What should $3 \cdot (-1)$ equal? Multiplication can also be considered repeated addition. As a result, the product $3 \cdot (-1)$ represents the sum

$$-1 + (-1) + (-1), \quad \text{which equals} \quad -3,$$

so the product $3 \cdot (-1)$ should be -3. This fits the pattern above. Also, $3 \cdot (-2)$ represents the sum

$$-2 + (-2) + (-2), \quad \text{which equals} \quad -6.$$

◀ **Work Problem 1** at the Side.

These results maintain the pattern above and suggest the following rule.

> **Multiplying Signed Numbers (Different Signs)**
>
> The product of a positive number and a negative number is negative.
>
> *Examples:* $6(-3) = -18$ and $(-6)3 = -18$

1 Find each product by finding the sum of three numbers.

(a) $3 \cdot (-3)$ **(b)** $3 \cdot (-4)$

(c) $3 \cdot (-5)$

2 Find each product.

(a) $7(-8)$ **(b)** $-9(2)$

(c) $-16\left(\dfrac{5}{32}\right)$ **(d)** $3.1(-2.5)$

EXAMPLE 1 Multiplying Signed Numbers (Different Signs)

Find each product.

(a) $8(-5)$
$= -(8 \cdot 5)$
$= -40$

(b) $-9\left(\dfrac{1}{3}\right)$
$= -3$

(c) $-6.2(4.1)$
$= -25.42$

The product of two numbers with *different* signs is *negative.*

◀ **Work Problem 2** at the Side.

Answers

1. **(a)** -9 **(b)** -12 **(c)** -15
2. **(a)** -56 **(b)** -18
   (c) $-\dfrac{5}{2}$ **(d)** -7.75

OBJECTIVE ❷ **Find the product of two negative numbers.** Look at another pattern.

$$-5(4) = -20$$
$$-5(3) = -15$$
$$-5(2) = -10$$
$$-5(1) = -5$$
$$-5(0) = 0$$
$$-5(-1) = ?$$

The products increase by 5.

The numbers in color on the left side of the equality symbols decrease by 1 for each step down the list. The products on the right increase by 5 for each step down the list. To maintain this pattern, $-5(-1)$ should be 5 more than $-5(0)$, or 5 more than 0, so

$$-5(-1) = 5.$$

The pattern continues with

$$-5(-2) = 10$$
$$-5(-3) = 15$$
$$-5(-4) = 20, \quad \text{and so on.}$$

These results suggest the next rule.

Multiplying Two Negative Numbers

The product of two negative numbers is positive.

Example: $-6(-3) = 18$

EXAMPLE 2 **Multiplying Two Negative Numbers**

Find each product.

(a) $-9(-2)$
$= 18$

(b) $-\dfrac{2}{3}\left(-\dfrac{3}{2}\right)$
$= 1$

(c) $-0.5(-1.25)$
$= 0.625$

The product of two numbers with the *same* sign is *positive*.

────────── Work Problem ❸ at the Side. ▶

Multiplying Signed Numbers

The product of two numbers with the *same* sign is *positive*.

The product of two numbers with *different* signs is *negative*.

OBJECTIVE ❸ **Use the reciprocal of a number to apply the definition of division.** The definition of division depends on the idea of a *reciprocal*, or *multiplicative inverse*, of a number.

Reciprocals

Pairs of numbers whose product is 1 are **reciprocals,** or **multiplicative inverses,** of each other.

---

❸ Find each product.

(a) $-5(-6)$

(b) $-7(-3)$

(c) $-\dfrac{1}{7}\left(-\dfrac{5}{2}\right)$

(d) $-1.2(-1.1)$

Answers

3. **(a)** 30 **(b)** 21 **(c)** $\dfrac{5}{14}$ **(d)** 1.32

4 Complete the table.

	Number	Reciprocal
(a)	6	___
(b)	−2	___
(c)	$\frac{2}{3}$	___
(d)	$-\frac{1}{4}$	___
(e)	0.75	___
(f)	0	___

RECIPROCALS

Number	Reciprocal
4	$\frac{1}{4}$
−5	$\frac{1}{-5}$, or $-\frac{1}{5}$
0.3, or $\frac{3}{10}$	$\frac{10}{3}$
$-\frac{5}{8}$	$-\frac{8}{5}$

A number and its reciprocal have a product of 1.

Example: $4 \cdot \frac{1}{4} = \frac{4}{4}$, or 1

0 has no reciprocal because the product of 0 and any number is 0, not 1.

◀ **Work Problem** **4** **at the Side.**

Recall that the answer to a division problem is a **quotient**. For example, we can write the quotient of 15 and 3 as **15 ÷ 3**, which equals 5. We obtain the same answer if we multiply **15 · $\frac{1}{3}$**, the reciprocal of 3. This suggests the next definition.

Definition of Division

For any real numbers x and y, where $y \neq 0$,

$$x \div y = x \cdot \frac{1}{y}.$$

To divide two numbers, multiply the first number (the **dividend**) by the reciprocal, or multiplicative inverse, of the second number (the **divisor**).

Example: $15 \div 3 = 15 \cdot \frac{1}{3} = 5$

Recall that an equivalent form of $x \div y$ is $\frac{x}{y}$, where the fraction bar represents division. *In algebra, quotients are usually represented with a fraction bar.* For example,

$$15 \div 3 \quad \text{is equivalent to} \quad \frac{15}{3}.$$

Note

The following forms all represent division, where $y \neq 0$.

$$x \div y, \quad \frac{x}{y}, \quad x/y, \quad \text{and} \quad y\overline{)x}$$

Example: $15 \div 3$, $\quad \frac{15}{3}$, $\quad 15/3$, $\quad$ and $\quad 3\overline{)15}$ $\quad$ are equivalent forms.

Because division is defined in terms of multiplication, the rules for multiplying signed numbers also apply to dividing them.

Dividing Signed Numbers

The quotient of two numbers with the *same* sign is *positive*.

The quotient of two numbers with *different* signs is *negative*.

Examples: $\dfrac{15}{3} = 5$, $\quad \dfrac{-15}{-3} = 5$, $\quad \dfrac{15}{-3} = -5$, $\quad$ and $\quad \dfrac{-15}{3} = -5$

Answers

4. (a) $\frac{1}{6}$ (b) $\frac{1}{-2}$, or $-\frac{1}{2}$ (c) $\frac{3}{2}$

(d) −4 (e) $\frac{4}{3}$ (f) none

EXAMPLE 3 Dividing Signed Numbers

Find each quotient.

(a) $\dfrac{8}{-2} = -4$ 　　**(b)** $\dfrac{-100}{5} = -20$ 　　**(c)** $\dfrac{-4.5}{-0.09} = 50$

(d) $-\dfrac{1}{8} \div \left(-\dfrac{3}{4}\right)$

　　$= -\dfrac{1}{8} \cdot \left(-\dfrac{4}{3}\right)$ 　Multiply by the reciprocal of the divisor.

　　$= \dfrac{1}{6}$ 　Multiply the fractions.
　　　　　Write in lowest terms.

──────────── **Work Problem ❺ at the Side.** ▶

Consider the quotient $\frac{12}{3}$.

$$\frac{12}{3} = 4 \quad \text{because} \quad 4 \cdot 3 = 12.$$ ⟵ Multiply to check a division problem.

This relationship between multiplication and division allows us to investigate division involving 0. Consider the quotient $\frac{0}{3}$.

$$\frac{0}{3} = 0 \quad \text{because} \quad 0 \cdot 3 = 0.$$

Now consider $\frac{3}{0}$.

$$\frac{3}{0} = \text{?}$$

We need to find a number that when multiplied by 0 will equal 3, that is,

$$\text{?} \cdot 0 = 3.$$

No real number satisfies this equation because the product of any real number and 0 must be 0. ***Thus, division by 0 is undefined.***

Division Involving 0

For any real number x, with $x \neq 0$,

$$\frac{0}{x} = 0 \quad \text{and} \quad \frac{x}{0} \text{ is undefined.}$$

Examples: $\dfrac{0}{-10} = 0$ and $\dfrac{-10}{0}$ is undefined.

Work Problem ❻ at the Side. ▶

From the definitions of multiplication and division of real numbers,

$$\frac{-40}{8} = -5 \quad \text{and} \quad \frac{40}{-8} = -5, \quad \text{so} \quad \frac{-40}{8} = \frac{40}{-8}.$$

Based on this example, the quotient of a positive number and a negative number can be expressed in different, yet equivalent, forms.

❺ Find each quotient.

(a) $\dfrac{-8}{-2}$

(b) $\dfrac{12}{-4}$

(c) $\dfrac{-1.44}{-0.12}$

(d) $\dfrac{1}{4} \div \left(-\dfrac{2}{3}\right)$

❻ Find each quotient if possible.

(a) $\dfrac{-3}{0}$

(b) $\dfrac{0}{-53}$

7 Label the order in which each operation should be performed. Then perform the operations.

GS **(a)** $-3(4) - 2(6)$

◯ ◯◯

= ____ − ____

= ____

GS **(b)** $-8[-1 - (-4)(-5)]$

◯ ◯ ◯

$= -8[-1 - \underline{\quad}]$

$= -8[\underline{\quad}]$

$= \underline{\quad}$

(c) $-4 - 2(7 - 10)$

(d) $6(-2) + |3(3) - 11|$

(e) $\dfrac{6(-4) - 2(5)}{3(2 - 7)}$

GS **(f)** $\dfrac{2^2 - 5^2}{3(7 - 8)}$

$= \dfrac{\underline{\quad} - \underline{\quad}}{3(\underline{\quad})}$

$= \dfrac{\underline{\quad}}{-3}$

$= \underline{\quad}$

Answers

7. (a) ①,③,②; −12; 12; −24
(b) ③,②,①; 20; −21; 168
(c) 2 (d) −10 (e) $\dfrac{34}{15}$
(f) 4; 25; −1; −21; 7

Also, $\dfrac{-40}{-8} = 5$ and $\dfrac{40}{8} = 5$, so $\dfrac{-40}{-8} = \dfrac{40}{8}$.

Equivalent Forms

For any positive real numbers x and y, the following are equivalent.

$\dfrac{-x}{y}$, $\dfrac{x}{-y}$, and $-\dfrac{x}{y}$ ← We generally use this form for negative final answers.

$\dfrac{-x}{-y}$ and $\dfrac{x}{y}$ ← We generally use this form for positive final answers.

OBJECTIVE ▶ 4 Use the rules for order of operations when multiplying and dividing real numbers.

EXAMPLE 4 Using the Rules for Order of Operations

Perform the indicated operations.

(a) $-9(2) - (-3)(2)$

$= -18 - (-6)$ Multiply.

$= -18 + 6$ Definition of subtraction

$= -12$ Add.

(b) $-6 + 2(3 - 5)$ ◁ Begin inside the parentheses.

Do *not* add first.

$= -6 + 2(-2)$ Subtract inside the parentheses.

$= -6 + (-4)$ Multiply.

$= -10$ Add.

(c) $|3 - 2(4)| - 2(-6)$

$= |3 - 8| - 2(-6)$ Multiply inside the absolute value bars.

$= |-5| - 2(-6)$ Subtract inside the absolute value bars.

$= 5 - 2(-6)$ Find the absolute value.

$= 5 - (-12)$ Multiply.

$= 17$ Subtract.

(d) $\dfrac{5(-2) - 3(4)}{2(1 - 6)}$ Simplify the numerator and denominator separately.

$= \dfrac{-10 - 12}{2(-5)}$ Multiply in the numerator.
Subtract in the denominator.

$= \dfrac{-22}{-10}$ Subtract in the numerator.
Multiply in the denominator.

$= \dfrac{11}{5}$ Write in lowest terms.

◀ **Work Problem 7** at the Side.

OBJECTIVE 5 Evaluate expressions involving variables.

EXAMPLE 5 Evaluating Algebraic Expressions

Evaluate each expression for $x = -1$, $y = -2$, and $m = -3$.

(a) $(3x + 4y)(-2m)$

> Use parentheses around substituted negative values to avoid errors.

$= [3(-1) + 4(-2)][-2(-3)]$ — Substitute the given values for the variables.

$= [-3 + (-8)][6]$ — Multiply.

$= [-11]6$ — Add inside the brackets.

$= -66$ — Multiply.

(b) $2x^2 - 3y^2$

> Think: $(-2)^2 = -2(-2)$

$= 2(-1)^2 - 3(-2)^2$ — Substitute -1 for x and -2 for y.

> Think: $(-1)^2 = -1(-1)$

$= 2(1) - 3(4)$ — Apply the exponents.

$= 2 - 12$ — Multiply.

$= -10$ — Subtract.

(c) $\dfrac{4y^2 + x}{m}$

$= \dfrac{4(-2)^2 + (-1)}{-3}$ — Substitute -2 for y, -1 for x, and -3 for m.

$= \dfrac{4(4) + (-1)}{-3}$ — Apply the exponent.

$= \dfrac{16 + (-1)}{-3}$ — Multiply.

$= \dfrac{15}{-3}$ — Add.

$= -5$ — Divide.

(d) $\left(\dfrac{3}{4}x + \dfrac{5}{8}y\right)\left(-\dfrac{1}{2}m\right)$

$= \left[\dfrac{3}{4}(-1) + \dfrac{5}{8}(-2)\right]\left[-\dfrac{1}{2}(-3)\right]$ — Substitute for x, y, and m.

$= \left[-\dfrac{3}{4} + \left(-\dfrac{5}{4}\right)\right]\left[\dfrac{3}{2}\right]$ — Multiply inside the brackets.

$= \left[-\dfrac{8}{4}\right]\left[\dfrac{3}{2}\right]$ — Add inside the brackets.

$= -2\left(\dfrac{3}{2}\right)$ — Divide.

$= -3$ — Multiply.

8 Evaluate each expression.

(a) $2x - 7(y + 1)$, for $x = -4$ and $y = 3$

$2x - 7(y + 1)$

$= 2(\underline{}) - 7(\underline{} + 1)$

$= \underline{} - 7(\underline{})$

$= -8 - \underline{}$

$= \underline{}$

(b) $2x^2 - 4y^2$, for $x = -2$ and $y = -3$

(c) $\dfrac{4x - 2y}{-3x}$, for $x = 2$ and $y = -1$

(d) $\left(\dfrac{2}{5}x - \dfrac{5}{6}y\right)\left(-\dfrac{1}{3}z\right)$, for $x = 10$, $y = 6$, and $z = -9$

Answers

8. (a) -4; 3; -8; 4; 28; -36

(b) -28 **(c)** $-\dfrac{5}{3}$ **(d)** -3

Work Problem **8** at the Side. ▶

9 Write a numerical expression for each phrase, and simplify the expression.

(a) The product of 6 and the sum of -5 and -4

(b) Three times the difference of 4 and -6

(c) Three-fifths of the sum of 2 and -7

(d) 20% of the sum of 9 and -4

(e) Triple the product of 5 and 6

OBJECTIVE **6** Translate words and phrases that indicate multiplication and division.

WORDS AND PHRASES THAT INDICATE MULTIPLICATION

Word or Phrase	Example	Numerical Expression and Simplification
Product of	The *product of* -5 and -2	$-5\,(-2)$, which equals 10
Times	13 *times* -4	$13\,(-4)$, which equals -52
Twice (meaning "2 times")	*Twice* 6	$2\,(6)$, which equals 12
Triple (meaning "3 times")	*Triple* 4	$3\,(4)$, which equals 12
Of (used with fractions)	$\frac{1}{2}$ *of* 10	$\frac{1}{2}(10)$, which equals 5
Percent of	12% *of* -16	$0.12\,(-16)$, which equals -1.92
As much as	$\frac{2}{3}$ *as much as* 30	$\frac{2}{3}(30)$, which equals 20

EXAMPLE 6 Translating Words and Phrases (Multiplication)

Write a numerical expression for each phrase, and simplify the expression.

(a) The **product of** 12 and the sum of 3 and -6

$\quad 12\,[3 + (-6)]$ simplifies to $12\,[-3]$, which equals -36.

(b) **Twice** the difference of 8 and -4

$\quad 2\,[8 - (-4)]$ simplifies to $2\,[12]$, which equals 24.

(c) **Two-thirds of** the sum of -5 and -3

$\quad \dfrac{2}{3}\,[-5 + (-3)]$ simplifies to $\dfrac{2}{3}\,[-8]$, which equals $-\dfrac{16}{3}$.

(d) **15% of** the difference of 14 and -2

$\quad 0.15\,[14 - (-2)]$ simplifies to $0.15\,[16]$, which equals 2.4.

> Remember that $15\% = 0.15$.

(e) **Double** the product of 3 and 4

> Double means "2 times."

$\quad 2 \cdot (3 \cdot 4)$ simplifies to $2\,(12)$, which equals 24.

◀ **Work Problem 9** at the Side.

PHRASES THAT INDICATE DIVISION

Phrase	Example	Numerical Expression and Simplification
Quotient of	The *quotient of* -24 and 3	$\frac{-24}{3}$, which equals -8
Divided by	-16 *divided by* -4	$\frac{-16}{-4}$, which equals 4
Ratio of	The *ratio of* 2 to 3	$\frac{2}{3}$

When translating a phrase involving division into a fraction, we write the first number named as the numerator and the second as the denominator.

Answers

9. **(a)** $6\,[(-5) + (-4)]$; -54
   (b) $3\,[4 - (-6)]$; 30
   (c) $\dfrac{3}{5}\,[2 + (-7)]$; -3
   (d) $0.20\,[9 + (-4)]$; 1
   (e) $3\,(5 \cdot 6)$; 90

EXAMPLE 7   **Translating Words and Phrases (Division)**

Write a numerical expression for each phrase, and simplify the expression.

(a) The **quotient of** 14 and the sum of -9 and 2

"Quotient" indicates division. $\dfrac{14}{-9+2}$ simplifies to $\dfrac{14}{-7}$, which equals -2.

(b) The product of 5 and -6, **divided by** the difference of -7 and 8

$\dfrac{5(-6)}{-7-8}$ simplifies to $\dfrac{-30}{-15}$, which equals 2.

———————————— **Work Problem ⑩ at the Side.** ▶

OBJECTIVE ▶ ⑦ Translate simple sentences into equations. We can use words and phrases to translate sentences into equations.

EXAMPLE 8   **Translating Sentences into Equations**

Write each sentence as an equation, using x as the variable.

(a) Three **times** a number **is** -18.

The word *times* indicates multiplication.   The word *is* translates as =.

$3 \cdot x = -18,$ or $3x = -18$ $3 \cdot x = 3x$

(b) The **sum** of a number and 9 **is** 12.

$$x + 9 = 12$$

(c) The **difference of** a number and 5 **is** 0.

$$x - 5 = 0$$

(d) The **quotient of** 24 and a number **is** -2.

$$\frac{24}{x} = -2$$

———————————— **Work Problem ⑪ at the Side.** ▶

⚠ **CAUTION**

In **Examples 6 and 7**, the *phrases* translate as *expressions*, while in **Example 8**, the *sentences* translate as *equations*.

- *An expression is a phrase.*

- *An equation is a sentence with something on the left side, an = symbol, and something on the right side.*

$\dfrac{5(-6)}{-7-8}$ $3x = -18$

↑ Expression   ↑ Equation

⑩ Write a numerical expression for each phrase, and simplify the expression.

(a) The quotient of 20 and the sum of 8 and -3

(b) The product of -9 and 2, divided by the difference of 5 and -1

⑪ Write each sentence as an equation, using x as the variable.

(a) Twice a number is -6.

(b) The difference of -8 and a number is -11.

(c) The sum of 5 and a number is 8.

(d) The quotient of a number and -2 is 6.

Answers

10. (a) $\dfrac{20}{8+(-3)}; 4$ **(b)** $\dfrac{-9(2)}{5-(-1)}; -3$

11. (a) $2x = -6$ **(b)** $-8 - x = -11$

(c) $5 + x = 8$ **(d)** $\dfrac{x}{-2} = 6$

1.6 Exercises

FOR EXTRA HELP

Go to MyMathLab *for worked-out, step-by-step solutions to exercises enclosed in a square and video solutions to ▶ exercises.*

CONCEPT CHECK *Fill in each blank with one of the following.*

> greater than 0, less than 0, *or* equal to 0

1. The product or the quotient of two numbers with the same sign is _____.

2. The product or the quotient of two numbers with different signs is _____.

3. If three negative numbers are multiplied together, the product is _____.

4. If two negative numbers are multiplied and then their product is divided by a negative number, the result is _____.

5. If a negative number is squared and the result is added to a positive number, the final answer is _____.

6. The reciprocal of a negative number is _____.

CONCEPT CHECK *Work each problem.*

7. Complete this statement: The quotient formed by any nonzero number divided
▶ by 0 is _____, and the quotient formed by 0 divided by any nonzero number is _____. Give an example of each quotient.

8. Which expression is undefined?

   A. $13 \div 0$ **B.** $13 \div 13$ **C.** $0 \div 13$ **D.** $13 \cdot 0$

Find each product. ***See Examples 1 and 2.***

9. $-7(4)$
▶

10. $-8(5)$

11. $-5(-6)$
▶

12. $-4(-20)$

13. $-8(0)$

14. $0(-12)$

15. $-\dfrac{3}{8}\left(-\dfrac{20}{9}\right)$
▶

16. $-\dfrac{5}{4}\left(-\dfrac{6}{25}\right)$

17. $-6.8(0.35)$
▶

18. $-4.6(0.24)$

19. $-6\left(-\dfrac{1}{4}\right)$

20. $-8\left(-\dfrac{1}{2}\right)$

Find each quotient. ***See Example 3*** *and the discussion of division involving 0.*

21. $\dfrac{-15}{5}$

22. $\dfrac{-18}{6}$

23. $\dfrac{96}{-16}$
▶

24. $\dfrac{38}{-19}$

25. $\dfrac{-8.8}{2.2}$

26. $\dfrac{-4.6}{0.23}$

27. $\dfrac{-160}{-10}$

28. $\dfrac{-260}{-20}$

29. $\dfrac{0}{-3}$

30. $\dfrac{0}{-5}$

31. $\dfrac{11.5}{0}$

32. $\dfrac{15.2}{0}$

33. $-\dfrac{5}{6} \div \dfrac{8}{9}$

34. $-\dfrac{7}{10} \div \dfrac{3}{4}$

35. $-\dfrac{3}{4} \div \left(-\dfrac{1}{2}\right)$

36. $-\dfrac{3}{16} \div \left(-\dfrac{5}{8}\right)$

*Perform the indicated operation. **See Example 4.***

37. $7 - 3 \cdot 6$

38. $8 - 2 \cdot 5$

39. $-2(5) - (-4)(2)$

40. $-4(3) - (-3)(6)$

41. $-7(3 - 8)$

42. $-5(4 - 7)$

43. $7 + 2(4 - 1)$

44. $5 + 3(6 - 4)$

45. $-4 + 3(2 - 8)$

46. $-8 + 4(5 - 7)$

47. $3(-5) + |3 - 10|$

48. $4(-8) + |4 - 15|$

49. $|8 - 7(2)| - 6(-2)$

50. $|5 - 3(9)| - 7(-4)$

51. $\dfrac{-5(-6)}{9 - (-1)}$

52. $\dfrac{-12(-5)}{7 - (-5)}$

53. $\dfrac{-21(3)}{-3 - 6}$

54. $\dfrac{-40(3)}{-2 - 3}$

55. $\dfrac{-10(2) + 6(2)}{-3 - (-1)}$

56. $\dfrac{8(-1) + 6(-2)}{-6 - (-1)}$

57. $\dfrac{-6 - |-9 + 5|}{2 - (-3)}$

58. $\dfrac{-8 - |-3 + 2|}{-3 - (-6)}$

59. $\dfrac{-27(-2) - (-12)(-2)}{-2(3) - 2(2)}$

60. $\dfrac{-13(-4) - (-8)(-2)}{(-10)(2) - 4(-2)}$

61. $\dfrac{3^2 - 4^2}{7(-8 + 9)}$

62. $\dfrac{5^2 - 7^2}{2(3 + 3)}$

63. $\dfrac{4(2^3 - 5) - 5(-3^3 + 21)}{3[6 - (-2)]}$

64. $\dfrac{-3(-2^4 + 10) + 4(2^5 - 12)}{-2[8 - (-7)]}$

*Evaluate each expression for $x = 6$, $y = -4$, and $a = 3$. **See Example 5.***

65. $6x - 5y + 4a$

66. $5x - 2y + 3a$

67. $(2x + y)(3a)$

68. $(5x - 2y)(-2a)$

69. $\left(\dfrac{5}{6}x + \dfrac{3}{2}y\right)\left(-\dfrac{1}{3}a\right)$

70. $\left(\dfrac{1}{3}x - \dfrac{4}{5}y\right)\left(-\dfrac{1}{5}a\right)$

71. $(6 - x)(5 + y)(3 + a)$ **72.** $(-5 + x)(-3 + y)(3 - a)$ **73.** $5x - 4a^2$
▶

74. $-2y^2 + 3a$ **75.** $\dfrac{2y - x}{a - 3}$ **76.** $\dfrac{xy + 8a}{x - 6}$

Write a numerical expression for each phrase, and simplify the expression.
See Examples 6 and 7.

77. The product of 4 and -7, added to -12 **78.** The product of -9 and 2, added to 9

79. Twice the product of -1 and 6, subtracted from -4 **80.** Twice the product of -8 and 2, subtracted from -1
▶

81. The product of -3 and the difference of 3 and -7 **82.** The product of 12 and the difference of 9 and -8

83. Three-tenths of the sum of -2 and -28 **84.** Four-fifths of the sum of -8 and -2

85. 20% of the product of -5 and 6   **86.** 30% of the product of -8 and 5

87. The quotient of -12 and the sum of -5 and -1 **88.** The quotient of -20 and the sum of -8 and -2
▶

89. The sum of -18 and -6, divided by the product of 2 and -4 **90.** The sum of 15 and -3, divided by the product of 4 and -3

91. The product of $-\frac{2}{3}$ and $-\frac{1}{5}$, divided by $\frac{1}{7}$ **92.** The product of $-\frac{1}{2}$ and $\frac{3}{4}$, divided by $-\frac{2}{3}$

Write each sentence as an equation, using x as the variable. ***See Example 8.***

93. Nine times a number is −36.

94. Seven times a number is −42.

95. The quotient of a number and 4 is −1.

96. The quotient of a number and 3 is −3.

97. $\frac{9}{11}$ less than a number is 5.

98. $\frac{1}{2}$ less than a number is 2.

99. When 6 is divided by a number, the result is −3.

100. When 15 is divided by a number, the result is −5.

A few years ago, the following question and expression appeared on boxes of Swiss Miss Hot Cocoa Mix: On average, how many mini-marshmallows are in one serving?

$$3 + 2 \times 4 \div 2 - 3 \times 7 - 4 + 47$$

101. The box gave 92 as the answer. What is the *correct* answer?

102. ***What Went Wrong?***   Explain the error that somebody at the company made in calculating the answer.

Relating Concepts (Exercises 103–108)   For Individual or Group Work

*To find the **average (mean)** of a group of numbers, we add the numbers and then divide the sum by the number of terms added.* ***Work Exercises 103–106 in order,*** *to find the average of* 23, 18, 13, −4, *and* −8.

103. Find the sum of the given group of numbers.

104. How many numbers are in the group?

105. Divide the answer for **Exercise 103** by the answer for **Exercise 104.** Give the quotient as a mixed number.

106. What is the average of the given group of numbers?

Find the average of each group of numbers.

107. All integers between −10 and 14, including both −10 and 14

108. All integers between −15 and −10, including both −15 and −10

Summary Exercises *Performing Operations with Real Numbers*

Operations with Signed Numbers

Addition

Same sign Add the absolute values of the numbers. The sum has the same sign as the addends.

Different signs Find the absolute values of the numbers, and subtract the lesser absolute value from the greater. The sum has the same sign as the addend with greater absolute value.

Subtraction

Add the additive inverse (or opposite) of the subtrahend to the minuend.

Multiplication and Division

Same sign The product or quotient of two numbers with the same sign is positive.

Different signs The product or quotient of two numbers with different signs is negative.

Division by 0 is undefined.

Perform operations with signed numbers using the rules for order of operations.

Order of Operations

If grouping symbols are present, work within them, innermost first (and above and below fraction bars separately), in the following order.

Step 1 Apply all **exponents**.

Step 2 Do any **multiplications** or **divisions** in order from left to right.

Step 3 Do any **additions** or **subtractions** in order from left to right.

If no grouping symbols are present, start with Step 1.

Perform the indicated operations.

1. $14 - 3 \cdot 10$

2. $-3(8) - 4(-7)$

3. $(3 - 8)(-2) - 10$

4. $-6(7 - 3)$

5. $7 + 3(2 - 10)$

6. $-4[(-2)(6) - 7]$

7. $(-4)(7) - (-5)(2)$

8. $-5[-4 - (-2)(-7)]$

9. $40 - (-2)[8 - 9]$

10. $\dfrac{5(-4)}{-7 - (-2)}$

11. $\dfrac{-3 - (-9 + 1)}{-7 - (-6)}$

12. $\dfrac{5(-8 + 3)}{13(-2) + (-7)(-3)}$

13. $\dfrac{6^2 - 8}{-2(2) + 4(-1)}$

14. $\dfrac{16(-8 + 5)}{15(-3) + (-7 - 4)(-3)}$

15. $\dfrac{9(-6)-3(8)}{4(-7)+(-2)(-11)}$

16. $\dfrac{2^2+4^2}{5^2-3^2}$

17. $\dfrac{(2+4)^2}{(5-3)^2}$

18. $\dfrac{4^3-3^3}{-5(-4+2)}$

19. $\dfrac{-9(-6)+(-2)(27)}{3(8-9)}$

20. $|-4(9)|-|-11|$

21. $\dfrac{6(-10+3)}{15(-2)-3(-9)}$

22. $\dfrac{(-9)^2-9^2}{3^2-5^2}$

23. $\dfrac{(-10)^2+10^2}{-10(5)}$

24. $-\dfrac{3}{4}\div\left(-\dfrac{5}{8}\right)$

25. $\dfrac{1}{2}\div\left(-\dfrac{1}{2}\right)$

26. $\dfrac{8^2-12}{(-5)^2+2(6)}$

27. $\left[\dfrac{5}{8}-\left(-\dfrac{1}{16}\right)\right]+\dfrac{3}{8}$

28. $\left(\dfrac{1}{2}-\dfrac{1}{3}\right)-\dfrac{5}{6}$

29. $-0.9(-3.7)$

30. $-5.1(-0.2)$

31. $|-2(3)+4|-|-2|$

32. $40+2(-5-3)$

Evaluate each expression for $x=-2$, $y=3$, and $a=4$.

33. $-x+y-3a$

34. $(x-y)-(a-2y)$

35. $\left(\dfrac{1}{2}x+\dfrac{2}{3}y\right)\left(-\dfrac{1}{4}a\right)$

36. $\dfrac{2x+3y}{a-xy}$

37. $\dfrac{x^2-y^2}{x^2+y^2}$

38. $-x^2+3y$

39. $\dfrac{-x+2y}{2x+a}$

40. $\dfrac{2x+a}{-x+2y}$

1.7 Properties of Real Numbers

OBJECTIVES

1. Use the commutative properties.
2. Use the associative properties.
3. Use the identity properties.
4. Use the inverse properties.
5. Use the distributive property.

In the basic properties in this section, *a*, *b*, and *c* represent real numbers.

OBJECTIVE ▶ 1 Use the commutative properties. The word *commute* means to go back and forth. We might commute to work or to school. If we travel from home to work and follow the same route from work to home, we travel the same distance each time.

The **commutative properties** say that if two numbers are added or multiplied in either order, the result is the same.

Commutative Properties	
$a + b = b + a$	Addition
$ab = ba$	Multiplication

EXAMPLE 1 Using the Commutative Properties

Use a commutative property to complete each statement.

(a) $-8 + 5 = 5 +$ ___?___   Notice that the "order" changed.

$-8 + 5 = 5 + (-8)$ Commutative property of addition

(b) $(-2)\,7 =$ ___?___ (-2)

$-2\,(7) = 7\,(-2)$ Commutative property of multiplication

◀ **Work Problem ❶ at the Side.**

OBJECTIVE ▶ 2 Use the associative properties. When we *associate* one object with another, we think of those objects as being grouped together.

The **associative properties** say that when we add or multiply three numbers, we can group the first two together or the last two together and obtain the same answer.

Associative Properties	
$(a + b) + c = a + (b + c)$	Addition
$(ab)\,c = a\,(bc)$	Multiplication

EXAMPLE 2 Using the Associative Properties

Use an associative property to complete each statement.

(a) $-8 + (1 + 4) = (-8 +$ ___?___ $) + 4$ The "order" is the same. The "grouping" changed.

$-8 + (1 + 4) = (-8 + 1) + 4$ Associative property of addition

(b) $[2 \cdot (-7)] \cdot 6 = 2 \cdot$ ___?___

$[2 \cdot (-7)] \cdot 6 = 2 \cdot [(-7) \cdot 6]$ Associative property of multiplication

◀ **Work Problem ❷ at the Side.**

---

❶ Use a commutative property to complete each statement.

(a) $x + 9 = 9 +$ _____

(b) $5x = x \cdot$ _____

❷ Use an associative property to complete each statement.

(a) $-5 + (2 + 8)$

$= ($ _____ $) + 8$

(b) $10 \cdot [-8 \cdot (-3)]$

$=$ _____

Answers

1. (a) x (b) 5
2. (a) $-5 + 2$ (b) $[10 \cdot (-8)] \cdot (-3)$

By the associative property, the sum (or product) of three numbers will be the same no matter how the numbers are "associated" in groups. Parentheses can be left out if a problem contains only addition (or multiplication). For example,

$(-1 + 2) + 3$ and $-1 + (2 + 3)$ can be written as $-1 + 2 + 3$.

EXAMPLE 3 Distinguishing between Properties

Decide whether each statement is an example of a *commutative property,* an *associative property,* or *both.*

(a) $(2 + 4) + 5 = 2 + (4 + 5)$

The order of the three numbers is the same on both sides of the equality symbol. The only change is in the *grouping*, or association, of the numbers. This is an example of the *associative property.*

(b) $6 \cdot (3 \cdot 10) = 6 \cdot (10 \cdot 3)$

The same numbers, 3 and 10, are grouped on each side. On the left, the 3 appears first, but on the right, the 10 appears first. The only change involves the *order* of the numbers, so this is an example of the *commutative property.*

(c) $(8 + 1) + 7 = 8 + (7 + 1)$

Both the order and the grouping are changed. On the left, the order of the three numbers is 8, 1, and 7. On the right, it is 8, 7, and 1. On the left, the 8 and 1 are grouped. On the right, the 7 and 1 are grouped. Therefore, *both* properties are used.

———————————— Work Problem ❸ at the Side. ▶

We can sometimes use the commutative and associative properties to rearrange and regroup numbers to simplify calculations.

EXAMPLE 4 Using the Commutative and Associative Properties

Find each sum or product.

(a) $23 + 41 + 2 + 9 + 25$

$= (41 + 9) + (23 + 2) + 25$

$= 50 + 25 + 25$ Use the commutative

$= 100$ and associative properties.

(b) $25(69)(4)$

$= 25(4)(69)$

$= 100(69)$

$= 6900$

———————————— Work Problem ❹ at the Side. ▶

OBJECTIVE ▶ ❸ Use the identity properties. If a child wears a costume on Halloween, the child's appearance is changed, but his or her *identity* is unchanged. The identity of a real number is left unchanged when identity properties are applied.

The **identity properties** say that the sum of 0 and any number equals that number, and the product of 1 and any number equals that number.

Identity Properties

$a + 0 = a$ and $0 + a = a$ Addition

$a \cdot 1 = a$ and $1 \cdot a = a$ Multiplication

---

❸ Decide whether each statement is an example of a *commutative property*, an *associative property*, or *both*.

(a) $2 \cdot (4 \cdot 6) = (2 \cdot 4) \cdot 6$

(b) $(2 \cdot 4) \cdot 6 = (4 \cdot 2) \cdot 6$

(c) $(2 + 4) + 6 = 4 + (2 + 6)$

❹ Find each sum or product.

(a) $5 + 18 + 29 + 31 + 12$

(b) $5(37)(20)$

Answers

3. (a) associative property
(b) commutative property   **(c)** both

4. (a) 95   **(b)** 3700

5 Use an identity property to complete each statement.

(a) $9 + 0 = $ _____

(b) _____ $+ (-7) = -7$

(c) _____ $\cdot 1 = 5$

The number 0 leaves the identity, or value, of any real number unchanged by addition, so 0 is the **identity element for addition,** or the **additive identity.** Because multiplication by 1 leaves any real number unchanged, 1 is the **identity element for multiplication,** or the **multiplicative identity.**

EXAMPLE 5 Using the Identity Properties

Use an identity property to complete each statement.

(a) $-3 + \underline{\ ?\ } = -3$
$-3 + \mathbf{0} = -3$
Identity property of addition

(b) $\underline{\ ?\ } \cdot \dfrac{1}{2} = \dfrac{1}{2}$
$\mathbf{1} \cdot \dfrac{1}{2} = \dfrac{1}{2}$
Identity property of multiplication

◀ **Work Problem 5** at the Side.

We use the identity property of multiplication to write fractions in lowest terms and to find common denominators.

EXAMPLE 6 Using the Identity Property to Simplify Expressions

In part (a), write in lowest terms. In part (b), perform the operation.

(a) $\dfrac{49}{35}$

$= \dfrac{7 \cdot 7}{5 \cdot 7}$ Factor.

$= \dfrac{7}{5} \cdot \dfrac{7}{7}$ Write as a product.

$= \dfrac{7}{5} \cdot 1$ Property of 1

$= \dfrac{7}{5}$ Identity property

(b) $\dfrac{3}{4} + \dfrac{5}{24}$

$= \dfrac{3}{4} \cdot 1 + \dfrac{5}{24}$ Identity property

$= \dfrac{3}{4} \cdot \dfrac{6}{6} + \dfrac{5}{24}$ Use $1 = \dfrac{6}{6}$ to obtain a common denominator.

$= \dfrac{18}{24} + \dfrac{5}{24}$ Multiply.

$= \dfrac{23}{24}$ Add.

◀ **Work Problem 6** at the Side.

6 In part (a), write in lowest terms. In part (b), perform the operation.

(a) $\dfrac{85}{105}$

(b) $\dfrac{9}{10} - \dfrac{53}{50}$

OBJECTIVE ▶ **4** **Use the inverse properties.** Each day before we go to work or school, we likely put on our shoes. Before we go to sleep at night, we likely take them off. These operations from everyday life are examples of *inverse* operations.

The **inverse properties** of addition and multiplication lead to the additive and multiplicative identities, respectively. Recall that $-a$ is the **additive inverse,** or **opposite,** of a, and $\frac{1}{a}$ is the **multiplicative inverse,** or **reciprocal,** of the nonzero number a.

Inverse Properties

$a + (-a) = 0$ and $-a + a = 0$ Addition

$a \cdot \dfrac{1}{a} = 1$ and $\dfrac{1}{a} \cdot a = 1$ $(a \neq 0)$ Multiplication

---

Answers

5. (a) 9 (b) 0 (c) 5

6. (a) $\dfrac{17}{21}$ (b) $-\dfrac{4}{25}$

EXAMPLE 7 Using the Inverse Properties

Use an inverse property to complete each statement.

(a) $\underline{\ ?\ } + \dfrac{1}{2} = 0$

$-\dfrac{1}{2} + \dfrac{1}{2} = 0$

(b) $4 + \underline{\ ?\ } = 0$

$4 + (-4) = 0$

(c) $-0.75 + \dfrac{3}{4} = \underline{\ ?\ }$

$-0.75 + \dfrac{3}{4} = \ 0$

The inverse property of addition is used in parts (a)–(c).

(d) $\underline{\ ?\ } \cdot \dfrac{5}{2} = 1$

$\dfrac{2}{5} \cdot \dfrac{5}{2} = 1$

(e) $-5\,(\underline{\ ?\ }) = 1$

$-5\left(-\dfrac{1}{5}\right) = 1$

(f) $4\,(0.25) = \underline{\ ?\ }$

$4\,(0.25) = \ 1$

The inverse property of multiplication is used in parts (d)–(f).

—————— **Work Problems 7 and 8 at the Side.** ▶

OBJECTIVE ▶ 5 **Use the distributive property.** The word *distribute* means "to give out from one to several." Consider the following expressions.

$2\,(5 + 8)$ equals $2\,(13)$, or 26.   Both expressions
$2\,(5) + 2\,(8)$ equals $10 + 16$, or 26.   equal 26.

Thus, $2\,(5 + 8) = 2\,(5) + 2\,(8).$

This result is an example of the *distributive property of multiplication with respect to addition,* the only property involving *both* addition and multiplication. With this property, a product can be changed to a sum or difference. This idea is illustrated by the divided rectangle in **Figure 15.**

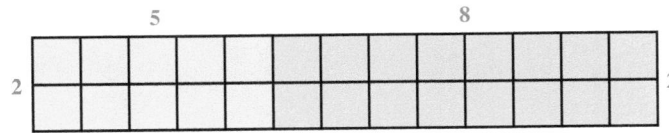

The area of the left part is 2(5) = 10.
The area of the right part is 2(8) = 16.
The total area is 2(5 + 8) = 26, or the total area is
2(5) + 2(8) = 10 + 16 = 26.
Thus, 2(5 + 8) = 2(5) + 2(8).

Figure 15

The **distributive property** says that multiplying a number a by a sum of two numbers $b + c$ gives the same result as multiplying a by b and a by c and then adding the two products.

Distributive Property

$$a\,(b + c) = ab + ac \quad \text{and} \quad (b + c)\,a = ba + ca$$

The a outside the parentheses is "distributed" over the b and c inside. The distributive property is valid for multiplication over subtraction.

$$a\,(b - c) = ab - ac \quad \text{and} \quad (b - c)\,a = ba - ca$$

7 Use an inverse property to complete each statement.

(a) $-6 + \underline{\ \ \ \ } = 0$

(b) $\dfrac{4}{3} \cdot \underline{\ \ \ \ } = 1$

(c) $-\dfrac{1}{9} \cdot (\underline{\ \ \ \ }) = 1$

8 Complete each statement so that it is an example of either an identity property or an inverse property. Tell which property is used.

(a) $275 + \underline{\ \ \ \ } = 275$

(b) $-0.6 + \dfrac{3}{5} = \underline{\ \ \ \ }$

(c) $0.2\,(5) = \underline{\ \ \ \ }$

(d) $\dfrac{2}{5} \cdot \underline{\ \ \ \ } = \dfrac{2}{5}$

Answers

7. (a) 6   **(b)** $\dfrac{3}{4}$ **(c)** -9

8. (a) 0; identity property
(b) 0; inverse property
(c) 1; inverse property
(d) 1; identity property

9 Use the distributive property to rewrite each expression. Simplify if possible.

GS (a) $2(p + 5)$

$$= 2 \cdot \underline{\hphantom{xx}} + 2 \cdot \underline{\hphantom{xx}}$$

$$= \underline{\hphantom{xx}} + \underline{\hphantom{xx}}$$

(b) $-4(y + 7)$

(c) $5(m - 4)$

(d) $-5(4x - 3)$

(e) $-\dfrac{2}{3}(6x - 3)$

(f) $7(2y + 7k - 9m)$

Answers

9. **(a)** p; 5; 2p; 10 **(b)** $-4y - 28$
 (c) $5m - 20$ **(d)** $-20x + 15$
 (e) $-4x + 2$ **(f)** $14y + 49k - 63m$

The distributive property can also be extended to more than two numbers.

$$a(b + c + d) = ab + ac + ad$$

EXAMPLE 8 Using the Distributive Property

Use the distributive property to rewrite each expression. Simplify if possible.

(a) $5(9 + 6)$ *We could write $5(9) + 5(6)$ here.*

$$= 5 \cdot 9 + 5 \cdot 6 \quad \text{The factor 5 is "distributed" over the 9 and 6.}$$

Multiply first.
$$= 45 + 30 \quad \text{Multiply.}$$
$$= 75 \quad \text{Add.}$$

(b) $4(x + 5 + y)$

$$= 4x + 4 \cdot 5 + 4y$$
$$= 4x + 20 + 4y$$

(c) $-2(x + 3)$

$$= -2x + (-2)(3)$$
$$= -2x + (-6)$$
$$= -2x - 6$$

(d) $-\dfrac{1}{2}(4x + 3)$

Think: $-\frac{1}{2}(4x) = \left(-\frac{1}{2} \cdot 4\right)x = \left(-\frac{1}{2} \cdot \frac{4}{1}\right)x$

$$= -\dfrac{1}{2}(4x) + \left(-\dfrac{1}{2}\right)(3) \quad \text{Distributive property}$$

This step is often omitted.
$$= -2x + \left(-\dfrac{3}{2}\right) \quad \text{Multiply.}$$
$$= -2x - \dfrac{3}{2} \quad \text{Definition of subtraction}$$

(e) $3(k - 9)$ *Be careful here.*

$$= 3[k + (-9)] \quad \text{Definition of subtraction}$$
$$= 3k + 3(-9) \quad \text{Distributive property}$$
$$= 3k - 27 \quad \text{Multiply.}$$

(f) $-2(3x - 4)$

$$= -2[3x + (-4)] \quad \text{Definition of subtraction}$$
$$= -2(3x) + (-2)(-4) \quad \text{Distributive property}$$
$$= (-2 \cdot 3)x + (-2)(-4) \quad \text{Associative property}$$
$$= -6x + 8 \quad \text{Multiply.}$$

(g) $8(3r + 11t + 5z)$

$$= 8(3r) + 8(11t) + 8(5z) \quad \text{Distributive property}$$

This step is often omitted.
$$= (8 \cdot 3)r + (8 \cdot 11)t + (8 \cdot 5)z \quad \text{Associative property}$$
$$= 24r + 88t + 40z \quad \text{Multiply.}$$

◀ **Work Problem 9** at the Side.

The expression $-a$ may be interpreted as $-1 \cdot a$. Using this result and the distributive property, we can *clear* (or *remove*) *parentheses*.

EXAMPLE 9 Using the Distributive Property to Clear Parentheses

Write each expression without parentheses.

(a) $-(2y + 3)$

> The $-$ symbol indicates a factor of -1.

$= -1 \cdot (2y + 3)$ $-a = -1 \cdot a$

$= -1 \cdot 2y + (-1) \cdot 3$ Distributive property

$= -2y - 3$ Multiply; definition of subtraction

(b) $-(-9w - 2)$

$= -1(-9w - 2)$

$= -1(-9w) - 1(-2)$

$= 9w + 2$

We can also interpret the negative sign in front of the parentheses to mean the *opposite* of each of the terms within the parentheses.

$$-1(-9w - 2)$$
$$\downarrow \qquad \downarrow$$
$$= +9w + 2$$

(c) $-(-x - 3y + 6z)$

$= -1(-1x - 3y + 6z)$

> Be careful with signs.

$-1(-1x)$
$= 1x$
$= x$

$= -1(-1x) - 1(-3y) - 1(6z)$ Distributive property

$= x + 3y - 6z$ Multiply.

———————— **Work Problem ⑩ at the Side.** ▶

Summary of the Properties of Addition and Multiplication

For any real numbers a, b, and c, the following properties hold true.

Commutative properties $a + b = b + a$ and $ab = ba$

Associative properties $(a + b) + c = a + (b + c)$

$(ab)c = a(bc)$

Identity properties   There is a real number 0 such that

$$a + 0 = a \quad \text{and} \quad 0 + a = a.$$

There is a real number 1 such that

$$a \cdot 1 = a \quad \text{and} \quad 1 \cdot a = a.$$

Inverse properties   For each real number a, there is a single real number $-a$ such that

$$a + (-a) = 0 \quad \text{and} \quad (-a) + a = 0.$$

For each nonzero real number a, there is a single real number $\frac{1}{a}$ such that

$$a \cdot \frac{1}{a} = 1 \quad \text{and} \quad \frac{1}{a} \cdot a = 1.$$

Distributive property $a(b + c) = ab + ac$

$(b + c)a = ba + ca$

---

⑩ Write each expression without parentheses.

GS (a) $-(3k - 5)$

$= \underline{} \cdot (3k - 5)$

$= \underline{} \cdot 3k + (-1)(\underline{})$

$= \underline{} + \underline{}$

(b) $-(2 - r)$

(c) $-(-5y + 8)$

(d) $-(-z + 4)$

(e) $-(-t - 4u + 5v)$

Answers

10. (a) $-1; -1; -5; -3k; 5$
    (b) $-2 + r$ **(c)** $5y - 8$
    (d) $z - 4$ **(e)** $t + 4u - 5v$

1.7 Exercises

FOR EXTRA HELP

Go to MyMathLab *for worked-out, step-by-step solutions to exercises enclosed in a square* ▢ *and video solutions to* ▶ *exercises.*

1. CONCEPT CHECK Match each item in Column I with the correct choice(s) from Column II. Choices may be used once, more than once, or not at all.

I	II
(a) Identity element for addition	A. $(5 \cdot 4) \cdot 3 = 5 \cdot (4 \cdot 3)$
(b) Identity element for multiplication	B. 0
(c) Additive inverse of a	C. $-a$
(d) Multiplicative inverse, or reciprocal, of the nonzero number a	D. -1
(e) The number that is its own additive inverse	E. $5 \cdot 4 \cdot 3 = 60$
(f) The two numbers that are their own multiplicative inverses	F. 1
(g) The only number that has no multiplicative inverse	G. $(5 \cdot 4) \cdot 3 = 3 \cdot (5 \cdot 4)$
(h) An example of the associative property	H. $5(4 + 3) = 5 \cdot 4 + 5 \cdot 3$
(i) An example of the commutative property	I. $\dfrac{1}{a}$
(j) An example of the distributive property	

2. CONCEPT CHECK Fill in the blanks: The commutative property allows us to change the _____ of the terms in a sum or the factors in a product. The associative property allows us to change the _____ of the terms in a sum or the factors in a product.

CONCEPT CHECK *Tell whether or not the following everyday activities are commutative.*

3. Washing your face and brushing your teeth

4. Putting on your left sock and putting on your right sock

5. Preparing a meal and eating a meal

6. Starting a car and driving away in a car

7. Putting on your socks and putting on your shoes

8. Getting undressed and taking a shower

9. CONCEPT CHECK Use parentheses to show how the associative property can be used to give two different meanings to the phrase "foreign sales clerk."

10. CONCEPT CHECK Use parentheses to show how the associative property can be used to give two different meanings to the phrase "defective merchandise counter."

Use a commutative or an associative property to complete each statement. State which property is used. **See Examples 1 and 2.**

11. $-15 + 9 = 9 +$ _____

12. $6 + (-2) = -2 +$ _____

13. $-8 \cdot 3 =$ _____ $\cdot (-8)$

14. $-12 \cdot 4 = 4 \cdot$ _____

15. $(3 + 6) + 7 = 3 + ($ _____ $+ 7)$

16. $(-2 + 3) + 6 = -2 + ($ _____ $+ 6)$

17. $7 \cdot (2 \cdot 5) = ($ _____ $\cdot 2) \cdot 5$

18. $8 \cdot (6 \cdot 4) = (8 \cdot$ _____ $) \cdot 4$

19. CONCEPT CHECK Evaluate $25 - (6 - 2)$ and evaluate $(25 - 6) - 2$. Does it appear that subtraction is associative?

20. CONCEPT CHECK Evaluate $180 \div (15 \div 3)$ and evaluate $(180 \div 15) \div 3$. Does it appear that division is associative?

21. CONCEPT CHECK Complete the table and each statement beside it.

Number	Additive Inverse	Multiplicative Inverse
5		
-10		
$-\frac{1}{2}$		
$\frac{3}{8}$		
x		
$-y$		

In general, a number and its additive inverse have (*the same/opposite*) signs.

A number and its multiplicative inverse have (*the same/opposite*) signs.

22. CONCEPT CHECK The following conversation took place between one of the authors of this text and his son, Jack, when Jack was 4 years old.

DADDY: "Jack, what is $3 + 0$?"
JACK: "3."
DADDY: "Jack, what is $4 + 0$?"
JACK: "4. And Daddy, *string* plus zero equals *string*!"

What property of addition did Jack recognize?

Decide whether each statement is an example of a commutative, *an* associative, *an* identity, *an* inverse *or the* distributive *property. **See Examples 1, 2, 3, and 5–8.***

23. $\frac{2}{3}(-4) = -4\left(\frac{2}{3}\right)$

24. $6\left(-\frac{5}{6}\right) = \left(-\frac{5}{6}\right)6$

25. $-6 + 6 = 0$

26. $12 + (-12) = 0$

27. $\frac{2}{3}\left(\frac{3}{2}\right) = 1$

28. $\frac{5}{8}\left(\frac{8}{5}\right) = 1$

29. $2.34 \cdot 1 = 2.34$

30. $-8.456 \cdot 1 = -8.456$

31. $6(x + y) = 6x + 6y$

32. $14(t + s) = 14t + 14s$

33. $-\frac{5}{9} = -\frac{5}{9} \cdot \frac{3}{3} = -\frac{15}{27}$

34. $\frac{13}{12} = \frac{13}{12} \cdot \frac{7}{7} = \frac{91}{84}$

35. $-6 + (12 + 7) = (-6 + 12) + 7$

36. $(-8 + 13) + 2 = -8 + (13 + 2)$

37. $(4 + 17) + 3 = 3 + (4 + 17)$

38. $(-8 + 4) + (-12) = -12 + (-8 + 4)$

39. $5(2x) + 5(3y) = 5(2x + 3y)$

40. $3(5t) - 3(7r) = 3(5t - 7r)$

Write a new expression that is equal to the given expression, using the given property. Then simplify the new expression if possible. **See Examples 1, 2, 5, 7, and 8.**

41. $r + 7$;   commutative   **42.** $t + 9$;   commutative   **43.** $s + 0$;   identity   **44.** $w + 0$;   identity

45. $-6(x + 7)$;   **46.** $-5(y + 2)$;   **47.** $(w + 5) + (-3)$;   **48.** $(b + 8) + (-10)$;
     distributive   distributive   associative   associative

Use the properties of this section to perform the operations. **See Example 4.**

49. $1999 + 2 + 1 + 8$ **50.** $2998 + 3 + 2 + 17$ **51.** $50(67)2$

52. $5(47)(2)$ **53.** $43 - 31 + 7 + 31$ **54.** $26 + 8 - 26 + 12$

55. $-\dfrac{3}{8} + \dfrac{2}{5} + \dfrac{8}{5} + \dfrac{3}{8}$ **56.** $-\dfrac{5}{12} - \dfrac{3}{7} + \dfrac{5}{12} + \dfrac{10}{7}$ **57.** $-\dfrac{8}{5}(0.77)\left(-\dfrac{5}{8}\right)$

58. $\dfrac{9}{7}(-0.38)\left(\dfrac{7}{9}\right)$ **59.** $6t + 8 - 6t + 3$ **60.** $9r + 12 - 9r + 1$

61. CONCEPT CHECK   A student used the distributive property to rewrite the expression $-3(4 - 6)$ as shown.

$$-3(4 - 6)$$
$$= -3(4) - 3(6)$$
$$= -12 - 18$$
$$= -30$$

What Went Wrong?   Rewrite the expression correctly.

62. CONCEPT CHECK   A student wrote the expression $-(3x + 4)$ without parentheses as shown.

$$-(3x + 4)$$
$$= -1(3x + 4)$$
$$= -1(3x) + 4$$
$$= -3x + 4$$

What Went Wrong?   Rewrite the expression correctly.

63. Explain how the procedure of changing $\frac{3}{4}$ to $\frac{9}{12}$ requires the use of the multiplicative identity element, 1.

64. Explain how the procedure for changing $\frac{9}{12}$ to $\frac{3}{4}$ requires the use of the multiplicative identity element, 1.

Use the distributive property to rewrite each expression. Simplify if possible. **See Example 8.**

65. $5\,(9 + 8)$

66. $6\,(11 + 8)$

67. $4\,(t + 3)$

68. $5\,(w + 4)$

69. $7\,(z - 8)$

70. $8\,(x - 6)$

71. $-8\,(r + 3)$

72. $-11\,(x + 4)$

73. $-\dfrac{1}{4}(8x + 3)$

74. $-\dfrac{1}{3}(9x + 5)$

75. $-5\,(y - 4)$

$= -5\,(\underline{}) - 5\,(\underline{})$

$= \underline{}$

76. $-9\,(g - 4)$

$= -9\,(\underline{}) - 9\,(\underline{})$

$= \underline{}$

77. $2\,(6x + 5)$

78. $3\,(3x + 4)$

79. $-3\,(2x - 5)$

80. $-4\,(3x - 2)$

81. $-6\,(8x + 1)$

82. $-5\,(4x + 1)$

83. $-\dfrac{4}{3}(12y + 15z)$

84. $-\dfrac{2}{5}(10b + 20a)$

85. $8\,(3r + 4s - 5y)$

86. $2\,(5u - 3v + 7w)$

87. $-3\,(8x + 3y + 4z)$

88. $-5\,(2x - 5y + 6z)$

Write each expression without parentheses. **See Example 9.**

89. $-\,(6x + 5)$

90. $-\,(8y + 7)$

91. $-\,(4t + 3m)$

92. $-\,(9x + 12y)$

93. $-\,(-5c - 4d)$

94. $-\,(-13x - 15y)$

95. $-\,(-3q + 5r - 8s)$

96. $-\,(-4z + 5w - 9y)$

1.8 | Simplifying Expressions

OBJECTIVES

1. Simplify expressions.
2. Identify terms and numerical coefficients.
3. Identify like terms.
4. Combine like terms.
5. Simplify expressions from word phrases.

OBJECTIVE ▶ **1** **Simplify expressions.** We now simplify expressions using the properties introduced in the previous section.

EXAMPLE 1 | **Simplifying Expressions**

Simplify each expression.

(a) $4x + 8 + 9$ simplifies to $4x + 17$.

(b) $4(3m - 2n)$ To simplify, we clear the parentheses.

$$= 4(3m) - 4(2n) \qquad \text{Distributive property}$$
$$= (4 \cdot 3)m - (4 \cdot 2)n \qquad \text{Associative property}$$
$$= 12m - 8n \qquad \text{Multiply.}$$

(c) $6 + 3(4k + 5)$

Do *not* start by adding.

$$= 6 + 3(4k) + 3(5) \qquad \text{Distributive property}$$
$$= 6 + (3 \cdot 4)k + 3(5) \qquad \text{Associative property}$$
$$= 6 + 12k + 15 \qquad \text{Multiply.}$$
$$= 6 + 15 + 12k \qquad \text{Commutative property}$$
$$= 21 + 12k \qquad \text{Add.}$$

(d) $5 - (2y - 8)$

$$= 5 - 1(2y - 8) \qquad -a = -1 \cdot a$$
$$= 5 - 1(2y) - 1(-8) \qquad \text{Distributive property}$$

Be careful with signs.

$$= 5 - 2y + 8 \qquad \text{Multiply.}$$
$$= 5 + 8 - 2y \qquad \text{Commutative property}$$
$$= 13 - 2y \qquad \text{Add.}$$

◀ **Work Problem** **1** **at the Side.**

---

1 Simplify each expression.

(a) $9k + 12 - 5$

(b) $7(3p + 2q)$

$$= 7(\underline{}) + 7(\underline{})$$

$$= \underline{} + \underline{}$$

(c) $2 + 5(3z - 1)$

(d) $-3 - (2 + 5y)$

Note

The steps using the commutative and associative properties will not be shown in the rest of the examples. However, be aware that they are usually involved.

OBJECTIVE ▶ **2** **Identify terms and numerical coefficients.** A **term** is a number (constant), a variable, or a product or quotient of a number and one or more variables raised to powers.

$$9x, \quad 15y^2, \quad -3, \quad -8m^2n, \quad \frac{2}{p}, \quad k \qquad \text{Terms}$$

In the term $9x$, the **numerical coefficient,** or simply the **coefficient,** of the variable x is 9. Additional examples are shown in the table on the next page.

Answers

1. **(a)** $9k + 7$ **(b)** $3p; 2q; 21p; 14q$
   (c) $15z - 3$ **(d)** $-5 - 5y$

TERMS AND THEIR COEFFICIENTS

Term	Numerical Coefficient
8	8
$-7y$	-7
$34r^3$	34
$-26x^5yz^4$	-26
$-k$, or $-1k$	-1
r, or $1r$	1
$\frac{3x}{8}$, or $\frac{3}{8}x$	$\frac{3}{8}$
$\frac{x}{3} = \frac{1x}{3}$, or $\frac{1}{3}x$	$\frac{1}{3}$

Work Problem ② at the Side. ▶

! CAUTION

It is important to be able to distinguish between *terms* and *factors*.

$8x^3 + 12x^2$ This expression has **two terms**, $8x^3$ and $12x^2$. **Terms** are separated by a $+$ or $-$ symbol.

$(8x^3)(12x^2)$ This is a **one-term** expression. The **factors** $8x^3$ and $12x^2$ are multiplied.

OBJECTIVE ▶ ③ Identify like terms. Terms with exactly the same variables that have the same exponents on the variables are **like terms.**

Like Terms	**Unlike Terms**	
$9t$ and $4t$	$4y$ and $7t$	Different variables
$6x^2$ and $-5x^2$	$17x$ and $-8x^2$	Different exponents
$-2pq$ and $11pq$	$4xy^2$ and $4xy$	Different exponents
$3x^2y$ and $5x^2y$	$-7wz^3$ and $2xz^3$	Different variables

Work Problem ③ at the Side. ▶

OBJECTIVE ▶ ④ Combine like terms. Recall the distributive property.

$a(b+c) = ab + ac$ can be written "in reverse" as $ba + ca = (b+c)a.$

This last form provides justification for **combining like terms.**

EXAMPLE 2   Combining Like Terms

Combine like terms in each expression.

(a) $-9m + 5m$
$= (-9+5)m$ Distributive property in reverse
$= -4m$

(b) $6r + 3r + 2r$
$= (6+3+2)r$
$= 11r$

(c) $4x + x$
$= 4x + 1x$ $x = 1x$
$= (4+1)x$
$= 5x$

(d) $16y^2 - 9y^2$
$= (16-9)y^2$
$= 7y^2$

(e) $32y + 10y^2$
These unlike terms cannot be combined.

Work Problem ④ at the Side. ▶

② Complete the table.

	Term	Numerical Coefficient
(a)	$15q$	_____
(b)	$-2m^3$	_____
(c)	$-18m^7q^4$	_____
(d)	$-r$	_____
(e)	$\frac{5x}{4}$	_____

③ Identify each pair of terms as *like* or *unlike*.

(a) $9x$, $4x$

(b) $-8y^3$, $12y^2$

(c) $5x^2y^4$, $5x^4y^2$

(d) $7x^2y^4$, $-7x^2y^4$

(e) $13kt$, $4tk$

④ Combine like terms.

(a) $4k + 7k$

(b) $4r - r$

(c) $5z + 9z - 4z$

(d) $8p + 8p^2$

Answers

2. (a) 15 **(b)** -2 **(c)** -18
  (d) -1 **(e)** $\frac{5}{4}$

3. (a) like **(b)** unlike **(c)** unlike
  (d) like **(e)** like

4. (a) $11k$ **(b)** $3r$ **(c)** $10z$
  (d) cannot be combined

> **!** **CAUTION**
> *Remember that only like terms may be combined.*

Simplifying an Expression

An expression has been simplified when the following conditions have been met.

- All grouping symbols have been removed.
- All like terms have been combined.
- Operations have been performed, when possible.

EXAMPLE 3 Simplifying Expressions Involving Like Terms

Simplify each expression.

(a)
$$14y + 2(6 + 3y)$$ Start by distributing the 2.

$$= 14y + 2(6) + 2(3y)$$ Distributive property

$$= 14y + 12 + 6y$$ Multiply.

$$= 20y + 12$$ Combine like terms.

$14y + 6y$
$= (14 + 6)y$
$= 20y$

(b) $9k - 6 - 3(2 - 5k)$ Be careful with signs.

$$= 9k - 6 - 3(2) - 3(-5k)$$ Distributive property

$$= 9k - 6 - 6 + 15k$$ Multiply.

$$= 24k - 12$$ Combine like terms.

(c)
$$-(2 - r) + 10r$$

$$= -1(2 - r) + 10r \qquad -(2 - r) = -1(2 - r)$$

$$= -1(2) - 1(-r) + 10r \qquad \text{Distributive property}$$

Be careful with signs.

$$= -2 + r + 10r \qquad \text{Multiply.}$$

$$= -2 + 11r \qquad \text{Combine like terms; } r = 1r.$$

Alternatively, $-(2 - r)$ can be thought of as the *opposite* of $(2 - r)$—that is, $-2 + r$—which can then be added to $10r$ to obtain $-2 + 11r$.

(d) $-\dfrac{2}{3}(x - 6) - \dfrac{1}{6}x$

$$= -\frac{2}{3}x - \frac{2}{3}(-6) - \frac{1}{6}x \qquad \text{Distributive property}$$

$$= -\frac{2}{3}x + 4 - \frac{1}{6}x \qquad \text{Multiply.}$$

$$= -\frac{4}{6}x + 4 - \frac{1}{6}x \qquad \text{Get a common denominator.}$$

$$= -\frac{5}{6}x + 4 \qquad \text{Combine like terms.}$$

Continued on Next Page

(e) $5(2a - 6) - 3(4a - 9)$

$= 5(2a) + 5(-6) - 3(4a) - 3(-9)$ Distributive property twice

$= 10a - 30 - 12a + 27$ Multiply.

$= -2a - 3$ Combine like terms.

───── **Work Problem ❺ at the Side.** ▶

Note

Examples 2 and 3 suggest that like terms may be combined by adding or subtracting the coefficients of the terms and keeping the same variable factors.

OBJECTIVE ▶ ❺ Simplify expressions from word phrases.

EXAMPLE 4   **Translating Words into a Mathematical Expression**

Write the phrase as a mathematical expression using x as the variable, and simplify.

The sum of 9, five times a number,

four times the number, and

six times the number

The word "sum" indicates that the terms should be added. Use x for the number.

$9 + 5x + 4x + 6x$ simplifies to $9 + 15x$.   Combine like terms.

This is an expression to be simplified, *not* an equation to be solved.

───── **Work Problem ❻ at the Side.** ▶

❺ Simplify each expression.

(a) $10p + 3(5 + 2p)$

$= 10p + \underline{\quad}(5) + 3(\underline{\quad})$

$= 10p + \underline{\quad} + \underline{\quad}$

$= \underline{\quad}$

(b) $7z - 2 - (1 + z)$

(c) $-(3k^2 + 5k) + 7(k^2 - 4k)$

(d) $-\dfrac{3}{4}(x - 8) - \dfrac{1}{3}x$

(e) $2(5r + 3) - 3(2r - 3)$

❻ Write each phrase as a mathematical expression using x as the variable, and simplify.

(a) Three times a number, subtracted from the sum of the number and 8

(b) Twice a number added to the sum of 6 and the number

Answers

5. (a) $3; 2p; 15; 6p; 16p + 15$
 (b) $6z - 3$ **(c)** $4k^2 - 33k$
 (d) $-\dfrac{13}{12}x + 6$ **(e)** $4r + 15$

6. (a) $(x + 8) - 3x; -2x + 8$
 (b) $(6 + x) + 2x; 3x + 6$

1.8 Exercises

FOR EXTRA HELP   Go to MyMathLab *for worked-out, step-by-step solutions to exercises enclosed in a square* ▢ *and video solutions to* ▶ *exercises.*

CONCEPT CHECK   *Choose the letter of the correct response.*

1. Which expression is a simplified form of $-(6x - 3)$?

A. $-6x - 3$ **B.** $-6x + 3$

C. $6x - 3$ **D.** $6x + 3$

2. Which is an example of a pair of like terms?

A. $6t, 6w$ **B.** $-8x^2y, 9xy^2$

C. $5ry, 6yr$ **D.** $-5x^2, 2x^3$

3. Which is an example of a term with numerical coefficient 5?

A. $5x^3y^7$ **B.** x^5

C. $\dfrac{x}{5}$ **D.** 5^2xy^3

4. Which is a correct translation for "six times a number, subtracted from the product of eleven and the number" (if x represents the number)?

A. $6x - 11x$ **B.** $11x - 6x$

C. $(11 + x) - 6x$ **D.** $6x - (11 + x)$

Simplify each expression. **See Example 1.**

5. $4r + 19 - 8$ ▶

6. $7t + 18 - 4$

7. $7(3x - 4y)$

8. $8(2p - 9q)$

9. $5 + 2(x - 3y)$ ▶

10. $8 + 3(s - 6t)$

11. $-2 - (5 - 3p)$ ▶

12. $-10 - (7 - 14r)$

13. $6 + (4 - 3x) - 8$

14. $-12 + (7 - 8x) + 6$

In each term, give the numerical coefficient of the variable(s). **See Objective 2.**

15. $-12k$ ▶

16. $-23y$

17. $5m^2$

18. $-3n^6$

19. xw

20. pq

21. $-x$

22. $-t$

23. 10

24. 15

25. $28xy^2$

26. $17a^2b$

27. $-\dfrac{3}{8}x$

28. $-\dfrac{5}{4}z$

29. $\dfrac{x}{2}$

30. $\dfrac{x}{6}$

31. $\dfrac{2x}{5}$

32. $\dfrac{8x}{9}$

33. $-1.28r^2$

34. $-2.985t^3$

Identify each group of terms as like *or* unlike. **See Objective 3.**

35. $8r, -13r$ ▶

36. $-7a, 12a$

37. $3x, 3y$

38. $9m, 9n$

39. $5z^4, 9z^3$

40. $8x^5, -10x^3$

41. $4, 9, -24$

42. $7, 17, -83$

43. x, y

44. t, s

Simplify each expression. **See Examples 1–3.**

45. $3x + 12x$

46. $4y + 9y$

47. $-6x - 3x$

48. $-4z - 8z$

49. $12b + b$ ▶

50. $19x + x$

51. $3k + 8 + 4k + 7$

52. $15z + 1 + 4z + 2$

53. $-2x + 3 + 4x - 17 + 20$

54. $r - 6 - 12r - 4 + 16$

55. $-\dfrac{4}{3} + 2t + \dfrac{1}{3}t - 8 - \dfrac{8}{3}t$

56. $-\dfrac{5}{6} + 8x + \dfrac{1}{6}x - 7 - \dfrac{7}{6}$

57. $6y^2 + 11y^2 - 8y^2$

58. $-9m^3 + 3m^3 - 7m^3$

59. $2p^2 + 3p^2 - 8p^3 - 6p^3$

60. $5y^3 + 6y^3 - 3y^2 - 4y^2$

61. $2y^2 - 7y^3 - 4y^2 + 10y^3$

62. $9x^4 - 7x^6 + 12x^4 + 14x^6$

63. $2(4x + 6) + 3$

64. $4(6y + 9) + 7$

65. $-\dfrac{5}{6}(y + 12) - \dfrac{1}{2}y$

66. $-\dfrac{2}{3}(w + 15) - \dfrac{1}{4}w$

67. $-\dfrac{4}{3}(y - 12) - \dfrac{1}{6}y$

68. $-\dfrac{7}{5}(t - 15) - \dfrac{1}{2}t$

69. $-5 - 2(x - 3)$

$\quad = -5 - 2(\underline{\quad}) - 2(\underline{\quad})$

$\quad = -5 - \underline{\quad} + \underline{\quad}$

$\quad = \underline{\qquad}$

70. $-8 - 3(2x + 4)$

$\quad = -8 - 3(\underline{\quad}) - 3(\underline{\quad})$

$\quad = -8 - \underline{\quad} - \underline{\quad}$

$\quad = \underline{\qquad}$

71. $13p + 4(4 - 8p)$

72. $5x + 3(7 - 2x)$

73. $-5(5y - 9) + 3(3y + 6)$

74. $-3(2t + 4) + 8(2t - 4)$

75. $-3(2r - 3) + 2(5r + 3)$

76. $-4(5y - 7) + 3(2y - 5)$

77. $8(2k - 1) - (4k - 3)$

78. $6(3p - 2) - (5p + 1)$

79. $\dfrac{1}{2}(2x + 4) - \dfrac{1}{3}(9x - 6)$

80. $\dfrac{1}{4}(8x + 16) - \dfrac{1}{5}(20x - 15)$

81. $-\dfrac{2}{3}(5x + 7) - \dfrac{1}{3}(4x + 8)$

82. $-\dfrac{3}{4}(7x + 9) - \dfrac{1}{4}(5x + 7)$

83. $-2(-3k + 2) - (5k - 6) - 3k - 5$

84. $-2(3r - 4) - (6 - r) + 2r - 5$

85. $-4(-3x + 3) - (6x - 4) - 2x + 1$

86. $-5(8x + 2) - (5x - 3) - 3x + 17$

87. $-5.3r + 4.9 - (2r + 0.7) + 3.2r$

88. $2.7b + 5.8 - (3b + 0.5) - 4.4b$

89. $-7.5(2y + 4) - 2.9(3y - 6)$

90. $8.4(6t - 6) + 2.4(9 - 3t)$

91. CONCEPT CHECK A student simplified the expression $7x - 2(3 - 2x)$ as shown.

$$7x - 2(3 - 2x)$$
$$= 7x - 2(3) - 2(2x)$$
$$= 7x - 6 - 4x$$
$$= 3x - 6$$

What Went Wrong? Find the correct simplified answer.

92. CONCEPT CHECK A student simplified the expression $3 + 2(4x - 5)$ as shown.

$$3 + 2(4x - 5)$$
$$= 5(4x - 5)$$
$$= 5(4x) + 5(-5)$$
$$= 20x - 25$$

What Went Wrong? Find the correct simplified answer.

Write each phrase as a mathematical expression using x as the variable, and simplify.
See Example 4.

93. Five times a number, added to the sum of the number and three

94. Six times a number, added to the sum of the number and six

95. A number multiplied by -7, subtracted from the sum of 13 and six times the number

96. A number multiplied by 5, subtracted from the sum of 14 and eight times the number

97. Six times a number added to -4, subtracted from twice the sum of three times the number and 4

98. Nine times a number added to 6, subtracted from triple the sum of 12 and 8 times the number

Relating Concepts (Exercises 99–102) For Individual or Group Work

A manufacturer has fixed costs of $1000 to produce gizmos. Each gizmo costs $5 to make. The fixed cost to produce gadgets is $750, and each gadget costs $3 to make.
Work Exercises 99–102 in order.

99. Write an expression for the cost to make x gizmos. (*Hint:* The cost will be the sum of the fixed cost and the cost per item times the number of items.)

100. Write an expression for the cost to make y gadgets.

101. Write an expression for the total cost to make x gizmos and y gadgets.

102. Simplify the expression from **Exercise 101.**

Study Skills

REVIEWING A CHAPTER

Your text provides material to help you prepare for quizzes or tests in this course. Refer to the **Chapter Summary** as you read through the following techniques.

Chapter Reviewing Techniques

▶ **Review the Key Terms.** Make a study card for each. Include a definition, an example, a sketch (if appropriate), and a section or page reference.

▶ **Review any New Symbols.** Cover the column with the symbol meanings and confirm that you know each symbol.

▶ **Take the Test Your Word Power quiz** to check your understanding of new vocabulary. The answers immediately follow.

▶ **Read the Quick Review.** Pay special attention to the headings. Study the explanations and examples given for each concept. Try to think about the whole chapter.

▶ **Reread your lecture notes.** Focus on what your instructor has emphasized in class, and review that material in your text.

▶ **Look over your homework and any quizzes.** Pay special attention to any trouble spots.

▶ **Work the Review Exercises.** They are grouped by section.
- ✓ Pay attention to direction words, such as *simplify*, *solve*, and *evaluate*.
- ✓ After you've done each section of exercises, check your answers in the answer section.
- ✓ Are your answers exact and complete? Did you include the correct labels, such as $, cm², ft, etc.?
- ✓ Make study cards for difficult problems.

▶ **Work the Mixed Review Exercises.** They are in mixed-up order. Check your answers in the answer section.

▶ **Take the Chapter Test under test conditions.**
- ✓ Time yourself.
- ✓ Use a calculator or notes (if your instructor permits them on tests).
- ✓ Take the test in one sitting.
- ✓ Show all your work.
- ✓ Check your answers in the back of the book.

Reviewing a chapter will take some time. Avoid rushing through your review in one night. Use the suggestions over a few days or evenings to better understand the material and remember it longer.

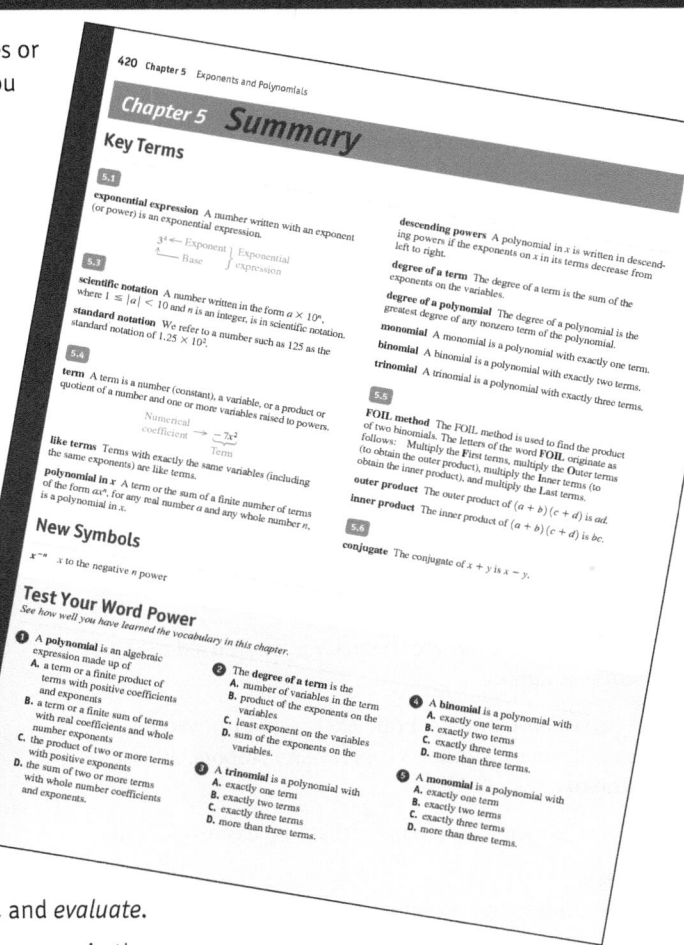

Now Try This

Follow these reviewing techniques to prepare for your next test. Then answer the questions below.

1 How much time did you spend reviewing for your test? Was it enough?

_____

2 How did the reviewing techniques work for you?

_____

3 What will you do differently when reviewing for your next test?

_____

Chapter 1 *Summary*

Key Terms

1.1

exponent An exponent, or **power**, is a number that indicates how many times a factor is repeated.

$$3^4 \leftarrow \text{Exponent}$$
$$\uparrow \quad \text{Base}$$

(Exponential expression)

base A base is the number that is a repeated factor when written with an exponent.

exponential expression A number written with an exponent is an exponential expression.

inequality An inequality is a statement that two expressions may not be equal.

1.2

constant A constant is a fixed, unchanging number.

variable A variable is a symbol, usually a letter, used to represent an unknown number.

algebraic expression An algebraic expression is a sequence of numbers (constants), variables, operation symbols, and/or grouping symbols.

equation An equation is a statement that two expressions are equal.

solution A solution of an equation is any value of the variable that makes the equation true.

1.3

set A set is a collection of objects.

element The objects that belong to a set are its elements.

natural numbers The set of natural numbers is $\{1, 2, 3, 4, \dots\}$.

whole numbers The set of whole numbers is $\{0, 1, 2, 3, 4, \dots\}$.

number line A number line shows the ordering of real numbers on a line.

additive inverse The additive inverse, or **opposite**, of a number x is the number that is the same distance from 0 on a number line as x, but on the opposite side of 0.

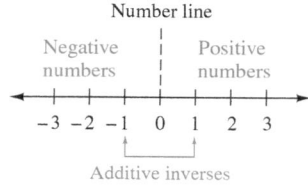

Number line

Negative numbers / Positive numbers

Additive inverses

integers The set of integers is $\{\dots, -3, -2, -1, 0, 1, 2, 3, \dots\}$.

negative number A negative number is located to the *left* of 0 on a number line.

positive number A positive number is located to the *right* of 0 on a number line.

signed numbers Positive numbers and negative numbers are signed numbers.

rational numbers A rational number is a number that can be written as the quotient of two integers, with denominator not 0.

set-builder notation Set-builder notation uses a variable and a description to describe a set. It is often used to describe sets whose elements cannot easily be listed.

coordinate The number that corresponds to a point on a number line is the coordinate of that point.

irrational numbers An irrational number is a real number that is not a rational number.

real numbers Real numbers are numbers that can be represented by points on a number line (that is, all rational and irrational numbers).

absolute value The absolute value of a number is the distance between 0 and the number on a number line.

1.4

sum The answer to an addition problem is the sum.

addends The numbers being added are the addends.

$$8 + 5 = 13 \leftarrow \text{Sum}$$
Addends

1.5

minuend In the operation $x - y$, x is the minuend.

subtrahend In the operation $x - y$, y is the subtrahend.

difference The answer to a subtraction problem is the difference.

$$15 - 7 = 8 \leftarrow \text{Difference}$$
Minuend   Subtrahend

1.6

product The answer to a multiplication problem is the product.

quotient The answer to a division problem is the quotient.

dividend In the division $x \div y$, x is the dividend.

divisor In the division $x \div y$, y is the divisor.

$$20 \div 4 = 5 \leftarrow \text{Quotient}$$

Dividend   Divisor

reciprocal Pairs of numbers whose product is 1 are reciprocals, or **multiplicative inverses,** of each other.

identity element for addition (additive identity) When the identity element for addition, which is 0, is added to a number, the number is unchanged.

identity element for multiplication (multiplicative identity) When a number is multiplied by the identity element for multiplication, which is 1, the number is unchanged.

term A term is a number (constant), a variable, or a product or quotient of a number and one or more variables raised to powers.

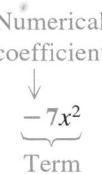

Numerical coefficient

$$-7x^2$$

Term

numerical coefficient The numerical factor of a term is its numerical coefficient, or **coefficient.**

like terms Terms with exactly the same variables (that have the same exponents on the variables) are like terms.

New Symbols

a^n	n factors of a	$>$	is greater than	$\{x \mid x \text{ has a certain property}\}$ set-builder notation
$(\ ), [\ ], \{ \ \}$	grouping symbols (parentheses, square brackets, braces)	$\geq$	is greater than or equal to	
		$x(y), (x)y, (x)(y), \ x \cdot y, \text{ or } xy$	x times y	$\lvert x \rvert$ absolute value of x
$=$	is equal to			$-x$ additive inverse, or opposite, of x
$\neq$	is not equal to	$x \div y, \dfrac{x}{y}, x/y, \text{ or } y\overline{)x}$		$\dfrac{1}{x}$ multiplicative inverse, or reciprocal, of x (where $x \neq 0$)
$<$	is less than		x divided by y	
$\leq$	is less than or equal to			

Test Your Word Power

See how well you have learned the vocabulary in this chapter.

1 A **product** is
A. the answer in an addition problem
B. the answer in a multiplication problem
C. one of two or more numbers that are added to obtain another number
D. one of two or more numbers that are multiplied to obtain another number.

2 An **exponent** is
A. a symbol that tells how many numbers are being multiplied
B. a number raised to a power
C. a number that tells how many times a factor is repeated
D. one of two or more numbers that are multiplied.

3 A **variable** is
A. a symbol used to represent an unknown number
B. a value that makes an equation true
C. a solution of an equation
D. the answer in a division problem.

4 An **integer** is
A. a positive or negative number
B. a natural number, its opposite, or zero
C. any number that can be graphed on a number line
D. the quotient of two numbers.

5 A **coordinate** is
A. the number that corresponds to a point on a number line
B. the graph of a number
C. any point on a number line
D. a distance on a number line.

6 The **absolute value** of a number is
A. the graph of the number
B. the reciprocal of the number
C. the opposite of the number
D. the distance between 0 and the number on a number line.

7 A **term** is
A. a numerical factor
B. a number, a variable, or a product or quotient of numbers and variables raised to powers
C. one of several variables with the same exponents
D. a sum of numbers and variables raised to powers.

8 The **subtrahend** in $a - b = c$ is
A. a
B. b
C. c
D. $a - b$.

Answers to Test Your Word Power

1. B; *Example:* The product of 2 and 5, or 2 times 5, is 10.

2. C; *Example:* In 2^3, the number 3 is the exponent (or power), so 2 is a factor three times; $2^3 = 2 \cdot 2 \cdot 2 = 8$.

3. A; *Examples:* x, y, z

4. B; *Examples:* $-9, 0, 6$

5. A; *Example:* The point graphed three units to the right of 0 on a number line has coordinate 3.

6. D; *Examples:* $|2| = 2$ and $|-2| = 2$

7. B; *Examples:* $6, \frac{x}{2}, -4ab^2$

8. B; *Example:* In $5 - 3 = 2$, 3 is the subtrahend.

Quick Review

Concepts	Examples

1.1 Exponents, Order of Operations, and Inequality

Order of Operations
Work within any parentheses or brackets and above and below fraction bars in the following order.

Step 1 Apply all exponents.

Step 2 Multiply or divide from left to right.

Step 3 Add or subtract from left to right.

Simplify.

$$36 - 4\left(2^2 + 3\right)$$
$$= 36 - 4\left(4 + 3\right) \quad \text{Apply the exponent.}$$
$$= 36 - 4\left(7\right) \quad \text{Add inside the parentheses.}$$
$$= 36 - 28 \quad \text{Multiply.}$$
$$= 8 \quad \text{Subtract.}$$

1.2 Variables, Expressions, and Equations

To evaluate an expression means to find its value. Evaluate an expression with a variable by substituting a given number for the variable.

A value of a variable that makes an equation true is a solution of the equation.

Evaluate $2x + y^2$ for $x = 3$ and $y = -4$.

$$2x + y^2$$
$$= 2\left(3\right) + \left(-4\right)^2 \quad \text{Substitute.}$$
$$= 6 + 16 \quad \text{Multiply. Apply the exponent.}$$
$$= 22 \quad \text{Add.}$$

Is 2 a solution of $5x + 3 = 18$?

$$5\left(2\right) + 3 \overset{?}{=} 18 \quad \text{Let } x = 2.$$
$$13 = 18 \quad \text{False}$$

2 is not a solution.

1.3 Real Numbers and the Number Line

Ordering Real Numbers
a is less than b if a lies to the left of b on a number line.

a is greater than b if a lies to the right of b on a number line.

The additive inverse, or opposite, of x is $-x$.

The absolute value of x, written $|x|$, is the distance between x and 0 on a number line.

Graph -2, 0, and 3.

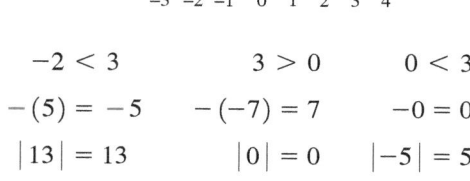

$-2 < 3$	$3 > 0$	$0 < 3$
$-(5) = -5$	$-(-7) = 7$	$-0 = 0$
$|13| = 13$	$|0| = 0$	$|-5| = 5$

1.4 Adding Real Numbers

Adding Two Signed Numbers
Same sign Add their absolute values. The sum has the same sign as the addends.

Different signs Subtract their absolute values. The sum has the sign of the addend with greater absolute value.

Add.

$$9 + 4 = 13$$
$$-8 + (-5) = -13$$
$$7 + (-12) = -5$$
$$-5 + 13 = 8$$

Concepts	**Examples**

1.5 Subtracting Real Numbers

Definition of Subtraction
For any real numbers x and y,

$$x - y \quad \text{is defined as} \quad x + (-y).$$

Subtract.

$$
\begin{array}{lll}
5 - (-2) & -3 - 4 & -2 - (-6) \\
= 5 + 2 & = -3 + (-4) & = -2 + 6 \\
= 7 & = -7 & = 4
\end{array}
$$

1.6 Multiplying and Dividing Real Numbers

Multiplying and Dividing Two Signed Numbers
Same sign The product (or quotient) is *positive*.

Different signs The product (or quotient) is *negative*.

Definition of Division
For any real numbers x and y,

$$x \div y = x \cdot \frac{1}{y} \quad (\text{where } y \neq 0).$$

0 divided by a nonzero number equals 0.

Division by 0 is undefined.

Multiply or divide.

$$6 \cdot 5 = 30 \qquad -7(-8) = 56 \qquad \frac{-24}{-6} = 4$$

$$-6(5) = -30 \qquad \frac{-18}{9} = -2 \qquad \frac{49}{-7} = -7$$

$$10 \div 2 = \frac{10}{2} = 10 \cdot \frac{1}{2} = 5$$

$$\frac{0}{5} = 0 \qquad \frac{5}{0} \text{ is undefined.}$$

1.7 Properties of Real Numbers

Commutative Properties
$$a + b = b + a$$
$$ab = ba$$

Associative Properties
$$(a + b) + c = a + (b + c)$$
$$(ab)c = a(bc)$$

Identity Properties
$$a + 0 = a \qquad 0 + a = a$$
$$a \cdot 1 = a \qquad 1 \cdot a = a$$

Inverse Properties
$$a + (-a) = 0 \qquad -a + a = 0$$
$$a \cdot \frac{1}{a} = 1 \qquad \frac{1}{a} \cdot a = 1 \quad (a \neq 0)$$

Distributive Properties
$$a(b + c) = ab + ac \quad \text{and} \quad (b + c)a = ba + ca$$
$$a(b - c) = ab - ac \quad \text{and} \quad (b - c)a = ba - ca$$

$$7 + (-1) = -1 + 7$$
$$5(-3) = (-3)5$$

$$(3 + 4) + 8 = 3 + (4 + 8)$$
$$[-2(6)]4 = -2[6(4)]$$

$$-7 + 0 = -7 \qquad 0 + (-7) = -7$$
$$9 \cdot 1 = 9 \qquad 1 \cdot 9 = 9$$

$$7 + (-7) = 0 \qquad -7 + 7 = 0$$
$$-2\left(-\frac{1}{2}\right) = 1 \qquad -\frac{1}{2}(-2) = 1$$

$$5(x + 2) = 5x + 5(2) \qquad (x + 2)5 = x \cdot 5 + 2(5)$$
$$9(5y - 4) = 9(5y) - 9(4) \qquad (5y - 4)9 = 5y(9) - 4(9)$$

1.8 Simplifying Expressions

Only like terms may be combined. We use a distributive property.

$$ba + ca = (b + c)a \quad \text{and} \quad a(b + c) = ab + ac$$

Simplify each expression.

$$
\begin{array}{l|l}
-3y^2 + 6y^2 & 4(3 + 2x) - 6(5 - x) \\
= (-3 + 6)y^2 & = 4(3) + 4(2x) - 6(5) - 6(-x) \\
= 3y^2 & = 12 + 8x - 30 + 6x \\
 & = 14x - 18
\end{array}
$$

Chapter 1 *Review Exercises*

If you need help with any of these Review Exercises, look in the section indicated.

1.1 *Find the value of each expression.*

1. 5^4

2. $(0.03)^4$

3. 0.21^3

4. $\left(\dfrac{5}{2}\right)^3$

Evaluate each expression.

5. $8 \cdot 5 - 13$

6. $5\left[4^2 + 3\left(2^3\right)\right]$

7. $16 + 12 \div 4 - 2$

8. $20 - 2\left(5 + 3\right)$

9. $\dfrac{7\left(3^2 - 5\right)}{16 - 2 \cdot 6}$

10. $\dfrac{5\left(6^2 - 2^4\right)}{3 \cdot 5 + 10}$

Write each word statement in symbols.

11. Thirteen is less than seventeen.

12. Five plus two is not equal to ten.

Write each statement in words, and decide whether it is true *or* false.

13. $6 < 15$

14. $\dfrac{2}{4} \neq \dfrac{3}{6}$

1.2 *Evaluate each expression for $x = 6$ and $y = 3$.*

15. $2x + 6y$

16. $4\left(3x - y\right)$

17. $\dfrac{x}{3} + 4y$

18. $\dfrac{x^2 + 3}{3y - x}$

Write each word phrase as an algebraic expression, using x as the variable.

19. Six added to a number

20. A number subtracted from eight

21. Nine subtracted from six times a number

22. Three-fifths of a number added to 12

Decide whether each equation has the given number as a solution.

23. $5x + 3\left(x + 2\right) = 22; \quad 2$

24. $\dfrac{x + 5}{3x} = 1; \quad 6$

Write each word sentence as an equation. Use x as the variable.

25. Six less than twice a number is 10.

26. The product of a number and 4 is 8.

Decide whether each of the following is an equation *or an* expression.

27. $5r - 8\left(r + 7\right) = 2$

28. $2y + \left(5y - 9\right) + 2$

1.3 *Graph each number on a number line.*

29. $-4, -\dfrac{1}{2}, 0, 2.5, 5$

30. $-3\dfrac{1}{4}, \dfrac{14}{5}, -1\dfrac{1}{8}, \dfrac{5}{6}$

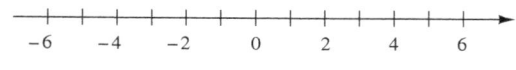

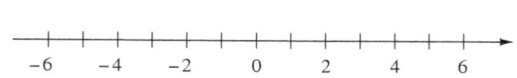

Classify each number, using the sets natural numbers, whole numbers, integers, rational numbers, irrational numbers, *and* real numbers.

31. $\dfrac{4}{3}$

32. 19

Select the lesser of the two given numbers.

33. $-10, 5$

34. $-8, -9$

35. $-\dfrac{2}{3}, -\dfrac{3}{4}$

36. $0, -|23|$

Decide whether each statement is true *or* false.

37. $12 > -13$

38. $0 > -5$

39. $-9 < -7$

40. $-13 > -13$

Find each absolute value and simplify if needed.

41. $-|3|$

42. $-|-19|$

43. $-|9 - 2|$

44. $|15 - 6|$

1.4 *Find each sum.*

45. $-10 + 4$

46. $14 + (-18)$

47. $-8 + (-9)$

48. $\dfrac{4}{9} + \left(-\dfrac{5}{4}\right)$

49. $-5 + \left[-6 + (-8) + 19\right]$

50. $|-12 + 3| + |-2 + (-4)|$

Write a numerical expression for each phrase, and simplify the expression.

51. 19 added to the sum of -31 and 12

52. 13 more than the sum of -4 and -8

Solve each problem.

53. Otis found that his checking account balance was $-\$23.75$, so he deposited $\$50.00$. What is his new balance?

54. The low temperature in Yellowknife, in the Canadian Northwest Territories, one January day was $-26°$F. It rose $16°$ that day. What was the high temperature?

1.5 *Find each difference.*

55. $-7 - 4$

56. $-12 - (-11)$

57. $5 - (-2)$

58. $-\dfrac{3}{7} - \dfrac{4}{5}$

59. $2.56 - (-7.75)$

60. $(-10 - 4) - (-2)$

61. $(-3 + 4) - (-1)$

62. $|5 - 9| - |-3 + 6|$

Write a numerical expression for each phrase, and simplify the expression.

63. The difference of -4 and -6

64. Five less than the sum of 4 and -8

65. The difference of 18 and -23, decreased by 15

66. Nineteen, decreased by 12 less than -7

Solve each problem.

67. A quarterback passed for a gain of 8 yd, was sacked for a loss of 12 yd, and then threw a 42 yd touchdown pass. Find the total net yardage for the plays.

68. On December 4, 2015, the Dow Jones Industrial Average closed at 17,847.63, up 370 points from the previous day. What was the closing price on December 3, 2015? (Data from *The Wall Street Journal*.)

The table shows the number of people naturalized in the United States (that is, made citizens of the United States) for the years 2008 through 2014. Use a signed number to represent the change in the number of people naturalized for each time period.

Year	Number of People (in thousands)
2008	1050
2009	742
2010	619
2011	691
2012	763
2013	777
2014	655

Data from Citizenship and Immigration Services.

69. 2008 to 2009   **70.** 2010 to 2011   **71.** 2012 to 2013   **72.** 2013 to 2014

1.6 *Perform the indicated operations.*

73. $(-12)(-3)$ **74.** $15(-7)$ **75.** $-\dfrac{4}{3}\left(-\dfrac{3}{8}\right)$ **76.** $-4.8(-2.1)$

77. $5(8-12)$ **78.** $(5-7)(8-3)$ **79.** $2(-6)-(-4)(-3)$ **80.** $3(-10)-5$

81. $\dfrac{-36}{-9}$ **82.** $\dfrac{220}{-11}$ **83.** $-\dfrac{1}{2}\div\dfrac{2}{3}$ **84.** $-33.9\div(-3)$

85. $\dfrac{-5(3)-1}{8-4(-2)}$ **86.** $\dfrac{5(-2)-3(4)}{-2[3-(-2)]+10}$ **87.** $\dfrac{10^2-5^2}{8^2+3^2-(-2)}$ **88.** $\dfrac{4^2-8\cdot2}{(-1.2)^2-(-0.56)}$

Evaluate each expression for $x=-5$, $y=4$, and $z=-3$.

89. $6x-4z$ **90.** $5x+y-z$ **91.** $5x^2$ **92.** $z^2(3x-8y)$

Write a numerical expression for each phrase, and simplify the expression.

93. Nine less than the product of -4 and 5

94. Five-sixths of the sum of 12 and -6

95. The quotient of 12 and the sum of 8 and -4

96. The product of -20 and 12, divided by the difference of 15 and -15

Write each sentence as an equation, using x as the variable.

97. The quotient of a number and the sum of the number and 5 is -2.

98. 3 less than 8 times a number is -7.

1.7 *Decide whether each statement is an example of a* commutative, *an* associative, *an* identity, *an* inverse, *or the* distributive property.

99. $6 + 0 = 6$

100. $5 \cdot 1 = 5$

101. $-\dfrac{2}{3}\left(-\dfrac{3}{2}\right) = 1$

102. $17 + (-17) = 0$

103. $3x + 3y = 3(x + y)$

104. $w(xy) = (wx)y$

105. $5 + (-9 + 2) = \left[5 + (-9)\right] + 2$

106. $(1 + 2) + 3 = 3 + (1 + 2)$

Use the distributive property to rewrite each expression. Simplify if possible.

107. $7(y + 2)$

108. $-12(4 - t)$

109. $3(2s + 5y)$

110. $-(-4r + 5s)$

1.8 *Simplify each expression.*

111. $7y + y$

112. $16p^2 - 8p^2 + 9p^2$

113. $4r^2 - 3r + 10r + 12r^2$

114. $-8(5k - 6) + 3(7k + 2)$

115. $2s - (-3s + 6)$

116. $-7(2t - 4) - 4(3t + 8) - 19(t + 1)$

Write each phrase as a mathematical expression using x as the variable, and simplify.

117. Seven times a number, subtracted from the product of -2 and three times the number

118. A number multiplied by 8, added to the sum of 5 and four times the number

Chapter 1 *Mixed Review Exercises*

Complete the table.

	Number	Absolute Value	Additive Inverse	Multiplicative Inverse
1.	−3	_____	_____	_____
2.	12	_____	_____	_____
3.	_____	_____	_____	$-\frac{3}{2}$
4.	_____	_____	−0.2	_____

5. To which of the following sets does $0.\overline{6}$ belong: natural numbers, whole numbers, integers, rational numbers, irrational numbers, real numbers?

6. Evaluate $(x + 6)^3 - y^3$ for $x = -2$ and $y = 3$.

Perform the indicated operations.

7. $\frac{15}{2} \cdot \left(-\frac{4}{5}\right)$

8. $\left(-\frac{5}{6}\right)^2$

9. $-|(-7)(-4)| - (-2)$

10. $\frac{6(-4) + 2(-12)}{5(-3) + (-3)}$

11. $\frac{3}{8} - \frac{5}{12}$

12. $\frac{12^2 + 2^2 - 8}{10^2 - (-4)(-15)}$

13. $\frac{8^2 + 6^2}{7^2 + 1^2}$

14. $-16(-3.5) - 7.2(-3)$

15. $2\frac{5}{6} - 4\frac{1}{3}$

16. $-8 + [(-4 + 17) - (-3 - 3)]$

17. $-\frac{12}{5} \div \frac{9}{7}$

18. $(-8 - 3) - 5(2 - 9)$

Solve each problem.

19. The highest temperature ever recorded in Iowa was 118°F. The lowest temperature ever recorded in the state was 165°F lower than the highest temperature. What is the record low temperature for Iowa? (Data from National Climatic Data Center.)

20. Humpback whales love to heave their 45-ton bodies out of the water. This is called *breaching*. A whale breached 15 ft above the surface of the ocean, while her mate cruised 12 ft below the surface. What is the difference between these two heights?

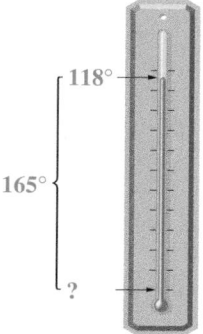

Decide whether each statement is true *or* false.

1. $4\left[-20 + 7(-2)\right] \le -135$

2. $\left(\dfrac{1}{2}\right)^2 + \left(\dfrac{2}{3}\right)^2 = \left(\dfrac{1}{2} + \dfrac{2}{3}\right)^2$

3. Graph the numbers $-1, -3, |-4|,$ and $|-1|$ on the number line.

4. To which of the following sets does $-\dfrac{2}{3}$ belong: natural numbers, whole numbers, integers, rational numbers, irrational numbers, real numbers?

Select the lesser of the two given numbers.

5. $6, -|-8|$

6. $-0.742, -1.277$

7. Write a numerical expression for the phrase, and simplify the expression.

The quotient of -6 and the sum of 2 and -8

8. If a and b are both negative, is $\dfrac{a + b}{a \cdot b}$ positive or negative?

Perform the indicated operations.

9. $-2 - (5 - 17) + (-6)$

10. $-5\dfrac{1}{2} + 2\dfrac{2}{3}$

11. $4^2 + (-8) - (2^3 - 6)$

12. $-6.2 - \left[-7.1 + (2.0 - 3.1)\right]$

13. $(-5)(-12) + 4(-4) + (-8)^2$

14. $\dfrac{-7 - |-6 + 2|}{-5 - (-4)}$

15. $\dfrac{30(-1 - 2)}{-9\left[3 - (-2)\right] - 12(-2)}$

Evaluate each expression for $x = -2$ and $y = 4$.

16. $3x - 4y^2$

17. $\dfrac{5x + 7y}{3(x + y)}$

Solve each problem.

18. The highest Fahrenheit temperature ever recorded in Idaho was 118°F, while the lowest was −60°F. What is the difference between these highest and lowest temperatures? (Data from *The World Almanac and Book of Facts*.)

19. For 2014, the U.S. federal government collected $3.02 trillion in revenues but spent $3.51 trillion. Write the federal budget deficit as a signed number. (Data from Office of Management and Budget.)

20. For a certain system of rating relief pitchers, 3 points are awarded for a save, 3 points are awarded for a win, 2 points are subtracted for a loss, and 2 points are subtracted for a blown save. If a pitcher has 4 saves, 3 wins, 2 losses, and 1 blown save, how many points does he have?

Match each statement in Column I with the property it illustrates in Column II.

	I		**II**
21.	$3x + 0 = 3x$	**A.**	Commutative property
22.	$(5 + 2) + 8 = 8 + (5 + 2)$	**B.**	Associative property
23.	$-3(x + y) = -3x + (-3y)$	**C.**	Inverse property
24.	$-5 + (3 + 2) = (-5 + 3) + 2$	**D.**	Identity property
25.	$-\dfrac{5}{3}\left(-\dfrac{3}{5}\right) = 1$	**E.**	Distributive property

Simplify each expression.

26. $8x + 4x - 6x + x + 14x$

27. $-(3x - 1)$

28. $-2(3x^2 + 4) - 3(x^2 + 2x)$

29. $5(2x - 1) - (x - 12) + 2(3x - 5)$

30. Consider the expression $-6[5 + (-2)]$.

    (a) Evaluate it by first working within the brackets.

    (b) Evaluate it using the distributive property.

    (c) Why must the answers in parts (a) and (b) be the same?

Equations, Inequalities, and Applications

Solving *linear equations*, the subject of this chapter, can be thought of in terms of the concept of balance.

2.1 The Addition Property of Equality

Study Skills *Managing Your Time*

2.2 The Multiplication Property of Equality

2.3 More on Solving Linear Equations

Study Skills *Using Study Cards Revisited*

Summary Exercises *Applying Methods for Solving Linear Equations*

2.4 An Introduction to Applications of Linear Equations

2.5 Formulas and Additional Applications from Geometry

2.6 Ratio, Proportion, and Percent

Summary Exercises *Applying Problem-Solving Techniques*

2.7 Solving Linear Inequalities

Study Skills *Taking Math Tests*

2.1 | The Addition Property of Equality

OBJECTIVES

1. Identify linear equations.
2. Use the addition property of equality.
3. Simplify, and then use the addition property of equality.

An *equation* is a statement asserting that two algebraic expressions are equal.

> **! CAUTION**
> *Remember that an equation always includes an equality symbol.*
>
> | Equation | Expression |
> |:---:|:---:|
> | ↓ | ↓ |
> | Left side → $x - 5 = 2$ ← Right side | $x - 5$ |
> | An equation can be solved. | An expression **cannot** be solved. (It can be *evaluated* for a given value or *simplified*.) |

OBJECTIVE ➊ Identify linear equations.

> **Linear Equation in One Variable**
>
> A **linear equation in one variable** (here x) can be written in the form
> $$Ax + B = C,$$
> where A, B, and C are real numbers and $A \neq 0$.
>
> *Examples:* $4x + 9 = 0$, $2x - 3 = 5$, $x = 7$ Linear equations
>
> $x^2 + 2x = 5$, $x^3 = -1$, $\dfrac{1}{x} = 6$, $|2x + 6| = 0$ *Non*linear equations

Recall that a **solution** of an equation is a number that makes the equation true when it replaces the variable. An equation is solved by finding its **solution set,** the set of all solutions. Equations that have exactly the same solution sets are **equivalent equations.**

A linear equation in x is solved by using a series of steps to produce a simpler equivalent equation of the form

$$x = \text{a number} \quad \text{or} \quad \text{a number} = x.$$

OBJECTIVE ➋ Use the addition property of equality. In the linear equation $x - 5 = 2$, both $x - 5$ and 2 represent the same number because that is the meaning of the equality symbol. To solve the equation, we change the left side from $x - 5$ to just x, as follows.

$x - 5 = 2$	Given equation
$x - 5 + 5 = 2 + 5$	Add 5 to *each* side to keep them equal.
$x + 0 = 7$	Additive inverse property
$x = 7$	Additive identity property

Add 5. It is the opposite (additive inverse) of -5, and $-5 + 5 = 0$.

To check that 7 is the solution, we replace x with 7 in the original equation.

CHECK	$x - 5 = 2$	Original equation
	$7 - 5 \overset{?}{=} 2$	Let $x = 7$.
	$2 = 2$ ✓	True

The left side equals the right side.

We write a solution set using set braces.

The final equation is true, so 7 is the solution and $\{7\}$ is the solution set.

To solve $x - 5 = 2$, we used the **addition property of equality.**

Addition Property of Equality

If A, B, and C represent real numbers, then the equations

$$A = B \quad \text{and} \quad A + C = B + C \quad \text{are equivalent.}$$

In words, the same number may be added to each side of an equation without changing the solution set.

In this property, any quantity that represents a real number C can be added to each side of an equation to obtain an equivalent equation.

Note

Equations can be thought of in terms of a balance. Thus, adding the *same* quantity to each side does not affect the balance. See **Figure 1.**

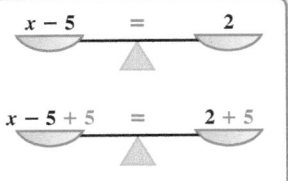

Figure 1

EXAMPLE 1   Applying the Addition Property of Equality

Solve $x - 16 = 7$.

Our goal is to get an equivalent equation of the form $x = \textbf{a number.}$

$$x - 16 = 7$$
$$x - 16 + \textbf{16} = 7 + \textbf{16} \qquad \text{Add 16 to each side.}$$
$$x = \textbf{23} \qquad \text{Combine like terms.}$$

CHECK   Substitute 23 for x in the *original* equation.

$$x - 16 = 7 \qquad \text{Original equation}$$
$$\textbf{23} - 16 \overset{?}{=} 7 \qquad \text{Let } x = 23.$$
$$7 = 7 \checkmark \qquad \text{True}$$

7 is *not* the solution.

A true statement results, so **23** is the solution and $\{\textbf{23}\}$ is the solution set.

— **Work Problem ① at the Side.** ▶

EXAMPLE 2   Applying the Addition Property of Equality

Solve $x - 2.9 = -6.4$.

Our goal is to isolate x.

$$x - 2.9 = -6.4$$
$$x - 2.9 + \textbf{2.9} = -6.4 + \textbf{2.9} \qquad \text{Add 2.9 to each side.}$$
$$x = -\textbf{3.5}$$

CHECK
$$x - 2.9 = -6.4 \qquad \text{Original equation}$$
$$-3.5 - 2.9 \overset{?}{=} -6.4 \qquad \text{Let } x = -3.5.$$
$$-6.4 = -6.4 \checkmark \qquad \text{True}$$

A true statement results, so the solution set is $\{-3.5\}$.

— **Work Problem ② at the Side.** ▶

---

① Solve.

GS **(a)** Fill in the blanks.

$$x - 12 = 9$$
$$x - 12 + \underline{\quad} = 9 + \underline{\quad}$$
$$x = \underline{\quad}$$

CHECK $x - 12 = 9$
$$\underline{\quad} - 12 \overset{?}{=} 9$$
$$\underline{\quad} = 9 \quad (True/False)$$

The solution set is $\underline{\quad}$.

(b) $x - 25 = -18$

(c) $x - 8 = -13$

② Solve.

(a) $x - 3.7 = -8.1$

(b) $a - 4.1 = 6.3$

Answers

1. **(a)** 12; 12; 21; 21; 9; True; $\{21\}$
   (b) $\{7\}$ **(c)** $\{-5\}$

2. **(a)** $\{-4.4\}$ **(b)** $\{10.4\}$

3 Solve.

GS **(a)** $-15 = a + 12$

Our goal is to isolate _____.

On each side of the equation, (*add / subtract*) 12.

Now solve.

Subtraction was previously defined as addition of the opposite. Thus, we can also use the following rule when solving an equation.

> **Addition Property of Equality Extended to Subtraction**
>
> **The same number may be *subtracted* from each side of an equation without changing the solution set.**

EXAMPLE 3 **Applying the Addition Property of Equality**

Solve $-7 = x + 22$.

Here, the variable x is on the right side of the equation.

$$-7 = x + 22 \quad \text{The variable can be isolated on } either \text{ side.}$$

$$-7 - 22 = x + 22 - 22 \qquad \text{Subtract 22 from each side.}$$

$$-29 = x, \quad \text{or} \quad x = -29 \qquad \begin{array}{l}\text{Rewrite; a number} = x, \\ \text{or } x = \text{a number.}\end{array}$$

CHECK $\qquad -7 = x + 22 \qquad$ Original equation

$$-7 \overset{?}{=} -29 + 22 \qquad \text{Let } x = -29.$$

$$-7 = -7 \checkmark \qquad \text{True}$$

The check confirms that the solution set is $\{-29\}$.

◀ **Work Problem ③ at the Side.**

> **Note**
>
> In **Example 3,** what would happen if we subtract $-7 - 22$ incorrectly, obtaining $x = -15$ (instead of $x = -29$) as the last line of the solution? A check should indicate an error.
>
> **CHECK** $\qquad -7 = x + 22 \qquad$ Original equation from **Example 3**
>
> $$-7 \overset{?}{=} -15 + 22 \qquad \text{Let } x = -15.$$
>
> The left side does *not* equal the right side. $\quad -7 = 7 \qquad$ False
>
> The false statement indicates that -15 is *not* a solution of the equation. If this happens, rework the problem.

(b) $22 = -16 + r$

EXAMPLE 4 **Subtracting a Variable Term**

Solve $6x - 8 = 7x$.

$$6x - 8 = 7x$$

$$6x - 8 - 6x = 7x - 6x \qquad \text{Subtract } 6x \text{ from each side.}$$

$$-8 = x \qquad \text{Combine like terms.}$$

CHECK $\qquad 6x - 8 = 7x \qquad$ Original equation

$$6(-8) - 8 \overset{?}{=} 7(-8) \qquad \text{Let } x = -8.$$

Use parentheses when substituting to avoid errors.

$$-48 - 8 \overset{?}{=} -56 \qquad \text{Multiply.}$$

$$-56 = -56 \checkmark \qquad \text{True}$$

A true statements results, so the solution set is $\{-8\}$.

Answers

3. **(a)** a; subtract; $\{-27\}$ **(b)** $\{38\}$

What happens in **Example 4** if we start by subtracting $7x$ from each side?

$$6x - 8 = 7x \qquad \text{Original equation from \textbf{Example 4}}$$

$$6x - 8 - 7x = 7x - 7x \qquad \text{Subtract } 7x \text{ from each side.}$$

$$-8 - x = 0 \qquad \text{Combine like terms.}$$

$$-8 - x + 8 = 0 + 8 \qquad \text{Add 8 to each side.}$$

$$-x = 8 \qquad \text{Combine like terms.}$$

This result gives the value of $-x$, but not of x itself. However, it does say that the additive inverse of x is 8, which means that x must be -8.

$$x = -8 \qquad \text{Same result as in \textbf{Example 4}}$$

We can make the following generalization.

If a is a number and $-x = a$, then $x = -a$.

Work Problem ④ at the Side. ▶

EXAMPLE 5   **Subtracting a Variable Term (Fractional Coefficients)**

Solve $\frac{3}{5}k + 15 = \frac{8}{5}k$.

$$\frac{3}{5}k + 15 = \frac{8}{5}k \qquad \boxed{\text{We must get the terms with } k \text{ on the same side of the} = \text{symbol.}}$$

$$\frac{3}{5}k + 15 - \frac{3}{5}k = \frac{8}{5}k - \frac{3}{5}k \qquad \text{Subtract } \tfrac{3}{5}k \text{ from each side.}$$

$\boxed{\text{From now on we will skip this step.}}$ $15 = 1k \qquad \tfrac{3}{5}k - \tfrac{3}{5}k = 0; \tfrac{8}{5}k - \tfrac{3}{5}k = \tfrac{5}{5}k = 1k$

$$15 = k \qquad \text{Multiplicative identity property}$$

Check by substituting 15 in the original equation. The solution set is $\{15\}$.

Work Problem ⑤ at the Side. ▶

EXAMPLE 6   **Applying the Addition Property of Equality Twice**

Solve $8 - 6p = -7p + 5$.

$$8 - 6p = -7p + 5$$

$$8 - 6p + 7p = -7p + 5 + 7p \qquad \text{Add } 7p \text{ to each side.}$$

$$8 + p = 5 \qquad \text{Combine like terms.}$$

$$8 + p - 8 = 5 - 8 \qquad \text{Subtract 8 from each side.}$$

$$p = -3 \qquad \text{Combine like terms.}$$

CHECK   Substitute -3 for p in the original equation.

$$8 - 6p = -7p + 5 \qquad \text{Original equation}$$

$$8 - 6(-3) \stackrel{?}{=} -7(-3) + 5 \qquad \text{Let } p = -3.$$

$$8 + 18 \stackrel{?}{=} 21 + 5 \qquad \text{Multiply.}$$

$$26 = 26 \ \checkmark \qquad \text{True}$$

The check results in a true statement, so the solution set is $\{-3\}$.

Work Problem ⑥ at the Side. ▶

---

④ (a) Solve $11z - 9 = 12z$.

(b) What is the solution set of $-x = 6$?

(c) What is the solution set of $-x = -12$?

⑤ Solve.

(a) $\dfrac{7}{2}m + 1 = \dfrac{9}{2}m$

(b) $\dfrac{2}{3}x - 4 = \dfrac{5}{3}x$

⑥ Solve.

GS (a) $10 - a = -2a + 9$

$$10 - a + \underline{\quad} = -2a + 9 + 2a$$

$$10 + a = 9$$

$$10 + a - \underline{\quad} = 9 - \underline{\quad}$$

$$a = \underline{\quad}$$

The solution set is $\underline{\quad}$.

(b) $6x - 8 = 12 + 5x$

Answers

4. (a) $\{-9\}$ **(b)** $\{-6\}$ **(c)** $\{12\}$

5. (a) $\{1\}$ **(b)** $\{-4\}$

6. (a) $2a$; 10; 10; -1; $\{-1\}$ **(b)** $\{20\}$

7 Solve.

(a) $9r + 4r + 6 - 2$
   $= 9r + 4 + 3r$

(b) $4x + 6 + 2x - 3$
   $= 9 + 5x - 4$

8 Solve.

(a) $3(2x - 1) - 5x = 8$

GS (b) $2(5 + 2m) - 3(m - 4) = 29$

   $2(5) + 2(2m) - \underline{\quad} m$

   $- \underline{\quad}(\underline{\quad}) = 29$

   $10 + 4m - \underline{\quad} + \underline{\quad} = 29$

   Now complete the solution.

Note

There are often several correct ways to solve an equation. We could begin by adding $6p$ (instead of $7p$) to each side of the equation

$$8 - 6p = -7p + 5. \quad \text{See Example 6.}$$

Combining like terms and subtracting 5 from each side gives $3 = -p$. (Try this.) If $3 = -p$, then $-3 = p$, and the variable has been isolated on the right side of the equation. The same solution results.

OBJECTIVE ▶ 3 Simplify, and then use the addition property of equality.

EXAMPLE 7 Combining Like Terms When Solving

Solve $3t - 12 + t + 2 = 5 + 3t - 15$.

$3t - 12 + t + 2 = 5 + 3t - 15$	
$4t - 10 = -10 + 3t$	Combine like terms on each side.
$4t - 10 - 3t = -10 + 3t - 3t$	Subtract $3t$ from each side.
$t - 10 = -10$	Combine like terms.
$t - 10 + 10 = -10 + 10$	Add 10 to each side.
$t = 0$	Combine like terms.

The real number 0 can be a solution of an equation.

CHECK $\quad 3t - 12 + t + 2 = 5 + 3t - 15$	Original equation
$3(0) - 12 + 0 + 2 \overset{?}{=} 5 + 3(0) - 15$	Let $t = 0$.
$0 - 12 + 0 + 2 \overset{?}{=} 5 + 0 - 15$	Multiply.
$-10 = -10$ ✓	True

The check results in a true statement, so the solution set is $\{0\}$.

◀ **Work Problem 7** at the Side.

! **CAUTION**

The final line of the CHECK does not give the solution of the equation. It gives a confirmation that the solution found is correct.

EXAMPLE 8 Using the Distributive Property When Solving

Solve $3(2 + 5x) - (1 + 14x) = 6$.

$3(2 + 5x) - (1 + 14x) = 6$	Begin by clearing (removing) the parentheses.
$3(2 + 5x) - 1(1 + 14x) = 6$	$-(1 + 14x) = -\mathbf{1}(1 + 14x)$
$3(2) + 3(5x) - 1(1) - 1(14x) = 6$	Distributive property
$6 + 15x - 1 - 14x = 6$	Multiply.
$x + 5 = 6$	Combine like terms.
$x + 5 - 5 = 6 - 5$	Subtract 5 from each side.
$x = 1$	Combine like terms.

Be careful here, or a sign error may result.

Check by substituting 1 in the original equation. The solution set is $\{1\}$.

◀ **Work Problem 8** at the Side.

2.1 Exercises

FOR EXTRA HELP

Go to MyMathLab *for worked-out, step-by-step solutions to exercises enclosed in a square* ▢ *and video solutions to* ▶ *exercises.*

CONCEPT CHECK *Complete each statement with the correct response. The following terms may be used once, more than once, or not at all.*

linear	expression	solution set	multiplication
equation	addition	equivalent equations	variable

1. A(n) _____ includes an equality symbol, while a(n) _____ does not.

2. A(n) _____ equation in one _____ (here x) can be written in the form $Ax + B \,(= / \ne)\, C$.

3. Equations that have exactly the same solution set are _____.

4. The _____ property of equality states that the same expression may be added to or subtracted from each side of an equation without changing the _____.

5. CONCEPT CHECK ▶ Which of the following are *not* linear equations in one variable?

   A. $x^2 - 5x + 6 = 0$ **B.** $x^3 = x$

   C. $3x - 4 = 0$ **D.** $7x - 6x = 3 + 9x$

6. CONCEPT CHECK Decide whether each is an *equation* or an *expression*. If it is an equation, solve it. If it is an expression, simplify it.

   (a) $5x + 8 - 4x + 7$ **(b)** $-6m + 12 + 7m - 5$

   (c) $5x + 8 - 4x = 7$ **(d)** $-6m + 12 + 7m = -5$

Solve each equation, and check the solution. **See Examples 1–6.**

7. $x - 4 = 8$

8. $x - 8 = 9$

9. $x - 5 = -8$

10. $x - 7 = -9$

11. $z - 12 = -8$

12. $z - 18 = -7$

13. $r + 9 = 13$

14. $t + 6 = 10$

15. $x + 26 = 17$

16. $x + 45 = 24$

17. $x - 8.4 = -2.1$

18. $x - 15.5 = -5.1$

19. $t - 12.7 = -19.2$

20. $t - 8.6 = -17.3$

21. $t + 12.3 = -4.6$

22. $x + 21.5 = -13.4$

23. $x + \dfrac{1}{4} = -\dfrac{1}{2}$

24. $x + \dfrac{2}{3} = -\dfrac{1}{6}$

25. $7 + r = -3$

26. $8 + k = -4$

27. $2 = p + 15$

28. $3 = z + 17$

29. $-4 = x - 14$

30. $-7 = x - 22$

31. $5.2 = z - 4.9$

32. $11.8 = z - 3.6$

33. $-\dfrac{1}{3} = x - \dfrac{3}{5}$

34. $-\dfrac{1}{4} = x - \dfrac{2}{3}$

35. $8x - 3 = 9x$

36. $4x - 1 = 5x$

37. $3x = 2x + 7$

38. $5x = 4x + 9$

39. $10x + 4 = 9x$

40. $8t + 5 = 7t$

41. $\dfrac{1}{3}x + 12 = \dfrac{4}{3}x$

42. $\dfrac{2}{9}x + 17 = \dfrac{11}{9}x$

43. $\dfrac{1}{2}x + 5 = -\dfrac{1}{2}x$

44. $\dfrac{1}{5}x + 7 = -\dfrac{4}{5}x$

45. $\dfrac{2}{5}w - 6 = \dfrac{7}{5}w$

46. $\dfrac{2}{7}r - 3 = \dfrac{9}{7}r$

47. $5.6x + 2 = 4.6x$ **48.** $9.1x + 5 = 8.1x$ **49.** $3p + 6 = 10 + 2p$ **50.** $8x + 4 = -6 + 7x$

51. $5 - x = -2x - 11$ **52.** $3 - 8x = -9x - 1$ **53.** $-4z + 7 = -5z + 9$ **54.** $-6q + 3 = -7q + 10$

Solve each equation, and check the solution. ***See Examples 7 and 8.***

55. $3x + 6 - 10 = 2x - 2$

56. $8k - 4 + 6 = 7k + 1$

57. $6x + 5 + 7x + 3 = 12x + 4$
▶

58. $4x - 3 - 8x + 1 = -5x + 9$

59. $10x + 5x + 7 - 4 = 12x + 3 + 2x$

60. $7p + 4p + 13 - 7 = 7p + 6 + 3p$

61. $5.2q - 4.6 - 7.1q = -0.9q - 4.6$

62. $-4.0x + 2.7 - 1.6x = -4.6x + 2.7$

63. $\dfrac{5}{7}x + \dfrac{1}{3} = \dfrac{2}{5} - \dfrac{2}{7}x + \dfrac{2}{5}$

64. $\dfrac{6}{7}s - \dfrac{3}{4} = \dfrac{4}{5} - \dfrac{1}{7}s + \dfrac{1}{6}$

65. $5(3x - 2) - 14x = 3$

66. $2(3x - 4) - 5x = 7$

67. $13p + 3(2 - 4p) = 4$

68. $21w + 4(6 - 5w) = 8$

69. $(5x + 6) - (3 + 4x) = 10$

70. $(8r - 3) - (7r + 1) = -6$

71. $2(p + 5) - (9 + p) = -3$

72. $4(k - 6) - (3k + 2) = -5$

73. $-6(2x - 1) + (13x - 6) = 0$

74. $-5(3w - 3) + (16w - 15) = 0$

75. $10(-2x + 1) = -19(x + 1)$

76. $2(-3r + 2) = -5(r - 3)$

77. $-2(8p + 2) - 3(2 - 7p) = 2(4 + 2p)$

78. $4(3 - z) - 5(1 - 2z) = 7(3 + z)$

Study Skills
MANAGING YOUR TIME

M any college students juggle a difficult schedule and multiple responsibilities, including school, work, and family demands.

Time Management Tips

► **Read the syllabus for each class.** Understand class policies, such as attendance, late homework, and make-up tests. Find out how you are graded.

► **Make a semester or quarter calendar.** Put test dates and major due dates for *all* your classes on the *same* calendar. Try using a different color pen for each class.

► **Make a weekly schedule.** After you fill in your classes and other regular responsibilities, block off some study periods. Aim for 2 hours of study for each 1 hour in class.

► **Choose a regular study time and place** (such as the campus library). Routine helps.

► **Keep distractions to a minimum.** Get the most out of the time you have set aside for studying by limiting interruptions. Turn off your cell phone. Take a break from social media. Avoid studying in front of the TV.

► **Make "to-do" lists.** Number tasks in order of importance. Cross off tasks as you complete them.

► **Break big assignments into smaller chunks**. Make deadlines for each smaller chunk so that you stay on schedule.

► **Take breaks when studying.** Do not try to study for hours at a time. Take a 10-minute break each hour or so.

► **Ask for help when you need it.** Talk with your instructor during office hours. Make use of the learning center, tutoring center, counseling office, or other resources available at your school.

Now Try This

Think through and answer each question.

1 Evaluate when and where you are currently studying. Are the places you named quiet and comfortable? Are you studying when you are most alert?

_____

2 How many hours do you have available for studying this week?

_____

3 Which two or three of the above suggestions will you try this week to improve your time management?

_____

4 Once the week is over, evaluate how these suggestions worked. What will you do differently next week?

_____

2.2 | The Multiplication Property of Equality

OBJECTIVES

1 Use the multiplication property of equality.

2 Simplify, and then use the multiplication property of equality.

---

1 Check that 5 is the solution
GS of $3x = 15$.

$$3x = 15$$
$$3(\underline{\hspace{1cm}}) \overset{?}{=} 15$$
$$\underline{\hspace{1cm}} = 15 \quad (True/False)$$

The solution set is _____.

OBJECTIVE ► 1 **Use the multiplication property of equality.** The addition property of equality is not sufficient to solve some equations.

$$3x + 2 = 17$$
$$3x + 2 - 2 = 17 - 2 \qquad \text{Subtract 2 from each side.}$$
$$3x = 15 \qquad \text{Combine like terms.}$$

The coefficient of x here is 3, not 1 as desired. The **multiplication property of equality** is needed to change $3x = 15$ to an equation of the form

$$x = \text{a number.}$$

Since $3x = 15$, both $3x$ and 15 must represent the same number. Multiplying both $3x$ and 15 by the same number will result in an equivalent equation.

Multiplication Property of Equality

If A, B, and C represent real numbers, where $C \neq 0$, then the equations

$$A = B \quad \text{and} \quad AC = BC \quad \text{are equivalent.}$$

In words, each side of an equation may be multiplied by the same nonzero number without changing the solution set.

In $3x = 15$, we must change $3x$ to $1x$, or x. To do this, we multiply each side of the equation by $\frac{1}{3}$, the *reciprocal* of 3, because $\frac{1}{3} \cdot 3 = \frac{3}{3} = 1$.

$$3x = 15$$

$$\frac{1}{3}(3x) = \frac{1}{3}(15) \qquad \text{Multiply each side by } \frac{1}{3}.$$

The product of a number and its reciprocal is 1.

$$\left(\frac{1}{3} \cdot 3\right)x = \frac{1}{3}(15) \qquad \text{Associative property}$$

$$1x = 5 \qquad \text{Multiplicative inverse property}$$

$$x = 5 \qquad \text{Multiplicative identity property}$$

The solution is 5. We can check this result in the original equation.

◄ Work Problem 1 at the Side

Just as the addition property of equality permits *subtracting* the same number from each side of an equation, the multiplication property of equality permits *dividing* each side of an equation by the same nonzero number.

$$3x = 15$$

$$\frac{3x}{3} = \frac{15}{3} \qquad \text{Divide each side by 3.}$$

$$x = 5 \qquad \text{Same result as above}$$

Multiplication Property of Equality Extended to Division

We can divide each side of an equation by the same nonzero number without changing the solution. *Do not, however, divide each side by a variable, because the variable might be equal to 0.*

Answer

1. 5; 15; True; {5}

Note

It is usually easier to multiply on each side of an equation if the coefficient of the variable is a fraction, and divide on each side if the coefficient is an integer.

To solve $\frac{3}{4}x = 12$, it is easier to multiply by $\frac{4}{3}$ than to divide by $\frac{3}{4}$.

To solve $5x = 20$, it is easier to divide by 5 than to multiply by $\frac{1}{5}$.

EXAMPLE 1 **Applying the Multiplication Property of Equality**

Solve $5x = 60$.

$$5x = 60 \quad \boxed{\text{Our goal is to isolate } x.}$$

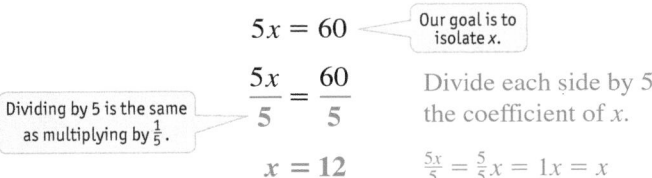

$$\frac{5x}{5} = \frac{60}{5} \qquad \text{Divide each side by 5, the coefficient of } x.$$

$$x = 12 \qquad \frac{5x}{5} = \frac{5}{5}x = 1x = x$$

CHECK Substitute 12 for x in the original equation.

$$5x = 60 \qquad \text{Original equation}$$

$$5(12) \overset{?}{=} 60 \qquad \text{Let } x = 12.$$

$\boxed{\text{60 is } not \text{ the solution.}}$ $\quad 60 = 60 \ \checkmark \quad$ True

A true statement results, so the solution set is $\{12\}$.

—————— **Work Problem 2 at the Side.** ▶

EXAMPLE 2 **Applying the Multiplication Property of Equality**

Solve $-25p = 30$.

$$-25p = 30$$

$$\frac{-25p}{-25} = \frac{30}{-25} \qquad \text{Divide each side by } -25, \text{ the coefficient of } p.$$

$$p = -\frac{30}{25} \qquad \frac{a}{-b} = -\frac{a}{b}$$

$$p = -\frac{6}{5} \qquad \text{Write in lowest terms.}$$

CHECK $\qquad -25p = 30 \qquad \text{Original equation}$

$$\frac{-25}{1}\left(-\frac{6}{5}\right) \overset{?}{=} 30 \qquad \text{Let } p = -\frac{6}{5}.$$

$$30 = 30 \ \checkmark \quad \text{True}$$

The check confirms that the solution set is $\left\{-\frac{6}{5}\right\}$.

—————— **Work Problem 3 at the Side.** ▶

---

2 Solve.

(GS) **(a)** Fill in the blanks.

$$7x = 91$$

$$\frac{7x}{\underline{}} = \frac{91}{\underline{}}$$

$$x = \underline{}$$

CHECK $\qquad 7x = 91$

$$7(\underline{}) \overset{?}{=} 91$$

$$\underline{} = 91 \quad (True/False)$$

The solution set is ____.

(b) $3r = -12$

(c) $15x = 75$

---

3 Solve.

(a) $2m = 15$

(b) $-6x = 14$

(c) $10z = -45$

Answers

2. **(a)** 7; 7; 13; 13; 91; True; $\{13\}$
   (b) $\{-4\}$ **(c)** $\{5\}$

3. **(a)** $\left\{\frac{15}{2}\right\}$ **(b)** $\left\{-\frac{7}{3}\right\}$ **(c)** $\left\{-\frac{9}{2}\right\}$

4 Solve.

(a) $-0.7m = -5.04$

(b) $-63.75 = 12.5k$

5 Solve.

GS (a) $\dfrac{x}{5} = 5$

What is the coefficient of x here? _____ By what number should we multiply each side? _____
Now solve.

(b) $\dfrac{p}{4} = -6$

6 Solve.

GS (a) $-\dfrac{5}{6}t = -15$

By what number should we multiply each side? _____
Now solve.

(b) $\dfrac{3}{5}k = -21$

Answers

4. (a) $\{7.2\}$ (b) $\{-5.1\}$

5. (a) $\dfrac{1}{5}$; 5; $\{25\}$ (b) $\{-24\}$

6. (a) $-\dfrac{6}{5}$; $\{18\}$ (b) $\{-35\}$

EXAMPLE 3 **Solving a Linear Equation (Decimal Coefficient)**

Solve $6.09 = -2.1x$.

$$6.09 = -2.1x \quad \boxed{\text{Isolate } x \text{ on the right.}}$$

$$\frac{6.09}{-2.1} = \frac{-2.1x}{-2.1} \qquad \text{Divide each side by } -2.1.$$

$$-2.9 = x, \quad \text{or} \quad x = -2.9$$

Check by replacing x with -2.9 in the original equation. The solution set is $\{-2.9\}$.

◀ **Work Problem 4 at the Side.**

EXAMPLE 4 **Solving a Linear Equation (Fractional Coefficient)**

Solve $\frac{x}{4} = 3$.

$$\frac{x}{4} = 3$$

$$\frac{1}{4}x = 3 \qquad \frac{x}{4} = \frac{1x}{4} = \frac{1}{4} \cdot x$$

$$4 \cdot \frac{1}{4}x = 4 \cdot 3 \qquad \begin{array}{l}\text{Multiply each side by 4,}\\ \text{the reciprocal of } \frac{1}{4}.\end{array}$$

$$\boxed{4 \cdot \frac{1}{4}x = 1x = x} \quad x = 12 \qquad \begin{array}{l}\text{Multiplicative inverse property;}\\ \text{multiplicative identity property}\end{array}$$

CHECK
$$\frac{x}{4} = 3 \qquad \text{Original equation}$$

$$\frac{12}{4} \overset{?}{=} 3 \qquad \text{Let } x = 12.$$

$$3 = 3 \checkmark \qquad \text{True}$$

A true statement results, so the solution set is $\{12\}$.

◀ **Work Problem 5 at the Side.**

EXAMPLE 5 **Solving a Linear Equation (Fractional Coefficient)**

Solve $\frac{3}{4}h = 6$.

$$\frac{3}{4}h = 6$$

$\boxed{\text{It is easier to multiply by } \frac{4}{3} \text{ than to divide by } \frac{3}{4}.}$ $\dfrac{4}{3} \cdot \dfrac{3}{4}h = \dfrac{4}{3} \cdot 6 \qquad \begin{array}{l}\text{Multiply each side by } \frac{4}{3},\\ \text{the reciprocal of } \frac{3}{4}.\end{array}$

$$1 \cdot h = \frac{4}{3} \cdot \frac{6}{1} \qquad \text{Multiplicative inverse property}$$

$$h = 8 \qquad \begin{array}{l}\text{Multiplicative identity property;}\\ \text{multiply fractions.}\end{array}$$

Check to confirm that the solution set is $\{8\}$.

◀ **Work Problem 6 at the Side.**

Note

We can use reasoning to solve an equation such as

$$-k = -15.$$

Because this equation says that the additive inverse (or opposite) of k is -15, k must equal 15. We can also use the multiplication property of equality to obtain the same result. This is done in **Example 6.**

EXAMPLE 6 **Applying the Multiplication Property of Equality When the Coefficient of the Variable Is -1**

Solve $-k = -15$.

$$-k = -15$$

$$-1 \cdot k = -15 \qquad -k = -1 \cdot k$$

$$-1(-1 \cdot k) = -1(-15) \qquad \text{Multiply each side by } -1.$$

$$[-1(-1)] \cdot k = 15 \qquad \text{Associative property; Multiply.}$$

$$1 \cdot k = 15 \qquad \text{Multiplicative inverse property}$$

$$k = 15 \qquad \text{Multiplicative identity property}$$

CHECK

$$-k = -15 \qquad \text{Original equation}$$

$$-(15) \overset{?}{=} -15 \qquad \text{Let } k = 15.$$

$$-15 = -15 \checkmark \qquad \text{True}$$

A true statement results, so the solution set is $\{15\}$.

———————— **Work Problem 7 at the Side.** ▶

OBJECTIVE ▶ 2 Simplify, and then use the multiplication property of equality.

EXAMPLE 7 **Combining Like Terms When Solving**

Solve $5m + 6m = 33$.

$$5m + 6m = 33$$

$$11m = 33 \qquad \text{Combine like terms.}$$

$$\frac{11m}{11} = \frac{33}{11} \qquad \text{Divide each side by 11.}$$

$$m = 3 \qquad \text{Multiplicative identity property}$$

CHECK

$$5m + 6m = 33 \qquad \text{Original equation}$$

$$5(3) + 6(3) \overset{?}{=} 33 \qquad \text{Let } m = 3.$$

$$15 + 18 \overset{?}{=} 33 \qquad \text{Multiply.}$$

$$33 = 33 \checkmark \qquad \text{True}$$

A true statement results, so the solution set is $\{3\}$.

———————— **Work Problem 8 at the Side.** ▶

---

7 Solve.

GS (a) Fill in the blanks.

$$-m = 2$$

$$\underline{\hspace{1cm}} \cdot m = 2$$

$$\underline{\hspace{1cm}}(-1 \cdot m) = \underline{\hspace{1cm}} \cdot 2$$

$$m = \underline{\hspace{1cm}}$$

CHECK $\quad -m = 2$

$$-(\underline{\hspace{1cm}}) \overset{?}{=} 2$$

$$\underline{\hspace{1cm}} = 2 \quad (True/False)$$

The solution set is $\underline{\hspace{1cm}}$.

(b) $-p = -7$

8 Solve.

(a) $7m - 5m = -12$

(b) $4r - 9r = 20$

Answers

7. (a) $-1; -1; -1; -2; -2; 2;$ True; $\{-2\}$
  (b) $\{7\}$

8. (a) $\{-6\}$ **(b)** $\{-4\}$

9 Solve.

GS **(a)** $3(2x - 2) + 6 = -24$

$3(2x) + 3(\underline{\quad}) + 6 = -24$

$\underline{\quad} - 6 + 6 = -24$

$6x = -24$

$\dfrac{6x}{\underline{\quad}} = \dfrac{-24}{\underline{\quad}}$

$x = \underline{\quad}$

Check by substituting $\underline{\quad}$ for x in the original equation.

The solution set is $\underline{\quad}$.

(b) $8 - 2(5x + 4) = 10$

(c) $5(x + 2) - (3x + 10) = 14$

EXAMPLE 8 Using the Distributive Property When Solving

Solve $4(x - 1) - 2(x - 2) = -12$.

Begin by clearing the parentheses.

$$4\,\overgroup{(x - 1)} - 2\,\overgroup{(x - 2)} = -12$$

$$4x + 4(-1) - 2x - 2(-2) = -12 \qquad \text{Distributive property}$$

$$4x - 4 - 2x + 4 = -12 \qquad \text{Multiply.}$$

$$2x = -12 \qquad \text{Combine like terms.}$$

$$\dfrac{2x}{2} = \dfrac{-12}{2} \qquad \text{Divide each side by 2.}$$

$$x = -6$$

CHECK

$$4(x - 1) - 2(x - 2) = -12 \qquad \text{Original equation}$$

$$4(-6 - 1) - 2(-6 - 2) \overset{?}{=} -12 \qquad \text{Let } x = -6.$$

$$4(-7) - 2(-8) \overset{?}{=} -12 \qquad \text{Subtract within the parentheses.}$$

$$-28 + 16 \overset{?}{=} -12 \qquad \text{Multiply.}$$

$$-12 = -12 \ \checkmark \qquad \text{True}$$

The check results in a true statement, so the solution set is $\{-6\}$.

◀ **Work Problem 9** at the Side.

Answers

9. **(a)** -2; $6x$; 6; 6; -4; -4; $\{-4\}$

(b) $\{-1\}$ **(c)** $\{7\}$

2.2 Exercises

FOR EXTRA HELP

Go to MyMathLab for worked-out, step-by-step solutions to exercises enclosed in a square [ ] and video solutions to ▶ exercises.

1. CONCEPT CHECK Indicate whether the addition or multiplication property of equality should be used to solve each equation. *Do not actually solve.*

(a) $3x = 12$ **(b)** $3 + x = 12$

(c) $-x = 4$ **(d)** $-12 = 6 + x$

2. CONCEPT CHECK Which equation does *not* require the use of the multiplication property of equality?

A. $3x - 5x = 6$ **B.** $-\dfrac{1}{4}x = 12$

C. $5x - 4x = 7$ **D.** $\dfrac{x}{3} = -2$

CONCEPT CHECK *By what number is it necessary to multiply each side of each equation in order to isolate x on the left side? Do not actually solve.*

3. $\dfrac{2}{3}x = 8$ **4.** $\dfrac{4}{5}x = 6$ **5.** $\dfrac{x}{10} = 3$ **6.** $\dfrac{x}{100} = 8$

7. $-\dfrac{9}{2}x = -4$ **8.** $-\dfrac{8}{3}x = -11$ **9.** $-x = 0.36$ **10.** $-x = 0.29$

CONCEPT CHECK *By what number is it necessary to divide each side of each equation in order to isolate x on the left side? Do not actually solve.*

11. $6x = 5$ **12.** $7x = 10$ **13.** $-4x = 13$ **14.** $-13x = 6$

15. $0.12x = 48$ **16.** $0.21x = 63$ **17.** $-x = 23$ **18.** $-x = 49$

19. CONCEPT CHECK In the solution of a linear equation, the next-to-the-last step reads "$-x = -\dfrac{3}{4}$." Which of the following would be the solution of this equation?

A. $-\dfrac{3}{4}$ **B.** $\dfrac{3}{4}$ **C.** -1 **D.** $\dfrac{4}{3}$

20. CONCEPT CHECK Which of the following is the solution of the equation

$$-x = -24?$$

A. 24   **B.** -24 **C.** 1   **D.** -1

Solve each equation, and check the solution. ***See Examples 1–8.***

21. $5x = 30$ **22.** $7x = 56$ **23.** $2m = 15$ **24.** $3m = 10$

25. $3a = -15$ ▶   **26.** $5k = -70$ **27.** $10t = -36$ ▶   **28.** $4s = -34$

29. $-6x = -72$ **30.** $-8x = -64$

31. GS $2r = 0$

$$\frac{2r}{\rule{1cm}{0.4pt}} = \frac{0}{\rule{1cm}{0.4pt}}$$

$$r = \underline{\hspace{1cm}}$$

Solution set: $\underline{\hspace{1cm}}$

32. GS 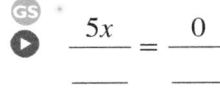 $5x = 0$

$$\frac{5x}{\rule{1cm}{0.4pt}} = \frac{0}{\rule{1cm}{0.4pt}}$$

$$x = \underline{\hspace{1cm}}$$

Solution set: $\underline{\hspace{1cm}}$

33. $-x = 12$

34. $-t = 14$

35. $0.2t = 8$

36. $0.9x = 18$

37. $-2.1m = 25.62$

38. $-3.9a = 31.2$

39. $\frac{1}{4}x = -12$

40. $\frac{1}{5}p = -3$

41. $\frac{z}{6} = 12$

42. $\frac{x}{5} = 15$

43. $\frac{x}{7} = -5$

44. $\frac{k}{8} = -3$

45. $\frac{2}{7}p = 4$

46. $\frac{3}{8}x = 9$

47. $-\frac{7}{9}c = \frac{3}{5}$

48. $-\frac{5}{6}d = \frac{4}{9}$

49. $4x + 3x = 21$

50. $9x + 2x = 121$

51. $3r - 5r = 10$

52. $9p - 13p = 24$

53. $\frac{2}{5}x - \frac{3}{10}x = 2$

54. $\frac{2}{3}x - \frac{5}{9}x = 4$

55. $5m + 6m - 2m = 63$

56. $11r - 5r + 6r = 168$

57. $x + x - 3x = 12$

58. $z - 3z + z = -16$

59. $-6x + 4x - 7x = 0$

60. $-5x + 4x - 8x = 0$

61. $4(3x - 1) + 4 = -36$

62. $5(3x + 2) - 10 = 30$

63. $8 - 4(x + 2) = 16$

64. $18 - 6(4x + 3) = -48$

65. $5(x + 4) - (3x + 20) = -10$

66. $8(x - 2) - (x - 16) = 35$

67. $-3(2p - 8) + 4(p - 6) = -2$

68. $-4(2p + 3) + 2(p + 6) = -18$

Write an equation using the information given in the problem. Use x as the variable.
Then solve the equation.

69. When a number is multiplied by -4, the result is 10. Find the number.

70. When a number is multiplied by 4, the result is 6. Find the number.

71. When a number is divided by -5, the result is 2. Find the number.

72. If twice a number is divided by 5, the result is 4. Find the number.

2.3 | More on Solving Linear Equations

We now apply *both* properties of equality to solve linear equations.

Work Problem **1** at the Side. ▶

OBJECTIVE ▶ 1 Learn and use the four steps for solving a linear equation.

OBJECTIVES

1 Learn and use the four steps for solving a linear equation.

2 Solve equations that have no solution or infinitely many solutions.

3 Solve equations with fractions or decimals as coefficients.

4 Write expressions for two related unknown quantities.

Solving a Linear Equation in One Variable

Step 1 **Simplify each side separately.** Use the distributive property as needed.
- Clear any parentheses.
- Clear any fractions or decimals.
- Combine like terms.

Step 2 **Isolate the variable terms on one side.** Use the addition property of equality so that all terms with variables are on one side of the equation and all constants (numbers) are on the other side.

Step 3 **Isolate the variable.** Use the multiplication property of equality to obtain an equation that has just the variable with coefficient 1 on one side.

Step 4 **Check.** Substitute the value found into the *original* equation. If a true statement results, write the solution set. If not, rework the problem.

Remember that when we solve an equation, our primary goal is to isolate the variable on one side of the equation.

1 As a review, tell whether the *addition* or *multiplication property of equality* should be used to solve each equation. *Do not actually solve.*

(a) $7 + x = -9$

(b) $-13x = 26$

(c) $-x = \dfrac{3}{4}$

(d) $-12 = x - 4$

EXAMPLE 1 **Solving a Linear Equation**

Solve $-6x + 5 = 17$.

Step 1 There are no parentheses, fractions, or decimals, nor are there like terms to combine on one side in this equation. This step is not necessary.

Our goal is to isolate x. ── $-6x + 5 = 17$

Step 2 $-6x + 5 - 5 = 17 - 5$ Subtract 5 from each side.

                         $-6x = 12$ Combine like terms.

Step 3 $\dfrac{-6x}{-6} = \dfrac{12}{-6}$ Divide each side by -6.

                         $x = -2$

Step 4 Check by substituting -2 for x in the original equation.

CHECK $-6x + 5 = 17$ Original equation

                  $-6(-2) + 5 \stackrel{?}{=} 17$ Let $x = -2$.

                       $12 + 5 \stackrel{?}{=} 17$ Multiply.

17 is *not* the solution. ── $17 = 17$ ✓   True

A true statement results, so the solution set is $\{-2\}$.

2 Solve.
(a) $-5p + 4 = 19$

(b) $7 + 2m = -3$

Answers

1. (a) and (d): addition property of equality
   (b) and (c): multiplication property of equality

2. (a) $\{-3\}$ (b) $\{-5\}$

Work Problem **2** at the Side. ▶

3 Solve.

(a) $5 - 8k = 2k - 5$

Begin with Step 2.

$$5 - 8k - 2k = 2k - 5 - \underline{\quad}$$

$$5 - \underline{\quad} = -5$$

$$5 - 10k - \underline{\quad} = -5 - \underline{\quad}$$

$$-10k = -10$$

$$\frac{-10k}{\underline{\quad}} = \frac{-10}{\underline{\quad}}$$

$$k = \underline{\quad}$$

Check by substituting _____
for k in the original equation.

The solution set is _____ .

(b) $2q + 3 = 4q - 9$

(c) $6x + 7 = -8 + 3x$

EXAMPLE 2 **Solving a Linear Equation**

Solve $3x + 2 = 5x - 8$.

Step 1 There are no parentheses, fractions, or decimals, nor are there like terms to combine on one side in this equation. We begin with Step 2.

$$3x + 2 = 5x - 8 \quad \text{← Our goal is to isolate } x.$$

Step 2 $3x + 2 - 5x = 5x - 8 - 5x$ Subtract $5x$ from each side.

$-2x + 2 = -8$ Combine like terms.

$-2x + 2 - 2 = -8 - 2$ Subtract 2 from each side.

$-2x = -10$ Combine like terms.

Step 3 $\dfrac{-2x}{-2} = \dfrac{-10}{-2}$ Divide each side by -2.

$x = 5$

Step 4 Check by substituting 5 for x in the original equation.

CHECK $3x + 2 = 5x - 8$ Original equation

$3(5) + 2 \stackrel{?}{=} 5(5) - 8$ Let $x = 5$.

$15 + 2 \stackrel{?}{=} 25 - 8$ Multiply.

$17 = 17$ ✓   True

The check confirms that 5 is the solution. The solution set is $\{5\}$.

Note

Remember that a variable can be isolated on either side of an equation. In **Example 2**, x will be isolated on the right if we begin by subtracting $3x$, instead of $5x$, from each side of the equation.

$3x + 2 = 5x - 8$ Equation from **Example 2**

$3x + 2 - 3x = 5x - 8 - 3x$ Subtract $3x$ from each side.

$2 = 2x - 8$ Combine like terms.

$2 + 8 = 2x - 8 + 8$ Add 8 to each side.

$10 = 2x$ Combine like terms.

$\dfrac{10}{2} = \dfrac{2x}{2}$ Divide each side by 2.

$5 = x$ The same solution results.

$5 = x$ is equivalent to $x = 5$.

There are often several equally correct ways to solve an equation.

◀ **Work Problem** **3** at the Side.

Answers

3. **(a)** $2k$; $10k$; 5; 5; -10; -10; 1; 1; $\{1\}$
    (b) $\{6\}$ **(c)** $\{-5\}$

EXAMPLE 3 Solving a Linear Equation

Solve $4(k - 3) - k = k - 6$.

Step 1 Clear the parentheses using the distributive property.

$$4(k - 3) - k = k - 6$$

$4(k) + 4(-3) - k = k - 6$	Distributive property
$4k - 12 - k = k - 6$	Multiply.
$3k - 12 = k - 6$	Combine like terms.

Step 2

$3k - 12 - k = k - 6 - k$	Subtract k.
$2k - 12 = -6$	Combine like terms.
$2k - 12 + 12 = -6 + 12$	Add 12.
$2k = 6$	Combine like terms.

Step 3

$\dfrac{2k}{2} = \dfrac{6}{2}$	Divide by 2.
$k = 3$	

Step 4 Check by substituting 3 for k in the original equation.

CHECK

$4(k - 3) - k = k - 6$	Original equation
$4(3 - 3) - 3 \overset{?}{=} 3 - 6$	Let $k = 3$.
$4(0) - 3 \overset{?}{=} 3 - 6$	Work inside the parentheses.
$-3 = -3$ ✓	True

A true statement results, so the solution set is $\{3\}$.

──────── **Work Problem ④ at the Side.** ▶

EXAMPLE 4 Solving a Linear Equation

Solve $8a - (3 + 2a) = 3a + 1$.

Step 1 $8a - (3 + 2a) = 3a + 1$

$8a - 1(3 + 2a) = 3a + 1$	Multiplicative identity property
$8a - 3 - 2a = 3a + 1$	Distributive property
Be careful with signs. $6a - 3 = 3a + 1$	Combine like terms.

Step 2

$6a - 3 - 3a = 3a + 1 - 3a$	Subtract $3a$.
$3a - 3 = 1$	Combine like terms.
$3a - 3 + 3 = 1 + 3$	Add 3.
$3a = 4$	Combine like terms.

Step 3

$\dfrac{3a}{3} = \dfrac{4}{3}$	Divide by 3.
$a = \dfrac{4}{3}$	

──────── **Continued on Next Page**

④ Solve.

GS (a) $7(p - 2) + p = 2p + 4$

Step 1 Clear the parentheses.

$$\underline{\quad}(p) + 7(\underline{\quad}) + p = 2p + 4$$

$$\underline{\quad} - \underline{\quad} + p = 2p + 4$$

$$\underline{\quad} - 14 = 2p + 4$$

Now complete the solution. Give the solution set.

(b) $11 + 3(x + 1) = 5x + 16$

Answers

4. **(a)** 7; −2; 7p; 14; 8p;
The solution set is $\{3\}$.

(b) $\{-1\}$

5 Solve.

(a) $7m - (2m - 9) = 39$

(b) $5x - (x + 9) = x - 4$

6 Solve.

(a) $2(4 + 3r) = 3(r + 1) + 11$

(b) $2 - 3(2 + 6z)$
$= 4(z + 1) - 8$

Step 4 **CHECK** $8a - (3 + 2a) = 3a + 1$ Original equation

$$8\left(\frac{4}{3}\right) - \left[3 + 2\left(\frac{4}{3}\right)\right] \stackrel{?}{=} 3\left(\frac{4}{3}\right) + 1 \quad \text{Let } a = \tfrac{4}{3}.$$

$$\frac{32}{3} - \left[3 + \frac{8}{3}\right] \stackrel{?}{=} 4 + 1 \quad \text{Multiply.}$$

$$\frac{32}{3} - \frac{17}{3} \stackrel{?}{=} 5 \quad \text{Add.}$$

$$5 = 5 \checkmark \quad \text{True}$$

A true statement results, so the solution set is $\left\{\frac{4}{3}\right\}$.

◀ **Work Problem 5 at the Side.**

> **! CAUTION**
>
> In an expression such as $8a - (3 + 2a)$, the $-$ sign acts like a factor of -1 and affects the sign of *every* term within the parentheses.
>
> $8a - (3 + 2a)$ ⟵ Left side of the equation in **Example 4**
>
> $= 8a - 1(3 + 2a)$
>
> $= 8a + (-1)(3 + 2a)$
>
> $= 8a - 3 - 2a$
>
> Change to $-$ in *both* terms.

EXAMPLE 5 **Solving a Linear Equation**

Solve $4(4 - 3x) = 32 - 8(x + 2)$. *Do not subtract 8 from 32 here.*

Step 1 $4(4 - 3x) = 32 - 8(x + 2)$ *Be careful with signs.*

$16 - 12x = 32 - 8x - 16$ Distributive property

$16 - 12x = 16 - 8x$ Combine like terms.

Step 2 $16 - 12x + 8x = 16 - 8x + 8x$ Add $8x$.

$16 - 4x = 16$ Combine like terms.

$16 - 4x - 16 = 16 - 16$ Subtract 16.

$-4x = 0$ Combine like terms.

Step 3 $\dfrac{-4x}{-4} = \dfrac{0}{-4}$ Divide by -4.

$x = 0$

Step 4 **CHECK** $4(4 - 3x) = 32 - 8(x + 2)$ Original equation

$4[4 - 3(0)] \stackrel{?}{=} 32 - 8(0 + 2)$ Let $x = 0$.

$4(4) \stackrel{?}{=} 32 - 8(2)$ Work inside the brackets and parentheses.

$16 = 16 \checkmark$ True

A true statement results, so the solution set is $\{0\}$. *{0} is a perfectly acceptable solution set.*

◀ **Work Problem 6 at the Side.**

OBJECTIVE ▶ ② Solve equations that have no solution or infinitely many solutions. Each equation so far has had exactly one solution. An equation with exactly one solution is a **conditional equation** because it is only true under certain conditions.

EXAMPLE 6 Solving an Equation That Has Infinitely Many Solutions

Solve $5x - 15 = 5(x - 3)$.

$$5x - 15 = 5(x - 3)$$
$$5x - 15 = 5x - 15 \quad \text{Distributive property}$$
$$5x - 15 - 5x = 5x - 15 - 5x \quad \text{Subtract } 5x.$$

Notice that the variable "disappeared." $\quad -15 = -15 \quad \text{Combine like terms.}$
$$-15 + 15 = -15 + 15 \quad \text{Add 15.}$$
$$0 = 0 \quad \text{True}$$

Solution set: **{all real numbers}**

Because the last statement $(0 = 0)$ is true, *any* real number is a solution. We could have predicted this from the second line in the solution,

$$5x - 15 = 5x - 15 \longleftarrow \text{This is true for } any \text{ value of } x.$$

Try several values for x in the original equation to see that they all satisfy it.

An equation with both sides exactly the same, like $0 = 0$, is an **identity.** An identity is true for all replacements of the variables. As shown above, we write the solution set as **{all real numbers}**.

⚠ CAUTION

In **Example 6,** do not write $\{0\}$ as the solution set of the equation. While 0 *is* a solution, there are infinitely many *other* solutions.
For $\{0\}$ to be the solution set, the last line must include a variable, such as x, and read x = 0 (as in Example 5), not 0 = 0.

EXAMPLE 7 Solving an Equation That Has No Solution

Solve $2x + 3(x + 1) = 5x + 4$.

$$2x + 3(x + 1) = 5x + 4$$
$$2x + 3x + 3 = 5x + 4 \quad \text{Distributive property}$$
$$5x + 3 = 5x + 4 \quad \text{Combine like terms.}$$
$$5x + 3 - 5x = 5x + 4 - 5x \quad \text{Subtract } 5x.$$

Again, the variable "disappeared." $\quad 3 = 4 \quad \text{False}$

There is no solution. Solution set: ∅

A false statement $(3 = 4)$ results. A **contradiction** is an equation that has no solution. Its solution set is the **empty set,** or **null set,** symbolized ∅.

Work Problem ⑦ at the Side. ▶

⚠ CAUTION

Do not write $\{\emptyset\}$ to represent the empty set.

⑦ Solve.

(a) $2(x - 6) = 2x - 12$

(b) $3x + 6(x + 1) = 9x - 4$

(c) $8(4 - x) = -8x + 32$

(d) $-4x + 12 = 3 - 4(x - 3)$

Answers
7. (a) {all real numbers} **(b)** ∅
(c) {all real numbers} **(d)** ∅

8 Solve.

(a) $\frac{1}{4}x - 4 = \frac{3}{2}x + \frac{3}{4}x$

(b) $\frac{1}{2}x + \frac{5}{8}x = \frac{3}{4}x - 6$

SOLUTION SETS OF EQUATIONS

Type of Equation	Final Equation in Solution	Number of Solutions	Solution Set
Conditional (See Examples 1–5.)	x = a number	One	{a number}
Identity (See Example 6.)	A true statement with no variable, such as $0 = 0$	Infinitely many	{all real numbers}
Contradiction (See Example 7.)	A false statement with no variable, such as $3 = 4$	None	$\varnothing$

OBJECTIVE ▸ 3 Solve equations with fractions or decimals as coefficients.
To avoid messy computations, we clear an equation of fractions by multiplying each side by the least common denominator (LCD) of all the fractions in the equation. Doing this will give an equation with only *integer* coefficients.

EXAMPLE 8   Solving a Linear Equation (Fractional Coefficients)

Solve $\frac{2}{3}x - \frac{1}{2}x = -\frac{1}{6}x - 2$.

Step 1

$$\frac{2}{3}x - \frac{1}{2}x = -\frac{1}{6}x - 2$$ — Pay particular attention here.

$$6\left(\frac{2}{3}x - \frac{1}{2}x\right) = 6\left(-\frac{1}{6}x - 2\right)$$ — Multiply each side by 6, the LCD.

$$6\left(\frac{2}{3}x\right) + 6\left(-\frac{1}{2}x\right) = 6\left(-\frac{1}{6}x\right) + 6(-2)$$ — Distributive property; Multiply *each* term inside the parentheses by 6.

The fractions have been cleared. → $4x - 3x = -x - 12$ — Multiply.

$$x = -x - 12$$ — Combine like terms.

Step 2 $x + x = -x - 12 + x$ — Add x.

$$2x = -12$$ — Combine like terms.

Step 3 $\frac{2x}{2} = \frac{-12}{2}$ — Divide by 2.

$$x = -6$$

Step 4 CHECK $\frac{2}{3}x - \frac{1}{2}x = -\frac{1}{6}x - 2$ — Original equation

$$\frac{2}{3}(-6) - \frac{1}{2}(-6) \stackrel{?}{=} -\frac{1}{6}(-6) - 2$$ — Let $x = -6$.

$$-4 + 3 \stackrel{?}{=} 1 - 2$$ — Multiply.

$$-1 = -1 \checkmark$$ — True

The check confirms that the solution set is $\{-6\}$.

◀ **Work Problem 8 at the Side.**

! CAUTION
When clearing an equation of fractions, be sure to multiply every term on each side of the equation by the LCD.

Answers
8. (a) $\{-2\}$ (b) $\{-16\}$

EXAMPLE 9 Solving a Linear Equation (Fractional Coefficients)

Solve $\frac{1}{3}(x + 5) - \frac{3}{5}(x + 2) = 1$.

Step 1 We clear the parentheses first. Then we clear the fractions.

$$\frac{1}{3}(x + 5) - \frac{3}{5}(x + 2) = 1 \quad \longleftarrow \boxed{\text{Study Step 1 carefully.}}$$

$$\frac{1}{3}(x) + \frac{1}{3}(5) - \frac{3}{5}(x) - \frac{3}{5}(2) = 1 \qquad \text{Distributive property}$$

$$\frac{1}{3}x + \frac{5}{3} - \frac{3}{5}x - \frac{6}{5} = 1 \qquad \text{Multiply.}$$

$\boxed{\text{Think: } 15\left(\frac{1}{3}x\right) \\ = \left(\frac{15}{1} \cdot \frac{1}{3}\right)x \\ = 5x}$ $15\left(\frac{1}{3}x + \frac{5}{3} - \frac{3}{5}x - \frac{6}{5}\right) = 15(1)$ Multiply each side by 15, the LCD.

$$15\left(\frac{1}{3}x\right) + 15\left(\frac{5}{3}\right) + 15\left(-\frac{3}{5}x\right) + 15\left(-\frac{6}{5}\right) = 15(1) \qquad \text{Distributive property}$$

$$5x + 25 - 9x - 18 = 15 \qquad \text{Multiply.}$$

$$-4x + 7 = 15 \qquad \text{Combine like terms.}$$

Step 2 $\qquad -4x + 7 - 7 = 15 - 7 \qquad$ Subtract 7.

$$-4x = 8 \qquad \text{Combine like terms.}$$

Step 3 $\qquad \dfrac{-4x}{-4} = \dfrac{8}{-4} \qquad$ Divide by -4.

$$x = -2$$

Step 4 Check to confirm that $\{-2\}$ is the solution set.

———————————————— **Work Problem ⑨ at the Side.** ▶

EXAMPLE 10 Solving a Linear Equation (Decimal Coefficients)

Solve $0.1t + 0.05(20 - t) = 0.09(20)$.

Step 1 $\qquad 0.1t + 0.05(20 - t) = 0.09(20) \quad \longleftarrow \boxed{\text{Clear the parentheses first.}}$

$$0.1t + 0.05(20) + 0.05(-t) = 0.09(20) \qquad \text{Distributive property}$$

$$0.1t + 1 - 0.05t = 1.8 \qquad (*) \quad \text{Multiply.}$$

$\boxed{\text{Now clear the decimals.}} \quad 100(0.1t + 1 - 0.05t) = 100(1.8) \qquad$ Multiply by 100.

$$100(0.1t) + 100(1) + 100(-0.05t) = 100(1.8) \qquad \text{Distributive property}$$

$$10t + 100 - 5t = 180 \qquad (**) \quad \text{Multiply.}$$

$$5t + 100 = 180 \qquad \text{Combine like terms.}$$

Step 2 $\qquad 5t + 100 - 100 = 180 - 100 \qquad$ Subtract 100.

$$5t = 80 \qquad \text{Combine like terms.}$$

Step 3 $\qquad \dfrac{5t}{5} = \dfrac{80}{5} \qquad$ Divide by 5.

$$t = 16$$

Step 4 Check to confirm that $\{16\}$ is the solution set.

———————————————— **Work Problem ⑩ at the Side.** ▶

⑨ Solve.

$$\frac{1}{4}(x + 3) - \frac{2}{3}(x + 1) = -2$$

⑩ Solve.

$$0.06(100 - x) + 0.04x \\ = 0.05(92)$$

Answers

9. $\{5\}$

10. $\{70\}$

11 Perform each translation.

(a) Two numbers have a sum of 36. One of the numbers is represented by r. Write an expression for the other number.

(b) Two numbers have a product of 18. One of the numbers is represented by x. Write an expression for the other number.

> **Note**
>
> In **Example 10,** the decimals are expressed as tenths (0.1 and 1.8) and hundredths (0.05). We chose the least exponent on 10 to eliminate the decimal points, which made all coefficients integers. So, we multiplied by 10^2—that is, 100.
>
> Multiplying by **100** is the same as moving the decimal point **two** places to the right.
>
> $$0.10t + 1.00 - 0.05t = 1.80$$
>
> Equation (*) from **Example 10** with 0s included as placeholders
>
> $$10t + 100 - 5t = 180$$
>
> Multiply by 100. Equation (**) results.

OBJECTIVE ▶ 4 Write expressions for two related unknown quantities.

> **Problem-Solving Hint**
>
> When we solve applied problems, we must often write *expressions* to relate unknown quantities. We then use these expressions to write the *equation* needed to solve the application. The next example provides preparation for doing this.

EXAMPLE 11 Translating Phrases into Algebraic Expressions

Perform each translation.

(a) Two numbers have a sum of 23. If one of the numbers is represented by x, find an expression for the other number.

First, suppose that the sum of two numbers is 23, and one of the numbers is **10**. To find the other number, we would subtract **10** from 23.

$$23 - 10 \longleftarrow \text{This gives 13 as the other number.}$$

Instead of using **10** as one of the numbers, we use x. The other number would be obtained in the same way—by subtracting x from 23.

$$23 - x \longleftarrow \begin{array}{l} x - 23 \text{ is } not \text{ correct.} \\ \text{Subtraction is } not \\ \text{commutative.} \end{array}$$

CHECK We find the sum of the two numbers.

$$x + (23 - x) = 23, \quad \text{as required. } \checkmark$$

(b) Two numbers have a product of 24. If one of the numbers is represented by x, find an expression for the other number.

Suppose that one of the numbers is **4**. To find the other number, we would divide 24 by **4**.

$$\frac{24}{4} \longleftarrow \begin{array}{l} \text{This gives 6 as the other number.} \\ \text{The product } 6 \cdot 4 \text{ is } 24. \end{array}$$

In the same way, if x is one of the numbers, then we divide 24 by x to find the other number.

$$\frac{24}{x} \longleftarrow \text{The other number}$$

Answers

11. (a) $36 - r$ (b) $\dfrac{18}{x}$

◀ Work Problem **11** at the Side.

2.3 Exercises

FOR EXTRA HELP

Go to MyMathLab *for worked-out, step-by-step solutions to exercises enclosed in a square* ▢ *and video solutions to* ▶ *exercises.*

CONCEPT CHECK *Based on the methods of this section, fill in each blank to indicate what we should do first to solve each equation. Do not actually solve.*

1. $7x + 8 = 1$

Use the _____ property of equality to _____ 8 from each side.

2. $7x - 5x + 15 = 8 + x$

On the _____ side, combine _____ terms.

3. $3(2t - 4) = 20 - 2t$

Use the _____ property to clear _____ on the left side of the equation.

4. $\frac{3}{4}z = -15$

Use the _____ property of equality to multiply each side by _____ to obtain z on the left.

5. $\frac{2}{3}x - \frac{1}{6} = \frac{3}{2}x + 1$

Clear _____ by multiplying by _____, the LCD.

6. $0.9x + 0.3x + 3.6 = 6$

Clear _____ by multiplying each side by _____ to obtain $9x$ as the first term on the left.

7. CONCEPT CHECK Suppose that when solving three linear equations, we obtain the final results shown in parts (a)–(c). Fill in the blanks in parts (a)–(c), and then match each result with the solution set in choices A–C for the *original* equation.

(a) $6 = 6$ (The original equation is a(n) _____.)

(b) $x = 0$ (The original equation is a(n) _____ equation.)

(c) $-5 = 0$ (The original equation is a(n) _____.)

A. $\{0\}$

B. $\{\text{all real numbers}\}$

C. $\varnothing$

CONCEPT CHECK *Give the letter of the correct choice.*

8. Which linear equation does *not* have all real numbers as solutions?

A. $5x = 4x + x$ **B.** $2(x + 6) = 2x + 12$ **C.** $\frac{1}{2}x = 0.5x$ **D.** $3x = 2x$

9. The expression $12\left(\frac{1}{6}x + \frac{1}{3} - \frac{2}{3}x - \frac{2}{3}\right)$ is equivalent to which of the following?

A. $-6x - 4$ **B.** $2x - 8$ **C.** $-6x + 1$ **D.** $-6x + 4$

10. The expression $100(0.03x - 0.3)$ is equivalent to which of the following?

A. $0.03x - 0.3$ **B.** $3x - 3$ **C.** $3x - 10$ **D.** $3x - 30$

Solve each equation, and check the solution. ***See Examples 1–7.***

11. $3x + 2 = 14$ **12.** $4x + 3 = 27$ **13.** $-5z - 4 = 21$ **14.** $-7w - 4 = 10$

15. $4p - 5 = 2p$

16. $6q - 2 = 3q$

17. $5m + 8 = 7 + 3m$

18. $4r + 2 = r - 6$

19. $10p + 6 = 12p - 4$

20. $-5x + 8 = -3x + 10$

21. $7r - 5r + 2 = 5r - r$

22. $9p - 4p + 6 = 7p - p$

23. $12h - 5 = 11h + 5 - h$

24. $-4x - 1 = -5x + 1 + 3x$

25. $x + 3 = -(2x + 2)$

26. $2x + 1 = -(x + 3)$

27. $3(4x + 2) + 5x = 30 - x$

28. $5(2m + 3) - 4m = 8m + 27$

29. $-2p + 7 = 3 - (5p + 1)$

30. $4x + 9 = 3 - (x - 2)$

31. $6(3w + 5) = 2(10w + 10)$

32. $4(2x - 1) = -6(x + 3)$

33. $-(8x - 2) + 5x - 6 = -4$

34. $-(7x - 5) + 4x - 7 = -2$

35. $24 - 4(7 - 2t) = 4(t - 1)$

36. $8 - 2(2 - x) = 4(x + 1)$

37. $6(3 - x) = -6x + 18$

38. $9(2 - p) = -9p + 18$

39. $3(2x - 4) = 6(x - 2)$

40. $3(6 - 4x) = 2(-6x + 9)$

41. $11x - 5(x + 2) = 6x + 5$

42. $6x - 4(x + 1) = 2x + 4$

43. $6(4x - 1) = 12(2x + 3)$

44. $6(2x + 8) = 4(3x - 6)$

Solve each equation, and check the solution. **See Examples 8–10.**

45. $\dfrac{3}{5}t - \dfrac{1}{10}t = t - \dfrac{5}{2}$

46. $-\dfrac{2}{7}r + 2r = \dfrac{1}{2}r + \dfrac{17}{2}$

47. $\dfrac{3}{4}x - \dfrac{1}{3}x + 5 = \dfrac{5}{6}x$

48. $\dfrac{1}{5}x - \dfrac{2}{3}x - 2 = -\dfrac{2}{5}x$

49. $\dfrac{1}{7}(3x + 2) - \dfrac{1}{5}(x + 4) = 2$

50. $\dfrac{1}{4}(3x - 1) + \dfrac{1}{6}(x + 3) = 3$

51. $\dfrac{1}{9}(x + 18) + \dfrac{1}{3}(2x + 3) = x + 3$

52. $-\dfrac{1}{4}(x - 12) + \dfrac{1}{2}(x + 2) = x + 4$

53. $-\dfrac{5}{6}q - \left(q - \dfrac{1}{2}\right) = \dfrac{1}{4}(q + 1)$

54. $\dfrac{2}{3}k - \left(k + \dfrac{1}{4}\right) = \dfrac{1}{12}(k + 4)$

55. $0.3\,(30) + 0.15x = 0.2\,(30) + 0.2x$

(*Hint:* Clear the decimals by multiplying each side of the equation by _____.)

56. $0.2\,(60) + 0.05x = 0.1\,(60) + 0.1x$

(*Hint:* Clear the decimals by multiplying each side of the equation by _____.)

57. $0.92x + 0.98\,(12 - x) = 0.96\,(12)$

58. $1.00x + 0.05\,(12 - x) = 0.10\,(63)$

59. $0.02\,(5000) + 0.03x = 0.025\,(5000 + x)$

60. $0.06\,(10{,}000) + 0.08x = 0.072\,(10{,}000 + x)$

Solve each equation, and check the solution. **See Examples 1–10.**

61. $-3\,(5z + 24) + 2 = 2\,(3 - 2z) - 4$

62. $-2\,(2s - 4) - 8 = -3\,(4s + 4) - 1$

63. $-(6k - 5) - (-5k + 8) = -3$

64. $-(4x + 2) - (-3x - 5) = 3$

65. $8\,(t - 3) + 4t = 6\,(2t + 1) - 10$

66. $9\,(v + 1) - 3v = 2\,(3v + 1) - 8$

67. $4(x + 3) = 2(2x + 8) - 4$

68. $4(x + 8) = 2(2x + 6) + 20$

69. $\dfrac{1}{3}(x + 3) + \dfrac{1}{6}(x - 6) = x + 3$

70. $\dfrac{1}{2}(x + 2) + \dfrac{3}{4}(x + 4) = x + 5$

71. $0.3(x + 15) + 0.4(x + 25) = 25$

72. $0.1(x + 80) + 0.2x = 14$

*Perform each translation. **See Example 11.***

73. Two numbers have a sum of 12. One of the numbers is q. What expression represents the other number?

74. Two numbers have a sum of 26. One of the numbers is r. What expression represents the other number?

75. The product of two numbers is 9. One of the numbers is z. What expression represents the other number?

76. The product of two numbers is 13. One of the numbers is k. What expression represents the other number?

77. A football player gained x yards rushing. On the next down, he gained 29 yd. What expression represents the number of yards he gained altogether?

78. A football player gained y yards on a punt return. On the next return, he gained 25 yd. What expression represents the number of yards he gained altogether?

79. Monica is m years old. What expression represents her age 12 yr from now? 2 yr ago?

80. Chandler is b years old. What expression represents his age 3 yr ago? 5 yr from now?

81. Tom has r quarters. Express the value of the quarters in cents.

82. Jean has y dimes. Express the value of the dimes in cents.

83. A bank teller has t dollars, all in \$5 bills. What expression represents the number of \$5 bills the teller has?

84. A store clerk has v dollars, all in \$10 bills. What expression represents the number of \$10 bills the clerk has?

85. A plane ticket costs x dollars for an adult and y dollars for a child. Find an expression that represents the total cost for 3 adults and 2 children.

86. A concert ticket costs p dollars for an adult and q dollars for a child. Find an expression that represents the total cost for 4 adults and 6 children.

Study Skills
USING STUDY CARDS REVISITED

Two additional types of study cards follow. Use challenging problem and practice quiz cards to do the following.

▶ To help you understand and learn the material

▶ To quickly review when you have a few minutes

▶ To review before a quiz or test

Challenging Problem Cards

When you are doing your homework and encounter a "difficult" problem, write the procedure to work the problem on the front of a card in words. Include special notes or tips (like what *not* to do). On the back of the card, work an example. Show all steps, and label what you are doing.

Front of Card

When solving a linear equation, be careful when clearing parentheses if there is a minus sign in front. p. 135

$$6x - (x + 3)$$

The minus sign acts like −1, so change the sign of every term inside the parentheses.

Back of Card

Solve.

	$6x - (x + 3) = 7$	
	$6x - 1(x + 3) = 7$	
Change both signs.	$6x - x - 3 = 7$	Distributive property
	$5x - 3 = 7$	Combine like terms.
	$5x - 3 + 3 = 7 + 3$	Add 3.
	$5x = 10$	Combine like terms.
	$\dfrac{5x}{5} = \dfrac{10}{5}$	Divide by 5.
	$x = 2$	

Solution set: {2}

Practice Quiz Cards

Write a problem with direction words (like *solve, simplify*) on the front of a card, and work the problem on the back. Make one for each type of problem you learn.

Front of Card

Solve 4 (3x − 4) = 2 (6x − 9) + 2. p. 137

Back of Card

	$4(3x - 4) = 2(6x - 9) + 2$	
	$12x - 16 = 12x - 18 + 2$	Distributive property
	$12x - 16 = 12x - 16$	Combine like terms.
	$12x - 16 + 16 = 12x - 16 + 16$	Add 16.
	$12x = 12x$	Combine like terms.
	$12x - 12x = 12x - 12x$	Subtract 12x.
When both sides of an equation are the same, it is called an identity.	$0 = 0$	True

Any real number will work, so the solution set is {all real numbers} (not just {0}).

Now Try This

Make a challenging problem card and a practice quiz card for material you are learning now.

Summary Exercises *Applying Methods for Solving Linear Equations*

CONCEPT CHECK *Decide whether each of the following is an* equation *or an* expression. *If it is an equation, solve it. If it is an expression, simplify it.*

1. $x + 2 = -3$

2. $4p - 6 + 3p - 8$

3. $-(m - 1) - (3 + 2m)$

4. $6q - 9 = 12 + 3q$

5. $5x - 9 = 3(x - 3)$

6. $\dfrac{1}{2}(x + 10) - \dfrac{2}{3}x$

Solve each equation, and check the solution.

7. $-6z = -14$

8. $2m + 8 = 16$

9. $12.5x = -63.75$

10. $-x = -12$

11. $\dfrac{4}{5}x = -20$

12. $7m - 5m = -12$

13. $-x = 6$

14. $\dfrac{x}{-2} = 8$

15. $4x + 2(3 - 2x) = 6$

16. $x - 16.2 = 7.5$

17. $7m - (2m - 9) = 39$

18. $2 - (m + 4) = 3m - 2$

19. $-3(m - 4) + 2(5 + 2m) = 29$

20. $-0.3x + 2.1(x - 4) = -6.6$

21. $0.08x + 0.06(x + 9) = 1.24$

22. $3(m + 5) - 1 + 2m = 5(m + 2)$

23. $-2t + 5t - 9 = 3(t - 4) - 5$

24. $2.3x + 13.7 = 1.3x + 2.9$

25. $0.2(50) + 0.8r = 0.4(50 + r)$

26. $r + 9 + 7r = 4(3 + 2r) - 3$

27. $2(3 + 7x) - (1 + 15x) = 2$

28. $0.6(100 - x) + 0.4x = 0.5(92)$

29. $\dfrac{1}{4}x - 4 = \dfrac{3}{2}x + \dfrac{3}{4}x$

30. $\dfrac{3}{4}(z - 2) - \dfrac{1}{3}(5 - 2z) = -2$

2.4   An Introduction to Applications of Linear Equations

OBJECTIVE ▶ 1 Learn the six steps for solving applied problems.

OBJECTIVES

1 Learn the six steps for solving applied problems.

2 Solve problems involving unknown numbers.

3 Solve problems involving sums of quantities.

4 Solve problems involving consecutive integers.

5 Solve problems involving complementary and supplementary angles.

Solving an Applied Problem

Step 1   Read the problem, several times if necessary. *What information is given? What is to be found?*

Step 2   Assign a variable to represent the unknown value. Use a sketch, diagram, or table, as needed. Express any other unknown values in terms of the variable.

Step 3   Write an equation using the variable expression(s).

Step 4   Solve the equation.

Step 5   State the answer. Label it appropriately. *Does the answer seem reasonable?*

Step 6   Check the answer in the words of the *original* problem.

OBJECTIVE ▶ 2 Solve problems involving unknown numbers.

| EXAMPLE 1 | Finding the Value of an Unknown Number |

The product of 4, and a number decreased by 7, is 100. What is the number?

Step 1   Read the problem carefully. We are asked to find a number.

Step 2   Assign a variable. Let x = the number.

Step 3   Write an equation.

> Writing a "word equation" is often helpful.

The product of 4,	and	a number	decreased by	7,	is	100.
↓		↓	↓	↓	↓	↓
4	·	(x	−	7)	=	100

Note the careful use of parentheses.

Because of the commas in the given problem, writing the equation as $4x - 7 = 100$ is *incorrect*. The equation $4x - 7 = 100$ corresponds to "*The product of* 4 *and a number, decreased by* 7, *is* 100."

Step 4   Solve the equation.

$$4(x - 7) = 100 \qquad \text{Equation from Step 3}$$
$$4x - 28 = 100 \qquad \text{Distributive property}$$
$$4x - 28 + 28 = 100 + 28 \qquad \text{Add 28.}$$
$$4x = 128 \qquad \text{Combine like terms.}$$
$$\frac{4x}{4} = \frac{128}{4} \qquad \text{Divide by 4.}$$
$$x = 32$$

Step 5   State the answer. The number is **32**.

Step 6   Check. The number **32** decreased by 7 is 25. The product of 4 and 25 is 100, as required. The answer, 32, is correct.

1 Solve each problem.

GS **(a)** If 5 is added to a number, the result is 7 less than 3 times the number. Find the number.

> **Step 1**
> We must find a _____.
>
> **Step 2**
> Let x = the _____.
>
> **Step 3**

If 5 is added to a number,	the result is	7 less than 3 times the number.
↓	↓	↓
_____	=	_____

Complete Steps 4–6 to solve the problem. Give the answer.

(b) The product of 9, and 4 more than twice a number, is 15 less than the number. Find the number.

Answers

1. **(a)** number; number; $x + 5$ (or $5 + x$); $3x - 7$; The number is 6.
   (b) −3

Work Problem **1** at the Side. ▶

2 Solve each problem.

(a) The 150-member Iowa legislature includes 12 fewer Democrats than Republicans. (No other parties are represented.) How many Democrats and Republicans are there in the legislature? (Data from www.legis.iowa.gov)

Step 1
We must find the number of Democrats and _____.

Step 2
Let x = the number of Republicans.

Then _____ = the number of _____.

Complete Steps 3–6 to solve the problem. Give the equation and the answer.

(b) At the 2014 Winter Olympics, Germany won 10 more medals than China. The two countries won a total of 28 medals. How many medals did each country win? (Data from *The World Almanac and Book of Facts.*)

Answers

2. **(a)** Republicans; $x - 12$; Democrats; $x + (x - 12) = 150$; Republicans: 81; Democrats: 69
(b) Germany: 19; China: 9

OBJECTIVE **3** **Solve problems involving sums of quantities.**

> **Problem-Solving Hint**
>
> In general, to solve problems involving sums of quantities, choose a variable to represent one of the unknowns. ***Then represent the other quantity in terms of the same variable.***

EXAMPLE 2 **Finding Numbers of Olympic Medals**

At the 2014 Winter Olympics in Sochi, Russia, the United States won 13 more medals than France. The two countries won a total of 43 medals. How many medals did each country win? (Data from *The World Almanac and Book of Facts.*)

Step 1 **Read** the problem. We are given the total number of medals and asked to find the number each country won.

Step 2 **Assign a variable.**

Let x = the number of medals France won.

Then $x + 13$ = the number of medals the United States won.

Step 3 **Write an equation.**

The total	is	the number of medals France won	plus	the number of medals the U.S. won.
↓	↓	↓	↓	↓
43	=	x	+	$(x + 13)$

Step 4 **Solve** the equation.

$$43 = 2x + 13 \qquad \text{Combine like terms.}$$
$$43 - 13 = 2x + 13 - 13 \qquad \text{Subtract 13.}$$
$$30 = 2x \qquad \text{Combine like terms.}$$
$$\frac{30}{2} = \frac{2x}{2} \qquad \text{Divide by 2.}$$
$$15 = x, \quad \text{or} \quad x = 15 \leftarrow \text{Medals France won}$$

Step 5 **State the answer.** The variable x represents the number of medals France won, so France won 15 medals.

$$x + 13$$
$$= 15 + 13$$
$$= 28 \leftarrow \text{Medals the United States won}$$

Step 6 **Check.** The United States won 28 medals and France won 15, so the total number of medals was

$$28 + 15 = 43.$$

The United States won 13 more medals than France, so the difference was

$$28 - 15 = 13.$$

All conditions of the problem are satisfied.

─────── ◄ **Work Problem** **2** **at the Side**

Problem-Solving Hint

The problem in **Example 2** could also be solved by letting x represent the number of medals the United States won. Then $x - 13$ would represent the number of medals France won. The equation would be different.

$$43 = x + (x - 13) \quad \text{Alternative equation for Example 2}$$

The solution of this equation is 28, which is the number of U.S. medals. The number of French medals would be $28 - 13 = 15$. ***The answers are the same,*** whichever approach is used, even though the equation and its solution are different.

EXAMPLE 3 **Analyzing a Gasoline/Oil Mixture**

A lawn trimmer uses a mixture of gasoline and oil. The mixture contains 16 oz of gasoline for each 1 oz of oil. If the tank holds 68 oz of the mixture, how many ounces of oil and how many ounces of gasoline does it require when it is full?

Step 1 **Read** the problem. We must find how many ounces of oil and gasoline are needed to fill the tank.

Step 2 **Assign a variable.**

Let x = the number of ounces of oil required.

Then $16x$ = the number of ounces of gasoline required.

A diagram like the following is sometimes helpful.

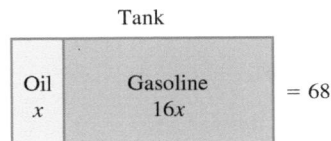

Step 3 **Write an equation.**

Amount of gasoline	plus	amount of oil	is	total amount in tank.
$\downarrow$	$\downarrow$	$\downarrow$	$\downarrow$	$\downarrow$
$16x$	$+$	x	$=$	68

Step 4 **Solve.**

$$17x = 68 \quad \text{Combine like terms.}$$
$$\frac{17x}{17} = \frac{68}{17} \quad \text{Divide by 17.}$$
$$x = 4$$

Step 5 **State the answer.** When full, the lawn trimmer requires 4 oz of oil, and

$$16x = 16(4)$$
$$= 64 \text{ oz of gasoline.}$$

Step 6 **Check.** Because $4 + 64 = 68$, and 64 is 16 times 4, the answer is correct.

Work Problem ❸ *at the Side.* ▶

❸ Solve each problem.

(a) At a club meeting, each member brought two nonmembers. If a total of 27 people attended, how many were members and how many were nonmembers?

Meeting

Members x	Nonmembers $2x$	= 27

Step 1
We must find the number of _____ and nonmembers.

Step 2
Let x = the number of members.

Then _____ = the number of _____.

Step 3
Write an equation.

$$\text{_____} = 27$$

Complete Steps 4–6 to solve the problem. Give the answer.

(b) A fly spray mixture requires 7 oz of water for each 1 oz of essential oil. To fill a quart bottle (32 oz), how many ounces of water and how many ounces of essential oil are required?

Answers

3. (a) members; $2x$; nonmembers; $x + 2x$; members: 9; nonmembers: 18
(b) water: 28 oz; essential oil: 4 oz

4 Solve each problem.

(a) Over a 6-hr period, a basketball player spent twice as much time lifting weights as practicing free throws and 2 hr longer watching game films than practicing free throws. How many hours did he spend on each task?

Steps 1 and 2
The unknown found in both pairs of comparisons is the time spent _____ .

Let x = the time spent practicing free throws.

Then _____ = the time spent lifting weights,

and _____ = the time spent watching game films.

Step 3
Write an equation.

_____ = 6

Complete Steps 4–6 to solve the problem. Give the answer.

(b) A piece of pipe is 50 in. long. It is cut into three pieces. The longest piece is 10 in. longer than the middle-sized piece, and the shortest piece measures 5 in. less than the middle-sized piece. Find the lengths of the three pieces.

Answers

4. **(a)** practicing free throws;
   $2x$; $x + 2$; $x + 2x + (x + 2)$;
   practicing free throws: 1 hr;
   lifting weights: 2 hr;
   watching game films: 3 hr
   (b) longest: 25 in.; middle: 15 in.;
   shortest: 10 in.

> **Problem-Solving Hint**
>
> Sometimes we must find three unknown quantities. *When the three unknown quantities are compared in pairs, let the variable represent the unknown found in both pairs.*

EXAMPLE 4 **Dividing a Board into Pieces**

A project calls for three pieces of wood. The longest piece must be twice the length of the middle-sized piece. The shortest piece must be 10 in. shorter than the middle-sized piece. If a board 70 in. long is to be used, how long must each piece be?

Step 1 **Read** the problem. Three lengths must be found.

Step 2 **Assign a variable.** The middle-sized piece appears in both pairs of comparisons, so let x represent the length, in inches, of the middle-sized piece.

Let x = the length of the middle-sized piece.

Then $2x$ = the length of the longest piece,

and $x - 10$ = the length of the shortest piece.

A sketch is helpful here. See **Figure 2.**

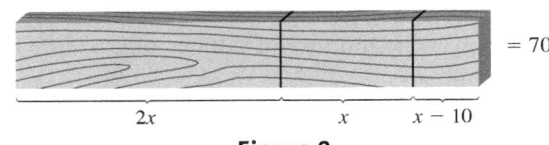

$= 70$

$2x$ x $x - 10$

Figure 2

Step 3 **Write an equation.**

Longest	plus	middle-sized	plus	shortest	is	total length.
↓	↓	↓	↓	↓	↓	↓
$2x$	$+$	x	$+$	$(x - 10)$	$=$	70

Step 4 **Solve.** $4x - 10 = 70$ Combine like terms.

$$4x - 10 + 10 = 70 + 10$$ Add 10.

$$4x = 80$$ Combine like terms.

$$\frac{4x}{4} = \frac{80}{4}$$ Divide by 4.

$$x = 20$$

Step 5 **State the answer.** The middle-sized piece is **20** in. long, the longest piece is

$$2\,(\mathbf{20}) = 40 \text{ in. long,}$$

and the shortest piece is

$$\mathbf{20} - 10 = 10 \text{ in. long.}$$

Step 6 **Check.** The sum of the lengths is 70 in. All conditions of the problem are satisfied.

◀ **Work Problem 4 at the Side.**

OBJECTIVE ▶ ④ **Solve problems involving consecutive integers.** Two integers that differ by 1 are **consecutive integers.** For example, 3 and 4, 6 and 7, and −2 and −1 are pairs of consecutive integers. See **Figure 3.**

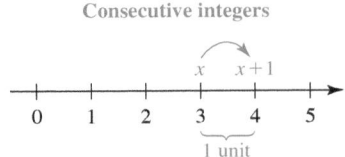

Consecutive integers

Figure 3

In general, if x represents an integer, then x + 1 represents the next greater consecutive integer.

EXAMPLE 5   **Finding Consecutive Integers**

Two pages that face each other in this book have 301 as the sum of their page numbers. What are the page numbers?

Step 1 **Read** the problem. Because the two pages face each other, they must have page numbers that are consecutive integers.

Step 2 **Assign a variable.**

Let x = the lesser page number.

Then $x + 1$ = the greater page number.

Figure 4 illustrates this situation.

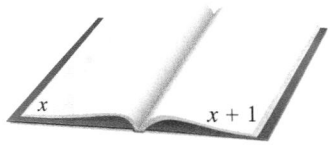

Figure 4

Step 3 **Write an equation.**

Lesser page number	plus	greater page number	is	the sum.
↓	↓	↓	↓	↓
x	$+$	$(x + 1)$	$=$	301

Step 4 **Solve.**

$$2x + 1 = 301 \qquad \text{Combine like terms.}$$
$$2x + 1 - 1 = 301 - 1 \qquad \text{Subtract 1.}$$
$$2x = 300 \qquad \text{Combine like terms.}$$
$$\frac{2x}{2} = \frac{300}{2} \qquad \text{Divide by 2.}$$
$$x = 150$$

Step 5 **State the answer.** The lesser page number is **150**, and the greater is

$$150 + 1 = 151.$$

(Your text is opened to these two pages.)

Step 6 **Check.** The sum of **150** and **151** is 301. The answer is correct.

⎯⎯⎯⎯⎯⎯⎯⎯ **Work Problem ⑤ at the Side.** ▶

⑤ Solve the problem.
   Two pages that face each other in this book have a sum of 569. What are the page numbers?

Answer

5. 284, 285

6 Solve each problem.

GS (a) The sum of two consecutive even integers is 254. Find the integers.

Step 1
We must find two consecutive _____.

Step 2
Let x = the lesser of the two _____ even integers.

Then _____ = the greater of the two consecutive even integers.

Step 3

The lesser consecutive even integer	+	the greater consecutive even integer	is	the total.
↓	↓	↓	↓	↓
_____	+	_____	=	_____

Complete Steps 4–6 to solve the problem. Give the answer.

(b) Find two consecutive odd integers such that the sum of twice the lesser and three times the greater is 191.

Consecutive *even* **integers,** such as 2 and 4, and 8 and 10, differ by 2. Similarly, **consecutive *odd* integers,** such as 1 and 3, and 9 and 11, also differ by 2. See **Figure 5.**

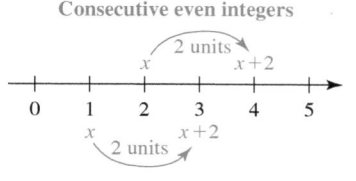

Figure 5

In general, if x represents an even (or odd) integer, then x + 2 represents the next greater consecutive even (or odd) integer, respectively.

Problem-Solving Hint

If x = the lesser (or least) integer in a consecutive integer problem, then the following apply.

- For two consecutive integers, use x, $x + 1$.
- For two consecutive *even* integers, use x, $x + 2$.
- For two consecutive *odd* integers, use x, $x + 2$.

EXAMPLE 6 **Finding Consecutive Odd Integers**

If the lesser of two consecutive odd integers is doubled, the result is 7 more than the greater of the two integers. Find the two integers.

Step 1 **Read** the problem. We must find two consecutive odd integers.

Step 2 **Assign a variable.**

Let x = the lesser consecutive odd integer.

Then $x + 2$ = the greater consecutive odd integer.

Step 3 **Write an equation.**

If the lesser is doubled,		the result is	7	more than	the greater.
↓		↓	↓	↓	↓
$2x$		$=$	7	$+$	$(x + 2)$

Step 4 **Solve.**
$$2x = 9 + x \qquad \text{Combine like terms.}$$
$$2x - x = 9 + x - x \qquad \text{Subtract } x.$$
$$x = 9 \qquad \text{Combine like terms.}$$

Step 5 **State the answer.** The lesser integer is 9. The greater is
$$9 + 2 = 11.$$

Step 6 **Check.** When 9 is doubled, we obtain 18, which is 7 more than the greater odd integer, 11. The answer is correct.

◀ **Work Problem 6 at the Side.**

Answers

6. (a) even integers; consecutive;
 $x + 2$; x; $x + 2$; 254; 126 and 128
 (b) 37, 39

OBJECTIVE ⑤ **Solve problems involving complementary and supplementary angles.** An angle can be measured using a unit called the degree (°), which is $\frac{1}{360}$ of a complete rotation. See **Figure 6.**

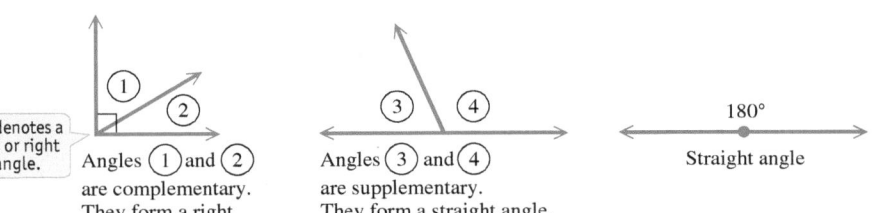

Figure 6

- Two angles whose sum is 90° are **complementary,** or *complements* of each other.

- An angle that measures 90° is a **right angle.**

- Two angles whose sum is 180° are **supplementary,** or *supplements* of each other.

- An angle that measures 180° is a **straight angle.**

Problem-Solving Hint

Let *x* represent the degree measure of an angle.

90 − *x* represents the degree measure of its complement.

180 − *x* represents the degree measure of its supplement.

EXAMPLE 7   **Finding the Measure of an Angle**

Find the measure of an angle whose complement is five times its measure.

Step 1   **Read** the problem. We must find the measure of an angle.

Step 2   **Assign a variable.**

Let x = the degree measure of the angle.

Then $90 - x$ = the degree measure of its complement.

Step 3   **Write an equation.**

Measure of the complement	is	5 times the measure of the angle.
↓	↓	↓
$90 - x$	=	$5x$

Step 4   **Solve.** $90 - x + x = 5x + x$ Add x.

$$90 = 6x$$ Combine like terms.

$$\frac{90}{6} = \frac{6x}{6}$$ Divide by 6.

$$15 = x, \quad \text{or} \quad x = 15$$

Step 5   **State the answer.** The measure of the angle is **15°.**

Step 6   **Check.** If the angle measures **15°,** then its complement measures $90° - 15° = 75°$, which is equal to five times **15°,** as required.

────── Work Problems ❼ and ❽ at the Side. ▶

❼ Fill in the blank below each figure. Then solve.

(a) Find the complement of an angle that measures 26°.

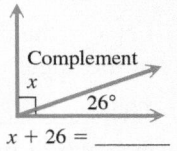

$x + 26 =$ _____

(b) Find the supplement of an angle that measures 92°.

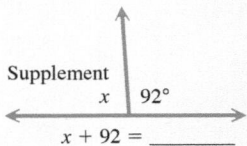

$x + 92 =$ _____

❽ Solve each problem. Give the equation and the answer.

Let x = the degree measure of the angle.

(a) Find the measure of an angle whose complement is eight times its measure.

(b) Find the measure of an angle whose supplement is twice its measure.

Answers

7. (a) 90; 64°   **(b)** 180; 88°

8. (a) $90 - x = 8x$; 10°

   (b) $180 - x = 2x$; 60°

9 Solve each problem.

GS **(a)** Find the measure of an angle such that twice its complement is 30° less than its supplement.

Let x = the degree measure of the angle.

Then _____ = the degree measure of its complement,

and _____ = the degree measure of its supplement.

Complete the solution. Give the equation and the answer.

EXAMPLE 8 **Finding the Measure of an Angle**

Find the measure of an angle whose supplement is 10° more than twice its complement.

Step 1 **Read** the problem. We must find the measure of an angle, given information about its complement and its supplement.

Step 2 **Assign a variable.**

Let x = the degree measure of the angle.

Then $90 - x$ = the degree measure of its complement,

and $180 - x$ = the degree measure of its supplement.

We can visualize this information using a sketch. See **Figure 7.**

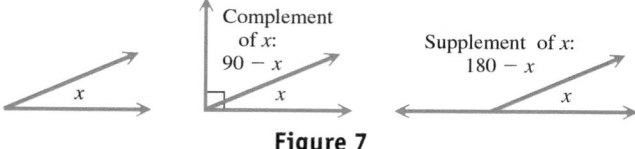

Complement of x: $90 - x$ Supplement of x: $180 - x$

Figure 7

Step 3 **Write an equation.**

Supplement	is	10	more than	twice	its complement.
↓	↓	↓	↓	↓	↓
$180 - x$	$=$	10	$+$	2 ·	$(90 - x)$

> Be sure to use parentheses here.

Step 4 **Solve.**

$$180 - x = 10 + 2(90 - x)$$
$$180 - x = 10 + 180 - 2x \qquad \text{Distributive property}$$
$$180 - x = 190 - 2x \qquad \text{Combine like terms.}$$
$$180 - x + 2x = 190 - 2x + 2x \qquad \text{Add } 2x.$$
$$180 + x = 190 \qquad \text{Combine like terms.}$$
$$180 + x - 180 = 190 - 180 \qquad \text{Subtract 180.}$$
$$x = 10$$

Step 5 **State the answer.** The measure of the angle is **10°**.

Step 6 **Check.** The complement of **10°** is 80° and the supplement of **10°** is 170°. Also, 170° is equal to **10°** more than twice 80° (that is, $170 = 10 + 2(80)$ is true). Therefore, the answer is correct.

◀ **Work Problem** **9** **at the Side.**

(b) Find the measure of an angle whose supplement is 46° less than three times its complement.

Answers

9. (a) $90 - x$; $180 - x$;
$2(90 - x) = (180 - x) - 30$;
30°

(b) 22°

2.4 Exercises

FOR EXTRA HELP *Go to* MyMathLab *for worked-out, step-by-step solutions to exercises enclosed in a square* ▢ *and video solutions to* ▶ *exercises.*

1. Give the six steps introduced in this section for solving application problems.

Step 1: _____ *Step 4:* _____

Step 2: _____ *Step 5:* _____

Step 3: _____ *Step 6:* _____

2. CONCEPT CHECK List some of the words that translate as "=" when writing an equation to solve an applied problem.

CONCEPT CHECK *Which choice would **not** be a reasonable answer? Justify your response.*

3. A problem requires finding the number of cars on a dealer's lot.

A. 0 **B.** 45 **C.** 1 **D.** $6\frac{1}{2}$

4. A problem requires finding the number of hours a light bulb is on during a day.

A. 0 **B.** 4.5 **C.** 13 **D.** 25

5. A problem requires finding the distance traveled in miles.

A. −10 **B.** 1.8 **C.** $10\frac{1}{2}$ **D.** 50

6. A problem requires finding the time in minutes.

A. 0 **B.** 10.5 **C.** −5 **D.** 90

CONCEPT CHECK *Fill in each blank with the correct response.*

7. Consecutive integers differ by _____, such as 15 and _____, and −8 and _____.

If x represents an integer, then _____ represents the next greater integer.

8. Consecutive odd integers are _____ integers that differ by _____, such as _____ and 13.

Consecutive even integers are _____ integers that differ by _____, such as 12 and _____.

9. Two angles whose measures sum to 90° are _____ angles. Two angles whose measures sum to 180° are _____ angles.

10. A right angle has measure _____. A straight angle has measure _____.

CONCEPT CHECK *Answer each question.*

11. Is there an angle that is equal to its supplement? Is there an angle that is equal to its complement? If the answer is yes to either question, give the measure of the angle.

12. If x represents an even integer, how can we express the next *smaller* consecutive integer in terms of x? The next *smaller* even integer?

Solve each problem. In each case, give the equation using x as the variable, and give the answer. **See Example 1.**

13. The product of 8, and a number increased by 6, is 104. What is the number?

14. The product of 5, and 3 more than twice a number, is 85. What is the number?

15. ⏵ If 2 is added to five times a number, the result is equal to 5 more than four times the number. Find the number.

16. If four times a number is added to 8, the result is three times the number, added to 5. Find the number.

17. ⏵ Two less than three times a number is equal to 14 more than five times the number. What is the number?

18. Nine more than five times a number is equal to 3 less than seven times the number. What is the number?

19. If 2 is subtracted from a number and this difference is tripled, the result is 6 more than the number. Find the number.

20. If 3 is added to a number and this sum is doubled, the result is 2 more than the number. Find the number.

21. The sum of three times a number and 7 more than the number is the same as the difference of -11 and twice the number. What is the number?

22. If 4 is added to twice a number and this sum is multiplied by 2, the result is the same as if the number is multiplied by 3 and 4 is added to the product. What is the number?

GS *Complete the six problem-solving steps to solve each problem.* **See Example 2.**

23. Pennsylvania and New York were among the states with the most remaining drive-in movie screens in 2015. Pennsylvania had 1 less screen than New York, and there were 55 screens total in the two states. How many drive-in movie screens remained in each state? (Data from www.Drive-Ins.com)

Step 1 **Read.** What are we asked to find?

_____

_____

Step 2 **Assign a variable.** Let $x =$ the number of screens in New York.

Then $x - 1 =$ _____

_____

Step 3 **Write an equation.**

____ + ____ = 55

Step 4 **Solve** the equation.

$x =$ ____

Step 5 **State the answer.** New York had ____ screens. Pennsylvania had ____ $- 1 =$ ____ screens.

Step 6 **Check.** The number of screens in Pennsylvania was ____ less than the number of _____. The total number of screens was $28 +$ ____ = ____ .

24. The total number of television viewers for the final episodes of *M*A*S*H* and *Cheers* was about 92 million, with 8 million more people watching the *M*A*S*H* episode than the *Cheers* episode. How many people watched each episode? (Data from Nielsen Media Research.)

Step 1 **Read.** What are we asked to find?

_____

_____

Step 2 **Assign a variable.** Let $x =$ the number of people who watched the *Cheers* episode.

Then $x + 8 =$ _____

_____

Step 3 **Write an equation.**

____ + ____ = ____

Step 4 **Solve** the equation.

$x =$ ____

Step 5 **State the answer.** ____ million people watched the *Cheers* episode, while ____ $+ 8 =$ ____ million watched *M*A*S*H*.

Step 6 **Check.** The number of people who watched the *M*A*S*H** episode was ____ million more than the number who watched the *Cheers* episode. The total number of viewers in millions was $42 +$ ____ = ____ .

Solve each problem. ***See Example 2.***

25. The total number of Democrats and Republicans in the U.S. House of Representatives during the 114th session (2015–2017) was 435. There were 59 more Republicans than Democrats. How many members of each party were there? (Data from *The World Almanac and Book of Facts*.)

26. During the 114th session, the U.S. Senate had a total of 98 Democrats and Republicans. There were 10 fewer Democrats than Republicans. How many Democrats and Republicans were there in the Senate? (Data from *The World Almanac and Book of Facts*.)

27. Taylor Swift and Kenny Chesney had the two top-grossing North American concert tours in 2015, together generating $315.8 million in ticket sales. If Kenny Chesney took in $83 million less than Taylor Swift, how much did each tour generate? (Data from Pollstar.)

28. In the United States in 2014, Honda Accord sales were 41 thousand less than Toyota Camry sales, and 817 thousand of these two cars were sold. How many of each make of car were sold? (Data from *The World Almanac and Book of Facts*.)

29. In the 2015–2016 NBA regular season, the Golden State Warriors won 1 more than eight times as many games as they lost. The Warriors played 82 games. How many wins and losses did the team have? (Data from www.nba.com)

30. In the 2015 regular MLB season, the Kansas City Royals won 39 fewer than twice as many games as they lost. The Royals played 162 regular season games. How many wins and losses did the team have? (Data from www.mlb.com)

31. A one-cup serving of orange juice contains 3 mg less than four times the amount of vitamin C as a one-cup serving of pineapple juice. Servings of the two juices contain a total of 122 mg of vitamin C. How many milligrams of vitamin C are in a serving of each type of juice? (Data from U.S. Agriculture Department.)

32. A one-cup serving of pineapple juice has 9 more than three times as many calories as a one-cup serving of tomato juice. Servings of the two juices contain a total of 173 calories. How many calories are in a serving of each type of juice? (Data from U.S. Agriculture Department.)

Solve each problem. ***See Example 3.***

33. A recipe for whole-grain bread calls for 1 oz of rye flour for every 4 oz of whole-wheat flour. How many ounces of each kind of flour should be used to make a loaf of bread weighing 32 oz?

34. U.S. five-cent coins are made from a combination of nickel and copper. For every 1 lb of nickel, 3 lb of copper are used. How many pounds of copper would be needed to make 560 lb of five-cent coins? (Data from The United States Mint.)

35. A medication contains 9 mg of active ingredients for every 1 mg of inert ingredients. How much of each kind of ingredient would be contained in a single 250-mg caplet?

36. A recipe for salad dressing uses 2 oz of olive oil for each 1 oz of red wine vinegar. If 42 oz of salad dressing are needed, how many ounces of each ingredient should be used?

37. The value of a "Mint State-63" (uncirculated) 1950 Jefferson nickel minted at Denver is $\frac{4}{3}$ the value of a similar condition 1944 nickel minted at Philadelphia. Together, the value of the two coins is $28.00. What is the value of each coin? (Data from Yeoman, R., *A Guide Book of United States Coins*.)

38. In one day, a store sold $\frac{8}{5}$ as many DVDs as Blu-ray discs. The total number of DVDs and Blu-ray discs sold that day was 273. How many DVDs were sold?

39. The world's largest taco contained approximately 1 kg of onion for every 6.6 kg of grilled steak. The total weight of these two ingredients was 617.6 kg. To the nearest tenth of a kilogram, how many kilograms of each ingredient were used? (Data from *Guinness World Records*.)

40. As of 2015, the combined population of China and India was estimated at 2.7 billion. If there were about 93% as many people living in India as China, what was the population of each country, to the nearest tenth of a billion? (Data from United Nations Population Division.)

*Solve each problem. **See Example 4.***

41. A party-length submarine sandwich is 59 in. long. It is to be cut into three pieces so that the middle piece is 5 in. longer than the shortest piece and the shortest piece is 9 in. shorter than the longest piece. How long should the three pieces be?

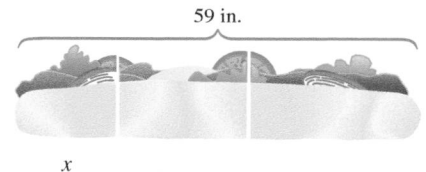

59 in.

x ____ ____

42. A three-foot-long deli sandwich must be split into three pieces so that the middle piece is twice as long as the shortest piece and the shortest piece is 8 in. shorter than the longest piece. How long should the three pieces be? (*Hint:* How many inches are in 3 ft?)

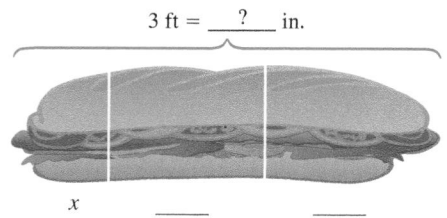

3 ft = __?__ in.

x ____ ____

43. An office manager booked 55 airline tickets. He booked 7 more tickets on American Airlines than United Airlines. On Southwest Airlines, he booked 4 more than twice as many tickets as on United. How many tickets did he book on each airline?

44. A mathematics textbook editor spent 7.5 hr making telephone calls, writing e-mails, and attending meetings. She spent twice as much time attending meetings as making telephone calls and 0.5 hr longer writing e-mails than making telephone calls. How many hours did she spend on each task?

45. The United States earned 28 medals at the 2014 Winter Olympics. The number of silver medals earned was 5 less than the number of bronze medals. The number of gold medals was 2 more than the number of silver medals. How many of each kind of medal did the United States earn? (Data from www.espn.go.com)

46. Russia earned 33 medals at the 2014 Winter Olympics. The number of gold medals earned was 4 more than the number of bronze medals. The number of silver medals earned was 2 more than the number of bronze medals. How many of each kind of medal did Russia earn? (Data from www.espn.go.com)

47. Venus is 31.2 million mi farther from the sun than Mercury, while Earth is 57 million mi farther from the sun than Mercury. If the total of the distances from these three planets to the sun is 196.2 million mi, how far away from the sun is Mercury? (All distances given here are mean (*average*) distances.) (Data from *The New York Times Almanac.*)

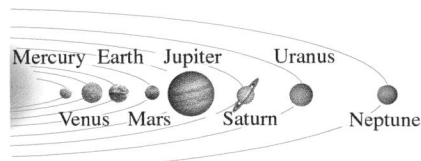

48. Saturn, Jupiter, and Uranus have a total of 156 known satellites (moons). Jupiter has 5 more satellites than Saturn, and Uranus has 35 fewer satellites than Saturn. How many known satellites does Uranus have? (Data from http://solarsystem.nasa.gov)

49. The sum of the measures of the angles of any triangle is 180°. In triangle *ABC,* angles *A* and *B* have the same measure, while the measure of angle *C* is 60° greater than each of *A* and *B*. What are the measures of the three angles?

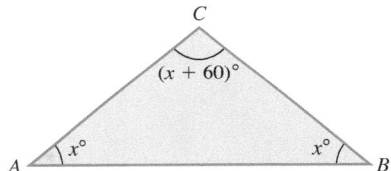

50. The sum of the measures of the angles of any triangle is 180°. In triangle *ABC,* the measure of angle *A* is 141° more than the measure of angle *B*. The measure of angle *B* is the same as the measure of angle *C*. Find the measure of each angle.

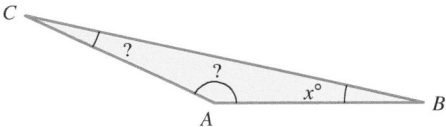

*Solve each problem. **See Examples 5 and 6.***

51. The numbers on two consecutively numbered gym lockers have a sum of 137. What are the locker numbers?

52. The sum of two consecutive check numbers is 357. Find the numbers.

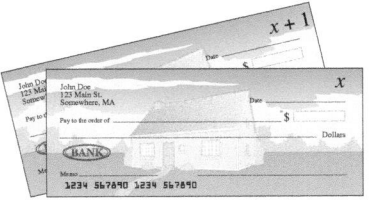

53. Two pages that are back-to-back in this book have 203 as the sum of their page numbers. What are the page numbers?

54. Two hotel rooms have room numbers that are consecutive integers. The sum of the numbers is 515. What are the two room numbers?

55. Find two consecutive even integers such that the lesser added to three times the greater gives a sum of 46.

56. Find two consecutive even integers such that six times the lesser added to the greater gives a sum of 86.

57. Find two consecutive odd integers such that 59 more than the lesser is four times the greater.

58. Find two consecutive odd integers such that twice the greater is 17 more than the lesser.

59. When the lesser of two consecutive integers is added to three times the greater, the result is 43. Find the integers.

60. If five times the lesser of two consecutive integers is added to three times the greater, the result is 59. Find the integers.

61. If the sum of three consecutive even integers is 60, what is the least of the three even integers? (*Hint:* If *x* and *x* + 2 represent the first two consecutive even integers, how would we represent the largest consecutive even integer?)

62. If the sum of three consecutive odd integers is 69, what is the largest of the three odd integers? (*Hint:* If *x* and *x* + 2 represent the first two consecutive odd integers, how would we represent the largest consecutive odd integer?)

Solve each problem. ***See Examples 7 and 8.***

63. Find the measure of an angle whose complement is four times its measure. (*Hint:* If *x* represents the measure of the unknown angle, how would we represent its complement?)

64. Find the measure of an angle whose complement is five times its measure.

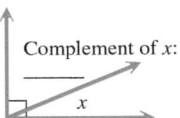

65. Find the measure of an angle whose supplement is eight times its measure. (*Hint:* If *x* represents the measure of the unknown angle, how would we represent its supplement?)

66. Find the measure of an angle whose supplement is three times its measure.

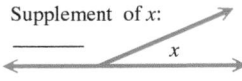

67. Find the measure of an angle whose supplement measures 39° more than twice its complement.

68. Find the measure of an angle whose supplement measures 38° less than three times its complement.

69. Find the measure of an angle such that the difference between the measures of its supplement and three times its complement is 10°.

70. Find the measure of an angle such that the sum of the measures of its complement and its supplement is 160°.

2.5 | Formulas and Additional Applications from Geometry

A **formula** is an equation in which variables are used to describe a relationship. For example, formulas exist for finding perimeters and areas of geometric figures, calculating money earned on bank savings, and converting among measurements.

$$P = 4s, \quad \mathcal{A}^* = \pi r^2, \quad I = prt, \quad F = \frac{9}{5}C + 32 \quad \text{Formulas}$$

Many of the formulas used in this text are given at the back of the text.

OBJECTIVE ▶ 1 Solve a formula for one variable, given the values of the other variables. The **area** of a plane (two-dimensional) geometric figure is a measure of the surface covered by the figure. Area is measured in square units.

OBJECTIVES

1 Solve a formula for one variable, given the values of the other variables.

2 Use a formula to solve an applied problem.

3 Solve problems involving vertical angles and straight angles.

4 Solve a formula for a specified variable.

EXAMPLE 1 Using Formulas to Evaluate Variables

Find the value of the remaining variable in each formula.

(a) $\mathcal{A} = LW$; $\mathcal{A} = 64, L = 10$

This formula gives the area of a rectangle. See **Figure 8.**

$\mathcal{A} = LW$ 〔Solve for W.〕

$64 = 10W$ Let $\mathcal{A} = 64$ and $L = 10$.

$\dfrac{64}{10} = \dfrac{10W}{10}$ Divide by 10.

$6.4 = W$

The width is **6.4**. Since $10\,(\mathbf{6.4}) = 64$, the given area, the answer checks.

(b) $\mathcal{A} = \dfrac{1}{2}h\,(b + B)$; $\mathcal{A} = 210, B = 27, h = 10$

This formula gives the area of a trapezoid. See **Figure 9.**

$\mathcal{A} = \dfrac{1}{2}h\,(b + B)$

〔Solve for b.〕

$210 = \dfrac{1}{2}\,(\mathbf{10})\,(b + 27)$ Let $\mathcal{A} = 210, h = 10, B = 27.$

$210 = 5\,(b + 27)$ Multiply $\frac{1}{2}(10)$.

$210 = 5b + 135$ Distributive property

$210 - 135 = 5b + 135 - 135$ Subtract 135.

$75 = 5b$ Combine like terms.

$\dfrac{75}{5} = \dfrac{5b}{5}$ Divide by 5.

$15 = b$

The length of the shorter parallel side, b, is **15**. Since $\frac{1}{2}(10)(\mathbf{15} + 27) = 210$, the given area, the answer checks.

──────────── **Work Problem 1 at the Side. ▶**

In this text, we use $\mathcal{A}$ to denote area.

---

1 Find the value of the remaining variable in each formula.

(a) $\mathcal{A} = bh$
(area of a parallelogram);
$\mathcal{A} = 96, h = 8$

(b) $I = prt$ (simple interest);
$I = 246, r = 0.06$ (that is, 6%), $t = 2$

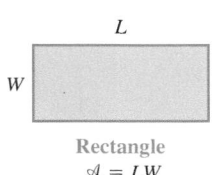

(c) $P = 2L + 2W$
(perimeter of a rectangle);
$P = 126, W = 25$

Answers

1. (a) $b = 12$
(b) 246; 0.06; 2; 0.12; 0.12; 2050
(c) $L = 38$

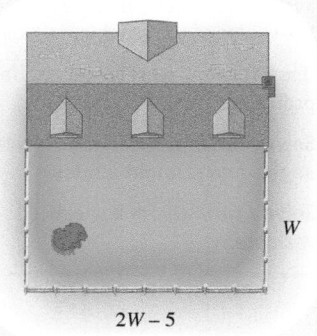

Figure 10

2 Solve the problem.
A farmer has 800 m of fencing material to enclose a rectangular field. The width of the field is 175 m. Find the length of the field.

OBJECTIVE ▶ 2 Use a formula to solve an applied problem. The **perimeter** of a plane (two-dimensional) geometric figure is the measure of the outer boundary of the figure. For a polygon (such as a rectangle, square, or triangle), it is the sum of the lengths of the sides.

EXAMPLE 2   Finding the Dimensions of a Rectangular Yard

A backyard is in the shape of a rectangle. The length is 5 m less than twice the width, and the perimeter is 80 m. Find the dimensions of the yard.

Step 1 **Read** the problem. We must find the dimensions of the yard.

Step 2 **Assign a variable.** Let $W =$ the width of the lot, in meters. The length is 5 m less than twice the width, so the length is given by $L = 2W - 5$. See **Figure 10.**

Step 3 **Write an equation.** Use the formula for the perimeter of a rectangle.

$$P = 2L + 2W$$

Perimeter $= 2 \cdot$ Length $+ 2 \cdot$ Width

$$80 = 2(2W - 5) + 2W$$

Substitute 80 for perimeter P and $2W - 5$ for length L.

Step 4 **Solve.**
$$80 = 4W - 10 + 2W \quad \text{Distributive property}$$
$$80 = 6W - 10 \quad \text{Combine like terms.}$$
$$80 + 10 = 6W - 10 + 10 \quad \text{Add 10.}$$
$$90 = 6W \quad \text{Combine like terms.}$$
$$\frac{90}{6} = \frac{6W}{6} \quad \text{Divide by 6.}$$
$$15 = W$$

Step 5 **State the answer.** The width is **15** m. The length is $2(15) - 5 = 25$ m.

Step 6 **Check.** If the width of the yard is **15** m and the length is **25** m, the perimeter is $2(25) + 2(15) = 80$ m, as required.

◀ **Work Problem 2 at the Side.**

EXAMPLE 3   Finding the Dimensions of a Triangle

The longest side of a triangle is 3 ft longer than the shortest side. The medium side is 1 ft longer than the shortest side. If the perimeter of the triangle is 16 ft, what are the lengths of the three sides?

Step 1 **Read** the problem. We are given the perimeter of a triangle and must find the lengths of the three sides.

Step 2 **Assign a variable.** The shortest side is mentioned in each pair of comparisons in the problem.

Let $s =$ the length of the shortest side, in feet,

$s + 1 =$ the length of the medium side, in feet, and

$s + 3 =$ the length of the longest side, in feet.

It is a good idea to draw a sketch. See **Figure 11.**

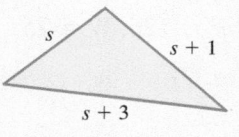

Figure 11

Answer
2. 225 m

Continued on Next Page

Step 3 **Write an equation.** Use the formula for the perimeter of a triangle.

$$P = a + b + c \qquad \text{Perimeter of a triangle}$$

$$16 = s + (s + 1) + (s + 3) \qquad \text{Substitute.}$$

Step 4 **Solve.** $16 = 3s + 4$ Combine like terms.

$$16 - 4 = 3s + 4 - 4 \qquad \text{Subtract 4.}$$

$$12 = 3s \qquad \text{Combine like terms.}$$

$$\frac{12}{3} = \frac{3s}{3} \qquad \text{Divide by 3.}$$

$$4 = s$$

Step 5 **State the answer.** The length of the shortest side, s, is **4** ft.

$$s + 1 = 4 + 1 = 5 \text{ ft} \qquad \text{Length of the medium side}$$

$$s + 3 = 4 + 3 = 7 \text{ ft} \qquad \text{Length of the longest side}$$

Step 6 **Check.** The medium side, 5 ft, is 1 ft longer than the shortest side, and the longest side, 7 ft, is 3 ft longer than the shortest side. The perimeter is

$$4 + 5 + 7 = 16 \text{ ft}, \quad \text{as required.}$$

────────────────────────── **Work Problem 3 at the Side.** ▶

③ Solve the problem.
     The longest side of a triangle is 1 in. longer than the medium side. The medium side is 5 in. longer than the shortest side. If the perimeter is 32 in., what are the lengths of the three sides?

EXAMPLE 4   **Finding the Height of a Triangular Sail**

The area of a triangular sail of a sailboat is 126 ft^2. (Recall that ft^2 means "square feet.") The base of the sail is 12 ft. Find the height of the sail.

Step 1 **Read** the problem. We must find the height of the triangular sail.

Step 2 **Assign a variable.** Let h = the height of the sail, in feet. See **Figure 12.**

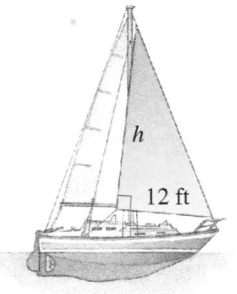

Step 3 **Write an equation.** Use the formula for the area of a triangle.

$$\mathcal{A} = \frac{1}{2}bh \qquad \begin{array}{l}\mathcal{A} \text{ is the area, } b \text{ is the}\\ \text{base, and } h \text{ is the height.}\end{array}$$

Figure 12

$$126 = \frac{1}{2}(12)h \qquad \text{Substitute } \mathcal{A} = 126, b = 12.$$

Step 4 **Solve.** $126 = 6h$ Multiply.

$$\frac{126}{6} = \frac{6h}{6} \qquad \text{Divide by 6.}$$

$$21 = h$$

Step 5 **State the answer.** The height of the sail is **21** ft.

Step 6 **Check** to see that the values $\mathcal{A} = 126$, $b = 12$, and $h = 21$ satisfy the formula for the area of a triangle.

$$126 = \frac{1}{2}(12)(21) \text{ is true.}$$

④ Solve the problem.
     The area of a triangle is 120 m^2. The height is 24 m. Find the length of the base of the triangle.

Answers

3. 7 in.; 12 in.; 13 in.

4. 10 m

────────────────────────── **Work Problem 4 at the Side.** ▶

5 Find the measure of each marked angle.

(a)

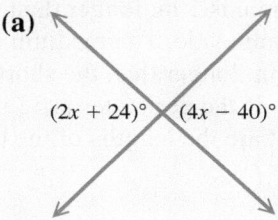

$(2x + 24)°$ $(4x - 40)°$

(b)

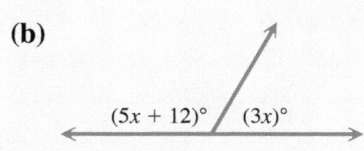

$(5x + 12)°$ $(3x)°$

GS **(c)**

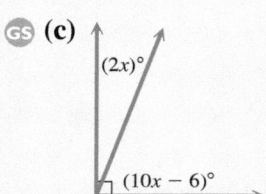

$(2x)°$

$(10x - 6)°$

Because of the ⌐ symbol, the marked angles are _____ angles and have a sum of _____. The equation to use is

_____ = 90.

Solve this equation to find that $x =$ _____. Then substitute to find the measure of each angle.

$2x = 2 ($ _____ $)$

= _____

$10x - 6 = 10 ($ _____ $) - 6$

= _____

The two angles measure _____.

OBJECTIVE **3** Solve problems involving vertical angles and straight angles. **Figure 13** shows two intersecting lines forming angles that are numbered ①, ②, ③, and ④. Angles ① and ③ lie "opposite" each other. They are **vertical angles.** Another pair of vertical angles is ② and ④. ***Vertical angles have equal measures.***

Consider angles ① and ②. When their measures are added, we obtain 180°, the measure of a **straight angle.** There are three other angle pairs that form straight angles:

② and ③, ③ and ④, and ① and ④.

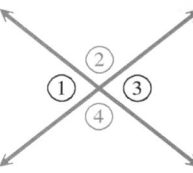

Figure 13

EXAMPLE 5 **Finding Angle Measures**

Refer to **Figure 14.**

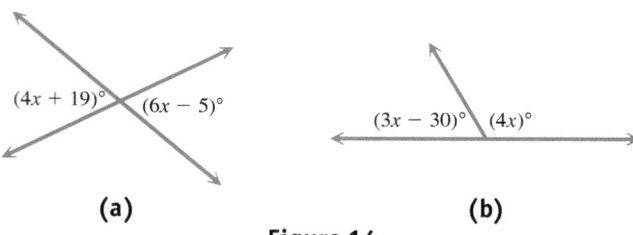

$(4x + 19)°$ $(6x - 5)°$ $(3x - 30)°$ $(4x)°$

(a) **(b)**

Figure 14

(a) Find the measure of each marked angle in **Figure 14(a).**

The marked angles are vertical angles, so they have equal measures.

$$4x + 19 = 6x - 5 \quad \text{Set } 4x + 19 \text{ equal to } 6x - 5.$$
$$19 = 2x - 5 \quad \text{Subtract } 4x.$$
$$24 = 2x \quad \text{Add 5.}$$

This is **not** the angle measure.

$$12 = x \quad \text{Divide by 2.}$$

Replace x with 12 in the expression for the measure of each angle.

$4x + 19$
$= 4(12) + 19 \quad$ Let $x = 12.$
$= 48 + 19 \quad$ Multiply.
$= 67 \quad$ Add.

$6x - 5$
$= 6(12) - 5 \quad$ Let $x = 12.$
$= 72 - 5 \quad$ Multiply.
$= 67 \quad$ Subtract.

Each angle measures **67°.**

(b) Find the measure of each marked angle in **Figure 14(b).**

The measures of the marked angles must add to 180° because together they form a straight angle. (They are also *supplements* of each other.)

$$(3x - 30) + 4x = 180 \quad \text{Supplementary angles sum to } 180°.$$
$$7x - 30 = 180 \quad \text{Combine like terms.}$$
$$7x = 210 \quad \text{Add 30.}$$

Don't stop here!

$$x = 30 \quad \text{Divide by 7.}$$

Replace x with 30 in the measure of each marked angle.

$$3x - 30 = 3(30) - 30 = 90 - 30 = 60$$
$$4x = 4(30) = 120$$

The measures of the angles add to 180°, as required.

The two angle measures are **60°** and **120°.**

Answers

5. (a) Both measure 88°. (b) 117° and 63°
(c) complementary; 90°; $2x + (10x - 6)$;
8; 8; 16; 8; 74; 16° and 74°

◀ **Work Problem 5** at the Side.

OBJECTIVE ▶ 4 Solve a formula for a specified variable. Sometimes we want to rewrite a formula in terms of a *different* variable in the formula. For example, consider $\mathcal{A} = LW$, the formula for the area of a rectangle.

How can we rewrite $\mathcal{A} = LW$ in terms of W?

The process whereby we do this involves **solving for a specified variable,** or **solving a literal equation.**

To solve a formula for a specified variable, we use the *same* steps that we used to solve an equation with just one variable. Consider the parallel reasoning to solve each of the following for x.

$3x + 4 = 13$	$ax + b = c$
$3x + 4 - 4 = 13 - 4$ Subtract 4.	$ax + b - b = c - b$ Subtract b.
$3x = 9$	$ax = c - b$
$\dfrac{3x}{3} = \dfrac{9}{3}$ Divide by 3.	$\dfrac{ax}{a} = \dfrac{c - b}{a}$ Divide by a.
$x = 3$	$x = \dfrac{c - b}{a}$

When we solve a formula for a specified variable, we treat the specified variable as if it were the ONLY variable in the equation, and treat the other variables as if they were constants (numbers).

EXAMPLE 6 Solving for a Specified Variable

Solve $\mathcal{A} = LW$ for W.

Think of undoing what has been done to W. Since W is multiplied by L, undo the multiplication by dividing each side of $\mathcal{A} = LW$ by L.

$$\mathcal{A} = LW \quad \text{Our goal is to isolate } W.$$

$$\frac{\mathcal{A}}{L} = \frac{LW}{L} \qquad \text{Divide by } L.$$

$$\frac{\mathcal{A}}{L} = W, \quad \text{or} \quad W = \frac{\mathcal{A}}{L} \qquad \tfrac{LW}{L} = \tfrac{L}{L} \cdot W = 1 \cdot W = W$$

—————————— **Work Problem 6 at the Side.** ▶

EXAMPLE 7 Solving for a Specified Variable

Solve $P = 2L + 2W$ for L.

$$P = 2L + 2W \quad \text{Our goal is to isolate } L.$$

$$P - 2W = 2L + 2W - 2W \qquad \text{Subtract } 2W.$$

$$P - 2W = 2L \qquad \text{Combine like terms.}$$

$$\frac{P - 2W}{2} = \frac{2L}{2} \qquad \text{Divide by 2.}$$

$$\frac{P - 2W}{2} = L, \quad \text{or} \quad L = \frac{P - 2W}{2} \qquad \tfrac{2L}{2} = \tfrac{2}{2} \cdot L = 1 \cdot L = L$$

—————————— **Work Problem 7 at the Side.** ▶

---

6 Solve each formula for the specified variable.

(a) $W = Fd$ for F

(b) $I = prt$ for t

Our goal is to isolate ____.

$$I = prt$$

$$\frac{I}{\rule{1.2cm}{0.4pt}} = \frac{prt}{\rule{1.2cm}{0.4pt}}$$

$$\rule{1.2cm}{0.4pt} = t$$

7 Solve for the specified variable.

(a) $Ax + By = C$ for A

Our goal is to isolate ____.
To do this, subtract ____ from each side. Then ____ each side by ____.

Show these steps and write the formula solved for A.

(b) $Ax + By = C$ for B

Answers

6. (a) $F = \dfrac{W}{d}$ (b) t; pr; pr; $\dfrac{I}{pr}$

7. (a) A; By; divide; x; $A = \dfrac{C - By}{x}$

(b) $B = \dfrac{C - Ax}{y}$

8 Solve each formula for the specified variable.

(a) $x = u + zs$ for z

(b) $A = p(1 + rt)$ for t

EXAMPLE 8 **Solving for a Specified Variable**

Solve $A = \frac{1}{2}h(b + B)$ for B.

> Our goal is to isolate B.

$$A = \frac{1}{2}h(b + B)$$

$$A = \frac{1}{2}hb + \frac{1}{2}hB \qquad \text{Clear the parentheses using the distributive property.}$$

$$2 \cdot A = 2\left(\frac{1}{2}hb + \frac{1}{2}hB\right) \qquad \text{Multiply each side by 2 to clear the fractions.}$$

$$2 \cdot A = 2 \cdot \frac{1}{2}hb + 2 \cdot \frac{1}{2}hB \qquad \text{Distributive property}$$

$$2A = hb + hB \qquad \text{Multiply; } 2 \cdot \frac{1}{2} = \frac{2}{2} = 1$$

$$2A - hb = hb + hB - hb \qquad \text{Subtract } hb.$$

$$2A - hb = hB \qquad \text{Combine like terms.}$$

$$\frac{2A - hb}{h} = \frac{hB}{h} \qquad \text{Divide by } h.$$

$$\frac{2A - hb}{h} = B, \quad \text{or} \quad B = \frac{2A - hb}{h}$$

◄ **Work Problem** **8** **at the Side.**

---

9 Solve each equation for y.

(a) $5x + y = 3$

(b) $x - 2y = 8$

EXAMPLE 9 **Solving for a Specified Variable**

Solve each equation for y.

(a) $\qquad 2x - y = 7$

> Our goal is to isolate y.

$$2x - y - 2x = 7 - 2x \qquad \text{Subtract } 2x.$$

$$-y = 7 - 2x \qquad \text{Combine like terms.}$$

$$-1(-y) = -1(7 - 2x) \qquad \text{Multiply by } -1.$$

$$y = -7 + 2x \qquad \text{Multiply; distributive property}$$

$$y = 2x - 7 \qquad -a + b = b - a$$

We could have added y and subtracted 7 from each side of the equation to isolate y on the right, giving $2x - 7 = y$, a different form of the same result.

(b) $\qquad -3x + 2y = 6$

$$-3x + 2y + 3x = 6 + 3x \qquad \text{Add } 3x.$$

$$2y = 3x + 6 \qquad \text{Combine like terms; commutative property}$$

$$\frac{2y}{2} = \frac{3x + 6}{2} \qquad \text{Divide by 2.}$$

> Be careful here.

$$y = \frac{3x}{2} + \frac{6}{2} \qquad \frac{a + b}{c} = \frac{a}{c} + \frac{b}{c}$$

> $\frac{3x}{2} = \frac{3}{2} \cdot \frac{x}{1} = \frac{3}{2}x$

$$y = \frac{3}{2}x + 3 \qquad \text{Simplify.}$$

Although we could have given the answer as $y = \frac{3x + 6}{2}$, we simplified further in preparation for later work.

Answers

8. **(a)** $z = \dfrac{x - u}{s}$ **(b)** $t = \dfrac{A - p}{pr}$

9. **(a)** $y = -5x + 3$ **(b)** $y = \dfrac{1}{2}x - 4$

◄ **Work Problem** **9** **at the Side.**

2.5 Exercises

FOR EXTRA HELP Go to MyMathLab for worked-out, step-by-step solutions to exercises enclosed in a square ☐ and video solutions to ▶ exercises.

CONCEPT CHECK *Give a one-sentence definition of each term.*

1. Perimeter of a plane geometric figure

2. Area of a plane geometric figure

CONCEPT CHECK *Decide whether* perimeter *or* area *would be used to solve a problem concerning the measure of the quantity.*

3. Sod for a lawn

4. Carpeting for a bedroom

5. Baseboards for a living room

6. Fencing for a yard

7. Fertilizer for a garden

8. Tile for a bathroom

9. Determining the cost of planting rye grass in a lawn for the winter

10. Determining the cost of replacing a linoleum floor with a wood floor

Find the value of the remaining variable in each formula. Use 3.14 as an approximation for π (pi). **See Example 1.**

11. $P = 2L + 2W$ (perimeter of a rectangle); $L = 8, W = 5$

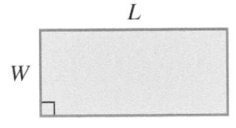

12. $P = 2L + 2W$; $L = 6, W = 4$

13. $\mathscr{A} = \dfrac{1}{2}bh$ (area of a triangle); ▶ $b = 8, h = 16$

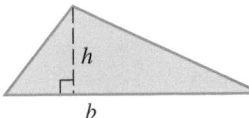

14. $\mathscr{A} = \dfrac{1}{2}bh$; $b = 10, h = 14$

15. $P = a + b + c$ (perimeter of a triangle); $P = 12, a = 3, c = 5$

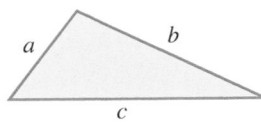

16. $P = a + b + c$; $P = 15, a = 3, b = 7$

17. $d = rt$ (distance formula); ▶ $d = 252, r = 45$

18. $d = rt$; $d = 100, t = 2.5$

19. $\mathscr{A} = \dfrac{1}{2}h(b + B)$ (area of a trapezoid); $\mathscr{A} = 91, b = 12, B = 14$

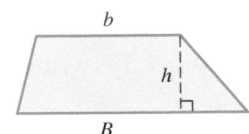

20. $\mathscr{A} = \dfrac{1}{2}h(b + B)$; $\mathscr{A} = 75, b = 19, B = 31$

21. $C = 2\pi r$ (circumference of a circle);
$C = 16.328$

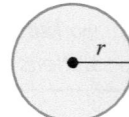

22. $C = 2\pi r$; $C = 8.164$

23. $\mathcal{A} = \pi r^2$ (area of a circle); $r = 4$

24. $\mathcal{A} = \pi r^2$; $r = 12$

*The **volume** of a three-dimensional object is a measure of the space occupied by the object. For example, we would need to know the volume of a gasoline tank in order to know how many gallons of gasoline it would take to completely fill the tank. Volume is measured in cubic units.*

In each exercise, a formula for the volume (V) of a three-dimensional object is given, along with values for the other variables. Evaluate V. (Use 3.14 as an approximation for π.) **See Example 1.**

25. $V = LWH$ (volume of a rectangular box);
$L = 10$, $W = 5$, $H = 3$

26. $V = LWH$; $L = 12$, $W = 8$, $H = 4$

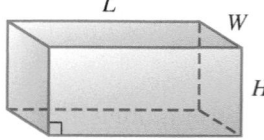

27. $V = \frac{1}{3}Bh$ (volume of a pyramid);
$B = 12$, $h = 13$

28. $V = \frac{1}{3}Bh$; $B = 36$, $h = 4$

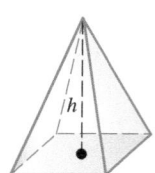

29. $V = \frac{4}{3}\pi r^3$ (volume of a sphere);
$r = 12$

30. $V = \frac{4}{3}\pi r^3$; $r = 6$

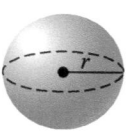

Simple interest I in dollars is calculated using the following formula.

$$I = prt \quad \text{Simple interest formula}$$

Here, p represents the principal, or amount, in dollars that is invested or borrowed, r represents the annual interest rate, expressed as a percent, and t represents time, in years.

In each problem, find the value of the remaining variable in the simple interest formula. **See Example 1.** *(Hint: Write percents as decimals.)*

31. $p = \$7500$, $r = 4\%$, $t = 2$ yr

32. $p = \$3600$, $r = 3\%$, $t = 4$ yr

33. $I = \$33$, $r = 2\%$, $t = 3$ yr

34. $I = \$270$, $r = 5\%$, $t = 6$ yr

35. $I = \$180$, $p = \$4800$, $r = 2.5\%$
(*Hint:* 2.5% written as a decimal is _____ .)

36. $I = \$162$, $p = \$2400$, $r = 1.5\%$
(*Hint:* 1.5% written as a decimal is _____ .)

Solve each problem. **See Examples 2 and 3.**

37. The length of a rectangle is 9 in. more than the width. The perimeter is 54 in. Find the length and the width of the rectangle.

38. The width of a rectangle is 3 ft less than the length. The perimeter is 62 ft. Find the length and the width of the rectangle.

39. The perimeter of a rectangle is 36 m. The length is 2 m more than three times the width. Find the length and the width of the rectangle.

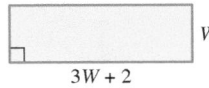

40. The perimeter of a rectangle is 36 yd. The width is 18 yd less than twice the length. Find the length and the width of the rectangle.

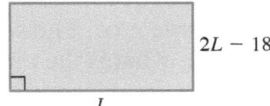

41. The longest side of a triangle is 3 in. longer than the shortest side. The medium side is 2 in. longer than the shortest side. If the perimeter of the triangle is 20 in., what are the lengths of the three sides?

42. The perimeter of a triangle is 28 ft. The medium side is 4 ft longer than the shortest side, while the longest side is twice as long as the shortest side. What are the lengths of the three sides?

43. Two sides of a triangle have the same length. The third side measures 4 m less than twice that length. The perimeter of the triangle is 24 m. Find the lengths of the three sides.

44. A triangle is such that its medium side is twice as long as its shortest side and its longest side is 7 yd less than three times its shortest side. The perimeter of the triangle is 47 yd. Find the lengths of the three sides.

Use a formula to write an equation for each application, and then solve. (Use 3.14 *as an approximation for* π.*)* **Formulas are found at the back of this text.** **See Examples 2–4.**

45. One of the largest fashion catalogues in the world was published in Hamburg, Germany. Each of the 212 pages in the catalogue measured 1.2 m by 1.5 m. What was the perimeter of a page? What was the area? (Data from *Guinness World Records.*)

46. One of the world's largest mandalas (sand paintings) measures 12.24 m by 12.24 m. What is the perimeter of the sand painting? To the nearest hundredth of a square meter, what is the area? (Data from *Guinness World Records.*)

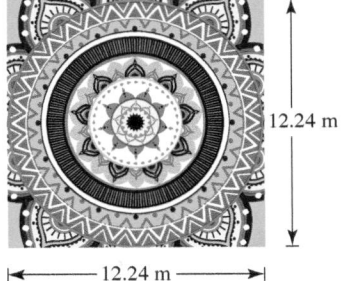

47. The area of a triangular road sign is 70 ft². If the base of the sign measures 14 ft, what is the height of the sign?

48. The area of a triangular advertising banner is 96 ft². If the height of the banner measures 12 ft, find the measure of the base.

49. A prehistoric ceremonial site dating to about 3000 B.C. was discovered at Stanton Drew in southwestern England. The site, which is larger than Stonehenge, is a nearly perfect circle, consisting of nine concentric rings that probably held upright wooden posts. Around this timber temple is a wide, encircling ditch enclosing an area with a diameter of 443 ft. Find this enclosed area to the nearest thousand square feet. (Data from *Archaeology*.)

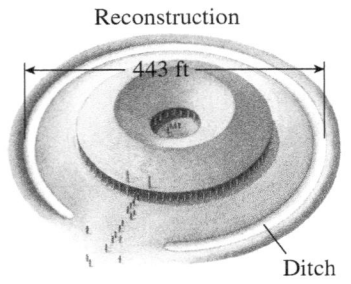

Reconstruction

443 ft

Ditch

50. The Rogers Centre in Toronto, Canada, is the first stadium with a hard-shell, retractable roof. The steel dome is 630 ft in diameter. To the nearest foot, what is the circumference of this dome? (Data from www.ballparks.com)

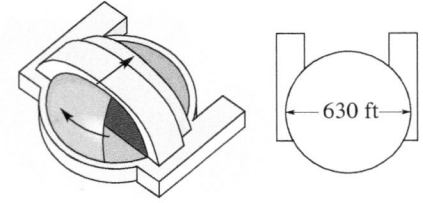

630 ft

51. One of the largest drums ever constructed was made from Japanese cedar and cowhide, with radius 7.87 ft. What was the area of the circular face of the drum? What was the circumference of the drum? Round answers to the nearest hundredth. (Data from *Guinness World Records*.)

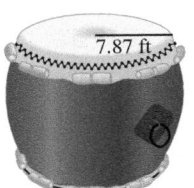

7.87 ft

52. A drum played at the Royal Festival Hall in London had radius 6.5 ft. What was the area of the circular face of the drum? What was the circumference of the drum? (Data from *Guinness World Records*.)

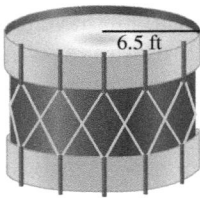

6.5 ft

53. The survey plat depicted here shows two lots that form a trapezoid. The measures of the parallel sides are 115.80 ft and 171.00 ft. The height of the trapezoid is 165.97 ft. Find the combined area of the two lots. Round the answer to the nearest hundredth of a square foot.

54. Lot A in the figure is in the shape of a trapezoid. The parallel sides measure 26.84 ft and 82.05 ft. The height of the trapezoid is 165.97 ft. Find the area of Lot A. Round the answer to the nearest hundredth of a square foot.

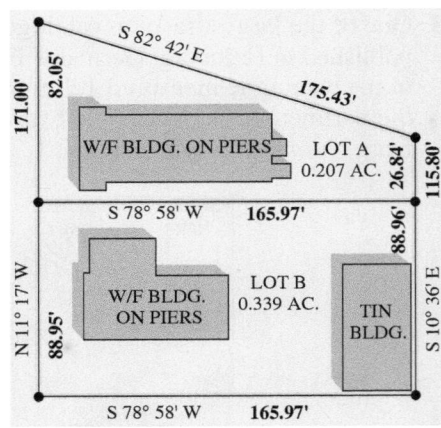

Data from property survey in New Roads, Louisiana.

55. The U.S. Postal Service requires that any box sent by Priority Mail® have length plus girth (distance around) totaling no more than 108 in. The maximum volume that meets this condition is contained by a box with a square end 18 in. on each side. What is the length of the box? What is the maximum volume? (Data from United States Postal Service.)

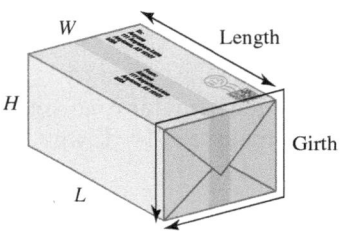

56. One of the world's largest sandwiches, made by Wild Woody's Chill and Grill in Roseville, Michigan, was 12 ft long, 12 ft wide, and $17\frac{1}{2}$ in. ($1\frac{11}{24}$ ft) thick. What was the volume of the sandwich? (Data from *Guinness World Records*.)

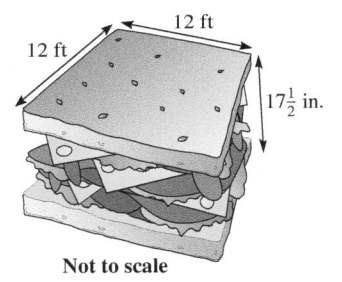

*Find the measure of each marked angle. **See Example 5.***

57.
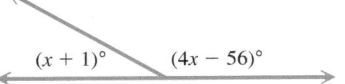
$(x + 1)°$ $(4x − 56)°$

58.
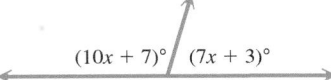
$(10x + 7)°$ $(7x + 3)°$

59.
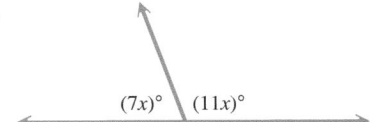
$(7x)°$ $(11x)°$

60.
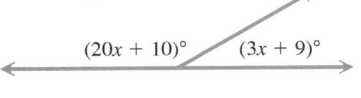
$(20x + 10)°$ $(3x + 9)°$

61.
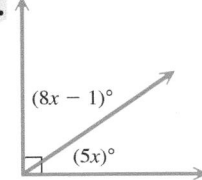
$(8x − 1)°$ $(5x)°$

62.
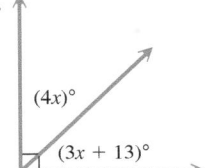
$(4x)°$ $(3x + 13)°$

63.
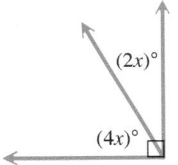
$(2x)°$ $(4x)°$

64.
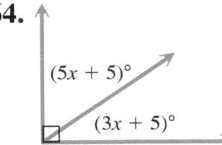
$(5x + 5)°$ $(3x + 5)°$

65.
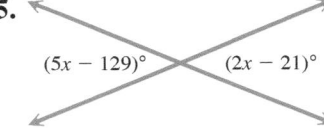
$(5x − 129)°$ $(2x − 21)°$

66.
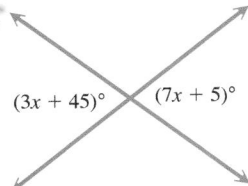
$(3x + 45)°$ $(7x + 5)°$

67.
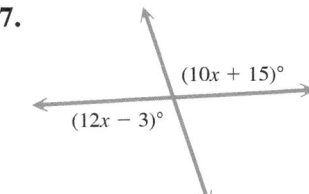
$(10x + 15)°$ $(12x − 3)°$

68.
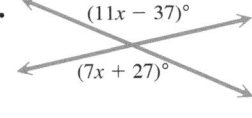
$(11x − 37)°$ $(7x + 27)°$

*Solve each formula for the specified variable. **See Examples 6–8.***

69. $d = rt$ for t

70. $d = rt$ for r

71. $V = LWH$ for H

72. $V = LWH$ for L

73. $P = a + b + c$ for b

74. $P = a + b + c$ for c

75. $C = 2\pi r$ for r

76. $C = \pi d$ for d

77. $I = prt$ for r

78. $I = prt$ for p

79. $\mathcal{A} = \dfrac{1}{2}bh$ for h

80. $\mathcal{A} = \dfrac{1}{2}bh$ for b

81. $V = \dfrac{1}{3}\pi r^2 h$ for h

82. $V = \pi r^2 h$ for h

83. $P = 2L + 2W$ for W

84. $A = p + prt$ for r

85. $y = mx + b$ for m

86. $y = mx + b$ for x

87. $Ax + By = C$ for y

88. $Ax + By = C$ for x

89. $M = C(1 + r)$ for r

90. $A = p(1 + rt)$ for r

91. $P = 2(a + b)$ for a

92. $P = 2(a + b)$ for b

93. $f = a(x - h)$ for x

94. $f = a(x - h)$ for h

95. $S = \dfrac{1}{2}(a + b + c)$ for b

96. $S = \dfrac{1}{2}(a + b + c)$ for c

97. $C = \dfrac{5}{9}(F - 32)$ for F

98. $\mathcal{A} = \dfrac{1}{2}h(b + B)$ for b

Solve each equation for y. ***See Example 9.***

99. $6x + y = 4$

100. $3x + y = 6$

101. $5x - y = 2$

102. $4x - y = 1$

103. $-3x + 5y = -15$

104. $-2x + 3y = -9$

105. $x - 3y = 12$

106. $x - 5y = 10$

Relating Concepts (Exercises 107–110) For Individual or Group Work

The climax of any sports season is the playoffs. Baseball fans eagerly debate predictions of which team will win the pennant for their division. The magic number for each first-place team is often reported in media outlets. The **magic number** (sometimes called the **elimination number**) is the combined number of wins by the first-place team and losses by the second-place team that would clinch the title for the first-place team.

To calculate the magic number, consider the following conditions.

The number of wins for the first-place team (W_1) plus the magic number (M) is one more than the sum of the number of wins to date (W_2) and the number of games remaining in the season (N_2) for the second-place team.

Work Exercises 107–110 in order, to see the relationships among these concepts.

107. Use the variable definitions to write an equation involving the magic number.

108. Solve the equation from **Exercise 107** for the magic number M and write a formula for it.

109. The American League standings on September 20, 2015, are shown in the table. There were 162 regulation games in the 2015 season. Find the magic number for each first-place team. The number of games remaining in the season for the second-place team is calculated as

$$N_2 = 162 - (W_2 + L_2),$$

where L_2 represents the number of losses for the second-place team.

(a) AL East: Toronto vs New York

Magic Number _____

(b) AL Central: Kansas City vs Minnesota

Magic Number _____

(c) AL West: Texas vs Houston

Magic Number _____

110. Calculate the magic number for Oakland vs Texas. (Treat Oakland as though it were the second-place team.) How can we interpret the result?

AMERICAN LEAGUE

East	W	L	PCT	GB
Toronto Blue Jays	85	64	.570	—
New York Yankees	82	66	.554	2.5
Baltimore Orioles	73	76	.490	12.0
Tampa Bay Rays	72	77	.483	13.0
Boston Red Sox	71	77	.480	13.5
Central	**W**	**L**	**PCT**	**GB**
Kansas City Royals	87	62	.584	—
Minnesota Twins	76	73	.510	11.0
Cleveland Indians	74	74	.500	12.5
Chicago White Sox	70	78	.473	16.5
Detroit Tigers	69	79	.466	17.5
West	**W**	**L**	**PCT**	**GB**
Texas Rangers	80	69	.537	—
Houston Astros	79	71	.527	1.5
Los Angeles Angels	76	73	.510	4.0
Seattle Mariners	73	77	.487	7.5
Oakland Athletics	64	86	.427	16.5

Data from mlb.com

2.6 Ratio, Proportion, and Percent

OBJECTIVES

1. Write ratios.
2. Solve proportions.
3. Solve applied problems using proportions.
4. Find percents and percentages.

OBJECTIVE **1** Write ratios. A **ratio** is a comparison of two quantities using a quotient.

Ratio

The ratio of the number a to the number b (where $b \neq 0$) is written as follows.

$$a \text{ to } b, \quad a:b, \quad \text{or} \quad \frac{a}{b}$$

Writing a ratio as a quotient $\frac{a}{b}$ is most common in algebra.

Examples: $2 \text{ to } 3, \quad 2:3, \quad \frac{2}{3}$

---

1 Write each ratio.

(a) 9 women to 5 women

EXAMPLE 1 Writing Word Phrases as Ratios

Write a ratio for each word phrase.

(a) 5 hr to 3 hr $\dfrac{5 \text{ hr}}{3 \text{ hr}} = \dfrac{5}{3}$

(b) 6 hr to 3 days

First convert 3 days to hours.

$$3 \text{ days} = 3 \cdot 24 = 72 \text{ hr} \quad 1 \text{ day} = 24 \text{ hr}$$

Now write the ratio using the common unit of measure, hours.

GS (b) 4 in. to 1 ft
First convert 1 ft to ____ in.
Then write a ratio.

$$\frac{6 \text{ hr}}{3 \text{ days}} = \frac{6 \text{ hr}}{72 \text{ hr}} = \frac{6}{72}, \quad \text{or} \quad \frac{1}{12} \quad \text{Write in lowest terms.}$$

◀ Work Problem **1** at the Side.

An application of ratios is in *unit pricing*, to see which size of an item offered in different sizes produces the best price per unit.

EXAMPLE 2 Finding Price per Unit

A Jewel-Osco supermarket charges the following prices for a jar of extra crunchy peanut butter.

(c) 8 months to 2 yr

PEANUT BUTTER

Size	Price
18 oz	$3.49
28 oz	$4.99
40 oz	$6.79

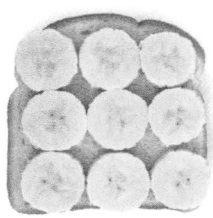 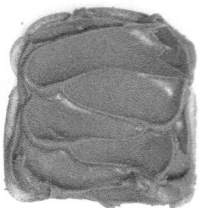

Answers

1. **(a)** $\dfrac{9}{5}$ **(b)** 12; $\dfrac{4}{12}$, or $\dfrac{1}{3}$

   (c) $\dfrac{8}{24}$, or $\dfrac{1}{3}$

Which size is the best buy? That is, which size has the lowest unit price?

Continued on Next Page

To find the best buy, write ratios comparing the price for each size jar to the number of units (ounces) per jar.

PEANUT BUTTER

Size	Price	Unit Price (dollars per ounce)
18 oz	$3.49	$\dfrac{\$3.49}{18} = \$0.194$
28 oz	$4.99	$\dfrac{\$4.99}{28} = \$0.178$
40 oz	$6.79	$\dfrac{\$6.79}{40} = \$0.170$ ← Best buy

To find the price per ounce, the number of ounces goes in the denominator.

(Results are rounded to the nearest thousandth.)

Because the 40-oz size produces the lowest unit price, it is the best buy. Buying the largest size does not always provide the best buy, although it often does, as in this case.

——————— **Work Problem 2 at the Side.** ▶

OBJECTIVE ▶ 2 Solve proportions. A ratio is used to compare two numbers or amounts. A **proportion** says that two ratios are equal. For example, the proportion

$$\frac{3}{4} = \frac{15}{20}$$

A proportion is a special type of equation.

says that the ratios $\frac{3}{4}$ and $\frac{15}{20}$ are equal. In the proportion

$$\frac{a}{b} = \frac{c}{d} \quad (\text{where } b, d \neq 0),$$

a, b, c, and d are the **terms** of the proportion. The a and d terms are the **extremes,** and the b and c terms are the **means.** We read the proportion $\frac{a}{b} = \frac{c}{d}$ as "*a* is to *b* as *c* is to *d*." Multiplying each side of this proportion by the common denominator, bd, gives the following.

$$bd \cdot \frac{a}{b} = bd \cdot \frac{c}{d} \qquad \text{Multiply each side by } bd.$$

$$\frac{b}{b}(d \cdot a) = \frac{d}{d}(b \cdot c) \qquad \text{Associative and commutative properties}$$

$$ad = bc \qquad \text{Commutative and identity properties}$$

We can also find the products ad and bc by multiplying diagonally.

$$ad = bc$$

$$\frac{a}{b} = \frac{c}{d}$$

For this reason, ad and bc are the **cross products of the proportion.**

Cross Products of a Proportion

If $\frac{a}{b} = \frac{c}{d}$, then the cross products ad and bc of the proportion are equal— that is, *the product of the extremes equals the product of the means.*

Also, if $ad = bc$, then $\frac{a}{b} = \frac{c}{d}$ (where $b, d \neq 0$).

2 Solve each problem.

(a) A supermarket charges the following prices for a popular brand of pork and beans.

PORK AND BEANS

Size	Price
8 oz	$0.76
28 oz	$1.00
53 oz	$1.99

Calculate the unit price to the nearest thousandth for each size.

8 oz: $\dfrac{\$0.76}{\rule{1cm}{0.4pt}} = \underline{\hspace{1cm}}$

28 oz: $\dfrac{\rule{1cm}{0.4pt}}{28} = \underline{\hspace{1cm}}$

53 oz: $\dfrac{\rule{1cm}{0.4pt}}{\rule{1cm}{0.4pt}} = \underline{\hspace{1cm}}$

Which size is the best buy? What is the unit price for that size?

(b) A supermarket charges the following prices for a certain brand of laundry detergent.

LAUNDRY DETERGENT

Size	Price
75 oz	$8.94
100 oz	$13.97
150 oz	$19.97

Which size is the best buy? What is the unit price to the nearest thousandth for that size?

Answers

2. **(a)** 8; $0.095; $1.00; $0.036; $1.99; 53; $0.038; 28 oz; $0.036 per oz
(b) 75 oz; $0.119 per oz

3 Solve each proportion.

GS **(a)** $\dfrac{y}{6} = \dfrac{35}{42}$

$y \cdot \underline{\hspace{1cm}} = \underline{\hspace{1cm}} \cdot 35$

$\underline{\hspace{1cm}} y = \underline{\hspace{1cm}}$

$y = \underline{\hspace{1cm}}$

The solution set is ____.

(b) $\dfrac{a}{24} = \dfrac{15}{16}$

Note

If $\dfrac{a}{c} = \dfrac{b}{d}$, then $ad = cb$, or $ad = bc$. This means that the two proportions are equivalent, and the proportion

$$\dfrac{a}{b} = \dfrac{c}{d} \quad \text{can also be written as} \quad \dfrac{a}{c} = \dfrac{b}{d} \quad \text{(where } c, d \neq 0\text{)}.$$

Sometimes one form is more convenient to work with than the other.

Four numbers are used in a proportion. If any three of these numbers are known, the fourth can be found.

EXAMPLE 3 **Finding an Unknown in a Proportion**

Solve the proportion $\frac{5}{9} = \frac{x}{63}$.

$$\dfrac{5}{9} = \dfrac{x}{63} \quad \boxed{\text{Solve for } x.}$$

$5 \cdot 63 = 9 \cdot x$ Cross products must be equal.

$315 = 9x$ Multiply.

$35 = x$ Divide by 9.

Check by substituting 35 for x in the proportion. The solution set is $\{35\}$.

◀ **Work Problem 3** at the Side.

---

4 Solve each equation.

(a) $\dfrac{z}{2} = \dfrac{z+1}{3}$

! **CAUTION**

The cross-product method cannot be used directly if there is more than one term on either side of the equality symbol.

$$\underbrace{\dfrac{m-1}{5} = \dfrac{m+1}{3} - 4,}_{\text{2 terms}} \qquad \underbrace{\dfrac{x}{3} + \dfrac{5}{4} = \dfrac{1}{2}}_{\text{2 terms}}$$

Do **not** use the cross-product method to solve equations in this form.

(b) $\dfrac{p+3}{3} = \dfrac{p-5}{4}$

EXAMPLE 4 **Solving an Equation Using Cross Products**

Solve the equation $\frac{m-2}{5} = \frac{m+1}{3}$.

$$\dfrac{m-2}{5} = \dfrac{m+1}{3} \quad \boxed{\text{Be sure to use parentheses.}}$$

$3(m-2) = 5(m+1)$ (*)   Cross products

$3m - 6 = 5m + 5$ Distributive property

$-2m - 6 = 5$ Subtract $5m$.

$-2m = 11$ Add 6.

$m = -\dfrac{11}{2}$ Divide by -2.

Check to confirm that the solution set is $\left\{-\frac{11}{2}\right\}$.

◀ **Work Problem 4** at the Side.

Answers

3. (a) 42; 6; 42; 210; 5; $\{5\}$ **(b)** $\left\{\dfrac{45}{2}\right\}$

4. (a) $\{2\}$ **(b)** $\{-27\}$

Note

When we set cross products equal to each other, we are actually multiplying each ratio in the proportion by a common denominator.

$$\frac{m-2}{5} = \frac{m+1}{3}$$ See **Example 4.**

$$15\left(\frac{m-2}{5}\right) = 15\left(\frac{m+1}{3}\right)$$ Multiply each ratio by 15, the LCD.

$$15\left(\frac{m-2}{5}\right)$$
$$= 15 \cdot \frac{1}{5}(m-2)$$
$$= 3(m-2)$$

$$3(m-2) = 5(m+1)$$ This is equation (*) from **Example 4.**

OBJECTIVE ❸ **Solve applied problems using proportions.**

EXAMPLE 5 **Applying Proportions**

After Lee Ann pumped 5.0 gal of gasoline, the display showing the price read $15.50. When she finished pumping the gasoline, the price display read $44.95. How many gallons did she pump?

To solve this problem, set up a proportion, with prices in the numerators and gallons in the denominators. Let x = the number of gallons pumped.

Price → $$\frac{\$15.50}{5.0} = \frac{\$44.95}{x}$$ ← Price
Gallons → ← Gallons

Be sure that numerators represent the *same* quantities and denominators represent the *same* quantities.

$$15.50x = 5.0(44.95)$$ Cross products
$$15.50x = 224.75$$ Multiply.
$$x = 14.5$$ Divide by 15.50.

She pumped a total of 14.5 gal. Check this answer. Notice that the way the proportion was set up uses the fact that the unit price is the same, no matter how many gallons are purchased.

—————— **Work Problem ❺ at the Side.** ▶

OBJECTIVE ❹ **Find percents and percentages.** *A percent is a ratio where the second number is always 100.*

50% represents the ratio of 50 to 100, that is, $\frac{50}{100}$, or, **0.50**.

27% represents the ratio of 27 to 100, that is, $\frac{27}{100}$, or, **0.27**.

The word **percent** means **"per 100."** One percent means "one per 100."

$$1\% = \frac{1}{100}, \quad \text{or} \quad 1\% = 0.01$$ Percent, decimal, and fraction equivalents

We can solve a percent problem involving $x\%$ by writing it as a proportion. The amount, or **percentage,** is compared to the **base** (the whole amount).

$$\frac{\text{amount}}{\text{base}} = \frac{x}{100}$$

We can also write this proportion as follows.

$$\frac{\text{amount}}{\text{base}} = \text{percent (as a decimal)}$$ $\frac{x}{100}$ or $0.01x$ is equivalent to x percent.

amount = percent (as a decimal) • base Basic percent equation

❺ Solve each problem.

(a) Twelve gallons of diesel fuel costs $40.80. To the nearest cent, how much would 16.5 gal of the same fuel cost?

(b) Eight quarts of oil cost $14.00. How much do 5 qt of oil cost?

Answers
5. **(a)** $56.10 **(b)** $8.75

6 Solve each problem.

(a) What is 20% of 70?

(b) 40% of what number is 130?

(c) 121 is what percent of 484?

7 Solve each problem.

(a) A winter coat is on a clearance sale for $48. The regular price is $120. What percent of the regular price is the savings?

GS (b) Mark scored 34 points on a test, which was 85% of the possible points. How many possible points were on the test?

Write the percent equation. Give the percent as a decimal.

$$\begin{array}{ccccc} & & & & \text{what} \\ 34 & \text{was} & 85\% & \text{of} & \text{number?} \\ \downarrow & \downarrow & \downarrow & \downarrow & \downarrow \\ 34 & \_\_\_ & \_\_\_ & \_\_\_ & n \end{array}$$

Complete the solution, and give the answer to the problem.

EXAMPLE 6   Solving Percent Equations

Solve each problem.

(a) What is 15% of 600?

Let n = the number. The word *of* indicates multiplication.

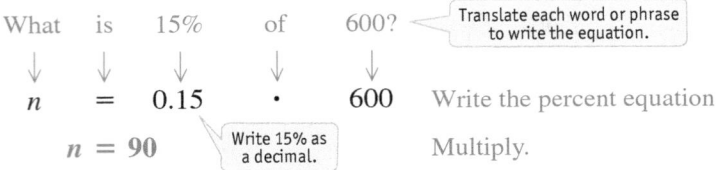

$$\begin{array}{ccccc} \text{What} & \text{is} & 15\% & \text{of} & 600? \\ \downarrow & \downarrow & \downarrow & \downarrow & \downarrow \\ n & = & 0.15 & \cdot & 600 \end{array}$$ Write the percent equation.

$n = 90$ Multiply. (Write 15% as a decimal.)

Thus, **90** is 15% of 600.

(b) 32% of what number is 64?

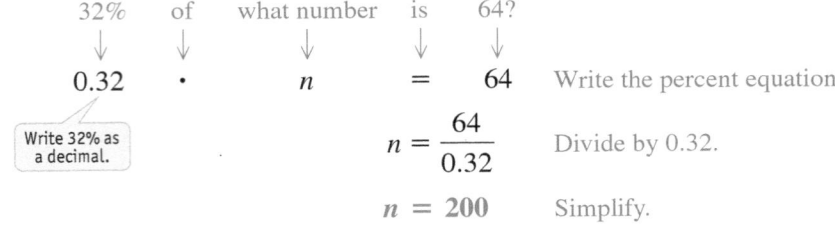

$$\begin{array}{ccccc} 32\% & \text{of} & \text{what number} & \text{is} & 64? \\ \downarrow & \downarrow & \downarrow & \downarrow & \downarrow \\ 0.32 & \cdot & n & = & 64 \end{array}$$ Write the percent equation.

(Write 32% as a decimal.)

$n = \dfrac{64}{0.32}$ Divide by 0.32.

$n = 200$ Simplify.

32% of **200** is 64.

(c) 90 is what percent of 360?

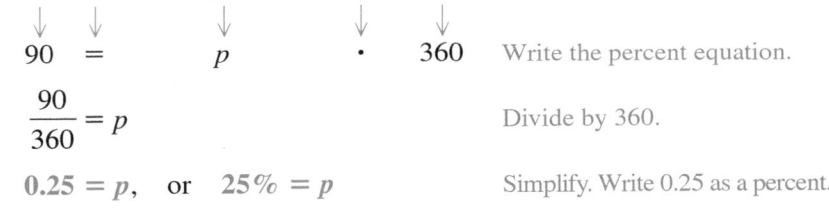

$$\begin{array}{ccccc} 90 & \text{is} & \text{what percent} & \text{of} & 360? \\ \downarrow & \downarrow & \downarrow & \downarrow & \downarrow \\ 90 & = & p & \cdot & 360 \end{array}$$ Write the percent equation.

$\dfrac{90}{360} = p$ Divide by 360.

$0.25 = p,$ or $25\% = p$ Simplify. Write 0.25 as a percent.

Thus, 90 is **25%** of 360.

◀ **Work Problem 6 at the Side**

EXAMPLE 7   Solving an Applied Percent Problem

A newspaper ad offered a set of tires at a sale price of $258. The regular price was $300. What percent of the regular price was the savings?

The savings amounted to $300 − $258 = $42. We can now restate the problem: *What percent of* 300 *is* 42?

$$\begin{array}{ccccc} \text{What percent} & \text{of} & 300 & \text{is} & 42? \\ \downarrow & \downarrow & \downarrow & \downarrow & \downarrow \\ p & \cdot & 300 & = & 42 \end{array}$$ Write the percent equation.

$p = \dfrac{42}{300}$ Divide by 300.

$p = 0.14,$ or 14% Simplify. Write 0.14 as a percent.

The sale price represents a 14% savings.

◀ **Work Problem 7 at the Side**

Answers

6. (a) 14 (b) 325 (c) 25%

7. (a) 60% (b) =; 0.85; ·; 40 points

2.6 Exercises

FOR EXTRA HELP   *Go to* MyMathLab *for worked-out, step-by-step solutions to exercises enclosed in a square* ☐ *and video solutions to* ▶ *exercises.*

1. CONCEPT CHECK Ratios are used to _____ two numbers or quantities. Which of the following indicate the ratio of *a* to *b*?

   A. $\dfrac{a}{b}$ **B.** $\dfrac{b}{a}$ **C.** $a \cdot b$ **D.** $a : b$

2. CONCEPT CHECK A proportion says that two _____ are equal. The equation

$$\frac{a}{b} = \frac{c}{d} \quad \text{(where } b, d \neq 0\text{)}$$

is a _____ , where *ad* and *bc* are the _____ .

3. CONCEPT CHECK Match each ratio in Column I with the ratio equivalent to it in Column II.

I	II
(a) 75 to 100	**A.** 80 to 100
(b) 5 to 4	**B.** 50 to 100
(c) $\dfrac{1}{2}$	**C.** 3 to 4
(d) 4 to 5	**D.** 15 to 12

4. CONCEPT CHECK Which of the following represent a ratio of 4 days to 2 weeks?

   A. $\dfrac{4}{2}$ **B.** $\dfrac{4}{7}$ **C.** $\dfrac{4}{14}$ **D.** $\dfrac{2}{1}$

   E. $\dfrac{2}{7}$ **F.** $\dfrac{1}{2}$ **G.** $\dfrac{2}{4}$ **H.** $\dfrac{7}{2}$

Write a ratio for each word phrase. Express fractions in lowest terms. ***See Example 1.***

5. 60 ft to 70 ft

6. 30 mi to 40 mi

7. 72 dollars to 220 dollars ▶

8. 80 people to 120 people

9. 30 in. to 8 ft

10. 8 ft to 20 yd

11. 16 min to 1 hr ▶

12. 24 min to 2 hr

13. 2 yd to 60 in.

14. 3 days to 40 hr

Find the best buy for each item. Give the unit price to the nearest thousandth for that size. ***See Example 2.*** *(Data from Jewel-Osco and HyVee.)*

15. GRANULATED SUGAR

Size	Price
4 lb	$3.29
10 lb	$7.49

16. APPLESAUCE

Size	Price
23 oz	$1.99
48 oz	$3.49

17. ORANGE JUICE

Size	Price
64 oz	$2.99
89 oz	$4.79
128 oz	$6.49

18. SALAD DRESSING

Size	Price
8 oz	$1.69
16 oz	$1.97
36 oz	$5.99

19. MAPLE SYRUP

Size	Price
8.5 oz	$5.79
12.5 oz	$7.99
32 oz	$16.99

20. MOUTHWASH

Size	Price
16.9 oz	$3.39
33.8 oz	$3.49
50.7 oz	$5.29

21. TOMATO KETCHUP

Size	Price
32 oz	$1.79
36 oz	$2.69
40 oz	$2.49
64 oz	$4.38

22. GRAPE JELLY

Size	Price
1 lb	$0.79
2 lb	$1.49
5 lb	$3.59
20 lb	$12.99

Solve each equation. ***See Examples 3 and 4.***

23. $\dfrac{k}{4} = \dfrac{175}{20}$

24. $\dfrac{x}{6} = \dfrac{18}{4}$

25. $\dfrac{49}{56} = \dfrac{z}{8}$

26. $\dfrac{20}{100} = \dfrac{z}{80}$

27. $\dfrac{x}{4} = \dfrac{12}{30}$

28. $\dfrac{x}{6} = \dfrac{5}{21}$

29. $\dfrac{8}{12} = \dfrac{12k}{18}$

30. $\dfrac{14}{10} = \dfrac{21t}{15}$

31. $\dfrac{z}{4} = \dfrac{z+1}{6}$

32. $\dfrac{m}{5} = \dfrac{m-2}{2}$

33. $\dfrac{3y-2}{5} = \dfrac{6y-5}{11}$

34. $\dfrac{2r+8}{4} = \dfrac{3r-9}{3}$

35. $\dfrac{5k+1}{6} = \dfrac{3k-2}{3}$

36. $\dfrac{x+4}{6} = \dfrac{x+10}{8}$

37. $\dfrac{2p+7}{3} = \dfrac{p-1}{4}$

38. $\dfrac{3m-2}{5} = \dfrac{4-m}{3}$

Solve each problem. ***See Example 5.***

39. If 16 candy bars cost $20.00, how much do 24 candy bars cost?

40. If 12 ring tones cost $30.00, how much do 8 ring tones cost?

41. If 6 gal of premium gasoline cost $22.74, how much would it cost to completely fill a 15-gal tank?

42. If sales tax on a $16.00 DVD is $1.32, how much would the sales tax be on a $120.00 DVD player?

43. Biologists tagged 500 fish in Grand Bay. At a later date, they found 7 tagged fish in a sample of 700. Estimate the total number of fish in Grand Bay to the nearest hundred.

44. Researchers at West Okoboji Lake tagged 840 fish. A later sample of 1000 fish contained 18 that were tagged. Approximate the fish population in West Okoboji Lake to the nearest hundred.

45. The distance between Kansas City, Missouri, and Denver is 600 mi. On a certain wall map, this is represented by a length of 2.4 ft. On the map, how many feet would there be between Memphis and Philadelphia, two cities that are actually 1000 mi apart?

46. The distance between Singapore and Tokyo is 3300 mi. On a certain wall map, this distance is represented by a length of 11 in. The actual distance between Mexico City and Cairo is 7700 mi. How far apart are they on the same map to the nearest tenth?

47. A wall map of the United States has a distance of 8.0 in. between New Orleans and Chicago, two cities that are actually 912 mi apart. The actual distance between Milwaukee and Seattle is 1940 mi. How far apart on this map are Milkwaukee and Seattle?

48. On a world globe, the distance between Capetown and Bangkok, two cities that are actually 10,080 km apart, is 12.4 in. The actual distance between Moscow and Berlin is 1610 km. How far apart on this globe are Moscow and Berlin?

49. According to the directions on the label of a bottle of Armstrong® Concentrated Floor Cleaner, for routine cleaning, $\frac{1}{4}$ cup of cleaner should be mixed with 1 gal of warm water. How much cleaner should be mixed with $10\frac{1}{2}$ gal of water?

50. The directions on the bottle mentioned in **Exercise 49** also specify that, for extra-strength cleaning, $\frac{1}{2}$ cup of cleaner should be used for each 1 gal of water. For extra-strength cleaning, how much cleaner should be mixed with $15\frac{1}{2}$ gal of water?

51. On January 18, 2016, the exchange rate between euros and U.S. dollars was 1 euro to $1.0889. Ashley went to Rome and exchanged her U.S. currency for euros, receiving 300 euros. How much in U.S. dollars did she exchange? (Data from www.exchange-rates.org)

52. If 12 U.S. dollars can be exchanged for 218.64 Mexican pesos, how many pesos can be obtained for $100?

*Two triangles are **similar** if they have the same shape (but not necessarily the same size). Similar triangles have sides that are proportional. The figure shows two similar triangles. Notice that the ratios of the corresponding sides all equal $\frac{3}{2}$.*

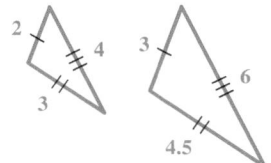

$$\frac{3}{2} = \frac{3}{2} \qquad \frac{4.5}{3} = \frac{3}{2} \qquad \frac{6}{4} = \frac{3}{2}$$

If we know that two triangles are similar, we can set up a proportion to solve for the length of an unknown side.
  Find the lengths x and y as needed in each pair of similar triangles.

53.

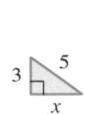 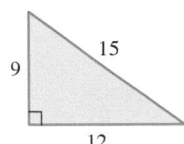

Complete the proportion and then solve for x.

$$\frac{x}{12} = \frac{3}{\underline{\quad}}$$

54.

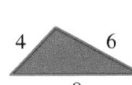 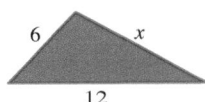

Complete the proportion and then solve for x.

$$\frac{x}{6} = \frac{12}{\underline{\quad}}$$

55.

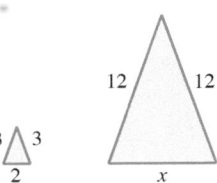

56.

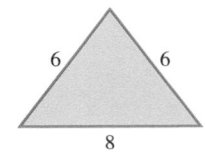

57.

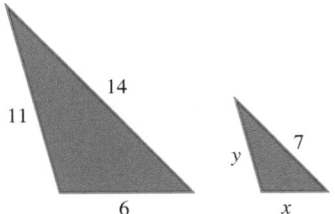

58.

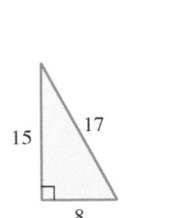 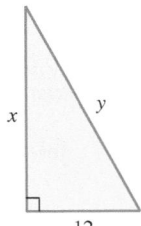

(GS) *Use the information in each problem to complete the diagram of similar triangles. Then write a proportion and solve the problem.*

59. An enlarged version of the chair used by George Washington at the Constitutional Convention casts a shadow 18 ft long at the same time a vertical pole 12 ft high casts a shadow 4 ft long. How tall is the chair?

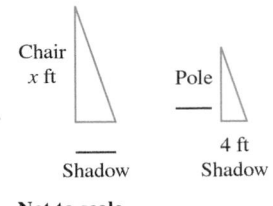

60. One of the tallest candles ever constructed was exhibited at the 1897 Stockholm Exhibition. If it cast a shadow 5 ft long at the same time a vertical pole 32 ft high cast a shadow 2 ft long, how tall was the candle?

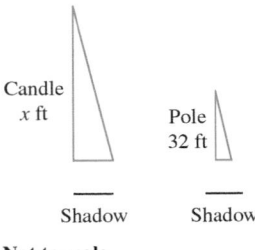

(GS) *Children are often given antibiotics in liquid form, called an oral suspension. Pharmacists make up these suspensions by mixing the medication in powder form with water. They use proportions to calculate the volume of the suspension for the amount of medication that has been prescribed. For each problem, do each of the following.*

(a) Find the total amount of medication in milligrams to be given over the full course of treatment.

(b) Write a proportion that can be solved to find the total volume of the liquid suspension that the pharmacist will prepare. Use x as the variable.

(c) Solve the proportion to determine the total volume of the oral suspension.

61. Logan's pediatric nurse practitioner has prescribed 375 mg of amoxil a day for 7 days to treat an infection. The pharmacist uses 125 mg of amoxil in each 5 mL of the suspension. (Data from www.drugs.com)

62. An amoxil oral suspension can also be made by using 250 mg for each 5 mL of suspension. Ava's pediatrician prescribed 900 mg a day for 10 days to treat her bronchitis. (Data from www.drugs.com)

The Consumer Price Index (CPI) provides a means of determining the purchasing power of the U.S. dollar from one year to the next. Using the period from 1982 to 1984 as a measure of 100.0, the CPI for selected years from 2002 to 2014 is shown in the table. To use the CPI to predict a price in a particular year, we set up a proportion and compare it with a known price in another year.

$$\frac{\text{price in year } A}{\text{index in year } A} = \frac{\text{price in year } B}{\text{index in year } B}$$

Use the CPI figures in the table to find the amount that would be charged for using the same amount of electricity that cost $225 in 2002. Give answers to the nearest dollar.

Year	Consumer Price Index
2002	179.9
2004	188.9
2006	201.6
2008	215.3
2010	218.1
2012	229.6
2014	236.7

Data from U.S. Bureau of Labor Statistics.

63. in 2004   **64.** in 2006   **65.** in 2010   **66.** in 2014

Solve each problem. See Examples 6 and 7.

67. What is 14% of 780?

68. What is 26% of 480?

69. What is 120% of 45?

70. What is 150% of 78?

71. 42% of what number is 294?

72. 18% of what number is 108?

73. 120% of what number is 510?

74. 140% of what number is 315?

75. 4 is what percent of 50?

76. 8 is what percent of 64?

77. What percent of 30 is 36?

78. What percent of 48 is 96?

79. Clayton earned 48 points on a 60-point geometry project. What percent of the total points did he earn?

80. On a 75-point algebra test, Grady scored 63 points. What percent of the total points did he score?

81. A laptop computer that has a regular price of $700 is on sale for $504. What percent of the regular price is the savings?

82. An all-in-one desktop computer that has a regular price of $980 is on sale for $833. What percent of the regular price is the savings?

83. Tyler has a monthly income of $1500. His rent is $480 per month. What percent of his monthly income is his rent?

84. Lily has a monthly income of $2200. She has budgeted $154 per month for entertainment. What percent of her monthly income did she budget for entertainment?

85. Anna saved $1950, which was 65% of the total amount she needed for a used car. What was the total amount she needed for the car?

86. Bryn had $525, which was 70% of the total amount she needed for a deposit on an apartment. What was the total deposit she needed?

Work each percent problem. Round all money amounts to the nearest dollar and percents to the nearest tenth, as needed. See Examples 5–7.

87. A family of four with a monthly income of $3800 plans to spend 8% of this amount on entertainment. How much will be spent on entertainment?

88. George earns $3200 per month. He saves 12% of this amount. How much does he save?

89. In 2014, the U.S. civilian labor force consisted of
155,922,000 persons. Of this total, 9,617,000 were
unemployed. What percent of the U.S. civilian labor
force was unemployed? (Data from U.S. Bureau of
Labor Statistics.)

The number unemployed	was	what percent	of	the total civilian labor force?
↓	↓	↓	↓	↓
_____	=	p	____	_____

90. In 2014, the U.S. civilian labor force consisted of
155,922,000 persons. Of this total, 2,237,000 were
employed in agricultural industries. What percent
were employed in agricultural industries? (Data from
U.S. Bureau of Labor Statistics.)

What percent	of	the total U.S. labor force	was	employed in agriculture?
↓	↓	↓	↓	↓
p	____	_____	=	_____

91. In 2015, U.S. households owned 312,100,000 pets.
Of these, 77,800,000 were dogs. What percent of the
pets were *not* dogs? (Data from American Pet Product
Manufacturers Association.)

92. Of the 1.79 million bachelor's degrees earned in
2011–12, 20.4% were earned in business. How many
degrees earned were *not* in business? (Data from
National Center for Education Statistics.)

93. The 1916 dime minted in Denver is quite rare. The
1979 edition of *A Guide Book of United States Coins*
listed its value in Extremely Fine condition as $625.
The 2015 value had increased to $6000. What was the
percent increase in the value of this coin? (*Hint:* First
subtract to find the increase in value. Then write a
percent equation that uses this increase.)

94. Here is a common business problem:

If the sales tax rate is 6.5% and we have collected
$3400 in sales tax, how much were sales?

(*Hint:* To solve using a percent equation, ask "6.5%
of what number is $3400?" Write 6.5% as a decimal.)

Relating Concepts (Exercises 95–98) For Individual or Group Work

*Work Exercises 95–98 in order. The steps justify the method of solving a proportion
using cross products.*

95. What is the LCD of the fractions in the following
equation?

$$\frac{x}{6} = \frac{2}{5}$$

96. Solve the equation in **Exercise 95** as follows.

   (a) Multiply each side by the LCD. What equation
results?

   (b) Solve the equation from part (a) by dividing
each side by the coefficient of x.

97. Solve the equation in **Exercise 95** using cross
products.

98. Compare the answers from **Exercises 96(b) and 97.**
What do you notice?

Summary Exercises *Applying Problem-Solving Techniques*

The following problems are of the various types discussed in this chapter. Solve each problem.

1. On an algebra test, the highest grade was 42 points more than the lowest grade. The sum of the two grades was 138. Find the lowest grade.

2. Find the measure of an angle whose supplement is 35° more than twice its complement.

3. If 2 is added to five times a number, the result is equal to 5 more than four times the number. Find the number.

4. Find two consecutive even integers such that four times the greater added to the lesser is 98.

5. Find the measures of the marked angles.

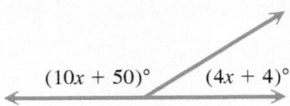

$(10x + 50)°$ $(4x + 4)°$

6. Find the measures of the marked angles.

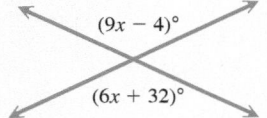

$(9x − 4)°$

$(6x + 32)°$

7. The perimeter of a certain square is seven times the length of a side, decreased by 12. Find the length of a side.

8. A store has 39 qt of milk, some in pint cartons and some in quart cartons. There are six times as many quart cartons as pint cartons. How many quart cartons are there? (*Hint:* 1 qt = 2 pt)

9. A music player that normally sells for $90 is on sale for $75. What is the percent discount on the player?

10. Two slices of bacon contain 85 calories. How many calories are there in twelve slices of bacon?

11. Athletes in vigorous training programs can eat 50 calories per day for every 2.2 lb of body weight. To the nearest hundred, how many calories can a 175 lb athlete consume per day? (Data from *The Gazette*.)

12. In the 2012 Summer Olympics in London, England, the United States won 16 more medals than China, and Russia won 6 fewer medals than China. The total number of medals won by the United States, China, and Russia was 274. How many medals did each country win? (Data from: www.espn.go.com)

13. Find the best buy (based on price per unit). Give the unit price to the nearest thousandth for that size. (Data from HyVee.)

SPAGHETTI SAUCE

Size	Price
14 oz	$1.79
24 oz	$1.77
48 oz	$3.65

14. A fully inflated professional basketball has a circumference of 78 cm. What is the radius of a circular cross section through the center of the ball? (Use 3.14 as the approximation for π.) Round the answer to the nearest hundredth.

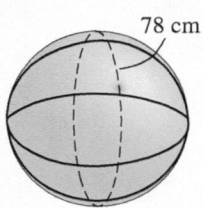

78 cm

2.7 | Solving Linear Inequalities

OBJECTIVES

1. Graph intervals on a number line.
2. Use the addition property of inequality.
3. Use the multiplication property of inequality.
4. Solve linear inequalities.
5. Solve applied problems using inequalities.
6. Solve linear inequalities with three parts.

An **inequality** relates algebraic expressions using the symbols

$<$ "is less than," $\le$ "is less than or equal to,"

$>$ "is greater than," $\ge$ "is greater than or equal to."

In each case, the interpretation is based on reading the symbol from left to right.

Linear Inequality in One Variable

A **linear inequality in one variable** (here x) can be written in the form

$$Ax + B < C, \quad Ax + B \le C, \quad Ax + B > C, \quad \text{or} \quad Ax + B \ge C,$$

where A, B, and C represent real numbers and $A \ne 0$.

Examples: $x + 5 < 2$, $z - \dfrac{3}{4} \ge 5$, and $2k + 5 \le 10$ Linear inequalities

---

We solve a linear inequality by finding all of its real number solutions. For example, the set

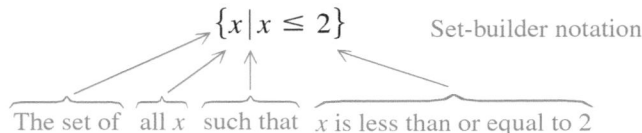

{x | x ≤ 2}   Set-builder notation

The set of   all x such that x is less than or equal to 2

includes *all real numbers* that are less than or equal to 2, not just the *integers* less than or equal to 2.

OBJECTIVE ▶ 1 Graph intervals on a number line. Graphing is a good way to show the solution set of an inequality. To graph all real numbers belonging to the set

$$\{x \mid x \le 2\},$$

we place a square bracket at 2 on a number line and draw an arrow extending from the bracket to the left (because all numbers *less than* 2 are also part of the graph). See **Figure 15**.

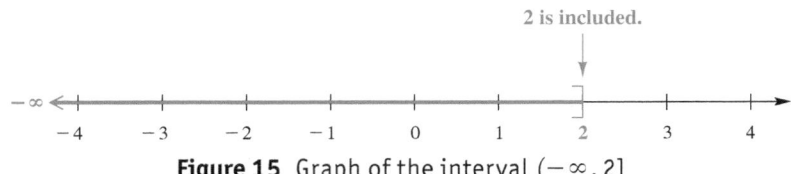

Figure 15 Graph of the interval $(-\infty, 2]$

The set of numbers less than or equal to 2 is an example of an **interval** on a number line. We can write this interval using **interval notation** as follows.

$$(-\infty, 2]$$ Interval notation

The **negative infinity symbol** $-\infty$ here does not indicate a number, but shows that the interval includes *all* real numbers less than 2. Again, the square bracket indicates that 2 is part of the solution. Intervals that continue indefinitely in the positive direction are written with the **positive infinity symbol** ∞.

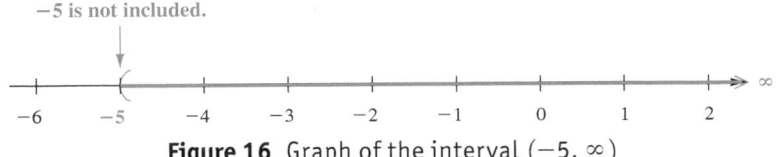

EXAMPLE 1 Graphing an Interval on a Number Line

Write the inequality $x > -5$ in interval notation, and graph the interval.

Here x can represent any value greater than -5 but *cannot* equal -5, written $(-5, \infty)$. We place a parenthesis at -5 and draw an arrow to the right, as in **Figure 16**. The parenthesis indicates that -5 is *not* part of the graph.

−5 is not included.

Figure 16 Graph of the interval $(-5, \infty)$

— Work Problem ❶ at the Side. ▶

Important Concepts Regarding Interval Notation

1. A parenthesis indicates that an endpoint is *not included* in a solution set.
2. A bracket indicates that an endpoint is *included* in a solution set.
3. A parenthesis is *always* used next to an infinity symbol, $-\infty$ or ∞.
4. The set of all real numbers is written in interval notation as $(-\infty, \infty)$.

EXAMPLE 2 Graphing an Interval on a Number Line

Write the inequality $3 > x$ in interval notation, and graph the interval.

The statement $3 > x$ means the same as $x < 3$. ***The inequality symbol continues to point to the lesser value.*** The graph of $x < 3$, written in interval notation as $(-\infty, 3)$, is shown in **Figure 17.**

Figure 17 Graph of the interval $(-\infty, 3)$

— Work Problem ❷ at the Side. ▶

METHODS OF EXPRESSING SOLUTION SETS OF LINEAR INEQUALITIES

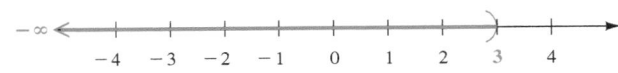

Set-Builder Notation	Interval Notation	Graph
$\{x \mid x < a\}$	$(-\infty, a)$	
$\{x \mid x \le a\}$	$(-\infty, a]$	
$\{x \mid x > a\}$	(a, ∞)	
$\{x \mid x \ge a\}$	$[a, \infty)$	
$\{x \mid x$ is a real number$\}$	$(-\infty, \infty)$	

OBJECTIVE ❷ Use the addition property of inequality. Consider the true inequality $2 < 5$. If 4 is added to each side, the result is also a true statement.

$$2 + 4 < 5 + 4 \quad \text{Add 4.}$$
$$6 < 9 \quad \text{True}$$

This example suggests the **addition property of inequality.**

❶ Write each inequality in interval notation, and graph the interval.

(a) $x \le 3$

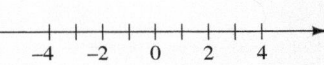

(b) $x > -4$

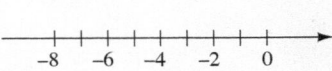

(c) $x \le -\dfrac{3}{4}$

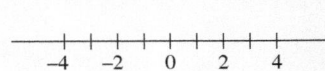

❷ Write each inequality in interval notation and graph the interval.

(a) $-4 \ge x$

(b) $0 < x$

Answers

1. **(a)** $(-\infty, 3]$
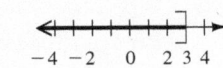
(b) $(-4, \infty)$
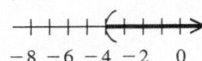
(c) $\left(-\infty, -\dfrac{3}{4}\right]$
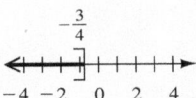

2. **(a)** $(-\infty, -4]$
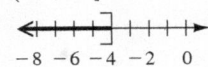
(b) $(0, \infty)$
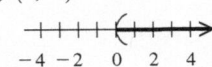

3 Solve each inequality, and graph the solution set.

(a) $-1 + 8r < 7r + 2$

_____→

(b) $5 + 5x \geq 4x + 3$

_____→

Addition Property of Inequality

If A, B, and C represent real numbers, then the inequalities

$$A < B \quad \text{and} \quad A + C < B + C \quad \text{are equivalent.}^*$$

 In words, the same number may be added to each side of an inequality without changing the solution set.

*This also applies to $A \leq B$, $A > B$, and $A \geq B$.

As with the addition property of equality, the same number may be subtracted from each side of an inequality.

EXAMPLE 3 Using the Addition Property of Inequality

Solve $7 + 3x \geq 2x - 5$, and graph the solution set.

$$7 + 3x \geq 2x - 5 \quad \boxed{\text{As with equations, our goal is to isolate } x.}$$

$$7 + 3x - 2x \geq 2x - 5 - 2x \quad \text{Subtract } 2x.$$

$$7 + x \geq -5 \quad \text{Combine like terms.}$$

$$7 + x - 7 \geq -5 - 7 \quad \text{Subtract 7.}$$

$$x \geq -12 \quad \text{Combine like terms.}$$

The solution set is $[-12, \infty)$. Its graph is shown in **Figure 18.**

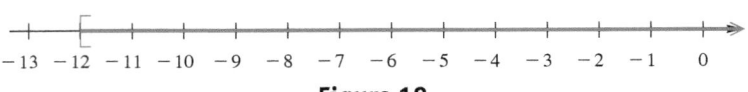

Figure 18

◀ **Work Problem ❸ at the Side.**

Note

Because an inequality has many solutions, we cannot check all of them by substitution as we did with the single solution of an equation. To check the solutions in the interval $[-12, \infty)$ in **Example 3,** we first substitute -12 for x in the related *equation.*

CHECK $\qquad\qquad 7 + 3x = 2x - 5 \qquad$ Related equation

$$7 + 3(-12) \overset{?}{=} 2(-12) - 5 \quad \text{Let } x = -12.$$

$$7 - 36 \overset{?}{=} -24 - 5 \quad \text{Multiply.}$$

$$-29 = -29 \checkmark \quad \text{True}$$

A true statement results, so -12 is indeed the "boundary" point. Now we test a number other than -12 from the interval $[-12, \infty)$. We choose 0.

CHECK $\qquad\qquad 7 + 3x \geq 2x - 5 \qquad$ Original inequality

$$7 + 3(0) \overset{?}{\geq} 2(0) - 5 \quad \text{Let } x = 0.$$

$\boxed{\text{0 is easy to substitute.}}\qquad 7 \geq -5 \checkmark \quad \text{True}$

Again, a true statement results, so the checks confirm that solutions to the inequality are in the interval $[-12, \infty)$. Any number "outside" the interval $[-12, \infty)$, that is, any number in $(-\infty, -12)$, will give a false statement when tested. (Try this with $x = -13$. A false statement, $-32 \geq -31$, results.)

Answers

3. (a) $(-\infty, 3)$

$-4\ -2\quad 0\quad 2\ 3\ 4$

(b) $[-2, \infty)$

$-4\ -2\quad 0\quad 2\quad 4$

OBJECTIVE ▶ ❸ Use the multiplication property of inequality. Consider the true inequality $3 < 7$. Multiply each side by the positive number 2.

$$3 < 7$$
$$\mathbf{2}(3) < \mathbf{2}(7) \qquad \text{Multiply by 2.}$$
$$6 < 14 \qquad \text{True}$$

The result is a true statement. Now multiply each side of $3 < 7$ by the negative number -5.

$$3 < 7$$
$$-\mathbf{5}(3) < -\mathbf{5}(7) \qquad \text{Multiply by } -5.$$
$$-15 < -35 \qquad \text{False}$$

To obtain a true statement when multiplying each side by -5, *we must reverse the direction of the inequality symbol.*

$$3 < 7$$
$$-\mathbf{5}(3) > -\mathbf{5}(7) \qquad \begin{array}{l}\text{Multiply by } -5. \text{ Reverse the}\\ \text{direction of the symbol.}\end{array}$$
$$-15 > -35 \qquad \text{True}$$

Work Problem ❹ at the Side. ▶

These examples suggest the **multiplication property of inequality.**

Multiplication Property of Inequality

Let A, B, and C represent real numbers, where $C \neq 0$.

1. If C is **positive**, then the inequalities

$$A < B \quad \text{and} \quad AC < BC \quad \text{are equivalent.*}$$

2. If C is **negative**, then the inequalities

$$A < B \quad \text{and} \quad AC > BC \quad \text{are equivalent.*}$$

In words, each side of an inequality may be multiplied by the same positive number without changing the direction of the inequality symbol. *If the multiplier is negative, we must reverse the direction of the inequality symbol.*

*This also applies to $A \leq B$, $A > B$, and $A \geq B$.

As with the multiplication property of equality, the same nonzero number may be divided into each side.

Note the following differences for positive and negative numbers.

1. When each side of an inequality is multiplied or divided by a *positive number,* the direction of the inequality symbol *does not change.*

2. When each side of an inequality is multiplied or divided by a *negative number, reverse the direction of the inequality symbol.*

❹ Work each of the following.

(a) Multiply each side of

$$-3 < 7$$

by 2 and then by -5. Reverse the direction of the inequality symbol if necessary to make a true statement.

(b) Multiply each side of

$$3 > -7$$

by 2 and then by -5. Reverse the direction of the inequality symbol if necessary to make a true statement.

(c) Multiply each side of

$$-7 < -3$$

by 2 and then by -5. Reverse the direction of the inequality symbol if necessary to make a true statement.

Answers

4. (a) $-6 < 14$; $15 > -35$
(b) $6 > -14$; $-15 < 35$
(c) $-14 < -6$; $35 > 15$

5 Solve each inequality, and graph the solution set.

(a) $9x < -18$

$$\frac{9x}{9} \; (</>) \; \frac{-18}{\underline{\hspace{1cm}}}$$

$$x \; (</>) \; \underline{\hspace{0.6cm}}$$

The solution set is ____.

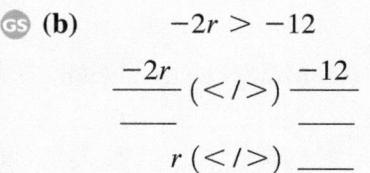

(b) $-2r > -12$

$$\frac{-2r}{\underline{\hspace{0.8cm}}} \; (</>) \; \frac{-12}{\underline{\hspace{0.8cm}}}$$

$$r \; (</>) \; \underline{\hspace{0.6cm}}$$

The solution set is ____.

(c) $-5p \le 0$

| EXAMPLE 4 | Using the Multiplication Property of Inequality |

Solve each inequality, and graph the solution set.

(a) $3x < -18$

We divide each side by 3, a positive number, so the direction of the inequality symbol *does not* change. (***It does not matter that the number on the right side of the inequality is negative.***)

$$3x < -18$$

3 is *positive*. Do NOT reverse the direction of the symbol.

$$\frac{3x}{3} < \frac{-18}{3} \qquad \text{Divide by 3.}$$

$$x < -6$$

The solution set is $(-\infty, -6)$. The graph is shown in **Figure 19.**

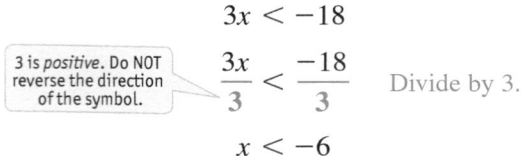

Figure 19

(b) $-4t \ge 8$

Each side of the inequality must be divided by -4, a negative number, which *does* require changing the direction of the inequality symbol.

$$-4t \ge 8 \qquad \text{To avoid errors, show the division as a separate step.}$$

$$\frac{-4t}{-4} \le \frac{8}{-4} \qquad \begin{array}{l} \text{Divide by } -4. \\ \text{Reverse the symbol.} \end{array}$$

-4 is *negative*. Change $\ge$ to $\le$.

$$t \le -2$$

The solution set $(-\infty, -2\,]$ is graphed in **Figure 20.**

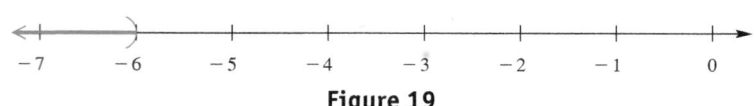

Figure 20

◀ **Work Problem 5 at the Side.**

OBJECTIVE ▶ 4 Solve linear inequalities.

Solving a Linear Inequality in One Variable

Step 1 **Simplify each side separately.** Use the distributive property as needed.
- Clear any parentheses.
- Clear any fractions or decimals.
- Combine like terms.

Step 2 **Isolate the variable terms on one side.** Use the addition property of inequality so that all terms with variables are on one side of the inequality and all constants (numbers) are on the other side.

Step 3 **Isolate the variable.** Use the multiplication property of inequality to obtain an inequality in one of the following forms, where k is a constant (number).

variable $< k$,   variable $\le k$,   variable $> k$,   or   variable $\ge k$

Remember: Reverse the direction of the inequality symbol only when multiplying or dividing each side of an inequality by a negative number.

Answers

5. (a) $<$; 9; $<$; -2; $(-\infty, -2)$

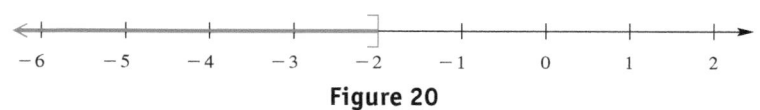

(b) -2; $<$; -2; $<$; 6; $(-\infty, 6)$

(c) $[0, \infty)$

| EXAMPLE 5 | Solving a Linear Inequality |

Solve $3x + 2 - 5 > -x + 7 + 2x$, and graph the solution set.

Step 1 Combine like terms and simplify.

$$3x + 2 - 5 > -x + 7 + 2x$$

$$3x - 3 > x + 7$$

Step 2 Use the addition property of inequality.

$$3x - 3 - x > x + 7 - x \qquad \text{Subtract } x.$$

$$2x - 3 > 7 \qquad \text{Combine like terms.}$$

$$2x - 3 + 3 > 7 + 3 \qquad \text{Add 3.}$$

$$2x > 10 \qquad \text{Combine like terms.}$$

Step 3 Use the multiplication property of inequality.

Because 2 is positive, keep the symbol >.

$$\frac{2x}{2} > \frac{10}{2} \qquad \text{Divide by 2.}$$

$$x > 5$$

The solution set is $(5, \infty)$. Its graph is shown in **Figure 21.**

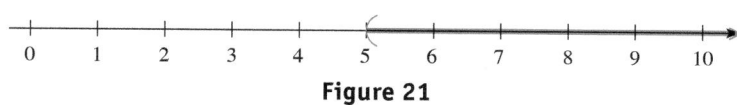

Figure 21

—————————— Work Problem **6** at the Side. ▶

| XAMPLE 6 | Solving a Linear Inequality |

Solve $5(k - 3) - 7k \geq 4(k - 3) + 9$, and graph the solution set.

Step 1 $5(k - 3) - 7k \geq 4(k - 3) + 9$ ← Start by clearing parentheses.

$$5k - 15 - 7k \geq 4k - 12 + 9 \qquad \text{Distributive property}$$

$$-2k - 15 \geq 4k - 3 \qquad \text{Combine like terms.}$$

Step 2 $-2k - 15 - 4k \geq 4k - 3 - 4k \qquad \text{Subtract } 4k.$

$$-6k - 15 \geq -3 \qquad \text{Combine like terms.}$$

$$-6k - 15 + 15 \geq -3 + 15 \qquad \text{Add 15.}$$

$$-6k \geq 12 \qquad \text{Combine like terms.}$$

Step 3 Because -6 is negative, change $\geq$ to $\leq$.

$$\frac{-6k}{-6} \leq \frac{12}{-6} \qquad \begin{array}{l}\text{Divide by } -6. \\ \text{Reverse the symbol.}\end{array}$$

$$k \leq -2$$

The solution set is $(-\infty, -2]$. Its graph is shown in **Figure 22.**

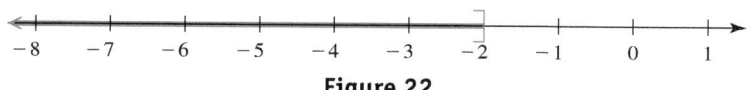

Figure 22

—————————— Work Problem **7** at the Side. ▶

6 Solve.

$$7x - 6 + 1 \geq 5x - x + 2$$

Graph the solution set.

————————————————▶

7 Solve.

$$-15 - (2x + 1) \geq 4(x - 1) - 3x$$

Graph the solution set.

————————————————▶

Answers

6. $\left[\frac{7}{3}, \infty\right)$

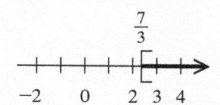

7. $(-\infty, -4]$

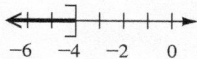

8 Solve each inequality, and graph the solution set.

(a) $\frac{1}{8}(x + 4) \geq \frac{1}{6}(2x + 8)$

(b) $\frac{1}{2}(3x - 1) > \frac{1}{5}(x + 4)$

EXAMPLE 7 Solving a Linear Inequality with Fractions

Solve $\frac{3}{4}(x - 6) < \frac{2}{3}(5x + 1)$, and graph the solution set.

Step 1
$$\frac{3}{4}(x - 6) < \frac{2}{3}(5x + 1)$$

Clear the parentheses first. Then clear the fractions.

$$\frac{3}{4}x - \frac{9}{2} < \frac{10}{3}x + \frac{2}{3}$$ Distributive property

$$12\left(\frac{3}{4}x - \frac{9}{2}\right) < 12\left(\frac{10}{3}x + \frac{2}{3}\right)$$ Multiply each side by the LCD, 12.

$$9x - 54 < 40x + 8$$ Distributive property

Step 2 $9x - 54 - \mathbf{40x} < 40x + 8 - \mathbf{40x}$ Subtract $40x$.

$$-31x - 54 < 8$$ Combine like terms.

$$-31x - 54 + \mathbf{54} < 8 + \mathbf{54}$$ Add 54.

$$-31x < 62$$ Combine like terms.

Step 3 $\dfrac{-31x}{-31} > \dfrac{62}{-31}$ Divide by -31. Reverse the symbol.

$$x > -2$$

The solution set is $(-2, \infty)$. Its graph is shown in **Figure 23.**

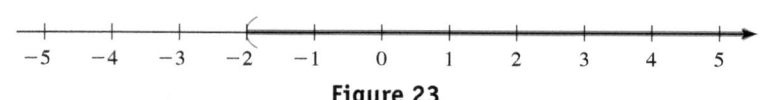

Figure 23

◄ **Work Problem 8** at the Side.

---

9 Translate each statement into an inequality, using x as the variable.

(a) The total cost is less than $10.

(b) Chicago received at most 5 in. of snow.

(c) The car's speed exceeded 60 mph.

(d) You must be at least 18 yr old to vote.

OBJECTIVE **5** Solve applied problems using inequalities.

WORDS AND PHRASES THAT INDICATE INEQUALITY

Phrase/Word	Example	Inequality
Is greater than	A number *is greater than* 4	$x > 4$
Is less than	A number *is less than* -12	$x < -12$
Exceeds	A number *exceeds* 3.5	$x > 3.5$
Is at least	A number *is at least* 6	$x \geq 6$
Is at most	A number *is at most* 8	$x \leq 8$

◄ **Work Problem 9** at the Side.

! CAUTION

Do not confuse statements such as "5 is more than a number" with the phrase "5 more than a number." The first of these is expressed as $5 > x$, while the second is expressed as $x + 5$, or $5 + x$.

The next example uses the idea of finding the average of a number of scores. ***In general, to find the average of n numbers, add the numbers and divide by n.*** We continue to use the six problem-solving steps, changing Step 3 to "Write an inequality."

Answers

8. (a) $(-\infty, -4]$

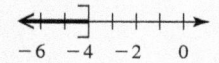

(b) $(1, \infty)$

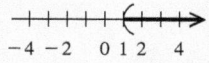

9. (a) $x < 10$ (b) $x \leq 5$
    (c) $x > 60$ (d) $x \geq 18$

EXAMPLE 8 Finding an Average Test Score	**10** Solve each problem.

Brent has scores of 86, 88, and 78 (out of a possible 100) on each of his first three tests in geometry. If he wants an average of at least 80 after his fourth test, what are the possible scores he can make on that test?

Step 1   **Read** the problem again.

Step 2   **Assign a variable.** Let x = Brent's score on his fourth test.

Step 3   **Write an inequality.**

$$\underset{\text{Average}}{\frac{86 + 88 + 78 + x}{4}} \geq \underset{\substack{\text{is at} \\ \text{least 80.}}}{80}$$

To find his average after four tests, add the test scores and divide by 4.

Step 4   **Solve.**

$$\frac{252 + x}{4} \geq 80 \qquad \text{Add the known scores.}$$

$$4\left(\frac{252 + x}{4}\right) \geq 4\,(80) \qquad \text{Multiply by 4.}$$

$$252 + x \geq 320$$

$$252 + x - 252 \geq 320 - 252 \qquad \text{Subtract 252.}$$

$$x \geq 68 \qquad \text{Combine like terms.}$$

Step 5   **State the answer.** He must score 68 or more on the fourth test to have an average of *at least* 80.

Step 6   **Check.**
$$\frac{86 + 88 + 78 + 68}{4} = \frac{320}{4} = 80$$

To complete the check, also show that any number greater than 68 (but less than or equal to 100) makes the average greater than 80.

— **Work Problem 10 at the Side.** ▶

OBJECTIVE ▶ 6 Solve linear inequalities with three parts. An inequality that says that one number is *between* two other numbers is a **three-part inequality.** For example,

$$-3 < 5 < 7 \quad \text{says that} \quad 5 \quad \text{is *between*} \quad -3 \text{ and 7.}$$

EXAMPLE 9   Graphing a Three-Part Inequality

Write the inequality $-3 \leq x < 2$ in interval notation, and graph the interval.

The statement is read "-3 *is less than or equal to x and x is less than* 2." We want the set of numbers that are *between* -3 and 2, with -3 included and 2 excluded. In interval notation, we write $[-3, 2)$, using a square bracket at -3 because -3 is part of the graph and a parenthesis at 2 because 2 is not part of the graph. See **Figure 24.**

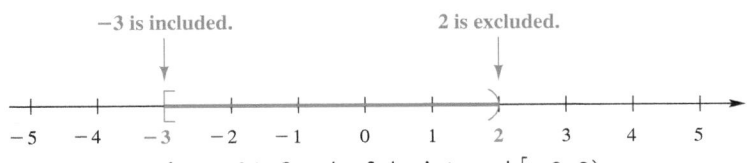

Figure 24 Graph of the interval $[-3, 2)$

— **Work Problem 11 at the Side.** ▶

(a) Matthew has grades of 98 and 85 on his first two tests in algebra. If he wants an average of at least 92 after his third test, what score must he make on that test?

(b) Maggie has scores of 98, 86, and 88 on her first three tests in algebra. If she wants an average of at least 90 after her fourth test, what score must she make on her fourth test?

11 Write each inequality in interval notation, and graph the interval.

(a) $-7 < x < -2$

(b) $-6 < x \leq -4$

Answers

10. (a) 93 or more   **(b)** 88 or more

11. (a) $(-7, -2)$

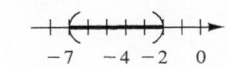

(b) $(-6, -4]$

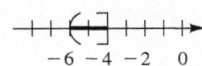

12 Solve each inequality, and graph the solution set.

(a) $2 \leq 3x - 1 \leq 8$

_____→

(b) $-4 < \dfrac{3}{2}x - 1 < 0$

_____→

The three-part inequality $3 < x + 2 < 8$ says that $x + 2$ is between 3 and 8. We solve this inequality as follows.

$$3 - 2 < x + 2 - 2 < 8 - 2 \quad \text{Subtract 2 from } each \text{ part.}$$
$$1 < \quad x \quad < 6$$

The idea is to obtain an inequality in the form

$$\text{a number} < x < \text{another number.}$$

> **⊘ CAUTION**
>
> **Three-part inequalities are written so that the symbols point in the same direction and both point toward the lesser number.** Do _not_ write $8 < x + 2 < 3$, which would imply that $8 < 3$, a **false** statement.

EXAMPLE 10 Solving a Three-Part Inequality

Solve each inequality, and graph the solution set.

(a)
$$4 < \quad 3x - 5 \quad < 10 \quad \boxed{\text{Work with all three parts at the same time.}}$$
$$4 + 5 < 3x - 5 + 5 < 10 + 5 \quad \text{Add 5 to each part.}$$
$$9 < \quad 3x \quad < 15 \quad \text{Combine like terms.}$$

$\boxed{\text{Remember to divide all } three \text{ parts by 3.}}$
$$\dfrac{9}{3} < \quad \dfrac{3x}{3} \quad < \dfrac{15}{3} \quad \text{Divide each part by 3.}$$
$$3 < \quad x \quad < 5$$

The solution set is $(3, 5)$. Its graph is shown in **Figure 25.**

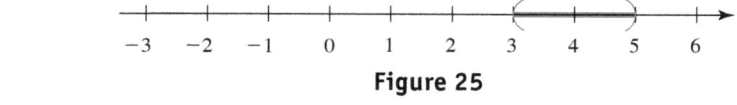

Figure 25

(b)
$$-4 \leq \quad \dfrac{2}{3}m - 1 \quad < 8 \quad \boxed{\text{Work with all three parts at the same time.}}$$

$$3(-4) \leq 3\left(\dfrac{2}{3}m - 1\right) < 3(8) \quad \begin{array}{l}\text{Multiply each part by 3} \\ \text{to clear the fraction.}\end{array}$$

$$-12 \leq \quad 2m - 3 \quad < 24 \quad \begin{array}{l}\text{Multiply. Use the} \\ \text{distributive property.}\end{array}$$

$$-12 + 3 \leq 2m - 3 + 3 < 24 + 3 \quad \text{Add 3 to each part.}$$

$$-9 \leq \quad 2m \quad < 27 \quad \text{Combine like terms.}$$

$$\dfrac{-9}{2} \leq \quad \dfrac{2m}{2} \quad < \dfrac{27}{2} \quad \text{Divide each part by 2.}$$

$$-\dfrac{9}{2} \leq \quad m \quad < \dfrac{27}{2}$$

The solution set is $\left[-\dfrac{9}{2}, \dfrac{27}{2}\right)$. Its graph is shown in **Figure 26.**

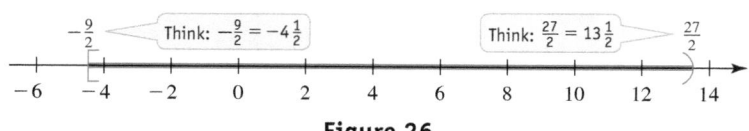

Figure 26

◄ **Work Problem 12** at the Side.

Answers

12. (a) $[1, 3]$

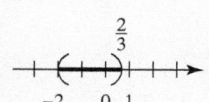

(b) $\left(-2, \dfrac{2}{3}\right)$

Note

The inequality in **Example 10(b)** could also be solved as follows.

$$-4 \leq \frac{2}{3}m - 1 < 8 \qquad \text{Inequality from \textbf{Example 10(b)}}$$

$$-4 + 1 \leq \frac{2}{3}m - 1 + 1 < 8 + 1 \qquad \text{Add 1 to each part.}$$

$$-3 \leq \frac{2}{3}m < 9$$

$$\frac{3}{2}(-3) \leq \frac{3}{2}\left(\frac{2}{3}m\right) < \frac{3}{2}(9) \qquad \text{Multiply each part by } \frac{3}{2}.$$

$$-\frac{9}{2} \leq m < \frac{27}{2}$$

The same solution set $\left[-\frac{9}{2}, \frac{27}{2}\right)$ results.

Be especially careful of whether to use parentheses or square brackets when writing and graphing solution sets of three part inequalities. The following table illustrates the four possibilities that may occur.

METHODS OF EXPRESSING SOLUTION SETS OF THREE-PART INEQUALITIES

Set-Builder Notation	Interval Notation	Graph
$\{x \mid a < x < b\}$	(a, b)	
$\{x \mid a < x \leq b\}$	$(a, b]$	
$\{x \mid a \leq x < b\}$	$[a, b)$	
$\{x \mid a \leq x \leq b\}$	$[a, b]$	

2.7 Exercises

FOR EXTRA HELP
Go to MyMathLab *for worked-out, step-by-step solutions to exercises enclosed in a square* ▢ *and video solutions to* ▶ *exercises.*

CONCEPT CHECK *Work each problem.*

1. When graphing an inequality, use a parenthesis if the inequality symbol is _____ or _____ . Use a square bracket if the inequality symbol is _____ or _____ .

2. *True* or *false*? In interval notation, a square bracket is sometimes used next to an infinity symbol.

3. In interval notation, the set $\{x \mid x > 0\}$ is written _____ .

4. In interval notation, the set of all real numbers is written _____ .

CONCEPT CHECK *Write an inequality using the variable x that corresponds to each graph of solutions on a number line.*

5.
```
  (+—+—+—+—+—+—+→
 -4 -3 -2 -1  0  1  2  3
```

6.
```
  [—+—+—+—+—+—+→
 -4 -3 -2 -1  0  1  2  3
```

7.
```
  ←+—+—+—+—+—+]—+→
 -2 -1  0  1  2  3  4  5
```

8.
```
  ←+—+—+—+—+—)—+→
 -2 -1  0  1  2  3  4  5
```

9.
```
  (—+—+—+—]—→
 -1     0     1     2
```

10.
```
  [—+—+—+—)—→
 -1     0     1     2
```

Write each inequality in interval notation, and graph the interval. **See Examples 1, 2, and 9.**

11. $k \le 4$ ▶
```
  +—+—+—+—+—+—+—+—+→
```

12. $r \le -10$
```
  +—+—+—+—+—+—+—+—+→
```

13. $x > -3$
```
  +—+—+—+—+—+—+—+—+→
```

14. $x > 3$
```
  +—+—+—+—+—+—+—+—+→
```

15. $8 \le x \le 10$
```
  +—+—+—+—+—+—+—+—+→
```

16. $3 \le x \le 5$
```
  +—+—+—+—+—+—+—+—+→
```

17. $0 < x \le 10$ ▶
```
  +—+—+—+—+—+—+—+—+→
```

18. $-3 \le x < 5$
```
  +—+—+—+—+—+—+—+—+→
```

Solve each inequality. Write the solution set in interval notation, and graph it. **See Example 3.**

19. $z - 8 > -7$
```
  +—+—+—+—+—+—+—+→
```

20. $p - 3 > -11$
```
  +—+—+—+—+—+—+—+→
```

21. $2k + 3 \ge k + 8$ ▶
```
  +—+—+—+—+—+—+—+→
```

22. $3x + 7 \ge 2x + 11$
```
  +—+—+—+—+—+—+—+→
```

23. $3n + 5 < 2n - 1$
```
  +—+—+—+—+—+—+—+→
```

24. $5x - 2 < 4x - 5$
```
  +—+—+—+—+—+—+—+→
```

25. Under what conditions must the inequality symbol be reversed when using the multiplication property of inequality?

26. Explain the steps you would use to solve the inequality $-5x > 20$.

Solve each inequality. Write the solution set in interval notation, and graph it.
See Example 4.

27. $3x < 18$

28. $5x < 35$

29. $2x \geq -20$

30. $6m \geq -24$

31. $-8t > 24$

32. $-7x > 49$

33. $-x \geq 0$

34. $-k < 0$

35. $-\dfrac{3}{4}r < -15$

36. $-\dfrac{7}{8}t < -14$

37. $-0.02x \leq 0.06$

38. $-0.03v \geq -0.12$

Solve each inequality. Write the solution set in interval notation, and graph it.
See Examples 3–7.

39. $8x + 9 \leq -15$

40. $6x + 7 \leq -17$

41. $-4x - 3 < 1$

42. $-5x - 4 < 6$

43. $5r + 1 \geq 3r - 9$

44. $6t + 3 < 3t + 12$

45. $6x + 3 + x < 2 + 4x + 4$

46. $-4w + 12 + 9w \geq w + 9 + w$

47. $x - 4 - 7x \geq 2 - 3x - 6$

48. $7x - 6 - 14x < 4 + 5x - 10$

49. $5(t - 1) > 3(t - 2)$

50. $7(m - 2) < 4(m - 4)$

51. $5(x + 3) - 6x \leq 3(2x + 1) - 4x$

52. $2(x - 5) + 3x < 4(x - 6) + 1$

53. $\dfrac{2}{3}(p + 3) > \dfrac{5}{6}(p - 4)$

54. $\dfrac{7}{9}(n - 4) \leq \dfrac{4}{3}(n + 5)$

55. $\dfrac{1}{3}(5x - 4) \geq \dfrac{2}{5}(x + 3)$

56. $\dfrac{5}{12}(5x - 7) < \dfrac{5}{6}(x - 5)$

57. $4x - (6x + 1) \le 8x + 2(x - 3)$

58. $2x - (4x + 3) < 6x + 3(x + 4)$

59. $5(2k + 3) - 2(k - 8) > 3(2k + 4) + k - 2$

60. $2(3z - 5) + 4(z + 6) \ge 2(3z + 2) + 3z - 15$

CONCEPT CHECK *Translate each statement into an inequality. Use x as the variable.*

61. You must be at least 16 yr old to drive.

62. Less than 1 in. of rain fell.

63. Denver received more than 8 in. of snow.

64. A full-time student must take at least 12 credits.

65. Tracy could spend at most $20 on a gift.

66. The wind speed exceeded 40 mph.

Solve each problem. ***See Example 8.***

67. John has grades of 84 and 98 on his first two history tests. What must he score on his third test so that his average is at least 90?

68. Elizabeth has scores of 74 and 82 on her first two algebra tests. What must she score on her third test so that her average is at least 80?

69. A student has scores of 87, 84, 95, and 79 on four quizzes. What must she score on the fifth quiz to have an average of at least 85?

70. Another student has scores of 82, 93, 94, and 86 on four quizzes. What must he score on the fifth quiz to have an average of at least 90?

71. When 2 is added to the difference of six times a number and 5, the result is greater than 13 added to 5 times the number. Find all such numbers.

72. When 8 is subtracted from the sum of three times a number and 6, the result is less than 4 more than the number. Find all such numbers.

73. The formula for converting Celsius temperature to Fahrenheit is $F = \frac{9}{5}C + 32$. The Fahrenheit temperature of Providence, Rhode Island, has never exceeded 104°. How would you describe this using Celsius temperature?

74. The formula for converting Fahrenheit temperature to Celsius is $C = \frac{5}{9}(F - 32)$. If the Celsius temperature on a certain day in San Diego, California, is never more than 25°, how would you describe the corresponding Fahrenheit temperature?

75. For what values of x would the rectangle have perimeter of at least 400?

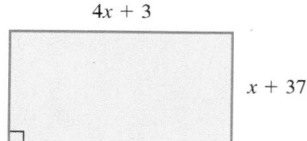

4x + 3

x + 37

76. For what values of x would the triangle have perimeter of at least 72?

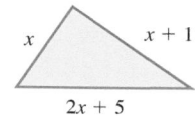

x   x + 11

2x + 5

77. An international phone call costs $2.00, plus $0.30 per minute or fractional part of a minute. If x represents the number of minutes of the length of the call, then $2 + 0.30x$ represents the cost of the call. If Jorge has $5.60 to spend on a call, what is the maximum total time he can use the phone?

78. At the Speedy Gas 'n Go, a car wash costs $4.50, and gasoline is selling for $3.40 per gal. Terri has $43.60 to spend, and her car is so dirty that she must have it washed. What is the maximum number of gallons of gasoline that she can purchase?

79. The average monthly precipitation in Houston, Texas, for October, November, and December is 4.6 in. If 5.7 in. falls in October and 4.3 in. falls in November, how many inches must fall in December so that the average monthly precipitation for these months exceeds 4.6 in.? (Data from National Climatic Data Center.)

80. The average monthly precipitation in New Orleans, Louisiana, for June, July, and August in 6.7 in. If 8.1 in. falls in June and 5.7 in. falls in July, how many inches must fall in August so that the average monthly precipitation for these months exceeds 6.7 in.? (Data from National Climatic Data Center.)

Solve each inequality. Write the solution set in interval notation, and graph it. See Example 10.

81. $-5 \leq 2x - 3 \leq 9$

82. $-7 \leq 3x - 4 \leq 8$

83. $10 < 7p + 3 < 24$

84. $-8 \leq 3r - 1 \leq -1$

85. $-12 < -1 + 6m \leq -5$

86. $-14 \leq 1 + 5q < 3$

87. $6 \leq 3(x - 1) < 18$

88. $-4 < 2(x + 1) \leq 6$

89. $-12 \leq \frac{1}{2}z + 1 \leq 4$

90. $-6 \leq 3 + \frac{1}{3}x \leq 5$

91. $1 \leq \frac{2}{3}p + 3 \leq 7$

92. $2 < \frac{3}{4}x + 6 < 12$

Relating Concepts (Exercises 93–96) For Individual or Group Work

Work Exercises 93–96 in order, *to see the connection between the solution of an equation and the solutions of the corresponding inequalities.*

In Exercises 93–95, solve, write the solution set in interval notation, and graph it.

93. $3x + 2 = 14$

94. $3x + 2 < 14$

95. $3x + 2 > 14$

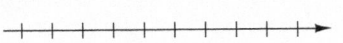

96. Based on the results from **Exercises 93–95,** if we were to graph the solutions of

$$-4x + 3 = -1, \quad -4x + 3 > -1, \quad \text{and} \quad -4x + 3 < -1$$

on the same number line, describe the graph. Give this solution set using interval notation.

Study Skills

TAKING MATH TESTS

Techniques to Improve Your Test Score	Comments
Come prepared with a pencil, eraser, paper, and calculator, if allowed.	Working in pencil lets you erase, keeping your work neat.
Scan the entire test, note the point values of different problems, and plan your time accordingly.	To do 20 problems in 50 minutes, allow $50 \div 20 = 2.5$ minutes per problem. Spend less time on the easier problems.
Do a "knowledge dump" when you get the test. Write important notes, such as formulas, in a corner of the test.	Writing down tips and information that you've learned at the beginning allows you to relax later.
Read directions carefully, and circle any significant words. When you finish a problem, reread the directions. Did you do what was asked?	Pay attention to any announcements written on the board or made by your instructor. Ask if you don't understand something.
Show all your work. Many teachers give partial credit if some steps are correct, even if the final answer is wrong. **Write neatly.**	If your teacher can't read your writing, you won't get credit for it. If you need more space to work, ask to use extra paper.
Write down anything that might help solve a problem: a formula, a diagram, etc. If necessary, circle the problem and come back to it later. Do **not** erase anything you wrote down.	If you know even a little bit about a problem, write it down. The answer may come to you as you work on it, or you may get partial credit. Don't spend too long on any one problem.
If you can't solve a problem, make a guess. Do not change it unless you find an obvious mistake.	Have a good reason for changing an answer. Your first guess is usually your best bet.
Check that the answer to an application problem is reasonable and makes sense. Reread the problem. Make sure you've answered the question.	Use common sense. Can the father really be seven years old? Would a month's rent be $32,140? Label answers, if needed: $, years, inches, etc.
Check for careless errors. Rework each problem without looking at your previous work. Then compare the two answers.	Reworking a problem from the beginning forces you to rethink it. If possible, use a different method to solve the problem.

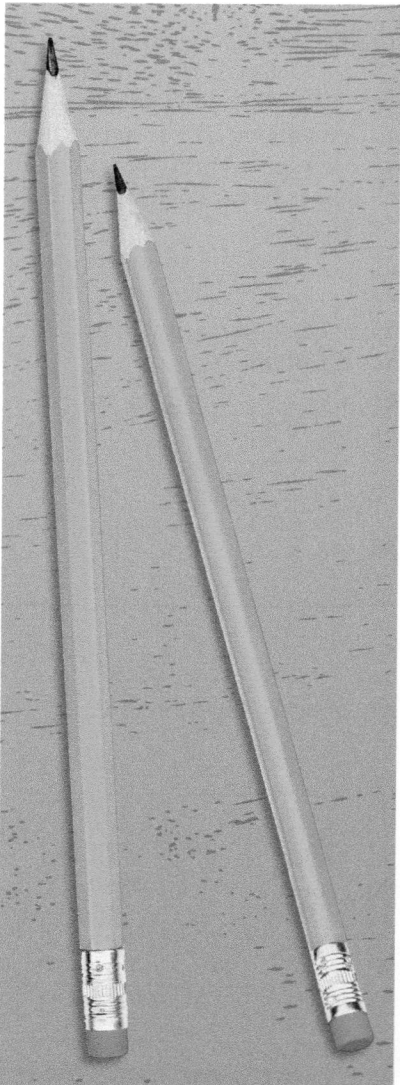

Now Try This

Think through and answer each question.

1 What two or three tips will you try when you take your next math test?

_____

2 How did the tips you selected work for you when you took your math test?

_____

3 What will you do differently when taking your next math test?

_____

Chapter 2   *Summary*

Key Terms

2.1

linear equation A linear equation in one variable (here x) is an equation that can be written in the form $Ax + B = C$, where A, B, and C are real numbers, and $A \neq 0$.

solution set The set of all solutions of an equation is its solution set.

equivalent equations Equations that have exactly the same solution sets are equivalent equations.

2.3

conditional equation A conditional equation is an equation that is true for some values of the variable and false for others.

identity An identity is an equation that is true for all values of the variable.

contradiction A contradiction is an equation that has no solution.

2.4

consecutive integers Two integers that differ by 1 are consecutive integers.

consecutive even (or odd) integers Two even (or odd) integers that differ by 2 are consecutive even (or odd) integers.

complementary angles Two angles whose measures have a sum of 90° are complementary angles.

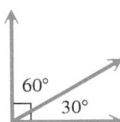

right angle A right angle measures 90°.

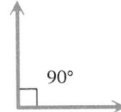

supplementary angles Two angles whose measures have a sum of 180° are supplementary angles.

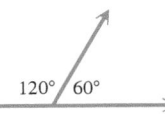

straight angle A straight angle measures 180°.

2.5

formula A formula is an equation in which variables are used to describe a relationship.

area The area of a plane geometric figure is a measure of the surface covered by the figure.

perimeter The perimeter of a plane geometric figure is the measure of the outer boundary of the figure.

vertical angles Vertical angles are angles formed by intersecting lines. They have the same measure. (In the figure, ① and ③ are vertical angles, as are ② and ④.)

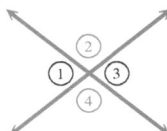

2.6

ratio A ratio is a comparison of two quantities using a quotient.

proportion A proportion is a statement that two ratios are equal.

cross products of a proportion The method of cross products provides a way of determining whether a proportion is true.

$$\frac{a}{b} = \frac{c}{d} \qquad ad \text{ and } bc \text{ are cross products.}$$

terms In the proportion $\frac{a}{b} = \frac{c}{d}$, the terms are a, b, c, and d. The a and d terms are the **extremes,** and the b and c terms are the **means.**

2.7

inequality An inequality is a statement that relates algebraic expressions using $<$, $\leq$, $>$, or $\geq$.

linear inequality A linear inequality in one variable (here x) can be written in the form $Ax + B < C$, $Ax + B \leq C$, $Ax + B > C$, or $Ax + B \geq C$, where A, B, and C are real numbers, and $A \neq 0$.

interval An interval is a portion of a number line.

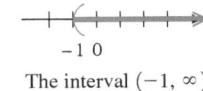

The interval $(-1, \infty)$

interval notation Interval notation is a special notation that uses parentheses ( ) and/or brackets [ ] to describe an interval on a number line.

three-part inequality An inequality that says that one number is between two other numbers is a three-part inequality.

New Symbols

∅	empty (null) set	a **to** b, $a:b$, **or** $\frac{a}{b}$	the ratio of a to b	∞	infinity
1°	one degree	(a, b)	interval notation for $a < x < b$	$-\infty$	negative infinity
⌐	right angle	$[a, b]$	interval notation for $a \leq x \leq b$	$(-\infty, \infty)$	set of all real numbers

Test Your Word Power

See how well you have learned the vocabulary in this chapter.

1 A **solution** of an equation is a number that
   A. makes an expression undefined
   B. makes the equation false
   C. makes the equation true
   D. makes an expression equal to 0.

2 **Complementary angles** are angles
   A. formed by two parallel lines
   B. whose sum is 90°
   C. whose sum is 180°
   D. formed by perpendicular lines.

3 **Supplementary angles** are angles
   A. formed by two parallel lines
   B. whose sum is 90°
   C. whose sum is 180°
   D. formed by perpendicular lines.

4 A **ratio**
   A. compares two quantities using a quotient
   B. says that two quotients are equal
   C. is a product of two quantities
   D. is a difference of two quantities.

5 A **proportion**
   A. compares two quantities using a quotient
   B. says that two ratios are equal
   C. is a product of two quantities
   D. is a difference of two quantities.

6 An **inequality** is
   A. a statement that two algebraic expressions are equal
   B. a point on a number line
   C. an equation with no solutions
   D. a statement that relates algebraic expressions using $<$, $\leq$, $>$, or $\geq$.

Answers to Test Your Word Power

1. C; *Example:* 8 is the solution of $2x + 5 = 21$.

2. B; *Example:* Angles with measures 35° and 55° are complementary angles.

3. C; *Example:* Angles with measures 112° and 68° are supplementary angles.

4. A; *Example:* $\frac{7 \text{ in.}}{12 \text{ in.}} = \frac{7}{12}$

5. B; *Example:* $\frac{2}{3} = \frac{8}{12}$

6. D; *Examples:* $x < 5, 7 + 2y \geq 11, -5 < 2z - 1 \leq 3$

Quick Review

Concepts	Examples

2.1 **The Addition Property of Equality**

The same number may be added to (or subtracted from) each side of an equation without changing the solution set.

Solve.
$$x - 6 = 12$$
$$x - 6 + 6 = 12 + 6 \quad \text{Add 6.}$$
$$x = 18 \quad \text{Combine like terms.}$$
Solution set: $\{18\}$

2.2 **The Multiplication Property of Equality**

Each side of an equation may be multiplied (or divided) by the same nonzero number without changing the solution set.

Solve.
$$\frac{3}{4}x = -9$$
$$\frac{4}{3} \cdot \frac{3}{4}x = \frac{4}{3} \cdot (-9) \quad \text{Multiply by } \frac{4}{3}.$$
$$x = -12$$
Solution set: $\{-12\}$

Concepts	Examples

2.3 **More on Solving Linear Equations**

Solving a Linear Equation in One Variable

Step 1 Simplify each side separately.
  - Clear any parentheses.
  - Clear any fractions or decimals.
  - Combine like terms.

Step 2 Isolate the variable terms on one side.

Step 3 Isolate the variable.

Step 4 Check.

Solve. $2x + 2(x + 1) = 14 + x$

$$2x + 2x + 2 = 14 + x \quad \text{Distributive property}$$

$$4x + 2 = 14 + x \quad \text{Combine like terms.}$$

$$4x + 2 - x - 2 = 14 + x - x - 2$$
$$\text{Subtract } x. \text{ Subtract 2.}$$

$$3x = 12 \quad \text{Combine like terms.}$$

$$\frac{3x}{3} = \frac{12}{3} \quad \text{Divide by 3.}$$

$$x = 4$$

CHECK $2(4) + 2(4 + 1) \stackrel{?}{=} 14 + 4$ Let $x = 4$.

$$18 = 18 \checkmark \quad \text{True}$$

Solution set: $\{4\}$

2.4 **An Introduction to Applications of Linear Equations**

Solving an Applied Problem

Step 1 Read.

Step 2 Assign a variable.

Step 3 Write an equation.

Step 4 Solve the equation.

Step 5 State the answer.

Step 6 Check.

One number is 5 more than another. Their sum is 21. What are the numbers?

We are looking for two numbers.

Let $x =$ the lesser number.

Then $x + 5 =$ the greater number.

$$x + (x + 5) = 21$$

$$2x + 5 = 21 \quad \text{Combine like terms.}$$

$$2x = 16 \quad \text{Subtract 5.}$$

$$x = 8 \quad \text{Divide by 2.}$$

The numbers are **8** and $8 + 5 = $ **13**.

13 is 5 more than **8**, and $8 + 13 = 21$, as required. The answer checks.

2.5 **Formulas and Additional Applications from Geometry**

To find the value of one of the variables in a formula, given values for the others, substitute the known values into the formula.

Find L if $\mathcal{A} = LW$, given that $\mathcal{A} = 24$ and $W = 3$.

$$\mathcal{A} = LW$$

$$24 = L \cdot 3 \quad \mathcal{A} = 24, W = 3$$

$$\frac{24}{3} = \frac{L \cdot 3}{3} \quad \text{Divide by 3.}$$

$$8 = L$$

To solve a formula for one of the variables, isolate that variable by treating the other variables as constants (numbers) and using the steps for solving equations.

Solve $P = 2a + 2b$ for b.

$$P - 2a = 2a + 2b - 2a \quad \text{Subtract } 2a.$$

$$P - 2a = 2b \quad \text{Combine like terms.}$$

$$\frac{P - 2a}{2} = \frac{2b}{2} \quad \text{Divide by 2.}$$

$$\frac{P - 2a}{2} = b, \quad \text{or} \quad b = \frac{P - 2a}{2}$$

Concepts	Examples

2.6 Ratio, Proportion, and Percent

To write a ratio, express quantities using the same units.

4 ft to 8 in. can be written **48 in.** to 8 in., which is the ratio

$$\frac{48}{8}, \quad \text{or} \quad \frac{6}{1}.$$

To solve a proportion, use the method of cross products.

Solve. $\dfrac{x}{12} = \dfrac{35}{60}$

$$60x = 12 \cdot 35 \qquad \text{Cross products}$$
$$60x = 420 \qquad \text{Multiply.}$$
$$x = 7 \qquad \text{Divide by 60.}$$

Solution set: $\{7\}$

To solve a percent problem, use the percent equation.

$$\textbf{amount} = \textbf{percent (as a decimal)} \cdot \textbf{base}$$

65 is what percent of 325?

$$65 = p \cdot 325$$

$$\frac{65}{325} = p$$

$$0.2 = p, \quad \text{or} \quad 20\% = p$$

65 is **20%** of 325.

2.7 Solving Linear Inequalities

Solving a Linear Inequality in One Variable

Step 1 Simplify each side separately.
- Clear any parentheses.
- Clear any fractions or decimals.
- Combine like terms.

Step 2 Isolate the variable terms on one side.

Step 3 Isolate the variable.

Be sure to reverse the direction of the inequality symbol when multiplying or dividing by a negative number.

Solve and graph the solution set.

$$3(1 - x) + 5 - 2x > 9 - 6$$
$$3 - 3x + 5 - 2x > 9 - 6 \qquad \text{Distributive property}$$
$$8 - 5x > 3 \qquad \text{Combine like terms.}$$
$$8 - 5x - 8 > 3 - 8 \qquad \text{Subtract 8.}$$
$$-5x > -5 \qquad \text{Combine like terms.}$$
$$\frac{-5x}{-5} < \frac{-5}{-5} \qquad \begin{array}{l}\text{Divide by } -5.\\ \text{Change } > \text{ to } <.\end{array}$$
$$x < 1$$

Solution set: $(-\infty, 1)$

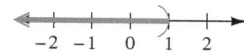

To solve a three-part inequality such as

$$4 < 2x + 6 \leq 8,$$

work with all three parts at the same time to obtain an inequality in the form

$$\text{a number} < x \leq \text{another number}.$$

Solve and graph the solution set.

$$4 < 2x + 6 \leq 8$$
$$4 - 6 < 2x + 6 - 6 \leq 8 - 6 \qquad \text{Subtract 6.}$$
$$-2 < 2x \leq 2$$
$$\frac{-2}{2} < \frac{2x}{2} \leq \frac{2}{2} \qquad \text{Divide by 2.}$$
$$-1 < x \leq 1$$

Solution set: $(-1, 1]$

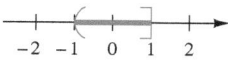

Chapter 2 Review Exercises

2.1–2.3 *Solve each equation. Check the solution.*

1. $x - 7 = 2$

2. $4r - 6 = 10$

3. $5x + 8 = 4x + 2$

4. $8t = 7t + \dfrac{3}{2}$

5. $4r + 12 - (3r + 12) = 0$

6. $7(2x + 1) = 6(2x - 9)$

7. $-\dfrac{6}{5}y = -18$

8. $\dfrac{1}{2}(r - 3) + 2 = \dfrac{1}{3}(r - 9)$

9. $3x - (-2x + 6) = 4(x - 4) + x$

10. $0.10(x + 80) + 0.20x = 8 + 0.30x$

2.4 *Solve each problem.*

11. If 7 is added to five times a number, the result is equal to three times the number. Find the number.

12. If 4 is subtracted from twice a number, the result is 36. Find the number.

13. The land area of Hawaii is 5213 mi² greater than that of Rhode Island. Together, the areas total 7637 mi². What is the area of each state?

14. The height of Seven Falls in Colorado is $\frac{5}{2}$ the height (in feet) of Twin Falls in Idaho. The sum of the heights is 420 ft. Find the height of each.

15. The supplement of an angle measures 10 times the measure of its complement. What is the measure of the angle (in degrees)?

16. Find two consecutive odd integers such that when the lesser is added to twice the greater, the result is 24 more than the greater integer.

17. A lawn mower uses a mixture of gasoline and oil. The mixture contains 1 oz of oil for every 32 oz of gasoline. How many ounces of oil and how many ounces of gasoline are required to fill a 132-oz tank completely?

18. A 72-in. board is to be cut into three pieces. The longest piece must be three times as long as the shortest piece. The middle-sized piece must be 7 in. longer than the shortest piece. How long must each piece be?

2.5 *Find the value of the remaining variable in each formula. Use 3.14 as an approximation for π.*

19. $\mathcal{A} = \dfrac{1}{2}bh$; $\mathcal{A} = 44, b = 8$

20. $\mathcal{A} = \dfrac{1}{2}h(b + B)$; $b = 3, B = 4, h = 8$

21. $C = 2\pi r$; $C = 29.83$

22. $V = \dfrac{4}{3}\pi r^3$; $r = 9$

Solve each formula for the specified variable.

23. $A = bh$ for h

24. $A = \dfrac{1}{2}h(b + B)$ for h

Solve each equation for y.

25. $x + y = 11$

26. $3x - 2y = 12$

Find the measure of each marked angle.

27.

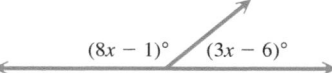

28.

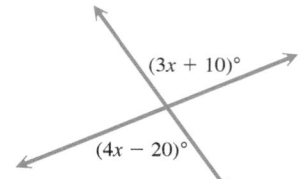

Solve each problem.

29. A cinema screen in Sydney, Australia, has length 97 ft and width 117 ft. What is the perimeter? What is the area? (Data from *Guinness World Records.*)

30. General Sherman, a giant sequoia growing in Sequoia National Park in California, is 271 ft tall and has a circumference of about 85 ft. What is the diameter of the tree? What is its radius? Use 3.14 as an approximation for π. Round answers to the nearest hundredth. (Data from *Guinness World Records.*)

2.6 *Write a ratio for each word phrase. Express fractions in lowest terms.*

31. 60 cm to 40 cm

32. 5 days to 2 weeks

33. 90 in. to 10 ft

Solve each equation.

34. $\dfrac{p}{21} = \dfrac{5}{30}$

35. $\dfrac{5 + x}{3} = \dfrac{2 - x}{6}$

36. $\dfrac{y}{5} = \dfrac{6y - 5}{11}$

Solve each problem.

37. If 2 lb of fertilizer will cover 150 ft^2 of lawn, how many pounds would be needed to cover 500 ft^2?

38. If 8 oz of medicine must be mixed with 20 oz of water, how many ounces of medicine must be mixed with 90 oz of water?

39. The distance between two cities on a road map is 32 cm. The two cities are actually 150 km apart. The distance on the map between two other cities is 80 cm. How far apart are these cities?

40. Find the best buy. Give the unit price to the nearest thousandth for that size. (Data from Jewel-Osco.)

CEREAL	
Size	Price
9 oz	$3.49
14 oz	$3.99
18 oz	$4.49

41. What is 8% of 75?

42. What percent of 12 is 21?

43. 6 is what percent of 18?

44. 36% of what number is 900?

45. Nicholas paid $22,870, including sales tax, for his 2016 Kia Optima. The sales tax rate where he lives is 6%. What was the actual price of the car to the nearest dollar? (Data from www.kia.com)

46. Maureen took the mathematics faculty from a community college out to dinner. The bill was $304.75. Maureen added a 15% tip and paid for the meal with her corporate credit card. What was the total price she paid to the nearest cent?

47. A laptop computer with a regular price of $680 is on sale for $510. What percent of the regular price is the savings?

48. Boyd has a monthly income of $3200. He has budgeted $560 per month for auto expenses. What percent of his monthly income did he budget for auto expenses?

2.7 *Write each inequality in interval notation, and graph it.*

49. $p \geq -4$

50. $x < 7$

51. $-5 \leq k < 6$

52. $r \geq \dfrac{1}{2}$

Solve each inequality. Write the solution set in interval notation, and graph it.

53. $x + 6 \geq 3$

54. $5t < 4t + 2$

55. $-6x \leq -18$

56. $-8(k - 5) + 2 + 7k \leq -4$

57. $4x - 3x > 10 - 4x + 7x$

58. $3(2w + 5) + 4(8 + 3w) < 5(3w + 2) + 2w$

59. $-3 \leq 2x + 1 < 4$

60. $8 < 3x + 5 \leq 20$

Solve each problem.

61. Justin has grades of 94 and 88 on his first two calculus tests. What possible scores on a third test will give him an average of at least 90?

62. If nine times a number is added to 6, the result is at most 3. Find all such numbers.

Chapter 2 Mixed Review Exercises

Solve.

1. $\dfrac{x}{7} = \dfrac{x-5}{2}$

2. $d = 2r$ for r

3. $-2x > -4$

4. $2k - 5 = 4k + 13$

5. $0.05x + 0.02x = 4.9$

6. $2 - 3(t - 5) = 4 + t$

7. $9x - (7x + 2) = 3x + (2 - x)$

8. $\dfrac{1}{3}s + \dfrac{1}{2}s + 7 = \dfrac{5}{6}s + 5 + 2$

9. On a world globe, the distance between Capetown and Bangkok, two cities that are actually 10,080 km apart, is 12.4 in. The actual distance between Moscow and Berlin is 1610 km. How far apart are Moscow and Berlin on this globe, to the nearest inch?

10. In triangle *DEF*, the measure of angle *E* is twice the measure of angle *D*. Angle *F* has measure 18° less than six times the measure of angle *D*. Find the measure of each angle.

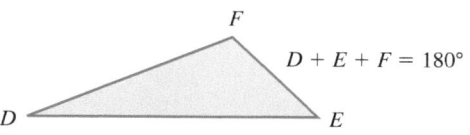

$D + E + F = 180°$

11. The perimeter of a triangle is 96 m. One side is twice as long as another, and the third side is 30 m long. What is the length of the longest side?

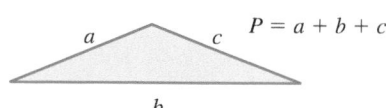

$P = a + b + c$

12. The perimeter of a rectangle is 288 ft. The length is 4 ft longer than the width. Find the width.

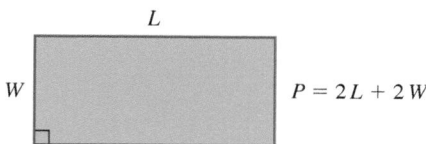

$P = 2L + 2W$

13. Find the best buy. Give the unit price to the nearest thousandth for that size. (Data from Jewel-Osco.)

LAUNDRY DETERGENT

Size	Price
50 oz	$3.99
100 oz	$7.29
160 oz	$9.99

14. Find the measure of each marked angle.

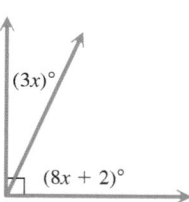

$(3x)°$

$(8x + 2)°$

15. Latarsha has grades of 82 and 96 on her first two English tests. What must she make on her third test so that her average will be at least 90?

16. If nine pairs of jeans cost $355.50, find the cost of five pairs. (Assume all are equally priced.)

Chapter 2 *Test*

The Chapter Test Prep Videos with step-by-step solutions are available in MyMathLab or on You Tube at *http://goo.gl/3rBuO5*

Solve each equation, and check the solution.

1. $3x - 7 = 11$

2. $5x + 9 = 7x + 21$

3. $2 - 3(x - 5) = 3 + (x + 1)$

4. $2.3x + 13.7 = 1.3x + 2.9$

5. $-\dfrac{4}{7}x = -12$

6. $-8(2x + 4) = -4(4x + 8)$

7. $0.06(x + 20) + 0.08(x - 10) = 4.6$

8. $7 - (m - 4) = -3m + 2(m + 1)$

Solve each problem.

9. Wilt Chamberlain and Michael Jordan are the two top NBA all-time point scorers for a single regular season. The total of the points for their best years is 7070. If Wilt Chamberlain scored 2053 points fewer than twice the number of points that Michael Jordan scored, how many points did each player score? (Data from www.landofbasketball.com)

10. Three islands in the Hawaiian island chain are Hawaii (the Big Island), Maui, and Kauai. Together, their areas total 5300 mi². The island of Hawaii is 3293 mi² larger than the island of Maui, and Maui is 177 mi² larger than Kauai. What is the area of each island?

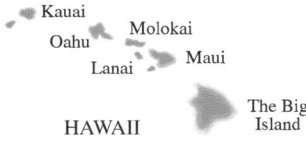

11. If the lesser of two consecutive even integers is tripled, the result is 20 more than twice the greater integer. Find the two integers.

12. Find the measure of an angle if its supplement measures 10° more than three times its complement.

13. The formula for the perimeter of a rectangle is $P = 2L + 2W$.

   (a) Solve for W.

   (b) If $P = 116$ and $L = 40$, find the value of W.

14. Solve the following equation for y.

$$5x - 4y = 8$$

Find the measure of each marked angle.

15.

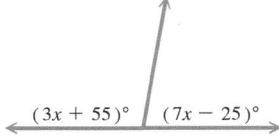

$(3x + 55)° \quad (7x - 25)°$

16.

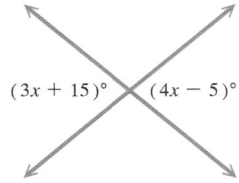

$(3x + 15)° \quad (4x - 5)°$

Solve each equation.

17. $\dfrac{z}{8} = \dfrac{12}{16}$

18. $\dfrac{x + 5}{3} = \dfrac{x - 3}{4}$

Solve each problem.

19. Find the best buy. Give the unit price to the nearest thousandth for that size. (Data from Jewel-Osco.)

PROCESSED CHEESE SLICES

Size	Price
8 oz	$2.99
16 oz	$3.99
48 oz	$14.69

20. The distance between Milwaukee and Boston is 1050 mi. On a certain map, this distance is represented by 42 in. On the same map, Seattle and Cincinnati are 92 in. apart. What is the actual distance between Seattle and Cincinnati?

21. Dawn has a monthly income of $2200 and plans to spend 12% of this amount on groceries. How much will be spent on groceries?

22. What percent of 65 is 26?

23. Write an inequality using the variable x that corresponds to each graph of solutions on a number line.

(a)

$-2 \; -1 \quad 0 \quad 1 \quad 2 \quad 3$

(b)

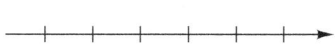

$-2 \; -1 \quad 0 \quad 1 \quad 2 \quad 3$

Solve each inequality. Write the solution set in interval notation, and graph it.

24. $-3x > -33$

25. $-0.04x \leq 0.12$

26. $-4x + 2(x - 3) \geq 4x - (3 + 5x) - 7$

27. $-10 < 3x - 4 \leq 14$

28. Shania has scores of 76 and 81 on her first two algebra tests. If she wants an average of at least 80 after her third test, what score must she make on her third test?

Chapters R–2 *Cumulative Review Exercises*

Write each fraction in lowest terms.

1. $\dfrac{15}{40}$

2. $\dfrac{108}{144}$

Perform the indicated operations.

3. $\dfrac{5}{6} + \dfrac{1}{4} + \dfrac{7}{15}$

4. $16\dfrac{7}{8} - 3\dfrac{1}{10}$

5. $\dfrac{9}{8} \cdot \dfrac{16}{3}$

6. $\dfrac{3}{4} \div \dfrac{5}{8}$

7. $4.8 + 12.5 + 16.73$

8. $56.3 - 28.99$

9. $67.8\,(0.45)$

10. $236.46 \div 4.2$

11. In making dresses, Earth Works uses $\frac{5}{8}$ yd of trim per dress. How many yards of trim would be used to make 56 dresses?

12. A cook wants to increase a recipe for Quaker Quick Grits that serves 4 to make enough for 10 people. The recipe calls for 3 cups of water. How much water will be needed to serve 10?

13. First published in 1953, the digest-sized *TV Guide* changed to a full-sized magazine in 2005. See the figure. The new magazine is 3 in. wider than the old guide. What is the difference in their heights? (Data from *TV Guide*.)

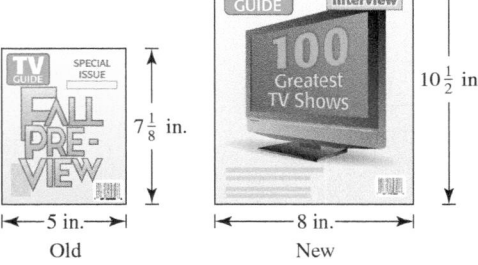

Old   New

14. A small business owner bought 3 business laptop computers for $529.99, $599.99, and $629.99 and 3 ergonomic office chairs for $279.99 each. What was the final bill (without tax)? (Data from www.staples.com)

Decide whether each inequality is true *or* false.

15. $\dfrac{8\,(7) - 5\,(6 + 2)}{3 \cdot 5 + 1} \geq 1$

16. $\dfrac{4\,(9 + 3) - 4^2}{2 + 3 \cdot 6} \geq 2$

Perform the indicated operations.

17. $-11 + 20 + (-2)$

18. $13 + (-19) + 7$

19. $9 - (-4)$

20. $-2\,(-5)\,(-4)$

21. $\dfrac{4 \cdot 9}{-3}$

22. $\dfrac{8}{7 - 7}$

23. $(-5 + 8) + (-2 - 7)$

24. $(-7 - 1)\,(-4) + (-4)$

25. $\dfrac{-3 - (-5)}{1 - (-1)}$

26. $\dfrac{6\,(-4) - (-2)\,(12)}{3^2 + 7^2}$

27. $\dfrac{(-3)^2 - (-4)\,(2^4)}{5 \cdot 2 - (-2)^3}$

28. $\dfrac{-2\,(5^3) - 6}{4^2 + 2\,(-5) + (-2)}$

Find the value of each expression for $x = -2$, $y = -4$, and $z = 3$.

29. $xz^3 - 5y^2$

30. $\dfrac{xz - y^3}{-4z}$

Name the property illustrated by each equation.

31. $7(k + m) = 7k + 7m$

32. $3 + (5 + 2) = 3 + (2 + 5)$

33. $7 + (-7) = 0$

34. $3.5(1) = 3.5$

Simplify each expression.

35. $4p - 6 + 3p - 8$

36. $-4(k + 2) + 3(2k - 1)$

Solve each equation, and check the solution.

37. $2r - 6 = 8$

38. $2(p - 1) = 3p + 2$

39. $4 - 5(a + 2) = 3(a + 1) - 1$

40. $2 - 6(z + 1) = 4(z - 2) + 10$

41. $-(m - 1) = 3 - 2m$

42. $\dfrac{x - 2}{3} = \dfrac{2x + 1}{5}$

43. $\dfrac{2x + 3}{5} = \dfrac{x - 4}{2}$

44. $\dfrac{2}{3}x + \dfrac{3}{4}x = -17$

Solve each formula for the indicated variable.

45. $P = a + b + c + B$ for c

46. $P = 4s$ for s

Solve each inequality. Write the solution set in interval notation, and graph it.

47. $-5z \geq 4z - 18$

48. $6(r - 1) + 2(3r - 5) < -4$

Solve each problem.

49. Abby bought textbooks at the college bookstore for $276.13, including 6% sales tax. What did the books cost before tax?

50. A used car has a price of $11,500. For trading in her old car, Shannon will get 25% off. Find the price of the car with the trade-in.

51. The perimeter of a rectangle is 98 cm. The width is 19 cm. Find the length.

52. The area of a triangle is 104 in.². The base is 13 in. Find the height.

?
19 cm

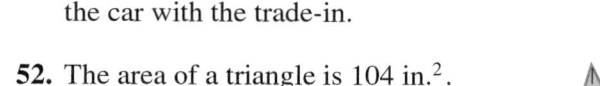
?
13 in.

Graphs of Linear Equations and Inequalities in Two Variables

We determine location on a map using *coordinates,* a concept that is based on a *rectangular coordinate system,* one of the topics of this chapter.

3.1 Linear Equations and Rectangular Coordinates

Study Skills *Analyzing Your Test Results*

3.2 Graphing Linear Equations in Two Variables

3.3 The Slope of a Line

3.4 Slope-Intercept Form of a Linear Equation

3.5 Point-Slope Form of a Linear Equation

Summary Exercises *Applying Graphing and Equation-Writing Techniques for Lines*

Study Skills *Preparing for Your Math Final Exam*

3.6 Graphing Linear Inequalities in Two Variables

3.1 | Linear Equations and Rectangular Coordinates

OBJECTIVES

1. Interpret line graphs.
2. Write a solution as an ordered pair.
3. Decide whether a given ordered pair is a solution of a given equation.
4. Complete ordered pairs for a given equation.
5. Complete a table of values.
6. Plot ordered pairs.

OBJECTIVE 1 Interpret line graphs. A **line graph** is used to show changes or trends in data over time. To form a line graph, we connect a series of points representing data with line segments.

EXAMPLE 1 | Interpreting a Line Graph

The line graph in **Figure 1** shows average prices of a gallon of regular unleaded gasoline in the United States for the years 2008 through 2015.

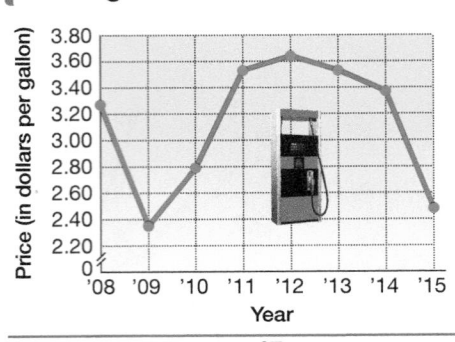

Data from U.S. Department of Energy.

Figure 1

(a) Between which years did the average price of a gallon of gasoline increase?

The line between 2009 and 2010 *rises* from left to right, as do the lines between 2010 and 2011 and between 2011 and 2012. This indicates that the average price of a gallon of gasoline *increased* between 2009 and 2012.

(b) What was the general trend in the average price of a gallon of gasoline from 2012 through 2015?

The line graph *falls* from left to right from 2012 to 2015, so the average price of a gallon of gasoline *decreased* over those years.

(c) Estimate the average price of a gallon of gasoline in 2012 and 2015. About how much did the price decrease between 2012 and 2015?

Move up from 2012 on the horizontal scale to the point plotted for 2012. This point is about one-fourth of the way between the lines on the vertical scale for $3.60 and $3.80—that is, about **$3.65** per gallon.

Locate the point plotted for 2015. Moving across to the vertical scale, this point is about halfway between the lines for $2.40 and $2.60—that is, about **$2.50** per gallon.

Between 2012 and 2015, the average price decreased about

◀ **Work Problem 1** at the Side.

---

1. Refer to the line graph in **Figure 1**.

   (a) Estimate the average price of a gallon of regular unleaded gasoline in 2009.

   (b) About how much did the average price of a gallon of gasoline increase between 2009 and 2012?

Answers

1. (a) $2.35   **(b)** $1.30

The line graph in **Figure 1** on the previous page relates years to average prices for a gallon of gasoline. We can also represent these two related quantities using a table of data, as shown in the margin. In table form, we can see more precise data rather than estimating it. Trends in the data are easier to see from the graph, which gives a "picture" of the data.

We can extend these ideas to the subject of this chapter, *linear equations in two variables*. A linear equation in two variables, one for each of the quantities being related, can be used to represent the data in a table or graph.

The graph of a linear equation in two variables is a line.

Year	Average Price (in dollars per gallon)
2008	3.27
2009	2.35
2010	2.79
2011	3.53
2012	3.64
2013	3.53
2014	3.37
2015	2.48

Data from U.S. Department of Energy.

Linear Equation in Two Variables

A **linear equation in two variables** (here x and y) can be written in the form

$$Ax + By = C,$$

where A, B, and C are real numbers and A and B are not both 0. This form is called *standard form*.

Examples: $3x + 4y = 9$, $x - y = 0$, $x + 2y = -8$

Linear equations in two variables in standard form

Note

Linear equations in two variables that are not written in standard form, such as

$$y = 4x + 5 \quad \text{and} \quad 3x = 7 - 2y,$$

can be algebraically rewritten in this form, as we will discuss later.

OBJECTIVE ▶ ② **Write a solution as an ordered pair.** Recall that a *solution* of an equation is a number that makes the equation true when it replaces the variable. For example, the linear equation in *one* variable

$$x - 2 = 5 \quad \text{has solution} \quad 7$$

because replacing x with 7 gives a true statement.

A solution of a linear equation in two variables requires two numbers, one for each variable. For example, a true statement results when we replace x with 2 and y with 13 in the equation $y = 4x + 5$.

$$13 = 4(2) + 5 \quad \text{Let } x = 2 \text{ and } y = 13.$$

The pair of numbers $x = 2$ and $y = 13$ gives one solution of the equation $y = 4x + 5$. The phrase "$x = 2$ and $y = 13$" can be abbreviated as a pair of numbers written inside parentheses. ***The x-value is always given first.*** Such a pair of numbers is an **ordered pair**.

x-value ⌐ ⌐ y-value

$$(2, 13)$$

Ordered pair

② Write each solution as an ordered pair.

(a) $x = 5$ and $y = 7$

x-value y-value
↓   ↓
(——, ——)

(b) $y = 6$ and $x = -1$

x-value y-value
↓   ↓
(——, ——)

(c) $x = \dfrac{2}{3}$ and $y = -12$

(d) $y = 1.5$ and $x = -2.4$

(e) $x = 0$ and $y = 0$

! CAUTION

The ordered pairs $(2, 13)$ and $(13, 2)$ are *not* the same. In the first pair, $x = 2$ and $y = 13$. In the second pair, $x = 13$ and $y = 2$. ***The order in which the numbers are written in an ordered pair is important.***

Answers

2. (a) $5; 7$ **(b)** $-1; 6$

(c) $\left(\dfrac{2}{3}, -12\right)$ **(d)** $(-2.4, 1.5)$

(e) $(0, 0)$

Work Problem ② at the Side. ▶

3 Decide whether each ordered pair is a solution of the equation

$$5x + 2y = 20.$$

GS **(a)** $(0, 10)$

In this ordered pair,

$x = $ _____ and $y = $ _____.

$$5x + 2y = 20$$
$$5(\underline{\hspace{0.4cm}}) + 2(\underline{\hspace{0.4cm}}) \overset{?}{=} 20$$
$$\underline{\hspace{0.6cm}} + 20 \overset{?}{=} 20$$
$$\underline{\hspace{0.6cm}} = 20$$

Is $(0, 10)$ a solution?

(b) $(2, -5)$

(c) $(-4, 20)$

4 Complete each ordered pair for the equation

$$y = 2x - 9.$$

GS **(a)** $(5, \underline{\hspace{0.4cm}})$

In this ordered pair,

$x = $ _____.

We must find the corresponding value of _____.

$$y = 2x - 9$$
$$y = 2(\underline{\hspace{0.4cm}}) - 9$$
$$y = \underline{\hspace{0.6cm}} - 9$$
$$y = \underline{\hspace{0.6cm}}$$

The ordered pair is _____.

(b) $(2, \underline{\hspace{0.4cm}})$

(c) $(\underline{\hspace{0.4cm}}, 7)$

Answers

3. **(a)** 0; 10; 0; 10; 0; 20; yes
   (b) no **(c)** yes
4. **(a)** 5; y; 5; 10; 1; (5, 1)
   (b) (2, −5) **(c)** (8, 7)

OBJECTIVE ▶ 3 Decide whether a given ordered pair is a solution of a given equation. We substitute the x- and y-values of an ordered pair into a linear equation in two variables to see whether the ordered pair is a solution.

EXAMPLE 2 Deciding Whether Ordered Pairs Are Solutions

Decide whether each ordered pair is a solution of the equation $2x + 3y = 12$.

(a) $(3, 2)$

$$2x + 3y = 12$$
$$2(3) + 3(2) \overset{?}{=} 12 \qquad \text{Let } x = 3 \text{ and } y = 2.$$
$$6 + 6 \overset{?}{=} 12 \qquad \text{Multiply.}$$
$$12 = 12 \checkmark \qquad \text{True}$$

This result is true, so $(3, 2)$ is a solution of $2x + 3y = 12$.

(b) $(-2, -7)$

$$2x + 3y = 12$$
$$2(-2) + 3(-7) \overset{?}{=} 12 \qquad \text{Let } x = -2 \text{ and } y = -7.$$

Use parentheses to avoid errors.

$$-4 + (-21) \overset{?}{=} 12 \qquad \text{Multiply.}$$
$$-25 = 12 \qquad \text{False}$$

This result is false, so $(-2, -7)$ is *not* a solution of $2x + 3y = 12$.

◀ **Work Problem 3 at the Side.**

OBJECTIVE ▶ 4 Complete ordered pairs for a given equation. We substitute a number for one variable to find the value of the other variable.

EXAMPLE 3 Completing Ordered Pairs

Complete each ordered pair for the equation $y = 4x + 5$.

(a) $(7, \underline{\hspace{0.4cm}})$ *The x-value always comes first.*

In this ordered pair, $x = 7$. To find the corresponding value of y, replace x with 7 in the given equation.

$$y = 4x + 5$$

Solve for the value of y.

$$y = 4(7) + 5 \qquad \text{Let } x = 7.$$
$$y = 28 + 5 \qquad \text{Multiply.}$$
$$y = 33 \qquad \text{Add.}$$

The ordered pair is $(7, 33)$.

(b) $(\underline{\hspace{0.6cm}}, -3)$

In this ordered pair, $y = -3$. Replace y with -3 in the given equation.

$$y = 4x + 5$$

Solve for the value of x.

$$-3 = 4x + 5 \qquad \text{Let } y = -3.$$
$$-8 = 4x \qquad \text{Subtract 5 from each side.}$$
$$-2 = x \qquad \text{Divide each side by 4.}$$

The ordered pair is $(-2, -3)$.

◀ **Work Problem 4 at the Side.**

OBJECTIVE ▶ ⑤ Complete a table of values. Ordered pairs are often displayed in a **table of values.** Although we usually write tables of values vertically, they may be written horizontally.

EXAMPLE 4   Completing Tables of Values

Complete each table of values for the given equation. Then write the results as ordered pairs.

(a) $x - 2y = 8$

x	y		Ordered Pairs
2		⟶	(2, ____)
10		⟶	(10, ____)
	0	⟶	(____ , 0)
	−2	⟶	(____ , −2)

From the first row of the table, let $x = 2$ in the equation. From the second row of the table, let $x = 10$.

If	$x = 2,$		If	$x = 10,$	
then	$x - 2y = 8$		then	$x - 2y = 8$	
becomes	$2 - 2y = 8$		becomes	$10 - 2y = 8$	
	$-2y = 6$			$-2y = -2$	
	$y = -3.$			$y = 1.$	

The first two ordered pairs are $(2, -3)$ and $(10, 1)$. From the third and fourth rows of the table, let $y = 0$ and $y = -2$, respectively.

If	$y = 0,$		If	$y = -2,$	
then	$x - 2y = 8$		then	$x - 2y = 8$	
becomes	$x - 2(0) = 8$		becomes	$x - 2(-2) = 8$	
	$x - 0 = 8$			$x + 4 = 8$	
	$x = 8.$			$x = 4.$	

The last two ordered pairs are $(8, 0)$ and $(4, -2)$. The completed table of values and corresponding ordered pairs follow.

Write *y*-values in the second column.

x	y		Ordered Pairs
2	−3	⟶	(2, −3)
10	1	⟶	(10, 1)
8	0	⟶	(8, 0)
4	−2	⟶	(4, −2)

Write *x*-values in the first column.

Each ordered pair is a solution of the given equation $x - 2y = 8$.

(b) $x = 5$ (Using two variables, $x = 5$ could be written $x + 0y = 5$.)

x	y
	−2
	6
	3

The given equation is $x = 5$. No matter which value of y is chosen, the value of x is *always* 5.

x	y		Ordered Pairs
5	−2	⟶	(5, −2)
5	6	⟶	(5, 6)
5	3	⟶	(5, 3)

René Descartes (1596–1650)

The rectangular coordinate system, shown in **Figure 3** on the next page, is also called the **Cartesian coordinate system,** in honor of René Descartes, the French mathematician credited with its invention.

Continued on Next Page

5 Complete each table of values for the given equation. Then write the results as ordered pairs.

(a) $2x - 3y = 12$

x	y
0	
	0
3	
	-3

From the first row of the table, let $x =$ _____.

$$2x - 3y = 12$$
$$2(\underline{\quad}) - 3y = 12$$
$$\underline{\quad} - 3y = 12$$
$$-3y = 12$$
$$\frac{-3y}{\underline{\quad}} = \frac{12}{\underline{\quad}}$$
$$y = \underline{\quad}$$

Write _____ for y in the first row of the table. Repeat this process to complete the rest of the table.

(b) $x = -1$

x	y
	-4
	0
-1	2

(c) $y = 4$

x	y
-3	4
2	
5	

(c) $y = -3$ (Using two variables, $y = -3$ could be written $0x + y = -3$.)

x	y
-5	
0	
2	

The given equation is $y = -3$. No matter which value of x is chosen, the value of y is *always* -3.

x	y	Ordered Pairs
-5	-3	$\longrightarrow (-5, -3)$
0	-3	$\longrightarrow (0, -3)$
2	-3	$\longrightarrow (2, -3)$

◀ **Work Problem 5 at the Side.**

OBJECTIVE 6 Plot ordered pairs. Recall that a linear equation in *one* variable can have zero, one, or an infinite number of real number solutions. These solutions can be graphed on *one* number line. For example, the linear equation in one variable

$$x - 2 = 5 \quad \text{has solution} \quad 7.$$

The solution 7 is graphed on the number line in **Figure 2.**

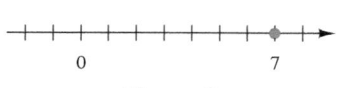

Figure 2

Every linear equation in *two* variables has an infinite number of ordered pairs (x, y) as solutions. To graph these solutions, we need *two* number lines, one for each variable, drawn at right angles as in **Figure 3.** The horizontal number line is the **x-axis,** and the vertical line is the **y-axis.** The point at which the x-axis and y-axis intersect is the **origin.** Together, the x-axis and y-axis form a **rectangular coordinate system.**

The rectangular coordinate system is divided into four regions, or **quadrants.** These quadrants are numbered counterclockwise. See **Figure 3.**

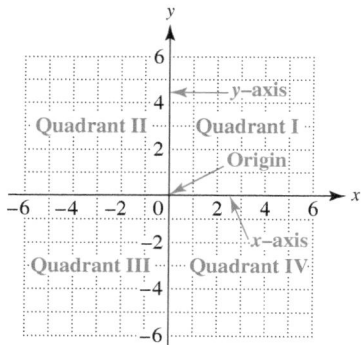

Rectangular coordinate system

Figure 3

The x-axis and y-axis determine a **plane**—a flat surface illustrated by a sheet of paper. By referring to the two axes, every point in the plane can be associated with an ordered pair. The numbers in the ordered pair are the **coordinates** of the point.

Answers

5. (a) 0; 0; 0; -3; -3; -4; -4

x	y
0	-4
6	0
3	-2
$\frac{3}{2}$	-3

$(0, -4), (6, 0), (3, -2), \left(\frac{3}{2}, -3\right)$

(b)

x	y
-1	-4
-1	0
-1	-2

$(-1, -4), (-1, 0),$ $(-1, 2)$

(c)

x	y
-3	4
2	4
5	4

$(-3, 4), (2, 4),$ $(5, 4)$

Note

In a plane, *both* numbers in the ordered pair are needed to locate a point. The ordered pair is a name for the point.

| EXAMPLE 5 | **Plotting Ordered Pairs** |

Plot the given points in a rectangular coordinate system.

(a) $(2, 3)$ **(b)** $(-1, -4)$ **(c)** $(-2, 3)$

(d) $(3, -2)$ **(e)** $\left(\frac{3}{2}, 2\right)$ **(f)** $(4, -3.75)$

(g) $(5, 0)$ **(h)** $(0, -3)$ **(i)** $(0, 0)$

The point $(2, 3)$ from part (a) is **plotted** (graphed) in **Figure 4.** The other points are plotted in **Figure 5.** In each case, we begin at the origin and follow this procedure.

Step 1 Move right or left the number of units that corresponds to the x-coordinate in the ordered pair—*right if the x-coordinate is positive or left if it is negative.*

Step 2 Then turn and move up or down the number of units that corresponds to the y-coordinate in the ordered pair—*up if the y-coordinate is positive or down if it is negative.*

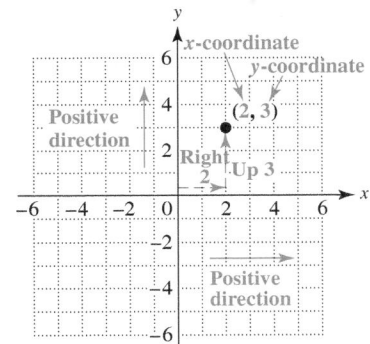

Figure 4

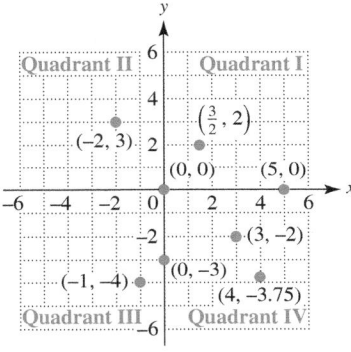

Figure 5

Notice in **Figure 5** that the point $(-2, 3)$ is in quadrant II, whereas the point $(3, -2)$ is in quadrant IV.

The order of the coordinates is important. The x-coordinate is always given first in an ordered pair.

To plot the point $\left(\frac{3}{2}, 2\right)$, think of the improper fraction $\frac{3}{2}$ as the mixed number $1\frac{1}{2}$ and move $\frac{3}{2}$ $\left(\text{or } 1\frac{1}{2}\right)$ units to the right along the x-axis. Then turn and go 2 units up, parallel to the y-axis.

The point $(4, -3.75)$ is plotted similarly, by approximating the location of the decimal y-coordinate.

The point $(5, 0)$ lies on the x-axis because the y-coordinate is 0. The point $(0, -3)$ lies on the y-axis because the x-coordinate is 0. The point $(0, 0)$ is at the origin.

Points on the axes themselves are not in any quadrant.

——————— Work Problem **6** at the Side. ▶

We can use a linear equation in two variables to mathematically describe, or *model*, certain real-life situations, as shown in the next example.

6 Plot the given points in a rectangular coordinate system.

(a) $(3, 5)$ **(b)** $(-2, 6)$

(c) $(-4.5, 0)$ **(d)** $(-5, -2)$

(e) $(6, -2)$ **(f)** $(0, -6)$

(g) $(0, 0)$ **(h)** $\left(-3, \frac{5}{2}\right)$

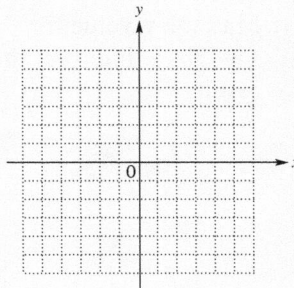

Indicate the points that lie in each quadrant.

quadrant I: _____

quadrant II: _____

quadrant III: _____

quadrant IV: _____

no quadrant: _____

Answers

6.

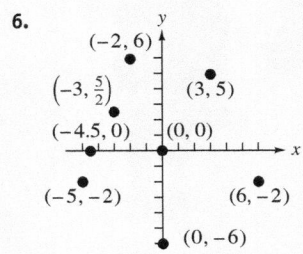

quadrant I: $(3, 5)$

quadrant II: $(-2, 6), \left(-3, \frac{5}{2}\right)$

quadrant III: $(-5, -2)$

quadrant IV: $(6, -2)$

no quadrant: $(-4.5, 0), (0, 0), (0, -6)$

7 Refer to the linear equation in **Example 6.** Round answers to the nearest whole number.

GS **(a)** Find the y-value for $x = 2011$.

$$y = -1.571x + 3294$$

$$y = -1.571(\underline{\quad}) + \underline{\quad}$$

$$y \approx \underline{\quad}$$

(b) Find the y-value for $x = 2013$. Interpret the result.

Answers

7. **(a)** 2011; 3294; 135
(b) 132; In 2013, there were about 132 thousand (or 132,000) twin births in the United States.

EXAMPLE 6 **Using a Linear Equation to Model Twin Births**

The annual number of twin births in the United States from 2008 through 2013 can be approximated by the linear equation

Number of twin births ———┐   ┌——— Year

$$y = -1.571x + 3294,$$

which relates x, the year, and y, the number of twin births in thousands. (Data from National Center for Health Statistics.)

(a) Complete the table of values for the given linear equation.

x (Year)	y (Number of Twin Births, in thousands)
2008	
2011	
2013	

To find y when $x = 2008$, we substitute into the equation.

$$y = -1.571x + 3294$$

$\approx$ means "is approximately equal to." $y = -1.571\,(\mathbf{2008}) + 3294$ Let $x = 2008$.

$$y \approx 139$$ Use a calculator.

In 2008, there were about 139 thousand (or 139,000) twin births.

◀ **Work Problem** **7** **at the Side.**

Including the results from **Margin Problem 7** gives the completed table.

x (Year)	y (Number of Twin Births, in thousands)		Ordered Pairs (x, y)
2008	139	⟶	(2008, 139)
2011	135	⟶	(2011, 135)
2013	132	⟶	(2013, 132)

Here each year x is paired with a number of twin births y (in thousands).

(b) Graph the ordered pairs found in part (a).

See **Figure 6.** A graph of ordered pairs of data is a **scatter diagram.** A scatter diagram enables us to describe how the two quantities are related. In **Figure 6,** the plotted points could be connected to approximate a straight *line,* so the variables x (year) and y (number of twin births) have a *linear* relationship. The decrease in the number of twin births is also reflected.

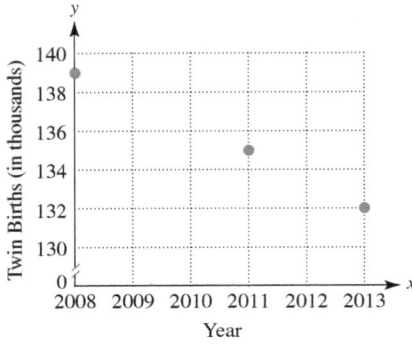

Notice the axis labels and scales. Each square represents 1 unit in the horizontal direction and 2 units in the vertical direction. We show a break in the y-axis, to indicate the jump from 0 to 130.

NUMBER OF TWIN BIRTHS

Figure 6

3.1 Exercises

FOR EXTRA HELP

Go to MyMathLab *for worked-out, step-by-step solutions to exercises enclosed in a square* ▢ *and video solutions to* ▶ *exercises.*

CONCEPT CHECK *Complete each statement.*

1. The symbol (x, y) (*does / does not*) represent an ordered pair, while the symbols $[x, y]$ and $\{x, y\}$ (*do / do not*) represent ordered pairs.

2. The origin is represented by the ordered pair _____.

3. In the ordered pair $(4, -1)$, $x =$ _____ and $y =$ _____. This ordered pair (*is / is not*) the same as the ordered pair $(-1, 4)$.

4. The point whose graph has coordinates $(-4, 2)$ is in quadrant _____.

5. The point whose graph has coordinates $(0, 5)$ lies on the _____-axis.

6. The ordered pair $(4,$ _____$)$ is a solution of the equation $y = 3$.

7. The ordered pair $($ _____$, -2)$ is a solution of the equation $x = 6$.

8. The ordered pair $(3, 2)$ is a solution of the equation $2x - 5y =$ _____.

CONCEPT CHECK *Fill in each blank with the word* positive *or the word* negative.

The point with coordinates (x, y) is in

9. quadrant III if x is _____ and y is _____ .

10. quadrant II if x is _____ and y is _____ .

11. quadrant IV if x is _____ and y is _____ .

12. quadrant I if x is _____ and y is _____ .

The line graph shows the overall unemployment rate in the U.S. civilian labor force for the years 2009 through 2015. Use the graph to work each problem. ***See Example 1.***

13. Between which years did the unemployment rate increase?

14. What was the general trend in the unemployment rate between 2010 and 2015?

15. Estimate the unemployment rate in 2010 and that in 2015. About how much did the unemployment rate decrease between 2010 and 2015?

16. About how much did the unemployment rate decrease between 2014 and 2015?

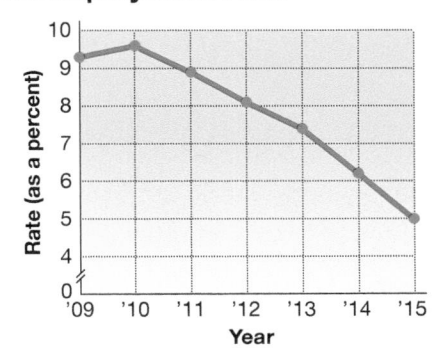

Unemployment Rate

Rate (as a percent)

Year

Data from Bureau of Labor Statistics.

The line graph shows the number of new and used passenger cars (in millions) imported into the United States for the years 2009 through 2014. Use the graph to work each problem. ***See Example 1.***

17. Over which two consecutive years did the number of imported cars increase the most? About how much was this increase?

18. Between which two consecutive years was the number of imported cars about the same? Estimate the number of cars imported during each of these years.

19. Describe what happened to sales of imported cars between 2012 and 2014.

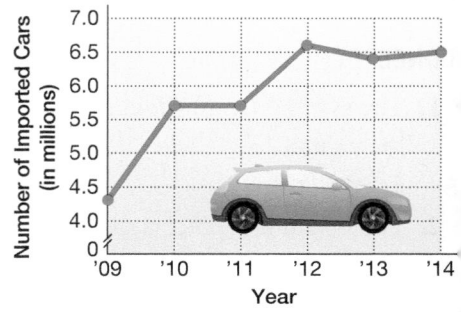

Passenger Cars Imported into the U.S.

Data from U.S. Census Bureau.

20. During which year(s) were fewer than 6 millions cars imported into the United States?

Decide whether each ordered pair is a solution of the given equation. ***See Example 2.***

21. $x + y = 8$; $(0, 8)$

22. $x + y = 9$; $(0, 9)$

23. $2x - y = 6$; $(4, 2)$

24. $2x + y = 5$; $(3, -1)$

25. $5x - 3y = 15$; $(5, 2)$

26. $4x - 3y = 6$; $(2, 1)$

27. $x = -4y$; $(-8, 2)$

28. $y = 3x$; $(2, 6)$

29. $x = -6$; $(5, -6)$

30. $x = -9$; $(8, -9)$

31. $y = 2$; $(2, 4)$

32. $y = 7$; $(7, -2)$

Complete each ordered pair for the equation $y = 2x + 7$. ***See Example 3.***

33. $(5, \underline{\quad})$

34. $(0, \underline{\quad})$

35. $(\underline{\quad}, 0)$

36. $(\underline{\quad}, -3)$

Complete each ordered pair for the equation $y = -4x - 4$. ***See Example 3.***

37. $(0, \underline{\quad})$

38. $(\underline{\quad}, 0)$

39. $(\underline{\quad}, 16)$

40. $(\underline{\quad}, 24)$

Complete each table of values for the given equation. Then write the results as ordered pairs. ***See Example 4.***

41. $4x + 3y = 24$

x	y
0	
	0
	4

42. $2x + 3y = 12$

x	y
0	
	0
	8

43. $3x - 5y = -15$

x	y
0	
	0
	-6

44. $4x - 9y = -36$

x	y
	0
0	
	8

45. $x = -9$

x	y
	6
	2
	-3

46. $x = 12$

x	y
	3
	8
	0

47. $y = 6$

x	y
8	
4	
−2	

48. $y = -10$

x	y
4	
0	
−4	

49. $x - 8 = 0$

x	y
	8
	3
	0

50. $x + 4 = 0$

x	y
	4
	0
	−4

51. $y + 2 = 0$

x	y
9	
2	
0	

52. $y - 1 = 0$

x	y
1	
0	
−1	

Give an ordered pair for each point labeled A–H in the figure. (Coordinates of the points shown are integers.) Identify the quadrant in which each point is located. ***See Example 5.***

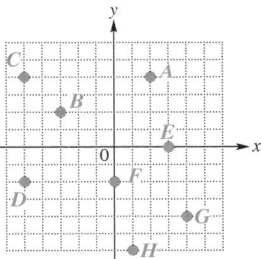

53. *A* **54.** *B* **55.** *C* **56.** *D*

57. *E* **58.** *F* **59.** *G* **60.** *H*

Answer each question.

61. A point (x, y) has the property that $xy < 0$. In which quadrant(s) must the point lie? Explain.

62. A point (x, y) has the property that $xy > 0$. In which quadrant(s) must the point lie? Explain.

Plot each point on the rectangular coordinate system provided. ***See Example 5.***

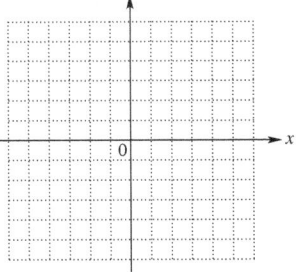

63. 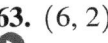 $(6, 2)$ **64.** $(5, 3)$ **65.** $(-4, 2)$ **66.** $(-3, 5)$

67. 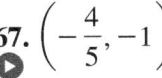 $\left(-\dfrac{4}{5}, -1\right)$ **68.** $\left(-\dfrac{3}{2}, -4\right)$ **69.** $(3, -1.75)$ **70.** $(5, -4.25)$

71. $(0, 4)$ **72.** $(0, -3)$ **73.** $(4, 0)$ **74.** $(-3, 0)$

Complete each table of values for the given equation. Then plot the ordered pairs. ***See Examples 4 and 5.***

75. $x - 2y = 6$

x	y
0	
	0
2	
	−1

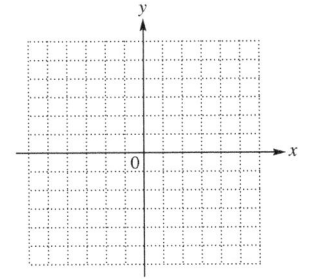

76. $2x - y = 4$

x	y
0	
	0
1	
	−6

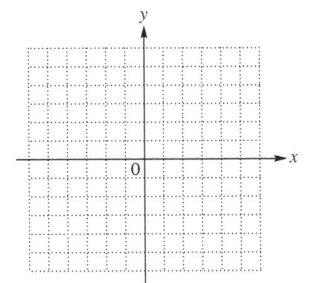

77. $3x - 4y = 12$

x	y
0	
	0
−4	
	−4

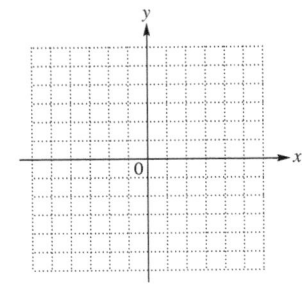

78. $2x - 5y = 10$

x	y
0	
	0
−5	
	−3

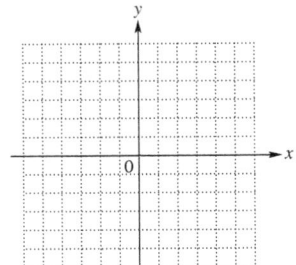

79. $y + 4 = 0$

x	y
0	
5	
−2	
−3	

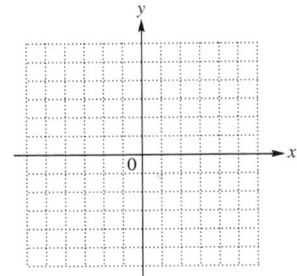

80. $x - 5 = 0$

x	y
	1
	0
	6
	−4

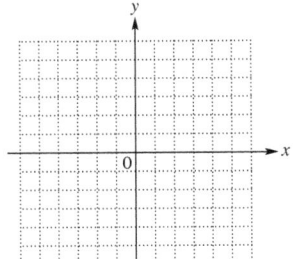

81. Describe the pattern indicated by the plotted points in **Exercises 75–80.**

82. Answer each question.

(a) A line through the plotted points in **Exercise 79** would be (*horizontal / vertical*). What do you notice about the *y*-coordinates of the ordered pairs?

(b) A line through the plotted points in **Exercise 80** would be (*horizontal / vertical*). What do you notice about the *x*-coordinates of the ordered pairs?

Work each problem. See Example 6.

83. Suppose that it costs a flat fee of $20 plus $5 per day to rent a pressure washer. Therefore, the cost *y* in dollars to rent the pressure washer for *x* days is given by

$$y = 5x + 20.$$

Express each of the following using an ordered pair (x, y).

(a) When the washer is rented for 5 days, the cost is $45. (*Hint:* What does *x* represent? What does *y* represent?)

(b) We paid $50 when we returned the washer, so we must have rented it for 6 days.

84. Suppose that it costs $5000 to start up a business selling snow cones. Furthermore, it costs $0.50 per cone in labor, ice, syrup, and overhead. Then the cost *y* in dollars to make *x* snow cones is given by

$$y = 0.50x + 5000.$$

Express each of the following using an ordered pair (x, y).

(a) When 100 snow cones are made, the cost is $5050. (*Hint:* What does *x* represent? What does *y* represent?)

(b) When the cost is $6000, the number of snow cones made is 2000.

85. The table shows the rate (in percent) at which 2-year college students (public) complete a degree within 3 years.

Year	Percent
2009	28.3
2010	28.0
2011	26.9
2012	25.4
2013	22.5
2014	21.9

Data from ACT.

(a) Write the data from the table as ordered pairs (x, y), where x represents the year and y represents the percent.

(b) What would the ordered pair $(2000, 32.4)$ mean in the context of this problem?

(c) Make a scatter diagram of the data using the ordered pairs from part (a).

2-YEAR COLLEGE STUDENTS COMPLETING A DEGREE WITHIN 3 YEARS

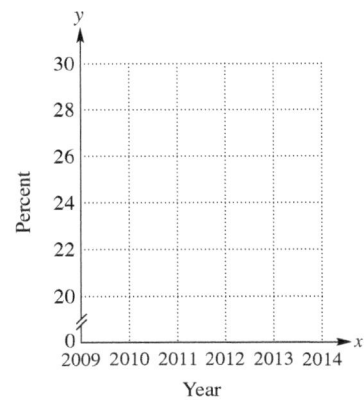

(d) Describe the pattern indicated by the points on the scatter diagram. What happened to the rates at which 2-year college students complete a degree within 3 years?

86. The table shows the number of U.S. students studying abroad (in thousands) for recent academic years.

Academic Year	Number of Students (in thousands)
2008	260
2009	271
2010	274
2011	283
2012	289
2013	304

Data from Institute of International Education.

(a) Write the data from the table as ordered pairs (x, y), where x represents the year and y represents the number of U.S. students studying abroad, in thousands.

(b) What does the ordered pair $(2000, 154)$ mean in the context of this problem?

(c) Make a scatter diagram of the data using the ordered pairs from part (a).

U.S. STUDENTS STUDYING ABROAD

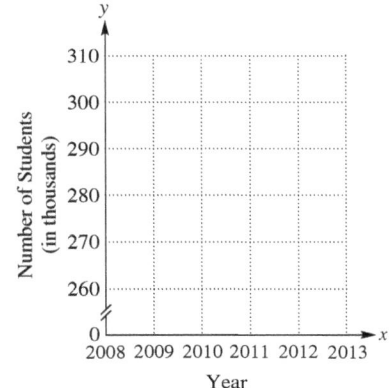

(d) Describe the pattern indicated by the points on the scatter diagram. What was the trend in the number of U.S. students studying abroad during these years?

87. The maximum benefit for the heart from exercising occurs if the heart rate is in the target heart rate zone. The lower limit of this target zone can be approximated by the linear equation

$$y = -0.5x + 108,$$

where x represents age and y represents heartbeats per minute. (Data from www.fitresource.com)

(a) Complete the table of values for this linear equation.

Age	Heartbeats (per minute)
20	
40	
60	
80	

(b) Write the data from the table of values as ordered pairs (x, y).

(c) Make a scatter diagram of the data. Do the points lie in a linear pattern?

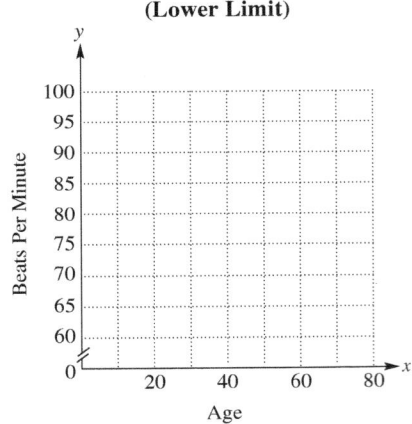

TARGET HEART RATE ZONE
(Lower Limit)

88. (See **Exercise 87.**) The upper limit of the target heart rate zone can be approximated by the linear equation

$$y = -0.8x + 173,$$

where x represents age and y represents heartbeats per minute. (Data from www.fitresource.com)

(a) Complete the table of values for this linear equation.

Age	Heartbeats (per minute)
20	
40	
60	
80	

(b) Write the data from the table of values as ordered pairs (x, y).

(c) Make a scatter diagram of the data. Describe the pattern indicated by the data.

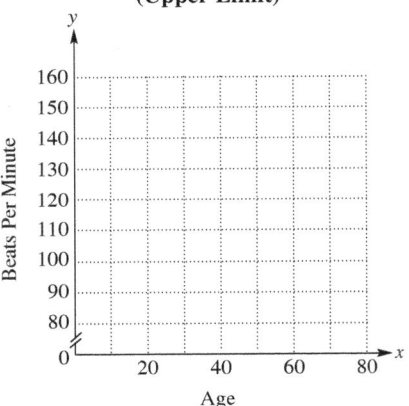

TARGET HEART RATE ZONE
(Upper Limit)

89. See **Exercises 87 and 88.** What is the target heart rate zone for age 20?   Age 40?

90. See **Exercises 87 and 88.** What is the target heart rate zone for age 60?   Age 80?

Study Skills
ANALYZING YOUR TEST RESULTS

*A*n exam is a learning opportunity—learn from your mistakes.* After a test is returned, do the following:

▶ **Note what you got wrong and why you had points deducted.**

▶ **Figure out how to solve the problems you missed.** Check your text or notes, or ask your instructor. Rework the problems correctly.

▶ **Keep all quizzes and tests that are returned to you.** Use them to study for future tests and the final exam.

Typical Reasons for Errors on Math Tests

1. You read the directions wrong.
2. You read the question wrong or skipped over something.
3. You made a computation error.
4. You made a careless error. (For example, you incorrectly copied a correct answer onto a separate answer sheet.)
5. Your answer was not complete.
6. You labeled your answer wrong. (For example, you labeled an answer "ft" instead of "ft^2".)
7. You didn't show your work.

These are test-taking errors. They are easy to correct if you read carefully, show all your work, proofread, and double-check units and labels.

8. You didn't understand a concept.
9. You were unable to set up the problem (in an application).
10. You were unable to apply a procedure.

These are test preparation errors. Be sure to practice all the kinds of problems that you will see on tests.

Now Try This

❶ Below are sample charts for tracking your test-taking progress. Refer to the tests you have taken so far in your course. For each test, check the appropriate box in the charts to indicate that you made an error in a particular category.

❷ What test-taking errors did you make? Do you notice any patterns?

_____

_____

❸ What test preparation errors did you make? Do you notice any patterns?

_____

_____

❹ What will you do to avoid these kinds of errors on your next test?

_____

_____

TEST-TAKING ERRORS

Test	Read directions wrong	Read question wrong	Computation error	Careless error	Not complete	Labeled wrong	Didn't show work
1							
2							
3							

TEST PREPARATION ERRORS

Test	Didn't understand concept	Didn't set up problem correctly	Couldn't apply a procedure to solve
1			
2			
3			

3.2 Graphing Linear Equations in Two Variables

OBJECTIVES

1. Graph linear equations by plotting ordered pairs.
2. Find intercepts.
3. Graph linear equations of the form $Ax + By = 0$.
4. Graph linear equations of the form $y = b$ or $x = a$.
5. Use a linear equation to model data.

OBJECTIVE ▸ 1 Graph linear equations by plotting ordered pairs. There are infinitely many ordered pairs that satisfy an equation in two variables. We find these ordered-pair solutions by choosing as many values of x (or y) as we wish and then completing each ordered pair.

For example, consider the equation $x + 2y = 7$. If we choose $x = 1$, then we can substitute to find the corresponding value of y.

$$x + 2y = 7 \quad \text{Given equation}$$
$$1 + 2y = 7 \quad \text{Let } x = 1.$$
$$2y = 6 \quad \text{Subtract 1.}$$
$$y = 3 \quad \text{Divide by 2.}$$

If $x = 1$, then $y = 3$, and the ordered pair $(1, 3)$ is a solution of the equation.

$$1 + 2(3) = 7 \checkmark \quad \begin{array}{l}\text{A true statement results, so}\\ (1, 3) \text{ is a solution.}\end{array}$$

◀ **Work Problem 1 at the Side.**

Figure 7 shows a graph of the ordered-pair solution found above and those in **Margin Problem 1** for $x + 2y = 7$.

1 Complete each ordered pair to find additional solutions of the equation

$$x + 2y = 7.$$

GS (a) $(-1, \underline{\quad})$

Substitute _____ for x in the equation and solve for the variable _____.

(b) $(3, \underline{\quad})$

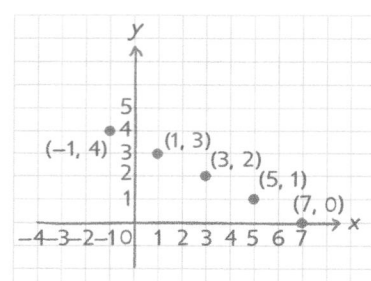

Figure 7

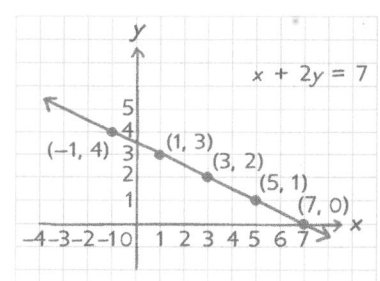

Figure 8

(c) $(5, \underline{\quad})$

Notice that the points plotted in **Figure 7** all appear to lie on a straight line, as shown in **Figure 8**. In fact, the following is true.

Every point on the line represents a solution of the equation $x + 2y = 7$, and every solution of the equation corresponds to a point on the line.

This line gives a "picture" of all the solutions of the equation

$$x + 2y = 7.$$

(d) $(7, \underline{\quad})$

The line extends indefinitely in both directions, as suggested by the arrowhead on each end, and is the **graph** of the equation $x + 2y = 7$. **Graphing** is the process of plotting ordered pairs and drawing a line (or curve) through the corresponding points.

Graph of a Linear Equation

The graph of any linear equation in two variables is a straight line.

Answers

1. **(a)** $-1; y; (-1, 4)$
   (b) $(3, 2)$ **(c)** $(5, 1)$ **(d)** $(7, 0)$

Notice that the word ***line*** appears in the term "***line***ar equation."

EXAMPLE 1 **Graphing a Linear Equation**

Graph $x - y = -3$.

At least two different ordered pairs are needed to draw the graph. To find them, we arbitrarily choose values for x or y and substitute them into the equation. We choose $x = 0$ to find one ordered pair and $y = 0$ to find another.

$x - y = -3$
$0 - y = -3$ 0 is easy to substitute.
$-y = -3$ Subtract.
$y = 3$ Multiply by -1.

One ordered pair is $(0, 3)$.

$x - y = -3$
$x - 0 = -3$ 0 is easy to substitute.
$x = -3$ Subtract.

One ordered pair is $(-3, 0)$.

We find a third ordered pair (as a check) by choosing some other value for x or y. We let $x = 2$.

$x - y = -3$ We arbitrarily let $x = 2$. Other numbers
$2 - y = -3$ could be used for x, or for y, instead.
$-y = -5$ Subtract 2.
$y = 5$ Multiply by -1.

This gives the ordered pair $(2, 5)$. We plot the three ordered-pair solutions and draw a line through them. See **Figure 9.**

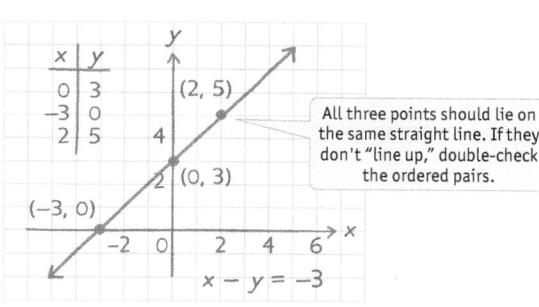

Figure 9

All three points should lie on the same straight line. If they don't "line up," double-check the ordered pairs.

─── Work Problem ② at the Side. ▶

EXAMPLE 2 **Graphing a Linear Equation**

Graph $4x - 5y = 20$.

To find three ordered pairs that are solutions of $4x - 5y = 20$, we choose three arbitrary values for x or y that we think will be easy to substitute.

Let $x = 0$.
$4x - 5y = 20$
$4(0) - 5y = 20$
$0 - 5y = 20$
$-5y = 20$
$y = -4$

Ordered pair: $(0, -4)$

Let $y = 0$.
$4x - 5y = 20$
$4x - 5(0) = 20$
$4x - 0 = 20$
$4x = 20$
$x = 5$

Ordered pair: $(5, 0)$

Let $y = 2$.
$4x - 5y = 20$
$4x - 5(2) = 20$
$4x - 10 = 20$
$4x = 30$
$\boxed{\frac{30}{4} = 7\frac{1}{2}} \rightarrow x = 7\frac{1}{2}$

Ordered pair: $\left(7\frac{1}{2}, 2\right)$

─── **Continued on Next Page**

② Graph the linear equation.
ⒼⓈ $x + y = 6$

x	y
0	
	0
4	

From the first row of the table, let $x = $ ____.

$x + y = 6$
____ $+ y = 6$
$y = $ ____

Write ____ for the y-value in the first row of the table.

The first ordered pair is ____.

Repeat this process to complete the table. Then plot the corresponding points, and draw the ____ through them.

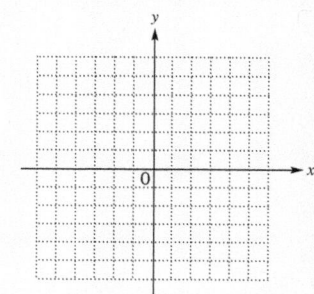

Answer

2. 0; 0; 6; 6; $(0, 6)$; line

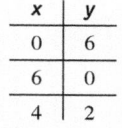

x	y
0	6
6	0
4	2

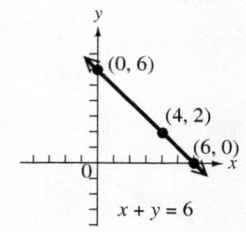

3 Graph $2x - 4y = 8$.

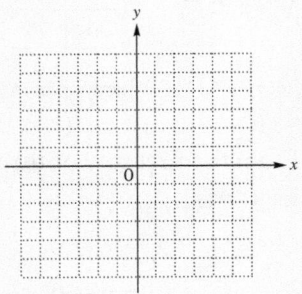

We plot the three ordered-pair solutions and draw a line through them. See **Figure 10.** Two points determine the line, and the third point is used to check that no errors have been made.

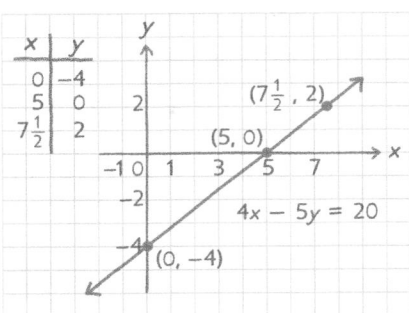

Figure 10

◀ **Work Problem 3 at the Side.**

Note

The ordered pairs that we find and use to graph an equation are *solutions* of the equation. For each value of x, there will be a corresponding value of y, and for each value of y, there will be a corresponding value of x. Substituting each ordered pair into the equation should produce a true statement.

OBJECTIVE ▶ **2** Find intercepts. In **Figure 10**, the graph intersects (crosses) the x-axis at $(5, 0)$ and the y-axis at $(0, -4)$. For this reason, $(5, 0)$ is the **x-intercept** and $(0, -4)$ is the **y-intercept** of the graph. The intercepts are convenient points to use when graphing a linear equation.

Finding Intercepts

To find the x-intercept, let $y = 0$ in the given equation and solve for x. Then $(x, 0)$ is the x-intercept.

To find the y-intercept, let $x = 0$ in the given equation and solve for y. Then $(0, y)$ is the y-intercept.

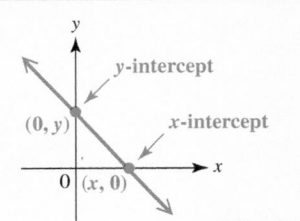

EXAMPLE 3 **Graphing a Linear Equation Using Intercepts**

Find the intercepts for the graph of $2x + y = 4$. Then draw the graph.

To find the intercepts, we first let $x = 0$ and then let $y = 0$. To find a third point, we arbitrarily let $x = 1$.

Let $x = 0$.	Let $y = 0$.	Let $x = 1$.
$2x + y = 4$	$2x + y = 4$	$2x + y = 4$
$2(0) + y = 4$	$2x + 0 = 4$	$2(1) + y = 4$
$0 + y = 4$	$2x = 4$	$2 + y = 4$
$y = 4$	$x = 2$	$y = 2$
y-intercept: $(0, 4)$	x-intercept: $(2, 0)$	Third point: $(1, 2)$

Answer

3.

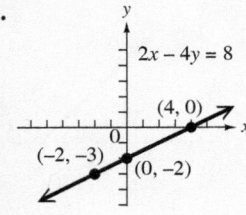

Continued on Next Page

The graph, with the two intercepts in red, is shown in **Figure 11.**

x	y
0	4
2	0
1	2

y-intercept ⟶ 0 | 4
x-intercept ⟶ 2 | 0
1 | 2

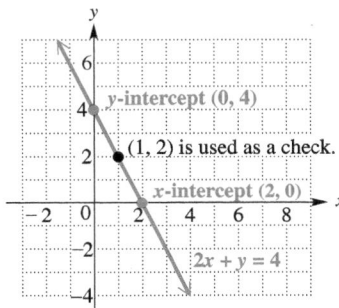

Figure 11

Work Problem ④ at the Side. ▶

EXAMPLE 4   **Graphing a Linear Equation Using Intercepts**

Graph $y = -\frac{3}{2}x + 3$.

Although this linear equation is not in standard form $Ax + By = C$, it *could* be written in that form. To find the intercepts, we first let $x = 0$ and then let $y = 0$.

$$y = -\frac{3}{2}x + 3 \qquad\qquad y = -\frac{3}{2}x + 3$$

$$y = -\frac{3}{2}(0) + 3 \quad \text{Let } x = 0. \qquad 0 = -\frac{3}{2}x + 3 \quad \text{Let } y = 0.$$

$$y = 0 + 3 \quad \text{Multiply.} \qquad \frac{3}{2}x = 3 \quad \text{Add } \frac{3}{2}x.$$

$$y = 3 \quad \text{Add.} \qquad x = 2 \quad \text{Multiply by } \frac{2}{3}.$$

y-intercept: $(0, 3)$ | x-intercept: $(2, 0)$

To find a third point, we arbitrarily let $x = -2$.

$$y = -\frac{3}{2}x + 3 \quad \boxed{\text{Choosing a multiple of 2 makes multiplying by } -\frac{3}{2} \text{ easier.}}$$

$$y = -\frac{3}{2}(-2) + 3 \quad \text{Let } x = -2.$$

$$y = 3 + 3 \quad \text{Multiply.}$$

$$y = 6 \quad \text{Add.}$$

Third point: $(-2, 6)$

We plot the three ordered-pair solutions and draw a line through them, as shown in **Figure 12.**

x	y
0	3
2	0
-2	6

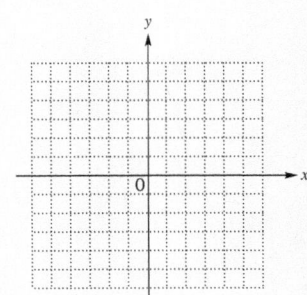

Figure 12

Work Problem ⑤ at the Side. ▶

---

④ GS Find the intercepts for the graph of
$$5x + 2y = 10.$$
Then draw the graph.

Find the y-intercept by letting $x = \underline{\quad}$ in the equation.
The y-intercept is $\underline{\quad}$.

Find the x-intercept by letting $y = \underline{\quad}$ in the equation.
The x-intercept is $\underline{\quad}$.

Find a third point with $x = 4$ as a check, and graph the equation.

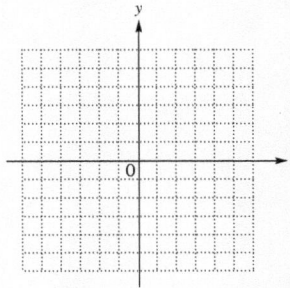

⑤ Graph $y = \frac{2}{3}x - 2$.

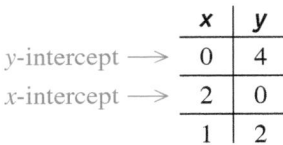

Answers

4. $0; (0, 5); 0; (2, 0)$

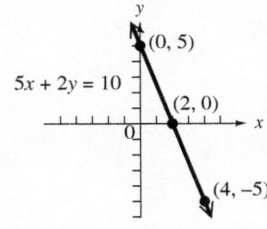

5.

6 Graph $2x - y = 0$.

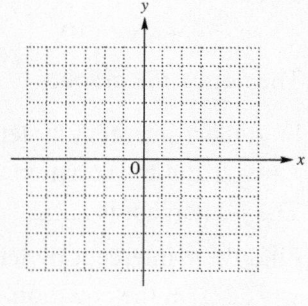

OBJECTIVE **3** Graph linear equations of the form $Ax + By = 0$.

EXAMPLE 5 Graphing an Equation with x- and y-Intercepts (0, 0)

Graph $x - 3y = 0$.

To find the y-intercept, let $x = 0$.

$$x - 3y = 0$$
$$0 - 3y = 0 \quad \text{Let } x = 0.$$
$$-3y = 0 \quad \text{Subtract.}$$
$$y = 0 \quad \text{Divide by } -3.$$

y-intercept: $(0, 0)$

To find the x-intercept, let $y = 0$.

$$x - 3y = 0$$
$$x - 3(0) = 0 \quad \text{Let } y = 0.$$
$$x - 0 = 0 \quad \text{Multiply.}$$
$$x = 0 \quad \text{Subtract.}$$

x-intercept: $(0, 0)$

The x- and y-intercepts are the *same* point, $(0, 0)$. We select *two other values* for x or y to find two other points. We choose $x = 6$ and $x = -3$.

$$x - 3y = 0$$
$$6 - 3y = 0 \quad \text{Let } x = 6.$$
$$-3y = -6 \quad \text{Subtract 6.}$$
$$y = 2 \quad \text{Divide by } -3.$$

Ordered pair: $(6, 2)$

$$x - 3y = 0$$
$$-3 - 3y = 0 \quad \text{Let } x = -3.$$
$$-3y = 3 \quad \text{Add 3.}$$
$$y = -1 \quad \text{Divide by } -3.$$

Ordered pair: $(-3, -1)$

We use the three ordered-pair solutions to draw the graph in **Figure 13**.

x	y
0	0
6	2
-3	-1

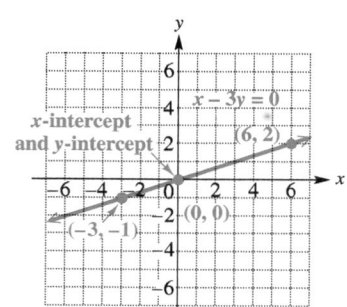

Figure 13

◀ **Work Problem 6** at the Side.

Line through the Origin

The graph of a linear equation of the form

$$Ax + By = 0,$$

where A and B are nonzero real numbers, passes through the origin $(0, 0)$.

Examples: $2x + 3y = 0$, $x = y$, $-4y = 3x$ — The last two can be written in $Ax + By = 0$ form.

Answer

6.

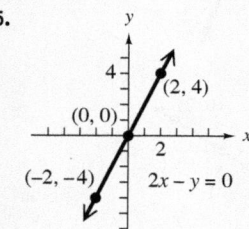

OBJECTIVE **4** Graph linear equations of the form $y = b$ or $x = a$. Consider the following linear equations.

$y = -4$ can be written as $0x + y = -4$.

$x = 3$ can be written as $x + 0y = 3$.

When the coefficient of x or y is 0, the graph is a horizontal or vertical line.

EXAMPLE 6 Graphing a Horizontal Line ($y = b$)

Graph $y = -4$.

For any value of x, the value of y is always -4. Three ordered-pair solutions of the equation are shown in the table of values. Drawing a line through these points gives the **horizontal line** in **Figure 14.**

The y-intercept is $(0, -4)$.

There is no x-intercept.

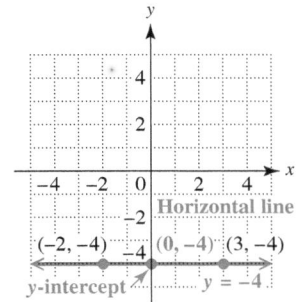

x	y
-2	-4
0	-4
3	-4

x can be any real number.

y must be -4.

Figure 14

Work Problem **7** at the Side. ▶

EXAMPLE 7 Graphing a Vertical Line ($x = a$)

Graph $x - 3 = 0$.

First we add 3 to each side of the equation $x - 3 = 0$ to obtain $x = 3$. All ordered-pair solutions of this equation have x-coordinate 3. Any number can be used for y. Three ordered pairs that satisfy the equation are given in the table of values. The graph is the **vertical line** in **Figure 15.**

The x-intercept is $(3, 0)$.

There is no y-intercept.

x	y
3	3
3	0
3	-2

y can be any real number.

x must be 3.

Figure 15

Work Problem **8** at the Side. ▶

From **Examples 6 and 7,** we make the following observations.

Horizontal and Vertical Lines

The graph of **$y = b$**, where b is a real number, is a **horizontal line** with y-intercept $(0, b)$ and no x-intercept (unless the horizontal line is the x-axis itself).

Examples: $y = 5$ and $y + 2 = 0$ (which can be written $y = -2$)

The graph of **$x = a$**, where a is a real number, is a **vertical line** with x-intercept $(a, 0)$ and no y-intercept (unless the vertical line is the y-axis itself).

Examples: $x = -1$ and $x - 6 = 0$ (which can be written $x = 6$)

Keep the following in mind regarding the x- and y-axes.

- *The x-axis is the horizontal line given by the equation $y = 0$.*
- *The y-axis is the vertical line given by the equation $x = 0$.*

7 Graph $y = -5$.

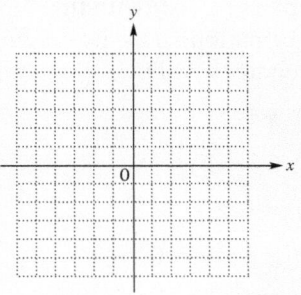

This is the graph of a (*horizontal / vertical*) line. There is no _____-intercept.

8 Graph $x + 4 = 6$.

GS First subtract _____ from each side to obtain the equivalent equation $x =$ _____.

Now graph this equation.

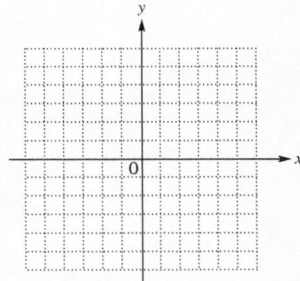

This is the graph of a (*horizontal / vertical*) line. There is no _____-intercept.

Answers

7.

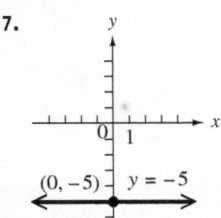

horizontal; x

8. 4; 2

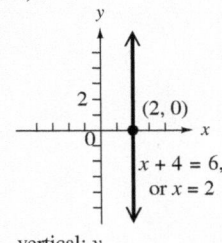

vertical; y

9 Match each linear equation in parts (a)–(d) with the information about its graph in choices A–D.

(a) $x = 5$

(b) $2x - 5y = 8$

(c) $y - 2 = 3$

(d) $x + 4y = 0$

A. The graph of the equation is a horizontal line.

B. The graph of the equation passes through the origin.

C. The graph of the equation is a vertical line.

D. The graph of the equation passes through the point $(9, 2)$.

> **! CAUTION**
> The equations of horizontal and vertical lines are often confused with each other.
> - The graph of $y = b$ is parallel to the x-axis (for $b \neq 0$).
> - The graph of $x = a$ is parallel to the y-axis (for $a \neq 0$).

A summary of the forms of linear equations from this section follows.

FORMS OF LINEAR EQUATIONS

Equation	To Graph	Example
$Ax + By = C$ (where A, B, and C are real numbers not equal to 0)	Find any two points on the line. A good choice is to find the intercepts. Let $x = 0$, and find the corresponding value of y. Then let $y = 0$, and find x. As a check, find a third point by choosing a value for x or y that has not yet been used.	
$Ax + By = 0$	The graph passes through $(0, 0)$. To find additional points that lie on the graph, choose any value for x or y, except 0.	
$y = b$	Draw a horizontal line, through the point $(0, b)$.	
$x = a$	Draw a vertical line, through the point $(a, 0)$.	

◀ **Work Problem 9 at the Side.**

OBJECTIVE ▶ 5 Use a linear equation to model data.

EXAMPLE 8 Using a Linear Equation to Model Credit Card Debt

The amount of credit card debt y in billions of dollars in the United States from 2010 through 2015 can be modeled by the linear equation

$$y = 179.0x + 2600,$$

where $x = 0$ represents the year 2010, $x = 1$ represents 2011, and so on. (Data from Board of Governors of the Federal Reserve System.)

——————————— **Continued on Next Page**

Answers

9. (a) C (b) D (c) A (d) B

(a) Use the equation to approximate credit card debt in the years 2010, 2013, and 2015.

Substitute the appropriate value for each year x to find credit card debt in that year.

$$y = 179.0x + 2600 \qquad \text{Given linear equation}$$

For 2010: $\quad y = 179.0(0) + 2600 \qquad$ Replace x with 0.

$y = 2600$ billion dollars $\quad$ Multiply, and then add.

For 2013: $\quad y = 179.0(3) + 2600 \qquad$ $2013 - 2010 = 3$

$y = 3137$ billion dollars $\quad$ Replace x with 3.

For 2015: $\quad y = 179.0(5) + 2600 \qquad$ $2015 - 2010 = 5$

$y = 3495$ billion dollars $\quad$ Replace x with 5.

(b) Write the information from part (a) as three ordered pairs, and use them to graph the given linear equation.

Because x represents the year and y represents the debt, the three ordered pairs are

$(0, 2600)$, $(3, 3137)$, and $(5, 3495)$.

See **Figure 16.** (Arrowheads are not included with the graphed line because the data are for the years 2010 to 2015 only—that is, from $x = 0$ to $x = 5$.)

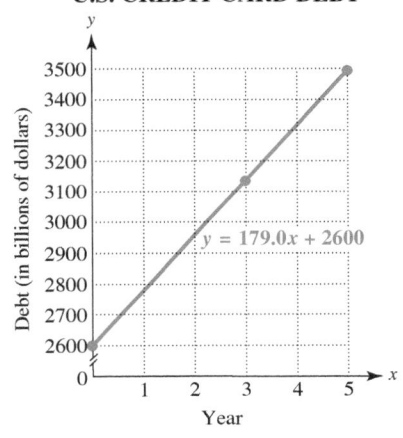

U.S. CREDIT CARD DEBT

$y = 179.0x + 2600$

Figure 16

(c) Use the graph and then the equation to determine the year when credit card debt was about $3300 billion.

Locate 3300 on the vertical axis in **Figure 16.** Move horizontally from 3300 to the graphed line, then down from the line to the value of x on the horizontal scale to find the year, here 4. Because $x = 0$ represents 2010, $x = 4$ represents the year

$$2010 + 4 = \mathbf{2014}. \leftarrow \begin{array}{l} \text{Year when credit card debt} \\ \text{was 3300 billion dollars} \end{array}$$

To use the equation to find the year, substitute 3300 for y and solve for x.

$$y = 179.0x + 2600 \qquad \text{Given linear equation}$$

$$\mathbf{3300} = 179.0x + 2600 \qquad \text{Let } y = 3300.$$

$$700 = 179.0x \qquad \text{Subtract 2600.}$$

$$3.9 \approx x \qquad \text{Divide by 179.0.}$$

Rounding up to the nearest year gives $x = 4$—that is, **2014**—which agrees with the graph.

Work Problem **10** at the Side. ▶

10 Refer to **Example 8.**

(a) Use the equation to approximate credit card debt in the year 2012.

(b) Use the graph and then the equation to determine the year when credit card debt was about $2800 billion. (Round down for the year.)

3.2 Exercises

FOR EXTRA HELP   *Go to* MyMathLab *for worked-out, step-by-step solutions to exercises enclosed in a square* ▢ *and video solutions to* ▶ *exercises.*

CONCEPT CHECK *Fill in each blank with the correct response.*

1. A linear equation in two variables can be written in the form $Ax +$ _____ $=$ _____, where A, B, and C are real numbers and A and B are not both _____.

2. The graph of any linear equation in two variables is a straight _____. Every point on the line represents a _____ of the equation.

3. **CONCEPT CHECK** Match the information about each graph in Column I with the correct linear equation in Column II.

I	II
(a) The graph of the equation has y-intercept $(0, -4)$.	**A.** $3x + y = -4$
(b) The graph of the equation has $(0, 0)$ as x-intercept and y-intercept.	**B.** $x - 4 = 0$
(c) The graph of the equation does not have an x-intercept.	**C.** $y = 4x$
(d) The graph of the equation has x-intercept $(4, 0)$.	**D.** $y = 4$

4. **CONCEPT CHECK** Which of these equations have a graph with only one intercept?

    A. $x + 8 = 0$ **B.** $x - y = 3$ **C.** $x + y = 0$ **D.** $y = 4$

CONCEPT CHECK *Identify the intercepts of each graph. (Coordinates of the points shown are integers.)*

5.
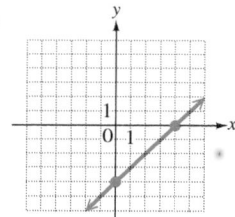

6.
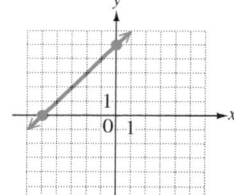

7.
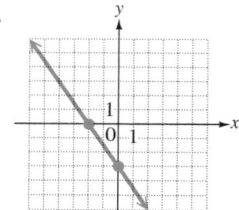

8.
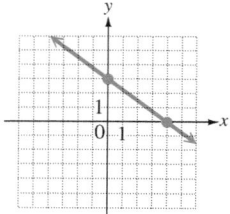

Complete the given ordered-pair solutions of each equation. Then graph the equation by plotting the points and drawing a line through them. **See Examples 1–4.**

9. $x + y = 5$ ▶

    $(0, \underline{\quad}), (\underline{\quad}, 0), (2, \underline{\quad})$

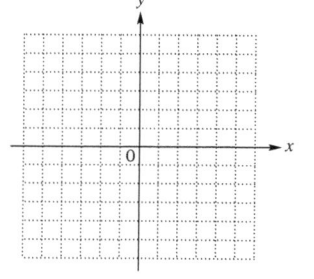

10. $x - y = 2$

    $(0, \underline{\quad}), (\underline{\quad}, 0), (5, \underline{\quad})$

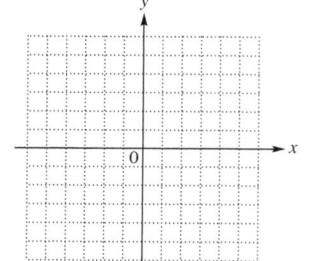

11. $y = \dfrac{2}{3}x + 1$ ▶

    $(0, \underline{\quad}), (3, \underline{\quad}), (-3, \underline{\quad})$

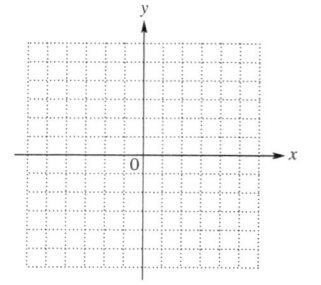

12. $y = -\dfrac{3}{4}x + 2$

$(0, \underline{\quad}), (4, \underline{\quad}), (-4, \underline{\quad})$

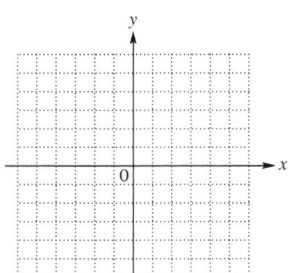

13. $3x = -y - 6$

$(0, \underline{\quad}), (\underline{\quad}, 0), (-\frac{1}{3}, \underline{\quad})$

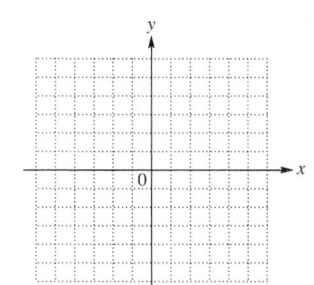

14. $x = 2y + 3$

$(\underline{\quad}, 0), (0, \underline{\quad}), (\underline{\quad}, \frac{1}{2})$

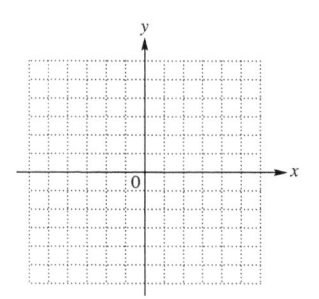

Find the x- and y-intercepts for the graph of each equation. ***See Examples 1–5.***

15. $x - y = 8$

To find the y-intercept, let $x = \underline{\quad\quad}$.
The y-intercept is $\underline{\quad\quad}$.

To find the x-intercept, let $y = \underline{\quad\quad}$.
The x-intercept is $\underline{\quad\quad}$.

16. $x - y = 10$

To find the y-intercept, let $x = \underline{\quad\quad}$.
The y-intercept is $\underline{\quad\quad}$.

To find the x-intercept, let $y = \underline{\quad\quad}$.
The x-intercept is $\underline{\quad\quad}$.

17. $2x - 3y = 24$

y-intercept: $\underline{\quad\quad}$

x-intercept: $\underline{\quad\quad}$

18. $-3x + 8y = 48$

y-intercept: $\underline{\quad\quad}$

x-intercept: $\underline{\quad\quad}$

19. $x + 6y = 0$

y-intercept: $\underline{\quad\quad}$

x-intercept: $\underline{\quad\quad}$

20. $3x - y = 0$

y-intercept: $\underline{\quad\quad}$

x-intercept: $\underline{\quad\quad}$

Graph each linear equation using intercepts. ***See Examples 1–7.***

21. $x - y = 4$

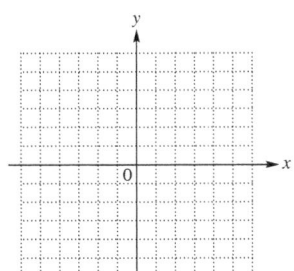

22. $x - y = 5$

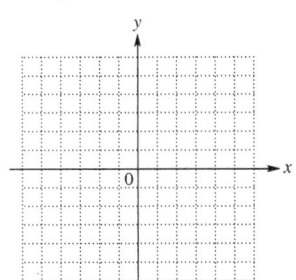

23. $2x + y = 6$

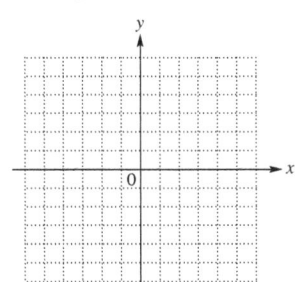

24. $-3x + y = -6$

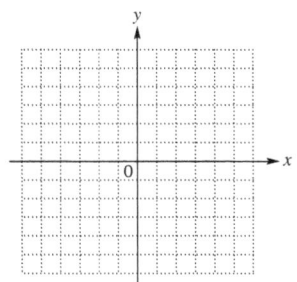

25. $y = x - 2$

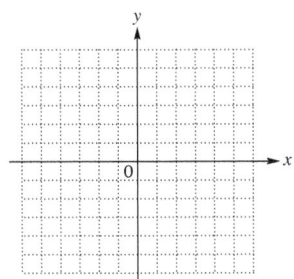

26. $y = -x + 6$

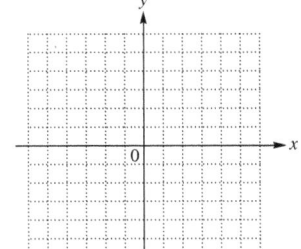

27. $y = 2x - 5$

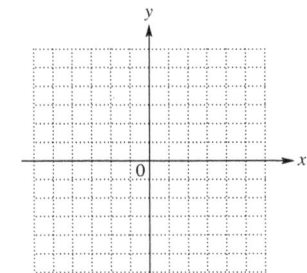

28. $y = 4x + 3$

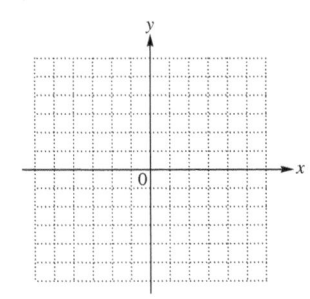

29. $3x + 7y = 14$

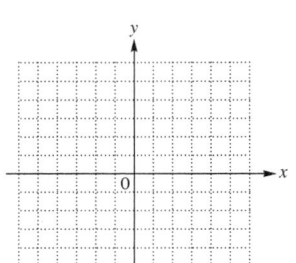

30. $6x - 5y = 18$

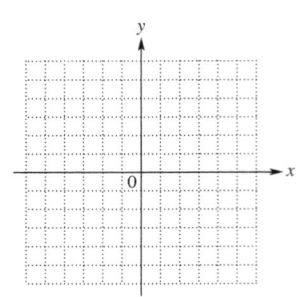

31. $y - 2x = 0$

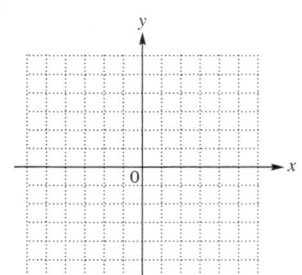

32. $y + 3x = 0$

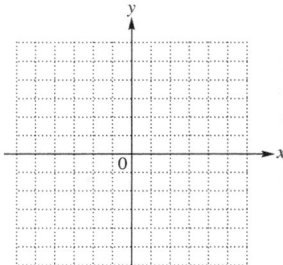

33. $y = -6x$

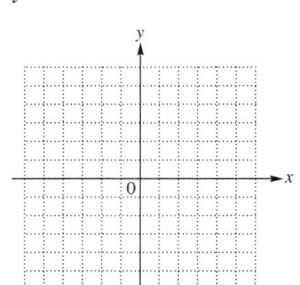

34. $y = 4x$

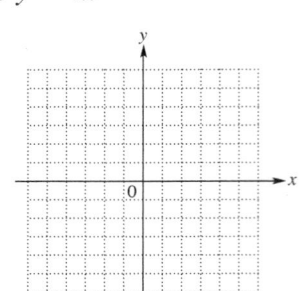

35. $y = -1$

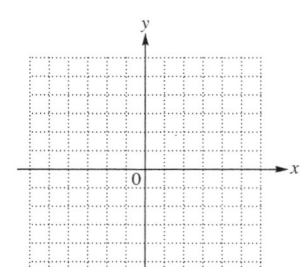

36. $y = 3$

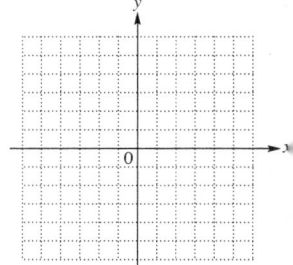

37. $x = -2$

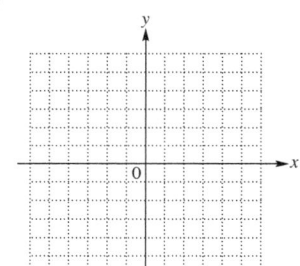

38. $x = 4$

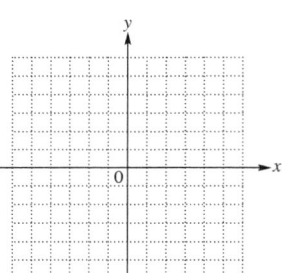

39. $y - 2 = 0$

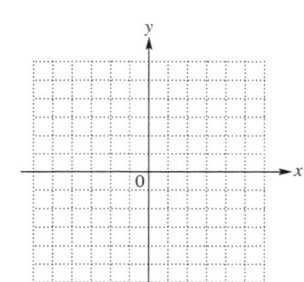

40. $y + 3 = 0$

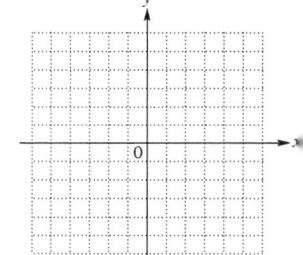

41. $x + 2 = 8$

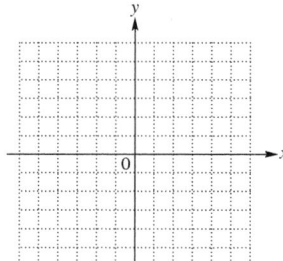

42. $x - 1 = -4$

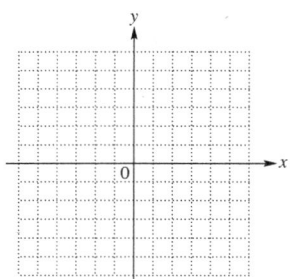

43. $-3y = 15$

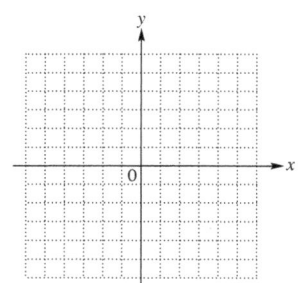

44. $-2y = 12$

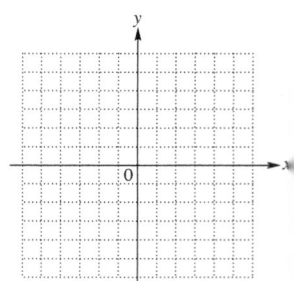

45. CONCEPT CHECK Match each equation in parts (a)–(d) with its graph in choices A–D.

(**a**) $x = -2$ (**b**) $y = -2$ (**c**) $x = 2$ (**d**) $y = 2$

A.

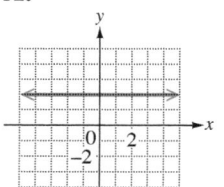

B.

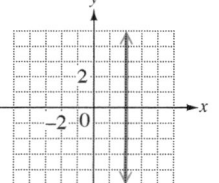

C.

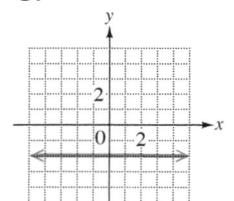

D.

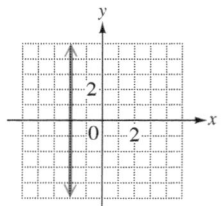

46. CONCEPT CHECK   What is the equation of the *x*-axis?   The *y*-axis?

Describe what the graph of each linear equation will look like in the coordinate plane.
(Hint: Rewrite the equation if necessary so that it is in a more recognizable form.)

47. $3x = y - 9$ **48.** $x - 10 = 1$ **49.** $3y = -6$ **50.** $2x = 4y$

Solve each problem. See Example 8.

51. The height *y* (in centimeters) of a woman can be approximated by the linear equation

$$y = 3.9x + 73.5,$$

where *x* is the length of her radius bone in centimeters.

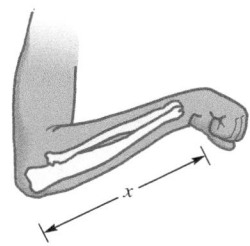

(a) Use the equation to approximate the heights of women with radius bones of lengths 20 cm, 22 cm, and 26 cm.

(b) Write the information from part (a) as three ordered pairs.

(c) Graph the equation for $x \geq 20$, using the data from part (b).

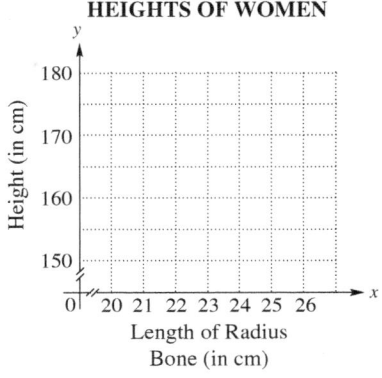

HEIGHTS OF WOMEN

(d) Use the graph to estimate the length of the radius bone in a woman who is 167 cm tall. Then use the equation to find the length of this radius bone to the nearest centimeter. (*Hint:* Substitute for *y* in the equation.)

52. The weight *y* (in pounds) of a man taller than 60 in. can be approximated by the linear equation

$$y = 5.5x - 220,$$

where *x* is the height of the man in inches.

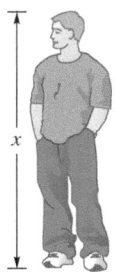

(a) Use the equation to approximate the weights of men whose heights are 62 in., 66 in., and 72 in.

(b) Write the information from part (a) as three ordered pairs.

(c) Graph the equation for $x \geq 62$, using the data from part (b).

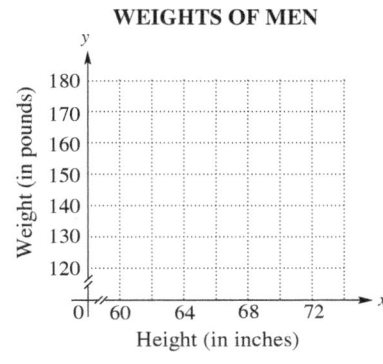

WEIGHTS OF MEN

(d) Use the graph to estimate the height of a man who weighs 155 lb. Then use the equation to find the height of this man to the nearest inch. (*Hint:* Substitute for *y* in the equation.)

53. As a fundraiser, a school club is selling posters. The printer charges a $25 set-up fee, plus $0.75 for each poster. The cost y in dollars to print x posters is given by the linear equation

$$y = 0.75x + 25.$$

(a) What is the cost y in dollars to print 50 posters? To print 100 posters?

(b) Find the number of posters x if the printer billed the club for costs of $175.

(c) Write the information from parts (a) and (b) as three ordered pairs.

(d) Use the data from part (c) to graph the equation for $x \geq 0$.

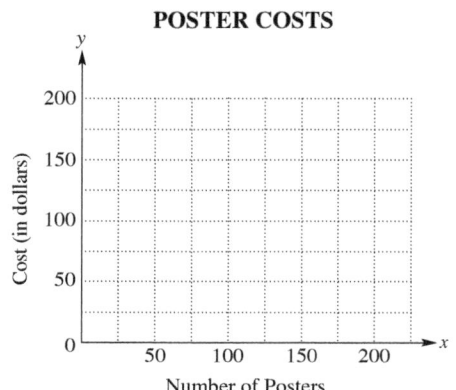

POSTER COSTS

(e) Use the graph in part (d) to estimate the cost to print 125 posters. Then find the actual cost using the given equation.

54. A gas station is selling gasoline for $3.50 per gal and charges $7 for a car wash. The cost y in dollars for x gallons of gasoline and a car wash is given by the linear equation

$$y = 3.50x + 7.$$

(a) What is the cost y in dollars for 9 gal of gasoline and a car wash? For 4 gal of gasoline and a car wash?

(b) Find the number of gallons of gasoline x if the cost for the gasoline and a car wash is $35.

(c) Write the information from parts (a) and (b) as three ordered pairs.

(d) Use the data from part (c) to graph the equation for $x \geq 0$.

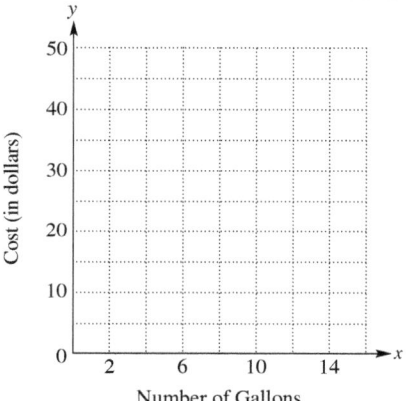

GASOLINE AND CAR WASH COSTS

(e) Use the graph in part (d) to estimate the cost of 12 gal of gasoline and a car wash. Then find the actual cost using the given equation.

55. The graph shows the value of a certain sport-utility vehicle over the first 5 yr of ownership. Use the graph to do the following.

(a) Determine the initial value of the SUV.

(b) Find the **depreciation** (loss in value) from the original value after the first 4 yr.

(c) What is the annual or yearly depreciation in each of the first 5 yr?

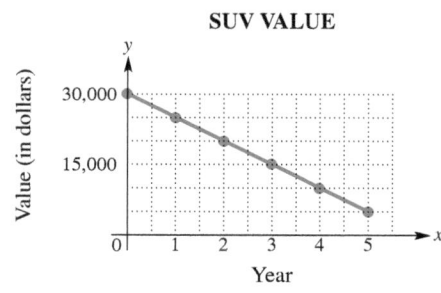

SUV VALUE

(d) What does the ordered pair (5, 5000) mean in the context of this problem?

56. Demand for an item is often closely related to its price. As price increases, demand decreases, and as price decreases, demand increases. Suppose demand for a video game is 2000 units when the price is $40, and demand is 2500 units when the price is $30.

(a) Let x be the price and y be the demand for the game. Graph the two given pairs of prices and demands on the graph to the right.

(b) Assume the relationship is linear. Draw a line through the two points from part (a). From the graph, estimate the demand if the price drops to $20.

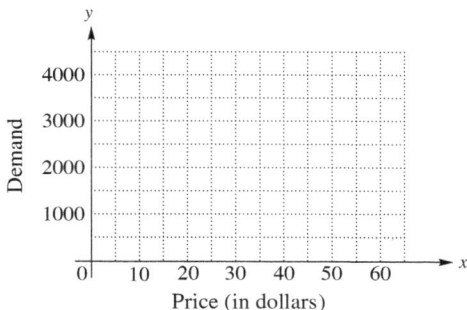

VIDEO GAME PRICE/DEMAND

(c) Use the graph to estimate the price if the demand is 3500 units.

(d) Write the prices and demands from parts (b) and (c) as ordered pairs.

57. U.S. per capita consumption y of cheese in pounds from 2000 through 2014 is shown in the graph and modeled by the linear equation

$$y = 0.307x + 30.1,$$

where $x = 0$ represents 2000, $x = 2$ represents 2002, and so on.

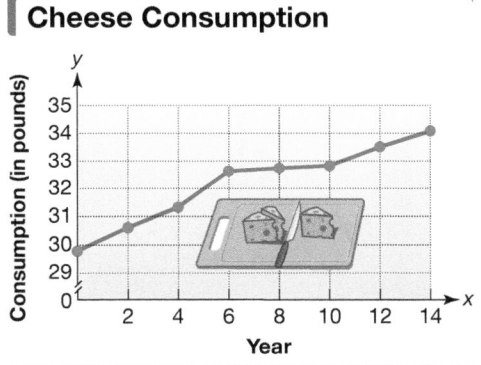

Cheese Consumption

Data from U.S. Department of Agriculture.

(a) Use the equation to approximate cheese consumption (to the nearest tenth) in 2000, 2010, and 2014.

(b) Use the graph to estimate cheese consumption for the same years.

(c) How do the approximations using the equation compare to the estimates from the graph?

(d) The USDA projects that per capita consumption of cheese in 2022 will be 36.8 lb. Use the equation to approximate per capita cheese consumption (to the nearest tenth) in 2022. How does the approximation compare to the USDA projection?

58. The number of U.S. marathon finishers y in thousands from 1990 through 2013 are shown in the graph and modeled by the linear equation

$$y = 13.8x + 224,$$

where $x = 0$ represents 1990, $x = 5$ represents to 1995, and so on.

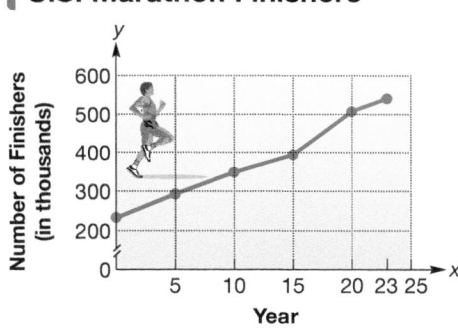

U.S. Marathon Finishers

Data from Running U.S.A.

(a) Use the equation to approximate the number of U.S. marathon finishers (to the nearest thousand) in 2000, 2010, and 2013.

(b) Use the graph to estimate the number of U.S. marathon finishers for the same years.

(c) How do the approximations using the equation compare to the estimates from the graph?

(d) Use the graph and then the equation to determine the year when there were about 400 thousand U.S. marathon finishers. Round up to the nearest year when using the equation.

3.3 The Slope of a Line

OBJECTIVES

1 Find the slope of a line given two points.

2 Find the slope from the equation of a line.

3 Use slope to determine whether two lines are parallel, perpendicular, or neither.

4 Solve problems involving average rate of change.

An important characteristic of the lines we graphed in the previous section is their slant or "steepness," as viewed from *left to right*. See **Figure 17.**

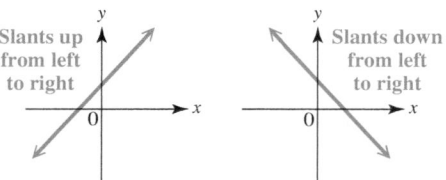

Figure 17

One way to measure the steepness of a line is to compare the vertical change in the line to the horizontal change while moving along the line from one fixed point to another. This measure of steepness is the *slope* of the line.

OBJECTIVE ▶ **1** **Find the slope of a line given two points.** To find the steepness, or slope, of the line in **Figure 18,** we begin at point Q and move to point P. The vertical change, or **rise,** is the change in the y-values, which is the difference

$$6 - 1 = 5 \text{ units.}$$

The horizontal change, or **run,** from Q to P is the change in the x-values, which is the difference

$$5 - 2 = 3 \text{ units.}$$

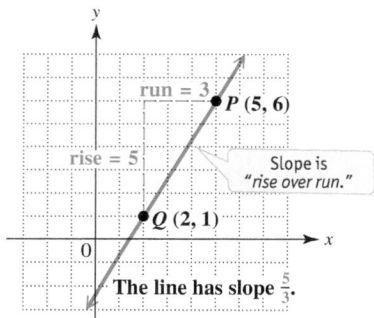

Figure 18

One way to compare two numbers is by using a ratio. **Slope** is the ratio of the vertical change in y to the horizontal change in x. The line in **Figure 18** has

$$\text{slope} = \frac{\text{vertical change in } y \text{ (rise)}}{\text{horizontal change in } x \text{ (run)}} = \frac{5}{3}.$$

To confirm this ratio, we can count grid squares. We start at point Q in **Figure 18** and count *up* 5 grid squares to find the vertical change (rise). To find the horizontal change (run) and arrive at point P, we count to the *right* 3 grid squares. The slope is $\frac{5}{3}$, as found above.

> **Slope of a Line**
>
> *Slope is a single number that allows us to determine the direction in which a line is slanting from left to right, as well as how much slant there is to the line.*

| EXAMPLE 1 | Finding the Slope of a Line |

Find the slope of the line in **Figure 19.**

We use the coordinates of the two points shown on the line. The vertical change is the difference of the y-values.

$$-1 - 3 = -4$$

The horizontal change is the difference of the x-values.

$$6 - 2 = 4$$

Thus, the line has

$$\text{slope} = \frac{\text{change in } y \text{ (rise)}}{\text{change in } x \text{ (run)}} = \frac{-4}{4}, \text{ or } -1.$$

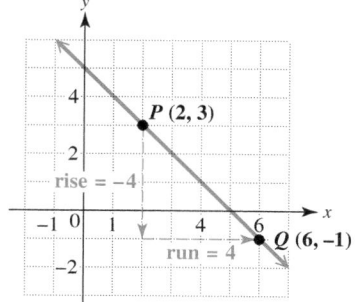

Figure 19

Counting grid squares, we begin at point P and count *down* 4 grid squares. Because we counted down, we write the vertical change as a negative number, -4 here. Then we count to the *right* 4 grid squares to reach point Q. The slope is $\frac{-4}{4}$, or -1.

──────── Work Problem ❶ at the Side. ▶

| Note |

The slope of a line is the same for any two points on the line. In **Figure 19,** locate the points $(3, 2)$ and $(5, 0)$, which also lie on the line. Start at $(3, 2)$ and count *down* 2 units and then to the *right* 2 units to arrive at the point $(5, 0)$.

$$\text{The slope is } \frac{-2}{2}, \text{ or } -1,$$

the same slope found in **Example 1** using the points $(2, 3)$ and $(6, -1)$.

The concept of slope is used in many everyday situations. See **Figure 20.**

- A highway with a 10%, or $\frac{1}{10}$, grade (or slope) rises 1 m for every 10 m of horizontal run.

- A roof with pitch (or slope) $\frac{5}{12}$ rises 5 ft for every 12 ft that it runs horizontally.

- A stairwell with slope $\frac{8}{12}$ $\left(\text{or } \frac{2}{3}\right)$ indicates a vertical rise of 8 ft for a horizontal run of 12 ft.

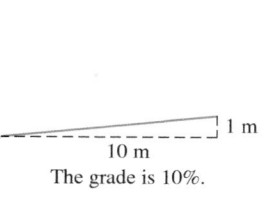

The grade is 10%.

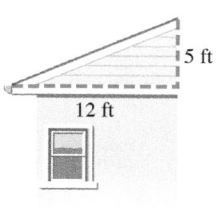

The roof has pitch $\frac{5}{12}$.

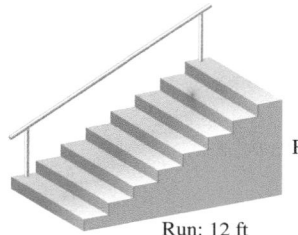

Rise: 8 ft

Run: 12 ft

The slope of these stairs is $\frac{8}{12} = \frac{2}{3}$.

Figure 20

We can generalize the preceding discussion and find the slope of a line through two nonspecific points (x_1, y_1) and (x_2, y_2). This notation is called **subscript notation.** Read x_1 as **"x-sub-one"** and x_2 as **"x-sub-two."**

❶ Find the slope of each line.

Ⓖⓢ **(a)**

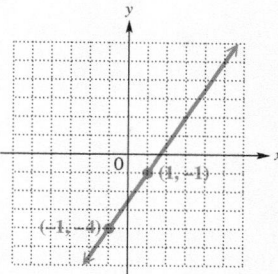

Begin at $(-1, -4)$.
Count (*up / down*) _____ units.
Then count to the (*right / left*) _____ units.

$$\text{slope} = \frac{\text{vertical change in } y}{\text{horizontal change in } x} = \frac{}{}$$

The slope is _____.

(b)

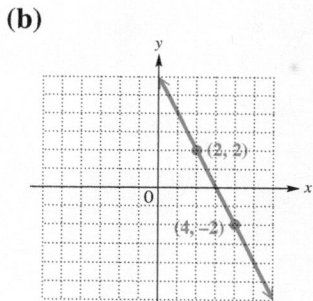

Answers

1. **(a)** up; 3; right; 2; 3; 2; $\frac{3}{2}$

   (b) -2

Moving along the line from the point (x_1, y_1) in **Figure 21** to the point (x_2, y_2), we see that y changes by $y_2 - y_1$ units. This is the vertical change (rise). Similarly, x changes by $x_2 - x_1$ units, which is the horizontal change (run). The slope of the line is the ratio of $y_2 - y_1$ to $x_2 - x_1$.

Figure 21

Slope Formula

The **slope m** of the line passing through the points (x_1, y_1) and (x_2, y_2) is defined as follows. (Traditionally, the letter m represents slope.)

$$m = \frac{\text{change in } y}{\text{change in } x} = \frac{y_2 - y_1}{x_2 - x_1} \quad \text{(where } x_1 \neq x_2\text{)}$$

The slope gives the change in y for each unit of change in x.

Note

Subscript notation is used to identify a point. It does *not* indicate an operation. *Notice the difference between x_2, which represents a nonspecific value, and x^2, which means $x \cdot x$.* Read x_2 as "x-sub-two," not "x squared."

EXAMPLE 2 **Finding Slopes of Lines Given Two Points**

Find the slope of each line.

(a) The line passing through $(-4, 7)$ and $(1, -2)$

Label the given points, and then apply the slope formula.

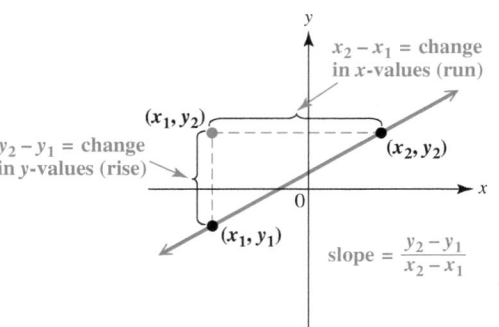

$$(\overset{\displaystyle (x_1, y_1)}{\downarrow \ \downarrow})\qquad (\overset{\displaystyle (x_2, y_2)}{\downarrow \ \downarrow})$$

$$(-4, 7) \quad \text{and} \quad (1, -2)$$

$$\text{slope } m = \frac{y_2 - y_1}{x_2 - x_1} = \frac{-2 - 7}{1 - (-4)} \quad \text{\small Substitute carefully.}$$

$$= \frac{-9}{5}, \quad \text{or} \quad -\frac{9}{5}$$

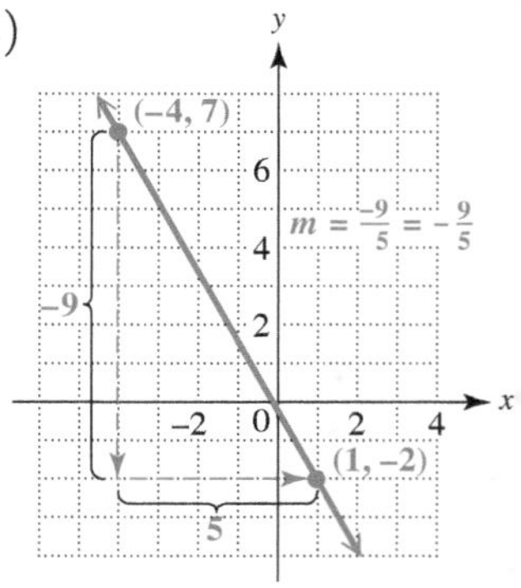

Figure 22

Begin at $(-4, 7)$ and count grid squares in **Figure 22** to confirm that the slope is $\frac{-9}{5}$, or $-\frac{9}{5}$.

Continued on Next Page

(b) The line passing through $(-9, -2)$ and $(12, 5)$

Label the points, and then apply the slope formula.

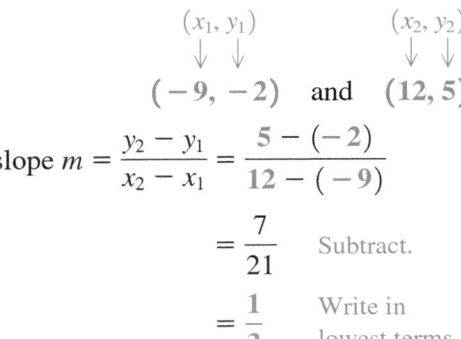

$$\begin{array}{cc} (x_1, y_1) & (x_2, y_2) \\ \downarrow\ \downarrow & \downarrow\ \downarrow \\ (-9, -2) & \text{and} \quad (12, 5) \end{array}$$

$$\text{slope } m = \frac{y_2 - y_1}{x_2 - x_1} = \frac{5 - (-2)}{12 - (-9)}$$

$$= \frac{7}{21} \qquad \text{Subtract.}$$

$$= \frac{1}{3} \qquad \begin{array}{l}\text{Write in}\\ \text{lowest terms.}\end{array}$$

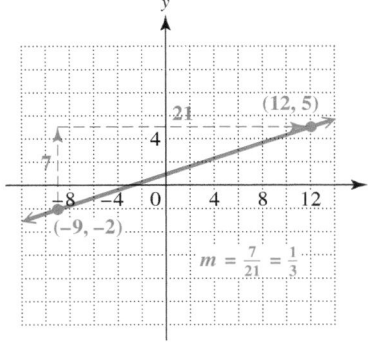

Figure 23

Confirm this calculation using **Figure 23.** (Note the scale on the axes.) The same slope is obtained if we label the points in reverse order.

$$\begin{array}{cc} (x_2, y_2) & (x_1, y_1) \\ \downarrow\ \downarrow & \downarrow\ \downarrow \\ (-9, -2) & \text{and} \quad (12, 5) \end{array}$$

It makes no difference which point is identified as (x_1, y_1) or (x_2, y_2).

$$\text{slope } m = \frac{y_2 - y_1}{x_2 - x_1} = \frac{-2 - 5}{-9 - 12} \qquad \text{Substitute.}$$

Start with the values of the *same* point. Subtract the values of the other point.

$$= \frac{1}{3} \qquad \begin{array}{l}\frac{-7}{-21} \text{ also equals } \frac{1}{3}.\\ \text{The same slope results.}\end{array}$$

─────────── **Work Problem ② at the Side.** ▶

The slopes of the lines in **Figures 22 and 23** suggest the following.

Orientation of Lines with Positive and Negative Slopes

A line with positive slope rises (slants up) from left to right.

A line with negative slope falls (slants down) from left to right.

| **EXAMPLE 3** | **Finding the Slope of a Horizontal Line** |

Find the slope of the line passing through $(-5, 4)$ and $(2, 4)$.

$$m = \frac{y_2 - y_1}{x_2 - x_1} = \frac{4 - 4}{-5 - 2} \qquad \begin{array}{l}\text{Subtract } y\text{-values.}\\ \text{Subtract } x\text{-values in the } same \text{ order.}\end{array}$$

$$= \frac{0}{-7}$$

$$= 0 \qquad \textbf{Slope 0}$$

The line passing through these two points is horizontal, with equation $y = 4$.

All horizontal lines have slope 0.

This is because the difference of the y-values for any two points on a horizontal line is always 0, which results in a 0 *numerator* when calculating slope. See **Figure 24.**

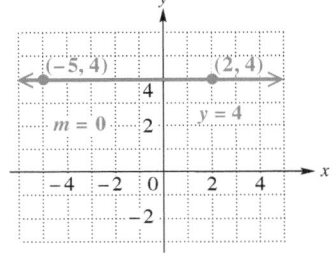

Figure 24

② Find the slope of each line.

ⓖⓢ **(a)** The line passing through $(6, -2)$ and $(5, 4)$

Label the points.

$$\begin{array}{cc} (x_1, y_1) & (\_\_\_, \_\_\_) \\ \downarrow\ \downarrow & \downarrow\ \ \downarrow \\ (6, -2) & \text{and} \quad (5, \ \ 4) \end{array}$$

$$\text{slope } m = \frac{y_2 - y_1}{x_2 - x_1}$$

$$= \frac{\_\_\_ - (\_\_\_)}{\_\_\_ - 6}$$

$$= \frac{6}{\_\_\_}$$

$$= -6$$

(b) The line passing through $(-3, 5)$ and $(-4, -7)$

(c) The line passing through $(6, -8)$ and $(-2, 4)$

(Find this slope in two different ways as in **Example 2(b).**)

Answers

2. (a) $x_2;\ y_2;\ 4;\ -2;\ 5;\ -1$

  (b) 12   **(c)** $-\dfrac{3}{2}; -\dfrac{3}{2}$

3 Find the slope of each line.

(a) The line passing through $(2, 5)$ and $(-1, 5)$

(b) The line passing through $(3, 1)$ and $(3, -4)$

EXAMPLE 4 Applying the Slope Concept to a Vertical Line

Find the slope of the line passing through $(6, 2)$ and $(6, -4)$.

$$m = \frac{y_2 - y_1}{x_2 - x_1} = \frac{2 - (-4)}{6 - 6} \quad \begin{array}{l}\text{Subtract } y\text{-values.} \\ \text{Subtract } x\text{-values in the } same \text{ order.}\end{array}$$

$$= \frac{6}{0} \quad \text{Undefined slope}$$

Because division by 0 is undefined, this line has undefined slope. (This is why the slope formula has the restriction $x_1 \neq x_2$.)

The graph in **Figure 25** shows that this line is vertical, with equation $x = 6$.

The slope of any vertical line is undefined.

This is because the difference of the x-values for any two points on a vertical line is always 0, which results in a 0 *denominator* when calculating slope.

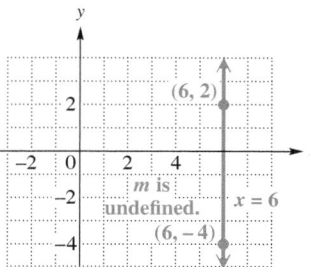

Figure 25

◀ **Work Problem** ③ **at the Side.**

---

4 Find the slope of each line.

GS (a) The line with equation $y = -1$

This is the equation of a (*horizontal / vertical*) line. It has (0 / *undefined*) slope.

(b) The line with equation $x - 4 = 0$

Rewrite this equation in an equivalent form.

$$x - 4 = 0$$

$$x = \underline{\hspace{1cm}}$$

This is the equation of a (*horizontal / vertical*) line. It has (0 / *undefined*) slope.

Slopes of Horizontal and Vertical Lines

A horizontal line, which has an equation of the form $y = b$ (where b is a constant (number)), has **slope 0.**

A vertical line, which has an equation of the form $x = a$ (where a is a constant (number)), has **undefined slope.**

◀ **Work Problem** ④ **at the Side.**

Figure 26 summarizes the four cases for slopes of lines.

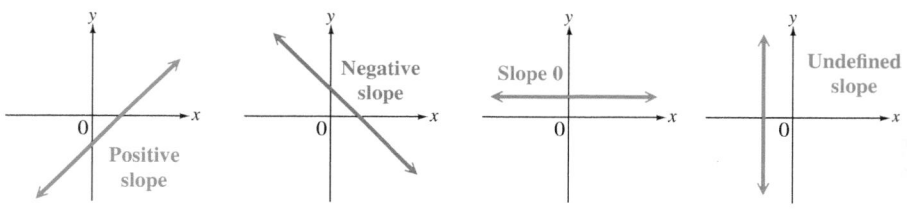

Slopes of lines

Figure 26

OBJECTIVE ❷ **Find the slope from the equation of a line.** Consider the linear equation

$$y = -3x + 5.$$

We can find the slope of this line using any two points on the line. Because the equation is solved for y, it involves less work to choose two different values of x and then find the corresponding values of y. We arbitrarily choose $x = -2$ and $x = 4$.

$y = -3x + 5$	$y = -3x + 5$
$y = -3(-2) + 5$ Let $x = -2$.	$y = -3(4) + 5$ Let $x = 4$.
$y = 11$ Multiply. Add.	$y = -7$ Multiply. Add.
Ordered pair: $(-2, 11)$	Ordered pair: $(4, -7)$

Answers

3. (a) 0   (b) undefined

4. (a) horizontal; 0

   (b) 4; vertical; undefined

Now we apply the slope formula using the two points $(-2, 11)$ and $(4, -7)$.

$$m = \frac{11 - (-7)}{-2 - 4} = \frac{18}{-6} = -3$$

The slope, -3, is the same number as the coefficient of x in the given equation $y = -3x + 5$. It can be shown that this always happens, *as long as the equation is solved for y.* This fact is used to find the slope of a line from its equation.

Finding the Slope of a Line from Its Equation

Step 1   Solve the equation for y.

Step 2   The slope is given by the coefficient of x.

EXAMPLE 5   **Finding Slopes from Equations**

Find the slope of each line.

(a) $2x - 5y = 4$

Step 1   Solve the equation for y.

$$2x - 5y = 4 \quad \boxed{\text{Isolate } y \text{ on one side.}}$$

$$-5y = 4 - 2x \qquad \text{Subtract } 2x.$$

$$-5y = -2x + 4 \qquad \text{Commutative property}$$

$$\boxed{\tfrac{-2x}{-5} = \tfrac{-2}{-5}x = \tfrac{2}{5}x} \quad y = \frac{2}{5}x - \frac{4}{5} \qquad \text{Divide } each \text{ term by } -5.$$

$$\uparrow \text{ Slope}$$

Step 2   The slope is given by the coefficient of x, so the slope is $\frac{2}{5}$.

(b)

$$8x + 4y = 1$$

$$\boxed{\text{Solve for } y.} \quad 4y = 1 - 8x \qquad \text{Subtract } 8x.$$

$$4y = -8x + 1 \qquad \text{Commutative property}$$

$$y = -2x + \frac{1}{4} \qquad \text{Divide } each \text{ term by } 4.$$

The slope of this line is given by the coefficient of x, which is -2.

(c)

$$3y + x = -3 \quad \boxed{\text{We omit the step showing the commutative property.}}$$

$$3y = -x - 3 \qquad \text{Subtract } x.$$

$$y = \frac{-x}{3} - 1 \qquad \text{Divide } each \text{ term by } 3.$$

$$\boxed{\text{The slope is } -\tfrac{1}{3}, \textit{ not } \tfrac{-x}{3} \text{ or } -\tfrac{x}{3}.} \quad y = -\frac{1}{3}x - 1 \qquad \tfrac{-x}{3} = \tfrac{-1x}{3} = -\tfrac{1}{3}x$$

The coefficient of x is $-\frac{1}{3}$, so the slope of this line is $-\frac{1}{3}$.

Work Problem ➎ **at the Side.** ▶

➎ Find the slope of each line.

ᴳˢ (a) $y = -\frac{7}{2}x + 1$

Because this equation is already solved for y, Step 1 is not needed. The slope, which is given by the _____ of _____, can be read directly from the equation. The slope is ____.

ᴳˢ (b) $4y = 4x - 3$

Solve for y here by dividing each term by ____ to obtain the equation

$$y = \text{_____}.$$

The coefficient of x is ____, so the slope is ____.

(c) $3x + 2y = 9$

(d) $5y - x = 10$

Answers

5. (a) coefficient; x; $-\dfrac{7}{2}$

(b) 4; $x - \dfrac{3}{4}$; 1; 1

(c) $-\dfrac{3}{2}$ **(d)** $\dfrac{1}{5}$

OBJECTIVE **3** **Use slope to determine whether two lines are parallel, perpendicular, or neither.** Two lines in a plane that never intersect are **parallel.** We use slopes to tell whether two lines are parallel.

Figure 27 shows the graphs of $x + 2y = 4$ and $x + 2y = -6$. These lines appear to be parallel. We solve each equation for y to find the slope.

$$x + 2y = 4$$
$$2y = -x + 4 \quad \text{Subtract } x.$$
$$y = \frac{-x}{2} + 2 \quad \text{Divide by 2.}$$
$$y = -\frac{1}{2}x + 2 \quad \tiny{\frac{-x}{2} = \frac{-1x}{2} = -\frac{1}{2}x}$$
$$\uparrow$$
$$\text{Slope}$$

$$x + 2y = -6$$
$$2y = -x - 6 \quad \text{Subtract } x.$$
$$y = \frac{-x}{2} - 3 \quad \text{Divide by 2.}$$
$$y = -\frac{1}{2}x - 3 \quad \boxed{\tiny{\text{The slope is } -\frac{1}{2}, \text{not} -\frac{x}{2}.}}$$
$$\uparrow$$
$$\text{Slope}$$

Each line has slope $-\frac{1}{2}$. *Nonvertical parallel lines always have equal slopes.*

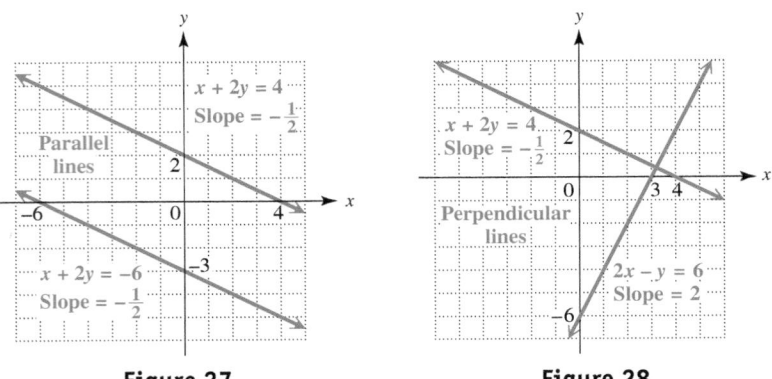

Figure 27   **Figure 28**

Figure 28 shows the graphs of $x + 2y = 4$ and $2x - y = 6$. These lines appear to be **perpendicular** (that is, they intersect at a 90° angle). As shown on the left above, solving $x + 2y = 4$ for y gives $y = -\frac{1}{2}x + 2$, with slope $-\frac{1}{2}$. We solve $2x - y = 6$ for y to find the slope.

$$2x - y = 6$$
$$-y = -2x + 6 \quad \text{Subtract } 2x.$$
$$y = 2x - 6 \quad \text{Multiply by } -1.$$
$$\uparrow$$
$$\text{Slope}$$

The product of the slopes of the two lines is

$$-\frac{1}{2}(2) = -1.$$

This condition is true in general.

The product of the slopes of two perpendicular lines, neither of which is vertical, is always −1.

This means that the slopes of perpendicular lines are negative (or opposite) reciprocals—if one slope is the nonzero number a, then the other is $-\frac{1}{a}$. (This is proved in more advanced courses.) The table in the margin shows several examples.

NEGATIVE RECIPROCALS

Number	Negative Reciprocal
$\frac{3}{4}$	$-\frac{4}{3}$
$\frac{1}{2}$	$-\frac{2}{1}$, or -2
-6, or $-\frac{6}{1}$	$\frac{1}{6}$
-0.4, or $-\frac{4}{10}$	$\frac{10}{4}$, or 2.5

The product of a number and its negative reciprocal is **−1.**

> **Slopes of Parallel and Perpendicular Lines**
>
> Two lines with the same slope are parallel.
>
> Two lines whose slopes have a product of -1 are perpendicular.

EXAMPLE 6 **Deciding Whether Two Lines Are Parallel or Perpendicular**

Decide whether each pair of lines is *parallel, perpendicular,* or *neither.*

(a) $x + 3y = 5$ and $-3x + y = 3$

Find the slope of each line by first solving each equation for y.

$$x + 3y = 5$$
$$3y = -x + 5 \qquad \text{Subtract } x.$$
$$y = -\frac{1}{3}x + \frac{5}{3} \qquad \text{Divide by 3.}$$

The slope is $-\frac{1}{3}$.

$$-3x + y = 3$$
$$y = 3x + 3 \qquad \text{Add } 3x.$$

The slope is 3.

Because the slopes are not equal, the lines are not parallel. Check the product of the slopes: $-\frac{1}{3}(3) = -1$. The two lines are *perpendicular* because the product of their slopes is -1. See **Figure 29.**

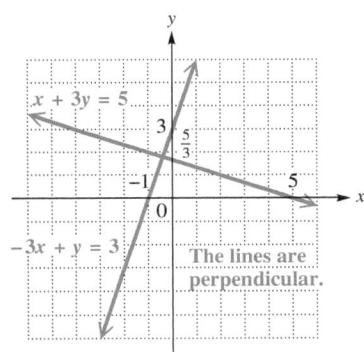

Figure 29

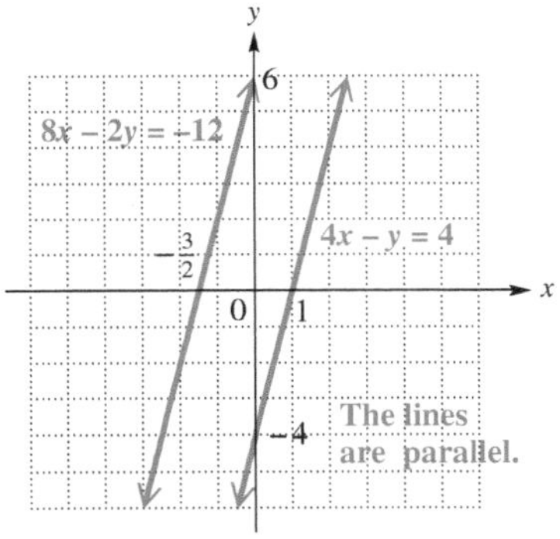

Figure 30

(b) $4x - y = 4$ → Solve each equation for y. → $y = 4x - 4$
$8x - 2y = -12$ → → $y = 4x + 6$

Both lines have slope 4, so the lines are *parallel.* See **Figure 30.**

(c) $4x + 3y = 6$ → Solve each equation for y. → $y = -\frac{4}{3}x + 2$
$2x - y = 5$ → → $y = 2x - 5$

The slopes are $-\frac{4}{3}$ and 2. They are not the same $\left(-\frac{4}{3} \neq 2\right)$, nor are they negative reciprocals $\left(-\frac{4}{3}(2) \neq -1\right)$. The two lines are *neither* parallel nor perpendicular.

(d) $5x - y = 1$ → Solve each equation for y. → $y = 5x - 1$
$x - 5y = -10$ → → $y = \frac{1}{5}x + 2$

$5\left(\frac{1}{5}\right) = 1, \text{not } -1.$

The slopes, 5 and $\frac{1}{5}$, neither are the same, nor are they negative reciprocals. The two lines are *neither* parallel nor perpendicular.

────── **Work Problem 6 at the Side.** ▶

6 Decide whether each pair of lines is *parallel, perpendicular,* or *neither.*

(a) $x + y = 6$
$x + y = 1$

(b) $3x - y = 4$
$x + 3y = 9$

(c) $2x - y = 5$
$2x + y = 3$

(d) $3x - 7y = 35$
$7x - 3y = -6$

Answers

6. (a) parallel **(b)** perpendicular
(c) neither **(d)** neither

7 There were approximately 40 million digital cable TV customers in the United States in 2008. (Data from SNL Kagan.)

   (a) Using this number for 2008 and the data for 2015 from the graph in **Figure 32,** find the average rate of change (to the nearest tenth) in number of customers per year from 2008 to 2015.

OBJECTIVE ▶ **4** **Solve problems involving average rate of change.** The slope formula applied to any two points on a line gives the **average rate of change** in y per unit change in x, where the value of y depends on the value of x.

For example, suppose the height of a boy increased from 60 to 68 in. between the ages of 12 and 16, as shown in **Figure 31.**

Change in height $y \rightarrow \dfrac{68 - 60}{16 - 12} = \dfrac{8}{4} = \mathbf{2 \textbf{ in. per yr}}$
Change in age $x \longrightarrow$

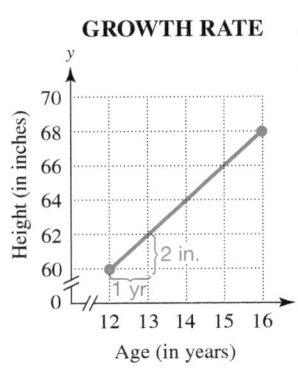

GROWTH RATE

Figure 31

The boy may have grown more than 2 in. during some years and less than 2 in. during others. If we plotted ordered pairs (age, height) for those years and drew a line connecting any two of the points, the average rate of change would likely be slightly different than that found above. However using the data for ages 12 and 16, the boy's *average* change in height was 2 in. per year over these years.

EXAMPLE 7 **Interpreting Slope as Average Rate of Change**

The graph in **Figure 32** approximates the number of digital cable TV customers in the United States during the years 2006 through 2015. Find the average rate of change in number of customers per year.

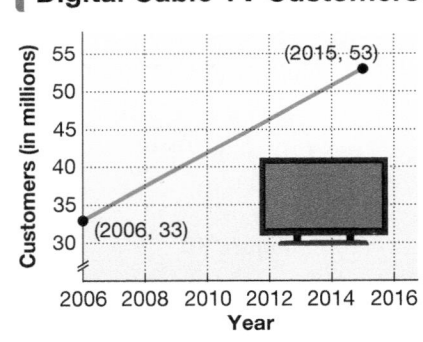

Digital Cable TV Customers

Data from SNL Kagan.

Figure 32

   (b) How does the average rate of change from part (a) compare to the average rate of change from 2006 to 2015 found in **Example 7?**

To find the average rate of change, we need two pairs of data. From the graph, we have the ordered pairs

$$(2006, 33) \quad \text{and} \quad (2015, 53).$$

We use the slope formula.

$$\text{average rate of change} = \frac{53 - 33}{2015 - 2006} = \frac{20}{9} \approx 2.2$$

> A positive slope indicates an increase.

This means that the number of digital cable TV customers *increased* by an average of 2.2 million customers per year from 2006 to 2015.

◀ **Work Problem 7** at the Side.

Answers

  7. (a) 1.9 million customers per year
    (b) It is less than the average rate of change for 2006–2015.

EXAMPLE 8   Interpreting Slope as Average Rate of Change

In 2006, there were 65 million basic cable TV customers in the United States. There were 54 million such customers in 2013. Find the average rate of change in the number of customers per year. (Data from Federal Communications Commission.)

To use the slope formula, we let one ordered pair be $(2006, 65)$ and the other be $(2013, 54)$.

$$\text{average rate of change} = \frac{54 - 65}{2013 - 2006} = \frac{-11}{7} \approx -1.6$$

> A negative slope indicates a decrease.

The graph in **Figure 33** confirms that the line through the ordered pairs falls from left to right and therefore has negative slope. Thus, the number of basic cable TV customers *decreased* by an average of 1.6 million customers per year from 2006 to 2013.

The negative sign in -1.6 denotes the *decrease*. (We say "The number of customers decreased by 1.6 million per year." It is *incorrect* to say "The number of customers decreased by -1.6 million per year.")

BASIC CABLE TV CUSTOMERS

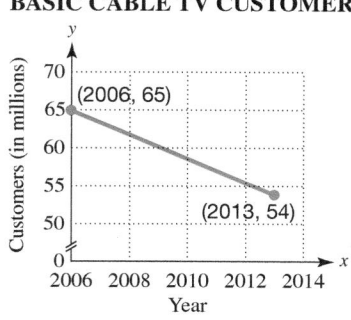

Figure 33

Work Problem **8** at the Side. ▶

8 In 2010, 226 million compact discs (CDs) were sold in the United States. In 2014, 141 million CDs were sold. Find the average rate of change (to the nearest tenth of a million) in CDs sold per year. (Data from Recording Industry Association of America.)

3.3 Exercises

FOR EXTRA HELP

Go to MyMathLab *for worked-out, step-by-step solutions to exercises enclosed in a square* ▢ *and video solutions to* ▶ *exercises.*

CONCEPT CHECK *Work each problem involving slope.*

1. Slope is used to measure the _____ of a line. Slope is the (*horizontal / vertical*) change compared to the (*horizontal / vertical*) change while moving along the line from one point to another.

2. Slope is the _____ of the vertical change in _____, called the (*rise / run*), to the horizontal change in _____, called the (*rise / run*).

3. Use at the graph at the right to answer the following.

(a) Start at the point $(-1, -4)$ and count vertically up to the horizontal line that goes through the other plotted point. What is this vertical change? (Remember: "up" means positive, "down" means negative.) _____

(b) From this new position, count horizontally to the other plotted point. What is this horizontal change? (Remember: "right" means positive, "left" means negative.) _____

(c) What is the ratio (quotient) of the numbers found in parts (a) and (b)? _____ What do we call this number? _____

(d) If we were to *start* at the point $(3, 2)$ and *end* at the point $(-1, -4)$, would the answer to part (c) be the same? Explain.

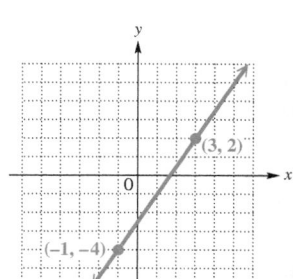

4. Match the graph of each line in parts (a)–(d) with its slope in choices A–D. (Coordinates of the points shown are integers.)

(a)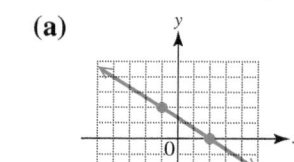

(b)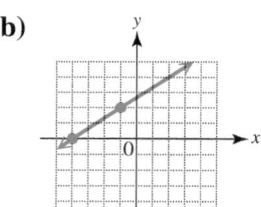

(c)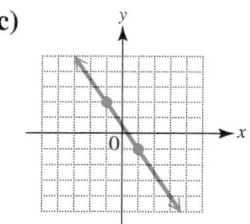

(d)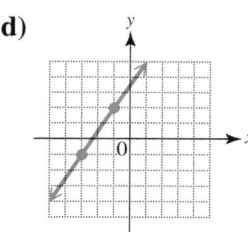

A. $\dfrac{2}{3}$ **B.** $\dfrac{3}{2}$ **C.** $-\dfrac{2}{3}$ **D.** $-\dfrac{3}{2}$

5. On the given axes, sketch the graph of a straight line having the indicated slope.

(a) Negative   (b) Positive   (c) Undefined   (d) 0

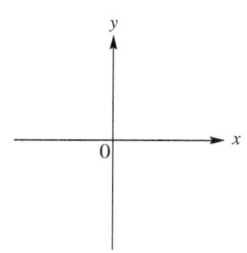

6. Decide whether the line with the given slope *m rises from left to right, falls from left to right*, is *horizontal*, or is *vertical*.

(a) $m = -4$ (b) $m = 0$ (c) m is undefined.   (d) $m = \dfrac{3}{7}$

CONCEPT CHECK   *The figure at the right shows a line that has a positive slope (because it rises from left to right) and a positive y-value for the y-intercept (because it intersects the y-axis above the origin).*

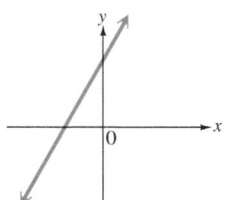

For each line graphed, decide whether

(a) the slope is positive, negative, *or* 0 *and*

(b) the y-value of the y-intercept is positive, negative, *or* 0.

7.

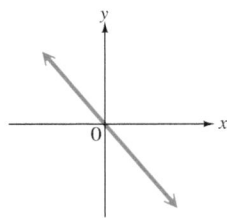

8.

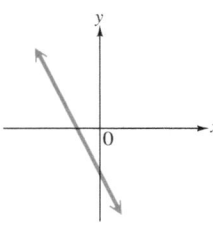

9.

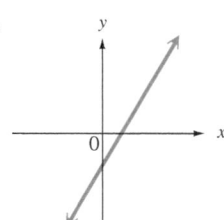

10.

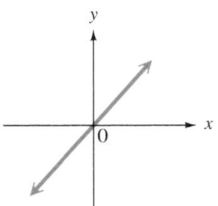

11.

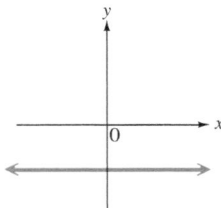

12.

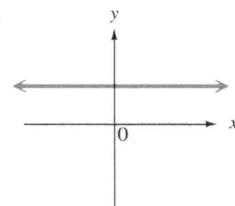

CONCEPT CHECK   *Answer each question.*

13. What is the slope (or grade) of this hill?

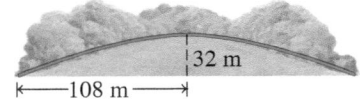

14. What is the slope (or pitch) of this roof?

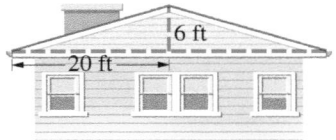

15. What is the slope of the slide? (*Hint:* The slide *drops* 8 ft vertically as it extends 12 ft horizontally.)

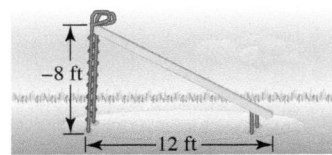

16. What is the slope (or grade) of this ski slope? (*Hint:* The ski slope *drops* 25 ft vertically as it extends 100 ft horizontally.)

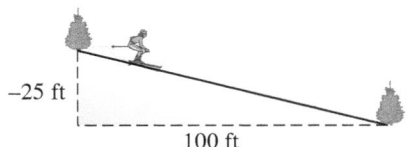

17. CONCEPT CHECK   A student found the slope of the line through the points $(2, 5)$ and $(-1, 3)$ as follows.

$$\frac{3 - 5}{2 - (-1)} = \frac{-2}{3}, \quad \text{or} \quad -\frac{2}{3} \leftarrow \text{His answer}$$

What Went Wrong?   Give the correct slope.

18. CONCEPT CHECK   A student found the slope of the line through the points $(-2, 4)$ and $(6, -1)$ as follows.

$$\frac{-2 - 6}{4 - (-1)} = \frac{-8}{5}, \quad \text{or} \quad -\frac{8}{5} \leftarrow \text{Her answer}$$

What Went Wrong?   Give the correct slope.

Use the coordinates of the indicated points to find the slope of each line. (Coordinates of the points shown are integers.) **See Examples 1–4.**

19.
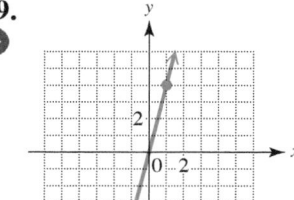

20.
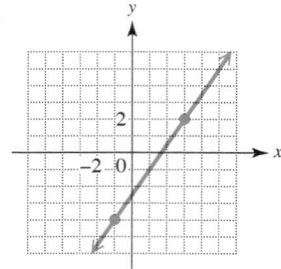

21.
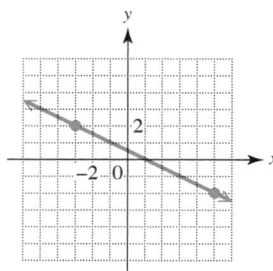

22.
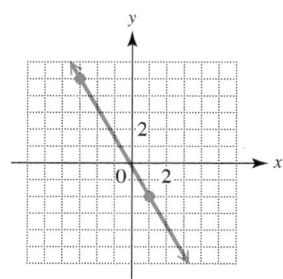

23.
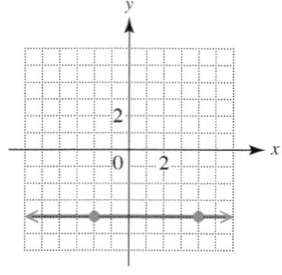

24.
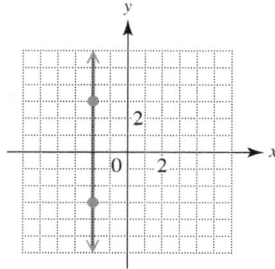

Find the slope of the line passing through each pair of points. **See Examples 2–4.**

25. $(1, -2)$ and $(-3, -7)$ **26.** $(4, -1)$ and $(-2, -8)$ **27.** $(0, 3)$ and $(-2, 0)$ **28.** $(-8, 0)$ and $(0, -5)$

29. $(-2, 4)$ and $(-3, 7)$ **30.** $(-4, -5)$ and $(-5, -8)$ **31.** $(4, 3)$ and $(-6, 3)$ **32.** $(6, -5)$ and $(-12, -5)$

33. $(-12, 3)$ and $(-12, -7)$ **34.** $(-8, 6)$ and $(-8, -1)$ **35.** $(4.8, 2.5)$ and $(3.6, 2.2)$

36. $(3.1, 2.6)$ and $(1.6, 2.1)$ **37.** $\left(-\dfrac{7}{5}, \dfrac{3}{10}\right)$ and $\left(\dfrac{1}{5}, -\dfrac{1}{2}\right)$ **38.** $\left(-\dfrac{4}{3}, \dfrac{1}{2}\right)$ and $\left(\dfrac{1}{3}, -\dfrac{5}{6}\right)$

Find the slope of each line. **See Example 5.**

39. $y = 5x + 12$ **40.** $y = 2x - 3$ **41.** $4y = x + 1$

42. $2y = -x + 4$ **43.** $3x - 2y = 3$ **44.** $6x - 4y = 4$

45. $-2y - 3x = 5$ **46.** $-4y - 3x = 2$ **47.** $y = 6$ **48.** $y = 4$

49. $x = -2$ **50.** $x = 5$ **51.** $x - y = 0$ **52.** $x + y = 0$

Find the slope of each line in two ways by doing the following.

(a) Give any two points that lie on the line, and use them to determine the slope.

(b) Solve the equation for y, and identify the slope from the equation.

See Objective 2 and Example 5.

53. $2x + y = 10$

54. $-4x + y = -8$

55. $5x - 3y = 15$

56. $3x + 2y = 12$

Each table of values gives several points that lie on a line.

(a) Use any two of the ordered pairs to find the slope of the line.

(b) What is the x-intercept of the line?   The y-intercept?

Then graph the line.

57.

x	y
-4	0
-2	2
0	4
1	5

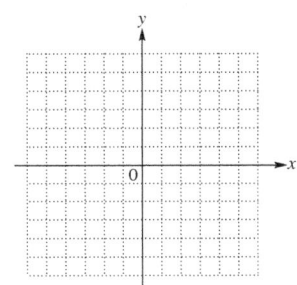

58.

x	y
-4	3
-1	0
0	-1
2	-3

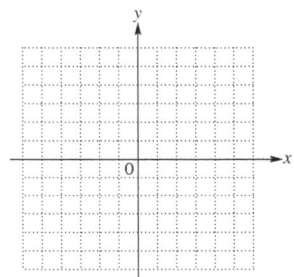

59.

x	y
3	-3
0	-2
-3	-1
-6	0

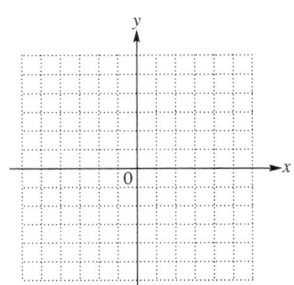

60.

x	y
-1	-6
0	-4
2	0
5	6

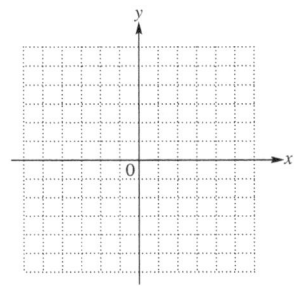

For each pair of equations, give the slopes of the lines, and then decide whether the two lines are parallel, perpendicular, *or* neither. **See Example 6.**

61. $-4x + 3y = 4$
$-8x + 6y = 0$

62. $2x + 5y = 4$
$4x + 10y = 1$

63. $5x - 3y = -2$
$3x - 5y = -8$

64. $8x - 9y = 6$
$8x + 6y = -5$

65. $3x - 5y = -1$
$5x + 3y = 2$

66. $3x - 2y = 6$
$2x + 3y = 3$

67. $6x + y = 1$
$x + 6y = 18$

68. $3x - 4y = 12$
$4x + 3y = 12$

Solve each problem.

69. The upper deck at U.S. Cellular Field in Chicago has produced, among other complaints, displeasure with its steepness. It is 160 ft from home plate to the front of the upper deck and 250 ft from home plate to the back. The top of the upper deck is 63 ft above the bottom. What is its slope? (Consider the slope as a positive number.)

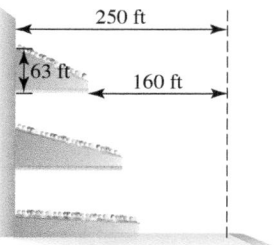

70. When designing the TD Bank North Garden arena in Boston, architects designed the ramps leading up to the entrances so that circus elephants would be able to march up the ramps. The maximum grade (or slope) that an elephant will walk on is 13%. Suppose that such a ramp were constructed with a horizontal run of 150 ft. What would be the maximum vertical rise the architects could use?

Find and interpret the average rate of change illustrated in each graph. **See Objective 4.**

71.

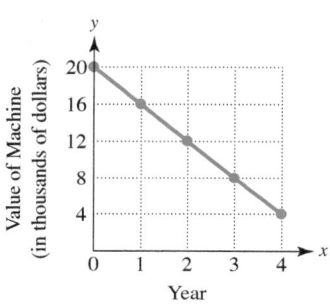

72.

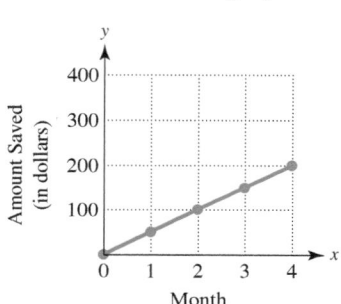

73.

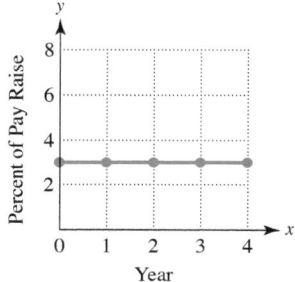

74. CONCEPT CHECK If the graph of a linear equation rises from left to right, then the average rate of change is (*positive / negative*). If the graph of a linear equation falls from left to right, then the average rate of change is (*positive / negative*).

Solve each problem. **See Examples 7 and 8.**

75. The graph shows the number of drive-in theaters in the United States from 2005 through 2016.

(a) Use the given ordered pairs to find the average rate of change in the number of drive-in theaters per year during this period. Round the answer to the nearest tenth.

(b) Explain how a negative slope is interpreted in this situation.

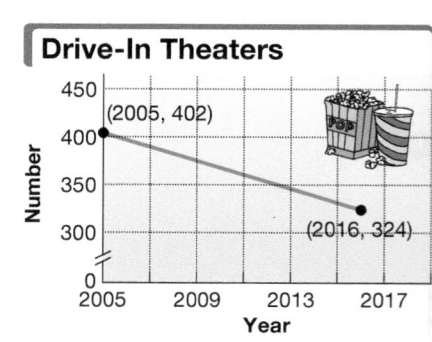

Drive-In Theaters

Data from United Drive-In Theatre Owners Association.

76. The graph shows the number of U.S. travelers to Canada (in thousands) from 2000 through 2014.

(a) Use the given ordered pairs to find the average rate of change in the number of U.S. travelers to Canada per year during this period. Round the answer to the nearest thousand.

(b) Explain how a negative slope is interpreted in this situation.

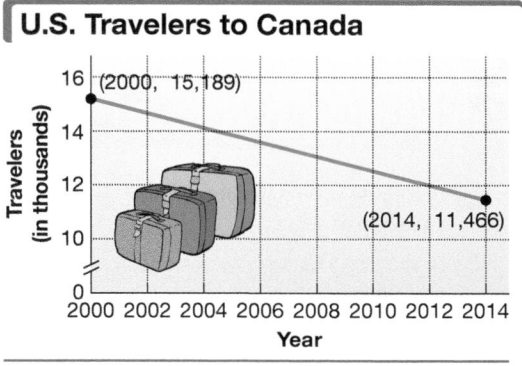

Data from U.S. Department of Commerce.

77. The graph shows the number of wireless subscriber connections (that is, active devices, including smartphones, feature phones, tablets, etc.) in millions in the United States for the years 2007 to 2014.

WIRELESS SUBSCRIBER CONNECTIONS

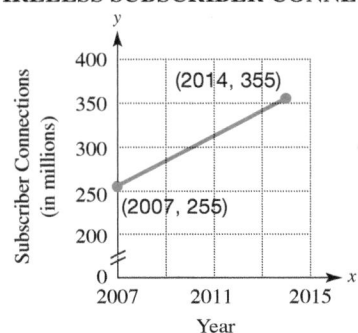

Data from CTIA.

(a) In the context of this graph, what does the ordered pair (2014, 355) mean?

(b) Use the given ordered pairs to find the slope of the line to the nearest million.

(c) Interpret the slope in the context of this problem.

78. The graph shows the percent of households in the United States that were wireless-only households for the years 2007 to 2014.

WIRELESS-ONLY HOUSEHOLDS

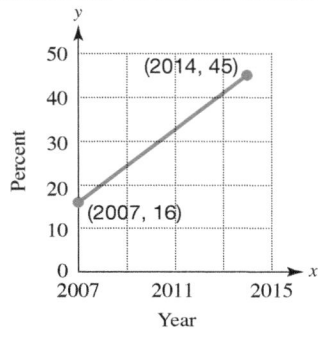

Data from CTIA.

(a) In the context of this graph, what does the ordered pair (2014, 45) mean?

(b) Use the given ordered pairs to find the slope of the line to the nearest tenth.

(c) Interpret the slope in the context of this problem.

Relating Concepts (Exercises 79–84) For Individual or Group Work

*Three points that lie on the same straight line are said to be **collinear**. Consider the points A (3, 1), B (6, 2), and C (9, 3). **Work Exercises 79–84 in order.***

79. Find the slope of segment AB.

80. Find the slope of segment BC.

81. Find the slope of segment AC.

82. If slope of AB = slope of BC = slope of AC, then A, B, and C are collinear. Use the results of **Exercises 79–81** to show that this statement is satisfied.

83. Use the slope formula to determine whether the points $(1, -2)$, $(3, -1)$, and $(5, 0)$ are collinear.

84. Repeat **Exercise 83** for the points $(0, 6)$, $(4, -5)$, and $(-2, 12)$.

3.4 | Slope-Intercept Form of a Linear Equation

OBJECTIVES

1. Use slope-intercept form of the equation of a line.

2. Graph a line using its slope and a point on the line.

3. Write an equation of a line using its slope and any point on the line.

4. Graph and write equations of horizontal and vertical lines.

5. Write an equation of a line that models real data.

---

1. Identify the slope and y-intercept of the line with each equation.

(a) $y = 2x - 6$

(b) $y = -\dfrac{x}{3} + \dfrac{7}{3}$

(c) $y = -x$

OBJECTIVE **1** **Use slope-intercept form of the equation of a line.** Recall that we can find the slope (steepness) of a line by solving the equation of the line for y. In that form, the slope is the coefficient of x. For example, the line with equation

$$y = 2x + 3 \quad \text{has slope} \quad 2.$$

What does the number **3** represent? To find out, suppose that a line has slope m and y-intercept $(0, b)$. We can find an equation of this line by choosing another point (x, y) on the line, as shown in **Figure 34.** Then we apply the slope formula.

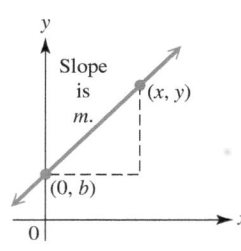

$$m = \dfrac{y - b}{x - 0} \quad \leftarrow \text{Change in } y\text{-values}$$
$$\phantom{m = \dfrac{y - b}{x - 0}} \quad \leftarrow \text{Change in } x\text{-values}$$

$$m = \dfrac{y - b}{x} \quad \begin{array}{l}\text{Subtract in the}\\\text{denominator.}\end{array}$$

$$mx = y - b \quad \text{Multiply by } x.$$

$$mx + b = y \quad \text{Add } b.$$

$$y = mx + b \quad \text{Interchange sides.}$$

Figure 34

This result is the *slope-intercept form* of the equation of a line. Both the *slope* and the *y-intercept* of the line can be read directly from this form. For the line with equation $y = 2x + 3$, the number 3 gives the y-intercept $(0, 3)$.

Slope-Intercept Form

The **slope-intercept form** of the equation of a line with slope m and y-intercept $(0, b)$ is

$$y = mx + b.$$

Slope $\nearrow$ $\quad$ $\nwarrow$ $(0, b)$ is the y-intercept.

The intercept given is the y-intercept.

EXAMPLE 1 **Identifying Slopes and y-Intercepts**

Identify the slope and y-intercept of the line with each equation.

(a) $y = -4x + 1$

Slope $\nearrow$ $\quad$ $\nwarrow$ y-intercept $(0, 1)$

(b) $y = x - 8$ can be written as $y = 1x + (-8).$
$\quad\quad\quad\quad\quad\quad\quad$ Slope $\nearrow$ $\quad\quad$ $\nwarrow$ y-intercept $(0, -8)$

(c) $y = 6x$ can be written as $y = 6x + 0.$
$\quad\quad\quad\quad\quad$ Slope $\nearrow$ $\quad$ $\nwarrow$ y-intercept $(0, 0)$

(d) $y = \frac{x}{4} - \frac{3}{4}$ can be written as $y = \frac{1}{4}x + \left(-\frac{3}{4}\right).$
$\quad\quad\quad\quad\quad\quad$ Slope $\nearrow$ $\quad\quad$ $\nwarrow$ y-intercept $\left(0, -\frac{3}{4}\right)$

◀ **Work Problem** **1** **at the Side.**

Answers

1. (a) slope: 2; y-intercept: $(0, -6)$

(b) slope: $-\dfrac{1}{3}$; y-intercept: $\left(0, \dfrac{7}{3}\right)$

(c) slope: -1; y-intercept: $(0, 0)$

Note

> Slope-intercept form is an especially useful form for a linear equation because of the information we can determine from it. It is also the form used by graphing calculators and the one that describes a *linear function*.

OBJECTIVE ▶ ② **Graph a line using its slope and a point on the line.** We can use the slope and y-intercept to graph a line.

Graphing a Line Using Its Slope and y-Intercept

Step 1 Write the equation in slope-intercept form

$$y = mx + b,$$

if necessary, by solving for y.

Step 2 Identify the y-intercept. Plot the point $(0, b)$.

Step 3 Identify the slope m of the line. Use the geometric interpretation of slope ("*rise over run*") to find another point on the graph by counting from the y-intercept.

Step 4 Join the two points with a line to obtain the graph. (If desired, obtain a third point, such as the x-intercept, as a check.)

EXAMPLE 2 **Graphing Lines Using Slopes and y-Intercepts**

Graph the equation of each line using the slope and y-intercept.

(a) $y = \dfrac{2}{3}x - 1$

Step 1 The equation is given in slope-intercept form.

$$y = \frac{2}{3}x - 1$$

↑ ↑
Slope   Value of b in y-intercept $(0, b)$

Step 2 The y-intercept is $(0, -1)$. Plot this point. See **Figure 35.**

Step 3 The slope is $\frac{2}{3}$. By definition,

$$\text{slope } m = \frac{\text{change in } y \text{ (rise)}}{\text{change in } x \text{ (run)}} = \frac{2}{3}.$$

From the y-intercept, count **up 2 units** and to the **right 3 units** to obtain the point $(3, 1)$.

Step 4 Draw the line through the two points $(0, -1)$ and $(3, 1)$ to obtain the graph in **Figure 35.**

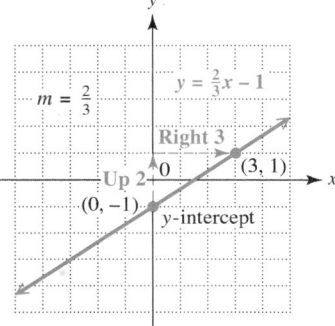

Figure 35

Continued on Next Page

② Graph $3x - 4y = 8$ using the slope and y-intercept.

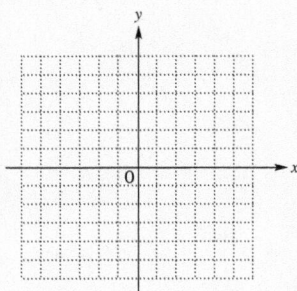

③ Graph the line passing through the point $(2, -3)$, with slope $-\frac{1}{3}$.

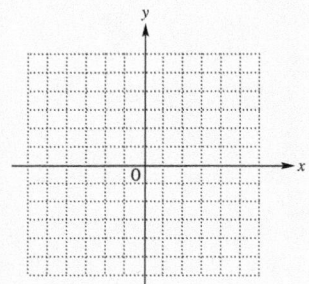

(b) $3x + 4y = 8$

Step 1 Solve for y to write the equation in slope-intercept form.

$$3x + 4y = 8$$

Isolate y on one side. $\quad 4y = -3x + 8 \quad$ Subtract $3x$.

Slope-intercept form $\longrightarrow y = -\dfrac{3}{4}x + 2 \quad$ Divide *each* term by 4.

Step 2 The y-intercept is $(0, 2)$. Plot this point. See **Figure 36**.

Step 3 The slope is $-\frac{3}{4}$, which can be written as either $\frac{-3}{4}$ or $\frac{3}{-4}$. We use $\frac{-3}{4}$ here.

$$m = \frac{\text{change in } y \text{ (rise)}}{\text{change in } x \text{ (run)}} = \frac{-3}{4}$$

From the y-intercept, count *down* **3 units** (because of the negative sign) and to the *right* **4 units** to obtain the point $(4, -1)$.

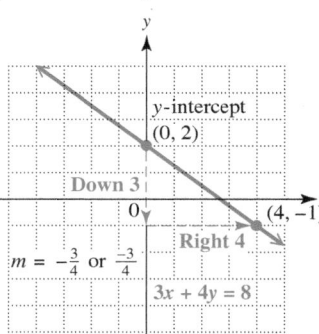

Figure 36

Step 4 Draw the line through the two points $(0, 2)$ and $(4, -1)$ to obtain the graph in **Figure 36**.

◀ **Work Problem ② at the Side.**

Note

In Step 3 of **Example 2(b),** we could use $\frac{3}{-4}$ for the slope. From the y-intercept $(0, 2)$ in **Figure 36**, count *up* **3 units** and to the *left* **4 units** (because of the negative sign) to obtain the point $(-4, 5)$. Verify that this produces the same line.

EXAMPLE 3 Graphing a Line Using Its Slope and a Point

Graph the line passing through the point $(-2, 3)$, with slope -4.

First, plot the point $(-2, 3)$. See **Figure 37**. Then write the slope -4 as

$$\text{slope } m = \frac{\text{change in } y}{\text{change in } x} = -4 = \frac{-4}{1}.$$

Locate another point on the line by counting *down* 4 units from the given point $(-2, 3)$ and then to the *right* 1 unit. Finally, draw the line through this new point $(-1, -1)$ and the given point $(-2, 3)$. See **Figure 37**.

We could have written the slope as $\frac{4}{-1}$ instead. In this case, we would move *up* 4 units from $(-2, 3)$ and then to the *left* 1 unit. Verify that this produces the same line.

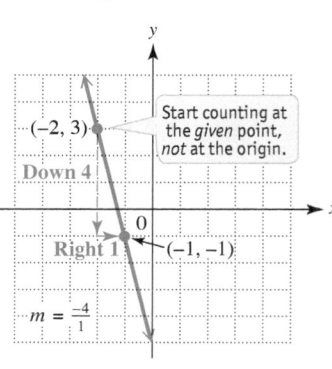

Figure 37

◀ **Work Problem ③ at the Side.**

Answers

2.

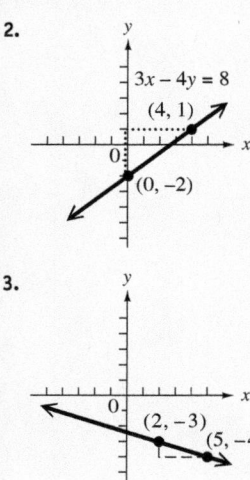

3.

OBJECTIVE ▶ **3** **Write an equation of a line using its slope and any point on the line.** We can use the slope-intercept form to do this.

EXAMPLE 4 **Using Slope-Intercept Form to Write Equations of Lines**

Write an equation in slope-intercept form of the line passing through the given point and having the given slope.

(a) $(0, -1)$, $m = \frac{2}{3}$

Because the point $(0, -1)$ is the y-intercept, $b = -1$. We can substitute this value for b and the given slope $m = \frac{2}{3}$ directly into slope-intercept form $y = mx + b$ to write an equation.

Slope ↘   ↙ y-intercept is $(0, b)$.

$$y = mx + b \qquad \text{Slope-intercept form}$$

$$y = \frac{2}{3}x + (-1) \qquad \text{Substitute.}$$

$$y = \frac{2}{3}x - 1 \qquad \text{Definition of subtraction}$$

(b) $(2, 5)$, $m = 4$

This line passes through the point $(2, 5)$, **which is not the y-intercept** because the x-coordinate is 2, **not 0. We cannot substitute for m and b directly as in part (a).**

We can find the y-intercept by substituting $x = 2$ and $y = 5$ from the given point, along with the given slope $m = 4$, into $y = mx + b$ and solving for b.

$$y = mx + b \qquad \text{Slope-intercept form}$$

$$5 = 4(2) + b \qquad \text{Let } y = 5, m = 4, \text{ and } x = 2.$$

$$5 = 8 + b \qquad \text{Multiply.}$$

$$-3 = b \qquad \text{Subtract 8.}$$

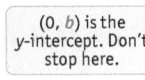 $(0, b)$ is the y-intercept. Don't stop here.

Now substitute the values of m and b into slope-intercept form.

$$y = mx + b \qquad \text{Slope-intercept form}$$

$$y = 4x - 3 \qquad \text{Let } m = 4 \text{ and } b = -3.$$

—————————————————— **Work Problem 4 at the Side.** ▶

OBJECTIVE ▶ **4** **Graph and write equations of horizontal and vertical lines.**

EXAMPLE 5 **Graphing Horizontal and Vertical Lines Using Slope and a Point**

Graph each line passing through the given point and having the given slope.

(a) $(4, -2)$, $m = 0$

Recall that a horizontal line has slope 0. To graph this line, plot the point $(4, -2)$ and draw the horizontal line through it. See **Figure 38.**

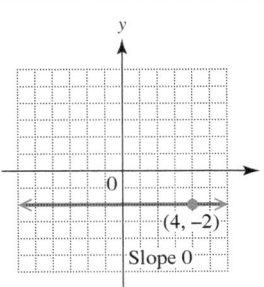

Figure 38

—————————————————— **Continued on Next Page**

4 Write an equation in slope-intercept form of the line passing through the given point and having the given slope.

(a) y-intercept $(0, -4)$, slope $\frac{1}{2}$

(b) $(0, 8)$, $m = -1$

(c) $(0, 0)$, $m = 3$

(d) $(-1, 4)$, $m = -2$

Substitute values and solve for b.

$$y = mx + b$$

$$\underline{\quad} = \underline{\quad}(\underline{\quad}) + b$$

$$4 = \underline{\quad} + b$$

$$\underline{\quad} = b$$

An equation of the line is $y = \underline{\qquad}$.

(e) $(-2, 1)$, $m = 3$

Answers

4. **(a)** $y = \frac{1}{2}x - 4$
   (b) $y = -x + 8$
   (c) $y = 3x$
   (d) $4; -2; -1; 2; 2; -2x + 2$
   (e) $y = 3x + 7$

5 Graph each line passing through the given point and having the given slope.

(a) $(-3, 3)$, undefined slope

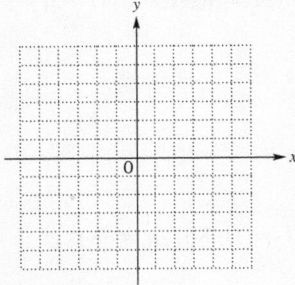

(b) $(3, -3)$, slope 0

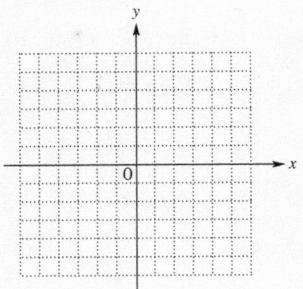

6 Write an equation of the line passing through the point $(-1, 1)$ and having the given slope.

(a) Undefined slope

(b) $m = 0$

Answers

5. (a)

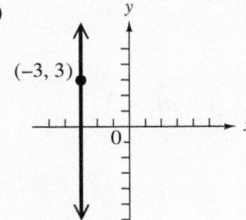

(b)

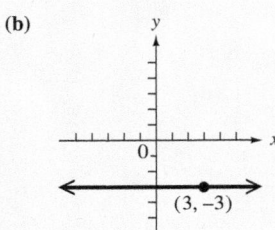

6. (a) $x = -1$ **(b)** $y = 1$

(b) $(2, -4)$, undefined slope

A vertical line has undefined slope. To graph this line, plot the point $(2, -4)$ and draw the vertical line through it. See **Figure 39.**

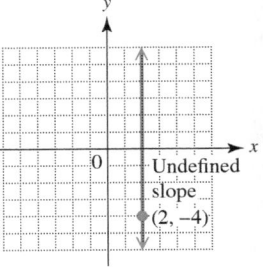

Figure 39

◀ Work Problem **5** at the Side.

EXAMPLE 6 **Writing Equations of Horizontal and Vertical Lines**

Write an equation of the line passing through the point $(2, -2)$ and having the given slope.

(a) Slope 0

This line is horizontal because it has slope 0. A horizontal line through the point (a, b) has equation $y = b$. The y-coordinate of the point $(2, -2)$ is -2, so the equation is $y = -2$. See **Figure 40.**

(b) Undefined slope

This line is vertical because it has undefined slope. A vertical line through the point (a, b) has equation $x = a$. The x-coordinate of $(2, -2)$ is 2, so the equation is $x = 2$. See **Figure 40.**

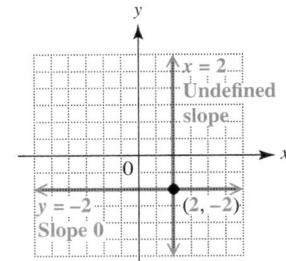

Figure 40

◀ Work Problem **6** at the Side.

OBJECTIVE ▶ 5 **Write an equation of a line that models real data.** If a given set of data changes at a fairly constant rate, the data may fit a linear pattern, where the rate of change is the slope of the line.

EXAMPLE 7 **Writing a Linear Equation to Describe Data**

A local gasoline station is selling 89-octane gas for $3.50 per gal.

(a) Write an equation that describes the cost y to buy x gallons of gas.

The total cost is determined by the number of gallons we buy multiplied by the price per gallon (in this case, $3.50). As the gas is pumped, two sets of numbers spin by:

the number of gallons pumped and the cost of that number of gallons.

The table illustrates this situation.

Number of Gallons Pumped	Cost of This Number of Gallons
0	$0 (\$3.50) = \$\ 0.00$
1	$1 (\$3.50) = \$\ 3.50$
2	$2 (\$3.50) = \$\ 7.00$
3	$3 (\$3.50) = \$10.50$
4	$4 (\$3.50) = \$14.00$

Continued on Next Page

If we let x denote the number of gallons pumped, then the total cost y in dollars can be found using the following linear equation.

Price per gallon

Total cost ⟶ ↓ ↓ ↓ ⟵ Number of gallons

$$y = 3.50x$$

This equation is graphed in **Figure 41.** The slope of the line is the price per gallon.

Theoretically, there are infinitely many ordered pairs (x, y) that satisfy this equation, but here we are limited to nonnegative values for x because we cannot have a negative number of gallons. There is also a practical maximum value for x in this situation, which varies from one car to another—the size of the gas tank.

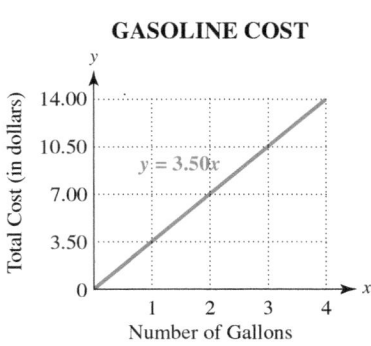

GASOLINE COST

Total Cost (in dollars)

$y = 3.50x$

Number of Gallons

Figure 41

(b) A car wash at this gas station costs an additional $3.00. Write an equation that defines the cost of gas and a car wash.

The cost will be $3.50x + 3.00$ dollars for x gallons of gas and a car wash.

$$y = 3.5x + 3 \quad \text{Final 0's need not be included.}$$

(c) Interpret the ordered pairs $(5, 20.5)$ and $(10, 38)$ in relation to the equation from part (b).

$(5, 20.5)$ indicates that 5 gal of gas and a car wash cost $20.50.

$(10, 38)$ indicates that 10 gal of gas and a car wash cost $38.00.

─── **Work Problem 7 at the Side.** ▶

Note

In **Example 7 (a),** the ordered pair $(0, 0)$ satisfied the equation, so the linear equation has the form

$$y = mx, \quad \text{where } b = 0.$$

If a situation involves an initial charge b plus a charge per unit m as in **Example 7 (b),** the equation has the form

$$y = mx + b, \quad \text{where } b \neq 0.$$

7 Solve each problem.

(a) A cell phone service provider offers unlimited calls, texts, and data for $95 per month. Write an equation to describe the cost y in dollars for x months of service.

(b) A cell phone plan costs $100 for the telephone plus $85 per month for service. Write an equation that gives the cost y in dollars for x months of cell phone service using this plan.

(c) Interpret the ordered pair $(11, 1035)$ in relation to the equation from part (b).

Answers

7. (a) $y = 95x$
   (b) $y = 85x + 100$
   (c) The ordered pair $(11, 1035)$ indicates that the cost for 11 months of service is $1035.

3.4 Exercises

FOR EXTRA HELP Go to MyMathLab *for worked-out, step-by-step solutions to exercises enclosed in a square* ___ *and video solutions to* ▶ *exercises.*

CONCEPT CHECK *Fill in each blank with the correct response.*

1. In slope-intercept form $y = mx + b$ of the equation of a line, the slope is _____ and the y-intercept is the point _____ .

2. The line with equation $y = -\frac{x}{2} - 3$ has slope _____ and y-intercept _____ .

CONCEPT CHECK *Work each problem.*

3. Match each equation in parts (a)–(d) with the graph in choices A–D that would most closely resemble its graph.

   (a) $y = x + 3$ **(b)** $y = -x + 3$ **(c)** $y = x - 3$ **(d)** $y = -x - 3$

   A. 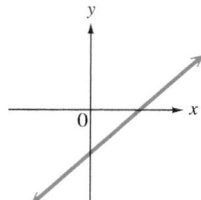   **B.** 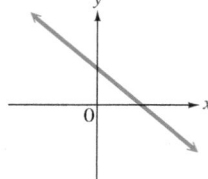   **C.** 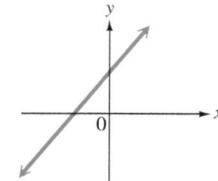   **D.**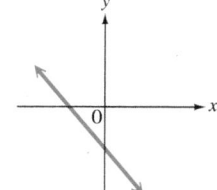

4. Match the description in Column I with the correct equation in Column II.

I	II
(a) Slope -2, passes through the point $(4, 1)$	**A.** $y = 4x$
(b) Slope -2, y-intercept $(0, 1)$	**B.** $y = \frac{1}{4}x$
(c) Passes through the points $(0, 0)$ and $(4, 1)$	**C.** $y = -4x$
(d) Passes through the points $(0, 0)$ and $(1, 4)$	**D.** $y = -2x + 1$
	E. $2x + y = 9$

5. What is the common name given to the vertical line whose x-intercept is the origin?

6. What is the common name given to the line with slope 0 whose y-intercept is the origin?

Identify the slope and y-intercept of the line with each equation. **See Example 1.**

7. $y = \frac{5}{2}x - 4$ 8. $y = \frac{7}{3}x - 6$ 9. $y = -x + 9$ 10. $y = x + 1$

11. $y = -8x$ 12. $y = 2x$ 13. $y = \frac{x}{5} - \frac{3}{10}$ 14. $y = \frac{x}{7} - \frac{5}{14}$

*Graph the equation of each line using the slope and y-intercept. **See Example 2.***

15. $y = 3x + 2$

16. $y = 4x - 4$

17. $y = \dfrac{3}{4}x - 1$

18. $y = \dfrac{3}{2}x + 2$

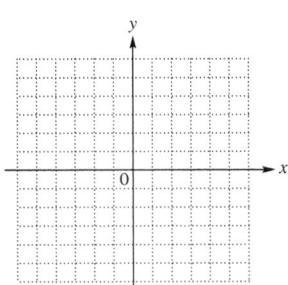 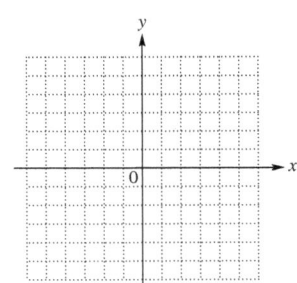 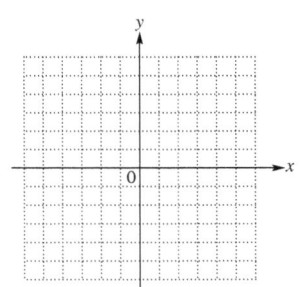 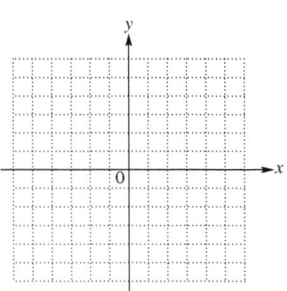

19. $2x + y = -5$

20. $3x + y = -2$

21. $x + 2y = 4$

22. $x + 3y = 12$

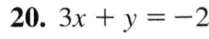

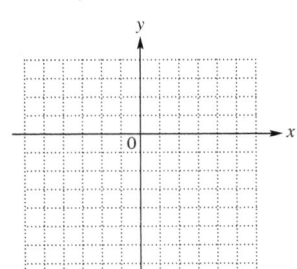 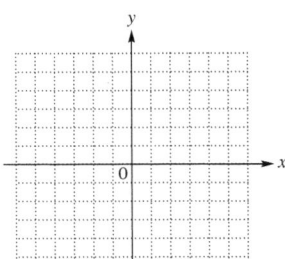 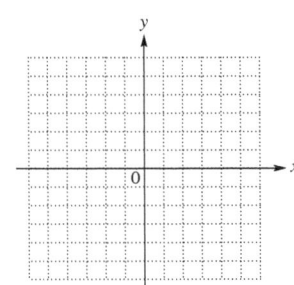 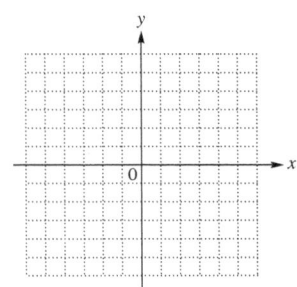

Graph each line passing through the given point and having the given slope.
See Examples 3 and 5.

23. $(0, 1)$, $m = 4$

24. $(0, -5)$, $m = -2$

25. $(-2, 3)$, $m = \dfrac{1}{2}$

26. $(-4, -1)$, $m = \dfrac{3}{4}$

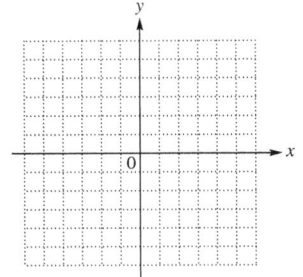 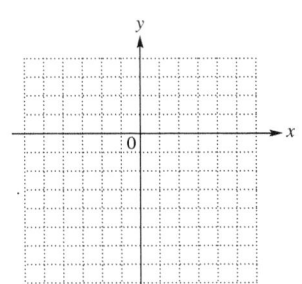 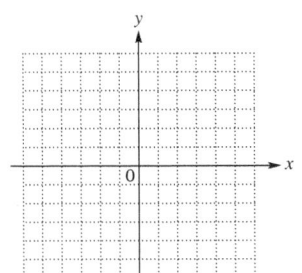 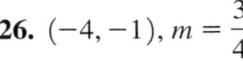 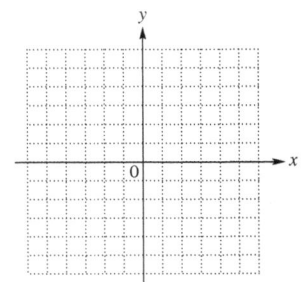

27. $(1, -5)$, $m = -\dfrac{2}{5}$

28. $(2, -1)$, $m = -\dfrac{1}{3}$

29. $(0, 0)$, $m = \dfrac{2}{3}$

30. $(0, 0)$, $m = \dfrac{5}{2}$

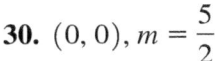

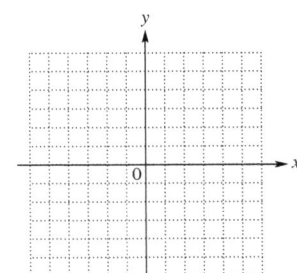 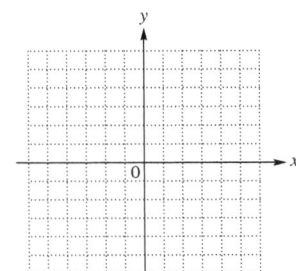 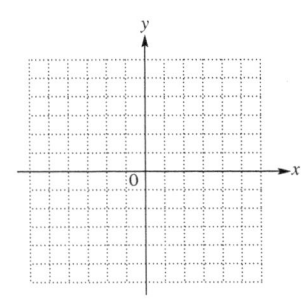

31. $(3, 2)$, $m = 0$

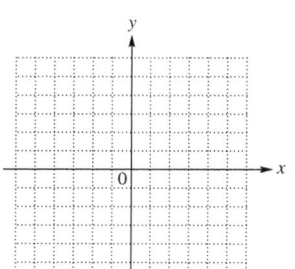

32. $(-2, 3)$, $m = 0$

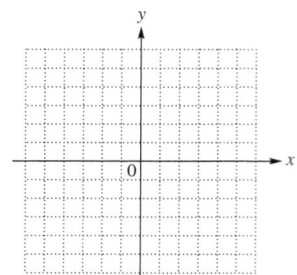

33. $(3, -2)$, undefined slope

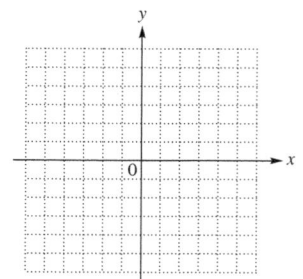

34. $(2, 4)$, undefined slope

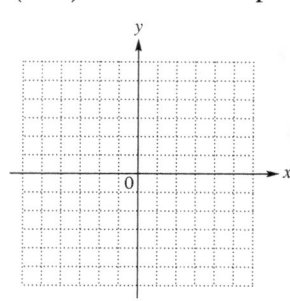

CONCEPT CHECK *Use the geometric interpretation of slope ("rise over run") to find the slope of each line. Then, by identifying the y-intercept from the graph, write the slope-intercept form of the equation of the line. (Coordinates of the points shown are integers.)*

35.

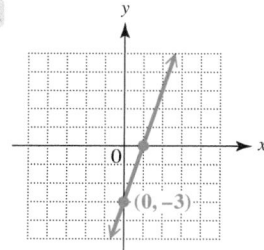

36.

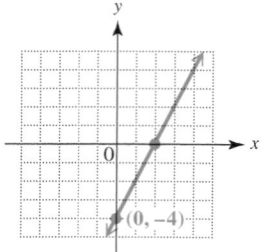

37.

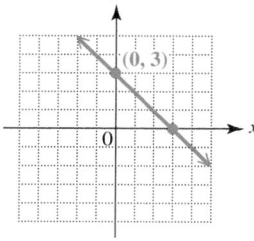

38.

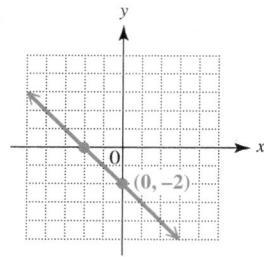

39.

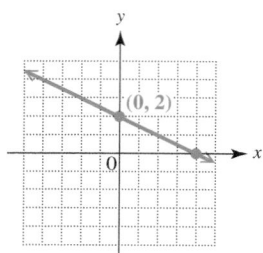

40.

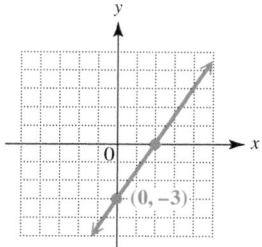

Write an equation in slope-intercept form (if possible) of the line passing through the given point and having the given slope. ***See Examples 4 and 6.***

41. slope 4,
y-intercept $(0, -3)$

42. slope -5,
y-intercept $(0, 6)$

43. $(0, -7)$, $m = -1$

44. $(0, -9)$, $m = 1$

45. $(4, 1)$, $m = 2$

46. $(2, 7)$, $m = 3$

47. $(-1, 3)$, $m = -4$

48. $(-3, 1)$, $m = -2$

49. $(3, -10)$, $m = -2$

50. $(2, -5)$, $m = -4$

51. $(-4, 1)$, $m = \dfrac{3}{4}$

52. $(2, 1)$, $m = \dfrac{5}{2}$

53. $(0, 3), m = 0$ **54.** $(0, -4), m = 0$ **55.** $(2, -6),$ undefined slope

56. $(-1, 7),$ undefined slope   **57.** $(6, -6),$ slope 0   **58.** $(-3, 3),$ slope 0

Each table of values gives several points that lie on a line.

(a) Use any two of the ordered pairs to find the slope of the line.

(b) Identify the y-intercept of the line.

(c) Use the slope and y-intercept from parts (a) and (b) to write an equation of the line in slope-intercept form.

(d) Then graph the equation.

59.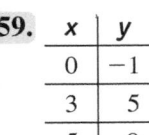

x	y
0	-1
3	5
5	9

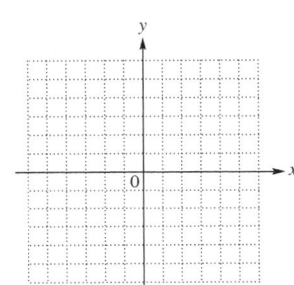

60.

x	y
-10	-1
0	3
5	5

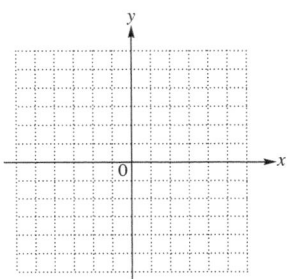

The cost y to produce x items is, in some cases, expressed in the form

$$y = mx + b.$$

*The value of b gives the **fixed cost** (the cost that is the same no matter how many items are produced), and the value of m gives the **variable cost** (the cost to produce an additional item). Use this information to work each problem.*

61. It costs \$400 to start up a business selling campaign buttons. Each button costs \$0.25 to produce.

    (a) What is the fixed cost?

    (b) What is the variable cost?

    (c) Write the cost equation.

    (d) What will be the cost of producing 100 campaign buttons, based on the cost equation?

    (e) How many campaign buttons will be produced if the total cost is \$775?

62. It costs \$2000 to purchase a copier, and each copy costs \$0.02 to make.

    (a) What is the fixed cost?

    (b) What is the variable cost?

    (c) Write the cost equation.

    (d) What will be the cost of producing 10,000 copies, based on the cost equation?

    (e) How many copies will be produced if the total cost is \$2600?

Solve each problem.

63. Andrew earns 5% commission on his sales, plus a base salary of $2000 per month. This is illustrated in the graph and can be modeled by the linear equation

$$y = 0.05x + 2000,$$

where y is his monthly salary in dollars and x is his sales, also in dollars.

(a) What is the slope? With what does the slope correspond in the problem?

(b) What is the y-intercept? With what does the y-value of the y-intercept correspond in the problem?

(c) Use the equation to determine Andrew's monthly salary if his sales are $10,000. Confirm this using the graph.

(d) Use the graph to determine his sales if he wants to earn a monthly salary of $3500. Confirm this using the equation.

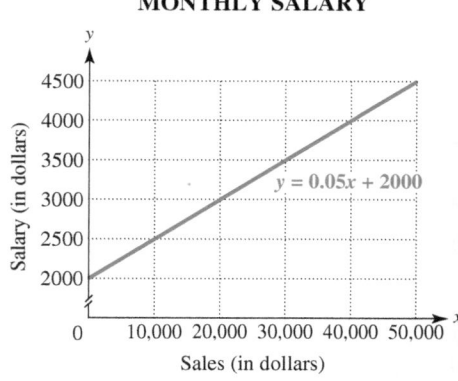

64. The cost to rent a moving van is $0.50 per mile, plus a flat fee of $100. This is illustrated in the graph and can be modeled by the linear equation

$$y = 0.50x + 100,$$

where y is the total rental cost in dollars and x is the number of miles driven.

(a) What is the slope? With what does the slope correspond in the problem?

(b) What is the y-intercept? With what does the y-value of the y-intercept correspond in the problem?

(c) Use the equation to determine the total charge if 400 mi are driven. Confirm this using the graph.

(d) Use the graph to determine the number of miles driven if the charge is $500. Confirm this using the equation.

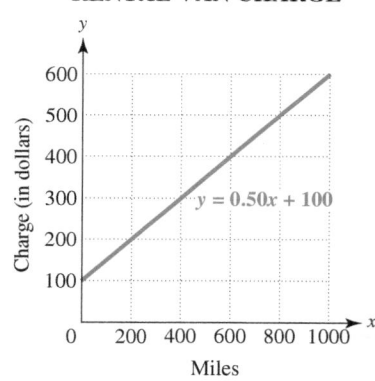

Write an equation in the form $y = mx$ for each situation. Then give three ordered pairs associated with the equation for x-values of 0, 5, and 10. **See Example 7(a).**

65. x represents the number of hours traveling at 45 mph, and y represents the distance traveled (in miles).

66. x represents the number of t-shirts sold at $26 each, and y represents the total cost of the t-shirts (in dollars).

67. x represents the number of gallons of gasoline sold at $3.00 per gal, and y represents the total cost of the gasoline (in dollars).

68. x represents the number of days a DVD movie is rented at $2.50 per day, and y represents the total charge for the rental (in dollars).

*For each situation, **(a)** write an equation in the form $y = mx + b$, **(b)** find and interpret the ordered pair associated with the equation for $x = 5$, and **(c)** answer the question. **See Examples 7(b) and 7(c).***

69. A membership to a health club costs $99, plus $41 per month. Let x represent the number of months and y represent the cost in dollars. How much does a one-year membership cost?

70. An Executive VIP/Gold membership to a health club costs $159, plus $57 per month. Let x represent the number of months and y represent the cost in dollars. How much does a one-year membership cost?

71. A wireless plan includes unlimited talk and text plus 5 GB of data for $90 per month, plus a one-time activation fee of $36. Let x represent the number of months and y represent the cost in dollars. Over a two-year contract, how much will this plan cost?

72. A wireless plan includes unlimited talk and text plus 4 GB of data for $80 per month, plus $99 for a cell phone and $36 for a one-time activation fee. Let x represent the number of months and y represent the cost in dollars. Over a two-year contract, how much will this plan cost?

73. A rental car costs $50, plus $0.20 per mile. Let x represent the number of miles driven and y represent the total charge to the renter in dollars. How many miles was the car driven if the renter paid $84.60?

74. There is a $30 fee to rent a chain saw, plus $6 per day. Let x represent the number of days the saw is rented and y represent the charge to the user in dollars. If the total charge is $138, for how many days is the saw rented?

Relating Concepts (Exercises 75–78) For Individual or Group Work

A line with equation written in slope-intercept form $y = mx + b$ has slope m and y-intercept $(0, b)$. Recall that the standard form of a linear equation in two variables is

$$Ax + By = C, \quad \text{Standard form}$$

*where A, B, and C are real numbers and A and B are not both 0. **Work Exercises 75–78 in order.***

75. Write the standard form of a linear equation in slope-intercept form—that is, solved for y—to show that, in general, the slope is given by $-\frac{A}{B}$ (where $B \neq 0$).

76. Use the fact that $m = -\frac{A}{B}$ to find the slope of the line with each equation.

   (a) $2x + 3y = 18$ **(b)** $4x - 2y = -1$ **(c)** $3x - 7y = 21$

77. Refer to the slope-intercept form found in **Exercise 75**. What is the y-intercept?

78. Use the result of **Exercise 77** to find the y-intercept of each line in **Exercise 76**.

3.5 | Point-Slope Form of a Linear Equation

OBJECTIVES

1. Use point-slope form to write an equation of a line.
2. Write an equation of a line using two points on the line.
3. Write an equation of a line parallel or perpendicular to a given line.
4. Write an equation of a line that models real data.

OBJECTIVE 1 Use point-slope form to write an equation of a line. There is another form that can be used to write an equation of a line. To develop this form, we let m represent the slope of a line and (x_1, y_1) represent a given point on the line. We let (x, y) represent any other point on the line. See **Figure 42.**

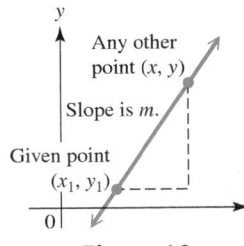

Figure 42

$$m = \frac{y - y_1}{x - x_1} \qquad \text{Definition of slope}$$

$$m(x - x_1) = y - y_1 \qquad \text{Multiply each side by } x - x_1.$$

$$y - y_1 = m(x - x_1) \qquad \text{Interchange sides.}$$

This result is the *point-slope form* of the equation of a line.

> **Point-Slope Form**
>
> The **point-slope form** of the equation of a line with slope m passing through the point (x_1, y_1) is
>
> $$y - y_1 = m(x - x_1).$$
>
> — Slope, Given point

EXAMPLE 1 Using Point-Slope Form to Write Equations

Write an equation of each line. Give the final answer in slope-intercept form.

(a) The line passing through $(-2, 4)$, with slope -3

The given point is $(-2, 4)$ so $x_1 = -2$ and $y_1 = 4$. Also, $m = -3$.

Only y_1, m, and x_1 are replaced with numbers.

$$y - y_1 = m(x - x_1) \qquad \text{Point-slope form}$$

$$y - 4 = -3[x - (-2)] \qquad \text{Let } y_1 = 4, m = -3, x_1 = -2.$$

$$y - 4 = -3(x + 2) \qquad \text{Definition of subtraction}$$

$$y - 4 = -3x - 6 \qquad \text{Distributive property}$$

The answer is in $y = mx + b$ form as specified.

$$y = -3x - 2 \qquad \text{Add 4.}$$

(b) The line passing through $(4, 2)$, with slope $\frac{3}{5}$

$$y - y_1 = m(x - x_1) \qquad \text{Point-slope form}$$

$$y - 2 = \frac{3}{5}(x - 4) \qquad \text{Let } y_1 = 2, m = \frac{3}{5}, x_1 = 4.$$

$$y - 2 = \frac{3}{5}x - \frac{12}{5} \qquad \text{Distributive property}$$

Do not clear fractions here because we want the answer in slope-intercept form—that is, solved for y.

$$y = \frac{3}{5}x - \frac{12}{5} + \frac{10}{5} \qquad \text{Add } 2 = \frac{10}{5} \text{ to each side.}$$

$$y = \frac{3}{5}x - \frac{2}{5} \qquad \text{Combine like terms.}$$

◀ **Work Problem 1 at the Side**

---

1 Write an equation of each line. Give the final answer in slope-intercept form.

GS (a) The line passing through $(-1, 3)$, with slope -2

$$y - y_1 = m(x - x_1)$$

$$y - \underline{\quad} = \underline{\quad}[x - (\underline{\quad})]$$

$$y - 3 = -2(x + \underline{\quad})$$

$$y - 3 = -2x - \underline{\quad}$$

$$y = \underline{\quad}$$

(b) The line passing through $(5, 2)$, with slope $-\frac{1}{3}$

Answers

1. (a) $3; -2; -1; 1; 2; -2x + 1$

(b) $y = -\frac{1}{3}x + \frac{11}{3}$

OBJECTIVE ▶ 2 **Write an equation of a line using two points on the line.**
Many of the linear equations we have worked with have been written in the form

$$Ax + By = C,$$

called **standard form,** where A, B, and C are real numbers and A and B are not both 0. In most cases, A, B, and C are rational numbers.

For consistency in this text, we give answers so that A, B, and C are integers with greatest common factor 1 and $A \geq 0$. (If $A = 0$, then we give $B > 0$.)

Note

The definition of standard form is not the same in all texts. A linear equation can be written in many different, yet equally correct, ways. For example,

$$3x + 4y = 12, \quad 6x + 8y = 24, \quad \text{and} \quad -9x - 12y = -36$$

all represent the same set of ordered pairs. When giving answers in standard form, $3x + 4y = 12$ is preferable to the other forms because the greatest common factor of 3, 4, and 12 is 1 and $A \geq 0$.

EXAMPLE 2   **Writing an Equation of a Line Using Two Points**

Write an equation of the line passing through the points $(3, 4)$ and $(-2, 5)$. Give the final answer in slope-intercept form and then in standard form.

First, find the slope of the line using the given points.

$$\text{slope } m = \frac{4 - 5}{3 - (-2)} \qquad \begin{array}{l}\text{Subtract } y\text{-values.}\\ \text{Subtract } x\text{-values in the same order.}\end{array}$$

$$= \frac{-1}{5} \qquad \text{Simplify the fraction.}$$

$$= -\frac{1}{5} \qquad \frac{-a}{b} = -\frac{a}{b}$$

Now use $m = -\frac{1}{5}$ and either $(-2, 5)$ or $(3, 4)$ as (x_1, y_1) in point-slope form. We choose $(3, 4)$.

$$y - y_1 = m(x - x_1) \qquad \text{Point-slope form}$$

$$y - 4 = -\frac{1}{5}(x - 3) \qquad \text{Let } y_1 = 4, m = -\frac{1}{5}, x_1 = 3.$$

$$y - 4 = -\frac{1}{5}x + \frac{3}{5} \qquad \text{Distributive property}$$

$$y = -\frac{1}{5}x + \frac{3}{5} + \frac{20}{5} \qquad \text{Add } 4 = \frac{20}{5} \text{ to each side.}$$

Slope-intercept form ⟶ $y = -\frac{1}{5}x + \frac{23}{5}$ Combine like terms.

$$5y = -x + 23 \qquad \begin{array}{l}\text{Multiply by 5 to clear}\\ \text{fractions.}\end{array}$$

Standard form ⟶ $x + 5y = 23$ Add x.

——————————— **Work Problem ❷ at the Side. ▶**

❷ Write an equation of the line passing through each pair of points. Give the final answer in slope-intercept form and then in standard form.

(a) $(2, 5)$ and $(-1, 6)$

(b) $(-3, 1)$ and $(2, 4)$

Answers

2. (a) $y = -\frac{1}{3}x + \frac{17}{3}$; $x + 3y = 17$

(b) $y = \frac{3}{5}x + \frac{14}{5}$; $3x - 5y = -14$

> **Note**
>
> There is often more than one way to write an equation of a line. Consider **Example 2.**
> - The same equation will result using the point $(-2, 5)$ for (x_1, y_1) in point-slope form.
> - We could also use slope-intercept form $y = mx + b$ and substitute the slope and either given point, solving for b.

OBJECTIVE ❸ **Write an equation of a line parallel or perpendicular to a given line.**

EXAMPLE 3   Writing Equations of Parallel or Perpendicular Lines

Write an equation of the line passing through the point $(-3, 6)$ that satisfies the given condition. Give final answers in slope-intercept form.

(a) The line is parallel to the line $2x + 3y = 6$.

We can find the slope of the given line by solving for y.

$$2x + 3y = 6$$
$$3y = -2x + 6 \qquad \text{Subtract } 2x.$$
$$y = -\frac{2}{3}x + 2 \qquad \text{Divide by 3.}$$

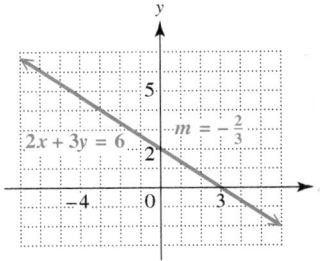

Figure 43

The slope is given by the coefficient of x, so $m = -\frac{2}{3}$. See **Figure 43.**

The required equation of the line through $(-3, 6)$ and *parallel* to $2x + 3y = 6$ must have the *same slope*, $-\frac{2}{3}$. To find this equation, we use the point-slope form, with $(x_1, y_1) = (-3, 6)$ and $m = -\frac{2}{3}$.

$$y - y_1 = m(x - x_1) \qquad \text{Point-slope form}$$

$$y - 6 = -\frac{2}{3}[x - (-3)] \qquad \begin{array}{l} y_1 = 6, \, m = -\frac{2}{3}, \\ x_1 = -3 \end{array}$$

$$y - 6 = -\frac{2}{3}(x + 3) \qquad \begin{array}{l}\text{Definition of}\\\text{subtraction}\end{array}$$

$$y - 6 = -\frac{2}{3}x - 2 \qquad \begin{array}{l}\text{Distributive}\\\text{property}\end{array}$$

$$y = -\frac{2}{3}x + 4 \qquad \text{Add 6.}$$

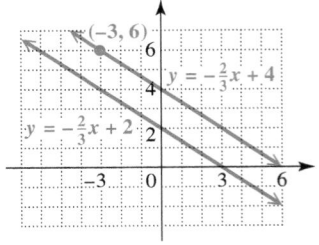

Figure 44

We did not clear the fraction here because we want the equation in slope-intercept form—that is, solved for y. Both lines are shown in **Figure 44.**

———— Continued on Next Page

(b) The line is perpendicular to the line $2x + 3y = 6$.

In part (a), we wrote the equation of the given line $2x + 3y = 6$ in slope-intercept form.

$$y = -\frac{2}{3}x + 2$$

$\uparrow$ Slope

To be *perpendicular* to the line $2x + 3y = 6$, a line must have slope $\frac{3}{2}$, the *negative reciprocal* of $-\frac{2}{3}$.

We use $(-3, 6)$ and slope $\frac{3}{2}$ in the point-slope form to find the equation of the perpendicular line shown in **Figure 45.**

$y - y_1 = m(x - x_1)$	Point-slope form	
$y - 6 = \frac{3}{2}\left[x - (-3)\right]$	$y_1 = 6, m = \frac{3}{2},$ $x_1 = -3$	
$y - 6 = \frac{3}{2}(x + 3)$	Definition of subtraction	
$y - 6 = \frac{3}{2}x + \frac{9}{2}$	Distributive property	
$y = \frac{3}{2}x + \frac{21}{2}$	Add $6 = \frac{12}{2}$.	

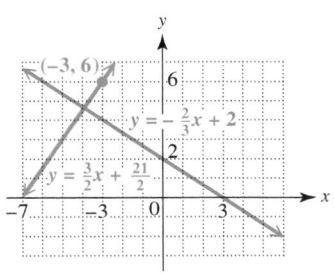

Figure 45

——————— Work Problem ③ at the Side. ▶

SUMMARY OF FORMS OF LINEAR EQUATIONS

Forms of Linear Equations		
Equation	**Description**	**When to Use**
$y = mx + b$	**Slope-Intercept Form** Slope is m. y-intercept is $(0, b)$.	The slope and y-intercept can be identified and used to quickly graph the equation.
$y - y_1 = m(x - x_1)$	**Point-Slope Form** Slope is m. Line passes through the point (x_1, y_1).	Use this form if the slope and a point on the line or two points on the line are known.
$Ax + By = C$	**Standard Form** (A, B, and C integers, with $A \geq 0$) Slope is $-\frac{A}{B}$ ($B \neq 0$). x-intercept is $\left(\frac{C}{A}, 0\right)$ ($A \neq 0$). y-intercept is $\left(0, \frac{C}{B}\right)$ ($B \neq 0$).	The x- and y-intercepts can be found quickly and used to graph the equation. The slope must be calculated.
$y = b$	**Horizontal Line** Slope is 0. y-intercept is $(0, b)$.	If the graph intersects only the y-axis, then y is the only variable in the equation.
$x = a$	**Vertical Line** Slope is undefined. x-intercept is $(a, 0)$.	If the graph intersects only the x-axis, then x is the only variable in the equation.

③ Write an equation of the line passing through the point $(-8, 3)$ that satisfies the given condition. Give final answers in slope-intercept form.

(a) The line is parallel to the line $2x - 3y = 10$.

(b) The line is perpendicular to the line $2x - 3y = 10$.

Answers

3. **(a)** $y = \frac{2}{3}x + \frac{25}{3}$ **(b)** $y = -\frac{3}{2}x - 9$

Year	x	Cost y (in dollars)
2001	1	3735
2003	3	4587
2005	5	5351
2007	7	5943
2009	9	6717
2011	11	7313
2013	13	8312

Data from National Center for Education Statistics.

4 Refer to **Example 4.** If we choose two different data points, we will obtain a slightly different equation.

(a) Use the points $(5, 5351)$ and $(11, 7313)$ to write an equation that approximates the data. Give the final equation in slope-intercept form.

(b) Use the equation found in part (a) to determine the cost of tuition and fees in 2009? How well does the equation approximate the 2009 data from the table?

Answers

4. (a) $y = 327x + 3716$
   (b) $6659; The corresponding value in the table for $x = 9$ is $6717, so the equation approximates the data reasonably well.

OBJECTIVE ▶ 4 Write an equation of a line that models real data. If a given set of data fits a linear pattern—that is, its graph consists of points lying close to a straight line—we can write a linear equation that models the data.

EXAMPLE 4 Writing an Equation of a Line That Models Data

The table in the margin lists average annual cost y (in dollars) of tuition and fees for instate students at public 4-year colleges and universities for selected years, where $x = 1$ represents 2001, $x = 3$ represents 2003, and so on.

(a) Plot the data and write an equation that approximates it.

We plot the data as shown in **Figure 46.**

AVERAGE ANNUAL COSTS AT PUBLIC 4-YEAR COLLEGES

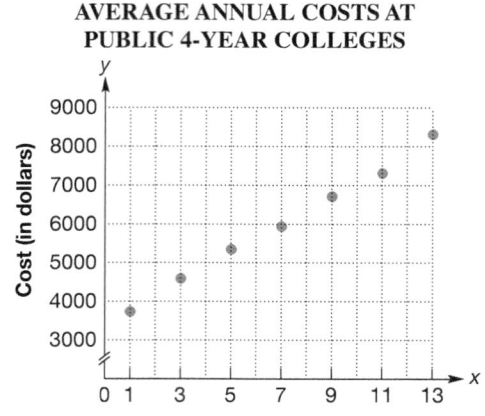

Figure 46

The points appear to lie approximately in a straight line. To find an equation of the line, we choose two ordered pairs $(3, 4587)$ and $(9, 6717)$ from the table and determine the slope of the line through these points.

$$m = \frac{y_2 - y_1}{x_2 - x_1} = \frac{6717 - 4587}{9 - 3} = 355 \qquad \text{Let } (9, 6717) = (x_2, y_2) \text{ and } (3, 4587) = (x_1, y_1).$$

The slope, 355, is positive, indicating that tuition and fees *increased* $355 each year. Now substitute this slope and the point $(3, 4587)$ in the point-slope form to find an equation of the line.

$$y - y_1 = m(x - x_1) \qquad \text{Point-slope form}$$
$$y - 4587 = 355(x - 3) \qquad \text{Let } (x_1, y_1) = (3, 4587), m = 355.$$
$$y - 4587 = 355x - 1065 \qquad \text{Distributive property}$$
$$y = 355x + 3522 \qquad \text{Add 4587.}$$

Thus, the equation $y = 355x + 3522$ can be used to model the data.

(b) Use the equation found in part (a) to determine the cost of tuition and fees in 2013.

$$y = 355x + 3522 \qquad \text{Equation found in part (a)}$$
$$y = 355(13) + 3522 \qquad \text{Let } x = 13 \text{ (for 2013).}$$
$$y = 8137 \qquad \text{Multiply, and then add.}$$

Using the equation, tuition and fees in 2013 were $8137. The corresponding value in the table for $x = 13$ is 8312, so the equation approximates the data reasonably well.

◀ **Work Problem 4 at the Side.**

3.5 Exercises

FOR EXTRA HELP

Go to MyMathLab *for worked-out, step-by-step solutions to exercises enclosed in a square* ▢ *and video solutions to* ▶ *exercises.*

CONCEPT CHECK *Work each problem.*

1. Match each form or description in Column I with the corresponding equation in Column II.

I	II
(a) Point-slope form	**A.** $x = a$
(b) Horizontal line	**B.** $y = mx + b$
(c) Slope-intercept form	**C.** $y = b$
(d) Standard form	**D.** $y - y_1 = m(x - x_1)$
(e) Vertical line	**E.** $Ax + By = C$

2. Write the equation $y + 1 = -2(x - 5)$ first in slope-intercept form and then in standard form.

3. Which equations are equivalent to $2x - 3y = 6$?

A. $y = \dfrac{2}{3}x - 2$ **B.** $-2x + 3y = -6$ **C.** $y = -\dfrac{3}{2}x + 3$ **D.** $y - 2 = \dfrac{2}{3}(x - 6)$

4. Consider the following equations, written in slope-intercept form and point-slope form, respectively.

$$y = \frac{3}{2}x - 6 \quad \text{and} \quad y + 3 = \frac{3}{2}(x - 2)$$

Write each of these equations in standard form. What do you notice?

Write an equation of the line passing through the given point and having the given slope. Give the final answer in slope-intercept form. **See Example 1.**

5. $(1, 7), m = 5$ **6.** $(2, 9), m = 6$ **7.** $(6, -3), m = 1$

8. $(-4, 4), m = 1$ **9.** $(1, -7), m = -3$ **10.** $(1, -5), m = -7$

11. $(3, -2), m = -1$ **12.** $(-5, 4), m = -1$ **13.** $(-2, 5), m = \dfrac{2}{3}$

14. $(4, 2), m = -\dfrac{1}{3}$ **15.** $(6, -3), m = -\dfrac{4}{5}$ **16.** $(7, -2), m = -\dfrac{7}{2}$

Write an equation of the line passing through the given pair of points. Give the final answer in (a) slope-intercept form and (b) standard form. See Example 2.

17. $(4, 10)$ and $(6, 12)$ **18.** $(8, 5)$ and $(9, 6)$ **19.** $(-1, -7)$ and $(-8, -2)$ **20.** $(-2, -1)$ and $(3, -4)$

21. $(0, -2)$ and $(-3, 0)$ **22.** $(-4, 0)$ and $(0, 2)$ **23.** $\left(\dfrac{1}{2}, \dfrac{3}{2}\right)$ and $\left(-\dfrac{1}{4}, \dfrac{5}{4}\right)$ **24.** $\left(-\dfrac{2}{3}, \dfrac{8}{3}\right)$ and $\left(\dfrac{1}{3}, \dfrac{7}{3}\right)$

Write an equation of the given line through the given points. Give the final answer in (a) slope-intercept form and (b) standard form.

25. 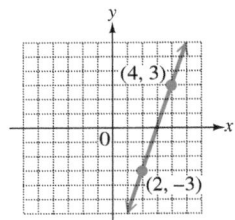   **26.** 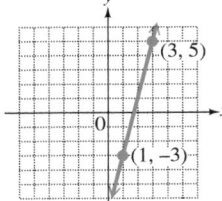   **27.** 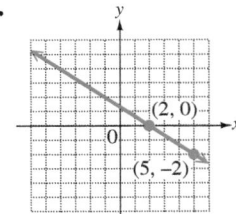   **28.**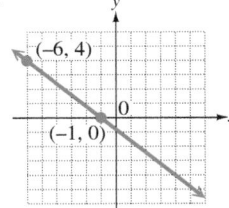

Write an equation of the line satisfying the given conditions. Give the final answer in slope-intercept form. See Example 3.

29. Passing through $(8, -1)$;   parallel to a line with slope $\frac{3}{4}$

30. Passing through $(-2, 1)$;   perpendicular to a line with slope $\frac{2}{3}$

31. Perpendicular to $x - 2y = 7$; y-intercept $(0, -3)$

32. Parallel to $5x = 2y + 10$; y-intercept $(0, 4)$

33. Passing through $(4, 2)$;   perpendicular to $x - 3y = 7$

34. Passing through $(2, 3)$;   parallel to $4x - y = -2$

35. Passing through $(2, -3)$;   parallel to $3x = 4y + 5$

36. Passing through $(-1, 4)$;   perpendicular to $2x + 3y = 8$

Solve each problem. See Example 4.

37. The table lists the average annual cost y (in dollars) of tuition and fees at 2-year public colleges for selected years x, where $x = 1$ represents 2009, $x = 2$ represents 2010, and so on.

   (a) Write five ordered pairs (x, y) for the data.

Year	x	Cost y (in dollars)
2009	1	2283
2010	2	2441
2011	3	2651
2012	4	2792
2013	5	2882

Data from National Center for Education Statistics.

   (b) Plot the ordered pairs (x, y). Do the points lie approximately in a straight line?

AVERAGE ANNUAL TUITION AND FEES AT 2-YEAR COLLEGES

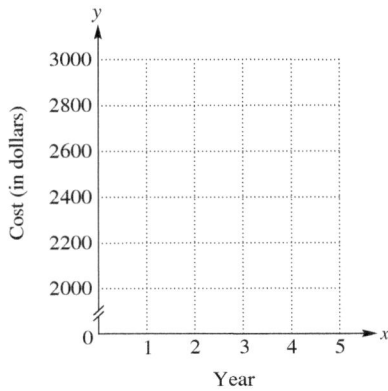

   (c) Use the ordered pairs $(2, 2441)$ and $(5, 2882)$ to write the equation of a line that approximates the data. Give the final equation in slope-intercept form.

   (d) Use the equation from part (c) to estimate the average annual cost at 2-year colleges in 2015 to the nearest dollar. (*Hint:* What is the value of x for 2015?)

38. The table gives heavy-metal nuclear waste y (in thousands of metric tons) from spent reactor fuel awaiting permanent storage. Here $x = 0$ represents 1995, $x = 5$ represents 2000, and so on.

   (a) Write four ordered pairs (x, y) for the data.

Year	x	Waste y (in thousands of tons)
1995	0	32
2000	5	42
2010	15	61
2020*	25	76

Data from *Scientific American.*

*Estimate by U.S. Department of Energy.

   (b) Plot the ordered pairs (x, y). Do the points lie approximately in a straight line?

HEAVY-METAL NUCLEAR WASTE AWAITING STORAGE

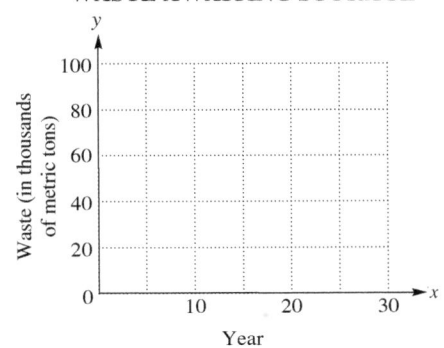

   (c) Use the ordered pairs $(0, 32)$ and $(25, 76)$ to write the equation of a line that approximates the data. Give the final equation in slope-intercept form.

   (d) Use the equation from part (c) to estimate the amount of nuclear waste in 2015. (*Hint:* What is the value of x for 2015?)

The points on the graph indicate years of life expected at birth y in the United States for selected years x. The graph of a linear equation that models the data is also shown. Here x = 0 represents 1930, x = 10 represents 1940, and so on.

39. Use the ordered pairs shown on the graph to write an equation of the line that models the data. Give the final equation in slope-intercept form.

40. Use the equation from **Exercise 39** to do the following.

(a) Find years of life expected at birth in 2000. (*Hint*: What is the value of x for 2000?) Round the answer to the nearest tenth.

(b) How does the answer in part (a) compare to the actual value of 76.8 yr?

(c) Project years of life expected at birth in 2020. (*Hint*: What is the value of x for 2020?) Round the answer to the nearest tenth. Does the answer seem reasonable?

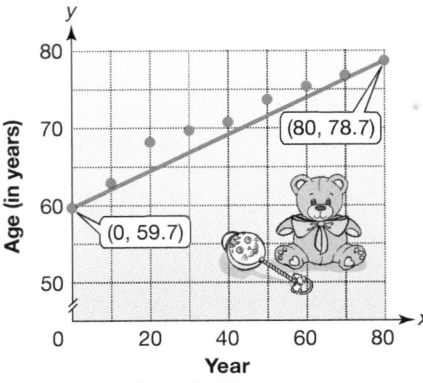

Life Expectancy

Points shown: $(0, 59.7)$ and $(80, 78.7)$

Data from National Center for Health Statistics.

Relating Concepts (Exercises 41–48) For Individual or Group Work

If we think of ordered pairs of the form (C, F), then the two most common methods of measuring temperature, Celsius and Fahrenheit, can be related as follows:

When $C = 0$, $F = 32$, and when $C = 100$, $F = 212$.

Work Exercises 41–48 in order.

41. Write two ordered pairs relating these two temperature scales.

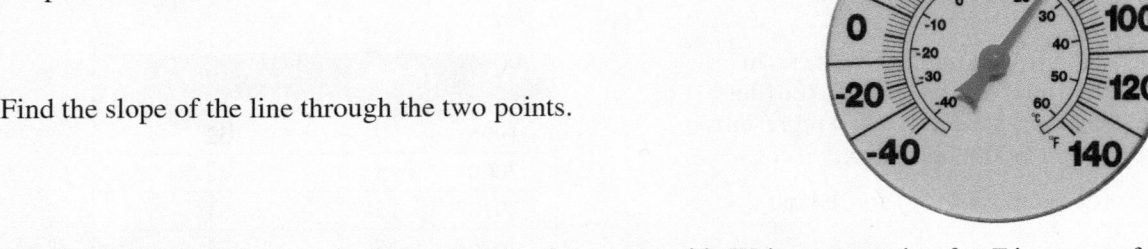

42. Find the slope of the line through the two points.

43. Use the point-slope form to find an equation of the line. (Your variables should be C and F rather than x and y.)

44. Write an equation for F in terms of C.

45. Use the equation from **Exercise 44** to write an equation for C in terms of F.

46. Use the equation from **Exercise 44** to find the Fahrenheit temperature when $C = 30$.

47. Use the equation from **Exercise 45** to find the Celsius temperature when $F = 50$.

48. For what temperature is $F = C$? (Use the thermometer shown above to confirm the answer.)

Summary Exercises *Applying Graphing and Equation-Writing Techniques for Lines*

1. CONCEPT CHECK   Match the description of a line in Column I with the correct equation in Column II.

I	II

I

(a) Slope -0.5, $b = -2$

(b) x-intercept $(4, 0)$, y-intercept $(0, 2)$

(c) Passes through $(4, -2)$ and $(0, 0)$

(d) $m = \frac{1}{2}$, passes through $(-2, -2)$

II

A. $y = -\frac{1}{2}x$

B. $y = -\frac{1}{2}x - 2$

C. $x - 2y = 2$

D. $x + 2y = 4$

E. $x = 2y$

2. CONCEPT CHECK   Which equations are equivalent to $2x + 5y = 20$?

A. $y = -\frac{2}{5}x + 4$ **B.** $y - 2 = -\frac{2}{5}(x - 5)$ **C.** $y = \frac{5}{2}x - 4$ **D.** $2x = 5y - 20$

Graph each line, using the given information or equation.

3. $m = 1$, $b = -2$

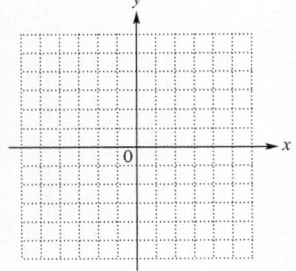

4. $m = 1$, y-intercept $(0, -4)$

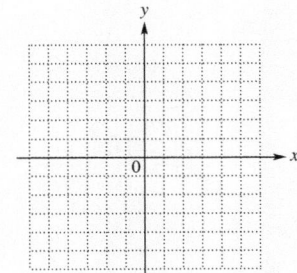

5. $y = -2x + 6$

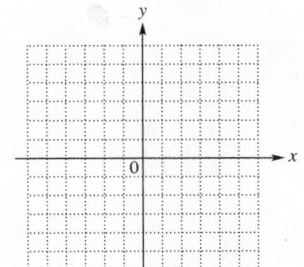

6. $x + 4 = 0$

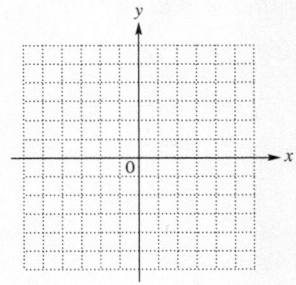

7. $m = -\frac{2}{3}$, passes through $(3, -4)$

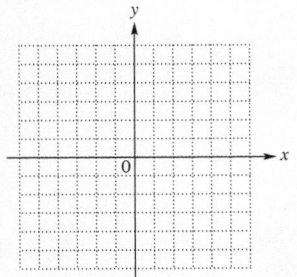

8. $y = -\frac{1}{2}x + 2$

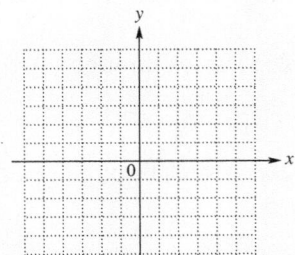

9. $y - 4 = -9$

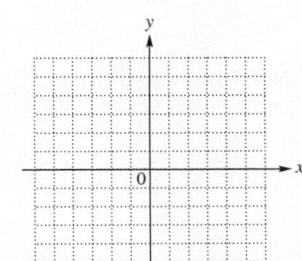

10. $m = -\frac{3}{4}$, passes through $(4, -4)$

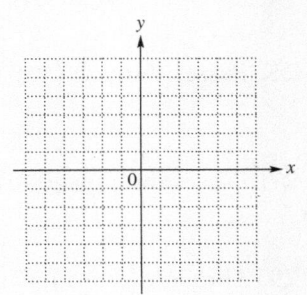

11. Undefined slope, passes through $(3.5, 0)$

12. Slope $-\frac{1}{5}$, passes through $(0, 0)$

13. $4x - 5y = 20$

14. $6x - 5y = 30$

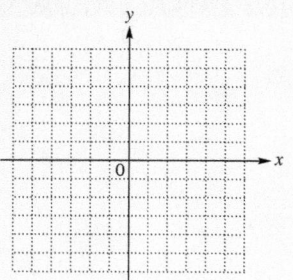 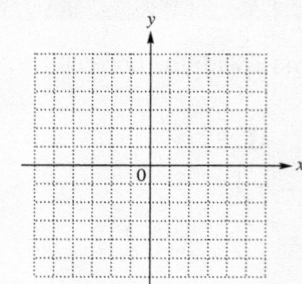 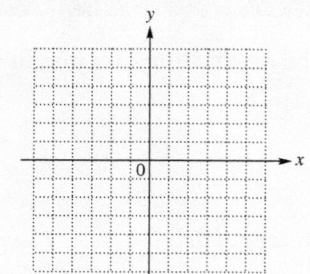 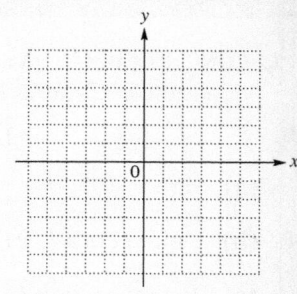

15. $x - 4y = 0$

16. $m = 0$, passes through $\left(0, \frac{3}{2}\right)$

17. $3y = 12 - 2x$

18. $8x = 6y + 24$

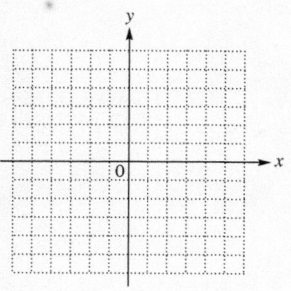 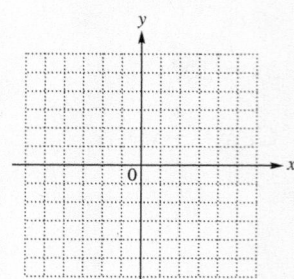 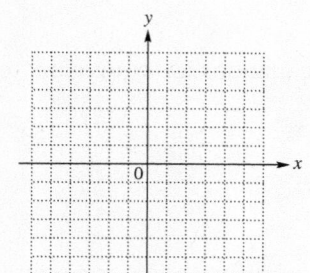 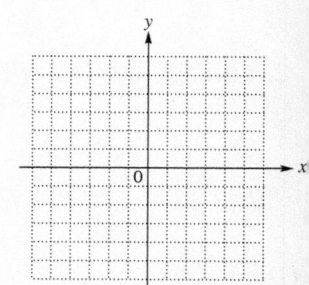

Write an equation in slope-intercept form of each line represented by the table of ordered pairs or the graph.

19.

x	y
3	0
1	4
−1	8

20.

x	y
−6	0
0	8
3	12

21.

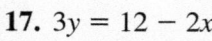

22.

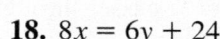

Write an equation of each line. Give the final answer in slope-intercept form if possible. In Exercises 29 and 30, also give the final answer in standard form.

23. $m = -3$, $b = -6$

24. Passes through $(1, -7)$ and $(-2, 5)$

25. Passes through $(0, 0)$ and $(5, 3)$

26. Passes through $(0, 0)$, undefined slope

27. Passes through $(0, 0)$, $m = 0$

28. $m = \frac{5}{3}$, through $(-3, 0)$

29. Through $(2, -1)$, parallel to the graph of $y = \frac{1}{5}x + \frac{7}{4}$

30. Through $(0, -6)$, perpendicular to the graph of $y = \frac{4}{3}x + \frac{3}{8}$

Study Skills

PREPARING FOR YOUR MATH FINAL EXAM

Your math final exam is likely to be a comprehensive exam, which means it will cover material from the entire term. **One way to prepare for it now is by working a set of Cumulative Review Exercises** each time your class finishes a chapter. This continual review will help you remember concepts and procedures as you progress through the course.

Final Exam Preparation Suggestions

1. **Figure out the grade you need to earn on the final exam to get the course grade you want.** Check your course syllabus for grading policies, or ask your instructor if you are not sure.

2. **Create a final exam week plan.** Set priorities that allow you to spend extra time studying. This may mean making adjustments, in advance, in your work schedule or enlisting extra help with family responsibilities.

3. **Use the following suggestions to guide your studying.**

   ▶ **Begin reviewing several days before the final exam.** DON'T wait until the last minute.

   ▶ **Know exactly which chapters and sections will be covered.**

   ▶ **Divide up the chapters.** Decide how much you will review each day.

   ▶ **Keep returned quizzes and tests. Use them to review.**

   ▶ **Practice all types of problems. Use the Cumulative Review Exercises** at the end of each chapter in your text beginning in Chapter 2. All answers are given in the answer section.

   ▶ **Review or rewrite your notes** to create summaries of key information.

   ▶ **Make study cards for all types of problems.** Carry the cards with you, and review them whenever you have a few minutes.

   ▶ **Take plenty of short breaks as you study to reduce physical and mental stress.** Exercising, listening to music, and enjoying a favorite activity are effective stress busters.

Finally, *DON'T* stay up all night the night before an exam—*get a good night's sleep.*

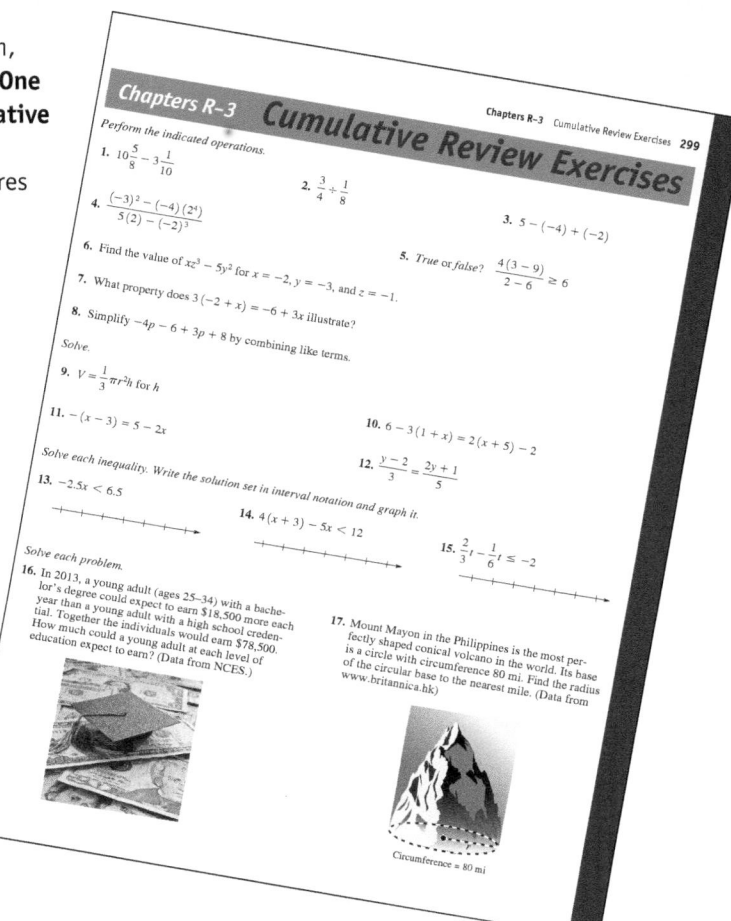

Now Try This

1 How many points do you need to earn on your math final exam to get the grade you want in your course?

_____

2 What adjustments to your usual routine or schedule do you need to make for final exam week? List two or three.

_____

_____

3 Which of the suggestions for studying will you use as you prepare for your math final exam?

_____

_____

3.6 | Graphing Linear Inequalities in Two Variables

OBJECTIVES

1 Graph linear inequalities in two variables.

2 Graph an inequality with a boundary line through the origin.

We have graphed linear equations, such as

$$2x + 3y = 6.$$

Now we extend this work to include *linear inequalities in two variables,* such as

$$2x + 3y \leq 6.$$

(Recall that $\leq$ is read "*is less than or equal to.*")

Linear Inequality in Two Variables

A **linear inequality in two variables** (here x and y) can be written in the form

$$Ax + By < C, \quad Ax + By \leq C, \quad Ax + By > C, \quad \text{or} \quad Ax + By \geq C,$$

where A, B, and C are real numbers and A and B are not both 0.

Examples: $\quad 3x - y < 9, \quad 2x + 5y \geq 0, \quad x > -2, \quad$ and $\quad y \leq 6$

OBJECTIVE **1** **Graph linear inequalities in two variables.** Consider the graph in **Figure 47.**

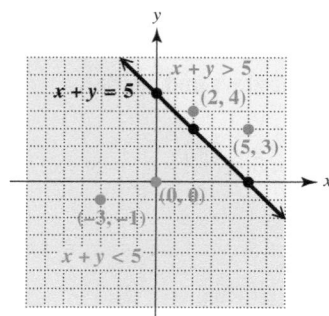

Figure 47

The graph of the line $x + y = 5$ in **Figure 47** divides the points in the rectangular coordinate system into three sets.

1. Those points that lie *on* the line itself and satisfy the equation $x + y = 5$ (such as $(0, 5)$, $(2, 3)$, and $(5, 0)$)

2. Those points that lie in the region *above* the line and satisfy the inequality $x + y > 5$ (such as $(5, 3)$ and $(2, 4)$)

3. Those points that lie in the region *below* the line and satisfy the inequality $x + y < 5$ (such as $(0, 0)$ and $(-3, -1)$)

The graph of the line $x + y = 5$ is the **boundary line** for the inequalities

$$x + y > 5 \quad \text{and} \quad x + y < 5.$$

Graphs of linear inequalities in two variables are regions in the real number plane that may or may not include boundary lines.

EXAMPLE 1   **Graphing a Linear Inequality**

Graph $2x + 3y \le 6$.

The inequality $2x + 3y \le 6$ means that

$$2x + 3y < 6 \quad \text{or} \quad 2x + 3y = 6.$$

We begin by graphing the equation $2x + 3y = 6$, a line with intercepts $(0, 2)$ and $(3, 0)$ as shown in **Figure 48.** This boundary line divides the plane into two regions, one of which satisfies the inequality. To find the correct region, we choose a test point *not* on the boundary line and substitute it into the inequality to see whether the resulting statement is true or false. The point $(0, 0)$ is a convenient choice.

$$2x + 3y < 6 \quad \text{We are testing the region.}$$

$$2(\mathbf{0}) + 3(\mathbf{0}) \overset{?}{<} 6 \quad \text{Let } x = 0 \text{ and } y = 0.$$

Use $(0, 0)$ as a test point.

$$0 + 0 \overset{?}{<} 6 \quad \text{Multiply.}$$

$$0 < 6 \quad \text{True}$$

Because a true statement results, we shade the region that includes the test point $(0, 0)$. See **Figure 48.** The shaded region, along with the boundary line because $\le$ includes equality, is the desired graph.

CHECK To confirm that the correct region is shaded, we select a test point in the region that is *not* shaded. We arbitrarily choose $(2, 5)$ and substitute it into the inequality.

$$2x + 3y < 6 \quad \text{Test the region.}$$

$$2(2) + 3(5) \overset{?}{<} 6 \quad \text{Let } x = 2 \text{ and } y = 5.$$

$$4 + 15 \overset{?}{<} 6 \quad \text{Multiply.}$$

$$19 < 6 \quad \text{False}$$

A false statement results, confirming that we shaded the correct region.

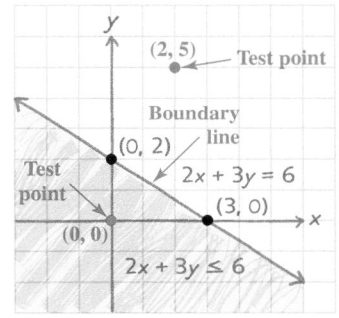

Figure 48

Work Problems ❶ and ❷ at the Side. ▶

Note

Alternatively in **Example 1,** we can find the required region by solving the given inequality for *y.*

$$2x + 3y \le 6 \quad \text{Inequality from \textbf{Example 1}}$$

$$3y \le -2x + 6 \quad \text{Subtract } 2x.$$

$$y \le -\frac{2}{3}x + 2 \quad \text{Divide each term by 3.}$$

Ordered pairs in which *y* is equal to $-\frac{2}{3}x + 2$ are on the boundary line, so pairs in which *y is less than* $-\frac{2}{3}x + 2$ will be *below* that line. (As we move *down* vertically, the *y*-values *decrease.*) This gives the same region that we shaded in **Figure 48.** (Ordered pairs in which *y is greater than* $-\frac{2}{3}x + 2$ will be *above* the boundary line.)

To solve for *y* in the inequality above, we divided each term by the positive number 3 in the last step. ***Remember to reverse the direction of the inequality symbol when multiplying or dividing an inequality by a negative number.***

❶ Use $(0, 0)$ as a test point, and shade the appropriate region for the linear inequality.

$$3x + 4y \le 12$$

$$3(\underline{}) + 4(\underline{}) \overset{?}{\le} 12$$

$$\underline{} \overset{?}{\le} 12 \quad (True / False)$$

Shade the region of the graph that (*includes / does not include*) the test point $(0, 0)$.

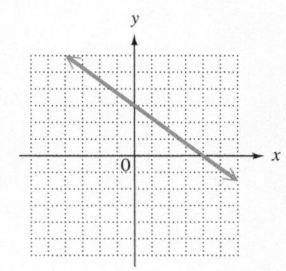

❷ Graph $4x - 5y \le 20$.

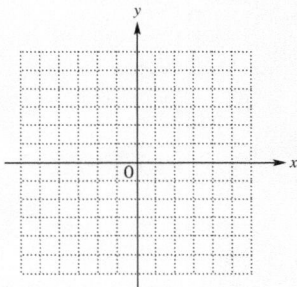

Answers

1. 0; 0; 0; True; includes

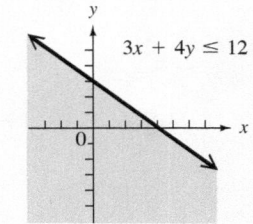

③ Use $(0, 0)$ as a test point and shade the appropriate region for the linear inequality.

$$3x + 5y > 15$$

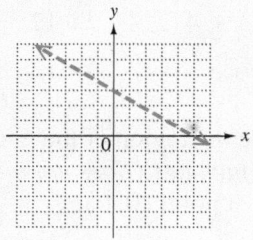

④ Graph $x + 2y > 6$.

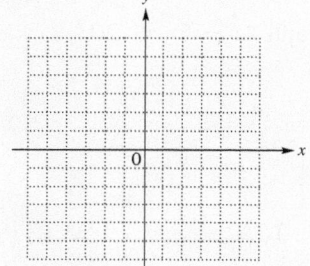

Answers

3.

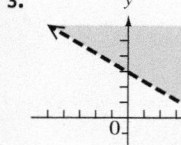

$3x + 5y > 15$

4.

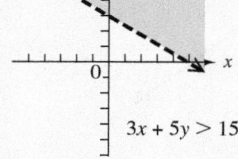

$x + 2y > 6$

EXAMPLE 2 Graphing a Linear Inequality

Graph $x - y > 5$.

This inequality does *not* involve equality. Therefore, the points on the line $x - y = 5$ do **not** belong to the graph. However, the line still serves as a boundary for two regions, one of which satisfies the inequality.

To graph the inequality, first graph the equation $x - y = 5$ using the intercepts $(5, 0)$ and $(0, -5)$. Use a *dashed line* to show that the points on the line are *not* solutions of the inequality $x - y > 5$. See **Figure 49.** Then choose a test point to see which region satisfies the inequality.

$$x - y > 5$$

$(0, 0)$ is a convenient test point. → $0 - 0 \overset{?}{>} 5$ Let $x = 0$ and $y = 0$.

$$0 > 5 \quad \text{False}$$

Because $0 > 5$ is false, the graph of the inequality is the region that *does not* include $(0, 0)$. Shade the *other* region, as shown in **Figure 49.**

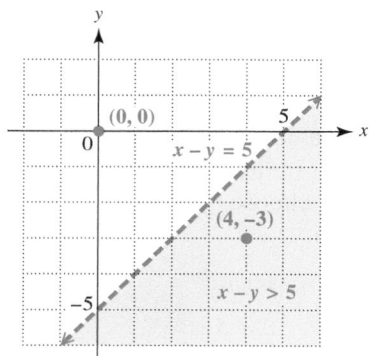

Figure 49

CHECK To confirm that the correct region is shaded, we select a test point in the shaded region. We arbitrarily choose $(4, -3)$.

$$x - y > 5$$

$$4 - (-3) \overset{?}{>} 5 \qquad \text{Let } x = 4 \text{ and } y = -3.$$

Use parentheses to avoid errors.

$$7 > 5 \checkmark \qquad \text{True}$$

This true statement confirms that the correct region is shaded in **Figure 49.**

◀ **Work Problems ③ and ④ at the Side.**

Graphing a Linear Inequality in Two Variables

Step 1 **Draw the graph of the straight line that is the boundary.**

• Make the line solid if the inequality involves $\leq$ or $\geq$.

• Make the line dashed if the inequality involves $<$ or $>$.

Step 2 **Choose a test point.** Choose any point not on the line, and substitute the coordinates of that point in the inequality.

Step 3 **Shade the appropriate region.** Shade the region that includes the test point if it satisfies the original inequality. Otherwise, shade the region on the other side of the boundary line.

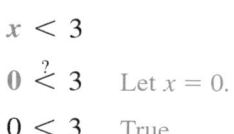

EXAMPLE 3 Graphing a Linear Inequality

Graph $x < 3$.

First, we graph $x = 3$, a vertical line passing through the point $(3, 0)$. We use a dashed line because $<$ does not include equality and choose $(0, 0)$ as a test point.

$$x < 3$$

$$0 \overset{?}{<} 3 \quad \text{Let } x = 0.$$

$$0 < 3 \quad \text{True}$$

Because $0 < 3$ is true, we shade the region containing $(0, 0)$, as in **Figure 50**. Intuitively this makes sense—all values of x along the x-axis in the shaded region are indeed less than 3.

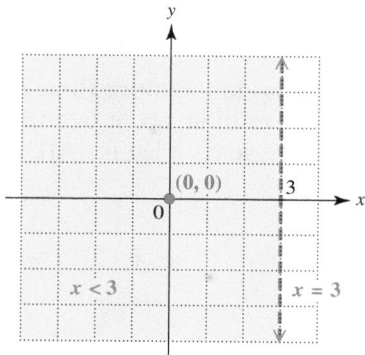

Figure 50

Work Problem **5** at the Side. ▶

OBJECTIVE ▶ **2** Graph an inequality with a boundary line through the origin. *If the graph of an inequality has a boundary line through the origin, $(0, 0)$ cannot be used as a test point.*

EXAMPLE 4 Graphing a Linear Inequality

Graph $x \leq 2y$.

We graph $x = 2y$ using a solid line by determining several ordered pairs that satisfy the equation.

$x = 2y$	$x = 2y$	$x = 2y$
$0 = 2y \quad$ Let $x = 0.$	$6 = 2y \quad$ Let $x = 6.$	$x = 2(2) \quad$ Let $y = 2.$
$0 = y$	$3 = y$	$x = 4$
Ordered pair: $(0, 0)$	Ordered pair: $(6, 3)$	Ordered pair: $(4, 2)$

The line through these three ordered pairs is shown in **Figure 51**. Because the point $(0, 0)$ is *on* the line $x = 2y$, it cannot be used as a test point. Instead, we choose a test point *off* the line, such as $(1, 3)$.

$$x < 2y \quad \text{Test the region.}$$

$$1 \overset{?}{<} 2(3) \quad \text{Let } x = 1 \text{ and } y = 3.$$

$$1 < 6 \quad \text{True}$$

A true statement results, so we shade the region containing the test point $(1, 3)$. See **Figure 51**.

CHECK To confirm that the correct region is shaded, choose a test point, such as $(5, 0)$, in the *other* region.

$$x < 2y \quad \text{Test the region.}$$

$$5 \overset{?}{<} 2(0) \quad \text{Let } x = 5 \text{ and } y = 0.$$

$$5 < 0 \quad \text{False}$$

A false statement results, confirming that we shaded the correct region.

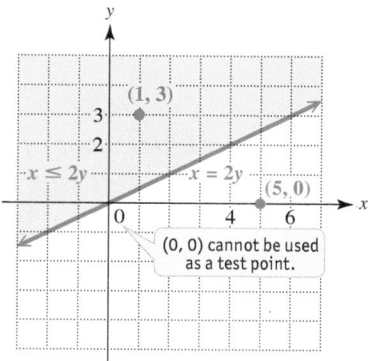

Figure 51

Work Problem **6** at the Side. ▶

5 Graph $y < 4$.

The graph of this equation has a (*horizontal / vertical*) boundary line.

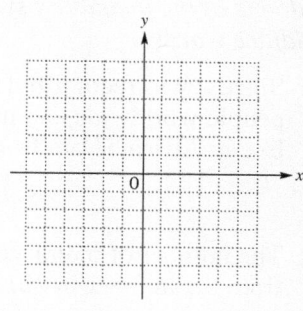

6 Graph $x \geq -3y$.

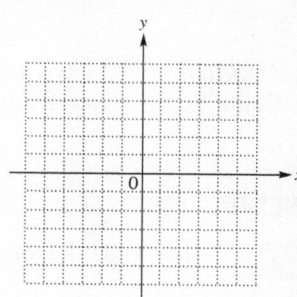

Can $(0, 0)$ be used as a test point here? (*Yes / No*)

Answers

5. horizontal

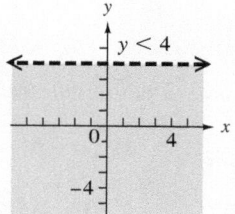

6.

No

CONCEPT CHECK *Each statement includes one or more phrases that can be symbolized with one of the inequality symbols* $<, \leq, >,$ *or* $\geq$. *Give the inequality symbol for the boldface words.*

1. Since it was recognized in 1981, HIV/AIDS has killed **more than** 25 million people worldwide and infected **more than** 60 million, about two-thirds of whom live in Africa. (Data from The President's Emergency Plan for AIDS Relief.)

2. The number of motor vehicle deaths in the United States in 2013 was 1063 **less than** the number in 2012. (Data from NHTSA.)

3. As of January 2016, American Airlines passengers were allowed one carry-on bag, with dimensions (length + width + height) of **at most** 45 in. (Data from www.aa.com)

4. A tornado must have winds of **at least** 65 mph to be rated using the Enhanced Fujita Scale. (Data from National Weather Service.)

CONCEPT CHECK *Decide whether each statement is* true *or* false. *If false, explain why.*

5. The point $(4, 0)$ lies on the graph of $3x - 4y < 12$.

6. The point $(4, 0)$ lies on the graph of $3x - 4y \leq 12$.

7. The point $(0, 0)$ can be used as a test point to determine which region to shade when graphing the linear inequality $x + 4y > 0$.

8. When graphing the linear inequality $3x + 2y \geq 12$, use a dashed line for the boundary line.

9. The points $(4, 1)$ and $(0, 0)$ lie on the graph of $3x - 2y \geq 0$.

10. The graph of $y > x$ does not contain points in quadrant IV.

CONCEPT CHECK *Decide whether the given ordered pair is a solution of the given inequality.*

11. $x - 4y \geq 8$
    (a) $(0, 0)$ (b) $(0, 2)$
    (c) $(4, -1)$ (d) $(-4, 1)$

12. $2x + 5y < 10$
    (a) $(0, 0)$ (b) $(5, 0)$
    (c) $(-5, 2)$ (d) $(-2, -3)$

13. Explain how to determine whether to use a dashed line or a solid line when graphing a linear inequality in two variables.

14. Explain why the point $(0, 0)$ is not an appropriate choice for a test point when graphing an inequality whose boundary passes through the origin.

For each inequality, the straight-line boundary has been drawn. Complete each graph by shading the correct region. ***See Examples 1–4.***

15. $x + y \geq 4$

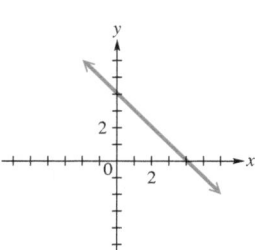

16. $x + y \leq 2$

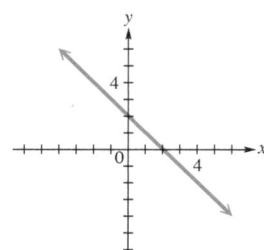

17. $x + 2y \geq 7$

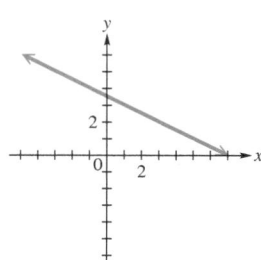

18. $2x + y \geq 5$

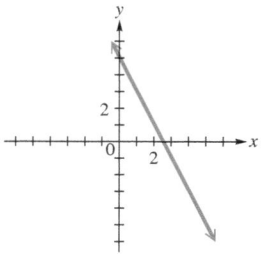

19. $-3x + 4y > 12$

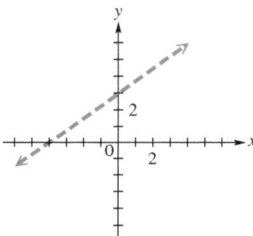

20. $4x - 5y < 20$

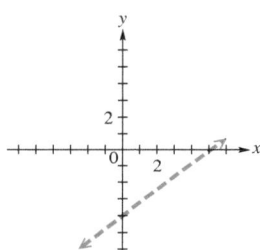

21. $x > 4$

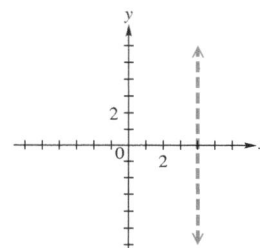

22. $x \leq 0$

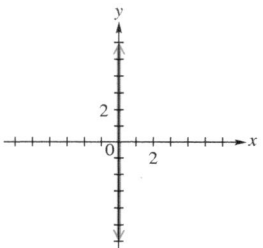

23. $y < 0$

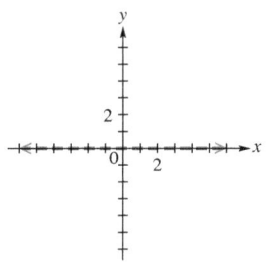

24. $y < -1$

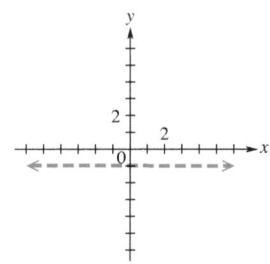

25. $x \geq -y$

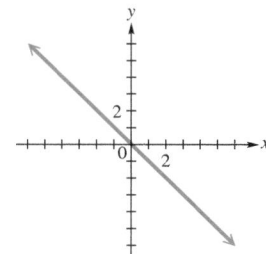

26. $x > 3y$

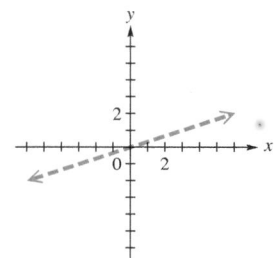

Graph each linear inequality. ***See Examples 1–4.***

27. $x + y \leq 5$

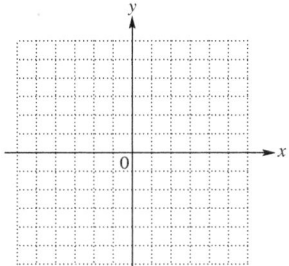

28. $x + y \geq 3$

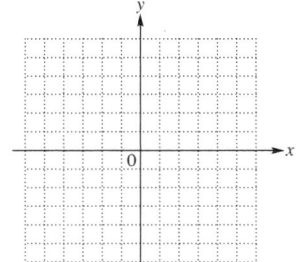

29. $x + 2y < 4$

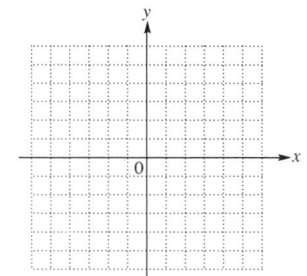

30. $x + 3y > 6$

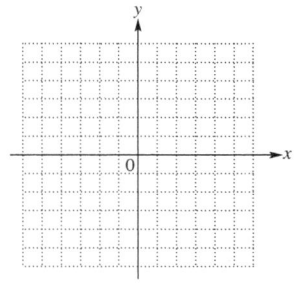

31. $2x + 3y > -6$

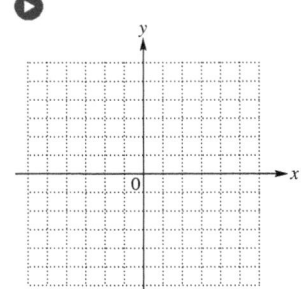

32. $3x + 4y < 12$

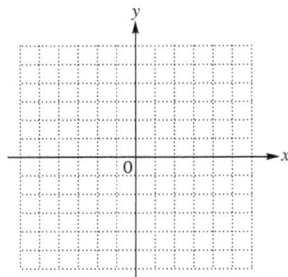

33. $y \geq 2x + 1$

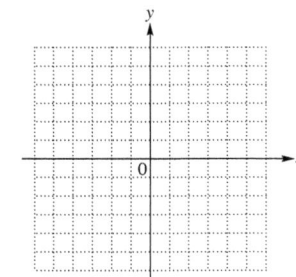

34. $y < -3x + 1$

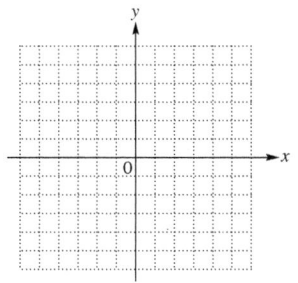

35. $x \leq -2$

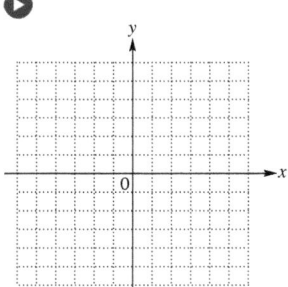

36. $x \geq 1$

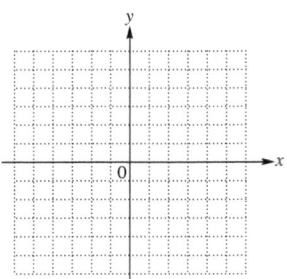

37. $y < 5$

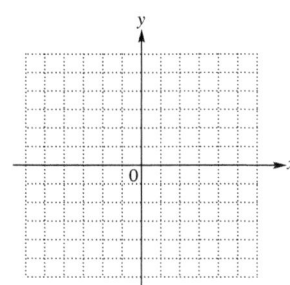

38. $y < -3$

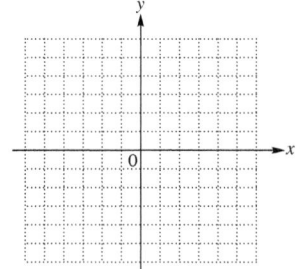

39. $x \geq 0$

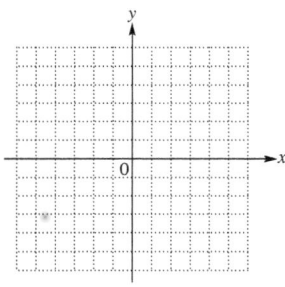

40. $y \geq 0$

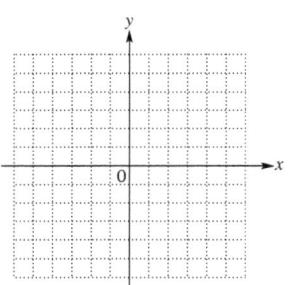

41. $y \geq 4x$

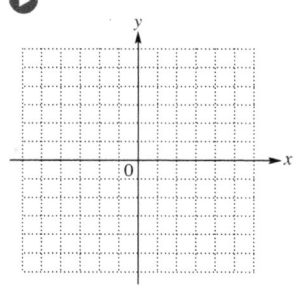

42. $y \leq 2x$

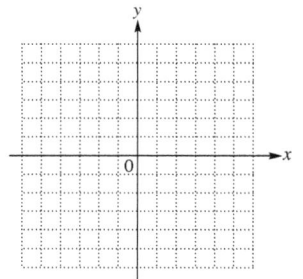

43. $x < -2y$

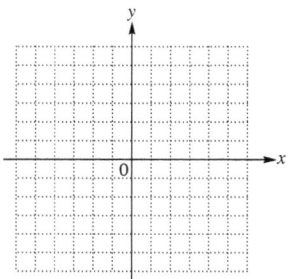

44. $x > -5y$

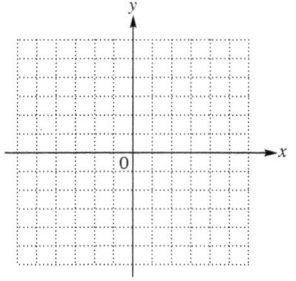

45. $x + y > 0$

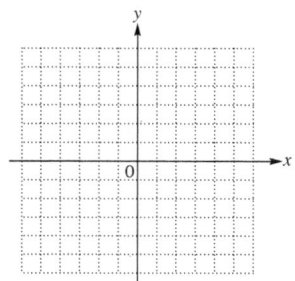

46. $x - 3y < 0$

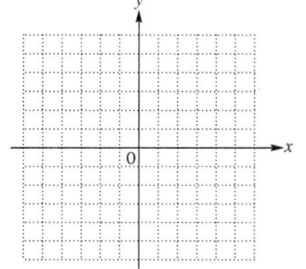

Chapter 3 *Summary*

Key Terms

3.1

line graph A line graph consists of a series of points that are connected with line segments and is used to show changes or trends in data over time.

linear equation in two variables An equation that can be written in the form $Ax + By = C$ is a linear equation in two variables (here x and y). A, B, and C are real numbers; A and B are not both 0.

ordered pair A pair of numbers written between parentheses in which order is important is an ordered pair.

table of values A table showing selected ordered pairs of numbers that satisfy an equation is a table of values.

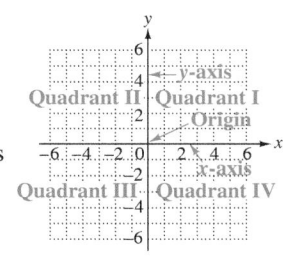

x	y
0	4	← Ordered pair (0, 4)
2	0
1	2

Table of values for $2x + y = 4$

x-axis The horizontal axis in a coordinate system is the x-axis.

y-axis The vertical axis in a coordinate system is the y-axis.

rectangular (Cartesian) coordinate system An x-axis and y-axis drawn at right angles form a coordinate system.

origin The point at which the x-axis and y-axis intersect is the origin.

quadrants A coordinate system divides the plane into four regions, or quadrants.

Rectangular coordinate system

plane A flat surface determined by two intersecting lines is a plane.

coordinates The numbers in an ordered pair are the coordinates of the corresponding point.

plot To plot an ordered pair is to find the corresponding point on a coordinate system.

scatter diagram A graph of ordered pairs of data is a scatter diagram.

3.2

graph The graph of an equation is the set of all points that correspond to the ordered pairs that satisfy the equation.

graphing The process of plotting the ordered pairs that satisfy an equation and drawing a line (or curve) through them is called graphing.

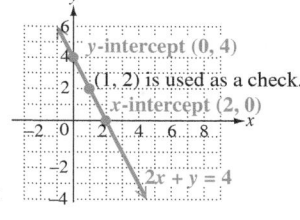

Graph of $2x + y = 4$

y-intercept If a graph intersects the y-axis at b, then the y-intercept is $(0, b)$.

x-intercept If a graph intersects the x-axis at a, then the x-intercept is $(a, 0)$.

3.3

rise Rise is the vertical change between two different points on a line.

run Run is the horizontal change between two different points on a line.

slope The slope of a line is the ratio of the change in y compared to the change in x when moving along the line from one point to another.

parallel lines Two lines in a plane that never intersect are parallel.

perpendicular lines Perpendicular lines intersect at a 90° angle.

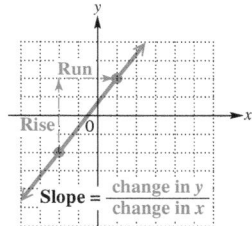

$$\text{Slope} = \frac{\text{change in } y}{\text{change in } x}$$

This line has slope $\frac{4}{3}$.

3.6

linear inequality in two variables An inequality that can be written in the form $Ax + By < C$, $Ax + By \le C$, $Ax + By > C$, or $Ax + By \ge C$ is a linear inequality in two variables (here x and y). A, B, and C are real numbers; A and B are not both 0.

boundary line In the graph of a linear inequality, the boundary line separates the region that satisfies the inequality from the region that does not satisfy the inequality.

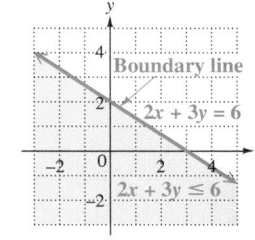

New Symbols

(x, y)	ordered pair		(x_1, y_1)	subscript notation (read "x-sub-one, y-sub-one")	m	slope

Test Your Word Power

See how well you have learned the vocabulary in this chapter.

1 An **ordered pair** is a pair of numbers written
  A. in numerical order between brackets
  B. between parentheses or brackets
  C. between parentheses in which order is important
  D. between parentheses in which order does not matter.

2 The **coordinates** of a point are
  A. the numbers in the corresponding ordered pair
  B. the solution of an equation
  C. the values of the x- and y-intercepts
  D. the graph of the point.

3 An **intercept** is
  A. the point where the x-axis and y-axis intersect
  B. a pair of numbers written in parentheses in which order is important
  C. one of the four regions determined by a rectangular coordinate system
  D. the point where a graph intersects the x-axis or the y-axis.

4 The **slope** of a line is
  A. the measure of the run over the rise of the line
  B. the distance between two points on the line
  C. the ratio of the change in y to the change in x along the line

  D. the horizontal change compared to the vertical change of two points on the line.

5 Two lines in a plane are **parallel** if
  A. they represent the same line
  B. they never intersect
  C. they intersect at a 90° angle
  D. one has a positive slope and one has a negative slope.

6 Two lines in a plane are **perpendicular** if
  A. they represent the same line
  B. they never intersect
  C. they intersect at a 90° angle
  D. one has a positive slope and one has a negative slope.

Answers to Test Your Word Power

1. C; *Examples:* $(0, 3)$, $(3, 8)$, $(4, 0)$

2. A; *Example:* The point associated with the ordered pair $(1, 2)$ has x-coordinate 1 and y-coordinate 2.

3. D; *Example:* The graph of the equation $4x - 3y = 12$ has x-intercept $(3, 0)$ and y-intercept $(0, -4)$.

4. C; *Example:* The line through $(3, 6)$ and $(5, 4)$ has slope
$$\frac{4 - 6}{5 - 3} = \frac{-2}{2} = -1.$$

5. B; *Example:* See **Figure A.**

6. C; *Example:* See **Figure B.**

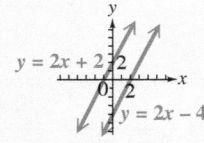

Figure A

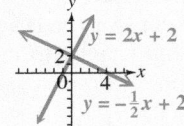

Figure B

Quick Review

Concepts	Examples

3.1 Linear Equations and Rectangular Coordinates

An ordered pair is a solution of an equation if it makes the equation a true statement.

Are $(2, -5)$ and $(0, -6)$ solutions of $4x - 3y = 18$?

$$4(2) - 3(-5) \stackrel{?}{=} 18 \qquad\qquad 4(0) - 3(-6) \stackrel{?}{=} 18$$
$$8 + 15 \stackrel{?}{=} 18 \qquad\qquad\qquad 0 + 18 \stackrel{?}{=} 18$$
$$23 = 18 \quad \text{False} \qquad\qquad 18 = 18 \checkmark \text{ True}$$

$(2, -5)$ is not a solution. $\qquad$ $(0, -6)$ is a solution.

If a value of either variable in an equation is given, the value of the other variable can be found by substitution.

Complete the ordered pair $(0, \underline{\quad})$ for the equation.

$$3x = y + 4$$
$$3(0) = y + 4 \qquad \text{Let } x = 0.$$
$$0 = y + 4 \qquad \text{Multiply.}$$
$$-4 = y \qquad \text{Subtract 4.}$$

The ordered pair is $(0, -4)$.

Chapter 3 Summary 291

Concepts	Examples

Concepts

To plot an ordered pair, begin at the origin.

Step 1   Move right or left the number of units that corresponds to the x-coordinate—right if it is positive or left if it is negative.

Step 2   Then turn and move up or down the number of units that corresponds to the y-coordinate—up if it is positive or down if it is negative.

Examples

Plot the ordered pair $(-3, 4)$.

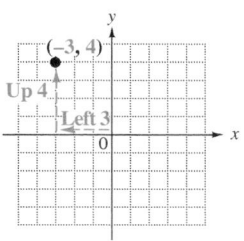

3.2 Graphing Linear Equations in Two Variables

Graphing a Linear Equation in Two Variables

Step 1   Find at least two ordered pairs that are solutions of the equation. (The intercepts are good choices.) It is good practice to find a third ordered pair as a check.

Step 2   Plot the corresponding points.

Step 3   Draw a straight line through the points.

The graph of $Ax + By = 0$ passes through the origin. In this case, find and plot at least one other point that satisfies the equation. Then draw the line through these points.

The graph of $y = b$ is a **horizontal line** through $(0, b)$.

The graph of $x = a$ is a **vertical line** through $(a, 0)$.

Graph $x - 2y = 4$.

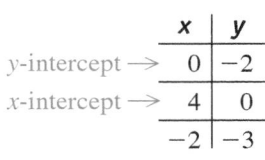

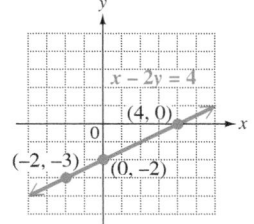

Graph $2x + 3y = 0$.   Graph $y = -3$ and $x = -3$.

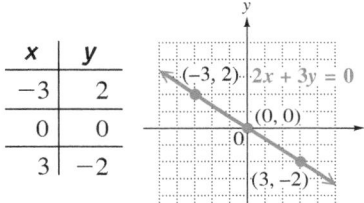

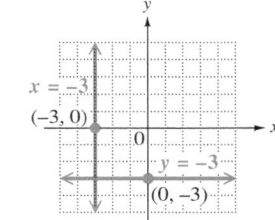

3.3 The Slope of a Line

The slope m of the line passing through the points (x_1, y_1) and (x_2, y_2) is defined as follows.

$$m = \frac{\text{change in } y}{\text{change in } x} = \frac{y_2 - y_1}{x_2 - x_1} \quad (\text{where } x_1 \neq x_2)$$

Horizontal lines have slope 0.

Vertical lines have undefined slope.

Finding the Slope of a Line from Its Equation

Step 1   Solve the equation for y.

Step 2   The slope is given by the coefficient of x.

Find each slope.

The line passing through $(-2, 3)$ and $(4, -5)$ has slope

$$m = \frac{-5 - 3}{4 - (-2)} = \frac{-8}{6} = -\frac{4}{3}.$$

The line $y = -2$ has slope 0.

The line $x = 4$ has **undefined slope**.

Find the slope of the line with the following equation.

$$3x - 4y = 12$$

$$-4y = -3x + 12 \qquad \text{Subtract } 3x.$$

$$y = \frac{3}{4}x - 3 \qquad \text{Divide by } -4.$$

$$\underset{\text{Slope}}{\uparrow}$$

Parallel lines have the same slope.

Perpendicular lines (neither of which is vertical) have slopes that are negative reciprocals—that is, their product is -1.

The lines $y = 3x - 1$ and $y = 3x + 4$ are parallel because both have slope 3.

The lines $y = -3x - 1$ and $y = \frac{1}{3}x + 4$ are perpendicular because their slopes are -3 and $\frac{1}{3}$, and $-3\left(\frac{1}{3}\right) = -1$.

Concepts	Examples

3.4 Slope-Intercept Form of a Linear Equation

Slope-Intercept Form
$y = mx + b$
m is the slope.
$(0, b)$ is the y-intercept.

Write an equation in slope-intercept form of the line with slope 2 and y-intercept $(0, -5)$.

$$y = mx + b \quad \text{Slope-intercept form}$$

$$y = 2x - 5$$

3.5 Point-Slope Form of a Linear Equation

Point-Slope Form
$y - y_1 = m(x - x_1)$
m is the slope.
(x_1, y_1) is a point on the line.

Write an equation of the line passing through $(-4, 5)$ with slope $-\frac{1}{2}$.

$$y - y_1 = m(x - x_1) \qquad \text{Point-slope form}$$

$$y - 5 = -\frac{1}{2}[x - (-4)] \quad \text{Substitute for } y_1, m, \text{ and } x_1.$$

$$y - 5 = -\frac{1}{2}(x + 4) \qquad \text{Definition of subtraction}$$

$$y - 5 = -\frac{1}{2}x - 2 \qquad \text{Distributive property}$$

$$y = -\frac{1}{2}x + 3 \qquad \text{Add 5.}$$

Standard Form
$Ax + By = C$
A, B, and C are real numbers and A and B are not both 0.

(In answers, we give A, B, and C as integers with greatest common factor 1 and $A \geq 0$.)

Write the above equation in standard form.

$$y = -\frac{1}{2}x + 3$$

$$2y = -x + 6 \qquad \text{Multiply each term by 2.}$$

$$x + 2y = 6 \qquad \text{Add } x.$$

3.6 Graphing Linear Inequalities in Two Variables

Graphing a Linear Inequality in Two Variables

Step 1 Draw the graph of the straight line that is the boundary.
- Make the line solid if the inequality involves $\leq$ or $\geq$.
- Make the line dashed if the inequality involves $<$ or $>$.

Step 2 Choose a test point not on the line, and substitute the coordinates of that point in the inequality.

Step 3 Shade the region that includes the test point if it satisfies the original inequality. Otherwise, shade the region on the other side of the boundary line.

Graph $2x + y \leq 5$.

Graph the boundary line

$$2x + y = 5$$

using the intercepts $(0, 5)$ and $\left(\frac{5}{2}, 0\right)$. Make it solid because the symbol $\leq$ includes equality.

Use $(0, 0)$ as a test point.

$$2x + y < 5$$

$$2(0) + 0 \stackrel{?}{\leq} 5$$

$$0 < 5 \qquad \text{True}$$

Shade the region that includes $(0, 0)$.

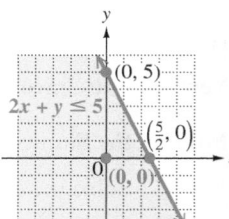

Chapter 3 *Review Exercises*

3.1 *The line graph shows the percent of 4-year college students at public institutions who earned a degree within 5 years. Use the graph to work each problem.*

1. Between the years 2010 and 2013, what was the general trend in the percent of students who earned a degree within 5 yr?

2. Estimate the percent of students earning a degree within 5 yr in 2010 and 2013.

3. About how much did the percent decrease between 2010 and 2013?

4. What does the ordered pair $(2015, 36.4)$ mean in the context of this problem?

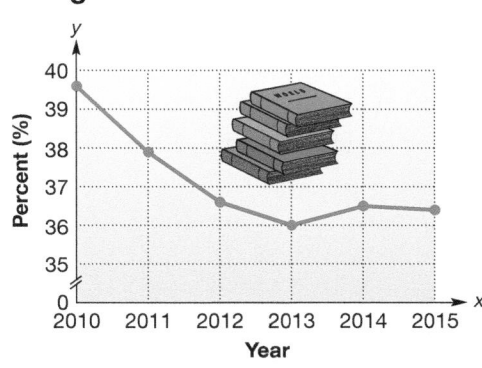

Percents of Students Earning a Degree within 5 Years

Data from ACT.

Complete the given ordered pairs for each equation.

5. $y = 3x + 2$; $(-1, \underline{\quad})$, $(0, \underline{\quad})$, $(\underline{\quad}, 5)$

6. $4x + 3y = 6$; $(0, \underline{\quad})$, $(\underline{\quad}, 0)$, $(-2, \underline{\quad})$

7. $x = 3y$; $(0, \underline{\quad})$, $(8, \underline{\quad})$, $(\underline{\quad}, -3)$

8. $x - 7 = 0$; $(\underline{\quad}, -3)$, $(\underline{\quad}, 0)$, $(\underline{\quad}, 5)$

Decide whether each ordered pair is a solution of the given equation.

9. $x + y = 7$; $(2, 5)$

10. $2x + y = 5$; $(-1, 3)$

11. $3x - y = 4$; $\left(\frac{1}{3}, -3\right)$

12. $x = -1$; $(0, -1)$

Identify the quadrant in which each point is located. Then plot the point on the rectangular coordinate system provided.

13. $(2, 3)$

14. $(-4, 2)$

15. $(3, 0)$

16. $(0, -6)$

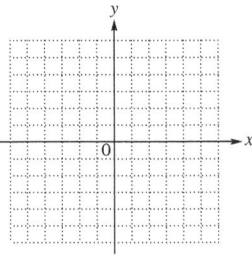

3.2 *Graph each linear equation using intercepts.*

17. $2x - y = 3$

18. $x + 2y = -4$

19. $x + y = 0$

20. $y = 3x + 4$

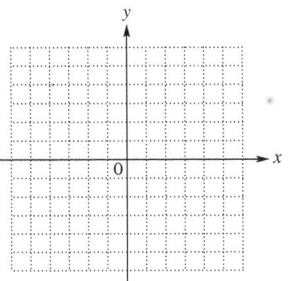

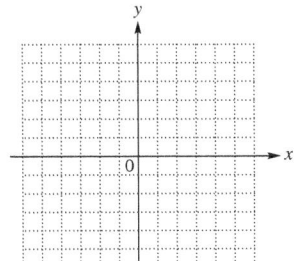

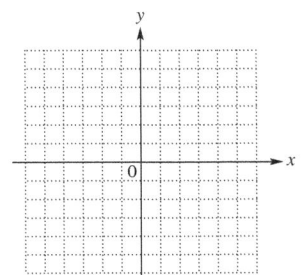

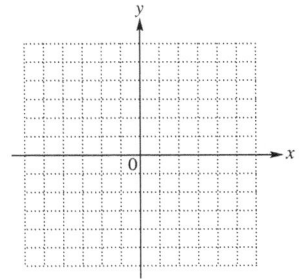

3.3 *Find the slope of each line. (In Exercises 24 and 25, coordinates of the points shown are integers.)*

21. The line passing through
$(2, 3)$ and $(-4, 6)$

22. The line passing through
$(2, 5)$ and $(2, 8)$

23. $y = 3x - 4$

24.

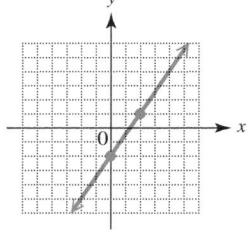

25.

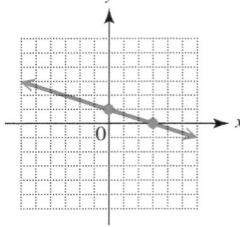

26. The line passing through these
points

x	y
0	1
2	4
6	10

27. $y = 4$

28. A line parallel to the graph of
$y = 2x + 3$

29. A line perpendicular to the graph
of $y = -3x + 3$

Decide whether each pair of lines is parallel, perpendicular, *or* neither.

30. $3x + 2y = 6$

$6x + 4y = 8$

31. $x - 3y = 1$

$3x + y = 4$

32. $x - 2y = 8$

$x + 2y = 8$

33. Family income in the United States has steadily increased for many years
(primarily due to inflation). In 1980 the median family income was about
$21,000 per year. In 2014 it was about $54,000 per year. Find the average rate
of change of median family income to the nearest dollar over that period. (Data
from U.S. Census Bureau.)

3.4, 3.5 *Write an equation of each line. Give the final answer in slope-intercept form (if possible).*

34. $m = -1, b = \frac{2}{3}$

35. The line in **Exercise 25**

36. The line passing through
$(4, -3), m = 1$

37. The line passing through
$(1, -1), m = -\frac{3}{4}$

38. The line passing through
$(2, 1)$ and $(-2, 2)$

39. The line passing through $(-4, 1)$,
slope 0

40. The line passing through $\left(\frac{1}{3}, -\frac{3}{4}\right)$,
undefined slope

41. Through $(6, -2)$,
parallel to $4x - y = 3$

42. Through $(0, 1)$,
perpendicular to $2x - 5y = 7$

43. Consider the linear equation $x + 3y = 15$.

   (a) Write it in the form $y = mx + b$.

   (b) What is the slope?   The y-intercept?

   (c) Use the slope and y-intercept to graph the line. Indicate two points on the graph.

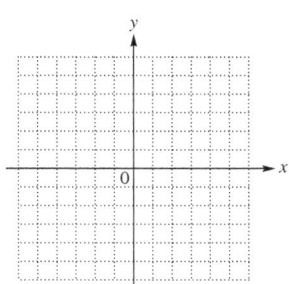

For each situation, write an equation in slope-intercept form. Then answer the question.

44. Resident tuition at a community college is $142 per credit hour. Let x represent the number of credit hours and y represent the cost. How much does it cost for a student to take 15 credit hours?

45. An Executive Regular/Silver membership to a health club costs $159, plus $47 per month. Let x represent the number of months and y represent the cost. How much will a one-year membership cost?

The points on the graph indicate sales y (in millions of dollars) of wearable fitness technology in the United States for selected years x. The graph of a linear equation that models the data is also shown. Here $x = 1$ represents 2011, $x = 2$ represents 2012, and so on.

46. Does the line that models the data have positive or negative slope? Explain.

47. Write two ordered pairs (x, y) for the data for 2011 and 2014. Then use these ordered pairs to write an equation of a line that models sales of wearable fitness technology. (Round the slope to the nearest whole number.) Give the final answer in slope-intercept form.

48. Use the equation from **Exercise 47** to approximate sales of wearable fitness technology in 2012, the year data were unavailable. (*Hint:* What is the value of x for 2012?)

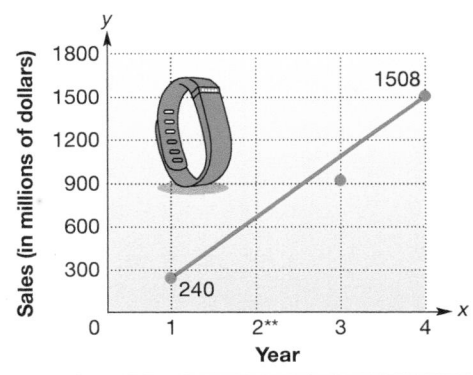

U.S. Sales of Wearable Fitness Technology*

* Includes devices containing pedometers, accelerometers, and heart-rate monitors

** Data for this year are unavailable.

Data from Consumer Electronics Association.

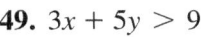 *Graph each linear inequality.*

49. $3x + 5y > 9$ **50.** $2x - 3y > -6$ **51.** $x \geq -4$ **52.** $y \leq -4x$

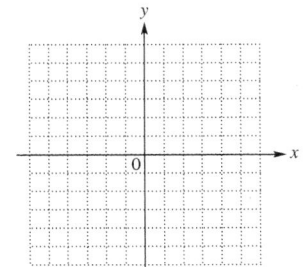 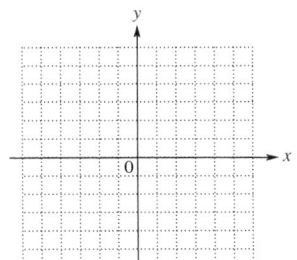 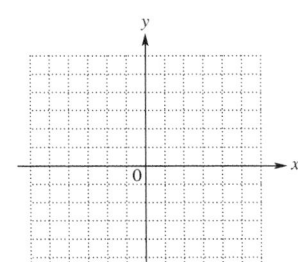 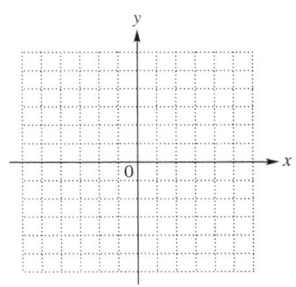

Chapter 3 Mixed Review Exercises

CONCEPT CHECK *Match each statement to the appropriate graph or graphs in choices A–D. Graphs may be used more than once.*

A. 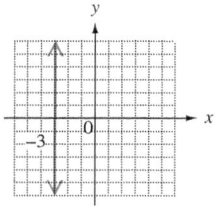   **B.** 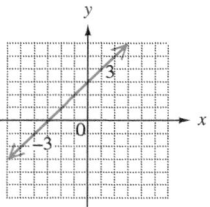   **C.** 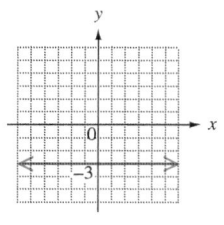   **D.**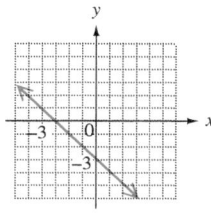

1. The line shown in the graph has undefined slope.

2. The graph of the equation has y-intercept $(0, -3)$.

3. The graph of the equation has x-intercept $(-3, 0)$.

4. The line shown in the graph has negative slope.

5. The graph is that of the equation $y = -3$.

6. The line shown in the graph has slope 1.

Find the intercepts and the slope of each line. Then use them to graph the line.

7. $y = -2x - 5$

    y-intercept: _____

    x-intercept: _____

    slope: _____

8. $x + 3y = 0$

    y-intercept: _____

    x-intercept: _____

    slope: _____

9. $y - 5 = 0$

    y-intercept: _____

    x-intercept: _____

    slope: _____

10. $x + 4 = 3$

    y-intercept: _____

    x-intercept: _____

    slope: _____

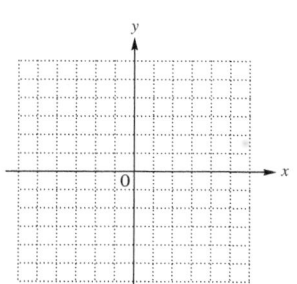   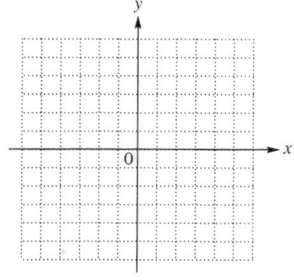   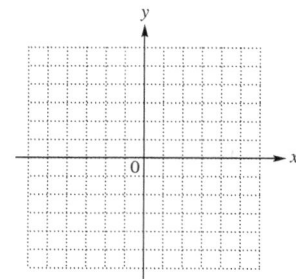 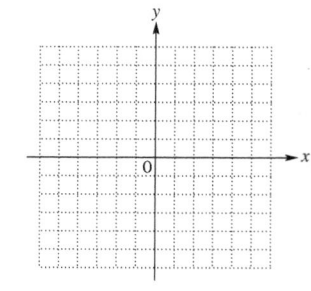

Write an equation of each line. Give the final answer in (a) slope-intercept form and (b) standard form.

11. $m = -\dfrac{1}{4}, b = -\dfrac{5}{4}$

12. The line passing through $(8, 6)$, $m = -3$

13. The line passing through $(3, -5)$ and $(-4, -1)$

14. Slope 0, through $(5, -5)$

| **Chapter 3 Test** | *The Chapter Test Prep Videos with step-by-step solutions are available in* MyMathLab *or on* YouTube *at **https://goo.gl/3rBuO5*** |

Work each problem.

1. Complete the ordered pairs $(0, \underline{})$, $(\underline{}, 0)$, and $(\underline{}, -3)$ for the equation $3x + 5y = -30$.

2. Is $(4, -1)$ a solution of $4x - 7y = 9$?

Graph each linear equation using the intercepts.

3. $3x + y = 6$ **4.** $y - 2x = 0$ **5.** $x + 3 = 0$ **6.** $y = 1$

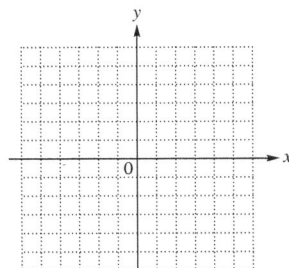   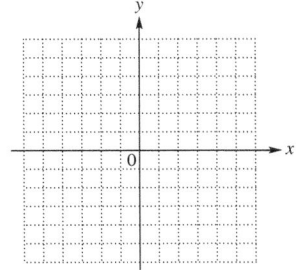   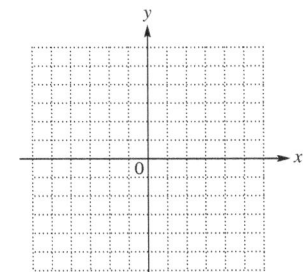   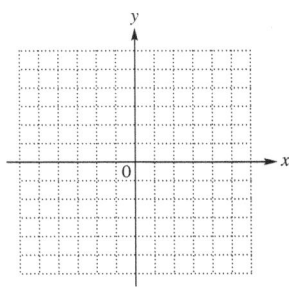

7. Give the slope and y-intercept of the graph of $y = x - 4$. Use them to graph the equation.

8. Graph the line passing through the point $(-2, 3)$, with slope $-\frac{1}{2}$.

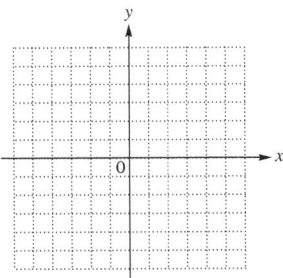   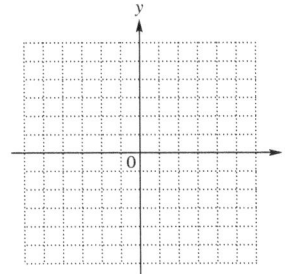

Find the slope of each line. (In Exercise 12, coordinates of the points shown are integers.)

9. The line passing through $(-4, 6)$ and $(-1, -2)$

10. $2x + y = 10$

11. $x + 12 = 0$

12.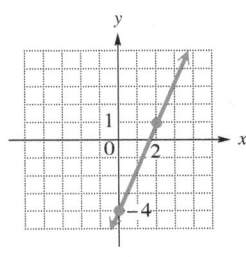

Solve each problem.

13. In 1980, there were 119,000 farms in Iowa. As of 2013, there were 89,000. Find and interpret the average rate of change in the number of farms per year to the nearest whole number. (Data from U.S. Department of Agriculture.)

14. Write an equation of the line having slope $-\frac{2}{5}$ and y-intercept $(0, 3)$. Give the equation in **(a)** slope-intercept form and **(b)** standard form.

Write an equation for each line. Give the final answer in slope-intercept form.

15. The line passing through $(-1, 4)$, $m = 2$

16. The line in **Exercise 12**

17. The line passing through $(2, -6)$ and $(1, 3)$

Write an equation of the line that satisfies the given conditions.

18. Through $(-3, 14)$; horizontal

19. Through $(5, -6)$; vertical

20. Write an equation in slope-intercept form of the line through $(-7, 2)$ and

(a) parallel to $3x + 5y = 6$.

(b) perpendicular to $y = 2x$.

Graph each linear inequality.

21. $x + y \leq 3$

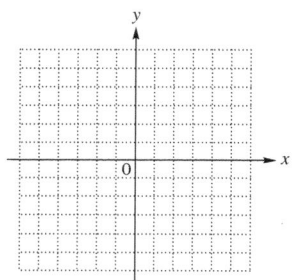

22. $3x - y > 0$

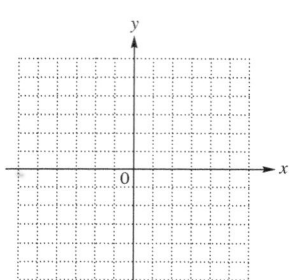

23. $x \leq 0$

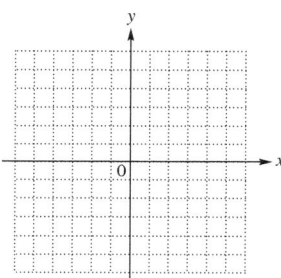

The graph shows worldwide snowmobile sales from 2000 through 2015, where $x = 0$ represents 2000, $x = 1$ represents 2001, and so on. Use the graph to work each problem.

24. Is the slope of the line in the graph positive or negative? Explain.

25. Write two ordered pairs (x, y) for the data points shown in the graph. Use the ordered pairs to find the slope of the line to the nearest tenth.

26. Use the ordered pairs and slope from **Exercise 25** to write an equation of a line that models the data. Give the final equation in slope-intercept form.

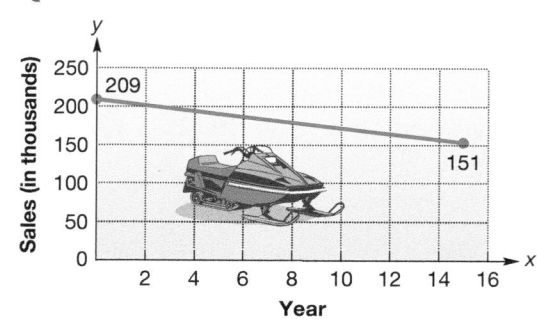

Worldwide Snowmobile Sales

Data from www.snowmobile.org

27. Use the equation from **Exercise 26** to approximate worldwide snowmobile sales in 2010.

28. What does the ordered pair $(15, 151)$ mean in the context of this problem?

Chapters R–3   *Cumulative Review Exercises*

Perform the indicated operations.

1. $10\frac{5}{8} - 3\frac{1}{10}$

2. $\frac{3}{4} \div \frac{1}{8}$

3. $5 - (-4) + (-2)$

4. $\dfrac{(-3)^2 - (-4)(2^4)}{5(2) - (-2)^3}$

5. *True* or *false?* $\dfrac{4(3-9)}{2-6} \geq 6$

6. Find the value of $xz^3 - 5y^2$ for $x = -2$, $y = -3$, and $z = -1$.

7. What property does $3(-2 + x) = -6 + 3x$ illustrate?

8. Simplify $-4p - 6 + 3p + 8$ by combining like terms.

Solve.

9. $V = \dfrac{1}{3}\pi r^2 h$ for h

10. $6 - 3(1 + x) = 2(x + 5) - 2$

11. $-(x - 3) = 5 - 2x$

12. $\dfrac{y - 2}{3} = \dfrac{2y + 1}{5}$

Solve each inequality. Write the solution set in interval notation and graph it.

13. $-2.5x < 6.5$

14. $4(x + 3) - 5x < 12$

15. $\dfrac{2}{3}t - \dfrac{1}{6}t \leq -2$

Solve each problem.

16. In 2013, a young adult (ages 25–34) with a bachelor's degree could expect to earn $18,500 more each year than a young adult with a high school credential. Together the individuals would earn $78,500. How much could a young adult at each level of education expect to earn? (Data from NCES.)

17. Mount Mayon in the Philippines is the most perfectly shaped conical volcano in the world. Its base is a circle with circumference 80 mi. Find the radius of the circular base to the nearest mile. (Data from www.britannica.hk)

Circumference = 80 mi

18. The winning times in seconds for the women's 1000 m speed skating event in the Winter Olympics for the years 1960 through 2014 can be closely approximated by the linear equation

$$y = -0.4336x + 94.30,$$

where x is the number of years since 1960. That is, $x = 4$ represents 1964, $x = 8$ represents 1968, and so on. (Data from *The World Almanac and Book of Facts.*)

(a) Use this equation to complete the table of values. Round times to the nearest hundredth of a second.

x	y
20	
38	
42	
	72.62

(b) Write ordered pairs for the data given in the table.

(c) In the context of this problem, what does the ordered pair (54, 70.89) mean?

19. In a recent year, approximately 60 million people from other countries visited the United States. The circle graph shows the distribution of these international visitors by their home countries or regions.

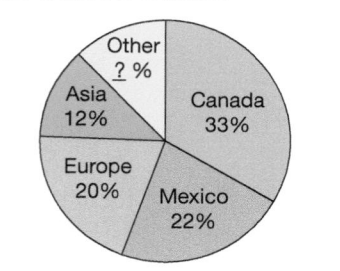

International Travelers to the United States

Data from U.S. Department of Commerce.

(a) About how many travelers visited the United States from Canada?

(b) About how many travelers visited the United States from Mexico?

(c) About how many travelers visited the United States from places other than Canada, Mexico, Europe, or Asia?

Consider the linear equation $-3x + 4y = 12$. Find the following.

20. The x- and y-intercepts

21. The slope

22. The y-value of the point having x-value 4

23. The graph

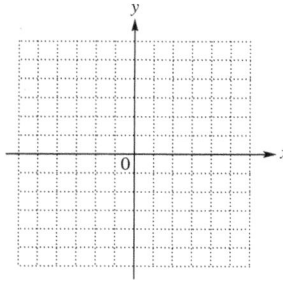

24. Are the lines with equations $x + 5y = -6$ and $y = 5x - 8$ *parallel, perpendicular,* or *neither?*

Write an equation of each line. Give the final answer in slope-intercept form if possible.

25. The line passing through $(2, -5)$, with slope 3

26. The line passing through $(0, 4)$ and $(2, 4)$

4

Systems of Linear Equations and Inequalities

The point of intersection of two lines can be found using a *system of linear equations*, the subject of this chapter.

4.1 Solving Systems of Linear Equations by Graphing

4.2 Solving Systems of Linear Equations by Substitution

4.3 Solving Systems of Linear Equations by Elimination

Summary Exercises *Applying Techniques for Solving Systems of Linear Equations*

4.4 Applications of Linear Systems

4.5 Solving Systems of Linear Inequalities

4.1 | Solving Systems of Linear Equations by Graphing

OBJECTIVES

1. Decide whether a given ordered pair is a solution of a system.
2. Solve linear systems by graphing.
3. Solve special systems by graphing.
4. Identify special systems without graphing.

A **system of linear equations,** or **linear system,** consists of two or more linear equations with the same variables.

$$2x + 3y = 4 \qquad x + 3y = 1 \qquad x - y = 1 \qquad \text{Linear}$$
$$3x - \ y = -5 \qquad -y = 4 - 2x \qquad y = 3 \qquad \text{systems}$$

In the system on the right, think of $y = 3$ as an equation in two variables by writing it as $0x + y = 3$.

OBJECTIVE ▶ **1** **Decide whether a given ordered pair is a solution of a system.** A **solution of a system** of linear equations is an ordered pair that makes both equations true at the same time. A solution of an equation is said to *satisfy* the equation.

1 Determine whether the given ordered pair is a solution of the system.

GS **(a)** $(2, 5)$

$$3x - 2y = -4$$
$$5x + \ y = 15$$

$$3x - 2y = -4$$
$$3(\underline{\quad}) - 2(\underline{\quad}) \overset{?}{=} -4$$
$$\underline{\quad} = -4$$

$$5x + y = 15$$
$$5(\underline{\quad}) + \underline{\quad} \overset{?}{=} 15$$
$$\underline{\quad} = 15$$

$(2, 5)$ (*is / is not*) a solution.

(b) $(1, -2)$

$$x - 3y = 7$$
$$4x + \ y = 5$$

$(1, -2)$ (*is / is not*) a solution.

EXAMPLE 1 **Determining Whether an Ordered Pair Is a Solution**

Determine whether the ordered pair $(4, -3)$ is a solution of each system.

(a) $x + 4y = -8$
$$3x + 2y = 6$$

To decide whether $(4, -3)$ is a solution of the system, substitute 4 for x and -3 for y in each equation.

$x + 4y = -8$		$3x + 2y = 6$	
$4 + 4(-3) \overset{?}{=} -8$	Substitute.	$3(4) + 2(-3) \overset{?}{=} 6$	Substitute.
$4 + (-12) \overset{?}{=} -8$	Multiply.	$12 + (-6) \overset{?}{=} 6$	Multiply.
$-8 = -8$ ✓ True		$6 = 6$ ✓ True	

Because $(4, -3)$ satisfies *both* equations, it is a solution of the system.

(b) $2x + 5y = -7$
$$3x + 4y = 2$$

Again, substitute 4 for x and -3 for y in each equation.

$2x + 5y = -7$		$3x + 4y = 2$	
$2(4) + 5(-3) \overset{?}{=} -7$	Substitute.	$3(4) + 4(-3) \overset{?}{=} 2$	Substitute.
$8 + (-15) \overset{?}{=} -7$	Multiply.	$12 + (-12) \overset{?}{=} 2$	Multiply.
$-7 = -7$ ✓ True		$0 = 2$	False

The ordered pair $(4, -3)$ is *not* a solution of this system because it does not satisfy the second equation.

◀ **Work Problem 1** at the Side.

OBJECTIVE ▶ **2** **Solve linear systems by graphing.** The set of all ordered pairs that are solutions of a system is its **solution set.** One way to find the solution set of a system of two linear equations is to graph both equations on the same axes. Any intersection point would be on both lines and would therefore be a solution of *both* equations. *Thus, the coordinates of any point where the lines intersect give a solution of the system.*

Answers

1. **(a)** 2; 5; −4; 2; 5; 15; is   **(b)** is not

The graph in **Figure 1** shows that the solution of the system in **Example 1(a)** is the intersection point $(4, -3)$.

The solution (point of intersection) is always written as an ordered pair.

Because *two different* straight lines can intersect at no more than one point, there can never be more than one solution for such a system.

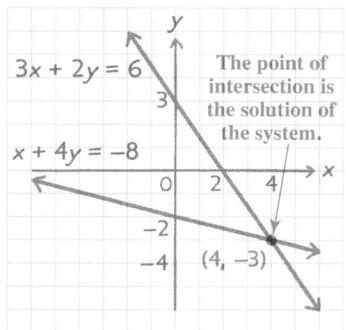

Figure 1

EXAMPLE 2   **Solving a System by Graphing**

Solve the system of equations by graphing both equations on the same axes.

$$2x + 3y = 4$$
$$3x - y = -5$$

We graph these two equations by plotting several points for each line. Recall that the intercepts are often convenient choices. As review, we show finding the intercepts for $2x + 3y = 4$.

To find the *y*-intercept, let $x = 0$.	To find the *x*-intercept, let $y = 0$.
$2x + 3y = 4$	$2x + 3y = 4$
$2(0) + 3y = 4$ Let $x = 0$.	$2x + 3(0) = 4$ Let $y = 0$.
$3y = 4$ Multiply.	$2x = 4$ Multiply.
$y = \dfrac{4}{3}$ Divide by 3.	$x = 2$ Divide by 2.

The tables show the intercepts and a check point for each graph.

$2x + 3y = 4$

x	y	
0	$\frac{4}{3}$	← *y*-intercept
2	0	← *x*-intercept
-2	$\frac{8}{3}$	

Find a third ordered pair as a check.

$3x - y = -5$

x	y	
0	5	← *y*-intercept
$-\frac{5}{3}$	0	← *x*-intercept
-2	-1	

The lines in **Figure 2** suggest that the graphs intersect at the point $(-1, 2)$. We check by substituting -1 for x and 2 for y in *both* equations.

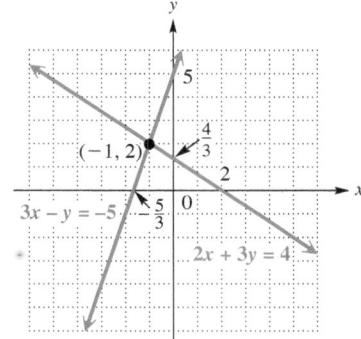

Figure 2

CHECK $2x + 3y = 4$

$2(-1) + 3(2) \overset{?}{=} 4$

$4 = 4$ ✓   True

$3x - y = -5$

$3(-1) - 2 \overset{?}{=} -5$

$-5 = -5$ ✓   True

Because $(-1, 2)$ satisfies both equations, the solution set of this system is $\{(-1, 2)\}$.

Work Problem ② at the Side. ▶

---

② Solve each system of equations by graphing both equations on the same axes.

(a) $5x - 3y = 9$

$x + 2y = 7$

One of the lines is already graphed. Complete the table, and graph the other line.

$5x - 3y = 9$

x	y
0	-3
$\frac{9}{5}$	0
3	2

$x + 2y = 7$

x	y
0	
	0
-1	

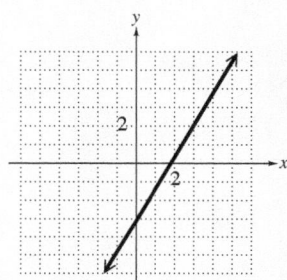

The point of intersection of the lines is the ordered pair _____, so the solution set of the system of equations is _____.

(b) $x + y = 4$

$2x - y = -1$

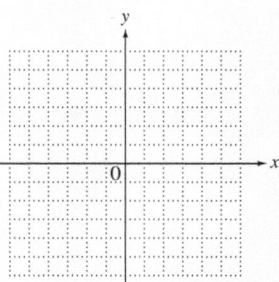

Answers

2. (a) $\frac{7}{2}$; 7; 4; (3, 2); $\{(3, 2)\}$ **(b)** $\{(1, 3)\}$

Note

We can also write each equation in a system in slope-intercept form and use the slope and y-intercept to graph each line. For **Example 2,**

$2x + 3y = 4$ becomes $y = -\frac{2}{3}x + \frac{4}{3}.$ y-intercept $\left(0, \frac{4}{3}\right)$; slope $-\frac{2}{3}$

$3x - y = -5$ becomes $y = 3x + 5.$ y-intercept $(0, 5)$; slope 3, or $\frac{3}{1}$

Confirm that graphing these equations results in the same lines and the same solution shown in **Figure 2** on the preceding page.

Solving a Linear System by Graphing

Step 1   **Graph each equation** of the system on the same coordinate axes.

Step 2   **Find the coordinates of the point of intersection** of the graphs if possible, and write it as an ordered pair.

Step 3   **Check** that the ordered pair is the solution by substituting it in *both* of the original equations. If it satisfies *both* equations, write the solution set.

---

❶ CAUTION

We recommend using graph paper and a straightedge when solving systems of equations graphically. It may not be possible to determine from the graph the exact coordinates of the point that represents the solution, particularly if those coordinates are not integers. The graphing method does, however, show geometrically how solutions are found and is useful when approximate answers will suffice.

OBJECTIVE ▶ ❸ Solve special systems by graphing. The graphs of the equations in a system may not intersect at all or may be the same line.

EXAMPLE 3   **Solving Special Systems**

Solve each system by graphing.

(a) $2x + y = 2$

      $2x + y = 8$

The graphs of these lines are shown in **Figure 3.** The two lines are parallel and have no points in common. For such a system, there is no solution. We write the solution set as $\varnothing$.

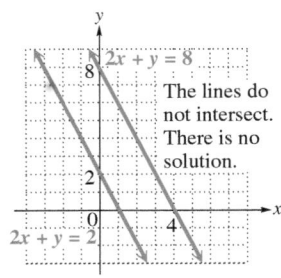

Figure 3

Continued on Next Page

(b) $2x + 5y = 1$

$6x + 15y = 3$

The graphs of these two equations are the same line. See **Figure 4.** We can obtain the second equation by multiplying each side of the first equation by 3. In this case, every point on the line is a solution of the system, and the solution set contains an infinite number of ordered pairs, each of which satisfies both equations of the system.

We write the solution set as

$$\{(x, y) \mid 2x + 5y = 1\},$$

read *"the set of ordered pairs (x, y) such that $2x + 5y = 1$."* Recall that this notation is called **set-builder notation.**

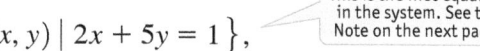

Both equations give the same graph. There is an infinite number of solutions.

Figure 4

> This is the first equation in the system. See the Note on the next page.

───────────────────── Work Problem ❸ at the Side. ▶

The system in **Example 2** has exactly one solution. A system with at least one solution is a **consistent system.** A system of equations with no solution, such as the one in **Example 3(a),** is an **inconsistent system.**

The equations in **Example 2** are **independent equations** with different graphs. The equations of the system in **Example 3(b)** have the same graph and are equivalent. Because they are different forms of the same equation, these equations are **dependent equations.**

Three Cases for Solutions of Linear Systems with Two Variables

Case 1   The graphs intersect at exactly one point, which gives the (single) ordered-pair solution of the system. The **system is consistent** and the **equations are independent. See Figure 5(a).**

Case 2   The graphs are parallel lines, so there is no solution and the solution set is ∅. The **system is inconsistent** and the **equations are independent. See Figure 5(b).**

Case 3   The graphs are the same line. There is an infinite number of solutions, and the solution set is written in set-builder notation as

$$\{(x, y) \mid \text{_____}\},$$

where one of the equations follows the | symbol. The **system is consistent** and the **equations are dependent. See Figure 5(c).**

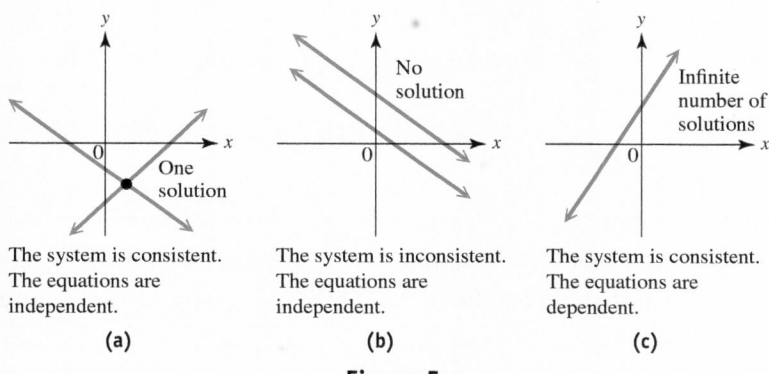

The system is consistent. The equations are independent.

(a)

The system is inconsistent. The equations are independent.

(b)

The system is consistent. The equations are dependent.

(c)

Figure 5

❸ Solve each system of equations by graphing.

(a) $3x - y = 4$

$6x - 2y = 12$

One of the lines is already graphed.

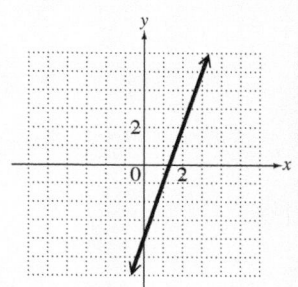

(b) $x - 3y = -2$

$2x - 6y = -4$

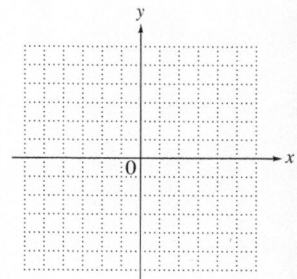

Answers

3. (a) ∅   **(b)** $\{(x, y) \mid x - 3y = -2\}$

Note

When a system has an infinite number of solutions, as in Case 3, either equation of the system can be used to write the solution set.

We prefer to use the equation in standard form with integer coefficients having greatest common factor 1 and positive coefficient of x.

If neither of the given equations is in this form, use an *equivalent* equation that is written this way.

Examples: For the system

$$-6x + 2y = -4$$
$$3x - y = 2,$$

This system has an infinite number of solutions.

we write the solution set using the second equation.

$$\{(x, y) \mid 3x - y = 2\}$$

For the system

$$2x - 4y = 8$$
$$-4x + 8y = -16,$$

This system has an infinite number of solutions.

we divide each term of the first equation by the common factor 2 and write the solution set as follows.

$$\{(x, y) \mid x - 2y = 4\}$$

OBJECTIVE **4** Identify special systems without graphing.

EXAMPLE 4 **Identifying the Three Cases by Using Slopes**

Describe each system without graphing. State the number of solutions.

(a) $3x + 2y = 6$

$ -2y = 3x - 5$

Write each equation in slope-intercept form, $y = mx + b$.

$$3x + 2y = 6 \quad \boxed{\text{Solve for } y.}$$

$$2y = -3x + 6 \qquad \text{Subtract } 3x.$$

$$y = -\frac{3}{2}x + 3 \qquad \text{Divide } each \text{ term by 2.}$$

$$-2y = 3x - 5 \quad \boxed{\text{Solve for } y.}$$

$$y = -\frac{3}{2}x + \frac{5}{2} \qquad \text{Divide } each \text{ term by } -2.$$

Both equations have slope $-\frac{3}{2}$ but they have different y-intercepts, $(0, 3)$ and $\left(0, \frac{5}{2}\right)$. Recall that lines with the same slope are parallel, so these equations have graphs that are parallel lines. Thus, the system has no solution.

—— **Continued on Next Page**

(b) $2x - y = 4$

$$x = \frac{y}{2} + 2$$

Again, write each equation in slope-intercept form.

$2x - y = 4$

$\quad -y = -2x + 4$ Subtract $2x$.

$\quad\quad y = 2x - 4$ Multiply by -1.

$x = \frac{y}{2} + 2$

$2x = y + 4$ Multiply by 2.

$\quad y = 2x - 4$ Subtract 4.
   Interchange sides.

The equations are exactly the same—their graphs are the same line. Any ordered-pair solution of one equation is also a solution of the other equation. Thus, the system has an infinite number of solutions.

(c) $x - 3y = 5$

$\quad 2x + y = 8$

Write each equation in slope-intercept form.

$x - 3y = 5$

$\quad -3y = -x + 5$ Subtract x.

$\quad\quad y = \frac{1}{3}x - \frac{5}{3}$ Divide by -3.
    ↑
    Slope

$2x + y = 8$

$\quad y = -2x + 8$ Subtract $2x$.
   ↑
   Slope

The graphs of these equations are neither parallel nor the same line because the slopes are different. The graphs will intersect in one point—thus, the system has exactly one solution.

——— **Work Problem ④ at the Side.** ▶

Note

The solution set of the system in **Example 4(a)** is $\varnothing$ because the graphs of the equations of the system are parallel lines. The solution set of the system in **Example 4(b)**, written using set-builder notation and the first equation, is

$$\{(x, y) \mid 2x - y = 4\}.$$

If we try to solve the system in **Example 4(c)** by graphing, we will have difficulty identifying the point of intersection of the graphs. We introduce an algebraic method for solving systems like this in the next section.

④ Describe each system without graphing. State the number of solutions.

(a) $2x - 3y = 5$

$\quad 3y = 2x - 7$

Solve the first equation for _____ .

$2x - 3y = 5$

$\quad -3y = \underline{\quad\quad} + 5$

$\quad\quad y = \underline{\quad\quad} - \frac{5}{3}$

The slope of this line is _____ , and the y-intercept is _____ .

Now solve the second equation for y, and complete the solution.

(b) $-x + 3y = 2$

$\quad 2x - 6y = -4$

(c) $6x + y = 3$

$\quad 2x - y = -11$

4.1 Exercises

FOR EXTRA HELP
Go to MyMathLab *for worked-out, step-by-step solutions to exercises enclosed in a square* and video solutions to ▶ exercises.

CONCEPT CHECK *Complete each statement. The following terms may be used once, more than once, or not at all.*

consistent	system of linear equations	inconsistent	solution
ordered pair	independent	linear equation	dependent

1. A(n) _____ consists of two or more linear equations with the (*same / different*) variables.

2. A solution of a system of linear equations is a(n) _____ that makes all equations of the system (*true / false*) at the same time.

3. The equations of two parallel lines form a(n) _____ system that has (*one / no / infinitely many*) solution(s). The equations are _____ because their graphs are different.

4. If the graphs of a linear system intersect in one point, the point of intersection is the _____ of the system. The system is _____ and the equations are independent.

5. If two equations of a linear system have the same graph, the equations are _____. The system is _____ and has (*one / no / infinitely many*) solution(s).

6. If a linear system is inconsistent, the graphs of the two equations are (*intersecting / parallel / the same*) line(s). The system has no _____.

CONCEPT CHECK *Work each problem.*

7. A student determined that the ordered pair $(1, -2)$ is a solution of the following system. His reasoning was that the ordered pair satisfies the first equation $x + y = -1$ because $1 + (-2) = -1$. **What Went Wrong?**

$$x + y = -1$$
$$2x + y = 4$$

8. The following system has infinitely many solutions. Write its solution set using set-builder notation.

$$6x - 4y = 8$$
$$3x - 2y = 4$$

9. Which ordered pair could be a solution of the system graphed? Why is it the only valid choice?

A. $(2, 2)$
B. $(-2, 2)$
C. $(-2, -2)$
D. $(2, -2)$

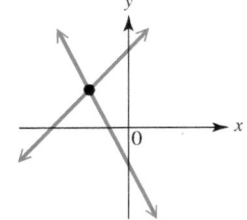

10. Which ordered pair could be a solution of the system graphed? Why is it the only valid choice?

A. $(2, 0)$
B. $(0, 2)$
C. $(-2, 0)$
D. $(0, -2)$

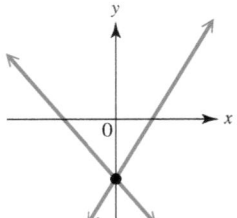

Determine whether the given ordered pair is a solution of the given system.
See Example 1.

11. 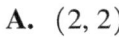 $\begin{aligned} x + y &= -1 \\ 2x + 5y &= 19 \end{aligned}$; $(2, -3)$

12. $\begin{aligned} x + 2y &= 10 \\ 3x + 5y &= 3 \end{aligned}$; $(4, 3)$

13. ▶ $\begin{aligned} 3x + 5y &= -18 \\ 4x + 2y &= -10 \end{aligned}$; $(-1, -3)$

14. $\begin{aligned} 2x - 5y &= -8 \\ 3x + 6y &= -39 \end{aligned}$; $(-9, -2$

15. $4x = 26 - y$
$3x = 29 + 4y$; $(7, -2)$

16. $2x = 23 - 5y$
$3x = 24 + 3y$; $(9, 1)$

17. $-2y = x + 10$
$3y = 2x + 30$; $(6, -8)$

18. $5y = 3x + 20$
$3y = -2x - 4$; $(-5, 2)$

19. $4x + 2y = 0$
$x + y = 0$; $(0, 0)$

20. $-4x + 4y = 0$
$x - y = 0$; $(-1, -1)$

21. $y = \dfrac{2}{3}x$
$y = \dfrac{1}{2}x$; $(1, 1)$

22. $y = -\dfrac{3}{2}x$
$y = -\dfrac{1}{3}x$; $(-2, 2)$

Solve each system of equations by graphing. If the system is inconsistent or the equations are dependent, say so. See Examples 2 and 3.

23. $x - y = 2$
$x + y = 6$

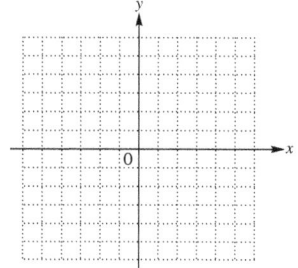

24. $x - y = 3$
$x + y = -1$

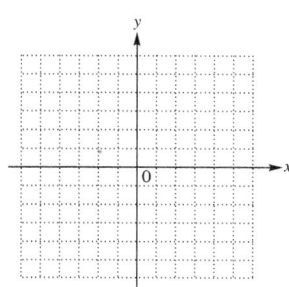

25. $x + y = 4$
$y - x = 4$

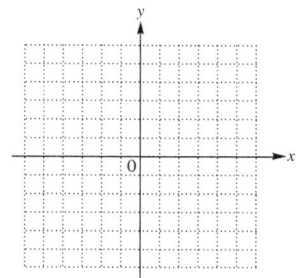

26. $x + y = -5$
$x - y = 5$

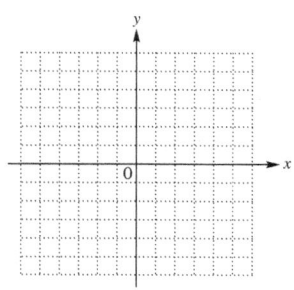

27. $x - 2y = 6$
$x + 2y = 2$

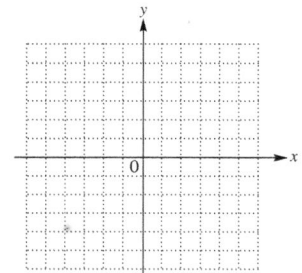

28. $2x - y = 4$
$4x + y = 2$

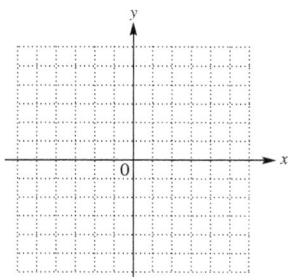

29. $3x - y = 0$
$-3x - y = -6$

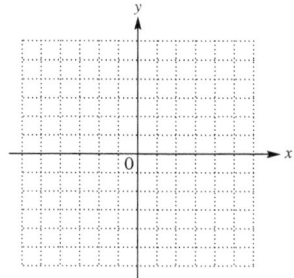

30. $2x - 3y = 0$
$2x + 3y = 12$

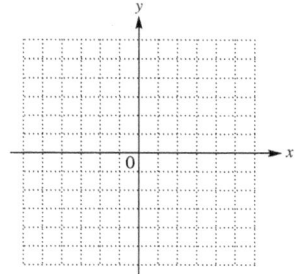

31. $2x - 3y = -6$
$y = -3x + 2$

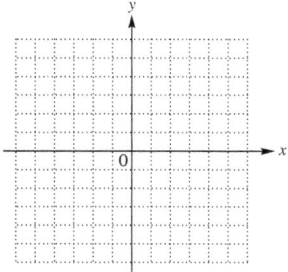

32. $-3x + y = -3$
$y = x - 3$

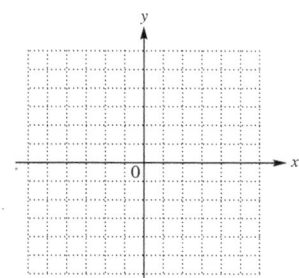

33. $x + 2y = 6$
$2x + 4y = 8$

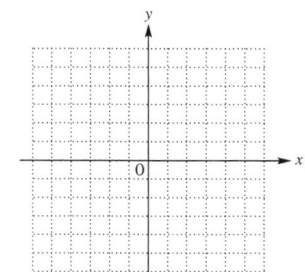

34. $2x - y = 6$
$6x - 3y = 12$

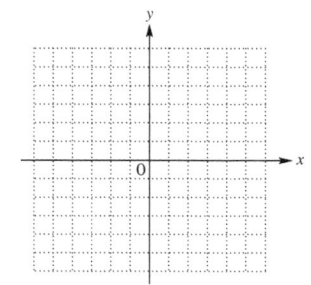

35. $5x - 3y = 2$
$10x - 6y = 4$

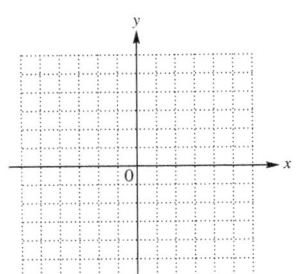

36. $2x - 5y = 8$
$4x - 10y = 16$

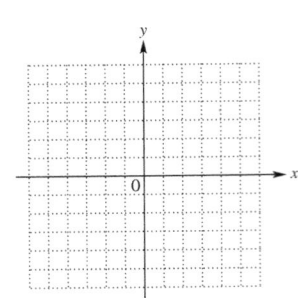

37. $3x - 4y = 24$
$y = -\dfrac{3}{2}x + 3$

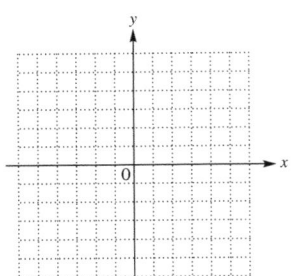

38. $3x - 2y = 12$
$y = -4x + 5$

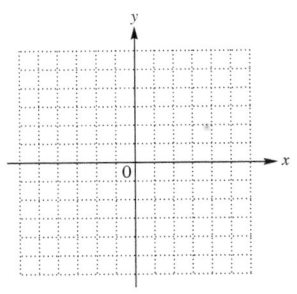

39. $4x - 2y = 8$
$2x = y + 4$

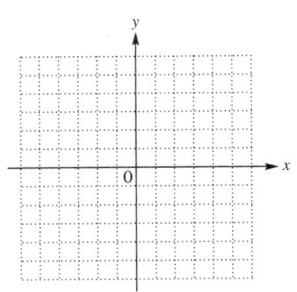

40. $3x = 5 - y$
$6x + 2y = 10$

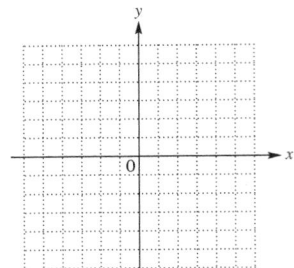

41. $3x = y + 5$
$6x - 5 = 2y$

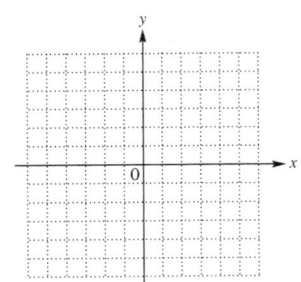

42. $2x = y - 4$
$4x - 2y = -4$

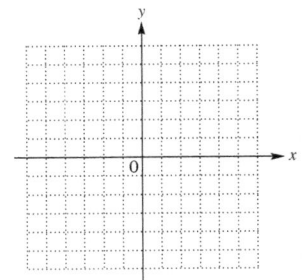

Without graphing, answer the following questions for each linear system. **See Example 4.**

(a) *Is the system inconsistent, are the equations dependent, or neither?*

(b) *Is the graph a pair of intersecting lines, a pair of parallel lines, or one line?*

(c) *Does the system have one solution, no solution, or an infinite number of solutions?*

43. $y - x = -5$
$x + y = 1$

44. $2x + y = 6$
$x - 3y = -4$

45. $x + 2y = 0$
$4y = -2x$

46. $4x - 6y = 10$
$-6x + 9y = -15$

47. $5x + 4y = 7$
$10x + 8y = 4$

48. $y = 3x$
$y + 3 = 3x$

49. $x - 3y = 5$
$2x + y = 8$

50. $2x + 3y = 12$
$2x - y = 4$

51. $5x = 10y$
$\dfrac{1}{2}x - y = 0$

52. $y = -3x$
$x + \dfrac{1}{3}y = 0$

53. $3x + 2y = 5$
$-6x - 4y = 10$

54. $2x - y = 6$
$-10x + 5y = -30$

*Economics deals with **supply and demand.** Typically, as the price of an item increases, the demand for the item decreases and the supply increases. If supply and demand can be described by straight-line equations, the point at which the lines intersect determines the **equilibrium supply** and **equilibrium demand.***

The price per unit, p, and the demand, x, for a particular aluminum siding are related by the linear equation $p = 60 - \frac{3}{4}x$, while the price and the supply are related by the linear equation $p = \frac{3}{4}x$. See the figure. Use the graph to work each problem.

SUPPLY AND DEMAND

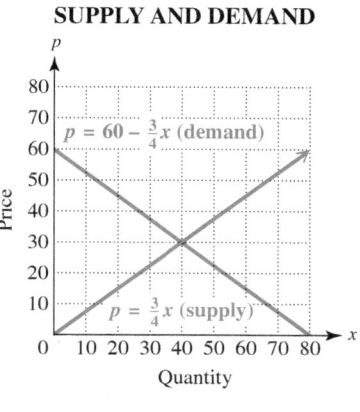

55. At what value of x does supply equal demand? At what value of p does supply equal demand?

56. Express the equilibrium supply and equilibrium demand as an ordered pair of the form (quantity, price).

57. When $x > 40$, does demand exceed supply or does supply exceed demand?

58. When $x < 40$, does demand exceed supply or does supply exceed demand?

The numbers of daily morning and evening newspapers in the United States in selected years over the period 1980–2013 are shown in the graph.

Number of Daily Newspapers

59. For which years were there more evening dailies than morning dailies?

60. Estimate the year in which the number of evening and morning dailies was closest to the same. About how many newspapers of each type were there in that year?

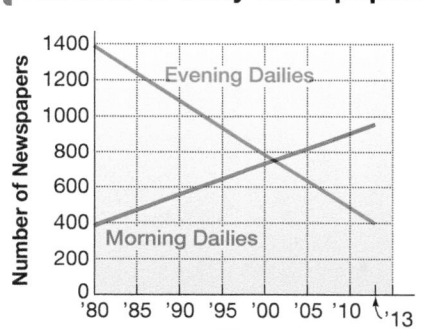

Data from *Editor & Publisher International Year Book.*

Relating Concepts (Exercises 61–64)   For Individual or Group Work

*The graph shows sales of music CDs and digital downloads of single songs (in millions) in the United States over selected years. Use the graph to work **Exercises 61–64 in order.***

Music Going Digital

61. In what year did Americans purchase about the same number of CDs as single digital downloads? How many units was this?

62. Express the point of intersection of the two graphs as an ordered pair of the form (year, units in millions).

63. Describe the trend in sales of music CDs over the years 2004 to 2013. If a straight line were used to approximate its graph, would the line have *positive, negative,* or *zero* slope? Explain.

64. If a straight line were used to approximate the graph of sales of digital downloads over the years 2004 to 2013, would the line have *positive, negative,* or *zero* slope? Explain.

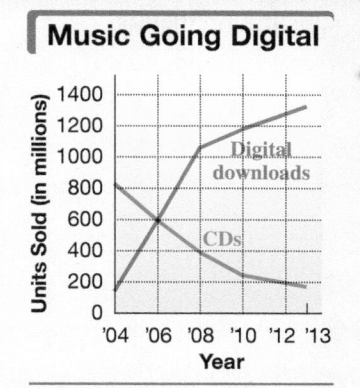

Data from Recording Industry Association of America.

4.2 | Solving Systems of Linear Equations by Substitution

OBJECTIVES

1 Solve linear systems by substitution.

2 Solve special systems by substitution.

3 Solve linear systems with fractions and decimals.

OBJECTIVE ▶ **1** Solve linear systems by substitution.

◀ Work Problem **1** at the Side.

As we see in **Margin Problem 1,** graphing to solve a system of equations has a serious drawback: It is difficult to accurately find a solution such as $\left(\frac{11}{3}, -\frac{4}{9}\right)$ from a graph.

As a result, there are algebraic methods for solving systems of equations. The **substitution method,** which gets its name from the fact that an expression in one variable is *substituted* for the other variable, is one such method.

EXAMPLE 1 | **Using the Substitution Method**

Solve the system by the substitution method.

$$3x + 5y = 26 \quad (1) \quad \text{We number the equations for reference in our discussion.}$$
$$y = 2x \quad (2)$$

Equation (2) is already solved for y. This equation says that $y = 2x$, so we substitute $2x$ for y in equation (1).

$$3x + 5y = 26 \quad (1)$$
$$3x + 5(\mathbf{2x}) = 26 \quad \text{Let } y = 2x.$$
$$3x + 10x = 26 \quad \text{Multiply.}$$
$$13x = 26 \quad \text{Combine like terms.}$$

Don't stop here. ▷ $\quad x = 2 \quad$ Divide by 13.

Now we can find the value of y by substituting 2 for x in either equation. We choose equation (2) because the substitution is easier.

$$y = 2x \quad (2)$$
$$y = 2(\mathbf{2}) \quad \text{Let } x = 2.$$
$$y = 4 \quad \text{Multiply.}$$

We check that the ordered pair $(\mathbf{2}, \mathbf{4})$ is the solution by substituting **2** for x and **4** for y in *both* equations.

CHECK
$$3x + 5y = 26 \quad (1) \qquad\qquad y = 2x \quad (2)$$
$$3(2) + 5(4) \overset{?}{=} 26 \quad \text{Substitute.} \qquad 4 \overset{?}{=} 2(2) \quad \text{Substitute.}$$
$$6 + 20 \overset{?}{=} 26 \quad \text{Multiply.} \qquad\qquad 4 = 4 \; ✓ \quad \text{True}$$
$$26 = 26 \; ✓ \; \text{True}$$

Since $(2, 4)$ satisfies both equations, the solution set of the system is $\{(2, 4)\}$.

◀ Work Problem **2** at the Side.

---

1 We solved the following system by graphing.

$$2x + 3y = 6$$
$$x - 3y = 5$$

Can we determine the solution? Why or why not?

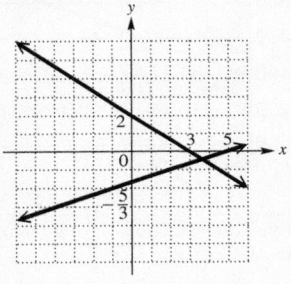

2 Solve the system by the substitution method.

$$3x + 5y = 69$$
$$y = 4x$$

⚠ **CAUTION**

A system is not completely solved until values for both x and y are found. Write the solution set as a set containing an ordered pair.

Answers

1. The solution cannot be determined from the graph because it is not possible to read the exact coordinates.

2. $\{(3, 12)\}$

EXAMPLE 2	Using the Substitution Method

Solve the system by the substitution method.

$$2x + 5y = 7 \quad (1)$$
$$x = -1 - y \quad (2)$$

Equation (2) gives x in terms of y. We substitute $-1 - y$ for x in equation (1).

$$2x + 5y = 7 \quad (1) \quad \text{←} \begin{array}{c}\text{Be sure to substitute in the}\\ \textit{other} \text{ equation.}\end{array}$$

$$2(-1 - y) + 5y = 7 \quad \text{Let } x = -1 - y.$$

Distribute 2 to both -1 and $-y$.

$$-2 - 2y + 5y = 7 \quad \text{Distributive property}$$
$$-2 + 3y = 7 \quad \text{Combine like terms.}$$
$$3y = 9 \quad \text{Add 2.}$$
$$y = 3 \quad \text{Divide by 3.}$$

To find x, substitute 3 for y in equation (2).

$$x = -1 - y \quad (2)$$
$$x = -1 - 3 \quad \text{Let } y = 3.$$

Write the x-coordinate first.

$$x = -4 \quad \text{Subtract.}$$

Check that $(-4, 3)$ is the solution.

CHECK

$$2x + 5y = 7 \quad (1) \qquad x = -1 - y \quad (2)$$
$$2(-4) + 5(3) \stackrel{?}{=} 7 \quad \text{Substitute.} \qquad -4 \stackrel{?}{=} -1 - 3 \quad \text{Substitute.}$$
$$-8 + 15 \stackrel{?}{=} 7 \quad \text{Multiply.} \qquad -4 = -4 \checkmark \quad \text{True}$$
$$7 = 7 \checkmark \text{ True}$$

Both results are true. The solution set of the system is $\{(-4, 3)\}$.

── **Work Problem ❸ at the Side.** ▶

❸ Solve each system by the substitution method.

(a) $2x + 7y = -12$
$x = 3 - 2y$

(b) $x = y - 3$
$4x + 9y = 1$

❶ CAUTION

Even though we found y first in **Example 2**, *the x-coordinate is always written first in the ordered-pair solution of a system.* The ordered pair $(-4, 3)$ is *not* the same as $(3, -4)$.

Solving a Linear System by Substitution

Step 1 **Solve one equation for either variable.** If one of the equations has a variable term with coefficient 1 or -1, choose it because the substitution method is usually easier.

Step 2 **Substitute** for that variable in the other equation. The result should be an equation with just one variable.

Step 3 **Solve** the equation from Step 2.

Step 4 **Find the other value.** Substitute the result from Step 3 into the equation from Step 1 and solve for the other variable.

Step 5 **Check** the values in *both* of the *original* equations. Then write the solution set as a set containing an ordered pair.

Answers

3. (a) $\{(15, -6)\}$ **(b)** $\{(-2, 1)\}$

4 Solve each system by the substitution method.

(a) Fill in the blanks to solve.

$$x + 4y = -1$$
$$2x - 5y = 11$$

Solve the first equation for x.

$$x = -1 - \underline{\quad}$$

Substitute into the second equation to find y.

$$2(\underline{\quad}) - 5y = 11$$
$$-2 - 8y - 5y = 11$$
$$-2 - \underline{\quad} y = 11$$
$$\underline{\quad} y = 13$$
$$y = -1$$

Find x.

$$x = -1 - 4y$$
$$x = -1 - 4(\underline{\quad})$$
$$x = \underline{\quad}$$

The solution set is $\underline{\quad}$.

(b) $2x + 5y = 4$
$\quad\; x + \; y = -1$

EXAMPLE 3 **Using the Substitution Method**

Solve the system by the substitution method.

$$2x = 4 - y \quad (1)$$
$$5x + 3y = 10 \quad (2)$$

Step 1 Because the coefficient of y in equation (1) is -1, we avoid fractions by choosing this equation and solving it for y.

$$2x = 4 - y \quad (1)$$
$$y + 2x = 4 \qquad \text{Add } y.$$
$$y = 4 - 2x \qquad \text{Subtract } 2x.$$

Step 2 Now substitute $4 - 2x$ for y in equation (2).

$$5x + 3y = 10 \quad (2)$$
$$5x + 3(4 - 2x) = 10 \qquad \text{Let } y = 4 - 2x.$$

Step 3 Solve the equation from Step 2.

$$5x + 12 - 6x = 10 \qquad \text{Distributive property}$$

Distribute 3 to *both* 4 and $-2x$.

$$-x + 12 = 10 \qquad \text{Combine like terms.}$$
$$-x = -2 \qquad \text{Subtract 12.}$$
$$x = 2 \qquad \text{Multiply by } -1.$$

Step 4 Equation (1) solved for y is $y = 4 - 2x$. Substitute 2 for x.

$$y = 4 - 2(2) \qquad \text{Substitute.}$$
$$y = 0 \qquad \text{Multiply, and then subtract.}$$

Step 5 Check that $(2, 0)$ is the solution.

CHECK

$$2x = 4 - y \quad (1) \qquad\qquad 5x + 3y = 10 \quad (2)$$
$$2(2) \overset{?}{=} 4 - 0 \quad \text{Substitute.} \qquad 5(2) + 3(0) \overset{?}{=} 10 \quad \text{Substitute.}$$
$$4 = 4 \checkmark \quad \text{True} \qquad\qquad 10 = 10 \checkmark \text{ True}$$

Because both results are true, the solution set of the system is $\{(2, 0)\}$.

◀ **Work Problem 4** at the Side.

OBJECTIVE ▶ 2 Solve special systems by substitution.

EXAMPLE 4 **Solving an Inconsistent System**

Solve the system by the substitution method.

$$x = 5 - 2y \quad (1)$$
$$2x + 4y = 6 \quad (2)$$

Equation (1) is solved for x, so we substitute $5 - 2y$ for x in equation (2).

$$2x + 4y = 6 \quad (2)$$
$$2(5 - 2y) + 4y = 6 \qquad \text{Let } x = 5 - 2y.$$
$$10 - 4y + 4y = 6 \qquad \text{Distributive property}$$
$$10 = 6 \qquad \text{False}$$

Continued on Next Page

Answers

4. (a) $4y; -1 - 4y; 13; -13; -1; 3;$
   $\{(3, -1)\}$
(b) $\{(-3, 2)\}$

The false result $10 = 6$ means that the equations in the system have graphs that are parallel lines. The system is inconsistent and has no solution, so the solution set is $\varnothing$.

CHECK We can confirm the solution set by writing each equation in slope-intercept form—that is, solved for y.

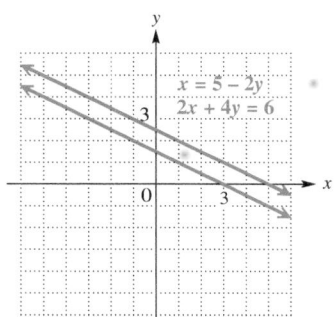

$$x = 5 - 2y \quad (1) \quad | \quad 2x + 4y = 6 \quad (2)$$
$$2y = -x + 5 \quad\quad\quad | \quad 4y = -2x + 6$$
$$y = -\frac{1}{2}x + \frac{5}{2} \quad | \quad y = -\frac{1}{2}x + \frac{3}{2}$$

The two lines have the same slope but different y-intercepts. Therefore, they are parallel and do not intersect, confirming that the solution set is $\varnothing$. See **Figure 6.** ✓

Figure 6

⟶ Work Problem ⑤ at the Side. ▶

EXAMPLE 5 **Solving a System with Dependent Equations**

Solve the system by the substitution method.

$$3x - y = 4 \quad (1)$$
$$-9x + 3y = -12 \quad (2)$$

Begin by solving equation (1) for y to obtain

$$y = 3x - 4. \quad \text{Equation (1) solved for } y$$

We substitute $3x - 4$ for y in equation (2) and solve the resulting equation.

$$-9x + 3y = -12 \quad (2)$$
$$-9x + 3(3x - 4) = -12 \quad \text{Let } y = 3x - 4.$$
$$-9x + 9x - 12 = -12 \quad \text{Distributive property}$$
$$\mathbf{0 = 0} \quad \text{Add 12. Combine like terms.}$$

The true result $0 = 0$ means that every solution of one equation is also a solution of the other, so the system has an infinite number of solutions. The solution set written in set-builder notation using equation (1) is

$$\left\{ (x, y) \mid 3x - y = 4 \right\}.$$

CHECK If we multiply equation (1) by -3, we obtain equation (2). Therefore,

$$3x - y = 4 \quad \text{and} \quad -9x + 3y = -12$$

are equivalent equations. They represent the same line. All of the ordered pairs corresponding to points that lie on the common graph are solutions. See **Figure 7.** ✓

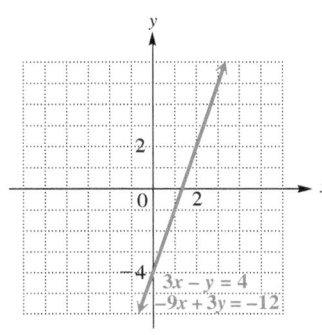

Figure 7

⟶ Work Problem ⑥ at the Side. ▶

---

⑤ Solve the system by the substitution method.

$$8x - 2y = 1$$
$$y = 4x - 8$$

⑥ Solve each system by the substitution method.

(a) $7x - 6y = 10$
$$-14x + 20 = -12y$$

(b) $8x - y = 4$
$$y = 8x + 4$$

> **⊘ CAUTION**
>
> Avoid these common mistakes.
>
> 1. Do not give "false" as the solution of an inconsistent system. The correct response is $\varnothing$. **(See Example 4.)**
>
> 2. Do not give "true" as the solution of a system of dependent equations. In this text, we write the solution set in set-builder notation using the equation in the system (or an equivalent equation) that is in standard form with integer coefficients having greatest common factor 1 and positive coefficient of *x*. **(See Example 5.)**

OBJECTIVE ▶ ③ Solve linear systems with fractions and decimals.

EXAMPLE 6 Using the Substitution Method (Fractional Coefficients)

Solve the system by the substitution method.

$$3x + \frac{1}{4}y = 2 \qquad (1)$$

$$\frac{1}{2}x + \frac{3}{4}y = -\frac{5}{2} \qquad (2)$$

Clear equation (1) of fractions by multiplying each side by 4.

$$4\left(3x + \frac{1}{4}y\right) = 4\,(2) \qquad \text{Multiply by 4, the common denominator.}$$

$$4\,(3x) + 4\left(\frac{1}{4}y\right) = 4\,(2) \qquad \text{Distributive property}$$

$$12x + y = 8 \qquad (3)$$

Now clear equation (2) of fractions by multiplying each side by 4.

$$\frac{1}{2}x + \frac{3}{4}y = -\frac{5}{2} \qquad (2)$$

$$4\left(\frac{1}{2}x + \frac{3}{4}y\right) = 4\left(-\frac{5}{2}\right) \qquad \text{Multiply by 4, the common denominator.}$$

$$4\left(\frac{1}{2}x\right) + 4\left(\frac{3}{4}y\right) = 4\left(-\frac{5}{2}\right) \qquad \text{Distributive property.}$$

$$2x + 3y = -10 \qquad (4)$$

The given system of equations has been simplified to an equivalent system.

$$12x + y = 8 \qquad (3)$$

$$2x + 3y = -10 \qquad (4)$$

To solve this system by substitution, solve equation (3) for *y*.

$$12x + y = 8 \qquad (3)$$

$$y = 8 - 12x \qquad \text{Subtract } 12x.$$

Now substitute this result for *y* in equation (4).

—————— **Continued on Next Page**

$$2x + 3y = -10 \quad (4)$$
$$2x + 3(8 - 12x) = -10 \quad \text{Let } y = 8 - 12x.$$
$$2x + 24 - 36x = -10 \quad \text{Distributive property}$$

Distribute 3 to both 8 and −12x.

$$-34x = -34 \quad \text{Combine like terms. Subtract 24.}$$
$$x = 1 \quad \text{Divide by } -34.$$

Substitute 1 for x in $y = 8 - 12x$ (equation (3) solved for y).

$$y = 8 - 12(1) \quad \text{Let } x = 1.$$
$$y = -4 \quad \text{Multiply, and then subtract.}$$

Check $(1, -4)$ in both of the original equations. The solution set of the system is $\{(1, -4)\}$.

─────── **Work Problem 7 at the Side.** ▶

EXAMPLE 7 **Using the Substitution Method (Decimal Coefficients)**

Solve the system by the substitution method.

$$0.5x + 2.4y = 4.2 \quad (1)$$
$$-0.1x + 1.5y = 5.1 \quad (2)$$

Clear each equation of decimals by multiplying by 10.

$$10(0.5x + 2.4y) = 10(4.2) \quad \text{Multiply equation (1) by 10.}$$
$$10(0.5x) + 10(2.4y) = 10(4.2) \quad \text{Distributive property}$$
$$5x + 24y = 42 \quad (3)$$

$$10(-0.1x + 1.5y) = 10(5.1) \quad \text{Multiply equation (2) by 10.}$$
$$10(-0.1x) + 10(1.5y) = 10(5.1) \quad \text{Distributive property}$$

$10(-0.1x) = -1x = -x$

$$-x + 15y = 51 \quad (4)$$

Now solve the equivalent system of equations by substitution.

$$5x + 24y = 42 \quad (3)$$
$$-x + 15y = 51 \quad (4)$$

Equation (4) can be solved for x.

$$x = 15y - 51 \quad \text{Equation (4) solved for } x$$

Substitute this result for x in equation (3).

$$5x + 24y = 42 \quad (3)$$
$$5(15y - 51) + 24y = 42 \quad \text{Let } x = 15y - 51.$$
$$75y - 255 + 24y = 42 \quad \text{Distributive property}$$
$$99y = 297 \quad \text{Combine like terms. Add 255.}$$
$$y = 3 \quad \text{Divide by 99.}$$

Equation (4) solved for x is $x = 15y - 51$. Substitute 3 for y.

$$x = 15(3) - 51 \quad \text{Let } y = 3.$$
$$x = -6 \quad \text{Multiply, and then subtract.}$$

Check $(-6, 3)$ in both of the original equations. The solution set is $\{(-6, 3)\}$.

─────── **Work Problem 8 at the Side.** ▶

7 Solve each system by the substitution method.

(a) $\dfrac{2}{3}x + \dfrac{1}{2}y = 6$

$\dfrac{1}{2}x - \dfrac{3}{4}y = 0$

(b) $x + \dfrac{1}{2}y = \dfrac{1}{2}$

$\dfrac{1}{6}x - \dfrac{1}{3}y = \dfrac{4}{3}$

8 Solve the system by the substitution method.

$$0.2x + 0.3y = 0.5$$
$$0.3x - 0.1y = 1.3$$

Answers

7. (a) $\{(6, 4)\}$ (b) $\{(2, -3)\}$
8. $\{(4, -1)\}$

4.2 Exercises

FOR EXTRA HELP   Go to MyMathLab for worked-out, step-by-step solutions to exercises enclosed in a square □ and video solutions to ▶ exercises.

1. **CONCEPT CHECK**   A student solves the following system and finds that $x = 3$, which is correct. The student gives $\{3\}$ as the solution set.

$$5x - y = 15$$
$$7x + y = 21$$

What Went Wrong?   Give the correct solution set.

2. **CONCEPT CHECK**   A student solves the following system and obtains the statement $0 = 0$. The student gives the solution set as $\{(0, 0)\}$.

$$x + y = 4$$
$$2x + 2y = 8$$

What Went Wrong?   Give the correct solution set.

CONCEPT CHECK   *Answer each question.*

3. When we use the substitution method, how can we tell that a system has no solution?

4. When we use the substitution method, how can we tell that a system has an infinite number of solutions?

Solve each system by the substitution method. Check each solution. **See Examples 1–5.**

5. ▶ $x + y = 12$
   $y = 3x$

6. $x + 3y = -28$
   $y = -5x$

7. ▶ $3x + 2y = 27$
   $x = y + 4$

8. $4x + 3y = -5$
   $x = y - 3$

9. $3x + 4 = -y$
   $2x + y = 0$

10. $2x - 5 = -y$
    $x + 3y = 0$

11. $7x + 4y = 13$
    $x + y = 1$

12. $3x - 2y = 19$
    $x + y = 8$

13. ▶ $3x + 5y = 25$
    $x - 2y = -10$

14. $5x + 2y = -15$
    $2x - y = -6$

15. $y = 6 - x$
    $y = 2x + 3$

16. $y = 4x - 4$
    $y = -3x - 11$

17. $3x - y = 5$
    $y = 3x - 5$

18. $4x - y = -3$
    $y = 4x + 3$

19. ▶ $2x + 8y = 3$
    $x = 8 - 4y$

20. $2x + 10y = 3$
    $x = 1 - 5y$

21. ▶ $2y = 4x + 24$
    $2x - y = -12$

22. $2y = 14 - 6x$
    $3x + y = 7$

23. $x + y = 0$
    $3x - 3y = 0$

24. $5x + y = 0$
    $x - y = 0$

25. $x = y - 4$
    $x - y = 1$

26. $x = 2 - y$
    $x + y = -5$

27. $6x - 8y = 6$
    $2y = -2 + 3x$

28. $3x + 2y = 6$
    $6x = 8 + 4y$

Solve each system by the substitution method. Check each solution. ***See Examples 6 and 7.***

29. $\dfrac{1}{5}x + \dfrac{2}{3}y = -\dfrac{8}{5}$

$3x - y = 9$

30. $\dfrac{1}{3}x - \dfrac{1}{2}y = -\dfrac{2}{3}$

$4x + y = 6$

31. $\dfrac{1}{2}x + \dfrac{1}{3}y = -\dfrac{1}{3}$

$\dfrac{1}{2}x + 2y = -7$

32. $\dfrac{1}{6}x + \dfrac{1}{6}y = 1$

$-\dfrac{1}{2}x - \dfrac{1}{3}y = -5$

33. $\dfrac{x}{5} + 2y = \dfrac{16}{5}$

$\dfrac{3x}{5} + \dfrac{y}{2} = -\dfrac{7}{5}$

34. $\dfrac{x}{2} + \dfrac{y}{3} = \dfrac{7}{6}$

$\dfrac{x}{4} - \dfrac{3y}{2} = \dfrac{9}{4}$

35. $-0.3x + 0.5y = -1.5$

$0.4x + 0.5y = 2$

36. $-0.1x + 0.1y = 0.2$

$0.3x + 0.1y = 0.2$

37. $0.1x + 0.9y = -2$

$0.5x - 0.2y = 4.1$

38. $0.2x - 1.3y = -3.2$

$-0.1x + 2.7y = 9.8$

39. $0.8x - 0.1y = 1.3$

$2.2x + 1.5y = 8.9$

40. $0.3x - 0.1y = 2.1$

$0.6x + 0.3y = -0.3$

Relating Concepts (Exercises 41–44) For Individual or Group Work

A system of linear equations can be used to model the cost and the revenue of a business. ***Work Exercises 41–44 in order.***

41. Suppose that it costs $5000 to start a business manufacturing and selling bicycles. Each bicycle will cost $400 to manufacture. Explain why the linear equation

$$y_1 = 400x + 5000 \quad (y_1 \text{ in dollars})$$

gives the *total* cost to manufacture x bicycles.

42. We decide to sell each bicycle for $600. Write an equation using y_2 (in dollars) to express the revenue when we sell x bicycles.

43. Form a system from the two equations in **Exercises 41 and 42.** Then solve the system, assuming $y_1 = y_2$, that is, cost = revenue.

44. The value of x in **Exercise 43** is the number of bicycles it takes to *break even*. Fill in the blanks:

When _____ bicycles are sold, the break-even point is reached. At that point, we have spent _____ dollars and taken in _____ dollars.

4.3 Solving Systems of Linear Equations by Elimination

OBJECTIVES

1. Solve linear systems by elimination.
2. Multiply when using the elimination method.
3. Use an alternative method to find the second value in a solution.
4. Solve special systems by elimination.

OBJECTIVE 1 **Solve linear systems by elimination.** Recall that adding the same quantity to each side of an equation results in equal sums.

$$\text{If} \quad A = B, \quad \text{then} \quad A + C = B + C.$$

We can take this addition a step further. Adding *equal* quantities, rather than the *same* quantity, to each side of an equation also results in equal sums.

$$\text{If} \quad A = B \quad \text{and} \quad C = D, \quad \text{then} \quad A + C = B + D.$$

The **elimination method** uses the addition property of equality to solve systems.

EXAMPLE 1 Using the Elimination Method

Solve the system by the elimination method.

$$x + y = 5 \quad (1)$$
$$x - y = 3 \quad (2)$$

Each equation in this system is a statement of equality, so the sum of the left sides equals the sum of the right sides. Adding vertically in this way gives the following.

The goal is to **eliminate** a variable.

$$x + y = 5 \quad (1)$$
$$\underline{x - y = 3} \quad (2)$$
$$2x \quad = 8 \quad \text{Add left sides and add right sides.}$$
$$x = 4 \quad \text{Divide by 2.}$$

Notice that y has been eliminated. The result, $x = 4$, gives the x-value of the ordered-pair solution of the given system. To find the y-value of the solution, substitute 4 for x in either of the two equations of the system. We choose equation (1).

$$x + y = 5 \quad (1)$$
$$4 + y = 5 \quad \text{Let } x = 4.$$
$$y = 1 \quad \text{Subtract 4.}$$

Check the ordered pair, $(4, 1)$, by substituting 4 for x and 1 for y in both equations of the given system.

CHECK

$x + y = 5$ (1)	$x - y = 3$ (2)
$4 + 1 \overset{?}{=} 5$ Substitute.	$4 - 1 \overset{?}{=} 3$ Substitute.
$5 = 5$ ✓ True	$3 = 3$ ✓ True

Because *both* results are true, the solution set of the system is $\{(4, 1)\}$.

◀ **Work Problem** 1 **at the Side.**

1 Solve each system by the elimination method.

(a) Fill in the blanks to solve the following system.

$$x + y = 8 \quad (1)$$
$$\underline{x - y = 2} \quad (2)$$
$$\underline{} = \underline{} \quad \text{Add.}$$
$$x = \underline{}$$

Find y.

$$x - y = 2 \quad (2)$$
$$\underline{} - y = 2$$
$$-y = \underline{}$$
$$y = \underline{}$$

The solution set is $\underline{}$.

(b) $3x - y = 7$
$2x + y = 3$

! **CAUTION**

A system is not completely solved until values for both x and y are found. Do not stop after finding the value of only one variable. Remember to write the solution set as a set containing an ordered pair.

Answers

1. **(a)** $2x$; 10; 5; 5; -3; 3; $\{(5, 3)\}$
   (b) $\{(2, -1)\}$

With the elimination method, the idea is to *eliminate* one of the two variables in a system. ***In order for us to do this, one pair of variable terms in the two equations must have coefficients that are opposites***.

Solving a Linear System by Elimination

Step 1 Write both equations in the form $Ax + By = C$.

Step 2 Transform the equations as needed so that the coefficients of one pair of variable terms are opposites. Multiply one or both equations by appropriate numbers so that the sum of the coefficients of either the x- or y-terms is 0.

Step 3 Add the new equations to *eliminate* a variable. The sum should be an equation with just one variable.

Step 4 Solve the equation from Step 3 for the remaining variable.

Step 5 Find the other value. Substitute the result from Step 4 into either of the original equations, and solve for the other variable.

Step 6 Check the values in *both* of the *original* equations. Then write the solution set as a set containing an ordered pair.

It does not matter which variable is eliminated first. Usually we choose the one that is more convenient to work with.

EXAMPLE 2 **Using the Elimination Method**

Solve the system.

$$y + 11 = 2x \quad (1)$$
$$5x = y + 26 \quad (2)$$

Step 1 Write both equations in the form $Ax + By = C$.

$$-2x + y = -11 \quad \text{Subtract } 2x \text{ and } 11 \text{ in equation (1).}$$
$$5x - y = 26 \quad \text{Subtract } y \text{ in equation (2).}$$

Step 2 Because the coefficients of y are 1 and -1, adding will eliminate y. It is not necessary to multiply either equation by a number.

Step 3 Add the two equations.

$$
\begin{array}{r}
-2x + y = -11 \\
\underline{5x - y = 26} \\
3x \phantom{{}- y} = 15
\end{array}
\quad \text{Add in columns.}
$$

Step 4 Solve. $\qquad\qquad x = 5 \qquad$ Divide by 3.

Step 5 Find the value of y by substituting 5 for x in either of the original equations.

$$y + 11 = 2x \qquad (1)$$
$$y + 11 = 2(5) \qquad \text{Let } x = 5.$$
$$y + 11 = 10 \qquad \text{Multiply.}$$
$$y = -1 \qquad \text{Subtract 11.}$$

—————— **Continued on Next Page**

2 Solve each system by the elimination method.

(a) $2x = y + 2$

$4x + y = 10$

(b) $-5y = -8x + 32$

$4 = 4x + 5y$

3 Solve each system by the elimination method.

GS (a) Fill in the blanks to solve the following system.

$$4x - 3y = 6 \quad (1)$$
$$2x - 7y = -8 \quad (2)$$

Multiply equation (2) by _____ and then add to eliminate the variable x.

$$4x - 3y = 6 \quad (1)$$
$$\underline{x + 14y = \underline{}}$$
$$11y = \underline{} \quad \text{Add.}$$
$$y = 2$$

Find the value of x by substituting _____ for y in either of the original equations. The value of x is _____.

The solution set is _____.

(b) $5x - y = 7$

$3x + 4y = -5$

Step 6 Check the ordered pair $(5, -1)$ by substituting $x = 5$ and $y = -1$ in both of the original equations.

CHECK
$$y + 11 = 2x \quad (1)$$
$$-1 + 11 \stackrel{?}{=} 2(5) \quad \text{Substitute.}$$
$$10 = 10 \checkmark \quad \text{True}$$

$$5x = y + 26 \quad (2)$$
$$5(5) \stackrel{?}{=} -1 + 26 \quad \text{Substitute.}$$
$$25 = 25 \checkmark \quad \text{True}$$

Because both results are true, the solution set is $\{(5, -1)\}$.

◀ **Work Problem 2 at the Side.**

OBJECTIVE 2 Multiply when using the elimination method. Sometimes we need to multiply each side of one or both equations in a system by some number so that adding the equations will eliminate a variable.

EXAMPLE 3 Using the Elimination Method

Solve the system.

$$3x - 2y = 10 \quad (1)$$
$$x + 5y = -8 \quad (2)$$

Step 1 The equations are already written in $Ax + By = C$ form.

Step 2 Adding the two equations gives $4x + 3y = 2$, which does not eliminate either variable. However, multiplying equation (2) by -3 and then adding will eliminate the variable x.

Step 3 Add the two equations.

$$3x - 2y = 10 \quad (1)$$
$$\underline{-3x - 15y = 24} \quad \text{Multiply equation (2) by } -3.$$
$$-17y = 34 \quad \text{Add.}$$

Step 4 Solve. $\qquad y = -2 \quad$ Divide by -17.

Step 5 Find the value of x by substituting -2 for y in either of the original equations.

$$x + 5y = -8 \quad (2)$$
$$x + 5(-2) = -8 \quad \text{Let } y = -2.$$
$$x - 10 = -8 \quad \text{Multiply.}$$
$$x = 2 \quad \text{Add 10.}$$

Step 6 Check the ordered pair $(2, -2)$ by substituting $x = 2$ and $y = -2$ in both of the original equations.

CHECK
$$3x - 2y = 10 \quad (1)$$
$$3(2) - 2(-2) \stackrel{?}{=} 10 \quad \text{Substitute.}$$
$$10 = 10 \checkmark \quad \text{True}$$

$$x + 5y = -8 \quad (2)$$
$$2 + 5(-2) \stackrel{?}{=} -8 \quad \text{Substitute.}$$
$$-8 = -8 \checkmark \quad \text{True}$$

Because both results are true, the solution set is $\{(2, -2)\}$.

◀ **Work Problem 3 at the Side.**

Answers

2. (a) $\{(2, 2)\}$ (b) $\left\{\left(3, -\dfrac{8}{5}\right)\right\}$

3. (a) -2; -4; 16; 22; 2; 3; $\{(3, 2)\}$
   (b) $\{(1, -2)\}$

❗ CAUTION

When using the elimination method, remember to *multiply both sides* of an equation by the same nonzero number.

EXAMPLE 4 Using the Elimination Method

Solve the system.

$$2x + 3y = -15 \quad (1)$$
$$5x + 2y = 1 \quad (2)$$

Adding the two equations gives $7x + 5y = -14$, which does not eliminate either variable. However, we can multiply each equation by a suitable number so that the coefficients of one of the two variables are opposites. For example, to eliminate x, multiply each side of equation (1) by 5, and each side of equation (2) by -2.

$$10x + 15y = -75 \quad \text{Multiply } both \text{ sides of equation (1) by 5.}$$
$$\underline{-10x - 4y = -2} \quad \text{Multiply } both \text{ sides of equation (2) by } -2.$$
$$11y = -77 \quad \text{Add.}$$
$$y = -7 \quad \text{Divide by 11.}$$

The coefficients of x are opposites.

Find the value of x by substituting -7 for y in either equation (1) or (2).

$$5x + 2y = 1 \quad (2)$$
$$5x + 2(-7) = 1 \quad \text{Let } y = -7.$$
$$5x - 14 = 1 \quad \text{Multiply.}$$
$$5x = 15 \quad \text{Add 14.}$$
$$x = 3 \quad \text{Divide by 5.}$$

CHECK $2x + 3y = -15 \quad (1)$ $\qquad 5x + 2y = 1 \quad (2)$

$2(3) + 3(-7) \stackrel{?}{=} -15$ Substitute. $\quad 5(3) + 2(-7) \stackrel{?}{=} 1$ Substitute.

$-15 = -15$ ✓ True $\qquad\qquad 1 = 1$ ✓ True

The solution set is $\{(3, -7)\}$. Write the x-value first.

— Work Problem **4** at the Side. ▶

OBJECTIVE ▶ **3** Use an alternative method to find the second value in a solution. Sometimes it is easier to find the value of the second variable in a solution by using the elimination method twice.

EXAMPLE 5 Finding the Second Value (Alternative Method)

Solve the system.

$$4x = 9 - 3y \quad (1)$$
$$5x - 2y = 8 \quad (2)$$

Write equation (1) in $Ax + By = C$ form by adding $3y$ to each side.

$$4x + 3y = 9 \quad (3)$$
$$5x - 2y = 8 \quad (2)$$

One way to proceed is to eliminate y. We multiply each side of equation (3) by 2 and each side of equation (2) by 3, and then add.

— Continued on Next Page

4 **(a)** Multiply each equation in the system in **Example 4** by a suitable number so that the variable y is eliminated.

$$2x + 3y = -15$$
$$5x + 2y = 1$$

Complete the solution, and give the solution set. Is it the same as in **Example 4**? (*Yes / No*)

(b) Solve the system.

$$6x + 7y = 4$$
$$5x + 8y = -1$$

Answers

4. (a) $\{(3, -7)\}$; Yes **(b)** $\{(3, -2)\}$

5 Solve each system of equations.

(a) $4x + 9y = 3$

$5y = 6 - 3x$

(b) $3y = 8 + 4x$

$6x = 9 - 2y$

6 Solve each system by the elimination method.

(a) $4x + 3y = 10$

$2x + \dfrac{3}{2}y = 12$

(b) $\quad 4x - 6y = 10$

$-10x + 15y = -25$

Answers

5. (a) $\left\{\left(\dfrac{39}{7}, -\dfrac{15}{7}\right)\right\}$ (b) $\left\{\left(\dfrac{11}{26}, \dfrac{42}{13}\right)\right\}$

6. (a) $\varnothing$

(b) $\{(x, y) \mid 2x - 3y = 5\}$

(*Note:* To write the solution set, we divided each term of the equation $4x - 6y = 10$ by 2 so that the coefficients would have greatest common factor 1.)

$$8x + 6y = 18 \quad \text{Multiply equation (3), } 4x + 3y = 9, \text{ by 2.}$$

$$\underline{15x - 6y = 24} \quad \text{Multiply equation (2), } 5x - 2y = 8, \text{ by 3.}$$

$$23x \qquad = 42 \quad \text{Add.}$$

The coefficients of y are opposites.

$$x = \dfrac{42}{23} \quad \text{Divide by 23.}$$

Substituting $\dfrac{42}{23}$ for x in one of the given equations would give y, but the arithmetic would be complicated. Instead, solve for y by starting again with the original equations in $Ax + By = C$ form (equations (3) and (2)) and eliminating x.

$$20x + 15y = \quad 45 \quad \text{Multiply equation (3), } 4x + 3y = 9, \text{ by 5.}$$

$$\underline{-20x + \quad 8y = -32} \quad \text{Multiply equation (2), } 5x - 2y = 8, \text{ by } -4.$$

$$23y = \quad 13 \quad \text{Add.}$$

The coefficients of x are opposites.

$$y = \dfrac{13}{23} \quad \text{Divide by 23.}$$

Check that the solution set is $\left\{\left(\dfrac{42}{23}, \dfrac{13}{23}\right)\right\}$.

◀ **Work Problem 5 at the Side.**

Note

When the value of the first variable is a fraction, the method used in **Example 5** helps avoid arithmetic errors. This method could be used to solve any system.

OBJECTIVE ▶ 4 Solve special systems by elimination.

EXAMPLE 6 Solve Special Systems Using the Elimination Method

Solve each system by the elimination method.

(a) $\qquad\qquad\quad 2x + 4y = 5 \qquad (1)$

$\qquad\qquad\quad 4x + 8y = -9 \qquad (2)$

Multiply each side of equation (1) by -2. Then add the two equations.

$$-4x - 8y = -10 \quad \text{Multiply equation (1) by } -2.$$

$$\underline{\quad 4x + 8y = \quad -9} \quad (2)$$

$$0 = -19 \quad \text{False}$$

The false statement $0 = -19$ indicates that the system has solution set $\varnothing$.

(b) $\qquad\qquad\quad 3x - \quad y = 4 \qquad (1)$

$\qquad\qquad -9x + 3y = -12 \qquad (2)$

Multiply each side of equation (1) by 3. Then add the two equations.

$$9x - 3y = \quad 12 \quad \text{Multiply equation (1) by 3.}$$

$$\underline{-9x + 3y = -12} \quad (2)$$

$$0 = 0 \quad \text{True}$$

A true statement occurs when the equations are equivalent. This indicates that every solution of one equation is also a solution of the other. The solution set is $\{(x, y) \mid 3x - y = 4\}$.

◀ **Work Problem 6 at the Side.**

4.3 Exercises

FOR EXTRA HELP

Go to MyMathLab *for worked-out, step-by-step solutions to exercises enclosed in a square* ☐ *and video solutions to* ▶ *exercises.*

CONCEPT CHECK *In Exercises 1 and 2, answer* true *or* false. *If false, tell why.*

1. To eliminate the *x*-terms in the following system, we should multiply equation (1) by −2 and then add the result to equation (2).

$$3x + 5y = 7 \quad (1)$$
$$6x + 3y = -10 \quad (2)$$

2. To eliminate the *y*-terms in the following system, we should multiply equation (2) by 3 and then add the result to equation (1).

$$2x + 12y = 7 \quad (1)$$
$$3x + 4y = 1 \quad (2)$$

3. CONCEPT CHECK When solving the system

$$x + y = 1 \quad (1)$$
$$-x - y = 2 \quad (2)$$

by elimination, a student obtained the false statement

$$0 = 3.$$

He then concluded that the solution set was $\{(0, 3)\}$. *What Went Wrong?* Give the correct solution set.

4. CONCEPT CHECK To eliminate the *y*-terms in the system

$$2x - y = 5 \quad (1)$$
$$-6x + 3y = -15, \quad (2)$$

a student multiplied equation (1) by 3 to obtain

$$6x - 3y = 5.$$

When she added this result to equation (2), she concluded that the solution set was ∅. *What Went Wrong?* Give the correct solution set.

Solve each system by the elimination method. Check each solution. ***See Examples 1 and 2.***

5. ▶ $x + y = 2$
$2x - y = -5$

6. $3x - y = -12$
$x + y = 4$

7. $2x + y = -5$
$x - y = 2$

8. $2x + y = -15$
$-x - y = 10$

9. $x + 2y = 11$
$-x + 3y = 4$

10. $-x - 4y = 10$
$x - 4y = 14$

11. ▶ $2y = -3x$
$-3x - y = 3$

12. $5x = y + 5$
$2y = 5x$

13. $6x - y = -1$
$5y = 17 + 6x$

14. $y = 9 - 6x$
$-6x + 3y = 15$

15. $2x - 6 = -3y$
$5x - 3y = -27$

16. $x - 2 = -y$
$2x = y + 10$

Solve each system by the elimination method. Check each solution. ***See Examples 3–5.***

17. ▶ $2x - y = 12$
$3x + 2y = -3$

18. $x + y = 3$
$-3x + 2y = -19$

19. $x + 3y = 19$
$2x - y = 10$

20. $4x - 3y = -19$
$2x + y = 13$

21. $x + 4y = 16$
$3x + 5y = 20$

22. $2x + y = 8$
$5x - 2y = -16$

23. $5x - 3y = -20$
$-3x + 6y = 12$

24. $4x + 3y = -28$
$5x - 6y = -35$

25. $2x - 8y = 0$
$4x + 5y = 0$

26. $3x - 15y = 0$
$6x + 10y = 0$

27. $x + y = 7$
$x + y = -3$

28. $x - y = 4$
$x - y = -3$

29. $-x + 3y = 4$
$-2x + 6y = 8$

30. $6x - 2y = 24$
$-3x + y = -12$

31. $2x + 3y = 21$
$5x - 2y = -14$

32. $5x + 4y = 12$
$3x + 5y = 15$

33. $3x - 7 = -5y$
$5x + 4y = -10$

34. $2x + 3y = 13$
$6 + 2y = -5x$

35. $4x - 3y = -2$
$5x + 3 = 2y$

36. $2x + 3y = 0$
$4x + 12 = 9y$

37. $24x + 12y = -7$
$16x - 17 = 18y$

38. $9x + 4y = -3$
$6x + 7 = -6y$

39. $5x - 2y = 3$
$10x - 4y = 5$

40. $3x - 5y = 1$
$6x - 10y = 4$

41. $6x + 3y = 0$
$-18x - 9y = 0$

42. $3x - 5y = 0$
$9x - 15y = 0$

43. $3x = 3 + 2y$
$-\frac{4}{3}x + y = \frac{1}{3}$

44. $3x = 27 + 2y$
$x - \frac{7}{2}y = -25$

45. $\dfrac{1}{5}x + y = \dfrac{6}{5}$

$\dfrac{1}{10}x + \dfrac{1}{3}y = \dfrac{5}{6}$

46. $\dfrac{1}{3}x + \dfrac{1}{2}y = \dfrac{13}{6}$

$\dfrac{1}{2}x - \dfrac{1}{4}y = -\dfrac{3}{4}$

47. $2.4x + 1.7y = 7.6$

$1.2x - 0.5y = 9.2$

48. $0.5x + 3.4y = 13$

$1.5x - 2.6y = -25$

Relating Concepts (Exercises 49–52) **For Individual or Group Work**

The graph shows average U.S. movie theater ticket prices from 2004 through 2014. In 2004 the average ticket price was $6.21, as represented on the graph by the point P(2004, 6.21). In 2014, the average ticket price was $8.17, as represented on the graph by the point Q(2014, 8.17). **Work Exercises 49–52 in order.**

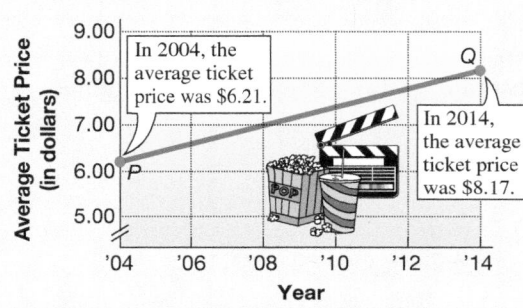

Data from Motion Picture Association of America.

49. The line segment has an equation that can be written in the form

$$y = ax + b.$$

Using the coordinates of point P with $x = 2004$ and $y = 6.21$, write an equation in the variables a and b.

50. Using the coordinates of point Q with $x = 2014$ and $y = 8.17$, write a second equation in the variables a and b.

51. Write the system of equations formed from the two equations in **Exercises 49 and 50.** Solve the system, giving the values of a and b to three decimal places. (*Hint:* Eliminate b using the elimination method.)

52. Answer each question.

(a) What is the equation of the segment PQ?

(b) Let $x = 2013$ in the equation from part (a), and solve for y (to two decimal places). How does the result compare with the actual figure of $8.13?

Summary Exercises *Applying Techniques for Solving Systems of Linear Equations*

EXAMPLE **Comparing the Substitution and Elimination Methods**

Consider the following system.

$$3x + y = -2 \quad (1)$$
$$5x + 2y = 4 \quad (2)$$

(a) Solve by the substitution method.

Solve equation (1) for y.

$$y = -2 - 3x \quad \text{Subtract } 3x.$$

Substitute $-2 - 3x$ for y in equation (2).

$$5x + 2y = 4 \quad (2)$$
$$5x + 2(-2 - 3x) = 4 \quad \text{Let } y = -2 - 3x.$$
$$5x - 4 - 6x = 4$$
$$-x = 8 \quad \begin{array}{l}\text{Combine like} \\ \text{terms. Add 4.}\end{array}$$
$$x = -8 \quad \text{Multiply by } -1.$$

Substitute -8 for x in $y = -2 - 3x$ (that is, equation (1) solved for y.)

$$y = -2 - 3(-8) \quad \text{Let } x = -8.$$
$$y = 22 \quad \text{Multiply. Subtract.}$$

Check that the solution set is $\{(-8, 22)\}$.

(b) Solve by the elimination method.

Multiply equation (1) by -2 and add the result to equation (2) to eliminate the y-terms.

$$-6x - 2y = 4 \quad \text{Multiply equation (1) by } -2.$$
$$\underline{5x + 2y = 4} \quad (2)$$
$$-x \quad\;\; = 8 \quad \text{Add.}$$
$$x = -8 \quad \text{Multiply by } -1.$$

Substitute -8 for x in either of the original equations.

$$3x + y = -2 \quad (1)$$
$$3(-8) + y = -2 \quad \text{Let } x = -8.$$
$$-24 + y = -2 \quad \text{Multiply.}$$
$$y = 22 \quad \text{Add 24.}$$

Check that the solution set is $\{(-8, 22)\}$.

Some systems are more easily solved using one method than using the other.

Guidelines for Choosing a Method to Solve a System of Linear Equations

1. If one of the equations of the system is already solved for one of the variables, the substitution method is the better choice.

$$\begin{array}{l}3x + 4y = 9 \\ y = 2x - 6\end{array} \quad \text{and} \quad \begin{array}{l}x = 3y - 7 \\ -5x + 3y = 9\end{array}$$

2. If both equations are in $Ax + By = C$ form and none of the variables has coefficient -1 or 1, the elimination method is the better choice.

$$4x - 11y = 3$$
$$-2x + 3y = 4$$

3. If one or both of the equations are in $Ax + By = C$ form and the coefficient of one of the variables is -1 or 1, either method is appropriate.

$$3x + y = -2$$
$$5x + 2y = 4$$

This system is solved by both methods in the example above for comparison.

CONCEPT CHECK *Use the preceding guidelines to solve each problem.*

1. To minimize the amount of work required, determine whether you would use the substitution or the elimination method to solve each system, and why. *Do not actually solve.*

(a) $3x + 2y = 18$ **(b)** $3x + y = -7$ **(c)** $3x - 2y = 0$

$y = 3x$ $x - y = -5$ $9x + 8y = 7$

2. Which system would be easier to solve using the substitution method? Why?

$\qquad$ *System A*: $5x - 3y = 7$ $\qquad$ *System B*: $7x + 2y = 4$

$\qquad\qquad\qquad\quad 2x + 8y = 3$ $\qquad\qquad\qquad\quad y = -3x + 1$

*In each problem, **(a)** solve the system by the substitution method, **(b)** solve the system by the elimination method, and **(c)** tell which method you prefer for that particular system and why.*

3. $4x - 3y = -8$ $\qquad\qquad\qquad\qquad\qquad$ 4. $2x + 5y = 0$

$x + 3y = 13$ $\qquad\qquad\qquad\qquad\qquadx = -3y + 1$

Solve each system by the method of your choice. (For Exercises 5–7, see your answers for **Exercise 1.**)

5. $3x + 2y = 18$ $\qquad$ 6. $3x + y = -7$ $\qquad$ 7. $3x - 2y = 0$ $\qquad$ 8. $x + y = 7$

$y = 3x$ $\qquad\qquadx - y = -5$ $\qquad\qquad9x + 8y = 7$ $\qquadx = -3 - y$

9. $5x - 4y = 15$ $\qquad$ 10. $4x + 2y = 3$ $\qquad$ 11. $3x = 7 - y$ $\qquad$ 12. $3x - 5y = 7$

$-3x + 6y = -9$ $\qquady = -x$ $\qquad\qquad2y = 14 - 6x$ $\qquad2x + 3y = 30$

13. $5x = 7 + 2y$ $\qquad\qquad$ 14. $4x + 3y = 1$ $\qquad\qquad\qquad$ 15. $2x - 3y = 7$

$5y = 5 - 3x$ $\qquad\qquad3x + 2y = 2$ $\qquad\qquad\qquad-4x + 6y = 14$

16. $7x - 4y = 0$ $\qquad\qquad$ 17. $6x + 5y = 13$ $\qquad\qquad\qquad$ 18. $x - 3y = 7$

$3x = 2y$ $\qquad\qquad\quad3x + 3y = 4$ $\qquad\qquad\qquad4x + y = 5$

Solve each system by any method. First clear all fractions or decimals.

19. $\dfrac{1}{4}x - \dfrac{1}{5}y = 9$ $\quad$ 20. $\dfrac{1}{5}x + \dfrac{2}{3}y = -\dfrac{8}{5}$ $\quad$ 21. $\dfrac{1}{6}x + \dfrac{1}{6}y = 2$ $\quad$ 22. $\dfrac{x}{5} + 2y = \dfrac{8}{5}$

$y = 5x$ $\qquad\qquad\qquadx - 5y = 17$ $\qquad\qquad-\dfrac{1}{2}x - \dfrac{1}{3}y = -8$ $\qquad\dfrac{3x}{5} + \dfrac{y}{2} = -\dfrac{7}{10}$

23. $\dfrac{x}{5} + y = 6$ $\qquad$ 24. $\dfrac{2}{5}x + \dfrac{4}{3}y = -8$ $\qquad$ 25. $0.2x + 0.3y = 1.0$ $\qquad$ 26. $0.3x - 0.2y = 0.9$

$\dfrac{x}{10} + \dfrac{y}{3} = \dfrac{5}{6}$ $\qquad\dfrac{7}{10}x - \dfrac{2}{9}y = 9$ $\qquad\qquad-0.3x + 0.1y = 1.8$ $\qquad0.2x - 0.3y = 0.1$

4.4 | Applications of Linear Systems

OBJECTIVES

1. Solve problems about unknown numbers.
2. Solve problems about quantities and their costs.
3. Solve problems about mixtures.
4. Solve problems about distance, rate (or speed), and time.

We modify the six-step problem-solving method used earlier to allow for two variables and two equations.

Solving an Applied Problem Using a System of Equations

Step 1 **Read** the problem carefully. *What information is given? What is to be found?*

Step 2 **Assign variables** to represent the unknown values. Make a sketch, diagram, or table, as needed. Write down what each variable represents.

Step 3 **Write two equations** using both variables.

Step 4 **Solve** the system of two equations.

Step 5 **State the answer.** Label it appropriately. *Does it seem reasonable?*

Step 6 **Check** the answer in the words of the *original* problem.

 **OBJECTIVE** ▶ **1** Solve problems about unknown numbers.

EXAMPLE 1 **Solving a Problem about Two Unknown Numbers**

In a recent year, consumer sales of sports equipment were $307 million more for snow skiing than for snowboarding. Together, total equipment sales for these two sports were $931 million. What were equipment sales for each sport? (Data from National Sporting Goods Association.)

Step 1 **Read** the problem carefully. We must find equipment sales (in millions of dollars) for snow skiing and for snowboarding. We know how much more equipment sales were for snow skiing than for snowboarding. Also, we know the total sales.

Step 2 **Assign variables.**

Let x = equipment sales for skiing (in millions of dollars),

and y = equipment sales for snowboarding (in millions of dollars).

Step 3 **Write two equations.**

$x = 307 + y$ Equipment sales for skiing were $307 million more than equipment sales for snowboarding. (1)

$x + y = 931$ Total sales were $931 million. (2)

Step 4 **Solve** the system of equations from Step 3. We use the substitution method because the first equation is already solved for x.

$$x + y = 931 \quad (2)$$

$$(307 + y) + y = 931 \quad \text{Let } x = 307 + y.$$

$$307 + 2y = 931 \quad \text{Combine like terms.}$$

$$2y = 624 \quad \text{Subtract 307.}$$

Don't stop here. ⟶ $y = 312$ Divide by 2.

—— **Continued on Next Page**

To find the value of x, we substitute 312 for y in equation (1) or (2).

$$x = 307 + y \qquad (1)$$
$$x = 307 + 312 \qquad \text{Let } y = 312 \text{ in equation (1).}$$
$$x = 619 \qquad \text{Add.}$$

Step 5 **State the answer.** Equipment sales for skiing were $619 million, and equipment sales for snowboarding were $312 million.

Step 6 **Check** the answer in the original problem. Because

$$619 = 307 + 312 \quad \text{and} \quad 619 + 312 = 931$$

are both true, the answer satisfies the information given.

──────────────── **Work Problem** ❶ **at the Side.** ▶

> ❗ **CAUTION**
> If an applied problem asks for *two* values as in **Example 1,** be sure to give both of them in the answer.

OBJECTIVE ▶ ❷ **Solve problems about quantities and their costs.**

EXAMPLE 2 **Solving a Problem about Quantities and Costs**

For a production of *Jersey Boys,* main floor tickets cost $127 and rear mezzanine tickets cost $97. Club members spent a total of $3150 for 30 tickets. How many tickets of each kind did they buy? (Data from www.broadway.com)

Step 1 **Read** the problem, several times if needed.

Step 2 **Assign variables.**

Let $x =$ the number of main floor tickets,

and $y =$ the number of rear mezzanine tickets.

Summarize the information given in the problem in a table.

	Number of Tickets	Price per Ticket (in dollars)	Total Value (in dollars)
Main Floor	x	127	$127x$
Mezzanine	y	97	$97y$
Total	30	XXXXXX	3150

Multiply Number of Tickets by Price per Ticket to find Total Value.

Step 3 **Write two equations.**

$$x + y = 30 \qquad \text{Total number of tickets was 30.} \quad (1)$$
$$127x + 97y = 3150 \qquad \text{Total value of tickets was \$3150.} \quad (2)$$

Step 4 **Solve** the system formed in Step 3. We use the elimination method, although the substitution method could be used if desired.

$$x + y = 30 \qquad (1)$$
$$127x + 97y = 3150 \qquad (2)$$

──────────────── **Continued on Next Page**

❶ Solve each problem.

 (a) In a recent year, consumer sales of sports equipment were $26 million less for tennis than for archery. Together, total equipment sales for these two sports were $876 million. What were equipment sales for each sport? (Data from National Sporting Goods Association.)

Step 1
We must find _____.

Step 2
Let $x =$ equipment sales for tennis (in millions of dollars), and $y =$ equipment sales for _____ (in millions of dollars).

Step 3
Write two equations.

$$x = \text{_____} \qquad (1)$$
(See the first sentence in the problem.)

$$\text{_____} \qquad (2)$$
(See the second sentence in the problem.)

Complete Steps 4–6 to solve the problem. Give the answer.

(b) Two of the most popular movies of 2015 were *Star Wars Episode VII* and *Jurassic World.* Together, their domestic gross was about $1394 million. *Jurassic World* grossed $90 million less than *Star Wars.* How much did each movie gross? (Data from www.the-numbers.com)

Answers
1. (a) equipment sales for each sport; archery; $y - 26$; $x + y = 876$; equipment sales for tennis: $425 million; equipment sales for archery: $451 million
 (b) *Star Wars Episode VII*: $742 million; *Jurassic World*: $652 million

2 For a production of *The Lion*
GS *King*, orchestra tickets cost
$209 and rear mezzanine tickets
cost $191. If a group of 18
people attended the show and
spent $3528 for their tickets,
how many of each kind of
ticket did they buy? (Data from
www.broadway.com)

(a) Complete the table.

	Number of Tickets	Price per Ticket (dollars)	Total Value (dollars)
Orchestra	x	___	___
Mezzanine	y	___	___
Total	___	✕✕✕	___

(b) Write a system of
equations.

(c) Use the system of equations
to solve the problem. Check
the answer in the words of
the original problem.

$$-97x - 97y = -2910 \quad \text{Multiply equation (1) by } -97.$$
$$\underline{127x + 97y = 3150} \quad \text{(2)}$$
$$30x = 240 \quad \text{Add.}$$

Main floor tickets $\rightarrow x = 8$ Divide by 30.

Substitute 8 for x in equation (1).

$$x + y = 30 \quad \text{(1)}$$
$$8 + y = 30 \quad \text{Let } x = 8.$$

Mezzanine tickets $\rightarrow y = 22$ Subtract 8.

Step 5 **State the answer.** Club members bought **8** main floor tickets and
22 rear mezzanine tickets.

Step 6 **Check.** The sum of **8** and **22** is 30, so the total number of tickets is
correct. Because **8** tickets were purchased at $127 each and **22** at $97
each, the amount spent on all the tickets is

$$\$127\,(8) + \$97\,(22) = \$3150, \quad \text{as required.}$$

◀ **Work Problem 2 at the Side.**

OBJECTIVE 3 **Solve problems about mixtures.** Previously, we solved percent problems using one variable. Mixture problems that involve percent can
be solved using a system of two equations in two variables.

EXAMPLE 3   **Solving a Mixture Problem Involving Percent**

A pharmacist needs 100 L of 50% alcohol solution. She has a 30% alcohol
solution and an 80% alcohol solution, which she can mix. How many liters
of each will be required to make the 100 L of a 50% alcohol solution?

Step 1 **Read** the problem. Note the percent of each solution and of the mixture.

Step 2 **Assign variables.**

Let x = the number of liters of 30% alcohol needed,

and y = the number of liters of 80% alcohol needed.

Liters of Mixture	Percent (as a decimal)	Liters of Pure Alcohol
x	0.30	$0.30x$
y	0.80	$0.80y$
100	0.50	$0.50\,(100)$

Summarize the
information in a
table. Percents
are written as
decimals.

Figure 8 gives an idea of what is happening in this problem.

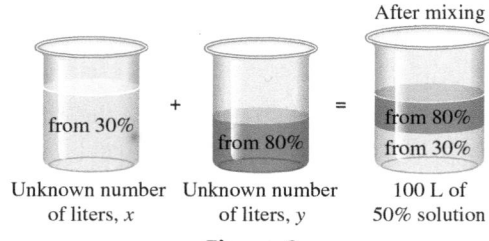

Figure 8

─────── **Continued on Next Page**

Step 3 **Write two equations.** The total number of liters in the final mixture will be 100, which gives one equation.

$$x + y = 100$$ Refer to the first column of the table.

To find the amount of pure alcohol in each mixture, multiply the number of liters by the concentration. (Refer to the table.) The amount of pure alcohol in the 30% solution added to the amount of pure alcohol in the 80% solution will equal the amount of pure alcohol in the final 50% solution. This gives a second equation.

$$0.30x + 0.80y = 0.50\,(100)$$ Refer to the last column of the table.

$$0.30x + 0.80y = 50$$ $0.50\,(100) = 50$

This is a simpler, yet equivalent, equation. — $3x + 8y = 500$ Multiply each side by 10 to clear the decimals.

These two equations form a system.

Be sure to write two equations. —

$$x + \ y = 100 \quad (1)$$
$$3x + 8y = 500 \quad (2)$$

Step 4 **Solve** the system. We use the substitution method, although the elimination method could also be used. Solving equation (1) for x gives

$$x = 100 - y.$$

Substitute $100 - y$ for x in equation (2).

$$3x + 8y = 500 \quad (2)$$
$$3\,(\mathbf{100 - y}) + 8y = 500 \quad \text{Let } x = 100 - y.$$
$$300 - 3y + 8y = 500 \quad \text{Distributive property}$$
$$300 + 5y = 500 \quad \text{Combine like terms.}$$
$$5y = 200 \quad \text{Subtract 300.}$$

Liters of 80% solution → $y = 40$ Divide by 5.

To find x, substitute 40 for y in $x = 100 - y$ (equation (1) solved for x).

$$x = 100 - \mathbf{40} \quad \text{Let } y = 40.$$

Liters of 30% solution → $x = 60$ Subtract.

Step 5 **State the answer.** The pharmacist should use 60 L of the 30% solution and 40 L of the 80% solution.

Step 6 **Check** the answer in the original problem. Because

Use the original equations written from the table. — $60 + 40 = 100$ and $0.30\,(\mathbf{60}) + 0.80\,(\mathbf{40}) = 0.50\,(100)$

are both true, this mixture will give the 100 L of 50% solution.

——— **Work Problems ③ and ④ at the Side.** ▶

Note

Whether to use the substitution or the elimination method to solve a system is often personal choice. In **Examples 2 and 3**, either method can be used efficiently because equation (1) has coefficients of 1 for both variables x and y.

---

③ **GS** How many liters of a 25% alcohol solution must be mixed with a 12% solution to obtain 13 L of a 15% solution?

(a) Complete the table.

Liters	Percent (as a decimal)	Liters of Pure Alcohol
x	0.25	$0.25x$
y	0.12	_____
13	0.15	_____

(b) Write a system of equations, and use it to solve the problem.

④ Solve the problem.
Joe needs 60 milliliters (mL) of 20% acid solution for a chemistry experiment. The lab has on hand only 10% and 25% solutions. How much of each should he mix to make the desired amount of 20% solution?

Answers

3. (a)

Liters	Percent (as a decimal)	Liters of Pure Alcohol
x	0.25	$0.25x$
y	0.12	$0.12y$
13	0.15	$0.15\,(13)$

(b) $x + \ y = 13$
$0.25x + 0.12y = 0.15\,(13)$;
3 L of 25%; 10 L of 12%

4. 20 mL of 10%; 40 mL of 25%

5 Solve using the distance formula $d = rt$.

A small plane traveled from Stockholm, Sweden, to Oslo, Norway, averaging 244 km per hr. The trip took 1.7 hr. To the nearest kilometer, what is the distance between the two cities?

6 Two cars that were 450 mi apart traveled toward each other. They met after 5 hr. If one car traveled twice as fast as the other, what were their rates?

(a) Complete this table.

	r	t	d
Faster Car	x	5	___
Slower Car	y	5	___

(b) Write a system of equations, and use it to solve the problem.

7 Solve the problem.

From a truck stop, two trucks travel in opposite directions on a straight highway. In 3 hr they are 405 mi apart. Find the rate of each truck if one travels 5 mph faster than the other.

Answers

5. 415 km

6. (a)

	r	t	d
Faster Car	x	5	$5x$
Slower Car	y	5	$5y$

(b) $5x + 5y = 450$
$x = 2y$;
faster car: 60 mph; slower car: 30 mph

7. faster truck: 70 mph; slower truck: 65 mph

OBJECTIVE **4** Solve problems about distance, rate (or speed), and time. If an automobile travels at an average rate of 50 mph for 2 hr, then it travels

$$50 \times 2 = 100 \text{ mi.}$$

This is an example of the basic relationship between distance, rate, and time.

distance = rate × time, given by the formula **$d = rt$.**

◀ Work Problem **5** at the Side.

EXAMPLE 4 Solving a Problem about Distance, Rate, and Time

Two executives in cities 400 mi apart drive to a business meeting at a location on the line between their cities. They meet after 4 hr. Find the rate (speed) of each car if one car travels 20 mph faster than the other.

Steps 1 and 2 **Read** the problem carefully. **Assign variables.**

Let x = the rate of the faster car, and y = the rate of the slower car.

Make a table using the formula $d = rt$, and draw a sketch. See **Figure 9.**

	r	t	d
Faster Car	x	4	$x \cdot 4$, or $4x$
Slower Car	y	4	$y \cdot 4$, or $4y$

Because each car travels for 4 hr, the time t for each car is 4. Find d, using $d = rt$ (or $rt = d$).

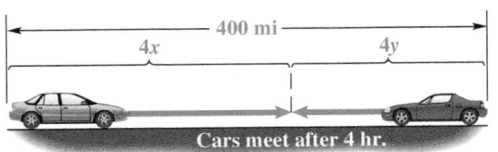

Figure 9

Step 3 **Write two equations.** The total distance traveled by both cars is 400 mi, which gives equation (1). The faster car travels 20 mph faster than the slower car, which gives equation (2).

$$4x + 4y = 400 \quad (1)$$
$$x = 20 + y \quad (2)$$

Step 4 **Solve** the system by substitution since equation (2) is already solved for x. Replace x with $20 + y$ in equation (1).

$$4x + 4y = 400 \quad (1)$$
$$4(20 + y) + 4y = 400 \quad \text{Let } x = 20 + y.$$
$$80 + 4y + 4y = 400 \quad \text{Distributive property}$$
$$80 + 8y = 400 \quad \text{Combine like terms.}$$

Slower car → $y = 40$ ⟵ Subtract 80. Divide by 8.

To find x, substitute 40 for y in equation (2), $x = 20 + y$.

$$x = 20 + 40 \quad \text{Let } y = 40.$$

Faster car → $x = 60$ ⟵ Add.

Step 5 **State the answer.** The rates of the cars are 40 mph and 60 mph.

Step 6 **Check** the answer. Each car travels for 4 hr, so total distance is

$$4(60) + 4(40) = 240 + 160 = 400 \text{ mi,} \quad \text{as required.}$$

◀ Work Problems **6** and **7** at the Side.

EXAMPLE 5   **Solving a Problem about Distance, Rate, and Time**

A plane flies 560 mi in 1.75 hr traveling with the wind. The return trip against the same wind takes the plane 2 hr. Find the rate (speed) of the plane and the wind speed.

Steps 1 and 2   **Read** the problem several times. **Assign variables.**

Let x = the rate of the plane in still air,

and y = the wind speed.

When the plane is traveling *with* the wind, the wind "pushes" the plane. In this case, the rate (speed) of the plane is the *sum* of the rate of the plane and the wind speed, $(x + y)$ mph. See **Figure 10**.

When the plane is traveling *against* the wind, the wind "slows" the plane down. In this case, the rate (speed) of the plane is the *difference* between the rate of the plane and the wind speed, $(x - y)$ mph. Again, see **Figure 10**.

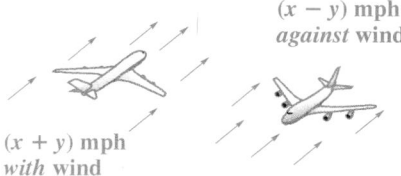

$(x - y)$ mph
against wind

$(x + y)$ mph
with wind

Figure 10

	r	t	d
With Wind	$x + y$	1.75	560
Against Wind	$x - y$	2	560

Summarize this information in a table. The distance is the same both ways.

Step 3   **Write two equations.** Refer to the table and use the formula $d = rt$ (or $rt = d$).

$(x + y)\,1.75 = 560 \xrightarrow{\text{Divide by 1.75.}} x + y = 320$ (1)

$(x - y)\,2 = 560 \xrightarrow{\text{Divide by 2.}} x - y = 280$ (2)

Step 4   **Solve** the system of equations using the elimination method.

$$x + y = 320 \quad (1)$$
$$\underline{x - y = 280} \quad (2)$$
$$2x = 600 \quad \text{Add.}$$
$$x = 300 \quad \text{Divide by 2.}$$

Because $x + y = 320$ and $x = 300$, it follows that $y = 20$.

Step 5   **State the answer.** The rate of the plane is 300 mph, and the wind speed is 20 mph.

Step 6   **Check.** Using equations (1) and (2), we see that $300 + 20 = 320$ and $300 - 20 = 280$ are both true. The answer is correct.

——————————— **Work Problem 8 at the Side.** ▶

> ❗ **CAUTION**
> Be careful. ***When we use two variables to solve a problem, we must write two equations.***

8 Solve each problem.

(a) In 1 hr, Gigi can row 2 mi against the current or 10 mi with the current. Find the rate of the current and Gigi's rate in still water.

Steps 1 and 2
Let x = the rate of the current, and y = _____ in still water.

Then her rate *against* the current is (_____) mph, and her rate with the current is (_____) mph.

Complete the table.

	r	t	d
Against Current	___	___	___
With Current	___	___	___

Step 3
Write two equations.

$(y - x) \cdot 1 =$ _____   (1)
(See the first row of the table.)

————————————   (2)
(See the second row of the table.)

Complete Steps 4–6 to solve the problem. Give the answer.

(b) In 1 hr, a boat travels 15 mi with the current and 9 mi against the current. Find the rate of the boat and the rate of the current.

Answers

8. (a) Gigi's rate; $y - x$; $y + x$

	r	t	d
Against Current	$y - x$	1	2
With Current	$y + x$	1	10

2; $(y + x) \cdot 1 = 10$;
rate of the current: 4 mph;
Gigi's rate: 6 mph

(b) rate of the boat: 12 mph;
rate of the current: 3 mph

4.4 Exercises

FOR EXTRA HELP

Go to MyMathLab *for worked-out, step-by-step solutions to exercises enclosed in a square* ⬚ *and video solutions to* ▶ *exercises.*

CONCEPT CHECK *Choose the correct response.*

1. Which expression represents the monetary value of x 20-dollar bills?

   A. $\dfrac{x}{20}$ dollars   **B.** $\dfrac{20}{x}$ dollars   **C.** $(20 + x)$ dollars   **D.** $20x$ dollars

2. Which expression represents the cost of t pounds of candy that sells for \$1.95 per lb?

   A. \$1.95t **B.** $\dfrac{\$1.95}{t}$ **C.** $\dfrac{t}{\$1.95}$ **D.** \$1.95 + t

3. Which expression represents the amount of interest earned on d dollars invested at an interest rate of 2% for 1 yr?

   A. $2d$ dollars   **B.** $0.02d$ dollars   **C.** $0.2d$ dollars   **D.** $200d$ dollars

4. Which expression represents the amount of pure alcohol in x liters of a 25% alcohol solution?

   A. $25x$ liters   **B.** $(25 + x)$ liters   **C.** $0.25x$ liters   **D.** $(0.25 + x)$ liters

5. According to *Natural History* magazine, the speed of a cheetah is 70 mph. If a cheetah runs for x hours, how many miles does the cheetah cover?

   A. $(70 + x)$ miles   **B.** $(70 - x)$ miles   **C.** $\dfrac{70}{x}$ miles   **D.** $70x$ miles

6. How far does a car travel in 2.5 hr if it travels at an average rate of x miles per hour?

   A. $(x + 2.5)$ miles   **B.** $\dfrac{2.5}{x}$ miles   **C.** $\dfrac{x}{2.5}$ miles   **D.** $2.5x$ miles

7. ▶ What is the rate of a plane that travels at 650 mph *with* a wind of r mph?

   A. $\dfrac{r}{650}$ mph   **B.** $(650 - r)$ mph   **C.** $(650 + r)$ mph   **D.** $(r - 650)$ mph

8. What is the rate of a plane that travels at 650 mph *against* a wind of r mph?

   A. $(650 + r)$ mph   **B.** $\dfrac{650}{r}$ mph   **C.** $(650 - r)$ mph   **D.** $(r - 650)$ mph

9. Suppose that x liters of a 40% acid solution are mixed with y liters of a 35% solution to obtain 100 L of a 38% solution. One equation in a system for solving this problem is

   $$x + y = 100.$$

   Which one of the following is the other equation?

   A. $0.35x + 0.40y = 0.38\,(100)$ **B.** $0.40x + 0.35y = 0.38\,(100)$

   C. $35x + 40y = 38$ **D.** $40x + 35y = 0.38\,(100)$

10. Suppose that two trucks leave a rest stop traveling in opposite directions on a straight highway. One truck travels 15 mph faster than the other, and in 8 hr they are 840 mi apart. If x and y represent the rates of the trucks, one equation in a system for solving this problem is

$$x = 15 + y.$$

Which one of the following is the other equation?

A. $8x + 8y = 840$ **B.** $8x + y = 840$

C. $x + y = 840$ **D.** $8x - 8y = 840$

GS *Refer to the six-step problem-solving method. Fill in the blanks for Steps 2 and 3 for each problem, and then complete the solution by applying Steps 4–6.*

11. The sum of two numbers is 98 and the difference between them is 48. Find the two numbers.

Step 1 **Read** the problem carefully.

Step 2 **Assign variables.**

Let $x =$ the first number

and $y =$ _____ .

Step 3 **Write two equations.**

First equation: $x + y = 98$

Second equation: _____

12. The sum of two numbers is 201 and the difference between them is 11. Find the two numbers.

Step 1 **Read** the problem carefully.

Step 2 **Assign variables.**

Let $x =$ _____

and $y =$ the second number.

Step 3 **Write two equations.**

First equation: _____

Second equation: $x - y = 11$

Solve each problem using a system of equations. **See Example 1.**

13. Two of the longest-running shows on Broadway are *The Phantom of the Opera* and *The Lion King.* As of February 10, 2016, there had been a total of 19,272 performances of the two shows, with 4066 more performances of *The Phantom of the Opera* than *The Lion King.* How many performances were there of each show? (Data from www.playbill.com)

14. During Broadway runs of *A Chorus Line* and *Beauty and the Beast,* there have been 676 fewer performances of *Beauty and the Beast* than of *A Chorus Line.* There were a total of 11,598 performances of the two shows. How many performances were there of each show? (Data from The Broadway League.)

15. Two domestic top-grossing movies of 2015 were *Furious 7* and *Minions.* *Minions* grossed $17 million less than *Furious 7,* and together the two films took in $689 million. How much did each of these movies earn? (Data from www.boxofficemojo.com)

16. During their opening weekends, the movies *Furious 7* and *Minions* grossed a total of $263 million, with *Furious 7* grossing $31 million more than *Minions.* How much did each of these movies earn during their opening weekends? (Data from www.boxofficemojo.com)

17. The Terminal Tower in Cleveland, Ohio, is 239 ft shorter than the Key Tower, also in Cleveland. The total of the heights of the two buildings is 1655 ft. Find the heights of the buildings. (Data from *The World Almanac and Book of Facts.*)

18. The total of the heights of the Chase Tower and the One America Tower, both in Indianapolis, Indiana, is 1234 ft. The Chase Tower is 168 ft taller than the One America Tower. Find the heights of the two buildings. (Data from *The World Almanac and Book of Facts.*)

19. An official playing field (including end zones) for the Indoor Football League has length 38 yd longer than its width. The perimeter of the rectangular field is 188 yd. Find the length and width of the field. (Data from Indoor Football League.)

Steps 1 and 2 **Read** carefully, and **assign** _____ .

Let x = the length (in yards),

and y = the _____ (in yards).

Step 3 **Write two equations.**

Equation (1): See the first sentence in the problem. Express the length in terms of the width.

$$x = \text{_____} \quad (1)$$

Equation (2): See the second sentence in the problem. Perimeter of a rectangle equals twice the _____ plus _____ the width.

$$2x + \text{_____} = \text{_____} \quad (2)$$

Now complete the solution.

20. Pickleball is a combination of badminton, tennis, and ping pong. The perimeter of the rectangular-shaped court is 128 ft. The width is 24 ft shorter than the length. Find the length and width of the court. (Data from www.sportsknowhow.com)

Steps 1 and 2 **Read** carefully, and **assign** _____ .

Let x = the _____ (in feet),

and y = the width (in feet).

Step 3 **Write two equations.**

Equation (1): Perimeter of a rectangle equals _____ the length plus twice the _____ .

$$\text{_____} + 2y = \text{_____} \quad (1)$$

Equation (2): See the third sentence in the problem. Express the width in terms of the length.

$$y = \text{_____} \quad (2)$$

Now complete the solution.

Suppose that x units of a product cost C dollars to manufacture and earn revenue of R dollars. The value of x, where the expressions for C and R are equal, is the **break-even quantity,** *the number of units that produce 0 profit.*

In each problem, (a) find the break-even quantity, and (b) decide whether the product should be produced, based on whether it will earn a profit. (Profit equals revenue minus cost.)

21. $C = 85x + 900$; $R = 105x$; No more than 38 units can be sold.

22. $C = 105x + 6000$; $R = 255x$; No more than 400 units can be sold.

For each problem, complete any tables. Then solve the problem using a system of equations. **See Example 2.**

23. A motel clerk counts his $1 and $10 bills at the end of a day. He finds that he has a total of 74 bills having a combined monetary value of $326. Find the number of bills of each denomination that he has.

Number of Bills	Denomination of Bill (in dollars)	Total Value (in dollars)
x	1	_____
y	10	_____
74	✕✕✕✕✕✕	326

24. Carly is a bank teller. At the end of a day, she has a total of 69 $5 and $10 bills. The total value of the money is $590. How many of each denomination does she have?

Number of Bills	Denomination of Bill (in dollars)	Total Value (in dollars)
x	5	$5x$
y	10	_____
_____	✕✕✕✕✕✕	_____

25. Tracy bought each of her seven nephews a DVD of *Ant-Man* or a Blu-ray disc of *The Martian*. Each DVD cost $16.99. Each Blu-ray disc cost $22.42. Tracy spent a total of $129.79. How many of each did she buy?

26. Terry bought each of his five nieces a DVD of *The Peanuts Movie* or a Blu-ray disc of *Frozen*. Each DVD cost $14.99. Each Blu-ray disc cost $24.99. Terry spent a total of $84.95. How many of each did he buy?

27. Maria has twice as much money invested at 5% simple annual interest as she does at 4%. If her yearly income from these two investments is $350, how much does she have invested at each rate?

Amount Invested (in dollars)	Rate of Interest	Interest for One Year (in dollars)
x	5%, or 0.05	$0.05x$
y	_____	_____
XXXXX	XXXXXX	350

Equation (1): $x =$ _____
Equation (2): $0.05x +$ _____ $=$ _____

28. Charles invested in two accounts, one paying 3% simple annual interest and the other paying 2%. He earned a total of $880 interest. If he invested three times as much in the 3% account as in the 2% account, how much did he invest at each rate?

Amount Invested (in dollars)	Rate of Interest	Interest for One Year (in dollars)
x	_____	_____
y	_____	_____
XXXXXX	XXXXXX	_____

Equation (1): _____ $+$ _____ $= 880$
Equation (2): $x =$ _____

29. The two top-grossing North American concert tours in 2015 were Taylor Swift and Kenny Chesney. Based on average ticket prices, it cost a total of $1097 to buy six tickets for Taylor Swift and five tickets for Kenny Chesney. Three tickets for Taylor Swift and four tickets for Kenny Chesney cost $676. How much did an average ticket cost for each tour? (Data from Pollstar.)

30. Two other popular North American concert tours in 2015 were the Rolling Stones and Garth Brooks. Based on average ticket prices, it cost a total of $1592 to buy eight tickets for the Rolling Stones and three tickets for Garth Brooks. Four tickets for the Rolling Stones and five tickets for Garth Brooks cost $1020. How much did an average ticket cost for each tour? (Data from Pollstar.)

For each problem, complete any tables. Then solve the problem using a system of equations. **See Example 3.**

31. A 40% dye solution is to be mixed with a 70% dye solution to make 120 L of a 50% solution. How many liters of the 40% and 70% solutions will be needed?

Liters of Solution	Percent (as a decimal)	Liters of Pure Dye
x	0.40	_____
y	0.70	_____
120	0.50	_____

32. A 90% antifreeze solution is to be mixed with a 75% solution to make 120 L of a 78% solution. How many liters of the 90% and 75% solutions will be used?

Liters of Solution	Percent (as a decimal)	Liters of Pure Antifreeze
x	0.90	_____
y	0.75	_____
120	0.78	_____

33. Ahmad wishes to mix coffee worth $6 per lb with coffee worth $3 per lb to obtain 90 lb of a mixture worth $4 per lb. How many pounds of the $6 and the $3 coffees will be needed?

Number of Pounds	Dollars per Pound	Cost (in dollars)
x	6	_____
y	_____	_____
90	_____	_____

34. Mariana wishes to blend candy selling for $1.20 per lb with candy selling for $1.80 per lb to obtain 45 lb of a mixture that will be sold for $1.40 per lb. How many pounds of the $1.20 and the $1.80 candies should be used to make the mixture?

Number of Pounds	Dollars per Pound	Cost (in dollars)
x	_____	_____
y	1.80	_____
45	_____	_____

35. How many pounds of nuts selling for $6 per lb and raisins selling for $3 per lb should Kelli combine to obtain 60 lb of a trail mix selling for $5 per lb?

36. Callie is preparing cheese trays. She uses some cheeses that sell for $8 per lb and others that sell for $12 per lb. How many pounds of each cheese should she use in order for the mixed cheeses on the trays to weigh a total of 56 lb and sell for $10.50 per lb?

For each problem, complete any tables. Then solve the problem using a system of equations. **See Examples 4 and 5.**

37. Two trains start from towns 495 mi apart and travel toward each other on parallel tracks. They pass each other 4.5 hr later. If one train travels 10 mph faster than the other, find the rate of each train.

	r	t	d
Train 1	x	_____	_____
Train 2	y	_____	_____

Equation (1): $4.5x +$ _____ $=$ _____

Equation (2): $x =$ _____ $+$ _____

38. Two trains that are 495 mi apart travel toward each other. They pass each other 5 hr later. If one train travels half as fast as the other, find the rate of each train.

	r	t	d
Train 1	x	_____	_____
Train 2	_____	_____	$5y$

Equation (1):   _____ $+ 5y =$ _____

Equation (2): $x =$ _____ y,   or   _____ $= y$

39. RAGBRAI®, the Des Moines **R**egister's **A**nnual **G**reat **B**icycle **R**ide **A**cross **I**owa, is the longest and oldest touring bicycle ride in the world. Suppose a cyclist began the 420-mi ride on July 23, 2016, in western Iowa at the same time that a car traveling toward it left eastern Iowa. If the bicycle and the car met after 7 hr and the car traveled 33 mph faster than the bicycle, find the average rate of each. (Data from www.ragbrai.com)

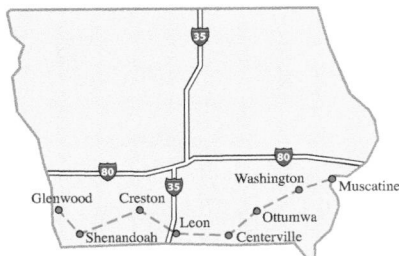

40. Suppose two planes leave Atlanta's Hartsfield Airport at the same time, one traveling east and the other traveling west. If the planes are 2100 mi apart after 2 hr and one plane travels 50 mph faster than the other, find the rate of each plane.

41. Toledo and Cincinnati are 200 mi apart. A car leaves Toledo traveling toward Cincinnati, and another car leaves Cincinnati at the same time, traveling toward Toledo. The car leaving Toledo averages 15 mph faster than the other, and they meet after 1 hr, 36 min. What are the rates of the cars?

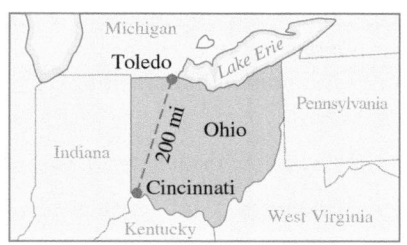

42. Kansas City and Denver are 600 mi apart. Two cars start from these cities, traveling toward each other. They meet after 6 hr. Find the rate of each car if one travels 30 mph slower than the other.

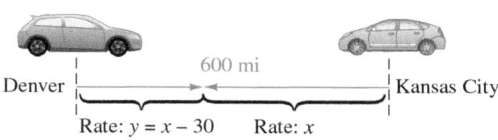

43. A boat takes 3 hr to go 24 mi upstream. It can go 36 mi downstream in the same time. Find the rate of the current and the rate of the boat in still water.

Let x = the rate of the boat in still water and y = the rate of the current.

	r	t	d
Downstream	$x + y$	_____	36
Upstream	$x - y$	_____	_____

44. It takes a boat $1\frac{1}{2}$ hr to go 12 mi downstream, and 6 hr to return. Find the rate of the boat in still water and the rate of the current.

Let x = the rate of the boat in still water and y = the rate of the current.

	r	t	d
Downstream	$x + y$	$\frac{3}{2}$	_____
Upstream	_____	_____	_____

45. If a plane can travel 440 mph against the wind and 500 mph with the wind, find the wind speed and the rate of the plane in still air.

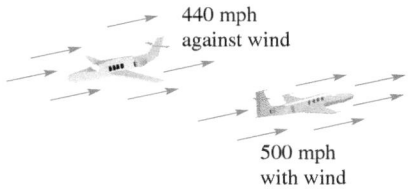

46. A small plane travels 200 mph with the wind and 120 mph against it. Find the wind speed and the rate of the plane in still air.

47. At the beginning of a bicycle ride for charity, Roberto and Juana are 30 mi apart. If they leave at the same time and ride in the same direction, Roberto overtakes Juana in 6 hr. If they ride toward each other, they meet in 1 hr. What are their rates?

48. Mr. Abbot left Farmersville in a plane at noon to travel to Exeter. Mr. Baker left Exeter in his automobile at 2 P.M. to travel to Farmersville. It is 400 mi from Exeter to Farmersville. If the sum of their rates was 120 mph, and if they crossed paths at 4 P.M., find the rate of each.

4.5 | Solving Systems of Linear Inequalities

1 Solve systems of linear inequalities by graphing.

Recall that to graph the solutions of $x + 3y > 12$, we first graph the boundary line $x + 3y = 12$ by finding and plotting a few ordered pairs that satisfy the equation. (The x- and y-intercepts are good choices.) Because the $>$ symbol does not include equality, the points on the line do *not* satisfy the inequality, and we graph it using a dashed line.

To decide which region includes the points that are solutions, we choose a test point not on the line.

$$x + 3y > 12 \qquad \text{Original inequality}$$

$$0 + 3(0) \overset{?}{>} 12 \qquad \text{Let } x = 0 \text{ and } y = 0.$$

$(0, 0)$ is a convenient test point.

$$0 > 12 \qquad \text{False}$$

This false result indicates that the solutions are those points on the side of the line that does *not* include $(0, 0)$, as shown in **Figure 11.**

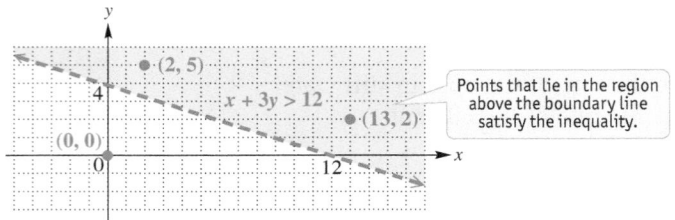

Points that lie in the region above the boundary line satisfy the inequality.

Figure 11

OBJECTIVE ▶ 1 Solve systems of linear inequalities by graphing. A **system of linear inequalities** consists of two or more linear inequalities. The **solution set of a system of linear inequalities** includes all points that make all inequalities of the system true at the same time.

Solving a System of Linear Inequalities

Step 1   **Graph each linear inequality on the same axes.**

Step 2   **Choose the intersection.** Indicate the solution set of the system by shading the intersection of the graphs—that is, the region where the graphs overlap.

EXAMPLE 1   **Solving a System of Linear Inequalities**

Graph the solution set of the system.

$$3x + 2y \leq 6$$

$$2x - 5y > 10$$

Step 1   Graph $3x + 2y \leq 6$ with the solid boundary line $3x + 2y = 6$ using the intercepts $(0, 3)$ and $(2, 0)$. Determine the region to shade.

$$3x + 2y < 6 \qquad \text{Test the region.}$$

$$3(0) + 2(0) \overset{?}{<} 6 \qquad \text{Use } (0, 0) \text{ as a test point.}$$

$$0 < 6 \qquad \text{True}$$

Shade the region containing $(0, 0)$. See **Figure 12(a)** on the next page.

Continued on Next Page

Now graph the inequality $2x - 5y > 10$ with dashed boundary line $2x - 5y = 10$ using the intercepts $(0, -2)$ and $(5, 0)$. Determine the region to shade.

$$2x - 5y > 10 \quad \text{Test the region.}$$
$$2(0) - 5(0) \overset{?}{>} 10 \quad \text{Use } (0, 0) \text{ as a test point.}$$
$$0 > 10 \quad \text{False}$$

Shade the region that does *not* contain $(0, 0)$. See **Figure 12(b).**

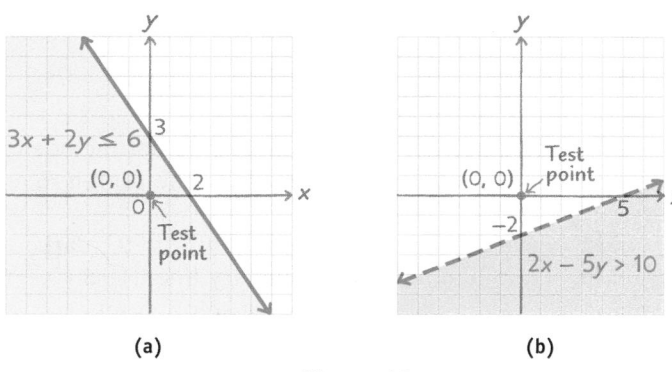

Figure 12

Step 2 The solution set of this system includes all points in the intersection (overlap) of the graphs of the two inequalities. As shown in **Figure 13,** this intersection is the purple shaded region and portion of the boundary line $3x + 2y = 6$ that surrounds it.

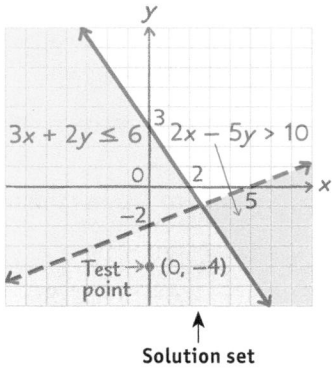

Figure 13

CHECK To confirm the solution set in **Figure 13**, select a test point in the gray shaded region, such as $(0, -4)$, and substitute it into *both* inequalities to make sure that true statements result. (Using an ordered pair that has one coordinate 0 makes the substitution easier.)

$3x + 2y < 6$	$2x - 5y > 10$
$3(0) + 2(-4) \overset{?}{<} 6$ Test $(0, -4)$.	$2(0) - 5(-4) \overset{?}{>} 10$ Test $(0, -4)$.
$-8 < 6$ True	$20 > 10$ True

True statements result, so we have shaded the correct region in **Figure 13**. Test points selected in the other three regions will satisfy only one of the inequalities or neither of them. (Verify this.) ✓

—————————————————————— **Work Problem ① at the Side.** ▶

① Graph the solution set of each system.

(a) $x - 2y \le 8$
       $3x + y > 6$

(The graphs of $x - 2y = 8$ and $3x + y = 6$ are shown.)

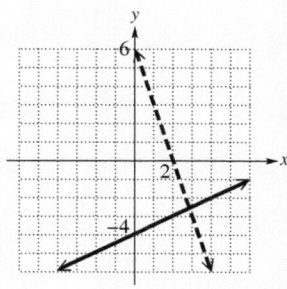

(b) $4x - 2y \le 8$
      $x + 3y \ge 3$

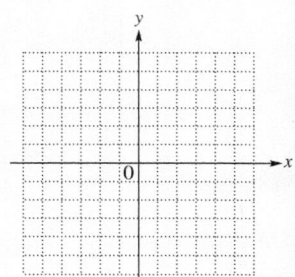

Answers

1. (a)

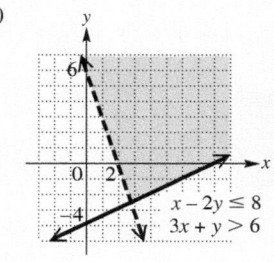

(b)

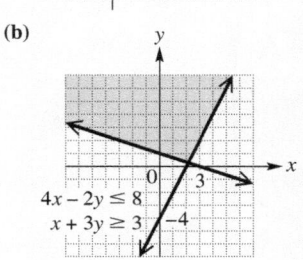

2 Graph the solution set of the system.

$$x + 2y < 0$$
$$3x - 4y < 12$$

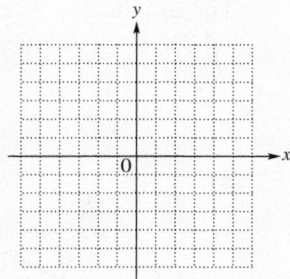

3 Graph the solution set of the system.

$$3x + 2y \leq 12$$
$$x \leq 2$$
$$y \leq 4$$

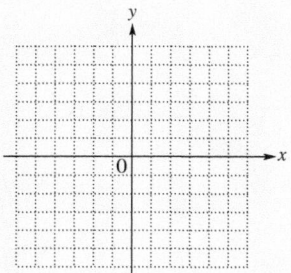

Answers

2.

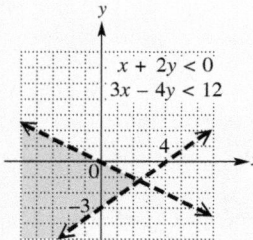

3.

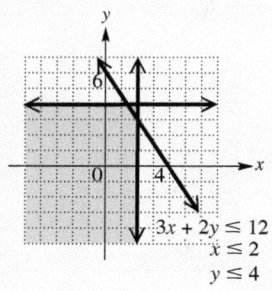

Note

We usually do all the work on one set of axes. In the remaining examples, only one graph is shown. Be sure that the region of the final solution set is clearly indicated.

EXAMPLE 2 Solving a System of Linear Inequalities

Graph the solution set of the system.

$$x - y > 5$$
$$2x + y < 2$$

Figure 14 shows the graphs of both $x - y > 5$ and $2x + y < 2$. Dashed lines show that the graphs of the inequalities do not include their boundary lines. Use $(0, 0)$ as a test point to determine the region to shade for each inequality.

The solution set of the system is the region with the darkest shading. The solution set does not include either boundary line. (Use $(0, -6)$ in the gray shaded region as a test point to confirm the solution set.)

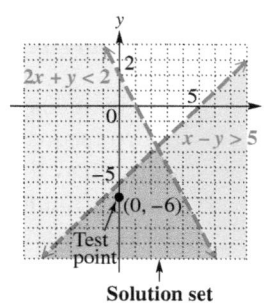

Figure 14

◄ Work Problem **2** at the Side.

EXAMPLE 3 Solving a System of Three Linear Inequalities

Graph the solution set of the system.

$$4x - 3y \leq 8$$
$$x \geq 2$$
$$y \leq 4$$

Graph the solid boundary line $4x - 3y = 8$ through the intercepts $(2, 0)$ and $\left(0, -\frac{8}{3}\right)$. (Because the y-intercept does not have integer coordinates, we also use the point $(-1, -4)$ to help draw an accurate line.) Recall that $x = 2$ is a vertical line through the point $(2, 0)$, and $y = 4$ is a horizontal line through the point $(0, 4)$. Use $(0, 0)$ as a test point to determine the region to shade for each inequality.

The graph of the solution set is the shaded region in **Figure 15,** including all boundary lines. (Here, use $(3, 2)$ as a test point to confirm that the correct region is shaded.)

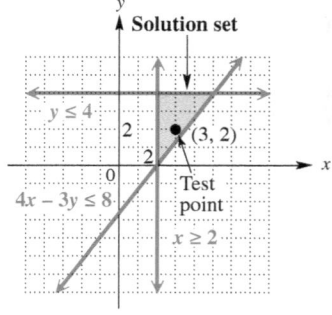

Figure 15

◄ Work Problem **3** at the Side.

4.5 Exercises

FOR EXTRA HELP Go to MyMathLab for worked-out, step-by-step solutions to exercises enclosed in a square 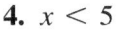 and video solutions to ▶ exercises.

CONCEPT CHECK *Match each system of inequalities with the correct graph from choices A–D.*

1. $x \geq 5$
  $y \leq -3$

2. $x \leq 5$
  $y \geq -3$

3. $x > 5$
  $y < -3$

4. $x < 5$
  $y > -3$

A. **B.** **C.** **D.**

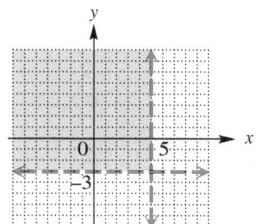

CONCEPT CHECK *Decide whether each ordered pair is a solution of the given system of inequalities. Then shade the solution set of each system. Boundary lines are already graphed.*

5. $x - 3y \leq 6$
  $x \geq -4$
  (a) $(5, -4)$ **(b)** $(0, 0)$

6. $x - 2y \geq 4$
  $x \leq -2$
  (a) $(0, 0)$ **(b)** $(-4, -5)$

7. $x + y > 4$
  $5x - 3y < 15$
  (a) $(3, 3)$ **(b)** $(5, 0)$

8. $3x - 2y > 12$
  $4x + 3y < 12$
  (a) $(3, -3)$ **(b)** $(6, 0)$

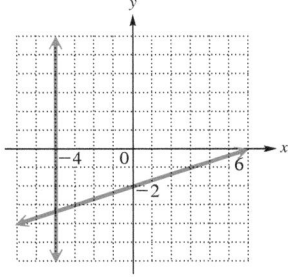 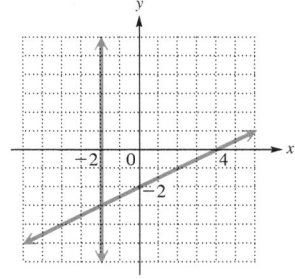 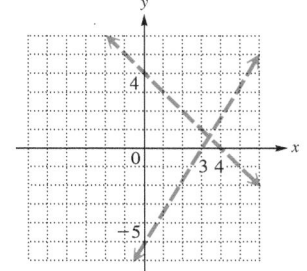 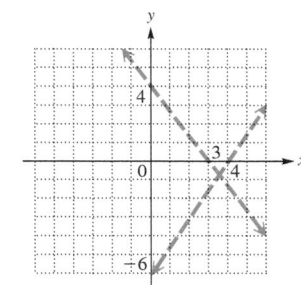

Graph the solution set of each system of linear inequalities. ***See Examples 1–3.***

9. $x + y \leq 6$
  $x - y \geq 1$

10. $x + y \leq 2$
  $x - y \geq 3$

11. $4x + 5y \geq 20$
  $x - 2y \leq 5$

12. $x + 4y \leq 8$
  $2x - y \geq 4$

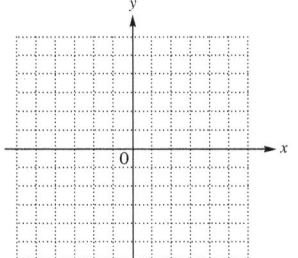 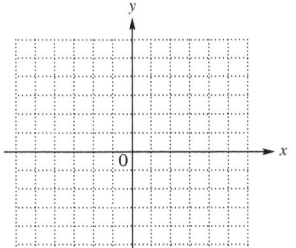 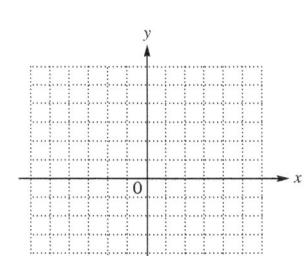 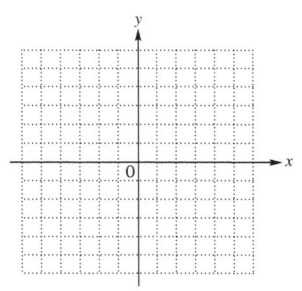

13. $2x + 3y < 6$

$\quad x - \ y < 5$

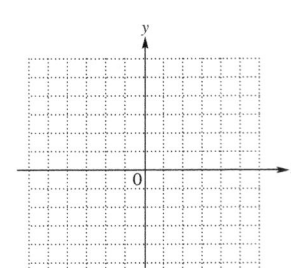

14. $x + 2y < 4$

$\quad x - \ y < -1$

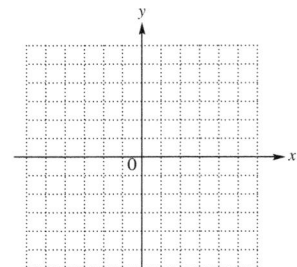

15. $y \le 2x - 5$

$\quad x < 3y + 2$

16. $x \ge 2y + 6$

$\quad y > -2x + 4$

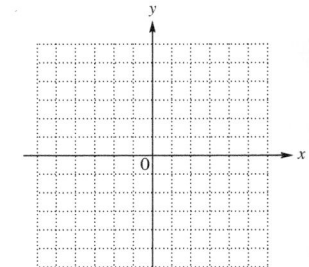

17. $4x + 3y < 6$

$\quad x - 2y > 4$

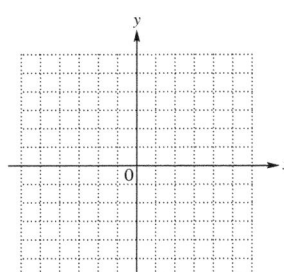

18. $3x + \ y > 4$

$\quad x + 2y < 2$

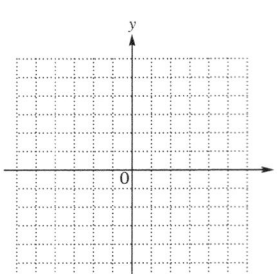

19. $x \le 2y + 3$

$\quad x + y < 0$

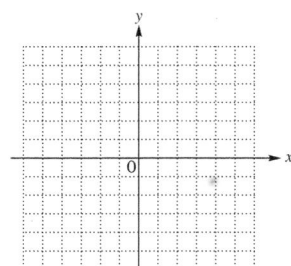

20. $x \le 4y + 3$

$\quad x + y > 0$

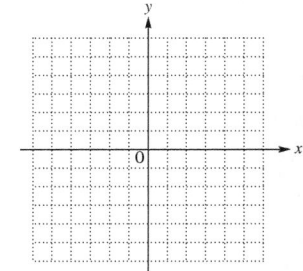

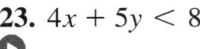

21. $x - 3y \le 6$

$\quad x \ge -5$

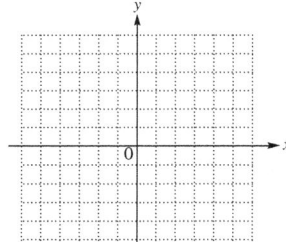

22. $x - 2y \ge 2$

$\quad x \le -3$

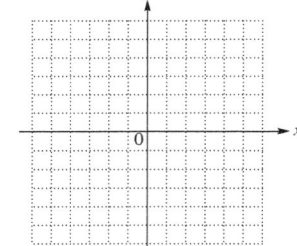

23. $4x + 5y < 8$

$\quad\quad y > -2$

$\quad\quad x > -4$

24. $x - 2y \ge -2$

$\quad\quad y \ge -2$

$\quad\quad x \le 3$

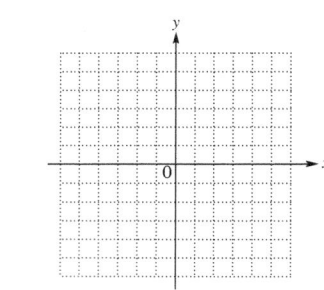

25. $x + y \ge -3$

$\quad x - y \le 3$

$\quad\quad y \le 3$

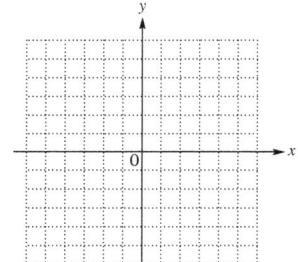

26. $x + y < 4$

$\quad x - y > -4$

$\quad\quad y > -1$

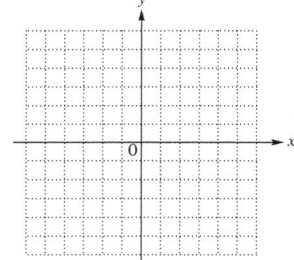

27. $3x - 2y \ge 6$

$\quad x + \ y \le 4$

$\quad\quad x \ge 0$

$\quad\quad y \ge -4$

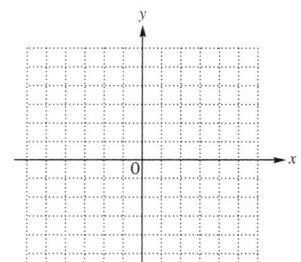

28. $2x - 3y < 6$

$\quad x + \ y > 3$

$\quad\quad x < 4$

$\quad\quad y < 4$

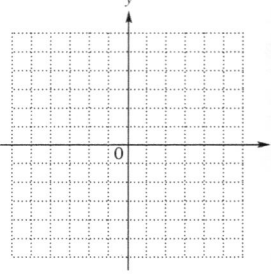

Chapter 4 Summary

Key Terms

4.1

system of linear equations A system of linear equations (or **linear system**) consists of two or more linear equations with the same variables.

solution of a system A solution of a system of linear equations is an ordered pair that makes all the equations of the system true at the same time.

solution set of a system The set of all ordered pairs that are solutions of a system is its solution set.

consistent system A system of equations with at least one solution is a consistent system.

inconsistent system An inconsistent system is a system of equations with no solution.

independent equations Equations of a system that have different graphs are independent equations.

dependent equations Equations of a system that have the same graph (because they are different forms of the same equation) are dependent equations.

4.5

system of linear inequalities A system of linear inequalities consists of two or more linear inequalities.

solution set of a system of linear inequalities The solution set of a system of linear inequalities includes all ordered pairs that make all inequalities of the system true at the same time.

Test Your Word Power

See how well you have learned the vocabulary in this chapter.

1 A **system of linear equations** consists of
  A. at least two linear equations with different variables
  B. two or more linear equations that have an infinite number of solutions
  C. two or more linear equations with the same variables
  D. two or more linear inequalities.

2 A **solution of a system** of linear equations is
  A. an ordered pair that makes one equation of the system true

  B. an ordered pair that makes all the equations of the system true at the same time
  C. any ordered pair that makes one or the other or both equations of the system true
  D. the set of values that make all the equations of the system false.

3 A **consistent system** is a system of equations
  A. with at least one solution
  B. with no solution
  C. with graphs that do not intersect
  D. with solution set $\varnothing$.

4 An **inconsistent system** is a system of equations
  A. with one solution
  B. with no solution
  C. with an infinite number of solutions
  D. that have the same graph.

5 **Dependent equations**
  A. have different graphs
  B. have no solution
  C. have one solution
  D. are different forms of the same equation.

Answers to Test Your Word Power

1. C; *Example:* $2x + y = 7$
$\qquad\qquad\quad 3x - y = 3$

2. B; *Example:* The ordered pair $(2, 3)$ satisfies both equations of the system in the Answer 1 example, so it is a solution of the system.

3. A; *Example:* The system in the Answer 1 example is consistent. The graphs of the equations intersect at exactly one point, in this case the solution $(2, 3)$.

4. B; *Example:* The equations of two parallel lines make up an inconsistent system. Their graphs never intersect, so there is no solution of the system.

5. D; *Example:* The equations $4x - y = 8$ and $8x - 2y = 16$ are dependent because their graphs are the same line. Multiplying the first equation by 2 gives a form that is equivalent to the second equation.

Quick Review

Concepts	**Examples**

4.1 Solving Systems of Linear Equations by Graphing

An ordered pair is a solution of a system if it makes all equations of the system true at the same time.

Is $(4, -1)$ a solution of the system $\begin{array}{l} x + y = 3 \\ 2x - y = 9 \end{array}$?

Because $4 + (-1) = 3$ and $2(4) - (-1) = 9$ are both true, $(4, -1)$ is a solution.

To solve a linear system by graphing, follow these steps.

Step 1 Graph each equation of the system on the same axes.

Step 2 Find the coordinates of the point of intersection.

Step 3 Check. Write the solution set.

Solve the system by graphing.
$$x + y = 5$$
$$2x - y = 4$$

The ordered pair $(3, 2)$ satisfies *both* equations, so $\{(3, 2)\}$ is the solution set.

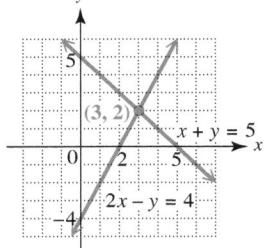

If the graphs of the equations do not intersect (that is, the lines are parallel), then the system has *no solution* and the solution set is $\varnothing$.

If the graphs of the equations are the same line, then the system has an *infinite number of solutions*. Use set-builder notation to write the solution set as
$$\{(x, y) \mid \underline{\hspace{1.5cm}}\},$$
where a form of the equation is written on the blank.

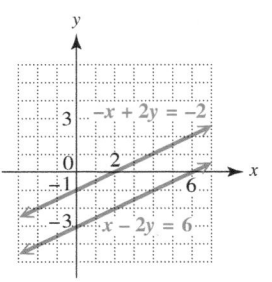

Solution set: $\varnothing$

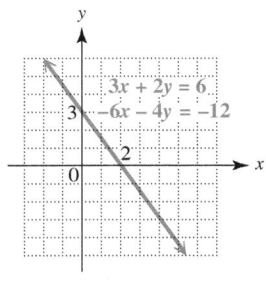

Solution set:
$\{(x, y) \mid 3x + 2y = 6\}$

4.2 Solving Systems of Linear Equations by Substitution

Step 1 Solve one equation for either variable.

Step 2 Substitute for that variable in the other equation to obtain an equation in one variable.

Step 3 Solve the equation from Step 2.

Step 4 Find the other value by substituting the result from Step 3 into the equation from Step 1 and solving for the remaining variable.

Step 5 Check. Write the solution set.

Solve the system by substitution.
$$x + 2y = -5 \quad (1)$$
$$y = -2x - 1 \quad (2)$$

Equation (2) is already solved for y.

Substitute $-2x - 1$ for y in equation (1).

$$\begin{align} x + 2y &= -5 \quad (1) \\ x + 2(-2x - 1) &= -5 \quad \text{Let } y = -2x - 1. \\ x - 4x - 2 &= -5 \quad \text{Distributive property} \\ -3x - 2 &= -5 \quad \text{Combine like terms.} \\ -3x &= -3 \quad \text{Add 2.} \\ x &= 1 \quad \text{Divide by } -3. \end{align}$$

To find y, let $x = 1$ in equation (2).
$$\begin{align} y &= -2x - 1 \quad (2) \\ y &= -2(1) - 1 \quad \text{Let } x = 1. \\ y &= -3 \quad \text{Multiply, and then subtract.} \end{align}$$

A check confirms that $\{(1, -3)\}$ is the solution set.

| **Concepts** | **Examples** |

4.3 Solving Systems of Linear Equations by Elimination

Step 1 Write both equations in standard form $Ax + By = C$.

Step 2 Multiply to transform the equations so that the coefficients of one pair of variable terms are opposites.

Step 3 Add the equations to *eliminate* a variable.

Step 4 Solve the equation from Step 3.

Step 5 Find the other value by substituting the result from Step 4 into either of the original equations and solving for the remaining variable.

Step 6 Check. Write the solution set.

Solve the system by elimination.

$$x + 3y = 7 \quad (1)$$
$$3x - y = 1 \quad (2)$$

Multiply equation (1) by -3 to eliminate the x-terms.

$$\begin{aligned} -3x - 9y &= -21 \quad \text{Multiply equation (1) by } -3. \\ \underline{3x - y = \quad 1} \quad &(2) \\ -10y &= -20 \quad \text{Add.} \\ y &= 2 \quad \text{Divide by } -10. \end{aligned}$$

Substitute to find the value of x.

$$\begin{aligned} x + 3y &= 7 \quad (1) \\ x + 3(2) &= 7 \quad \text{Let } y = 2. \\ x + 6 &= 7 \quad \text{Multiply.} \\ x &= 1 \quad \text{Subtract 6.} \end{aligned}$$

Because $1 + 3(2) = 7$ and $3(1) - 2 = 1$, the solution $(1, 2)$ checks. The solution set is $\{(1, 2)\}$.

4.4 Applications of Linear Systems

Use the modified six-step method.

Step 1 Read the problem carefully.

Step 2 Assign variables to represent the unknown values. Make a sketch, diagram, or table, as needed.

Step 3 Write two equations using both variables.

Step 4 Solve the system of two equations.

Step 5 State the answer.

Step 6 Check the answer in the words of the *original* problem.

The sum of two numbers is 30. Their difference is 6. Find the numbers.

Let x = one number, and let y = the other number.

$$\begin{aligned} x + y &= 30 \quad (1) \\ \underline{x - y = \quad 6} \quad &(2) \\ 2x &= 36 \quad \text{Add.} \\ x &= 18 \quad \text{Divide by 2.} \end{aligned}$$

Let $x = 18$ in equation (1), $x + y = 30$.

$$\begin{aligned} 18 + y &= 30 \quad \text{Let } x = 18. \\ y &= 12 \quad \text{Subtract 18.} \end{aligned}$$

The two numbers are 18 and 12.

The sum of 18 and 12 is 30, and the difference of 18 and 12 is 6, so the answer checks.

4.5 Solving Systems of Linear Inequalities

To solve a system of linear inequalities, follow these steps.

Step 1 Graph each inequality on the same axes.

Step 2 Choose the intersection. The solution set of the system is formed by the overlap of the regions of the two graphs.

Graph the solution set of the system.

$$2x + 4y \geq 5$$
$$x \geq 1$$

First graph the solid boundary lines $2x + 4y = 5$ and $x = 1$. Then use a test point, such as $(0, 0)$, to determine the region to shade for each inequality. The intersection, the gray shaded region, is the solution set of the system.

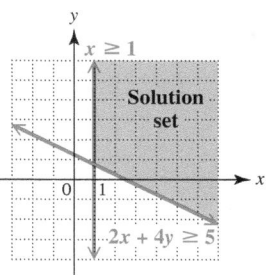

Chapter 4 *Review Exercises*

4.1 *Determine whether the given ordered pair is a solution of the given system.*

1. $\begin{array}{l} 4x - 2y = 4 \\ 5x + \ y = 19 \end{array}$; $(3, 4)$

2. $\begin{array}{l} x - 4y = -13 \\ 2x + 3y = 4 \end{array}$; $(-5, 2)$

Solve each system by graphing.

3. $\begin{array}{l} x + y = 4 \\ 2x - y = 5 \end{array}$

4. $\begin{array}{l} x - 2y = 4 \\ 2x + \ y = -2 \end{array}$

5. $\begin{array}{l} x - 2 \ = 2y \\ 2x - 4y = 4 \end{array}$

6. $\begin{array}{l} 2x + 4 = 2y \\ y - x = -3 \end{array}$

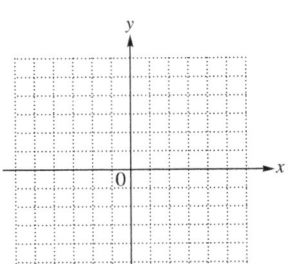
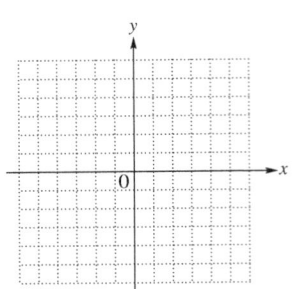
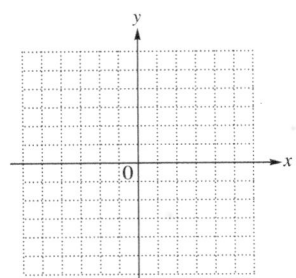
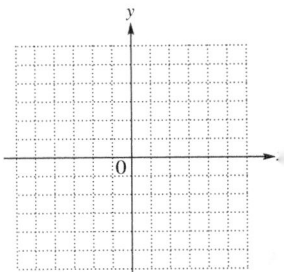

4.2 *Solve each system by the substitution method.*

7. $\begin{array}{l} 3x + y = 7 \\ x = 2y \end{array}$

8. $\begin{array}{l} 2x - 5y = -19 \\ y = x + 2 \end{array}$

9. $\begin{array}{l} 4x + 5y = 44 \\ x + 2 \ = 2y \end{array}$

10. $\begin{array}{l} 5x + 15y = 3 \\ x + \ 3y = 2 \end{array}$

4.3 *Solve each system by the elimination method.*

11. $\begin{array}{l} 2x - y = 13 \\ x + y = 8 \end{array}$

12. $\begin{array}{l} 3x - \ y = -13 \\ x - 2y = -1 \end{array}$

13. $\begin{array}{l} -4x + 3y = 25 \\ 6x - 5y = -39 \end{array}$

14. $\begin{array}{l} 3x - 4y = 9 \\ 6x - 8y = 18 \end{array}$

4.1–4.3 *Solve each system by any method.*

15. $\begin{array}{l} x - 2y = 5 \\ y = x - 7 \end{array}$

16. $\begin{array}{l} 5x - 3y = 11 \\ 2y = x - 4 \end{array}$

17. $\begin{array}{l} 5x - 4y = 0 \\ -3x + 2y = 0 \end{array}$

18. $\begin{array}{l} 6y = 10x - 15 \\ 14x - \ 8y = 21 \end{array}$

19. $\begin{array}{l} \dfrac{x}{2} + \dfrac{y}{3} = 7 \\[2mm] \dfrac{x}{4} + \dfrac{2y}{3} = 8 \end{array}$

20. $\begin{array}{l} \dfrac{3x}{4} - \dfrac{y}{3} = \dfrac{7}{6} \\[2mm] \dfrac{x}{2} + \dfrac{2y}{3} = \dfrac{5}{3} \end{array}$

21. $\begin{array}{l} 0.2x + 1.2y = -1 \\ 0.1x + 0.3y = 0.1 \end{array}$

22. $\begin{array}{l} 0.1x + \ \ y = 1.6 \\ 0.6x + 0.5y = -1.4 \end{array}$

4.4 *For each problem, complete any tables. Then solve the problem using a system of equations.*

23. The two leading pizza chains in the United States are Pizza Hut and Domino's. In 2015, Pizza Hut had 3976 more locations than Domino's, and together the two chains had 27,234 locations. How many locations did each chain have? (Data from www.pizzatoday.com)

24. Together, the average paid circulation for *Reader's Digest* and *People* magazines in 2014 was 6.2 million. The circulation for *People* was 0.8 million more than that of *Reader's Digest*. What were the circulation figures for each magazine? (Data from Audit Bureau of Circulations.)

25. Candy that sells for $1.30 per lb is to be mixed with candy selling for $0.90 per lb to make 100 lb of a mix that will sell for $1 per lb. How much of each type candy should be used?

Number of Pounds	Cost per Pound (in dollars)	Total Value (in dollars)
_____	1.30	$1.30x$
y	_____	_____
100	1.00	_____

26. A cashier has 20 bills, all of which are $10 or $20 bills. The total value of the money is $330. How many of each type of bill does the cashier have?

Number of Bills	Denomination of Bills (in dollars)	Total Value (in dollars)
x	10	_____
_____	_____	$20y$
_____	XXXXXXXXX	330

27. The perimeter of a rectangle is 90 m. Its length is $1\frac{1}{2}$ times its width. Find the length and width of the rectangle.

28. A certain plane flying with the wind travels 540 mi in 2 hr. Later, flying against the same wind, the plane travels 690 mi in 3 hr. Find the rate of the plane in still air and the wind speed.

29. After taxes, Ms. Cesar's game show winnings were $18,000. She invested part of it at 3% annual simple interest and the rest at 4%. Her interest income for the first year was $650. How much did she invest at each rate?

Amount Invested (in dollars)	Percent (as a decimal)	Interest (in dollars)
x	0.03	_____
y	_____	_____
18,000	XXXXXXX	_____

30. A 40% antifreeze solution is to be mixed with a 70% solution to make 90 L of a 50% solution. How many liters of the 40% and 70% solutions will be needed?

Number of Liters	Percent (as a decimal)	Amount of Pure Antifreeze
x	0.40	_____
y	_____	_____
90	0.50	_____

Graph the solution set of each system of linear inequalities.

31. $x + y \geq 2$
$x - y \leq 4$

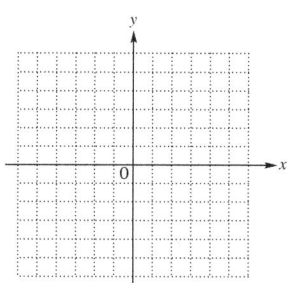

32. $y \geq 2x$
$2x + 3y \leq 6$

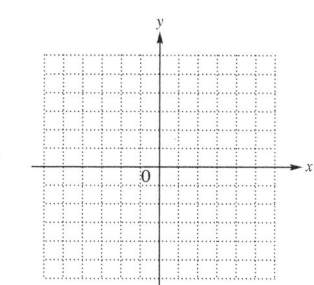

33. $x + y < 3$
$2x > y$

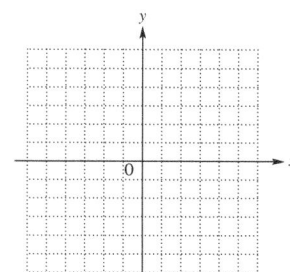

34. $y < -4x$
$y < -2$

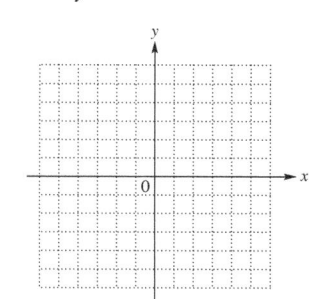

Chapter 4 *Mixed Review Exercises*

Solve.

1. $3x + 4y = 6$
$4x - 5y = 8$

2. $\dfrac{3x}{2} + \dfrac{y}{5} = -3$

$4x + \dfrac{y}{3} = -11$

3. $x + 6y = 3$
$2x + 12y = 2$

4. $x + y < 5$
$x - y \geq 2$

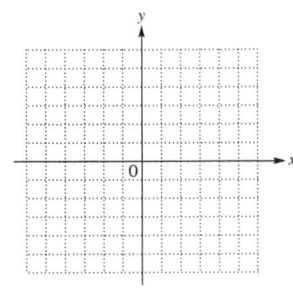

5. $y \leq 2x$
$x + 2y > 4$

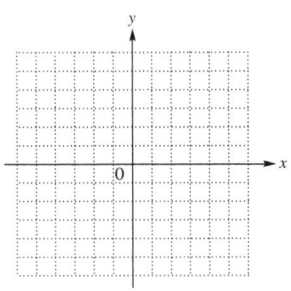

6. The perimeter of an isosceles triangle is 29 in. One side of the triangle is 5 in. longer than each of the two equal sides. Find the lengths of the sides of the triangle.

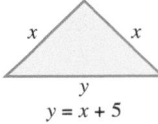

$y = x + 5$

7. In Super Bowl 50, the Denver Broncos beat the Carolina Panthers by 14 points, and the winning score was 4 points more than twice the losing score. What was the final score of the game? (Data from NFL.)

8. Eboni compared the monthly payments she would incur for two types of mortgages: fixed-rate and variable-rate. Her observations led to the graph shown.

  (a) For which years would the monthly payment be more for the fixed-rate mortgage than for the variable-rate mortgage?

  (b) In what year would the payments be the same, and what would those payments be?

Mortgage Shopping

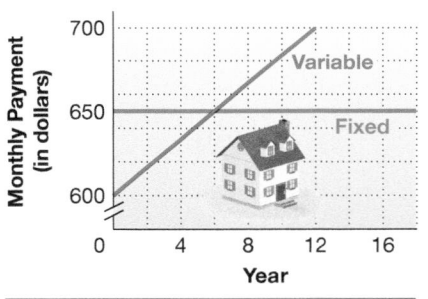

CONCEPT CHECK *Answer each question.*

9. Which system of linear inequalities is graphed in the figure?

  A. $x \leq 3$
      $y \leq 1$

  B. $x \leq 3$
      $y \geq 1$

  C. $x \geq 3$
      $y \leq 1$

  D. $x \geq 3$
      $y \geq 1$

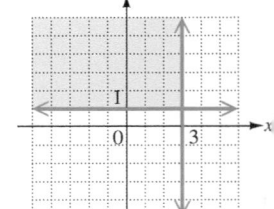

10. Which system of linear inequalities has no solution? (Do not graph.)

  A. $x \geq 4$
      $y \leq 3$

  B. $x + y > 4$
      $x + y < 3$

  C. $x > 2$
      $y < 1$

  D. $x + y < 4$
      $x - y < 3$

1. Decide whether each ordered pair is a solution of the system.

$$2x + y = -3$$
$$x - y = -9$$

(a) $(1, -5)$ (b) $(1, 10)$ (c) $(-4, 5)$

2. Solve the system by graphing.

$$2x + y = 1$$
$$3x - y = 9$$

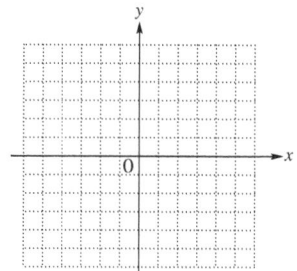

3. Suppose that the graph of a system of two linear equations consists of lines
that have the same slope but different *y*-intercepts. How many solutions does
the system have?

Solve each system by the substitution method.

4. $2x + y = -4$
    $x = y + 7$

5. $4x + 3y = -35$
    $x + y = 0$

6. $y = 6x - 8$
    $y = -3x - 11$

Solve each system by the elimination method.

7. $2x - y = 4$
    $3x + y = 21$

8. $4x + 2y = 2$
    $5x + 4y = 7$

9. $3x + 4y = 9$
    $2x + 5y = 13$

10. $6x - 5y = 0$
    $-2x + 3y = 0$

11. $4x + 5y = 2$
    $-8x - 10y = 6$

12. $-2x + 5y = 14$
    $7x + 6y = -2$

Solve each system by any method.

13. $3x = 6 + y$

$\quad 6x - 2y = 12$

14. $\quad \dfrac{6}{5}x - \dfrac{1}{3}y = -20$

$\quad\quad -\dfrac{2}{3}x + \dfrac{1}{6}y = 11$

Solve each problem.

15. The distance between Memphis and Atlanta is 782 mi less than the distance between Minneapolis and Houston. Together, the two distances total 1570 mi. How far is it between Memphis and Atlanta? How far is it between Minneapolis and Houston? (Data from *Rand McNally Road Atlas.*)

16. In 2015, a total of 6.7 million people visited the Statue of Liberty and the Mount Rushmore National Memorial. The Statue of Liberty had 1.9 million more visitors than the Mount Rushmore National Memorial. How many visitors did each of these attractions have? (Data from National Park Service, Department of the Interior.)

17. A 15% solution of alcohol is to be mixed with a 40% solution to make 50 L of a final mixture that is 30% alcohol. How much of each of the original solutions should be used?

Liters of Solution	Percent (as a decimal)	Liters of Pure Alcohol

18. Two cars leave from Perham, Minnesota, and travel in the same direction. One car travels $1\frac{1}{3}$ times as fast as the other. After 3 hr they are 45 mi apart. What are the rates of the cars?

	r	*t*	*d*
Faster Car			
Slower Car			

Graph the solution set of each system of linear inequalities.

19. $2x + 7y \leq 14$

$\quad x - y \geq 1$

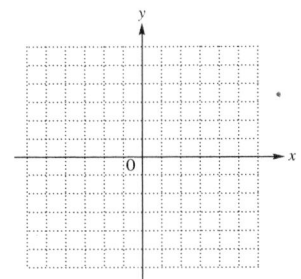

20. $2x - y > 6$

$\quad 4y + 12 \geq -3x$

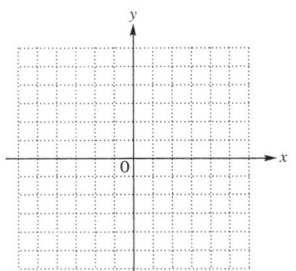

Chapters R-4 Cumulative Review Exercises

1. List all integer factors of 40.

2. Find the value of the expression for $x = 1$ and $y = 5$.

$$\frac{3x^2 + 2y^2}{10y + 3}$$

Name the property that justifies each statement.

3. $5 + (-4) = (-4) + 5$

4. $r(s - k) = rs - rk$

5. $-\frac{2}{3} + \frac{2}{3} = 0$

6. Evaluate $-2 + 6[3 - (4 - 9)]$.

7. Solve the formula $P = \frac{kT}{V}$ for T.

Solve each linear equation.

8. $2 - 3(6x + 2) = 4(x + 1) + 18$

9. $\frac{3}{2}\left(\frac{1}{3}x + 4\right) = 6\left(\frac{1}{4} + x\right)$

Solve each linear inequality. Write the solution set in interval notation.

10. $-\frac{5}{6}x < 15$

11. $-8 < 2x + 3$

12. The iPad Pro tablet computer has a perimeter of 41.4 in., and its width is 3.3 in. less than its length. What are its dimensions? (Data from www.apple.com)

Graph each linear equation.

13. $x - y = 4$

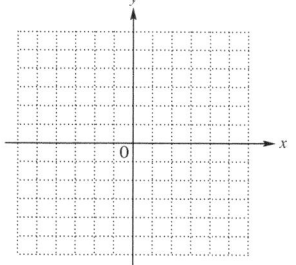

14. $3x + y = 6$

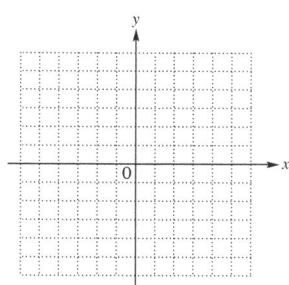

Find the slope of each line.

15. Through $(-5, 6)$ and $(1, -2)$

16. Perpendicular to the line $y = 4x - 3$

Write an equation in slope-intercept form for each line.

17. Through $(-4, 1)$ with slope $\frac{1}{2}$

18. Through the points $(1, 3)$ and $(-2, -3)$

19. Write an equation for each line described.

    (a) Vertical, through $(9, -2)$

    (b) Horizontal, through $(4, -1)$

Solve each system by any method.

20. $2x - y = -8$
$\ x + 2y = 11$

21. $4x + 5y = -8$
$\ 3x + 4y = -7$

22. $3x + 4y = 2$
$\ 6x + 8y = 1$

Solve each problem using a system of equations.

23. Admission prices at a high school football game were $6 for adults and $2 for children. The total value of the tickets sold was $2528, and 454 tickets were sold. How many adults and how many children attended the game?

Kind of Ticket	Number Sold	Cost of Each (in dollars)	Total Value (in dollars)
Adult	x	6	$6x$
Child	y	_____	_____
Total	454	XXXX	_____

24. The perimeter of a triangle is 53 in. If two sides are of equal length, and the third side measures 4 in. less than each of the equal sides, what are the lengths of the three sides?

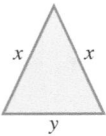

25. Graph the solution set of the system.

$$x + 2y \leq 12$$
$$2x - y \leq 8$$

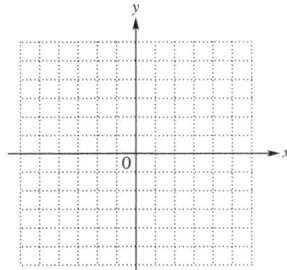

5

Exponents and Polynomials

Exponents and *scientific notation,* two of the topics of this chapter, are often used to express very large or very small numbers. Using this notation, one light-year, which is about 6 trillion miles, is written

$$6 \times 10^{12}.$$

5.1 The Product Rule and Power Rules for Exponents

5.2 Integer Exponents and the Quotient Rule

Summary Exercises *Applying the Rules for Exponents*

5.3 An Application of Exponents: Scientific Notation

5.4 Adding and Subtracting Polynomials

5.5 Multiplying Polynomials

5.6 Special Products

5.7 Dividing a Polynomial by a Monomial

5.8 Dividing a Polynomial by a Polynomial

5.1 | The Product Rule and Power Rules for Exponents

OBJECTIVES

1. Use exponents.
2. Use the product rule for exponents.
3. Use the rule $(a^m)^n = a^{mn}$.
4. Use the rule $(ab)^m = a^m b^m$.
5. Use the rule $\left(\dfrac{a}{b}\right)^m = \dfrac{a^m}{b^m}$.
6. Use combinations of the rules for exponents.
7. Use the rules for exponents in a geometry problem.

OBJECTIVE ▶ 1 **Use exponents.** Recall that we can use exponents to write repeated products. In the expression 5^2, the number 5 is the **base** and 2 is the **exponent,** or **power.** The expression 5^2 is an **exponential expression.** Although we do not usually write the exponent when it is 1, in general,

$$a^1 = a, \quad \text{for any quantity } a.$$

EXAMPLE 1 Using Exponents

Write $3 \cdot 3 \cdot 3 \cdot 3 \cdot 3$ in exponential form and evaluate.

Since 3 occurs as a factor five times, the base is **3** and the exponent is **5.** The exponential expression is 3^5, read "3 *to the fifth power,*" or simply "3 *to the fifth.*"

$$\underbrace{3 \cdot 3 \cdot 3 \cdot 3 \cdot 3}_{5 \text{ factors of } 3} \quad \text{means} \quad 3^5, \quad \text{which equals} \quad 243.$$

◀ **Work Problem ➊ at the Side.**

➊ Write each product in exponential form and evaluate.

(a) $2 \cdot 2 \cdot 2 \cdot 2$

(b) $(-3)(-3)(-3)$

EXAMPLE 2 Evaluating Exponential Expressions

Identify the base and the exponent of each expression. Then evaluate.

Expression	Base	Exponent	Value
(a) 5^4	5	4	$5 \cdot 5 \cdot 5 \cdot 5,$ which equals 625
(b) -5^4	5	4	$-1 \cdot (5 \cdot 5 \cdot 5 \cdot 5),$ which equals -625
(c) $(-5)^4$	-5	4	$(-5)(-5)(-5)(-5),$ which equals 625

◀ **Work Problem ➋ at the Side.**

➋ Identify the base and the exponent of each expression. Then evaluate.

(a) 2^5　　(b) -2^5

(c) $(-2)^5$　　(d) 4^2

(e) -4^2　　(f) $(-4)^2$

! CAUTION

Compare **Examples 2(b) and 2(c).** In -5^4, the absence of parentheses means that the exponent 4 applies only to the base 5, not -5. In $(-5)^4$, the parentheses mean that the exponent 4 applies to the base -5.
In summary, $-a^n$ and $(-a)^n$ are not necessarily the same.

Expression	Base	Exponent	Example
$-a^n$	a	n	$-3^2 = -(3 \cdot 3) = -9$
$(-a)^n$	$-a$	n	$(-3)^2 = (-3)(-3) = 9$

OBJECTIVE ▶ 2 **Use the product rule for exponents.** To develop the product rule, we use the definition of an exponent. Consider the following.

$$2^4 \cdot 2^3$$

$$= \underbrace{(2 \cdot 2 \cdot 2 \cdot 2)}_{4 \text{ factors}} \underbrace{(2 \cdot 2 \cdot 2)}_{3 \text{ factors}}$$

$$= \underbrace{2 \cdot 2 \cdot 2 \cdot 2 \cdot 2 \cdot 2 \cdot 2}_{4 + 3 = 7 \text{ factors}}$$

$$= 2^7$$

Answers

1. (a) 2^4; 16　(b) $(-3)^3$; -27
2. (a) 2; 5; 32　(b) 2; 5; -32
　(c) -2; 5; -32　(d) 4; 2; 16
　(e) 4; 2; -16　(f) -4; 2; 16

Also, consider that

$$6^2 \cdot 6^3$$
$$= (6 \cdot 6)(6 \cdot 6 \cdot 6)$$
$$= 6 \cdot 6 \cdot 6 \cdot 6 \cdot 6$$
$$= 6^5.$$

Generalizing from these examples, we have the following.

$2^4 \cdot 2^3$ is equal to 2^{4+3}, which equals 2^7.
$6^2 \cdot 6^3$ is equal to 6^{2+3}, which equals 6^5.

In each case, adding the exponents gives the exponent of the product, suggesting the **product rule for exponents.**

Product Rule for Exponents

For any positive integers m and n, $\quad a^m \cdot a^n = a^{m+n}$.
(Keep the same base and add the exponents.)

Example: $6^2 \cdot 6^5 = 6^{2+5} = 6^7$

❗ CAUTION
When using the product rule, keep the same base and add the exponents.
Do *not* multiply the bases.

$$6^2 \cdot 6^5 \text{ is equal to } 6^7, \textbf{ not } 36^7.$$

EXAMPLE 3 Using the Product Rule

Use the product rule for exponents to simplify each expression, if possible.

(a) $6^3 \cdot 6^5$
$= 6^{3+5}$ Product rule
$= 6^8$ Add the exponents.

(b) $(-4)^7(-4)^2$
$= (-4)^{7+2}$ Product rule
$= (-4)^9$ Add the exponents.

(c) $x^2 \cdot x$
$= x^2 \cdot x^1$ $a = a^1$, for all a.
$= x^{2+1}$ Product rule
$= x^3$ Add the exponents.

(d) $m^4 m^3 m^5$
$= m^{4+3+5}$ Product rule
$= m^{12}$ Add the exponents.

(e) $2^3 \cdot 3^2$ Think: 3^2 means $3 \cdot 3$. **The bases are different.**
Think: 2^3 means $2 \cdot 2 \cdot 2$.
$= 8 \cdot 9$ Evaluate 2^3 and 3^2.
$= 72$ Multiply.
The product rule does not apply.

(f) $2^3 + 2^4$ **This is a sum, not a product.**
$= 8 + 16$ Evaluate 2^3 and 2^4.
$= 24$ Add.
The product rule does not apply.

Work Problem ❸ at the Side. ▶

---

❸ Use the product rule for exponents to simplify each expression, if possible.

(a) $8^2 \cdot 8^5$
$= 8^{—+—}$
$= \underline{\quad}$

(b) $(-7)^5(-7)^3$

(c) $y^3 \cdot y$
$= y^3 \cdot y—$
$= y^{—+—}$
$= \underline{\quad}$

(d) $z^2 z^5 z^6$

(e) $4^2 \cdot 3^5$

(f) $6^4 + 6^2$

Answers
3. **(a)** 2; 5; 8^7 **(b)** $(-7)^8$
(c) 1; 3; 1; y^4 **(d)** z^{13}
(e) The product rule does not apply.
(The product is 3888.)
(f) The product rule does not apply.
(The sum is 1332.)

4 Multiply.

(a) $5m^2 \cdot 2m^6$

$= (5 \cdot \underline{\quad}) \cdot (m\text{—} \cdot m\text{—})$

$= \underline{\quad} m\text{—}^{+}\text{—}$

$= \underline{\quad}$

(b) $3p^5 \cdot 9p^4$

(c) $-7p^5(3p^8)$

5 Use power rule (a) for exponents to simplify each expression.

(a) $(5^3)^4$

$= 5\text{—} \cdot \text{—}$

$= \underline{\quad}$

(b) $(6^2)^5$

(c) $(a^6)^5$

Answers

4. (a) 2; 2; 6; 10; 2; 6; $10m^8$
(b) $27p^9$ (c) $-21p^{13}$
5. (a) 3; 4; 5^{12} (b) 6^{10} (c) a^{30}

EXAMPLE 4 Using the Product Rule

Multiply $2x^3$ and $3x^7$.

$2x^3 \cdot 3x^7$ — $2x^3 = 2 \cdot x^3; 3x^7 = 3 \cdot x^7$

$= (2 \cdot 3) \cdot (x^3 \cdot x^7)$ Commutative and associative properties

$= 6x^{3+7}$ Multiply; product rule

$= 6x^{10}$ Add the exponents.

◀ **Work Problem 4 at the Side.**

⚠ CAUTION

Note the important difference between *adding* and *multiplying* exponential expressions.

$8x^3 + 5x^3$ means $(8+5)x^3$,   which equals $13x^3$.

$(8x^3)(5x^3)$ means $(8 \cdot 5)x^{3+3}$,   which equals $40x^6$.

OBJECTIVE 3 Use the rule $(a^m)^n = a^{mn}$. We can simplify an expression such as $(5^2)^4$ with the product rule for exponents, as follows.

$(5^2)^4$

$= 5^2 \cdot 5^2 \cdot 5^2 \cdot 5^2$ Definition of exponent

$= 5^{2+2+2+2}$ Product rule

$= 5^8$ Add.

Observe that $2 \cdot 4 = 8$. This example suggests **power rule (a) for exponents.**

Power Rule (a) for Exponents

For any positive integers m and n, $(a^m)^n = a^{mn}$.
(Raise a power to a power by multiplying exponents.)

Example: $(3^4)^2 = 3^{4 \cdot 2} = 3^8$

EXAMPLE 5 Using Power Rule (a)

Use power rule (a) for exponents to simplify each expression.

(a) $(2^5)^3$ **(b)** $(5^7)^2$ **(c)** $(x^2)^5$

$= 2^{5 \cdot 3}$ $= 5^{7 \cdot 2}$ $= x^{2 \cdot 5}$ Power rule (a)

$= 2^{15}$ $= 5^{14}$ $= x^{10}$ Multiply.

◀ **Work Problem 5 at the Side.**

OBJECTIVE 4 Use the rule $(ab)^m = a^m b^m$. Consider the following.

$(4x)^3$

$= (4x)(4x)(4x)$ Definition of exponent

$= 4 \cdot 4 \cdot 4 \cdot x \cdot x \cdot x$ Commutative and associative properties

$= 4^3 x^3$ Definition of exponent

The example $(4x)^3 = 4^3x^3$ suggests **power rule (b) for exponents.**

Power Rule (b) for Exponents

For any positive integer m, $(ab)^m = a^m b^m$.

(Raise a product to a power by raising each factor to the power.)

Example: $(2p)^5 = 2^5 p^5$

EXAMPLE 6 **Using Power Rule (b)**

Use power rule (b) for exponents to simplify each expression.

(a) $(3xy)^2$

$= 3^2 x^2 y^2$ Power rule (b)

$= 9x^2 y^2$ $3^2 = 3 \cdot 3 = 9$

(b) $3(xy)^2$

$= 3(x^2 y^2)$ Power rule (b)

$= 3x^2 y^2$ Multiply.

> Compare parts (a) and (b). Pay attention to the use of parentheses.

(c) $(2m^2 p^3)^4$

$= 2^4 (m^2)^4 (p^3)^4$ Power rule (b)

$= 2^4 m^8 p^{12}$ Power rule (a)

$= 16m^8 p^{12}$ $2^4 = 2 \cdot 2 \cdot 2 \cdot 2 = 16$

(d) $(-5^6)^3$

$= (-1 \cdot 5^6)^3$ $-a = -1 \cdot a$

$= (-1)^3 (5^6)^3$ Power rule (b)

> Raise -1 to the designated power.

$= -1 \cdot 5^{18}$ Power rule (a)

$= -5^{18}$ Multiply.

―――――――――――――――― **Work Problem 6 at the Side.** ▶

⚠ **CAUTION**

Power rule (b) does not apply to a sum.

$$(4x)^2 = 4^2 x^2, \quad but \quad (4 + x)^2 \ne 4^2 + x^2.$$

OBJECTIVE ▶ **5** **Use the rule** $\left(\frac{a}{b}\right)^m = \frac{a^m}{b^m}$. Because the quotient $\frac{a}{b}$ can be written as $a \cdot \frac{1}{b}$, we use this fact, power rule (b), and properties of real numbers to obtain **power rule (c) for exponents.**

Power Rule (c) for Exponents

For any positive integer m, $\left(\dfrac{a}{b}\right)^m = \dfrac{a^m}{b^m}$ **(where $b \ne 0$).**

(Raise a quotient to a power by raising both numerator and denominator to that power.)

Example: $\left(\dfrac{5}{3}\right)^2 = \dfrac{5^2}{3^2}$

---

6 Use power rule (b) for exponents to simplify each expression.

GS (a) $(2ab)^4$

$= 2{\rule{1cm}{0.4pt}}\, a {\rule{0.6cm}{0.4pt}}\, b {\rule{0.6cm}{0.4pt}}$

$= {\rule{1.5cm}{0.4pt}}$

(b) $5(mn)^3$

(c) $(3a^2 b^4)^5$

(d) $(-5m^2)^3$

7 Use power rule (c) for exponents to simplify each expression. Assume that all variables represent nonzero real numbers.

(a) $\left(\dfrac{5}{2}\right)^4$

$= \dfrac{5—}{2—}$

$= \underline{\quad}$

(b) $\left(\dfrac{1}{3}\right)^5$

(c) $\left(\dfrac{p}{q}\right)^2$

(d) $\left(\dfrac{r}{t}\right)^3$

(e) $\left(\dfrac{1}{x}\right)^{10}$

Answers

7. (a) $4; 4; \dfrac{625}{16}$ **(b)** $\dfrac{1}{243}$
(c) $\dfrac{p^2}{q^2}$ **(d)** $\dfrac{r^3}{t^3}$ **(e)** $\dfrac{1}{x^{10}}$

EXAMPLE 7 Using Power Rule (c)

Use power rule (c) for exponents to simplify each expression.

(a) $\left(\dfrac{2}{3}\right)^5$

$= \dfrac{2^5}{3^5}$ Power rule (c)

$= \dfrac{32}{243}$ Simplify.

(b) $\left(\dfrac{1}{5}\right)^4$

$= \dfrac{1^4}{5^4}$

$= \dfrac{1}{625}$

(c) $\left(\dfrac{m}{n}\right)^4$

$= \dfrac{m^4}{n^4}$

(where $n \neq 0$)

◀ **Work Problem 7 at the Side.**

Note

In **Example 7(b)**, we used the fact that $1^4 = 1$ because $1 \cdot 1 \cdot 1 \cdot 1 = 1$.

In general, $1^n = 1$, *for any integer n.*

Rules for Exponents

For positive integers m and n, the following hold true.

                                                  Examples

Product rule $a^m \cdot a^n = a^{m+n}$ $6^2 \cdot 6^5 = 6^{2+5} = 6^7$

Power rules (a) $(a^m)^n = a^{mn}$ $(3^4)^2 = 3^{4 \cdot 2} = 3^8$

         (b) $(ab)^m = a^m b^m$ $(2p)^5 = 2^5 p^5$

         (c) $\left(\dfrac{a}{b}\right)^m = \dfrac{a^m}{b^m}$ $(b \neq 0)$ $\left(\dfrac{5}{3}\right)^2 = \dfrac{5^2}{3^2}$

OBJECTIVE ▶ 6 Use combinations of the rules for exponents.

EXAMPLE 8 Using Combinations of the Rules

Simplify each expression.

(a) $\left(\dfrac{2}{3}\right)^2 \cdot 2^3$

$= \dfrac{2^2}{3^2} \cdot \dfrac{2^3}{1}$ Power rule (c)

$= \dfrac{2^2 \cdot 2^3}{3^2 \cdot 1}$ Multiply fractions.

$= \dfrac{2^{2+3}}{3^2}$ Product rule Multiply.

$= \dfrac{2^5}{3^2}$ Add.

$= \dfrac{32}{9}$ Apply the exponents.

(b) $(5x)^3 (5x)^4$

$= (5x)^7$ Product rule

$= 5^7 x^7$ Power rule (b)

An equally correct way to simplify this expression follows.

$(5x)^3 (5x)^4$ **Alternative solution**

$= 5^3 x^3 5^4 x^4$ Power rule (b)

$= 5^3 \cdot 5^4 \cdot x^3 x^4$ Commutative property

$= 5^{3+4} x^{3+4}$ Product rule

$= 5^7 x^7$ Add the exponents.

Continued on Next Page

(c) $(2x^2y^3)^4 (3xy^2)^3$

$= 2^4 (x^2)^4 (y^3)^4 \cdot 3^3 x^3 (y^2)^3$ Power rule (b)

$= 2^4 x^8 y^{12} \cdot 3^3 x^3 y^6$ Power rule (a)

$= 2^4 \cdot 3^3 \cdot x^8 x^3 y^{12} y^6$ Commutative and associative properties

$= 16 \cdot 27 \cdot x^{11} y^{18}$ Apply the exponents; product rule

$= 432 x^{11} y^{18}$ Multiply $16 \cdot 27$.

Notice that $(2x^2y^3)^4$ means $2^4 x^{2 \cdot 4} y^{3 \cdot 4}$, **not** $(2 \cdot 4) x^{2 \cdot 4} y^{3 \cdot 4}$.

(d) $(-x^3y)^2 (-x^5y^4)^3$

> **Think of the negative sign in each factor as -1.**

$= (-1x^3y)^2 \cdot (-1x^5y^4)^3$ $-a = -1 \cdot a$

$= (-1)^2 (x^3)^2 (y^2) \cdot (-1)^3 (x^5)^3 (y^4)^3$ Power rule (b)

$= (-1)^2 x^6 y^2 \cdot (-1)^3 x^{15} y^{12}$ Power rule (a)

$= (-1)^5 x^{21} y^{14}$ Product rule

$= -x^{21} y^{14}$ Simplify; $(-1)^5 = -1$

— **Work Problem 8 at the Side.** ▶

OBJECTIVE 7 Use the rules for exponents in a geometry problem.

EXAMPLE 9   Using Area Formulas

Find an expression that represents, in appropriate units, the area of each figure.

(a)

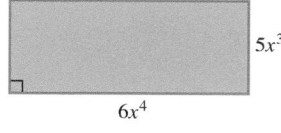

5x^3

6x^4

Figure 1

(b)

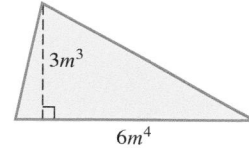

3m^3

6m^4

Figure 2

For **Figure 1,** use the formula for the area of a rectangle.

$\mathcal{A} = LW$ Area formula

$\mathcal{A} = (6x^4)(5x^3)$ Substitute.

$\mathcal{A} = 6 \cdot 5 \cdot x^{4+3}$ Commutative property; product rule

$\mathcal{A} = 30x^7$ Multiply. Add the exponents.

Figure 2 is a triangle with base $6m^4$ and height $3m^3$.

$\mathcal{A} = \dfrac{1}{2}bh$ Area formula

$\mathcal{A} = \dfrac{1}{2}(6m^4)(3m^3)$ Substitute.

$\mathcal{A} = \dfrac{1}{2}(6 \cdot 3 \cdot m^{4+3})$ Properties of real numbers; product rule

$\mathcal{A} = 9m^7$ Multiply. Add the exponents.

— **Work Problem 9 at the Side.** ▶

8 Simplify each expression.

GS (a) $(2m)^5 (2m)^3$

$= (2m)—$

$= \underline{}$

(b) $\left(\dfrac{5k^3}{3}\right)^2$

(c) $\left(\dfrac{1}{5}\right)^4 (2x)^2$

(d) $(-3xy^2)^3 (x^2y)^4$

9 Find an expression that represents, in appropriate units, the area of each figure.

(a)

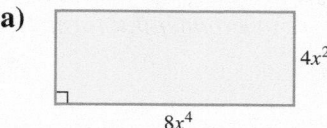

4x^2

8x^4

(b)

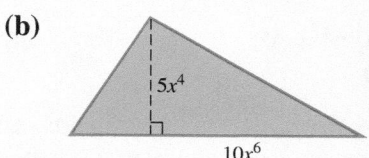

5x^4

10x^6

Answers

8. **(a)** 8; $2^8 m^8$, or $256m^8$

    (b) $\dfrac{25k^6}{9}$ **(c)** $\dfrac{4x^2}{625}$ **(d)** $-27x^{11}y^{10}$

9. **(a)** $32x^6$ **(b)** $25x^{10}$

5.1 Exercises

FOR EXTRA HELP

Go to MyMathLab *for worked-out, step-by-step solutions to exercises enclosed in a square* ☐ *and video solutions to* ▶ *exercises.*

CONCEPT CHECK *Decide whether each statement is* true *or* false. *If false, correct the right-hand side of the statement.*

1. $3^3 = 9$

2. $(-2)^4 = 2^4$

3. $(a^2)^3 = a^5$

4. $\left(\dfrac{1}{4}\right)^2 = \dfrac{1}{4^2}$

5. $-2^2 = 4$

6. $2^3 \cdot 2^4 = 4^7$

7. $(3x)^2 = 6x^2$

8. $(-x)^2 = x^2$

Write each expression in exponential form. ***See Example 1.***

9. $t \cdot t \cdot t \cdot t \cdot t \cdot t \cdot t$

10. $w \cdot w \cdot w \cdot w \cdot w \cdot w$

11. $\left(\dfrac{1}{2}\right)\left(\dfrac{1}{2}\right)\left(\dfrac{1}{2}\right)\left(\dfrac{1}{2}\right)\left(\dfrac{1}{2}\right)$

12. $\left(-\dfrac{1}{4}\right)\left(-\dfrac{1}{4}\right)\left(-\dfrac{1}{4}\right)\left(-\dfrac{1}{4}\right)$

13. $(-8p)(-8p)$

14. $(-7x)(-7x)(-7x)$

Identify the base and the exponent of each expression. Then evaluate, if possible. ***See Example 2.***

15. 3^5 ▶

16. 2^7

17. $(-3)^5$ ▶

18. $(-2)^7$

19. $(-6)^2$

20. $(-9)^2$

21. -6^2

22. -9^2

23. $(-2x)^4$

24. $(-4x)^4$

25. $-2x^4$

26. $-4x^4$

Use the product rule for exponents to simplify each expression, if possible. Write answers in exponential form. ***See Examples 3 and 4.***

27. $5^2 \cdot 5^6$ ▶

28. $3^6 \cdot 3^7$

29. $4^2 \cdot 4^7 \cdot 4^3$

30. $5^3 \cdot 5^8 \cdot 5^2$

31. $(-7)^3(-7)^6$

32. $(-9)^8(-9)^5$

33. $t^3 t^8 t^{13}$ ▶

34. $n^5 n^6 n^9$

35. $-8r^4(7r^3)$

36. $10a^7(-4a^3)$

37. $(-6p^5)(-7p^5)$ ▶

38. $(-5w^8)(-9w^8)$

39. $3^8 + 3^9$ ▶

40. $4^{12} + 4^5$

41. $5^8 \cdot 3^8$

42. $6^3 \cdot 8^3$

Use the power rules for exponents to simplify each expression. Evaluate coefficients in answers if the exponent on them is 4 or less. ***See Examples 5–7.***

43. $(4^3)^2$ ▶

44. $(8^3)^6$

45. $(t^4)^5$ ▶

46. $(y^6)^5$

47. $(7r)^3$

48. $(5x)^4$

49. $(-5^2)^6$

50. $(-9^4)^8$

51. $(-8^3)^5$

52. $(-7^5)^7$

53. $(5xy)^5$ ▶

54. $(9pq)^6$

55. $8(qr)^3$

56. $4(vw)^5$

57. $\left(\dfrac{9}{5}\right)^8$

58. $\left(\dfrac{12}{7}\right)^6$

59. $\left(\dfrac{1}{2}\right)^3$

60. $\left(\dfrac{1}{3}\right)^3$

61. $\left(\dfrac{a}{b}\right)^3$ $(b \neq 0)$

62. $\left(\dfrac{r}{t}\right)^4$ $(t \neq 0)$

63. $(-2x^2y)^3$

64. $(-5m^4p^2)^3$

65. $(3a^3b^2)^2$

66. $(4x^3y^5)^4$

Simplify each expression. (Do not evaluate the exponents on coefficients in answers in Exercises 67–76.) **See Example 8.**

67. $\left(\dfrac{5}{2}\right)^3 \cdot \left(\dfrac{5}{2}\right)^2$

68. $\left(\dfrac{3}{4}\right)^5 \cdot \left(\dfrac{3}{4}\right)^6$

69. $\left(\dfrac{9}{8}\right)^3 \cdot 9^2$

70. $\left(\dfrac{8}{5}\right)^4 \cdot 8^3$

71. $(2x)^9(2x)^3$

72. $(6y)^5(6y)^8$

73. $(-6p)^4(-6p)$

74. $(-13q)^6(-13q)$

75. $(6x^2y^3)^5$

76. $(5r^5t^6)^7$

77. $(x^2)^3(x^3)^5$

78. $(y^4)^5(y^3)^5$

79. $(2w^2x^3y)^2(x^4y)^5$

80. $(3x^4y^2z)^3(yz^4)^5$

81. $(-r^4s)^2(-r^2s^3)^5$

82. $(-ts^6)^4(-t^3s^5)^3$

83. $\left(\dfrac{4x^2}{5}\right)^3$

84. $\left(\dfrac{3z^5}{4}\right)^2$

85. $\left(\dfrac{5a^2b^5}{c^6}\right)^3$ $(c \neq 0)$

86. $\left(\dfrac{6x^3y^9}{z^5}\right)^4$ $(z \neq 0)$

87. $(-5m^3p^4q)^2(p^2q)^3$

88. $(-a^4b^5)(-6a^3b^3)^2$

89. $(2x^2y^3z)^4(xy^2z^3)^2$

90. $(4q^2r^3s^5)^3(qr^2s^3)^4$

91. CONCEPT CHECK   A student simplified $(10^2)^3$ as 1000^6. *What Went Wrong?* Simplify correctly.

92. CONCEPT CHECK   A student simplified $(3x^2y^3)^4$ as $12x^8y^{12}$. *What Went Wrong?* Simplify correctly.

Find an expression that represents, in appropriate units, the area of each figure. In Exercise 96, leave π in the answer. **See Example 9.** *(If necessary, refer to the formulas at the back of this text. The ⌐ in the figures indicates 90° (right) angles.)*

93.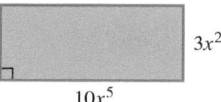

94.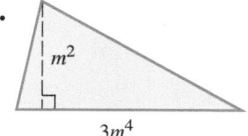

95.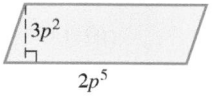

96.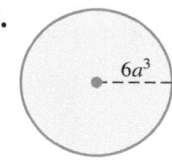

Find an expression that represents the volume of each figure. (If necessary, refer to the formulas at the back of this text.)

97.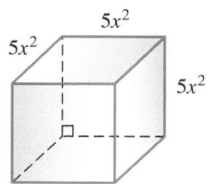

98.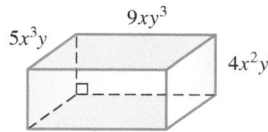

5.2 | Integer Exponents and the Quotient Rule

OBJECTIVES

1. Use 0 as an exponent.
2. Use negative numbers as exponents.
3. Use the quotient rule for exponents.
4. Use combinations of the rules for exponents.

Consider the following list.

$$2^4 = 16$$
$$2^3 = 8$$
$$2^2 = 4$$

As exponents decrease by 1, the results are divided by 2 each time.

Each time we decrease the exponent by 1, the value is divided by 2 (the base). We can continue the list to lesser and lesser integer exponents.

$$2^1 = 2$$
$$2^0 = 1$$
$$2^{-1} = \frac{1}{2}$$

We continue the pattern here.

◀ Work Problem **1** at the Side

From the preceding list and the answers to **Margin Problem 1**, i appears that we should define 2^0 as 1 and bases raised to negative exponent as reciprocals of those bases.

OBJECTIVE ▶ 1 Use 0 as an exponent. The definitions of 0 and negative exponents must be consistent with the rules for exponents developed earlier For example, if we define 6^0 to be 1, then

$$6^0 \cdot 6^2 = 1 \cdot 6^2 = 6^2 \quad \text{and} \quad 6^0 \cdot 6^2 = 6^{0+2} = 6^2.$$

The product rule is satisfied. The power rules are also valid for a 0 exponent Thus, we define a 0 exponent as follows.

① Continue the list of exponentials using −2, −3, and −4 as exponents.

$$2^{-2} = \underline{\qquad}$$
$$2^{-3} = \underline{\qquad}$$
$$2^{-4} = \underline{\qquad}$$

② Evaluate. Assume that all variables represent nonzero real numbers.

(a) 28^0　　　**(b)** $(-16)^0$

(c) -7^0　　　**(d)** m^0

(e) $-2p^0$　　　**(f)** $(5r)^0$

(g) $13^0 + 2^0$　**(h)** $14^0 - 12^0$

Zero Exponent

For any nonzero real number a, $\quad a^0 = 1$.

Example: $17^0 = 1$

EXAMPLE 1　**Using Zero Exponents**

Evaluate.

(a) $60^0 = 1$

(b) $(-60)^0 = 1$

(c) $-60^0 = -(1) = -1$

(d) $y^0 = 1 \quad (y \neq 0)$

(e) $6y^0 = 6(1) = 6 \quad (y \neq 0)$

(f) $(6y)^0 = 1 \quad (y \neq 0)$

(g) $8^0 + 11^0 = 1 + 1 = 2$

(h) $-8^0 - 11^0 = -1 - 1 = -2$

◀ Work Problem **2** at the Side

Answers

1. $2^{-2} = \frac{1}{4}; 2^{-3} = \frac{1}{8}; 2^{-4} = \frac{1}{16}$
2. **(a)** 1　**(b)** 1　**(c)** −1　**(d)** 1
   (e) −2　**(f)** 1　**(g)** 2　**(h)** 0

! CAUTION

Look again at **Examples 1(b) and 1(c).** In $(-60)^0$, the base is −60, and since any nonzero base raised to the 0 exponent is 1, $(-60)^0 = 1$. In -60^0, which can be written $-(60)^0$, the base is 60, so $-60^0 = -1$.

OBJECTIVE ▶ 2 **Use negative numbers as exponents.** Review the list of exponentials in the margin. Because $2^{-2} = \frac{1}{4}$ and $2^{-3} = \frac{1}{8}$, we can make a conjecture that 2^{-n} should equal $\frac{1}{2^n}$. *Is the product rule valid in such cases?* For example, if we multiply 6^{-2} by 6^2, we obtain

$$6^{-2} \cdot 6^2 = 6^{-2+2} = 6^0 = 1.$$

The expression 6^{-2} behaves as if it were the reciprocal of 6^2—that is, their product is 1. The reciprocal of 6^2 may be written $\frac{1}{6^2}$, leading us to define 6^{-2} as $\frac{1}{6^2}$, and generalize accordingly.

$$2^4 = 16$$
$$2^3 = 8$$
$$2^2 = 4$$
$$2^1 = 2$$
$$2^0 = 1$$
$$2^{-1} = \frac{1}{2}$$
$$2^{-2} = \frac{1}{4}$$
$$2^{-3} = \frac{1}{8}$$
$$2^{-4} = \frac{1}{16}$$

Negative Exponents

For any nonzero real number a and any integer n, $\quad a^{-n} = \dfrac{1}{a^n}.$

Example: $\quad 3^{-2} = \dfrac{1}{3^2}$

By definition, a^{-n} and a^n are reciprocals.

$$a^n \cdot a^{-n} = a^n \cdot \frac{1}{a^n} = 1$$

Because $1^n = 1$, the definition of a^{-n} can also be written as follows.

$$a^{-n} = \frac{1}{a^n} = \frac{1^n}{a^n} = \left(\frac{1}{a}\right)^n$$

For example, $\qquad 6^{-3} = \left(\dfrac{1}{6}\right)^3 \quad \text{and} \quad \left(\dfrac{1}{3}\right)^{-2} = 3^2.$

EXAMPLE 2 Using Negative Exponents

Write with positive exponents and simplify. Assume that all variables represent nonzero real numbers.

(a) $3^{-2} = \dfrac{1}{3^2} = \dfrac{1}{9} \quad a^{-n} = \frac{1}{a^n}$
    (b) $5^{-3} = \dfrac{1}{5^3} = \dfrac{1}{125} \quad a^{-n} = \frac{1}{a^n}$

(c) $\left(\dfrac{1}{2}\right)^{-3} = 2^3 = 8 \qquad \frac{1}{2}$ and 2 are reciprocals.
    (Reciprocals have a product of 1.)

Notice that we can change the base to its reciprocal if we also change the sign of the exponent.

(d) $\left(\dfrac{2}{5}\right)^{-4}$
    (e) $\left(\dfrac{4}{3}\right)^{-5}$

$= \left(\dfrac{5}{2}\right)^4 \quad \frac{2}{5}$ and $\frac{5}{2}$ are reciprocals.
    $= \left(\dfrac{3}{4}\right)^5 \quad \frac{4}{3}$ and $\frac{3}{4}$ are reciprocals.

$= \dfrac{5^4}{2^4} \quad$ Power rule (c)
    $= \dfrac{3^5}{4^5} \quad$ Power rule (c)

$= \dfrac{625}{16} \quad$ Apply the exponents.
    $= \dfrac{243}{1024} \quad$ Apply the exponents.

Continued on Next Page

3 Write with positive exponents and simplify. Assume that all variables represent nonzero real numbers.

(a) 4^{-3}

(b) 6^{-2}

(c) $\left(\dfrac{1}{4}\right)^{-2}$

(d) $\left(\dfrac{2}{3}\right)^{-2}$

(e) $2^{-1} + 5^{-1}$

(f) $7m^{-5}$

(g) $\dfrac{1}{z^{-6}}$

(h) p^2q^{-5}

(f) $4^{-1} - 2^{-1}$

$= \dfrac{1}{4} - \dfrac{1}{2}$ Apply the exponents.

$= \dfrac{1}{4} - \dfrac{2}{4}$ Find a common denominator.

$= -\dfrac{1}{4}$ Subtract.

(h) $\dfrac{1}{x^{-4}}$

$= \dfrac{1^{-4}}{x^{-4}}$ $1^n = 1$, for any integer n

$= \left(\dfrac{1}{x}\right)^{-4}$ Power rule (c)

$= x^4$ $\frac{1}{x}$ and x are reciprocals.

In general, $\dfrac{1}{a^{-n}} = a^n.$

(g) $3p^{-2}$

$= \dfrac{3}{1} \cdot \dfrac{1}{p^2}$ $a^{-n} = \frac{1}{a^n}$

$= \dfrac{3}{p^2}$ Multiply.

(i) x^3y^{-4}

$= \dfrac{x^3}{1} \cdot \dfrac{1}{y^4}$ $a^{-n} = \frac{1}{a^n}$

$= \dfrac{x^3}{y^4}$ Multiply.

◀ **Work Problem 3 at the Side.**

> **⚠ CAUTION**
>
> *A negative exponent does not indicate a negative number. Negative exponents lead to reciprocals.*
>
> | Expression | Example | |
> |---|---|---|
> | a^{-n} | $3^{-2} = \dfrac{1}{3^2} = \dfrac{1}{9}$ | Not negative |
> | $-a^{-n}$ | $-3^{-2} = -\dfrac{1}{3^2} = -\dfrac{1}{9}$ | Negative |

Consider the following.

$$\dfrac{2^{-3}}{3^{-4}}$$

$= \dfrac{\dfrac{1}{2^3}}{\dfrac{1}{3^4}}$ Definition of negative exponent

$= \dfrac{1}{2^3} \div \dfrac{1}{3^4}$ $\frac{a}{b}$ means $a \div b$.

$= \dfrac{1}{2^3} \cdot \dfrac{3^4}{1}$ To divide, multiply by the reciprocal of the divisor.

$= \dfrac{3^4}{2^3}$ Multiply.

Therefore, $\dfrac{2^{-3}}{3^{-4}} = \dfrac{3^4}{2^3}.$

Answers

3. **(a)** $\dfrac{1}{64}$ **(b)** $\dfrac{1}{36}$ **(c)** 16   **(d)** $\dfrac{9}{4}$

   (e) $\dfrac{7}{10}$ **(f)** $\dfrac{7}{m^5}$ **(g)** z^6 **(h)** $\dfrac{p^2}{q^5}$

Negative-to-Positive Rules for Exponents

For any nonzero real numbers a and b and any integers m and n,

$$\frac{a^{-m}}{b^{-n}} = \frac{b^n}{a^m} \quad \text{and} \quad \left(\frac{a}{b}\right)^{-m} = \left(\frac{b}{a}\right)^m.$$

Examples: $\dfrac{3^{-5}}{2^{-4}} = \dfrac{2^4}{3^5}$ and $\left(\dfrac{4}{5}\right)^{-3} = \left(\dfrac{5}{4}\right)^3$

EXAMPLE 3 Changing from Negative to Positive Exponents

Write with positive exponents and simplify. Assume that all variables represent nonzero real numbers.

(a) $\dfrac{4^{-2}}{5^{-3}} = \dfrac{5^3}{4^2} = \dfrac{125}{16}$

(b) $\dfrac{m^{-5}}{p^{-1}} = \dfrac{p^1}{m^5} = \dfrac{p}{m^5}$

(c) $\dfrac{a^{-2}b}{3d^{-3}} = \dfrac{bd^3}{3a^2}$ Notice that b in the numerator and the coefficient 3 in the denominator are not affected.

(d) $\left(\dfrac{x}{2y}\right)^{-4}$

$= \left(\dfrac{2y}{x}\right)^4$ Negative-to-positive rule

$= \dfrac{2^4 y^4}{x^4}$ Power rules (b) and (c)

$= \dfrac{16y^4}{x^4}$ Apply the exponent.

——— Work Problem **4** at the Side. ▶

! CAUTION

We cannot use the rule $\dfrac{a^{-m}}{b^{-n}} = \dfrac{b^n}{a^m}$ to change negative exponents to positive exponents if the exponents occur in a *sum* or *difference* of terms.

Example: $\dfrac{5^{-2} + 3^{-1}}{7 - 2^{-3}}$ written with positive exponents is $\dfrac{\frac{1}{5^2} + \frac{1}{3}}{7 - \frac{1}{2^3}}$.

OBJECTIVE ▶ 3 Use the quotient rule for exponents. Consider a quotient of two exponential expressions with the same base.

$$\frac{6^5}{6^3} = \frac{6 \cdot 6 \cdot 6 \cdot 6 \cdot 6}{6 \cdot 6 \cdot 6} = 6^2$$ Divide out the common factors.

The difference of the exponents, $5 - 3 = 2$, is the exponent in the quotient. Also,

$$\frac{6^2}{6^4} = \frac{6 \cdot 6}{6 \cdot 6 \cdot 6 \cdot 6} = \frac{1}{6^2} = 6^{-2}.$$ Divide out the common factors.

Here, $2 - 4 = -2$. These examples suggest the **quotient rule for exponents.**

4 Write with positive exponents and simplify. Assume that all variables represent nonzero real numbers.

GS (a) $\dfrac{7^{-1}}{5^{-4}}$

$= \dfrac{5\text{——}}{7\text{——}}$

$= \underline{\quad\quad}$

(b) $\dfrac{x^{-3}}{y^{-2}}$

(c) $\dfrac{4h^{-5}}{m^{-2}k}$

GS (d) $\left(\dfrac{3m}{p}\right)^{-2}$

$= \left(\dfrac{p}{3m}\right)^{\text{——}}$

$= \dfrac{p\text{——}}{3\text{——}m\text{——}}$

$= \underline{\quad\quad}$

Answers

4. (a) $4; 1; \dfrac{625}{7}$

(b) $\dfrac{y^2}{x^3}$ (c) $\dfrac{4m^2}{h^5k}$

(d) $2; 2; 2; 2; \dfrac{p^2}{9m^2}$

5 Simplify. Assume that all variables represent nonzero real numbers.

GS **(a)** $\dfrac{5^{11}}{5^8}$

$= 5^{\underline{} - \underline{}}$

$= 5^{\underline{}}$

$= \underline{}$

(b) $\dfrac{4^7}{4^{10}}$

GS **(c)** $\dfrac{6^{-5}}{6^{-2}}$

$= 6^{\underline{} - (\underline{})}$

$= 6^{\underline{}}$

$= \dfrac{1}{6^{\underline{}}}$

$= \underline{}$

(d) $\dfrac{8^4 m^9}{8^5 m^{10}}$

(e) $\dfrac{(x+y)^{-3}}{(x+y)^{-4}}$ $(x \neq -y)$

Answers

5. (a) 11; 8; 3; 125   **(b)** $\dfrac{1}{64}$

(c) $-5; -2; -3; 3; \dfrac{1}{216}$

(d) $\dfrac{1}{8m}$ **(e)** $x + y$

Quotient Rule for Exponents

For any nonzero real number a and any integers m and n,

$$\frac{a^m}{a^n} = a^{m-n}.$$

(Keep the same base and subtract the exponents.)

Example: $\dfrac{5^8}{5^4} = 5^{8-4} = 5^4$

⚠ **CAUTION**

A common **error** is to write $\dfrac{5^8}{5^4} = 1^{8-4} = 1^4$. **This is incorrect.**

$\dfrac{5^8}{5^4} = 5^{8-4} = 5^4$ The quotient must have the *same base*, which is 5 here.

We can confirm this by writing out the factors.

$$\frac{5^8}{5^4} = \frac{5 \cdot 5 \cdot 5 \cdot 5 \cdot 5 \cdot 5 \cdot 5 \cdot 5}{5 \cdot 5 \cdot 5 \cdot 5} = 5^4$$

EXAMPLE 4   **Using the Quotient Rule**

Simplify. Assume that all variables represent nonzero real numbers.

(a) $\dfrac{5^8}{5^6} = 5^{8-6} = 5^2 = 25$
   Keep the same base.

(b) $\dfrac{4^2}{4^9} = 4^{2-9} = 4^{-7} = \dfrac{1}{4^7}$

(c) $\dfrac{5^{-3}}{5^{-7}} = 5^{-3-(-7)} = 5^4 = 625$
   Be careful with signs.

(d) $\dfrac{q^5}{q^{-3}} = q^{5-(-3)} = q^8$

(e) $\dfrac{3^2 x^5}{3^4 x^3}$

$= \dfrac{3^2}{3^4} \cdot \dfrac{x^5}{x^3}$

$= 3^{2-4} \cdot x^{5-3}$ Quotient rule

$= 3^{-2} x^2$ Subtract.

$= \dfrac{x^2}{3^2}$ Definition of negative exponent

$= \dfrac{x^2}{9}$ Apply the exponent.

(f) $\dfrac{(m+n)^{-2}}{(m+n)^{-4}}$

$= (m+n)^{-2-(-4)}$

$= (m+n)^{-2+4}$

$= (m+n)^2$ $(m \neq -n)$

The restriction $m \neq -n$ is necessary to prevent a denominator of 0 in the original expression. Division by 0 is undefined.

(g) $\dfrac{7x^{-3}y^2}{2^{-1}x^2 y^{-5}}$

$= \dfrac{7 \cdot 2^1 \cdot y^2 y^5}{x^2 x^3}$ Negative-to-positive rule

$= \dfrac{14y^7}{x^5}$ Multiply; product rule

◀ **Work Problem** 5 **at the Side.**

Summary of Definitions and Rules for Exponents

For all integers m and n and all real numbers a and b for which the following are defined, these definitions and rules hold true.

		Examples
Product rule	$a^m \cdot a^n = a^{m+n}$	$7^4 \cdot 7^5 = 7^{4+5} = 7^9$
Zero exponent	$a^0 = 1$	$(-3)^0 = 1$
Negative exponent	$a^{-n} = \dfrac{1}{a^n}$	$5^{-3} = \dfrac{1}{5^3}$
Quotient rule	$\dfrac{a^m}{a^n} = a^{m-n}$	$\dfrac{2^2}{2^5} = 2^{2-5} = 2^{-3} = \dfrac{1}{2^3}$
Power rules (a)	$(a^m)^n = a^{mn}$	$(4^2)^3 = 4^{2 \cdot 3} = 4^6$
(b)	$(ab)^m = a^m b^m$	$(3k)^4 = 3^4 k^4$
(c)	$\left(\dfrac{a}{b}\right)^m = \dfrac{a^m}{b^m}$	$\left(\dfrac{2}{3}\right)^2 = \dfrac{2^2}{3^2}$
Negative-to-positive rules	$\dfrac{a^{-m}}{b^{-n}} = \dfrac{b^n}{a^m}$	$\dfrac{2^{-4}}{5^{-3}} = \dfrac{5^3}{2^4}$
	$\left(\dfrac{a}{b}\right)^{-m} = \left(\dfrac{b}{a}\right)^m$	$\left(\dfrac{4}{7}\right)^{-2} = \left(\dfrac{7}{4}\right)^2$

OBJECTIVE ▶ **4** Use combinations of the rules for exponents.

EXAMPLE 5 Using a Combination of the Rules

Simplify. Assume that all variables represent nonzero real numbers.

(a) $\dfrac{(4^2)^3}{4^5}$

$= \dfrac{4^6}{4^5}$ Power rule (a)

$= 4^{6-5}$ Quotient rule

$= 4^1$ Subtract.

$= 4$ $a^1 = a$, for all a.

(b) $x^2 \cdot x^{-6} \cdot x^{-1}$

$= x^{2+(-6)+(-1)}$ Product rule

$= x^{-5}$ Add.

$= \dfrac{1}{x^5}$ Definition of negative exponent

(c) $(2x)^3(2x)^2$

$= (2x)^5$ Product rule

$= 2^5 x^5$ Power rule (b)

$= 32x^5$ $2^5 = 32$

$(2x)^3(2x)^2$ **Alternative solution**

$= 2^3 x^3 \cdot 2^2 x^2$ Power rule (b)

$= 2^{3+2} x^{3+2}$ Product rule

$= 2^5 x^5$ Add exponents.

$= 32x^5$ $2^5 = 32$

Continued on Next Page

6 Simplify. Assume that all variables represent nonzero real numbers.

(a) $\dfrac{(3^4)^2}{3^3}$

(b) $z^{-2} \cdot z^{-1} \cdot z^4$

(c) $(4t)^5 (4t)^{-3}$

(d) $\left(\dfrac{5}{2z^4}\right)^{-3}$

(e) $\left(\dfrac{6y^{-4}}{7^{-1}z^5}\right)^{-2}$

(f) $\dfrac{(6x)^{-1}}{(3x^2)^{-2}}$

(d) $\left(\dfrac{2x^3}{5}\right)^{-4}$

$= \left(\dfrac{5}{2x^3}\right)^4$ Negative-to-positive rule

$= \dfrac{5^4}{2^4 x^{12}}$ Power rules (a)–(c)

$= \dfrac{625}{16x^{12}}$ Apply the exponents.

(e) $\left(\dfrac{3x^{-2}}{4^{-1}y^3}\right)^{-3}$

$= \dfrac{3^{-3}x^6}{4^3 y^{-9}}$ Power rules (a)–(c)

$= \dfrac{x^6 y^9}{4^3 \cdot 3^3}$ Negative-to-positive rule

$= \dfrac{x^6 y^9}{1728}$ $4^3 \cdot 3^3 = 64 \cdot 27$ $= 1728$

(f) $\dfrac{(4m)^{-3}}{(3m)^{-4}}$

$= \dfrac{4^{-3}m^{-3}}{3^{-4}m^{-4}}$ Power rule (b)

$= \dfrac{3^4 m^4}{4^3 m^3}$ Negative-to-positive rule

$= \dfrac{3^4 m^{4-3}}{4^3}$ Quotient rule

$= \dfrac{3^4 m}{4^3}$ Subtract.

$= \dfrac{81m}{64}$ Apply the exponents.

$\dfrac{(4m)^{-3}}{(3m)^{-4}}$ **Alternative solution**

$= \dfrac{(3m)^4}{(4m)^3}$ Use negative-to-positive rule first, followed by power rule (b).

$= \dfrac{3^4 m^4}{4^3 m^3}$

The rest of the solution can be done as shown at the left.

◄ **Work Problem 6 at the Side.**

> **Note**
>
> Because steps can be done in several different orders, there are many correct ways to simplify expressions like those in **Example 5.** See the alternative solutions shown.

Answers

6. (a) 243   **(b)** z **(c)** $16t^2$

    (d) $\dfrac{8z^{12}}{125}$ **(e)** $\dfrac{y^8 z^{10}}{1764}$ **(f)** $\dfrac{3x^3}{2}$

5.2 Exercises

FOR EXTRA HELP

Go to MyMathLab *for worked-out, step-by-step solutions to exercises enclosed in a square* ▢ *and video solutions to* ▶ *exercises.*

CONCEPT CHECK *Decide whether each expression is* positive, negative, *or* 0.

1. $(-2)^{-3}$

2. $(-3)^{-2}$

3. -2^4

4. -3^6

5. $\left(\dfrac{1}{4}\right)^{-2}$

6. $\left(\dfrac{1}{5}\right)^{-2}$

7. $1 - 5^0$

8. $1 - 7^0$

CONCEPT CHECK *Match each expression in Column I with the equivalent expression in Column II. Choices in Column II may be used once, more than once, or not at all. (In Exercise 9, $x \neq 0$.)*

I	II	I	II
9. (a) x^0	**A.** 0	**10. (a)** -2^{-4}	**A.** 8
(b) $-x^0$	**B.** 1	**(b)** $(-2)^{-4}$	**B.** 16
(c) $7x^0$	**C.** -1	**(c)** 2^{-4}	**C.** $-\dfrac{1}{16}$
(d) $(7x)^0$	**D.** 7	**(d)** $\dfrac{1}{2^{-4}}$	**D.** -8
(e) $-7x^0$	**E.** -7	**(e)** $\dfrac{1}{-2^{-4}}$	**E.** -16
(f) $(-7x)^0$	**F.** $\dfrac{1}{7}$	**(f)** $\dfrac{1}{(-2)^{-4}}$	**F.** $\dfrac{1}{16}$

Decide whether each expression is equal to 0, 1, *or* -1. ***See Example 1.***

11. 9^0

12. 5^0

13. $(-4)^0$

14. $(-10)^0$

15. -9^0

16. -5^0

17. $(-2)^0 - 2^0$

18. $(-8)^0 - 8^0$

19. $\dfrac{0^{10}}{10^0}$

20. $\dfrac{0^5}{5^0}$

Evaluate each expression. ***See Examples 1 and 2.***

21. 4^{-3} ▶

22. 5^{-4}

23. $\left(\dfrac{1}{2}\right)^{-4}$

24. $\left(\dfrac{1}{3}\right)^{-3}$

25. $\left(\dfrac{6}{7}\right)^{-2}$ ▶

26. $\left(\dfrac{2}{3}\right)^{-3}$

27. $(-3)^{-4}$

28. $(-4)^{-3}$

29. $3x^0$ $(x \neq 0)$

30. $-5t^0$ $(t \neq 0)$

31. $(3x)^0$ $(x \neq 0)$

32. $(-5t)^0$ $(t \neq 0)$

33. $7^0 + 9^0$

34. $8^0 + 6^0$

35. $5^{-1} + 3^{-1}$

36. $6^{-1} + 2^{-1}$

37. $-2^{-1} + 3^{-2}$

38. $(-3)^{-2} + (-4)^{-1}$

Simplify each expression. Evaluate coefficients if the exponent is 4 or less. Assume that all variables represent nonzero real numbers and no denominators are equal to 0.
See Examples 2–4.

39. $\dfrac{5^8}{5^5}$ ▶

40. $\dfrac{11^6}{11^4}$

41. $\dfrac{9^4}{9^5}$ ▶

42. $\dfrac{7^3}{7^4}$

43. $\dfrac{6^{-3}}{6^2}$ ▶

44. $\dfrac{4^{-2}}{4^3}$

45. $\dfrac{3^{-4}}{3^{-7}}$

46. $\dfrac{2^{-5}}{2^{-9}}$

47. $\dfrac{1}{6^{-3}}$

48. $\dfrac{1}{5^{-2}}$

49. $\dfrac{2}{r^{-4}}$

50. $\dfrac{3}{s^{-8}}$

51. $\dfrac{3^{-2}}{5^{-3}}$ ▶

52. $\dfrac{6^{-2}}{5^{-4}}$

53. $-4x^{-3}$

54. $-8z^{-5}$

55. $p^5 q^{-8}$

56. $x^{-8}y^4$

57. $\dfrac{r^5}{r^{-4}}$

58. $\dfrac{a^6}{a^{-4}}$

59. $\dfrac{6^4 x^8}{6^5 x^3}$ ▶

60. $\dfrac{3^8 y^5}{3^{10} y^2}$

61. $\dfrac{6y^3}{2y}$

62. $\dfrac{15m^2}{3m}$

63. $\dfrac{3x^5}{3x^2}$

64. $\dfrac{10p^8}{10p^4}$

65. $\dfrac{x^{-3}y}{4z^{-2}}$

66. $\dfrac{p^{-5}q^4}{9r^{-3}}$

67. $\dfrac{(a+b)^{-3}}{(a+b)^{-4}}$

68. $\dfrac{(x+y)^{-8}}{(x+y)^{-9}}$

Simplify each expression. Evaluate coefficients if the exponent is 4 or less. Assume that all variables represent nonzero real numbers. **See Example 5.**

69. $\dfrac{(7^4)^3}{7^9}$ ▶

70. $\dfrac{(5^3)^2}{5^2}$

71. $x^{-3} \cdot x^5 \cdot x^{-4}$

72. $y^{-8} \cdot y^5 \cdot y^{-2}$

73. $\dfrac{(3x)^{-2}}{(4x)^{-3}}$

74. $\dfrac{(2y)^{-3}}{(5y)^{-4}}$

75. $\left(\dfrac{x^{-1}y}{z^2}\right)^{-2}$ ▶

76. $\left(\dfrac{p^{-4}q}{r^{-3}}\right)^{-3}$

77. $(6x)^4 (6x)^{-3}$

78. $(10y)^9 (10y)^{-8}$

79. $\dfrac{(m^7 n)^{-2}}{m^{-4}n^3}$ ▶

80. $\dfrac{(m^2 n^4)^{-3}}{m^{-2}n^5}$

81. $\dfrac{5x^{-3}}{(4x)^2}$

82. $\dfrac{-3k^{-5}}{(2k)^2}$

83. $\left(\dfrac{2p^{-1}q}{3^{-1}m^2}\right)^2$

84. $\left(\dfrac{3xy^{-2}}{2^{-1}y}\right)^2$

85. CONCEPT CHECK A student simplified $\frac{16^3}{2^2}$ as shown.

$$\dfrac{16^3}{2^2} = \left(\dfrac{16}{2}\right)^{3-2} = 8^1 = 8 \quad \text{Incorrect}$$

What Went Wrong? Give the correct answer.

86. CONCEPT CHECK A student simplified 5^{-4} as shown.

$$5^{-4} = -5^4 = -625 \quad \text{Incorrect}$$

What Went Wrong? Give the correct answer.

Summary Exercises *Applying the Rules for Exponents*

CONCEPT CHECK *Decide whether each expression is* positive *or* negative.

1. $(-5)^4$

2. -5^4

3. $(-2)^5$

4. -2^5

5. $\left(-\dfrac{3}{7}\right)^2$

6. $\left(-\dfrac{3}{7}\right)^3$

7. $\left(-\dfrac{3}{7}\right)^{-2}$

8. $\left(-\dfrac{3}{7}\right)^{-5}$

Simplify each expression. Evaluate coefficients if the exponent is 6 or less. Assume that all variables represent nonzero real numbers.

9. $\left(\dfrac{6x^2}{5}\right)^{12}$

10. $\left(\dfrac{rs^2t^3}{3t^4}\right)^6$

11. $(10x^2y^4)^2(10xy^2)^3$

12. $(-2ab^3c)^4(-2a^2b)^2$

13. $\left(\dfrac{9wx^3}{y^4}\right)^3$

14. $(4x^{-2}y^{-3})^{-2}$

15. $\dfrac{c^{11}(c^2)^4}{(c^3)^3(c^2)^{-6}}$

16. $\left(\dfrac{k^4t^2}{k^2t^{-4}}\right)^{-2}$

17. $5^{-1}+6^{-1}$

18. $\dfrac{(3y^{-1}z^3)^{-1}(3y^2)}{(y^3z^2)^{-3}}$

19. $\dfrac{(2xy^{-1})^3}{2^3x^{-3}y^2}$

20. $-8^0+(-8)^0$

21. $(z^4)^{-3}(z^{-2})^{-5}$

22. $\left(\dfrac{r^2st^5}{3r}\right)^{-2}$

23. $\dfrac{(3^{-1}x^{-3}y)^{-1}(2x^2y^{-3})^2}{(5x^{-2}y^2)^{-2}}$

24. $\left(\dfrac{5x^2}{3x^{-4}}\right)^{-1}$

25. $\left(\dfrac{-2x^{-2}}{2x^2}\right)^{-2}$

26. $\dfrac{(x^{-4}y^2)^3(x^2y)^{-1}}{(xy^2)^{-3}}$

27. $\dfrac{\left(a^{-2}b^3\right)^{-4}}{\left(a^{-3}b^2\right)^{-2}\left(ab\right)^{-4}}$

28. $\left(2a^{-30}b^{-29}\right)\left(3a^{31}b^{30}\right)$

29. $5^{-2} + 6^{-2}$

30. $\left(\dfrac{\left(x^{47}y^{23}\right)^2}{x^{-26}y^{-42}}\right)^0$

31. $\left(\dfrac{7a^2b^3}{2}\right)^3$

32. $-\left(-12^0\right)$

33. $-\left(-12\right)^0$

34. $\dfrac{0^{12}}{12^0}$

35. $\dfrac{\left(2xy^{-3}\right)^{-2}}{\left(3x^{-2}y^4\right)^{-3}}$

36. $\left(\dfrac{a^2b^3c^4}{a^{-2}b^{-3}c^{-4}}\right)^{-2}$

37. $\left(6x^{-5}z^3\right)^{-3}$

38. $\left(2p^{-2}qr^{-3}\right)\left(2p\right)^{-4}$

39. $\dfrac{\left(xy\right)^{-3}\left(xy\right)^5}{\left(xy\right)^{-4}}$

40. $42^0 - \left(-12\right)^0$

41. $\dfrac{\left(7^{-1}x^{-3}\right)^{-2}\left(x^4\right)^{-6}}{7^{-1}x^{-3}}$

42. $\left(\dfrac{3^{-4}x^{-3}}{3^{-3}x^{-6}}\right)^{-2}$

43. $\left(5p^{-2}q\right)^{-3}\left(5pq^3\right)^4$

44. $8^{-1} + 6^{-1}$

45. $\left(\dfrac{4r^{-6}s^{-2}t}{2r^8s^{-4}t^2}\right)^{-1}$

46. $\left(13x^{-6}y\right)\left(13x^{-6}y\right)^{-1}$

47. $\dfrac{\left(8pq^{-2}\right)^4}{\left(8p^{-2}q^{-3}\right)^3}$

48. $\left(\dfrac{mn^{-2}p}{m^2np^4}\right)^{-2}\left(\dfrac{mn^{-2}p}{m^2np^4}\right)^3$

49. $-\left(-3^0\right)^0$

50. $5^{-1} - 8^{-1}$

5.3 | An Application of Exponents: Scientific Notation

OBJECTIVE ▶ ❶ Express numbers in scientific notation. Numbers occurring in science are often extremely large (such as the distance from Earth to the sun, 93,000,000 mi) or extremely small (the wavelength of blue light, approximately 0.000000475 m). Because of the difficulty of working with many zeros, scientists often express such numbers with exponents using *scientific notation*.

OBJECTIVES

❶ Express numbers in scientific notation.

❷ Convert numbers in scientific notation to standard notation.

❸ Use scientific notation in calculations.

Scientific Notation

A number is written in **scientific notation** when it is expressed in the form

$$a \times 10^n,$$

where $1 \leq |a| < 10$ and n is an integer.

In **scientific notation,** there is *always* one nonzero digit to the left of the decimal point.

Scientific
notation

3.19×10^1	$= 3.19 \times 10 = 31.9$	Decimal point moves 1 place to the right.
3.19×10^2	$= 3.19 \times 100 = 319.$	Decimal point moves 2 places to the right.
3.19×10^3	$= 3.19 \times 1000 = 3190.$	Decimal point moves 3 places to the right.
3.19×10^{-1}	$= 3.19 \times 0.1 = 0.319$	Decimal point moves 1 place to the left.
3.19×10^{-2}	$= 3.19 \times 0.01 = 0.0319$	Decimal point moves 2 places to the left.
3.19×10^{-3}	$= 3.19 \times 0.001 = 0.00319$	Decimal point moves 3 places to the left.

Note

In scientific notation, a multiplication cross $\times$ is commonly used.

A number in scientific notation is always written with the decimal point after the first nonzero digit and then multiplied by the appropriate power of 10.

Example: 56,200 is written 5.62×10^4 because

$$56,200 = 5.62 \times 10,000 = 5.62 \times 10^4.$$

Additional examples:

42,000,000	is written	4.2×10^7.
0.000586	is written	5.86×10^{-4}.
2,000,000,000	is written	2×10^9.

It is not necessary to write 2.0.

To write a positive number in scientific notation, follow the steps given on the next page. (For a negative number, follow these steps using the *absolute value* of the number. Then make the result negative.)

1 Write each number in scientific notation.

(a) 7500

The first nonzero digit is

_____ .

The decimal point should be moved _____ places.

$$7500 = \underline{\quad} \times 10^{\underline{\quad}}$$

(b) 5,870,000

(c) 0.057102

The first nonzero digit is

_____ .

The decimal point should be moved _____ places.

$$0.057102 = \underline{\quad} \times 10^{\underline{\quad}}$$

(d) −0.00062

Converting a Positive Number to Scientific Notation

Step 1 **Position the decimal point.** Place a caret ^ to the right of the first nonzero digit, where the decimal point will be placed.

Step 2 **Determine the numeral for the exponent.** Count the number of digits from the decimal point to the caret. This number gives the absolute value of the exponent on 10.

Step 3 **Determine the sign for the exponent.** Decide whether multiplying by 10^n should make the result of Step 1 greater or less.

- The exponent should be positive to make the result greater.
- The exponent should be negative to make the result less.

EXAMPLE 1 **Using Scientific Notation**

Write each number in scientific notation.

(a) 93,000,000

Step 1 Place a caret to the right of the 9 (the first nonzero digit) to mark the new location of the decimal point.

$$9{}_\wedge 3{,}000{,}000$$

Step 2 Count from the decimal point, which is understood to be after the last 0, to the caret.

$$9.3,000,000. \leftarrow \text{Decimal point}$$
Count 7 places.

Step 3 Here 9.3 is to be made greater, so the exponent on 10 is positive.

$$93{,}000{,}000 = 9.3 \times 10^7$$

(b) $63{,}200{,}000{,}000 = 6.3200000000 = 6.32 \times 10^{10}$
10 places

(c) 0.00462

Move the decimal point to the right of the first nonzero digit and count the number of places the decimal point was moved.

$$0.00462 \qquad 3 \text{ places}$$

Because 0.00462 is *less* than 4.62, the exponent must be *negative*.

$$0.00462 = 4.62 \times 10^{-3}$$

(d) $-0.0000762 = -7.62 \times 10^{-5}$
5 places
Remember the negative sign.

◀ **Work Problem 1 at the Side.**

Note

When writing a positive number in scientific notation, think as follows.

- If the original number is "large," like 93,000,000, use a *positive* exponent on 10 because positive is greater than negative.

- If the original number is "small," like 0.00462, use a *negative* exponent on 10 because negative is less than positive.

Answers

1. (a) 7; 3; 7.5; 3   **(b)** 5.87×10^6
(c) 5; 2; 5.7102; −2
(d) -6.2×10^{-4}

OBJECTIVE ▶ 2 Convert numbers in scientific notation to standard nota-tion. To convert a number written in scientific notation to a number without exponents, work in reverse.

> *Multiplying a positive number by a positive power of 10 will make the number greater. Multiplying by a negative power of 10 will make the number less.*

We refer to a number such as 475 as the **standard notation** of 4.75×10^2.

EXAMPLE 2   Writing Numbers in Standard Notation

Write each number in standard notation.

(a) 6.2×10^3

Because the exponent is positive, make 6.2 greater by moving the deci-mal point 3 places to the right. It is necessary to attach two 0s.

$$6.2 \times 10^3 = 6.200 = 6200$$

(b) $4.283 \times 10^5 = 4.28300 = 428{,}300$ Move 5 places to the right.
Attach 0s as necessary.

(c) $5.41 \times 10^0 = 5.41$ $10^0 = 1$

(d) $-9.73 \times 10^{-2} = -09.73 = -0.0973$ Move 2 places to the left.

> *The exponent tells the number of places and the direction in which the decimal point is moved.*

Work Problem 2 at the Side. ▶

OBJECTIVE ▶ 3 Use scientific notation in calculations.

EXAMPLE 3   Multiplying and Dividing with Scientific Notation

Perform each calculation. Write answers in both scientific notation and stan-dard notation.

a)
$$(7 \times 10^3)(5 \times 10^4)$$

$= (7 \times 5)(10^3 \times 10^4)$ Commutative and associative properties

$= 35 \times 10^7$ Multiply. Use the product rule.

> Don't stop. This number is *not* in scientific notation because 35 is not between 1 and 10.

$= (3.5 \times 10^1) \times 10^7$ Write 35 in scientific notation.

$= 3.5 \times (10^1 \times 10^7)$ Associative property

$= 3.5 \times 10^8$ Answer in scientific notation

$= 350{,}000{,}000$ Answer in standard notation

b)
$$\frac{4 \times 10^{-5}}{2 \times 10^3}$$

$= \dfrac{4}{2} \times \dfrac{10^{-5}}{10^3}$

$= 2 \times 10^{-8}$ Answer in scientific notation

$= 0.00000002$ Answer in standard notation

Work Problem 3 at the Side. ▶

---

2 Write each number in standard notation.

GS (a) 1.2×10^4

Move the decimal point ____ places to the ____ .

$1.2 \times 10^4 =$ _____

(b) 8.7×10^5

(c) 7.004×10^0

GS (d) 5.49×10^{-3}

Move the decimal point ____ places to the ____ .

$5.49 \times 10^{-3} =$ _____

(e) -5.27×10^{-1}

3 Perform each calculation. Write answers in both scientific notation and standard notation.

(a) $(2.6 \times 10^4)(2 \times 10^{-6})$

(b) $(3 \times 10^5)(5 \times 10^{-2})$

(c) $\dfrac{4.8 \times 10^2}{2.4 \times 10^{-3}}$

Answers

2. **(a)** 4; right; 12,000
   (b) 870,000 **(c)** 7.004
   (d) 3; left; 0.00549 **(e)** −0.527
3. **(a)** 5.2×10^{-2}; 0.052
   (b) 1.5×10^4; 15,000
   (c) 2×10^5; 200,000

④ Solve the problem.
See **Example 4.** About how much would 8,000,000 nanometers measure in inches?

| Note |

Multiplying or dividing numbers written in scientific notation may produce an answer in the form $a \times 10^0$. Because $10^0 = 1$, $a \times 10^0 = a$.

Example: $(8 \times 10^{-4})(5 \times 10^4) = 40 \times 10^0 = 40$ $10^0 = 1$

Also, if $a = 1$, then $a \times 10^n = 10^n$.

Example: 1,000,000 could be written as 10^6 instead of 1×10^6.

⑤ Solve the problem.
If the speed of light is approximately 3.0×10^5 km per sec, how many seconds does it take light to travel approximately 1.5×10^8 km from the sun to Earth? (Data from *The World Almanac and Book of Facts.*)

EXAMPLE 4 Using Scientific Notation to Solve an Application

A *nanometer* is a very small unit of measure that is equivalent to about 0.00000003937 in. About how much would 700,000 nanometers measure in inches? (Data from *The World Almanac and Book of Facts.*)

Write each number in scientific notation, and then multiply.

$$700{,}000\,(0.00000003937)$$

$= (7 \times 10^5)(3.937 \times 10^{-8})$ Write in scientific notation.

$= (7 \times 3.937)(10^5 \times 10^{-8})$ Properties of real numbers

$= 27.559 \times 10^{-3}$ Multiply; product rule

Don't stop here.

$= (2.7559 \times 10^1) \times 10^{-3}$ Write 27.559 in scientific notation.

$= 2.7559 \times 10^{-2}$ Product rule

$= 0.027559$ Write in standard notation.

Thus, 700,000 nanometers would measure

$$2.7559 \times 10^{-2} \text{ in.,} \quad \text{or} \quad 0.027559 \text{ in.}$$

◀ **Work Problem ④ at the Side.**

EXAMPLE 5 Using Scientific Notation to Solve an Application

In 2016, outstanding public debt was $\$1.9008 \times 10^{13}$ (which is more than \$19 trillion). The population of the United States was approximately 323 million that year. What was each citizen's share of this debt? (Data from U.S. Department of the Treasury; U.S. Census Bureau.)

Divide to obtain each citizen's share.

$$\frac{1.9008 \times 10^{13}}{323{,}000{,}000}$$

$= \dfrac{1.9008 \times 10^{13}}{3.23 \times 10^8}$ Write 323 million in scientific notation.

$= \dfrac{1.9008}{3.23} \times 10^5$ Quotient rule

$\approx 0.5885 \times 10^5$ Divide. Round to 4 decimal places.

$= 58{,}850$ Write in standard notation.

Each citizen would have to pay about \$58,850.

◀ **Work Problem ⑤ at the Side.**

Answers

4. 3.1496×10^{-1} in., or 0.31496 in.
5. 5×10^2 sec, or 500 sec

5.3 Exercises

FOR EXTRA HELP Go to MyMathLab for worked-out, step-by-step solutions to exercises enclosed in a square and video solutions to ▶ exercises.

CONCEPT CHECK *Match each number written in scientific notation in Column I with the correct choice from Column II. Not all choices in Column II will be used.*

I	II	I	II
1. (a) 4.6×10^{-4}	**A.** 46,000	**2. (a)** 1×10^9	**A.** 1 billion
(b) 4.6×10^4	**B.** 460,000	**(b)** 1×10^6	**B.** 100 million
(c) 4.6×10^5	**C.** 0.00046	**(c)** 1×10^8	**C.** 1 million
(d) 4.6×10^{-5}	**D.** 0.000046	**(d)** 1×10^{10}	**D.** 10 billion
	E. 4600		**E.** 100 billion

CONCEPT CHECK *Determine whether or not the given number is written in scientific notation as defined in **Objective 1**. If it is not, write it as such.*

3. 4.56×10^3 **4.** 7.34×10^5 **5.** 5,600,000   **6.** 34,000

7. 0.004   **8.** 0.0007   **9.** 0.8×10^2 **10.** 0.9×10^3

Complete each of the following.

11. Write each number in scientific notation.

(a) 63,000

The first nonzero digit is _____. The decimal point should be moved _____ places.

$63{,}000 =$ _____ $\times$ 10—

(b) 0.0571

The first nonzero digit is _____. The decimal point should be moved _____ places.

$0.0571 =$ _____ $\times$ 10—

12. Write each number in standard notation.

(a) 4.2×10^3

Move the decimal point _____ places to the (*right/left*).

$4.2 \times 10^3 =$ _____

(b) 6.42×10^{-3}

Move the decimal point _____ places to the (*right/left*).

$6.42 \times 10^{-3} =$ _____

Write each number in scientific notation. See Example 1.

13. 5,876,000,000   **14.** 9,994,000,000   **15.** 82,350   **16.** 78,330

17. 0.000007   **18.** 0.0000004   **19.** −0.00203   **20.** −0.0000578

Write each number in standard notation. See Example 2.

21. 7.5×10^5 **22.** 8.8×10^6 **23.** 5.677×10^{12} **24.** 8.766×10^9

25. 1×10^{12} **26.** 1×10^7 **27.** -6.21×10^0 **28.** -8.56×10^0

29. 7.8×10^{-4} **30.** 8.9×10^{-5} **31.** 5.134×10^{-9} **32.** 7.123×10^{-10}

*Each statement contains a number in **boldface italic** type. If the number is in scientific notation, write it in standard notation. If the number is not in scientific notation, write it as such. **See Examples 1 and 2.***

33. A *muon* is an atomic particle related to an electron. The half-life of a muon is about 2 millionths (2×10^{-6}) of a second. (Data from www.schoolphysics.co.uk)

34. There are 13 red balls and 39 black balls in a box. Mix them up and draw 13 out one at a time without returning any ball . . . the probability that the 13 drawings each will produce a red ball is . . . *1.6×10^{-12}.*

35. An electron and a positron attract each other in two ways: the electromagnetic attraction of their opposite electric charges, and the gravitational attraction of their two masses. The electromagnetic attraction is

$$4,200,000,000,000,000,000,000,000,000,000,000,000,000,000$$

times as strong as the gravitational. (Data from Asimov, I., *Isaac Asimov's Book of Facts.*)

36. The name "googol" applies to the number

$$10,000,000,000,000,000,000,000,000,000,000,000,000,000,000,000,000,$$
$$000,000,000,000,000,000,000,000,000,000,000,000,000,000.$$

The Web search engine Google honors this number. Sergey Brin, president and cofounder of Google, Inc., was a mathematics major. He chose the name Google to describe the vast reach of this search engine. (Data from *The Gazette.*)

*Perform the indicated operations. Write each answer in (**a**) scientific notation and (**b**) standard notation. **See Example 3.***

37. $(2 \times 10^8)(3 \times 10^3)$

38. $(3 \times 10^7)(3 \times 10^3)$

39. $(5 \times 10^4)(3 \times 10^2)$

40. $(8 \times 10^5)(2 \times 10^3)$

41. $(4 \times 10^{-6})(2 \times 10^3)$

42. $(3 \times 10^{-7})(2 \times 10^2)$

43. $(6 \times 10^3)(4 \times 10^{-2})$

44. $(7 \times 10^5)(3 \times 10^{-4})$

45. $(3 \times 10^{-4})(-2 \times 10^8)$

46. $(4 \times 10^{-3})(-2 \times 10^7)$

47. $(9 \times 10^4)(7 \times 10^{-7})$

48. $(6 \times 10^4)(8 \times 10^{-8})$

49. $\dfrac{9 \times 10^{-5}}{3 \times 10^{-1}}$

50. $\dfrac{12 \times 10^{-4}}{4 \times 10^{-3}}$

51. $\dfrac{8 \times 10^3}{2 \times 10^2}$

52. $\dfrac{15 \times 10^4}{3 \times 10^3}$

53. $\dfrac{2.6 \times 10^{-3}}{2 \times 10^2}$

54. $\dfrac{9.5 \times 10^{-1}}{5 \times 10^3}$

55. $\dfrac{4 \times 10^5}{8 \times 10^2}$

56. $\dfrac{3 \times 10^9}{6 \times 10^5}$

57. $\dfrac{15 \times 10^{-4} \times 12 \times 10^5}{5 \times 10^3 \times 4 \times 10^{-8}}$

58. $\dfrac{24 \times 10^{-3} \times 18 \times 10^4}{6 \times 10^6 \times 9 \times 10^{-2}}$

59. $\dfrac{2.6 \times 10^{-3} \times 7.0 \times 10^{-1}}{2 \times 10^2 \times 3.5 \times 10^{-3}}$

60. $\dfrac{9.5 \times 10^{-1} \times 2.4 \times 10^4}{5 \times 10^3 \times 1.2 \times 10^{-2}}$

Use scientific notation to calculate the answer to each problem. ***See Examples 4 and 5.***

61. The Double Helix Nebula, a conglomeration of dust and gas stretching across the center of the Milky Way galaxy, is 25,000 light-years from Earth. If one light-year is about 6,000,000,000,000 mi, about how many miles is the Double Helix Nebula from Earth? (Data from www.spitzer.caltech.edu)

62. Pollux, one of the brightest stars in the night sky, is 33.7 light-years from Earth. If one light-year is about 6,000,000,000,000 mi, about how many miles is Pollux from Earth? (Data from *The World Almanac and Book of Facts.*)

63. In 2016, the population of the United States was about 322.9 million. To the nearest dollar, calculate how much each person in the United States would have had to contribute in order to make one person a trillionaire (that is, to give that person $1,000,000,000,000). (Data from U.S. Census Bureau.)

64. In 2015, Congress raised the debt limit to 1.81×10^{13}. To the nearest dollar, about how much was this for every man, woman, and child in the country? Use 321 million as the population of the United States. (Data from U.S. Census Bureau.)

65. In 2014, the U.S. government collected about $4372 per person in individual income taxes. If the population at that time was 319,000,000, how much did the government collect in taxes for 2014? (Data from *The World Almanac and Book of Facts.*)

66. In 2014, the state of Iowa had about 8.8×10^4 farms with an average of 3.47×10^2 acres per farm. What was the total number of acres devoted to farmland in Iowa that year? (Data from U.S. Department of Agriculture.)

67. Light travels at a speed of 1.86×10^5 mi per sec. When Venus is 6.68×10^7 mi from the sun, how long does it take light to travel from the sun to Venus? Round to two decimal places. (Data from *The World Almanac and Book of Facts.*)

68. The distance to Earth from Pluto is 4.58×10^9 km. *Pioneer 10* transmitted radio signals from Pluto to Earth at the speed of light, 3.00×10^5 km per sec. How long (in seconds) did it take for the signals to reach Earth? Round to two decimal places.

69. One of the world's fastest computers can perform 10,000,000,000,000,000 calculations per second. How many can it perform per minute? Per hour? (Data from www.japantimes.co.jp)

70. One of the world's fastest computers can perform 33.86 quadrillion calculations per second. (*Hint:* 1 quadrillion $= 1 \times 10^{15}$) How many can it perform per minute? Per hour? (Data from www.top500.org)

Calculators can express numbers in scientific notation using notation such as

$$5.4\text{E}3 \quad to\ represent \quad 5.4 \times 10^3.$$

Similarly, 5.4E^-3 represents 5.4×10^{-3}. Predict the display the calculator would give for the expression shown in each screen.

71. | .00000047 |

72. | .000021 |

73. | (8E5)/(4E-2) |

74. | (9E-4)/(3E3) |

Relating Concepts (Exercises 75–78) For Individual or Group Work

*In 1935, Charles F. Richter devised a scale to compare the intensities, or relative powers, of earthquakes. The **intensity** of an earthquake is measured relative to the intensity of a standard **zero-level** earthquake of intensity I_0. The relationship is equivalent to*

$$I = I_0 \times 10^R, \quad where\ R\ is\ the\ \textbf{Richter scale}\ measure.$$

For example, if an earthquake has magnitude 5.0 on the Richter scale, then its intensity is calculated as

$$I = I_0 \times 10^{5.0} = I_0 \times 100{,}000,$$

which is 100,000 times as intense as a zero-level earthquake.

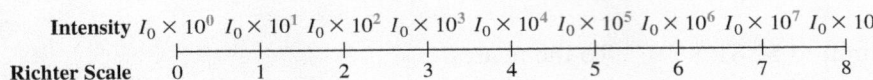

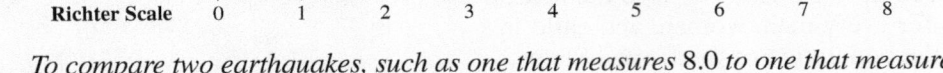

To compare two earthquakes, such as one that measures 8.0 to one that measures 5.0, calculate the ratio of their intensities.

$$\frac{intensity\ 8.0}{intensity\ 5.0} = \frac{I_0 \times 10^{8.0}}{I_0 \times 10^{5.0}} = \frac{10^8}{10^5} = 10^{8-5} = 10^3 = 1000$$

An earthquake that measures 8.0 is 1000 times as intense as one that measures 5.0.

*Use the information in the table to **work Exercises 75–78 in order.***

Year	Earthquake Location	Richter Scale Measurement
1960	Chile	9.5
2011	NE Japan	9.0
2007	Southern Sumatra, Indonesia	8.5
2013	Solomon Islands region	8.0
2013	Falkland Islands region	7.0

Data from earthquake.usgs.gov

75. Compare the intensity of the 1960 Chile earthquake with the 2007 Southern Sumatra earthquake.

76. Compare the intensity of the 2013 Solomon Islands earthquake with the 2013 Falkland Islands earthquake.

77. Compare the intensity of the 2011 NE Japan earthquake with the 2013 Falkland Islands earthquake.

78. Suppose an earthquake measures 5.5 on the Richter scale. How would the intensity of the 1960 Chile earthquake compare to it?

5.4 Adding and Subtracting Polynomials

OBJECTIVES

1 Identify terms and coefficients.
2 Combine like terms.
3 Know the vocabulary for polynomials.
4 Evaluate polynomials.
5 Add polynomials.
6 Subtract polynomials.
7 Add and subtract polynomials with more than one variable.

OBJECTIVE ▶ **1** **Identify terms and coefficients.** Recall that in an algebraic expression such as

$$4x^3 + 6x^2 + 5x + 8,$$

the quantities that are added, $4x^3$, $6x^2$, $5x$, and 8, are **terms.** In the term $4x^3$, the number **4** is the **numerical coefficient,** or simply the **coefficient,** of x^3. In the same way, **6** is the coefficient of x^2 in the term $6x^2$, and **5** is the coefficient of x in the term $5x$. The constant term 8 can be thought of as

$$8 \cdot 1 = 8x^0, \quad \text{By definition, } x^0 = 1.$$

so 8 is the coefficient in the term 8. Other examples are given in the table.

TERMS AND THEIR COEFFICIENTS

Term	Numerical Coefficient
8	8
$-7y$	-7
$34r^3$	34
$-26x^5yz^4$	-26
$-k = -1k$	-1
$r = 1r$	1
$\frac{3x}{8} = \frac{3}{8}x$	$\frac{3}{8}$
$\frac{x}{3} = \frac{1x}{3} = \frac{1}{3}x$	$\frac{1}{3}$

1 Identify the coefficient of each term in the expression. Then give the number of terms.

$$2x^3 - x + 10$$

EXAMPLE 1 **Identifying Coefficients**

Identify the coefficient of each term in the expression. Then give the number of terms.

(a) $-6x^4 + x - 3$ can be written as $-6x^4 + 1x + (-3x^0).$

There are three terms:

$$-6x^4, \quad x, \quad \text{and} \quad -3.$$

The coefficients are $-6, 1,$ and $-3.$

(b) $5 - v^3$ can be written as $5v^0 + (-1v^3).$

There are two terms.

The coefficients are 5 and $-1.$

Work Problem ❶ **at the Side.** ▶

OBJECTIVE ▶ **2** **Combine like terms.** Recall that **like terms** have exactly the same combination of variables, with the same exponents on the variables. *Only the coefficients may differ.*

$19m^5$ and $14m^5$	
$-37y^9$ and y^9	Examples of like terms
$3pq$ and $-2pq$	
$2xy^2$ and $-xy^2$	

$7x$ and $7y$	
z^4 and z	Examples of unlike terms
$2pq$ and $2p$	
$-4xy^2$ and $5x^2y$	

Using the distributive property, we combine like terms by adding or subtracting their coefficients.

2 Simplify each expression by combining like terms, if possible.

(a) $5x^4 + 7x^4$

(b) $9pq + 3pq - 2pq$

(c) $r^2 + 3r + 5r^2$

(d) $x + \frac{1}{2}x$

(e) $8t + 6w$

(f) $3x^4 - 3x^2$

Answers

2. (a) $12x^4$ (b) $10pq$ (c) $6r^2 + 3r$ (d) $\frac{3}{2}x$
   (e) These are unlike terms. They cannot be combined.
   (f) These are unlike terms. They cannot be combined.

EXAMPLE 2 Combining Like Terms

Simplify each expression by combining like terms, if possible.

(a) $-4x^3 + 6x^3$ $ac + bc$
$= (-4 + 6)x^3$ $= (a + b)c$
$= 2x^3$

(b) $9x^6 - 14x^6 + x^6$ $x^6 = 1x^6$
$= (9 - 14 + 1)x^6$
$= -4x^6$

(c) $y + \frac{2}{3}y$
$= 1y + \frac{2}{3}y$ $y = 1y$
$= \left(\frac{3}{3} + \frac{2}{3}\right)y$ $1 = \frac{3}{3}$; Distributive property
$= \frac{5}{3}y$ Add the fractions.

(d) $8rs - 13rs + 9rs$
$= (8 - 13 + 9)rs$
$= 4rs$

(e) $12m^2 + 5m + 4m^2$
$= (12 + 4)m^2 + 5m$
$= 16m^2 + 5m$ Stop here. These are unlike terms.

(f) $5u + 11v$
These are unlike terms. They cannot be combined.

◀ **Work Problem 2 at the Side.**

⚠ CAUTION

In **Example 2(e)**, we cannot combine $16m^2$ and $5m$ because the exponents on the variables are different. *Unlike terms have different variables or different exponents on the same variables.*

OBJECTIVE 3 Know the vocabulary for polynomials.

Polynomial in x

A **polynomial in x** is a term or the sum of a finite number of terms of the form

$$ax^n, \quad \text{for any real number } a \text{ and any whole number } n.$$

For example, the expression

$$\underbrace{16x^8 - 7x^6 + 5x^4 - 3x^2 + 4}_{\text{Descending powers of } x}$$ Polynomial in x (The 4 can be written as $4x^0$.)

is a polynomial in x. It is written in **descending powers,** because the exponents on x decrease from left to right. By contrast, the expression

$$2x^3 - x^2 + \frac{4}{x}, \quad \text{or} \quad 2x^3 - x^2 + 4x^{-1}, \quad \text{Not a polynomial}$$

is *not* a polynomial in x. A variable appears in a denominator, which can be written as a factor to a negative power.

Note *

A polynomial can use any variable, not just x (see **Example 2(c)**), and have terms with more than one variable (see **Example 2(d)**).

Work Problem ③ at the Side. ▶

The **degree of a term** is the sum of the exponents on the variables. The **degree of a polynomial** is the greatest degree of any nonzero term of the polynomial. The table gives several examples.

DEGREES OF TERMS AND POLYNOMIALS

Term	Degree	Polynomial	Degree
$3x^4$	4	$3x^4 - 5x^2 + 6$	4
$5x$, or $5x^1$	1	$5x + 7$	1
-7, or $-7x^0$	0	$x^5 + 3x^6 - 7$	6
$2x^2y$, or $2x^2y^1$	$2 + 1 = 3$	$xy - 5y^2 + 2x^2y$	3

Some polynomials with a specific number of terms have special names.

• A polynomial with exactly one term is a **monomial.** (*Mono-* means "one," as in *mono*rail.)

$$9m, \quad -6y^5, \quad x^2, \quad \text{and} \quad 6 \quad \text{Monomials}$$

• A polynomial with exactly two terms is a **binomial.** (*Bi-* means "two," as in *bi*cycle.)

$$-9x^4 + 9x^3, \quad 8m^2 + 6m, \quad \text{and} \quad 3t - 10 \quad \text{Binomials}$$

• A polynomial with exactly three terms is a **trinomial.** (*Tri-* means "three," as in *tri*angle.)

$$9m^3 - 4m^2 + 6, \quad \frac{19}{3}y^2 + \frac{8}{3}y + 5, \quad \text{and} \quad -3z^5 - z^2 + z \quad \text{Trinomials}$$

EXAMPLE 3 **Classifying Polynomials**

For each polynomial, first simplify, if possible. Then give the degree and tell whether the simplified polynomial is a *monomial*, a *binomial*, a *trinomial*, or *none of these*.

(a) $2x^3 + 5$

The polynomial cannot be simplified. It is a *binomial* of degree **3**.

(b) $6x - 8x + 13x$

$= 11x$ Combine like terms to simplify.

The degree is **1** (here $x = x^1$). The simplified polynomial is a *monomial*.

(c) $4xy - 5xy + 2xy$

$= xy$ Combine like terms.

The degree is 2 (because $xy = x^1y^1$, and $1 + 1 = 2$). The simplified polynomial is a *monomial*.

(d) $2x^2 - 3x + 8x - 12$

$= 2x^2 + 5x - 12$ Combine like terms.

The degree is 2. The simplified polynomial is a *trinomial*.

Work Problem ④ at the Side. ▶

③ Choose all descriptions that apply for each of the expressions in parts (a)–(d).

A. Polynomial

B. Polynomial written in descending powers

C. Not a polynomial

(a) $3m^5 + 5m^2 - 2m + 1$

(b) $2p^4 + p^6$

(c) $\dfrac{1}{x} + 2x^2 + 3$

(d) $x - 3$

④ For each polynomial, first simplify, if possible. Then give the degree and tell whether the simplified polynomial is a *monomial*, a *binomial*, a *trinomial*, or *none of these*.

(a) $3x^2 + 2x - 4$

(b) $x^3 + 4x^3$

(c) $x^8 - x^7 + 2x^8$

(d) $6ab - 7ab + 3ab$

Answers

3. **(a)** A, B **(b)** A **(c)** C **(d)** A, B
4. **(a)** The polynomial cannot be simplified; degree 2; trinomial
    (b) $5x^3$; degree 3; monomial
    (c) $3x^8 - x^7$; degree 8; binomial
    (d) $2ab$; degree 2; monomial

5 Find the value of $2x^3 + 8x - 6$ in each case.

GS **(a)** For $x = -1$

$$2x^3 + 8x - 6$$
$$= 2(\underline{\hspace{0.3cm}})^3 + 8(\underline{\hspace{0.3cm}}) - 6$$
$$= 2(\underline{\hspace{0.3cm}}) + 8(-1) - 6$$
$$= \underline{\hspace{0.5cm}} - \underline{\hspace{0.5cm}} - 6$$
$$= \underline{\hspace{0.5cm}}$$

(b) For $x = 4$

(c) For $x = -2$

6 Find each sum.

(a) Add $4x^3 - 3x^2 + 2x$ and $6x^3 + 2x^2 - 3x$.

(b) Add $x^2 - 2x + 5$ and $4x^2 - 2$.

Answers

5. **(a)** $-1; -1; -1; -2; 8; -16$
   (b) 154   **(c)** -38
6. **(a)** $10x^3 - x^2 - x$
   (b) $5x^2 - 2x + 3$

OBJECTIVE ▶ **4** **Evaluate polynomials.** When we *evaluate* an expression, we find its *value*. A polynomial usually represents different numbers for different values of the variable.

EXAMPLE 4 **Evaluating a Polynomial**

Find the value of $3x^4 + 5x^3 - 4x - 4$ for **(a)** $x = -2$ and for **(b)** $x = 3$.

(a) $3x^4 + 5x^3 - 4x - 4$

$$= 3(-2)^4 + 5(-2)^3 - 4(-2) - 4 \quad \text{Substitute } -2 \text{ for } x.$$

[Use parentheses to avoid errors.] $= 3(16) + 5(-8) - 4(-2) - 4 \quad \text{Apply the exponents.}$

$$= 48 - 40 + 8 - 4 \quad \text{Multiply.}$$

$$= 12 \quad \text{Add and subtract.}$$

(b) $3x^4 + 5x^3 - 4x - 4$

$$= 3(3)^4 + 5(3)^3 - 4(3) - 4 \quad \text{Let } x = 3.$$

$$= 3(81) + 5(27) - 4(3) - 4 \quad \text{Apply the exponents.}$$

$$= 243 + 135 - 12 - 4 \quad \text{Multiply.}$$

$$= 362 \quad \text{Add and subtract.}$$

◀ **Work Problem 5 at the Side.**

OBJECTIVE ▶ **5** **Add polynomials.**

Adding Polynomials

To add two polynomials, combine (add) like terms.

EXAMPLE 5 **Adding Polynomials Vertically**

Find each sum.

(a) Add $6x^3 - 4x^2 + 3$ and $-2x^3 + 7x^2 - 5$.

$$6x^3 - 4x^2 + 3 \quad \text{Write like terms}$$
$$+ \underline{(-2x^3 + 7x^2 - 5)} \quad \text{in columns.}$$

Now add, column by column.

[Add the coefficients only. Do **not** add the exponents.]

$$\begin{array}{ccc} 6x^3 & -4x^2 & 3 \\ -2x^3 & 7x^2 & -5 \\ \hline 4x^3 & 3x^2 & -2 \end{array}$$

Add the three sums together to obtain the answer.

$$4x^3 + 3x^2 + (-2) = 4x^3 + 3x^2 - 2$$

(b) Add $2x^2 - 4x + 3$ and $x^3 + 5x$.

Write like terms in columns and add column by column.

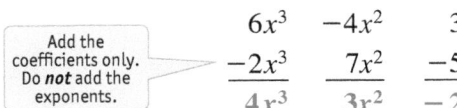

$$2x^2 - 4x + 3 \qquad \text{[Leave spaces for missing terms.]}$$
$$+ \underline{(x^3 \qquad + 5x \qquad)}$$
$$x^3 + 2x^2 + x + 3$$

◀ **Work Problem 6 at the Side.**

The polynomials in **Example 5** also could be added horizontally.

EXAMPLE 6   **Adding Polynomials Horizontally**

Find each sum.

(a) Add $6x^3 - 4x^2 + 3$ and $-2x^3 + 7x^2 - 5$.

$(6x^3 - 4x^2 + 3) + (-2x^3 + 7x^2 - 5) = 4x^3 + 3x^2 - 2$ Same answer as found in
Combine like terms.   **Example 5(a)**

(b) Add $2x^2 - 4x + 3$ and $x^3 + 5x$.

$(2x^2 - 4x + 3) + (x^3 + 5x)$

$= x^3 + 2x^2 - 4x + 5x + 3$ Commutative property

$= x^3 + 2x^2 + x + 3$ See **Example 5(b)**.

────────────────────── **Work Problem 7 at the Side.** ▶

OBJECTIVE ▶ 6 Subtract polynomials. Recall that the difference $x - y$ is defined as $x + (-y)$. (We find the difference $x - y$ by adding x and the *opposite* of y.)

$7 - 2$ is equivalent to $7 + (-2)$,   which equals 5.

$-8 - (-2)$ is equivalent to $-8 + 2$,   which equals -6.

A similar method is used to subtract polynomials.

Subtracting Polynomials

To subtract two polynomials, change the sign of each term in the subtrahend (second polynomial) and add the result to the minuend (first polynomial)—that is, add the *opposite* of each term of the second polynomial to the first polynomial.

EXAMPLE 7   **Subtracting Polynomials Horizontally**

Perform each subtraction.

(a) $(5x - 2) - (3x - 8)$

$= (5x - 2) + \left[-(3x - 8) \right]$ Definition of subtraction

$= (5x - 2) + \left[-1(3x - 8) \right]$ $-a = -1a$

$= (5x - 2) + (-3x + 8)$ Distributive property

$= 2x + 6$ Combine like terms.

CHECK   To check a subtraction problem, use the fact that

if $a - b = c$,   then $a = b + c$.

$(3x - 8) + (2x + 6) = 5x - 2$ ✓

(b) Subtract $6x^3 - 4x^2 + 2$ from $11x^3 + 2x^2 - 8$.

$(11x^3 + 2x^2 - 8) - (6x^3 - 4x^2 + 2)$ Be careful to write the problem in the correct order.

$= (11x^3 + 2x^2 - 8) + (-6x^3 + 4x^2 - 2)$

Check as above. $= 5x^3 + 6x^2 - 10$ Combine like terms.

────────────────────── **Work Problem 8 at the Side.** ▶

7 Find each sum.

(a) Add $2x^4 - 6x^2 + 7$ and $-3x^4 + 5x^2 + 2$.

(b) Add $3x^2 + 4x + 2$ and $6x^3 - 5x - 7$.

8 Perform each subtraction.

(a) $(3x - 8) - (5x - 9)$

(b) $(14y^3 - 6y^2 + 2y - 5)$
$- (2y^3 - 7y^2 - 4y + 6)$

(c) Subtract $-3y^2 + 4y + 6$ from $7y^2 - 11y + 8$.

Answers

7. **(a)** $-x^4 - x^2 + 9$
   (b) $6x^3 + 3x^2 - x - 5$
8. **(a)** $-2x + 1$
   (b) $12y^3 + y^2 + 6y - 11$
   (c) $10y^2 - 15y + 2$

9 Subtract by columns.

$(4y^3 - 16y^2 + 2y + 1)$

$- (12y^3 - 9y^2 - 3y + 16)$

10 Perform the indicated operations.

$(6p^4 - 8p^3 + 2p - 1)$

$- (-7p^4 + 6p^2 - 12)$

$+ (p^4 - 3p + 8)$

11 Add or subtract as indicated.

(a) $(3mn + 2m - 4n)$

$+ (-mn + 4m + n)$

(b) $(5p^2q^2 - 4p^2 + 2q)$

$- (2p^2q^2 - p^2 - 3q)$

Subtraction also can be done in columns. We will use vertical subtraction when we study polynomial division.

EXAMPLE 8 **Subtracting Polynomials Vertically**

Subtract by columns. $(14y^3 - 6y^2 + 2y - 5) - (2y^3 - 7y^2 - 4y + 6)$

$$\begin{array}{r} 14y^3 - 6y^2 + 2y - 5 \\ - (2y^3 - 7y^2 - 4y + 6) \end{array}$$ Arrange like terms in columns.

Change all signs in the second polynomial (the subtrahend), and then add.

$$\begin{array}{r} 14y^3 - 6y^2 + 2y - 5 \\ + (-2y^3 + 7y^2 + 4y - 6) \\ \hline 12y^3 + y^2 + 6y - 11 \end{array}$$ Change each sign.

Add.

◀ **Work Problem 9** at the Side.

EXAMPLE 9 **Adding and Subtracting More Than Two Polynomials**

Perform the indicated operations.

$$(4 - x + 3x^2) - (2 - 3x + 5x^2) + (8 + 2x - 4x^2)$$

Rewrite, changing subtraction to adding the opposite.

$(4 - x + 3x^2) - (2 - 3x + 5x^2) + (8 + 2x - 4x^2)$

$= (4 - x + 3x^2) + (-2 + 3x - 5x^2) + (8 + 2x - 4x^2)$

$= (2 + 2x - 2x^2) + (8 + 2x - 4x^2)$ Combine like terms.

$= 10 + 4x - 6x^2$ Combine like terms.

◀ **Work Problem 10** at the Side.

OBJECTIVE 7 **Add and subtract polynomials with more than one variable.** Polynomials in more than one variable are added and subtracted by combining like terms, just as with single-variable polynomials.

EXAMPLE 10 **Adding and Subtracting Multivariable Polynomials**

Add or subtract as indicated.

(a) $(4a + 2ab - b) + (3a - ab + b)$

$= 4a + 2ab - b + 3a - ab + b$

$= 7a + ab$ Combine like terms.

(b) $(2x^2y + 3xy + y^2) - (3x^2y - xy - 2y^2)$

$= 2x^2y + 3xy + y^2 - 3x^2y + xy + 2y^2$ Be careful with signs. The coefficient of xy is 1.

$= -x^2y + 4xy + 3y^2$

◀ **Work Problem 11** at the Side.

Answers

9. $-8y^3 - 7y^2 + 5y - 15$
10. $14p^4 - 8p^3 - 6p^2 - p + 19$
11. (a) $2mn + 6m - 3n$
(b) $3p^2q^2 - 3p^2 + 5q$

5.4 Exercises

FOR EXTRA HELP

Go to MyMathLab *for worked-out, step-by-step solutions to exercises enclosed in a square* ▢ *and video solutions to* ▶ *exercises.*

CONCEPT CHECK *Complete each statement.*

1. In the term $7x^5$, the coefficient is _____ and the exponent is _____ .

2. The expression $5x^3 - 4x^2$ has (*one* / *two* / *three*) term(s).

3. The degree of the term $-4x^8$ is _____ .

4. The polynomial $4x^2 - y^2$ (*is* / *is not*) an example of a trinomial.

5. When $x^2 + 10$ is evaluated for $x = 4$, the result is _____ .

6. _____ is an example of a monomial with coefficient 5, in the variable x, having degree 9.

Identify the coefficient of each term in the expression. Then give the number of terms. ***See Example 1.***

7. $6x^4$ ▶

8. $-9y^5$

9. t^4

10. s^7

11. $\dfrac{x}{5}$

12. $\dfrac{z}{8}$

13. $-19r^2 - r$

14. $2y^3 - y$

15. $x - 8x^2 + \dfrac{2}{3}x^3$

16. $v - 2v^3 + \dfrac{3}{4}v^2$

Simplify each expression by combining like terms, if possible. Write results with more than one term in descending powers of the variable. ***See Example 2 and Objective 3.***

17. $-3m^5 + 5m^5$ ▶

18. $-4y^3 + 3y^3$

19. $2r^5 + (-3r^5)$

20. $-19y^2 + 9y^2$

21. $\dfrac{1}{2}x^4 + \dfrac{1}{6}x^4$

22. $\dfrac{3}{10}x^6 + \dfrac{1}{5}x^6$

23. $-0.5m^2 + 0.2m^5$

24. $-0.9y + 0.9y^2$

25. $-3x^5 + 2x^5 - 4x^5$

26. $6x^3 - 8x^3 + 9x^3$

27. $-4p^7 + 8p^7 + 5p^9$ ▶

28. $-3a^8 + 4a^8 - 3a^2$

29. $-4y^2 + 3y^2 - 2y^2 + y^2$ ▶

30. $3r^5 - 8r^5 + r^5 + 2r^5$

31. $3xy + 5xy - 12xy$

32. $2ab - 4ab - 7ab$

For each polynomial, first simplify if possible, and write the result in descending powers of the variable. Then give the degree, and tell whether the simplified polynomial is a monomial, *a* binomial, *a* trinomial, *or* none of these. ***See Example 3.***

33. $6x^4 - 9x$ ▶

34. $7t^3 - 3t$

35. $x^2 + 3x + 6x - 3$

36. $y^2 - 2y - 6y + 5$

37. $5xy + 13xy - 12xy$

38. $-11ab + 2ab - 4ab$

39. $5m^4 - 3m^2 + 6m^5 - 7m^3$

40. $6p^5 + 4p^3 - 8p^4 + 10p^2$

41. $\dfrac{5}{3}x^4 - \dfrac{2}{3}x^4$

42. $\dfrac{4}{5}r^6 + \dfrac{1}{5}r^6$

43. $0.8x^4 - 0.3x^4 - 0.5x^4 + 7$

44. $1.2t^3 - 0.9t^3 - 0.3t^3 + 9$

Find the value of each polynomial for (a) $x = 2$ and for (b) $x = -1$. See Example 4.

45. $-2x + 3$

46. $5x - 4$

47. $2x^2 + 5x + 1$

48. $-3x^2 + 14x - 2$

49. $2x^5 - 4x^4 + 5x^3 - x^2$

50. $x^4 - 6x^3 + x^2 + 1$

51. $-4x^5 + x^2$

52. $2x^6 - 4x$

Add. See Example 5.

53.
$$2x^2 - 4x$$
$$+ \ \underline{(3x^2 + 2x)}$$

54.
$$-5y^3 + 3y$$
$$+ \ \underline{(\ 8y^3 - 4y)}$$

55.
$$3m^2 + 5m + 6$$
$$+ \ \underline{(2m^2 - 2m - 4)}$$

56.
$$4a^3 - 4a^2 - 4$$
$$+ \ \underline{(6a^3 + 5a^2 - 8)}$$

57.
$$\tfrac{2}{3}x^2 + \tfrac{1}{5}x + \tfrac{1}{6}$$
$$+ \ \underline{\left(\tfrac{1}{2}x^2 - \tfrac{1}{3}x + \tfrac{2}{3}\right)}$$

58.
$$\tfrac{4}{7}y^2 - \tfrac{1}{5}y + \tfrac{7}{9}$$
$$+ \ \underline{\left(\tfrac{1}{3}y^2 - \tfrac{1}{3}y + \tfrac{2}{5}\right)}$$

Subtract. See Example 8.

59.
$$5y^3 - 3y^2$$
$$- \ \underline{(2y^3 + 8y^2)}$$

60.
$$-6t^3 + 4t^2$$
$$- \ \underline{(\ 8t^3 - 6t^2)}$$

61.
$$12x^4 - \ x^2 + \ x$$
$$- \ \underline{(\ 8x^4 + 3x^2 - 3x)}$$

62.
$$13y^5 - \ y^3 - 8y^2$$
$$- \ \underline{(7y^5 + 5y^3 + \ y^2)}$$

63.
$$12m^3 - 8m^2 + 6m + 7$$
$$- \ \underline{(-3m^3 + 5m^2 - 2m - 4)}$$

64.
$$5a^4 - 3a^3 + 2a^2 - a$$
$$- \ \underline{(-6a^4 + \ a^3 - \ a^2 + a)}$$

Perform the indicated operations. ***See Examples 6, 7, and 9.***

65. $(2r^2 + 3r - 12) + (6r^2 + 2r)$

66. $(3r^2 + 5r - 6) + (2r - 5r^2)$

67. $(8m^2 - 7m) - (3m^2 + 7m - 6)$

68. $(x^2 + x) - (3x^2 + 2x - 1)$

69. $(16x^3 - x^2 + 3x) + (-12x^3 + 3x^2 + 2x)$

70. $(-2b^6 + 3b^4 - b^2) + (b^6 + 2b^4 + 2b^2)$

71. $(7y^4 + 3y^2 + 2y) - (18y^5 - 5y^3 + y)$

72. $(8t^5 + 3t^3 + 5t) - (19t^4 - 6t^2 + t)$

73. $(-4x^2 + 2x - 3) - (-2x^2 + x - 1)$
$+ (-8x^2 + 3x - 4)$

74. $(-8x^2 - 3x + 2) + (4x^2 - 3x + 8)$
$- (-2x^2 - x + 7)$

75. $\left[(8m^2 + 4m - 7) - (2m^3 - 5m + 2) \right]$
$- (m^2 + m)$

76. $\left[(9b^3 - 4b^2 + 3b + 2) - (-2b^3 + b) \right]$
$- (8b^3 + 6b + 4)$

77. Add $9m^3 - 5m^2 + 4m - 8$ and $-3m^3 + 6m^2 - 6$.

78. Add $12r^5 + 11r^4 - 2r^2$ and $-8r^5 + 3r^3 + 2r^2$.

79. Subtract $9x^2 - 3x + 7$ from $-2x^2 - 6x + 4$.

80. Subtract $-5w^3 + 5w^2 - 7$ from $6w^3 + 8w + 5$.

Find a polynomial that represents, in appropriate units, the perimeter of each square, rectangle, or triangle.

81.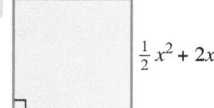
$\frac{1}{2}x^2 + 2x$

82.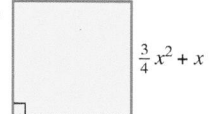
$\frac{3}{4}x^2 + x$

83.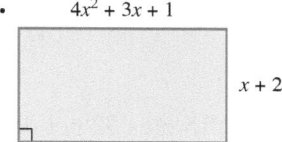
$4x^2 + 3x + 1$
$x + 2$

84.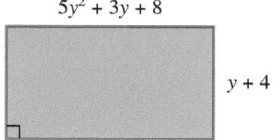
$5y^2 + 3y + 8$
$y + 4$

85.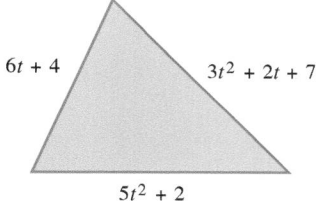
$6t + 4$
$3t^2 + 2t + 7$
$5t^2 + 2$

86.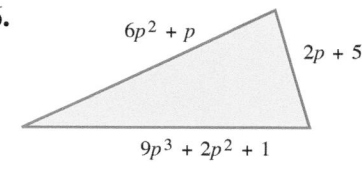
$6p^2 + p$
$2p + 5$
$9p^3 + 2p^2 + 1$

Add or subtract as indicated. See Example 10.

87. $(4x + 2xy - 3) - (-2x + 3xy + 4)$

88. $(8ab + 2a - 3b) - (6ab - 2a + 3b)$

89. $(9a^2b - 3a^2 + 2b) + (4a^2b - 4a^2 - 3b)$

90. $(4xy^3 - 3x + y) + (5xy^3 + 13x - 4y)$

91. $(2c^4d + 3c^2d^2 - 4d^2) - (c^4d + 8c^2d^2 - 5d^2)$

92. $(3k^2h^3 + 5kh + 6k^3h^2) - (2k^2h^3 - 9kh + k^3h^2)$

*Find **(a)** a polynomial that represents the perimeter of each triangle and **(b)** the measures of the angles of the triangle. (Hint: The sum of the measures of the angles of any triangle is 180°.)*

93.

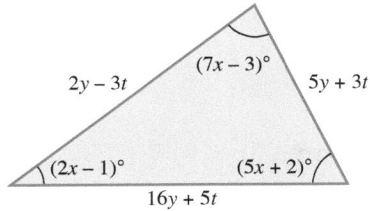

$2y - 3t$ $(7x - 3)°$ $5y + 3t$
$(2x - 1)°$ $(5x + 2)°$
$16y + 5t$

94.

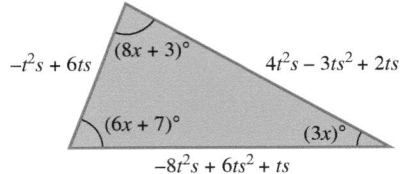

$-t^2s + 6ts$ $(8x + 3)°$ $4t^2s - 3ts^2 + 2ts$
$(6x + 7)°$ $(3x)°$
$-8t^2s + 6ts^2 + ts$

Relating Concepts (Exercises 95–98) For Individual or Group Work

The following binomial models the distance in feet that a car going approximately 68 mph will skid in t seconds.

$$100t - 13t^2$$

*When we evaluate this binomial for a value of t, we obtain a value for distance. This illustrates the concept of a **function**—for each input of a time, we obtain one and only one output for distance.*

*Exercises 95–98 further illustrate the function concept with polynomials. **Work them in order.***

95. Evaluate the given binomial

$$100t - 13t^2$$

for $t = 5$. Use the result to fill in the blanks:

In _____ seconds, the car will skid _____ feet.

96. If one "dog" year is estimated to be about seven "human" years, the monomial

$$7x$$

gives the dog's age in human years for x dog years. Evaluate this monomial for $x = 9$. Use the result to fill in the blanks:

If a dog is _____ in dog years, then it is _____ in human years.

97. If it costs $15 plus $2 per day to rent a chain saw, the binomial

$$2x + 15$$

gives the cost in dollars to rent the chain saw for x days. Evaluate this binomial for $x = 6$. Use the result to fill in the blanks:

If the saw is rented for _____ days, then the cost is _____ dollars.

98. If an object is projected upward under certain conditions, its height in feet is given by the trinomial

$$-16t^2 + 60t + 80,$$

where t is in seconds. Evaluate this trinomial for $t = 2.5$. Use the result to fill in the blanks:

If _____ seconds have elapsed, then the height of the object is _____ feet.

5.5 | Multiplying Polynomials

OBJECTIVE ▶ 1 Multiply monomials. Recall that we multiply monomials using the product rule for exponents.

OBJECTIVES

1 Multiply monomials.

2 Multiply a monomial and a polynomial.

3 Multiply two polynomials.

4 Multiply binomials using the FOIL method.

EXAMPLE 1   Multiplying Monomials

Find each product.

(a) $8m^2(-9m)$

$= 8(-9) \cdot m^2 m^1$

$= -72m^{2+1}$

$= -72m^3$

(b) $4x^3 y^2(2x^2 y)$

$= 4(2) \cdot x^3 x^2 \cdot y^2 y^1$ Commutative and associative properties

$= 8x^{3+2} y^{2+1}$ Multiply; product rule

$= 8x^5 y^3$ Add.

——————————— **Work Problem 1 at the Side.** ▶

OBJECTIVE ▶ 2 Multiply a monomial and a polynomial. We use the distributive property and multiplication of monomials.

EXAMPLE 2   Multiplying Monomials and Polynomials

Find each product.

a) $4x^2(3x + 5)$ $a(b + c) = ab + ac$

$= 4x^2(3x) + 4x^2(5)$ Distributive property

$= 12x^3 + 20x^2$ Multiply monomials.

b) $-8m^3(4m^3 + 3m^2 + 2m - 1)$

$= -8m^3(4m^3) + (-8m^3)(3m^2)$
$\quad + (-8m^3)(2m) + (-8m^3)(-1)$ Distributive property

$= -32m^6 - 24m^5 - 16m^4 + 8m^3$ Multiply monomials.

——————————— **Work Problem 2 at the Side.** ▶

OBJECTIVE ▶ 3 Multiply two polynomials. To find the product of the polynomials $x^2 + 3x + 5$ and $x - 4$, think of $x - 4$ as a single quantity and use the distributive property as follows.

$(x^2 + 3x + 5)(x - 4)$

$= x^2(x - 4) + 3x(x - 4) + 5(x - 4)$ Distributive property

$= x^2(x) + x^2(-4) + 3x(x) + 3x(-4) + 5(x) + 5(-4)$

   Distributive property again

$= x^3 - 4x^2 + 3x^2 - 12x + 5x - 20$ Multiply monomials.

$= x^3 - x^2 - 7x - 20$ Combine like terms.

Multiplying Polynomials

To multiply two polynomials, multiply each term of the first polynomial by each term of the second polynomial. Then combine like terms.

1 Find each product.

(a) $2x(3x)$

(b) $-6x(5x^3)$

(c) $10x^2(-8xy^2)$

(d) $6mn^3(12mn)$

2 Find each product.

GS (a) $5m^3(2m + 7)$

$= 5m^3(\underline{\quad}) + 5m^3(\underline{\quad})$

$= \underline{\qquad\qquad}$

(b) $2x^4(3x^2 + 2x - 5)$

(c) $-4y^2(3y^3 + 2y^2 - 4y + 8)$

Answers

1. (a) $6x^2$ (b) $-30x^4$
   (c) $-80x^3 y^2$ (d) $72m^2 n^4$
2. (a) $2m$; 7; $10m^4 + 35m^3$
   (b) $6x^6 + 4x^5 - 10x^4$
   (c) $-12y^5 - 8y^4 + 16y^3 - 32y^2$

3 Multiply.

(a) $(m + 3)(m^2 - 2m + 1)$

(b) $(6p^2 + 2p - 4)(3p^2 - 5)$

EXAMPLE 3 Multiplying Two Polynomials

Multiply $(m^2 + 5)(4m^3 - 2m^2 + 4m)$.

$(m^2 + 5)(4m^3 - 2m^2 + 4m)$ Multiply each term of the first polynomial by each term of the second.

$= m^2(4m^3) + m^2(-2m^2) + m^2(4m) + 5(4m^3) + 5(-2m^2) + 5(4m)$ Distributive property

$= 4m^5 - 2m^4 + 4m^3 + 20m^3 - 10m^2 + 20m$ Distributive property again

$= 4m^5 - 2m^4 + 24m^3 - 10m^2 + 20m$ Combine like terms.

◀ **Work Problem 3 at the Side.**

---

4 Multiply vertically.

$$3x^2 + 4x - 5$$
$$\underline{x + 4}$$

EXAMPLE 4 Multiplying Polynomials Vertically

Multiply $(x^3 + 2x^2 + 4x + 1)(3x + 5)$ vertically.

$$x^3 + 2x^2 + 4x + 1$$
$$\underline{3x + 5}$$ Write the polynomials vertically.

Begin by multiplying each of the terms in the top row by 5.

$$x^3 + 2x^2 + 4x + 1$$
$$\underline{3x + 5}$$
$$5x^3 + 10x^2 + 20x + 5 \quad 5(x^3 + 2x^2 + 4x + 1)$$

Now multiply each term in the top row by $3x$. Then add like terms.

$$x^3 + 2x^2 + 4x + 1$$
$$\underline{3x + 5}$$ This process is similar to multiplication of whole numbers.

Place *like* terms in columns so they can be added.

$$5x^3 + 10x^2 + 20x + 5$$
$$\underline{3x^4 + \ 6x^3 + 12x^2 + \ \ 3x} \quad 3x(x^3 + 2x^2 + 4x + 1)$$
$$3x^4 + 11x^3 + 22x^2 + 23x + 5 \quad \text{Add in columns.}$$

◀ **Work Problem 4 at the Side.**

---

5 Use the rectangle method to find each product.

GS (a) $(4x + 3)(x + 2)$

	x	2
$4x$	$4x^2$	
3		

(b) $(x + 5)(x^2 + 3x + 1)$

We can use a rectangle to model polynomial multiplication. For example, to find the product

$$(2x + 1)(3x + 2),$$

we label a rectangle with each term as shown below on the left. Then we write the product of each pair of monomials in the appropriate box as shown on the right.

	$3x$	2
$2x$		
1		

	$3x$	2
$2x$	$6x^2$	$4x$
1	$3x$	2

The product of the binomials is the sum of these four monomial products.

$(2x + 1)(3x + 2)$

$= 6x^2 + 4x + 3x + 2$

$= 6x^2 + 7x + 2$ Combine like terms.

◀ **Work Problem 5 at the Side.**

Answers

3. (a) $m^3 + m^2 - 5m + 3$
   (b) $18p^4 + 6p^3 - 42p^2 - 10p + 20$

4. $3x^3 + 16x^2 + 11x - 20$

5. (a)
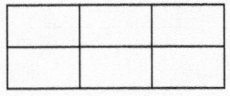

	x	2
$4x$	$4x^2$	$8x$
3	$3x$	6

   $4x^2 + 11x + 6$
   (b) $x^3 + 8x^2 + 16x + 5$

OBJECTIVE ▶ **4** **Multiply binomials using the FOIL method.** When multiplying binomials, the **FOIL method** reduces the rectangle method to a systematic approach without the rectangle. Consider this example.

$$(x + 3)(x + 5)$$

$$= x(x + 5) + 3(x + 5) \qquad \text{Distributive property}$$

$$= x(x) + x(5) + 3(x) + 3(5) \qquad \text{Distributive property again}$$

$$= x^2 + 5x + 3x + 15 \qquad \text{Multiply.}$$

$$= x^2 + 8x + 15 \qquad \text{Combine like terms.}$$

The letters of the word FOIL refer to the positions of the terms.

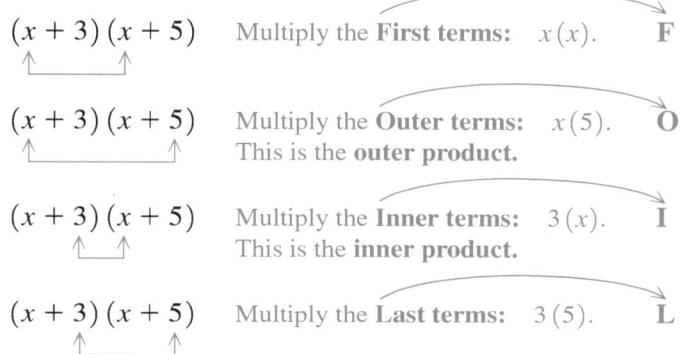

$(x + 3)(x + 5)$ Multiply the **First terms:** $x(x)$.   **F**

$(x + 3)(x + 5)$ Multiply the **Outer terms:** $x(5)$.   **O**
                   This is the **outer product.**

$(x + 3)(x + 5)$ Multiply the **Inner terms:** $3(x)$.   **I**
                   This is the **inner product.**

$(x + 3)(x + 5)$ Multiply the **Last terms:** $3(5)$.   **L**

We add the outer product, $5x$, and the inner product, $3x$, mentally so that the three terms of the answer can be written without extra steps.

$$(x + 3)(x + 5)$$
$$= x^2 + 8x + 15$$

FOIL Method for Multiplying Binomials

Step 1   Multiply the two **F**irst terms of the binomials to obtain the first term of the product.

Step 2   Find the **O**uter product and the **I**nner product and combine them (when possible) to obtain the middle term of the product.

Step 3   Multiply the two **L**ast terms of the binomials to obtain the last term of the product.

Step 4   Add the terms found in Steps 1–3.

Example:

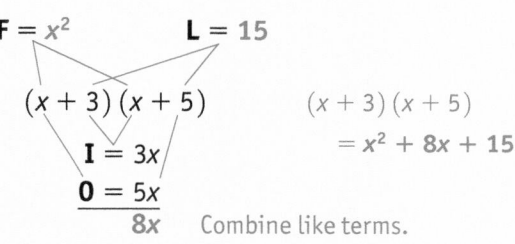

$F = x^2$ $L = 15$

$(x + 3)(x + 5)$ $(x + 3)(x + 5)$

$I = 3x$ $= x^2 + 8x + 15$

$O = 5x$
_____
$8x$ Combine like terms.

Work Problem ⑥ at the Side. ▶

---

⑥ **GS** For the product

$$(2p - 5)(3p + 7),$$

find and simplify the following.

(a) Product of first terms

____(____)

= ____

(b) Outer product

____(____)

= ____

(c) Inner product

____(____)

= ____

(d) Product of last terms

____(____)

= ____

(e) Complete product in simplified form

_____

Answers

6. **(a)** $2p$; $3p$; $6p^2$ **(b)** $2p$; 7; $14p$
   (c) -5; $3p$; $-15p$ **(d)** -5; 7; -35
   (e) $6p^2 - p - 35$

7 Use the FOIL method to find each product.

(a) $(m + 4)(m - 3)$

$$= m(\underline{\quad}) + m(\underline{\quad})$$
$$+ 4(\underline{\quad}) + 4(\underline{\quad})$$
$$= \underline{\hspace{3cm}}$$

(b) $(y + 7)(y + 2)$

(c) $(r - 8)(r - 5)$

8 Multiply.
$$(4x - 3)(2y + 5)$$

9 Find each product.

(a) $(6m + 5)(m - 4)$

$$= 6m(\underline{\quad}) + 6m(\underline{\quad})$$
$$+ 5(\underline{\quad}) + 5(\underline{\quad})$$
$$= \underline{\hspace{3cm}}$$

(b) $(3r + 2t)(3r + 4t)$

(c) $y^2(8y + 3)(2y + 1)$

$$= y^2(\underline{\hspace{2.5cm}})$$
$$= \underline{\hspace{3cm}}$$

EXAMPLE 5   Using the FOIL Method

Use the FOIL method to find the product $(x + 8)(x - 6)$.

Step 1 **F** Multiply the **first** terms: $x(x) = x^2$.

Step 2 **O** Find the **outer** product: $x(-6) = -6x$. ⎫ Combine.
         I Find the **inner** product: $8(x) = 8x$. ⎭ $-6x + 8x = 2x$

Step 3 **L** Multiply the **last** terms: $8(-6) = -48$.

Step 4 The product $(x + 8)(x - 6)$ is $x^2 + 2x - 48$.   Add the terms found in Steps 1–3.

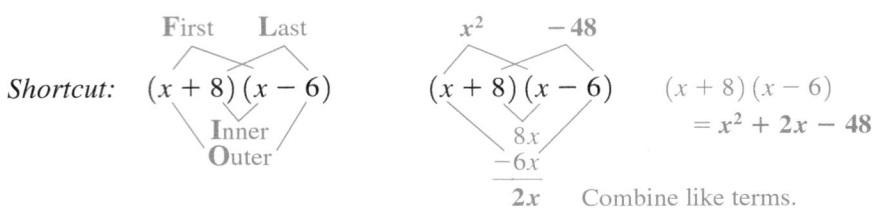

Shortcut:

$2x$ Combine like terms.

◀ **Work Problem 7** at the Side

EXAMPLE 6   Using the FOIL Method

Multiply $(9x - 2)(3y + 1)$.

First	$(9x - 2)(3y + 1)$	$27xy$
Outer	$(9x - 2)(3y + 1)$	$9x$
Inner	$(9x - 2)(3y + 1)$	$-6y$
Last	$(9x - 2)(3y + 1)$	-2

These unlike terms *cannot* be combined.

The product $(9x - 2)(3y + 1)$ is $27xy + 9x - 6y - 2$.

◀ **Work Problem 8** at the Side

EXAMPLE 7   Using the FOIL Method

Find each product.

(a) $(2k + 5y)(k + 3y)$

$$= 2k(k) + 2k(3y) + 5y(k) + 5y(3y) \quad \text{FOIL method}$$
$$= 2k^2 + 6ky + 5ky + 15y^2 \quad \text{Multiply.}$$
$$= 2k^2 + 11ky + 15y^2 \quad \text{Combine like terms.}$$

(b) $(7p + 2q)(3p - q)$

$$= 21p^2 - 7pq + 6pq - 2q^2$$
$$= 21p^2 - pq - 2q^2$$

(c) $2x^2(x - 3)(3x + 4)$

$$= 2x^2(3x^2 - 5x - 12)$$
$$= 6x^4 - 10x^3 - 24x^2$$

◀ **Work Problem 9** at the Side

Answers

7. **(a)** $m; -3; m; -3; m^2 + m - 12$
   (b) $y^2 + 9y + 14$
   (c) $r^2 - 13r + 40$
8. $8xy + 20x - 6y - 15$
9. **(a)** $m; -4; m; -4; 6m^2 - 19m - 20$
   (b) $9r^2 + 18rt + 8t^2$
   (c) $16y^2 + 14y + 3; 16y^4 + 14y^3 + 3y^2$

Note

Alternatively, multiply in **Example 7 (c)** as follows.

$$2x^2(x - 3)(3x + 4) \quad \text{Multiply } 2x^2 \text{ and } x - 3 \text{ first.}$$
$$= (2x^3 - 6x^2)(3x + 4) \quad \text{Multiply that product and } 3x + 4.$$
$$= 6x^4 - 10x^3 - 24x^2 \quad \text{The same answer results.}$$

5.5 Exercises

FOR EXTRA HELP

Go to MyMathLab *for worked-out, step-by-step solutions to exercises enclosed in a square* and *video solutions to* ▶ *exercises.*

CONCEPT CHECK *Match each product in Column I with the correct polynomial in Column II.*

I	II
1. (a) $5x^3(6x^7)$	**A.** $125x^{21}$
(b) $-5x^7(6x^3)$	**B.** $30x^{10}$
(c) $(5x^7)^3$	**C.** $-216x^9$
(d) $(-6x^3)^3$	**D.** $-30x^{10}$

I	II
2. (a) $(x-5)(x+4)$	**A.** $x^2+9x+20$
(b) $(x+5)(x+4)$	**B.** $x^2-9x+20$
(c) $(x-5)(x-4)$	**C.** x^2-x-20
(d) $(x+5)(x-4)$	**D.** x^2+x-20

CONCEPT CHECK *Complete each statement.*

3. In multiplying a monomial by a polynomial, such as in $4x(3x^2+7x^3)=4x(3x^2)+4x(7x^3)$, the first property that is used is the _____ property.

4. The FOIL method can only be used to multiply two polynomials when both polynomials are (*monomials / binomials / trinomials*).

Find each product. **See Example 1.**

5. $4x(3x^2)$

6. $6x(7x^4)$

7. $5y^4(-3y^7)$

8. $10p^2(-5p^3)$

9. $-15a^4(-2a^5)$

10. $-3m^6(-5m^4)$

11. $-6m^3(3n^2)$

12. $-2s^2(9r^3)$

13. $4a(5ab)$

14. $7y(3xy)$

15. $2m^2n(-6mn^3)$

16. $8xy^3(-9xy^2)$

Find each product. **See Example 2.**

17. $2m(3m+2)$ ▶

18. $4x(5x+3)$

19. $2y^5(5y^4+2y+3)$

20. $2m^4(3m^2+5m+6)$

21. $2y^3(3y^3+2y+1)$

22. $2m^4(3m^2+5m+1)$

23. $\frac{3}{4}p(8-6p+12p^3)$

24. $\frac{4}{3}x(3+2x+5x^3)$

25. $-4r^3(-7r^2+8r-9)$

26. $-9a^5(-3a^6-2a^4+8a^2)$

27. $3a^2(2a^2-4ab+5b^2)$

28. $4z^3(8z^2+5zy-3y^2)$

29. $7m^3n^2(3m^2+2mn-n^3)$
$= 7m^3n^2(\_\_\_) + 7m^3n^2(\_\_\_) + 7m^3n^2(\_\_\_)$
$= \underline{}$

30. $2p^2q(3p^2q^2-5p+2q^2)$
$= \_\_\_(3p^2q^2) + \_\_\_(-5p) + \_\_\_(2q^2)$
$= \underline{}$

Find each product. ***See Examples 3 and 4.***

31. $(6x + 1)(2x^2 + 4x + 1)$
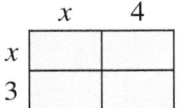

32. $(9a + 2)(9a^2 + a + 1)$

33. $(2r - 1)(3r^2 + 4r - 4)$

34. $(9y - 2)(8y^2 - 6y + 1)$

35. $(4m + 3)(5m^3 - 4m^2 + m - 5)$

36. $(y + 4)(3y^3 - 2y^2 + y + 3)$

37. $(5x^2 + 2x + 1)(x^2 - 3x + 5)$

38. $(2m^2 + m - 3)(m^2 - 4m + 5)$

39. $(6x^4 - 4x^2 + 8x)\left(\frac{1}{2}x + 3\right)$

40. $(8y^6 + 4y^4 - 12y^2)\left(\frac{3}{4}y^2 + 2\right)$

GS *Find each product using the rectangle method shown in the text. Determine the individual terms that should appear on the blanks or in the rectangles, and then give the final product.*

41. $(x + 3)(x + 4)$

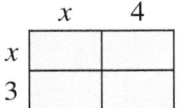

Product: _____

42. $(x + 5)(x + 2)$

Product: _____

43. $(2x + 1)(x^2 + 3x + 2)$

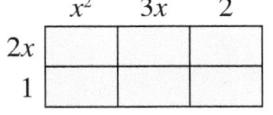

Product: _____

44. $(x + 4)(3x^2 + 2x + 1)$

Product: _____

Find each product. ***See Examples 5–7.***

45. $(m + 7)(m + 5)$

46. $(x + 4)(x + 7)$

47. $(n - 2)(n + 3)$

48. $(r - 6)(r + 8)$

49. $(4r + 1)(2r - 3)$

50. $(5x + 2)(2x - 7)$

51. $(3x + 2)(3x - 2)$

52. $(7x + 3)(7x - 3)$

53. $(3q + 1)(3q + 1)$

54. $(4w + 7)(4w + 7)$

55. $(4x + 3)(2y - 1)$

56. $(5x + 7)(3y - 8)$

57. $(3x + 2y)(5x - 3y)$

58. $(5a + 3b)(5a - 4b)$

59. $(3t + 4s)(2t + 5s)$

60. $(8v + 5w)(2v + 3w)$

61. $(-0.3t + 0.4)(t + 0.6)$

62. $(-0.5x + 0.9)(x - 0.2)$

63. $\left(x - \dfrac{2}{3}\right)\left(x + \dfrac{1}{4}\right)$
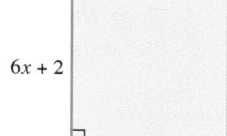

64. $\left(y + \dfrac{3}{5}\right)\left(y - \dfrac{1}{2}\right)$

65. $\left(-\dfrac{5}{4} + 2r\right)\left(-\dfrac{3}{4} - r\right)$

66. $\left(-\dfrac{8}{3} + 3k\right)\left(-\dfrac{2}{3} - k\right)$

67. $x(2x - 5)(x + 3)$

68. $m(4m - 1)(2m + 3)$

69. $3y^3(2y + 3)(y - 5)$

70. $5t^4(t + 3)(3t - 1)$

71. $-8r^3(5r^2 + 2)(5r^2 - 2)$

72. $-5t^4(2t^4 + 1)(2t^4 - 1)$

Find polynomials that represent, in appropriate units, (a) the area and (b) the perimeter of each square or rectangle. (If necessary, refer to the formulas at the back of this text.)

73.
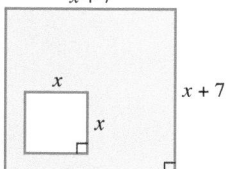

74.

Find a polynomial that represents, in appropriate units, the area of each shaded region. (If necessary, refer to the formulas at the back of this text.)

75.

76.
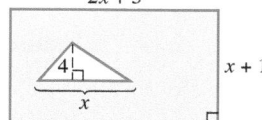

Relating Concepts (Exercises 77–82) For Individual or Group Work

Work Exercises 77–82 in order. (All units are in feet.)

77. Find a polynomial that represents the area, in square feet, of the rectangle.

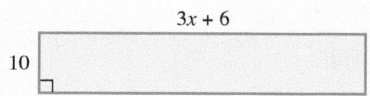

78. Suppose we know that the area of the rectangle is 600 ft². Use this information and the polynomial from **Exercise 77** to write an equation in x, and solve it.

79. Refer to **Exercise 78.** What are the dimensions of the rectangle?

80. Use the result of **Exercise 79** to find the perimeter of the rectangle.

81. Suppose the rectangle represents a lawn and it costs $1.50 per square foot for sod. How much will it cost to sod the entire lawn?

82. Again, suppose the rectangle represents a lawn and it costs $20.50 per linear foot for fencing. How much will it cost to fence the entire lawn?

5.6 | Special Products

OBJECTIVES

1. Square binomials.
2. Find the product of the sum and difference of two terms.
3. Find greater powers of binomials.

---

1. Consider the binomial $x + 4$.

GS (a) What is the first term of the binomial? ____

   Square it. ____

(b) What is the last term of the binomial? ____

   Square it. ____

(c) Find twice the product of the two terms of the binomial.

   $2($____$)($____$) = $____

(d) Use the results of parts (a)–(c) to find $(x + 4)^2$.

   _____

OBJECTIVE 1 **Square binomials.**

EXAMPLE 1 **Squaring a Binomial**

Find $(m + 3)^2$. $(m + 3)^2$ means $(m + 3)(m + 3)$.

$$(m + 3)(m + 3)$$
$$= m^2 + m(3) + 3(m) + 9 \quad \text{FOIL method}$$
$$= m^2 + 6m + 9 \quad \text{Combine like terms.}$$

Compare the result, $m^2 + 6m + 9$, to the binomial $m + 3$. The trinomial result includes the squares of the first and last terms of the binomial.

$$m^2 = m^2 \quad \text{and} \quad 3^2 = 9$$

The middle term of the trinomial, 6m, is twice the product of the two terms of the binomial, m and 3. This is true because when we used the FOIL method above, the outer and inner products were $m(3)$ and $3(m)$, and

$$m(3) + 3(m) \quad \text{equals} \quad 2(m)(3).$$

Thus, $(m + 3)^2 = m^2 + 6m + 9.$

Square m. $\quad$ $2(m)(3)$ $\quad$ Square 3.

◀ **Work Problem** 1 **at the Side.**

Example 1 suggests the following rules.

Square of a Binomial

The square of a binomial is a *trinomial* consisting of

$$\begin{array}{c} \text{the square of} \\ \text{the first term} \end{array} + \begin{array}{c} \text{twice the product} \\ \text{of the two terms} \end{array} + \begin{array}{c} \text{the square of} \\ \text{the last term.} \end{array}$$

For x and y, the following hold true.

$$(x + y)^2 = x^2 + 2xy + y^2$$
$$(x - y)^2 = x^2 - 2xy + y^2$$

EXAMPLE 2 **Squaring Binomials**

Square each binomial.

$$(x - y)^2 = x^2 - 2 \cdot x \cdot y + y^2$$

(a) $(t - 8)^2 = t^2 - 2(t)(8) + 8^2$
$$= t^2 - 16t + 64$$

Continued on Next Page

Answers

1. (a) x; x^2 (b) 4; 16 (c) x; 4; $8x$
   (d) $x^2 + 8x + 16$

(b) $(5z - 1)^2$

$\begin{aligned} &= (5z)^2 - 2(5z)(1) + 1^2 \qquad (x - y)^2 = x^2 - 2xy + y^2 \\ &= 5^2z^2 - 10z + 1 \qquad\qquad (5z)^2 = 5^2z^2 = 25z^2 \\ &= 25z^2 - 10z + 1 \qquad\qquad \text{by power rule (b).} \end{aligned}$

> Be careful to square 5z correctly.

(c) $(3b + 5r)^2$

$\begin{aligned} &= (3b)^2 + 2(3b)(5r) + (5r)^2 \qquad (x + y)^2 = x^2 + 2xy + y^2 \\ &= 9b^2 + 30br + 25r^2 \qquad\qquad (3b)^2 = 3^2b^2 = 9b^2 \text{ and} \\ &\qquad\qquad\qquad\qquad\qquad\qquad (5r)^2 = 5^2r^2 = 25r^2 \end{aligned}$

(d) $(2a - 9x)^2$

$\begin{aligned} &= (2a)^2 - 2(2a)(9x) + (9x)^2 \qquad (x - y)^2 = x^2 - 2xy + y^2 \\ &= 4a^2 - 36ax + 81x^2 \qquad\qquad (2a)^2 = 2^2a^2 = 4a^2 \text{ and} \\ &\qquad\qquad\qquad\qquad\qquad\qquad (9x)^2 = 9^2x^2 = 81x^2 \end{aligned}$

(e) $\left(4m + \dfrac{1}{2} \right)^2$

$\begin{aligned} &= (4m)^2 + 2(4m)\left(\dfrac{1}{2}\right) + \left(\dfrac{1}{2}\right)^2 \qquad (x + y)^2 = x^2 + 2xy + y^2 \\ \\ &= 16m^2 + 4m + \dfrac{1}{4} \qquad\qquad (4m)^2 = 4^2m^2 = 16m^2 \text{ and } \left(\tfrac{1}{2}\right)^2 = \tfrac{1}{4} \end{aligned}$

(f) $x(4x - 3)^2$

> Remember the middle term, $2(4x)(3)$.

$\begin{aligned} &= x(16x^2 - 24x + 9) \qquad \text{Square the binomial.} \\ &= 16x^3 - 24x^2 + 9x \qquad \text{Distributive property} \end{aligned}$

——————————— **Work Problem ❷ at the Side.** ▶

In the square of a sum, all of the terms are positive. (See Examples 2(c) and (e).) In the square of a difference, the middle term is negative. (See Examples 2(a), (b), and (d).)

> ❗ **CAUTION**
> A common error in squaring a binomial is to forget the middle term of the product. In general, remember the following.
> $$(x + y)^2 = x^2 + 2xy + y^2, \quad \textbf{\textit{not}} \quad x^2 + y^2.$$
> $$(x - y)^2 = x^2 - 2xy + y^2, \quad \textbf{\textit{not}} \quad x^2 - y^2.$$

OBJECTIVE ▶ **2** **Find the product of the sum and difference of two terms.**
In binomial products of the form $(x + y)(x - y)$, one binomial is the sum of two terms, and the other is the difference of the *same* two terms. Consider the following.

$$(x + 2)(x - 2)$$
$$= x^2 - 2x + 2x - 4 \qquad \text{FOIL method}$$
$$= x^2 - 4 \qquad \text{Combine like terms.}$$

Thus, the product of $x + y$ and $x - y$ is a **difference of two squares**.

❷ Square each binomial.

ⓖⓢ (a) $(t + 6)^2$

$= (\underline{\quad})^2 + 2(\underline{\quad})(\underline{\quad})$
$\quad + (\underline{\quad})^2$

$= \underline{\hspace{4cm}}$

(b) $(2m - p)^2$

ⓖⓢ (c) $(4p + 3q)^2$

$= (\underline{\quad})^2 + \underline{\quad}(\underline{\quad})\,3q$
$\quad + (\underline{\quad})^2$

$= \underline{\hspace{4cm}}$

(d) $(5r - 6s)^2$

(e) $\left(3k - \dfrac{1}{2} \right)^2$

(f) $x(2x + 7)^2$

Answers
2. **(a)** $t; t; 6; 6; t^2 + 12t + 36$
   (b) $4m^2 - 4mp + p^2$
   (c) $4p; 2; 4p; 3q; 16p^2 + 24pq + 9q^2$
   (d) $25r^2 - 60rs + 36s^2$
   (e) $9k^2 - 3k + \dfrac{1}{4}$
   (f) $4x^3 + 28x^2 + 49x$

3 Find each product.

GS **(a)** $(y + 3)(y - 3)$

$= (\underline{\quad})^2 - (\underline{\quad})^2$

$= \underline{\hspace{3cm}}$

(b) $(8 - x)(8 + x)$

(c) $2x^2(x + 5)(x - 5)$

Product of a Sum and Difference of Two Terms

The product of a sum and difference of two terms is a *binomial* consisting of

the square of __ the square of
the first term   the second term.

For *x* and *y*, the following holds true.

$$(x + y)(x - y) = x^2 - y^2$$

Note

The expressions $x + y$ and $x - y$, the sum and difference of the *same* two terms, are **conjugates**.

Example: $x + 2$ and $x - 2$ are conjugates.

EXAMPLE 3 Finding the Product of a Sum and Difference of Two Terms

Find each product.

(a) $(x + 4)(x - 4)$

$= x^2 - 4^2 \qquad (x + y)(x - y) = x^2 - y^2$

$= x^2 - 16 \qquad$ Square 4.

(b) $(10 - w)(10 + w)$

$= (10 + w)(10 - w) \qquad$ Commutative property

$= 10^2 - w^2 \qquad (x + y)(x - y) = x^2 - y^2$

$= 100 - w^2 \qquad$ Square 10.

(c) $x(x + 2)(x - 2)$

$= x(x^2 - 4) \qquad$ Find the product of the sum and difference of two terms.

$= x^3 - 4x \qquad$ Distributive property

◀ **Work Problem 3 at the Side.**

EXAMPLE 4 Finding the Product of a Sum and Difference of Two Terms

Find each product.

$$(x \; + \; y) \; (x \; - \; y)$$
$$\downarrow \quad \downarrow \quad \downarrow \quad \downarrow$$

(a) $(5m + 3)(5m - 3)$

$= (5m)^2 - 3^2 \qquad (x + y)(x - y) = x^2 - y^2$

Be careful to square 5*m* correctly.

$= 25m^2 - 9 \qquad$ Apply the exponents.

(b) $(4x + y)(4x - y)$

$= (4x)^2 - y^2$

$= 16x^2 - y^2 \qquad (4x)^2 = 4^2x^2 = 16x^2$

Continued on Next Page

Answers

3. **(a)** y; 3; $y^2 - 9$
    (b) $64 - x^2$ **(c)** $2x^4 - 50x^2$

(c) $\left(z - \dfrac{1}{4} \right)\left(z + \dfrac{1}{4} \right)$

$= z^2 - \left(\dfrac{1}{4} \right)^2 \qquad \begin{array}{l} (x - y)(x + y) = (x + y)(x - y) \\ \qquad\qquad\qquad = x^2 - y^2 \end{array}$

$= z^2 - \dfrac{1}{16}$

(d) $p\,(2p + 1)(2p - 1)$

$= p\,(4p^2 - 1)$

$= 4p^3 - p \qquad\qquad$ Distributive property

(e) $-3\,(x + y^2)(x - y^2)$

$= -3\,(x^2 - y^4)$

$= -3x^2 + 3y^4$

―――――――――――――― Work Problem ④ at the Side. ▶

Work Problem ④ at the Side. ▶

OBJECTIVE ▶ 3 **Find greater powers of binomials.** The methods used in the previous section and this section can be combined to find greater powers of binomials.

EXAMPLE 5 **Finding Greater Powers of Binomials**

Find each product.

(a) $(x + 5)^3$

$= (x + 5)(x + 5)^2 \qquad\qquad a^3 = a \cdot a^2$

$= (x + 5)(x^2 + 10x + 25) \qquad$ Square the binomial.

$= x^3 + 10x^2 + 25x + 5x^2 + 50x + 125 \qquad$ Multiply polynomials.

$= x^3 + 15x^2 + 75x + 125 \qquad$ Combine like terms.

(b) $(2y - 3)^4$

$= (2y - 3)^2 (2y - 3)^2 \qquad\qquad a^4 = a^2 \cdot a^2$

$= (4y^2 - 12y + 9)(4y^2 - 12y + 9) \qquad$ Square each binomial.

$= 16y^4 - 48y^3 + 36y^2 - 48y^3 + 144y^2 \qquad$ Multiply polynomials.
$\quad - 108y + 36y^2 - 108y + 81$

$= 16y^4 - 96y^3 + 216y^2 - 216y + 81 \qquad$ Combine like terms.

(c) $-2r\,(r + 2)^3$

$= -2r\,(r + 2)(r + 2)^2 \qquad\qquad a^3 = a \cdot a^2$

$= -2r\,(r + 2)(r^2 + 4r + 4) \qquad$ Square the binomial.

$= -2r\,(r^3 + 4r^2 + 4r + 2r^2 + 8r + 8) \qquad$ Multiply polynomials.

$= -2r\,(r^3 + 6r^2 + 12r + 8) \qquad$ Combine like terms.

$= -2r^4 - 12r^3 - 24r^2 - 16r \qquad$ Distributive property

―――――――――――――― Work Problem ⑤ at the Side. ▶

Work Problem ⑤ at the Side. ▶

④ Find each product.

(a) $(10m + 7)(10m - 7)$

GS (b) $(7p + 2q)(7p - 2q)$

$= (\underline{\quad})^2 - (\underline{\quad})^2$

$= \underline{\qquad\qquad}$

(c) $\left(3r - \dfrac{1}{2} \right)\left(3r + \dfrac{1}{2} \right)$

(d) $-7\,(t^2 - q)(t^2 + q)$

⑤ Find each product.

GS (a) $(m + 3)^3$

$= (\underline{\quad})\,(\underline{\quad})^2$

$= (m + 3)\,(\underline{\qquad})$

$= \underline{\qquad\qquad}$

(b) $(3k - 2)^4$

(c) $-3x\,(x - 4)^3$

Answers

4. (a) $100m^2 - 49$ **(b)** $7p;\ 2q;\ 49p^2 - 4q^2$

   (c) $9r^2 - \dfrac{1}{4}$ **(d)** $-7t^4 + 7q^2$

5. (a) $m + 3;\ m + 3;\ m^2 + 6m + 9;$
   $m^3 + 9m^2 + 27m + 27$

   (b) $81k^4 - 216k^3 + 216k^2 - 96k + 16$

   (c) $-3x^4 + 36x^3 - 144x^2 + 192x$

5.6 Exercises

FOR EXTRA HELP Go to MyMathLab *for worked-out, step-by-step solutions to exercises enclosed in a square* ☐ *and video solutions to* ▶ *exercises.*

CONCEPT CHECK *Fill in each blank with the correct response.*

1. The square of a binomial is a trinomial consisting of the _____ of the first term + _____ the _____ of the two terms + the _____ of the last term.

2. The product of a sum and difference of two terms is the _____ of the _____ of the two terms.

3. Consider the square of the binomial $2x + 3$:

ⒼⓈ
$$(2x + 3)^2.$$

(a) What is the first term of the binomial? Square it.

(b) Find twice the product of the two terms of the binomial: $2(\_\_\_)(\_\_\_) = \_\_\_.$

(c) What is the last term of the binomial? Square it.

(d) Use the results of parts (a)–(c) to find $(2x + 3)^2$.

4. Repeat **Exercise 3** for the binomial square $(3x - 2)^2$.

ⒼⓈ

Square each binomial. ***See Examples 1 and 2.***

5. $(p + 2)^2$

6. $(r + 5)^2$

7. $(z - 5)^2$

8. $(x - 3)^2$

9. $\left(x - \dfrac{3}{4}\right)^2$

10. $\left(y + \dfrac{5}{8}\right)^2$

11. $(v + 0.4)^2$

12. $(w - 0.9)^2$

13. $(4x - 3)^2$

14. $(9y - 4)^2$

15. $(10z + 6)^2$

16. $(5y + 2)^2$

17. $(x + 2y)^2$
▶

18. $(p + 3m)^2$

19. $(2p + 5q)^2$

20. $(8a + 3b)^2$

21. $(4a - 5b)^2$

22. $(9y - 4z)^2$

23. $(0.8t + 0.7s)^2$

24. $(0.7z - 0.3w)^2$

25. $\left(6m - \dfrac{4}{5}n\right)^2$
▶

26. $\left(5x + \dfrac{2}{5}y\right)^2$

27. $t(3t - 1)^2$

28. $x(2x + 5)^2$

29. $3t(4t + 1)^2$

30. $2x(7x - 2)^2$

31. $-(4r - 2)^2$

32. $-(3y - 8)^2$

33. Consider the product of the conjugates $(7x + 3y)$ and $(7x - 3y)$:

$$(7x + 3y)(7x - 3y).$$

(a) What is the first term of each binomial factor? Square it.

(b) What is the product of the outer terms? The inner terms? Add them.

(c) What are the last terms of the binomial factors? Multiply them.

(d) Use the results of parts (a)–(c) to find $(7x + 3y)(7x - 3y)$.

34. Repeat **Exercise 33** for the product $(5x + 7y)(5x - 7y)$.

Find each product. See Examples 3 and 4.

35. $(k + 5)(k - 5)$

36. $(x + 8)(x - 8)$

37. $\left(r - \dfrac{3}{4}\right)\left(r + \dfrac{3}{4}\right)$

38. $\left(q - \dfrac{7}{8}\right)\left(q + \dfrac{7}{8}\right)$

39. $(s + 2.5)(s - 2.5)$

40. $(t + 1.4)(t - 1.4)$

41. $(2w + 5)(2w - 5)$

42. $(3z + 8)(3z - 8)$

43. $(3x + 4y)(3x - 4y)$

44. $(5y + 3x)(5y - 3x)$

45. $(10x + 3y)(10x - 3y)$

46. $(13r + 2z)(13r - 2z)$

47. $\left(7x + \dfrac{3}{7}\right)\left(7x - \dfrac{3}{7}\right)$

48. $\left(9y + \dfrac{2}{3}\right)\left(9y - \dfrac{2}{3}\right)$

49. $(2x^2 - 5)(2x^2 + 5)$

50. $(9y^2 - 2)(9y^2 + 2)$

51. $q(5q - 1)(5q + 1)$

52. $p(3p + 7)(3p - 7)$

53. $-5(a - b^3)(a + b^3)$

54. $-6(r - s^4)(r + s^4)$

Find each product. See Example 5.

55. $(x + 1)^3$

56. $(y + 2)^3$

57. $(m - 5)^3$

58. $(x - 7)^3$

59. $(2a + 1)^3$

60. $(3m + 1)^3$

61. $(4x - 1)^4$

62. $(2x - 1)^4$

63. $(3r - 2t)^4$

64. $(2z + 5y)^4$

65. $3x^2(x - 3)^3$

66. $4p^3(p + 4)^3$

67. $-8x^2y(x + y)^4$

68. $-5uv^2(u - v)^4$

Find a polynomial that represents, in appropriate units, the area of each figure.
(In Exercise 73, leave π in the answer. If necessary, refer to the formulas at the
back of this text.)

69.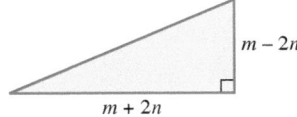
$m - 2n$
$m + 2n$

70.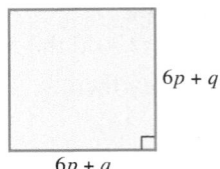
$6p + q$
$6p + q$

71.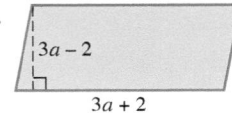
$3a - 2$
$3a + 2$

72.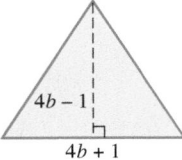
$4b - 1$
$4b + 1$

73.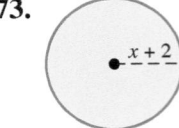
$x + 2$

74.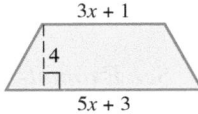
$3x + 1$
4
$5x + 3$

Refer to the figure shown here.

75. Find a polynomial that represents the volume of the cube (in cubic units).

76. If the value of x is 6, what is the volume of the cube (in cubic units)?

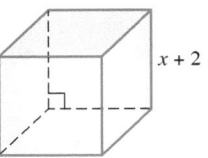
$x + 2$

Relating Concepts (Exercises 77–86) For Individual or Group Work

*Use the figure and **work Exercises 77–82 in order**, to justify the special product*
$$(x + y)^2 = x^2 + 2xy + y^2.$$

77. Express the area of the large square as the square of a binomial.

78. Give the monomial that represents the area of the red square.

79. Give the monomial that represents the sum of the areas of the blue rectangles.

80. Give the monomial that represents the area of the yellow square.

81. What is the sum of the monomials obtained in **Exercises 78–80?**

82. Explain why the binomial square found in **Exercise 77** must equal the polynomial found in **Exercise 81.**

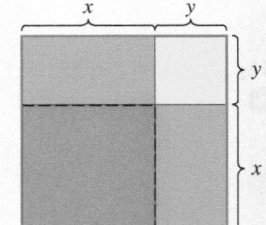
x y
y
x

To apply the above special product to a purely numerical problem,
*work **Exercises 83–86 in order.***

83. Using either traditional paper-and-pencil methods or a calculator, evaluate 35^2.

84. The number 35 can be written as $30 + 5$. Therefore, $35^2 = (30 + 5)^2$. Use the special product for squaring a binomial with $x = 30$ and $y = 5$ to write an expression for $(30 + 5)^2$. Do not simplify yet.

85. Use the rules for order of operations to simplify the expression found in **Exercise 84.**

86. Compare the answers to **Exercises 83 and 85.**

5.7   Dividing a Polynomial by a Monomial

OBJECTIVE ▸ ❶ Divide a polynomial by a monomial. We add two fractions with a common denominator as follows.

$$\frac{a}{c} + \frac{b}{c} = \frac{a+b}{c}$$

In reverse, this statement gives a rule for dividing a polynomial by a monomial.

> **Dividing a Polynomial by a Monomial**
>
> To divide a polynomial by a monomial, divide each term of the polynomial by the monomial.
>
> $$\frac{a+b}{c} = \frac{a}{c} + \frac{b}{c} \quad \textbf{(where } c \neq 0\textbf{)}$$
>
> *Examples:* $\dfrac{2+5}{3} = \dfrac{2}{3} + \dfrac{5}{3}$ and $\dfrac{x+3z}{2y} = \dfrac{x}{2y} + \dfrac{3z}{2y} \quad (y \neq 0)$

The parts of a division problem are named as follows.

$$\text{Dividend} \rightarrow \frac{12x^2 + 6x}{6x} = 2x + 1 \leftarrow \text{Quotient}$$
$$\text{Divisor} \rightarrow$$

EXAMPLE 1   Dividing a Polynomial by a Monomial

Divide $5m^5 - 10m^3$ by $5m^2$.

$$\frac{5m^5 - 10m^3}{5m^2} \quad \boxed{\text{A fraction bar means division.}}$$

$$= \frac{5m^5}{5m^2} - \frac{10m^3}{5m^2} \quad \text{Use the preceding rule, with + replaced by } -.$$

$$= m^3 - 2m \quad \text{Quotient rule}$$

CHECK   Multiply. $5m^2 \cdot (m^3 - 2m) = 5m^5 - 10m^3 \leftarrow ✔$

$\qquad\qquad\qquad \uparrow \qquad\qquad \uparrow \qquad\qquad$ Original polynomial
$\qquad\quad$ Divisor   Quotient $\qquad$ (Dividend)

Because division by 0 is undefined, the quotient $\frac{5m^5 - 10m^3}{5m^2}$ is undefined if $m = 0$. From now on, we assume that no denominators are 0.

————— **Work Problem ❶ at the Side. ▶**

EXAMPLE 2   Dividing a Polynomial by a Monomial

Divide.

$$\frac{16a^5 - 12a^4 + 8a^2}{4a^3} \quad \boxed{\text{Be careful simplifying this expression.}}$$

$$= \frac{16a^5}{4a^3} - \frac{12a^4}{4a^3} + \frac{8a^2}{4a^3} \quad \text{Divide each term by } 4a^3.$$

$$= 4a^2 - 3a + \frac{2}{a} \qquad \frac{8a^2}{4a^3} = \frac{8}{4}a^{2-3} = 2a^{-1} = 2\left(\frac{1}{a}\right) = \frac{2}{a}$$

————— **Continued on Next Page**

OBJECTIVE

> ❶ Divide a polynomial by a monomial.

❶ Divide.

GS (a) $\dfrac{6p^4 + 18p^7}{3p^2}$

$$= \frac{\overline{}}{3p^2} + \frac{\overline{}}{3p^2}$$

$$= \underline{}$$

(b) $\dfrac{12m^6 + 18m^5 + 30m^4}{6m^2}$

(c) $(18r^7 - 9r^2) \div (3r)$

Answers

1. (a) $6p^4$; $18p^7$; $2p^2 + 6p^5$
   (b) $2m^4 + 3m^3 + 5m^2$
   (c) $6r^6 - 3r$

2 Divide.

(GS) **(a)** $\dfrac{20x^4 - 25x^3 + 5x}{5x^2}$

$= \dfrac{20x^4}{\underline{}} - \dfrac{}{5x^2} + \dfrac{5x}{\underline{}}$

$= \underline{}$

(b) $\dfrac{50m^4 - 30m^3 + 20m}{10m^3}$

3 Divide.

(a) $\dfrac{-8p^4 - 6p^3 - 12p^5}{-3p^3}$

(b) $\dfrac{-9y^6 + 8y^7 - 11y - 4}{y^2}$

4 Divide.

$\dfrac{45x^4y^3 + 30x^3y^2 - 60x^2y}{15x^2y^2}$

Answers

2. (a) $5x^2$; $25x^3$; $5x$; $4x^2 - 5x + \dfrac{1}{x}$

(b) $5m - 3 + \dfrac{2}{m^2}$

3. (a) $4p^2 + \dfrac{8p}{3} + 2$

(b) $8y^5 - 9y^4 - \dfrac{11}{y} - \dfrac{4}{y^2}$

4. $3x^2y + 2x - \dfrac{4}{y}$

The quotient $4a^2 - 3a + \dfrac{2}{a}$ is *not* a polynomial because of the expression $\dfrac{2}{a}$, which has a variable in the denominator. While the sum, difference, and product of two polynomials are always polynomials, the quotient of two polynomials may not be.

CHECK $4a^3\left(4a^2 - 3a + \dfrac{2}{a}\right)$ Divisor × Quotient should equal Dividend.

$= 4a^3(4a^2) + 4a^3(-3a) + 4a^3\left(\dfrac{2}{a}\right)$ Distributive property

$= 16a^5 - 12a^4 + 8a^2$ ✓   Dividend

◀ **Work Problem 2 at the Side.**

EXAMPLE 3 Dividing a Polynomial by a Monomial

Divide $-7x^3 + 12x^4 - 4x$ by $-4x$.

Write the dividend polynomial in descending powers.

$\dfrac{12x^4 - 7x^3 - 4x}{-4x}$ Write in descending powers before dividing.

$= \dfrac{12x^4}{-4x} - \dfrac{7x^3}{-4x} - \dfrac{4x}{-4x}$ Divide each term by $-4x$.

$= -3x^3 - \dfrac{7x^2}{-4} - (-1)$ Quotient rule

$= -3x^3 + \dfrac{7x^2}{4} + 1$ Be careful with signs, and be sure to include 1 in the answer.

CHECK $-4x\left(-3x^3 + \dfrac{7x^2}{4} + 1\right)$ Divisor × Quotient should equal Dividend.

$= -4x(-3x^3) - 4x\left(\dfrac{7x^2}{4}\right) - 4x(1)$ Distributive property

$= 12x^4 - 7x^3 - 4x$ ✓   Dividend

◀ **Work Problem 3 at the Side.**

EXAMPLE 4 Dividing a Polynomial by a Monomial

Divide $180x^4y^{10} - 150x^3y^8 + 120x^2y^6 - 90xy^4 + 100y$ by $-30xy^2$.

Divide each term of the polynomial by $-30xy^2$.

$\dfrac{180x^4y^{10} - 150x^3y^8 + 120x^2y^6 - 90xy^4 + 100y}{-30xy^2}$

$= \dfrac{180x^4y^{10}}{-30xy^2} - \dfrac{150x^3y^8}{-30xy^2} + \dfrac{120x^2y^6}{-30xy^2} - \dfrac{90xy^4}{-30xy^2} + \dfrac{100y}{-30xy^2}$

$= -6x^3y^8 + 5x^2y^6 - 4xy^4 + 3y^2 - \dfrac{10}{3xy}$

Check by multiplying the divisor by the quotient.

◀ **Work Problem 4 at the Side.**

5.7 Exercises

FOR EXTRA HELP   Go to MyMathLab for worked-out, step-by-step solutions to exercises enclosed in a square   and video solutions to ▶ exercises.

CONCEPT CHECK   *Complete each statement.*

1. In the division $\dfrac{6x^2 + 8}{2} = 3x^2 + 4$, _____ is the dividend, _____ is the divisor, and _____ is the quotient.

2. To check the division shown in **Exercise 1,** multiply _____ by _____ and show that the product is _____ .

3. The expression $5x^2 - 3x + 6 + \dfrac{2}{x}$ (*is /is not*) a polynomial.

4. The expression $\dfrac{3x + 12}{x}$ is undefined if $x =$ _____ .

Perform each division. See Examples 1–3.

5. $\dfrac{12m^4 - 6m^3}{6m^2}$

6. $\dfrac{35n^5 - 5n^2}{5n}$

7. $\dfrac{60x^4 - 20x^2 + 10x}{2x}$

8. $\dfrac{120x^6 - 60x^3 + 80x^2}{2x}$

9. $\dfrac{20m^5 - 10m^4 + 5m^2}{-5m^2}$

10. $\dfrac{12t^5 - 6t^3 + 6t^2}{-6t^2}$

11. $\dfrac{8t^5 - 4t^3 + 4t^2}{2t}$

12. $\dfrac{8r^4 - 4r^3 + 6r^2}{2r}$

13. $\dfrac{4a^5 - 4a^2 + 8}{4a}$

14. $\dfrac{5t^8 + 5t^7 + 15}{5t}$

15. $\dfrac{12x^5 - 4x^4 + 6x^3}{-6x^2}$

16. $\dfrac{24x^6 - 14x^5 + 32x^4}{-4x^2}$

17. $\dfrac{4x^2 + 20x^3 - 36x^4}{4x^2}$

18. $\dfrac{5x^2 - 30x^4 + 30x^5}{5x^2}$

19. $\dfrac{-7r^7 + 6r^5 - r^4}{-r^5}$

20. $\dfrac{-13t^9 + 8t^6 - t^5}{-t^6}$

21. $\dfrac{-3x^3 - 4x^4 + 2x}{-3x^2}$

22. $\dfrac{-8x + 6x^3 - 5x^4}{-3x^2}$

23. CONCEPT CHECK   What polynomial, when divided by $5x^3$, yields $3x^2 - 7x + 7$ as a quotient?

24. CONCEPT CHECK   The quotient of a certain polynomial and $-12y^3$ is $6y^3 - 5y^2 + 2y - 3 + \dfrac{7}{y}$. What is this polynomial?

Perform each division. **See Example 1–4.**

25. $\dfrac{27r^4 - 36r^3 - 6r^2 + 3r - 2}{3r}$

$= \dfrac{\quad\quad}{3r} - \dfrac{\quad\quad}{3r} - \dfrac{\quad\quad}{3r} + \dfrac{\quad\quad}{3r} - \dfrac{\quad\quad}{3r}$

$=$

_____

26. $\dfrac{8k^4 - 12k^3 - 2k^2 - 2k - 3}{2k}$

$= \dfrac{8k^4}{\quad\quad} - \dfrac{12k^3}{\quad\quad} - \dfrac{2k^2}{\quad\quad} - \dfrac{2k}{\quad\quad} - \dfrac{3}{\quad\quad}$

$=$

_____

27. $\dfrac{2m^5 - 6m^4 + 8m^2}{-2m^3}$

28. $\dfrac{6r^5 - 8r^4 + 10r^2}{-2r^3}$

29. $(120x^{11} - 60x^{10} + 140x^9 - 100x^8) \div (10x^{12})$

30. $(120x^{12} - 84x^9 + 60x^8 - 36x^7) \div (12x^9)$

31. $(20a^4b^3 - 15a^5b^2 + 25a^3b) \div (-5a^4b)$

32. $(16y^5z - 8y^2z^2 + 12yz^3) \div (-4y^2z^2)$

33. $(120x^5y^4 - 80x^2y^3 + 40x^2y^4 - 20x^5y^3) \div (20xy^2)$

34. $(200a^5b^6 - 160a^4b^7 - 120a^3b^9 + 40a^2b^2) \div (40a^2b)$

Relating Concepts (Exercises 35–38) For Individual or Group Work

Our system of numeration is a decimal system, based on powers of 10. *Consider the following whole number.*

$$2846$$

Each digit represents the number of powers of 10 *for its place value. The* 2 *represents two thousands* (2×10^3), *the* 8 *represents eight hundreds* (8×10^2), *the* 4 *represents four tens* (4×10^1), *and the* 6 *represents six ones (or units)* (6×10^0). *In expanded form, we write*

$$2846 = (2 \times 10^3) + (8 \times 10^2) + (4 \times 10^1) + (6 \times 10^0).$$

Keeping this information in mind, **work Exercises 35–38 in order.**

35. Divide 2846 by 2, using paper-and-pencil methods.

$$2\overline{)2846}$$

36. Write the answer from **Exercise 35** in expanded form.

37. Divide the polynomial $2x^3 + 8x^2 + 4x + 6$ by 2.

38. Compare the answers in **Exercises 36 and 37.** For what value of x does the answer in **Exercise 37** equal the answer in **Exercise 36?**

5.8 | Dividing a Polynomial by a Polynomial

OBJECTIVE ▸ **1** **Divide a polynomial by a polynomial.** We use a method of "long division" to do this.

OBJECTIVES

1 Divide a polynomial by a polynomial.

2 Apply polynomial division to a geometry problem.

Dividing Whole Numbers	Dividing Polynomials

Step 1

Divide 6696 by 27.

$$27\overline{)6696}$$

Divide $8x^3 - 4x^2 - 14x + 15$ by $2x + 3$.

$$2x + 3\overline{)8x^3 - 4x^2 - 14x + 15}$$

Step 2

66 divided by 27 = 2.

$2 \cdot 27 = 54$

$$\begin{array}{r} 2 \\ 27\overline{)6696} \\ 54 \end{array}$$

$8x^3$ divided by $2x = 4x^2$.

$4x^2(2x + 3) = 8x^3 + 12x^2$

$$\begin{array}{r} 4x^2 \\ 2x + 3\overline{)8x^3 - 4x^2 - 14x + 15} \\ 8x^3 + 12x^2 \end{array}$$

Step 3

Subtract.

$$\begin{array}{r} 2 \\ 27\overline{)6696} \\ -54 \\ \hline 12 \end{array}$$

Subtract.

$$\begin{array}{r} 4x^2 \\ 2x + 3\overline{)8x^3 - 4x^2 - 14x + 15} \\ -(8x^3 + 12x^2) \\ \hline -16x^2 \end{array}$$

Bring down the next digit.

$$\begin{array}{r} 2 \\ 27\overline{)6696} \\ -54\downarrow \\ \hline 129 \end{array}$$

Bring down the next term.

$$\begin{array}{r} 4x^2 \\ 2x + 3\overline{)8x^3 - 4x^2 - 14x + 15} \\ -(8x^3 + 12x^2)\downarrow \\ \hline -16x^2 - 14x \end{array}$$

Step 4

129 divided by 27 = 4.

$4 \cdot 27 = 108$

$$\begin{array}{r} 24 \\ 27\overline{)6696} \\ -54 \\ \hline 129 \\ 108 \end{array}$$

$-16x^2$ divided by $2x = -8x$.

$-8x(2x + 3) = -16x^2 - 24x$

$$\begin{array}{r} 4x^2 - 8x \\ 2x + 3\overline{)8x^3 - 4x^2 - 14x + 15} \\ -(8x^3 + 12x^2) \\ \hline -16x^2 - 14x \\ -16x^2 - 24x \end{array}$$

Step 5

Subtract. Bring down.

$$\begin{array}{r} 24 \\ 27\overline{)6696} \\ -54 \\ \hline 129 \\ -108\downarrow \\ \hline 216 \end{array}$$

Subtract. Bring down.

$$\begin{array}{r} 4x^2 - 8x \\ 2x + 3\overline{)8x^3 - 4x^2 - 14x + 15} \\ -(8x^3 + 12x^2) \\ \hline -16x^2 - 14x \\ -(-16x^2 - 24x)\downarrow \\ \hline 10x + 15 \end{array}$$

1 Divide.

(a) $\dfrac{4x^2 + x - 18}{x - 2}$

Dividing Whole Numbers	Dividing Polynomials

Step 6

216 divided by 27 = 8.

8 · 27 = 216

$$\begin{array}{r} 248 \\ 27\overline{)6696} \\ -54 \\ \hline 129 \\ -108 \\ \hline 216 \\ -216 \\ \hline \text{Remainder} \rightarrow 0 \end{array}$$

6696 divided by 27 is 248.

10x divided by 2x = 5.

5(2x + 3) = 10x + 15

$$\begin{array}{r} 4x^2 - 8x + 5 \\ 2x + 3\overline{)8x^3 - 4x^2 - 14x + 15} \\ -(8x^3 + 12x^2) \\ \hline -16x^2 - 14x \\ -(-16x^2 - 24x) \\ \hline 10x + 15 \\ -(10x + 15) \leftarrow \\ \hline \text{Remainder} \rightarrow 0 \end{array}$$

$8x^3 - 4x^2 - 14x + 15$ divided by $2x + 3$ is $4x^2 - 8x + 5$.

Step 7 Multiply to check.

CHECK 27 · 248 = 6696 ✓

Multiply to check.

CHECK $(2x + 3)(4x^2 - 8x + 5)$
$= 8x^3 - 4x^2 - 14x + 15$ ✓

(b) $\dfrac{2x^2 + 5x - 25}{x + 5}$

EXAMPLE 1   **Dividing a Polynomial by a Polynomial**

Divide. $\dfrac{3x^2 - 5x - 28}{x - 4}$

$$\begin{array}{r} 3x + 7 \quad \leftarrow \text{Quotient} \\ x - 4\overline{)3x^2 - 5x - 28} \quad \leftarrow \text{Dividend} \\ -(3x^2 - 12x) \quad\quad \leftarrow (3x^2 - 5x) - (3x^2 - 12x) = 7x \\ \hline 7x - 28 \\ -(7x - 28) \leftarrow (7x - 28) - (7x - 28) = 0 \\ \hline 0 \end{array}$$

Step 1 $3x^2$ divided by x is $3x$. $3x(x - 4) = 3x^2 - 12x$

Step 2 Subtract $3x^2 - 12x$ from $3x^2 - 5x$. Bring down -28.

Step 3 $7x$ divided by x is 7. $7(x - 4) = 7x - 28$

Step 4 Subtract $7x - 28$ from $7x - 28$. The remainder is 0.

CHECK Multiply the divisor, $x - 4$, by the quotient, $3x + 7$. The product must be the original dividend, $3x^2 - 5x - 28$.

$$(x - 4)(3x + 7) = 3x^2 + 7x - 12x - 28 \quad \text{FOIL method}$$
$$= 3x^2 - 5x - 28 \checkmark \quad \text{Combine like terms.}$$

◀ Work Problem **1** at the Side

◀ Work Problem **1** at the Side

Answers

1. (a) $4x + 9$ (b) $2x - 5$

EXAMPLE 2   **Dividing a Polynomial by a Polynomial**

Divide. $\dfrac{5x + 4x^3 - 8 - 4x^2}{2x - 1}$

When we divide two polynomials, we must write both in descending powers of the variable. We must rewrite the dividend polynomial here. Then we divide by $2x - 1$.

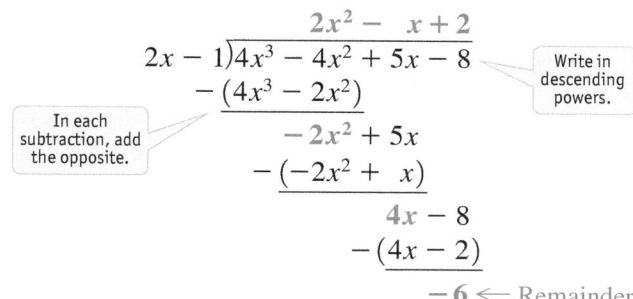

Step 1 $4x^3$ divided by $2x$ is $2x^2$. $2x^2(2x - 1) = 4x^3 - 2x^2$

Step 2   Subtract $4x^3 - 2x^2$ from $4x^3 - 4x^2$. Bring down the next term, $5x$.

Step 3 $-2x^2$ divided by $2x$ is $-x$. $-x(2x - 1) = -2x^2 + x$

Step 4   Subtract $-2x^2 + x$ from $-2x^2 + 5x$. Bring down the next term, -8.

Step 5 $4x$ divided by $2x$ is 2. $2(2x - 1) = 4x - 2$

Step 6   Subtract $4x - 2$ from $4x - 8$. The remainder is -6. Write the remainder as the numerator of a fraction that has the divisor $2x - 1$ as its denominator. Because there is a nonzero remainder, the answer is not a polynomial.

Dividend $\rightarrow$ $\dfrac{4x^3 - 4x^2 + 5x - 8}{2x - 1}$ $=$ $\underbrace{2x^2 - x + 2}_{\substack{\text{Quotient}\\ \text{polynomial}}} + \underbrace{\dfrac{-6}{2x - 1}}_{\substack{\text{Fractional}\\ \text{part of}\\ \text{quotient}}}$ $\leftarrow$ Remainder
Divisor $\rightarrow$ $\qquad\qquad\qquad\qquad\qquad\qquad\qquad\qquad\quad\ \leftarrow$ Divisor

Step 7   Multiply to check.

CHECK $(2x - 1)\left(2x^2 - x + 2 + \dfrac{-6}{2x - 1}\right)$ Multiply Divisor $\times$ (Quotient including the Remainder).

$= (2x - 1)(2x^2) + (2x - 1)(-x) + (2x - 1)(2)$
$\quad + (2x - 1)\left(\dfrac{-6}{2x - 1}\right)$

$= 4x^3 - 2x^2 - 2x^2 + x + 4x - 2 - 6$

$= 4x^3 - 4x^2 + 5x - 8$ ✓   Divisor $\times$ Quotient = Dividend

──────── **Work Problem ② at the Side.** ▶

⚠ CAUTION

Remember to include " $+ \frac{\text{remainder}}{\text{divisor}}$ " as part of the answer.

② Divide.

(a) $(x^2 + x^3 + 4x - 6)$
$\div (x - 1)$

(b) $\dfrac{p^3 - 2p^2 + 9 - 5p}{p + 2}$

(c) $\dfrac{6k^3 - 20k - k^2 + 1}{2k - 3}$

Answers

2. **(a)** $x^2 + 2x + 6$

(b) $p^2 - 4p + 3 + \dfrac{3}{p + 2}$

(c) $3k^2 + 4k - 4 + \dfrac{-11}{2k - 3}$

3 Divide.

(a) $(x^3 - 8) \div (x - 2)$

(b) $\dfrac{r^2 - 5}{r + 4}$

4 Divide.

(a)

$$\frac{2m^5 + m^4 + 6m^3 - 3m^2 - 18}{m^2 + 3}$$

(b) $(2x^4 + 3x^3 - x^2 + 6x + 5)$
$\div (x^2 - 1)$

Answers

3. (a) $x^2 + 2x + 4$
   (b) $r - 4 + \dfrac{11}{r + 4}$

4. (a) $2m^3 + m^2 - 6$
   (b) $2x^2 + 3x + 1 + \dfrac{9x + 6}{x^2 - 1}$

EXAMPLE 3 Dividing into a Polynomial with Missing Terms

Divide $x^3 - 1$ by $x - 1$.

Here the dividend, $x^3 - 1$, is missing the x^2-term and the x-term. We use 0 as the coefficient for each missing term. Thus, we write

$$x^3 - 1 \quad \text{as} \quad x^3 + 0x^2 + 0x - 1.$$

$$
\begin{array}{r}
x^2 + x + 1 \\
x - 1 \overline{)x^3 + 0x^2 + 0x - 1} \\
-(x^3 - x^2) \\
\hline
x^2 + 0x \\
-(x^2 - x) \\
\hline
x - 1 \\
-(x - 1) \\
\hline
0
\end{array}
$$

Insert placeholders for the missing terms.

The remainder is 0. The quotient is $x^2 + x + 1$.

CHECK $(x - 1)(x^2 + x + 1)$
$= x^3 + x^2 + x - x^2 - x - 1$
$= x^3 - 1$ ✓   Divisor × Quotient = Dividend

◀ Work Problem **3** at the Side.

EXAMPLE 4 Dividing by a Polynomial with Missing Terms

Divide $x^4 + 2x^3 + 2x^2 - x - 1$ by $x^2 + 1$.

The divisor $x^2 + 1$ has a missing x-term, so we write it as $x^2 + 0x + 1$.

$$
\begin{array}{r}
x^2 + 2x + 1 \\
x^2 + 0x + 1 \overline{)x^4 + 2x^3 + 2x^2 - x - 1} \\
-(x^4 + 0x^3 + x^2) \\
\hline
2x^3 + x^2 - x \\
-(2x^3 + 0x^2 + 2x) \\
\hline
x^2 - 3x - 1 \\
-(x^2 + 0x + 1) \\
\hline
-3x - 2 \leftarrow \text{Remainder}
\end{array}
$$

Insert a placeholder for the missing term.

When the result of subtracting (here $-3x - 2$) is a polynomial of degree *less* than the divisor ($x^2 + 0x + 1$, in this case), that polynomial is the remainder. We write the answer as follows.

$$x^2 + 2x + 1 + \frac{-3x - 2}{x^2 + 1}$$

Remember to include "+ $\frac{\text{remainder}}{\text{divisor}}$."

CHECK Show that multiplying $(x^2 + 1)\left(x^2 + 2x + 1 + \dfrac{-3x - 2}{x^2 + 1}\right)$ gives the original dividend, $x^4 + 2x^3 + 2x^2 - x - 1$. ✓

◀ Work Problem **4** at the Side.

EXAMPLE 5 Dividing a Polynomial When the Quotient Has Fractional Coefficients

Divide $4x^3 + 2x^2 + 3x + 2$ by $4x - 4$.

$$\frac{6x^2}{4x} = \frac{3}{2}x$$

$$x^2 + \frac{3}{2}x + \frac{9}{4} \leftarrow \frac{9x}{4x} = \frac{9}{4}$$

$$4x - 4)\overline{4x^3 + 2x^2 + 3x + 2}$$
$$\underline{-(4x^3 - 4x^2)}$$
$$6x^2 + 3x$$
$$\underline{-(6x^2 - 6x)}$$
$$9x + 2$$
$$\underline{-(9x - 9)}$$
$$11$$

The answer is $x^2 + \frac{3}{2}x + \frac{9}{4} + \frac{11}{4x - 4}$.

─────── **Work Problem ⑤ at the Side.** ▶

OBJECTIVE ▶ **②** Apply polynomial division to a geometry problem.

EXAMPLE 6 Using an Area Formula

The area of the rectangle in **Figure 3** is given by $(x^3 + 4x^2 + 8x + 8)$ sq. units. The width is given by $(x + 2)$ units. What is its length?

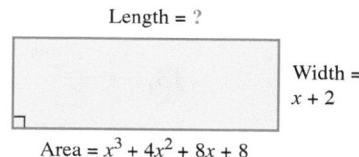

Length = ?

Width = $x + 2$

Area = $x^3 + 4x^2 + 8x + 8$

Figure 3

For a rectangle, $\mathcal{A} = LW$. Solving for L gives $L = \frac{\mathcal{A}}{W}$. Divide the area, $x^3 + 4x^2 + 8x + 8$, by the width, $x + 2$.

$$x + 2)\overline{x^3 + 4x^2 + 8x + 8}$$
$$\frac{x^2 + 2x + 4}{}$$
$$\underline{-(x^3 + 2x^2)}$$
$$2x^2 + 8x$$
$$\underline{-(2x^2 + 4x)}$$
$$4x + 8$$
$$\underline{-(4x + 8)}$$
$$0$$

The quotient $(x^2 + 2x + 4)$ units represents the length of the rectangle.

─────── **Work Problem ⑥ at the Side.** ▶

⑤ Divide $3x^3 + 7x^2 + 7x + 11$ by $3x + 6$.

⑥ The area of a rectangle is given by $(x^3 + 7x^2 + 17x + 20)$ sq. units. The width is given by $(x + 4)$ units. What is its length?

Length = ?

Width = $x + 4$

Area = $x^3 + 7x^2 + 17x + 20$

Answers

5. $x^2 + \dfrac{1}{3}x + \dfrac{5}{3} + \dfrac{1}{3x + 6}$

6. $(x^2 + 3x + 5)$ units

5.8 Exercises

FOR EXTRA HELP

Go to MyMathLab *for worked-out, step-by-step solutions to exercises enclosed in a square* ▢ *and video solutions to* ▶ *exercises.*

CONCEPT CHECK *Complete the statement or answer the question.*

1. Label the parts of the division problem using the words *quotient*, *divisor*, and *dividend*.

$$(x^3 - 2x^2 - 9) \div (x - 3) = x^2 + x + 3$$

2. When dividing one polynomial by another, how do we know when to stop dividing?

3. In dividing $12m^2 - 20m + 3$ by $2m - 3$, what is the first step?

4. In the division in **Exercise 3,** what is the second step?

Perform each division. See Examples 1–5.

5. $\dfrac{x^2 - x - 6}{x - 3}$

6. $\dfrac{m^2 - 2m - 24}{m - 6}$

7. $\dfrac{2y^2 + 9y - 35}{y + 7}$

8. $\dfrac{2y^2 + 9y + 7}{y + 1}$

9. $\dfrac{p^2 + 2p + 20}{p + 6}$

10. $\dfrac{x^2 + 11x + 16}{x + 8}$

11. $(r^2 - 8r + 15) \div (r - 3)$

12. $(t^2 + 2t - 35) \div (t - 5)$

13. $\dfrac{4a^2 - 22a + 32}{2a + 3}$

14. $\dfrac{9w^2 + 6w + 10}{3w - 2}$

15. $\dfrac{8x^3 - 10x^2 - x + 3}{2x + 1}$

16. $\dfrac{12t^3 - 11t^2 + 9t + 18}{4t + 3}$

17. $\dfrac{2r^3 - 6r - 5r^2 + 15}{r - 3}$

18. $\dfrac{2y^2 + 5y^3 - y - 8}{y + 1}$

19. $\dfrac{3y^3 + y^2 + 2}{y + 1}$

20. $\dfrac{2r^3 - 6r - 36}{r - 3}$

21. $\dfrac{2x^3 + x + 2}{x + 3}$

22. $\dfrac{3x^3 + x + 5}{x + 1}$

23. $\dfrac{3k^3 - 4k^2 - 6k + 10}{k^2 - 2}$

24. $\dfrac{5z^3 - z^2 + 10z + 2}{z^2 + 2}$

25. $(x^4 - x^2 - 2) \div (x^2 - 2)$

26. $(r^4 + 2r^2 - 3) \div (r^2 - 1)$

27. $\dfrac{x^4 - 1}{x^2 - 1}$

28. $\dfrac{y^3 + 1}{y + 1}$

29. $\dfrac{6p^4 - 15p^3 + 14p^2 - 5p + 10}{3p^2 + 1}$

30. $\dfrac{6r^4 - 10r^3 - r^2 + 15r - 8}{2r^2 - 3}$

31. $(10x^3 + 13x^2 + 4x + 1) \div (5x + 5)$

32. $(6x^3 - 19x^2 - 19x - 4) \div (2x - 8)$

33. $\dfrac{3x^3 + 5x^2 - 9x + 5}{3x - 3}$

34. $\dfrac{5x^3 + 4x^2 + 10x + 20}{5x + 5}$

35. $\dfrac{2x^5 + x^4 + 11x^3 - 8x^2 - 13x + 7}{2x^2 + x - 1}$

36. $\dfrac{4t^5 - 11t^4 - 6t^3 + 5t^2 - t + 3}{4t^2 + t - 3}$

Work each problem. Give answers in units (or as specified). **See Example 6.** *(If necessary, refer to the formulas at the back of this text.)*

37. What expression represents the length of the rectangle?

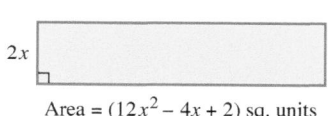

Area = $(12x^2 - 4x + 2)$ sq. units

38. What expression represents the length of the base of the triangle?

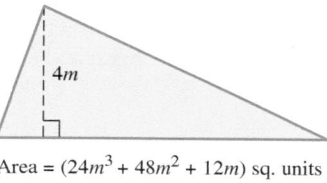

Area = $(24m^3 + 48m^2 + 12m)$ sq. units

39. Find the measure of the length of the rectangle.

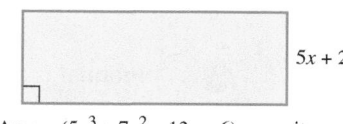

Area = $(5x^3 + 7x^2 - 13x - 6)$ sq. units

40. Find the measure of the base of the parallelogram.

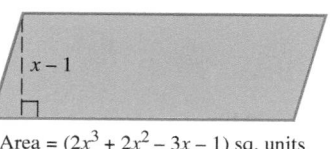

Area = $(2x^3 + 2x^2 - 3x - 1)$ sq. units

41. If the distance traveled is

$$(5x^3 - 6x^2 + 3x + 14) \text{ miles}$$

and the rate is $(x + 1)$ mph, write an expression, in hours, for the time traveled.

42. If the cost to fertilize a garden is

$$(4x^5 + 3x^4 + 2x^3 + 9x^2 - 29x + 2) \text{ dollars}$$

and fertilizer costs $(x + 2)$ dollars per square yard, write an expression, in square yards, for the area of the garden.

Chapter 5 **Summary**

Key Terms

5.1

exponential expression A number written with an exponent (or power) is an exponential expression.

$$3^4 \leftarrow \text{Exponent} \quad \} \text{ Exponential}$$
$$\text{\textasciicircum}\!\!\!\!\underline{\quad}\text{ Base} \quad \} \text{ expression}$$

5.3

scientific notation A number written in the form $a \times 10^n$, where $1 \leq |a| < 10$ and n is an integer, is in scientific notation.

standard notation We refer to a number such as 125 as the standard notation of 1.25×10^2.

5.4

term A term is a number (constant), a variable, or a product or quotient of a number and one or more variables raised to powers.

$$\begin{array}{c}\text{Numerical} \\ \text{coefficient}\end{array} \longrightarrow \underbrace{-7x^2}_{\text{Term}}$$

like terms Terms with exactly the same variables (including the same exponents) are like terms.

polynomial in x A term or the sum of a finite number of terms of the form ax^n, for any real number a and any whole number n, is a polynomial in x.

descending powers A polynomial in x is written in descending powers if the exponents on x in its terms decrease from left to right.

degree of a term The degree of a term is the sum of the exponents on the variables.

degree of a polynomial The degree of a polynomial is the greatest degree of any nonzero term of the polynomial.

monomial A monomial is a polynomial with exactly one term.

binomial A binomial is a polynomial with exactly two terms.

trinomial A trinomial is a polynomial with exactly three terms.

5.5

FOIL method The FOIL method is used to find the product of two binomials. The letters of the word **FOIL** originate as follows: Multiply the **F**irst terms, multiply the **O**uter terms (to obtain the outer product), multiply the **I**nner terms (to obtain the inner product), and multiply the **L**ast terms.

outer product The outer product of $(a + b)(c + d)$ is ad.

inner product The inner product of $(a + b)(c + d)$ is bc.

5.6

conjugate The conjugate of $x + y$ is $x - y$.

New Symbols

x^{-n} x to the negative n power

Test Your Word Power
See how well you have learned the vocabulary in this chapter.

1 A **polynomial** is an algebraic expression made up of
  A. a term or a finite product of terms with positive coefficients and exponents
  B. a term or a finite sum of terms with real coefficients and whole number exponents
  C. the product of two or more terms with positive exponents
  D. the sum of two or more terms with whole number coefficients and exponents.

2 The **degree of a term** is the
  A. number of variables in the term
  B. product of the exponents on the variables
  C. least exponent on the variables
  D. sum of the exponents on the variables.

3 A **trinomial** is a polynomial with
  A. exactly one term
  B. exactly two terms
  C. exactly three terms
  D. more than three terms.

4 A **binomial** is a polynomial with
  A. exactly one term
  B. exactly two terms
  C. exactly three terms
  D. more than three terms.

5 A **monomial** is a polynomial with
  A. exactly one term
  B. exactly two terms
  C. exactly three terms
  D. more than three terms.

Answers to Test Your Word Power

1. B; *Example:* $5x^3 + 2x^2 - 7$

2. D; *Examples:* The term 6 has degree 0, $3x$ has degree 1, $-2x^8$ has degree 8, and $5x^2y^4$ has degree 6.

3. C; *Example:* $2a^2 - 3ab + b^2$

4. B; *Example:* $3t^3 + 5t$

5. A; *Examples:* -5 and $4xy^5$

Quick Review

Concepts	Examples

5.1 The Product Rule and Power Rules for Exponents

For any integers m and n, the following hold true.

Product rule $\quad a^m \cdot a^n = a^{m+n}$

Power rules (a) $\quad (a^m)^n = a^{mn}$

(b) $\quad (ab)^m = a^m b^m$

(c) $\quad \left(\dfrac{a}{b}\right)^m = \dfrac{a^m}{b^m}$ (where $b \neq 0$)

Simplify using the rules for exponents.

$$2^4 \cdot 2^5 = 2^{4+5} = 2^9$$

$$(3^4)^2 = 3^{4 \cdot 2} = 3^8$$

$$(6a)^5 = 6^5 a^5$$

$$\left(\frac{2}{3}\right)^4 = \frac{2^4}{3^4}$$

5.2 Integer Exponents and the Quotient Rule

For any nonzero real numbers a and b and any integers m and n, the following hold true.

Zero exponent $\quad a^0 = 1$

Negative exponent $\quad a^{-n} = \dfrac{1}{a^n}$

Quotient rule $\quad \dfrac{a^m}{a^n} = a^{m-n}$

Negative-to-positive rules $\quad \dfrac{a^{-m}}{b^{-n}} = \dfrac{b^n}{a^m} \quad \left(\dfrac{a}{b}\right)^{-m} = \left(\dfrac{b}{a}\right)^m$

Simplify using the rules for exponents.

$$15^0 = 1$$

$$5^{-2} = \frac{1}{5^2} = \frac{1}{25}$$

$$\frac{4^8}{4^3} = 4^{8-3} = 4^5$$

$$\frac{6^{-2}}{7^{-3}} = \frac{7^3}{6^2} \quad \left(\frac{5}{3}\right)^{-4} = \left(\frac{3}{5}\right)^4$$

5.3 An Application of Exponents: Scientific Notation

To write a positive number in scientific notation

$$a \times 10^n, \quad \text{where} \quad 1 \leq |a| < 10,$$

move the decimal point to follow the first nonzero digit.

1. If moving the decimal point makes the number less, then n is positive.

2. If moving the decimal point makes the number greater, then n is negative.

3. If the decimal point is not moved, then n is 0.

For a negative number, follow these steps using the *absolute value* of the number. Then make the result negative.

Write in scientific notation.

$$247 = 2.47 \times 10^2$$

$$0.0051 = 5.1 \times 10^{-3}$$

Write in standard notation.

$$3.25 \times 10^5 = 325,000$$

$$8.44 \times 10^{-6} = 0.00000844$$

$$-4.8 \times 10^0 = -4.8$$

Concepts	Examples

5.4 Adding and Subtracting Polynomials

Adding Polynomials
Combine (add) like terms.

Subtracting Polynomials
Change the sign of each term in the subtrahend (second polynomial) and add the result to the minuend (first polynomial).

Add.
$$\begin{array}{r} 2x^2 + 5x - 3 \\ + (5x^2 - 2x + 7) \\ \hline 7x^2 + 3x + 4 \end{array}$$

Subtract. $(2x^2 + 5x - 3) - (5x^2 - 2x + 7)$
$$= (2x^2 + 5x - 3) + (-5x^2 + 2x - 7)$$
$$= -3x^2 + 7x - 10$$

5.5 Multiplying Polynomials

Multiply each term of the first polynomial by each term of the second polynomial. Then combine like terms.

FOIL Method for Multiplying Binomials

Step 1 Multiply the two **F**irst terms to obtain the first term of the product.

Step 2 Find the **O**uter product and the **I**nner product and combine them (when possible) to obtain the middle term of the product.

Step 3 Multiply the two **L**ast terms to obtain the last term of the product.

Step 4 Add the terms found in Steps 1–3.

Multiply.
$$\begin{array}{r} 3x^3 - 4x^2 + 2x - 7 \\ 4x + 3 \\ \hline 9x^3 - 12x^2 + 6x - 21 \\ 12x^4 - 16x^3 + 8x^2 - 28x \\ \hline 12x^4 - 7x^3 - 4x^2 - 22x - 21 \end{array}$$

Multiply. $(2x + 3)(5x - 4)$
$$2x(5x) = 10x^2 \quad \text{F}$$
$$2x(-4) + 3(5x) = 7x \quad \text{O, I}$$
$$3(-4) = -12 \quad \text{L}$$
The product is $10x^2 + 7x - 12$.

5.6 Special Products

Square of a Binomial
$$(x + y)^2 = x^2 + 2xy + y^2$$
$$(x - y)^2 = x^2 - 2xy + y^2$$

Product of a Sum and Difference of Two Terms
$$(x + y)(x - y) = x^2 - y^2$$

Multiply.

$(3x + 1)^2$
$= (3x)^2 + 2(3x)(1) + 1^2$
$= 9x^2 + 6x + 1$

$(2m - 5n)^2$
$= (2m)^2 - 2(2m)(5n) + (5n)^2$
$= 4m^2 - 20mn + 25n^2$

$(4a + 3)(4a - 3)$
$= (4a)^2 - 3^2$
$= 16a^2 - 9 \quad (4a)^2 = 4^2a^2 = 16a^2$

5.7 Dividing a Polynomial by a Monomial

Divide each term of the polynomial by the monomial.
$$\frac{a + b}{c} = \frac{a}{c} + \frac{b}{c} \quad (\text{where } c \neq 0)$$

Divide. $\dfrac{4x^3 - 2x^2 + 6x - 8}{2x}$
$$= \frac{4x^3}{2x} - \frac{2x^2}{2x} + \frac{6x}{2x} - \frac{8}{2x}$$
$$= 2x^2 - x + 3 - \frac{4}{x}$$

Divide each term in the dividend by $2x$, the divisor.
$\frac{8}{2x} = \frac{8 \cdot 1}{2 \cdot x} = \frac{4}{x}$

5.8 Dividing a Polynomial by a Polynomial

Use "long division."

Divide.
$$\begin{array}{r} 2x - 5 \\ 3x + 4 \overline{)6x^2 - 7x - 21} \\ - (6x^2 + 8x) \\ \hline -15x - 21 \\ - (-15x - 20) \\ \hline -1 \leftarrow \text{Remainder} \end{array}$$

The answer is $2x - 5 + \dfrac{-1}{3x + 4}$.

Chapter 5 *Review Exercises*

5.1 *Use the product rule, power rules, or both to simplify each expression. Evaluate coefficients if the exponent is 4 or less.*

1. $4^3 \cdot 4^8$

2. $(-5)^6(-5)^5$

3. $-8x^4(9x^3)$

4. $(2x^2)(5x^3)(x^9)$

5. $(19x)^5$

6. $(-4y)^7$

7. $5(pt)^4$

8. $\left(\dfrac{7}{5}\right)^6$

9. $(3x^2y^3)^3$

10. $(t^4)^8(t^2)^5$

11. $(6x^2z^4)^2(x^3yz^2)^4$

12. $\left(\dfrac{2m^3n}{p^2}\right)^3$

Solve each problem.

13. Find an expression that represents, in appropriate units, the volume of the figure. (If necessary, refer to the formulas at the back of this text.)

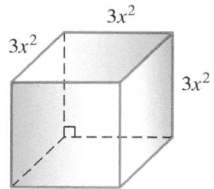

14. CONCEPT CHECK A student incorrectly simplified the expression

$$7^2 + 7^3 \quad \text{as} \quad 7^5.$$

What Went Wrong? Give the correct answer.

5.2 *Evaluate each expression.*

15. -10^0

16. $(-23)^0$

17. $5^0 + 8^0$

18. 2^{-5}

19. $\left(\dfrac{6}{5}\right)^{-2}$

20. $4^{-2} - 4^{-1}$

Simplify each expression. Assume that all variables represent nonzero real numbers. Evaluate coefficients if the exponent is 4 or less.

21. $\dfrac{6^{-3}}{6^{-5}}$

22. $\dfrac{x^{-7}}{x^{-9}}$

23. $\dfrac{p^{-8}}{p^4}$

24. $\dfrac{r^{-2}}{r^{-6}}$

25. $(2^4)^2$

26. $(9^3)^{-2}$

27. $(5^{-2})^{-4}$

28. $(8^{-3})^4$

29. $\dfrac{(m^2)^3}{(m^4)^2}$

30. $\dfrac{y^4 \cdot y^{-2}}{y^{-5}}$

31. $\dfrac{r^9 \cdot r^{-5}}{r^{-2} \cdot r^{-7}}$

32. $(-5m^3)^2$

33. $(2y^{-4})^{-3}$

34. $\dfrac{ab^{-3}}{a^4b^2}$

35. $\dfrac{(6r^{-1})^2 \cdot (2r^{-4})}{r^{-5}(r^2)^{-3}}$

36. $\dfrac{(2m^{-5}n^2)^3(3m^2)^{-1}}{m^{-2}n^{-4}(m^{-1})^2}$

5.3 *Write each number in scientific notation.*

37. 48,000,000 **38.** 28,988,000,000 **39.** 0.000065 **40.** 0.0000000824

Write each number in standard notation.

41. 2.4×10^4 **42.** 7.83×10^7 **43.** 8.97×10^{-7} **44.** 9.95×10^{-12}

*Perform the indicated operations. Write each answer in (**a**) scientific notation and (**b**) standard notation.*

45. $(2 \times 10^{-3})(4 \times 10^5)$

46. $\dfrac{8 \times 10^4}{2 \times 10^{-2}}$

47. $\dfrac{12 \times 10^{-5} \times 16 \times 10^4}{4 \times 10^3 \times 8 \times 10^{-2}}$

48. $\dfrac{2.5 \times 10^5 \times 4.8 \times 10^{-4}}{7.5 \times 10^8 \times 1.6 \times 10^{-5}}$

Use scientific notation to calculate the answer to each problem.

49. A computer can perform 466,000,000 calculations per second. How many calculations can it perform per minute? Per hour?

50. In theory, there are 1×10^9 possible Social Security numbers. The population of the United States is about 3×10^8. How many Social Security numbers are available for each person? (Data from U.S. Census Bureau.)

5.4 *For each polynomial, first simplify if possible, and write the result in descending powers of the variable. Then give the degree, and tell whether the simplified polynomial is a* monomial, *a* binomial, *a* trinomial, *or* none of these.

51. $9m^2 + 11m^2 + 2m^2$

52. $-4p + p^3 - p^2 + 8p + 2$

53. $12a^5 - 9a^4 + 8a^3 + 2a^2 - a + 3$

54. $-7y^5 - 8y^4 - y^5 + y^4 + 9y$

Add or subtract as indicated.

55. $\begin{array}{r} -2a^3 + 5a^2 \\ + (-3a^3 - a^2) \\ \hline \end{array}$

56. $\begin{array}{r} 4r^3 - 8r^2 + 6r \\ + (-2r^3 + 5r^2 + 3r) \\ \hline \end{array}$

57. $\begin{array}{r} 6y^2 - 8y + 2 \\ - (-5y^2 + 2y - 7) \\ \hline \end{array}$

58. $\begin{array}{r} -12k^4 - 8k^2 + 7k - 5 \\ - (\quad k^4 + 7k^2 + 11k + 1) \\ \hline \end{array}$

59. $(2m^3 - 8m^2 + 4) + (8m^3 + 2m^2 - 7)$

60. $(-5y^2 + 3y + 11) + (4y^2 - 7y + 15)$

61. $(6p^2 - p - 8) - (-4p^2 + 2p + 3)$

62. $(12r^4 - 7r^3 + 2r^2) - (5r^4 - 3r^3 + 2r^2 + 1)$

5.5 *Find each product.*

63. $5x(2x + 14)$

64. $-3p^3(2p^2 - 5p)$

65. $(3r - 2)(2r^2 + 4r - 3)$

66. $(2y + 3)(4y^2 - 6y + 9)$

67. $(5p^2 + 3p)(p^3 - p^2 + 5)$

68. $(x + 6)(x - 3)$

69. $(3k - 6)(2k + 1)$

70. $(6p - 3q)(2p - 7q)$

71. $(m^2 + m - 9)(2m^2 + 3m - 1)$

5.6 *Find each product.*

72. $(a + 4)^2$

73. $(3p - 2)^2$

74. $(2r + 5s)^2$

75. $(r + 2)^3$

76. $(2x - 1)^3$

77. $(2z + 7)(2z - 7)$

78. $(6m - 5)(6m + 5)$

79. $(5a + 6b)(5a - 6b)$

80. $3(2x^2 + 5)(2x^2 - 5)$

Work each problem.

81. CONCEPT CHECK The square of a binomial leads to a polynomial with how many terms? The product of a sum and difference of two terms leads to a polynomial with how many terms?

82. Explain why $(a + b)^2$ is not equivalent to $a^2 + b^2$.

5.7 *Perform each division.*

83. $\dfrac{-15y^4}{-9y^2}$

84. $\dfrac{-12x^3y^2}{6xy}$

85. $\dfrac{6y^4 - 12y^2 + 18y}{-6y}$

86. $\dfrac{2p^3 - 6p^2 + 5p}{2p^2}$

87. $(5x^{13} - 10x^{12} + 20x^7 - 35x^5) \div (-5x^4)$

88. $(-10m^4n^2 + 5m^3n^3 + 6m^2n^4) \div (5m^2n)$

5.8 *Perform each division.*

89. $(2r^2 + 3r - 14) \div (r - 2)$

90. $\dfrac{12m^2 - 11m - 10}{3m - 5}$

91. $\dfrac{10a^3 + 5a^2 - 14a + 9}{5a^2 - 3}$

92. $\dfrac{2k^4 + 4k^3 + 9k^2 - 8}{2k^2 + 1}$

Chapter 5 Mixed Review Exercises

Perform each indicated operation, or simplify each expression. Evaluate coefficients if the exponent is 4 or less. Assume that all variables represent nonzero real numbers.

1. $19^0 - 3^0$

2. $(3p)^4(3p^{-7})$

3. 7^{-2}

4. $(2k - 7)^2$

5. $\dfrac{2y^3 + 17y^2 + 37y + 7}{2y + 7}$

6. $\left(\dfrac{6r^2s}{5}\right)^4$

7. $-m^5(8m^2 + 10m + 6)$

8. $\left(\dfrac{1}{2}\right)^{-5}$

9. $(25x^2y^3 - 8xy^2 + 15x^3y) \div (5x)$

10. $(6r^{-2})^{-1}$

11. $(2x + y)^3$

12. $2^{-1} + 4^{-1}$

13. $(a + 2)(a^2 - 4a + 1)$

14. $(5y^3 - 8y^2 + 7) - (-3y^3 + y^2 + 2)$

15. $(2r + 5)(5r - 2)$

16. $(12a + 1)(12a - 1)$

*Find polynomials that represent, in appropriate units, **(a)** the perimeter and **(b)** the area of each square or rectangle.*

17.

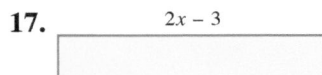

2x – 3

x + 2

18.

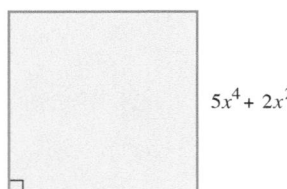

$5x^4 + 2x^2$

19. CONCEPT CHECK   A friend incorrectly simplified

$$\dfrac{6x^2 - 12x}{6} \quad \text{as} \quad x^2 - 12x.$$

What Went Wrong?   Give the correct answer.

20. CONCEPT CHECK   What polynomial, when multiplied by $6m^2n$, gives the following product?

$$12m^3n^2 + 18m^6n^3 - 24m^2n^2$$

Chapter 5 Test

The Chapter Test Prep Videos with step-by-step solutions are available in MyMathLab or on YouTube at **https://goo.gl/3rBuO5**

Evaluate each expression.

1. $(-2)^3(-2)^2$

2. 5^{-4}

3. $(-3)^0 + 4^0$

4. $4^{-1} + 3^{-1}$

Simplify each expression. Evaluate coefficients if the exponent is 4 or less. Assume that all variables represent nonzero real numbers.

5. $\left(\dfrac{6}{m^2}\right)^3$

6. $\dfrac{(3x^2y)^2(xy^3)^2}{(xy)^3}$

7. $\dfrac{8^{-1} \cdot 8^4}{8^{-2}}$

8. $\dfrac{(x^{-3})^{-2}(x^{-1}y)^2}{(xy^{-2})^2}$

9. Determine whether each expression represents a number that is *positive, negative,* or *zero.*

  (a) 3^{-4} **(b)** $(-3)^4$ **(c)** -3^4 **(d)** 3^0 **(e)** $(-3)^0 - 3^0$ **(f)** $(-3)^{-3}$

10. Write each number in scientific notation.

  (a) 344,000,000,000   **(b)** 0.00000557

11. Write each number in standard notation.

  (a) 2.96×10^7 **(b)** 6.07×10^{-8}

12. A satellite galaxy of the Milky Way, known as the Large Magellanic Cloud, is **1000** light-years across. A light-year is equal to **5,890,000,000,000** mi. (Data from *USA Today.*)

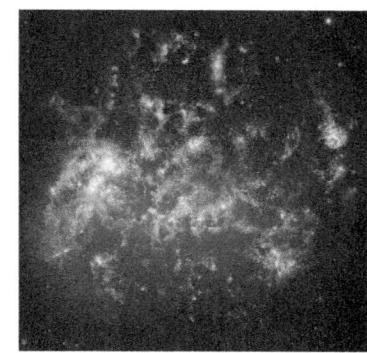

  (a) Write the two boldface italic numbers in scientific notation.

  (b) How many miles across is the Large Magellanic Cloud?

For each polynomial, first simplify if possible, and write the result in descending powers of the variable. Then give the degree, and tell whether the simplified polynomial is a monomial, *a* binomial, *a* trinomial, *or* none of these.

13. $5x^2 + 8x - 12x^2$

14. $13n^3 - n^2 + n^4 + 3n^4 - 9n^2$

Perform the indicated operations.

15. $(5t^4 - 3t^2 + 7t + 3) - (t^4 - t^3 + 3t^2 + 8t + 3)$

16. $(2y^2 - 8y + 8) + (-3y^2 + 2y + 3) - (y^2 + 3y - 6)$

17. $\begin{array}{r} -6r^5 + 4r^2 - 3 \\ + (\ 6r^5 + 12r^2 - 16) \\ \hline \end{array}$

18. $\begin{array}{r} 9t^3 - 4t^2 + 2t + 2 \\ - (9t^3 + 8t^2 - 3t - 6) \\ \hline \end{array}$

19. $3x^2(-9x^3 + 6x^2 - 2x + 1)$

20. $(2r - 3)(r^2 + 2r - 5)$

21. $(t - 8)(t + 3)$

22. $(4x + 3y)(2x - y)$

23. $(5x - 2y)^2$

24. $(10v + 3w)(10v - 3w)$

25. $(x + 1)^3$

26. What polynomial represents, in appropriate units, the perimeter of this square?   The area?

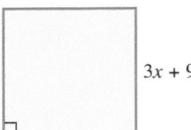

$3x + 9$

Perform each division.

27. $\dfrac{8y^3 - 6y^2 + 4y + 10}{2y}$

28. $(-9x^2y^3 + 6x^4y^3 + 12xy^3) \div (3xy)$

29. $\dfrac{2x^2 + x - 36}{x - 4}$

30. $(3x^3 - x + 4) \div (x - 2)$

Chapters R–5 *Cumulative Review Exercises*

Perform each operation.

1. $\dfrac{2}{3} + \dfrac{1}{8}$

2. $\dfrac{7}{4} - \dfrac{9}{5}$

3. $8.32 - 4.6$

4. 0.07×0.0006

5. A retailer has $34,000 invested in her business. She finds that last year she earned 5.4% on this investment. How much did she earn?

Find the value of each expression for $x = -2$ and $y = 4$.

6. $\dfrac{4x - 2y}{x + y}$

7. $x^3 - 4xy$

Perform the indicated operations.

8. $\dfrac{(-13 + 15) - (3 + 2)}{6 - 12}$

9. $-7 - 3[2 + (5 - 8)]$

Decide what property justifies each statement.

10. $(9 + 2) + 3 = 9 + (2 + 3)$

11. $-7 + 7 = 0$

12. $6(4 + 2) = 6(4) + 6(2)$

Solve each equation.

13. $2x - 7x + 8x = 30$

14. $2 - 3(t - 5) = 4 + t$

15. $2(5h + 1) = 10h + 4$

16. $d = rt$ for r

17. $\dfrac{x}{5} = \dfrac{x - 2}{7}$

18. $\dfrac{1}{3}p - \dfrac{1}{6}p = -2$

19. $0.05x + 0.15(50 - x) = 5.50$

20. $4 - (3x + 12) = -9 - (3x - 1)$

Solve each problem.

21. In any given time period, a 1-oz mouse takes about 16 times as many breaths as a 3-ton elephant. If the two animals take a combined total of 170 breaths per minute, how many breaths does each take during that time? (Data from *Dinosaurs, Spitfires, and Sea Dragons*, McGowan, C., Harvard University Press.)

22. If a number is subtracted from 8 and this difference is tripled, the result is three times the number. Find this number to learn how many times a dolphin rests during a 24-hr period.

Solve each inequality. Write the solution set in interval notation.

23. $-8x \leq -80$

24. $-2(x + 4) > 3x + 6$

25. $-3 \leq 2x + 5 < 9$

Given $2x - 3y = -6$, find the following.

26. The intercepts of the graph

28. The graph of the equation

27. The slope of the line

Consider the two points $(-1, 5)$ and $(2, 8)$.

29. Find the slope of the line passing through them.

30. Write, in slope-intercept form, the equation of the line passing through them.

Solve each system of equations using the method indicated.

31. $y = 2x + 5$

$x + y = -4$ (Substitution)

32. $3x + 2y = 2$

$2x + 3y = -7$ (Elimination)

Evaluate each expression.

33. $4^{-1} + 3^0$

34. $2^{-4} \cdot 2^5$

35. $\dfrac{8^{-5} \cdot 8^7}{8^2}$

36. Write $\dfrac{(a^{-3}b^2)^2}{(2a^{-4}b^{-3})^{-1}}$ with positive exponents only.

37. Write 34,500 in scientific notation.

Perform the indicated operations.

38. $(7x^3 - 12x^2 - 3x + 8) + (6x^2 + 4) - (-4x^3 + 8x^2 - 2x - 2)$

39. $6x^5(3x^2 - 9x + 10)$

40. $(7x + 4)(9x + 3)$

41. $(5x + 8)^2$

42. $\dfrac{y^3 - 3y^2 + 8y - 6}{y - 1}$

6

Factoring and Applications

The motion of a freely falling object or of an object that is projected upward can be described using a *quadratic equation*. *Factoring*, a key topic of this chapter, is used when solving some such equations.

6.1 Greatest Common Factors; Factor by Grouping

6.2 Factoring Trinomials

6.3 Factoring Trinomials by Grouping

6.4 Factoring Trinomials Using the FOIL Method

6.5 Special Factoring Techniques

6.6 A General Approach to Factoring

6.7 Solving Quadratic Equations Using the Zero-Factor Property

6.8 Applications of Quadratic Equations

6.1 Greatest Common Factors; Factor by Grouping

OBJECTIVES

1. Find the greatest common factor of a list of numbers.
2. Find the greatest common factor of a list of variable terms.
3. Factor out the greatest common factor.
4. Factor by grouping.

To **factor** a number means to write it as the product of two or more numbers.

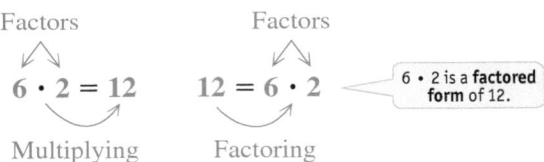

Factoring is a process that "undoes" multiplying. We multiply $6 \cdot 2$ to obtain 12, but we factor 12 by writing it as $6 \cdot 2$.

OBJECTIVE 1 Find the greatest common factor of a list of numbers. An integer that is a factor of two or more integers is a **common factor** of those integers. For example, 6 is a common factor of 18 and 24 because 6 is a factor of both 18 and 24. Other common factors of 18 and 24 are 1, 2, and 3.

The **greatest common factor (GCF)** of a list of integers is the largest common factor of those integers. This means 6 is the greatest common factor of 18 and 24 because it is the largest of their common factors.

> **Note**
>
> *Factors* of a number are also *divisors* of the number. The *greatest common* factor is the same as the *greatest common divisor*. Here are some divisibility rules for deciding what numbers divide into a given number.
>
> **DIVISIBILITY TESTS**
>
> | A Whole Number Divisible by | Must Have the Following Property |
> |---|---|
> | 2 | Ends in 0, 2, 4, 6, or 8 |
> | 3 | Sum of digits divisible by 3 |
> | 4 | Last two digits form a number divisible by 4 |
> | 5 | Ends in 0 or 5 |
> | 6 | Divisible by both 2 and 3 |
> | 8 | Last three digits form a number divisible by 8 |
> | 9 | Sum of digits divisible by 9 |
> | 10 | Ends in 0 |

EXAMPLE 1 **Finding the Greatest Common Factor for Numbers**

Find the greatest common factor for each list of numbers.

(a) 30, 45

$$30 = 2 \cdot 3 \cdot 5$$
$$45 = 3 \cdot 3 \cdot 5$$

Write the prime factored form of each number.

Use each prime the least number of times it appears in all the factored forms. There is no 2 in the prime factored form of 45, so there will be no 2 in the greatest common factor. The least number of times 3 appears in all the factored forms is 1. The least number of times 5 appears is also 1.

$$\text{GCF} = 3^1 \cdot 5^1 = 15 \qquad 3^1 = 3 \text{ and } 5^1 = 5.$$

Continued on Next Page

(b) 72, 120, 432

$$72 = 2 \cdot 2 \cdot 2 \cdot 3 \cdot 3$$
$$120 = 2 \cdot 2 \cdot 2 \cdot 3 \cdot 5$$
$$432 = 2 \cdot 2 \cdot 2 \cdot 2 \cdot 3 \cdot 3 \cdot 3$$

Write the prime factored form of each number.

The least number of times 2 appears in all the factored forms is 3, and the least number of times 3 appears is 1. There is no 5 in the prime factored form of either 72 or 432.

$$GCF = 2^3 \cdot 3^1 = 24 \quad 2^3 = 8 \text{ and } 3^1 = 3.$$

We can also align factors vertically and use exponents in the prime factorizations to organize the lists of factors.

$$72 = 2^3 \cdot 3^2$$
$$120 = 2^3 \cdot 3^1 \cdot 5$$
$$432 = 2^4 \cdot 3^3$$
$$\overline{GCF = 2^3 \cdot 3^1 = 24}$$

The exponent on a factor in the GCF is the least exponent that appears on a factor in all the terms.

(c) 10, 11, 14

$$10 = 2 \cdot 5$$
$$11 = 11$$
$$14 = 2 \cdot 7$$

Write the prime factored form of each number.

There are no primes common to all three numbers. In such cases,

$$GCF = 1.$$

—————— Work Problem ❶ at the Side. ▶

OBJECTIVE ▶ ❷ **Find the greatest common factor of a list of variable terms.** The terms x^4, x^5, x^6, and x^7 have x^4 as the greatest common factor because the least exponent on the variable x in the factored forms is 4.

$$x^4 = 1 \cdot x^4, \quad x^5 = x \cdot x^4, \quad x^6 = x^2 \cdot x^4, \quad x^7 = x^3 \cdot x^4$$
$$GCF = x^4$$

Finding the Greatest Common Factor (GCF)

Step 1 **Factor.** Write each number in prime factored form.

Step 2 **List common factors.** List each prime number or each variable that is a factor of every term in the list. (If a prime does not appear in one of the prime factored forms, it *cannot* appear in the greatest common factor.)

Step 3 **Choose least exponents.** Use as exponents on the common prime factors the *least* exponents from the prime factored forms.

Step 4 **Multiply** the primes from Step 3. If there are no primes left after Step 3, the greatest common factor is 1.

❶ Find the greatest common factor for each list of numbers.

(a) 30, 20, 15

$$30 = 2 \cdot 3 \cdot 5$$
$$20 = 2 \cdot \underline{\quad} \cdot \underline{\quad}$$
$$15 = 3 \cdot \underline{\quad}$$
$$GCF = \underline{\quad}$$

(b) 42, 28, 35

(c) 12, 18, 26, 32

(d) 10, 15, 21

2 Find the greatest common factor for each list of terms.

(a) $6m^4$, $9m^2$, $12m^5$

$6m^4 = 2 \cdot \underline{\hspace{0.5cm}} \cdot m^4$

$9m^2 = 3 \cdot \underline{\hspace{0.5cm}} \cdot \underline{\hspace{0.5cm}}$

$12m^5 = 2 \cdot 2 \cdot \underline{\hspace{0.5cm}} \cdot \underline{\hspace{0.5cm}}$

GCF = $\underline{\hspace{0.5cm}}$

(b) $12p^5$, $18q^4$

(c) y^4z^2, y^6z^8, z^9

(d) $12p^{11}$, $17q^5$

EXAMPLE 2 **Finding the Greatest Common Factor for Variable Terms**

Find the greatest common factor for each list of terms.

(a) $21m^7$, $18m^6$, $45m^8$, $24m^5$

$21m^7 = 3 \cdot 7 \cdot m^7$

$18m^6 = 2 \cdot 3 \cdot 3 \cdot m^6$

$45m^8 = 3 \cdot 3 \cdot 5 \cdot m^8$

$24m^5 = 2 \cdot 2 \cdot 2 \cdot 3 \cdot m^5$

Here, **3** is the greatest common factor of the coefficients 21, 18, 45, and 24. The least exponent on m is **5**.

GCF = $3m^5$

(b) x^4y^2, x^7y^5, x^3y^7, y^{15}

$x^4y^2 = x^4 \cdot y^2$

$x^7y^5 = x^7 \cdot y^5$

$x^3y^7 = x^3 \cdot y^7$

$y^{15} = y^{15}$

There is no x in the last term, y^{15}, so x will not appear in the greatest common factor. There is a y in each term, however, and **2** is the least exponent on y.

GCF = y^2

◀ **Work Problem 2 at the Side.**

OBJECTIVE **3** **Factor out the greatest common factor.** **Factoring** a polynomial is the process of writing a polynomial sum in factored form as a product. For example, the polynomial

$$3m + 12$$

has two terms, $3m$ and 12. The greatest common factor of these two terms is 3. We can write $3m + 12$ so that each term is a product with 3 as one factor.

$$3m + 12$$
$$= 3 \cdot m + 3 \cdot 4 \quad \text{GCF} = 3$$
$$= 3(m + 4) \quad \text{Distributive property,}$$
$$a \cdot b + a \cdot c = a(b + c)$$

The factored form of $3m + 12$ is $3(m + 4)$. This process is called **factoring out the greatest common factor.**

! CAUTION
The polynomial $3m + 12$ is *not* in factored form when written as

$$3 \cdot m + 3 \cdot 4. \quad \text{Not in factored form}$$

The terms are factored, but the polynomial is not. The factored form of $3m + 12$ is the *product*

The factors are 3 and $(m + 4)$. $\quad 3(m + 4). \quad$ In factored form

EXAMPLE 3 **Factoring Out the Greatest Common Factor**

Write in factored form by factoring out the greatest common factor.

(a) $5y^2 + 10y$

$= 5y(y) + 5y(2) \quad \text{GCF} = 5y$

$= 5y(y + 2) \quad \text{Distributive property}$

Answers

2. **(a)** 3; 3; m^2; 3; m^5; $3m^2$
(b) 6 **(c)** z^2 **(d)** 1

─────── **Continued on Next Page**

CHECK   Multiply the factored form.

$5y\,(y + 2)$

$= 5y\,(y) + 5y\,(2)$ Distributive property, $a\,(b + c) = ab + ac$

$= 5y^2 + 10y$ ✓   Original polynomial

(b) $20m^5 + 10m^4 - 15m^3$

$= 5m^3(4m^2) + 5m^3(2m) - 5m^3(3)$ GCF $= 5m^3$

$= 5m^3(4m^2 + 2m - 3)$ Factor out $5m^3$.

CHECK $5m^3(4m^2 + 2m - 3)$

$= 5m^3(4m^2) + 5m^3(2m) + 5m^3(-3)$ Distributive property

$= 20m^5 + 10m^4 - 15m^3$ ✓   Original polynomial

(c) $x^5 + x^3$

$= x^3(x^2) + x^3(1)$ GCF $= x^3$

$= x^3(x^2 + 1)$ ⟵ Don't forget the 1.

Check mentally by distributing x^3 over each term inside the parentheses.

(d) $20m^7p^2 - 36m^3p^4$

$= 4m^3p^2(5m^4) - 4m^3p^2(9p^2)$ GCF $= 4m^3p^2$

$= 4m^3p^2(5m^4 - 9p^2)$ Factor out $4m^3p^2$.

Check mentally by distributing $4m^3p^2$ over each term inside the parentheses.

—————— **Work Problem 3 at the Side.** ▶

| **EXAMPLE 4** | **Factoring Out a Negative Common Factor** |

Write $-8x^4 + 16x^3 - 4x^2$ in factored form.

We can factor out either $4x^2$ or $-4x^2$ here. So that the coefficient of the first term in the trinomial factor will be positive, we factor out $-4x^2$.

$-8x^4 + 16x^3 - 4x^2$ *Be careful with signs.*

$= -4x^2(2x^2) - 4x^2(-4x) - 4x^2(1)$ $-4x^2$ is a common factor.

$= -4x^2(2x^2 - 4x + 1)$ Factor out $-4x^2$.

CHECK $-4x^2(2x^2 - 4x + 1)$

$= -4x^2(2x^2) - 4x^2(-4x) - 4x^2(1)$ Distributive property

$= -8x^4 + 16x^3 - 4x^2$ ✓   Original polynomial

—————— **Work Problem 4 at the Side.** ▶

Note

When the coefficient of the first term in a polynomial is negative, we will often factor out the negative common factor, even if it is just -1. It would also be correct to factor out $4x^2$ in **Example 4** to obtain

$$4x^2(-2x^2 + 4x - 1).$$

---

3 Write in factored form by factoring out the greatest common factor.

(a) $4x^2 + 6x$

$= 2x\,(\underline{\quad}) + 2x\,(\underline{\quad})$

$= \underline{\quad}(\underline{\quad} + \underline{\quad})$

(b) $10y^5 - 8y^4 + 6y^2$

(c) $m^7 + m^9$

$= m^7\,(\underline{\quad}) + \underline{\quad}(m^2)$

$= \underline{\quad}(\underline{\quad} + \underline{\quad})$

(d) $15x^3 - 10x^2 + 5x$

(e) $8p^5q^2 + 16p^6q^3 - 12p^4q^7$

4 Write

$$-14a^3 - 21a^2 + 7a$$

in factored form by factoring out a negative common factor.

Answers

3. **(a)** $2x$; 3; $2x$; $2x$; 3

  (b) $2y^2\,(5y^3 - 4y^2 + 3)$

  (c) 1; m^7; m^7; 1; m^2

  (d) $5x\,(3x^2 - 2x + 1)$

  (e) $4p^4q^2\,(2p + 4p^2q - 3q^5)$

4. $-7a\,(2a^2 + 3a - 1)$

5 Write in factored form by factoring out the greatest common factor.

(a) $r(t - 4) + 5(t - 4)$

$= (t - 4)(\underline{\hspace{1cm}})$

(b) $x(x + 2) + 7(x + 2)$

(c) $y^2(y + 2) - 3(y + 2)$

(d) $x(x - 1) - 5(x - 1)$

EXAMPLE 5 **Factoring Out a Common Binomial Factor**

Write in factored form by factoring out the greatest common factor.

Same

(a) $a(a + 3) + 4(a + 3)$ The binomial $a + 3$ is the greatest common factor.

$= (a + 3)(a + 4)$ Factor out $a + 3$.

(b) $x^2(x + 1) - 5(x + 1)$

$= (x + 1)(x^2 - 5)$ Factor out $x + 1$.

◀ **Work Problem 5 at the Side.**

Note

In factored forms like those in **Example 5**, the order of the factors does not matter because of the commutative property of multiplication, $ab = ba$.

$(a + 3)(a + 4)$ can also be written $(a + 4)(a + 3)$.

OBJECTIVE ▶ 4 Factor by grouping. *When a polynomial has four terms, common factors can sometimes be used to factor by grouping.*

EXAMPLE 6 **Factoring by Grouping**

Factor by grouping.

(a) $2x + 6 + ax + 3a$

Group the first two terms and the last two terms because the first two terms have a common factor of 2 and the last two terms have a common factor of a.

$$2x + 6 + ax + 3a$$

$$= (2x + 6) + (ax + 3a)$$ Group the terms.

$$= 2(x + 3) + a(x + 3)$$ Factor each group.

The expression is still not in factored form because it is the *sum* of two terms. Now, however, $x + 3$ is a common factor and can be factored out.

$$= 2(x + 3) + a(x + 3)$$ $x + 3$ is a common factor.

$(2 + a)(x + 3)$ is also correct.

$$= (x + 3)(2 + a)$$ Factor out $x + 3$.

The final result is in factored form because it is a ***product.***

CHECK $(x + 3)(2 + a)$

$$= x(2) + x(a) + 3(2) + 3(a)$$ Multiply using the FOIL method

$$= 2x + ax + 6 + 3a$$ Simplify.

$$= 2x + 6 + ax + 3a ✓$$ Rearrange terms to obtain the original polynomial.

─── **Continued on Next Page**

Answers

5. **(a)** $r + 5$ **(b)** $(x + 2)(x + 7)$

(c) $(y + 2)(y^2 - 3)$

(d) $(x - 1)(x - 5)$

(b) $6ax + 24x + a + 4$

$= (6ax + 24x) + (a + 4)$ Group the terms.

$= 6x(a + 4) + 1(a + 4)$ Factor each group.

> Remember the 1.

$= (a + 4)(6x + 1)$ Factor out $a + 4$.

CHECK $(a + 4)(6x + 1)$

$= 6ax + a + 24x + 4$ FOIL method

$= 6ax + 24x + a + 4$ ✓   Rearrange terms to obtain the original polynomial.

(c) $2x^2 - 10x + 3xy - 15y$

$= (2x^2 - 10x) + (3xy - 15y)$ Group the terms.

$= 2x(x - 5) + 3y(x - 5)$ Factor each group.

$= (x - 5)(2x + 3y)$ Factor out the common factor, $x - 5$.

CHECK $(x - 5)(2x + 3y)$

$= 2x^2 + 3xy - 10x - 15y$ FOIL method

$= 2x^2 - 10x + 3xy - 15y$ ✓   Original polynomial

(d) $t^3 + 2t^2 - 3t - 6$

> Write a + sign between the groups.

$= (t^3 + 2t^2) + (-3t - 6)$ Group the terms.

$= t^2(t + 2) - 3(t + 2)$ Factor out -3 so there is a common factor, $t + 2$. **Check:** $-3(t + 2) = -3t - 6$

> Be careful with signs.

$= (t + 2)(t^2 - 3)$ Factor out $t + 2$.

Check by multiplying using the FOIL method.

─────────────────── **Work Problem** ⑥ **at the Side.** ▶

---

❶ CAUTION

Be careful with signs when grouping in a problem like **Example 6(d).** It is wise to check the factoring in the second step, as shown in the example side comment, before continuing.

Factoring a Polynomial with Four Terms by Grouping

Step 1 **Group terms.** Collect the terms into two groups so that each group has a common factor.

Step 2 **Factor within groups.** Factor out the greatest common factor from each group.

Step 3 **If possible, factor the entire polynomial.** Factor out a common binomial factor from the results of Step 2.

Step 4 **If necessary, rearrange terms.** If Step 2 does not result in a common binomial factor, try a different grouping.

Always check the factored form by multiplying.

⑥ Factor by grouping.

Ⓖ **(a)** $pq + 5q + 2p + 10$

$= (\_\_ + 5q) + (\_\_ + 10)$

$= \_\_(p + 5) + \_\_(p + 5)$

$= (p + 5)(\_\_\_\_\_)$

(b) $2xy + 3y + 2x + 3$

(c) $2a^2 - 4a + 3ab - 6b$

(d) $x^3 + 3x^2 - 5x - 15$

Answers

6. **(a)** pq; $2p$; q; 2; $q + 2$
    (b) $(2x + 3)(y + 1)$
    (c) $(a - 2)(2a + 3b)$
    (d) $(x + 3)(x^2 - 5)$

7 Factor by grouping.

(a) $6y^2 - 20w + 15y - 8yw$

(b) $9mn - 4 + 12m - 3n$

(c) $12p^2 - 28q - 16pq + 21p$

EXAMPLE 7   **Rearranging Terms before Factoring by Grouping**

Factor by grouping.

(a) $10x^2 - 12y + 15x - 8xy$

Factoring out the common factor 2 from the first two terms and the common factor x from the last two terms gives the following.

$$(10x^2 - 12y) + (15x - 8xy) \qquad \text{Group the terms.}$$
$$= 2(5x^2 - 6y) + x(15 - 8y) \qquad \text{Factor each group.}$$

This does not lead to a common factor, so we try rearranging the terms. There is usually more than one way to do this. We try the following.

$$10x^2 - 12y + 15x - 8xy$$
$$= 10x^2 - 8xy - 12y + 15x \qquad \text{Commutative property}$$
$$= (10x^2 - 8xy) + (-12y + 15x) \qquad \text{Group the terms.}$$
$$= 2x(5x - 4y) + 3(-4y + 5x) \qquad \text{Factor each group.}$$
$$= 2x(5x - 4y) + 3(5x - 4y) \qquad \text{Rewrite } -4y + 5x.$$
$$= (5x - 4y)(2x + 3) \qquad \text{Factor out } 5x - 4y.$$

CHECK $(5x - 4y)(2x + 3)$
$$= 10x^2 + 15x - 8xy - 12y \qquad \text{FOIL method}$$
$$= 10x^2 - 12y + 15x - 8xy ✓ \qquad \text{Original polynomial}$$

(b) $2xy + 12 - 3y - 8x$

We must rearrange the terms to obtain two groups that each have a common factor. Trial and error suggests the following grouping.

$$2xy + 12 - 3y - 8x \qquad \text{\small Write a + sign between the two groups.}$$
$$= (2xy - 3y) + (-8x + 12) \qquad \text{Group the terms.}$$
$$= y(2x - 3) - 4(2x - 3) \qquad \text{Factor each group;} \quad Check: -4(2x - 3) = -8x + 12$$
           Be careful with signs.
$$= (2x - 3)(y - 4) \qquad \text{Factor out } 2x - 3.$$

Because the quantities in parentheses in the second step must be the same, we factored out -4 rather than 4.

CHECK $(2x - 3)(y - 4)$
$$= 2xy - 8x - 3y + 12 \qquad \text{FOIL method}$$
$$= 2xy + 12 - 3y - 8x ✓ \qquad \text{Original polynomial}$$

◄ **Work Problem** **7** **at the Side.**

> **⚠ CAUTION**
> Use negative signs carefully when grouping, as in **Example 7(b),** or a sign error will occur. ***Always check by multiplying.***

Answers

7. (a) $(2y + 5)(3y - 4w)$
   (b) $(3m - 1)(3n + 4)$
   (c) $(3p - 4q)(4p + 7)$

6.1 Exercises

FOR EXTRA HELP   Go to MyMathLab for worked-out, step-by-step solutions to exercises enclosed in a square ▢ and video solutions to ▶ exercises.

CONCEPT CHECK   *Complete each statement.*

1. To factor a number or quantity means to write it as a _____. Factoring is the opposite, or inverse, process of _____.

2. An integer or variable expression that is a factor of two or more terms is a _____ _____. For example, 12 (*is /is not*) a common factor of both 36 and 72 since it _____ evenly into both integers.

Find the greatest common factor for each list of numbers. **See Example 1.**

3. 12, 16

4. 18, 24

5. 40, 20, 4 ▶

6. 50, 30, 5

7. 18, 24, 36, 48

8. 15, 30, 45, 75

9. 4, 9, 12 ▶

10. 9, 16, 24

Find the greatest common factor for each list of terms. **See Example 2.**

11. $16y$, 24 ▶

12. $18w$, 27

13. $30x^3$, $40x^6$, $50x^7$

14. $60z^4$, $70z^8$, $90z^9$

15. $15m^2$, $30m^4$, $60m^2$

16. $12y^5$, $36y^5$, $72y^7$

17. x^4y^3, xy^2 ▶

18. a^4b^5, a^3b

19. $42ab^3$, $36a$, $90b$, $48ab$

20. $45c^3d$, $75c$, $90d$, $105cd$

21. $12m^3n^2$, $18m^5n^4$, $36m^8n^3$

22. $25p^5r^7$, $30p^7r^8$, $50p^5r^3$

CONCEPT CHECK   *An expression is factored when it is written as a product, not a sum. Determine whether each expression is* factored *or* not factored.

23. $2k^2(5k)$

24. $2k^2(5k + 1)$

25. $2k^2 + (5k + 1)$

26. $(2k^2 + 5k) + 1$

27. **CONCEPT CHECK**   A student incorrectly factored
$$18x^3y^2 + 9xy \quad \text{as} \quad 9xy(2x^2y).$$
What Went Wrong?   Factor correctly.

28. **CONCEPT CHECK**   When asked to factor completely, a student incorrectly factored
$$12x^2y - 24xy \quad \text{as} \quad 3xy(4x - 8).$$
What Went Wrong?   Factor correctly.

ⒼⓈ *Complete each factoring by writing each polynomial as the product of two factors.* **See Example 3.**

29. $9m^4$
$= 3m^2(\underline{\quad\quad})$

30. $12p^5$
$= 6p^3(\underline{\quad\quad})$

31. $-8z^9$
$= -4z^5(\underline{\quad\quad})$

32. $-15k^{11}$
$= -5k^8(\underline{\quad\quad})$

33. $6m^4n^5$
$= 3m^3n(\underline{\quad\quad})$

34. $27a^3b^2$
$= 9a^2b(\underline{\quad\quad})$

35. $12y + 24$
$= 12(\underline{\quad\quad})$

36. $18p + 36$
$= 18(\underline{\quad\quad})$

37. $10a^2 - 20a$
$= 10a(\underline{\quad\quad})$

38. $15x^2 - 30x$
$= 15x(\underline{\quad\quad})$

39. $8x^2y + 12x^3y^2$
$= 4x^2y(\underline{\quad\quad})$

40. $18s^3t^2 + 10st$
$= 2st(\underline{\quad\quad})$

Write in factored form by factoring out the greatest common factor (or a negative common factor if the coefficient of the term of greatest degree is negative).
See Examples 3–5.

41. $x^2 - 4x$

42. $m^2 - 7m$

43. $6t^2 + 15t$

44. $8x^2 + 6x$

45. $m^3 - m^2$

46. $p^3 - p^2$

47. $-12x^3 - 6x^2$

48. $-21b^3 - 7b^2$

49. $16z^4 + 24z^2$

50. $100a^5 + 16a^3$

51. $11w^3 - 100$

52. $13z^5 - 80$

53. $8mn^3 + 24m^2n^3$

54. $19p^2y + 38p^2y^3$

55. $-4x^3 + 10x^2 - 6x$

56. $-9z^3 + 6z^2 - 12z$

57. $13y^8 + 26y^4 - 39y^2$

58. $5x^5 + 25x^4 - 20x^3$

59. $45q^4p^5 - 36qp^6 + 81q^2p^3$

60. $125a^3z^5 + 60a^4z^4 - 85a^5z^2$

61. $c(x + 2) + d(x + 2)$

62. $r(5 - x) + t(5 - x)$

63. $a^2(2a + b) - b(2a + b)$

64. $3x(x^2 + 5) - y(x^2 + 5)$

65. $q(p + 4) - 1(p + 4)$

66. $y^2(x - 4) + 1(x - 4)$

CONCEPT CHECK *Students often have difficulty when factoring by grouping because they are not able to tell when the polynomial is completely factored. For example,*

$$5y(2x - 3) + 8t(2x - 3) \quad \text{Not in factored form}$$

*is not in factored form because it is the **sum** of two terms:* $5y(2x - 3)$ *and* $8t(2x - 3)$. *However, because* $2x - 3$ *is a common factor of these two terms, the expression can now be factored.*

$$(2x - 3)(5y + 8t) \quad \text{In factored form}$$

*The factored form is a **product** of the two factors* $2x - 3$ *and* $5y + 8t$.

Determine whether each expression is in factored form or is not in factored form. If it is not in factored form, factor it if possible.

67. $8(7t + 4) + x(7t + 4)$

68. $3r(5x - 1) + 7(5x - 1)$

69. $(8 + x)(7t + 4)$

70. $(3r + 7)(5x - 1)$

71. $18x^2(y + 4) + 7(y - 4)$

72. $12k^3(s - 3) + 7(s + 3)$

Factor by grouping. See Examples 6 and 7.

73. $5m + mn + 20 + 4n$

74. $ts + 5t + 2s + 10$

75. $6xy - 21x + 8y - 28$
▶

76. $2mn - 8n + 3m - 12$

77. $a^2 - 2a + ab - 2b$
▶

78. $y^2 - 6y + yw - 6w$

79. $7z^2 + 14z - az - 2a$

80. $2b^2 + 3b - 8ab - 12a$

81. $18r^2 + 12ry - 3xr - 2xy$

82. $5m^2 + 15mp - 2mr - 6pr$

83. $w^3 + w^2 + 9w + 9$

84. $y^3 + y^2 + 6y + 6$

85. $3a^3 + 6a^2 - 2a - 4$

86. $10x^3 + 15x^2 - 8x - 12$

87. $16m^3 - 4m^2p^2 - 4mp + p^3$

88. $10t^3 - 2t^2s^2 - 5ts + s^3$

89. $y^2 + 3x + 3y + xy$

90. $m^2 + 14p + 7m + 2mp$

91. $2z^2 + 6w - 4z - 3wz$

92. $2a^2 + 20b - 8a - 5ab$

93. $5m - 6p - 2mp + 15$
▶

94. $7y - 9x - 3xy + 21$

95. $18r^2 - 2ty + 12ry - 3rt$

96. $12a^2 - 4bc + 16ac - 3ab$

Relating Concepts (Exercises 97–100) For Individual or Group Work

In many cases, the choice of which pairs of terms to group when factoring by grouping can be made in different ways. To see this for **Example 7(b),** *work Exercises 97–100 in order.*

97. Start with the polynomial from **Example 7(b),** $2xy + 12 - 3y - 8x$, and rearrange the terms as follows: $2xy - 8x - 3y + 12$. What property allows this?

98. Group the first two terms and the last two terms of the rearranged polynomial in **Exercise 97.** Then factor each group.

99. Is the result from **Exercise 98** in factored form? Explain.

100. If the answer to **Exercise 99** is *no,* factor the polynomial. Is the result the same as the one shown for **Example 7(b)?**

6.2 | Factoring Trinomials

OBJECTIVES

1. Factor trinomials with coefficient 1 for the second-degree term.

2. Factor such trinomials after factoring out the greatest common factor.

Using the FOIL method, we can find the product of the binomials $k - 3$ and $k + 1$.

$$(k - 3)(k + 1) = k^2 - 2k - 3 \quad \text{Multiplying}$$

Suppose instead that we are given the polynomial $k^2 - 2k - 3$ and want to rewrite it as the product $(k - 3)(k + 1)$.

$$k^2 - 2k - 3 = (k - 3)(k + 1) \quad \text{Factoring}$$

Recall that this process is called *factoring* the polynomial. Factoring reverses, or "undoes," multiplying.

OBJECTIVE ▸ **1** **Factor trinomials with coefficient 1 for the second-degree term.** When factoring polynomials with integer coefficients, we use only integers in the factors. For example, we can factor $x^2 + 5x + 6$ by finding two integers m and n such that

$$x^2 + 5x + 6 \quad \text{is written as} \quad (x + m)(x + n).$$

To find these integers m and n, we multiply the two binomials on the right.

$$(x + m)(x + n)$$
$$= x^2 + nx + mx + mn \quad \text{FOIL method}$$
$$= x^2 + (n + m)x + mn \quad \text{Distributive property}$$

Comparing this result with $x^2 + 5x + 6$ shows that we must find integers m and n having a sum of 5 and a product of 6.

Product of m and n is 6.

$$x^2 + 5x + 6 = x^2 + (n + m)x + mn$$

Sum of m and n is 5.

Because many pairs of integers have a sum of **5**, it is best to begin by listing those pairs of integers whose product is **6**. Both 5 and 6 are positive, so we consider only pairs in which both integers are positive.

◀ **Work Problem** ❶ **at the Side.**

1. **(a)** Complete the table to find pairs of positive integers whose product is 6. Then find the sum of each pair.

Factors of 6	Sums of Factors
6, ___	6 + ___ = ___
___, 2	___ + 2 = ___

(b) Which pair of factors from the table in part (a) has a sum of 5?

From **Margin Problem 1,** we see that the numbers 6 and 1 and the numbers 3 and 2 both have a product of 6, but only the pair 3 and 2 has a sum of 5. So 3 and 2 are the required integers.

$$x^2 + 5x + 6 \quad \text{is factored as} \quad (x + 3)(x + 2).$$

Check by using the FOIL method to multiply the binomials. *Make sure that the sum of the outer and inner products produces the correct middle term.*

CHECK
$$(x + 3)(x + 2) = x^2 + 5x + 6 \checkmark \quad \text{Correct}$$

$$\begin{array}{c} 3x \\ 2x \\ \hline 5x \quad \text{Add.} \end{array}$$

This method of factoring can be used only for trinomials that have 1 as the coefficient of the second-degree (squared) term.

Note

Consider all possible sign combinations for multiplying two bionomials to understand the resulting signs of the terms of a trinomial.

$(x + 3)(x + 2) = x^2 + 5x + 6$
Both signs positive

All signs in the trinomial product are positive.

$(x - 3)(x - 2) = x^2 - 5x + 6$
Both signs negative

The last term of the trinomial product is positive and the middle term is negative.

$(x + 3)(x - 2) = x^2 + x - 6$
$(x - 3)(x + 2) = x^2 - x - 6$
Different signs

The last term of the trinomial product is negative and the middle term has the same sign as the number in the binomials with the greater absolute value.

EXAMPLE 1   Factoring a Trinomial (All Positive Terms)

Factor $m^2 + 9m + 14$.

Look for two integers whose product is **14** and whose sum is **9**. List the pairs of integers whose products are 14, and examine the sums. Only positive integers are needed because all signs in $m^2 + 9m + 14$ are positive.

Factors of 14	Sums of Factors
14, 1	14 + 1 = 15
7, 2	7 + 2 = 9

Sum is 9.

The required integers are **7** and **2**.

$m^2 + 9m + 14$ factors as $(m + 7)(m + 2)$. $(m+2)(m+7)$ is also correct.

CHECK $(m + 7)(m + 2)$

$= m^2 + 2m + 7m + 14$ FOIL method

$= m^2 + 9m + 14$ ✓   Original polynomial

— Work Problem ❷ at the Side. ▶

EXAMPLE 2   Factoring a Trinomial (Negative Middle Term)

Factor $x^2 - 9x + 20$.

Find two integers whose product is **20** and whose sum is -9. Because the numbers we are looking for have a *positive product* and a *negative sum*, we consider only pairs of negative integers.

Factors of 20	Sums of Factors
−20, −1	−20 + (−1) = −21
−10, −2	−10 + (−2) = −12
−5, −4	−5 + (−4) = −9

Sum is −9.

The required integers are -5 and -4.

$x^2 - 9x + 20$ factors as $(x - 5)(x - 4)$. The order of the factors does not matter.

CHECK $(x - 5)(x - 4)$

$= x^2 - 4x - 5x + 20$ FOIL method

$= x^2 - 9x + 20$ ✓   Original polynomial

— Work Problem ❸ at the Side. ▶

❷ Factor each trinomial.

(a) $y^2 + 12y + 20$

Find two integers whose product is ____ and whose sum is ____. Complete the table.

Factors of 20	Sums of Factors
20, 1	20 + 1 = 21
10, ___	10 + ___ = ___
5, ___	5 + ___ = ___

Which pair of factors has the required sum? _____
Now factor the trinomial.

(b) $x^2 + 9x + 18$

❸ Factor each trinomial.

(a) $t^2 - 12t + 32$

Find two integers whose product is ____ and whose sum is ____. Complete the table.

Factors of 32	Sums of Factors
−32, −1	−32 + (−1) = −33
−16, ___	−16 + (___) = ___
−8, ___	−8 + (___) = ___

Which pair of factors has the required sum? _____
Now factor the trinomial.

(b) $y^2 - 10y + 24$

Answers

2. **(a)** 20; 12; 2; 2; 12; 4; 4; 9; 10 and 2; $(y + 10)(y + 2)$
   (b) $(x + 3)(x + 6)$

3. **(a)** 32; −12; −2; −2; −18; −4; −4; −12; −8 and −4; $(t - 8)(t - 4)$
   (b) $(y - 6)(y - 4)$

4 Factor each trinomial.

(a) $z^2 + z - 30$

Factors of -30	Sums of Factors

(b) $x^2 + x - 42$

EXAMPLE 3 Factoring a Trinomial (Negative Last (Constant) Term)

Factor $x^2 + x - 6$.

We must find two integers whose product is -6 and whose sum is 1 (since the coefficient of x, or $1x$, is 1). To obtain a *negative product*, the pairs of integers must have different signs.

Once we find the required pair, we can stop listing factors.

Factors of -6	Sums of Factors
6, -1	$6 + (-1) = 5$
-6, 1	$-6 + 1 = -5$
3, -2	$3 + (-2) = 1$ Sum is 1.

The required integers are 3 and -2.

$$x^2 + x - 6 \quad \text{factors as} \quad (x + 3)(x - 2).$$

CHECK $(x + 3)(x - 2)$

$$= x^2 - 2x + 3x - 6 \quad \text{FOIL method}$$

$$= x^2 + x - 6 \checkmark \quad \text{Original polynomial}$$

◀ **Work Problem 4 at the Side.**

Note

Remember that because of the commutative property of multiplication, the order of the factors does not matter. ***Always check by multiplying.***

5 Factor each trinomial.

(a) $a^2 - 9a - 22$

Factors of -22	Sums of Factors

(b) $r^2 - 6r - 16$

EXAMPLE 4 Factoring a Trinomial (Two Negative Terms)

Factor $p^2 - 2p - 15$.

Find two integers whose product is -15 and whose sum is -2. Because the constant term, -15, is negative, we need pairs of integers with different signs.

Factors of -15	Sums of Factors
15, -1	$15 + (-1) = 14$
-15, 1	$-15 + 1 = -14$
5, -3	$5 + (-3) = 2$
-5, 3	$-5 + 3 = -2$ Sum is -2.

The required integers are -5 and 3.

$$p^2 - 2p - 15 \quad \text{factors as} \quad (p - 5)(p + 3).$$

CHECK Multiply $(p - 5)(p + 3)$ to obtain $p^2 - 2p - 15$. $\checkmark$

◀ **Work Problem 5 at the Side.**

Note

In **Examples 1–4**, we listed factors in descending order (disregarding their signs) when we were looking for the required pair of integers. This helps avoid skipping the correct combination.

Answers

4. (a) $(z + 6)(z - 5)$ **(b)** $(x + 7)(x - 6)$

5. (a) $(a - 11)(a + 2)$ **(b)** $(r - 8)(r + 2)$

Guidelines for Factoring $x^2 + bx + c$

Find two integers whose product is c and whose sum is b.

1. Both integers must be positive if b and c are positive. (See **Example 1.**)

2. Both integers must be negative if c is positive and b is negative. (See **Example 2.**)

3. One integer must be positive and one must be negative if c is negative. (See **Examples 3 and 4.**)

Some trinomials cannot be factored using only integers. Such trinomials are **prime polynomials.**

EXAMPLE 5   Deciding Whether Polynomials Are Prime

Factor each trinomial if possible.

(a) $x^2 - 5x + 12$

As in **Example 2,** both factors must be negative to give a positive product, 12, and a negative sum, -5. List pairs of negative integers whose product is 12, and examine the sums.

Factors of 12	Sums of Factors
$-12, -1$	$-12 + (-1) = -13$
$-6, -2$	$-6 + (-2) = -8$
$-4, -3$	$-4 + (-3) = -7$

No sum is -5.

None of the pairs of integers has a sum of -5. Therefore, the trinomial $x^2 - 5x + 12$ *cannot be factored using only integers.* It is a prime polynomial.

(b) $k^2 - 8k + 11$

There is no pair of integers whose product is 11 and whose sum is -8, so $k^2 - 8k + 11$ is a prime polynomial.

—————— Work Problem ⑥ at the Side. ▶

EXAMPLE 6   Factoring a Trinomial with Two Variables

Factor $z^2 - 2bz - 3b^2$.

Here, the coefficient of z in the middle term is $-2b$, so we need to find two expressions whose product is $-3b^2$ and whose sum is $-2b$.

Factors of $-3b^2$	Sums of Factors
$3b, -b$	$3b + (-b) = 2b$
$-3b, b$	$-3b + b = -2b$

Sum is $-2b$.

$z^2 - 2bz - 3b^2$ factors as $(z - 3b)(z + b)$.

CHECK $(z - 3b)(z + b)$

$= z^2 + zb - 3bz - 3b^2$ FOIL method

$= z^2 + 1bz - 3bz - 3b^2$ Identity and commutative properties

$= z^2 - 2bz - 3b^2$ ✓   Combine like terms.

—————— Work Problem ⑦ at the Side. ▶

⑥ Factor each trinomial if possible.

(a) $x^2 + 5x + 8$

(b) $r^2 - 3r - 4$

(c) $m^2 - 2m + 5$

⑦ Factor each trinomial.

ⓖⓢ **(a)** $b^2 - 3ab - 4a^2$

We need two expressions whose product is ____ and whose sum is ____. Complete the table.

Factors of $-4a^2$	Sums of Factors
$4a,$ ___	$4a + (\_\_) = \_\_$
$-4a,$ ___	$-4a + \_\_ = \_\_$
$2a, -2a$	$2a + (-2a) = 0$

Which pair of factors has the required sum? _____

Now factor the trinomial.

(b) $r^2 - 6rs + 8s^2$

Answers

6. (a) prime
   (b) $(r - 4)(r + 1)$
   (c) prime
7. (a) $-4a^2; -3a; -a; -a; 3a; a; a; -3a;$
      $-4a$ and $a; (b - 4a)(b + a)$
   (b) $(r - 4s)(r - 2s)$

8 Factor each trinomial completely.

GS (a) $2p^3 + 6p^2 - 8p$

$$= \underline{\quad}(\underline{\quad} + 3p - \underline{\quad})$$
$$= \underline{\quad}(\underline{\quad\quad})(p - 1)$$

(b) $3y^4 - 27y^3 + 60y^2$

(c) $-3x^4 + 15x^3 - 18x^2$

(d) $-5y^5 - 15y^4 + 90y^3$

OBJECTIVE **2** **Factor such trinomials after factoring out the greatest common factor.** If the terms of a trinomial have a common factor, first factor it out. Then factor the remaining trinomial as in **Examples 1–6.**

EXAMPLE 7 **Factoring a Trinomial with a Common Factor**

Factor completely.

(a) $4x^5 - 28x^4 + 40x^3$

There is no second-degree term. Look for a common factor.

$$4x^5 - 28x^4 + 40x^3$$
$$= 4x^3(x^2 - 7x + 10) \qquad \text{Factor out the greatest common factor, } 4x^3.$$

Now factor $x^2 - 7x + 10$. The integers -5 and -2 have a product of 10 and a sum of -7.

$$\boxed{\text{Include } 4x^3.} \quad = 4x^3(x - 5)(x - 2) \qquad \text{Completely factored form}$$

CHECK $4x^3(x - 5)(x - 2)$
$$= 4x^3(x^2 - 2x - 5x + 10) \qquad \text{FOIL method}$$
$$= 4x^3(x^2 - 7x + 10) \qquad \text{Combine like terms.}$$
$$= 4x^5 - 28x^4 + 40x^3 \checkmark \qquad \text{Distributive property}$$

(b) $-3y^8 - 18y^7 + 21y^6$

The coefficient of the first term is negative, so we factor out $-3y^6$.

$$-3y^8 - 18y^7 + 21y^6$$
$$= -3y^6(y^2 + 6y - 7) \qquad \text{Factor out the greatest common factor, } -3y^6.$$

Now factor $y^2 + 6y - 7$. The integers 7 and -1 have a product of -7 and a sum of 6.

$$= -3y^6(y + 7)(y - 1) \qquad \text{Completely factored form}$$

CHECK $-3y^6(y + 7)(y - 1)$
$$= -3y^6(y^2 - y + 7y - 7) \qquad \text{FOIL method}$$
$$= -3y^6(y^2 + 6y - 7) \qquad \text{Combine like terms.}$$
$$= -3y^8 - 18y^7 + 21y^6 \checkmark \qquad \text{Distributive property}$$

◀ **Work Problem** **8** **at the Side**

⚠ CAUTION

When factoring, always look for a common factor first. If the coefficient of the leading term is negative, we will factor out the negative common factor.

Remember to include the common factor as part of the answer, and check by multiplying out the completely factored form.

Answers

8. (a) $2p; p^2; 4; 2p; p + 4$
(b) $3y^2(y - 5)(y - 4)$
(c) $-3x^2(x - 3)(x - 2)$
(d) $-5y^3(y + 6)(y - 3)$

6.2 Exercises

FOR EXTRA HELP Go to MyMathLab for worked-out, step-by-step solutions to exercises enclosed in a square ▢ and video solutions to ▶ exercises.

CONCEPT CHECK *Answer each question.*

1. When factoring a trinomial in x as $(x + a)(x + b)$, what must be true of a and b, if the coefficient of the constant term of the trinomial is negative?

2. When factoring a trinomial in x as $(x + a)(x + b)$ what must be true of a and b if the coefficient of the constant term is positive?

3. Which one of the following is the correct factored form of $x^2 - 12x + 32$?

   A. $(x - 8)(x + 4)$ **B.** $(x + 8)(x - 4)$

   C. $(x - 8)(x - 4)$ **D.** $(x + 8)(x + 4)$

4. What would be the first step in factoring
$$2x^3 + 8x^2 - 10x? \quad \text{(See Example 7.)}$$

5. What polynomial can be factored as
$$(a + 9)(a + 4)?$$

6. What polynomial can be factored as
$$(y - 7)(y + 3)?$$

7. CONCEPT CHECK A student factored as follows.
$$x^3 + 3x^2 - 28x$$
$$= x(x^2 + 3x - 28x)$$
$$= (x + 7)(x - 4) \qquad \text{Incorrect}$$
What Went Wrong? Factor correctly.

8. CONCEPT CHECK A student incorrectly factored
$$x^2 + x + 6 \quad \text{as} \quad (x + 6)(x - 1).$$
What Went Wrong? Factor correctly if possible.

List all pairs of integers with the given product. Then find the pair whose sum is given. See the tables in Examples 1–4.

9. Product: 12; Sum: 7

10. Product: 18; Sum: 9

11. Product: -24; Sum: -5

12. Product: -36; Sum: -16

GS *Complete each factoring. See Examples 1–4.*

13. $p^2 + 11p + 30$
$$= (p + 5)(\underline{\hspace{1cm}})$$

14. $x^2 + 10x + 21$
$$= (x + 7)(\underline{\hspace{1cm}})$$

15. $x^2 + 15x + 44$
$$= (x + 4)(\underline{\hspace{1cm}})$$

16. $r^2 + 15r + 56$
$$= (r + 7)(\underline{\hspace{1cm}})$$

17. $x^2 - 9x + 8$
$$= (x - 1)(\underline{\hspace{1cm}})$$

18. $t^2 - 14t + 24$
$$= (t - 2)(\underline{\hspace{1cm}})$$

19. $y^2 - 2y - 15$
$$= (y + 3)(\underline{\hspace{1cm}})$$

20. $t^2 - t - 42$
$$= (t + 6)(\underline{\hspace{1cm}})$$

21. $x^2 + 9x - 22$
$$= (x - 2)(\underline{\hspace{1cm}})$$

22. $x^2 + 6x - 27$
$$= (x - 3)(\underline{\hspace{1cm}})$$

23. $y^2 - 7y - 18$
$$= (y + 2)(\underline{\hspace{1cm}})$$

24. $y^2 - 2y - 24$
$$= (y + 4)(\underline{\hspace{1cm}})$$

Factor completely. If a polynomial cannot be factored, write prime.
See Examples 1–5.

25. $y^2 + 9y + 8$

26. $a^2 + 9a + 20$

27. $b^2 + 8b + 15$

28. $x^2 + 6x + 8$

29. $m^2 + m - 20$

30. $p^2 + 4p - 5$

31. $x^2 + 3x - 40$

32. $d^2 + 4d - 45$

33. $x^2 + 4x + 5$

34. $t^2 + 11t + 12$

35. $y^2 - 8y + 15$

36. $y^2 - 6y + 8$

37. $z^2 - 15z + 56$

38. $x^2 - 13x + 36$

39. $r^2 - r - 30$

40. $q^2 - q - 42$

41. $a^2 - 8a - 48$

42. $m^2 - 10m - 24$

Factor completely. **See Example 6.**

43. $r^2 + 3ra + 2a^2$

44. $x^2 + 5xa + 4a^2$

45. $x^2 + 4xy + 3y^2$

46. $p^2 + 9pq + 8q^2$

47. $t^2 - tz - 6z^2$

48. $a^2 - ab - 12b^2$

49. $v^2 - 11vw + 30w^2$

50. $v^2 - 11vx + 24x^2$

51. $a^2 + 2ab - 15b^2$

52. $m^2 + 4mn - 12n^2$

53. $a^2 - 9ab + 18b^2$

54. $h^2 - 11hk + 28k^2$

Factor completely. **See Example 7.**

55. $4x^2 + 12x - 40$

56. $5y^2 - 5y - 30$

57. $2t^3 + 8t^2 + 6t$

58. $3t^3 + 27t^2 + 24t$

59. $-2x^6 - 8x^5 + 42x^4$

60. $-4y^5 - 12y^4 + 40y^3$

61. $-a^5 - 3a^4b + 4a^3b^2$

62. $-z^{10} + 4z^9y + 21z^8y^2$

63. $5m^5 + 25m^4 - 40m^2$

64. $12k^5 - 6k^3 + 10k^2$

65. $m^3n - 10m^2n^2 + 24mn^3$

66. $y^3z + 3y^2z^2 - 54yz^3$

6.3 | Factoring Trinomials by Grouping

OBJECTIVE ▶ 1 Factor trinomials by grouping when the coefficient of the second-degree term is not 1. We now extend our work to factor a trinomial such as $2x^2 + 7x + 6$, where the coefficient of x^2 is *not* 1.

OBJECTIVE

1 Factor trinomials by grouping when the coefficient of the second-degree term is not 1.

EXAMPLE 1 Factoring a Trinomial by Grouping (Coefficient of the Second-Degree Term Not 1)

Factor $2x^2 + 7x + 6$.

To factor this trinomial, we look for two positive integers whose product is $2 \cdot 6 = 12$ and whose sum is 7.

$$\underset{\text{Product is } 2 \cdot 6 = 12.}{\overset{\text{Sum is 7.}}{2x^2 + 7x + 6}}$$

The required integers are 3 and 4, since $3 \cdot 4 = 12$ and $3 + 4 = 7$. We use these integers to write the middle term $7x$ as $3x + 4x$.

$$2x^2 + 7x + 6$$
$$= 2x^2 + \underbrace{3x + 4x}_{7x} + 6$$
$$= (2x^2 + 3x) + (4x + 6) \qquad \text{Group the terms.}$$
$$= x(2x + 3) + 2(2x + 3) \qquad \text{Factor each group.}$$

Must be the same factor

$$= (2x + 3)(x + 2) \qquad \text{Factor out } 2x + 3.$$

CHECK Multiply $(2x + 3)(x + 2)$ to obtain $2x^2 + 7x + 6$. ✓

—————————— Work Problem **1** at the Side. ▶

EXAMPLE 2 Factoring Trinomials by Grouping

Factor each trinomial.

(a) $6r^2 + r - 1$

We must find two integers with a product of $6(-1) = -6$ and a sum of **1** (because the coefficient of r, or $1r$, is 1). The integers are -2 and 3. We write the middle term r as $-2r + 3r$.

$$6r^2 + r - 1$$
$$= 6r^2 - 2r + 3r - 1 \qquad r = -2r + 3r$$
$$= (6r^2 - 2r) + (3r - 1) \qquad \text{Group the terms.}$$
$$= 2r(3r - 1) + 1(3r - 1) \qquad \text{The binomials must be the same. Remember the 1.}$$
$$= (3r - 1)(2r + 1) \qquad \text{Factor out } 3r - 1.$$

CHECK Multiply $(3r - 1)(2r + 1)$ to obtain $6r^2 + r - 1$. ✓

—————————— **Continued on Next Page**

1 (a) In **Example 1**, we factored
$$2x^2 + 7x + 6$$
by writing $7x$ as $3x + 4x$. This trinomial can also be factored by writing $7x$ as $4x + 3x$.

Complete the following.

$$2x^2 + 7x + 6$$
$$= 2x^2 + 4x + 3x + 6$$
$$= (2x^2 + \underline{}) + (3x + \underline{})$$
$$= 2x(x + \underline{}) + 3(x + \underline{})$$
$$= (\underline{})(2x + 3)$$

(b) Is the answer in part (a) the same as in **Example 1**? (Remember that the order of the factors does not matter.)

(c) Factor $2z^2 + 5z + 3$ by grouping.

Answers
1. (a) $4x$; 6; 2; 2; $x + 2$ **(b)** yes
(c) $(2z + 3)(z + 1)$

2 Factor each trinomial by grouping.

(a) $2m^2 + 7m + 3$

(b) $5p^2 - 2p - 3$

(c) $15k^2 - km - 2m^2$

3 Factor the trinomial completely.

GS $4x^2 - 2x - 30$

$= \underline{\quad}(2x^2 - x - 15)$

$= \underline{\quad}(2x^2 - \underline{\quad} + \underline{\quad} - 15)$

$= 2[(2x^2 - \underline{\quad}) + (5x - 15)]$

$= 2[2x(\underline{\quad}) + 5(x - 3)]$

$= \underline{\qquad\qquad}$

4 Factor each trinomial completely.

(a) $18p^4 + 63p^3 + 27p^2$

(b) $6a^2 + 3ab - 18b^2$

Answers

2. (a) $(2m + 1)(m + 3)$
   (b) $(5p + 3)(p - 1)$
   (c) $(5k - 2m)(3k + m)$
3. $2; 2; 6x; 5x; 6x; x - 3$;
   $2(x - 3)(2x + 5)$
4. (a) $9p^2(2p + 1)(p + 3)$
   (b) $3(2a - 3b)(a + 2b)$

(b) $12z^2 - 5z - 2$

   Look for two integers whose product is $12(-2) = -24$ and whose sum is -5. The required integers are 3 and -8.

$$12z^2 - 5z - 2$$
$$= 12z^2 + 3z - 8z - 2 \qquad -5z = 3z - 8z$$
$$= (12z^2 + 3z) + (-8z - 2) \qquad \text{Group the terms.}$$
$$= 3z(4z + 1) - 2(4z + 1) \qquad \text{Factor each group.}$$
$$= (4z + 1)(3z - 2) \qquad \text{Factor out } 4z + 1.$$

> Be careful with signs.

CHECK Multiply $(4z + 1)(3z - 2)$ to obtain $12z^2 - 5z - 2$. ✓

(c) $10m^2 + mn - 3n^2$

   Two integers whose product is $10(-3) = -30$ and whose sum is 1 are -5 and 6. Rewrite the trinomial with four terms.

$$10m^2 + mn - 3n^2$$
$$= 10m^2 - 5mn + 6mn - 3n^2 \qquad mn = -5mn + 6mn$$
$$= (10m^2 - 5mn) + (6mn - 3n^2) \qquad \text{Group the terms.}$$
$$= 5m(2m - n) + 3n(2m - n) \qquad \text{Factor each group.}$$
$$= (2m - n)(5m + 3n) \qquad \text{Factor out } 2m - n.$$

CHECK Multiply $(2m - n)(5m + 3n)$ to obtain $10m^2 + mn - 3n^2$. ✓

◀ **Work Problem 2** at the Side.

EXAMPLE 3 Factoring a Trinomial with a Common Factor by Grouping

Factor $28x^5 - 58x^4 - 30x^3$.

$$28x^5 - 58x^4 - 30x^3$$
$$= 2x^3(14x^2 - 29x - 15) \qquad \begin{array}{l}\text{Factor out the greatest}\\\text{common factor, } 2x^3.\end{array}$$

To factor $14x^2 - 29x - 15$, find two integers whose product is $14(-15) = -210$ and whose sum is -29. Factoring 210 into prime factors helps find these integers.

$$210 = 2 \cdot 3 \cdot 5 \cdot 7$$

Combine the prime factors in pairs in different ways, using one positive factor and one negative factor to obtain -210. The factors 6 and -35 have the correct sum, -29.

$$28x^5 - 58x^4 - 30x^3$$
$$= 2x^3(14x^2 - 29x - 15) \qquad \text{From above}$$
$$= 2x^3(14x^2 + 6x - 35x - 15) \qquad -29x = 6x - 35x$$
$$= 2x^3[(14x^2 + 6x) + (-35x - 15)] \qquad \text{Group the terms.}$$
$$= 2x^3[2x(7x + 3) - 5(7x + 3)] \qquad \text{Factor each group.}$$
$$= 2x^3[(7x + 3)(2x - 5)] \qquad \text{Factor out } 7x + 3.$$
$$= 2x^3(7x + 3)(2x - 5) \qquad \text{Check by multiplying.}$$

> Remember the common factor.

◀ **Work Problem 3** and **4** at the Side.

6.3 Exercises

FOR EXTRA HELP

Go to MyMathLab *for worked-out, step-by-step solutions to exercises enclosed in a square* ▢ *and video solutions to* ▶ *exercises.*

1. CONCEPT CHECK Which pair of integers would be used to rewrite the middle term when factoring $12y^2 + 5y - 2$ by grouping?

A. $-8, 3$ **B.** $8, -3$ **C.** $-6, 4$ **D.** $6, -4$

2. CONCEPT CHECK Which pair of integers would be used to rewrite the middle term when factoring $20b^2 - 13b + 2$ by grouping?

A. $10, 3$ **B.** $-10, -3$ **C.** $8, 5$ **D.** $-8, -5$

⒢ *The middle term of each trinomial has been rewritten. Now factor by grouping.*
See Examples 1 and 2.

3. $m^2 + 8m + 12$
$= m^2 + 6m + 2m + 12$

4. $x^2 + 9x + 14$
$= x^2 + 7x + 2x + 14$

5. $a^2 + 3a - 10$
$= a^2 + 5a - 2a - 10$

6. $y^2 + 2y - 24$
$= y^2 - 4y + 6y - 24$

7. $10t^2 + 9t + 2$
$= 10t^2 + 5t + 4t + 2$

8. $6x^2 + 13x + 6$
$= 6x^2 + 9x + 4x + 6$

9. $15z^2 - 19z + 6$
$= 15z^2 - 10z - 9z + 6$

10. $12p^2 - 17p + 6$
$= 12p^2 - 9p - 8p + 6$

11. $8s^2 - 2st - 3t^2$
$= 8s^2 + 4st - 6st - 3t^2$

12. $3x^2 - xy - 14y^2$
$= 3x^2 - 7xy + 6xy - 14y^2$

13. $15a^2 + 22ab + 8b^2$
$= 15a^2 + 10ab + 12ab + 8b^2$

14. $25m^2 + 25mn + 6n^2$
$= 25m^2 + 15mn + 10mn + 6n^2$

⒢ *Complete the steps to factor each trinomial by grouping.* **See Examples 1 and 2.**

15. $2m^2 + 11m + 12$

  (a) Find two integers whose product is
    ____ · ____ = ____ and whose sum is ____ .

  (b) The required integers are ____ and ____ .

  (c) Write the middle term $11m$ as ____ + ____ .

  (d) Rewrite the given trinomial using four terms.

  (e) Factor the polynomial in part (d) by grouping.

  (f) Check by multiplying.

16. $6y^2 - 19y + 10$

  (a) Find two integers whose product is
    ____ · ____ = ____ and whose sum is ____ .

  (b) The required integers are ____ and ____ .

  (c) Write the middle term $-19y$ as ____ + _____ .

  (d) Rewrite the given trinomial using four terms.

  (e) Factor the polynomial in part (d) by grouping.

  (f) Check by multiplying.

Factor each trinomial completely. ***See Examples 1–3.***

17. $2x^2 + 7x + 3$

18. $3y^2 + 13y + 4$

19. $4r^2 + r - 3$

20. $4r^2 + 3r - 10$

21. $8m^2 - 10m - 3$

22. $20x^2 - 28x - 3$

23. $21m^2 + 13m + 2$

24. $38x^2 + 23x + 2$

25. $3a^2 + 10a + 7$

26. $6w^2 + 19w + 10$

27. $12y^2 - 13y + 3$

28. $15a^2 - 16a + 4$

29. $16 + 16x + 3x^2$

30. $18 + 65x + 7x^2$

31. $24x^2 - 42x + 9$

32. $48b^2 - 86b + 10$

33. $2m^3 + 2m^2 - 40m$

34. $3x^3 + 12x^2 - 36x$

35. $-32z^5 + 20z^4 + 12z^3$

36. $-18x^5 - 15x^4 + 75x^3$

37. $12p^2 + 7pq - 12q^2$

38. $6m^2 + 5mn - 6n^2$

39. $6a^2 - 7ab - 5b^2$

40. $25g^2 - 5gh - 2h^2$

41. CONCEPT CHECK On a quiz, a student factored $16x^2 - 24x + 5$ by grouping as follows.

$$16x^2 - 24x + 5$$
$$= 16x^2 - 4x - 20x + 5$$
$$= 4x(4x - 1) - 5(4x - 1) \quad \text{His answer}$$

He did not receive credit for this answer.
What Went Wrong? What is the correct factored form?

42. CONCEPT CHECK On a quiz, a student factored $3k^3 - 12k^2 - 15k$ by first factoring out the common factor $3k$ to obtain $3k(k^2 - 4k - 5)$. Then she wrote the following.

$$k^2 - 4k - 5$$
$$= k^2 - 5k + k - 5$$
$$= k(k - 5) + 1(k - 5)$$
$$= (k - 5)(k + 1) \quad \text{Her answer}$$

What Went Wrong? What is the correct factored form?

6.4 Factoring Trinomials Using the FOIL Method

OBJECTIVE ▸ 1 **Factor trinomials using the FOIL method.** This section shows an alternative method of factoring trinomials that uses trial and error.

OBJECTIVE

1 Factor trinomials using the FOIL method.

EXAMPLE 1 Factoring a Trinomial Using FOIL (Coefficient of the Second-Degree Term Not 1)

Factor $2x^2 + 7x + 6$.

We want to write $2x^2 + 7x + 6$ as the product of two binomials.

$$2x^2 + 7x + 6$$
$$= (\underline{\quad})(\underline{\quad})$$

We use the FOIL method in reverse.

The product of the two first terms of the binomials is $2x^2$. The possible factors of $2x^2$ are $2x$ and x, or $-2x$ and $-x$. Because all terms of the trinomial are positive, we consider only positive factors. Thus, we have the following.

$$2x^2 + 7x + 6$$
$$= (2x\underline{\quad})(x\underline{\quad})$$

The product of the two last terms of the binomials must be 6. It can be factored as $1 \cdot 6$, $6 \cdot 1$, $2 \cdot 3$, or $3 \cdot 2$. We try each pair of factors in $(2x\underline{\quad})(x\underline{\quad})$ to find the pair that gives the correct middle term, $7x$. Begin with 1 and 6 and then try 6 and 1.

   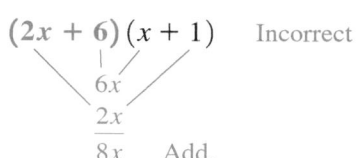

On the right above, $2x + 6 = 2(x + 3)$. The terms of the binomial $2x + 6$ have a common factor of 2, while the terms of $2x^2 + 7x + 6$ have no common factor other than 1. The product $(2x + 6)(x + 1)$ cannot be correct.

If the terms of the original polynomial have greatest common factor 1, then each of its factors will also have terms with GCF 1.

We try the pair 2 and 3 in $(2x\underline{\quad})(x\underline{\quad})$. Because of the common factor 2 in the terms of $2x + 2$, the product $(2x + 2)(x + 3)$ will not work. Finally, we try the pair 3 and 2 in $(2x\underline{\quad})(x\underline{\quad})$.

$$(2x + 3)(x + 2) = 2x^2 + 7x + 6 \quad \text{Correct}$$
(with $3x$, $4x$, $7x$ Add.)

Thus, $2x^2 + 7x + 6$ factors as $(2x + 3)(x + 2)$.

CHECK Multiply $(2x + 3)(x + 2)$ to obtain $2x^2 + 7x + 6$. ✓

— Work Problem ① at the Side. ▶

1 Factor each trinomial.

(a) $2p^2 + 9p + 9$
Try various combinations of factors of $2p^2$ with factors of 9 to find the pair of factors that gives the correct middle term, _____.

Possible Pairs of Factors	Middle Term	Correct?
$(2p + 9)(p + 1)$	$11p$	(Yes/No)
$(2p + 1)(p + 9)$	_____	(Yes/No)
$(2p + 3)(p + 3)$	_____	(Yes/No)

$2p^2 + 9p + 9$ factors as _____.

(b) $8y^2 + 22y + 5$

Answers
1. (a) $9p$; No; $19p$; No; $9p$; Yes;
$(2p + 3)(p + 3)$
(b) $(4y + 1)(2y + 5)$

2 Factor each trinomial.

(a) $8x^2 + 10x + 3$

(b) $6p^2 + 19p + 10$

EXAMPLE 2 **Factoring a Trinomial Using FOIL (All Positive Terms)**

Factor $8p^2 + 14p + 5$.

The number 8 has several possible pairs of factors, but 5 has only 1 and 5 or -1 and -5, so we begin by considering the factors of 5. We ignore the negative factors because all coefficients in the trinomial are positive. If $8p^2 + 14p + 5$ can be factored, the factors will have this form.

$$(\underline{} + 5)(\underline{} + 1)$$

The possible pairs of factors of $8p^2$ are $8p$ and p, or $4p$ and $2p$. We try various combinations, checking to see if the middle term is **14p**.

$(8p + 5)(p + 1)$ Incorrect
$5p$
$8p$
$13p$ Add.

$(p + 5)(8p + 1)$ Incorrect
$40p$
p
$41p$ Add.

$(4p + 5)(2p + 1)$ Correct
$10p$
$4p$
$14p$ Add.

This last combination produces **14p**, the correct middle term.

$$8p^2 + 14p + 5 \quad \text{factors as} \quad (4p + 5)(2p + 1).$$

CHECK Multiply $(4p + 5)(2p + 1)$ to obtain $8p^2 + 14p + 5$. ✓

◀ Work Problem **2** at the Side.

---

3 Factor each trinomial.

(a) $4y^2 - 11y + 7$

(b) $9x^2 - 21x + 10$

EXAMPLE 3 **Factoring a Trinomial Using FOIL (Negative Middle Term)**

Factor $6x^2 - 11x + 3$.

Because 3 has only 1 and 3 or -1 and -3 as factors, it is better here to begin by considering the factors of 3. The last term of the trinomial $6x^2 - 11x + 3$ is positive and the middle term has a negative coefficient, so we consider only negative factors. We need two negative factors because the *product* of two negative factors is positive and their *sum* is negative, as required.

We try -3 and -1 as factors of 3.

$$(\underline{} - 3)(\underline{} - 1)$$

The factors of $6x^2$ may be either $6x$ and x, or $2x$ and $3x$.

$(6x - 3)(x - 1)$ Incorrect
$-3x$
$-6x$
$-9x$ Add.

$(2x - 3)(3x - 1)$ Correct
$-9x$
$-2x$
$-11x$ Add.

The factors $2x$ and $3x$ produce $-11x$, the correct middle term.

$$6x^2 - 11x + 3 \quad \text{factors as} \quad (2x - 3)(3x - 1).$$

CHECK Multiply $(2x - 3)(3x - 1)$ to obtain $6x^2 - 11x + 3$. ✓

◀ Work Problem **3** at the Side.

Answers

2. **(a)** $(4x + 3)(2x + 1)$
     (b) $(3p + 2)(2p + 5)$
3. **(a)** $(4y - 7)(y - 1)$
     (b) $(3x - 5)(3x - 2)$

Note

Our initial attempt to factor $6x^2 - 11x + 3$ as $(6x - 3)(x - 1)$ in **Example 3** *cannot* be correct because the terms of $6x - 3$ have a common factor of 3, while those of the original polynomial do not.

EXAMPLE 4   **Factoring a Trinomial Using FOIL (Negative Constant Term)**

Factor $8x^2 + 6x - 9$.

The integer 8 has several possible pairs of factors, as does -9. Because the constant term is negative, one positive factor and one negative factor of -9 are needed. The coefficient of the middle term is relatively small, so we avoid large factors, such as 8 or 9. We try $4x$ and $2x$ as factors of $8x^2$, and 3 and -3 as factors of -9, and check the middle term.

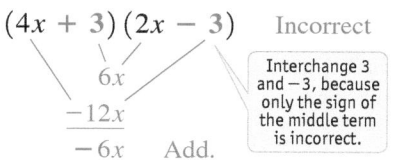   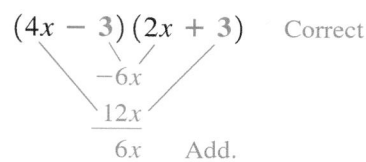

The combination on the right produces $6x$, the correct middle term.

$8x^2 + 6x - 9$ factors as $(4x - 3)(2x + 3)$.   *Check by multiplying.*

────────────────────── **Work Problem 4 at the Side.** ▶

EXAMPLE 5   **Factoring a Trinomial with Two Variables**

Factor $12a^2 - ab - 20b^2$.

There are several pairs of factors of $12a^2$, including

$$12a \text{ and } a, \quad 6a \text{ and } 2a, \quad \text{and} \quad 4a \text{ and } 3a.$$

There are also many possible pairs of factors of $-20b^2$, including

$$20b \text{ and } -b, \quad -20b \text{ and } b, \quad 10b \text{ and } -2b,$$
$$-10b \text{ and } 2b, \quad 4b \text{ and } -5b, \quad \text{and} \quad -4b \text{ and } 5b.$$

Once again, because the coefficient of the middle term is relatively small, avoid the larger factors. Try the factors $3a$ and $4a$, and $4b$ and $-5b$.

$(3a - 5b)(4a + 4b)$ Incorrect

This cannot be correct because the terms of $(4a + 4b)$ have 4 as a common factor, while the terms of the given trinomial do not.

$(3a + 4b)(4a - 5b)$ Incorrect

$16ab$
$-15ab$
ab Add.

In the factorization attempt on the right above, the middle term is ab, rather than $-ab$. We interchange the signs of the last two terms in the factors to obtain the correct result.

$$(3a - 4b)(4a + 5b)$$
$$= 12a^2 - ab - 20b^2 \quad \text{Correct}$$

Thus, $12a^2 - ab - 20b^2$ factors as $(3a - 4b)(4a + 5b)$.   *Check by multiplying.*

────────────────────── **Work Problem 5 at the Side.** ▶

---

4 Factor each trinomial if possible.

(a) $6x^2 + 5x - 4$
$$= (3x + \underline{\quad})(2x - \underline{\quad})$$

(b) $6m^2 - 11m - 10$

(c) $4x^2 - 3x - 7$

(d) $3y^2 + 8y - 6$

5 Factor each trinomial.

(a) $2x^2 - 5xy - 3y^2$
$$= (2x + \underline{\quad})(x - \underline{\quad})$$

(b) $8a^2 + 2ab - 3b^2$

Answers
4. (a) 4; 1
   (b) $(2m - 5)(3m + 2)$
   (c) $(4x - 7)(x + 1)$
   (d) prime
5. (a) y; $3y$
   (b) $(4a + 3b)(2a - b)$

6 Factor each trinomial.

(a) $36z^3 + 102z^2 + 72z$

$= \underline{\quad}(\underline{\quad} + \underline{\quad} + 12)$

$= 6z(3z + 4)(\underline{\quad})$

(b) $10x^3 + 45x^2 - 90x$

(c) $-24x^3 + 32x^2 + 6x$

EXAMPLE 6 **Factoring Trinomials with Common Factors**

Factor each trinomial.

(a) $15y^3 + 55y^2 + 30y$

$$15y^3 + 55y^2 + 30y$$

$$= 5y(3y^2 + 11y + 6) \quad \text{Factor out the greatest common factor, } 5y.$$

Now factor $3y^2 + 11y + 6$. Try $3y$ and y as factors of $3y^2$ and 2 and 3 as factors of 6. We know that

$$(3y + 3)(y + 2) \text{ is incorrect}$$

because the terms of $(3y + 3)$ have a common factor of **3**. So we switch the 3 and 2 and try the following factors.

$$(3y + 2)(y + 3)$$

$$= 3y^2 + 11y + 6 \quad \text{Correct}$$

This leads to the completely factored form.

$$15y^3 + 55y^2 + 30y$$

$$= 5y(3y + 2)(y + 3)$$

> Remember the common factor.

CHECK $5y(3y + 2)(y + 3)$

$$= 5y(3y^2 + 9y + 2y + 6) \quad \text{FOIL method}$$

$$= 5y(3y^2 + 11y + 6) \quad \text{Combine like terms.}$$

$$= 15y^3 + 55y^2 + 30y \checkmark \quad \text{Distributive property}$$

(b) $-24a^3 - 42a^2 + 45a$

The common factor could be $3a$ or $-3a$. If we factor out $-3a$, the first term of the trinomial will be positive, which makes it easier to factor the remaining trinomial.

$$-24a^3 - 42a^2 + 45a$$

> It is easier here to factor the trinomial if the first term is $8a^2$ rather than $-8a^2$.

$$= -3a(8a^2 + 14a - 15) \quad \text{Factor out } -3a.$$

$$= -3a(4a - 3)(2a + 5) \quad \text{Use trial and error.}$$

CHECK $-3a(4a - 3)(2a + 5)$

$$= -3a(8a^2 + 20a - 6a - 15) \quad \text{FOIL method}$$

$$= -3a(8a^2 + 14a - 15) \quad \text{Combine like terms.}$$

$$= -24a^3 - 42a^2 + 45a \checkmark \quad \text{Distributive property}$$

◀ **Work Problem 6 at the Side.**

⊘ CAUTION

Remember to include the common factor in the final factored form.

Answers

6. (a) $6z$; $6z^2$; $17z$; $2z + 3$

(b) $5x(2x - 3)(x + 6)$

(c) $-2x(6x + 1)(2x - 3)$

6.4 Exercises

FOR EXTRA HELP Go to MyMathLab for worked-out, step-by-step solutions to exercises enclosed in a square ▢ and video solutions to ▶ exercises.

CONCEPT CHECK *Decide which is the correct factored form of the given polynomial.*

1. $2x^2 - x - 1$

   A. $(2x - 1)(x + 1)$ **B.** $(2x + 1)(x - 1)$

2. $3a^2 - 5a - 2$

   A. $(3a + 1)(a - 2)$ **B.** $(3a - 1)(a + 2)$

3. $4y^2 + 17y - 15$

   A. $(y + 5)(4y - 3)$ **B.** $(2y - 5)(2y + 3)$

4. $12c^2 - 7c - 12$

   A. $(6c - 2)(2c + 6)$ **B.** $(4c + 3)(3c - 4)$

5. $4k^2 + 13mk + 3m^2$

   A. $(4k + m)(k + 3m)$ **B.** $(4k + 3m)(k + m)$

6. $2x^2 + 11x + 12$

   A. $(2x + 3)(x + 4)$ **B.** $(2x + 4)(x + 3)$

Ⓖ️Ⓢ *Complete each factoring.* **See Examples 1–6.**

7. $6a^2 + 7ab - 20b^2$

   $= (3a - 4b)(\underline{\hspace{1.5cm}})$

8. $9m^2 - 3mn - 2n^2$

   $= (3m + n)(\underline{\hspace{1.5cm}})$

9. $2x^2 + 6x - 8$

   $= 2(\underline{\hspace{2cm}})$

   $= 2(\underline{\hspace{1cm}})(\underline{\hspace{1cm}})$

10. $3x^2 - 9x - 30$

   $= 3(\underline{\hspace{2cm}})$

   $= 3(\underline{\hspace{1cm}})(\underline{\hspace{1cm}})$

11. $-4z^3 + 10z^2 + 6z$

   $= -2z(\underline{\hspace{2cm}})$

   $= -2z(\underline{\hspace{1cm}})(\underline{\hspace{1cm}})$

12. $-15r^3 - 39r^2 + 18r$

   $= -3r(\underline{\hspace{2cm}})$

   $= -3r(\underline{\hspace{1cm}})(\underline{\hspace{1cm}})$

13. CONCEPT CHECK A student factoring the trinomial
$$12x^2 + 7x - 12$$
wrote $(4x + 4)$ as one binomial factor. *What Went Wrong?* Factor the trinomial correctly.

14. CONCEPT CHECK A student factoring the trinomial
$$4x^2 + 10x - 6$$
wrote $(4x - 2)(x + 3)$. *What Went Wrong?* Factor the trinomial correctly.

Factor each trinomial completely. **See Examples 1–6.**

15. $3a^2 + 10a + 7$

16. $7r^2 + 8r + 1$

17. $2y^2 + 7y + 6$

18. $5z^2 + 12z + 4$

19. $15m^2 + m - 2$

20. $6x^2 + x - 1$

21. $12s^2 + 11s - 5$

22. $20x^2 + 11x - 3$

23. $10m^2 - 23m + 12$

24. $6x^2 - 17x + 12$

25. $8w^2 - 14w + 3$

26. $9p^2 - 18p + 8$

27. $20y^2 - 39y - 11$

28. $10x^2 - 11x - 6$

29. $3x^2 - 15x + 16$

30. $2t^2 + 13t - 18$

31. $20x^2 + 22x + 6$

32. $36y^2 + 81y + 45$

33. $-40m^2q - mq + 6q$

34. $-15a^2b - 22ab - 8b$

35. $15n^4 - 39n^3 + 18n^2$

36. $24a^4 + 10a^3 - 4a^2$

37. $-15x^2y^2 + 7xy^2 + 4y^2$

38. $-14a^2b^3 - 15ab^3 + 9b^3$

39. $5a^2 - 7ab - 6b^2$

40. $6x^2 - 5xy - y^2$

41. $12s^2 + 11st - 5t^2$

42. $25a^2 + 25ab + 6b^2$

43. $6m^6n + 7m^5n^2 + 2m^4n^3$

44. $12k^3q^4 - 4k^2q^5 - kq^6$

If a trinomial has a negative coefficient for the second-degree term, such as
$-2x^2 + 11x - 12$, *it may be easier to factor by first factoring out* -1.

$$-2x^2 + 11x - 12$$
$$= -1(2x^2 - 11x + 12) \quad \text{Factor out } -1.$$
$$= -1(2x - 3)(x - 4) \quad \text{Factor the trinomial.}$$

Use this method to factor each trinomial.

45. $-x^2 - 4x + 21$

46. $-x^2 + x + 72$

47. $-3x^2 - x + 4$

48. $-5x^2 + 2x + 16$

49. $-2a^2 - 5ab - 2b^2$

50. $-3p^2 + 13pq - 4q^2$

Relating Concepts (Exercises 51–56) For Individual or Group Work

Often there are several different equivalent forms of an answer that are all correct.
Work Exercises 51–56 in order, *to see this for factoring problems.*

51. Factor the integer 35 as the product of two prime numbers.

52. Factor the integer 35 as the product of the negatives of two prime numbers.

53. Verify that $6x^2 - 11x + 4$ factors as $(3x - 4)(2x - 1)$.

54. Verify that $6x^2 - 11x + 4$ factors as $(4 - 3x)(1 - 2x)$.

55. Compare the two valid factored forms in **Exercises 53 and 54.** How do the factors in each case compare?

56. Suppose we know that the correct factored form of a particular trinomial is $(7t - 3)(2t - 5)$. From **Exercises 51–55,** what is another valid factored form?

6.5 | Special Factoring Techniques

OBJECTIVE **1** **Factor a difference of squares.** The rule for finding the product of the sum and difference of the same two terms is

$$(x + y)(x - y) = x^2 - y^2.$$

Reversing this rule leads to the following special factoring rule.

OBJECTIVES

1 Factor a difference of squares.
2 Factor a perfect square trinomial.
3 Factor a difference of cubes.
4 Factor a sum of cubes.

Factoring a Difference of Squares

$$x^2 - y^2 = (x + y)(x - y)$$

For example, $m^2 - 4$

$$= m^2 - 2^2$$

$$= (m + 2)(m - 2).$$

Two conditions must be true for a binomial to be a difference of squares.

1. Both terms of the binomial must be **perfect squares,** such as

$$x^2, \quad 9y^2 = (3y)^2, \quad m^4 = (m^2)^2, \quad 25 = 5^2, \quad 1 = 1^2.$$

2. The binomial terms must have different signs (one positive, one negative).

1 Factor each binomial, if possible.

(GS) **(a)** $x^2 - 81$

$$= (x + \underline{\quad})(x - \underline{\quad})$$

(b) $p^2 - 100$

EXAMPLE 1   **Factoring Differences of Squares**

Factor each binomial if possible.

$$\begin{array}{ccccccc} x^2 & - & y^2 & = & (x & + & y)(x & - & y) \\ \downarrow & & \downarrow & & \downarrow & & \downarrow & & \downarrow & & \downarrow \end{array}$$

(a) $p^2 - 16 = p^2 - 4^2 = (p + 4)(p - 4)$

(b) $x^2 - 8$

Because 8 is not the square of an integer, the binomial $x^2 - 8$ does not satisfy Condition 1 above. It cannot be factored using integers, so it is a prime polynomial.

(c) $p^2 + 16$

The binomial $p^2 + 16$ does not satisfy Condition 2 above. It is a *sum* of squares—it is *not* equal to $(p + 4)(p - 4)$. (See part (a).) We can use the FOIL method and try the following.

$(p - 4)(p - 4)$	$(p + 4)(p + 4)$
$= p^2 - 8p + 16,$ not $p^2 + 16.$	$= p^2 + 8p + 16,$ not $p^2 + 16.$

Thus, $p^2 + 16$ is a prime polynomial.

(c) $y^2 - 10$

(d) $x^2 + 36$

(e) $4x^2 + 16$

———————————— **Work Problem** **1** **at the Side.** ▶

Sum of Squares

If x and y have no common factors (except 1), the following holds true.

A sum of squares $x^2 + y^2$ cannot be factored using real numbers.

That is, $x^2 + y^2$ is prime. (See **Example 1(c).**)

Answers
1. (a) 9; 9
   (b) $(p + 10)(p - 10)$
   (c) prime   **(d)** prime   **(e)** $4(x^2 + 4)$

② Factor each binomial.

GS **(a)** $9m^2 - 49$

$$= (\underline{\quad})^2 - \underline{\quad}^2$$

$$= (\underline{\quad})(\underline{\quad})$$

(b) $64a^2 - 25$

(c) $25a^2 - 64b^2$

③ Factor each binomial completely.

GS **(a)** $50r^2 - 32$

$$= 2(\underline{\quad})$$

$$= 2[(\underline{\quad})^2 - 4^2]$$

$$= \underline{\quad}(\underline{\quad})(\underline{\quad})$$

(b) $27y^2 - 75$

(c) $k^4 - 49$

(d) $81r^4 - 16$

Answers

2. (a) $3m$; 7; $3m + 7$; $3m - 7$

(b) $(8a + 5)(8a - 5)$

(c) $(5a + 8b)(5a - 8b)$

3. (a) $25r^2 - 16$; $5r$; 2; $5r + 4$; $5r - 4$

(b) $3(3y + 5)(3y - 5)$

(c) $(k^2 + 7)(k^2 - 7)$

(d) $(9r^2 + 4)(3r + 2)(3r - 2)$

EXAMPLE 2 **Factoring Differences of Squares**

Factor each binomial.

$$x^2 \ - \ y^2 = \ (x \ + \ y) \ (x \ - \ y)$$
$$\downarrow \qquad \downarrow \qquad \downarrow \qquad \downarrow \qquad \downarrow \qquad \downarrow$$

(a) $25m^2 - 4 = (5m)^2 - 2^2 = (5m + 2)(5m - 2)$

(b) $49z^2 - 64$

$$= (7z)^2 - 8^2 \qquad \text{Write each term as a square.}$$

$$= (7z + 8)(7z - 8) \quad \text{Factor the difference of squares.}$$

(c) $9x^2 - 4z^2$

$$= (3x)^2 - (2z)^2 \qquad \text{Write each term as a square.}$$

$$= (3x + 2z)(3x - 2z) \quad \text{Factor the difference of squares.}$$

CHECK $(3x + 2z)(3x - 2z)$

$$= 9x^2 - 6xz + 6zx - 4z^2 \quad \text{FOIL method}$$

$$= 9x^2 - 4z^2 \ \checkmark \qquad \begin{array}{l}\text{Commutative property;}\\ \text{Combine like terms.}\end{array}$$

◀ **Work Problem ②** at the Side.

Note

It is a good idea to check a factored form by multiplying.

EXAMPLE 3 **Factoring More Complex Differences of Squares**

Factor each binomial completely.

(a) $81y^2 - 36$

$$= 9(9y^2 - 4) \qquad \text{Factor out the GCF, 9.}$$

$$= 9[(3y)^2 - 2^2] \qquad \text{Write each term as a square.}$$

$$= 9(3y + 2)(3y - 2) \quad \text{Factor the difference of squares.}$$

(b) $\qquad p^4 - 36$

Neither binomial can be factored further.

$$= (p^2)^2 - 6^2 \qquad \text{Write each term as a square.}$$

$$= (p^2 + 6)(p^2 - 6) \quad \text{Factor the difference of squares.}$$

(c) $\quad m^4 - 16$

$$= (m^2)^2 - 4^2 \qquad \text{Write each term as a square.}$$

Don't stop here.

$$= (m^2 + 4)(m^2 - 4) \qquad \text{Factor the difference of squares.}$$

$$= (m^2 + 4)(m + 2)(m - 2) \quad \begin{array}{l}\text{Factor the difference of squares}\\ \text{again.}\end{array}$$

◀ **Work Problem ③** at the Side.

⚠ CAUTION

Factor again when any of the factors is a difference of squares, as in **Example 3(c).** Check by multiplying.

OBJECTIVE ▶ 2 Factor a perfect square trinomial. Recall the rules for squaring binomials.

$(x + y)^2$ — Squared binomial

$= (x + y)(x + y)$

$= x^2 + 2xy + y^2$ — Perfect square trinomial

$(x - y)^2$ — Squared binomial

$= (x - y)(x - y)$

$= x^2 - 2xy + y^2$ — Perfect square trinomial

A **perfect square trinomial** is a trinomial that is the square of a binomial. For example, $x^2 + 8x + 16$ is a perfect square trinomial because it is the square of the binomial $x + 4$.

$(x + 4)^2$ — Squared binomial

$= (x + 4)(x + 4)$ — Apply the exponent.

$= x^2 + 8x + 16$ — Perfect square trinomial

Two conditions must be true for a trinomial to be a perfect square trinomial.

1. Two of its terms must be perfect squares. In the perfect square trinomial $x^2 + 8x + 16$, the terms x^2 and $16 = 4^2$ are perfect squares.

2. *The remaining (middle) term of a perfect square trinomial is always twice the product of the two terms in the squared binomial.*

$x^2 + 8x + 16$

$= x^2 + 2(x)(4) + 4^2$ $8x = 2(x)(4)$

$= (x + 4)^2$ — Factor.

The following are *not* perfect square trinomials.

$16x^2 + 4x + 15$ — Violates Condition 1 (Only $16x^2 = (4x)^2$ is a perfect square; 15 is not.)

$x^2 + 6x + 36$ — Violates Condition 2 (x^2 and $36 = 6^2$ are perfect squares, but $2(x)(6) = 12x$, *not* 6x.)

Reversing the rules for squaring binomials leads to the following.

Factoring Perfect Square Trinomials

$$x^2 + 2xy + y^2 = (x + y)^2$$
$$x^2 - 2xy + y^2 = (x - y)^2$$

EXAMPLE 4   Factoring a Perfect Square Trinomial

Factor $x^2 + 10x + 25$.

The x^2-term is a perfect square, and so is 25, which equals 5^2.

Try to factor the trinomial $x^2 + 10x + 25$ as $(x + 5)^2$.

To check, take twice the product of the two terms in the squared binomial.

$2 \cdot x \cdot 5 = 10x$ ← Middle term of $x^2 + 10x + 25$

Twice First term / Last term of binomial

Because $10x$ is the middle term of the given trinomial $x^2 + 10x + 25$, the trinomial is a perfect square and factors as $(x + 5)^2$.

Work Problem ④ at the Side. ▶

④ Factor each trinomial.

(a) $p^2 + 14p + 49$

The term p^2 is a perfect square. Since $49 = $ ____^{2}, 49 (*is/is not*) a perfect square. Try to factor the trinomial

$p^2 + 14p + 49$

as $(p + $ ____$)^2$.

Check by taking twice the product of the two terms of the squared binomial.

$2 \cdot p \cdot$ ____ $=$ ____

The result (*is/is not*) the middle term of the given trinomial. The trinomial is a perfect square and factors as _____.

(b) $x^2 + 6x + 9$

(c) $y^2 + 22y + 121$

Answers

4. (a) 7; is; 7; 7; 14p; is; $(p + 7)^2$
   (b) $(x + 3)^2$ (c) $(y + 11)^2$

5 Factor each trinomial.

(a) $p^2 - 18p + 81$

(b) $16a^2 - 56a + 49$

(c) $121z^2 + 110z + 100$

(d) $64x^2 - 48x + 9$

(e) $27y^3 + 72y^2 + 48y$

EXAMPLE 5 **Factoring Perfect Square Trinomials**

Factor each trinomial.

(a) $x^2 - 22x + 121$

The first and last terms are perfect squares ($121 = 11^2$ or $(-11)^2$). Check to see whether the middle term of $x^2 - 22x + 121$ is twice the product of the first and last terms of the binomial $x - 11$.

$$2\,(x)\,(-11) = -22x \leftarrow \text{Middle term of } x^2 - 22x + 121$$

Twice — First term — Last term

Thus, $x^2 - 22x + 121$ is a perfect square trinomial.

Check by squaring the binomial.

$$x^2 - 22x + 121 \quad \text{factors as} \quad (x - 11)^2.$$

Same sign

Notice that the sign of the second term in the squared binomial is the same as the sign of the middle term in the trinomial.

(b) $9m^2 - 24m + 16 = (3m)^2 + 2\,(3m)\,(-4) + (-4)^2 = (3m - 4)^2$

Perfect Squares — Twice — First term — Last Term

(c) $25y^2 + 20y + 16$

The first and last terms are perfect squares.

$$25y^2 = (5y)^2 \quad \text{and} \quad 16 = 4^2$$

Twice the product of the first and last terms of the binomial $5y + 4$ is

$$2\,(5y)\,4 = 40y,$$

which is *not* the middle term of

$$25y^2 + 20y + 16.$$

This trinomial is not a perfect square. In fact, the trinomial cannot be factored even with the methods of the previous sections. It is a prime polynomial.

(d) $12z^3 + 60z^2 + 75z$

$$= 3z\,(4z^2 + 20z + 25) \qquad \text{Factor out the common factor, } 3z.$$

$$= 3z\,[(2z)^2 + 2\,(2z)\,(5) + 5^2] \qquad 4z^2 + 20z + 25 \text{ is a perfect square trinomial.}$$

$$= 3z\,(2z + 5)^2 \qquad \text{Factor.}$$

◀ **Work Problem 5 at the Side**

Note

1. The sign of the second term in a squared binomial is always the same as the sign of the middle term in the trinomial.

2. The first and last terms of a perfect square trinomial must be *positive* because they are squares. For example, the polynomial $x^2 - 2x - 1$ cannot be a perfect square because the last term is negative.

3. Perfect square trinomials can also be factored using grouping or the FOIL method. Using the method of this section is often easier.

Answers

5. **(a)** $(p - 9)^2$ **(b)** $(4a - 7)^2$ **(c)** prime
(d) $(8x - 3)^2$ **(e)** $3y\,(3y + 4)^2$

OBJECTIVE ❸ **Factor a difference of cubes.** In a *difference of cubes* $x^3 - y^3$, both terms of the binomial must be **perfect cubes**, such as

$$x^3, \quad 8p^3 = (2p)^3, \quad s^6 = (s^2)^3, \quad 1 = 1^3, \quad 27 = 3^3, \quad 216 = 6^3.$$

We can factor a **difference of cubes** using the following rule.

Factoring a Difference of Cubes

$$x^3 - y^3 = (x - y)(x^2 + xy + y^2)$$

Notice the pattern of the terms in the factored form of $x^3 - y^3$.

- $x^3 - y^3$ factors as (a binomial factor) · (a trinomial factor).
- The binomial factor has the difference of the cube roots of the given terms. (*Note*: A **cube root** of 1 is 1 because $1^3 = 1$, a **cube root** of 8 is 2 because $2^3 = 8$, and so on.)
- The terms in the trinomial factor are all positive.
- The terms in the binomial factor help determine the trinomial factor.

$$x^3 - y^3 = (x - y)(\underset{\text{First term squared}}{x^2} + \underset{\substack{\text{Positive}\\\text{product of}\\\text{the terms}}}{xy} + \underset{\text{Second term squared}}{y^2})$$

⚠ CAUTION

A common error in factoring $x^3 - y^3 = (x - y)(x^2 + xy + y^2)$ is to try to factor $x^2 + xy + y^2$. This is usually not possible.

EXAMPLE 6 **Factoring Differences of Cubes**

Factor each binomial.

$$x^3 - y^3 = (x - y)(x^2 + xy + y^2)$$

(a) $m^3 - 125 = m^3 - 5^3 = (m - 5)(m^2 + 5m + 5^2)$ Let $x = m$ and $y = 5$.

$$= (m - 5)(m^2 + 5m + 25) \quad 5^2 = 25$$

(b) $8p^3 - 27$

$$= (2p)^3 - 3^3 \qquad\qquad 8p^3 = (2p)^3 \text{ and } 27 = 3^3.$$

$$= (2p - 3)\left[(2p)^2 + (2p)3 + 3^2\right] \quad \text{Let } x = 2p \text{ and } y = 3.$$

$$= (2p - 3)(4p^2 + 6p + 9) \qquad \text{Apply the exponents. Multiply.}$$

$(2p)^2 = 2^2p^2 = 4p^2, \textbf{not } 2p^2.$

To see that the rule for factoring a difference of cubes is correct, multiply

$$(x - y)(x^2 + xy + y^2).$$

$$\begin{array}{r} x^2 + xy + y^2 \\ x - y \\ \hline -x^2y - xy^2 - y^3 \\ x^3 + x^2y + xy^2 \\ \hline x^3 \qquad\qquad - y^3 \end{array}$$

Multiply vertically.

Add.

──── **Continued on Next Page**

6 Factor each binomial.

(a) $t^3 - 64$

$= \underline{}^3 - \underline{}^3$

$= (\underline{} - \underline{}) \cdot$

$(\underline{}^2 + \underline{} + \underline{}^2)$

$= \underline{}$

(b) $27x^3 - 8$

(c) $2x^3 - 432y^3$

7 Factor each binomial.

(a) $x^3 + 8$

$= \underline{}^3 + \underline{}^3$

$= (\underline{} + \underline{}) \cdot$

$(\underline{}^2 - \underline{} + \underline{}^2)$

$= \underline{}$

(b) $64y^3 + 1$

(c) $27m^3 + 343n^3$

Answers

6. (a) $t; 4; t; 4; t; 4t; 4;$
   $(t - 4)(t^2 + 4t + 16)$
   (b) $(3x - 2)(9x^2 + 6x + 4)$
   (c) $2(x - 6y)(x^2 + 6xy + 36y^2)$
7. (a) $x; 2; x; 2; x; 2x; 2;$
   $(x + 2)(x^2 - 2x + 4)$
   (b) $(4y + 1)(16y^2 - 4y + 1)$
   (c) $(3m + 7n)(9m^2 - 21mn + 49n^2)$

(c) $4m^3 - 32n^3$

$= 4(m^3 - 8n^3)$ \hfill Factor out the common factor.

$= 4[m^3 - (2n)^3]$ \hfill $8n^3 = (2n)^3$

$= 4(m - 2n)[m^2 + m(2n) + (2n)^2]$ \hfill Let $x = m$ and $y = 2n$.

$= 4(m - 2n)(m^2 + 2mn + 4n^2)$ \hfill Apply the exponents. Multiply.

◀ **Work Problem 6 at the Side.**

OBJECTIVE 4 **Factor a sum of cubes.** A *sum of squares*, such as $m^2 + 25$, *cannot* be factored using real numbers, but **a sum of cubes** can.

Factoring a Sum of Cubes

$$x^3 + y^3 = (x + y)(x^2 - xy + y^2)$$

Compare the rule for the *sum* of cubes with that for the *difference* of cubes.

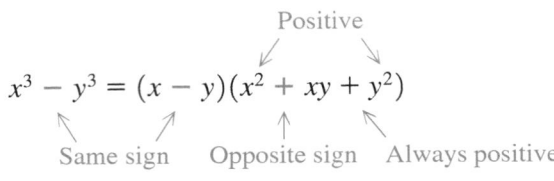

	Positive	
$x^3 - y^3 = (x - y)(x^2 + xy + y^2)$		**Difference of cubes**
Same sign Opposite sign Always positive		The only difference between the rules is the positive and negative signs.

	Positive	
$x^3 + y^3 = (x + y)(x^2 - xy + y^2)$		**Sum of cubes**
Same sign Opposite sign Always positive		

EXAMPLE 7 **Factoring Sums of Cubes**

Factor each binomial.

(a) $k^3 + 27$

$= k^3 + 3^3$ \hfill $27 = 3^3$

$= (k + 3)(k^2 - 3k + 3^2)$ \hfill Let $x = k$ and $y = 3$.

$= (k + 3)(k^2 - 3k + 9)$ \hfill Apply the exponent.

(b) $8m^3 + 125p^3$

$= (2m)^3 + (5p)^3$ \hfill $8m^3 = (2m)^3; 125p^3 = (5p)^3$

$= (2m + 5p)[(2m)^2 - (2m)(5p) + (5p)^2]$ \hfill Let $x = 2m$ and $y = 5p$.

$= (2m + 5p)(4m^2 - 10mp + 25p^2)$ \hfill Apply the exponents. Multiply.

◀ **Work Problem 7 at the Side.**

6.5 Exercises

FOR EXTRA HELP

Go to MyMathLab *for worked-out, step-by-step solutions to exercises enclosed in a square* and video solutions to ▶ exercises.

CONCEPT CHECK *Work each problem.*

1. To help factor a difference of squares, complete the following list of squares.

$1^2 =$ _____ $2^2 =$ _____ $3^2 =$ _____ $4^2 =$ _____ $5^2 =$ _____

$6^2 =$ _____ $7^2 =$ _____ $8^2 =$ _____ $9^2 =$ _____ $10^2 =$ _____

$11^2 =$ _____ $12^2 =$ _____ $13^2 =$ _____ $14^2 =$ _____ $15^2 =$ _____

$16^2 =$ _____ $17^2 =$ _____ $18^2 =$ _____ $19^2 =$ _____ $20^2 =$ _____

2. To use the factoring techniques described in this section, it is helpful to recognize fourth powers of integers. Complete the following list of fourth powers.

$1^4 =$ _____ $2^4 =$ _____ $3^4 =$ _____ $4^4 =$ _____ $5^4 =$ _____

3. Which of the following binomials are differences of squares?

  A. $x^2 - 4$ **B.** $y^2 + 9$

  C. $2a^2 - 25$ **D.** $9m^2 - 1$

4. Which of the following binomial sums can be factored?

  A. $x^2 + 36$ **B.** $x^3 + x$

  C. $3x^2 + 12$ **D.** $25x^2 + 49$

5. CONCEPT CHECK On a quiz, a student indicated *prime* when asked to factor the binomial

$$4x^2 + 16,$$

because she said that a sum of squares cannot be factored. *What Went Wrong?* Give the correct answer.

6. CONCEPT CHECK When directed to factor $k^4 - 81$ completely, a student did not earn full credit.

$$(k^2 + 9)(k^2 - 9) \quad \text{His answer}$$

The student argued that because his answer does indeed give $k^4 - 81$ when multiplied out, he should be given full credit. *What Went Wrong?* Give the correct factored form.

Factor each binomial completely. ***See Examples 1–3.***

7. $y^2 - 25$ **8.** $t^2 - 36$ **9.** $x^2 - 144$ **10.** $y^2 - 400$

11. $m^2 - 12$ **12.** $k^2 - 18$ **13.** $m^2 + 64$ **14.** $k^2 + 49$

15. $9r^2 - 4$ **16.** $4x^2 - 9$ **17.** $36x^2 - 16$ **18.** $32a^2 - 8$

19. $196p^2 - 225$ **20.** $361q^2 - 400$ **21.** $16r^2 - 25a^2$ **22.** $49m^2 - 100p^2$

23. $16m^2 + 64$ **24.** $9x^2 + 81$ **25.** $p^4 - 49$ **26.** $r^4 - 25$

27. $x^4 - 1$ **28.** $y^4 - 10{,}000$ **29.** $p^4 - 256$ **30.** $x^4 - 625$

31. CONCEPT CHECK Which of the following are perfect square trinomials?

    A. $y^2 - 13y + 36$ **B.** $x^2 + 6x + 9$ **C.** $4z^2 - 4z + 1$ **D.** $16m^2 + 8m - 1$

32. In the polynomial $9y^2 + 14y + 25$, the first and last terms are perfect squares. Can the polynomial be factored? If it can, factor it. If it cannot, explain why it is not a perfect square trinomial.

*Factor each trinomial completely. **See Examples 4 and 5.***

33. $w^2 + 2w + 1$ **34.** $p^2 + 4p + 4$ **35.** $x^2 - 8x + 16$
▶   ▶

36. $x^2 - 10x + 25$ **37.** $x^2 - 10x + 100$ **38.** $x^2 - 18x + 36$

39. $2x^2 + 24x + 72$ **40.** $3y^2 + 48y + 192$ **41.** $4x^2 + 12x + 9$

42. $25x^2 + 10x + 1$ **43.** $16x^3 - 40x^2 + 25x$ **44.** $36y^3 - 60y^2 + 25y$

45. $49x^2 - 28xy + 4y^2$ **46.** $4z^2 - 12zw + 9w^2$ **47.** $64x^2 + 48xy + 9y^2$

48. $9t^2 + 24tr + 16r^2$ **49.** $-50h^3 + 40h^2y - 8hy^2$ **50.** $-18x^3 - 48x^2y - 32xy^2$
                              ▶

Although we usually factor polynomials using integers, we can apply the same concepts to factoring using fractions and decimals.

$$z^2 - \frac{9}{16}$$

$$= z^2 - \left(\frac{3}{4}\right)^2 \qquad \tfrac{9}{16} = \left(\tfrac{3}{4}\right)^2$$

$$= \left(z + \frac{3}{4}\right)\left(z - \frac{3}{4}\right) \qquad \text{Factor the difference of squares.}$$

$$x^2 + \frac{2}{5}x + \frac{1}{25}$$

$$= x^2 + 2\,(x)\left(\frac{1}{5}\right) + \left(\frac{1}{5}\right)^2 \qquad \tfrac{1}{25} = \left(\tfrac{1}{5}\right)^2$$

$$= \left(x + \frac{1}{5}\right)^2 \qquad \text{Factor the perfect square trinomial.}$$

Factor each binomial or trinomial.

51. $p^2 - \dfrac{1}{9}$ **52.** $q^2 - \dfrac{1}{4}$ **53.** $4m^2 - \dfrac{9}{25}$ **54.** $100b^2 - \dfrac{4}{49}$

55. $x^2 - 0.64$ **56.** $y^2 - 0.36$ **57.** $t^2 + t + \dfrac{1}{4}$ **58.** $m^2 + \dfrac{2}{3}m + \dfrac{1}{9}$

59. $a^2 - \dfrac{4}{7}a + \dfrac{4}{49}$ **60.** $b^2 - \dfrac{10}{9}b + \dfrac{25}{81}$ **61.** $x^2 - 1.0x + 0.25$ **62.** $y^2 - 1.4y + 0.49$

CONCEPT CHECK *Work each problem.*

63. To help factor the sum or difference of cubes, complete the list of perfect cubes.

$1^3 = \underline{\hspace{1cm}}$ $2^3 = \underline{\hspace{1cm}}$ $3^3 = \underline{\hspace{1cm}}$ $4^3 = \underline{\hspace{1cm}}$ $5^3 = \underline{\hspace{1cm}}$

$6^3 = \underline{\hspace{1cm}}$ $7^3 = \underline{\hspace{1cm}}$ $8^3 = \underline{\hspace{1cm}}$ $9^3 = \underline{\hspace{1cm}}$ $10^3 = \underline{\hspace{1cm}}$

64. The following powers of x are all perfect cubes: $x^3, x^6, x^9, x^{12}, x^{15}$. Based on this observation, we may make a conjecture that if the power of a variable is divisible by $\underline{\hspace{1cm}}$ (with 0 remainder), then we have a perfect cube.

65. Which of the following are differences of cubes?

 A. $9x^3 - 125$ **B.** $x^3 - 16$ **C.** $x^3 - 1$ **D.** $8x^3 - 27y^3$

66. Which of the following are sums of cubes?

 A. $x^3 - 1$ **B.** $x^3 + 36$ **C.** $12x^3 + 27$ **D.** $64x^3 + 216y^3$

Factor each binomial completely. ***See Examples 6 and 7.***

67. $a^3 - 1$ **68.** $m^3 - 8$ **69.** $m^3 + 8$ **70.** $x^3 + 1$

71. $y^3 - 216$ **72.** $x^3 - 343$ **73.** $k^3 + 1000$ **74.** $p^3 + 512$

75. $27x^3 - 1$ **76.** $64y^3 - 27$ **77.** $125x^3 + 8$

78. $216x^3 + 125$ **79.** $y^3 - 8x^3$ **80.** $w^3 - 216z^3$

81. $27x^3 - 64y^3$ **82.** $125m^3 - 8n^3$ **83.** $8p^3 + 729q^3$

84. $27x^3 + 1000y^3$ **85.** $16t^3 - 2$ **86.** $3p^3 - 81$

87. $40w^3 + 135$ **88.** $32z^3 + 500$ **89.** $x^3 + y^6$

90. $p^9 + q^3$ **91.** $125k^3 - 8m^9$ **92.** $125c^6 - 216d^3$

6.6 A General Approach to Factoring

OBJECTIVE

1 Factor any polynomial.

OBJECTIVE 1 **Factor any polynomial.** A polynomial is *completely factored* when it is written as a product of prime polynomials with integer coefficients.

Factoring a Polynomial

Step 1 **Factor out any common factor.**

Step 2 **How many terms are in the polynomial?**

If the polynomial is a binomial, check to see whether it is a difference of squares, a difference of cubes, or a sum of cubes.

If the polynomial is a trinomial, check to see whether it is a perfect square trinomial. If it is not, use one of the following methods.

- To factor $x^2 + bx + c$, find two integers whose product is c and whose sum is b, the coefficient of the middle term.

- To factor $ax^2 + bx + c$, find two integers having product ac and sum b. Use these integers to rewrite the middle term, and factor by grouping.

 Alternatively, use the FOIL method and try various combinations of the factors until the correct middle term is found.

If the polynomial has more than three terms, try to factor it by grouping.

Step 3 **If any of the factors can be factored further, do so.**

Step 4 **Check the factored form by multiplying.**

1 Factor each polynomial.

(a) $8x - 80$

(b) $2x^3 + 10x^2 - 2x$

(c) $12m(p - q) - 7n(p - q)$

(d) $(y - 1)(2y + 1)$
$- (y - 1)(y + 4)$

EXAMPLE 1 Factoring Out a Common Factor

Factor each polynomial.

(a) $9p + 45$
 $= 9(p + 5)$ GCF = 9

(b) $8m^2p^2 + 4mp$
 $= 4mp(2mp + 1)$ GCF = $4mp$

(c) $5x(a + b) - y(a + b)$
 $= (a + b)(5x - y)$ Factor out $a + b$.

(d) $(x - 4)(x + 2) + (x - 4)(2x - 1)$
 $= (x - 4)[(x + 2) + (2x - 1)]$ Factor out $x - 4$.
 $= (x - 4)(3x + 1)$ Combine like terms inside the brackets.

◀ **Work Problem 1 at the Side.**

Factoring a Binomial

For a **binomial** (two terms), check for the following patterns.

Difference of squares $x^2 - y^2 = (x + y)(x - y)$

Difference of cubes $x^3 - y^3 = (x - y)(x^2 + xy + y^2)$

Sum of cubes $x^3 + y^3 = (x + y)(x^2 - xy + y^2)$

Answers

1. (a) $8(x - 10)$
 (b) $2x(x^2 + 5x - 1)$
 (c) $(p - q)(12m - 7n)$
 (d) $(y - 1)(y - 3)$

EXAMPLE 2	Factoring Binomials

Factor each binomial if possible.

(a) $64m^2 - 9n^2$

$\quad = (8m)^2 - (3n)^2 \qquad$ Difference of squares

$\quad = (8m + 3n)(8m - 3n) \qquad x^2 - y^2 = (x + y)(x - y)$

(b) $8p^3 - 27$

$\quad = (2p)^3 - 3^3 \qquad$ Difference of cubes

$\quad = (2p - 3)[(2p)^2 + (2p)(3) + 3^2] \qquad x^3 - y^3 = (x - y)(x^2 + xy + y^2)$

$\quad = (2p - 3)(4p^2 + 6p + 9) \qquad (2p)^2 = 2^2p^2 = 4p^2$

(c) $1000m^3 + 1$

$\quad = (10m)^3 + 1^3 \qquad$ Sum of cubes

$\quad = (10m + 1)[(10m)^2 - (10m)(1) + 1^2]$

$\qquad\qquad x^3 + y^3 = (x + y)(x^2 - xy + y^2)$

$\quad = (10m + 1)(100m^2 - 10m + 1) \qquad (10m)^2 = 10^2m^2 = 100m^2$

(d) $25m^2 + 121$ $\qquad$ This *sum* of squares is prime. There is no common factor (except 1).

─────────────── **Work Problem ❷ at the Side. ▶**

Note

Although the binomial $25m^2 + 625$ is a sum of squares, it can be factored because the greatest common factor of the terms is *not* 1.

$\qquad\qquad 25m^2 + 625 = \mathbf{25}(m^2 + 25)$ $\quad$ Factor out the common factor 25. The sum of squares $m^2 + 25$ cannot be factored further.

Factoring a Trinomial

For a **trinomial** (three terms), decide whether it is a perfect square trinomial of either of these forms.

$$x^2 + 2xy + y^2 = (x + y)^2 \quad \text{or} \quad x^2 - 2xy + y^2 = (x - y)^2$$

If not, use the methods shown in **Examples 3(c)–(f)**.

EXAMPLE 3	Factoring Trinomials

Factor each trinomial.

(a) $p^2 + 10p + 25$ $\quad$ Perfect square

$\quad = (p + 5)^2$ $\quad$ trinomial

(b) $49z^2 - 42z + 9$ $\quad$ Perfect square

$\quad = (7z - 3)^2$ $\quad$ trinomial

(c) $y^2 - 5y - 6$ $\qquad$ The numbers -6 and 1 have a product

$\quad = (y - 6)(y + 1)$ $\qquad$ of -6 and a sum of -5.

(d) $2k^2 - k - 6 = (2k + 3)(k - 2)$

$\overset{\displaystyle -4k}{}$

$\underset{\displaystyle 3k}{}$

$-4k + 3k = -k$

Use the FOIL method and try various combinations of the factors until the correct middle term is found.

─────────────── **Continued on Next Page**

❷ Factor each binomial if possible.

(a) $36x^2 - y^2$

(b) $4t^2 + 1$

(c) $125x^3 - 27y^3$

(d) $x^3 + 343y^3$

Answers

2. (a) $(6x + y)(6x - y)$

$\quad$ **(b)** prime

$\quad$ **(c)** $(5x - 3y)(25x^2 + 15xy + 9y^2)$

$\quad$ **(d)** $(x + 7y)(x^2 - 7xy + 49y^2)$

3 Factor each trinomial.

(a) $16m^2 + 56m + 49$

(b) $r^2 + 18r + 72$

(c) $8t^2 - 13t + 5$

(d) $8a^2 + 2ab - 3b^2$

(e) $6x^2 - 3x - 63$

4 Factor each polynomial.

(a) $20 - 5m - 12n + 3mn$

(b) $5a^3 + 5a^2b - ab^2 - b^3$

(c) $9x^2 + 24x + 16 - y^2$

Answers

3. (a) $(4m + 7)^2$

  (b) $(r + 6)(r + 12)$

  (c) $(8t - 5)(t - 1)$

  (d) $(4a + 3b)(2a - b)$

  (e) $3(2x - 7)(x + 3)$

4. (a) $(4 - m)(5 - 3n)$

  (b) $(a + b)(5a^2 - b^2)$

  (c) $(3x + 4 + y)(3x + 4 - y)$

(e) $10x^2 + xy - 3y^2$

$= 10x^2 - \underbrace{5xy + 6xy}_{xy} - 3y^2$ The integers -5 and 6 have a product of $10(-3) = -30$ and a sum of 1, the coefficient of the middle term.

$= (10x^2 - 5xy) + (6xy - 3y^2)$ Group the terms.

$= 5x(2x - y) + 3y(2x - y)$ Factor each group.

$= (2x - y)(5x + 3y)$ Factor out the common factor.

(f) $28z^2 + 6z - 10$

$= 2(14z^2 + 3z - 5)$ Factor out the common factor.

Remember the common factor. $= 2(7z + 5)(2z - 1)$ Factor the trinomial.

Remember to check each factored form by multiplying.

◀ **Work Problem 3** at the Side.

If a polynomial has more than three terms, consider factoring by grouping.

EXAMPLE 4   **Factoring Polynomials with More Than Three Terms**

Factor each polynomial.

(a) $4 - 2q - 6p + 3pq$

$= (4 - 2q) + (-6p + 3pq)$ Group the terms.

$= 2(2 - q) - 3p(2 - q)$ Factor each group.

$= (2 - q)(2 - 3p)$ Factor out $2 - q$.

(b) $20k^3 + 4k^2 - 45k - 9$ Be careful with signs.

$= (20k^3 + 4k^2) + (-45k - 9)$ Group the terms.

$= 4k^2(5k + 1) - 9(5k + 1)$ Factor each group.

$= (5k + 1)(4k^2 - 9)$ $5k + 1$ is a common factor.

$= (5k + 1)(2k + 3)(2k - 3)$ Factor the difference of squares.

(c) $4a^2 + 4a + 1 - b^2$ The first three terms form a perfect square trinomial. $4a^2 = (2a)^2$, $1 = 1^2$, and $2(2a)(1) = 4a$, as required.

$= (4a^2 + 4a + 1) - b^2$

$= (2a + 1)^2 - b^2$ Factor the perfect square trinomial.

$= (2a + 1 + b)(2a + 1 - b)$ Factor the difference of squares.

Remember to check each factored form by multiplying.

◀ **Work Problem 4** at the Side.

6.6 Exercises

FOR EXTRA HELP

Go to MyMathLab *for worked-out, step-by-step solutions to exercises enclosed in a square* and video solutions to ▶ *exercises.*

CONCEPT CHECK *Match each polynomial in Column I with the method or methods for factoring it in Column II. The choices in Column II may be used once, more than once, or not at all.*

I	II
1. (a) $49x^2 - 81y^2$	**A.** Factor out the GCF.
(b) $125z^6 + 1$	**B.** Factor a difference of squares.
(c) $88r^2 - 55s^2$	**C.** Factor a difference of cubes.
(d) $64a^3 - 8b^9$	**D.** Factor a sum of cubes.
(e) $50x^2 - 128y^4$	**E.** The polynomial is prime.

I	II
2. (a) $ab - 5a + 3b - 15$	**A.** Factor out the GCF.
(b) $z^2 - 3z + 6$	**B.** Factor a perfect square trinomial.
(c) $25x^2 + 100$	**C.** Factor by grouping.
(d) $r^2 - 24r + 144$	**D.** Factor into two distinct binomials.
(e) $2y^2 + 36y + 162$	**E.** The polynomial is prime.

The following exercises are of mixed variety. Factor each polynomial.
See Examples 1–4.

3. $6b^2 - 17b - 3$
▶

4. $10r^2 + 13r - 3$

5. $12p^6 + 18p^5 - 24p^3$

6. $15x^2 - 5x$

7. $x^2 + 2x - 35$

8. $4k^2 + 28k + 49$

9. $225p^2 + 256$
▶

10. $x^3 + 1000$

11. $100a^2 - 9b^2$

12. $k^2 - 6k + 16$

13. $18m^3n + 3m^2n^2 - 6mn^3$

14. $6t^2 + 19tu - 77u^2$

15. $2p^2 + 11pq + 15q^2$

16. $9m^2 - 45m + 18m^3$

17. $9m^2 - 30m + 25 - p^2$

18. $54m^3 - 2000$

19. $kq - 9q + kr - 9r$
▶

20. $a^2 - 2a + 1 - b^2$

21. $x^3 + 3x^2 - 9x - 27$

22. $56k^3 - 875$

23. $4(p + 2) + m(p + 2)$
⏵

24. $8p^3 - 125$

25. $6k^2 - k - 1$

26. $27m^2 + 144mn + 192n^2$

27. $x^2 - 225$

28. $p^3 + 64$

29. $ab + 6b + ac + 6c$

30. $4y^2 - 8y$

31. $x^2 - 12x + 36 - 4p^2$

32. $12z^3 - 6z^2 + 18z$

33. $256b^2 - 400c^2$

34. $z^2 - zp + 20p^2$

35. $1000z^3 + 512$

36. $64m^2 - 25n^2$

37. $10r^2 + 23rs - 5s^2$

38. $m^3 + 4m^2 - 6m - 24$

39. $-8x^2 + 16x^3 - 24x^5$

40. $48k^4 - 243$

41. $14x^2 - 25xq - 25q^2$

42. $5p^2 - 10p$

43. $y^2 + 3y - 10$

44. $b^2 - 7ba - 18a^2$

45. $18p^2 + 53pr - 35r^2$

46. $12m^2rx + 4mnrx + 40n^2rx$

47. $z^2 - 9z + 20$

48. $21a^2 - 5ab - 4b^2$

49. $9r^2 + 100$

50. $mn - 2n + 5m - 10$

51. $50p^2 - 162$

52. $25x^2 - 20x + 4$

53. $16a^2 + 8ab + b^2$

54. $x^2 + 4 + x^2y + 4y$

55. $4x^2 + 16$

56. $(x - 2)(x + 1) + (x - 2)(x - 4)$

6.7 Solving Quadratic Equations Using the Zero-Factor Property

Galileo Galilei developed theories to explain physical phenomena. According to legend, Galileo dropped objects of different weights from the Leaning Tower of Pisa to disprove the belief that heavier objects fall faster than lighter objects. He developed a formula for freely falling objects described by

$$d = 16t^2,$$

where d is the distance in feet that an object falls (disregarding air resistance) in t seconds, regardless of weight.

The equation $d = 16t^2$ is a *quadratic equation*.

**Galileo Galilei
(1564–1642)**

OBJECTIVES

1 Solve quadratic equations using the zero-factor property.

2 Solve other equations using the zero-factor property.

Quadratic Equation

A **quadratic equation** (in x here) can be written in the form

$$ax^2 + bx + c = 0,$$

where a, b, and c are real numbers and $a \neq 0$. The given form is called **standard form.**

Examples: $x^2 + 5x + 6 = 0$, $2x^2 - 5x = 3$, $x^2 = 4$ Quadratic equations

---

A quadratic equation has a second-degree (squared) term and no terms of greater degree. Of the above examples, only $x^2 + 5x + 6 = 0$ is in standard form.

Work Problems ❶ and ❷ at the Side. ▶

We have factored many quadratic *expressions* of the form

$$ax^2 + bx + c.$$

In this section, we use factored quadratic expressions to solve quadratic *equations*.

OBJECTIVE ▶ **1** Solve quadratic equations using the zero-factor property.
We can use the following property to solve some quadratic equations.

Zero-Factor Property

If a and b are real numbers and $ab = 0$, then $a = 0$ or $b = 0$.

In words, if the product of two numbers is 0, then at least one of the numbers must be 0. One number *must* be 0, but both *may* be 0.

---

❶ Which of the following equations are quadratic equations?

A. $y^2 - 4y - 5 = 0$

B. $x^3 - x^2 + 16 = 0$

C. $2z^2 + 7z = -3$

D. $x + 2y = -4$

❷ Write each quadratic equation in standard form.

(a) $x^2 - 3x = 4$

(b) $y^2 = 9y - 8$

Answers

1. A, C

2. (a) $x^2 - 3x - 4 = 0$
   (b) $y^2 - 9y + 8 = 0$

3 Solve each equation.

(a) $(x + 2)(x - 5) = 0$

To solve, use the zero-factor property.

_____ = 0   or   _____ = 0

Solve these two equations, obtaining

$x = $ ___   or $x = $ ___.

Check each value in the original equation.

The solution set is {___, ___}.

(b) $(3x - 2)(x + 6) = 0$

(c) $z(2z + 5) = 0$

Answers

3. (a) $x + 2$; $x - 5$; -2; 5; -2; 5

   (b) $\left\{-6, \frac{2}{3}\right\}$ **(c)** $\left\{-\frac{5}{2}, 0\right\}$

EXAMPLE 1 Using the Zero-Factor Property

Solve each equation.

(a) $(x + 3)(2x - 1) = 0$

The product $(x + 3)(2x - 1)$ is equal to 0. By the zero-factor property, the only way that the product of these two factors can be 0 is if at least one of the factors equals 0. Therefore, $x + 3 = 0$ or $2x - 1 = 0$.

$$x + 3 = 0 \quad \text{or} \quad 2x - 1 = 0 \quad \text{Zero-factor property}$$
$$x = -3 \quad \text{or} \quad 2x = 1 \quad \text{Solve each equation.}$$
$$x = \frac{1}{2} \quad \text{Divide each side by 2.}$$

Check these two values by substituting -3 for x in the original equation. ***Then start over*** and substitute $\frac{1}{2}$ for x.

CHECK Let $x = -3$.
$$(x + 3)(2x - 1) = 0$$
$$(-3 + 3)[2(-3) - 1] \overset{?}{=} 0$$
$$0(-7) \overset{?}{=} 0$$
$$0 = 0 \ \checkmark \ \text{True}$$

Let $x = \frac{1}{2}$.
$$(x + 3)(2x - 1) = 0$$
$$\left(\frac{1}{2} + 3\right)\left(2 \cdot \frac{1}{2} - 1\right) \overset{?}{=} 0$$
$$\frac{7}{2}(1 - 1) \overset{?}{=} 0$$
$$0 = 0 \ \checkmark \ \text{True}$$

Because true statements result, the solution set is $\left\{-3, \frac{1}{2}\right\}$.

(b)
$$y(3y - 4) = 0$$
$$y = 0 \quad \text{or} \quad 3y - 4 = 0 \quad \text{Zero-factor property}$$
$$3y = 4 \quad \text{Add 4.}$$
$$y = \frac{4}{3} \quad \text{Divide by 3.}$$

Don't forget that 0 is a solution.

Check each value in the original equation. The solution set is $\left\{0, \frac{4}{3}\right\}$.

◀ **Work Problem 3 at the Side.**

EXAMPLE 2 Solving Quadratic Equations

Solve each equation.

(a) $x^2 - 5x = -6$

First, write the equation in standard form by adding 6 to each side.

Don't factor x out at this step.
$$x^2 - 5x = -6$$
$$x^2 - 5x + 6 = 0 \quad \text{Add 6.}$$

Now factor $x^2 - 5x + 6$. Find two numbers whose product is 6 and whose sum is -5. These two numbers are -2 and -3, so we factor as follows.

$$(x - 2)(x - 3) = 0 \quad \text{Factor.}$$
$$x - 2 = 0 \quad \text{or} \quad x - 3 = 0 \quad \text{Zero-factor property}$$
$$x = 2 \quad \text{or} \quad x = 3 \quad \text{Solve each equation.}$$

— **Continued on Next Page**

CHECK Let $x = 2$.

$$x^2 - 5x = -6$$
$$2^2 - 5(2) \stackrel{?}{=} -6$$
$$4 - 10 \stackrel{?}{=} -6$$
$$-6 = -6 \ \checkmark \ \text{True}$$

Let $x = 3$.

$$x^2 - 5x = -6$$
$$3^2 - 5(3) \stackrel{?}{=} -6$$
$$9 - 15 \stackrel{?}{=} -6$$
$$-6 = -6 \ \checkmark \ \text{True}$$

Both values check, so the solution set is $\{2, 3\}$.

(b)

$$y^2 = y + 20 \quad \text{Write this equation in standard form.}$$

Standard form $\longrightarrow y^2 - y - 20 = 0$ Subtract y and 20.

$$(y - 5)(y + 4) = 0 \quad \text{Factor.}$$

$$y - 5 = 0 \quad \text{or} \quad y + 4 = 0 \quad \text{Zero-factor property}$$

$$y = 5 \quad \text{or} \quad y = -4 \quad \text{Solve each equation.}$$

Check each value in the original equation. The solution set is $\{-4, 5\}$.

—————— Work Problem **4** at the Side. ▶

Solving a Quadratic Equation Using the Zero-Factor Property

Step 1 **Write the equation in standard form**—that is, with all terms on one side of the equality symbol in descending powers of the variable and 0 on the other side.

Step 2 **Factor** completely.

Step 3 **Apply the zero-factor property.** Set each factor with a variable equal to 0.

Step 4 **Solve** the resulting equations.

Step 5 **Check** each value in the original equation. Write the solution set.

EXAMPLE 3   Solving a Quadratic Equation (Common Factor)

Solve $4p^2 + 40 = 26p$.

$$4p^2 + 40 = 26p \quad \text{Write this equation in the form } ax^2 + bx + c = 0.$$

Step 1 $4p^2 - 26p + 40 = 0$ Subtract $26p$.

This 2 is not a solution of the equation. $\ 2(2p^2 - 13p + 20) = 0$ Factor out 2.

$$2p^2 - 13p + 20 = 0 \quad \text{Divide each side by 2.}$$

Step 2 $(2p - 5)(p - 4) = 0$ Factor.

Step 3 $2p - 5 = 0 \quad \text{or} \quad p - 4 = 0$ Zero-factor property

Step 4 $p = \dfrac{5}{2} \quad \text{or} \quad p = 4$ Solve each equation.

Step 5   Substitute to check $\frac{5}{2}$ and 4. The solution set is $\left\{\frac{5}{2}, 4\right\}$.

—————— Work Problem **5** at the Side. ▶

ⓘ CAUTION

A common error is to include the common factor **2** as a solution in **Example 3**. *Only factors containing variables lead to solutions.*

---

4 Solve each equation.

(a) $m^2 - 3m - 10 = 0$

(b) $r^2 + 2r = 8$

5 Solve each equation.

GS (a) $10x^2 - 5x - 15 = 0$

$$\underline{\quad}(\underline{\quad} - x - 3) = 0$$

Divide each side by $\underline{\quad}$.

$$2x^2 - x - 3 = 0$$

$$(2x - 3)(\underline{\quad}) = 0$$

$$2x - 3 = 0 \quad \text{or} \quad \underline{\quad} = 0$$

$$x = \underline{\quad} \quad \text{or} \quad x = \underline{\quad}$$

Check by substituting in the original equation.

The solution set is $\underline{\quad}$.

(b) $4x^2 - 2x = 42$

Answers

4. (a) $\{-2, 5\}$ **(b)** $\{-4, 2\}$

5. (a) $5; 2x^2; 5; x + 1; x + 1; \dfrac{3}{2}; -1;$

$$\left\{-1, \frac{3}{2}\right\}$$

(b) $\left\{-3, \frac{7}{2}\right\}$

⑥ Solve each equation.

(a) $49x^2 - 9 = 0$

(b) $m^2 = 3m$

(c) $p(4p + 7) = 2$

EXAMPLE 4 **Solving Quadratic Equations**

Solve each equation.

(a) $$16m^2 - 25 = 0$$

> This equation is in standard form $ax^2 + bx + c = 0$. There is no first-degree term because $b = 0$.

$$(4m + 5)(4m - 5) = 0$$ Factor the difference of squares.

$4m + 5 = 0$ or $4m - 5 = 0$ Zero-factor property

$4m = -5$ or $4m = 5$ Solve each equation.

$m = -\dfrac{5}{4}$ or $m = \dfrac{5}{4}$ Divide by 4.

Check $-\frac{5}{4}$ and $\frac{5}{4}$ in the original equation. The solution set is $\left\{ -\frac{5}{4}, \frac{5}{4} \right\}$.

(b) $$y^2 = 2y$$
$$y^2 - 2y = 0$$

> This equation is in the form $ax^2 + bx + c = 0$. Here, $c = 0$.

> Don't forget to set the variable factor y equal to 0.

$$y(y - 2) = 0$$ Factor.

$y = 0$ or $y - 2 = 0$ Zero-factor property

$y = 2$ Add 2.

A check confirms that the solution set is $\{0, 2\}$.

(c) $$k(2k + 5) = 3$$

> To be in standard form, 0 must be on one side.

$$2k^2 + 5k = 3$$ Multiply.

Standard form $\rightarrow$ $2k^2 + 5k - 3 = 0$ Subtract 3.

$$(2k - 1)(k + 3) = 0$$ Factor.

$2k - 1 = 0$ or $k + 3 = 0$ Zero-factor property

$2k = 1$ or $k = -3$ Solve each equation.

$k = \dfrac{1}{2}$

A check confirms that the solution set is $\left\{ -3, \frac{1}{2} \right\}$.

◀ **Work Problem** ⑥ **at the Side.**

❗ CAUTION

In **Example 4(b),** it is tempting to begin by dividing both sides of
$$y^2 = 2y$$
by y to obtain $y = 2$. We do not find the solution 0 if we divide by a variable. (We *may* divide each side of an equation by a *nonzero* real number, however. In **Example 3** we divided each side by 2.)

In **Example 4(c),** we cannot use the zero-factor property to solve
$$k(2k + 5) = 3$$
in its given form because of the 3 on the right side of the equation. *The zero-factor property applies only to a product that equals 0.*

Answers

6. **(a)** $\left\{ -\frac{3}{7}, \frac{3}{7} \right\}$ **(b)** $\{0, 3\}$ **(c)** $\left\{ -2, \frac{1}{4} \right\}$

EXAMPLE 5 Solving Quadratic Equations (Double Solutions)

Solve each equation.

(a) $z^2 - 22z + 121 = 0$ ← [This is a perfect square trinomial.]

$(z - 11)^2 = 0$ Factor.

$(z - 11)(z - 11) = 0$ $a^2 = a \cdot a$

$z - 11 = 0 \quad \text{or} \quad z - 11 = 0$ Zero-factor property

$z = 11$ Add 11.

The *same* factor appears twice, which leads to the *same* solution, called a **double solution.**

CHECK $z^2 - 22z + 121 = 0$ Original equation

$11^2 - 22(11) + 121 \overset{?}{=} 0$ Let $z = 11$.

$121 - 242 + 121 \overset{?}{=} 0$ Apply the exponent. Multiply.

$0 = 0 \checkmark$ True

The solution set is $\{11\}$.

(b) $9t^2 + 30t = -25$

$9t^2 + 30t + 25 = 0$ Standard form

$(3t + 5)^2 = 0$ Factor the perfect square trinomial.

$3t + 5 = 0 \quad \text{or} \quad 3t + 5 = 0$ Zero-factor property

$3t = -5$ Subtract 5.

$t = -\dfrac{5}{3}$ $\frac{5}{3}$ is a double solution.

CHECK $9t^2 + 30t = -25$ Original equation

$9\left(-\dfrac{5}{3}\right)^2 + 30\left(-\dfrac{5}{3}\right) \overset{?}{=} -25$ Let $t = -\frac{5}{3}$.

$9\left(\dfrac{25}{9}\right) + 30\left(-\dfrac{5}{3}\right) \overset{?}{=} -25$ Apply the exponent.

$25 - 50 \overset{?}{=} -25$ Multiply.

$-25 = -25 \checkmark$ True

The solution set is $\left\{-\frac{5}{3}\right\}$.

─────── **Work Problem ⑦ at the Side.** ▶

❗ CAUTION

Each equation in **Example 5** *has only* one *distinct solution.* ***We write a double solution only once in a solution set.***

⑦ Solve each equation.

🅖🅢 **(a)** $x^2 + 16x = -64$

$x^2 + 16x + \underline{\quad} = 0$

$(\underline{\quad})^2 = 0$

$\underline{\quad} = 0 \quad \text{or} \quad \underline{\quad} = 0$

Solve to obtain $x = \underline{\quad}$.

Check by substituting in the original equation. -8 is a $\underline{\quad}$ solution.

The solution set is $\underline{\quad}$.

(b) $4x^2 - 4x + 1 = 0$

(c) $4z^2 + 20z = -25$

Answers

7. (a) $64; x + 8; x + 8; x + 8; -8;$ double; $\{-8\}$

     (b) $\left\{\dfrac{1}{2}\right\}$ **(c)** $\left\{-\dfrac{5}{2}\right\}$

8 Solve each equation.

(a) $2r^3 - 32r = 0$

(b) $x^3 - 3x^2 - 18x = 0$

9 Solve each equation.

(a) $(m + 3)(m^2 - 11m + 10) = 0$

(b) $(2x + 5)(4x^2 - 9) = 0$

Note

Not all quadratic equations can be solved by factoring. A more general method for solving such equations is given later in the text.

OBJECTIVE ▶ 2 Solve other equations using the zero-factor property. We can extend the zero-factor property to solve equations that involve more than two factors with variables. (These equations will have at least one term greater than second degree. They are *not* quadratic equations.)

EXAMPLE 6 Solving an Equation with More Than Two Variable Factors

Solve $6z^3 - 6z = 0$.

$$6z^3 - 6z = 0 \quad \text{This is not a quadratic equation because of the degree 3 term.}$$
$$6z(z^2 - 1) = 0 \quad \text{Factor out } 6z.$$
$$6z(z + 1)(z - 1) = 0 \quad \text{Factor } z^2 - 1.$$

By an extension of the zero-factor property, this product can equal 0 only if at least one of the factors equals 0. Write and solve three equations, one for each factor with a variable.

$$6z = 0 \quad \text{or} \quad z + 1 = 0 \quad \text{or} \quad z - 1 = 0 \quad \text{Zero-factor property}$$
$$z = 0 \quad \text{or} \quad z = -1 \quad \text{or} \quad z = 1 \quad \text{Solve each equation.}$$

Check by substituting, in turn, 0, −1, and 1 into the original equation. The solution set is $\{-1, 0, 1\}$.

◀ **Work Problem 8** at the Side

EXAMPLE 7 Solving an Equation with a Quadratic Factor

Solve $(2x - 1)(x^2 - 9x + 20) = 0$.

$$(2x - 1)(x^2 - 9x + 20) = 0 \quad \text{The product of the factors is 0, as required. Do \textbf{not} multiply.}$$
$$(2x - 1)(x - 5)(x - 4) = 0 \quad \text{Factor } x^2 - 9x + 20.$$
$$2x - 1 = 0 \quad \text{or} \quad x - 5 = 0 \quad \text{or} \quad x - 4 = 0 \quad \text{Zero-factor property}$$
$$x = \frac{1}{2} \quad \text{or} \quad x = 5 \quad \text{or} \quad x = 4 \quad \text{Solve each equation.}$$

Check to verify that the solution set is $\left\{\frac{1}{2}, 4, 5\right\}$.

◀ **Work Problem 9** at the Side

! CAUTION

In **Example 7**, it would be unproductive to begin by multiplying the two factors together. The zero-factor property requires the *product* of two or more factors to equal 0. *Always consider first whether an equation is given in the appropriate form to apply the zero-factor property.*

Answers

8. (a) $\{-4, 0, 4\}$ (b) $\{-3, 0, 6\}$

9. (a) $\{-3, 1, 10\}$ (b) $\left\{-\frac{5}{2}, -\frac{3}{2}, \frac{3}{2}\right\}$

6.7 Exercises	FOR EXTRA HELP

Go to MyMathLab *for worked-out, step-by-step solutions to exercises enclosed in a square* and video solutions to ▶ exercises.

CONCEPT CHECK *Fill in each blank with the correct response.*

1. A quadratic equation in x is an equation that can be written in the form _____ = 0.

2. The form $ax^2 + bx + c = 0$ is called _____ form.

3. If a quadratic equation is in standard form, to solve the equation we should begin by attempting to _____ the polynomial.

4. If the product of two numbers is 0, then at least one of the numbers is _____ . This is the _____-_____ property.

CONCEPT CHECK *Work each problem.*

5. Identify each equation as *linear* or *quadratic*.

    (a) $2x - 5 = 6$ **(b)** $x^2 - 5 = -4$

    (c) $x^2 + 2x - 1 = 2x^2$ **(d)** $2^2 + 5x = 0$

6. The number 9 is a *double solution* of the equation
$$(x - 9)^2 = 0.$$
Why is this so?

7. CONCEPT CHECK Look at this "solution."
$$2x(3x - 4) = 0$$
$$x = 2 \quad \text{or} \quad x = 0 \quad \text{or} \quad 3x - 4 = 0$$
$$x = \frac{4}{3}$$

The solution set is $\left\{2, 0, \frac{4}{3}\right\}$.

What Went Wrong? Solve the equation correctly.

8. CONCEPT CHECK Look at this "solution."
$$7x^2 - x = 0$$
$$7x - 1 = 0 \quad \text{Divide by } x.$$
$$x = \frac{1}{7} \quad \text{Solve the equation.}$$

The solution set is $\left\{\frac{1}{7}\right\}$.

What Went Wrong? Solve the equation correctly.

Solve each equation, and check the solutions. ***See Example 1.***

9. $(x + 5)(x - 2) = 0$

10. $(x - 1)(x + 8) = 0$

11. $(2m - 7)(m - 3) = 0$ ▶

12. $(6k + 5)(k + 4) = 0$

13. $(2x + 1)(6x - 1) = 0$

14. $(3x - 2)(10x + 1) = 0$

15. $t(6t + 5) = 0$

16. $w(4w + 1) = 0$

17. $2x(3x - 4) = 0$

18. $6x(4x - 9) = 0$

19. $(x - 9)(x - 9) = 0$

20. $(y + 1)(y + 1) = 0$

*Solve each equation, and check the solutions. **See Examples 2–7.***

21. $y^2 + 5y + 4 = 0$

22. $p^2 + 8p + 7 = 0$

23. $y^2 - 3y + 2 = 0$

24. $r^2 - 4r + 3 = 0$

25. $x^2 = 24 - 5x$

26. $t^2 = 2t + 15$

27. $x^2 = 3 + 2x$

28. $m^2 = 4 + 3m$

29. $z^2 + 3z = -2$

30. $p^2 - 2p = 3$

31. $m^2 + 8m + 16 = 0$

32. $x^2 + 6x + 9 = 0$

33. $16x^2 = 8x - 1$

34. $25y^2 = 10y - 1$

35. $3x^2 + 5x - 2 = 0$

36. $6r^2 - r - 2 = 0$

37. $12p^2 = 8 - 10p$

38. $18x^2 = 12 + 15x$

39. $9k^2 + 12k = -4$

40. $36x^2 - 60x = -25$

41. $y^2 - 9 = 0$

42. $m^2 - 100 = 0$

43. $16k^2 - 49 = 0$

44. $4w^2 - 9 = 0$

45. $n^2 = 169$

46. $x^2 = 400$

47. $x^2 = 7x$

48. $t^2 = 9t$

49. $6r^2 = 3r$

50. $10y^2 = -5y$

51. $g(g - 7) = -10$

52. $r(r - 5) = -6$

53. $z(2z + 7) = 4$

54. $b(2b + 3) = 9$

55. $2(y^2 - 66) = -13y$

56. $3(t^2 + 4) = 20t$

57. $3z(2z + 7) = 12$

58. $4x(2x + 3) = 36$

59. $5x^3 - 20x = 0$

60. $3x^3 - 48x = 0$

61. $9y^3 - 49y = 0$

62. $16r^3 - 9r = 0$

63. $(2r + 5)(3r^2 - 16r + 5) = 0$

64. $(3m + 4)(6m^2 + m - 2) = 0$

65. $(2x + 7)(x^2 + 2x - 3) = 0$

66. $(x + 1)(6x^2 + x - 12) = 0$

67. $x^3 + x^2 - 20x = 0$

68. $y^3 - 6y^2 + 8y = 0$

69. $r^4 = 2r^3 + 15r^2$

70. $x^4 = 3x^2 + 2x^3$

71. $(x - 8)(x + 6) = 6x$

72. $(x - 2)(x + 9) = 4x$

73. $3x(x + 1) = (2x + 3)(x + 1)$

74. $2x(x + 3) = (3x + 1)(x + 3)$

Galileo's formula describing the motion of freely falling objects is

$$d = 16t^2.$$

*The distance d in feet an object falls depends on the time t elapsed, in seconds. (This is an example of an important mathematical concept, a **function**.)*

75. (a) Use Galileo's formula and complete the following table. (*Hint:* Substitute each given value into the formula and solve for the unknown value.)

t in seconds	0	1	2	3	___	___
d in feet	0	16	___	___	256	576

(b) When $t = 0$, $d = 0$. Explain this in the context of the problem.

76. Refer to **Exercise 75.** When 256 was substituted for d and the formula was solved for t, there should have been two solutions: 4 and -4. Why doesn't -4 make sense as an answer?

6.8 | Applications of Quadratic Equations

OBJECTIVES

1. Solve problems involving geometric figures.
2. Solve problems involving consecutive integers.
3. Solve problems by applying the Pythagorean theorem.
4. Solve problems using given quadratic models.

Solving an Applied Problem

Step 1 **Read** the problem carefully. *What information is given? What is to be found?*

Step 2 **Assign a variable** to represent the unknown value. Use a sketch, diagram, or table, as needed. Express any other unknown values in terms of the variable.

Step 3 **Write an equation** using the variable expression(s).

Step 4 **Solve** the equation.

Step 5 **State the answer.** Label it appropriately. *Does it seem reasonable?*

Step 6 **Check** the answer in the words of the *original* problem.

Problem-Solving Hint

Refer to the formulas at the back of the text as needed when solving application problems.

OBJECTIVE **1** Solve problems involving geometric figures.

EXAMPLE 1 Solving an Area Problem

The Monroes want to plant a rectangular garden in their yard. The width of the garden will be 4 ft less than its length, and they want it to have an area of 96 ft². (ft² means square feet.) Find the length and width of the garden.

Step 1 **Read** the problem carefully. We need to find the dimensions of a garden with area 96 ft².

Step 2 **Assign a variable.** See **Figure 1.**

Let x = the length of the garden.

Then $x - 4$ = the width. (The width is 4 ft less than the length.)

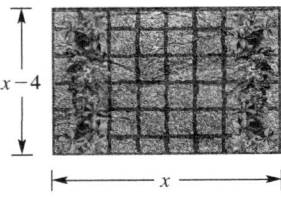

Figure 1

Step 3 **Write an equation.** The area of a rectangle is given by

$$\text{Area} = \text{Length} \cdot \text{Width}. \quad \text{Area formula}$$

Substitute 96 for area, x for length, and $x - 4$ for width.

$$\mathcal{A} = L \cdot W$$
$$\downarrow \quad \downarrow \quad \downarrow$$
$$96 = x(x - 4) \quad \text{Let } \mathcal{A} = 96, L = x, W = x - 4.$$

—— **Continued on Next Page**

Step 4 **Solve.**

$$96 = x(x - 4) \quad \text{Equation from Step 3}$$
$$96 = x^2 - 4x \quad \text{Distributive property}$$
$$x^2 - 4x - 96 = 0 \quad \text{Standard form}$$
$$(x - 12)(x + 8) = 0 \quad \text{Factor.}$$
$$x - 12 = 0 \quad \text{or} \quad x + 8 = 0 \quad \text{Zero-factor property}$$
$$x = 12 \quad \text{or} \quad x = -8 \quad \text{Solve each equation.}$$

Step 5 **State the answer.** The solutions are **12** and -8. A rectangle cannot have a side of negative length, so we discard -8. The length of the garden will be **12** ft. The width will be

$$12 - 4 = 8 \text{ ft.}$$

Step 6 **Check.** The width of the garden is 4 ft less than the length, and the area is

$$12 \cdot 8 = 96 \text{ ft}^2, \quad \text{as required.}$$

—————————————— **Work Problem ① at the Side.** ▶

> **⚠ CAUTION**
>
> ***When solving applied problems, always check solutions against physical facts and discard any answers that are not appropriate.***

OBJECTIVE ▶ ② **Solve problems involving consecutive integers.** Recall that **consecutive integers** (see **Figure 2**) are integers that are next to each other on a number line, such as 1 and 2, or -11 and -10.

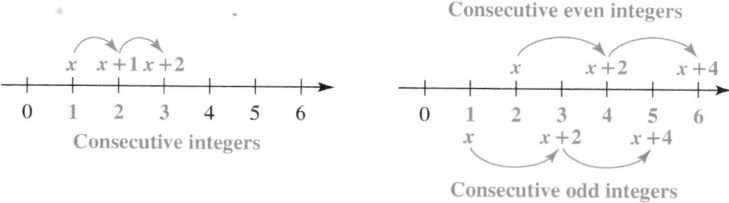

| Figure 2 | Figure 3 |

Consecutive even integers are *even* integers that are next to each other on a number line, such as

$$4 \text{ and } 6, \quad \text{or} \quad -10 \text{ and} -8.$$

Consecutive odd integers are defined similarly—for example, 3 and 5 are consecutive *odd* integers, as are -13 and -11. See **Figure 3.**

> **Problem-Solving Hint**
>
> If x = the lesser (least) integer in a consecutive integer problem, then the following apply.
>
> - For two consecutive integers, use $\quad$ ***x, x + 1.***
> - For three consecutive integers, use $\quad$ ***x, x + 1, x + 2.***
> - For two consecutive even or odd integers, use $\quad$ ***x, x + 2.***
> - For three consecutive even or odd integers, use $\quad$ ***x, x + 2, x + 4.***

In this text, we list consecutive integers in increasing order.

① Solve each problem.

(a) 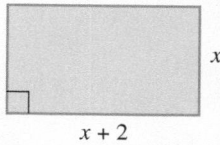 The length of a rectangular room is 2 m more than the width. The area of the floor is 48 m². Find the length and width of the room.

Give the equation using x as the variable, and give the answer.

(b) The length of each side of a square is increased by 4 in. The sum of the areas of the original square and the larger square is 106 in². What is the length of a side of the original square?

2 Solve the problem.

The product of the numbers on two consecutively-numbered lockers at a health club is 132. Find the locker numbers.

EXAMPLE 2 Solving a Consecutive Integer Problem

The product of the numbers on two consecutively-numbered post-office boxes is 210. Find the box numbers.

Step 1 **Read** the problem. Note that the boxes are numbered consecutively.

Step 2 **Assign a variable.** See **Figure 4.**

Let x = the first box number.

Then $x + 1$ = the next consecutive box number.

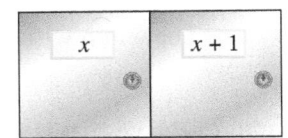

Figure 4

Step 3 **Write an equation.** The product of the box numbers is 210.

$$\underset{\downarrow}{\text{The product}} \quad \underset{\downarrow}{\text{is}} \quad \underset{\downarrow}{210.}$$

$$x(x+1) \quad = \quad 210$$

Step 4 **Solve.**

$$x^2 + x = 210 \qquad \text{Distributive property}$$
$$x^2 + x - 210 = 0 \qquad \text{Standard form}$$
$$(x + 15)(x - 14) = 0 \qquad \text{Factor.}$$
$$x + 15 = 0 \quad \text{or} \quad x - 14 = 0 \qquad \text{Zero-factor property}$$
$$x = -15 \quad \text{or} \quad x = 14 \qquad \text{Solve each equation.}$$

Step 5 **State the answer.** The solutions are -15 and 14. We discard -15 because a box number cannot be negative. If $x = 14$, then

$$x + 1 = 15,$$

so the boxes have numbers **14** and **15.**

Step 6 **Check.** The numbers 14 and 15 are consecutive and their product is

$$14 \cdot 15 = 210, \quad \text{as required.}$$

◀ **Work Problem 2 at the Side.**

EXAMPLE 3 Solving a Consecutive Integer Problem

The product of two consecutive odd integers is 1 less than five times their sum. Find the integers.

Step 1 **Read** carefully. This problem is a little more complicated.

Step 2 **Assign a variable.** We must find two consecutive *odd* integers.

Let x = the lesser integer.

Then $x + 2$ = the next greater odd integer.

Step 3 **Write an equation.**

$$\underset{\downarrow}{\substack{\text{The} \\ \text{product}}} \quad \underset{\downarrow}{\text{is}} \quad \underset{\downarrow}{\substack{\text{five times} \\ \text{the sum}}} \quad \underset{\downarrow}{\text{less}} \quad \underset{\downarrow}{\substack{1.}}$$

$$x(x+2) \quad = \quad 5(x + x + 2) \quad - \quad 1$$

Answer

2. 11 and 12

Continued on Next Page

Step 4 **Solve.**

$$x(x + 2) = 5(x + x + 2) - 1 \qquad \text{Equation from Step 3}$$
$$x^2 + 2x = 5x + 5x + 10 - 1 \qquad \text{Distributive property}$$
$$x^2 + 2x = 10x + 9 \qquad \text{Combine like terms.}$$
$$x^2 - 8x - 9 = 0 \qquad \text{Standard form}$$
$$(x - 9)(x + 1) = 0 \qquad \text{Factor.}$$
$$x - 9 = 0 \quad \text{or} \quad x + 1 = 0 \qquad \text{Zero-factor property}$$
$$x = 9 \quad \text{or} \quad x = -1 \qquad \text{Solve each equation.}$$

Step 5 **State the answer.** We need to find two consecutive odd integers.

If $x = 9$ is the lesser, then $x + 2 = 9 + 2 = 11$ is the greater.

If $x = -1$ is the lesser, then $x + 2 = -1 + 2 = 1$ is the greater.

Do not discard the solution -1 here. There are two sets of answers since integers can be positive *or* negative.

Step 6 **Check.** The product of the first pair of integers is

$$9 \cdot 11 = 99.$$

One less than five times their sum is

$$5(9 + 11) - 1 = 99.$$

Thus, 9 and 11 satisfy the problem. Repeat the check with -1 and 1.

───────────── **Work Problem ③ at the Side.** ▶

> ⚠ **CAUTION**
>
> Do *not* use $x, x + 1, x + 3$ to represent consecutive odd integers. To see why, let $x = 3$.
>
> $$\text{Then } x + 1 = 3 + 1 \text{ or } 4, \quad \text{and} \quad x + 3 = 3 + 3 \text{ or } 6.$$
>
> The numbers 3, 4, and 6 are not consecutive odd integers.

OBJECTIVE ▶ ③ Solve problems by applying the Pythagorean theorem.
Although there is evidence of the discovery of the Pythagorean relationship in earlier civilizations, the Greek mathematician and philosopher Pythagoras generally receives credit for being the first to prove it. This famous theorem from geometry relates the lengths of the sides of a right triangle.

Pythagorean Theorem

If a and b are the lengths of the two shorter sides of a right triangle (a triangle with a 90° angle) and c is the length of the longest side, then

$$a^2 + b^2 = c^2.$$

The two shorter sides are the **legs** of the triangle, and the longest side, opposite the right angle, is the **hypotenuse**.

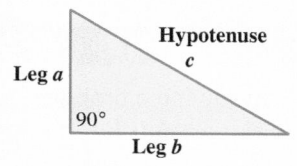

③
Ⓖ Solve each problem. Give the equation using x to represent the least integer, and give the answer.

(a) The product of two consecutive even integers is 4 more than two times their sum. Find the integers.

(b) Find three consecutive odd integers such that the product of the least and greatest is 16 more than the middle integer.

Pythagoras (c. 580–500 B.C.)

Answers

3. **(a)** $x(x + 2) = 4 + 2(x + x + 2)$;
     4 and 6 or -2 and 0
   (b) $x(x + 4) = 16 + (x + 2)$;
     3, 5, 7

④ Solve the problem.

The hypotenuse of a right triangle is 3 in. longer than the longer leg. The shorter leg is 3 in. shorter than the longer leg. Find the lengths of the sides of the triangle.

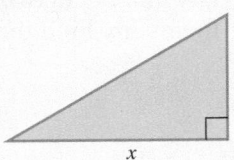

EXAMPLE 4 **Applying the Pythagorean Theorem**

Amy and Kevin leave their office, with Amy traveling north and Kevin traveling east. When Kevin is 1 mi farther than Amy from the office, the distance between them is 2 mi more than Amy's distance from the office. Find their distances from the office and the distance between them.

Step 1 **Read** the problem again. We must find three distances.

Step 2 **Assign a variable.**

Let x = Amy's distance from the office.

Then $x + 1$ = Kevin's distance from the office,

and $x + 2$ = the distance between them.

Label a right triangle with these expressions, as in **Figure 5.**

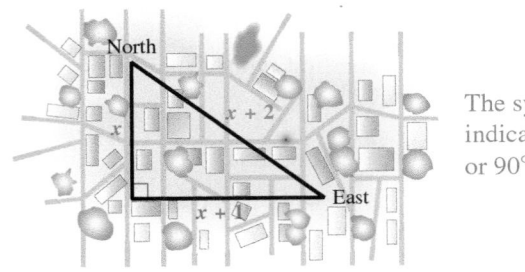

The symbol ∟ indicates a right, or 90°, angle.

Figure 5

Step 3 **Write an equation.** Substitute into the Pythagorean theorem.

$$a^2 + b^2 = c^2$$

$$x^2 + (x + 1)^2 = (x + 2)^2 \quad \leftarrow \boxed{\text{Be careful to substitute properly.}}$$

Step 4 **Solve.**

$$x^2 + x^2 + 2x + 1 = x^2 + 4x + 4 \qquad \text{Square each binomial.}$$

$$x^2 - 2x - 3 = 0 \qquad \text{Standard form}$$

$$(x - 3)(x + 1) = 0 \qquad \text{Factor.}$$

$$x - 3 = 0 \quad \text{or} \quad x + 1 = 0 \qquad \text{Zero-factor property}$$

$$x = 3 \quad \text{or} \qquad x = -1 \qquad \text{Solve each equation.}$$

Step 5 **State the answer.** Because -1 cannot represent a distance, 3 is the only possible answer. Amy's distance is **3** mi, Kevin's distance is

$$3 + 1 = 4 \text{ mi,}$$

and the distance between them is

$$3 + 2 = 5 \text{ mi.}$$

Step 6 **Check.** Because $3^2 + 4^2 = 5^2$ is true, the answer is correct.

◀ **Work Problem** ④ **at the Side.**

Problem-Solving Hint

When solving a problem involving the Pythagorean theorem, be sure that the expressions for the sides of the triangle are properly placed.

$$\textbf{(one leg)}^2 + \textbf{(other leg)}^2 = \textbf{hypotenuse}^2$$

Answer

4. 9 in., 12 in., 15 in.

OBJECTIVE ▶ **4** Solve problems using given quadratic models. In **Examples 1–4,** we wrote quadratic equations to model, or mathematically describe, various situations and then solved the equations. Now we are given the quadratic models and must use them to determine data.

EXAMPLE 5   **Finding the Height of a Ball**

A tennis player can hit a ball 180 ft per sec (123 mph). If she hits a ball directly upward, the height h of the ball in feet at time t in seconds is modeled by the quadratic equation

$$h = -16t^2 + 180t + 6.$$

How long will it take for the ball to reach a height of 206 ft?

A height of 206 ft means $h = 206$, so we substitute 206 for h in the equation and then solve for t.

$$h = -16t^2 + 180t + 6$$

$$206 = -16t^2 + 180t + 6 \qquad \text{Let } h = 206.$$

$$-16t^2 + 180t + 6 = 206 \qquad \text{Interchange sides.}$$

$$-16t^2 + 180t - 200 = 0 \qquad \text{Standard form}$$

$$4t^2 - 45t + 50 = 0 \qquad \text{Divide by } -4.$$

$$(4t - 5)(t - 10) = 0 \qquad \text{Factor.}$$

$$4t - 5 = 0 \quad \text{or} \quad t - 10 = 0 \qquad \text{Zero-factor property}$$

$$t = \frac{5}{4} \quad \text{or} \qquad t = 10 \qquad \text{Solve each equation.}$$

Both answers are acceptable. The ball will be 206 ft above the ground twice—once on its way up and once on its way down—at $\frac{5}{4}$ sec and at 10 sec after it is hit. See **Figure 6.**

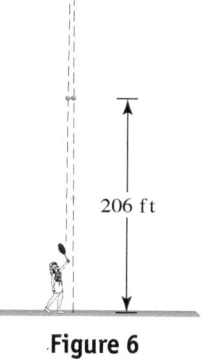

206 ft

Figure 6

───── Work Problem **5** at the Side. ▶

EXAMPLE 6   **Modeling Foreign-Born Population of the United States**

The foreign-born population of the United States over the years 1930–2010 can be modeled by the quadratic equation

$$y = 0.009665x^2 - 0.4942x + 15.12,$$

where $x = 0$ represents 1930, $x = 10$ represents 1940, and so on, and y is the number of people in millions. (Data from U.S. Census Bureau.)

(a) Use the model to find the foreign-born population in 1980 to the nearest tenth of a million.

Because $x = 0$ represents 1930, $x = 50$ represents 1980. Substitute 50 for x in the equation.

$$y = 0.009665x^2 - 0.4942x + 15.12 \qquad \text{Given model}$$

$$y = 0.009665\,(50)^2 - 0.4942\,(50) + 15.12 \qquad \text{Let } x = 50.$$

$$y \approx 14.6 \qquad \text{Round to the nearest tenth.}$$

In 1980, the foreign-born population of the United States was about 14.6 million.

───── Continued on Next Page

5 Solve each problem.

(a) Refer to **Example 5.** How long will it take for the ball to reach a height of 50 ft?

(b) The number of impulses y fired after a nerve has been stimulated is modeled by the quadratic equation

$$y = -x^2 + 2x + 60,$$

where x is in milliseconds (ms) after the stimulation. When will 45 impulses occur? How many solutions do we obtain? Why is only one answer acceptable?

Answers

5. (a) $\frac{1}{4}$ sec and 11 sec

(b) After 5 ms; There are two solutions, -3 and 5; Only one answer makes sense here because a negative answer is not appropriate.

6 Use the model in **Example 6** to find the foreign-born population of the United States in 1990. Give the answer to the nearest tenth of a million. How does it compare to the actual value from the table?

(b) Repeat part (a) for 2010.

$$y = 0.009665\,x^2 - 0.4942x + 15.12 \qquad \text{Given model}$$

$$y = 0.009665\,(80)^2 - 0.4942\,(80) + 15.12 \qquad \text{For 2010, let } x = 80.$$

$$y \approx 37.4 \qquad \text{Round to the nearest tenth.}$$

In 2010, the foreign-born population of the United States was about 37.4 million.

(c) The model used in parts (a) and (b) was developed using the data in the table below. How do the results in parts (a) and (b) compare to the actual data from the table?

Year	Foreign-Born Population (millions)
1930	14.2
1940	11.6
1950	10.3
1960	9.7
1970	9.6
1980	14.1
1990	19.8
2000	28.4
2010	37.6

From the table, the actual value for 1980 is 14.1 million. By comparison, our answer in part (a), 14.6 million, is slightly high.

For 2010, the actual value is 37.6 million. Our answer of 37.4 million in part (b) is slightly low, but a good estimate.

◄ **Work Problem 6 at the Side.**

Answer

6. 20.3 million; The actual value is 19.8 million, so the answer using the model is slightly high.

6.8 Exercises

FOR EXTRA HELP Go to MyMathLab *for worked-out, step-by-step solutions to exercises enclosed in a square* ▢ *and video solutions to* ▶ *exercises.*

1. **CONCEPT CHECK** Complete each statement to review the six problem-solving steps.

   Step 1: _____ the problem carefully.

   Step 2: Assign a _____ to represent the unknown value.

   Step 3: Write a(n) _____ using the variable expression(s).

   Step 4: _____ the equation.

   Step 5: State the _____ .

   Step 6: _____ the answer in the words of the _____ problem.

2. **CONCEPT CHECK** A student solves an applied problem and gets 6 or −3 for the length of the side of a square. Which of these answers is reasonable? Why?

GS *A geometric figure is given in each exercise. Write the indicated formula. Then, using x as the variable, complete Steps 3–6 for each problem. (Refer to the steps in **Exercise 1** as needed.)*

3.

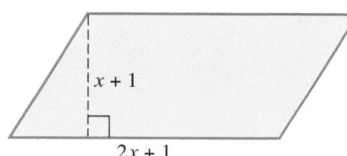

$x + 1$

$2x + 1$

The area of this parallelogram is 45 sq. units. Find its base and height.

Formula for the area of a parallelogram: _____

Step 3: 45 = _____

Step 4: $x =$ _____ or $x =$ _____

Step 5: base: _____ units;

   height: _____ units

Step 6: _____ = 45

4.

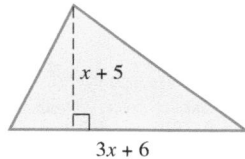

$x + 5$

$3x + 6$

The area of this triangle is 60 sq. units. Find its base and height.

Formula for the area of a triangle: _____

Step 3: 60 = _____

Step 4: $x =$ _____ or $x =$ _____

Step 5: base: _____ units;

   height: _____ units

Step 6: _____ = 60

5.

4

$x + 2$ x

The volume of this box is 192 cu. units. Find its length and width.

Formula for the volume of a rectangular solid: _____

Step 3: _____ = _____ $(x + 2)$

Step 4: $x =$ _____ or $x =$ _____

Step 5: length: _____ units;

   width: _____ units

Step 6: _____ · 4 = _____

6.

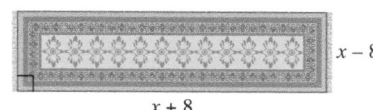

$x - 8$

$x + 8$

The area of this rug is 80 sq. units. Find its length and width.

Formula for the area of a rectangle: _____

Step 3: _____ = $(x + 8)$ _____

Step 4: $x =$ _____ or $x =$ _____

Step 5: length: _____ units;

   width: _____ units

Step 6: _____ = 80

Solve each problem. Check answers to be sure they are reasonable. (If necessary, refer to the formulas at the back of this text.) **See Example 1.**

7. The length of a standard jewel case is 2 cm more than its width. The area of the rectangular top of the case is 168 cm². Find the length and width of the jewel case.

8. A standard DVD case is 6 cm longer than it is wide. The area of the rectangular top of the case is 247 cm². Find the length and width of the case.

9. The area of a triangle is 30 in.². The base of the triangle measures 2 in. more than twice the height of the triangle. Find the measures of the base and the height.

10. A certain triangle has its base equal in measure to its height. The area of the triangle is 72 m². Find the equal base and height measure.

11. The dimensions of a rectangular monitor screen are such that its length is 3 in. more than its width. If the length were doubled and if the width were decreased by 1 in., the area would be increased by 150 in.². What are the length and width of the screen?

12. A computer keyboard is 11 in. longer than it is wide. If the length were doubled and if 2 in. were added to the width, the area would be increased by 198 in.². What are the length and width of the keyboard?

13. A 10-gal aquarium is 3 in. higher than it is wide. Its length is 21 in., and its volume is 2730 in.³. What are the height and width of the aquarium?

14. A toolbox is 2 ft high, and its width is 3 ft less than its length. If its volume is 80 ft³, find the length and width of the box.

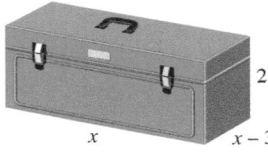

15. A square mirror has sides measuring 2 ft less than the sides of a square painting. If the difference between their areas is 32 ft², find the lengths of the sides of the mirror and the painting.

16. The sides of one square have length 3 m more than the sides of a second square. If the area of the larger square is subtracted from 4 times the area of the smaller square, the result is 36 m². What are the lengths of the sides of each square?

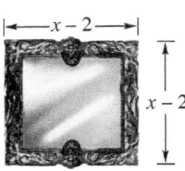

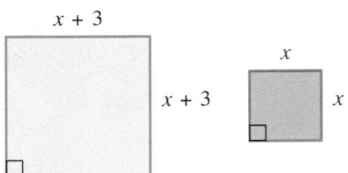

Solve each problem. See Examples 2 and 3.

17. The product of the numbers on two consecutive volumes of research data is 420. Find the volume numbers.

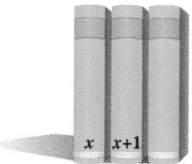

18. The product of the page numbers on two facing pages of a book is 600. Find the page numbers.

19. The product of two consecutive integers is 11 more than their sum. Find the integers.

20. The product of two consecutive integers is 4 less than four times their sum. Find the integers.

21. Find two consecutive odd integers such that their product is 15 more than three times their sum.

22. Find two consecutive odd integers such that five times their sum is 23 less than their product.

23. Find three consecutive even integers such that the sum of the squares of the lesser two integers is equal to the square of the greatest.

24. Find three consecutive even integers such that the square of the sum of the lesser two integers is equal to twice the greatest.

25. Find three consecutive odd integers such that 3 times the sum of all three is 18 more than the product of the lesser two integers.

26. Find three consecutive odd integers such that the sum of all three is 42 less than the product of the greater two integers.

Solve each problem. See Example 4.

27. The hypotenuse of a right triangle is 1 cm longer than the longer leg. The shorter leg is 7 cm shorter than the longer leg. Find the length of the longer leg.

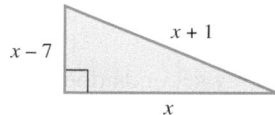

28. The longer leg of a right triangle is 1 m longer than the shorter leg. The hypotenuse is 1 m shorter than twice the shorter leg. Find the length of the shorter leg.

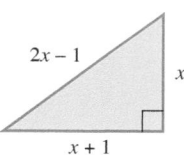

29. Terri works due north of home. Her husband Denny works due east. They leave for work at the same time. By the time Terri is 5 mi from home, the distance between them is 1 mi more than Denny's distance from home. How far from home is Denny?

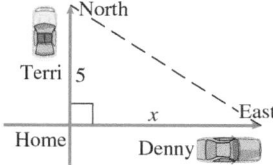

30. Two cars left an intersection at the same time. One traveled north. The other traveled 14 mi farther, but to the east. How far apart were they then, if the distance between them was 4 mi more than the distance traveled east?

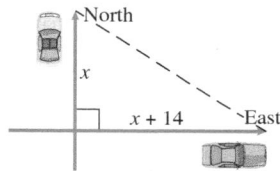

31. The length of a rectangle is 5 in. longer than its width. The diagonal is 5 in. shorter than twice the width. Find the length, width, and diagonal measures.

32. The length of a rectangle is 4 in. longer than its width. The diagonal is 8 in. longer than the width. Find the length, width, and diagonal measures.

33. A ladder is leaning against a building. The distance from the bottom of the ladder to the building is 4 ft less than the length of the ladder. How high up the side of the building is the top of the ladder if that distance is 2 ft less than the length of the ladder?

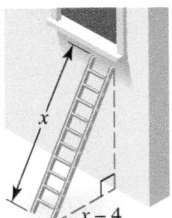

34. A lot has the shape of a right triangle with one leg 2 m longer than the other. The hypotenuse is 2 m less than twice the length of the shorter leg. Find the length of the shorter leg.

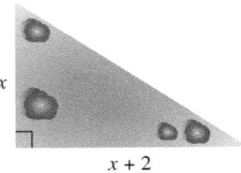

Solve each problem. See Example 5.

35. An object projected from a height of 48 ft with an initial velocity of 32 ft per sec after t seconds has height $h = -16t^2 + 32t + 48$.

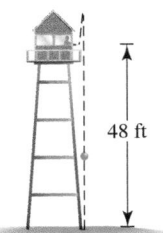

48 ft

(a) After how many seconds is the height 64 ft? (*Hint:* Let $h = 64$ and solve.)

(b) After how many seconds is the height 60 ft?

(c) After how many seconds does the object hit the ground? (*Hint:* When the object hits the ground, $h = 0$.)

(d) The quadratic equation from part (c) has two solutions, yet only one of them is appropriate for answering the question. Why is this so?

36. If an object is projected upward from ground level with an initial velocity of 64 ft per sec, its height h in feet t seconds later is $h = -16t^2 + 64t$.

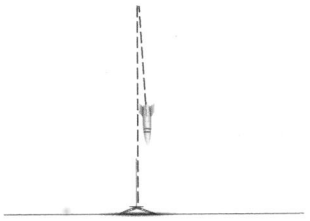

(a) After how many seconds is the height 48 ft? (*Hint:* Let $h = 48$ and solve.)

(b) The object reaches its maximum height 2 sec after it is projected. What is this maximum height?

(c) After how many seconds does the object hit the ground? (*Hint:* When the object hits the ground, $h = 0$.)

(d) The quadratic equation from part (c) has two solutions, yet only one of them is appropriate for answering the question. Why is this so?

If an object is projected upward with an initial velocity of 128 ft per sec, its height h in feet after t seconds is

$$h = 128t - 16t^2.$$

Find the height of the object after each period of time. See Example 5.

37. 1 sec   **38.** 2 sec   **39.** 4 sec

40. How long does it take the object just described to return to the ground?

Solve each problem. See Example 6.

41. The table shows the number of cellular phone subscribers (in millions) in the United States.

Year	Subscribers (in millions)
2000	109
2002	141
2004	182
2006	233
2008	286
2010	303
2012	326
2014	355

Data from CTIA-The Wireless Association.

We used the data to develop the quadratic equation

$$y = -0.4985x^2 + 25.21x + 100.3,$$

which models the number of cellular phone subscribers y (in millions) in the year x, where $x = 0$ represents 2000, $x = 2$ represents 2002, and so on.

(a) Use the model to find the number of subscribers in 2000 to the nearest million. How does the result compare to the actual data in the table?

(b) What value of x corresponds to 2010?

(c) Use the model to find the number of subscribers in 2010 to the nearest million. How does the result compare to the actual data in the table?

(d) Assuming that the trend in the data continues, use the quadratic equation to estimate the number of subscribers in 2018 to the nearest million.

42. Annual revenue in billions of dollars for eBay is shown in the table.

Year	Revenue (in billions of dollars)
2007	7.67
2008	8.54
2009	8.73
2010	9.16
2011	11.65
2012	14.07
2013	16.05
2014	17.90

Data from Statista—the Statistics Portal.

We used the data to develop the quadratic equation

$$y = 0.185x^2 + 0.223x + 7.70,$$

which models eBay revenues y (in billion of dollars) in the year x, where $x = 0$ represents 2007, $x = 1$ represents 2008, and so on.

(a) Use the model to find eBay revenue in 2011 to the nearest hundredth of a billion. How does the result compare to the actual data in the table?

(b) What value of x corresponds to 2014?

(c) Use the model to find eBay revenue in 2014 to the nearest hundredth of a billion. How does the result compare to the actual revenue in 2014?

(d) Assuming that the trend in the data continues, use the quadratic equation to estimate the number of subscribers in 2016 to the nearest hundredth of a billion.

Relating Concepts (Exercises 43–46) For Individual or Group Work

A proof of the Pythagorean theorem is based on the figures shown. *Work Exercises 43–46 in order.*

43. What is an expression for the area of the dark square labeled ③ in **Figure A?**

44. The five regions in **Figure A** are equal in area to the six regions in **Figure B.** What is an expression for the area of the square labeled ① in **Figure B?**

45. What is an expression for the area of the square labeled ② in **Figure B?**

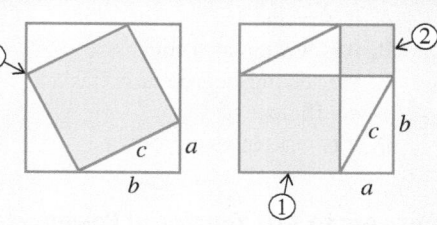

Figure A **Figure B**

46. Represent this statement using algebraic expressions: The sum of the areas of the shaded regions in **Figure B** is equal to the area of the shaded region in **Figure A.** What does this equation represent?

Chapter 6	*Summary*

Key Terms

6.1

factor For integers a and b, if $a \cdot b = c$, then a and b are factors of c.

factored form An expression is in factored form when it is written as a product.

$$\overset{\text{Factors}}{\overbrace{20 = 4 \cdot 5}}$$
Factored form

greatest common factor (GCF) The greatest common factor is the largest quantity that is a factor of each of a group of quantities.

factoring The process of writing a polynomial as a product is called factoring.

6.2

prime polynomial A prime polynomial is a polynomial that cannot be factored using only integers.

6.5

perfect square trinomial A perfect square trinomial is a trinomial that can be factored as the square of a binomial.

6.7

quadratic equation A quadratic equation is an equation that can be written in the form $ax^2 + bx + c = 0$, where a, b, and c are real numbers and $a \neq 0$.

standard form The form $ax^2 + bx + c = 0$ is the standard form of a quadratic equation.

6.8

hypotenuse The longest side of a right triangle, opposite the right angle, is the hypotenuse.

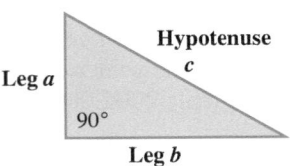

legs The two shorter sides of a right triangle are the legs.

Test Your Word Power

See how well you have learned the vocabulary in this chapter.

1 **Factoring** is
  A. a method of multiplying polynomials
  B. the process of writing a polynomial as a product
  C. the answer in a multiplication problem
  D. a way to add the terms of a polynomial.

2 A polynomial is in **factored form** when
  A. it is prime
  B. it is written as a sum
  C. the second-degree term has a coefficient of 1
  D. it is written as a product.

3 The greatest common factor of a polynomial is
  A. the least integer that divides evenly into all its terms
  B. the least expression that is a factor of all its terms
  C. the greatest expression that is a factor of all its terms
  D. the variable that is common to all its terms.

4 A **perfect square trinomial** is a trinomial
  A. that can be factored as the square of a binomial
  B. that cannot be factored
  C. that is multiplied by a binomial

D. where all terms are perfect squares.

5 A **quadratic equation** is an equation that can be written in the form
  A. $y = mx + b$
  B. $ax^2 + bx + c = 0$ $(a \neq 0)$
  C. $Ax + By = C$
  D. $x = k$.

6 A **hypotenuse** is
  A. either of the two shorter sides of a triangle
  B. the shortest side of a right triangle
  C. the side opposite the right angle in a right triangle
  D. the longest side in any triangle.

Answers to Test Your Word Power

1. B; *Example:* $7t^5 - 14t^{10}$ factors as $7t^5(1 - 2t^5)$.

2. D; *Example:* The factored form of $x^2 + 2x - 7x - 14$ is $(x - 7)(x + 2)$.

3. C; *Example:* The greatest common factor of $8x^2$, $22xy$, and $16x^3y^2$ is $2x$.

4. A; *Example:* $a^2 + 2a + 1$ is a perfect square trinomial. its factored form is $(a + 1)^2$.

5. B; *Examples:* $y^2 - 3y + 2 = 0$, $x^2 - 9 = 0$, $2m^2 = 6m + 8$

6. C; *Example:* See the triangle included in the Key Terms above.

Quick Review

Concepts	Examples

6.1 Greatest Common Factors; Factor by Grouping

Finding the Greatest Common Factor (GCF)

Step 1 Write each number in prime factored form.

Step 2 List each prime number or each variable that is a factor of every term in the list.

Step 3 Use as exponents on the common prime factors the *least* exponents from the prime factored forms.

Step 4 Multiply the primes from Step 3.

Factoring by Grouping

Step 1 Collect the terms into two groups so that each group has a common factor.

Step 2 Factor out the greatest common factor from each group.

Step 3 Factor out a common binomial factor from the results of Step 2.

Step 4 If necessary, rearrange terms and try a different grouping.

Find the greatest common factor of $4x^2y$, $6x^2y^3$, and $2xy^2$.

$$4x^2y = 2 \cdot 2 \cdot x^2 \cdot y$$
$$6x^2y^3 = 2 \cdot 3 \cdot x^2 \cdot y^3$$
$$2xy^2 = 2 \cdot x \cdot y^2$$
$$\text{GCF} = 2xy$$

Factor by grouping.

$$2a^2 + 2ab + a + b$$
$$= (2a^2 + 2ab) + (a + b) \qquad \text{Group the terms.}$$
$$= 2a(a + b) + 1(a + b) \qquad \text{Factor each group.}$$
$$= (a + b)(2a + 1) \qquad \text{Factor out } a + b.$$

6.2 Factoring Trinomials

To factor $x^2 + bx + c$, find m and n such that $mn = c$ and $m + n = b$.

$$\underset{\underset{m+n=b}{\uparrow}}{\overset{\overset{mn=c}{\downarrow}}{x^2 + bx + c}}$$

Then $x^2 + bx + c$ factors as $(x + m)(x + n)$.

Check by multiplying.

Factor $x^2 + 6x + 8$.

$$\underset{\underset{m+n=6}{\uparrow}}{\overset{\overset{mn=8}{\downarrow}}{x^2 + 6x + 8}} \quad \begin{array}{l} \text{Find two integers } m \text{ and } n \text{ whose} \\ \text{product is 8 and whose sum is 6.} \\ \text{Here, } m = 2 \text{ and } n = 4. \end{array}$$

$x^2 + 6x + 8$ factors as $(x + 2)(x + 4)$.

CHECK $(x + 2)(x + 4)$
$$= x^2 + 4x + 2x + 8 \qquad \text{FOIL method}$$
$$= x^2 + 6x + 8 \checkmark \qquad \text{Combine like terms.}$$

6.3 Factoring Trinomials by Grouping

To factor $ax^2 + bx + c$, find m and n such that $mn = ac$ and $m + n = b$.

$$\underset{\underset{mn=ac}{\uparrow}}{\overset{\overset{m+n=b}{\downarrow}}{ax^2 + bx + c}}$$

Then factor $ax^2 + mx + nx + c$ by grouping.

Factor $3x^2 + 14x - 5$. Here, $mn = -15$ and $m + n = 14$.

$$\overset{\uparrow \quad \overline{\quad\quad\quad} \quad \uparrow}{\underset{-15}{}}$$

Find two integers with a product of $3(-5) = -15$ and a sum of 14. The integers are -1 and 15.

$$3x^2 + 14x - 5$$
$$= 3x^2 - x + 15x - 5 \qquad 14x = -x + 15x$$
$$= (3x^2 - x) + (15x - 5) \qquad \text{Group the terms.}$$
$$= x(3x - 1) + 5(3x - 1) \qquad \text{Factor each group.}$$
$$= (3x - 1)(x + 5) \qquad \text{Factor out } 3x - 1.$$

Concepts	Examples

6.4 **Factoring Trinomials Using the FOIL Method**

To factor $ax^2 + bx + c$ using trial and error, apply the FOIL method in reverse.

Factor $3x^2 + 14x - 5$.

Because the only positive factors of 3 are 3 and 1, and -5 has possible factors of 1 and -5, or -1 and 5, the only possible factored forms for this trinomial follow.

$$(3x + 1)(x - 5) \quad \text{Incorrect}$$
$$(3x - 5)(x + 1) \quad \text{Incorrect}$$
$$(3x + 5)(x - 1) \quad \text{Incorrect}$$
$$(3x - 1)(x + 5) \quad \text{Correct}$$

6.5 **Special Factoring Techniques**

Difference of Squares
$$x^2 - y^2 = (x + y)(x - y)$$

Perfect Square Trinomials
$$x^2 + 2xy + y^2 = (x + y)^2$$
$$x^2 - 2xy + y^2 = (x - y)^2$$

Difference of Cubes
$$x^3 - y^3 = (x - y)(x^2 + xy + y^2)$$

Sum of Cubes
$$x^3 + y^3 = (x + y)(x^2 - xy + y^2)$$

Factor.

$$4x^2 - 9 \qquad\qquad 100y^4 - 49$$
$$= (2x + 3)(2x - 3) \quad\quad = (10y^2 + 7)(10y^2 - 7)$$

$$9x^2 + 6x + 1 \qquad\qquad 4x^2 - 20x + 25$$
$$= (3x + 1)^2 \qquad\qquad = (2x - 5)^2$$

$$8 - 27a^3$$
$$= (2 - 3a)(4 + 6a + 9a^2)$$
$$64z^3 + 1$$
$$= (4z + 1)(16z^2 - 4z + 1)$$

6.7 **Solving Quadratic Equations Using the Zero-Factor Property**

Quadratic Equation
A **quadratic equation** (in x here) can be written in the form

$$ax^2 + bx + c = 0 \quad \text{Standard form}$$

where a, b, and c are real numbers and $a \neq 0$.

Zero-Factor Property
If a and b are real numbers and $ab = 0$, then

$$a = 0 \quad \text{or} \quad b = 0.$$

Solving a Quadratic Equation Using the Zero-Factor Property

Step 1 Write the equation in standard form.

Step 2 Factor.

Step 3 Apply the zero-factor property.

Step 4 Solve the resulting equations.

Step 5 Check. Write the solution set.

The following are examples of quadratic equations.

$$x^2 - 144 = 0, \quad 2x^2 + 11x - 21 = 0 \quad \text{Both are in standard form.}$$

If $(x - 2)(x + 3) = 0$, then

$$x - 2 = 0 \quad \text{or} \quad x + 3 = 0,$$

leading to $\quad x = 2 \quad$ or $\quad x = -3.$

Solve. $\qquad 2x^2 = 7x + 15$

$$2x^2 - 7x - 15 = 0 \qquad \text{Standard form}$$
$$(2x + 3)(x - 5) = 0 \qquad \text{Factor.}$$
$$2x + 3 = 0 \quad \text{or} \quad x - 5 = 0 \quad \text{Zero-factor property}$$
$$x = -\frac{3}{2} \quad \text{or} \quad x = 5 \quad \text{Solve each equation.}$$

A check confirms that $-\frac{3}{2}$ and 5 satisfy the original equation.

Solution set: $\left\{-\frac{3}{2}, 5\right\}$

Concepts	Examples

6.8 Applications of Quadratic Equations

Step 1 Read the problem.

In a right triangle, one leg measures 2 ft longer than the other. The hypotenuse measures 4 ft longer than the shorter leg. Find the lengths of the three sides of the triangle.

Step 2 Assign a variable.

Let $x =$ the length of the shorter leg.

Then $x + 2 =$ the length of the longer leg,

and $x + 4 =$ the length of the hypotenuse.

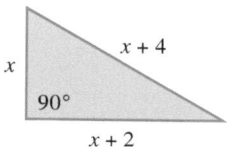

Step 3 Write an equation.

Step 4 Solve the equation.

$$\underset{\downarrow}{a^2} + \underset{\downarrow}{b^2} = \underset{\downarrow}{c^2}$$

$x^2 + (x + 2)^2 = (x + 4)^2$ Pythagorean theorem

$x^2 + x^2 + 4x + 4 = x^2 + 8x + 16$ Square each binomial.

$x^2 - 4x - 12 = 0$ Standard form

$(x - 6)(x + 2) = 0$ Factor.

$x - 6 = 0$ or $x + 2 = 0$ Zero-factor property

$x = 6$ or $x = -2$ Solve each equation.

Step 5 State the answer.

Because -2 cannot represent a length of a triangle, 6 is the only possible answer. The length of the shorter leg is 6 ft, the length of the longer leg is

$$6 + 2 = 8 \text{ ft,}$$

and the length of the hypotenuse is

$$6 + 4 = 10 \text{ ft.}$$

Step 6 Check.

Because $6^2 + 8^2 = 10^2$ is true, the answer is correct.

Chapter 6 *Review Exercises*

6.1 *Factor out the greatest common factor or factor by grouping.*

1. $15t + 45$

2. $60z^3 - 30z$

3. $44x^3 + 55x^2$

4. $100m^2n^3 - 50m^3n^4 + 150m^2n^2$

5. $2xy - 8y + 3x - 12$

6. $6y^2 + 9y + 4xy + 6x$

6.2 *Factor completely.*

7. $x^2 + 10x + 21$

8. $y^2 - 13y + 40$

9. $q^2 + 6q - 27$

10. $r^2 - r - 56$

11. $x^2 + x + 1$

12. $3x^2 + 6x + 6$

13. $r^2 - 4rs - 96s^2$

14. $p^2 + 2pq - 120q^2$

15. $-8p^3 + 24p^2 + 80p$

16. $3x^4 + 30x^3 + 48x^2$

17. $m^2 - 3mn - 18n^2$

18. $y^2 - 8yz + 15z^2$

19. $p^7 - p^6q - 2p^5q^2$

20. $-3r^5 + 6r^4s + 45r^3s^2$

6.3–6.4

21. CONCEPT CHECK To begin factoring
$$6r^2 - 5r - 6,$$
what are the possible first terms of the two binomial factors, if we consider only positive integer coefficients?

22. CONCEPT CHECK What is the first step we would use to factor the following trinomial?
$$2z^3 + 9z^2 - 5z$$

Factor completely.

23. $2k^2 - 5k + 2$

24. $3r^2 + 11r - 4$

25. $6r^2 - 5r - 6$

26. $10z^2 - 3z - 1$

27. $5t^2 - 11t + 12$

28. $24x^5 - 20x^4 + 4x^3$

29. $-6x^2 + 3x + 30$

30. $10r^3s + 17r^2s^2 + 6rs^3$

31. $-30y^3 - 5y^2 + 10y$

32. $4z^2 - 5z + 7$

33. $-3m^3n + 19m^2n + 40mn$

34. $14a^2 - 27ab - 20b^2$

6.5

35. CONCEPT CHECK   Which one of the following is a difference of squares?

   A. $32x^2 - 1$ **B.** $4x^2y^2 - 25z^2$

   C. $x^2 + 36$ **D.** $25y^3 - 1$

36. CONCEPT CHECK   Which one of the following is a perfect square trinomial?

   A. $x^2 + x + 1$ **B.** $y^2 - 4y + 9$

   C. $4x^2 + 10x + 25$ **D.** $x^2 - 20x + 100$

Factor completely.

37. $n^2 - 64$

38. $25b^2 - 121$

39. $49y^2 - 25w^2$

40. $9m^2 + 81$

41. $144p^2 - 36q^2$

42. $v^4 - 1$

43. $x^2 + 100$

44. $z^2 + 10z + 25$

45. $9t^2 - 42t + 49$

46. $16m^2 + 40mn + 25n^2$

47. $125x^3 - 1$

48. $1000p^3 + 27$

6.7

Solve each equation, and check the solutions.

49. $(4t + 3)(t - 1) = 0$

50. $(x + 7)(x - 4)(x + 3) = 0$

51. $x(2x - 5) = 0$

52. $z^2 + 4z + 3 = 0$

53. $m^2 - 5m + 4 = 0$

54. $x^2 = -15 + 8x$

55. $3z^2 - 11z - 20 = 0$

56. $81t^2 - 64 = 0$

57. $y^2 = 8y$

58. $n(n-5) = 6$

59. $t^2 + 14t + 49 = 0$

60. $t^2 = 12(t-3)$

61. $(5z + 2)(z^2 + 3z + 2) = 0$

62. $x^2 = 9$

63. $(x + 2)(x - 3) = 4x$

64. $(2r + 1)(12r^2 + 5r - 3) = 0$

65. $25w^2 - 90w + 81 = 0$

66. $r(r - 7) = 30$

6.8

Solve each problem. (If necessary, refer to the formulas at the back of this text.)

67. The length of a rectangular rug is 6 ft more than the width. The area is 40 ft^2. Find the length and width of the rug.

68. A treasure chest from a sunken galleon has dimensions (in feet) as shown in the figure. Its surface area is 650 ft^2. Find its width.

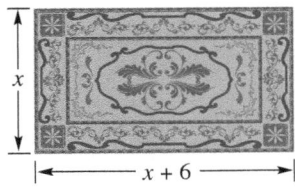

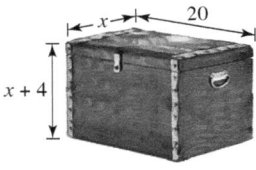

69. The product of two consecutive integers is 29 more than their sum. What are the integers?

70. The product of the lesser two of three consecutive integers is equal to 23 plus the greatest. Find the integers.

71. Two cars left an intersection at the same time. One traveled west, and the other traveled 14 mi less, but to the south. How far apart were they then, if the distance between them was 16 mi more than the distance traveled south?

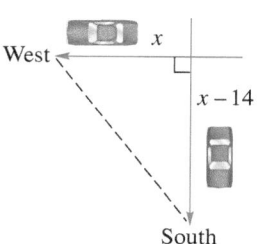

West ← x

$x - 14$

South

72. The triangular sail of a schooner has an area of 30 m². The height of the sail is 4 m more than the base. Find the length of the base of the sail.

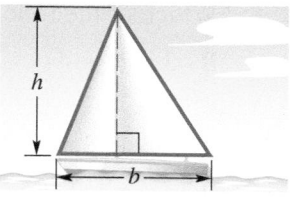

h

b

73. The floor plan for a house is a rectangle with length 7 m more than its width. The area is 170 m². Find the width and length of the house.

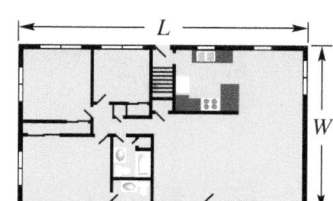

L

W

74. If an object is dropped, the distance d in feet it falls in t seconds (disregarding air resistance) is given by the quadratic equation

$$d = 16t^2.$$

Find the distance an object would fall in each of the following times.

(a) 4 sec   **(b)** 8 sec

The table shows the number of alternative fuel vehicles, in thousands, in use in the United States.

Year	Number (in thousands)
2001	425
2003	534
2005	592
2007	696
2009	826
2011	1192

Data from U.S. Department of Energy.

We used the data to develop the quadratic equation

$$y = 7.02x^2 - 15.5x + 469,$$

which models the number of vehicles y (in thousands) in year x, where x = 1 represents 2001, x = 2 represents 2002, and so on.

75. Use the model to find the number of alternative fuel vehicles in 2007, to the nearest thousand. How does the result compare with the actual data in the table?

76. Assuming that the trend in the data continues, use the quadratic equation to estimate the number of alternative fuel vehicles in 2013 to the nearest thousand.

Chapter 6   Mixed Review Exercises

1. CONCEPT CHECK   Which of the following is *not* factored completely?

A. $3(7 + t)$ **B.** $3x(7t + 4)$ **C.** $(3 + x)(7t + 4)$ **D.** $3(7t + 4) + x(7t + 4)$

2. CONCEPT CHECK   A student factored $6x^2 + 16x - 32$ as

$$(2x + 8)(3x - 4)$$

What Went Wrong?   Factor the trinomial correctly.

Factor completely.

3. $15m^2 + 20mp - 12m - 16p$ **4.** $24ab^3 - 56a^2bc^3 + 72a^2b^2$ **5.** $k^2 + 400$

6. $z^2 - 11zx + 10x^2$ **7.** $3k^2 + 11k + 10$ **8.** $y^4 - 625$

9. $6m^3 - 21m^2 - 45m$ **10.** $25a^2 + 15ab + 9b^2$ **11.** $8z^3 + 64y^3$

12. $-12r^2 - 8rq + 15q^2$ **13.** $100a^2 - 9$ **14.** $49t^2 + 56t + 16$

Solve each equation, and check the solutions.

15. $t(t - 7) = 0$ **16.** $x^2 + 3x = 10$ **17.** $25x^2 + 20x + 4 = 0$

18. $64x^3 - 9x = 0$ **19.** $6r^2 = 15 - r$ **20.** $(t + 1)(3t^2 + 19t + 6) = 0$

Solve each problem.

21. A lot is in the shape of a right triangle. The hypotenuse is 3 m longer than the longer leg. The longer leg is 6 m longer than twice the length of the shorter leg. Find the lengths of the sides of the lot.

22. A pyramid has a rectangular base with a length that is 2 m more than the width. The height of the pyramid is 6 m, and its volume is 48 m^3. Find the length and width of the base.

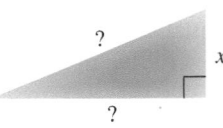

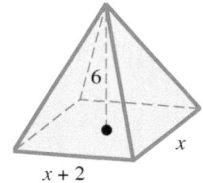

1. Which one of the following is the correct, completely factored form of
$2x^2 - 2x - 24$?

A. $(2x + 6)(x - 4)$ **B.** $(x + 3)(2x - 8)$

C. $2(x + 4)(x - 3)$ **D.** $2(x + 3)(x - 4)$

Factor completely.

2. $12x^2 - 30x$

3. $2m^3n^2 + 3m^3n - 5m^2n^2$

4. $2ax - 2bx + ay - by$

5. $x^2 - 9x + 14$

6. $t^2 + 7t + 10$

7. $6x^2 - 19x - 7$

8. $3x^2 - 12x - 15$

9. $10z^2 - 17z + 3$

10. $t^2 + 6t + 10$

11. $x^2 + 36$

12. $y^2 - 49$

13. $81a^2 - 121b^2$

14. $x^2 + 16x + 64$

15. $4x^2 - 28xy + 49y^2$

16. $-2x^2 - 4x - 2$

17. $4t^3 + 32t^2 + 64t$

18. $x^4 - 81$

19. $x^3 - 512$

20. $8k^3 + 64$

Solve each equation.

21. $(x + 3)(x - 9) = 0$

22. $2r^2 - 13r + 6 = 0$

23. $25x^2 - 4 = 0$

24. $x(x - 20) = -100$

25. $t^2 = 3t$

26. $(x + 8)(6x^2 + 13x - 5) = 0$

Solve each problem.

27. The length of a rectangular flower bed is 3 ft less than twice its width. The area of the bed is 54 ft². Find the dimensions of the flower bed.

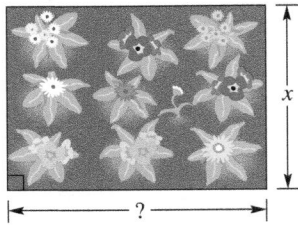

28. Find two consecutive integers such that the square of the sum of the two integers is 11 more than the lesser integer.

29. A carpenter needs to cut a brace to support a wall stud, as shown in the figure. The brace should be 7 ft less than three times the length of the stud. If the brace will be anchored on the floor 15 ft away from the stud, how long should the brace be?

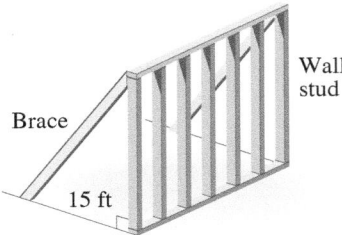

30. The public debt y (in billions of dollars) of the United States from 2000 through 2014 can be approximated by the quadratic equation

$$y = 57.53x^2 - 72.93x + 3417,$$

where $x = 0$ represents 2000, $x = 1$ represents 2001, and so on. Use the model to estimate the public debt, to the nearest billion dollars, in the year 2018. (Data from Bureau of Public Debt.)

Chapters R–6 *Cumulative Review Exercises*

Solve each equation.

1. $3x + 2(x - 4) = 4(x - 2)$

2. $0.3x + 0.9x = 0.06$

3. $\dfrac{2}{3}n - \dfrac{1}{2}(n - 4) = 3$

4. Solve for t: $A = P + Prt$

Solve each problem.

5. From a list of "technology-related items," 500 adults were surveyed as to those items they couldn't live without. Complete the results shown in the table.

Item	Percent That Couldn't Live Without	Number That Couldn't Live Without
Personal computer	46%	_____
Cell phone	41%	_____
High-speed Internet	_____	190
MP3 player	_____	60

(Other items included digital cable, HDTV, and electronic gaming console.)
Data from Ipsos for AP.

6. At the 2014 Winter Olympics in Sochi, Russia, the United States won a total of 28 medals. The United States won 2 more gold medals than silver and 5 fewer silver medals than bronze. Find the number of each type of medal won. (Data from *The Gazette*.)

7. In 2014, American women working full time earned, on average, 79 cents for every dollar earned by men working full time. The median annual salary for full-time male workers was $50,383. To the nearest dollar, what was the median annual salary for full-time female workers? (Data from U.S. Bureau of Labor Statistics.)

8. Find the measures of the marked angles.

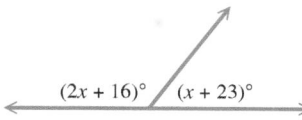

9. Fill in each blank with *positive* or *negative*. The point with coordinates (a, b) is in

   (a) quadrant II if a is _____ and b is _____ .

   (b) quadrant III if a is _____ and b is _____ .

Consider the equation $y = 4x + 3$. Find the following.

10. The x- and y-intercepts

11. The slope

12. The graph

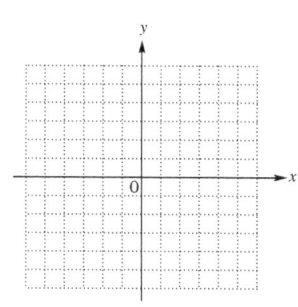

13. The points on the graph show total revenue, in billions of dollars, for Amazon in selected years (2011–2015), along with a graph of a linear equation that models the data.

(a) Use the ordered pairs shown on the graph to find the slope of the line. Interpret this slope.

(b) Use the graph to estimate revenue in the year 2014. Write the answer as an ordered pair of the form (year, sales in billions of dollars).

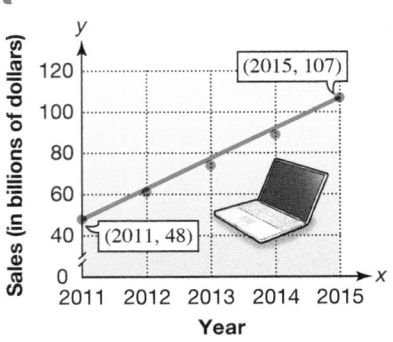

Amazon Revenues

(2015, 107)

(2011, 48)

Data from Market Watch.

Solve each system of equations.

14. $4x - y = -6$
$2x + 3y = 4$

15. $5x + 3y = 10$
$2x + \dfrac{6}{5}y = 5$

Evaluate each expression.

16. $2^{-3} \cdot 2^5$

17. $\left(\dfrac{3}{4}\right)^{-2}$

18. $\dfrac{6^5 \cdot 6^{-2}}{6^3}$

19. $\left(\dfrac{4^{-3} \cdot 4^4}{4^5}\right)^{-1}$

Simplify each expression and write the answer using only positive exponents. Assume no denominators are 0.

20. $\dfrac{(p^2)^3 p^{-4}}{(p^{-3})^{-1}p}$

21. $\dfrac{(m^{-2})^3 m}{m^5 m^{-4}}$

Perform the indicated operations.

22. $(2k^2 + 4k) - (5k^2 - 2) - (k^2 + 8k - 6)$

23. $(9x + 6)(5x - 3)$

24. $(3p + 2)^2$

25. $\dfrac{8x^4 + 12x^3 - 6x^2 + 20x}{2x}$

Factor completely.

26. $2a^2 + 7a - 4$

27. $10m^2 + 19m + 6$

28. $8t^2 + 10tv + 3v^2$

29. $4p^2 - 12p + 9$

30. $25r^2 - 81t^2$

31. $2pq + 6p^3q + 8p^2q$

Solve each equation.

32. $6m^2 + m - 2 = 0$

33. $8x^2 = 64x$

34. $49x^2 - 56x + 16 = 0$

35. The length of the hypotenuse of a right triangle is 3 m more than twice the length of the shorter leg. The longer leg is 7 m longer than the shorter leg. Find the lengths of the sides.

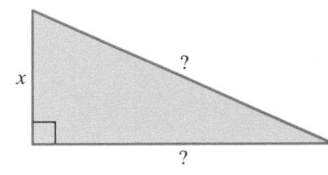

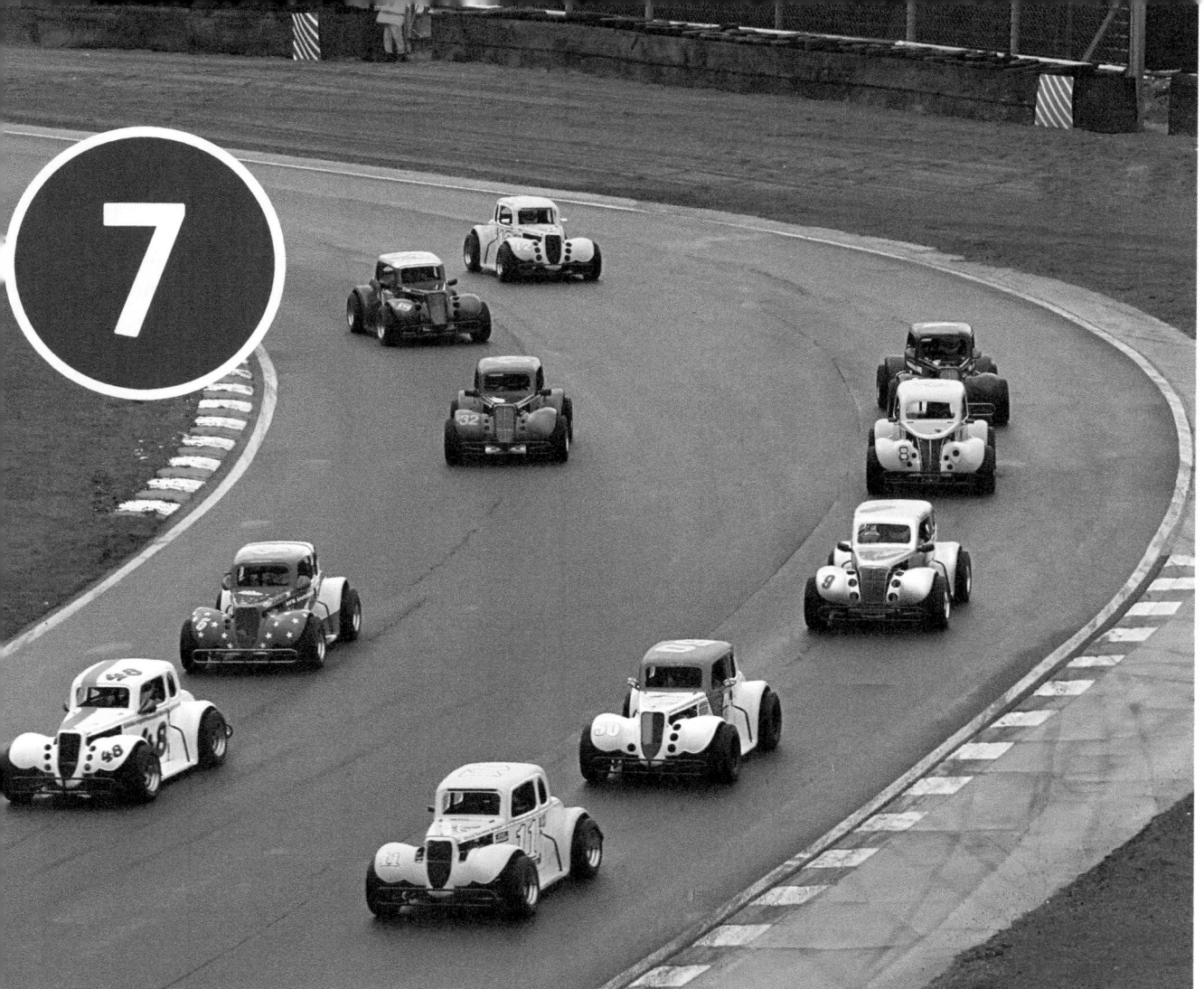

7

Rational Expressions and Applications

The formula $r = \frac{d}{t}$ gives the rate r of a speeding car in terms of its distance d and its time t traveled. This formula involves a *rational expression* (or *algebraic fraction*), the subject of this chapter.

7.1 The Fundamental Property of Rational Expressions

7.2 Multiplying and Dividing Rational Expressions

7.3 Least Common Denominators

7.4 Adding and Subtracting Rational Expressions

7.5 Complex Fractions

7.6 Solving Equations with Rational Expressions

Summary Exercises *Simplifying Rational Expressions vs. Solving Rational Equations*

7.7 Applications of Rational Expressions

7.1 The Fundamental Property of Rational Expressions

OBJECTIVES

1. Find the numerical value of a rational expression.

2. Find the values of the variable for which a rational expression is undefined.

3. Write rational expressions in lowest terms.

4. Recognize equivalent forms of rational expressions.

The quotient of two integers (with denominator not 0), such as $\frac{2}{3}$ or $-\frac{3}{4}$, is a *rational number*. In the same way, the quotient of two polynomials with denominator not equal to 0 is a *rational expression*.

Rational Expression

A **rational expression** is an expression of the form $\frac{P}{Q}$, where P and Q are polynomials and $Q \neq 0$.

Examples: $\dfrac{-6x}{x^3 + 8}$, $\dfrac{9x}{y + 3}$, and $\dfrac{2m^3}{8}$ Rational expressions

---

Our work with rational expressions will require much of what we learned on polynomials and factoring, as well as the rules for arithmetic fractions.

OBJECTIVE ▶ 1 Find the numerical value of a rational expression. Remember that to *evaluate* an expression means to find its *value*. We use substitution to evaluate a rational expression for a given value of the variable.

---

1 Find the numerical value of each rational expression for $x = -3$, $x = 0$, and $x = 3$.

(GS) (a) $\dfrac{x}{2x + 1}$

For $x = -3$:

$$\dfrac{x}{2x + 1}$$

$$= \dfrac{\underline{}}{2(\underline{}) + 1}$$

$$= \dfrac{-3}{\underline{} + 1}$$

$$= \underline{}$$

(b) $\dfrac{2x + 6}{x - 3}$

EXAMPLE 1   Evaluating Rational Expressions

Find the numerical value of $\frac{3x + 6}{2x - 4}$ for each value of x.

(a) $x = 1$

$$\dfrac{3x + 6}{2x - 4}$$

$$= \dfrac{3(1) + 6}{2(1) - 4} \quad \text{Let } x = 1.$$

$$= \dfrac{9}{-2}$$

$$= -\dfrac{9}{2} \qquad \frac{a}{-b} = -\frac{a}{b}$$

(b) $x = 0$

$$\dfrac{3x + 6}{2x - 4}$$

$$= \dfrac{3(0) + 6}{2(0) - 4} \quad \text{Let } x = 0.$$

$$= \dfrac{6}{-4}$$

$$= -\dfrac{3}{2} \qquad \text{Lowest terms}$$

(c) $x = 2$

$$\dfrac{3x + 6}{2x - 4}$$

$$= \dfrac{3(2) + 6}{2(2) - 4} \quad \text{Let } x = 2.$$

$$= \dfrac{12}{0} \quad \boxed{\begin{array}{c}\text{The expression}\\\text{is undefined for}\\ x = 2.\end{array}}$$

(d) $x = -2$

$$\dfrac{3x + 6}{2x - 4}$$

$$= \dfrac{3(-2) + 6}{2(-2) - 4} \quad \text{Let } x = -2.$$

$$= \dfrac{0}{-8}$$

$$= 0 \qquad \frac{0}{b} = 0$$

◀ **Work Problem 1 at the Side.**

Answers

1. (a) For $x = -3$: -3; -3; -6; $\dfrac{3}{5}$;

for $x = 0$, final answer 0;

for $x = 3$, final answer $\dfrac{3}{7}$

(b) 0; -2; undefined

Note

> *The numerator of a rational expression may be any real number.* If the numerator equals 0 and the denominator does not equal 0, then the rational expression equals 0. **See Example 1(d).**

OBJECTIVE ▶ ❷ **Find the values of the variable for which a rational expression is undefined.** In the definition of a rational expression $\frac{P}{Q}$, Q cannot equal 0. *The denominator of a rational expression cannot equal 0 because division by 0 is undefined.* For example, in the rational expression

$$\frac{8x^2}{x - 3},\ \leftarrow \text{Denominator cannot equal 0.}$$

the variable x can take on any real number value except 3. When x is 3, the denominator becomes $3 - 3 = 0$, making the expression undefined. Thus, x cannot equal 3. We indicate this restriction by writing $x \neq 3$.

Determining When a Rational Expression Is Undefined

Step 1   Set the denominator of the rational expression equal to 0.

Step 2   Solve this equation.

Step 3   The solutions of the equation are the values that make the rational expression undefined. The variable *cannot* equal these values.

EXAMPLE 2   **Finding Values That Make Rational Expressions Undefined**

Find values of the variable for which each rational expression is undefined.

(a) $\dfrac{x + 5}{3x + 2}$ We must find any value of x that makes the *denominator* equal to **0** because division by 0 is undefined.

Step 1 $3x + 2 = 0$ Set the denominator equal to 0.

Step 2   Solve. $3x = -2$ Subtract 2.

$$x = -\frac{2}{3}\qquad \text{Divide by 3.}$$

Step 3   The given expression is undefined for $-\frac{2}{3}$, so $x \neq -\frac{2}{3}$.

(b) $\dfrac{9m^2}{m^2 - 5m + 6}$

$m^2 - 5m + 6 = 0$ Set the denominator equal to 0.

$(m - 2)(m - 3) = 0$ Factor.

$m - 2 = 0$ or $m - 3 = 0$ Zero-factor property

$m = 2$ or $m = 3$ Solve for m.

The given expression is undefined for 2 and 3, so $m \neq 2$, $m \neq 3$.

(c) $\dfrac{2r}{r^2 + 1}$ This denominator will not equal 0 for any value of r, because r^2 is always greater than or equal to 0, and adding 1 makes the sum greater than or equal to 1. There are no values for which this expression is undefined.

——— **Work Problem** ❷ **at the Side.** ▶

❷ Find values of the variable for which each rational expression is undefined. Write answers with the symbol $\neq$.

GS (a) $\dfrac{x + 2}{x - 5}$

Step 1 _____ $= 0$

Step 2 $x =$ ____

Step 3 The given expression is undefined for ____ . Thus,

$$x\,(=/\neq)\,5.$$

(b) $\dfrac{3r}{r^2 + 6r + 8}$

(c) $\dfrac{-5m}{m^2 + 4}$

Answers

2. (a) $x - 5$; 5; 5; $\neq$
(b) $r \neq -4$, $r \neq -2$
(c) The expression is never undefined.

510 Chapter 7 Rational Expressions and Applications

3 Write each expression in lowest terms.

(a) $\dfrac{15}{40}$

(b) $\dfrac{5x^4}{15x^2}$

(c) $\dfrac{6p^3}{2p^2}$

OBJECTIVE **3** **Write rational expressions in lowest terms.** A common fraction such as $\frac{2}{3}$ is said to be in *lowest terms*.

> **Lowest Terms**
>
> A rational expression $\frac{P}{Q}$ (where $Q \neq 0$) is in **lowest terms** if the greatest common factor of its numerator and denominator is 1.

We use the **fundamental property of rational expressions** to write a rational expression in lowest terms.

> **Fundamental Property of Rational Expressions**
>
> If $\frac{P}{Q}$ (where $Q \neq 0$) is a rational expression and if K represents any polynomial (where $K \neq 0$), then the following holds true.
>
> $$\frac{PK}{QK} = \frac{P}{Q}$$

This property is based on the identity property of multiplication.

$$\frac{PK}{QK} = \frac{P}{Q} \cdot \frac{K}{K} = \frac{P}{Q} \cdot 1 = \frac{P}{Q}$$

EXAMPLE 3 Writing in Lowest Terms

Write each expression in lowest terms.

(a) $\dfrac{30}{72}$ Rational number

Begin by factoring.

$$= \frac{2 \cdot 3 \cdot 5}{2 \cdot 2 \cdot 2 \cdot 3 \cdot 3}$$

(b) $\dfrac{14k^2}{2k^3}$ Rational expression

Write k^2 as $k \cdot k$ and k^3 as $k \cdot k \cdot k$.

$$= \frac{2 \cdot 7 \cdot k \cdot k}{2 \cdot k \cdot k \cdot k}$$

Group any factors common to the numerator and denominator.

$$= \frac{5 \cdot (2 \cdot 3)}{2 \cdot 2 \cdot 3 \cdot (2 \cdot 3)}$$

$$= \frac{7 (2 \cdot k \cdot k)}{k (2 \cdot k \cdot k)}$$

Use the fundamental property.

$$= \frac{5}{2 \cdot 2 \cdot 3}$$

$$= \frac{7}{k}$$

$$= \frac{5}{12}$$

◀ **Work Problem 3** at the Side

> **Writing a Rational Expression in Lowest Terms**
>
> *Step 1*   **Factor** the numerator and denominator completely.
>
> *Step 2*   **Use the fundamental property** to divide out any common factors.

Answers

3. (a) $\dfrac{3}{8}$ (b) $\dfrac{x^2}{3}$ (c) $3p$

| EXAMPLE 4 | Writing in Lowest Terms |

Write each rational expression in lowest terms.

(a) $\dfrac{3x - 12}{5x - 20}$

> $x \neq 4$ because the denominator is 0 for this value.

Step 1 $= \dfrac{3(x - 4)}{5(x - 4)}$ Factor.

Step 2 $= \dfrac{3}{5}$ $\frac{x-4}{x-4} = 1$; Fundamental property

The given expression is equal to $\frac{3}{5}$ for all values of x, where $x \neq 4$ (because the denominator of the original rational expression is 0 when x is 4).

(b) $\dfrac{2y^2 - 8}{2y + 4}$

> $y \neq -2$ because the denominator is 0 for this value.

Step 1 $= \dfrac{2(y^2 - 4)}{2(y + 2)}$ Factor.

$= \dfrac{2(y + 2)(y - 2)}{2(y + 2)}$ Factor the numerator completely. $y^2 - 4$ is a difference of squares.

Step 2 $= y - 2$ $\frac{2(y+2)}{2(y+2)} = 1$; Fundamental property

(c) $\dfrac{m^2 + 2m - 8}{2m^2 - m - 6}$

Step 1 $= \dfrac{(m + 4)(m - 2)}{(2m + 3)(m - 2)}$

> $m \neq -\frac{3}{2}, m \neq 2$
> Factor.

Step 2 $= \dfrac{m + 4}{2m + 3}$ $\frac{m-2}{m-2} = 1$; Fundamental property

From now on, we write statements of equality of rational expressions with the understanding that they apply only to those real numbers that make neither denominator equal to 0.

(d) $\dfrac{4m + 12 - mp - 3p}{5m + mp + 15 + 3p}$ The numerator and denominator each have four terms, so try to factor by grouping.

Step 1 $= \dfrac{(4m + 12) + (-mp - 3p)}{(5m + mp) + (15 + 3p)}$ Group terms in the numerator.
      Group terms in the denominator.

$= \dfrac{4(m + 3) - p(m + 3)}{m(5 + p) + 3(5 + p)}$ Factor each group.

$= \dfrac{(m + 3)(4 - p)}{(5 + p)(m + 3)}$ Factor out $m + 3$.
      Factor out $5 + p$.

Step 2 $= \dfrac{4 - p}{5 + p}$ $\frac{m+3}{m+3} = 1$; Fundamental property

— Work Problem ④ at the Side. ▶

---

④ Write each rational expression in lowest terms.

(a) $\dfrac{4y + 2}{6y + 3}$

$= \dfrac{2(\underline{\qquad})}{3(\underline{\qquad})}$

$= \underline{\qquad}$

(b) $\dfrac{8p + 8q}{5p + 5q}$

(c) $\dfrac{x^2 + 4x + 4}{4x + 8}$

(d) $\dfrac{a^2 - b^2}{a^2 + 2ab + b^2}$

(e) $\dfrac{xy + 5y - 2x - 10}{xy + 3x + 5y + 15}$

Answers

4. **(a)** $2y + 1; 2y + 1; \dfrac{2}{3}$ **(b)** $\dfrac{8}{5}$

   (c) $\dfrac{x + 2}{4}$ **(d)** $\dfrac{a - b}{a + b}$ **(e)** $\dfrac{y - 2}{y + 3}$

5 Write $\frac{m-n}{n-m}$ in lowest terms.

Rational expressions cannot be written in lowest terms until after the numerator and denominator have been factored. Only common factors can be divided out, not common terms.

$$\frac{6x+9}{4x+6} = \frac{3(2x+3)}{2(2x+3)} = \frac{3}{2} \qquad \Big| \qquad \frac{6+x}{4x} \quad \leftarrow \text{Numerator cannot be factored.}$$

Divide out the common factor.   Already in lowest terms

EXAMPLE 5 **Writing in Lowest Terms (Factors Are Opposites)**

Write $\frac{x-y}{y-x}$ in lowest terms.

To find a common factor, the denominator $y-x$ can be factored as follows.

$y-x$ We are factoring out -1, **NOT** multiplying by it.

$= -1(-y+x)$ Factor out -1.

$= -1(x-y)$ Commutative property, $a+b=b+a$

With this result in mind, we simplify as follows.

$$\frac{x-y}{y-x}$$

$$= \frac{1(x-y)}{-1(x-y)} \qquad y-x = -1(x-y) \text{ from above.}$$

$$= \frac{1}{-1} \qquad \text{Fundamental property}$$

$$= -1 \qquad \text{Lowest terms}$$

Alternatively, we could factor -1 from the numerator $x-y$.

$$\frac{x-y}{y-x} \qquad \text{Alternative solution}$$

$$= \frac{-1(-x+y)}{y-x} \qquad \text{Factor out } -1 \text{ in the numerator.}$$

$$= \frac{-1(y-x)}{y-x} \qquad \text{Commutative property}$$

$$= -1 \qquad \text{The result is the same.}$$

◀ **Work Problem 5 at the Side.**

Although x and y appear in both the numerator and denominator in **Example 5**, we cannot use the fundamental property right away because they are *terms*, not *factors*. ***Terms are added, while factors are multiplied.***

Answer

5. -1

In **Example 5,** notice that $y - x$ is the **opposite** (or **additive inverse**) of $x - y$. A general rule for this situation follows.

> #### Quotient of Opposites
>
> If the numerator and the denominator of a rational expression are opposites, such as in $\frac{x-y}{y-x}$, then the rational expression is equal to -1.

Based on this result, the following are true.

Numerator and denominator are opposites. $\longrightarrow$ $\dfrac{q-7}{7-q} = -1$ and $\dfrac{-5a+2b}{5a-2b} = -1$

However, the following expression cannot be simplified further.

$$\dfrac{x-2}{x+2} \longleftarrow \text{Numerator and denominator} \atop \longleftarrow \text{are } not \text{ opposites.}$$

EXAMPLE 6 Writing in Lowest Terms (Factors Are Opposites)

Write each rational expression in lowest terms.

(a) $\dfrac{2-m}{m-2}$

Because $2 - m$ and $m - 2$ (or $-2 + m$) are opposites, this expression equals -1.

(b) $\dfrac{4x^2 - 9}{6 - 4x}$

$= \dfrac{(2x+3)(2x-3)}{2(3-2x)}$ Factor the numerator and denominator.

$= \dfrac{(2x+3)(2x-3)}{2(-1)(2x-3)}$ Write $3 - 2x$ in the denominator as $-1(2x-3)$.

$= \dfrac{2x+3}{2(-1)}$ Fundamental property

$= \dfrac{2x+3}{-2}$ Multiply in the denominator.

$= -\dfrac{2x+3}{2}$ $\frac{a}{-b} = -\frac{a}{b}$

(c) $\dfrac{3+r}{3-r}$ $3 - r$ is *not* the opposite of $3 + r$.

The rational expression is already in lowest terms.

─────────────────── **Work Problem** ⑥ **at the Side.** ▶

OBJECTIVE ▶ ④ **Recognize equivalent forms of rational expressions.** It is important to recognize equivalent forms of expressions. For example,

$$0.5, \quad \frac{1}{2}, \quad 50\%, \quad \text{and} \quad \frac{50}{100} \quad \text{Equivalent expressions}$$

all represent the *same* real number. On a number line, the exact same point would apply to all four of them.

⑥ Write each rational expression in lowest terms.

(a) $\dfrac{5-y}{y-5}$

(b) $\dfrac{25x^2 - 16}{12 - 15x}$

$= \dfrac{(5x+4)(\underline{\hspace{1cm}})}{3(\underline{\hspace{1cm}})}$

$= \dfrac{(5x+4)(5x-4)}{3(\underline{\hspace{0.5cm}})(5x-4)}$

$= \underline{\hspace{1.5cm}}$

(c) $\dfrac{9-k}{9+k}$

Answers

6. **(a)** -1

    (b) $5x - 4; \ 4 - 5x; \ -1; \ \dfrac{5x+4}{-3}$, or $-\dfrac{5x+4}{3}$

    (c) It is already in lowest terms.

7 Which rational expressions are equivalent to

$$-\frac{2x - 6}{x + 3}?$$

A. $\dfrac{-(2x - 6)}{x + 3}$

B. $\dfrac{-2x + 6}{x + 3}$

C. $\dfrac{-2x - 6}{x + 3}$

D. $\dfrac{2x - 6}{-(x + 3)}$

E. $\dfrac{2x - 6}{-x - 3}$

F. $\dfrac{2x - 6}{x - 3}$

A similar situation exists with negative common fractions. The common fraction $-\frac{5}{6}$ can also be written $\frac{-5}{6}$ and $\frac{5}{-6}$, with the negative sign appearing in any of three different positions. All represent the *same* rational number.

Consider the following rational expression.

$$-\frac{2x + 3}{2} \quad \begin{array}{l} \text{Final result from \textbf{Example 6(b)}} \\ \text{in the form } -\frac{a}{b} \end{array}$$

The $-$ sign representing the factor -1 is in front of the expression, aligned with the fraction bar. Although we usually give answers in this form, it is important to be able to recognize other equivalent forms of a rational expression. The factor -1 may instead be placed in the numerator or in the denominator.

Use parentheses.

$$\frac{-(2x + 3)}{2} \quad \text{and} \quad \frac{2x + 3}{-2}$$

In the first of these two expressions, the distributive property can be applied. Thus,

$$\frac{-(2x + 3)}{2} \quad \text{can also be written} \quad \frac{-2x - 3}{2}. \quad \begin{array}{l}\text{Multiply \textit{each} term in}\\\text{the binomial by } -1.\end{array}$$

> **! CAUTION**
> $\frac{-2x + 3}{2}$ is *not* an equivalent form of $\frac{-(2x + 3)}{2}$. **Be careful to apply the distributive property correctly.**

> **EXAMPLE 7** Writing Equivalent Forms of a Rational Expression
>
> Write four equivalent forms of the following rational expression.
>
> $$-\frac{3x + 2}{x - 6}$$
>
> If we apply the negative sign to the numerator, we obtain these equivalent forms.
>
> $$① \rightarrow \frac{-(3x + 2)}{x - 6}, \quad \text{and, by the distributive property,} \quad \frac{-3x - 2}{x - 6} \leftarrow ②$$
>
> If we apply the negative sign to the denominator, we obtain two additional forms.
>
> $$③ \rightarrow \frac{3x + 2}{-(x - 6)} \quad \text{and, by distributing once again,} \quad \frac{3x + 2}{-x + 6} \leftarrow ④$$

◀ **Work Problem 7 at the Side.**

> **! CAUTION**
> Recall that $-\frac{5}{6} \neq \frac{-5}{-6}$. Thus, in **Example 7**, it would be incorrect to distribute the negative sign in $-\frac{3x + 2}{x - 6}$ to *both* the numerator *and* the denominator. (Doing this would actually lead to the *opposite* of the original expression.)

Answer

7. A, B, D, E

7.1 Exercises

FOR EXTRA HELP

Go to MyMathLab for worked-out, step-by-step solutions to exercises enclosed in a square ▢ and video solutions to ▶ exercises.

CONCEPT CHECK *Fill in each blank with the correct response.*

1. The rational expression $\frac{x-5}{x+3}$ is undefined when x is _____ , so $x \neq$ _____ .
This rational expression is equal to 0 when $x =$ _____ .

2. The rational expression $\frac{p-q}{q-p}$ is undefined when the values of p and _____ are
the same, so $p \neq$ _____ . In all other cases, $\frac{p-q}{q-p}$ is equal to _____ .

3. CONCEPT CHECK Which rational expressions are equivalent to $-\frac{a}{b}$?

A. $\dfrac{a}{b}$ **B.** $\dfrac{a}{-b}$ **C.** $\dfrac{-a}{b}$ **D.** $\dfrac{-a}{-b}$ **E.** $-\dfrac{a}{-b}$ **F.** $-\dfrac{-a}{b}$

4. CONCEPT CHECK Make the correct choice to complete each statement.

(a) $\dfrac{4-r^2}{4+r^2}$ *(is/is not)* equal to -1.

(b) $\dfrac{5+2x}{3-x}$ and $\dfrac{-5-2x}{x-3}$ *(are/are not)* equivalent rational expressions.

5. Define *rational expression,* and give an example.

6. Why can't the denominator of a rational expression equal 0?

Find the numerical value of each rational expression for **(a)** $x = 2$ *and* **(b)** $x = -3$.
See Example 1.

7. $\dfrac{3x+1}{5x}$ **8.** $\dfrac{5x-2}{4x}$ **9.** $\dfrac{x^2-4}{2x+1}$ **10.** $\dfrac{2x^2-4x}{3x-1}$

11. $\dfrac{(-3x)^2}{4x+12}$ **12.** $\dfrac{(-2x)^3}{3x+9}$ **13.** $\dfrac{5x+2}{2x^2+11x+12}$ **14.** $\dfrac{7-3x}{3x^2-7x+2}$

Find any value(s) of the variable for which each rational expression is undefined.
Write answers with the symbol $\neq$. See Example 2.

15. $\dfrac{2}{5y}$ **16.** $\dfrac{7}{3z}$ **17.** $\dfrac{x+1}{x+6}$ **18.** $\dfrac{m+2}{m+5}$

19. $\dfrac{4x^2}{3x-5}$ **20.** $\dfrac{2x^3}{3x-4}$ **21.** $\dfrac{m+2}{m^2+m-6}$ **22.** $\dfrac{r-5}{r^2-5r+4}$

23. $\dfrac{x^2-3x}{4}$ **24.** $\dfrac{x^2-4x}{6}$ **25.** $\dfrac{3x}{x^2+2}$ **26.** $\dfrac{4q}{q^2+9}$

Write each rational number in lowest terms. **See Example 3(a).**

27. $\dfrac{36}{84}$

28. $\dfrac{16}{60}$

29. $\dfrac{54}{198}$

30. $\dfrac{48}{108}$

Write each rational expression in lowest terms. **See Examples 3(b) and 4.**

31. $\dfrac{18r^3}{6r}$

32. $\dfrac{27p^2}{3p}$

33. $\dfrac{4(y-2)}{10(y-2)}$

34. $\dfrac{15(m-1)}{9(m-1)}$

35. $\dfrac{(x+1)(x-1)}{(x+1)^2}$

36. $\dfrac{(t+5)(t-3)}{(t-1)(t+5)}$

37. $\dfrac{7m+14}{5m+10}$

38. $\dfrac{5r+20}{3r+12}$

39. $\dfrac{16x-8}{14x-7}$

40. $\dfrac{21x-7}{9x-3}$

41. $\dfrac{m^2-n^2}{m+n}$

42. $\dfrac{a^2-b^2}{a-b}$

43. $\dfrac{12m^2-3}{8m-4}$

44. $\dfrac{20p^2-45}{6p-9}$

45. $\dfrac{3m^2-3m}{5m-5}$

46. $\dfrac{6t^2-6t}{2t-2}$

47. $\dfrac{9r^2-4s^2}{9r+6s}$

48. $\dfrac{16x^2-9y^2}{12x-9y}$

49. $\dfrac{2x^2-3x-5}{2x^2-7x+5}$

50. $\dfrac{3x^2+8x+4}{3x^2-4x-4}$

51. $\dfrac{zw+4z-3w-12}{zw+4z+5w+20}$

52. $\dfrac{km+4k+4m+16}{km+4k+5m+20}$

53. $\dfrac{ac-ad+bc-bd}{ac-ad-bc+bd}$

54. $\dfrac{rt-ru-st+su}{rt-ru+st-su}$

Write each rational expression in lowest terms. **See Examples 5 and 6.**

55. $\dfrac{6-t}{t-6}$

56. $\dfrac{2-k}{k-2}$

57. $\dfrac{m^2-1}{1-m}$

58. $\dfrac{a^2-b^2}{b-a}$

59. $\dfrac{q^2-4q}{4q-q^2}$

60. $\dfrac{z^2-5z}{5z-z^2}$

61. $\dfrac{p+6}{p-6}$

62. $\dfrac{5-x}{5+x}$

Write four equivalent forms of each rational expression. **See Example 7.**

63. $-\dfrac{x+4}{x-3}$

64. $-\dfrac{x+6}{x-1}$

65. $-\dfrac{2x-3}{x+3}$

66. $-\dfrac{5x-6}{x+4}$

67. $-\dfrac{3x-1}{5x-6}$

68. $-\dfrac{2x-9}{7x-1}$

Solve each problem. (Assume all measures are given in appropriate units.)

69. The area of the rectangle is represented by
$$x^4 + 10x^2 + 21.$$

Find the polynomial that represents the width of the rectangle. $\left(\text{ Hint: Use } W = \frac{A}{L}.\right)$

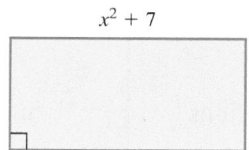

$x^2 + 7$

70. The volume of the box is represented by
$$(x^2 + 8x + 15)(x + 4).$$

Find the polynomial that represents the area of the bottom of the box.

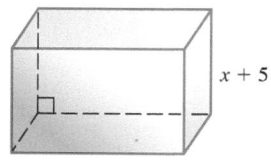

$x + 5$

The percent of deaths caused by smoking is modeled by the rational expression
$$\frac{x - 1}{x},$$

*where x is the number that tells how many times more likely a smoker is than a nonsmoker to die of lung cancer. This is called the **incidence rate.** (Data from Walker, A., Observation and Inference: An Introduction to the Methods of Epidemiology, Epidemiology Resources Inc.) For example, x = 10 means that a smoker is 10 times more likely than a nonsmoker to die of lung cancer.*

71. Find the percent of deaths if the incidence rate is the given number.

(a) 5   (b) 10   (c) 20

72. Can the incidence rate equal 0? Explain.

Relating Concepts (Exercises 73–75) For Individual or Group Work

We have used long division to find a quotient of two polynomials. We obtain the same quotient by expressing a division problem as a rational expression (algebraic fraction) and writing this rational expression in lowest terms, as shown below.

$$\begin{array}{r} x + 4 \\ 2x - 3\overline{)2x^2 + 5x - 12} \\ -(2x^2 - 3x) \\ \hline 8x - 12 \\ -(8x - 12) \\ \hline 0 \end{array}$$

$$\frac{2x^2 + 5x - 12}{2x - 3}$$

$$= \frac{(2x - 3)(x + 4)}{2x - 3} \qquad \text{Factor.}$$

$$= x + 4 \qquad \text{Fundamental property}$$

Perform the long division. Then simplify the rational expression to show that the result is the same.

73. $4x + 7\overline{)8x^2 + 26x + 21}$

and $\dfrac{8x^2 + 26x + 21}{4x + 7}$

74. $6x + 5\overline{)12x^2 + 16x + 5}$

and $\dfrac{12x^2 + 16x + 5}{6x + 5}$

75. $x + 1\overline{)x^3 + x^2 + x + 1}$

and $\dfrac{x^3 + x^2 + x + 1}{x + 1}$

7.2 Multiplying and Dividing Rational Expressions

OBJECTIVES

1. Multiply rational expressions.
2. Find reciprocals.
3. Divide rational expressions.

OBJECTIVE ▶ **1** **Multiply rational expressions.** The product of two common fractions is found by multiplying the numerators and multiplying the denominators. Rational expressions are multiplied in the same way.

Multiplying Rational Expressions

The product of the rational expressions $\frac{P}{Q}$ and $\frac{R}{S}$ is defined as follows.

$$\frac{P}{Q} \cdot \frac{R}{S} = \frac{PR}{QS}$$

In words: **To multiply rational expressions, multiply the numerators and multiply the denominators.**

1 Multiply. Write each answer in lowest terms.

(a) $\frac{2}{7} \cdot \frac{5}{10}$

(b) $\frac{3m^2}{2} \cdot \frac{10}{m}$

2 Multiply. Write each answer in lowest terms.

(a) $\frac{a+b}{5} \cdot \frac{30}{2(a+b)}$

(b) $\frac{3(p-q)}{q^2} \cdot \frac{q}{2(p-q)^2}$

EXAMPLE 1 Multiplying Rational Expressions

Multiply. Write each answer in lowest terms.

(a) $\frac{3}{10} \cdot \frac{5}{9}$ Rational numbers

(b) $\frac{6}{x} \cdot \frac{x^2}{12}$ Rational expressions

Indicate the product of the numerators and the product of the denominators.

$$= \frac{3 \cdot 5}{10 \cdot 9} \qquad\qquad = \frac{6 \cdot x^2}{x \cdot 12}$$

Leave the products in factored form. Factor the numerator and denominator to further identify any common factors. Then use the fundamental property to divide out any common factors and write each product in lowest terms.

$$= \frac{3 \cdot 5}{2 \cdot 5 \cdot 3 \cdot 3} \qquad\qquad = \frac{6 \cdot x \cdot x}{2 \cdot 6 \cdot x}$$

$$= \frac{1}{6} \quad \boxed{\text{Remember to write 1 in the numerator.}} \qquad = \frac{x}{2}$$

◀ **Work Problem** **1** **at the Side.**

EXAMPLE 2 Multiplying Rational Expressions

Multiply. Write the answer in lowest terms.

$$\frac{x+y}{2x} \cdot \frac{x^2}{(x+y)^2}$$

$\boxed{\text{Use parentheses here around } x+y.}$

$$= \frac{(x+y)x^2}{2x(x+y)^2} \qquad \text{Multiply numerators.}$$
$$\text{Multiply denominators.}$$

$$= \frac{(x+y)x \cdot x}{2x(x+y)(x+y)} \qquad \text{Factor. Identify the common factors.}$$

$$= \frac{x}{2(x+y)} \qquad \frac{(x+y)x}{x(x+y)} = 1; \text{ Write in lowest terms.}$$

◀ **Work Problem** **2** **at the Side.**

Answers

1. **(a)** $\frac{1}{7}$ **(b)** $15m$

2. **(a)** 3 **(b)** $\frac{3}{2q(p-q)}$

EXAMPLE 3 **Multiplying Rational Expressions**

Multiply. Write the answer in lowest terms.

$$\frac{x^2 + 3x}{x^2 - 3x - 4} \cdot \frac{x^2 - 5x + 4}{x^2 + 2x - 3}$$

$$= \frac{(x^2 + 3x)(x^2 - 5x + 4)}{(x^2 - 3x - 4)(x^2 + 2x - 3)} \qquad \text{Definition of multiplication}$$

$$= \frac{x(x + 3)(x - 4)(x - 1)}{(x - 4)(x + 1)(x + 3)(x - 1)} \qquad \text{Factor.}$$

$$= \frac{x}{x + 1} \qquad \qquad \begin{array}{l}\text{Divide out the common factors.}\\ \text{The result is in lowest terms.}\end{array}$$

The quotients $\frac{x+3}{x+3}$, $\frac{x-4}{x-4}$, and $\frac{x-1}{x-1}$ are all equal to 1, justifying the final product $\frac{x}{x+1}$.

───────── **Work Problem ③ at the Side.** ▶

OBJECTIVE ▶ ② Find reciprocals. If the product of two rational expressions is 1, the rational expressions are **reciprocals** (or **multiplicative inverses**) of each other. The reciprocal of a rational expression is found by interchanging the numerator and the denominator.

$$\frac{2x - 1}{x - 5} \quad \text{has reciprocal} \quad \frac{x - 5}{2x - 1}.$$

EXAMPLE 4 **Finding Reciprocals of Rational Expressions**

Find the reciprocal of each rational expression.

(a) $\dfrac{4p^3}{9q}$ has reciprocal $\dfrac{9q}{4p^3}.$ Interchange the numerator and denominator.

(b) $\dfrac{k^2 - 9}{k^2 - k - 20}$ has reciprocal $\dfrac{k^2 - k - 20}{k^2 - 9}.$ Reciprocals have product 1.

───────── **Work Problem ④ at the Side.** ▶

OBJECTIVE ▶ ③ Divide rational expressions. Suppose we have $\frac{7}{8}$ gal of milk and want to find how many quarts we have. Because 1 qt is $\frac{1}{4}$ gal, we ask, "*How many $\frac{1}{4}$s are there in $\frac{7}{8}$?*" This would be interpreted as follows.

$$\frac{7}{8} \div \frac{1}{4}, \quad \text{which can be written} \quad \frac{\frac{7}{8}}{\frac{1}{4}} \leftarrow \text{The fraction bar means division.}$$

The fundamental property of rational expressions can be applied to rational number values of P, Q, and K.

$$\frac{P}{Q} = \frac{P \cdot K}{Q \cdot K} = \frac{\frac{7}{8} \cdot \frac{4}{1}}{\frac{1}{4} \cdot \frac{4}{1}} = \frac{\frac{7}{8} \cdot \frac{4}{1}}{1} = \frac{7}{8} \cdot \frac{4}{1} \qquad \begin{array}{l}\text{Let } P = \frac{7}{8}, Q = \frac{1}{4}, \text{ and } K = \frac{4}{1}.\\ (K \text{ is the reciprocal of } Q.)\end{array}$$

So, to divide $\frac{7}{8}$ by $\frac{1}{4}$, we multiply $\frac{7}{8}$ by the reciprocal of $\frac{1}{4}$, namely $\frac{4}{1}$ (or 4). Because $\frac{7}{8} \cdot \frac{4}{1} = \frac{7}{2}$, there are $\frac{7}{2}$ qt, or $3\frac{1}{2}$ qt, in $\frac{7}{8}$ gal.

---

③ Multiply. Write each answer in lowest terms.

(a) $\dfrac{x^2 + 7x + 10}{3x + 6} \cdot \dfrac{6x - 6}{x^2 + 2x - 15}$

(b)
$$\dfrac{m^2 + 4m - 5}{m + 5} \cdot \dfrac{m^2 + 8m + 15}{m - 1}$$

④ Find the reciprocal of each rational expression.

(a) $\dfrac{5}{8}$

(b) $\dfrac{6b^5}{3r^2b}$

(c) $\dfrac{t^2 - 4t}{t^2 + 2t - 3}$

Answers

3. (a) $\dfrac{2(x - 1)}{x - 3}$ **(b)** $(m + 5)(m + 3)$

4. (a) $\dfrac{8}{5}$ **(b)** $\dfrac{3r^2b}{6b^5}$ **(c)** $\dfrac{t^2 + 2t - 3}{t^2 - 4t}$

5 Divide. Write each answer in lowest terms.

(a) $\dfrac{3}{4} \div \dfrac{5}{16}$

(b) $\dfrac{r}{r-1} \div \dfrac{3r}{r+4}$

GS (c) $\dfrac{6x-4}{3} \div \dfrac{15x-10}{9}$

$= \dfrac{6x-4}{3} \cdot \dfrac{\rule{1cm}{0.4pt}}{\rule{1cm}{0.4pt}}$

$= \dfrac{2(\rule{0.6cm}{0.4pt})}{3} \cdot \dfrac{9}{5(\rule{0.6cm}{0.4pt})}$

$= \dfrac{2(3x-2)\cdot 3\cdot 3}{3\cdot 5(3x-2)}$

$= \rule{1cm}{0.4pt}$

6 Divide. Write each answer in lowest terms.

(a) $\dfrac{5a^2b}{2} \div \dfrac{10ab^2}{8}$

(b) $\dfrac{(3t)^2}{w} \div \dfrac{3t^2}{5w^4}$

Answers

5. (a) $\dfrac{12}{5}$ (b) $\dfrac{r+4}{3(r-1)}$

(c) $9; 15x-10; 3x-2; 3x-2; \dfrac{6}{5}$

6. (a) $\dfrac{2a}{b}$ (b) $15w^3$

The preceding discussion illustrates dividing common fractions. Division of rational expressions is defined in the same way.

Dividing Rational Expressions

If $\frac{P}{Q}$ and $\frac{R}{S}$ are any two rational expressions where $\frac{R}{S} \neq 0$, then their quotient is defined as follows.

$$\frac{P}{Q} \div \frac{R}{S} = \frac{P}{Q} \cdot \frac{S}{R} = \frac{PS}{QR}$$

In words: To divide one rational expression by another rational expression, multiply the first rational expression (dividend) by the reciprocal of the second rational expression (divisor).

EXAMPLE 5 Dividing Rational Expressions

Divide. Write each answer in lowest terms.

(a) $\dfrac{5}{8} \div \dfrac{7}{16}$ Rational numbers

(b) $\dfrac{y}{y+3} \div \dfrac{4y}{y+5}$ Rational expressions

Multiply the dividend by the reciprocal of the divisor.

$= \dfrac{5}{8} \cdot \dfrac{16}{7}$ ← Reciprocal of $\frac{7}{16}$

$= \dfrac{5\cdot 16}{8\cdot 7}$ Multiply.

$= \dfrac{5\cdot 8\cdot 2}{8\cdot 7}$ Factor 16.

$= \dfrac{10}{7}$ Lowest terms

$= \dfrac{y}{y+3} \cdot \dfrac{y+5}{4y}$ ← Reciprocal of $\frac{4y}{y+5}$

$= \dfrac{y(y+5)}{(y+3)(4y)}$ Multiply.

$= \dfrac{y+5}{4(y+3)}$ Lowest terms

◀ **Work Problem 5** at the Side.

EXAMPLE 6 Dividing Rational Expressions

Divide. Write the answer in lowest terms.

$$\frac{(3m)^2}{(2p)^3} \div \frac{6m^3}{16p^2}$$

$= \dfrac{(3m)^2}{(2p)^3} \cdot \dfrac{16p^2}{6m^3}$ Multiply by the reciprocal of the divisor.

$= \dfrac{9m^2}{8p^3} \cdot \dfrac{16p^2}{6m^3}$ [$(3m)^2 = 3^2m^2$; $(2p)^3 = 2^3p^3$] Power rule for exponents, $(ab)^2 = a^2b^2$

$= \dfrac{9\cdot 16m^2p^2}{8\cdot 6p^3m^3}$ Multiply numerators. Multiply denominators.

$= \dfrac{3\cdot 3\cdot 8\cdot 2\cdot m^2\cdot p^2}{8\cdot 3\cdot 2\cdot p^2\cdot p\cdot m^2\cdot m}$ Factor.

$= \dfrac{3}{pm}$, or $\dfrac{3}{mp}$ Lowest terms; Either form is correct.

◀ **Work Problem 6** at the Side.

EXAMPLE 7 Dividing Rational Expressions

Divide. Write the answer in lowest terms.

$$\frac{x^2 - 4}{(x + 3)(x - 2)} \div \frac{(x + 2)(x + 3)}{-2x}$$

$$= \frac{x^2 - 4}{(x + 3)(x - 2)} \cdot \frac{-2x}{(x + 2)(x + 3)}$$ Multiply by the reciprocal of the divisor.

$$= \frac{-2x(x^2 - 4)}{(x + 3)(x - 2)(x + 2)(x + 3)}$$ Multiply numerators.

   Multiply denominators.

$$= \frac{-2x(x + 2)(x - 2)}{(x + 3)(x - 2)(x + 2)(x + 3)}$$ Factor the numerator.

$$= -\frac{2x}{(x + 3)^2}$$ Divide out the common factors; $a \cdot a = a^2$; $\frac{-a}{b} = -\frac{a}{b}$

—————————————— **Work Problem ⑦ at the Side.** ▶

EXAMPLE 8 Dividing Rational Expressions (Factors Are Opposites)

Divide. Write the answer in lowest terms.

$$\frac{m^2 - 4}{m^2 - 1} \div \frac{2m^2 + 4m}{1 - m}$$

$$= \frac{m^2 - 4}{m^2 - 1} \cdot \frac{1 - m}{2m^2 + 4m}$$ Multiply by the reciprocal of the divisor.

$$= \frac{(m^2 - 4)(1 - m)}{(m^2 - 1)(2m^2 + 4m)}$$ Multiply numerators.

   Multiply denominators.

$$= \frac{(m + 2)(m - 2)(1 - m)}{(m + 1)(m - 1)(2m)(m + 2)}$$ Factor. $1 - m$ and $m - 1$ are opposites.

$$= \frac{-1(m - 2)}{2m(m + 1)}$$ Divide out the common factors. Recall that $\frac{1 - m}{m - 1} = -1$.

$$= \frac{-m + 2}{2m(m + 1)}$$ Distribute -1 in the numerator.

$$= \frac{2 - m}{2m(m + 1)}$$ Rewrite $-m + 2$ as $2 - m$.

—————————————— **Work Problem ⑧ at the Side.** ▶

Multiplying or Dividing Rational Expressions

Step 1 **Note the operation.** If the operation is division, use the definition of division to rewrite it as multiplication.

Step 2 **Multiply** numerators and multiply denominators.

Step 3 **Factor** all numerators and denominators completely.

Step 4 **Write in lowest terms** using the fundamental property.

Steps 2 and 3 may be interchanged based on personal preference.

---

⑦ Divide. Write each answer in lowest terms.

(GS) (a) $\dfrac{y^2 + 4y + 3}{y + 3} \div \dfrac{y^2 - 4y - 5}{y - 3}$

Rewrite as multiplication, and complete the problem.

$$\underline{\hspace{3cm}} \cdot \underline{\hspace{3cm}}$$

(b) $\dfrac{4x(x + 3)}{2x + 1} \div \dfrac{-x^2(x + 3)}{4x^2 - 1}$

⑧ Divide. Write each answer in lowest terms.

(a) $\dfrac{ab - a^2}{a^2 - 1} \div \dfrac{a - b}{a - 1}$

(b) $\dfrac{x^2 - 9}{2x + 6} \div \dfrac{9 - x^2}{4x - 12}$

Answers

7. **(a)** $\dfrac{y^2 + 4y + 3}{y + 3} \cdot \dfrac{y - 3}{y^2 - 4y - 5}; \dfrac{y - 3}{y - 5}$

   (b) $-\dfrac{4(2x - 1)}{x}$

8. **(a)** $\dfrac{-a}{a + 1}$ **(b)** $\dfrac{6 - 2x}{3 + x}$

7.2 Exercises

FOR EXTRA HELP

Go to MyMathLab *for worked-out, step-by-step solutions to exercises enclosed in a square* ☐ *and video solutions to* ▶ *exercises.*

1. CONCEPT CHECK Match each multiplication problem in Column I with the correct product in Column II.

I

(a) $\dfrac{5x^3}{10x^4} \cdot \dfrac{10x^7}{2x}$

(b) $\dfrac{10x^4}{5x^3} \cdot \dfrac{10x^7}{2x}$

(c) $\dfrac{5x^3}{10x^4} \cdot \dfrac{2x}{10x^7}$

(d) $\dfrac{10x^4}{5x^3} \cdot \dfrac{2x}{10x^7}$

II

A. $\dfrac{2}{5x^5}$

B. $\dfrac{5x^5}{2}$

C. $\dfrac{1}{10x^7}$

D. $10x^7$

2. CONCEPT CHECK Match each division problem in Column I with the correct quotient in Column II.

I

(a) $\dfrac{5x^3}{10x^4} \div \dfrac{10x^7}{2x}$

(b) $\dfrac{10x^4}{5x^3} \div \dfrac{10x^7}{2x}$

(c) $\dfrac{5x^3}{10x^4} \div \dfrac{2x}{10x^7}$

(d) $\dfrac{10x^4}{5x^3} \div \dfrac{2x}{10x^7}$

II

A. $\dfrac{5x^5}{2}$

B. $10x^7$

C. $\dfrac{2}{5x^5}$

D. $\dfrac{1}{10x^7}$

Multiply. Write each answer in lowest terms. **See Examples 1 and 2.**

3. $\dfrac{4}{9} \cdot \dfrac{15}{16}$

4. $\dfrac{10}{21} \cdot \dfrac{3}{5}$

5. $\dfrac{15a^2}{14} \cdot \dfrac{7}{5a}$

6. $\dfrac{21b^6}{18} \cdot \dfrac{9}{7b^4}$

7. $\dfrac{16y^4}{18y^5} \cdot \dfrac{15y^5}{y^2}$

8. $\dfrac{20x^5}{-2x^2} \cdot \dfrac{8x^4}{35x^3}$

9. $\dfrac{2(c+d)}{3} \cdot \dfrac{18}{6(c+d)^2}$

10. $\dfrac{4(y-2)}{x} \cdot \dfrac{3x}{6(y-2)^2}$

11. $\dfrac{(x-y)^2}{2} \cdot \dfrac{24}{3(x-y)}$

12. $\dfrac{(a+b)^2}{5} \cdot \dfrac{30}{2(a+b)}$

Find the reciprocal of each rational expression. **See Example 4.**

13. $\dfrac{3p^3}{16q}$

14. $\dfrac{6x^4}{9y^2}$

15. $\dfrac{r^2+rp}{7}$

16. $\dfrac{16}{9a^2+36a}$

17. $\dfrac{z^2+7z+12}{z^2-9}$

18. $\dfrac{p^2-4p+3}{p^2-3p}$

Divide. Write each answer in lowest terms. **See Examples 5 and 6.**

19. $\dfrac{4}{5} \div \dfrac{13}{20}$

20. $\dfrac{7}{8} \div \dfrac{3}{4}$

21. $\dfrac{9z^4}{3z^5} \div \dfrac{3z^2}{5z^3}$

22. $\dfrac{35q^8}{9q^5} \div \dfrac{25q^6}{10q^5}$

23. $\dfrac{4t^4}{2t^5} \div \dfrac{(2t)^3}{-6}$

24. $\dfrac{-12a^6}{3a^2} \div \dfrac{(2a)^3}{27a}$

25. $\dfrac{3}{2y-6} \div \dfrac{6}{y-3}$

26. $\dfrac{4m+16}{10} \div \dfrac{3m+12}{18}$

27. $\dfrac{(x-3)^2}{6x} \div \dfrac{x-3}{x^2}$

28. $\dfrac{2a}{a+4} \div \dfrac{a^2}{(a+4)^2}$

Multiply or divide. Write each answer in lowest terms. ***See Examples 3, 7, and 8.***

29. $\dfrac{5x - 15}{3x + 9} \cdot \dfrac{4x + 12}{6x - 18}$

30. $\dfrac{8r + 16}{24r - 24} \cdot \dfrac{6r - 6}{3r + 6}$

31. $\dfrac{2 - t}{8} \div \dfrac{t - 2}{6}$

32. $\dfrac{4}{m - 2} \div \dfrac{16}{2 - m}$

33. $\dfrac{5 - 4x}{5 + 4x} \cdot \dfrac{4x + 5}{4x - 5}$

34. $\dfrac{5 - x}{5 + x} \cdot \dfrac{x + 5}{x - 5}$

35. $\dfrac{6(m - 2)^2}{5(m + 4)^2} \cdot \dfrac{15(m + 4)}{2(2 - m)}$

36. $\dfrac{7(q - 1)}{3(q + 1)^2} \cdot \dfrac{6(q + 1)}{3(1 - q)^2}$

37. $\dfrac{m^2 - 4}{16 - 8m} \div \dfrac{m + 2}{8}$

38. $\dfrac{r^2 - 36}{54 - 9r} \div \dfrac{r + 6}{9}$

39. $\dfrac{p^2 + 4p - 5}{p^2 + 7p + 10} \div \dfrac{p - 1}{p + 4}$

40. $\dfrac{z^2 - 3z + 2}{z^2 + 4z + 3} \div \dfrac{z - 1}{z + 1}$

41. $\dfrac{2k^2 - k - 1}{2k^2 + 5k + 3} \div \dfrac{4k^2 - 1}{2k^2 + k - 3}$

42. $\dfrac{3t^2 - 4t - 4}{3t^2 + 10t + 8} \div \dfrac{9t^2 + 21t + 10}{3t^2 - t - 10}$

43. $\dfrac{2k^2 + 3k - 2}{6k^2 - 7k + 2} \cdot \dfrac{4k^2 - 5k + 1}{k^2 + k - 2}$

44. $\dfrac{2m^2 - 5m - 12}{m^2 - 10m + 24} \cdot \dfrac{m^2 - 9m + 18}{4m^2 - 9}$

45. $\dfrac{m^2 + 2mp - 3p^2}{m^2 - 3mp + 2p^2} \div \dfrac{m^2 + 4mp + 3p^2}{m^2 + 2mp - 8p^2}$

46. $\dfrac{r^2 + rs - 12s^2}{r^2 - rs - 20s^2} \div \dfrac{r^2 - 2rs - 3s^2}{r^2 + rs - 30s^2}$

47. $\left(\dfrac{x^2 + 10x + 25}{x^2 + 10x} \cdot \dfrac{10x}{x^2 + 15x + 50} \right) \div \dfrac{x + 5}{x + 10}$

48. $\left(\dfrac{m^2 - 12m + 32}{8m} \cdot \dfrac{m^2 - 8m}{m^2 - 8m + 16} \right) \div \dfrac{m - 8}{m - 4}$

Solve each problem. (Assume all measures are given in appropriate units.)

49. If the rational expression $\frac{5x^2y^3}{2pq}$ represents the area of a rectangle and $\frac{2xy}{p}$ represents the length, what rational expression represents the width?

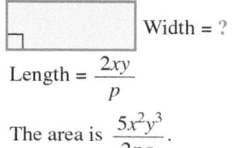

Width = ?

Length = $\dfrac{2xy}{p}$

The area is $\dfrac{5x^2y^3}{2pq}$.

50. If the rational expression $\frac{12a^3b^4}{5cd}$ represents the area of a rectangle and $\frac{9ab^2}{c}$ represents the width, what rational expression represents the length?

Width = $\dfrac{9ab^2}{c}$

Length = ?

The area is $\dfrac{12a^3b^4}{5cd}$.

7.3 | Least Common Denominators

OBJECTIVES

1 Find the least common denominator for a list of fractions.

2 Write equivalent rational expressions.

OBJECTIVE ▶ 1 Find the least common denominator for a list of fractions.
Adding or subtracting rational expressions often requires finding a **least common denominator (LCD)**. The LCD is the simplest expression that is divisible by all of the denominators in all of the expressions. For example,

$$\frac{2}{9} \quad \text{and} \quad \frac{5}{12} \quad \text{have LCD} \quad 36,$$

because 36 is the least positive number divisible by both 9 and 12.

We can often find least common denominators by inspection. In other cases, we find the LCD using the following procedure.

Finding the Least Common Denominator (LCD)

Step 1 **Factor** each denominator into prime factors.

Step 2 **List each different denominator factor** the *greatest* number of times it appears in any of the denominators.

Step 3 **Multiply** the denominator factors from Step 2 to find the LCD.

When each denominator is factored into prime factors, every prime factor must be a factor of the least common denominator.

1 Find the LCD for each pair of fractions.

(a) $\frac{7}{10}, \frac{1}{25}$

(b) $\frac{7}{20p}, \frac{11}{30p}$

(c) $\frac{4}{5x}, \frac{12}{10x}$

EXAMPLE 1 Finding Least Common Denominators

Find the LCD for each pair of fractions.

(a) $\frac{1}{24}, \frac{7}{15}$ Rational numbers

(b) $\frac{1}{8x}, \frac{3}{10x}$ Rational expressions

Step 1 Write each denominator in factored form with numerical coefficients in prime factored form.

$24 = 2 \cdot 2 \cdot 2 \cdot 3 = 2^3 \cdot 3$ $8x = 2 \cdot 2 \cdot 2 \cdot x = 2^3 \cdot x$

$15 = 3 \cdot 5$ $10x = 2 \cdot 5 \cdot x$

Step 2 We find the LCD by taking each different factor the *greatest* number of times it appears as a factor in any of the denominators.

The factor 2 appears three times in one product and not at all in the other, so the greatest number of times 2 appears is three. The greatest number of times both 3 and 5 appear in either product is one.

Here, 2 appears three times in one product and once in the other, so the greatest number of times 2 appears is three. The greatest number of times 5 appears is one. The greatest number of times x appears in either product is one.

Step 3 LCD $= 2 \cdot 2 \cdot 2 \cdot 3 \cdot 5$
$= 2^3 \cdot 3 \cdot 5$
$= 120$

LCD $= 2 \cdot 2 \cdot 2 \cdot 5 \cdot x$
$= 2^3 \cdot 5 \cdot x$
$= 40x$

◀ Work Problem **1** at the Side.

Answers

1. **(a)** 50 **(b)** 60p **(c)** 10x

EXAMPLE 2   **Finding the LCD**

Find the LCD for $\dfrac{5}{6r^2}$ and $\dfrac{3}{4r^3}$.

Step 1
$$6r^2 = 2 \cdot 3 \cdot r^2$$
$$4r^3 = 2^2 \cdot r^3$$
⎫ Factor each denominator.

Step 2   The greatest number of times 2 appears is two, the greatest number of times 3 appears is one, and the greatest number of times r appears is three.

Step 3
$$\text{LCD} = 2^2 \cdot 3 \cdot r^3 = 12r^3$$

───────────────────────── **Work Problem ❷ at the Side.** ▶

❶ CAUTION

When finding the LCD, use each factor the **greatest** number of times it appears in any *single* denominator, not the **total** number of times it appears. For instance, the greatest number of times r appears as a factor in one denominator in **Example 2** is 3, *not* 5.

EXAMPLE 3   **Finding LCDs**

Find the LCD for the fractions in each list.

(a) $\dfrac{6}{5m}, \dfrac{4}{m^2 - 3m}$

$$5m = 5 \cdot m$$
$$m^2 - 3m = m(m - 3)$$
⎫ Factor each denominator.

Use each different factor the greatest number of times it appears.

$$\text{LCD} = 5 \cdot m \cdot (m - 3) = 5m(m - 3)$$ ◁ Be sure to include m as a factor in the LCD.

Because m is not a *factor* of $m - 3$, **both** factors, m and $m - 3$ must appear in the LCD.

(b) $\dfrac{1}{r^2 - 4r - 5}, \dfrac{3}{r^2 - r - 20}, \dfrac{1}{r^2 - 10r + 25}$

$$r^2 - 4r - 5 = (r - 5)(r + 1)$$
$$r^2 - r - 20 = (r - 5)(r + 4)$$
$$r^2 - 10r + 25 = (r - 5)^2$$
⎫ Factor each denominator.

Use each different factor the greatest number of times it appears as a factor.

$$\text{LCD} = (r + 1)(r + 4)(r - 5)^2$$ ◁ Be sure to include the exponent 2 on the factor $r - 5$.

(c) $\dfrac{1}{q - 5}, \dfrac{3}{5 - q}$

The expressions $q - 5$ and $5 - q$ are opposites of each other because

$$-(q - 5) = -q + 5 = 5 - q$$

Therefore, either $q - 5$ or $5 - q$ can be used as the LCD.

───────────────────────── **Work Problem ❸ at the Side.** ▶

---

❷ Find the LCD for each pair of fractions.

(a) $\dfrac{4}{16m^3}, \dfrac{5}{9m^5}$

(b) $\dfrac{3}{25a^2}, \dfrac{2}{10a^3 b}$

❸ Find the LCD for the fractions in each list.

(a) $\dfrac{7}{3a}, \dfrac{11}{a^2 - 4a}$

(b) $\dfrac{1}{x^2 + 7x + 12}, \dfrac{2}{x^2 + 6x + 9},$ $\dfrac{5}{x^2 + 2x - 8}$

(c) $\dfrac{6}{x - 4}, \dfrac{3x - 1}{4 - x}$

Answers

2. (a) $144m^5$ (b) $50a^3 b$
3. (a) $3a(a - 4)$
   (b) $(x + 3)^2 (x + 4)(x - 2)$
   (c) either $x - 4$ or $4 - x$

4 Write each rational expression as an equivalent expression with the indicated denominator.

(a) $\dfrac{3}{4} = \dfrac{?}{36}$

GS (b) $\dfrac{7k}{5} = \dfrac{?}{30k}$

Step 1 Factor the denominator on the right.

$$\dfrac{7k}{5} = \dfrac{?}{5 \cdot \underline{\hspace{1cm}}}$$

Step 2 Factors of _____ and _____ are missing.

Step 3

$$\dfrac{7k}{5} = \dfrac{7k}{5} \cdot \dfrac{\underline{\hspace{0.7cm}}}{\underline{\hspace{0.7cm}}} = \dfrac{\underline{\hspace{0.7cm}}}{30k}$$

(c) $\dfrac{4t}{11} = \dfrac{?}{33t}$

OBJECTIVE ▶ **2** **Write equivalent rational expressions.** Once the LCD has been found, the next step in preparing to add or subtract two rational expressions is to use the fundamental property to write equivalent rational expressions.

Writing a Rational Expression with a Specified Denominator

Step 1 **Factor** both denominators.

Step 2 **Decide what factor(s) the denominator must be multiplied by** in order to equal the specified denominator.

Step 3 **Multiply** the rational expression by that factor divided by itself. (That is, multiply by 1.)

EXAMPLE 4 **Writing Equivalent Rational Expressions**

Write each fraction as an equivalent expression with the indicated denominator.

(a) $\dfrac{3}{8} = \dfrac{?}{40}$ Rational numbers

(b) $\dfrac{9k}{25} = \dfrac{?}{50k}$ Rational expressions

Step 1 For each example, first factor the denominator on the right. Then compare the denominator on the left with the one on the right to decide what factors are missing.

$$\dfrac{3}{8} = \dfrac{?}{5 \cdot 8}$$

$$\dfrac{9k}{25} = \dfrac{?}{25 \cdot 2k}$$

Step 2 A factor of 5 is missing.

Factors of 2 and k are missing.

Step 3 Multiply $\frac{3}{8}$ by $\frac{5}{5}$.

Multiply $\frac{9k}{25}$ by $\frac{2k}{2k}$.

$$\dfrac{3}{8} = \dfrac{3}{8} \cdot \dfrac{5}{5} = \dfrac{15}{40}$$

$$\dfrac{9k}{25} = \dfrac{9k}{25} \cdot \dfrac{2k}{2k} = \dfrac{18k^2}{50k}$$

$\frac{5}{5} = 1$ ⟶

$\frac{2k}{2k} = 1$ ⟶

◀ **Work Problem 4 at the Side**

EXAMPLE 5 **Writing Equivalent Rational Expressions**

Write each rational expression as an equivalent expression with the indicated denominator.

(a) $\dfrac{8}{3x + 1} = \dfrac{?}{12x + 4}$

$$\dfrac{8}{3x + 1} = \dfrac{?}{4(3x + 1)}$$ Factor the denominator on the right.

The missing factor is 4, so multiply the fraction on the left by $\frac{4}{4}$.

$$\dfrac{8}{3x + 1} \cdot \dfrac{4}{4} = \dfrac{32}{12x + 4}$$ $\frac{4}{4} = 1$; Fundamental property

Continued on Next Page

Answers

4. (a) $\dfrac{27}{36}$ (b) $6k$; 6; k; $6k$; $6k$; $42k^2$

(c) $\dfrac{12t^2}{33t}$

(b) $\dfrac{12p}{p^2 + 8p} = \dfrac{?}{p^3 + 4p^2 - 32p}$

Factor the denominator in each rational expression.

$$\dfrac{12p}{p(p + 8)} = \dfrac{?}{p(p + 8)(p - 4)}$$

$$\begin{aligned} p^3 + 4p^2 - 32p \\ = p(p^2 + 4p - 32) \\ = p(p + 8)(p - 4) \end{aligned}$$

The factor $p - 4$ is missing, so multiply $\dfrac{12p}{p(p + 8)}$ by $\dfrac{p - 4}{p - 4}$.

$$= \dfrac{12p}{p(p + 8)} \cdot \dfrac{p - 4}{p - 4} \qquad \dfrac{p - 4}{p - 4} = 1; \text{ Fundamental property}$$

$$= \dfrac{12p(p - 4)}{p(p + 8)(p - 4)} \qquad \begin{aligned}\text{Multiply numerators.}\\ \text{Multiply denominators.}\end{aligned}$$

$$= \dfrac{12p^2 - 48p}{p^3 + 4p^2 - 32p} \qquad \text{Multiply the factors.}$$

—— **Work Problem ⑤ at the Side.** ▶

> **Note**
>
> In the last step in **Example 5(b),** we multiplied the factors of the numerator and denominator in
>
> $$\dfrac{12p(p - 4)}{p(p + 8)(p - 4)} \quad \text{to obtain} \quad \dfrac{12p^2 - 48p}{p^3 + 4p^2 - 32p}.$$
>
> We did this to match the form of the fractions in the original statement of the problem. In actuality, these are equivalent expressions, and either form is acceptable as the answer.

⑤ Write each rational expression as an equivalent expression with the indicated denominator.

(a) $\dfrac{9}{2a + 5} = \dfrac{?}{6a + 15}$

(b) $\dfrac{5k + 1}{k^2 + 2k} = \dfrac{?}{k^3 + k^2 - 2k}$

Answers

5. (a) $\dfrac{27}{6a + 15}$

(b) $\dfrac{(5k + 1)(k - 1)}{k^3 + k^2 - 2k}$, or $\dfrac{5k^2 - 4k - 1}{k^3 + k^2 - 2k}$

CONCEPT CHECK *Choose the correct response.*

1. The least common denominator for $\frac{11}{20}$ and $\frac{1}{2}$ is

A. 40 **B.** 2 **C.** 20 **D.** none of these.

2. The least common denominator for $\frac{1}{a}$ and $\frac{1}{5a}$ is

A. a **B.** $5a$ **C.** $5a^2$ **D.** 5.

3. CONCEPT CHECK To find the LCD for $\frac{4}{25x^2}$ and $\frac{7}{10x^4}$, a student factored each denominator as follows.

$$25x^2 = 5^2 \cdot x^2$$
$$10x^4 = 2 \cdot 5 \cdot x^4$$

He multiplied the factors $2 \cdot 5^2 \cdot x^6$ to obtain $50x^6$ as the LCD. *What Went Wrong?* Give the correct LCD.

4. CONCEPT CHECK A student was asked to find the LCD for

$$\frac{2}{x-1} \quad \text{and} \quad \frac{5}{x+1}.$$

She answered that because the denominator expressions are opposites, either $x-1$ or $x+1$ could be used as the LCD. *What Went Wrong?* Give the correct LCD.

Find the LCD for the fractions in each list. **See Examples 1 and 2.**

5. $\frac{7}{15}, \frac{21}{20}$

6. $\frac{9}{10}, \frac{13}{25}$

7. $\frac{2}{15}, \frac{3}{10}, \frac{7}{30}$

8. $\frac{5}{24}, \frac{7}{12}, \frac{9}{28}$

9. $\frac{3}{x^4}, \frac{5}{x^7}$

10. $\frac{2}{y^5}, \frac{3}{y^6}$

11. $\frac{2}{5p}, \frac{13}{6p}$

12. $\frac{14}{15k}, \frac{11}{4k}$

13. $\frac{5}{36q}, \frac{17}{24q}$

14. $\frac{4}{30p}, \frac{9}{50p}$

15. $\frac{6}{21r^3}, \frac{8}{12r^5}$

16. $\frac{9}{35t^2}, \frac{5}{49t^6}$

17. $\frac{13}{5a^2b^3}, \frac{29}{15a^5b}$

18. $\frac{7}{3r^4s^5}, \frac{23}{9r^6s^8}$

19. $\frac{5}{12x^2y}, \frac{7}{24x^3y^2}, \frac{-11}{6xy^4}$

20. $\frac{3}{10a^4b}, \frac{7}{15ab}, \frac{-7}{30ab^7}$

Find the LCD for the fractions in each list. **See Examples 1–3.**

21. $\frac{7}{6p}, \frac{15}{4p-8}$

22. $\frac{7}{8k}, \frac{28}{12k-24}$

23. $\frac{9}{28m^2}, \frac{3}{12m-20}$

24. $\frac{15}{27a^3}, \frac{8}{9a-45}$

25. $\frac{7}{5b-10}, \frac{11}{6b-12}$

26. $\frac{3}{7x+21}, \frac{1}{5x+15}$

27. $\dfrac{5}{c-d}, \dfrac{8}{d-c}$

28. $\dfrac{4}{y-x}, \dfrac{7}{x-y}$

29. $\dfrac{13}{x^2-1}, \dfrac{-5}{2x+2}$

30. $\dfrac{9}{y^2-9}, \dfrac{-2}{2y+6}$

31. $\dfrac{3}{k^2+5k}, \dfrac{2}{k^2+3k-10}$

32. $\dfrac{1}{z^2-4z}, \dfrac{4}{z^2-3z-4}$

33. $\dfrac{6}{a^2+6a}, \dfrac{-5}{a^2+3a-18}$

34. $\dfrac{8}{y^2-5y}, \dfrac{-5}{y^2-2y-15}$

35. $\dfrac{5}{p^2+8p+15}, \dfrac{3}{p^2-3p-18}, \dfrac{2}{p^2-p-30}$

36. $\dfrac{10}{y^2-10y+21}, \dfrac{2}{y^2-2y-3}, \dfrac{5}{y^2-6y-7}$

Write each rational expression as an equivalent expression with the indicated denominator. **See Examples 4 and 5.**

37. $\dfrac{4}{11} = \dfrac{?}{55}$

38. $\dfrac{6}{7} = \dfrac{?}{42}$

39. $\dfrac{-5}{k} = \dfrac{?}{9k}$

40. $\dfrac{-3}{q} = \dfrac{?}{6q}$

41. $\dfrac{13}{40y} = \dfrac{?}{80y^3}$

42. $\dfrac{5}{27p} = \dfrac{?}{108p^4}$

43. $\dfrac{5t^2}{6r} = \dfrac{?}{42r^4}$

44. $\dfrac{8y^2}{3x} = \dfrac{?}{30x^3}$

45. $\dfrac{5}{2(m+3)} = \dfrac{?}{8(m+3)}$

46. $\dfrac{7}{4(y-1)} = \dfrac{?}{16(y-1)}$

47. $\dfrac{19z}{2z-6} = \dfrac{?}{6z-18}$

48. $\dfrac{3r}{5r-5} = \dfrac{?}{15r-15}$

49. $\dfrac{-4t}{3t-6} = \dfrac{?}{12-6t}$

50. $\dfrac{-7k}{5k-20} = \dfrac{?}{40-10k}$

51. $\dfrac{14}{z^2-3z} = \dfrac{?}{z(z-3)(z-2)}$

52. $\dfrac{12}{x(x+4)} = \dfrac{?}{x(x+4)(x-9)}$

53. $\dfrac{2(b-1)}{b^2+b} = \dfrac{?}{b^3+3b^2+2b}$

54. $\dfrac{3(c+2)}{c(c-1)} = \dfrac{?}{c^3-5c^2+4c}$

7.4 | Adding and Subtracting Rational Expressions

OBJECTIVES

1. Add rational expressions having the same denominator.
2. Add rational expressions having different denominators.
3. Subtract rational expressions.

OBJECTIVE ▶ 1 Add rational expressions having the same denominator.
We find the sum of two such rational expressions using the procedure for adding two common fractions having the same denominator.

Adding Rational Expressions (Same Denominator)

The rational expressions $\frac{P}{Q}$ and $\frac{R}{Q}$ (where $Q \neq 0$) are added as follows.

$$\frac{P}{Q} + \frac{R}{Q} = \frac{P+R}{Q}$$

In words: To add rational expressions with the same denominator, add the numerators and keep the same denominator.

---

1 Add. Write each answer in lowest terms.

(a) $\dfrac{7}{15} + \dfrac{3}{15}$

(b) $\dfrac{3}{y+4} + \dfrac{2}{y+4}$

(c) $\dfrac{a}{a+b} + \dfrac{b}{a+b}$

(d) $\dfrac{x^2}{x+1} + \dfrac{x}{x+1}$

EXAMPLE 1 Adding Rational Expressions (Same Denominator)

Add. Write each answer in lowest terms.

(a) $\dfrac{4}{9} + \dfrac{2}{9}$ Rational numbers

(b) $\dfrac{3x}{x+1} + \dfrac{3}{x+1}$ Rational expressions

The denominators are the same, so the sum is found by adding the two numerators and keeping the same (common) denominator.

$= \dfrac{4+2}{9}$ Add.

$= \dfrac{6}{9}$

$= \dfrac{2 \cdot 3}{3 \cdot 3}$ Factor.

$= \dfrac{2}{3}$ Lowest terms

$= \dfrac{3x+3}{x+1}$ Add.

$= \dfrac{3(x+1)}{x+1}$ Factor.

$= 3$ Lowest terms

◀ **Work Problem 1 at the Side.**

OBJECTIVE ▶ 2 Add rational expressions having different denominators.
We use the following steps to add two rational expressions having different denominators.

Adding Rational Expressions (Different Denominators)

Step 1 **Find the least common denominator (LCD).**

Step 2 **Write each rational expression** as an equivalent rational expression with the LCD as the denominator.

Step 3 **Add** the numerators to obtain the numerator of the sum. The LCD is the denominator of the sum.

Step 4 **Write in lowest terms** using the fundamental property.

Answers

1. (a) $\dfrac{2}{3}$ (b) $\dfrac{5}{y+4}$ (c) 1   (d) x

EXAMPLE 2 **Adding Rational Expressions (Different Denominators)**

Add. Write each answer in lowest terms.

(a) $\dfrac{1}{12} + \dfrac{7}{15}$ **(b)** $\dfrac{2}{3y} + \dfrac{1}{4y}$

Step 1 First find the LCD, using the methods of the previous section.

$$12 = 2 \cdot 2 \cdot 3 = 2^2 \cdot 3 \qquad\qquad 3y = 3 \cdot y$$
$$15 = 3 \cdot 5 \qquad\qquad\qquad\qquad 4y = 2 \cdot 2 \cdot y = 2^2 \cdot y$$
$$\text{LCD} = 2^2 \cdot 3 \cdot 5 = \mathbf{60} \qquad \text{LCD} = 2^2 \cdot 3 \cdot y = \mathbf{12y}$$

Step 2 Now write each rational expression as an equivalent expression with the LCD (60 or 12y, respectively) as the denominator.

$\dfrac{1}{12} + \dfrac{7}{15}$ The LCD is 60. $\dfrac{2}{3y} + \dfrac{1}{4y}$ The LCD is 12y.

$$= \dfrac{1}{12} \cdot \dfrac{5}{5} + \dfrac{7}{15} \cdot \dfrac{4}{4} \qquad = \dfrac{2}{3y} \cdot \dfrac{4}{4} + \dfrac{1}{4y} \cdot \dfrac{3}{3}$$

$$= \dfrac{5}{60} + \dfrac{28}{60} \qquad\qquad = \dfrac{8}{12y} + \dfrac{3}{12y}$$

Step 3 Add the numerators. The LCD is the denominator.

Step 4 Write in lowest terms if necessary.

$$= \dfrac{5 + 28}{60} \qquad\qquad\qquad = \dfrac{8 + 3}{12y}$$

$$= \dfrac{33}{60} \qquad\qquad\qquad\qquad = \dfrac{11}{12y}$$

$$= \dfrac{11}{20}$$

─────── Work Problem **2** at the Side. ▶

EXAMPLE 3 **Adding Rational Expressions**

Add. Write the answer in lowest terms.

$$\dfrac{2x}{x^2 - 1} + \dfrac{-1}{x + 1}$$

Step 1 The denominators are different, so find the LCD.

$$\left.\begin{array}{l} x^2 - 1 = (x + 1)(x - 1) \\ x + 1 \text{ is prime.} \end{array}\right\} \text{ The LCD is } (x + 1)(x - 1).$$

Step 2 Write each rational expression with the LCD as the denominator.

$$\dfrac{2x}{x^2 - 1} + \dfrac{-1}{x + 1} \qquad\qquad \text{The LCD is } (x + 1)(x - 1).$$

$$= \dfrac{2x}{(x + 1)(x - 1)} + \dfrac{-1(x - 1)}{(x + 1)(x - 1)} \qquad \text{Multiply the second fraction by } \tfrac{x-1}{x-1}.$$

$$= \dfrac{2x}{(x + 1)(x - 1)} + \dfrac{-x + 1}{(x + 1)(x - 1)} \qquad \text{Distributive property}$$

2 Add. Write each answer in lowest terms.

(a) $\dfrac{1}{10} + \dfrac{1}{15}$

(b) $\dfrac{6}{5x} + \dfrac{9}{2x}$

$$= \dfrac{6}{5x} \cdot \dfrac{\underline{}}{\underline{}} + \dfrac{9}{2x} \cdot \dfrac{\underline{}}{\underline{}}$$

$$= \dfrac{12 + 45}{\underline{}}$$

$$= \underline{}$$

(c) $\dfrac{m}{3n} + \dfrac{2}{7n}$

Answers

2. (a) $\dfrac{1}{6}$ **(b)** 2; 2; 5; 5; 10x; $\dfrac{57}{10x}$

(c) $\dfrac{7m + 6}{21n}$

─────── **Continued on Next Page**

3 Add. Write each answer in lowest terms.

(a) $\dfrac{2p}{3p+3}+\dfrac{5p}{2p+2}$

(b) $\dfrac{4}{y^2-1}+\dfrac{6}{y+1}$

(c) $\dfrac{-2}{p+1}+\dfrac{4p}{p^2-1}$

4 Add. Write each answer in lowest terms.

(a) $\dfrac{2k}{k^2-5k+4}+\dfrac{3}{k^2-1}$

(b)
$\dfrac{4m}{m^2+3m+2}+\dfrac{2m-1}{m^2+6m+5}$

5 Add. Write the answer in lowest terms.

$$\dfrac{2k}{k-7}+\dfrac{5}{7-k}$$

Answers

3. (a) $\dfrac{19p}{6(p+1)}$ (b) $\dfrac{2(3y-1)}{(y+1)(y-1)}$

(c) $\dfrac{2}{p-1}$

4. (a) $\dfrac{(2k-3)(k+4)}{(k-4)(k-1)(k+1)}$

(b) $\dfrac{6m^2+23m-2}{(m+2)(m+1)(m+5)}$

5. $\dfrac{2k-5}{k-7}$, or $\dfrac{5-2k}{7-k}$

Step 3

$=\dfrac{2x-x+1}{(x+1)(x-1)}$ Add numerators.

Keep the same denominator.

$=\dfrac{x+1}{(x+1)(x-1)}$ Combine like terms in the numerator.

Step 4

$=\dfrac{1(x+1)}{(x+1)(x-1)}$ Identity property of multiplication

Remember to write 1 in the numerator.

$=\dfrac{1}{x-1}$ Divide out the common factors. The result is in lowest terms.

◀ **Work Problem 3** at the Side.

EXAMPLE 4 Adding Rational Expressions

Add. Write the answer in lowest terms.

$$\dfrac{2x}{x^2+5x+6}+\dfrac{x+1}{x^2+2x-3}$$

$=\dfrac{2x}{(x+2)(x+3)}+\dfrac{x+1}{(x+3)(x-1)}$ Factor the denominators.

$=\dfrac{2x(x-1)}{(x+2)(x+3)(x-1)}+\dfrac{(x+1)(x+2)}{(x+2)(x+3)(x-1)}$

The LCD is $(x+2)(x+3)(x-1)$.

$=\dfrac{2x(x-1)+(x+1)(x+2)}{(x+2)(x+3)(x-1)}$ Add numerators. Keep the same denominator.

$=\dfrac{2x^2-2x+x^2+3x+2}{(x+2)(x+3)(x-1)}$ Multiply.

$=\dfrac{3x^2+x+2}{(x+2)(x+3)(x-1)}$ Combine like terms.

The numerator cannot be factored here, so the expression is in lowest terms.

◀ **Work Problem 4** at the Side.

EXAMPLE 5 Adding Rational Expressions (Denominators Are Opposites)

Add. Write the answer in lowest terms.

$$\dfrac{y}{y-2}+\dfrac{8}{2-y}$$ The denominators are opposites.

$=\dfrac{y}{y-2}+\dfrac{8(-1)}{(2-y)(-1)}$ Multiply $\dfrac{8}{2-y}$ by 1 in the form $\dfrac{-1}{-1}$ to find a common denominator.

$=\dfrac{y}{y-2}+\dfrac{-8}{-2+y}$ Multiply. Apply the distributive property in the denominator.

$=\dfrac{y}{y-2}+\dfrac{-8}{y-2}$ Rewrite $-2+y$ as $y-2$.

$=\dfrac{y-8}{y-2}$ Add numerators. Keep the same denominator.

◀ **Work Problem 5** at the Side.

Note

If we had chosen to use $2 - y$ as the common denominator in **Example 5,** we would have obtained a different, yet equivalent, form of the answer $\frac{y-8}{y-2}$.

$$\frac{y}{y-2} + \frac{8}{2-y}$$

See Example 5.

$$= \frac{y(-1)}{(y-2)(-1)} + \frac{8}{2-y}$$

Multiply $\frac{y}{y-2}$ by 1 in the form $\frac{-1}{-1}$.

$$= \frac{-y}{2-y} + \frac{8}{2-y}$$

In the first denominator, $(y-2)(-1) = -y + 2 = 2 - y$.

$$= \frac{-y+8}{2-y}$$

Add numerators. Keep the same denominator.

$$= \frac{8-y}{2-y}$$

Multiply $\frac{8-y}{2-y}$ by $\frac{-1}{-1}$ to confirm that it is equivalent to $\frac{y-8}{y-2}$.

OBJECTIVE ▶ **3** Subtract rational expressions.

Subtracting Rational Expressions (Same Denominator)

The rational expressions $\frac{P}{Q}$ and $\frac{R}{Q}$ (where $Q \neq 0$) are subtracted as follows.

$$\frac{P}{Q} - \frac{R}{Q} = \frac{P-R}{Q}$$

In words: To subtract rational expressions with the same denominator, subtract the numerators and keep the same denominator.

EXAMPLE 6   **Subtracting Rational Expressions (Same Denominator)**

Subtract. Write the answer in lowest terms.

$$\frac{2m}{m-1} - \frac{m+3}{m-1}$$

Use parentheses around the numerator of the subtrahend.

$$= \frac{2m - (m+3)}{m-1}$$

Subtract numerators. Keep the same denominator.

Be careful with signs.

$$= \frac{2m - m - 3}{m-1}$$

Distributive property

$$= \frac{m-3}{m-1}$$

Combine like terms.

——————— **Work Problem 6 at the Side.** ▶

⊗ CAUTION

In subtraction problems like the one in **Example 6,** the numerator of the fraction being subtracted must be treated as a single quantity. *Be sure to use parentheses after the subtraction symbol. Subtract each term within the parentheses, or a sign error may occur.*

6 Subtract. Write each answer in lowest terms.

(a) $\dfrac{3}{m^2} - \dfrac{2}{m^2}$

GS (b) $\dfrac{x}{2x+3} - \dfrac{3x+4}{2x+3}$

$$= \frac{x - (\underline{})}{2x+3}$$

$$= \frac{x - \underline{} - \underline{}}{2x+3}$$

$$= \frac{\overline{}}{2x+3}$$

If the numerator is factored, the answer can be written as _____.

(c) $\dfrac{5t}{t-1} - \dfrac{5+t}{t-1}$

Answers

6. (a) $\dfrac{1}{m^2}$

(b) $3x + 4$; $3x$; 4; $-2x - 4$; $\dfrac{-2(x+2)}{2x+3}$

(c) $\dfrac{4t-5}{t-1}$

7 Subtract. Write each answer in lowest terms.

(a) $\dfrac{1}{k+4} - \dfrac{2}{k}$

(b) $\dfrac{6}{a+2} - \dfrac{1}{a-3}$

EXAMPLE 7 **Subtracting Rational Expressions (Different Denominators)**

Subtract. Write the answer in lowest terms.

$$\frac{9}{x-2} - \frac{3}{x} \qquad \text{The LCD is } x(x-2).$$

$$= \frac{9x}{x(x-2)} - \frac{3(x-2)}{x(x-2)} \qquad \begin{array}{l}\text{Write each expression with}\\ \text{the LCD.}\end{array}$$

$$= \frac{9x - 3(x-2)}{x(x-2)} \qquad \begin{array}{l}\text{Subtract numerators.}\\ \text{Keep the same denominator.}\end{array}$$

$$\boxed{\begin{array}{l}\text{Be careful}\\ \text{with signs.}\end{array}} = \frac{9x - 3x + 6}{x(x-2)} \qquad \text{Distributive property}$$

$$= \frac{6x+6}{x(x-2)}, \quad \text{or} \quad \frac{6(x+1)}{x(x-2)} \qquad \begin{array}{l}\text{Combine like terms.}\\ \text{Factor the numerator.}\end{array}$$

We factored in the last step to determine whether there were any common factors to divide out. There were not, so the expression is in lowest terms. The two final forms are equivalent. Either form can be given as the answer.

◀ **Work Problem 7 at the Side.**

---

8 Subtract. Write each answer in lowest terms.

(a) $\dfrac{5}{x-1} - \dfrac{3x}{1-x}$

(b) $\dfrac{2y}{y-2} - \dfrac{1+y}{2-y}$

EXAMPLE 8 **Subtracting Rational Expressions (Denominators Are Opposites)**

Subtract. Write the answer in lowest terms.

$$\frac{3x}{x-5} - \frac{2x-25}{5-x} \qquad \begin{array}{l}\text{The denominators are opposites.}\\ \text{We choose } x-5 \text{ as the common}\\ \text{denominator.}\end{array}$$

$$= \frac{3x}{x-5} - \frac{(2x-25)(-1)}{(5-x)(-1)} \qquad \begin{array}{l}\text{Multiply } \frac{2x-25}{5-x} \text{ by } \frac{-1}{-1} \text{ to find}\\ \text{a common denominator.}\end{array}$$

$$= \frac{3x}{x-5} - \frac{-2x+25}{x-5} \qquad \begin{array}{l}(2x-25)(-1) = -2x+25;\\ (5-x)(-1) = -5+x = x-5\end{array}$$

$$= \frac{3x - (-2x+25)}{x-5} \qquad \boxed{\text{Use parentheses.}} \quad \text{Subtract numerators.}$$

$$= \frac{3x + 2x - 25}{x-5} \qquad \boxed{\begin{array}{l}\text{Be careful}\\ \text{with signs.}\end{array}} \quad \text{Distributive property}$$

$$= \frac{5x - 25}{x-5} \qquad \text{Combine like terms.}$$

$$= \frac{5(x-5)}{x-5} \qquad \text{Factor.}$$

$$= 5 \qquad \text{Lowest terms}$$

◀ **Work Problem 8 at the Side.**

Answers

7. (a) $\dfrac{-k-8}{k(k+4)}$ **(b)** $\dfrac{5(a-4)}{(a+2)(a-3)}$

8. (a) $\dfrac{5+3x}{x-1}$, or $\dfrac{-5-3x}{1-x}$

   (b) $\dfrac{3y+1}{y-2}$, or $\dfrac{-3y-1}{2-y}$

EXAMPLE 9 **Subtracting Rational Expressions**

Subtract. Write the answer in lowest terms.

$$\frac{6x}{x^2 - 2x + 1} - \frac{1}{x^2 - 1}$$

$$= \frac{6x}{(x-1)^2} - \frac{1}{(x-1)(x+1)} \qquad \text{Factor the denominators.}$$

From the factored denominators, we identify the LCD, $(x-1)^2(x+1)$. **We use the factor $x - 1$ twice** because it appears twice in the first denominator.

$$= \frac{6x(x+1)}{(x-1)^2(x+1)} - \frac{1(x-1)}{(x-1)(x-1)(x+1)} \qquad \text{Fundamental property}$$

$$= \frac{6x(x+1) - 1(x-1)}{(x-1)^2(x+1)} \qquad \text{Subtract numerators.}$$

$$= \frac{6x^2 + 6x - x + 1}{(x-1)^2(x+1)} \qquad \text{Distributive property}$$

$$= \frac{6x^2 + 5x + 1}{(x-1)^2(x+1)}, \quad \text{or} \quad \frac{(3x+1)(2x+1)}{(x-1)^2(x+1)} \qquad \begin{array}{l}\text{Combine like terms.}\\ \text{Factor the numerator.}\end{array}$$

The two final forms are equivalent. The factored form indicates that the expression is in lowest terms—there are no common factors to divide out. Either form can be given as the answer.

——————————— **Work Problem 9 at the Side.** ▶

EXAMPLE 10 **Subtracting Rational Expressions**

Subtract. Write the answer in lowest terms.

$$\frac{q}{q^2 - 4q - 5} - \frac{3}{2q^2 - 13q + 15}$$

$$= \frac{q}{(q+1)(q-5)} - \frac{3}{(q-5)(2q-3)} \qquad \begin{array}{l}\text{Factor the denominators. The}\\ \text{LCD is } (q+1)(q-5)(2q-3).\end{array}$$

$$= \frac{q(2q-3)}{(q+1)(q-5)(2q-3)} - \frac{3(q+1)}{(q+1)(q-5)(2q-3)}$$

$$\qquad\qquad\qquad\qquad\qquad\qquad\qquad\qquad \text{Fundamental property}$$

$$= \frac{q(2q-3) - 3(q+1)}{(q+1)(q-5)(2q-3)} \qquad \text{Subtract numerators.}$$

$$= \frac{2q^2 - 3q - 3q - 3}{(q+1)(q-5)(2q-3)} \qquad \text{Distributive property}$$

$$= \frac{2q^2 - 6q - 3}{(q+1)(q-5)(2q-3)} \qquad \text{Combine like terms.}$$

The numerator cannot be factored, so the final answer is in lowest terms.

——————————— **Work Problem 10 at the Side.** ▶

9 Subtract. Write each answer in lowest terms.

(a) $\dfrac{4y}{y^2 - 1} - \dfrac{5}{y^2 + 2y + 1}$

GS **(b)** $\dfrac{3r}{r - 5} - \dfrac{4}{r^2 - 10r + 25}$

The LCD is _____.

Complete the subtraction.

10 Subtract. Write each answer in lowest terms.

(a) $\dfrac{2}{p^2 - 5p + 4} - \dfrac{3}{p^2 - 1}$

(b)

$\dfrac{q}{2q^2 + 5q - 3} - \dfrac{3q + 4}{3q^2 + 10q + 3}$

Answers

9. (a) $\dfrac{4y^2 - y + 5}{(y+1)^2(y-1)}$

   (b) $(r-5)^2; \dfrac{3r^2 - 15r - 4}{(r-5)^2}$

10. (a) $\dfrac{14 - p}{(p-4)(p-1)(p+1)}$

   (b) $\dfrac{-3q^2 - 4q + 4}{(2q-1)(q+3)(3q+1)}$

7.4 Exercises

FOR EXTRA HELP

Go to MyMathLab for worked-out, step-by-step solutions to exercises enclosed in a square ▢ and video solutions to ▶ exercises.

CONCEPT CHECK *Match each expression in Column I with the correct sum or difference in Column II.*

I

1. $\dfrac{x}{x+6} + \dfrac{6}{x+6}$

2. $\dfrac{2x}{x-6} - \dfrac{12}{x-6}$

3. $\dfrac{6}{x-6} - \dfrac{x}{x-6}$

4. $\dfrac{6}{x+6} - \dfrac{x}{x+6}$

5. $\dfrac{x}{x+6} - \dfrac{6}{x+6}$

6. $\dfrac{1}{x} + \dfrac{1}{6}$

7. $\dfrac{1}{6} - \dfrac{1}{x}$

8. $\dfrac{1}{6x} - \dfrac{1}{6x}$

II

A. 2

B. $\dfrac{x-6}{x+6}$

C. -1

D. $\dfrac{6+x}{6x}$

E. 1

F. 0

G. $\dfrac{x-6}{6x}$

H. $\dfrac{6-x}{x+6}$

9. CONCEPT CHECK A student subtracted the following rational expressions incorrectly as shown.

$$\dfrac{2x}{x+5} - \dfrac{x+1}{x+5}$$
$$= \dfrac{2x - x + 1}{x+5}$$
$$= \dfrac{x+1}{x+5}$$

What Went Wrong? Give the correct answer.

10. CONCEPT CHECK A student subtracted the following rational expressions incorrectly as shown.

$$\dfrac{7x}{2x-3} - \dfrac{3x-5}{2x-3}$$
$$= \dfrac{7x - (3x-5)}{2x-3}$$
$$= \dfrac{7x - 3x - 5}{2x-3}$$
$$= \dfrac{4x-5}{2x-3}$$

What Went Wrong? Give the correct answer.

Add or subtract. Write each answer in lowest terms. ***See Examples 1 and 6.***

11. $\dfrac{5}{18} + \dfrac{7}{18}$

12. $\dfrac{11}{24} + \dfrac{7}{24}$

13. ▶ $\dfrac{4}{m} + \dfrac{7}{m}$

14. $\dfrac{5}{p} + \dfrac{11}{p}$

15. $\dfrac{5}{y+4} - \dfrac{1}{y+4}$

16. $\dfrac{4}{y+3} - \dfrac{1}{y+3}$

17. $\dfrac{4y}{y+3} + \dfrac{12}{y+3}$

18. $\dfrac{2x}{x+4} + \dfrac{8}{x+4}$

19. $\dfrac{a+b}{2} - \dfrac{a-b}{2}$

20. $\dfrac{x-y}{2} - \dfrac{x+y}{2}$

21. ▶ $\dfrac{5m}{m+1} - \dfrac{1+4m}{m+1}$

22. $\dfrac{4x}{x+2} - \dfrac{2+3x}{x+2}$

23. $\dfrac{6x}{x-4} - \dfrac{4x-3}{x-4}$

24. $\dfrac{8x}{x-2} - \dfrac{5x-4}{x-2}$

25. $\dfrac{x^2}{x+5} + \dfrac{5x}{x+5}$

26. $\dfrac{t^2}{t-3} + \dfrac{-3t}{t-3}$

27. $\dfrac{y^2-3y}{y+3} + \dfrac{-18}{y+3}$

28. $\dfrac{r^2-8r}{r-5} + \dfrac{15}{r-5}$

Add or subtract. Write each answer in lowest terms. ***See Examples 2, 3, 4, and 7.***

29. $\dfrac{5}{12} + \dfrac{3}{20}$

30. $\dfrac{7}{30} + \dfrac{2}{45}$

31. $\dfrac{z}{5} + \dfrac{1}{3}$

32. $\dfrac{p}{8} + \dfrac{3}{5}$

33. $\dfrac{5}{7} - \dfrac{r}{2}$

34. $\dfrac{10}{9} - \dfrac{z}{3}$

35. $-\dfrac{3}{4} - \dfrac{1}{2x}$

36. $-\dfrac{5}{8} - \dfrac{3}{2a}$

37. $\dfrac{3}{5x} + \dfrac{9}{4x}$

38. $\dfrac{3}{2x} + \dfrac{4}{7x}$

39. $\dfrac{x+1}{6} + \dfrac{3x+3}{9}$

40. $\dfrac{2x-6}{4} + \dfrac{x+5}{6}$

41. $\dfrac{x+3}{3x} + \dfrac{2x+2}{4x}$

42. $\dfrac{x+2}{5x} + \dfrac{6x+3}{3x}$

43. $\dfrac{2}{x+3} + \dfrac{1}{x}$

44. $\dfrac{3}{x-4} + \dfrac{2}{x}$

45. $\dfrac{1}{k+4} - \dfrac{2}{k}$

46. $\dfrac{3}{m+1} - \dfrac{4}{m}$

47. $\dfrac{x}{x-2} + \dfrac{-8}{x^2-4}$

48. $\dfrac{2x}{x-1} + \dfrac{-4}{x^2-1}$

49. $\dfrac{x}{x-2} + \dfrac{4}{x+2}$

50. $\dfrac{2x}{x-1} + \dfrac{3}{x+1}$

51. $\dfrac{4m}{m^2+3m+2} + \dfrac{2m-1}{m^2+6m+5}$

52. $\dfrac{a}{a^2+3a-4} + \dfrac{4a}{a^2+7a+12}$

53. $\dfrac{t}{t+2} + \dfrac{5-t}{t} - \dfrac{4}{t^2+2t}$

54. $\dfrac{2p}{p-3} + \dfrac{2+p}{p} - \dfrac{-6}{p^2-3p}$

55. CONCEPT CHECK What are the two possible LCDs that could be used for the following sum?

$$\frac{10}{m-2}+\frac{5}{2-m}$$

56. CONCEPT CHECK If one form of the correct answer to a sum or difference of rational expressions is $\frac{4}{k-3}$, what would be an alternative form of the answer if the denominator is $3-k$?

Add or subtract. Write each answer in lowest terms. **See Examples 5 and 8.**

57. $\dfrac{4}{x-5}+\dfrac{6}{5-x}$

58. $\dfrac{10}{m-2}+\dfrac{5}{2-m}$

59. $\dfrac{-1}{1-y}-\dfrac{4y-3}{y-1}$

60. $\dfrac{-4}{p-3}-\dfrac{p+1}{3-p}$

61. $\dfrac{2}{x-y^2}+\dfrac{7}{y^2-x}$

62. $\dfrac{-8}{p-q^2}+\dfrac{3}{q^2-p}$

63. $\dfrac{x}{5x-3y}-\dfrac{y}{3y-5x}$

64. $\dfrac{t}{8t-9s}-\dfrac{s}{9s-8t}$

65. $\dfrac{3}{4p-5}+\dfrac{9}{5-4p}$

66. $\dfrac{8}{3-7y}-\dfrac{2}{7y-3}$

67. $\dfrac{15x}{5x-7}-\dfrac{-21}{7-5x}$

68. $\dfrac{24y}{6y-5}-\dfrac{-20}{5-6y}$

In each subtraction problem, the rational expression that follows the subtraction sign has a numerator with more than one term. **Be careful with signs** *and find each difference.* **See Examples 6–10.**

69. $\dfrac{2m}{m-n}-\dfrac{5m+n}{2m-2n}$

70. $\dfrac{5p}{p-q}-\dfrac{3p+1}{4p-4q}$

71. $\dfrac{y^2}{y-2}-\dfrac{9y-14}{y-2}$

72. $\dfrac{y^2}{y-4}-\dfrac{y+12}{y-4}$

73. $\dfrac{5}{x^2-9}-\dfrac{x+2}{x^2+4x+3}$

74. $\dfrac{1}{a^2-1}-\dfrac{a-1}{a^2+3a-4}$

75. $\dfrac{2q + 1}{3q^2 + 10q - 8} - \dfrac{3q + 5}{2q^2 + 5q - 12}$

76. $\dfrac{4y - 1}{2y^2 + 5y - 3} - \dfrac{y + 3}{6y^2 + y - 2}$

Perform the indicated operations. ***See Examples 1–10.***

77. $\dfrac{4}{r^2 - r} + \dfrac{6}{r^2 + 2r} - \dfrac{1}{r^2 + r - 2}$

78. $\dfrac{6}{k^2 + 3k} - \dfrac{1}{k^2 - k} + \dfrac{2}{k^2 + 2k - 3}$

79. $\dfrac{x + 3y}{x^2 + 2xy + y^2} + \dfrac{x - y}{x^2 + 4xy + 3y^2}$

80. $\dfrac{m}{m^2 - 1} + \dfrac{m - 1}{m^2 + 2m + 1}$

81. $\dfrac{r + y}{18r^2 + 9ry - 2y^2} + \dfrac{3r - y}{36r^2 - y^2}$

82. $\dfrac{2x - z}{2x^2 + xz - 10z^2} - \dfrac{x + z}{x^2 - 4z^2}$

Find an expression that represents ***(a)*** *the perimeter and* ***(b)*** *the area of each figure.*
Give answers in simplified form. (Assume all measures are given in appropriate units.
If necessary, refer to the formulas at the back of this text.)

83.
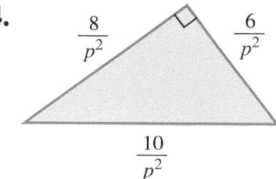

$\dfrac{3k + 1}{10}$

$\dfrac{5}{6k + 2}$

84.

$\dfrac{8}{p^2}$ $\dfrac{6}{p^2}$

$\dfrac{10}{p^2}$

A Concours d'Elégance is a competition in which a maximum of 100 *points is
awarded to a car based on its general attractiveness. The rational expression*

$$\dfrac{9010}{49(101 - x)} - \dfrac{10}{49}$$

*approximates the cost, in thousands of dollars, of restoring a car so that it will
win x points.*

85. Simplify the given expression by performing the indicated subtraction.

86. Use the simplified expression from **Exercise 85** to determine, to two decimal places, how much it would cost to win 95 points.

7.5 | Complex Fractions

OBJECTIVES

1. Define and recognize a complex fraction.
2. Simplify a complex fraction by writing it as a division problem (Method 1).
3. Simplify a complex fraction by multiplying numerator and denominator by the least common denominator (Method 2).
4. Simplify rational expressions with negative exponents.

OBJECTIVE 1 Define and recognize a complex fraction. The quotient of two mixed numbers in arithmetic, such as $2\frac{1}{2} \div 3\frac{1}{4}$, can be written as a fraction.

$$2\frac{1}{2} \div 3\frac{1}{4}$$

$$= \frac{2\frac{1}{2}}{3\frac{1}{4}} \qquad a \div b = \frac{a}{b}$$

We do this to illustrate a complex fraction.

$$= \frac{2+\frac{1}{2}}{3+\frac{1}{4}} \qquad \text{Definition of mixed number}$$

In algebra, some rational expressions also have fractions in the numerator, or denominator, or both.

Complex Fraction

A quotient with one or more fractions in the numerator, or denominator, or both, is a **complex fraction.**

Examples: $\dfrac{2+\frac{1}{2}}{3+\frac{1}{4}}$, $\dfrac{\frac{3x^2-5x}{6x^2}}{2x-\frac{1}{x}}$, and $\dfrac{3+x}{5-\frac{2}{x}}$ Complex fractions

---

The parts of a complex fraction are named as follows.

$$\frac{\dfrac{2}{p}-\dfrac{1}{q}}{\dfrac{3}{p}+\dfrac{5}{q}}$$

← Numerator of complex fraction
← Main fraction bar
← Denominator of complex fraction

OBJECTIVE 2 Simplify a complex fraction by writing it as a division problem (Method 1). The main fraction bar represents division in a complex fraction, so one method of simplifying a complex fraction involves division.

Method 1 for Simplifying a Complex Fraction

Step 1 Write both the numerator and denominator as single fractions.

Step 2 Change the complex fraction to a division problem.

Step 3 Perform the indicated division.

EXAMPLE 1   **Simplifying Complex Fractions (Method 1)**

Simplify each complex fraction.

(a) $\dfrac{\dfrac{2}{3}+\dfrac{5}{9}}{\dfrac{1}{4}+\dfrac{1}{12}}$

(b) $\dfrac{6+\dfrac{3}{x}}{\dfrac{x}{4}+\dfrac{1}{8}}$

Step 1   First, write each numerator as a single fraction.

$$\frac{2}{3}+\frac{5}{9}$$

$$=\frac{2}{3}\cdot\frac{3}{3}+\frac{5}{9}$$

$$=\frac{6}{9}+\frac{5}{9}$$

$$=\frac{11}{9}$$

$$6+\frac{3}{x}$$

$$=\frac{6}{1}\cdot\frac{x}{x}+\frac{3}{x}$$

$$=\frac{6x}{x}+\frac{3}{x}$$

$$=\frac{6x+3}{x}$$

Repeat the process for each denominator.

$$\frac{1}{4}+\frac{1}{12}$$

$$=\frac{1}{4}\cdot\frac{3}{3}+\frac{1}{12}$$

$$=\frac{3}{12}+\frac{1}{12}$$

$$=\frac{4}{12}$$

$$\frac{x}{4}+\frac{1}{8}$$

$$=\frac{x}{4}\cdot\frac{2}{2}+\frac{1}{8}$$

$$=\frac{2x}{8}+\frac{1}{8}$$

$$=\frac{2x+1}{8}$$

Step 2   Write the equivalent complex fraction as a division problem.

$$\frac{\dfrac{11}{9}}{\dfrac{4}{12}}$$

$$=\frac{11}{9}\div\frac{4}{12}$$

$$\frac{\dfrac{6x+3}{x}}{\dfrac{2x+1}{8}}$$

$$=\frac{6x+3}{x}\div\frac{2x+1}{8}$$

Step 3   Now use the definition of division and multiply by the reciprocal. Then write in lowest terms using the fundamental property.

$$=\frac{11}{9}\cdot\frac{12}{4}$$

$$=\frac{11\cdot 3\cdot 4}{3\cdot 3\cdot 4}$$

$$=\frac{11}{3}$$

$$=\frac{6x+3}{x}\cdot\frac{8}{2x+1}$$

$$=\frac{3(2x+1)}{x}\cdot\frac{8}{2x+1}$$

$$=\frac{24}{x}$$

───────────── Work Problem **1** at the Side. ▶

1 Simplify each complex fraction using Method 1.

GS (a) $\dfrac{\dfrac{2}{5}+\dfrac{1}{4}}{\dfrac{1}{2}+\dfrac{1}{3}}$

Step 1
Write the numerator as a single fraction. ____

Write the denominator as a single fraction. ____

Step 2
Write the equivalent fraction as a division problem.

────────

Step 3
Write the division problem as a multiplication problem.

────────

Multiply and write the answer in lowest terms. ____

(b) $\dfrac{6+\dfrac{1}{x}}{5-\dfrac{2}{x}}$

(c) $\dfrac{9-\dfrac{4}{p}}{\dfrac{2}{p}+1}$

Answers

1. (a) $\dfrac{13}{20};\dfrac{5}{6};\dfrac{13}{20}\div\dfrac{5}{6};\dfrac{13}{20}\cdot\dfrac{6}{5};\dfrac{39}{50}$

(b) $\dfrac{6x+1}{5x-2}$ **(c)** $\dfrac{9p-4}{2+p}$

2 Simplify each complex fraction using Method 1.

(a) $\dfrac{\dfrac{rs^2}{t}}{\dfrac{r^2s}{t^2}}$

(b) $\dfrac{\dfrac{m^2n^3}{p}}{\dfrac{m^4n}{p^2}}$

3 Simplify using Method 1.

$$\dfrac{5+\dfrac{2}{a-3}}{\dfrac{1}{a-3}-2}$$

Answers

2. **(a)** $\dfrac{st}{r}$ **(b)** $\dfrac{n^2p}{m^2}$

3. $\dfrac{5a-13}{7-2a}$

EXAMPLE 2 **Simplifying a Complex Fraction (Method 1)**

Simplify the complex fraction.

$\dfrac{\dfrac{xp}{q^3}}{\dfrac{p^2}{qx^2}}$ The numerator and denominator are single fractions, so use the definition of division and then the fundamental property.

$$\dfrac{xp}{q^3} \div \dfrac{p^2}{qx^2}$$

$$= \dfrac{xp}{q^3} \cdot \dfrac{qx^2}{p^2} \qquad (*)$$

$$= \dfrac{x \cdot p \cdot q \cdot x^2}{q \cdot q^2 \cdot p \cdot p}$$

$$= \dfrac{x^3}{pq^2}$$

◄ **Work Problem 2** at the Side.

Note

Alternatively, we can simplify equation $(*)$ in **Example 2** as follows.

$$\dfrac{xp}{q^3} \cdot \dfrac{qx^2}{p^2} = x^{1+2}p^{1-2}q^{1-3}$$ Product and quotient rules for exponents; Confirm that the same answer results.

EXAMPLE 3 **Simplifying a Complex Fraction (Method 1)**

Simplify the complex fraction.

$$\dfrac{\dfrac{3}{x+2} - 4}{\dfrac{2}{x+2} + 1}$$ Find a common denominator before subtracting in the numerator or adding in the denominator.

$$= \dfrac{\dfrac{3}{x+2} - \dfrac{4(x+2)}{x+2}}{\dfrac{2}{x+2} + \dfrac{1(x+2)}{x+2}}$$ Write both second terms with a denominator of $x+2$.

$$= \dfrac{\dfrac{3 - 4(x+2)}{x+2}}{\dfrac{2 + 1(x+2)}{x+2}}$$ Subtract in the numerator.

Add in the denominator.

$$= \dfrac{\dfrac{3 - 4x - 8}{x+2}}{\dfrac{2 + x + 2}{x+2}}$$ Be careful with signs.

Distributive property

$$= \dfrac{\dfrac{-5 - 4x}{x+2}}{\dfrac{4 + x}{x+2}}$$ Combine like terms.

$$= \dfrac{-5 - 4x}{x+2} \cdot \dfrac{x+2}{4+x}$$ Multiply by the reciprocal of the denominator (divisor).

$$= \dfrac{-5 - 4x}{4+x}$$ Divide out the common factor.

◄ **Work Problem 3** at the Side

OBJECTIVE ▶ ③ Simplify a complex fraction by multiplying numerator and denominator by the least common denominator (Method 2). If we multiply both the numerator and the denominator of a complex fraction by the LCD of all the fractions within the complex fraction, the result will no longer be complex. This is Method 2.

Method 2 for Simplifying a Complex Fraction

Step 1 Find the LCD of all fractions within the complex fraction.

Step 2 Multiply both the numerator and the denominator of the complex fraction by this LCD using the distributive property as necessary. Write in lowest terms.

EXAMPLE 4 **Simplifying Complex Fractions (Method 2)**

Simplify each complex fraction.

(a) $\dfrac{\frac{2}{3}+\frac{5}{9}}{\frac{1}{4}+\frac{1}{12}}$ (In **Example 1,** we simplified these same complex fractions using Method 1.)

(b) $\dfrac{6+\frac{3}{x}}{\frac{x}{4}+\frac{1}{8}}$

Step 1 Find the LCD for all denominators in the complex fraction.

The LCD for 3, 9, 4, and 12 is **36**. | The LCD for x, 4, and 8 is $8x$.

Step 2 Multiply both numerator and denominator by the LCD.

$\dfrac{\frac{2}{3}+\frac{5}{9}}{\frac{1}{4}+\frac{1}{12}}$

$= \dfrac{36\left(\frac{2}{3}+\frac{5}{9}\right)}{36\left(\frac{1}{4}+\frac{1}{12}\right)}$

$= \dfrac{36\left(\frac{2}{3}\right)+36\left(\frac{5}{9}\right)}{36\left(\frac{1}{4}\right)+36\left(\frac{1}{12}\right)}$ Multiply *each* term by 36.

$= \dfrac{24+20}{9+3}$ Multiply.

$= \dfrac{44}{12}$ Add.

$= \dfrac{4\cdot 11}{4\cdot 3}$ Factor.

$= \dfrac{11}{3}$ Same answer as in **Example 1(a)**

$\dfrac{6+\frac{3}{x}}{\frac{x}{4}+\frac{1}{8}}$

$= \dfrac{8x\left(6+\frac{3}{x}\right)}{8x\left(\frac{x}{4}+\frac{1}{8}\right)}$

$= \dfrac{8x(6)+8x\left(\frac{3}{x}\right)}{8x\left(\frac{x}{4}\right)+8x\left(\frac{1}{8}\right)}$ Multiply *each* term by 8x.

$= \dfrac{48x+24}{2x^2+x}$ Multiply.

$= \dfrac{24(2x+1)}{x(2x+1)}$ Factor.

$= \dfrac{24}{x}$ Same answer as in **Example 1(b)**

---

④ Simplify each complex fraction using Method 2.

GS **(a)** $\dfrac{\frac{2}{3}-\frac{1}{4}}{\frac{4}{9}+\frac{1}{2}}$

Step 1
The LCD for ____, ____, ____, and ____ is ____.

Refer to Step 2 in **Example 4,** and simplify the complex fraction.

(b) $\dfrac{2-\frac{6}{a}}{3+\frac{4}{a}}$

(c) $\dfrac{9-\frac{4}{p}}{\frac{2}{p}+1}$

(This is the same complex fraction simplified in **Margin Problem 1(c)** using Method 1. Compare the answers.)

Answers

4. (a) $3; 4; 9; 2; 36; \dfrac{15}{34}$

  (b) $\dfrac{2a-6}{3a+4}$ (c) $\dfrac{9p-4}{2+p}$

Work Problem ④ at the Side. ▶

⑤ Simplify using Method 2.

$$\dfrac{\dfrac{2}{5x} - \dfrac{3}{x^2}}{\dfrac{7}{4x} + \dfrac{1}{2x^2}}$$

The LCD for ____, ____, ____, and ____ is ____.

Simplify the complex fraction.

EXAMPLE 5 Simplifying a Complex Fraction (Method 2)

Simplify the complex fraction.

$$\dfrac{\dfrac{3}{5m} - \dfrac{2}{m^2}}{\dfrac{9}{2m} + \dfrac{3}{4m^2}}$$ The LCD for $5m$, m^2, $2m$, and $4m^2$ is $20m^2$.

$$= \dfrac{20m^2\left(\dfrac{3}{5m} - \dfrac{2}{m^2}\right)}{20m^2\left(\dfrac{9}{2m} + \dfrac{3}{4m^2}\right)}$$ Multiply numerator and denominator by $20m^2$.

$$= \dfrac{20m^2\left(\dfrac{3}{5m}\right) - 20m^2\left(\dfrac{2}{m^2}\right)}{20m^2\left(\dfrac{9}{2m}\right) + 20m^2\left(\dfrac{3}{4m^2}\right)}$$ Distributive property

$$= \dfrac{12m - 40}{90m + 15}, \quad \text{or} \quad \dfrac{4(3m - 10)}{5(18m + 3)}$$ Multiply and factor.

The factored form indicates that there are no common factors to divide out. The two forms are equivalent, so either can be given as the answer.

◀ **Work Problem ⑤ at the Side.**

Note

Either method can be used to simplify a complex fraction. A little more or less work may be involved based on the method selected, but the same answer will result if the method is applied correctly **(Examples 1 and 3).**

- We prefer Method 1 for problems that involve the quotient of two fractions, like **Example 2.**

- We prefer Method 2 for complex fractions that have sums or differences in the numerators or denominators, like **Examples 1, 3, 4, and 5.**

EXAMPLE 6 Simplifying Complex Fractions

Simplify each complex fraction. Use either method.

(a) $\dfrac{\dfrac{x + 2}{x - 3}}{\dfrac{x^2 - 4}{x^2 - 9}}$ This is a quotient of two rational expressions. We use Method 1.

$$= \dfrac{x + 2}{x - 3} \div \dfrac{x^2 - 4}{x^2 - 9}$$ Write as a division problem.

$$= \dfrac{x + 2}{x - 3} \cdot \dfrac{x^2 - 9}{x^2 - 4}$$ Multiply by the reciprocal.

$$= \dfrac{(x + 2)(x + 3)(x - 3)}{(x - 3)(x + 2)(x - 2)}$$ Multiply, and then factor.

$$= \dfrac{x + 3}{x - 2}$$ Divide out the common factors.

Continued on Next Page

Answer

5. $5x$; x^2; $4x$; $2x^2$; $20x^2$;

$\dfrac{8x - 60}{35x + 10}$, or $\dfrac{4(2x - 15)}{5(7x + 2)}$

(b) $\dfrac{\dfrac{1}{y} + \dfrac{2}{y+2}}{\dfrac{4}{y} - \dfrac{3}{y+2}}$ There are sums and differences in the numerator and denominator. We use Method 2.

$$= \frac{\left(\dfrac{1}{y} + \dfrac{2}{y+2}\right) y\,(y+2)}{\left(\dfrac{4}{y} - \dfrac{3}{y+2}\right) y\,(y+2)}$$ Multiply numerator and denominator by the LCD, $y\,(y+2)$. Because y appears in two denominators, it must be a factor in the LCD.

$$= \frac{\left(\dfrac{1}{y}\right) y\,(y+2) + \left(\dfrac{2}{y+2}\right) y\,(y+2)}{\left(\dfrac{4}{y}\right) y\,(y+2) - \left(\dfrac{3}{y+2}\right) y\,(y+2)}$$ Distributive property

$$= \frac{1\,(y+2) + 2y}{4\,(y+2) - 3y}$$ Multiply and simplify.

$$= \frac{y + 2 + 2y}{4y + 8 - 3y}$$ Distributive property

$$= \frac{3y + 2}{y + 8}$$ Combine like terms.

(c) $\dfrac{1 - \dfrac{2}{x} - \dfrac{3}{x^2}}{1 - \dfrac{5}{x} + \dfrac{6}{x^2}}$ As in **Example 6(b),** there are sums and differences in the numerator and denominator. We use Method 2.

$$= \frac{\left(1 - \dfrac{2}{x} - \dfrac{3}{x^2}\right) x^2}{\left(1 - \dfrac{5}{x} + \dfrac{6}{x^2}\right) x^2}$$ Multiply numerator and denominator by the LCD, x^2.

$$= \frac{(1)\,x^2 - \left(\dfrac{2}{x}\right) x^2 - \left(\dfrac{3}{x^2}\right) x^2}{(1)\,x^2 - \left(\dfrac{5}{x}\right) x^2 + \left(\dfrac{6}{x^2}\right) x^2}$$ Distributive property

$$= \frac{x^2 - 2x - 3}{x^2 - 5x + 6}$$ Multiply and simplify.

$$= \frac{(x-3)\,(x+1)}{(x-3)\,(x-2)}$$ Factor.

$$= \frac{x+1}{x-2}$$ Divide out the common factor.

— **Work Problem 6 at the Side.** ▶

6 Simplify each complex fraction. Use either method.

(a) $\dfrac{\dfrac{2x+3}{x-4}}{\dfrac{4x^2-9}{x^2-16}}$

(b) $\dfrac{\dfrac{1}{x} + \dfrac{2}{x-1}}{\dfrac{2}{x} - \dfrac{4}{x-1}}$

(c) $\dfrac{1 - \dfrac{2}{x} - \dfrac{15}{x^2}}{1 + \dfrac{5}{x} + \dfrac{6}{x^2}}$

Answers

6. (a) $\dfrac{x+4}{2x-3}$ **(b)** $\dfrac{3x-1}{-2x-2}$ **(c)** $\dfrac{x-5}{x+2}$

7 Simplify each expression, using only positive exponents in the answer.

(a) $\dfrac{r^{-2} - s^{-1}}{4r^{-1} + s^{-2}}$

We begin by rewriting these expressions with only positive exponents. Recall that for any nonzero real number a and any integer n,

$$a^{-n} = \frac{1}{a^n}. \qquad \text{Definition of negative exponent}$$

⚠ CAUTION

$$a^{-1} + b^{-1} = \frac{1}{a} + \frac{1}{b}, \quad \textbf{not} \quad \frac{1}{a+b}. \qquad \text{Avoid this common error.}$$

EXAMPLE 7 **Simplifying a Rational Expression with Negative Exponents**

Simplify the expression, using only positive exponents in the answer.

$$\frac{m^{-1} + p^{-2}}{2m^{-2} - p^{-1}} \qquad a^{-n} = \frac{1}{a^n}$$

The base of $2m^{-2}$ is m, not $2m$: $2m^{-2} = \frac{2}{m^2}$.

$$= \frac{\dfrac{1}{m} + \dfrac{1}{p^2}}{\dfrac{2}{m^2} - \dfrac{1}{p}} \qquad \begin{array}{l}\text{Write with positive exponents.}\\ 2m^{-2} = 2 \cdot m^{-2} = \frac{2}{1} \cdot \frac{1}{m^2} = \frac{2}{m^2}\end{array}$$

(b) $\dfrac{x^{-2} - 2y^{-1}}{y - 2x^2}$

$$= \frac{m^2 p^2 \left(\dfrac{1}{m} + \dfrac{1}{p^2} \right)}{m^2 p^2 \left(\dfrac{2}{m^2} - \dfrac{1}{p} \right)} \qquad \begin{array}{l}\text{Simplify by Method 2.}\\ \text{Multiply the numerator and}\\ \text{denominator by the LCD, } m^2 p^2.\end{array}$$

$$= \frac{m^2 p^2 \cdot \dfrac{1}{m} + m^2 p^2 \cdot \dfrac{1}{p^2}}{m^2 p^2 \cdot \dfrac{2}{m^2} - m^2 p^2 \cdot \dfrac{1}{p}} \qquad \text{Distributive property}$$

$$= \frac{mp^2 + m^2}{2p^2 - m^2 p} \qquad \text{Write in lowest terms.}$$

◀ **Work Problem 7 at the Side.**

Answers

7. (a) $\dfrac{s^2 - r^2 s}{4rs^2 + r^2}$ (b) $\dfrac{1}{x^2 y}$

7.5 Exercises

FOR EXTRA HELP

Go to MyMathLab *for worked-out, step-by-step solutions to exercises enclosed in a square* ▢ *and video solutions to* ▶ *exercises.*

CONCEPT CHECK   *Answer each question.*

1. In a fraction, what operation does the fraction bar represent?

2. What property of real numbers justifies Method 2 of simplifying complex fractions?

ⓖⓢ *Consider the following complex fraction.*

$$\dfrac{\dfrac{1}{2} - \dfrac{1}{3}}{\dfrac{5}{6} - \dfrac{1}{12}}$$

3. Answer each part, outlining Method 1 for simplifying this complex fraction.

   (a) To combine the terms in the numerator, we must find the LCD of $\frac{1}{2}$ and $\frac{1}{3}$.
   What is this LCD? _____
   Determine the simplified form of the numerator of the complex fraction. _____

   (b) To combine the terms in the denominator, we must find the LCD of $\frac{5}{6}$ and $\frac{1}{12}$.
   What is this LCD? _____
   Determine the simplified form of the denominator of the complex fraction. _____

   (c) Now use the results from parts (a) and (b) to write the complex fraction as a division problem using the symbol ÷. _____

   (d) Perform the operation from part (c) to obtain the final simplification. _____

4. Answer each part, outlining Method 2 for simplifying this complex fraction.

   (a) We must determine the LCD of all the fractions within the complex fraction.
   What is this LCD? _____

   (b) Multiply every term in the complex fraction by the LCD found in part (a), but at this time do not combine the terms in the numerator and the denominator. _____

   (c) Now combine the terms from part (b) to obtain the simplified form of the complex fraction. _____

CONCEPT CHECK   *Recall that slope measures the steepness of a line and is calculated using the formula*

$$\textbf{slope } m = \frac{\textbf{change in } y}{\textbf{change in } x} = \frac{y_2 - y_1}{x_2 - x_1} \quad (\textbf{where } x_1 \neq x_2).$$

Find the slope of the line that passes through each pair of points. This will involve simplifying complex fractions.

5. $\left(\dfrac{3}{4}, \dfrac{1}{3}\right)$ and $\left(\dfrac{5}{4}, \dfrac{10}{3}\right)$

6. $\left(-\dfrac{4}{5}, \dfrac{1}{2}\right)$ and $\left(-\dfrac{3}{10}, -\dfrac{1}{5}\right)$

Simplify each complex fraction. Use either method. ***See Examples 1–6.***

7. $\dfrac{-\dfrac{4}{3}}{\dfrac{2}{9}}$

8. $\dfrac{-\dfrac{5}{6}}{\dfrac{5}{4}}$

9. $\dfrac{\dfrac{5}{8}+\dfrac{2}{3}}{\dfrac{7}{3}-\dfrac{1}{4}}$

10. $\dfrac{\dfrac{6}{5}-\dfrac{1}{9}}{\dfrac{2}{5}+\dfrac{5}{3}}$

11. $\dfrac{\dfrac{x}{y^2}}{\dfrac{x^2}{y}}$

12. $\dfrac{\dfrac{p^4}{r}}{\dfrac{p^2}{r^2}}$

13. $\dfrac{\dfrac{p}{6q^2}}{\dfrac{p^2}{q}}$

14. $\dfrac{\dfrac{a}{x}}{\dfrac{a^2}{2x}}$

15. $\dfrac{\dfrac{4a^4b^3}{3a}}{\dfrac{2ab^4}{b^2}}$

16. $\dfrac{\dfrac{2r^4t^2}{3t}}{\dfrac{5r^2t^5}{3r}}$

17. $\dfrac{\dfrac{m+2}{3}}{\dfrac{m-4}{m}}$

18. $\dfrac{\dfrac{q-5}{q}}{\dfrac{q+5}{3}}$

19. $\dfrac{\dfrac{2}{x}-3}{\dfrac{2-3x}{2}}$

20. $\dfrac{6+\dfrac{2}{r}}{\dfrac{3r+1}{4}}$

21. $\dfrac{\dfrac{1}{x}+x}{\dfrac{x^2+1}{8}}$

22. $\dfrac{\dfrac{3}{m}-m}{\dfrac{3-m^2}{4}}$

23. $\dfrac{a-\dfrac{5}{a}}{a+\dfrac{1}{a}}$

24. $\dfrac{q+\dfrac{1}{q}}{q+\dfrac{4}{q}}$

25. $\dfrac{\dfrac{1}{2}+\dfrac{1}{p}}{\dfrac{2}{3}+\dfrac{1}{p}}$

26. $\dfrac{\dfrac{3}{4}-\dfrac{1}{r}}{\dfrac{1}{5}+\dfrac{1}{r}}$

27. $\dfrac{\dfrac{1}{4}-\dfrac{1}{a^2}}{\dfrac{1}{2}+\dfrac{1}{a}}$

28. $\dfrac{\dfrac{1}{9}-\dfrac{1}{m^2}}{\dfrac{1}{3}+\dfrac{1}{m}}$

29. $\dfrac{\dfrac{2}{p^2}-\dfrac{3}{5p}}{\dfrac{4}{p}+\dfrac{1}{4p}}$

30. $\dfrac{\dfrac{2}{m^2}-\dfrac{3}{m}}{\dfrac{2}{5m^2}+\dfrac{1}{3m}}$

31. $\dfrac{\dfrac{t}{t+2}}{\dfrac{4}{t^2-4}}$

32. $\dfrac{\dfrac{m}{m+1}}{\dfrac{3}{m^2-1}}$

33. $\dfrac{\dfrac{1}{m+1}-1}{\dfrac{1}{m+1}+1}$

34. $\dfrac{\dfrac{2}{p-1}+2}{\dfrac{3}{p-1}-2}$

35. $\dfrac{2 + \dfrac{1}{x} - \dfrac{28}{x^2}}{3 + \dfrac{13}{x} + \dfrac{4}{x^2}}$

36. $\dfrac{4 - \dfrac{11}{x} - \dfrac{3}{x^2}}{2 - \dfrac{1}{x} - \dfrac{15}{x^2}}$

37. $\dfrac{\dfrac{1}{m-1} + \dfrac{2}{m+2}}{\dfrac{2}{m+2} - \dfrac{1}{m-3}}$

38. $\dfrac{\dfrac{5}{r+3} - \dfrac{1}{r-1}}{\dfrac{2}{r+2} + \dfrac{3}{r+3}}$

Simplify each expression, using only positive exponents in the answer. **See Example 7.**

39. $\dfrac{1}{x^{-2} + y^{-2}}$

40. $\dfrac{1}{p^{-2} - q^{-2}}$

41. $\dfrac{x^{-2} + y^{-2}}{x^{-1} + y^{-1}}$

42. $\dfrac{x^{-1} - y^{-1}}{x^{-2} - y^{-2}}$

43. $\dfrac{2y^{-1} - 3y^{-2}}{y^{-2} + 3x^{-1}}$

44. $\dfrac{k^{-1} + p^{-2}}{k^{-1} - 3p^{-2}}$

45. $\dfrac{x^{-1} + 2y^{-1}}{2y + 4x}$

46. $\dfrac{a^{-2} - 4b^{-2}}{3b - 6a}$

Relating Concepts (Exercises 47–52) For Individual or Group Work

Simplifying a complex fraction by Method 1 is a good way to review the methods of adding, subtracting, multiplying, and dividing rational expressions. Method 2 gives a good review of the fundamental property of rational numbers.

Refer to the following complex fraction, and **work Exercises 47–52 in order.**

$$\dfrac{\dfrac{4}{m} + \dfrac{m+2}{m-1}}{\dfrac{m+2}{m} - \dfrac{2}{m-1}}$$

47. Add the fractions in the numerator.

48. Subtract as indicated in the denominator.

49. Divide the answer from **Exercise 47** by the answer from **Exercise 48.**

50. Go back to the original complex fraction and find the LCD of all denominators.

51. Multiply the numerator and denominator of the complex fraction by the answer from **Exercise 50.**

52. The answers for **Exercises 49 and 51** should be the same. Which method do you prefer? Explain why.

7.6 | Solving Equations with Rational Expressions

OBJECTIVES

1 Distinguish between operations with rational expressions and equations with terms that are rational expressions.

2 Solve equations with rational expressions.

3 Solve a formula for a specified variable.

OBJECTIVE ▶ **1** Distinguish between operations with rational expressions and equations with terms that are rational expressions. We emphasize the distinction between sums and differences of terms with rational coefficients—that is, rational *expressions*—and *equations* with terms that are rational expressions.

Sums and differences are expressions to simplify. Equations are solved.

EXAMPLE 1 | Distinguishing between an Expression and an Equation

Identify each of the following as an *expression* or an *equation*. Then *simplify the expression* or *solve the equation*.

(a) $\dfrac{3}{4}x - \dfrac{2}{3}x$ This is a difference of two terms. It represents an *expression* to simplify—there is no equality symbol.

$$= \frac{3 \cdot 3}{3 \cdot 4}x - \frac{4 \cdot 2}{4 \cdot 3}x$$ The LCD is 12. Write each coefficient with this LCD.

$$= \frac{9}{12}x - \frac{8}{12}x$$ Multiply.

$$= \frac{1}{12}x$$ Combine like terms, using the distributive property: $\frac{9}{12}x - \frac{8}{12}x = \left(\frac{9}{12} - \frac{8}{12}\right)x.$

(b) $\qquad \dfrac{3}{4}x - \dfrac{2}{3}x = \dfrac{1}{2}$ Because there is an equality symbol, this is an *equation* to be solved.

$$12\left(\frac{3}{4}x - \frac{2}{3}x\right) = 12\left(\frac{1}{2}\right)$$ Use the multiplication property of equality to clear the fractions. Multiply by 12, the LCD.

$$12\left(\frac{3}{4}x\right) - 12\left(\frac{2}{3}x\right) = 12\left(\frac{1}{2}\right)$$ Distributive property

Multiply *each* term by 12.

$$9x - 8x = 6$$ Multiply.

$$x = 6$$ Combine like terms.

CHECK $\qquad \dfrac{3}{4}x - \dfrac{2}{3}x = \dfrac{1}{2}$ Original equation

$$\frac{3}{4}(6) - \frac{2}{3}(6) \overset{?}{=} \frac{1}{2}$$ Let $x = 6$.

$$\frac{9}{2} - 4 \overset{?}{=} \frac{1}{2}$$ Multiply.

$$\frac{1}{2} = \frac{1}{2} \checkmark$$ True

A true statement results, so $\{6\}$ is the solution set of the equation.

◀ **Work Problem** 1 at the Side.

1 Identify each of the following as an *expression* or an *equation*. Then *simplify the expression* or *solve the equation*.

(a) $\dfrac{2}{3}x - \dfrac{4}{9}x$

(b) $\dfrac{2}{3}x - \dfrac{4}{9}x = 2$

Answers

1. **(a)** expression; $\dfrac{2}{9}x$

   (b) equation; $\{9\}$

The ideas of **Example 1** can be summarized as follows.

Uses of the LCD

When adding or subtracting rational expressions, keep the LCD throughout the simplification. **(See Example 1(a).)**

When solving an equation with terms that are rational expressions, multiply each side by the LCD so that denominators are eliminated. **(See Example 1(b).)**

OBJECTIVE ▶ **2** **Solve equations with rational expressions.** When an equation involves fractions as in **Example 1(b),** we use the multiplication property of equality to clear the fractions. We choose the LCD of all denominators as the multiplier so the resulting equation contains no fractions.

EXAMPLE 2 **Solving an Equation with Rational Expressions**

Solve, and check the solution.

$$\frac{x}{3} + \frac{x}{4} = 10 + x$$

$$12\left(\frac{x}{3} + \frac{x}{4}\right) = 12\,(10 + x) \qquad \text{Multiply by the LCD, 12, to clear the fractions.}$$

$$12\left(\frac{x}{3}\right) + 12\left(\frac{x}{4}\right) = 12\,(10) + 12x \qquad \text{Distributive property}$$

$$4x + 3x = 120 + 12x \qquad \text{Multiply.}$$

$$7x = 120 + 12x \qquad \text{Combine like terms.}$$

$$-5x = 120 \qquad \text{Subtract } 12x.$$

$$x = -24 \qquad \text{Divide by } -5.$$

CHECK

$$\frac{x}{3} + \frac{x}{4} = 10 + x \qquad \text{Original equation}$$

$$\frac{-24}{3} + \frac{-24}{4} \overset{?}{=} 10 + (-24) \qquad \text{Let } x = -24.$$

$$-8 + (-6) \overset{?}{=} -14 \qquad \text{Divide. Add.}$$

$$-14 = -14 \ \checkmark \qquad \text{True}$$

A true statement results, so the solution set is $\{-24\}$.

──────────── **Work Problem ② at the Side.** ▶

❗ CAUTION

Be careful not to confuse the following procedures.

- In **Examples 2 and 3,** we use the multiplication property of equality to multiply each side of an *equation* by the LCD.

- In our work with complex fractions, we used the fundamental property to multiply a *fraction* (an *expression*) by another fraction that had the LCD as both its numerator and denominator.

2 Solve each equation, and check the solutions.

(a) $\dfrac{x}{2} - \dfrac{x}{3} = \dfrac{5}{6}$

(b) $\dfrac{x}{6} + \dfrac{x}{3} = 6 + x$

Answers

2. (a) $\{5\}$ **(b)** $\{-12\}$

3 Solve each equation, and check the solutions.

GS **(a)** $\dfrac{k}{6} - \dfrac{k+1}{4} = -\dfrac{1}{2}$

Multiply by the LCD, ____.

$\underline{}\left(\dfrac{k}{6} - \dfrac{k+1}{4}\right) = \underline{}\left(-\dfrac{1}{2}\right)$

Complete the solution.

(b) $\dfrac{2m-3}{5} - \dfrac{m}{3} = -\dfrac{6}{5}$

4 Solve the equation, and check the proposed solution.

$1 - \dfrac{2}{x+1} = \dfrac{2x}{x+1}$

Answers

3. **(a)** 12; 12; 12; $\{3\}$ **(b)** $\{-9\}$

4. $\varnothing$ (When the equation is solved, -1 is a proposed solution. However, because $x = -1$ leads to a 0 denominator in the original equation, there is no solution.)

EXAMPLE 3 Solving an Equation with Rational Expressions

Solve, and check the solution.

$$\frac{p}{2} - \frac{p-1}{3} = 1$$

$$6\left(\frac{p}{2} - \frac{p-1}{3}\right) = 6\,(1) \qquad \text{Multiply by the LCD, 6, to clear the fractions.}$$

$$6\left(\frac{p}{2}\right) - 6\left(\frac{p-1}{3}\right) = 6\,(1) \qquad \text{Distributive property}$$

$$3p - 2\,(p-1) = 6 \qquad \boxed{\text{Use parentheses around } p-1 \text{ to avoid errors.}}$$

$$3p - 2\,(p) - 2\,(-1) = 6 \qquad \text{Distributive property}$$

$$\boxed{\text{Be careful with signs.}} \qquad 3p - 2p + 2 = 6 \qquad \text{Multiply.}$$

$$p = 4 \qquad \text{Combine like terms. Subtract 2.}$$

Check that $\{4\}$ is the solution set by replacing p with 4 in the original equation.

◀ **Work Problem** **3** at the Side.

Recall that division by 0 is undefined. *Therefore, when solving an equation with rational expressions that have variables in the denominator, the solution cannot be a number that makes the denominator equal* **0.**

A value of the variable that appears to be a solution after both sides of an equation with rational expressions are multiplied by a variable expression is a **proposed solution.** *All proposed solutions must be checked.*

EXAMPLE 4 Solving an Equation with Rational Expressions

Solve, and check the proposed solution.

$$\frac{x}{x-2} = \frac{2}{x-2} + 2 \qquad \begin{array}{l} x \textit{ cannot} \text{ equal 2 because 2 causes} \\ \text{both denominators to equal 0.} \end{array}$$

$$(x-2)\left(\frac{x}{x-2}\right) = (x-2)\left(\frac{2}{x-2} + 2\right) \qquad \begin{array}{l} \text{Multiply each side} \\ \text{by the LCD, } x-2. \end{array}$$

$$(x-2)\left(\frac{x}{x-2}\right) = (x-2)\left(\frac{2}{x-2}\right) + (x-2)\,(2) \qquad \text{Distributive property}$$

$$x = 2 + 2x - 4 \qquad \text{Simplify.}$$

$$x = -2 + 2x \qquad \text{Combine like terms.}$$

$$-x = -2 \qquad \text{Subtract } 2x.$$

$$\begin{array}{l} \text{Proposed} \\ \text{solution} \end{array} \rightarrow x = 2 \qquad \text{Multiply by } -1.$$

CHECK $\qquad \dfrac{x}{x-2} = \dfrac{2}{x-2} + 2 \qquad$ Original equation

$$\frac{2}{2-2} \overset{?}{=} \frac{2}{2-2} + 2 \qquad \text{Let } x = 2.$$

$\boxed{\text{Division by 0 is undefined.}} \quad \dfrac{2}{0} \overset{?}{=} \dfrac{2}{0} + 2 \qquad$ Subtract in the denominators.

Thus, the proposed solution 2 must be rejected. The solution set is $\varnothing$.

◀ **Work Problem** **4** at the Side.

A proposed solution that is not an actual solution of the original equation, such as 2 in **Example 4,** is an **extraneous solution,** or **extraneous value.** Some students like to determine which numbers cannot be solutions *before* solving the equation, as we did at the beginning of **Example 4.**

Solving an Equation with Rational Expressions

Step 1 **Multiply each side of the equation by the LCD** (This clears the equation of fractions.) Be sure to distribute to *every* term on *both* sides of the equation.

Step 2 **Solve** the resulting equation for proposed solutions.

Step 3 **Check** each proposed solution by substituting it in the original equation. Reject any value that causes a denominator to equal 0.

EXAMPLE 5 Solving an Equation with Rational Expressions

Solve, and check the proposed solution.

$$\frac{2}{x^2 - x} = \frac{1}{x^2 - 1}$$

Step 1 $\qquad \dfrac{2}{x(x-1)} = \dfrac{1}{(x+1)(x-1)} \qquad$ Factor the denominators to find the LCD.

The LCD is $x(x+1)(x-1)$. *Notice that* 0, -1, *and* 1 *cannot be solutions of this equation.* Otherwise, a denominator will equal 0.

$$x(x+1)(x-1)\frac{2}{x(x-1)} = x(x+1)(x-1)\frac{1}{(x+1)(x-1)}$$

Multiply by the LCD to clear the fractions.

Step 2 $\qquad\qquad 2(x+1) = x \qquad$ Divide out the common factors.

$\qquad\qquad\qquad 2x + 2 = x \qquad$ Distributive property

$\qquad\qquad\qquad\quad x + 2 = 0 \qquad$ Subtract x.

Proposed solution $\rightarrow x = -2 \qquad$ Subtract 2.

Step 3 The proposed solution is -2, which does not make any denominator equal 0.

CHECK $\qquad \dfrac{2}{x^2 - x} = \dfrac{1}{x^2 - 1} \qquad$ Original equation

$$\frac{2}{(-2)^2 - (-2)} \overset{?}{=} \frac{1}{(-2)^2 - 1} \qquad \text{Let } x = -2.$$

$$\frac{2}{4 + 2} \overset{?}{=} \frac{1}{4 - 1} \qquad \begin{array}{l}\text{Apply the exponents;}\\ \text{Definition of subtraction}\end{array}$$

$$\frac{1}{3} = \frac{1}{3} \checkmark \qquad \text{True}$$

A true statement results, so the solution set is $\{-2\}$.

Work Problem **5** *at the Side.* ▶

5 Solve each equation, and check the proposed solutions.

(a) $\dfrac{4}{x^2 - 3x} = \dfrac{1}{x^2 - 9}$

(b) $\dfrac{2}{p^2 - 2p} = \dfrac{3}{p^2 - p}$

Step 1
Factor the denominators.

$p^2 - 2p = p(\underline{\hspace{1cm}})$

$p^2 - p = p(\underline{\hspace{1cm}})$

The LCD is $\underline{\hspace{1.5cm}}$.

The numbers $\underline{\hspace{0.6cm}}$, $\underline{\hspace{0.6cm}}$, and $\underline{\hspace{0.6cm}}$ cannot be solutions.

Complete the steps to solve the equation.

Answers

5. (a) $\{-4\}$
 (b) $p - 2$; $p - 1$; $p(p-2)(p-1)$; 0; 1; 2 (Order of the numbers 0, 1, and 2 does not matter.); $\{4\}$

⑥ Solve each equation, and check the proposed solutions.

(a) $\dfrac{2y}{y^2 - 25} = \dfrac{8}{y + 5} - \dfrac{1}{y - 5}$

(b) $\dfrac{8r}{4r^2 - 1} = \dfrac{3}{2r + 1} + \dfrac{3}{2r - 1}$

EXAMPLE 6 Solving an Equation with Rational Expressions

Solve, and check the proposed solution.

$$\frac{2m}{m^2 - 4} + \frac{1}{m - 2} = \frac{2}{m + 2}$$

$$\frac{2m}{(m + 2)(m - 2)} + \frac{1}{m - 2} = \frac{2}{m + 2}$$

Factor the first denominator on the left to find the LCD, $(m + 2)(m - 2)$.

Notice that -2 and 2 cannot be solutions of the equation.

$$(m + 2)(m - 2)\left(\frac{2m}{(m + 2)(m - 2)} + \frac{1}{m - 2}\right)$$

$$= (m + 2)(m - 2)\frac{2}{m + 2} \quad \text{Multiply by the LCD.}$$

$$(m + 2)(m - 2)\frac{2m}{(m + 2)(m - 2)} + (m + 2)(m - 2)\frac{1}{m - 2}$$

$$= (m + 2)(m - 2)\frac{2}{m + 2} \quad \text{Distributive property}$$

$$2m + m + 2 = 2(m - 2) \quad \text{Divide out the common factors.}$$

$$3m + 2 = 2m - 4 \quad \text{Combine like terms; distributive property}$$

$$m + 2 = -4 \quad \text{Subtract } 2m.$$

$$m = -6 \quad \text{Subtract 2.}$$

CHECK $\quad \dfrac{2m}{m^2 - 4} + \dfrac{1}{m - 2} = \dfrac{2}{m + 2} \quad$ Original equation

$$\frac{2(-6)}{(-6)^2 - 4} + \frac{1}{-6 - 2} \stackrel{?}{=} \frac{2}{-6 + 2} \quad \text{Let } m = -6.$$

$$\frac{-12}{32} + \frac{1}{-8} \stackrel{?}{=} \frac{2}{-4} \quad \begin{array}{l}\text{Apply the exponent.}\\ \text{Subtract and add.}\end{array}$$

$$-\frac{1}{2} = -\frac{1}{2} \checkmark \quad \text{True}$$

The solution set is $\{-6\}$.

◀ **Work Problem ⑥ at the Side.**

EXAMPLE 7 Solving an Equation with Rational Expressions

Solve, and check the proposed solution(s).

$$\frac{1}{x - 1} + \frac{1}{2} = \frac{2}{x^2 - 1}$$

$$\frac{1}{x - 1} + \frac{1}{2} = \frac{2}{(x + 1)(x - 1)} \quad \boxed{x \neq 1, -1 \text{ or a}\\ \text{denominator is 0.}}$$

Factor the denominator on the right. The LCD is $2(x + 1)(x - 1)$.

Continued on Next Page

Answers

6. (a) $\{9\}$ **(b)** $\{0\}$

$$2(x+1)(x-1)\left(\frac{1}{x-1}+\frac{1}{2}\right) = 2(x+1)(x-1)\frac{2}{(x+1)(x-1)}$$

Multiply by the LCD.

$$2(x+1)(x-1)\frac{1}{x-1} + 2(x+1)(x-1)\frac{1}{2}$$

$$= 2(x+1)(x-1)\frac{2}{(x+1)(x-1)}$$

Distributive property

$2(x+1)+(x+1)(x-1) = 2(2)$ Divide out the common factors.

$2x+2+x^2-1 = 4$ Distributive property; Multiply.

Write in standard form. $\rightarrow x^2+2x-3=0$ Subtract 4. Combine like terms.

$(x+3)(x-1)=0$ Factor.

$x+3=0 \quad$ or $\quad x-1=0$ Zero-factor property

$x=-3 \quad$ or $\quad x=1 \leftarrow$ Proposed solutions

Because 1 makes an original denominator equal 0, the proposed solution 1 is an extraneous value. Check that -3 is a solution.

CHECK
$$\frac{1}{x-1}+\frac{1}{2}=\frac{2}{x^2-1}$$
Original equation

$$\frac{1}{-3-1}+\frac{1}{2} \overset{?}{=} \frac{2}{(-3)^2-1}$$
Let $x=-3$.

$$\frac{1}{-4}+\frac{1}{2} \overset{?}{=} \frac{2}{9-1}$$
Subtract. Apply the exponent.

$$\frac{1}{4}=\frac{1}{4} \checkmark$$
True

The check shows that the solution set is $\{-3\}$.

— **Work Problem 7 at the Side.** ▶

7 Solve each equation, and check the proposed solution(s).

(a) $\dfrac{3}{m^2-9}=\dfrac{1}{2(m-3)}-\dfrac{1}{4}$

(b) $\dfrac{1}{x-1}-\dfrac{2}{x+3}=\dfrac{x^2+3x}{x^2+2x-3}$

EXAMPLE 8 Solving an Equation with Rational Expressions

Solve, and check the proposed solution(s).

$$\frac{1}{k^2+4k+3}+\frac{1}{2k+2}=\frac{3}{4k+12}$$

$$\frac{1}{(k+1)(k+3)}+\frac{1}{2(k+1)}=\frac{3}{4(k+3)}$$
Factor each denominator. The LCD is $4(k+1)(k+3)$.

$k \neq -1,-3$

$$4(k+1)(k+3)\left(\frac{1}{(k+1)(k+3)}+\frac{1}{2(k+1)}\right)$$

$$= 4(k+1)(k+3)\frac{3}{4(k+3)}$$
Multiply by the LCD.

— **Continued on Next Page**

Answers
7. (a) $\{-1\}$ (b) $\{-5\}$

8 Solve each equation, and check the proposed solution(s).

(a)

$$\frac{5}{k^2 + k - 2} = \frac{1}{3k - 3} - \frac{1}{k + 2}$$

(b) $\dfrac{1}{x - 2} + \dfrac{1}{5} = \dfrac{2}{5(x^2 - 4)}$

9 Solve each formula for the specified variable.

(GS) (a) $r = \dfrac{A - p}{pt}$ for A

The goal is to isolate _____.
Multiply by pt to obtain the equation _____.

Add _____ to obtain the equation

_____ $= A$, or _____.

(b) $p = \dfrac{x - y}{z}$ for y

$$4(k + 1)(k + 3)\frac{1}{(k + 1)(k + 3)} + 2 \cdot 2(k + 1)(k + 3)\frac{1}{2(k + 1)}$$

Do *not* add 4 + 2 here.

$$= 4(k + 1)(k + 3)\frac{3}{4(k + 3)} \quad \text{Distributive property}$$

$$4 + 2(k + 3) = 3(k + 1) \quad \text{Divide out the common factors.}$$

$$4 + 2k + 6 = 3k + 3 \quad \text{Distributive property}$$

$$2k + 10 = 3k + 3 \quad \text{Combine like terms.}$$

$$10 = k + 3 \quad \text{Subtract } 2k.$$

$$7 = k \quad \text{Subtract 3.}$$

The proposed solution, 7, does not make an original denominator equal 0. A check shows that the algebra is correct, so the solution set is $\{7\}$.

◀ **Work Problem 8 at the Side.**

OBJECTIVE 3 Solve a formula for a specified variable.

When solving a formula for a specified variable, remember to treat the variable for which you are solving as if it were the only variable, and all others as if they were constants.

EXAMPLE 9 Solving for a Specified Variable

Solve the following formula for v.

$$a = \frac{v - w}{t} \quad \boxed{\text{Our goal is to isolate } v.}$$

$$at = \left(\frac{v - w}{t}\right)t \quad \text{Multiply by } t \text{ to clear the fraction.}$$

$$at = v - w \quad \text{Divide out the common factor.}$$

$$at + w = v \quad \text{Add } w.$$

$$v = at + w \quad \text{Interchange sides.}$$

CHECK Substitute $at + w$ for v in the original equation.

$$a = \frac{v - w}{t} \quad \text{Original equation}$$

$$a = \frac{at + w - w}{t} \quad \text{Let } v = at + w.$$

$$a = \frac{at}{t} \quad \text{Combine like terms.}$$

$$a = a \checkmark \quad \text{True}$$

A true statement results, so $v = at + w$.

◀ **Work Problem 9 at the Side.**

Answers

8. **(a)** $\{-5\}$ **(b)** $\{-4, -1\}$
9. **(a)** A; $rpt = A - p$; p; $p + prt$;
   $A = p + prt$
   (b) $y = x - pz$

EXAMPLE 10 Solving for a Specified Variable

Solve the following formula for d.

$$F = \frac{k}{d - D}$$ We must isolate d.

$$F(d - D) = \frac{k}{d - D}(d - D)$$ Multiply by $d - D$ to clear the fraction.

$$F(d - D) = k$$ Divide out the common factor.

$$Fd - FD = k$$ Distributive property

$$Fd = k + FD$$ Add FD.

$$d = \frac{k + FD}{F}$$ Divide by F.

We can write an equivalent form of this answer as follows.

$$d = \frac{k + FD}{F}$$ Answer from above

$$d = \frac{k}{F} + \frac{FD}{F}$$ Definition of addition of fractions: $\frac{a + b}{c} = \frac{a}{c} + \frac{b}{c}$

This form of the answer is also correct. $\quad d = \frac{k}{F} + D$ Divide out the common factor from $\frac{FD}{F}$.

—————— **Work Problem 10 at the Side.** ▶

EXAMPLE 11 Solving for a Specified Variable

Solve the following formula for c.

$$\frac{1}{a} = \frac{1}{b} + \frac{1}{c}$$ Goal: Isolate c, the specified variable.

$$abc\left(\frac{1}{a}\right) = abc\left(\frac{1}{b} + \frac{1}{c}\right)$$ Multiply by the LCD, abc, to clear the fractions.

$$abc\left(\frac{1}{a}\right) = abc\left(\frac{1}{b}\right) + abc\left(\frac{1}{c}\right)$$ Distributive property

$$bc = ac + ab$$ Divide out the common factors.

Pay careful attention here. $\quad bc - ac = ab \quad (*)$ Subtract ac so that both terms with c are on the same side.

$$c(b - a) = ab$$ Factor out c.

$$c = \frac{ab}{b - a}$$ Divide by $b - a$.

—————— **Work Problem 11 at the Side.** ▶

❗ **CAUTION**

In **Example 11,** we transformed to obtain equation $(*)$ that has *both* terms with c on the same side of the equality symbol. This key step enabled us to factor out c on the left and ultimately isolate it.

When solving an equation for a specified variable, be sure that the specified variable appears alone on only one side of the equality symbol in the final equation.

10 Solve the following formula for y.

$$z = \frac{x}{x + y}$$

11 Solve the formula

$$\frac{2}{x} = \frac{1}{y} + \frac{1}{z}$$

for the specified variable.

(a) for z

(b) for y

Answers

10. $y = \dfrac{x - zx}{z}$, or $y = \dfrac{x}{z} - x$

11. (a) $z = \dfrac{xy}{2y - x}$ **(b)** $y = \dfrac{xz}{2z - x}$

7.6 Exercises

FOR EXTRA HELP

Go to MyMathLab *for worked-out, step-by-step solutions to exercises enclosed in a square* ▢ *and video solutions to* ▶ *exercises.*

CONCEPT CHECK *Fill in each blank with the correct response.*

1. A value of the variable that appears to be a solution after both sides of an equation with rational expressions are multiplied by a variable expression is a(n) _____ solution. It must be checked in the _____ equation to determine whether it is an actual solution.

2. A proposed solution that is not an actual solution of an original equation is a(n) _____ solution, or _____ value.

Identify each as an expression *or an* equation. *Then* simplify the expression *or* solve the equation. *See Example 1.*

3. $\dfrac{7}{8}x + \dfrac{1}{5}x$ ▶

4. $\dfrac{4}{7}x + \dfrac{3}{5}x$

5. $\dfrac{7}{8}x + \dfrac{1}{5}x = 1$

6. $\dfrac{4}{7}x + \dfrac{3}{5}x = 1$

7. $\dfrac{3}{5}y - \dfrac{7}{10}y$

8. $\dfrac{3}{5}y - \dfrac{7}{10}y = 1$

9. $\dfrac{2}{3}x - \dfrac{9}{4}x = -19$

10. $\dfrac{2}{3}x - \dfrac{9}{4}x$

Solve each equation, and check the solutions. See Examples 2 and 3.

11. $\dfrac{2}{3}x + \dfrac{1}{2}x = -7$

12. $\dfrac{1}{4}x - \dfrac{1}{3}x = 1$

13. $\dfrac{3x}{5} - 6 = x$

14. $\dfrac{5t}{4} + t = 9$

15. $\dfrac{4m}{7} + m = 11$

16. $a - \dfrac{3a}{2} = 1$

17. $\dfrac{z-1}{4} = \dfrac{z+3}{3}$

18. $\dfrac{r-5}{2} = \dfrac{r+2}{3}$

19. $\dfrac{3p+6}{8} = \dfrac{3p-3}{16}$

20. $\dfrac{2z+1}{5} = \dfrac{7z+5}{15}$

21. $\dfrac{2x+3}{-6} = \dfrac{3}{2}$

22. $\dfrac{4x+3}{6} = \dfrac{5}{2}$

23. $\dfrac{r}{6} - \dfrac{r-2}{3} = -\dfrac{4}{3}$

24. $\dfrac{p}{2} - \dfrac{p-1}{4} = \dfrac{5}{4}$

25. $\dfrac{q+2}{3} + \dfrac{q-5}{5} = \dfrac{7}{3}$

26. $\dfrac{x-6}{6} + \dfrac{x+2}{8} = \dfrac{11}{4}$

27. $\dfrac{a + 7}{8} - \dfrac{a - 2}{3} = \dfrac{4}{3}$ **28.** $\dfrac{x + 3}{7} - \dfrac{x + 2}{6} = \dfrac{1}{6}$ **29.** $\dfrac{3m}{5} - \dfrac{3m - 2}{4} = \dfrac{1}{5}$ **30.** $\dfrac{8p}{5} - \dfrac{3p - 4}{2} = \dfrac{5}{2}$

When solving an equation with variables in denominators, we must determine the values that cause these denominators to equal 0, so that we can reject these values if they appear as proposed solutions. Find all values for which at least one denominator is equal to 0. Write answers using the symbol $\neq$. Do not solve. **See Examples 4–8.**

31. $\dfrac{3}{x + 2} - \dfrac{5}{x} = 1$ **32.** $\dfrac{7}{x} + \dfrac{9}{x - 4} = 5$ **33.** $\dfrac{-1}{(x + 3)(x - 4)} = \dfrac{1}{2x + 1}$

34. $\dfrac{8}{(x - 7)(x + 3)} = \dfrac{7}{3x - 10}$ **35.** $\dfrac{4}{x^2 + 8x - 9} + \dfrac{1}{x^2 - 4} = 0$ **36.** $\dfrac{-3}{x^2 + 9x - 10} - \dfrac{12}{x^2 - 49} = 0$

Solve each equation, and check the solutions. **See Examples 4–8.**

37. $\dfrac{5}{m} - \dfrac{3}{m} = 8$ **38.** $\dfrac{4}{y} + \dfrac{1}{y} = 2$ **39.** $\dfrac{5}{y} + 4 = \dfrac{2}{y}$

40. $\dfrac{11}{q} - 3 = \dfrac{1}{q}$ **41.** $\dfrac{5 - 2x}{x} = \dfrac{1}{4}$ **42.** $\dfrac{2x + 3}{x} = \dfrac{3}{2}$

43. $\dfrac{k}{k - 4} - 5 = \dfrac{4}{k - 4}$ **44.** $\dfrac{-5}{a + 5} = \dfrac{a}{a + 5} + 2$ **45.** $\dfrac{3}{x - 1} + \dfrac{2}{4x - 4} = \dfrac{7}{4}$

46. $\dfrac{2}{p + 3} + \dfrac{3}{8} = \dfrac{5}{4p + 12}$ **47.** $\dfrac{x}{3x + 3} = \dfrac{2x - 3}{x + 1} - \dfrac{2x}{3x + 3}$ **48.** $\dfrac{2k + 3}{k + 1} - \dfrac{3k}{2k + 2} = \dfrac{-2k}{2k + 2}$

49. $\dfrac{2}{m} = \dfrac{m}{5m + 12}$ **50.** $\dfrac{x}{4 - x} = \dfrac{2}{x}$ **51.** $\dfrac{5x}{14x + 3} = \dfrac{1}{x}$

52. $\dfrac{m}{8m + 3} = \dfrac{1}{3m}$ **53.** $\dfrac{2}{z - 1} - \dfrac{5}{4} = \dfrac{-1}{z + 1}$ **54.** $\dfrac{5}{p - 2} = 7 - \dfrac{10}{p + 2}$

55. $\dfrac{4}{x^2 - 3x} = \dfrac{1}{x^2 - 9}$

56. $\dfrac{2}{t^2 - 4} = \dfrac{3}{t^2 - 2t}$

57. $\dfrac{-2}{z + 5} + \dfrac{3}{z - 5} = \dfrac{20}{z^2 - 25}$

58. $\dfrac{3}{r + 3} - \dfrac{2}{r - 3} = \dfrac{-12}{r^2 - 9}$

59. $\dfrac{1}{x + 4} + \dfrac{x}{x - 4} = \dfrac{-8}{x^2 - 16}$

60. $\dfrac{x}{x - 3} + \dfrac{4}{x + 3} = \dfrac{18}{x^2 - 9}$

61. $\dfrac{2p}{p^2 - 1} = \dfrac{2}{p + 1} - \dfrac{1}{p - 1}$

62. $\dfrac{2x}{x^2 - 16} - \dfrac{2}{x - 4} = \dfrac{4}{x + 4}$

63. $\dfrac{4}{3x + 6} - \dfrac{3}{x + 3} = \dfrac{8}{x^2 + 5x + 6}$

64. $\dfrac{-13}{t^2 + 6t + 8} + \dfrac{4}{t + 2} = \dfrac{3}{2t + 8}$

65. $\dfrac{3x}{x^2 + 5x + 6} = \dfrac{5x}{x^2 + 2x - 3} - \dfrac{2}{x^2 + x - 2}$

66. $\dfrac{m}{m^2 + m - 2} = \dfrac{m}{m^2 + 3m + 2} - \dfrac{m}{m^2 - 1}$

67. CONCEPT CHECK   A student simplified the following expression as shown.

$$\frac{3}{2}t + \frac{5}{7}t$$
$$= 14\left(\frac{3}{2}t + \frac{5}{7}t\right)$$
$$= 21t + 10t$$
$$= 31t \quad \text{Incorrect}$$

What Went Wrong?   Give the correct answer.

68. CONCEPT CHECK   A student solved the following formula for r as shown.

$$\frac{1}{r} - \frac{1}{m} = \frac{1}{k}$$
$$rmk\left(\frac{1}{r} - \frac{1}{m}\right) = rmk\left(\frac{1}{k}\right)$$
$$mk - rk = rm$$
$$\frac{mk - rk}{m} = r \quad \text{Incorrect}$$

What Went Wrong?   Give the correct answer.

*Solve each formula for the specified variable. **See Examples 9–11.***

69. $m = \dfrac{kF}{a}$ for F

70. $I = \dfrac{kE}{R}$ for E

71. $m = \dfrac{kF}{a}$ for a

72. $I = \dfrac{kE}{R}$ for R

73. $m = \dfrac{y - b}{x}$ for y

74. $y = \dfrac{C - Ax}{B}$ for C

75. $I = \dfrac{E}{R + r}$ for R

76. $I = \dfrac{E}{R + r}$ for r

77. $h = \dfrac{2\mathcal{A}}{B + b}$ for b

78. $h = \dfrac{2\mathcal{A}}{B + b}$ for B

79. $d = \dfrac{2S}{n(a + L)}$ for a

80. $d = \dfrac{2S}{n(a + L)}$ for L

81. $\dfrac{1}{x} = \dfrac{1}{y} - \dfrac{1}{z}$ for y

82. $\dfrac{3}{k} = \dfrac{1}{p} + \dfrac{1}{q}$ for q

83. $\dfrac{2}{r} + \dfrac{3}{s} + \dfrac{1}{t} = 1$ for t

84. $\dfrac{5}{p} + \dfrac{2}{q} + \dfrac{3}{r} = 1$ for r

85. $\dfrac{1}{a} - \dfrac{1}{b} - \dfrac{1}{c} = 2$ for c

86. $\dfrac{-1}{x} + \dfrac{1}{y} + \dfrac{1}{z} = 4$ for y

87. $9x + \dfrac{3}{z} = \dfrac{5}{y}$ for z

88. $-3t - \dfrac{4}{p} = \dfrac{6}{s}$ for p

Relating Concepts (Exercises 89–94) For Individual or Group Work

In these exercises, we summarize various concepts involving rational expressions.
Work Exercises 89–94 in order.

Let P, Q, and R be rational expressions defined as follows.

$$P = \dfrac{6}{x + 3}, \qquad Q = \dfrac{5}{x + 1}, \qquad R = \dfrac{4x}{x^2 + 4x + 3}$$

89. Find the values for which each expression is undefined. Write answers using the symbol $\neq$.

(a) P (b) Q (c) R

90. Find and express $(P \cdot Q) \div R$ in lowest terms.

91. Find the LCD for P, Q, and R.

92. Perform the operations and express $P + Q - R$ in lowest terms.

93. Simplify the complex fraction $\dfrac{P + Q}{R}$.

94. Solve the equation $P + Q = R$.

Summary Exercises *Simplifying Rational Expressions vs. Solving Rational Equations*

Students often confuse *simplifying expressions* with *solving equations*. We review the four operations to *simplify* the rational expressions $\frac{1}{x}$ and $\frac{1}{x-2}$ as follows.

Add:

$$\frac{1}{x} + \frac{1}{x-2}$$

$$= \frac{1(x-2)}{x(x-2)} + \frac{x(1)}{x(x-2)} \qquad \text{Write with a common denominator.}$$

$$= \frac{x-2+x}{x(x-2)} \qquad \text{Add numerators.}$$
$$\qquad \qquad \qquad \text{Keep the same denominator.}$$

$$= \frac{2x-2}{x(x-2)} \qquad \text{Combine like terms.}$$

Subtract:

$$\frac{1}{x} - \frac{1}{x-2}$$

$$= \frac{1(x-2)}{x(x-2)} - \frac{x(1)}{x(x-2)} \qquad \text{Write with a common denominator.}$$

$$= \frac{x-2-x}{x(x-2)} \qquad \text{Subtract numerators.}$$
$$\qquad \qquad \qquad \text{Keep the same denominator.}$$

$$= \frac{-2}{x(x-2)} \qquad \text{Combine like terms.}$$

Multiply:

$$\frac{1}{x} \cdot \frac{1}{x-2}$$

$$= \frac{1}{x(x-2)} \qquad \text{Multiply numerators.}$$
$$\qquad \qquad \text{Multiply denominators.}$$

Divide:

$$\frac{1}{x} \div \frac{1}{x-2}$$

$$= \frac{1}{x} \cdot \frac{x-2}{1} \qquad \text{Multiply by the reciprocal of the divisor.}$$

$$= \frac{x-2}{x} \qquad \text{Multiply numerators.}$$
$$\qquad \qquad \text{Multiply denominators.}$$

By contrast, consider the following *equation*.

$$\frac{1}{x} + \frac{1}{x-2} = \frac{3}{4} \qquad \boxed{x \neq 0, 2 \text{ because a denominator is 0 for these values.}}$$

$$4x(x-2)\left(\frac{1}{x} + \frac{1}{x-2}\right) = 4x(x-2)\frac{3}{4} \qquad \text{Multiply each side by the LCD, } 4x(x-2), \text{ to clear the fractions.}$$

$$4x(x-2)\frac{1}{x} + 4x(x-2)\frac{1}{x-2} = 4x(x-2)\frac{3}{4} \qquad \text{Distributive property}$$

$$4(x-2) + 4x = 3x(x-2) \qquad \text{Divide out the common factors.}$$

$$4x - 8 + 4x = 3x^2 - 6x \qquad \text{Distributive property}$$

$$3x^2 - 14x + 8 = 0 \qquad \text{Standard form}$$

$$(3x-2)(x-4) = 0 \qquad \text{Factor.}$$

$$3x - 2 = 0 \quad \text{or} \quad x - 4 = 0 \qquad \text{Zero-factor property}$$

$$\text{Proposed solutions} \rightarrow x = \frac{2}{3} \quad \text{or} \quad x = 4 \qquad \text{Solve for } x.$$

The proposed solutions are $\frac{2}{3}$ and 4. Neither makes a denominator equal 0. Check by substituting each proposed solution into the original equation to confirm that the solution set is $\left\{\frac{2}{3}, 4\right\}$.

Points to Remember when Working with Rational Expressions and Equations
1. When simplifying rational expressions, the fundamental property is applied only after numerators and denominators have been *factored*.
2. When adding and subtracting rational expressions, the common denominator must be kept throughout the problem and in the final result.
3. When simplifying rational expressions, check to see if the answer is in lowest terms. If it is not, use the fundamental property.
4. When solving equations with rational expressions, the LCD is used to clear fractions. Multiply each side by the LCD. (Notice how this use differs from that of the common denominator in Point 2.)
5. When solving equations with rational expressions, reject any proposed solution that causes an original denominator to equal 0.

For each exercise, indicate "expression" *if an expression is to be* simplified *or* "equation" *if an equation is to be* solved. *Then simplify the expression or solve the equation.*

1. $\dfrac{4}{p} + \dfrac{6}{p}$

2. $\dfrac{3x}{x+7} - \dfrac{x+1}{x+7}$

3. $\dfrac{1}{x^2+x-2} \div \dfrac{4x^2}{2x-2}$

4. $\dfrac{8}{m-5} = 2$

5. $\dfrac{2x^2+x-6}{2x^2-9x+9} \cdot \dfrac{x^2-2x-3}{x^2-1}$

6. $\dfrac{2}{k^2-4k} + \dfrac{3}{k^2-16}$

7. $\dfrac{x-4}{5} = \dfrac{x+3}{6}$

8. $\dfrac{3t^2-t}{6t^2+15t} \div \dfrac{6t^2+t-1}{2t^2-5t-25}$

9. $\dfrac{4}{p+2} + \dfrac{1}{3p+6}$

10. $\dfrac{1}{x} + \dfrac{1}{x-3} = -\dfrac{5}{4}$

11. $\dfrac{3}{t-1} + \dfrac{1}{t} = \dfrac{7}{2}$

12. $\dfrac{5}{4z} - \dfrac{2}{3z}$

13. $\dfrac{2m}{m-4} - \dfrac{m-12}{4-m}$

14. $\dfrac{k+2}{3} = \dfrac{2k-1}{5}$

15. $\dfrac{1}{m^2+5m+6} + \dfrac{2}{m^2+4m+3}$

16. $\dfrac{2k^2-3k}{20k^2-5k} \cdot \dfrac{4k^2+11k-3}{2k^2-5k+3}$

17. $\dfrac{2}{x+1} + \dfrac{5}{x-1} = \dfrac{10}{x^2-1}$

18. $\dfrac{x}{x-2} + \dfrac{3}{x+2} = \dfrac{8}{x^2-4}$

7.7 Applications of Rational Expressions

OBJECTIVES

1. Solve problems about numbers.
2. Solve problems about distance, rate, and time.
3. Solve problems about work.

We continue to use the six-step problem-solving method introduced earlier.

Solving an Applied Problem

Step 1 **Read** the problem, several times if necessary. *What information is given? What is to be found?*

Step 2 **Assign a variable** to represent the unknown value. Use a sketch, diagram, or table, as needed. Express any other unknown values in terms of the variable.

Step 3 **Write an equation** using the variable expression(s).

Step 4 **Solve** the equation.

Step 5 **State the answer.** Label it appropriately. *Does the answer seem reasonable?*

Step 6 **Check** the answer in the words of the *original* problem.

---

1 A certain number is added to the numerator and subtracted from the denominator of $\frac{5}{8}$. The new fraction equals the reciprocal of $\frac{5}{8}$. Find the number.

Step 1
We are trying to find a(n) _____.

Step 2
Let x = the number added to the numerator and _____ from the denominator.

Step 3
The expression _____ represents the new fraction. The reciprocal of $\frac{5}{8}$ is ____. Write an equation.

_____

Complete Steps 4–6 to solve the problem. Give the answer.

OBJECTIVE 1 Solve problems about numbers.

EXAMPLE 1 Solving a Problem about an Unknown Number

If the same number is added to both the numerator and the denominator of the fraction $\frac{2}{5}$, the result is equivalent to $\frac{2}{3}$. Find the number.

Step 1 **Read** the problem carefully. We are trying to find a number.

Step 2 **Assign a variable.**

Let x = the number added to the numerator and the denominator.

Step 3 **Write an equation.** The fraction $\frac{2}{5}$ is given. The expression

$$\frac{2 + x}{5 + x}$$

represents the result of adding the same number x to both the numerator and the denominator. This result is equivalent to $\frac{2}{3}$.

$$\frac{2 + x}{5 + x} = \frac{2}{3}$$

Step 4 **Solve.** $3(5 + x)\dfrac{2 + x}{5 + x} = 3(5 + x)\dfrac{2}{3}$ $\quad$ Multiply by the LCD, $3(5 + x)$.

$$3(2 + x) = (5 + x)2 \qquad \text{Divide out the common factors.}$$

$$6 + 3x = 10 + 2x \qquad \text{Distributive property}$$

$$x = 4 \qquad \text{Subtract } 2x. \text{ Subtract } 6.$$

Step 5 **State the answer.** The number is 4.

Step 6 **Check.** If 4 is added to both the numerator and the denominator of $\frac{2}{5}$, the result is $\frac{2+4}{5+4} = \frac{6}{9}$, which in lowest terms is $\frac{2}{3}$, as required.

◀ **Work Problem ❶ at the Side**

Answer

1. number; subtracted;
$\dfrac{5+x}{8-x}; \dfrac{8}{5}; \dfrac{5+x}{8-x} = \dfrac{8}{5}$;
The number is 3.

OBJECTIVE ▸ ② Solve problems about distance, rate, and time. If an automobile travels at an average rate of 65 mph for 2 hr, then it travels

$$65 \times 2 = 130 \text{ mi.} \qquad rt = d, \text{ or } d = rt \text{ (Relationship between distance, rate, and time)}$$

By solving, in turn, for r and t in the distance formula $d = rt$, we obtain two other equivalent forms of the formula.

Forms of the Distance Formula

$$d = rt \qquad r = \frac{d}{t} \qquad t = \frac{d}{r}$$

EXAMPLE 2 | **Finding Distance, Rate, or Time**

Solve each problem using a form of the distance formula.

(a) The speed (rate) of sound is 1088 ft per sec at sea level at 32°F. Find the distance sound travels in 5 sec under these conditions.

We must find distance, given rate and time, using $d = rt$ (or $rt = d$).

$$\underset{\text{Rate}}{1088} \quad \cdot \quad \underset{\text{Time}}{5} \quad = \quad \underset{\text{Distance}}{5440 \text{ ft}}$$

(b) Ray Harroun won the first Indianapolis 500 race (in 1911), driving a Marmon Wasp at an average rate of 74.60 mph. How long did it take him to complete the 500 mi? (Data from *The World Almanac and Book of Facts*.)

We must find time, given rate and distance, using $t = \frac{d}{r}$ (or $\frac{d}{r} = t$).

$$\underset{\text{Rate}}{\overset{\text{Distance}}{\frac{500}{74.60}}} = 6.70 \text{ hr (rounded)} \leftarrow \text{Time}$$

To convert 0.70 hr to minutes, we multiply by 60 to obtain $0.70\,(60) = 42$. It took Harroun about 6 hr, **42** min, to complete the race.

(c) At the 2016 Olympic Games, U.S. swimmer Michael Phelps won the men's 100-m butterfly swimming event in 51.14 sec. Find his rate. (Data from www.olympic.org)

We must find rate, given distance and time, using $r = \frac{d}{t}$ (or $\frac{d}{t} = r$).

$$\underset{\text{Time}}{\overset{\text{Distance}}{\frac{100}{51.14}}} = 1.96 \text{ m per sec (rounded)} \leftarrow \text{Rate}$$

Work Problem ② at the Side. ▶

Problem-Solving Hint

Many applied problems use forms of the distance formula. The following two strategies are especially helpful in setting up equations to solve such problems.

- ***Make a sketch*** to visualize what is happening in the problem.

- ***Make a table*** to organize the information given in the problem and the unknown quantities.

---

② Solve each problem using a form of the distance formula.

(a) A small plane flew from Chicago to St. Louis averaging 145 mph. The trip took 2 hr. What is the distance between Chicago and St. Louis?

(b) Usain Bolt of Jamaica ran the men's 100-m dash in 9.63 sec. What was his rate in meters per second, to the nearest hundredth? (Data from *The World Almanac and Book of Facts*.)

(c) The world record for the women's 3000-m steeplechase is held by Gulnara Samitova of Russia. Her rate was 5.568 m per sec. To the nearest second, what was her time? (Data from *The World Almanac and Book of Facts*.)

Answers

2. (a) 290 mi **(b)** 10.38 m per sec
(c) 539 sec, or 8 min, 59 sec

3 Solve each problem.

(GS) (a) From a point on a straight road, Lupe and Maria ride bicycles in *opposite* directions. Lupe rides 10 mph and Maria rides 12 mph. In how many hours will they be 55 mi apart?

Steps 1 and 2
Let x = the number of
_____ until the distance
between Lupe and Maria is

_____ .

Step 3
Complete the table.

	Rate	Time	Distance
Maria	10	t	_____
Lupe	_____	t	_____

Because Lupe and Maria are traveling in *opposite* directions, we must (*add/subtract*) the distances they travel to find the distance between them. Write an equation.

_____

Complete Steps 4–6 to solve the problem. Give the answer.

(b) At a given hour, two steamboats leave a city in the same direction on a straight canal. One travels at 18 mph, and the other travels at 25 mph. In how many hours will the boats be 35 mi apart?

EXAMPLE 3 **Solving a Distance-Rate-Time Problem**

Two cars leave Iowa City, Iowa, at the same time and travel east on Interstate 80. One travels at a constant rate of 55 mph. The other travels at a constant rate of 63 mph. In how many hours will the distance between them be 24 mi?

Step 1 **Read** the problem again.

Step 2 **Assign a variable.** We are looking for time.

Let t = the number of hours until the distance between the cars is 24 mi.

The sketch in **Figure 1** shows what is happening in the problem.

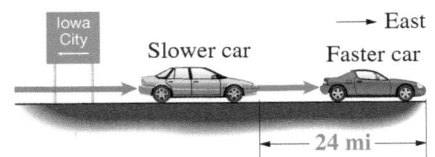

Figure 1

To construct a table, we fill in the rates given in the problem, using t for the time traveled by each car. Because $rt = d$, we multiply rate by time to find expressions for the distances traveled.

	Rate	Time	Distance	
Faster Car	63	t	$63t$	⟵ The quantities $63t$ and $55t$
Slower Car	55	t	$55t$	⟵ represent the two distances.

Step 3 **Write an equation.**

$$63t - 55t = 24$$

The *difference* between the larger distance and the smaller distance is 24 mi.

Step 4 **Solve.** $8t = 24$ Combine like terms.

$t = 3$ Divide by 8.

Step 5 **State the answer.** It will take the cars 3 hr to be 24 mi apart.

Step 6 **Check.** After 3 hr, the faster car will have traveled

$$63 \cdot 3 = 189 \text{ mi}$$

and the slower car will have traveled

$$55 \cdot 3 = 165 \text{ mi.}$$

The difference is

$$189 - 165 = 24, \quad \text{as required.}$$

◀ **Work Problem** **3** **at the Side.**

Problem-Solving Hint

In distance-rate-time problems like the one in **Example 3**, once we have filled in two pieces of information in each row of a table, we can automatically fill in the third piece of information, using the appropriate form of the distance formula. Then we set up an equation based on our sketch and the information in the table.

Answers

3. (a) hours; 55 mi

	Rate	Time	Distance
Maria	10	t	$10t$
Lupe	12	t	$12t$

add; $10t + 12t = 55$;

$2\frac{1}{2}$ hr

(b) 5 hr

EXAMPLE 4 Solving a Distance-Rate-Time Problem

The Tickfaw River has a current of 3 mph. A motorboat takes as long to travel 12 mi downstream as to travel 8 mi upstream. What is the rate of the boat in still water?

Step 1 **Read** the problem. We want the rate (speed) of the boat in still water.

Step 2 **Assign a variable.**

Let x = the rate of the boat in still water.

Because the current pushes the boat when the boat is going downstream, the rate of the boat downstream will be the *sum* of the rate of the boat and the rate of the current, $(x + 3)$ mph.

Because the current slows down the boat when the boat is going upstream, the boat's rate upstream will be the *difference* between the rate of the boat in still water and the rate of the current, $(x - 3)$ mph. See **Figure 2.**

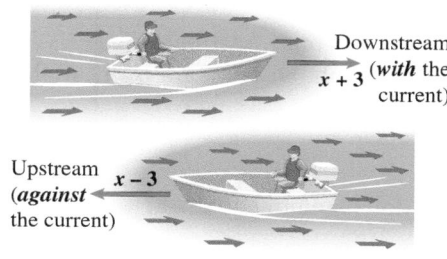

Downstream
$x + 3$ (*with* the current)

Upstream
(*against* the current) $x - 3$

Figure 2

This information is summarized in the following table.

	d	r	t
Downstream	12	$x + 3$	
Upstream	8	$x - 3$	

Fill in the times using the formula $t = \frac{d}{r}$.

The time downstream is the distance divided by the rate.

$$t = \frac{d}{r} = \frac{12}{x + 3} \quad \text{Time downstream}$$

The time upstream is also the distance divided by the rate.

$$t = \frac{d}{r} = \frac{8}{x - 3} \quad \text{Time upstream}$$

	d	r	t
Downstream	12	$x + 3$	$\frac{12}{x + 3}$
Upstream	8	$x - 3$	$\frac{8}{x - 3}$

Enter each time using $t = \frac{d}{r}$.

Step 3 **Write an equation.**

$$\frac{12}{x + 3} = \frac{8}{x - 3}$$

The time downstream equals the time upstream, so the two times from the table must be equal.

Continued on Next Page

4 Solve each problem.

GS (a) A boat travels 10 mi against the current in the same time it travels 30 mi with the current. The current is flowing at 4 mph. Find the rate of the boat in still water.

Steps 1 and 2
Let x = the _____ of the boat with no current.

Step 3
Complete the table.

	d	r	t
Against the Current	10	____	____
With the Current	30	____	____

How are the times traveling with the current and against the current related?

_____

Write an equation.

_____

Complete Steps 4–6 to solve the problem. Give the answer.

(b) An airplane, maintaining a constant airspeed, takes as long to travel 450 mi with the wind as it does to travel 375 mi against the wind. If the wind is blowing at 15 mph, what is the rate of the plane?

Answers

4. **(a)** rate

	d	r	t
Against the Current	10	$x - 4$	$\frac{10}{x-4}$
With the Current	30	$x + 4$	$\frac{30}{x+4}$

They are the same; $\dfrac{10}{x-4} = \dfrac{30}{x+4}$;
8 mph
(b) 165 mph

Step 4 **Solve.** $\dfrac{12}{x+3} = \dfrac{8}{x-3}$ Equation from Step 3

$(x+3)(x-3)\dfrac{12}{x+3} = (x+3)(x-3)\dfrac{8}{x-3}$ Multiply by the LCD, $(x+3)(x-3)$.

$12(x-3) = 8(x+3)$ Divide out the common factors.

$12x - 36 = 8x + 24$ Distributive property

$4x = 60$ Subtract $8x$. Add 36.

$x = 15$ Divide by 4.

Step 5 **State the answer.** The rate of the boat in still water is 15 mph.

Step 6 **Check.** The rate of the boat downstream is $(x+3)$ mph, which would be $15 + 3 = 18$ mph. Divide 12 mi by 18 mph to find the time.

$$t = \frac{d}{r} = \frac{12}{18} = \frac{2}{3} \text{ hr}$$

The rate of the boat upstream is $(x-3)$ mph, which would be $15 - 3 = 12$ mph. Divide 8 mi by 12 mph to find the time.

$$t = \frac{d}{r} = \frac{8}{12} = \frac{2}{3} \text{ hr}$$

The time downstream equals the time upstream, as required.

◀ **Work Problem ④ at the Side.**

OBJECTIVE ③ Solve problems about work. Suppose that we can mow a lawn in 4 hr. Then after 1 hr, we will have mowed $\frac{1}{4}$ of the lawn. After 2 hr, we will have mowed $\frac{2}{4}$, or $\frac{1}{2}$, of the lawn, and so on. This idea is generalized as follows.

Rate of Work

If a job can be completed in t units of time, then the rate of work is

$\dfrac{1}{t}$ **job per unit of time.**

Problem-Solving Hint

The amount of work accomplished W is equal to rate of work r multiplied by time worked t—that is, **$W = rt$.** Note the similarity to the distance formula $d = rt$.

In the lawn mowing example, the amount of work done after 3 hr, is found as follows.

$$\underset{\substack{\text{Rate of}\\\text{work}}}{\frac{1}{4}} \cdot \underset{\substack{\text{Time}\\\text{worked}}}{3} = \underset{\substack{\text{Fractional part}\\\text{of job done}}}{\frac{3}{4}}$$

After 4 hr, $\frac{1}{4}(4) = 1$ whole job has been done.

EXAMPLE 5 **Solving a Problem about Work Rates**

With spraying equipment, Mateo can paint the trim on a small house in 10 hr. Chet needs 15 hr to complete the same job by hand. If both Mateo and Chet work together, how long will it take them to paint the trim?

Step 1 **Read** the problem again. We are looking for time working together.

Step 2 **Assign a variable.**

Let x = the number of hours it will take for Mateo and Chet to paint the trim, working together.

Making a table is helpful. Based on the previous discussion on work rates, Mateo's rate alone is $\frac{1}{10}$ job per hour, and Chet's rate alone is $\frac{1}{15}$ job per hour.

	Rate	Time Working Together	Fractional Part of the Job Done When Working Together
Mateo	$\frac{1}{10}$	x	$\frac{1}{10}x$
Chet	$\frac{1}{15}$	x	$\frac{1}{15}x$

Because $rt = W$, the quantities $\frac{1}{10}x$ and $\frac{1}{15}x$ represent the two amounts of work.

Step 3 **Write an equation.**

$$\underbrace{\text{Fractional part}}_{\text{done by Mateo}} + \underbrace{\text{Fractional part}}_{\text{done by Chet}} = \text{1 whole job}$$

$$\frac{1}{10}x + \frac{1}{15}x = 1$$

Together, Mateo and Chet complete **1 whole job.** Add the fractional parts and set the sum equal to **1.**

Step 4 **Solve.** $30\left(\frac{1}{10}x + \frac{1}{15}x\right) = 30(1)$ Multiply by the LCD, 30.

$$30\left(\frac{1}{10}x\right) + 30\left(\frac{1}{15}x\right) = 30(1)$$ Distributive property

$$3x + 2x = 30 \quad (*) \quad \text{Multiply.}$$

$$5x = 30 \quad \text{Combine like terms.}$$

$$x = 6 \quad \text{Divide by 6.}$$

Step 5 **State the answer.** Working together, Mateo and Chet can paint the trim in 6 hr.

Step 6 **Check.** The value of x must be *less than* 10 due to the fact that Mateo can complete the job *alone* in 10 hr. So 6 hr seems reasonable.

In 6 hr, Mateo completes

$$\frac{1}{10}x = \frac{1}{10}(6) = \frac{6}{10} = \frac{3}{5} \text{ of the job.}$$

In 6 hr, Chet completes

$$\frac{1}{15}x = \frac{1}{15}(6) = \frac{6}{15} = \frac{2}{5} \text{ of the job.}$$

Working together, they complete $\frac{3}{5} + \frac{2}{5} = 1$ **whole job,** as required. The answer, 6 hr, is correct.

— **Work Problem** ⑤ **at the Side.** ▶

---

⑤ Solve the problem.
 Michael can paint a room, working alone, in 6 hr. Lindsay can paint the same room, working alone, in 12 hr. How long will it take them if they work together?

Steps 1 and 2
Let x = the number of _____ it will take for Michael and Lindsay to paint the room, working _____.

Step 3
Complete the table.

	Rate	Time Working Together	Fractional Part of the Job Done When Working Together
Michael	_____	x	_____
Lindsay	_____	x	_____

Together, Michael and Lindsay complete _____ whole job(s). Write an equation.

_____

Complete Steps 4–6 to solve the problem. Give the answer.

Answer

5. hours; together

	Rate	Time Working Together	Fractional Part of the Job Done When Working Together
Michael	$\frac{1}{6}$	x	$\frac{1}{6}x$
Lindsay	$\frac{1}{12}$	x	$\frac{1}{12}x$

$1; \frac{1}{6}x + \frac{1}{12}x = 1;$

4 hr

6 Solve the problem using either the method of **Example 5** or the alternative approach discussed at the right.

Roberto can detail his Camaro in 2 hr working alone. His brother Marco can do the job in 3 hr working alone. How long would it take them if they worked together?

An alternative approach when solving work problems is to consider the part of the job that can be done in 1 hr. For instance, in **Example 5** Mateo can do the entire job in 10 hr, and Chet can do it in 15 hr. Thus, their work rates, as we saw in **Example 5,** are $\frac{1}{10}$ and $\frac{1}{15}$, respectively. Since it takes them x hours to complete the job working together, in 1 hr they can paint $\frac{1}{x}$ of the trim.

The amount painted by Mateo in 1 hr plus the amount painted by Chet in 1 hr must equal the amount they can paint *together* in 1 hr. This leads to the following alternative equation.

Amount by Chet

Amount by Mateo $\rightarrow \dfrac{1}{10} + \dfrac{1}{15} = \dfrac{1}{x} \leftarrow$ Amount together

Compare this alternative equation with the equation

$$\frac{1}{10}x + \frac{1}{15}x = 1$$

in Step 3 of **Example 5.** If we multiply each side of the alternative equation by the LCD $30x$, we obtain the following.

$$\frac{1}{10} + \frac{1}{15} = \frac{1}{x} \qquad \text{Alternative equation}$$

$$30x\left(\frac{1}{10} + \frac{1}{15}\right) = 30x\left(\frac{1}{x}\right) \qquad \text{Multiply by the LCD, } 30x.$$

$$30x\left(\frac{1}{10}\right) + 30x\left(\frac{1}{15}\right) = 30x\left(\frac{1}{x}\right) \qquad \text{Distributive property}$$

$$3x + 2x = 30 \qquad \text{Multiply.}$$

This is equation $(*)$ in **Example 5.** The same solution, $x = 6$, results.

◀ **Work Problem 6** at the Side.

Answer

6. $\dfrac{6}{5}$ hr, or $1\dfrac{1}{5}$ hr

(that is, 1 hr, 12 min)

7.7 Exercises

FOR EXTRA HELP

Go to MyMathLab *for worked-out, step-by-step solutions to exercises enclosed in a square* ☐ *and video solutions to* ▶ *exercises.*

1. **CONCEPT CHECK** If a migrating hawk travels m mph in still air, what is its rate when it flies into a steady headwind of 5 mph? What is its rate with a tailwind of 5 mph?

2. **CONCEPT CHECK** Suppose Stephanie walks D miles at R mph in the same time that Wally walks d miles at r mph. Give an equation relating D, R, d, and r.

3. **CONCEPT CHECK** If it takes Elayn 10 hr to do a job, what is her rate?

4. **CONCEPT CHECK** If it takes Clay 12 hr to do a job, how much of the job does he do in 8 hr?

GS *Use Steps 2 and 3 of the six-step problem solving method to set up an equation to use to solve each problem. (Remember that Step 1 is to read the problem carefully.) Do not actually solve the equation.* **See Example 1.**

5. The numerator of the fraction $\frac{5}{6}$ is increased by an amount so that the value of the resulting fraction is equivalent to $\frac{13}{3}$. By what amount was the numerator increased?

    (a) Let $x =$ _____ . (*Step 2*)

    (b) Write an expression for "the numerator of the fraction $\frac{5}{6}$ is increased by an amount." _____

    (c) Set up an equation to solve the problem.

    (*Step 3*) _____

6. If the same number is added to the numerator and subtracted from the denominator of $\frac{23}{12}$, the resulting fraction is equivalent to $\frac{3}{2}$. What is the number?

    (a) Let $x =$ _____ . (*Step 2*)

    (b) Write an expression for "a number is added to the numerator of $\frac{23}{12}$." _____ Then write an expression for "the same number is subtracted from the denominator of $\frac{23}{12}$." _____

    (c) Set up an equation to solve the problem.

    (*Step 3*) _____

In each problem, state what x represents, write an equation, and answer the question. **See Example 1.**

7. ▶ In a certain fraction, the denominator is 6 more than the numerator. If 3 is added to both the numerator and the denominator, the resulting fraction is equivalent to $\frac{5}{7}$. What was the original fraction (*not* written in lowest terms)?

8. In a certain fraction, the denominator is 4 less than the numerator. If 3 is added to both the numerator and the denominator, the resulting fraction is equivalent to $\frac{3}{2}$. What was the original fraction?

9. The denominator of a certain fraction is three times the numerator. If 2 is added to the numerator and subtracted from the denominator, the resulting fraction is equivalent to 1. What was the original fraction (*not* written in lowest terms)?

10. The numerator of a certain fraction is four times the denominator. If 6 is added to both the numerator and the denominator, the resulting fraction is equivalent to 2. What was the original fraction (*not* written in lowest terms)?

11. One-sixth of a number is 5 more than the same number. What is the number?

12. One-third of a number is 2 more than one-sixth of the same number. What is the number?

13. "A quantity, its $\frac{3}{4}$, its $\frac{1}{2}$, and its $\frac{1}{3}$, added together, become 93." What is the quantity? (Data from *Rhind Mathematical Papyrus.*)

14. "A quantity, its $\frac{2}{3}$, its $\frac{1}{2}$, and its $\frac{1}{7}$, added together, become 33." What is the quantity? (Data from *Rhind Mathematical Papyrus.*)

Solve each problem. **See Example 2.**

15. British explorer and endurance swimmer Lewis Gordon Pugh was the first person to swim at the North Pole. He swam 0.6 mi at 0.0319 mi per min in waters created by melted sea ice. What was his time (to three decimal places)? (Data from *The Gazette.*)

16. In the 2012 Olympics, Missy Franklin of the United States won the women's 100-m backstroke swimming event. Her rate was 1.7143 m per sec. What was her time (to two decimal places)? (Data from *The World Almanac and Book of Facts.*)

17. Caroline Rotich of Kenya won the women's 26.2 mi Boston Marathon in 2015 with a time of 2.4153 hr. What was her rate (to three decimal places)? (Data from *The World Almanac and Book of Facts.*)

18. Ireen Wüst of the Netherlands won the women's 3000-m speed skating event in the 2014 Olympics with a time of 4.009 min. What was her rate (to three decimal places)? (Data from *The World Almanac and Book of Facts.*)

19. The winner of the 2015 Daytona 500 (mile) race was Joey Logano, who drove his Ford to victory with a rate of 161.939 mph. What was his time (to the nearest thousandth of an hour)? (Data from *The World Almanac and Book of Facts.*)

20. In 2015, Kyle Busch drove his Toyota to victory in the Brickyard 400 (mile) race. His rate was 131.656 mph. What was his time (to the nearest thousandth of an hour)? (Data from *The World Almanac and Book of Facts.*)

Complete the table and write an equation to use to solve each problem. Do not actually solve the equation. **See Examples 3 and 4.**

21. Luvenia can row 4 mph in still water. She takes as long to row 8 mi upstream as 24 mi downstream. How fast is the current?

Let x = the rate of the current.

	d	r	t
Upstream	8	$4 - x$	_____
Downstream	24	$4 + x$	_____

22. Julio flew his airplane 500 mi against the wind in the same time it took him to fly it 600 mi with the wind. If the rate of the wind was 10 mph, what was the average rate of his plane in still air?

Let x = the rate of the plane in still air.

	d	r	t
Against the Wind	500	$x - 10$	_____
With the Wind	600	$x + 10$	_____

*Solve each problem. **See Examples 3 and 4.***

23. From a point on a straight road, Marco and Celeste ride bicycles in the same direction. Marco rides at 10 mph and Celeste rides at 12 mph. In how many hours will they be 15 mi apart?

24. Two steamboats leaves a city on a river at the same time, traveling in the same direction. One travels at 18 mph and the other travels at 24 mph. In how many hours will the boats be 9 mi apart?

25. A train leaves Kansas City and travels north at 85 km per hr. Another train leaves at the same time and travels south at 95 km per hour. How long will it take before they are 315 km apart? (*Hint*: **See Margin Problem 3(a).**)

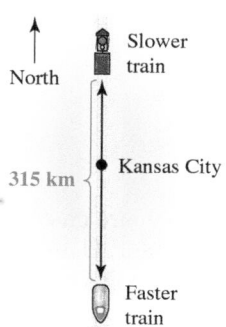

26. Two planes leave Boston at 12:00 noon and fly in opposite directions. If one flies at 410 mph and the other flies at 530 mph, how long will it take them to be 3290 mi apart? (*Hint*: **See Margin Problem 3(a).**)

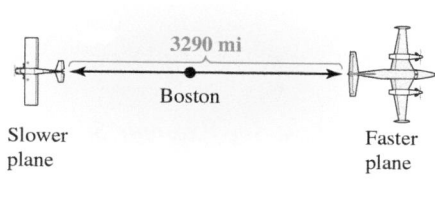

27. A boat can travel 20 mi against a current in the same time that it can travel 60 mi with the current. The rate of the current is 4 mph. Find the rate of the boat in still water.

28. Vince can fly his plane 200 mi against the wind in the same time it takes him to fly 300 mi with the wind. The wind blows at 30 mph. Find the rate of his plane in still air.

29. The sanderling is a small shorebird about 6.5 in. long, with a thin, dark bill and a wide, white wing stripe. If a sanderling can fly 30 mi with the wind in the same time it can fly 18 mi against the wind when the wind speed is 8 mph, what is the rate of the bird in still air? (Data from U.S. Geological Survey.)

30. Airplanes usually fly faster from west to east than from east to west because the prevailing winds go from west to east. The air distance between Chicago and London is about 4000 mi, while the air distance between New York and London is about 3500 mi. If a jet can fly eastbound from Chicago to London in the same time it can fly westbound from London to New York in a 35-mph wind, what is the rate of the plane in still air? (Data from www.geobytes.com)

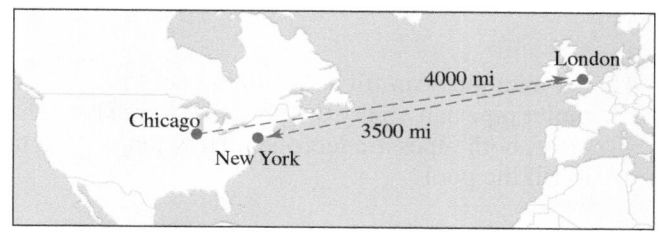

31. Perian's boat travels at 12 mph. Find the rate of the current of the river if she can travel 6 mi upstream in the same amount of time she can travel 10 mi downstream.

32. Bridget can travel 8 mi upstream in the same time it takes her to travel 12 mi downstream. Her boat travels 15 mph in still water. What is the rate of the current?

Complete the table and write an equation to use to solve each problem. Do not actually solve the equation. ***See Example 5.***

33. Eric can tune up his Chevy in 2 hr working alone. His son Oscar can do the job in 3 hr working alone. How long would it take them if they worked together?

Let t = the time working together.

	Rate	Time Working Together	Fractional Part of the Job Done When Working Together
Eric	____	t	____
Oscar	____	t	____

34. Working alone, Kyle can paint a room in 8 hr. Julianne can paint the same room working alone in 6 hr. How long will it take them if they work together?

Let t = the time working together.

	Rate	Time Working Together	Fractional Part of the Job Done When Working Together
Kyle	____	t	____
Julianne	____	t	____

Solve each problem. ***See Example 5.***

35. A copier can do a large printing job in 20 hr. An older model can do the same job in 30 hr. How long would it take to do the job using both copiers?

36. A company can prepare customer statements in 8 hr using a new computer. Using an older computer requires 24 hr to do the same job. How long would it take to prepare the statements using both computers?

37. A high school mathematics teacher gave a geometry test. Working alone, it would take her 4 hr to grade the tests. Her student teacher would take 6 hr to grade the same tests. How long would it take them to grade these tests if they work together?

38. A pump can pump the water out of a flooded basement in 10 hr. A smaller pump takes 12 hr. How long would it take to pump the water from the basement using both pumps?

39. Hilda can paint a room in 6 hr. Working together with Brenda, they can paint the room in $3\frac{3}{4}$ hr. How long would it take Brenda to paint the room by herself?

40. Grant can completely mess up his room in 15 min. If his cousin Wade helps him, they can completely mess up the room in $8\frac{4}{7}$ min. How long would it take Wade to mess up the room by himself?

41. An inlet pipe can fill a swimming pool in 9 hr, and an outlet pipe can empty the pool in 12 hr. Through an error, both pipes are left open. How long will it take to fill the pool?

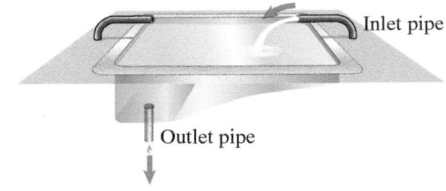
Inlet pipe
Outlet pipe

42. One pipe can fill a swimming pool in 6 hr, and another pipe can do it in 9 hr. How long will it take the two pipes working together to fill the pool $\frac{3}{4}$ full?

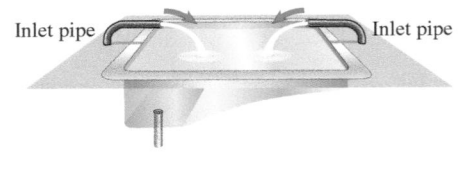
Inlet pipe   Inlet pipe

Solve each problem. (Data from Mary Jo Boyer, Math for Nurses, Wolter Kluwer.)

43. Nurses use Young's Rule to calculate the pediatric (child's) dose P of a medication, given a child's age c in years and a normal adult dose a.

$$P = \frac{c}{c + 12} \cdot a$$

The normal adult dose for milk of magnesia is 30 mL. Use Young's Rule to calculate the correct dose to give a 6-yr-old boy.

44. Nurses use Clark's Rule to calculate the pediatric (child's) dose P of a medication, given a child's weight w in pounds and a normal adult dose a.

$$P = \frac{w}{150} \cdot a$$

The normal adult dose for ibuprofen is 200 mg. Use Clark's Rule to calculate the correct dose to give a 4-yr-old girl who weighs 30 lb.

Relating Concepts (Exercises 45–48) For Individual or Group Work

In the movie Little Big League, *young Billy Heywood inherits the Minnesota Twins baseball team and becomes its manager. Before the biggest game of the year, he can't keep his mind on his job because a homework problem is giving him trouble.*

> *If Joe can paint a house in 3 hr, and Sam can paint the same house in 5 hr, how long does it take for them to do it together?*

With the help of one of his players, Billy solves the problem.

45. Use the method of **Example 5** of this section to solve this problem.

46. Billy got "help" from some of the other players. The incorrect answers they gave him follow. Explain the faulty reasoning behind each of these answers.

   (a) 15 hr   **(b)** 8 hr   **(c)** 4 hr

47. The player who gave Billy the correct answer solved the problem as follows:

> *Using the simple formula a times b over a plus b, we get our answer of one and seven-eighths.*

Show that if it takes one person a hours to complete a job and another b hours to complete the same job, then the expression stated by the player,

$$\frac{a \cdot b}{a + b},$$

actually does give the number of hours it would take them to do the job together. (*Hint:* Refer to **Example 5** and use a and b rather than 10 and 15 to write a formula. Then solve the formula for x.)

48. Solve the following problem using the method of **Example 5.** Then solve it using the formula obtained in **Exercise 47.** How do the answers compare?

> *A screen printer can complete a t-shirt order for a Little League baseball organization in 15 hr using a large machine. The same order would take 30 hr using a smaller machine. How long would it take to complete the order using both machines together?*

Chapter 7 *Summary*

Key Terms

7.1

rational expression The quotient of two polynomials with denominator not 0 is a rational expression.

lowest terms A rational expression is written in lowest terms if the greatest common factor of its numerator and denominator is 1.

7.2

reciprocal (multiplicative inverse) Two rational expressions are reciprocals of each other if the product of the two rational expressions is 1.

7.3

least common denominator (LCD) The simplest expression that is divisible by all denominators is the least common denominator.

7.5

complex fraction A quotient with one or more fractions in the numerator, or denominator, or both, is a complex fraction.

7.6

proposed solution A value of the variable that appears to be a solution after both sides of an equation with rational expressions are multiplied by a variable expression is a proposed solution.

extraneous solution (extraneous value) A proposed solution that is not an actual solution of a given equation is an extraneous solution, or extraneous value.

Test Your Word Power

See how well you have learned the vocabulary in this chapter.

1 A **rational expression** is
 A. an algebraic expression made up of a term or the sum of a finite number of terms with real coefficients and whole number exponents
 B. a polynomial equation of degree 2
 C. an expression with one or more fractions in the numerator, or denominator, or both
 D. the quotient of two polynomials with denominator not 0.

2 In a given set of fractions, the **least common denominator** is
 A. the smallest denominator of all the denominators
 B. the smallest expression that is divisible by all the denominators
 C. the largest integer that evenly divides the numerator and denominator of all the fractions
 D. the largest denominator of all the denominators.

3 A **complex fraction** is
 A. an algebraic expression made up of a term or the sum of a finite number of terms with real coefficients and whole number exponents
 B. a polynomial equation of degree 2
 C. a rational expression with one or more fractions in the numerator, or denominator, or both
 D. the quotient of two polynomials with denominator not 0.

Answers to Test Your Word Power

1. D; *Examples:* $-\dfrac{3}{4y}$, $\dfrac{5x^3}{x+2}$, $\dfrac{a+3}{a^2-4a-5}$

2. B; *Example:* The LCD of $\dfrac{1}{x}$, $\dfrac{2}{3}$, and $\dfrac{5}{x+1}$ is $3x(x+1)$.

3. C; *Examples:* $\dfrac{\frac{2}{3}}{\frac{4}{7}}$, $\dfrac{x-\frac{1}{y}}{x+\frac{1}{y}}$, $\dfrac{\frac{2}{a+1}}{a^2-1}$

Quick Review

Concepts

7.1 The Fundamental Property of Rational Expressions

Determining When a Rational Expression Is Undefined

Step 1 Set the denominator equal to 0.

Step 2 Solve this equation.

Step 3 The solutions of the equation are the values that make the rational expression undefined. The variable *cannot* equal these values.

Writing a Rational Expression in Lowest Terms

Step 1 Factor the numerator and denominator completely.

Step 2 Use the fundamental property to divide out any common factors.

Writing Equivalent Forms of a Rational Expression

There are often several different equivalent forms of a rational expression.

Examples

Find the values for which $\dfrac{x-4}{x^2-16}$ is undefined.

$$x^2 - 16 = 0$$

$$(x-4)(x+4) = 0 \qquad \text{Factor.}$$

$$x - 4 = 0 \quad \text{or} \quad x + 4 = 0 \qquad \text{Zero-factor property}$$

$$x = 4 \quad \text{or} \qquad x = -4 \qquad \text{Solve for } x.$$

The rational expression is undefined for 4 and -4, so $x \neq 4$ and $x \neq -4$.

Write the rational expression in lowest terms.

$$\frac{x^2 - 1}{(x-1)^2}$$

$$= \frac{(x-1)(x+1)}{(x-1)(x-1)} \qquad \text{Factor.}$$

$$= \frac{x+1}{x-1} \qquad \text{Lowest terms}$$

Write four equivalent forms of $-\dfrac{x-1}{x+2}$.

$$① \rightarrow \frac{-(x-1)}{x+2}, \quad \text{or} \quad \frac{-x+1}{x+2} \leftarrow ②$$

Distribute the negative sign in the numerator.

$$③ \rightarrow \frac{x-1}{-(x+2)}, \quad \text{or} \quad \frac{x-1}{-x-2} \leftarrow ④$$

Distribute the negative sign in the denominator.

7.2 Multiplying and Dividing Rational Expressions

Multiplying or Dividing Rational Expressions

Step 1 Note the operation. If the operation is division, use the definition of division to rewrite it as multiplication.

Step 2 Multiply numerators and multiply denominators.

Step 3 Factor numerators and denominators completely.

Step 4 Write in lowest terms using the fundamental property.

Steps 2 and 3 may be interchanged based on personal preference.

Multiply. $\dfrac{3x+9}{x-5} \cdot \dfrac{x^2-3x-10}{x^2-9}$

$$= \frac{(3x+9)(x^2-3x-10)}{(x-5)(x^2-9)} \qquad \begin{array}{l}\text{Multiply}\\ \text{numerators and}\\ \text{denominators.}\end{array}$$

$$= \frac{3(x+3)(x-5)(x+2)}{(x-5)(x+3)(x-3)} \qquad \text{Factor.}$$

$$= \frac{3(x+2)}{x-3} \qquad \text{Lowest terms}$$

Divide. $\dfrac{2x+1}{x+5} \div \dfrac{6x^2-x-2}{x^2-25}$

$$= \frac{2x+1}{x+5} \cdot \frac{x^2-25}{6x^2-x-2} \qquad \begin{array}{l}\text{Multiply by the}\\ \text{reciprocal of the}\\ \text{divisor.}\end{array}$$

$$= \frac{(2x+1)(x+5)(x-5)}{(x+5)(2x+1)(3x-2)} \qquad \begin{array}{l}\text{Multiply and}\\ \text{factor.}\end{array}$$

$$= \frac{x-5}{3x-2} \qquad \text{Lowest terms}$$

Concepts

Examples

7.3 Least Common Denominators

Finding the LCD

Step 1 Factor each denominator into prime factors.

Step 2 List each different denominator factor the *greatest* number of times it appears in any of the denominators.

Step 3 Multiply the factors from Step 2 to find the LCD.

Writing a Rational Expression with a Specified Denominator

Step 1 Factor both denominators.

Step 2 Decide what factors the denominator must be multiplied by in order to equal the specified denominator.

Step 3 Multiply the rational expression by that factor divided by itself. (That is, multiply by 1.)

Find the LCD for $\dfrac{3}{k^2 - 8k + 16}$ and $\dfrac{1}{4k^2 - 16k}$.

$$\left.\begin{array}{l} k^2 - 8k + 16 = (k-4)^2 \\ 4k^2 - 16k = 4k(k-4) \end{array}\right\} \text{Factor each denominator.}$$

$$\begin{aligned} \text{LCD} &= (k-4)^2 \cdot 4 \cdot k \\ &= 4k(k-4)^2 \end{aligned}$$

Write the rational expression as an equivalent expression with the indicated denominator.

$$\frac{5}{2z^2 - 6z} = \frac{?}{4z^3 - 12z^2}$$

$$\frac{5}{2z(z-3)} = \frac{?}{4z^2(z-3)}$$

$2z(z-3)$ must be multiplied by $2z$ to obtain $4z^2(z-3)$.

$$\frac{5}{2z(z-3)} \cdot \frac{2z}{2z} \qquad \tfrac{2z}{2z} = 1$$

$$= \frac{10z}{4z^2(z-3)}, \quad \text{or} \quad \frac{10z}{4z^3 - 12z^2}$$

7.4 Adding and Subtracting Rational Expressions

Adding Rational Expressions

Step 1 Find the LCD.

Step 2 Write each rational expression as an equivalent rational expression with the LCD as denominator.

Step 3 Add the numerators to obtain the numerator of the sum. The LCD is the denominator of the sum.

Step 4 Write in lowest terms using the fundamental property.

Add. $\dfrac{2}{3m + 6} + \dfrac{m}{m^2 - 4}$

$$\left.\begin{array}{l} 3m + 6 = 3(m+2) \\ m^2 - 4 = (m+2)(m-2) \end{array}\right\} \begin{array}{l}\text{The LCD is}\\ 3(m+2)(m-2).\end{array}$$

$$= \frac{2(m-2)}{3(m+2)(m-2)} + \frac{3m}{3(m+2)(m-2)} \quad \text{Write with the LCD.}$$

$$= \frac{2m - 4 + 3m}{3(m+2)(m-2)} \quad \begin{array}{l}\text{Add numerators.}\\\text{Keep the same}\\\text{denominator.}\end{array}$$

$$= \frac{5m - 4}{3(m+2)(m-2)} \quad \text{Combine like terms.}$$

Subtracting Rational Expressions

Follow the steps above for addition, but subtract in Step 3.

Subtract. $\dfrac{6}{k+4} - \dfrac{2}{k}$ The LCD is $k(k+4)$.

$$= \frac{6k}{(k+4)k} - \frac{2(k+4)}{k(k+4)} \quad \text{Write with the LCD.}$$

$$= \frac{6k - 2(k+4)}{k(k+4)} \quad \begin{array}{l}\text{Subtract numerators.}\\\text{Keep the same}\\\text{denominator.}\end{array}$$

$$= \frac{6k - 2k - 8}{k(k+4)} \quad \text{Distributive property}$$

$$= \frac{4k - 8}{k(k+4)}, \quad \text{or} \quad \frac{4(k-2)}{k(k+4)} \quad \begin{array}{l}\text{Either form is}\\\text{correct.}\end{array}$$

Concepts

Examples

7.5 Complex Fractions

Simplifying a Complex Fraction

Method 1

Step 1 Write both the numerator and the denominator as single fractions.

Step 2 Change the complex fraction to a division problem.

Step 3 Perform the indicated division.

Method 2

Step 1 Find the LCD of all fractions within the complex fraction.

Step 2 Multiply both the numerator and the denominator of the complex fraction by this LCD using the distributive property as necessary. Write in lowest terms.

Which method to use is a matter of individual preference.

Simplify the complex fraction.

Method 1

$$\frac{\frac{1}{a} - a}{1 - a}$$

$$= \frac{\frac{1}{a} - \frac{a^2}{a}}{1 - a}$$

$$= \frac{\frac{1 - a^2}{a}}{1 - a}$$

$$= \frac{1 - a^2}{a} \div (1 - a)$$

$$= \frac{1 - a^2}{a} \cdot \frac{1}{1 - a}$$

$$= \frac{(1 - a)(1 + a)}{a(1 - a)}$$

$$= \frac{1 + a}{a}$$

Method 2

$$\frac{\frac{1}{a} - a}{1 - a}$$

$$= \frac{a\left(\frac{1}{a} - a\right)}{a(1 - a)}$$

$$= \frac{\frac{a}{a} - a^2}{(1 - a)a}$$

$$= \frac{1 - a^2}{(1 - a)a}$$

$$= \frac{(1 + a)(1 - a)}{(1 - a)a}$$

$$= \frac{1 + a}{a}$$

The same answer results using either method.

7.6 Solving Equations with Rational Expressions

Solving an Equation with Rational Expressions

Step 1 Multiply each side of the equation by the LCD. (This clears the equation of fractions.) Be sure to distribute to *every* term on *both* sides of the equation.

Step 2 Solve the resulting equation for proposed solutions.

Step 3 Check each proposed solution by substituting it in the original equation. Reject any value that causes a denominator to equal 0.

Solve.

$$\frac{x}{x - 3} + \frac{4}{x + 3} = \frac{18}{x^2 - 9}$$

$$\frac{x}{x - 3} + \frac{4}{x + 3} = \frac{18}{(x - 3)(x + 3)} \quad \text{Factor.}$$

The LCD is $(x - 3)(x + 3)$. *Note that 3 and -3 cannot be solutions, as they cause a denominator to equal 0.*

$$(x - 3)(x + 3)\left(\frac{x}{x - 3} + \frac{4}{x + 3}\right)$$

$$= (x - 3)(x + 3)\frac{18}{(x - 3)(x + 3)}$$

Multiply by the LCD.

$$x(x + 3) + 4(x - 3) = 18 \quad \text{Distributive property}$$

$$x^2 + 3x + 4x - 12 = 18 \quad \text{Distributive property}$$

$$x^2 + 7x - 30 = 0 \quad \text{Standard form}$$

$$(x - 3)(x + 10) = 0 \quad \text{Factor.}$$

$$x - 3 = 0 \quad \text{or} \quad x + 10 = 0 \quad \text{Zero-factor property}$$

Reject $\rightarrow x = 3$ or $x = -10$ Solve for x.

Because 3 causes denominators to equal 0, it is an extraneous value. Check that the only solution is -10. Thus, $\{-10\}$ is the solution set.

Concepts

| **Examples** |

7.7 Applications of Rational Expressions

Solving a Distance-Rate-Time Problem
Use the formulas relating d, r, and t.

$$d = rt, \quad r = \frac{d}{t}, \quad t = \frac{d}{r}$$

Solving a Work Problem

Step 1 Read the problem, several times if necessary.

Step 2 Assign a variable. State what the variable represents. Organize the information from the problem in a table.

If a job can be completed in t units of time, then the rate of work is

$$\frac{1}{t} \text{ job per unit of time.}$$

Step 3 Write an equation. The sum of the fractional parts should equal 1 (whole job).

Step 4 Solve the equation.

Step 5 State the answer.

Step 6 Check.

Examples

A small plane flew from Chicago to Kansas City averaging 145 mph. The trip took 3.5 hr. What is the distance between Chicago and Kansas City?

$$\underset{\text{Rate}}{145} \quad \cdot \quad \underset{\text{Time}}{3.5} \quad = \quad \underset{\text{Distance}}{507.5 \text{ mi}}$$

It takes the regular mail carrier 6 hr to cover her route. A substitute takes 8 hr to cover the same route. How long would it take them to cover the route together?

Let x = the number of hours to cover the route together.

The rate of the regular carrier is $\frac{1}{6}$ job per hour, and the rate of the substitute is $\frac{1}{8}$ job per hour.

	Rate	Time	Part of the Job Done
Regular	$\frac{1}{6}$	x	$\frac{1}{6}x$
Substitute	$\frac{1}{8}$	x	$\frac{1}{8}x$

Multiply rate by time to find the fractional part of the job done.

$$\frac{1}{6}x + \frac{1}{8}x = 1 \qquad \text{The parts add to 1 whole job.}$$

$$24\left(\frac{1}{6}x + \frac{1}{8}x\right) = 24\,(1) \quad \text{Multiply by the LCD, 24.}$$

$$24\left(\frac{1}{6}x\right) + 24\left(\frac{1}{8}x\right) = 24\,(1) \quad \text{Distributive property}$$

$$4x + 3x = 24 \qquad \text{Multiply.}$$

$$7x = 24 \qquad \text{Combine like terms.}$$

$$x = \frac{24}{7} \qquad \text{Divide by 7.}$$

It would take them $\frac{24}{7}$ hr, or $3\frac{3}{7}$ hr, to cover the route together.

This answer makes sense. The time together is *less than* the time of the regular carrier working alone. Also,

$$\frac{1}{6}\left(\frac{24}{7}\right) + \frac{1}{8}\left(\frac{24}{7}\right) = 1.$$

Chapter 7 *Review Exercises*

7.1 *Find the numerical value of each rational expression for* **(a)** $x = -2$ *and*
(b) $x = 4$.

1. $\dfrac{x^2}{x - 5}$

2. $\dfrac{4x - 3}{5x + 2}$

3. $\dfrac{3x}{x^2 - 4}$

4. $\dfrac{x - 1}{x + 2}$

Find any value(s) of the variable for which each rational expression is undefined.
Write answers with the symbol $\neq$.

5. $\dfrac{4}{x - 3}$

6. $\dfrac{x + 3}{2x}$

7. $\dfrac{m - 2}{m^2 - 2m - 3}$

8. $\dfrac{2k + 1}{3k^2 + 17k + 10}$

Write each rational expression in lowest terms.

9. $\dfrac{5a^3b^3}{15a^4b^2}$

10. $\dfrac{m - 4}{4 - m}$

11. $\dfrac{4x^2 - 9}{6 - 4x}$

12. $\dfrac{4p^2 + 8pq - 5q^2}{10p^2 - 3pq - q^2}$

Write four equivalent forms of each rational expression.

13. $-\dfrac{4x - 9}{2x + 3}$

14. $-\dfrac{8 - 3x}{3 - 6x}$

7.2 *Multiply or divide. Write each answer in lowest terms.*

15. $\dfrac{8x^2}{12x^5} \cdot \dfrac{6x^4}{2x}$

16. $\dfrac{9m^2}{(3m)^4} \div \dfrac{6m^5}{36m}$

17. $\dfrac{x - 3}{4} \cdot \dfrac{5}{2x - 6}$

18. $\dfrac{2r + 3}{r - 4} \cdot \dfrac{r^2 - 16}{6r + 9}$

19. $\dfrac{3q + 3}{5 - 6q} \div \dfrac{4q + 4}{2(5 - 6q)}$

20. $\dfrac{y^2 - 6y + 8}{y^2 + 3y - 18} \div \dfrac{y - 4}{y + 6}$

21. $\dfrac{2p^2 + 13p + 20}{p^2 + p - 12} \cdot \dfrac{p^2 + 2p - 15}{2p^2 + 7p + 5}$

22. $\dfrac{3z^2 + 5z - 2}{9z^2 - 1} \cdot \dfrac{9z^2 + 6z + 1}{z^2 + 5z + 6}$

7.3 *Find the LCD for the fractions in each list.*

23. $\dfrac{1}{8}, \dfrac{5}{12}, \dfrac{7}{32}$

24. $\dfrac{4}{9y}, \dfrac{7}{12y^2}, \dfrac{5}{27y^4}$

25. $\dfrac{1}{m^2 + 2m}, \dfrac{4}{m^2 + 7m + 10}$

26. $\dfrac{3}{x^2 + 4x + 3}, \dfrac{5}{x^2 + 5x + 4}, \dfrac{2}{x^2 + 7x + 12}$

Write each rational expression as an equivalent expression with the indicated denominator.

27. $\dfrac{5}{8} = \dfrac{?}{56}$

28. $\dfrac{10}{k} = \dfrac{?}{4k}$

29. $\dfrac{3}{2a^3} = \dfrac{?}{10a^4}$

30. $\dfrac{9}{x - 3} = \dfrac{?}{18 - 6x}$

31. $\dfrac{-3y}{2y - 10} = \dfrac{?}{50 - 10y}$

32. $\dfrac{4b}{b^2 + 2b - 3} = \dfrac{?}{(b + 3)(b - 1)(b + 2)}$

7.4 *Add or subtract. Write each answer in lowest terms.*

33. $\dfrac{10}{x} + \dfrac{5}{x}$

34. $\dfrac{6}{3p} - \dfrac{12}{3p}$

35. $\dfrac{9}{k} - \dfrac{5}{k - 5}$

36. $\dfrac{4}{y} + \dfrac{7}{7 + y}$

37. $\dfrac{m}{3} - \dfrac{2 + 5m}{6}$

38. $\dfrac{12}{x^2} - \dfrac{3}{4x}$

39. $\dfrac{5}{a - 2b} + \dfrac{2}{a + 2b}$

40. $\dfrac{4}{k^2 - 9} - \dfrac{k + 3}{3k - 9}$

41. $\dfrac{8}{z^2 + 6z} - \dfrac{3}{z^2 + 4z - 12}$

42. $\dfrac{11}{2p - p^2} - \dfrac{2}{p^2 - 5p + 6}$

7.5 *Simplify each complex fraction.*

43. $\dfrac{\dfrac{a^4}{b^2}}{\dfrac{a^3}{b}}$

44. $\dfrac{\dfrac{y - 3}{y}}{\dfrac{y + 3}{4y}}$

45. $\dfrac{\dfrac{3m + 2}{m}}{\dfrac{2m - 5}{6m}}$

46. $\dfrac{\dfrac{1}{p} - \dfrac{1}{q}}{\dfrac{1}{q - p}}$

47. $\dfrac{x + \dfrac{1}{w}}{x - \dfrac{1}{w}}$

48. $\dfrac{\dfrac{1}{r + t} - 1}{\dfrac{1}{r + t} + 1}$

Simplify each expression, using only positive exponents in the answer.

49. $\dfrac{a^{-2} + b^{-1}}{a^{-1} - 5b^{-3}}$

50. $\dfrac{x^{-3} + 2y^{-1}}{y + 2x^3}$

7.6 *Solve each equation, and check the solutions.*

51. $\dfrac{k}{5} - \dfrac{2}{3} = \dfrac{1}{2}$

52. $\dfrac{4 - z}{z} + \dfrac{3}{2} = \dfrac{-4}{z}$

53. $\dfrac{x}{2} - \dfrac{x - 3}{7} = -1$

54. $\dfrac{3y - 1}{y - 2} = \dfrac{5}{y - 2} + 1$

55. $\dfrac{3}{x + 4} - \dfrac{2x}{5} = \dfrac{3}{x + 4}$

56. $\dfrac{3}{m - 2} + \dfrac{1}{m - 1} = \dfrac{7}{m^2 - 3m + 2}$

Solve each formula for the specified variable.

57. $m = \dfrac{Ry}{t}$ for t

58. $b = \dfrac{s + t}{r}$ for s

59. $a = \dfrac{b}{c + d}$ for d

60. $\dfrac{1}{r} - \dfrac{1}{s} = \dfrac{1}{t}$ for t

7.7 *Solve each problem.*

61. In a certain fraction, the denominator is 5 less than the numerator. If 5 is added to both the numerator and the denominator, the resulting fraction is equivalent to $\frac{5}{4}$. Find the original fraction (*not* written in lowest terms).

62. The denominator of a certain fraction is six times the numerator. If 3 is added to the numerator and subtracted from the denominator, the resulting fraction is equivalent to $\frac{2}{5}$. Find the original fraction (*not* written in lowest terms).

63. Ryan Hunter-Reay won the Iowa Corn Indy 300. He drove a Dallara-Honda the 262.5 mi distance with an average rate of 129.943 mph. What was his time (to the nearest thousandth of an hour)? (Data from www.indycar.com)

64. In the 2014 Winter Olympics in Sochi, Russia, Sven Kramer of the Netherlands won the men's 5000-m speed skating event in 6.179 min. What was his rate (to three decimal places)? (Data from *The World Almanac and Book of Facts*.)

65. Zachary and Samuel are brothers who share a bedroom. By himself, Zachary can completely mess up their room in 20 min, while it would take Samuel only 12 min to do the same thing. How long would it take them to mess up the room together?

66. A man can plant his garden in 5 hr, working alone. His daughter can do the same job in 8 hr. How long would it take them if they worked together?

Chapter 7 Mixed Review Exercises

Perform the indicated operations. Write each answer in lowest terms.

1. $\dfrac{4}{m-1} - \dfrac{3}{m+1}$

2. $\dfrac{8p^5}{5} \div \dfrac{2p^3}{10}$

3. $\dfrac{r-3}{8} \div \dfrac{3r-9}{4}$

4. $\dfrac{\dfrac{5}{x} - 1}{\dfrac{5-x}{3x}}$

5. $\dfrac{4}{z^2 - 2z + 1} - \dfrac{3}{z^2 - 1}$

6. $\dfrac{2x^2 + 5x - 12}{4x^2 - 9} \cdot \dfrac{x^2 - 3x - 28}{x^2 + 8x + 16}$

Solve each equation, and check the solutions.

7. $\dfrac{5t}{6} = \dfrac{2t-1}{3} + 1$

8. $\dfrac{2}{z} - \dfrac{z}{z+3} = \dfrac{1}{z+3}$

9. $\dfrac{2x}{x^2 - 16} - \dfrac{2}{x-4} = \dfrac{4}{x+4}$

10. Solve $a = \dfrac{v-w}{t}$ for w.

Solve each problem.

11. If the same number is added to both the numerator and denominator of the fraction $\frac{4}{11}$, the result is equivalent to $\frac{1}{2}$. Find the number.

12. Seema can clean the house in 3 hr. Satish can clean the house in 6 hr. Working together, how long will it take them to clean the house?

13. Anne flew her plane 400 km with the wind in the same time it took her to go 200 km against the wind. The wind speed is 50 km per hr. Find the rate of the plane in still air. Use x as the variable.

14. At a given hour, two steamboats leave a city in the same direction on a straight canal. One travels at 18 mph, and the other travels at 25 mph. In how many hours will the boats be 70 mi apart?

	d	*r*	*t*
With the Wind	400	_____	_____
Against the Wind	200	_____	_____

1. Find the numerical value of $\dfrac{6r + 1}{2r^2 - 3r - 20}$ for each value of r.

  (a) $r = -2$ **(b)** $r = 4$

2. Find any values for which $\dfrac{3x - 1}{x^2 - 2x - 8}$ is undefined. Write the answer with the symbol $\neq$.

3. Write four equivalent forms of the rational expression $-\dfrac{6x - 5}{2x + 3}$.

Write each rational expression in lowest terms.

4. $\dfrac{-15x^6y^4}{5x^4y}$

5. $\dfrac{6a^2 + a - 2}{2a^2 - 3a + 1}$

Multiply or divide. Write each answer in lowest terms.

6. $\dfrac{5(d - 2)}{9} \div \dfrac{3(d - 2)}{5}$

7. $\dfrac{6k^2 - k - 2}{8k^2 + 10k + 3} \cdot \dfrac{4k^2 + 7k + 3}{3k^2 + 5k + 2}$

8. $\dfrac{4a^2 + 9a + 2}{3a^2 + 11a + 10} \div \dfrac{4a^2 + 17a + 4}{3a^2 + 2a - 5}$

9. $\dfrac{x^2 - 10x + 25}{9 - 6x + x^2} \cdot \dfrac{x - 3}{5 - x}$

Find the LCD for the fractions in each list.

10. $\dfrac{-3}{10p^2}, \dfrac{21}{25p^3}, \dfrac{-7}{30p^5}$

11. $\dfrac{r + 1}{2r^2 + 7r + 6}, \dfrac{-2r + 1}{2r^2 - 7r - 15}$

Write each rational expression as an equivalent expression with the indicated denominator.

12. $\dfrac{15}{4p} = \dfrac{?}{64p^3}$

13. $\dfrac{3}{6m - 12} = \dfrac{?}{42m - 84}$

Add or subtract. Write each answer in lowest terms.

14. $\dfrac{4x + 2}{x + 5} + \dfrac{-2x + 8}{x + 5}$

15. $\dfrac{-4}{y + 2} + \dfrac{6}{5y + 10}$

16. $\dfrac{x + 1}{3 - x} - \dfrac{x^2}{x - 3}$

17. $\dfrac{3}{2m^2 - 9m - 5} - \dfrac{m + 1}{2m^2 - m - 1}$

Simplify each complex fraction.

18. $\dfrac{\dfrac{2p}{k^2}}{\dfrac{3p^2}{k^3}}$

19. $\dfrac{\dfrac{x^2-25}{x+3}}{\dfrac{x+5}{x^2-9}}$

20. $\dfrac{\dfrac{1}{x+3}-1}{1+\dfrac{1}{x+3}}$

21. Simplify $\dfrac{2x^{-2}+y^{-2}}{x^{-1}-y^{-1}}$, using only positive exponents in the answer.

Decide whether each of the following is an expression *or an* equation. *Simplify the one that is an expression, and solve the one that is an equation.*

22. $\dfrac{2x}{3}+\dfrac{x}{4}-\dfrac{11}{2}$

23. $\dfrac{2x}{3}+\dfrac{x}{4}=\dfrac{11}{2}$

Solve each equation.

24. $\dfrac{3x}{x+1}=\dfrac{3}{2x}$

25. $\dfrac{2}{x-1}-\dfrac{2}{3}=\dfrac{-1}{x+1}$

26. $4+\dfrac{6}{x-3}=\dfrac{2x}{x-3}$

27. $\dfrac{2x}{x-3}+\dfrac{1}{x+3}=\dfrac{-6}{x^2-9}$

28. Solve the formula $F=\dfrac{k}{d-D}$ for D.

Solve each problem.

29. A man can paint a room in his house, working alone, in 5 hr. His wife can do the job in 4 hr. How long will it take them to paint the room if they work together?

	Rate	Time Working Together	Fractional Part of the Job Done When Working Together
Man			
Wife			

30. A boat travels 7 mph in still water. It takes as long to go 20 mi upstream as 50 mi downstream. Find the rate of the current.

		d	r	t
Upstream				
Downstream				

Chapters R–7 *Cumulative Review Exercises*

1. Evaluate $3 + 4\left(\dfrac{1}{2} - \dfrac{3}{4}\right)$.

Solve each equation.

2. $3(2t - 5) = 2 + 5t$

3. $A = \dfrac{1}{2}bh$ for b

4. $\dfrac{2 + m}{2 - m} = \dfrac{3}{4}$

Solve each inequality. Write the solution set in interval notation, and graph it.

5. $5x \le 6x + 8$

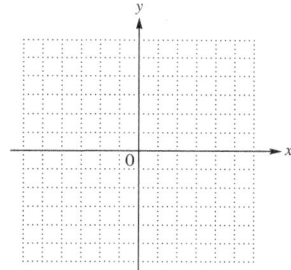

6. $5m - 9 > 2m + 3$

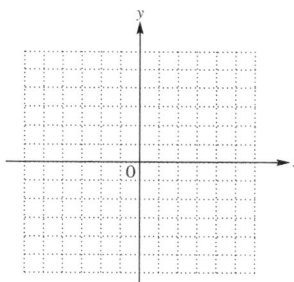

Graph each equation or inequality.

7. $y = -3x + 2$

8. $y \ge 2x + 3$

Solve each system using the method indicated.

9. $3x + 4y = 5$
   $6x + 7y = 8$ (elimination)

10. $y = -3x + 1$
   $x + 2y = -3$ (substitution)

Simplify each expression.

11. $\dfrac{(2x^3)^{-1} \cdot x}{2^3 x^5}$

12. $\dfrac{(m^{-2})^3 m}{m^5 m^{-4}}$

13. $\dfrac{2p^3 q^4}{8p^5 q^3}$

Perform the indicated operations.

14. $(2k^2 + 3k) - (k^2 + k - 1)$

15. $8x^2 y^2 (9x^4 y^5)$

16. $(2a - b)^2$

17. $(y^2 + 3y + 5)(3y - 1)$

18. $\dfrac{12p^3 + 2p^2 - 12p + 4}{2p - 2}$

Factor completely.

19. $8t^2 + 10tv + 3v^2$

20. $8r^2 - 9rs + 12s^2$

21. $16x^4 - 1$

Solve each equation.

22. $r^2 = 2r + 15$

23. $y^2 - 121 = 0$

24. $(r - 5)(2r + 1)(3r - 2) = 0$

Solve each problem.

25. One number is 4 greater than another. The product of the numbers is 2 less than the lesser number. Find the lesser number.

26. The length of a rectangle is 2 m less than twice the width. The area is 60 m². Find the width of the rectangle.

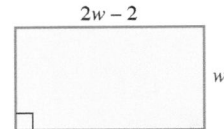

27. For what value(s) of t is $\frac{2 + t}{t^2 - 4}$ undefined? Write the answer with the symbol $\neq$.

28. Which one of the following rational expressions is *not* equivalent to $\frac{4 - 3x}{7}$?

A. $-\dfrac{-4 + 3x}{7}$ **B.** $-\dfrac{4 - 3x}{-7}$ **C.** $\dfrac{-4 + 3x}{-7}$ **D.** $\dfrac{-(3x + 4)}{7}$

Perform the indicated operations. Write each answer in lowest terms.

29. $\dfrac{5}{q} - \dfrac{1}{q}$

30. $\dfrac{3}{7} + \dfrac{4}{r}$

31. $\dfrac{4}{5q - 20} - \dfrac{1}{3q - 12}$

32. $\dfrac{2}{k^2 + k} - \dfrac{3}{k^2 - k}$

33. $\dfrac{7z^2 + 49z + 70}{16z^2 + 72z - 40} \div \dfrac{3z + 6}{4z^2 - 1}$

34. $\dfrac{\dfrac{4}{a} + \dfrac{5}{2a}}{\dfrac{7}{6a} - \dfrac{1}{5a}}$

Solve.

35. $\dfrac{r + 2}{5} = \dfrac{r - 3}{3}$

36. $\dfrac{1}{x} = \dfrac{1}{x + 1} + \dfrac{1}{2}$

37. $\dfrac{1}{f} = \dfrac{1}{p} + \dfrac{1}{q}$ for q

38. Len can weed the yard in 3 hr. Bruno can weed the yard in 2 hr. How long would it take them if they worked together?

8

Equations, Inequalities, Graphs, and Systems Revisited

A centered bubble in a carpenter's level indicates a level surface (suggesting *equality*), while a surface that is not level causes the bubble to be off center (suggesting *inequality*).

8.1 Review of Solving Linear Equations and Inequalities in One Variable

8.2 Set Operations and Compound Inequalities

8.3 Absolute Value Equations and Inequalities

Summary Exercises *Solving Linear and Absolute Value Equations and Inequalities*

8.4 Review of Graphing Linear Equations in Two Variables; Slope

8.5 Review of Systems of Linear Equations in Two Variables

8.6 Systems of Linear Equations in Three Variables; Applications

8.1 Review of Solving Linear Equations and Inequalities in One Variable

OBJECTIVES

1. Distinguish between expressions and equations.
2. Solve linear equations.
3. Review interval notation.
4. Solve linear inequalities.
5. Solve three-part inequalities.

1 Decide whether each of the following is an *expression* or an *equation*.

(a) $9x = 10$

(b) $9x + 10$

(c) $3 + 5x - 8x + 9$

(d) $3 + 5x = -8x + 9$

OBJECTIVE 1 **Distinguish between expressions and equations.** Recall that an *algebraic expression* is a collection of constants, variables, operation symbols, and/or grouping symbols.

$$8x + 9, \quad y - 4, \quad \text{and} \quad \frac{x^3 y^3}{z} \qquad \text{Algebraic expressions}$$

An *equation* is a statement that two algebraic expressions are equal. *An equation always contains an equality symbol, while an expression does not.*

EXAMPLE 1 **Distinguishing between Expressions and Equations**

Decide whether each of the following is an *expression* or an *equation*.

(a) $3x - 7 = 2$ (b) $3x - 7$

In part (a) we have an equation, because there is an equality symbol. In part (b), there is no equality symbol, so it is an expression.

Equation
Left side | Right side
$3x - 7 = 2$
An equation can be *solved.*

Expression
$3x - 7$
An expression **cannot** be solved. It can often be *evaluated* or *simplified.*

◀ **Work Problem 1 at the Side.**

OBJECTIVE 2 **Solve linear equations.**

Linear Equation in One Variable

A **linear equation in one variable** (here x) can be written in the form

$$Ax + B = C,$$

where A, B, and C are real numbers and $A \neq 0$.

Examples: $x + 1 = -2$, $x - 3 = 5$, $2x + 5 = 10$ Linear equations in one variable

A linear equation is a **first-degree equation** because the greatest power on the variable is 1. The following are not linear (that is, *nonlinear*).

$$x^2 + 3y = 5, \quad \frac{8}{x} = -22, \quad \text{and} \quad \sqrt{x} = 6 \qquad \text{Nonlinear equations}$$

If the variable in an equation can be replaced by a real number that makes the statement true, then that number is a **solution** of the equation. An equation is *solved* by finding its **solution set,** the set of all solutions. The solution set of $x - 3 = 5$ is $\{8\}$.

Equivalent equations are related equations that have the same solution set. The following are all equivalent because each has solution set $\{3\}$.

$$5x + 2 = 17, \quad 5x = 15, \quad \text{and} \quad x = 3 \qquad \text{Equivalent equations}$$

Answers
1. (a) equation (b) expression (c) expression (d) equation

We use two important properties of equality to produce equivalent equations.

Addition and Multiplication Properties of Equality

Addition Property of Equality

If A, B, and C represent real numbers, then the equations

$$A = B \quad \text{and} \quad A + C = B + C \quad \text{are equivalent.}$$

In words, the same number may be added to each side of an equation without changing the solution set.

Multiplication Property of Equality

If A, B, and C represent real numbers and $C \neq 0$, then the equations

$$A = B \quad \text{and} \quad AC = BC \quad \text{are equivalent.}$$

In words, each side of an equation may be multiplied by the same nonzero number without changing the solution set.

Because subtraction and division are defined in terms of addition and multiplication, respectively, these properties can be extended.

> *The same number may be subtracted from each side of an equation, and each side of an equation may be divided by the same nonzero number, without changing the solution set.*

EXAMPLE 2 **Solving a Linear Equation**

Solve $4x - 2x - 5 = 4 + 6x + 3$.

The goal is to isolate x on one side of the equation.

$4x - 2x - 5 = 4 + 6x + 3$	
$2x - 5 = 7 + 6x$	Combine like terms.
$2x - 5 - 6x = 7 + 6x - 6x$	Subtract $6x$ from each side.
$-4x - 5 = 7$	Combine like terms.
$-4x - 5 + 5 = 7 + 5$	Add 5 to each side.
$-4x = 12$	Combine like terms.
$\dfrac{-4x}{-4} = \dfrac{12}{-4}$	Divide each side by -4.
$x = -3$	

CHECK Substitute -3 for x in the *original* equation.

$4x - 2x - 5 = 4 + 6x + 3$	Original equation
$4(-3) - 2(-3) - 5 \stackrel{?}{=} 4 + 6(-3) + 3$	Let $x = -3$.
$-12 + 6 - 5 \stackrel{?}{=} 4 - 18 + 3$	Multiply.
$-11 = -11$ ✓	True

> Use parentheses around substituted values to avoid errors.

> This is **not** the solution.

The true statement indicates that $\{-3\}$ is the solution set.

Work Problem 2 at the Side. ▶

---

2 Solve each equation.

(a) $3p + 2p + 1 = -24$

$$\underline{} + 1 = -24$$
$$5p + 1 - \underline{} = -24 - \underline{}$$
$$5p = -25$$
$$\frac{5p}{\underline{}} = \frac{-25}{\underline{}}$$
$$p = \underline{}$$

CHECK Substitute _____ in the original equation. Does the solution check? (*Yes / No*)

The solution set is $\{ \underline{} \}$.

(b) $3p = 2p + 4p + 5$

(c) $4x + 8x = 17x - 9 - 1$

(d) $-7 + 3t - 9t = 12t - 5$

Answers

2. **(a)** $5p$; 1; 1; 5; 5; -5; -5; Yes; -5

   (b) $\left\{ -\dfrac{5}{3} \right\}$ **(c)** $\{2\}$ **(d)** $\left\{ -\dfrac{1}{9} \right\}$

③ Solve each equation.

(a) $5p + 4(3 - 2p)$
$= 2 + p - 10$

(b) $3(z - 2) + 5z = 2$

(c) $-2 + 3(x + 4) = 8x$

Solving a Linear Equation in One Variable

Step 1 **Simplify each side separately.** Use the distributive property as needed.

- Clear any parentheses.
- Clear any fractions or decimals.
- Combine like terms.

Step 2 **Isolate the variable terms on one side.** Use the addition property of equality so that all terms with variables are on one side of the equation and all constants (numbers) are on the other side.

Step 3 **Isolate the variable.** Use the multiplication property of equality to obtain an equation that has just the variable with coefficient 1 on one side.

Step 4 **Check.** Substitute the value found into the *original* equation. If a true statement results, write the solution set. If not, rework the problem.

EXAMPLE 3 **Solving a Linear Equation**

Solve $2(k - 5) + 3k = k + 6$.

Step 1 Clear parentheses on the left. Then combine like terms.

> Be sure to distribute over *all* terms within parentheses.

$2(k - 5) + 3k = k + 6$

$2k + 2(-5) + 3k = k + 6$ Distributive property

$2k - 10 + 3k = k + 6$ Multiply.

$5k - 10 = k + 6$ Combine like terms.

Step 2 Isolate the variable terms on one side and constants on the other.

$5k - 10 - k = k + 6 - k$ Subtract k.

$4k - 10 = 6$ Combine like terms.

$4k - 10 + 10 = 6 + 10$ Add 10.

$4k = 16$ Combine like terms.

Step 3 Use the multiplication property of equality to isolate k on the left.

$$\frac{4k}{4} = \frac{16}{4}$$ Divide by 4.

$$k = 4$$

Step 4 Check by substituting 4 for k in the original equation.

CHECK

> Always check your work.

$2(k - 5) + 3k = k + 6$ Original equation

$2(4 - 5) + 3(4) \overset{?}{=} 4 + 6$ Let $k = 4$.

$2(-1) + 12 \overset{?}{=} 10$ Perform operations.

$10 = 10$ ✓   True

A true statement results, so the solution set is $\{4\}$.

◀ **Work Problem ③ at the Side.**

Answers

3. (a) $\{5\}$ **(b)** $\{1\}$ **(c)** $\{2\}$

EXAMPLE 4 Solving a Linear Equation

Solve. $\qquad 4(3x - 2) = 38 - 2(2x - 1)$ | Clear parentheses using the distributive property.

Step 1 $\quad 4(3x) + 4(-2) = 38 - 2(2x) - 2(-1)$ | Clear parentheses using the distributive property.

> Be careful with signs when distributing.

$12x - 8 = 38 - 4x + 2$ | Multiply.

$12x - 8 = 40 - 4x$ | Combine like terms.

Step 2 $\quad 12x - 8 + 4x = 40 - 4x + 4x$ | Add $4x$.

$16x - 8 = 40$ | Combine like terms.

$16x - 8 + 8 = 40 + 8$ | Add 8.

$16x = 48$ | Combine like terms.

Step 3 $\quad \dfrac{16x}{16} = \dfrac{48}{16}$ | Divide by 16.

$x = 3$

Step 4 CHECK $\quad 4(3x - 2) = 38 - 2(2x - 1)$ | Original equation

$4[3(3) - 2] \overset{?}{=} 38 - 2[2(3) - 1]$ | Let $x = 3$.

$4[7] \overset{?}{=} 38 - 2[5]$ | Work inside the brackets.

$28 = 28 \checkmark$ | True

A true statement results, so the solution set is $\{3\}$.

—————————— **Work Problem 4 at the Side.** ▶

EXAMPLE 5 Solving a Linear Equation with Fractions

Solve. $\qquad \dfrac{x + 7}{6} + \dfrac{2x - 8}{2} = -4$

Step 1 $\quad 6\left(\dfrac{x + 7}{6} + \dfrac{2x - 8}{2}\right) = 6(-4)$ | Eliminate the fractions. Multiply each side by the LCD, 6.

$6\left(\dfrac{x + 7}{6}\right) + 6\left(\dfrac{2x - 8}{2}\right) = 6(-4)$ | Distributive property

> his equivalent equation has integer coefficients.

$(x + 7) + 3(2x - 8) = -24$ | Multiply.

$x + 7 + 3(2x) + 3(-8) = -24$ | Distributive property

$x + 7 + 6x - 24 = -24$ | Multiply.

$7x - 17 = -24$ | Combine like terms.

Step 2 $\quad 7x - 17 + 17 = -24 + 17$ | Add 17.

$7x = -7$ | Combine like terms.

Step 3 $\quad \dfrac{7x}{7} = \dfrac{-7}{7}$ | Divide by 7.

$x = -1$

Step 4 Check that the solution set is $\{-1\}$.

—————————— **Work Problem 5 at the Side.** ▶

4 Solve each equation.

(GS) **(a)** $2(2x + 1) - 3(2x - 1) = 9$

$2(\underline{\quad}) + 2(1) - 3(2x) - 3(\underline{\quad})$
$= 9$

$4x + 2 - \underline{\quad} + \underline{\quad} = 9$

$\underline{\quad} + 5 = 9$

Now complete the solution. Give the solution set.

(b) $2 - 3(2 + 6x)$
$\quad = 4(x + 1) + 18$

5 Solve each equation.

(a) $\dfrac{2p}{7} - \dfrac{p}{2} = -3$

(b) $\dfrac{k + 1}{2} + \dfrac{k + 3}{4} = \dfrac{1}{2}$

Answers

4. (a) $2x; -1; 6x; 3; -2x; \{-2\}$

(b) $\left\{-\dfrac{13}{11}\right\}$

5. (a) $\{14\}$ **(b)** $\{-1\}$

6 Solve each equation.

(a) $0.04x + 0.06(20 - x)$
$= 0.05(50)$

EXAMPLE 6 **Solving a Linear Equation with Decimals**

Solve. $0.06x + \mathbf{0.09}(15 - x) = 0.07(15)$ Clear parentheses first using the distributive property.

Step 1 $0.06x + \mathbf{0.09}(15) + \mathbf{0.09}(-x) = 0.07(15)$

$0.06x + 1.35 - 0.09x = 1.05$ Multiply.

To clear the decimals, multiply by a power of 10. Each decimal number is given in hundredths here, so we multiply by 100 (that is, by 10^2). This is done by moving each decimal point two places to the right.

$0.06x + 1.35 - 0.09x = 1.05$ **Multiply each term by 100.**

Move decimal points 2 places to the right.

$6x + 135 - 9x = 105$ This is an equivalent equation without decimals.

$-3x + 135 = 105$ Combine like terms.

Step 2 $-3x + 135 - \mathbf{135} = 105 - \mathbf{135}$ Subtract 135.

$-3x = -30$ Combine like terms.

Step 3 $\dfrac{-3x}{-3} = \dfrac{-30}{-3}$ Divide by -3.

$x = 10$

Step 4 Check that the solution set is $\{10\}$.

◀ **Work Problem** **6** **at the Side.**

(b) $0.10(x - 6) + 0.05x$
$= 0.06(50)$

Note

Some students prefer to solve an equation with decimal coefficients without clearing the decimals.

$0.06x + \mathbf{0.09}(15 - x) = 0.07(15)$ Equation from **Example 6**

$0.06x + \mathbf{0.09}(15) + \mathbf{0.09}(-x) = 0.07(15)$ Distributive property

$0.06x + 1.35 - 0.09x = 1.05$ Multiply.

Be careful with decimal points. $-0.03x + 1.35 = 1.05$ Combine like terms.

$-0.03x = -0.3$ Subtract 1.35.

The same solution results. $x = 10$ Divide by -0.03.

An equation can have one solution, an infinite number of solutions, or no solution. The table below summarizes these types of equations.

SOLUTION SETS OF EQUATIONS

Type of Linear Equation	Number of Solutions	Indication When Solving
Conditional	One solution; solution set {a number}	Final line is $x = $ a number. (See **Examples 2–6, 7(a)**.)
Identity	Infinitely many solutions; solution set {all real numbers}	Final line is true, such as $0 = 0$. (See **Example 7(b)**.)
Contradiction	No solution; solution set $\varnothing$	Final line is false, such as $-15 = -20$. (See **Example 7(c)**.)

Answers

6. **(a)** $\{-65\}$ **(b)** $\{24\}$

EXAMPLE 7 **Recognizing Conditional Equations, Identities, and Contradictions**

Solve each equation. Decide whether it is a *conditional equation*, an *identity*, or a *contradiction*.

(a)

$$5(2x + 6) - 2 = 7(x + 4)$$

$10x + 30 - 2 = 7x + 28$	Distributive property
$10x + 28 = 7x + 28$	Combine like terms.
$10x + 28 - 7x - 28 = 7x + 28 - 7x - 28$	Subtract $7x$. Subtract 28.
$3x = 0$	Combine like terms.
$\dfrac{3x}{3} = \dfrac{0}{3}$	Divide by 3.
$x = 0$	$\frac{0}{3} = 0$

The last line has a variable. The number following "=" is a solution.

CHECK

$5(2x + 6) - 2 = 7(x + 4)$	Original equation
$5[2(0) + 6] - 2 \overset{?}{=} 7(0 + 4)$	Let $x = 0$.
$5(6) - 2 \overset{?}{=} 7(4)$	Multiply, and then add.
$28 = 28 \checkmark$	True

The value 0 checks, so the solution set is $\{0\}$. Because the solution set has only one element, $5(2x + 6) - 2 = 7(x + 4)$ is a conditional equation.

(b)

$5x - 15 = 5(x - 3)$	
$5x - 15 = 5x - 15$	Distributive property
$5x - 15 - 5x + 15 = 5x - 15 - 5x + 15$	Subtract $5x$. Add 15.
$0 = 0$	True

The variable has "disappeared."

The *true* statement $0 = 0$ indicates that the solution set is {all real numbers}. The equation $5x - 15 = 5(x - 3)$ is an identity. Notice that the first step yielded

$$5x - 15 = 5x - 15, \quad \text{which is true for } all \text{ values of } x.$$

We could have identified the equation as an identity at that point.

(c)

$5x - 15 = 5(x - 4)$	
$5x - 15 = 5x - 20$	Distributive property
$5x - 15 - 5x = 5x - 20 - 5x$	Subtract $5x$.
$-15 = -20$	False

The variable has "disappeared."

Because the result, $-15 = -20$, is *false*, the equation has no solution. The solution set is $\varnothing$, so the equation $5x - 15 = 5(x - 4)$ is a contradiction.

─────── **Work Problem 7 at the Side.** ▶

⚠ CAUTION

A common error in solving an equation like that in **Example 7(a)** is to think that the equation has no solution and write the solution set as $\varnothing$. This equation has one solution, the number 0, so it is a conditional equation with solution set $\{0\}$.

7 Solve each equation. Decide whether it is a *conditional equation*, an *identity*, or a *contradiction*.

(a) $5(x + 2) - 2(x + 1)$
$= 3x + 1$

(b) $9x - 3(x + 4) = 6(x - 2)$

(c) $5(3x + 1) = x + 5$

(d) $3(2x - 4) = 20 - 2x$

Answers

7. **(a)** $\varnothing$; contradiction
  (b) {all real numbers}; identity
  (c) $\{0\}$; conditional
  (d) $\{4\}$; conditional

OBJECTIVE ▶ 3 **Review interval notation.** An **inequality** consists of algebraic expressions related by one of the following symbols. (The symbols are read as shown when the inequality is read from left to right.)

$<$ "is less than" $\leq$ "is less than or equal to"

$>$ "is greater than" $\geq$ "is greater than or equal to"

Linear Inequality in One Variable

A **linear inequality in one variable** (here x) can be written in the form

$$Ax + B < C, \quad Ax + B \leq C, \quad Ax + B > C, \quad \text{or} \quad Ax + B \geq C,$$

where A, B, and C are real numbers and $A \neq 0$.

Examples: $x + 5 < 2$, $x - 3 \geq 5$, $2k + 5 \leq 10$ *Linear inequalities in one variable*

We write and graph solution sets of linear inequalities in one variable using **interval notation.** For example, the solution set of $x \leq 2$ is an **interval** on a number line and is written $(-\infty, 2]$. The negative infinity symbol $-\infty$ shows that the interval includes *all* real numbers less than 2. The square bracket indicates that 2 is included in the solution set.

Remember the following important concepts regarding interval notation.

- A parenthesis indicates that an endpoint is *not* included.
- A square bracket indicates that an endpoint is included.
- A parenthesis is always used next to an infinity symbol, $-\infty$ or ∞.
- The set of real numbers is written in interval notation as $(-\infty, \infty)$.

SUMMARY OF TYPES OF INTERVALS

Type of Interval	Set-Builder Notation	Interval Notation	Graph
Open interval	$\{x \mid a < x < b\}$	(a, b)	
Closed interval	$\{x \mid a \leq x \leq b\}$	$[a, b]$	
Half-open (or half-closed) interval	$\{x \mid a \leq x < b\}$	$[a, b)$	
	$\{x \mid a < x \leq b\}$	$(a, b]$	
Disjoint intervals*	$\{x \mid x < a \text{ or } x > b\}$	$(-\infty, a) \cup (b, \infty)$	
Infinite interval	$\{x \mid x > a\}$	(a, ∞)	
	$\{x \mid x \geq a\}$	$[a, \infty)$	
	$\{x \mid x < a\}$	$(-\infty, a)$	
	$\{x \mid x \leq a\}$	$(-\infty, a]$	
	$\{x \mid x \text{ is a real number}\}$	$(-\infty, \infty)$	

---

*We use disjoint intervals with set operations and compound inequalities.

OBJECTIVE ▶ **4** **Solve linear inequalities.** We solve an inequality by finding all numbers that make the inequality true. Usually, an inequality has an infinite number of solutions. These solutions, like solutions of equations, are found by producing a series of simpler equivalent inequalities. **Equivalent inequalities** are inequalities with the same solution set.

We use two important properties to produce equivalent inequalities.

Addition Property of Inequality

If A, B, and C represent real numbers, then the inequalities

$$A < B \quad \text{and} \quad A + C < B + C \quad \text{are equivalent.}^*$$

In words, the same number may be added to each side of an inequality without changing the solution set.

*This also applies to $A \leq B$, $A > B$, and $A \geq B$.

EXAMPLE 8 Using the Addition Property of Inequality

Solve $x - 7 < -12$, and graph the solution set.

$$x - 7 < -12$$
$$x - 7 + 7 < -12 + 7 \qquad \text{Add 7.}$$
$$x < -5 \qquad \text{Combine like terms.}$$

CHECK Substitute -5 for x in the *equation* $x - 7 = -12$.

$$x - 7 = -12$$
$$-5 - 7 \overset{?}{=} -12 \qquad \text{Let } x = -5.$$
$$-12 = -12 \checkmark \text{ True}$$

The result, a true statement, shows that -5 is the boundary point. Now we test a value on each side of -5 to verify that values *less than* -5 make the *inequality* true. We choose -6 and -4.

$$x - 7 < -12$$

$-6 - 7 \overset{?}{<} -12 \qquad \text{Let } x = -6.$	$-4 - 7 \overset{?}{<} -12 \qquad \text{Let } x = -4.$
$-13 < -12 \checkmark \text{ True}$	$-11 < -12 \qquad \text{False}$
-6 is in the solution set.	-4 is *not* in the solution set.

The check confirms that $x < 5$, written as the interval $(-\infty, -5)$, is the solution set. See **Figure 1**.

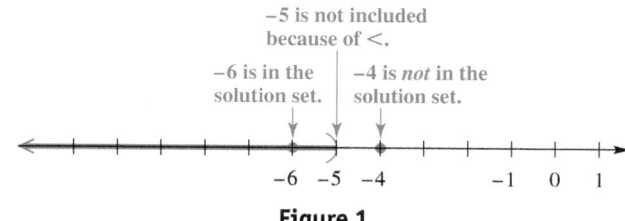

−5 is not included because of <.

−6 is in the solution set. −4 is *not* in the solution set.

Figure 1

—————————————————————— Work Problem **8** at the Side. ▶

As with equations, the addition property of inequality can be used to *subtract* the same number from each side of an inequality.

---

8 Solve each inequality, and graph the solution set.

(a) $x - 3 < -9$

————————————————▶

(b) $p - 2 < 0$

————————————————▶

Answers

8. **(a)** $(-\infty, -6)$

————————————————▶
$-6 \quad -2 \; 0 \; 2$

(b) $(-\infty, 2)$

————————————————▶
$-2 \quad 0 \quad 2$

The multiplication property of inequality has two parts.

⑨ Solve each inequality, and graph the solution set.

(a) $2x < -10$

Multiplication Property of Inequality

Let A, B, and C represent real numbers, where $C \neq 0$.

(a) If C is *positive*, then the inequalities

$$A < B \quad \text{and} \quad AC < BC \quad \text{are equivalent.}^*$$

(b) If C is *negative*, then the inequalities

$$A < B \quad \text{and} \quad AC > BC \quad \text{are equivalent.}^*$$

In words, each side of an inequality may be multiplied (or divided) by the same *positive* number without changing the direction of the inequality symbol. **If the multiplier is negative, we must reverse the direction of the inequality symbol.**

* This also applies to $A \leq B$, $A > B$, and $A \geq B$.

GS (b) $-7x \geq 8$

Divide each side by _____.
Because $-7 \ (</>) \ 0$,
(reverse / do not reverse)
the direction of the
inequality symbol.

$$x \ (\leq/\geq) \ -\frac{8}{7}$$

The solution set is _____.

EXAMPLE 9 Using the Multiplication Property of Inequality

Solve each inequality, and graph the solution set.

(a) $5m \leq -30$

Divide each side by 5. **Because $5 > 0$, do not reverse the direction of the inequality symbol.**

$$5m \leq -30$$

$$\frac{5m}{5} \leq \frac{-30}{5} \qquad \text{Divide by 5.}$$

$$m \leq -6$$

Check that the solution set is the interval $(-\infty, -6]$, graphed in **Figure 2**.

(c) $-9x < -81$

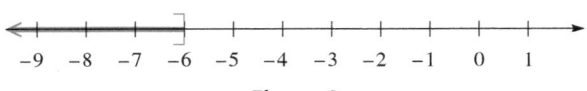

Figure 2

(b) $-4x \leq 32$

Divide each side by -4. **Because $-4 < 0$, reverse the direction of the inequality symbol.**

$$-4x \leq 32$$

| Reverse the inequality symbol when dividing by a negative number. | $\dfrac{-4x}{-4} \geq \dfrac{32}{-4}$ | Divide by -4. Reverse the direction of the symbol. |

$$x \geq -8$$

Check that the solution set is the interval $[-8, \infty)$. See **Figure 3**.

Answers

9. (a) $(-\infty, -5)$

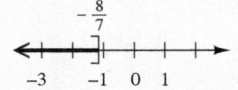

(b) -7; $<$; reverse; $\leq$; $\left(-\infty, -\dfrac{8}{7}\right]$

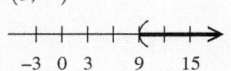

(c) $(9, \infty)$

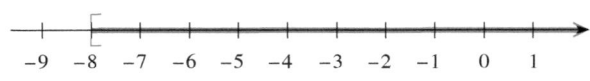

Figure 3

◀ **Work Problem ⑨ at the Side.**

Solving a Linear Inequality in One Variable

Step 1   **Simplify each side separately.** Use the distributive property as needed.
   - Clear any parentheses.
   - Clear any fractions or decimals.
   - Combine like terms.

Step 2   **Isolate the variable terms on one side.** Use the addition property of inequality so that all terms with variables are on one side of the inequality and all constants (numbers) are on the other side.

Step 3   **Isolate the variable.** Use the multiplication property of inequality to obtain an inequality in one of the following forms, where k is a constant (number).

variable $< k$,   variable $\leq k$,   variable $> k$,   or   variable $\geq k$

Remember: Reverse the direction of the inequality symbol only when multiplying or dividing each side of an inequality by a negative number.

EXAMPLE 10   **Solving a Linear Inequality**

Solve $-3(x + 4) + 2 \geq 7 - x$, and graph the solution set.

Step 1 $-3(x + 4) + 2 \geq 7 - x$ Clear parentheses using the distributive property:
$$-3x - 12 + 2 \geq 7 - x$$ $-3(x + 4) = -3x - 3(4).$
$$-3x - 10 \geq 7 - x$$ Combine like terms.

Step 2 $-3x - 10 + x \geq 7 - x + x$ Add x.
$$-2x - 10 \geq 7$$ Combine like terms.
$$-2x - 10 + 10 \geq 7 + 10$$ Add 10.
$$-2x \geq 17$$ Combine like terms.

Step 3 $\dfrac{-2x}{-2} \leq \dfrac{17}{-2}$ Divide by -2.
   Change $\geq$ to $\leq$.

> Be sure to reverse the direction of the inequality symbol.

$$x \leq -\frac{17}{2}$$ $-\frac{17}{2} = -8\frac{1}{2}$

Figure 4 shows the graph of the solution set, the interval $\left(-\infty, -\frac{17}{2}\right]$.

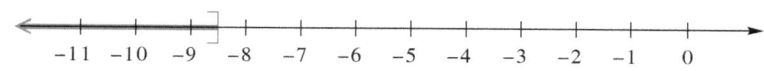

Figure 4

——— **Work Problem ⑩ at the Side.** ▶

Note

In Step 2 of **Example 10**, we could add $3x$ (instead of x) to both sides.

$$-3x - 10 + 3x \geq 7 - x + 3x$$ Add $3x$.
$$-10 \geq 2x + 7$$ Combine like terms.
$$-10 - 7 \geq 2x + 7 - 7$$ Subtract 7.
$$-17 \geq 2x$$ Combine like terms.
$$-\frac{17}{2} \geq x, \quad \text{or} \quad x \leq -\frac{17}{2}$$ Divide by 2. Rewrite.
   The same solution results.

> The inequality symbol points to x in each case.

---

⑩ Solve each inequality, and graph the solution set.

Ⓖ **(a)** $x + 4(2x - 1) \geq x + 2$

Step 1
Use the distributive property to clear parentheses.

———————————

Combine like terms.

———————————

Complete the solution.

The solution set is _____.

———————————→

(b) $5 - 2(x - 4) < 11 - 4x$

———————————→

(c) $2(x + 2) - 1 \leq 6x - 5$

———————————→

Answers

10. **(a)** $x + 8x - 4 \geq x + 2$; $9x - 4 \geq x + 2$;
$$\left[\frac{3}{4}, \infty\right)$$

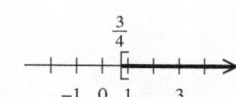

(b) $(-\infty, -1)$

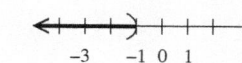

(c) $[2, \infty)$

11 Solve each inequality, and graph the solution set.

(a) $5 < 3x - 4 < 9$

(b) $-2 < -4x - 5 \le 7$

OBJECTIVE **5** **Solve three-part inequalities.** An inequality that says that one number is *between* two other numbers is a **three-part inequality.**

$$-1 < t < 8 \quad \text{and} \quad 4 \le 3x - 5 < 6 \qquad \text{Three-part inequalities}$$

To solve a three-part inequality, we work with all three parts at the same time.

EXAMPLE 11 **Solving a Three-Part Inequality**

Solve $-2 \le -3k - 1 \le 5$, and graph the solution set.

$$-2 \le \quad -3k - 1 \quad \le 5$$

$$-2 + 1 \le -3k - 1 + 1 \le 5 + 1 \qquad \text{Add 1 to each part.}$$

$$-1 \le \quad -3k \quad \le 6$$

$$\frac{-1}{-3} \ge \frac{-3k}{-3} \ge \frac{6}{-3} \qquad \begin{array}{l}\text{Divide each part by } -3. \\ \text{Reverse the direction of the} \\ \text{inequality symbols.}\end{array}$$

$$\frac{1}{3} \ge \quad k \quad \ge -2$$

$$-2 \le \quad k \quad \le \frac{1}{3} \quad \boxed{\begin{array}{l}\text{Rewrite in the} \\ \text{order on the} \\ \text{number line.}\end{array}}$$

Check that the solution set is the closed interval $\left[-2, \frac{1}{3}\right]$. See **Figure 5.**

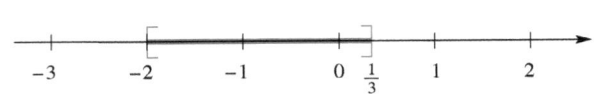

Figure 5

◀ **Work Problem** **11** **at the Side.**

! **CAUTION**

We write three-part inequalities so that the symbols point in the same direction and both point toward the lesser number.

SOLUTIONS OF LINEAR EQUATIONS AND INEQUALITIES*

Equation or Inequality	Solution Set	Graph of Solution Set
Linear equation $5x + 4 = 14$	$\{2\}$	(number line: point at 2; marks at 0, 2)
Linear inequality $5x + 4 < 14$	$(-\infty, 2)$	(number line: open ray left of 2; marks at 0, 2)
$5x + 4 > 14$	$(2, \infty)$	(number line: open ray right of 2; marks at 0, 2)
Three-part inequality $-1 \le 5x + 4 \le 14$	$[-1, 2]$	(number line: closed segment from −1 to 2; marks at −1, 0, 2)

---

*We use set notation for equations that have all real numbers as solutions—that is, {all real numbers}— and interval notation for similar inequalities—that is, $(-\infty, \infty)$.

Answers

11. (a) $\left(3, \dfrac{13}{3}\right)$

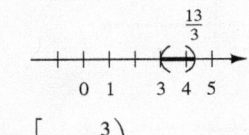

(b) $\left[-3, -\dfrac{3}{4}\right)$

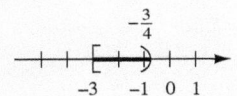

8.1 Exercises

FOR EXTRA HELP Go to MyMathLab for worked-out, step-by-step solutions to exercises enclosed in a square ⬚ and video solutions to ▶ exercises.

CONCEPT CHECK *Complete each statement. The following key terms may be used once, more than once, or not at all.*

linear equation	solution	algebraic expression	contradiction	all real numbers
solution set	identity	conditional equation	first-degree equation	empty set ∅

1. A collection of numbers, variables, operation symbols, and grouping symbols, such as $2(8x - 15)$, is a(n) _____. While an equation (*does / does not*) include an equality symbol, there (*is / is not*) an equality symbol in an algebraic expression.

2. A(n) _____ in one variable can be written in the form $Ax + B (= / > / <) C$, with $A \neq 0$. Another name for a linear equation is a(n) _____, since the greatest power on the variable is (*one / two / three*).

3. If we let $x = 2$ in the linear equation $2x + 5 = 9$, a (*true / false*) statement results. The number 2 is a(n) _____ of the equation, and $\{2\}$ is the _____.

4. A linear equation with one solution in its _____, such as the equation in **Exercise 3**, is a(n) _____.

5. A linear equation with an infinite number of solutions is a(n) _____. Its solution set is $\{$_____$\}$.

6. A linear equation with no solution is a(n) _____. Its solution set is the _____.

Decide whether each of the following is an expression *or an* equation. *See Example 1.*

7. $-3x + 2 - 4 = x$

8. $-3x + 2 - 4 - x = 4$

9. $4(x + 3) - 2(x + 1) - 10$

10. $4(x + 3) - 2(x + 1) + 10$

11. $-10x + 12 - 4x = -3$

12. $-10x + 12 - 4x + 3 = 0$

13. CONCEPT CHECK This incorrect work contains a common error.

$$8x - 2(2x - 3) = 3x + 7$$
$$8x - 4x - 6 = 3x + 7 \quad \text{Distributive property}$$
$$4x - 6 = 3x + 7 \quad \text{Combine like terms.}$$
$$x = 13 \quad \text{Subtract } 3x. \text{ Add 6.}$$

What Went Wrong? Give the correct solution.

14. CONCEPT CHECK When clearing parentheses in the expression

$$-5m - (2m - 4) + 5,$$

the $-$ sign before the parenthesis acts like a factor representing what number? Clear parentheses and simplify this expression.

Solve each equation. See Examples 2–4 and 7(a).

15. $9x + 10 = 1$

16. $7x - 4 = 31$

17. $5x + 2 = 3x - 6$

18. $9p + 1 = 7p - 9$

19. $7x - 5x + 15 = x + 8$
▶

20. $2x + 4 - x = 4x - 5$

21. $12w + 15w - 9 + 5 = -3w + 5 - 9$
⊙

22. $-4t + 5t - 8 + 4 = 6t - 4$

23. $3(2t - 4) = 20 - 2t$
⊙

24. $2(3 - 2x) = x - 4$

25. $-5(x + 1) + 3x + 2 = 6x + 4$

26. $5(x + 3) + 4x - 5 = 4 - 2x$

27. $3(2w + 1) - 2(w - 2) = 5$

28. $4(x + 2) - 2(x + 3) = 5$

29. $6p - 4(3 - 2p) = 5(p - 4) - 10$

30. $-2k - 3(4 - 2k) = 2(k - 3) + 2$

31. $2\left[w - (2w + 4) + 3\right] = 2(w + 1)$

32. $4\left[2t - (3 - t) + 5\right] = -(2 + 7t)$

*Solve each equation. **See Examples 5 and 6.***

33. $\dfrac{3}{4}x + \dfrac{5}{2}x = 13$

34. $\dfrac{8}{3}x - \dfrac{1}{2}x = -13$

35. $\dfrac{x - 8}{5} + \dfrac{8}{5} = -\dfrac{x}{3}$

36. $\dfrac{2r - 3}{7} + \dfrac{3}{7} = -\dfrac{r}{3}$

37. $\dfrac{3x - 1}{4} + \dfrac{x + 3}{6} = 3$
⊙

38. $\dfrac{3x + 2}{7} - \dfrac{x + 4}{5} = 2$

39. $0.05x + 0.12(x + 5000) = 940$
⊙

40. $0.09k + 0.13(k + 300) = 61$

41. $0.02(50) + 0.08r = 0.04(50 + r)$

42. $0.20(14{,}000) + 0.14t = 0.18(14{,}000 + t)$

43. $0.006(x + 2) = 0.007x + 0.009$

44. $0.004x + 0.006(50 - x) = 0.004(68)$

Solve each equation. Decide whether it is a conditional equation, *an* identity, *or a* contradiction. ***See Example 7.***

45. $-x + 4x - 9 = 3(x - 4) - 5$

46. $-12x + 2x - 11 = -2(5x - 3) + 4$

47. $-11x + 4(x - 3) + 6x = 4x - 12$

48. $3x - 5(x + 4) + 9 = -11 + 15x$

49. $-2(t + 3) - t - 4 = -3(t + 4) + 2$
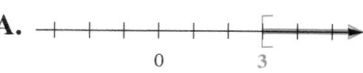

50. $4(2d + 7) = 2d + 25 + 3(2d + 1)$

CONCEPT CHECK *Match each inequality in Column I with the correct graph or interval in Column II.*

I	II
51. $x \leq 3$	**A.**
52. $x > 3$	
53. $x < 3$	**B.**
54. $x \geq 3$	
55. $-3 \leq x \leq 3$	**C.** $(3, \infty)$ **D.** $(-\infty, 3]$
56. $-3 < x < 3$	**E.** $(-3, 3)$ **F.** $[-3, 3]$

57. CONCEPT CHECK A student solved the following inequality incorrectly as shown.

$$4x \geq -64$$
$$\frac{4x}{4} \leq \frac{-64}{4}$$
$$x \leq -16$$

Solution set: $(-\infty, -16]$

What Went Wrong? Give the correct solution set.

58. CONCEPT CHECK A student solved the following inequality incorrectly as shown.

$$-2x < -18$$
$$\frac{-2x}{-2} < \frac{-18}{-2}$$
$$x < 9$$

Solution set: $(-\infty, 9)$

What Went Wrong? Give the correct solution set.

Solve each inequality. Give solution sets in both interval and graph forms.
See Examples 8–10.

59. $x - 4 \leq 3$

60. $t - 3 \leq 1$

61. $4x + 1 \geq 21$

62. $5t + 2 \geq 52$

63. $4x < -16$

64. $5x > -25$

65. $-4x < 16$

66. $-5x > 25$

67. $3k + 1 < -20$

68. $5z + 6 > -29$

69. $\dfrac{3k - 1}{4} > 5$

70. $\dfrac{5z - 6}{8} < 8$

71. $\dfrac{2k - 5}{-4} > 5$

72. $\dfrac{3z - 2}{-5} < 6$

73. $-(4 + r) + 2 - 3r < -14$

74. $-(9 + k) - 5 + 4k \geq 4$

75. $-3(z - 6) > 2z - 2$

76. $-2(x + 4) \leq 6x + 16$

Solve each inequality. Give solution sets in both interval and graph forms.
See Example 11.

77. $-4 < x - 5 < 6$

78. $-1 < x + 1 < 8$

79. $-6 \leq 2(z + 2) \leq 16$

80. $-15 < 3(p + 2) < 24$

81. $-16 < 3t + 2 < -10$

82. $-19 < 3x - 5 \leq 1$

83. $4 < -9x + 5 \leq 8$

84. $4 < -2x + 3 \leq 8$

8.2 | Set Operations and Compound Inequalities

OBJECTIVE ▸ ① Recognize set intersection and union. Consider the two sets A and B, defined as follows.

$$A = \{1, 2, 3\}, \qquad B = \{2, 3, 4\}$$

The set of all elements that belong to both A **and** B, called their *intersection* and symbolized $A \cap B$, is given by

$$A \cap B = \{2, 3\}. \qquad \text{Intersection}$$

The set of all elements that belong to either A **or** B, or both, called their *union* and symbolized $A \cup B$, is given by

$$A \cup B = \{1, 2, 3, 4\}. \qquad \text{Union}$$

OBJECTIVE ▸ ② Find the intersection of two sets. The intersection of two sets is defined using the word *and*.

Intersection of Sets

For any two sets A and B, the **intersection** of A and B, symbolized $A \cap B$, is defined as follows.

$$A \cap B = \{x \mid x \text{ is an element of } A \text{ and } x \text{ is an element of } B\}$$

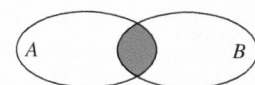

EXAMPLE 1   Finding the Intersection of Two Sets

Let $A = \{1, 2, 3, 4\}$ and $B = \{2, 4, 6\}$. Find $A \cap B$.

The set $A \cap B$ contains those elements that belong to both A *and* B.

$$A \cap B = \{1, 2, 3, 4\} \cap \{2, 4, 6\}$$
$$= \{2, 4\}$$

—————————————————— **Work Problem ① at the Side. ▸**

OBJECTIVE ▸ ③ Solve compound inequalities with the word *and*. A **compound inequality** consists of two inequalities linked by a connective word.

$$x + 1 \le 9 \quad \text{and} \quad x - 2 \ge 3$$
$$2x > 4 \quad \text{or} \quad 3x - 6 < 5$$

Compound inequalities

Solving a Compound Inequality with *and*

Step 1   Solve each inequality individually.

Step 2   The solution set of the compound inequality includes all numbers that satisfy both of the inequalities in Step 1—that is, the *intersection* of the solution sets.

OBJECTIVES

① Recognize set intersection and union.

② Find the intersection of two sets.

③ Solve compound inequalities with the word *and*.

④ Find the union of two sets.

⑤ Solve compound inequalities with the word *or*.

---

① List the elements in each set.

(a) $A \cap B$, if $A = \{3, 4, 5, 6\}$ and $B = \{5, 6, 7\}$

(b) $R \cap S$, if $R = \{1, 3, 5\}$ and $S = \{2, 4, 6\}$

Answers

1. (a) $\{5, 6\}$ **(b)** $\varnothing$

2 Solve each compound inequality, and graph the solution set.

(a) $x < 10$ and $x > 2$

(b) $x + 3 \leq 1$ and
$x - 4 \geq -12$

EXAMPLE 2 **Solving a Compound Inequality with *and***

Solve the compound inequality, and graph the solution set.

$$x + 1 \leq 9 \quad \text{and} \quad x - 2 \geq 3$$

Step 1 Solve each inequality individually.

$$x + 1 \leq 9 \qquad \text{and} \qquad x - 2 \geq 3$$
$$x + 1 - 1 \leq 9 - 1 \quad \text{and} \quad x - 2 + 2 \geq 3 + 2$$
$$x \leq 8 \qquad \text{and} \qquad x \geq 5$$

Step 2 The solution set includes all numbers that satisfy *both* inequalities in Step 1. The compound inequality is true whenever $x \leq 8$ and $x \geq 5$ are both true. See the graphs in **Figure 6.**

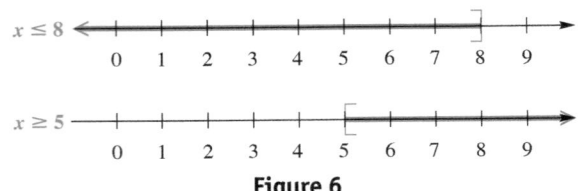

The set of points where the graphs "overlap" represents the intersection.

Figure 6

The intersection of the two graphs in **Figure 6** is the solution set. **Figure 7** shows this solution set, the closed interval $[5, 8]$.

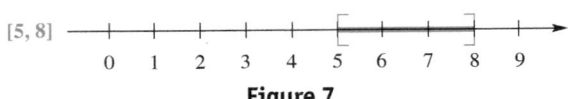

Figure 7

◄ **Work Problem ② at the Side.**

---

3 Solve the compound inequality, and graph the solution set.

$$2x - 3 \geq 1 \quad \text{and}$$
$$-3x + 1 \leq -8$$

EXAMPLE 3 **Solving a Compound Inequality with *and***

Solve the compound inequality, and graph the solution set.

Step 1 $\qquad -3x - 2 > 5 \quad \text{and} \quad 5x - 1 \leq -21$ Solve each inequality individually.

$$-3x > 7 \qquad \text{and} \qquad 5x \leq -20$$

Remember to reverse the direction of the inequality symbol.

$$x < -\frac{7}{3} \quad \text{and} \qquad x \leq -4$$

The graphs of $x < -\frac{7}{3}$ and $x \leq -4$ are shown in **Figure 8.**

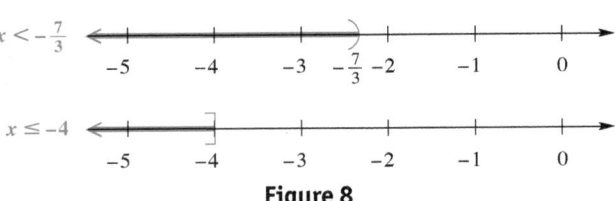

Figure 8

Step 2 Now find all values of x that are less than $-\frac{7}{3}$ and also less than or equal to -4. As shown in **Figure 9,** the solution set is $(-\infty, -4]$.

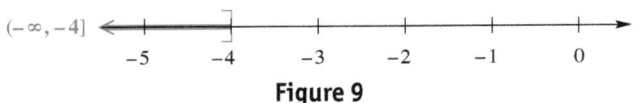

Figure 9

◄ **Work Problem ③ at the Side.**

Answers

2. (a) $(2, 10)$

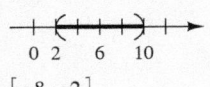

(b) $[-8, -2]$

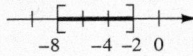

3. $[3, \infty)$

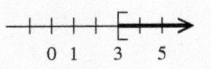

EXAMPLE 4 Solving a Compound Inequality with *and*

Solve the compound inequality, and graph the solution set.

Step 1 $x + 2 < 5$ and $x - 10 > 2$ Solve each inequality
                $x < 3$ and $x > 12$ individually.

The graphs of $x < 3$ and $x > 12$ are shown in **Figure 10.**

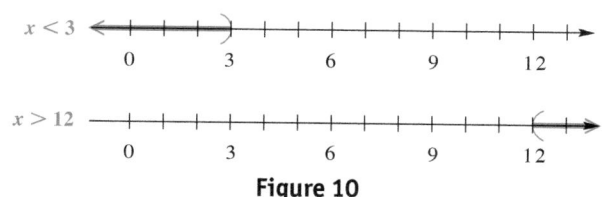

Figure 10

Step 2   No number is both less than 3 *and* greater than 12, so the compound
inequality has no solution. The solution set is $\varnothing$. See **Figure 11.**

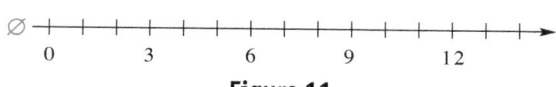

Figure 11

──────────── **Work Problem 4 at the Side.** ▶

OBJECTIVE ▶ 4 Find the union of two sets. The union of two sets is defined
using the word *or.*

Union of Sets

For any two sets A and B, the **union** of A and B, symbolized $A \cup B$, is
defined as follows.

$A \cup B = \{x \mid x \text{ is an element of } A \text{ or } x \text{ is an element of } B \text{ (or both)}\}$

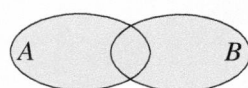

EXAMPLE 5 Finding the Union of Two Sets

Let $A = \{1, 2, 3, 4\}$ and $B = \{2, 4, 6\}$. Find $A \cup B$.

Begin by listing all the elements of set A: 1, 2, 3, 4. Then list any additional
elements from set B. In this case the elements 2 and 4 are already listed, so the
only additional element is 6.

$$A \cup B = \{1, 2, 3, 4\} \cup \{2, 4, 6\}$$
$$= \{1, 2, 3, 4, 6\}$$

The union consists of all elements in A *or* B (or both).

──────────── **Work Problem 5 at the Side.** ▶

Note

In **Example 5,** although the elements 2 and 4 appeared in both sets A
and B, they are written only once in $A \cup B$.

---

4 Solve each compound
inequality.

(a) $x < 5$ and $x > 5$

(b) $x + 2 > 3$ and
          $2x + 1 < -3$

Step 1
Solve each inequality individually.

$x + 2 > 3$ and $2x + 1 < -3$

$x > \underline{\quad}$ and $x < \underline{\quad}$

Step 2
There is no number that is
both greater than ____ and
less than ____.

The solution set is _____.

5 List the elements in each set.

(a) $A \cup B$, if $A = \{3, 4, 5, 6\}$
and $B = \{5, 6, 7\}$

(b) $R \cup S$, if $R = \{1, 3, 5\}$
and $S = \{2, 4, 6\}$

Answers

4. (a) $\varnothing$ (b) $1; -2; 1; -2; \varnothing$

5. (a) $\{3, 4, 5, 6, 7\}$ (b) $\{1, 2, 3, 4, 5, 6\}$

6 Solve each compound inequality, and graph the solution set.

(a) $x - 1 > 2$ or
$3x + 5 < 2x + 6$

_____→

(b) $x + 2 > 3$ or
$-2x > 4$

_____→

7 Solve each compound inequality, and graph the solution set.

(a) $2x + 1 \leq 9$ or
$2x + 3 \leq 5$

_____→

(b) $3x - 4 > 2$ or
$-2x + 5 < 3$

_____→

Answers

6. (a) $(-\infty, 1) \cup (3, \infty)$

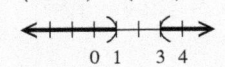

(b) $(-\infty, -2) \cup (1, \infty)$

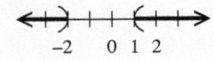

7. (a) $(-\infty, 4]$

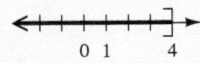

(b) $(1, \infty)$

0 1 2

OBJECTIVE ▶ 5 Solve compound inequalities with the word _or_.

Solving a Compound Inequality with _or_

Step 1 Solve each inequality individually.

Step 2 The solution set of the compound inequality includes all numbers that satisfy one or the other (or both) of the inequalities in Step 1—that is, the _union_ of the solution sets.

EXAMPLE 6 Solving a Compound Inequality with _or_

Solve the compound inequality, and graph the solution set.

Step 1 $6x - 4 < 2x$ or $-3x \leq -9$ Solve each inequality individually.

$\quad\quad\quad\quad 4x < 4$

$\quad\quad\quad\quad x < 1$ or $x \geq 3$ ← Reverse the inequality symbol.

The graphs of these two inequalities are shown in **Figure 12.**

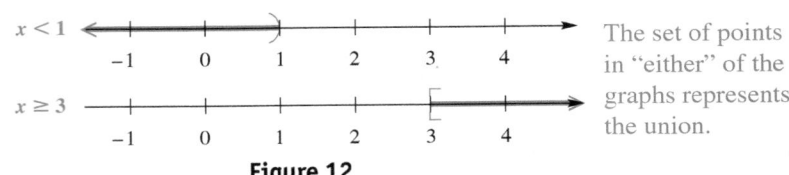

The set of points in "either" of the graphs represents the union.

Figure 12

Step 2 Because the inequalities are joined with _or_, find the union of the two solution sets to obtain the disjoint intervals in **Figure 13.**

$$(-\infty, 1) \cup [3, \infty)$$

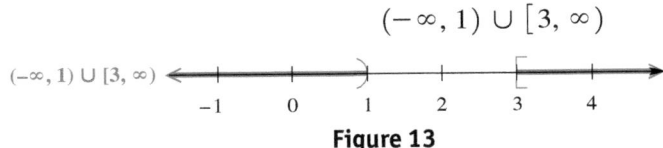

Figure 13

◀ **Work Problem 6** at the Side.

EXAMPLE 7 Solving a Compound Inequality with _or_

Solve the compound inequality, and graph the solution set.

Step 1 $-4x + 1 \geq 9$ or $5x + 3 \leq -12$ Solve each inequality individually.

$\quad\quad\quad -4x \geq 8$ or $\quad 5x \leq -15$

$\quad\quad\quad\quad x \leq -2$ or $\quad\quad x \leq -3$

The graphs of these two inequalities are shown in **Figure 14.**

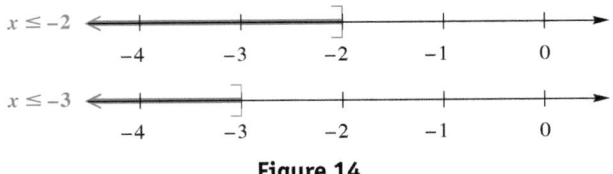

Figure 14

Step 2 We take the union to obtain $(-\infty, -2]$. See **Figure 15.**

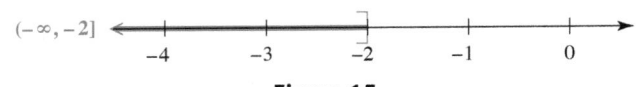

Figure 15

◀ **Work Problem 7** at the Side.

EXAMPLE 8   Solving a Compound Inequality with *or*

Solve the compound inequality, and graph the solution set.

Step 1 $-2x + 5 \geq 11$ or $4x - 7 \geq -27$ Solve each

$-2x \geq 6$ or $4x \geq -20$ inequality individually.

$x \leq -3$ or $x \geq -5$

The graphs of these two inequalities are shown in **Figure 16**.

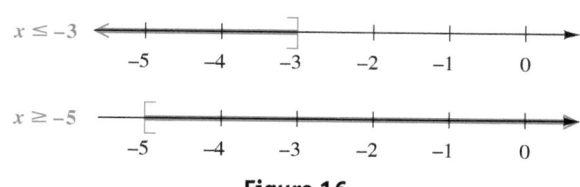

Figure 16

Step 2   By taking the union, we obtain every real number as a solution, because every real number satisfies one or the other (or both) of the inequalities. The solution set is $(-\infty, \infty)$. See **Figure 17**.

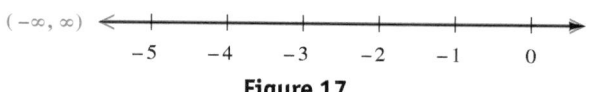

Figure 17

—————— Work Problem **8** at the Side. ▶

EXAMPLE 9   Applying Intersection and Union

The table shows number of tickets sold and domestic box office receipts for top-grossing movies in the United States in recent years.

Movie	Tickets Sold (in millions)	Box Office Receipts (in millions of dollars)
Star Wars Episode VII: The Force Awakens	88	936
Guardians of the Galaxy	41	333
Iron Man 3	50	409
The Avengers	78	623
Harry Potter and the Deathly Hallows	48	381

Data from www.the-numbers.com

List the elements of each set.

(a) The set of movies with greater than 75 million tickets sold *and* less than $900 million in box office receipts

The only movie that satisfies *both* conditions is *The Avengers,* so the set is $\{The\ Avengers\}$.

(b) The set of movies with less than 50 million tickets sold *or* less than $500 million in box office receipts

Guardians and *Harry Potter* satisfy the first condition.

Guardians, Iron Man, and *Harry Potter* satisfy the second condition.

The movies that satisfy *one or the other* (or both) of the conditions are $\{Guardians\ of\ the\ Galaxy,\ Iron\ Man\ 3,\ Harry\ Potter\ and\ the\ Deathly\ Hallows\}$.

—————— Work Problem **9** at the Side. ▶

8 Solve the compound inequality, and graph the solution set.

$3x - 2 \leq 13$ or $x + 5 \geq 7$

9 Refer to **Example 9.** List the elements of each set.

(a) The set of movies with greater than 50 million tickets sold *and* greater than $950 million in box office receipts

(b) The set of movies with greater than 80 million tickets sold *or* less than $350 million in box office receipts

Answers

8. $(-\infty, \infty)$

9. (a) ∅

(b) {*Star Wars Episode VII: The Force Awakens, Guardians of the Galaxy*}

8.2 Exercises

FOR EXTRA HELP Go to MyMathLab for worked-out, step-by-step solutions to exercises enclosed in a square ▢ and video solutions to ▶ exercises.

CONCEPT CHECK *Decide whether each statement is* true *or* false. *If it is* false, *explain why.*

1. The union of the solution sets of $2x + 1 = 3$, $2x + 1 > 3$, and $2x + 1 < 3$ is $(-\infty, \infty)$.

2. The intersection of the sets $\{x \mid x \leq 5\}$ and $\{x \mid x \geq 5\}$ is $\varnothing$.

3. The union of the sets $(-\infty, 6)$ and $(6, \infty)$ is $\{6\}$.

4. The intersection of the sets $(-\infty, 6]$ and $[6, \infty)$ is $\{6\}$.

Let $A = \{1, 2, 3, 4, 5, 6\}$, $B = \{1, 3, 5\}$, $C = \{1, 6\}$, and $D = \{4\}$. Find each set.
See Examples 1 and 5.

5. ▶ $A \cap D$

6. $B \cap C$

7. ▶ $B \cap A$

8. $C \cap A$

9. $B \cap \varnothing$

10. $A \cap \varnothing$

11. ▶ $A \cup B$

12. $B \cup D$

13. ▶ $B \cup C$

14. $C \cup D$

CONCEPT CHECK *Two sets are specified by graphs. Graph the intersection of the two sets.*

15. ▶

16.

17.

CONCEPT CHECK *Two sets are specified by graphs. Graph the union of the two sets.*

18.

19.

20.

Solve each compound inequality. Give solution sets in both interval and graph forms.
See Examples 2–4.

21. $x < 2$ and $x > -3$

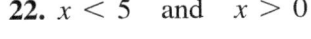

22. $x < 5$ and $x > 0$

23. $x \leq 2$ and $x \leq 5$

24. $x \geq 3$ and $x \geq 6$

25. ▶ $x \leq 3$ and $x \geq 6$

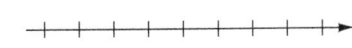

26. $x \leq -1$ and $x \geq 3$

27. $x - 3 \le 6$ and $x + 2 \ge 7$

28. $x + 5 \le 11$ and $x - 3 \ge -1$

29. $-3x > 3$ and $x + 3 > 0$

30. $-3x < 3$ and $x + 2 < 6$

31. $3x - 4 \le 8$ and $-4x + 1 \ge -15$

32. $7x + 6 \le 48$ and $-4x \ge -24$

Solve each compound inequality. Give solution sets in both interval and graph forms.
See Examples 6–8.

33. $x \le 1$ or $x \le 8$

34. $x \ge 1$ or $x \ge 8$

35. $x \ge -2$ or $-x \le -1$

36. $-x \ge 1$ or $x \le 6$

37. $x + 3 \ge 1$ or $x - 8 \le -4$

38. $x + 6 \ge 11$ or $x - 4 \le 3$

39. $x + 2 > 7$ or $1 - x > 6$

40. $7 - x < 5$ or $x + 4 < 2$

41. $x + 1 > 3$ or $-4x + 1 \ge 5$

42. $-2x + 3 > -9$ or $x + 1 > 10$

43. $4x + 1 \ge -7$ or $-2x + 3 \ge 5$

44. $3x + 2 \le -7$ or $-2x + 1 \le 9$

45. $4x - 8 > 0$ or $4x - 1 < 7$

46. $3x < x + 12$ or $3x - 8 > 10$

Express each set in simplest interval form. (Hint: Graph each set and look for the intersection or union.)

47. $(-\infty, -1] \cap [-4, \infty)$

48. $[-1, \infty) \cap (-\infty, 9]$

49. $(-\infty, -6] \cap [-9, \infty)$

50. $(5, 11] \cap [6, \infty)$

51. $(-\infty, 3) \cup (-\infty, -2)$

52. $[-9, 1] \cup (-\infty, -3)$

53. $[3, 6] \cup (4, 9)$

54. $[-1, 2] \cup (0, 5)$

Solve each compound inequality. Give solution sets in both interval and graph forms.
See Examples 2–4 and 6–8.

55. $x < -1$ and $x > -5$

56. $x > -1$ and $x < 7$

57. $x < 4$ or $x < -2$

58. $x < 5$ or $x < -3$

59. $-3x \leq -6$ or $-3x \geq 0$

60. $-8x \leq -24$ or $-5x \geq 15$

61. $x + 1 \geq 5$ and $x - 2 \leq 10$

62. $2x - 6 \leq -18$ and $2x \geq -18$

Average expenses for full-time college students at 4-year institutions in the
United States during the 2012–2013 academic year are shown in the table.

Type of Expense	Public Schools	Private Schools
Tuition and fees	8070	24,525
Board rates	4163	4712
Dormitory charges	5241	5837

Data from National Center for Education Statistics.

List the elements of each set. **See Example 9.**

63. The set of expenses that are less than $10,000 for public schools *and* are greater than $10,000 for private schools

64. The set of expenses that are greater than $4000 for public schools *and* are less than $5000 for private schools

65. The set of expenses that are less than $6000 for public schools *or* are greater than $20,000 for private schools

66. The set of expenses that are greater than $23,000 for private schools *or* are less than $4000 for public schools

The figures represent the backyards of neighbors Luigi, Mario, Than, and Joe. Suppose
that each resident has 150 ft of fencing and enough sod to cover 1400 ft² of lawn.
Give the name or names of the residents whose yards satisfy each description.
(Hint: Find and use the perimeter and area of each yard to help answer.)

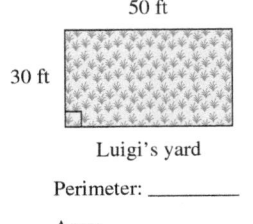

50 ft

30 ft

Luigi's yard

Perimeter: _____

Area: _____

40 ft

35 ft

Mario's yard

Perimeter: _____

Area: _____

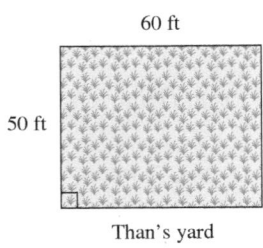

60 ft

50 ft

Than's yard

Perimeter: _____

Area: _____

40 ft

30 ft   50 ft

Joe's yard

Perimeter: _____

Area: _____

67. The yard can be fenced *and* the yard can be sodded.

68. The yard can be fenced *and* the yard cannot be sodded

69. The yard cannot be fenced *and* the yard can be sodded.

70. The yard cannot be fenced *and* the yard cannot be sodded.

71. The yard can be fenced *or* the yard can be sodded.

72. The yard cannot be fenced *or* the yard can be sodded.

Relating Concepts (Exercises 73–76) For Individual or Group Work

An intermediate algebra teacher bases final grades on points earned for activities as given in the Graded Classwork table on the left. To determine final grades, the teacher strictly adheres to the point ranges given in the Grade Distribution table on the right.

GRADED CLASSWORK

Activity	Points Available
Homework and vocabulary	45
Daily activities (scaled)	55
Lab participation and completion	100
Major exams (3 at 100 points)	300
Final Exam	150
Total points	**650**

GRADE DISTRIBUTION

Grade	Points Required
A	585–650
B	520–584
C	455–519
IP*	< 455 and active
F	< 455 and inactive

*In Progress

Use this information to **work Exercises 73–76 in order.**

73. Suppose Lauren earns all of the homework and vocabulary points, 50 points for daily activities, and 90 points for lab participation and completion.

Let x = points to be earned on exams.

(a) Write three inequalities to find the minimum number of points she needs on exams to earn grades no lower than A, B, and C.

(b) Solve each inequality from part (a) to find the minimum number of points she needs for each grade. What "test average" (as a percent) corresponds to this number of points, given that exams account for 450 possible points? (Round up to the nearest whole number.)

74. **See Exercise 73.** Write and solve a compound inequality to find the range of points Lauren needs in exam scores to earn a B average. What range of "test averages" (as percents) correspond to these scores, given that exams account for 450 possible points? (Round up to the nearest whole number.)

75. Suppose Mark earns only 15 points in homework and vocabulary, 40 points in daily activities, and 50 points in lab participation. Repeat **Exercise 73** using these values.

76. Repeat **Exercise 74** given that Mark wants to earn a C average. (Use his classwork points given in **Exercise 75.**)

8.3 | Absolute Value Equations and Inequalities

OBJECTIVES

1 Use the distance definition of absolute value.

2 Solve equations of the form $|ax + b| = k$, for $k > 0$.

3 Solve inequalities of the form $|ax + b| < k$ and of the form $|ax + b| > k$, for $k > 0$.

4 Solve absolute value equations and inequalities that involve rewriting.

5 Solve equations of the form $|ax + b| = |cx + d|$.

6 Solve special cases of absolute value equations and inequalities.

7 Solve an application involving relative error.

Suppose a government will impose a restriction on greenhouse gas emissions *within* 3 years of 2025. This means that the *difference* between the year it will comply and 2025 is less than 3, *without regard to sign*. We state this mathematically as follows, where x represents the year in which it complies.

$$|x - 2025| < 3 \quad \text{Absolute value inequality}$$

We can intuitively reason that the year must be between 2022 and 2028, and thus $2022 < x < 2028$ makes this inequality true.

OBJECTIVE ▶ 1 **Use the distance definition of absolute value.** Recall that the **absolute value** of a number x, written $|x|$, represents the undirected distance from x to 0 on a number line. For example, the solution set of $|x| = 4$ is $\{-4, 4\}$, which means $x = -4$ or $x = 4$, as shown in **Figure 18.**

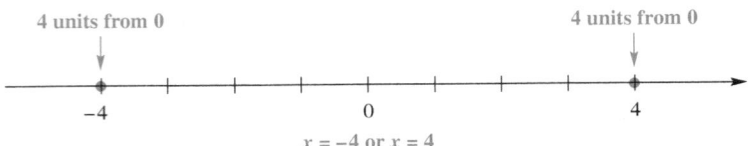

$$x = -4 \text{ or } x = 4$$
Figure 18

The solution set of $|x| > 4$ consists of all numbers that are *more* than 4 units from 0 on a number line. The set $(-\infty, -4) \cup (4, \infty)$ fits this description. The graph consists of disjoint intervals, which means $x < -4 \text{ or } x > 4$, as shown in **Figure 19.**

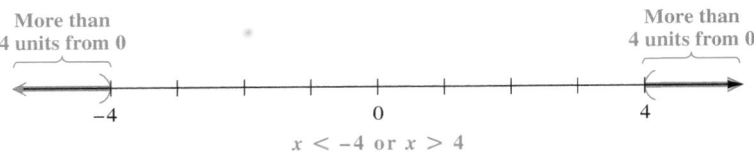

$$x < -4 \text{ or } x > 4$$
Figure 19

The solution set of $|x| < 4$ consists of all numbers that are *less* than 4 units from 0 on a number line. This is represented by all numbers *between* -4 and 4, which is given by the open interval $(-4, 4)$, as shown in **Figure 20.** Here, $-4 < x < 4$, which means $x > -4 \text{ and } x < 4$.

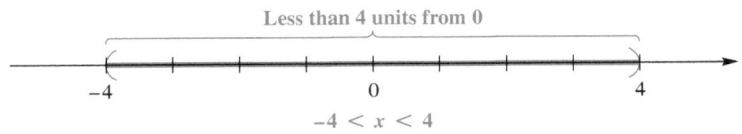

$$-4 < x < 4$$
Figure 20

◀ **Work Problem 1** at the Side.

Absolute value equations and inequalities generally take the form

$$|ax + b| = k, \quad |ax + b| > k, \quad \text{or} \quad |ax + b| < k,$$

where k is a positive number. From **Figures 18–20,** we see that

$|x| = 4$	has the same solution set as	$x = -4$	or	$x = 4$,
$|x| > 4$	has the same solution set as	$x < -4$	or	$x > 4$,
$|x| < 4$	has the same solution set as	$x > -4$	and	$x < 4$.

1 Graph the solution set of each equation or inequality.

(a) $|x| = 3$

_____→

(b) $|x| > 3$

_____→

(c) $|x| < 3$

_____→

Answers

1. (a)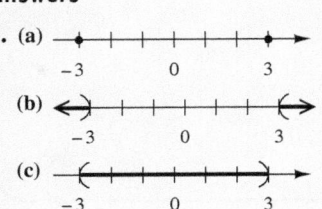

Solving Absolute Value Equations and Inequalities

Let k be a positive real number, and p and q be real numbers.

Case 1   To solve $|ax + b| = k$, solve the compound equation

$$ax + b = k \quad \text{or} \quad ax + b = -k.$$

The solution set is usually of the form $\{p, q\}$, which includes two numbers.

Case 2   To solve $|ax + b| > k^*$, solve the compound inequality

$$ax + b > k \quad \text{or} \quad ax + b < -k.$$

The solution set is of the form $(-\infty, p) \cup (q, \infty)$, which consists of disjoint intervals.

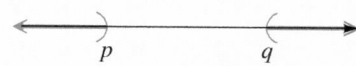

Case 3   To solve $|ax + b| < k^{**}$, solve the three-part inequality

$$-k < ax + b < k.$$

The solution set is of the form (p, q), which consists of a single interval.

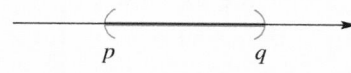

* This also applies to $|ax + b| \geq k$. The solution set *includes* the endpoints, using brackets rather than parentheses.

** This also applies to $|ax + b| \leq k$. The solution set *includes* the endpoints, using brackets rather than parentheses.

Note

It is also acceptable to write the compound statements in Cases 1 and 2 of the box as the following equivalent forms.

$$ax + b = k \quad \text{or} \quad -(ax + b) = k \qquad \text{Alternative for Case 1}$$

$$ax + b > k \quad \text{or} \quad -(ax + b) > k \qquad \text{Alternative for Case 2}$$

These forms produce the same results.

OBJECTIVE ❷ Solve equations of the form $|ax + b| = k$, for $k > 0$. *Remember that because absolute value refers to distance from the origin, an absolute value equation (with $k > 0$) will have two parts.*

EXAMPLE 1   Solving an Absolute Value Equation

Solve $|2x + 1| = 7$. Graph the solution set.

For $|2x + 1|$ to equal 7, $2x + 1$ must be 7 units from 0 on a number line. This happens only when $2x + 1 = 7$ or $2x + 1 = -7$. This is ***Case 1***.

$$2x + 1 = 7 \quad \text{or} \quad 2x + 1 = -7$$

$$2x = 6 \quad \text{or} \quad 2x = -8 \qquad \text{Subtract 1.}$$

$$x = 3 \quad \text{or} \quad x = -4 \qquad \text{Divide by 2.}$$

Continued on Next Page

2 Solve each equation. Graph the solution set.

(a) $|x + 2| = 3$

For $|x + 2|$ to equal 3, $x + 2$ must be _____ units from 0 on a number line.

$x + 2 = 3$ or $x + 2 =$ _____

$x = 1$ or $x =$ _____

The solution set is _____.

(b) $|3x - 4| = 11$

3 Solve each inequality. Graph the solution set.

(a) $|x + 2| > 3$

(b) $|3x - 4| \geq 11$

Answers

2. (a) $3; -3; -5; \{-5, 1\}$

(b) $\left\{-\dfrac{7}{3}, 5\right\}$

3. (a) $(-\infty, -5) \cup (1, \infty)$

(b) $\left(-\infty, -\dfrac{7}{3}\right] \cup [5, \infty)$

CHECK $|2x + 1| = 7$

$|2(3) + 1| \overset{?}{=} 7$ Let $x = 3$.
$|6 + 1| \overset{?}{=} 7$
$|7| \overset{?}{=} 7$
$7 = 7$ ✓ True

$|2(-4) + 1| \overset{?}{=} 7$ Let $x = -4$.
$|-8 + 1| \overset{?}{=} 7$
$|-7| \overset{?}{=} 7$
$7 = 7$ ✓ True

The solution set is $\{-4, 3\}$. A graph of the two points is shown in **Figure 21.**

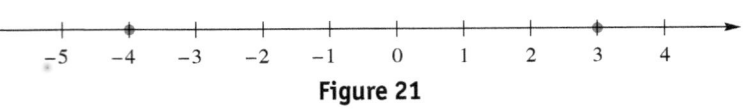

Figure 21

◄ **Work Problem 2 at the Side.**

OBJECTIVE 3 Solve inequalities of the form $|ax + b| < k$ and of the form $|ax + b| > k$, for $k > 0$.

EXAMPLE 2   **Solving an Absolute Value Inequality Involving >**

Solve $|2x + 1| > 7$. Graph the solution set.

Because $2x + 1$ must represent a number that is *more* than 7 units from 0 on either side of a number line, this absolute value inequality is rewritten as the following compound inequality. This is *Case 2.*

$2x + 1 > 7$ or $2x + 1 < -7$
$2x > 6$ or $2x < -8$ Subtract 1.
$x > 3$ or $x < -4$ Divide by 2.

The solution set, shown in **Figure 22,** consists of disjoint intervals and is written $(-\infty, -4) \cup (3, \infty)$.

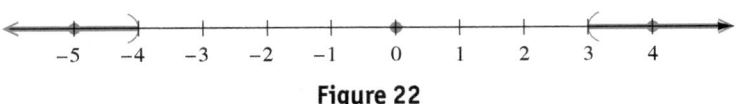

Figure 22

CHECK   The excluded endpoints -4 and 3 are correct because from **Example 1** we know that -4 and 3 are the solutions of the related equation. Equality is not part of the symbol $>$. Referring to **Figure 22,** we select and test a value in each of the three intervals $(-\infty, -4)$, $(-4, 3)$, and $(3, \infty)$.

Let $x = -5$.
$|2x + 1| > 7$
$|2(-5) + 1| \overset{?}{>} 7$
$|-9| \overset{?}{>} 7$
$9 > 7$ ✓ True

Let $x = 0$.
$|2x + 1| > 7$
$|2(0) + 1| \overset{?}{>} 7$
$|1| \overset{?}{>} 7$
$1 > 7$ False

Let $x = 4$.
$|2x + 1| > 7$
$|2(4) + 1| \overset{?}{>} 7$
$|9| \overset{?}{>} 7$
$9 > 7$ ✓ True

The check confirms that the solution set is $(-\infty, -4) \cup (3, \infty)$.

◄ **Work Problem 3 at the Side.**

EXAMPLE 3   Solving an Absolute Value Inequality Involving $<$

Solve $|2x + 1| < 7$. Graph the solution set.

The expression $2x + 1$ must represent a number that is less than 7 units from 0 on either side of a number line. Another way of thinking of this is to realize that $2x + 1$ must be between -7 and 7, which is written as a three-part inequality. This is **Case 3.**

$$-7 < 2x + 1 < 7$$
$$-8 < \quad 2x \quad < 6 \qquad \text{Subtract 1 from each part.}$$
$$-4 < \quad x \quad < 3 \qquad \text{Divide each part by 2.}$$

Check that the solution set is $(-4, 3)$. The graph consists of the open interval shown in **Figure 23.**

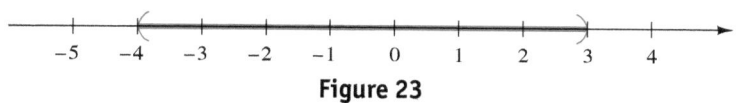

Figure 23

─────────────────────── Work Problem **4** at the Side. ▶

Look back at **Figures 21, 22, and 23,** with the graphs of

$$|2x + 1| = 7, \quad |2x + 1| > 7, \quad \text{and} \quad |2x + 1| < 7.$$

If we find the union of the three sets, we obtain the set of all real numbers. This is because, for any value of x, $|2x + 1|$ will satisfy one and only one of the following: It is either equal to 7, greater than 7, or less than 7.

❗ CAUTION

Refer to **Examples 1, 2, and 3,** and remember the following.

1. The methods described apply when the constant is alone on one side of the equation or inequality and is *positive.*

2. Absolute value equations $|ax + b| = k$ and absolute value inequalities $|ax + b| > k$ translate into **"or"** compound statements.

3. Absolute value inequalities $|ax + b| < k$ translate into **"and"** compound statements. *Only "and" compound statements may be written as three-part inequalities.*

EXAMPLE 4   Solving an Absolute Value Inequality Involving $\geq$

Solve $|5 - 2x| \geq 5$. Graph the solution set.

Case 2 is applied. Notice that the endpoints are included because equality is part of the symbol $\geq$.

$$5 - 2x \geq 5 \quad \text{or} \quad 5 - 2x \leq -5 \qquad \text{Case 2}$$
$$-2x \geq 0 \quad \text{or} \quad -2x \leq -10 \qquad \text{Subtract 5.}$$
$$x \leq 0 \quad \text{or} \quad x \geq 5 \qquad \begin{array}{l}\text{Divide by } -2. \text{ Reverse the} \\ \text{direction of the inequality symbols.}\end{array}$$

Check that the solution set is $(-\infty, 0] \cup [5, \infty)$. See **Figure 24.**

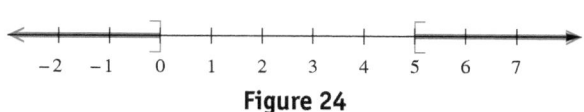

Figure 24

─────────────────────── Work Problem **5** at the Side. ▶

---

4 Solve each inequality. Graph the solution set.

(a) $|x + 2| < 3$

_____

(b) $|3x - 4| \leq 11$

_____

5 Solve the inequality. Graph the solution set.

$$|7 - 4x| \geq 7$$

_____

Answers

4. (a) $(-5, 1)$

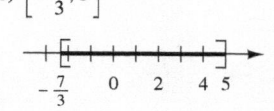

(b) $\left[-\dfrac{7}{3}, 5\right]$

5. $(-\infty, 0] \cup \left[\dfrac{7}{2}, \infty\right)$

6 Solve each equation.

GS (a) $|5x + 2| - 9 = -7$

Isolate the absolute value on one side of the equality symbol.

$$|5x + 2| = \underline{\qquad}$$

$5x + 2 = 2$ or $5x + 2 = \underline{\qquad}$

$5x = 0$ or $5x = \underline{\qquad}$

$x = 0$ or $x = \underline{\qquad}$

Check these solutions in the original equation.

The solution set is \underline{\qquad}.

(b) $|10x - 2| - 2 = 12$

7 Solve each inequality.

(a) $|x + 2| - 3 > 2$

(b) $|3x + 2| + 4 \le 15$

Answers

6. (a) $2; -2; -4; -\frac{4}{5}; \left\{-\frac{4}{5}, 0\right\}$

(b) $\left\{-\frac{6}{5}, \frac{8}{5}\right\}$

7. (a) $(-\infty, -7) \cup (3, \infty)$

(b) $\left[-\frac{13}{3}, 3\right]$

OBJECTIVE 4 Solve absolute value equations and inequalities that involve rewriting.

EXAMPLE 5 Solving an Absolute Value Equation That Requires Rewriting

Solve $|x + 3| + 5 = 12$.

Isolate the absolute value alone on one side of the equality symbol.

$$|x + 3| + 5 = 12$$
$$|x + 3| + 5 - 5 = 12 - 5 \quad \text{Subtract 5.}$$
$$|x + 3| = 7 \quad \text{Combine like terms.}$$
$$x + 3 = 7 \quad \text{or} \quad x + 3 = -7 \quad \text{Case 1}$$
$$x = 4 \quad \text{or} \quad x = -10 \quad \text{Subtract 3.}$$

CHECK $|x + 3| + 5 = 12$

$|4 + 3| + 5 \stackrel{?}{=} 12$ Let $x = 4$. | $|-10 + 3| + 5 \stackrel{?}{=} 12$ Let $x = -10$.

$|7| + 5 \stackrel{?}{=} 12$ | $|-7| + 5 \stackrel{?}{=} 12$

$12 = 12$ ✓ True | $12 = 12$ ✓ True

The check confirms that the solution set is $\{-10, 4\}$.

◀ **Work Problem 6** at the Side.

EXAMPLE 6 Solving Absolute Value Inequalities That Require Rewriting

Solve each inequality.

(a) $\quad |x + 3| + 5 \ge 12$

$\quad |x + 3| \ge 7$ Case 2

$x + 3 \ge 7$ or $x + 3 \le -7$

$x \ge 4$ or $x \le -10$

The solution set is

$(-\infty, -10] \cup [4, \infty)$.

(b) $\quad |x + 3| + 5 \le 12$

$\quad |x + 3| \le 7$ Case 3

$-7 \le x + 3 \le 7$

$-10 \le x \le 4$

The solution set is

$[-10, 4]$.

◀ **Work Problem 7** at the Side.

OBJECTIVE 5 Solve equations of the form $|ax + b| = |cx + d|$. *If two expressions have the same absolute value, they must either be equal or be negatives of each other.*

Solving $|ax + b| = |cx + d|$

To solve an absolute value equation of the form

$$|ax + b| = |cx + d|,$$

solve the compound equation

$$ax + b = cx + d \quad \text{or} \quad ax + b = -(cx + d).$$

EXAMPLE 7 Solving an Equation with Two Absolute Values

Solve $|z + 6| = |2z - 3|$.

This equation is satisfied either if $z + 6$ and $2z - 3$ are equal to each other, or if $z + 6$ and $2z - 3$ are negatives of each other.

$$z + 6 = 2z - 3 \quad \text{or} \quad z + 6 = -(2z - 3)$$
$$z + 9 = 2z \quad \text{or} \quad z + 6 = -2z + 3$$
$$9 = z \quad \text{or} \quad 3z = -3$$
$$z = 9 \quad \text{or} \quad z = -1$$

CHECK $\qquad |z + 6| = |2z - 3|$

$|9 + 6| \overset{?}{=} |2(9) - 3|$ Let $z = 9$. $\qquad |-1 + 6| \overset{?}{=} |2(-1) - 3|$ Let $z = -1$.

$|15| \overset{?}{=} |18 - 3| \qquad\qquad |5| \overset{?}{=} |-2 - 3|$

$|15| \overset{?}{=} |15| \qquad\qquad |5| \overset{?}{=} |-5|$

$15 = 15$ ✓ True $\qquad\qquad 5 = 5$ ✓ True

The check confirms that the solution set is $\{-1, 9\}$.

Work Problem ❽ *at the Side.* ▶

OBJECTIVE ❻ **Solve special cases of absolute value equations and inequalities.** When an absolute value equation or inequality involves a *negative constant or 0* alone on one side, we use the following properties to solve it.

Special Properties of Absolute Value

Property 1 The absolute value of an expression can never be negative—that is, $|a| \geq 0$ for all real numbers a.

Property 2 The absolute value of an expression equals 0 only when the expression is equal to 0.

EXAMPLE 8 Solving Special Cases of Absolute Value Equations

Solve each equation.

(a) $|5r - 3| = -4$ See Property 1.

The absolute value of an expression can never be negative, so there are no solutions for this equation. The solution set is $\varnothing$.

(b) $|7x - 3| = 0$ See Property 2.

The expression $|7x - 3|$ will equal 0 *only* if $7x - 3$ equals 0.

$$7x - 3 = 0 \quad |a| = 0 \text{ implies } a = 0.$$
$$7x = 3 \quad \text{Add 3.}$$

Check by substituting in the original equation.

$$x = \frac{3}{7} \quad \text{Divide by 7.}$$

The solution set $\left\{\frac{3}{7}\right\}$ consists of just one element.

Work Problem ❾ *at the Side.* ▶

❽ Solve each equation.

(a) $|k - 1| = |5k + 7|$

(b) $|4r - 1| = |3r + 5|$

❾ Solve each equation.

(a) $|6x + 7| = -5$

(b) $|7x + 12| = 0$

(c) $\left|\dfrac{1}{4}x - 3\right| = 0$

Answers

8. (a) $\{-1, -2\}$ (b) $\left\{-\frac{4}{7}, 6\right\}$

9. (a) $\varnothing$ (b) $\left\{-\frac{12}{7}\right\}$ (c) $\{12\}$

⓾ Solve each inequality.

(a) $|x| > -1$

(b) $|x| < -5$

(c) $|x + 2| \le 0$

(d) $|t - 10| - 2 \le -3$

⓫ A machine filling *quart* milk cartons is set for a relative error that is *no greater than* 0.03. How many ounces may a filled carton contain?

EXAMPLE 9 **Solving Special Cases of Absolute Value Inequalities**

Solve each inequality.

(a) $|x| \ge -4$ See Property 1.

The absolute value of a number is always greater than or equal to 0. Thus, $|x| \ge -4$ is true for *all* real numbers. The solution set is $(-\infty, \infty)$.

(b)
$$|x + 6| - 3 < -5$$
$$|x + 6| < -2 \quad \text{Add 3 to each side.}$$

By Property 1, there is no number whose absolute value is less than -2, so this inequality has no solution. The solution set is $\varnothing$.

(c)
$$|x - 7| + 4 \le 4$$
$$|x - 7| \le 0 \quad \text{Subtract 4 from each side.}$$

The value of $|x - 7|$ will never be less than 0 (Property 1). However, $|x - 7|$ will *equal* 0 when $x = 7$ (Property 2). Therefore, the solution set is $\{7\}$.

◀ **Work Problem ⓾ at the Side.**

OBJECTIVE ▶ ⑦ Solve an application involving relative error. Absolute value is used to find **relative error,** or **tolerance,** in a measurement. If x represents actual measurement and x_t represents expected measurement, then the absolute value of the difference of x and x_t, divided by x_t, gives the relative error in x.

$$\left| \frac{x - x_t}{x_t} \right| = \text{relative error in } x$$

In quality control situations, relative error must often be *less than* some predetermined amount.

EXAMPLE 10 **Solving an Application Involving Relative Error**

A machine filling *quart* milk cartons is set for a relative error that *is no greater than* 0.05. How many ounces may a filled carton contain?

Here $x_t = 32$ oz (because 1 qt = 32 oz), and relative error = 0.05. We must find x, the actual measurement of a filled carton.

$$\left| \frac{x - 32}{32} \right| \le 0.05 \quad \begin{array}{l}\text{Substitute the given values.}\\ \text{"Is no greater than" translates as } \le.\end{array}$$

$$-0.05 \le \frac{x - 32}{32} \le 0.05 \quad \text{Case 3}$$

$$-1.6 \le x - 32 \le 1.6 \quad \text{Multiply by 32.}$$

$$30.4 \le x \le 33.6 \quad \text{Add 32.}$$

The filled carton may contain between 30.4 and 33.6 oz, inclusive.

◀ **Work Problem ⓫ at the Side.**

Answers

10. (a) $(-\infty, \infty)$ (b) $\varnothing$
(c) $\{-2\}$ (d) $\varnothing$

11. Between 31.04 and 32.96 oz, inclusive

8.3 Exercises

FOR EXTRA HELP Go to MyMathLab for worked-out, step-by-step solutions to exercises enclosed in a square □ and video solutions to ▶ exercises.

CONCEPT CHECK *Match each absolute value equation or inequality in Column I with the graph of its solution set in Column II.*

I   **II**

1. $|x| = 5$ **A.**

$|x| < 5$ **B.**

$|x| > 5$ **C.**

$|x| \le 5$ **D.**

$|x| \ge 5$ **E.**

I   **II**

2. $|x| = 9$ **A.**

$|x| > 9$ **B.**

$|x| \ge 9$ **C.**

$|x| < 9$ **D.**

$|x| \le 9$ **E.**

3. CONCEPT CHECK For each of the following conditions, how many solutions will $|ax + b| = k$ have?

   (a) $k = 0$ **(b)** $k > 0$ **(c)** $k < 0$

4. CONCEPT CHECK If $k < 0$, find the solution set of each of the following.

   (a) $|x - 1| < k$ **(b)** $|x - 1| > k$ **(c)** $|x - 1| = k$

Solve each equation. See Example 1.

5. $|x| = 12$ **6.** $|x| = 14$ **7.** $|4x| = 20$ **8.** $|5x| = 30$

9. $|x - 3| = 9$ **10.** $|p - 5| = 13$ **11.** ▶ $|2x - 1| = 11$ **12.** $|2x + 3| = 19$

13. $|4r - 5| = 17$ **14.** $|5t - 1| = 21$ **15.** $|2x + 5| = 14$ **16.** $|2x - 9| = 18$

17. $\left|\dfrac{1}{2}x + 3\right| = 2$ **18.** $\left|\dfrac{2}{3}q - 1\right| = 5$ **19.** $\left|1 - \dfrac{3}{4}k\right| = 7$ **20.** $\left|2 - \dfrac{5}{2}m\right| = 14$

Solve each inequality. Graph the solution set. See Examples 2 and 4.

21. $|x| > 3$ **22.** $|x| > 2$ **23.** $|k| \ge 4$

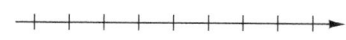   

24. $|r| \geq 1$

25. $|r + 5| \geq 20$

26. $|t + 2| > 8$

27. $|3x - 1| \geq 8$

28. $|4x + 1| \geq 21$

29. $|3 - x| > 5$

30. $|5 - x| > 3$

31. $|-5x + 3| \geq 12$

32. $|-2x - 4| \geq 5$

33. CONCEPT CHECK The graph of the solution set of $|2x + 1| = 9$ is given here.

Without doing any algebraic work, graph the solution set of each inequality, referring to the graph above.

(a) $|2x + 1| < 9$

(b) $|2x + 1| > 9$

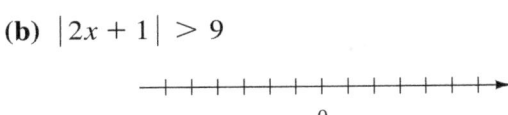

34. CONCEPT CHECK The graph of the solution set of $|3x - 4| < 5$ is given here.

Without doing any algebraic work, graph the solution set of the equation and the inequality, referring to the graph above.

(a) $|3x - 4| = 5$

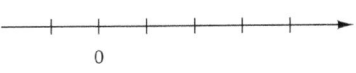

(b) $|3x - 4| > 5$

Solve each inequality. Graph the solution set. ***See Example 3.*** *(Hint: Compare answers to those in* ***Exercises 21–32.****)*

35. $|x| \leq 3$

36. $|x| \leq 2$

37. $|k| < 4$

38. $|r| < 1$

39. $|r + 5| < 20$

40. $|t + 2| \leq 8$

41. $|3x - 1| < 8$

42. $|4x + 1| < 21$

43. $|3 - x| \leq 5$

44. $|5 - x| \le 3$

45. $|-5x + 3| < 12$

46. $|-2x - 4| < 5$

*The following exercises represent a sampling of the various types of absolute value equations and inequalities. Solve, and graph the solution set. **See Examples 1–4.***

47. $|-4 + k| > 6$

48. $|-3 + t| > 5$

49. $|7 + 2z| = 5$

50. $|9 - 3p| = 3$

51. $|3r - 1| \le 11$

52. $|2s - 6| \le 6$

53. $|-8 - 3x| \le 4$

54. $|-6 - 2x| \le 5$

*Solve each equation or inequality. Give the solution set using set notation for equations and interval notation for inequalities. **See Examples 5 and 6.***

55. $|x| - 1 = 4$

56. $|x| + 3 = 10$

57. $|x + 4| + 1 = 2$

58. $|x + 5| - 2 = 12$

59. $|2x + 1| + 3 > 8$

60. $|6x - 1| - 2 > 6$

61. $|x + 5| - 6 \le -1$

62. $|r - 2| - 3 \le 4$

*Solve each equation. **See Example 7.***

63. $|3x + 1| = |2x + 4|$

64. $|7x + 12| = |x - 8|$

65. $\left| m - \dfrac{1}{2} \right| = \left| \dfrac{1}{2}m - 2 \right|$

66. $\left| \dfrac{2}{3}r - 2 \right| = \left| \dfrac{1}{3}r + 3 \right|$

67. $|6x| = |9x + 1|$

68. $|13x| = |2x + 1|$

69. $|2p - 6| = |2p + 11|$

70. $|3x - 1| = |3x + 9|$

Solve each equation or inequality. ***See Examples 8 and 9.***

71. $|x| \geq -10$

72. $|x| \geq -15$

73. $|12t - 3| = -8$

74. $|13w + 1| = -3$

75. $|4x + 1| = 0$

76. $|6r - 2| = 0$

77. $|2q - 1| < -6$

78. $|8n + 4| < -4$

79. $|x + 5| > -9$

80. $|x + 9| > -3$

81. $|7x + 3| \leq 0$

82. $|4x - 1| \leq 0$

83. $|5x - 2| \geq 0$

84. $|4 + 7x| \geq 0$

85. $|10z + 7| > 0$

86. $|4x + 1| > 0$

87. $|x - 2| + 3 \geq 2$

88. $|k - 4| + 5 \geq 4$

89. $|10x + 7| + 3 < 1$

90. $|4x + 1| - 2 < -5$

Determine the number of ounces a filled carton of the given size may contain for the given relative error. ***See Example 10.***

91. 64 oz carton; relative error no greater than 0.05

92. 24 oz carton; relative error no greater than 0.05

93. 32 oz carton; relative error no greater than 0.02

94. 36 oz carton; relative error no greater than 0.03

Solve each problem.

95. The recommended daily intake (RDI) of calcium for females aged 19–50 is 1000 mg. Actual needs vary from person to person. Write an absolute value inequality in x to express the RDI plus or minus 100 mg and solve it. (Data from National Academy of Sciences—Institute of Medicine.)

96. The average clotting time of blood is 7.45 sec with a variation of plus or minus 3.6 sec. Write this statement as an absolute value inequality in x and solve it.

Relating Concepts (Exercises 97–100) For Individual or Group Work

The 10 tallest buildings in Houston, Texas, are listed along with their heights.

Building	Height (in feet)
JPMorgan Chase Tower	1002
Wells Fargo Plaza	992
Williams Tower	901
Bank of America Center	780
Texaco Heritage Plaza	762
Enterprise Plaza	756
Centerpoint Energy Plaza	741
Continental Center I	732
Fulbright Tower	725
One Shell Plaza	714

Data from *The World Almanac and Book of Facts.*

Use this information to **work Exercises 97–100 in order.**

97. To find the average of a group of numbers, we add the numbers and then divide by the number of numbers added. Find the average of the heights.

98. Let k represent the average height of these buildings. If a height x satisfies the inequality

$$|x - k| < t,$$

then the height is said to be within t feet of the average. Using the result from **Exercise 97,** list the buildings that are within 50 ft of the average.

99. Repeat **Exercise 98,** but list the buildings that are within 95 ft of the average.

100. Answer each of the following.

(a) Write an absolute value inequality that describes the height of a building that is *not* within 95 ft of the average.

(b) Solve the inequality from part (a).

(c) Use the result of part (b) to list the buildings that are not within 95 ft of the average.

(d) Confirm that the answer to part (c) makes sense by comparing it with the answer to **Exercise 99.**

Summary Exercises *Solving Linear and Absolute Value Equations and Inequalities*

Solve each equation or inequality. Give the solution set using set notation for equations and interval notation for inequalities.

1. $4z + 1 = 49$

2. $|m - 1| = 6$

3. $6q - 9 = 12 + 3q$

4. $3p + 7 = 9 + 8p$

5. $|a + 3| = -4$

6. $2m + 1 \leq m$

7. $8r + 2 \geq 5r$

8. $4(a - 11) + 3a = 20a - 31$

9. $2q - 1 = -7$

10. $|3q - 7| - 4 = 0$

11. $6z - 5 \leq 3z + 10$

12. $|5z - 8| + 9 \geq 7$

13. $9x - 3(x + 1) = 8x - 7$

14. $|x| \geq 8$

15. $9x - 5 \geq 9x + 3$

16. $13p - 5 > 13p - 8$

17. $|q| < 5.5$

18. $4z - 1 = 12 + z$

19. $\frac{2}{3}x + 8 = \frac{1}{4}x$

20. $-\frac{5}{8}x \geq -20$

21. $\frac{1}{4}p < -6$

22. $7z - 3 + 2z = 9z - 8z$

23. $\frac{3}{5}q - \frac{1}{10} = 2$

24. $|r - 1| < 7$

25. $r + 9 + 7r = 4(3 + 2r) - 3$

26. $6 - 3(2 - p) < 2(1 + p) + 3$

27. $|2p - 3| > 11$

28. $\dfrac{x}{4} - \dfrac{2x}{3} = -10$

29. $|5a + 1| \le 0$

30. $5z - (3 + z) \ge 2(3z + 1)$

31. $-2 \le 3x - 1 \le 8$

32. $-1 \le 6 - x \le 5$

33. $|7z - 1| = |5z + 3|$

34. $|p + 2| = |p + 4|$

35. $|1 - 3x| \ge 4$

36. $\dfrac{1}{2} \le \dfrac{2}{3}r \le \dfrac{5}{4}$

37. $-(m + 4) + 2 = 3m + 8$

38. $\dfrac{p}{6} - \dfrac{3p}{5} = p - 86$

39. $-6 \le \dfrac{3}{2} - x \le 6$

40. $|5 - x| < 4$

41. $|x - 1| \ge -6$

42. $|2r - 5| = |r + 4|$

43. $8q - (1 - q) = 3(1 + 3q) - 4$

44. $8x - (x + 3) = -(2x + 1) - 12$

45. $|r - 5| = |r + 9|$

46. $|r + 2| < -3$

47. $2x + 1 > 5$ or $3x + 4 < 1$

48. $1 - 2x \ge 5$ and $7 + 3x \ge -2$

8.4 Review of Graphing Linear Equations in Two Variables; Slope

OBJECTIVES

1. Plot ordered pairs.
2. Find ordered pairs that satisfy a given equation.
3. Graph lines and find intercepts.
4. Recognize equations of horizontal and vertical lines.
5. Find the slope of a line.
6. Graph a line given its slope and a point on the line.

OBJECTIVE 1 Plot ordered pairs. In the context of linear equations in two variables, introduced earlier in this text, each of the pairs of numbers

$$(3, 2), \quad (-5, 6), \quad \text{and} \quad (4, -1)$$

is an example of an **ordered pair**—that is, a pair of numbers written within parentheses. The *order* in which the numbers are written is important. We graph an ordered pair using two perpendicular number lines that intersect at their 0 points, as shown in **Figure 25**. The common 0 point is the **origin.**

The position of any point in this plane is determined by referring to the horizontal number line, or **x-axis,** and the vertical number line, or **y-axis.** The x-axis and the y-axis make up a **rectangular** (or **Cartesian,** for mathematician René Descartes) **coordinate system.**

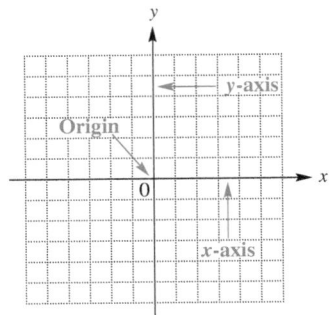

Rectangular coordinate system
Figure 25

① Plot each point. Name the quadrant (if any) in which each point is located.

(a) $(-4, 2)$ (b) $(3, -2)$

(c) $(-5, -6)$ (d) $(4, 6)$

(e) $(-3, 0)$ (f) $(0, -5)$

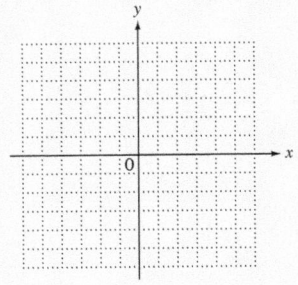

The numbers in an ordered pair are its **components.** The first component indicates position relative to the x-axis, and the second component indicates position relative to the y-axis.

For example, to locate, or **plot,** the point on the graph that corresponds to the ordered pair $(3, 2)$, we move 3 units from 0 to the right along the x-axis and then 2 units up parallel to the y-axis. See **Figure 26.** The numbers in an ordered pair are the **coordinates** of the corresponding point.

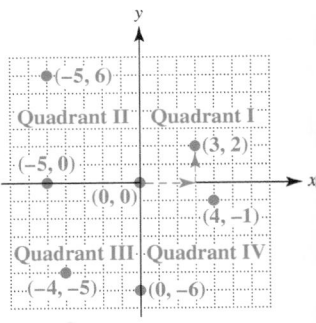

Figure 26

❗ CAUTION
The parentheses used with an ordered pair are also used to represent an open interval. The context of the discussion tells whether ordered pairs or open intervals are being represented.

The four regions of the graph shown in **Figure 26** are **quadrants I, II III,** and **IV,** reading counterclockwise from the upper-right quadrant. *The points on the x-axis and y-axis do not belong to any quadrant.*

Answers

1.

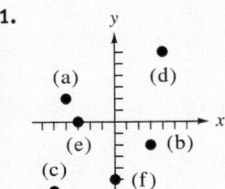

(a) II (b) IV (c) III (d) I
(e) no quadrant (f) no quadrant

◀ **Work Problem 1 at the Side**

OBJECTIVE ▶ 2 **Find ordered pairs that satisfy a given equation.** Each solution of an equation with two variables, such as

$$2x + 3y = 6, \qquad \text{Equation with two variables } x \text{ and } y$$

will include two numbers, one for each variable. To keep track of which number goes with which variable, we write the solutions as ordered pairs. (*If x and y are used as the variables, the x-value is given first.*) For example, we can show that $(6, -2)$ is a solution of $2x + 3y = 6$ by substitution.

$$2x + 3y = 6$$

$$2(6) + 3(-2) \overset{?}{=} 6 \qquad \text{Let } x = 6, y = -2.$$

> Use parentheses to avoid errors.

$$12 - 6 \overset{?}{=} 6 \qquad \text{Multiply.}$$

$$6 = 6 \checkmark \text{ True}$$

Because the pair of numbers $(6, -2)$ makes the equation true, it is a solution. On the other hand, $(5, 1)$ is *not* a solution of $2x + 3y = 6$.

$$2x + 3y = 6$$

$$2(5) + 3(1) \overset{?}{=} 6 \qquad \text{Let } x = 5, y = 1.$$

$$10 + 3 \overset{?}{=} 6 \qquad \text{Multiply.}$$

$$13 = 6 \qquad \text{False}$$

To find ordered pairs that satisfy an equation, we select any number for either one of the variables, substitute it into the equation for that variable, and then solve for the other variable.

Because any real number could be selected for one variable and would lead to a real number for the other variable, an equation with two variables such as $2x + 3y = 6$ has an infinite number of solutions.

EXAMPLE 1 **Completing Ordered Pairs**

Complete each ordered pair for the equation $2x + 3y = 6$.

(a) $(0, \underline{\quad})$

$$2x + 3y = 6$$

$$2(0) + 3y = 6 \qquad \text{Let } x = 0.$$

$$3y = 6 \qquad \text{Multiply. Add.}$$

$$y = 2 \qquad \text{Divide by 3.}$$

The ordered pair is $(0, 2)$.

(b) $(\underline{\quad}, 0)$

$$2x + 3y = 6$$

$$2x + 3(0) = 6 \qquad \text{Let } y = 0.$$

$$2x = 6 \qquad \text{Multiply. Add.}$$

$$x = 3 \qquad \text{Divide by 2.}$$

The ordered pair is $(3, 0)$.

(c) $(-3, \underline{\quad})$

$$2x + 3y = 6$$

$$2(-3) + 3y = 6 \qquad \text{Let } x = -3.$$

$$-6 + 3y = 6 \qquad \text{Multiply.}$$

$$3y = 12 \qquad \text{Add 6.}$$

$$y = 4 \qquad \text{Divide by 3.}$$

The ordered pair is $(-3, 4)$.

(d) $(\underline{\quad}, -4)$

$$2x + 3y = 6$$

$$2x + 3(-4) = 6 \qquad \text{Let } y = -4.$$

$$2x - 12 = 6 \qquad \text{Multiply.}$$

$$2x = 18 \qquad \text{Add 12.}$$

$$x = 9 \qquad \text{Divide by 2.}$$

The ordered pair is $(9, -4)$.

—————— **Work Problem ❷ at the Side.** ▶

❷ Complete each ordered pair for the equation $3x - 4y = 12$.

(a) $(0, \underline{\quad})$

(b) $(\underline{\quad}, 0)$

(c) $(\underline{\quad}, -2)$

(d) $(-4, \underline{\quad})$

Answers

2. (a) $(0, -3)$ **(b)** $(4, 0)$

   (c) $\left(\dfrac{4}{3}, -2\right)$ **(d)** $(-4, -6)$

3 Graph $3x - 4y = 12$. Use the points from **Margin Problem 2.**

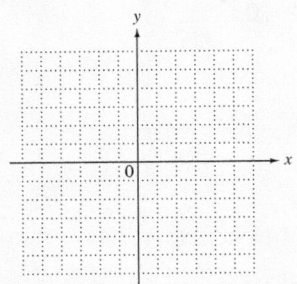

OBJECTIVE ▶ 3 **Graph lines and find intercepts.** The **graph of an equation** is the set of points corresponding to *all* ordered pairs that satisfy the equation. It gives a "picture" of the equation. The graph of $2x + 3y = 6$ is shown in **Figure 27** along with a **table of ordered pairs** (or a **table of values**) that includes the ordered pairs found in **Objective 2** and **Example 1.**

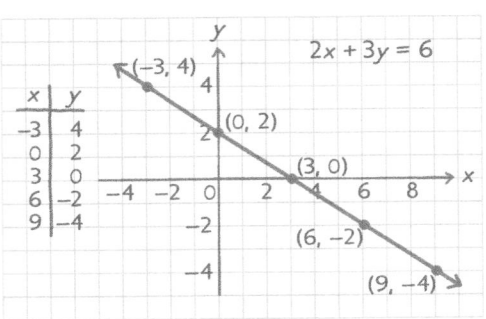

Figure 27

◀ Work Problem **3** at the Side.

The equation $2x + 3y = 6$ is a **first-degree equation** because it has no term with a variable to a power greater than one.

> *The graph of any first-degree equation in two variables is a straight line.*

Since first-degree equations with two variables have straight-line graphs, they are called *linear equations in two variables.*

Linear Equation in Two Variables

A **linear equation in two variables** (here x and y) can be written in the form

$$Ax + By = C,$$

where A, B, and C are real numbers, and A and B are not both 0. This form is called **standard form.**

Examples: $3x + 4y = 9$, $x - y = 0$, $x + 2y = -8$ Linear equations in two variables

---

A straight line is determined if any two different points on the line are known. Therefore, finding two different points is sufficient to graph the line.

Two useful points for graphing are the x- and y-intercepts. The **x-intercept** is the point (if any) where the line intersects the x-axis. The **y-intercept** is the point (if any) where the line intersects the y-axis.* See **Figure 28.**

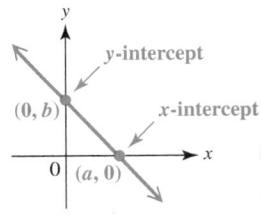

Figure 28

Finding Intercepts

When graphing the equation of a line, find the intercepts as follows.

Let $y = 0$ to find the x-intercept.

Let $x = 0$ to find the y-intercept.

Answer

3.

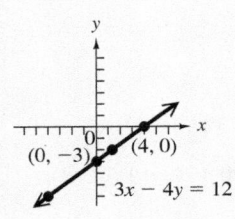

---

*Some texts define an intercept as a number, not a point. For example, "y-intercept $(0, 4)$" would be given as "y-intercept 4."

EXAMPLE 2 Finding Intercepts and Graphing a Line

Find the x- and y-intercepts of $4x - y = -3$, and graph the equation.

To find the x-intercept, let $y = 0$.

$4x - y = -3$

$4x - 0 = -3$ Let $y = 0$.

$\quad 4x = -3$ Subtract.

$\quad\quad x = -\dfrac{3}{4}$ Divide by 4.

The x-intercept is $\left(-\frac{3}{4}, 0\right)$.

To find the y-intercept, let $x = 0$.

$4x - y = -3$

$4(0) - y = -3$ Let $x = 0$.

$\quad -y = -3$ Subtract.

$\quad\quad y = 3$ Multiply by -1.

The y-intercept is $(0, 3)$.

To guard against errors when graphing the equation, it is a good idea to find a third point. We arbitrarily choose $x = -2$ and substitute this value in the equation to find the corresponding value of y.

$$4x - y = -3$$
$$4(-2) - y = -3 \quad \text{Let } x = -2.$$
$$-8 - y = -3 \quad \text{Multiply.}$$
$$-y = 5 \quad \text{Add 8.}$$
$$y = -5 \quad \text{Multiply by } -1.$$

The ordered pair $(-2, -5)$ lies on the graph. We plot the three ordered pairs and draw a line through them. See **Figure 29.**

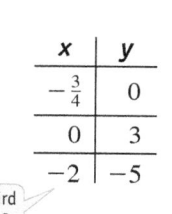

x	y
$-\frac{3}{4}$	0
0	3
-2	-5

Find a third point as a check.

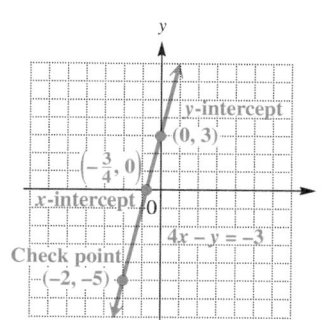

Figure 29

A linear equation with both x and y variables will have both x- and y-intercepts. Its graph will be a "slanted" line.

─── **Work Problem ④ at the Side.** ▶

Some lines have both the x- and y-intercepts at the origin.

EXAMPLE 3 Graphing a Line That Passes through the Origin

Graph $x + 2y = 0$.

Find the x-intercept.

$x + 2y = 0$

$x + 2(0) = 0$ Let $y = 0$.

$x + 0 = 0$ Multiply.

$\quad x = 0$ x-intercept is $(0, 0)$.

Find the y-intercept.

$x + 2y = 0$

$0 + 2y = 0$ Let $x = 0$.

$2y = 0$ Add.

$\quad y = 0$ y-intercept is $(0, 0)$.

─── **Continued on Next Page**

④ Find the x- and y-intercepts of $2x - y = 4$, and graph the equation.

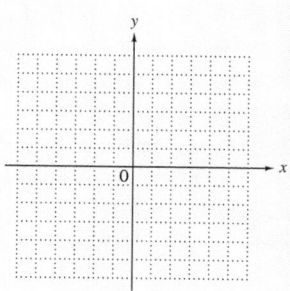

Answer

4. x-intercept: $(2, 0)$; y-intercept: $(0, -4)$

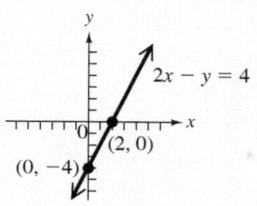

5 Find the intercepts, and graph $3x - y = 0$.

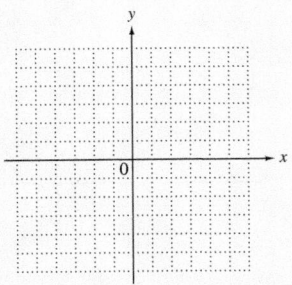

Both intercepts are the same ordered pair, $(0, 0)$, which means that the graph passes through the origin. To find a second point to graph the line, choose any nonzero number for x or y and solve for the other variable. We arbitrarily choose $x = 4$.

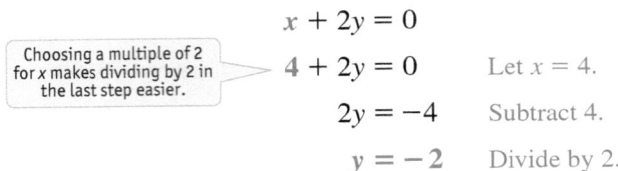

Choosing a multiple of 2 for x makes dividing by 2 in the last step easier.

$$x + 2y = 0$$
$$4 + 2y = 0 \qquad \text{Let } x = 4.$$
$$2y = -4 \qquad \text{Subtract 4.}$$
$$y = -2 \qquad \text{Divide by 2.}$$

This gives the ordered pair $(4, -2)$. As a final check, verify that the ordered pair $(-2, 1)$ also lies on the line. The graph is shown in **Figure 30.**

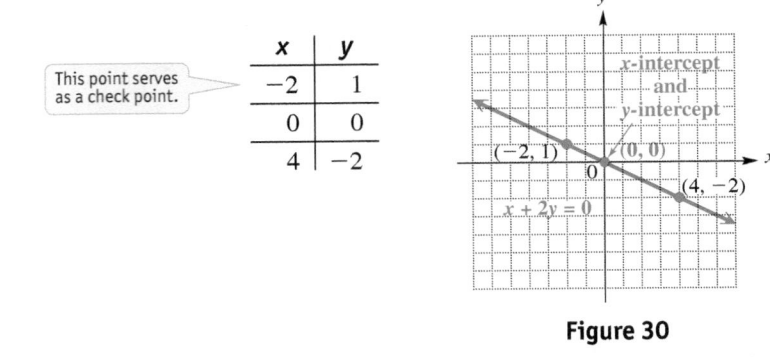

This point serves as a check point.

x	y
-2	1
0	0
4	-2

Figure 30

◀ **Work Problem 5 at the Side.**

OBJECTIVE 4 **Recognize equations of horizontal and vertical lines.** A line parallel to the x-axis will not have an x-intercept. Similarly, a line parallel to the y-axis will not have a y-intercept. This is why we included the phrase "if any" when we discussed intercepts.

EXAMPLE 4 **Graphing Horizontal and Vertical Lines**

Graph each equation.

(a) $y = 2$ (This equation can be written as $0x + y = 2$.)

Because y *always* equals 2, there is no value of x corresponding to $y = 0$, and the graph has no x-intercept. One value where $y = 2$ is on the y-axis, so the y-intercept is $(0, 2)$. Plot any two other points with y-coordinate 2, such as $(-1, 2)$ and $(3, 2)$.

The graph is shown in **Figure 31.** It is a horizontal line.

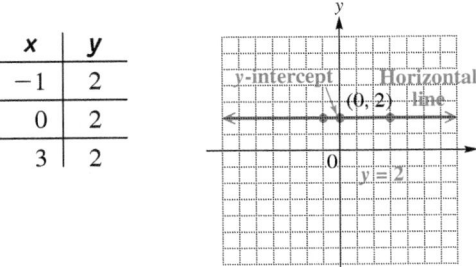

x	y
-1	2
0	2
3	2

Figure 31

Answer

5. Both intercepts are $(0, 0)$.

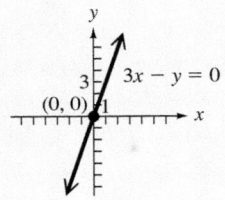

— **Continued on Next Page**

(b) $x + 1 = 0$ (This equation can be written as $x = -1$ or $x + 0y = -1$.)

Because x *always* equals -1, there is no value of y that makes $x = 0$, and the graph has no y-intercept. One value where $x = -1$ is on the x-axis, so the x-intercept is $(-1, 0)$. Plot any two other points with x-coordinate -1, such as $(-1, -4)$ and $(-1, 5)$.

The graph shown in **Figure 32** is a vertical line.

x	y
-1	-4
-1	0
-1	5

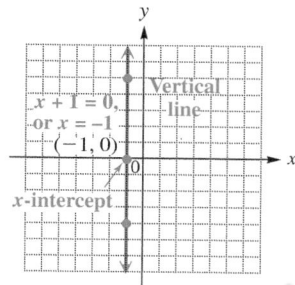

Figure 32

————————— **Work Problem ⑥ at the Side.** ▶

OBJECTIVE ▶ ⑤ Find the slope of a line. Slope (steepness) is used in many practical ways. The slope of a highway (sometimes called the *grade*) is often given as a percent. For example, a 10% (or $\frac{10}{100} = \frac{1}{10}$) slope means the highway rises 1 vertical unit for every 10 horizontal units. Stairs and roofs have slopes too, as shown in **Figure 33.**

Not to scale

Slope (or grade) is $\frac{1}{10}$.

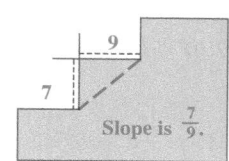

Slope is $\frac{7}{9}$.

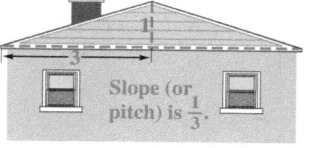

Slope (or pitch) is $\frac{1}{3}$.

Figure 33

Slope is the ratio of vertical change, or **rise,** to horizontal change, or **run.** A simple way to remember this is to think, ***"Slope is rise over run."***

To obtain a formal definition of the slope of a line, we designate two different points on the line using **subscript notation** as (x_1, y_1) and (x_2, y_2). (Read (x_1, y_1) as "*x-sub-one, y-sub-one*.") See **Figure 34.**

As we move along the line in **Figure 34** from (x_1, y_1) to (x_2, y_2), the y-value changes (vertically) from y_1 to y_2, an amount equal to $y_2 - y_1$. As y changes from y_1 to y_2, the value of x changes (horizontally) from x_1 to x_2 by the amount $x_2 - x_1$.

The ratio of the change in y to the change in x (the rise over the run, or $\frac{\text{rise}}{\text{run}}$) is the *slope* of the line, with the letter m traditionally used for slope.

Slope Formula

The **slope m** of the line passing through the distinct points (x_1, y_1) and (x_2, y_2) is defined as follows.

$$m = \frac{\text{rise}}{\text{run}} = \frac{\text{change in } y}{\text{change in } x} = \frac{y_2 - y_1}{x_2 - x_1} \quad (\text{where } x_1 \neq x_2)$$

⑥ Find the intercepts, and graph each equation.

(a) $y + 4 = 0$

Write $y + 4 = 0$ as $y = $ _____.

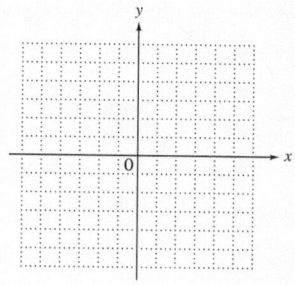

(b) $x = 2$

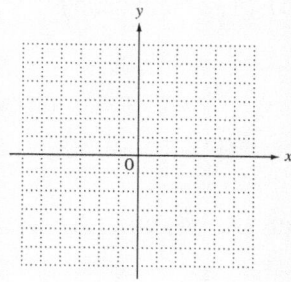

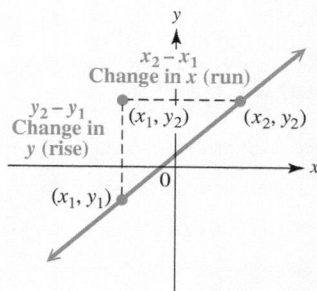

Figure 34

Answers

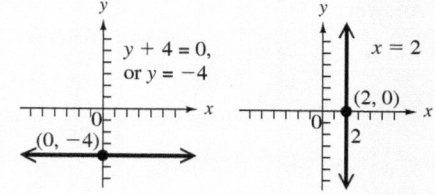

7 Find the slope of the line passing through each pair of points.

GS **(a)** $(-2, 7)$ and $(4, -3)$

Label the points.

$$(x_1, y_1) \qquad (\underline{\quad}, \underline{\quad})$$
$$\downarrow \downarrow \qquad\qquad \downarrow \downarrow$$
$$(-2, 7) \quad \text{and} \quad (4, -3)$$

$$m = \frac{y_2 - y_1}{x_2 - x_1} = \frac{\underline{\quad} - \underline{\quad}}{\underline{\quad} - (-2)}$$

$$= \frac{\underline{\quad}}{6}$$

$$= \underline{\quad}$$

(b) $(1, 2)$ and $(8, 5)$

(c) $(8, -4)$ and $(3, -2)$

8 Find the slope of each line.

(a) $2x + y = 6$

(b) $3x - 4y = 12$

Answers

7. (a) $x_2; y_2; -3; 7; 4; -10; -\dfrac{5}{3}$

   (b) $\dfrac{3}{7}$ **(c)** $-\dfrac{2}{5}$

8. (a) -2 **(b)** $\dfrac{3}{4}$

EXAMPLE 5 **Finding the Slope of a Line**

Find the slope of the line passing through the points $(2, -1)$ and $(-5, 3)$.

Label the points, and then apply the slope formula.

$$(x_1, \quad y_1) \qquad\qquad (x_2, \quad y_2)$$
$$\downarrow \quad \downarrow \qquad\qquad\quad \downarrow \quad \downarrow$$
$$(2, -1) \quad \text{and} \quad (-5, 3)$$

> Be careful to subtract the x- and y-values in the same order.

$$\text{slope } m = \frac{y_2 - y_1}{x_2 - x_1} = \frac{3 - (-1)}{-5 - 2} \qquad \text{Substitute.}$$

$$= \frac{4}{-7}, \quad \text{or} \quad -\frac{4}{7} \qquad \text{Subtract; } \frac{a}{-b} = -\frac{a}{b}$$

The slope is $-\dfrac{4}{7}$. See **Figure 35**.

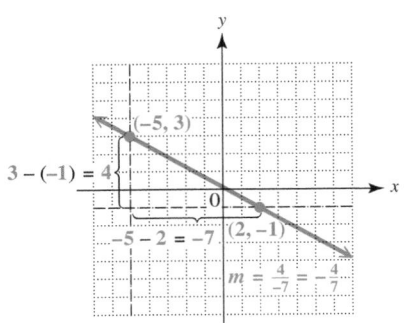

Figure 35

The same slope is obtained if we label the points in reverse order. *It makes no difference which point is identified as (x_1, y_1) or (x_2, y_2).*

$$(x_2, \quad y_2) \qquad\qquad (x_1, \quad y_1)$$
$$\downarrow \quad \downarrow \qquad\qquad\quad \downarrow \quad \downarrow$$
$$(2, -1) \quad \text{and} \quad (-5, 3)$$

> y-values are in the numerator, x-values in the denominator.

$$\text{slope } m = \frac{y_2 - y_1}{x_2 - x_1} = \frac{-1 - 3}{2 - (-5)} \qquad \text{Substitute.}$$

$$= \frac{-4}{7}, \quad \text{or} \quad -\frac{4}{7} \qquad \text{Subtract; } \frac{-a}{b} = -\frac{a}{b}$$

◀ **Work Problem 7 at the Side.**

EXAMPLE 6 **Finding the Slope of a Line**

Find the slope of the line $4x - y = -8$.

The intercepts can be used as the two points needed to find the slope. Let $y = 0$ to find that the x-intercept is $(-2, 0)$. Then let $x = 0$ to find that the y-intercept is $(0, 8)$. Use these two points in the slope formula.

$$\text{slope } m = \frac{y_2 - y_1}{x_2 - x_1} = \frac{8 - 0}{0 - (-2)} \qquad \begin{array}{l}(x_1, y_1) = (-2, 0) \\ (x_2, y_2) = (0, 8)\end{array}$$

$$= \frac{8}{2} \qquad \text{Subtract.}$$

$$= 4 \qquad \text{Divide.}$$

◀ **Work Problem 8 at the Side.**

The slope of a line can also be found directly from its equation. Consider the equation $4x - y = -8$ from **Example 6.** Solve this equation for y.

$$4x - y = -8 \qquad \text{Equation from \textbf{Example 6}}$$

Going forward, we combine these steps.

$$-y = -8 - 4x \qquad \text{Subtract } 4x.$$

$$-y = -4x - 8 \qquad \text{Commutative property}$$

$$y = 4x + 8 \qquad \text{Multiply by } -1.$$

The slope, 4, found using the slope formula in **Example 6,** is the same number as the coefficient of x in the equation $y = 4x + 8$. This always happens, *as long as the equation is solved for y.*

EXAMPLE 7 **Finding the Slope from an Equation**

Find the slope of the graph of $3x - 5y = 8$.

$$3x - 5y = 8 \qquad \boxed{\text{Solve for } y.}$$

$$-5y = -3x + 8 \qquad \text{Subtract } 3x.$$

$$\frac{-5y}{-5} = \frac{-3x + 8}{-5} \qquad \text{Divide each side by } -5.$$

$$\frac{-3x}{-5} = \frac{-3}{-5} \cdot \frac{x}{1} = \frac{3}{5}x$$

$$y = \frac{3}{5}x - \frac{8}{5} \qquad \frac{a + b}{c} = \frac{a}{c} + \frac{b}{c}$$

The slope is given by the coefficient of x, so the slope is $\frac{3}{5}$.

Work Problem ⑨ at the Side. ▶

We review the special cases of slope.

Horizontal and Vertical Lines

- An equation of the form **$y = b$** always intersects the y-axis at the point $(0, b)$. A line with that equation is **horizontal** and has **slope 0.** See **Figure 36** for the line with equation $y = 2$.

- An equation of the form **$x = a$** always intersects the x-axis at the point $(a, 0)$. A line with that equation is **vertical** and has **undefined slope.** See **Figure 37** for the line with equation $x = -1$.

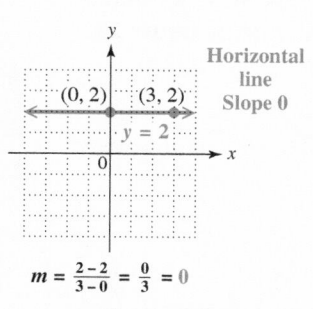

$$m = \frac{2 - 2}{3 - 0} = \frac{0}{3} = 0$$

Figure 36

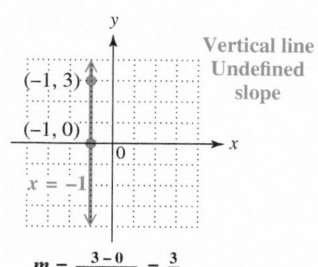

$$m = \frac{3 - 0}{-1 - (-1)} = \frac{3}{0}$$

Figure 37

Work Problem ⑩ at the Side. ▶

---

⑨ Find the slope of the graph of each line.

(a) $3x + 4y = 9$

(b) $2x - 5y = 8$

⑩ Find the slope of each line.

(a) $x = -6$

(b) $y + 5 = 0$

Answers

9. (a) $-\dfrac{3}{4}$ (b) $\dfrac{2}{5}$

10. (a) undefined (b) 0

11 Graph each line described.

(a) Through $(1, -3)$; $m = -\frac{3}{4}$

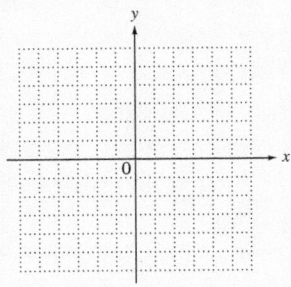

(b) Through $(-1, -4)$; $m = 2$

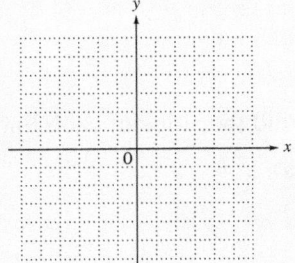

Answers

11. (a)

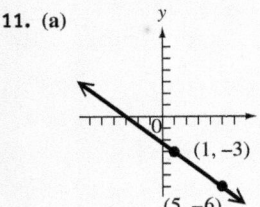

(b)

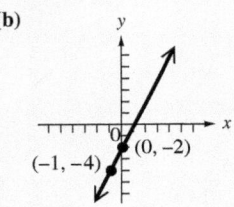

OBJECTIVE ▶ 6 Graph a line given its slope and a point on the line.

EXAMPLE 8   **Using the Slope and a Point to Graph Lines**

Graph each line described.

(a) With slope $\frac{2}{3}$ and y-intercept $(0, -4)$

Begin by plotting the point $P(0, -4)$, as shown in **Figure 38.** Then use the geometric interpretation of slope to find a second point.

$$m = \frac{\text{change in } y}{\text{change in } x} = \frac{2}{3} \begin{array}{l} \leftarrow \text{rise} \\ \leftarrow \text{run} \end{array}$$

We move **2** units *up* from $(0, -4)$ and then **3** units to the *right* to locate another point, $R(3, -2)$. The line through $P(0, -4)$ and R is the graph.

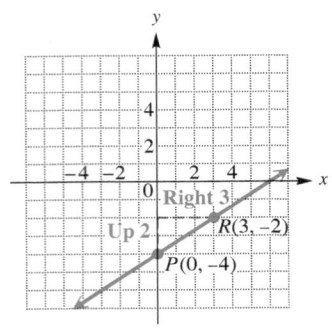

Figure 38

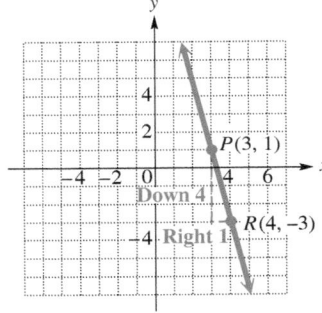

Figure 39

(b) Through $(3, 1)$ with slope -4

Start by locating the point $P(3, 1)$ on a graph. See **Figure 39.** Find a second point R on the line by writing -4 as $\frac{-4}{1}$.

$$m = \frac{\text{change in } y}{\text{change in } x} = \frac{-4}{1} \begin{array}{l} \leftarrow \text{rise} \\ \leftarrow \text{run} \end{array}$$

We move 4 units *down* from $(3, 1)$, and then 1 unit to the *right* to locate a second point $R(4, -3)$. The line through $P(3, 1)$ and R is the graph.

The slope -4 also could be written as

$$m = \frac{\text{change in } y}{\text{change in } x} = \frac{4}{-1}. \begin{array}{l} \leftarrow \text{rise} \\ \leftarrow \text{run} \end{array}$$

In this case, the second point R is located 4 units *up* and 1 unit to the *left*. Verify that this approach also produces the line in **Figure 39.**

◀ **Work Problem 11 at the Side.**

Figure 40 summarizes the four cases for slopes of lines.

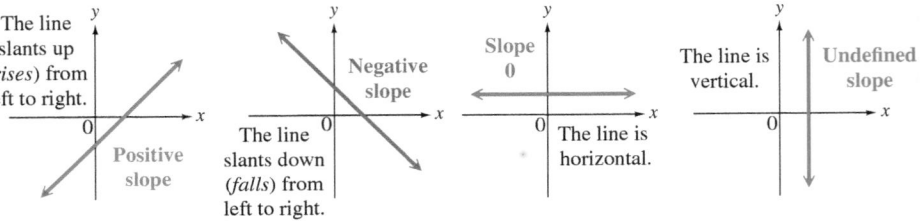

Slopes of lines

Figure 40

8.4 Exercises

FOR EXTRA HELP

Go to MyMathLab *for worked-out, step-by-step solutions to exercises enclosed in a square* and *video solutions to ▶ exercises.*

CONCEPT CHECK *Fill in each blank with the correct response.*

1. The point with coordinates $(0, 0)$ is the _____ of a rectangular coordinate system.

2. For any value of x, the point $(x, 0)$ lies on the _____ -axis.

3. To find the x-intercept of a line, we let _____ equal 0 and solve for _____ .

4. The equation $y = 4$ has a _____ line as its graph, while $x = 4$ has a _____ line as its graph.

5. CONCEPT CHECK A student plotted the point with coordinates $(-4, 2)$ incorrectly by moving 2 units from 0 to the right along the x-axis and then 4 units down parallel to the y-axis. *What Went Wrong?*

6. CONCEPT CHECK Use the given information to determine the possible quadrants in which the point (x, y) must lie. (*Hint:* Consider the signs of the coordinates in each quadrant, and the signs of their product and quotient.)

(a) $xy > 0$ **(b)** $xy < 0$

(c) $\dfrac{x}{y} < 0$ **(d)** $\dfrac{x}{y} > 0$

Complete the given table for each equation, and then graph the equation.
See Example 1 and **Figure 27.**

7. $x - y = 3$

x	y
0	
	0
5	
2	

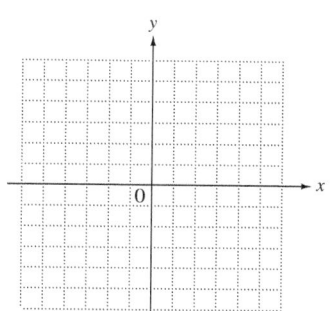

8. $x - y = 5$

x	y
0	
	0
1	
3	

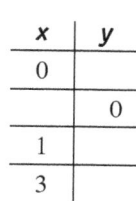
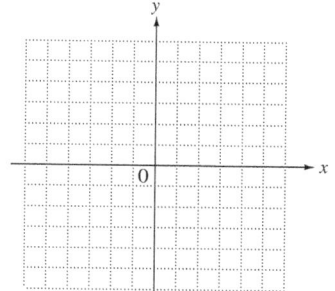

9. $x + 2y = 5$

x	y
0	
	0
2	
	4

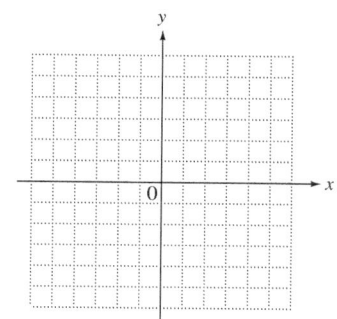

10. $x + 3y = -5$

x	y
0	
	0
1	
	-1

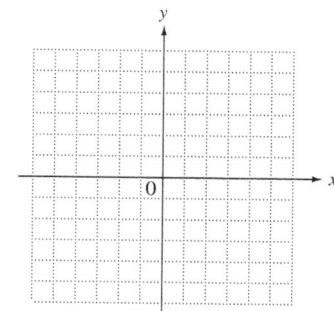

Find the x- and y-intercepts. Then graph each equation. **See Examples 2–4.**

11. $2x + 3y = 12$

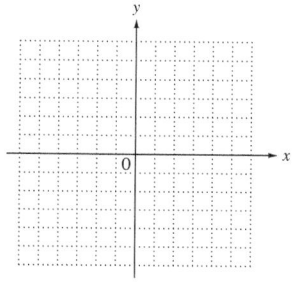

12. $5x + 2y = 10$

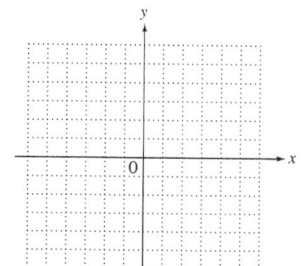

13. $x - 3y = 6$

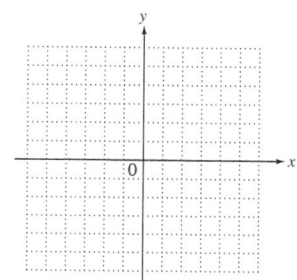

14. $x - 2y = -4$

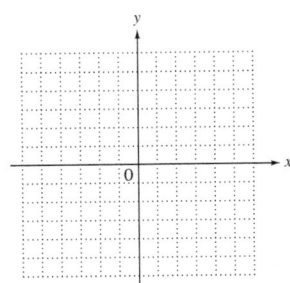

15. $x + 5y = 0$

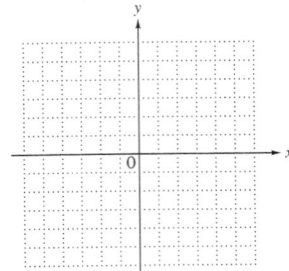

16. $x - 3y = 0$

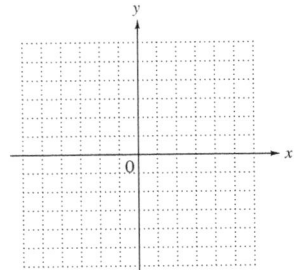

17. $2x + y = 0$

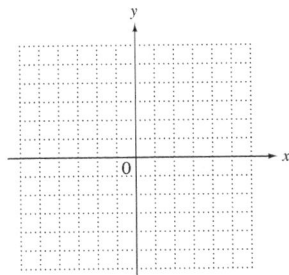

18. $4x - y = 0$

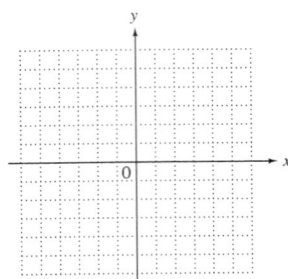

19. $y = 5$

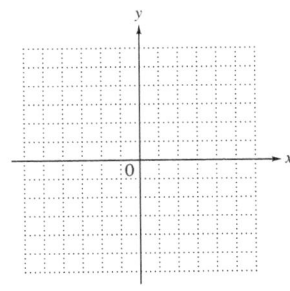

20. $y = -3$

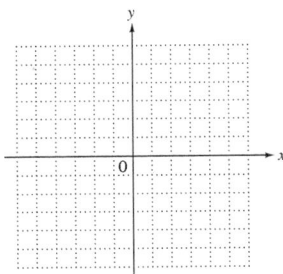

21. $x + 4 = 0$

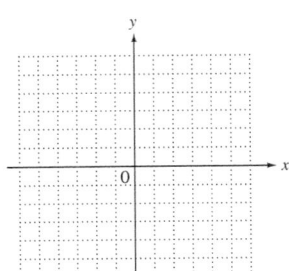

22. $x - 5 = 0$

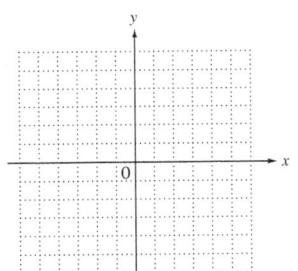

CONCEPT CHECK *Based on the figure shown here, determine which line satisfies the given description.*

23. The line has positive slope.

24. The line has negative slope.

25. The line has slope 0.

26. The line has undefined slope.

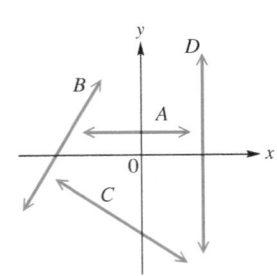

*In each exercise, **(a)** find the slope of the line through each pair of points, if possible, and **(b)** based on the slope, indicate whether the line through the points rises from left to right, falls from left to right, is horizontal, or is vertical. **See Example 5 and the discussion on slopes of horizontal and vertical lines.***

27. $(-2, -3)$ and $(-1, 5)$

28. $(-4, 1)$ and $(-3, 4)$

29. $(2, 4)$ and $(-4, 4)$

30. $(-6, 3)$ and $(2, 3)$

31. $(-2, 2)$ and $(4, -1)$

32. $(-3, 1)$ and $(6, -2)$

33. $(5, -3)$ and $(5, 2)$

34. $(4, -1)$ and $(4, 3)$

Find the slope of each line, and sketch the graph. ***See Examples 2–4, 6, and 7.***

35. $x + 2y = 4$

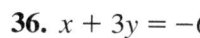

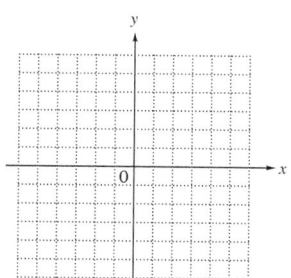

36. $x + 3y = -6$

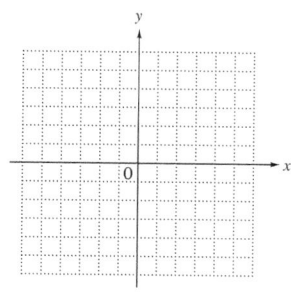

37. $-x + y = 4$

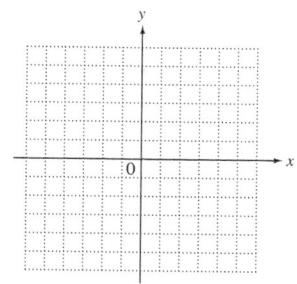

38. $-x + y = 6$

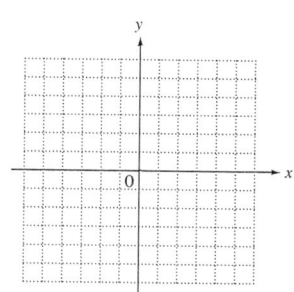

39. $x - 3 = 0$

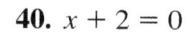

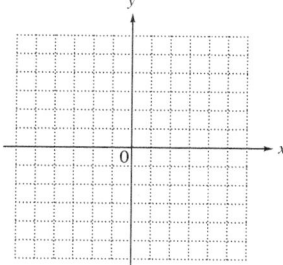

40. $x + 2 = 0$

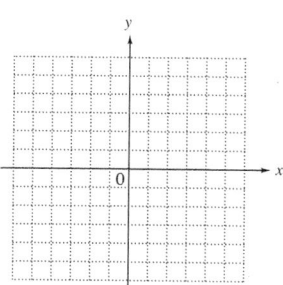

41. $y + 5 = 0$

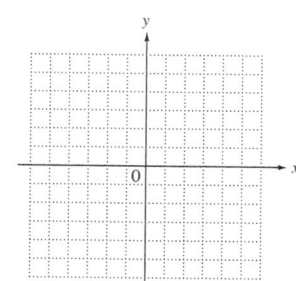

42. $y - 3 = 0$

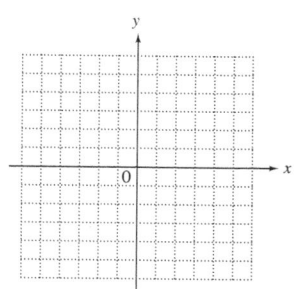

Graph each line described. ***See Example 8.***

43. Through $(-4, 2)$; $m = \frac{1}{2}$

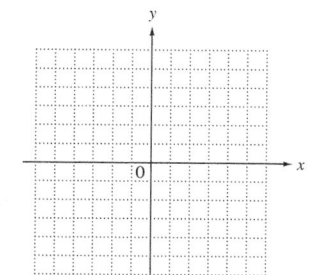

44. Through $(-2, -3)$; $m = \frac{5}{4}$

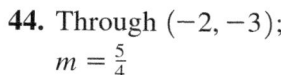

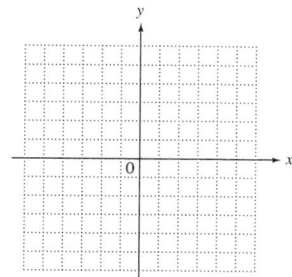

45. y-intercept $(0, -2)$; $m = -\frac{2}{3}$

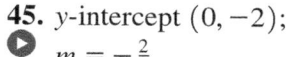

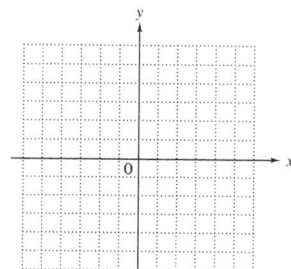

46. y-intercept $(0, -4)$; $m = -\frac{3}{2}$

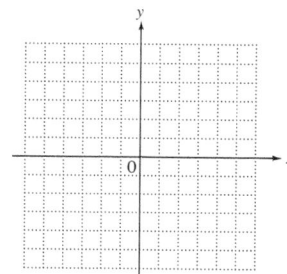

47. Through $(-1, -2)$; $m = 3$

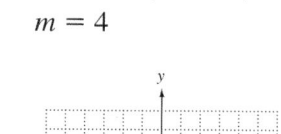

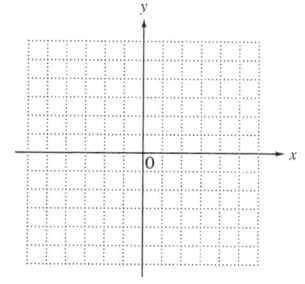

48. Through $(-2, -4)$; $m = 4$

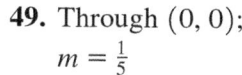

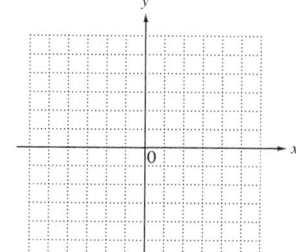

49. Through $(0, 0)$; $m = \frac{1}{5}$

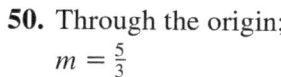

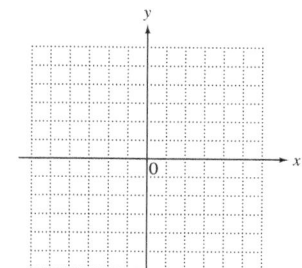

50. Through the origin; $m = \frac{5}{3}$

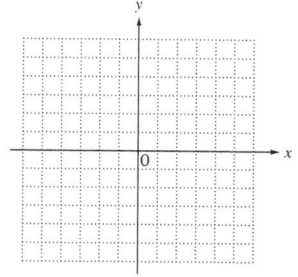

8.5 Review of Systems of Linear Equations in Two Variables

OBJECTIVES

1. Solve linear systems with two equations and two variables.
2. Solve special systems.

OBJECTIVE ▶ 1 Solve linear systems with two equations and two variables. Recall that a **system of linear equations** (often called a **linear system**) consists of two or more linear equations with the same variables.

$$x + y = 5 \quad \text{System of linear equations}$$
$$2x - y = 4 \quad \text{in two variables}$$

The **solution set of a system of linear equations** contains all ordered pairs that satisfy all equations of the system *at the same time*.

We review three methods for solving linear systems:

(1) The *graphing method*,

(2) The *substitution method*, and

(3) The *elimination method*.

The **graphing method** involves graphing each equation of a system on the same set of axes and finding the point where the graphs intersect.

EXAMPLE 1 **Solving a System by Graphing**

Solve the system of equations by graphing.

$$x + y = 5 \quad (1)$$
$$2x - y = 4 \quad (2)$$

To graph these linear equations, we plot several points for each line.

$$x + y = 5 \qquad\qquad 2x - y = 4$$

The intercepts are a convenient choice.

x	y
0	5
5	0
2	3

x	y
0	−4
2	0
4	4

Find a third ordered pair as a check.

As shown in **Figure 41,** the graph suggests that the point of intersection is the ordered pair $(3, 2)$.

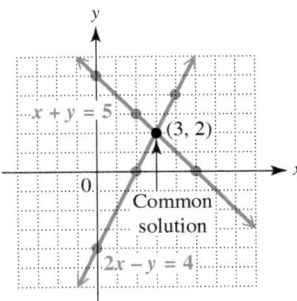

Figure 41

To confirm that $(3, 2)$ is a solution of *both* equations, we check by substituting 3 for *x* and 2 for *y* in each equation.

———— Continued on Next Page

CHECK

$$x + y = 5 \quad (1)$$
$$3 + 2 \overset{?}{=} 5$$
$$5 = 5 \checkmark \text{ True}$$

$$2x - y = 4 \quad (2)$$
$$2(3) - 2 \overset{?}{=} 4$$
$$6 - 2 \overset{?}{=} 4$$
$$4 = 4 \checkmark \text{ True}$$

The ordered pair $(3, 2)$ makes both equations true, so $\{(3, 2)\}$ is the solution set of the system.

——————— Work Problem **1** at the Side. ▶

There are three possibilities for the number of elements in the solution set of a linear system in two variables. **Example 1** illustrates Case 1.

Graphs of Linear Systems in Two Variables

Case 1 **The two graphs intersect in a single point.**

The coordinates of this point give the only solution of the system. Because the system has a solution, it is **consistent**. The equations are *not* equivalent, so they are **independent**. See **Figure 42(a).**

Case 2 **The graphs are parallel lines—that is, they do not intersect.**

There is no solution common to both equations, so the solution set is ∅ and the system is **inconsistent.** Because the equations are *not* equivalent, they are **independent.** See **Figure 42(b).**

Case 3 **The graphs are the same line—that is, they coincide.**

Because any solution of one equation of the system is a solution of the other, the solution set is an infinite set of ordered pairs representing the points on the line. This type of system is **consistent** because there is a solution. The equations are equivalent, so they are **dependent.** See **Figure 42(c).**

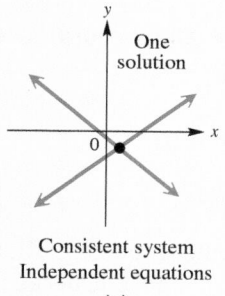
Consistent system
Independent equations
(a)

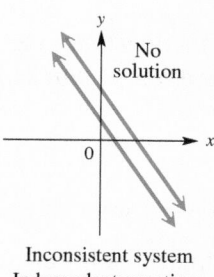
No solution

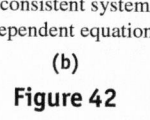
Inconsistent system
Independent equations
(b)

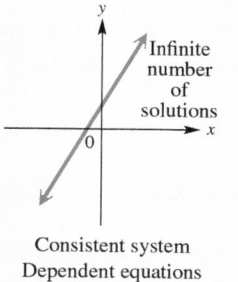
Infinite number of solutions
Consistent system
Dependent equations
(c)

Figure 42

It can be difficult to read exact coordinates from a graph, especially if they are not integers, so we generally use algebraic methods to solve systems. One such method, the **substitution method,** is well suited for solving linear systems in which one equation is solved or can be easily solved for one variable in terms of the other.

1 Solve each system of equations by graphing.

(a) $x - y = 3 \quad (1)$
$\quad\quad 2x - y = 4 \quad (2)$

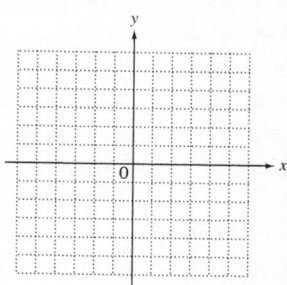

(b) $2x + y = -5 \quad (1)$
$\quad\quad -x + 3y = 6 \quad (2)$

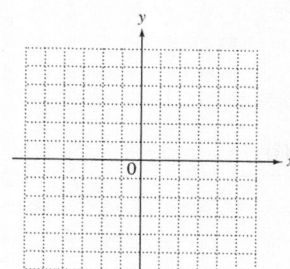

Answers

1. (a) $\{(1, -2)\}$

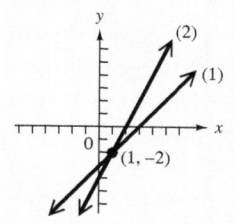

(b) $\{(-3, 1)\}$

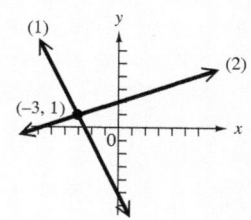

2 Solve each system.

(a) $7x - 2y = -2$
$y = 3x$

| EXAMPLE 2 | Solving a System by Substitution |

Solve the system.

$$2x - y = 6 \quad (1)$$
$$x = y + 2 \quad (2)$$

Equation (2) is solved for x, so we substitute $y + 2$ for x in equation (1).

$$2x - y = 6 \quad (1) \quad \longleftarrow \boxed{\text{Substitute in the } \textit{other} \text{ equation.}}$$
$$\boxed{\text{Be sure to use parentheses here.}} \longrightarrow 2(y + 2) - y = 6 \quad \text{Let } x = y + 2.$$
$$2y + 4 - y = 6 \quad \text{Distributive property}$$
$$y + 4 = 6 \quad \text{Combine like terms.}$$
$$y = 2 \quad \text{Subtract 4.}$$

Now we find x by substituting 2 for y in either equation (1) or (2).

$$x = y + 2 \quad (2)$$
$$x = 2 + 2 \quad \text{Let } y = 2.$$
$$x = 4 \quad \text{Add.} \quad \boxed{\text{Write the } x\text{-value first in the ordered pair.}}$$

Thus, $x = 4$ and $y = 2$, giving the ordered pair $(4, 2)$. Check these values in both equations of the original system.

CHECK

$2x - y = 6 \quad (1)$	$x = y + 2 \quad (2)$
$2(4) - 2 \overset{?}{=} 6$	$4 \overset{?}{=} 2 + 2$
$8 - 2 \overset{?}{=} 6$	$4 = 4 \checkmark \quad$ True
$6 = 6 \checkmark \quad$ True	

(b) $5x - 3y = -6$
$x = 2 - y$

Because $(4, 2)$ makes both equations true, the solution set is $\{(4, 2)\}$.

◀ **Work Problem ❷ at the Side.**

❗ CAUTION

Be careful. Even though we found *y* first in **Example 2,** *the x-coordinate is always written first in the ordered-pair solution of a system.*

Solving a Linear System by Substitution

Step 1 **Solve one of the equations for either variable.** If one equation has a variable term with coefficient 1 or −1, choose it because the substitution method is usually easier.

Step 2 **Substitute** for that variable in the other equation. The result should be an equation with just one variable.

Step 3 **Solve** the equation from Step 2.

Step 4 **Find the other value.** Substitute the result from Step 3 into the equation from Step 1 and solve for the value of the other variable.

Step 5 **Check** the values in *both* of the *original* equations. Then write the solution set as a set containing an ordered pair.

Answers

2. (a) $\{(-2, -6)\}$ **(b)** $\{(0, 2)\}$

EXAMPLE 3 Solving a System by Substitution

Solve the system.

$$3x + 2y = 13 \quad (1)$$
$$4x - y = -1 \quad (2)$$

Step 1 First solve one of the equations for x or y. Because the coefficient of y in equation (2) is -1, it is easiest to solve for y in this equation.

$$4x - y = -1 \quad (2)$$
$$-y = -1 - 4x \quad \text{Subtract } 4x.$$
$$y = 1 + 4x \quad \text{Multiply by } -1.$$

Step 2 Substitute $1 + 4x$ for y in equation (1).

$$3x + 2y = 13 \quad (1)$$
$$3x + 2(\mathbf{1 + 4x}) = 13 \quad \text{Let } y = 1 + 4x.$$

Step 3 Solve. $\quad 3x + 2 + 8x = 13 \quad \text{Distributive property}$
$$11x + 2 = 13 \quad \text{Combine like terms.}$$
$$11x = 11 \quad \text{Subtract 2.}$$
$$x = 1 \quad \text{Divide by 11.}$$

Step 4 Now find y. From Step 1, $y = 1 + 4x$. Substitute 1 for x.

$$y = 1 + 4(\mathbf{1}) \quad \text{Let } x = 1.$$
$$y = 5 \quad \text{Multiply, and then add.}$$

Step 5 Check 1 for x and 5 for y in both equations (1) and (2).

CHECK $\quad 3x + 2y = 13 \quad (1) \quad \bigg| \quad 4x - y = -1 \quad (2)$
$$3(\mathbf{1}) + 2(\mathbf{5}) \stackrel{?}{=} 13 \quad \bigg| \quad 4(\mathbf{1}) - 5 \stackrel{?}{=} -1$$
$$3 + 10 \stackrel{?}{=} 13 \quad \bigg| \quad 4 - 5 \stackrel{?}{=} -1$$
$$13 = 13 \checkmark \text{ True} \quad \bigg| \quad -1 = -1 \checkmark \text{ True}$$

The solution set is $\{(1, 5)\}$.

───────────────── **Work Problem ③ at the Side.** ▶

The **elimination method** involves combining the two equations in a system so that one variable is eliminated. This is done using the following logic.

$$\textbf{If } a = b \textbf{ and } c = d, \textbf{ then } a + c = b + d.$$

EXAMPLE 4 Solving a System by Elimination

Solve the system.

$$2x + 3y = -6 \quad (1)$$
$$4x - 3y = 6 \quad (2)$$

Notice that adding the equations together will eliminate the variable y.

$$\begin{array}{ll} 2x + 3y = -6 & (1) \\ \underline{4x - 3y = 6} & (2) \\ 6x = 0 & \text{Add.} \end{array}$$

Solve for x.
$$x = 0 \quad \text{Divide by 6.}$$

───────────────── **Continued on Next Page**

③ Solve each system.

(a) $\quad 4x - 5y = -11 \quad (1)$
$$x + 2y = 7 \quad (2)$$

Step 1
Solve equation (2) for x.

$$x = \underline{\hspace{2cm}}$$

Step 2
Substitute $7 - 2y$ for x in equation (1).

$$4(\underline{\hspace{1.5cm}}) - 5y = -11$$

Step 3
Solve for y.

$$y = \underline{\hspace{1cm}}$$

Step 4
Now find x.

$$x = 7 - 2y$$
$$x = 7 - 2(\underline{\hspace{0.7cm}})$$
$$x = \underline{\hspace{1cm}}$$

Step 5
Check 1 for x and 3 for y in both equations (1) and (2).

The solution set is $\underline{\hspace{1.5cm}}$.

(b) $\quad 3x - y = 10$
$$2x + 5y = 1$$

Answers

3. **(a)** $7 - 2y$; $7 - 2y$; 3; 3; 1; $\{(1, 3)\}$
   (b) $\{(3, -1)\}$

④ Solve each system.

(a) $3x - y = -7$

$2x + y = -3$

(b) $-2x + 3y = -10$

$2x + 2y = 5$

To find y, substitute 0 for x in either equation (1) or equation (2).

$$2x + 3y = -6 \quad (1)$$
$$2(0) + 3y = -6 \quad \text{Let } x = 0.$$
$$0 + 3y = -6 \quad \text{Multiply.}$$
$$3y = -6 \quad \text{Add.}$$
$$y = -2 \quad \text{Divide by 3.}$$

Check by substituting 0 for x and -2 for y in both equations of the original system. The solution set is $\{(0, -2)\}$.

◀ **Work Problem ④ at the Side.**

By adding the equations in **Example 4,** we eliminated the variable y because the coefficients of the y-terms were opposites. In many cases the coefficients will *not* be opposites, and we must transform one or both equations so that the coefficients of one pair of variable terms are opposites.

Solving a Linear System by Elimination

Step 1 Write both equations in the form $Ax + By = C$.

Step 2 **Transform the equations as needed so that the coefficients of one pair of variable terms are opposites.** Multiply one or both equations by appropriate numbers so that the sum of the coefficients of either the x- or y-terms is 0.

Step 3 **Add** the new equations to eliminate a variable. The sum should be an equation with just one variable.

Step 4 **Solve** the equation from Step 3 for the remaining variable.

Step 5 **Find the other value.** Substitute the result from Step 4 into either of the original equations and solve for the other variable.

Step 6 **Check** the values in *both* of the *original* equations. Then write the solution set as a set containing an ordered pair.

EXAMPLE 5 Solving a System by Elimination

Solve the system.

$$5x - 2y = 4 \quad (1)$$
$$2x + 3y = 13 \quad (2)$$

Step 1 Both equations are in $Ax + By = C$ form.

Step 2 Suppose that we wish to eliminate the variable x. One way to do this is to multiply equation (1) by 2 and equation (2) by -5.

The goal is to have *opposite* coefficients.

$$10x - 4y = 8 \quad \text{2 times each side of equation (1)}$$
$$-10x - 15y = -65 \quad \text{-5 times each side of equation (2)}$$

Step 3 Now add.

$$\begin{array}{r} 10x - 4y = 8 \\ -10x - 15y = -65 \\ \hline -19y = -57 \end{array} \quad \text{Add.}$$

Step 4 Solve for y.

$$y = 3 \quad \text{Divide by } -19.$$

Answers

4. **(a)** $\{(-2, 1)\}$ **(b)** $\left\{\left(\frac{7}{2}, -1\right)\right\}$

Continued on Next Page

Step 5 To find x, substitute 3 for y in either equation (1) or (2).

$$2x + 3y = 13 \quad (2)$$
$$2x + 3(3) = 13 \quad \text{Let } y = 3.$$
$$2x + 9 = 13 \quad \text{Multiply.}$$
$$2x = 4 \quad \text{Subtract 9.}$$
$$x = 2 \quad \text{Divide by 2.}$$

Step 6 To check, substitute 2 for x and 3 for y in equations (1) and (2).

CHECK

$$5x - 2y = 4 \quad (1)$$
$$5(2) - 2(3) \overset{?}{=} 4$$
$$10 - 6 \overset{?}{=} 4$$
$$4 = 4 \ \checkmark \ \text{True}$$

$$2x + 3y = 13 \quad (2)$$
$$2(2) + 3(3) \overset{?}{=} 13$$
$$4 + 9 \overset{?}{=} 13$$
$$13 = 13 \ \checkmark \ \text{True}$$

The solution set is $\{(2, 3)\}$.

———— Work Problem **5** at the Side. ▶

| OBJECTIVE ▶ 2 | Solve special systems. |

| EXAMPLE 6 | Solving a System of Dependent Equations |

Solve the system.

$$2x - y = 3 \quad (1)$$
$$6x - 3y = 9 \quad (2)$$

We multiply equation (1) by -3, and then add the result to equation (2).

$$-6x + 3y = -9 \quad \text{-3 times each side of equation (1)}$$
$$\underline{6x - 3y = 9} \quad (2)$$
$$0 = 0 \quad \text{True}$$

The result of the addition step is a true statement $0 = 0$. In the original system, we could obtain equation (2) from equation (1) by multiplying equation (1) by 3. Equations (1) and (2) are equivalent and have the same graph, as shown in **Figure 43**. The equations are dependent.

The solution set is the set of all points on the line with equation $2x - y = 3$, written in set-builder notation as

$$\{(x, y) \mid 2x - y = 3\}$$

and read *"the set of all ordered pairs (x, y), such that $2x - y = 3$."*

Either equation of the system or an equivalent equation could be used to write the solution set.

We use the equation in standard form with coefficients that are integers having greatest common factor 1 and positive coefficient of x.

———— Work Problem **6** at the Side. ▶

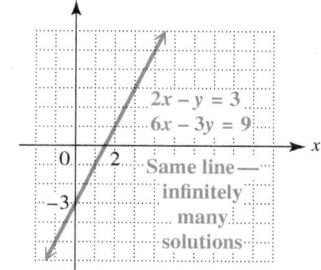

Figure 43

5 Solve each system.

(a) $\quad x + 3y = 8$
$\quad 2x - 5y = -17$

(b) $\quad 6x - 2y = -21$
$\quad -3x + 4y = 36$

(c) $\quad 2x + 3y = 19$
$\quad 3x - 7y = -6$

6 Solve the system. Then graph both equations.

$$2x + y = 6 \quad (1)$$
$$-8x - 4y = -24 \quad (2)$$

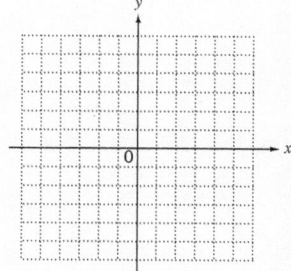

Answers

5. (a) $\{(-1, 3)\}$ (b) $\left\{\left(-\frac{2}{3}, \frac{17}{2}\right)\right\}$
(c) $\{(5, 3)\}$

6. $\{(x, y) \mid 2x + y = 6\}$

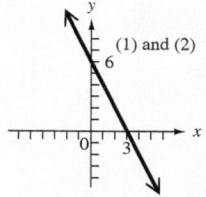

7 Solve the system. Then graph both equations.

$$2x - y = 4$$
$$-6x + 3y = 0$$

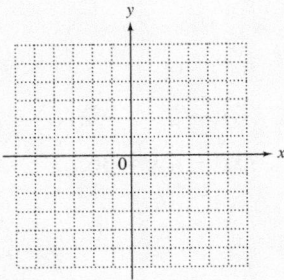

EXAMPLE 7 **Solving an Inconsistent System**

Solve the system.

$$x + 3y = 4 \quad (1)$$
$$-2x - 6y = 3 \quad (2)$$

Multiply equation (1) by 2, and then add the result to equation (2).

$$2x + 6y = 8 \quad \text{Equation (1) multiplied by 2}$$
$$\underline{-2x - 6y = 3} \quad (2)$$
$$0 = 11 \quad \text{False}$$

The result of the addition step is a false statement, $0 = 11$, which indicates that the system is inconsistent. As shown in **Figure 44,** the graphs of the equations are parallel lines.

There are no ordered pairs that satisfy both equations, so there is no solution for the system. The solution set is $\varnothing$.

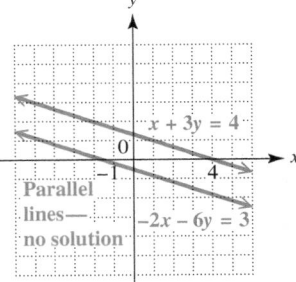

Figure 44

◀ **Work Problem 7 at the Side.**

Note

Solving the system in **Example 6**

$$2x - y = 3 \quad (1)$$
$$6x - 3y = 9 \quad (2)$$

using the substitution method gives the same true statement $0 = 0$. To see this, solve equation (1) for y to obtain

$$y = 2x - 3. \quad \text{Equation (1) solved for } y$$

Substitute this result for y into equation (2).

$$6x - 3y = 9 \quad (2)$$
$$6x - 3(2x - 3) = 9 \quad \text{Let } y = 2x - 3.$$
$$6x - 6x + 9 = 9 \quad \text{Distributive property}$$
$$0 = 0 \quad \text{Simplify.}$$

The same solution set results, written using set-builder notation as

$$\{(x, y) \mid 2x - y = 3\}.$$

Solve **Example 7** using the substitution method to see that the false statement $0 = 11$ again results, indicating solution set $\varnothing$.

Answer

7. $\varnothing$

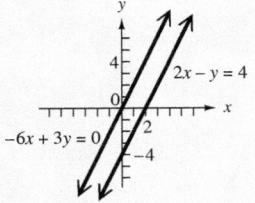

8.5 Exercises

1. CONCEPT CHECK Which ordered pair could possibly be a solution of the graphed system of equations? Why?

  A. $(3, 3)$

  B. $(-3, 3)$

  C. $(-3, -3)$

  D. $(3, -3)$

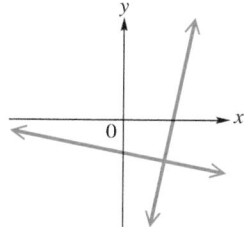

2. CONCEPT CHECK Which ordered pair could possibly be a solution of the graphed system of equations? Why?

  A. $(3, 0)$

  B. $(-3, 0)$

  C. $(0, 3)$

  D. $(0, -3)$

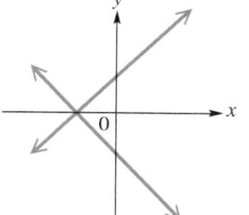

3. CONCEPT CHECK Match each system with the correct graph.

  (a) $x + y = 6$
     $x - y = 0$

  (b) $x + y = -6$
     $x - y = 0$

  (c) $x + y = 0$
     $x - y = -6$

  (d) $x + y = 0$
     $x - y = 6$

A.
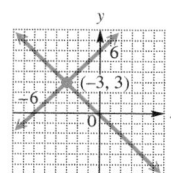

B.
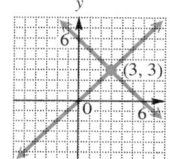

C.
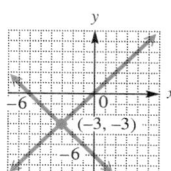

D.
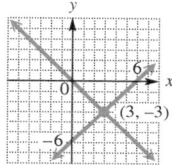

4. CONCEPT CHECK To minimize the amount of work required, tell whether to use the substitution or the elimination method to solve each system. Then solve.

  (a) $6x - y = 5$
     $y = 11x$

  (b) $3x + y = -7$
     $x - y = -5$

  (c) $3x - 2y = 0$
     $9x + 8y = 7$

Solve each system by graphing. ***See Example 1.***

5. $\quad x + y = -5$
   $-2x + y = 1$

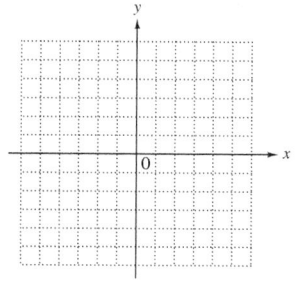

6. $\quad x + y = 4$
   $2x - y = 2$

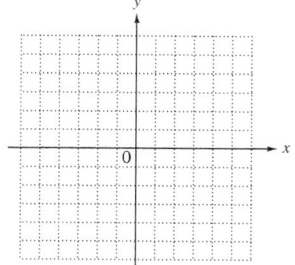

7. $\quad x - 4y = -4$
   $3x + \ y = 1$

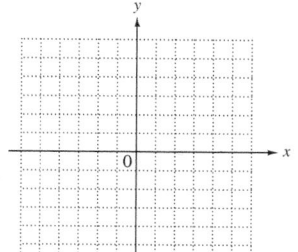

8. $2x + 3y = -6$
   $x - 3y = -3$

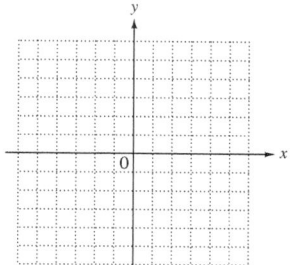

Solve each system by substitution. If the system is inconsistent or has dependent equations, say so. ***See Examples 2, 3, 6, and 7.***

9. $4x + y = 6$
$y = 2x$

10. $2x - y = 6$
$y = 5x$

11. $-x - 4y = -14$
$y = 2x - 1$

12. $-3x - 5y = -17$
$y = 4x + 8$

13. $3x - 4y = -22$
$-3x + y = 0$

14. $-3x + y = -5$
$x + 2y = 0$

15. $2x - y = 4$
$5x - 2y = 8$

16. $3x + 2y = 6$
$4x + y = 3$

17. $x = 3y + 5$
$x = \dfrac{3}{2}y$

18. $x = 6y - 2$
$x = \dfrac{3}{4}y$

19. $\dfrac{1}{2}x + \dfrac{1}{3}y = 3$
$-3x + y = 0$

20. $\dfrac{1}{4}x - \dfrac{1}{5}y = 9$
$5x - y = 0$

21. $y = 2x$
$4x - 2y = 0$

22. $x = 3y$
$3x - 9y = 0$

23. $5x - 25y = 5$
$x = 5y$

24. $8x + 2y = 4$
$y = -4x$

Solve each system by elimination. If the system is inconsistent or has dependent equations, say so. ***See Examples 4–7.***

25. $-2x + 3y = -16$
$2x - 5y = 24$

26. $6x + 5y = -7$
$-6x - 11y = 1$

27. $2x - 5y = 11$
$3x + y = 8$

28. $-2x + 3y = 1$
$-4x + y = -3$

29. $3x + 4y = -6$
$5x + 3y = 1$

30. $4x + 3y = 1$
$3x + 2y = 2$

31. $3x + 3y = 0$
$4x + 2y = 3$

32. $8x + 4y = 0$
$4x - 2y = 2$

33. $7x + 2y = 6$
$-14x - 4y = -12$

34. $x - 4y = 2$
$4x - 16y = 8$

35. $3x - 2y = -3$
$4x + 3y = -4$

36. $5x - 2y = 10$
$3x + 5y = 6$

37. $5x - 5y = 3$
$x - y = 12$

38. $2x - 3y = 7$
$-4x + 6y = 14$

39. $\dfrac{x}{2} + \dfrac{y}{3} = -\dfrac{1}{3}$
$\dfrac{x}{2} + 2y = -7$

40. $\dfrac{x}{4} + \dfrac{y}{3} = -\dfrac{1}{3}$
$\dfrac{x}{3} - \dfrac{y}{4} = -6$

8.6 Systems of Linear Equations in Three Variables; Applications

A solution of an equation in three variables, such as

$$2x + 3y - z = 4,$$ Linear equation in three variables

is an **ordered triple** and is written (x, y, z). For example, the ordered triple $(0, 1, -1)$ is a solution of the equation, because

$$2(0) + 3(1) - (-1) = 4$$ is a true statement.

Verify that another solution of this equation is $(10, -3, 7)$.

We now extend the term *linear equation* to equations of the form

$$Ax + By + Cz + \ldots + Dw = K,$$

where not all the coefficients $A, B, C, \ldots, D$ equal 0. For example,

$$2x + 3y - 5z = 7 \quad \text{and} \quad x - 2y - z + 3u - 2w = 8$$

are linear equations, the first with three variables and the second with five.

OBJECTIVES

1. Understand the geometry of systems of three equations in three variables.
2. Solve linear systems with three equations and three variables by elimination.
3. Solve linear systems with three equations and three variables in which some of the equations have missing terms.
4. Solve special systems.
5. Solve application problems with three variables using a system of three equations.

OBJECTIVE ▶ 1 Understand the geometry of systems of three equations in three variables. Consider the solution of a system such as the following.

$$4x + 8y + z = 2$$
$$x + 7y - 3z = -14$$ System of linear equations in three variables
$$2x - 3y + 2z = 3$$

Theoretically, a system of this type can be solved by graphing. However, the graph of a linear equation with three variables is a *plane,* not a line. Because visualizing a plane requires three-dimensional graphing, the graphing method is not practical with these systems. However, it does illustrate the number of solutions possible for such systems, as shown in **Figure 45.**

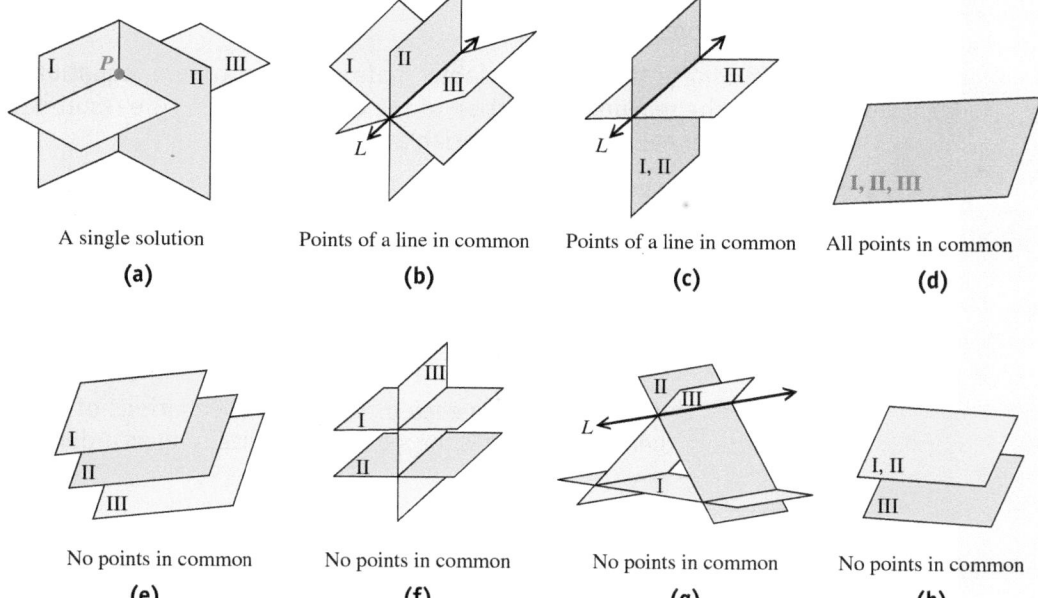

A single solution **(a)**   Points of a line in common **(b)**   Points of a line in common **(c)**   All points in common **(d)**

No points in common **(e)**   No points in common **(f)**   No points in common **(g)**   No points in common **(h)**

Figure 45

Figure 45 on the preceding page illustrates the following cases.

Graphs of Linear Systems in Three Variables

Case 1   **The three planes may meet at a single, common point.**
This point is the solution set of the system. See **Figure 45(a).**

Case 2   **The three planes may have the points of a line in common.**
The infinite set of points that satisfy the equation of the line is the solution of the system. See **Figures 45(b) and (c).**

Case 3   **The three planes may coincide.**
The solution set of the system is the set of all points in a plane. See **Figure 45(d).**

Case 4   **The planes may have no points common to all three.**
There is no solution of the system. See **Figures 45(e)–(h).**

OBJECTIVE ▶ 2 Solve linear systems with three equations and three variables by elimination. Because graphing to find the solution set of a system of three equations in three variables is impractical, these systems are solved with an extension of the elimination method.

In the steps that follow, we use the term **focus variable** to identify the first variable to be eliminated. The focus variable will always be present in the **working equation,** which will be used twice to eliminate this variable.

Solving a Linear System in Three Variables*

Step 1   **Select a variable and an equation.** A good choice for the variable, which we call the *focus variable,* is one that has coefficient 1 or −1. Then select an equation, one that contains the focus variable, as the *working equation*.

Step 2   **Eliminate the focus variable.** Use the working equation and one of the other two equations of the original system. The result is an equation in two variables.

Step 3   **Eliminate the focus variable again.** Use the working equation and the remaining equation of the original system. The result is another equation in two variables.

Step 4   **Write the equations in two variables from Steps 2 and 3 as a system, and solve it.** Doing this gives the values of two of the variables.

Step 5   **Find the value of the remaining variable.** Substitute the values of the two variables found in Step 4 into the working equation to obtain the value of the focus variable.

Step 6   **Check** the three values in *each* of the *original* equations of the system. Then write the solution set as a set containing an ordered triple.

---

*The authors wish to thank Christine Heinecke Lehmann of Purdue University North Central for her suggestions here.

| EXAMPLE 1 | Solving a System in Three Variables |

Solve the system.

$$4x + 8y + z = 2 \quad (1)$$
$$x + 7y - 3z = -14 \quad (2)$$
$$2x - 3y + 2z = 3 \quad (3)$$

Step 1 Because z in equation (1) has coefficient 1, we choose z as the focus variable and (1) as the working equation. (Another option would be to choose x as the focus variable—it also has coefficient 1—and use (2) as the working equation.)

$$\overset{\text{Focus variable}}{4x + 8y + z = 2} \quad (1) \longleftarrow \text{Working equation}$$

Step 2 Multiply working equation (1) by 3 and add the result to equation (2).

$$\begin{array}{ll} 12x + 24y + 3z = 6 & \text{Multiply each side of (1) by 3.} \\ \underline{x + 7y - 3z = -14} & (2) \\ 13x + 31y = -8 & \text{Add.} \quad (4) \end{array}$$

Focus variable z was eliminated.

Step 3 Multiply working equation (1) by -2 and add the result to remaining equation (3) to again eliminate focus variable z.

$$\begin{array}{ll} -8x - 16y - 2z = -4 & \text{Multiply each side of (1) by } -2. \\ \underline{2x - 3y + 2z = 3} & (3) \\ -6x - 19y = -1 & \text{Add.} \quad (5) \end{array}$$

Focus variable z was eliminated.

Step 4 Write the equations that result in Steps 2 and 3 as a system.

Make sure these equations have the same two variables.

$$13x + 31y = -8 \quad (4) \quad \text{The result from Step 2}$$
$$-6x - 19y = -1 \quad (5) \quad \text{The result from Step 3}$$

Now solve this system. We choose to eliminate x.

$$\begin{array}{ll} 78x + 186y = -48 & \text{Multiply each side of (4) by 6.} \\ \underline{-78x - 247y = -13} & \text{Multiply each side of (5) by 13.} \\ -61y = -61 & \text{Add.} \\ y = 1 & \text{Divide by } -61. \end{array}$$

Substitute 1 for y in either equation (4) or (5) to find x.

$$\begin{array}{ll} -6x - 19y = -1 & (5) \\ -6x - 19(1) = -1 & \text{Let } y = 1. \\ -6x - 19 = -1 & \text{Multiply.} \\ -6x = 18 & \text{Add 19.} \\ x = -3 & \text{Divide by } -6. \end{array}$$

Step 5 Now substitute the two values we found in Step 4 in working equation (1) to find the value of the remaining variable, focus variable z.

$$\begin{array}{ll} 4x + 8y + z = 2 & (1) \\ 4(-3) + 8(1) + z = 2 & \text{Let } x = -3 \text{ and } y = 1. \\ -4 + z = 2 & \text{Multiply, and then add.} \\ z = 6 & \text{Add 4.} \end{array}$$

Continued on Next Page

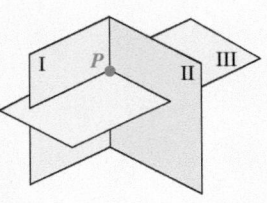

A single solution

Figure 45(a) (repeated)

1 Solve each system.

(a)
$$x + y + z = 2$$
$$x - y + 2z = 2$$
$$-x + 2y - z = 1$$

(b)
$$x - y + 2z = 1$$
$$3x + 2y + 7z = 8$$
$$-3x - 4y + 9z = -10$$

Write the values of x, y, and z in the correct order

Step 6 It appears that $(-3, 1, 6)$ is the only solution of the system. We must check that this ordered triple satisfies all three original equations of the system. We begin with equation (1).

CHECK

$$4x + 8y + z = 2 \qquad (1)$$
$$4(-3) + 8(1) + 6 \overset{?}{=} 2 \qquad \text{Substitute.}$$
$$-12 + 8 + 6 \overset{?}{=} 2 \qquad \text{Multiply.}$$
$$2 = 2 \checkmark \quad \text{True}$$

The check of these values in equations (2) and (3) is done similarly. Because $(-3, 1, 6)$ satisfies all three original equations, the solution set is $\{(-3, 1, 6)\}$. This is Case 1, illustrated earlier in **Figure 45(a)** and repeated in the margin.

◀ **Work Problem 1** at the Side.

OBJECTIVE **3** Solve linear systems with three equations and three variables in which some of the equations have missing terms.

EXAMPLE 2 Solving a System with Missing Terms

Solve the system.

$$6x - 12y = -5 \quad (1) \quad \text{Missing } z$$
$$8y + z = 0 \quad (2) \quad \text{Missing } x$$
$$9x - z = 12 \quad (3) \quad \text{Missing } y$$

Because equation (3) is missing the variable y, one way to begin is to use y as the focus variable and eliminate y using equations (1) and (2).

$$12x - 24y = -10 \qquad \text{Multiply each side of (1) by 2.}$$

Leave space for the missing terms.

$$\underline{\qquad 24y + 3z = \quad 0} \qquad \text{Multiply each side of (2) by 3.}$$
$$12x \qquad + 3z = -10 \qquad \text{Add.} \quad (4)$$

Now use resulting equation (4) in x and z, together with equation (3), $9x - z = 12$, to eliminate z. Multiply equation (3) by 3.

$$27x - 3z = \quad 36 \qquad \text{Multiply each side of (3) by 3.}$$

These equations have the same variables.

$$\underline{12x + 3z = -10} \qquad (4)$$
$$39x \qquad = \quad 26 \qquad \text{Add.}$$

$$x = \frac{26}{39} \qquad \text{Divide by 39.}$$

$$x = \frac{2}{3} \qquad \text{Write in lowest terms.}$$

We can find z by substituting this value for x in equation (3).

$$9x - z = 12 \qquad (3)$$
$$9\left(\frac{2}{3}\right) - z = 12 \qquad \text{Let } x = \tfrac{2}{3}.$$
$$6 - z = 12 \qquad \text{Multiply.}$$
$$z = -6 \qquad \text{Subtract 6. Multiply by } -1.$$

Answers

1. **(a)** $\{(-1, 1, 2)\}$ **(b)** $\{(2, 1, 0)\}$

Continued on Next Page

We can find y by substituting -6 for z in equation (2).

$$8y + z = 0 \quad \text{(2)}$$

$$8y - 6 = 0 \quad \text{Let } z = -6.$$

$$y = \frac{6}{8} \quad \text{Add 6. Divide by 8.}$$

$$y = \frac{3}{4} \quad \text{Write in lowest terms.}$$

Thus $x = \frac{2}{3}$, $y = \frac{3}{4}$, and $z = -6$. Check these values in equations (1), (2), and (3) to verify that the solution set is $\left\{\left(\frac{2}{3}, \frac{3}{4}, -6\right)\right\}$. This is also an example of Case 1.

─────── **Work Problem ② at the Side.** ▶

> **Note**
>
> Another way to solve the system in **Example 2** is to begin by eliminating the variable z from equations (2) and (3). The resulting equation together with equation (1) forms a system of two equations in the variables x and y. Try working **Example 2** this way to see that the same solution results.
>   There are often multiple ways to solve a system of equations. Some ways may involve more work than others.

OBJECTIVE ▶ ④ Solve special systems. Linear systems with three variables may include dependent equations or may be inconsistent.

EXAMPLE 3 Solving a System of Dependent Equations

Solve the system.

$$2x - 3y + 4z = 8 \quad \text{(1)}$$

$$-x + \frac{3}{2}y - 2z = -4 \quad \text{(2)} \quad \boxed{\text{Use as the working equation, with focus variable } x.}$$

$$6x - 9y + 12z = 24 \quad \text{(3)}$$

Eliminate focus variable x using equations (1) and (2).

$$-2x + 3y - 4z = -8 \quad \text{Multiply each side of (2) by 2.}$$

$$\underline{2x - 3y + 4z = 8} \quad \text{(1)}$$

$$0 = 0 \quad \text{True}$$

Eliminating x from equations (2) and (3) gives the same result.

$$-6x + 9y - 12z = -24 \quad \text{Multiply each side of (2) by 6.}$$

$$\underline{6x - 9y + 12z = 24} \quad \text{(3)}$$

$$0 = 0 \quad \text{True}$$

When solving a system such as this, attempting to eliminate one variable results in elimination of *all* variables. The equations are dependent—that is, they are equivalent forms of the *same* equation—and have the same graph. This is Case 3, as illustrated in **Figure 45(d)**. The solution set is written

$$\{(x, y, z) \mid 2x - 3y + 4z = 8\}. \quad \text{Set-builder notation}$$

Although any one of the three equations could be used to write the solution set, we use the equation with integer coefficients having greatest common factor 1 and positive coefficient of x, as in the previous section.

─────── **Work Problem ③ at the Side.** ▶

② Solve each system.

(a) $\quad x - y = 6$

$\qquad\quad 2y + 5z = 1$

$\qquad\quad 3x - 4z = 8$

(b) $\quad 3x - z = -10$

$\qquad\quad 4y + 5z = 24$

$\qquad\quad x - 6y = -8$

③ Solve each system.

(a) $\quad x - y + z = 4$

$\qquad -3x + 3y - 3z = -12$

$\qquad2x - 2y + 2z = 8$

(b) $\quad x - 3y + 2z = 10$

$\qquad -2x + 6y - 4z = -20$

$\qquad \dfrac{1}{2}x - \dfrac{3}{2}y + z = 5$

I, II, III

All points in common

Figure 45(d) (repeated)

Answers

2. (a) $\{(4, -2, 1)\}$ **(b)** $\{(-2, 1, 4)\}$

3. (a) $\{(x, y, z) \mid x - y + z = 4\}$

$\quad$ **(b)** $\{(x, y, z) \mid x - 3y + 2z = 10\}$

④ Solve the system.

$$3x - 5y + 2z = 1$$
$$5x + 8y - z = 4$$
$$-6x + 10y - 4z = 5$$

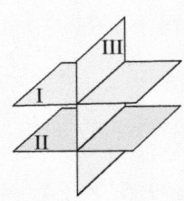

No points in common

Figure 45(f) (repeated)

⑤ Solve the system.

$$2x + 3y - z = 8$$
$$\frac{1}{2}x + \frac{3}{4}y - \frac{1}{4}z = 2$$
$$x + \frac{3}{2}y - \frac{1}{2}z = -6$$

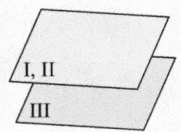

No points in common

Figure 45(h) (repeated)

EXAMPLE 4 Solving an Inconsistent System

Solve the system.

$$2x - 4y + 6z = 5 \quad (1)$$
$$-x + 3y - 2z = -1 \quad (2)$$
$$x - 2y + 3z = 1 \quad (3) \quad \text{← Use as the working equation, with focus variable } x.$$

Eliminate focus variable x using equations (1) and (3).

$$-2x + 4y - 6z = -2 \quad \text{Multiply each side of (3) by } -2.$$
$$\underline{2x - 4y + 6z = 5} \quad (1)$$
$$0 = 3 \quad \text{False}$$

The resulting false statement indicates that equations (1) and (3) have no common solution. Thus, the system is inconsistent and the solution set is $\varnothing$. The graph of this system would show these two planes parallel to one another and a third plane that intersects both, as illustrated in **Figure 45(f)**. This is Case 4.

◀ **Work Problem ④ at the Side.**

Note

If a false statement results when adding, as in **Example 4,** it is not necessary to go any further with the solution. Because two of the three planes are parallel, it is not possible for the three planes to have any points in common.

EXAMPLE 5 Solving Another Special System

Solve the system.

$$2x - y + 3z = 6 \quad (1)$$
$$x - \frac{1}{2}y + \frac{3}{2}z = 3 \quad (2)$$
$$4x - 2y + 6z = 1 \quad (3)$$

Equations (1) and (2) are equivalent. If we multiply each side of equation (2) by 2, we obtain equation (1). These two equations are dependent and have the same graph.

Equations (1) and (3) are *not* equivalent, however. If we multiply equation (3) by $\frac{1}{2}$, we obtain

$$2x - y + 3z = \frac{1}{2}.$$

This equation has the same coefficients as equation (1), but a different constant term. Therefore, the graphs of equations (1) and (3) have *no* points in common—that is, the planes are parallel.

Thus, this system is inconsistent and the solution set is $\varnothing$, as illustrated in **Figure 45(h)**. This is another example of Case 4.

◀ **Work Problem ⑤ at the Side.**

Answers

4. $\varnothing$

5. $\varnothing$

OBJECTIVE ▶ ⑤ Solve application problems with three variables using a system of three equations.

EXAMPLE 6   Solving a Geometry Problem

The sum of the measures of the angles of a triangle is 180°. The smallest angle measures 36° less than the middle-sized angle. The largest angle measures 16° more than twice the smallest angle. Find the measure of each angle.

Step 1   **Read** the problem again. There are three angles, so there will be three unknowns.

Step 2   **Assign variables.** Make a sketch, as in **Figure 46.**

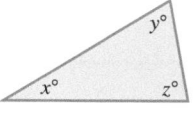

Let x = the measure of the smallest angle,

   y = the measure of the middle-sized angle,

and z = the measure of the largest angle.

Figure 46

Step 3   **Write a system of three equations.** The sum of the measures of the angles of a triangle is 180°.

$$x + y + z = 180$$

We can write two more equations from the information given.

Smallest angle	is	36° less than middle-sized angle.
↓	↓	↓
x	$=$	$y - 36$

Largest angle	is	16° more than twice smallest angle.
↓	↓	↓
z	$=$	$16 + 2x$

These three equations form a system.

$$x + y + z = 180 \qquad (1)$$
$$x = y - 36 \qquad (2)$$
$$z = 16 + 2x \qquad (3)$$

Step 4   **Solve** the system of equations. If we write equation (2) in terms of y, then equations (2) and (3) will give both y and z in terms of x.

$$x = y - 36 \qquad (2)$$
$$y = x + 36 \qquad \text{Add 36. Interchange sides.}$$

Now substitute $x + 36$ for y and $16 + 2x$ (from equation (3)) for z in equation (1).

$$x + y + z = 180 \qquad (1)$$
$$x + (x + 36) + (16 + 2x) = 180 \qquad \text{Let } y = x + 36 \text{ and } z = 16 + 2x.$$
$$4x + 52 = 180 \qquad \text{Combine like terms.}$$
$$4x = 128 \qquad \text{Subtract 52.}$$
$$x = 32 \qquad \text{Divide by 4.}$$

Substitute 32 for x in $y = x + 36$ (equation (2) solved for y) to find y.

$$y = 32 + 36 \qquad \text{Let } x = 32.$$
$$y = 68 \qquad \text{Add.}$$

Continued on Next Page

6 Solve the problem.

The sum of the measures of the angles of a triangle is 180°. The measure of the third angle is four times that of the first angle. The sum of the measures of the first and second angles is 84°. Find the measure of each angle.

Substitute **32** for x in $z = 16 + 2x$ (equation (3)) to find z.

$$z = 16 + 2\,(\mathbf{32}) \qquad \text{Let } x = 32.$$

$$z = 80 \qquad\qquad \text{Multiply, and then add.}$$

Step 5 **State the answer.** The three angles measure 32°, 68°, and 80°.

Step 6 **Check.** The sum of the measures of the three angles is

$$32° + 68° + 80° = 180°, \quad \text{as required.}$$

Also, each of the following is a true statement.

$32° = 68° - 36°$ Smallest measures 36° less than middle-sized.

$80° = 16° + 2\,(32°)$ Largest measures 16° more than twice smallest.

◀ **Work Problem 6 at the Side.**

Problem-Solving Hint

In Step 4 of **Example 6,** we could also have substituted $16 + 2x$ (from equation (3)) for z in equation (1) as follows.

$$x + y + z = 180 \qquad (1)$$

$$x + y + (\mathbf{16 + 2x}) = 180 \qquad \text{Let } z = 16 + 2x.$$

$$3x + y = 164 \qquad \text{Combine like terms. Subtract 16.} \quad (4)$$

This gives a system of two equations in x and y.

$$x - y = -36 \qquad \text{(2) in standard form}$$

$$3x + y = 164 \qquad (4)$$

Eliminating y gives $x = 32$, which can be used to obtain $y = 68$ and $z = 80$. There is often more than one way to solve applications involving systems of three equations.

EXAMPLE 7 **Solving a Problem Involving Prices**

At Panera Bread, a loaf of honey wheat bread costs $3.89, a loaf of tomato basil bread costs $5.39, and a loaf of French bread costs $3.19. On a recent day, three times as many loaves of honey wheat were sold as tomato basil. The number of loaves of French sold was 5 less than the number of loaves of honey wheat sold. Total receipts for these breads were $90.57. How many loaves of each type of bread were sold? (Data from Panera Bread.)

Step 1 **Read** the problem again. There are three unknowns.

Step 2 **Assign variables** to represent the three unknowns.

    Let x = the number of loaves of honey wheat bread,

          y = the number of loaves of tomato basil bread,

    and z = the number of loaves of French bread.

Step 3 **Write a system of three equations.** Three times as many loaves of honey wheat were sold as of tomato basil.

$$x = 3y$$

$$x - 3y = 0 \qquad \text{Subtract } 3y.$$

Continued on Next Page

Answer

6. first: 24°; second: 60°; third: 96°

Also, we have the information needed for another equation.

Number of loaves of French	equals	5 less than the number of loaves of honey wheat.
↓	↓	↓
z	$=$	$x - 5$

$$x - z = 5 \quad \text{Rewrite.}$$

Multiplying the cost of a loaf of each kind of bread by the number of loaves of that kind sold and adding gives the total receipts.

$$3.89x + 5.39y + 3.19z = 90.57$$
$$389x + 539y + 319z = 9057 \quad \begin{array}{l}\text{Multiply by 100 to clear}\\ \text{decimals.}\end{array}$$

These three equations form a system.

$$x - 3y = 0 \qquad (1)$$
$$x - z = 5 \qquad (2)$$
$$389x + 539y + 319z = 9057 \qquad (3)$$

Step 4 **Solve** the system of equations. Equation (1) is missing the variable z, so one way to begin is to eliminate z again, using equations (2) and (3).

$$
\begin{array}{ll}
319x \qquad\quad - 319z = \quad 1595 & \text{Multiply (2) by 319.}\\
\underline{389x + 539y + 319z = \quad 9057} & (3)\\
708x + 539y \qquad\quad = 10{,}652 & \text{Add.} \quad (4)
\end{array}
$$

Use resulting equation (4) in x and y, together with equation (1), $x - 3y = 0$, to eliminate x.

$$
\begin{array}{ll}
-708x + 2124y = 0 & \text{Multiply (1) by } -708.\\
\underline{708x + 539y = 10{,}652} & (4)\\
2663y = 10{,}652 & \text{Add.}\\
y = 4 & \text{Divide by 2663.}
\end{array}
$$

We can find x by substituting this value for y in equation (1).

$$
\begin{array}{ll}
x - 3y = 0 & \\
x - 3(4) = 0 & \text{Let } y = 4.\\
x = 12 & \text{Multiply. Add 12.}
\end{array}
$$

We can find z by substituting this value for x in equation (2).

$$
\begin{array}{ll}
x - z = 5 & (2)\\
12 - z = 5 & \text{Let } x = 12.\\
z = 7 & \text{Subtract 12. Multiply by } -1.
\end{array}
$$

Step 5 **State the answer.** There were **12** loaves of honey wheat bread, **4** loaves of tomato basil bread, and **7** loaves of French bread sold.

Step 6 **Check.** Each of the following is a true statement.

$$
\begin{array}{ll}
12 = 3 \cdot 4 & \text{Honey wheat is three times tomato basil.}\\
7 = 12 - 5 & \text{French is 5 less than honey wheat.}
\end{array}
$$

Multiply cost per loaf by number of loaves and add to confirm total receipts.

$$\$3.89(12) + \$5.39(4) + \$3.19(7) = \$90.57, \quad \text{as required.}$$

Work Problem ❼ at the Side. ▶

❼ Solve the problem.

A department store display features three kinds of perfume: Felice, Vivid, and Joy. There are 10 more bottles of Felice than Vivid, and 3 fewer bottles of Joy than Vivid. Each bottle of Felice costs $8, Vivid costs $15, and Joy costs $32. The total value of all the perfume is $589. How many bottles of each are there?

| $8 | $15 | $32 |

8.6 Exercises

FOR EXTRA HELP Go to MyMathLab for worked-out, step-by-step solutions to exercises enclosed in a square ☐ and video solutions to ▶ exercises.

1. **CONCEPT CHECK** Using your immediate surroundings, give an example of three planes that satisfy the condition.

   (a) They intersect in a single point.

   (b) They do not intersect.

   (c) They intersect in infinitely many points.

2. **CONCEPT CHECK** The two equations

   $$x + y + z = 6$$
   $$2x - y + z = 3$$

   have a common solution of $(1, 2, 3)$. Which equation would complete a system of three linear equations in three variables having solution set $\{(1, 2, 3)\}$?

   A. $3x + 2y - z = 1$ **B.** $3x + 2y - z = 4$

   C. $3x + 2y - z = 5$ **D.** $3x + 2y - z = 6$

Solve each system of equations. **See Example 1.**

3. ▶ $2x - 5y + 3z = -1$
   $x + 4y - 2z = 9$
   $x - 2y - 4z = -5$

4. $x + 3y - 6z = 1$
   $2x - y + z = 7$
   $x + 2y + 2z = 14$

5. $3x + 2y + z = 8$
   $2x - 3y + 2z = -16$
   $x + 4y - z = 20$

6. $-3x + y - z = -10$
   $-4x + 2y + 3z = -1$
   $2x + 3y - 2z = -5$

7. $x + 2y + z = 4$
   $2x + y - z = -1$
   $x - y - z = -2$

8. $x - 2y + 5z = -7$
   $-2x - 3y + 4z = -14$
   $-3x + 5y - z = -7$

9. $2x + 5y + 2z = 0$
   $4x - 7y - 3z = 1$
   $3x - 8y - 2z = -6$

10. $5x - 2y + 3z = -9$
   $4x + 3y + 5z = 4$
   $2x + 4y - 2z = 14$

11. $-x + 2y + 6z = 2$
   $3x + 2y + 6z = 6$
   $x + 4y - 3z = 1$

12. $2x + y + 2z = 1$
   $x + 2y + z = 2$
   $x - y - z = 0$

13. $x - 2y + z = 5$
   $-x - y + 2z = 1$
   $2x + y - 7z = -1$

14. $x + y - z = -2$
   $2x - y + z = -5$
   $-x + 2y - 3z = -4$

Solve each system of equations. **See Example 2.**

15. $2x - 3y + 2z = -1$
   $x + 2y + z = 17$
   $2y - z = 7$

16. $2x - y + 3z = 6$
   $x + 2y - z = 8$
   $2y + z = 1$

17. $4x + 2y - 3z = 6$
   $x - 4y + z = -4$
   $-x + 2z = 2$

18. $2x + 3y - 4z = 4$
$x - 6y + z = -16$
$-x + 3z = 8$

19. $2x + y = 6$
$3y - 2z = -4$
$3x - 5z = -7$

20. $4x - 8y = -7$
$4y + z = 7$
$-8x + z = -4$

21. $-5x + 2y + z = 5$
$-3x - 2y - z = 3$
$-x + 6y = 1$

22. $-4x + 3y - z = 4$
$-5x - 3y + z = -4$
$-2x - 3z = 12$

23. $7x - 3z = -34$
$2y + 4z = 20$
$\dfrac{3}{4}x + \dfrac{1}{6}y = -2$

24. $5x - 2z = 8$
$4y + 3z = -9$
$\dfrac{1}{2}x + \dfrac{2}{3}y = -1$

25. $4x - z = -6$
$\dfrac{3}{5}y + \dfrac{1}{2}z = 0$
$\dfrac{1}{3}x + \dfrac{2}{3}z = -5$

26. $5x - z = 38$
$\dfrac{2}{3}y + \dfrac{1}{4}z = -17$
$\dfrac{1}{5}y + \dfrac{5}{6}z = 4$

Solve each system of equations. If the system is inconsistent or has dependent equations, say so. ***See Examples 1, 3, 4, and 5.***

27. $2x + 2y - 6z = 5$
$-3x + y - z = -2$
$-x - y + 3z = 4$

28. $-2x + 5y + z = -3$
$5x + 14y - z = -11$
$7x + 9y - 2z = -5$

29. $-5x + 5y - 20z = -40$
$x - y + 4z = 8$
$3x - 3y + 12z = 24$

30. $x + 4y - z = 3$
$-2x - 8y + 2z = -6$
$3x + 12y - 3z = 9$

31. $x + 5y - 2z = -1$
$-2x + 8y + z = -4$
$3x - y + 5z = 19$

32. $x + 3y + z = 2$
$4x + y + 2z = -4$
$5x + 2y + 3z = -2$

33. $2x + y - z = 6$
$4x + 2y - 2z = 12$
$-x - \dfrac{1}{2}y + \dfrac{1}{2}z = -3$

34. $2x - 8y + 2z = -10$
$-x + 4y - z = 5$
$\dfrac{1}{8}x - \dfrac{1}{2}y + \dfrac{1}{8}z = -\dfrac{5}{8}$

35. $x + y - 2z = 0$
$3x - y + z = 0$
$4x + 2y - z = 0$

36. $2x + 3y - z = 0$
$x - 4y + 2z = 0$
$3x - 5y - z = 0$

37. $x - 2y + \frac{1}{3}z = 4$
$3x - 6y + z = 12$
$-6x + 12y - 2z = -3$

38. $4x + y - 2z = 3$
$x + \frac{1}{4}y - \frac{1}{2}z = \frac{3}{4}$
$2x + \frac{1}{2}y - z = 1$

Solve each problem involving three unknowns. ***See Examples 6 and 7.***

39. In the figure, $z = x + 10$ and $x + y = 100$. Determine a third equation involving x, y, and z, and then find the measures of the three angles. (Recall that the sum of the measures of the angles of a triangle is 180°.)

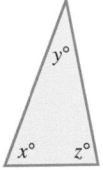

40. In the figure, x is 10 less than y and x is 20 less than z. Write a system of three equations and find the measures of the three angles. (Recall that the sum of the measures of the angles of a triangle is 180°.)

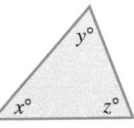

41. In a certain triangle, the measure of the second angle is 10° more than three times the first. The third angle measure is equal to the sum of the measures of the other two. Find the measures of the three angles.

42. The measure of the largest angle of a triangle is 12° less than the sum of the measures of the other two. The smallest angle measures 58° less than the largest. Find the measures of the three angles.

43. The perimeter of a triangle is 70 cm. The longest side is 4 cm less than the sum of the other two sides. Twice the shortest side is 9 cm less than the longest side. Find the length of each side of the triangle.

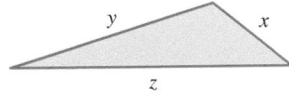

44. The perimeter of a triangle is 56 in. The longest side measures 4 in. less than the sum of the other two sides. Three times the shortest side is 4 in. more than the longest side. Find the lengths of the three sides.

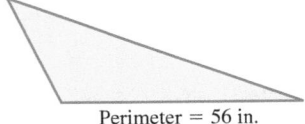

Perimeter = 56 in.

45. In a random sample of Americans of voting age, 16% more people identified themselves as Independents than as Republicans, while 3% fewer people identified themselves as Republicans than as Democrats. Of those sampled, 3% did not identify with any of the three categories. What percent identified themselves with each of the three political affiliations? (Data from Gallup, Inc.)

46. In the 2014 Winter Olympics, Russia earned 4 more gold medals than bronze. The number of silver medals earned was 7 less than twice the number of bronze medals. Russia earned a total of 33 medals. How many of each kind of medal did Russia earn? (Data from www.sochi.com)

47. Tickets for a Harlem Globetrotters game cost $28 general admission, $43 courtside, or $173 bench seats. Nine times as many general admission tickets were sold as bench tickets, and the number of general admission tickets sold was 55 more than the sum of the number of courtside tickets and bench tickets. Sales of all three kinds of tickets totaled $97,605. How many of each kind of ticket were sold? (Data from www.harlemglobetrotters.com)

48. Three kinds of tickets are available for a rock concert: "up close," "in the middle," and "far out." "Up close" tickets cost $10 more than "in the middle" tickets. "In the middle" tickets cost $10 more than "far out" tickets. Twice the cost of an "up close" ticket is $20 more than 3 times the cost of a "far out" ticket. Find the price of each kind of ticket.

49. A wholesaler supplies college t-shirts to three college bookstores: A, B, and C. The wholesaler recently shipped a total of 800 t-shirts to the three bookstores. Twice as many t-shirts were shipped to bookstore B as to bookstore A, and the number shipped to bookstore C was 40 less than the sum of the numbers shipped to the other two bookstores. How many t-shirts were shipped to each bookstore?

50. An office supply store sells three models of computer desks: A, B, and C. In one month, the store sold a total of 85 computer desks. The number of model B desks was five more than the number of model C desks, and the number of model A desks was four more than twice the number of model C desks. How many of each model did the store sell that month?

Relating Concepts (Exercises 51–56) For Individual or Group Work

A circle *has an equation of the following form.*

$$x^2 + y^2 + ax + by + c = 0 \quad \text{Equation of a circle}$$

It is a fact from geometry that given three **noncollinear points**—*that is, points that do not all lie on the same straight line—there will be a circle that contains them. For example, the points* $(4, 2)$, $(-5, -2)$, *and* $(0, 3)$ *lie on the circle whose equation is shown in the figure.*

   Work Exercises 51–55 in order, *to find an equation of the circle passing through the points*

$$(2, 1), \quad (-1, 0), \quad and \quad (3, 3).$$

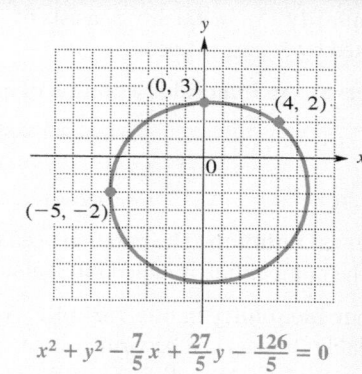

$$x^2 + y^2 - \frac{7}{5}x + \frac{27}{5}y - \frac{126}{5} = 0$$

51. Let $x = 2$ and $y = 1$ in the general equation $x^2 + y^2 + ax + by + c = 0$ to find an equation in a, b, and c.

52. Let $x = -1$ and $y = 0$ to find a second equation in a, b, and c.

53. Let $x = 3$ and $y = 3$ to find a third equation in a, b, and c.

54. Form a system of three equations using the answers from **Exercises 51–53.** Solve the system to find the values of a, b, and c.

55. Use the values of a, b, and c from **Exercise 54** and the form of the equation of a circle given above to write an equation of the circle passing through the given points.

56. Use the concepts of **Exercises 51–55** to find an equation of the circle passing through the points $(-1, 5)$, $(6, 6)$, and $(7, -1)$.

Chapter 8 *Summary*

Key Terms

8.1

linear (first-degree) equation in one variable A linear equation in one variable (here x) can be written in the form $Ax + B = C$, where A, B, and C are real numbers and $A \neq 0$.

solution A solution of an equation is a number that makes the equation true when substituted for the variable.

solution set The solution set of an equation is the set of all its solutions.

equivalent equations Equivalent equations are equations that have the same solution set.

conditional equation An equation that is true only for certain value(s) of the variable is a conditional equation.

identity An equation that is satisfied by every valid replacement of the variable is an identity.

contradiction An equation that has no solution (that is, its solution set is $\varnothing$) is a contradiction.

inequality An inequality consists of algebraic expressions related by $<$, $>$, $\leq$, or $\geq$.

interval An **interval** is a portion of a number line.

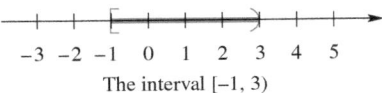

The interval $[-1, 3)$

interval notation The notation used to indicate an interval on the number line is called interval notation.

linear inequality in one variable A linear inequality in one variable (here x) can be written in the form $Ax + B < C$, $Ax + B \leq C$, $Ax + B > C$, or $Ax + B \geq C$, where A, B, and C are real numbers and $A \neq 0$.

equivalent inequalities Equivalent inequalities are inequalities with the same solution set.

8.2

intersection The intersection of two sets A and B is the set of elements that belong to both A and B.

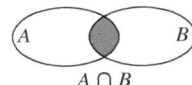

$A \cap B$

compound inequality A compound inequality is formed by joining two inequalities with a connective word such as *and* or *or*.

union The union of two sets A and B is the set of elements that belong to either A or B (or both).

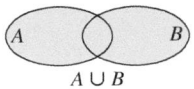

$A \cup B$

8.3

absolute value equation; absolute value inequality Absolute value equations and inequalities involve the absolute value of a variable expression and generally take the form $|ax + b| = k$, $|ax + b| > k$, or $|ax + b| < k$.

8.4

ordered pair An ordered pair is a pair of numbers written within parentheses. The *order* in which the numbers are written is important.

origin When two number lines intersect at a right angle, the origin is the common 0 point, with coordinates $(0, 0)$.

x-axis The horizontal number line in a rectangular coordinate system is the x-axis.

y-axis The vertical number line in a rectangular coordinate system is the y-axis.

rectangular coordinate system Two number lines that intersect at a right angle at their 0 points form a rectangular (Cartesian) coordinate system.

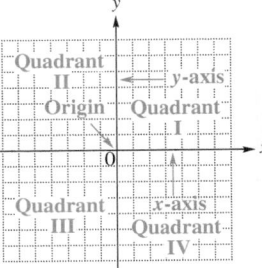

Rectangular coordinate system

components The two numbers in an ordered pair are the components of the ordered pair.

plot To plot an ordered pair is to locate it on a rectangular coordinate system.

coordinate Each number in an ordered pair represents a coordinate of the corresponding point.

quadrant A quadrant is one of the four regions in the plane determined by a rectangular coordinate system.

graph of an equation The graph of an equation is the set of points corresponding to all ordered pairs that satisfy the equation.

first-degree equation A first-degree equation has no term with a variable to a power greater than one.

linear equation in two variables A first-degree equation with two variables is a linear equation in two variables.

x-intercept The point where a line intersects the x-axis is the x-intercept.

y-intercept The point where a line intersects the y-axis is the y-intercept.

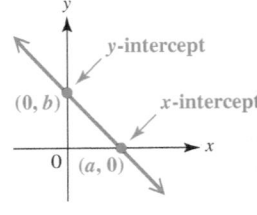

rise The rise of a line is the vertical change between two points on the line.

run The run of a line is the horizontal change between two points on the line.

slope The ratio of the change in y compared to the change in x $\left(\frac{\text{rise}}{\text{run}}\right)$ along a line is the slope of the line.

8.5

system of equations Two or more equations that are to be solved at the same time form a system of equations.

linear system A linear system is a system of equations that contains only linear equations.

solution set of a system All ordered pairs that satisfy all the equations of a system at the same time make up the solution set of the system.

consistent system A system is consistent if it has a solution.

independent equations Independent equations are equations whose graphs are different lines.

inconsistent system A system is inconsistent if it has no solution.

dependent equations Dependent equations are equations whose graphs are the same line.

New Symbols

$\varnothing$	empty (null) set	$\cap$	set intersection	(x_1, y_1)	subscript notation
∞	infinity	$\cup$	set union		(read "x-sub-one, y-sub-one")
$-\infty$	negative infinity	(x, y)	ordered pair	m	slope
$(-\infty, \infty)$	set of real numbers			(x, y, z)	ordered triple

Test Your Word Power

See how well you have learned the vocabulary in this chapter.

1 An **equation** is
A. an algebraic expression
B. an expression with fractions
C. an expression that uses any of the four basic operations or the operations of raising to powers or taking roots on any collection of variables and numbers
D. a statement that two algebraic expressions are equal.

2 A **solution set** is the set of numbers that make
A. an expression undefined
B. an equation false
C. an equation true
D. an expression equal to 0.

3 An **inequality** is
A. a statement that two algebraic expressions are equal
B. a point on a number line
C. an equation with no solutions

D. a statement consisting of algebraic expressions related by $<$, $\le$, $>$, or $\ge$.

4 The **intersection** of two sets A and B is the set of elements that belong
A. to both A and B
B. to either A or B, or both
C. to either A or B, but not both
D. to just A.

5 The **union** of two sets A and B is the set of elements that belong
A. to both A and B
B. to either A or B, or both
C. to either A or B, but not both
D. to just B.

6 A **linear equation in two variables** is an equation that can be written in the form
A. $Ax + By < C$
B. $ax = b$

C. $y = x^2$
D. $Ax + By = C$.

7 The **slope** of a line is
A. the measure of the run over the rise of the line
B. the distance between two points on the line
C. the ratio of the change in y to the change in x along the line
D. the horizontal change compared to the vertical change of two points on the line.

8 A **system of equations** consists of
A. at least two equations with different variables
B. two or more equations that have an infinite number of solutions
C. two or more equations that are to be solved at the same time
D. two or more inequalities that are to be solved.

Answers to Test Your Word Power

1. D; *Examples:* $2a + 3 = 7$, $3y = -8$, $x^2 = 4$

2. C; *Example:* $\{8\}$ is the solution set of $2x + 5 = 21$.

3. D; *Examples:* $x < 5, 7 + 2k \ge 11, -5 < 2z - 1 \le 3$

4. A; *Example:* If $A = \{2, 4, 6, 8\}$ and $B = \{1, 2, 3\}$, $A \cap B = \{2\}$.

5. B; *Example:* Using sets A and B from Answer 4, $A \cup B = \{1, 2, 3, 4, 6, 8\}$.

6. D; *Examples:* $3x + 2y = 6, x = y - 7, 4x = y$

7. C; *Example:* The line through $(3, 6)$ and $(5, 4)$ has slope $\frac{4 - 6}{5 - 3} = \frac{-2}{2} = -1$.

8. C; *Example:* $\begin{array}{l} 3x - y = 3 \\ 2x + y = 7 \end{array}$

Quick Review

Concepts

8.1 Review of Solving Linear Equations and Inequalities in One Variable

Solving a Linear Equation in One Variable

Step 1 Simplify each side separately.
- Clear any parentheses.
- Clear any fractions or decimals.
- Combine like terms.

Step 2 Isolate the variable terms on one side.

Step 3 Isolate the variable.

Step 4 Check.

Solving a Linear Inequality in One Variable

Step 1 Simplify each side separately.
- Clear any parentheses.
- Clear any fractions or decimals.
- Combine like terms.

Step 2 Isolate the variable terms on one side.

Step 3 Isolate the variable (here x) to write the inequality in one of these forms, where k is a constant.

$$x < k, \quad x \leq k, \quad x > k, \quad \text{or} \quad x \geq k$$

If an inequality is multiplied or divided by a negative number, then the direction of the inequality symbol must be reversed.

8.2 Set Operations and Compound Inequalities

Solving a Compound Inequality

Step 1 Solve each inequality in the compound inequality individually.

Step 2 If the inequalities are joined with *and*, the solution set is the intersection of the two individual solution sets.

If the inequalities are joined with *or*, the solution set is the union of the two individual solution sets.

Examples

Solve each equation or inequality.

$$4(8 - 3t) = 32 - 8(t + 2)$$

$32 - 12t = 32 - 8t - 16$	Distributive property
$32 - 12t = 16 - 8t$	Combine like terms.
$32 - 12t + 12t = 16 - 8t + 12t$	Add $12t$.
$32 = 16 + 4t$	Combine like terms.
$32 - 16 = 16 + 4t - 16$	Subtract 16.
$16 = 4t$	Combine like terms.
$\dfrac{16}{4} = \dfrac{4t}{4}$	Divide by 4.
$4 = t$	

To check, substitute 4 for t in the original equation.
Solution set: $\{4\}$

$3(x + 2) - 5x \leq 12$	
$3x + 6 - 5x \leq 12$	Distributive property
$-2x + 6 \leq 12$	Combine like terms.
$-2x + 6 - 6 \leq 12 - 6$	Subtract 6.
$-2x \leq 6$	Combine like terms.
$\dfrac{-2x}{-2} \geq \dfrac{6}{-2}$	Divide by -2. Change $\leq$ to $\geq$.
$x \geq -3$	

Solution set: $[-3, \infty)$

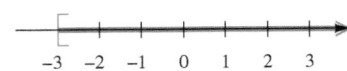

Solve each compound inequality.

$$x + 1 > 2 \quad \text{and} \quad 2x < 6$$
$$x > 1 \quad \text{and} \quad x < 3$$

Solution set: $(1, 3)$

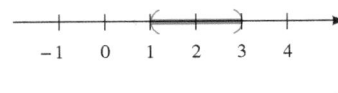

$$2x \leq -2 \quad \text{or} \quad -4x \leq -16$$
$$\frac{2x}{2} \leq \frac{-2}{2} \quad \text{or} \quad \frac{-4x}{-4} \geq \frac{-16}{-4}$$
$$x \leq -1 \quad \text{or} \quad x \geq 4$$

Solution set: $(-\infty, -1] \cup [4, \infty)$

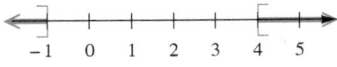

| **Concepts** | **Examples** |

8.3 Absolute Value Equations and Inequalities

Solving Absolute Value Equations and Inequalities

Let k be a positive number.

Case 1 To solve $|ax + b| = k$, solve the compound equation

$$ax + b = k \quad \text{or} \quad ax + b = -k.$$

Case 2 To solve $|ax + b| > k$, solve the compound inequality

$$ax + b > k \quad \text{or} \quad ax + b < -k.$$

Case 3 To solve $|ax + b| < k$, solve the compound inequality

$$-k < ax + b < k.$$

To solve an absolute value equation of the form

$$|ax + b| = |cx + d|,$$

solve the compound equation

$$ax + b = cx + d \quad \text{or} \quad ax + b = -(cx + d).$$

Solve each equation or inequality.

$$|x - 7| = 3 \qquad \text{Case 1}$$

$$x - 7 = 3 \quad \text{or} \quad x - 7 = -3$$

$$x = 10 \quad \text{or} \qquad x = 4 \qquad \text{Add 7.}$$

Solution set: $\{4, 10\}$

$$|x - 7| > 3 \qquad \text{Case 2}$$

$$x - 7 > 3 \quad \text{or} \quad x - 7 < -3$$

$$x > 10 \quad \text{or} \qquad x < 4 \qquad \text{Add 7.}$$

Solution set: $(-\infty, 4) \cup (10, \infty)$

$$|x - 7| < 3 \qquad \text{Case 3}$$

$$-3 < x - 7 < 3$$

$$4 < \quad x \quad < 10 \qquad \text{Add 7 to each part.}$$

Solution set: $(4, 10)$

$$|x + 2| = |2x - 6|$$

$$x + 2 = 2x - 6 \quad \text{or} \quad x + 2 = -(2x - 6)$$

$$-x = -8 \qquad \qquad x + 2 = -2x + 6$$

$$x = 8 \qquad \qquad \qquad 3x = 4$$

$$x = \frac{4}{3}$$

Solution set: $\left\{ \frac{4}{3}, 8 \right\}$

8.4 Review of Graphing Linear Equations in Two Variables; Slope

Finding Intercepts

To find the x-intercept, let $y = 0$ and solve for x.

To find the y-intercept, let $x = 0$ and solve for y.

Find the intercepts and graph the equation $2x + 3y = 12$.

$2x + 3(0) = 12$ Let $y = 0$. | $2(0) + 3y = 12$ Let $x = 0$.

$\qquad 2x = 12 \qquad\qquad\qquad\qquad 3y = 12$

$\qquad\; x = 6 \qquad\qquad\qquad\qquad\; y = 4$

The x-intercept is $(6, 0)$. | The y-intercept is $(0, 4)$.

x	y
0	4
3	2
6	0

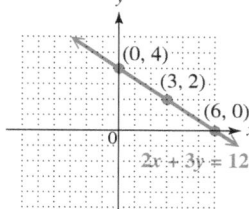

Concepts

The slope m of the line passing through the points (x_1, y_1) and (x_2, y_2) is defined as follows.

$$\text{slope } m = \frac{\text{rise}}{\text{run}} = \frac{\text{change in } y}{\text{change in } x} = \frac{y_2 - y_1}{x_2 - x_1}$$
$$(\text{where } x_1 \neq x_2)$$

A horizontal line has slope 0.

A vertical line has undefined slope.

8.5 Review of Systems of Linear Equations in Two Variables

Solving a Linear System by Substitution

Step 1 Solve one of the equations for either variable.

Step 2 Substitute for that variable in the other equation. The result should be an equation with just one variable.

Step 3 Solve the equation from Step 2.

Step 4 Find the value of the other variable by substituting the result from Step 3 into the equation from Step 1.

Step 5 Check the values in *both* of the *original* equations. Then write the solution set as a set containing an ordered pair.

Solving a Linear System by Elimination

Step 1 Write both equations in standard form.

Step 2 Transform the equations as needed so that the coefficients of one pair of variable terms are opposites.

Step 3 Add the new equations. The sum should be an equation with just one variable.

Step 4 Solve the equation from Step 3.

Step 5 Find the value of the other variable by substituting the result from Step 4 into either of the original equations.

Step 6 Check the values in *both* of the *original* equations. Then write the solution set as a set containing an ordered pair.

Examples

Find the slope of the graph of $2x + 3y = 12$.
Use the intercepts $(6, 0)$ and $(0, 4)$ and the slope formula.

$$m = \frac{4 - 0}{0 - 6} = \frac{4}{-6} = -\frac{2}{3} \qquad \begin{array}{l} (x_1, y_1) = (6, 0) \\ (x_2, y_2) = (0, 4) \end{array}$$

The graph of the line $y = -5$ has slope $m = 0$.

The graph of the line $x = 3$ has undefined slope.

Solve by substitution.

$$\begin{array}{ll} 4x - y = 7 & (1) \\ 3x + 2y = 30 & (2) \end{array}$$

Solve for y in equation (1).

$$y = 4x - 7$$

Substitute $4x - 7$ for y in equation (2), and solve for x.

$$\begin{array}{ll} 3x + 2y = 30 & (2) \\ 3x + 2(4x - 7) = 30 & \text{Let } y = 4x - 7. \\ 3x + 8x - 14 = 30 & \text{Distributive property} \\ 11x - 14 = 30 & \text{Combine like terms.} \\ 11x = 44 & \text{Add 14.} \\ x = 4 & \text{Divide by 11.} \end{array}$$

Substitute 4 for x in the equation $y = 4x - 7$ to find y.

$$\begin{array}{ll} y = 4(4) - 7 & \text{Let } x = 4. \\ y = 9 & \text{Multiply. Subtract.} \end{array}$$

Check to verify that $\{(4, 9)\}$ is the solution set.

Solve by elimination.

$$\begin{array}{ll} 5x + y = 2 & (1) \\ 2x - 3y = 11 & (2) \end{array}$$

To eliminate y, multiply equation (1) by 3, and add the result to equation (2).

$$\begin{array}{ll} 15x + 3y = 6 & \text{3 times equation (1)} \\ \underline{2x - 3y = 11} & (2) \\ 17x = 17 & \text{Add.} \\ x = 1 & \text{Divide by 17.} \end{array}$$

Let $x = 1$ in equation (1), and solve for y.

$$\begin{array}{ll} 5(1) + y = 2 & (1) \\ y = -3 & \text{Multiply. Subtract 5.} \end{array}$$

Check to verify that $\{(1, -3)\}$ is the solution set.

Concepts

Examples

Special Systems

If the result of the addition step (Step 3) is a false statement, such as $0 = 4$, the graphs are parallel lines and *there is no solution. The solution set is* $\varnothing$.

If the result is a true statement, such as $0 = 0$, the graphs are the same line, and an *infinite number of ordered pairs are solutions. The solution set is written in set-builder notation as*

$$\{(x, y) \mid \underline{\hspace{2cm}}\},$$

where a form of the equation is written in the blank.

$$\begin{array}{r} x - 2y = 6 \\ -x + 2y = -2 \\ \hline 0 = 4 \end{array}$$

Inconsistent system

Solution set: $\varnothing$

$$\begin{array}{r} x - 2y = 6 \\ -x + 2y = -6 \\ \hline 0 = 0 \end{array}$$

Dependent equations

Solution set: $\{(x, y) \mid x - 2y = 6\}$

8.6 Systems of Linear Equations in Three Variables; Applications

Solving a Linear System in Three Variables

Step 1   Select a focus variable, preferably one with coefficient 1 or -1, and a working equation.

Step 2   Eliminate the focus variable, using the working equation and one of the equations of the system.

Step 3   Eliminate the focus variable again, using the working equation and the remaining equation of the system.

Step 4   Solve the system of two equations in two variables formed by the equations from Steps 2 and 3.

Step 5   Find the value of the remaining variable.

Step 6   Check the values in *each* of the *original* equations of the system. Then write the solution set as a set containing an ordered triple.

Solve the system.

$$\begin{array}{rl} x + 2y - z = 6 & (1) \\ x + y + z = 6 & (2) \\ 2x + y - z = 7 & (3) \end{array}$$

We choose z as the focus variable and (2) as the working equation.

Add equations (1) and (2).

$$2x + 3y = 12 \quad (4)$$

Add equations (2) and (3).

$$3x + 2y = 13 \quad (5)$$

Use equations (4) and (5) to eliminate x.

$$\begin{array}{rl} -6x - 9y = -36 & \text{Multiply (4) by } -3. \\ 6x + 4y = 26 & \text{Multiply (5) by 2.} \\ \hline -5y = -10 & \text{Add.} \\ y = 2 & \text{Divide by } -5. \end{array}$$

To find x, substitute 2 for y in equation (4).

$$\begin{array}{rl} 2x + 3(2) = 12 & \text{Let } y = 2 \text{ in (4).} \\ 2x + 6 = 12 & \text{Multiply.} \\ 2x = 6 & \text{Subtract 6.} \\ x = 3 & \text{Divide by 2.} \end{array}$$

Substitute 3 for x and 2 for y in working equation (2).

$$\begin{array}{rl} x + y + z = 6 & (2) \\ 3 + 2 + z = 6 & \text{Substitute.} \\ z = 1 & \text{Subtract 5.} \end{array}$$

Check to verify that $\{(3, 2, 1)\}$ is the solution set.

Chapter 8 Review Exercises

8.1 *Solve each equation.*

1. $-(8 + 3x) + 5 = 2x + 6$

2. $-3x + 2(4x + 5) = 10$

3. $\dfrac{m-2}{4} + \dfrac{m+2}{2} = 8$

4. $0.05x + 0.03(1200 - x) = 42$

Solve each equation. Decide whether it is a conditional equation, *an* identity, *or a* contradiction.

5. $7r - 3(2r - 5) + 5 + 3r = 4r + 20$

6. $8p - 4p - (p - 7) + 9p + 13 = 12p$

7. $-2r + 6(r - 1) + 3r - (4 - r) = -(r + 5) - 5$

8. $\dfrac{2}{3}x + \dfrac{5}{8}x = \dfrac{31}{24}x$

Solve each inequality. Give solution sets in both interval and graph forms.

9. $-\dfrac{2}{3}x < 6$

10. $4x - 3 \le -19$

11. $-5x - 4 \ge 11$

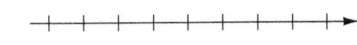

12. $5 - (6 - 4t) \ge 2t - 7$

13. $8 \le 3x - 1 < 14$

14. $-4 < -2z + 3 < 9$

8.2 *Let* $A = \{1, 2, 3, 4\}$, $B = \{1, 3, 6, 8\}$, *and* $C = \{1, 6, 8, 9\}$. *Find each set.*

15. $A \cap B$

16. $A \cap C$

17. $B \cup C$

18. $A \cup C$

Solve each compound inequality. Give solution sets in both interval and graph forms.

19. $x > 4$ and $x < 7$

20. $x + 4 > 12$ and $x - 2 < 12$

21. $x > 5$ or $x \leq -3$

22. $x \geq -2$ or $x < 2$

23. $x - 4 > 6$ and $x + 3 \leq 10$

24. $-5x + 1 \geq 11$ or $3x + 5 \geq 26$

Express each set in simplest interval form.

25. $(-3, \infty) \cap (-\infty, 4)$

26. $(-\infty, 6) \cap (-\infty, 2)$

27. $(4, \infty) \cup (9, \infty)$

28. $(1, 2) \cup (1, \infty)$

8.3 *Solve each absolute value equation.*

29. $|x| = 7$

30. $|x + 2| = 9$

31. $|3k - 7| = 8$

32. $|z - 4| = -12$

33. $|2k - 7| + 4 = 11$

34. $|4a + 2| - 7 = -3$

35. $|3p + 1| = |p + 2|$

36. $|5x + 8| = 0$

Solve each absolute value inequality. Give solution sets in both interval and graph forms.

37. $|x| < 12$

38. $|-x + 6| \leq 7$

39. $|2p + 5| \leq 1$

40. $|x + 1| \geq -3$

41. $|5r - 1| > 9$

42. $|3x + 6| \geq 0$

8.4 *Find the x- and y-intercepts. Then graph each equation.*

43. $4x + 3y = 12$

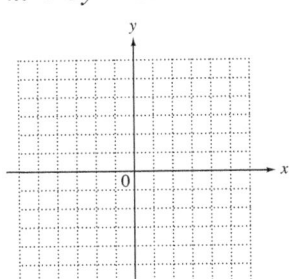

44. $x = 5$

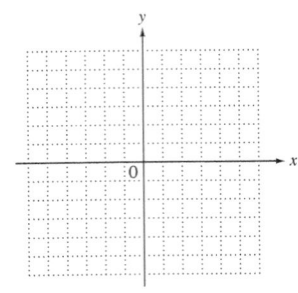

45. $y - 2x = 0$

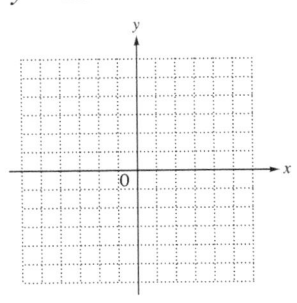

46. CONCEPT CHECK Determine whether the slope of the line is *positive, negative,* 0, *or undefined.*

(a)

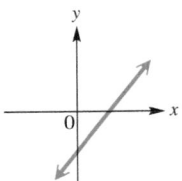

(b)

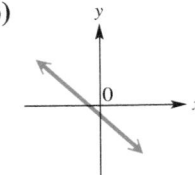

(c)

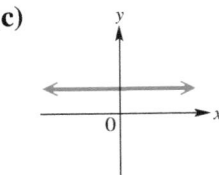

(d)

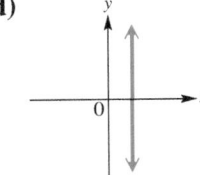

Find the slope of each line.

47. Through $(-1, 2)$ and $(4, -6)$

48. $y = 2x + 3$

49. $-3x + 4y = 5$

50. $y = 4$

8.5 *Solve each system by graphing.*

51. $\begin{aligned} x + 3y &= 8 \\ 2x - y &= 2 \end{aligned}$

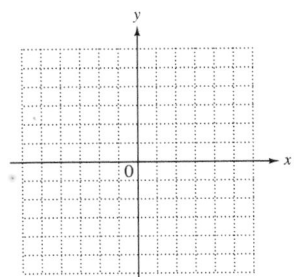

52. $\begin{aligned} 2x + y &= -8 \\ x - 4y &= -4 \end{aligned}$

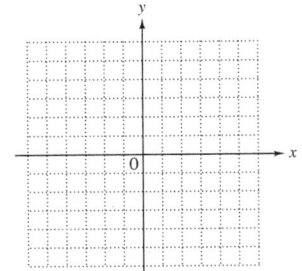

53. $\begin{aligned} x - y &= 2 \\ x + 2y &= -1 \end{aligned}$

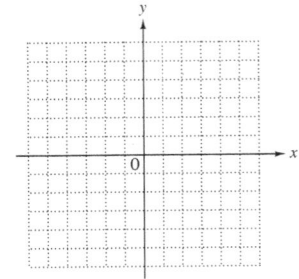

54. CONCEPT CHECK Which ordered pair is a solution of the following system?

$$3x + 2y = 6$$
$$2x - y = 11$$

A. $(2, 0)$ **B.** $(0, -11)$ **C.** $(4, -3)$ **D.** $(3, -2)$

Solve each system using the substitution method.

55. $3x + y = -4$

$\quad x = \dfrac{2}{3}y$

56. $9x - y = -4$

$\quad y = x + 4$

57. $-5x + 2y = -2$

$\quad x + 6y = 26$

58. $5x + \ y = 12$

$\quad 2x - 2y = 0$

Solve each system using the elimination method. If a system is inconsistent or has dependent equations, say so.

59. $\ 6x + 5y = 4$

$\quad -4x + 2y = 8$

60. $\dfrac{1}{6}x + \dfrac{1}{6}y = -\dfrac{1}{2}$

$\quad x - \ y = -9$

61. $4x + 5y = 9$

$\quad 3x + 7y = -1$

62. $-3x + y = 6$

$\quad 2y = 12 + 6x$

63. $\quad 5x - 4y = 2$

$\quad -10x + 8y = 7$

64. $\quad x - 4y = -4$

$\quad 3x + \ y = 1$

8.6   *Solve each system of equations. If a system is inconsistent or has dependent equations, say so.*

65. $\quad 2x + 3y - \ z = -16$

$\quad\ \ x + 2y + 2z = -3$

$\quad -3x + \ y + \ z = -5$

66. $\quad 3x - \ y - \ z = -8$

$\quad\ \ 4x + 2y + 3z = 15$

$\quad -6x + 2y + 2z = 10$

67. $5x - \ y = 26$

$\quad 4y + 3z = -4$

$\quad x + \ z = 5$

68. $4x - \ y = 2$

$\quad 3y + \ z = 9$

$\quad x + 2z = 7$

69. $\quad 3x - 4y + \ z = 8$

$\quad -6x + 8y - 2z = -16$

$\quad \dfrac{3}{2}x - 2y + \dfrac{1}{2}z = 4$

70. $\quad 2x - \ y + 3z = 0$

$\quad\ \ 5x + \ y - \ z = 0$

$\quad -2x + 3y + 4z = 0$

Solve each problem using a system of equations.

71. The sum of the measures of the angles of a triangle is 180°. The largest angle measures 10° less than the sum of the other two. The measure of the middle-sized angle is the average of the other two. Find the measures of the three angles.

72. In the 2016 Summer Olympics, China, the United States, and Great Britain won a combined total of 258 medals. China won 51 fewer medals than the United States, while Great Britain won 54 fewer medals than the United States. How many medals did each country win? (Data from www.rio2016.com)

Chapter 8 *Mixed Review Exercises*

Solve each equation or inequality.

1. $(7 - 2k) + 3(5 - 3k) = k + 8$

2. $-5(6p + 4) - 2p = -32p + 14$

3. $x < 5$ and $x \geq -4$

4. $-5r \geq -10$

5. $|7x - 2| > 9$

6. $|2x - 10| = 20$

7. $|m + 3| \leq 13$

8. $x \geq -2$ or $x < 4$

9. $|m - 1| = |2m + 3|$

10. CONCEPT CHECK If $k < 0$, find the solution set of each of the following.

    (a) $|5x + 3| > k$

    (b) $|5x + 3| < k$

    (c) $|5x + 3| = k$

11. Complete the table for $3x + 2y = 6$ and then graph the equation.

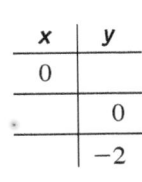

x	y
0	
	0
	-2

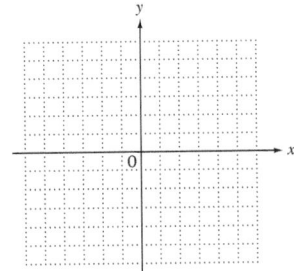

12. CONCEPT CHECK Which system, A or B, would be easier to solve using the substitution method? Why?

    A. $5x - 3y = 7$
          $2x + 8y = 3$

    B. $7x + 2y = 4$
          $y = -3x + 1$

Solve each system using the method of your choice.

13. $x = 7y + 10$
    $2x + 3y = 3$

14. $x + 4y = 17$
    $-3x + 2y = -9$

15. $-7x + 3y = 12$
    $5x + 2y = 8$

16. $x + 3y - 6z = 7$
    $2x - y + z = 1$
    $x + 2y + 2z = -1$

17. $x + y - z = 0$
    $2y - z = 1$
    $2x + 3y - 4z = -4$

18. $2x + 5y - z = 12$
    $-x + y - 4z = -10$
    $-8x - 20y + 4z = 31$

Solve each equation. In Problems 4–6, decide whether the equation is a conditional *equation,* an identity, *or a* contradiction.

1. $3(2x - 2) - 4(x + 6) = 4x + 8$

2. $0.08x + 0.06(x + 9) = 1.24$

3. $\dfrac{x + 6}{10} + \dfrac{x - 4}{15} = 1$

4. $3x - (2 - x) + 4x + 2 = 8x + 3$

5. $\dfrac{x}{3} + 7 = \dfrac{5x}{6} - 2 - \dfrac{x}{2} + 9$

6. $-4(2x - 6) = 5x + 24 - 7x$

Solve each inequality. Give solution sets in both interval and graph forms.

7. $2 + 4x \le 5x$

8. $4 - 6(x + 3) \le -2 - 3(x + 6) + 3x$

9. $-\dfrac{4}{7}x > -16$

10. $-1 < 3x - 4 < 2$

Let $A = \{1, 2, 5, 7\}$ *and* $B = \{1, 5, 9, 12\}$. *Find each set.*

11. $A \cap B$

12. $A \cup B$

Solve each compound or absolute value inequality. Give solution sets in both interval and graph forms.

13. $3k \ge 6$ and $k - 4 < 5$

14. $-4x \le -24$ or $4x - 2 < 10$

15. $|4x + 3| \le 7$

16. $|5 - 6x| > 12$

17. $|-3x + 4| - 4 < -1$

18. $|7 - x| \le -1$

Solve each absolute value equation.

19. $|3x - 9| = 6$

20. $|3 - 5x| = |2x + 8|$

21. $|4x + 3| + 5 = 4$

22. If $k < 0$, find the solution set of each of the following.

(a) $|8x - 5| < k$

(b) $|8x - 5| > k$

(c) $|8x - 5| = k$

23. Which line has positive slope and negative y-coordinate for its y-intercept?

A.

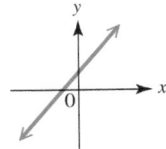

B.

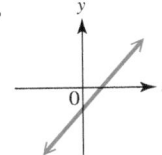

C.

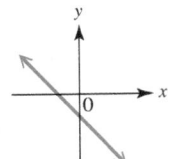

D.

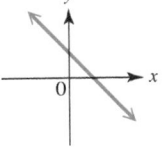

24. Find the x- and y-intercepts of $4x - 3y = -12$. Then graph the equation.

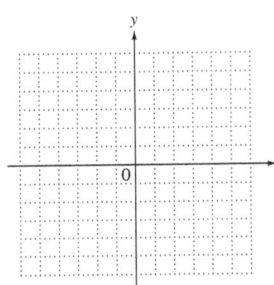

25. Use a graph to solve the system.

$$x + y = 7$$
$$x - y = 5$$

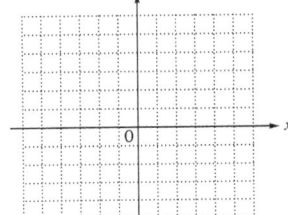

Solve each system of equations. If a system is inconsistent or has dependent equations, say so.

26. $3x + y = 12$
$2x - y = 3$

27. $-5x + 2y = -4$
$6x + 3y = -6$

28. $3x + 4y = 8$
$8y = 7 - 6x$

29. $12x - 5y = 8$
$3x = \dfrac{5}{4}y + 2$

30. $3x + 5y + 3z = 2$
$6x + 5y + z = 0$
$3x + 10y - 2z = 6$

31. $4x + y + z = 11$
$x - y - z = 4$
$y + 2z = 0$

32. The largest angle of a triangle measures 10° less than twice the middle-sized angle. The middle-sized angle measures 5° more than twice the smallest angle. The sum of the measures of the angles of a triangle is 180°. Find the measure of each angle.

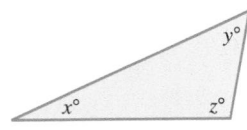

Chapters R–8 *Cumulative Review Exercises*

Simplify each expression.

1. $-2(m - 3)$

2. $-(-4m + 3)$

3. $3x^2 - 4x + 4 + 9x - x^2$

Evaluate for $p = -4$, $q = -2$, and $r = 5$.

4. $-3(2q - 3p)$

5. $8r^2 + q^2$

6. $\dfrac{r}{-p + 2q}$

7. $\dfrac{rp + 6r^2}{p^2 + q - 1}$

Solve.

8. $2z - 5 + 3z = 4 - (z + 2)$

9. $\dfrac{3a - 1}{5} + \dfrac{a + 2}{2} = -\dfrac{3}{10}$

10. $-\dfrac{4}{3}d \geq -5$

11. $3 - 2(m + 3) < 4m$

12. $2k + 4 < 10$ and $3k - 1 > 5$

13. $2k + 4 > 10$ or $3k - 1 < 5$

14. $|5x + 3| - 10 = 3$

15. $|x + 2| < 9$

16. $|2y - 5| \geq 9$

17. $V = lwh$ for h

18. Two planes leave the Dallas–Fort Worth airport at the same time. One travels east at 550 mph, and the other travels west at 500 mph. Assuming no wind, how long will it take for the planes to be 2100 mi apart?

	r	t	d
Eastbound plane	550	x	___
Westbound plane	500	x	___

19. Graph $4x + 2y = -8$.

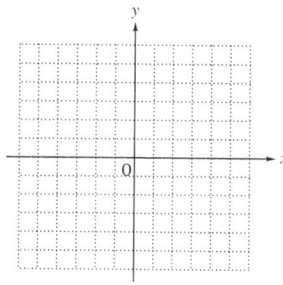

20. Find the slope of the line through the points $(-4, 8)$ and $(-2, 6)$.

21. What is the slope of the line shown here?

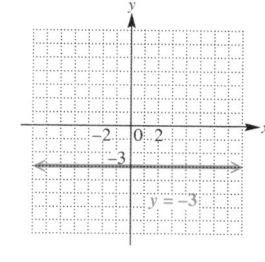

Find the following for the equation $y = 2x + 7$.

22. The slope

23. The x-intercept of its graph

24. The y-intercept of its graph

Solve each system.

25. $3x - 2y = -7$

$\quad 2x + 3y = 17$

26. $2x + 3y - 6z = 5$

$\quad 8x - \ y + 3z = 7$

$\quad 3x + 4y - 3z = 7$

Perform the indicated operations. Assume that variables represent nonzero real numbers.

27. $(3x^2y^{-1})^{-2}(2x^{-3}y)^{-1}$

28. $\dfrac{5m^{-2}y^3}{3m^{-3}y^{-1}}$

Perform the indicated operations.

29. $(3x^3 + 4x^2 - 7)$
$\quad - (2x^3 - 8x^2 + 3x)$

30. $(7x + 3y)^2$

31. $(2p + 3)(5p^2 - 4p - 8)$

Factor.

32. $16w^2 + 50wz - 21z^2$

33. $4y^2 - 36y + 81$

34. $8p^3 + 27$

Solve.

35. $9q^2 = 6q - 1$

36. $6x^2 - 19x - 7 = 0$

37. $\dfrac{1}{x} = \dfrac{1}{x+1} + \dfrac{1}{2}$

Perform the indicated operations, and write the answer in lowest terms.

38. $\dfrac{5}{q} - \dfrac{1}{q}$

39. $\dfrac{3}{7} + \dfrac{4}{r}$

40. $\dfrac{4}{5q - 20} - \dfrac{1}{3q - 12}$

41. $\dfrac{7z^2 + 49z + 70}{16z^2 + 72z - 40} \div \dfrac{3z + 6}{4z^2 - 1}$

42. Simplify the complex fraction $\dfrac{\dfrac{4}{a} + \dfrac{5}{2a}}{\dfrac{7}{6a} - \dfrac{1}{5a}}$.

9

Relations and Functions

Linear equations with graphs that are straight (nonvertical) lines define *linear functions*, one of the topics of this chapter. We use the concept of slope, or steepness, to graph such functions.

9.1 Introduction to Relations and Functions

9.2 Function Notation and Linear Functions

9.3 Polynomial Functions, Operations, and Graphs

9.4 Variation

9.1 | Introduction to Relations and Functions

OBJECTIVES

1. Define and identify relations and functions.
2. Find the domain and range.
3. Identify functions defined by graphs and equations.

OBJECTIVE ▸ 1 Define and identify relations and functions. Consider the relationship illustrated in the following table between number of hours worked and paycheck amount for an hourly worker.

Number of Hours Worked	Paycheck Amount (in dollars)	Ordered Pairs
5	40	⟶ (5, 40)
10	80	⟶ (10, 80)
20	160	⟶ (20, 160)
40	320	⟶ (40, 320)

The data from the table can be represented by a set of ordered pairs.

$$\{(5, 40), (10, 80), (20, 160), (40, 320)\}$$

Number of hours worked ↑ ↑ Paycheck amount in dollars

Each first component of the ordered pairs represents a number of hours worked, and each second component represents the corresponding paycheck amount. Such a set of ordered pairs is a *relation*.

Relation

A **relation** is any set of ordered pairs.

1. Write the relation as a set of ordered pairs.

Year	Average Gas Price per Gallon (in dollars)
2000	1.56
2005	2.34
2010	2.84
2015	3.39

Data from Energy Information Administration.

EXAMPLE 1 Writing Ordered Pairs for a Relation

Write the relation as a set of ordered pairs.

Number of Gallons of Gas	Cost (in dollars)
0	0
1	3.50
2	7.00
3	10.50
4	14.00

The data in the table defines a relation between number of gallons of gas and cost and can be written as the following set of ordered pairs.

$$\{(0, 0), (1, 3.50), (2, 7.00), (3, 10.50), (4, 14.00)\}$$

Number of gallons of gas ↑ ↑ Cost in dollars

◀ Work Problem 1 at the Side.

Answer

1. {(2000, 1.56), (2005, 2.34), (2010, 2.84), (2015, 3.39)}

A *function* is a special kind of relation.

Function

A **function** is a relation in which, for each distinct value of the first component of the ordered pairs of the relation, there is *exactly one* value of the second component.

EXAMPLE 2 Determining Whether Relations Are Functions

Determine whether each relation defines a function.

(a) $F = \{(1, 2), (-2, 4), (3, -1)\}$

Look at the ordered pairs that defined this relation.

For $x = 1$, there is only one value of y, 2.

For $x = -2$, there is only one value of y, 4.

For $x = 3$, there is only one value of y, -1.

Relation F is a function—for each distinct x-value, there is *exactly one* y-value.

(b) $G = \{(-2, -1), (-1, 0), (0, 1), (1, 2), (2, 2)\}$

Relation G is also a function. Although the last two ordered pairs have the same y-value (1 is paired with 2, and 2 is paired with 2), this does not violate the definition of a function. The first components (x-values) are distinct, and each is paired with only one second component (y-value).

(c) $H = \{(-4, 1), (-2, 1), (-2, 0)\}$

In relation H, the last two ordered pairs have the **same** x-value paired with **two different** y-values (-2 is paired with both 1 and 0). H is a relation, but *not* a function.

In a function, no two ordered pairs have the same first component and different second components.

Different y-values

Relation $H = \{(-4, 1), (-2, 1), (-2, 0)\}$ Not a function

Same x-value

——————————————— **Work Problem 2 at the Side.** ▶

Relations may be defined in several different ways.

• **A relation may be defined as a set of ordered pair. (See Example 2.)**

Relation $F = \{(1, 2), (-2, 4), (3, -1)\}$ Function

Relation $H = \{(-4, 1), (-2, 1), (-2, 0)\}$ Not a function

• **A relation may be defined as a correspondence or *mapping*.**

See **Figure 1.** In the mapping for relation F from **Example 2(a)**, 1 is mapped to 2, -2 is mapped to 4, and 3 is mapped to -1. Thus, F is a function—each first component of an ordered pair is paired with exactly one second component.

In the mapping for relation H from **Example 2(c)**, which is *not* a function, the first component -2 is paired with two different second components.

2 Determine whether each relation defines a function.

(a) $\{(0, 3), (-1, 2), (-1, 3)\}$

The x-value _____ is paired with both _____ and _____. This relation (*is / is not*) a function.

(b) $\{(2, -2), (4, -4), (6, -6)\}$

(c) $\{(-1, 5), (0, 5)\}$

(d) $\{(1, 5), (2, 3), (1, 7), (-2, 3)\}$

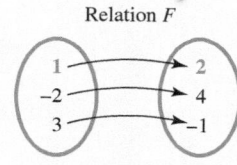

Relation F

F is a function.

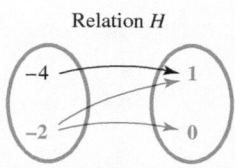

Relation H

H is not a function.

Figure 1

Answers

2. (a) -1; 2; 3; is not **(b)** function
(c) function **(d)** not a function

- **A relation may be defined as a table.**
- **A relation may be defined as a graph.**

  Figure 2 includes a table and graph for relation F from **Example 2(a).**

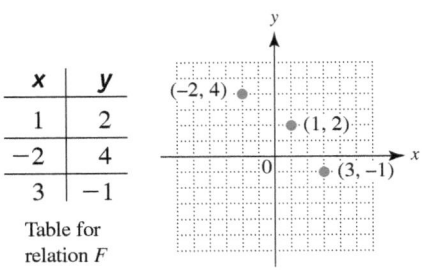

x	y
1	2
−2	4
3	−1

Table for
relation F

Graph of relation F

Figure 2

- **A relation may be defined as an equation (or rule).**

  The solutions of an equation give an infinite set of ordered pairs. For example, if the value of y is twice the value of x, the equation is

  $$y = 2x.$$

  There are an infinite number of ordered-pair solutions (x, y), which can be represented by the graph in **Figure 3.**

  In the equation $y = 2x$, the value of y *depends* on the value of x. Thus, the variable y is the **dependent variable.** The variable x is the **independent variable.**

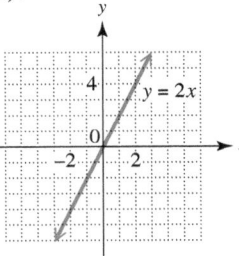

Graph of the relation
$y = 2x$

Figure 3

$$\text{Dependent variable} \longrightarrow y = 2x \longleftarrow \text{Independent variable}$$

An equation tells how to determine the value of the dependent variable for a specific value of the independent variable.

> **Note**
>
> An equation that describes the relationship given at the beginning of this section between number of hours worked and paycheck amount is
>
> $$y = 8x. \qquad \text{8 represents the hourly rate, \$8.}$$
>
> Paycheck amount y depends on number of hours worked x. Thus, paycheck amount is the dependent variable, and number of hours worked is the independent variable.

In a function, there is exactly one value of the dependent variable, the second component, for each value of the independent variable, the first component.

> **Note**
>
> Another way to think of a function relationship is to think of the independent variable as an **input** and the dependent variable as an **output.** This **input-output (function) machine** illustrates the relationship between number of hours worked and paycheck amount.
>
>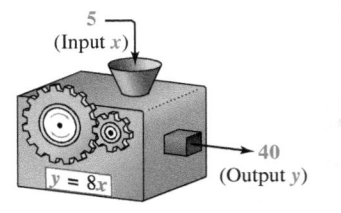
>
> Function machine

OBJECTIVE ▶ ② Find the domain and range.

Domain and Range

For every relation defined by a set of ordered pairs (x, y), there are two important sets of elements.

- The set of all values of the independent variable (x) is the **domain.**
- The set of all values of the dependent variable (y) is the **range.**

EXAMPLE 3   **Finding Domains and Ranges of Relations**

Give the domain and range of each relation. Decide whether the relation defines a function.

(a) $\{(3, -1), (4, 2), (4, 5), (6, 8)\}$

> List 4 only once.

Domain: $\{3, 4, 6\}$ Set of x-values

Range: $\{-1, 2, 5, 8\}$ Set of y-values

This relation is not a function because the same x-value 4 is paired with two different y-values, 2 and 5.

(b)
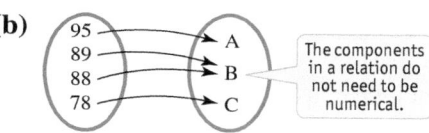

The components in a relation do not need to be numerical.

This mapping represents the following set of ordered pairs.

$\{(95, A), (89, B), (88, B), (78, C)\}$

Domain: $\{95, 89, 88, 78\}$ Set of first components

Range: $\{A, B, C\}$ Set of second components

The mapping defines a function—each domain value corresponds to exactly one range value.

(c)

x	y
−5	2
0	2
5	2

This table represents the following set of ordered pairs.

$\{(-5, 2), (0, 2), (5, 2)\}$

Domain: $\{-5, 0, 5\}$ Set of x-values

Range: $\{2\}$ Set of y-values

The table defines a function—each distinct x-value corresponds to exactly one y-value (even though it is the same y-value).

——————————————— **Work Problem** ❸ **at the Side.** ▶

③ Give the domain and range of each relation. Decide whether the relation defines a function.

(a) $\{(2, 2), (2, 5), (4, 8)\}$

(b)
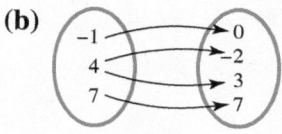

(c)

Number of Hours Worked	Paycheck Amount (in dollars)
5	40
10	80
20	160
40	320

Answers

3. **(a)** domain: $\{2, 4\}$;
    range: $\{2, 5, 8\}$;
    not a function
   (b) domain: $\{-1, 4, 7\}$;
    range: $\{0, -2, 3, 7\}$;
    not a function
   (c) domain: $\{5, 10, 20, 40\}$;
    range: $\{40, 80, 160, 320\}$;
    function

④ Give the domain and range of each relation.

(a)

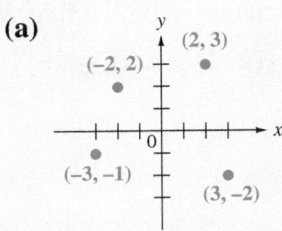

A graph gives a "picture" of a relation and can be used to determine its domain and range.

> **Note**
>
> Pay particular attention to the use of color to interpret domain and range in **Example 4**—blue for domain and red for range.

EXAMPLE 4 Finding Domains and Ranges from Graphs

Give the domain and range of each relation.

(a)

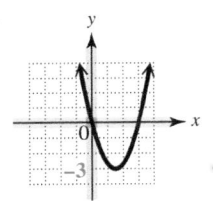

This relation includes the five ordered pairs that are graphed.

$$\{(-1, 1), (0, -1), (1, 2), (4, -3), (5, 2)\}$$

Domain: $\{-1, 0, 1, 4, 5\}$ Set of x-values

Range: $\{1, -1, 2, -3\}$ Set of y-values

> List 2 only once.

(b)

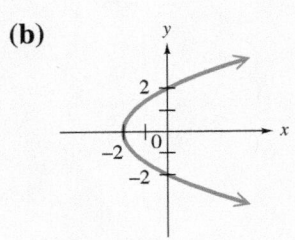

(b)

The x-values of the ordered pairs that form the graph include all numbers between -4 and 4, inclusive, as shown in blue. The y-values include all numbers between -6 and 6, inclusive, as shown in red.

Domain: $[-4, 4]$ Use interval
Range: $[-6, 6]$ notation.

(c)

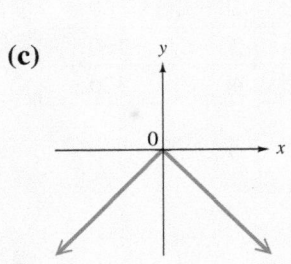

(c)

The arrowheads on the graphed line indicate that the line extends indefinitely left and right, as well as up and down. Therefore, both the domain, shown in blue, (the set of x-values) and the range, shown in red, (the set of y-values) include all real numbers.

Domain: $(-\infty, \infty)$ Range: $(-\infty, \infty)$

(d)

The graphed curve extends indefinitely left and right, as well as upward. The domain, shown in blue, includes all real numbers. Because there is a least y-value, -3, the range, shown in red, includes all numbers greater than or equal to -3.

Domain: $(-\infty, \infty)$ Range: $[-3, \infty)$

◀ **Work Problem ④ at the Side.**

Answers

4. (a) domain: $\{-3, -2, 2, 3\}$;
   range: $\{-2, -1, 2, 3\}$
   (b) domain: $[-2, \infty)$; range: $(-\infty, \infty)$
   (c) domain: $(-\infty, \infty)$; range: $(-\infty, 0]$

OBJECTIVE ③ Identify functions defined by graphs and equations. Because each value of x in a function corresponds to only one value of y, any vertical line drawn through the graph of a function must intersect the graph in at most one point. This is the *vertical line test* for a function.

Figure 4 illustrates the vertical line test with the graphs of two relations.

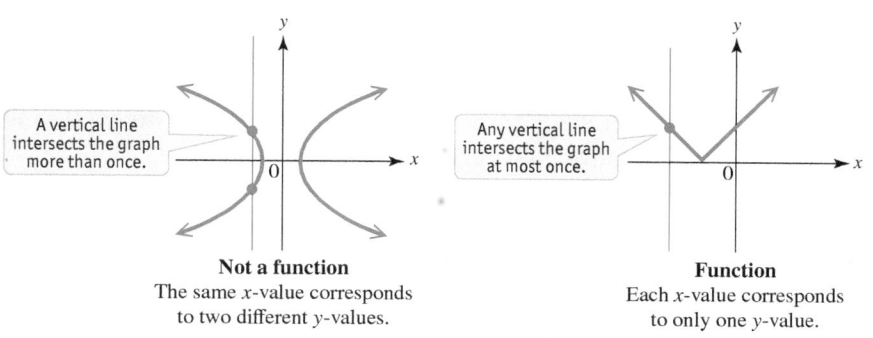

A vertical line intersects the graph more than once.

Any vertical line intersects the graph at most once.

Not a function
The same *x*-value corresponds to two different *y*-values.

Function
Each *x*-value corresponds to only one *y*-value.

Figure 4

Vertical Line Test

If every vertical line intersects the graph of a relation in no more than one point, then the relation represents a function.

EXAMPLE 5   Using the Vertical Line Test

Use the vertical line test to determine whether each relation graphed in **Example 4** is a function. (We repeat the graphs here.)

(a)

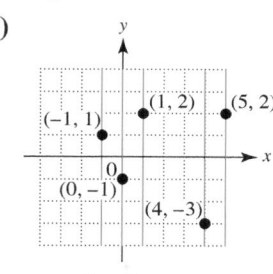

Function

(b)

Not a function

(c)

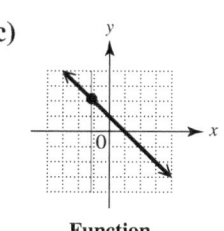

Function

(d)

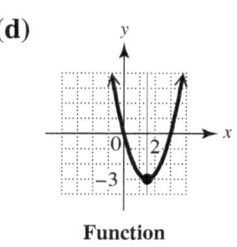

Function

The graphs in (a), (c), and (d) satisfy the vertical line test and represent functions. The graph in (b) fails the vertical line test because a vertical line intersects the graph more than once—that is, the same *x*-value corresponds to two different *y*-values. This is not the graph of a function.

Work Problem ⑤ at the Side. ▶

Note

Graphs that do not represent functions are still relations. *All equations and graphs represent relations, and all relations have a domain and range.*

⑤ Use the vertical line test to decide which graphs represent functions.

A.

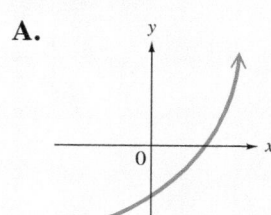

B.

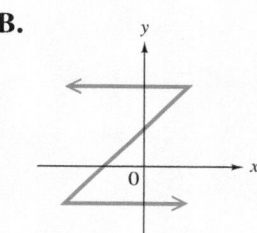

C.

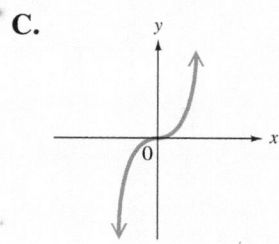

Answer

5. A and C are graphs of functions.

If a relation is defined by an equation involving a fraction, keep the following in mind when finding its domain.

Exclude from the domain any values that make the denominator equal to 0.

Example: The function $y = \frac{1}{x}$ has the set of all real numbers *except* 0 as its domain because division by 0 is undefined.

> **Note**
>
> As we will see in a later chapter, we must also exclude from the domain any values that result in an even root of a negative number.
>
> *Example:* The function $y = \sqrt{x}$ has all *nonnegative* real numbers as its domain because the square root of a negative number is not real.

> **Agreement on Domain**
>
> Unless specified otherwise, the domain of a relation is assumed to be all real numbers that produce real numbers when substituted for the independent variable.

EXAMPLE 6 Identifying Functions from Their Equations

Decide whether each relation defines y as a function of x. Give the domain.

(a) $y = x + 4$

In this equation, y is found by adding 4 to x. Thus, each value of x corresponds to just one value of y, and the relation defines a function.

Because x can be any real number, the domain is $(-\infty, \infty)$.

(b) $y^2 = x$

The ordered pairs $(16, 4)$ and $(16, -4)$ both satisfy this equation. One value of x, 16, corresponds to two values of y, 4 and -4, so this equation does not define a function.

Because x is equal to the square of y, the values of x must always be nonnegative. The domain of the relation is $[0, \infty)$.

(c) $y \leq x - 1$

By definition, y is a function of x if every value of x leads to exactly one value of y. Here a particular value of x, such as 1, corresponds to many values of y. The ordered pairs

$$(1, 0), \quad (1, -1), \quad (1, -2), \quad (1, -3), \quad \text{and so on,}$$

all satisfy the inequality. Thus, this relation does not define a function.

Any number can be used for x, so the domain of this relation is the set of all real numbers, $(-\infty, \infty)$.

Continued on Next Page

(d) $y = \dfrac{5}{x - 1}$

Given any value of x in the domain, we find y by subtracting 1 and then dividing the result into 5. This process produces exactly one value of y for each value in the domain, so the given equation defines a function.

The domain includes all real numbers *except* those that make the denominator of the fraction 0.

$$x - 1 = 0 \quad \text{Set the denominator equal to 0.}$$

$$x = 1 \quad \text{Add 1.}$$

Thus, the domain includes all real numbers *except* 1, written

$$(-\infty, 1) \cup (1, \infty).$$

──────────── **Work Problem ⑥ at the Side.** ▶

In summary, we give three variations of the definition of function.

Variations of the Definition of Function

1. A **function** is a relation in which, for each distinct value of the first component of the ordered pairs, there is exactly one value of the second component.

2. A **function** is a set of distinct ordered pairs in which no first component is repeated.

3. A **function** is a correspondence (mapping) or an equation (rule) that assigns exactly one range value to each distinct domain value.

---

⑥ Decide whether each relation defines y as a function of x. Give the domain.

(a) $y = 6x + 12$

(b) $y \leq 4x$

(c) $y^2 = 25x$

(d) $y = \dfrac{1}{x + 2}$

Answers

6. (a) function; $(-\infty, \infty)$
  (b) not a function; $(-\infty, \infty)$
  (c) not a function; $[0, \infty)$
  (d) function; $(-\infty, -2) \cup (-2, \infty)$

9.1 Exercises

FOR EXTRA HELP Go to MyMathLab *for worked-out, step-by-step solutions to exercises enclosed in a square* ⬜ *and video solutions to* ▶ *exercises.*

CONCEPT CHECK *Complete each statement. Choices may be used more than once.*

function	independent variable	vertical line test	relation
domain	ordered pairs	dependent variable	range

1. A _____ is any set of _____ $\{(x, y)\}$.

2. In a relation $\{(x, y)\}$, the _____ is the set of x-values, and the _____ is the set of y-values.

3. A _____ is a relation in which, for each distinct value of the first component of the _____, there is exactly one value of the second component.

4. The relation $\{(0, -2), (2, -1), (2, -4), (5, 3)\}$ (*does / does not*) define a function. The set $\{0, 2, 5\}$ is its _____, and the set $\{-2, -1, -4, 3\}$ is its _____.

5. Consider the function $d = 50t$, where d represents distance and t represents time. The value of d depends on the value of t, so the variable t is the _____, and the variable d is the _____.

6. The _____ is used to determine whether a graph is that of a function. It says that any vertical line can intersect the graph of a _____ in no more than (*zero / one / two*) point(s).

CONCEPT CHECK *Write each relation as a set of ordered pairs. See Example 1.*

7.

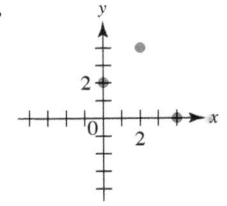

8.

x	y
-1	-3
0	-1
1	1
3	3

9.

Year	Salary (in dollars)
2012	36,300
2013	37,389
2014	38,511
2015	39,665

10.

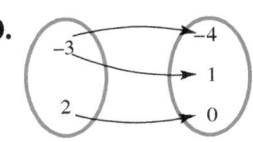

Determine whether each relation defines a function, and give the domain and range. See Examples 2–5.

11. $\{(5, 1), (3, 2), (4, 9), (7, 3)\}$ ▶

12. $\{(8, 0), (5, 4), (9, 3), (3, 9)\}$

13. $\{(2, 4), (0, 2), (2, 5)\}$ ▶

14. $\{(9, -2), (-3, 5), (9, 1)\}$

15. $\{(-3, 1), (4, 1), (-2, 7)\}$

16. $\{(-12, 5), (-10, 3), (8, 3)\}$

17. $\{(1, 1), (1, -1), (0, 0), (2, 4), (2, -4)\}$ ▶

18. $\{(2, 5), (3, 7), (4, 9), (5, 11)\}$

19.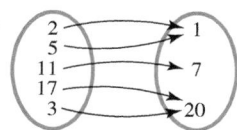

20.

21.

x	y
1	5
1	2
1	−1
1	−4

22.

x	y
−4	−4
−4	0
−4	4
−4	8

23.

x	y
4	−3
2	−3
0	−3
−2	−3

24.

x	y
−3	−6
−1	−6
1	−6
3	−6

25.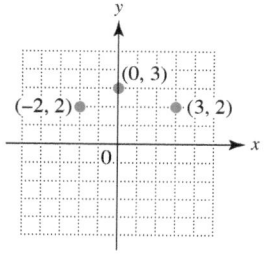

26.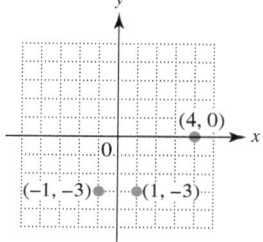

27.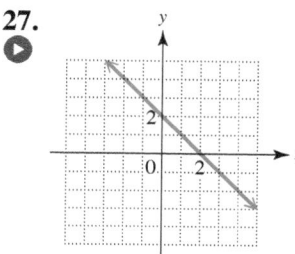

28.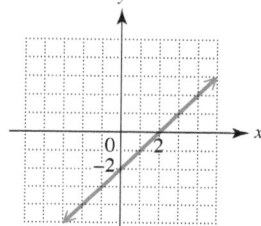

29.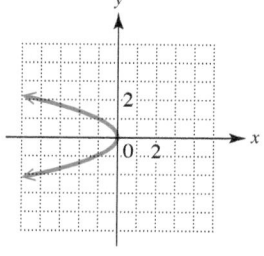

30.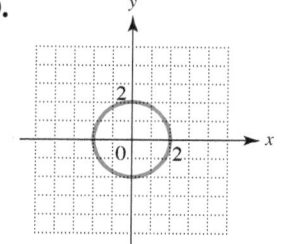

31.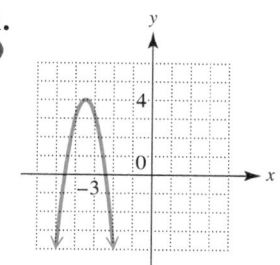

32.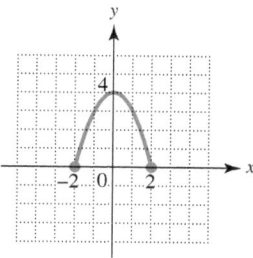

33.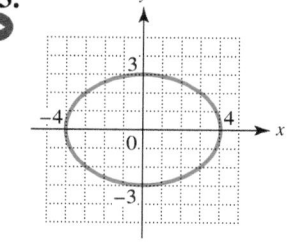

34.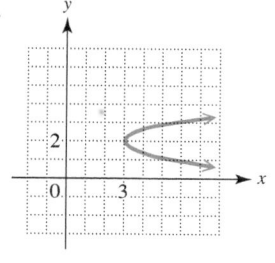

35.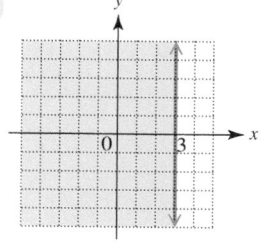

36.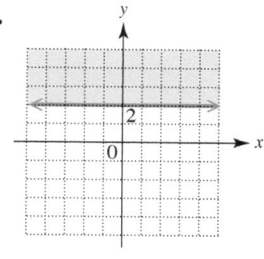

Determine whether each relation defines y as a function of x. Give the domain.
See Example 6.

37. $y = -6x$

38. $y = -9x$

39. $y = 2x - 6$
▶

40. $y = 6x + 8$

41. $y = x^2$

42. $y = x^3$

43. $x = y^6$

44. $x = y^4$

45. $x + y < 4$

46. $x - y < 3$

47. $x = y$

48. $x = -y$

49. $y = \dfrac{x + 4}{5}$

50. $y = \dfrac{x - 3}{2}$

51. $y = -\dfrac{2}{x}$

52. $y = -\dfrac{6}{x}$

53. $y = \dfrac{2}{x - 4}$

54. $y = \dfrac{7}{x - 2}$

55. $y = \dfrac{1}{4x + 2}$

56. $y = \dfrac{1}{2x + 9}$

57. $x = y^2 + 1$

58. $x = y^2 - 3$

59. $xy = 1$

60. $xy = 3$

Solve each problem.

61. The table shows the percentage of ACT-tested high school graduates meeting ACT college readiness benchmarks.

Year	Percentage
2011	25
2012	25
2013	26
2014	26
2015	28

Data from ACT.

    (a) Does the table define a function?

    (b) What are the domain and range?

    (c) Call this function f. Give two ordered pairs that belong to f.

62. The table shows the percentage of full-time college freshmen who said that they frequently smoked cigarettes in the last year.

Year	Percentage
2011	2.8
2012	2.6
2013	2.2
2014	1.7
2015	1.4

Data from Higher Education Research Institute.

    (a) Does the table define a function?

    (b) What are the domain and range?

    (c) Call this function g. Give two ordered pairs that belong to g.

9.2 | Function Notation and Linear Functions

OBJECTIVE ▶ **1 Use function notation.** When a function f is defined with a rule or an equation using x and y for the independent and dependent variables, we say "y is a function of x" to emphasize that y depends on x. We use the notation $y = f(x)$, called **function notation,** to express this and read $f(x)$ as "**f of x,**" or "**f at x.**" The letter f is a name for this particular function.

For example, if $y = 9x - 5$, we can name this function f and write

$$f(x) = 9x - 5.$$

    f is the name of the function.
    x is a value from the domain.
    $f(x)$ is the function value (or y-value) that corresponds to x.

$f(x)$ is just another name for the dependent variable y.

We evaluate a function at different values of x by substituting x-values from the domain into the function.

EXAMPLE 1   Evaluating a Function

Let $f(x) = 9x - 5$. Find the value of function f for each value of x.

(a) $x = 2$

$f(x) = 9x - 5$	Given function
$f(2) = 9 \cdot 2 - 5$	Replace x with 2.
$f(2) = 18 - 5$	Multiply.
$f(2) = 13$	Subtract.

Read $f(2)$ as "f of 2" or "f at 2".

Thus, for $x = 2$, the corresponding function value (or y-value) is **13**. $f(2) = 13$ is an abbreviation for the statement "*If $x = 2$ in the function f, then $y = 13$*" and is represented by the ordered pair $(2, 13)$.

(b) $x = -3$

$f(x) = 9x - 5$	Use parentheses to avoid errors.
$f(-3) = 9(-3) - 5$	Replace x with -3.
$f(-3) = -32$	Multiply, and then subtract.

Thus, $f(-3) = -32$ and the ordered pair $(-3, -32)$ belongs to f.

————————— **Work Problem 1 at the Side.** ▶

⚠ CAUTION

The symbol $f(x)$ *does not* indicate "f times x," but represents the y-value associated with the indicated x-value. As shown in **Example 1(a)**, $f(2)$ is the y-value that corresponds to the x-value 2 in f.

These ideas can be illustrated as follows.

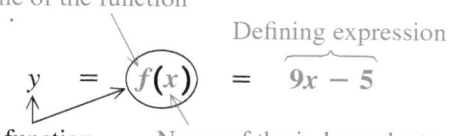

Name of the function

Defining expression

$$y = f(x) = 9x - 5$$

Value of the function   Name of the independent variable

OBJECTIVES

1 Use function notation.
2 Graph linear and constant functions.

1 Let $f(x) = 6x - 2$. Find the value of function f for each value of x.

GS (a) $x = -2$

$$f(x) = 6x - 2$$
$$f(\underline{\quad}) = 6(\underline{\quad}) - 2$$
$$f(-2) = \underline{\quad} - 2$$
$$f(-2) = \underline{\quad}$$

Thus, $f(-2) = -14$
and the ordered pair
$(\underline{\quad}, \underline{\quad})$ belongs to f.

(b) $x = 0$

(c) $x = 11$

Answers

1. **(a)** $-2; -2; -12; -14; -2; -14$
   (b) -2 **(c)** 64

2 Let $f(x) = -x^2 - 4x + 1$.
Find the following.

(a) $f(-2)$

(b) $f(a)$

3 Find the following.

GS (a) Let $g(x) = 5x - 1$.
Find and simplify $g(m + 2)$.

$$g(x) = 5x - 1$$
$$g(m + 2) = 5(\underline{\quad}) - 1$$
$$g(m + 2) = \underline{\quad} + \underline{\quad} - 1$$
$$g(m + 2) = \underline{\quad}$$

(b) Let $f(x) = 8x - 5$.
Find and simplify $f(a - 2)$.

4 For each function, find $f(-2)$.

(a) $f = \{(0, 5), (-1, 3), (-2, 1)\}$

(b)
x	y = f(x)
-4	16
-2	4
0	0
2	4

Answers

2. (a) 5 (b) $-a^2 - 4a + 1$
3. (a) $m + 2$; $5m$; 10; $5m + 9$ (b) $8a - 21$
4. (a) 1 (b) 4

EXAMPLE 2 Evaluating a Function

Let $f(x) = -x^2 + 5x - 3$. Find the following.

(a) $f(4)$

$$f(x) = -x^2 + 5x - 3 \quad \text{The base in } -x^2 \text{ is } x, \text{ not } (-x).$$
$$f(4) = -4^2 + 5 \cdot 4 - 3 \quad \text{Replace } x \text{ with 4.}$$
$$f(4) = -16 + 20 - 3 \quad \text{Apply the exponent. Multiply.}$$
$$f(4) = 1 \quad \text{Add and subtract.}$$

Do not read this as "f times 4." Read it as "f of 4," or "f at 4."

Because $f(4) = 1$, the ordered pair $(4, 1)$ belongs to f.

(b) $f(q)$

$$f(x) = -x^2 + 5x - 3$$
$$f(q) = -q^2 + 5q - 3 \quad \text{Replace } x \text{ with } q.$$

The replacement of one variable with another is important in later courses.

◀ **Work Problem 2** at the Side.

Sometimes letters other than f, such as g, h, or capital letters F, G, and H, are used to name functions.

EXAMPLE 3 Evaluating a Function

Let $g(x) = 2x + 3$. Find and simplify $g(a + 1)$.

$$g(x) = 2x + 3$$
$$g(a + 1) = 2(a + 1) + 3 \quad \text{Replace } x \text{ with } a + 1.$$
$$g(a + 1) = 2a + 2 + 3 \quad \text{Distributive property}$$
$$g(a + 1) = 2a + 5 \quad \text{Add.}$$

◀ **Work Problem 3** at the Side.

EXAMPLE 4 Evaluating Functions

For each function, find $f(3)$.

(a) $f(x) = 3x - 7$

$$f(3) = 3(3) - 7 \quad \text{Replace } x \text{ with 3.}$$
$$f(3) = 9 - 7 \quad \text{Multiply.}$$
$$f(3) = 2 \quad \text{Subtract.}$$

(b)
x	y = f(x)
6	-12
3	-6	←$f(3) = -6$
0	0
-3	6

(c) $f = \{(-3, 5), (0, 3), (3, 1), (6, -1)\}$

We want $f(3)$, the y-value of the ordered pair whose first component is 3. As indicated by the ordered pair $(3, 1)$, for $x = 3$, $y = 1$. Thus, $f(3) = 1$.

(d)

The domain element 3 is paired with 5 in the range, so $f(3) = 5$.

◀ **Work Problem 4** at the Side.

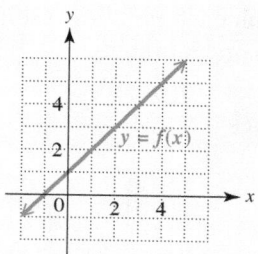

Figure 5

EXAMPLE 5 Finding Function Values from a Graph

Refer to the function f graphed in **Figure 5** in the margin.

(a) Find $f(3)$.

Locate 3 on the x-axis. See **Figure 6.** Moving up to the graph of f and over to the y-axis gives 4 for the corresponding y-value. Thus, $f(3) = 4$, which corresponds to the ordered pair $(3, 4)$.

(b) Find $f(0)$.   Refer to **Figure 6** to see that $f(0) = 1$.

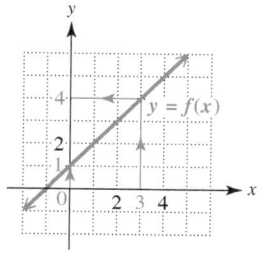

Figure 6

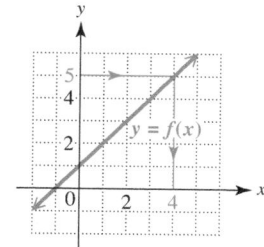

Figure 7

(c) For what value of x is $f(x) = 5$?

Because $f(x) = y$, we want the value of x that corresponds to $y = 5$. Locate 5 on the y-axis. See **Figure 7.** Moving across to the graph of f and down to the x-axis gives $x = 4$. Thus, $f(4) = 5$, which corresponds to the ordered pair $(4, 5)$.

⑤ Refer to the function graphed above in **Figure 5.**

(a) Find $f(2)$.

(b) Find $f(-1)$.

(c) For what value of x is $f(x) = 2$?

─── **Work Problem ⑤ at the Side.** ▶

If a function f is defined by an equation with x and y instead of with function notation, use the following steps to find $f(x)$.

⑥ Write each equation defining a function f using function notation $f(x)$. Then find $f(-1)$.

(a) $y = -3x + 6$

Writing an Equation Using Function Notation

Step 1 Solve the equation for y if it is not given in that form.

Step 2 Replace y with $f(x)$.

EXAMPLE 6 Writing Equations Using Function Notation

Write each equation using function notation $f(x)$. Then find $f(-2)$.

(b) $2x - 5y = 4$

(a) $y = x^2 + 1$ ⟵ This equation is already solved for y.

$f(x) = x^2 + 1$ Replace y with $f(x)$. (Step 2)

Now find $f(-2)$. ⟶ $f(-2) = (-2)^2 + 1$ Let $x = -2$.

$f(-2) = 4 + 1$ $(-2)^2 = -2(-2)$

$f(-2) = 5$ Add.

(c) $x^2 - 4y = 3$

(b) $x - 4y = 5$

Step 1 $-4y = -x + 5$ Subtract x.

$y = \dfrac{1}{4}x - \dfrac{5}{4}$ Divide by -4.

Step 2 $f(x) = \dfrac{1}{4}x - \dfrac{5}{4}$, so $f(-2) = \dfrac{1}{4}(-2) - \dfrac{5}{4} = -\dfrac{7}{4}$

Answers

5. (a) 3 (b) 0 (c) 1

6. (a) $f(x) = -3x + 6$; 9

(b) $f(x) = \dfrac{2}{5}x - \dfrac{4}{5}$; $-\dfrac{6}{5}$

(c) $f(x) = \dfrac{1}{4}x^2 - \dfrac{3}{4}$; $-\dfrac{1}{2}$

─── **Work Problem ⑥ at the Side.** ▶

7 Graph each function. Give the domain and range.

(a) $f(x) = \dfrac{3}{4}x - 2$

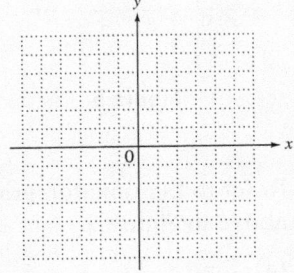

(b) $g(x) = 3$

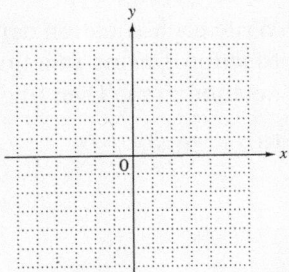

Answers

7. (a)

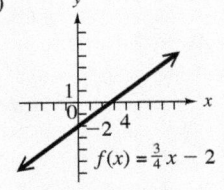

domain: $(-\infty, \infty)$; range: $(-\infty, \infty)$

(b)

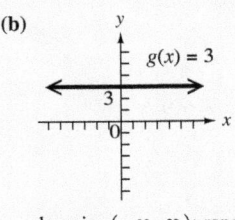

domain: $(-\infty, \infty)$; range: $\{3\}$

OBJECTIVE ▶ **2** **Graph linear and constant functions.** Linear equations (except for the case of vertical lines with equations of the form $x = a$) define *linear functions*.

Linear Function

A function f that can be written in the form

$$f(x) = ax + b,$$

where a and b are real numbers, is a **linear function.** The value of a is the slope m of the graph of the function. The domain of a linear function is $(-\infty, \infty)$ unless specified otherwise.

A linear function whose graph is a horizontal line has the form

$$f(x) = b \quad \text{Constant function}$$

and is a **constant function.** While the range of any nonconstant linear function is $(-\infty, \infty)$, the range of a constant function $f(x) = b$ is $\{b\}$.

EXAMPLE 7 **Graphing Linear and Constant Functions**

Graph each function. Give the domain and range.

(a) $f(x) = \dfrac{1}{4}x - \dfrac{5}{4}$ From **Example 6(b)**

Slope ⟵   ⟶ The y-intercept is $\left(0, -\dfrac{5}{4}\right)$.

To graph this function, plot the y-intercept $\left(0, -\dfrac{5}{4}\right)$. Use the geometric definition of slope as $\frac{\text{rise}}{\text{run}}$ to find a second point on the line. The slope is $\frac{1}{4}$, so we move 1 unit up from $\left(0, -\dfrac{5}{4}\right)$ and 4 units to the right to the point $\left(4, -\dfrac{1}{4}\right)$. Draw the straight line through these points to obtain the graph shown in **Figure 8.** The domain and range are both $(-\infty, \infty)$.

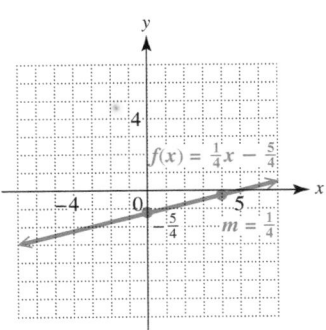

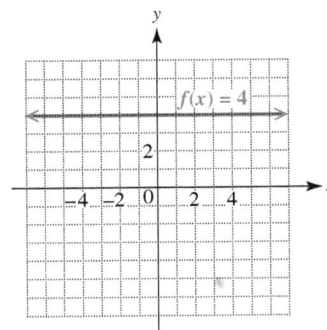

Figure 8

Figure 9

(b) $f(x) = 4$

The graph of this constant function is the horizontal line containing all points with y-coordinate 4. See **Figure 9.** The domain is $(-\infty, \infty)$ and the range is $\{4\}$.

◀ **Work Problem** **7** **at the Side**

9.2 Exercises

FOR EXTRA HELP Go to MyMathLab for worked-out, step-by-step solutions to exercises enclosed in a square ▢ and video solutions to ▶ exercises.

1. **CONCEPT CHECK** To emphasize that "y is a function of x" for a given function f, we use function notation and write $y =$ _____ . Here, f is the name of the _____ , x is a value from the _____ , and $f(x)$ is the function value (or y-value) that corresponds to _____ . We read $f(x)$ as "_____ ."

2. **CONCEPT CHECK** Choose the correct response:

   For a function f, the notation $f(3)$ means _____ .

   A. the variable f times 3 or $3f$

   B. the value of the dependent variable when the independent variable is 3

   C. the value of the independent variable when the dependent variable is 3

   D. f equals 3

Let $f(x) = -3x + 4$ and $g(x) = -x^2 + 4x + 1$. Find the following.
See Examples 1–3.

3. ▶ $f(0)$

4. $g(0)$

5. $f(-5)$

6. $f(-3)$

7. $g(10)$

8. $g(3)$

9. $f\left(\dfrac{1}{3}\right)$

10. $f\left(\dfrac{7}{3}\right)$

11. $g(0.5)$

12. $g(1.5)$

13. $f(p)$

14. $g(k)$

15. $f(-x)$

16. $g(-x)$

17. ▶ $f(x + 2)$

18. $f(x - 2)$

19. $f(2t + 1)$

20. $f(3t - 2)$

21. $g\left(\dfrac{p}{3}\right)$

22. $g\left(\dfrac{1}{x}\right)$

For each function, find (a) $f(2)$ and (b) $f(-1)$. **See Examples 4, 5(a), and 5(b).**

23. $f = \{(-2, 2), (-1, -1), (2, -1)\}$

24. $f = \{(-1, -5), (0, 5), (2, -5)\}$

25. ▶ $f = \{(-1, 3), (4, 7), (0, 6), (2, 2)\}$

26. $f = \{(2, 5), (3, 9), (-1, 11), (5, 3)\}$

27.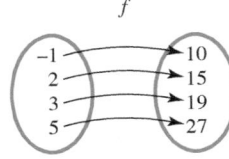

28.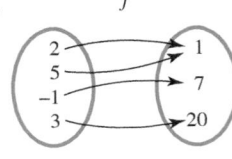

29.

x	y = f(x)
2	4
1	1
0	0
−1	1
−2	4

30.

x	y = f(x)
8	6
5	3
2	0
−1	−3
−4	−6

31.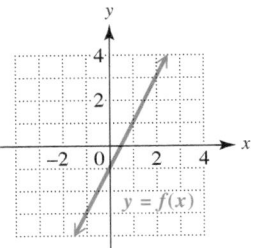

32.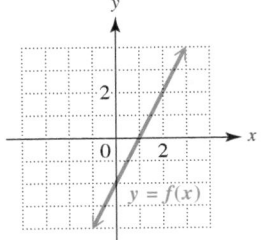

33.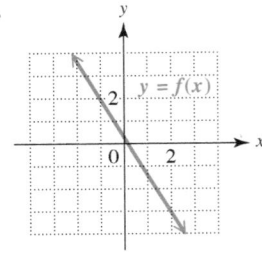

34.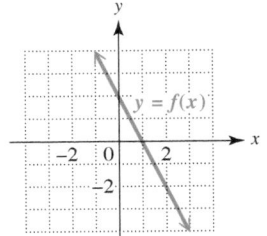

Refer to the given graph. Find the value of x for each value of f(x). ***See Example 5(c).***

35.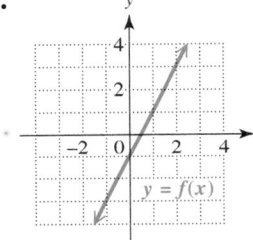

(a) $f(x) = 3$

(b) $f(x) = -1$

(c) $f(x) = -3$

36.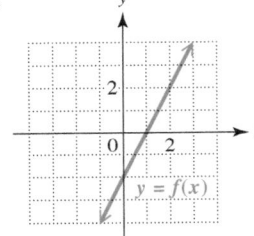

(a) $f(x) = 4$

(b) $f(x) = -2$

(c) $f(x) = 0$

An equation that defines y as a function f of x is given. ***(a)*** *Solve for y in terms of x, and replace y with the function notation f(x).* ***(b)*** *Find f(3).* ***See Example 6.***

37. $x + 3y = 12$

38. $x - 4y = 8$

39. $y + 2x^2 = 3$

40. $y - 3x^2 = 2$

41. $4x - 3y = 8$

42. $-2x + 5y = 9$

CONCEPT CHECK *Fill in each blank with the correct response.*

43. The equation $2x + y = 4$ has a straight _____ as its graph. One point that lies on the graph is $(3, \_\_\_)$. If we solve the equation for y and use function notation, we have a _____ function $f(x) = $ _____. For this function, $f(3) = $ _____, meaning that the point $(\_\_\_,\_\_\_)$ lies on the graph of the function.

44. A linear function f can be written in the form
$f(x) = $ _____, for real numbers a and b. The graph of a linear function is a _____. The value of a is the _____ of the line and $(0, b)$ is the _____. The domain of a linear function is _____ unless specified otherwise.

Graph each linear or constant function. Give the domain and range. See Example 7.

45. $f(x) = -2x + 5$

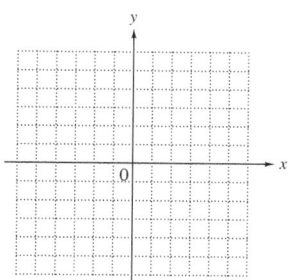

46. $g(x) = 4x - 1$

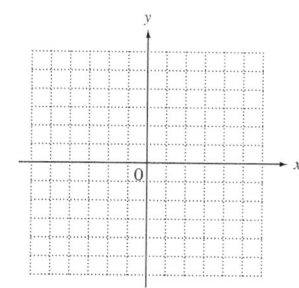

47. $h(x) = \frac{1}{2}x + 2$

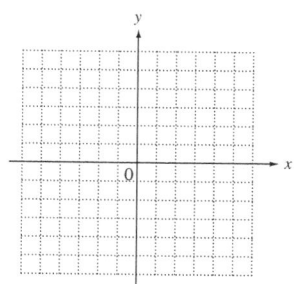

48. $F(x) = -\frac{1}{4}x + 1$

49. $g(x) = -4$

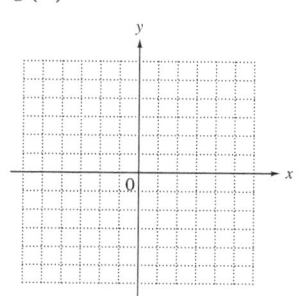

50. $f(x) = 5$

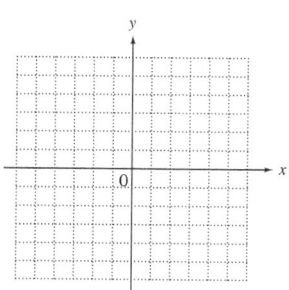

51. $f(x) = 0$

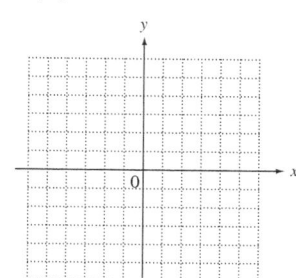

52. $f(x) = 2.5$

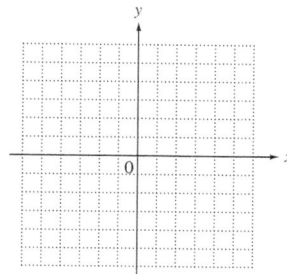

Solve each problem.

53. A taxi company charges $2.50 per mi.

(a) Fill in the table with the correct response for the price $f(x)$ charged for a trip of x miles.

x	f(x)
0	
1	
2	
3	

(b) The linear function that gives a rule for the amount charged in dollars is $f(x) = $ _____ .

(c) Graph this function for the domain $\{0, 1, 2, 3\}$.

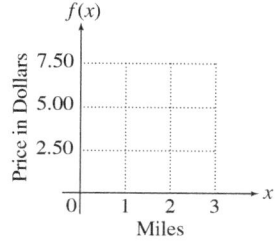

54. A package weighing x pounds costs $f(x)$ dollars to ship to a given location, where $f(x) = 3.75x$.

(a) Evaluate $f(3)$.

(b) Describe what 3 and the value $f(3)$ mean in part (a), using the terms *independent variable* and *dependent variable*.

(c) How much would it cost to mail a 5-lb package? Express this situation using function notation.

55. To print t-shirts, there is a $100 set-up fee, plus a $12 charge per t-shirt. Let x represent the number of t-shirts printed and $f(x)$ represent the total charge.

(a) Write a linear function that models this situation.

(b) Find $f(125)$. Interpret the answer in the context of this problem.

(c) Find the value of x if $f(x) = 1000$. Express this situation using function notation, and interpret it in the context of this problem.

56. Rental on a car is $150, plus $0.50 per mile. Let x represent the number of miles the car is driven and $f(x)$ represent the total cost to rent the car.

(a) Write a linear function that models this situation.

(b) How much would it cost to drive 250 mi? Interpret the answer in the context of this problem.

(c) Find the value of x if $f(x) = 400$. Express this situation using function notation, and interpret it in the context of this problem.

57. The table represents a linear function.

x	$y = f(x)$
0	3.5
1	2.3
2	1.1
3	−0.1
4	−1.3

(a) What is $f(2)$?

(b) If $f(x) = -1.3$, what is the value of x?

(c) What is the slope of the line?

(d) What is the y-intercept?

(e) Using the answers from parts (c) and (d), write an equation for $f(x)$.

58. The table represents a linear function.

x	$y = f(x)$
−1	−3.9
0	−2.4
1	−0.9
2	0.6
3	2.1

(a) What is $f(2)$?

(b) If $f(x) = 2.1$, what is the value of x?

(c) What is the slope of the line?

(d) What is the y-intercept?

(e) Using the answers from parts (c) and (d), write an equation for $f(x)$.

59. Refer to the graph to answer the questions.

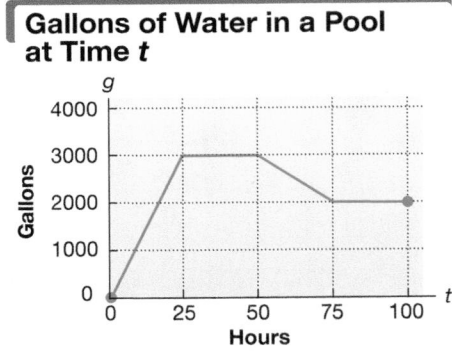

Gallons of Water in a Pool at Time t

(a) What numbers are possible values of the independent variable? The dependent variable?

(b) For how long is the water level increasing? Decreasing?

(c) How many gallons are in the pool after 90 hr?

(d) Call this function g. What is $g(0)$? What does it mean in this example?

60. The graph shows electricity use on a summer day.

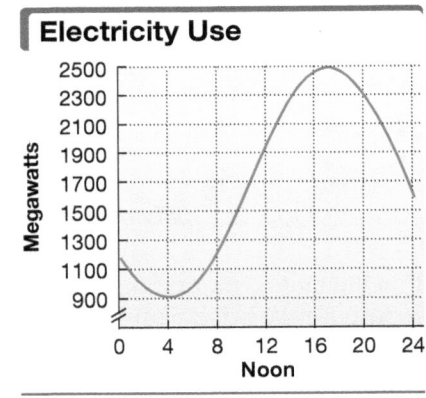

Electricity Use

(a) Is this the graph of a function?

(b) What is the domain?

(c) Estimate the number of megawatts used at 8 A.M.

(d) At what time was the most electricity used? The least electricity?

9.3 | Polynomial Functions, Operations, and Graphs

OBJECTIVE ▶ 1 **Recognize and evaluate polynomial functions.** We have studied linear (first-degree polynomial) functions $f(x) = ax + b$. Now we consider more general polynomial functions.

Polynomial Function

A **polynomial function of degree n** is defined by

$$f(x) = a_n x^n + a_{n-1} x^{n-1} + \cdots + a_1 x + a_0,$$

for real numbers $a_n, a_{n-1}, \ldots, a_1,$ and $a_0,$ where $a_n \neq 0$ and n is a whole number.

Another way of describing a polynomial function is to say that it is a function defined by a polynomial in one variable, consisting of one or more terms. It is usually written in descending powers of the variable, and its degree is the degree of the polynomial that defines it.

We can evaluate a polynomial function $f(x)$ at different values of the variable x.

EXAMPLE 1   **Evaluating Polynomial Functions**

Let $f(x) = 4x^3 - x^2 + 5$. Find each value.

(a) $f(3)$

$f(x) = 4x^3 - x^2 + 5$	Given function
$f(3) = 4(3)^3 - 3^2 + 5$	Substitute 3 for x.
$f(3) = 4(27) - 9 + 5$	Apply the exponents.
$f(3) = 108 - 9 + 5$	Multiply.
$f(3) = 104$	Subtract, and then add.

Read this as "f of 3," not "f times 3."

Thus, $f(3) = 104$ and the ordered pair $(3, 104)$ belongs to f.

(b) $f(-4)$

$f(x) = 4x^3 - x^2 + 5$	Use parentheses.
$f(-4) = 4(-4)^3 - (-4)^2 + 5$	Let $x = -4$.
$f(-4) = 4(-64) - 16 + 5$	Be careful with signs.
$f(-4) = -256 - 16 + 5$	Multiply.
$f(-4) = -267$	Subtract, and then add.

So, $f(-4) = -267$. The ordered pair $(-4, -267)$ belongs to f.

——————————————— **Work Problem ① at the Side. ▶**

While f is the most common letter used to represent functions, recall that other letters such as g and h are also used. ***The capital letter P is often used for polynomial functions.*** The function

$$P(x) = 4x^3 - x^2 + 5$$

yields the same ordered pairs as the function f in **Example 1**.

OBJECTIVES

① Recognize and evaluate polynomial functions.

② Perform operations on polynomial functions.

③ Graph basic polynomial functions.

---

① Let $f(x) = -x^2 + 5x - 11$.
Find each value.

GS **(a)** $f(-1)$

$f(x) = -x^2 + 5x - 11$

$f(-1) = -(\underline{\quad})^2 + 5(\underline{\quad}) - 11$

$f(-1) = \underline{\quad} - \underline{\quad} - 11$

$f(-1) = \underline{\quad}$

(b) $f(1)$

(c) $f(-4)$

(d) $f(0)$

Answers

1. (a) $-1; -1; -1; 5; -17$
   (b) -7 **(c)** -47 **(d)** -11

OBJECTIVE ▶ **2** **Perform operations on polynomial functions.** The graph in **Figure 10** shows dollars (in billions) spent for general science and for space/other technologies over a 20-year period.

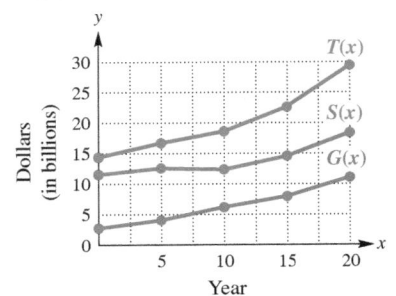

SCIENCE AND SPACE SPENDING

$G(x)$ represents dollars spent for general science.

$S(x)$ represents dollars spent for space/other technologies.

$T(x)$ represents total expenditures for these two categories.

Data from U.S. Office of Management and Budget.

Figure 10

The total expenditures function can be found by *adding* the spending functions for the two individual categories.

$$T(x) = G(x) + S(x)$$

As another example, businesses use the equation "profit equals revenue minus cost," which can be written using function notation.

$$P(x) = R(x) - C(x)$$

x is the number of items produced and sold.

Profit   Revenue   Cost
function   function   function

The profit function is found by *subtracting* the cost function from the revenue function.

We define the following **operations on functions.**

Operations on Functions

If $f(x)$ and $g(x)$ define functions, then

$$(f + g)(x) = f(x) + g(x),$$ Sum function

$$(f - g)(x) = f(x) - g(x),$$ Difference function

$$(fg)(x) = f(x) \cdot g(x),$$ Product function

and $$\left(\frac{f}{g}\right)(x) = \frac{f(x)}{g(x)}.$$ Quotient function

In each case, the domain of the new function is the intersection of the domains of $f(x)$ and $g(x)$. The domain of the quotient function must exclude any values of *x* for which $g(x) = 0$.

EXAMPLE 2 Adding and Subtracting Polynomial Functions

Find each of the following for polynomial functions f and g as defined.

$$f(x) = x^2 - 3x + 7 \quad \text{and} \quad g(x) = -3x^2 - 7x + 7$$

(a) $(f + g)(x)$ — *This notation does not indicate the distributive property.*

$$= f(x) + g(x) \qquad \text{Sum function}$$
$$= (x^2 - 3x + 7) + (-3x^2 - 7x + 7) \qquad \text{Substitute.}$$
$$= -2x^2 - 10x + 14 \qquad \text{Combine like terms.}$$

(b) $(f - g)(x)$

$$= f(x) - g(x) \qquad \text{Difference function}$$
$$= (x^2 - 3x + 7) - (-3x^2 - 7x + 7) \qquad \text{Substitute.}$$
$$= x^2 - 3x + 7 + 3x^2 + 7x - 7 \qquad \text{Definition of subtraction}$$
$$= 4x^2 + 4x \qquad \text{Combine like terms.}$$

— **Work Problem ② at the Side.** ▶

EXAMPLE 3 Adding and Subtracting Polynomial Functions

Find each of the following for polynomial functions f and g as defined.

$$f(x) = 10x^2 - 2x \quad \text{and} \quad g(x) = 2x.$$

(a) $(f + g)(2)$

$$= f(2) + g(2) \qquad \text{Sum function}$$

$f(x) = 10x^2 - 2x$ $g(x) = 2x$

$$= [10(2)^2 - 2(2)] + 2(2) \qquad \text{Substitute.}$$

This is a key step.

$$= [40 - 4] + 4 \qquad \text{Order of operations}$$
$$= 40 \qquad \text{Subtract, and then add.}$$

Alternative method: $(f + g)(x)$

$$= f(x) + g(x) \qquad \text{Sum function}$$
$$= (10x^2 - 2x) + 2x \qquad \text{Substitute.}$$
$$= 10x^2 \qquad \text{Combine like terms.}$$
$$(f + g)(2)$$
$$= 10(2)^2 \qquad \text{Substitute.}$$
$$= 40 \qquad \text{The result is the same.}$$

(b) $(f - g)(x)$ and $(f - g)(1)$

$$(f - g)(x) = f(x) - g(x) \qquad \text{Difference function}$$
$$= (10x^2 - 2x) - 2x \qquad \text{Substitute.}$$
$$= 10x^2 - 4x \qquad \text{Combine like terms.}$$
$$(f - g)(1) = 10(1)^2 - 4(1) \qquad \text{Substitute.}$$

Confirm that $f(1) - g(1)$ gives the same result.

$$= 6 \qquad \text{Perform the operations.}$$

— **Work Problem ③ at the Side.** ▶

② For

$$f(x) = 3x^2 + 8x - 6$$
and $g(x) = -4x^2 + 4x - 8$,

find each of the following.

(a) $(f + g)(x)$
$$= f(x) + \underline{\quad}$$
$$= (\underline{\quad}) + (\underline{\quad})$$
$$= \underline{\quad}$$

(b) $(f - g)(x)$

③ For

$$f(x) = 18x^2 - 24x$$
and $g(x) = 3x$,

find each of the following.

(a) $(f + g)(x)$ and $(f + g)(-1)$

(b) $(f - g)(x)$ and $(f - g)(1)$

Answers
2. (a) $g(x)$; $3x^2 + 8x - 6$; $-4x^2 + 4x - 8$; $-x^2 + 12x - 14$
(b) $7x^2 + 4x + 2$
3. (a) $18x^2 - 21x$; 39
(b) $18x^2 - 27x$; -9

④ For
$$f(x) = 2x + 7$$
and $\quad g(x) = x^2 - 4,$
find $(fg)(x)$ and $(fg)(2)$.

EXAMPLE 4   Multiplying Polynomial Functions

For $f(x) = 3x + 4$ and $g(x) = 2x^2 + x$, find $(fg)(x)$ and $(fg)(-1)$.

$(fg)(x)$
$\quad = f(x) \cdot g(x)$ Use the definition.
$\quad = (3x + 4)(2x^2 + x)$ Substitute.
$\quad = 6x^3 + 3x^2 + 8x^2 + 4x$ FOIL method
$\quad = 6x^3 + 11x^2 + 4x$ Combine like terms.

$(fg)(-1)$
$\quad = 6(-1)^3 + 11(-1)^2 + 4(-1)$ Let $x = -1$.
$\quad = -6 + 11 - 4$ Apply the exponents. Multiply.
$\quad = 1$ Add and subtract.

Be careful with signs.

An alternative method for finding $(fg)(-1)$ is to find $f(-1)$ and $g(-1)$ and then multiply the results. Verify this by showing that $f(-1) \cdot g(-1)$ equals **1**. This follows from the definition.

◀ **Work Problem ④ at the Side.**

⚠ CAUTION
Write the product $f(x) \cdot g(x)$ as $(fg)(x)$, **not** $f(g(x))$, which has a different mathematical meaning, as discussed later in the text.

⑤ For
$$f(x) = 2x^2 + 17x + 30$$
and $\quad g(x) = 2x + 5,$
find $\left(\frac{f}{g}\right)(x)$ and $\left(\frac{f}{g}\right)(-1)$.

EXAMPLE 5   Dividing Polynomial Functions

For $f(x) = 2x^2 + x - 10$ and $g(x) = x - 2$, find $\left(\frac{f}{g}\right)(x)$ and $\left(\frac{f}{g}\right)(-3)$.

$\left(\frac{f}{g}\right)(x)$

$\quad = \dfrac{f(x)}{g(x)}$ Use the definition.

$\quad = \dfrac{2x^2 + x - 10}{x - 2}$ Substitute.

$\quad = \dfrac{(2x + 5)(x - 2)}{x - 2}$ Factor.

$\quad$ $g(x) \neq 0$, so $x \neq 2$

$\quad = 2x + 5, \quad x \neq 2$ Divide out the common factor.

$\left(\frac{f}{g}\right)(-3)$

$\quad = 2(-3) + 5$ Let $x = -3$.

$\quad = -1$ Multiply and then add.

As an alternative method, verify that the same value is found by evaluating $\frac{f(-3)}{g(-3)}$.

◀ **Work Problem ⑤ at the Side.**

Answers
4. $2x^3 + 7x^2 - 8x - 28; 0$
5. $x + 6, \quad x \neq -\dfrac{5}{2}; 5$

OBJECTIVE ▶ ❸ Graph basic polynomial functions. Recall that each input (or x-value) of a function results in one output (or y-value). The set of input values (for x) defines the domain of the function, and the set of output values (for y) defines the range.

The simplest polynomial function is the **identity function** $f(x) = x$, graphed in **Figure 11.** This function pairs each real number with itself.

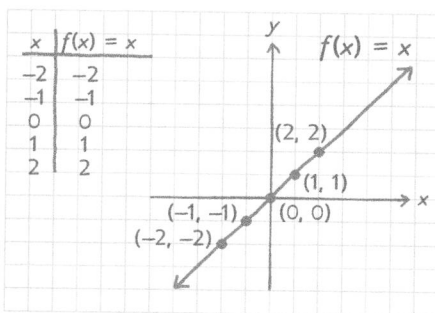

Identity function
$$f(x) = x$$
Domain: $(-\infty, \infty)$
Range: $(-\infty, \infty)$

Figure 11

> **Note**
>
> The identity function $f(x) = x$ shown in **Figure 11** is a *linear function* of the form $f(x) = ax + b$, where the slope a is 1 and the y-value of the y-intercept b is 0.

Another polynomial function, the **squaring function** $f(x) = x^2$, is graphed in **Figure 12.** For this function, every real number is paired with its square. The graph of the squaring function is a *parabola*.

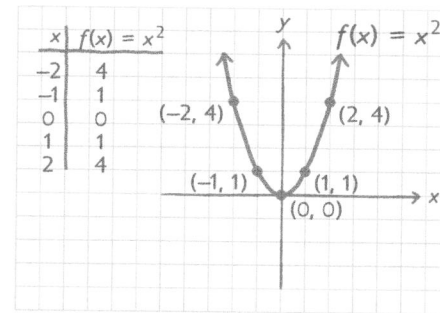

Squaring function
$$f(x) = x^2$$
Domain: $(-\infty, \infty)$
Range: $[0, \infty)$

Figure 12

The **cubing function** $f(x) = x^3$ is graphed in **Figure 13.** This function pairs every real number with its cube.

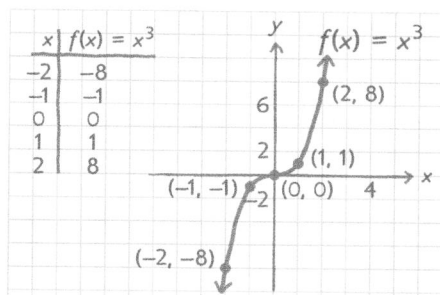

Cubing function
$$f(x) = x^3$$
Domain: $(-\infty, \infty)$
Range: $(-\infty, \infty)$

Figure 13

6 Graph each function. Give the domain and range.

(a) $f(x) = -2x^2$

x	$f(x) = -2x^2$
-2	___
-1	___
0	___
1	___
2	___

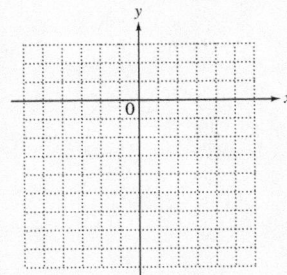

(b) $f(x) = x^3 + 2$

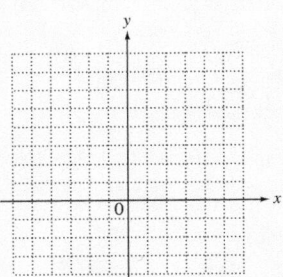

Answers

6. (a)

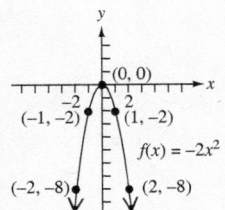

domain: $(-\infty, \infty)$; range: $(-\infty, 0]$

(b)

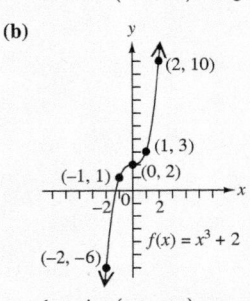

domain: $(-\infty, \infty)$; range: $(-\infty, \infty)$

EXAMPLE 6 **Graphing Variations of Polynomial Functions**

Graph each function. Give the domain and range.

(a) $f(x) = 2x$

To find each range value, multiply the domain value by 2. Plot the points and join them with a straight line. See **Figure 14.** The domain and the range are both $(-\infty, \infty)$.

x	$f(x) = 2x$
-2	-4
-1	-2
0	0
1	2
2	4

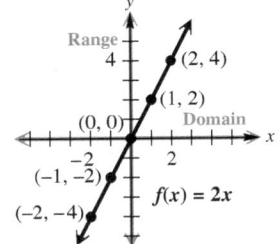

Figure 14

(b) $f(x) = -x^2$

For each input x, square it and then take its opposite. Plotting and joining the points gives a parabola that opens down. It is a *reflection* of the graph of the squaring function across the x-axis. See the table and **Figure 15.** The domain is $(-\infty, \infty)$, and the range is $(-\infty, 0]$.

x	$f(x) = -x^2$
-2	-4
-1	-1
0	0
1	-1
2	-4

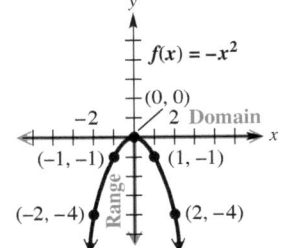

Figure 15

(c) $f(x) = x^3 - 2$

For this function, cube the input and then subtract 2 from the result. The graph is that of the cubing function *shifted* 2 units down. See the table and **Figure 16.** The domain and the range are both $(-\infty, \infty)$.

x	$f(x) = x^3 - 2$
-2	-10
-1	-3
0	-2
1	-1
2	6

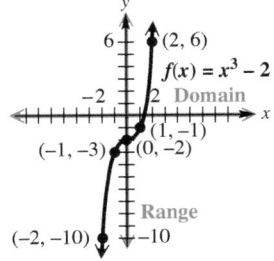

Figure 16

◀ **Work Problem 6 at the Side**

9.3 Exercises

FOR EXTRA HELP Go to MyMathLab *for worked-out, step-by-step solutions to exercises enclosed in a square* ▢ *and video solutions to* ▶ *exercises.*

1. CONCEPT CHECK A polynomial function is a function defined by a _____ in (*one / two / three*) variable(s), consisting of one or more (*factors / terms*) and usually written in descending _____ of the variable.

2. CONCEPT CHECK Which of the following are *not* polynomial functions?

A. $P(x) = x^{-2} - 2x$

B. $f(x) = \dfrac{1}{2}x^2 + x - 1$

C. $g(x) = -4x + 1.5$

D. $p(x) = x^3 - x^2 - \dfrac{5}{x}$

For each polynomial function, find **(a)** $f(-1)$, **(b)** $f(2)$, *and* **(c)** $f(0)$. ***See Example 1.***

3. $f(x) = 6x - 4$

4. $f(x) = 2x + 5$

5. $f(x) = x^2 - 7x$

6. $f(x) = x^2 + 5x$

7. $f(x) = 2x^2 - 3x + 4$

8. $f(x) = 3x^2 + x - 5$

9. $f(x) = 5x^4 - 3x^2 + 6$

10. $f(x) = 4x^4 + 2x^2 - 1$

11. $f(x) = -x^2 + 2x^3 - 8$

12. $f(x) = -x^2 - x^3 + 11$

CONCEPT CHECK *Find two polynomial functions* $f(x)$ *and* $g(x)$ *such that each statement is true.*

13. $(f + g)(x) = 3x^3 - x + 3$

14. $(f - g)(x) = -x^2 + x - 5$

Let $f(x) = x^2 - 9$, $g(x) = 2x$, *and* $h(x) = x - 3$. *Find each of the following.* ***See Examples 2–5.***

15. $(f + g)(x)$

16. $(f - g)(x)$

17. $(f + g)(3)$

18. $(f - g)(-3)$

19. $(f - h)(x)$

20. $(f + h)(x)$

21. $(f - h)(-3)$

22. $(f + h)(-2)$

23. $(g - h)(-3)$

24. $(g + h)(1)$

25. $(g + h)\left(\dfrac{1}{4}\right)$

26. $(g + h)\left(\dfrac{1}{3}\right)$

27. $(fg)(x)$

28. $(fh)(x)$

29. $(fg)(2)$

30. $(fh)(1)$

31. $(fh)(-1)$

32. $(gh)(-3)$

33. $(fg)(0)$

34. $(fh)(0)$

35. $(fg)\left(-\dfrac{1}{2}\right)$

36. $(fg)\left(-\dfrac{1}{3}\right)$

37. $\left(\dfrac{f}{g}\right)(x)$

38. $\left(\dfrac{f}{h}\right)(x)$

39. $\left(\dfrac{f}{g}\right)(2)$

40. $\left(\dfrac{f}{h}\right)(1)$

41. $\left(\dfrac{h}{g}\right)(x)$

42. $\left(\dfrac{g}{h}\right)(x)$

43. $\left(\dfrac{h}{g}\right)(3)$

44. $\left(\dfrac{f}{g}\right)(-1)$

45. $\left(\dfrac{h}{g}\right)\left(-\dfrac{1}{2}\right)$

46. $\left(\dfrac{h}{g}\right)\left(-\dfrac{3}{2}\right)$

*Solve each problem. **See Objective 2.***

47. The cost in dollars to produce x t-shirts is $C(x) = 2.5x + 50$. The revenue in dollars from sales of x t-shirts is $R(x) = 10.99x$.

   (a) Write and simplify a function P that gives profit in terms of x.

   (b) Find the profit if 100 t-shirts are produced and sold.

48. The cost in dollars to produce x baseball caps is $C(x) = 4.3x + 75$. The revenue in dollars from sales of x caps is $R(x) = 25x$.

   (a) Write and simplify a function P that gives profit in terms of x.

   (b) Find the profit if 50 caps are produced and sold.

*Graph each function. Give the domain and range. **See Example 6.***

49. $f(x) = 3x$

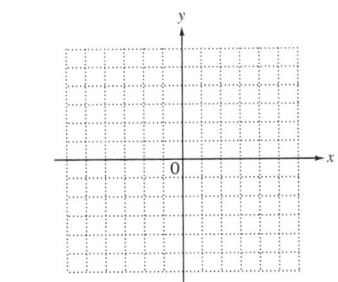

50. $f(x) = -4x$

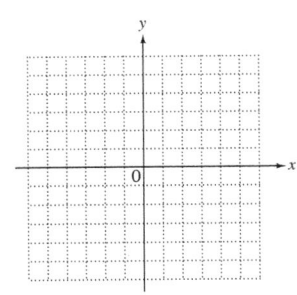

51. $f(x) = -2x + 1$

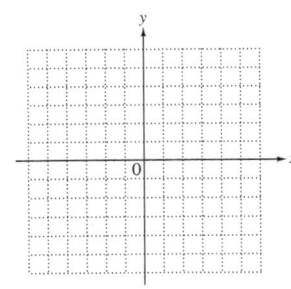

52. $f(x) = 3x + 2$

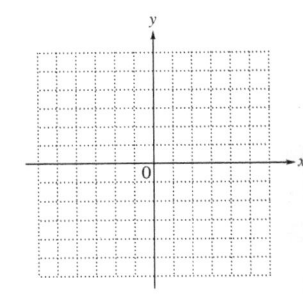

53. $f(x) = -3x^2$

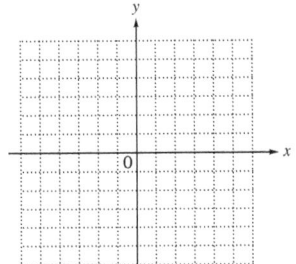

54. $f(x) = \dfrac{1}{2}x^2$

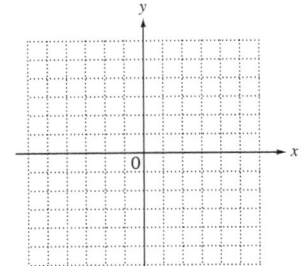

55. $f(x) = x^2 - 2$

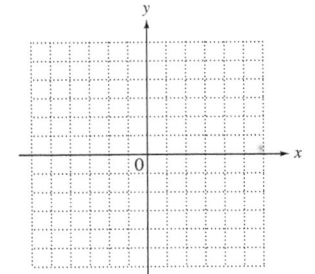

56. $f(x) = -x^2 + 2$

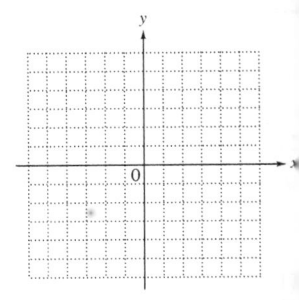

57. $f(x) = x^3 + 1$

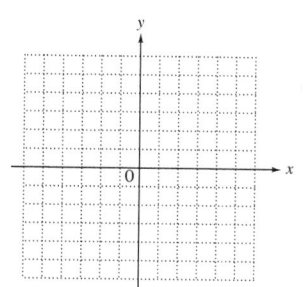

58. $f(x) = -x^3 + 2$

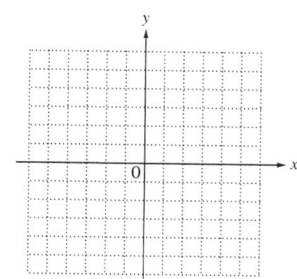

59. $f(x) = -2x^3 - 1$

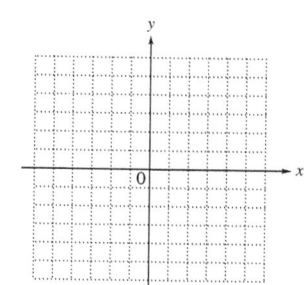

60. $f(x) = \frac{1}{2}x^3 + 3$

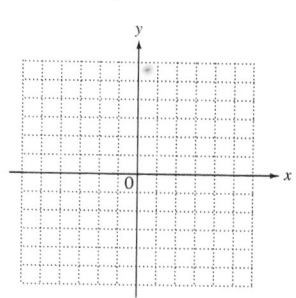

Relating Concepts (Exercises 61–64) For Individual or Group Work

The polynomial function

$$f(x) = \frac{1}{24}x^4 - \frac{1}{4}x^3 + \frac{23}{24}x^2 - \frac{3}{4}x + 1$$

will give the maximum number of interior regions formed in a circle if x points on the circumference are joined by all possible chords. For x = 1, 2, 3, 4, and 5, see **Figures A–E.**

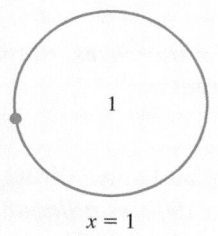

$x = 1$

Figure A

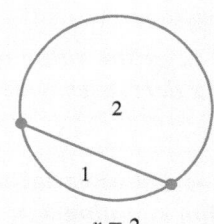

$x = 2$

Figure B

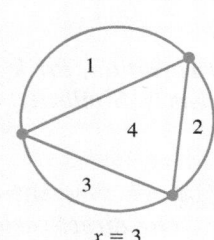

$x = 3$

Figure C

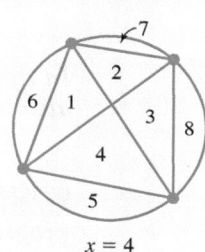

$x = 4$

Figure D

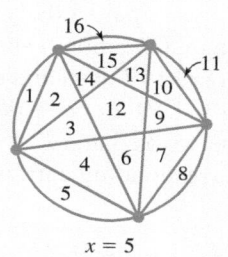

$x = 5$

Figure E

For example, in **Figure A** *we have 1 point, and because no chords can be drawn, we have only 1 interior region. In* **Figure B** *there are 2 points, and 2 interior regions are formed.*

    Apply this information and **work Exercises 61–64 in order.**

61. Use the given polynomial function to verify that $f(1) = 1$ and $f(2) = 2$.

62. Based on the appropriate figure alone, what is a logical prediction for the value of $f(3)$? $f(4)$? $f(5)$?

63. Verify the answers in **Exercise 62** by evaluating $f(3)$, $f(4)$, and $f(5)$.

64. Observe a pattern in the results of **Exercises 61–63.** Use the pattern to make a logical prediction for the value of $f(6)$. Does the prediction equal $f(6)$?

9.4 | Variation

OBJECTIVES

1. Write an equation expressing direct variation.
2. Find the constant of variation, and solve direct variation problems.
3. Solve inverse variation problems.
4. Solve joint variation problems.
5. Solve combined variation problems.

OBJECTIVE 1 **Write an equation expressing direct variation.** Functions in which *y depends on a multiple of x or y depends on a number divided by x* occur in business, mathematics, and the physical sciences.

For example, the circumference of a circle is given by the formula $C = 2\pi r$, where r is the radius of the circle. See **Figure 17.** The circumference is always a constant multiple of the radius—that is, C is always found by multiplying r by the constant 2π.

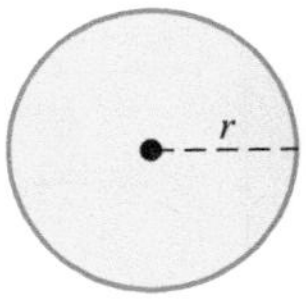

$C = 2\pi r$

Figure 17

As the **radius increases,** the **circumference increases.**

As the **radius decreases,** the **circumference decreases.**

As a result, the circumference is said to *vary directly* as the radius.

Direct Variation

y varies directly as x if there exists a real number k such that

$$y = kx.$$

Stated another way, **y is proportional to x.** The number k is the **constant of variation.**

In direct variation, for k > 0, as the value of x increases, the value of y also increases. Similarly, as x decreases, y decreases.

OBJECTIVE 2 **Find the constant of variation, and solve direct variation problems.** *The direct variation equation y = kx defines a linear function, where the constant of variation k is the slope of the line.* For example, the equation $y = 3.50x$ describes the cost y to buy x gallons of gasoline. The cost varies directly as the number of gallons of gasoline purchased.

As the *number* of gallons of gasoline *increases,* the *cost increases.*

As the *number* of gallons of gasoline *decreases,* the *cost decreases.*

The constant of variation k is **3.50,** the cost of 1 gallon of gasoline.

EXAMPLE 1 Solving a Direct Variation Problem

Eva is paid an hourly wage. One week she worked 43 hr and was paid $795.50. How much does she earn per hour?

Let h = the number of hours she works

and P = her corresponding pay.

k represents Eva's hourly wage. → $P = kh$ P varies directly as h.

$795.50 = k \cdot 43$ Let $P = 795.50$ and $h = 43$.

This is the constant of variation. → $18.50 = k$ Divide by 43.

Her hourly wage is $18.50, and P and h are related by $P = 18.50h$.

◄ **Work Problem** 1 **at the Side.**

---

1. Find the constant of variation k, and write a direct variation equation.

(a) Ginny is paid a daily wage. One month she worked 17 days and earned $1334.50. Let d = days she worked and E = her corresponding earnings.

(b) Distance varies directly as time (at a constant rate). A car travels 100 mi at a constant rate in 2 hr.

Answers

1. (a) $k = 78.50$; $E = 78.50d$
   (b) $k = 50$; Let d represent the distance traveled in h hours. Then $d = 50h$.

EXAMPLE 2   **Solving a Direct Variation Problem**

Hooke's law for an elastic spring states that the distance a spring stretches is directly proportional to the force applied. If a force of 150 newtons* stretches a certain spring 8 cm, how much will a force of 400 newtons stretch the spring? See **Figure 18.**

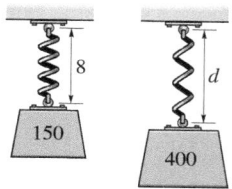

Figure 18

Let d = the distance the spring stretches

and f = the force applied.

Then $d = kf$ for some constant k. A force of 150 newtons stretches the spring 8 cm, so use these values to find k.

$$d = kf \qquad \text{Variation equation}$$

$\boxed{\text{Solve for } k.}$ $\quad 8 = k \cdot 150 \qquad$ Let $d = 8$ and $f = 150$.

$$k = \frac{8}{150} \qquad \text{Solve for } k.$$

$$k = \frac{4}{75} \qquad \text{Write in lowest terms.}$$

Substitute $\frac{4}{75}$ for k in the variation equation $d = kf$.

$$d = \frac{4}{75}f \qquad \text{Here, } k = \frac{4}{75}.$$

For a force of 400 newtons, substitute 400 for f.

$$d = \frac{4}{75}(400) = \frac{64}{3} \qquad \text{Let } f = 400.$$

The spring will stretch $\frac{64}{3}$ cm, or $21\frac{1}{3}$ cm, if a force of 400 newtons is applied.

─────────── **Work Problem ❷ at the Side.** ▶

Solving a Variation Problem

Step 1   Write the variation equation.

Step 2   Substitute the initial values and solve for k.

Step 3   Rewrite the variation equation with the value of k from Step 2.

Step 4   Substitute the remaining values, solve for the unknown, and find the required answer.

One variable can be proportional to a power of another variable.

Direct Variation as a Power

y varies directly as the nth power of x if there exists a real number k such that

$$y = kx^n.$$

❷ Solve the problem.
   The charge (in dollars) to customers for electricity (in kilowatt-hours) varies directly as the number of kilowatt-hours used. It costs $52 to use 800 kilowatt-hours. Find the cost to use 1000 kilowatt-hours.

---

*A newton is a unit of measure of force used in physics.

Answer

2. $65

3 The area $\mathscr{A}$ of a circle varies directly as the square of its radius r. A circle with radius 3 in. has area 28.278 in.^{2}.

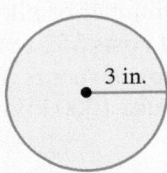

3 in.

(a) Write a variation equation and give the value of k.

An example of direct variation as a power is the formula for the area of a circle,

$$\mathscr{A} = \pi r^2.$$

See **Figure 19.** Here, π is the constant of variation, and the area varies directly as the square of the radius.

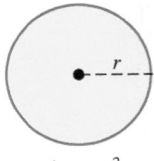

$\mathscr{A} = \pi r^2$

Figure 19

EXAMPLE 3 **Solving a Direct Variation Problem**

The distance a body falls from rest varies directly as the square of the time it falls (disregarding air resistance). If a skydiver falls 64 ft in 2 sec, how far will she fall in 8 sec?

Step 1 Let d = the distance the skydiver falls

and t = the time it takes to fall.

Then d is proportional to t for some constant k.

$d = kt^2$ *d varies directly as the square of t.*

Step 2 To find the value of k, substitute the given values 64 ft and 2 sec.

$d = kt^2$ Variation equation

$64 = k(2)^2$ Let $d = 64$ and $t = 2$.

$k = 16$ Solve for k.

Step 3 Rewrite the variation equation $d = kt^2$ using 16 for k.

$d = 16t^2$ Here, $k = 16$.

Step 4 Let $t = 8$ to find the number of feet the skydiver will fall in 8 sec.

$d = 16(8)^2 = 1024$ Let $t = 8$.

The skydiver will fall 1024 ft in 8 sec.

(b) What is the area of a circle with radius 4.1 in.? (Use the answers from part (a).)

◀ **Work Problem** **3** **at the Side.**

OBJECTIVE **3** **Solve inverse variation problems.**
With inverse variation, where $k > 0$, as one variable increases, the other variable decreases.

For example, in a closed space, volume decreases as pressure increases, as illustrated by a trash compactor. See **Figure 20.** As the compactor presses down, the pressure on the trash increases, and in turn, the trash occupies a smaller space.

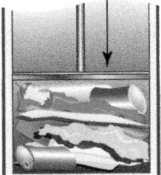

As pressure on trash increases, volume of trash decreases.

Figure 20

Inverse Variation

y **varies inversely as** *x* if there exists a real number k such that

$$y = \frac{k}{x}.$$

y **varies inversely as the** *n***th power of** *x* if there exists a real number k such that

$$y = \frac{k}{x^n}.$$

The inverse variation equation $y = \frac{k}{x}$ defines a rational function.

Another example of inverse variation comes from the distance formula.

$$d = rt \quad \text{Distance formula}$$

$$t = \frac{d}{r} \quad \text{Divide each side by } r.$$

Here, t (time) varies inversely as r (rate or speed), with d (distance) serving as the constant of variation. For example, if the distance between Chicago and Des Moines is 300 mi, then

$$t = \frac{300}{r}.$$

The values of r and t might be any of the following.

$\left.\begin{array}{l} r = 50, t = 6 \\ r = 60, t = 5 \\ r = 75, t = 4 \end{array}\right\}$ As r increases, t decreases. $\quad \left.\begin{array}{l} r = 30, t = 10 \\ r = 25, t = 12 \\ r = 20, t = 15 \end{array}\right\}$ As r decreases, t increases.

If we *increase* the rate (speed) at which we drive, time *decreases*. If we *decrease* the rate (speed) at which we drive, time *increases*.

EXAMPLE 4 **Solving an Inverse Variation Problem**

In the manufacture of a phone-charging device, the cost of producing the device varies inversely as the number produced. If 10,000 units are produced, the cost is $2 per unit. Find the cost per unit to produce 25,000 units.

Let x = the number of units produced

and c = the cost per unit.

Here, as production increases, cost decreases, and as production decreases, cost increases. We write a variation equation using the variables c and x and the constant k.

$$c = \frac{k}{x} \quad c \text{ varies inversely as } x.$$

To find k, we replace c with 2 and x with 10,000.

$$2 = \frac{k}{10,000} \quad \text{Substitute in the variation equation.}$$

$$20,000 = k \quad \text{Multiply by 10,000.}$$

Thus, $c = \frac{k}{x}$ becomes $c = \frac{20,000}{x}$. When $x = 25,000$,

$$c = \frac{20,000}{25,000} = 0.80. \quad \text{Let } x = 25,000.$$

The cost per unit to make 25,000 units is $0.80.

―――――― **Work Problem** 4 **at the Side.** ▶

④ Solve each problem.

(a) For a constant area, the height of a triangle varies inversely as the base. If the height is 7 cm when the base is 8 cm, find the height when the base is 14 cm.

(b) The current in a simple electrical circuit varies inversely as the resistance. If the current is 80 amps when the resistance is 10 ohms, find the current when the resistance is 16 ohms.

Answers
4. **(a)** 4 cm **(b)** 50 amps

5 If the temperature is constant, the volume of a gas varies inversely as the pressure. For a certain gas, the volume is 10 cm³ when the pressure is 6 kg per cm².

(a) Find the variation equation.

(b) Find the volume when the pressure is 12 kg per cm².

EXAMPLE 5 Solving an Inverse Variation Problem

The weight of an object above Earth varies inversely as the square of its distance from the center of Earth. A space shuttle in an elliptical orbit has a maximum distance from the center of Earth (**apogee**) of 6700 mi. Its minimum distance from the center of Earth (**perigee**) is 4090 mi. See **Figure 21.** If an astronaut in the shuttle weighs 57 lb at its apogee, what does the astronaut weigh at its perigee?

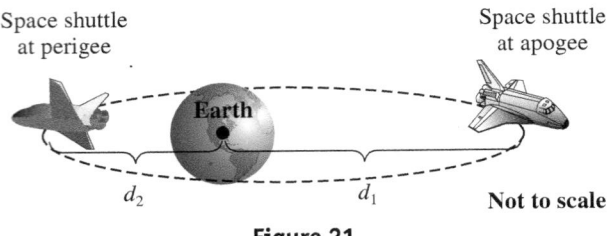

Space shuttle at perigee · Earth · Space shuttle at apogee

d_2 d_1 **Not to scale**

Figure 21

Let w = the weight and d = the distance from the center of Earth, for some constant k.

$$w = \frac{k}{d^2} \qquad w \text{ varies inversely as the square of } d.$$

At the apogee, the astronaut weighs 57 lb, and the distance from the center of Earth is 6700 mi. Use these values to find k.

$$57 = \frac{k}{(6700)^2} \qquad \text{Let } w = 57 \text{ and } d = 6700.$$

$$k = 57(6700)^2 \qquad \text{Solve for } k.$$

Substitute $k = 57(6700)^2$ and $d = 4090$ to find the weight at the perigee.

$$w = \frac{57(6700)^2}{(4090)^2} \approx 153 \text{ lb} \qquad \text{Round to the nearest pound.}$$

◀ **Work Problem 5 at the Side.**

OBJECTIVE ▶ 4 Solve joint variation problems. If one variable varies directly as the *product* of several other variables (perhaps raised to powers), the first variable is said to *vary jointly* as the others.

> **Joint Variation**
>
> ***y* varies jointly as *x* and *z*** if there exists a real number *k* such that
>
> $$y = kxz.$$

An example of joint variation is the formula for the volume of a right pyramid, $V = \frac{1}{3}Bh$. See **Figure 22.** Here, $\frac{1}{3}$ is the constant of variation, and the volume varies jointly as the area of the base and the height.

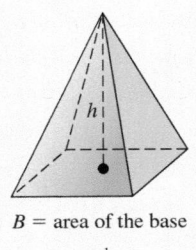

B = area of the base

$V = \frac{1}{3}Bh$

Figure 22

> **❗ CAUTION**
>
> Note that *and* in the expression "*y* varies jointly as *x and z*" translates as a product in
>
> $$y = kxz.$$
>
> The word *and* does not indicate addition here.

Answers

5. **(a)** $V = \dfrac{60}{P}$ **(b)** 5 cm³

EXAMPLE 6 Solving a Joint Variation Problem

The interest on a loan or an investment is given by the formula $I = prt$. Here, for a given principal p, the interest earned I varies jointly as the interest rate r and the time t that the principal is left earning interest. If an investment earns \$100 interest at 5% for 2 yr, how much interest will the same principal earn at 4.5% for 3 yr?

We use the formula $I = prt$, where p is the constant of variation because it is the same for both investments.

$$I = prt$$
$$100 = p\,(0.05)\,(2) \qquad \text{Let } I = 100, r = 0.05, \text{ and } t = 2.$$
$$100 = 0.1p \qquad \text{Multiply.}$$
$$p = 1000 \qquad \text{Divide by 0.1. Rewrite.}$$

Now we find I when $p = 1000$, $r = 0.045$, and $t = 3$.

$$I = 1000\,(0.045)\,(3) = 135 \qquad \text{Let } p = 1000, r = 0.045, \text{ and } t = 3.$$

The interest will be \$135.

——————— **Work Problem 6 at the Side.** ▶

OBJECTIVE ▶ **5** **Solve combined variation problems.** There are combinations of direct and inverse variation, called **combined variation.**

EXAMPLE 7 Solving a Combined Variation Problem

Body mass index (BMI) is used to assess whether a person's level of weight is healthy. A BMI from 19 through 25 is considered desirable. BMI varies directly as an individual's weight in pounds and inversely as the square of the individual's height in inches. (Data from *Washington Post*.)

A person who weighs 118 lb and is 64 in. tall has a BMI of 20. (BMI is rounded to the nearest whole number.) Find the BMI of a man who weighs 165 lb and is 70 in. tall.

Let B represent the BMI, w the weight, and h the height.

$$B = \frac{kw}{h^2} \quad \begin{array}{l} \longleftarrow \text{ BMI varies directly as the weight.} \\ \longleftarrow \text{ BMI varies inversely as the square of the height.} \end{array}$$

To find k, let $B = 20$, $w = 118$, and $h = 64$.

$$20 = \frac{k\,(118)}{64^2} \qquad B = \frac{kw}{h^2}$$

$$k = \frac{20\,(64^2)}{118} \qquad \begin{array}{l} \text{Multiply by } 64^2. \\ \text{Divide by 118.} \end{array}$$

$$k \approx 694 \qquad \begin{array}{l} \text{Nearest whole} \\ \text{number} \end{array}$$

Now find B when $k = 694$, $w = 165$, and $h = 70$.

$$B = \frac{694\,(165)}{70^2} \approx 23 \qquad \begin{array}{l} \text{Nearest whole} \\ \text{number} \end{array}$$

The man's BMI is 23.

——————— **Work Problem 7 at the Side.** ▶

6 Solve the problem.

The volume of a rectangular box of a given height is proportional to its width and length. A box with width 2 ft and length 4 ft has volume 12 ft³. Find the volume of a box with the same height that is 3 ft wide and 5 ft long.

7 Solve the problem.

The maximum load that a cylindrical column with a circular cross section can hold varies directly as the fourth power of the diameter of the cross section and inversely as the square of the height. A 9-m column 1 m in diameter will support 8 metric tons. How many metric tons can be supported by a column 12 m high and $\frac{2}{3}$ m in diameter?

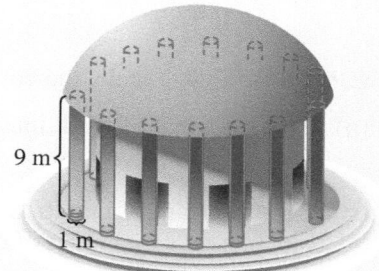

Load = 8 metric tons

Answers

6. 22.5 ft³

7. $\frac{8}{9}$ metric ton

9.4 Exercises

FOR EXTRA HELP

Go to MyMathLab *for worked-out, step-by-step solutions to exercises enclosed in a square* ☐ *and video solutions to* ▶ *exercises.*

CONCEPT CHECK *Use personal experience or intuition to determine whether the situation suggests* direct *or* inverse *variation.**

1. The rate and the distance traveled by a pickup truck in 3 hr

2. The amount of pressure placed on the accelerator of a truck and the rate of the truck

3. The amount of gasoline pumped and the amount of empty space in the tank

4. A person's age and the probability that the person believes in the tooth fairy

5. The surface area of a balloon and its diameter

6. The intensity of a light source (such as a light bulb) and the distance from which a person views the light

7. The loudness of a sound source (such as a car horn) and the distance from which a person hears the sound

8. The number of different lottery tickets purchased and the probability of winning that lottery

9. **CONCEPT CHECK** Refer to **Exercises 1–8.** Give an example of direct variation from everyday life.

10. **CONCEPT CHECK** Refer to **Exercises 1–8.** Give an example of inverse variation from everyday life.

11. **CONCEPT CHECK** Make the correct choice.

    (a) If the constant of variation is positive and y varies directly as x, then as x increases, y (*increases / decreases*).

    (b) If the constant of variation is positive and y varies inversely as x, then as x increases, y (*increases / decreases*).

12. Bill Veeck was the owner of several major league baseball teams in the 1950s and 1960s. He was known to often sit in the stands and enjoy games with his paying customers. Here is a quote attributed to him:

    "I have discovered in 20 years of moving around a ballpark, that the knowledge of the game is usually in inverse proportion to the price of the seats."

    Explain the meaning of this statement.

---

*The authors thank Linda Kodama for suggesting these exercises.

CONCEPT CHECK *Determine whether each equation represents* direct, inverse, joint, *or* combined *variation.*

13. $y = \dfrac{3}{x}$

14. $y = \dfrac{8}{x}$

15. $y = 10x^2$

16. $y = 2x^3$

17. $y = 3xz^4$

18. $y = 6x^3z^2$

19. $y = \dfrac{4x}{wz}$

20. $y = \dfrac{6x}{st}$

CONCEPT CHECK *Write each formula using the "language" of variation. For example, the formula for the circumference of a circle, $C = 2\pi r$, can be written as*

"The circumference of a circle varies directly as the length of its radius."

21. $P = 4s$, where P is the perimeter of a square with side of length s

22. $d = 2r$, where d is the diameter of a circle with radius r

23. $S = 4\pi r^2$, where S is the surface area of a sphere with radius r

24. $V = \frac{4}{3}\pi r^3$, where V is the volume of a sphere with radius r

25. $\mathcal{A} = \frac{1}{2}bh$, where $\mathcal{A}$ is the area of a triangle with base b and height h

26. $V = \frac{1}{3}\pi r^2 h$, where V is the volume of a cone with radius r and height h

CONCEPT CHECK *Write a variation equation for each situation. Use k as the constant of variation.*

27. A varies directly as b.

28. h varies inversely as t.

29. P varies inversely as the cube of x.

30. M varies directly as the square of d.

31. I varies jointly as g and h.

32. C varies jointly as a and the square of b.

Solve each problem. **See Examples 1–6.**

33. If x varies directly as y, and $x = 9$ when $y = 3$, find x when $y = 12$.

34. If x varies directly as y, and $x = 10$ when $y = 7$, find y when $x = 50$.

35. If a varies directly as the square of b, and $a = 4$ when $b = 3$, find a when $b = 2$.

36. If h varies directly as the square of m, and $h = 15$ when $m = 5$, find h when $m = 7$.

37. If z varies inversely as w, and $z = 10$ when $w = 0.5$, find z when $w = 8$.

38. If t varies inversely as s, and $t = 3$ when $s = 5$, find s when $t = 5$.

39. If m varies inversely as the square of p, and $m = 20$ when $p = 2$, find m when $p = 5$.

40. If a varies inversely as the square of b, and $a = 48$ when $b = 4$, find a when $b = 7$.

41. p varies jointly as q and the square of r, and $p = 200$ when $q = 2$ and $r = 3$. Find p when $q = 5$ and $r = 2$.

42. f varies jointly as h and the square of g, and $f = 50$ when $h = 2$ and $g = 4$. Find f when $h = 6$ and $g = 3$.

Solve each problem. ***See Examples 1–7.***

43. Matt bought 8 gal of gasoline and paid $26.39. To the nearest tenth of a cent, what is the price of gasoline per gallon?

44. Nora gives horseback rides at Shadow Mountain Ranch. A 2.5-hr ride costs $50.00. What is the price per hour?

45. The weight of an object on Earth is directly proportional to the weight of that same object on the moon. A 200-lb astronaut would weigh 32 lb on the moon. How much would a 50-lb dog weigh on the moon?

46. The pressure exerted by a certain liquid at a given point is directly proportional to the depth of the point beneath the surface of the liquid. The pressure at 30 m is 80 newtons. What pressure is exerted at 50 m?

47. The volume of a can of tomatoes is directly proportional to the height of the can. If the volume of the can is 300 cm³ when its height is 10.62 cm, find the volume of a can (to the nearest whole number) with height 15.92 cm.

48. The force required to compress a spring is directly proportional to the change in length of the spring. If a force of 20 newtons is required to compress a certain spring 2 cm, how much force is required to compress the spring from 20 cm to 8 cm?

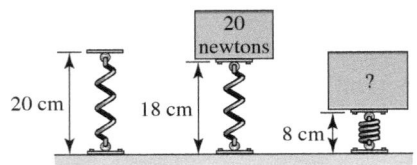

49. The current in a simple electrical circuit is inversely proportional to the resistance. If the current is 20 amperes (an **ampere** is a unit for measuring current) when the resistance is 5 ohms, find the current when the resistance is 7.5 ohms.

50. The frequency (number of vibrations per second) of a vibrating string varies inversely as its length. That is, a longer string vibrates fewer times in a second than a shorter string. Suppose a piano string 2 ft long vibrates 250 cycles per sec. What frequency would a string 5 ft long have?

51. For a constant area, the length of a rectangle varies inversely as the width. The length of a rectangle is 27 ft when the width is 10 ft. Find the width of a rectangle with the same area if the length is 18 ft.

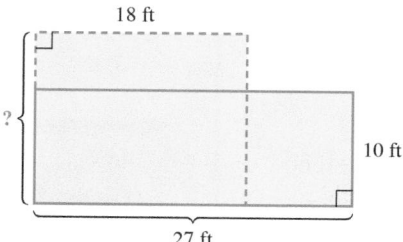

52. The speed of a pulley varies inversely as its diameter. One kind of pulley, with diameter 6 in., turns at 150 revolutions per minute. Find the number of revolutions per minute for a similar pulley with diameter 10 in.

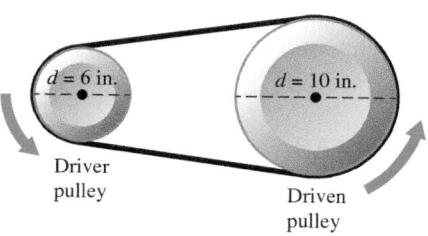

53. For a body falling freely from rest (disregarding air resistance), the distance the body falls varies directly as the square of the time. If an object is dropped from the top of a tower 576 ft high and hits the ground in 6 sec, how far did it fall in the first 4 sec?

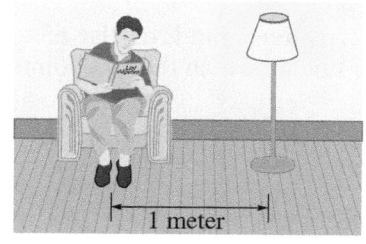

54. The amount of water emptied by a pipe varies directly as the square of the diameter of the pipe. For a certain constant water flow, a pipe will allow 200 gal of water to escape in an hour. The diameter of the pipe is 6 in. How much water would a 12-in. pipe empty in an hour, assuming the same water flow?

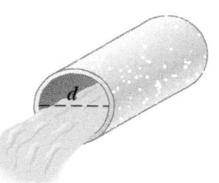

55. The amount of light (measured in foot-candles) produced by a light source varies inversely as the square of the distance from the source. If the illumination produced 1 m from a light source is 768 foot-candles, find the illumination produced 6 m from the same source.

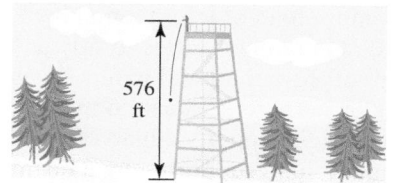

56. The force with which Earth attracts an object above Earth's surface varies inversely as the square of the distance of the object from the center of Earth. If an object 4000 mi from the center of Earth is attracted with a force of 160 lb, find the force of attraction if the object were 6000 mi from the center of Earth.

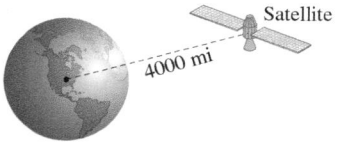

57. For a given interest rate, simple interest varies jointly as principal and time. If $2000 left in an account for 4 yr earned interest of $280, how much interest would be earned in 6 yr?

58. The collision impact of an automobile varies jointly as its weight and the square of its speed. Suppose a 2000-lb car traveling at 55 mph has a collision impact of 6.1. What is the collision impact (to the nearest tenth) of the same car at 65 mph?

59. The force needed to keep a car from skidding on a curve varies inversely as the radius of the curve and jointly as the weight of the car and the square of the speed. If 242 lb of force keep a 2000-lb car from skidding on a curve of radius 500 ft at 30 mph, what force (to the nearest tenth) would keep the same car from skidding on a curve of radius 750 ft at 50 mph?

60. The volume of gas varies inversely as the pressure and directly as the temperature. (Temperature must be measured in *Kelvin* (K), a unit of measurement used in physics.) If a certain gas occupies a volume of 1.3 L at 300 K and a pressure of 18 newtons, find the volume at 340 K and a pressure of 24 newtons.

61. The weight of a bass varies jointly as its girth and the square of its length. (**Girth** is the distance around the body of a fish.) A prize-winning bass weighed in at 22.7 lb and measured 36 in. long with a 21-in. girth. How much would a bass 28 in. long with an 18-in. girth weigh (to the nearest tenth)? (Data from *The Sacramento Bee.*)

62. See **Exercise 61.** The weight of a trout varies jointly as its length and the square of its girth. One angler caught a trout that weighed 10.5 lb and measured 26 in. long with an 18-in. girth. Find the weight of a trout that is 22 in. long with a 15-in. girth (to the nearest tenth). (Data from *The Sacramento Bee.*)

63. A body mass index from 27 through 29 carries a slight risk of weight-related health problems, while one of 30 or more indicates a great increase in risk. Use your own height and weight and the information in **Example 7** to determine your BMI and whether you are at risk.

64. The maximum load of a horizontal beam that is supported at both ends varies jointly as the width and the square of the height and inversely as the length between the supports. A beam 6 m long, 0.1 m wide, and 0.06 m high supports a load of 360 kg. What is the maximum load supported by a beam 16 m long, 0.2 m wide, and 0.08 m high?

Relating Concepts (Exercises 65–70) For Individual or Group Work

A routine activity such as pumping gasoline can be related to many of the concepts we have studied. Suppose that premium unleaded costs $3.35 per gal.
Work Exercises 65–70 in order.

65. 0 gal of gasoline cost $0.00, while 1 gal costs $3.35. Represent these two pieces of information as ordered pairs of the form (gallons, price).

66. Use the information from **Exercise 65** to find the slope of the line on which the two points lie.

67. Write the slope-intercept form of the equation of the line on which the two points lie.

68. Using function notation, if $f(x) = ax + b$ represents the line from **Exercise 67,** what are the values of a and b?

69. How does the value of a from **Exercise 68** relate to gasoline in this situation? With relationship to the line, what do we call this number?

70. Why does the equation from **Exercise 68** satisfy the conditions for direct variation? In the context of variation, what do we call the value of a?

Chapter 9   *Summary*

Key Terms

9.1

relation   A relation is any set of ordered pairs.

function   A function is a relation in which, for each distinct value of the first component of the ordered pairs of the relation, there is *exactly one* value of the second component.

dependent variable   If the quantity y depends on x, then y is the dependent variable in a relation between x and y.

independent variable   If y depends on x, then x is the independent variable in a relation between x and y.

domain   The domain of a relation is the set of all values of the independent variable (x) of the ordered pairs of the relation.

range   The range of a relation is the set of all values of the dependent variable (y) of the ordered pairs of the relation.

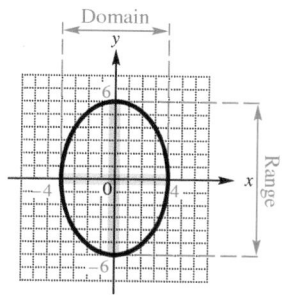

Graph of a relation

9.2

function notation   Function notation $f(x)$ is another way to represent the dependent variable y for the function f.

Name of the function

Defining expression

$$y \;=\; f(x) \;=\; \overbrace{9x - 5}$$

Value of the function   Name of the independent variable

linear function   A function of the form $f(x) = ax + b$ is a linear function.

constant function   A constant function is a linear function of the form $f(x) = b$, for a real number b.

9.3

polynomial function of degree n   A function defined by $f(x) = a_n x^n + a_{n-1} x^{n-1} + \cdots + a_1 x + a_0$, where $a_n \neq 0$ and n is a whole number, is a polynomial function of degree n.

identity function   The simplest polynomial function is the identity function $f(x) = x$.

squaring function   The polynomial function $f(x) = x^2$ is the squaring function.

cubing function   The polynomial function $f(x) = x^3$ is the cubing function.

9.4

varies directly y varies directly as x if there exists a real number k such that $y = kx$. The number k is the **constant of variation.**

varies inversely y varies inversely as x if there exists a real number k such that $y = \frac{k}{x}$.

joint variation y varies jointly as x and z if there exists a real number k such that $y = kxz$.

combined variation   Combined variation occurs when both direct and inverse variation are involved in the same equation.

New Symbols

$f(x)$ function notation; function f evaluated at x (read "f *of* x" or "f *at* x")

Test Your Word Power

See how well you have learned the vocabulary in this chapter.

1 A **relation** is
A. a set of ordered pairs
B. the ratio of the change in y to the change in x along a line
C. the set of all possible values of the independent variable
D. all the second components of a set of ordered pairs.

2 A **function** is
A. the numbers in an ordered pair
B. a set of ordered pairs in which each distinct x-value corresponds to exactly one y-value
C. a pair of numbers written within parentheses in which order matters
D. the set of all ordered pairs that satisfy an equation.

(continued)

Test Your Word Power (*continued*)

3 In a relationship between two variables x and y, the **independent variable** is
  A. x, if x depends on y
  B. x, if y depends on x
  C. either x or y
  D. the larger of x and y.

4 In a relationship between two variables x and y, the **dependent variable** is
  A. y, if y depends on x

  B. y, if x depends on y
  C. either x or y
  D. the smaller of x and y.

5 The **domain** of a function is
  A. the set of all possible values of the dependent variable y
  B. a set of ordered pairs
  C. the difference of the x-values
  D. the set of all possible values of the independent variable x.

6 The **range** of a function is
  A. the set of all possible values of the dependent variable y
  B. a set of ordered pairs
  C. the difference of the y-values
  D. the set of all possible values of the independent variable x.

Answers to Test Your Word Power

1. A; *Example:* The set $\{(2,0),(4,3),(6,6),(8,9)\}$ defines a relation.

2. B; *Example:* The relation given in Answer 1 is a function because each distinct x-value corresponds to exactly one y-value.

3. B; *Example:* See Answer 4, which follows.

4. A; *Example:* When borrowing money, the amount you borrow (independent variable) determines the size of your payments (dependent variable).

5. D; *Example:* In the function in Answer 1, the domain is the set of x-values, $\{2,4,6,8\}$.

6. A; *Example:* In the function in Answer 1, the range is the set of y-values, $\{0,3,6,9\}$.

Quick Review

Concepts	Examples

9.1 Introduction to Relations and Functions

A **relation** is any set of ordered pairs (x, y). A **function** is a set of ordered pairs in which, for each distinct value of the first component, there is *exactly one* value of the second component.

The set of first components (x-values) is the **domain.**

The set of second components (y-values) is the **range.**

The set of ordered pairs $\{(-1,4),(0,6),(1,4)\}$ defines a function.

  Domain: $\{-1,0,1\}$ Set of x-values
  Range: $\{4,6\}$ Set of y-values

The equation $y = x^2$ defines a function.

  Domain: $(-\infty, \infty)$ Range: $[0, \infty)$

9.2 Function Notation and Linear Functions

To evaluate a function f, where $f(x)$ defines the range value for a given value of x in the domain, substitute the domain value wherever x appears.

Let $f(x) = x^2 - 7x + 12$. Find $f(1)$.

$$f(x) = x^2 - 7x + 12$$
$$f(1) = 1^2 - 7(1) + 12 \quad \text{Let } x = 1.$$
$$f(1) = 6$$

To write an equation that defines a function f in function notation, follow these steps.

Step 1 Solve the equation for y if it is not given in that form.

Step 2 Replace y with $f(x)$.

Write $2x + 3y = 12$ in function notation for function f.

$$3y = -2x + 12 \quad \text{Subtract } 2x.$$
$$y = -\frac{2}{3}x + 4 \quad \text{Divide by 3.}$$
$$f(x) = -\frac{2}{3}x + 4 \quad \text{Replace } y \text{ with } f(x).$$

Concepts	**Examples**

9.3 Polynomial Functions, Operations, and Graphs

Operations on Functions

If $f(x)$ and $g(x)$ define functions, then

$$(f + g)(x) = f(x) + g(x),$$
$$(f - g)(x) = f(x) - g(x),$$
$$(fg)(x) = f(x) \cdot g(x),$$

and $$\left(\frac{f}{g}\right)(x) = \frac{f(x)}{g(x)}, \quad \text{where } g(x) \neq 0.$$

Let $f(x) = x^2$ and $g(x) = 2x + 1$.

$(f + g)(x)$
$\qquad = f(x) + g(x)$
$\qquad = x^2 + 2x + 1$

$(f - g)(x)$
$\qquad = f(x) - g(x)$
$\qquad = x^2 - (2x + 1)$
$\qquad = x^2 - 2x - 1$

$(fg)(x)$
$\qquad = f(x) \cdot g(x)$
$\qquad = x^2(2x + 1)$
$\qquad = 2x^3 + x^2$

$\left(\dfrac{f}{g}\right)(x)$
$\qquad = \dfrac{f(x)}{g(x)}$
$\qquad = \dfrac{x^2}{2x + 1}, \quad x \neq -\dfrac{1}{2}$

Graphs of Basic Polynomial Functions

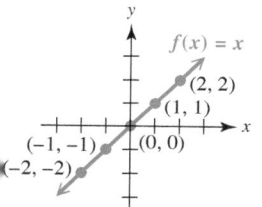

Identity function
$f(x) = x$
Domain: $(-\infty, \infty)$
Range: $(-\infty, \infty)$

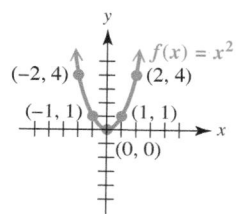

Squaring function
$f(x) = x^2$
Domain: $(-\infty, \infty)$
Range: $[0, \infty)$

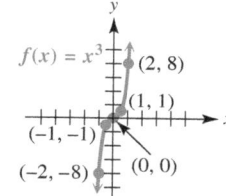

Cubing function
$f(x) = x^3$
Domain: $(-\infty, \infty)$
Range: $(-\infty, \infty)$

9.4 Variation

Let k be a real number.

If $\quad y = kx,\quad$ then y varies directly as x.

If $\quad y = kx^n,\quad$ then y varies directly as x^n.

If $\quad y = \dfrac{k}{x^n},\quad$ then y varies inversely as x^n.

If $\quad y = kxz,\quad$ then y varies jointly as x and z.

The diameter of a circle **varies directly as** the radius.

$$d = kr \qquad \text{Here, } k = 2.$$

The area of a circle **varies directly as** the square of the radius.

$$\mathscr{A} = kr^2 \qquad \text{Here, } k = \pi.$$

Pressure **varies inversely as** volume.

$$P = \frac{k}{V}$$

For a given principal, interest **varies jointly as** interest rate and time.

$$I = krt \qquad k \text{ is the given principal.}$$

Chapter 9 Review Exercises

9.1, 9.2 *Determine whether each relation defines a function, and give the domain and range.*

1. $\{(-4, 2), (-4, -2), (1, 5), (1, -5)\}$

2.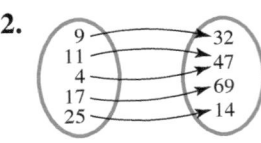

3.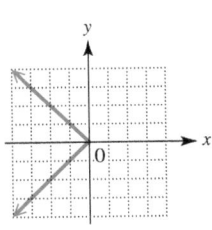

4.

Determine whether each relation defines y as a function of x. Identify any linear functions. Give the domain.

5. $y = 3x - 3$

6. $y < x + 2$

7. $x = y^2$

8. $y = \dfrac{7}{x - 36}$

Given $f(x) = -2x^2 + 3x - 6$, find each of the following.

9. $f(0)$

10. $f(3)$

11. $f(p)$

12. $f(-k)$

13. The equation $2x^2 - y = 0$ defines y as a function of x. Write it using $f(x)$ notation, and find $f(3)$.

14. Describe the graph of a constant function.

9.3 *Let $f(x) = 12x^2 - 3x$ and $g(x) = 3x$. Find each of the following.*

15. $(f + g)(x)$

16. $(f - g)(-2)$

17. $(fg)(x)$

18. $(fg)(-1)$

19. $\left(\dfrac{f}{g}\right)(x)$

20. $\left(\dfrac{f}{g}\right)(2)$

Graph each function. Give the domain and range.

21. $f(x) = -2x + 5$

22. $f(x) = x^2 - 6$

23. $f(x) = -x^3 + 1$

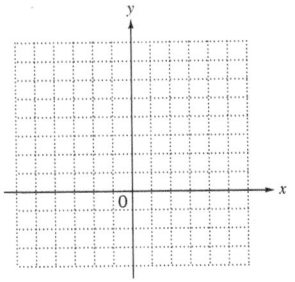

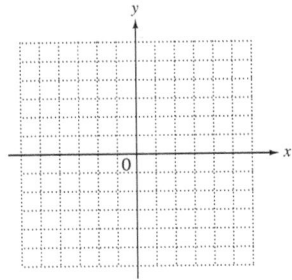

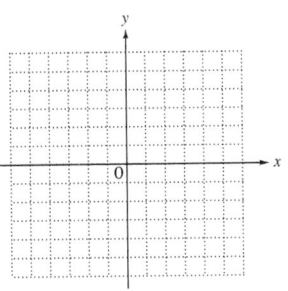

9.4 *Solve each problem.*

24. For a particular camera, the viewing distance varies directly as the amount of enlargement. A picture taken with this camera that is enlarged 5 times should be viewed from a distance of 250 mm. A print 8.6 times the size of the negative is made. From what distance should it be viewed?

25. The frequency (number of vibrations per second) of a vibrating guitar string varies inversely as its length. That is, a longer string vibrates fewer times in a second than a shorter string. A guitar string 0.65 m long vibrates 4.3 cycles per sec. What frequency would a string 0.5 m long have?

Chapter 9 Mixed Review Exercises

1. The table shows life expectancy at birth in the United States for selected years.

   (a) Does the table define a function?

   (b) What are the domain and range?

   (c) Call this function f. Give two ordered pairs that belong to f.

   (d) Find $f(2010)$. What does it mean?

   (e) If $f(x) = 75.4$, what does x equal?

Year	Life Expectancy at Birth (in years)
1950	68.2
1960	69.7
1970	70.8
1980	73.7
1990	75.4
2000	77.0
2010	78.7

Data from National Center for Health Statistics.

2. **CONCEPT CHECK** The linear equation $2x - 5y = 7$ defines y as a function of x. If $y = f(x)$, which of the following defines the same function?

   A. $f(x) = -\dfrac{2}{5}x + \dfrac{7}{5}$ **B.** $f(x) = -\dfrac{2}{5}x - \dfrac{7}{5}$

   C. $f(x) = \dfrac{2}{5}x - \dfrac{7}{5}$ **D.** $f(x) = \dfrac{2}{5}x + \dfrac{7}{5}$

3. **CONCEPT CHECK** Which of the following defines a linear function?

   A. $y = \dfrac{2}{5}x - 3$ **B.** $y = \dfrac{1}{x}$

   C. $y = x^2$ **D.** $y = x^3$

Let $f(x) = 2x^2 - 4$ and $g(x) = 3x + 1$. Find each of the following.

4. $f(-1)$

5. $(f + g)(3)$

6. $(gf)(-3)$

7. $\left(\dfrac{g}{f}\right)(-1)$

8. Graph the function

$$f(x) = \dfrac{1}{2}x^2 - 1.$$

Give the domain and range.

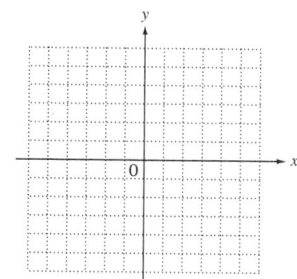

Solve each problem.

9. In which one of the following does y vary inversely as x?

   A. $y = 2x$ **B.** $y = \dfrac{x}{3}$ **C.** $y = \dfrac{3}{x}$ **D.** $y = x^2$

10. If p varies inversely as the cube of q, and $p = 100$ when $q = 3$, find p when $q = 5$.

11. The volume of a rectangular box of a given height is proportional to its width and length. A box with width 4 ft and length 8 ft has volume 64 ft^3. Find the volume of a box with the same height that is 3 ft wide and 6 ft long.

12. The area of a triangle varies jointly as the lengths of the base and height. A triangle with base 10 ft and height 4 ft has area 20 ft^2. Find the area of a triangle with base 3 ft and height 8 ft.

Chapter 9 Test

The Chapter Test Prep Videos with step-by-step solutions are available in MyMathLab or on YouTube at **https://goo.gl/3rBuO5**

1. Which of the following is the graph of a function? Give its domain and range.

A.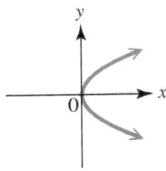

B.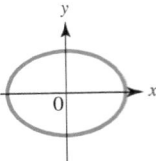

C.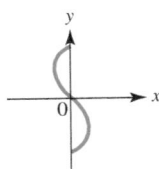

D.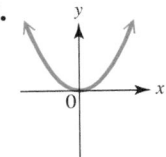

2. Which of the following does not define a function? Give its domain and range.

A. $\{(0, 1), (-2, 3), (4, 8)\}$

B. $y = 2x - 6$

C.

x	y
0	1
3	2
0	2
6	3

Let $f(x) = -2x^2 + 5x - 6$ and $g(x) = 7x - 3$. Find each of the following.

3. $f(4)$

4. $(f + g)(x)$

5. $(f - g)(x)$

6. $(f - g)(-2)$

Let $f(x) = x^2 + 3x + 2$ and $g(x) = x + 1$. Find each of the following.

7. $(fg)(x)$

8. $(fg)(-2)$

9. $\left(\dfrac{f}{g}\right)(x)$

10. $\left(\dfrac{f}{g}\right)(-2)$

Graph each function. Give the domain and range.

11. $f(x) = -2x^2 + 3$

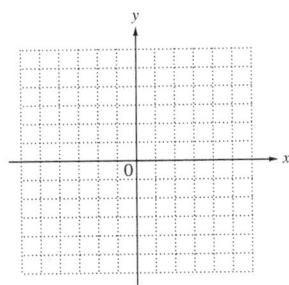

12. $f(x) = 3x - 4$

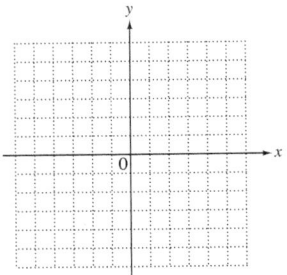

Solve each problem.

13. The current in a simple electrical circuit is inversely proportional to the resistance. If the current is 80 amps when the resistance is 30 ohms, find the current when the resistance is 12 ohms.

14. The force of the wind blowing on a vertical surface varies jointly as the area of the surface and the square of the velocity. If a wind blowing at 40 mph exerts a force of 50 lb on a surface of 500 ft², how much force will a wind of 80 mph place on a surface of 2 ft²?

Chapters R–9 *Cumulative Review Exercises*

Solve each equation or inequality.

1. $7(2x+3) - 4(2x+1)$
$= 2(x+1)$

2. $|6x-8| - 4 = 0$

3. $\dfrac{2}{3}x + \dfrac{5}{12}x \le 20$

4. $3x^2 + 4x = 7$

5. $\dfrac{-3x}{x+1} + \dfrac{4x+1}{x} = \dfrac{-3}{x^2+x}$

6. $\dfrac{1}{f} = \dfrac{1}{p} + \dfrac{1}{q}$ for q

Solve each problem.

7. Otis invested some money at 4% interest and twice as much at 3% interest. His interest for the first year was $400. How much did he invest at each rate?

8. A triangle has an area of 42 m². The base is 14 m long. Find the height of the triangle.

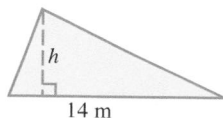

14 m

9. Find the slope of the line passing through the points $(-1, -3)$ and $(-2, 3)$.

10. Give the slope and y-intercept of the line with equation $y = x - 5$.

11. Find the $y = mx + b$ form of the equation of the line through $(1, 6)$ and parallel to the graph of the line through $(-5, 8)$ and $(-1, 2)$.

12. Find the $y = mx + b$ form of the equation of the line through $(5, 2)$ and perpendicular to the graph of $4x + 3y = 12$.

Graph.

13. $-4x + 2y = 8$
(Give the intercepts.)

14. $2x + 5y > 10$

15. $3x + 4y \le 12$

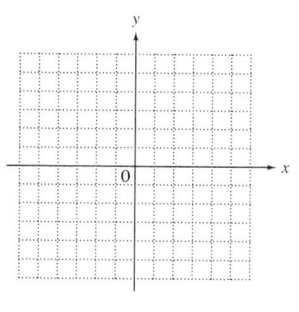

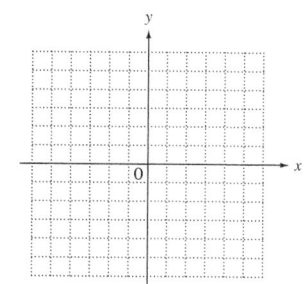

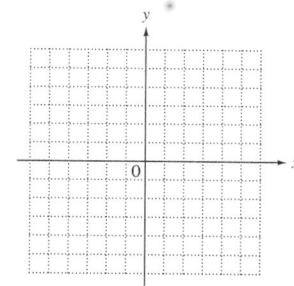

Solve each system.

16. $4x - y = -7$
$5x + 2y = 1$

17. $x + y - 2z = -1$
$2x - y + z = -6$
$3x + 2y - 3z = -3$

18. $x + 2y + z = 5$
$x - y + z = 3$
$2x + 4y + 2z = 11$

Perform the indicated operations. Write answers in lowest terms as needed.

19. $(3y^2 - 2y + 6) - (-y^2 + 5y + 12)$

20. $(3x^3 + 13x^2 - 17x - 7) \div (3x + 1)$

21. $(4x + 3)(3x - 1)$

22. $(7t + 8)(7t - 8)$

23. $(4x + 5)^2$

24. $\dfrac{2a^2}{a + b} \cdot \dfrac{a - b}{4a}$

25. $\dfrac{x + 4}{x - 2} + \dfrac{2x - 10}{x - 2}$

26. $\dfrac{2x}{2x - 1} + \dfrac{4}{2x + 1} + \dfrac{8}{4x^2 - 1}$

Factor each polynomial completely.

27. $2x^2 - 13x - 45$

28. $100t^2 - 25$

29. $8p^3 + 125$

30. $4x^2 - 4x + 1$

Solve each problem.

31. Consider the equation $5x - 3y = 8$.

   (a) Write y as a function f of x, using function notation $f(x)$.

   (b) Find $f(1)$.

32. Consider the relation $y = -x + 2$.

   (a) Does it define a function?

   (b) Give its domain and range.

33. Find each of the following for the polynomial functions

$$f(x) = x^2 + 2x - 3 \quad \text{and} \quad g(x) = 2x^3 - 3x^2 + 4x - 1.$$

   (a) $(f + g)(x)$

   (b) $(g - f)(x)$

   (c) $(f + g)(-1)$

34. The cost of a pizza varies directly as the square of its radius. It a pizza with a 4-in. radius costs $6.00, how much should a pizza with a 6-in. radius cost?

Roots, Radicals, and Root Functions

The formula for calculating the distance one can see to the horizon from the top of a tall building involves a *square root radical,* one of the topics covered in this chapter.

10.1 Radical Expressions and Graphs

10.2 Rational Exponents

10.3 Simplifying Radical Expressions

10.4 Adding and Subtracting Radical Expressions

10.5 Multiplying and Dividing Radical Expressions

Summary Exercises *Performing Operations with Radicals and Rational Exponents*

10.6 Solving Equations with Radicals

10.7 Complex Numbers

10.1 Radical Expressions and Graphs

OBJECTIVES

1. Find square roots.
2. Decide whether a given root is rational, irrational, or not a real number.
3. Find cube, fourth, and other roots.
4. Graph functions defined by radical expressions.
5. Find nth roots of nth powers.
6. Use a calculator to find roots.

OBJECTIVE ▶ 1 Find square roots. Recall that *squaring* a number means multiplying the number by itself.

7^2 means $7 \cdot 7$,   which equals   49.   The square of 7 is 49.

The opposite (inverse) of squaring a number is taking its *square root.* This is equivalent to asking

"*What number when multiplied by itself equals* 49?"

For the example above, one answer is 7 because $7 \cdot 7 = 49$.

Square Root

A number b is a **square root** of a if $b^2 = a$ (that is, $b \cdot b = a$).

EXAMPLE 1   Finding All Square Roots of a Number

Find all square roots of 49.

We ask, "*What number when multiplied by itself equals* 49?" As mentioned above, one square root is 7. Another square root of 49 is -7, because

$$(-7)(-7) = 49.$$

Thus, the number 49 has *two* square roots: 7 and -7. One square root is positive, and one is negative.

◀ **Work Problem 1 at the Side.**

---

1. Find all square roots of each number.

(a) 100

Ask "*What number when multiplied by itself equals* 100?" There are two answers.

(b) 25   **(c)** 36   **(d)** $\dfrac{25}{36}$

Leonardo of Pisa (c. 1170–1250)

Answers

1. (a) $10, -10$ **(b)** $5, -5$

   (c) $6, -6$ **(d)** $\dfrac{5}{6}, -\dfrac{5}{6}$

The **positive** or **principal square root** of a number is written with the symbol $\sqrt{}$. For example, the positive square root of 121 is 11.

$$\sqrt{121} = 11 \qquad 11^2 = 121$$

The symbol $-\sqrt{}$ is used for the **negative square root** of a number. For example, the negative square root of 121 is -11.

$$-\sqrt{121} = -11 \qquad (-11)^2 = 121$$

The **radical symbol** $\sqrt{}$ always represents the positive square root (except that $\sqrt{0} = 0$). The number inside the radical symbol is the **radicand,** and the entire expression—radical symbol and radicand—is a **radical.**

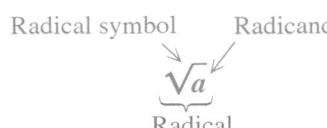

Radical symbol   Radicand

$\sqrt{a}$

Radical

An algebraic expression containing a radical is a **radical expression.**

The radical symbol $\sqrt{}$ has been used since sixteenth-century Germany and was probably derived from the letter R. The radical symbol at the right comes from the Latin word *radix,* for root. It was first used by Leonardo of Pisa (Fibonacci) in 1220.

Early radical symbol

We summarize our discussion of square roots as follows.

Square Roots of a

Let a be a positive real number.

$\sqrt{a}$ is the positive or principal square root of a.

$-\sqrt{a}$ is the negative square root of a.

For nonnegative a, the following hold true.

$$\sqrt{a} \cdot \sqrt{a} = \left(\sqrt{a}\right)^2 = a \quad \text{and} \quad -\sqrt{a} \cdot \left(-\sqrt{a}\right) = \left(-\sqrt{a}\right)^2 = a$$

Also, $\sqrt{0} = 0$.

EXAMPLE 2 **Finding Square Roots**

Find each square root.

(a) $\sqrt{144}$

The radical $\sqrt{144}$ represents the positive or principal square root of 144. Think of a positive number whose square is 144.

$$12^2 = 144, \quad \text{so} \quad \sqrt{144} = 12.$$

(b) $-\sqrt{1024}$

This symbol represents the negative square root of 1024. A calculator with a square root key can be used to find $\sqrt{1024} = 32$. Therefore,

$$-\sqrt{1024} = -32.$$

$(0.9)^2 = 0.9 \cdot 0.9$
$= 0.81$

(c) $\sqrt{\dfrac{4}{9}} = \dfrac{2}{3}$ **(d)** $-\sqrt{\dfrac{16}{49}} = -\dfrac{4}{7}$ **(e)** $\sqrt{0.81} = 0.9$

———————— **Work Problem ② at the Side.** ▶

❗ CAUTION

By definition, $\sqrt{4} = 2$ because $2^2 = 4$. ***In general, however, the square root of a number is not half the number.***

As noted above, when the square root of a positive real number is squared, the result is that positive real number. $\left(\text{Also, } \left(\sqrt{0}\right)^2 = 0.\right)$

EXAMPLE 3 **Squaring Radical Expressions**

Find the *square* of each radical expression.

(a) $\sqrt{13}$ The square of $\sqrt{13}$ is $\left(\sqrt{13}\right)^2 = 13$.   Definition of square root

(b) $-\sqrt{29}$
$\left(-\sqrt{29}\right)^2 = 29$

(c) $\sqrt{p^2 + 1}$
$\left(\sqrt{p^2 + 1}\right)^2 = p^2 + 1$

The square of a *negative* number is positive.

———————— **Work Problem ③ at the Side.** ▶

---

② Find each square root.

GS (a) $\sqrt{16}$

$4^2 =$ _____ , so

$\sqrt{16} =$ _____ .

GS (b) $-\sqrt{169}$

$13^2 =$ _____ , so

$-\sqrt{169} =$ _____ .

(c) $-\sqrt{225}$ **(d)** $\sqrt{729}$

(e) $-\sqrt{\dfrac{36}{25}}$ **(f)** $\sqrt{0.49}$

③ Find the *square* of each radical expression.

GS (a) $\sqrt{41}$

$\left(\sqrt{41}\right)^2 =$ _____

GS (b) $-\sqrt{39}$

$\left(-\sqrt{39}\right)^2 =$ _____

(c) $\sqrt{120}$

(d) $\sqrt{2x^2 + 3}$

Answers

2. (a) 16; 4   **(b)** 169; −13   **(c)** −15
(d) 27   **(e)** $-\dfrac{6}{5}$ **(f)** 0.7

3. (a) 41   **(b)** 39   **(c)** 120   **(d)** $2x^2 + 3$

4 Determine whether each square root is *rational*, *irrational*, or *not a real number.*

(a) $\sqrt{9}$

(b) $\sqrt{7}$

(c) $\sqrt{\dfrac{9}{16}}$

(d) $\sqrt{72}$

(e) $\sqrt{-43}$

OBJECTIVE **2** **Decide whether a given root is rational, irrational, or not a real number.** Numbers with rational square roots are **perfect squares.**

Perfect squares $\left\{\begin{array}{l}25 \\ 144 \\ \dfrac{4}{9}\end{array}\right.$ are perfect squares because $\left.\begin{array}{l}\sqrt{25}=5 \\ \sqrt{144}=12 \\ \sqrt{\dfrac{4}{9}}=\dfrac{2}{3}\end{array}\right\}$ Rational square roots

A number that is not a perfect square has a square root that is not a rational number. For example, $\sqrt{5}$ is not a rational number because it cannot be written as the ratio of two integers. Its decimal equivalent (or approximation) neither terminates nor repeats. However, $\sqrt{5}$ is a real number and corresponds to a point on the number line.

A real number that is not rational is an **irrational number.** The number $\sqrt{5}$ is irrational. *Many square roots of integers are irrational.*

If a is a **positive** real number that is **not** a perfect square, then
$$\sqrt{a} \text{ is irrational.}$$

Not every number has a real number square root. For example, there is no real number that can be squared to obtain -36. (The square of a real number can never be negative.) Because of this, $\sqrt{-36}$ *is not a real number.*

If a is a **negative** real number, then $\sqrt{a}$ is *not* a real number.

⚠ CAUTION
Do not confuse $\sqrt{-36}$ and $-\sqrt{36}$. $\sqrt{-36}$ is not a real number because there is no real number that can be squared to obtain -36. However, $-\sqrt{36}$ is the negative square root of 36, which is -6.

EXAMPLE 4 **Identifying Types of Square Roots**

Determine whether each square root is *rational*, *irrational*, or *not a real number.*

(a) $\sqrt{17}$ — Because 17 is not a perfect square, $\sqrt{17}$ is irrational.

(b) $\sqrt{64}$ — 64 is a perfect square, 8^2, so $\sqrt{64}=8$ is a rational number.

(c) $\sqrt{-25}$ — There is no real number whose square is -25. Therefore, $\sqrt{-25}$ is not a real number.

◀ Work Problem **4** at the Side.

Note
Not all irrational numbers are square roots of integers. For example, the number π (approximately 3.14159) is an irrational number that is not a square root of any integer.

OBJECTIVE ▶ **3** **Find cube, fourth, and other roots.** Finding the square root of a number is the inverse (opposite) of squaring a number. There are inverses to finding the cube of a number and to finding the fourth or greater power of a number. These inverses are, respectively, the **cube root, $\sqrt[3]{a}$,** and the **fourth root, $\sqrt[4]{a}$.** Similar symbols are used for other roots.

$\sqrt[n]{a}$

The *n*th root of *a*, written $\sqrt[n]{a}$, is a number whose *n*th power equals *a*. That is,

$$\sqrt[n]{a} = b \quad \text{means} \quad b^n = a.$$

In $\sqrt[n]{a}$, the number *n* is the **index,** or **order,** of the radical.

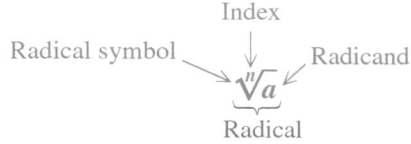

We could write $\sqrt[2]{a}$ instead of $\sqrt{a}$, but the simpler symbol $\sqrt{a}$ is customary since the square root is the most commonly used root.

When working with cube roots or fourth roots, it is helpful to memorize the first few **perfect cubes** ($1^3 = 1$, $2^3 = 8$, $3^3 = 27$, and so on) and the first few **perfect fourth powers** ($1^4 = 1$, $2^4 = 16$, $3^4 = 81$, and so on).

Work Problem 5 at the Side. ▶

EXAMPLE 5 **Finding Cube Roots**

Find each cube root.

(a) $\sqrt[3]{8}$

Ask *"What number can be cubed to give 8?"* Because $2^3 = 8$, $\sqrt[3]{8} = 2$. $\quad$ $2^3 = 2 \cdot 2 \cdot 2$

(b) $\sqrt[3]{-8}$ $\quad$ Because $(-2)^3 = -8$, $\sqrt[3]{-8} = -2$.

(c) $\sqrt[3]{216}$ $\quad$ Because $6^3 = 216$, $\sqrt[3]{216} = 6$.

─────── **Work Problem 6 at the Side.** ▶

Notice in **Example 5(b)** that we can find the cube root of a negative number. (Contrast this with the square root of a negative number, which is not real.) In fact, the cube root of a positive number is positive, and the cube root of a negative number is negative. ***There is only one real number cube root for each real number.***

When a radical has an *even index* (square root, fourth root, and so on), *the radicand must be nonnegative* to yield a real number root. Also, for $a > 0$,

$$\sqrt{a}, \ \sqrt[4]{a}, \ \sqrt[6]{a}, \text{ and so on are positive (principal) roots.}$$

$$-\sqrt{a}, \ -\sqrt[4]{a}, \ -\sqrt[6]{a}, \text{ and so on are negative roots.}$$

5 Complete the following list of perfect cubes and perfect fourth powers.

Perfect Cubes	Perfect Fourth Powers
$1^3 = 1$	$1^4 = 1$
$2^3 = 8$	$2^4 = 16$
$3^3 = 27$	$3^4 = 81$
$4^3 = $____	$4^4 = $____
$5^3 = $____	$5^4 = $____
$6^3 = $____	$6^4 = $____
$7^3 = $____	$7^4 = $____
$8^3 = $____	$8^4 = $____
$9^3 = $____	$9^4 = $____
$10^3 = $____	$10^4 = $____

6 Find each cube root.

GS (a) $\sqrt[3]{27}$

____$^3 = 27$, so

$\sqrt[3]{27} = $____.

(b) $\sqrt[3]{1}$

(c) $\sqrt[3]{-125}$

Answers

5. Perfect cubes: 64; 125; 216; 343; 512; 729; 1000
Perfect fourth powers: 256; 625; 1296; 2401; 4096; 6561; 10,000

6. (a) 3; 3 (b) 1 (c) −5

7 Find each root.

(a) $\sqrt[4]{81}$ (b) $\sqrt[4]{-81}$

(c) $-\sqrt[4]{81}$ (d) $\sqrt[5]{243}$

(e) $\sqrt[5]{-243}$ (f) $-\sqrt[5]{-243}$

EXAMPLE 6 Finding Other Roots

Find each root.

$2^4 = 2 \cdot 2 \cdot 2 \cdot 2$

(a) $\sqrt[4]{16}$ Because 2 is positive and $2^4 = 16$, $\sqrt[4]{16} = 2$.

(b) $-\sqrt[4]{16}$
From part (a), $\sqrt[4]{16} = 2$, so the negative root is $-\sqrt[4]{16} = -2$.

(c) $\sqrt[4]{-16}$
For a real number fourth root, the radicand must be nonnegative. There is no real number that equals $\sqrt[4]{-16}$.

(d) $-\sqrt[5]{32}$
First find $\sqrt[5]{32}$. Because 2 is the number whose fifth power is 32, $\sqrt[5]{32} = 2$. Since $\sqrt[5]{32} = 2$, it follows that

$$-\sqrt[5]{32} = -2.$$

(e) $\sqrt[5]{-32}$ Because $(-2)^5 = -32$, $\sqrt[5]{-32} = -2$.

(f) $-\sqrt[5]{-32}$
From part (e), $\sqrt[5]{-32} = -2$ because $(-2)^5 = -32$. So it follows that

$$-\sqrt[5]{-32} = -(-2) = 2.$$

◀ **Work Problem 7 at the Side.**

OBJECTIVE ▶ **4** Graph functions defined by radical expressions. A **radical expression** is an algebraic expression that contains a radical.

$$3 - \sqrt{x}, \quad \sqrt[3]{x}, \quad \text{and} \quad \sqrt{2x - 1} \quad \text{Radical expressions}$$

In earlier chapters we graphed functions defined by polynomial and rational expressions. Now we examine the graphs of functions defined by the radical expressions $f(x) = \sqrt{x}$ and $f(x) = \sqrt[3]{x}$.

Figure 1 shows the graph of the **square root function**

$$f(x) = \sqrt{x},$$

together with a table of selected points. Only nonnegative values can be used for x, so the domain is $[0, \infty)$. Because $\sqrt{x}$ is the principal square root of x, it always has a nonnegative value, so the range is also $[0, \infty)$.

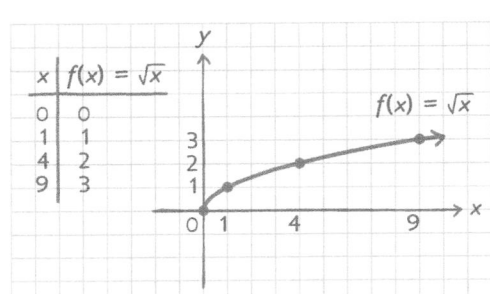

Square root function

$$f(x) = \sqrt{x}$$

Domain: $[0, \infty)$
Range: $[0, \infty)$

Figure 1

Figure 2 shows the graph of the **cube root function**

$$f(x) = \sqrt[3]{x}.$$

Any real number (positive, negative, or 0) can be used for x in the cube root function, so $\sqrt[3]{x}$ can be positive, negative, or 0. Thus, both the domain and the range of the cube root function are $(-\infty, \infty)$.

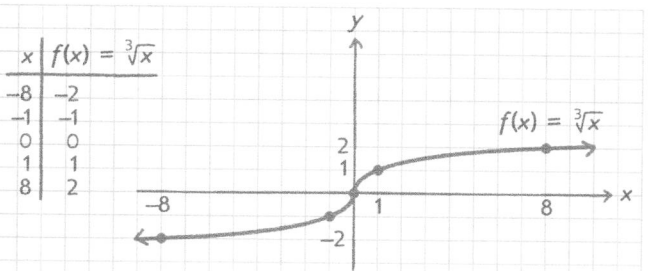

Cube root function

$$f(x) = \sqrt[3]{x}$$

Domain: $(-\infty, \infty)$
Range: $(-\infty, \infty)$

Figure 2

EXAMPLE 7 **Graphing Functions Defined with Radicals**

Graph each function, and give its domain and range.

(a) $f(x) = \sqrt{x - 3}$

A table of values is given with the graph in **Figure 3.** The x-values were chosen so that the function values are all integers. For the radicand to be nonnegative, we must have

$$x - 3 \geq 0$$

$$x \geq 3.$$

Therefore, the domain is $[3, \infty)$. Function values are positive or 0, so the range is $[0, \infty)$.

x	$f(x) = \sqrt{x-3}$
3	$\sqrt{3-3} = 0$
4	$\sqrt{4-3} = 1$
7	$\sqrt{7-3} = 2$

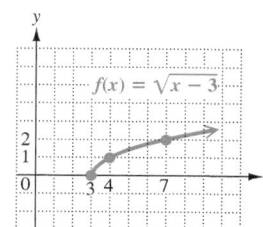

This graph is shifted 3 units to the right compared to the graph of $y = \sqrt{x}$.

Figure 3

(b) $f(x) = \sqrt[3]{x} + 2$

See **Figure 4.** Both the domain and the range are $(-\infty, \infty)$.

x	$f(x) = \sqrt[3]{x} + 2$
-8	$\sqrt[3]{-8} + 2 = 0$
-1	$\sqrt[3]{-1} + 2 = 1$
0	$\sqrt[3]{0} + 2 = 2$
1	$\sqrt[3]{1} + 2 = 3$
8	$\sqrt[3]{8} + 2 = 4$

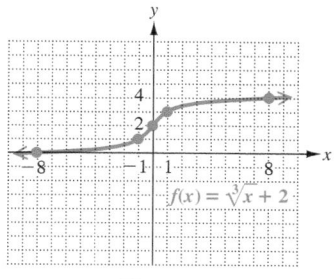

This graph is shifted 2 units up compared to the graph of $y = \sqrt[3]{x}$.

Figure 4

Work Problem 8 at the Side. ▶

---

8 Graph each function, and give its domain and range.

(a) $f(x) = \sqrt{x} + 2$

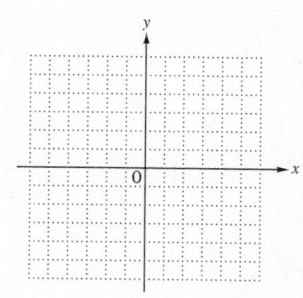

(b) $f(x) = \sqrt[3]{x} - 1$

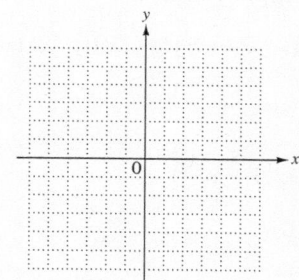

Answers

8. (a)

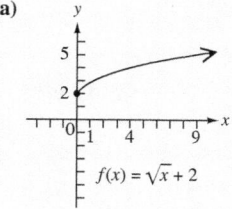

domain: $[0, \infty)$; range: $[2, \infty)$

(b)

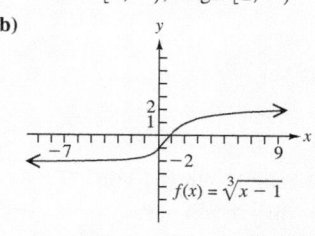

domain: $(-\infty, \infty)$; range: $(-\infty, \infty)$

9 Find each square root. In parts (c) and (d), r is a real number.

(a) $\sqrt{15^2}$ (b) $\sqrt{(-12)^2}$

(c) $\sqrt{r^2}$ (d) $\sqrt{(-r)^2}$

10 Simplify each root.

(a) $\sqrt[4]{(-5)^4}$ (b) $\sqrt[5]{(-7)^5}$

(c) $-\sqrt[6]{(-3)^6}$ (d) $-\sqrt[4]{m^8}$

(e) $\sqrt[3]{x^{24}}$ (f) $\sqrt[6]{y^{18}}$

OBJECTIVE **5** **Find *n*th roots of *n*th powers.** Consider the expression $\sqrt{a^2}$. At first glance, we may think that it is equivalent to a. However, this is not necessarily true. For example, consider the following.

If $a = 6$, then $\sqrt{a^2} = \sqrt{6^2} = \sqrt{36} = 6$.

If $a = -6$, then $\sqrt{a^2} = \sqrt{(-6)^2} = \sqrt{36} = 6$. ← Instead of -6, we get 6, the *absolute value* of -6.

The symbol $\sqrt{a^2}$ represents the *nonnegative* square root, so we write $\sqrt{a^2}$ with absolute value bars, as $|a|$, because a may be a negative number.

Meaning of $\sqrt{a^2}$

For any real number a, $\qquad \sqrt{a^2} = |a|.$

In words, the principal square root of a^2 is the absolute value of a.

EXAMPLE 8 **Simplifying Square Roots Using Absolute Value**

Find each square root. In parts (c) and (d), k is a real number.

(a) $\sqrt{7^2} = |7| = 7$ (b) $\sqrt{(-7)^2} = |-7| = 7$

(c) $\sqrt{k^2} = |k|$ (d) $\sqrt{(-k)^2} = |-k| = |k|$

◀ **Work Problem 9 at the Side.**

We can generalize this idea to any *n*th root.

Meaning of $\sqrt[n]{a^n}$

If n is an *even* positive integer, then $\sqrt[n]{a^n} = |a|.$

If n is an *odd* positive integer, then $\sqrt[n]{a^n} = a.$

In words, use absolute value when n is even. Absolute value is not necessary when n is odd.

EXAMPLE 9 **Simplifying Higher Roots Using Absolute Value**

Simplify each root.

(a) $\sqrt[6]{(-3)^6} = |-3| = 3$ n is even. Use absolute value.

(b) $\sqrt[5]{(-4)^5} = -4$ n is odd.

(c) $-\sqrt[4]{(-9)^4} = -|-9| = -9$ n is even. Use absolute value.

(d) $-\sqrt{m^4} = -|m^2| = -m^2$ For all m, $|m^2| = m^2$.
No absolute value bars are needed here because m^2 is nonnegative for any real number value of m.

(e) $\sqrt[3]{a^{12}} = a^4$, because $a^{12} = (a^4)^3$.

(f) $\sqrt[4]{x^{12}} = |x^3|$
Absolute value bars guarantee that the result is not negative (because x^3 is negative when x is negative). Also, $|x^3|$ can be written as $x^2 \cdot |x|$.

◀ **Work Problem 10 at the Side.**

OBJECTIVE 6 Use a calculator to find roots. Radical expressions often represent irrational numbers. To find approximations of such radicals, we usually use a calculator. For example,

$$\sqrt{15} \approx 3.872983346, \quad \sqrt[3]{10} \approx 2.15443469, \quad \text{and} \quad \sqrt[4]{2} \approx 1.189207115,$$

where the symbol $\approx$ means **"is approximately equal to."** In this text, we often give approximations rounded to three decimal places. Thus,

$$\sqrt{15} \approx 3.873, \quad \sqrt[3]{10} \approx 2.154, \quad \text{and} \quad \sqrt[4]{2} \approx 1.189.$$

There is a simple way to check that a calculator approximation is "in the ballpark." For example, because 16 is slightly larger than 15, $\sqrt{16} = 4$ should be slightly larger than $\sqrt{15}$. Thus, 3.873 is a reasonable approximation for $\sqrt{15}$.

Note

Methods for finding approximations differ among makes and models of calculators. **Consult your owner's guide for keystroke instructions.** Be aware that graphing calculators often differ from scientific calculators in the order in which keystrokes are made.

EXAMPLE 10 Finding Approximations for Roots

Use a calculator to approximate each radical to three decimal places.

(a) $\sqrt{39} \approx 6.245$

(b) $-\sqrt{72} \approx -8.485$

(c) $\sqrt[3]{93} \approx 4.531$

(d) $\sqrt[4]{39} \approx 2.499$

—————————————— **Work Problem 11 at the Side.** ▶

EXAMPLE 11 Using Roots to Calculate Resonant Frequency

The resonant frequency f of a circuit may be found using the formula

$$f = \frac{1}{2\pi\sqrt{LC}}, \quad \text{Electronics formula}$$

where f is in cycles per second, L is in henrys, and C is in farads. (Henrys and farads are units of measure in electronics.) Find the resonant frequency f if $L = 5 \times 10^{-4}$ and $C = 3 \times 10^{-10}$. Give the answer to the nearest thousand.

Find the value of f when $L = 5 \times 10^{-4}$ and $C = 3 \times 10^{-10}$.

$$f = \frac{1}{2\pi\sqrt{LC}} \qquad \text{Given formula}$$

$$f = \frac{1}{2\pi\sqrt{(5 \times 10^{-4})(3 \times 10^{-10})}} \qquad \text{Substitute for } L \text{ and } C.$$

$$f \approx 411,000 \qquad \text{Use a calculator.}$$

The resonant frequency f is approximately 411,000 cycles per sec.

—————————————— **Work Problem 12 at the Side.** ▶

11 Use a calculator to approximate each radical to three decimal places.

(a) $\sqrt{17}$ **(b)** $-\sqrt{362}$

(c) $\sqrt[3]{9482}$ **(d)** $\sqrt[4]{6825}$

12 Use the formula in **Example 11** to approximate f to the nearest thousand if

$$L = 6 \times 10^{-5}$$

and $C = 4 \times 10^{-9}$.

Answers
11. (a) 4.123 **(b)** -19.026
   (c) 21.166 **(d)** 9.089
12. 325,000 cycles per sec

10.1 Exercises

FOR EXTRA HELP Go to MyMathLab for worked-out, step-by-step solutions to exercises enclosed in a square ☐ and video solutions to ▶ exercises.

CONCEPT CHECK *Decide whether each statement is* true *or* false. *If false, tell why.*

1. Every positive number has two real square roots.

2. A negative number has negative square roots.

3. Every nonnegative number has two real square roots.

4. The positive square root of a positive number is its principal square root.

5. The cube root of every real number has the same sign as the number itself.

6. Every positive number has three real cube roots.

CONCEPT CHECK *Match each expression from Column I with the equivalent choice from Column II. Answers may be used once, more than once, or not at all.*

I		II	
7. $-\sqrt{16}$	**8.** $\sqrt{-16}$	**A.** 3	**B.** -2
9. $\sqrt[3]{-27}$	**10.** $\sqrt[5]{-32}$	**C.** 2	**D.** -3
11. $\sqrt[4]{16}$	**12.** $-\sqrt[3]{64}$	**E.** -4	**F.** Not a real number

CONCEPT CHECK *Choose the closest approximation of each square root. Do not use a calculator.*

13. $\sqrt{123.5}$
   A. 9   **B.** 10   **C.** 11   **D.** 12

14. $\sqrt{67.8}$
   A. 7   **B.** 8   **C.** 9   **D.** 10

CONCEPT CHECK *Refer to the figure to answer each question.*

15. Which one of the following is the best estimate of its area?
   A. 50   **B.** 100   **C.** 250   **D.** 2500

16. Which one of the following is the best estimate of its perimeter?
   A. 15   **B.** 30   **C.** 100   **D.** 250

17. CONCEPT CHECK Consider the expression $-\sqrt{-a}$. Decide whether it is positive, negative, 0, or not a real number in each case.
   (a) $a > 0$ **(b)** $a < 0$ **(c)** $a = 0$

18. CONCEPT CHECK If n is odd, under what conditions is $\sqrt[n]{a}$ the following?
   (a) positive   **(b)** negative   **(c)** 0

Find all square roots of each number. ***See Example 1.***

19. 9

20. 16

21. 64

22. 121

23. 169

24. 225

25. $\dfrac{25}{196}$

26. $\dfrac{81}{400}$

27. 900

28. 1600

Find each square root. ***See Examples 2 and 4(c).***

29. $\sqrt{1}$

30. $\sqrt{4}$

31. $\sqrt{64}$

32. $\sqrt{9}$

33. $\sqrt{49}$

34. $\sqrt{81}$

35. $-\sqrt{81}$

36. $-\sqrt{121}$

37. $-\sqrt{256}$

38. $-\sqrt{196}$

39. $\sqrt{\dfrac{64}{81}}$

40. $\sqrt{\dfrac{100}{9}}$

41. $-\sqrt{\dfrac{144}{121}}$

42. $-\sqrt{\dfrac{49}{36}}$

43. $\sqrt{0.64}$

44. $\sqrt{0.16}$

45. $\sqrt{-121}$

46. $\sqrt{-64}$

47. $-\sqrt{-49}$

48. $-\sqrt{-100}$

Find the square of each radical expression. ***See Example 3.***

49. $\sqrt{100}$
$\left(\sqrt{100}\right)^2 =$ ____

50. $\sqrt{36}$
$\left(\sqrt{36}\right)^2 =$ ____

51. $-\sqrt{19}$

52. $-\sqrt{99}$

53. $\sqrt{\dfrac{2}{3}}$

54. $\sqrt{\dfrac{5}{7}}$

55. $\sqrt{3x^2 + 4}$

56. $\sqrt{9y^2 + 3}$

Determine whether each number is rational, irrational, *or* not a real number. *If a number is rational, give its exact value. If a number is irrational, give a decimal approximation to the nearest thousandth. Use a calculator as necessary.* ***See Examples 4 and 10.***

57. $\sqrt{25}$

58. $\sqrt{169}$

59. $\sqrt{29}$

60. $\sqrt{33}$

61. $-\sqrt{64}$

62. $-\sqrt{81}$

63. $-\sqrt{300}$

64. $-\sqrt{500}$

65. $\sqrt{-29}$

66. $\sqrt{-47}$

67. $\sqrt{1200}$

68. $\sqrt{1500}$

Find each root. ***See Examples 5 and 6.***

69. $\sqrt[3]{216}$

70. $\sqrt[3]{343}$

71. $\sqrt[3]{-64}$

72. $\sqrt[3]{-125}$

73. $-\sqrt[3]{512}$

74. $-\sqrt[3]{1000}$

75. $-\sqrt[3]{-27}$

76. $-\sqrt[3]{-64}$

77. $\sqrt[4]{1296}$

78. $\sqrt[4]{625}$

79. $-\sqrt[4]{16}$

80. $-\sqrt[4]{256}$

81. $\sqrt[4]{-625}$

82. $\sqrt[4]{-256}$

83. $\sqrt[6]{64}$

84. $\sqrt[6]{729}$

85. $\sqrt[6]{-64}$

86. $\sqrt[6]{-1}$

87. $\sqrt[3]{\dfrac{64}{27}}$

88. $\sqrt[4]{\dfrac{81}{16}}$

89. $-\sqrt[6]{\dfrac{1}{64}}$

90. $-\sqrt[5]{\dfrac{1}{32}}$

91. $\sqrt[3]{0.001}$

92. $\sqrt[3]{0.125}$

Graph each function, and give its domain and range. ***See Example 7.***

93. $f(x) = \sqrt{x+3}$

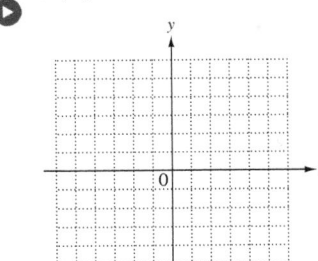

94. $f(x) = \sqrt{x-2}$

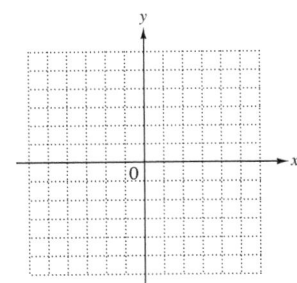

95. $f(x) = \sqrt{x}-2$

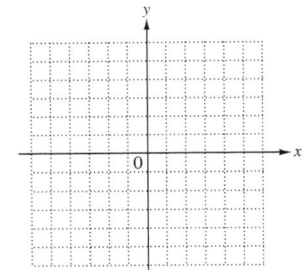

96. $f(x) = \sqrt{x}+1$

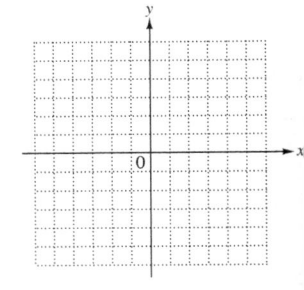

97. $f(x) = \sqrt[3]{x}-3$

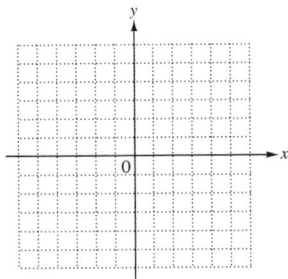

98. $f(x) = \sqrt[3]{x}+1$

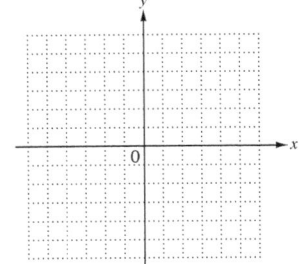

99. $f(x) = \sqrt[3]{x-2}$

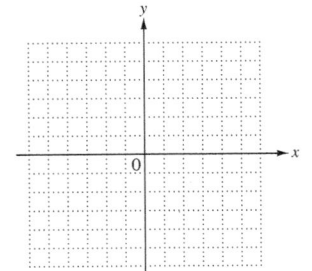

100. $f(x) = \sqrt[3]{x+1}$

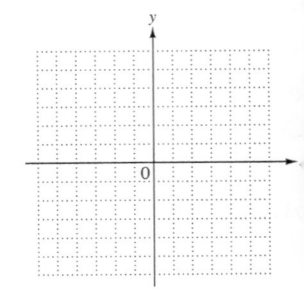

Simplify each root. See Examples 8 and 9.

101. $\sqrt{12^2}$

102. $\sqrt{19^2}$

103. $\sqrt{(-10)^2}$

104. $\sqrt{(-13)^2}$

105. $\sqrt[6]{(-2)^6}$

106. $\sqrt[6]{(-4)^6}$

107. $\sqrt[5]{(-9)^5}$

108. $\sqrt[5]{(-8)^5}$

109. $-\sqrt[6]{(-5)^6}$

110. $-\sqrt[6]{(-7)^6}$

111. $\sqrt{x^2}$

112. $-\sqrt{x^2}$

113. $\sqrt{(-z)^2}$

114. $\sqrt{(-q)^2}$

115. $\sqrt[3]{x^3}$

116. $-\sqrt[3]{x^3}$

117. $\sqrt[3]{x^{15}}$

118. $\sqrt[3]{m^9}$

119. $\sqrt[6]{x^{30}}$

120. $\sqrt[4]{k^{20}}$

Use a calculator to approximate each radical to three decimal places. See Example 10.

121. $\sqrt{9483}$

122. $\sqrt{6825}$

123. $\sqrt{284.361}$

124. $\sqrt{846.104}$

125. $-\sqrt{82}$

126. $-\sqrt{91}$

127. $\sqrt[3]{423}$

128. $\sqrt[3]{555}$

129. $\sqrt[4]{100}$

130. $\sqrt[4]{250}$

131. $\sqrt[5]{23.8}$

132. $\sqrt[5]{98.4}$

Solve each problem. See Example 11.

133. Use the electronics formula

$$f = \frac{1}{2\pi\sqrt{LC}}$$

to calculate the resonant frequency f of a circuit to the nearest thousand for the following values of L and C.

(a) $L = 7.237 \times 10^{-5}$ and $C = 2.5 \times 10^{-10}$

(b) $L = 5.582 \times 10^{-4}$ and $C = 3.245 \times 10^{-9}$

134. The threshold weight T for a person is the weight above which the risk of death increases greatly. The threshold weight in pounds for men aged 40–49 is related to height in inches by the formula

$$h = 12.3\sqrt[3]{T}.$$

What height corresponds to a threshold weight of 216 lb for a 43-yr-old man? Round the answer to the nearest inch and then to the nearest tenth of a foot.

135. According to an article in *The World Scanner Report*, the distance D, in miles, to the horizon from an observer's point of view over water or "flat" earth is given by

$$D = \sqrt{2H},$$

where H is the height of the point of view, in feet. If a person whose eyes are 6 ft above ground level is standing at the top of a hill 44 ft above "flat" earth, how far to the horizon will she be able to see?

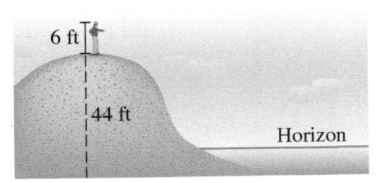

136. The time for one complete swing of a simple pendulum is given by

$$t = 2\pi\sqrt{\frac{L}{g}},$$

where t is time in seconds, L is the length of the pendulum in feet, and g, the force due to gravity, is about 32 ft per sec^2. Find the time of a complete swing of a 2-ft pendulum to the nearest tenth of a second.

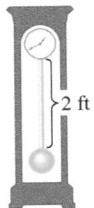

Heron's formula gives a method of finding the area of a triangle if the lengths of its sides are known. Suppose that a, b, and c are the lengths of the sides. Let s denote one-half of the perimeter of the triangle (called the semiperimeter)—that is,

$$s = \frac{1}{2}(a + b + c).$$

Then the area $\mathscr{A}$ of the triangle is

$$\mathscr{A} = \sqrt{s(s - a)(s - b)(s - c)}.$$

Use Heron's formula to solve each problem.

137. Find the area of the Bermuda Triangle, to the nearest thousand square miles, if the "sides" of this triangle measure approximately 960 mi, 1030 mi, and 1030 mi.

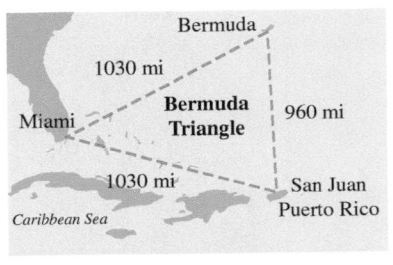

138. The Vietnam Veterans Memorial in Washington, D.C., is in the shape of an unenclosed isosceles triangle with equal sides of length 246.75 ft. If the triangle were enclosed, the third side would have length 438.14 ft. Find the area of this enclosure to the nearest hundred square feet. (Data from a pamphlet obtained at the Vietnam Veterans Memorial.)

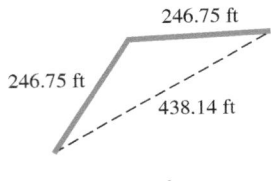

Not to scale

139. Find the area of a triangle with sides of lengths $a = 11$ m, $b = 60$ m, and $c = 61$ m.

140. Find the area of a triangle with sides of lengths $a = 20$ ft, $b = 34$ ft, and $c = 42$ ft.

The coefficient of self-induction L (in henrys), the energy P stored in an electronic circuit (in joules), and the current I (in amps) are related by the formula

$$I = \sqrt{\frac{2P}{L}}.$$

Use this formula to work each problem. Give answers to the nearest thousandth.

141. Find I if $P = 120$ and $L = 80$.

142. Find I if $P = 100$ and $L = 40$.

10.2 | Rational Exponents

OBJECTIVE ▶ 1 Use exponential notation for *n*th roots. Consider the expression $(3^{1/2})^2$. We can simplify it as follows.

$$(3^{1/2})^2$$

$$= 3^{1/2} \cdot 3^{1/2} \qquad a^2 = a \cdot a$$

$$= 3^{1/2+1/2} \qquad \text{Product rule: } a^m \cdot a^n = a^{m+n}$$

$$= 3^1 \qquad \text{Add exponents.}$$

$$= 3 \qquad a^1 = a$$

Also, by definition,

$$\left(\sqrt{3}\right)^2 = \sqrt{3} \cdot \sqrt{3} = 3.$$

Because both $(3^{1/2})^2$ and $\left(\sqrt{3}\right)^2$ equal 3, it seems reasonable to define

$$3^{1/2} = \sqrt{3}.$$

This discussion suggests the following generalization.

Meaning of $a^{1/n}$

If $\sqrt[n]{a}$ is a real number, then $a^{1/n} = \sqrt[n]{a}.$

Examples: $4^{1/2} = \sqrt{4}$, $8^{1/3} = \sqrt[3]{8}$,   and $16^{1/4} = \sqrt[4]{16}$

The denominator of the rational exponent is the index of the radical.

EXAMPLE 1   Evaluating Exponentials of the Form $a^{1/n}$

Evaluate each exponential.

The denominator is the index, or root.

The denominator is the index, or root. $\sqrt{}$ means $\sqrt[2]{}$.

(a) $64^{1/3} = \sqrt[3]{64} = 4$ **(b)** $100^{1/2} = \sqrt{100} = 10$

(c) $-256^{1/4} = -\sqrt[4]{256} = -4$

(d) $(-256)^{1/4} = \sqrt[4]{-256}$ is not a real number because the radicand, -256, is negative and the index is even.

(e) $(-32)^{1/5} = \sqrt[5]{-32} = -2$ **(f)** $\left(\dfrac{1}{8}\right)^{1/3} = \sqrt[3]{\dfrac{1}{8}} = \dfrac{1}{2}$

──────── **Work Problem 1 at the Side.** ▶

⚠ CAUTION

Notice the distinction between **Examples 1(c) and (d).** The radical in part (c) is the ***negative fourth root of a positive number,*** while the radical in part (d) is the ***principal fourth root of a negative number,*** which is not a real number.

OBJECTIVES

1 Use exponential notation for *n*th roots.

2 Define and use expressions of the form $a^{m/n}$.

3 Convert between radicals and rational exponents.

4 Use the rules for exponents with rational exponents.

---

1 Evaluate each exponential.

(a) $8^{1/3}$ **(b)** $9^{1/2}$

(c) $-81^{1/4}$ **(d)** $(-81)^{1/4}$

(e) $(-64)^{1/3}$ **(f)** $\left(\dfrac{1}{32}\right)^{1/5}$

Answers

1. **(a)** 2   **(b)** 3   **(c)** -3
    (d) not a real number
    (e) -4 **(f)** $\dfrac{1}{2}$

2 Evaluate each exponential.

(a) $25^{3/2}$

$$= (25^{1/\underline{}})^{\underline{}}$$

$$= \underline{}$$

$$= \underline{}$$

(b) $27^{2/3}$

(c) $-16^{3/2}$

(d) $(-64)^{2/3}$

(e) $(-36)^{3/2}$

OBJECTIVE ▶ 2 Define and use expressions of the form $a^{m/n}$. We know that $8^{1/3} = \sqrt[3]{8}$. Now we define a number like $8^{2/3}$, where the numerator of the exponent is *not* 1. For past rules of exponents to be valid,

$$8^{2/3} = 8^{(1/3)2} = (8^{1/3})^2.$$

Because $8^{1/3} = \sqrt[3]{8}$,

$$8^{2/3} = (\sqrt[3]{8})^2 = 2^2 = 4.$$

Generalizing from this example, we define $a^{m/n}$ as follows.

Meaning of $a^{m/n}$

If m and n are positive integers with m/n in lowest terms, then

$$a^{m/n} = (a^{1/n})^m,$$

provided that $a^{1/n}$ is a real number. If $a^{1/n}$ is not a real number, then $a^{m/n}$ is not a real number.

EXAMPLE 2 Evaluating Exponentials of the Form $a^{m/n}$

Evaluate each exponential.

Think:
$36^{1/2} = \sqrt{36} = 6$

Think:
$125^{1/3} = \sqrt[3]{125} = 5$

(a) $36^{3/2} = (36^{1/2})^3 = 6^3 = 216$ **(b)** $125^{2/3} = (125^{1/3})^2 = 5^2 = 25$

Be careful.
The base is 4.

(c) $-4^{5/2} = -(4^{5/2}) = -(4^{1/2})^5 = -(2)^5 = -32$

Because the base is 4, the negative sign is *not* affected by the exponent.

(d) $(-27)^{2/3} = [(-27)^{1/3}]^2 = (-3)^2 = 9$

Notice in part (c) that we first evaluate the exponential and then find its negative. In part (d), the $-$ sign is part of the base, -27.

(e) $(-100)^{3/2} = [(-100)^{1/2}]^3$, which is *not* a real number, because

$$(-100)^{1/2}, \quad \text{or} \quad \sqrt{-100}, \quad \text{is not a real number.}$$

◀ **Work Problem 2 at the Side.**

Recall that for any natural number n,

$$a^{-n} = \frac{1}{a^n} \quad (\text{where } a \neq 0). \qquad \text{Definition of negative exponent}$$

When a rational exponent is negative, we apply this interpretation of negative exponents.

Meaning of $a^{-m/n}$

If $a^{m/n}$ is a real number, then

$$a^{-m/n} = \frac{1}{a^{m/n}} \quad (\text{where } a \neq 0).$$

Answers

2. **(a)** 2; 3; 5; 125   **(b)** 9   **(c)** -64
   (d) 16   **(e)** not a real number

EXAMPLE 3 Evaluating Exponentials of the Form $a^{-m/n}$

Evaluate each exponential.

(a) $16^{-3/4} = \dfrac{1}{16^{3/4}} = \dfrac{1}{(16^{1/4})^3} = \dfrac{1}{(\sqrt[4]{16})^3} = \dfrac{1}{2^3} = \dfrac{1}{8}$

> The denominator of 3/4 is the index and the numerator is the exponent.

(b) $25^{-3/2} = \dfrac{1}{25^{3/2}} = \dfrac{1}{(25^{1/2})^3} = \dfrac{1}{(\sqrt{25})^3} = \dfrac{1}{5^3} = \dfrac{1}{125}$

(c) $\left(\dfrac{8}{27}\right)^{-2/3} = \dfrac{1}{\left(\frac{8}{27}\right)^{2/3}} = \dfrac{1}{\left(\sqrt[3]{\frac{8}{27}}\right)^2} = \dfrac{1}{\left(\frac{2}{3}\right)^2} = \dfrac{1}{\frac{4}{9}} = \dfrac{9}{4}$

> $\frac{1}{\frac{4}{9}} = 1 \div \frac{4}{9} = 1 \cdot \frac{9}{4}$

We could also use the rule $\left(\frac{b}{a}\right)^{-m} = \left(\frac{a}{b}\right)^m$ here, as follows.

$\left(\dfrac{8}{27}\right)^{-2/3} = \left(\dfrac{27}{8}\right)^{2/3} = \left(\sqrt[3]{\dfrac{27}{8}}\right)^2 = \left(\dfrac{3}{2}\right)^2 = \dfrac{9}{4}$ The result is the same.

> Take the reciprocal only of the base, *not* the exponent.

─── Work Problem ③ at the Side. ▶

❗ CAUTION

Be careful to distinguish between exponential expressions like the following.

$16^{-1/4}$, which equals $\dfrac{1}{2}$, $-16^{1/4}$, which equals -2, and

$-16^{-1/4}$, which equals $-\dfrac{1}{2}$

A negative exponent does not necessarily lead to a negative result. Negative exponents lead to reciprocals, which may be positive.

We obtain an alternative meaning of $a^{m/n}$ by applying the power rule a little differently than in the earlier definition.

Alternative Meaning of $a^{m/n}$

If all indicated roots are real numbers, then
$$a^{m/n} = (a^{1/n})^m = (a^m)^{1/n}.$$

As a result, we can evaluate an expression such as $27^{2/3}$ in two ways.

$27^{2/3} = (27^{1/3})^2 = 3^2 = 9$ The result is the same.

or $27^{2/3} = (27^2)^{1/3} = 729^{1/3} = 9$

In most cases, it is easier to use $(a^{1/n})^m$.

③ Evaluate each exponential.

(a) $36^{-3/2}$

$= \dfrac{1}{36^{\underline{}}}$

$= \dfrac{1}{(36^{\underline{}})^{\underline{}}}$

$= \dfrac{1}{(\sqrt{36})^3}$

$= \dfrac{1}{\underline{}^3}$

$= \underline{}$

(b) $32^{-4/5}$

(c) $\left(\dfrac{4}{9}\right)^{-5/2}$

Answers

3. (a) 3/2; 1/2; 3; 6; $\dfrac{1}{216}$

  (b) $\dfrac{1}{16}$ (c) $\dfrac{243}{32}$

4 Write each exponential as a radical. Assume that all variables represent positive real numbers. Use the definition that takes the root first.

(a) $19^{1/2}$

(b) $5^{2/3}$

(c) $4k^{3/5}$

(d) $5x^{3/5} - (2x)^{3/5}$

(e) $x^{-5/7}$

(f) $(m^3 + n^3)^{1/3}$

5 Write each radical as an exponential and simplify. Assume that all variables represent positive real numbers.

(a) $\sqrt{37}$ **(b)** $\sqrt{2^8}$

(c) $\sqrt[4]{9^8}$ **(d)** $\sqrt[4]{t^4}$

Radical Form of $a^{m/n}$

If all indicated roots are real numbers, then

$$a^{m/n} = \sqrt[n]{a^m} = \left(\sqrt[n]{a}\right)^m.$$

In words, raise a to the mth power and then take the nth root, or take the nth root of a and then raise to the mth power.

For example,

$$8^{2/3} = \sqrt[3]{8^2} = \sqrt[3]{64} = 4, \quad \text{and} \quad 8^{2/3} = \left(\sqrt[3]{8}\right)^2 = 2^2 = 4,$$

so

$$8^{2/3} = \sqrt[3]{8^2} = \left(\sqrt[3]{8}\right)^2.$$

OBJECTIVE 3 **Convert between radicals and rational exponents.** Using the definition of rational exponents, we can simplify many problems involving radicals by converting the radicals to numbers with rational exponents. After simplifying, we convert the answer back to radical form if required.

EXAMPLE 4	Converting Exponentials to Radicals

Write each exponential as a radical. Assume that all variables represent positive real numbers. Use the definition that takes the root first.

(a) $13^{1/2} = \sqrt{13}$ **(b)** $6^{3/4} = \left(\sqrt[4]{6}\right)^3$ **(c)** $9m^{5/8} = 9\left(\sqrt[8]{m}\right)^5$

(d) $6x^{2/3} - (4x)^{3/5} = 6\left(\sqrt[3]{x}\right)^2 - \left(\sqrt[5]{4x}\right)^3$

(e) $r^{-2/3} = \dfrac{1}{r^{2/3}} = \dfrac{1}{\left(\sqrt[3]{r}\right)^2}$

(f) $(a^2 + b^2)^{1/2} = \sqrt{a^2 + b^2}$ ◁ $\sqrt{a^2 + b^2} \neq a + b$

◀ Work Problem **4** at the Side.

EXAMPLE 5	Simplifying Radicals Using Rational Exponents

Write each radical as an exponential and simplify. Assume that all variables represent positive real numbers.

(a) $\sqrt{10} = 10^{1/2}$ **(b)** $\sqrt{5^4} = 5^{4/2} = 5^2 = 25$

(c) $\sqrt[4]{3^8} = 3^{8/4} = 3^2 = 9$

(d) $\sqrt[6]{z^6} = z^{6/6} = z^1 = z$, because z is positive.

◀ Work Problem **5** at the Side.

Answers

4. **(a)** $\sqrt{19}$ **(b)** $\left(\sqrt[3]{5}\right)^2$ **(c)** $4\left(\sqrt[5]{k}\right)^3$
   (d) $5\left(\sqrt[5]{x}\right)^3 - \left(\sqrt[5]{2x}\right)^3$
   (e) $\dfrac{1}{\left(\sqrt[7]{x}\right)^5}$ **(f)** $\sqrt[3]{m^3 + n^3}$

5. **(a)** $37^{1/2}$ **(b)** 16 **(c)** 81 **(d)** t

Note

In **Example 5(d)**, it was not necessary to use absolute value bars because the directions specifically stated that the variable represents a positive real number. The absolute value of the positive real number z is z itself, so the answer is simply z.

OBJECTIVE ▶ 4 **Use the rules for exponents with rational exponents.** The definition of rational exponents allows us to apply the rules for exponents, summarized below.

Rules for Rational Exponents

Let r and s be rational numbers. For all real numbers a and b for which the indicated expressions exist, the following hold true.

$$a^r \cdot a^s = a^{r+s} \qquad a^{-r} = \frac{1}{a^r} \qquad \frac{a^r}{a^s} = a^{r-s} \qquad \left(\frac{a}{b}\right)^{-r} = \frac{b^r}{a^r}$$

$$(a^r)^s = a^{rs} \qquad (ab)^r = a^r b^r \qquad \left(\frac{a}{b}\right)^r = \frac{a^r}{b^r} \qquad a^{-r} = \left(\frac{1}{a}\right)^r$$

EXAMPLE 6 **Applying Rules for Rational Exponents**

Simplify each expression. Assume that all variables represent positive real numbers.

(a) $2^{1/2} \cdot 2^{1/4}$

$\quad = 2^{1/2 + 1/4}$ Product rule

$\quad = 2^{3/4}$ Add exponents.

(b) $\dfrac{5^{2/3}}{5^{7/3}}$

$\quad = 5^{2/3 - 7/3}$ Quotient rule

$\quad = 5^{-5/3}$ Subtract exponents.

$\quad = \dfrac{1}{5^{5/3}}$ $\quad a^{-r} = \frac{1}{a^r}$

(c) $\dfrac{\left(x^{1/2} y^{2/3}\right)^4}{y}$

$\quad = \dfrac{\left(x^{1/2}\right)^4 \left(y^{2/3}\right)^4}{y}$ Power rule

$\quad = \dfrac{x^2 y^{8/3}}{y^1}$ Power rule; $y = y^1$

$\quad = x^2 y^{8/3 - 1}$ Quotient rule

$\quad = x^2 y^{5/3}$ $\quad \frac{8}{3} - 1 = \frac{8}{3} - \frac{3}{3} = \frac{5}{3}$

(d) $\left(\dfrac{x^4 y^{-6}}{x^{-2} y^{1/3}}\right)^{-2/3}$

$\quad = \dfrac{\left(x^4\right)^{-2/3} \left(y^{-6}\right)^{-2/3}}{\left(x^{-2}\right)^{-2/3} \left(y^{1/3}\right)^{-2/3}}$ Power rule

$\quad = \dfrac{x^{-8/3} y^4}{x^{4/3} y^{-2/9}}$ Power rule

$\quad = x^{-8/3 - 4/3} y^{4-(-2/9)}$ Quotient rule

$\quad = x^{-4} y^{38/9}$ ⟶ Use parentheses to avoid errors. $\quad 4 - \left(-\frac{2}{9}\right) = \frac{36}{9} + \frac{2}{9} = \frac{38}{9}$

$\quad = \dfrac{y^{38/9}}{x^4}$ Definition of negative exponent

---

Continued on Next Page

6 Simplify each expression. Assume that all variables represent positive real numbers.

(a) $11^{3/4} \cdot 11^{5/4}$

(b) $\dfrac{7^{3/4}}{7^{7/4}}$

(c) $\dfrac{9^{2/3}\,(x^{1/3})^4}{9^{-1/3}}$

(d) $\left(\dfrac{a^3 b^{-4}}{a^{-2} b^{1/5}}\right)^{-1/2}$

(e) $a^{2/3}\,(a^{7/3} + a^{1/3})$

7 Write each radical as an exponential and simplify. Leave answers in exponential form. Assume that all variables represent positive real numbers.

(a) $\sqrt[5]{x^3} \cdot \sqrt[3]{x}$

(b) $\dfrac{\sqrt{x^5}}{\sqrt[3]{x}}$

(c) $\sqrt{\sqrt[3]{x}}$

Answers

6. (a) 121 (b) $\frac{1}{7}$ (c) $9x^{4/3}$
   (d) $\dfrac{b^{21/10}}{a^{5/2}}$ (e) $a^3 + a$
7. (a) $x^{14/15}$ (b) $x^{13/6}$ (c) $x^{1/6}$

The same result is obtained if we simplify within the parentheses first.

$$\left(\frac{x^4 y^{-6}}{x^{-2} y^{1/3}}\right)^{-2/3}$$

$$= (x^{4-(-2)} y^{-6-1/3})^{-2/3} \quad \text{Quotient rule}$$

$$= (x^6 y^{-19/3})^{-2/3} \quad -6 - \tfrac{1}{3} = -\tfrac{18}{3} - \tfrac{1}{3} = -\tfrac{19}{3}$$

$$= (x^6)^{-2/3} (y^{-19/3})^{-2/3} \quad \text{Power rule}$$

$$= x^{-4} y^{38/9} \quad \text{Power rule}$$

$$= \frac{y^{38/9}}{x^4} \quad \text{Definition of negative exponent}$$

(e) $m^{3/4}(m^{5/4} - m^{1/4})$

$$= m^{3/4}(m^{5/4}) - m^{3/4}(m^{1/4}) \quad \text{Distributive property}$$

$$= m^{3/4+5/4} - m^{3/4+1/4} \quad \text{Product rule}$$

$$= m^{8/4} - m^{4/4} \quad \text{Add exponents.}$$

$$= m^2 - m \quad \text{Write the exponents in lowest terms.}$$

Do not make the common mistake of multiplying exponents in the first step.

◀ **Work Problem 6 at the Side.**

! CAUTION
Use the rules of exponents in problems like those in **Example 6**. Do not convert the expressions to radical form.

EXAMPLE 7 Applying Rules for Rational Exponents

Write each radical as an exponential and simplify. Leave answers in exponential form. Assume that all variables represent positive real numbers.

(a) $\sqrt[3]{x^2} \cdot \sqrt[4]{x}$

$$= x^{2/3} \cdot x^{1/4} \quad \text{Convert to rational exponents.}$$

$$= x^{2/3+1/4} \quad \text{Product rule}$$

$$= x^{8/12+3/12} \quad \text{Write exponents with a common denominator.}$$

$$= x^{11/12} \quad \text{Add exponents.}$$

(b) $\dfrac{\sqrt{x^3}}{\sqrt[3]{x^2}}$

$$= \frac{x^{3/2}}{x^{2/3}} \quad \text{Convert to rational exponents.}$$

$$= x^{3/2-2/3} \quad \text{Quotient rule}$$

$$= x^{9/6-4/6} \quad \text{Write exponents with a common denominator.}$$

$$= x^{5/6} \quad \text{Subtract exponents.}$$

(c) $\sqrt{\sqrt[4]{z}}$

$$= \sqrt{z^{1/4}} \quad \text{Convert the inside radical to rational exponents.}$$

$$= (z^{1/4})^{1/2} \quad \text{Convert the square root to a rational exponent.}$$

$$= z^{1/8} \quad \text{Power rule}$$

◀ **Work Problem 7 at the Side.**

10.2 Exercises

FOR EXTRA HELP

Go to MyMathLab *for worked-out, step-by-step solutions to exercises enclosed in a square* ☐ *and video solutions to* ▶ *exercises.*

CONCEPT CHECK *Match each expression from Column I with the equivalent choice from Column II.*

I

1. $3^{1/2}$　　**2.** $(-27)^{1/3}$

3. $-16^{1/2}$　　**4.** $(-16)^{1/2}$

5. $(-32)^{1/5}$　　**6.** $(-32)^{2/5}$

7. $4^{3/2}$　　**8.** $6^{2/4}$

9. $-6^{2/4}$　　**10.** $36^{0.5}$

II

A. -4　　**B.** 8

C. $\sqrt{3}$　　**D.** $-\sqrt{6}$

E. -3　　**F.** $\sqrt{6}$

G. 4　　**H.** -2

I. 6　　**J.** Not a real number

Evaluate each exponential. **See Examples 1–3.**

11. $169^{1/2}$　　**12.** $121^{1/2}$　　**13.** $729^{1/3}$　　**14.** $512^{1/3}$

15. $16^{1/4}$　　**16.** $625^{1/4}$　　**17.** $\left(\dfrac{64}{81}\right)^{1/2}$　　**18.** $\left(\dfrac{8}{27}\right)^{1/3}$

19. $(-27)^{1/3}$　　**20.** $(-32)^{1/5}$　　**21.** $(-144)^{1/2}$　　**22.** $(-36)^{1/2}$

23. $100^{3/2}$　　**24.** $64^{3/2}$　　**25.** $81^{3/4}$　　**26.** $216^{2/3}$

27. $-16^{5/2}$　　**28.** $-32^{3/5}$　　**29.** $(-8)^{4/3}$　　**30.** $(-243)^{2/5}$

31. $32^{-3/5}$　　**32.** $27^{-4/3}$　　**33.** $64^{-3/2}$　　**34.** $81^{-3/2}$

35. $\left(\dfrac{125}{27}\right)^{-2/3}$　　**36.** $\left(\dfrac{64}{125}\right)^{-2/3}$　　**37.** $\left(\dfrac{16}{81}\right)^{-3/4}$　　**38.** $\left(\dfrac{729}{64}\right)^{-5/6}$

Write each exponential as a radical. Assume that all variables represent positive real numbers. Use the definition that takes the root first. See Example 4.

39. $10^{1/2}$
⏵

40. $3^{1/2}$

41. $8^{3/4}$

42. $7^{2/3}$

43. $5x^{2/3}$

44. $8x^{3/4}$

45. $(9q)^{5/8} - (2x)^{2/3}$
⏵

46. $(3p)^{3/4} + (4x)^{2/3}$

47. $x^{-3/5}$

48. $z^{-4/9}$

49. $(2m)^{-3/2}$

50. $(5y)^{-3/5}$

51. $(2y + x)^{2/3}$

52. $(r + 2z)^{3/2}$

53. $(3m^4 + 2k^2)^{-2/3}$

54. $(5x^2 + 3z^3)^{-5/6}$

Write each radical as an exponential and simplify. Assume that all variables represent positive real numbers. See Example 5.

55. $\sqrt{15}$

56. $\sqrt{26}$

57. $\sqrt{2^{12}}$

58. $\sqrt{5^{10}}$

59. $\sqrt[3]{4^9}$

60. $\sqrt[4]{6^8}$

61. $\sqrt[8]{x^8}$

62. $\sqrt{t^2}$

63. $\sqrt{x^{20}}$

64. $\sqrt{r^{50}}$

65. CONCEPT CHECK Replace a with 3 and b with 4 to show that, in general,
$$\sqrt{a^2 + b^2} \neq a + b.$$

66. Suppose someone claims that $\sqrt[n]{a^n + b^n}$ must equal $a + b$, because when $a = 1$ and $b = 0$, a true statement results.
$$\sqrt[n]{a^n + b^n} = \sqrt[n]{1^n + 0^n} = \sqrt[n]{1^n} = 1 = 1 + 0 = a + b.$$
Why is this faulty reasoning?

Simplify each expression. Assume that all variables represent positive real numbers. See Example 6.

67. $3^{1/2} \cdot 3^{3/2}$
⏵

68. $6^{4/3} \cdot 6^{2/3}$

69. $\dfrac{64^{5/3}}{64^{4/3}}$

70. $\dfrac{125^{7/3}}{125^{5/3}}$

71. $y^{7/3} \cdot y^{-4/3}$

72. $r^{-8/9} \cdot r^{17/9}$

73. $x^{2/3} \cdot x^{-1/4}$

74. $x^{2/5} \cdot x^{-1/3}$

75. $\dfrac{k^{1/3}}{k^{2/3} \cdot k^{-1}}$

76. $\dfrac{z^{3/4}}{z^{5/4} \cdot z^{-2}}$

77. $\dfrac{(x^{1/4}y^{2/5})^{20}}{x^2}$

78. $\dfrac{(r^{1/5}s^{2/3})^{15}}{r^2}$

79. $\dfrac{(x^{2/3})^2}{(x^2)^{7/3}}$

80. $\dfrac{(p^3)^{1/4}}{(p^{5/4})^2}$

81. $\dfrac{m^{3/4}n^{-1/4}}{(m^2 n)^{1/2}}$

82. $\dfrac{(a^2 b^5)^{-1/4}}{(a^{-3}b^2)^{1/6}}$

83. $\dfrac{p^{1/5}p^{7/10}p^{1/2}}{(p^3)^{-1/5}}$

84. $\dfrac{z^{1/3}z^{-2/3}z^{1/6}}{(z^{-1/6})^3}$

85. $\left(\dfrac{b^{-3/2}}{c^{-5/3}}\right)^2 (b^{-1/4}c^{-1/3})^{-1}$

86. $\left(\dfrac{m^{-2/3}}{a^{-3/4}}\right)^4 (m^{-3/8}a^{1/4})^{-2}$

87. $\left(\dfrac{p^{-1/4}q^{-3/2}}{3^{-1}p^{-2}q^{-2/3}}\right)^{-2}$

88. $\left(\dfrac{2^{-2}w^{-3/4}x^{-5/8}}{w^{3/4}x^{-1/2}}\right)^{-3}$

89. $p^{2/3}\left(p^{1/3} + 2p^{4/3}\right)$

90. $z^{5/8}\left(3z^{5/8} + 5z^{11/8}\right)$

91. $k^{1/4}\left(k^{3/2} - k^{1/2}\right)$

92. $r^{3/5}\left(r^{1/2} + r^{3/4}\right)$

93. $6a^{7/4}\left(a^{-7/4} + 3a^{-3/4}\right)$

94. $4m^{5/3}\left(m^{-2/3} - 4m^{-5/3}\right)$

95. $5m^{-2/3}\left(m^{2/3} + m^{-7/3}\right)$

96. $7z^{-4/5}\left(z^{4/5} - z^{-6/5}\right)$

Write each radical as an exponential and simplify. Leave answers in exponential form. Assume that all variables represent positive real numbers. See Example 7.

97. $\sqrt[5]{x^3} \cdot \sqrt[4]{x}$

98. $\sqrt[6]{y^5} \cdot \sqrt[3]{y^2}$

99. $\dfrac{\sqrt[3]{t^4}}{\sqrt[5]{t^4}}$

100. $\dfrac{\sqrt[4]{w^3}}{\sqrt[6]{w}}$

101. $\dfrac{\sqrt[3]{k^5}}{\sqrt[3]{k^7}}$

102. $\dfrac{\sqrt{x^5}}{\sqrt{x^8}}$

103. $\sqrt[3]{xz} \cdot \sqrt{z}$

104. $\sqrt{y} \cdot \sqrt[3]{yz}$

105. $\sqrt[4]{\sqrt[3]{m}}$

106. $\sqrt[5]{\sqrt{k}}$

107. $\sqrt[3]{\sqrt[5]{\sqrt{y}}}$

108. $\sqrt{\sqrt[3]{\sqrt[4]{x}}}$

Solve each problem.

109. The threshold weight T, in pounds, for a person is the weight above which the risk of death increases greatly. The threshold weight in pounds for men aged 40–49 is related to height in inches by the function

$$h(T) = (1860.867T)^{1/3}.$$

What height corresponds to a threshold weight of 200 lb for a 46-yr-old man? Round the answer to the nearest inch and then to the nearest tenth of a foot.

110. Meteorologists can determine the duration of a storm by using the function

$$T(D) = 0.07D^{3/2},$$

where D is the diameter of the storm in miles and T is the time in hours. Find the duration of a storm with a diameter of 16 mi. Round the answer to the nearest tenth of an hour.

*The **windchill factor** is a measure of the cooling effect that the wind has on a person's skin. It calculates the equivalent cooling temperature if there were no wind. The National Weather Service uses the formula*

$$\text{Windchill temperature} = 35.74 + 0.6215T - 35.75V^{4/25} + 0.4275TV^{4/25},$$

where T is the temperature in °F and V is the wind speed in miles per hour, to calculate windchill. The table gives the windchill factor for various wind speeds and temperatures at which frostbite is a risk, and how quickly it may occur.

	Temperature (°F)								
Calm	**40**	**30**	**20**	**10**	**0**	**–10**	**–20**	**–30**	**–40**
5	36	25	13	1	–11	–22	–34	–46	–57
10	34	21	9	–4	–16	–28	–41	–53	–66
15	32	19	6	–7	–19	–32	–45	–58	–71
20	30	17	4	–9	–22	–35	–48	–61	–74
25	29	16	3	–11	–24	–37	–51	–64	–78
30	28	15	1	–12	–26	–39	–53	–67	–80
35	28	14	0	–14	–27	–41	–55	–69	–82
40	27	13	–1	–15	–29	–43	–57	–71	–84

Wind speed (mph)

Frostbites times: ☐ 30 minutes ☐ 10 minutes ☐ 5 minutes

Data from National Oceanic and Atmospheric Administration, National Weather Service.

Use the formula to determine the windchill temperature to the nearest tenth of a degree, given the following conditions. Compare answers with the appropriate entries in the table.

111. 10°F, 30-mph wind

112. 30°F, 15-mph wind

113. 20°F, 20-mph wind

114. 40°F, 10-mph wind

115. Refer to the given formula for calculating windchill temperature.

    (a) Write a simplified version of the formula that can be used when the temperature is 0°—that is, when $T = 0$.

    (b) Use the formula from part (a) to determine the windchill temperature to the nearest tenth of a degree when there is a 25-mph wind. Compare the answer with the appropriate table entry.

10.3 | Simplifying Radical Expressions

OBJECTIVE ▸ 1 Use the product rule for radicals. Consider the expressions $\sqrt{36 \cdot 4}$ and $\sqrt{36} \cdot \sqrt{4}$.

$$\sqrt{36 \cdot 4} = \sqrt{144} = 12$$
$$\sqrt{36} \cdot \sqrt{4} = 6 \cdot 2 = 12$$

The result is the same.

This is an example of the **product rule for radicals.**

OBJECTIVES

① Use the product rule for radicals.
② Use the quotient rule for radicals.
③ Simplify radicals.
④ Simplify products and quotients of radicals with different indexes.
⑤ Use the Pythagorean theorem.
⑥ Use the distance formula.

Product Rule for Radicals

If n is a natural number and $\sqrt[n]{a}$ and $\sqrt[n]{b}$ are real numbers, then the following holds true.

$$\sqrt[n]{a} \cdot \sqrt[n]{b} = \sqrt[n]{ab}$$

In words, the product of two nth roots is the nth root of the product.

We justify the product rule using the rules for rational exponents. Because $\sqrt[n]{a} = a^{1/n}$ and $\sqrt[n]{b} = b^{1/n}$,

$$\sqrt[n]{a} \cdot \sqrt[n]{b} = a^{1/n} \cdot b^{1/n} = (ab)^{1/n} = \sqrt[n]{ab}.$$

❶ CAUTION

Use the product rule only when the radicals have the same index.

EXAMPLE 1 Using the Product Rule

Multiply. Assume that all variables represent positive real numbers.

(a) $\sqrt{5} \cdot \sqrt{7}$

$= \sqrt{5 \cdot 7}$

$= \sqrt{35}$

(b) $\sqrt{11} \cdot \sqrt{p}$

$= \sqrt{11p}$

(c) $\sqrt{7} \cdot \sqrt{11xyz}$

$= \sqrt{77xyz}$

— **Work Problem ❶ at the Side. ▶**

EXAMPLE 2 Using the Product Rule

Multiply. Assume that all variables represent positive real numbers.

(a) $\sqrt[3]{3} \cdot \sqrt[3]{12}$

$= \sqrt[3]{3 \cdot 12}$

$= \sqrt[3]{36}$ ⟵ Remember to write the index.

(b) $\sqrt[4]{8y} \cdot \sqrt[4]{3r^2}$

$= \sqrt[4]{24yr^2}$

(c) $\sqrt[6]{10m^4} \cdot \sqrt[6]{5m}$

$= \sqrt[6]{50m^5}$

(d) $\sqrt[4]{2} \cdot \sqrt[5]{2}$ This product cannot be found directly using the product rule for radicals because the indexes (4 and 5) are different.

— **Work Problem ❷ at the Side. ▶**

① Multiply. Assume that all variables represent positive real numbers.

(a) $\sqrt{5} \cdot \sqrt{13}$

(b) $\sqrt{10y} \cdot \sqrt{3k}$

② Multiply. Assume that all variables represent positive real numbers.

(a) $\sqrt[3]{2} \cdot \sqrt[3]{7}$

(b) $\sqrt[6]{8r^2} \cdot \sqrt[6]{2r^3}$

(c) $\sqrt{7} \cdot \sqrt[3]{5}$

Answers

1. **(a)** $\sqrt{65}$ **(b)** $\sqrt{30yk}$
2. **(a)** $\sqrt[3]{14}$ **(b)** $\sqrt[6]{16r^5}$
   (c) This product cannot be found directly using the product rule.

3 Simplify. Assume that all variables represent positive real numbers.

(a) $\sqrt{\dfrac{100}{81}}$

(b) $\sqrt{\dfrac{11}{25}}$

(c) $\sqrt[3]{-\dfrac{125}{216}}$

(d) $\sqrt{\dfrac{y^8}{16}}$

(e) $-\sqrt[3]{\dfrac{x^2}{r^{12}}}$

OBJECTIVE **2** **Use the quotient rule for radicals.** The **quotient rule for radicals** is similar to the product rule.

Quotient Rule for Radicals

If n is a natural number and $\sqrt[n]{a}$ and $\sqrt[n]{b}$ are real numbers, then the following holds true.

$$\sqrt[n]{\dfrac{a}{b}} = \dfrac{\sqrt[n]{a}}{\sqrt[n]{b}} \quad \text{(where } b \neq 0\text{)}$$

In words, the nth root of a quotient is the quotient of the nth roots.

EXAMPLE 3 **Using the Quotient Rule**

Simplify. Assume that all variables represent positive real numbers.

(a) $\sqrt{\dfrac{16}{25}} = \dfrac{\sqrt{16}}{\sqrt{25}} = \dfrac{4}{5}$

(b) $\sqrt{\dfrac{7}{36}} = \dfrac{\sqrt{7}}{\sqrt{36}} = \dfrac{\sqrt{7}}{6}$

(c) $\sqrt[3]{-\dfrac{8}{125}} = \sqrt[3]{\dfrac{-8}{125}} = \dfrac{\sqrt[3]{-8}}{\sqrt[3]{125}} = \dfrac{-2}{5} = -\dfrac{2}{5}$ $\quad \dfrac{-a}{b} = -\dfrac{a}{b}$

(d) $\sqrt[3]{\dfrac{7}{216}} = \dfrac{\sqrt[3]{7}}{\sqrt[3]{216}} = \dfrac{\sqrt[3]{7}}{6}$

(e) $\sqrt[5]{\dfrac{x}{32}} = \dfrac{\sqrt[5]{x}}{\sqrt[5]{32}} = \dfrac{\sqrt[5]{x}}{2}$

(f) $-\sqrt[3]{\dfrac{m^6}{125}} = -\dfrac{\sqrt[3]{m^6}}{\sqrt[3]{125}} = -\dfrac{m^2}{5}$ $\quad$ Think: $\sqrt[3]{m^6} = m^{6/3} = m^2$

◀ **Work Problem** **3** **at the Side.**

OBJECTIVE **3** **Simplify radicals.** We use the product and quotient rules to simplify radicals. A radical is **simplified** if the following four conditions are met.

Conditions for a Simplified Radical

1. The radicand has no factor raised to a power greater than or equal to the index.
2. The radicand has no fractions.
3. No denominator contains a radical.
4. Exponents in the radicand and the index of the radical have greatest common factor 1.

Examples:

$\sqrt{22}, \quad \sqrt{15xy}, \quad \sqrt[3]{18}, \quad \dfrac{\sqrt[4]{m^3}}{m}$ These radicals are simplified.

$\sqrt{28}, \quad \sqrt[3]{\dfrac{3}{5}}, \quad \dfrac{7}{\sqrt{7}}, \quad \sqrt[3]{r^{12}}$ These radicals are not simplified. Each violates one of the above conditions.

Answers

3. (a) $\dfrac{10}{9}$ (b) $\dfrac{\sqrt{11}}{5}$ (c) $-\dfrac{5}{6}$

(d) $\dfrac{y^4}{4}$ (e) $-\dfrac{\sqrt[3]{x^2}}{r^4}$

EXAMPLE 4 Simplifying Roots of Numbers

Simplify.

(a) $\sqrt{24}$

Check to see whether 24 is divisible by a perfect square (the square of a natural number) such as 4, 9, 16, ... The greatest perfect square that divides into 24 is 4.

$$\sqrt{24}$$
$$= \sqrt{4 \cdot 6} \quad \text{Factor. 4 is a perfect square.}$$
$$= \sqrt{4} \cdot \sqrt{6} \quad \text{Product rule}$$
$$= 2\sqrt{6} \quad \sqrt{4} = 2$$

(b) $\sqrt{108}$

As shown on the left below, the number 108 is divisible by the perfect square 36. If this perfect square is not immediately apparent, try factoring 108 into its prime factors, as shown on the right.

$$\sqrt{108} \qquad \qquad \sqrt{108}$$
$$= \sqrt{36 \cdot 3} \qquad = \sqrt{2^2 \cdot 3^3} \qquad \text{Factor into prime factors.}$$
$$= \sqrt{36} \cdot \sqrt{3} \qquad = \sqrt{2^2 \cdot 3^2 \cdot 3} \qquad a^3 = a^2 \cdot a$$
$$= 6\sqrt{3} \qquad = \sqrt{2^2} \cdot \sqrt{3^2} \cdot \sqrt{3} \qquad \text{Product rule}$$
$$\qquad \qquad = 2 \cdot 3 \cdot \sqrt{3} \qquad \sqrt{2^2} = 2, \sqrt{3^2} = 3$$
$$\qquad \qquad = 6\sqrt{3} \qquad \text{Multiply.}$$

(c) $\sqrt{10}$ No perfect square (other than 1) divides into 10, so $\sqrt{10}$ cannot be simplified further.

(d)
$$\sqrt[3]{16} \qquad \text{Look for the greatest perfect } cube \text{ that divides into 16.}$$

Remember to write the index.

$$= \sqrt[3]{8 \cdot 2} \qquad \text{Factor; 8 is a perfect cube.}$$
$$= \sqrt[3]{8} \cdot \sqrt[3]{2} \qquad \text{Product rule}$$
$$= 2\sqrt[3]{2} \qquad \sqrt[3]{8} = 2$$

(e)
$$-\sqrt[4]{162}$$

Remember the negative sign in each line.

$$= -\sqrt[4]{81 \cdot 2} \qquad \text{81 is a perfect 4th power.}$$
$$= -\sqrt[4]{81} \cdot \sqrt[4]{2} \qquad \text{Product rule}$$
$$= -3\sqrt[4]{2} \qquad \sqrt[4]{81} = 3$$

———— Work Problem **4** at the Side. ▶

⚠ CAUTION

Be careful with which factors belong outside the radical symbol and which belong inside. In **Example 4(b)**, the **2 · 3** is written **outside** because $\sqrt{2^2} = 2$ and $\sqrt{3^2} = 3$. The remaining 3 is left inside.

4 Simplify.

(a) $\sqrt{32}$

The greatest perfect square that divides into 32 is ____.

$$\sqrt{32}$$
$$= \sqrt{\underline{} \cdot 2}$$
$$= \sqrt{\underline{}} \cdot \sqrt{2}$$
$$= \underline{}$$

(b) $\sqrt{45}$

(c) $\sqrt{300}$

(d) $\sqrt{35}$

(e) $-\sqrt[3]{54}$

(f) $\sqrt[4]{243}$

Answers
4. (a) 16; 16; 16; $4\sqrt{2}$
   (b) $3\sqrt{5}$ (c) $10\sqrt{3}$
   (d) This radical cannot be simplified further.
   (e) $-3\sqrt[3]{2}$ (f) $3\sqrt[4]{3}$

⑤ Simplify. Assume that all variables represent positive real numbers.

(a) $\sqrt{25p^7}$

(b) $\sqrt{72xy^3}$

(c) $\sqrt[3]{-27x^5y^7z^6}$

(d) $-\sqrt[4]{32a^5b^7}$

⑥ Simplify. Assume that all variables represent positive real numbers.

(a) $\sqrt[12]{2^3}$

(b) $\sqrt[6]{t^2}$

(c) $\sqrt[6]{x^{15}}$

Answers

5. (a) $5p^3\sqrt{p}$ (b) $6y\sqrt{2xy}$

   (c) $-3xy^2z^2\sqrt[3]{x^2y}$ (d) $-2ab\sqrt[4]{2ab^3}$

6. (a) $\sqrt[4]{2}$ (b) $\sqrt[3]{t}$ (c) $x^2\sqrt{x}$

EXAMPLE 5 Simplifying Radicals Involving Variables

Simplify. Assume that all variables represent positive real numbers.

(a) $\sqrt{16m^3}$

$= \sqrt{16m^2 \cdot m}$ Factor.

$= \sqrt{16m^2} \cdot \sqrt{m}$ Product rule

$= 4m\sqrt{m}$ Take the square root.

Absolute value bars are not needed around the m in color because all the variables represent *positive* real numbers.

(b) $\sqrt{200k^7q^8}$

$= \sqrt{10^2 \cdot 2 \cdot (k^3)^2 \cdot k \cdot (q^4)^2}$ Factor into perfect squares.

$= 10k^3q^4\sqrt{2k}$ Take the square root.

(c) $\sqrt[3]{-8x^4y^5}$

$= \sqrt[3]{(-8x^3y^3)(xy^2)}$ Choose $-8x^3y^3$ as the perfect cube that divides into $-8x^4y^5$.

$= \sqrt[3]{-8x^3y^3} \cdot \sqrt[3]{xy^2}$ Product rule

$= -2xy\sqrt[3]{xy^2}$ Take the cube root.

(d) $-\sqrt[4]{32y^9}$

$= -\sqrt[4]{(16y^8)(2y)}$ $16y^8$ is the greatest 4th power that divides into $32y^9$.

$= -\sqrt[4]{16y^8} \cdot \sqrt[4]{2y}$ Product rule

$= -2y^2\sqrt[4]{2y}$ Take the fourth root.

◀ **Work Problem ⑤ at the Side.**

Note

If a variable is raised to a power with an exponent divisible by 2, it is a perfect square. If it is raised to a power with an exponent divisible by 3, it is a perfect cube. *In general, if it is raised to a power with an exponent divisible by n, it is a perfect nth power.*

EXAMPLE 6 Simplifying Radicals Using Lesser Indexes

Simplify. Assume that all variables represent positive real numbers.

(a) $\sqrt[9]{5^6}$ Exponents in the radicand and the index must have GCF 1.

We can write this radical using rational exponents and then write the exponent in lowest terms. We then express the answer as a radical.

$$\sqrt[9]{5^6} = (5^6)^{1/9} = 5^{6/9} = 5^{2/3} = \sqrt[3]{5^2} = \sqrt[3]{25}$$

(b) $\sqrt[4]{p^2} = p^{2/4} = p^{1/2} = \sqrt{p}$ (Recall the assumption that $p > 0$.)

(c) $\sqrt[4]{x^{18}} = (x^{18})^{1/4} = x^{18/4} = x^{9/2} = \sqrt{x^9} = \sqrt{x^8 \cdot x} = \sqrt{x^8} \cdot \sqrt{x} = x^4\sqrt{x}$

◀ **Work Problem ⑥ at the Side.**

These examples suggest the following rule.

Meaning of $\sqrt[kn]{a^{km}}$

If m is an integer, n and k are natural numbers, and all indicated roots exist, then

$$\sqrt[kn]{a^{km}} = \sqrt[n]{a^m}.$$

OBJECTIVE 4 Simplify products and quotients of radicals with different indexes. We multiply and divide radicals with different indexes using rational exponents.

EXAMPLE 7 Multiplying Radicals with Different Indexes

Multiply $\sqrt{7} \cdot \sqrt[3]{2}$.

The indexes, 2 and 3, have least common multiple **6**, so we use rational exponents to write each radical as a **sixth** root.

$$\sqrt{7} = 7^{1/2} = 7^{3/6} = \sqrt[6]{7^3} = \sqrt[6]{343}$$
$$\sqrt[3]{2} = 2^{1/3} = 2^{2/6} = \sqrt[6]{2^2} = \sqrt[6]{4}$$

Now we can multiply.

$$\sqrt{7} \cdot \sqrt[3]{2}$$
$$= \sqrt[6]{343} \cdot \sqrt[6]{4} \quad \text{Substitute; } \sqrt{7} = \sqrt[6]{343},\ \sqrt[3]{2} = \sqrt[6]{4}$$
$$= \sqrt[6]{1372} \quad \text{Product rule}$$

——————————— **Work Problem 7 at the Side.** ▶

OBJECTIVE 5 Use the Pythagorean theorem. The **Pythagorean theorem** gives an equation that relates the lengths of the three sides of a right triangle.

Pythagorean Theorem

If a and b are the lengths of the shorter sides of a right triangle and c is the length of the longest side, then the following holds true.

$$a^2 + b^2 = c^2$$

Hypotenuse
c

Leg a

⌐ denotes a 90°
or right angle

Leg b

The two shorter sides are the **legs** of the triangle, and the longest side is the **hypotenuse.** The hypotenuse is the side opposite the right angle.

$$\text{leg}^2 + \text{leg}^2 = \text{hypotenuse}^2$$

Later we will see that an equation such as $x^2 = 7$ has two solutions: $\sqrt{7}$ (the principal, or positive, square root of 7) and $-\sqrt{7}$. Similarly, $c^2 = 15$ has two solutions, $\pm\sqrt{15}$. In applications we often choose only the positive square root.

7 Multiply.

GS (a) $\sqrt{5} \cdot \sqrt[3]{4}$

The indexes of $\sqrt{5}$ and $\sqrt[3]{4}$ are _____ and 3, which have least common multiple _____. We use rational exponents to write each radical as a sixth root.

$$\sqrt{5} = 5^{1/2} = 5^{—/6} = \sqrt[6]{5^{—}} = \sqrt[6]{125}$$
$$\sqrt[3]{4} = 4^{1/3} = 4^{—/6} = \sqrt[6]{4^{—}} = \sqrt[6]{16}$$

$$\sqrt{5} \cdot \sqrt[3]{4}$$
$$= \sqrt[6]{125} \cdot \sqrt[6]{16}$$
$$= \underline{\hspace{2cm}}$$

(b) $\sqrt[3]{3} \cdot \sqrt{6}$

8 Find the length of the unknown side in each right triangle.

(a)

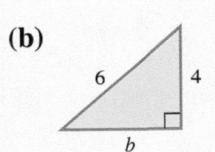

(b)

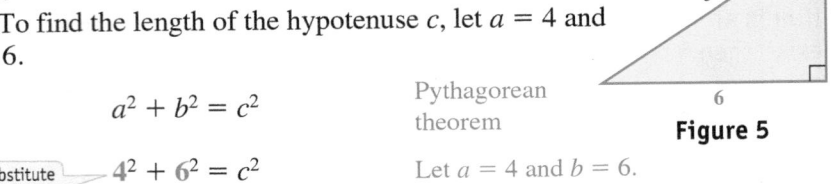

EXAMPLE 8 **Using the Pythagorean Theorem**

Find the length of the unknown side in the right triangle in **Figure 5**.

To find the length of the hypotenuse c, let $a = 4$ and $b = 6$.

$a^2 + b^2 = c^2$	Pythagorean theorem	
$4^2 + 6^2 = c^2$	Let $a = 4$ and $b = 6$.	
$16 + 36 = c^2$	Apply the exponents.	
$c^2 = 52$	Add. Interchange sides.	
$c = \sqrt{52}$	Choose the principal root.	
$c = \sqrt{4 \cdot 13}$	Factor.	
$c = \sqrt{4} \cdot \sqrt{13}$	Product rule	
$c = 2\sqrt{13}$	Simplify.	

Substitute carefully.

Figure 5

The length of the hypotenuse is $2\sqrt{13}$.

◀ **Work Problem 8 at the Side.**

OBJECTIVE 6 **Use the distance formula.** The *distance formula* allows us to find the distance between two points in the coordinate plane, or the length of the line segment joining those two points.

Figure 6 shows the points $(3, -4)$ and $(-5, 3)$. The vertical line through $(-5, 3)$ and the horizontal line through $(3, -4)$ intersect at the point $(-5, -4)$. Thus, the point $(-5, -4)$ becomes the vertex of the right angle in a right triangle.

By the Pythagorean theorem, the sum of the squares of the lengths of the two legs a and b of the right triangle in **Figure 6** is equal to the square of the length of the hypotenuse, c.

$$a^2 + b^2 = c^2, \quad \text{or} \quad c^2 = a^2 + b^2.$$

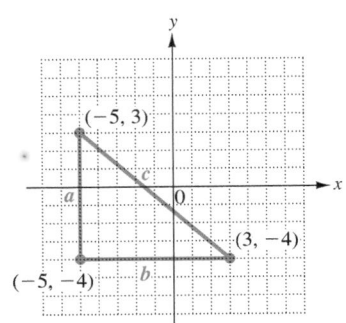

Figure 6

Because the x-coordinate of two of the points in **Figure 6** is -5, side a is vertical. We can find a by finding the difference of the y-coordinates. We subtract -4 from 3 to obtain a positive value for a.

$$a = 3 - (-4) = 7$$

Similarly, we find b by subtracting -5 from 3.

$$b = 3 - (-5) = 8$$

Now substitute these values for a and b into the equation.

$$c^2 = a^2 + b^2 \qquad \text{Pythagorean theorem}$$
$$c^2 = 7^2 + 8^2 \qquad \text{Let } a = 7 \text{ and } b = 8.$$
$$c^2 = 49 + 64 \qquad \text{Apply the exponents.}$$
$$c^2 = 113 \qquad \text{Add.}$$
$$c = \sqrt{113} \qquad \text{Choose the principal root.}$$

We choose the principal root because distance cannot be negative. Therefore, the distance between $(-5, 3)$ and $(3, -4)$ is $\sqrt{113}$.

> **Note**
>
> It is customary to leave the distance in radical form. Do not use a calculator to get an approximation unless specifically directed to do so.

This work can be generalized. **Figure 7** shows the two points (x_1, y_1) and (x_2, y_2). The distance a between (x_1, y_1) and (x_2, y_1) is given by

$$a = |x_2 - x_1|.$$

The distance b between (x_2, y_2) and (x_2, y_1) is given by

$$b = |y_2 - y_1|.$$

From the Pythagorean theorem, we obtain the following.

$$c^2 = a^2 + b^2$$
$$c^2 = (x_2 - x_1)^2 + (y_2 - y_1)^2$$

For all real numbers a, $|a|^2 = a^2$.

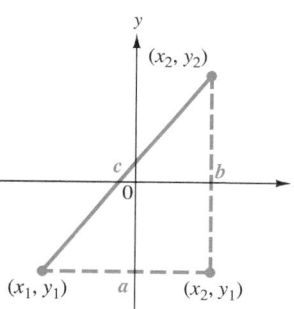

Figure 7

Choosing the principal square root gives the **distance formula.** In this formula, we use d (to denote distance) rather than c.

> **Distance Formula**
>
> The distance d between the points (x_1, y_1) and (x_2, y_2) is given by
>
> $$d = \sqrt{(x_2 - x_1)^2 + (y_2 - y_1)^2}.$$

EXAMPLE 9 Using the Distance Formula

Find the distance between the points $(-3, 5)$ and $(6, 4)$.

We arbitrarily choose to let $(x_1, y_1) = (-3, 5)$ and $(x_2, y_2) = (6, 4)$.

$$d = \sqrt{(x_2 - x_1)^2 + (y_2 - y_1)^2} \qquad \text{Distance formula}$$
$$d = \sqrt{[6 - (-3)]^2 + (4 - 5)^2} \qquad \text{Let } x_2 = 6, y_2 = 4, x_1 = -3, y_1 = 5.$$

Substitute carefully.

$$d = \sqrt{9^2 + (-1)^2}$$
$$d = \sqrt{82} \qquad \text{Leave in radical form.}$$

Work Problem 9 at the Side. ▶

9 Find the distance between each pair of points.

(**a**) $(2, -1)$ and $(5, 3)$

(**b**) $(-3, 2)$ and $(0, -4)$

Answers

9. (**a**) 5 (**b**) $3\sqrt{5}$

10.3 Exercises

FOR EXTRA HELP

Go to MyMathLab *for worked-out, step-by-step solutions to exercises enclosed in a square* ▢ *and video solutions to* ▶ *exercises.*

CONCEPT CHECK *Choose the correct response.*

1. Which is the greatest perfect square factor of 128?

    A. 12   **B.** 16   **C.** 32   **D.** 64

2. Which is the greatest perfect cube factor of $81a^7$?

    A. $8a^3$ **B.** $27a^3$ **C.** $81a^6$ **D.** $27a^6$

3. Which radical *can* be simplified?

    A. $\sqrt{21}$ **B.** $\sqrt{48}$ **C.** $\sqrt[3]{12}$ **D.** $\sqrt[4]{10}$

4. Which radical *cannot* be simplified?

    A. $\sqrt[3]{30}$ **B.** $\sqrt[3]{27a^2b}$ **C.** $\sqrt{\dfrac{25}{81}}$ **D.** $\dfrac{2}{\sqrt{7}}$

5. Which one of the following is *not* equal to $\sqrt{\frac{1}{2}}$? (Do not use calculator approximations.)

    A. $\sqrt{0.5}$ **B.** $\sqrt{\dfrac{2}{4}}$ **C.** $\sqrt{\dfrac{3}{6}}$ **D.** $\dfrac{\sqrt{4}}{\sqrt{16}}$

6. Which one of the following is *not* equal to $\sqrt[3]{\frac{2}{5}}$? (Do not use calculator approximations.)

    A. $\sqrt[3]{\dfrac{6}{15}}$ **B.** $\dfrac{\sqrt[3]{50}}{5}$ **C.** $\dfrac{\sqrt[3]{10}}{\sqrt[3]{25}}$ **D.** $\dfrac{\sqrt[3]{10}}{5}$

7. CONCEPT CHECK A student multiplied incorrectly as follows.

$$\sqrt[3]{13} \cdot \sqrt[3]{5}$$
$$= \sqrt{13 \cdot 5} \qquad \text{Product rule}$$
$$= \sqrt{65} \qquad \text{Multiply.}$$

What Went Wrong? Give the correct product.

8. CONCEPT CHECK A student multiplied incorrectly as follows.

$$\sqrt[3]{x} \cdot \sqrt[3]{x} = x$$

What Went Wrong? What does $\sqrt[3]{x} \cdot \sqrt[3]{x}$ equal?

Multiply, if possible, using the product rule. Assume that all variables represent positive real numbers. ***See Examples 1 and 2.***

9. $\sqrt{3} \cdot \sqrt{3}$

10. $\sqrt{5} \cdot \sqrt{5}$

11. $\sqrt{18} \cdot \sqrt{2}$

12. $\sqrt{12} \cdot \sqrt{3}$

13. ▶ $\sqrt{5} \cdot \sqrt{6}$

14. $\sqrt{10} \cdot \sqrt{3}$

15. $\sqrt{14} \cdot \sqrt{x}$

16. $\sqrt{23} \cdot \sqrt{t}$

17. $\sqrt{14} \cdot \sqrt{3pqr}$

18. $\sqrt{7} \cdot \sqrt{5xt}$

19. ▶ $\sqrt[3]{7x} \cdot \sqrt[3]{2y}$

20. $\sqrt[3]{9x} \cdot \sqrt[3]{4y}$

21. $\sqrt[4]{11} \cdot \sqrt[4]{3}$

22. $\sqrt[4]{6} \cdot \sqrt[4]{9}$

23. $\sqrt[4]{2x} \cdot \sqrt[4]{3y^2}$

24. $\sqrt[4]{3y^2} \cdot \sqrt[4]{6yz}$

25. $\sqrt[3]{7} \cdot \sqrt[4]{3}$ **26.** $\sqrt[5]{8} \cdot \sqrt[6]{12}$ **27.** $\sqrt{12} \cdot \sqrt[3]{3}$ **28.** $\sqrt[4]{5} \cdot \sqrt[5]{4}$

Simplify. Assume that all variables represent positive real numbers. **See Example 3.**

29. $\sqrt{\dfrac{64}{121}}$ **30.** $\sqrt{\dfrac{16}{49}}$ **31.** $\sqrt{\dfrac{3}{25}}$ **32.** $\sqrt{\dfrac{13}{49}}$

33. $\sqrt{\dfrac{x}{25}}$ **34.** $\sqrt{\dfrac{k}{100}}$ **35.** $\sqrt{\dfrac{p^6}{81}}$ **36.** $\sqrt{\dfrac{w^{10}}{36}}$

37. $\sqrt[3]{-\dfrac{27}{64}}$ **38.** $\sqrt[3]{-\dfrac{216}{125}}$ **39.** $\sqrt[3]{\dfrac{r^2}{8}}$ **40.** $\sqrt[3]{\dfrac{t}{125}}$

41. $-\sqrt[4]{\dfrac{81}{x^4}}$ **42.** $-\sqrt[4]{\dfrac{625}{y^4}}$ **43.** $\sqrt[5]{\dfrac{1}{x^{15}}}$ **44.** $\sqrt[5]{\dfrac{32}{y^{20}}}$

45. CONCEPT CHECK A student incorrectly simplified $\sqrt{48}$ as follows.

$$\sqrt{48}$$
$$= \sqrt{4 \cdot 12}$$
$$= \sqrt{4} \cdot \sqrt{12}$$
$$= 2\sqrt{12}$$

What Went Wrong? Give the correct simplified form.

46. CONCEPT CHECK A student incorrectly claimed that the following radical is in simplified form.

$$\sqrt[3]{k^4}$$

What Went Wrong? Give the correct simplified form.

Simplify. **See Example 4.**

47. $\sqrt{12}$ **48.** $\sqrt{18}$ **49.** $\sqrt{288}$ **50.** $\sqrt{72}$

51. $-\sqrt{32}$ **52.** $-\sqrt{48}$ **53.** $-\sqrt{28}$ **54.** $-\sqrt{24}$

55. $\sqrt{30}$ **56.** $\sqrt{46}$ **57.** $\sqrt[3]{128}$ **58.** $\sqrt[3]{24}$

59. $\sqrt[3]{40}$

60. $\sqrt[3]{375}$

61. $\sqrt[3]{-16}$

62. $\sqrt[3]{-250}$

63. $-\sqrt[4]{512}$

64. $-\sqrt[4]{1250}$

65. $\sqrt[5]{64}$

66. $\sqrt[5]{128}$

Simplify. Assume that all variables represent positive real numbers. ***See Example 5.***

67. $\sqrt{72k^2}$

68. $\sqrt{18m^2}$

69. $\sqrt{144x^3y^9}$

70. $\sqrt{169s^5t^{10}}$

71. $\sqrt{121x^6}$

72. $\sqrt{256z^{12}}$

73. $-\sqrt[3]{27t^{12}}$

74. $-\sqrt[3]{64y^{18}}$

75. $-\sqrt{100m^8z^4}$

76. $-\sqrt{25t^6s^{20}}$

77. $-\sqrt[3]{-125a^6b^9c^{12}}$

78. $-\sqrt[3]{-216x^6y^{15}z^3}$

79. $\sqrt[4]{\dfrac{1}{16}r^8t^{20}}$

80. $\sqrt[4]{\dfrac{81}{256}t^{12}u^8}$

81. $\sqrt{50x^3}$

82. $\sqrt{300z^3}$

83. $-\sqrt{500r^{11}}$

84. $-\sqrt{200p^{13}}$

85. $\sqrt{13x^7y^8}$

86. $\sqrt{23k^9p^{14}}$

87. $\sqrt[3]{8z^6w^9}$

88. $\sqrt[3]{64a^{15}b^{12}}$

89. $\sqrt[3]{-16z^5t^7}$

90. $\sqrt[3]{-81m^4n^{10}}$

91. $\sqrt[4]{81x^{12}y^{16}}$

92. $\sqrt[4]{81t^8u^{28}}$

93. $-\sqrt[4]{162r^{15}s^{10}}$

94. $-\sqrt[4]{32k^5m^{10}}$

95. $\sqrt{\dfrac{y^{11}}{36}}$

96. $\sqrt{\dfrac{v^{13}}{49}}$

97. $\sqrt[3]{\dfrac{x^{16}}{27}}$

98. $\sqrt[3]{\dfrac{y^{17}}{125}}$

Simplify. Assume that $x \geq 0$. See Example 6.

99. $\sqrt[4]{48^2}$

100. $\sqrt[4]{50^2}$

101. $\sqrt[4]{25}$

102. $\sqrt[6]{8}$

103. $\sqrt[10]{x^{25}}$

104. $\sqrt[12]{x^{44}}$

105. $\sqrt[10]{x^{16}}$

106. $\sqrt[12]{x^{38}}$

Multiply. Assume that $x \geq 0$. See Example 7.

107. $\sqrt[3]{4} \cdot \sqrt{3}$

108. $\sqrt[3]{5} \cdot \sqrt{6}$

109. $\sqrt[4]{3} \cdot \sqrt[3]{4}$

110. $\sqrt[3]{2} \cdot \sqrt[5]{3}$

111. $\sqrt{x} \cdot \sqrt[3]{x}$

112. $\sqrt[3]{x} \cdot \sqrt[4]{x}$

Find the length of the unknown side in each right triangle. Simplify answers if possible.
See Example 8.

113.
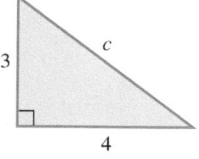

114.
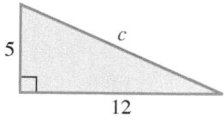

115.
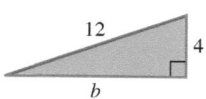

116.
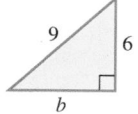

117.
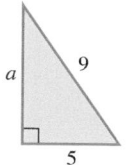

118.
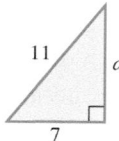

Find the distance between each pair of points. ***See Example 9.***

119. $(6, 13)$ and $(1, 1)$

120. $(8, 13)$ and $(2, 5)$

121. $(-6, 5)$ and $(3, -4)$
▶

122. $(-1, 5)$ and $(-7, 7)$

123. $(-8, 2)$ and $(-4, 1)$

124. $(-1, 2)$ and $(5, 3)$

125. $(4.7, 2.3)$ and $(1.7, -1.7)$

126. $(-2.9, 18.2)$ and $(2.1, 6.2)$

127. $\left(\sqrt{2}, \sqrt{6}\right)$ and $\left(-2\sqrt{2}, 4\sqrt{6}\right)$

128. $\left(\sqrt{7}, 9\sqrt{3}\right)$ and $\left(-\sqrt{7}, 4\sqrt{3}\right)$

129. $(x + y, y)$ and $(x - y, x)$

130. $(c, c - d)$ and $(d, c + d)$

Solve each problem.

131. A Panasonic Smart Viera E50 LCD HDTV has a rectangular screen with a 36.5-in. width. Its height is 20.8 in. What is the length of the diagonal of the screen to the nearest tenth of an inch? (Data from measurements of the author's television.)

36.5 in.

20.8 in.

132. The length of the diagonal of a box is given by

$$D = \sqrt{L^2 + W^2 + H^2},$$

where L, W, and H are the length, width, and height of the box. Find the length of the diagonal D of a box that is 4 ft long, 3 ft high, and 2 ft wide. Give the exact value, and then round to the nearest tenth of a foot.

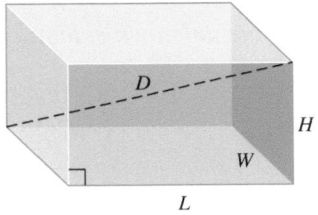

133. A formula from electronics dealing with impedance of parallel resonant circuits is

$$I = \frac{E}{\sqrt{R^2 + \omega^2 L^2}},$$

where the variables are in appropriate units. Find I if $E = 282$, $R = 100$, $L = 264$, and $\omega = 120\pi$. Give the answer to the nearest thousandth.

134. In the study of sound, one version of the law of tensions is

$$f_1 = f_2 \sqrt{\frac{F_1}{F_2}}.$$

Find f_1 to the nearest unit if $F_1 = 300$, $F_2 = 60$, and $f_2 = 260$.

The following letter appeared in the column "Ask Tom Why," written by Tom Skilling of the Chicago Tribune.

Dear Tom,

I cannot remember the formula to calculate the distance to the horizon. I have a stunning view from my 14th floor condo, 150 feet above the ground. How far can I see?

Ted Fleischaker; Indianapolis, Indiana
(Used by permission of Ted Fleischaker.)

Skilling's answer was as follows.

To find the distance to the horizon in miles, take the square root of the height of your view in feet and multiply that result by 1.224. Your answer will be the number of miles to the horizon. (Data from *Chicago Tribune*.)

Use this information to work each problem.

135. **(a)** Write a formula for calculating the distance *d* to the horizon in terms of the height *h* of the view.

(b) Assuming Ted's eyes are 6 ft above the ground, the total height from the ground is 150 + 6 = 156 ft. Use the formula from part (a) to find the distance, to the nearest tenth of a mile, that Ted can see to the horizon.

136. Ted's neighbor Sheri lives on a floor that is 100 ft above the ground. Assuming that her eyes are 5 ft above the ground, how far, to the nearest tenth of a mile, can she see to the horizon?

Relating Concepts (Exercises 137–142)   For Individual or Group Work

Heron's formula for finding the area $\mathcal{A}$ of a triangle with sides a, b, and c is

$$\mathcal{A} = \sqrt{s(s-a)(s-b)(s-c)},$$

where s is the semiperimeter, and $s = \frac{1}{2}(a + b + c)$.

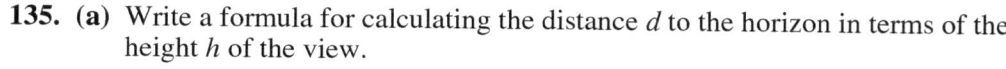

Consider the triangle at the right, and **work Exercises 137–142 in order.**

137. The lengths of the sides of the entire triangle shown are 7, 7, and 12. Find the semiperimeter *s*.

138. Use Heron's formula to find the area of the entire triangle. Write it as a simplified radical.

139. Find the height *h* of the triangle using the Pythagorean theorem.

140. Find the area of each congruent right triangle forming the entire triangle, using the common area formula, $\mathcal{A} = \frac{1}{2}bh$.

141. Double the result from **Exercise 140** to determine the area of the entire triangle.

142. How do the answers in **Exercises 138 and 141** compare?

10.4 | Adding and Subtracting Radical Expressions

OBJECTIVE

1 Simplify radical expressions involving addition and subtraction.

OBJECTIVE ▶ 1 Simplify radical expressions involving addition and subtraction. We do so using the distributive property,

$$ac + bc = (a + b)c.$$

EXAMPLE 1 Adding and Subtracting Radicals

Add or subtract to simplify each radical expression.

(a) $4\sqrt{2} + 3\sqrt{2}$

$= (4 + 3)\sqrt{2}$ ⎫ This is similar to

$= 7\sqrt{2}$ ⎭ simplifying $4x + 3x$ as $7x$.

(b) $2\sqrt{3} - 5\sqrt{3}$

$= (2 - 5)\sqrt{3}$ ⎫ This is similar to

$= -3\sqrt{3}$ ⎭ simplifying $2x - 5x$ as $-3x$.

(c) $3\sqrt{24} + \sqrt{54}$ ⟵ Simplify each individual radical.

$= 3\sqrt{4 \cdot 6} + \sqrt{9 \cdot 6}$ Factor the radicands so that one factor is a perfect square.

$= 3\sqrt{4} \cdot \sqrt{6} + \sqrt{9} \cdot \sqrt{6}$ Product rule

$= 3 \cdot 2\sqrt{6} + 3\sqrt{6}$ Find the square roots.

$= 6\sqrt{6} + 3\sqrt{6}$ Multiply.

$= (6 + 3)\sqrt{6}$ Distributive property

$= 9\sqrt{6}$ Add.

(d) $2\sqrt{20x} - \sqrt{45x}, \quad x \geq 0$

$= 2\sqrt{4} \cdot \sqrt{5x} - \sqrt{9} \cdot \sqrt{5x}$ Product rule

$= 2 \cdot 2\sqrt{5x} - 3\sqrt{5x}$ Find the square roots.

$= 4\sqrt{5x} - 3\sqrt{5x}$ Multiply.

$= (4 - 3)\sqrt{5x}$ Distributive property

$= \sqrt{5x}$ ⟵ $1\sqrt{5x} = \sqrt{5x}$ Subtract.

(e) $2\sqrt{3} - 4\sqrt{5}$

The radicands differ and are already simplified, so this expression cannot be simplified further.

◀ **Work Problem 1 at the Side.**

1 Add or subtract to simplify each radical expression.

(a) $3\sqrt{5} + 7\sqrt{5}$

(b) $2\sqrt{7} - 3\sqrt{7}$

(c) $2\sqrt{11} + 3\sqrt{44}$

(d) $5\sqrt{12y} + 6\sqrt{75y}, \quad y \geq 0$

(e) $9\sqrt{5} - 4\sqrt{10}$

(f) $3\sqrt{8} - 6\sqrt{50} + 2\sqrt{200}$

Answers

1. **(a)** $10\sqrt{5}$ **(b)** $-\sqrt{7}$
   (c) $8\sqrt{11}$ **(d)** $40\sqrt{3y}$
   (e) This expression cannot be simplified further.
   (f) $-4\sqrt{2}$

⚠ **CAUTION**

Only radical expressions with the same index and the same radicand may be combined into a single radical.

⊘ CAUTION

In general, the root of a sum does not equal the sum of the roots.
For example,

$$\sqrt{9 + 16} \neq \sqrt{9} + \sqrt{16}$$

because $\sqrt{9 + 16} = \sqrt{25} = 5$,   but $\sqrt{9} + \sqrt{16} = 3 + 4 = 7$.

EXAMPLE 2   Adding and Subtracting Radicals with Higher Indexes

Add or subtract to simplify each radical expression. Assume that all variables represent positive real numbers.

(a) $2\sqrt[3]{16} - 5\sqrt[3]{54}$ *Remember to write the index with each radical.*

$$= 2\sqrt[3]{8 \cdot 2} - 5\sqrt[3]{27 \cdot 2} \qquad \text{Factor.}$$

$$= 2\sqrt[3]{8} \cdot \sqrt[3]{2} - 5\sqrt[3]{27} \cdot \sqrt[3]{2} \qquad \text{Product rule}$$

$$= 2 \cdot 2 \cdot \sqrt[3]{2} - 5 \cdot 3 \cdot \sqrt[3]{2} \qquad \text{Find the cube roots.}$$

$$= 4\sqrt[3]{2} - 15\sqrt[3]{2} \qquad \text{Multiply.}$$

$$= (4 - 15)\sqrt[3]{2} \qquad \text{Distributive property}$$

$$= -11\sqrt[3]{2} \qquad \text{Subtract.}$$

In practice, the step indicating $(4 - 15)\sqrt[3]{2}$ can be done mentally, giving the final answer $-11\sqrt[3]{2}$ directly.

(b)
$$2\sqrt[3]{x^2y} + \sqrt[3]{8x^5y^4}$$

$$= 2\sqrt[3]{x^2y} + \sqrt[3]{8x^3y^3 \cdot x^2y} \qquad \text{Factor.}$$

$$= 2\sqrt[3]{x^2y} + \sqrt[3]{8x^3y^3} \cdot \sqrt[3]{x^2y} \qquad \text{Product rule}$$

$$= 2\sqrt[3]{x^2y} + 2xy\sqrt[3]{x^2y} \qquad \text{Find the cube root.}$$

This result cannot be simplified further.
$$= (2 + 2xy)\sqrt[3]{x^2y} \qquad \text{Distributive property}$$

Although we were able to use the distributive property in the last step, 2 and $2xy$ are not like terms and cannot be combined into a single term.

(c) $5\sqrt{4x^3} + 3\sqrt[3]{64x^4}$ *Be careful. The indexes are different.*

$$= 5\sqrt{4x^2 \cdot x} + 3\sqrt[3]{64x^3 \cdot x} \qquad \text{Factor.}$$

$$= 5\sqrt{4x^2} \cdot \sqrt{x} + 3\sqrt[3]{64x^3} \cdot \sqrt[3]{x} \qquad \text{Product rule}$$

$$= 5 \cdot 2x\sqrt{x} + 3 \cdot 4x\sqrt[3]{x} \qquad \textit{Keep track of the indexes.}$$

$$= 10x\sqrt{x} + 12x\sqrt[3]{x} \qquad \text{Multiply.}$$

The two terms in the final expression cannot be combined into a single term—the indexes are different.

———————— **Work Problem ② at the Side.** ▶

② Add or subtract to simplify each radical expression. Assume that all variables represent positive real numbers.

(a) $7\sqrt[3]{81} + 3\sqrt[3]{24}$

(b) $-2\sqrt[4]{32} - 7\sqrt[4]{162}$

(c) $\sqrt[3]{p^4q^7} - \sqrt[3]{64pq}$

(d) $\sqrt[3]{128t^4} - 2\sqrt{72t^3}$

Answers

2. **(a)** $27\sqrt[3]{3}$ **(b)** $-25\sqrt[4]{2}$
   (c) $(pq^2 - 4)\sqrt[3]{pq}$
   (d) $4t\sqrt[3]{2t} - 12t\sqrt{2t}$

③ Perform the indicated operations. Assume that all variables represent positive real numbers.

(a) $2\sqrt{\dfrac{8}{9}} - 2\dfrac{\sqrt{27}}{\sqrt{108}}$

(b) $\sqrt{\dfrac{80}{y^4}} + \sqrt{\dfrac{81}{y^{10}}}$

EXAMPLE 3	Adding and Subtracting Radicals with Fractions

Perform the indicated operations. Assume that all variables represent positive real numbers.

(a) $2\sqrt{\dfrac{75}{16}} + 4\dfrac{\sqrt{8}}{\sqrt{32}}$

$= 2\dfrac{\sqrt{25 \cdot 3}}{\sqrt{16}} + 4\dfrac{\sqrt{4 \cdot 2}}{\sqrt{16 \cdot 2}}$ Quotient rule; Factor.

$= 2\left(\dfrac{5\sqrt{3}}{4}\right) + 4\left(\dfrac{2\sqrt{2}}{4\sqrt{2}}\right)$ Product rule; Take square roots.

$= \dfrac{5\sqrt{3}}{2} + 2$ Multiply; $\dfrac{\sqrt{2}}{\sqrt{2}} = 1$

$= \dfrac{5\sqrt{3}}{2} + \dfrac{4}{2}$ Write with a common denominator; $2 = \dfrac{4}{2}$

$= \dfrac{5\sqrt{3} + 4}{2}$ $\dfrac{a}{c} + \dfrac{b}{c} = \dfrac{a + b}{c}$

(b) $10\sqrt[3]{\dfrac{5}{x^6}} - 3\sqrt[3]{\dfrac{4}{x^9}}$

$= 10\dfrac{\sqrt[3]{5}}{\sqrt[3]{x^6}} - 3\dfrac{\sqrt[3]{4}}{\sqrt[3]{x^9}}$ Quotient rule

$= \dfrac{10\sqrt[3]{5}}{x^2} - \dfrac{3\sqrt[3]{4}}{x^3}$ Simplify denominators.

$= \dfrac{10\sqrt[3]{5} \cdot x}{x^2 \cdot x} - \dfrac{3\sqrt[3]{4}}{x^3}$ Write with a common denominator.

$= \dfrac{10x\sqrt[3]{5} - 3\sqrt[3]{4}}{x^3}$ $\dfrac{a}{c} - \dfrac{b}{c} = \dfrac{a - b}{c}$

◀ **Work Problem ③ at the Side.**

Answers

3. (a) $\dfrac{4\sqrt{2} - 3}{3}$ **(b)** $\dfrac{4y^3\sqrt{5} + 9}{y^5}$

10.4 Exercises

FOR EXTRA HELP Go to MyMathLab for worked-out, step-by-step solutions to exercises enclosed in a square ▢ and video solutions to ▶ exercises.

CONCEPT CHECK *Choose the correct response.*

1. Which sum can be simplified without first simplifying the individual radical expressions?

   A. $\sqrt{50} + \sqrt{32}$ **B.** $3\sqrt{6} + 9\sqrt{6}$

   C. $\sqrt[3]{32} - \sqrt[3]{108}$ **D.** $\sqrt[5]{6} - \sqrt[5]{192}$

2. Which difference can be simplified without first simplifying the individual radical expressions?

   A. $\sqrt{81} - \sqrt{18}$ **B.** $\sqrt[3]{8} - \sqrt[3]{16}$

   C. $4\sqrt[3]{7} - 9\sqrt[3]{7}$ **D.** $\sqrt{75} - \sqrt{12}$

3. **CONCEPT CHECK** A student gave the difference

   $$28 - 4\sqrt{2} \quad \text{as} \quad 24\sqrt{2}.$$

   Her teacher did not give her any credit for this answer. *What Went Wrong?*

4. **CONCEPT CHECK** A student gave the sum

   $$(3 + 3xy)\sqrt[3]{xy^2} \quad \text{as} \quad 6xy\sqrt[3]{xy^2}.$$

   His teacher did not give him any credit for this answer. *What Went Wrong?*

Simplify. Assume that all variables represent positive real numbers.
See Examples 1 and 2.

5. $\sqrt{36} - \sqrt{100}$ 6. $\sqrt{25} - \sqrt{81}$ 7. $6\sqrt{10} + 2\sqrt{10}$ 8. $5\sqrt{6} + 4\sqrt{6}$

9. $6\sqrt{5} - 7\sqrt{5}$ 10. $3\sqrt{2} - 4\sqrt{2}$ 11. $-2\sqrt{48} + 3\sqrt{75}$ 12. $4\sqrt{32} - 2\sqrt{8}$

13. $5\sqrt{6} + 2\sqrt{10}$ 14. $3\sqrt{11} - 5\sqrt{13}$ 15. $\sqrt[3]{16} + 4\sqrt[3]{54}$ 16. $3\sqrt[3]{24} - 2\sqrt[3]{192}$

17. $2\sqrt[3]{16} - \sqrt[3]{54}$ 18. $3\sqrt[3]{81} - 4\sqrt[3]{24}$ 19. $\sqrt[4]{32} + 3\sqrt[4]{2}$

20. $\sqrt[4]{405} - 2\sqrt[4]{5}$ 21. $5\sqrt[4]{32} + 3\sqrt[4]{162}$ 22. $2\sqrt[4]{512} + 4\sqrt[4]{32}$

23. $6\sqrt{18} - \sqrt{32} + 2\sqrt{50}$ 24. $5\sqrt{8} + 3\sqrt{72} - 3\sqrt{50}$ 25. $2\sqrt{5} + 3\sqrt{20} + 4\sqrt{45}$

26. $5\sqrt{54} - 2\sqrt{24} - 2\sqrt{96}$ 27. $8\sqrt{2x} - \sqrt{8x} + \sqrt{72x}$ 28. $4\sqrt{18k} - \sqrt{72k} + \sqrt{50k}$

29. $3\sqrt{72m^2} - 5\sqrt{32m^2}$ 30. $9\sqrt{27p^2} - 14\sqrt{108p^2}$ 31. $2\sqrt[3]{27x} - 2\sqrt[3]{8x}$

32. $6\sqrt[3]{128m} + 3\sqrt[3]{16m}$ 33. $\sqrt[3]{x^2y} - \sqrt[3]{8x^2y}$ 34. $3\sqrt[3]{x^2y^2} - 2\sqrt[3]{64x^2y^2}$

35. $3x\sqrt[3]{xy^2} - 2\sqrt[3]{8x^4y^2}$

36. $6q^2\sqrt[3]{5q} - 2q\sqrt[3]{40q^4}$

37. $3\sqrt[4]{x^5y} - 2x\sqrt[4]{xy}$

38. $2\sqrt[4]{m^9p^6} - 3m^2p\sqrt[4]{mp^2}$

39. $2\sqrt[4]{32a^3} + 5\sqrt[4]{2a^3}$

40. $-\sqrt[4]{16r} + 5\sqrt[4]{r}$

41. $\sqrt[3]{64xy^2} + \sqrt[3]{27x^4y^5}$

42. $\sqrt[4]{625s^3t} + \sqrt[4]{81s^7t^5}$

43. $2\sqrt[3]{8x^4} + 3\sqrt[4]{16x^5}$

44. $3\sqrt[3]{64m^4} + 5\sqrt[4]{81m^5}$

45. $\sqrt[3]{192st^4} - \sqrt{27s^3t}$

46. $\sqrt{125a^5b^5} + \sqrt[3]{125a^4b^4}$

Perform the indicated operations. Assume that all variables represent positive real numbers. ***See Example 3.***

47. $\dfrac{2\sqrt{5}}{3} + \dfrac{\sqrt{5}}{6}$

48. $\dfrac{4\sqrt{3}}{3} + \dfrac{2\sqrt{3}}{9}$

49. $\sqrt{\dfrac{8}{9}} + \sqrt{\dfrac{18}{36}}$

50. $\sqrt{\dfrac{12}{16}} + \sqrt{\dfrac{48}{64}}$

51. $\dfrac{\sqrt{32}}{3} + \dfrac{2\sqrt{2}}{3} - \dfrac{\sqrt{2}}{\sqrt{9}}$

52. $\dfrac{\sqrt{27}}{2} - \dfrac{3\sqrt{3}}{2} + \dfrac{\sqrt{3}}{\sqrt{4}}$

53. $3\sqrt{\dfrac{50}{9}} + 8\dfrac{\sqrt{2}}{\sqrt{8}}$

54. $5\sqrt{\dfrac{288}{25}} + 21\dfrac{\sqrt{2}}{\sqrt{18}}$

55. $3\sqrt{\dfrac{50}{49}} - \dfrac{\sqrt{27}}{\sqrt{12}}$

56. $9\sqrt{\dfrac{48}{25}} - 2\dfrac{\sqrt{2}}{\sqrt{98}}$

57. $\sqrt{\dfrac{25}{x^8}} + \sqrt{\dfrac{9}{x^6}}$

58. $\sqrt{\dfrac{100}{y^4}} + \sqrt{\dfrac{81}{y^{10}}}$

59. $3\sqrt[3]{\dfrac{m^5}{27}} - 2m\sqrt[3]{\dfrac{m^2}{64}}$

60. $2a\sqrt[4]{\dfrac{a}{16}} - 5a\sqrt[4]{\dfrac{a}{81}}$

61. $3\sqrt[3]{\dfrac{2}{x^6}} - 4\sqrt[3]{\dfrac{5}{x^9}}$

62. $-4\sqrt[3]{\dfrac{4}{t^9}} + 3\sqrt[3]{\dfrac{9}{t^{12}}}$

Find the perimeter of each figure. Give answers as simplified radical expressions.

63.

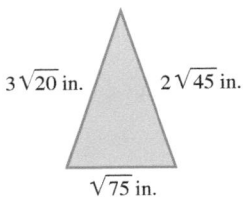

$3\sqrt{20}$ in.　　$2\sqrt{45}$ in.

$\sqrt{75}$ in.

64.

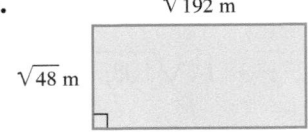

$\sqrt{192}$ m

$\sqrt{48}$ m

65.

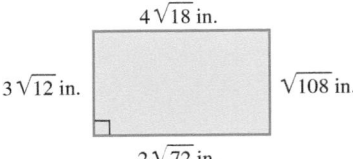

$4\sqrt{18}$ in.

$3\sqrt{12}$ in.　　$\sqrt{108}$ in.

$2\sqrt{72}$ in.

10.5 | Multiplying and Dividing Radical Expressions

OBJECTIVE ▶ **1** **Multiply radical expressions.** The distributive property may be used when multiplying radical expressions.

OBJECTIVES

1 Multiply radical expressions.

2 Rationalize denominators with one radical term.

3 Rationalize denominators with binomials involving radicals.

4 Write radical quotients in lowest terms.

EXAMPLE 1 Using the Distributive Property with Radicals

Multiply.

(a) $\sqrt{5}\left(2 + \sqrt{6}\right)$

$= \sqrt{5} \cdot 2 + \sqrt{5} \cdot \sqrt{6}$ Distributive property, $a\left(b + c\right) = ab + ac$

$= 2\sqrt{5} + \sqrt{30}$ Commutative property; product rule

(b) $4\left(\sqrt{12} - \sqrt{27}\right)$

$= 4\sqrt{12} - 4\sqrt{27}$ Distributive property

$= 4\sqrt{4 \cdot 3} - 4\sqrt{9 \cdot 3}$ Factor the radicands so that one factor is a perfect square.

$= 4 \cdot 2\sqrt{3} - 4 \cdot 3\sqrt{3}$ $\sqrt{4} = 2; \sqrt{9} = 3$

$= 8\sqrt{3} - 12\sqrt{3}$ Multiply.

$= \left(8 - 12\right)\sqrt{3}$ Distributive property

$= -4\sqrt{3}$ Subtract.

─────── **Work Problem 1 at the Side.** ▶

1 Multiply.

(a) $\sqrt{10}\left(4 + \sqrt{7}\right)$

We multiply binomial expressions involving radicals using the FOIL method. Recall that the acronym **FOIL** refers to the positions of the terms. We multiply

First terms, **O**uter terms, **I**nner terms, and **L**ast terms.

EXAMPLE 2 Multiplying Binomials Involving Radical Expressions

Multiply using the FOIL method.

(a) $\left(\sqrt{5} + 3\right)\left(\sqrt{6} + 1\right)$

$\overset{\text{First}}{} \quad \overset{\text{Outer}}{} \quad \overset{\text{Inner}}{} \quad \overset{\text{Last}}{}$

$= \sqrt{5} \cdot \sqrt{6} + \sqrt{5} \cdot 1 + 3 \cdot \sqrt{6} + 3 \cdot 1$ FOIL method

$= \sqrt{30} + \sqrt{5} + 3\sqrt{6} + 3$ This result cannot be simplified further.

(b) $\left(7 - \sqrt{3}\right)\left(\sqrt{5} + \sqrt{2}\right)$

$\overset{\text{F}}{} \quad \overset{\text{O}}{} \quad \overset{\text{I}}{} \quad \overset{\text{L}}{}$

$= 7\sqrt{5} + 7\sqrt{2} - \sqrt{3} \cdot \sqrt{5} - \sqrt{3} \cdot \sqrt{2}$ FOIL method

$= 7\sqrt{5} + 7\sqrt{2} - \sqrt{15} - \sqrt{6}$ Product rule

(b) $3\left(\sqrt{20} - \sqrt{45}\right)$

─────── **Continued on Next Page**

Answers

1. **(a)** $4\sqrt{10} + \sqrt{70}$ **(b)** $-3\sqrt{5}$

2 Multiply using the FOIL method.

(a) $\left(2 + \sqrt{3}\right)\left(1 + \sqrt{5}\right)$

$$= 2 \cdot \underline{\hspace{1cm}} + 2 \cdot \underline{\hspace{1cm}}$$
$$+ \sqrt{3} \cdot \underline{\hspace{1cm}} + \sqrt{3} \cdot \underline{\hspace{1cm}}$$
$$= \underline{\hspace{3cm}}$$

(b) $\left(4 + \sqrt{3}\right)\left(4 - \sqrt{3}\right)$

(c) $\left(\sqrt{13} - 2\right)^2$

(d) $\left(4 + \sqrt[3]{7}\right)\left(4 - \sqrt[3]{7}\right)$

(e) $\left(\sqrt{p} + \sqrt{s}\right)\left(\sqrt{p} - \sqrt{s}\right)$, $p \geq 0$ and $s \geq 0$

Answers

2. (a) 1; $\sqrt{5}$; 1; $\sqrt{5}$;
$2 + 2\sqrt{5} + \sqrt{3} + \sqrt{15}$
   (b) 13 (c) $17 - 4\sqrt{13}$
   (d) $16 - \sqrt[3]{49}$ (e) $p - s$

(c) $\left(\sqrt{10} + \sqrt{3}\right)\left(\sqrt{10} - \sqrt{3}\right)$

$$= \sqrt{10} \cdot \sqrt{10} - \sqrt{10} \cdot \sqrt{3} + \sqrt{3} \cdot \sqrt{10} - \sqrt{3} \cdot \sqrt{3} \quad \text{FOIL method}$$

$$= 10 - 3 \quad \text{Product rule; } -\sqrt{30} + \sqrt{30} = 0$$

$$= 7 \quad \text{Subtract.}$$

A product such as

$$\left(\sqrt{10} + \sqrt{3}\right)\left(\sqrt{10} - \sqrt{3}\right) = \left(\sqrt{10}\right)^2 - \left(\sqrt{3}\right)^2$$

is a difference of squares. Recall that

$$(x + y)(x - y) = x^2 - y^2. \quad \text{Here, } x = \sqrt{10} \text{ and } y = \sqrt{3}.$$

(d) $\left(\sqrt{7} - 3\right)^2$

$$= \left(\sqrt{7} - 3\right)\left(\sqrt{7} - 3\right) \quad a^2 = a \cdot a$$

$$= \sqrt{7} \cdot \sqrt{7} - 3\sqrt{7} - 3\sqrt{7} + 3 \cdot 3 \quad \text{FOIL method}$$

$$= 7 - 6\sqrt{7} + 9 \quad \text{Multiply. Combine like terms.}$$

$$= 16 - 6\sqrt{7} \quad \boxed{\text{Be careful. These terms cannot be combined.}} \quad \text{Add.}$$

The expression $16 - 6\sqrt{7}$ *cannot* be simplified further because 16 and $6\sqrt{7}$ are not like terms.

(e) $\left(5 - \sqrt[3]{3}\right)\left(5 + \sqrt[3]{3}\right)$

$$= 5 \cdot 5 + 5\sqrt[3]{3} - 5\sqrt[3]{3} - \sqrt[3]{3} \cdot \sqrt[3]{3} \quad \boxed{\text{Remember to write the index 3 in } \textit{each} \text{ radical.}}$$

$$= 25 - \sqrt[3]{3^2} \quad \text{Multiply. Combine like terms.}$$

$$= 25 - \sqrt[3]{9} \quad \text{Apply the exponent.}$$

(f) $\left(\sqrt{k} + \sqrt{y}\right)\left(\sqrt{k} - \sqrt{y}\right), \quad k \geq 0 \text{ and } y \geq 0$

$$= \left(\sqrt{k}\right)^2 - \left(\sqrt{y}\right)^2 \quad \text{Difference of squares}$$

$$= k - y$$

◀ **Work Problem 2 at the Side.**

Note

In **Example 2(d)**, we could have used the formula for the square of a binomial to obtain the same result.

$$\left(\sqrt{7} - 3\right)^2$$

$$= \left(\sqrt{7}\right)^2 - 2\left(\sqrt{7}\right)(3) + 3^2 \quad (x - y)^2 = x^2 - 2xy + y^2$$

$$= 7 - 6\sqrt{7} + 9 \quad \text{Apply the exponents. Multiply.}$$

$$= 16 - 6\sqrt{7} \quad \text{Add.}$$

OBJECTIVE ▶ ② Rationalize denominators with one radical term. As defined earlier, a simplified radical expression will have no radical in the denominator. The origin of this agreement no doubt occurred before the days of high-speed calculation, when computation was a tedious process performed by hand.

Consider the radical expression $\frac{1}{\sqrt{2}}$. To find a decimal approximation by hand, it is necessary to divide 1 by a decimal approximation for $\sqrt{2}$, such as 1.414. The division is much easier if the divisor is a whole number. This can be accomplished by multiplying $\frac{1}{\sqrt{2}}$ by 1 in the form $\frac{\sqrt{2}}{\sqrt{2}}$. *Multiplying by 1 in any form does not change the value of the original expression.*

$$\frac{1}{\sqrt{2}} \cdot \frac{\sqrt{2}}{\sqrt{2}} = \frac{\sqrt{2}}{2} \qquad \text{Multiply by 1; } \tfrac{\sqrt{2}}{\sqrt{2}} = 1$$

Now the computation requires dividing 1.414 by 2 to obtain 0.707, a much easier task.

Rationalizing a Denominator

The process of removing radicals from a denominator so that the denominator contains only rational numbers is called **rationalizing the denominator.** This is done by multiplying by a form of 1.

EXAMPLE 3   Rationalizing Denominators with Square Roots

Rationalize each denominator.

(a) $\dfrac{3}{\sqrt{7}}$

Multiply by $\frac{\sqrt{7}}{\sqrt{7}}$. This is an application of the identity property of multiplication—in effect, we are multiplying by 1.

$$\frac{3}{\sqrt{7}} = \frac{3 \cdot \sqrt{7}}{\sqrt{7} \cdot \sqrt{7}} = \frac{3\sqrt{7}}{7} \qquad \begin{array}{l}\text{In the denominator,} \\ \sqrt{7} \cdot \sqrt{7} = \sqrt{7 \cdot 7} = \sqrt{49} = 7. \\ \text{The final denominator is a rational number.}\end{array}$$

(b) $\dfrac{5\sqrt{2}}{\sqrt{5}} = \dfrac{5\sqrt{2} \cdot \sqrt{5}}{\sqrt{5} \cdot \sqrt{5}} = \dfrac{5\sqrt{10}}{5} = \sqrt{10}$

(c) $\dfrac{-6}{\sqrt{12}}$

Less work is involved if the radical in the denominator is simplified first.

$$\frac{-6}{\sqrt{12}} = \frac{-6}{\sqrt{4 \cdot 3}} = \frac{-6}{2\sqrt{3}} = \frac{-3}{\sqrt{3}}$$

Now we rationalize the denominator.

$$\frac{-3}{\sqrt{3}} = \frac{-3 \cdot \sqrt{3}}{\sqrt{3} \cdot \sqrt{3}} = \frac{-3\sqrt{3}}{3} = -\sqrt{3}$$

———— Work Problem ③ at the Side. ▶

③ Rationalize each denominator.

(a) $\dfrac{8}{\sqrt{3}}$

(b) $\dfrac{9\sqrt{7}}{\sqrt{3}}$

(c) $\dfrac{3}{\sqrt{48}}$

(d) $\dfrac{-16}{\sqrt{32}}$

Answers

3. (a) $\dfrac{8\sqrt{3}}{3}$ **(b)** $3\sqrt{21}$ **(c)** $\dfrac{\sqrt{3}}{4}$

(d) $-2\sqrt{2}$

4 Simplify. Assume that all variables represent positive real numbers.

(a) $\sqrt{\dfrac{8}{45}}$

(b) $\sqrt{\dfrac{72}{y}}$

(c) $\sqrt{\dfrac{200k^6}{y^7}}$

EXAMPLE 4 Rationalizing Denominators in Roots of Fractions

Simplify.

(a) $-\sqrt{\dfrac{18}{125}}$

$= -\dfrac{\sqrt{18}}{\sqrt{125}}$ Quotient rule

$= -\dfrac{\sqrt{9\cdot 2}}{\sqrt{25\cdot 5}}$ Factor.

$= -\dfrac{3\sqrt{2}}{5\sqrt{5}}$ Product rule

$= -\dfrac{3\sqrt{2}\cdot\sqrt{5}}{5\sqrt{5}\cdot\sqrt{5}}$ Multiply by $\frac{\sqrt5}{\sqrt5}$.

$= -\dfrac{3\sqrt{10}}{5\cdot 5}$ Product rule

$= -\dfrac{3\sqrt{10}}{25}$ Multiply.

(b) $\sqrt{\dfrac{50m^4}{p^5}},\quad p>0.$

$= \dfrac{\sqrt{50m^4}}{\sqrt{p^5}}$ Quotient rule

$= \dfrac{\sqrt{25m^4\cdot 2}}{\sqrt{p^4\cdot p}}$ Factor.

$= \dfrac{5m^2\sqrt{2}}{p^2\sqrt{p}}$ Product rule

$= \dfrac{5m^2\sqrt{2}\cdot\sqrt{p}}{p^2\sqrt{p}\cdot\sqrt{p}}$ Multiply by $\frac{\sqrt p}{\sqrt p}$.

$= \dfrac{5m^2\sqrt{2p}}{p^2\cdot p}$ Product rule

$= \dfrac{5m^2\sqrt{2p}}{p^3}$ Multiply.

◀ **Work Problem ④ at the Side.**

EXAMPLE 5 Rationalizing Denominators with Higher Roots

Simplify.

(a) $\sqrt[3]{\dfrac{27}{16}}$

Use the quotient rule, and simplify the numerator and denominator.

$$\sqrt[3]{\dfrac{27}{16}}=\dfrac{\sqrt[3]{27}}{\sqrt[3]{16}}=\dfrac{3}{\sqrt[3]{8}\cdot\sqrt[3]{2}}=\dfrac{3}{2\sqrt[3]{2}}$$

Because $2\cdot 4=8$, a perfect cube, multiply the numerator and denominator by $\sqrt[3]{4}$.

$\dfrac{3}{2\sqrt[3]{2}}$ $\sqrt[3]{\frac{27}{16}}=\frac{3}{2\sqrt[3]{2}}$ from above

$=\dfrac{3\cdot\sqrt[3]{4}}{2\sqrt[3]{2}\cdot\sqrt[3]{4}}$ Multiply by $\sqrt[3]{4}$ in numerator and denominator. This will give $\sqrt[3]{8}=2$ in the denominator.

$=\dfrac{3\sqrt[3]{4}}{2\sqrt[3]{8}}$ Multiply.

$=\dfrac{3\sqrt[3]{4}}{2\cdot 2}$ $\sqrt[3]{8}=2$

$=\dfrac{3\sqrt[3]{4}}{4}$ Multiply.

Answers

4. (a) $\dfrac{2\sqrt{10}}{15}$ (b) $\dfrac{6\sqrt{2y}}{y}$ (c) $\dfrac{10k^3\sqrt{2y}}{y^4}$

Continued on Next Page

(b) $\sqrt[4]{\dfrac{5x}{z}}, \quad x \ge 0, z > 0$

$= \dfrac{\sqrt[4]{5x}}{\sqrt[4]{z}}$ Quotient rule

$\boxed{\sqrt[4]{z} \cdot \sqrt[4]{z^3} \text{ will give } \sqrt[4]{z^4}.}$

$= \dfrac{\sqrt[4]{5x}}{\sqrt[4]{z}} \cdot \dfrac{\sqrt[4]{z^3}}{\sqrt[4]{z^3}}$ Multiply by 1.

$= \dfrac{\sqrt[4]{5xz^3}}{\sqrt[4]{z^4}}$ Product rule

$= \dfrac{\sqrt[4]{5xz^3}}{z}$ $\sqrt[4]{z^4} = z$

─────────── Work Problem **5** at the Side. ▶

> ⚠ **CAUTION**
>
> In **Example 5(a)**, a typical error is to multiply the numerator and denominator by $\sqrt[3]{2}$, forgetting that
>
> $$\sqrt[3]{2} \cdot \sqrt[3]{2} = \sqrt[3]{2^2}, \quad \text{which does } \textbf{\textit{not}} \text{ equal } 2.$$
>
> We need **three** factors of 2 to obtain 2^3 under the radical.
>
> $$\sqrt[3]{2} \cdot \sqrt[3]{2} \cdot \sqrt[3]{2} = \sqrt[3]{2^3}, \quad \text{which does equal } 2.$$

OBJECTIVE ▶ **3** **Rationalize denominators with binomials involving radicals.** To rationalize a denominator that contains a binomial expression (one that contains exactly two terms) involving radicals, such as

$$\frac{3}{1 + \sqrt{2}},$$

we use the special product

$$(x + y)(x - y) = x^2 - y^2$$

and the concept of *conjugates*. The conjugate of $1 + \sqrt{2}$ is $1 - \sqrt{2}$. In general,

$$x + y \text{ and } x - y \text{ are } \textbf{conjugates.}$$

Specifically, if x and y represent nonnegative rational numbers, the product

$$\left(\sqrt{x} + \sqrt{y}\right)\left(\sqrt{x} - \sqrt{y}\right) \quad \text{produces the rational number } \quad x - y.$$

> **Rationalizing a Binomial Denominator**
>
> Whenever a radical expression has a sum or difference with square root radicals in the denominator, rationalize the denominator by multiplying both the numerator and denominator by the conjugate of the denominator.

5 Simplify.

(a) $\sqrt[3]{\dfrac{15}{32}}$

(b) $\sqrt[3]{\dfrac{m^{12}}{n}}, \quad n \ne 0$

(c) $\sqrt[4]{\dfrac{6y}{w^2}}, \quad y \ge 0, w \ne 0$

Answers

5. **(a)** $\dfrac{\sqrt[3]{30}}{4}$ **(b)** $\dfrac{m^4 \sqrt[3]{n^2}}{n}$ **(c)** $\dfrac{\sqrt[4]{6yw^2}}{w}$

6 Rationalize each denominator.

(a) $\dfrac{-4}{\sqrt{5}+2}$

(b) $\dfrac{3}{5-\sqrt{6}}$

(c) $\dfrac{\sqrt{3}+\sqrt{5}}{\sqrt{2}-\sqrt{7}}$

(d) $\dfrac{2}{\sqrt{k}+\sqrt{z}}$,
$k \neq z, k > 0, z > 0$

Answers

6. (a) $-4\left(\sqrt{5}-2\right)$ **(b)** $\dfrac{3\left(5+\sqrt{6}\right)}{19}$

(c) $\dfrac{-\left(\sqrt{6}+\sqrt{21}+\sqrt{10}+\sqrt{35}\right)}{5}$

(d) $\dfrac{2\left(\sqrt{k}-\sqrt{z}\right)}{k-z}$

EXAMPLE 6 Rationalizing Binomial Denominators

Rationalize each denominator.

(a) $\dfrac{3}{1+\sqrt{2}}$

Again, we are multiplying by a form of 1.

$= \dfrac{3\left(1-\sqrt{2}\right)}{\left(1+\sqrt{2}\right)\left(1-\sqrt{2}\right)}$

Multiply the numerator and denominator by $1-\sqrt{2}$, the conjugate of the denominator.

$= \dfrac{3\left(1-\sqrt{2}\right)}{-1}$

$\begin{aligned}\left(1+\sqrt{2}\right)\left(1-\sqrt{2}\right)\\ = 1^2 - \left(\sqrt{2}\right)^2\\ = 1 - 2, \text{ or } -1\end{aligned}$

$= \dfrac{3}{-1}\left(1-\sqrt{2}\right)$

$\dfrac{a \cdot b}{c} = \dfrac{a}{c} \cdot b$

Either form is correct. $= -3\left(1-\sqrt{2}\right)$, or $-3+3\sqrt{2}$ $\dfrac{a}{-1} = -a$; Distributive property

(b) $\dfrac{5}{4-\sqrt{3}}$

$= \dfrac{5\left(4+\sqrt{3}\right)}{\left(4-\sqrt{3}\right)\left(4+\sqrt{3}\right)}$

Multiply the numerator and denominator by $4+\sqrt{3}$.

$= \dfrac{5\left(4+\sqrt{3}\right)}{16-3}$

Multiply in the denominator.

$= \dfrac{5\left(4+\sqrt{3}\right)}{13}$

Subtract in the denominator.

We leave the numerator in factored form. This makes it easier to determine whether the expression is written in lowest terms.

(c) $\dfrac{\sqrt{2}-\sqrt{3}}{\sqrt{5}+\sqrt{3}}$

$= \dfrac{\left(\sqrt{2}-\sqrt{3}\right)\left(\sqrt{5}-\sqrt{3}\right)}{\left(\sqrt{5}+\sqrt{3}\right)\left(\sqrt{5}-\sqrt{3}\right)}$

Multiply the numerator and denominator by $\sqrt{5}-\sqrt{3}$.

$= \dfrac{\sqrt{10}-\sqrt{6}-\sqrt{15}+3}{5-3}$

Multiply.

$= \dfrac{\sqrt{10}-\sqrt{6}-\sqrt{15}+3}{2}$

Subtract in the denominator.

(d) $\dfrac{3}{\sqrt{5m}-\sqrt{p}}$, $5m \neq p, m > 0, p > 0$

$= \dfrac{3\left(\sqrt{5m}+\sqrt{p}\right)}{\left(\sqrt{5m}-\sqrt{p}\right)\left(\sqrt{5m}+\sqrt{p}\right)}$

Multiply the numerator and denominator by $\sqrt{5m}+\sqrt{p}$.

$= \dfrac{3\left(\sqrt{5m}+\sqrt{p}\right)}{5m-p}$

Multiply in the denominator.

◄ **Work Problem 6 at the Side.**

OBJECTIVE ▶ **4** Write radical quotients in lowest terms.

EXAMPLE 7 Writing Radical Quotients in Lowest Terms

Write each quotient in lowest terms.

(a) $\dfrac{6 + 2\sqrt{5}}{4}$

> This is a key step.

$= \dfrac{2(3 + \sqrt{5})}{2 \cdot 2}$ Factor the numerator and denominator.

$= \dfrac{3 + \sqrt{5}}{2}$ Divide out the common factor.

Alternatively, we could write this expression in lowest terms as follows.

$$\frac{6 + 2\sqrt{5}}{4} = \frac{6}{4} + \frac{2\sqrt{5}}{4} = \frac{3}{2} + \frac{\sqrt{5}}{2} = \frac{3 + \sqrt{5}}{2}$$

(b) $\dfrac{5y - \sqrt{8y^2}}{6y}, \quad y > 0$

$= \dfrac{5y - 2y\sqrt{2}}{6y}$ $\sqrt{8y^2} = \sqrt{4y^2 \cdot 2} = 2y\sqrt{2}$

$= \dfrac{y(5 - 2\sqrt{2})}{6y}$ Factor the numerator.

$= \dfrac{5 - 2\sqrt{2}}{6}$ Divide out the common factor.

────────────── Work Problem **7** at the Side. ▶

⚠ CAUTION
Be careful to factor before writing a quotient in lowest terms.

7 Write each quotient in lowest terms.

(a) $\dfrac{24 - 36\sqrt{7}}{16}$

(b) $\dfrac{2x + \sqrt{32x^2}}{6x}, \quad x > 0$

Answers

7. **(a)** $\dfrac{6 - 9\sqrt{7}}{4}$ **(b)** $\dfrac{1 + 2\sqrt{2}}{3}$

10.5 Exercises

FOR EXTRA HELP

Go to MyMathLab for worked-out, step-by-step solutions to exercises enclosed in a square ▢ and video solutions to ▶ exercises.

CONCEPT CHECK *Match each part of a rule for a special product in Column I with the part it equals in Column II.*

I

1. $\left(x + \sqrt{y}\right)\left(x - \sqrt{y}\right)$

2. $\left(\sqrt{x} + y\right)\left(\sqrt{x} - y\right)$

3. $\left(\sqrt{x} + \sqrt{y}\right)\left(\sqrt{x} - \sqrt{y}\right)$

4. $\left(\sqrt{x} + \sqrt{y}\right)^2$

5. $\left(\sqrt{x} - \sqrt{y}\right)^2$

6. $\left(\sqrt{x} + y\right)^2$

II

A. $x - y$

B. $x + 2y\sqrt{x} + y^2$

C. $x - y^2$

D. $x - 2\sqrt{xy} + y$

E. $x^2 - y$

F. $x + 2\sqrt{xy} + y$

Multiply, and then simplify each product. Assume that all variables represent positive real numbers. **See Examples 1 and 2.**

7. $\sqrt{3}\left(4 + \sqrt{5}\right)$

8. $\sqrt{6}\left(2 + \sqrt{7}\right)$

9. $\sqrt{3}\left(\sqrt{12} - 4\right)$

10. $\sqrt{5}\left(\sqrt{125} - 6\right)$

11. $5\left(\sqrt{72} - \sqrt{8}\right)$

12. $7\left(\sqrt{50} - \sqrt{18}\right)$

13. $\sqrt{2}\left(\sqrt{18} - \sqrt{3}\right)$

14. $\sqrt{5}\left(\sqrt{15} + \sqrt{5}\right)$

15. $\left(\sqrt{3} + 2\right)\left(\sqrt{6} - 5\right)$

16. $\left(\sqrt{7} + 1\right)\left(\sqrt{2} - 4\right)$

17. $\left(\sqrt{7} - 5\right)\left(\sqrt{3} + \sqrt{2}\right)$

18. $\left(\sqrt{2} + \sqrt{10}\right)\left(\sqrt{3} - 4\right)$

19. $\left(\sqrt{6} + 2\right)\left(\sqrt{6} - 2\right)$

20. $\left(\sqrt{7} + 8\right)\left(\sqrt{7} - 8\right)$

21. $\left(\sqrt{2} - \sqrt{3}\right)\left(\sqrt{2} + \sqrt{3}\right)$

22. $\left(\sqrt{7} + \sqrt{14}\right)\left(\sqrt{7} - \sqrt{14}\right)$

23. $\left(\sqrt{3x} + 2\right)\left(\sqrt{3x} - 2\right)$

24. $\left(\sqrt{6y} - 4\right)\left(\sqrt{6y} + 4\right)$

25. $\left(\sqrt{5} + 2\right)^2$

26. $\left(\sqrt{11} - 1\right)^2$

27. $\left(4\sqrt{x} + 3\right)^2$

28. $\left(5\sqrt{p} - 6\right)^2$

29. $\left(9 - \sqrt[3]{2}\right)\left(9 + \sqrt[3]{2}\right)$

30. $\left(7 + \sqrt[3]{6}\right)\left(7 - \sqrt[3]{6}\right)$

31. $\left(2\sqrt{x} + \sqrt{y}\right)\left(2\sqrt{x} - \sqrt{y}\right)$

32. $\left(\sqrt{p} + 5\sqrt{s}\right)\left(\sqrt{p} - 5\sqrt{s}\right)$

33. CONCEPT CHECK A student incorrectly simplified the radical expression

$$6 - 4\sqrt{3} \quad \text{as} \quad 2\sqrt{3}.$$

What Went Wrong?

34. CONCEPT CHECK A student rationalized the following denominator as shown.

$$\frac{5}{\sqrt[3]{2}} = \frac{5 \cdot \sqrt[3]{2}}{\sqrt[3]{2} \cdot \sqrt[3]{2}} = \frac{5\sqrt[3]{2}}{2} \quad \text{Incorrect}$$

What Went Wrong? Give the correct answer.

*Rationalize each denominator. **See Example 3.***

35. $\dfrac{7}{\sqrt{7}}$

36. $\dfrac{11}{\sqrt{11}}$

37. $\dfrac{15}{\sqrt{3}}$

38. $\dfrac{12}{\sqrt{6}}$

39. $\dfrac{\sqrt{3}}{\sqrt{2}}$

40. $\dfrac{\sqrt{7}}{\sqrt{6}}$

41. $\dfrac{9\sqrt{3}}{\sqrt{5}}$

42. $\dfrac{3\sqrt{2}}{\sqrt{11}}$

43. $\dfrac{-6}{\sqrt{18}}$

44. $\dfrac{-5}{\sqrt{24}}$

Simplify. Assume that all variables represent positive real numbers.
*****See Examples 4 and 5.*****

45. $\sqrt{\dfrac{7}{2}}$

46. $\sqrt{\dfrac{10}{3}}$

47. $-\sqrt{\dfrac{7}{50}}$

48. $-\sqrt{\dfrac{13}{75}}$

49. $\sqrt{\dfrac{24}{x}}$

50. $\sqrt{\dfrac{52}{y}}$

51. $-\sqrt{\dfrac{98r^3}{s}}$

52. $-\sqrt{\dfrac{150m^5}{n}}$

53. $\sqrt{\dfrac{288x^7}{y^9}}$

54. $\sqrt{\dfrac{242t^9}{u^{11}}}$

55. $\sqrt[3]{\dfrac{2}{3}}$

56. $\sqrt[3]{\dfrac{4}{5}}$

57. $\sqrt[3]{\dfrac{4}{9}}$

58. $\sqrt[3]{\dfrac{5}{16}}$

59. $-\sqrt[3]{\dfrac{2p}{r^2}}$

60. $-\sqrt[3]{\dfrac{6x}{y^2}}$

61. $\sqrt[4]{\dfrac{16}{x}}$

62. $\sqrt[4]{\dfrac{81}{y}}$

63. $\sqrt[4]{\dfrac{2y}{z}}$

64. $\sqrt[4]{\dfrac{7t}{s^2}}$

Rationalize each denominator. Assume that all variables represent positive real numbers and that no denominators are 0. **See Example 6.**

65. $\dfrac{3}{4 + \sqrt{5}}$

66. $\dfrac{6}{5 + \sqrt{2}}$

67. $\dfrac{6}{\sqrt{5} + \sqrt{3}}$

68. $\dfrac{12}{\sqrt{6} + \sqrt{3}}$

69. $\dfrac{-4}{\sqrt{3} - \sqrt{7}}$

70. $\dfrac{-3}{\sqrt{2} + \sqrt{5}}$

71. $\dfrac{1 - \sqrt{2}}{\sqrt{7} + \sqrt{6}}$

72. $\dfrac{-1 - \sqrt{3}}{\sqrt{6} + \sqrt{5}}$

73. $\dfrac{\sqrt{2} - \sqrt{3}}{\sqrt{6} - \sqrt{5}}$

74. $\dfrac{\sqrt{5} + \sqrt{6}}{\sqrt{3} - \sqrt{2}}$

75. $\dfrac{4}{\sqrt{x} - 2\sqrt{y}}$

76. $\dfrac{5}{3\sqrt{r} + \sqrt{s}}$

Write each quotient in lowest terms. Assume that all variables represent positive real numbers. **See Example 7.**

77. $\dfrac{25 + 10\sqrt{6}}{20}$

78. $\dfrac{12 - 6\sqrt{2}}{24}$

79. $\dfrac{30 - 20\sqrt{6}}{10}$

80. $\dfrac{24 + 12\sqrt{5}}{12}$

81. $\dfrac{16 - 4\sqrt{8}}{12}$

82. $\dfrac{12 - 9\sqrt{72}}{18}$

83. $\dfrac{6x + \sqrt{24x^3}}{3x}$

84. $\dfrac{11y + \sqrt{242y^5}}{22y}$

Relating Concepts (Exercises 85–88) For Individual or Group Work

In calculus, it is sometimes desirable to rationalize the numerator. To rationalize a numerator, we multiply the numerator and the denominator by the conjugate of the numerator. For example,

$$\frac{6 - \sqrt{2}}{4} = \frac{(6 - \sqrt{2})(6 + \sqrt{2})}{4(6 + \sqrt{2})} = \frac{36 - 2}{4(6 + \sqrt{2})} = \frac{34}{4(6 + \sqrt{2})} = \frac{17}{2(6 + \sqrt{2})}.$$

Rationalize each numerator. Assume that all variables represent positive real numbers.

85. $\dfrac{6 - \sqrt{3}}{8}$

86. $\dfrac{2\sqrt{5} - 3}{2}$

87. $\dfrac{2\sqrt{x} - \sqrt{y}}{3x}$

88. $\dfrac{\sqrt{p} - 3\sqrt{q}}{4q}$

Summary Exercises *Performing Operations with Radicals and Rational Exponents*

Recall that a simplified radical satisfies the following conditions.

Conditions for a Simplified Radical

1. The radicand has no factor raised to a power greater than or equal to the index.

2. The radicand has no fractions.

3. No denominator contains a radical.

4. Exponents in the radicand and the index of the radical have greatest common factor 1.

CONCEPT CHECK *Give the reason why each radical is not simplified.*

1. $\sqrt{\dfrac{2}{5}}$

2. $\sqrt[15]{x^5}$

3. $\dfrac{5}{\sqrt[3]{10}}$

4. $\sqrt[3]{x^5y^6}$

Perform the indicated operations, and express each answer in simplest form. Assume that all variables represent positive real numbers.

5. $6\sqrt{10} - 12\sqrt{10}$

6. $\sqrt{7}\left(\sqrt{7} - \sqrt{2}\right)$

7. $\dfrac{-3}{\sqrt{6}}$

8. $\dfrac{8}{\sqrt{7} + \sqrt{5}}$

9. $\left(1 - \sqrt{3}\right)\left(2 + \sqrt{6}\right)$

10. $\sqrt{50} - \sqrt{98} + \sqrt{72}$

11. $\left(3\sqrt{5} + 2\sqrt{7}\right)^2$

12. $\sqrt[3]{16x^2} - \sqrt[3]{54x^2}$

13. $\dfrac{1 - \sqrt{2}}{1 + \sqrt{2}}$

14. $\left(\sqrt{5} + 7\right)\left(\sqrt{5} - 7\right)$

15. $\dfrac{1}{\sqrt{x} - \sqrt{5}}, \quad x \neq 5$

16. $\sqrt[3]{8a^3b^5c^9}$

17. $\dfrac{15}{\sqrt[3]{9}}$

18. $\dfrac{3}{\sqrt{5} + 2}$

19. $\sqrt{\dfrac{3}{5x}}$

20. $\dfrac{16\sqrt{3}}{5\sqrt{12}}$

21. $\dfrac{2\sqrt{25}}{8\sqrt{50}}$

22. $\dfrac{-10}{\sqrt[3]{10}}$

23. $\dfrac{\sqrt{6}+\sqrt{5}}{\sqrt{6}-\sqrt{5}}$

24. $\sqrt{12x}-\sqrt{75x}$

25. $\left(5-3\sqrt{3}\right)^2$

26. $\left(\sqrt{74}-\sqrt{73}\right)\left(\sqrt{74}+\sqrt{73}\right)$

27. $\sqrt[3]{\dfrac{13}{81}}$

28. $-t^2\sqrt[4]{t}+3\sqrt[4]{t^9}-t\sqrt[4]{t^5}$

29. $\dfrac{\sqrt{3}+\sqrt{7}}{\sqrt{6}-\sqrt{5}}$

30. $\dfrac{6}{\sqrt[4]{3}}$

31. $\sqrt{12}-\sqrt{108}-\sqrt[3]{27}$

32. $\left(6-\sqrt{5}\right)\left(\sqrt{7}+\sqrt{5}\right)$

Simplify each expression. Write answers with positive exponents. Assume that all variables represent positive real numbers.

33. $3^{1/2}\cdot 3^{1/3}$

34. $\left(\dfrac{x^2y}{x^{-3}y^4}\right)^{1/3}$

35. $\dfrac{x^{-2/3}y^{4/5}}{x^{-5/3}y^{-2/5}}$

36. $\left(\dfrac{x^{3/4}y^{2/3}}{x^{1/3}y^{5/8}}\right)^{24}$

37. $\left(125x^3\right)^{-2/3}$

38. $\left(3x^{-2/3}y^{1/2}\right)\left(-2x^{5/8}y^{-1/3}\right)$

Solve each problem. Give answers as simplified radical expressions. (If necessary, refer to the formulas at the back of this text.)

39. Find the perimeter and area of the rectangle.

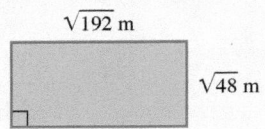

$\sqrt{192}$ m

$\sqrt{48}$ m

40. Find the area of the trapezoid.

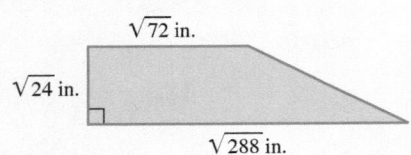

$\sqrt{72}$ in.

$\sqrt{24}$ in.

$\sqrt{288}$ in.

10.6 | Solving Equations with Radicals

OBJECTIVE ▶ 1 Solve radical equations using the power rule. An equation that includes one or more radical expressions with a variable in a radicand is a **radical equation.**

$$\sqrt{x-4} = 8, \quad \sqrt{5x+12} = 3\sqrt{2x-1}, \quad \sqrt[3]{6+x} = 27$$

Radical equations

Consider the equation $x = 1$, which has only one solution. Its solution set is $\{1\}$. If we square both sides of this equation, we obtain $x^2 = 1$. This new equation has *two* solutions, -1 and 1. Notice that the solution of the original equation is also a solution of the "squared" equation. However, that equation has another solution, -1, that is *not* a solution of the original equation.

When solving radical equations, we use this idea of raising both sides to a power. This is an application of the **power rule.**

Power Rule for Solving a Radical Equation

If both sides of an equation are raised to the same power, all solutions of the original equation are also solutions of the new equation.

The power rule does not say that all solutions of the new equation are solutions of the original equation. They may or may not be. A value of the variable that appears to be a solution is a **proposed solution.** Such values that do not satisfy the original equation are **extraneous solutions.** They must be rejected.

❗ CAUTION

When the power rule is used to solve an equation, every solution of the new equation **must** *be checked in the original equation.*

EXAMPLE 1   Using the Power Rule

Solve $\sqrt{3x+4} = 8$.

$$\left(\sqrt{3x+4}\right)^2 = 8^2 \quad \text{Use the power rule and square each side.}$$

$(\sqrt{a})^2 = \sqrt{a} \cdot \sqrt{a} = a,$
for $a \geq 0$.

$$3x + 4 = 64 \quad \text{Apply the exponents.}$$
$$3x = 60 \quad \text{Subtract 4.}$$
$$x = 20 \quad \text{Divide by 3.}$$

CHECK
$$\sqrt{3x+4} = 8 \quad \text{Original equation}$$
$$\sqrt{3 \cdot 20 + 4} \stackrel{?}{=} 8 \quad \text{Let } x = 20.$$
$$\sqrt{64} \stackrel{?}{=} 8 \quad \text{Evaluate the radicand.}$$
$$8 = 8 \checkmark \quad \text{True}$$

Because 20 satisfies the *original* equation, the solution set is $\{20\}$.

——————— **Work Problem 1 at the Side. ▶**

OBJECTIVES

1 Solve radical equations using the power rule.

2 Solve radical equations that require additional steps.

3 Solve radical equations with indexes greater than 2.

4 Use the power rule to solve a formula for a specified variable.

1 Solve each equation.

(a) $\sqrt{r} = 3$

(b) $\sqrt{5x+1} = 4$

Answers

1. (a) $\{9\}$ (b) $\{3\}$

2 Solve each equation.

(a) $\sqrt{5x+3}+2=0$

Step 1 Isolate the radical on the left side.

$$\sqrt{5x+3}=\underline{\quad}$$

Step 2 To apply the power rule, square each side.

$$(\sqrt{5x+3})^2=(\underline{\quad})^2$$

Step 3 Solve.

$$5x+3=\underline{\quad}$$
$$5x=\underline{\quad}$$
$$x=\underline{\quad}$$

Step 4 Check the proposed solution in the original equation.

The result is a (*true / false*) statement, so the solution set is _____.

(b) $\sqrt{x-9}-3=0$

(c) $\sqrt{3x+4}+5=0$

The method used in the solution of the equation in **Example 1** can be generalized.

Solving a Radical Equation

Step 1 **Isolate the radical.** Make sure that one radical term is alone on one side of the equation.

Step 2 **Apply the power rule.** Raise each side of the equation to a power that is the same as the index of the radical.

Step 3 **Solve** the resulting equation. If it still contains a radical, repeat Steps 1 and 2.

Step 4 **Check** all proposed solutions in the *original* equation. Discard any values that are not solutions of the original equation.

! CAUTION

Remember to check all proposed solutions (Step 4) or an incorrect solution set may result.

EXAMPLE 2 **Using the Power Rule**

Solve $\sqrt{5x-1}+3=0$.

Step 1 $\quad\sqrt{5x-1}=-3\quad$ To isolate the radical on one side, subtract 3 from each side.

Step 2 $\quad(\sqrt{5x-1})^2=(-3)^2\quad$ Square each side.

Step 3 $\quad5x-1=9\quad$ Apply the exponents.

$\quad5x=10\quad$ Add 1.

$\quad x=2\quad$ Divide by 5.

Step 4 Check the proposed solution in the original equation.

CHECK $\quad\sqrt{5x-1}+3=0\quad$ Original equation

$\sqrt{5\cdot2-1}+3\stackrel{?}{=}0\quad$ Let $x=2$.

$\sqrt{9}+3\stackrel{?}{=}0\quad$ Evaluate the radicand.

$3+3\stackrel{?}{=}0\quad$ Take the square root.

$6=0\quad$ False

This false result shows that the *proposed solution* 2 is *not* a solution of the original equation. It is extraneous. The solution set is $\varnothing$.

◀ **Work Problem 2 at the Side.**

Note

We could have determined after Step 1 that the equation in **Example 2** has no solution because the expression on the left cannot equal a negative number.

$$\sqrt{5x-1}=-3\quad$$ A square root radical cannot be negative.

Answers

2. **(a)** -2; -2; 4; 1; $\frac{1}{5}$; false; $\varnothing$

(b) $\{18\}$ **(c)** $\varnothing$

OBJECTIVE ▶ **2** Solve radical equations that require additional steps. Recall the following rule for squaring a binomial.

$$(x + y)^2 = x^2 + 2xy + y^2$$

EXAMPLE 3 Using the Power Rule (Squaring a Binomial)

Solve $\sqrt{4 - x} = x + 2$.

Step 1 The radical is isolated on the left side of the equation.

Step 2 Square each side. On the right, $(x + 2)^2 = x^2 + 2(x)(2) + 2^2$.

$$\left(\sqrt{4 - x}\right)^2 = (x + 2)^2 \quad \boxed{\text{Remember the middle term.}}$$
$$4 - x = x^2 + 4x + 4$$
↑ Twice the product of 2 and x

Step 3 The new equation is quadratic, so write it in standard form.

$$x^2 + 5x = 0 \qquad \text{Subtract 4, add } x, \text{ and interchange sides.}$$
$$x(x + 5) = 0 \qquad \text{Factor.}$$

$\boxed{\text{Set } each \text{ factor equal to 0.}}$ → $x = 0$ or $x + 5 = 0$ — Zero-factor property

$$x = -5 \qquad \text{Solve.}$$

Step 4 Check each proposed solution in the original equation.

CHECK $\sqrt{4 - x} = x + 2$

$\sqrt{4 - 0} \overset{?}{=} 0 + 2$ Let $x = 0$.

$\sqrt{4} \overset{?}{=} 2$

$2 = 2$ ✓ True

$\sqrt{4 - x} = x + 2$

$\sqrt{4 - (-5)} \overset{?}{=} -5 + 2$ Let $x = -5$.

$\sqrt{9} \overset{?}{=} -3$

$3 = -3$ False

The solution set is $\{0\}$. The proposed solution -5 is extraneous.

———————— Work Problem **3** at the Side. ▶

EXAMPLE 4 Using the Power Rule (Squaring a Binomial)

Solve $\sqrt{x^2 - 4x + 9} = x - 1$.

Square each side. On the right, $(x - 1)^2 = x^2 - 2(x)(1) + 1^2$.

$$\left(\sqrt{x^2 - 4x + 9}\right)^2 = (x - 1)^2 \quad \boxed{\text{Remember the middle term.}}$$
$$x^2 - 4x + 9 = x^2 - 2x + 1$$
↑ Twice the product of x and -1

$$-2x = -8 \qquad \text{Subtract } x^2 \text{ and 9. Add } 2x.$$
$$x = 4 \qquad \text{Divide by } -2.$$

CHECK $\sqrt{x^2 - 4x + 9} = x - 1$ Original equation

$\sqrt{4^2 - 4 \cdot 4 + 9} \overset{?}{=} 4 - 1$ Let $x = 4$.

$3 = 3$ ✓ True

The solution set is $\{4\}$.

———————— Work Problem **4** at the Side. ▶

3 Solve.

(a) $\sqrt{-2x - 2} = x + 1$

(b) $\sqrt{3x - 5} = x - 1$

4 Solve each equation.

(a) $\sqrt{4x^2 + 2x - 3} = 2x + 7$

(b) $\sqrt{1 - 2x - x^2} = x + 1$

Answers

3. (a) $\{-1\}$ (b) $\{2, 3\}$
4. (a) $\{-2\}$ (b) $\{0\}$

5 Solve each equation.

(a) $\sqrt{2x + 3} + \sqrt{x + 1} = 1$

(b) $\sqrt{3x + 1} - \sqrt{x + 4} = 1$

EXAMPLE 5 **Using the Power Rule (Squaring Twice)**

Solve $\sqrt{5x + 6} + \sqrt{3x + 4} = 2$.

Isolate one radical on one side of the equation by subtracting $\sqrt{3x + 4}$ from each side.

$$\sqrt{5x + 6} = 2 - \sqrt{3x + 4} \qquad \text{Subtract } \sqrt{3x + 4}.$$

$$\left(\sqrt{5x + 6}\right)^2 = \left(2 - \sqrt{3x + 4}\right)^2 \qquad \text{Square each side.}$$

$$5x + 6 = 4 - 4\sqrt{3x + 4} + (3x + 4) \qquad \boxed{\text{Be careful here.}}$$

$\boxed{\text{Remember the middle term.}}$ ⌐ Twice the product of 2 and $-\sqrt{3x + 4}$

This equation still contains a radical. Isolate this radical term on the right.

$$5x + 6 = 8 + 3x - 4\sqrt{3x + 4} \qquad \text{Combine like terms.}$$

$$2x - 2 = -4\sqrt{3x + 4} \qquad \text{Subtract 8 and } 3x.$$

$\boxed{\text{Divide } \textit{each} \text{ term by 2.}}$ $\quad x - 1 = -2\sqrt{3x + 4} \qquad$ Divide by 2 to make the numbers smaller.

$$(x - 1)^2 = \left(-2\sqrt{3x + 4}\right)^2 \qquad \text{Square each side again.}$$

$$x^2 - 2x + 1 = (-2)^2\left(\sqrt{3x + 4}\right)^2 \qquad \text{On the right, } (ab)^2 = a^2b^2.$$

$$x^2 - 2x + 1 = 4(3x + 4) \qquad \text{Apply the exponents.}$$

$$x^2 - 2x + 1 = 12x + 16 \qquad \text{Distributive property}$$

$$x^2 - 14x - 15 = 0 \qquad \text{Standard form}$$

$$(x + 1)(x - 15) = 0 \qquad \text{Factor.}$$

$$x + 1 = 0 \quad \text{or} \quad x - 15 = 0 \qquad \text{Zero-factor property}$$

$$x = -1 \quad \text{or} \qquad x = 15 \qquad \text{Solve each equation.}$$

CHECK Check the proposed solution -1.

$$\sqrt{5x + 6} + \sqrt{3x + 4} = 2 \qquad \text{Original equation}$$

$$\sqrt{5(-1) + 6} + \sqrt{3(-1) + 4} \stackrel{?}{=} 2 \qquad \text{Let } x = -1.$$

$$\sqrt{1} + \sqrt{1} \stackrel{?}{=} 2 \qquad \text{Evaluate the radicands.}$$

$$1 + 1 \stackrel{?}{=} 2 \qquad \text{Take square roots.}$$

$$2 = 2 \checkmark \quad \text{True}$$

Now check the proposed solution 15.

$$\sqrt{5x + 6} + \sqrt{3x + 4} = 2 \qquad \text{Original equation}$$

$$\sqrt{5(15) + 6} + \sqrt{3(15) + 4} \stackrel{?}{=} 2 \qquad \text{Let } x = 15.$$

$$\sqrt{81} + \sqrt{49} \stackrel{?}{=} 2 \qquad \text{Evaluate the radicands.}$$

$$9 + 7 \stackrel{?}{=} 2 \qquad \text{Take square roots.}$$

$$16 = 2 \qquad \text{False}$$

The proposed solution -1 is valid, but 15 is extraneous and must be rejected. Thus, the solution set is $\{-1\}$.

◀ **Work Problem** **5** **at the Side**

Answers

5. (a) $\{-1\}$ **(b)** $\{5\}$

OBJECTIVE 3 **Solve radical equations with indexes greater than 2.** The power rule also applies to powers greater than 2.

EXAMPLE 6 Using the Power Rule for a Power Greater than 2

Solve $\sqrt[3]{x + 5} = \sqrt[3]{2x - 6}$.

$$\left(\sqrt[3]{x + 5}\right)^3 = \left(\sqrt[3]{2x - 6}\right)^3 \quad \text{Cube each side.}$$

$$x + 5 = 2x - 6 \qquad \left(\sqrt[3]{a}\right)^3 = a$$

$$11 = x \qquad \text{Subtract } x. \text{ Add 6.}$$

CHECK $\sqrt[3]{x + 5} = \sqrt[3]{2x - 6}$ Original equation

$$\sqrt[3]{11 + 5} \stackrel{?}{=} \sqrt[3]{2 \cdot 11 - 6} \quad \text{Let } x = 11.$$

$$\sqrt[3]{16} = \sqrt[3]{16} \checkmark \qquad \text{True}$$

The solution set is $\{11\}$.

——————— Work Problem **6** at the Side. ▶

OBJECTIVE 4 **Use the power rule to solve a formula for a specified variable.**

EXAMPLE 7 Solving a Formula for a Specified Variable

An important property of a radio-frequency transmission line is its **characteristic impedance,** represented by Z and measured in ohms. If L and C are the inductance and capacitance, respectively, per unit of length of the line, then these quantities are related by the formula

$$Z = \sqrt{\frac{L}{C}}.$$

Solve this formula for C.

$$Z = \sqrt{\frac{L}{C}} \quad \text{Our goal is to isolate } C \text{ on one side of the equality symbol.}$$

$$Z^2 = \left(\sqrt{\frac{L}{C}}\right)^2 \quad \text{Square each side.}$$

$$Z^2 = \frac{L}{C} \qquad \left(\sqrt{a}\right)^2 = a$$

$$CZ^2 = L \qquad \text{Multiply by } C.$$

$$C = \frac{L}{Z^2} \qquad \text{Divide by } Z^2.$$

——————— Work Problem **7** at the Side. ▶

6 Solve each equation.

(a) $\sqrt[3]{2x + 7} = \sqrt[3]{3x - 2}$

(b) $\sqrt[4]{2x + 5} + 1 = 0$

7 Solve the formula for R.

$$Z = \sqrt{\frac{R}{T}}$$

Answers

6. (a) $\{9\}$ (b) $\varnothing$

7. $R = TZ^2$

CONCEPT CHECK *Check each equation to see if the given value for x is a solution.*

1. $\sqrt{3x + 18} = x$

   (a) 6   **(b)** −3

2. $\sqrt{3x - 3} = x - 1$

   (a) 1   **(b)** 4

3. $\sqrt{x + 2} = \sqrt{9x - 2} - 2\sqrt{x - 1}$

   (a) 2   **(b)** 7

4. $\sqrt{8x - 3} = 2x$

   (a) $\dfrac{3}{2}$ **(b)** $\dfrac{1}{2}$

5. CONCEPT CHECK A student claimed that 9 is a solution of the following equation.

$$\sqrt{x} = -3$$

He received no credit for his answer. *What Went Wrong?* Give the correct solution set.

6. CONCEPT CHECK A student solved the following equation and obtained the proposed solutions $x = -3$ and $x = 6$.

$$\sqrt{3x + 18} = x$$

She gave $\{-3, 6\}$ as the solution set. *What Went Wrong?* Give the correct solution set.

Solve each equation. See Examples 1–4.

7. $\sqrt{x - 2} = 3$

8. $\sqrt{x + 1} = 7$

9. $\sqrt{6x - 1} = 1$

10. $\sqrt{7x - 3} = 5$

11. $\sqrt{4x + 3} + 1 = 0$

12. $\sqrt{5x - 3} + 2 = 0$

13. $\sqrt{3k + 1} - 4 = 0$

14. $\sqrt{5z + 1} - 11 = 0$

15. $4 - \sqrt{x - 2} = 0$

16. $9 - \sqrt{4k + 1} = 0$

17. $\sqrt{9a - 4} = \sqrt{8a + 1}$

18. $\sqrt{4p - 2} = \sqrt{3p + 5}$

19. $2\sqrt{x} = \sqrt{3x + 4}$

20. $2\sqrt{m} = \sqrt{5m - 16}$

21. $3\sqrt{z - 1} = 2\sqrt{2z + 2}$

22. $5\sqrt{4x + 1} = 3\sqrt{10x + 25}$

23. $k = \sqrt{k^2 + 4k - 20}$

24. $p = \sqrt{p^2 - 3p + 18}$

25. $x = \sqrt{x^2 + 3x + 9}$

26. $z = \sqrt{z^2 - 4z - 8}$

27. $\sqrt{9 - x} = x + 3$

28. $\sqrt{16 - x} = x + 4$

29. $\sqrt{5 - x} = x + 1$

30. $\sqrt{3 - x} = x + 3$

31. $\sqrt{6x + 7} = x + 2$

32. $\sqrt{4x + 13} = x + 4$

33. $\sqrt{k^2 + 2k + 9} = k + 3$

34. $\sqrt{x^2 - 3x + 3} = x - 1$

35. $\sqrt{m^2 + 3m + 12} = m + 2$

36. $\sqrt{r^2 + 9r + 15} = r + 4$

37. $\sqrt{z^2 + 12z - 4} + 4 - z = 0$

38. $\sqrt{p^2 - 15p + 15} + 5 - p = 0$

39. CONCEPT CHECK When solving the equation
$$\sqrt{3x + 4} = 8 - x,$$
a student wrote the following as his first step.
$$3x + 4 = 64 + x^2$$
What Went Wrong? Solve the given equation correctly.

40. CONCEPT CHECK When solving the equation
$$\sqrt{5x + 6} = \sqrt{x + 3} + 3,$$
a student wrote the following as her first step.
$$5x + 6 = x + 3 + 9$$
What Went Wrong? Solve the given equation correctly.

*Solve each equation. **See Example 5.***

41. $\sqrt{k + 2} - \sqrt{k - 3} = 1$

42. $\sqrt{r + 6} - \sqrt{r - 2} = 2$

43. $\sqrt{2r + 11} - \sqrt{5r + 1} = -1$

44. $\sqrt{3x - 2} - \sqrt{x + 3} = 1$

45. $\sqrt{3p + 4} - \sqrt{2p - 4} = 2$

46. $\sqrt{4x + 5} - \sqrt{2x + 2} = 1$

47. $\sqrt{3 - 3p} - 3 = \sqrt{3p + 2}$

48. $\sqrt{4x + 7} - 4 = \sqrt{4x - 1}$

49. $\sqrt{2\sqrt{x + 11}} = \sqrt{4x + 2}$

50. $\sqrt{3\sqrt{-x + 21}} = \sqrt{6x + 9}$

Solve each equation. ***See Example 6.***

51. $\sqrt[3]{p - 1} = 2$

52. $\sqrt[3]{x + 8} = 3$

53. $\sqrt[3]{2x + 5} = \sqrt[3]{6x + 1}$

54. $\sqrt[3]{p + 5} = \sqrt[3]{2p - 4}$

55. $\sqrt[3]{2m - 1} = \sqrt[3]{m + 13}$

56. $\sqrt[3]{2k - 11} - \sqrt[3]{5k + 1} = 0$

57. $\sqrt[3]{a^2 + 5a + 1} = \sqrt[3]{a^2 + 4a}$

58. $\sqrt[3]{r^2 + 3r + 8} = \sqrt[3]{r^2 + r}$

59. $\sqrt[4]{a + 8} = \sqrt[4]{2a}$

60. $\sqrt[4]{x + 5} = \sqrt[4]{6x}$

61. $\sqrt[4]{z + 11} = \sqrt[4]{2z + 6}$

62. $\sqrt[4]{x + 12} = \sqrt[4]{3x - 4}$

63. $\sqrt[3]{x - 8} + 2 = 0$

64. $\sqrt[3]{r + 1} + 1 = 0$

65. $\sqrt[4]{2k - 5} + 4 = 0$

66. $\sqrt[4]{8z - 3} + 2 = 0$

67. $\sqrt[3]{r^2 + 2r + 8} = \sqrt[3]{r^2 + 3r + 12}$

68. $\sqrt[3]{x^2 + 7x + 2} = \sqrt[3]{x^2 + 6x + 1}$

For each equation, write the expressions with rational exponents as radical expressions, and then solve using the procedures explained in this section.

69. $(2x - 9)^{1/2} = 2 + (x - 8)^{1/2}$

70. $(3w + 7)^{1/2} = 1 + (w + 2)^{1/2}$

71. $(2w - 1)^{2/3} - w^{1/3} = 0$

72. $(x^2 - 2x)^{1/3} - x^{1/3} = 0$

*Solve each formula for the specified variable. **See Example 7.** (Data from Cooke, Nelson M., and Joseph B. Orleans, Mathematics Essential to Electricity and Radio, McGraw-Hill.)*

73. $Z = \sqrt{\dfrac{L}{C}}$ for L

74. $r = \sqrt{\dfrac{\mathscr{A}}{\pi}}$ for $\mathscr{A}$

75. $V = \sqrt{\dfrac{2K}{m}}$ for K

76. $V = \sqrt{\dfrac{2K}{m}}$ for m

77. $r = \sqrt{\dfrac{Mm}{F}}$ for M

78. $r = \sqrt{\dfrac{Mm}{F}}$ for F

To find the rotational rate N of a space station, the formula

$$N = \frac{1}{2\pi}\sqrt{\frac{a}{r}}$$

can be used. Here, a is the acceleration and r represents the radius of the space station in meters. To find the value of r that will make N simulate the effect of gravity on Earth, the equation must be solved for r, using the required value of N. (Data from Kastner, Bernice, Space Mathematics, NASA.)

79. Solve the equation for the indicated variable.

 (a) for r

 (b) for a

80. If $a = 9.8$ m per sec^2, find the value of r (to the nearest tenth) using each value of N.

 (a) $N = 0.063$ rotation per sec

 (b) $N = 0.04$ rotation per sec

10.7 Complex Numbers

OBJECTIVES

1. Simplify numbers of the form $\sqrt{-b}$, where $b > 0$.
2. Recognize subsets of the complex numbers.
3. Add and subtract complex numbers.
4. Multiply complex numbers.
5. Divide complex numbers.
6. Simplify powers of i.

Recall that the set of real numbers includes many other number sets—the rational numbers, integers, and natural numbers, for example. In this section, we introduce a new set of numbers that includes the set of real numbers, as well as numbers that are even roots of negative numbers, like $\sqrt{-2}$.

OBJECTIVE 1 Simplify numbers of the form $\sqrt{-b}$, where $b > 0$. The equation $x^2 + 1 = 0$ has no real number solution because any solution must be a number whose square is -1. In the set of real numbers, all squares are *nonnegative* numbers because the product of two positive numbers or two negative numbers is positive and $0^2 = 0$. To provide a solution for the equation $x^2 + 1 = 0$, we introduce a new number i.

> **Imaginary Unit i**
>
> The **imaginary unit i** is defined as follows.
> $$i = \sqrt{-1}, \quad \text{and thus} \quad i^2 = -1.$$
> In words, i is the principal square root of -1.

This definition of i makes it possible to define any square root of a negative number as follows.

> **Meaning of $\sqrt{-b}$**
>
> For any positive number b, $\qquad \sqrt{-b} = i\sqrt{b}.$

1. Write each number as a product of a real number and i.

(a) $\sqrt{-16}$

(b) $-\sqrt{-81}$

(c) $\sqrt{-7}$

(d) $\sqrt{-32}$

EXAMPLE 1 Simplifying Square Roots of Negative Numbers

Write each number as a product of a real number and i.

(a) $\sqrt{-100} = i\sqrt{100} = 10i$

(b) $-\sqrt{-36} = -i\sqrt{36} = -6i$

(c) $\sqrt{-2} = i\sqrt{2}$

(d) $\sqrt{-8} = i\sqrt{8} = i\sqrt{4 \cdot 2} = 2i\sqrt{2}$

◀ Work Problem **1** at the Side.

> **⚠ CAUTION**
>
> It is easy to mistake $\sqrt{2}i$ for $\sqrt{2i}$, with the i under the radical. For this reason, we usually write $\sqrt{2}i$ as $i\sqrt{2}$, as in the definition of $\sqrt{-b}$.

When finding a product such as $\sqrt{-4} \cdot \sqrt{-9}$, we cannot use the product rule for radicals because it applies only to nonnegative radicands.

For this reason, we change $\sqrt{-b}$ to the form $i\sqrt{b}$ before performing any multiplications or divisions.

Answers

1. (a) $4i$ (b) $-9i$ (c) $i\sqrt{7}$ (d) $4i\sqrt{2}$

EXAMPLE 2   **Multiplying Square Roots of Negative Numbers**

Multiply.

(a)
$$\sqrt{-4} \cdot \sqrt{-9}$$

First write all square roots in terms of i.

$$= i\sqrt{4} \cdot i\sqrt{9} \qquad \sqrt{-b} = i\sqrt{b}$$
$$= i \cdot 2 \cdot i \cdot 3 \qquad \text{Take square roots.}$$
$$= 6i^2 \qquad \text{Multiply.}$$
$$= 6(-1) \qquad \text{Substitute } -1 \text{ for } i^2.$$
$$= -6 \qquad \text{Multiply.}$$

(b)
$$\sqrt{-3} \cdot \sqrt{-7}$$

First write all square roots in terms of i.

$$= i\sqrt{3} \cdot i\sqrt{7} \qquad \sqrt{-b} = i\sqrt{b}$$
$$= i^2\sqrt{3 \cdot 7} \qquad \text{Product rule}$$
$$= (-1)\sqrt{21} \qquad \text{Substitute } -1 \text{ for } i^2.$$
$$= -\sqrt{21} \qquad (-1)a = -a$$

(c) $\sqrt{-2} \cdot \sqrt{-8}$

$$= i\sqrt{2} \cdot i\sqrt{8}$$
$$= i^2\sqrt{2 \cdot 8}$$
$$= (-1)\sqrt{16}$$
$$= -4$$

(d) $\sqrt{-5} \cdot \sqrt{6}$

$$= i\sqrt{5} \cdot \sqrt{6}$$
$$= i\sqrt{30}$$

──────── **Work Problem 2 at the Side.** ▶

❗ **CAUTION**

Use the definition of $\sqrt{-b}$ **before** the product rule for radicals.

$$\sqrt{-4} \cdot \sqrt{-9} = i\sqrt{4} \cdot i\sqrt{9} = -6, \text{ but } \sqrt{-4(-9)} = \sqrt{36} = 6.$$

Thus,
$$\sqrt{-4} \cdot \sqrt{-9} \neq \sqrt{-4(-9)}.$$

EXAMPLE 3   **Dividing Square Roots of Negative Numbers**

Divide.

(a) $\dfrac{\sqrt{-75}}{\sqrt{-3}}$

First write all square roots in terms of i.

$$= \frac{i\sqrt{75}}{i\sqrt{3}}$$
$$= \sqrt{\frac{75}{3}} \qquad \frac{i}{i} = 1; \text{ Quotient rule}$$
$$= \sqrt{25} \qquad \text{Divide.}$$
$$= 5$$

(b) $\dfrac{\sqrt{-32}}{\sqrt{8}}$

$$= \frac{i\sqrt{32}}{\sqrt{8}} \qquad \sqrt{-32} = i\sqrt{32}$$
$$= i\sqrt{\frac{32}{8}} \qquad \text{Quotient rule}$$
$$= i\sqrt{4} \qquad \text{Divide.}$$
$$= 2i$$

──────── **Work Problem 3 at the Side.** ▶

2 Multiply.

(a) $\sqrt{-16} \cdot \sqrt{-4}$

(b) $\sqrt{-5} \cdot \sqrt{-10}$

(c) $\sqrt{-15} \cdot \sqrt{2}$

3 Divide.

(a) $\dfrac{\sqrt{-32}}{\sqrt{-2}}$

(b) $\dfrac{\sqrt{-27}}{\sqrt{-3}}$

(c) $\dfrac{\sqrt{-40}}{\sqrt{10}}$

Answers

2. (a) -8 (b) $-5\sqrt{2}$ (c) $i\sqrt{30}$
3. (a) 4 (b) 3 (c) $2i$

OBJECTIVE **2** **Recognize subsets of the complex numbers.** A new set of numbers, the *complex numbers*, is defined as follows.

Complex Number

If a and b are real numbers, then any number of the form

$$a + bi$$

↑   ↑
Real part   Imaginary part

is a **complex number.** In the complex number $a + bi$, the number a is the **real part** and b is the **imaginary part.***

The following important concepts apply to a complex number $a + bi$.

1. If $b = 0$, then $a + bi = a$, which is a real number.
   Thus, the set of real numbers is a subset of the set of complex numbers. See **Figure 8.**

2. If $b \neq 0$, then $a + bi$ is a **nonreal complex number.**
   Examples: $7 + 2i$, $-1 - i$

3. If $a = 0$ and $b \neq 0$, then the nonreal complex number is a **pure imaginary number.**
   Examples: $3i$, $-16i$

A complex number written in the form $a + bi$ is in **standard form.** In this section, most answers will be given in standard form, but if $a = 0$ or $b = 0$, we consider answers such as a or bi to be in standard form.

The relationships among the subsets of the complex numbers are shown in **Figure 8.**

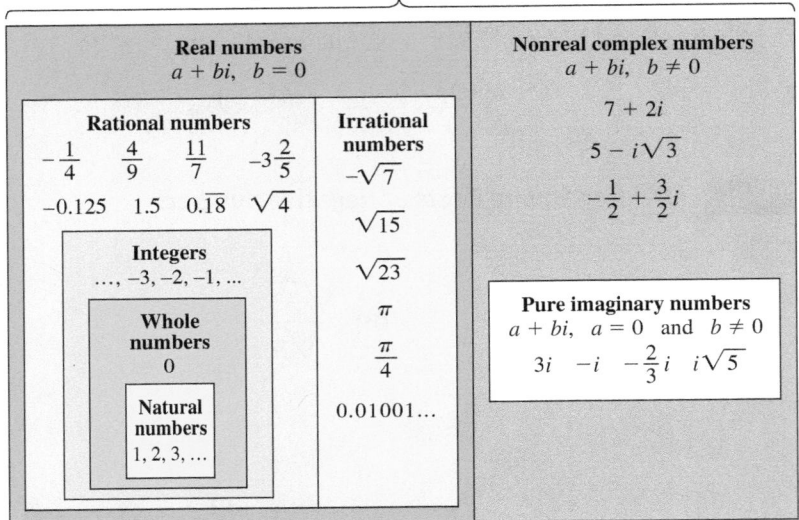

Figure 8

---

*Some texts define bi as the imaginary part of the complex number $a + bi$.

OBJECTIVE ▶ ❸ Add and subtract complex numbers. The commutative, associative, and distributive properties for real numbers are also valid for complex numbers.

To add complex numbers, we add their real parts and add their imaginary parts.

EXAMPLE 4   Adding Complex Numbers

Add.

(a) $(2 + 3i) + (6 + 4i)$ Commutative, associative,
$= (2 + 6) + (3 + 4)i$ and distributive properties
$= 8 + 7i$ Add real parts. Add imaginary parts.

(b) $(4 + 2i) + (3 - i) + (-6 + 3i)$ Commutative, associative,
$= [4 + 3 + (-6)] + [2 + (-1) + 3]i$ and distributive properties
$= 1 + 4i$ Add real parts.
Add imaginary parts.

——— **Work Problem ❹ at the Side.** ▶

To subtract complex numbers, we subtract their real parts and subtract their imaginary parts.

EXAMPLE 5   Subtracting Complex Numbers

Subtract.

(a) $(6 + 5i) - (3 + 2i)$ Commutative, associative,
$= (6 - 3) + (5 - 2)i$ and distributive properties
$= 3 + 3i$ Subtract real parts. Subtract imaginary parts.

(b) $(7 - 3i) - (8 - 6i)$ **(c)** $(-9 + 4i) - (-9 + 8i)$
$= (7 - 8) + [-3 - (-6)]i$ $= (-9 + 9) + (4 - 8)i$
$= -1 + 3i$ $= 0 - 4i$ Be careful.
       $= -4i$

——— **Work Problem ❺ at the Side.** ▶

OBJECTIVE ▶ ❹ Multiply complex numbers. We multiply complex numbers in the same way that we multiply polynomials.

EXAMPLE 6   Multiplying Complex Numbers

Multiply.

(a) $4i(2 + 3i)$

$= 4i(2) + 4i(3i)$ Distributive property
$= 8i + 12i^2$ Multiply.
$= 8i + 12(-1)$ Substitute -1 for i^2.
$= -12 + 8i$ Standard form

——— **Continued on Next Page**

❹ Add.

(a) $(4 + 6i) + (-3 + 5i)$

(b) $(5 - i) + (-3 + 3i)$
$+ (6 - 4i)$

❺ Subtract.

(a) $(7 + 3i) - (4 + 2i)$

(b) $(5 - 2i) - (9 - 7i)$

(c) $(-1 + 12i) - (-1 - i)$

Answers

4. **(a)** $1 + 11i$ **(b)** $8 - 2i$
5. **(a)** $3 + i$ **(b)** $-4 + 5i$ **(c)** $13i$

6 Multiply.

   (a) $6i(4 + 3i)$

(b) $(3 + 5i)(4 - 2i)$

$$= \underbrace{3(4)}_{\text{First}} + \underbrace{3(-2i)}_{\text{Outer}} + \underbrace{5i(4)}_{\text{Inner}} + \underbrace{5i(-2i)}_{\text{Last}} \quad \text{FOIL method}$$

$$= 12 - 6i + 20i - 10i^2 \qquad \text{Multiply.}$$

$$= 12 + 14i - 10(-1) \qquad \text{Add imaginary parts; } i^2 = -1$$

$$= 12 + 14i + 10 \qquad \text{Multiply.}$$

$$= 22 + 14i \qquad \text{Add real parts.}$$

(c) $(2 + 3i)(1 - 5i)$

$$= 2(1) + 2(-5i) + 3i(1) + 3i(-5i) \quad \text{FOIL method}$$

$$= 2 - 10i + 3i - 15i^2 \qquad \text{Multiply.}$$

$$= 2 - 7i - 15(-1) \quad \boxed{\text{Use parentheses around } -1 \text{ to avoid errors.}} \quad \text{Add imaginary parts; } i^2 = -1$$

$$= 2 - 7i + 15 \qquad \text{Multiply.}$$

$$= 17 - 7i \qquad \text{Add real parts.}$$

◀ **Work Problem 6 at the Side.**

(b) $(6 - 4i)(2 + 4i)$

The two complex numbers $a + bi$ and $a - bi$ are **complex conjugates,** or simply *conjugates*, of each other. ***The product of a complex number and its conjugate is always a real number,*** as shown here.

$$(a + bi)(a - bi)$$

$$= a^2 - abi + abi - b^2i^2 \qquad \text{FOIL method}$$

$$= a^2 - b^2(-1) \qquad \text{Combine like terms; } i^2 = -1$$

$$= a^2 + b^2 \quad \boxed{\text{The product eliminates } i.}$$

Example: $(3 + 7i)(3 - 7i) = 3^2 + 7^2 = 9 + 49 = 58$

(c) $(3 - 2i)(3 + 2i)$

OBJECTIVE ▶ **5** **Divide complex numbers.**

EXAMPLE 7 **Dividing Complex Numbers**

Divide.

(a) $\dfrac{8 + 9i}{5 + 2i}$ $\boxed{\frac{5 - 2i}{5 - 2i} = 1}$

$$= \frac{(8 + 9i)(5 - 2i)}{(5 + 2i)(5 - 2i)} \qquad \begin{array}{l}\text{Multiply numerator and}\\ \text{denominator by } 5 - 2i, \text{ the}\\ \text{conjugate of the denominator.}\end{array}$$

$$= \frac{40 - 16i + 45i - 18i^2}{5^2 + 2^2} \qquad \begin{array}{l}\text{In the denominator,}\\ (a + bi)(a - bi) = a^2 + b^2.\end{array}$$

$$= \frac{40 + 29i - 18(-1)}{25 + 4} \qquad \begin{array}{l}\text{In the numerator, add imaginary}\\ \text{parts; } i^2 = -1\end{array}$$

$$= \frac{58 + 29i}{29} \qquad \begin{array}{l}\text{Multiply. Add real parts.}\\ \text{Add in the denominator.}\end{array}$$

$$= \frac{29(2 + i)}{29} \quad \boxed{\begin{array}{l}\text{Factor first. Then}\\ \text{divide out the}\\ \text{common factor.}\end{array}} \qquad \text{Factor the numerator.}$$

$$= 2 + i \qquad \text{Lowest terms}$$

Answers

6. (a) $-18 + 24i$ **(b)** $28 + 16i$ **(c)** 13

———— Continued on Next Page

(b) $\dfrac{1+i}{i}$

$= \dfrac{(1+i)(-i)}{i(-i)}$ — Multiply numerator and denominator by $-i$, the conjugate of i.

$= \dfrac{-i - i^2}{-i^2}$ — Use the distributive property in the numerator. Multiply in the denominator.

$= \dfrac{-i - (-1)}{-(-1)}$ — Substitute -1 for i^2.

$= \dfrac{-i + 1}{1}$ — Use parentheses to avoid errors.

$= 1 - i$ — $\frac{a}{1} = a$

— **Work Problem 7 at the Side.** ▶

OBJECTIVE 6 Simplify powers of i. Powers of i can be simplified using the facts

$$i^2 = -1 \quad \text{and} \quad i^4 = (i^2)^2 = (-1)^2 = 1.$$

Consider the following powers of i.

$i^1 = i$ $i^5 = i^4 \cdot i = 1 \cdot i = i$

$i^2 = -1$ $i^6 = i^4 \cdot i^2 = 1(-1) = -1$

$i^3 = i^2 \cdot i = (-1) \cdot i = -i$ $i^7 = i^4 \cdot i^3 = 1 \cdot (-i) = -i$

$i^4 = i^2 \cdot i^2 = (-1)(-1) = 1$ $i^8 = i^4 \cdot i^4 = 1 \cdot 1 = 1,$ and so on.

Powers of i cycle through the same four outcomes

$$i, \quad -1, \quad -i, \quad \text{and} \quad 1$$

because i^4 has the same multiplicative property as 1. Also, any power of i with an exponent that is a multiple of 4 has value 1. As with real numbers, $i^0 = 1$.

EXAMPLE 8   Simplifying Powers of i

Find each power of i.

(a) $i^{12} = (i^4)^3 = 1^3 = 1$ $i^4 = 1$

(b) $i^{39} = i^{36} \cdot i^3 = (i^4)^9 \cdot i^3 = 1^9 \cdot (-i) = 1 \cdot (-i) = -i$

(c) $i^{-2} = \dfrac{1}{i^2} = \dfrac{1}{-1} = -1$

(d) $i^{-1} = \dfrac{1}{i} = \dfrac{1(-i)}{i(-i)} = \dfrac{-i}{-i^2} = \dfrac{-i}{-(-1)} = \dfrac{-i}{1} = -i$

— **Work Problem 8 at the Side.** ▶

7 Divide.

(a) $\dfrac{8 - 4i}{1 - i}$

(b) $\dfrac{5}{3 - 2i}$

(c) $\dfrac{5 - i}{i}$

8 Find each power of i.

(a) i^{21}

$= i\text{—} \cdot i$

$= (i^4)\text{—} \cdot i$

$= \underline{\quad}^5 \cdot i$

$= \underline{\quad}$

(b) i^{36}

(c) i^{50}

(d) i^{-9}

Answers

7. (a) $6 + 2i$ (b) $\dfrac{15}{13} + \dfrac{10}{13}i$ (c) $-1 - 5i$

8. (a) $20; 5; 1; i$ (b) 1 (c) -1 (d) $-i$

10.7 Exercises   FOR EXTRA HELP   Go to MyMathLab *for worked-out, step-by-step solutions to exercises enclosed in a square* ▢ *and video solutions to* ▶ *exercises.*

CONCEPT CHECK   *List all of the following sets to which each number belongs. A number may belong to more than one set.*

real numbers   pure imaginary numbers   nonreal complex numbers   complex numbers

1. $3 + 5i$

2. $-7i$

3. $\sqrt{2}$

4. $\dfrac{13}{3}$

5. $\sqrt{-49}$

6. $-\sqrt{-8}$

CONCEPT CHECK   *Decide whether each expression is equal to* $1, -1, i,$ *or* $-i$.

7. $\sqrt{-1}$ **8.** $-\sqrt{-1}$ **9.** i^2 **10.** $-i^2$ **11.** $\dfrac{1}{i}$ **12.** $(-i)^2$

Write each number as a product of a real number and i. Simplify all radical expressions. **See Example 1.**

13. $\sqrt{-169}$ ▶   **14.** $\sqrt{-225}$ **15.** $-\sqrt{-144}$ **16.** $-\sqrt{-196}$

17. $\sqrt{-5}$ **18.** $\sqrt{-21}$ **19.** $\sqrt{-48}$ **20.** $\sqrt{-96}$

Multiply or divide as indicated. **See Examples 2 and 3.**

21. $\sqrt{-15} \cdot \sqrt{-15}$ **22.** $\sqrt{-19} \cdot \sqrt{-19}$ **23.** $\sqrt{-7} \cdot \sqrt{-15}$ ▶   **24.** $\sqrt{-3} \cdot \sqrt{-19}$

25. $\sqrt{-4} \cdot \sqrt{-25}$ **26.** $\sqrt{-9} \cdot \sqrt{-81}$ **27.** $\sqrt{-3} \cdot \sqrt{11}$ **28.** $\sqrt{-5} \cdot \sqrt{13}$

29. $\dfrac{\sqrt{-300}}{\sqrt{-100}}$ ▶   **30.** $\dfrac{\sqrt{-40}}{\sqrt{-10}}$ **31.** $\dfrac{\sqrt{-75}}{\sqrt{3}}$ ▶   **32.** $\dfrac{\sqrt{-160}}{\sqrt{10}}$

Add or subtract as indicated. Give answers in standard form. **See Examples 4 and 5.**

33. $(3 + 2i) + (-4 + 5i)$ ▶   **34.** $(7 + 15i) + (-11 + 14i)$ **35.** $(5 - i) + (-5 + i)$

36. $(-2 + 6i) + (2 - 6i)$ **37.** $(4 + i) - (-3 - 2i)$ ▶   **38.** $(9 + i) - (3 + 2i)$

39. $(-3 - 4i) - (-1 - 4i)$

40. $(-2 - 3i) - (-5 - 3i)$

41. $(-4 + 11i) + (-2 - 4i) + (7 + 6i)$

42. $(-1 + i) + (2 + 5i) + (3 + 2i)$

43. $\left[(7 + 3i) - (4 - 2i)\right] + (3 + i)$

44. $\left[(7 + 2i) + (-4 - i)\right] - (2 + 5i)$

CONCEPT CHECK *Fill in the blank with the correct response.*

45. Because $(4 + 2i) - (3 + i) = 1 + i$, using the definition of subtraction we can check this to find that

$$(1 + i) + (3 + i) = \text{_____} .$$

46. Because $\frac{-5}{2 - i} = -2 - i$, using the definition of division we can check this to find that

$$(-2 - i)(2 - i) = \text{_____} .$$

Multiply. Give answers in standard form. ***See Example 6.***

47. $(3i)(27i)$

48. $(5i)(125i)$

49. $(-8i)(-2i)$

50. $(-32i)(-2i)$

51. $5i(-6 + 2i)$

52. $6i(-7 + 3i)$

53. $2i(3 + 5i)$

54. $3i(4 + 9i)$

55. $(4 + 3i)(1 - 2i)$

56. $(7 - 2i)(3 + i)$

57. $(2 - 5i)(3 - i)$

58. $(6 + 5i)(2 + 3i)$

59. $(4 + 5i)^2$

60. $(3 + 2i)^2$

61. $(7 + 2i)(7 - 2i)$

62. $(6 + 7i)(6 - 7i)$

CONCEPT CHECK *Answer each of the following.*

63. Let a and b represent real numbers.
   (a) What is the conjugate of $a + bi$?
   (b) If we multiply $a + bi$ by its conjugate, we obtain
   _____ + _____ , which is always a real number.

64. By what complex number should we multiply the numerator and denominator of $\frac{2 + i\sqrt{2}}{2 - i\sqrt{2}}$ to write the quotient in standard form?

   A. $\sqrt{2}$ **B.** $i\sqrt{2}$

   C. $2 + i\sqrt{2}$ **D.** $2 - i\sqrt{2}$

Divide. Give answers in standard form. ***See Example 7.***

65. $\dfrac{2}{1 - i}$

66. $\dfrac{29}{5 + 2i}$

67. $\dfrac{-7 + 4i}{3 + 2i}$

68. $\dfrac{-38 - 8i}{7 + 3i}$

69. $\dfrac{8i}{2 + 2i}$

70. $\dfrac{-8i}{1 + i}$

71. $\dfrac{2 - 3i}{2 + 3i}$

72. $\dfrac{-1 + 5i}{3 + 2i}$

73. $\dfrac{3 - i}{i}$

74. $\dfrac{4 + i}{i}$

75. $\dfrac{2 + 5i}{-i}$

76. $\dfrac{3 + 2i}{-i}$

*Find each power of i. **See Example 8.***

77. i^{18} **78.** i^{26} **79.** i^{89} **80.** i^{45} **81.** i^{96} **82.** i^{48}

83. i^{43} **84.** i^{83} **85.** i^{-5} **86.** i^{-17} **87.** i^{-20} **88.** i^{-27}

Ohm's law *for the current I in a circuit with voltage E, resistance R, capacitance reactance X_c, and inductive reactance X_L is*

$$I = \frac{E}{R + (X_L - X_c)i}.$$

Use this law to work each problem.

89. Find I if $E = 2 + 3i$, $R = 5$, $X_L = 4$, and $X_c = 3$.

90. Find E if $I = 1 - i$, $R = 2$, $X_L = 3$, and $X_c = 1$.

Relating Concepts (Exercises 91–95) For Individual or Group Work

Some equations have nonreal complex solutions. **Work Exercises 91–95 in order,** *to see how these nonreal complex solutions are related.*

91. Show that $1 + 5i$ is a solution of $x^2 - 2x + 26 = 0$.

92. Show that $1 - 5i$ is a solution of $x^2 - 2x + 26 = 0$.

93. From **Exercises 91 and 92,** the nonreal complex solutions of the equation

$$x^2 - 2x + 26 = 0$$

are $1 + 5i$ and $1 - 5i$. What do we call two complex numbers $a + bi$ and $a - bi$?

94. Show that $3 + 2i$ is a solution of the equation

$$x^2 - 6x + 13 = 0.$$

95. Using the results of **Exercises 91–94,** make a conjecture about another nonreal complex solution of the equation $x^2 - 6x + 13 = 0$, and verify it.

Chapter 10 *Summary*

Key Terms

10.1

square root A number b is a square root of a if $b^2 = a$.

principal square root The positive square root of a number is its principal square root.

radicand, index In the expression $\sqrt[n]{a}$, a is the radicand and n is the index **(order)**.

radical The expression $\sqrt[n]{a}$ is a radical.

Index → Radical symbol ↘

$$\sqrt[n]{a} \leftarrow \text{Radicand}$$

Radical

radical expression A radical expression is an algebraic expression that contains a radical.

perfect square A number with a rational square root is a perfect square.

irrational number A real number that is not rational is an irrational number.

cube root A number b is a cube root of a if $b^3 = a$.

perfect cube A number with a rational cube root is a perfect cube.

10.5

conjugate The conjugate of $x + y$ is $x - y$.

10.6

radical equation A radical equation is an equation that includes one or more radical expressions with a variable in a radicand.

proposed solution A value of the variable that appears to be a solution of an equation is a proposed solution.

extraneous solution (of a radical equation) An extraneous solution of a radical equation is a value found after applying the power rule that is not a solution of the original equation.

10.7

complex number A complex number is a number that can be written in the form $a + bi$, where a and b are real numbers.

real part The real part of $a + bi$ is a.

imaginary part The imaginary part of $a + bi$ is b.

pure imaginary number A complex number $a + bi$ with $a = 0$ and $b \neq 0$ is a pure imaginary number.

nonreal complex number A complex number $a + bi$ with $b \neq 0$ is a nonreal complex number.

standard form (of a complex number) A complex number is in standard form if it is written in the form $a + bi$.

complex conjugate The complex conjugate of $a + bi$ is $a - bi$.

New Symbols

$\sqrt{}$	radical symbol	$\approx$	is approximately equal to
$\sqrt[n]{a}$	radical; principal nth root of a	$a^{1/n}$	a to the power $\frac{1}{n}$
$\pm$	*"positive or negative,"* or *"plus or minus"*		

$a^{m/n}$	a to the power $\frac{m}{n}$
i	imaginary unit

Test Your Word Power

See how well you have learned the vocabulary in this chapter.

1 A **square root** of a number is
   A. the number raised to the second power
   B. the number under a radical symbol
   C. a number that when multiplied by itself gives the original number
   D. the inverse of the number.

2 A **radicand** is
   A. the index of a radical
   B. the number or expression under the radical symbol
   C. the positive root of a number
   D. the radical symbol.

3 An **extraneous solution** is a value
   A. that does not satisfy the original equation
   B. that makes an equation true

   C. that makes an expression equal 0
   D. that checks in the original equation.

4 A **complex number** is
   A. a real number that includes a complex fraction
   B. a zero multiple of i
   C. a number of the form $a + bi$, where a and b are real numbers
   D. the square root of -1.

Quick Review

Concepts	Examples
10.1 **Radical Expressions and Graphs**	Find each root.

10.1 Radical Expressions and Graphs

$\sqrt[n]{a} = b$ means $b^n = a$.

$\sqrt[n]{a}$ is the **principal nth root** of a.

$\sqrt[n]{a^n} = |a|$ if n is even. $\sqrt[n]{a^n} = a$ if n is odd.

Functions Defined by Radical Expressions

The square root function is

$$f(x) = \sqrt{x}.$$

The cube root function is

$$f(x) = \sqrt[3]{x}.$$

Find each root.

$$\sqrt{64} = 8 \quad \text{Principal square root}$$

$$-\sqrt{64} = -8 \quad \sqrt{-64} \text{ is not a real number.}$$

$$\sqrt[4]{(-2)^4} = |-2| = 2 \quad \sqrt[3]{-27} = -3$$

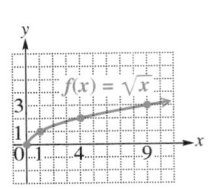

Square root function
Domain and range: $[0, \infty)$

Cube root function
Domain and range: $(-\infty, \infty)$

10.2 Rational Exponents

$a^{1/n} = \sqrt[n]{a}$ whenever $\sqrt[n]{a}$ exists.

If m and n are positive integers with m/n in lowest terms, then $a^{m/n} = (a^{1/n})^m$, provided that $a^{1/n}$ is a real number.

All of the usual definitions and rules for exponents are valid for rational exponents.

Apply the rules for rational exponents.

$$81^{1/2} = \sqrt{81} = 9 \qquad -64^{1/3} = -\sqrt[3]{64} = -4$$

$$8^{5/3} = (8^{1/3})^5 = 2^5 = 32 \qquad (y^{2/5})^{10} = y^4$$

Write with positive exponents.

$$5^{-1/2} \cdot 5^{1/4} = 5^{-1/2 + 1/4}$$
$$= 5^{-1/4}$$
$$= \frac{1}{5^{1/4}}$$

$$\frac{x^{-1/3}}{x^{-1/2}} = x^{-1/3 - (-1/2)}$$
$$= x^{-1/3 + 1/2}$$
$$= x^{1/6}, \quad x > 0$$

10.3 Simplifying Radical Expressions

Product and Quotient Rules for Radicals

If n is a natural number and $\sqrt[n]{a}$ and $\sqrt[n]{b}$ are real numbers, then the following hold true.

$$\sqrt[n]{a} \cdot \sqrt[n]{b} = \sqrt[n]{ab} \quad \text{and} \quad \sqrt[n]{\frac{a}{b}} = \frac{\sqrt[n]{a}}{\sqrt[n]{b}} \quad (\text{where } b \neq 0)$$

Conditions for a Simplified Radical

1. The radicand has no factor raised to a power greater than or equal to the index.

2. The radicand has no fractions.

3. No denominator contains a radical.

4. Exponents in the radicand and the index of the radical have greatest common factor 1.

Simplify.

$$\sqrt{3} \cdot \sqrt{7} = \sqrt{21} \qquad \sqrt[5]{x^3 y} \cdot \sqrt[5]{xy^2} = \sqrt[5]{x^4 y^3}$$

$$\frac{\sqrt{x^5}}{\sqrt{x^4}} = \sqrt{\frac{x^5}{x^4}} = \sqrt{x}, \quad x > 0$$

$$\sqrt{18} = \sqrt{9 \cdot 2} = 3\sqrt{2}$$

$$\sqrt[3]{54x^5 y^3} = \sqrt[3]{27x^3 y^3 \cdot 2x^2} = 3xy\sqrt[3]{2x^2}$$

$$\sqrt{\frac{7}{4}} = \frac{\sqrt{7}}{\sqrt{4}} = \frac{\sqrt{7}}{2}$$

$$\sqrt[9]{x^3} = x^{3/9} = x^{1/3}, \quad \text{or} \quad \sqrt[3]{x}$$

Concepts	Examples
Pythagorean Theorem If a and b are the lengths of the shorter sides (**legs**) of a right triangle and c is the length of the longest side (**hypotenuse**), then the following holds true. $$a^2 + b^2 = c^2$$	Find the length of the unknown side in the right triangle. $$10^2 + b^2 = \left(2\sqrt{61}\right)^2$$ $$b^2 = 4(61) - 100$$ $$b^2 = 144$$ $$b = 12$$

Find the length of the unknown side in the right triangle.

$$10^2 + b^2 = \left(2\sqrt{61}\right)^2$$
$$b^2 = 4(61) - 100$$
$$b^2 = 144$$
$$b = 12$$

(triangle with legs labeled $2\sqrt{61}$ and b, hypotenuse 10)

Distance Formula

The distance d between the points (x_1, y_1) and (x_2, y_2) is given by

$$d = \sqrt{(x_2 - x_1)^2 + (y_2 - y_1)^2}.$$

Find the distance between $(3, -2)$ and $(-1, 1)$.

$$d = \sqrt{(-1 - 3)^2 + [1 - (-2)]^2}$$ Substitute.
$$d = \sqrt{(-4)^2 + 3^2}$$ Subtract.
$$d = \sqrt{25}$$ Simplify the radicand.
$$d = 5$$ Take the square root.

10.4 Adding and Subtracting Radical Expressions

Add or subtract radical expressions using the distributive property.

$$ac + bc = (a + b)c$$

Only radical expressions with the same index and the same radicand may be combined into a single radical.

Simplify. $2\sqrt{28} - 3\sqrt{63}$

$$= 2\sqrt{4 \cdot 7} - 3\sqrt{9 \cdot 7}$$
$$= 2 \cdot 2\sqrt{7} - 3 \cdot 3\sqrt{7}$$
$$= 4\sqrt{7} - 9\sqrt{7}$$
$$= (4 - 9)\sqrt{7}$$
$$= -5\sqrt{7}$$

$\left.\sqrt{15} + \sqrt{30}, \quad \sqrt{3} + \sqrt[3]{9}\right\}$ Cannot be simplified further

10.5 Multiplying and Dividing Radical Expressions

Multiply binomial radical expressions using the FOIL method. Special product rules may apply.

$$(x + y)(x - y) = x^2 - y^2$$
$$(x + y)^2 = x^2 + 2xy + y^2$$
$$(x - y)^2 = x^2 - 2xy + y^2$$

Multiply.

$$\left(\sqrt{2} + \sqrt{7}\right)\left(\sqrt{3} - \sqrt{6}\right)$$

$$\quad\quad \overset{F}{} \quad \overset{O}{} \quad \overset{I}{} \quad \overset{L}{}$$
$$= \sqrt{6} - 2\sqrt{3} + \sqrt{21} - \sqrt{42} \quad \sqrt{12} = 2\sqrt{3}$$

$$\left(\sqrt{5} - \sqrt{10}\right)\left(\sqrt{5} + \sqrt{10}\right) \quad\bigg|\quad \left(\sqrt{3} - \sqrt{2}\right)^2$$
$$= 5 - 10 \quad\quad\quad\quad\quad\quad\quad\bigg|\quad = 3 - 2\sqrt{3} \cdot \sqrt{2} + 2$$
$$= -5 \quad\quad\quad\quad\quad\quad\quad\quad\bigg|\quad = 5 - 2\sqrt{6}$$

Rationalizing a Denominator

Rationalize the denominator by multiplying both the numerator and denominator by the same expression, one that will yield a rational number in the final denominator.

$$\frac{\sqrt{7}}{\sqrt{5}} = \frac{\sqrt{7} \cdot \sqrt{5}}{\sqrt{5} \cdot \sqrt{5}} = \frac{\sqrt{35}}{5}$$

$$\frac{4}{\sqrt{5} - \sqrt{2}} = \frac{4\left(\sqrt{5} + \sqrt{2}\right)}{\left(\sqrt{5} - \sqrt{2}\right)\left(\sqrt{5} + \sqrt{2}\right)}$$

$$= \frac{4\left(\sqrt{5} + \sqrt{2}\right)}{5 - 2} = \frac{4\left(\sqrt{5} + \sqrt{2}\right)}{3}$$

To write a radical quotient in lowest terms, factor the numerator and denominator, and then divide out any common factor(s).

$$\frac{5 + 15\sqrt{6}}{10} = \frac{5\left(1 + 3\sqrt{6}\right)}{5 \cdot 2} = \frac{1 + 3\sqrt{6}}{2}$$

Concepts

Examples

10.6 Solving Equations with Radicals

Solving a Radical Equation

Step 1 Isolate one radical on one side of the equation.

Step 2 Raise each side of the equation to a power that is the same as the index of the radical.

Step 3 Solve the resulting equation. If it still contains a radical, repeat Steps 1 and 2.

Step 4 Check all proposed solutions in the *original* equation. Discard any values that are not solutions of the original equation.

Solve.

$$\sqrt{2x + 3} - x = 0$$

$$\sqrt{2x + 3} = x \qquad \text{Add } x.$$

$$(\sqrt{2x + 3})^2 = x^2 \qquad \text{Square each side.}$$

$$2x + 3 = x^2 \qquad \text{Apply the exponent.}$$

$$x^2 - 2x - 3 = 0 \qquad \text{Standard form}$$

$$(x + 1)(x - 3) = 0 \qquad \text{Factor.}$$

$$x + 1 = 0 \quad \text{or} \quad x - 3 = 0 \qquad \text{Zero-factor property}$$

$$x = -1 \quad \text{or} \qquad x = 3 \qquad \text{Solve each equation.}$$

A check shows that 3 is a solution, but -1 is extraneous (as it leads to $2 = 0$, a false statement). The solution set is $\{3\}$.

10.7 Complex Numbers

$i = \sqrt{-1},$ and thus $i^2 = -1.$

For any positive number b, $\sqrt{-b} = i\sqrt{b}.$

To multiply radicals with negative radicands, first change each factor to the form $i\sqrt{b}$, and then multiply. The same procedure applies to quotients.

Simplify.

$$\sqrt{-25} = i\sqrt{25} = 5i$$

$$\sqrt{-3} \cdot \sqrt{-27}$$

$$= i\sqrt{3} \cdot i\sqrt{27} \qquad \sqrt{-b} = i\sqrt{b}$$

$$= i^2\sqrt{81} \qquad \text{Product rule}$$

$$= -1 \cdot 9 \qquad i^2 = -1; \text{ Take the square root.}$$

$$= -9 \qquad \text{Multiply.}$$

$$\frac{\sqrt{-18}}{\sqrt{-2}} = \frac{i\sqrt{18}}{i\sqrt{2}} = \sqrt{\frac{18}{2}} = \sqrt{9} = 3$$

Adding and Subtracting Complex Numbers

Add (or subtract) the real parts and add (or subtract) the imaginary parts.

Perform the operations.

$$(5 + 3i) + (8 - 7i) \qquad (5 + 3i) - (8 - 7i)$$

$$= 13 - 4i \qquad = -3 + 10i$$

Multiplying Complex Numbers

Multiply complex numbers using the FOIL method.

$$(2 + i)(5 - 3i)$$

$$= 10 - 6i + 5i - 3i^2 \qquad \text{FOIL method}$$

$$= 10 - i - 3(-1) \qquad \text{Add imaginary parts; } i^2 = -1$$

$$= 10 - i + 3 \qquad \text{Multiply.}$$

$$= 13 - i \qquad \text{Add real parts.}$$

Dividing Complex Numbers

Divide complex numbers by multiplying the numerator and the denominator by the conjugate of the denominator.

Use the fact that the product of a complex number and its conjugate is a real number.

$$(a + bi)(a - bi) = a^2 + b^2$$

$$\frac{10}{3 + i}$$

$$= \frac{10(3 - i)}{(3 + i)(3 - i)} \qquad \begin{array}{l}\text{Multiply both numerator} \\ \text{and denominator by the} \\ \text{conjugate of the denominator.}\end{array}$$

$$= \frac{10(3 - i)}{3^2 + 1^2} \qquad (a + bi)(a - bi) = a^2 + b^2$$

$$= \frac{10(3 - i)}{10} \qquad \text{Apply the exponents. Add.}$$

$$= 3 - i \qquad \text{Divide out the common factor.}$$

Chapter 10 **Review Exercises**

10.1 *Find each root.*

1. $\sqrt{144}$

2. $-\sqrt{289}$

3. $-\sqrt{-841}$

4. $\sqrt[3]{216}$

5. $\sqrt[5]{-32}$

6. $\sqrt{x^2}$

7. $\sqrt[3]{x^3}$

8. $\sqrt[4]{x^{20}}$

Graph each function, and give its domain and range.

9. $f(x) = \sqrt{x-1}$

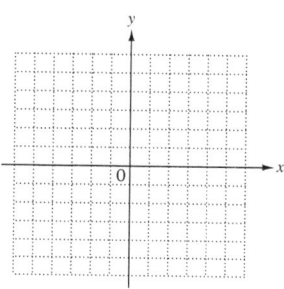

10. $f(x) = \sqrt[3]{x} - 2$

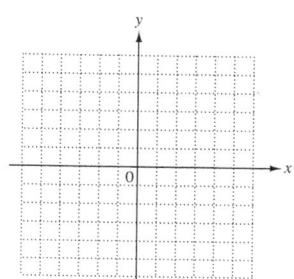

Use a calculator to approximate each radical to three decimal places.

11. $\sqrt{40}$

12. $\sqrt{77}$

13. $\sqrt{310}$

14. CONCEPT CHECK Under what conditions is $\sqrt[n]{a}$ not a real number?

Solve each problem.

15. The time t in seconds for one complete swing of a pendulum is given by

$$t = 2\pi\sqrt{\frac{L}{g}},$$

where L is the length of the pendulum in feet, and g, the force due to gravity, is about 32 ft per sec². Find the time of a complete swing of a 3-ft pendulum to the nearest tenth of a second.

16. Use Heron's formula

$$\mathscr{A} = \sqrt{s(s-a)(s-b)(s-c)},$$

where $s = \frac{1}{2}(a+b+c)$, to find the area of a triangle with sides of lengths 11 in., 13 in., and 20 in.

10.2 *Evaluate each exponential.*

17. $49^{1/2}$

18. $-8^{1/3}$

19. $(-16)^{1/4}$

20. $16^{5/4}$

21. $-8^{2/3}$

22. $\left(\dfrac{36}{25}\right)^{3/2}$

23. $\left(-\dfrac{1}{8}\right)^{-5/3}$

24. $\left(\dfrac{81}{10,000}\right)^{-3/4}$

Write each radical as an exponential and simplify. Leave answers in radical form as possible. Assume that all variables represent positive real numbers.

25. $\sqrt{3^{18}}$

26. $\sqrt[3]{7^9}$

27. $\sqrt[5]{y} \cdot \sqrt[3]{y}$

28. $\dfrac{\sqrt[3]{y^2}}{\sqrt[4]{y}}$

Simplify each expression. Assume that all variables represent positive real numbers.

29. $5^{1/4} \cdot 5^{7/4}$

30. $\dfrac{96^{2/3}}{96^{-1/3}}$

31. $\dfrac{(a^{1/3})^4}{a^{2/3}}$

32. $\dfrac{y^{-1/3} \cdot y^{5/6}}{y}$

33. $\left(\dfrac{z^{-1}x^{-3/5}}{2^{-2}z^{-1/2}x}\right)^{-1}$

34. $r^{-1/2}(r + r^{3/2})$

Write each radical as an exponential and simplify. Leave answers in exponential form. Assume that all variables represent positive real numbers.

35. $\sqrt[8]{s^4}$

36. $\sqrt[6]{r^9}$

37. $\dfrac{\sqrt{p^5}}{p^2}$

38. $\sqrt[4]{k^3} \cdot \sqrt{k^3}$

39. $\sqrt[3]{m^5} \cdot \sqrt[3]{m^8}$

40. $\sqrt[4]{\sqrt[3]{z}}$

10.3 *Simplify. Assume that all variables represent positive real numbers.*

41. $\sqrt{6} \cdot \sqrt{11}$

42. $\sqrt{5} \cdot \sqrt{r}$

43. $\sqrt[3]{6} \cdot \sqrt[3]{5}$

44. $\sqrt[4]{7} \cdot \sqrt[4]{3}$

45. $\sqrt{20}$

46. $-\sqrt{125}$

47. $\sqrt[3]{-108x^4y}$

48. $\sqrt[3]{64p^4q^6}$

49. $\sqrt{\dfrac{49}{81}}$

50. $\sqrt{\dfrac{y^3}{144}}$

51. $\sqrt[3]{\dfrac{m^{15}}{27}}$

52. $\sqrt[3]{\dfrac{r^2}{8}}$

53. $\dfrac{\sqrt[3]{2^4}}{\sqrt[4]{32}}$

54. $\dfrac{\sqrt{x}}{\sqrt[5]{x}}$

55. $\sqrt[4]{2} \cdot \sqrt{10}$

56. $\sqrt{5} \cdot \sqrt[3]{3}$

Find the distance between each pair of points.

57. $(2, 7)$ and $(-1, -4)$

58. $(-3, -5)$ and $(4, -3)$

10.4 *Perform the indicated operations. Assume that all variables represent positive real numbers.*

59. $2\sqrt{8} - 3\sqrt{50}$

60. $8\sqrt{80} - 3\sqrt{45}$

61. $-\sqrt{27y} + 2\sqrt{75y}$

62. $2\sqrt{54m^3} + 5\sqrt{96m^3}$

63. $3\sqrt[3]{54} + 5\sqrt[3]{16}$

64. $-6\sqrt[4]{32} + \sqrt[4]{512}$

10.5 *Multiply, and then simplify each product.*

65. $3\left(\sqrt{20} - \sqrt{45}\right)$

66. $\left(\sqrt{3} + 1\right)\left(\sqrt{3} - 2\right)$

67. $\left(\sqrt{7} + \sqrt{5}\right)\left(\sqrt{7} - \sqrt{5}\right)$

68. $\left(3\sqrt{2} + 1\right)\left(2\sqrt{2} - 3\right)$

69. $\left(\sqrt{13} - 2\right)^2$

70. $\left(\sqrt{5} + \sqrt{7}\right)^2$

Rationalize each denominator. Assume that all variables represent positive real numbers.

71. $\dfrac{\sqrt{6}}{\sqrt{5}}$

72. $\dfrac{-6\sqrt{3}}{\sqrt{2}}$

73. $-\sqrt[3]{\dfrac{9}{25}}$

74. $\sqrt[3]{\dfrac{108m^3}{n^5}}$

75. $\dfrac{1}{\sqrt{2} + \sqrt{7}}$

76. $\dfrac{-5}{\sqrt{6} - 3}$

Write each quotient in lowest terms.

77. $\dfrac{2 - 2\sqrt{5}}{8}$

78. $\dfrac{-18 + \sqrt{27}}{6}$

10.6 *Solve each equation.*

79. $\sqrt{8x + 9} = 5$

80. $\sqrt{2z - 3} - 3 = 0$

81. $\sqrt{3m + 1} = -1$

82. $\sqrt{7z + 1} = z + 1$

83. $3\sqrt{m} = \sqrt{10m - 9}$

84. $\sqrt{p^2 + 3p + 7} = p + 2$

85. $\sqrt{x + 2} - \sqrt{x - 3} = 1$

86. $\sqrt[3]{5m - 1} = \sqrt[3]{3m - 2}$

87. $\sqrt[4]{x + 6} = \sqrt[4]{2x}$

10.7 *Write as a product of a real number and i.*

88. $\sqrt{-25}$

89. $\sqrt{-200}$

90. $\sqrt{-160}$

Perform the indicated operations. Give answers in standard form.

91. $(2 + 5i) + (8 - 7i)$

92. $(5 + 4i) - (-9 - 3i)$

93. $\sqrt{-5} \cdot \sqrt{-7}$

94. $\sqrt{-25} \cdot \sqrt{-81}$

95. $\dfrac{\sqrt{-72}}{\sqrt{-8}}$

96. $(2 + 3i)(1 - i)$

97. $(6 - 2i)^2$

98. $\dfrac{3 - i}{2 + i}$

Simplify each power of i.

99. i^{11}

100. i^{52}

101. i^{-13}

102. i^{-10}

Chapter 10 Mixed Review Exercises

Simplify. Assume that all variables represent positive real numbers.

1. $-\sqrt{169a^2b^4}$

2. $1000^{-2/3}$

3. $\dfrac{y^{-1/3} \cdot y^{5/6}}{y}$

4. $\dfrac{z^{-1/4}x^{1/2}}{z^{1/2}x^{-1/4}}$

5. $\sqrt[4]{k^{24}}$

6. $\sqrt[3]{54z^9t^8}$

7. $5i(3 - 7i)$

8. $\sqrt[3]{2} \cdot \sqrt[4]{5}$

9. $\left(7\sqrt{a} - 5\right)^2$

10. $-5\sqrt{18} + 12\sqrt{72}$

11. $8\sqrt[3]{x^3y^2} - 2x\sqrt[3]{y^2}$

12. $\left(\sqrt{5} - \sqrt{3}\right)\left(\sqrt{7} + \sqrt{3}\right)$

13. $\dfrac{-1}{\sqrt{12}}$

14. $\sqrt[3]{\dfrac{12}{25}}$

15. $\dfrac{2\sqrt{z}}{\sqrt{z} - 2}, \quad z \neq 4$

16. $\sqrt{-49}$

17. $(4 - 9i) + (-1 + 2i)$

18. $\dfrac{\sqrt{50}}{\sqrt{-2}}$

Solve each equation.

19. $\sqrt{x + 4} = x - 2$

20. $\sqrt{6 + 2x} - 1 = \sqrt{7 - 2x}$

Solve each problem.

21. Carpenters stabilize wall frames with a diagonal brace, as shown in the figure. The length of the brace is given by

$$L = \sqrt{H^2 + W^2}.$$

(a) Solve this formula for H.

(b) If the bottom of the brace is attached 9 ft from the corner and the brace is 12 ft long, how far up the corner post should it be nailed? Give the answer to the nearest tenth of a foot.

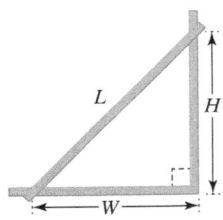

22. Find the perimeter of a triangular electronic highway road sign having the dimensions shown in the figure.

Chapter 10 *Test*

The Chapter Test Prep Videos with step-by-step solutions are available in MyMathLab or on YouTube at **https://goo.gl/3rBuO5**

Find each root.

1. $-\sqrt{841}$

2. $\sqrt[3]{-512}$

3. $125^{1/3}$

4. For $\sqrt{146.25}$, which choice gives the best estimate?

   A. 10   **B.** 11   **C.** 12   **D.** 13

Use a calculator to approximate each radical to three decimal places.

5. $\sqrt{478}$

6. $\sqrt[3]{-832}$

7. Graph the function, and give its domain and range.

$$f(x) = \sqrt{x+6}$$

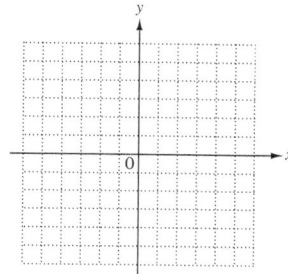

8. Use the Pythagorean theorem to find the exact length of side b in the figure.

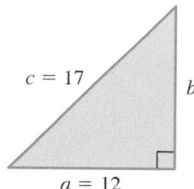

$c = 17$, b, $a = 12$

Simplify each expression. Assume that all variables represent positive real numbers.

9. $(-64)^{-4/3}$

10. $\left(\dfrac{16}{25}\right)^{-3/2}$

11. $7^{3/4} \cdot 7^{-1/4}$

12. $\left(\dfrac{x^{-4}y^{-6}}{x^{-2}y^3}\right)^{-2/3}$

13. $\dfrac{3^{2/5}x^{-1/4}y^{2/5}}{3^{-8/5}x^{7/4}y^{1/10}}$

14. $\sqrt{54x^5y^6}$

15. $\sqrt[4]{32a^7b^{13}}$

16. $\sqrt{2} \cdot \sqrt[3]{5}$
(Express as a radical.)

17. $2\sqrt{300} + 5\sqrt{48}$

18. $3\sqrt{20} - 5\sqrt{80} + 4\sqrt{500}$ **19.** $\left(7\sqrt{5} + 4\right)\left(2\sqrt{5} - 1\right)$ **20.** $\left(\sqrt{3} - 2\sqrt{5}\right)^2$

21. $\dfrac{-5}{\sqrt{40}}$ **22.** $\dfrac{2}{\sqrt[3]{5}}$ **23.** $\dfrac{-4}{\sqrt{7} + \sqrt{5}}$

24. Write $\dfrac{6 + \sqrt{24}}{2}$ in lowest terms.   **25.** Find the distance between the points $(-3, 8)$ and $(2, 7)$.

Solve each equation.

26. $\sqrt[3]{5x} = \sqrt[3]{2x - 3}$ **27.** $\sqrt{7 - x} + 5 = x$ **28.** $\sqrt{x + 4} - \sqrt{1 - x} = -1$

29. The following formula from physics relates the velocity V of sound to the temperature T.

$$V = \frac{V_0}{\sqrt{1 - kT}}$$

(a) Approximate V to the nearest tenth if $V_0 = 50$, $k = 0.01$, and $T = 30$.

(b) Solve the formula for T.

Perform the indicated operations. Give answers in standard form.

30. $(-2 + 5i) - (3 + 6i) - 7i$ **31.** $(-4 + 2i)(3 - i)$ **32.** $\dfrac{7 + i}{1 - i}$

33. Simplify i^{35}.

34. Answer *true* or *false* to each of the following.

(a) $i^2 = -1$ (b) $i = \sqrt{-1}$ (c) $i = -1$ (d) $\sqrt{-3} = i\sqrt{3}$

Chapters R–10 *Cumulative Review Exercises*

Solve each equation or inequality.

1. $7 - (4 + 3t) + 2t = -6(t - 2) - 5$

2. $\frac{1}{3}x + \frac{1}{4}(x + 8) = x + 7$

3. $|6x - 9| = |-4x + 2|$

4. $-5 - 3(x - 2) < 11 - 2(x + 2)$

5. $1 + 4x > 5$ and $-2x > -6$

6. $-2 < 1 - 3x < 7$

Work each problem.

7. Write the standard form of the equation of the line through the points $(-4, 6)$ and $(7, -6)$.

8. Choose the correct response: The lines with equations $2x + 3y = 8$ and $6y = 4x + 16$ are

    A. parallel   **B.** perpendicular   **C.** neither.

9. Consider the graph of $f(x) = -3x + 6$. Give the intercepts.

10. What is the slope of the line described in **Exercise 9?**

11. Graph the inequality $-2x + y < -6$.

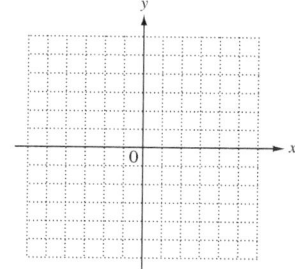

12. Find the measures of the marked angles.

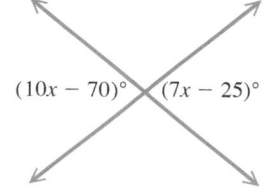

$(10x - 70)°$ $(7x - 25)°$

Solve each system.

13. $3x - y = 23$
$2x + 3y = 8$

14. $5x + 2y = 7$
$10x + 4y = 12$

15. $2x + y - z = 5$
$6x + 3y - 3z = 15$
$4x + 2y - 2z = 10$

16. At one time, sending five 2-oz letters and three 3-oz letters by first-class mail cost $5.80. Sending three 2-oz letters and five 3-oz letters cost $6.20. What was the postage rate for one 2-oz letter and for one 3-oz letter? (Data from U.S. Postal Service.)

Perform the indicated operations.

17. $(3k^3 - 5k^2 + 8k - 2) - (4k^3 + 11k + 7)$
$\ + (2k^2 - 5k)$

18. $(8x - 7)(x + 3)$

19. $\dfrac{8z^3 - 16z^2 + 24z}{8z^2}$

20. $\dfrac{6y^4 - 3y^3 + 5y^2 + 6y - 9}{2y + 1}$

Factor each polynomial completely.

21. $2p^2 - 5pq + 3q^2$

22. $18k^4 + 9k^2 - 20$

23. $x^3 + 512$

Perform each operation and express answers in lowest terms.

24. $\dfrac{y^2 + y - 12}{y^3 + 9y^2 + 20y} \div \dfrac{y^2 - 9}{y^3 + 3y^2}$

25. $\dfrac{1}{x + y} + \dfrac{3}{x - y}$

26. $\dfrac{x^2 - 12x + 36}{x^2 + 2x - 8} \cdot \dfrac{x^2 + 4x}{x^2 - 6x}$

Simplify.

27. $\dfrac{\dfrac{-6}{x - 2}}{\dfrac{8}{3x - 6}}$

28. $\dfrac{\dfrac{1}{a} - \dfrac{1}{b}}{\dfrac{a}{b} - \dfrac{b}{a}}$

29. $\dfrac{\dfrac{5r^2 s^3}{9}}{\dfrac{10 r^4 s^5}{27}}$

30. $27^{-5/3}$

31. $\dfrac{x^{-2/3}}{x^{-3/4}}, \quad x \neq 0$

32. $8\sqrt{20} + 3\sqrt{80} - 2\sqrt{500}$

33. $\dfrac{-9}{\sqrt{80}}$

34. $\dfrac{4}{\sqrt{6} - \sqrt{5}}$

35. $\dfrac{12}{\sqrt[3]{2}}$

36. Find the distance between the points $(-4, 4)$ and $(-2, 9)$.

Solve.

37. $2x^2 + 11x + 15 = 0$

38. $5t(t - 1) = 2(1 - t)$

39. $4x^2 - 28x = -49$

40. $\sqrt{8x - 4} - \sqrt{7x + 2} = 0$

Solve each problem.

41. The current of a river runs at 3 mph. Brent's boat can travel 36 mi downstream in the same time that it takes to travel 24 mi upstream. Find the rate of the boat in still water.

42. How many liters of pure alcohol must be mixed with 40 L of 18% alcohol to obtain a 22% alcohol solution?

43. A jar containing only dimes and quarters has 29 coins with a face value of $4.70. How many of each denomination are there?

44. Brenda rides her bike 4 mph faster than her husband, Chuck. If Brenda can ride 48 mi in the same time that Chuck can ride 24 mi, what are their rates?

11

Quadratic Equations, Inequalities, and Functions

Quadratic functions, one of the topics of this chapter, have graphs that are *parabolas.* Cross sections of telescopes, satellite dishes, and automobile headlights form parabolas, as do the cables that support suspension bridges. The trajectory of a water spout follows a *parabolic* path.

11.1 Solving Quadratic Equations by the Square Root Property

11.2 Solving Quadratic Equations by Completing the Square

11.3 Solving Quadratic Equations by the Quadratic Formula

11.4 Equations Quadratic in Form

Summary Exercises *Applying Methods for Solving Quadratic Equations*

11.5 Formulas and Further Applications

11.6 Graphs of Quadratic Functions

11.7 More about Parabolas and Their Applications

11.8 Polynomial and Rational Inequalities

11.1 Solving Quadratic Equations by the Square Root Property

OBJECTIVES

1 Review the zero-factor property.

2 Solve equations of the form $x^2 = k$, where $k > 0$.

3 Solve equations of the form $(ax + b)^2 = k$, where $k > 0$.

4 Solve quadratic equations with nonreal complex solutions.

OBJECTIVE ▸ **1** **Review the zero-factor property.** Recall that a *quadratic equation* is defined as follows.

Quadratic Equation

A **quadratic equation** (in x here) can be written in the form

$$ax^2 + bx + c = 0,$$

where a, b, and c are real numbers and $a \neq 0$. The given form is called **standard form**.

Examples: $4x^2 + 4x - 5 = 0$ and $3x^2 = 4x - 8$ Quadratic equations (The first equation is in standard form.)

A quadratic equation is a *second-degree equation*—that is, an equation with a squared variable term and no terms of greater degree.

The **zero-factor property** can be used to solve some quadratic equations.

Zero-Factor Property

If a and b are real numbers and if $ab = 0$, then $a = 0$ or $b = 0$.

In words, if the product of two numbers is 0, then at least one of the numbers must be 0. One number must be 0, but both *may* be 0.

---

1 Solve each equation using the zero-factor property.

(GS) **(a)** $x^2 - 2x - 15 = 0$

$(x + \underline{\hspace{0.5cm}})(x - \underline{\hspace{0.5cm}}) = 0$

$x + \underline{\hspace{0.5cm}} = 0$ or $x - 5 = 0$

$x = -3$ or $x = \underline{\hspace{0.5cm}}$

The solution set is $\{\underline{\hspace{0.5cm}}, \underline{\hspace{0.5cm}}\}$.

(b) $2x^2 - 3x + 1 = 0$

(c) $x^2 = 4$

EXAMPLE 1   **Solving Quadratic Equations by the Zero-Factor Property**

Solve each equation using the zero-factor property.

(a) $x^2 + 4x + 3 = 0$

$(x + 3)(x + 1) = 0$ Factor.

$x + 3 = 0$ or $x + 1 = 0$ Zero-factor property

$x = -3$ or $x = -1$ Solve each equation.

The solution set is $\{-3, -1\}$.

(b) $x^2 = 9$

$x^2 - 9 = 0$ Subtract 9.

$(x + 3)(x - 3) = 0$ Factor.

$x + 3 = 0$ or $x - 3 = 0$ Zero-factor property

$x = -3$ or $x = 3$ Solve each equation.

The solution set is $\{-3, 3\}$.

◀ **Work Problem** **1** **at the Side.**

Answers

1. (a) 3; 5; 3; 5; −3; 5

(b) $\left\{\frac{1}{2}, 1\right\}$ **(c)** $\{-2, 2\}$

Not all quadratic expressions can easily be factored, so we develop other methods for solving quadratic equations.

OBJECTIVE **2** **Solve equations of the form** $x^2 = k$, **where** $k > 0$. In **Example 1(b),** we might also have solved $x^2 = 9$ by noticing that x must be a number whose square is 9. Thus we have

$$x = \sqrt{9} = 3 \quad \text{or} \quad x = -\sqrt{9} = -3.$$

This is generalized as the **square root property.**

Square Root Property

If k is a positive number and if $x^2 = k$, then

$$x = \sqrt{k} \quad \text{or} \quad x = -\sqrt{k}.$$

The solution set is $\left\{ -\sqrt{k}, \sqrt{k} \right\}$, which can be written $\left\{ \pm\sqrt{k} \right\}$. (The symbol $\pm$ is read "*positive or negative*" or "*plus or minus.*")

EXAMPLE 2 **Solving Quadratic Equations of the Form** $x^2 = k$

Solve each equation. Express radicals in simplified form.

(a) $x^2 = 16$

By the square root property, if $x^2 = 16$, then

$$x = \sqrt{16} = 4 \quad \text{or} \quad x = -\sqrt{16} = -4.$$

Check each value by substituting it for x in the original equation. The solution set is $\{-4, 4\}$, or $\{\pm 4\}$. — This $\pm$ notation indicates *two* solutions, one *positive* and one *negative.*

(b)
$$x^2 - 5 = 0$$
$$x^2 = 5 \qquad \text{Add 5.}$$
$$x = \sqrt{5} \quad \text{or} \quad x = -\sqrt{5} \qquad \text{Square root property}$$

The solution set is $\left\{ -\sqrt{5}, \sqrt{5} \right\}$, or $\left\{ \pm\sqrt{5} \right\}$.

(c)
$$5m^2 - 32 = 8$$
$$5m^2 = 40 \qquad \text{Add 32.}$$
$$m^2 = 8 \qquad \text{Divide by 5.}$$

Don't stop here. Simplify the radicals.

$$m = \sqrt{8} \quad \text{or} \quad m = -\sqrt{8} \qquad \text{Square root property}$$
$$m = 2\sqrt{2} \quad \text{or} \quad m = -2\sqrt{2} \qquad \sqrt{8} = \sqrt{4} \cdot \sqrt{2} = 2\sqrt{2}$$

CHECK
$$5m^2 - 32 = 8 \qquad \text{Original equation}$$
$$5\left(2\sqrt{2}\right)^2 - 32 \overset{?}{=} 8 \qquad \text{Let } m = 2\sqrt{2}.$$
$$5(8) - 32 \overset{?}{=} 8 \qquad \left(2\sqrt{2}\right)^2 = 2^2 \cdot \left(\sqrt{2}\right)^2 = 4 \cdot 2 = 8$$
$$40 - 32 \overset{?}{=} 8 \qquad \text{Multiply.}$$
$$8 = 8 \;\checkmark\; \text{True}$$

The check of the other value is similar. The solution set is

$$\left\{ -2\sqrt{2}, 2\sqrt{2} \right\}, \quad \text{or} \quad \left\{ \pm 2\sqrt{2} \right\}.$$

Work Problem **2** **at the Side.** ▶

---

2 Solve each equation. Express radicals in simplified form.

(a) $x^2 = 49$

(b) $x^2 - 11 = 0$

(c) $3x^2 - 8 = 88$

Answers

2. **(a)** $\{-7, 7\}$ **(b)** $\left\{ -\sqrt{11}, \sqrt{11} \right\}$
(c) $\left\{ -4\sqrt{2}, 4\sqrt{2} \right\}$

3 Solve the problem.

Tim is dropping roofing nails from the top of a roof 25 ft high into a large bucket on the ground. Use the formula in **Example 3** to determine how long it will take a nail dropped from 25 ft to hit the bottom of the bucket.

EXAMPLE 3 **Using the Square Root Property in an Application**

Galileo Galilei developed a formula for freely falling objects,

$$d = 16t^2,$$

where d is the distance in feet that an object falls (disregarding air resistance) in t seconds, regardless of weight. The Leaning Tower of Pisa is about 180 ft tall. Use the formula to determine how long it would take an object dropped from the top of the tower to fall to the ground. (Data from www.brittanica.com)

$d = 16t^2$	Galileo's formula
$180 = 16t^2$	Let $d = 180$.
$11.25 = t^2$	Divide by 16.
$t = \sqrt{11.25}$ or $t = -\sqrt{11.25}$	Square root property

Time cannot be negative, so we discard $t = -\sqrt{11.25}$. Using a calculator, $\sqrt{11.25} \approx 3.4$ so $t \approx 3.4$. The object would fall to the ground in about 3.4 sec.

◀ **Work Problem 3 at the Side.**

OBJECTIVE **3** Solve equations of the form $(ax + b)^2 = k$, where $k > 0$.
We can extend the square root property to solve equations in which the base is a binomial.

---

4 Solve each equation.

(a) $(x + 2)^2 = 36$

EXAMPLE 4 **Solving Quadratic Equations of the Form $(x + b)^2 = k$**

Solve each equation.

(a) $\boxed{\text{Use } x - 3 \text{ as the base.}}$ $(x - 3)^2 = 16$

$x - 3 = \sqrt{16}$	or $x - 3 = -\sqrt{16}$	Square root property
$x - 3 = 4$	or $x - 3 = -4$	$\sqrt{16} = 4$
$x = 7$	or $x = -1$	Add 3.

CHECK

$(x - 3)^2 = 16$		$(x - 3)^2 = 16$	
$(7 - 3)^2 \overset{?}{=} 16$	Let $x = 7$.	$(-1 - 3)^2 \overset{?}{=} 16$	Let $x = -1$.
$4^2 \overset{?}{=} 16$	Subtract.	$(-4)^2 \overset{?}{=} 16$	Subtract.
$16 = 16$ ✓	True	$16 = 16$ ✓	True

True statements result, so the solution set is $\{-1, 7\}$.

(b) $(x + 1)^2 = 6$

$x + 1 = \sqrt{6}$	or $x + 1 = -\sqrt{6}$	Square root property
$x = -1 + \sqrt{6}$	or $x = -1 - \sqrt{6}$	Add -1.

CHECK $\left(-1 + \sqrt{6} + 1\right)^2 = \left(\sqrt{6}\right)^2 = 6$ ✓ Let $x = -1 + \sqrt{6}$.

$\left(-1 - \sqrt{6} + 1\right)^2 = \left(-\sqrt{6}\right)^2 = 6$ ✓ Let $x = -1 - \sqrt{6}$.

The solution set is $\left\{-1 + \sqrt{6}, -1 - \sqrt{6}\right\}$, or $\left\{-1 \pm \sqrt{6}\right\}$.

◀ **Work Problem 4 at the Side.**

GS (b) $(x - 4)^2 = 3$

$x - 4 = $ _____ or $x - 4 = $ _____

$x = $ _____ or $x = $ _____

The solution set is _____.

Answers

3. 1.25 sec

4. (a) $\{-8, 4\}$

(b) $\sqrt{3}; -\sqrt{3}; 4 + \sqrt{3}; 4 - \sqrt{3};$
$\left\{4 + \sqrt{3}, 4 - \sqrt{3}\right\}$

EXAMPLE 5 Solving a Quadratic Equation of the Form $(ax + b)^2 = k$

Solve $(3r - 2)^2 = 27$.

$$(3r - 2)^2 = 27$$

$3r - 2 = \sqrt{27}$ or $3r - 2 = -\sqrt{27}$ Square root property

$3r - 2 = 3\sqrt{3}$ or $3r - 2 = -3\sqrt{3}$ $\sqrt{27} = \sqrt{9} \cdot \sqrt{3}$
$= 3\sqrt{3}$

$3r = 2 + 3\sqrt{3}$ or $\quad 3r = 2 - 3\sqrt{3}$ Add 2.

$r = \dfrac{2 + 3\sqrt{3}}{3}$ or $\quad r = \dfrac{2 - 3\sqrt{3}}{3}$ Divide by 3.

CHECK $\qquad\qquad (3r - 2)^2 = 27$ Original equation

$$\left(3 \cdot \frac{2 + 3\sqrt{3}}{3} - 2\right)^2 \overset{?}{=} 27 \qquad \text{Let } r = \frac{2 + 3\sqrt{3}}{3}.$$

$$\left(2 + 3\sqrt{3} - 2\right)^2 \overset{?}{=} 27 \qquad \text{Multiply.}$$

$(ab)^2 = a^2 b^2$ → $\left(3\sqrt{3}\right)^2 \overset{?}{=} 27$ Subtract.

$$27 = 27 \checkmark \quad \text{True}$$

The check of the other value is similar. The solution set is

$$\left\{\frac{2 + 3\sqrt{3}}{3}, \frac{2 - 3\sqrt{3}}{3}\right\}.$$

These fractions **cannot** be simplified. 3 is **not** a common factor in the numerator.

—— **Work Problem ⑤ at the Side.** ▶

OBJECTIVE ▶ ④ Solve quadratic equations with nonreal complex solutions.
If $k < 0$ in the equation $x^2 = k$, then there will be two nonreal complex solutions.

EXAMPLE 6 Solving for Nonreal Complex Solutions

Solve each equation.

(a) $\qquad\qquad x^2 = -15$

$x = \sqrt{-15}$ or $x = -\sqrt{-15}$ Square root property

$x = i\sqrt{15}$ or $x = -i\sqrt{15}$ $\sqrt{-a} = i\sqrt{a}$

The solution set is $\left\{i\sqrt{15}, -i\sqrt{15}\right\}$.

(b) $\qquad (t + 2)^2 = -16$

$t + 2 = \sqrt{-16}$ or $t + 2 = -\sqrt{-16}$ Square root property

$t + 2 = 4i$ or $t + 2 = -4i$ $\sqrt{-16} = 4i$

$t = -2 + 4i$ or $t = -2 - 4i$ Add -2.

The solution set is $\{-2 + 4i, -2 - 4i\}$.

—— **Work Problem ⑥ at the Side.** ▶

⑤ Solve each equation.

(a) $(2x - 5)^2 = 18$

(b) $(5x + 1)^2 = 7$

⑥ Solve each equation.

(a) $x^2 = -17$

(b) $(k + 5)^2 = -100$

Answers

5. (a) $\left\{\dfrac{5 + 3\sqrt{2}}{2}, \dfrac{5 - 3\sqrt{2}}{2}\right\}$

   (b) $\left\{\dfrac{-1 + \sqrt{7}}{5}, \dfrac{-1 - \sqrt{7}}{5}\right\}$

6. (a) $\left\{i\sqrt{17}, -i\sqrt{17}\right\}$

   (b) $\{-5 + 10i, -5 - 10i\}$

11.1 Exercises | FOR EXTRA HELP | Go to MyMathLab *for worked-out, step-by-step solutions to exercises enclosed in a square* ▢ *and video solutions to* ▶ *exercises.*

1. CONCEPT CHECK Which of the following are quadratic equations?

   A. $x + 2y = 0$ **B.** $x^2 - 8x + 16 = 0$ **C.** $2x^2 - 5x = 3$ **D.** $x^3 + x^2 + 4 = 0$

2. CONCEPT CHECK Which quadratic equation identified in **Exercise 1** is in standard form?

CONCEPT CHECK *Match each equation in Column I with the correct description of its solution(s) in Column II.*

I		II	
3. $x^2 = 12$	**4.** $x^2 = -36$	**A.** Two nonreal complex solutions	**B.** Two integer solutions
5. $x^2 = \dfrac{25}{36}$	**6.** $x^2 = 25$	**C.** Two irrational solutions	**D.** Two rational solutions that are not integers

7. CONCEPT CHECK When a student was asked to solve

$$x^2 = 81,$$

she wrote $\{9\}$ as the solution set. Her teacher did not give her full credit. The student argued that because $9^2 = 81$, her answer had to be correct. *What Went Wrong?* Give the correct solution set.

8. CONCEPT CHECK When solving a quadratic equation, a student obtained the solutions

$$x = \frac{3 + 2\sqrt{5}}{2} \quad \text{or} \quad x = \frac{3 - 2\sqrt{5}}{2},$$

and wrote the solution set incorrectly as

$$\{3 + \sqrt{5},\ 3 - \sqrt{5}\}.$$

What Went Wrong? Give the correct solution set.

Solve each equation using the zero-factor property. **See Example 1.**

  9. $x^2 - x - 56 = 0$ **10.** $x^2 - 2x - 99 = 0$ **11.** $x^2 - 8x + 15 = 0$ **12.** $x^2 - 6x + 5 = 0$

 13. $x^2 = 121$ **14.** $x^2 = 144$ **15.** $3x^2 - 13x = 30$ **16.** $5x^2 - 14x = 3$

Solve each equation using the square root property. Express radicals in simplified form. **See Example 2.**

 17. $x^2 = 81$ ▶   **18.** $x^2 = 36$ **19.** $k^2 = 14$ ▶   **20.** $m^2 = 22$

 21. $t^2 = 48$ **22.** $x^2 = 54$ **23.** $x^2 = \dfrac{25}{4}$ **24.** $m^2 = \dfrac{36}{121}$

 25. $z^2 = 0.25$ **26.** $x^2 = 0.49$ **27.** $x^2 - 64 = 0$ **28.** $x^2 - 100 = 0$

29. $r^2 - 3 = 0$ **30.** $x^2 - 13 = 0$ **31.** $4x^2 - 72 = 0$ **32.** $5z^2 - 200 = 0$

33. $2x^2 + 7 = 61$ **34.** $2x^2 + 8 = 32$ **35.** $3x^2 - 8 = 64$ **36.** $2x^2 - 5 = 35$

37. $7x^2 = 4$ **38.** $3x^2 = 10$ **39.** $5x^2 + 4 = 8$ **40.** $4x^2 - 3 = 7$

*Solve each equation using the square root property. Express radicals in simplified form. **See Examples 4 and 5.***

41. $(x - 3)^2 = 25$ **42.** $(x - 7)^2 = 16$ **43.** $(x - 6)^2 = 49$

44. $(x - 4)^2 = 64$ **45.** $(x - 4)^2 = 3$ **46.** $(x + 3)^2 = 11$

47. $(x - 8)^2 = 27$ **48.** $(x - 5)^2 = 40$ **49.** $(3x + 2)^2 = 49$

50. $(5x + 3)^2 = 36$ **51.** $(4x - 3)^2 = 9$ **52.** $(7x - 5)^2 = 25$

53. $(5 - 2x)^2 = 30$ **54.** $(3 - 2x)^2 = 70$ **55.** $(3k + 1)^2 = 18$

56. $(5x + 6)^2 = 75$ **57.** $(4x - 1)^2 - 48 = 0$ **58.** $(2x - 5)^2 - 180 = 0$

*Solve each equation. (All solutions for these equations are nonreal complex numbers.) **See Example 6.***

59. $x^2 = -100$ **60.** $x^2 = -64$ **61.** $x^2 = -12$ **62.** $x^2 = -18$

63. $(x + 3)^2 = -4$ **64.** $(x - 5)^2 = -36$ **65.** $(r - 5)^2 = -3$

66. $(t + 6)^2 = -5$ **67.** $(6k - 1)^2 = -8$ **68.** $(4m - 7)^2 = -27$

Use Galileo's formula, $d = 16t^2$, to solve each problem. Round answers to the nearest tenth. **See Example 3.**

69. The sculpture of American presidents at Mount Rushmore National Memorial is 500 ft above the valley floor. How long would it take a rock dropped from the top of the sculpture to fall to the ground? (Data from www.travelsd.com)

70. The Gateway Arch in St. Louis, Missouri, is 630 ft tall. How long would it take an object dropped from the top of the arch to fall to the ground? (Data from www.gatewayarch.com)

Solve each problem. **See Example 3.**

71. An expert marksman can hold a silver dollar at forehead level, drop it, draw his gun, and shoot the coin as it passes waist level. The distance traveled by a falling object is given by

$$d = 16t^2,$$

where d is the distance (in feet) the object falls in t seconds. If the coin falls 4 ft, use the formula to find the time that elapses between the dropping of the coin and the shot.

72. The illumination produced by a light source depends on the distance from the source. For a particular light source, this relationship can be expressed as

$$I = \frac{4050}{d^2},$$

where I is the amount of illumination in footcandles and d is the distance from the light source (in feet). How far from the source is the illumination equal to 50 footcandles?

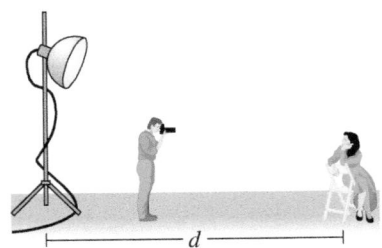

73. The area $\mathcal{A}$ of a circle with radius r is given by the formula

$$\mathcal{A} = \pi r^2.$$

If a circle has area 81π in.², what is its radius?

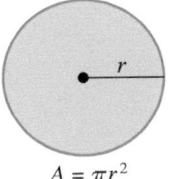

$A = \pi r^2$

74. The surface area S of a sphere with radius r is given by the formula

$$S = 4\pi r^2.$$

If a sphere has surface area 36π ft², what is its radius?

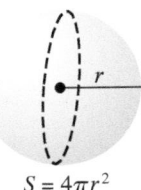

$S = 4\pi r^2$

11.2 Solving Quadratic Equations by Completing the Square

OBJECTIVE ① Solve quadratic equations by completing the square when the coefficient of the second-degree term is 1. The methods we have studied so far are not enough to solve an equation such as

$$x^2 + 8x + 10 = 0.$$

We could use the square root property to solve this equation if it was written in the form

Square of a binomial → $(x + k)^2 = n.$ ← Constant

The left side of the equation must be a perfect square trinomial that can be factored as $(x + k)^2$, the square of a binomial, and the right side must be a constant. This process is called **completing the square.**

Recall that the perfect square trinomial

$$x^2 + 8x + 16 \quad \text{can be factored as} \quad (x + 4)^2.$$

In the trinomial, the coefficient of x (the first-degree term) is 8 and the constant term is 16. If we take half of 8 and square it, we get the constant term, 16.

$$\left[\frac{1}{2}(8)\right]^2 = 4^2 = 16$$

Coefficient of x Constant

Similarly, in $\quad x^2 + 12x + 36, \quad \left[\frac{1}{2}(12)\right]^2 = 6^2 = 36,$

and in $\quad m^2 - 6m + 9, \quad \left[\frac{1}{2}(-6)\right]^2 = (-3)^2 = 9.$

This relationship is true in general and is the idea behind completing the square.

Work Problem ① at the Side. ▶

EXAMPLE 1   Completing the Square to Solve a Quadratic Equation

Solve $x^2 + 8x + 10 = 0$.

The trinomial on the left is nonfactorable, so this quadratic equation cannot be solved using the zero-factor property. It is not in the correct form to solve using the square root property. We can solve it by completing the square.

$$x^2 + 8x + 10 = 0 \qquad \text{Original equation}$$

Only terms with variables remain on the left side. → $x^2 + 8x = -10 \qquad$ Subtract 10.

$$\underbrace{x^2 + 8x + \underline{\ ?\ }}_{\text{Needs to be a perfect square trinomial}} = -10 \qquad \text{We must add a constant.}$$

Continued on Next Page

OBJECTIVES

① Solve quadratic equations by completing the square when the coefficient of the second-degree term is 1.

② Solve quadratic equations by completing the square when the coefficient of the second-degree term is not 1.

③ Simplify the terms of an equation before solving.

① Find the constant that must be added to make each expression a perfect square trinomial. Then factor the trinomial.

(a) $x^2 + 4x$

The coefficient of the first-degree term is ____.

$$\left[\frac{1}{2}(4)\right]^2 = \underline{\ \ } = \underline{\ \ }^2$$

The perfect square trinomial would be

$$x^2 + 4x + \underline{\ \ }.$$

It factors as _____.

(b) $t^2 - 2t + \underline{\ \ }$

It factors as _____.

(c) $m^2 + 5m + \underline{\ \ }$

It factors as _____.

Answers

1. (a) 4; 2; 4; 4; $(x + 2)^2$ **(b)** 1; $(t - 1)^2$

(c) $\frac{25}{4}$; $\left(m + \frac{5}{2}\right)^2$

2 Solve each equation.

(a) $n^2 + 6n + 4 = 0$

Isolate the terms with variables on the left side.

$$n^2 + 6n = \text{\underline{\hspace{1cm}}}$$

Take half the coefficient of the first-degree term and square the result.

$$\left[\frac{1}{2}(\text{\underline{\hspace{0.5cm}}})\right]^2 = \text{\underline{\hspace{0.5cm}}}^2 = \text{\underline{\hspace{0.5cm}}}$$

Add this result to each side of the equation, and factor on the left.

$$n^2 + 6n + 9 = -4 + \text{\underline{\hspace{1cm}}}$$

$$(\text{\underline{\hspace{1cm}}})^2 = 5$$

Complete the solution.

The solution set is

$$\{\text{\underline{\hspace{1cm}}}, \text{\underline{\hspace{1cm}}}\}.$$

(b) $x^2 + 2x - 10 = 0$

3 Solve $x^2 - 4x = 1$ by completing the square.

Answers

2. **(a)** -4; 6; 3; 9; 9; $n + 3$;
   $-3 + \sqrt{5}$; $-3 - \sqrt{5}$
   (b) $\{-1 + \sqrt{11}, -1 - \sqrt{11}\}$
3. $\{2 + \sqrt{5}, 2 - \sqrt{5}\}$

Take half the coefficient of the first-degree term, $8x$, and square the result.

$$\left[\frac{1}{2}(8)\right]^2 = 4^2 = 16 \leftarrow \text{Desired constant}$$

We add this constant, 16, to *each* side of the equation.

$$x^2 + 8x + 16 = -10 + 16 \qquad \text{Add 16 to each side.}$$

> This is a key step.

$$(x + 4)^2 = 6 \qquad \begin{array}{l}\text{Factor on the left.}\\\text{Add on the right.}\end{array}$$

$$x + 4 = \sqrt{6} \qquad \text{or} \quad x + 4 = -\sqrt{6} \qquad \text{Square root property}$$

$$x = -4 + \sqrt{6} \quad \text{or} \qquad x = -4 - \sqrt{6} \qquad \text{Add } -4.$$

CHECK $\qquad x^2 + 8x + 10 = 0 \qquad$ Original equation

$$(-4 + \sqrt{6})^2 + 8(-4 + \sqrt{6}) + 10 \stackrel{?}{=} 0 \qquad \text{Let } x = -4 + \sqrt{6}.$$

$$16 - 8\sqrt{6} + 6 - 32 + 8\sqrt{6} + 10 \stackrel{?}{=} 0 \qquad \text{Multiply.}$$

$$0 = 0 \checkmark \qquad \text{True}$$

> Remember the middle term when squaring $-4 + \sqrt{6}$.

The check of $-4 - \sqrt{6}$ is similar. The solution set is

$$\{-4 + \sqrt{6}, -4 - \sqrt{6}\}.$$

◀ **Work Problem 2** at the Side.

The process of completing the square in **Example 1** to write

$$x^2 + 8x + 10 = 0 \quad \text{as} \quad (x + 4)^2 = 6$$

changes only the form of the equation. To see this, multiply out the left side of $(x + 4)^2 = 6$, and write the equation in standard form to obtain the original equation $x^2 + 8x + 10 = 0$.

> **EXAMPLE 2** **Completing the Square to Solve a Quadratic Equation**

Solve $x^2 - 6x = 12$ by completing the square.

To complete the square, take half the coefficient of x and square it.

$$\frac{1}{2}(-6) = -3 \quad \text{and} \quad (-3)^2 = 9$$

Coefficient of x

Add the result, **9**, to each side of the equation.

$$x^2 - 6x = 12 \qquad \text{Given equation}$$

$$x^2 - 6x + 9 = 12 + 9 \qquad \text{Add 9.}$$

$$(x - 3)^2 = 21 \qquad \begin{array}{l}\text{Factor on the left.}\\\text{Add on the right.}\end{array}$$

$$x - 3 = \sqrt{21} \qquad \text{or} \quad x - 3 = -\sqrt{21} \qquad \text{Square root property}$$

$$x = 3 + \sqrt{21} \quad \text{or} \qquad x = 3 - \sqrt{21} \qquad \text{Add 3.}$$

A check confirms that the solution set is $\{3 + \sqrt{21}, 3 - \sqrt{21}\}$.

◀ **Work Problem 3** at the Side.

Completing the Square to Solve $ax^2 + bx + c = 0$ (Where $a \neq 0$)

Step 1 **Be sure the second-degree term has coefficient 1.**

- If the coefficient of the second-degree term is 1, go to Step 2.
- If it is not 1, but some other nonzero number a, divide each side of the equation by a.

Step 2 **Write the equation in correct form.** Make sure that all variable terms are on one side of the equality symbol and the constant term is on the other side.

Step 3 **Complete the square.**

- Take half the coefficient of the first-degree term, and square it.
- Add the square to each side of the equation.
- Factor the variable side, which should be a perfect square trinomial, as the square of a binomial. Add on the other side.

Step 4 **Solve** the equation using the square root property.

EXAMPLE 3 Completing the Square ($a = 1$)

Solve $k^2 + 5k - 1 = 0$.

   The coefficient of the second-degree term is 1, so begin with Step 2.

Step 2 $k^2 + 5k = 1$ Add 1 to each side.

Step 3   Take half the coefficient of the first-degree term. Square the result.

$$\left[\frac{1}{2}(5)\right]^2 = \left(\frac{5}{2}\right)^2 = \frac{25}{4}$$

$$k^2 + 5k + \frac{25}{4} = 1 + \frac{25}{4} \quad \boxed{\text{Add the square to each side of the equation.}}$$

$$\left(k + \frac{5}{2}\right)^2 = \frac{29}{4} \quad \begin{array}{l}\text{Factor on the left.}\\ \text{Add on the right.}\end{array}$$

Step 4 $k + \dfrac{5}{2} = \sqrt{\dfrac{29}{4}}$ or $k + \dfrac{5}{2} = -\sqrt{\dfrac{29}{4}}$ Square root property

$k + \dfrac{5}{2} = \dfrac{\sqrt{29}}{2}$ or $k + \dfrac{5}{2} = -\dfrac{\sqrt{29}}{2}$ $\sqrt{\dfrac{a}{b}} = \dfrac{\sqrt{a}}{\sqrt{b}}$

$k = -\dfrac{5}{2} + \dfrac{\sqrt{29}}{2}$ or $k = -\dfrac{5}{2} - \dfrac{\sqrt{29}}{2}$ Add $-\dfrac{5}{2}$.

$k = \dfrac{-5 + \sqrt{29}}{2}$ or $k = \dfrac{-5 - \sqrt{29}}{2}$ $\dfrac{a}{c} \pm \dfrac{b}{c} = \dfrac{a \pm b}{c}$

The solution set is $\left\{\dfrac{-5 + \sqrt{29}}{2}, \dfrac{-5 - \sqrt{29}}{2}\right\}$.

—————— **Work Problem** ❹ **at the Side.** ▶

❹ Solve each equation.

(a) $x^2 + x - 3 = 0$

(b) $r^2 + 3r - 1 = 0$

Answers

4. (a) $\left\{\dfrac{-1 + \sqrt{13}}{2}, \dfrac{-1 - \sqrt{13}}{2}\right\}$

   (b) $\left\{\dfrac{-3 + \sqrt{13}}{2}, \dfrac{-3 - \sqrt{13}}{2}\right\}$

5 Solve each equation by completing the square.

(a) $9x^2 + 18x + 5 = 0$

(b) $4t^2 - 24t + 11 = 0$

OBJECTIVE 2 **Solve quadratic equations by completing the square when the coefficient of the second-degree term is not 1.** If a quadratic equation has the form $ax^2 + bx + c = 0$, where $a \neq 1$, we obtain 1 as the coefficient of x^2 by dividing each side by a.

EXAMPLE 4 Completing the Square ($a \neq 1$)

Solve $4x^2 + 16x - 9 = 0$.

Step 1 *Before completing the square, the coefficient of x^2 must be 1,* not 4.

$$4x^2 + 16x - 9 = 0 \qquad \text{Given equation}$$

$$x^2 + 4x - \frac{9}{4} = 0 \qquad \begin{array}{l} \text{Divide by 4 to obtain 1} \\ \text{as the coefficient of } x^2. \end{array}$$

Step 2 Write the equation so that all variable terms are on one side of the equation and all constant terms are on the other side.

$$x^2 + 4x = \frac{9}{4} \qquad \text{Add } \tfrac{9}{4}.$$

Step 3 Complete the square. Take half the coefficient of x and square it.

$$\left[\frac{1}{2}(4) \right]^2 = 2^2 = 4$$

$$x^2 + 4x + 4 = \frac{9}{4} + 4 \qquad \text{Add 4 to each side.}$$

$$(x + 2)^2 = \frac{25}{4} \qquad \text{Factor; } \tfrac{9}{4} + 4 = \tfrac{9}{4} + \tfrac{16}{4} = \tfrac{25}{4}.$$

Step 4 $\quad x + 2 = \sqrt{\dfrac{25}{4}} \quad$ or $\quad x + 2 = -\sqrt{\dfrac{25}{4}} \qquad$ Square root property

$$x + 2 = \frac{5}{2} \quad \text{or} \quad x + 2 = -\frac{5}{2} \qquad \text{Take square roots.}$$

$$x = \frac{5}{2} - 2 \quad \text{or} \quad x = -\frac{5}{2} - 2 \qquad \text{Subtract 2.}$$

$$x = \frac{5}{2} - \frac{4}{2} \quad \text{or} \quad x = -\frac{5}{2} - \frac{4}{2} \qquad 2 = \tfrac{4}{2}$$

$$x = \frac{1}{2} \quad \text{or} \quad x = -\frac{9}{2} \qquad \text{Subtract fractions.}$$

CHECK $\qquad\qquad 4x^2 + 16x - 9 = 0$

$$4\left(\frac{1}{2}\right)^2 + 16\left(\frac{1}{2}\right) - 9 \overset{?}{=} 0 \qquad \bigg| \qquad 4\left(-\frac{9}{2}\right)^2 + 16\left(-\frac{9}{2}\right) - 9 \overset{?}{=} 0$$

$$\text{Let } x = \tfrac{1}{2}. \qquad\qquad\qquad\qquad \text{Let } x = -\tfrac{9}{2}$$

$$4\left(\frac{1}{4}\right) + 8 - 9 \overset{?}{=} 0 \qquad \bigg| \qquad 4\left(\frac{81}{4}\right) - 72 - 9 \overset{?}{=} 0$$

$$1 + 8 - 9 \overset{?}{=} 9 \qquad\qquad\qquad \bigg| \qquad 81 - 72 - 9 \overset{?}{=} 0$$

$$0 = 0 \checkmark \text{ True} \qquad\qquad\qquad \bigg| \qquad\qquad 0 = 0 \checkmark \text{ True}$$

The two values $\frac{1}{2}$ and $-\frac{9}{2}$ check, so the solution set is $\left\{ -\frac{9}{2}, \frac{1}{2} \right\}$.

◀ **Work Problem 5 at the Side.**

Answers

5. (a) $\left\{ -\frac{1}{3}, -\frac{5}{3} \right\}$ (b) $\left\{ \frac{11}{2}, \frac{1}{2} \right\}$

| EXAMPLE 5 | Completing the Square ($a \neq 1$) |

Solve $2x^2 - 4x - 5 = 0$.

$$x^2 - 2x - \frac{5}{2} = 0 \qquad \text{Divide by 2. (Step 1)}$$

$$x^2 - 2x = \frac{5}{2} \qquad \text{Add } \tfrac{5}{2}. \text{ (Step 2)}$$

$$\left[\frac{1}{2}(-2)\right]^2 = (-1)^2 = 1 \qquad \begin{array}{l}\text{Complete the square.}\\ \text{(Step 3)}\end{array}$$

$$x^2 - 2x + 1 = \frac{5}{2} + 1 \qquad \text{Add 1 to each side.}$$

$$(x - 1)^2 = \frac{7}{2} \qquad \begin{array}{l}\text{Factor on the left.}\\ \text{Add on the right.}\end{array}$$

$$x - 1 = \sqrt{\frac{7}{2}} \quad \text{or} \quad x - 1 = -\sqrt{\frac{7}{2}} \qquad \text{Square root property (Step 4)}$$

$$x = 1 + \sqrt{\frac{7}{2}} \quad \text{or} \quad x = 1 - \sqrt{\frac{7}{2}} \qquad \text{Add 1.}$$

$$x = 1 + \frac{\sqrt{14}}{2} \quad \text{or} \quad x = 1 - \frac{\sqrt{14}}{2} \qquad \begin{array}{l}\text{Rationalize denominators;}\\ \sqrt{\frac{7}{2}} = \frac{\sqrt{7}}{\sqrt{2}} = \frac{\sqrt{7}}{\sqrt{2}} \cdot \frac{\sqrt{2}}{\sqrt{2}} = \frac{\sqrt{14}}{2}.\end{array}$$

$$x = \frac{2}{2} + \frac{\sqrt{14}}{2} \quad \text{or} \quad x = \frac{2}{2} - \frac{\sqrt{14}}{2} \qquad 1 = \tfrac{2}{2}$$

$$x = \frac{2 + \sqrt{14}}{2} \quad \text{or} \quad x = \frac{2 - \sqrt{14}}{2} \qquad \begin{array}{l}\text{Add and subtract}\\ \text{fractions.}\end{array}$$

The solution set is $\left\{\frac{2 + \sqrt{14}}{2}, \frac{2 - \sqrt{14}}{2}\right\}$.

─────────────── **Work Problem 6 at the Side.** ▶

6 Solve each equation.

  (a) $2r^2 - 4r + 1 = 0$

  (b) $3z^2 - 6z - 2 = 0$

| EXAMPLE 6 | Solving for Nonreal Complex Solutions |

Solve each equation.

(a) $x^2 - 8x + 21 = 0$

$$x^2 - 8x = -21 \qquad \text{Subtract 21.}$$

$$x^2 - 8x + 16 = -21 + 16 \qquad [\tfrac{1}{2}(-8)]^2 = (-4)^2 = 16; \text{ Add 16 to each side.}$$

$$(x - 4)^2 = -5 \qquad \text{Factor on the left. Add on the right.}$$

Because the constant term on the right side of the equation is negative, this equation will have nonreal complex solutions.

$$x - 4 = \sqrt{-5} \quad \text{or} \quad x - 4 = -\sqrt{-5} \qquad \text{Square root property}$$

$$x - 4 = i\sqrt{5} \quad \text{or} \quad x - 4 = -i\sqrt{5} \qquad \sqrt{-a} = i\sqrt{a}$$

$$x = 4 + i\sqrt{5} \quad \text{or} \quad x = 4 - i\sqrt{5} \qquad \text{Add 4.}$$

The solution set is $\left\{4 + i\sqrt{5}, 4 - i\sqrt{5}\right\}$.

Answers

6. (a) $\left\{\frac{2 + \sqrt{2}}{2}, \frac{2 - \sqrt{2}}{2}\right\}$

  (b) $\left\{\frac{3 + \sqrt{15}}{3}, \frac{3 - \sqrt{15}}{3}\right\}$

─────────────── **Continued on Next Page**

7 Solve each equation.

(a) $x^2 + 2x + 7 = 0$

(b) $2t^2 - 2t + 3 = 0$

8 Solve each equation.

(a) $(x - 5)(x + 1) = 2$

(b) $(x + 6)(x + 2) = 1$

(c) $x(x + 5) = 3$

(b)
$$4p^2 + 8p + 5 = 0$$

> The coefficient of the second-degree term must be 1.

$$p^2 + 2p + \frac{5}{4} = 0 \qquad \text{Divide by 4.}$$

$$p^2 + 2p = -\frac{5}{4} \qquad \text{Subtract } \tfrac{5}{4}.$$

$$p^2 + 2p + 1 = -\frac{5}{4} + 1 \qquad \begin{array}{l}\text{Complete the square. Add}\\ \left[\tfrac{1}{2}(2)\right]^2 = 1^2 = 1 \text{ to each side.}\end{array}$$

> There will be nonreal complex solutions because of $-\tfrac{1}{4}$.

$$(p + 1)^2 = -\frac{1}{4} \qquad \text{Factor; } -\tfrac{5}{4} + 1 = -\tfrac{5}{4} + \tfrac{4}{4} = -\tfrac{1}{4}.$$

$$p + 1 = \sqrt{-\frac{1}{4}} \quad \text{or} \quad p + 1 = -\sqrt{-\frac{1}{4}} \qquad \text{Square root property}$$

$$p + 1 = \frac{1}{2}i \quad \text{or} \quad p + 1 = -\frac{1}{2}i \qquad \sqrt{-\tfrac{1}{4}} = \tfrac{1}{2}i$$

$$p = -1 + \frac{1}{2}i \quad \text{or} \quad p = -1 - \frac{1}{2}i \qquad \text{Add} -1.$$

The solution set is $\left\{-1 + \tfrac{1}{2}i, -1 - \tfrac{1}{2}i\right\}$.

◀ **Work Problem 7 at the Side.**

OBJECTIVE 3 Simplify the terms of an equation before solving.

EXAMPLE 7 Simplifying before Completing the Square

Solve $(x + 3)(x - 1) = 2$.

$$(x + 3)(x - 1) = 2$$

$$x^2 + 2x - 3 = 2 \qquad \text{Multiply using the FOIL method.}$$

$$x^2 + 2x = 5 \qquad \text{Add 3.}$$

$$x^2 + 2x + 1 = 5 + 1 \qquad \text{Add } \left[\tfrac{1}{2}(2)\right]^2 = 1^2 = 1.$$

$$(x + 1)^2 = 6 \qquad \text{Factor on the left. Add on the right.}$$

$$x + 1 = \sqrt{6} \quad \text{or} \quad x + 1 = -\sqrt{6} \qquad \text{Square root property}$$

$$x = -1 + \sqrt{6} \quad \text{or} \quad x = -1 - \sqrt{6} \qquad \text{Subtract 1.}$$

The solution set is $\left\{-1 + \sqrt{6}, -1 - \sqrt{6}\right\}$.

◀ **Work Problem 8 at the Side.**

Answers

7. (a) $\left\{-1 + i\sqrt{6}, -1 - i\sqrt{6}\right\}$

   (b) $\left\{\dfrac{1}{2} + \dfrac{\sqrt{5}}{2}i, \dfrac{1}{2} - \dfrac{\sqrt{5}}{2}i\right\}$

8. (a) $\left\{2 + \sqrt{11}, 2 - \sqrt{11}\right\}$

   (b) $\left\{-4 + \sqrt{5}, -4 - \sqrt{5}\right\}$

   (c) $\left\{\dfrac{-5 + \sqrt{37}}{2}, \dfrac{-5 - \sqrt{37}}{2}\right\}$

11.2 Exercises

FOR EXTRA HELP

Go to MyMathLab *for worked-out, step-by-step solutions to exercises enclosed in a square* and video solutions to ▶ *exercises.*

1. CONCEPT CHECK Which one of the two equations

$$(2x + 1)^2 = 5 \quad \text{and} \quad x^2 + 4x = 12$$

is more suitable for solving by the square root property? By completing the square?

2. CONCEPT CHECK What would be the first step in solving the equation

$$2x^2 + 8x = 9$$

by completing the square?

CONCEPT CHECK *Find the constant that must be added to make each expression a perfect square trinomial. Then factor the trinomial.*

3. $x^2 + 6x + $ _____

It factors as _____.

4. $x^2 + 14x + $ _____

It factors as _____.

5. $p^2 - 12p + $ _____

It factors as _____.

6. $x^2 - 20x + $ _____

It factors as _____.

7. $q^2 + 9q + $ _____

It factors as _____.

8. $t^2 + 3t + $ _____

It factors as _____.

Solve each equation by completing the square. **See Examples 1–3.**

9. $x^2 + 5x + 6 = 0$

10. $x^2 + 6x + 5 = 0$

11. $x^2 - 4x = -3$
▶

12. $x^2 - 2x = 8$

13. $x^2 + 2x - 5 = 0$
▶

14. $x^2 + 4x + 1 = 0$

15. $x^2 + 10x + 18 = 0$

16. $x^2 + 8x + 11 = 0$

17. $x^2 - 8x = -4$

18. $m^2 - 4m = 14$

19. $x^2 + x - 1 = 0$

20. $x^2 + x - 3 = 0$

21. $r^2 - 3r = 2$

22. $x^2 - 3x = 6$

Solve each equation by completing the square. **See Examples 4, 5, and 7.**

23. $3w^2 - w - 24 = 0$

24. $4z^2 - z - 39 = 0$

25. $4x^2 + 4x = 3$
▶

26. $9x^2 + 3x = 2$

27. $2k^2 + 5k - 2 = 0$

28. $3r^2 + 2r - 2 = 0$

29. $3k^2 + 7k = 4$
▶

30. $2k^2 + 5k = 1$

31. $5x^2 - 10x + 2 = 0$
▶

32. $2x^2 - 16x + 25 = 0$

33. $2x^2 - 4x = 3$

34. $2x^2 - 4x = 1$

35. $(x + 3)(x - 1) = 5$
▶

36. $(x - 8)(x + 2) = 24$

37. $(r - 3)(r - 5) = 2$

38. $(k - 1)(k - 7) = 1$

39. $x(x - 3) = 1$

40. $x(x - 5) = 2$

Solve each equation. (All solutions for these equations are nonreal complex numbers.)
See Example 6.

41. $m^2 + 4m + 13 = 0$

42. $t^2 + 6t + 10 = 0$

43. $m^2 + 6m + 12 = 0$

44. $x^2 + 10x + 27 = 0$

45. $k^2 + 5k + 10 = 0$

46. $x^2 + 3x + 8 = 0$

47. $3r^2 + 4r + 4 = 0$

48. $4x^2 + 5x + 5 = 0$

Relating Concepts (Exercises 49–52) For Individual or Group Work

We have discussed "completing the square" in an algebraic sense. This procedure can literally be applied to a geometric figure so that it becomes a square.

For example, to complete the square for $x^2 + 8x$, begin with a square having a side of length x. Add four rectangles of width 1 to the right side and to the bottom, as shown in the top figure. To "complete the square," fill in the bottom right corner with 16 squares of area 1, as shown in the bottom figure.

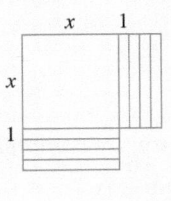
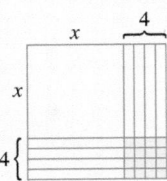

Work Exercises 49–52 in order.

49. What is the area of the original square?

50. What is the area of the figure after the 8 rectangles are added?

51. What is the area of the figure after the 16 small squares are added?

52. At what point did we "complete the square"?

11.3 | Solving Quadratic Equations by the Quadratic Formula

In this section, we complete the square to solve the general quadratic equation

$$ax^2 + bx + c = 0,$$

where a, b, and c are complex numbers and $a \neq 0$. The solution gives a formula for finding the solution of *any* specific quadratic equation.

OBJECTIVES

1. Derive the quadratic formula.
2. Solve quadratic equations using the quadratic formula.
3. Use the discriminant to determine the number and type of solutions.

OBJECTIVE ① **Derive the quadratic formula.** We solve $ax^2 + bx + c = 0$ by completing the square (where $a > 0$) as follows.

$$ax^2 + bx + c = 0$$

$$x^2 + \frac{b}{a}x + \frac{c}{a} = 0 \qquad \text{Divide by } a. \text{ (Step 1)}$$

$$x^2 + \frac{b}{a}x = -\frac{c}{a} \qquad \text{Subtract } \frac{c}{a}. \text{ (Step 2)}$$

$$\left[\frac{1}{2}\left(\frac{b}{a}\right)\right]^2 = \left(\frac{b}{2a}\right)^2 = \frac{b^2}{4a^2} \qquad \text{Complete the square. (Step 3)}$$

$$x^2 + \frac{b}{a}x + \frac{b^2}{4a^2} = -\frac{c}{a} + \frac{b^2}{4a^2} \qquad \text{Add } \frac{b^2}{4a^2} \text{ to each side.}$$

$$\left(x + \frac{b}{2a}\right)^2 = \frac{b^2}{4a^2} + \frac{-c}{a} \qquad \begin{array}{l}\text{Write the left side as a perfect square.}\\ \text{Rearrange the terms on the right.}\end{array}$$

$$\left(x + \frac{b}{2a}\right)^2 = \frac{b^2}{4a^2} + \frac{-4ac}{4a^2} \qquad \text{Write with a common denominator.}$$

$$\left(x + \frac{b}{2a}\right)^2 = \frac{b^2 - 4ac}{4a^2} \qquad \text{Add fractions.}$$

$$x + \frac{b}{2a} = \sqrt{\frac{b^2 - 4ac}{4a^2}} \quad \text{or} \quad x + \frac{b}{2a} = -\sqrt{\frac{b^2 - 4ac}{4a^2}} \qquad \begin{array}{l}\text{Square root}\\ \text{property (Step 4)}\end{array}$$

We can simplify $\sqrt{\dfrac{b^2 - 4ac}{4a^2}}$ as $\dfrac{\sqrt{b^2 - 4ac}}{\sqrt{4a^2}}$, or $\dfrac{\sqrt{b^2 - 4ac}}{2a}$.

The right side of each equation can be expressed as follows.

$$x + \frac{b}{2a} = \frac{\sqrt{b^2 - 4ac}}{2a} \qquad \text{or} \qquad x + \frac{b}{2a} = -\frac{\sqrt{b^2 - 4ac}}{2a}$$

$$x = \frac{-b}{2a} + \frac{\sqrt{b^2 - 4ac}}{2a} \qquad \text{or} \qquad x = \frac{-b}{2a} - \frac{\sqrt{b^2 - 4ac}}{2a}$$

$$x = \frac{-b + \sqrt{b^2 - 4ac}}{2a} \qquad \text{or} \qquad x = \frac{-b - \sqrt{b^2 - 4ac}}{2a}$$

If $a < 0$, the same two solutions are obtained. The result is the **quadratic formula,** which is abbreviated as shown on the next page.

① Identify the values of a, b, and c. (*Hint:* If necessary, first write the equation in standard form with 0 on the right side.) *Do not actually solve.*

(a) $-3x^2 + 9x - 4 = 0$

(b) $3x^2 = 6x + 2$

② Solve $4x^2 - 11x - 3 = 0$.

Quadratic Formula

The solutions of $ax^2 + bx + c = 0$ (where $a \neq 0$) are given by

$$x = \frac{-b \pm \sqrt{b^2 - 4ac}}{2a}.$$

⚠ CAUTION

In the quadratic formula, the square root is added to or subtracted from the value of $-b$ before dividing by $2a$.

OBJECTIVE ❷ Solve quadratic equations using the quadratic formula.
To use the quadratic formula, first write the equation in standard form

$$ax^2 + bx + c = 0.$$

Then identify the values of a, b, and c and substitute them into the quadratic formula.

◀ **Work Problem ❶ at the Side.**

EXAMPLE 1 Using the Quadratic Formula (Two Rational Solutions)

Solve $6x^2 - 5x - 4 = 0$.

This equation is in standard form, so we identify the values of a, b, and c. Here a, the coefficient of the second-degree term, is **6**, and b, the coefficient of the first-degree term, is -5. The constant c is -4.

Substitute these values into the quadratic formula.

$$x = \frac{-b \pm \sqrt{b^2 - 4ac}}{2a} \quad \text{Quadratic formula}$$

$$x = \frac{-(-5) \pm \sqrt{(-5)^2 - 4(6)(-4)}}{2(6)} \quad a = 6, b = -5, c = -4$$

Use parentheses and substitute carefully to avoid errors.

$$x = \frac{5 \pm \sqrt{25 + 96}}{12}$$

$$x = \frac{5 \pm \sqrt{121}}{12} \quad \text{Add under the radical.}$$

$$x = \frac{5 \pm 11}{12} \quad \text{Take the square root.}$$

There are two solutions, one from the $+$ sign and one from the $-$ sign.

$$x = \frac{5 + 11}{12} = \frac{16}{12} = \frac{4}{3} \quad \text{or} \quad x = \frac{5 - 11}{12} = \frac{-6}{12} = -\frac{1}{2}$$

Check each value in the original equation. The solution set is $\left\{-\frac{1}{2}, \frac{4}{3}\right\}$.

◀ **Work Problem ❷ at the Side.**

Answers

1. (a) $-3; 9; -4$ **(b)** $3; -6; -2$

2. $\left\{-\frac{1}{4}, 3\right\}$

Note

We could have factored the trinomial and then used the zero-factor property to solve the equation in **Example 1**.

$$6x^2 - 5x - 4 = 0$$

$$(3x - 4)(2x + 1) = 0 \qquad \text{Factor.}$$

$$3x - 4 = 0 \quad \text{or} \quad 2x + 1 = 0 \qquad \text{Zero-factor property}$$

$$3x = 4 \quad \text{or} \qquad 2x = -1 \qquad \text{Solve each equation.}$$

$$x = \frac{4}{3} \quad \text{or} \qquad x = -\frac{1}{2} \qquad \text{Same solutions as in \textbf{Example 1}}$$

When solving a quadratic equation, it is a good idea to try to factor the quadratic expression first. If it can be factored, then apply the zero-factor property. If it cannot be factored or if factoring is difficult, then use the quadratic formula.

③ Solve $4x^2 - 20x + 25 = 0$.

EXAMPLE 2 Using the Quadratic Formula (One Rational Solution)

Solve $9x^2 + 12x + 4 = 0$.

The trinomial on the left side of the equality symbol can be factored, so this equation could be solved using the zero-factor property. However, if we did not recognize this and solved using the quadratic formula, our work might look similar to that shown below.

$$x = \frac{-b \pm \sqrt{b^2 - 4ac}}{2a} \qquad \text{Quadratic formula}$$

$$x = \frac{-12 \pm \sqrt{12^2 - 4(9)(4)}}{2(9)} \qquad a = 9, b = 12, c = 4$$

$$x = \frac{-12 \pm \sqrt{144 - 144}}{18} \qquad \text{Simplify.}$$

$$x = \frac{-12 \pm 0}{18} \qquad \sqrt{0} = 0$$

$$x = -\frac{2}{3} \qquad \text{Write } \tfrac{-12}{18} \text{ in lowest terms.}$$

When applying the quadratic formula in this case, $b^2 - 4ac = 0$ because

$$9x^2 + 12x + 4 \quad \text{is a perfect square trinomial.}$$

There is one *distinct* solution, $-\frac{2}{3}$. The solution set is $\left\{-\frac{2}{3}\right\}$.

Work Problem ③ at the Side. ▶

Note

Solve the equation in **Example 2** by factoring

$$9x^2 + 12x + 4$$

and using the zero-factor property to confirm that the same solution, $-\frac{2}{3}$, results.

Answer

3. $\left\{\frac{5}{2}\right\}$

4 Solve each equation.

(a) $6x^2 + 4x - 1 = 0$

Here, $a = $ ____, $b = 4$, and $c = $ ____.

$$x = \frac{-b \pm \sqrt{b^2 - 4ac}}{2a}$$

$$x = \frac{-4 \pm \sqrt{\underline{}^2 - 4(6)(\underline{})}}{2(6)}$$

$$x = \frac{-4 \pm \sqrt{16 + \underline{}}}{12}$$

$$x = \frac{-4 \pm \sqrt{40}}{12}$$

$$x = \frac{-4 \pm \underline{}\sqrt{10}}{12}$$

$$x = \frac{\underline{}(-2 \pm \sqrt{10})}{2(6)}$$

$$x = \underline{}$$

The solution set is _____.

(b) $2x^2 + 19 = 14x$

EXAMPLE 3 Using the Quadratic Formula (Two Irrational Solutions)

Solve $4x^2 = 8x - 1$.

Write the equation in standard form as $4x^2 - 8x + 1 = 0$. *(This is a key step.)*

$$x = \frac{-b \pm \sqrt{b^2 - 4ac}}{2a}$$ Quadratic formula

$$x = \frac{-(-8) \pm \sqrt{(-8)^2 - 4(4)(1)}}{2(4)}$$ $a = 4$, $b = -8$, $c = 1$

$$x = \frac{8 \pm \sqrt{64 - 16}}{8}$$ Simplify in the numerator and denominator.

$$x = \frac{8 \pm \sqrt{48}}{8}$$ Subtract under the radical.

$$x = \frac{8 \pm 4\sqrt{3}}{8}$$ $\sqrt{48} = \sqrt{16} \cdot \sqrt{3} = 4\sqrt{3}$

$$x = \frac{4(2 \pm \sqrt{3})}{4(2)}$$ Factor.

$$x = \frac{2 \pm \sqrt{3}}{2}$$ Divide out the common factor 4 to write in lowest terms.

The solution set is $\left\{\frac{2 + \sqrt{3}}{2}, \frac{2 - \sqrt{3}}{2}\right\}$.

◀ **Work Problem 4 at the Side.**

❗ CAUTION

1. *Before solving, every quadratic equation must be expressed in standard form $ax^2 + bx + c = 0$,* whether we use the zero-factor property or the quadratic formula.

2. *When writing solutions in lowest terms, factor first. Then divide out the common factor.* See the last two steps in **Example 3**.

EXAMPLE 4 Using the Quadratic Formula (Two Nonreal Complex Solutions)

Solve $(9x + 3)(x - 1) = -8$.

This is a quadratic equation—when the first terms $9x$ and x are multiplied, we get a second-degree term, $9x^2$. We must write the equation in standard form.

$$(9x + 3)(x - 1) = -8$$

$$9x^2 - 6x - 3 = -8$$ Multiply using the FOIL method.

Standard form → $9x^2 - 6x + 5 = 0$ Add 8.

From the standard form of the equation, we identify $a = 9$, $b = -6$, and $c = 5$.

Answers

4. **(a)** $6; -1; 4; -1; 24; 2; 2; \dfrac{-2 \pm \sqrt{10}}{6}$;

$\left\{\dfrac{-2 + \sqrt{10}}{6}, \dfrac{-2 - \sqrt{10}}{6}\right\}$

(b) $\left\{\dfrac{7 + \sqrt{11}}{2}, \dfrac{7 - \sqrt{11}}{2}\right\}$

Continued on Next Page

$$x = \frac{-b \pm \sqrt{b^2 - 4ac}}{2a}$$

Quadratic formula

$$x = \frac{-(-6) \pm \sqrt{(-6)^2 - 4(9)(5)}}{2(9)}$$

$a = 9, b = -6, c = 5$

$$x = \frac{6 \pm \sqrt{-144}}{18}$$

Simplify.

$$x = \frac{6 \pm 12i}{18}$$

$\sqrt{-144} = 12i$

$$x = \frac{6(1 \pm 2i)}{6(3)}$$

> Factor first. Then divide out the common factor.

Factor.

$$x = \frac{1 \pm 2i}{3}$$

Divide out the common factor 6 to write in lowest terms.

$$x = \frac{1}{3} \pm \frac{2}{3}i$$

Standard form $a + bi$ for a complex number

The solution set is $\left\{ \frac{1}{3} + \frac{2}{3}i, \frac{1}{3} - \frac{2}{3}i \right\}$.

──────── **Work Problem ⑤ at the Side.** ▶

OBJECTIVE ▶ ❸ **Use the discriminant to determine the number and type of solutions.** The solutions of the quadratic equation $ax^2 + bx + c = 0$ are given by

$$x = \frac{-b \pm \sqrt{b^2 - 4ac}}{2a}. \quad \leftarrow \text{Discriminant}$$

The expression under the radical, $b^2 - 4ac$, is called the **discriminant** because it distinguishes among the numbers of solutions—one or two—and the types of solutions—rational, irrational, or nonreal complex—of a quadratic equation.

Discriminant

If a, b, and c are integers in a quadratic equation $ax^2 + bx + c = 0$, then the discriminant $b^2 - 4ac$ can be used to determine the number and type of solutions of the equation as follows.

Discriminant $b^2 - 4ac$	Number and Type of Solutions
Positive, and the square of an integer	Two rational solutions
Positive, but not the square of an integer	Two irrational solutions
Zero	One rational solution
Negative	Two nonreal complex solutions

We can use the discriminant to help decide how to solve a quadratic equation.

If a, b, and c are integers and the discriminant is a perfect square (including 0), then the equation can be solved using the zero-factor property. Otherwise, the quadratic formula should be used.

⑤ Solve each equation.

(a) $x^2 + x + 1 = 0$

(b) $(x + 2)(x - 6) = -17$

Answers

5. (a) $\left\{ -\frac{1}{2} + \frac{\sqrt{3}}{2}i, -\frac{1}{2} - \frac{\sqrt{3}}{2}i \right\}$

(b) $\{2 + i, 2 - i\}$

6 Find the discriminant. Use it to predict the number and type of solutions for each equation. Then tell whether the equation can be solved using the zero-factor property or whether the quadratic formula should be used.

(a) $2x^2 + 3x = 4$

(b) $2x^2 + 3x + 4 = 0$

(c) $x^2 + 20x + 100 = 0$

(d) $15x^2 - 14 = -11x$

Answers

6. **(a)** 41; two irrational solutions; quadratic formula
(b) −23; two nonreal complex solutions; quadratic formula
(c) 0; one rational solution; zero-factor property
(d) 961; two rational solutions; zero-factor property

EXAMPLE 5 Using the Discriminant

Find the discriminant. Use it to predict the number and type of solutions for each equation. Then tell whether the equation can be solved using the zero-factor property or whether the quadratic formula should be used.

(a) $6x^2 - x - 15 = 0$

First identify the values of a, b, and c. Because $-x = -1x$, the value of b is -1. We find the discriminant by evaluating $b^2 - 4ac$.

$$b^2 - 4ac$$

> Use parentheses and substitute carefully.

$$= (-1)^2 - 4(6)(-15) \quad a = 6, b = -1, c = -15 \text{ (all integers)}$$
$$= 1 + 360 \quad \text{Apply the exponent. Multiply.}$$
$$= 361 \quad \text{Add.}$$
$$= 19^2, \quad \text{which is a perfect square.}$$

The discriminant 361 is a perfect square, so referring to the table we see that there will be two rational solutions. We can solve using the zero-factor property.

(b) $3x^2 - 4x = 5$

Write the equation in standard form as $3x^2 - 4x - 5 = 0$.

$$b^2 - 4ac \quad \text{Discriminant}$$
$$= (-4)^2 - 4(3)(-5) \quad a = 3, b = -4, c = -5 \text{ (all integers)}$$
$$= 16 + 60 \quad \text{Apply the exponent. Multiply.}$$
$$= 76 \quad \text{Add.}$$

Because 76 is positive but *not* the square of an integer, and a, b, and c are integers, this quadratic equation will have two irrational solutions and is best solved using the quadratic formula.

(c) $4x^2 + 9 = 12x$

First write the equation in standard form as $4x^2 - 12x + 9 = 0$.

$$b^2 - 4ac \quad \text{Discriminant}$$
$$= (-12)^2 - 4(4)(9) \quad a = 4, b = -12, c = 9 \text{ (all integers)}$$
$$= 144 - 144 \quad \text{Apply the exponent. Multiply.}$$
$$= 0 \quad \text{Subtract.}$$

The discriminant is 0, so this quadratic equation will have only one rational solution. We can solve using the zero-factor property.

(d) $4x^2 + x + 1 = 0$

> $x = 1x$, so $b = 1$.

$$b^2 - 4ac \quad \text{Discriminant}$$
$$= 1^2 - 4(4)(1) \quad a = 4, b = 1, c = 1 \text{ (all integers)}$$
$$= 1 - 16 \quad \text{Apply the exponent. Multiply.}$$
$$= -15 \quad \text{Subtract.}$$

Because the discriminant is negative, this quadratic equation will have two nonreal complex solutions. The quadratic formula should be used to solve it.

◀ Work Problem **6** at the Side

11.3 Exercises

FOR EXTRA HELP   Go to MyMathLab *for worked-out, step-by-step solutions to exercises enclosed in a square*   *and video solutions to* ▶ *exercises.*

CONCEPT CHECK *Answer each question.*

1. The documentation for an early version of Microsoft *Word* for Windows used the following for the quadratic formula. Was this correct? If not, correct it.

$$x = -b \pm \frac{\sqrt{b^2 - 4ac}}{2a}$$ Correct or incorrect?

2. One patron wrote the quadratic formula, as shown here, on a wall at the Cadillac Bar in Houston, Texas. Was this correct? If not, correct it.

$$x = \frac{-b\sqrt{b^2 - 4ac}}{2a}$$ Correct or incorrect?

3. **CONCEPT CHECK** A student solved $5x^2 - 5x + 1 = 0$ incorrectly as follows.

$$x = \frac{-(-5) \pm \sqrt{(-5)^2 - 4(5)(1)}}{2(5)}$$ $a = 5,$ $b = -5,$ $c = 1$

$$x = \frac{5 \pm \sqrt{5}}{10}$$ Simplify.

$$x = \frac{1}{2} \pm \sqrt{5}$$ Write in lowest terms.

What Went Wrong? Give the correct solution set.

4. **CONCEPT CHECK** A student claimed that the following equation cannot be solved using the quadratic formula because there is no first-degree x-term.

$$2x^2 - 5 = 0$$

What Went Wrong? Give the values of a, b, and c, and solve the equation.

Solve each equation using the quadratic formula. (All solutions for these equations are real numbers.) **See Examples 1–3.**

5. ▶ $x^2 - 8x + 15 = 0$

6. $x^2 + 3x - 28 = 0$

7. $6x^2 + 11x - 10 = 0$

8. $8x^2 + 10x - 3 = 0$

9. $4x^2 + 12x + 9 = 0$

10. $16x^2 + 40x + 25 = 0$

11. $36x^2 - 12x + 1 = 0$

12. $9x^2 - 6x + 1 = 0$

13. $2x^2 + 4x + 1 = 0$

14. $2x^2 + 3x - 1 = 0$

15. ▶ $2x^2 - 2x = 1$

16. $9x^2 + 6x = 1$

17. $x^2 + 18 = 10x$

18. $x^2 - 4 = 2x$

19. $4k^2 + 4k - 1 = 0$

20. $4r^2 - 4r - 19 = 0$

21. $2 - 2x = 3x^2$

22. $26r - 2 = 3r^2$

23. $\dfrac{x^2}{4} - \dfrac{x}{2} = 1$

(*Hint:* First clear the fractions.)

24. $p^2 + \dfrac{p}{3} = \dfrac{1}{6}$

(*Hint:* First clear the fractions.)

25. $-2t(t + 2) = -3$

26. $-3x(x + 2) = -4$

27. $(r - 3)(r + 5) = 2$

28. $(k + 1)(k - 7) = 1$

Solve each equation using the quadratic formula. (All solutions for these equations are nonreal complex numbers.) **See Example 4.**

29. $r^2 - 6r + 14 = 0$

30. $t^2 + 4t + 11 = 0$

31. $x^2 - 3x + 17 = 0$

32. $x^2 - 5x + 20 = 0$

33. $4x^2 - 4x = -7$

34. $9x^2 - 6x = -7$

35. $x(3x + 4) = -2$

36. $p(2p + 3) = -2$

37. $(2x - 1)(8x - 4) = -1$

38. $(x - 1)(9x - 3) = -2$

Find the discriminant. Use it to determine whether the solutions for each equation are

A. *two rational numbers,*

B. *two irrational numbers,*

C. *one rational number,*

D. *two nonreal complex numbers.*

Then tell whether the equation can be solved using the zero-factor property or whether the quadratic formula should be used. Do not actually solve. **See Example 5.**

39. $25x^2 + 70x + 49 = 0$

40. $4k^2 - 28k + 49 = 0$

41. $x^2 + 4x + 2 = 0$

42. $9x^2 - 12x - 1 = 0$

43. $3x^2 = 5x + 2$

44. $4x^2 = 4x + 3$

45. $3m^2 - 10m + 15 = 0$

46. $18x^2 + 60x + 82 = 0$

Refer to the answers in **Exercises 39–42,** *and solve each equation.*

47. $25x^2 + 70x + 49 = 0$

48. $4k^2 - 28k + 49 = 0$

49. $x^2 + 4x + 2 = 0$

50. $9x^2 - 12x - 1 = 0$

11.4 | Equations Quadratic in Form

OBJECTIVE ▶ 1 Solve rational equations that lead to quadratic equations.
A variety of nonquadratic equations can be written in the form of a quadratic equation and solved using the methods of this chapter.

EXAMPLE 1 Solving a Rational Equation That Leads to a Quadratic Equation

Solve $\dfrac{1}{x} + \dfrac{1}{x-1} = \dfrac{7}{12}$.

Clear fractions by multiplying each side by the least common denominator, $12x(x-1)$. (The domain is $\{x \mid x \text{ is a real number}, x \neq 0, 1\}$.)

$$12x(x-1)\left(\frac{1}{x} + \frac{1}{x+1}\right) = 12x(x-1)\left(\frac{7}{12}\right) \quad \text{Multiply by the LCD.}$$

$$12x(x-1)\frac{1}{x} + 12x(x-1)\frac{1}{x+1} = 12x(x-1)\left(\frac{7}{12}\right) \quad \text{Distributive property}$$

$$12(x-1) + 12x = 7x(x-1) \quad \text{Multiply.}$$

$$12x - 12 + 12x = 7x^2 - 7x \quad \text{Distributive property}$$

$$24x - 12 = 7x^2 - 7x \quad \text{Combine like terms.}$$

This trinomial is factorable. ▶ $7x^2 - 31x + 12 = 0$ Standard form

$$(7x - 3)(x - 4) = 0 \quad \text{Factor.}$$

$$7x - 3 = 0 \quad \text{or} \quad x - 4 = 0 \quad \text{Zero-factor property}$$

$$x = \frac{3}{7} \quad \text{or} \quad x = 4 \quad \text{Solve each equation.}$$

These values are in the domain. Check them in the original equation. The solution set is $\left\{\frac{3}{7}, 4\right\}$.

—— **Work Problem 1 at the Side.** ▶

OBJECTIVE ▶ 2 Solve applied problems involving quadratic equations.
Some distance-rate-time problems lead to quadratic equations.

EXAMPLE 2 Solving a Motion Problem

A riverboat for tourists averages 12 mph in still water. It takes the boat 1 hr, 4 min to travel 6 mi upstream and return. Find the rate of the current.

Step 1 **Read** the problem carefully.

Step 2 **Assign a variable.**

Let x = the rate of the current.

The current slows down the boat when it travels upstream, so the rate of the boat traveling upstream is its rate in still water *less* the rate of the current, or $(12 - x)$ mph. See **Figure 1** on the next page.

—— **Continued on Next Page**

OBJECTIVES

1 Solve rational equations that lead to quadratic equations.

2 Solve applied problems involving quadratic equations.

3 Solve radical equations that lead to quadratic equations.

4 Solve equations that are quadratic in form.

1 Solve each equation.

(a) $\dfrac{5}{m} + \dfrac{12}{m^2} = 2$

(b) $\dfrac{2}{x} + \dfrac{1}{x-2} = \dfrac{5}{3}$

Answers

1. (a) $\left\{-\frac{3}{2}, 4\right\}$ (b) $\left\{\frac{4}{5}, 3\right\}$

2 Solve each problem.

(a) In 4 hr, Kerrie can travel 15 mi upriver and come back. The rate of the current is 5 mph. Find the rate of her boat in still water.

Let $x = $ _____.

The rate traveling upriver (*against* the current) is ____ mph.

The rate traveling back downriver (*with* the current) is ____ mph.

Complete the table.

	d	r	t
Up	___	___	___
Down	___	___	___

Write an equation, and complete the solution.

(b) In $1\frac{3}{4}$ hr, Ken rows his boat 5 mi upriver and comes back. The rate of the current is 3 mph. How fast does Ken row?

Riverboat traveling *upstream*—the current slows it down.

Figure 1

Similarly, the current speeds up the boat as it travels downstream, so its rate downstream is $(12 + x)$ mph. Thus,

$$12 - x = \text{the rate upstream in miles per hour,}$$

and $12 + x = $ the rate downstream in miles per hour.

	d	r	t
Upstream	6	$12 - x$	$\frac{6}{12-x}$
Downstream	6	$12 + x$	$\frac{6}{12+x}$

Complete a table. Use the distance formula, $d = rt$, solved for time t, $t = \frac{d}{r}$, to write expressions for t.

Step 3 **Write an equation.** We use the total time, written as a fraction.

$$1 \text{ hr, } 4 \text{ min} = 1 + \frac{4}{60} = 1 + \frac{1}{15} = \frac{16}{15} \text{ hr} \quad \text{Total time}$$

Time upstream $\quad + \quad$ time downstream $\quad = \quad$ total time.

$$\frac{6}{12 - x} \quad + \quad \frac{6}{12 + x} \quad = \quad \frac{16}{15}$$

Step 4 **Solve** the equation. The LCD is $15(12 - x)(12 + x)$.

$$15(12 - x)(12 + x)\left(\frac{6}{12 - x} + \frac{6}{12 + x}\right)$$

$$= 15(12 - x)(12 + x)\left(\frac{16}{15}\right)$$

Multiply by the LCD.

$$15(12 + x)6 + 15(12 - x)6 = (12 - x)(12 + x)16$$

Distributive property; Multiply.

$$90(12 + x) + 90(12 - x) = 16(144 - x^2) \quad \text{Multiply.}$$

$$1080 + 90x + 1080 - 90x = 2304 - 16x^2 \quad \text{Distributive property}$$

$$2160 = 2304 - 16x^2 \quad \text{Combine like terms.}$$

$$16x^2 = 144 \quad \text{Add } 16x^2. \text{ Subtract 2160.}$$

$$x^2 = 9 \quad \text{Divide by 16.}$$

$$x = 3 \quad \text{or} \quad x = -3 \quad \text{Square root property}$$

Step 5 **State the answer.** The rate cannot be -3, so the answer is **3 mph.**

Step 6 **Check** that this value satisfies the original problem.

◄ **Work Problem 2 at the Side.**

> **❶ CAUTION**
> As shown in **Example 2,** when a quadratic equation is used to solve an applied problem, sometimes only *one* answer satisfies the application. ***Always check each answer in the words of the original problem.***

Recall that a person's work rate is $\frac{1}{t}$ part of the job per hour, where t is the time in hours required to complete the job. Thus, the part of the job the person will do in x hours is $\frac{1}{t}x$.

EXAMPLE 3 **Solving a Work Problem**

It takes two carpet layers 4 hr to carpet a room. If each worked alone, one of them could do the job in 1 hr less time than the other. How long would it take each carpet layer to complete the job alone?

Step 1 **Read** the problem again. There will be two answers.

Step 2 **Assign a variable.**

Let $x =$ the number of hours for the slower carpet layer to complete the job.

Then $x - 1 =$ the number of hours for the faster carpet layer to complete the job.

The slower worker's rate is thus $\frac{1}{x}$, and the faster worker's rate is $\frac{1}{x-1}$. Together they can do the job in 4 hr. Complete a table as shown.

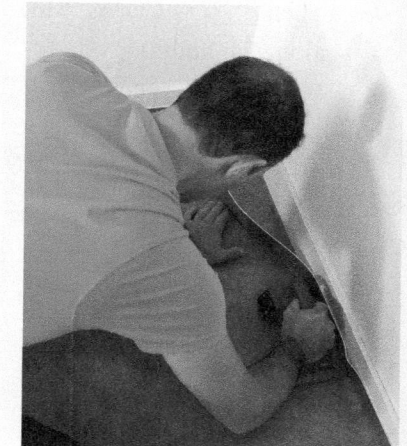

	Rate	Time Working Together	Fractional Part of the Job Done	
Slower Worker	$\frac{1}{x}$	4	$\frac{1}{x}(4)$	← Sum is 1 whole job.
Faster Worker	$\frac{1}{x-1}$	4	$\frac{1}{x-1}(4)$	←

Step 3 **Write an equation.**

$$\begin{array}{ccccc} \text{Part done by} & & \text{part done by} & & \\ \text{slower worker} & + & \text{faster worker} & = & \text{1 whole job.} \\ \downarrow & & \downarrow & & \downarrow \\ \dfrac{4}{x} & + & \dfrac{4}{x-1} & = & 1 \end{array}$$

Step 4 **Solve** the equation.

$$x(x-1)\left(\frac{4}{x}+\frac{4}{x-1}\right)=x(x-1)(1) \qquad \text{Multiply by the LCD, } x(x-1).$$

$$4(x-1)+4x=x(x-1) \qquad \text{Distributive property}$$

$$4x-4+4x=x^2-x \qquad \text{Distributive property}$$

$$x^2-9x+4=0 \qquad \text{Standard form}$$

The trinomial on the left cannot be factored, so the equation cannot be solved using the zero-factor property. We use the quadratic formula.

Continued on Next Page

3 Solve each problem. Round answers to the nearest tenth.

(GS) (a) Carlos can complete a certain lab test in 2 hr less time than Jaime can. If they can finish the job together in 2 hr, how long would it take each of them working alone?

Let x = Jaime's time alone (in hours).

Then _____ = Carlos' time alone (in hours).

Complete the table.

	Rate	Time Working Together	Fractional Part of the Job Done
Carlos	_____	_____	_____
Jaime	_____	_____	_____

Write an equation, and complete the solution.

(b) Two chefs are preparing a banquet. One chef could prepare the banquet in 2 hr less time than the other. Together, they complete the job in 5 hr. How long would it take the faster chef working alone?

Answers

3. **(a)** $x - 2$;

row 1 of table: $\dfrac{1}{x-2}$; 2; $\dfrac{2}{x-2}$;

row 2 of table: $\dfrac{1}{x}$; 2; $\dfrac{2}{x}$;

$\dfrac{2}{x-2} + \dfrac{2}{x} = 1$;

Jaime: 5.2 hr; Carlos: 3.2 hr

(b) 9.1 hr

$$x = \frac{-b \pm \sqrt{b^2 - 4ac}}{2a} \qquad \text{Quadratic formula}$$

$$x = \frac{-(-9) \pm \sqrt{(-9)^2 - 4(1)(4)}}{2(1)} \qquad \begin{array}{l}\text{In } x^2 - 9x + 4 = 0, \\ a = 1, b = -9, \text{ and } c = 4.\end{array}$$

$$x = \frac{9 \pm \sqrt{65}}{2} \qquad \text{Simplify.}$$

$$x = \frac{9 + \sqrt{65}}{2} \approx 8.5 \quad \text{or} \quad x = \frac{9 - \sqrt{65}}{2} \approx 0.5 \qquad \text{Use a calculator.}$$

Step 5 **State the answer.** Only the solution 8.5 makes sense in the original problem. If $x = 0.5$, then

$$x - 1 = 0.5 - 1 = -0.5, \qquad \text{Time cannot be negative.}$$

which cannot represent the time for the faster worker. The slower worker could do the job in about 8.5 hr and the faster in about

$$8.5 - 1 = 7.5 \text{ hr.}$$

Step 6 **Check** that these values satisfy the original problem.

◀ **Work Problem 3 at the Side.**

OBJECTIVE 3 Solve radical equations that lead to quadratic equations.

EXAMPLE 4 Solving Radical Equations That Lead to Quadratic Equations

Solve each equation.

(a) $k = \sqrt{6k - 8}$

This equation is not quadratic. However, squaring each side gives a quadratic equation.

$$k^2 = \left(\sqrt{6k - 8}\right)^2 \qquad \text{Square each side.}$$

$$k^2 = 6k - 8 \qquad \left(\sqrt{a}\right)^2 = a$$

$$k^2 - 6k + 8 = 0 \qquad \text{Standard form}$$

This trinomial is factorable.

$$(k - 4)(k - 2) = 0 \qquad \text{Factor.}$$

$$k - 4 = 0 \quad \text{or} \quad k - 2 = 0 \qquad \text{Zero-factor property}$$

$$k = 4 \quad \text{or} \quad k = 2 \qquad \text{Proposed solutions}$$

Recall that squaring each side of a radical equation can introduce extraneous solutions that do not satisfy the original equation. ***All proposed solutions must be checked in the original (not the squared) equation.***

CHECK $\quad k = \sqrt{6k - 8} \qquad\qquad\qquad k = \sqrt{6k - 8}$

$\qquad 4 \stackrel{?}{=} \sqrt{6(4) - 8} \quad \text{Let } k = 4. \qquad 2 \stackrel{?}{=} \sqrt{6(2) - 8} \quad \text{Let } k = 2.$

$\qquad 4 \stackrel{?}{=} \sqrt{16} \qquad\qquad\qquad\qquad 2 \stackrel{?}{=} \sqrt{4}$

$\qquad 4 = 4 \checkmark \qquad \text{True} \qquad\qquad 2 = 2 \checkmark \qquad \text{True}$

Both proposed solutions check, so the solution set is $\{2, 4\}$.

───────── **Continued on Next Page**

(b)

$$x + \sqrt{x} = 6$$

$$\sqrt{x} = 6 - x \qquad \text{Isolate the radical on one side.}$$

$$\left(\sqrt{x}\right)^2 = (6 - x)^2 \qquad \text{Square each side.}$$

$$x = 36 - 12x + x^2 \qquad (x - y)^2 = x^2 - 2xy + y^2$$

$$x^2 - 13x + 36 = 0 \qquad \begin{array}{l} \text{Subtract } x. \text{ Interchange sides to} \\ \text{write in standard form.} \end{array}$$

$$(x - 4)(x - 9) = 0 \qquad \text{Factor.}$$

$$x - 4 = 0 \quad \text{or} \quad x - 9 = 0 \qquad \text{Zero-factor property}$$

$$x = 4 \quad \text{or} \quad x = 9 \qquad \text{Proposed solutions}$$

CHECK

$x + \sqrt{x} = 6$	$x + \sqrt{x} = 6$
$4 + \sqrt{4} \overset{?}{=} 6$ Let $x = 4$.	$9 + \sqrt{9} \overset{?}{=} 6$ Let $x = 9$.
$6 = 6$ ✓ True	$12 = 6$ False

Only the proposed solution 4 checks, so the solution set is $\{4\}$.

―――――――――――――― **Work Problem ④ at the Side.** ▶

OBJECTIVE ▶ ④ Solve equations that are quadratic in form. A nonquadratic equation that can be written in the form

$$au^2 + bu + c = 0,$$

for $a \neq 0$ and an algebraic expression u, is **quadratic in form.**

Many equations that are quadratic in form can be solved more easily by defining and substituting a "temporary" variable u for an expression involving the variable in the original equation.

EXAMPLE 5　**Defining Substitution Variables**

Define a variable u in terms of x, and write each equation in quadratic form $au^2 + bu + c = 0$.

(a) $x^4 - 13x^2 + 36 = 0$

Look at the two terms involving the variable x, ignoring their coefficients. Try to find one variable expression that is the square of the other. Because $x^4 = (x^2)^2$, we can define $u = x^2$, and rewrite the original equation as a quadratic equation in u.

$$u^2 - 13u + 36 = 0 \qquad \text{Here, } u = x^2.$$

(b) $2(4x - 3)^2 + 7(4x - 3) + 5 = 0$

Because this equation involves both $(4x - 3)^2$ and $(4x - 3)$, we choose $u = 4x - 3$. Substituting u for $4x - 3$ gives a quadratic equation in u.

$$2u^2 + 7u + 5 = 0 \qquad \text{Here, } u = 4x - 3.$$

(c) $2x^{2/3} - 11x^{1/3} + 12 = 0$

In this case, we apply a power rule for exponents, $(a^m)^n = a^{mn}$. Because $(x^{1/3})^2 = x^{2/3}$, we define $u = x^{1/3}$. With this substitution, the original equation can be written as follows.

$$2u^2 - 11u + 12 = 0 \qquad \text{Here, } u = x^{1/3}.$$

―――――――――――――― **Work Problem ⑤ at the Side.** ▶

---

④ Solve each equation.

(a) $x = \sqrt{7x - 10}$

(b) $2x = \sqrt{x} + 1$

---

⑤ Define a variable u in terms of x, and write each equation in quadratic form

$$au^2 + bu + c = 0.$$

(a) $2x^4 + 5x^2 - 12 = 0$

(b) $2(x + 5)^2 - 7(x + 5) + 6 = 0$

(c) $x^{4/3} - 8x^{2/3} + 16 = 0$

Answers

4. (a) $\{2, 5\}$ (b) $\{1\}$

5. (a) $u = x^2$; $2u^2 + 5u - 12 = 0$
(b) $u = x + 5$; $2u^2 - 7u + 6 = 0$
(c) $u = x^{2/3}$; $u^2 - 8u + 16 = 0$

EXAMPLE 6 Solving Equations That Are Quadratic in Form

Solve each equation.

(a)
$$x^4 - 13x^2 + 36 = 0$$

> Think of this as a "disguised" quadratic equation. See **Example 5(a).**

$$(x^2)^2 - 13x^2 + 36 = 0 \qquad x^4 = (x^2)^2$$

> Quadratic in form

$$u^2 - 13u + 36 = 0 \qquad \text{Let } u = x^2.$$

$$(u - 4)(u - 9) = 0 \qquad \text{Factor.}$$

$$u - 4 = 0 \qquad \text{or} \qquad u - 9 = 0 \qquad \text{Zero-factor property}$$

> Don't stop here.

$$u = 4 \qquad \text{or} \qquad u = 9 \qquad \text{Solve each equation.}$$

$$x^2 = 4 \qquad \text{or} \qquad x^2 = 9 \qquad \text{Substitute } x^2 \text{ for } u.$$

$$x = \pm 2 \qquad \text{or} \qquad x = \pm 3 \qquad \text{Square root property}$$

Each value can be checked by substituting it into the original equation for x. The equation $x^4 - 13x^2 + 36 = 0$, is a *fourth*-degree equation and has *four* solutions.* The solution set is

$$\{-3, -2, 2, 3\}.$$

(b)
$$4x^4 + 1 = 5x^2$$

$$4x^4 - 5x^2 + 1 = 0 \qquad \text{Subtract } 5x^2.$$

$$4(x^2)^2 - 5x^2 + 1 = 0 \qquad x^4 = (x^2)^2$$

$$4u^2 - 5u + 1 = 0 \qquad \text{Let } u = x^2.$$

$$(4u - 1)(u - 1) = 0 \qquad \text{Factor.}$$

$$4u - 1 = 0 \qquad \text{or} \quad u - 1 = 0 \qquad \text{Zero-factor property}$$

$$u = \frac{1}{4} \qquad \text{or} \qquad u = 1 \qquad \text{Solve each equation.}$$

> This is a key step.

$$x^2 = \frac{1}{4} \qquad \text{or} \qquad x^2 = 1 \qquad \text{Substitute } x^2 \text{ for } u.$$

$$x = \pm\frac{1}{2} \qquad \text{or} \qquad x = \pm 1 \qquad \text{Square root property}$$

Check that the solution set is $\left\{-1, -\frac{1}{2}, \frac{1}{2}, 1\right\}$.

(c)
$$x^4 = 6x^2 - 3$$

$$x^4 - 6x^2 + 3 = 0 \qquad \text{Subtract } 6x^2. \text{ Add } 3.$$

$$(x^2)^2 - 6x^2 + 3 = 0 \qquad x^4 = (x^2)^2$$

$$u^2 - 6u + 3 = 0 \qquad \text{Let } u = x^2.$$

The trinomial on the left cannot be factored, so the equation cannot be solved using the zero-factor property. We use the quadratic formula.

——— **Continued on Next Page**

---

* In general, an equation in which an nth-degree polynomial equals 0 has n complex solutions, although they may not all be distinct—that is, some may be repeated.

$$u = \frac{-(-6) \pm \sqrt{(-6)^2 - 4(1)(3)}}{2(1)}$$

In $u^2 - 6u + 3 = 0$, $a = 1$, $b = -6$, and $c = 3$.

$$u = \frac{6 \pm \sqrt{24}}{2}$$

Simplify.

$$u = \frac{6 \pm 2\sqrt{6}}{2}$$

$\sqrt{24} = \sqrt{4} \cdot \sqrt{6}$
$= 2\sqrt{6}$

$$u = \frac{2(3 \pm \sqrt{6})}{2}$$

Factor.

$$u = 3 \pm \sqrt{6}$$

Divide out the common factor 2.

$$x^2 = 3 + \sqrt{6} \qquad \text{or} \qquad x^2 = 3 - \sqrt{6}$$

Substitute x^2 for u.

Find both square roots in each case.

$$x = \pm\sqrt{3 + \sqrt{6}} \quad \text{or} \quad x = \pm\sqrt{3 - \sqrt{6}}$$

Square root property

The solution set contains four numbers, written as follows.

$$\left\{ \sqrt{3 + \sqrt{6}}, -\sqrt{3 + \sqrt{6}}, \sqrt{3 - \sqrt{6}}, -\sqrt{3 - \sqrt{6}} \right\}$$

Work Problem ⑥ at the Side. ▶

Note

Quadratic expressions in equations like those in **Examples 6(a) and (b)** can be factored directly.

$$x^4 - 13x^2 + 36 = 0 \qquad \text{Example 6(a) equation}$$
$$(x^2 - 9)(x^2 - 4) = 0 \qquad \text{Factor.}$$
$$(x + 3)(x - 3)(x + 2)(x - 2) = 0 \qquad \text{Factor again.}$$

Using the zero-factor property gives the same solutions that we obtained in **Example 6(a).** Equations that include nonfactorable quadratic expressions (as in **Example 6(c)**) must be solved using substitution and the quadratic formula.

Solving an Equation That Is Quadratic in Form by Substitution

Step 1   **Define a temporary variable u,** based on the relationship between the variable expressions in the given equation. Substitute u in the original equation and rewrite the equation in the form

$$au^2 + bu + c = 0.$$

Step 2   **Solve the quadratic equation obtained in Step 1** either by factoring the trinomial and applying the zero-factor property or by using the quadratic formula.

Step 3   **Replace u with the expression it defined in Step 1.**

Step 4   **Solve the resulting equations for the original variable.**

Step 5   **Check** all values by substituting them in the original equation. Write the solution set.

---

⑥ Solve each equation.

GS (a) $m^4 - 10m^2 + 9 = 0$

$$(\underline{\quad})^2 - 10m^2 + 9 = 0$$

Let $u = m^2$.

$$\underline{\quad}^2 - 10\underline{\quad} + 9 = 0$$

$$(u - 9)(\underline{\quad}) = 0$$

$$u - 9 = 0 \quad \text{or} \quad \underline{\quad} = 0$$

$$u = 9 \quad \text{or} \quad u = \underline{\quad}$$

Substitute m^2 for u.

$$m^2 = 9 \qquad \text{or} \qquad m^2 = 1$$

$$m = \underline{\quad} \qquad \text{or} \qquad m = \pm 1$$

The solution set is $\underline{\quad\quad}$.

(b) $9k^4 - 37k^2 + 4 = 0$

(c) $x^4 - 4x^2 = -2$

Answers

6. (a) m^2; u; u; $u - 1$; $u - 1$; 1; ± 3;
$\{-3, -1, 1, 3\}$

(b) $\left\{ -2, -\dfrac{1}{3}, \dfrac{1}{3}, 2 \right\}$

(c) $\left\{ \sqrt{2 + \sqrt{2}}, -\sqrt{2 + \sqrt{2}}, \sqrt{2 - \sqrt{2}}, -\sqrt{2 - \sqrt{2}} \right\}$

7 Solve each equation.

(a) $5(r+3)^2 + 9(r+3) = 2$

(b) $4m^{2/3} = 3m^{1/3} + 1$

EXAMPLE 7 **Solving Equations That Are Quadratic in Form**

Solve each equation.

(a) $2(4x-3)^2 + 7(4x-3) + 5 = 0$

Step 1 Because of the repeated quantity $4x-3$, substitute u for $4x-3$.

$$2(4x-3)^2 + 7(4x-3) + 5 = 0 \qquad \text{See Example 5(b).}$$
$$2u^2 + 7u + 5 = 0 \qquad \text{Let } u = 4x-3.$$

Step 2 $(2u+5)(u+1) = 0$ Factor.

$2u+5 = 0 \quad$ or $\quad u+1 = 0 \qquad$ Zero-factor property

~Don't stop here.~ $\quad u = -\dfrac{5}{2} \quad$ or $\quad u = -1 \qquad$ Solve for u.

Step 3 $\quad 4x-3 = -\dfrac{5}{2} \quad$ or $\quad 4x-3 = -1 \qquad$ Substitute $4x-3$ for u.

Step 4 $\quad 4x = \dfrac{1}{2} \quad$ or $\quad 4x = 2 \qquad$ Add 3.

$x = \dfrac{1}{8} \quad$ or $\quad x = \dfrac{1}{2} \qquad$ Divide by 4.

Step 5 Check that the solution set of the original equation is $\left\{\frac{1}{8}, \frac{1}{2}\right\}$.

(b) $\qquad 2x^{2/3} - 11x^{1/3} + 12 = 0 \qquad$ See Example 5(c).

Step 1 $2(x^{1/3})^2 - 11x^{1/3} + 12 = 0 \qquad x^{2/3} = (x^{1/3})^2,$

$2u^2 - 11u + 12 = 0 \qquad \text{Let } u = x^{1/3}.$

Step 2 $(2u-3)(u-4) = 0 \qquad$ Factor.

$2u-3 = 0 \quad$ or $\quad u-4 = 0 \qquad$ Zero-factor property

$u = \dfrac{3}{2} \quad$ or $\quad u = 4 \qquad$ Solve for u.

Step 3 $x^{1/3} = \dfrac{3}{2} \quad$ or $\quad x^{1/3} = 4 \qquad$ Substitute $x^{1/3}$ for u.

Step 4 $(x^{1/3})^3 = \left(\dfrac{3}{2}\right)^3 \quad$ or $\quad (x^{1/3})^3 = 4^3 \qquad$ Cube each side.

$x = \dfrac{27}{8} \quad$ or $\quad x = 64 \qquad$ Apply the exponents.

Step 5 Because the original equation involves variables with rational exponents, check that neither of these solutions is extraneous. The solution set is $\left\{\frac{27}{8}, 64\right\}$.

◀ **Work Problem 7 at the Side.**

! CAUTION
A common error when solving problems like those in **Examples 6 and 7** is to stop too soon. *Once we have solved for u, we must remember to substitute and solve for the values of the original variable.*

Answers

7. (a) $\left\{-5, -\frac{14}{5}\right\}$ **(b)** $\left\{-\frac{1}{64}, 1\right\}$

11.4 Exercises

Go to MyMathLab *for worked-out, step-by-step solutions to exercises enclosed in a square* and video solutions to ▶ *exercises.*

CONCEPT CHECK *Based on the discussion and examples of this section, give the first step to solve each equation. Do not actually solve.*

1. $\dfrac{14}{x} = x - 5$

2. $\sqrt{1 + x} + x = 5$

3. $(r^2 + r)^2 - 8(r^2 + r) + 12 = 0$

4. $3t = \sqrt{16 - 10t}$

5. CONCEPT CHECK Study this incorrect "solution."

$$x = \sqrt{3x + 4}$$
$$x^2 = 3x + 4 \qquad \text{Square each side.}$$
$$x^2 - 3x - 4 = 0$$
$$(x - 4)(x + 1) = 0$$
$$x - 4 = 0 \quad \text{or} \quad x + 1 = 0$$
$$x = 4 \quad \text{or} \quad x = -1$$

Solution set: $\{4, -1\}$

What Went Wrong? Give the correct solution set.

6. CONCEPT CHECK Study this incorrect "solution."

$$2(m - 1)^2 - 3(m - 1) + 1 = 0$$
$$2u^2 - 3u + 1 = 0 \qquad \text{Let } u = m - 1.$$
$$(2u - 1)(u - 1) = 0$$
$$2u - 1 = 0 \quad \text{or} \quad u - 1 = 0$$
$$u = \frac{1}{2} \quad \text{or} \quad u = 1$$

Solution set: $\left\{\frac{1}{2}, 1\right\}$

What Went Wrong? Give the correct solution set.

Solve each equation. **See Example 1.**

7. $1 - \dfrac{3}{x} - \dfrac{28}{x^2} = 0$

8. $4 - \dfrac{7}{r} - \dfrac{2}{r^2} = 0$

9. $3 - \dfrac{1}{t} = \dfrac{2}{t^2}$

10. $1 + \dfrac{2}{k} = \dfrac{3}{k^2}$

11. ▶ $\dfrac{1}{x} + \dfrac{2}{x + 2} = \dfrac{17}{35}$

12. $\dfrac{2}{m} + \dfrac{3}{m + 9} = \dfrac{11}{4}$

13. ▶ $\dfrac{2}{x + 1} + \dfrac{3}{x + 2} = \dfrac{7}{2}$

14. $\dfrac{4}{3 - p} + \dfrac{2}{5 - p} = \dfrac{26}{15}$

15. $\dfrac{3}{2x} - \dfrac{1}{2(x + 2)} = 1$

16. $\dfrac{4}{3x} - \dfrac{1}{2(x + 1)} = 1$

17. $\dfrac{6}{p} = 2 + \dfrac{p}{p + 1}$

18. $\dfrac{k}{2 - k} + \dfrac{2}{k} = 5$

19. CONCEPT CHECK A boat travels 20 mph in still water, and the rate of the current is t mph. What is the rate of the boat when it travels each direction?

(a) Upstream   **(b)** Downstream

20. CONCEPT CHECK It takes m hours to grade a set of papers.

(a) What is the grader's rate (in job per hour)?

(b) How much of the job will the grader do in 2 hr?

Complete any tables. Then solve each problem. ***See Examples 2 and 3.***

21. On a windy day Yoshiaki found that he could travel 16 mi downstream and then 4 mi back upstream at top speed in a total of 48 min. What was the top speed of Yoshiaki's boat if the rate of the current was 15 mph? (Let x represent the rate of the boat in still water.)

	d	r	t
Upstream	4	$x - 15$	_____
Downstream	16	_____	_____

22. Lekesha flew her plane for 6 hr at a constant rate. She traveled 810 mi with the wind, then turned around and traveled 720 mi against the wind. The wind speed was a constant 15 mph. Find the rate of the plane. (Let x represent the rate of the plane in still air.)

	d	r	t
With Wind	810	_____	_____
Against Wind	720	_____	_____

23. Medicine Hat and Cranbrook are 300 km apart. Harry rides his Honda 20 km per hr faster than Sally rides her Yamaha. Find Harry's average rate if he travels from Cranbrook to Medicine Hat in $1\frac{1}{4}$ hr less time than Sally. (Data from *State Farm Road Atlas.*)

ALBERTA

BRITISH COLUMBIA

Medicine Hat

300 km

Cranbrook

24. The distance from Jackson to Lodi is 40 mi, as is the distance from Lodi to Manteca. Rico drove from Jackson to Lodi, stopped in Lodi for a root beer, and then drove to Manteca at 10 mph faster. Total driving time was 88 min. Find his rate from Jackson to Lodi. (Data from *State Farm Road Atlas.*)

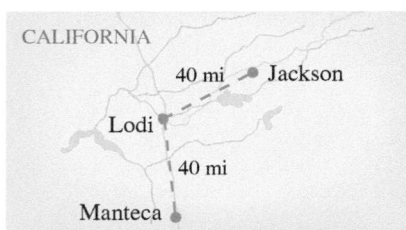

CALIFORNIA

40 mi — Jackson

Lodi

40 mi

Manteca

25. Working together, two people can cut a large lawn in 2 hr. One person can do the job alone in 1 hr less time than the other. How long (to the nearest tenth) would it take the faster person to do the job? (Let x represent the time of the faster person.)

	Rate	Time Working Together	Fractional Part of the Job Done
Faster Worker	$\frac{1}{x}$	2	_____
Slower Worker	_____	2	_____

26. Working together, two people can clean an office building in 5 hr. One person takes 2 hr longer than the other to clean the building alone. How long (to the nearest tenth) would it take the slower worker alone? (Let x represent the time of the slower worker.)

	Rate	Time Working Together	Fractional Part of the Job Done
Faster Worker	_____	_____	_____
Slower Worker	$\frac{1}{x}$	_____	_____

27. Rusty and Nancy are planting flats of spring flowers. Working alone, Rusty would take 2 hr longer than Nancy to plant the flowers. Working together, they do the job in 12 hr. How long (to the nearest tenth) would it have taken each person working alone?

28. Joel can work through a stack of invoices in 1 hr less time than Noel can. Working together they take $1\frac{1}{2}$ hr. How long (to the nearest tenth) would it take each person working alone?

29. A washing machine can be filled in 6 min if both the hot and cold water taps are fully opened. Filling the washer with hot water alone takes 9 min longer than filling it with cold water alone. How long does it take to fill the washer with cold water?

30. Two pipes together can fill a large tank in 2 hr. One of the pipes, used alone, takes 3 hr longer than the other to fill the tank. How long would each pipe take to fill the tank alone?

*Solve each equation. **See Example 4.***

31. $z = \sqrt{5z - 4}$

32. $x = \sqrt{9x - 14}$

33. $2x = \sqrt{11x + 3}$

34. $4x = \sqrt{6x + 1}$

35. $3x = \sqrt{16 - 10x}$

36. $4t = \sqrt{8t + 3}$

37. $k + \sqrt{k} = 12$

38. $p - \sqrt{p} = 12$

39. $m = \sqrt{\dfrac{6 - 13m}{5}}$

40. $r = \sqrt{\dfrac{20 - 19r}{6}}$

41. $-x = \sqrt{\dfrac{8 - 2x}{3}}$

42. $-x = \sqrt{\dfrac{3x + 7}{4}}$

*Solve each equation. **See Examples 5–7.***

43. $x^4 - 29x^2 + 100 = 0$

44. $x^4 - 37x^2 + 36 = 0$

45. $t^4 - 18t^2 + 81 = 0$

46. $x^4 - 8x^2 + 16 = 0$

47. $4k^4 - 13k^2 + 9 = 0$

48. $9x^4 - 25x^2 + 16 = 0$

49. $x^4 + 48 = 16x^2$

50. $z^4 = 17z^2 - 72$

51. $2x^4 - 9x^2 = -2$

52. $8x^4 + 1 = 11x^2$

53. $(x + 3)^2 + 5(x + 3) + 6 = 0$

54. $(k - 4)^2 + (k - 4) - 20 = 0$

55. $3(m + 4)^2 - 8 = 2(m + 4)$

56. $(t + 5)^2 + 6 = 7(t + 5)$

57. $2 + \dfrac{5}{3k - 1} = \dfrac{-2}{(3k - 1)^2}$

58. $3 - \dfrac{7}{2p + 2} = \dfrac{6}{(2p + 2)^2}$

59. $x^{2/3} + x^{1/3} - 2 = 0$

60. $x^{2/3} - 2x^{1/3} - 3 = 0$

61. $r^{2/3} + r^{1/3} - 12 = 0$

62. $3x^{2/3} - x^{1/3} - 24 = 0$

63. $4x^{4/3} - 13x^{2/3} + 9 = 0$

64. $9t^{4/3} - 25t^{2/3} + 16 = 0$

Summary Exercises *Applying Methods for Solving Quadratic Equations*

We have introduced four methods for solving quadratic (second-degree) equations.

METHODS FOR SOLVING QUADRATIC EQUATIONS

Method	Advantages	Disadvantages
Zero-factor property	This is usually the fastest method.	Not all polynomials are factorable. Some factorable polynomials are difficult to factor.
Square root property	This is the simplest method for solving equations of the form $(ax + b)^2 = c$.	Few equations are given in this form.
Completing the square	This method can always be used.	It requires more steps than other methods.
Quadratic formula	This method can always be used.	Sign errors may occur when evaluating $\sqrt{b^2 - 4ac}$.

A quadratic equation can be solved using more than one method, although one may be more direct than another. The following example compares several of the methods.

EXAMPLE   **Solving a Quadratic Equation**

Solve $x^2 - 64 = 0$ using the method specified.

Zero-factor property

$$x^2 - 64 = 0$$
$$(x + 8)(x - 8) = 0$$
$$x + 8 = 0 \quad \text{or} \quad x - 8 = 0$$
$$x = -8 \quad \text{or} \quad x = 8$$

Solution set: $\{-8, 8\}$

Square root property

$$x^2 - 64 = 0$$
$$x^2 = 64$$
$$x = \sqrt{64} \quad \text{or} \quad x = -\sqrt{64}$$
$$x = 8 \quad \text{or} \quad x = -8$$

Solution set: $\{-8, 8\}$

Quadratic formula

$$x = \frac{-b \pm \sqrt{b^2 - 4ac}}{2a}$$

$$x = \frac{-0 \pm \sqrt{0^2 - 4(1)(-64)}}{2(1)}$$

In $x^2 - 64 = 0$, $a = 1$, $b = 0$, and $c = -64$.

$$x = \frac{\pm\sqrt{256}}{2}$$

$$x = \frac{\pm 16}{2}$$

$$x = \pm 8$$

Solution set: $\{-8, 8\}$

CONCEPT CHECK   *Decide whether the* zero-factor property, *the* square root property, *or the* quadratic formula *is most appropriate for solving each quadratic equation. Do not actually solve.*

1. $(2x + 3)^2 = 4$ **2.** $4x^2 - 3x = 1$ **3.** $z^2 + 5z - 8 = 0$

4. $2k^2 + 3k = 1$ **5.** $3m^2 = 2 - 5m$ **6.** $p^2 = 5$

Solve each quadratic equation by the method of your choice.

7. $p^2 = 7$

8. $6x^2 - x - 15 = 0$

9. $n^2 + 8n + 6 = 0$

10. $(x - 4)^2 = 49$

11. $\dfrac{9}{m} + \dfrac{5}{m^2} = 2$

12. $3m^2 = 3 - 8m$

13. $3x^2 - 9x + 4 = 0$

*14. $x^2 = -12$

15. $x\sqrt{2} = \sqrt{5x - 2}$

16. $12x^4 - 11x^2 + 2 = 0$

17. $(2k + 5)^2 = 12$

18. $\dfrac{2}{x} + \dfrac{1}{x - 2} - \dfrac{5}{3} = 0$

19. $t^4 + 14 = 9t^2$

20. $2x^2 + 4x = 5$

*21. $z^2 + z + 2 = 0$

22. $x^4 - 8x^2 = -1$

23. $4t^2 - 12t + 9 = 0$

24. $x\sqrt{3} = \sqrt{2 - x}$

25. $r^2 - 72 = 0$

26. $-3x^2 + 4x = -4$

27. $x^2 - 5x - 36 = 0$

28. $w^2 = 169$

*29. $3p^2 = 6p - 4$

30. $z = \sqrt{\dfrac{5z + 3}{2}}$

31. $2(3k - 1)^2 + 5(3k - 1) = -2$

*32. $\dfrac{4}{r^2} + 3 = \dfrac{1}{r}$

33. $x - \sqrt{15 - 2x} = 0$

34. $3 = \dfrac{1}{t + 2} + \dfrac{2}{(t + 2)^2}$

*35. $4k^4 + 5k^2 + 1 = 0$

36. $(x + 1)^{2/3} - (x + 1)^{1/3} = 2$

---

*This exercise requires knowledge of complex numbers.

11.5 | Formulas and Further Applications

OBJECTIVES

1. Solve formulas involving squares and square roots for specified variables.
2. Solve applied problems using the Pythagorean theorem.
3. Solve applied problems using area formulas.
4. Solve applied problems using quadratic functions as models.

OBJECTIVE 1 Solve formulas involving squares and square roots for specified variables.

EXAMPLE 1   Solving for Specified Variables

Solve each formula for the specified variable. Keep $\pm$ in the answer in part (a).

(a) $w = \dfrac{kFr}{v^2}$ for v [The goal is to isolate v on one side.]

$v^2w = kFr$ Multiply by v^2.

$v^2 = \dfrac{kFr}{w}$ Divide by w.

[Include both positive and negative roots.] $v = \pm\sqrt{\dfrac{kFr}{w}}$ Square root property

$v = \dfrac{\pm\sqrt{kFr}}{\sqrt{w}} \cdot \dfrac{\sqrt{w}}{\sqrt{w}}$ Rationalize the denominator.

$v = \dfrac{\pm\sqrt{kFrw}}{w}$ $\sqrt{a} \cdot \sqrt{b} = \sqrt{ab};\ \sqrt{a} \cdot \sqrt{a} = a$

(b) $d = \sqrt{\dfrac{4\mathcal{A}}{\pi}}$ for $\mathcal{A}$ [The goal is to isolate $\mathcal{A}$ on one side.]

$d^2 = \dfrac{4\mathcal{A}}{\pi}$ Square each side.

$\pi d^2 = 4\mathcal{A}$ Multiply by π.

$\dfrac{\pi d^2}{4} = \mathcal{A}$ Divide by 4.

$\mathcal{A} = \dfrac{\pi d^2}{4}$ Interchange sides.

◀ **Work Problem 1** at the Side

---

1. Solve each formula for the specified variable. Keep $\pm$ in the answer in part (a).

(a) $n = \dfrac{ab}{E^2}$ for E

(b) $S = \sqrt{\dfrac{pq}{n}}$ for p

EXAMPLE 2   Solving for a Specified Variable

Solve $s = 2t^2 + kt$ for t.

Because the equation has terms with t^2 and t, we write it in standard form $ax^2 + bx + c = 0$, with t as the variable instead of x.

$s = 2t^2 + kt$

$0 = 2t^2 + kt - s$ Subtract s.

$2t^2 + kt - s = 0$ Standard form

To solve $2t^2 + kt - s = 0$ for t, we use the quadratic formula.

Continued on Next Page

Answers

1. (a) $E = \dfrac{\pm\sqrt{abn}}{n}$ **(b)** $p = \dfrac{nS^2}{q}$

$$t = \frac{-b \pm \sqrt{b^2 - 4ac}}{2a}$$ Quadratic formula

$$t = \frac{-k \pm \sqrt{k^2 - 4(2)(-s)}}{2(2)}$$ In $2t^2 + kt - s = 0$, $a = 2$, $b = k$, and $c = -s$.

$$t = \frac{-k \pm \sqrt{k^2 + 8s}}{4}$$ Simplify.

The two solutions are $t = \dfrac{-k + \sqrt{k^2 + 8s}}{4}$ and $t = \dfrac{-k - \sqrt{k^2 + 8s}}{4}$.

———————— **Work Problem ② at the Side.** ▶

OBJECTIVE ② Solve applied problems using the Pythagorean theorem.
The Pythagorean theorem is represented by the equation

$$a^2 + b^2 = c^2.$$ See Figure 2.

EXAMPLE 3 Using the Pythagorean Theorem

Two cars left an intersection at the same time, one heading due north, the other due west. Some time later, they were exactly 100 mi apart. The car headed north had gone 20 mi farther than the car headed west. How far had each car traveled?

Step 1 **Read** the problem carefully.

Step 2 **Assign a variable.**

Let x = the distance traveled by the car headed west.

Then $x + 20$ = the distance traveled by the car headed north.

See **Figure 3.** The cars are 100 mi apart, so the hypotenuse of the right triangle equals 100.

Step 3 **Write an equation.** Use the Pythagorean theorem.

$$a^2 + b^2 = c^2$$ Pythagorean theorem

$(x+y)^2 = x^2 + 2xy + y^2$ ⟍ $x^2 + (x + 20)^2 = 100^2$ See Figure 3.

Step 4 **Solve.** $x^2 + x^2 + 40x + 400 = 10{,}000$ Square the binomial.

$$2x^2 + 40x - 9600 = 0$$ Standard form

$$x^2 + 20x - 4800 = 0$$ Divide by 2.

$$(x + 80)(x - 60) = 0$$ Factor.

$$x + 80 = 0 \quad \text{or} \quad x - 60 = 0$$ Zero-factor property

$$x = -80 \quad \text{or} \quad x = 60$$ Solve for x.

Step 5 **State the answer.** Distance cannot be negative, so discard the negative solution. The distances are **60** mi and **60 + 20 = 80** mi.

Step 6 **Check.** Here $60^2 + 80^2 = 100^2$, as required.

———————— **Work Problem ③ at the Side.** ▶

② Solve $2t^2 - 5t + k = 0$ for t.

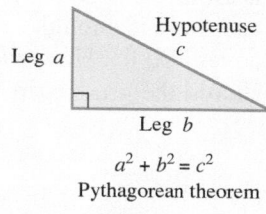

$a^2 + b^2 = c^2$
Pythagorean theorem
Figure 2

③ Solve the problem.
    A ladder is learning against a house. The distance from the bottom of the ladder to the house is 5 ft. The distance from the top of the ladder to the ground is 1 ft less than the length of the ladder. How long is the ladder?

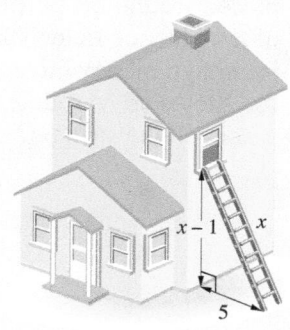

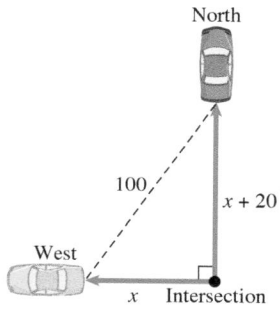

North

100

$x + 20$

West

x Intersection

Figure 3

Answers

2. $t = \dfrac{5 + \sqrt{25 - 8k}}{4}$, $t = \dfrac{5 - \sqrt{25 - 8k}}{4}$

3. 13 ft

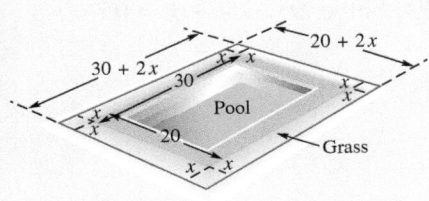

Figure 4

4 Solve each problem.

(a) Suppose the pool in **Example 4** is 20 ft by 40 ft and there is enough seed to cover 700 ft². How wide should the grass strip be?

(b) A football practice field is 30 yd wide and 40 yd long. A strip of grass sod of uniform width is to be placed around the perimeter of the practice field. There is enough money budgeted for 296 sq yd of sod. How wide will the strip be?

OBJECTIVE ▶ **3** Solve applied problems using area formulas.

EXAMPLE 4 Solving an Area Problem

A rectangular reflecting pool in a park is 20 ft wide and 30 ft long. The park gardener wants to plant a strip of grass of uniform width around the edge of the pool. She has enough seed to cover 336 ft². How wide will the strip be?

Step 1 **Read** the problem carefully.

Step 2 **Assign a variable.** The pool is shown in **Figure 4.**

Let x = the unknown width of the grass strip.

Then $20 + 2x$ = the width of the large rectangle (which is the width of the pool plus two grass strips),

and $30 + 2x$ = the length of the large rectangle.

Step 3 **Write an equation.** Refer to **Figure 4.**

$(30 + 2x)(20 + 2x)$ Area of large rectangle (length · width)

$30 \cdot 20,$ or 600 Area of pool (in square feet)

The area of the large rectangle minus the area of the pool should equal 336 ft², the area of the grass strip.

$$\begin{array}{ccc} \text{Area of large} & \text{area of} & \text{area of} \\ \text{rectangle} & - \quad \text{pool} & = \text{grass.} \\ \downarrow & \downarrow & \downarrow \end{array}$$

$$(30 + 2x)(20 + 2x) - 600 = 336$$

Step 4 **Solve.**

$$\begin{aligned} 600 + 100x + 4x^2 - 600 &= 336 & \text{Multiply.} \\ 4x^2 + 100x - 336 &= 0 & \text{Standard form} \\ x^2 + 25x - 84 &= 0 & \text{Divide by 4.} \\ (x + 28)(x - 3) &= 0 & \text{Factor.} \end{aligned}$$

$x + 28 = 0$ or $x - 3 = 0$ Zero-factor property

$x = -28$ or $x = 3$ Solve each equation.

Step 5 **State the answer.** The width cannot be -28 ft, so the grass strip will be 3 ft wide.

Step 6 **Check.** If $x = 3$, we can find the area of the large rectangle (which includes the grass strip).

$$(30 + 2 \cdot 3)(20 + 2 \cdot 3) = 36 \cdot 26 = 936 \text{ ft}^2 \quad \text{Area of pool and strip}$$

The area of the pool is

$$30 \cdot 20 = 600 \text{ ft}^2.$$

So, the area of the grass strip is

$$936 - 600 = 336 \text{ ft}^2, \quad \text{as required.}$$

The answer is correct.

◀ **Work Problem** **4** at the Side

Answers

4. (a) 5 ft (b) 2 yd

OBJECTIVE 4 Solve applied problems using quadratic functions as models. Some applied problems can be modeled by *quadratic functions,* which for real numbers a, b, and c can be written in the form

$$f(x) = ax^2 + bx + c \quad (\text{where } a \neq 0).$$

EXAMPLE 5 Solving an Applied Problem Using a Quadratic Function

If an object is projected upward from the top of a 144-ft building at 112 ft per sec, its position (in feet above the ground) is given by

$$s(t) = -16t^2 + 112t + 144,$$

where t is time in seconds after it was projected. When does it hit the ground?

When the object hits the ground, its distance above the ground is 0. We must find the value of t that makes $s(t) = 0$.

$s(t) = -16t^2 + 112t + 144$	Given model
$0 = -16t^2 + 112t + 144$	Let $s(t) = 0$.
$0 = t^2 - 7t - 9$	Divide by -16.
$t = \dfrac{-b \pm \sqrt{b^2 - 4ac}}{2a}$	Quadratic formula
$t = \dfrac{-(-7) \pm \sqrt{(-7)^2 - 4(1)(-9)}}{2(1)}$	Let $a = 1$, $b = -7$, and $c = -9$.
$t = \dfrac{7 \pm \sqrt{85}}{2}$	Simplify.
$t \approx \dfrac{7 \pm 9.2}{2}$	Approximate the square root to the nearest tenth.
$t \approx 8.1$ or $t \approx -1.1$	Find the two solutions.

Time cannot be negative, so discard -1.1.

The object will hit the ground about **8.1** sec after it is projected.

Work Problem **5** at the Side. ▶

EXAMPLE 6 Using a Quadratic Function to Model the CPI

The Consumer Price Index (CPI) is used to measure trends in prices for a "basket" of goods purchased by typical American families. This index uses a base period of 1982–1984, which means that the index number for that period is 100. The quadratic function

$$f(x) = -0.002x^2 + 4.58x + 83.7$$

approximates the CPI for the years 1980–2014, where x is the number of years since 1980. (Data from Bureau of Labor Statistics.)

(a) Use the model to approximate the CPI for 2014.

For 2014, $x = 2014 - 1980 = 34$, so find $f(34)$.

$f(x) = -0.002x^2 + 4.58x + 83.7$	Given model
$f(34) = -0.002(34)^2 + 4.58(34) + 83.7$	Let $x = 34$.
$f(34) = 237$	Nearest whole number

According to the model, the CPI for 2014 was 237.

Continued on Next Page

5 Solve the problem.

A ball is projected vertically upward from the ground. Its distance in feet above the ground at t seconds is

$$s(t) = -16t^2 + 64t.$$

After how many seconds (to the nearest tenth) will the ball be 32 ft above the ground? (*Hint:* There are two answers.)

Answer
5. 0.6 sec and 3.4 sec

6 Refer to **Example 6.**

(a) Use the model

$$f(x) = -0.002x^2 + 4.58x + 83.7$$

to approximate the CPI for 2010, to the nearest whole number.

(b) In what year did the CPI reach 175? (Round down for the year.)

(b) In what year did the CPI reach 200?

Find the value of x that makes $f(x) = 200$.

$f(x) = -0.002x^2 + 4.58x + 83.7$	Given model
$200 = -0.002x^2 + 4.58x + 83.7$	Let $f(x) = 200$.
$0 = -0.002x^2 + 4.58x - 116.3$	Subtract 200.
$x = \dfrac{-b \pm \sqrt{b^2 - 4ac}}{2a}$	Use $a = -0.002$, $b = 4.58$, and $c = -116.3$ in the quadratic formula.
$x = \dfrac{-4.58 \pm \sqrt{4.58^2 - 4(-0.002)(-116.3)}}{2(-0.002)}$	
$x \approx 25.7$ or $x \approx 2264.3$	Use a calculator. Round to the nearest tenth.

Rounding the first value 25.7 down to 25, the CPI first reached 200 in

$$1980 + 25 = 2005.$$

(Reject the proposed solution $x \approx 2264.3$ because it corresponds to a totally unreasonable year.)

◀ **Work Problem 6 at the Side.**

Answers

6. (a) 219 (b) 2000

11.5 Exercises

CONCEPT CHECK *Answer each question.*

1. What is the first step in solving a formula like
$$gw^2 = 2r \quad \text{for } w?$$

2. What is the first step in solving a formula like
$$gw^2 = kw + 24 \quad \text{for } w?$$

For each triangle, solve for m in terms of the other variables (where m > 0).

3.

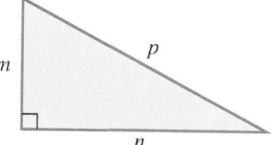

4.

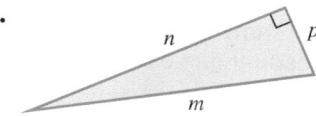

Solve each equation for the indicated variable. (Leave ± in the answers as needed.)
See Examples 1 and 2.

5. $d = kt^2$ for t

6. $S = 6e^2$ for e

7. $s = kwd^2$ for d

8. $S = \pi r^2 h$ for r

9. $I = \dfrac{ks}{d^2}$ for d

10. $R = \dfrac{k}{d^2}$ for d

11. $F = \dfrac{kA}{v^2}$ for v

12. $L = \dfrac{kd^4}{h^2}$ for h

13. $V = \pi r^2 h$ for r

14. $V = \dfrac{1}{3}\pi r^2 h$ for r

15. $At^2 + Bt = -C$ for t

16. $S = 2\pi rh + \pi r^2$ for r

17. $D = \sqrt{kh}$ for h

18. $F = \dfrac{k}{\sqrt{d}}$ for d

19. $p = \sqrt{\dfrac{k\ell}{g}}$ for ℓ

20. $p = \sqrt{\dfrac{k\ell}{g}}$ for g

Solve each problem. Round answers to the nearest tenth as needed. ***See Example 3.***

21. Find the lengths of the sides of the triangle.

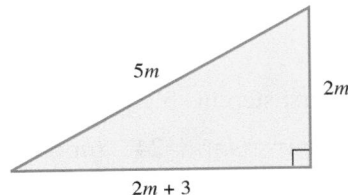

22. Find the lengths of the sides of the triangle.

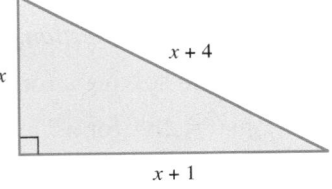

23. Two ships leave port at the same time, one heading due south and the other heading due east. Several hours later, they are 170 mi apart. If the ship traveling south traveled 70 mi farther than the other, how many miles did they each travel?

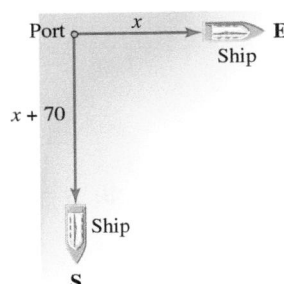

24. Faith is flying a kite that is 30 ft farther above her hand than its horizontal distance from her. The string from her hand to the kite is 150 ft long. How high is the kite?

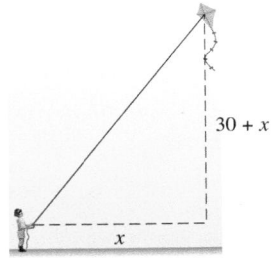

25. A game board is in the shape of a right triangle. The hypotenuse is 2 in. longer than the longer leg, and the longer leg is 1 in. less than twice as long as the shorter leg. How long is each side of the game board?

26. Manuel is planting a garden in the shape of a right triangle. The longer leg is 3 ft longer than the shorter leg. The hypotenuse is 3 ft longer than the longer leg. Find the lengths of the three sides of the garden.

27. The diagonal of a rectangular rug measures 26 ft, and the length is 4 ft more than twice the width. Find the length and width of the rug.

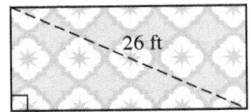

28. A 15-ft ladder is leaning against a house. The distance from the bottom of the ladder to the house is 3 ft less than the distance from the top of the ladder to the ground. How far is the bottom of the ladder from the house?

Solve each problem. See Example 4.

29. A club swimming pool is 30 ft wide and 40 ft long. The club members want an exposed aggregate border in a strip of uniform width around the pool. They have enough material for 296 ft². How wide can the strip be?

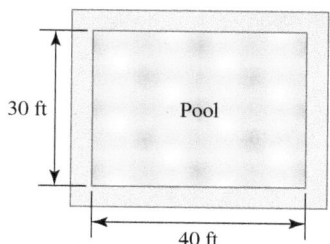

30. A couple wants to buy a rug for a room that is 20 ft long and 15 ft wide. They want to leave an even strip of flooring uncovered around the edges of the room. How wide a strip will they have if they buy a rug with an area of 234 ft²?

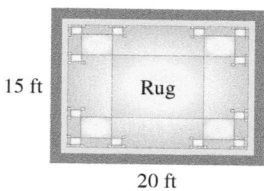

31. Mariana's backyard measures 20 m by 30 m. She wants to put a flower garden in the middle of the yard, leaving a strip of grass of uniform width around the flower garden. Mariana must have 184 m² of grass. Under these conditions, what will the length and width of the garden be?

32. A rectangle has a length 2 m less than twice its width. When 5 m are added to the width, the resulting figure is a square with an area of 144 m². Find the dimensions of the original rectangle.

33. A rectangular piece of sheet metal has a length that is 4 in. less than twice the width. A square piece 2 in. on a side is cut from each corner. The sides are then turned up to form an uncovered box of volume 256 in.³. Find the length and width of the original piece of metal.

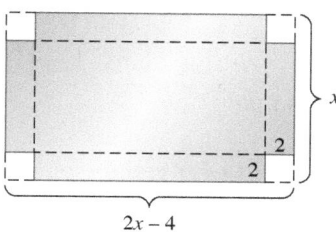

34. A rectangular piece of cardboard is 2 in. longer than it is wide. A square piece 3 in. on a side is cut from each corner. The sides are then turned up to form an uncovered box of volume 765 in.³. Find the dimensions of the original piece of cardboard.

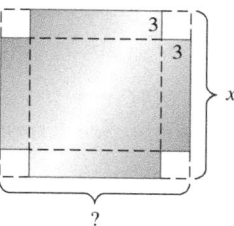

Solve each problem. Round answers to the nearest tenth as needed. See Example 5.

35. An object is projected directly upward from the ground. After t seconds its distance in feet above the ground is

$$s(t) = -16t^2 + 144t.$$

After how many seconds will the object be 128 ft above the ground? (*Hint:* Look for a common factor before solving the equation.)

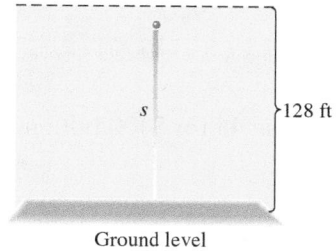

36. A toy rocket is launched from ground level. After t seconds its distance in feet above the ground is

$$s(t) = -16t^2 + 208t.$$

After how many seconds will the rocket be 550 ft above the ground?

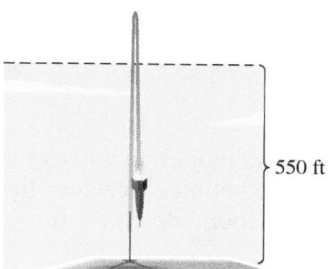

37. The following function gives the distance in feet a car going approximately 68 mph will skid in t seconds.

$$D(t) = 13t^2 - 100t$$

Find the time it would take for the car to skid 180 ft.

38. Refer to the function in **Exercise 37.** Find the time it would take for the car to skid 500 ft.

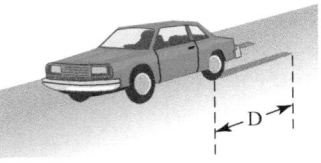

A ball is projected upward from ground level, and its distance in feet from the ground in t seconds is given by

$$s(t) = -16t^2 + 160t.$$

39. After how many seconds does the ball reach a height of 400 ft? Describe in words its position at this height.

40. After how many seconds does it reach a height of 425 ft? Interpret the mathematical result here.

Solve each problem using a quadratic equation.

41. A certain bakery has found that the daily demand for blueberry muffins is $\frac{6000}{p}$, where p is the price of a muffin in cents. The daily supply is $3p - 410$. Find the price at which supply and demand are equal.

42. In one area the demand for Blu-ray discs is $\frac{1900}{P}$ per day, where P is the price in dollars per disc. The supply is $5P - 1$ per day. At what price, to the nearest cent, does supply equal demand?

Total spending (in billions of dollars) in the United States from all sources on physician and clinical services for the years 2000–2014 are shown in the bar graph and can be modeled by the quadratic function

$$f(x) = -0.2901x^2 + 25.90x + 291.6.$$

*Here, $x = 0$ represents 2000, $x = 1$ represents 2001, and so on. Use the graph and the model to work each problem. **See Example 6.***

43. Approximate spending on physician and clinical services in 2012 to the nearest $10 billion using

  (a) the graph and   **(b)** the model.

  (c) How do the two approximations compare?

44. Repeat **Exercise 43** for the year 2008.

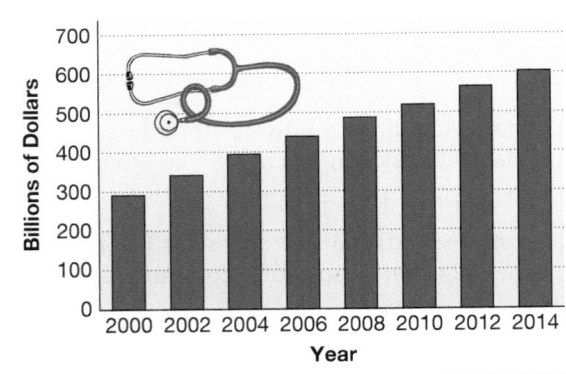

Spending on Physician and Clinical Services

Data from Centers for Medicare and Medicaid Services.

45. According to the model, in what year did spending on physician and clinical services first exceed $500 billion? (Round down for the year.)

46. Repeat **Exercise 45** for $400 billion.

William Froude was a 19th-century naval architect who used the expression

$$\frac{v^2}{g\ell}$$

in shipbuilding. This expression, known as the **Froude number,** was also used by R. McNeill Alexander in his research on dinosaurs. (*Data from* "How Dinosaurs Ran," *Scientific American.*)

Use this expression to find the value of *v* (in meters per second) to the nearest tenth, given *g* = 9.8 m per sec².

47. Rhinoceros: ℓ = 1.2; Froude number = 2.57

48. Triceratops: ℓ = 2.8; Froude number = 0.16

Recall that corresponding sides of similar triangles are proportional. Use this fact to find the lengths of the indicated sides of each pair of similar triangles. Check all possible solutions in both triangles. Sides of a triangle cannot be negative (and are not drawn to scale here).

49. Side *AC*

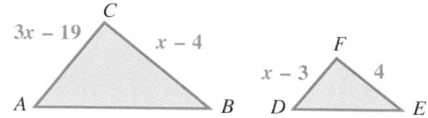

50. Side *RQ*

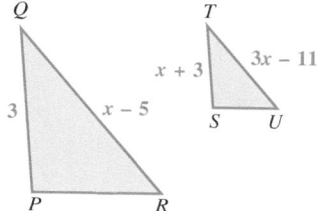

Relating Concepts (Exercises 51–54) For Individual or Group Work

In the 1939 classic movie The Wizard of Oz, *Ray Bolger's character, the Scarecrow, wants a brain. When the Wizard grants him his "Th.D." (Doctor of Thinkology), the Scarecrow replies with the following statement.*

Scarecrow: The sum of the square roots of any two sides of an isosceles triangle is equal to the square root of the remaining side.

His statement sounds like the formula for the Pythagorean theorem. To see why it is incorrect, **work Exercises 51–54 in order.**

51. To what kind of triangle does the Scarecrow refer in his statement? To what kind of triangle does the Pythagorean theorem actually refer?

52. In the Scarecrow's statement, he refers to square roots. In applying the formula for the Pythagorean theorem, do we find square roots of the sides? If not, what do we find?

53. An isosceles triangle has two sides of equal length. Draw an isosceles triangle with two sides of length 9 units and remaining side of length 4 units. Show that this triangle does not satisfy the Scarecrow's statement. (This is a *counterexample* and is sufficient to show that his statement is false in general.)

54. Use wording similar to that of the Scarecrow, but state the Pythagorean theorem correctly.

11.6 | Graphs of Quadratic Functions

OBJECTIVES

1. Graph a quadratic function.
2. Graph parabolas with horizontal and vertical shifts.
3. Use the coefficient of x^2 to predict the shape and direction in which a parabola opens.
4. Find a quadratic function to model data.

OBJECTIVE 1 Graph a quadratic function. **Figure 5** gives a graph of the simplest *quadratic function* $y = x^2$.

x	y
-2	4
-1	1
0	0
1	1
2	4

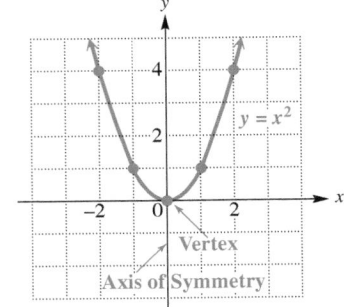

Figure 5

This graph is a parabola. The point $(0, 0)$, the lowest point on the curve, is the vertex of this parabola. The vertical line through the vertex is the **axis of symmetry,** or simply the **axis,** of the parabola. Here, its equation is $x = 0$. A parabola is **symmetric about its axis**—that is, if the graph were folded along the axis, the two portions of the curve would coincide.

As **Figure 5** suggests, x can be any real number, so the domain of the function $y = x^2$, written in interval notation, is $(-\infty, \infty)$. Values of y are always nonnegative, so the range is $[0, \infty)$.

Quadratic Function

A function that can be written in the form

$$f(x) = ax^2 + bx + c$$

for real numbers a, b, and c, where $a \neq 0$, is a **quadratic function.**

The graph of any quadratic function is a parabola with a vertical axis.

Note

We use the variable y and function notation $f(x)$ interchangeably. Although the letter f is most often used to name quadratic functions, other letters can be used. We use the capital letter F to distinguish between different parabolas graphed on the same coordinate axes.

Parabolas have a special reflecting property that makes them useful in the design of telescopes, radar equipment, solar furnaces, and automobile headlights. See **Figure 6.**

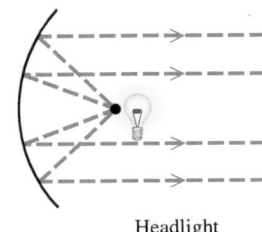

Headlight

Figure 6

OBJECTIVE ▶ **2** Graph parabolas with horizontal and vertical shifts. Parabolas need not have their vertices at the origin, as is the case with the graph of $f(x) = x^2$.

EXAMPLE 1 Graphing a Parabola (Vertical Shift)

Graph $F(x) = x^2 - 2$.

If $x = 0$, then $F(x) = -2$, which gives the vertex $(0, -2)$. The graph of $F(x) = x^2 - 2$ has the same shape as that of $f(x) = x^2$, but is *shifted*, or *translated*, 2 units down. Every function value is 2 less than the corresponding function value of $f(x) = x^2$. Plotting points on both sides of the vertex gives the graph in **Figure 7**.

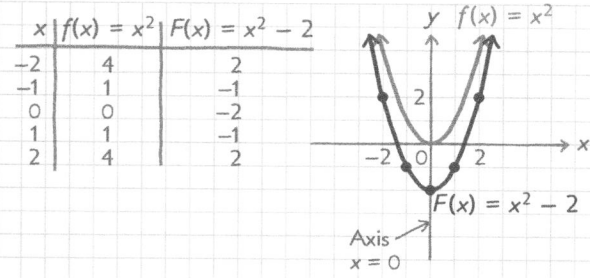

$F(x) = x^2 - 2$

Vertex: $(0, -2)$

Axis of symmetry: $x = 0$

Domain: $(-\infty, \infty)$

Range: $[-2, \infty)$

The graph of $f(x) = x^2$ is shown for comparison.

Figure 7

This parabola is symmetric about its axis $x = 0$, so the plotted points are "mirror images" of each other. Because x can be any real number, the domain is $(-\infty, \infty)$. The value of y (or $F(x)$) is always greater than or equal to -2, so the range is $[-2, \infty)$.

─────────── **Work Problem ① at the Side.** ▶

Parabola with a Vertical Shift

The graph of **$F(x) = x^2 + k$** is a parabola.

- The graph has the same shape as the graph of $f(x) = x^2$.
- The parabola is shifted k units up if $k > 0$, and $|k|$ units down if $k < 0$.
- The vertex of the parabola is $(0, k)$.

EXAMPLE 2 Graphing a Parabola (Horizontal Shift)

Graph $F(x) = (x - 2)^2$.

If $x = 2$, then $F(x) = 0$, which gives the vertex $(2, 0)$. The graph of

$$F(x) = (x - 2)^2$$

has the same shape as that of $f(x) = x^2$, but is shifted 2 units *to the right*. We plot several points on one side of the vertex. Then we use symmetry about the axis $x = 2$ to find corresponding points on the other side of the vertex. If $x = 0$, for example, then

$$F(0) = (0 - 2)^2 = 4,$$

and the point $(0, 4)$ lies on the graph. The corresponding point two units on the "other" side of the axis $x = 2$ is the point $(4, 4)$, which also lies on the graph. See **Figure 8** on the next page.

─────────── **Continued on Next Page**

① Graph the parabola.

$$f(x) = x^2 - 3$$

Give the vertex, axis of symmetry, domain, and range.

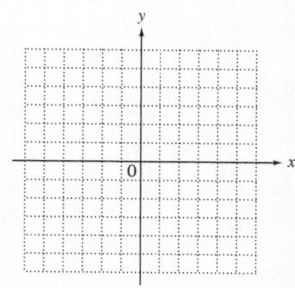

Answer

1.

vertex: $(0, -3)$; axis: $x = 0$;

domain: $(-\infty, \infty)$; range: $[-3, \infty)$

2 Graph the parabola.

$$f(x) = (x - 3)^2$$

Give the vertex, axis of symmetry, domain, and range.

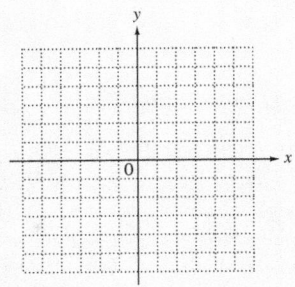

3 Graph the parabola.

$$f(x) = (x - 2)^2 + 5$$

Give the vertex, axis of symmetry, domain, and range.

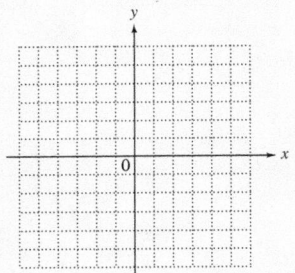

Answers

2.

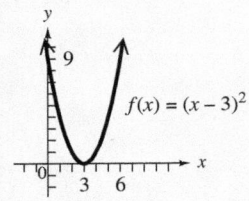

vertex: $(3, 0)$; axis: $x = 3$;
domain: $(-\infty, \infty)$; range: $[0, \infty)$

3.

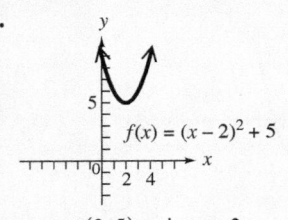

vertex: $(2, 5)$; axis: $x = 2$;
domain: $(-\infty, \infty)$; range: $[5, \infty)$

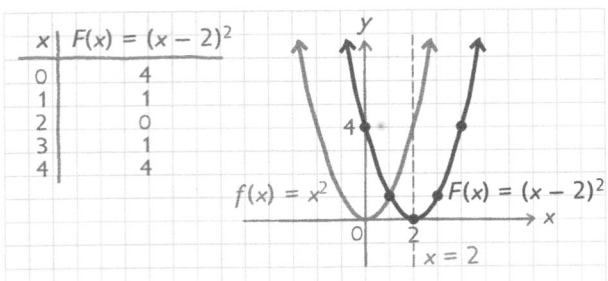

x	$F(x) = (x - 2)^2$
0	4
1	1
2	0
3	1
4	4

$F(x) = (x - 2)^2$
Vertex: $(2, 0)$
Axis of symmetry: $x = 2$
Domain: $(-\infty, \infty)$
Range: $[0, \infty)$

Figure 8

◀ **Work Problem 2 at the Side.**

Parabola with a Horizontal Shift

The graph of $F(x) = (x - h)^2$ is a parabola.

- The graph has the same shape as the graph of $f(x) = x^2$.
- The parabola is shifted h units to the right if $h > 0$, and $|h|$ units to the left if $h < 0$.
- The vertex of the parabola is $(h, 0)$.

⚠ **CAUTION**

Errors frequently occur when horizontal shifts are involved. To determine the direction and magnitude of a horizontal shift, find the value that causes the expression $x - h$ to equal 0, as shown below.

$$F(x) = (x - 5)^2 \qquad\qquad F(x) = (x + 5)^2$$

Because **+5** causes $x - 5$ to equal 0, the graph of $F(x)$ illustrates a shift of

Because **−5** causes $x + 5$ to equal 0, the graph of $F(x)$ illustrates a shift of

5 units *to the right*.   **5 units *to the left*.**

EXAMPLE 3   **Graphing a Parabola (Horizontal and Vertical Shifts)**

Graph $F(x) = (x + 3)^2 - 2$.

This graph has the same shape as that of $f(x) = x^2$, but is shifted 3 units *to the left* (because $x + 3 = 0$ when $x = -3$) and 2 units *down* (because of the negative sign in -2). This gives the vertex $(-3, -2)$. Find and plot several ordered pairs, using symmetry as needed, to obtain the graph in **Figure 9**.

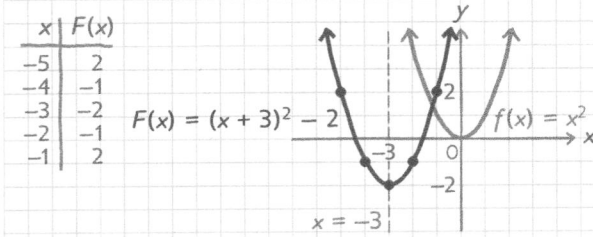

x	$F(x)$
−5	2
−4	−1
−3	−2
−2	−1
−1	2

$F(x) = (x + 3)^2 - 2$
Vertex: $(-3, -2)$
Axis of symmetry: $x = -$
Domain: $(-\infty, \infty)$
Range: $[-2, \infty)$

Figure 9

◀ **Work Problem 3 at the Side.**

Parabola with Horizontal and Vertical Shifts

The graph of $F(x) = (x - h)^2 + k$ is a parabola.

- The graph has the same shape as the graph of $f(x) = x^2$.
- The vertex of the parabola is (h, k).
- The axis of symmetry is the vertical line $x = h$.

OBJECTIVE ▶ ③ **Use the coefficient of x^2 to predict the shape and direction in which a parabola opens.** Not all parabolas open up, and not all parabolas have the same shape as the graph of $f(x) = x^2$.

EXAMPLE 4   Graphing a Parabola That Opens Down

Graph $f(x) = -\frac{1}{2}x^2$.

This parabola is shown in **Figure 10.** The coefficient of x^2, $-\frac{1}{2}$, affects the shape of the graph—the $\frac{1}{2}$ makes the parabola wider (because the values of $\frac{1}{2}x^2$ increase more slowly than those of x^2), and the negative sign makes the parabola open down.

The graph is not shifted in any direction, so the vertex is $(0, 0)$. Unlike the parabolas graphed in **Examples 1–3,** the vertex $(0, 0)$ has the *greatest* function value of any point on the graph.

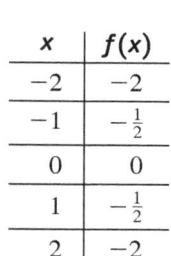

x	$f(x)$
-2	-2
-1	$-\frac{1}{2}$
0	0
1	$-\frac{1}{2}$
2	-2

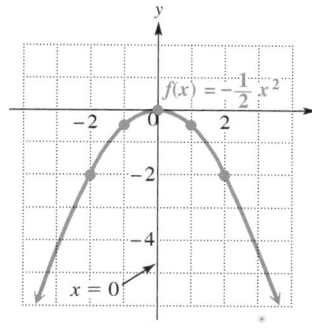

$f(x) = -\frac{1}{2}x^2$
Vertex: $(0, 0)$
Axis of symmetry: $x = 0$
Domain: $(-\infty, \infty)$
Range: $(-\infty, 0]$

Figure 10

──────── Work Problem ④ at the Side. ▶

This discussion can be summarized as follows.

General Characteristics of the Graph of a Vertical Parabola

The graph of the quadratic function $F(x) = a(x - h)^2 + k$ (where $a \neq 0$) is a parabola.

- The vertex of the parabola is (h, k).
- The axis of symmetry is the vertical line $x = h$.
- The graph opens up if $a > 0$ and down if $a < 0$.
- The graph is wider than that of $f(x) = x^2$ if $0 < |a| < 1$.
  The graph is narrower than that of $f(x) = x^2$ if $|a| > 1$.

④ Graph the parabola.

$$f(x) = -\frac{2}{3}x^2$$

Give the vertex, axis of symmetry, domain, and range.

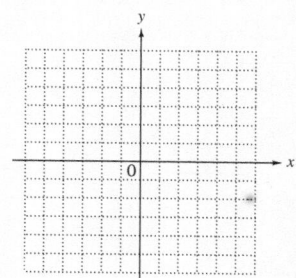

Answer

4.

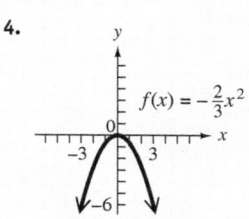

vertex: $(0, 0)$; axis: $x = 0$;
domain: $(-\infty, \infty)$; range: $(-\infty, 0]$

⑤ Graph the parabola.

$$f(x) = \frac{1}{2}(x - 2)^2 + 1$$

Give the vertex, axis of symmetry, domain, and range.

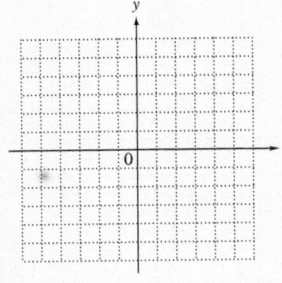

EXAMPLE 5 **Using the General Characteristics to Graph a Parabola**

Graph $F(x) = -2(x + 3)^2 + 4$.

The parabola opens down (because $a = -2$ and $-2 < 0$) and is narrower than the graph of $f(x) = x^2$ (because $|-2| = 2$ and $2 > 1$). This causes values of $F(x)$ to decrease more quickly than those of $f(x) = -x^2$.

The graph is shifted 3 units *to the left* (because $x + 3 = 0$ when $x = -3$) and 4 units *up* (because of the $+4$), which gives the vertex $(-3, 4)$. To complete the graph, we plotted the ordered pairs $(-4, 2)$ and, by symmetry, $(-2, 2)$. Symmetry can be used to find additional ordered pairs that satisfy the equation. See **Figure 11**.

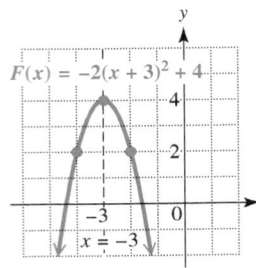

$F(x) = -2(x + 3)^2 + 4$
Vertex: $(-3, 4)$
Axis of symmetry: $x = -3$
Domain: $(-\infty, \infty)$
Range: $(-\infty, 4]$

Figure 11

◀ Work Problem **⑤** at the Side.

OBJECTIVE ▶ **④** Find a quadratic function to model data.

EXAMPLE 6 **Modeling the Number of Multiple Births**

The number of higher-order multiple births (triplets or more) in the United States is shown in the table. Here, x represents the number of years since 1996 and y represents the number of higher-order multiple births (to the nearest hundred).

Year	x	y
1996	0	5900
2000	4	7300
2002	6	7400
2004	8	7300
2006	10	6500
2008	12	6300
2010	14	5500
2012	16	4900
2014	18	4500

Data from National Center for Health Statistics.

Find a quadratic function that models the data.

A scatter diagram of the ordered pairs (x, y) is shown in **Figure 12** on the next page. The general shape suggested by the scatter diagram indicates that a parabola should approximate these points, as shown by the dashed curve in **Figure 13**. The equation for such a parabola would have a negative coefficient for x^2 because the graph opens down.

Answer

5.

$f(x) = \frac{1}{2}(x - 2)^2 + 1$

vertex: $(2, 1)$; axis: $x = 2$;
domain: $(-\infty, \infty)$; range: $[1, \infty)$

Continued on Next Page

U.S. HIGHER-ORDER
MULTIPLE BIRTHS

Figure 12

U.S. HIGHER-ORDER
MULTIPLE BIRTHS

Figure 13

6 Using the points $(0, 5900)$, $(4, 7300)$, and $(12, 6300)$, find another quadratic model for the data on higher-order multiple births in **Example 6.** (Round values of a and b to the nearest tenth.)

To find a quadratic function of the form

$$y = ax^2 + bx + c$$

that models, or *fits,* these data, we choose three representative ordered pairs and use them to write a system of three equations.

$(0, 5900)$, $(6, 7400)$,   and $(12, 6300)$ Three ordered pairs (x, y)

We substitute the x- and y-values from each ordered pair into the quadratic form $y = ax^2 + bx + c$ to obtain three equations.

$$a(0)^2 + b(0) + c = 5900 \xrightarrow{\text{Simplify.}} c = 5900 \quad (1)$$

$$a(6)^2 + b(6) + c = 7400 \longrightarrow 36a + 6b + c = 7400 \quad (2)$$

$$a(12)^2 + b(12) + c = 6300 \longrightarrow 144a + 12b + c = 6300 \quad (3)$$

We can find the values of a, b, and c, by solving this system of three equations in three variables. From equation (1), $c = 5900$, so we substitute 5900 for c in equations (2) and (3) to obtain two equations in two variables.

$$36a + 6b + 5900 = 7400 \xrightarrow[\text{5900.}]{\text{Subtract}} 36a + 6b = 1500 \quad (4)$$

$$144a + 12b + 5900 = 6300 \longrightarrow 144a + 12b = 400 \quad (5)$$

We eliminate b from this system of equations in two variables.

$$-72a - 12b = -3000 \quad \text{Multiply equation (4) by } -2.$$

$$\underline{144a + 12b = 400 \quad (5)}$$

$$72a = -2600 \quad \text{Add.}$$

$$a \approx -36.1 \quad \text{Use a calculator. Round to one decimal place.}$$

We substitute -36.1 for a in equation (4) to find that $b \approx 466.6$. (Substituting in equation (5) will give $b \approx 466.5$ due to rounding procedures.) Using the values we found for a, b, and c, the model is

$$y = \overset{a}{\underset{\downarrow}{-36.1}}x^2 + \overset{b}{\underset{\downarrow}{466.6}}x + \overset{c}{\underset{\downarrow}{5900}}.$$

——————— **Work Problem 6 at the Side.** ▶

Note

If we had chosen three different ordered pairs of data in **Example 6,** a slightly different model would have resulted, as in **Margin Problem 6.**

Answer

6. $y = -39.6x^2 + 508.4x + 5900$
(Answers may vary slightly due to rounding.)

11.6 Exercises

FOR EXTRA HELP

Go to MyMathLab *for worked-out, step-by-step solutions to exercises enclosed in a square* [ ] *and video solutions to* ▶ *exercises.*

CONCEPT CHECK *Match each quadratic function in parts (a)–(d) with its graph from choices A–D.*

1. (a) $f(x) = (x + 2)^2 - 1$ **(b)** $f(x) = (x + 2)^2 + 1$ **(c)** $f(x) = (x - 2)^2 - 1$ **(d)** $f(x) = (x - 2)^2 + 1$

A.
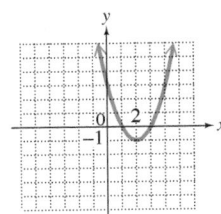

B.
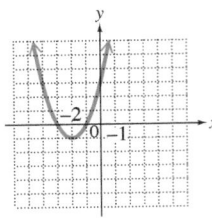

C.
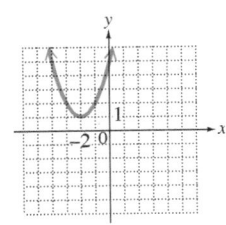

D.
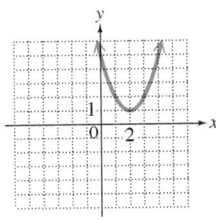

2. (a) $f(x) = -x^2 + 2$ **(b)** $f(x) = -x^2 - 2$ **(c)** $f(x) = -(x + 2)^2$ **(d)** $f(x) = -(x - 2)^2$

A.
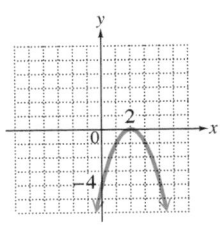

B.
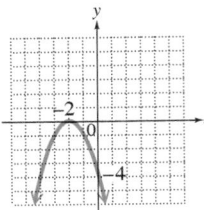

C.
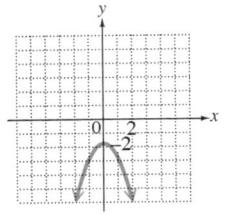

D.
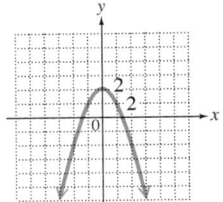

3. CONCEPT CHECK For the quadratic function

$$f(x) = a(x - h)^2 + k,$$

in what quadrant is the vertex if the values of h and k are as follows?

(a) $h > 0, k > 0$ **(b)** $h > 0, k < 0$

(c) $h < 0, k > 0$ **(d)** $h < 0, k < 0$

Consider the value of a.

(e) If $a > 0$, then the graph opens (*up / down*).

(f) If $a < 0$, then the graph opens (*up / down*)

(g) If $|a| > 1$, then the graph is (*narrower / wider*) than the graph of $f(x) = x^2$.

(h) If $0 < |a| < 1$, then the graph is (*narrower / wider*) than the graph of $f(x) = x^2$.

4. CONCEPT CHECK Match each quadratic function in Column I with the description of the parabola that is its graph in Column II.

I	II
(a) $f(x) = (x - 4)^2 - 2$	**A.** Vertex $(2, -4)$, opens down
(b) $f(x) = (x - 2)^2 - 4$	**B.** Vertex $(2, -4)$, opens up
(c) $f(x) = (x + 4)^2 + 2$	**C.** Vertex $(4, -2)$, opens down
(d) $f(x) = -(x - 4)^2 - 2$	**D.** Vertex $(4, -2)$, opens up
(e) $f(x) = -(x - 2)^2 - 4$	**E.** Vertex $(4, 2)$, opens down
(f) $f(x) = -(x - 4)^2 + 2$	**F.** Vertex $(-4, 2)$, opens up

Identity the vertex of each parabola. ***See Examples 1–4.***

5. $f(x) = -3x^2$ **6.** $f(x) = \frac{1}{2}x^2$ **7.** $f(x) = x^2 + 4$ **8.** $f(x) = x^2 - 4$

9. $f(x) = (x - 1)^2$ **10.** $f(x) = (x + 3)^2$ **11.** $f(x) = (x + 3)^2 - 4$

12. $f(x) = (x - 5)^2 - 8$ **13.** $f(x) = -(x - 5)^2 + 6$ **14.** $f(x) = -(x - 2)^2 + 1$

For each quadratic function, tell whether the graph opens up *or* down *and whether the graph is* wider, narrower, *or the* same shape *as the graph of* $f(x) = x^2$.
See Examples 4 and 5.

15. $f(x) = -\dfrac{2}{5}x^2$

16. $f(x) = -2x^2$

17. $f(x) = 3x^2 + 1$

18. $f(x) = \dfrac{2}{3}x^2 - 4$

19. $f(x) = -4(x + 2)^2 + 5$

20. $f(x) = -\dfrac{1}{3}(x + 6)^2 + 3$

Graph each parabola. Give the vertex, axis of symmetry, domain, and range.
See Examples 1–5.

21. $f(x) = 3x^2$

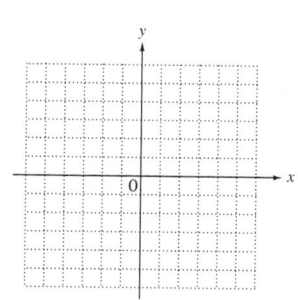

22. $f(x) = \dfrac{1}{2}x^2$

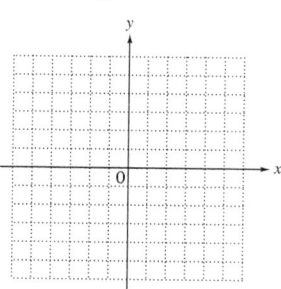

23. $f(x) = -2x^2$

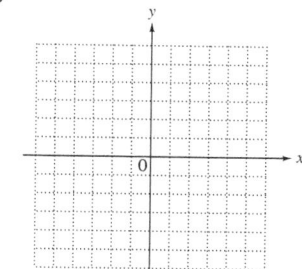

24. $f(x) = -\dfrac{1}{3}x^2$

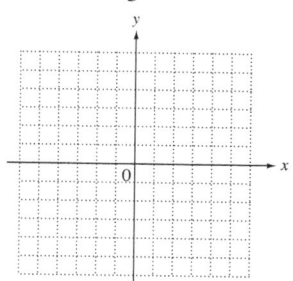

25. $f(x) = x^2 - 1$

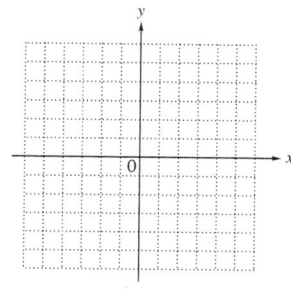

26. $f(x) = x^2 + 3$

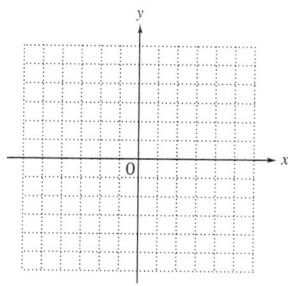

27. $f(x) = -x^2 + 2$

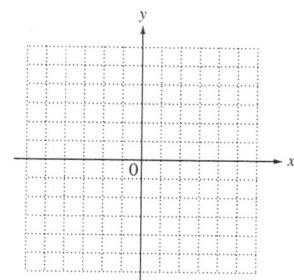

28. $f(x) = -x^2 - 2$

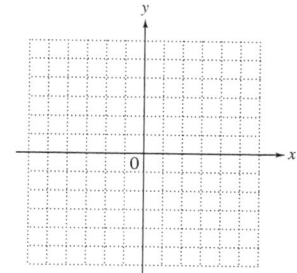

29. $f(x) = (x - 4)^2$

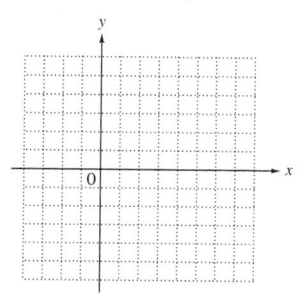

30. $f(x) = (x + 1)^2$

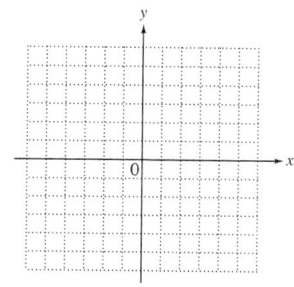

31. $f(x) = (x + 2)^2 - 1$

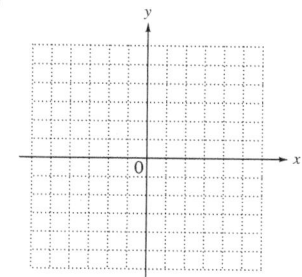

32. $f(x) = (x - 1)^2 + 2$

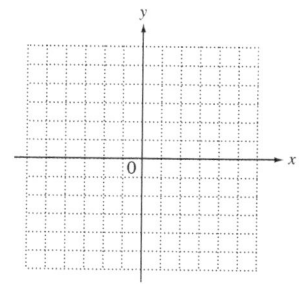

33. $f(x) = (x - 1)^2 - 3$　　**34.** $f(x) = (x + 1)^2 + 1$　　**35.** $f(x) = 2(x - 2)^2 - 3$　　**36.** $f(x) = 3(x - 2)^2 + 1$

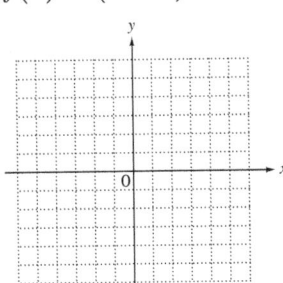 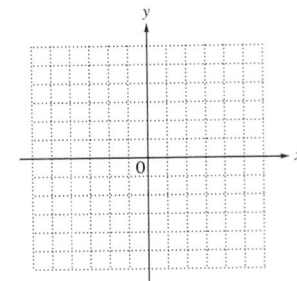 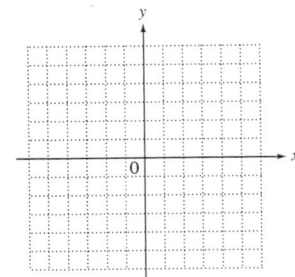 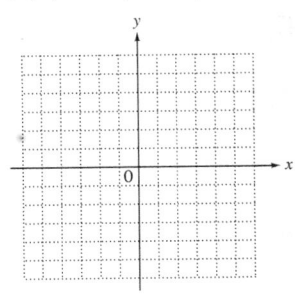

37. $f(x) = -2(x - 3)^2 + 2$　**38.** $f(x) = -2(x - 2)^2 - 3$　**39.** $f(x) = -\dfrac{1}{2}(x + 1)^2 + 2$　**40.** $f(x) = -\dfrac{2}{3}(x + 2)^2 + 1$

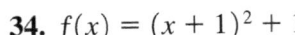

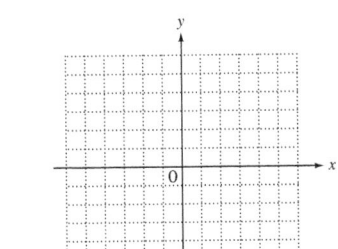 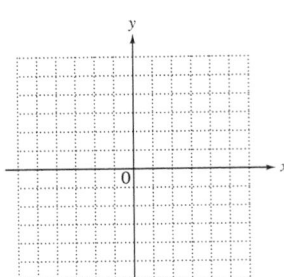 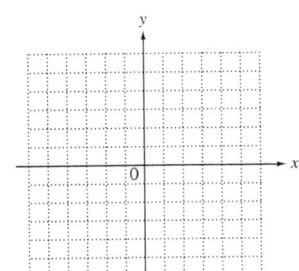 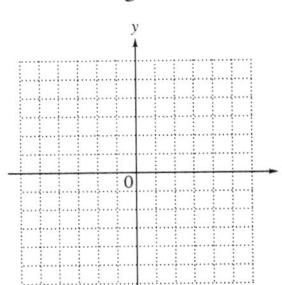

Decide whether a linear function *or a* quadratic function *would be a more appropriate model for each set of graphed data. If linear, tell whether the slope should be* positive *or* negative. *If quadratic, tell whether the coefficient of x^2 should be* positive *or* negative. ***See Example 6.***

41. **TIME SPENT PLAYING VIDEO GAMES**

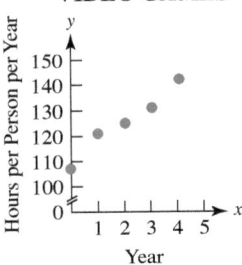

Data from www.statisca.com

42. **AVERAGE DAILY VOLUME OF FIRST-CLASS MAIL**

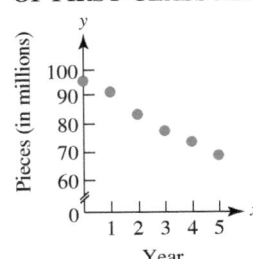

Data from USPS.

43. **FOOD ASSISTANCE SPENDING IN IOWA**

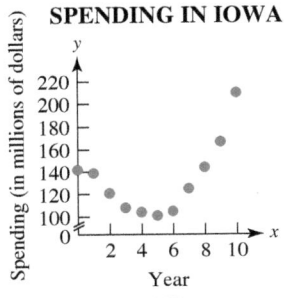

Data from Iowa DHS.

44. **U.S. FOREIGN-BORN POPULATION**

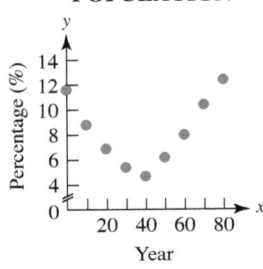

Data from U.S. Census Bureau.

45. **HIGH SCHOOL STUDENTS WHO SMOKE**

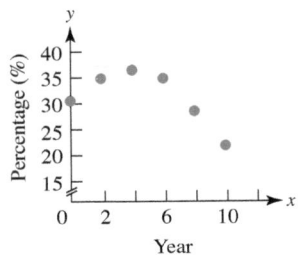

Data from www.cdc.gov

46. **SOCIAL SECURITY ASSETS**

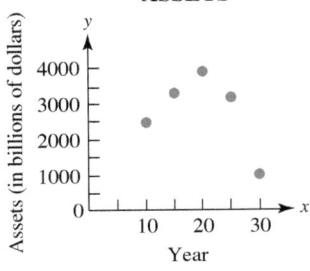

Data from SSA.

Solve each problem. See Example 6.

47. Federal student loans (in billions of dollars) are shown in the table, where *x* represents the number of years since 2009 and *y* represents total student loans.

Year	x	y
2009	0	93
2010	1	110
2011	2	116
2012	3	112
2013	4	106
2014	5	103
2015	6	96

Data from The College Board.

(a) Use the ordered pairs (x, y) to make a scatter diagram of the data.

FEDERAL STUDENT LOANS

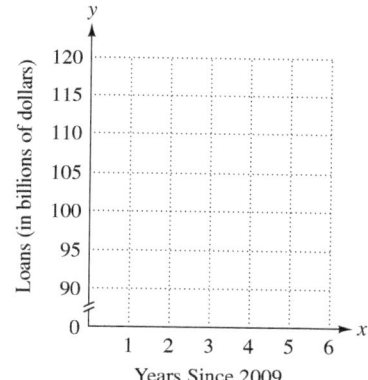

Years Since 2009

(b) Would a *linear function* or a *quadratic function* better model the data?

(c) Should the coefficient *a* of x^2 in a quadratic model $y = ax^2 + bx + c$ be *positive* or *negative?*

(d) Use the ordered pairs $(0, 93)$, $(2, 116)$, and $(4, 106)$ to find a quadratic function that models the data.

(e) Use the model from part (d) to approximate total federal student loans to the nearest billion dollars for 2012 and 2014. How well does the model approximate the actual data from the table?

48. The number (in thousands) of new, privately owned housing units started in the United States is shown in the table. Here *x* represents years since 2006 and *y* represents total housing starts.

Year	x	y
2006	0	1800
2007	1	1360
2008	2	910
2009	3	550
2010	4	590
2011	5	610
2012	6	780
2013	7	925
2014	8	1003

Data from U.S. Census Bureau.

(a) Use the ordered pairs (x, y) to make a scatter diagram of the data.

HOUSING STARTS

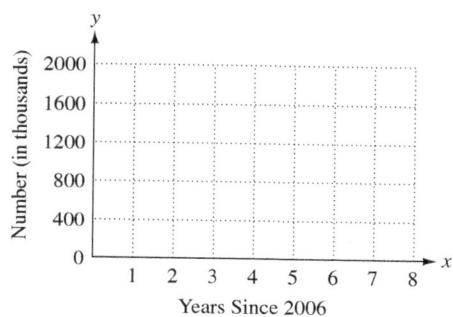

Years Since 2006

(b) Would a *linear function* or a *quadratic function* better model the data?

(c) Should the coefficient *a* of x^2 in a quadratic model $y = ax^2 + bx + c$ be *positive* or *negative?*

(d) Use the ordered pairs $(0, 1800)$, $(4, 590)$, and $(6, 780)$ to find a quadratic function that models the data.

(e) Use the model from part (d) to approximate the number of housing starts in 2011 and 2013 to the nearest thousand. How well does the model approximate the actual data from the table?

11.7 | More about Parabolas and Their Applications

OBJECTIVES

1. Find the vertex of a vertical parabola.

2. Graph a quadratic function.

3. Use the discriminant to find the number of x-intercepts of a parabola with a vertical axis.

4. Use quadratic functions to solve problems involving maximum or minimum value.

5. Graph parabolas with horizontal axes.

OBJECTIVE 1 **Find the vertex of a vertical parabola.** When the equation of a parabola is given in the form $f(x) = ax^2 + bx + c$, there are two ways to locate the vertex.

1. Complete the square (**See Examples 1 and 2.**)

2. Use a formula derived by completing the square (**See Example 3.**)

EXAMPLE 1 Completing the Square to Find the Vertex ($a = 1$)

Find the vertex of the graph of $f(x) = x^2 - 4x + 5$.

To find the vertex, we need to write the expression $x^2 - 4x + 5$ in the form $(x - h)^2 + k$. We do this by completing the square on $x^2 - 4x$. The process is slightly different here than in earlier work because we want to keep $f(x)$ alone on one side of the equation. Instead of adding the appropriate number to each side, we *add and subtract* it on the right.

$$f(x) = x^2 - 4x + 5$$

$$f(x) = (x^2 - 4x \qquad) + 5 \qquad \text{Group the variable terms.}$$

This is equivalent to adding 0. $\quad \left[\frac{1}{2}(-4)\right]^2 = (-2)^2 = 4 \qquad$ Square half the coefficient of the first-degree term.

$$f(x) = (x^2 - 4x + 4 - 4) + 5 \qquad \text{Add and subtract 4.}$$

$$f(x) = (x^2 - 4x + 4) - 4 + 5 \qquad \text{Bring } -4 \text{ outside the parentheses.}$$

$$f(x) = (x - 2)^2 + 1 \qquad \text{Factor. Combine like terms.}$$

The vertex of this parabola is $(2, 1)$.

◀ **Work Problem** 1 **at the Side.**

---

1. Find the vertex of the graph of each quadratic function.

   (a) $f(x) = x^2 - 6x + 7$

   (b) $f(x) = x^2 + 4x - 9$

EXAMPLE 2 Completing the Square to Find the Vertex ($a \neq 1$)

Find the vertex of the graph of $f(x) = -3x^2 + 6x - 1$.

Because the x^2-term has a coefficient other than 1, we factor that coefficient out of the first two terms before completing the square.

$$f(x) = -3x^2 + 6x - 1$$

$$f(x) = (-3x^2 + 6x) - 1 \qquad \text{Group the variable terms.}$$

$$f(x) = -3(x^2 - 2x) - 1 \qquad \text{Factor out } -3.$$

$$f(x) = -3(x^2 - 2x \qquad) - 1 \qquad \text{Prepare to complete the square.}$$

$\quad \left[\frac{1}{2}(-2)\right]^2 = (-1)^2 = 1 \qquad$ Square half the coefficient of the first-degree term.

$$f(x) = -3(x^2 - 2x + 1 - 1) - 1 \qquad \text{Add and subtract 1.}$$

Now bring -1 outside the parentheses. Be sure to multiply it by -3.

$$f(x) = -3(x^2 - 2x + 1) + (-3)(-1) - 1 \qquad \text{Distributive property}$$

$$f(x) = -3(x^2 - 2x + 1) + 3 - 1 \qquad \text{This is a key step.}$$

$$f(x) = -3(x - 1)^2 + 2 \qquad \text{Factor. Combine like terms.}$$

The vertex of this parabola is $(1, 2)$.

◀ **Work Problem** 2 **at the Side.**

---

2. Find the vertex of the graph of each quadratic function.

   (a) $f(x) = 2x^2 - 4x + 1$

   (b) $f(x) = -4x^2 + 16x - 10$

Answers

1. (a) $(3, -2)$ (b) $(-2, -13)$
2. (a) $(1, -1)$ (b) $(2, 6)$

We complete the square to derive a formula for the vertex of the graph of the quadratic function $f(x) = ax^2 + bx + c$ (where $a \neq 0$).

$f(x) = ax^2 + bx + c$ — Standard form

$f(x) = (ax^2 + bx) + c$ — Group the terms with x.

$f(x) = a\left(x^2 + \dfrac{b}{a}x\right) + c$ — Factor a from the first two terms.

$\left[\dfrac{1}{2}\left(\dfrac{b}{a}\right)\right]^2 = \left(\dfrac{b}{2a}\right)^2 = \dfrac{b^2}{4a^2}$ — Square half the coefficient of the first-degree term.

$f(x) = a\left(x^2 + \dfrac{b}{a}x + \dfrac{b^2}{4a^2} - \dfrac{b^2}{4a^2}\right) + c$ — Add and subtract $\dfrac{b^2}{4a^2}$.

$f(x) = a\left(x^2 + \dfrac{b}{a}x + \dfrac{b^2}{4a^2}\right) + a\left(-\dfrac{b^2}{4a^2}\right) + c$ — Distributive property

$f(x) = a\left(x^2 + \dfrac{b}{a}x + \dfrac{b^2}{4a^2}\right) - \dfrac{b^2}{4a} + c$ — $-\dfrac{ab^2}{4a^2} = -\dfrac{b^2}{4a}$

$f(x) = a\left(x + \dfrac{b}{2a}\right)^2 + \dfrac{4ac - b^2}{4a}$ — Factor. Rewrite terms with a common denominator.

$f(x) = a\left[x - \left(\dfrac{-b}{2a}\right)\right]^2 + \dfrac{4ac - b^2}{4a}$ — $f(x) = a(x - h)^2 + k$; The vertex (h, k) can be expressed in terms of $a, b,$ and c.

$\underbrace{\phantom{x - \left(\dfrac{-b}{2a}\right)}}_{h} \quad \underbrace{\phantom{\dfrac{4ac - b^2}{4a}}}_{k}$

The expression for k can be found by replacing x with $\dfrac{-b}{2a}$. Using function notation, if $y = f(x)$, then the y-value of the vertex is $f\left(\dfrac{-b}{2a}\right)$.

Vertex Formula

The graph of the quadratic function $f(x) = ax^2 + bx + c$ has vertex
$$\left(\dfrac{-b}{2a}, f\left(\dfrac{-b}{2a}\right)\right).$$
The axis of symmetry of the parabola is the line having equation
$$x = \dfrac{-b}{2a}.$$

EXAMPLE 3   Using the Vertex Formula

Use the vertex formula to find the vertex of the graph of $f(x) = x^2 - x - 6$.

The x-coordinate of the vertex of the parabola is given by $\dfrac{-b}{2a}$.

$$\dfrac{-b}{2a} = \dfrac{-(-1)}{2(1)} = \dfrac{1}{2} \leftarrow \text{x-coordinate of vertex}$$

$a = 1, b = -1,$ and $c = -6$

The y-coordinate of the vertex is $f\left(\dfrac{-b}{2a}\right) = f\left(\dfrac{1}{2}\right)$.

$$f\left(\dfrac{1}{2}\right) = \left(\dfrac{1}{2}\right)^2 - \dfrac{1}{2} - 6 = \dfrac{1}{4} - \dfrac{1}{2} - 6 = -\dfrac{25}{4} \leftarrow \text{y-coordinate of vertex}$$

$\dfrac{1}{4} - \dfrac{1}{2} - 6 = \dfrac{1}{4} - \dfrac{2}{4} - \dfrac{24}{4};$

The vertex is $\left(\dfrac{1}{2}, -\dfrac{25}{4}\right)$.

Work Problem ③ at the Side. ▶

③ Use the vertex formula to find the vertex of the graph of each quadratic function.

(a) $f(x) = 3x^2 - 2x + 8$

(b) $f(x) = -2x^2 + 3x - 1$

Answers

3. (a) $\left(\dfrac{1}{3}, \dfrac{23}{3}\right)$ **(b)** $\left(\dfrac{3}{4}, \dfrac{1}{8}\right)$

4 Graph the quadratic function.

$$f(x) = x^2 - 6x + 5$$

Give the vertex, axis of symmetry, domain, and range.

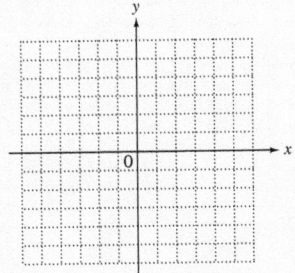

Graphing a Quadratic Function $f(x) = ax^2 + bx + c$

Step 1 **Determine whether the graph opens up or down.**
- If $a > 0$, then the parabola opens up.
- If $a < 0$, then the parabola opens down.

Step 2 **Find the vertex.** Use the vertex formula or complete the square.

Step 3 **Find any intercepts.**
- To find the x-intercepts (if any), solve $f(x) = 0$.
- To find the y-intercept, evaluate $f(0)$.

Step 4 **Complete the graph.** Plot the points found so far. Find and plot additional points as needed, using symmetry about the axis.

EXAMPLE 4 **Graphing a Quadratic Function**

Graph the quadratic function $f(x) = x^2 - x - 6$.

Step 1 From the equation, $a = 1$, so the graph of the function opens up.

Step 2 The vertex, $\left(\frac{1}{2}, -\frac{25}{4}\right)$, was found in **Example 3.**

Step 3 The vertex lies in quadrant IV and the graph opens up, so there will be two x-intercepts. Let $f(x) = 0$ and solve to find them.

$$f(x) = x^2 - x - 6$$
$$0 = x^2 - x - 6 \qquad \text{Let } f(x) = 0.$$
$$0 = (x - 3)(x + 2) \qquad \text{Factor.}$$
$$x - 3 = 0 \quad \text{or} \quad x + 2 = 0 \qquad \text{Zero-factor property}$$
$$x = 3 \quad \text{or} \qquad x = -2 \qquad \text{Solve each equation.}$$

The x-intercepts are $(3, 0)$ and $(-2, 0)$. Find the y-intercept by evaluating $f(0)$.

$$f(x) = x^2 - x - 6$$
$$f(0) = 0^2 - 0 - 6 \qquad \text{Let } x = 0.$$
$$f(0) = -6 \qquad \text{Apply the exponent. Subtract.}$$

The y-intercept is $(0, -6)$.

Step 4 Plot the above points and others using symmetry. See **Figure 14.**

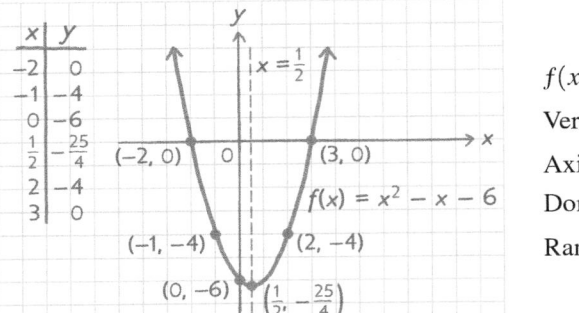

$$f(x) = x^2 - x - 6$$
Vertex: $\left(\frac{1}{2}, -\frac{25}{4}\right)$
Axis of symmetry: $x = \frac{1}{2}$
Domain: $(-\infty, \infty)$
Range: $\left[-\frac{25}{4}, \infty\right)$

Figure 14

Answer

4.

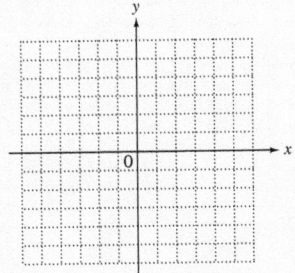

$f(x) = x^2 - 6x + 5$

vertex: $(3, -4)$; axis: $x = 3$;
domain: $(-\infty, \infty)$; range: $[-4, \infty)$

◀ **Work Problem** 4 **at the Side**

OBJECTIVE ▶ ③ **Use the discriminant to find the number of x-intercepts of a parabola with a vertical axis.** Recall that

$$b^2 - 4ac \qquad \text{Discriminant}$$

is the *discriminant* of the quadratic equation $ax^2 + bx + c = 0$ and that we can use it to determine the number of real solutions of a quadratic *equation*.

In a similar way, we can use the discriminant of a quadratic *function* to determine the number of x-intercepts of its graph. See **Figure 15.**

1. If the discriminant is positive, the parabola will have two x-intercepts.
2. If the discriminant is 0, there will be only one x-intercept, and it will be the vertex of the parabola.
3. If the discriminant is negative, the graph will have no x-intercepts.

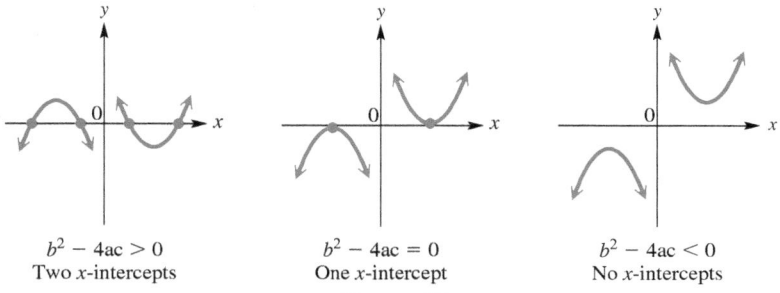

| $b^2 - 4ac > 0$ | $b^2 - 4ac = 0$ | $b^2 - 4ac < 0$ |
| Two x-intercepts | One x-intercept | No x-intercepts |

Figure 15

EXAMPLE 5 **Determining the Number of x-Intercepts**

Find the discriminant and use it to determine the number of x-intercepts of the graph of each quadratic function.

(a) $f(x) = 2x^2 + 3x - 5$

$$b^2 - 4ac \qquad \text{Discriminant}$$
$$= 3^2 - 4(2)(-5) \qquad a = 2, b = 3, c = -5$$
$$= 9 - (-40) \qquad \text{Apply the exponent. Multiply.}$$
$$= 49 \qquad \text{Subtract.}$$

Because the discriminant is positive, the parabola has two x-intercepts.

(b) $f(x) = -3x^2 - 1$ (which can be written as $f(x) = -3x^2 + 0x - 1$)

$$b^2 - 4ac$$
$$= 0^2 - 4(-3)(-1) \qquad a = -3, b = 0, c = -1$$
$$= 0 - 12 \qquad \text{Apply the exponent. Multiply.}$$
$$= -12 \qquad \text{Subtract.}$$

The discriminant is negative, so the graph has no x-intercepts.

(c) $f(x) = 9x^2 + 6x + 1$

$$b^2 - 4ac$$
$$= 6^2 - 4(9)(1) \qquad a = 9, b = 6, c = 1$$
$$= 36 - 36 \qquad \text{Apply the exponent. Multiply.}$$
$$= 0 \qquad \text{Subtract.}$$

Because the value of the discriminant is 0, the parabola has only one x-intercept.

⸻ **Work Problem ⑤ at the Side.** ▶

⑤ Find the discriminant and use it to determine the number of x-intercepts of the graph of each quadratic function.

(a) $f(x) = 4x^2 - 20x + 25$

(b) $f(x) = 2x^2 + 3x + 5$

(c) $f(x) = -3x^2 - x + 2$

Answers

5. (a) 0; one x-intercept
(b) −31; no x-intercepts
(c) 25; two x-intercepts

6 Solve **Example 6** if the farmer has only 100 ft of fencing.

OBJECTIVE ▶ **4** Use quadratic functions to solve problems involving maximum or minimum value. The vertex of the graph of a quadratic function is either the highest or the lowest point on the parabola. It provides the following information.

1. The y-value of the vertex gives the maximum or minimum value of y.

2. The x-value tells where the maximum or minimum occurs.

Problem-Solving Hint

In many applied problems we must find the least or greatest value of some quantity. When we can express that quantity as a quadratic function, the value of k in the vertex (h, k) gives that optimum value.

EXAMPLE 6 Finding Maximum Area

A farmer has 120 ft of fencing to enclose a rectangular area next to a building. See **Figure 16.** Find the maximum area he can enclose and the dimensions of the field when the area is maximized.

Figure 16

Let x = the width of the rectangle.

$x + x + \text{length} = 120$	Sum of the sides is 120 ft.
$2x + \text{length} = 120$	Combine like terms.
$\text{length} = \mathbf{120 - 2x}$	Subtract $2x$.

The area $\mathcal{A}(x)$ is given by the product of the length and width.

$\mathcal{A}(x) = (\mathbf{120 - 2x})x$	Area = length · width
$\mathcal{A}(x) = 120x - 2x^2$	Distributive property
$\mathcal{A}(x) = -2x^2 + 120x$	Standard form

The graph is a parabola that opens down. To determine the maximum area, use the vertex formula to find the vertex of the parabola.

$$x = \frac{-b}{2a} = \frac{-120}{2(-2)} = \frac{-120}{-4} = 30 \qquad \text{Vertex formula;} \atop a = -2, b = 120, c = 0$$

$$\mathcal{A}(30) = -2(30)^2 + 120(30)$$

$$\mathcal{A}(30) = -2(900) + 3600$$

$$\mathcal{A}(30) = \mathbf{1800}$$

The vertex is $(\mathbf{30, 1800})$. The maximum area will be $\mathbf{1800}$ ft^2 when x, the width of the rectangle, is $\mathbf{30}$ ft and the length is

$$120 - 2(30) = \mathbf{60} \text{ ft.}$$

Answer

6. The field should be 25 ft by 50 ft with maximum area 1250 ft^2.

◀ **Work Problem 6 at the Side.**

⚠️ **CAUTION**

Be careful when interpreting the meanings of the coordinates of the vertex. The first coordinate, x, gives the value for which the *function value*, y or $f(x)$, is a maximum or a minimum.

Read the problem carefully to determine whether to find the value of the independent variable, the function value, or both.

EXAMPLE 7 **Finding Maximum Height**

If air resistance is neglected, a projectile on Earth shot straight upward with an initial velocity of 40 m per sec will be at a height s in meters given by

$$s(t) = -4.9t^2 + 40t,$$

where t is the number of seconds elapsed after projection. After how many seconds will it reach its maximum height, and what is this maximum height?

For this function, $a = -4.9$, $b = 40$, and $c = 0$. Use the vertex formula.

$$t = \frac{-b}{2a} = \frac{-40}{2(-4.9)} \approx 4.1 \qquad \text{Use a calculator. Round to the nearest tenth.}$$

This indicates that the maximum height is attained at 4.1 sec. To find this maximum height, calculate $s(4.1)$.

$$s(t) = -4.9t^2 + 40t$$

$$s(4.1) = -4.9(4.1)^2 + 40(4.1) \qquad \text{Let } t = 4.1.$$

$$s(4.1) \approx 81.6 \qquad \text{Use a calculator. Round to the nearest tenth.}$$

The projectile will attain a maximum height of approximately 81.6 m.

──────── **Work Problem 7 at the Side.** ▶

OBJECTIVE ▶ 5 Graph parabolas with horizontal axes. If x and y are interchanged in the equation

$$y = ax^2 + bx + c,$$

the equation becomes

$$x = ay^2 + by + c.$$

Because of the interchange of the roles of x and y, these parabolas are horizontal (with horizontal lines as axes of symmetry).

General Characteristics of the Graph of a Horizontal Parabola

The graph of an equation of the form

$$x = ay^2 + by + c \quad \text{or} \quad x = a(y - k)^2 + h$$

is a horizontal parabola.

- The vertex of the parabola is (h, k).
- The axis of symmetry is the horizontal line $y = k$.
- The graph opens to the right if $a > 0$ and to the left if $a < 0$.

---

7 Solve the problem.

A toy rocket is launched from the ground so that its distance in feet above the ground after t seconds is

$$s(t) = -16t^2 + 208t.$$

Find the maximum height it reaches and the number of seconds it takes to reach that height.

Answer

7. 676 ft; 6.5 sec

8 Graph the equation.

$$x = (y + 1)^2 - 4$$

Give the vertex, axis of symmetry, domain, and range.

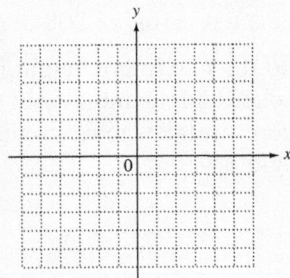

9 Graph the equation.

$$x = -y^2 + 2y + 5$$

Give the vertex, axis of symmetry, domain, and range.

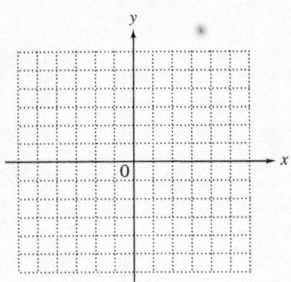

Answers

8.

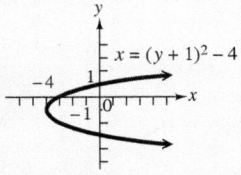

vertex: $(-4, -1)$; axis: $y = -1$;
domain: $[-4, \infty)$; range: $(-\infty, \infty)$

9.

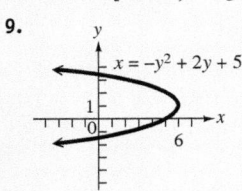

vertex: $(6, 1)$; axis: $y = 1$;
domain: $(-\infty, 6]$; range: $(-\infty, \infty)$

EXAMPLE 8 **Graphing a Horizontal Parabola ($a = 1$)**

Graph $x = (y - 2)^2 - 3$.

This graph has its vertex at $(-3, 2)$ because the roles of x and y are interchanged. It opens to the right (the positive x-direction) because $a = 1$ and $1 > 0$, and has the same shape as $y = x^2$ (but situated horizontally).

To find additional points to plot, it is easiest to substitute a value for y and find the corresponding value for x. For example, let $y = 3$. Then

$$x = (3 - 2)^2 - 3 = -2, \quad \text{giving the point} \quad (-2, 3). \quad \boxed{\text{Write the } x\text{-value first.}}$$

Using symmetry, we can locate the point $(-2, 1)$. See **Figure 17**.

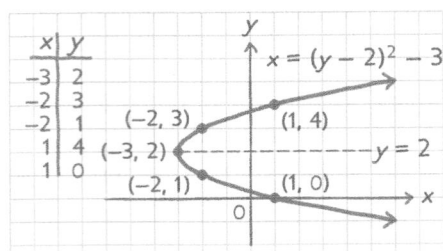

$x = (y - 2)^2 - 3$
Vertex: $(-3, 2)$
Axis of symmetry: $y = 2$
Domain: $[-3, \infty)$
Range: $(-\infty, \infty)$

Figure 17

◀ **Work Problem 8 at the Side.**

EXAMPLE 9 **Graphing a Horizontal Parabola ($a \neq 1$)**

Graph $x = -2y^2 + 4y - 3$.

$$x = -2y^2 + 4y - 3$$

$$x = (-2y^2 + 4y) - 3 \qquad \text{Group the variable terms.}$$

$$x = -2(y^2 - 2y) - 3 \qquad \text{Factor out } -2.$$

$$x = -2(y^2 - 2y \qquad) - 3$$

$$\qquad \qquad \longrightarrow \left[\tfrac{1}{2}(-2)\right]^2 = (-1)^2 = 1 \qquad \begin{array}{l}\text{Square half the coefficient}\\\text{of the first-degree term.}\end{array}$$

$$x = -2(y^2 - 2y + 1 - 1) - 3 \qquad \begin{array}{l}\text{Complete the square within the}\\\text{parentheses. Add and subtract 1.}\end{array}$$

$$x = -2(y^2 - 2y + 1) + (-2)(-1) - 3 \qquad \text{Distributive property}$$

$\boxed{\text{Be careful here.}}$

$$x = -2(y - 1)^2 - 1 \qquad \text{Factor. Simplify.}$$

The vertex is $(-1, 1)$. The graph opens to the left (the negative x-direction) because of the negative coefficient -2 in $x = -2(y - 1)^2 - 1$. The graph is narrower than the graph of $y = x^2$ because $|-2| = 2$ and $2 > 1$. See **Figure 18**.

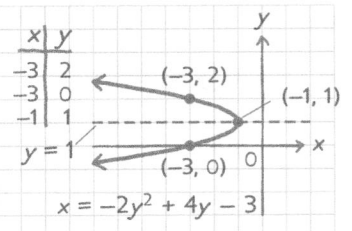

$x = -2y^2 + 4y - 3$
Vertex: $(-1, 1)$
Axis of symmetry: $y = 1$
Domain: $(-\infty, -1]$
Range: $(-\infty, \infty)$

Figure 18

◀ **Work Problem 9 at the Side.**

⚠ CAUTION

Only quadratic equations solved for y (whose graphs are vertical parabolas) are examples of functions. The horizontal parabolas given in **Examples 8 and 9** are *not* graphs of functions because they do not satisfy the conditions of the vertical line test.

In summary, the graphs of parabolas fall into the following categories.

GRAPHS OF PARABOLAS

Equation	Graph
$y = ax^2 + bx + c$ **or** $y = a(x - h)^2 + k$	 These graphs represent functions.
$x = ay^2 + by + c$ **or** $x = a(y - k)^2 + h$	 These graphs are not graphs of functions.

Work Problems ⑩ and ⑪ at the Side. ▶

⑩ Find the vertex of each parabola. Tell whether the graph opens to the right or to the left. Give the domain and range.

(a) $x = 2y^2 - 6y + 5$

(b) $x = -3y^2 - 6y - 5$

⑪ Refer to the table on graphs of parabolas as needed.

(a) Tell whether each equation has a vertical or horizontal parabola as its graph.

A. $y = -x^2 + 20x + 80$

B. $x = 2y^2 + 6y + 5$

C. $x + 1 = (y + 2)^2$

D. $f(x) = (x - 4)^2$

(b) Which of the equations in part (a) represent functions?

Answers

10. (a) $\left(\dfrac{1}{2}, \dfrac{3}{2}\right)$; right; domain: $\left[\dfrac{1}{2}, \infty\right)$; range: $(-\infty, \infty)$

(b) $(-2, -1)$; left; domain: $(-\infty, -2]$; range: $(-\infty, \infty)$

11. (a) A, D are vertical parabolas. B, C are horizontal parabolas.

(b) A, D

11.7 Exercises

FOR EXTRA HELP

Go to MyMathLab *for worked-out, step-by-step solutions to exercises enclosed in a square* ☐ *and video solutions to* ▶ *exercises.*

CONCEPT CHECK *Answer each question.*

1. How can we determine just by looking at the equation of a parabola whether it has a vertical or a horizontal axis of symmetry?

2. Why can't the graph of a quadratic function be a parabola with a horizontal axis of symmetry?

Find the vertex of each parabola. **See Examples 1–3.**

3. ▶ $f(x) = x^2 + 8x + 10$

4. $f(x) = x^2 + 10x + 23$

5. ▶ $f(x) = -2x^2 + 4x - 5$

6. $f(x) = -3x^2 + 12x - 8$

7. ▶ $f(x) = x^2 + x - 7$

8. $f(x) = x^2 - x + 5$

Find the vertex of each parabola. For each equation, decide whether the graph opens up, down, to the left, or to the right, and whether it is wider, narrower, or the same shape as the graph of $y = x^2$. If it is a parabola with a vertical axis of symmetry, use the discriminant to determine the number of x-intercepts. **See Examples 1–3, 5, 8, and 9.**

9. ▶ $f(x) = 2x^2 + 4x + 5$

10. $f(x) = 3x^2 - 6x + 4$

11. $f(x) = -x^2 + 5x + 3$

12. $f(x) = -x^2 + 7x - 2$

13. $x = \frac{1}{3}y^2 + 6y + 24$

14. $x = \frac{1}{2}y^2 + 10y - 5$

CONCEPT CHECK *Match each equation with its graph in choices A–F.*

15. $y = 2x^2 + 4x - 3$

16. $y = -x^2 + 3x + 5$

17. $y = -\frac{1}{2}x^2 - x + 1$

18. $x = y^2 + 6y + 3$

19. $x = -y^2 - 2y + 4$

20. $x = 3y^2 + 6y + 5$

A.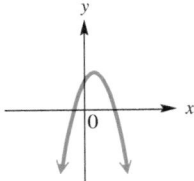

B.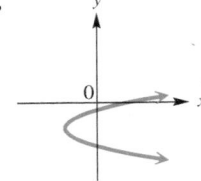

C.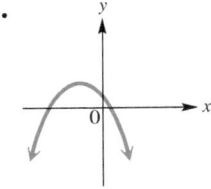

D.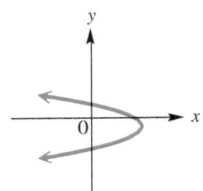

E.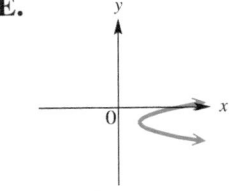

F.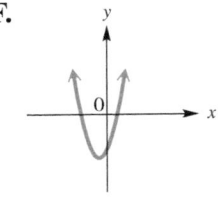

Graph each parabola. Give the vertex, axis of symmetry, domain, and range.
See Examples 4, 8, and 9.

21. $f(x) = x^2 + 4x + 3$

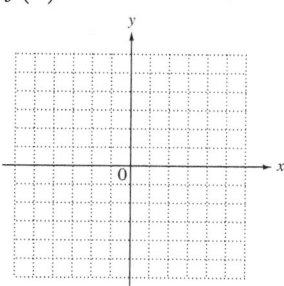

22. $f(x) = x^2 + 2x - 2$

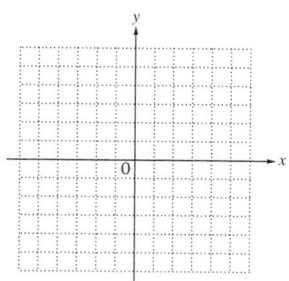

23. $f(x) = x^2 + 8x + 10$

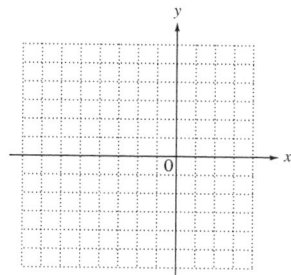

24. $f(x) = x^2 + 10x + 23$

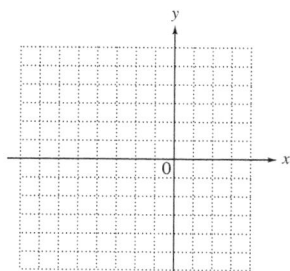

25. $f(x) = -2x^2 + 4x - 5$

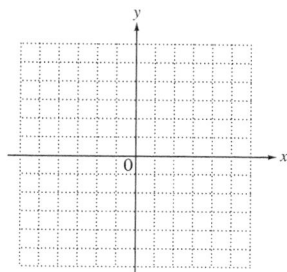

26. $f(x) = -3x^2 + 12x - 8$

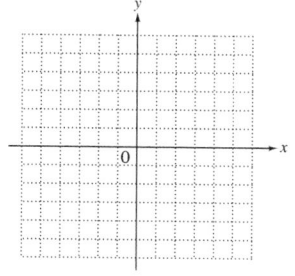

27. $x = (y + 2)^2 + 1$

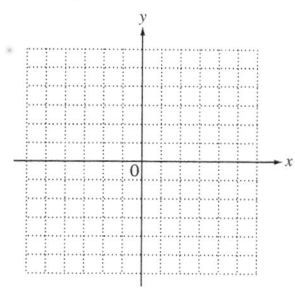

28. $x = (y + 3)^2 - 2$

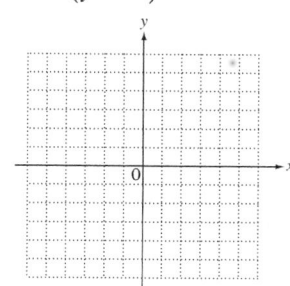

29. $x = -(y - 3)^2 - 1$

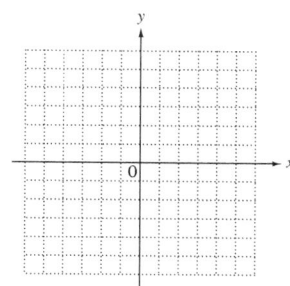

30. $x = -(y - 2)^2 + 4$

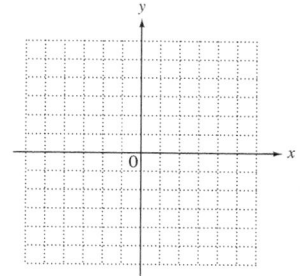

31. $x = -\dfrac{1}{5}y^2 + 2y - 4$

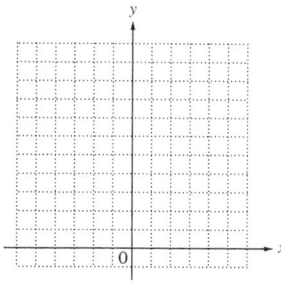

32. $x = -\dfrac{1}{2}y^2 - 4y - 6$

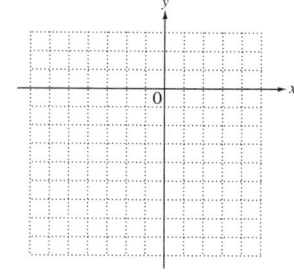

33. $x = 3y^2 + 12y + 5$

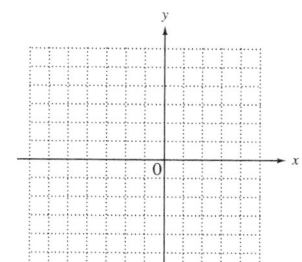

34. $x = 4y^2 + 16y + 11$

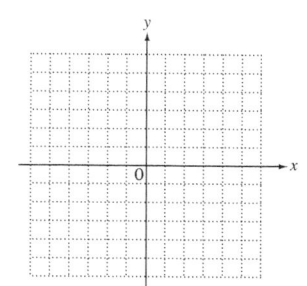

CONCEPT CHECK *Given the following information about the graph of a quadratic function, how many x-intercepts does the graph have?*

35. Vertex $(-4, 0)$, opens up

36. Vertex $(1, -3)$, opens down

*Solve each problem. **See Examples 6 and 7.***

37. Find the pair of numbers whose sum is 60 and whose product is a maximum. (*Hint:* Let x and $60 - x$ represent the two numbers.)

38. Find the pair of numbers whose sum is 10 and whose product is a maximum.

39. Polk Community College wants to construct a rectangular parking lot on land bordered on one side by a highway. It has 280 ft of fencing to fence off the other three sides. What should be the dimensions of the lot if the enclosed area is to be a maximum? What is the maximum area?

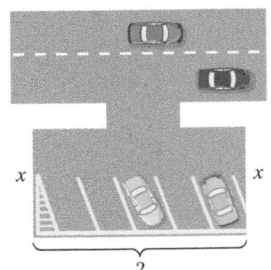

40. Bonnie has 100 ft of fencing material to enclose a rectangular exercise run for her dog. One side of the run will border her house, so she will only need to fence three sides. What dimensions will give the enclosure the maximum area? What is the maximum area?

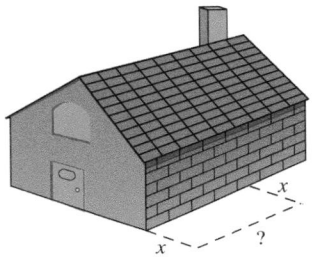

41. Klaus has a taco stand. He has found that his daily costs are approximated by

$$C(x) = x^2 - 40x + 610,$$

where $C(x)$ is the cost, in dollars, to sell x units of tacos. Find the number of units of tacos he should sell to minimize his costs. What is the minimum cost?

42. Mohammad has a frozen yogurt cart. His daily costs are approximated by

$$C(x) = x^2 - 70x + 1500,$$

where $C(x)$ is the cost, in dollars, to sell x units of frozen yogurt. Find the number of units of frozen yogurt he must sell to minimize his costs. What is the minimum cost?

43. If an object on Earth is projected upward with an initial velocity of 32 ft per sec, then its height (in feet) after t seconds is given by

$$h(t) = -16t^2 + 32t.$$

Find the maximum height attained by the object and the number of seconds it takes to hit the ground.

44. A projectile on Earth is fired straight upward so that its distance (in feet) above the ground t seconds after firing is given by

$$s(t) = -16t^2 + 400t.$$

Find the maximum height it reaches and the number of seconds it takes to reach that height.

45. The percent of the U.S. population that was foreign-born during the years 1930–2010 can be modeled by the quadratic function

$$f(x) = 0.0043x^2 - 0.3245x + 11.53,$$

where $x = 0$ represents 1930, $x = 10$ represents 1940, and so on. (Data from U.S. Census Bureau.)

(a) The coefficient of x^2 in the model is positive, so the graph of this quadratic function is a parabola that opens up. Will the y-value of the vertex of this graph be a maximum or a minimum?

(b) According to the model, in what year during this period was the percent of foreign-born population a minimum? (Round down for the year.) Use the actual x-value of the vertex, to the nearest tenth, to find this percent, also to the nearest tenth.

46. The percent of births in the United States to teenage mothers during the years 2005–2012 can be modeled by the quadratic function

$$f(x) = -0.3661x^2 + 1.565x + 39.21,$$

where $x = 0$ represents 2005, $x = 1$ represents 2006, and so on. (Data from CDC.)

(a) The coefficient of x^2 in the model is negative, so the graph of this quadratic function is a parabola that opens down. Will the y-value of the vertex of this graph be a maximum or a minimum?

(b) According to the model, in what year during this period was the percent of births in the United States to teenage mothers a maximum? (Round down for the year.) Use the actual x-value of the vertex, to the nearest tenth, to find this percent, also to the nearest tenth.

The graph shows how Social Security trust fund assets are expected to change, and suggests that a quadratic function would be a good fit to the data. The data are approximated by the function

$$f(x) = -20.57x^2 + 758.9x - 3140.$$

In the model, $x = 10$ represents 2010, $x = 15$ represents 2015, and so on, and $f(x)$ is in billions of dollars.

47. Algebraically determine the vertex of the graph of the function, with coordinates to four significant digits. Interpret the answer as it applies to the application.

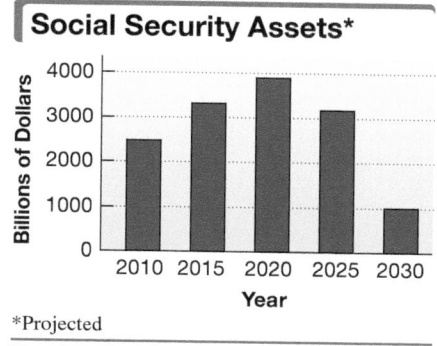

*Projected

Data from Social Security Administration.

48. How could we have predicted that this quadratic model would have a negative coefficient for x^2, based only on the graph shown?

49. A charter flight charges a fare of $200 per person, plus $4 per person for each unsold seat on the plane. If the plane holds 100 passengers and if x represents the number of unsold seats, find the following.

(a) A function $R(x)$ that describes the total revenue received for the flight (*Hint:* To find $R(x)$, multiply the number of people flying, $100 - x$, by the price per ticket, $200 + 4x$.)

(b) The number of unsold seats that will produce the maximum revenue

(c) The maximum revenue

50. A charter bus company charges a fare of $48 per person, plus $2 per person for each unsold seat on the bus. If the bus has 42 seats and if x represents the number of unsold seats, find the following.

(a) A function $R(x)$ that describes the total revenue from the trip (*Hint:* To find $R(x)$, multiply the number of people riding, $42 - x$, by the price per ticket, $48 + 2x$.)

(b) The number of unsold seats that will produce the maximum revenue

(c) The maximum revenue

11.8 | Polynomial and Rational Inequalities

OBJECTIVES

1 Solve quadratic inequalities.

2 Solve polynomial inequalities of degree 3 or greater.

3 Solve rational inequalities.

We can combine methods of solving linear inequalities and methods of solving quadratic equations to solve *quadratic inequalities*.

Quadratic Inequality

A **quadratic inequality** (in x here) can be written in the form

$$ax^2 + bx + c < 0, \qquad ax^2 + bx + c > 0,$$

$$ax^2 + bx + c \leq 0, \quad \text{or} \quad ax^2 + bx + c \geq 0,$$

where a, b, and c are real numbers and $a \neq 0$.

OBJECTIVE ▶ 1 **Solve quadratic inequalities.** One method for solving a quadratic inequality is by graphing the related quadratic function.

EXAMPLE 1 **Solving Quadratic Inequalities by Graphing**

Solve each inequality.

(a) $x^2 - x - 12 > 0$

We graph the related quadratic function $f(x) = x^2 - x - 12$. We are particularly interested in the x-intercepts, which are found by letting $f(x) = 0$ and solving the quadratic equation.

$$x^2 - x - 12 = 0 \qquad \text{Let } f(x) = 0.$$
$$(x - 4)(x + 3) = 0 \qquad \text{Factor.}$$
$$x - 4 = 0 \quad \text{or} \quad x + 3 = 0 \qquad \text{Zero-factor property}$$
$$x = 4 \quad \text{or} \quad x = -3 \leftarrow \text{The } x\text{-intercepts are } (4, 0) \text{ and } (-3, 0).$$

The graph, which opens up because the coefficient of x^2 is positive, is shown in **Figure 19(a).** Notice that x-values less than -3 or greater than 4 result in y-values *greater than* 0. Thus, the solution set of $x^2 - x - 12 > 0$, written in interval notation, is

$$(-\infty, -3) \cup (4, \infty).$$

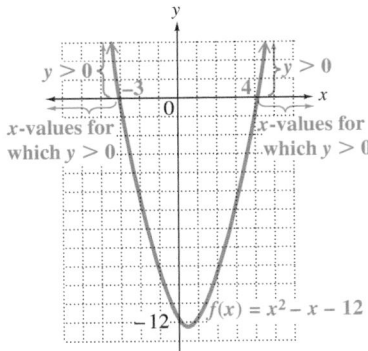

The graph is *above* the x-axis for
$(-\infty, -3) \cup (4, \infty)$.

(a)

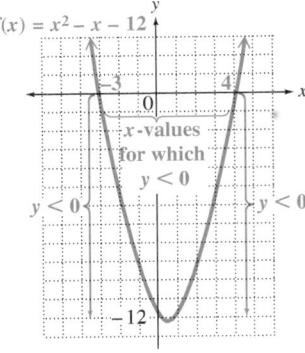

The graph is *below* the x-axis for
$(-3, 4)$.

(b)

Figure 19

———— **Continued on Next Page**

(b) $x^2 - x - 12 < 0$

We want values of y that are *less than* 0. See **Figure 19(b)** on the previous page. Notice from the graph that x-values between -3 and 4 result in y-values less than 0. Thus, the solution set of the inequality $x^2 - x - 12 < 0$, written in interval notation, is $(-3, 4)$.

─────────── Work Problem ❶ at the Side. ▶

> **Note**
>
> If the inequalities in **Example 1** had used $\geq$ and $\leq$, the solution sets would have included the x-values of the intercepts, which make the quadratic expression equal to 0. They would have been written in interval notation as
>
> $$(-\infty, -3] \cup [4, \infty) \quad \text{and} \quad [-3, 4].$$
>
> Square brackets would indicate that the endpoints -3 and 4 are *included* in the solution sets.

Work Problem ❷ at the Side. ▶

Another method for solving a quadratic inequality uses these basic ideas without actually graphing the related quadratic function.

EXAMPLE 2 Solving a Quadratic Inequality Using Test Values

Solve and graph the solution set of $x^2 - x - 12 > 0$. (See **Example 1(a)**).
Solve the quadratic equation $x^2 - x - 12 = 0$.

$$x^2 - x - 12 = 0 \qquad \text{Let } f(x) = 0.$$
$$(x - 4)(x + 3) = 0 \qquad \text{Factor.}$$
$$x - 4 = 0 \quad \text{or} \quad x + 3 = 0 \qquad \text{Zero-factor property}$$
$$x = 4 \quad \text{or} \quad x = -3 \qquad \text{Solve each equation.}$$

The numbers 4 and -3 divide a number line into Intervals A, B, and C, as shown in **Figure 20**. *Be careful to put the lesser number on the left.*

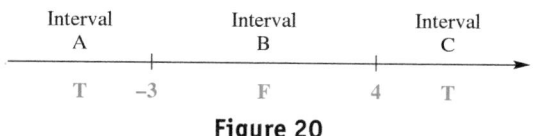

Figure 20

Notice the similarity between **Figure 20** and the x-axis with intercepts $(-3, 0)$ and $(4, 0)$ in **Figure 19(a)**.

The numbers 4 and -3 are the only values that make the quadratic expression $x^2 - x - 12$ equal to 0. All other numbers make the expression either positive or negative. The sign of the expression can change from positive to negative or from negative to positive only at a number that makes it 0.

Therefore, if one number in an interval satisfies the inequality, then all the numbers in that interval will satisfy the inequality.

To see if the numbers in Interval A satisfy the inequality, choose any number from Interval A in **Figure 20** (that is, any number less than -3). Substitute this test value for x in the original inequality $x^2 - x - 12 > 0$.

─────────── **Continued on Next Page**

❶ Use the graph to solve each quadratic inequality.

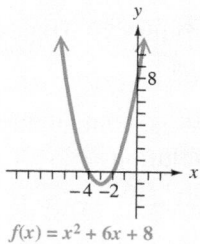

$f(x) = x^2 + 6x + 8$

(a) $x^2 + 6x + 8 > 0$

(b) $x^2 + 6x + 8 < 0$

❷ Graph $f(x) = x^2 + 3x - 4$ and use the graph to solve each quadratic inequality.

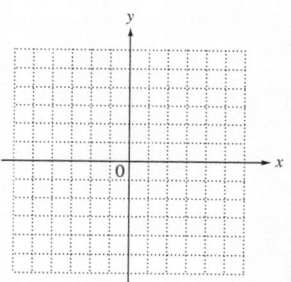

(a) $x^2 + 3x - 4 \geq 0$

(b) $x^2 + 3x - 4 \leq 0$

Answers

1. (a) $(-\infty, -4) \cup (-2, \infty)$ (b) $(-4, -2)$
2. (a) $(-\infty, -4] \cup [1, \infty)$ (b) $[-4, 1]$

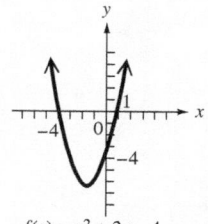

$f(x) = x^2 + 3x - 4$

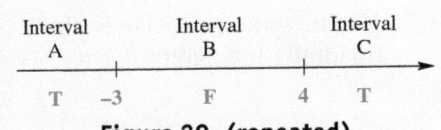

Figure 20 (repeated)

3 Solve each inequality, and graph the solution set.

(a) $x^2 + x - 6 > 0$

_____→

(b) $3m^2 - 13m - 10 \leq 0$

_____→

We choose -5 from Interval A, and substitute -5 for x.

> Use parentheses to avoid sign errors.

$$x^2 - x - 12 > 0 \quad \text{Original inequality}$$
$$(-5)^2 - (-5) - 12 \overset{?}{>} 0 \quad \text{Let } x = -5.$$
$$25 + 5 - 12 \overset{?}{>} 0 \quad \text{Simplify.}$$
$$18 > 0 \quad \text{True}$$

Because -5 satisfies the inequality, *all* numbers from Interval A are solutions. (The **T** (for True) in **Figure 20** indicates this.)

Now try 0 from Interval B in **Figure 20**.

$$x^2 - x - 12 > 0 \quad \text{Original inequality}$$
$$0^2 - 0 - 12 \overset{?}{>} 0 \quad \text{Let } x = 0.$$
$$-12 > 0 \quad \text{False}$$

The numbers in Interval B are *not* solutions (indicated by the **F** in **Figure 20**). Now try 5 from Interval C in **Figure 20**.

$$x^2 - x - 12 > 0 \quad \text{Original inequality}$$
$$5^2 - 5 - 12 \overset{?}{>} 0 \quad \text{Let } x = 5.$$
$$8 > 0 \quad \text{True}$$

All numbers in Interval C are solutions.

The solution set includes the numbers in Intervals A and C, as shown in **Figure 21**. The solution set is written in interval notation as

$$(-\infty, -3) \cup (4, \infty). \quad \begin{array}{l}\text{This agrees with the solution}\\ \text{set in \textbf{Example 1(a)}.}\end{array}$$

Figure 21

◀ **Work Problem** ③ **at the Side.**

Solving a Quadratic Inequality

Step 1 **Write the inequality as an equation and solve it.**

Step 2 **Use the solutions from Step 1 to determine intervals.** Graph the values found in Step 1 on a number line. These values divide the number line into intervals.

Step 3 **Find the intervals that satisfy the inequality.** Substitute a test value from each interval into the original inequality to determine the intervals that satisfy the inequality. All numbers in those intervals are in the solution set. A graph of the solution set will usually look like one of these.

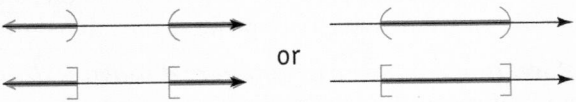

Step 4 **Consider the endpoints separately.** The values from Step 1 are included in the solution set if the inequality is $\leq$ or $\geq$. They are not included if it is $<$ or $>$.

Answers

3. **(a)** $(-\infty, -3) \cup (2, \infty)$

(b) $\left[-\dfrac{2}{3}, 5\right]$

| EXAMPLE 3 | Solving a Quadratic Inequality |

Solve and graph the solution set of $2x^2 + 5x \leq 12$.

Step 1

$$2x^2 + 5x = 12 \qquad \text{Related quadratic equation}$$

$$2x^2 + 5x - 12 = 0 \qquad \text{Standard form}$$

$$(2x - 3)(x + 4) = 0 \qquad \text{Factor.}$$

$$2x - 3 = 0 \quad \text{or} \quad x + 4 = 0 \qquad \text{Zero-factor property}$$

$$x = \frac{3}{2} \quad \text{or} \qquad x = -4 \qquad \text{Solve each equation.}$$

Step 2 The numbers $\frac{3}{2}$ and -4 divide a number line into three intervals. See **Figure 22.**

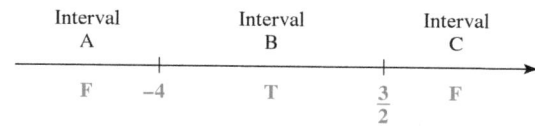

Figure 22

Steps 3 and 4 Substitute a test value from each interval in the *original* inequality $2x^2 + 5x \leq 12$ to determine which intervals satisfy the inequality.

Interval	Test Value	Test of Inequality	True or False?
A	-5	$25 \leq 12$	F
B	0	$0 \leq 12$	T
C	2	$18 \leq 12$	F

We use a table to organize this information. (Verify it.)

The numbers in Interval B are solutions. See **Figure 23.** The solution set is the interval

$$\left[-4, \frac{3}{2} \right].$$

-4 and $\frac{3}{2}$ are included because the symbol $\leq$ includes equality.

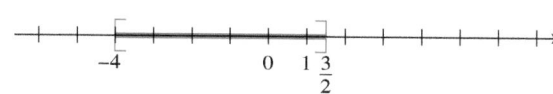

Figure 23

—————— **Work Problem** 4 **at the Side.** ▶

| EXAMPLE 4 | Solving Special Cases |

Solve each inequality.

(a) $(2x - 3)^2 > -1$

Because $(2x - 3)^2$ is never negative, it is *always* greater than -1. Thus, the solution set of $(2x - 3)^2 > -1$ is the set of all real numbers, $(-\infty, \infty)$.

(b) $(2x - 3)^2 < -1$

Using similar reasoning as in part (a), there is no solution for this inequality. The solution set is $\varnothing$.

—————— **Work Problem** 5 **at the Side.** ▶

4 Solve and graph the solution set.

$$3x^2 - 11x \leq 4$$

⟶

5 Solve each inequality.

(a) $(3x - 2)^2 > -2$

(b) $(3x - 2)^2 < -2$

Answers

4. $\left[-\frac{1}{3}, 4 \right]$

$-\frac{1}{3}$

$-1\ 0 \qquad 4$

5. (a) $(-\infty, \infty)$ **(b)** $\varnothing$

6 Solve each inequality, and graph the solution set.

(a) $(x - 3)(x + 2)(x + 1) > 0$

OBJECTIVE ▶ **2** Solve polynomial inequalities of degree 3 or greater.

EXAMPLE 5 **Solving a Third-Degree Polynomial Inequality**

Solve and graph the solution set of $(x - 1)(x + 2)(x - 4) \leq 0$.

This *cubic* (third-degree) inequality can be solved by extending the zero-factor property to more than two factors (Step 1).

$$(x - 1)(x + 2)(x - 4) = 0$$ Set the factored polynomial *equal* to 0.

$x - 1 = 0$ or $x + 2 = 0$ or $x - 4 = 0$ Zero-factor property

$x = 1$ or $x = -2$ or $x = 4$ Solve each equation.

Locate the numbers -2, 1, and 4 on a number line, as in **Figure 24**, to determine the Intervals A, B, C, and D (Step 2).

Interval A		Interval B		Interval C		Interval D
T	-2	F	1	T	4	F

Figure 24

Substitute a test value from each interval in the *original* inequality to determine which intervals satisfy the inequality (Step 3).

Interval	Test Value	Test of Inequality	True or False?
A	-3	$-28 \leq 0$	T
B	0	$8 \leq 0$	F
C	2	$-8 \leq 0$	T
D	5	$28 \leq 0$	F

The numbers in Intervals A and C are in the solution set, which is written as

$$(-\infty, -2] \cup [1, 4],$$

and graphed in **Figure 25**. The three endpoints are included because the inequality symbol involves equality (Step 4).

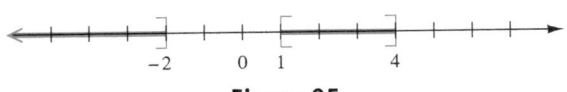

Figure 25

◀ **Work Problem 6** at the Side.

(b) $(x - 5)(x + 1)(x - 3) \leq 0$

OBJECTIVE ▶ **3** Solve rational inequalities. **Rational inequalities** involve rational expressions and are solved similarly using the following steps.

Solving a Rational Inequality

Step 1 **Write the inequality** so that 0 is on one side and there is a single fraction on the other side.

Step 2 **Determine the numbers that make the numerator or denominator equal to 0.**

Step 3 **Divide a number line into intervals.** Use the values from Step 2.

Step 4 **Find the intervals that satisfy the inequality.** Test a value from each interval by substituting it into the *original* inequality.

Step 5 **Consider the endpoints separately.** Exclude any values that make the denominator 0.

Answers

6. (a) $(-2, -1) \cup (3, \infty)$

‑2 ‑1 0   3

(b) $(-\infty, -1] \cup [3, 5]$

‑1 0   3 5

EXAMPLE 6 Solving a Rational Inequality

Solve and graph the solution set of $\dfrac{-1}{x-3} > 1$.

Write the inequality so that 0 is on one side (Step 1).

$$\frac{-1}{x-3} - 1 > 0 \qquad \text{Subtract 1.}$$

$$\frac{-1}{x-3} - \frac{x-3}{x-3} > 0 \qquad \text{Use } x-3 \text{ as the common denominator.}$$

$$\frac{-1-(x-3)}{x-3} > 0 \qquad \text{Write as a single fraction.}$$

> **Be careful with signs.**

$$\frac{-1-x+3}{x-3} > 0 \qquad \text{Distributive property}$$

$$\frac{-x+2}{x-3} > 0 \qquad \text{Combine like terms in the numerator.}$$

The sign of $\frac{-x+2}{x-3}$ will change from positive to negative or negative to positive only at those values that make the numerator or denominator 0. The number 2 makes the numerator 0, and 3 makes the denominator 0 (Step 2). These two numbers, 2 and 3, divide a number line into three intervals. See **Figure 26** (Step 3).

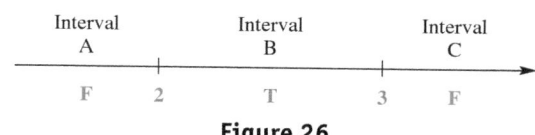

Figure 26

Substitute a test value from each interval in the *original* inequality $\frac{-1}{x-3} > 1$ to determine which intervals satisfy the inequality (Step 4).

Interval	Test Value	Test of Inequality	True or False?
A	0	$\frac{1}{3} > 1$	F
B	2.5	$2 > 1$	T
C	4	$-1 > 1$	F

The numbers in Interval B are solutions, so the solution set is the interval $(2, 3)$. This interval does not include 3 because it would make the denominator of the original inequality 0. The number 2 is not included either because the inequality symbol $>$ does not involve equality (Step 5). See **Figure 27.**

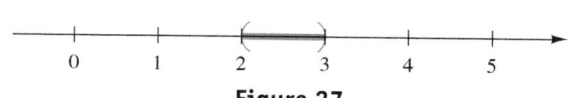

Figure 27

—— **Work Problem 7 at the Side.** ▶

> **! CAUTION**
> **When solving a rational inequality, any number that makes the denominator 0 must be excluded from the solution set.**

7 Solve each inequality, and graph the solution set.

(a) $\dfrac{2}{x-4} < 3$

(b) $\dfrac{5}{x+1} > 4$

Answers

7. (a) $(-\infty, 4) \cup \left(\dfrac{14}{3}, \infty\right)$

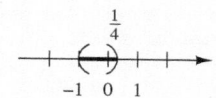

(b) $\left(-1, \dfrac{1}{4}\right)$

8 Solve and graph the solution set.

$$\frac{x+2}{x-1} \le 5$$

⟶

EXAMPLE 7 **Solving a Rational Inequality**

Solve and graph the solution set of $\frac{x-2}{x+2} \le 2$.

Write the inequality so that 0 is on one side (Step 1).

$$\frac{x-2}{x+2} - 2 \le 0 \quad \text{Subtract 2.}$$

$$\frac{x-2}{x+2} - \frac{2(x+2)}{x+2} \le 0 \quad \text{Use } x+2 \text{ as the common denominator.}$$

$$\frac{x-2}{x+2} - \frac{2x+4}{x+2} \le 0 \quad \text{Distributive property}$$

$$\frac{x-2-(2x+4)}{x+2} \le 0 \quad \text{Write as a single fraction.}$$

Be careful with signs. → $$\frac{x-2-2x-4}{x+2} \le 0 \quad \text{Distributive property}$$

$$\frac{-x-6}{x+2} \le 0 \quad \text{Combine like terms in the numerator.}$$

The number -6 makes the numerator 0, and -2 makes the denominator 0 (Step 2). These two numbers determine three intervals on a number line. See **Figure 28.** (Step 3)

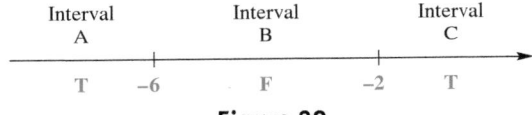

Figure 28

Substitute a test value from each interval in the *original* inequality $\frac{x-2}{x+2} \le 2$ (Step 4).

Interval	Test Value	Test of Inequality	True or False?
A	-8	$\frac{5}{3} \le 2$	T
B	-4	$3 \le 2$	F
C	0	$-1 \le 2$	T

The numbers in Intervals A and C are solutions. The solution set is the interval

$$(-\infty, -6] \cup (-2, \infty).$$

The number -6 satisfies the original inequality, but -2 does not because it makes the denominator 0 (Step 5). See **Figure 29.**

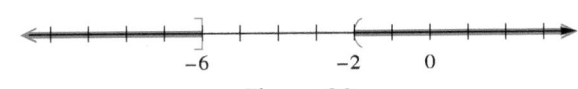

Figure 29

◀ **Work Problem 8** at the Side

Answer

8. $(-\infty, 1) \cup \left[\frac{7}{4}, \infty\right)$

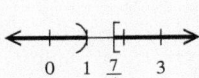

11.8 Exercises

FOR
EXTRA
HELP

Go to MyMathLab *for worked-out, step-by-step solutions to exercises enclosed in a square* ☐ *and video solutions to* ▶ *exercises.*

1. Explain how to determine whether to include or exclude endpoints when solving a quadratic or higher-degree inequality.

2. **CONCEPT CHECK** The solution set of the inequality $x^2 + x - 12 < 0$ is the interval $(-4, 3)$. Without actually performing any work, give the solution set of the inequality

$$x^2 + x - 12 \geq 0.$$

In each problem, the graph of a quadratic function f is given. Use the graph to find the solution set of each equation or inequality. See Example 1.

3. (a) $x^2 - 4x + 3 = 0$
   ▶
   (b) $x^2 - 4x + 3 > 0$
   (c) $x^2 - 4x + 3 < 0$

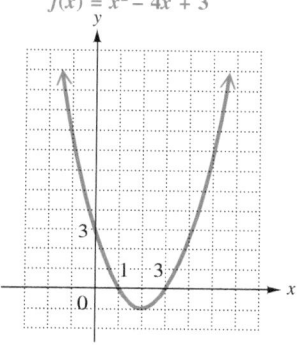

$f(x) = x^2 - 4x + 3$

4. (a) $3x^2 + 10x - 8 = 0$
   (b) $3x^2 + 10x - 8 \geq 0$
   (c) $3x^2 + 10x - 8 < 0$

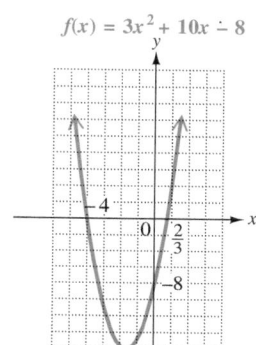

$f(x) = 3x^2 + 10x - 8$

5. (a) $-2x^2 - x + 15 = 0$
   (b) $-2x^2 - x + 15 \geq 0$
   (c) $-2x^2 - x + 15 \leq 0$

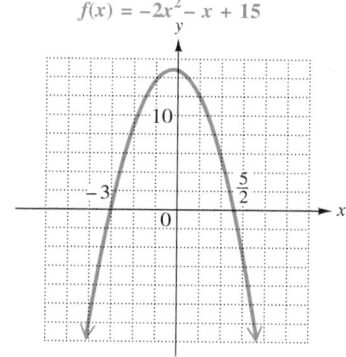

$f(x) = -2x^2 - x + 15$

6. (a) $-x^2 + 3x + 10 = 0$
   (b) $-x^2 + 3x + 10 \geq 0$
   (c) $-x^2 + 3x + 10 \leq 0$

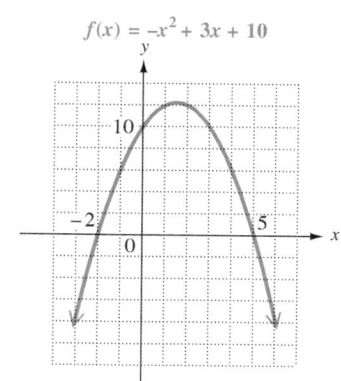

$f(x) = -x^2 + 3x + 10$

Solve each inequality, and graph the solution set. See Examples 2 and 3.

7. $(x + 1)(x - 5) > 0$

8. $(m + 6)(m - 2) > 0$

9. $(r + 4)(r - 6) < 0$

10. $(x + 4)(x - 8) < 0$

11. $x^2 - 4x + 3 \geq 0$

12. $m^2 - 3m - 10 \geq 0$

13. $10t^2 + 9t \geq 9$

14. $3r^2 + 10r \geq 8$

15. $9p^2 + 3p < 2$

16. $2x^2 + x < 15$

17. $6x^2 + x \geq 1$

18. $4m^2 + 7m \geq -3$

19. $4x^2 - 9 \leq 0$

20. $9x^2 - 25 \leq 0$

21. $z^2 - 4z > 0$

22. $x^2 + 2x > 0$

23. $x^2 - 6x + 6 \geq 0$
(*Hint:* Use the quadratic formula.)

24. $3k^2 - 6k + 2 \leq 0$
(*Hint:* Use the quadratic formula.)

Solve each inequality. ***See Example 4.***

25. $(4 - 3x)^2 \geq -2$

26. $(7 - 6x)^2 \geq -1$

27. $(3x + 5)^2 \leq -4$

28. $(8t + 5)^2 \leq -5$

29. $(2x + 5)^2 < 0$

30. $(3x - 7)^2 < 0$

31. $(5x - 1)^2 \geq 0$

32. $(4x + 1)^2 \geq 0$

Solve each inequality, and graph the solution set. ***See Example 5.***

33. $(p - 1)(p - 2)(p - 4) < 0$

34. $(2r + 1)(3r - 2)(4r + 7) < 0$

35. $(x - 4)(2x + 3)(3x - 1) \geq 0$

36. $(z + 2)(4z - 3)(2z + 7) \geq 0$

Solve each inequality, and graph the solution set. ***See Examples 6 and 7.***

37. $\dfrac{x - 1}{x - 4} > 0$

38. $\dfrac{x + 1}{x - 5} > 0$

39. $\dfrac{2n + 3}{n - 5} \leq 0$

40. $\dfrac{3t + 7}{t - 3} \leq 0$

41. $\dfrac{8}{x - 2} \geq 2$

42. $\dfrac{20}{x - 1} \geq 1$

43. $\dfrac{3}{2t - 1} < 2$

44. $\dfrac{6}{m - 1} < 1$

45. $\dfrac{w}{w + 2} \geq 2$

46. $\dfrac{m}{m + 5} \geq 2$

47. $\dfrac{4k}{2k - 1} < k$

48. $\dfrac{r}{r + 2} < 2r$

49. $\dfrac{x-3}{x+2} \geq 2$

50. $\dfrac{m+4}{m+5} \geq 2$

51. $\dfrac{x-8}{x-4} \leq 3$

52. $\dfrac{2t-3}{t+1} \geq 4$

53. $\dfrac{2x-3}{x^2+1} \geq 0$

54. $\dfrac{9x-8}{4x^2+25} < 0$

Relating Concepts (Exercises 55–58) For Individual or Group Work

A toy rocket is projected vertically upward from the ground. Its distance s in feet above the ground after t seconds is given by the quadratic function

$$s(t) = -16t^2 + 256t.$$

Work Exercises 55–58 in order, *to see how quadratic equations and inequalities are related.*

55. At what times will the rocket be 624 ft above the ground? (*Hint:* Let $s(t) = 624$ and solve the quadratic *equation.*)

56. At what times will the rocket be more than 624 ft above the ground? (*Hint:* Let $s(t) > 624$ and solve the quadratic *inequality.*)

57. At what times will the rocket be at ground level? (*Hint:* Let $s(t) = 0$ and solve the quadratic *equation.*)

58. At what times will the rocket be less than 624 ft above the ground? (*Hint:* Let $s(t) < 624$, solve the quadratic *inequality,* and observe the solutions in **Exercises 56 and 57** to determine the least and greatest possible values of t.)

Key Terms

11.1

quadratic equation A quadratic equation (in x here) is an equation that can be written in the form $ax^2 + bx + c = 0$, where a, b, and c are real numbers and $a \neq 0$. This form is called **standard form.**

second-degree equation An equation with a second-degree term and no terms of greater degree is a second-degree (or quadratic) equation.

11.3

quadratic formula The solutions of any quadratic equation $ax^2 + bx + c = 0$ (where $a \neq 0$) are given by the quadratic formula $x = \dfrac{-b \pm \sqrt{b^2 - 4ac}}{2a}$.

discriminant The discriminant is the expression $b^2 - 4ac$ under the radical in the quadratic formula.

11.4

quadratic in form A nonquadratic equation that can be written in the form $au^2 + bu + c = 0$, for $a \neq 0$ and an algebraic expression u, is quadratic in form.

11.6

quadratic function A function that can be written in the form $f(x) = ax^2 + bx + c$, for real numbers a, b, and c, where $a \neq 0$, is a quadratic function.

parabola The graph of a quadratic function is a parabola.

vertex The point on a parabola that has the least y-value (if the parabola opens up) or the greatest y-value (if the parabola opens down) is the vertex of the parabola.

axis of symmetry The vertical (or horizontal) line through the vertex of a vertical (or horizontal) parabola is its axis of symmetry.

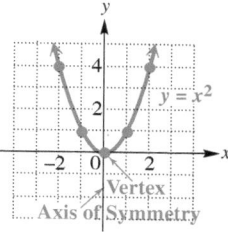

11.8

quadratic inequality A quadratic inequality (in x here) is an inequality that can be written in the form $ax^2 + bx + c < 0$ or $ax^2 + bx + c > 0$ (or with $\leq$ or $\geq$), where a, b, and c are real numbers and $a \neq 0$.

rational inequality An inequality that involves a rational expression is a rational inequality.

Test Your Word Power

See how well you have learned the vocabulary in this chapter.

1 The **quadratic formula** is
   A. a formula to find the number of solutions of a quadratic equation
   B. a formula to find the type of solutions of a quadratic equation
   C. the standard form of a quadratic equation
   D. a general formula for solving any quadratic equation.

2 A **quadratic function** is a function that can be written in the form
   A. $f(x) = mx + b$, for real numbers m and b
   B. $f(x) = \dfrac{P(x)}{Q(x)}$, where $Q(x) \neq 0$

   C. $f(x) = ax^2 + bx + c$, for real numbers a, b, and c $(a \neq 0)$
   D. $f(x) = \sqrt{x}$, for $x \geq 0$.

3 A **parabola** is the graph of
   A. any equation in two variables
   B. a linear equation
   C. an equation of degree 3
   D. a quadratic equation in two variables.

4 The **vertex** of a parabola is
   A. the point where the graph intersects the y-axis
   B. the point where the graph intersects the x-axis

   C. the lowest point on a parabola that opens up or the highest point on a parabola that opens down
   D. the origin.

5 The **axis of symmetry** of a parabola is
   A. either the x-axis or the y-axis
   B. the vertical line (of a vertical parabola) or the horizontal line (of a horizontal parabola) through the vertex
   C. the lowest or highest point on the graph of a parabola
   D. a line through the origin.

Answers to Test Your Word Power

1. D; *Example:* The solutions of $ax^2 + bx + c = 0$ (where $a \neq 0$) are given by $x = \dfrac{-b \pm \sqrt{b^2 - 4ac}}{2a}$.

2. C; *Examples:* $f(x) = x^2 - 2$, $f(x) = (x + 4)^2 + 1$, $f(x) = x^2 - 4x + 5$

3. D; *Example:* The quadratic equation $y = x^2$ has a parabola as its graph.

4. C; *Example:* The graph of $y = (x + 3)^2$ has vertex $(-3, 0)$, which is the lowest point on the graph.

5. B; *Example:* The axis of symmetry of $y = (x + 3)^2$ is the vertical line $x = -3$.

Quick Review

Concepts	Examples

11.1 Solving Quadratic Equations by the Square Root Property

Square Root Property
If x and k are complex numbers and $x^2 = k$, then
$$x = \sqrt{k} \quad \text{or} \quad x = -\sqrt{k}.$$

Solve $(x-1)^2 = 8$.
$$x - 1 = \sqrt{8} \quad \text{or} \quad x - 1 = -\sqrt{8}$$
$$x = 1 + 2\sqrt{2} \quad \text{or} \quad x = 1 - 2\sqrt{2}$$
Solution set: $\left\{1 + 2\sqrt{2}, 1 - 2\sqrt{2}\right\}$

11.2 Solving Quadratic Equations by Completing the Square

Completing the Square
To solve $ax^2 + bx + c = 0$ (where $a \neq 0$), follow these steps.

Step 1 If $a \neq 1$, divide each side by a.

Step 2 Write the equation with the variable terms on one side of the equality symbol and the constant on the other.

Step 3 Complete the square.
- Take half the coefficient of x and square it.
- Add the square to each side.
- Factor the perfect square trinomial, and write it as the square of a binomial. Combine terms on the other side.

Step 4 Use the square root property to solve.

Solve $2x^2 - 4x - 18 = 0$.
$$x^2 - 2x - 9 = 0 \qquad \text{Divide by 2.}$$
$$x^2 - 2x = 9 \qquad \text{Add 9.}$$
$$\left[\tfrac{1}{2}(-2)\right]^2 = (-1)^2 = 1$$
$$x^2 - 2x + 1 = 9 + 1 \qquad \text{Add 1.}$$
$$(x-1)^2 = 10 \qquad \text{Factor. Add.}$$
$$x - 1 = \sqrt{10} \quad \text{or} \quad x - 1 = -\sqrt{10} \quad \text{Square root}$$
$$x = 1 + \sqrt{10} \quad \text{or} \quad x = 1 - \sqrt{10} \quad \text{property}$$
Solution set: $\left\{1 + \sqrt{10}, 1 - \sqrt{10}\right\}$

11.3 Solving Quadratic Equations by the Quadratic Formula

Quadratic Formula
The solutions of $ax^2 + bx + c = 0$ (where $a \neq 0$) are given by
$$x = \frac{-b \pm \sqrt{b^2 - 4ac}}{2a}.$$

Solve $3x^2 + 5x + 2 = 0$.
$$x = \frac{-5 \pm \sqrt{5^2 - 4(3)(2)}}{2(3)} \qquad a = 3, b = 5, c = 2$$
$$x = \frac{-5 \pm 1}{6} \qquad \text{Simplify.}$$
$$x = -\frac{2}{3} \quad \text{or} \quad x = -1$$
Solution set: $\left\{-1, -\frac{2}{3}\right\}$

The Discriminant
The discriminant $b^2 - 4ac$ of $ax^2 + bx + c = 0$ (where a, b, and c are integers) can be used to determine the number and type of solutions.

Discriminant $b^2 - 4ac$	Number and Type of Solutions
Positive, and the square of an integer	Two rational solutions
Positive, but not the square of an integer	Two irrational solutions
Zero	One rational solution
Negative	Two nonreal complex solutions

For $x^2 + 3x - 10 = 0$, the discriminant is
$$b^2 - 4ac$$
$$= 3^2 - 4(1)(-10) \qquad a = 1, b = 3, c = -10$$
$$= 49 \qquad \text{Simplify.}$$
$$= 7^2. \leftarrow \text{The equation has two rational solutions.}$$

Concepts	**Examples**

11.4 Equations Quadratic in Form

A nonquadratic equation that can be written in the form

$$au^2 + bu + c = 0,$$

for $a \neq 0$ and an algebraic expression u, is quadratic in form.

Solving an Equation Quadratic in Form (Substitution)
Substitute u for the expression, solve for u, and then solve for the variable in the expression.

Solve $3(x + 5)^2 + 7(x + 5) + 2 = 0$.

$$3u^2 + 7u + 2 = 0 \qquad \text{Let } u = x + 5.$$

$$(3u + 1)(u + 2) = 0 \qquad \text{Factor.}$$

$$u = -\frac{1}{3} \quad \text{or} \quad u = -2 \quad \text{Solve for } u.$$

$$x + 5 = -\frac{1}{3} \quad \text{or} \quad x + 5 = -2 \quad x + 5 = u$$

$$x = -\frac{16}{3} \quad \text{or} \quad x = -7 \quad \text{Subtract 5.}$$

Solution set: $\left\{-7, -\frac{16}{3}\right\}$

11.5 Formulas and Further Applications

Solving a Formula for a Squared Variable

- **If the variable appears only to the second power:**
  Isolate the second-degree variable on one side of the equation, and then use the square root property.

- **If the variable appears to the first and second powers:**
  Write the equation in standard form, and then use the quadratic formula.

Solve $A = \dfrac{2mp}{r^2}$ for r.

$$r^2 A = 2mp$$

$$r^2 = \frac{2mp}{A}$$

$$r = \pm\sqrt{\frac{2mp}{A}}$$

Square root property

$$r = \frac{\pm\sqrt{2mpA}}{A}$$

Rationalize denominator.

Solve $x^2 + rx = t$ for x.

$$x^2 + rx - t = 0 \qquad \begin{array}{l}\text{Standard}\\\text{form}\end{array}$$

$$x = \frac{-r \pm \sqrt{r^2 - 4(1)(-t)}}{2(1)}$$

$$a = 1, b = r, c = -t$$

$$x = \frac{-r \pm \sqrt{r^2 + 4t}}{2}$$

Simplify.

11.6 Graphs of Quadratic Functions

The graph of the quadratic function $F(x) = a(x - h)^2 + k$ (where $a \neq 0$) is a parabola.

- The vertex of the parabola is (h, k).

- The axis of symmetry is the vertical line $x = h$.

- The graph opens up if $a > 0$ and down if $a < 0$.

- The graph is wider than the graph of $f(x) = x^2$ if $0 < |a| < 1$ and narrower if $|a| > 1$.

Graph $f(x) = -(x + 3)^2 + 1$.

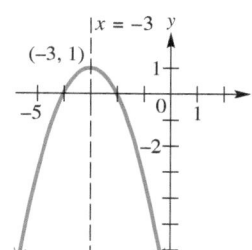

The graph opens down since $a < 0$.

Vertex: $(-3, 1)$

Axis of symmetry: $x = -3$

Domain: $(-\infty, \infty)$

Range: $(-\infty, 1]$

11.7 More about Parabolas and Their Applications

The vertex of the graph of $f(x) = ax^2 + bx + c$ (where $a \neq 0$) may be found by completing the square or using the vertex formula $\left(\frac{-b}{2a}, f\left(\frac{-b}{2a}\right)\right)$.

Graphing a Quadratic Function

Step 1 Determine whether the graph opens up or down.

Step 2 Find the vertex.

Step 3 Find any intercepts.

Step 4 Find and plot additional points as needed.

Graph $f(x) = x^2 + 4x + 3$.

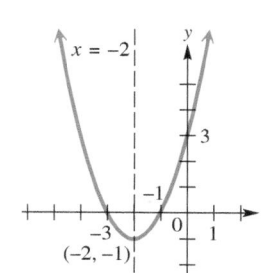

The graph opens up since $a > 0$.

Vertex: $(-2, -1)$

The solutions of $x^2 + 4x + 3 = 0$ are -1 and -3, so the x-intercepts are $(-1, 0)$ and $(-3, 0)$.

$f(0) = 3$, so the y-intercept is $(0, 3)$.

Axis of symmetry: $x = -2$

Domain: $(-\infty, \infty)$

Range: $[-1, \infty)$

Concepts	Examples

Horizontal Parabolas

The graph of an equation of the form

$$x = ay^2 + by + c \quad \text{or} \quad x = a(y - k)^2 + h$$

is a horizontal parabola.

- The vertex of the parabola is (h, k).

- The axis of symmetry is the horizontal line $y = k$.

- The graph opens to the right if $a > 0$ and to the left if $a < 0$.

Horizontal parabolas do not represent functions.

Graph $x = 2y^2 + 6y + 5$.

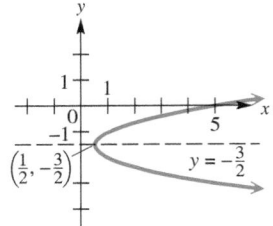

The graph opens to the right since $a > 0$.

Vertex: $\left(\frac{1}{2}, -\frac{3}{2}\right)$

Axis of symmetry: $y = -\frac{3}{2}$

Domain: $\left[\frac{1}{2}, \infty\right)$

Range: $(-\infty, \infty)$

11.8 Polynomial and Rational Inequalities

Solving a Quadratic (or Higher-Degree Polynomial) Inequality

Step 1 Write the inequality as an equation and solve.

Step 2 Use the values found in Step 1 to divide a number line into intervals.

Step 3 Substitute a test value from each interval into the original inequality to determine the intervals that belong to the solution set.

Step 4 Consider the endpoints separately.

Solve $2x^2 + 5x + 2 < 0$.

$$2x^2 + 5x + 2 = 0 \qquad \text{Related equation}$$

$$(2x + 1)(x + 2) = 0 \qquad \text{Factor.}$$

$$2x + 1 = 0 \quad \text{or} \quad x + 2 = 0 \qquad \text{Zero-factor property}$$

$$x = -\frac{1}{2} \quad \text{or} \qquad x = -2 \qquad \text{Solve each equation.}$$

Intervals: $(-\infty, -2)$, $\left(-2, -\frac{1}{2}\right)$, $\left(-\frac{1}{2}, \infty\right)$

Test values: -3 (Interval A), -1 (Interval B), 0 (Interval C)
$x = -3$ makes the original inequality false, $x = -1$ makes it true, and $x = 0$ makes it false.

Solution set: $\left(-2, -\frac{1}{2}\right)$ (Endpoints are not included because the symbol $<$ does not include equality.)

Solving a Rational Inequality

Step 1 Write the inequality so that 0 is on one side and there is a single fraction on the other side.

Step 2 Determine the values that make the numerator or denominator 0.

Step 3 Use the values from Step 2 to divide a number line into intervals.

Step 4 Substitute a test value from each interval into the original inequality to determine the intervals that satisfy the inequality.

Step 5 Consider the endpoints separately. Exclude any values that make the denominator 0.

Solve $\dfrac{x}{x + 2} \geq 4$.

$$\frac{x}{x + 2} - 4 \geq 0 \qquad \text{Subtract 4.}$$

$$\frac{x}{x + 2} - \frac{4(x + 2)}{x + 2} \geq 0 \qquad \begin{array}{l}\text{Write with a common}\\ \text{denominator.}\end{array}$$

$$\frac{-3x - 8}{x + 2} \geq 0 \qquad \text{Subtract fractions.}$$

$-\frac{8}{3}$ makes the numerator 0 and -2 makes the denominator 0.

Intervals: $\left(-\infty, -\frac{8}{3}\right)$, $\left(-\frac{8}{3}, -2\right)$, $(-2, \infty)$

Test values: -4 from Interval A makes the original inequality false, $-\frac{7}{3}$ from Interval B makes it true, and 0 from Interval C makes it false.

Solution set: $\left[-\frac{8}{3}, -2\right)$ (The endpoint -2 is not included because it makes the denominator 0.)

Chapter 11 *Review Exercises*

11.1, 11.2 *Solve each equation using the zero-factor property.*

1. $x^2 + 3x - 10 = 0$ **2.** $6x^2 + 7x + 2 = 0$ **3.** $4x^2 = 11x + 3$ **4.** $2x^2 - 13x + 15 = 0$

Solve each equation using the square root property or by completing the square.

5. $t^2 = 121$ **6.** $p^2 = 3$ **7.** $(2x + 5)^2 = 100$

*8. $(3k - 2)^2 = -25$ **9.** $x^2 + 4x = 15$ **10.** $2m^2 - 3m = -1$

Solve each problem.

11. CONCEPT CHECK A student gave the following incorrect "solution."

$x^2 = 12$

$x = \sqrt{12}$ Square root property

$x = 2\sqrt{3}$ $\sqrt{12} = \sqrt{4} \cdot \sqrt{3} = 2\sqrt{3}$

Solution set: $\{2\sqrt{3}\}$

What Went Wrong? Give the correct solution set.

12. The High Roller observation wheel in Las Vegas has a height of 168 m. Use the metric version of Galileo's formula,

$$d = 4.9t^2$$

(where d is in meters and t is in seconds), to find how long, to the nearest tenth of a second, it would take a wallet dropped from the top of the High Roller to reach the ground. (Data from www.caesars.com)

11.3 *Solve each equation using the quadratic formula.*

13. $2x^2 + x - 21 = 0$ **14.** $k^2 + 5k = 7$ **15.** $(t + 3)(t - 4) = -2$

16. $2x^2 + 3x + 4 = 0$ ***17.** $3p^2 = 2(2p - 1)$ **18.** $m(2m - 7) = 3m^2 + 3$

Find the discriminant. Use it to predict whether the solutions for each equation are

A. *two rational numbers,* **B.** *two irrational numbers,*

C. *one rational number,* **D.** *two nonreal complex numbers.*

Tell whether the equation can be solved using the zero-factor property or whether the quadratic formula should be used. Do not actually solve.

19. $x^2 + 5x + 2 = 0$ **20.** $4t^2 = 3 - 4t$ **21.** $9z^2 + 30z + 25 = 0$ **22.** $4x^2 = 6x - 8$

---

*This exercise requires knowledge of complex numbers.

11.4 *Solve each equation.*

23. $\dfrac{15}{x} = 2x - 1$

24. $\dfrac{1}{n} + \dfrac{2}{n+1} = 2$

25. $-2r = \sqrt{\dfrac{48 - 20r}{2}}$

26. $8(3x + 5)^2 + 2(3x + 5) - 1 = 0$ **27.** $2x^{2/3} - x^{1/3} - 28 = 0$

28. $p^4 - 5p^2 + 4 = 0$

Solve each problem. Round answers to the nearest tenth, as necessary.

29. Matthew drove 8 mi to pick up his cousin Jack, and then drove 11 mi to a mall at a rate 15 mph faster. If Matthew's total travel time was 24 min, what was his rate on the trip to pick up Jack?

30. An old machine processes a batch of checks in 1 hr more time than a new one. How long would it take the old machine to process a batch of checks that the two machines together process in 2 hr?

11.5 *Solve each formula for the indicated variable. (Leave $\pm$ in the answers as needed.)*

31. $k = \dfrac{rF}{wv^2}$ for v

32. $mt^2 = 3mt + 6$ for t

Solve each problem. Round answers to the nearest tenth, as necessary.

33. A large machine requires a part in the shape of a right triangle with a hypotenuse 9 ft less than twice the length of the longer leg. The shorter leg must be $\frac{3}{4}$ the length of the longer leg. Find the lengths of the three sides of the part.

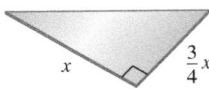

34. A square has an area of 256 cm². If the same amount is removed from one dimension and added to the other, the resulting rectangle has an area 16 cm² less. Find the dimensions of the rectangle.

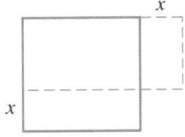

35. Nancy wants to buy a mat for a photograph that measures 14 in. by 20 in. She wants to have an even border around the picture when it is mounted on the mat. If the area of the mat she chooses is 352 in.², how wide will the border be?

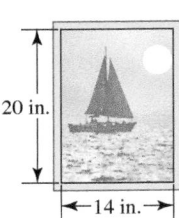

36. Lewis Tower in Philadelphia, Pennsylvania, is 400 ft high. Suppose that a ball is projected upward from the top of the Tower, and its position in feet above the ground is given by the quadratic function

$$f(t) = -16t^2 + 45t + 400,$$

where t is the number of seconds elapsed. How long will it take for the ball to reach a height of 200 ft above the ground? (Data from *The World Almanac and Book of Facts*.)

11.6, 11.7   *Identify the vertex of the graph of each parabola.*

37. $f(x) = -(x - 1)^2$ **38.** $f(x) = (x - 3)^2 + 7$ **39.** $y = -3x^2 + 4x - 2$ **40.** $x = (y - 3)^2 - 4$

Graph each parabola. Give the vertex, axis of symmetry, domain, and range.

41. $y = 2(x - 2)^2 - 3$ **42.** $f(x) = -2x^2 + 8x - 5$ **43.** $x = 2(y + 3)^2 - 4$ **44.** $x = -\dfrac{1}{2}y^2 + 6y - 14$

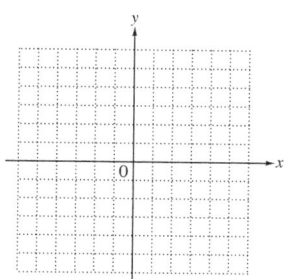   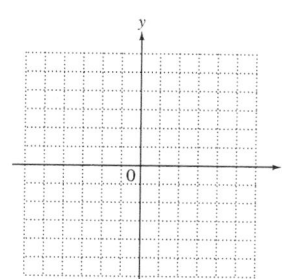   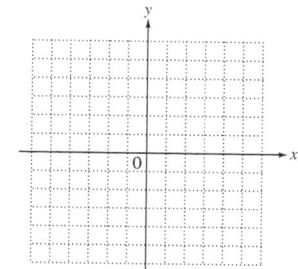   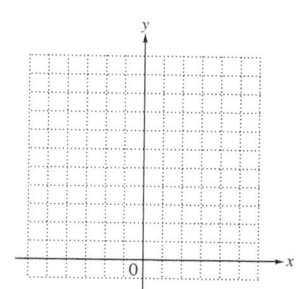

Solve each problem.

45. The height (in feet) of a projectile t seconds after being fired from ground level into the air is given by

$$f(t) = -16t^2 + 160t.$$

Find the number of seconds required for the projectile to reach maximum height. What is the maximum height?

46. Find the length and width of a rectangle having a perimeter of 200 m if the area is to be a maximum. What is the maximum area?

11.8   *Solve each inequality, and graph the solution set.*

47. $(x - 4)(2x + 3) > 0$ **48.** $x^2 + x \le 12$ **49.** $(x + 2)(x - 3)(x + 5) \le 0$

50. $(4m + 3)^2 \le -4$ **51.** $\dfrac{6}{2z - 1} < 2$ **52.** $\dfrac{3t + 4}{t - 2} \le 1$

Chapter 11 *Mixed Review Exercises*

Solve each equation or inequality.

1. $V = r^2 + R^2 h$ for R
(Leave $\pm$ in the answer.)

*2. $3t^2 - 6t = -4$

3. $(3k + 11)^2 = 7$

4. $S = \dfrac{Id^2}{k}$ for d
(Leave $\pm$ in the answer.)

5. $2x - \sqrt{x} = 6$

6. $6 + \dfrac{15}{s^2} = -\dfrac{19}{s}$

7. $\dfrac{-2}{x + 5} \le -5$

8. $(8x - 7)^2 \ge -1$

9. $25x^2 - 10x + 1 = 0$

10. $(x^2 - 2x)^2 = 11(x^2 - 2x) - 24$

11. $(r - 1)(2r + 3)(r + 6) < 0$

Work each problem.

12. CONCEPT CHECK   Match each equation in parts (a)–(f) with the figure that most closely resembles its graph in choices A–F.

(a) $g(x) = x^2 - 5$

(b) $h(x) = -x^2 + 4$

(c) $F(x) = (x - 1)^2$

(d) $G(x) = (x + 1)^2$

(e) $H(x) = (x - 1)^2 + 1$

(f) $K(x) = (x + 1)^2 + 1$

A.
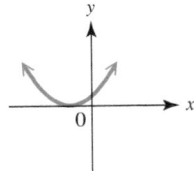

B.
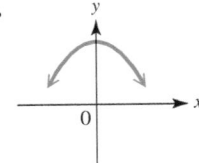

C.
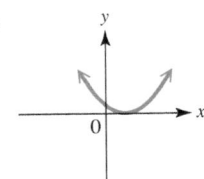

D.
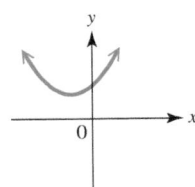

E.
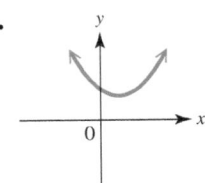

F.
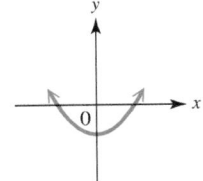

13. In 4 hr, Rajeed can travel 15 mi upriver and come back. The rate of the current is 5 mph. Find the rate of the boat in still water.

14. Two pieces of a large wooden puzzle fit together to form a rectangle with length 1 cm less than twice the width. The diagonal, where the two pieces meet, is 2.5 cm in length. Find the length and width of the rectangle.

---

*This exercise requires knowledge of complex numbers.

1. Solve $5x^2 + 13x = 6$ using the zero-factor property.

Solve each equation using the square root property or by completing the square.

2. $t^2 = 54$

3. $(7x + 3)^2 = 25$

4. $x^2 + 2x = 1$

Solve each equation using the quadratic formula.

5. $2x^2 - 3x - 1 = 0$

***6.** $3t^2 - 4t = -5$

7. $3x = \sqrt{\dfrac{9x + 2}{2}}$

8. What is the discriminant for $2x^2 - 8x - 3 = 0$? How many and what type of solutions does this equation have? (Do not actually solve.)

Solve each equation by any method.

9. $3 - \dfrac{16}{x} - \dfrac{12}{x^2} = 0$

10. $4x^2 + 7x - 3 = 0$

11. $9x^4 + 4 = 37x^2$

12. $12 = (2n + 1)^2 + (2n + 1)$

13. $S = 4\pi r^2$ for r (Leave $\pm$ in the answer.)

Solve each problem.

14. Andrew and Kent do desktop publishing. Kent can prepare a certain prospectus 2 hr faster than Andrew. If they work together, they can do the entire prospectus in 5 hr. How long will it take each of them working alone to prepare the prospectus? Round answers to the nearest tenth of an hour.

15. Bryn paddled her canoe 10 mi upstream, and then paddled back to her starting point. If the rate of the current was 3 mph and the entire trip took $3\frac{1}{2}$ hr, what was Bryn's rate?

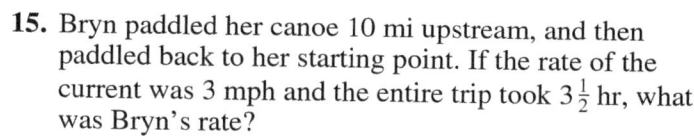

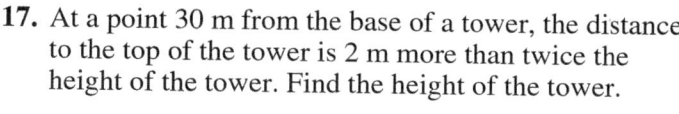

16. Tyler has a pool 24 ft long and 10 ft wide. He wants to construct a concrete walk around the pool. If he plans for the walk to be of uniform width and cover 152 ft², what will the width of the walk be?

17. At a point 30 m from the base of a tower, the distance to the top of the tower is 2 m more than twice the height of the tower. Find the height of the tower.

Pool

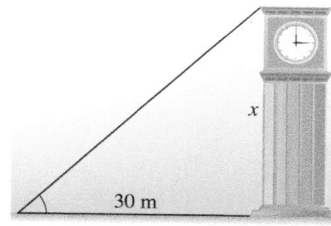

30 m

18. Professor Bernstein has found that the number of students attending her intermediate algebra class is approximated by

$$S(x) = -x^2 + 20x + 80,$$

where x is the number of hours that the Campus Center is open daily.

(a) Find the number of hours that the center should be open so that the number of students attending class is a maximum.

(b) What is this maximum number of students?

19. Houston Community College is planning to construct a rectangular parking lot on land bordered on one side by a highway. The plan is to use 640 ft of fencing to fence off the other three sides. What should the dimensions of the lot be if the enclosed area is to be a maximum? What is the maximum area?

20. Which one of the following most closely resembles the graph of $f(x) = a(x - h)^2 + k$ if $a < 0, h > 0,$ and $k < 0$?

A.
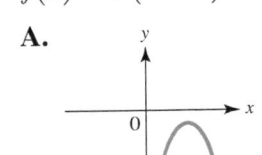

B.
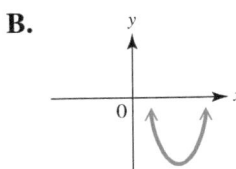

C.
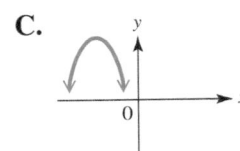

D.
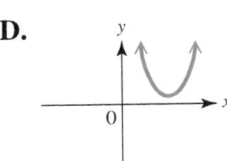

Graph each parabola. Give the vertex, axis of symmetry, domain, and range.

21. $f(x) = \dfrac{1}{2}x^2 - 2$

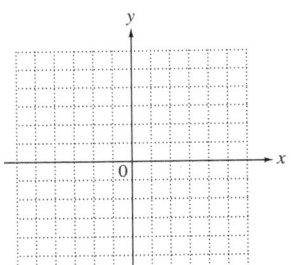

22. $f(x) = -x^2 + 4x - 1$

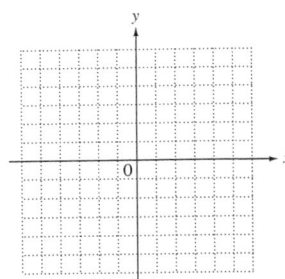

23. $x = 2y^2 + 8y + 3$

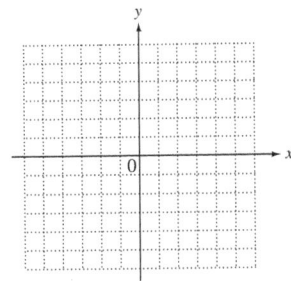

Solve each inequality, and graph the solution set.

24. $2x^2 + 7x > 15$

25. $\dfrac{5}{t - 4} \leq 1$

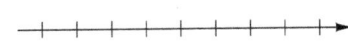

Chapters R–11 *Cumulative Review Exercises*

1. Let $S = \left\{ -\frac{7}{3}, -2, -\sqrt{3}, 0, 0.7, \sqrt{12}, \sqrt{-8}, 7, \frac{32}{3} \right\}$. List the elements of S that are elements of each set.

   (a) Integers   **(b)** Rational numbers   **(c)** Real numbers   **(d)** Complex numbers

Solve each equation or inequality.

2. $-2x + 4 = 5(x - 4) + 17$ **3.** $-2x + 4 \le -x + 3$ **4.** $|3x - 7| \le 1$

5. $|6x - 9| = |-4x + 2|$ **6.** $2x^2 - 4x - 3 = 0$ **7.** $z^2 - 2z = 15$

8. $\dfrac{3}{x - 3} - \dfrac{2}{x - 2} = \dfrac{3}{x^2 - 5x + 6}$ **9.** $p^4 - 10p^2 + 9 = 0$ **10.** $2x = \sqrt{\dfrac{5x + 2}{3}}$

Solve each problem.

11. Find the slope and y-intercept of the line with equation $2x - 4y = 7$.

12. Write the equation in standard form of the line through $(2, -1)$ and perpendicular to $-3x + y = 5$.

Graph each relation. Tell whether or not each is a function, and if it is, give its domain and range.

13. $4x - 5y = 15$ **14.** $4x - 5y < 15$ **15.** $y = -2(x - 1)^2 + 3$

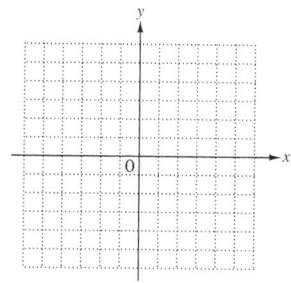   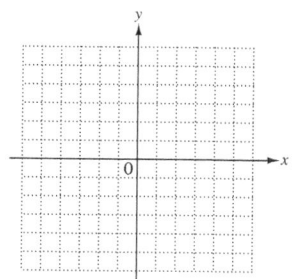   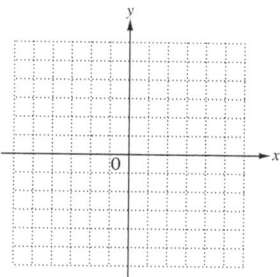

Solve each system of equations.

16. $2x - 4y = 10$
    $9x + 3y = 3$

17. $x - y = 5$
    $2x - 10 = 2y$

18. $x + y + 2z = 3$
    $-x + y + z = -5$
    $2x + 3y - z = -8$

Write with positive exponents only. Assume that variables represent positive real numbers.

19. $\left(\dfrac{x^{-3}y^2}{x^5y^{-2}}\right)^{-1}$

20. $\dfrac{(4x^{-2})^2(2y^3)}{8x^{-3}y^5}$

21. Multiply $(2t + 9)^2$.

22. Divide $4x^3 + 2x^2 - x + 26$ by $x + 2$.

Factor completely.

23. $16x - x^3$

24. $24m^2 + 2m - 15$

25. $9x^2 - 30xy + 25y^2$

Perform the indicated operations, and express answers in lowest terms. Assume that denominators represent nonzero real numbers.

26. $\dfrac{5t + 2}{-6} \div \dfrac{15t + 6}{5}$

27. $\dfrac{3}{2 - k} - \dfrac{5}{k} + \dfrac{6}{k^2 - 2k}$

28. $\dfrac{\dfrac{r}{s} - \dfrac{s}{r}}{\dfrac{r}{s} + 1}$

Simplify each radical expression.

29. $\sqrt[3]{\dfrac{27}{16}}$

30. $\dfrac{2}{\sqrt{7} - \sqrt{5}}$

Solve each problem.

31. Clark's rule, a formula used in reducing drug dosage according to weight from the recommended adult dosage to a child dosage, is

$$\dfrac{\text{weight of child in pounds}}{150} \times \text{adult dose} = \text{child's dose}.$$

Find a child's dosage if the child weighs 55 lb and the recommended adult dosage is 120 mg.

32. Two cars left an intersection at the same time, one heading due south and the other due east. Later they were exactly 95 mi apart. The car heading east had gone 38 mi less than twice as far as the car heading south. How far had each car traveled?

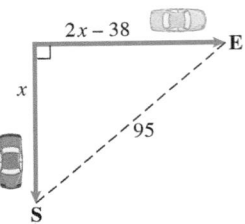

12

Inverse, Exponential, and Logarithmic Functions

The magnitudes of earthquakes, intensities of sounds, and population growth and decay are some examples of applications of *exponential* and *logarithmic functions*.

12.1 Composition of Functions
12.2 Inverse Functions
12.3 Exponential Functions
12.4 Logarithmic Functions

12.5 Properties of Logarithms
12.6 Common and Natural Logarithms
12.7 Exponential and Logarithmic Equations and Their Applications

12.1 Composition of Functions

OBJECTIVE

1 Find the composition of functions.

OBJECTIVE ▶ **1** **Find the composition of functions.** The diagram in **Figure 1** shows a function g that assigns, to each element x of set X, some element y of set Y. Suppose that a function f takes each element of set Y and assigns a value z of set Z. Then g and f together assign an element x in X to an element z in Z.

The result of this process is a new function h, which takes an element x in X and assigns it an element z in Z.

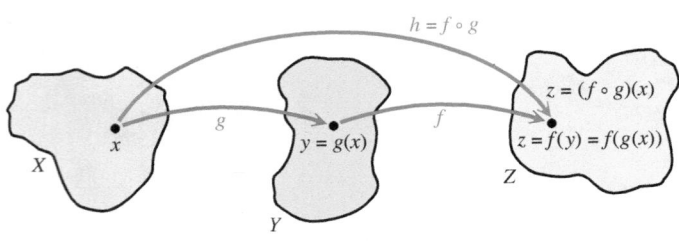

Figure 1

This function h is the *composition* of functions f and g, written $f \circ g$.

Composition of Functions

The **composite function,** or **composition,** of functions f and g is defined by
$$(f \circ g)(x) = f(g(x)),$$
for all x in the domain of g such that $g(x)$ is in the domain of f.

Read $f \circ g$ as "f of g" (or "f compose g").

As a real-life example of how composite functions occur, consider the following retail situation.

A $40 pair of blue jeans is on sale for 25% off. If we purchase the jeans before noon, the retailer offers an additional 10% off. What is the final sale price of the blue jeans?

We might be tempted to say that the jeans are 35% off and calculate as follows.

$$\$40 - 0.35\,(\$40) \quad \text{Original price} - \text{Discount}$$
$$= \$40 - \$14 \qquad = \text{Sale price}$$
$$= \$26 \longleftarrow \text{This is not correct.}$$

To find the correct final sale price, we must first find the price after taking 25% off, and then take an additional 10% off *that* price.

Take 25% off the original price.

$$\$40 - 0.25\,(\$40)$$
$$= \$40 - \$10$$
$$= \$30$$

Take an additional 10% off.

$$\$30 - 0.10\,(\$30)$$
$$= \$30 - \$3$$
$$= \$27$$

This is the idea behind composition of functions.

As another real-life example of composition, suppose an oil well off the coast is leaking, with the leak spreading oil in a circular layer over the surface. See **Figure 2.**

At any time t, in minutes, after the beginning of the leak, the radius of the circular oil slick is given by $r(t) = 5t$ feet. Because $\mathcal{A}(r) = \pi r^2$ gives the area of a circle of radius r, the area can be expressed as a function of time.

Figure 2

$$\mathcal{A}(r) = \pi r^2 \qquad \text{Area of a circle}$$

$$\mathcal{A}(r(t)) = \pi (5t)^2 \qquad \text{Substitute } 5t \text{ for } r.$$

$$\mathcal{A}(r(t)) = 25\pi t^2 \qquad \begin{array}{l}\text{Apply the exponent;} \\ \text{commutative property}\end{array}$$

The function $\mathcal{A}(r(t))$ is a composite function of the functions $\mathcal{A}$ and r.

EXAMPLE 1 **Finding a Composite Function**

Let $f(x) = x^2$ and $g(x) = x + 3$. Find $(f \circ g)(4)$.

$(f \circ g)(4)$ Evaluate the "inside" function value first.

$= f(g(4))$ Definition of composition

$= f(4 + 3)$ Use the rule for $g(x)$; $g(4) = 4 + 3$

$= f(7)$ Add.   *Now evaluate the "outside" function.*

$= 7^2$ Use the rule for $f(x)$; $f(7) = 7^2$

$= 49$ Square 7.

In this composition, g is the innermost "operation" and acts on x (here 4) first. Then the output value of g (here 7) becomes the input (domain) value of f.

— **Work Problem ❶ at the Side.** ▶

If we interchange the order of the functions f and g, the composition $g \circ f$, which is read "g *of* f" (or "g *compose* f"), is defined by

$$(g \circ f)(x) = g(f(x)), \quad \text{for all } x \text{ in the domain of } f \text{ such that } f(x) \text{ is in the domain of } g.$$

EXAMPLE 2 **Finding a Composite Function**

Let $f(x) = x^2$ and $g(x) = x + 3$ as in **Example 1.** Find $(g \circ f)(4)$.

$(g \circ f)(4)$ Evaluate the "inside" function value first.

$= g(f(4))$ Definition of composition

$= g(4^2)$ Use the rule for $f(x)$; $f(4) = 4^2$

$= g(16)$ Square 4.

$= 16 + 3$ Use the rule for $g(x)$; $g(16) = 16 + 3$ *Now evaluate the "outside" function.*

$= 19$ Add.

In this composition, f is the innermost "operation" and acts on x (again 4) first. Then the output value of f (here 16) becomes the input (domain) value of g.

— **Work Problem ❷ at the Side.** ▶

---

❶ Let $f(x) = x - 4$ and $g(x) = x^2$.

⑤⑤ (a) Find $(f \circ g)(3)$.

Apply the definition of composition of functions.

$(f \circ g)(3)$

$= f(\underline{\quad}(\underline{\quad}))$

Use the rule for $g(x)$.

$= f(\underline{\quad}^2)$

Apply the exponent.

$= f(\underline{\quad})$

Use the rule for $f(x)$.

$= \underline{\quad} - 4$

$= \underline{\quad}$

(b) Find $(f \circ g)(7)$.

❷ Let $f(x) = x - 4$ and $g(x) = x^2$ as in **Margin Problem 1.**

(a) Find $(g \circ f)(3)$.

(b) Find $(g \circ f)(7)$.

Answers

1. **(a)** g; 3; 3; 9; 9; 5   **(b)** 45

2. **(a)** 1   **(b)** 9

3 Let $f(x) = 3x + 6$ and $g(x) = x^3$. Find each of the following.

(a) $(f \circ g)(2)$

(b) $(g \circ f)(2)$

(c) $(f \circ g)(x)$

(d) $(g \circ f)(x)$

We see in **Examples 1 and 2** that

$$(f \circ g)(4) \neq (g \circ f)(4) \quad \text{because} \quad 49 \neq 19.$$

In general,

$$(f \circ g)(x) \neq (g \circ f)(x).$$

EXAMPLE 3 **Finding Composite Functions**

Let $f(x) = 4x - 1$ and $g(x) = x^2 + 5$. Find each of the following.

(a) $\qquad (f \circ g)(2)$

$\qquad = f(g(2)) \qquad$ Definition of composition

$\qquad = f(2^2 + 5) \qquad g(x) = x^2 + 5$

$\qquad = f(9) \qquad$ Work inside the parentheses.

$\qquad = 4(9) - 1 \qquad f(x) = 4x - 1$

$\qquad = 35 \qquad$ Multiply, and then subtract.

(b) $\qquad (f \circ g)(x)$

$\qquad = f(g(x)) \qquad$ Use $g(x)$ as the input for the function f.

$\qquad = 4(g(x)) - 1 \qquad$ Use the rule for $f(x)$; $f(x) = 4x - 1$

$\qquad = 4(x^2 + 5) - 1 \qquad g(x) = x^2 + 5$

$\qquad = 4x^2 + 20 - 1 \qquad$ Distributive property

$\qquad = 4x^2 + 19 \qquad$ Combine like terms.

(c) Find $(f \circ g)(2)$ again, this time using the rule obtained in part (b).

$$(f \circ g)(x) = 4x^2 + 19 \qquad \text{From part (b)}$$

$$(f \circ g)(2) = 4(2)^2 + 19 \qquad \text{Let } x = 2.$$

$$= 4(4) + 19 \qquad \text{Square 2.}$$

$$= 16 + 19 \qquad \text{Multiply.}$$

Same result as in part (a) $\longrightarrow = 35 \qquad$ Add.

(d) $\qquad (g \circ f)(x)$

$\qquad = g(f(x)) \qquad$ Use $f(x)$ as the input for the function g.

$\qquad = (f(x))^2 + 5 \qquad$ Use the rule for $g(x)$; $g(x) = x^2 + 5$

$\qquad = (4x - 1)^2 + 5 \qquad f(x) = 4x - 1$

$\qquad = 16x^2 - 8x + 1 + 5 \qquad (x - y)^2 = x^2 - 2xy + y^2$

$\qquad = 16x^2 - 8x + 6 \qquad$ Combine like terms.

Compare this result to that in part (b). Again,

$$(f \circ g)(x) \neq (g \circ f)(x).$$

◀ **Work Problem 3 at the Side.**

Answers

3. **(a)** 30 **(b)** 1728 **(c)** $3x^3 + 6$
  (d) $(3x + 6)^3$

12.1 Exercises

FOR EXTRA HELP

Go to MyMathLab for worked-out, step-by-step solutions to exercises enclosed in a square ▢ and video solutions to ▶ exercises.

CONCEPT CHECK Let $f(x) = x^2$ and $g(x) = 2x - 1$. Match each expression in Column I with the description of how to evaluate it in Column II.

I

1. $(f \circ g)(5)$

2. $(g \circ f)(5)$

3. $(f \circ f)(5)$

4. $(g \circ g)(5)$

II

A. Square 5. Take the result and square it.

B. Double 5 and subtract 1. Take the result and square it.

C. Double 5 and subtract 1. Take the result, double it, and subtract 1.

D. Square 5. Take the result, double it, and subtract 1.

5. CONCEPT CHECK For $f(x) = x - 8$ and $g(x) = 2x^2$, a student found $(f \circ g)(x)$ incorrectly as follows.

$$(f \circ g)(x) = 2x^2(x - 8)$$
$$= 2x^3 - 16x^2$$

What Went Wrong? Give the correct composition.

6. CONCEPT CHECK For $f(x) = 2x + 3$ and $g(x) = x + 5$, a student found $(f \circ g)(x)$ correctly as

$$(f \circ g)(x) = 2x + 13.$$

When asked to find $(g \circ f)(x)$, he gave the same result. *What Went Wrong?* Give the correct composition.

Let $f(x) = x^2 + 4$, $g(x) = 2x + 3$, and $h(x) = x + 5$. Find each value or expression. *See Examples 1–3.*

7. ▶ $(h \circ g)(4)$

8. $(g \circ h)(4)$

9. $(g \circ f)(6)$

10. $(f \circ g)(6)$

11. $(f \circ h)(-2)$

12. $(h \circ g)(-2)$

13. ▶ $(g \circ h)(x)$

14. $(f \circ g)(x)$

15. $(f \circ h)(x)$

16. $(h \circ f)(x)$

17. ▶ $(h \circ g)(x)$

18. $(g \circ f)(x)$

19. $(f \circ h)\left(\dfrac{1}{2}\right)$

20. $(h \circ f)\left(\dfrac{1}{2}\right)$

21. $(f \circ g)\left(-\dfrac{1}{2}\right)$

22. $(g \circ f)\left(-\dfrac{1}{2}\right)$

CONCEPT CHECK The tables give some selected ordered pairs for functions f and g.

x	3	4	6
f(x)	1	3	9

x	2	7	1	9
g(x)	3	6	9	12

Tables like these can be used to evaluate composite functions. For example, to evaluate $(g \circ f)(6)$, use the first table to find $f(6) = 9$. Then use the second table to find $g(9) = 12$. Find each of the following.

23. ▶ $(f \circ g)(2)$

24. $(f \circ g)(7)$

25. $(g \circ f)(3)$

26. $(g \circ f)(6)$

27. ▶ $(f \circ f)(4)$

28. $(g \circ g)(1)$

Solve each problem.

29. The function

$$f(x) = 12x$$

computes the number of inches in x feet, and the function

$$g(x) = 5280x$$

computes the number of feet in x miles. Find and simplify $(f \circ g)(x)$. What does it compute?

30. The function

$$f(x) = 60x$$

computes the number of minutes in x hours, and the function

$$g(x) = 24x$$

computes the number of hours in x days. Find and simplify $(f \circ g)(x)$. What does it compute?

31. The perimeter x of a square with sides of length s is given by the formula $x = 4s$.

(a) Solve for s in terms of x.

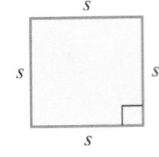

(b) If y represents the area of this square, write y as a function of the perimeter x.

(c) Use the composite function of part (b) to find the area of a square with perimeter 6.

32. The perimeter x of an equilateral triangle with sides of length s is given by the formula $x = 3s$.

(a) Solve for s in terms of x.

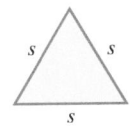

(b) The area y of an equilateral triangle with sides of length s is given by the formula $y = \frac{s^2\sqrt{3}}{4}$. Write y as a function of the perimeter x.

(c) Use the composite function of part (b) to find the area of an equilateral triangle with perimeter 12.

33. When a thermal inversion layer is over a city (as happens often in Los Angeles), pollutants cannot rise vertically but are trapped below the layer and must disperse horizontally.

Assume that a factory smokestack begins emitting a pollutant at 8 A.M. and that the pollutant disperses horizontally over a circular area. Suppose that t represents the time, in hours, since the factory began emitting pollutants ($t = 0$ represents 8 A.M), and assume that the radius of the circle of pollution is $r(t) = 2t$ miles. Let $\mathscr{A}(r) = \pi r^2$ represent the area of a circle of radius r. Find and interpret $(\mathscr{A} \circ r)(t)$.

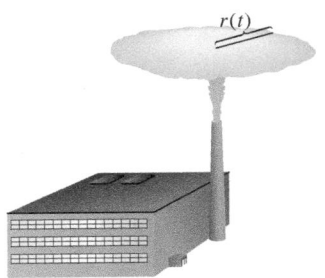

34. An oil well off the Gulf Coast is leaking, with the leak spreading oil over the surface as a circle. At any time t, in minutes, after the beginning of the leak, the radius of the circular oil slick on the surface is $r(t) = 4t$ feet. Let

$$\mathscr{A}(r) = \pi r^2$$

represent the area of a circle of radius r. Find and interpret $(\mathscr{A} \circ r)(5)$.

12.2 | Inverse Functions

In this chapter we will study two important types of functions, *exponential* and *logarithmic*. These functions are related: They are *inverses* of one another.

> **Note**
>
> A calculator with the following keys will be essential in this chapter.
>
> , or , or LN

OBJECTIVE 1 Decide whether a function is one-to-one, and if it is, find its inverse. Suppose we define the function

$$G = \{(-2, 2), (-1, 1), (0, 0), (1, 3), (2, 5)\}.$$

We can form another set of ordered pairs from G by interchanging the x- and y-values of each pair in G. We can call this set F, so

$$F = \{(2, -2), (1, -1), (0, 0), (3, 1), (5, 2)\}.$$

To show that these two sets are related as just described, F is called the *inverse* of G. For a function f to have an inverse function, f must be *one-to-one*.

> **One-to-One Function**
>
> In a **one-to-one function,** each x-value corresponds to just one y-value, and each y-value corresponds to just one x-value.

The function shown in **Figure 3(a)** is not one-to-one because the y-value 7 corresponds to *two* x-values, 2 and 3. That is, the ordered pairs $(2, 7)$ and $(3, 7)$ both appear in the function. The function in **Figure 3(b)** is one-to-one.

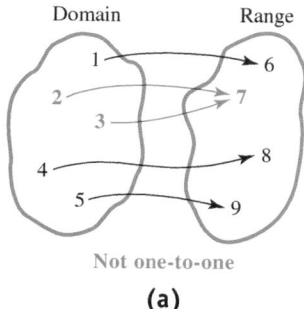

(a) Not one-to-one

(b) One-to-one

Figure 3

The *inverse* of any one-to-one function f is found by interchanging the components of the ordered pairs of f. The inverse of f is written $\mathbf{f^{-1}}$. Read f^{-1} as *"the inverse of f"* or *"f-inverse."*

> ❗ **CAUTION**
>
> The symbol $f^{-1}(x)$ does not represent $\dfrac{1}{f(x)}$.

1 Decide whether each function is one-to-one. If it is, find the inverse.

(a) $\{(1, 2), (2, 4), (3, 3), (4, 5)\}$

(b) $\{(0, 3), (-1, 2), (1, 3)\}$

(c) A Norwegian physiologist has developed a rule for predicting running times based on the time to run 5 km (5K). An example for one runner is shown here. (Data from Stephen Seiler, Agder College, Kristiansand, Norway.)

Distance	Time
1.5K	4:22
3K	9:18
5K	16:00
10K	33:40

Answers

4. (a) $\{(2, 1), (4, 2), (3, 3), (5, 4)\}$

(b) not a one-to-one function

(c)

Time	Distance
4:22	1.5K
9:18	3K
16:00	5K
33:40	10K

The definition of the inverse of a function follows.

Inverse of a Function

The **inverse** of a one-to-one function f, written f^{-1}, is the set of all ordered pairs of the form (y, x), where (x, y) belongs to f. *The inverse is formed by interchanging x and y, so the domain of f becomes the range of f^{-1} and the range of f becomes the domain of f^{-1}.*

For inverses f and f^{-1}, it follows that for all x in their domains,

$$(f \circ f^{-1})(x) = x \quad \text{and} \quad (f^{-1} \circ f)(x) = x.$$

EXAMPLE 1 **Finding Inverses of One-to-One Functions**

Decide whether each function is one-to-one. If it is, find the inverse.

(a) $F = \{(-2, 1), (-1, 0), (0, 1), (1, 2), (2, 2)\}$

Each x-value in F corresponds to just one y-value. However, the y-value 1 corresponds to two x-values, -2 and 0. Also, the y-value 2 corresponds to both 1 and 2. Because some y-values correspond to more than one x-value, F is not one-to-one and does not have an inverse function.

(b) $G = \{(3, 1), (0, 2), (2, 3), (4, 0)\}$

Every x-value in G corresponds to only one y-value, and every y-value corresponds to only one x-value, so G is a one-to-one function. The inverse function is found by interchanging the x- and y-values in each ordered pair.

$$G^{-1} = \{(1, 3), (2, 0), (3, 2), (0, 4)\}$$

The domain and range of G become the range and domain, respectively, of G^{-1}.

(c) The U.S. National Trails System is a network of scenic, historic, and recreation trails. The table shows the length in miles of several national trails, along with the year that each was designated as such.

Trail Name	Year	Length (in miles)
Appalachian	1968	2200
Continental Divide	1978	3100
Nez Perce	1986	1200
Trail of Tears	1987	5000
Pony Express	1992	2000
Pacific Northwest	2009	1200

Data from *The World Almanac and Book of Facts.*

Let f be the function defined in the table, with the years designated forming the domain and the lengths in miles forming the range. Then f is not a one-to-one function because in two different years (1986 and 2009), the lengths of the trails designated were the same, 1200 mi.

◀ **Work Problem 1** at the Side.

OBJECTIVE ▶ 2 **Use the horizontal line test to determine whether a function is one-to-one.** By graphing a function and observing the graph, we can use the *horizontal line test* to tell whether the function is one-to-one.

Horizontal Line Test

A function is one-to-one if every horizontal line intersects the graph of the function at most once.

The horizontal line test follows from the definition of a one-to-one function. Any two points that lie on the same horizontal line have the same *y*-coordinate. No two ordered pairs that belong to a one-to-one function may have the same *y*-coordinate. Therefore, no horizontal line will intersect the graph of a one-to-one function more than once.

EXAMPLE 2 **Using the Horizontal Line Test**

Use the horizontal line test to determine whether each graph is the graph of a one-to-one function.

(a)

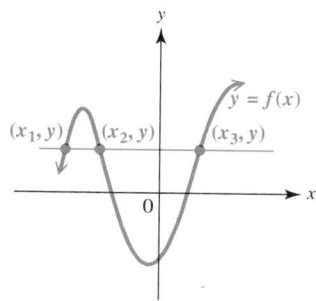

Figure 4

(b)

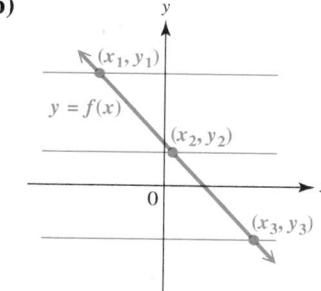

Figure 5

Because the red horizontal line shown in **Figure 4** intersects the graph in more than one point (actually three points), the function is not one-to-one.

Every horizontal line will intersect the graph in **Figure 5** in exactly one point. This function is one-to-one.

—————— **Work Problem 2 at the Side.** ▶

OBJECTIVE ▶ 3 **Find the equation of the inverse of a function.** The inverse of a one-to-one function is found by interchanging the *x*- and *y*-values of each of its ordered pairs. The equation of the inverse of a function defined by $y = f(x)$ is found in the same way.

Finding the Equation of the Inverse of $y = f(x)$

For a one-to-one function f defined by an equation $y = f(x)$, find the defining equation of the inverse as follows.

Step 1 Interchange *x* and *y*.

Step 2 Solve for *y*.

Step 3 Replace *y* with $f^{-1}(x)$.

---

2 Use the horizontal line test to determine whether each graph is the graph of a one-to-one function.

(a)

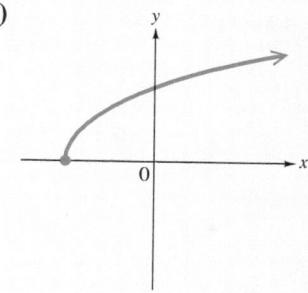

(b)

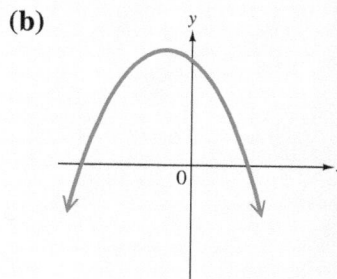

Answers

2. (a) one-to-one **(b)** not one-to-one

3 Decide whether each equation represents a one-to-one function. If so, find the equation that defines the inverse.

(a) $f(x) = 3x - 4$

(b) $f(x) = x^3 + 1$

(c) $f(x) = (x - 3)^2$

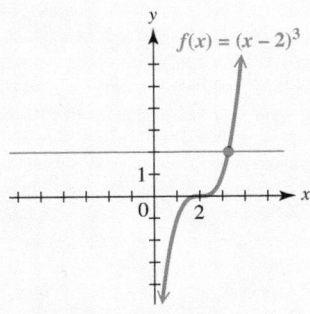

Figure 6

Answers

3. **(a)** one-to-one function;

$f^{-1}(x) = \dfrac{x + 4}{3}$, or $f^{-1}(x) = \dfrac{1}{3}x + \dfrac{4}{3}$

(b) one-to-one function; $f^{-1}(x) = \sqrt[3]{x - 1}$

(c) not a one-to-one function

EXAMPLE 3 **Finding Equations of Inverses**

Decide whether each equation represents a one-to-one function. If so, find the equation that defines the inverse.

(a) $f(x) = 2x + 5$

The graph of $y = 2x + 5$ is a nonvertical line, so by the horizontal line test, f is a one-to-one function. Find the inverse as follows.

$$y = 2x + 5 \quad \text{Let } y = f(x).$$

Step 1 $\quad x = 2y + 5 \quad$ Interchange x and y.

Step 2 $\quad 2y = x - 5 \quad$ Subtract 5. Interchange sides. } Solve for y.

$$y = \frac{x - 5}{2} \quad \text{Divide by 2.}$$

Step 3 $\quad f^{-1}(x) = \dfrac{x - 5}{2} \quad$ Replace y with $f^{-1}(x)$.

$$f^{-1}(x) = \frac{x}{2} - \frac{5}{2}, \quad \text{or} \quad f^{-1}(x) = \frac{1}{2}x - \frac{5}{2} \qquad \frac{a - b}{c} = \frac{a}{c} - \frac{b}{c}$$

Thus, f^{-1} is a linear function. In the function $y = 2x + 5$, the value of y is found by starting with a value of x, multiplying by 2, and adding 5. The equation $f^{-1}(x) = \frac{x - 5}{2}$ for the inverse has us *subtract* 5, and then *divide* by 2. An inverse is used to "undo" what a function does to the variable x.

(b) $y = x^2 + 2$

This equation has a vertical parabola as its graph, so some horizontal lines will intersect the graph at two points. For example, both $x = 3$ and $x = -3$ correspond to $y = 11$. Because of the x^2-term, there are many pairs of x-values that correspond to the same y-value. This means that the function $y = x^2 + 2$ is not one-to-one and does not have an inverse.

Alternatively, apply the steps for finding the equation of an inverse.

$$y = x^2 + 2$$

$$x = y^2 + 2 \quad \text{Interchange } x \text{ and } y.$$

$$y^2 = x - 2 \quad \text{Solve for } y.$$

Remember *both* roots.

$$y = \pm\sqrt{x - 2} \quad \text{Square root property}$$

The last step shows that there are two y-values for each choice of x in $(2, \infty)$, so the given function is not one-to-one. It does not have an inverse.

(c) $f(x) = (x - 2)^3$

A cubing function like this is one-to-one. See the graph in **Figure 6.**

$$y = (x - 2)^3 \quad \text{Replace } f(x) \text{ with } y.$$

Step 1 $\quad x = (y - 2)^3 \quad$ Interchange x and y.

Step 2 $\quad \sqrt[3]{x} = \sqrt[3]{(y - 2)^3} \quad$ Take the cube root on each side.

$$\sqrt[3]{x} = y - 2 \qquad \sqrt[3]{a^3} = a \quad \Bigg\} \text{ Solve for } y.$$

$$y = \sqrt[3]{x} + 2 \quad \text{Add 2. Interchange sides.}$$

Step 3 $\quad f^{-1}(x) = \sqrt[3]{x} + 2 \quad$ Replace y with $f^{-1}(x)$.

◀ **Work Problem** **3** **at the Side**

OBJECTIVE ▸ 4 Graph f^{-1}, given the graph of f. One way to graph the inverse of a function f whose equation is given is as follows.

Graphing the Inverse

1. Find several ordered pairs that belong to f.
2. Interchange x and y to obtain ordered pairs that belong to f^{-1}.
3. Plot those points, and sketch the graph of f^{-1} through them.

We can also select points on the graph of f and use symmetry to find corresponding points on the graph of f^{-1}. For example, suppose the point (a, b) shown in **Figure 7** belongs to a one-to-one function f. Then the point (b, a) belongs to f^{-1}. The line segment connecting (a, b) and (b, a) is perpendicular to, and cut in half by, the line $y = x$. The points (a, b) and (b, a) are "mirror images" of each other with respect to $y = x$.

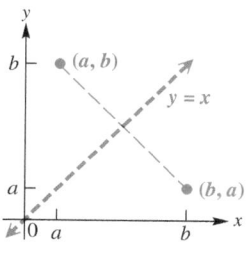

Figure 7

We can find the graph of f^{-1} from the graph of f by locating the mirror image of each point in f with respect to the line $y = x$.

EXAMPLE 4 Graphing the Inverse

Graph the inverse of each function labeled f in the figures.

(a) **Figure 8(a)** shows the graph of a one-to-one function f. The points $\left(-1, \frac{1}{2}\right)$, $(0, 1)$, $(1, 2)$, and $(2, 4)$ lie on its graph. Interchange x and y to obtain ordered pairs that belong to f^{-1}.

$$\left(\tfrac{1}{2}, -1\right), (1, 0), (2, 1), \text{ and } (4, 2) \quad \text{Points on } f^{-1}$$

Plot these points, and sketch the graph of f^{-1} through them. See **Figure 8(b)**.

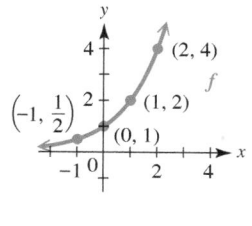 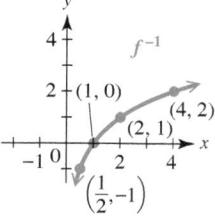

(a) (b)

Figure 8

(b) Each function f (shown in blue) in **Figure 9** is a one-to-one function.

Each inverse f^{-1} is shown in red. In both cases, the graph of f^{-1} is a reflection of the graph of f across the line $y = x$.

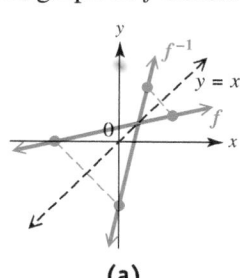 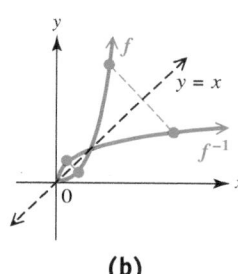

(a) (b)

Figure 9

Work Problem **4** at the Side. ▶

4 Graph the inverse of each function.

(a)

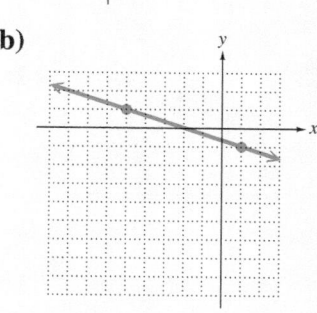

(b)

(c)

Answers

4. (a)

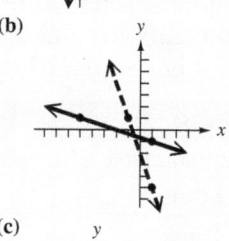

(b)

(c)

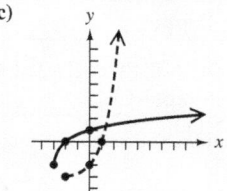

12.2 Exercises

FOR EXTRA HELP Go to MyMathLab *for worked-out, step-by-step solutions to exercises enclosed in a square* ▢ *and video solutions to* ▶ *exercises.*

1. CONCEPT CHECK Which graph illustrates a one-to-one function?

A.
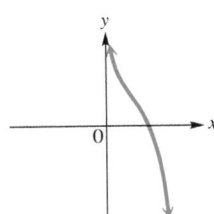

B.
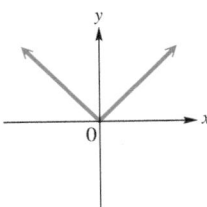

C.
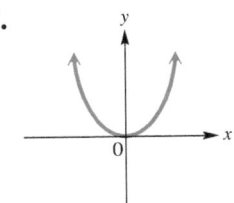

D.
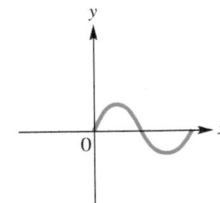

2. CONCEPT CHECK When asked to find the inverse, if it exists, of the function $f(x) = x^2 - 1$, a student did the following.

$$y = x^2 - 1 \qquad \text{Let } y = f(x).$$

$$x = y^2 - 1 \qquad \text{Interchange } x \text{ and } y.$$

$$\left.\begin{array}{c} y^2 = x + 1 \\ y = \pm\sqrt{x + 1} \end{array}\right\} \text{ Solve for } y.$$

$$f^{-1}(x) = \pm\sqrt{x + 1} \qquad \text{Replace } y \text{ with } f^{-1}(x).$$

The student's answer, $f^{-1}(x) = \pm\sqrt{x + 1}$, is incorrect. ***What Went Wrong?***

*Answer each question. **See Example 1.***

3. The table shows trans fat content in a fast-food product in various countries, based on type of frying oil used. If the set of countries is the domain and the set of trans fat percentages is the range of the function, is it one-to-one? Why or why not?

Country	Percentage of Trans Fat in McDonald's Chicken
Scotland	14
France	11
United States	11
Peru	9
Russia	5
Denmark	1

Data from *New England Journal of Medicine.*

4. The table shows concentrations of carbon monoxide in the United States for the years 2010–2015. If this correspondence is considered to be a function that pairs each year with its concentration, is it one-to-one? Why or why not?

Year	Concentration (in parts per million)
2010	1.61
2011	1.58
2012	1.50
2013	1.45
2014	1.39
2015	1.40

Data from E.P.A.

5. The table lists caffeine amounts in several popular 12-oz soft drinks. If the set of sodas is the domain and the set of caffeine amounts is the range of the function, is it one-to-one? Why or why not?

Soda	Caffeine (in mg)
Mountain Dew	55
Diet Coke	45
Dr. Pepper	41
Sunkist Orange Soda	41
Diet Pepsi-Cola	36

Data from National Soft Drink Association.

6. The road mileage between Denver, Colorado, and several selected U.S. cities is shown in the table. If we consider this as a function that pairs each city with a distance, is it one-to-one? How could we change the answer to this question by adding 1 mile to one of the distances shown?

City	Distance to Denver (in miles)
Atlanta	1398
Indianapolis	1058
Kansas City, MO	600
Los Angeles	1059

CONCEPT CHECK   *Choose the correct response.*

7. Which function is one-to-one?

A. $f(x) = x$ **B.** $f(x) = x^2$

C. $f(x) = |x|$ **D.** $f(x) = -x^2 + 2x - 1$

8. If a function f is one-to-one and the point (p, q) lies on the graph of f, then which point *must* lie on the graph of f^{-1}?

A. $(-p, q)$ **B.** $(-q, -p)$

C. $(p, -q)$ **D.** (q, p)

If the function is one-to-one, find its inverse. **See Examples 1 and 3.**

9. $\{(3, 6), (2, 10), (5, 12)\}$

10. $\{(-1, 3), (0, 5), (7, -2)\}$

11. $\{(-1, 3), (2, 7), (4, 3), (5, 8)\}$

12. $\{(-8, 6), (-4, 3), (0, 6)\}$

13. $\{(0, 4.5), (2, 8.6), (4, 12.7)\}$

14. $\{(1, 5.8), (2, 8.8), (3, 8.5)\}$

15. $f(x) = x + 3$

16. $f(x) = x + 8$

17. $f(x) = 2x + 4$

18. $f(x) = 3x + 1$

19. $g(x) = -4x + 3$

20. $g(x) = -6x - 8$

21. $g(x) = \sqrt{x - 3}, \quad x \geq 3$

22. $g(x) = \sqrt{x + 2}, \quad x \geq -2$

23. $f(x) = \sqrt{x + 6}, \quad x \geq -6$

24. $f(x) = \sqrt{x - 4}, \quad x \geq 4$

25. $f(x) = 3x^2 + 2$

26. $f(x) = -4x^2 - 1$

27. $g(x) = (x + 1)^3$

28. $g(x) = (x - 4)^3$

29. $f(x) = x^3 - 4$

30. $f(x) = x^3 - 3$

31. $f(x) = 5$

32. $f(x) = -7$

Let $f(x) = 2^x$. This function is one-to-one. Find each value, always working part (a) before part (b).

33. (a) $f(3)$

34. (a) $f(4)$

35. (a) $f(0)$

36. (a) $f(-2)$

(b) $f^{-1}(8)$

(b) $f^{-1}(16)$

(b) $f^{-1}(1)$

(b) $f^{-1}\left(\dfrac{1}{4}\right)$

Graphs of selected functions are given in the following exercises.

(a) *Use the horizontal line test to determine whether each function is one-to-one.*

(b) *If the function is one-to-one, then graph its inverse on the same set of axes as a dashed line or curve.* ***See Examples 2 and 4.***

37.
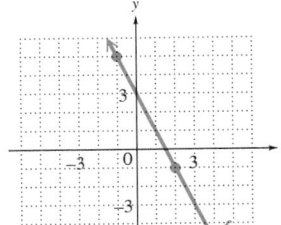

38.
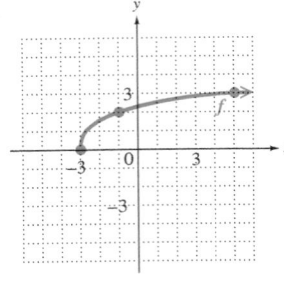

39.
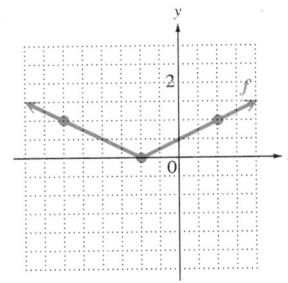

40.
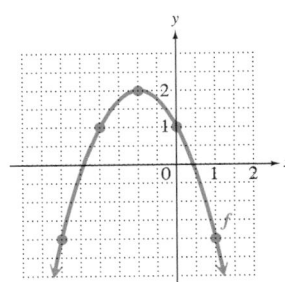

41.
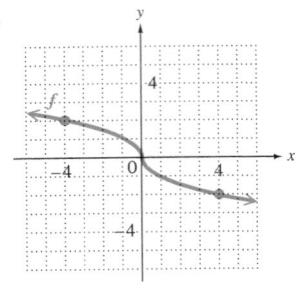

42.
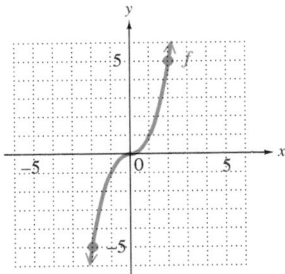

Each of the following functions is one-to-one. Graph the function as a solid line or curve, and then graph its inverse on the same set of axes as a dashed line or curve. In Exercises 47–50, complete the table so that graphing the function will be easier. ***See Example 4.***

43. $f(x) = 2x - 1$

44. $f(x) = 2x + 3$

45. $g(x) = -4x$

46. $g(x) = -2x$

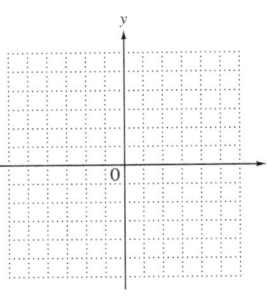 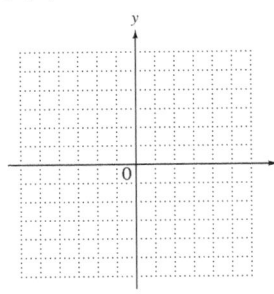 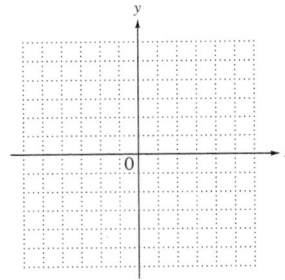 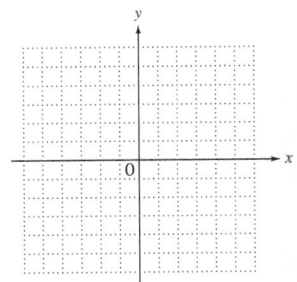

47. $f(x) = \sqrt{x},\ x \geq 0$

x	f(x)
0	
1	
4	

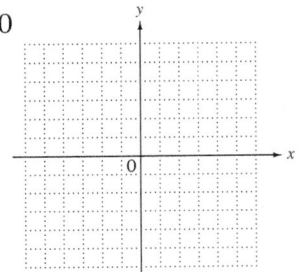

48. $f(x) = -\sqrt{x},\ x \geq 0$

x	f(x)
0	
1	
4	

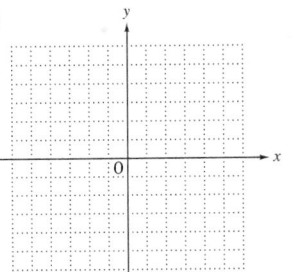

49. $f(x) = x^3 - 2$

x	f(x)
−1	
0	
1	
2	

50. $f(x) = x^3 + 3$

x	f(x)
−2	
−1	
0	
1	

Relating Concepts (Exercises 51–54) For Individual or Group Work

Inverse functions can be used to send and receive coded information. A simple example might use the function

$$f(x) = 2x + 5.$$

(Note that it is one-to-one.) Suppose that each letter of the alphabet is assigned a numerical value according to its position, as follows.

A	1	E	5	I	9	M	13	Q	17	U	21	Y	25
B	2	F	6	J	10	N	14	R	18	V	22	Z	26
C	3	G	7	K	11	O	15	S	19	W	23		
D	4	H	8	L	12	P	16	T	20	X	24		

Using the function, the word ALGEBRA *would be encoded as*

$$7 \quad 29 \quad 19 \quad 15 \quad 9 \quad 41 \quad 7,$$

because

$$f(A) = f(1) = 2(1) + 5 = 7, \quad f(L) = f(12) = 2(12) + 5 = 29, \quad \text{and so on.}$$

The message would then be decoded by using the inverse of f, which is

$$f^{-1}(x) = \frac{x - 5}{2} \quad \left(\text{or } f^{-1}(x) = \frac{1}{2}x - \frac{5}{2} \right).$$

For example,

$$f^{-1}(7) = \frac{7 - 5}{2} = 1 = A, \quad f^{-1}(29) = \frac{29 - 5}{2} = 12 = L, \quad \text{and so on.}$$

This is an **Enigma machine** used by the Germans in World War II to send coded messages.

Work Exercises 51–54 in order.

51. Suppose that you are an agent for a detective agency. Today's function for your code is $f(x) = 4x - 5$. Find the rule for f^{-1} algebraically.

52. You receive the following coded message today. (Read across from left to right.)

47 95 7 −1 43 7 79 43 −1 75 55 67 31 71 75 27

15 23 67 15 −1 75 15 71 75 75 27 31 51 23 71

31 51 7 15 71 43 31 7 15 11 3 67 15 −1 11

Use the letter/number assignment described earlier to decode the message.

53. Why is a one-to-one function essential in this encoding/decoding process?

54. Use $f(x) = x^3 + 4$ to encode your name, using the letter/number assignment described earlier.

12.3 | Exponential Functions

OBJECTIVES

1. Define exponential functions.
2. Graph exponential functions.
3. Solve exponential equations of the form $a^x = a^k$ for x.
4. Use exponential functions in applications involving growth or decay.

OBJECTIVE **1** **Define exponential functions.** Consider the expression 2^x evaluated for rational values of x.

$$2^3 = 8, \quad 2^{-1} = \frac{1}{2}, \quad 2^{1/2} = \sqrt{2}, \quad 2^{3/4} = \sqrt[4]{2^3} = \sqrt[4]{8}$$

Examples of 2^x for rational x

In more advanced courses it is shown that 2^x exists for all real number values of x, both rational and irrational. The following definition of an exponential function assumes that a^x exists for all real numbers x.

Exponential Function

For $a > 0$, $a \neq 1$, and all real numbers x,

$$f(x) = a^x$$

defines the **exponential function with base a**.

Note

The two restrictions on the value of the base a in the definition of an exponential function $f(x) = a^x$ are important.

1. The restriction $a > 0$ is necessary so that the function can be defined for all real numbers x. Letting a be negative ($a = -2$, for instance) and letting $x = \frac{1}{2}$ would give $(-2)^{1/2}$, which is not a real number.

2. The restriction $a \neq 1$ is necessary because 1 raised to any power is equal to 1, resulting in the linear function $f(x) = 1$.

OBJECTIVE **2** **Graph exponential functions.** When graphing exponential functions of the form $f(x) = a^x$, pay particular attention to whether $a > 1$ or $0 < a < 1$.

EXAMPLE 1 Graphing an Exponential Function ($a > 1$)

Graph $f(x) = 2^x$. Then compare it to the graph of $F(x) = 5^x$.

Choose some values of x, and find the corresponding values of $f(x)$. Plotting these points and drawing a smooth curve through them gives the graph of $f(x) = 2^x$ shown in **Figure 10.**

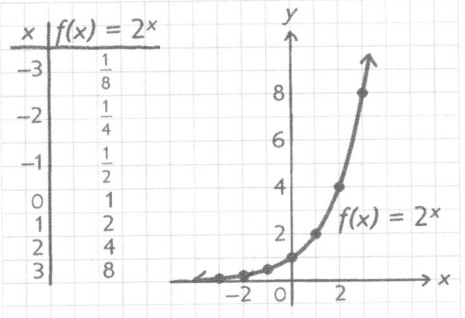

x	$f(x) = 2^x$
-3	$\frac{1}{8}$
-2	$\frac{1}{4}$
-1	$\frac{1}{2}$
0	1
1	2
2	4
3	8

Exponential function with base $a > 1$

Domain: $(-\infty, \infty)$

Range: $(0, \infty)$

y-intercept: $(0, 1)$

The function is one-to-one, and its graph rises from left to right.

Figure 10

Continued on Next Page

The graph of $f(x) = 2^x$ is typical of the graphs of exponential functions of the form $f(x) = a^x$, where $a > 1$.

The larger the value of a, the faster the graph rises.

To see this, compare the graph of $F(x) = 5^x$ with the graph of $f(x) = 2^x$ in **Figure 11.** When graphing such functions, be sure to plot a sufficient number of points to see how rapidly the graph rises.

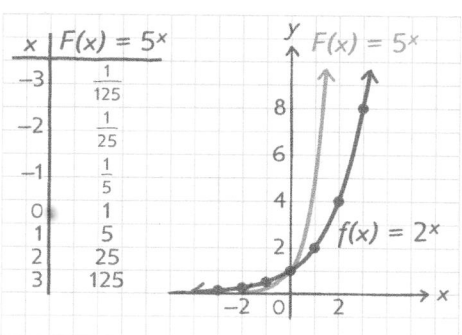

Figure 11

The vertical line test assures us that the graphs in **Figures 10 and 11** represent functions. These graphs also show an important characteristic of exponential functions where $a > 1$:

As x gets larger, y increases at a faster and faster rate.

——————————— Work Problem **1** at the Side. ▶

EXAMPLE 2 Graphing an Exponential Function $(0 < a < 1)$

Graph $g(x) = \left(\dfrac{1}{2}\right)^x$.

Find some points on the graph. The graph in **Figure 12** is similar to that of $f(x) = 2^x$ **(Figure 10)** with the same domain and range, except that here ***as x gets larger, y decreases.*** This graph is typical of the graph of an exponential function of the form $f(x) = a^x$, where $0 < a < 1$.

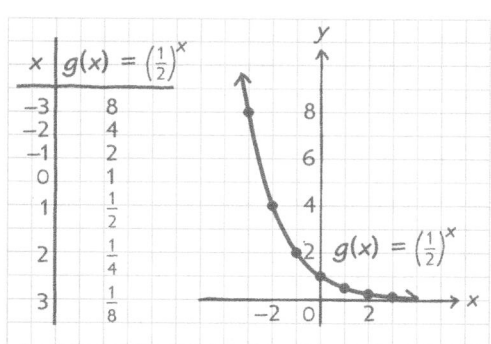

Figure 12

Exponential function with base $0 < a < 1$

Domain: $(-\infty, \infty)$

Range: $(0, \infty)$

y-intercept: $(0, 1)$

The function is one-to-one, and its graph falls from left to right.

——————————— Work Problem **2** at the Side. ▶

❗ **CAUTION**

The graph of an exponential function of the form $f(x) = a^x$ *approaches* the *x*-axis, but does ***not*** touch it.

1 Graph $f(x) = 10^x$.

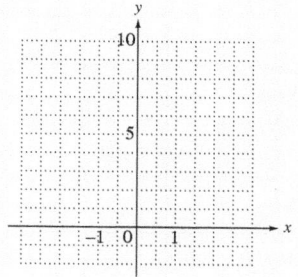

2 Graph $g(x) = \left(\dfrac{1}{10}\right)^x$.

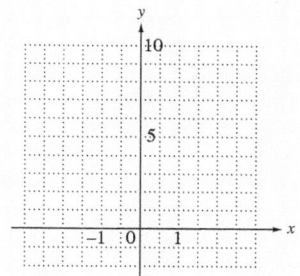

Answers

1.

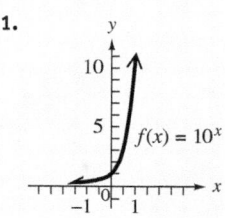

2.

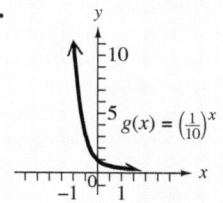

3 Graph $f(x) = 2^{4x-3}$.

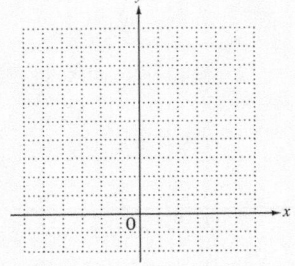

Characteristics of the Graph of $f(x) = a^x$

1. The graph contains the point $(0, 1)$, which is the y-intercept.
2. The function is one-to-one.
   - When $a > 1$, the graph *rises* from left to right. (See **Figures 10 and 11.**)
   - When $0 < a < 1$, the graph *falls* from left to right. (See **Figure 12.**)

   In both cases, the graph goes from the second quadrant to the first.
3. The graph approaches the x-axis, but never touches it. (Recall that such a line is an **asymptote.**)
4. The domain is $(-\infty, \infty)$, and the range is $(0, \infty)$.

EXAMPLE 3 **Graphing a More Complicated Exponential Function**

Graph $f(x) = 3^{2x-4}$.

Find several ordered pairs. We let $x = 0$ and $x = 2$ and substitute to find values of $f(x)$, or y.

$y = 3^{2(0)-4}$ Let $x = 0$.

$y = 3^{-4}$

$y = \dfrac{1}{81}$ $a^{-n} = \frac{1}{a^n}$

$y = 3^{2(2)-4}$ Let $x = 2$.

$y = 3^0$

$y = 1$ $a^0 = 1$

These ordered pairs, $\left(0, \frac{1}{81}\right)$ and $(2, 1)$, along with the other ordered pairs shown in the table, lead to the graph in **Figure 13.**

x	y
0	$\frac{1}{81}$
1	$\frac{1}{9}$
2	1
3	9

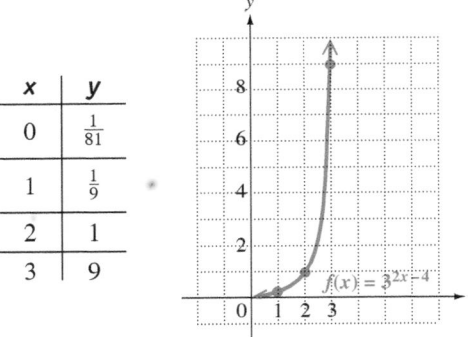

Figure 13

The graph of $f(x) = 3^{2x-4}$ is similar to the graph of $f(x) = 3^x$ except that it is shifted to the right and rises more rapidly.

◀ **Work Problem 3** at the Side.

OBJECTIVE 3 Solve exponential equations of the form $a^x = a^k$ for x. Until this chapter, we have solved only equations that had the variable as a base, like $x^2 = 8$. In these equations, all exponents have been constants. An **exponential equation** is an equation that has a variable in an exponent, such as

$$9^x = 27.$$

We can use the following property to solve many exponential equations.

Property for Solving an Exponential Equation

For $a > 0$ and $a \neq 1$, if $a^x = a^y$ then $x = y$.

Answer

3.

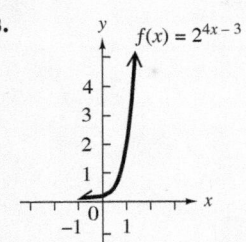

Solving an Exponential Equation

Step 1   **Each side must have the same base.** If the two sides of the equation do not have the same base, express each as a power of the same base if possible.

Step 2   **Simplify exponents** if necessary, using the rules of exponents.

Step 3   **Set exponents equal** using the property given in this section.

Step 4   **Solve** the equation obtained in Step 3.

Note

These steps cannot be applied to an exponential equation like $3^x = 12$ because Step 1 cannot easily be done. A method for solving such equations is given later in the chapter.

EXAMPLE 4   Solving an Exponential Equation

Solve $9^x = 27$.

$$9^x = 27$$

Step 1 $(3^2)^x = 3^3$ Write with the same base; $9 = 3^2$ and $27 = 3^3$.

Step 2 $3^{2x} = 3^3$ Power rule for exponents

Step 3 $2x = 3$ If $a^x = a^y$, then $x = y$.

Step 4 $x = \dfrac{3}{2}$ Solve for x.

CHECK   Substitute $\frac{3}{2}$ for x: $9^x = 9^{3/2} = (9^{1/2})^3 = 3^3 = 27$. ✓   True

The solution set is $\left\{\frac{3}{2}\right\}$.

─── **Work Problem ④ at the Side.** ▶

EXAMPLE 5   Solving Exponential Equations

Solve each equation.

(a) $4^{3x-1} = 16^{x+2}$ ⟨Be careful multiplying the exponents.⟩

$4^{3x-1} = (4^2)^{x+2}$ Write with the same base; $16 = 4^2$. (Step 1)

$4^{3x-1} = 4^{2x+4}$ Power rule for exponents (Step 2)

$3x - 1 = 2x + 4$ Set the exponents equal. (Step 3)

$x = 5$ Subtract $2x$. Add 1. (Step 4)

CHECK $4^{3x-1} = 16^{x+2}$

$4^{3(5)-1} \stackrel{?}{=} 16^{5+2}$ Substitute. Let $x = 5$.

$4^{14} \stackrel{?}{=} 16^7$ Perform the operations in the exponents.

$4^{14} \stackrel{?}{=} (4^2)^7$ $16 = 4^2$

$4^{14} = 4^{14}$ ✓   True

The solution set is $\{5\}$.

─── **Continued on Next Page**

④ Solve each equation.

(a) $25^x = 125$

Step 1   Write each side as a power of the same base.
$(5^{—})^x = 5^{—}$

Step 2   Use the power rule for exponents to simplify exponents on the left.
$5^{—} = 5^3$

Step 3   Set the exponents equal.
$\underline{\quad} = \underline{\quad}$

Step 4   Solve for x.
$x = \underline{\quad}$

Verify that the solution set is $\underline{\quad}$.

(b) $4^x = 32$

(c) $81^x = 27$

Answers

4. (a) $2; 3; 2x; 2x; 3; \dfrac{3}{2}; \left\{\dfrac{3}{2}\right\}$

(b) $\left\{\dfrac{5}{2}\right\}$ **(c)** $\left\{\dfrac{3}{4}\right\}$

5 Solve each equation and check the solution.

(GS) **(a)** $$25^{x-2} = 125^x$$

Step 1
Write each side as a power of the same base.
$$(5\text{---})^{x-2} = (5\text{---})^x$$

Step 2
Use the power rule for exponents to simplify exponents on each side.
$$5\text{---} = 5\text{---}$$

Step 3
Set the exponents equal.
$$\text{----} = \text{----}$$

Step 4
Solve for x.
$$x = \text{----}$$

Verify that the solution set is ____ .

(b) $$3^{2x-1} = 27^{x+4}$$

(c) $$4^x = \frac{1}{32}$$

(d) $$\left(\frac{3}{4}\right)^x = \frac{16}{9}$$

(b) $$6^x = \frac{1}{216}$$

$$6^x = \frac{1}{6^3} \qquad 216 = 6^3$$

$$6^x = 6^{-3} \qquad \text{Write with the same base; } \tfrac{1}{6^3} = 6^{-3}$$

$$x = -3 \qquad \text{Set the exponents equal.}$$

CHECK Substitute -3 for x.
$$6^x = 6^{-3} = \frac{1}{6^3} = \frac{1}{216} \checkmark \quad \text{True}$$

The solution set is $\{-3\}$.

(c) $$\left(\frac{2}{3}\right)^x = \frac{9}{4}$$

$$\left(\frac{2}{3}\right)^x = \left(\frac{4}{9}\right)^{-1} \qquad \tfrac{9}{4} = \left(\tfrac{4}{9}\right)^{-1}$$

$$\left(\frac{2}{3}\right)^x = \left[\left(\frac{2}{3}\right)^2\right]^{-1} \qquad \text{Write with the same base.}$$

$$\left(\frac{2}{3}\right)^x = \left(\frac{2}{3}\right)^{-2} \qquad \text{Power rule for exponents}$$

$$x = -2 \qquad \text{Set the exponents equal.}$$

Check that the solution set is $\{-2\}$.

◀ **Work Problem** **5** **at the Side.**

OBJECTIVE ▶ **4** **Use exponential functions in applications involving growth or decay.**

EXAMPLE 6 **Applying an Exponential Growth Function**

The graph in **Figure 14** shows the concentration of carbon dioxide (in parts per million) in the air. This concentration is increasing exponentially.

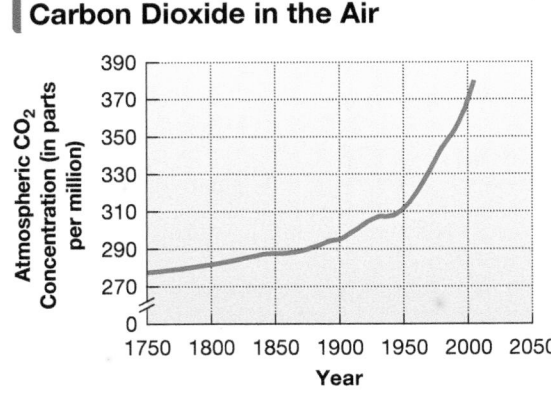

Carbon Dioxide in the Air

Data from *The Sacramento Bee*; National Oceanic and Atmospheric Administration.

Figure 14

Answers

5. **(a)** 2; 3; $2x - 4$; $3x$; $2x - 4$; $3x$; -4; $\{-4\}$
(b) $\{-13\}$ **(c)** $\left\{-\frac{5}{2}\right\}$ **(d)** $\{-2\}$

Continued on Next Page

The data graphed in **Figure 14** are approximated by the exponential function

$$f(x) = 266\,(1.001)^x,$$

where x is the number of years since 1750. Use this function and a calculator to approximate the concentration of carbon dioxide in parts per million, to the nearest unit, for each year.

(a) 1900

Because x represents the number of years since 1750,

$$x = 1900 - 1750 = 150.$$

$$f(x) = 266\,(1.001)^x \qquad \text{Given function}$$

$$f(\mathbf{150}) = 266\,(1.001)^{150} \qquad \text{Let } x = 150.$$

$$f(150) \approx 309 \qquad\qquad \text{Evaluate with a calculator.}$$

The concentration in 1900 was approximately 309 parts per million.

(b) 1950

$$f(x) = 266\,(1.001)^x \qquad \text{Given function}$$

$$f(\mathbf{200}) = 266\,(1.001)^{200} \qquad x = 1950 - 1750 = 200$$

$$f(200) \approx 325 \qquad\qquad \text{Evaluate with a calculator.}$$

The concentration in 1950 was approximately 325 parts per million.

——————————— **Work Problem ⑥ at the Side.** ▶

⑥ Use the exponential function in **Example 6** to approximate the carbon dioxide concentration in 2000.

EXAMPLE 7   Applying an Exponential Decay Function

The atmospheric pressure (in millibars) at a given altitude x, in meters, can be approximated by the exponential function

$$f(x) = 1038\,(1.000134)^{-x},$$

for values of x between 0 and 10,000. Because the base is greater than 1 and the coefficient of x in the exponent is negative, the function values decrease as x increases. This means that as the altitude increases, the atmospheric pressure decreases. (Data from Miller, A. and J. Thompson, *Elements of Meteorology,* Fourth Edition, Charles E. Merrill Publishing Company.)

(a) According to this function, what is the pressure at ground level?

$$f(x) = 1038\,(1.000134)^{-x} \qquad \text{Given function}$$

$$f(\mathbf{0}) = 1038\,(1.000134)^{-0} \qquad \text{Let } x = 0.$$

At ground level, $x = 0$.

$$f(0) = 1038\,(1) \qquad\qquad a^0 = 1$$

$$f(0) = 1038$$

The pressure is 1038 millibars.

(b) What is the pressure at 5000 m?

$$f(x) = 1038\,(1.000134)^{-x} \qquad \text{Given function}$$

$$f(\mathbf{5000}) = 1038\,(1.000134)^{-5000} \qquad \text{Let } x = 5000.$$

$$f(5000) \approx 531 \qquad\qquad \text{Evaluate with a calculator.}$$

The pressure is approximately 531 millibars.

——————————— **Work Problem ⑦ at the Side.** ▶

⑦ Use the exponential function in **Example 7** to approximate the pressure at 8000 m.

Answers

6. 342 parts per million

7. 355 millibars

12.3 Exercises

FOR EXTRA HELP

Go to MyMathLab *for worked-out, step-by-step solutions to exercises enclosed in a square* and *video solutions to* ▶ *exercises.*

CONCEPT CHECK *Choose the correct response.*

1. Which point lies on the graph of $f(x) = 2^x$?

A. $(1, 0)$ **B.** $(2, 1)$

C. $(0, 1)$ **D.** $\left(\sqrt{2}, \frac{1}{2}\right)$

2. The asymptote of the graph of $f(x) = a^x$

A. is the x-axis.   **B.** is the y-axis.

C. has equation $x = 1$.   **D.** has equation $y = 1$.

3. Which statement is true?

A. The y-intercept of the graph of $f(x) = 10^x$ is $(0, 10)$.

B. For any $a > 1$, the graph of $f(x) = a^x$ falls from left to right.

C. The point $\left(\frac{1}{2}, \sqrt{5}\right)$ lies on the graph of $f(x) = 5^x$.

4. Which statement is false?

A. The domain of the function $f(x) = \left(\frac{1}{4}\right)^x$ is $(-\infty, \infty)$.

B. The graph of the function $f(x) = \left(\frac{1}{4}\right)^x$ has one x-intercept.

C. The range of the function $f(x) = \left(\frac{1}{4}\right)^x$ is $(0, \infty)$.

Graph each function. **See Examples 1–3.**

5. $f(x) = 3^x$ ▶

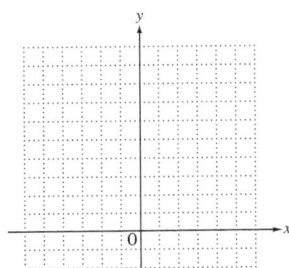

6. $f(x) = 5^x$

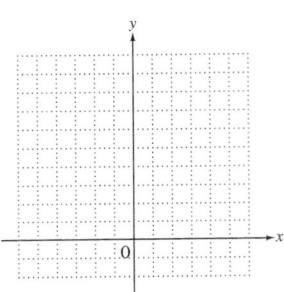

7. $g(x) = \left(\frac{1}{3}\right)^x$ ▶

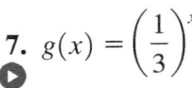
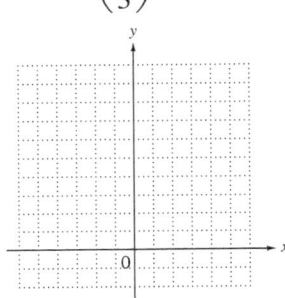

8. $g(x) = \left(\frac{1}{5}\right)^x$

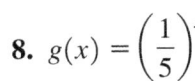
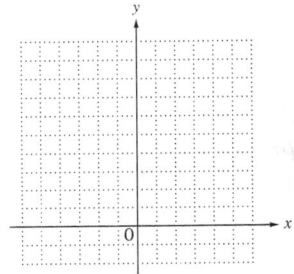

9. $f(x) = 4^{-x}$

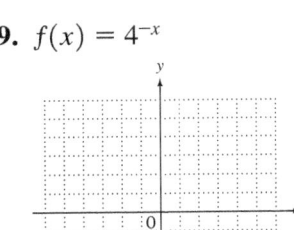

10. $f(x) = 6^{-x}$

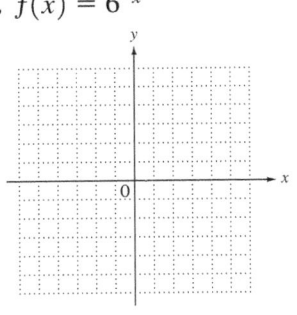

11. $g(x) = 2^{2x-2}$ ▶

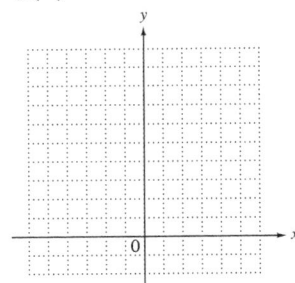

12. $g(x) = 2^{2x+1}$

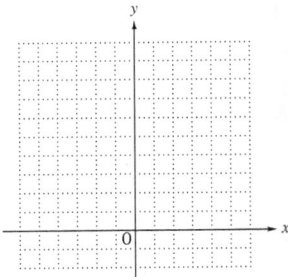

13. CONCEPT CHECK A student incorrectly solved the following equation as shown.

$$2^x = 32 \quad \text{Given equation}$$

$$\frac{2^x}{2} = \frac{32}{2} \quad \text{Divide by 2.}$$

$$x = 16$$

What Went Wrong? Give the correct solution set.

14. CONCEPT CHECK A student incorrectly solved the following equation as shown.

$$3^x = 81 \quad \text{Given equation}$$

$$3^x - 3 = 81 - 3 \quad \text{Subtract 3.}$$

$$x = 78$$

What Went Wrong? Give the correct solution set.

*Solve each equation. **See Examples 4 and 5.***

15. $6^x = 36$

16. $8^x = 64$

17. $100^x = 1000$

18. $8^x = 4$

19. $16^x = 64$

20. $8^x = 32$

21. $4^{x-5} = 64^{2x}$

22. $125^{3x} = 5^{2x-7}$

23. $16^{2x+1} = 64^{x+3}$

24. $9^{2x-8} = 27^{x-4}$

25. $5^x = \dfrac{1}{125}$

26. $3^x = \dfrac{1}{81}$

27. $9^x = \dfrac{1}{27}$

28. $8^x = \dfrac{1}{32}$

29. $5^x = 0.2$

30. $10^x = 0.1$

31. $\left(\dfrac{3}{2}\right)^x = \dfrac{8}{27}$

32. $\left(\dfrac{4}{3}\right)^x = \dfrac{27}{64}$

33. $\left(\dfrac{5}{4}\right)^x = \dfrac{16}{25}$

34. $\left(\dfrac{3}{2}\right)^x = \dfrac{16}{81}$

*Solve each problem. **See Examples 6 and 7.***

A major scientific periodical published an article in 1990 dealing with the problem of global warming. The article provided two possible scenarios.

(a) The warming might be modeled by an exponential function of the form

$$f(x) = (1.046 \times 10^{-38})(1.0444^x).$$

(b) The warming might be modeled by a linear function of the form

$$f(x) = 0.009x - 17.67.$$

In both cases, x represents the year, and the function value represents the increase in degrees Celsius due to the warming. Use these functions to approximate the increase in temperature for each year, to the nearest tenth.

35. 2000

36. 2010

37. 2020

38. 2040

The amount of radioactive material in an ore sample is given by the function

$$A(t) = 100\,(3.2)^{-0.5t},$$

where $A(t)$ is the amount present, in grams, of the sample t months after the initial measurement.

39. How much was present at the initial measurement? (*Hint:* $t = 0$.)

40. How much, to the nearest hundredth, was present 2 months later?

41. How much, to the nearest hundredth, was present 10 months later?

42. Graph the function on the axes at the right.

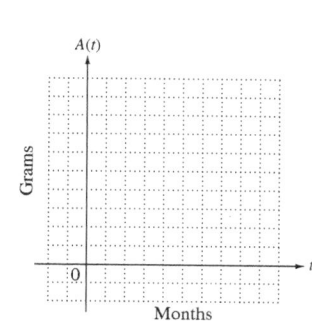

12.4 | Logarithmic Functions

OBJECTIVES

1. Define a logarithm.
2. Convert between exponential and logarithmic forms.
3. Solve logarithmic equations of the form $\log_a b = k$ for a, b, or k.
4. Define and graph logarithmic functions.
5. Use logarithmic functions in applications involving growth or decay.

OBJECTIVE ▶ 1 Define a logarithm. The graph of $y = 2^x$ is the curve shown in blue in **Figure 15**. Because $y = 2^x$ defines a one-to-one function, it has an inverse function. Interchanging x and y gives

$$x = 2^y, \quad \text{the inverse of} \quad y = 2^x.$$

The graph of the inverse is found by reflecting the graph of $y = 2^x$ across the line $y = x$. The graph of the inverse $x = 2^y$ is the curve shown in red in **Figure 15**.

We can also write the equation of the red curve using a new notation that involves the concept of *logarithm*.

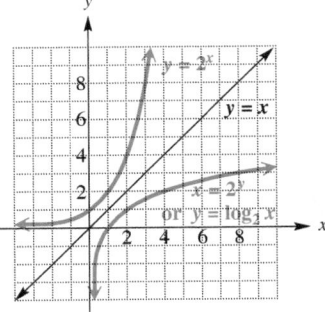

Figure 15

Logarithm

For all positive numbers a, where $a \neq 1$, and all positive numbers x,

$$y = \log_a x \quad \text{means the same as} \quad x = a^y.$$

The abbreviation **log** is used for **logarithm**. Read $\log_a x$ as *"the logarithm of x with base a"* or *"the base a logarithm of x."* To remember the location of the base and the exponent in each form, refer to the following diagrams.

Logarithmic form: $\overset{\text{Exponent}}{\underset{\text{Base}}{y = \log_a x}}$ Exponential form: $\overset{\text{Exponent}}{\underset{\text{Base}}{x = a^y}}$

Meaning of $\log_a x$

A logarithm is an exponent. *The expression $\log_a x$ represents the exponent to which the base a must be raised to obtain x.*

OBJECTIVE ▶ 2 Convert between exponential and logarithmic forms. We use the definition of a logarithm to convert between these forms.

EXAMPLE 1   Converting between Exponential and Logarithmic Forms

The table shows several pairs of equivalent forms.

Exponential Form	Logarithmic Form
$3^2 = 9$	$\log_3 9 = 2$
$\left(\frac{1}{5}\right)^{-2} = 25$	$\log_{1/5} 25 = -2$
$10^5 = 100{,}000$	$\log_{10} 100{,}000 = 5$
$4^{-3} = \frac{1}{64}$	$\log_4 \frac{1}{64} = -3$

$y = \log_a x$
means
$x = a^y$.

◀ **Work Problem ① at the Side.**

---

① Complete the table.

Exponential Form	Logarithmic Form
$2^5 = 32$	
$100^{1/2} = 10$	
	$\log_8 4 = \frac{2}{3}$
	$\log_6 \frac{1}{1296} = -4$

Answer

1. $\log_2 32 = 5$; $\log_{100} 10 = \frac{1}{2}$;

   $8^{2/3} = 4$; $6^{-4} = \frac{1}{1296}$

OBJECTIVE **3** **Solve logarithmic equations of the form** $\log_a b = k$ **for** a, b, **or** k. A **logarithmic equation** is an equation with a logarithm in at least one term.

EXAMPLE 2 **Solving Logarithmic Equations**

Solve each equation.

(a) $\log_4 x = -2$

$\qquad$ $\log_a x = y$

$x = 4^{-2}$ $\qquad$ means $x = a^y$.

$x = \dfrac{1}{4^2}$

$x = \dfrac{1}{16}$

CHECK $\log_4 \frac{1}{16} = -2$ because $4^{-2} = \frac{1}{16}$. ✓

The solution set is $\left\{\frac{1}{16}\right\}$.

(b) $\log_x 3 = 2$

$\qquad$ $\log_a x = y$

$x^2 = 3$ $\qquad$ means $x = a^y$.

$x = \pm\sqrt{3}$

The base must be positive, so only the *principal* square root satisfies this equation. The solution set is $\left\{\sqrt{3}\right\}$.

(c) $\log_{1/2}(3x + 1) = 2$

$3x + 1 = \left(\dfrac{1}{2}\right)^2$ $\qquad$ | This is a key step.

$\qquad\qquad\qquad\qquad$ Write in exponential form.

$3x + 1 = \dfrac{1}{4}$ $\qquad$ Apply the exponent.

$12x + 4 = 1$ $\qquad$ Multiply each term by 4.

$x = -\dfrac{1}{4}$ $\qquad$ Subtract 4, divide by 12, and write in lowest terms.

CHECK $\log_{1/2}\left[3\left(-\dfrac{1}{4}\right) + 1\right] \overset{?}{=} 2$ $\qquad$ Let $x = -\frac{1}{4}$ in the original equation.

$\log_{1/2}\dfrac{1}{4} \overset{?}{=} 2$ $\qquad$ Simplify within the parentheses.

$\left(\dfrac{1}{2}\right)^2 \overset{?}{=} \dfrac{1}{4}$ $\qquad$ Write in exponential form.

$\dfrac{1}{4} = \dfrac{1}{4}$ ✓ True

The solution set is $\left\{-\frac{1}{4}\right\}$.

(d) $\log_{49}\sqrt[3]{7} = x$

$49^x = \sqrt[3]{7}$ $\qquad$ Write in exponential form.

$(7^2)^x = 7^{1/3}$ $\qquad$ Write with the same base.

$7^{2x} = 7^{1/3}$ $\qquad$ Power rule for exponents

$2x = \dfrac{1}{3}$ $\qquad$ Set the exponents equal.

$x = \dfrac{1}{6}$ $\qquad$ Divide by 2 (or multiply by $\frac{1}{2}$).

Check to confirm that the solution set is $\left\{\frac{1}{6}\right\}$.

Work Problem **2** **at the Side.** ▶

2 Solve each equation.

(a) $\log_5 x = 2$

(b) $\log_3 27 = x$

(c) $\log_x 12 = 4$

(d) $\log_x \dfrac{1}{16} = -4$

(e) $\log_2 (3x - 2) = 4$

(f) $\log_9 \sqrt[4]{3} = x$

Answers

2. (a) $\{25\}$ **(b)** $\{3\}$ **(c)** $\left\{\sqrt[4]{12}\right\}$

(d) $\{2\}$ **(e)** $\{6\}$ **(f)** $\left\{\frac{1}{8}\right\}$

For any real positive number b, we know that $b^1 = b$ and $b^0 = 1$. Writing these two statements in logarithmic form gives the following properties.

③ Evaluate each logarithm.

(a) $\log_\pi \pi$

Properties of Logarithms

For any positive real number b, with $b \neq 1$, the following hold true.

$$\log_b b = 1 \quad \text{and} \quad \log_b 1 = 0$$

(b) $\log_{2/5} \dfrac{2}{5}$

EXAMPLE 3 Using Properties of Logarithms

Evaluate each logarithm.

(a) $\log_7 7 = 1$ $\quad \log_b b = 1$ $\qquad$ **(b)** $\log_{\sqrt{2}} \sqrt{2} = 1$

(c) $\log_9 1 = 0$ $\quad \log_b 1 = 0$ $\qquad$ **(d)** $\log_{0.2} 1 = 0$

◀ **Work Problem ③ at the Side.**

(c) $\log_6 1$

OBJECTIVE ④ Define and graph logarithmic functions. Now we define the logarithmic function with base a.

Logarithmic Function

If a and x are positive numbers, where $a \neq 1$, then

$$g(x) = \log_a x$$

defines the **logarithmic function with base a.**

(d) $\log_{0.4} 1$

EXAMPLE 4 Graphing a Logarithmic Function ($a > 1$)

Graph $f(x) = \log_2 x$.

By writing $y = f(x) = \log_2 x$ in exponential form as

$$x = 2^y,$$

we can identify ordered pairs that satisfy the equation. It is easier to choose values for y and find the corresponding values of x. Plotting the points in the table and connecting them with a smooth curve gives the graph in **Figure 16.** This graph is typical of logarithmic functions with base $a > 1$.

④ Graph $f(x) = \log_{10} x$.

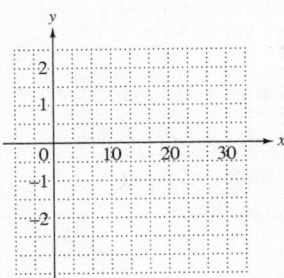

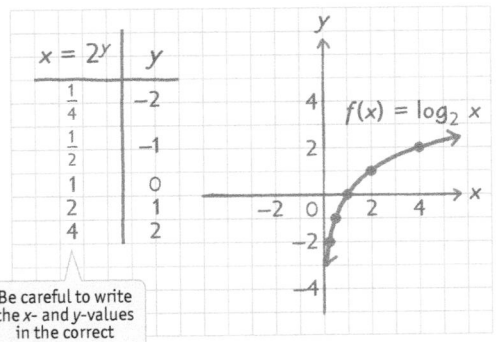

$x = 2^y$	y
$\frac{1}{4}$	-2
$\frac{1}{2}$	-1
1	0
2	1
4	2

Be careful to write the x- and y-values in the correct order.

Figure 16

Logarithmic function with base $a > 1$

Domain: $(0, \infty)$

Range: $(-\infty, \infty)$

x-intercept: $(1, 0)$

The function is one-to-one, and its graph rises from left to right.

Answers

3. (a) 1 **(b)** 1 **(c)** 0 **(d)** 0

4.

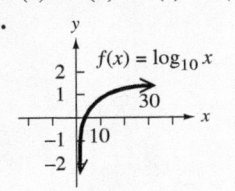

◀ **Work Problem ④ at the Side**

EXAMPLE 5 Graphing a Logarithmic Function $(0 < a < 1)$

Graph $g(x) = \log_{1/2} x$.

We write $y = g(x) = \log_{1/2} x$ in exponential form as $x = \left(\frac{1}{2}\right)^y$. Then we choose values for y and find the corresponding values of x. Plotting these points and connecting them with a smooth curve gives the graph in **Figure 17.** This graph is typical of logarithmic functions with $0 < a < 1$.

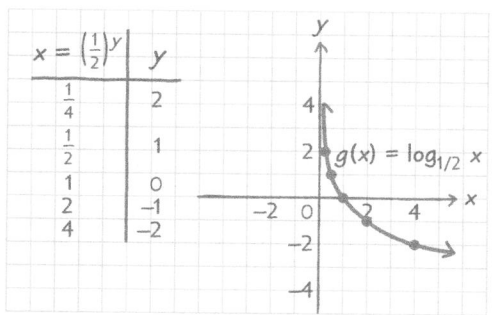

Logarithmic function with base $0 < a < 1$

Domain: $(0, \infty)$

Range: $(-\infty, \infty)$

x-intercept: $(1, 0)$

The function is one-to-one, and its graph falls from left to right.

Figure 17

─────── **Work Problem ❺ at the Side.** ▶

Characteristics of the Graph of $g(x) = \log_a x$

1. The graph contains the point $(1, 0)$, which is the x-intercept.

2. The function is one-to-one.

   • When $a > 1$, the graph *rises* from left to right, from the fourth quadrant to the first. (See **Figure 16.**)

   • When $0 < a < 1$, the graph *falls* from left to right, from the first quadrant to the fourth. (See **Figure 17.**)

3. The graph approaches the y-axis, but never touches it. (The y-axis is an asymptote.)

4. The domain is $(0, \infty)$, and the range is $(-\infty, \infty)$.

OBJECTIVE ▶ ❺ Use logarithmic functions in applications involving growth or decay.

EXAMPLE 6 Solving an Application of a Logarithmic Function

The barometric pressure in inches of mercury at a distance of x miles from the eye of a typical hurricane can be approximated by the logarithmic function

$$f(x) = 27 + 1.105 \log_{10} (x + 1).$$

(Data from Miller, A. and R. Anthes, *Meteorology*, Fifth Edition, Charles E. Merrill Publishing Company.)

Approximate the pressure 9 mi from the eye of the hurricane.

$f(9) = 27 + 1.105 \log_{10} (9 + 1)$ Let $x = 9$ in the given function.

$f(9) = 27 + 1.105 \log_{10} 10$ Add inside the parentheses.

$f(9) = 27 + 1.105 (1)$ $\log_{10} 10 = 1$

$f(9) = 28.105$ Add.

The pressure 9 mi from the eye of the hurricane is 28.105 in.

─────── **Work Problem ❻ at the Side.** ▶

❺ Graph $g(x) = \log_{1/10} x$.

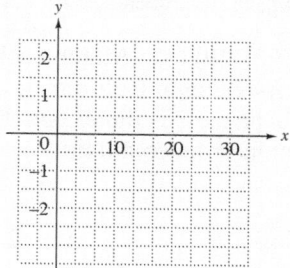

❻ Solve the problem.

A population of mites in a laboratory is growing according to the logarithmic function

$$P(t) = 80 \log_{10} (t + 10),$$

where t is the number of days after a study is begun.

(a) Find the number of mites at the beginning of the study.

(b) Find the number present after 90 days.

Answers

5.

$g(x) = \log_{1/10} x$

6. (a) 80   **(b)** 160

12.4 Exercises

FOR EXTRA HELP

Go to MyMathLab *for worked-out, step-by-step solutions to exercises enclosed in a square* and video solutions to ▶ *exercises.*

1. **CONCEPT CHECK**   Match each logarithm in Column I with its value in Column II. (*Example:* $\log_3 9$ is equal to 2 because 2 is the exponent to which 3 must be raised in order to obtain 9.)

I	II
(a) $\log_4 16$	**A.** -2
(b) $\log_3 81$	**B.** -1
(c) $\log_3\left(\dfrac{1}{3}\right)$	**C.** 2
(d) $\log_{10} 0.01$	**D.** 0
(e) $\log_5 \sqrt{5}$	**E.** $\dfrac{1}{2}$
(f) $\log_{13} 1$	**F.** 4

2. **CONCEPT CHECK**   Match each logarithmic equation in Column I with the corresponding exponential equation in Column II.

I	II
(a) $\log_{1/3} 3 = -1$	**A.** $8^{1/3} = \sqrt[3]{8}$
(b) $\log_5 1 = 0$	**B.** $\left(\dfrac{1}{3}\right)^{-1} = 3$
(c) $\log_2 \sqrt{2} = \dfrac{1}{2}$	**C.** $4^1 = 4$
(d) $\log_{10} 1000 = 3$	**D.** $2^{1/2} = \sqrt{2}$
(e) $\log_8 \sqrt[3]{8} = \dfrac{1}{3}$	**E.** $5^0 = 1$
(f) $\log_4 4 = 1$	**F.** $10^3 = 1000$

Write in logarithmic form. **See Example 1.**

3. $4^5 = 1024$
▶

4. $3^6 = 729$

5. $\left(\dfrac{1}{2}\right)^{-3} = 8$

6. $\left(\dfrac{1}{6}\right)^{-3} = 216$

7. $10^{-3} = 0.001$

8. $10^{-1} = 0.1$

9. $\sqrt[4]{625} = 5$

10. $\sqrt[3]{343} = 7$

11. $8^{-2/3} = \dfrac{1}{4}$

12. $16^{-3/4} = \dfrac{1}{8}$

13. $5^0 = 1$

14. $7^0 = 1$

Write in exponential form. **See Example 1.**

15. $\log_4 64 = 3$
▶

16. $\log_2 512 = 9$

17. $\log_{12} 12 = 1$

18. $\log_{100} 100 = 1$

19. $\log_6 1 = 0$

20. $\log_\pi 1 = 0$

21. $\log_9 3 = \dfrac{1}{2}$

22. $\log_{64} 2 = \dfrac{1}{6}$

23. $\log_{1/4} \dfrac{1}{2} = \dfrac{1}{2}$

24. $\log_{1/8} \dfrac{1}{2} = \dfrac{1}{3}$

25. $\log_5 5^{-1} = -1$

26. $\log_{10} 10^{-2} = -2$

27. CONCEPT CHECK Match each logarithm in Column I with its value in Column II.

I	II
(a) $\log_8 8$	**A.** -1
(b) $\log_{16} 1$	**B.** 0
(c) $\log_{0.3} 1$	**C.** 1
(d) $\log_{\sqrt{7}} \sqrt{7}$	**D.** 0.1

28. When a student asked his teacher to explain how to evaluate

$$\log_9 3$$

without showing any work, his teacher told him, *"Think radically."* Explain what the teacher meant by this hint.

Solve each equation. See Examples 2 and 3.

29. $x = \log_{27} 3$

30. $x = \log_{125} 5$

31. $\log_5 x = -3$

32. $\log_{10} x = -2$

33. $\log_x 9 = \dfrac{1}{2}$

34. $\log_x 5 = \dfrac{1}{2}$

35. $\log_x 125 = -3$

36. $\log_x 64 = -6$

37. $\log_{12} x = 0$

38. $\log_4 x = 0$

39. $\log_x x = 1$

40. $\log_x 1 = 0$

41. $\log_x \dfrac{1}{25} = -2$

42. $\log_x \dfrac{1}{10} = -1$

43. $\log_8 32 = x$

44. $\log_{81} 27 = x$

45. $\log_\pi \pi^4 = x$

46. $\log_{\sqrt{2}} \left(\sqrt{2}\right)^9 = x$

47. $\log_6 \sqrt{216} = x$

48. $\log_4 \sqrt{64} = x$

49. $\log_4 (2x + 4) = 3$

50. $\log_3 (2x + 7) = 4$

51. $\log_{1/3} (x - 4) = 2$

52. $\log_{1/2} (2x - 1) = 3$

Graph each function. ***See Examples 4 and 5.***

53. $g(x) = \log_3 x$

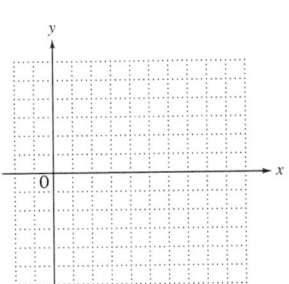

54. $g(x) = \log_5 x$

55. $f(x) = \log_4 x$

56. $f(x) = \log_6 x$

57. $f(x) = \log_{1/3} x$

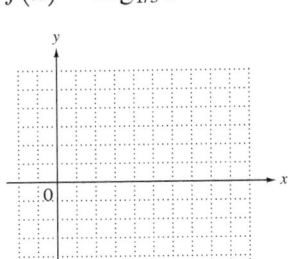

58. $f(x) = \log_{1/5} x$

59. $g(x) = \log_{1/4} x$

60. $g(x) = \log_{1/6} x$

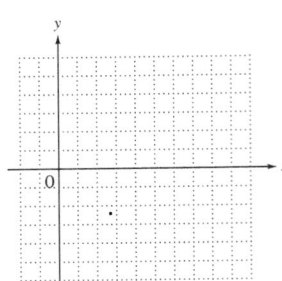

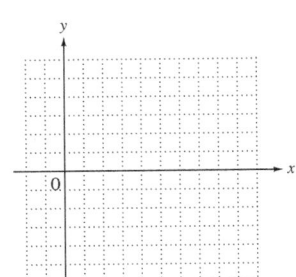

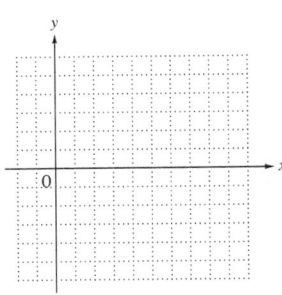

CONCEPT CHECK   *Use the graph to predict the value of* $f(t)$ *for each value of* t.

61. $t = 0$

62. $t = 10$

63. $t = 60$

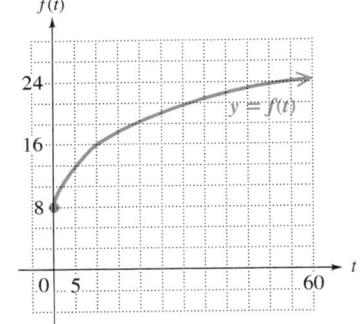

64. Show that the points determined in **Exercises 61–63** lie on the graph of

$$f(t) = 8 \log_5 (2t + 5).$$

CONCEPT CHECK   *Answer each question.*

65. Why is 1 not allowed as a base for a logarithmic function?

66. Why is a negative number not allowed as a base for a logarithmic function?

67. Why is $\log_a 1 = 0$ true for any value of a that is allowed as the base of a logarithm? Use a rule of exponents introduced earlier in the explanation.

68. Why is $\log_a a = 1$ true for any value of a that is allowed as the base of a logarithm?

Solve each problem. See Example 6.

69. Sales (in thousands of units) of a new product are approximated by the function

$$S(t) = 100 + 30 \log_3 (2t + 1),$$

where t is the number of years after the product is introduced. Use this function to approximate the sales after each period of time.

(a) 1 yr

(b) 4 yr

(c) 13 yr

70. A study showed that the number of mice in an old abandoned house was approximated by the function

$$M(t) = 6 \log_4 (2t + 4),$$

where t is measured in months and $t = 0$ corresponds to January 2016. Use this function to approximate the number of mice in the house in each month.

(a) January 2016

(b) July 2016

(c) July 2018

71. An online sales company finds that its sales in millions of dollars are approximated by the function

$$S(x) = \log_2 (3x + 1),$$

where x is the number of advertisements placed on a popular website. How many advertisements must be placed to earn sales of $4 million?

72. The population of deer, in thousands, in a certain area is approximated by the function

$$f(x) = \log_5 (100x - 75),$$

where x is the number of years since 2017. During what year is the population expected to be 4 thousand deer?

Relating Concepts (Exercises 73–76) For Individual or Group Work

To see how exponential and logarithmic functions are related, **work Exercises 73–76 in order.**

73. Complete the table of values, and sketch the graph of $y = 10^x$. Give the domain and range of the function.

x	y
−2	___
−1	___
0	___
1	___
2	___

74. Complete the table of values, and sketch the graph of $y = \log_{10} x$. Give the domain and range of the function.

x	y
$\frac{1}{100}$	___
$\frac{1}{10}$	___
1	___
10	___
100	___

75. Describe the symmetry between the graphs in **Exercises 73 and 74.**

76. What can we conclude about the functions

$$y = f(x) = 10^x \quad \text{and} \quad y = g(x) = \log_{10} x?$$

12.5 Properties of Logarithms

OBJECTIVES

1. Use the product rule for logarithms.
2. Use the quotient rule for logarithms.
3. Use the power rule for logarithms.
4. Use properties to write alternative forms of logarithmic expressions.

Logarithms have been used as an aid to numerical calculation for several hundred years. Today the widespread use of calculators has made the use of logarithms for calculation obsolete. However, logarithms are still very important in applications and in further work in mathematics.

OBJECTIVE 1 Use the product rule for logarithms. One way in which logarithms are used is to change a problem of multiplication into one of addition. For example, we know that

$$\log_2 4 = 2, \quad \log_2 8 = 3, \quad \text{and} \quad \log_2 32 = 5.$$

Therefore, we can make the following statements.

$$\log_2 32 = \log_2 4 + \log_2 8 \quad 5 = 2 + 3$$
$$\log_2 (4 \cdot 8) = \log_2 4 + \log_2 8 \quad 32 = 4 \cdot 8$$

This is an example of the product rule for logarithms.

Product Rule for Logarithms

If x, y, and b are positive real numbers, where $b \neq 1$, then the following holds true.

$$\log_b xy = \log_b x + \log_b y$$

In words, the logarithm of a product is the sum of the logarithms of the factors.

Examples:

$$\log_3 (4 \cdot 7) = \log_3 4 + \log_3 7 \quad \text{and} \quad \log_{10} 8 + \log_{10} 9 = \log_{10} (8 \cdot 9)$$

To prove this rule, let $m = \log_b x$ and $n = \log_b y$, and recall that

$$\log_b x = m \quad \text{means} \quad b^m = x.$$
$$\log_b y = n \quad \text{means} \quad b^n = y.$$

Now consider the product xy.

$xy = b^m \cdot b^n$	Substitute.
$xy = b^{m+n}$	Product rule for exponents
$\log_b xy = m + n$	Write in logarithmic form.
$\log_b xy = \log_b x + \log_b y$	Substitute for m and n.

The last statement is the result we wished to prove.

Note

The word statement of the product rule for logarithms above can be restated by replacing the word "logarithm" with the word "exponent." The rule then becomes the familiar rule for multiplying exponential expressions:

The *exponent* of a product is equal to the sum of the *exponents* of the factors.

EXAMPLE 1 Using the Product Rule

Use the product rule to rewrite each logarithm. Assume $x > 0$.

(a) $\log_5 (6 \cdot 9)$

$= \log_5 6 + \log_5 9$ Product rule

(b) $\log_7 8 + \log_7 12$

$= \log_7 (8 \cdot 12)$ Product rule

$= \log_7 96$ Multiply.

(c) $\log_3 (3x)$

$= \log_3 3 + \log_3 x$

     Product rule

$= 1 + \log_3 x$

     $\log_3 3 = 1$

(d) $\log_4 x^3$

$= \log_4 (x \cdot x \cdot x)$ $x^3 = x \cdot x \cdot x$

$= \log_4 x + \log_4 x + \log_4 x$

     Product rule

$= 3 \log_4 x$ Combine like terms.

Work Problem ① at the Side. ▶

OBJECTIVE ② Use the quotient rule for logarithms.

Quotient Rule for Logarithms

If x, y, and b are positive real numbers, where $b \neq 1$, then the following holds true.

$$\log_b \frac{x}{y} = \log_b x - \log_b y$$

In words, the logarithm of a quotient is the difference of the logarithm of the numerator and the logarithm of the denominator.

Examples: $\log_5 \frac{2}{3} = \log_5 2 - \log_5 3$ and $\log_7 3 - \log_7 5 = \log_7 \frac{3}{5}$

EXAMPLE 2 Using the Quotient Rule

Use the quotient rule to rewrite each logarithm. Assume $x > 0$.

(a) $\log_4 \frac{7}{9}$

$= \log_4 7 - \log_4 9$ Quotient rule

(b) $\log_5 6 - \log_5 x$

$= \log_5 \frac{6}{x}$ Quotient rule

(c) $\log_3 \frac{27}{5}$

$= \log_3 27 - \log_3 5$ Quotient rule

$= 3 - \log_3 5$ $\log_3 27 = 3$

(d) $\log_6 28 - \log_6 7$

$= \log_6 \frac{28}{7}$ Quotient rule

$= \log_6 4$ $\frac{28}{7} = 4$

Work Problem ② at the Side. ▶

❗ CAUTION

There is no property of logarithms to rewrite the logarithm of a sum.

$$\log_b (x + y) \neq \log_b x + \log_b y$$

Also, $\log_b x \cdot \log_b y \neq \log_b xy$,   and $\dfrac{\log_b x}{\log_b y} \neq \log_b \dfrac{x}{y}$.

---

① Use the product rule to rewrite each logarithm.

(a) $\log_6 (5 \cdot 8)$

(b) $\log_4 3 + \log_4 7$

(c) $\log_8 8k$, $k > 0$

(d) $\log_5 m^2$, $m > 0$

② Use the quotient rule to rewrite each logarithm.

(a) $\log_7 \dfrac{9}{4}$

(b) $\log_3 p - \log_3 10$, $p > 0$

(c) $\log_4 \dfrac{3}{16}$

(d) $\log_7 32 - \log_7 4$

Answers

1. **(a)** $\log_6 5 + \log_6 8$ **(b)** $\log_4 21$
    (c) $1 + \log_8 k$ **(d)** $2 \log_5 m$
2. **(a)** $\log_7 9 - \log_7 4$ **(b)** $\log_3 \dfrac{p}{10}$
    (c) $\log_4 3 - 2$ **(d)** $\log_7 8$

OBJECTIVE 3 **Use the power rule for logarithms.** Consider the exponential expression 2^3.

$$2^3 \quad \text{means} \quad 2 \cdot 2 \cdot 2.$$

The base 2 is used as a factor 3 times. Similarly, the product rule can be extended to rewrite the logarithm of a power as the product of the exponent and the logarithm of the base.

$\log_5 2^3$	$\log_2 7^4$
$= \log_5 (2 \cdot 2 \cdot 2)$	$= \log_2 (7 \cdot 7 \cdot 7 \cdot 7)$
$= \log_5 2 + \log_5 2 + \log_5 2$	$= \log_2 7 + \log_2 7 + \log_2 7 + \log_2 7$
$= 3 \log_5 2$	$= 4 \log_2 7$

Furthermore, we saw in **Example 1(d)** that $\log_4 x^3 = 3 \log_4 x$. These examples suggest the power rule for logarithms.

Power Rule for Logarithms

If x and b are positive real numbers, where $b \neq 1$, and if r is any real number, then the following holds true.

$$\log_b x^r = r \log_b x$$

In words, the logarithm of a number to a power equals the exponent times the logarithm of the number.

Examples: $\log_b m^5 = 5 \log_b m$ and $\log_3 5^4 = 4 \log_3 5$

To prove the power rule, let $\log_b x = m$.

$\log_b x = m$	
$b^m = x$	Write in exponential form.
$(b^m)^r = x^r$	Raise each side to the power r.
$b^{mr} = x^r$	Power rule for exponents
$\log_b x^r = mr$	Write in logarithmic form.
$\log_b x^r = rm$	Commutative property
$\log_b x^r = r \log_b x$	$m = \log_b x$

This is the statement to be proved.

As a special case of the power rule, let $r = \frac{1}{p}$, so

$$\log_b \sqrt[p]{x} = \log_b x^{1/p} = \frac{1}{p} \log_b x.$$

For example, using this result, with $x > 0$,

$$\log_b \sqrt[5]{x} = \log_b x^{1/5} = \frac{1}{5} \log_b x \quad \text{and} \quad \log_b \sqrt[3]{x^4} = \log_b x^{4/3} = \frac{4}{3} \log_b x.$$

Another special case is

$$\log_b \frac{1}{x} = \log_b x^{-1} = -\log_b x. \quad -a = -1 \cdot a$$

For example,

$$\log_9 \frac{1}{5} = \log_9 5^{-1} = -\log_9 5.$$

EXAMPLE 3   **Using the Power Rule**

Use the power rule to rewrite each logarithm. Assume that $b > 0, x > 0$, and $b \neq 1$.

(a) $\log_5 4^2$

$= 2 \log_5 4$ Power rule

(b) $\log_b x^5$

$= 5 \log_b x$ Power rule

(c) $\log_b \sqrt{7}$

When using the power rule with logarithms of expressions involving radicals, begin by rewriting the radical expression with a rational exponent.

$$\log_b \sqrt{7}$$
$$= \log_b 7^{1/2} \quad \sqrt{x} = x^{1/2}$$
$$= \frac{1}{2} \log_b 7 \quad \text{Power rule}$$

(d) $\log_2 \sqrt[5]{x^2}$

$= \log_2 x^{2/5}$ $\sqrt[5]{x^2} = x^{2/5}$

$= \frac{2}{5} \log_2 x$ Power rule

(e) $\log_3 \dfrac{1}{x^4}$

$= \log_3 x^{-4}$ Definition of negative exponent

$= -4 \log_3 x$ Power rule

──────────── **Work Problem** ❸ **at the Side.** ▶

Two special properties involving both exponential and logarithmic expressions come directly from the fact that logarithmic and exponential functions are inverses of each other.

> **Special Properties**
>
> For any positive real number b, where $b \neq 1$, the following hold true.
>
> $$b^{\log_b r} = r, \quad r > 0 \quad \text{and} \quad \log_b b^r = r, \quad r \text{ is real.}$$
>
> *Examples:* $10^{\log_{10} 4} = 4$ and $\log_{12} 12^2 = 2$

To prove the first statement, let $x = \log_b r$.

$$x = \log_b r$$
$$b^x = r \qquad \text{Write in exponential form.}$$
$$b^{\log_b r} = r \qquad \text{Replace } x \text{ with } \log_b r.$$

The proof of the second statement is similar.

EXAMPLE 4   **Using the Special Properties**

Find the value of each logarithmic expression.

(a) $\log_5 5^4 = 4$ $\log_b b^r = r$

(b) $\log_3 9$

$= \log_3 3^2$ $9 = 3^2$

$= 2$ $\log_b b^r = r$

(c) $4^{\log_4 10} = 10$ $b^{\log_b r} = r$

(d) $8^{\log_8 \sqrt{2}} = \sqrt{2}$ $b^{\log_b r} = r$

──────────── **Work Problem** ❹ **at the Side.** ▶

❸ Use the power rule to rewrite each logarithm. Assume that $a > 0, x > 0$, and $a \neq 1$.

(a) $\log_3 5^2$

(b) $\log_a x^4$

(c) $\log_a \sqrt{8}$

(d) $\log_2 \sqrt[3]{2}$

(e) $\log_3 \dfrac{1}{x^5}$

❹ Find the value of each logarithmic expression.

(a) $\log_{10} 10^3$

(b) $\log_2 8$

(c) $5^{\log_5 3}$

(d) $6^{\log_6 \sqrt{3}}$

Answers

3. **(a)** $2 \log_3 5$ **(b)** $4 \log_a x$ **(c)** $\dfrac{1}{2} \log_a 8$

   (d) $\dfrac{1}{3}$ **(e)** $-5 \log_3 x$

4. **(a)** 3   **(b)** 3   **(c)** 3   **(d)** $\sqrt{3}$

We summarize the properties of logarithms from this section and the previous one.

Properties of Logarithms

If x, y, and b are positive real numbers, where $b \neq 1$, and r is any real number, then the following hold true.

Product Rule $\qquad\qquad \log_b xy = \log_b x + \log_b y$

Quotient Rule $\qquad\qquad \log_b \dfrac{x}{y} = \log_b x - \log_b y$

Power Rule $\qquad\qquad \log_b x^r = r \log_b x$

Special Properties $\qquad b^{\log_b r} = r,\ \ r > 0 \quad$ and $\quad \log_b b^r = r$

$\qquad\qquad\qquad\qquad\qquad \log_b b = 1 \qquad\qquad$ and $\quad \log_b 1 = 0$

OBJECTIVE ▶ **4** **Use properties to write alternative forms of logarithmic expressions.**

EXAMPLE 5 **Writing Logarithms in Alternative Forms**

Use the properties of logarithms to rewrite each expression if possible. Assume that all variables represent positive real numbers.

(a) $\log_4 4x^3$

$\qquad = \log_4 4 + \log_4 x^3 \qquad$ Product rule

$\qquad = 1 + 3 \log_4 x \qquad\quad$ $\log_4 4 = 1$; Power rule

(b) $\log_7 \sqrt{\dfrac{m}{n}}$

$\qquad = \log_7 \left(\dfrac{m}{n}\right)^{1/2} \qquad$ Write the radical expression with a rational exponent.

$\qquad = \dfrac{1}{2} \log_7 \dfrac{m}{n} \qquad\qquad$ Power rule

$\qquad = \dfrac{1}{2} \left(\log_7 m - \log_7 n\right) \qquad$ Quotient rule

(c) $\log_5 \dfrac{a^2}{bc}$

$\qquad = \log_5 a^2 - \log_5 bc \qquad\qquad$ Quotient rule

$\qquad = 2 \log_5 a - \log_5 bc \qquad\qquad$ Power rule

$\qquad = 2 \log_5 a - \left(\log_5 b + \log_5 c\right) \qquad$ Product rule

$\qquad = 2 \log_5 a - \log_5 b - \log_5 c \qquad$ Parentheses are necessary here.

(d) $4 \log_b m - \log_b n, \quad b \neq 1$

$\qquad = \log_b m^4 - \log_b n \qquad$ Power rule

$\qquad = \log_b \dfrac{m^4}{n} \qquad\qquad$ Quotient rule

Continued on Next Page

(e) $\log_b (x + 1) + \log_b (2x + 1) - \dfrac{2}{3} \log_b x, \quad b \neq 1$

$= \log_b (x + 1) + \log_b (2x + 1) - \log_b x^{2/3}$ Power rule

$= \log_b \dfrac{(x + 1)(2x + 1)}{x^{2/3}}$ Product and quotient rules

$= \log_b \dfrac{2x^2 + 3x + 1}{x^{2/3}}$ Multiply in the numerator.

(f) $\log_8 (2p + 3r)$

This expression cannot be rewritten using the properties of logarithms. ***There is no property of logarithms to rewrite the logarithm of a sum.***

—————————————————————— **Work Problem ⑤ at the Side.** ▶

| EXAMPLE 6 | **Deciding Whether Statements about Logarithms Are True** |

Decide whether each statement is *true* or *false*.

(a) $\log_2 8 - \log_2 4 = \log_2 4$

Evaluate each side.

$\log_2 8 - \log_2 4$	Left side	$\log_2 4$	Right side
$= \log_2 2^3 - \log_2 2^2$	Write 8 and 4 as powers of 2.	$= \log_2 2^2$	Write 4 as a power of 2.
$= 3 - 2$	$\log_b b^r = r$	$= 2$	$\log_b b^r = r$
$= 1$	Subtract.		

The statement is false because $1 \neq 2$.

(b) $\log_3 (\log_2 8) = \dfrac{\log_7 49}{\log_8 64}$

Evaluate each side.

$\log_3 (\log_2 8)$	Left side	$\dfrac{\log_7 49}{\log_8 64}$	Right side
$= \log_3 (\log_2 2^3)$	Write 8 as a power of 2.	$= \dfrac{\log_7 7^2}{\log_8 8^2}$	Write 49 and 64 using exponents.
$= \log_3 3$	$\log_b b^r = r$	$= \dfrac{2}{2}$	$\log_b b^r = r$
$= 1$	$3 = 3^1$	$= 1$	Simplify.

The statement is true because $1 = 1$.

—————————————————————— **Work Problem ⑥ at the Side.** ▶

---

⑤ Use the properties of logarithms to rewrite each expression if possible. Assume that all variables represent positive real numbers.

(a) $\log_6 36m^5$

(b) $\log_2 \sqrt{9z}$

(c) $\log_q \dfrac{8r^2}{m^2 + 1}, \quad q \neq 1$

(d) $2 \log_a x + 3 \log_a y, \quad a \neq 1$

(e) $\log_4 (3x + y)$

⑥ Decide whether each statement is *true* or *false*.

(a) $\log_6 36 - \log_6 6 = \log_6 30$

(b) $\log_4 (\log_2 16) = \dfrac{\log_6 6}{\log_6 36}$

Answers

5. **(a)** $2 + 5 \log_6 m$ **(b)** $\log_2 3 + \dfrac{1}{2} \log_2 z$

   (c) $\log_q 8 + 2 \log_q r - \log_q (m^2 + 1)$
   (d) $\log_a x^2 y^3$ **(e)** cannot be rewritten

6. **(a)** false   **(b)** false

12.5 Exercises

FOR EXTRA HELP Go to MyMathLab *for worked-out, step-by-step solutions to exercises enclosed in a square* ▢ *and video solutions to* ▶ *exercises.*

CONCEPT CHECK *Use the indicated rule of logarithms to complete each equation.*

1. $\log_{10}(7 \cdot 8) =$ _____ Product rule

2. $\log_{10}\dfrac{7}{8} =$ _____ Quotient rule

3. $3^{\log_3 4} =$ _____ Special property

4. $\log_{10} 3^6 =$ _____ Power rule

CONCEPT CHECK *Decide whether each statement of a logarithmic property is* true *or* false. *If it is false, correct it by changing the right side of the equation.*

5. $\log_b x + \log_b y = \log_b(x + y)$

6. $\log_b \dfrac{x}{y} = \log_b x - \log_b y$

7. $\log_b xy = \log_b x + \log_b y$

8. $b^{\log_b r} = 1$

9. $\log_b b^r = r$

10. $\log_b x^r = \log_b rx$

Use the properties of logarithms to express each logarithm as a sum or difference of logarithms. Assume that all variables represent positive real numbers. See Examples 1–5.

11. $\log_7(4 \cdot 5)$
▶

12. $\log_8(9 \cdot 11)$

13. $\log_5 \dfrac{8}{3}$
▶

14. $\log_3 \dfrac{7}{5}$

15. $\log_4 6^2$
▶

16. $\log_5 7^4$

17. $\log_3 \dfrac{\sqrt[3]{4}}{x^2 y}$
▶

18. $\log_7 \dfrac{\sqrt[3]{13}}{pq^2}$

19. $\log_3 \sqrt{\dfrac{xy}{5}}$

20. $\log_6 \sqrt{\dfrac{pq}{7}}$

21. $\log_2 \dfrac{\sqrt[3]{x} \cdot \sqrt[5]{y}}{r^2}$
▶

22. $\log_4 \dfrac{\sqrt[4]{z} \cdot \sqrt[5]{w}}{s^2}$

23. CONCEPT CHECK A student incorrectly wrote

$$\log_a(x + y) = \log_a x + \log_a y.$$

When his teacher explained that this was wrong, the student claimed he had used the distributive property. *What Went Wrong?*

24. CONCEPT CHECK Consider the following "proof" that $\log_2 16$ does not exist.

$$\log_2 16$$
$$= \log_2(-4)(-4)$$
$$= \log_2(-4) + \log_2(-4)$$

The logarithm of a negative number is not defined, so the final step cannot be evaluated. Thus $\log_2 16$ does not exist. *What Went Wrong?*

Use the properties of logarithms to rewrite each expression as a single logarithm.
Assume that all variables are defined in such a way that the variable expressions
are positive, and bases are positive numbers not equal to 1. ***See Examples 1–5.***

25. $\log_b x + \log_b y$

26. $\log_b 2 + \log_b z$

27. $3 \log_a m - \log_a n$

28. $5 \log_b x - \log_b y$

29. $(\log_a r - \log_a s) + 3 \log_a t$

30. $(\log_a p - \log_a q) + 2 \log_a r$

31. $3 \log_a 5 - 4 \log_a 3$

32. $3 \log_a 5 + \dfrac{1}{2} \log_a 9$

33. $\log_{10} (x + 3) + \log_{10} (x - 3)$

34. $\log_{10} (y + 4) + \log_{10} (y - 4)$

35. $3 \log_p x + \dfrac{1}{2} \log_p y - \dfrac{3}{2} \log_p z - 3 \log_p a$

36. $\dfrac{1}{3} \log_b x + \dfrac{2}{3} \log_b y - \dfrac{3}{4} \log_b s - \dfrac{2}{3} \log_b t$

Decide whether each statement is true *or* false. ***See Example 6.***

37. $\log_2 (8 + 32) = \log_2 8 + \log_2 32$

38. $\log_2 (64 - 16) = \log_2 64 - \log_2 16$

39. $\log_3 7 + \log_3 7^{-1} = 0$

40. $\log_9 14 - \log_{14} 9 = 0$

41. $\log_6 60 - \log_6 10 = 1$

42. $\log_3 8 + \log_3 \dfrac{1}{8} = 0$

43. $\dfrac{\log_{10} 7}{\log_{10} 14} = \dfrac{1}{2}$

44. $\dfrac{\log_{10} 10}{\log_{10} 100} = \dfrac{1}{10}$

Relating Concepts (Exercises 45–50) For Individual or Group Work

Work Exercises 45–50 in order.

45. Evaluate $\log_3 81$.

46. Write the *meaning* of the expression $\log_3 81$.

47. Evaluate $3^{\log_3 81}$.

48. Write the *meaning* of the expression $\log_2 19$.

49. Evaluate $2^{\log_2 19}$.

50. Keeping in mind that a logarithm is an exponent, and using the results from **Exercises 45–49,** what is the simplest form of the expression $k^{\log_k m}$?

12.6 | Common and Natural Logarithms

OBJECTIVES

1 Evaluate common logarithms using a calculator.

2 Use common logarithms in applications.

3 Evaluate natural logarithms using a calculator.

4 Use natural logarithms in applications.

OBJECTIVE ▶ 1 Evaluate common logarithms using a calculator. Logarithms are important in applications in biology, engineering, economics, and social science. In this section we find numerical approximations for logarithms. Traditionally, base 10 logarithms were used most often because our number system is base 10. Logarithms with base 10 are **common logarithms.**

$$\log_{10} x \quad \text{is abbreviated as} \quad \log x,$$

where the base is understood to be 10.

In **Example 1,** we evaluate some common logarithms using a calculator with a (LOG) key. We express calculator approximations for logarithms to four decimal places.

EXAMPLE 1   **Evaluating Common Logarithms**

Evaluate each logarithm to four decimal places using a calculator as needed.

(a) $\log 327.1 \approx 2.5147$

(b) $\log 437{,}000 \approx 5.6405$

(c) $\log 0.0615 \approx -1.2111$

(d) $\log 10^{6.1988} = 6.1988$
Special property $\log_b b^r = r$

In part (c), $\log 0.0615 \approx -1.2111$ is a negative number. ***The common logarithm of a number between 0 and 1 is always negative*** because the logarithm is the exponent on 10 that produces the number. In this case, we have

$$10^{-1.2111} \approx 0.0615.$$

If the exponent (the logarithm) were positive, the result would be greater than 1 because $10^0 = 1$. The graph in **Figure 18** illustrates these concepts.

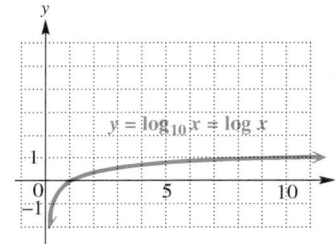

Figure 18

◀ **Work Problem ❶ at the Side.**

---

❶ Evaluate each logarithm to four decimal places using a calculator as needed.

(a) $\log 41{,}600$

(b) $\log 43.5$

(c) $\log 0.442$

(d) $\log 10^{0.5766}$

OBJECTIVE ▶ 2 Use common logarithms in applications. In chemistry, pH is a measure of the acidity or alkalinity of a solution. Water, for example, has pH 7. In general, acids have pH numbers less than 7, and alkaline solutions have pH values greater than 7.

Figure 19 illustrates the pH scale.

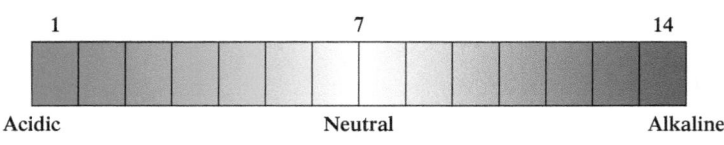

Figure 19 pH Scale

The **pH** of a solution is defined as

$$\text{pH} = -\log [\text{H}_3\text{O}^+],$$

where $[\text{H}_3\text{O}^+]$ is the hydronium ion concentration in moles per liter. It is customary to round pH values to the nearest tenth.

Answers

1. (a) 4.6191 **(b)** 1.6385
(c) −0.3546 **(d)** 0.5766

| EXAMPLE 2 | Using pH in an Application |

Wetlands are classified as *bogs, fens, marshes,* and *swamps* on the basis of pH values. A pH value between 6.0 and 7.5, such as that of Summerby Swamp in Michigan's Hiawatha National Forest, indicates that the wetland is a "rich fen." When the pH is between 3.0 and 6.0, the wetland is a "poor fen," and if the pH falls to 3.0 or less, it is a "bog." (Data from Mohlenbrock, R., "Summerby Swamp, Michigan," *Natural History.*)

Suppose that the hydronium ion concentration of a sample of water from a wetland is 6.3×10^{-3} mole per liter. How would this wetland be classified?

Use the definition of pH.

$$\text{pH} = -\log\left[H_3O^+\right] \qquad \text{Definition of pH}$$

$$\text{pH} = -\log\left(6.3 \times 10^{-3}\right) \qquad \text{Let } [H_3O^+] = 6.3 \times 10^{-3}.$$

$$\text{pH} = -\left(\log 6.3 + \log 10^{-3}\right) \qquad \text{Product rule}$$

$$\text{pH} \approx -\left[0.7993 - 3\right] \qquad \begin{array}{l}\text{Use a calculator to approximate log 6.3;} \\ \log_b b^r = r\end{array}$$

$$\text{pH} = -0.7993 + 3 \qquad \text{Distributive property}$$

$$\text{pH} \approx 2.2 \qquad \text{Add.}$$

The pH is less than 3.0, so the wetland is a bog.

———————————— **Work Problem 2 at the Side.** ▶

| EXAMPLE 3 | Finding Hydronium Ion Concentration |

Find the hydronium ion concentration of drinking water with pH 6.5.

$$\textbf{pH} = -\log\left[H_3O^+\right] \qquad \text{Definition of pH}$$

$$\textbf{6.5} = -\log\left[H_3O^+\right] \qquad \text{Let pH} = 6.5.$$

$$\log\left[H_3O^+\right] = -6.5 \qquad \text{Multiply by} -1.$$

Solve for $[H_3O^+]$ by writing the equation in exponential form using base 10.

$$\left[H_3O^+\right] = 10^{-6.5} \qquad \text{Write in exponential form.}$$

$$\left[H_3O^+\right] \approx 3.2 \times 10^{-7} \qquad \text{Evaluate with a calculator.}$$

The hydronium ion concentration of the drinking water is approximately 3.2×10^{-7} mole per liter.

———————————— **Work Problem 3 at the Side.** ▶

2 Solve the problem.
Find the pH of water with a hydronium ion concentration of 1.2×10^{-3} mole per liter. If this water had been taken from a wetland, is the wetland a *rich fen,* a *poor fen,* or a *bog*?

3 Find the hydronium ion concentrations of solutions with the following pH values.

GS **(a)** 3.6

$$\text{pH} = -\log\left[H_3O^+\right]$$

Let pH = 3.6.

$$\underline{\quad} = -\log\left[H_3O^+\right]$$

$$\log\left[H_3O^+\right] = \underline{\quad}$$

Solve for $[H_3O^+]$ by writing the equation in exponential form.

$$\left[H_3O^+\right] = 10 \underline{\quad}$$

$$\left[H_3O^+\right] \approx \underline{\quad}$$

(b) 7.5

LOUDNESS OF COMMON SOUNDS

Decibel Level	Examples
60	Normal conversation
90	Rush hour traffic, lawn mower
100	Garbage truck, chain saw, pneumatic drill
120	Rock concert, thunderclap
140	Gunshot blast, jet engine
180	Rocket launching pad

Data from Deafness Research Foundation.

④ Find the decibel level D to the nearest whole number of each sound.

GS **(a)** A whisper with intensity I of $115\,I_0$

$$D = 10 \log \left(\frac{I}{I_0} \right)$$

$$D = 10 \log \left(\frac{\underline{\quad} I_0}{I_0} \right)$$

$$D = 10 \log \underline{\quad}$$

$$D \approx \underline{\quad}$$

To the nearest whole number, the decibel level is ____ .

(b) A jet engine with intensity I of $(6.312 \times 10^{13})\,I_0$

The loudness of sound is measured in a unit called a **decibel,** abbreviated **dB.** To measure with this unit, we first assign an intensity of I_0 to a very faint sound, called the **threshold sound.** If a particular sound has intensity I, then the decibel level D of this louder sound is given by this formula.

$$D = 10 \log \left(\frac{I}{I_0} \right)$$

Any sound over 85 dB exceeds what hearing experts consider safe. Permanent hearing damage can be suffered at levels above 150 dB.

EXAMPLE 4 **Measuring the Loudness of Sound**

If rock music delivered through Bluetooth headphones has intensity I of $(3.162 \times 10^9)\,I_0$, find the decibel level D to the nearest whole number.

$$D = 10 \log \left(\frac{I}{I_0} \right)$$

$$D = 10 \log \left(\frac{(3.162 \times 10^9)\,I_0}{I_0} \right) \quad \text{Substitute the given value for } I.$$

$$D = 10 \log (3.162 \times 10^9) \quad \text{Divide: } \tfrac{I_0}{I_0} = 1.$$

$$D \approx 95 \text{ dB} \quad \text{Evaluate with a calculator.}$$

◀ **Work Problem ④ at the Side.**

OBJECTIVE ▶ ③ **Evaluate natural logarithms using a calculator.** Logarithms used in applications are often **natural logarithms,** which have as base the number *e*. The letter *e* was chosen to honor the mathematician Leonhard Euler, who published extensive results on the number in 1748. It is an irrational number, so its decimal expansion never terminates and never repeats.

Approximation for *e*

$$e \approx 2.718281828459$$

A scientific calculator with an $\boxed{e^x}$ key can approximate powers of *e*. For example, a calculator gives

$$e^2 \approx 7.389056099, \quad e^3 \approx 20.08553692, \quad \text{and} \quad e^{0.6} \approx 1.8221188.$$

Logarithms with base *e* are called natural logarithms because they occur in natural situations that involve growth or decay.

The base *e* logarithm of x is written **ln x** (read *"el en x"*).

A graph of $y = \ln x$ is given in **Figure 20.**

Answers

4. (a) 115; 115; 21; 21 dB
(b) 138 dB

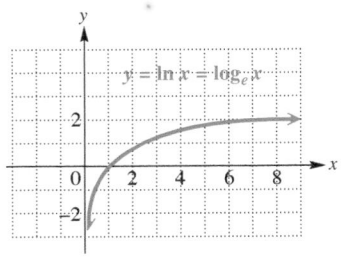

Figure 20

A calculator key labeled $\boxed{\text{LN}}$ is used to evaluate natural logarithms.

| EXAMPLE 5 | Evaluating Natural Logarithms |

Evaluate each logarithm to four decimal places using a calculator as needed.

(a) $\ln 0.5841 \approx -0.5377$ **(b)** $\ln 0.9215 \approx -0.0818$

As with common logarithms, a number between 0 and 1 has a negative natural logarithm.

(c) $\ln 192.7 \approx 5.2611$ **(d)** $\ln e^{4.6832} = 4.6832$

                     Special property $\log_b b^r = r$

——————————— Work Problem **5** at the Side. ▶

| OBJECTIVE ▶ 4 | Use natural logarithms in applications. |

| EXAMPLE 6 | Applying a Natural Logarithmic Function |

The altitude in meters that corresponds to an atmospheric pressure of x millibars can be approximated by the natural logarithmic function

$$f(x) = 51{,}600 - 7457 \ln x.$$

(Data from Miller, A. and J. Thompson, *Elements of Meteorology,* Fourth Edition, Charles E. Merrill Publishing Company.) Use this function to find the altitude when atmospheric pressure is 400 millibars. Round to the nearest hundred.

Let $x = 400$ and substitute in the expression for $f(x)$.

$f(x) = 51{,}600 - 7457 \ln x$ Given function

$f(400) = 51{,}600 - 7457 \ln 400$ Let $x = 400$.

$f(400) \approx 6900$ Evaluate with a calculator.

Atmospheric pressure is 400 millibars at 6900 m.

——————————— Work Problem **6** at the Side. ▶

| Note |

In Example 6, the final answer was obtained using a calculator *without* rounding the intermediate values. In general, it is best to wait until the final step to round the answer. Otherwise, a buildup of round-off error may cause the final answer to have an incorrect final decimal place digit or digits.

5 Evaluate each logarithm to four decimal places using a calculator as needed.

    (a) $\ln 0.01$ **(b)** $\ln 0.2711$

    (c) $\ln 529$ **(d)** $\ln e^{-1.2136}$

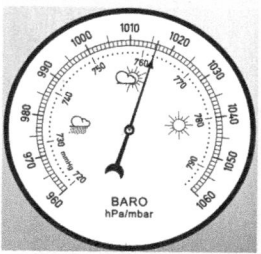

A barometer is an instrument that measures atmospheric pressure.

6 Use the natural logarithmic function in **Example 6** to approximate the altitude at 700 millibars of pressure. Round to the nearest hundred.

Answers

5. **(a)** -4.6052 **(b)** -1.3053
    (c) 6.2710 **(d)** -1.2136

6. 2700 m

12.6 Exercises

FOR EXTRA HELP Go to MyMathLab *for worked-out, step-by-step solutions to exercises enclosed in a square* ⬜ *and video solutions to* ▶ *exercises.*

CONCEPT CHECK *Choose the correct response.*

1. What is the base in the expression log x?

   A. e **B.** 1   **C.** 10   **D.** x

2. What is the base in the expression ln x?

   A. e **B.** 1   **C.** 10   **D.** x

3. Given $10^0 = 1$ and $10^1 = 10$, between what two consecutive integers is the value of log 5.6?

   A. 5 and 6   **B.** 10 and 11
   C. 1 and 10   **D.** 0 and 1

4. Given $e^1 \approx 2.718$ and $e^2 \approx 7.389$, between what two consecutive integers is the value of ln 5.6?

   A. 5 and 6   **B.** 2 and 7
   C. 1 and 2   **D.** 0 and 1

CONCEPT CHECK *Without using a calculator, give the value of each expression.*

5. log $10^{19.2}$

6. ln $e^{\sqrt{2}}$

7. $10^{\log \sqrt{3}}$

8. $e^{\ln 75.2}$

Use a calculator for the remaining exercises in this set.

Evaluate each logarithm to four decimal places. **See Examples 1 and 5.**

9. log 328.4 ▶

10. log 457.2

11. log 0.0326 ▶

12. log 0.1741

13. log (4.76×10^9) ▶

14. log (2.13×10^4)

15. ln 7.84 ▶

16. ln 8.32

17. ln 0.0556 ▶

18. ln 0.0217

19. ln 10 ▶

20. log e

Suppose that water from a wetland is sampled and found to have the given hydronium ion concentration. Is the wetland a rich fen, *a* poor fen, *or a* bog? **See Example 2.**

21. 2.5×10^{-5}

22. 3.1×10^{-5}

23. 2.5×10^{-2} ▶

24. 3.6×10^{-2}

25. 2.5×10^{-7}

26. 2.7×10^{-7}

Find the pH *(to the nearest tenth) of the substance with the given hydronium ion concentration.* **See Example 2.**

27. Ammonia, 2.5×10^{-12}

28. Egg white, 1.6×10^{-8}

29. Sodium bicarbonate, 4.0×10^{-9}

30. Tuna, 1.3×10^{-6}

31. Grapes, 5.0×10^{-5}

32. Grapefruit, 6.3×10^{-4}

Find the hydronium ion concentration of the substance with the given pH.
See Example 3.

33. Human gastric contents, 2.0

34. Milk, 6.4

35. Human blood plasma, 7.4

36. Spinach, 5.4

37. Bananas, 4.6

38. Milk of magnesia, 10.5

Solve each problem. See Examples 4 and 6.

39. The time t in years for an amount increasing at a rate r (in decimal form) to double is given by

$$t = \frac{\ln 2}{\ln(1 + r)}.$$

This is the **doubling time.** Find the doubling time to the nearest tenth for an investment at each interest rate.

(a) 2% (or 0.02)　　**(b)** 5% (or 0.05)

40. The number of years, $N(r)$, since two independently evolving languages split off from a common ancestral language is approximated by

$$N(r) = -5000 \ln r,$$

where r is the percent of words (as a decimal) from the ancestral language common to both languages now. Find the number of years (to the nearest hundred) since the split for each percent of common words.

(a) 85% (or 0.85)　　**(b)** 35% (or 0.35)

41. Managements of sports stadiums and arenas often encourage fans to make as much noise as possible. Find the average decibel level

$$D = 10 \log\left(\frac{I}{I_0}\right)$$

for each venue with the given intensity I.

(a) NFL fans, Kansas City Chiefs at Arrowhead Stadium: $I = (1.58 \times 10^{14})I_0$

(b) NBA fans, Sacramento Kings at Sleep Train Arena: $I = (3.9 \times 10^{12})I_0$

(c) MLB fans, Baltimore Orioles at Camden Yards: $I = (1.1 \times 10^{12})I_0$
(Data from www.guinessworldrecords.com and www.baltimoresportsreport.com)

42. Find the decibel level of each sound. (Data from The Canadian Society of Otolaryngology.)

(a) noisy restaurant: $I = 10^8 I_0$

(b) farm tractor: $I = (5.340 \times 10^9)I_0$

(c) snowmobile: $I = 31{,}622{,}776{,}600 I_0$

43. In the central Sierra Nevada of California, the percent of moisture p that falls as snow rather than rain is approximated reasonably well by

$$p(h) = 86.3 \ln h - 680,$$

where h is the altitude in feet.

(a) Approximately what percent of the moisture at 5000 ft falls as snow?

(b) Approximately what percent at 7500 ft falls as snow?

44. The **cost-benefit equation**

$$T = -0.642 - 189 \ln(1 - 0.01p)$$

describes the approximate tax T, in dollars per ton, that would result in a p% reduction in carbon dioxide emissions.

(a) What tax (to the nearest dollar) will reduce emissions 25%?

(b) Explain why the equation is not valid for $p = 0$.

12.7 Exponential and Logarithmic Equations and Their Applications

OBJECTIVES

1 Solve equations involving variables in the exponents.

2 Solve equations involving logarithms.

3 Solve applications of compound interest.

4 Solve applications involving base e exponential growth and decay.

5 Use the change-of-base rule.

General methods for solving exponential and logarithmic equations follow.

Properties for Solving Exponential and Logarithmic Equations

For all real numbers $b > 0$, $b \neq 1$, and any real numbers x and y, the following hold true.

1. If $x = y$, then $b^x = b^y$.
2. If $b^x = b^y$, then $x = y$.
3. If $x = y$, and $x > 0$, $y > 0$, then $\log_b x = \log_b y$.
4. If $x > 0$, $y > 0$, and $\log_b x = \log_b y$, then $x = y$.

OBJECTIVE **1** Solve equations involving variables in the exponents.

EXAMPLE 1 Solving an Exponential Equation (Property 3)

Solve $3^x = 12$. Approximate the solution to three decimal places.

$$3^x = 12$$

$$\log 3^x = \log 12 \qquad \text{Property 3 (common logarithms)}$$

$$x \log 3 = \log 12 \qquad \text{Power rule}$$

Exact solution $\longrightarrow$ $x = \dfrac{\log 12}{\log 3} \qquad$ Divide by $\log 3$.

Decimal approximation $\longrightarrow$ $x \approx 2.262 \qquad$ Evaluate with a calculator.

Check that $3^{2.262} \approx 12$. The solution set is $\{2.262\}$.

◀ **Work Problem** **1** at the Side.

---

1 Solve $2^x = 9$. Approximate the solution to three decimal places.

! CAUTION

Be careful: $\dfrac{\log 12}{\log 3}$ is **not** equal to log 4. Check to see that

$$\log 4 \approx 0.6021, \quad \text{but} \quad \frac{\log 12}{\log 3} \approx 2.262.$$

---

2 Solve $e^{-0.01t} = 0.38$. Approximate the solution to three decimal places.

EXAMPLE 2 Solving an Exponential Equation (Base e)

Solve $e^{0.003x} = 40$. Approximate the solution to three decimal places.

$$\ln e^{0.003x} = \ln 40 \qquad \text{Property 3 (natural logarithms)}$$

$$0.003x \ln e = \ln 40 \qquad \text{Power rule}$$

$$0.003x = \ln 40 \qquad \ln e = \ln e^1 = 1$$

$$x = \frac{\ln 40}{0.003} \qquad \text{Divide by 0.003.}$$

$$x \approx 1229.626 \qquad \text{Evaluate with a calculator.}$$

Check that $e^{0.003\,(1229.626)} \approx 40$. The solution set is $\{1229.626\}$.

◀ **Work Problem** **2** at the Side.

Answers

1. $\{3.170\}$ **2.** $\{96.758\}$

> **General Method for Solving an Exponential Equation**
>
> Take logarithms with the same base on both sides and then use the power rule of logarithms or the special property $\log_b b^r = r$. (See **Examples 1 and 2**.)
>
> As a special case, if both sides can be written as exponentials with the same base, do so, and then set the exponents equal.

3 Solve $\log_3 (x + 1)^5 = 3$. Give the exact solution.

OBJECTIVE **2** Solve equations involving logarithms.

EXAMPLE 3 Solving a Logarithmic Equation

Solve $\log_2 (x + 5)^3 = 4$. Give the exact solution.

$\log_2 (x + 5)^3 = 4$

$(x + 5)^3 = 2^4$ — Write in exponential form.

$(x + 5)^3 = 16$ — $2^4 = 16$

$x + 5 = \sqrt[3]{16}$ — Take the cube root on each side.

$x = -5 + \sqrt[3]{16}$ — Add -5.

$x = -5 + 2\sqrt[3]{2}$ — $\sqrt[3]{16} = \sqrt[3]{8 \cdot 2} = \sqrt[3]{8} \cdot \sqrt[3]{2} = 2\sqrt[3]{2}$

CHECK $\log_2 (x + 5)^3 = 4$ — Original equation

$\log_2 \left(-5 + 2\sqrt[3]{2} + 5\right)^3 \overset{?}{=} 4$ — Let $x = -5 + 2\sqrt[3]{2}$.

$\log_2 \left(2\sqrt[3]{2}\right)^3 \overset{?}{=} 4$ — Work inside the parentheses.

$\log_2 16 \overset{?}{=} 4$ — $\left(2\sqrt[3]{2}\right)^3 = 2^3 \left(\sqrt[3]{2}\right)^3 = 8 \cdot 2 = 16$

$2^4 \overset{?}{=} 16$ — Write in exponential form.

$16 = 16$ ✓ True

A true statement results, so the solution set is $\left\{-5 + 2\sqrt[3]{2}\right\}$.

Work Problem 3 at the Side. ▶

EXAMPLE 4 Solving a Logarithmic Equation (Property 4)

Solve $\log_2 (x + 1) - \log_2 x = \log_2 7$.

$\log_2 (x + 1) - \log_2 x = \log_2 7$

(Transform the left side to an expression with only *one* logarithm.)

$\log_2 \dfrac{x + 1}{x} = \log_2 7$ — Quotient rule

$\dfrac{x + 1}{x} = 7$ — Property 4

$x + 1 = 7x$ — Multiply by x.

$1 = 6x$ — Subtract x.

(This proposed solution must be checked.)

$\dfrac{1}{6} = x$ — Divide by 6.

Continued on Next Page

Answer

3. $\left\{-1 + \sqrt[5]{27}\right\}$

4 Solve.

$$\log_8 (2x + 5) + \log_8 3 = \log_8 33$$

5 Solve each equation.

(a) $\log_3 2x - \log_3 (3x + 15) = -2$

Apply the quotient rule to obtain a single logarithm on the left.

$$\log_3 \frac{2x}{\underline{\quad}} = -2$$

Write the equation in exponential form.

$$\frac{2x}{\underline{\quad}} = 3 \text{—}$$

Solve this equation, and verify that the solution set is _____.

(b) $\log x + \log (x + 15) = 2$

CHECK

$$\log_2 (x + 1) - \log_2 x = \log_2 7 \quad \text{Original equation}$$

$$\log_2 \left(\frac{1}{6} + 1\right) - \log_2 \frac{1}{6} \stackrel{?}{=} \log_2 7 \quad \text{Let } x = \frac{1}{6}.$$

$$\log_2 \frac{7}{6} - \log_2 \frac{1}{6} \stackrel{?}{=} \log_2 7 \quad \frac{1}{6} + 1 = \frac{1}{6} + \frac{6}{6} = \frac{7}{6}$$

$$\log_2 \frac{\frac{7}{6}}{\frac{1}{6}} \stackrel{?}{=} \log_2 7 \quad \text{Quotient rule}$$

$$\frac{\frac{7}{6}}{\frac{1}{6}} = \frac{7}{6} \div \frac{1}{6} = \frac{7}{6} \cdot \frac{6}{1} = 7$$

$$\log_2 7 = \log_2 7 \ \checkmark \quad \text{True}$$

A true statement results, so the solution set is $\left\{\frac{1}{6}\right\}$.

◀ **Work Problem 4** at the Side.

⚠ CAUTION

Do not reject a proposed solution just because it is nonpositive. Reject any value that leads to the logarithm of a nonpositive number.

EXAMPLE 5 Solving a Logarithmic Equation

Solve $\log x + \log (x - 21) = 2$.

$$\log x + \log (x - 21) = 2$$

$$\log x (x - 21) = 2 \quad \text{Product rule}$$

The base is 10. $\quad x (x - 21) = 10^2 \quad$ Write in exponential form.

$$x^2 - 21x = 100 \quad \text{Distributive property; } 10^2 = 100$$

$$x^2 - 21x - 100 = 0 \quad \text{Standard form}$$

$$(x - 25)(x + 4) = 0 \quad \text{Factor.}$$

$$x - 25 = 0 \quad \text{or} \quad x + 4 = 0 \quad \text{Zero-factor property}$$

$$x = 25 \quad \text{or} \quad x = -4 \quad \text{Solve each equation.}$$

The value -4 must be rejected as a solution because it leads to the logarithm of a negative number in the original equation.

$$\log (-4) + \log (-4 - 21) = 2 \quad \text{The left side is undefined.}$$

Check that the only solution is 25, so the solution set is $\{25\}$.

◀ **Work Problem 5** at the Side.

Solving a Logarithmic Equation

Step 1 **Transform the equation so that a single logarithm appears on one side** using the product or quotient rule of logarithms.

Step 2 **Do one of the following.**

(a) **Use Property 4.**
If $\log_b x = \log_b y$, then $x = y$. (See **Example 4.**)

(b) **Write the equation in exponential form.**
If $\log_b x = k$, then $x = b^k$. (See **Examples 3 and 5.**)

Answers

4. $\{3\}$

5. **(a)** $3x + 15; 3x + 15; -2; \{1\}$
(b) $\{5\}$

OBJECTIVE ▶ **3** **Solve applications of compound interest.** We have solved simple interest problems using the formula

$$I = prt. \quad \text{Simple interest formula}$$

Most cases involve **compound interest** (interest paid on both principal and interest). *In this text, monetary amounts are given to the nearest cent.*

Compound Interest Formula (for a Finite Number of Periods)

If a principal of P dollars is deposited at an annual rate of interest r compounded (paid) n times per year, the account will contain

$$A = P\left(1 + \frac{r}{n}\right)^{nt}$$

dollars after t years. (In this formula, r is expressed as a decimal.)

EXAMPLE 6   **Solving a Compound Interest Problem for A**

How much money will there be in an account at the end of 5 yr if $1000 is deposited at 3% compounded quarterly? (Assume no withdrawals are made.)

Because interest is compounded quarterly, $n = 4$.

$$A = P\left(1 + \frac{r}{n}\right)^{nt} \quad \text{Compound interest formula}$$

$$A = 1000\left(1 + \frac{0.03}{4}\right)^{4 \cdot 5} \quad \begin{array}{l}\text{Substitute } P = 1000, r = 0.03 \text{ (because}\\ 3\% = 0.03), n = 4, \text{ and } t = 5.\end{array}$$

$$A = 1000\,(1.0075)^{20} \quad \text{Simplify.}$$

$$A = 1161.18 \quad \text{Evaluate with a calculator.}$$

The account will contain $1161.18.

─────────────────── **Work Problem** **6** **at the Side.** ▶

EXAMPLE 7   **Solving a Compound Interest Problem for t**

Suppose inflation is averaging 3% per year. To the nearest hundredth, how many years will it take for prices to double? (This is the **doubling time.**)

We want to find the number of years t for P dollars to grow to $2P$ dollars.

$$A = P\left(1 + \frac{r}{n}\right)^{nt} \quad \text{Compound interest formula}$$

$$2P = P\left(1 + \frac{0.03}{1}\right)^{1t} \quad \text{Substitute } A = 2P, r = 0.03, \text{ and } n = 1.$$

$$2 = (1.03)^{t} \quad \text{Divide by } P. \text{ Simplify.}$$

$$\log 2 = \log(1.03)^{t} \quad \text{Property 3}$$

$$\log 2 = t \log 1.03 \quad \text{Power rule}$$

$$t = \frac{\log 2}{\log 1.03} \quad \text{Divide by } \log 1.03. \text{ Interchange sides.}$$

$$t \approx 23.45 \quad \text{Evaluate with a calculator.}$$

Prices will double in 23.45 yr. To check, verify that $1.03^{23.45} \approx 2$.

─────────────────── **Work Problem** **7** **at the Side.** ▶

6 Solve the problem.
How much money will there be in an account at the end of 10 yr if $10,000 is deposited at 2.5% compounded monthly?

7 Solve the problem.
Find the number of years, to the nearest hundredth, it will take for money deposited in an account paying 2% interest compounded semiannually to double.

Answers
6. $12,836.92
7. 34.83 yr

⑧ Suppose that $2000 is invested at 5% interest for 10 yr.

(a) How much will the investment grow to if compounded continuously?

Interest can be compounded annually, semiannually, quarterly, daily, and so on. If the number of compounding periods n is allowed to approach infinity, we have an example of **continuous compounding.**

Continuous Compound Interest Formula

If a principal of P dollars is deposited at an annual rate of interest r compounded continuously for t years, the final amount A on deposit is given by

$$A = Pe^{rt}.$$

EXAMPLE 8 **Solving a Continuous Interest Problem**

In **Example 6,** we found that $1000 invested for 5 yr at 3% interest compounded quarterly would grow to $1161.18.

(a) How much would this investment grow to if compounded continuously?

$$A = Pe^{rt} \qquad \text{Continuous compounding formula}$$
$$A = 1000e^{(0.03)5} \qquad \text{Let } P = 1000, r = 0.03, \text{ and } t = 5.$$
$$A = 1161.83 \qquad \text{Evaluate with a calculator.}$$

The account will grow to $1161.83 (which is $0.65 more than the amount in **Example 6** when interest was compounded quarterly).

(b) How long would it take for the initial investment to double? Round to the nearest hundredth.

(b) How long would it take for the initial investment amount to double?
We must find the value of t that will cause A to be $2\,(\$1000) = \$2000$.

$$A = Pe^{rt} \qquad \text{Continuous compounding formula}$$
$$2000 = 1000e^{0.03t} \qquad \text{Let } A = 2P = 2000, P = 1000, \text{ and } r = 0.03.$$
$$2 = e^{0.03t} \qquad \text{Divide by 1000.}$$
$$\ln 2 = 0.03t \qquad \text{Take natural logarithms; } \ln e^k = k.$$
$$t = \frac{\ln 2}{0.03} \qquad \text{Divide by 0.03. Interchange sides.}$$
$$t \approx 23.10 \qquad \text{Evaluate with a calculator to the nearest hundredth.}$$

It would take 23.10 yr for the original investment to double.

◀ **Work Problem ⑧ at the Side.**

OBJECTIVE ④ Solve applications involving base e exponential growth and decay.

EXAMPLE 9 **Solving an Exponential Decay Application**

After a plant or animal dies, the amount of radioactive carbon-14 that is present disintegrates according to the natural logarithmic function

$$y = y_0 e^{-0.000121t},$$

where t is time in years, y is the amount of the sample at time t, and y_0 is the initial amount present at $t = 0$.

(a) If an initial sample contains $y_0 = 10$ g of carbon-14, how many grams, to the nearest hundredth, will be present after 3000 yr?

$$y = 10e^{-0.000121\,(3000)} \approx 6.96 \text{ g} \qquad \begin{array}{l}\text{Let } y_0 = 10 \text{ and } t = 3000 \\ \text{in the formula.}\end{array}$$

Continued on Next Page

Answers

8. (a) $3297.44 **(b)** 13.86 yr

(b) How long would it take to the nearest year for the initial sample to decay to half of its original amount? (This is the **half-life.**)
Let $y = \frac{1}{2}(10) = 5$, and solve for t.

$$y = y_0 e^{-0.000121t} \qquad \text{Exponential decay formula}$$

$$5 = 10 e^{-0.000121t} \qquad \text{Let } y = 5 \text{ and } y_0 = 10.$$

$$\frac{1}{2} = e^{-0.000121t} \qquad \text{Divide by 10.}$$

$$\ln \frac{1}{2} = -0.000121t \qquad \text{Take natural logarithms; } \ln e^k = k.$$

$$t = \frac{\ln \frac{1}{2}}{-0.000121} \qquad \text{Divide by } -0.000121. \text{ Interchange sides.}$$

$$t \approx 5728 \qquad \text{Evaluate with a calculator.}$$

The half-life is 5728 yr.

───────────── Work Problem **9** at the Side. ▶

OBJECTIVE ▶ 5 **Use the change-of-base rule.** The *change-of-base rule* is used to convert logarithms from one base to another.

Change-of-Base Rule

If $a > 0, a \neq 1, b > 0, b \neq 1$, and $x > 0$, then the following holds true.

$$\log_a x = \frac{\log_b x}{\log_b a}$$

Any positive number other than 1 can be used for base b in the change-of-base rule, but usually the only practical bases are e and 10 because calculators give logarithms for these two bases.

To derive the change-of-base rule, let $\log_a x = m$.

$$\log_a x = m$$

$$a^m = x \qquad \text{Write in exponential form.}$$

$$\log_b (a^m) = \log_b x \qquad \text{Property 3}$$

$$m \log_b a = \log_b x \qquad \text{Power rule}$$

$$(\log_a x)(\log_b a) = \log_b x \qquad \text{Substitute for } m.$$

This is the change-of-base rule. $\rightarrow \log_a x = \frac{\log_b x}{\log_b a} \qquad \text{Divide by } \log_b a.$

EXAMPLE 10 **Using the Change-of-Base Rule**

Use the change-of-base rule to approximate $\log_5 12$ to four decimal places.

$$\log_5 12 = \frac{\log 12}{\log 5} \approx 1.5440$$

$$\log_5 12 = \frac{\ln 12}{\ln 5} \approx 1.5440$$

Either common or natural logarithms can be used.

───────────── Work Problem **10** at the Side. ▶

9 Radioactive strontium decays according to the natural logarithmic function

$$y = y_0 e^{-0.0239t},$$

where t is time in years.

(a) If an initial sample contains $y_0 = 12$ g of radioactive strontium, how many grams, to the nearest hundredth, will be present after 35 yr?

(b) How long (to the nearest year) would it take for the initial sample to decay to half its original amount?

10 Use the change-of-base rule to approximate each logarithm to four decimal places.

(a) $\log_3 17$, using common logarithms

(b) $\log_3 17$, using natural logarithms

Answers

9. (a) 5.20 g (b) 29 yr
10. (a) 2.5789 (b) 2.5789

12.7 Exercises

FOR EXTRA HELP — Go to MyMathLab for worked-out, step-by-step solutions to exercises enclosed in a square ☐ and video solutions to ▶ exercises.

CONCEPT CHECK *Tell whether* common logarithms *or* natural logarithms *would be a better choice to use for solving each equation. Do not actually solve.*

1. $10^{0.0025x} = 75$

2. $10^{3x+1} = 13$

3. $e^{x-2} = 24$

4. $e^{-0.28x} = 30$

Many of the problems in the remaining exercises require a scientific calculator.
Solve each equation. Approximate solutions to three decimal places. **See Example 1.**

5. $7^x = 5$ ▶

6. $4^x = 3$

7. $3^{2x} = 14$

8. $5^{0.3x} = 11$

9. $9^{-x+2} = 13$

10. $6^{-x+1} = 22$

11. $2^{x+3} = 5^x$

12. $6^{x+3} = 4^x$

13. $2^{x+3} = 3^{x-4}$ ▶

14. $4^{x-2} = 5^{3x+2}$

15. $4^{2x+3} = 6^{x-1}$

16. $3^{2x+1} = 5^{x-1}$

Solve each equation. Use natural logarithms. Approximate solutions to three decimal places as necessary. **See Example 2.**

17. $e^{0.012x} = 23$ ▶

18. $e^{0.006x} = 30$

19. $e^{-0.205x} = 9$

20. $e^{-0.103x} = 7$

21. $\ln e^{3x} = 9$

22. $\ln e^{5x} = 20$

23. $\ln e^{0.45x} = \sqrt{7}$

24. $\ln e^{0.04x} = \sqrt{3}$

25. $\ln e^{-2x} = \pi$

26. $\ln e^{-x} = \pi$

27. $e^{\ln 2x} = e^{\ln(x+1)}$

28. $e^{\ln(6-x)} = e^{\ln(4+2x)}$

Solve each equation. Give exact solutions. **See Example 3.**

29. $\log_3(6x+5) = 2$

30. $\log_5(12x-8) = 3$

31. $\log_2(2x-1) = 5$

32. $\log_6(4x+2) = 2$

33. $\log_7(x+1)^3 = 2$ ▶

34. $\log_4(x-3)^3 = 4$

35. $\log_6(x-4)^5 = 3$

36. $\log_5(x+8)^5 = 2$

37. CONCEPT CHECK Suppose that in solving a logarithmic equation having the term
$$\log (x - 3),$$
we obtain the proposed solution 2. We know that our algebraic work is correct, so we give $\{2\}$ as the solution set. *What Went Wrong?*

38. CONCEPT CHECK Suppose that in solving a logarithmic equation having the term
$$\log (3 - x),$$
we obtain the proposed solution -4. We know that our algebraic work is correct, so we reject -4 and give $\varnothing$ as the solution set. *What Went Wrong?*

Solve each equation. Give exact solutions. **See Examples 4 and 5.**

39. $\log (6x + 1) = \log 3$

40. $\log (2x - 3) = \log 12$

41. $\log_5 (3x + 2) - \log_5 x = \log_5 4$

42. $\log_2 (x + 5) - \log_2 (x - 1) = \log_2 3$

43. $\log 4x - \log (x - 3) = \log 2$

44. $\log (-x) + \log 3 = \log (2x - 15)$

45. $\log_2 x + \log_2 (x - 7) = 3$

46. $\log_3 x + \log_3 (2x + 5) = 1$

47. $\log 5x - \log (2x - 1) = \log 4$

48. $\log (2x + 1) - \log 10x = \log 10$

49. $\log_2 x + \log_2 (x - 6) = 4$

50. $\log_2 x + \log_2 (x + 4) = 5$

Solve each problem. **See Examples 6–8.**

51. Suppose that $2000 is deposited at 4% compounded quarterly.

  (a) How much money will be in the account at the end of 6 yr? (Assume no withdrawals are made.)

  (b) To two decimal places, how long will it take for the account to grow to $3000?

52. Suppose that $3000 is deposited at 3.5% compounded quarterly.

  (a) How much money will be in the account at the end of 7 yr? (Assume no withdrawals are made.)

  (b) To two decimal places, how long will it take for the account to grow to $5000?

53. What will be the amount A in an account with initial principal $4000 if interest is compounded continuously at an annual rate of 3.5% for 6 yr?

54. What will be the amount A in an account with initial principal $10,000 if interest is compounded continuously at an annual rate of 2.5% for 5 yr?

55. How long, to the nearest hundredth of a year, would it take an initial principal P to double if it is invested at 2.5% compounded continuously?

56. How long, to the nearest hundredth of a year, would it take $4000 to double at 3.25% compounded continuously?

*Solve each problem. **See Example 9.***

57. A sample of 400 g of lead-210 decays to polonium-210 according to the function

$$y = 400e^{-0.032t},$$

where t is time in years. Approximate answers to the nearest hundredth.

   (a) How much lead will be left in the sample after 25 yr?

   (b) How long will it take the initial sample to decay to half of its original amount?

58. The amount, in grams, of radium-226 present in a given sample is determined by the function

$$y = 3.25e^{-0.00043t},$$

where t is time in years. Approximate answers to the nearest hundredth.

   (a) How much radium is present after 100 yr?

   (b) How long will it take the initial sample to decay to half its original amount?

*Use the change-of-base rule (with either common or natural logarithms) to approximate each logarithm to four decimal places. **See Example 10.***

59. $\log_6 13$

60. $\log_7 19$

61. $\log_{\sqrt{2}} \pi$

62. $\log_\pi \sqrt{2}$

63. $\log_{21} 0.7496$

64. $\log_{19} 0.8325$

65. $\log_{1/2} 5$

66. $\log_{1/3} 7$

Relating Concepts (Exercises 67–70) For Individual or Group Work

Previously, we solved an equation such as $5^x = 125$ as follows.

$$5^x = 125 \qquad \text{Original equation}$$
$$5^x = 5^3 \qquad 125 = 5^3$$
$$x = 3 \qquad \text{Set exponents equal.}$$

Solution set: $\{3\}$

The method described in this section can also be used to solve this equation.
***Work Exercises 67–70 in order,** to see how this is done.*

67. Take common logarithms on both sides, and write this equation.

68. Apply the power rule for logarithms on the left.

69. Write the equation so that x is alone on the left.

70. Use a calculator to find the decimal form of the solution. What is the solution set?

Chapter 12 *Summary*

Key Terms

composition of functions The composite function, or composition, of functions f and g is defined by $(f \circ g)(x) = f(g(x))$, for all x in the domain of g such that $g(x)$ is in the domain of f.

one-to-one function A one-to-one function is a function in which each x-value corresponds to just one y-value, and each y-value corresponds to just one x-value.

Domain   Range

inverse of a function f If f is a one-to-one function, then the inverse of f is the set of all ordered pairs of the form (y, x), where (x, y) belongs to f.

exponential equation An equation involving an exponential, where the variable is in the exponent, is an exponential equation.

logarithm A logarithm is an exponent. The expression $\log_a x$ represents the exponent to which the base a must be raised to obtain x.

logarithmic equation A logarithmic equation is an equation with a logarithm in at least one term.

common logarithm A common logarithm is a logarithm with base 10.

natural logarithm A natural logarithm is a logarithm with base e.

New Symbols

$(f \circ g)(x) = f(g(x))$	composite function of f and g
f^{-1}	inverse of f
$\log_a x$	logarithm of x with base a
$\log x$	common (base 10) logarithm of x
$\ln x$	natural (base e) logarithm of x
e	a constant, approximately 2.718281828459

Test Your Word Power

See how well you have learned the vocabulary in this chapter.

1 In a **one-to-one function**
   A. each x-value corresponds to only two y-values
   B. each x-value corresponds to one or more y-values
   C. each x-value is the same as each y-value
   D. each x-value corresponds to only one y-value, and each y-value corresponds to only one x-value.

2 If f is a one-to-one function, then the **inverse** of f is
   A. the set of all solutions of f
   B. the set of all ordered pairs formed by interchanging the coordinates of the ordered pairs of f

   C. an equation involving an exponential expression
   D. the set of all ordered pairs that are the opposite (negative) of the coordinates of the ordered pairs of f.

3 An **exponential function** is a function defined by an expression of the form
   A. $f(x) = ax^2 + bx + c$, for real numbers a, b, c $(a \neq 0)$
   B. $f(x) = \log_a x$, for a and x positive numbers $(a \neq 1)$
   C. $f(x) = a^x$, for all real numbers x $(a > 0, a \neq 1)$
   D. $f(x) = \sqrt{x}$, for $x \geq 0$.

4 A **logarithm is**
   A. an exponent
   B. a base
   C. an equation
   D. a radical expression.

5 A **logarithmic function** is a function defined by an expression of the form
   A. $f(x) = ax^2 + bx + c$, for real numbers a, b, c $(a \neq 0)$
   B. $f(x) = \log_a x$, for a and x positive numbers $(a \neq 1)$
   C. $f(x) = a^x$, for all real numbers x $(a > 0, a \neq 1)$
   D. $f(x) = \sqrt{x}$, for $x \geq 0$.

Answers to Test Your Word Power

1. D; *Example:* The function $f = \{(0, 2), (1, -1), (3, 5), (-2, 3)\}$ is one-to-one.

2. B; *Example:* The inverse of the one-to-one function f defined in Answer 1 is $f^{-1} = \{(2, 0), (-1, 1), (5, 3), (3, -2)\}$.

3. C; *Examples:* $f(x) = 4^x$, $g(x) = \left(\frac{1}{2}\right)^x$

4. A; *Example:* $\log_a x$ is the exponent to which a must be raised to obtain x. For instance, $\log_3 9 = 2$ because $3^2 = 9$.

5. B; *Examples:* $y = \log_3 x$, $y = \log_{1/3} x$

Quick Review

Concepts	Examples

12.1 Composition of Functions

Composition of f and g

$$(f \circ g)(x) = f(g(x))$$
$$(g \circ f)(x) = g(f(x))$$

Let $f(x) = x^2$ and $g(x) = 2x + 1$.

$$
\begin{aligned}
(f \circ g)(x) &= f(g(x)) \\
&= f(2x + 1) \\
&= (2x + 1)^2 \\
&= 4x^2 + 4x + 1
\end{aligned}
\qquad
\begin{aligned}
(g \circ f)(x) &= g(f(x)) \\
&= g(x^2) \\
&= 2x^2 + 1
\end{aligned}
$$

12.2 Inverse Functions

Horizontal Line Test

A function is one-to-one if every horizontal line intersects the graph of the function at most once.

Inverse Functions

For a one-to-one function f defined by an equation $y = f(x)$, find the defining equation of the inverse f^{-1} as follows.

Step 1 Interchange x and y.

Step 2 Solve for y.

Step 3 Replace y with $f^{-1}(x)$.

In general, the graph of f^{-1} is the mirror image of the graph of f with respect to the line $y = x$. If the point (a, b) lies on the graph of f, then the point (b, a) lies on the graph of f^{-1}.

Find f^{-1} if $f(x) = 2x - 3$. The graph of f is a slanted straight line, so f is one-to-one by the horizontal line test.

$$y = 2x - 3 \qquad \text{Let } y = f(x).$$
$$x = 2y - 3 \qquad \text{Interchange } x \text{ and } y.$$
$$y = \frac{x + 3}{2} \qquad \text{Solve for } y.$$
$$f^{-1}(x) = \frac{1}{2}x + \frac{3}{2} \qquad \text{Replace } y \text{ with } f^{-1}(x); \frac{a + b}{c} = \frac{a}{c} + \frac{b}{c}.$$

The graphs of a function f and its inverse f^{-1} are shown here.

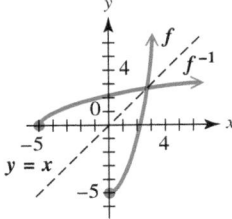

12.3 Exponential Functions

For $a > 0$, $a \neq 1$, and all real numbers x, $\boldsymbol{f(x) = a^x}$ defines the exponential function with base a.

Graph of $f(x) = a^x$

1. The graph contains the point $(0, 1)$, which is the y-intercept.

2. When $a > 1$, the graph rises from left to right. When $0 < a < 1$, the graph falls from left to right.

3. The x-axis is an asymptote.

4. The domain is $(-\infty, \infty)$, and the range is $(0, \infty)$.

$f(x) = 3^x$ is the exponential function with base 3.

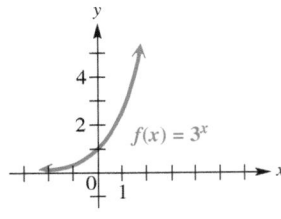

Concepts

12.4 Logarithmic Functions

For all positive real numbers a, where $a \neq 1$, and all positive real numbers x,

$$y = \log_a x \quad \text{means} \quad x = a^y.$$

If a and x are positive real numbers, where $a \neq 1$, then

$$g(x) = \log_a x$$

defines the logarithmic function with base a.

Graph of $g(x) = \log_a x$

1. The graph contains the point $(1, 0)$, which is the x-intercept.

2. When $a > 1$, the graph rises from left to right.
   When $0 < a < 1$, the graph falls from left to right.

3. The y-axis is an asymptote.

4. The domain is $(0, \infty)$, and the range is $(-\infty, \infty)$.

12.5 Properties of Logarithms

If x, y, and b are positive real numbers, where $b \neq 1$, and r is any real number, then the following hold true.

Product Rule

$$\log_b xy = \log_b x + \log_b y$$

Quotient Rule

$$\log_b \frac{x}{y} = \log_b x - \log_b y$$

Power Rule

$$\log_b x^r = r \log_b x$$

Special Properties

$$b^{\log_b r} = r, \ r > 0 \quad \text{and} \quad \log_b b^r = r$$
$$\log_b b = 1 \quad \text{and} \quad \log_b 1 = 0$$

12.6 Common and Natural Logarithms

Common logarithms (base 10) are used in applications such as pH, sound level, and intensity of an earthquake. Use the LOG key of a calculator to evaluate common logarithms.

Natural logarithms (base e) are most often used in applications of growth and decay, such as continuous compounding of money, decay of chemical compounds, and biological growth. Use the LN key of a calculator to evaluate natural logarithms.

Examples

$$y = \log_2 x \quad \text{means} \quad x = 2^y.$$

$g(x) = \log_3 x$ is the logarithmic function with base 3.

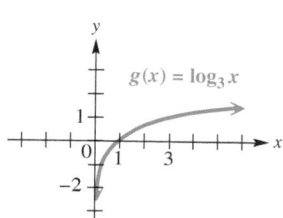

Rewrite each logarithm.

$$\log_2 3m = \log_2 3 + \log_2 m \quad \text{Product rule}$$

$$\log_5 \frac{9}{4} = \log_5 9 - \log_5 4 \quad \text{Quotient rule}$$

$$\log_{10} 2^3 = 3 \log_{10} 2 \quad \text{Power rule}$$

$$6^{\log_6 10} = 10 \qquad \log_3 3^4 = 4$$
$$\log_3 3 = 1 \qquad \log_5 1 = 0 \qquad \text{Special properties}$$

Use the formula $\mathbf{pH} = -\log [\mathbf{H_3O^+}]$ to find the pH (to one decimal place) of grapes with hydronium ion concentration 5.0×10^{-5}.

$$\text{pH} = -\log (5.0 \times 10^{-5}) \quad \text{Substitute.}$$
$$\text{pH} \approx 4.3 \quad \text{Evaluate with a calculator.}$$

Use the formula for doubling time (in years)

$$t = \frac{\ln 2}{\ln (1 + r)}$$

to find the doubling time, to the nearest hundredth of a year, for an interest rate of 4%.

$$t = \frac{\ln 2}{\ln (1 + 0.04)} \quad \text{Let } r = 0.04.$$

$$t \approx 17.67 \quad \text{Evaluate with a calculator.}$$

The doubling time is 17.67 yr.

Concepts	Examples

12.7 Exponential and Logarithmic Equations and Their Applications

To solve exponential equations, use these properties (where $b > 0$, $b \neq 1$).

1. If $b^x = b^y$, then $x = y$.

Solve. $\qquad 2^{3x} = 2^5$

$\qquad\qquad 3x = 5 \qquad$ Set the exponents equal.

$\qquad\qquad x = \dfrac{5}{3} \qquad$ Divide by 3.

Solution set: $\left\{ \dfrac{5}{3} \right\}$

2. If $x = y$ $(x > 0, y > 0)$, then $\log_b x = \log_b y$.

Solve. $\qquad 5^x = 8$

$\qquad \log 5^x = \log 8 \qquad$ Take common logarithms.

$\qquad x \log 5 = \log 8 \qquad$ Power rule

$\qquad\qquad x = \dfrac{\log 8}{\log 5} \qquad$ Divide by log 5.

$\qquad\qquad x \approx 1.2920 \qquad$ Evaluate with a calculator.

Solution set: $\{1.2920\}$

To solve logarithmic equations, use these properties (where $b > 0$, $b \neq 1$, $x > 0$, $y > 0$). First use the product rule, quotient rule, power rule, or special properties, if necessary, to write the equation in the proper form.

1. If $\log_b x = \log_b y$, then $x = y$.

Solve. $\qquad \log_3 2x = \log_3 (x + 1)$

$\qquad\qquad 2x = x + 1 \qquad$ Property 1

$\qquad\qquad x = 1 \qquad$ Subtract x.

This value checks, so the solution set is $\{1\}$.

Solve.

$\log x + \log (x + 15) = 2$

$\qquad \log x (x + 15) = 2 \qquad$ Product rule

$\qquad \log (x^2 + 15x) = 2 \qquad$ Distributive property

2. If $\log_b x = y$, then $b^y = x$.

$\qquad\qquad x^2 + 15x = 10^2 \qquad$ Write in exponential form.

$\qquad\qquad x^2 + 15x = 100 \qquad 10^2 = 100$

$\qquad x^2 + 15x - 100 = 0 \qquad$ Standard form

$\qquad (x + 20)(x - 5) = 0 \qquad$ Factor.

$x + 20 = 0 \quad$ or $\quad x - 5 = 0 \qquad$ Zero-factor property

$\qquad x = -20 \quad$ or $\qquad x = 5 \qquad$ Solve each equation.

The value -20 must be rejected as a solution because it leads to the logarithm of at least one negative number in the original equation. Check that the only solution is 5, so the solution set is $\{5\}$.

Change-of-Base Rule

If $a > 0$, $a \neq 1$, $b > 0$, $b \neq 1$, $x > 0$, then the following holds true.

$$\log_a x = \frac{\log_b x}{\log_b a}$$

Approximate $\log_3 37$ to four decimal places.

$$\log_3 37 = \frac{\ln 37}{\ln 3} = \frac{\log 37}{\log 3} \approx 3.2868$$

Chapter 12   *Review Exercises*

12.1 *Let $f(x) = 3x^2 + 2x - 1$ and $g(x) = 5x + 7$. Find each value or expression.*

1. (a) $(g \circ f)(3)$
  (b) $(f \circ g)(3)$

2. (a) $(f \circ g)(-2)$
  (b) $(g \circ f)(-2)$

3. (a) $(f \circ g)(x)$
  (b) $(g \circ f)(x)$

4. Based on the answers to **Exercises 1–3**, discuss whether composition of functions is a commutative operation.

12.2 *Determine whether each graph is the graph of a one-to-one function.*

5.

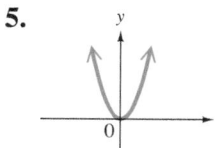

6.

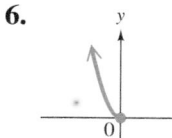

7.

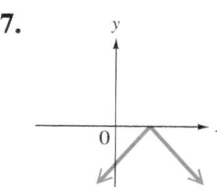

Determine whether each function is one-to-one. If it is, find its inverse.

8. $\{(-2, 4), (-1, 1), (0, 0), (1, 1), (2, 4)\}$

9. $\{(-2, -8), (-1, -1), (0, 0), (1, 1), (2, 8)\}$

10. $f(x) = -3x + 7$

11. $f(x) = \sqrt[3]{6x - 4}$

12. $f(x) = -x^2 + 3$

Each function graphed is one-to-one. Graph its inverse on the same set of axes as a dashed line or curve.

13.

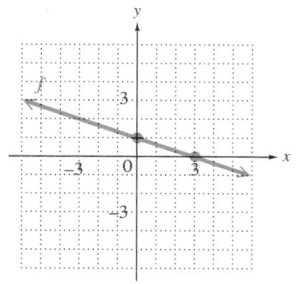

14.

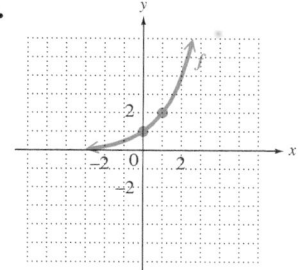

15.

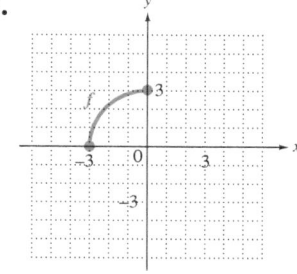

12.3 *Graph each function.*

16. $f(x) = 4^x$

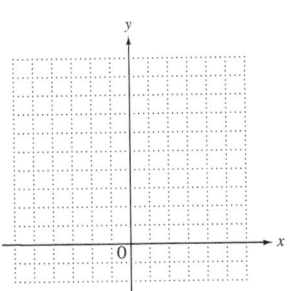

17. $f(x) = \left(\dfrac{1}{4}\right)^x$

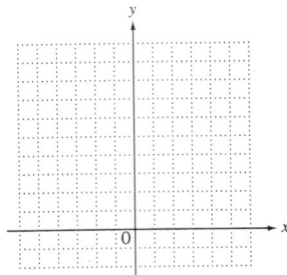

18. $f(x) = 4^{x+1}$

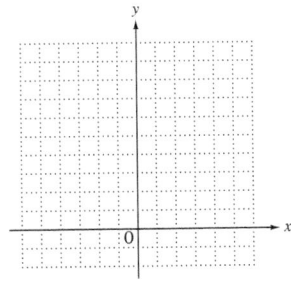

Solve each equation.

19. $4^{3x} = 8^{x+4}$

20. $\left(\dfrac{1}{27}\right)^{x-1} = 9^{2x}$

21. $5^x = 1$

22. $\left(\dfrac{2}{5}\right)^x = \dfrac{125}{8}$

Many of the remaining exercises will require a scientific calculator. We do not mark each such exercise.

23. The U.S. Hispanic population can be approximated by

$$f(x) = 46.9 \cdot 2^{0.035811x},$$

where x represents the number of years since 2008. Use this function to approximate, to the nearest tenth, the Hispanic population in each year. (Data from U.S. Census Bureau.)

(a) 2015

(b) 2030

12.4 **CONCEPT CHECK** *Work each problem.*

24. Convert each equation to the indicated form.

    (a) Write in exponential form: $\log_5 625 = 4$.

    (b) Write in logarithmic form: $5^{-2} = 0.04$.

25. Fill in the blanks with the correct responses:

The value of $\log_2 32$ is _____. This means that if we raise _____ to the _____ power, the result is _____.

Graph each function.

26. $g(x) = \log_4 x$

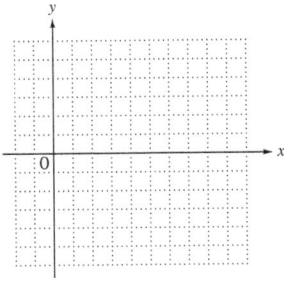

27. $g(x) = \log_{1/4} x$

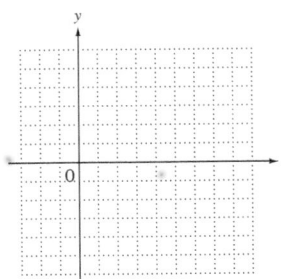

28. $g(x) = \ln x$

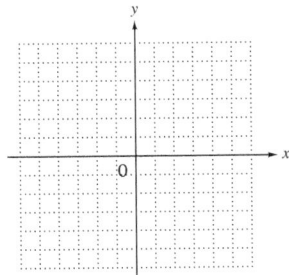

Solve each equation.

29. $\log_8 64 = x$

30. $\log_7 \dfrac{1}{49} = x$

31. $\log_4 x = \dfrac{3}{2}$

32. $\log_b b^2 = 2$

12.5 *Use the properties of logarithms to express each logarithm as a sum or difference of logarithms. Assume that all variables represent positive real numbers.*

33. $\log_4 3x^2$

34. $\log_5 \dfrac{a^3 b^2}{c^4}$

35. $\log_4 \dfrac{\sqrt{x} \cdot w^2}{z}$

36. $\log_2 \dfrac{p^2 r}{\sqrt{z}}$

Use the properties of logarithms to rewrite each expression as a single logarithm. Assume that all variables are defined in such a way that the variable expressions are positive, and bases are positive numbers not equal to 1.

37. $2 \log_a 7 - 4 \log_a 2$

38. $3 \log_a 5 + \dfrac{1}{3} \log_a 8$

39. $\log_b 3 + \log_b x - 2 \log_b y$

40. $\log_3 (x + 7) - \log_3 (4x + 6)$

12.6 *Evaluate each logarithm to four decimal places.*

41. $\log 28.9$

42. $\log 0.257$

43. $\ln 28.9$

44. $\ln 0.257$

Find the pH (to the nearest tenth) of the substance with the given hydronium ion concentration.

45. Milk, 4.0×10^{-7}

46. Crackers, 3.8×10^{-9}

47. If vinegar has pH 2.2, what is its hydronium ion concentration?

12.7 *Solve each equation. Approximate solutions to three decimal places.*

48. $3^x = 9.42$

49. $2^{x-1} = 15$

50. $e^{0.06x} = 3$

Solve each equation. Give exact solutions.

51. $\log_3 (9x + 8) = 2$

52. $\log_5 (x + 6)^3 = 2$

53. $\log_3 (p + 2) - \log_3 p = \log_3 2$

54. $\log (2x + 3) - \log x = 1$

55. $\log_4 x + \log_4 (8 - x) = 2$

56. $\log_2 x + \log_2 (x + 15) = 4$

Solve each problem.

57. How much would be in an account after 3 yr if $6500.00 was invested at 3% annual interest, compounded daily? (Use $n = 365$.)

58. Which plan is better? How much more would it pay?

Plan A: Invest $1000.00 at 4% compounded quarterly for 3 yr

Plan B: Invest $1000.00 at 3.9% compounded monthly for 3 yr

Use the change-of-base rule (with either common or natural logarithms) to approximate each logarithm to four decimal places.

59. $\log_{16} 13$

60. $\log_4 12$

61. $\log_{\sqrt{6}} \sqrt{13}$

62. $\log_{1/4} 17$

Chapter 12 *Mixed Review Exercises*

Evaluate.

1. $\log_2 128$

2. $\log_{12} 1$

3. $\log_{2/3} \dfrac{27}{8}$

4. $5^{\log_5 36}$

5. $e^{\ln 4}$

6. $10^{\log e}$

7. $\log_3 3^{-5}$

8. $\ln e^{5.4}$

Evaluate each logarithm to four decimal places.

9. $\log 385$

10. $\ln 0.68$

11. $\log_2 25$

12. $\log_{1/3} 14$

Solve.

13. $\log_3 (x + 9) = 4$

14. $\log_2 32 = x$

15. $\log_x \dfrac{1}{81} = 2$

16. $27^x = 81$

17. $2^{2x-3} = 8$

18. $\log_3 (x + 1) - \log_3 x = 2$

19. $\log (3x - 1) = \log 10$

20. $5^{x+2} = 25^{2x+1}$

21. $\log_4 (x + 2) - \log_4 x = 3$

22. $\ln (x^2 + 3x + 4) = \ln 2$

*A machine purchased for business use **depreciates,** or loses value, over a period of years. The value of the machine at the end of its useful life is its **scrap value.** By one method of depreciation the scrap value, S, is given by*

$$S = C(1 - r)^n,$$

where C is the original cost, n is the useful life in years, and r is the constant percent of depreciation.

23. Find the scrap value, to the nearest dollar, of a machine costing $30,000, having a useful life of 12 yr and a constant annual rate of depreciation of 15%.

24. A machine has a "half-life" of 6 yr. Find the constant annual rate of depreciation to the nearest unit of percent.

*One measure of the diversity of species in an ecological community is the **index of diversity,** given by the logarithmic expression*

$$-(p_1 \ln p_1 + p_2 \ln p_2 + \ldots + p_n \ln p_n),$$

where $p_1, p_2, \ldots, p_n$ are the proportions of a sample belonging to each of n species in the sample. (Data from Ludwig, John and James Reynolds, Statistical Ecology: A Primer on Methods and Computing, *New York, John Wiley and Sons.)*

Approximate the index of diversity to the nearest thousandth if a sample of 100 from a community produces the following numbers.

25. 90 of one species, 10 of another

26. 60 of one species, 40 of another

Chapter 12   Test   The Chapter Test Prep Videos with step-by-step solutions are available in MyMathLab or on YouTube at **https://goo.gl/3rBuO5**

1. For $f(x) = 3x + 5$ and $g(x) = x^2 + 2$, find each of the following.

  (a) $(f \circ g)(-2)$

  (b) $(f \circ g)(x)$

  (c) $(g \circ f)(x)$

2. Determine whether each function is one-to-one.

  (a) $f(x) = x^2 + 9$

  (b)

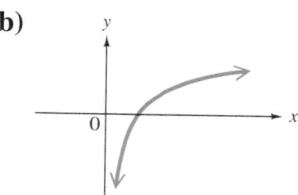

3. Find $f^{-1}(x)$ for the one-to-one function

$$f(x) = \sqrt[3]{x + 7}.$$

4. The graph of a one-to-one function f is given. Graph f^{-1} on the same set of axes as a dashed curve.

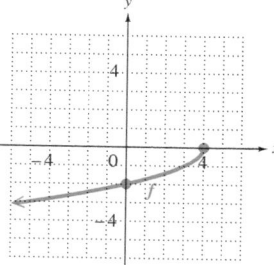

Graph each function.

5. $f(x) = 6^x$

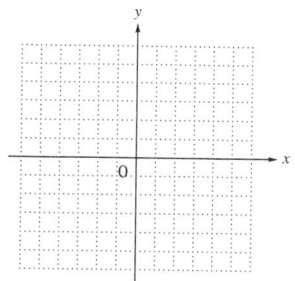

6. $g(x) = \log_6 x$

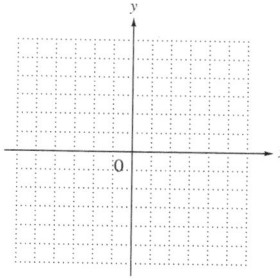

7. Explain how the graph of the function in **Exercise 6** can be obtained from the graph of the function in **Exercise 5.**

Solve each equation. Give exact solutions.

8. $5^x = \dfrac{1}{625}$

9. $2^{3x-7} = 8^{2x+2}$

10. The atmospheric pressure (in millibars) at a given altitude x (in meters) is approximated by

$$f(x) = 1013e^{-0.0001341x}.$$

Use this function to approximate the atmospheric pressure, to the nearest unit, at each altitude.

  (a) 2000 m   **(b)** 10,000 m

11. Write in logarithmic form: $4^{-2} = 0.0625$.

12. Write in exponential form: $\log_7 49 = 2$.

Solve each equation.

13. $\log_{1/2} x = -5$

14. $x = \log_9 3$

15. $\log_x 16 = 4$

Use the properties of logarithms to express each logarithm as a sum or difference of logarithms. Assume that all variables represent positive real numbers.

16. $\log_3 x^2 y$

17. $\log_5 \left(\dfrac{\sqrt{x}}{yz} \right)$

Use the properties of logarithms to rewrite each expression as a single logarithm. Assume that all variables represent positive real numbers, and that bases are positive numbers not equal to 1.

18. $3 \log_b s - \log_b t$

19. $\dfrac{1}{4} \log_b r + 2 \log_b s - \dfrac{2}{3} \log_b t$

Work each problem.

20. Use a calculator to approximate each logarithm to four decimal places.

   (a) $\log 21.3$ **(b)** $\ln 0.43$ **(c)** $\log_6 45$

21. Solve $3^x = 78$, giving the solution to four decimal places.

22. Solve $\log_8 (x + 5) + \log_8 (x - 2) = \log_8 8$.

23. Suppose that \$10,000 is invested at 3.5% annual interest, compounded quarterly.

   (a) How much will be in the account in 5 yr if no money is withdrawn?

   (b) How long, to the nearest tenth of a year, will it take for the initial principal to double?

24. Suppose that \$15,000 is invested at 3% annual interest, compounded continuously.

   (a) How much will be in the account in 5 yr if no money is withdrawn?

   (b) How long, to the nearest tenth of a year, will it take for the initial principal to double?

25. Use the change-of-base rule to express $\log_3 19$ as described.

   (a) in terms of common logarithms

   (b) in terms of natural logarithms

   (c) approximated to four decimal places

Chapters R–12 *Cumulative Review Exercises*

Let $S = \left\{ -\frac{9}{4}, -2, -\sqrt{2}, 0, 0.6, \sqrt{11}, \sqrt{-8}, 6, \frac{30}{3} \right\}$. *List the elements of S that are elements of each set.*

1. Integers

2. Rational numbers

3. Irrational numbers

Solve each equation or inequality.

4. $7 - (3 + 4x) + 2x = -5(x - 1) - 3$

5. $2x + 2 \le 5x - 1$

6. $|2x - 5| = 9$

7. $|4x + 2| > 10$

8. The graph projects that the number of international travelers to the United States will increase from 51.2 million in 2000 to 90.3 million in 2020.

    (a) Is this the graph of a function?

    (b) What is the slope of the line in the graph? Interpret the slope in the context of international travelers to the United States.

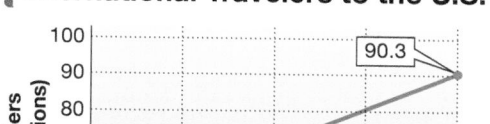

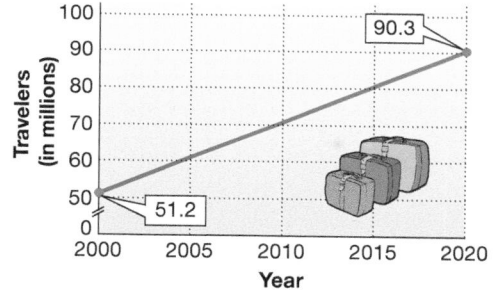

Data from U.S. Department of Commerce.

Solve each system of equations.

9. $5x - 3y = 14$
    $2x + 5y = 18$

10. $x + 2y + 3z = 11$
    $3x - \;\;y + \;\;z = 8$
    $2x + 2y - 3z = -12$

Perform the indicated operations.

11. $(2p + 3)(3p - 1)$

12. $(4k - 3)^2$

13. $(3m^3 + 2m^2 - 5m) - (8m^3 + 2m - 4)$

14. Divide $6t^4 + 17t^3 - 4t^2 + 9t + 4$ by $3t + 1$.

Factor completely.

15. $5z^3 - 19z^2 - 4z$

16. $16a^2 - 25b^4$

17. $8c^3 + d^3$

Perform the indicated operations.

18. $\dfrac{(5p^3)^4(-3p^7)}{2p^2(4p^4)}$

19. $\dfrac{x^2 - 9}{x^2 + 7x + 12} \div \dfrac{x - 3}{x + 5}$

20. $\dfrac{2}{k + 3} - \dfrac{5}{k - 2}$

Simplify.

21. $\sqrt{288}$

22. $\dfrac{-8^{4/3}}{8^2}$

23. $2\sqrt{32} - 5\sqrt{98}$

24. Multiply $(5 + 4i)(5 - 4i)$.

25. Simplify i^{-21}.

Solve each equation or inequality.

26. $\sqrt{2x + 1} - \sqrt{x} = 1$

27. $3x^2 = x + 1$

28. $x^2 + 2x - 8 > 0$

29. $x^4 - 5x^2 + 4 = 0$

30. $5^{x+3} = \left(\dfrac{1}{25}\right)^{3x+2}$

31. $\log_5 x + \log_5 (x + 4) = 1$

32. Write $\log_5 125 = 3$ in exponential form.

33. Rewrite the following using the product, quotient, and power rules for logarithms.

$$\log \dfrac{x^3 \sqrt{y}}{z}$$

Graph.

34. $y = \dfrac{1}{3}(x - 1)^2 + 2$

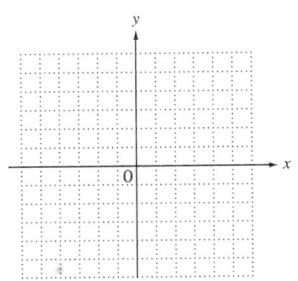

35. $f(x) = 2^x$

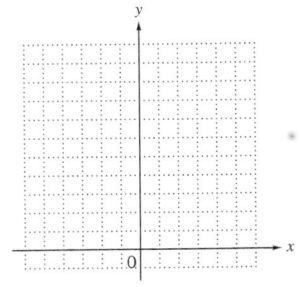

36. $f(x) = \log_3 x$

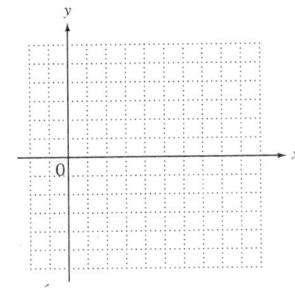

13

Nonlinear Functions, Conic Sections, and Nonlinear Systems

An *ellipse*, one of a group of curves known as *conic sections*, has a special reflecting property responsible for "whispering galleries" like that in the Old House Chamber of the U.S. Capitol. We investigate ellipses in this chapter.

13.1 Additional Graphs of Functions

13.2 Circles and Ellipses

13.3 Hyperbolas and Functions Defined by Radicals

13.4 Nonlinear Systems of Equations

13.5 Second-Degree Inequalities and Systems of Inequalities

13.1 | Additional Graphs of Functions

OBJECTIVES

1. Recognize graphs of the absolute value, reciprocal, and square root functions, and graph their translations.

2. Recognize and graph step functions.

OBJECTIVE ▸ 1 Recognize graphs of the absolute value, reciprocal, and square root functions, and graph their translations. The elementary function $f(x) = |x|$ is the **absolute value function**. This function pairs each real number with its absolute value. Its graph is shown in **Figure 1**.

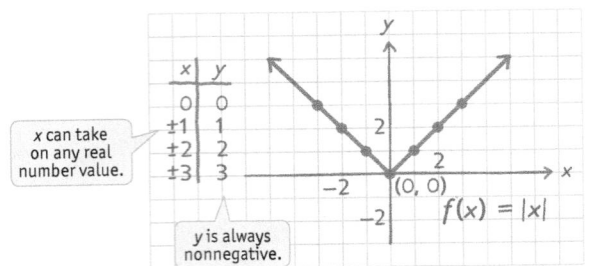

Absolute value function
$$f(x) = |x|$$
Domain: $(-\infty, \infty)$
Range: $[0, \infty)$

Figure 1

Recall that the **reciprocal function** $f(x) = \frac{1}{x}$ pairs every real number except 0 with its reciprocal. Its graph is shown in **Figure 2**. Because x can never equal 0, as x gets closer and closer to 0, $\frac{1}{x}$ approaches either ∞ or $-\infty$. Also, $\frac{1}{x}$ can never equal 0, and as x approaches ∞ or $-\infty$, $\frac{1}{x}$ approaches 0. The axes are **asymptotes** for the function.

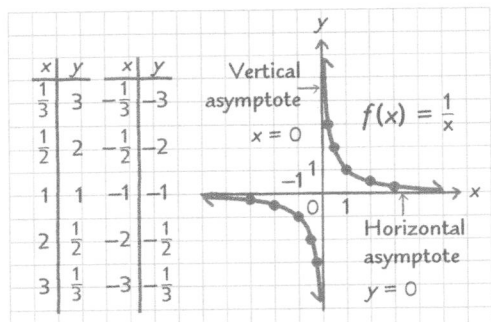

Reciprocal function
$$f(x) = \frac{1}{x}$$
Domain: $(-\infty, 0) \cup (0, \infty)$
Range: $(-\infty, 0) \cup (0, \infty)$

Figure 2

The **square root function** $f(x) = \sqrt{x}$, also introduced earlier, pairs every nonnegative real number with its principal square root. See **Figure 3**.

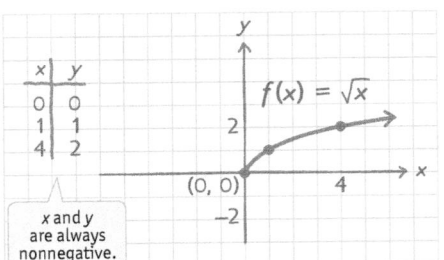

Square root function
$$f(x) = \sqrt{x}$$
Domain: $[0, \infty)$
Range: $[0, \infty)$

Figure 3

The graphs of these elementary functions can be shifted, or translated.

EXAMPLE 1 Applying a Horizontal Shift

Graph $f(x) = |x - 2|$. Give the domain and range.

If $x = 2$, then $f(x) = 0$, which gives the lowest point on the graph $(2, 0)$. The graph of $f(x) = |x - 2|$ has the same shape as that of $f(x) = |x|$ but is *shifted*, or *translated*, 2 units to the right, as shown in **Figure 4.**

x	y
0	2
1	1
2	0
3	1
4	2

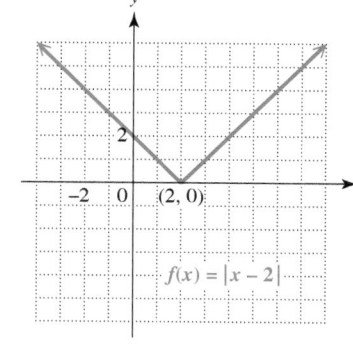

Compare this table of values to that with **Figure 1.**

Domain: $(-\infty, \infty)$
Range: $[0, \infty)$

Figure 4

── Work Problem ❶ at the Side. ▶

As seen in **Example 1,** the graph of

$$y = f(x + h)$$

is a *horizontal* translation of the graph of $y = f(x)$. In **Example 2,** we use the fact that the graph of

$$y = f(x) + k$$

is a *vertical* translation of the graph of $y = f(x)$.

EXAMPLE 2 Applying a Vertical Shift

Graph $f(x) = \frac{1}{x} + 3$. Give the domain and range.

The graph of this function is found by shifting the graph of $y = \frac{1}{x}$ up 3 units. See **Figure 5.**

x	y		x	y
$\frac{1}{3}$	6		$-\frac{1}{3}$	0
$\frac{1}{2}$	5		$-\frac{1}{2}$	1
1	4		-1	2
2	3.5		-2	2.5

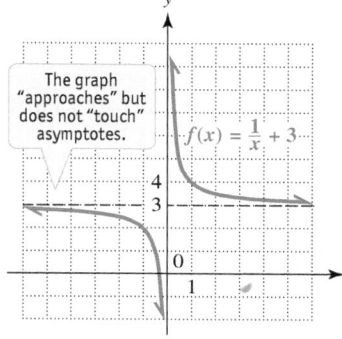

The graph "approaches" but does not "touch" asymptotes.

Compare this table of values to that with **Figure 2.**

Domain:
$(-\infty, 0) \cup (0, \infty)$

Range:
$(-\infty, 3) \cup (3, \infty)$

Vertical asymptote: $x = 0$

Horizontal asymptote: $y = 3$

Figure 5

── Work Problem ❷ at the Side. ▶

❶ Graph $f(x) = \sqrt{x + 4}$. Give the domain and range.

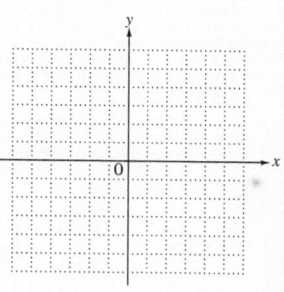

❷ Graph $f(x) = \frac{1}{x} - 2$. Give the domain and range.

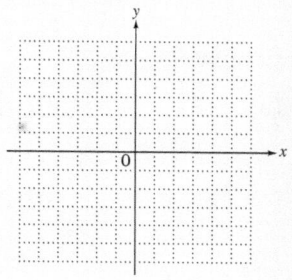

Answers

1.

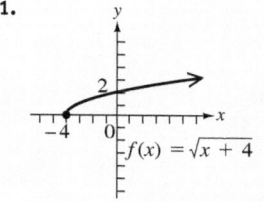

domain: $[-4, \infty)$; range: $[0, \infty)$

2.

$f(x) = \frac{1}{x} - 2$

domain: $(-\infty, 0) \cup (0, \infty)$;
range: $(-\infty, -2) \cup (-2, \infty)$

③ Graph $f(x) = |x + 2| + 1$. Give the domain and range.

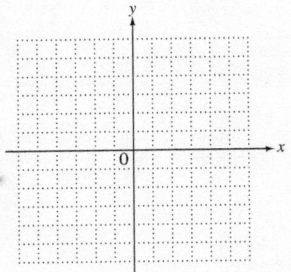

④ Evaluate.

(a) $[\![18]\!]$ (b) $[\![-5]\!]$

(c) $[\![8.7]\!]$ (d) $[\![-6.9]\!]$

(e) $\left[\!\left[1\dfrac{1}{2}\right]\!\right]$ (f) $[\![\pi]\!]$

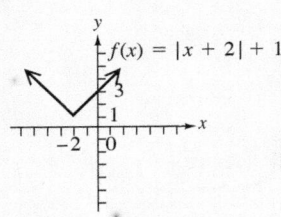
EXAMPLE 3 Applying Both Horizontal and Vertical Shifts

Graph $f(x) = \sqrt{x + 1} - 4$. Give the domain and range.

This graph has the same shape as that of $f(x) = \sqrt{x}$ but is shifted 1 unit to the left (because $x + 1 = 0$ if $x = -1$) and 4 units down (because of the negative sign in -4). See **Figure 6**.

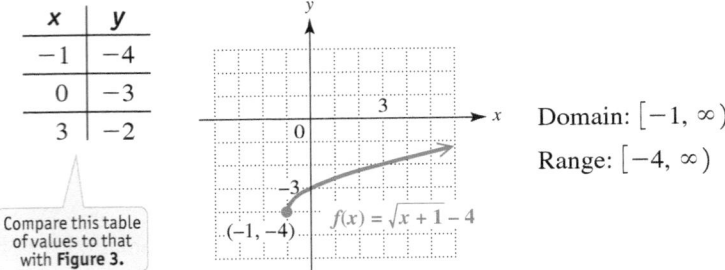

x	y
−1	−4
0	−3
3	−2

Compare this table of values to that with **Figure 3**.

Domain: $[-1, \infty)$

Range: $[-4, \infty)$

$f(x) = \sqrt{x + 1} - 4$

Figure 6

◀ Work Problem **③** at the Side.

OBJECTIVE ➤ ② Recognize and graph step functions. The greatest integer function is defined as follows.

$f(x) = [\![x]\!]$

The **greatest integer function**

$$f(x) = [\![x]\!]$$

pairs every real number x with the greatest integer less than or equal to x.

EXAMPLE 4 Finding the Greatest Integer

Evaluate.

(a) $[\![8]\!] = 8$ (b) $[\![-1]\!] = -1$ (c) $[\![0]\!] = 0$ If x is an integer, then $[\![x]\!] = x$.

(d) $[\![7.45]\!] = 7$ The greatest integer *less than or equal to* 7.45 is 7. This is like "rounding down."

(e) $[\![-2.6]\!] = -3$ Think of a number line with -2.6 graphed on it. Because -3 is to the *left of* (and therefore *less than*) -2.6, the greatest integer less than or equal to -2.6 is -3, **not** -2.

−2.6

◀ Work Problem **④** at the Side.

EXAMPLE 5 Graphing the Greatest Integer Function

Graph $f(x) = [\![x]\!]$. Give the domain and range.

For $[\![x]\!]$, if $-1 \le x < 0$, then $[\![x]\!] = -1$;

if $0 \le x < 1$, then $[\![x]\!] = 0$;

if $1 \le x < 2$, then $[\![x]\!] = 1$;

if $2 \le x < 3$, then $[\![x]\!] = 2$;

if $3 \le x < 4$, then $[\![x]\!] = 3$,   and so on.

Continued on Next Page

The graph, as shown in **Figure 7,** consists of a series of horizontal line segments. In each segment, the left endpoint is included and the right endpoint is excluded. These segments continue indefinitely following this pattern to the left and right. The appearance of the graph is the reason why this function is called a **step function.**

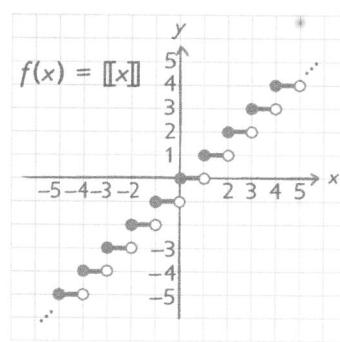

Figure 7

Greatest integer function

$$f(x) = [\![x]\!]$$

Domain: $(-\infty, \infty)$

Range: $\{\ldots, -3, -2, -1, 0, 1, 2, 3, \ldots\}$
(the set of integers)

The ellipsis points indicate that the graph continues indefinitely in the same pattern.

The graph of a step function also may be shifted. For example, the graph of $h(x) = [\![x - 2]\!]$ is the same as the graph of $f(x) = [\![x]\!]$ shifted 2 units to the right. Similarly, the graph of $g(x) = [\![x]\!] + 2$ is the graph of $f(x)$ shifted 2 units up.

—————— Work Problem ⑤ at the Side. ▶

EXAMPLE 6 **Applying a Greatest Integer Function**

An overnight delivery service charges $25 for a package weighing up to 2 lb. For each additional pound or fraction of a pound, there is an additional charge of $3. Let $y = D(x)$ represent the cost to send a package weighing x pounds. Graph $y = D(x)$ for x in the interval $(0, 6]$.

For x in the interval $(0, 2]$, $y = 25$.

For x in the interval $(2, 3]$, $y = 25 + 3 = 28$.

For x in the interval $(3, 4]$, $y = 28 + 3 = 31$.

For x in the interval $(4, 5]$, $y = 31 + 3 = 34$.

For x in the interval $(5, 6]$, $y = 34 + 3 = 37$.

The graph, which is that of a step function, is shown in **Figure 8.**

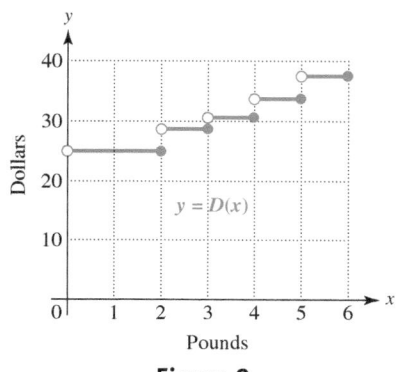

Figure 8

—————— Work Problem ⑥ at the Side. ▶

⑤ Graph $f(x) = [\![x + 1]\!]$. Give the domain and range.

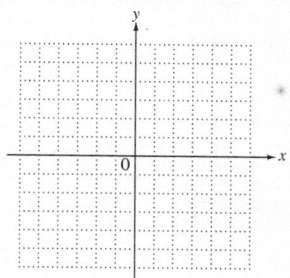

⑥ Suppose that the post office charges $0.80 per oz (or fraction of an ounce) to mail a letter to Europe. Let $y = f(x)$ represent the cost to mail a letter weighing x ounces. Graph $y = f(x)$ for x in the interval $(0, 4]$.

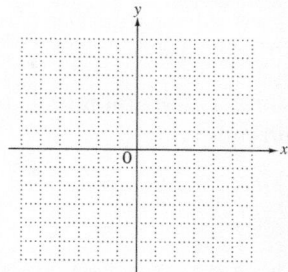

Answers

5.

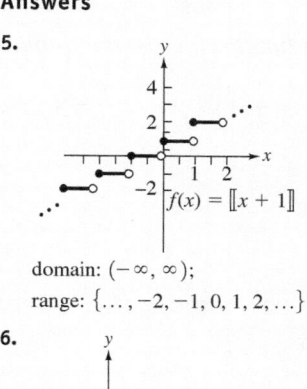

domain: $(-\infty, \infty)$;
range: $\{\ldots, -2, -1, 0, 1, 2, \ldots\}$

6.

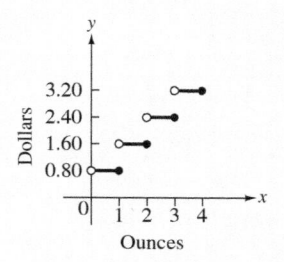

13.1 Exercises

FOR EXTRA HELP

Go to MyMathLab *for worked-out, step-by-step solutions to exercises enclosed in a square* ▢ *and video solutions to* ▶ *exercises.*

CONCEPT CHECK *Refer to the basic graphs in A–F to answer each of the following.*

A.
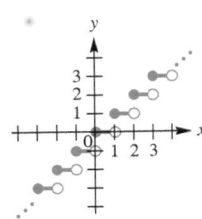

B.
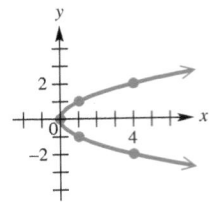

C.
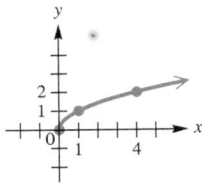

D.
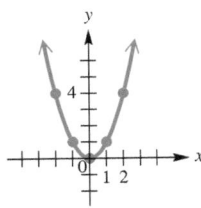

E.
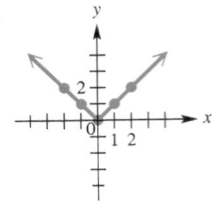

F.
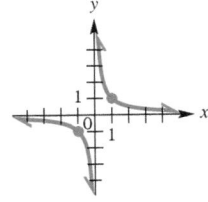

1. Which is the graph of $f(x) = |x|$? The lowest point on its graph has coordinates (____, ____).

2. Which is the graph of $f(x) = x^2$? Give the domain and range.

3. Which is the graph of $f(x) = [\![x]\!]$? Give the domain and range.

4. Which is the graph of $f(x) = \sqrt{x}$? Give the domain and range.

5. Which is not the graph of a function? Why?

6. Which is the graph of $f(x) = \frac{1}{x}$? The lines with equations $x = 0$ and $y = 0$ are its _____.

Graph each function. Give the domain and range. ***See Examples 1–3.***

7. $f(x) = |x + 1|$
▶
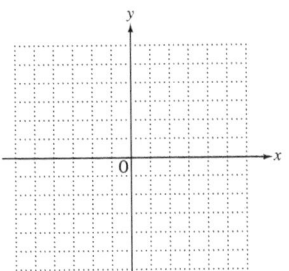

8. $f(x) = |x - 1|$
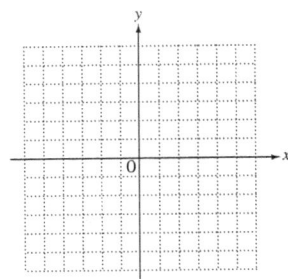

9. $f(x) = \frac{1}{x} + 1$
▶
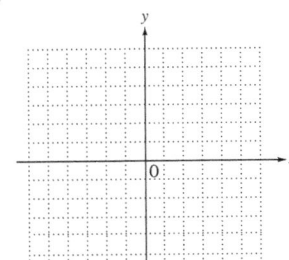

10. $f(x) = \frac{1}{x} - 1$
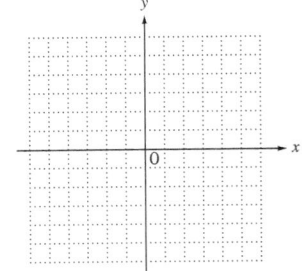

11. $f(x) = \sqrt{x - 2}$

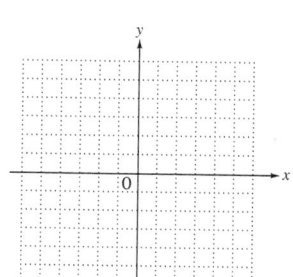

12. $f(x) = \sqrt{x + 5}$

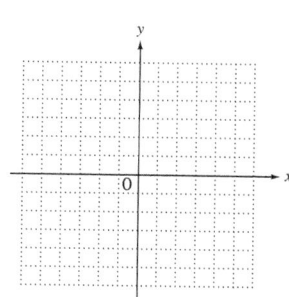

13. $f(x) = \dfrac{1}{x - 2}$

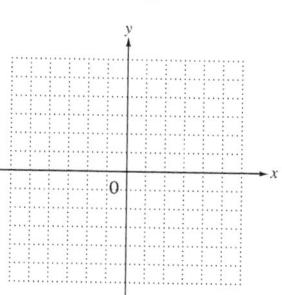

14. $f(x) = \dfrac{1}{x + 2}$

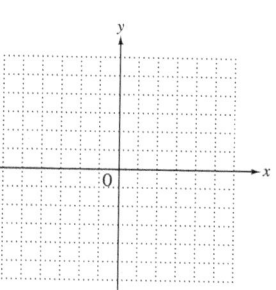

15. $f(x) = \sqrt{x + 3} - 3$

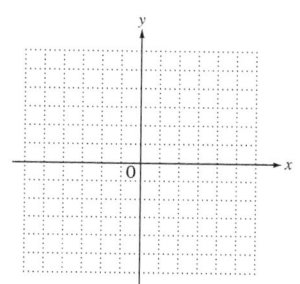

16. $f(x) = \sqrt{x - 2} + 2$

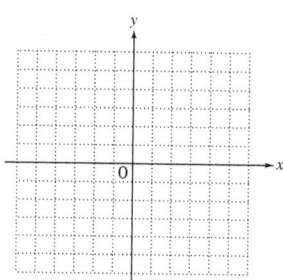

17. $f(x) = |x - 3| + 1$

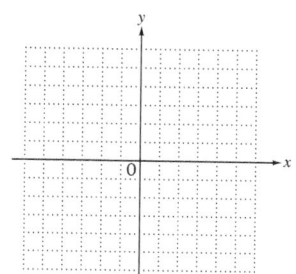

18. $f(x) = |x + 1| - 4$

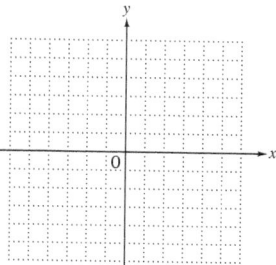

CONCEPT CHECK *Without actually plotting points, match each function with its graph from choices A–D.*

19. $f(x) = |x - 2| + 2$

20. $f(x) = |x + 2| + 2$

21. $f(x) = |x - 2| - 2$

22. $f(x) = |x + 2| - 2$

A.

B.

C.

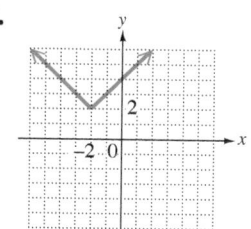

D.

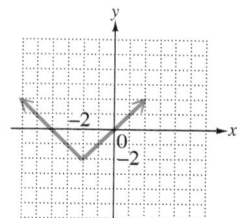

23. CONCEPT CHECK How is the graph of
$$f(x) = \dfrac{1}{x - 3} + 2$$
obtained from the graph of $g(x) = \frac{1}{x}$?

24. CONCEPT CHECK How is the graph of
$$f(x) = \dfrac{1}{x + 5} - 3$$
obtained from the graph of $g(x) = \frac{1}{x}$?

Evaluate each expression. ***See Example 4.***

25. $[\![3]\!]$

26. $[\![28]\!]$

27. $[\![4.5]\!]$

28. $[\![7.6]\!]$

29. $\left[\!\!\left[\dfrac{1}{2}\right]\!\!\right]$

30. $\left[\!\!\left[\dfrac{3}{4}\right]\!\!\right]$

31. $\left[\!\!\left[\dfrac{8}{3}\right]\!\!\right]$

32. $\left[\!\!\left[\dfrac{5}{2}\right]\!\!\right]$

33. $[\![-14]\!]$

34. $[\![-10]\!]$

35. $[\![-10.1]\!]$

36. $[\![-6.5]\!]$

Graph each step function. ***See Example 5.***

37. $f(x) = [\![x - 3]\!]$

38. $g(x) = [\![x + 2]\!]$

39. $f(x) = [\![x]\!] - 1$

40. $f(x) = [\![x]\!] + 1$

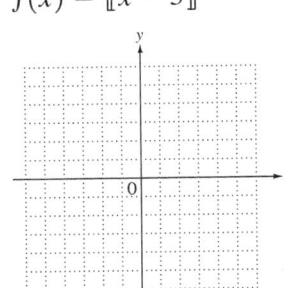
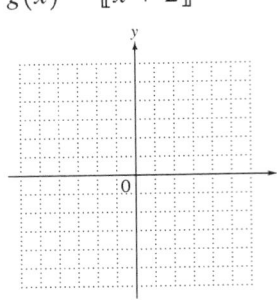
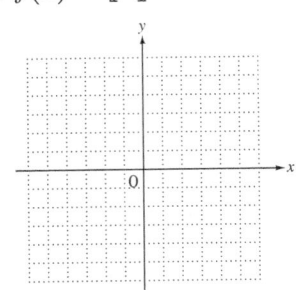
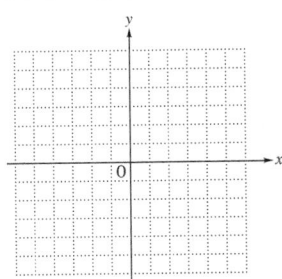

Solve each problem. ***See Example 6.***

41. Suppose that postage rates are $0.55 for the first ounce, plus $0.24 for each additional ounce, and that each letter carries one $0.55 stamp and as many $0.24 stamps as necessary. Graph the function

$$y = p(x) = \text{the number of stamps}$$

on a letter weighing x ounces. Use the interval $(0, 5\,]$.

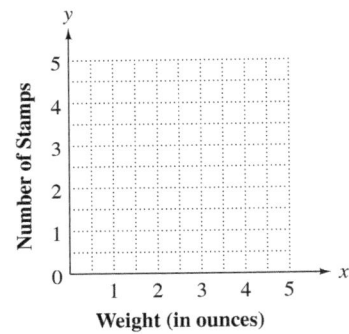

42. The cost of parking a car at an airport hourly parking lot is $3 for the first half-hour and $2 for each additional half-hour or fraction thereof. Graph the function

$$y = f(x) = \text{the cost of parking a car}$$

for x hours. Use the interval $(0, 2\,]$.

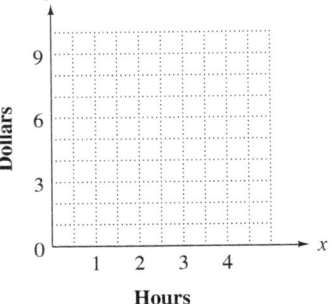

43. A certain long-distance carrier provides service between Podunk and Nowhereville. If x represents the number of minutes for the call, where $x > 0$, then the function

$$f(x) = 0.40 [\![x]\!] + 0.75$$

gives the total cost of the call in dollars. Find the cost of a 5.5-minute call.

44. Total rental cost in dollars for a power washer, where x represents the number of hours with $x > 0$, can be represented by the function

$$f(x) = 12 [\![x]\!] + 25.$$

Find the cost of a $7\frac{1}{2}$ hr rental.

13.2 | Circles and Ellipses

When an infinite cone is intersected by a plane, the resulting figure is a **conic section.** A parabola is one example of a conic section. Circles, ellipses, and hyperbolas may also result. See **Figure 9.**

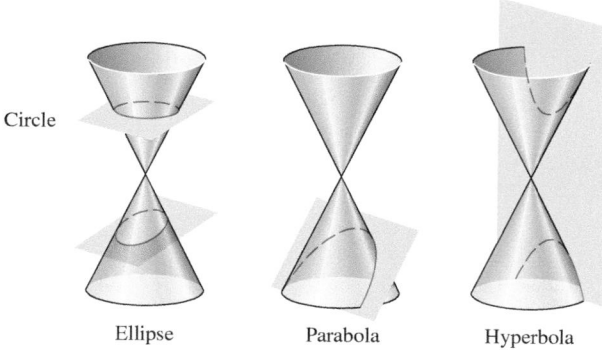

Circle

Ellipse   Parabola   Hyperbola

Figure 9

OBJECTIVE ▸ 1 **Find an equation of a circle given its center and radius.** A **circle** is the set of all points in a plane that lie a fixed distance from a fixed point. The fixed point is the **center,** and the fixed distance is the **radius.** We use the distance formula to find an equation of a circle.

EXAMPLE 1   Finding an Equation of a Circle and Graphing It

Find an equation of the circle with radius 3 and center at $(0, 0)$, and graph it.

If the point (x, y) is on the circle, then the distance from (x, y) to the center $(0, 0)$ is the radius 3.

$$\sqrt{(x_2 - x_1)^2 + (y_2 - y_1)^2} = d \quad \text{Distance formula}$$

$$\sqrt{(x - 0)^2 + (y - 0)^2} = 3 \quad \text{Let } x_1 = 0, y_1 = 0, \text{ and } d = 3.$$

$$\left(\sqrt{x^2 + y^2}\right)^2 = 3^2 \quad \text{Square each side.}$$

$$x^2 + y^2 = 9 \quad \left(\sqrt{a}\right)^2 = a$$

An equation of this circle is $x^2 + y^2 = 9$. The graph is shown in **Figure 10.**

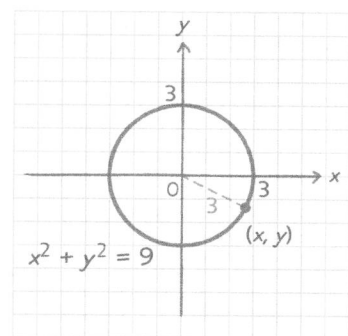

Figure 10

───── Work Problem **1** at the Side. ▸

OBJECTIVES

1 Find an equation of a circle given its center and radius.

2 Determine the center and radius of a circle given its equation.

3 Recognize the equation of an ellipse.

4 Graph ellipses.

1 Find an equation of the circle with radius 4 and center $(0, 0)$, and graph it.

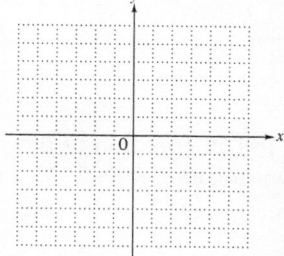

Answer

1. $x^2 + y^2 = 16$

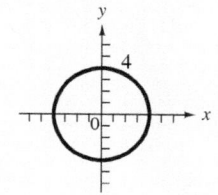

2 Find an equation of the circle with center at $(3, -2)$ and radius 3, and graph it.

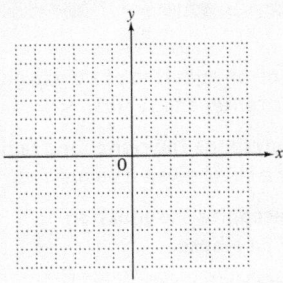

3 Find an equation of the circle with center at $(-5, 4)$ and radius $\sqrt{6}$.

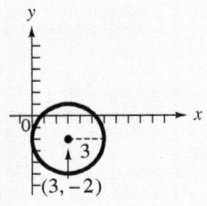

EXAMPLE 2 Finding an Equation of a Circle and Graphing It

Find an equation of the circle with center at $(4, -3)$ and radius 5, and graph it.

$$\sqrt{(x_2 - x_1)^2 + (y_2 - y_1)^2} = d \qquad \text{Distance formula}$$

$$\sqrt{(x - 4)^2 + [y - (-3)]^2} = 5 \qquad \text{Let } x_1 = 4, y_1 = -3, \text{ and } d = 5.$$

$$(x - 4)^2 + (y + 3)^2 = 25 \qquad \text{Square each side.}$$

To graph the circle, locate the center $(4, -3)$, and then, because the radius is 5, move 5 units right, left, up, and down from the center, plotting the points

$$(9, -3), \quad (-1, -3), \quad (4, 2), \quad \text{and} \quad (4, -8).$$

Draw a smooth curve through these four points. When graphing by hand, it is helpful to sketch one quarter of the circle at a time. See **Figure 11.**

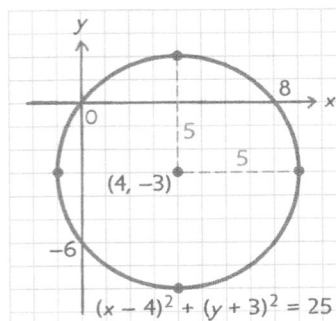

Figure 11

When graphing a circle, the center is not part of the actual graph. It provides help in drawing a more accurate graph.

◀ **Work Problem 2** at the Side.

Examples 1 and 2 suggest the form of an equation of a circle with radius r and center at (h, k). If (x, y) is a point on the circle, then the distance from the center (h, k) to the point (x, y) is r. See **Figure 12.** By the distance formula,

$$\sqrt{(x - h)^2 + (y - k)^2} = r.$$

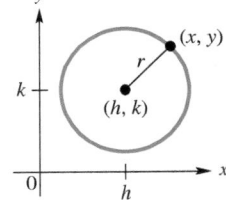

Figure 12

Squaring each side gives the **center-radius form** of the equation of a circle.

Equation of a Circle (Center-Radius Form)

A circle with center (h, k) and radius $r > 0$ has an equation of the form
$$(x - h)^2 + (y - k)^2 = r^2.$$

EXAMPLE 3 Using the Center-Radius Form of the Equation of a Circle

Find an equation of the circle with center at $(-1, 2)$ and radius $\sqrt{7}$.

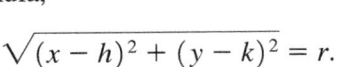
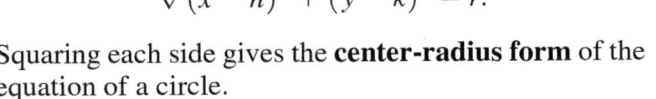

$$(x - h)^2 + (y - k)^2 = r^2 \qquad \text{Center-radius form}$$

$$[x - (-1)]^2 + (y - 2)^2 = (\sqrt{7})^2 \qquad \text{Let } h = -1, k = 2, \text{ and } r = \sqrt{7}.$$

$$(x + 1)^2 + (y - 2)^2 = 7 \qquad \text{Simplify; } (\sqrt{a})^2 = a$$

Pay attention to signs here.

◀ **Work Problem 3** at the Side

Note

If a circle has its center at the origin $(0, 0)$ and radius r, then its equation is as follows.

$$(x - 0)^2 + (y - 0)^2 = r^2 \quad \text{Let } h = 0, k = 0 \text{ in the center-radius form.}$$

$$\boldsymbol{x^2 + y^2 = r^2} \quad \text{See Example 1.}$$

OBJECTIVE **2** **Determine the center and radius of a circle given its equation.** In the equation found in **Example 2,** multiplying out $(x - 4)^2$ and $(y + 3)^2$ and then combining like terms gives the following.

$$(x - 4)^2 + (y + 3)^2 = 25 \quad \text{Circle from \textbf{Example 2}}$$

$$x^2 - 8x + 16 + y^2 + 6y + 9 = 25 \quad \text{Square each binomial.}$$

$$x^2 + y^2 - 8x + 6y = 0 \quad \text{Subtract 25.}$$

This general form suggests that an equation with both x^2- and y^2-terms that have equal coefficients may represent a circle.

EXAMPLE 4 **Completing the Square to Find the Center and Radius**

Find the center and radius of the circle $x^2 + y^2 + 2x + 6y - 15 = 0$, and graph it.

Since the equation has an x^2-term and a y^2-term with equal coefficients, its graph might be that of a circle. To find the center and radius, complete the squares on x and y.

$$x^2 + y^2 + 2x + 6y = 15 \qquad \text{Transform so that the constant is on the right.}$$

$$(x^2 + 2x \quad) + (y^2 + 6y \quad) = 15 \qquad \text{Rewrite in anticipation of completing the square.}$$

$$\left[\frac{1}{2}(2)\right]^2 = 1 \quad \left[\frac{1}{2}(6)\right]^2 = 9 \qquad \text{Square half the coefficient of each middle term.}$$

$$(x^2 + 2x + 1) + (y^2 + 6y + 9) = 15 + 1 + 9 \qquad \text{Complete the squares on both } x \text{ and } y.$$

$$(x + 1)^2 + (y + 3)^2 = 25 \qquad \text{Factor on the left. Add on the right.}$$

$$[x - (-1)]^2 + [y - (-3)]^2 = 5^2 \qquad \text{Center-radius form}$$

The graph is a circle with center at $(-1, -3)$ and radius 5. See **Figure 13.**

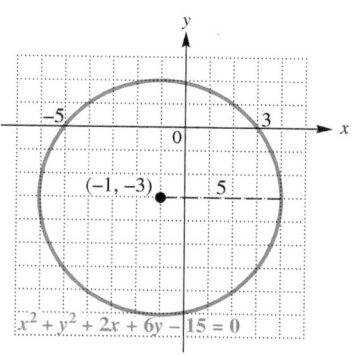

Figure 13

Work Problem **4** at the Side. ▶

4 Find the center and radius of the circle with equation

$$x^2 + y^2 - 10x + 4y + 20 = 0,$$

and graph it.

Answer

4. center: $(5, -2)$; radius: 3

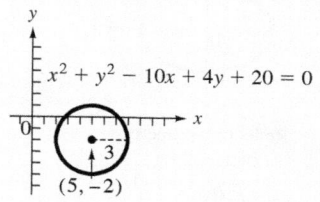

Note

There are three possibilities for the graph of an equation of the form

$$(x - h)^2 + (y - k)^2 = m, \quad \text{where } m \text{ is a constant.}$$

1. If $m > 0$, then $r^2 = m$, and the graph of the equation is a circle with radius $\sqrt{m}$.
2. If $m = 0$, then the graph of the equation is the single point (h, k).
3. If $m < 0$, then no points satisfy the equation, and the graph is non-existent.

OBJECTIVE ▸ 3 **Recognize the equation of an ellipse.** An **ellipse** is the set of all points in a plane the *sum* of whose distances from two fixed points is constant. These fixed points are the **foci** (singular: *focus*). The ellipse in **Figure 14** has foci $(c, 0)$ and $(-c, 0)$, with x-intercepts $(a, 0)$ and $(-a, 0)$ and y-intercepts $(0, b)$ and $(0, -b)$. It can be shown in more advanced courses that $c^2 = a^2 - b^2$ for an ellipse of this type. The origin is the **center** of the ellipse.

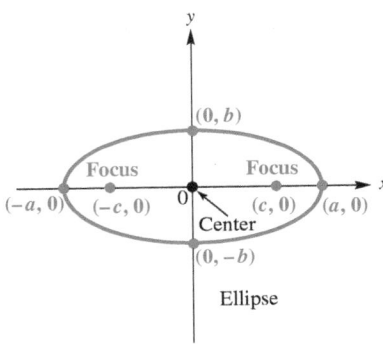

Figure 14

An ellipse centered at the origin has the following equation.

Equation of an Ellipse

An ellipse with x-intercepts $(a, 0)$ and $(-a, 0)$ and y-intercepts $(0, b)$ and $(0, -b)$ has an equation of the form

$$\frac{x^2}{a^2} + \frac{y^2}{b^2} = 1.$$

Note

A circle is a special case of an ellipse, where $a^2 = b^2$.

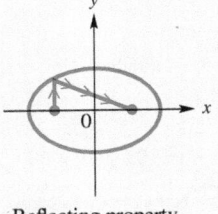

Reflecting property
of an ellipse

Figure 15

When a ray of light or sound emanating from one focus of an ellipse bounces off the ellipse, it passes through the other focus. See **Figure 15**. This reflecting property is responsible for whispering galleries. In the Old House Chamber of the U.S. Capitol, John Quincy Adams was able to listen in on his opponents' conversations—his desk was positioned at one of the foci beneath the ellipsoidal ceiling, and his opponents were located across the room at the other focus. (See the chapter opener photo.)

Elliptical bicycle gears are designed to respond to the legs' natural strengths and weaknesses. At the top and bottom of the powerstroke, where the legs have the least leverage, the gear offers little resistance, but as the gear rotates, the resistance increases. This allows the legs to apply more power where it is most naturally available. See **Figure 16.**

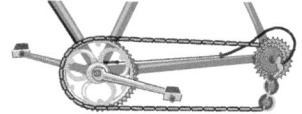

Figure 16

OBJECTIVE ▶ **4** **Graph ellipses.** To graph an ellipse centered at the origin, we plot the four intercepts and sketch the ellipse through those points.

EXAMPLE 5 **Graphing Ellipses**

Graph each ellipse.

(a) $\dfrac{x^2}{49} + \dfrac{y^2}{36} = 1$

Here, $a^2 = 49$, so $a = 7$, and the x-intercepts for this ellipse are $(7, 0)$ and $(-7, 0)$. Similarly, $b^2 = 36$, so $b = 6$, and the y-intercepts for this ellipse are $(0, 6)$ and $(0, -6)$. Plotting the intercepts and sketching the ellipse through them gives the graph in **Figure 17.**

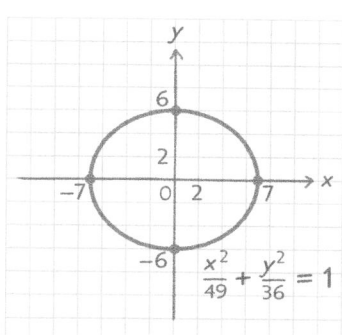

Figure 17

(b) $\dfrac{x^2}{36} + \dfrac{y^2}{121} = 1$

The x-intercepts for this ellipse are $(6, 0)$ and $(-6, 0)$, and the y-intercepts are $(0, 11)$ and $(0, -11)$. Join these intercepts with the smooth curve of an ellipse. See **Figure 18.**

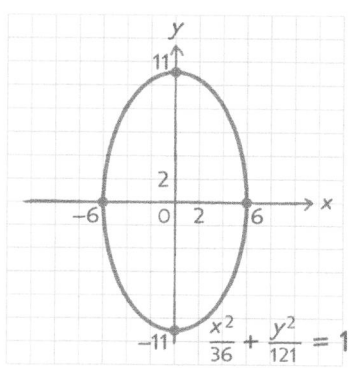

Figure 18

Work Problem **5** at the Side. ▶

5 Graph each ellipse.

(a) $\dfrac{x^2}{64} + \dfrac{y^2}{49} = 1$

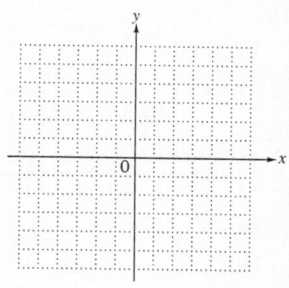

(b) $\dfrac{x^2}{4} + \dfrac{y^2}{25} = 1$

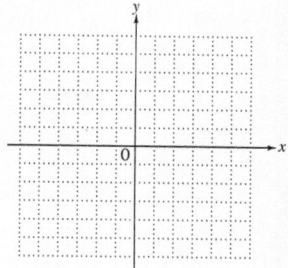

Answers

5. (a)

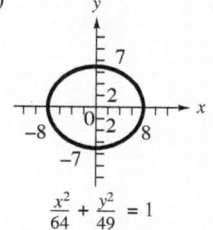

$\dfrac{x^2}{64} + \dfrac{y^2}{49} = 1$

(b)

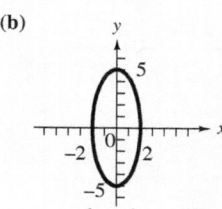

$\dfrac{x^2}{4} + \dfrac{y^2}{25} = 1$

6 Graph

$$\frac{(x+4)^2}{16} + \frac{(y-1)^2}{36} = 1.$$

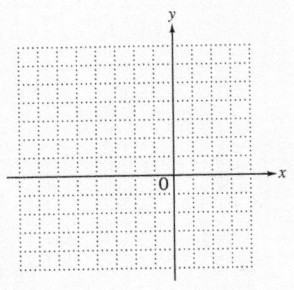

> **!** **CAUTION**
> Hand-drawn graphs of ellipses are smooth curves that show symmetry with respect to the center.

EXAMPLE 6 **Graphing an Ellipse Shifted Horizontally and Vertically**

Graph $\dfrac{(x-2)^2}{25} + \dfrac{(y+3)^2}{49} = 1.$

Just as $(x-2)^2$ and $(y+3)^2$ would indicate that the center of a circle would be $(2, -3)$, so it is with this ellipse. **Figure 19** shows that the graph goes through the four points

$$(2, 4), \quad (7, -3), \quad (2, -10), \quad \text{and} \quad (-3, -3).$$

The x-values of these points are found by adding $\pm a = \pm 5$ to 2 (the x-value of the center). The y-values are found by adding $\pm b = \pm 7$ to -3 (the y-value of the center).

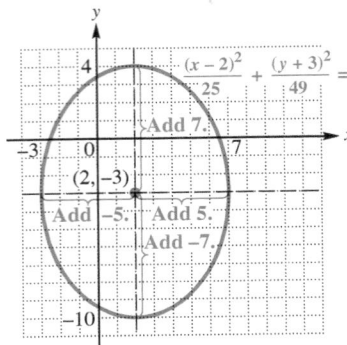

Figure 19

Again, the center is not part of the actual graph, but provides help in drawing a more accurate graph.

◄ **Work Problem 6** at the Side.

> **Note**
>
> ***Graphs of circles and ellipses are not graphs of functions**—they fail to* meet the conditions of the vertical line test. The only conic section whose graph represents a function is the vertical parabola with equation
>
> $$f(x) = ax^2 + bx + c.$$

Answer

6.

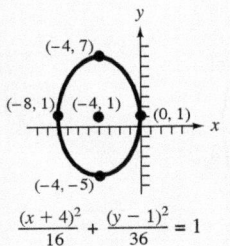

$$\frac{(x+4)^2}{16} + \frac{(y-1)^2}{36} = 1$$

13.2 Exercises

FOR EXTRA HELP

Go to MyMathLab *for worked-out, step-by-step solutions to exercises enclosed in a square* [ ] *and video solutions to* ▶ *exercises.*

CONCEPT CHECK *Match each equation with the correct graph.*

1. $(x - 3)^2 + (y - 2)^2 = 25$

A.
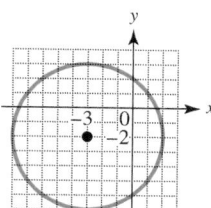

B.
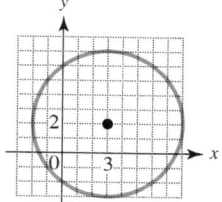

2. $(x - 3)^2 + (y + 2)^2 = 25$

3. $(x + 3)^2 + (y - 2)^2 = 25$

C.
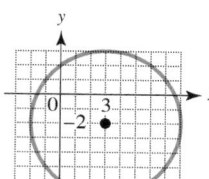

D.
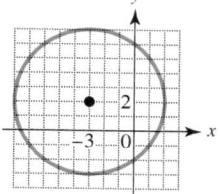

4. $(x + 3)^2 + (y + 2)^2 = 25$

5. Consider the circle whose equation is
$$x^2 + y^2 = 25.$$

(a) What are the coordinates of its center?

(b) What is its radius?

(c) Sketch its graph.

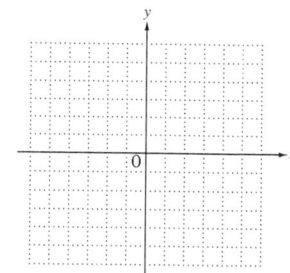

6. Why does a set of points defined by a circle *not* satisfy the definition of a function.

Find an equation of a circle satisfying the given conditions. ***See Examples 1–3.***

7. Center: $(0, 0)$; radius: 1

8. Center: $(0, 0)$; radius: 6

9. Center: $(0, 0)$; radius: $\sqrt{3}$

10. Center: $(0, 0)$; radius: $\sqrt{11}$

11. Center: $(-4, 3)$; radius: 2

12. Center: $(5, -2)$; radius: 4

13. Center: $(1, 0)$; radius: 3

14. Center: $(3, 0)$; radius: 2

15. Center: $(0, 4)$; radius: 6

16. Center: $(0, 7)$; radius: 10

17. Center: $(-8, -5)$; radius: $\sqrt{5}$

18. Center: $(-12, 13)$; radius: $\sqrt{7}$

Find the center and radius of each circle. (Hint: In Exercises 23 and 24, divide each side by a common factor.) ***See Example 4.***

19. $x^2 + y^2 + 4x + 6y + 9 = 0$

20. $x^2 + y^2 - 8x - 12y + 3 = 0$

21. $x^2 + y^2 + 10x - 14y - 7 = 0$

22. $x^2 + y^2 - 2x + 4y - 4 = 0$

23. $3x^2 + 3y^2 - 12x - 24y + 12 = 0$

24. $2x^2 + 2y^2 + 20x + 16y + 10 = 0$

Graph each circle. Identify the center and the radius. ***See Examples 1, 2, and 4.***

25. $x^2 + y^2 = 4$

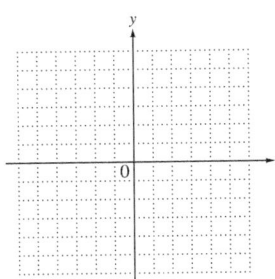

26. $x^2 + y^2 = 16$

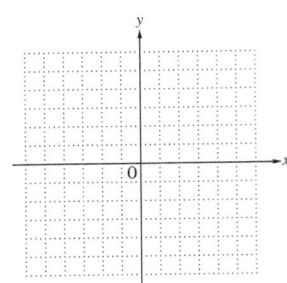

27. $3x^2 = 30 - 3y^2$

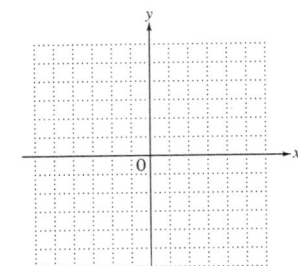

28. $2y^2 = 10 - 2x^2$

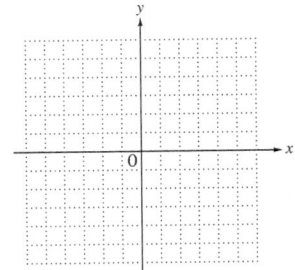

29. $(x - 1)^2 + (y + 2)^2 = 16$

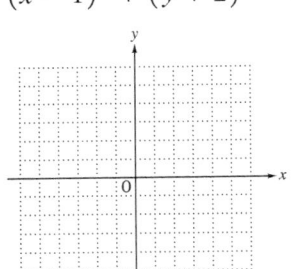

30. $(x + 3)^2 + (y - 2)^2 = 9$

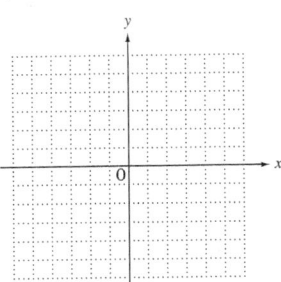

31. $(x + 2)^2 + y^2 = 9$

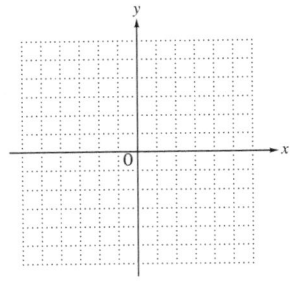

32. $x^2 + (y - 1)^2 = 4$

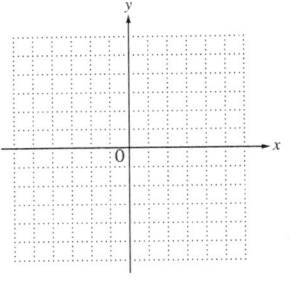

33. $x^2 + y^2 + 2x + 2y - 23 = 0$

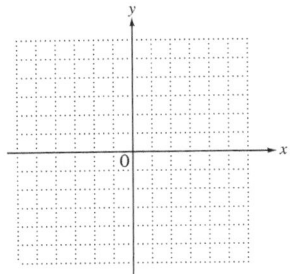

34. $x^2 + y^2 - 4x - 6y + 9 = 0$

35. $x^2 + y^2 + 6x - 6y + 9 = 0$

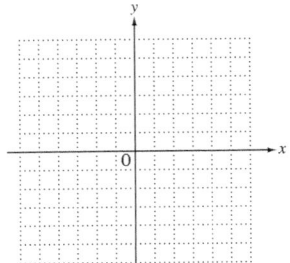

36. $x^2 + y^2 - 4x + 6y + 4 = 0$

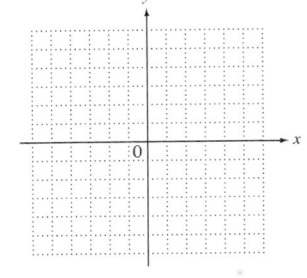

Write a short answer to each question.

37. A circle can be drawn on a piece of posterboard by fastening one end of a length of string with a thumbtack, pulling the string taut with a pencil, and tracing a curve, as shown in the figure. Why does this method work?

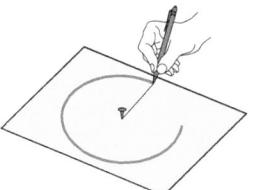

38. An ellipse can be drawn on a piece of posterboard by fastening two ends of a length of string with thumbtacks, pulling the string taut with a pencil, and tracing a curve, as shown in the figure. Why does this method work?

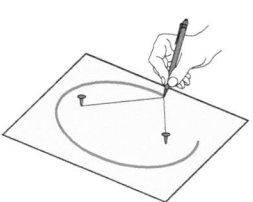

Graph each ellipse. **See Examples 5 and 6.**

39. $\dfrac{x^2}{9} + \dfrac{y^2}{25} = 1$

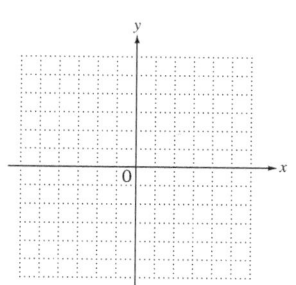

40. $\dfrac{x^2}{9} + \dfrac{y^2}{16} = 1$

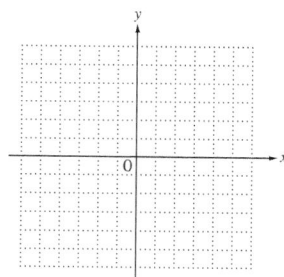

41. $\dfrac{x^2}{36} + \dfrac{y^2}{16} = 1$

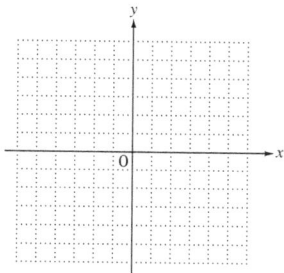

42. $\dfrac{x^2}{9} + \dfrac{y^2}{4} = 1$

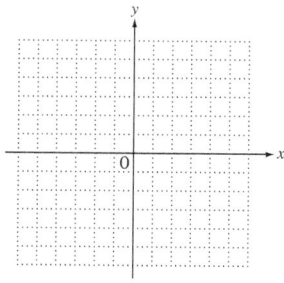

43. $\dfrac{x^2}{25} + \dfrac{y^2}{4} = 1$

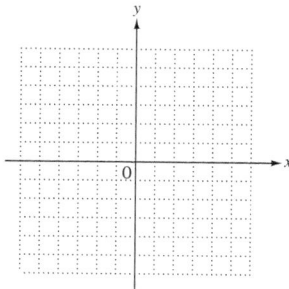

44. $\dfrac{x^2}{16} + \dfrac{y^2}{9} = 1$

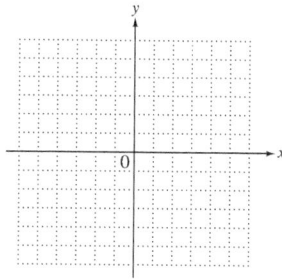

45. $\dfrac{(x-2)^2}{16} + \dfrac{(y-1)^2}{9} = 1$

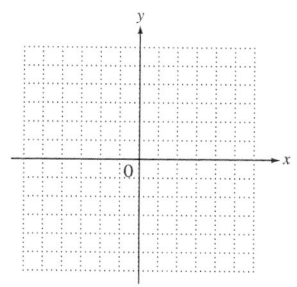

46. $\dfrac{(x-3)^2}{9} + \dfrac{(y+2)^2}{4} = 1$

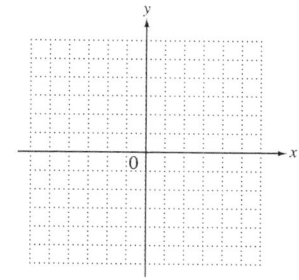

47. $\dfrac{(x+1)^2}{16} + \dfrac{y^2}{4} = 1$

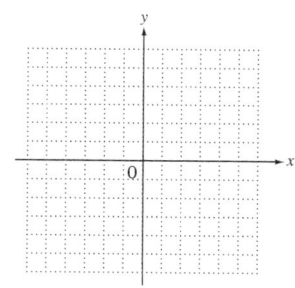

48. $\dfrac{x^2}{9} + \dfrac{(y+1)^2}{25} = 1$

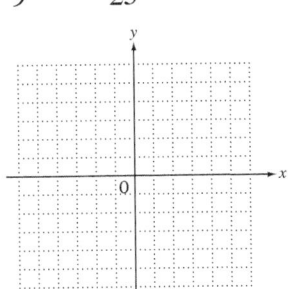

49. $\dfrac{(x+3)^2}{4} + \dfrac{(y-1)^2}{25} = 1$

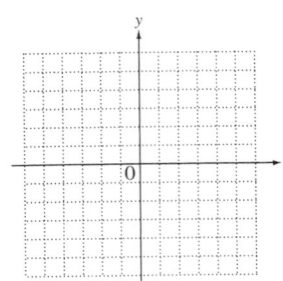

50. $\dfrac{(x+2)^2}{16} + \dfrac{(y+1)^2}{25} = 1$

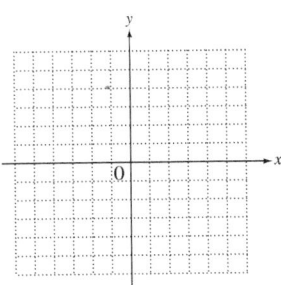

Solve each problem.

51. An arch has the shape of half an ellipse. The equation of the complete ellipse, where x and y are in meters, is $100x^2 + 324y^2 = 32,400$.

    (a) How high is the center of the arch?

    (b) How wide is the arch across the bottom?

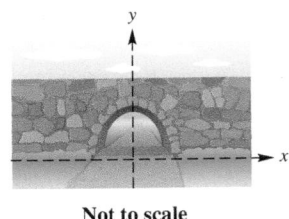

Not to scale

52. A one-way street passes under an overpass, which is in the form of the top half of an ellipse, as shown in the figure. Suppose that a truck 12 ft wide passes directly under the overpass. What is the maximum possible height of this truck?

15 ft

20 ft

Not to scale

*A **lithotripter** is a machine used to crush kidney stones using shock waves. The patient is placed in an elliptical tub with the kidney stone at one focus of the ellipse. A beam is projected from the other focus to the tub, so that it reflects to hit the kidney stone. See the figure.*

53. Suppose a lithotripter is based on the ellipse with equation

$$\frac{x^2}{36} + \frac{y^2}{9} = 1.$$

How far from the center of the ellipse must the kidney stone and the source of the beam be placed? (*Hint:* Use the fact that $c^2 = a^2 - b^2$, because $a > b$ here.)

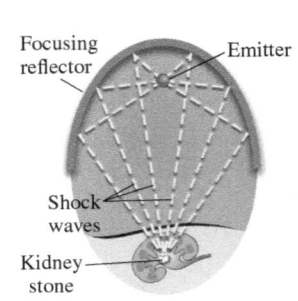

Focusing reflector   Emitter

Shock waves

Kidney stone

The top of an ellipse is illustrated in this depiction of how a lithotripter crushes a kidney stone.

54. Rework **Exercise 53** if the equation of the ellipse is

$$9x^2 + 4y^2 = 36.$$

(*Hint:* Write the equation in fractional form by dividing each term by 36, and use $c^2 = b^2 - a^2$ because $b > a$ here.)

13.3 Hyperbolas and Functions Defined by Radicals

OBJECTIVE ➊ Recognize the equation of a hyperbola. A **hyperbola** is the set of all points in a plane such that the absolute value of the *difference* of the distances from two fixed points (the *foci*) is constant. The graph of a hyperbola has two parts, or *branches,* and two intercepts (or *vertices*) that lie on its axis, called the **transverse axis.**

The hyperbola in **Figure 20** has a horizontal transverse axis, with foci $(c, 0)$ and $(-c, 0)$ and x-intercepts $(a, 0)$ and $(-a, 0)$. (A hyperbola with vertical transverse axis would have its intercepts on the y-axis.)

A hyperbola centered at the origin has one of the following equations. (It is shown in more advanced courses that for a hyperbola, $c^2 = a^2 + b^2$.)

OBJECTIVES

➊ **Recognize the equation of a hyperbola.**

➋ **Graph hyperbolas by using asymptotes.**

➌ **Identify conic sections by their equations.**

➍ **Graph generalized square root functions.**

Equations of Hyperbolas

A hyperbola with x-intercepts $(a, 0)$ and $(-a, 0)$ has equation

$$\frac{x^2}{a^2} - \frac{y^2}{b^2} = 1. \quad \text{Transverse axis on } x\text{-axis}$$

A hyperbola with y-intercepts $(0, b)$ and $(0, -b)$ has equation

$$\frac{y^2}{b^2} - \frac{x^2}{a^2} = 1. \quad \text{Transverse axis on } y\text{-axis}$$

OBJECTIVE ➋ Graph hyperbolas by using asymptotes. The two branches of the graph of a hyperbola approach a pair of intersecting straight lines, which are its *asymptotes.* (See **Figures 21 and 22** on the next page.)

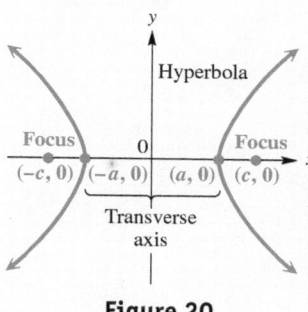

Figure 20

Asymptotes of Hyperbolas

The extended diagonals of a rectangle, called the **fundamental rectangle,** with vertices (corners) at the points (a, b), $(-a, b)$, $(-a, -b)$, and $(a, -b)$ are the **asymptotes** of the hyperbolas

$$\frac{x^2}{a^2} - \frac{y^2}{b^2} = 1 \quad \text{and} \quad \frac{y^2}{b^2} - \frac{x^2}{a^2} = 1.$$

Graphing a Hyperbola

Step 1 Find and locate the intercepts.
- At $(a, 0)$ and $(-a, 0)$ if the x^2-term has a positive coefficient
- At $(0, b)$ and $(0, -b)$ if the y^2-term has a positive coefficient

Step 2 Find the fundamental rectangle. Its vertices will be located at the points (a, b), $(-a, b)$, $(-a, -b)$, and $(a, -b)$.

Step 3 Sketch the asymptotes. The extended diagonals of the fundamental rectangle are the asymptotes of the hyperbola. They have equations $y = \pm\frac{b}{a}x$.

Step 4 Draw the graph. Sketch each branch of the hyperbola through an intercept, approaching (but not touching) the asymptotes.

1 Graph $\dfrac{x^2}{4} - \dfrac{y^2}{25} = 1$.

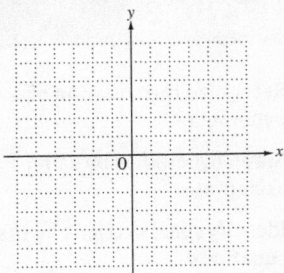

EXAMPLE 1 Graphing a Horizontal Hyperbola

Graph $\dfrac{x^2}{16} - \dfrac{y^2}{25} = 1$.

Step 1 Here $a = 4$ and $b = 5$. The x-intercepts are $(4, 0)$ and $(-4, 0)$.

Step 2 The vertices of the fundamental rectangle are the four points

$$(a, b) \quad (-a, b) \quad (-a, -b) \quad (a, -b)$$
$$\downarrow\downarrow \quad\quad \downarrow\downarrow \quad\quad \downarrow\downarrow \quad\quad \downarrow\downarrow$$
$$(4, 5), \quad (-4, 5), \quad (-4, -5), \quad \text{and} \quad (4, -5).$$

Steps 3 and 4 The equations of the asymptotes are $y = \pm\dfrac{b}{a}x$, or $y = \pm\dfrac{5}{4}x$. The hyperbola approaches these lines as x and y get larger and larger in absolute value. See **Figure 21.**

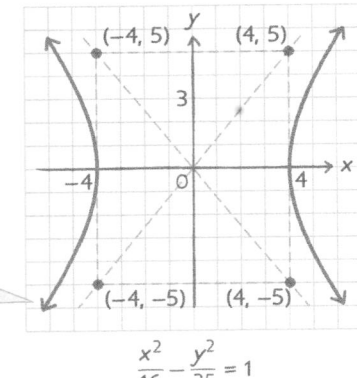

When graphing a hyperbola, the fundamental rectangle and the asymptotes are not part of the actual graph. They provide help in drawing a more accurate graph.

Be sure that the branches do not touch the asymptotes.

$$\dfrac{x^2}{16} - \dfrac{y^2}{25} = 1$$

Figure 21

◀ Work Problem **1** at the Side.

---

2 Graph $\dfrac{y^2}{81} - \dfrac{x^2}{64} = 1$.

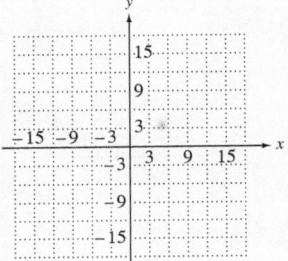

EXAMPLE 2 Graphing a Vertical Hyperbola

Graph $\dfrac{y^2}{49} - \dfrac{x^2}{16} = 1$.

This hyperbola has y-intercepts $(0, 7)$ and $(0, -7)$. The asymptotes are the extended diagonals of the fundamental rectangle with vertices at

$$(4, 7), \quad (-4, 7), \quad (-4, -7), \quad \text{and} \quad (4, -7).$$

Their equations are $y = \pm\dfrac{7}{4}x$. See **Figure 22.**

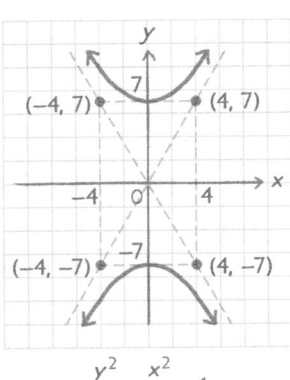

$$\dfrac{y^2}{49} - \dfrac{x^2}{16} = 1$$

Figure 22

◀ Work Problem **2** at the Side.

Answers

1.

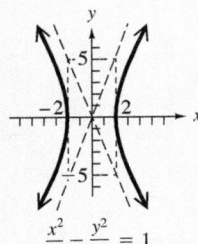

$$\dfrac{x^2}{4} - \dfrac{y^2}{25} = 1$$

2.

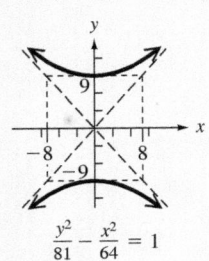

$$\dfrac{y^2}{81} - \dfrac{x^2}{64} = 1$$

OBJECTIVE ▶ **3** **Identify conic sections by their equations.** Rewriting a second-degree equation in one of the forms given for ellipses, hyperbolas, circles, or parabolas makes it possible to identify the graph of the equation.

SUMMARY OF CONIC SECTIONS

Equation	Graph	Description	Identification
$y = ax^2 + bx + c$ or $y = a(x-h)^2 + k$	*Parabola*	It opens up if $a > 0$, down if $a < 0$. The vertex is (h, k).	It has an x^2-term. y is not squared.
$x = ay^2 + by + c$ or $x = a(y-k)^2 + h$	*Parabola*	It opens to the right if $a > 0$, to the left if $a < 0$. The vertex is (h, k).	It has a y^2-term. x is not squared.
$(x-h)^2 + (y-k)^2 = r^2$	*Circle*	The center is (h, k), and the radius is r.	x^2- and y^2-terms have the same positive coefficient.
$\dfrac{x^2}{a^2} + \dfrac{y^2}{b^2} = 1$	*Ellipse*	The x-intercepts are $(a, 0)$ and $(-a, 0)$. The y-intercepts are $(0, b)$ and $(0, -b)$.	x^2- and y^2-terms have different positive coefficients.
$\dfrac{x^2}{a^2} - \dfrac{y^2}{b^2} = 1$	*Hyperbola*	The x-intercepts are $(a, 0)$ and $(-a, 0)$. The asymptotes are found from (a, b), $(-a, b)$ $(-a, -b)$, and $(a, -b)$.	x^2 has a positive coefficient. y^2 has a negative coefficient.
$\dfrac{y^2}{b^2} - \dfrac{x^2}{a^2} = 1$	*Hyperbola*	The y-intercepts are $(0, b)$ and $(0, -b)$. The asymptotes are found from (a, b), $(-a, b)$ $(-a, -b)$, and $(a, -b)$.	y^2 has a positive coefficient. x^2 has a negative coefficient.

③ Identify the graph of each equation.

(a) $3x^2 = 27 - 4y^2$

(b) $6x^2 = 100 + 2y^2$

(c) $3x^2 = 27 - 4y$

(d) $3x^2 = 27 - 3y^2$

EXAMPLE 3 **Identifying the Graphs of Equations**

Identify the graph of each equation.

(a) $9x^2 = 108 + 12y^2$

Both variables are squared, so the graph is either an ellipse or a hyperbola. (This situation also occurs for a circle, which is a special case of an ellipse.) To see which conic section it is, rewrite the equation so that both the x^2-term and y^2-term are on one side of the equation and 1 is on the other side.

$$9x^2 - 12y^2 = 108 \quad \text{Subtract } 12y^2.$$

$$\frac{x^2}{12} - \frac{y^2}{9} = 1 \quad \text{Divide by 108.}$$

Because of the subtraction symbol, the graph of this equation is a hyperbola.

(b) $x^2 = y - 3$ \quad Only one of the two variables, x, is squared, so this is the vertical parabola with equation $y = x^2 + 3$.

(c) $x^2 = 9 - y^2$

Write the variable terms on the same side of the equation.

$$x^2 + y^2 = 9 \quad \text{Add } y^2.$$

The graph of this equation is a circle with center at the origin and radius 3.

◀ **Work Problem ③ at the Side.**

OBJECTIVE ▶ ④ Graph generalized square root functions. Recall that no vertical line will intersect the graph of a function in more than one point. Thus, horizontal parabolas and all circles, ellipses, and hyperbolas with horizontal or vertical axes are examples of graphs that do not satisfy the conditions of a function. However, by considering only a part of the graph of each of these, we have the graph of a function, as seen in **Figure 23.**

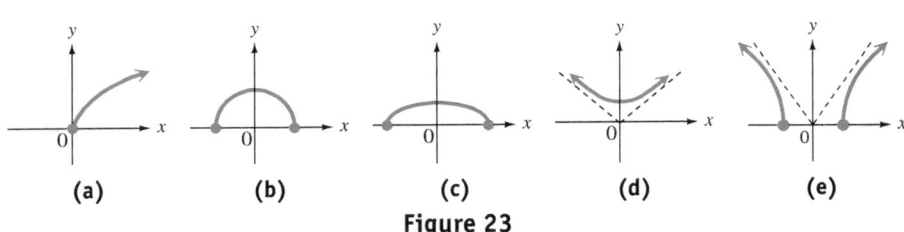

Figure 23

In parts (a)–(d) of **Figure 23,** the top portion of a conic section is shown (parabola, circle, ellipse, and hyperbola, respectively). In part (e), the top two portions of a hyperbola are shown. In each case, the graph is that of a function because the graph satisfies the conditions of the vertical line test.

Previously, we worked with the square root function $f(x) = \sqrt{x}$. To find equations for the types of graphs shown in **Figure 23,** we extend its definition.

Generalized Square Root Function

For an algebraic expression in x defined by u, with $u \geq 0$, a function of the form

$$f(x) = \sqrt{u}$$

is a **generalized square root function.**

Answers

3. (a) ellipse (b) hyperbola (c) parabola
   (d) circle

EXAMPLE 4 Graphing a Semicircle

Graph $f(x) = \sqrt{25 - x^2}$. Give the domain and range.

$$f(x) = \sqrt{25 - x^2} \qquad \text{Given function}$$

$$y = \sqrt{25 - x^2} \qquad \text{Replace } f(x) \text{ with } y.$$

$$y^2 = \left(\sqrt{25 - x^2}\right)^2 \qquad \text{Square each side.}$$

$$y^2 = 25 - x^2 \qquad \left(\sqrt{a}\right)^2 = a$$

$$x^2 + y^2 = 25 \qquad \text{Add } x^2.$$

This is the equation of a circle with center at $(0, 0)$ and radius 5.

Because $f(x)$, or y, represents a principal square root in the original equation, $f(x)$ must be nonnegative. This restricts the graph to the upper half of the circle.

See **Figure 24.**

Use the graph and the vertical line test to verify that it is indeed a function. The domain is $[-5, 5]$, and the range is $[0, 5]$.

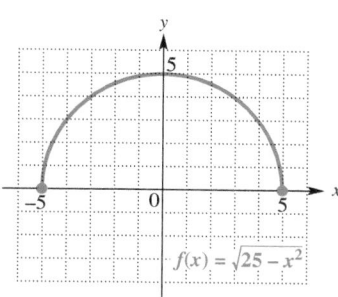

$$f(x) = \sqrt{25 - x^2}$$

Figure 24

─────── Work Problem **4** at the Side. ▶

EXAMPLE 5 Graphing a Portion of an Ellipse

Graph $\dfrac{y}{6} = -\sqrt{1 - \dfrac{x^2}{16}}$. Give the domain and range.

$$\frac{y}{6} = -\sqrt{1 - \frac{x^2}{16}} \qquad \text{Given equation}$$

$$\left(\frac{y}{6}\right)^2 = \left(-\sqrt{1 - \frac{x^2}{16}}\right)^2 \qquad \text{Square each side.}$$

$$\frac{y^2}{36} = 1 - \frac{x^2}{16} \qquad \text{Apply the exponents.}$$

$$\frac{x^2}{16} + \frac{y^2}{36} = 1 \qquad \text{Add } \tfrac{x^2}{16}.$$

This is the equation of an ellipse with center at $(0, 0)$. The x-intercepts are $(4, 0)$ and $(-4, 0)$. The y-intercepts are $(0, 6)$ and $(0, -6)$.

Because $\frac{y}{6}$ equals a negative square root in the original equation, y must be nonpositive, restricting the graph to the lower half of the ellipse.

See **Figure 25.** The domain is $[-4, 4]$, and the range is $[-6, 0]$.

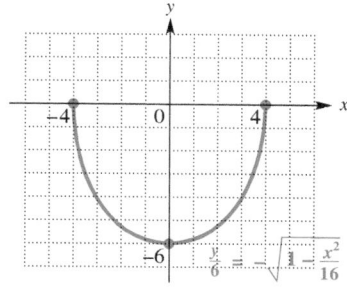

$$\frac{y}{6} = -\sqrt{1 - \frac{x^2}{16}}$$

Figure 25

─────── Work Problem **5** at the Side. ▶

4 Graph $f(x) = \sqrt{36 - x^2}$. Give the domain and range.

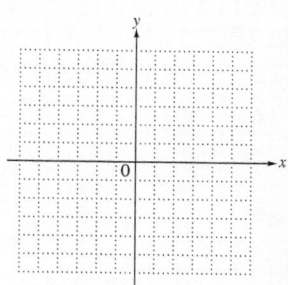

5 Graph

$$\frac{y}{3} = -\sqrt{1 - \frac{x^2}{4}}.$$

Give the domain and range.

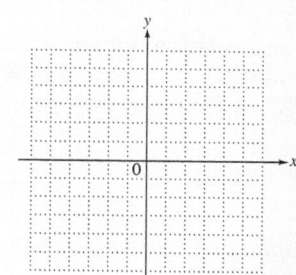

Answers

4.

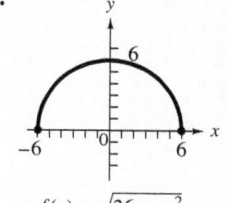

$$f(x) = \sqrt{36 - x^2}$$

domain: $[-6, 6]$; range: $[0, 6]$

5.

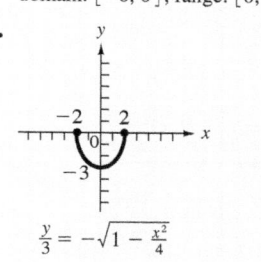

$$\frac{y}{3} = -\sqrt{1 - \frac{x^2}{4}}$$

domain: $[-2, 2]$; range: $[-3, 0]$

13.3 Exercises

FOR EXTRA HELP   Go to MyMathLab *for worked-out, step-by-step solutions to exercises enclosed in a square* ☐ *and video solutions to* ▶ *exercises.*

CONCEPT CHECK   *Based on the discussions of ellipses in the previous section and of hyperbolas in this section, match each equation with its graph.*

1. $\dfrac{x^2}{25} + \dfrac{y^2}{9} = 1$

2. $\dfrac{x^2}{9} + \dfrac{y^2}{25} = 1$

3. $\dfrac{x^2}{9} - \dfrac{y^2}{25} = 1$

4. $\dfrac{x^2}{25} - \dfrac{y^2}{9} = 1$

A.
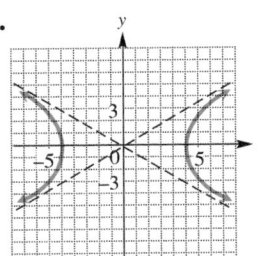

B.
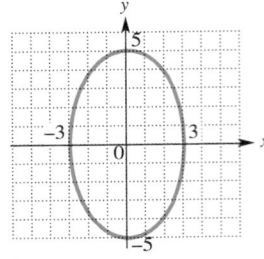

C.
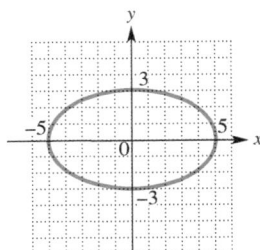

D.
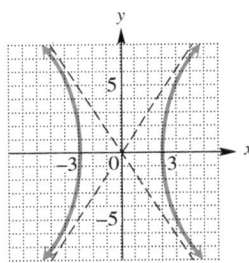

5. CONCEPT CHECK   A student incorrectly described the graph of the equation

$$\frac{x^2}{9} - \frac{y^2}{16} = 1$$

as a vertical hyperbola with y-intercepts $(0, -4)$ and $(0, 4)$. **What Went Wrong?** Give the correct description of the graph.

6. CONCEPT CHECK   A student incorrectly described the graph of the function

$$f(x) = \sqrt{49 - x^2}$$

as a circle centered at the origin with radius 7. **What Went Wrong?** Give the correct description of the graph.

Graph each hyperbola. **See Examples 1 and 2.**

7. $\dfrac{x^2}{16} - \dfrac{y^2}{9} = 1$
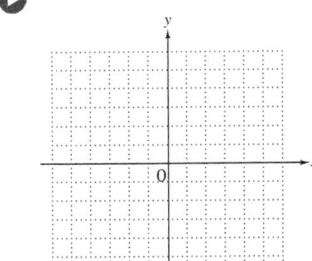

8. $\dfrac{x^2}{25} - \dfrac{y^2}{4} = 1$
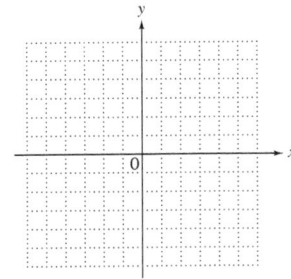

9. $\dfrac{y^2}{4} - \dfrac{x^2}{25} = 1$
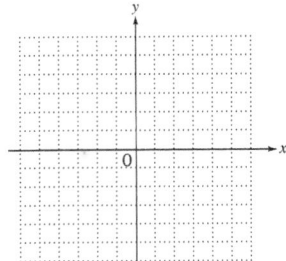

10. $\dfrac{y^2}{9} - \dfrac{x^2}{4} = 1$
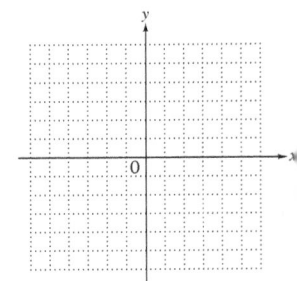

11. $\dfrac{x^2}{25} - \dfrac{y^2}{36} = 1$
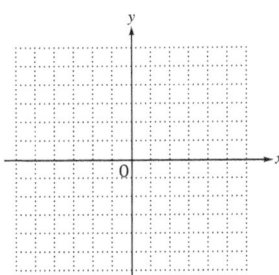

12. $\dfrac{x^2}{49} - \dfrac{y^2}{16} = 1$
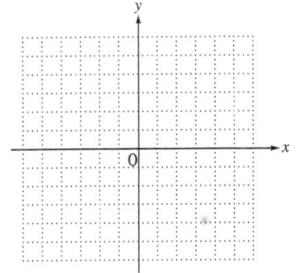

13. $\dfrac{y^2}{9} - \dfrac{x^2}{9} = 1$
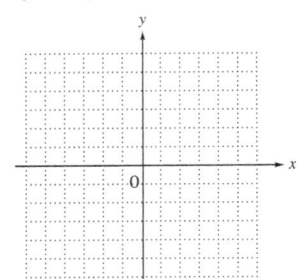

14. $\dfrac{y^2}{16} - \dfrac{x^2}{16} = 1$
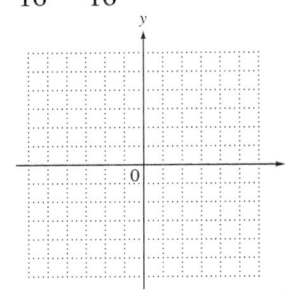

Identify the graph of each equation as a parabola, circle, ellipse, *or* hyperbola, *and then sketch its graph.* ***See Example 3.***

15. $x^2 - y^2 = 16$

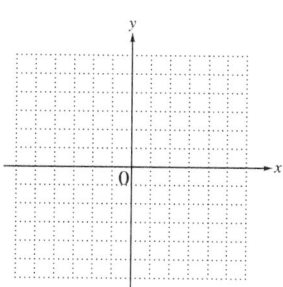

16. $x^2 + y^2 = 16$

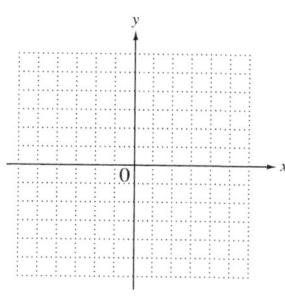

17. $4x^2 + y^2 = 16$

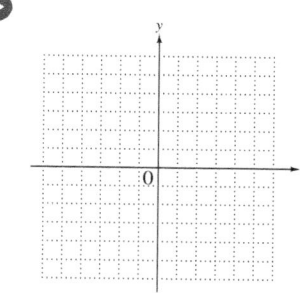

18. $x^2 - 2y = 0$

19. $y^2 = 36 - x^2$

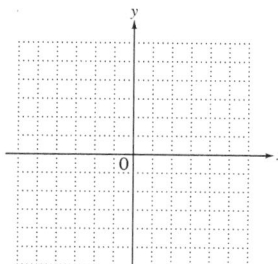

20. $9x^2 + 25y^2 = 225$

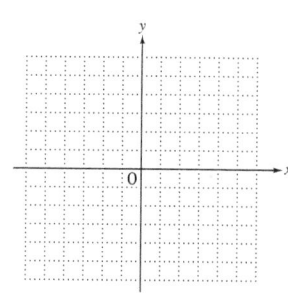

21. $x^2 + 9y^2 = 9$

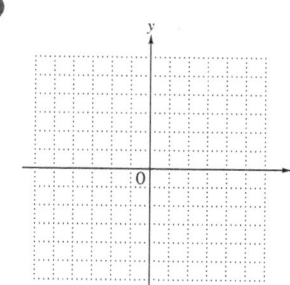

22. $y^2 = 4 + x^2$

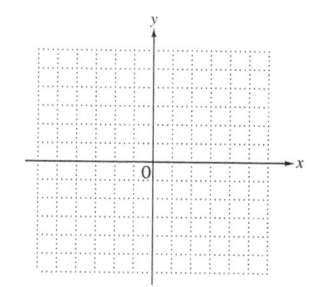

Graph each generalized square root function. Give the domain and range. ***See Examples 4 and 5.***

23. $f(x) = \sqrt{16 - x^2}$

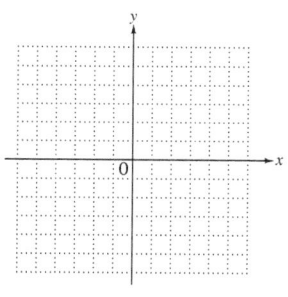

24. $f(x) = \sqrt{9 - x^2}$

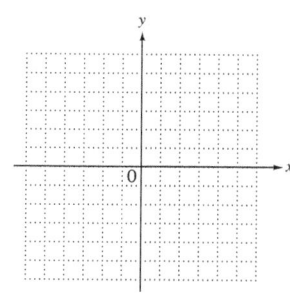

25. $f(x) = -\sqrt{36 - x^2}$

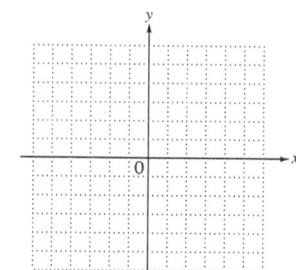

26. $f(x) = -\sqrt{25 - x^2}$

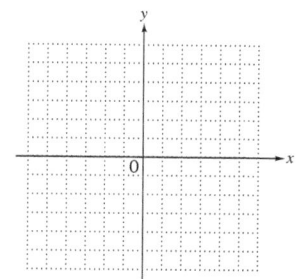

27. $y = \sqrt{\dfrac{x + 4}{2}}$

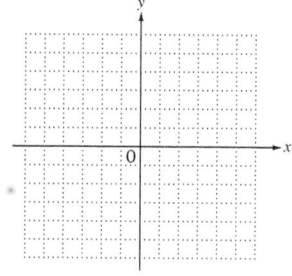

28. $\dfrac{y}{3} = \sqrt{1 + \dfrac{x^2}{9}}$

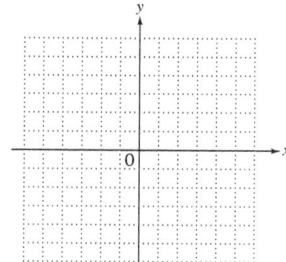

29. $y = -2\sqrt{\dfrac{9 - x^2}{9}}$

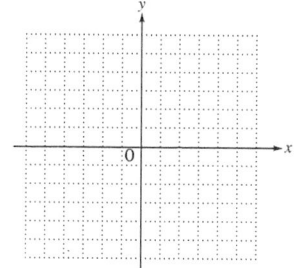

30. $y = -3\sqrt{1 - \dfrac{x^2}{25}}$

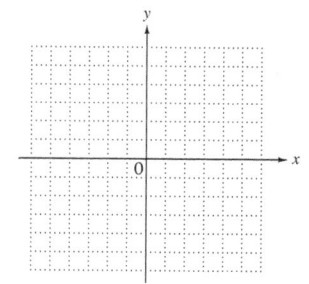

Solve each problem.

31. Two buildings in a sports complex are shaped and positioned like a portion of the branches of the hyperbola with equation

$$400x^2 - 625y^2 = 250{,}000,$$

where x and y are in meters.

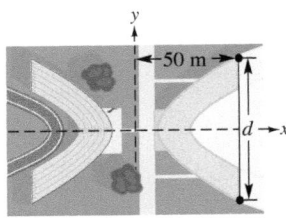

Not to scale

  (a) How far apart are the buildings at their closest point?

  (b) Find the distance d in the figure to the nearest tenth of a meter.

32. Using LORAN, a location-finding system, a radio transmitter at M sends out a series of pulses. When each pulse is received at transmitter S, it then sends out a pulse. A ship at P receives pulses from both M and S. A receiver on the ship measures the difference in the arrival times of the pulses. A special map gives hyperbolas that correspond to the differences in arrival times (which give the distances d_1 and d_2 in the figure). The ship can then be located as lying on a branch of a particular hyperbola.

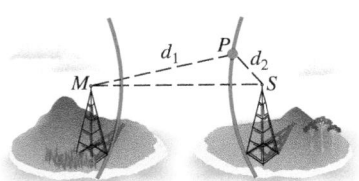

Suppose $d_1 = 80$ mi and $d_2 = 30$ mi, and the distance between transmitters M and S is 100 mi. Use the definition to find an equation of the hyperbola on which the ship is located.

Relating Concepts (Exercises 33–36)   For Individual or Group Work

We have seen that the center of a circle or ellipse may be shifted away from the origin. The same process can be applied to hyperbolas. For example, the hyperbola,

$$\frac{(x+5)^2}{4} - \frac{(y-2)^2}{9} = 1$$

has the same graph as

$$\frac{x^2}{4} - \frac{y^2}{9} = 1,$$

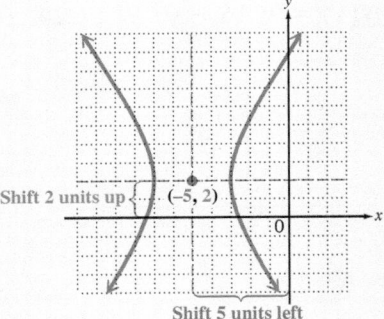

Shift 2 units up   (−5, 2)

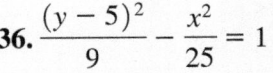

Shift 5 units left

but it is centered at $(-5, 2)$, as shown at the right. Graph each hyperbola with center shifted away from the origin.

33. $\dfrac{(x-2)^2}{4} - \dfrac{(y+1)^2}{9} = 1$ **34.** $\dfrac{(x+3)^2}{16} - \dfrac{(y-2)^2}{4} = 1$ **35.** $\dfrac{y^2}{36} - \dfrac{(x-2)^2}{49} = 1$ **36.** $\dfrac{(y-5)^2}{9} - \dfrac{x^2}{25} = 1$

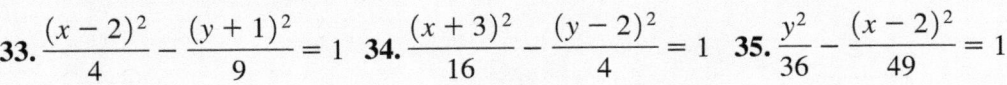

13.4 Nonlinear Systems of Equations

An equation in which some terms have more than one variable or a variable of degree 2 or greater is a **nonlinear equation**. A **nonlinear system of equations** includes at least one nonlinear equation.

When solving a nonlinear system, it helps to visualize the types of graphs of the equations of the system to determine the possible number of points of intersection. For example, if a system includes two equations where the graph of one is a circle and the graph of the other is a line, then there may be zero, one, or two points of intersection, as illustrated in **Figure 26.**

OBJECTIVES

1. Solve a nonlinear system using substitution.
2. Solve a nonlinear system with two second-degree equations using elimination.
3. Solve a nonlinear system that requires a combination of methods.

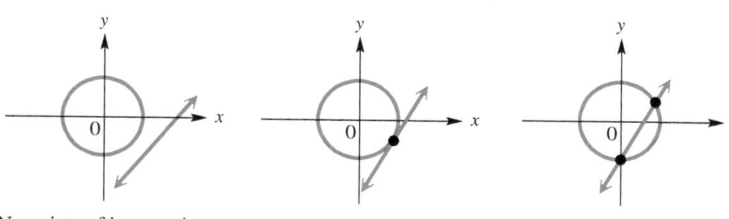

| No points of intersection | One point of intersection | Two points of intersection |

Figure 26

OBJECTIVE ▶ 1 Solve a nonlinear system using substitution. We can usually solve a nonlinear system by the substitution method if one of the equations is linear.

EXAMPLE 1 Solving a Nonlinear System Using Substitution

Solve the system.

$$x^2 + y^2 = 9 \quad (1)$$
$$2x - y = 3 \quad (2)$$

The graph of (1) is a circle and the graph of (2) is a line. The graphs could intersect in zero, one, or two points, as shown in **Figure 26.** We begin by solving the linear equation (2) for one of its two variables.

$$2x - y = 3 \quad (2)$$
$$y = 2x - 3 \quad \text{Solve for } y. \quad (3)$$

Then we substitute $2x - 3$ for y in the nonlinear equation (1).

$$x^2 + y^2 = 9 \quad (1)$$
$$x^2 + (2x - 3)^2 = 9 \quad \text{Let } y = 2x - 3.$$
$$x^2 + 4x^2 - 12x + 9 = 9 \quad \text{Square } 2x - 3.$$
$$5x^2 - 12x = 0 \quad \text{Combine like terms. Subtract 9.}$$
$$x(5x - 12) = 0 \quad \text{Factor. The GCF is } x.$$

> Set *both* factors equal to 0.

$$x = 0 \quad \text{or} \quad 5x - 12 = 0 \quad \text{Zero-factor property}$$
$$x = \frac{12}{5} \quad \text{Solve for } x.$$

If we let $x = 0$ in equation (3), $y = 2x - 3$, we obtain $y = -3$. If $x = \frac{12}{5}$ in equation (3), then $y = \frac{9}{5}$. The solution set of the system is $\left\{(0, -3), \left(\frac{12}{5}, \frac{9}{5}\right)\right\}$. The graph in **Figure 27** confirms the two points of intersection.

——— Work Problem **1** at the Side. ▶

1. Solve each system.

(a) $x^2 + y^2 = 10$
$x = y + 2$

(b) $x^2 - 2y^2 = 8$
$x + y = 6$

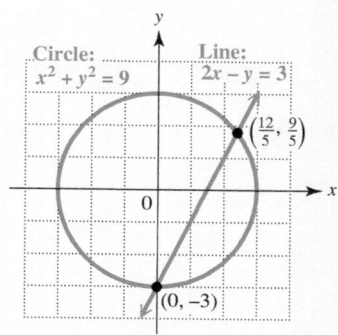

Figure 27

Answers

1. (a) $\{(3, 1), (-1, -3)\}$
(b) $\{(4, 2), (20, -14)\}$

2 Solve each system.

(a) $xy = 8$

  $x + y = 6$

(b) $xy + 10 = 0$

  $4x + 9y = -2$

EXAMPLE 2 **Solving a Nonlinear System Using Substitution**

Solve the system.

$$6x - y = 5 \quad (1)$$

$$xy = 4 \quad (2)$$

The graph of (1) is a line. It can be shown by plotting points that the graph of (2) is a hyperbola. Visualizing a line and a hyperbola indicates that there may be zero, one, or two points of intersection.

Solving $xy = 4$ for x gives $x = \frac{4}{y}$. We substitute $\frac{4}{y}$ for x in equation (1).

$$6x - y = 5 \qquad (1)$$

$$6\left(\frac{4}{y}\right) - y = 5 \qquad \text{Let } x = \frac{4}{y}.$$

$$\frac{24}{y} - y = 5 \qquad \text{Multiply.}$$

$$24 - y^2 = 5y \qquad \text{Multiply by } y, y \neq 0.$$

$$y^2 + 5y - 24 = 0 \qquad \text{Standard form}$$

$$(y - 3)(y + 8) = 0 \qquad \text{Factor.}$$

$$y - 3 = 0 \quad \text{or} \quad y + 8 = 0 \qquad \text{Zero-factor property.}$$

$$y = 3 \quad \text{or} \qquad y = -8 \qquad \text{Solve each equation.}$$

We substitute these results into $x = \frac{4}{y}$ to obtain the corresponding values of x.

If $y = 3$, then $x = \frac{4}{3}$.

If $y = -8$, then $x = -\frac{1}{2}$.

The solution set of the system is

$$\left\{\left(\frac{4}{3}, 3\right), \left(-\frac{1}{2}, -8\right)\right\}.$$

> Write the x-coordinates first in the ordered-pair solutions.

See the graph in **Figure 28**.

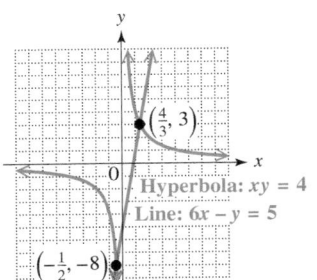

Figure 28

◀ **Work Problem 2 at the Side.**

Note

In **Example 2,** we could solve the *linear* equation for one of its variables and substitute for this variable in the *nonlinear* equation. There is often more than one way to solve a nonlinear system of equations.

OBJECTIVE ▶ 2 **Solve a nonlinear system with two second-degree equations using elimination.** If a system consists of two second-degree equations, then there may be zero, one, two, three, or four solutions. **Figure 29** shows a case where a system consisting of a circle and a parabola has four solutions, all made up of ordered pairs of real numbers.

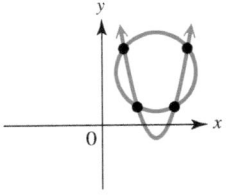

This system has four solutions because there are four points of intersection.

Figure 29

Answers

2. (a) $\{(4, 2), (2, 4)\}$

  (b) $\left\{(-5, 2), \left(\frac{9}{2}, -\frac{20}{9}\right)\right\}$

The elimination method is often used when both equations of a nonlinear system are second degree.

EXAMPLE 3 **Solving a Nonlinear System Using Elimination**

Solve the system.

$$x^2 + y^2 = 9 \qquad (1)$$
$$2x^2 - y^2 = -6 \qquad (2)$$

The graph of (1) is a circle, while the graph of (2) is a hyperbola. By analyzing the possibilities, we conclude that there may be zero, one, two, three, or four points of intersection. Adding the two equations will eliminate y.

$$
\begin{array}{llll}
x^2 + y^2 = 9 & (1) \\
\underline{2x^2 - y^2 = -6} & (2) \\
3x^2 = 3 & \text{Add.} \\
x^2 = 1 & \text{Divide by 3.} \\
x = 1 \quad \text{or} \quad x = -1 & \text{Square root property}
\end{array}
$$

Each value of x gives corresponding values for y when substituted into one of the original equations. Using equation (1) is easier because the coefficients of the x^2- and y^2-terms are 1.

$x^2 + y^2 = 9$ (1)	$x^2 + y^2 = 9$ (1)
$1^2 + y^2 = 9$ Let $x = 1$.	$(-1)^2 + y^2 = 9$ Let $x = -1$.
$y^2 = 8$	$y^2 = 8$
$y = \sqrt{8}$ or $y = -\sqrt{8}$	$y = \sqrt{8}$ or $y = -\sqrt{8}$
$y = 2\sqrt{2}$ or $y = -2\sqrt{2}$	$y = 2\sqrt{2}$ or $y = -2\sqrt{2}$

The solution set is

$$\left\{ \left(1, 2\sqrt{2}\right), \left(1, -2\sqrt{2}\right), \left(-1, 2\sqrt{2}\right), \left(-1, -2\sqrt{2}\right) \right\}.$$

Figure 30 shows the four points of intersection.

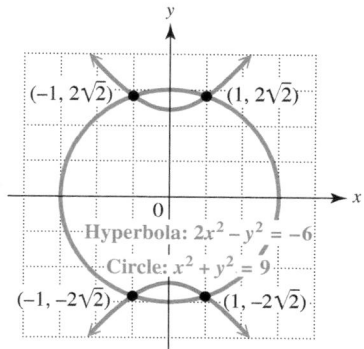

Figure 30

—————— **Work Problem ③ at the Side.** ▶

③ Solve each system.

(a) $x^2 + y^2 = 41$
$x^2 - y^2 = 9$

(b) $x^2 + 3y^2 = 40$
$4x^2 - y^2 = 4$

Answers

3. (a) $\{(5, 4), (5, -4), (-5, 4), (-5, -4)\}$

(b) $\{(2, 2\sqrt{3}), (2, -2\sqrt{3}),$
$(-2, 2\sqrt{3}), (-2, -2\sqrt{3})\}$

OBJECTIVE ▸ ❸ Solve a nonlinear system that requires a combination of methods.

EXAMPLE 4 | Solving a Nonlinear System Using a Combination of Methods

Solve the system.

$$x^2 + 2xy - y^2 = 7 \quad (1)$$
$$x^2 - y^2 = 3 \quad (2)$$

While we have not graphed equations like (1), its graph is a hyperbola. The graph of (2) is also a hyperbola. Two hyperbolas may have zero, one, two, three, or four points of intersection. We use the elimination method here in combination with the substitution method.

$$
\begin{aligned}
x^2 + 2xy - y^2 &= 7 \quad (1) \\
-x^2 \qquad\quad + y^2 &= -3 \quad \text{Multiply (2) by } -1. \\
\hline
2xy \qquad &= 4 \quad \text{Add.}
\end{aligned}
$$

The x^2- and y^2-terms were eliminated.

Next, we solve $2xy = 4$ for one of the variables. We choose y.

$$2xy = 4$$
$$y = \frac{2}{x} \quad (3)$$

Now, we substitute $y = \frac{2}{x}$ into one of the original equations.

$$x^2 - y^2 = 3 \qquad\qquad \text{The substitution is easier in (2).}$$

$$x^2 - \left(\frac{2}{x}\right)^2 = 3 \qquad\qquad \text{Let } y = \frac{2}{x}.$$

$$x^2 - \frac{4}{x^2} = 3 \qquad\qquad \text{Square } \frac{2}{x}.$$

$$x^4 - 4 = 3x^2 \qquad\qquad \text{Multiply by } x^2, x \neq 0.$$

$$x^4 - 3x^2 - 4 = 0 \qquad\qquad \text{Subtract } 3x^2.$$

$$(x^2 - 4)(x^2 + 1) = 0 \qquad\qquad \text{Factor.}$$

$$x^2 - 4 = 0 \quad \text{or} \quad x^2 + 1 = 0 \qquad \text{Zero-factor property}$$

$$x^2 = 4 \quad \text{or} \quad x^2 = -1 \qquad \text{Solve each equation.}$$

$$x = 2 \quad \text{or} \quad x = -2 \quad x = i \quad \text{or} \quad x = -i$$

Substituting these four values of x into $y = \frac{2}{x}$ (equation (3)) gives the corresponding values for y.

If $x = 2$, then $y = \frac{2}{2} = 1$.

If $x = -2$, then $y = \frac{2}{-2} = -1$.

> Multiply by the complex conjugate of the denominator. $i(-i) = 1$

If $x = i$, then $y = \frac{2}{i} = \frac{2}{i} \cdot \frac{-i}{-i} = -2i$.

If $x = -i$, then $y = \frac{2}{-i} = \frac{2}{-i} \cdot \frac{i}{i} = 2i$.

—— **Continued on Next Page**

If we substitute the x-values we found into equation (1) or (2) instead of into equation (3), we get extraneous solutions. ***It is always wise to check all solutions in both of the given equations.*** We show a check for the ordered pair $(i, -2i)$.

CHECK Let $x = i$ and $y = -2i$ in both equations (1) and (2).

$$x^2 + 2xy - y^2 = 7 \quad (1) \qquad\qquad x^2 - y^2 = 3 \quad (2)$$

$$i^2 + 2(i)(-2i) - (-2i)^2 \overset{?}{=} 7 \qquad\qquad i^2 - (-2i)^2 \overset{?}{=} 3$$

$$i^2 - 4i^2 - 4i^2 \overset{?}{=} 7 \qquad\qquad i^2 - 4i^2 \overset{?}{=} 3$$

$$-1 - 4(-1) - 4(-1) \overset{?}{=} 7 \quad i^2 = -1 \qquad -1 - 4(-1) \overset{?}{=} 3 \quad i^2 = -1$$

$$7 = 7 \checkmark \text{ True} \qquad\qquad 3 = 3 \checkmark \text{ True}$$

The other ordered pairs would be checked similarly. There are four ordered pairs in the solution set, two with real values and two with nonreal complex values. The solution set is

$$\{(2, 1), (-2, -1), (i, -2i), (-i, 2i)\}.$$

The graph of the system, shown in **Figure 31,** shows only the two real intersection points because the graph is in the real number plane. In general, if solutions contain nonreal complex numbers as components, they do not appear on the graph.

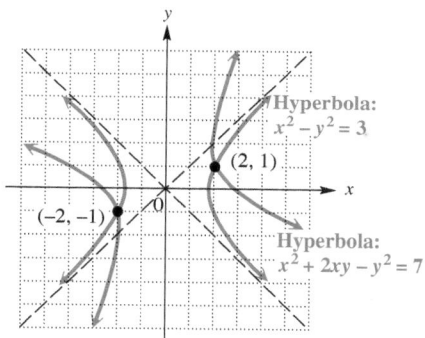

Hyperbola: $x^2 - y^2 = 3$

$(2, 1)$

$(-2, -1)$

Hyperbola: $x^2 + 2xy - y^2 = 7$

Figure 31

───────── Work Problem **4** at the Side. ▶

Note

It is not essential to visualize the number of points of intersection of the graphs in order to solve a nonlinear system. Sometimes we are unfamiliar with the graphs or, as in **Example 4,** there are nonreal complex solutions that do not appear as points of intersection in the real plane. Visualizing the geometry of the graphs is only an aid to solving these systems.

4 Solve each system.

(a) $x^2 + xy + y^2 = 3$
$x^2 + y^2 = 5$

(b) $x^2 + 7xy - 2y^2 = -8$
$-2x^2 + 4y^2 = 16$

Answers

4. (a) $\{(1, -2), (-1, 2), (2, -1), (-2, 1)\}$
  (b) $\{(0, 2), (0, -2), (2i\sqrt{2}, 0), (-2i\sqrt{2}, 0)\}$

13.4 Exercises

FOR EXTRA HELP

Go to MyMathLab for worked-out, step-by-step solutions to exercises enclosed in a square ☐ and video solutions to ▶ exercises.

CONCEPT CHECK *Each sketch represents the graphs of a pair of equations in a system. How many ordered pairs of real numbers are in each solution set?*

1.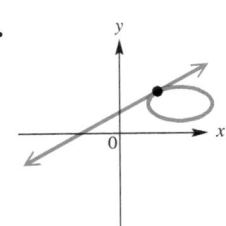

2.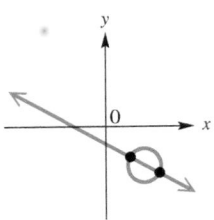

3.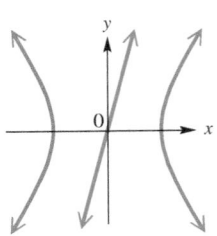

4.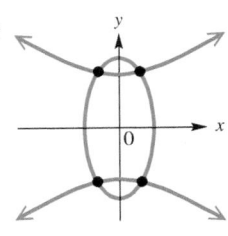

CONCEPT CHECK *Suppose that a nonlinear system is composed of equations whose graphs are those described, and the number of points of intersection of the two graphs is as given. Make a sketch satisfying these conditions. (There may be more than one way to do this.)*

5. A line and a circle; no points

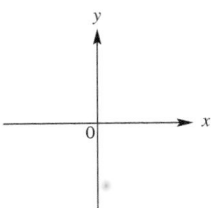

6. A line and a circle; one point

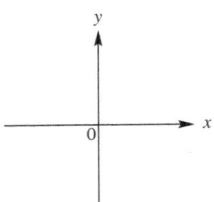

7. A line and an ellipse; two points

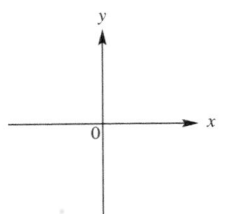

8. A line and a hyperbola; no points

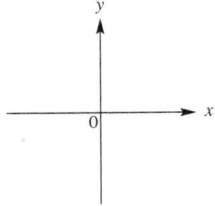

9. A circle and an ellipse; four points

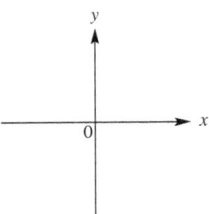

10. A parabola and an ellipse; one point

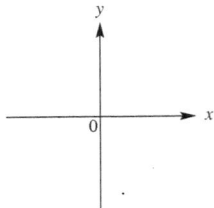

11. A parabola and an ellipse; four points

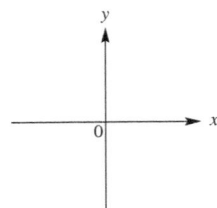

12. A parabola and a hyperbola; two points

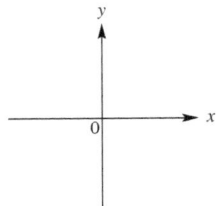

Solve each system using the substitution method. **See Examples 1 and 2.**

13. $y = 4x^2 - x$
$y = x$

14. $y = x^2 + 6x$
$3y = 12x$

15. $y = x^2 + 6x + 9$
$x + y = 3$

16. $y = x^2 + 8x + 16$
$x - y = -4$

17. $x^2 + y^2 = 2$
$2x + y = 1$

18. $2x^2 + 4y^2 = 4$
$x = 4y$

19. $xy = 4$
$3x + 2y = -10$

20. $xy = -5$
$2x + y = 3$

21. $xy = -3$
$x + y = -2$

22. $xy = 12$
$x + y = 8$

23. $y = 3x^2 + 6x$
$y = x^2 - x - 6$

24. $y = 2x^2 + 1$
$y = 5x^2 + 2x - 7$

25. $2x^2 - y^2 = 6$
$y = x^2 - 3$

26. $x^2 + y^2 = 4$
$y = x^2 - 2$

*Solve each system using the elimination method or a combination of the elimination and substitution methods. **See Examples 3 and 4.***

27. $3x^2 + 2y^2 = 12$
$x^2 + 2y^2 = 4$

28. $6x^2 + y^2 = 9$
$3x^2 + 4y^2 = 36$

29. $2x^2 + 3y^2 = 6$
$x^2 + 3y^2 = 3$

30. $x^2 + y^2 = 14$
$-x^2 + 5y^2 = 16$

31. $2x^2 + y^2 = 28$
$4x^2 - 5y^2 = 28$

32. $5x^2 - 2y^2 = -13$
$3x^2 + 4y^2 = 39$

33. $xy = 6$
$3x^2 - y^2 = 12$

34. $xy = 5$
$2y^2 - x^2 = 5$

35. $2x^2 + 2y^2 = 8$
$3x^2 + 4y^2 = 24$

36. $5x^2 + 5y^2 = 20$
$x^2 + 2y^2 = 2$

37. $x^2 + xy + y^2 = 15$
$x^2 + y^2 = 10$

38. $2x^2 + 3xy + 2y^2 = 21$
$x^2 + y^2 = 6$

39. $x^2 + xy - y^2 = 11$
$x^2 - y^2 = 8$

40. $x^2 + xy - y^2 = 29$
$x^2 - y^2 = 24$

Solve each problem using a nonlinear system.

41. The area of a rectangular rug is 84 ft² and its perimeter is 38 ft. Find the length and width of the rug.

42. Find the length and width of a rectangular room whose perimeter is 50 m and whose area is 100 m².

13.5 | Second-Degree Inequalities and Systems of Inequalities

OBJECTIVES

1. Graph second-degree inequalities.
2. Graph the solution set of a system of inequalities.

OBJECTIVE ▸ 1   Graph second-degree inequalities. An inequality with at least one variable of degree 2 and no variable with degree greater than 2 is a **second-degree inequality.**

---

1. Graph $x^2 + y^2 \geq 9$.

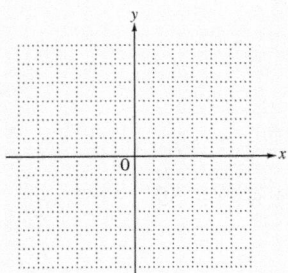

---

2. Graph $y > (x + 1)^2 - 5$.

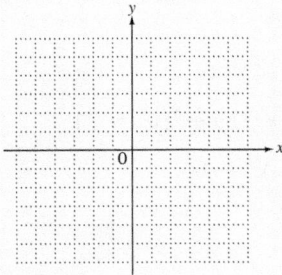

Answers

1.
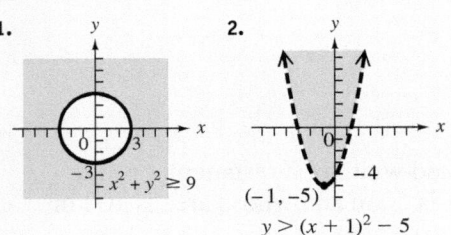
$x^2 + y^2 \geq 9$

2.
$(-1, -5)$
$y > (x + 1)^2 - 5$

EXAMPLE 1   Graphing a Second-Degree Inequality

Graph $x^2 + y^2 \leq 36$.

The boundary of the inequality $x^2 + y^2 \leq 36$ is the graph of the equation $x^2 + y^2 = 36$, a circle with radius 6 and center at the origin, as shown in **Figure 32.**

The inequality $x^2 + y^2 \leq 36$ includes the points of the boundary (because the symbol $\leq$ includes equality) and either the points "outside" the circle or the points "inside" the circle. To decide which region to shade, we substitute any test point not on the circle.

$x^2 + y^2 < 36$ ◁ We are testing the region.

$0^2 + 0^2 \overset{?}{<} 36$ Use $(0, 0)$ as a test point.

$0 < 36$ True

Because a true statement results, the original inequality includes the points *inside* the circle, the shaded region in **Figure 32,** and the boundary.

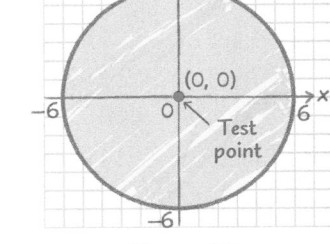

Figure 32

◀ **Work Problem ❶ at the Side.**

EXAMPLE 2   Graphing a Second-Degree Inequality

Graph $y < -2(x - 4)^2 - 3$.

The boundary, $y = -2(x - 4)^2 - 3$, is a parabola that opens down with vertex at $(4, -3)$. Decide whether to shade the region "inside" or "outside" the parabola.

$y < -2(x - 4)^2 - 3$ Original inequality

$0 \overset{?}{<} -2(0 - 4)^2 - 3$ Use $(0, 0)$ as a test point.

$0 \overset{?}{<} -32 - 3$ Simplify.

$0 < -35$ False

Because the final inequality is a false statement, the points in the region containing $(0, 0)$ do not satisfy the inequality. In **Figure 33,** the parabola is drawn as a dashed curve because the points of the parabola itself do not satisfy the inequality. The region inside (or below) the parabola is shaded.

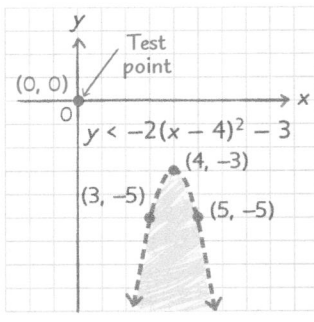

Figure 33

◀ **Work Problem ❷ at the Side.**

Note

Because the substitution is easy, the origin is the test point of choice unless the graph actually passes through $(0, 0)$.

EXAMPLE 3 Graphing a Second-Degree Inequality

Graph $16y^2 \leq 144 + 9x^2$.

Rewrite the inequality as follows.

$$16y^2 - 9x^2 \leq 144 \qquad \text{Subtract } 9x^2.$$

$$\frac{y^2}{9} - \frac{x^2}{16} \leq 1 \qquad \text{Divide by } 144.$$

This form shows that the boundary is the following hyperbola.

$$\frac{y^2}{9} - \frac{x^2}{16} = 1$$

Because the graph is a vertical hyperbola, the desired region will be either the region between the branches or the regions "above" the top branch and "below" the bottom branch. We choose $(0, 0)$ as a test point.

$$16y^2 < 144 + 9x^2$$

$$16(0)^2 \overset{?}{<} 144 + 9(0)^2$$

$$0 < 144 \qquad \text{True}$$

Because a true statements results, we shade the region between the branches containing $(0, 0)$. See **Figure 34.**

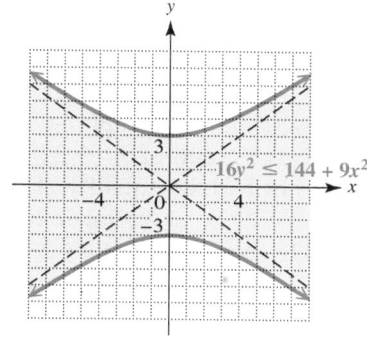

Figure 34

③ Graph $x^2 + 4y^2 > 36$.

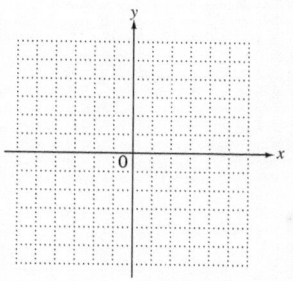

—————— Work Problem ③ at the Side. ▶

OBJECTIVE ▶ ② Graph the solution set of a system of inequalities. If two or more inequalities are considered at the same time, we have a **system of inequalities.** To find the solution set of the system, we find the intersection of the graphs (solution sets) of the inequalities in the system.

EXAMPLE 4 Graphing a System of Two Inequalities

Graph the solution set of the system.

$$x - y \leq 4$$

$$x + 2y < 2$$

We begin by graphing the solution set of $x - y \leq 4$. The inequality includes the points of the boundary line $x - y = 4$ because the symbol $\leq$ includes equality. The test point $(0, 0)$ leads to a true statement in $x - y < 4$, so we shade the region above the line. See **Figure 35** on the next page.

The graph of the solution set of $x + 2y < 2$ does not include the boundary line $x + 2y = 2$. Testing the point $(0, 0)$ leads to a true statement, indicating that we should shade the region below the dashed boundary line. See **Figure 36** on the next page.

Answer

3.

$$x^2 + 4y^2 > 36$$

—————— Continued on Next Page

4 Graph the solution set of the system.

$$2x + 3y \geq 6$$
$$x - 5y \geq 5$$

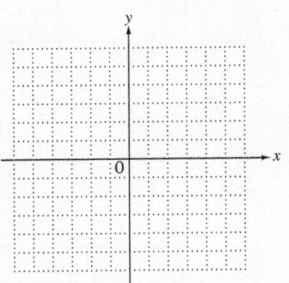

5 Graph the solution set of the system.

$$x^2 + y^2 \leq 25$$
$$x + y \leq 3$$

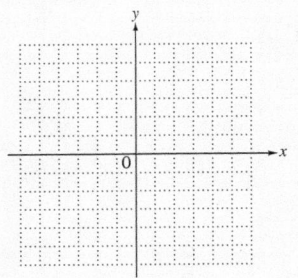

The graph of the solution set of the system is the intersection of the graphs of the two inequalities. See the overlapping region shown in **Figure 37,** which includes one boundary line.

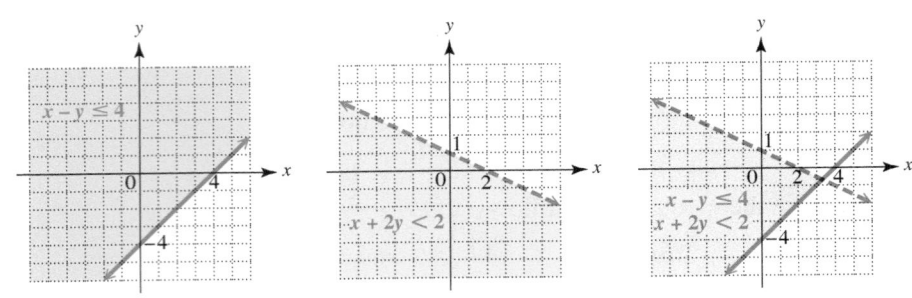

| Figure 35 | Figure 36 | Figure 37 |

◀ **Work Problem 4 at the Side.**

EXAMPLE 5 Graphing a System of Two Inequalities

Graph the solution set of the system.

$$2x + 3y > 6$$
$$x^2 + y^2 < 16$$

We begin by graphing the solution set of $2x + 3y > 6$. The boundary line is the graph of $2x + 3y = 6$ and is a dashed line because the symbol $>$ does not include equality. The test point $(0, 0)$ leads to a false statement in $2x + 3y > 6$, so we shade the region above the line, as shown in **Figure 38.**

The graph of $x^2 + y^2 < 16$ is the region inside of a dashed circle centered at the origin with radius 4. See **Figure 39.**

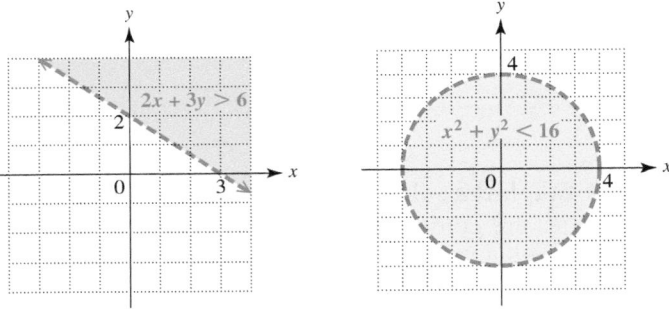

| Figure 38 | Figure 39 |

The graph of the solution set of the system is the intersection of the graphs of the two inequalities. The overlapping region in **Figure 40** is the solution set.

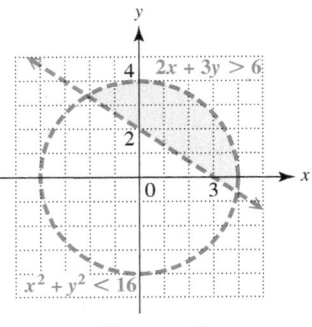

Figure 40

Answers

4.

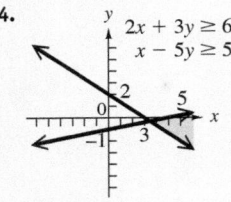

5.

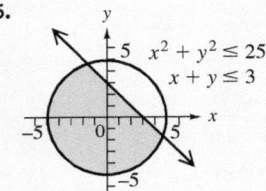

◀ **Work Problem 5 at the Side.**

EXAMPLE 6 Graphing a System of Three Inequalities

Graph the solution set of the system.

$$x + y < 1$$
$$y \le 2x + 3$$
$$y \ge -2$$

We graph each inequality separately, on the same axes.

• The graph of $x + y < 1$ is the region that lies below the dashed line $x + y = 1$.

• The graph of $y \le 2x + 3$ is the region that lies below the solid line $y = 2x + 3$.

• The graph of $y \ge -2$ is the region above the solid horizontal line $y = -2$.

Verify that the test point $(0, 0)$ satisfies all three inequalities. Thus, the graph of the system, the intersection of these three graphs, is the triangular region enclosed by the three boundary lines in **Figure 41**, including two of its boundary lines.

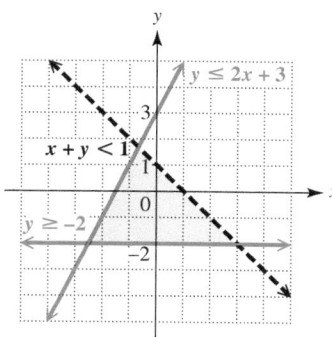

Figure 41

—————— Work Problem **6** at the Side. ▶

EXAMPLE 7 Graphing a System of Three Inequalities

Graph the solution set of the system.

$$y \ge x^2 - 2x + 1$$
$$2x^2 + y^2 > 4$$
$$y < 4$$

We graph each inequality separately, on the same axes.

• The graph of $y = x^2 - 2x + 1$ is a parabola with vertex at $(1, 0)$. Those points inside (or above) the parabola satisfy the condition $y > x^2 - 2x + 1$. Thus, the solution set of $y \ge x^2 - 2x + 1$ includes points on or inside the parabola.

• The graph of the equation $2x^2 + y^2 = 4$ is an ellipse. We draw it as a dashed curve. To satisfy the inequality $2x^2 + y^2 > 4$, a point must lie outside the ellipse.

• The graph of $y < 4$ includes all points below the dashed line $y = 4$.

The graph of the system is the region shaded in **Figure 42**, which lies outside the ellipse, inside or on the boundary of the parabola, and below the line $y = 4$.

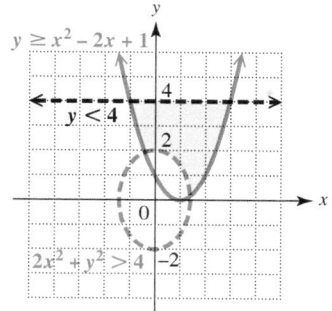

Figure 42

—————— Work Problem **7** at the Side. ▶

6 Graph the solution set of the system.

$$3x - 4y \ge 12$$
$$x + 3y > 6$$
$$y \le 2$$

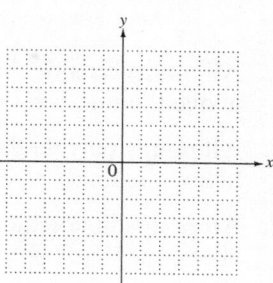

7 Graph the solution set of the system.

$$y > x^2 + 1$$
$$\frac{x^2}{9} + \frac{y^2}{4} \ge 1$$
$$y \le 5$$

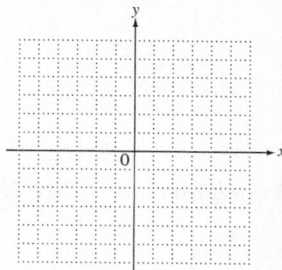

Answers

6.

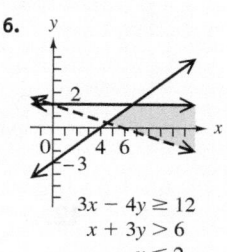

$$3x - 4y \ge 12$$
$$x + 3y > 6$$
$$y \le 2$$

7.

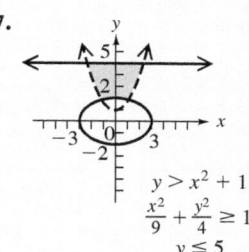

$$y > x^2 + 1$$
$$\frac{x^2}{9} + \frac{y^2}{4} \ge 1$$
$$y \le 5$$

13.5 Exercises

FOR EXTRA HELP   Go to MyMathLab *for worked-out, step-by-step solutions to exercises enclosed in a square* ☐ *and video solutions to* ▶ *exercises.*

1. **CONCEPT CHECK**   Which is a description of the graph of the solution set of the following system?

$$x^2 + y^2 < 25$$
$$y > -2$$

A. All points outside the circle $x^2 + y^2 = 25$ and above the line $y = -2$

B. All points outside the circle $x^2 + y^2 = 25$ and below the line $y = -2$

C. All points inside the circle $x^2 + y^2 = 25$ and above the line $y = -2$

D. All points inside the circle $x^2 + y^2 = 25$ and below the line $y = -2$

2. **CONCEPT CHECK**   The graph of the system

$$y > x^2 + 1$$
$$\frac{x^2}{9} + \frac{y^2}{4} > 1$$
$$y < 5$$

consists of all points (*above/below*) the parabola $y = x^2 + 1$, (*inside/outside*) the ellipse $\frac{x^2}{9} + \frac{y^2}{4} = 1$, and (*above/below*) the line $y = 5$.

CONCEPT CHECK   *Match each nonlinear inequality with its graph.*

3. $y \geq x^2 + 4$

4. $y \leq x^2 + 4$

5. $y < x^2 + 4$

6. $y > x^2 + 4$

A.
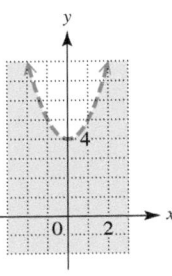

B.
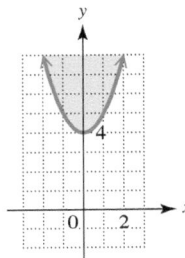

C.
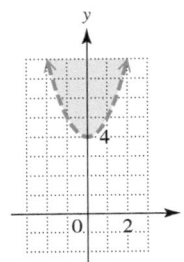

D.
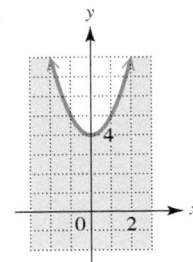

Graph each inequality. See Examples 1–3.

7. $y > x^2 - 1$
▶
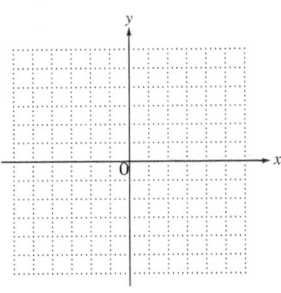

8. $y > x^2 - 2$
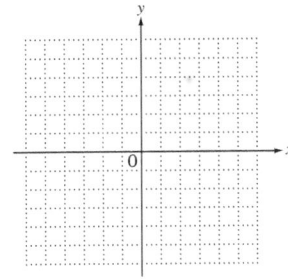

9. $y^2 \leq 4 - 2x^2$
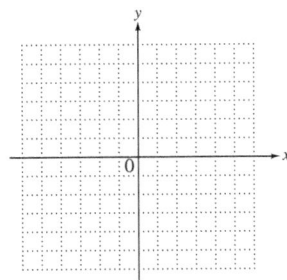

10. $2y^2 \geq 8 - x^2$
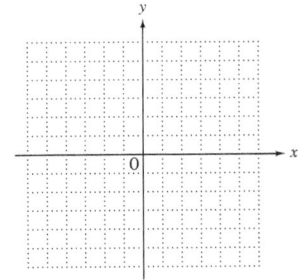

11. $x^2 \leq 16 - y^2$
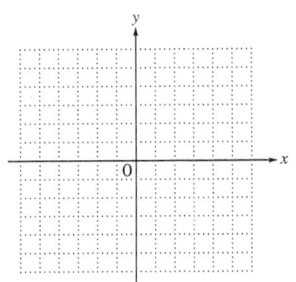

12. $x^2 > 4 - y^2$
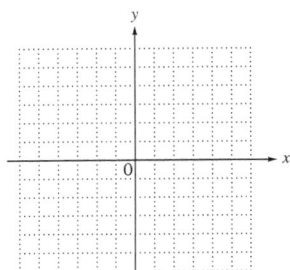

13. $9x^2 > 16y^2 + 144$
▶
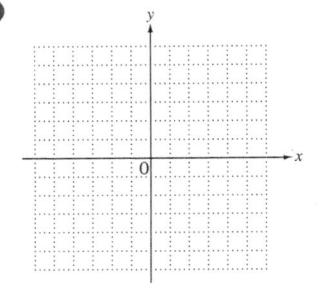

14. $y^2 > 4 + x^2$
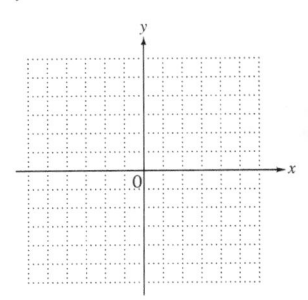

15. $9x^2 < 16y^2 - 144$

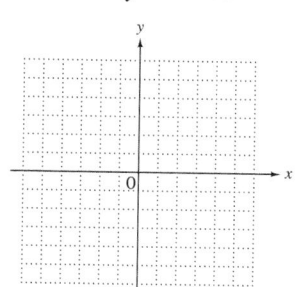

16. $x^2 \le 16 + 4y^2$

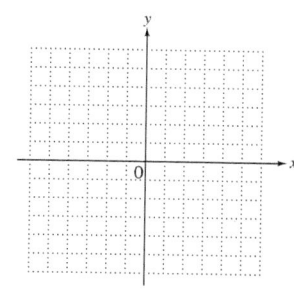

17. $4y^2 \le 36 - 9x^2$

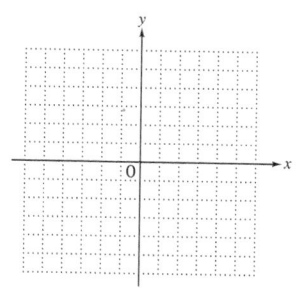

18. $x^2 - 4 \ge -4y^2$

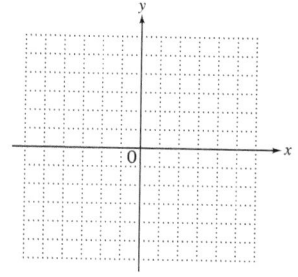

19. $x \ge y^2 - 8y + 14$

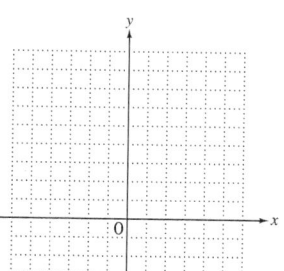

20. $x \le -y^2 + 6y - 7$

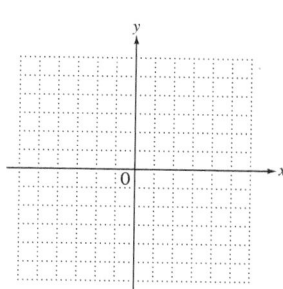

21. $25x^2 \le 9y^2 + 225$

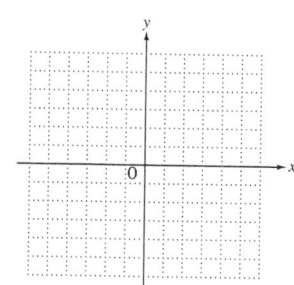

22. $y^2 - 16x^2 \le 16$

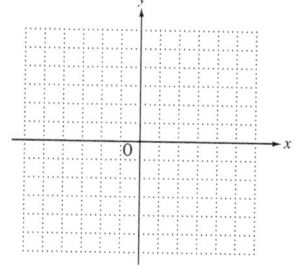

Graph each system of inequalities. ***See Examples 4–7.***

23. $3x - y > -6$
$4x + 3y > 12$

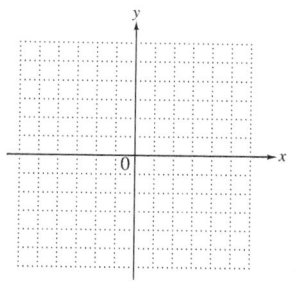

24. $2x + 5y < 10$
$x - 2y < 4$

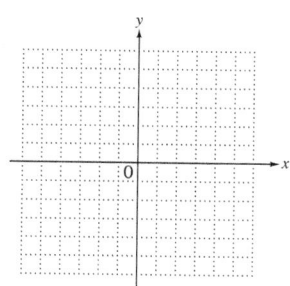

25. $4x - 3y \le 0$
$x + y \le 5$

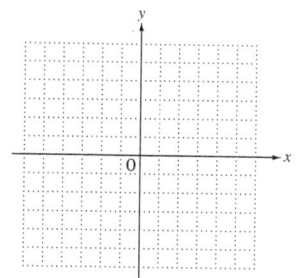

26. $5x - 3y \le 15$
$4x + y \ge 4$

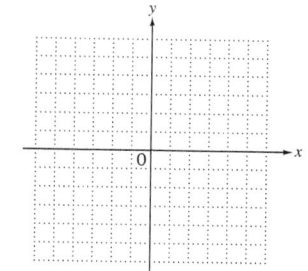

27. $x^2 - y^2 \ge 9$
$\dfrac{x^2}{16} + \dfrac{y^2}{9} \le 1$

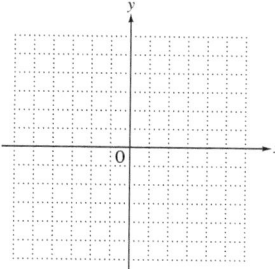

28. $y^2 - x^2 \ge 4$
$-5 \le y \le 5$

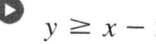

29. $y \le -x^2$
$y \ge x - 3$
$y \le -1$
$x < 1$

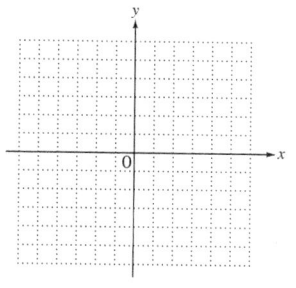

30. $y < x^2$
$y \ge -2$
$x + y < 3$
$3x - 2y > -6$

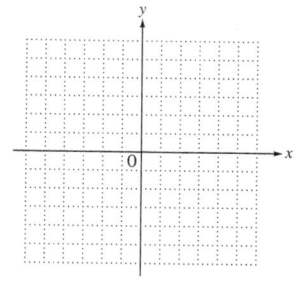

Chapter 13 Summary

Key Terms

13.1

asymptotes Lines that a graph approaches, such as the x- and y-axes for the graph of the reciprocal function, are the asymptotes of the graph.

greatest integer function The function $f(x) = [\![x]\!]$, where the symbol $[\![x]\!]$ represents the greatest integer less than or equal to x, is the greatest integer function.

step function A step function is a function with a graph that looks like a series of steps.

13.2

conic section When a plane intersects an infinite cone at different angles, the figures formed by the intersections are conic sections.

circle A circle is the set of all points in a plane that lie a fixed distance from a fixed point.

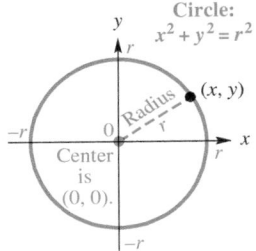

center The fixed point discussed in the definition of a circle is the center of the circle.

radius The radius of a circle is the fixed distance between the center and any point on the circle.

ellipse An ellipse is the set of all points in a plane the sum of whose distances from two fixed points (**foci**) is constant.

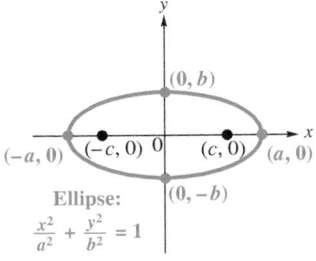

13.3

hyperbola A hyperbola is the set of all points in a plane such that the absolute value of the difference of the distances from two fixed points (foci) is constant.

transverse axis The line segment joining the two vertices of a hyperbola is the transverse axis.

asymptotes of a hyperbola The two intersecting lines that the branches of a hyperbola approach are the asymptotes of the hyperbola.

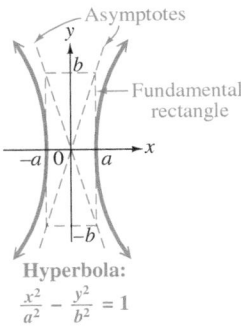

fundamental rectangle The asymptotes of a hyperbola are the extended diagonals of its fundamental rectangle.

13.4

nonlinear equation An equation in which some terms have more than one variable or a variable of degree 2 or greater is a nonlinear equation.

nonlinear system of equations A nonlinear system of equations is a system with at least one nonlinear equation.

13.5

second-degree inequality A second-degree inequality is an inequality with at least one variable of degree 2 and no variable with degree greater than 2.

system of inequalities A system of inequalities consists of two or more inequalities to be solved at the same time.

New Symbols

$[\![x]\!]$ greatest integer less than or equal to x

Test Your Word Power

See how well you have learned the vocabulary in this chapter.

1 **Conic sections** are
A. graphs of first-degree equations
B. the result of two or more intersecting planes
C. graphs of first-degree inequalities
D. figures that result from the intersection of an infinite cone with a plane.

2 A **circle** is the set of all points in a plane
A. such that the absolute value of the difference of the distances from two fixed points is constant
B. that lie a fixed distance from a fixed point
C. the sum of whose distances from two fixed points is constant
D. that make up the graph of any second-degree equation.

3 An **ellipse** is the set of all points in a plane
A. such that the absolute value of the difference of the distances from two fixed points is constant
B. that lie a fixed distance from a fixed point
C. the sum of whose distances from two fixed points is constant
D. that make up the graph of any second-degree equation.

4 A **hyperbola** is the set of all points in a plane
A. such that the absolute value of the difference of the distances from two fixed points is constant
B. that lie a fixed distance from a fixed point
C. the sum of whose distances from two fixed points is constant
D. that make up the graph of any second-degree equation.

5 A **nonlinear equation** is an equation
A. in which some terms have more than one variable or a variable of degree 2 or greater
B. in which the terms have only one variable
C. of degree 1
D. of a linear function.

6 A **nonlinear system of equations** is a system
A. with at least one linear equation
B. with two or more inequalities
C. with at least one nonlinear equation
D. with at least two linear equations.

Answers to Test Your Word Power

1. D; *Example:* Parabolas, circles, ellipses, and hyperbolas are conic sections.

2. B; *Example:* The graph of $x^2 + y^2 = 9$ is a circle centered at the origin with radius 3.

3. C; *Example:* The graph of $\frac{x^2}{49} + \frac{y^2}{36} = 1$ is an ellipse centered at the origin with x-intercepts $(7, 0)$ and $(-7, 0)$ and y-intercepts $(0, 6)$ and $(0, -6)$.

4. A; *Example:* The graph of $\frac{x^2}{16} - \frac{y^2}{25} = 1$ is a horizontal parabola centered at the origin with vertices $(4, 0)$ and $(-4, 0)$.

5. A; *Examples:* $y = x^2 + 8x + 16$, $xy = 5$, $2x^2 - y^2 = 6$

6. C; *Example:* $x^2 + y^2 = 2$
   $2x + y = 1$

Quick Review

Concepts

13.1 Additional Graphs of Functions

In addition to the squaring function, some other elementary functions include the following.

• Absolute value function $f(x) = |x|$

• Reciprocal function $f(x) = \frac{1}{x}$

• Square root function $f(x) = \sqrt{x}$

• Greatest integer function $f(x) = [\![x]\!]$, which is a step function

Their graphs can be translated, as shown in the first three examples at the right.

Examples

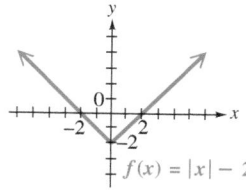

$f(x) = |x| - 2$

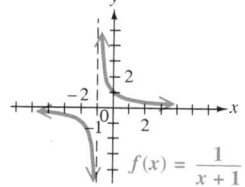

$f(x) = \frac{1}{x + 1}$

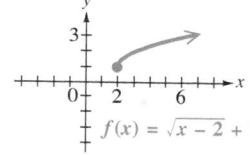

$f(x) = \sqrt{x - 2} + 1$

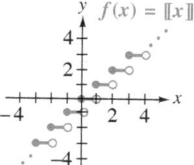

$f(x) = [\![x]\!]$

Concepts	Examples

13.2 Circles and Ellipses

Circle
A circle with center (h, k) and radius $r > 0$ has an equation of the form

$$(x - h)^2 + (y - k)^2 = r^2. \quad \text{Center-radius form}$$

If its center is $(0, 0)$, then this equation becomes

$$x^2 + y^2 = r^2.$$

Graph $(x + 2)^2 + (y - 3)^2 = 25$.

This equation, which can be written

$$[x - (-2)]^2 + (y - 3)^2 = 5^2,$$

represents a circle with center $(-2, 3)$ and radius 5.

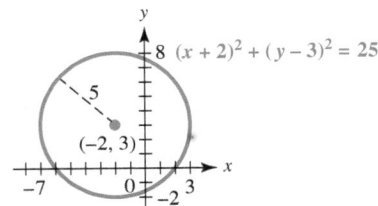

The general form of the equation of this circle is as follows.

$$(x + 2)^2 + (y - 3)^2 = 25 \quad \text{Center-radius form}$$
$$x^2 + 4x + 4 + y^2 - 6y + 9 = 25 \quad \text{Square each binomial.}$$
$$x^2 + y^2 + 4x - 6y - 12 = 0 \quad \text{General form}$$

Ellipse
An ellipse with x-intercepts $(a, 0)$ and $(-a, 0)$ and y-intercepts $(0, b)$ and $(0, -b)$ has an equation of the form

$$\frac{x^2}{a^2} + \frac{y^2}{b^2} = 1.$$

Graph $\dfrac{x^2}{9} + \dfrac{y^2}{4} = 1$.

x-intercepts: $(3, 0)$ and $(-3, 0)$

y-intercepts: $(0, 2)$ and $(0, -2)$

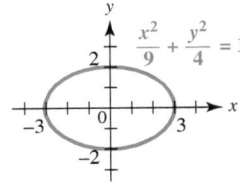

13.3 Hyperbolas and Functions Defined by Radicals

Hyperbola
A hyperbola with x-intercepts $(a, 0)$ and $(-a, 0)$ has an equation of the form

$$\frac{x^2}{a^2} - \frac{y^2}{b^2} = 1.$$

A hyperbola with y-intercepts $(0, b)$ and $(0, -b)$ has an equation of the form

$$\frac{y^2}{b^2} - \frac{x^2}{a^2} = 1.$$

The extended diagonals of the fundamental rectangle with vertices at the points $(a, b), (-a, b), (-a, -b)$, and $(a, -b)$ are the asymptotes of these hyperbolas.

Graph $\dfrac{x^2}{4} - \dfrac{y^2}{4} = 1$.

x-intercepts: $(2, 0)$ and $(-2, 0)$

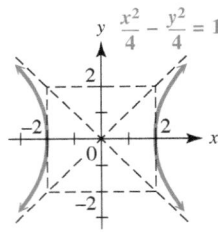

The fundamental rectangle has vertices at

$$(2, 2), \quad (-2, 2), \quad (-2, -2), \quad \text{and} \quad (2, -2).$$

Generalized Square Root Function
For an algebraic expression in x defined by u, with $u \geq 0$, a function of the form

$$f(x) = \sqrt{u}$$

is a generalized square root function.

Graph $y = -\sqrt{4 - x^2}$.
Square each side and rearrange terms.

$$x^2 + y^2 = 4$$

This equation has a circle as its graph. However, graph only the lower half of the circle because the original equation indicates that y cannot be positive.

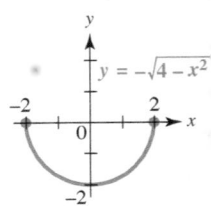

Concepts

Examples

13.4 Nonlinear Systems of Equations

Solving a Nonlinear System
A nonlinear system can be solved by the substitution method, the elimination method, or a combination of the two.

Solve the system.

$$x^2 + 2xy - y^2 = 14 \quad (1)$$
$$x^2 - y^2 = -16 \quad (2)$$

Multiply equation (2) by -1 and use the elimination method.

$$x^2 + 2xy - y^2 = 14$$
$$\underline{-x^2 \qquad + y^2 = 16}$$
$$2xy \qquad = 30$$
$$xy = 15$$

Geometric Interpretation
If, for example, a nonlinear system includes two second-degree equations, then there may be zero, one, two, three, or four solutions of the system.

Solve for y to obtain $y = \frac{15}{x}$, and substitute into equation (2).

$$x^2 - y^2 = -16 \quad (2)$$
$$x^2 - \left(\frac{15}{x}\right)^2 = -16 \quad \text{Let } y = \frac{15}{x}.$$
$$x^2 - \frac{225}{x^2} = -16 \quad \text{Apply the exponent.}$$
$$x^4 + 16x^2 - 225 = 0 \quad \text{Multiply by } x^2. \text{ Add } 16x^2.$$
$$(x^2 - 9)(x^2 + 25) = 0 \quad \text{Factor.}$$
$$x^2 - 9 = 0 \quad \text{or} \quad x^2 + 25 = 0 \quad \text{Zero-factor property}$$
$$x = \pm 3 \quad \text{or} \qquad x = \pm 5i \quad \text{Solve each equation.}$$

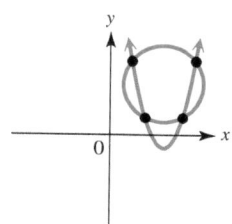

This system has four solutions because there are four points of intersection.

Find corresponding y-values to obtain the solution set.

$$\{(3, 5), (-3, -5), (5i, -3i), (-5i, 3i)\}$$

13.5 Second-Degree Inequalities and Systems of Inequalities

Graphing a Second-Degree Inequality
To graph a second-degree inequality, graph the corresponding equation as a boundary and use test points to determine which region(s) form the solution set. Shade the appropriate region(s).

Graphing a System of Inequalities
The solution set of a system of inequalities is the intersection of the graphs (solution sets) of the inequalities in the system.

Graph $y \geq x^2 - 2x + 3$.
The boundary is a parabola that opens up with vertex $(1, 2)$. Use $(0, 0)$ as a test point. Substituting into the inequality $y > x^2 - 2x + 3$ gives a false statement,

$$0 > 3. \quad \text{False}$$

Shade the region inside (or above) the parabola.

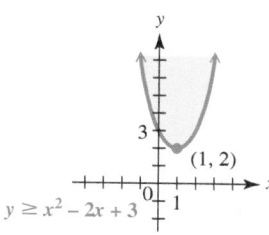

Graph the solution set of the system.

$$3x - 5y > -15$$
$$x^2 + y^2 \leq 25$$

Graph each inequality separately, on the same axes. The graph of the system is the region that lies below the dashed line *and* inside the solid circle.

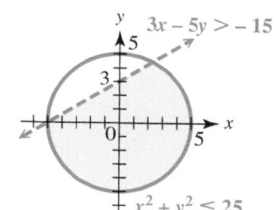

Chapter 13 *Review Exercises*

13.1 *Graph each function. Give the domain and range.*

1. $f(x) = |x + 4|$

2. $f(x) = \dfrac{1}{x - 4}$

3. $f(x) = \sqrt{x} + 3$

4. $f(x) = [\![-x]\!]$

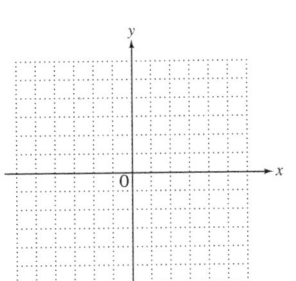 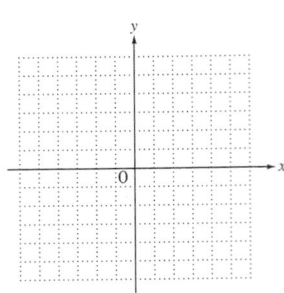 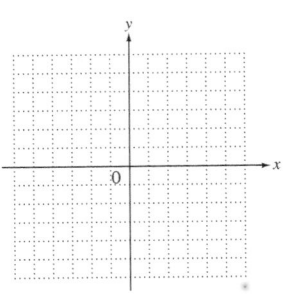 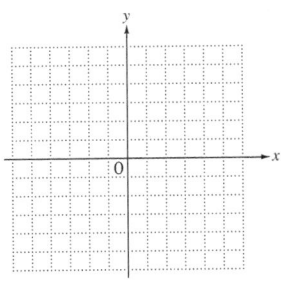

Evaluate each expression.

5. $[\![12]\!]$

6. $\left[\!\!\left[2\dfrac{3}{4} \right]\!\!\right]$

7. $[\![-21]\!]$

8. $[\![-4.75]\!]$

13.2 *Find an equation of a circle satisfying the given conditions.*

9. Center: $(0, 0)$; radius: 7

10. Center: $(-2, 4)$; radius: 3

11. Center: $(-1, -3)$; radius: 5

12. Center: $(4, 2)$; radius: 6

Find the center and radius of each circle.

13. $x^2 + y^2 + 6x - 4y - 3 = 0$

14. $x^2 + y^2 - 8x - 2y + 13 = 0$

15. $2x^2 + 2y^2 + 4x + 20y = -34$

16. $4x^2 + 4y^2 - 24x + 16y = 48$

Graph each equation.

17. $x^2 + y^2 = 16$

18. $\dfrac{x^2}{16} + \dfrac{y^2}{9} = 1$

19. $\dfrac{x^2}{36} + \dfrac{y^2}{25} = 1$

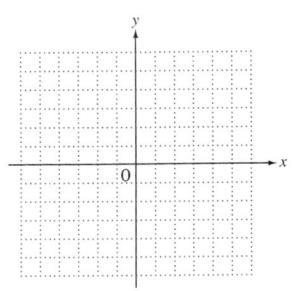 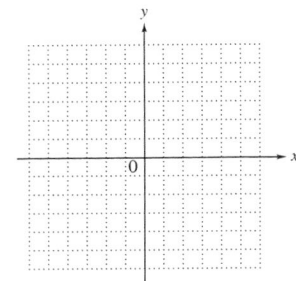 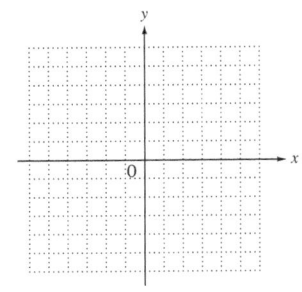

13.3 *Graph each equation.*

20. $\dfrac{x^2}{16} - \dfrac{y^2}{25} = 1$

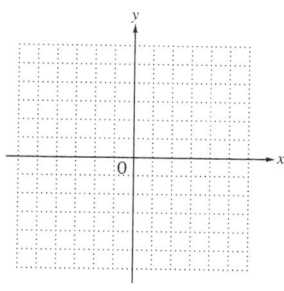

21. $\dfrac{y^2}{25} - \dfrac{x^2}{4} = 1$

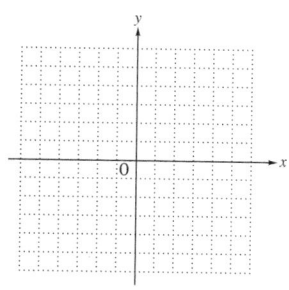

22. $f(x) = -\sqrt{16 - x^2}$

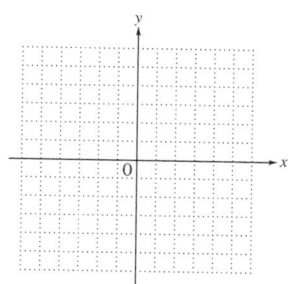

Identify the graph of each equation as a parabola, circle, ellipse, *or* hyperbola.

23. $x^2 + y^2 = 64$

24. $y = 2x^2 - 3$

25. $y^2 = 2x^2 - 8$

26. $y^2 = 8 - 2x^2$

27. $x = y^2 + 4$

28. $x^2 - y^2 = 64$

13.4 *Solve each system.*

29. $2y = 3x - x^2$
$\quad x + 2y = -12$

30. $y + 1 = x^2 + 2x$
$\quad y + 2x = 4$

31. $x^2 + 3y^2 = 28$
$\quad y - x = -2$

32. $xy = 8$
$\quad x - 2y = 6$

33. $x^2 + y^2 = 6$
$\quad x^2 - 2y^2 = -6$

34. $3x^2 - 2y^2 = 12$
$\quad x^2 + 4y^2 = 18$

CONCEPT CHECK *Answer each question.*

35. How many solutions are possible for a system of two equations whose graphs are a circle and a line?

36. How many solutions are possible for a system of two equations whose graphs are a parabola and a hyperbola?

13.5 *Graph each inequality or system of inequalities.*

37. $9x^2 \geq 16y^2 + 144$

38. $4x^2 + y^2 \geq 16$

39. $2x + 5y \leq 10$
$\quad 3x - y \leq 6$

40. $|x| \leq 2$
$\quad |y| > 1$
$\quad 4x^2 + 9y^2 \leq 36$

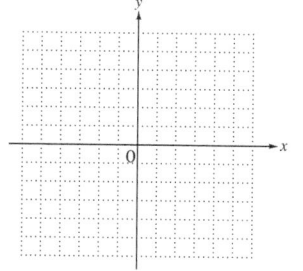

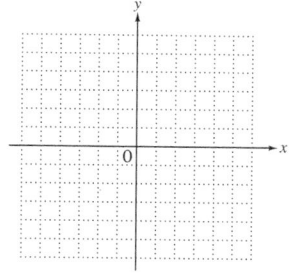

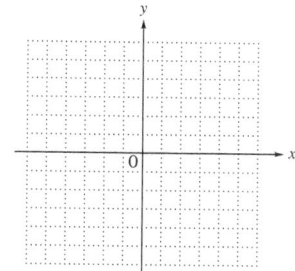

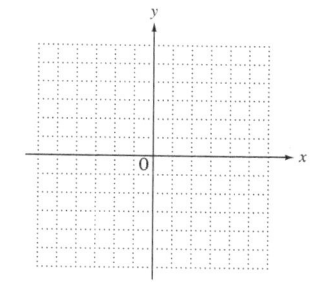

Chapter 13 *Mixed Review Exercises*

1. Find the center and radius of the circle with equation $x^2 + y^2 + 4x - 10y - 7 = 0$.

Graph.

2. $(x + 1)^2 + (y - 2)^2 = 4$

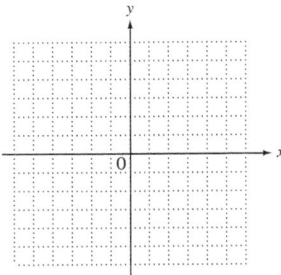

3. $x^2 + 9y^2 = 9$

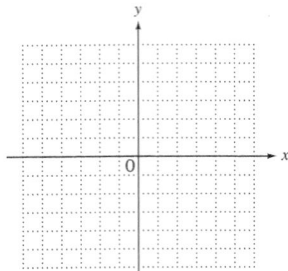

4. $\dfrac{(x - 1)^2}{16} + \dfrac{(y + 3)^2}{9} = 1$

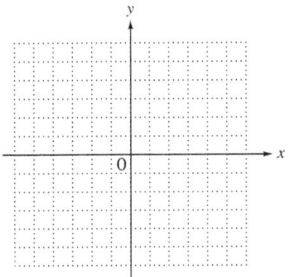

5. $x^2 - 9y^2 = 9$

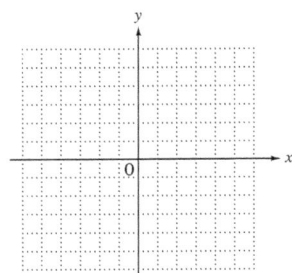

6. $f(x) = \sqrt{x + 2}$

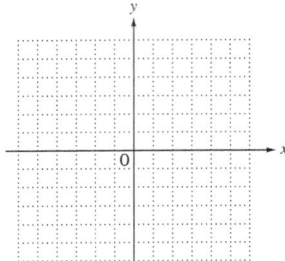

7. $f(x) = [\![x]\!] - 1$

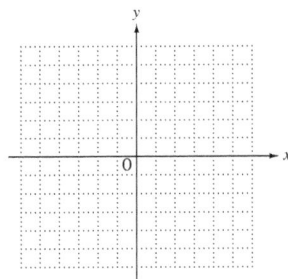

8. $y < -(x + 2)^2 + 1$

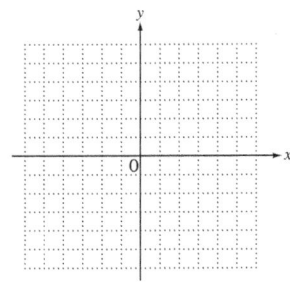

9. $4y > 3x - 12$
$x^2 < 16 - y^2$

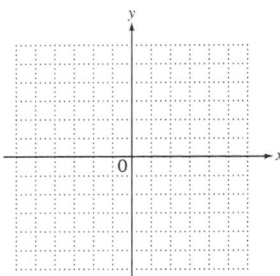

10. $9x^2 \le 4y^2 + 36$
$x^2 + y^2 \le 16$

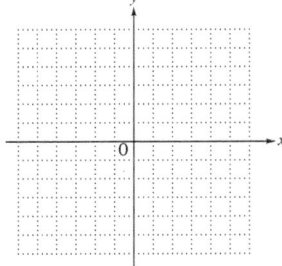

Solve each system.

11. $y = x^2 - 84$
$4y = 20x$

12. $x^2 - xy - y^2 = -5$
$x^2 - y^2 = -3$

| **Chapter 13** | **Test** | *The Chapter Test Prep Videos with step-by-step solutions are available in* MyMathLab *or on* You Tube *at **https://goo.gl/3rBuO5*** |

Fill in each blank with the correct response.

1. For the reciprocal function $f(x) = \frac{1}{x}$, _____ is the only real number not in the domain.

2. The range of the square root function $f(x) = \sqrt{x}$ is _____ .

3. The range of $f(x) = [\![x]\!]$, the greatest integer function, is _____ .

4. Match each function in parts (a)–(d) with its graph from choices A–D.

   (a) $f(x) = \sqrt{x} - 2$ **(b)** $f(x) = \sqrt{x+2}$ **(c)** $f(x) = \sqrt{x} + 2$ **(d)** $f(x) = \sqrt{x-2}$

A. 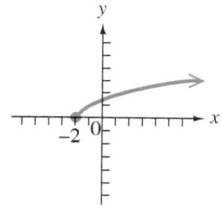   **B.** 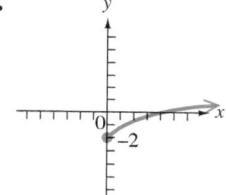   **C.** 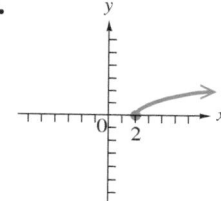   **D.**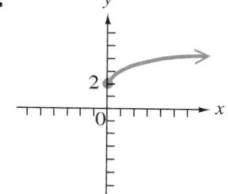

5. Graph $f(x) = |x - 3| + 4$. Give the domain and range.

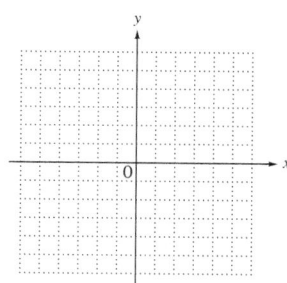

6. Find the center and radius of the circle with equation $(x - 2)^2 + (y + 3)^2 = 16$. Graph it.

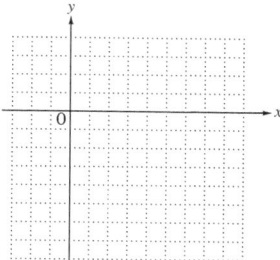

7. Which one of the following equations is represented by the graph of a circle?

   A. $x^2 + y^2 = 0$ **B.** $x^2 + y^2 = -1$ **C.** $x^2 + y^2 = x^2 - y^2$ **D.** $x^2 + y^2 = 1$

8. For the equation in **Exercise 7** that is represented by a circle, what are the coordinates of the center? What is the radius?

9. Find the center and radius of the circle with equation $x^2 + y^2 + 8x - 2y = 8$.

Graph.

10. $f(x) = \sqrt{9 - x^2}$

11. $4x^2 + 9y^2 = 36$

12. $16y^2 - 4x^2 = 64$

13. $\dfrac{y}{2} = -\sqrt{1 - \dfrac{x^2}{9}}$

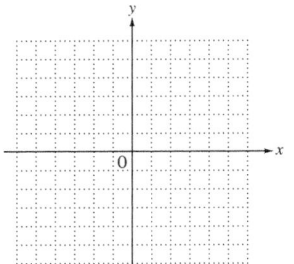
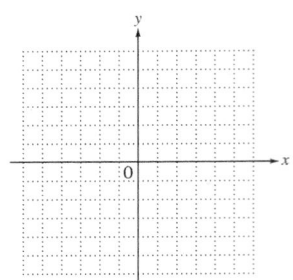
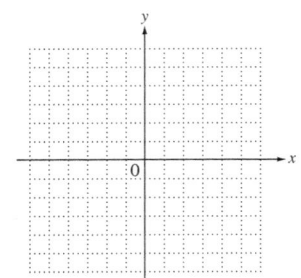
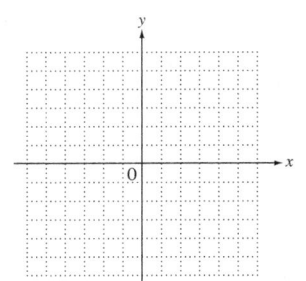

Identify the graph of each equation as a parabola, circle, ellipse, *or* hyperbola.

14. $6x^2 + 4y^2 = 12$

15. $16x^2 = 144 + 9y^2$

16. $4y^2 + 4x = 9$

17. $y^2 = 20 - x^2$

Solve each system.

18. $2x - y = 9$
   $xy = 5$

19. $x - 4 = 3y$
   $x^2 + y^2 = 8$

20. $x^2 + y^2 = 25$
   $x^2 - 2y^2 = 16$

21. Graph the inequality $y < x^2 - 2$.

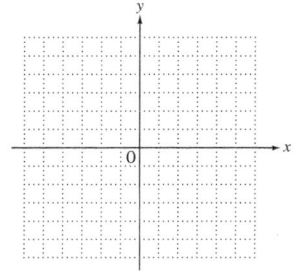

22. Graph the system $\begin{array}{l} x^2 + 25y^2 \le 25 \\ x^2 + y^2 \le 9 \end{array}$.

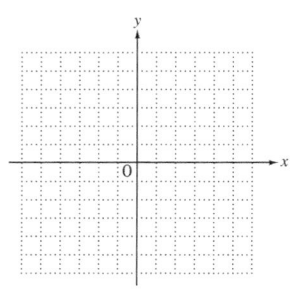

Chapters R–13 *Cumulative Review Exercises*

Solve.

1. $4 - (2x + 3) + x = 5x - 3$

2. $-4k + 7 \geq 6k + 1$

3. $|5m| - 6 = 14$

4. Find the slope of the line through $(2, 5)$ and $(-4, 1)$.

5. Find an equation in standard form of the line passing through the point $(-3, -2)$ and perpendicular to the graph of $2x - 3y = 7$.

Solve each system.

6. $3x - y = 12$
$\quad 2x + 3y = -3$

7. $x + y - 2z = 9$
$\quad 2x + y + z = 7$
$\quad 3x - y - z = 13$

8. $xy = -5$
$\quad 2x + y = 3$

Simplify. Assume that all variables represent positive real numbers.

9. $\dfrac{(2a)^{-2}a^4}{a^{-3}}$

10. $4\sqrt[3]{16} - 2\sqrt[3]{54}$

11. $\dfrac{3\sqrt{5x}}{\sqrt{2x}}$

12. Write the number -0.000276 in scientific notation.

Perform the indicated operations.

13. $(5y - 3)^2$

14. $\dfrac{8x^4 - 4x^3 + 2x^2 + 13x + 8}{2x + 1}$

15. $\dfrac{5 + 3i}{2 - i}$

16. $\dfrac{y^2 - 4}{y^2 - y - 6} \div \dfrac{y^2 - 2y}{y - 1}$

17. $\dfrac{5}{c + 5} - \dfrac{2}{c + 3}$

18. $\dfrac{p}{p^2 + p} + \dfrac{1}{p^2 + p}$

Factor.

19. $12x^2 - 7x - 10$

20. $z^4 - 1$

21. $a^3 - 27b^3$

22. Kareem and Jamal want to clean their office. Kareem can do the job alone in 3 hr, and Jamal can do it alone in 2 hr. How long will it take them if they work together?

Solve.

23. $2\sqrt{k} = \sqrt{5k + 3}$

24. $10q^2 + 13q = 3$

25. $3k^2 - 3k - 2 = 0$

26. $2(x^2 - 3)^2 - 5(x^2 - 3) = 12$

27. $\log(x + 2) + \log(x - 1) = 1$

28. $F = \dfrac{kwv^2}{r}$ for v

(Leave $\pm$ in the answer.)

29. If $f(x) = x^2 + 2x - 4$ and $g(x) = 3x + 2$, find the following.

  (a) $(g \circ f)(1)$

  (b) $(f \circ g)(x)$

30. If $f(x) = x^3 + 4$, find $f^{-1}(x)$.

31. Evaluate.

  (a) $3^{\log_3 4}$

  (b) $e^{\ln 7}$

32. Use properties of logarithms to write the following as a single logarithm.

$$2 \log(3x + 7) - \log 4$$

Graph.

33. $f(x) = -3x + 5$

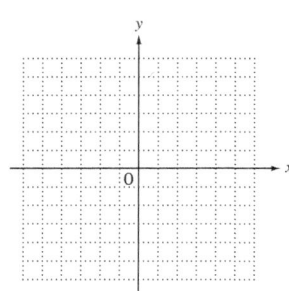

34. $f(x) = -2(x - 1)^2 + 3$

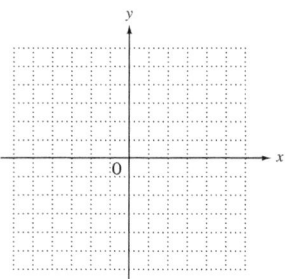

35. $\dfrac{x^2}{25} + \dfrac{y^2}{16} \leq 1$

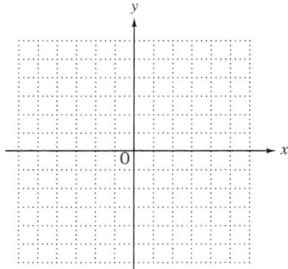

36. $f(x) = \sqrt{x - 2}$

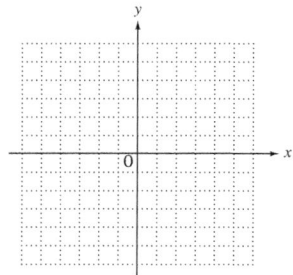

37. $\dfrac{x^2}{4} - \dfrac{y^2}{16} = 1$

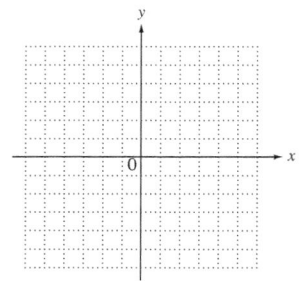

38. $f(x) = 3^x$

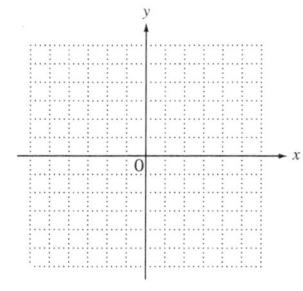

Appendix: Review of Exponents, Polynomials, and Factoring
Transition from Introductory to Intermediate Algebra

OBJECTIVE ▶ **1** Review the basic rules for exponents.

OBJECTIVES

1 Review the basic rules for exponents.

2 Review addition, subtraction, and multiplication of polynomials.

3 Review factoring techniques.

Definitions and Rules for Exponents

For all integers m and n and all real numbers a and b for which the following are defined, these definitions and rules hold true.

		Examples
Product rule	$a^m \cdot a^n = a^{m+n}$	$7^4 \cdot 7^3 = 7^{4+3} = 7^7$
Zero exponent	$a^0 = 1$	$(-3)^0 = 1$
Negative exponent	$a^{-n} = \dfrac{1}{a^n}$	$5^{-3} = \dfrac{1}{5^3}$
Quotient rule	$\dfrac{a^m}{a^n} = a^{m-n}$	$\dfrac{2^2}{2^5} = 2^{2-5} = 2^{-3} = \dfrac{1}{2^3}$
Power rules (a)	$(a^m)^n = a^{mn}$	$(4^2)^3 = 4^{2\cdot3} = 4^6$
(b)	$(ab)^m = a^m b^m$	$(3k)^4 = 3^4 k^4$
(c)	$\left(\dfrac{a}{b}\right)^m = \dfrac{a^m}{b^m}$	$\left(\dfrac{2}{3}\right)^2 = \dfrac{2^2}{3^2}$
Negative-to-positive rules	$\dfrac{a^{-m}}{b^{-n}} = \dfrac{b^n}{a^m}$	$\dfrac{2^{-4}}{5^{-3}} = \dfrac{5^3}{2^4}$
	$\left(\dfrac{a}{b}\right)^{-m} = \left(\dfrac{b}{a}\right)^m$	$\left(\dfrac{4}{7}\right)^{-2} = \left(\dfrac{7}{4}\right)^2$

EXAMPLE 1 Applying Definitions and Rules for Exponents

Simplify. Write answers using only positive exponents. Assume that all variables represent nonzero real numbers.

(a) $(x^2 y^{-3})(x^{-5} y^7)$

$= (x^{2+(-5)})(y^{-3+7})$ Product rule

$= x^{-3} y^4$

$= \dfrac{1}{x^3} y^4$ Definition of negative exponent

$= \dfrac{y^4}{x^3}$

$\frac{1}{x^3} y^4 = \frac{1}{x^3} \cdot \frac{y^4}{1} = \frac{y^4}{x^3}$

(b) $-5^0 + (-5)^0$ Notice the use of parentheses.

    ↑   ↑

The base is 5.   The base is -5.

$= -1 + 1$ $a^0 = 1$

$= 0$ Add.

Continued on Next Page

1017

1 Simplify. Write answers using only positive exponents. Assume that all variables represent nonzero real numbers.

(a) $(m^{-8}n^4)(m^4n^{-3})$

(b) $4^0 + (-4)^0$

(c) $\dfrac{(x^3y^{-2})^3}{(x^4y^{-3})^2}$

(d) $\left(\dfrac{2x^2y^{-2}}{x^{-4}y}\right)^{-3}$

(e) $(3ab^4c^2)^3(b^2c)^2$

2 Add or subtract as indicated.

(a) $(5x^3 - 3x^2 + x + 4)$
$\quad + (2x^3 - x^2 - 3x - 1)$

(b) $(7y^2 - 11y + 8)$
$\quad - (-3y^2 + 4y + 6)$

(c) Subtract.
$$4x^2 + 7x - 5$$
$$- (-5x^2 - 2x + 3)$$

Answers

1. (a) $\dfrac{n}{m^4}$ (b) 2 (c) x (d) $\dfrac{y^9}{8x^{18}}$
   (e) $27a^3b^{16}c^8$
2. (a) $7x^3 - 4x^2 - 2x + 3$
   (b) $10y^2 - 15y + 2$
   (c) $9x^2 + 9x - 8$

(c) $\dfrac{(t^5s^{-4})^2}{(t^{-3}s^5)^3}$

$= \dfrac{t^{10}s^{-8}}{t^{-9}s^{15}}$ Power rules (a) and (b)

$= \dfrac{t^{10}t^9}{s^{15}s^8}$ Definition of negative exponent

$= \dfrac{t^{19}}{s^{23}}$ Product rule

(d) $\left(\dfrac{-3x^{-4}y}{x^5y^{-4}}\right)^{-2}$

$= \left(\dfrac{x^5y^{-4}}{-3x^{-4}y}\right)^2$ Negative-to-positive rule

$= \dfrac{x^{10}y^{-8}}{9x^{-8}y^2}$ Power rules (a), (b), and (c)

$= \dfrac{x^{18}}{9y^{10}}$ Quotient rule

(e) $(2x^2y^3z)^2(x^4y^2)^3$

$= (4x^4y^6z^2)(x^{12}y^6)$ Power rules (a) and (b)

$= 4x^{16}y^{12}z^2$ Product rule

◀ **Work Problem ① at the Side.**

OBJECTIVE ② Review addition, subtraction, and multiplication of polynomials.

Adding and Subtracting Polynomials

To add two polynomials, add (combine) like terms.

To subtract two polynomials, change all signs in the subtrahend (second polynomial) and add the result to the minuend (first polynomial).

EXAMPLE 2 Adding and Subtracting Polynomials

Add or subtract as indicated.

(a) $(-4x^3 + 3x^2 - 8x + 2) + (5x^3 - 8x^2 + 12x - 3)$

$= (-4x^3 + 5x^3) + (3x^2 - 8x^2) + (-8x + 12x) + (2 - 3)$
$\qquad$ Commutative and associative properties

$= (-4 + 5)x^3 + (3 - 8)x^2 + (-8 + 12)x + (2 - 3)$
$\qquad$ Distributive property

$= x^3 - 5x^2 + 4x - 1$ Add and subtract.

(b) $-4(x^2 + 3x - 6) - (2x^2 - 3x + 7)$

$= -4(x^2 + 3x - 6) - 1(2x^2 - 3x + 7)$ $-a = -1a$

$= -4(x^2) - 4(3x) - 4(-6) - 1(2x^2) - 1(-3x) - 1(7)$
$\qquad$ Distributive property

$= -4x^2 - 12x + 24 - 2x^2 + 3x - 7$ Multiply.

$= -6x^2 - 9x + 17$ Combine like terms.

(c) Subtract.

$$2t^2 - 3t - 4 \qquad\qquad 2t^2 - 3t - 4$$
$$- (-8t^2 + 4t - 1) \longrightarrow + (8t^2 - 4t + 1) \quad \text{Change each sign.}$$
$$\qquad\qquad\qquad\qquad 10t^2 - 7t - 3 \quad \text{Add.}$$

◀ **Work Problem ② at the Side.**

Multiplying Polynomials

To multiply two polynomials, multiply each term of the second polynomial by each term of the first polynomial and add the products.

To multiply two binomials, use the FOIL method.

Also recall the special product rules. For x and y, the following hold true.

$$\left.\begin{array}{l}(x + y)^2 = x^2 + 2xy + y^2 \\ (x - y)^2 = x^2 - 2xy + y^2\end{array}\right\} \text{Square of a binomial}$$

$$(x + y)(x - y) = x^2 - y^2 \quad \begin{array}{l}\text{Product of a sum and} \\ \text{difference of two terms}\end{array}$$

EXAMPLE 3   Multiplying Polynomials

Find each product.

(a) $(4y - 1)(3y + 2)$

$$\underbrace{\text{First}}_{\text{terms}} \quad \underbrace{\text{Outer}}_{\text{terms}} \quad \underbrace{\text{Inner}}_{\text{terms}} \quad \underbrace{\text{Last}}_{\text{terms}}$$

$= 4y(3y) + 4y(2) - 1(3y) - 1(2)$ FOIL method

$= 12y^2 + 8y - 3y - 2$ Multiply.

$= 12y^2 + 5y - 2$ Combine like terms.

(b) $(3x + 5y)(3x - 5y)$ $(ab)^2 = a^2b^2, \textbf{ not } ab^2.$

$= (3x)^2 - (5y)^2$ $(x + y)(x - y) = x^2 - y^2$

$= 9x^2 - 25y^2$ $(3x)^2 = 3^2x^2 = 9x^2; (5y)^2 = 5^2y^2 = 25y^2$

(c) $(2t + 3)^2$

$= (2t)^2 + 2(2t)(3) + 3^2$ $(x + y)^2 = x^2 + 2xy + y^2$

$= 4t^2 + 12t + 9$ Remember the middle term.

(d) $(5x - 1)^2$

$= (5x)^2 - 2(5x)(1) + 1^2$ $(x - y)^2 = x^2 - 2xy + y^2$

$= 25x^2 - 10x + 1$ $(5x)^2 = 5^2x^2 = 25x^2$

(e) $(3x + 2)(9x^2 - 6x + 4)$

$$\begin{array}{r}9x^2 - 6x + 4 \\ 3x + 2\end{array} \quad \text{Multiply vertically.}$$

$$\begin{array}{l}18x^2 - 12x + 8 \leftarrow 2(9x^2 - 6x + 4) \\ \underline{27x^3 - 18x^2 + 12x} \quad\; \leftarrow 3x(9x^2 - 6x + 4) \\ 27x^3 \qquad\qquad\quad + 8 \quad \text{Add like terms.}\end{array}$$

Be sure to write like terms in columns.

The product is a sum of cubes, $27x^3 + 8$.

───────────── Work Problem ③ at the Side. ▶

③ Find each product.

(a) $(2x + 5)(3x - 2)$

(b) $(2t + 7y)(2t - 7y)$

(c) $(6r - 5)^2$

(d) $(3x + 7)^2$

(e) $(2x - 3)(4x^2 + 6x + 9)$

Answers

3. **(a)** $6x^2 + 11x - 10$ **(b)** $4t^2 - 49y^2$
(c) $36r^2 - 60r + 25$ **(d)** $9x^2 + 42x + 49$
(e) $8x^3 - 27$

OBJECTIVE ▸ ③ Review factoring techniques. Recall that factoring involves writing a polynomial as a product.

Guidelines for Factoring a Polynomial

Question 1 **Is there a common factor other than 1?** If so, factor it out.

Question 2 **How many terms are in the polynomial?**

Two terms: The polynomial is a binomial. Is it a difference of squares or a sum or difference of cubes? If so, factor using the appropriate rule.

$$x^2 - y^2 = (x + y)(x - y) \qquad \text{Difference of squares}$$

$$x^3 - y^3 = (x - y)(x^2 + xy + y^2) \qquad \text{Difference of cubes}$$

$$x^3 + y^3 = (x + y)(x^2 - xy + y^2) \qquad \text{Sum of cubes}$$

Three terms: The polynomial is a trinomial. Is it a perfect square trinomial? If so, factor as follows.

$$x^2 + 2xy + y^2 = (x + y)^2$$
$$x^2 - 2xy + y^2 = (x - y)^2$$

Perfect square trinomials

If the trinomial is not a perfect square trinomial, use one of the following methods.

- To factor $x^2 + bx + c$, find two integers whose product is c and whose sum is b, the coefficient of the middle term.

- To factor $ax^2 + bx + c$, find two integers having product ac and sum b. Use these integers to rewrite the middle term, and factor by grouping.

  Alternatively, use the FOIL method and try various combinations of the factors until the correct middle term is found.

Four terms: Try to factor by grouping.

Question 3 **Can any factors be factored further?** If so, factor them.

EXAMPLE 4 Factoring Polynomials

Factor each polynomial completely.

(a) $6x^2y^3 - 12x^3y^2$

$$= 6x^2y^2(y) - 6x^2y^2(2x) \qquad 6x^2y^2 \text{ is the greatest common factor.}$$

$$= 6x^2y^2(y - 2x) \qquad \text{Distributive property}$$

(b) $3x^2 - x - 2$

To find the factors, find two terms that multiply to give $3x^2$ (here $3x$ and x) and two terms that multiply to give -2 (here $+2$ and -1). Make sure that the sum of the outer and inner products in the factored form is $-x$.

$$3x^2 - x - 2 \quad \text{factors as} \quad (3x + 2)(x - 1).$$

CHECK $(3x + 2)(x - 1)$

$$= 3x(x) + 3x(-1) + 2(x) + 2(-1) \qquad \text{Multiply using the FOIL method.}$$

$$= 3x^2 - x - 2 \checkmark \qquad \text{Original polynomial}$$

Continued on Next Page

(c) $3x^2 - 27x + 42$

$\qquad = 3(x^2 - 9x + 14)$ Factor out the common factor.

$\qquad = 3(x - 7)(x - 2)$ Factor the trinomial.

(d) $100t^2 - 81$

$\qquad = (10t)^2 - 9^2$ Difference of squares

$\qquad = (10t + 9)(10t - 9)$ $x^2 - y^2 = (x + y)(x - y)$

(e) $4x^2 + 20xy + 25y^2$

The terms $4x^2$ and $25y^2$ are both perfect squares, so this trinomial might factor as a perfect square trinomial.

$\qquad$ Try to factor $4x^2 + 20xy + 25y^2$ as $(2x + 5y)^2$.

CHECK   Take twice the product of the two terms in the squared binomial.

$\qquad 2 \cdot 2x \cdot 5y = 20xy \leftarrow$ Middle term of $4x^2 + 20xy + 25y^2$

Twice $\longrightarrow$ First term $\longrightarrow$ Last term

Because $20xy$ is the middle term of the trinomial, the trinomial is a perfect square. ✓

$\qquad 4x^2 + 20xy + 25y^2$ factors as $(2x + 5y)^2$.

(f) $1000x^3 - 27$

$\qquad = (10x)^3 - 3^3$ Difference of cubes

$\qquad = (10x - 3)[(10x)^2 + 10x(3) + 3^2]$

$\qquad\qquad\qquad x^3 - y^3 = (x - y)(x^2 + xy + y^2)$

$\qquad = (10x - 3)(100x^2 + 30x + 9)$ $(10x)^2 = 10^2x^2 = 100x^2$

(g) $6xy - 3x + 4y - 2$

Because there are four terms, try factoring by grouping.

$\qquad 6xy - 3x + 4y - 2$

$\qquad = (6xy - 3x) + (4y - 2)$ Group the terms.

$\qquad = 3x(2y - 1) + 2(2y - 1)$ Factor each group.

$\qquad = (2y - 1)(3x + 2)$ Factor out $2y - 1$.

In the final step, factor out the greatest common factor, the binomial $2y - 1$.

$\qquad\qquad\qquad$ **Work Problem ④ at the Side.** ▶

❗ CAUTION

When a polynomial has been factored, it is wise to do the following.

1. *Check* that the product of all the factors does indeed yield the original polynomial.

2. *Check* that the original polynomial has been factored **completely**.

④ Factor each polynomial completely.

(a) $10s^3t^6 + 5s^9t^2$

(b) $12x^2 - 5x - 2$

(c) $5x^2 - 20x - 60$

(d) $49z^2 - 36$

(e) $4x^2 - 28x + 49$

(f) $8p^3 + 125$

(g) $xy + 6y + xz + 6z$

Answers

4. (a) $5s^3t^2(2t^4 + s^6)$
$\quad$ **(b)** $(4x + 1)(3x - 2)$
$\quad$ **(c)** $5(x - 6)(x + 2)$
$\quad$ **(d)** $(7z + 6)(7z - 6)$
$\quad$ **(e)** $(2x - 7)^2$
$\quad$ **(f)** $(2p + 5)(4p^2 - 10p + 25)$
$\quad$ **(g)** $(x + 6)(y + z)$

Appendix A Exercises

FOR EXTRA HELP

Go to MyMathLab *for worked-out, step-by-step solutions to exercises enclosed in a square* ▢ *and video solutions to* ▶ *exercises.*

Simplify each expression. Write the answers using only positive exponents. Assume that all variables represent positive real numbers. **See Example 1.**

1. $(a^4 b^{-3})(a^{-6} b^2)$

2. $(t^{-3} s^{-5})(t^8 s^{-2})$

3. $(5x^{-2}y)^2 (2xy^4)^2$

4. $(7x^{-3}y^4)^3 (2x^{-1}y^{-4})^2$

5. $-6^0 + (-6)^0$

6. $(-12)^0 - 12^0$

7. $\dfrac{(2w^{-1}x^2y^{-1})^3}{(4w^5 x^{-2}y)^2}$

8. $\dfrac{(5p^{-3}q^2 r^{-4})^2}{(10p^4 q^{-1} r^5)^{-1}}$

9. $\left(\dfrac{-4a^{-2}b^4}{a^3 b^{-1}}\right)^{-3}$

10. $\left(\dfrac{r^{-3}s^{-8}}{-6r^2 s^{-4}}\right)^{-2}$

11. $(7x^{-4}y^2 z^{-2})^{-2} (7x^4 y^{-1} z^3)^2$

12. $(3m^{-5}n^2 p^{-4})^3 (3m^4 n^{-3} p^5)^{-2}$

Add or subtract as indicated. **See Example 2.**

13. $(2a^4 + 3a^3 - 6a^2 + 5a - 12)$
$\quad + (-8a^4 + 8a^3 - 14a^2 + 21a - 3)$

14. $(-6r^4 - 3r^3 + 12r^2 - 9r + 9)$
$\quad + (8r^4 - 13r^3 - 14r^2 - 10r - 3)$

15. $(6x^3 - 12x^2 + 3x - 4) - (-2x^3 + 6x^2 - 3x + 12)$

16. $(10y^3 - 4y^2 + 8y + 7) - (7y^3 + 5y^2 - 2y - 13)$

17. $\quad 5x^2 y + 2xy^2 + y^3$
$+ \underline{(-4x^2 y - 3xy^2 + 5y^3)}$

18. $\quad 6ab^3 - 2a^2 b^2 + 3b^5$
$+ \underline{(8ab^3 + 12a^2 b^2 - 8b^5)}$

19. $3(5x^2 - 12x + 4) - 2(9x^2 + 13x - 10)$

20. $-4(2t^3 - 3t^2 + 4t - 1)$
$\quad - 3(-8t^3 + 3t^2 - 2t + 9)$

21. $\quad 6x^3 - 2x^2 + 3x - 1$
$- \underline{(-4x^3 + 2x^2 - 6x + 3)}$

22. $\quad -9y^3 - 2y^2 + 3y - 8$
$- \underline{(-8y^3 + 4y^2 + 3y + 1)}$

*Find each product. **See Example 3.***

23. $(3x + 1)(2x - 7)$

24. $(5z + 3)(2z - 3)$

25. $(4x - 1)(x - 2)$

26. $(7t - 3)(t - 4)$

27. $(4t + 3)(4t - 3)$

28. $(6x + 1)(6x - 1)$

29. $(2y^2 + 4)(2y^2 - 4)$

30. $(3b^3 + 2t)(3b^3 - 2t)$

31. $(4x - 3)^2$

32. $(9t + 2)^2$

33. $(6r + 5y)^2$

34. $(8m - 3n)^2$

35. $(c + 2d)(c^2 - 2cd + 4d^2)$

36. $(f + 3g)(f^2 - 3fg + 9g^2)$

37. $(4x - 1)(16x^2 + 4x + 1)$

38. $(5r - 2)(25r^2 + 10r + 4)$

39. $(7t + 5s)(2t^2 + 5st - s^2)$

40. $(8p + 3q)(2p^2 - 4pq + q^2)$

CONCEPT CHECK   *Match each polynomial in Column I with the best choice for factoring it in Column II. The choices in Column II may be used once, more than once, or not at all.*

I	II
41. $12x^2 + 20x + 8$	**A.** Factor out the GCF. No further factoring is possible.
42. $x^2 - 17x + 72$	**B.** Factor a difference of squares once.
43. $-16m^2n + 24mn - 40mn^2$	**C.** Factor a difference of squares twice.
44. $64a^2 - 121b^2$	**D.** Factor a perfect square trinomial.
45. $36p^2 - 60pq + 25q^2$	**E.** Factor by grouping.
46. $2z^2 - 4z + 6$	**F.** Factor out the GCF. Then factor a trinomial by grouping or the FOIL method with various combinations of factors.
47. $625 - r^4$	
48. $x^6 + 4x^4 - 3x^2 - 12$	**G.** Factor into two binomials by finding two integers whose product is the constant in the trinomial and whose sum is the coefficient of the middle term.
49. $8x^3 - 27$	
50. $144 - 24z + z^2$	**H.** Factor as a difference of cubes.

Factor each polynomial completely. ***See Example 4.***

51. $40ab - 16a$

52. $25xy - 15y$

53. $8x^3y^4 + 12x^2y^3 + 36xy^4$

54. $10m^5n + 4m^2n^3 + 18m^3n^2$

55. $x^2 - 2x - 15$

56. $x^2 + x - 12$

57. $2x^2 - 9x - 18$

58. $3x^2 + 2x - 8$

59. $4x^2 - 28x + 40$

60. $2x^2 - 18x + 36$

61. $36t^2 - 25$

62. $49r^2 - 9$

63. $16t^2 + 24t + 9$

64. $25t^2 + 90t + 81$

65. $4m^2p - 12mnp + 9n^2p$

66. $16p^2r - 40pqr + 25q^2r$

67. $x^3 + 1$

68. $x^3 + 27$

69. $8t^3 + 125$

70. $27s^3 + 64$

71. $t^6 - 125$

72. $w^6 - 27$

73. $20 + 5m + 12n + 3mn$

74. $4 + 2q + 6p + 3pq$

75. $5xt + 15xr + 2yt + 6yr$

76. $3am + 18mb + 2an + 12nb$

77. $6ar + 12br - 5as - 10bs$

78. $7mt + 35ms - 2nt - 10ns$

79. $t^4 - 1$

80. $r^4 - 81$

We begin by reviewing the terminology for the parts of a division problem. The *divisor* is the quantity we are dividing by, the *dividend* is the quantity we are dividing into, and the *quotient* is the result of the division.

$$\text{Divisor} \longrightarrow 247\overline{)385{,}814} \xleftarrow{\hspace{1cm}} \begin{array}{l} \text{Quotient} \\ \text{Dividend} \end{array}$$

with $1\,562$ shown above the bracket as the Quotient.

OBJECTIVES

1. Use synthetic division to divide by a polynomial of the form $x - k$.

2. Use the remainder theorem to evaluate a polynomial.

3. Decide whether a given number is a solution of an equation.

OBJECTIVE 1 Use synthetic division to divide by a polynomial of the form $x - k$. If a polynomial in x is divided by a binomial of the form $x - k$, a shortcut method called **synthetic division** can be used. For an illustration, look at the division on the left below.

Polynomial Division

$$
\begin{array}{r}
3x^2 + 9x + 25 \\
x-3\overline{)3x^3 + 0x^2 - 2x + 5} \\
\underline{3x^3 - 9x^2} \\
9x^2 - 2x \\
\underline{9x^2 - 27x} \\
25x + 5 \\
\underline{25x - 75} \\
80
\end{array}
$$

Synthetic Division

$$
\begin{array}{r}
3 \quad 9 \quad 25 \\
1-3\overline{)3 \quad 0 \quad -2 \quad 5} \\
\underline{3 \quad -9} \\
9 \quad -2 \\
\underline{9 \quad -27} \\
25 \quad 5 \\
\underline{25 \quad -75} \\
80
\end{array}
$$

On the right above, the same division is shown written without the variables. This is why it is *essential* to use 0 as a placeholder in synthetic division. All the numbers in color on the right are repetitions of the numbers directly above them, so we omit them to condense the work, as shown on the left below.

$$
\begin{array}{r}
3 \quad 9 \quad 25 \\
1-3\overline{)3 \quad 0 \quad -2 \quad 5} \\
-9 \\
\overline{9 \quad -2} \\
-27 \\
\overline{25 \quad 5} \\
-75 \\
\overline{80}
\end{array}
$$

$$
\begin{array}{r}
3 \quad 9 \quad 25 \\
1-3\overline{)3 \quad 0 \quad -2 \quad 5} \\
-9 \\
\overline{9} \\
-27 \\
\overline{25} \\
-75 \\
\overline{80}
\end{array}
$$

The numbers in color on the left are again repetitions of the numbers directly above them. They too are omitted, as shown on the right above. If we bring the 3 in the dividend down to the beginning of the bottom row, the top row can be omitted because it duplicates the bottom row.

1 Use synthetic division to divide each of the following.

(a) $3x^2 + 10x - 8$ by $x + 4$

$$
\begin{array}{r}
1 - 3\overline{)3 \quad0 \quad -2 \quad5} \\
\underline{-9 \;\; -27 \;\; -75} \\
3 \quad9 \quad25 \quad80
\end{array}
$$

We omit the 1 at the upper left—it represents $1x$, which will *always* be the first term in the divisor. To simplify the arithmetic, we replace subtraction in the second row by addition. To compensate, we change the -3 at the upper left to its additive inverse, 3.

Additive inverse of $-3 \longrightarrow$

$$
\begin{array}{r}
3\overline{)3 \quad0 \quad -2 \quad5} \\
 9 \quad27 \quad75 \;\; \longleftarrow \text{Signs changed}\\
\underline{3 \quad9 \quad25 \quad80} \;\; \longleftarrow \text{Remainder}
\end{array}
$$

The quotient is read from the bottom row.

$$3x^2 + 9x + 25 + \frac{80}{x - 3}$$

The first three numbers in the bottom row are the coefficients of the quotient polynomial with degree 1 less than the degree of the dividend. The last number gives the remainder.

> *Synthetic division is used only when dividing a polynomial $P(x)$ by a binomial of the form $x - k$.*

EXAMPLE 1 **Using Synthetic Division**

Use synthetic division to divide $5x^2 + 16x + 15$ by $x + 2$.

We change $x + 2$ into the form $x - k$ by writing it as

$$x + 2 = x - (-2), \quad \text{where } k = -2.$$

Now we write the coefficients of $5x^2 + 16x + 15$, placing -2 to the left.

$x + 2$ leads to -2. $\longrightarrow$ $-2\overline{)5 \quad 16 \quad 15}$ $\leftarrow$ Coefficients

$$
\begin{array}{r}
-2\overline{)5 \quad16 \quad 15} \\
\downarrow \quad -10 \\
5
\end{array}
$$
Bring down the 5, and multiply: $-2 \cdot 5 = -10$.

$$
\begin{array}{r}
-2\overline{)5 \quad16 \quad 15} \\
-10 \;\; -12 \\
5 \quad6
\end{array}
$$
Add 16 and -10, getting 6. Multiply -2 and 6 to obtain -12.

$$
\begin{array}{r}
-2\overline{)5 \quad16 \quad 15} \\
-10 \;\; -12 \\
\underline{5 \quad6 \quad3}
\end{array}
$$
Add 15 and -12, getting 3.

Read the result from the bottom row. $\longrightarrow$ $5 \quad 6 \quad 3$ $\leftarrow$ Remainder

Remember that a fraction bar means division.

$$\frac{5x^2 + 16x + 15}{x + 2} = 5x + 6 + \frac{3}{x + 2}$$

◀ **Work Problem 1 at the Side.**

(b) $2x^2 + 3x - 5$ by $x + 1$

Answers

1. **(a)** $3x - 2$

(b) $2x + 1 + \dfrac{-6}{x + 1}$

EXAMPLE 2   Using Synthetic Division (Missing Term)

Use synthetic division to divide $-4x^5 + x^4 + 6x^3 + 2x^2 + 50$ by $x - 2$.

$$
\begin{array}{r|rrrrrr}
2) & -4 & 1 & 6 & 2 & 0 & 50 \\
   &   & -8 & -14 & -16 & -28 & -56 \\
\hline
   & -4 & -7 & -8 & -14 & -28 & -6
\end{array}
$$

Use the steps given earlier, first inserting a 0 for the missing x-term.

Read the result from the bottom row.

$$\frac{-4x^5 + x^4 + 6x^3 + 2x^2 + 50}{x - 2}$$

$$= -4x^4 - 7x^3 - 8x^2 - 14x - 28 + \frac{-6}{x - 2}$$

——————————————— **Work Problem ② at the Side.** ▶

OBJECTIVE ▶ ② Use the remainder theorem to evaluate a polynomial. We can use synthetic division to evaluate polynomials. For example, in the synthetic division of **Example 2,** where the polynomial was divided by $x - 2$, the remainder was -6.

Replacing x in the polynomial with 2 gives the following.

$$-4x^5 + x^4 + 6x^3 + 2x^2 + 50 \qquad \text{From \textbf{Example 2}}$$
$$= -4 \cdot 2^5 + 2^4 + 6 \cdot 2^3 + 2 \cdot 2^2 + 50 \qquad \text{Replace } x \text{ with 2.}$$
$$= -4 \cdot 32 + 16 + 6 \cdot 8 + 2 \cdot 4 + 50 \qquad \text{Evaluate the powers.}$$
$$= -128 + 16 + 48 + 8 + 50 \qquad \text{Multiply.}$$
$$= -6 \qquad \text{Add.}$$

This number, -6, is the same number as the remainder. Dividing by $x - 2$ produced a remainder equal to the result when x is replaced with 2. This always happens, as the following **remainder theorem** states. This result is proved in more advanced courses.

Remainder Theorem

If the polynomial $P(x)$ is divided by $x - k$, then the remainder is equal to $P(k)$.

EXAMPLE 3   Using the Remainder Theorem

Let $P(x) = 2x^3 - 5x^2 - 3x + 11$. Use the remainder theorem to evaluate $P(-2)$.

Divide $P(x)$ by $x - (-2)$, using synthetic division.

$$
\begin{array}{r|rrrr}
\text{Value of } k \rightarrow -2) & 2 & -5 & -3 & 11 \\
 & & -4 & 18 & -30 \\
\hline
 & 2 & -9 & 15 & -19 \leftarrow \text{Remainder}
\end{array}
$$

Thus, $P(-2) = -19$.

——————————————— **Work Problem ③ at the Side.** ▶

② Use synthetic division to divide each of the following.

(a) $\dfrac{3x^3 - 2x + 21}{x + 2}$

(b) $(-4x^4 + 3x^3 + 18x + 2)$
$\div (x - 2)$

③ Let $P(x) = x^3 - 5x^2 + 7x - 3$. Use the remainder theorem to find each value.

(a) $P(1)$ (Divide by $x - 1$.)

(b) $P(-2)$

Answers

2. (a) $3x^2 - 6x + 10 + \dfrac{1}{x + 2}$

   (b) $-4x^3 - 5x^2 - 10x - 2 + \dfrac{-2}{x - 2}$

3. (a) 0   (b) -45

4 Use the remainder theorem to decide whether 2 is a solution of each equation.

(a) $3x^3 - 11x^2 + 17x - 14 = 0$

We can use the remainder theorem to do this.

EXAMPLE 4 Using the Remainder Theorem

Use the remainder theorem to decide whether -5 is a solution of the equation.

$$2x^4 + 12x^3 + 6x^2 - 5x + 75 = 0$$

If synthetic division gives a remainder of 0, then -5 is a solution. Otherwise, it is not.

Proposed solution →
$$-5)\overline{\begin{array}{ccccc} 2 & 12 & 6 & -5 & 75 \\ & -10 & -10 & 20 & -75 \\ \hline 2 & 2 & -4 & 15 & 0 \end{array}} \leftarrow \text{Remainder}$$

The remainder is 0, so the polynomial has a value of 0 when $x = -5$. Therefore, -5 is a solution of the given equation.

◀ **Work Problem 4 at the Side.**

The synthetic division in **Example 4** shows that $x - (-5)$ divides the polynomial with 0 remainder. Thus

$$x - (-5) = x + 5$$

is a *factor* of the polynomial and

$$2x^4 + 12x^3 + 6x^2 - 5x + 75$$

(b) $4x^5 - 7x^4 - 11x^2 + 2x + 6 = 0$

factors as

$$(x + 5)(2x^3 + 2x^2 - 4x + 15).$$

The second factor is the quotient polynomial found in the last row of the synthetic division.

Answers

4. (a) yes (b) no

Appendix B Exercises

FOR EXTRA HELP   Go to MyMathLab for worked-out, step-by-step solutions to exercises enclosed in a square ▢ and video solutions to ▶ exercises.

CONCEPT CHECK   *Choose the letter of the correct setup to perform synthetic division on the indicated quotient.*

1. $\dfrac{x^2 + 3x - 6}{x - 2}$

    A. $-2\overline{)1 \quad 3 \quad -6}$ **B.** $-2\overline{)-1 \quad -3 \quad 6}$

    C. $2\overline{)1 \quad 3 \quad -6}$ **D.** $2\overline{)-1 \quad -3 \quad 6}$

2. $\dfrac{x^3 - 3x^2 + 2}{x - 1}$

    A. $1\overline{)1 \quad -3 \quad 2}$ **B.** $-1\overline{)1 \quad -3 \quad 2}$

    C. $1\overline{)1 \quad -3 \quad 0 \quad 2}$ **D.** $1\overline{)-1 \quad 3 \quad 0 \quad -2}$

Use synthetic division to find each quotient. **See Examples 1 and 2.**

3. $\dfrac{x^2 - 6x + 5}{x - 1}$

4. $\dfrac{x^2 - 4x - 21}{x + 3}$

5. $\dfrac{4m^2 + 19m - 5}{m + 5}$

6. $\dfrac{3k^2 - 5k - 12}{k - 3}$

7. $\dfrac{2a^2 + 8a + 13}{a + 2}$

8. $\dfrac{4y^2 - 5y - 20}{y - 4}$

9. $(p^2 - 3p + 5) \div (p + 1)$

10. $(z^2 + 4z - 6) \div (z - 5)$

11. $\dfrac{4a^3 - 3a^2 + 2a - 3}{a - 1}$

12. $\dfrac{5p^3 - 6p^2 + 3p + 14}{p + 1}$

13. $(x^5 - 2x^3 + 3x^2 - 4x - 2) \div (x - 2)$

14. $(2y^5 - 5y^4 - 3y^2 - 6y - 23) \div (y - 3)$

15. $(-4r^6 - 3r^5 - 3r^4 + 5r^3 - 6r^2 + 3r) \div (r - 1)$

16. $(-3t^5 + 2t^4 - 5t^3 + 6t^2 - 3t - 2) \div (t - 2)$

17. $(-3y^5 + 2y^4 - 5y^3 - 6y^2 - 1) \div (y + 2)$

18. $(m^6 + 2m^4 - 5m + 11) \div (m - 2)$

19. $\dfrac{y^3 + 1}{y - 1}$

20. $\dfrac{z^4 + 81}{z - 3}$

Use the remainder theorem to find $P(k)$. **See Example 3.**

21. $P(x) = 2x^3 - 4x^2 + 5x - 3; \quad k = 2$

22. $P(x) = x^3 + 3x^2 - x + 5; \quad k = -1$

23. $P(r) = -r^3 - 5r^2 - 4r - 2; \quad k = -4$

24. $P(z) = -z^3 + 5z^2 - 3z + 4; \quad k = 3$

25. $P(x) = 2x^3 - 4x^2 + 5x - 33; \quad k = 3$

26. $P(x) = x^3 - 3x^2 + 4x - 4; \quad k = 2$

Use the remainder theorem to decide whether the given number is a solution of the equation. **See Example 4.**

27. $x^3 - 2x^2 - 3x + 10 = 0; \quad x = -2$

28. $x^3 - 3x^2 - x + 10 = 0; \quad x = -2$

29. $3x^3 + 2x^2 - 2x + 11 = 0; \quad x = -2$

30. $3z^3 + 10z^2 + 3z - 9 = 0; \quad z = -2$

31. $2x^3 - x^2 - 13x + 24 = 0; \quad x = -3$

32. $5x^3 + 22x^2 + x - 28 = 0; \quad x = -4$

33. $m^4 + 2m^3 - 3m^2 + 8m - 8 = 0; \quad m = -2$

34. $r^4 - r^3 - 6r^2 + 5r + 10 = 0; \quad r = -2$

Relating Concepts (Exercises 35–40) For Individual or Group Work

We can show a connection between dividing one polynomial by another and factoring the first polynomial. Let $P(x) = 2x^2 + 5x - 12$. **Work Exercises 35–40 in order.**

35. Factor $P(x)$.

36. Solve $P(x) = 0$.

37. Evaluate $P(-4)$.

38. Evaluate $P\left(\frac{3}{2}\right)$.

39. Complete the sentence:

If $P(a) = 0$, then $x -$ _____ is a factor of $P(x)$.

40. Use the conclusion reached in **Exercise 39** to decide whether $x - 3$ is a factor of

$$Q(x) = 3x^3 - 4x^2 - 17x + 6.$$

Factor $Q(x)$ completely.

Appendix: Solving Systems of Linear Equations by Matrix Methods

OBJECTIVE 1 Define a matrix. An ordered array of numbers is a **matrix.**

Columns

$$\text{Rows} \begin{bmatrix} 2 & 3 & 5 \\ 7 & 1 & 2 \end{bmatrix} \quad \text{Matrix}$$

The numbers are the **elements** of the matrix. *Matrices* (the plural of *matrix*) are named according to the number of **rows** and **columns** they contain. The rows are read horizontally, and the columns are read vertically. This matrix is a 2×3 (read "*two by three*") matrix because it has 2 rows and 3 columns. The number of rows followed by the number of columns gives the **dimensions** of the matrix.

$$\begin{bmatrix} -1 & 0 \\ 1 & -2 \end{bmatrix} \quad \begin{matrix} 2 \times 2 \\ \text{matrix} \end{matrix} \qquad \begin{bmatrix} 8 & -1 & -3 \\ 2 & 1 & 6 \\ 0 & 5 & -3 \\ 5 & 9 & 7 \end{bmatrix} \quad \begin{matrix} 4 \times 3 \\ \text{matrix} \end{matrix}$$

A **square matrix** has the same number of rows as columns. The 2×2 matrix above is a square matrix.

We now discuss a matrix method of solving linear systems that is a structured way of using the elimination method. The advantage of this new method is that it can be done by a graphing calculator or a computer.

OBJECTIVE 2 Write the augmented matrix of a system. To solve a linear system using matrices, we begin by writing an *augmented matrix* for the system. An **augmented matrix** has a vertical bar that separates the columns of the matrix into two groups. For example, to solve the system

$$x - 3y = 1$$
$$2x + y = -5,$$

we start by writing the augmented matrix

$$\left[\begin{array}{cc|c} 1 & -3 & 1 \\ 2 & 1 & -5 \end{array} \right]. \quad \text{Augmented matrix}$$

Place the coefficients of the variables to the left of the bar, and the constants to the right.

A matrix is just a shorthand way of writing a system of equations, so the rows of an augmented matrix can be treated the same as the equations of a system of equations.

OBJECTIVES

1. Define a matrix.
2. Write the augmented matrix of a system.
3. Use row operations to solve a system with two equations.
4. Use row operations to solve a system with three equations.
5. Use row operations to solve special systems.

System of equations:

$$x - 3y = 1$$
$$2x + y = -5$$

Augmented matrix:

$$\begin{bmatrix} 1 & -3 & | & 1 \\ 2 & 1 & | & -5 \end{bmatrix}$$

Coefficients   The bar   Constants
of the   separates
variables   coefficients
              from constants.

Exchanging the position of two equations in a system does not change the system. Also, multiplying any equation in a system by a nonzero number does not change the system. Comparable changes to the augmented matrix of a system of equations produce new matrices that correspond to systems with the same solutions as the original system.

The following **row operations** produce new matrices that lead to systems having the same solutions as the original system.

Matrix Row Operations

1. Any two rows of the matrix may be interchanged.

2. The elements of any row may be multiplied by any nonzero real number.

3. Any row may be transformed by adding to the elements of the row the product of a real number and the corresponding elements of another row.

Example of row operation 1

$$\begin{bmatrix} 2 & 3 & 9 \\ 4 & 8 & -3 \\ 1 & 0 & 7 \end{bmatrix} \quad \text{becomes} \quad \begin{bmatrix} 1 & 0 & 7 \\ 4 & 8 & -3 \\ 2 & 3 & 9 \end{bmatrix}$$

Interchange row 1 and row 3.

Example of row operation 2

$$\begin{bmatrix} 2 & 3 & 9 \\ 4 & 8 & -3 \\ 1 & 0 & 7 \end{bmatrix} \quad \text{becomes} \quad \begin{bmatrix} 6 & 9 & 27 \\ 4 & 8 & -3 \\ 1 & 0 & 7 \end{bmatrix}$$

Multiply the numbers in row 1 by 3.

Example of row operation 3

$$\begin{bmatrix} 2 & 3 & 9 \\ 4 & 8 & -3 \\ 1 & 0 & 7 \end{bmatrix} \quad \text{becomes} \quad \begin{bmatrix} 0 & 3 & -5 \\ 4 & 8 & -3 \\ 1 & 0 & 7 \end{bmatrix}$$

Multiply the numbers in row 3 by −2. Add them to the corresponding numbers in row 1.

The third row operation corresponds to the way we eliminated a variable from a pair of equations to solve a system by the elimination method.

OBJECTIVE ▶ 3 Use row operations to solve a system with two equations. Row operations can be used to rewrite a matrix until it is the matrix of a system whose solution is easy to find. The goal is a matrix in the form

$$\begin{bmatrix} 1 & a & | & b \\ 0 & 1 & | & c \end{bmatrix} \quad \text{or} \quad \begin{bmatrix} 1 & a & b & | & c \\ 0 & 1 & d & | & e \\ 0 & 0 & 1 & | & f \end{bmatrix}$$

for systems with two or three equations, respectively. Notice that there are 1s down the diagonal from upper left to lower right and 0s below the 1s. A matrix written this way is said to be in **row echelon form.**

EXAMPLE 1 **Using Row Operations to Solve a System**

Use row operations to solve the system.

$$x - 3y = 1$$
$$2x + y = -5$$

We start by writing the augmented matrix of the system.

$$\begin{bmatrix} 1 & -3 & | & 1 \\ 2 & 1 & | & -5 \end{bmatrix} \quad \text{Augmented matrix}$$

Our goal is to use the various row operations to change this matrix into one that leads to a system that is easier to solve. It is best to work by columns.

We start with the first column and make sure that there is a 1 in the first row, first column position. There is already a 1 in this position.

Next, we introduce 0 in every position below the first. To obtain 0 in row two, column one, we add to the numbers in row two the result of multiplying each number in row one by -2. (We abbreviate this as $-2R_1 + R_2$.) Row one remains unchanged.

$$\begin{bmatrix} 1 & -3 & | & 1 \\ 2 + 1(-2) & 1 + -3(-2) & | & -5 + 1(-2) \end{bmatrix}$$

Original number from row two -2 times number from row one

1 in the first position of column one $\rightarrow \begin{bmatrix} 1 & -3 & | & 1 \\ 0 & 7 & | & -7 \end{bmatrix}$ $-2R_1 + R_2$
0 in every position below the first $\rightarrow$

Now we go to column two. The number 1 is needed in row two, column two. We use the second row operation, multiplying each number of row two by $\frac{1}{7}$.

Stop here—this matrix is in row echelon form. $\begin{bmatrix} 1 & -3 & | & 1 \\ 0 & 1 & | & -1 \end{bmatrix}$ $\frac{1}{7}R_2$

This augmented matrix leads to the following system of equations.

$$1x - 3y = 1 \qquad x - 3y = 1$$
$$0x + 1y = -1, \quad \text{or} \quad y = -1$$

From the second equation, $y = -1$, we substitute -1 for y in the first equation to find x.

$$x - 3y = 1$$
$$x - 3(-1) = 1 \qquad \text{Let } y = -1.$$
$$x + 3 = 1 \qquad \text{Multiply.}$$
$$x = -2 \qquad \text{Subtract 3.}$$

Check by substituting $x = -2$ and $y = -1$ in both equations of the *original* system. The solution set is $\{(-2, -1)\}$.

Write the values of x and y in the correct order.

Work Problem ❶ at the Side. ▶

❶ Use row operations to solve the system.

$$x - 2y = 9$$
$$3x + y = 13$$

Answer

1. $\{(5, -2)\}$

EXAMPLE 2   Using Row Operations to Solve a System

Use row operations to solve the system.

$$x - y + 5z = -6$$
$$3x + 3y - z = 10$$
$$x + 3y + 2z = 5$$

Start by writing the augmented matrix of the system.

$$\begin{bmatrix} 1 & -1 & 5 & | & -6 \\ 3 & 3 & -1 & | & 10 \\ 1 & 3 & 2 & | & 5 \end{bmatrix} \quad \text{Augmented matrix}$$

This matrix already has 1 in row one, column one. Next obtain 0s in the rest of column one. First, add to row two the results of multiplying each number of row one by -3.

$$\begin{bmatrix} 1 & -1 & 5 & | & -6 \\ 0 & 6 & -16 & | & 28 \\ 1 & 3 & 2 & | & 5 \end{bmatrix} \quad -3R_1 + R_2$$

Now add to the numbers in row three the results of multiplying each number of row one by -1.

$$\begin{bmatrix} 1 & -1 & 5 & | & -6 \\ 0 & 6 & -16 & | & 28 \\ 0 & 4 & -3 & | & 11 \end{bmatrix} \quad -1R_1 + R_3$$

Obtain 1 in row two, column two by multiplying each number in row two by $\frac{1}{6}$.

$$\begin{bmatrix} 1 & -1 & 5 & | & -6 \\ 0 & 1 & -\frac{8}{3} & | & \frac{14}{3} \\ 0 & 4 & -3 & | & 11 \end{bmatrix} \quad \frac{1}{6}R_2$$

To obtain 0 in row three, column two, add to row three the results of multiplying each number in row two by -4.

$$\begin{bmatrix} 1 & -1 & 5 & | & -6 \\ 0 & 1 & -\frac{8}{3} & | & \frac{14}{3} \\ 0 & 0 & \frac{23}{3} & | & -\frac{23}{3} \end{bmatrix} \quad -4R_2 + R_3$$

Obtain 1 in row three, column three by multiplying each number in row three by $\frac{3}{23}$.

$$\begin{bmatrix} 1 & -1 & 5 & | & -6 \\ 0 & 1 & -\frac{8}{3} & | & \frac{14}{3} \\ 0 & 0 & 1 & | & -1 \end{bmatrix} \quad \frac{3}{23}R_3$$

This matrix leads to the system of equations given at the top of the next page.

Continued on Next Page

$$x - y + 5z = -6$$
$$y - \frac{8}{3}z = \frac{14}{3}$$
$$z = -1$$

Substitute -1 for z in the second equation, $y - \frac{8}{3}z = \frac{14}{3}$, to find that $y = 2$. Finally, substitute 2 for y and -1 for z in the first equation,

$$x - y + 5z = -6,$$

to determine that $x = 1$. Check by substituting $x = 1$, $y = 2$, and $z = -1$ in the three equations of the *original* system. The solution set is $\{(1, 2, -1)\}$.

— Work Problem ➋ at the Side. ▶

OBJECTIVE ➎ Use row operations to solve special systems.

EXAMPLE 3 Recognizing Inconsistent Systems or Dependent Equations

Use row operations to solve each system.

(a) $\begin{aligned} 2x - 3y &= 8 \\ -6x + 9y &= 4 \end{aligned}$ ⟶ $\begin{bmatrix} 2 & -3 & | & 8 \\ -6 & 9 & | & 4 \end{bmatrix}$ Write the augmented matrix.

$\begin{bmatrix} 1 & -\frac{3}{2} & | & 4 \\ -6 & 9 & | & 4 \end{bmatrix}$ $\frac{1}{2}R_1$

$\begin{bmatrix} 1 & -\frac{3}{2} & | & 4 \\ 0 & 0 & | & 28 \end{bmatrix}$ $6R_1 + R_2$

The corresponding system of equations is

$$x - \frac{3}{2}y = 4$$
$$0 = 28. \quad \text{False}$$

The original system has no solution and is inconsistent. The solution set is $\varnothing$.

(b) $\begin{aligned} -10x + 12y &= 30 \\ 5x - 6y &= -15 \end{aligned}$ ⟶ $\begin{bmatrix} -10 & 12 & | & 30 \\ 5 & -6 & | & -15 \end{bmatrix}$ Write the augmented matrix.

$\begin{bmatrix} 1 & -\frac{6}{5} & | & -3 \\ 5 & -6 & | & -15 \end{bmatrix}$ $-\frac{1}{10}R_1$

$\begin{bmatrix} 1 & -\frac{6}{5} & | & -3 \\ 0 & 0 & | & 0 \end{bmatrix}$ $-5R_1 + R_2$

The corresponding system of equations is

$$x - \frac{6}{5}y = -3$$
$$0 = 0. \quad \text{True}$$

The original system has dependent equations. We use the second equation of the original system, which is in standard form, to express the solution set.

$$\{(x, y) \mid 5x - 6y = -15\}$$

— Work Problem ➌ at the Side. ▶

➋ Use row operations to solve the system.
$$\begin{aligned} 2x - y + z &= 7 \\ x - 3y - z &= 7 \\ -x + y - 5z &= -9 \end{aligned}$$

➌ Use row operations to solve each system.

(a) $\begin{aligned} x - y &= 2 \\ -2x + 2y &= 2 \end{aligned}$

(b) $\begin{aligned} x - y &= 2 \\ -2x + 2y &= -4 \end{aligned}$

Answers
2. $\{(2, -2, 1)\}$
3. (a) $\varnothing$ (b) $\{(x, y) \mid x - y = 2\}$

Appendix C Exercises

FOR EXTRA HELP

Go to MyMathLab *for worked-out, step-by-step solutions to exercises enclosed in a square* ⬚ *and video solutions to* ▶ *exercises.*

1. CONCEPT CHECK Consider the matrix $\begin{bmatrix} -2 & 3 & 1 \\ 0 & 5 & -3 \\ 1 & 4 & 8 \end{bmatrix}$, and answer the following.

(a) What are the elements of the second row?

(b) What are the elements of the third column?

(c) Is this a square matrix? Why?

(d) Give the matrix obtained by interchanging the first and third rows.

(e) Give the matrix obtained by multiplying the first row by $-\frac{1}{2}$.

(f) Give the matrix obtained by multiplying the third row by 3 and adding it to the first row.

2. CONCEPT CHECK Give the dimensions of each matrix.

(a) $\begin{bmatrix} 3 & -7 \\ 4 & 5 \\ -1 & 0 \end{bmatrix}$

(b) $\begin{bmatrix} 4 & 9 & 0 \\ -1 & 2 & -4 \end{bmatrix}$

(c) $\begin{bmatrix} 6 & 3 \\ -2 & 5 \\ 4 & 10 \\ 1 & -11 \end{bmatrix}$

GS *Complete the steps in the matrix solution of each system by filling in the blanks. Give the final system and the solution set. See Example 1.*

3. $4x + 8y = 44$
$2x - y = -3$

$\begin{bmatrix} 4 & 8 & | & 44 \\ 2 & -1 & | & -3 \end{bmatrix}$

$\begin{bmatrix} 1 & \underline{} & | & \underline{} \\ 2 & -1 & | & -3 \end{bmatrix}$ $\frac{1}{4}R_1$

$\begin{bmatrix} 1 & 2 & | & 11 \\ 0 & \underline{} & | & \underline{} \end{bmatrix}$ $-2R_1 + R_2$

$\begin{bmatrix} 1 & 2 & | & 11 \\ 0 & 1 & | & \underline{} \end{bmatrix}$ $-\frac{1}{5}R_2$

4. $2x - 5y = -1$
$3x + y = 7$

$\begin{bmatrix} 2 & -5 & | & -1 \\ 3 & 1 & | & 7 \end{bmatrix}$

$\begin{bmatrix} 1 & -\frac{5}{2} & | & \underline{} \\ 3 & 1 & | & 7 \end{bmatrix}$ $\frac{1}{2}R_1$

$\begin{bmatrix} 1 & -\frac{5}{2} & | & -\frac{1}{2} \\ 0 & \underline{} & | & \underline{} \end{bmatrix}$ $-3R_1 + R_2$

$\begin{bmatrix} 1 & -\frac{5}{2} & | & -\frac{1}{2} \\ 0 & 1 & | & \underline{} \end{bmatrix}$ $\frac{2}{17}R_2$

Use row operations to solve each system. See Examples 1 and 3.

5. $x + y = 5$
$x - y = 3$

6. $x + 2y = 7$
$x - y = -2$

7. $2x + 4y = 6$
▶ $3x - y = 2$

8. $4x + 5y = -7$
$x - y = 5$

9. $3x + 4y = 13$
$2x - 3y = -14$

10. $5x + 2y = 8$
$3x - y = 7$

11. $-4x + 12y = 36$
▶ $x - 3y = 9$

12. $2x - 4y = 8$
$-3x + 6y = 5$

13. $2x + y = 4$
$4x + 2y = 8$

14. $3x + 4y = -1$
$6x + 8y = -2$

15. $\frac{1}{2}x + \frac{1}{3}y = 0$
$\frac{2}{3}x + \frac{3}{4}y = 0$

16. $1.2x + 0.3y = 0$
$2.9x - 0.6y = 0$

GS *Complete the steps in the matrix solution of each system by filling in the blanks. Give the final system and the solution set. See Example 2.*

17. $x + y - z = -3$
$2x + y + z = 4$
$5x - y + 2z = 23$

$$\begin{bmatrix} 1 & 1 & -1 & | & -3 \\ 2 & 1 & 1 & | & 4 \\ 5 & -1 & 2 & | & 23 \end{bmatrix}$$

$$\begin{bmatrix} 1 & 1 & -1 & | & -3 \\ 0 & \_\_ & \_\_ & | & \_\_ \\ 0 & \_\_ & \_\_ & | & \_\_ \end{bmatrix} \begin{array}{l} -2R_1 + R_2 \\ -5R_1 + R_3 \end{array}$$

$$\begin{bmatrix} 1 & 1 & -1 & | & -3 \\ 0 & 1 & \_\_ & | & \_\_ \\ 0 & -6 & 7 & | & 38 \end{bmatrix} -1R_2$$

$$\begin{bmatrix} 1 & 1 & -1 & | & -3 \\ 0 & 1 & -3 & | & -10 \\ 0 & 0 & \_\_ & | & \_\_ \end{bmatrix} 6R_2 + R_3$$

$$\begin{bmatrix} 1 & 1 & -1 & | & -3 \\ 0 & 1 & -3 & | & -10 \\ 0 & 0 & 1 & | & \_\_ \end{bmatrix} -\frac{1}{11}R_3$$

18. $2x + y + 2z = 11$
$2x - y - z = -3$
$3x + 2y + z = 9$

$$\begin{bmatrix} 2 & 1 & 2 & | & 11 \\ 2 & -1 & -1 & | & -3 \\ 3 & 2 & 1 & | & 9 \end{bmatrix}$$

$$\begin{bmatrix} 1 & \_\_ & \_\_ & | & \_\_ \\ 2 & -1 & -1 & | & -3 \\ 3 & 2 & 1 & | & 9 \end{bmatrix} \frac{1}{2}R_1$$

$$\begin{bmatrix} 1 & \frac{1}{2} & 1 & | & \frac{11}{2} \\ 0 & \_\_ & \_\_ & | & \_\_ \\ 0 & \_\_ & \_\_ & | & \_\_ \end{bmatrix} \begin{array}{l} -2R_1 + R_2 \\ -3R_1 + R_3 \end{array}$$

$$\begin{bmatrix} 1 & \frac{1}{2} & 1 & | & \frac{11}{2} \\ 0 & 1 & \_\_ & | & \_\_ \\ 0 & \frac{1}{2} & -2 & | & -\frac{15}{2} \end{bmatrix} -\frac{1}{2}R_2$$

$$\begin{bmatrix} 1 & \frac{1}{2} & 1 & | & \frac{11}{2} \\ 0 & 1 & \frac{3}{2} & | & 7 \\ 0 & 0 & \_\_ & | & \_\_ \end{bmatrix} -\frac{1}{2}R_2 + R_3$$

$$\begin{bmatrix} 1 & \frac{1}{2} & 1 & | & \frac{11}{2} \\ 0 & 1 & \frac{3}{2} & | & 7 \\ 0 & 0 & 1 & | & \_\_ \end{bmatrix} -\frac{4}{11}R_3$$

Use row operations to solve each system. See Examples 2 and 3.

19. $x + y - 3z = 1$
$2x - y + z = 9$
$3x + y - 4z = 8$

20. $2x + 4y - 3z = -18$
$3x + y - z = -5$
$x - 2y + 4z = 14$

21. $x + y - z = 6$
$2x - y + z = -9$
$x - 2y + 3z = 1$

22. $x + 3y - 6z = 7$
$2x - y + 2z = 0$
$x + y + 2z = -1$

23. $x - y = 1$
$y - z = 6$
$x + z = -1$

24. $x + y = 1$
$2x - z = 0$
$y + 2z = -2$

25. $4x + 8y + 4z = 9$
$x + 3y + 4z = 10$
$5x + 10y + 5z = 12$

26. $x + 2y + 3z = -2$
$2x + 4y + 6z = -5$
$x - y + 2z = 6$

27. $x - 2y + z = 4$
$3x - 6y + 3z = 12$
$-2x + 4y - 2z = -8$

28. $x + 3y + z = 1$
$2x + 6y + 2z = 2$
$3x + 9y + 3z = 3$

29. $5x + 3y - z = 0$
$2x - 3y + z = 0$
$x + 4y - 2z = 0$

30. $4x + 5y - z = 0$
$7x - 5y + z = 0$
$x + 3y - 2z = 0$

Answers to Selected Exercises

In this section we provide the answers that we think most students will obtain when they work the exercises using the methods explained in the text. If your answer does not look exactly like the one given here, it is not necessarily wrong. In many cases there are equivalent forms of the answer that are correct. For example, if the answer section shows $\frac{3}{4}$ and your answer is 0.75, you have obtained the correct answer but written it in a different (yet equivalent) form. Unless the directions specify otherwise, 0.75 is just as valid an answer as $\frac{3}{4}$.

In general, if your answer does not agree with the one given in the text, see whether it can be transformed into the other form. If it can, then it is the correct answer. If you still have doubts, talk with your instructor.

CHAPTER R Prealgebra Review

SECTION R.1

1. true **2.** true **3.** false; This is an improper fraction. Its value is 1.
4. false; The number 1 is neither prime nor composite. **5.** false; The fraction $\frac{17}{51}$ can be simplified to $\frac{1}{3}$. **6.** false; The reciprocal of $\frac{8}{2} = 4$ is $\frac{2}{8} = \frac{1}{4}$. **7.** false; *Product* indicates multiplication, so the product of 8 and 2 is 16. **8.** false; *Difference* indicates subtraction, so the difference of 12 and 2 is 10. **9.** prime **11.** composite **13.** composite
15. prime **17.** $2 \cdot 3 \cdot 5$ **19.** $3 \cdot 19$ **21.** $2 \cdot 2 \cdot 31$
23. $2 \cdot 2 \cdot 3 \cdot 3 \cdot 7$ **25.** $2 \cdot 2 \cdot 5 \cdot 5 \cdot 5$ **27.** $\frac{5}{6}$ **29.** $\frac{1}{2}$ **31.** $\frac{3}{10}$
33. $\frac{1}{5}$ **35.** $\frac{3}{5}$ **37.** $6\frac{5}{12}$ **39.** $7\frac{6}{11}$ **41.** $1\frac{5}{7}$ **43.** $\frac{13}{5}$ **45.** $\frac{83}{8}$
47. $\frac{51}{5}$ **49.** A **50.** C **51.** $\frac{24}{35}$ **53.** $\frac{1}{8}$ **55.** $\frac{6}{25}$ **57.** $\frac{6}{5}$, or $1\frac{1}{5}$
59. $\frac{65}{12}$, or $5\frac{5}{12}$ **61.** $\frac{38}{5}$, or $7\frac{3}{5}$ **63.** $\frac{18}{35}$ **65.** $\frac{10}{3}$, or $3\frac{1}{3}$ **67.** 12
69. $\frac{1}{16}$ **71.** $\frac{24}{35}$ **73.** $\frac{84}{47}$, or $1\frac{37}{47}$ **75.** $\frac{11}{15}$ **77.** $\frac{2}{3}$ **79.** $\frac{8}{9}$
81. $\frac{29}{24}$, or $1\frac{5}{24}$ **83.** $\frac{43}{8}$, or $5\frac{3}{8}$ **85.** $\frac{5}{9}$ **87.** $\frac{2}{3}$ **89.** $\frac{17}{36}$ **91.** $\frac{11}{12}$
93. $\frac{4}{3}$, or $1\frac{1}{3}$ **95.** 2 cups **97.** $618\frac{3}{4}$ ft **99.** $\frac{9}{16}$ in. **101.** $\frac{5}{16}$ in.
103. 8 cakes (There will be some sugar left over.) **105.** $16\frac{5}{8}$ yd
107. 10 million, or 10,000,000 **109.** $4\frac{4}{5}$ million, or 4,800,000 **111.** $\frac{3}{50}$

SECTION R.2

1. (a) 6 (b) 9 (c) 1 (d) 7 (e) 4 **2.** (a) 46.25 (b) 46.2
(c) 46 (d) 50 **3.** (a) 0.889 (b) 0.556 (c) 0.976 (d) 0.864
4. (a) 254 (b) 2540 (c) 0.254 (d) 0.0254 **5.** $\frac{4}{10}$ **7.** $\frac{64}{100}$
9. $\frac{138}{1000}$ **11.** $\frac{43}{1000}$ **13.** $\frac{3805}{1000}$ **15.** 143.094 **17.** 25.61 **19.** 15.33
21. 21.77 **23.** 81.716 **25.** 15.211 **27.** 116.48 **29.** 0.006 **31.** 7.15
33. 2.05 **35.** 5711.6 **37.** 94 **39.** 0.162 **41.** 0.2403 **43.** 1%
44. 0.02 **45.** $\frac{1}{20}$ **46.** 0.1; 10% **47.** $12\frac{1}{2}$%, or 12.5% **48.** $\frac{1}{5}$; 0.2

49. 0.25; 25% **50.** $0.\overline{3}$; $33\frac{1}{3}$%, or $33.\overline{3}$% **51.** $\frac{1}{2}$; 0.5 **52.** $0.\overline{6}$
53. $\frac{3}{4}$; 75% **54.** 100% **55.** 0.125 **57.** 1.25 **59.** $0.\overline{5}$; 0.556
61. $0.1\overline{6}$; 0.167 **63.** 0.54 **65.** 0.07 **67.** 0.9 **69.** 1.17 **71.** 0.024
73. 0.0625 **75.** 0.008 **77.** 73% **79.** 2% **81.** 0.4% **83.** 128%
85. 30% **87.** 600% **89.** $\frac{51}{100}$ **91.** $\frac{3}{20}$ **93.** $\frac{1}{50}$ **95.** $\frac{7}{5}$, or $1\frac{2}{5}$
97. $\frac{3}{40}$ **99.** 80% **101.** 14% **103.** $18\frac{2}{11}$%, or $18.\overline{18}$% **105.** 225%
107. $216\frac{2}{3}$%, or $216.\overline{6}$% **109.** 160 **111.** 4.8 **113.** 109.2
115. $17.80; $106.80 **117.** $119.25; $675.75 **119.** 19.8 million, or 19,800,000 **121.** 13%

CHAPTER 1 The Real Number System

SECTION 1.1

1. false; $3^2 = 3 \cdot 3 = 9$ **2.** false; 1 raised to *any* power is 1. Here, $1^3 = 1 \cdot 1 \cdot 1 = 1$. **3.** false; A number raised to the first power is that number, so $3^1 = 3$. **4.** false; 6^2 means that 6 is used as a factor 2 times, so $6^2 = 6 \cdot 6 = 36$. **5.** 49 **7.** 9 **9.** 144 **11.** 64 **13.** 1000
15. 81 **17.** 1024 **19.** $\frac{16}{81}$ **21.** $\frac{1}{36}$ **23.** 0.000064 **25.** ② ①; 45; 58
27. ② ① ③; 12; 8; 13 **29.** ① ②; 32 **31.** ① ②; 19 **33.** 32 **35.** 12
37. $\frac{49}{30}$ **39.** 22.2 **41.** 26 **43.** 4 **45.** 42 **47.** 5 **49.** 95 **51.** 90
53. 41 **55.** 14 **57.** $\frac{19}{2}$ **59.** $3 \cdot (6 + 4) \cdot 2$ **60.** $2 \cdot (8 - 1) \cdot 3$
61. $10 - (7 - 3)$ **62.** $15 - (10 - 2)$ **63.** $(8 + 2)^2$ **64.** $(4 + 2)^2$
65. false **67.** true **69.** true **71.** true **73.** true **75.** false **77.** false
79. true **81.** $15 = 5 + 10$ **83.** $9 > 5 - 4$ **85.** $16 \neq 19$ **87.** $2 \leq 3$
89. Seven is less than nineteen; true **91.** Eight is greater than or equal to eleven; false **93.** One-third is not equal to three-tenths; true
95. $30 > 5$ **97.** $3 \leq 12$ **99.** $1.3 \leq 2.5$ **101.** $\frac{3}{4} < \frac{4}{5}$
103. (a) $14.7 - 40 \cdot 0.13$ (b) 9.5 (c) 8.075; walking (5 mph)
(d) $14.7 - 55 \cdot 0.11$; 8.65; 7.3525, swimming **105.** Alaska, Texas, California, Idaho **107.** Alaska, Texas, California, Idaho, Missouri

SECTION 1.2

1. B **2.** C **3.** A **4.** B, C **5.** 11 **6.** 10 **7.** $13 + x$; 16
8. expression; equation **9.** (a) 11 (b) 13 **11.** (a) 16 (b) 24
13. (a) 22 (b) 32 **15.** (a) 64 (b) 144 **17.** (a) $\frac{5}{3}$ (b) $\frac{7}{3}$
19. (a) $\frac{7}{8}$ (b) $\frac{13}{12}$ **21.** (a) 25.836 (b) 38.754 **23.** (a) 52 (b) 114
25. (a) 24 (b) 3 **27.** (a) 24 (b) 28 **29.** (a) 12 (b) 33
31. (a) $\frac{4}{3}$ (b) $\frac{13}{6}$ **33.** (a) $\frac{2}{7}$ (b) $\frac{16}{27}$ **35.** (a) 12 (b) 55
37. (a) 1 (b) $\frac{28}{17}$ **39.** (a) 3.684 (b) 8.841 **41.** $12x$ **43.** $x + 13$
45. $x - 2$ **47.** $2x - 6$ **49.** $7 - \frac{1}{3}x$ **51.** $\frac{12}{x + 3}$ **53.** $6(x - 4)$

55. no **57.** yes **59.** yes **61.** no **63.** yes **65.** yes **67.** $x + 8 = 18$
69. $2x + 5 = 5$ **71.** $16 - \frac{3}{4}x = 13$ **73.** $3x = 2x + 8$ **75.** $\frac{x}{3} = x - 4$
77. expression **79.** equation **81.** equation **83.** expression **85.** 70 yr
86. 73 yr **87.** 76 yr **88.** 79 yr

SECTION 1.3

1. 0 **2.** integers **3.** positive **4.** right **5.** quotient; denominator
6. irrational **7.** 1,212,795 **9.** -3413 **11.**

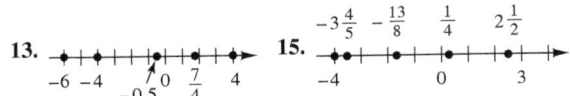
-6 -5 $\quad$ 0 $\quad$ 3

13.
-6 -4 $\quad$ 0 $\frac{7}{4}$ $\quad$ 4
-0.5

15.
$-3\frac{4}{5}$ $-\frac{13}{8}$ $\frac{1}{4}$ $2\frac{1}{2}$
-4 $\quad$ 0 $\quad$ 3

17. (a) 3, 7 (b) 0, 3, 7 (c) $-9, 0, 3, 7$ (d) $-9, -1\frac{1}{4}, -\frac{3}{5}, 0, 3, 5.9, 7$
(e) $-\sqrt{7}, \sqrt{5}$ (f) All are real numbers. **19.** (a) 11 (b) 0, 11
(c) $0, 11, -6$ (d) $\frac{7}{9}, -2.\overline{3}, 0, -8\frac{3}{4}, 11, -6$ (e) $\sqrt{3}, \pi$
(f) All are real numbers. **21.** 4 **22.** One example is 2.85. There are
others. **23.** 0 **24.** One example is 4. There are others. **25.** One
example is $\sqrt{13}$. There are others. **26.** 0 **27.** true **28.** false
29. true **30.** true **31.** false **32.** true *In Exercises 33–38, answers*
will vary. **33.** $\frac{1}{2}, \frac{5}{8}, 1\frac{3}{4}$ **34.** $-1, -\frac{3}{4}, -5$ **35.** $-3\frac{1}{2}, -\frac{2}{3}, \frac{3}{7}$
36. $\frac{1}{2}, -\frac{2}{3}, \frac{2}{7}$ **37.** $\sqrt{5}, \pi, -\sqrt{3}$ **38.** $\frac{2}{3}, \frac{5}{6}, \frac{5}{2}$ **39.** -11 **41.** -21
43. -100 **45.** $-\frac{2}{3}$ **47.** false **49.** true **51.** false **53.** false
55. (a) 2 (b) 2 **57.** (a) -6 (b) 6 **59.** (a) $\frac{3}{4}$ (b) $\frac{3}{4}$
61. (a) -4.95 (b) 4.95 **63.** (a) A (b) A (c) B (d) B
64. $5; 5; 5; -5$ **65.** 6 **67.** -12 **69.** $-\frac{2}{3}$ **71.** 9 **73.** -3 **75.** false
77. true **79.** true **81.** false **83.** Energy, 2014 to 2015 **85.** Apparel,
2013 to 2014

SECTION 1.4

1. negative; -5 **2.** negative; -2 **3.** zero (0)

-3
-2
-5 -2 0

2
-4
-4 -2 0

4. $-3; 5$ **5.** -10 **7.** -13 **9.** 2 **11.** -3 **13.** -9 **15.** 0 **17.** $-\frac{3}{5}$
19. $\frac{1}{2}$ **21.** $-\frac{19}{40}$ **23.** $-\frac{3}{4}$ **25.** -15.9 **27.** -1.6 **29.** 5 **31.** 13
33. 0 **35.** -8 **37.** -8.7 **39.** $-11; -14; -25$ **41.** 6 **43.** 22
45. $-\frac{1}{4}$, or -0.25 **47.** false **49.** true **51.** false **53.** true **55.** false
57. $-5 + 12 + 6; 13$ **59.** $[-19 + (-4)] + 14; -9$
61. $[-4 + (-10)] + 12; -2$ **63.** $\left[\frac{5}{7} + \left(-\frac{9}{7}\right)\right] + \frac{2}{7}; -\frac{2}{7}$ **65.** -12
67. $+4$ **69.** -184 m **71.** -12 **73.** 17 **75.** 37 yd **77.** 120°F

SECTION 1.5

1. $-8; -6; 2$ **2.** additive; inverse; opposite **3.** $5; -4$
4. $7 - 12; 12 - 7$ **5.** -4 **7.** -3 **9.** $-3; -10$ **11.** -16 **13.** 4; 11
15. 19 **17.** -4 **19.** 9 **21.** $\frac{3}{4}$ **23.** $-\frac{11}{8}$ **25.** 13.6 **27.** -11.9
29. 10 **31.** -5 **33.** 5 **35.** 0 **37.** 8 **39.** -4 **41.** -20 **43.** 22

45. -2 **47.** -21 **49.** $-\frac{5}{8}$ **51.** $\frac{37}{12}$ **53.** -2.8 **55.** -6.3 **57.** -28
59. -42.04 **61.** negative **62.** positive **63.** positive **64.** negative
65. positive **66.** negative **67.** $4 - (-8); 12$ **69.** $-2 - 8; -10$
71. $[9 + (-4)] - 7; -2$ **73.** $[8 - (-5)] - 12; 1$ **75.** -69°F
77. 14,776 ft **79.** -176.9°F **81.** $\$1045.55$ **83.** $\$323.83$ **85.** 14 ft
87. $\$710$ billion **89.** $-\$22,600$ **91.** $-\$6900$ **93.** 50,395 ft
95. 1345 ft **97.** 136 ft

SECTION 1.6

1. greater than 0 **2.** less than 0 **3.** less than 0 **4.** less than 0
5. greater than 0 **6.** less than 0 **7.** undefined; 0; Examples will vary.
For instance, $\frac{1}{0}$ is undefined, and $\frac{0}{1}$ equals 0. **8.** A **9.** -28 **11.** 30
13. 0 **15.** $\frac{5}{6}$ **17.** -2.38 **19.** $\frac{3}{2}$ **21.** -3 **23.** -6 **25.** -4
27. 16 **29.** 0 **31.** undefined **33.** $-\frac{15}{16}$ **35.** $\frac{3}{2}$ **37.** -11
39. -2 **41.** 35 **43.** 13 **45.** -22 **47.** -8 **49.** 18 **51.** 3
53. 7 **55.** 4 **57.** -2 **59.** -3 **61.** -1 **63.** $\frac{7}{4}$ **65.** 68
67. 72 **69.** 1 **71.** 0 **73.** -6 **75.** undefined
77. $-12 + 4(-7); -40$ **79.** $-4 - 2(-1)(6); 8$
81. $-3[3 - (-7)]; -30$ **83.** $\frac{3}{10}[-2 + (-28)]; -9$
85. $0.20(-5 \cdot 6); -6$ **87.** $\frac{-12}{-5 + (-1)}; 2$ **89.** $\frac{-18 + (-6)}{2(-4)}; 3$
91. $\frac{-\frac{2}{3}\left(-\frac{1}{5}\right)}{\frac{1}{7}}; \frac{14}{15}$ **93.** $9x = -36$ **95.** $\frac{x}{4} = -1$ **97.** $x - \frac{9}{11} = 5$
99. $\frac{6}{x} = -3$ **101.** 29 **102.** The incorrect answer, 92, was obtained by
performing all of the operations in order from left to right rather than
following the rules for order of operations. The multiplications and
divisions need to be done in order, before the additions and subtractions.
103. 42 **104.** 5 **105.** $8\frac{2}{5}$ **106.** $8\frac{2}{5}$ **107.** 2 **108.** $-12\frac{1}{2}$

SUMMARY EXERCISES Performing Operations With Real Numbers

1. -16 **2.** 4 **3.** 0 **4.** -24 **5.** -17 **6.** 76 **7.** -18 **8.** 90 **9.** 38
10. 4 **11.** -5 **12.** 5 **13.** $-\frac{7}{2}$, or $-3\frac{1}{2}$ **14.** 4 **15.** 13 **16.** $\frac{5}{4}$, or $1\frac{1}{4}$
17. 9 **18.** $\frac{37}{10}$, or $3\frac{7}{10}$ **19.** 0 **20.** 25 **21.** 14 **22.** 0 **23.** -4
24. $\frac{6}{5}$, or $1\frac{1}{5}$ **25.** -1 **26.** $\frac{52}{37}$, or $1\frac{15}{37}$ **27.** $\frac{17}{16}$, or $1\frac{1}{16}$ **28.** $-\frac{2}{3}$
29. 3.33 **30.** 1.02 **31.** 0 **32.** 24 **33.** -7 **34.** -3 **35.** -1 **36.** $\frac{1}{2}$
37. $-\frac{5}{13}$ **38.** 5 **39.** undefined **40.** 0

SECTION 1.7

1. (a) B (b) F (c) C (d) I (e) B (f) D, F (g) B (h) A
(i) G (j) H **2.** order; grouping **3.** yes **4.** yes **5.** no **6.** no
7. no **8.** no **9.** (foreign sales) clerk; foreign (sales clerk) **10.** (defective
merchandise) counter; defective (merchandise counter) **11.** -15;
commutative property **13.** 3; commutative property **15.** 6; associative
property **17.** 7; associative property **19.** Subtraction is not associative.

20. Division is not associative. **21.** row 1: $-5, \frac{1}{5}$; row 2: $10, -\frac{1}{10}$;

row 3: $\frac{1}{2}, -2$; row 4: $-\frac{3}{8}, \frac{8}{3}$; row 5: $-x, \frac{1}{x} (x \neq 0)$;

row 6: $y, -\frac{1}{y} (y \neq 0)$; opposite; the same **22.** identity property

23. commutative property **25.** inverse property **27.** inverse property
29. identity property **31.** distributive property **33.** identity property
35. associative property **37.** commutative property **39.** distributive
property **41.** $7 + r$ **43.** s **45.** $-6x + (-6)7; -6x - 42$
47. $w + [5 + (-3)]; w + 2$ **49.** 2010 **51.** 6700 **53.** 50 **55.** 2
57. 0.77 **59.** 11 **61.** The expression following the first equality symbol
should be $-3(4) - 3(-6)$. This simplifies to $-12 + 18$, which equals 6.
62. The expression following the second equality symbol should be
$-1(3x) + (-1)4$. This simplifies to $-3x - 4$. **63.** We must multiply $\frac{3}{4}$

by 1 in the form of a fraction, $\frac{3}{3}$: $\frac{3}{4} \cdot \frac{3}{3} = \frac{9}{12}$. **64.** This is the reverse of

the procedure in **Exercise 63.** We factor the numerator and denominator,

writing the identity element 1 as $\frac{3}{3}$: $\frac{9}{12} = \frac{3}{4} \cdot \frac{3}{3} = \frac{3}{4} \cdot 1 = \frac{3}{4}$.

65. 85 **67.** $4t + 12$ **69.** $7z - 56$ **71.** $-8r - 24$ **73.** $-2x - \frac{3}{4}$

75. $y; -4; -5y + 20$ **77.** $12x + 10$ **79.** $-6x + 15$ **81.** $-48x - 6$
83. $-16y - 20z$ **85.** $24r + 32s - 40y$ **87.** $-24x - 9y - 12z$
89. $-6x - 5$ **91.** $-4t - 3m$ **93.** $5c + 4d$ **95.** $3q - 5r + 8s$

SECTION 1.8

1. B **2.** C **3.** A **4.** B **5.** $4r + 11$ **7.** $21x - 28y$ **9.** $5 + 2x - 6y$
11. $-7 + 3p$ **13.** $2 - 3x$ **15.** -12 **17.** 5 **19.** 1 **21.** -1 **23.** 10
25. 28 **27.** $-\frac{3}{8}$ **29.** $\frac{1}{2}$ **31.** $\frac{2}{5}$ **33.** -1.28 **35.** like **37.** unlike
39. unlike **41.** like **43.** unlike **45.** $15x$ **47.** $-9x$ **49.** $13b$
51. $7k + 15$ **53.** $2x + 6$ **55.** $-\frac{1}{3}t - \frac{28}{3}$ **57.** $9y^2$ **59.** $5p^2 - 14p^3$
61. $-2y^2 + 3y^3$ **63.** $8x + 15$ **65.** $-\frac{4}{3}y - 10$ **67.** $-\frac{3}{2}y + 16$
69. $x; -3; 2x; 6; 1 - 2x$ **71.** $-19p + 16$ **73.** $-16y + 63$ **75.** $4r + 15$
77. $12k - 5$ **79.** $-2x + 4$ **81.** $-\frac{14}{3}x - \frac{22}{3}$ **83.** $-2k - 3$ **85.** $4x - 7$
87. $-4.1r + 4.2$ **89.** $-23.7y - 12.6$ **91.** The student made a sign
error when applying the distributive property. $7x - 2(3 - 2x)$ means
$7x - 2(3) - 2(-2x)$, which simplifies to $7x - 6 + 4x$, or $11x - 6$.
92. The student incorrectly started by adding $3 + 2$. As the first step, 2
must be multiplied by $4x - 5$. Thus, $3 + 2(4x - 5)$ equals $3 + 8x - 10$,
which simplifies to $8x - 7$. **93.** $(x + 3) + 5x; 6x + 3$
95. $(13 + 6x) - (-7x); 13 + 13x$ **97.** $2(3x + 4) - (-4 + 6x); 12$
99. $1000 + 5x$ (dollars) **100.** $750 + 3y$ (dollars)
101. $1000 + 5x + 750 + 3y$ (dollars) **102.** $1750 + 5x + 3y$ (dollars)

Chapter 1 REVIEW EXERCISES

1. 625 **2.** 0.00000081 **3.** 0.009261 **4.** $\frac{125}{8}$ **5.** 27 **6.** 200 **7.** 17
8. 4 **9.** 7 **10.** 4 **11.** $13 < 17$ **12.** $5 + 2 \neq 10$ **13.** Six is less
than fifteen; true **14.** Two-fourths is not equal to three-sixths; false
15. 30 **16.** 60 **17.** 14 **18.** 13 **19.** $x + 6$ **20.** $8 - x$ **21.** $6x - 9$
22. $12 + \frac{3}{5}x$ **23.** yes **24.** no **25.** $2x - 6 = 10$ **26.** $4x = 8$

27. equation **28.** expression
29.
30.

31. rational numbers, real numbers **32.** natural numbers, whole
numbers, integers, rational numbers, real numbers **33.** -10 **34.** -9
35. $-\frac{3}{4}$ **36.** $-|23|$ **37.** true **38.** true **39.** true **40.** false **41.** -3
42. -19 **43.** -7 **44.** 9 **45.** -6 **46.** -4 **47.** -17 **48.** $-\frac{29}{36}$
49. 0 **50.** 15 **51.** $(-31 + 12) + 19; 0$ **52.** $[-4 + (-8)] + 13; 1$
53. \$26.25 **54.** $-10°F$ **55.** -11 **56.** -1 **57.** 7 **58.** $-\frac{43}{35}$
59. 10.31 **60.** -12 **61.** 2 **62.** 1 **63.** $-4 - (-6); 2$
64. $[4 + (-8)] - 5; -9$ **65.** $[18 - (-23)] - 15; 26$
66. $19 - (-7 - 12); 38$ **67.** 38 yd **68.** 17,477.63 **69.** -308 thousand
70. 72 thousand **71.** 14 thousand **72.** -122 thousand **73.** 36
74. -105 **75.** $\frac{1}{2}$ **76.** 10.08 **77.** -20 **78.** -10 **79.** -24
80. -35 **81.** 4 **82.** -20 **83.** $-\frac{3}{4}$ **84.** 11.3 **85.** -1
86. undefined **87.** 1 **88.** 0 **89.** -18 **90.** -18 **91.** 125 **92.** -423
93. $-4(5) - 9; -29$ **94.** $\frac{5}{6}[12 + (-6)]; 5$ **95.** $\frac{12}{8 + (-4)}; 3$
96. $\frac{-20(12)}{15 - (-15)}; -8$ **97.** $\frac{x}{x + 5} = -2$ **98.** $8x - 3 = -7$
99. identity property **100.** identity property **101.** inverse property
102. inverse property **103.** distributive property **104.** associative
property **105.** associative property **106.** commutative property
107. $7y + 14$ **108.** $-48 + 12t$ **109.** $6s + 15y$ **110.** $4r - 5s$
111. $8y$ **112.** $17p^2$ **113.** $16r^2 + 7r$ **114.** $-19k + 54$ **115.** $5s - 6$
116. $-45t - 23$ **117.** $-2(3x) - 7x; -13x$ **118.** $(5 + 4x) + 8x; 5 + 12x$

Chapter 1 MIXED REVIEW EXERCISES

1. $3; 3; -\frac{1}{3}$ **2.** $12; -12; \frac{1}{12}$ **3.** $-\frac{2}{3}; \frac{2}{3}; \frac{2}{3}$ **4.** $0.2; 0.2; 5$ **5.** rational
numbers, real numbers **6.** 37 **7.** -6 **8.** $\frac{25}{36}$ **9.** -26 **10.** $\frac{8}{3}$
11. $-\frac{1}{24}$ **12.** $\frac{7}{2}$ **13.** 2 **14.** 77.6 **15.** $-1\frac{1}{2}$ **16.** 11 **17.** $-\frac{28}{15}$
18. 24 **19.** $-47°F$ **20.** 27 ft

Chapter 1 TEST

1. true **2.** false **3.** **4.** rational numbers, real
numbers **5.** $-|-8|$ (or -8) **6.** -1.277 **7.** $\frac{-6}{2 + (-8)}; 1$ **8.** negative
9. 4 **10.** $-2\frac{5}{6}$ **11.** 6 **12.** 2 **13.** 108 **14.** 11 **15.** $\frac{30}{7}$ **16.** -70
17. 3 **18.** $178°F$ **19.** $-\$0.49$ trillion **20.** 15 **21.** D **22.** A
23. E **24.** B **25.** C **26.** $21x$ **27.** $-3x + 1$ **28.** $-9x^2 - 6x - 8$
29. $15x - 3$ **30.** **(a)** -18 **(b)** -18 **(c)** The distributive property tells
us that the answers must be the same because $a(b + c) = ab + ac$ for all
a, b, c.

CHAPTER 2 Equations, Inequalities, and Applications

SECTION 2.1

1. equation; expression **2.** linear; variable; = **3.** equivalent equations
4. addition; solution set **5.** A, B **6. (a)** expression; $x + 15$
(b) expression; $m + 7$ **(c)** equation; $\{-1\}$ **(d)** equation; $\{-17\}$
7. $\{12\}$ **9.** $\{-3\}$ **11.** $\{4\}$ **13.** $\{4\}$ **15.** $\{-9\}$ **17.** $\{6.3\}$
19. $\{-6.5\}$ **21.** $\{-16.9\}$ **23.** $\left\{-\dfrac{3}{4}\right\}$ **25.** $\{-10\}$ **27.** $\{-13\}$
29. $\{10\}$ **31.** $\{10.1\}$ **33.** $\left\{\dfrac{4}{15}\right\}$ **35.** $\{-3\}$ **37.** $\{7\}$ **39.** $\{-4\}$
41. $\{12\}$ **43.** $\{-5\}$ **45.** $\{-6\}$ **47.** $\{-2\}$ **49.** $\{4\}$ **51.** $\{-16\}$
53. $\{2\}$ **55.** $\{2\}$ **57.** $\{-4\}$ **59.** $\{0\}$ **61.** $\{0\}$ **63.** $\left\{\dfrac{7}{15}\right\}$
65. $\{13\}$ **67.** $\{-2\}$ **69.** $\{7\}$ **71.** $\{-4\}$ **73.** $\{0\}$
75. $\{29\}$ **77.** $\{18\}$

SECTION 2.2

1. (a) and **(c)**: multiplication property of equality; **(b)** and **(d)**: addition
property of equality **2.** C **3.** $\dfrac{3}{2}$ **4.** $\dfrac{5}{4}$ **5.** 10 **6.** 100 **7.** $-\dfrac{2}{9}$
8. $-\dfrac{3}{8}$ **9.** -1 **10.** -1 **11.** 6 **12.** 7 **13.** -4 **14.** -13 **15.** 0.12
16. 0.21 **17.** -1 **18.** -1 **19.** B **20.** A **21.** $\{6\}$ **23.** $\left\{\dfrac{15}{2}\right\}$
25. $\{-5\}$ **27.** $\left\{-\dfrac{18}{5}\right\}$ **29.** $\{12\}$ **31.** 2; 2; 0; $\{0\}$ **33.** $\{-12\}$
35. $\{40\}$ **37.** $\{-12.2\}$ **39.** $\{-48\}$ **41.** $\{72\}$ **43.** $\{-35\}$
45. $\{14\}$ **47.** $\left\{-\dfrac{27}{35}\right\}$ **49.** $\{3\}$ **51.** $\{-5\}$ **53.** $\{20\}$ **55.** $\{7\}$
57. $\{-12\}$ **59.** $\{0\}$ **61.** $\{-3\}$ **63.** $\{-4\}$ **65.** $\{-5\}$ **67.** $\{1\}$
69. $-4x = 10; -\dfrac{5}{2}$ **71.** $\dfrac{x}{-5} = 2; -10$

SECTION 2.3

1. addition; subtract **2.** left; like **3.** distributive; parentheses
4. multiplication; $\dfrac{4}{3}$ **5.** fractions; 6 **6.** decimals; 10 **7. (a)** identity; B
(b) conditional; A **(c)** contradiction; C **8.** D **9.** A **10.** D **11.** $\{4\}$
13. $\{-5\}$ **15.** $\left\{\dfrac{5}{2}\right\}$ **17.** $\left\{-\dfrac{1}{2}\right\}$ **19.** $\{5\}$ **21.** $\{1\}$ **23.** $\{5\}$
25. $\left\{-\dfrac{5}{3}\right\}$ **27.** $\left\{\dfrac{4}{3}\right\}$ **29.** $\left\{-\dfrac{5}{3}\right\}$ **31.** $\{5\}$ **33.** $\{0\}$ **35.** $\{0\}$
37. $\{$all real numbers$\}$ **39.** $\{$all real numbers$\}$ **41.** $\varnothing$ **43.** $\varnothing$
45. $\{5\}$ **47.** $\{12\}$ **49.** $\{11\}$ **51.** $\{0\}$ **53.** $\left\{\dfrac{3}{25}\right\}$ **55.** 100; $\{60\}$
57. $\{4\}$ **59.** $\{5000\}$ **61.** $\left\{-\dfrac{72}{11}\right\}$ **63.** $\{0\}$ **65.** $\varnothing$
67. $\{$all real numbers$\}$ **69.** $\{-6\}$ **71.** $\{15\}$ **73.** $12 - q$ **75.** $\dfrac{9}{z}$
77. $x + 29$ **79.** $m + 12; m - 2$ **81.** $25r$ **83.** $\dfrac{t}{5}$ **85.** $3x + 2y$

SUMMARY EXERCISES Applying Methods for Solving Linear Equations

1. equation; $\{-5\}$ **2.** expression; $7p - 14$ **3.** expression; $-3m - 2$
4. equation; $\{7\}$ **5.** equation; $\{0\}$ **6.** expression; $-\dfrac{1}{6}x + 5$ **7.** $\left\{\dfrac{7}{3}\right\}$
8. $\{4\}$ **9.** $\{-5.1\}$ **10.** $\{12\}$ **11.** $\{-25\}$ **12.** $\{-6\}$ **13.** $\{-6\}$
14. $\{-16\}$ **15.** $\{$all real numbers$\}$ **16.** $\{23.7\}$ **17.** $\{6\}$ **18.** $\{0\}$
19. $\{7\}$ **20.** $\{1\}$ **21.** $\{5\}$ **22.** $\varnothing$ **23.** $\varnothing$ **24.** $\{-10.8\}$ **25.** $\{25\}$
26. $\{$all real numbers$\}$ **27.** $\{3\}$ **28.** $\{70\}$ **29.** $\{-2\}$ **30.** $\left\{\dfrac{14}{17}\right\}$

SECTION 2.4

1. *Step 1:* Read the problem carefully; *Step 2:* Assign a variable to represent the unknown; *Step 3:* Write an equation; *Step 4:* Solve the equation;
Step 5: State the answer; *Step 6:* Check the answer. **2.** Some examples
are *is, are, was,* and *were.* **3.** D; There cannot be a fractional number
of cars. **4.** D; A day cannot have more than 24 hr. **5.** A; Distance
cannot be negative. **6.** C; Time cannot be negative. **7.** 1; 16 (or 14);
-7 (or -9); $x + 1$ **8.** odd; 2; 11 (or 15); even; 2; 14 (or 10)
9. complementary; supplementary **10.** 90°; 180° **11.** yes, 90°; yes, 45°
12. $x - 1; x - 2$ **13.** $8 \cdot (x + 6) = 104; 7$ **15.** $5x + 2 = 4x + 5; 3$
17. $3x - 2 = 5x + 14; -8$ **19.** $3(x - 2) = x + 6; 6$
21. $3x + (x + 7) = -11 - 2x; -3$ **23.** *Step 1:* We are asked to find the
number of drive-in movie screens in the two states; *Step 2:* the number
of screens in Pennsylvania; *Step 3:* $x; x - 1$; *Step 4:* 28; *Step 5:* 28;
28; 27; *Step 6:* 1; screens in New York; 27; 55 **25.** Democrats: 188;
Republicans: 247 **27.** Kenny Chesney: $116.4 million; Taylor Swift:
$199.4 million **29.** wins: 73; losses: 9 **31.** orange: 97 mg; pineapple:
25 mg **33.** whole wheat: 25.6 oz; rye: 6.4 oz **35.** active: 225 mg;
inert: 25 mg **37.** 1950 Denver nickel: $16.00; 1944 Philadelphia nickel:
$12.00 **39.** onions: 81.3 kg; grilled steak: 536.3 kg **41.** $x + 5; x + 9$;
shortest piece: 15 in.; middle piece: 20 in.; longest piece: 24 in.
43. American: 18; United: 11; Southwest: 26 **45.** gold: 9; silver: 7;
bronze: 12 **47.** 36 million mi **49.** *A* and *B*: 40°; *C*: 100° **51.** 68, 69
53. 101, 102 **55.** 10, 12 **57.** 17, 19 **59.** 10, 11 **61.** 18 **63.** 18°
65. 20° **67.** 39° **69.** 50°

SECTION 2.5

1. The perimeter of a plane geometric figure is the measure of the outer
boundary of the figure. **2.** The area of a plane geometric figure is the
measure of the surface covered or enclosed by the figure. **3.** area
4. area **5.** perimeter **6.** perimeter **7.** area **8.** area **9.** area
10. area **11.** $P = 26$ **13.** $\mathcal{A} = 64$ **15.** $b = 4$ **17.** $t = 5.6$
19. $h = 7$ **21.** $r = 2.6$ **23.** $\mathcal{A} = 50.24$ **25.** $V = 150$ **27.** $V = 52$
29. $V = 7234.56$ **31.** $I = \$600$ **33.** $p = \$550$ **35.** 0.025; $t = 1.5$ yr
37. length: 18 in.; width: 9 in. **39.** length: 14 m; width: 4 m
41. shortest: 5 in.; medium: 7 in.; longest: 8 in. **43.** two equal sides: 7 m;
third side: 10 m **45.** perimeter: 5.4 m; area: 1.8 m^2 **47.** 10 ft
49. 154,000 ft^2 **51.** 194.48 ft^2; 49.42 ft **53.** 23,800.10 ft^2
55. length: 36 in.; maximum volume: 11,664 in.^{3} **57.** 48°, 132°
59. 70°, 110° **61.** 55°, 35° **63.** 30°, 60° **65.** 51°, 51°
67. 105°, 105° **69.** $t = \dfrac{d}{r}$ **71.** $H = \dfrac{V}{LW}$ **73.** $b = P - a - c$

75. $r = \dfrac{C}{2\pi}$ **77.** $r = \dfrac{I}{pt}$ **79.** $h = \dfrac{2\mathcal{A}}{b}$ **81.** $h = \dfrac{3V}{\pi r^2}$ **83.** $W = \dfrac{P - 2L}{2}$

85. $m = \dfrac{y - b}{x}$ **87.** $y = \dfrac{C - Ax}{B}$ **89.** $r = \dfrac{M - C}{C}$ **91.** $a = \dfrac{P - 2b}{2}$

93. $x = \dfrac{f + ah}{a}$ **95.** $b = 2S - a - c$ **97.** $F = \dfrac{9}{5}C + 32$

We give one possible answer for Exercises 99–105. There are other correct forms.

99. $y = -6x + 4$ **101.** $y = 5x - 2$ **103.** $y = \dfrac{3}{5}x - 3$

105. $y = \dfrac{1}{3}x - 4$ **107.** $W_1 + M = W_2 + N_2 + 1$

108. $M = W_2 + N_2 + 1 - W_1$ **109. (a)** 12 **(b)** 3 **(c)** 12

110. $M = -3$; A negative magic number indicates that Oakland has been eliminated from winning the division.

SECTION 2.6

1. compare; A, D **2.** ratios; proportion; cross products **3. (a)** C
(b) D **(c)** B **(d)** A **4.** C, E **5.** $\dfrac{6}{7}$ **7.** $\dfrac{18}{55}$ **9.** $\dfrac{5}{16}$ **11.** $\dfrac{4}{15}$

13. $\dfrac{6}{5}$ **15.** 10 lb; $0.749 **17.** 64 oz; $0.047 **19.** 32 oz; $0.531

21. 32 oz; $0.056 **23.** $\{35\}$ **25.** $\{7\}$ **27.** $\left\{\dfrac{8}{5}\right\}$ **29.** $\{1\}$ **31.** $\{2\}$

33. $\{-1\}$ **35.** $\{5\}$ **37.** $\left\{-\dfrac{31}{5}\right\}$ **39.** $30.00 **41.** $56.85

43. 50,000 fish **45.** 4 ft **47.** 17.0 in. **49.** $2\dfrac{5}{8}$ cups **51.** $326.67

53. 9; $x = 4$ **55.** $x = 8$ **57.** $x = 3$; $y = 5.5$ **59.** side of triangle labeled Chair: 18 ft; side of triangle labeled Pole: 12 ft; One proportion is $\dfrac{x}{12} = \dfrac{18}{4}$; 54 ft **61. (a)** 2625 mg **(b)** $\dfrac{125\,\text{mg}}{5\,\text{mL}} = \dfrac{2625\,\text{mg}}{x\,\text{mL}}$ **(c)** 105 mL

63. $236 **65.** $273 **67.** 109.2 **69.** 54 **71.** 700 **73.** 425 **75.** 8%

77. 120% **79.** 80% **81.** 28% **83.** 32% **85.** $3000 **87.** $304

89. 9,617,000; · ; 155,922,000; 6.2% **91.** 75.1% **93.** 860%

95. 30 **96. (a)** $5x = 12$ **(b)** $\left\{\dfrac{12}{5}\right\}$ **97.** $\left\{\dfrac{12}{5}\right\}$ **98.** Both methods give the same solution set.

SUMMARY EXERCISES Applying Problem-Solving Techniques

1. 48 **2.** 35° **3.** 3 **4.** 18, 20 **5.** 140°, 40° **6.** 104°, 104° **7.** 4

8. 36 quart cartons **9.** $16\dfrac{2}{3}$% **10.** 510 calories **11.** 4000 calories

12. U.S.: 104; China: 88; Russia: 82 **13.** 24 oz; $0.074 **14.** 12.42 cm

SECTION 2.7

1. < (or >); > (or <); ≤ (or ≥); ≥ (or ≤) **2.** false **3.** $(0, \infty)$
4. $(-\infty, \infty)$ **5.** $x > -4$ **6.** $x \geq -4$ **7.** $x \leq 4$ **8.** $x < 4$
9. $-1 < x \leq 2$ **10.** $-1 \leq x < 2$
11. $(-\infty, 4]$ **13.** $(-3, \infty)$

15. $[8, 10]$ **17.** $(0, 10]$

19. $(1, \infty)$ **21.** $[5, \infty)$

23. $(-\infty, -6)$
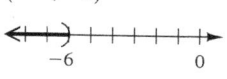

25. The inequality symbol must be reversed when multiplying or dividing by a negative number.

26. Divide by -5 and reverse the direction of the inequality symbol to get $x < -4$.

27. $(-\infty, 6)$

29. $[-10, \infty)$
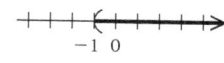

31. $(-\infty, -3)$
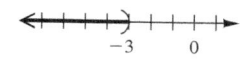

33. $(-\infty, 0]$
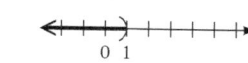

35. $(20, \infty)$
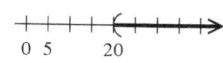

37. $[-3, \infty)$
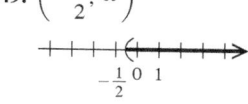

39. $(-\infty, -3]$
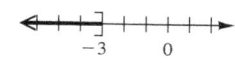

41. $(-1, \infty)$

43. $[-5, \infty)$
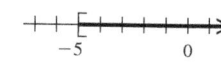

45. $(-\infty, 1)$

47. $(-\infty, 0]$

49. $\left(-\dfrac{1}{2}, \infty\right)$
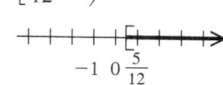

51. $[4, \infty)$
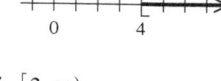

53. $(-\infty, 32)$

55. $[2, \infty)$

57. $\left[\dfrac{5}{12}, \infty\right)$

59. $(-21, \infty)$

61. $x \geq 16$ **62.** $x < 1$
63. $x > 8$ **64.** $x \geq 12$
65. $x \leq 20$ **66.** $x > 40$

67. 88 or more **69.** 80 or more **71.** all numbers greater than 16
73. It has never exceeded 40°C. **75.** 32 or greater
77. 12 min **79.** more than 3.8 in.

81. $[-1, 6]$
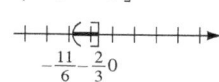

83. $(1, 3)$
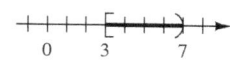

85. $\left(-\dfrac{11}{6}, -\dfrac{2}{3}\right]$

87. $[3, 7)$

89. $[-26, 6]$
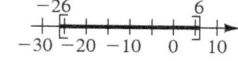

91. $[-3, 6]$
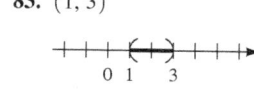

93. $\{4\}$

94. $(-\infty, 4)$

95. $(4, \infty)$

96. The graph would be the set of all real numbers; $(-\infty, \infty)$

Chapter 2 REVIEW EXERCISES

1. $\{9\}$ **2.** $\{4\}$ **3.** $\{-6\}$ **4.** $\left\{\dfrac{3}{2}\right\}$ **5.** $\{0\}$ **6.** $\left\{-\dfrac{61}{2}\right\}$ **7.** $\{15\}$

8. $\{-21\}$ **9.** $\varnothing$ **10.** $\{\text{all real numbers}\}$ **11.** $-\dfrac{7}{2}$ **12.** 20

13. Hawaii: 6425 mi^2; Rhode Island: 1212 mi^2 **14.** Seven Falls: 300 ft; Twin Falls: 120 ft **15.** 80° **16.** 11, 13 **17.** oil: 4 oz; gasoline: 128 oz

18. shortest piece: 13 in.; middle-sized piece: 20 in.; longest piece: 39 in.

19. $h = 11$ **20.** $\mathcal{A} = 28$ **21.** $r = 4.75$ **22.** $V = 3052.08$

23. $h = \dfrac{\mathcal{A}}{b}$ **24.** $h = \dfrac{2\mathcal{A}}{b + B}$

We give one possible answer for Exercises 25 and 26. There are other correct forms.

25. $y = -x + 11$ **26.** $y = \dfrac{3}{2}x - 6$ **27.** 135°, 45° **28.** 100°, 100°

29. perimeter: 428 ft; area: 11,349 ft^2 **30.** diameter: 27.07 ft; radius: 13.54 ft **31.** $\dfrac{3}{2}$ **32.** $\dfrac{5}{14}$ **33.** $\dfrac{3}{4}$ **34.** $\left\{\dfrac{7}{2}\right\}$ **35.** $\left\{-\dfrac{8}{3}\right\}$

36. $\left\{\dfrac{25}{19}\right\}$ **37.** $6\dfrac{2}{3}$ lb **38.** 36 oz **39.** 375 km **40.** 18 oz; $0.249

41. 6 **42.** 175% **43.** $33\dfrac{1}{3}$% **44.** 2500 **45.** $21,575 **46.** $350.46

47. 25% **48.** 17.5%

49. $[-4, \infty)$

50. $(-\infty, 7)$

51. $[-5, 6)$

52. $\left[\dfrac{1}{2}, \infty\right)$

53. $[-3, \infty)$

54. $(-\infty, 2)$

55. $[3, \infty)$

56. $[46, \infty)$

57. $(-\infty, -5)$

58. $(-\infty, -37)$

59. $\left[-2, \dfrac{3}{2}\right)$

60. $(1, 5]$

61. 88 or more **62.** all numbers less than or equal to $-\dfrac{1}{3}$

Chapter 2 MIXED REVIEW EXERCISES

1. $\{7\}$ **2.** $r = \dfrac{d}{2}$ **3.** $(-\infty, 2)$ **4.** $\{-9\}$ **5.** $\{70\}$ **6.** $\left\{\dfrac{13}{4}\right\}$

7. $\varnothing$ **8.** $\{\text{all real numbers}\}$ **9.** 2.0 in. **10.** D: 22°; E: 44°; F: 114°

11. 44 m **12.** 70 ft **13.** 160 oz; $0.062 **14.** 24°, 66° **15.** 92 or more

16. $197.50

Chapter 2 TEST

1. $\{6\}$ **2.** $\{-6\}$ **3.** $\left\{\dfrac{13}{4}\right\}$ **4.** $\{-10.8\}$ **5.** $\{21\}$

6. $\{\text{all real numbers}\}$ **7.** $\{30\}$ **8.** $\varnothing$ **9.** Chamberlain: 4029; Jordan: 3041 **10.** Hawaii: 4021 mi^2; Maui: 728 mi^2; Kauai: 551 mi^2

11. 24, 26 **12.** 50° **13.** (a) $W = \dfrac{P - 2L}{2}$ (b) 18 **14.** $y = \dfrac{5}{4}x - 2$

(Other correct forms of the answer are possible.) **15.** 100°, 80°

16. 75°, 75° **17.** $\{6\}$ **18.** $\{-29\}$ **19.** 16 oz; $0.249 **20.** 2300 mi

21. $264 **22.** 40% **23.** (a) $x < 0$ (b) $-2 < x \le 3$

24. $(-\infty, 11)$

25. $[-3, \infty)$

26. $(-\infty, 4]$

27. $(-2, 6]$

28. 83 or more

Chapters R–2 CUMULATIVE REVIEW EXERCISES

1. $\dfrac{3}{8}$ **2.** $\dfrac{3}{4}$ **3.** $\dfrac{31}{20}$ **4.** $\dfrac{551}{40}$, or $13\dfrac{31}{40}$ **5.** 6 **6.** $\dfrac{6}{5}$ **7.** 34.03

8. 27.31 **9.** 30.51 **10.** 56.3 **11.** 35 yd **12.** $7\dfrac{1}{2}$ cups **13.** $3\dfrac{3}{8}$ in.

14. $2599.94 **15.** true **16.** false **17.** 7 **18.** 1 **19.** 13 **20.** -40

21. -12 **22.** undefined **23.** -6 **24.** 28 **25.** 1 **26.** 0 **27.** $\dfrac{73}{18}$

28. -64 **29.** -134 **30.** $-\dfrac{29}{6}$ **31.** distributive property

32. commutative property **33.** inverse property **34.** identity property

35. $7p - 14$ **36.** $2k - 11$ **37.** $\{7\}$ **38.** $\{-4\}$ **39.** $\{-1\}$

40. $\left\{-\dfrac{3}{5}\right\}$ **41.** $\{2\}$ **42.** $\{-13\}$ **43.** $\{26\}$ **44.** $\{-12\}$

45. $c = P - a - b - B$ **46.** $s = \dfrac{P}{4}$

47. $(-\infty, 2]$

48. $(-\infty, 1)$

49. $260.50 **50.** $8625 **51.** 30 cm **52.** 16 in.

CHAPTER 3 Graphs of Linear Equations and Inequalities in Two Variables

SECTION 3.1

1. does; do not **2.** $(0, 0)$ **3.** 4; -1; is not **4.** II **5.** y **6.** 3 **7.** 6

8. -4 **9.** negative; negative **10.** negative; positive **11.** positive; negative **12.** positive; positive **13.** 2009 and 2010 **14.** The unemployment rate was decreasing. **15.** 2010: 9.5%; 2015: 5%; 4.5% **17.** 2009 and 2010; 1.5 million **19.** Sales decreased slightly between 2012 and 2013 and then increased slightly between 2013 and 2014. **21.** yes

23. yes **25.** no **27.** yes **29.** no **31.** no **33.** 17 **35.** $-\dfrac{7}{2}$ **37.** -4

39. -5 **41.** 8, 6, 3; $(0, 8)$, $(6, 0)$, $(3, 4)$ **43.** 3, -5, -15; $(0, 3)$, $(-5, 0)$, $(-15, -6)$ **45.** -9, -9, -9; $(-9, 6)$, $(-9, 2)$, $(-9, -3)$

47. 6, 6, 6; $(8, 6)$, $(4, 6)$, $(-2, 6)$ **49.** 8, 8, 8; $(8, 8)$, $(8, 3)$, $(8, 0)$

51. -2, -2, -2; $(9, -2)$, $(2, -2)$, $(0, -2)$ **53.** $(2, 4)$; I

55. $(-5, 4)$; II   **57.** $(3, 0)$; no quadrant   **59.** $(4, -4)$; IV   **61.** If $xy < 0$, then either $x < 0$ and $y > 0$ or $x > 0$ and $y < 0$. If $x < 0$ and $y > 0$, then the point lies in quadrant II. If $x > 0$ and $y < 0$, then the point lies in quadrant IV.   **62.** If $xy > 0$, then either $x > 0$ and $y > 0$ or $x < 0$ and $y < 0$. If $x > 0$ and $y > 0$, then the point lies in quadrant I. If $x < 0$ and $y < 0$, then the point lies in quadrant III.

63.–74.

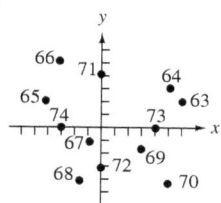

75. $-3, 6, -2, 4$

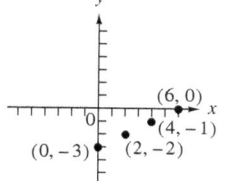

77. $-3, 4, -6, -\dfrac{4}{3}$

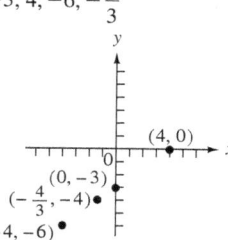

79. $-4, -4, -4, -4$

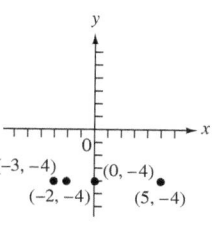

81. The points in each graph appear to lie on a straight line.
82. (a) horizontal; They are the same (all -4).   **(b)** vertical; They are the same (all 5).   **83. (a)** $(5, 45)$ **(b)** $(6, 50)$ **85. (a)** $(2009, 28.3)$, $(2010, 28.0)$, $(2011, 26.9)$, $(2012, 25.4)$, $(2013, 22.5)$, $(2014, 21.9)$
(b) $(2000, 32.4)$ means that 32.4 percent of 2-yr college students in 2000 received a degree within 3 yr.

(c)
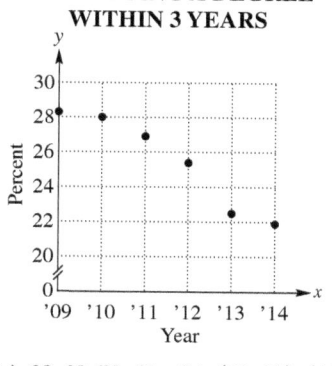

(d) The points lie approximately in a linear pattern. Rates at which 2-yr college students complete a degree within 3 yr were decreasing.

87. (a) $98, 88, 78, 68$ **(b)** $(20, 98), (40, 88), (60, 78), (80, 68)$

(c)
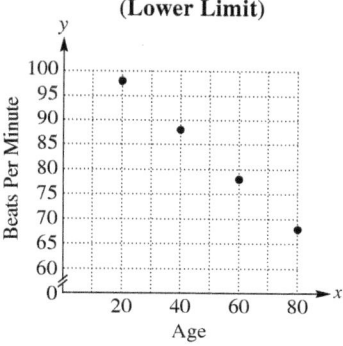

Yes, the points lie in a linear pattern.

89. between 98 and 157 beats per minute; between 88 and 141 beats per minute

SECTION 3.2

1. By; C; 0 **2.** line; solution   **3. (a)** A   **(b)** C   **(c)** D   **(d)** B
4. A, C, D   **5.** x-intercept: $(4, 0)$; y-intercept: $(0, -4)$
6. x-intercept: $(-5, 0)$; y-intercept: $(0, 5)$ **7.** x-intercept: $(-2, 0)$; y-intercept: $(0, -3)$ **8.** x-intercept: $(4, 0)$; y-intercept: $(0, 3)$
9. $5, 5, 3$

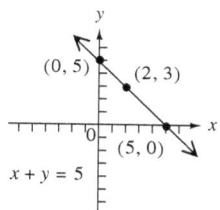

11. $1, 3, -1$

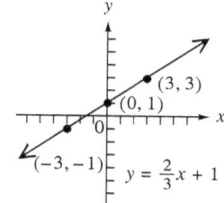

13. $-6, -2, -5$

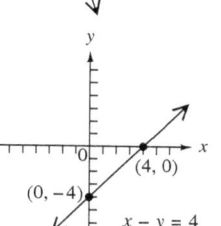

15. 0; $(0, -8)$; 0; $(8, 0)$
17. $(0, -8)$; $(12, 0)$
19. $(0, 0)$; $(0, 0)$

21.
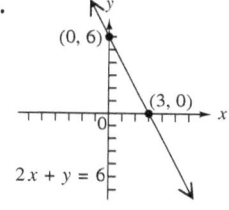

23.
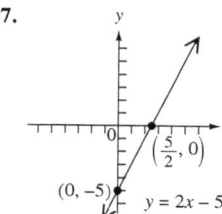

25.

27.

29.
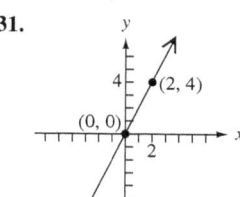

31.

33.
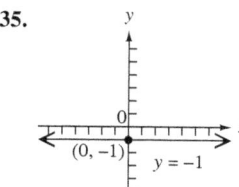

35.

37.
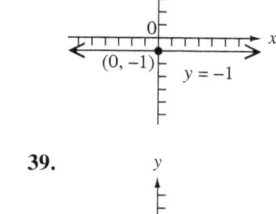

39.
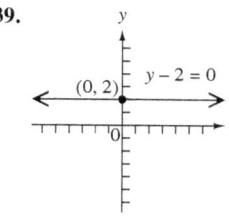

41.

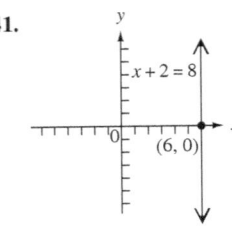

43.

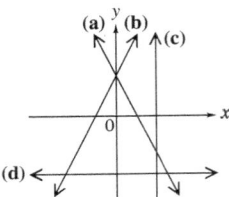

45. (a) D **(b)** C **(c)** B **(d)** A **46.** $y = 0$; $x = 0$

In Exercises 47–50, descriptions may vary.

47. The graph is a line with x-intercept $(-3, 0)$ and y-intercept $(0, 9)$.
48. The graph is a vertical line with x-intercept $(11, 0)$. **49.** The graph is a horizontal line with y-intercept $(0, -2)$. **50.** The graph passes through the origin $(0, 0)$ and the points $(2, 1)$ and $(4, 2)$.

51. (a) 151.5 cm, 159.3 cm, 174.9 cm
(b) $(20, 151.5)$, $(22, 159.3)$, $(26, 174.9)$
(c) **HEIGHTS OF WOMEN** **(d)** 24 cm; 24 cm

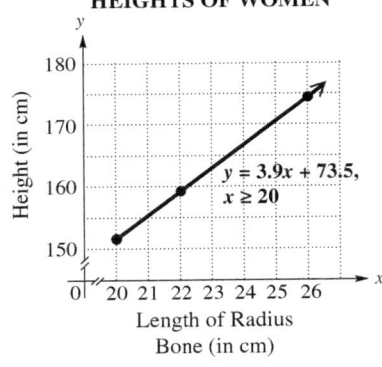

53. (a) $62.50; $100 **(b)** 200 **(c)** $(50, 62.50)$, $(100, 100)$, $(200, 175)$
(d) **POSTER COSTS** **(e)** $120; $118.75

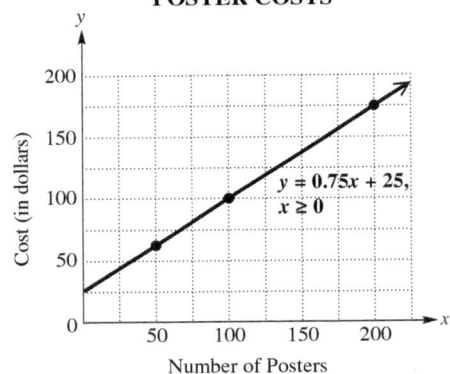

55. (a) $30,000 **(b)** $20,000 **(c)** $5000 **(d)** After 5 yr, the SUV has a value of $5000. **57. (a)** 2000: 30.1 lb; 2010: 33.2 lb; 2014: 34.4 lb
(b) 2000: 30 lb; 2010: 33 lb; 2014: 34 lb **(c)** The values are quite close.
(d) 36.9 lb; It is very close to the USDA projection.

SECTION 3.3

1. steepness; vertical; horizontal **2.** ratio; y; rise; x; run **3. (a)** 6
(b) 4 **(c)** $\frac{6}{4}$, or $\frac{3}{2}$; slope of the line **(d)** Yes, it doesn't matter which point we start with. The slope would be expressed as the quotient of -6 and -4, which simplifies to $\frac{3}{2}$. **4. (a)** C **(b)** A **(c)** D **(d)** B

5. Answers will vary. **6. (a)** falls from left to right
(b) horizontal **(c)** vertical
(d) rises from left to right
7. (a) negative **(b)** 0
8. (a) negative **(b)** negative
9. (a) positive **(b)** negative
10. (a) positive **(b)** 0 **11. (a)** 0
(b) negative **12. (a)** 0 **(b)** positive

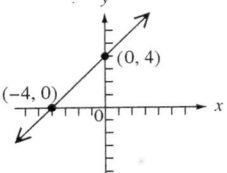

13. $\frac{8}{27}$ **14.** $\frac{3}{10}$ **15.** $-\frac{2}{3}$ **16.** $-\frac{1}{4}$ **17.** Because the student found the difference $3 - 5 = -2$ in the numerator, he should have subtracted in the *same* order in the denominator, $-1 - 2 = -3$. The correct slope is $\frac{-2}{-3} = \frac{2}{3}$.

18. Slope is defined as $\frac{\text{change in } y}{\text{change in } x}$, but the student found $\frac{\text{change in } x}{\text{change in } y}$.
The correct slope is $\frac{5}{-8} = -\frac{5}{8}$. **19.** 4 **21.** $-\frac{1}{2}$ **23.** 0 **25.** $\frac{5}{4}$ **27.** $\frac{3}{2}$

29. -3 **31.** 0 **33.** undefined **35.** $\frac{1}{4}$ **37.** $-\frac{1}{2}$ **39.** 5 **41.** $\frac{1}{4}$ **43.** $\frac{3}{2}$

45. $-\frac{3}{2}$ **47.** 0 **49.** undefined **51.** 1

In part (a) of Exercises 53 and 55, we used the intercepts. Other points can be used.
53. (a) $(5, 0)$ and $(0, 10)$; -2 **(b)** $y = -2x + 10$; -2 **55. (a)** $(3, 0)$ and $(0, -5)$; $\frac{5}{3}$ **(b)** $y = \frac{5}{3}x - 5$; $\frac{5}{3}$

57. (a) 1 **(b)** $(-4, 0)$; $(0, 4)$ **59. (a)** $-\frac{1}{3}$ **(b)** $(-6, 0)$; $(0, -2)$
(c) **(c)**

61. $\frac{4}{3}$; $\frac{4}{3}$; parallel **63.** $\frac{5}{3}$; $\frac{3}{5}$; neither **65.** $\frac{3}{5}$; $-\frac{5}{3}$; perpendicular
67. -6; $-\frac{1}{6}$; neither **69.** $\frac{7}{10}$ **71.** $-$$4000 per year;
The value of the machine is decreasing $4000 per year during these years.
72. $50 per month; The amount saved is increasing $50 per month during these months. **73.** 0% per year (or no change); The percent of pay raise is not changing—it is 3% per year during these years. **74.** positive; negative
75. (a) -7.1 theaters per year **(b)** The negative slope -7.1 means that the number of drive-in theaters decreased by an average of 7.1 per year from 2005 to 2016. **77. (a)** In 2014, there were 355 million wireless subscriber connections in the U.S. **(b)** 14.3 **(c)** The number of subscribers increased by an average of 14.3 million per year from 2007 to 2014.

79. $\frac{1}{3}$ **80.** $\frac{1}{3}$ **81.** $\frac{1}{3}$ **82.** $\frac{1}{3} = \frac{1}{3} = \frac{1}{3}$ is true. **83.** They are collinear.
84. They are not collinear.

SECTION 3.4

1. m; $(0, b)$ **2.** $-\frac{1}{2}$; $(0, -3)$ **3. (a)** C **(b)** B **(c)** A **(d)** D
4. (a) E **(b)** D **(c)** B **(d)** A **5.** y-axis **6.** x-axis **7.** $\frac{5}{2}$; $(0, -4)$

9. -1; $(0, 9)$ **11.** -8; $(0, 0)$ **13.** $\dfrac{1}{5}$; $\left(0, -\dfrac{3}{10}\right)$

15.
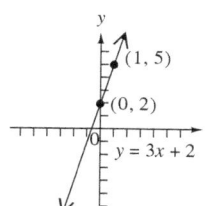

17.
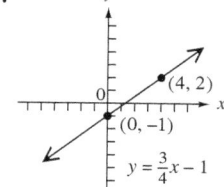

19.
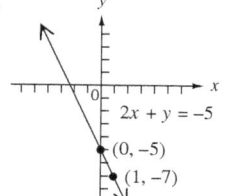

21.
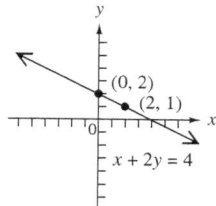

23.
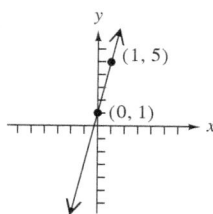

25.
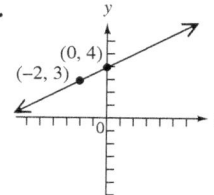

27.
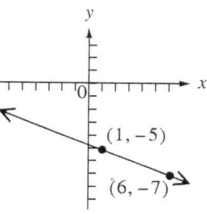

29.
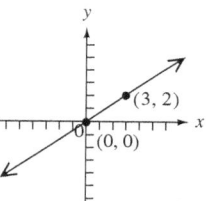

31.
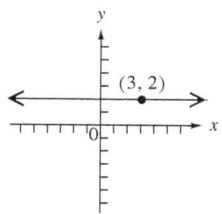

33.
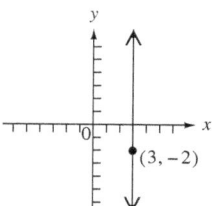

35. $y = 3x - 3$ **36.** $y = 2x - 4$ **37.** $y = -x + 3$ **38.** $y = -x - 2$
39. $y = -\dfrac{1}{2}x + 2$ **40.** $y = \dfrac{3}{2}x - 3$ **41.** $y = 4x - 3$ **43.** $y = -x - 7$
45. $y = 2x - 7$ **47.** $y = -4x - 1$ **49.** $y = -2x - 4$ **51.** $y = \dfrac{3}{4}x + 4$
53. $y = 3$ **55.** $x = 2$ **57.** $y = -6$ **59. (a)** 2 **(b)** $(0, -1)$
(c) $y = 2x - 1$ **(d)**

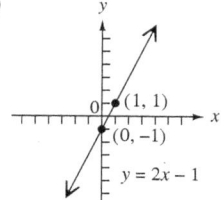

61. (a) \$400 **(b)** \$0.25 **(c)** $y = 0.25x + 400$ **(d)** \$425 **(e)** 1500
63. (a) 0.05; commission rate **(b)** $(0, 2000)$; base salary per month
(c) \$2500 **(d)** \$30,000 **65.** $y = 45x$; $(0, 0)$, $(5, 225)$, $(10, 450)$
67. $y = 3.00x$; $(0, 0)$, $(5, 15.00)$, $(10, 30.00)$ **69. (a)** $y = 41x + 99$
(b) $(5, 304)$; The cost of a 5-month membership is \$304. **(c)** \$591

71. (a) $y = 90x + 36$ **(b)** $(5, 486)$; The cost of the plan for 5 months is
\$486. **(c)** \$2196 **73. (a)** $y = 0.20x + 50$ **(b)** $(5, 51)$; The charge for
driving 5 mi is \$51. **(c)** 173 mi **75.** $y = -\dfrac{A}{B}x + \dfrac{C}{B}$ **76. (a)** $-\dfrac{2}{3}$
(b) 2 **(c)** $\dfrac{3}{7}$ **77.** $\left(0, \dfrac{C}{B}\right)$ **78. (a)** $(0, 6)$ **(b)** $\left(0, \dfrac{1}{2}\right)$ **(c)** $(0, -3)$

SECTION 3.5

1. (a) D **(b)** C **(c)** B **(d)** E **(e)** A **2.** $y = -2x + 9$; $2x + y = 9$
3. A, B, D **4.** In standard form, both equations are written $3x - 2y = 12$.
They are different, but equivalent, forms of the same equation.
5. $y = 5x + 2$ **7.** $y = x - 9$ **9.** $y = -3x - 4$
11. $y = -x + 1$ **13.** $y = \dfrac{2}{3}x + \dfrac{19}{3}$ **15.** $y = -\dfrac{4}{5}x + \dfrac{9}{5}$
17. (a) $y = x + 6$ **(b)** $x - y = -6$ **19. (a)** $y = -\dfrac{5}{7}x - \dfrac{54}{7}$
(b) $5x + 7y = -54$ **21. (a)** $y = -\dfrac{2}{3}x - 2$ **(b)** $2x + 3y = -6$
23. (a) $y = \dfrac{1}{3}x + \dfrac{4}{3}$ **(b)** $x - 3y = -4$ **25. (a)** $y = 3x - 9$
(b) $3x - y = 9$ **27. (a)** $y = -\dfrac{2}{3}x + \dfrac{4}{3}$ **(b)** $2x + 3y = 4$
29. $y = \dfrac{3}{4}x - 7$ **31.** $y = -2x - 3$ **33.** $y = -3x + 14$
35. $y = \dfrac{3}{4}x - \dfrac{9}{2}$ **37. (a)** $(1, 2283)$, $(2, 2441)$, $(3, 2651)$,
$(4, 2792)$, $(5, 2882)$
(b) yes

**AVERAGE ANNUAL COSTS AT
2-YEAR COLLEGES**

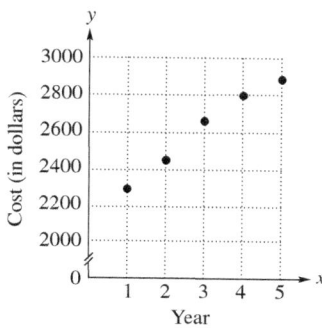

(c) $y = 147x + 2147$ **(d)** \$3176 $(x = 7)$

39. $y = 0.2375x + 59.7$ **41.** $(0, 32)$; $(100, 212)$ **42.** $\dfrac{9}{5}$
43. $F - 32 = \dfrac{9}{5}(C - 0)$ **44.** $F = \dfrac{9}{5}C + 32$ **45.** $C = \dfrac{5}{9}(F - 32)$
46. 86° **47.** 10° **48.** $-40°$

SUMMARY EXERCISES Applying Graphing and Equation-Writing Techniques for Lines

1. (a) B **(b)** D **(c)** A **(d)** C **2.** A, B
3.
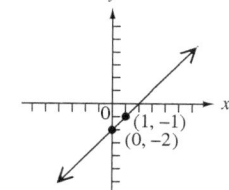

4.
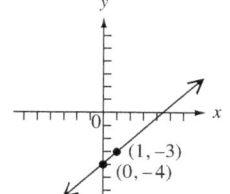

5.
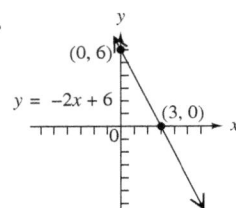

6.
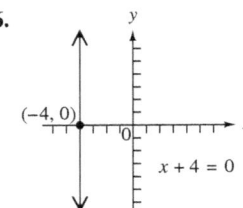

7.
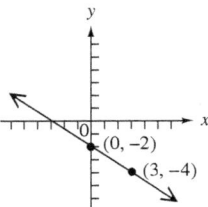

8.
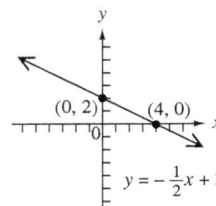

9.
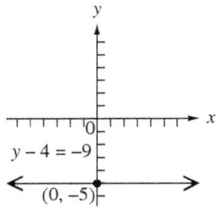

10.
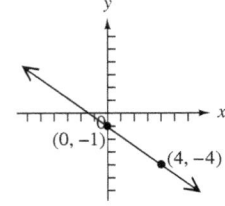

11.
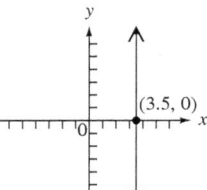

12.
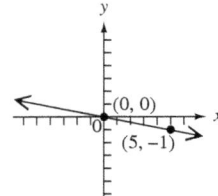

13.
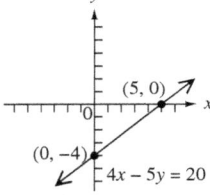

14.
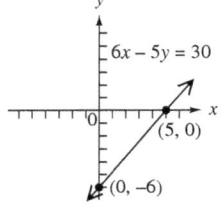

15.
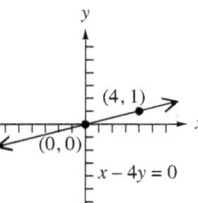

16.
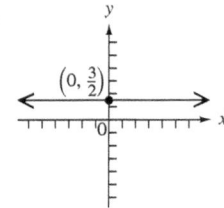

17.
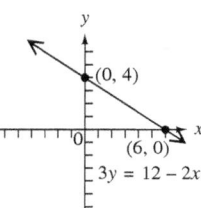

18.
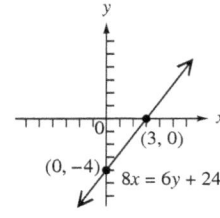

19. $y = -2x + 6$ **20.** $y = \frac{4}{3}x + 8$ **21.** $y = \frac{1}{2}x - 2$ **22.** $y = -\frac{2}{3}x + 5$

23. $y = -3x - 6$ **24.** $y = -4x - 3$ **25.** $y = \frac{3}{5}x$ **26.** $x = 0$

27. $y = 0$ **28.** $y = \frac{5}{3}x + 5$ **29.** $y = \frac{1}{5}x - \frac{7}{5}$; $x - 5y = 7$

30. $y = -\frac{3}{4}x - 6$; $3x + 4y = -24$

SECTION 3.6

1. $>, >$ **2.** $<$ **3.** $\le$ **4.** $\ge$ **5.** false; The point $(4, 0)$ lies on the boundary line $3x - 4y = 12$, which is *not* part of the graph because the symbol $<$ does not involve equality. **6.** true **7.** false; Because $(0, 0)$ is on the boundary line $x + 4y = 0$, it cannot be used as a test point. Use a test point *off* the line. **8.** false; Use a solid line for the boundary line because the symbol $\ge$ involves equality. **9.** true **10.** true **11. (a)** no **(b)** no **(c)** yes **(d)** no **12. (a)** yes **(b)** no **(c)** yes **(d)** yes **13.** Use a dashed line if the symbol is $<$ or $>$. Use a solid line if the symbol is $\le$ or $\ge$. **14.** A test point cannot lie on the boundary line. It must lie on one side of the boundary.

15.
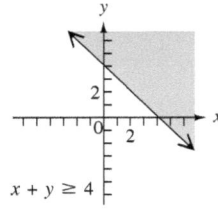

17.
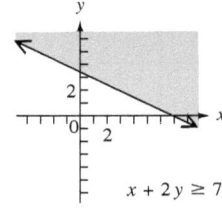

19.
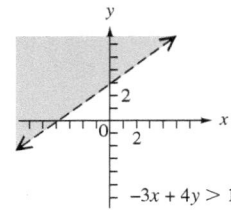

21.
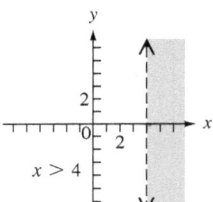

23.
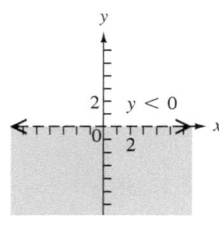

25.
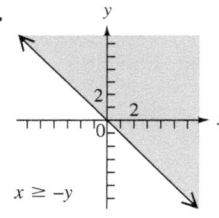

27.
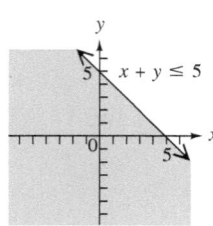

29.
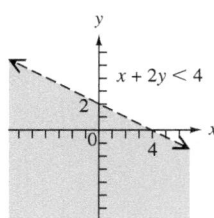

31.
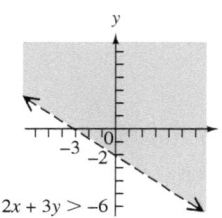

33.
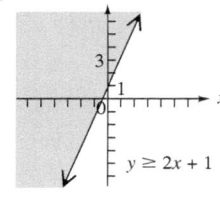

35.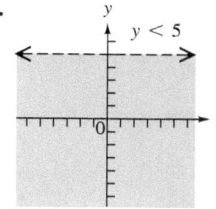
$x \le -2$

37.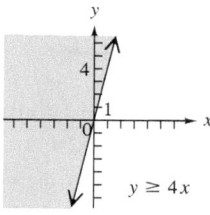
$y < 5$

39.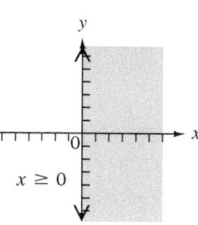
$x \ge 0$

41.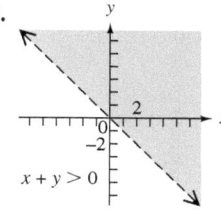
$y \ge 4x$

43.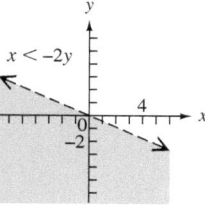
$x < -2y$

45.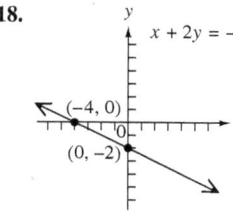
$x + y > 0$

37. $y = -\frac{3}{4}x - \frac{1}{4}$ **38.** $y = -\frac{1}{4}x + \frac{3}{2}$ **39.** $y = 1$ **40.** $x = \frac{1}{3}$

41. $y = 4x - 26$ **42.** $y = -\frac{5}{2}x + 1$ **43.** **(a)** $y = -\frac{1}{3}x + 5$

(b) slope: $-\frac{1}{3}$; y-intercept: $(0, 5)$

(c)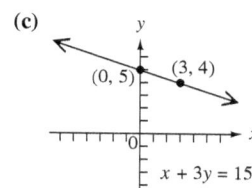
$x + 3y = 15$

44. $y = 142x$; $2130
45. $y = 47x + 159$; $723 **46.** positive;
The graph of the line rises from left to
right, so the slope is positive.
47. $(1, 240), (4, 1508)$; $y = 423x - 183$
48. $663 million $(x = 2)$

49.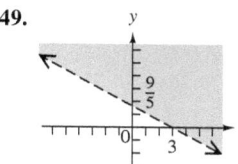
$3x + 5y > 9$

50.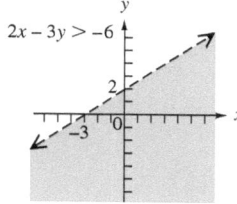
$2x - 3y > -6$

51.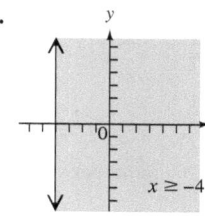
$x \ge -4$

52.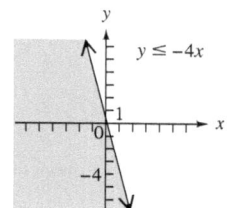
$y \le -4x$

Chapter 3 REVIEW EXERCISES

1. The percent was decreasing. **2.** 2010: 39.5%; 2013: 36% **3.** 3.5%
4. In the year 2015, 36.4% of students at 4-yr public institutions earned a
degree within 5 yr. **5.** -1; 2; 1 **6.** 2; $\frac{3}{2}$; $\frac{14}{3}$ **7.** 0; $\frac{8}{3}$; -9 **8.** 7; 7; 7
9. yes **10.** no **11.** yes **12.** no **13.** quadrant I **14.** quadrant II
15. no quadrant **16.** no quadrant

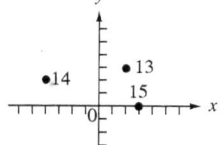

Graph for Exercises 13–16

17.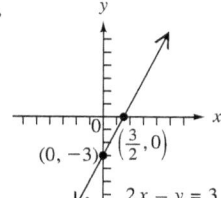
$(0, -3)$ $\left(\frac{3}{2}, 0\right)$
$2x - y = 3$

18.
$x + 2y = -4$
$(-4, 0)$
$(0, -2)$

19.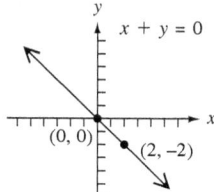
$x + y = 0$
$(0, 0)$
$(2, -2)$

20.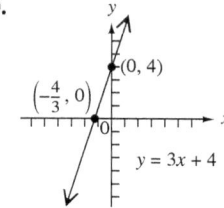
$\left(-\frac{4}{3}, 0\right)$ $(0, 4)$
$y = 3x + 4$

21. $-\frac{1}{2}$ **22.** undefined **23.** 3 **24.** $\frac{3}{2}$ **25.** $-\frac{1}{3}$ **26.** $\frac{3}{2}$ **27.** 0
28. 2 **29.** $\frac{1}{3}$ **30.** parallel **31.** perpendicular **32.** neither
33. $971 per year **34.** $y = -x + \frac{2}{3}$ **35.** $y = -\frac{1}{3}x + 1$ **36.** $y = x - 7$

Chapter 3 MIXED REVIEW EXERCISES

1. A **2.** C, D **3.** A, B, D **4.** D **5.** C **6.** B
7. $(0, -5)$; $\left(-\frac{5}{2}, 0\right)$; -2 **8.** $(0, 0)$; $(0, 0)$; $-\frac{1}{3}$

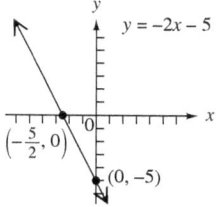
$y = -2x - 5$
$\left(-\frac{5}{2}, 0\right)$
$(0, -5)$

$x + 3y = 0$
$(-3, 1)$
$(0, 0)$

9. $(0, 5)$; no x-intercept; 0 **10.** no y-intercept; $(-1, 0)$; undefined

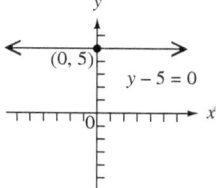
$(0, 5)$
$y - 5 = 0$

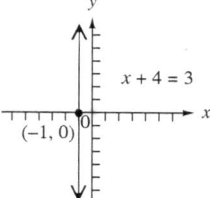
$x + 4 = 3$
$(-1, 0)$

11. **(a)** $y = -\frac{1}{4}x - \frac{5}{4}$ **(b)** $x + 4y = -5$ **12.** **(a)** $y = -3x + 30$
(b) $3x + y = 30$ **13.** **(a)** $y = -\frac{4}{7}x - \frac{23}{7}$ **(b)** $4x + 7y = -23$
14. **(a)** $y = -5$ **(b)** $y = -5$

Chapter 3 TEST

1. $-6; -10; -5$ **2.** no

3.
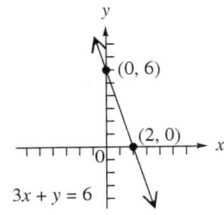

4.
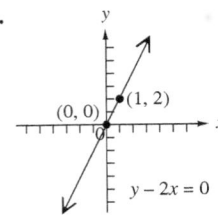

5.
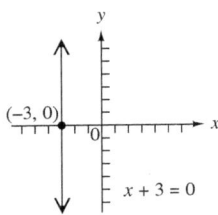

6.
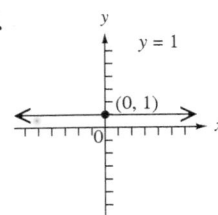

7. $1; (0, -4)$

8.
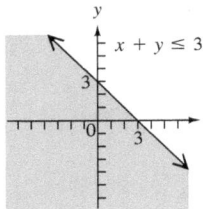
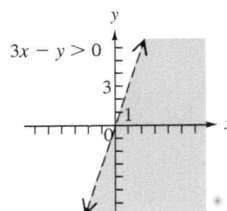

9. $-\dfrac{8}{3}$ **10.** -2 **11.** undefined   **12.** $\dfrac{5}{2}$ **13.** -909 farms per year; The number of farms decreased by an average of 909 per year from 1980 to 2013.

14. (a) $y = -\dfrac{2}{5}x + 3$ **(b)** $2x + 5y = 15$ **15.** $y = 2x + 6$

16. $y = \dfrac{5}{2}x - 4$ **17.** $y = -9x + 12$ **18.** $y = 14$ **19.** $x = 5$

20. (a) $y = -\dfrac{3}{5}x - \dfrac{11}{5}$ **(b)** $y = -\dfrac{1}{2}x - \dfrac{3}{2}$

21.
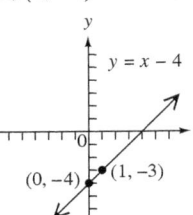

22.
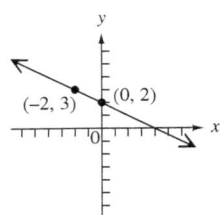

23.
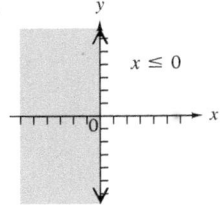

24. The graph falls from left to right, so the slope is negative.
25. $(0, 209), (15, 151); -3.9$ **26.** $y = -3.9x + 209$
27. 170 thousand   **28.** In 2015, worldwide snowmobile sales were 151 thousand.

Chapters R–3 CUMULATIVE REVIEW EXERCISES

1. $\dfrac{301}{40}$, or $7\dfrac{21}{40}$ **2.** 6   **3.** 7   **4.** $\dfrac{73}{18}$ **5.** true   **6.** -43

7. distributive property   **8.** $-p + 2$ **9.** $h = \dfrac{3V}{\pi r^2}$ **10.** $\{-1\}$ **11.** $\{2\}$

12. $\{-13\}$ **13.** $(-2.6, \infty)$
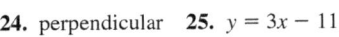

14. $(0, \infty)$ **15.** $(-\infty, -4\,]$

16. high school credential: \$30,000; bachelor's degree: \$48,500   **17.** 13 mi
18. (a) $85.63; 77.82; 76.09; 50$ **(b)** $(20, 85.63), (38, 77.82), (42, 76.09),$
$(50, 72.62)$ **(c)** In 2014, the winning time was approximately 70.89 sec.
19. (a) 19.8 million   **(b)** 13.2 million   **(c)** 7.8 million
20. $(-4, 0); (0, 3)$ **21.** $\dfrac{3}{4}$ **22.** 6

23.
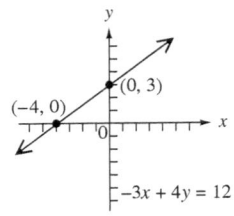

24. perpendicular   **25.** $y = 3x - 11$
26. $y = 4$

CHAPTER 4 Systems of Linear Equations and Inequalities

SECTION 4.1

1. system of linear equations; same   **2.** ordered pair; true   **3.** inconsistent; no; independent   **4.** solution; consistent   **5.** dependent; consistent; infinitely many   **6.** parallel; solution   **7.** It is not a solution of the system because it is not a solution of the second equation, $2x + y = 4$.
8. $\{(x, y) \mid 3x - 2y = 4\}$ **9.** B; The ordered pair must be in quadrant II.
10. D; The ordered pair must be on the y-axis, with $y < 0$.   **11.** no
13. yes   **15.** yes   **17.** no   **19.** yes   **21.** no

We show the graphs here only for Exercises 23–27.

23. $\{(4, 2)\}$
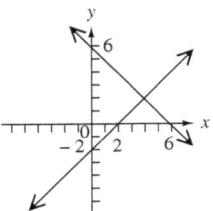

25. $\{(0, 4)\}$
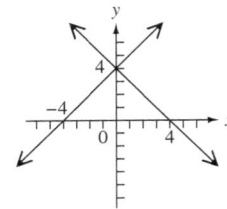

27. $\{(4, -1)\}$
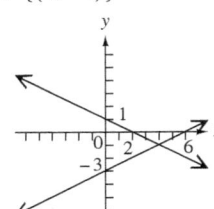

29. $\{(1, 3)\}$ **31.** $\{(0, 2)\}$
33. $\varnothing$ (inconsistent system)
35. $\{(x, y) \mid 5x - 3y = 2\}$
(dependent equations)
37. $\{(4, -3)\}$
39. $\{(x, y) \mid 2x - y = 4\}$
(dependent equations)

41. $\varnothing$ (inconsistent system)   **43. (a)** neither   **(b)** intersecting lines
(c) one solution   **45. (a)** dependent   **(b)** one line   **(c)** infinite number
of solutions   **47. (a)** inconsistent   **(b)** parallel lines   **(c)** no solution
49. (a) neither   **(b)** intersecting lines   **(c)** one solution
51. (a) dependent   **(b)** one line   **(c)** infinite number of solutions
53. (a) inconsistent   **(b)** parallel lines   **(c)** no solution
55. 40; 30   **57.** Supply exceeds demand.   **59.** 1980–2000   **61.** 2006;
600 (million) units   **62.** (2006, 600)   **63.** The slope would be negative.
Sales of CDs were decreasing during this period.   **64.** The slope would be
positive. Sales of digital downloads were increasing during this period.

SECTION 4.2

1. The student must find the value of y and write the solution as an
ordered pair. The solution set is $\{(3, 0)\}$.   **2.** The true result $0 = 0$ means
that the system has an infinite number of solutions. The solution set is
$\{(x, y) \mid x + y = 4\}$.   **3.** A false statement, such as $0 = 3$, occurs.
4. A true statement, such as $0 = 0$, occurs.   **5.** $\{(3, 9)\}$ **7.** $\{(7, 3)\}$
9. $\{(-4, 8)\}$ **11.** $\{(3, -2)\}$ **13.** $\{(0, 5)\}$ **15.** $\{(1, 5)\}$
17. $\{(x, y) \mid 3x - y = 5\}$ **19.** $\varnothing$ **21.** $\{(x, y) \mid 2x - y = -12\}$
23. $\{(0, 0)\}$ **25.** $\varnothing$ **27.** $\left\{\left(\dfrac{1}{3}, -\dfrac{1}{2}\right)\right\}$ **29.** $\{(2, -3)\}$
31. $\{(2, -4)\}$ **33.** $\{(-4, 2)\}$ **35.** $\{(5, 0)\}$ **37.** $\{(7, -3)\}$
39. $\{(2, 3)\}$ **41.** To find the total cost, multiply the number of
bicycles (x) by the cost per bicycle $(400$ dollars$)$ and add the fixed cost
$(5000$ dollars$)$. Thus $y_1 = 400x + 5000$ gives this total cost (in dollars).
42. $y_2 = 600x$ **43.** $y_1 = 400x + 5000$, $y_2 = 600x$; solution set:
$\{(25, 15,000)\}$ **44.** 25; 15,000; 15,000

SECTION 4.3

1. true   **2.** false; Multiply by -3.   **3.** The student incorrectly stated the
solution set. A false statement indicates that the solution set is $\varnothing$.
4. The student did not multiply *both* sides of equation (1) by 3. The correct solution set is $\{(x, y) \mid 2x - y = 5\}$.   **5.** $\{(-1, 3)\}$ **7.** $\{(-1, -3)\}$
9. $\{(5, 3)\}$ **11.** $\{(-2, 3)\}$ **13.** $\left\{\left(\dfrac{1}{2}, 4\right)\right\}$ **15.** $\{(-3, 4)\}$
17. $\{(3, -6)\}$ **19.** $\{(7, 4)\}$ **21.** $\{(0, 4)\}$ **23.** $\{(-4, 0)\}$
25. $\{(0, 0)\}$ **27.** $\varnothing$ **29.** $\{(x, y) \mid x - 3y = -4\}$ **31.** $\{(0, 7)\}$
33. $\{(-6, 5)\}$ **35.** $\left\{\left(-\dfrac{5}{7}, -\dfrac{2}{7}\right)\right\}$ **37.** $\left\{\left(\dfrac{1}{8}, -\dfrac{5}{6}\right)\right\}$ **39.** $\varnothing$
41. $\{(x, y) \mid 2x + y = 0\}$ **43.** $\{(11, 15)\}$ **45.** $\left\{\left(13, -\dfrac{7}{5}\right)\right\}$
47. $\{(6, -4)\}$ **49.** $6.21 = 2004a + b$ **50.** $8.17 = 2014a + b$
51. $2004a + b = 6.21$, $2014a + b = 8.17$; solution set:
$\{(0.196, -386.574)\}$ **52. (a)** $y = 0.196x - 386.574$
(b) \$7.97; This is a bit less than the actual figure.

SUMMARY EXERCISES   Applying Techniques for Solving
Systems of Linear Equations

1. (a) Use substitution because the second equation is solved for y.
(b) Use elimination because the coefficients of the y-terms are opposites.
(c) Use elimination because the equations are in $Ax + By = C$ form with
no coefficients of 1 or -1. Solving by substitution would involve fractions.
2. System B is easier to solve by substitution because the second equation
is already solved for y.   **3. (a)** $\{(1, 4)\}$ **(b)** $\{(1, 4)\}$

(c) Answers will vary.   **4. (a)** $\{(-5, 2)\}$ **(b)** $\{(-5, 2)\}$
(c) Answers will vary.   **5.** $\{(2, 6)\}$ **6.** $\{(-3, 2)\}$ **7.** $\left\{\left(\dfrac{1}{3}, \dfrac{1}{2}\right)\right\}$
8. $\varnothing$ **9.** $\{(3, 0)\}$ **10.** $\left\{\left(\dfrac{3}{2}, -\dfrac{3}{2}\right)\right\}$ **11.** $\{(x, y) \mid 3x + y = 7\}$
12. $\{(9, 4)\}$ **13.** $\left\{\left(\dfrac{45}{31}, \dfrac{4}{31}\right)\right\}$ **14.** $\{(4, -5)\}$ **15.** $\varnothing$ **16.** $\{(0, 0)\}$
17. $\left\{\left(\dfrac{19}{3}, -5\right)\right\}$ **18.** $\left\{\left(\dfrac{22}{13}, -\dfrac{23}{13}\right)\right\}$ **19.** $\{(-12, -60)\}$
20. $\{(2, -3)\}$ **21.** $\{(24, -12)\}$ **22.** $\{(-2, 1)\}$ **23.** $\{(-35, 13)\}$
24. $\{(10, -9)\}$ **25.** $\{(-4, 6)\}$ **26.** $\{(5, 3)\}$

SECTION 4.4

1. D   **2.** A   **3.** B   **4.** C   **5.** D   **6.** D   **7.** C   **8.** C   **9.** B   **10.** A
11. the second number; $x - y = 48$ (or $y - x = 48$); The two numbers are
73 and 25.   **13.** *The Phantom of the Opera*: 11,669; *The Lion King*: 7603
15. *Furious 7*: \$353 million; *Minions*: \$336 million   **17.** Terminal Tower:
708 ft; Key Tower: 947 ft   **19.** variables; width; Equation (1): $x = 38 + y$;
length; twice; Equation (2): $2x + 2y = 188$; length: 66 yd; width: 28 yd
21. (a) 45 units   **(b)** Do not produce—the product will lead to a loss.
23. table entries: (third column) $1x$ (or x), $10y$; 46 ones; 28 tens
25. 5 DVDs of *Ant-Man*; 2 Blu-ray discs of *The Martian*
27. table entries: (second column) 4%, or 0.04; (third column) $0.04y$;
Equation (1): $x = 2y$; Equation (2): $0.05x + 0.04y = 350$; \$2500 at 4%;
\$5000 at 5%   **29.** Taylor Swift: \$112; Kenny Chesney: \$85   **31.** table
entries: (third column) $0.40x$, $0.70y$, $0.50(120)$, or 60; 80 L of 40%
solution; 40 L of 70% solution   **33.** table entries: (second column) 3, 4;
(third column) $6x$, $3y$, $4(90)$, or 360; 30 lb at \$6 per lb; 60 lb at \$3 per lb
35. nuts: 40 lb; raisins: 20 lb   **37.** table entries: (third column) 4.5, 4.5;
(fourth column) $4.5x$, $4.5y$; Equation (1): $4.5x + 4.5y = 495$;
Equation (2): $x = 10 + y$; 60 mph; 50 mph   **39.** bicycle: 13.5 mph;
car: 46.5 mph   **41.** car leaving Cincinnati: 55 mph; car leaving Toledo:
70 mph   **43.** table entries: (third column) 3, 3; (fourth column) 24;
boat: 10 mph; current: 2 mph   **45.** plane: 470 mph; wind: 30 mph
47. Roberto: 17.5 mph; Juana: 12.5 mph

SECTION 4.5

1. C   **2.** A   **3.** B   **4.** D
5. (a) no   **(b)** yes

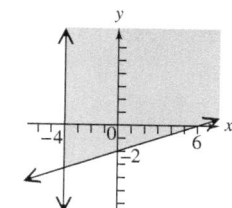

6. (a) no   **(b)** yes

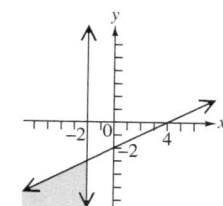

7. (a) yes   **(b)** no

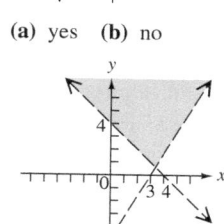

8. (a) yes   **(b)** no

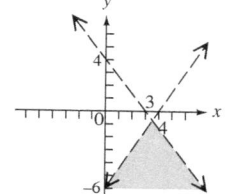

9.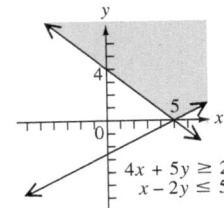

$x + y \le 6$
$x - y \ge 1$

11.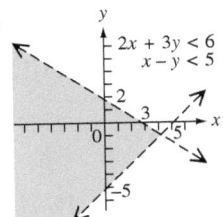

$4x + 5y \ge 20$
$x - 2y \le 5$

13.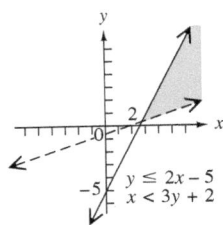

$2x + 3y < 6$
$x - y < 5$

15.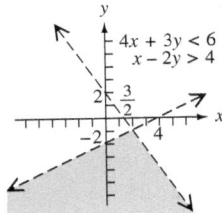

$y \le 2x - 5$
$x < 3y + 2$

17.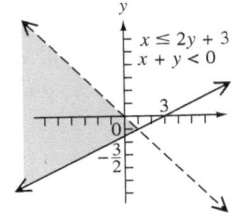

$4x + 3y < 6$
$x - 2y > 4$

19.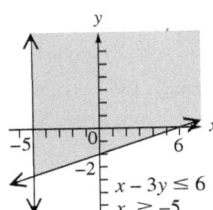

$x \le 2y + 3$
$x + y < 0$

21.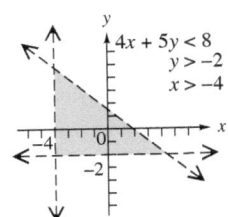

$x - 3y \le 6$
$x \ge -5$

23.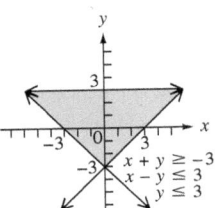

$4x + 5y < 8$
$y > -2$
$x > -4$

25.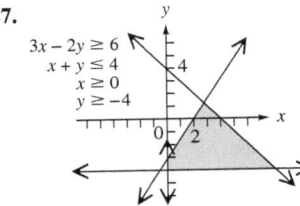

$x + y \ge -3$
$x - y \le 3$
$y \le 3$

27.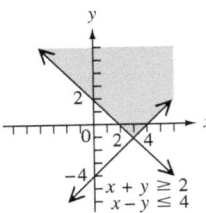

$3x - 2y \ge 6$
$x + y \le 4$
$x \ge 0$
$y \ge -4$

30. table entries: (second column) 0.70; (third column) 0.40x, 0.70y, 0.50(90), or 45; 60 L of 40% solution; 30 L of 70% solution

31.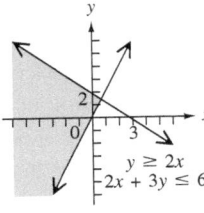

$x + y \ge 2$
$x - y \le 4$

32.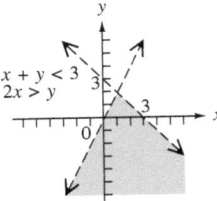

$y \ge 2x$
$2x + 3y \le 6$

33.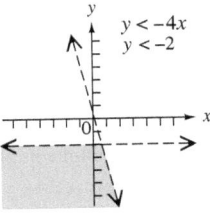

$x + y < 3$
$2x > y$

34.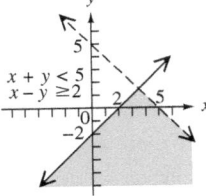

$y < -4x$
$y < -2$

Chapter 4 MIXED REVIEW EXERCISES

1. $\{(2, 0)\}$ **2.** $\{(-4, 15)\}$ **3.** $\varnothing$

4.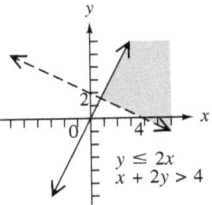

$x + y < 5$
$x - y \ge 2$

5.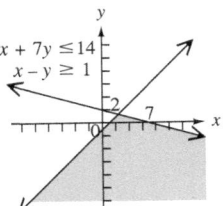

$y \le 2x$
$x + 2y > 4$

6. 8 in., 8 in., and 13 in.   **7.** Broncos: 24; Panthers: 10   **8. (a)** years 0–6
(b) year 6; $650   **9.** B   **10.** B

Chapter 4 TEST

1. (a) no   **(b)** no   **(c)** yes   **2.** $\{(2, -3)\}$ **3.** It has no solution.
4. $\{(1, -6)\}$ **5.** $\{(-35, 35)\}$ **6.** $\left\{\left(-\dfrac{1}{3}, -10\right)\right\}$ **7.** $\{(5, 6)\}$
8. $\{(-1, 3)\}$ **9.** $\{(-1, 3)\}$ **10.** $\{(0, 0)\}$ **11.** $\varnothing$ **12.** $\{(-2, 2)\}$
13. $\{(x, y) \mid 3x - y = 6\}$ **14.** $\{(-15, 6)\}$
15. Memphis and Atlanta: 394 mi; Minneapolis and Houston: 1176 mi
16. Statue of Liberty: 4.3 million: Mount Rushmore National Memorial:
2.4 million   **17.** 20 L of 15% solution; 30 L of 40% solution
18. slower car: 45 mph; faster car: 60 mph

19.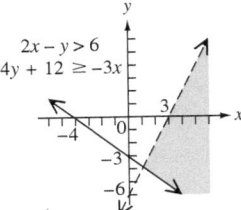

$2x + 7y \le 14$
$x - y \ge 1$

20.

$2x - y > 6$
$4y + 12 \ge -3x$

Chapter 4 REVIEW EXERCISES

1. yes   **2.** no
We do not show the graphs for Exercises 3–6.
3. $\{(3, 1)\}$ **4.** $\{(0, -2)\}$ **5.** $\{(x, y) \mid x - 2y = 2\}$ **6.** $\varnothing$
7. $\{(2, 1)\}$ **8.** $\{(3, 5)\}$ **9.** $\{(6, 4)\}$ **10.** $\varnothing$ **11.** $\{(7, 1)\}$
12. $\{(-5, -2)\}$ **13.** $\{(-4, 3)\}$ **14.** $\{(x, y) \mid 3x - 4y = 9\}$
15. $\{(9, 2)\}$ **16.** $\left\{\left(\dfrac{10}{7}, -\dfrac{9}{7}\right)\right\}$ **17.** $\{(0, 0)\}$ **18.** $\left\{\left(\dfrac{3}{2}, 0\right)\right\}$
19. $\{(8, 9)\}$ **20.** $\{(2, 1)\}$ **21.** $\{(7, -2)\}$ **22.** $\{(-4, 2)\}$
23. Pizza Hut: 15,605 locations; Domino's: 11,629 locations
24. *Reader's Digest*: 2.7 million; *People*: 3.5 million
25. table entries: (first column) x; (second column) 0.90; (third column)
0.90y, 100(1), or 100; 25 lb of $1.30 candy; 75 lb of $0.90 candy
26. table entries: (first column) y, 20; (second column) 20; (third column)
10x; 13 twenties; 7 tens   **27.** length: 27 m; width: 18 m   **28.** plane:
250 mph; wind: 20 mph   **29.** table entries: (second column) 0.04;
(third column) 0.03x, 0.04y, 650; $7000 at 3%; $11,000 at 4%

Chapters R-4 CUMULATIVE REVIEW EXERCISES

1. $-1, 1, -2, 2, -4, 4, -5, 5, -8, 8, -10, 10, -20, 20, -40, 40$ **2.** 1
3. commutative property   **4.** distributive property   **5.** inverse property
6. 46   **7.** $T = \dfrac{PV}{k}$ **8.** $\left\{-\dfrac{13}{11}\right\}$ **9.** $\left\{\dfrac{9}{11}\right\}$ **10.** $(-18, \infty)$
11. $\left(-\dfrac{11}{2}, \infty\right)$ **12.** length: 12 in.; width: 8.7 in.

13.

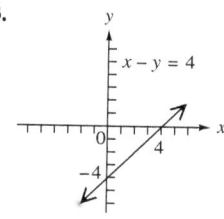

$x - y = 4$

14.

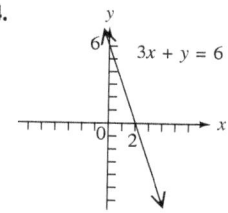

$3x + y = 6$

15. $-\dfrac{4}{3}$ **16.** $-\dfrac{1}{4}$ **17.** $y = \dfrac{1}{2}x + 3$ **18.** $y = 2x + 1$

19. (a) $x = 9$ (b) $y = -1$ **20.** $\{(-1, 6)\}$ **21.** $\{(3, -4)\}$ **22.** $\varnothing$

23. table entries: (third column) 2; (fourth column) $2y$, 2528; 405 adults, 49 children **24.** 19 in., 19 in., 15 in.

25.

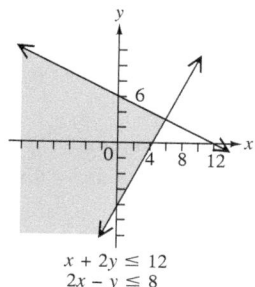

$x + 2y \le 12$
$2x - y \le 8$

CHAPTER 5 Exponents and Polynomials

SECTION 5.1

1. false; $3^3 = 3 \cdot 3 \cdot 3 = 27$ **2.** true **3.** false; $(a^2)^3 = a^{2 \cdot 3} = a^6$
4. true **5.** false; $-2^2 = -(2 \cdot 2) = -4$ **6.** false; $2^3 \cdot 2^4 = 2^7$
7. false; $(3x)^2 = 3^2 x^2 = 9x^2$ **8.** true **9.** t^7 **11.** $\left(\dfrac{1}{2}\right)^5$ **13.** $(-8p)^2$
15. base: 3; exponent: 5; 243 **17.** base: -3; exponent: 5; -243
19. base: -6; exponent: 2; 36 **21.** base: 6; exponent: 2; -36
23. base: $-2x$; exponent: 4; $16x^4$ **25.** base: x; exponent: 4 **27.** 5^8
29. 4^{12} **31.** $(-7)^9$ **33.** t^{24} **35.** $-56r^7$ **37.** $42p^{10}$
39. The product rule does not apply. **41.** The product rule does not apply.
43. 4^6 **45.** t^{20} **47.** $343r^3$ **49.** 5^{12} **51.** -8^{15} **53.** $5^5 x^5 y^5$ **55.** $8q^3 r^3$
57. $\dfrac{9^8}{5^8}$ **59.** $\dfrac{1}{8}$ **61.** $\dfrac{a^3}{b^3}$ **63.** $-8x^6 y^3$ **65.** $9a^6 b^4$ **67.** $\dfrac{5^5}{2^5}$ **69.** $\dfrac{9^5}{8^3}$
71. $2^{12} x^{12}$ **73.** $-6^5 p^5$ **75.** $6^5 x^{10} y^{15}$ **77.** x^{21} **79.** $4w^4 x^{26} y^7$
81. $-r^{18} s^{17}$ **83.** $\dfrac{64x^6}{125}$ **85.** $\dfrac{125a^6 b^{15}}{c^{18}}$ **87.** $25m^6 p^{14} q^5$ **89.** $16x^{10} y^{16} z^{10}$
91. Using power rule (a), raise a power to a power by multiplying *exponents*. The base remains the same. Simplify as follows: $(10^2)^3 = 10^{2 \cdot 3} = 10^6 = $ 1,000,000. **92.** The 4 is used as an *exponent* on 3. It is *not* multiplied by 3. The correct simplification is $3^4 \cdot x^8 \cdot y^{12} = 81x^8 y^{12}$. **93.** $30x^7$ **95.** $6p^7$
97. $125x^6$

SECTION 5.2

1. negative **2.** positive **3.** negative **4.** negative **5.** positive
6. positive **7.** 0 **8.** 0 **9.** (a) B (b) C (c) D (d) B (e) E
(f) B **10.** (a) C (b) F (c) F (d) B (e) E (f) B **11.** 1 **13.** 1
15. -1 **17.** 0 **19.** 0 **21.** $\dfrac{1}{64}$ **23.** 16 **25.** $\dfrac{49}{36}$ **27.** $\dfrac{1}{81}$ **29.** 3
31. 1 **33.** 2 **35.** $\dfrac{8}{15}$ **37.** $-\dfrac{7}{18}$ **39.** 125 **41.** $\dfrac{1}{9}$ **43.** $\dfrac{1}{6^5}$ **45.** 27
47. 216 **49.** $2r^4$ **51.** $\dfrac{125}{9}$ **53.** $-\dfrac{4}{x^3}$ **55.** $\dfrac{p^5}{q^8}$ **57.** r^9 **59.** $\dfrac{x^5}{6}$

61. $3y^2$ **63.** x^3 **65.** $\dfrac{yz^2}{4x^3}$ **67.** $a + b$ **69.** 343 **71.** $\dfrac{1}{x^2}$ **73.** $\dfrac{64x}{9}$
75. $\dfrac{x^2 z^4}{y^2}$ **77.** $6x$ **79.** $\dfrac{1}{m^{10} n^5}$ **81.** $\dfrac{5}{16x^5}$ **83.** $\dfrac{36q^2}{m^4 p^2}$
85. The student attempted to use the quotient rule with unequal bases. The correct way to simplify is $\dfrac{16^3}{2^2} = \dfrac{(2^4)^3}{2^2} = \dfrac{2^{12}}{2^2} = 2^{12-2} = 2^{10} = 1024$.
86. The student incorrectly assumed that the negative exponent indicated a negative number. The correct way to simplify is $5^{-4} = \dfrac{1}{5^4} = \dfrac{1}{625}$.

SUMMARY EXERCISES Applying the Rules for Exponents

1. positive **2.** negative **3.** negative **4.** negative **5.** positive
6. negative **7.** positive **8.** negative **9.** $\dfrac{6^{12} x^{24}}{5^{12}}$ **10.** $\dfrac{r^6 s^{12}}{729t^6}$
11. $100{,}000x^7 y^{14}$ **12.** $64a^8 b^{14} c^4$ **13.** $\dfrac{729w^3 x^9}{y^{12}}$ **14.** $\dfrac{x^4 y^6}{16}$ **15.** c^{22}
16. $\dfrac{1}{k^4 t^{12}}$ **17.** $\dfrac{11}{30}$ **18.** $y^{12} z^3$ **19.** $\dfrac{x^6}{y^5}$ **20.** 0 **21.** $\dfrac{1}{z^2}$ **22.** $\dfrac{9}{r^2 s^2 t^{10}}$
23. $\dfrac{300x^3}{y^3}$ **24.** $\dfrac{3}{5x^6}$ **25.** x^8 **26.** $\dfrac{y^{11}}{x^{11}}$ **27.** $\dfrac{a^6}{b^4}$ **28.** $6ab$ **29.** $\dfrac{61}{900}$
30. 1 **31.** $\dfrac{343a^6 b^9}{8}$ **32.** 1 **33.** -1 **34.** 0 **35.** $\dfrac{27y^{18}}{4x^8}$ **36.** $\dfrac{1}{a^8 b^{12} c^{16}}$
37. $\dfrac{x^{15}}{216z^9}$ **38.** $\dfrac{q}{8p^6 r^3}$ **39.** $x^6 y^6$ **40.** 0 **41.** $\dfrac{343}{x^{15}}$ **42.** $\dfrac{9}{x^6}$ **43.** $5p^{10} q^9$
44. $\dfrac{7}{24}$ **45.** $\dfrac{r^{14} t}{2s^2}$ **46.** 1 **47.** $8p^{10} q$ **48.** $\dfrac{1}{mn^3 p^3}$ **49.** -1 **50.** $\dfrac{3}{40}$

SECTION 5.3

1. (a) C (b) A (c) B (d) D **2.** (a) A (b) C (c) B (d) D
3. in scientific notation **4.** in scientific notation **5.** not in scientific notation; 5.6×10^6 **6.** not in scientific notation; 3.4×10^4
7. not in scientific notation; 4×10^{-3} **8.** not in scientific notation; 7×10^{-4}
9. not in scientific notation; 8×10^1 **10.** not in scientific notation; 9×10^2 **11.** (a) 6; 4; 6.3; 4 (b) 5; 2; 5.71; -2 **13.** 5.876×10^9
15. 8.235×10^4 **17.** 7×10^{-6} **19.** -2.03×10^{-3} **21.** 750,000
23. 5,677,000,000,000 **25.** 1,000,000,000,000 **27.** -6.21
29. 0.00078 **31.** 0.000000005134 **33.** 0.000002 **35.** 4.2×10^{42}
37. (a) 6×10^{11} (b) 600,000,000,000 **39.** (a) 1.5×10^7
(b) 15,000,000 **41.** (a) 8×10^{-3} (b) 0.008 **43.** (a) 2.4×10^2 (b) 240
45. (a) -6×10^4 (b) $-60,000$ **47.** (a) 6.3×10^{-2} (b) 0.063
49. (a) 3×10^{-4} (b) 0.0003 **51.** (a) 4×10^1 (b) 40
53. (a) 1.3×10^{-5} (b) 0.000013 **55.** (a) 5×10^2 (b) 500
57. (a) 9×10^6 (b) 9,000,000 **59.** (a) 2.6×10^{-3} (b) 0.0026
61. 1.5×10^{17} mi **63.** $3097 **65.** $1,394,668,000,000
67. 3.59×10^2 sec, or 359 sec **69.** 6×10^{17}, or
600,000,000,000,000,000; 3.6×10^{19}, or 36,000,000,000,000,000,000
71. 4.7E-7 **73.** 2E7 **75.** The Chile earthquake was 10 times as intense as the Southern Sumatra earthquake. **76.** The Solomon Islands earthquake was 10 times as intense as the Falkland Islands earthquake.
77. The NE Japan earthquake was 100 times as intense as the Falkland Islands earthquake. **78.** The Chile earthquake would be 10,000 times as intense.

SECTION 5.4

1. 7; 5 **2.** two **3.** 8 **4.** is not **5.** 26 **6.** $5x^9$ **7.** 6; 1 **9.** 1; 1
11. $\dfrac{1}{5}$; 1 **13.** $-19, -1$; 2 **15.** $1, -8, \dfrac{2}{3}$; 3 **17.** $2m^5$ **19.** $-r^5$
21. $\dfrac{2}{3}x^4$ **23.** cannot be simplified; $0.2m^5 - 0.5m^2$ **25.** $-5x^5$
27. $5p^9 + 4p^7$ **29.** $-2y^2$ **31.** $-4xy$ **33.** already simplified; 4;
binomial **35.** $x^2 + 9x - 3$; 2; trinomial **37.** $6xy$; 2; monomial
39. already simplified; $6m^5 + 5m^4 - 7m^3 - 3m^2$; 5; none of these
41. x^4; 4; monomial **43.** 7; 0; monomial **45.** (a) -1 (b) 5
47. (a) 19 (b) -2 **49.** (a) 36 (b) -12 **51.** (a) -124 (b) 5
53. $5x^2 - 2x$ **55.** $5m^2 + 3m + 2$ **57.** $\dfrac{7}{6}x^2 - \dfrac{2}{15}x + \dfrac{5}{6}$
59. $3y^3 - 11y^2$ **61.** $4x^4 - 4x^2 + 4x$ **63.** $15m^3 - 13m^2 + 8m + 11$
65. $8r^2 + 5r - 12$ **67.** $5m^2 - 14m + 6$ **69.** $4x^3 + 2x^2 + 5x$
71. $-18y^5 + 7y^4 + 5y^3 + 3y^2 + y$ **73.** $-10x^2 + 4x - 6$
75. $-2m^3 + 7m^2 + 8m - 9$ **77.** $6m^3 + m^2 + 4m - 14$
79. $-11x^2 - 3x - 3$ **81.** $2x^2 + 8x$ **83.** $8x^2 + 8x + 6$
85. $8t^2 + 8t + 13$ **87.** $6x - xy - 7$ **89.** $13a^2b - 7a^2 - b$
91. $c^4d - 5c^2d^2 + d^2$ **93.** (a) $23y + 5t$ (b) $25°, 67°, 88°$ **95.** 5; 175
96. 9; 63 **97.** 6; 27 **98.** 2.5; 130

SECTION 5.5

1. (a) B (b) D (c) A (d) C **2.** (a) C (b) A (c) B (d) D
3. distributive **4.** binomials **5.** $12x^3$ **7.** $-15y^{11}$ **9.** $30a^9$
11. $-18m^3n^2$ **13.** $20a^2b$ **15.** $-12m^3n^4$ **17.** $6m^2 + 4m$
19. $10y^9 + 4y^6 + 6y^5$ **21.** $6y^6 + 4y^4 + 2y^3$ **23.** $6p - \dfrac{9}{2}p^2 + 9p^4$
25. $28r^5 - 32r^4 + 36r^3$ **27.** $6a^4 - 12a^3b + 15a^2b^2$ **29.** $3m^2$; $2mn$; $-n^3$;
$21m^5n^2 + 14m^4n^3 - 7m^3n^5$ **31.** $12x^3 + 26x^2 + 10x + 1$
33. $6r^3 + 5r^2 - 12r + 4$ **35.** $20m^4 - m^3 - 8m^2 - 17m - 15$
37. $5x^4 - 13x^3 + 20x^2 + 7x + 5$ **39.** $3x^5 + 18x^4 - 2x^3 - 8x^2 + 24x$
41. first row: x^2; $4x$; second row: $3x$; 12; Product: $x^2 + 7x + 12$
43. first row: $2x^3$; $6x^2$; $4x$; second row: x^2; $3x$; 2; Product: $2x^3 + 7x^2 + 7x + 2$
45. $m^2 + 12m + 35$ **47.** $n^2 + n - 6$ **49.** $8r^2 - 10r - 3$ **51.** $9x^2 - 4$
53. $9q^2 + 6q + 1$ **55.** $8xy - 4x + 6y - 3$ **57.** $15x^2 + xy - 6y^2$
59. $6t^2 + 23st + 20s^2$ **61.** $-0.3t^2 + 0.22t + 0.24$ **63.** $x^2 - \dfrac{5}{12}x - \dfrac{1}{6}$
65. $\dfrac{15}{16} - \dfrac{1}{4}r - 2r^2$ **67.** $2x^3 + x^2 - 15x$ **69.** $6y^5 - 21y^4 - 45y^3$
71. $-200r^7 + 32r^3$ **73.** (a) $3y^2 + 10y + 7$ (b) $8y + 16$ **75.** $14x + 49$
77. $30x + 60$ **78.** $30x + 60 = 600$; {18} **79.** 10 ft by 60 ft
80. 140 ft **81.** \$900 **82.** \$2870

SECTION 5.6

1. square; twice; product; square **2.** difference; squares **3.** (a) $2x$; $4x^2$
(b) $2x$; 3; $12x$ (c) 3; 9 (d) $4x^2 + 12x + 9$ **5.** $p^2 + 4p + 4$
7. $z^2 - 10z + 25$ **9.** $x^2 - \dfrac{3}{2}x + \dfrac{9}{16}$ **11.** $v^2 + 0.8v + 0.16$
13. $16x^2 - 24x + 9$ **15.** $100z^2 + 120z + 36$ **17.** $x^2 + 4xy + 4y^2$
19. $4p^2 + 20pq + 25q^2$ **21.** $16a^2 - 40ab + 25b^2$
23. $0.64t^2 + 1.12ts + 0.49s^2$ **25.** $36m^2 - \dfrac{48}{5}mn + \dfrac{16}{25}n^2$
27. $9t^3 - 6t^2 + t$ **29.** $48t^3 + 24t^2 + 3t$ **31.** $-16r^2 + 16r - 4$
33. (a) $7x$; $49x^2$ (b) $-21xy$; $21xy$; 0 (c) $3y$ and $-3y$; $-9y^2$
(d) $49x^2 - 9y^2$ **35.** $k^2 - 25$ **37.** $r^2 - \dfrac{9}{16}$ **39.** $s^2 - 6.25$ **41.** $4w^2 - 25$

43. $9x^2 - 16y^2$ **45.** $100x^2 - 9y^2$ **47.** $49x^2 - \dfrac{9}{49}$ **49.** $4x^4 - 25$
51. $25q^3 - q$ **53.** $-5a^2 + 5b^6$ **55.** $x^3 + 3x^2 + 3x + 1$
57. $m^3 - 15m^2 + 75m - 125$ **59.** $8a^3 + 12a^2 + 6a + 1$
61. $256x^4 - 256x^3 + 96x^2 - 16x + 1$
63. $81r^4 - 216r^3t + 216r^2t^2 - 96rt^3 + 16t^4$
65. $3x^5 - 27x^4 + 81x^3 - 81x^2$
67. $-8x^6y - 32x^5y^2 - 48x^4y^3 - 32x^3y^4 - 8x^2y^5$
69. $\dfrac{1}{2}m^2 - 2n^2$ **71.** $9a^2 - 4$ **73.** $\pi x^2 + 4\pi x + 4\pi$
75. $x^3 + 6x^2 + 12x + 8$ **77.** $(x + y)^2$ **78.** x^2 **79.** $2xy$ **80.** y^2
81. $x^2 + 2xy + y^2$ **82.** They both represent the area of the entire large
square. **83.** 1225 **84.** $30^2 + 2(30)(5) + 5^2$ **85.** 1225
86. They are equal.

SECTION 5.7

1. $6x^2 + 8$; 2; $3x^2 + 4$ **2.** $3x^2 + 4$; 2 (These may be reversed.); $6x^2 + 8$
3. is not **4.** 0 **5.** $2m^2 - m$ **7.** $30x^3 - 10x + 5$ **9.** $-4m^3 + 2m^2 - 1$
11. $4t^4 - 2t^2 + 2t$ **13.** $a^4 - a + \dfrac{2}{a}$ **15.** $-2x^3 + \dfrac{2x^2}{3} - x$
17. $-9x^2 + 5x + 1$ **19.** $7r^2 - 6 + \dfrac{1}{r}$ **21.** $\dfrac{4x^2}{3} + x - \dfrac{2}{3x}$
23. $15x^5 - 35x^4 + 35x^3$ **24.** $-72y^6 + 60y^5 - 24y^4 + 36y^3 - 84y^2$
25. $27r^4$; $36r^3$; $6r^2$; $3r$; 2; $9r^3 - 12r^2 - 2r + 1 - \dfrac{2}{3r}$ **27.** $-m^2 + 3m - \dfrac{4}{m}$
29. $\dfrac{12}{x} - \dfrac{6}{x^2} + \dfrac{14}{x^3} - \dfrac{10}{x^4}$ **31.** $-4b^2 + 3ab - \dfrac{5}{a}$
33. $6x^4y^2 - 4xy + 2xy^2 - x^4y$ **35.** 1423
36. $(1 \times 10^3) + (4 \times 10^2) + (2 \times 10^1) + (3 \times 10^0)$
37. $x^3 + 4x^2 + 2x + 3$ **38.** The coefficients of the powers of 10 are
equal to the coefficients of the powers of x. One is a constant, while the other
is a polynomial. They are equal if $x = 10$ (which is the base of our decimal
system).

SECTION 5.8

1. dividend; divisor; quotient **2.** Stop when the degree of the remainder
is less than the degree of the divisor, or when the remainder is 0.
3. Divide $12m^2$ by $2m$ to obtain $6m$. **4.** Multiply $6m$ by $2m - 3$ to obtain
$12m^2 - 18m$. **5.** $x + 2$ **7.** $2y - 5$ **9.** $p - 4 + \dfrac{44}{p + 6}$ **11.** $r - 5$
13. $2a - 14 + \dfrac{74}{2a + 3}$ **15.** $4x^2 - 7x + 3$ **17.** $2r^2 + r - 3 + \dfrac{6}{r - 3}$
19. $3y^2 - 2y + 2$ **21.** $2x^2 - 6x + 19 + \dfrac{-55}{x + 3}$ **23.** $3k - 4 + \dfrac{2}{k^2 - 2}$
25. $x^2 + 1$ **27.** $x^2 + 1$ **29.** $2p^2 - 5p + 4 + \dfrac{6}{3p^2 + 1}$
31. $2x^2 + \dfrac{3}{5}x + \dfrac{1}{5}$ **33.** $x^2 + \dfrac{8}{3}x - \dfrac{1}{3} + \dfrac{4}{3x - 3}$ **35.** $x^3 + 6x - 7$
37. $\left(6x - 2 + \dfrac{1}{x}\right)$ units **39.** $(x^2 + x - 3)$ units
41. $(5x^2 - 11x + 14)$ hours

CHAPTER 5 Review Exercises

1. 4^{11} **2.** -5^{11} **3.** $-72x^7$ **4.** $10x^{14}$ **5.** 19^5x^5 **6.** -4^7y^7 **7.** $5p^4x^7$
8. $\dfrac{7^6}{5^6}$ **9.** $27x^6y^9$ **10.** t^{42} **11.** $36x^{16}y^4z^{16}$ **12.** $\dfrac{8m^9n^3}{p^6}$ **13.** $27x^6$

14. The product rule for exponents does not apply here because we want the sum of 7^2 and 7^3, not their product; $7^2 + 7^3 = 49 + 343 = 392$

15. -1 **16.** 1 **17.** 2 **18.** $\dfrac{1}{32}$ **19.** $\dfrac{25}{36}$ **20.** $-\dfrac{3}{16}$ **21.** 36 **22.** x^2

23. $\dfrac{1}{p^{12}}$ **24.** r^4 **25.** 2^8 **26.** $\dfrac{1}{9^6}$ **27.** 5^8 **28.** $\dfrac{1}{8^{12}}$ **29.** $\dfrac{1}{m^2}$ **30.** y^7

31. r^{13} **32.** $25m^6$ **33.** $\dfrac{y^{12}}{8}$ **34.** $\dfrac{1}{a^3 b^5}$ **35.** $72r^5$ **36.** $\dfrac{8n^{10}}{3m^{13}}$

37. 4.8×10^7 **38.** 2.8988×10^{10} **39.** 6.5×10^{-5} **40.** 8.24×10^{-8}

41. 24,000 **42.** 78,300,000 **43.** 0.000000897 **44.** 0.00000000000995

45. (a) 8×10^2 (b) 800 **46.** (a) 4×10^6 (b) 4,000,000

47. (a) 6×10^{-2} (b) 0.06 **48.** (a) 1×10^{-2} (b) 0.01

49. 2.796×10^{10} calculations; 1.6776×10^{12} calculations **50.** about 3.3

51. $22m^2$; 2; monomial **52.** $p^3 - p^2 + 4p + 2$; 3; none of these

53. already simplified; 5; none of these **54.** $-8y^5 - 7y^4 + 9y$; 5; trinomial

55. $-5a^3 + 4a^2$ **56.** $2r^3 - 3r^2 + 9r$ **57.** $11y^2 - 10y + 9$

58. $-13k^4 - 15k^2 - 4k - 6$ **59.** $10m^3 - 6m^2 - 3$ **60.** $-y^2 - 4y + 26$

61. $10p^2 - 3p - 11$ **62.** $7r^4 - 4r^3 - 1$ **63.** $10x^2 + 70x$

64. $-6p^5 + 15p^4$ **65.** $6r^3 + 8r^2 - 17r + 6$ **66.** $8y^3 + 27$

67. $5p^5 - 2p^4 - 3p^3 + 25p^2 + 15p$ **68.** $x^2 + 3x - 18$

69. $6k^2 - 9k - 6$ **70.** $12p^2 - 48pq + 21q^2$

71. $2m^4 + 5m^3 - 16m^2 - 28m + 9$ **72.** $a^2 + 8a + 16$

73. $9p^2 - 12p + 4$ **74.** $4r^2 + 20rs + 25s^2$ **75.** $r^3 + 6r^2 + 12r + 8$

76. $8x^3 - 12x^2 + 6x - 1$ **77.** $4z^2 - 49$ **78.** $36m^2 - 25$

79. $25a^2 - 36b^2$ **80.** $12x^4 - 75$ **81.** three; two

82. $(a+b)^2 = (a+b)(a+b) = a^2 + 2ab + b^2$. The term $2ab$ is not in $a^2 + b^2$. **83.** $\dfrac{5y^2}{3}$ **84.** $-2x^2 y$ **85.** $-y^3 + 2y - 3$ **86.** $p - 3 + \dfrac{5}{2p}$

87. $-x^9 + 2x^8 - 4x^3 + 7x$ **88.** $-2m^2 n + mn^2 + \dfrac{6n^3}{5}$ **89.** $2r + 7$

90. $4m + 3 + \dfrac{5}{3m - 5}$ **91.** $2a + 1 + \dfrac{-8a + 12}{5a^2 - 3}$

92. $k^2 + 2k + 4 + \dfrac{-2k - 12}{2k^2 + 1}$

CHAPTER 5 Mixed Review Exercises

1. 0 **2.** $\dfrac{243}{p^3}$ **3.** $\dfrac{1}{49}$ **4.** $4k^2 - 28k + 49$ **5.** $y^2 + 5y + 1$

6. $\dfrac{1296 r^8 s^4}{625}$ **7.** $-8m^7 - 10m^6 - 6m^5$ **8.** 32 **9.** $5xy^3 - \dfrac{8y^2}{5} + 3x^2 y$

10. $\dfrac{r^2}{6}$ **11.** $8x^3 + 12x^2 y + 6xy^2 + y^3$ **12.** $\dfrac{3}{4}$ **13.** $a^3 - 2a^2 - 7a + 2$

14. $8y^3 - 9y^2 + 5$ **15.** $10r^2 + 21r - 10$ **16.** $144a^2 - 1$

17. (a) $6x - 2$ (b) $2x^2 + x - 6$ **18.** (a) $20x^4 + 8x^2$

(b) $25x^8 + 20x^6 + 4x^4$ **19.** The second term of the quotient should be $-2x$, not $-12x$. Simplify as follows: $\dfrac{6x^2 - 12x}{6} = \dfrac{6x^2}{6} - \dfrac{12x}{6} = x^2 - 2x$.

20. $2mn + 3m^4 n^2 - 4n$

CHAPTER 5 Test

1. -32 **2.** $\dfrac{1}{625}$ **3.** 2 **4.** $\dfrac{7}{12}$ **5.** $\dfrac{216}{m^6}$ **6.** $9x^3 y^5$ **7.** 8^5 **8.** $x^2 y^6$

9. (a) positive (b) positive (c) negative (d) positive (e) zero

(f) negative **10.** (a) 3.44×10^{11} (b) 5.57×10^{-6} **11.** (a) 29,600,000

(b) 0.0000000607 **12.** (a) 1×10^3; 5.89×10^{12} (b) 5.89×10^{15} mi

13. $-7x^2 + 8x$; 2; binomial **14.** $4n^4 + 13n^3 - 10n^2$; 4; trinomial

15. $4t^4 + t^3 - 6t^2 - t$ **16.** $-2y^2 - 9y + 17$ **17.** $16r^2 - 19$

18. $-12t^2 + 5t + 8$ **19.** $-27x^5 + 18x^4 - 6x^3 + 3x^2$

20. $2r^3 + r^2 - 16r + 15$ **21.** $t^2 - 5t - 24$ **22.** $8x^2 + 2xy - 3y^2$

23. $25x^2 - 20xy + 4y^2$ **24.** $100v^2 - 9w^2$ **25.** $x^3 + 3x^2 + 3x + 1$

26. $12x + 36$; $9x^2 + 54x + 81$ **27.** $4y^2 - 3y + 2 + \dfrac{5}{y}$

28. $-3xy^2 + 2x^3 y^2 + 4y^2$ **29.** $2x + 9$ **30.** $3x^2 + 6x + 11 + \dfrac{26}{x - 2}$

CHAPTERS R–5 Cumulative Review Exercises

1. $\dfrac{19}{24}$ **2.** $-\dfrac{1}{20}$ **3.** 3.72 **4.** 0.000042 **5.** $1836 **6.** -8 **7.** 24 **8.** $\dfrac{1}{2}$

9. -4 **10.** associative property **11.** inverse property

12. distributive property **13.** $\{10\}$ **14.** $\left\{\dfrac{13}{4}\right\}$ **15.** $\varnothing$ **16.** $r = \dfrac{d}{t}$

17. $\{-5\}$ **18.** $\{-12\}$ **19.** $\{20\}$ **20.** {all real numbers}

21. mouse: 160; elephant: 10 **22.** 4 **23.** $[10, \infty)$ **24.** $\left(-\infty, -\dfrac{14}{5}\right)$

25. $[-4, 2)$ **26.** $(0, 2)$ and $(-3, 0)$ **27.** $\dfrac{2}{3}$

28.

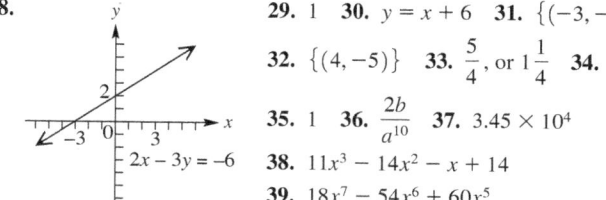

29. 1 **30.** $y = x + 6$ **31.** $\{(-3, -1)\}$

32. $\{(4, -5)\}$ **33.** $\dfrac{5}{4}$, or $1\dfrac{1}{4}$ **34.** 2

35. 1 **36.** $\dfrac{2b}{a^{10}}$ **37.** 3.45×10^4

38. $11x^3 - 14x^2 - x + 14$

39. $18x^7 - 54x^6 + 60x^5$

40. $63x^2 + 57x + 12$ **41.** $25x^2 + 80x + 64$ **42.** $y^2 - 2y + 6$

CHAPTER 6 Factoring and Applications

SECTION 6.1

1. product; multiplying **2.** common factor; is; divides **3.** 4 **5.** 4

7. 6 **9.** 1 **11.** 8 **13.** $10x^3$ **15.** $15m^2$ **17.** xy^2 **19.** 6 **21.** $6m^3 n^2$

23. factored **24.** factored **25.** not factored **26.** not factored

27. $18x^3 y^2 + 9xy = 9xy(2x^2 y + 1)$; If a polynomial has two terms, the product of the factors must have two terms. $9xy(2x^2 y) = 18x^3 y^2$ is just one term.

28. $12x^2 y - 24xy = 12xy(x - 2)$; The polynomial is *completely* factored when each factor has no common factor greater than 1. **29.** $3m^2$ **31.** $2z^4$

33. $2mn^4$ **35.** $y + 2$ **37.** $a - 2$ **39.** $2 + 3xy$ **41.** $x(x - 4)$

43. $3t(2t + 5)$ **45.** $m^2(m - 1)$ **47.** $-6x^2(2x + 1)$ **49.** $8z^2(2z^2 + 3)$

51. no common factor (except 1) **53.** $8mn^3(1 + 3m)$

55. $-2x(2x^2 - 5x + 3)$ **57.** $13y^2(y^6 + 2y^2 - 3)$

59. $9qp^3(5q^3 p^2 - 4p^3 + 9q)$ **61.** $(x + 2)(c + d)$ **63.** $(2a + b)(a^2 - b)$

65. $(p + 4)(q - 1)$ **67.** not in factored form; $(7t + 4)(8 + x)$

68. not in factored form; $(5x - 1)(3r + 7)$ **69.** in factored form

70. in factored form **71.** not in factored form **72.** not in factored form

73. $(5 + n)(m + 4)$ **75.** $(2y - 7)(3x + 4)$ **77.** $(a - 2)(a + b)$

79. $(z + 2)(7z - a)$ **81.** $(3r + 2y)(6r - x)$ **83.** $(w + 1)(w^2 + 9)$

85. $(a + 2)(3a^2 - 2)$ **87.** $(4m - p^2)(4m^2 - p)$ **89.** $(y + 3)(y + x)$

91. $(z - 2)(2z - 3w)$ **93.** $(5 - 2p)(m + 3)$ **95.** $(3r + 2y)(6r - t)$

97. commutative property **98.** $2x(y - 4) - 3(y - 4)$ **99.** No, because it is not a product. It is the difference of $2x(y - 4)$ and $3(y - 4)$.

100. $(y - 4)(2x - 3)$, or $(2x - 3)(y - 4)$; yes

SECTION 6.2

1. a and b must have different signs.   **2.** a and b must have the same sign.
3. C   **4.** Factor out the greatest common factor, $2x$.   **5.** $a^2 + 13a + 36$
6. $y^2 - 4y - 21$ **7.** The greatest common factor must be included in the
factorization; $x^3 + 3x^2 - 28x = x(x + 7)(x - 4)$ **8.** The polynomial
cannot be factored. It is prime.   **9.** 1 and 12, -1 and -12, 2 and 6, -2 and
-6, 3 and 4, -3 and -4; The pair with a sum of 7 is 3 and 4.   **11.** 1 and
-24, -1 and 24, 2 and -12, -2 and 12, 3 and -8, -3 and 8, 4 and -6, -4
and 6; The pair with a sum of -5 is 3 and -8.   **13.** $p + 6$ **15.** $x + 11$
17. $x - 8$ **19.** $y - 5$ **21.** $x + 11$ **23.** $y - 9$ **25.** $(y + 8)(y + 1)$
27. $(b + 3)(b + 5)$ **29.** $(m + 5)(m - 4)$ **31.** $(x + 8)(x - 5)$
33. prime   **35.** $(y - 5)(y - 3)$ **37.** $(z - 8)(z - 7)$
39. $(r - 6)(r + 5)$ **41.** $(a - 12)(a + 4)$ **43.** $(r + 2a)(r + a)$
45. $(x + y)(x + 3y)$ **47.** $(t + 2z)(t - 3z)$ **49.** $(v - 5w)(v - 6w)$
51. $(a + 5b)(a - 3b)$ **53.** $(a - 6b)(a - 3b)$ **55.** $4(x + 5)(x - 2)$
57. $2t(t + 1)(t + 3)$ **59.** $-2x^4(x - 3)(x + 7)$
61. $-a^3(a + 4b)(a - b)$ **63.** $5m^2(m^3 + 5m^2 - 8)$
65. $mn(m - 6n)(m - 4n)$

SECTION 6.3

1. B   **2.** D   **3.** $(m + 6)(m + 2)$ **5.** $(a + 5)(a - 2)$
7. $(2t + 1)(5t + 2)$ **9.** $(3z - 2)(5z - 3)$ **11.** $(2s + t)(4s - 3t)$
13. $(3a + 2b)(5a + 4b)$ **15. (a)** 2; 12; 24; 11   **(b)** 3; 8 (Order is
irrelevant.)   **(c)** $3m$; $8m$ **(d)** $2m^2 + 3m + 8m + 12$
(e) $(2m + 3)(m + 4)$ **(f)** $(2m + 3)(m + 4) = 2m^2 + 8m + 3m + 12$;
Combine like terms to obtain $2m^2 + 11m + 12$.   **17.** $(2x + 1)(x + 3)$
19. $(4r - 3)(r + 1)$ **21.** $(4m + 1)(2m - 3)$ **23.** $(3m + 1)(7m + 2)$
25. $(3a + 7)(a + 1)$ **27.** $(4y - 3)(3y - 1)$ **29.** $(4 + x)(4 + 3x)$, or
$(x + 4)(3x + 4)$ **31.** $3(4x - 1)(2x - 3)$ **33.** $2m(m - 4)(m + 5)$
35. $-4z^3(z - 1)(8z + 3)$ **37.** $(3p + 4q)(4p - 3q)$
39. $(3a - 5b)(2a + b)$ **41.** The student stopped too soon. He needs to
factor out the common factor $4x - 1$ to obtain $(4x - 1)(4x - 5)$ as the
correct answer.   **42.** The student forgot to include the common factor $3k$
in her answer. The correct answer is $3k(k - 5)(k + 1)$.

SECTION 6.4

1. B   **2.** A   **3.** A   **4.** B   **5.** A   **6.** A   **7.** $2a + 5b$
9. $x^2 + 3x - 4$; $x + 4$, $x - 1$ **11.** $2z^2 - 5z - 3$; $2z + 1$, $z - 3$
13. $(4x + 4)$ cannot be a factor because its terms have a common factor
of 4, but those of the polynomial do not. The correct factored form is
$(4x - 3)(3x + 4)$.   **14.** The student forgot to factor out the common
factor 2 from the terms of the trinomial. The *completely* factored form is
$2(2x - 1)(x + 3)$.   **15.** $(3a + 7)(a + 1)$ **17.** $(2y + 3)(y + 2)$
19. $(3m - 1)(5m + 2)$ **21.** $(3s - 1)(4s + 5)$ **23.** $(5m - 4)(2m - 3)$
25. $(4w - 1)(2w - 3)$ **27.** $(4y + 1)(5y - 11)$ **29.** prime
31. $2(5x + 3)(2x + 1)$ **33.** $-q(5m + 2)(8m - 3)$
35. $3n^2(5n - 3)(n - 2)$ **37.** $-y^2(5x - 4)(3x + 1)$
39. $(5a + 3b)(a - 2b)$ **41.** $(4s + 5t)(3s - t)$
43. $m^4n(3m + 2n)(2m + n)$ **45.** $-1(x + 7)(x - 3)$
47. $-1(3x + 4)(x - 1)$ **49.** $-1(a + 2b)(2a + b)$ **51.** $5 \cdot 7$
52. $(-5)(-7)$ **53.** The product of $3x - 4$ and $2x - 1$ is $6x^2 - 11x + 4$.
54. The product of $4 - 3x$ and $1 - 2x$ is $6x^2 - 11x + 4$.   **55.** The factors
in **Exercise 53** are the opposites of the factors in **Exercise 54.**
56. $(3 - 7t)(5 - 2t)$

SECTION 6.5

1. 1; 4; 9; 16; 25; 36; 49; 64; 81; 100; 121; 144; 169; 196; 225; 256; 289;
324; 361; 400   **2.** 1; 16; 81; 256; 625   **3.** A, D   **4.** B, C   **5.** The binomial
$4x^2 + 16$ can be factored as $4(x^2 + 4)$. After any common factor is removed,
a sum of squares (like $x^2 + 4$ here) *cannot* be factored.   **6.** $k^2 - 9$ can
be factored further as $(k + 3)(k - 3)$. The completely factored form is
$(k^2 + 9)(k + 3)(k - 3)$.   **7.** $(y + 5)(y - 5)$ **9.** $(x + 12)(x - 12)$
11. prime   **13.** prime   **15.** $(3r + 2)(3r - 2)$ **17.** $4(3x + 2)(3x - 2)$
19. $(14p + 15)(14p - 15)$ **21.** $(4r + 5a)(4r - 5a)$ **23.** $16(m^2 + 4)$
25. $(p^2 + 7)(p^2 - 7)$ **27.** $(x^2 + 1)(x + 1)(x - 1)$
29. $(p^2 + 16)(p + 4)(p - 4)$ **31.** B, C   **32.** This polynomial is prime.
It is not a perfect square trinomial because the middle term would have to
be $30y$.   **33.** $(w + 1)^2$ **35.** $(x - 4)^2$ **37.** prime   **39.** $2(x + 6)^2$
41. $(2x + 3)^2$ **43.** $x(4x - 5)^2$ **45.** $(7x - 2y)^2$ **47.** $(8x + 3y)^2$
49. $-2h(5h - 2y)^2$ **51.** $\left(p + \dfrac{1}{3}\right)\left(p - \dfrac{1}{3}\right)$ **53.** $\left(2m + \dfrac{3}{5}\right)\left(2m - \dfrac{3}{5}\right)$
55. $(x + 0.8)(x - 0.8)$ **57.** $\left(t + \dfrac{1}{2}\right)^2$ **59.** $\left(a - \dfrac{2}{7}\right)^2$ **61.** $(x - 0.5)^2$
63. 1; 8; 27; 64; 125; 216; 343; 512; 729; 1000   **64.** 3   **65.** C, D
66. A, D   **67.** $(a - 1)(a^2 + a + 1)$ **69.** $(m + 2)(m^2 - 2m + 4)$
71. $(y - 6)(y^2 + 6y + 36)$ **73.** $(k + 10)(k^2 - 10k + 100)$
75. $(3x - 1)(9x^2 + 3x + 1)$ **77.** $(5x + 2)(25x^2 - 10x + 4)$
79. $(y - 2x)(y^2 + 2xy + 4x^2)$ **81.** $(3x - 4y)(9x^2 + 12xy + 16y^2)$
83. $(2p + 9q)(4p^2 - 18pq + 81q^2)$ **85.** $2(2t - 1)(4t^2 + 2t + 1)$
87. $5(2w + 3)(4w^2 - 6w + 9)$ **89.** $(x + y^2)(x^2 - xy^2 + y^4)$
91. $(5k - 2m^3)(25k^2 + 10km^3 + 4m^6)$

SECTION 6.6

1. (a) B   **(b)** D   **(c)** A   **(d)** A, C   **(e)** A, B   **2. (a)** C   **(b)** E
(c) A   **(d)** B   **(e)** A, B   **3.** $(6b + 1)(b - 3)$ **5.** $6p^3(2p^3 + 3p^2 - 4)$
7. $(x + 7)(x - 5)$ **9.** prime   **11.** $(10a + 3b)(10a - 3b)$
13. $3mn(3m + 2n)(2m - n)$ **15.** $(2p + 5q)(p + 3q)$
17. $(3m - 5 + p)(3m - 5 - p)$ **19.** $(k - 9)(q + r)$
21. $(x + 3)^2(x - 3)$ **23.** $(p + 2)(4 + m)$ **25.** $(3k + 1)(2k - 1)$
27. $(x + 15)(x - 15)$ **29.** $(a + 6)(b + c)$
31. $(x - 6 + 2p)(x - 6 - 2p)$ **33.** $16(4b + 5c)(4b - 5c)$
35. $8(5z + 4)(25z^2 - 20z + 16)$ **37.** $(5r - s)(2r + 5s)$
39. $-8x^2(1 - 2x + 3x^3)$ **41.** $(2x - 5q)(7x + 5q)$ **43.** $(y + 5)(y - 2)$
45. $(9p - 5r)(2p + 7r)$ **47.** $(z - 5)(z - 4)$ **49.** prime
51. $2(5p + 9)(5p - 9)$ **53.** $(4a + b)^2$ **55.** $4(x^2 + 4)$

SECTION 6.7

1. $ax^2 + bx + c$ **2.** standard   **3.** factor   **4.** 0; zero; factor
5. (a) linear   **(b)** quadratic   **(c)** quadratic   **(d)** linear
6. Because $(x - 9)^2 = (x - 9)(x - 9)$, applying the zero-factor property
leads to two solutions of 9. Thus, 9 is a double solution.   **7.** Set each
variable factor equal to 0, to obtain $2x = 0$ or $3x - 4 = 0$. The solution set
is $\left\{0, \dfrac{4}{3}\right\}$.   **8.** The student should not divide by a variable because this
causes the solution 0 to be eliminated. The solution set is $\left\{0, \dfrac{1}{7}\right\}$.
9. $\{-5, 2\}$ **11.** $\left\{3, \dfrac{7}{2}\right\}$ **13.** $\left\{-\dfrac{1}{2}, \dfrac{1}{6}\right\}$ **15.** $\left\{-\dfrac{5}{6}, 0\right\}$ **17.** $\left\{0, \dfrac{4}{3}\right\}$
19. $\{9\}$ **21.** $\{-4, -1\}$ **23.** $\{1, 2\}$ **25.** $\{-8, 3\}$ **27.** $\{-1, 3\}$

29. $\{-2, -1\}$ **31.** $\{-4\}$ **33.** $\left\{\frac{1}{4}\right\}$ **35.** $\left\{-2, \frac{1}{3}\right\}$ **37.** $\left\{-\frac{4}{3}, \frac{1}{2}\right\}$

39. $\left\{-\frac{2}{3}\right\}$ **41.** $\{-3, 3\}$ **43.** $\left\{-\frac{7}{4}, \frac{7}{4}\right\}$ **45.** $\{-13, 13\}$

47. $\{0, 7\}$ **49.** $\left\{0, \frac{1}{2}\right\}$ **51.** $\{2, 5\}$ **53.** $\left\{-4, \frac{1}{2}\right\}$ **55.** $\left\{-12, \frac{11}{2}\right\}$

57. $\left\{-4, \frac{1}{2}\right\}$ **59.** $\{-2, 0, 2\}$ **61.** $\left\{-\frac{7}{3}, 0, \frac{7}{3}\right\}$ **63.** $\left\{-\frac{5}{2}, \frac{1}{3}, 5\right\}$

65. $\left\{-\frac{7}{2}, -3, 1\right\}$ **67.** $\{-5, 0, 4\}$ **69.** $\{-3, 0, 5\}$ **71.** $\{-4, 12\}$

73. $\{-1, 3\}$ **75.** **(a)** 64; 144; 4; 6 **(b)** No time has elapsed, so the object hasn't fallen (been released) yet. **76.** Time cannot be negative.

SECTION 6.8

1. Read; variable; equation; Solve; answer; Check; original **2.** Only 6 is reasonable because a square cannot have a side of negative length.

3. $\mathcal{A} = bh$; *Step 3:* $(2x + 1)(x + 1)$; *Step 4:* 4; $-\frac{11}{2}$; *Step 5:* 9; 5; *Step 6:* $9 \cdot 5$ **5.** $V = LWH$; *Step 3:* 192; $4x$; *Step 4:* 6; -8; *Step 5:* 8; 6; *Step 6:* $8 \cdot 6$; 192 **7.** length: 14 cm; width: 12 cm **9.** base: 12 in.; height: 5 in. **11.** length: 15 in.; width: 12 in. **13.** height: 13 in.; width: 10 in. **15.** mirror: 7 ft; painting: 9 ft **17.** 20, 21 **19.** $-3, -2$ or 4, 5 **21.** $-3, -1$ or 7, 9 **23.** $-2, 0, 2$ or 6, 8, 10 **25.** 7, 9, 11 **27.** 12 cm **29.** 12 mi **31.** length: 20 in.; width: 15 in.; diagonal: 25 in. **33.** 8 ft

35. **(a)** 1 sec **(b)** $\frac{1}{2}$ sec and $1\frac{1}{2}$ sec **(c)** 3 sec **(d)** The negative solution, -1, does not make sense because t represents time, which cannot be negative.

37. 112 ft **39.** 256 ft **41.** **(a)** 100 million; The result is less than 109 million, the actual number from the table for 2000. **(b)** 10 **(c)** 303 million; The result using the model is the same as the actual number for 2010. **(d)** 393 million **43.** c^2 **44.** b^2 **45.** a^2

46. $a^2 + b^2 = c^2$; This is the equation of the Pythagorean theorem.

Chapter 6 REVIEW EXERCISES

1. $15(t + 3)$ **2.** $30z(2z^2 - 1)$ **3.** $11x^2(4x + 5)$ **4.** $50m^2n^2(2n - mn^2 + 3)$ **5.** $(x - 4)(2y + 3)$ **6.** $(2y + 3)(3y + 2x)$ **7.** $(x + 3)(x + 7)$ **8.** $(y - 5)(y - 8)$ **9.** $(q + 9)(q - 3)$ **10.** $(r - 8)(r + 7)$ **11.** prime **12.** $3(x^2 + 2x + 2)$ **13.** $(r + 8s)(r - 12s)$ **14.** $(p + 12q)(p - 10q)$ **15.** $-8p(p + 2)(p - 5)$ **16.** $3x^2(x + 2)(x + 8)$ **17.** $(m + 3n)(m - 6n)$ **18.** $(y - 3z)(y - 5z)$ **19.** $p^5(p - 2q)(p + q)$ **20.** $-3r^3(r + 3s)(r - 5s)$ **21.** r and $6r, 2r$ and $3r$ **22.** Factor out z. **23.** $(2k - 1)(k - 2)$ **24.** $(3r - 1)(r + 4)$ **25.** $(3r + 2)(2r - 3)$ **26.** $(5z + 1)(2z - 1)$ **27.** prime **28.** $4x^3(3x - 1)(2x - 1)$ **29.** $-3(x + 2)(2x - 5)$ **30.** $rs(5r + 6s)(2r + s)$ **31.** $-5y(3y + 2)(2y - 1)$ **32.** prime **33.** $-mn(3m + 5)(m - 8)$ **34.** $(2a - 5b)(7a + 4b)$ **35.** B **36.** D **37.** $(n + 8)(n - 8)$ **38.** $(5b + 11)(5b - 11)$ **39.** $(7y + 5w)(7y - 5w)$ **40.** $9(m^2 + 9)$ **41.** $36(2p + q)(2p - q)$ **42.** $(v^2 + 1)(v + 1)(v - 1)$ **43.** prime **44.** $(z + 5)^2$ **45.** $(3t - 7)^2$ **46.** $(4m + 5n)^2$ **47.** $(5x - 1)(25x^2 + 5x + 1)$ **48.** $(10p + 3)(100p^2 - 30p + 9)$ **49.** $\left\{-\frac{3}{4}, 1\right\}$ **50.** $\{-7, -3, 4\}$ **51.** $\left\{0, \frac{5}{2}\right\}$ **52.** $\{-3, -1\}$ **53.** $\{1, 4\}$ **54.** $\{3, 5\}$ **55.** $\left\{-\frac{4}{3}, 5\right\}$

56. $\left\{-\frac{8}{9}, \frac{8}{9}\right\}$ **57.** $\{0, 8\}$ **58.** $\{-1, 6\}$ **59.** $\{-7\}$ **60.** $\{6\}$

61. $\left\{-\frac{2}{5}, -2, -1\right\}$ **62.** $\{-3, 3\}$ **63.** $\{-1, 6\}$ **64.** $\left\{-\frac{3}{4}, -\frac{1}{2}, \frac{1}{3}\right\}$

65. $\left\{\frac{9}{5}\right\}$ **66.** $\{-3, 10\}$ **67.** length: 10 ft; width: 4 ft **68.** 5 ft

69. 6, 7 or $-5, -4$ **70.** $-5, -4, -3$ or 5, 6, 7 **71.** 26 mi **72.** 6 m **73.** width: 10 m; length: 17 m **74.** **(a)** 256 ft **(b)** 1024 ft **75.** 704 thousand; The result is a little higher than the 696 thousand given in the table. **76.** 1454 thousand

Chapter 6 MIXED REVIEW EXERCISES

1. D **2.** The student forgot to factor out the common factor 2 from the terms of the trinomial. The completely factored form is $2(x + 4)(3x - 4)$. **3.** $(3m + 4p)(5m - 4)$ **4.** $8ab(3b^2 - 7ac^3 + 9ab)$ **5.** prime **6.** $(z - x)(z - 10x)$ **7.** $(3k + 5)(k + 2)$ **8.** $(y^2 + 25)(y + 5)(y - 5)$ **9.** $3m(2m + 3)(m - 5)$ **10.** prime **11.** $8(z + 2y)(z^2 - 2zy + 4y^2)$ **12.** $-1(2r + 3q)(6r - 5q)$ **13.** $(10a + 3)(10a - 3)$ **14.** $(7t + 4)^2$ **15.** $\{0, 7\}$ **16.** $\{-5, 2\}$ **17.** $\left\{-\frac{2}{5}\right\}$ **18.** $\left\{-\frac{3}{8}, 0, \frac{3}{8}\right\}$ **19.** $\left\{-\frac{5}{3}, \frac{3}{2}\right\}$ **20.** $\left\{-6, -1, -\frac{1}{3}\right\}$

21. 15 m, 36 m, 39 m **22.** length: 6 m; width: 4 m

Chapter 6 TEST

1. D **2.** $6x(2x - 5)$ **3.** $m^2n(2mn + 3m - 5n)$ **4.** $(2x + y)(a - b)$ **5.** $(x - 7)(x - 2)$ **6.** $(t + 2)(t + 5)$ **7.** $(3x + 1)(2x - 7)$ **8.** $3(x + 1)(x - 5)$ **9.** $(5z - 1)(2z - 3)$ **10.** prime **11.** prime **12.** $(y + 7)(y - 7)$ **13.** $(9a + 11b)(9a - 11b)$ **14.** $(x + 8)^2$ **15.** $(2x - 7y)^2$ **16.** $-2(x + 1)^2$ **17.** $4t(t + 4)^2$ **18.** $(x^2 + 9)(x + 3)(x - 3)$ **19.** $(x - 8)(x^2 + 8x + 64)$ **20.** $8(k + 2)(k^2 - 2k + 4)$ **21.** $\{-3, 9\}$ **22.** $\left\{\frac{1}{2}, 6\right\}$ **23.** $\left\{-\frac{2}{5}, \frac{2}{5}\right\}$ **24.** $\{10\}$ **25.** $\{0, 3\}$ **26.** $\left\{-8, -\frac{5}{2}, \frac{1}{3}\right\}$ **27.** 6 ft by 9 ft **28.** $-2, -1$ **29.** 17 ft **30.** $20,744 billion

Chapters R–6 CUMULATIVE REVIEW EXERCISES

1. $\{0\}$ **2.** $\{0.05\}$ **3.** $\{6\}$ **4.** $t = \frac{A - P}{Pr}$ **5.** second column: 38%, 12%; third column: 230, 205 **6.** gold: 9; silver: 7; bronze: 12 **7.** $39,803 **8.** 110° and 70° **9.** **(a)** negative; positive **(b)** negative; negative

10. $\left(-\frac{3}{4}, 0\right), (0, 3)$ **11.** 4

12.

13. **(a)** 14.75; A slope of 14.75 means that revenue increased by about $14.75 billion per year. **(b)** (2014, 90) **14.** $\{(-1, 2)\}$ **15.** $\varnothing$ **16.** 4 **17.** $\frac{16}{9}$ **18.** 1 **19.** 256 **20.** $\frac{1}{p^2}$ **21.** $\frac{1}{m^6}$ **22.** $-4k^2 - 4k + 8$ **23.** $45x^2 + 3x - 18$ **24.** $9p^2 + 12p + 4$ **25.** $4x^3 + 6x^2 - 3x + 10$ **26.** $(2a - 1)(a + 4)$ **27.** $(2m + 3)(5m + 2)$ **28.** $(4t + 3v)(2t + v)$ **29.** $(2p - 3)^2$ **30.** $(5r + 9t)(5r - 9t)$ **31.** $2pq(3p + 1)(p + 1)$ **32.** $\left\{-\frac{2}{3}, \frac{1}{2}\right\}$ **33.** $\{0, 8\}$ **34.** $\left\{\frac{4}{7}\right\}$ **35.** 5 m, 12 m, 13 m

CHAPTER 7 Rational Expressions and Applications

Note: In work with rational expressions, several different equivalent forms of the answer often exist. If your answer does not look exactly like the one given here, check to see if you have written an equivalent form.

SECTION 7.1

1. $-3; -3; 5$ **2.** $q; q; -1$ **3.** B, C **4. (a)** is not **(b)** are
5. A rational expression is a quotient of polynomials, such as $\dfrac{x+3}{x^2-4}$, with denominator not equal to 0. **6.** Division by 0 is undefined, so if the denominator of a rational expression equals 0, the expression is undefined.
7. (a) $\dfrac{7}{10}$ **(b)** $\dfrac{8}{15}$ **9. (a)** 0 **(b)** -1 **11. (a)** $\dfrac{9}{5}$ **(b)** undefined
13. (a) $\dfrac{2}{7}$ **(b)** $\dfrac{13}{3}$ **15.** $y \neq 0$ **17.** $x \neq -6$ **19.** $x \neq \dfrac{5}{3}$
21. $m \neq -3, m \neq 2$ **23.** It is never undefined. **25.** It is never undefined. **27.** $\dfrac{3}{7}$ **29.** $\dfrac{3}{11}$ **31.** $3r^2$ **33.** $\dfrac{2}{5}$ **35.** $\dfrac{x-1}{x+1}$ **37.** $\dfrac{7}{5}$
39. $\dfrac{8}{7}$ **41.** $m-n$ **43.** $\dfrac{3(2m+1)}{4}$ **45.** $\dfrac{3m}{5}$ **47.** $\dfrac{3r-2s}{3}$ **49.** $\dfrac{x+1}{x-1}$
51. $\dfrac{z-3}{z+5}$ **53.** $\dfrac{a+b}{a-b}$ **55.** -1 **57.** $-(m+1)$ **59.** -1
61. It is already in lowest terms.

Answers may vary in Exercises 63–67.
63. $\dfrac{-(x+4)}{x-3}, \dfrac{-x-4}{x-3}, \dfrac{x+4}{-(x-3)}, \dfrac{x+4}{-x+3}$
65. $\dfrac{-(2x-3)}{x+3}, \dfrac{-2x+3}{x+3}, \dfrac{2x-3}{-(x+3)}, \dfrac{2x-3}{-x-3}$
67. $\dfrac{-(3x-1)}{5x-6}, \dfrac{-3x+1}{5x-6}, \dfrac{3x-1}{-(5x-6)}, \dfrac{3x-1}{-5x+6}$ **69.** x^2+3
71. (a) 80% **(b)** 90% **(c)** 95% **72.** No. If x is 0, then the expression is undefined. **73.** Both yield $2x+3$. **74.** Both yield $2x+1$.
75. Both yield x^2+1.

SECTION 7.2

1. (a) B **(b)** D **(c)** C **(d)** A **2. (a)** D **(b)** C **(c)** A **(d)** B
3. $\dfrac{5}{12}$ **5.** $\dfrac{3a}{2}$ **7.** $\dfrac{40y^2}{3}$ **9.** $\dfrac{2}{c+d}$ **11.** $4(x-y)$ **13.** $\dfrac{16q}{3p^3}$
15. $\dfrac{7}{r^2+rp}$ **17.** $\dfrac{z^2-9}{z^2+7z+12}$ **19.** $\dfrac{16}{13}$ **21.** 5 **23.** $-\dfrac{3}{2t^4}$ **25.** $\dfrac{1}{4}$
27. $\dfrac{x(x-3)}{6}$ **29.** $\dfrac{10}{9}$ **31.** $-\dfrac{3}{4}$ **33.** -1 **35.** $\dfrac{9(m-2)}{-(m+4)}$, or $\dfrac{-9(m-2)}{m+4}$ **37.** -1 **39.** $\dfrac{p+4}{p+2}$ **41.** $\dfrac{(k-1)^2}{(k+1)(2k-1)}$
43. $\dfrac{4k-1}{3k-2}$ **45.** $\dfrac{m+4p}{m+p}$ **47.** $\dfrac{10}{x+10}$ **49.** $\dfrac{5xy^2}{4q}$

SECTION 7.3

1. C **2.** B **3.** The factor x should appear in the LCD the *greatest* number of times it appears in any single denominator, not the *total* number of times. The correct LCD is $50x^4$. **4.** The expressions are not opposites. The opposite of $x-1$ is $1-x$. The correct LCD is $(x-1)(x+1)$. **5.** 60
7. 30 **9.** x^7 **11.** $30p$ **13.** $72q$ **15.** $84r^5$ **17.** $15a^5b^3$
19. $24x^3y^4$ **21.** $12p(p-2)$ **23.** $28m^2(3m-5)$ **25.** $30(b-2)$
27. $c-d$ or $d-c$ **29.** $2(x+1)(x-1)$ **31.** $k(k+5)(k-2)$
33. $a(a+6)(a-3)$ **35.** $(p+3)(p+5)(p-6)$ **37.** $\dfrac{20}{55}$

39. $\dfrac{-45}{9k}$ **41.** $\dfrac{26y^2}{80y^3}$ **43.** $\dfrac{35t^2r^3}{42r^4}$ **45.** $\dfrac{20}{8(m+3)}$ **47.** $\dfrac{57z}{6z-18}$
49. $\dfrac{8t}{12-6t}$ **51.** $\dfrac{14(z-2)}{z(z-3)(z-2)}$ **53.** $\dfrac{2(b-1)(b+2)}{b^3+3b^2+2b}$

SECTION 7.4

1. E **2.** A **3.** C **4.** H **5.** B **6.** D **7.** G **8.** F
9. *Each* term in the numerator of the second expression must be subtracted. Using parentheses will help avoid this error.
$$\frac{2x}{x+5} - \frac{x+1}{x+5} = \frac{2x-(x+1)}{x+5} = \frac{2x-x-1}{x+5} = \frac{x-1}{x+5}$$
10. The student did not apply the distributive property correctly. In the third line, the numerator should be $7x-3x+5$. The correct answer is $\dfrac{4x+5}{2x-3}$. **11.** $\dfrac{2}{3}$ **13.** $\dfrac{11}{m}$ **15.** $\dfrac{4}{y+4}$ **17.** 4 **19.** b **21.** $\dfrac{m-1}{m+1}$
23. $\dfrac{2x+3}{x-4}$ **25.** x **27.** $y-6$ **29.** $\dfrac{17}{30}$ **31.** $\dfrac{3z+5}{15}$ **33.** $\dfrac{10-7r}{14}$
35. $\dfrac{-3x-2}{4x}$ **37.** $\dfrac{57}{20x}$ **39.** $\dfrac{x+1}{2}$ **41.** $\dfrac{5x+9}{6x}$ **43.** $\dfrac{3x+3}{x(x+3)}$
45. $\dfrac{-k-8}{k(k+4)}$ **47.** $\dfrac{x+4}{x+2}$ **49.** $\dfrac{x^2+6x-8}{(x-2)(x+2)}$
51. $\dfrac{6m^2+23m-2}{(m+2)(m+1)(m+5)}$ **53.** $\dfrac{3}{t}$ **55.** $m-2$ or $2-m$
56. $\dfrac{-4}{3-k}$, or $-\dfrac{4}{3-k}$ **57.** $\dfrac{-2}{x-5}$, or $\dfrac{2}{5-x}$ **59.** -4 **61.** $\dfrac{-5}{x-y^2}$,
or $\dfrac{5}{y^2-x}$ **63.** $\dfrac{x+y}{5x-3y}$, or $\dfrac{-x-y}{3y-5x}$ **65.** $\dfrac{-6}{4p-5}$, or $\dfrac{6}{5-4p}$ **67.** 3
69. $\dfrac{-(m+n)}{2(m-n)}$ **71.** $y-7$ **73.** $\dfrac{-x^2+6x+11}{(x+3)(x-3)(x+1)}$
75. $\dfrac{-5q^2-13q+7}{(3q-2)(q+4)(2q-3)}$ **77.** $\dfrac{9r+2}{r(r+2)(r-1)}$
79. $\dfrac{2x^2+6xy+8y^2}{(x+y)(x+y)(x+3y)}$, or $\dfrac{2x^2+6xy+8y^2}{(x+y)^2(x+3y)}$
81. $\dfrac{15r^2+10ry-y^2}{(3r+2y)(6r-y)(6r+y)}$ **83. (a)** $\dfrac{9k^2+6k+26}{5(3k+1)}$ **(b)** $\dfrac{1}{4}$
85. $\dfrac{8000+10x}{49(101-x)}$

SECTION 7.5

1. division **2.** identity property of multiplication
3. (a) $6; \dfrac{1}{6}$ **(b)** $12; \dfrac{3}{4}$ **(c)** $\dfrac{1}{6} \div \dfrac{3}{4}$ **(d)** $\dfrac{2}{9}$ **5.** 6 **6.** $-\dfrac{7}{5}$ **7.** -6
9. $\dfrac{31}{50}$ **11.** $\dfrac{1}{xy}$ **13.** $\dfrac{1}{6pq}$ **15.** $\dfrac{2a^2b}{3}$ **17.** $\dfrac{m(m+2)}{3(m-4)}$ **19.** $\dfrac{2}{x}$
21. $\dfrac{8}{x}$ **23.** $\dfrac{a^2-5}{a^2+1}$ **25.** $\dfrac{3(p+2)}{2(2p+3)}$ **27.** $\dfrac{a-2}{2a}$
29. $\dfrac{40-12p}{85p}$, or $\dfrac{4(10-3p)}{85p}$ **31.** $\dfrac{t(t-2)}{4}$ **33.** $\dfrac{-m}{2+m}$
35. $\dfrac{2x-7}{3x+1}$ **37.** $\dfrac{3m(m-3)}{(m-1)(m-8)}$ **39.** $\dfrac{x^2y^2}{y^2+x^2}$
41. $\dfrac{y^2+x^2}{xy^2+x^2y}$, or $\dfrac{y^2+x^2}{xy(y+x)}$ **43.** $\dfrac{2xy-3x}{x+3y^2}$ **45.** $\dfrac{1}{2xy}$
47. $\dfrac{m^2+6m-4}{m(m-1)}$ **48.** $\dfrac{m^2-m-2}{m(m-1)}$ **49.** $\dfrac{m^2+6m-4}{m^2-m-2}$
50. $m(m-1)$ **51.** $\dfrac{m^2+6m-4}{m^2-m-2}$ **52.** Answers will vary.

SECTION 7.6

1. proposed; original   **2.** extraneous; extraneous   **3.** expression; $\dfrac{43}{40}x$

5. equation; $\left\{\dfrac{40}{43}\right\}$ **7.** expression; $-\dfrac{1}{10}y$ **9.** equation; $\{12\}$

11. $\{-6\}$ **13.** $\{-15\}$ **15.** $\{7\}$ **17.** $\{-15\}$ **19.** $\{-5\}$ **21.** $\{-6\}$

23. $\{12\}$ **25.** $\{5\}$ **27.** $\{1\}$ **29.** $\{2\}$ **31.** $x \neq -2, x \neq 0$

33. $x \neq -3, x \neq 4, x \neq -\dfrac{1}{2}$ **35.** $x \neq -9, x \neq 1, x \neq -2, x \neq 2$

37. $\left\{\dfrac{1}{4}\right\}$ **39.** $\left\{-\dfrac{3}{4}\right\}$ **41.** $\left\{\dfrac{20}{9}\right\}$ **43.** $\varnothing$ **45.** $\{3\}$ **47.** $\{3\}$

49. $\{-2, 12\}$ **51.** $\left\{-\dfrac{1}{5}, 3\right\}$ **53.** $\left\{-\dfrac{3}{5}, 3\right\}$ **55.** $\{-4\}$ **57.** $\varnothing$

59. $\{-1\}$ **61.** $\{-3\}$ **63.** $\{-6\}$ **65.** $\left\{-6, \dfrac{1}{2}\right\}$

67. This is an expression, *not* an equation. The student multiplied by the LCD, 14, instead of writing each coefficient with the LCD.

$$\frac{7}{7} \cdot \frac{3}{2}t + \frac{2}{2} \cdot \frac{5}{7}t$$
$$= \frac{21}{14}t + \frac{10}{14}t$$
$$= \frac{31}{14}t$$

68. The specified variable r appears on *both* sides of the final equation. Add rk in the third line, factor, and then divide to isolate r.

$$mk - rk = rm$$
$$mk = rm + rk$$
$$mk = r(m + k)$$
$$\frac{mk}{m + k} = r$$

69. $F = \dfrac{ma}{k}$ **71.** $a = \dfrac{kF}{m}$ **73.** $y = mx + b$ **75.** $R = \dfrac{E - Ir}{I}$, or

$R = \dfrac{E}{I} - r$ **77.** $b = \dfrac{2\mathscr{A} - hB}{h}$, or $b = \dfrac{2\mathscr{A}}{h} - B$ **79.** $a = \dfrac{2S - dnL}{dn}$, or

$a = \dfrac{2S}{dn} - L$ **81.** $y = \dfrac{xz}{x + z}$ **83.** $t = \dfrac{rs}{rs - 2s - 3r}$, or

$t = \dfrac{-rs}{-rs + 2s + 3r}$ **85.** $c = \dfrac{ab}{b - a - 2ab}$, or $c = \dfrac{-ab}{-b + a + 2ab}$

87. $z = \dfrac{3y}{5 - 9xy}$, or $z = \dfrac{-3y}{9xy - 5}$ **89. (a)** $x \neq -3$ **(b)** $x \neq -1$

(c) $x \neq -3, x \neq -1$ **90.** $\dfrac{15}{2x}$ **91.** $(x + 3)(x + 1)$ **92.** $\dfrac{7}{x + 1}$

93. $\dfrac{11x + 21}{4x}$ **94.** $\varnothing$

SUMMARY EXERCISES   Simplifying Rational Expressions vs. Solving Rational Equations

1. expression; $\dfrac{10}{p}$ **2.** expression; $\dfrac{2x - 1}{x + 7}$ **3.** expression; $\dfrac{1}{2x^2(x + 2)}$

4. equation; $\{9\}$ **5.** expression; $\dfrac{x + 2}{x - 1}$ **6.** expression; $\dfrac{5k + 8}{k(k - 4)(k + 4)}$

7. equation; $\{39\}$ **8.** expression; $\dfrac{t - 5}{3(2t + 1)}$ **9.** expression; $\dfrac{13}{3(p + 2)}$

10. equation; $\left\{-1, \dfrac{12}{5}\right\}$ **11.** equation; $\left\{\dfrac{1}{7}, 2\right\}$ **12.** expression; $\dfrac{7}{12z}$

13. expression; 3   **14.** equation; $\{13\}$ **15.** expression;

$\dfrac{3m + 5}{(m + 2)(m + 3)(m + 1)}$ **16.** expression; $\dfrac{k + 3}{5(k - 1)}$ **17.** equation; $\varnothing$

18. equation; $\{-7\}$

SECTION 7.7

1. into a headwind: $(m - 5)$ mph; with a tailwind: $(m + 5)$ mph

2. $\dfrac{D}{R} = \dfrac{d}{r}$ **3.** $\dfrac{1}{10}$ job per hr   **4.** $\dfrac{2}{3}$ of the job   **5. (a)** the amount

(b) $5 + x$ **(c)** $\dfrac{5 + x}{6} = \dfrac{13}{3}$ **7.** x represents the original numerator;

$\dfrac{x + 3}{(x + 6) + 3} = \dfrac{5}{7}; \dfrac{12}{18}$ **9.** x represents the original numerator;

$\dfrac{x + 2}{3x - 2} = 1; \dfrac{2}{6}$ **11.** x represents the number; $\dfrac{1}{6}x = x + 5; -6$

13. x represents the quantity; $x + \dfrac{3}{4}x + \dfrac{1}{2}x + \dfrac{1}{3}x = 93; 36$

15. 18.809 min   **17.** 10.848 mph   **19.** 3.088 hr

21. table entries: (fourth column) $\dfrac{8}{4 - x}, \dfrac{24}{4 + x}; \dfrac{8}{4 - x} = \dfrac{24}{4 + x}$

23. $7\dfrac{1}{2}$ hr   **25.** $1\dfrac{3}{4}$ hr   **27.** 8 mph   **29.** 32 mph   **31.** 3 mph

33. table entries: (second column) $\dfrac{1}{2}, \dfrac{1}{3}$; (fourth column) $\dfrac{1}{2}t, \dfrac{1}{3}t$;

$\dfrac{1}{2}t + \dfrac{1}{3}t = 1$ **35.** 12 hr   **37.** $2\dfrac{2}{5}$ hr   **39.** 10 hr   **41.** 36 hr   **43.** 10 mL

45. $\dfrac{15}{8}$ hr, or $1\dfrac{7}{8}$ hr   **46. (a)** The player multiplied: $5 \cdot 3 = 15$.

(b) The player added: $5 + 3 = 8$.   **(c)** The player added the two times and divided by 2—that is, he averaged the times: $\dfrac{5 + 3}{2} = 4$.

47.
$$\frac{1}{a}x + \frac{1}{b}x = 1$$
$$ab\left(\frac{1}{a}x + \frac{1}{b}x\right) = ab(1)$$
$$bx + ax = ab$$
$$x(b + a) = ab$$
$$x = \frac{ab}{b + a}$$
$$x = \frac{a \cdot b}{a + b}$$

48. 10 hr; 10 hr; The same answer results.

Chapter 7 REVIEW EXERCISES

1. (a) $-\dfrac{4}{7}$ **(b)** -16 **2. (a)** $\dfrac{11}{8}$ **(b)** $\dfrac{13}{22}$ **3. (a)** undefined   **(b)** 1

4. (a) undefined   **(b)** $\dfrac{1}{2}$ **5.** $x \neq 3$ **6.** $x \neq 0$ **7.** $m \neq -1, m \neq 3$

8. $k \neq -5, k \neq -\dfrac{2}{3}$ **9.** $\dfrac{b}{3a}$ **10.** -1 **11.** $\dfrac{-(2x + 3)}{2}$ **12.** $\dfrac{2p + 5q}{5p + q}$

Answers may vary in Exercises 13 and 14.

13. $\dfrac{-(4x - 9)}{2x + 3}, \dfrac{-4x + 9}{2x + 3}, \dfrac{4x - 9}{-(2x + 3)}, \dfrac{4x - 9}{-2x - 3}$ **14.** $\dfrac{-(8 - 3x)}{3 - 6x},$

$\dfrac{-8 + 3x}{3 - 6x}, \dfrac{8 - 3x}{-(3 - 6x)}, \dfrac{8 - 3x}{-3 + 6x}$ **15.** 2   **16.** $\dfrac{2}{3m^6}$ **17.** $\dfrac{5}{8}$

18. $\dfrac{r + 4}{3}$ **19.** $\dfrac{3}{2}$ **20.** $\dfrac{y - 2}{y - 3}$ **21.** $\dfrac{p + 5}{p + 1}$ **22.** $\dfrac{3z + 1}{z + 3}$ **23.** 96

24. $108y^4$ **25.** $m(m + 2)(m + 5)$ **26.** $(x + 3)(x + 1)(x + 4)$

27. $\dfrac{35}{56}$ **28.** $\dfrac{40}{4k}$ **29.** $\dfrac{15a}{10a^4}$ **30.** $\dfrac{-54}{18 - 6x}$ **31.** $\dfrac{15y}{50 - 10y}$

32. $\dfrac{4b(b + 2)}{(b + 3)(b - 1)(b + 2)}$ **33.** $\dfrac{15}{x}$ **34.** $-\dfrac{2}{p}$ **35.** $\dfrac{4k - 45}{k(k - 5)}$

36. $\dfrac{28 + 11y}{y(7 + y)}$ **37.** $\dfrac{-2 - 3m}{6}$ **38.** $\dfrac{3(16 - x)}{4x^2}$ **39.** $\dfrac{7a + 6b}{(a - 2b)(a + 2b)}$

40. $\dfrac{-k^2 - 6k + 3}{3(k + 3)(k - 3)}$ **41.** $\dfrac{5z - 16}{z(z + 6)(z - 2)}$ **42.** $\dfrac{-13p + 33}{p(p - 2)(p - 3)}$

43. $\dfrac{a}{b}$ **44.** $\dfrac{4(y - 3)}{y + 3}$ **45.** $\dfrac{6(3m + 2)}{2m - 5}$ **46.** $\dfrac{(q - p)^2}{pq}$ **47.** $\dfrac{xw + 1}{xw - 1}$

48. $\dfrac{1 - r - t}{1 + r + t}$ **49.** $\dfrac{b^3 + a^2b^2}{ab^3 - 5a^2}$ **50.** $\dfrac{1}{x^3y}$ **51.** $\left\{\dfrac{35}{6}\right\}$ **52.** $\{-16\}$

53. $\{-4\}$ **54.** $\varnothing$ **55.** $\{0\}$ **56.** $\{3\}$ **57.** $t = \dfrac{Ry}{m}$ **58.** $s = br - t$

59. $d = \dfrac{b - ac}{a}$, or $d = \dfrac{b}{a} - c$ **60.** $t = \dfrac{rs}{s - r}$ **61.** $\dfrac{20}{15}$ **62.** $\dfrac{3}{18}$

63. 2.020 hr **64.** 809.192 m per min **65.** $7\dfrac{1}{2}$ min **66.** $3\dfrac{1}{13}$ hr

Chapter 7 MIXED REVIEW EXERCISES

1. $\dfrac{m + 7}{(m - 1)(m + 1)}$ **2.** $8p^2$ **3.** $\dfrac{1}{6}$ **4.** 3 **5.** $\dfrac{z + 7}{(z + 1)(z - 1)^2}$

6. $\dfrac{x - 7}{2x + 3}$ **7.** $\{4\}$ **8.** $\{-2, 3\}$ **9.** $\{2\}$ **10.** $w = v - at$ **11.** 3

12. 2 hr **13.** table entries: (third column) $x + 50, x - 50$; (fourth column)

$\dfrac{400}{x + 50}, \dfrac{200}{x - 50}$; 150 km per hr **14.** 10 hr

Chapter 7 TEST

1. (a) $\dfrac{11}{6}$ (b) undefined **2.** $x \neq -2, x \neq 4$ **3.** (Answers may vary.)

$\dfrac{-(6x - 5)}{2x + 3}, \dfrac{-6x + 5}{2x + 3}, \dfrac{6x - 5}{-(2x + 3)}, \dfrac{6x - 5}{-2x - 3}$ **4.** $-3x^2y^3$ **5.** $\dfrac{3a + 2}{a - 1}$

6. $\dfrac{25}{27}$ **7.** $\dfrac{3k - 2}{3k + 2}$ **8.** $\dfrac{a - 1}{a + 4}$ **9.** $\dfrac{x - 5}{3 - x}$ **10.** $150p^5$

11. $(2r + 3)(r + 2)(r - 5)$ **12.** $\dfrac{240p^2}{64p^3}$ **13.** $\dfrac{21}{42m - 84}$

14. 2 **15.** $\dfrac{-14}{5(y + 2)}$ **16.** $\dfrac{x^2 + x + 1}{3 - x}$, or $\dfrac{-x^2 - x - 1}{x - 3}$

17. $\dfrac{-m^2 + 7m + 2}{(2m + 1)(m - 5)(m - 1)}$ **18.** $\dfrac{2k}{3p}$ **19.** $(x - 5)(x - 3)$, or

$x^2 - 8x + 15$ **20.** $\dfrac{-2 - x}{4 + x}$ **21.** $\dfrac{2y^2 + x^2}{xy(y - x)}$ **22.** expression; $\dfrac{11(x - 6)}{12}$

23. equation; $\{6\}$ **24.** $\left\{-\dfrac{1}{2}, 1\right\}$ **25.** $\left\{-\dfrac{1}{2}, 5\right\}$ **26.** $\varnothing$ **27.** $\left\{-\dfrac{1}{2}\right\}$

28. $D = \dfrac{dF - k}{F}$, or $D = d - \dfrac{k}{F}$ **29.** $2\dfrac{2}{9}$ hr **30.** 3 mph

Chapters R–7 CUMULATIVE REVIEW EXERCISES

1. 2 **2.** $\{17\}$ **3.** $b = \dfrac{2\mathcal{A}}{h}$ **4.** $\left\{-\dfrac{2}{7}\right\}$

5. $[-8, \infty)$

6. $(4, \infty)$

7.

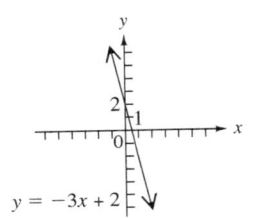

$y = -3x + 2$

8.

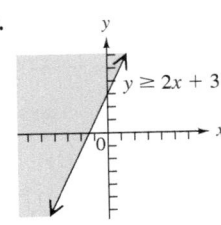

$y \geq 2x + 3$

9. $\{(-1, 2)\}$ **10.** $\{(1, -2)\}$ **11.** $\dfrac{1}{16x^7}$ **12.** $\dfrac{1}{m^6}$ **13.** $\dfrac{q}{4p^2}$

14. $k^2 + 2k + 1$ **15.** $72x^6y^7$ **16.** $4a^2 - 4ab + b^2$

17. $3y^3 + 8y^2 + 12y - 5$ **18.** $6p^2 + 7p + 1 + \dfrac{3}{p - 1}$

19. $(4t + 3v)(2t + v)$ **20.** prime **21.** $(4x^2 + 1)(2x + 1)(2x - 1)$

22. $\{-3, 5\}$ **23.** $\{-11, 11\}$ **24.** $\left\{-\dfrac{1}{2}, \dfrac{2}{3}, 5\right\}$ **25.** -2 or -1

26. 6 m **27.** $t \neq -2, t \neq 2$ **28.** D **29.** $\dfrac{4}{q}$ **30.** $\dfrac{3r + 28}{7r}$

31. $\dfrac{7}{15(q - 4)}$ **32.** $\dfrac{-k - 5}{k(k + 1)(k - 1)}$ **33.** $\dfrac{7(2z + 1)}{24}$ **34.** $\dfrac{195}{29}$

35. $\left\{\dfrac{21}{2}\right\}$ **36.** $\{-2, 1\}$ **37.** $q = \dfrac{fp}{p - f}$, or $q = \dfrac{-fp}{f - p}$ **38.** $1\dfrac{1}{5}$ hr

CHAPTER 8 Equations, Inequalities, Graphs, and Systems Revisited

SECTION 8.1

1. algebraic expression; does; is not **2.** linear equation; $=$; first-degree equation; one **3.** true; solution; solution set **4.** solution set; conditional equation **5.** identity; all real numbers **6.** contradiction; empty set $\varnothing$ **7.** equation **9.** expression **11.** equation **13.** A sign error was made when the distributive property was applied. The left side of the second line should be $8x - 4x + 6$. The correct solution is 1. **14.** $-1; -7m + 9$

15. $\{-1\}$ **17.** $\{-4\}$ **19.** $\{-7\}$ **21.** $\{0\}$ **23.** $\{4\}$ **25.** $\left\{-\dfrac{7}{8}\right\}$

27. $\left\{-\dfrac{1}{2}\right\}$ **29.** $\{-2\}$ **31.** $\{-1\}$ **33.** $\{4\}$ **35.** $\{0\}$ **37.** $\{3\}$

39. $\{2000\}$ **41.** $\{25\}$ **43.** $\{3\}$ **45.** $\varnothing$; contradiction **47.** $\{0\}$; conditional equation **49.** $\{$all real numbers$\}$; identity **51.** D **52.** C **53.** B **54.** A **55.** F **56.** E **57.** The student divided by 4, a *positive* number. Reverse the direction of the inequality symbol only when multiplying or dividing by a *negative* number. The solution set is $[-16, \infty)$. **58.** The student divided by -2, a *negative* number, which requires reversing the direction of the inequality symbol. The solution set is $(9, \infty)$.

59. $(-\infty, 7]$

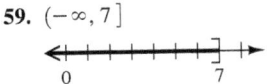

61. $[5, \infty)$

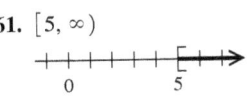

63. $(-\infty, -4)$

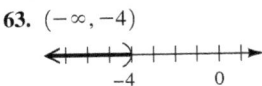

65. $(-4, \infty)$

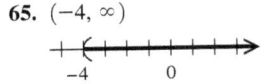

67. $(-\infty, -7)$

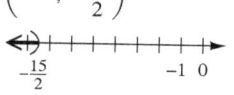

69. $(7, \infty)$

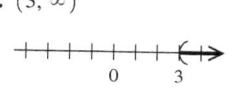

71. $\left(-\infty, -\dfrac{15}{2}\right)$

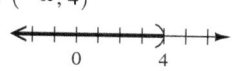

73. $(3, \infty)$

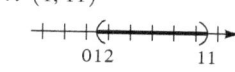

75. $(-\infty, 4)$

77. $(1, 11)$

79. $[-5, 6]$

81. $(-6, -4)$

83. $\left[-\dfrac{1}{3}, \dfrac{1}{9}\right)$

SECTION 8.2

1. true **2.** false; The intersection is $\{5\}$. **3.** false; The union is $(-\infty, 6) \cup (6, \infty)$. **4.** true **5.** $\{4\}$, or D **7.** $\{1, 3, 5\}$, or B **9.** $\varnothing$ **11.** $\{1, 2, 3, 4, 5, 6\}$, or A **13.** $\{1, 3, 5, 6\}$

15.

16.

17.

18.

19.

20.

21. $(-3, 2)$

23. $(-\infty, 2]$

25. $\varnothing$

27. $[5, 9]$

29. $(-3, -1)$

31. $(-\infty, 4]$

33. $(-\infty, 8]$

35. $[-2, \infty)$

37. $(-\infty, \infty)$

39. $(-\infty, -5) \cup (5, \infty)$

41. $(-\infty, -1] \cup (2, \infty)$

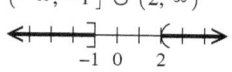

43. $(-\infty, \infty)$

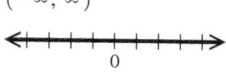

45. $(-\infty, 2) \cup (2, \infty)$

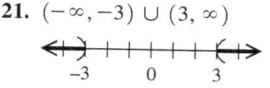

47. $[-4, -1]$ **49.** $[-9, -6]$
51. $(-\infty, 3)$ **53.** $[3, 9)$

55. $(-5, -1)$

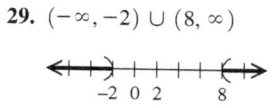

57. $(-\infty, 4)$

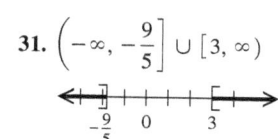

59. $(-\infty, 0] \cup [2, \infty)$

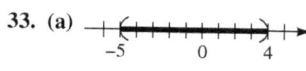

61. $[4, 12]$

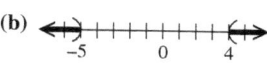

63. $\{$Tuition and fees$\}$ **65.** $\{$Tuition and fees, Board rates, Dormitory charges$\}$

For Exercises 67–71, refer to the following information.
Luigi's yard: Perimeter 160 ft, Area 1500 ft²; Mario's yard: Perimeter 150 ft, Area 1400 ft²; Than's yard: Perimeter 220 ft, Area 3000 ft²; Joe's yard: Perimeter 120 ft, Area 600 ft² **67.** Mario, Joe **69.** none of them
71. Mario, Joe **73. (a)** A: $185 + x \geq 585$; B: $185 + x \geq 520$;
C: $185 + x \geq 455$ **(b)** A: $x \geq 400$; 89%; B: $x \geq 335$; 75%;
C: $x \geq 270$; 60% **74.** $520 \leq 185 + x \leq 584$; $335 \leq x \leq 399$;
75% $\leq$ average $\leq$ 89% **75.** A: $105 + x \geq 585$; $x \geq 480$; impossible;
B: $105 + x \geq 520$; $x \geq 415$; 93%; C: $105 + x \geq 455$; $x \geq 350$; 78%
76. $455 \leq 105 + x \leq 519$; $350 \leq x \leq 414$; 78% $\leq$ average $\leq$ 92%

SECTION 8.3

1. E; C; D; B; A **2.** E; D; A; C; B **3. (a)** one **(b)** two
(c) none **4. (a)** $\varnothing$ **(b)** $(-\infty, \infty)$ **(c)** $\varnothing$ **5.** $\{-12, 12\}$ **7.** $\{-5, 5\}$

9. $\{-6, 12\}$ **11.** $\{-5, 6\}$ **13.** $\left\{-3, \dfrac{11}{2}\right\}$ **15.** $\left\{-\dfrac{19}{2}, \dfrac{9}{2}\right\}$

17. $\{-10, -2\}$ **19.** $\left\{-8, \dfrac{32}{3}\right\}$

21. $(-\infty, -3) \cup (3, \infty)$

23. $(-\infty, -4] \cup [4, \infty)$

25. $(-\infty, -25] \cup [15, \infty)$

27. $\left(-\infty, -\dfrac{7}{3}\right] \cup [3, \infty)$

29. $(-\infty, -2) \cup (8, \infty)$

31. $\left(-\infty, -\dfrac{9}{5}\right] \cup [3, \infty)$

33. (a)

(b)

34. (a)

(b)

35. $[-3, 3]$

37. $(-4, 4)$

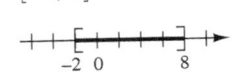

39. $(-25, 15)$

41. $\left(-\dfrac{7}{3}, 3\right)$

43. $[-2, 8]$

45. $\left(-\dfrac{9}{5}, 3\right)$

47. $(-\infty, -2) \cup (10, \infty)$

49. $\{-6, -1\}$

51. $\left[-\dfrac{10}{3}, 4\right]$

53. $\left[-4, -\dfrac{4}{3}\right]$

55. $\{-5, 5\}$ **57.** $\{-5, -3\}$ **59.** $(-\infty, -3) \cup (2, \infty)$ **61.** $[-10, 0]$

63. $\{-1, 3\}$ **65.** $\left\{-3, \dfrac{5}{3}\right\}$ **67.** $\left\{-\dfrac{1}{3}, -\dfrac{1}{15}\right\}$ **69.** $\left\{-\dfrac{5}{4}\right\}$

71. $(-\infty, \infty)$ **73.** $\varnothing$ **75.** $\left\{-\dfrac{1}{4}\right\}$ **77.** $\varnothing$ **79.** $(-\infty, \infty)$

81. $\left\{-\dfrac{3}{7}\right\}$ **83.** $(-\infty, \infty)$ **85.** $\left(-\infty, -\dfrac{7}{10}\right) \cup \left(-\dfrac{7}{10}, \infty\right)$

87. $(-\infty, \infty)$ **89.** $\varnothing$ **91.** between 60.8 and 67.2 oz, inclusive

93. between 31.36 and 32.64 oz, inclusive

95. $|x - 1000| \le 100;\ 900 \le x \le 1100$ **97.** 810.5 ft

98. Bank of America Center, Texaco Heritage Plaza **99.** Williams Tower, Bank of America Center, Texaco Heritage Plaza, Enterprise Plaza, Centerpoint Energy Plaza, Continental Center I, Fulbright Tower

100. (a) $|x - 810.5| > 95$ **(b)** $x > 905.5$ or $x < 715.5$ **(c)** JPMorgan Chase Tower, Wells Fargo Plaza, One Shell Plaza **(d)** It makes sense because it includes all buildings *not* listed in the answer to **Exercise 99.**

SUMMARY EXERCISES Solving Linear and Absolute Value Equations and Inequalities

1. $\{12\}$ **2.** $\{-5, 7\}$ **3.** $\{7\}$ **4.** $\left\{-\dfrac{2}{5}\right\}$ **5.** $\varnothing$ **6.** $(-\infty, -1]$

7. $\left[-\dfrac{2}{3}, \infty\right)$ **8.** $\{-1\}$ **9.** $\{-3\}$ **10.** $\left\{1, \dfrac{11}{3}\right\}$ **11.** $(-\infty, 5]$

12. $(-\infty, \infty)$ **13.** $\{2\}$ **14.** $(-\infty, -8] \cup [8, \infty)$ **15.** $\varnothing$

16. $(-\infty, \infty)$ **17.** $(-5.5, 5.5)$ **18.** $\left\{\dfrac{13}{3}\right\}$ **19.** $\left\{-\dfrac{96}{5}\right\}$

20. $(-\infty, 32]$ **21.** $(-\infty, -24)$ **22.** $\left\{\dfrac{3}{8}\right\}$ **23.** $\left\{\dfrac{7}{2}\right\}$ **24.** $(-6, 8)$

25. $\{\text{all real numbers}\}$ **26.** $(-\infty, 5)$ **27.** $(-\infty, -4) \cup (7, \infty)$

28. $\{24\}$ **29.** $\left\{-\dfrac{1}{5}\right\}$ **30.** $\left(-\infty, -\dfrac{5}{2}\right]$ **31.** $\left[-\dfrac{1}{3}, 3\right]$ **32.** $[1, 7]$

33. $\left\{-\dfrac{1}{6}, 2\right\}$ **34.** $\{-3\}$ **35.** $(-\infty, -1] \cup \left[\dfrac{5}{3}, \infty\right)$ **36.** $\left[\dfrac{3}{4}, \dfrac{15}{8}\right]$

37. $\left\{-\dfrac{5}{2}\right\}$ **38.** $\{60\}$ **39.** $\left[-\dfrac{9}{2}, \dfrac{15}{2}\right]$ **40.** $(1, 9)$ **41.** $(-\infty, \infty)$

42. $\left\{\dfrac{1}{3}, 9\right\}$ **43.** $\{\text{all real numbers}\}$ **44.** $\left\{-\dfrac{10}{9}\right\}$ **45.** $\{-2\}$

46. $\varnothing$ **47.** $(-\infty, -1) \cup (2, \infty)$ **48.** $[-3, -2]$

SECTION 8.4

1. origin **2.** x **3.** $y; x$ **4.** horizontal; vertical **5.** The student interchanged the x- and y-coordinates. To plot this point correctly, move 4 units from 0 to the left on the x-axis and then 2 units up parallel to the y-axis. **6. (a)** I or III **(b)** II or IV **(c)** II or IV **(d)** I or III

7. $-3; 3; 2; -1$

9. $\dfrac{5}{2}; 5; \dfrac{3}{2}; -3$

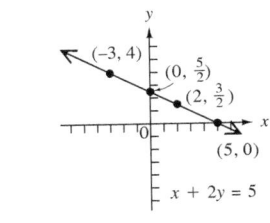

11. $(6, 0); (0, 4)$

13. $(6, 0); (0, -2)$

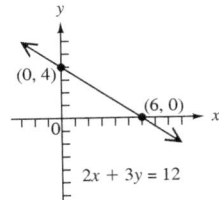

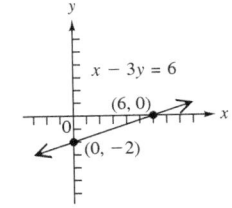

15. $(0, 0); (0, 0)$

17. $(0, 0); (0, 0)$

19. none; $(0, 5)$

21. $(-4, 0)$; none

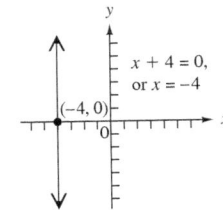

23. B **24.** C **25.** A **26.** D **27. (a)** 8 **(b)** rises **29. (a)** 0 **(b)** horizontal **31. (a)** $-\dfrac{1}{2}$ **(b)** falls **33. (a)** undefined **(b)** vertical

35. $-\dfrac{1}{2}$

37. 1

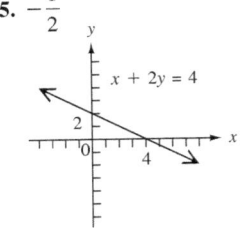

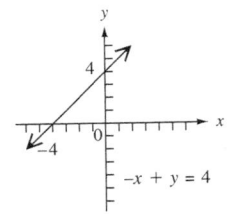

39. undefined

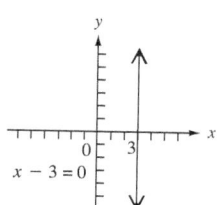

41. 0

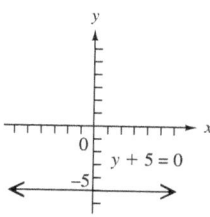

SECTION 8.6

1. Answers will vary. Some possible answers are   **(a)** two perpendicular walls and the ceiling in a normal room,   **(b)** the floors of three different levels of an office building, and   **(c)** three pages of a book (since they intersect in the spine).   **2.** B   **3.** $\{(3, 2, 1)\}$ **5.** $\{(1, 4, -3)\}$
7. $\{(1, 0, 3)\}$ **9.** $\{(0, 2, -5)\}$ **11.** $\left\{\left(1, \frac{3}{10}, \frac{2}{5}\right)\right\}$
13. $\left\{\left(\frac{5}{4}, -\frac{7}{4}, \frac{1}{4}\right)\right\}$ **15.** $\{(4, 5, 3)\}$ **17.** $\{(2, 2, 2)\}$
19. $\left\{\left(\frac{8}{3}, \frac{2}{3}, 3\right)\right\}$ **21.** $\{(-1, 0, 0)\}$ **23.** $\{(-4, 6, 2)\}$
25. $\{(-3, 5, -6)\}$ **27.** $\varnothing$; inconsistent system
29. $\{(x, y, z) \mid x - y + 4z = 8\}$; dependent equations   **31.** $\{(3, 0, 2)\}$
33. $\{(x, y, z) \mid 2x + y - z = 6\}$; dependent equations   **35.** $\{(0, 0, 0)\}$
37. $\varnothing$; inconsistent system   **39.** $x + y + z = 180$; angle measures: $70°, 30°, 80°$ **41.** first: $20°$; second: $70°$; third: $90°$ **43.** shortest: 12 cm; middle: 25 cm; longest: 33 cm   **45.** Independent: 42%; Democrat: 29%; Republican: 26%   **47.** general admission: 1170; courtside: 985; bench: 130   **49.** bookstore A: 140; bookstore B: 280; bookstore C: 380   **51.** $2a + b + c = -5$ **52.** $a - c = 1$
53. $3a + 3b + c = -18$ **54.** $a = 1, b = -7, c = 0$
55. $x^2 + y^2 + x - 7y = 0$ **56.** $x^2 + y^2 - 6x - 4y - 12 = 0$

43.

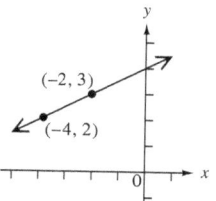

45.

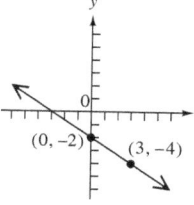

47.

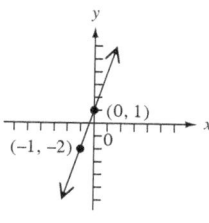

49.

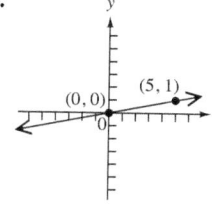

Chapter 8 REVIEW EXERCISES

1. $\left\{-\frac{9}{5}\right\}$ **2.** $\{0\}$ **3.** $\{10\}$ **4.** $\{300\}$ **5.** $\{\text{all real numbers}\}$; identity   **6.** $\varnothing$; contradiction   **7.** $\{0\}$; conditional equation
8. $\{\text{all real numbers}\}$; identity
9. $(-9, \infty)$

10. $(-\infty, -4]$

11. $(-\infty, -3]$

12. $[-3, \infty)$

13. $[3, 5)$

14. $\left(-3, \frac{7}{2}\right)$

15. $\{1, 3\}$ **16.** $\{1\}$ **17.** $\{1, 3, 6, 8, 9\}$ **18.** $\{1, 2, 3, 4, 6, 8, 9\}$
19. $(4, 7)$

20. $(8, 14)$

21. $(-\infty, -3] \cup (5, \infty)$

22. $(-\infty, \infty)$

23. $\varnothing$

24. $(-\infty, -2] \cup [7, \infty)$

25. $(-3, 4)$ **26.** $(-\infty, 2)$ **27.** $(4, \infty)$ **28.** $(1, \infty)$
29. $\{-7, 7\}$ **30.** $\{-11, 7\}$ **31.** $\left\{-\frac{1}{3}, 5\right\}$ **32.** $\varnothing$
33. $\{0, 7\}$ **34.** $\left\{-\frac{3}{2}, \frac{1}{2}\right\}$ **35.** $\left\{-\frac{3}{4}, \frac{1}{2}\right\}$ **36.** $\left\{-\frac{8}{5}\right\}$

SECTION 8.5

1. D; The ordered-pair solution must be in quadrant IV because that is where the graphs of the equations intersect.   **2.** B; The ordered-pair solution must be on the x-axis, with $x < 0$, because that is where the graphs of the equations intersect.   **3.** **(a)** B   **(b)** C   **(c)** A   **(d)** D   **4.** **(a)** Use substitution since the second equation is solved for y; $\{(-1, -11)\}$ **(b)** Use elimination since the coefficients of the y-terms are opposites; $\{(-3, 2)\}$ **(c)** Use elimination since the equations are in $Ax + By = C$ form with no coefficients of 1 or -1. Solving by substitution would involve fractions; $\left\{\left(\frac{1}{3}, \frac{1}{2}\right)\right\}$

5. $\{(-2, -3)\}$ **7.** $\{(0, 1)\}$

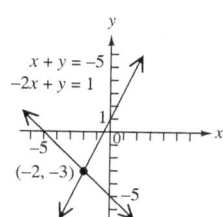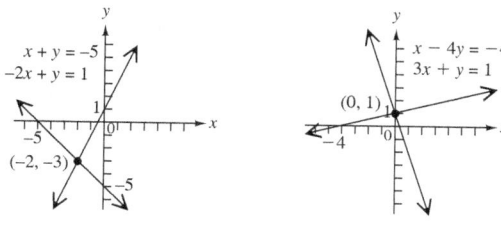

9. $\{(1, 2)\}$ **11.** $\{(2, 3)\}$ **13.** $\left\{\left(\frac{22}{9}, \frac{22}{3}\right)\right\}$ **15.** $\{(0, -4)\}$
17. $\left\{\left(-5, -\frac{10}{3}\right)\right\}$ **19.** $\{(2, 6)\}$ **21.** $\{(x, y) \mid 2x - y = 0\}$; dependent equations   **23.** $\varnothing$; inconsistent system   **25.** $\{(2, -4)\}$
27. $\{(3, -1)\}$ **29.** $\{(2, -3)\}$ **31.** $\left\{\left(\frac{3}{2}, -\frac{3}{2}\right)\right\}$
33. $\{(x, y) \mid 7x + 2y = 6\}$; dependent equations   **35.** $\{(-1, 0)\}$
37. $\varnothing$; inconsistent system   **39.** $\{(2, -4)\}$

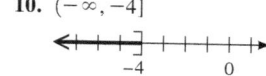

37. $(-12, 12)$

38. $[-1, 13]$

39. $[-3, -2]$

40. $(-\infty, \infty)$

41. $\left(-\infty, -\dfrac{8}{5}\right) \cup (2, \infty)$

42. $(-\infty, \infty)$

43. $(3, 0); (0, 4)$

44. $(5, 0);$ none

45. $(0, 0); (0, 0)$

46. (a) positive **(b)** negative **(c)** 0 **(d)** undefined
47. $-\dfrac{8}{5}$ **48.** 2 **49.** $\dfrac{3}{4}$ **50.** 0
51. $\{(2, 2)\}$ **52.** $\{(-4, 0)\}$
53. $\{(1, -1)\}$ **54.** C
55. $\left\{\left(-\dfrac{8}{9}, -\dfrac{4}{3}\right)\right\}$ **56.** $\{(0, 4)\}$

57. $\{(2, 4)\}$ **58.** $\{(2, 2)\}$ **59.** $\{(-1, 2)\}$ **60.** $\{(-6, 3)\}$
61. $\left\{\left(\dfrac{68}{13}, -\dfrac{31}{13}\right)\right\}$ **62.** $\{(x, y) \mid 3x - y = -6\};$ dependent equations
63. $\varnothing;$ inconsistent system **64.** $\{(0, 1)\}$ **65.** $\{(1, -5, 3)\}$
66. $\varnothing;$ inconsistent system **67.** $\{(5, -1, 0)\}$ **68.** $\{(1, 2, 3)\}$
69. $\{(x, y, z) \mid 3x - 4y + z = 8\};$ dependent equations **70.** $\{(0, 0, 0)\}$
71. $85°, 35°, 60°$ **72.** United States: 121; China: 70; Great Britain: 67

Chapter 8 MIXED REVIEW EXERCISES

1. $\left\{\dfrac{7}{6}\right\}$ **2.** $\varnothing$ **3.** $[-4, 5)$ **4.** $(-\infty, 2]$ **5.** $(-\infty, -1) \cup \left(\dfrac{11}{7}, \infty\right)$

6. $\{-5, 15\}$ **7.** $[-16, 10]$ **8.** $(-\infty, \infty)$ **9.** $\left\{-4, -\dfrac{2}{3}\right\}$

10. (a) $(-\infty, \infty)$ **(b)** $\varnothing$ **(c)** $\varnothing$

11. $3; 2; \dfrac{10}{3}$

12. B; The second equation is already solved for y. **13.** $\{(3, -1)\}$
14. $\{(5, 3)\}$ **15.** $\{(0, 4)\}$
16. $\{(1, 0, -1)\}$ **17.** $\{(1, 2, 3)\}$
18. $\varnothing$

Chapter 8 TEST

1. $\{-19\}$ **2.** $\{5\}$ **3.** $\{4\}$ **4.** $\varnothing;$ contradiction **5.** $\{$all real numbers$\};$ identity **6.** $\{0\};$ conditional equation

7. $[2, \infty)$

8. $[1, \infty)$

9. $(-\infty, 28)$

10. $(1, 2)$

11. $\{1, 5\}$ **12.** $\{1, 2, 5, 7, 9, 12\}$

13. $[2, 9)$

14. $(-\infty, 3) \cup [6, \infty)$

15. $\left[-\dfrac{5}{2}, 1\right]$

16. $\left(-\infty, -\dfrac{7}{6}\right) \cup \left(\dfrac{17}{6}, \infty\right)$

17. $\left(\dfrac{1}{3}, \dfrac{7}{3}\right)$

18. $\varnothing$

19. $\{1, 5\}$ **20.** $\left\{-\dfrac{5}{7}, \dfrac{11}{3}\right\}$ **21.** $\varnothing$ **22. (a)** $\varnothing$ **(b)** $(-\infty, \infty)$ **(c)** $\varnothing$ **23.** B

24. $(-3, 0); (0, 4)$

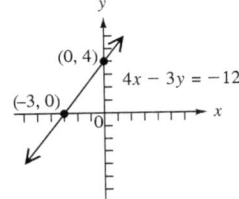

25. $\{(6, 1)\}$

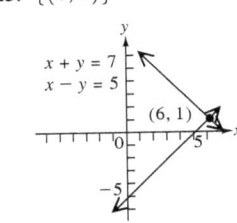

26. $\{(3, 3)\}$ **27.** $\{(0, -2)\}$ **28.** $\varnothing;$ inconsistent system
29. $\{(x, y) \mid 12x - 5y = 8\};$ dependent equations **30.** $\left\{\left(-\dfrac{2}{3}, \dfrac{4}{5}, 0\right)\right\}$
31. $\{(3, -2, 1)\}$ **32.** smallest: $25°;$ middle-sized: $55°;$ largest: $100°$

Chapters R–8 CUMULATIVE REVIEW EXERCISES

1. $-2m + 6$ **2.** $4m - 3$ **3.** $2x^2 + 5x + 4$ **4.** -24 **5.** 204

6. undefined **7.** 10 **8.** $\left\{\dfrac{7}{6}\right\}$ **9.** $\{-1\}$ **10.** $\left(-\infty, \dfrac{15}{4}\right]$

11. $\left(-\dfrac{1}{2}, \infty\right)$ **12.** $(2, 3)$ **13.** $(-\infty, 2) \cup (3, \infty)$ **14.** $\left\{-\dfrac{16}{5}, 2\right\}$

15. $(-11, 7)$ **16.** $(-\infty, -2] \cup [7, \infty)$ **17.** $h = \dfrac{V}{lw}$

18. table entries: (fourth column) $550x, 500x;$ 2 hr

19.

20. -1 **21.** 0 **22.** 2
23. $\left(-\dfrac{7}{2}, 0\right)$ **24.** $(0, 7)$ **25.** $\{(1, 5)\}$
26. $\{(1, 1, 0)\}$ **27.** $\dfrac{y}{18x}$ **28.** $\dfrac{5my^4}{3}$
29. $x^3 + 12x^2 - 3x - 7$
30. $49x^2 + 42xy + 9y^2$

31. $10p^3 + 7p^2 - 28p - 24$ **32.** $(2w + 7z)(8w - 3z)$

33. $(2y - 9)^2$ **34.** $(2p + 3)(4p^2 - 6p + 9)$ **35.** $\left\{\dfrac{1}{3}\right\}$ **36.** $\left\{-\dfrac{1}{3}, \dfrac{7}{2}\right\}$

37. $\{-2, 1\}$ **38.** $\dfrac{4}{q}$ **39.** $\dfrac{3r + 28}{7r}$ **40.** $\dfrac{7}{15(q - 4)}$

41. $\dfrac{7(2z + 1)}{24}$ **42.** $\dfrac{195}{29}$

CHAPTER 9 Relations and Functions

SECTION 9.1

1. relation; ordered pairs   **2.** domain; range   **3.** function; ordered pairs
4. does not; domain; range   **5.** independent variable; dependent variable
6. vertical line test; function; one   **7.** $\{(0, 2), (2, 4), (4, 0)\}$
8. $\{(-1, -3), (0, -1), (1, 1), (3, 3)\}$ **9.** $\{(2012, 36{,}300), (2013, 37{,}389),$
$(2014, 38{,}511), (2015, 39{,}665)\}$ **10.** $\{(-3, -4), (-3, 1), (2, 0)\}$
11. function; domain: $\{5, 3, 4, 7\}$; range: $\{1, 2, 9, 3\}$ **13.** not a
function; domain: $\{2, 0\}$; range: $\{4, 2, 5\}$ **15.** function; domain:
$\{-3, 4, -2\}$; range: $\{1, 7\}$ **17.** not a function; domain: $\{1, 0, 2\}$;
range: $\{1, -1, 0, 4, -4\}$ **19.** function; domain: $\{2, 5, 11, 17, 3\}$;
range: $\{1, 7, 20\}$ **21.** not a function; domain: $\{1\}$; range: $\{5, 2, -1, -4\}$
23. function; domain: $\{4, 2, 0, -2\}$; range: $\{-3\}$ **25.** function;
domain: $\{-2, 0, 3\}$; range: $\{2, 3\}$ **27.** function; domain: $(-\infty, \infty)$;
range: $(-\infty, \infty)$ **29.** not a function; domain: $(-\infty, 0]$; range: $(-\infty, \infty)$
31. function; domain: $(-\infty, \infty)$; range: $(-\infty, 4]$ **33.** not a function;
domain: $[-4, 4]$; range: $[-3, 3]$ **35.** not a function; domain: $(-\infty, 3]$;
range: $(-\infty, \infty)$ **37.** function; $(-\infty, \infty)$ **39.** function; $(-\infty, \infty)$
41. function; $(-\infty, \infty)$ **43.** not a function; $[0, \infty)$ **45.** not a function;
$(-\infty, \infty)$ **47.** function; $(-\infty, \infty)$ **49.** function; $(-\infty, \infty)$ **51.** function;
$(-\infty, 0) \cup (0, \infty)$ **53.** function; $(-\infty, 4) \cup (4, \infty)$ **55.** function;
$\left(-\infty, -\dfrac{1}{2}\right) \cup \left(-\dfrac{1}{2}, \infty\right)$ **57.** not a function; $[1, \infty)$ **59.** function;
$(-\infty, 0) \cup (0, \infty)$ **61. (a)** yes   **(b)** domain: $\{2011, 2012, 2013, 2014,$
$2015\}$; range: $\{25, 26, 28\}$ **(c)** Answers will vary. Two possible answers
are $(2011, 25)$ and $(2015, 28)$.

SECTION 9.2

1. $f(x)$; function; domain; x; f of x (or "f at x")   **2.** B   **3.** 4   **5.** 19
7. -59 **9.** 3   **11.** 2.75   **13.** $-3p + 4$ **15.** $3x + 4$ **17.** $-3x - 2$
19. $-6t + 1$ **21.** $-\dfrac{p^2}{9} + \dfrac{4p}{3} + 1$ **23. (a)** -1 **(b)** -1 **25. (a)** 2
(b) 3   **27. (a)** 15   **(b)** 10   **29. (a)** 4   **(b)** 1   **31. (a)** 3   **(b)** -3
33. (a) -3 **(b)** 2   **35. (a)** 2   **(b)** 0   **(c)** -1

37. (a) $f(x) = -\dfrac{1}{3}x + 4$ **(b)** 3   **39. (a)** $f(x) = 3 - 2x^2$ **(b)** -15

41. (a) $f(x) = \dfrac{4}{3}x - \dfrac{8}{3}$ **(b)** $\dfrac{4}{3}$ **43.** line; -2; linear; $-2x + 4$; -2; 3; -2

44. $ax + b$; line; slope; y-intercept; $(-\infty, \infty)$

45.
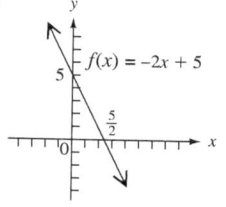
domain: $(-\infty, \infty)$;
range: $(-\infty, \infty)$

47.
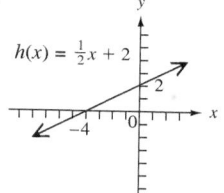
domain: $(-\infty, \infty)$;
range: $(-\infty, \infty)$

49.
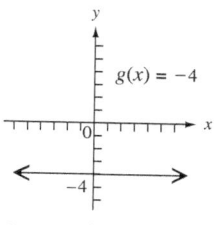
domain: $(-\infty, \infty)$;
range: $\{-4\}$

51.
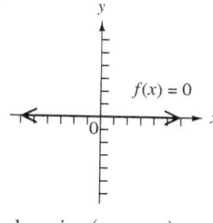
domain: $(-\infty, \infty)$;
range: $\{0\}$

53. (a) \$0; \$2.50; \$5.00; \$7.50
(b) $2.50x$
(c)
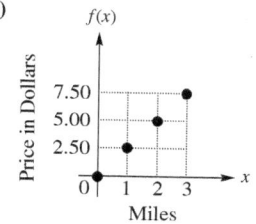

55. (a) $f(x) = 12x + 100$ **(b)** 1600;
The cost to print 125 t-shirts is \$1600.
(c) 75; $f(75) = 1000$; The cost to
print 75 t-shirts is \$1000.
57. (a) 1.1   **(b)** 4   **(c)** -1.2
(d) $(0, 3.5)$ **(e)** $f(x) = -1.2x + 3.5$
59. (a) $[0, 100]$; $[0, 3000]$
(b) 25 hr; 25 hr   **(c)** 2000 gal
(d) $g(0) = 0$; The pool is empty
at time 0.

SECTION 9.3

1. polynomial; one; terms; powers   **2.** A, D   **3. (a)** -10 **(b)** 8
(c) -4 **5. (a)** 8   **(b)** -10 **(c)** 0   **7. (a)** 9   **(b)** 6   **(c)** 4
9. (a) 8   **(b)** 74   **(c)** 6   **11. (a)** -11 **(b)** 4   **(c)** -8 **13.** $f(x)$ and
$g(x)$ can be any two polynomials that have a sum of $3x^3 - x + 3$, such as
$f(x) = 3x^3 + 1$ and $g(x) = -x + 2$.   **14.** $f(x)$ and $g(x)$ can be any two
polynomials whose difference is $-x^2 + x - 5$, such as $f(x) = 2x^2 + 3x - 2$
and $g(x) = 3x^2 + 2x + 3$.   **15.** $x^2 + 2x - 9$ **17.** 6   **19.** $x^2 - x - 6$
21. 6   **23.** 0   **25.** $-\dfrac{9}{4}$ **27.** $2x^3 - 18x$ **29.** -20 **31.** 32   **33.** 0

35. $\dfrac{35}{4}$ **37.** $\dfrac{x^2 - 9}{2x}, x \neq 0$ **39.** $-\dfrac{5}{4}$ **41.** $\dfrac{x - 3}{2x}, x \neq 0$ **43.** 0

45. $\dfrac{7}{2}$ **47. (a)** $P(x) = 8.49x - 50$ **(b)** \$799

49.
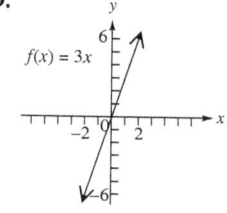
domain: $(-\infty, \infty)$;
range: $(-\infty, \infty)$

51.
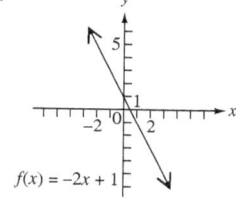
domain: $(-\infty, \infty)$;
range: $(-\infty, \infty)$

53.

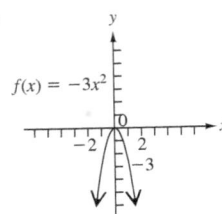

$f(x) = -3x^2$

domain: $(-\infty, \infty)$;
range: $(-\infty, 0]$

55.

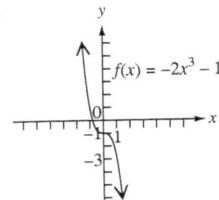

$f(x) = x^2 - 2$

domain: $(-\infty, \infty)$;
range: $[-2, \infty)$

57.

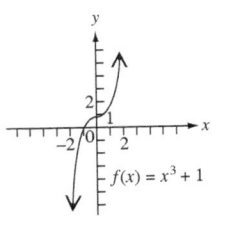

$f(x) = x^3 + 1$

domain: $(-\infty, \infty)$;
range: $(-\infty, \infty)$

59.

$f(x) = -2x^3 - 1$

domain: $(-\infty, \infty)$;
range: $(-\infty, \infty)$

61. $f(1) = 1$; $f(2) = 2$ **62.** $f(3) = 4$; $f(4) = 8$; $f(5) = 16$
63. $f(3) = 4$; $f(4) = 8$; $f(5) = 16$ **64.** The pattern 1, 2, 4, 8, 16
emerges, so most students predict 32 because the terms are doubling each
time. However, $f(6) = 31$ (not 32). See the figure.

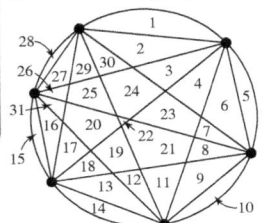

SECTION 9.4

1. direct **2.** direct **3.** inverse **4.** inverse **5.** direct **6.** inverse
7. inverse **8.** direct **9.** Answers will vary; for example, number of
movie tickets purchased and total price paid for the tickets. **10.** Answers
will vary; for example, percentage off an item that is on sale and price paid
for the item. **11. (a)** increases **(b)** decreases **12.** The customers in
the lower-priced seats know more about the game than those in the
higher-priced seats. **13.** inverse **14.** inverse **15.** direct **16.** direct
17. joint **18.** joint **19.** combined **20.** combined
21. The perimeter of a square varies directly as the length of its side.
22. The diameter of a circle varies directly as the length of its radius.
23. The surface area of a sphere varies directly as the square of its radius.
24. The volume of a sphere varies directly as the cube of its radius.
25. The area of a triangle varies jointly as the length of its base and its height.
26. The volume of a cone varies jointly as the square of its radius and its
height. **27.** $A = kb$ **28.** $h = \dfrac{k}{t}$ **29.** $P = \dfrac{k}{x^3}$ **30.** $M = kd^2$

31. $I = kgh$ **32.** $C = kab^2$ **33.** 36 **35.** $\dfrac{16}{9}$ **37.** 0.625

39. $\dfrac{16}{5}$ **41.** $222\dfrac{2}{9}$ **43.** $\$3.29\dfrac{9}{10}$ **45.** 8 lb **47.** 450 cm³

49. $13\dfrac{1}{3}$ amperes **51.** 15 ft **53.** 256 ft **55.** $21\dfrac{1}{3}$ foot-candles

57. $420 **59.** 448.1 lb **61.** 11.8 lb **63.** Answers will vary.
65. $(0, 0), (1, 3.35)$ **66.** 3.35 **67.** $y = 3.35x + 0$, or $y = 3.35x$
68. $a = 3.35, b = 0$ **69.** It is the price per gallon and the slope of the
line. **70.** It can be written in the form $y = kx$ (where $k = a$). The value of
a is the constant of variation.

Chapter 9 REVIEW EXERCISES
1. not a function; domain: $\{-4, 1\}$; range: $\{2, -2, 5, -5\}$
2. function; domain: $\{9, 11, 4, 17, 25\}$; range: $\{32, 47, 69, 14\}$
3. function; domain: $[-3, 3]$; range: $[0, 2]$ **4.** not a function; domain;
$(-\infty, 0]$; range: $(-\infty, \infty)$ **5.** function; linear function; domain:
$(-\infty, \infty)$ **6.** not a function; domain: $(-\infty, \infty)$ **7.** not a function;
domain: $[0, \infty)$ **8.** function; domain: $(-\infty, 36) \cup (36, \infty)$ **9.** -6
10. -15 **11.** $-2p^2 + 3p - 6$ **12.** $-2k^2 - 3k - 6$ **13.** $f(x) = 2x^2$; 18
14. It is a horizontal line. **15.** $12x^2$ **16.** 60 **17.** $36x^3 - 9x^2$
18. -45 **19.** $4x - 1$, $x \neq 0$ **20.** 7

21.

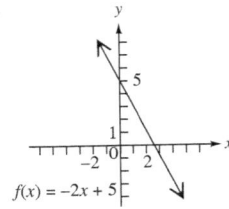

$f(x) = -2x + 5$

domain: $(-\infty, \infty)$;
range: $(-\infty, \infty)$

22.

$f(x) = x^2 - 6$

domain: $(-\infty, \infty)$;
range: $[-6, \infty)$

23.

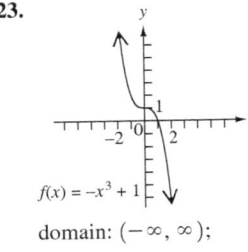

$f(x) = -x^3 + 1$

domain: $(-\infty, \infty)$;
range: $(-\infty, \infty)$

24. 430 mm
25. 5.59 cycles per sec

Chapter 9 MIXED REVIEW EXERCISES
1. (a) yes **(b)** domain: $\{1950, 1960, 1970, 1980, 1990, 2000, 2010\}$;
range: $\{68.2, 69.7, 70.8, 73.7, 75.4, 77.0, 78.7\}$ **(c)** Answers will vary.
Two possible ordered pairs are $(1960, 69.7)$ and $(2010, 78.7)$. **(d)** 78.7;
In 2010, life expectancy at birth was 78.7 yr. **(e)** 1990 **2.** C **3.** A
4. -2 **5.** 24 **6.** -112 **7.** 1

8.

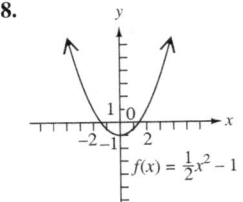

$f(x) = \frac{1}{2}x^2 - 1$

domain: $(-\infty, \infty)$;
range: $[-1, \infty)$

9. C **10.** $\dfrac{108}{5}$ **11.** 36 ft³
12. 12 ft²

Chapter 9 TEST

1. D; domain: $(-\infty, \infty)$; range: $[0, \infty)$ **2.** C; domain: $\{0, 3, 6\}$;
range: $\{1, 2, 3\}$ **3.** -18 **4.** $-2x^2 + 12x - 9$ **5.** $-2x^2 - 2x - 3$
6. -7 **7.** $x^3 + 4x^2 + 5x + 2$ **8.** 0 **9.** $x + 2, x \neq -1$ **10.** 0
11.   **12.**

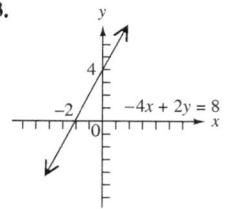
$f(x) = -2x^2 + 3$

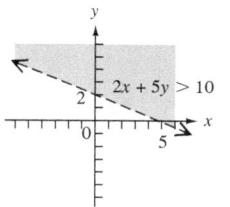
$f(x) = 3x - 4$

domain: $(-\infty, \infty)$;   domain: $(-\infty, \infty)$;
range: $(-\infty, 3]$ range: $(-\infty, \infty)$

13. 200 amps   **14.** 0.8 lb

Chapters R–9 CUMULATIVE REVIEW EXERCISES

1. $\left\{-\dfrac{15}{4}\right\}$ **2.** $\left\{\dfrac{2}{3}, 2\right\}$ **3.** $\left(-\infty, \dfrac{240}{13}\right]$ **4.** $\left\{-\dfrac{7}{3}, 1\right\}$

5. $\{-4\}$ **6.** $q = \dfrac{fp}{p - f}$, or $q = \dfrac{-fp}{f - p}$ **7.** \$4000 at 4%; \$8000 at 3%

8. 6 m   **9.** -6 **10.** $1; (0, -5)$ **11.** $y = -\dfrac{3}{2}x + \dfrac{15}{2}$ **12.** $y = \dfrac{3}{4}x - \dfrac{7}{4}$

13.   **14.**

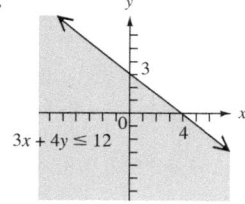
$-4x + 2y = 8$

$2x + 5y > 10$

$(-2, 0)$ and $(0, 4)$

15.

$3x + 4y \leq 12$

16. $\{(-1, 3)\}$ **17.** $\{(-2, 3, 1)\}$
18. $\varnothing$ **19.** $4y^2 - 7y - 6$
20. $x^2 + 4x - 7$ **21.** $12x^2 + 5x - 3$
22. $49t^2 - 64$ **23.** $16x^2 + 40x + 25$
24. $\dfrac{a(a - b)}{2(a + b)}$ **25.** 3 **26.** $\dfrac{2(x + 2)}{2x - 1}$

27. $(2x + 5)(x - 9)$ **28.** $25(2t + 1)(2t - 1)$
29. $(2p + 5)(4p^2 - 10p + 25)$ **30.** $(2x - 1)^2$
31. (a) $f(x) = \dfrac{5}{3}x - \dfrac{8}{3}$ **(b)** -1 **32. (a)** yes
(b) domain: $(-\infty, \infty)$; range: $(-\infty, \infty)$ **33. (a)** $2x^3 - 2x^2 + 6x - 4$
(b) $2x^3 - 4x^2 + 2x + 2$ **(c)** -14 **34.** \$13.50

CHAPTER 10 Roots, Radicals, and Root Functions

SECTION 10.1

1. true   **2.** false; A negative number has no real square roots.   **3.** false;
Zero has only one square root.   **4.** true   **5.** true   **6.** false; A positive
number has just one real cube root.   **7.** E   **8.** F   **9.** D   **10.** B
11. C   **12.** E   **13.** C   **14.** B   **15.** A   **16.** B   **17. (a)** not a real
number   **(b)** negative   **(c)** 0   **18. (a)** a must be positive $(a > 0)$.
(b) a must be negative $(a < 0)$.   **(c)** a must be 0 $(a = 0)$.   **19.** $-3, 3$

21. $-8, 8$ **23.** $-13, 13$ **25.** $-\dfrac{5}{14}, \dfrac{5}{14}$ **27.** $-30, 30$ **29.** 1

31. 8 **33.** 7 **35.** -9 **37.** -16 **39.** $\dfrac{8}{9}$ **41.** $-\dfrac{12}{11}$ **43.** 0.8

45. not a real number   **47.** not a real number   **49.** 100 **51.** 19 **53.** $\dfrac{2}{3}$

55. $3x^2 + 4$ **57.** rational; 5   **59.** irrational; 5.385   **61.** rational; -8
63. irrational; -17.321 **65.** not a real number   **67.** irrational; 34.641
69. 6 **71.** -4 **73.** -8 **75.** 3 **77.** 6 **79.** -2
81. not a real number   **83.** 2 **85.** not a real number   **87.** $\dfrac{4}{3}$

89. $-\dfrac{1}{2}$ **91.** 0.1

93.   **95.**

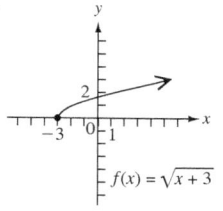
$f(x) = \sqrt{x + 3}$

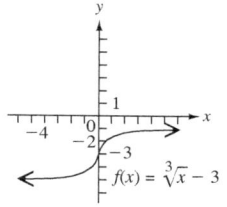
$f(x) = \sqrt{x} - 2$

domain: $[-3, \infty)$;   domain: $[0, \infty)$;
range: $[0, \infty)$ range: $[-2, \infty)$

97.   **99.**

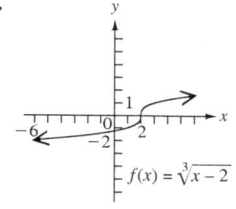
$f(x) = \sqrt[3]{x} - 3$

$f(x) = \sqrt[3]{x - 2}$

domain: $(-\infty, \infty)$;   domain: $(-\infty, \infty)$;
range: $(-\infty, \infty)$ range: $(-\infty, \infty)$

101. 12 **103.** 10 **105.** 2 **107.** -9 **109.** -5 **111.** $|x|$ **113.** $|z|$
115. x **117.** x^5 **119.** $|x^5|$ (or $|x|^5$)   **121.** 97.381 **123.** 16.863
125. -9.055 **127.** 7.507 **129.** 3.162 **131.** 1.885
133. (a) 1,183,000 cycles per sec   **(b)** 118,000 cycles per sec
135. 10 mi   **137.** $437{,}000 \text{ mi}^2$ **139.** 330 m^2 **141.** 1.732 amps

SECTION 10.2

1. C   **2.** E   **3.** A   **4.** J   **5.** H   **6.** G   **7.** B   **8.** F   **9.** D   **10.** I
11. 13 **13.** 9 **15.** 2 **17.** $\dfrac{8}{9}$ **19.** -3 **21.** not a real number

23. 1000 **25.** 27 **27.** -1024 **29.** 16 **31.** $\dfrac{1}{8}$ **33.** $\dfrac{1}{512}$ **35.** $\dfrac{9}{25}$

37. $\dfrac{27}{8}$ **39.** $\sqrt[3]{10}$ **41.** $\left(\sqrt[4]{8}\right)^3$ **43.** $5\left(\sqrt[3]{x}\right)^2$ **45.** $\left(\sqrt[8]{9q}\right)^5 - \left(\sqrt[3]{2x}\right)^2$

47. $\dfrac{1}{\left(\sqrt[5]{x}\right)^3}$ **49.** $\dfrac{1}{\left(\sqrt{2m}\right)^3}$ **51.** $\left(\sqrt[3]{2y + x}\right)^2$ **53.** $\dfrac{1}{\left(\sqrt[3]{3m^4 + 2k^2}\right)^2}$

55. $15^{1/2}$ **57.** 64 **59.** 64 **61.** x **63.** x^{10}
65. $\sqrt{a^2 + b^2} = \sqrt{3^2 + 4^2} = 5; a + b = 3 + 4 = 7; 5 \neq 7$
66. The statement is true for this particular choice of values for a and b.
However, it is not true *in general*. For example, let $a = 3$, $b = 4$, and $n = 2$.

67. 9 **69.** 4 **71.** y **73.** $x^{5/12}$ **75.** $k^{2/3}$ **77.** x^3y^8 **79.** $\dfrac{1}{x^{10/3}}$

81. $\dfrac{1}{m^{1/4}n^{3/4}}$ **83.** p^2 **85.** $\dfrac{c^{11/3}}{b^{11/4}}$ **87.** $\dfrac{q^{5/3}}{9p^{7/2}}$ **89.** $p + 2p^2$

91. $k^{7/4} - k^{3/4}$ **93.** $6 + 18a$ **95.** $5 + \dfrac{5}{m^3}$ **97.** $x^{17/20}$ **99.** $t^{8/15}$

101. $\dfrac{1}{k^{2/3}}$ **103.** $x^{1/3}z^{5/6}$ **105.** $m^{1/12}$ **107.** $y^{1/30}$ **109.** 72 in.; 6.0 ft

111. $-12.3°$; The table gives $-12°$. **113.** $4.2°$; The table gives $4°$.

115. (a) Windchill temperature $= 35.74 - 35.75V^{4/25}$

(b) $-24.1°$; The table gives $-24°$.

SECTION 10.3

1. D **2.** D **3.** B **4.** A **5.** D **6.** D **7.** The student "dropped" the index, 3. The correct product is $\sqrt[3]{65}$. **8.** Because there are only two factors of $\sqrt[3]{x}$, $\sqrt[3]{x} \cdot \sqrt[3]{x} = \left(\sqrt[3]{x}\right)^2$, or $\sqrt[3]{x^2}$. **9.** 3 **11.** 6 **13.** $\sqrt{30}$

15. $\sqrt{14x}$ **17.** $\sqrt{42pqr}$ **19.** $\sqrt[3]{14xy}$ **21.** $\sqrt[4]{33}$ **23.** $\sqrt[4]{6xy^2}$

25. This product cannot be found directly using the product rule.

27. This product cannot be found directly using the product rule.

29. $\dfrac{8}{11}$ **31.** $\dfrac{\sqrt{3}}{5}$ **33.** $\dfrac{\sqrt{x}}{5}$ **35.** $\dfrac{p^3}{9}$ **37.** $-\dfrac{3}{4}$ **39.** $\dfrac{\sqrt[3]{r^2}}{2}$ **41.** $-\dfrac{3}{x}$

43. $\dfrac{1}{x^3}$ **45.** $\sqrt{12}$ can be simplified further. The *greatest* perfect square factor that divides into 48 is 16, not 4. Thus, $\sqrt{48} = \sqrt{16 \cdot 3} = \sqrt{16} \cdot \sqrt{3} = 4\sqrt{3}$. **46.** It is not simplified because the power of k is greater than the index of the radical. The simplified form is $k\sqrt[3]{k}$.

47. $2\sqrt{3}$ **49.** $12\sqrt{2}$ **51.** $-4\sqrt{2}$ **53.** $-2\sqrt{7}$ **55.** This radical cannot be simplified further. **57.** $4\sqrt[3]{2}$ **59.** $2\sqrt[3]{5}$ **61.** $-2\sqrt[3]{2}$

63. $-4\sqrt[4]{2}$ **65.** $2\sqrt[5]{2}$ **67.** $6k\sqrt{2}$ **69.** $12xy^4\sqrt{xy}$ **71.** $11x^3$

73. $-3t^4$ **75.** $-10m^4z^2$ **77.** $5a^2b^3c^4$ **79.** $\dfrac{1}{2}r^2t^5$ **81.** $5x\sqrt{2x}$

83. $-10r^5\sqrt{5r}$ **85.** $x^3y^4\sqrt{13x}$ **87.** $2z^2w^3$ **89.** $-2zt^2\sqrt[3]{2z^2t}$

91. $3x^3y^4$ **93.** $-3r^3s^2\sqrt[4]{2r^3s^2}$ **95.** $\dfrac{y^5\sqrt{y}}{6}$ **97.** $\dfrac{x^5\sqrt[3]{x}}{3}$ **99.** $4\sqrt{3}$

101. $\sqrt[6]{5}$ **103.** $x^2\sqrt[4]{x}$ **105.** $x\sqrt[5]{x^3}$ **107.** $\sqrt[6]{432}$ **109.** $\sqrt[12]{6912}$

111. $\sqrt[6]{x^5}$ **113.** 5 **115.** $8\sqrt{2}$ **117.** $2\sqrt{14}$ **119.** 13 **121.** $9\sqrt{2}$

123. $\sqrt{17}$ **125.** 5 **127.** $6\sqrt{2}$ **129.** $\sqrt{5y^2 - 2xy + x^2}$ **131.** 42.0 in.

133. 0.003 **135. (a)** $d = 1.224\sqrt{h}$ **(b)** 15.3 mi **137.** $s = 13$ units

138. $6\sqrt{13}$ sq. units **139.** $h = \sqrt{13}$ units **140.** $3\sqrt{13}$ sq. units

141. $6\sqrt{13}$ sq. units **142.** The answers are equal, both $6\sqrt{13}$ sq. units, as expected.

SECTION 10.4

1. B **2.** C **3.** The terms 28 and $4\sqrt{2}$ are not like terms and cannot be combined. The expression $28 - 4\sqrt{2}$ cannot be simplified further.

4. The terms 3 and $3xy$ are not like terms and cannot be combined. The expression $(3 + 3xy)\sqrt[3]{xy^2}$ cannot be simplified further. **5.** -4

7. $8\sqrt{10}$ **9.** $-\sqrt{5}$ **11.** $7\sqrt{3}$ **13.** This expression cannot be simplified further. **15.** $14\sqrt[3]{2}$ **17.** $\sqrt[3]{2}$ **19.** $5\sqrt[4]{2}$ **21.** $19\sqrt[4]{2}$ **23.** $24\sqrt{2}$

25. $20\sqrt{5}$ **27.** $12\sqrt{2x}$ **29.** $-2m\sqrt{2}$ **31.** $2\sqrt[3]{x}$ **33.** $-\sqrt[3]{x^2y}$

35. $-x\sqrt[3]{xy^2}$ **37.** $x\sqrt[4]{xy}$ **39.** $9\sqrt[4]{2a^3}$ **41.** $(4 + 3xy)\sqrt[3]{xy^2}$

43. $4x\sqrt[3]{x} + 6x\sqrt[4]{x}$ **45.** $4t\sqrt[3]{3st} - 3s\sqrt{3st}$ **47.** $\dfrac{5\sqrt{5}}{6}$ **49.** $\dfrac{7\sqrt{2}}{6}$

51. $\dfrac{5\sqrt{2}}{3}$ **53.** $5\sqrt{2} + 4$ **55.** $\dfrac{30\sqrt{2} - 21}{14}$ **57.** $\dfrac{5 + 3x}{x^4}$ **59.** $\dfrac{m\sqrt[3]{m^2}}{2}$

61. $\dfrac{3x\sqrt[3]{2} - 4\sqrt[3]{5}}{x^3}$ **63.** $\left(12\sqrt{5} + 5\sqrt{3}\right)$ in. **65.** $\left(24\sqrt{2} + 12\sqrt{3}\right)$ in.

SECTION 10.5

1. E **2.** C **3.** A **4.** F **5.** D **6.** B **7.** $4\sqrt{3} + \sqrt{15}$ **9.** $6 - 4\sqrt{3}$

11. $20\sqrt{2}$ **13.** $6 - \sqrt{6}$ **15.** $3\sqrt{2} - 5\sqrt{3} + 2\sqrt{6} - 10$

17. $\sqrt{21} + \sqrt{14} - 5\sqrt{3} - 5\sqrt{2}$ **19.** 2 **21.** -1 **23.** $3x - 4$

25. $9 + 4\sqrt{5}$ **27.** $16x + 24\sqrt{x} + 9$ **29.** $81 - \sqrt[3]{4}$ **31.** $4x - y$

33. Because 6 and $4\sqrt{3}$ are not like terms, they cannot be combined. The expression $6 - 4\sqrt{3}$ cannot be simplified further.

34. In the denominator, $\sqrt[3]{2} \cdot \sqrt[3]{2} = \sqrt[3]{4}$, so the denominator is not rationalized. Multiply numerator and denominator by $\sqrt[3]{2^2}$, or $\sqrt[3]{4}$. Thus,

$\dfrac{5}{\sqrt[3]{2}} = \dfrac{5 \cdot \sqrt[3]{4}}{\sqrt[3]{2} \cdot \sqrt[3]{4}} = \dfrac{5\sqrt[3]{4}}{\sqrt[3]{8}} = \dfrac{5\sqrt[3]{4}}{2}$. **35.** $\sqrt{7}$ **37.** $5\sqrt{3}$ **39.** $\dfrac{\sqrt{6}}{2}$

41. $\dfrac{9\sqrt{15}}{5}$ **43.** $-\sqrt{2}$ **45.** $\dfrac{\sqrt{14}}{2}$ **47.** $-\dfrac{\sqrt{14}}{10}$ **49.** $\dfrac{2\sqrt{6x}}{x}$

51. $-\dfrac{7r\sqrt{2rs}}{s}$ **53.** $\dfrac{12x^3\sqrt{2xy}}{y^5}$ **55.** $\dfrac{\sqrt[3]{18}}{3}$ **57.** $\dfrac{\sqrt[3]{12}}{3}$ **59.** $-\dfrac{\sqrt[3]{2pr}}{r}$

61. $\dfrac{2\sqrt[4]{x^3}}{x}$ **63.** $\dfrac{\sqrt[4]{2yz^3}}{z}$ **65.** $\dfrac{3(4 - \sqrt{5})}{11}$ **67.** $3\left(\sqrt{5} - \sqrt{3}\right)$

69. $\sqrt{3} + \sqrt{7}$ **71.** $\sqrt{7} - \sqrt{6} - \sqrt{14} + 2\sqrt{3}$

73. $2\sqrt{3} + \sqrt{10} - 3\sqrt{2} - \sqrt{15}$ **75.** $\dfrac{4(\sqrt{x} + 2\sqrt{y})}{x - 4y}$ **77.** $\dfrac{5 + 2\sqrt{6}}{4}$

79. $3 - 2\sqrt{6}$ **81.** $\dfrac{4 - 2\sqrt{2}}{3}$ **83.** $\dfrac{6 + 2\sqrt{6x}}{3}$ **85.** $\dfrac{33}{8(6 + \sqrt{3})}$

86. $\dfrac{11}{2(2\sqrt{5} + 3)}$ **87.** $\dfrac{4x - y}{3x(2\sqrt{x} + \sqrt{y})}$ **88.** $\dfrac{p - 9q}{4q(\sqrt{p} + 3\sqrt{q})}$

SUMMARY EXERCISES   Performing Operations with Radicals and Rational Exponents

1. The radicand is a fraction, $\dfrac{2}{5}$. **2.** The exponent in the radicand and the index of the radical have greatest common factor 5. **3.** The denominator contains a radical, $\sqrt[3]{10}$. **4.** The radicand has two factors x and y, that are raised to powers greater than the index, 3. **5.** $-6\sqrt{10}$ **6.** $7 - \sqrt{14}$

7. $\dfrac{-\sqrt{6}}{2}$ **8.** $4\left(\sqrt{7} - \sqrt{5}\right)$ **9.** $2 + \sqrt{6} - 2\sqrt{3} - 3\sqrt{2}$ **10.** $4\sqrt{2}$

11. $73 + 12\sqrt{35}$ **12.** $-\sqrt[3]{2x^2}$ **13.** $-3 + 2\sqrt{2}$ **14.** -44

15. $\dfrac{\sqrt{x} + \sqrt{5}}{x - 5}$ **16.** $2abc^3\sqrt[3]{b^2}$ **17.** $5\sqrt[3]{3}$ **18.** $3\left(\sqrt{5} - 2\right)$

19. $\dfrac{\sqrt{15x}}{5x}$ **20.** $\dfrac{8}{5}$ **21.** $\dfrac{\sqrt{2}}{8}$ **22.** $-\sqrt[3]{100}$ **23.** $11 + 2\sqrt{30}$

24. $-3\sqrt{3x}$ **25.** $52 - 30\sqrt{3}$ **26.** 1 **27.** $\dfrac{\sqrt[3]{117}}{9}$ **28.** $t^2\sqrt[4]{t}$

29. $3\sqrt{2} + \sqrt{15} + \sqrt{42} + \sqrt{35}$ **30.** $2\sqrt[4]{27}$ **31.** $-4\sqrt{3} - 3$

32. $6\sqrt{7} + 6\sqrt{5} - \sqrt{35} - 5$ **33.** $3^{5/6}$ **34.** $\dfrac{x^{5/3}}{y}$ **35.** $xy^{6/5}$ **36.** $x^{10}y$

37. $\dfrac{1}{25x^2}$ **38.** $\dfrac{-6y^{1/6}}{x^{1/24}}$ **39.** $24\sqrt{3}$ m; 96 m² **40.** $36\sqrt{3}$ in.²

SECTION 10.6

1. (a) yes **(b)** no **2. (a)** yes **(b)** yes **3. (a)** yes **(b)** no

4. (a) yes **(b)** yes **5.** There is no solution. The radical expression, which is nonnegative, cannot equal a negative number. The solution set is $\varnothing$.

6. The proposed solution -3 is extraneous. Because the radical on the left side cannot be negative, and it must equal x, x cannot be negative. The solution set is $\{6\}$. **7.** $\{11\}$ **9.** $\left\{\dfrac{1}{3}\right\}$ **11.** $\varnothing$ **13.** $\{5\}$ **15.** $\{18\}$ **17.** $\{5\}$ **19.** $\{4\}$ **21.** $\{17\}$ **23.** $\{5\}$ **25.** $\varnothing$ **27.** $\{0\}$ **29.** $\{1\}$ **31.** $\{-1, 3\}$ **33.** $\{0\}$ **35.** $\{8\}$ **37.** $\varnothing$ **39.** We cannot just square each term. The right side should be $(8 - x)^2 = 64 - 16x + x^2$. The correct first step is $3x + 4 = 64 - 16x + x^2$. The solution set is $\{4\}$.

40. We cannot just square each term. The right side should be $x + 3 + 2\sqrt{x + 3} \cdot 3 + 9$. The correct first step is $5x + 6 = x + 3 + 2\sqrt{x + 3} \cdot 3 + 9$. The solution set is $\{6\}$.

41. $\{7\}$ **43.** $\{7\}$ **45.** $\{4, 20\}$ **47.** $\varnothing$ **49.** $\left\{\dfrac{5}{4}\right\}$ **51.** $\{9\}$ **53.** $\{1\}$ **55.** $\{14\}$ **57.** $\{-1\}$ **59.** $\{8\}$ **61.** $\{5\}$ **63.** $\{0\}$ **65.** $\varnothing$ **67.** $\{-4\}$ **69.** $\{9, 17\}$ **71.** $\left\{\dfrac{1}{4}, 1\right\}$ **73.** $L = CZ^2$ **75.** $K = \dfrac{V^2 m}{2}$ **77.** $M = \dfrac{r^2 F}{m}$ **79. (a)** $r = \dfrac{a}{4\pi^2 N^2}$ **(b)** $a = 4\pi^2 N^2 r$

SECTION 10.7

1. nonreal complex, complex **2.** pure imaginary, nonreal complex, complex **3.** real, complex **4.** real, complex **5.** pure imaginary, nonreal complex, complex **6.** pure imaginary, nonreal complex, complex **7.** i **8.** $-i$ **9.** -1 **10.** 1 **11.** $-i$ **12.** -1 **13.** $13i$ **15.** $-12i$ **17.** $i\sqrt{5}$ **19.** $4i\sqrt{3}$ **21.** -15 **23.** $-\sqrt{105}$ **25.** -10 **27.** $i\sqrt{33}$ **29.** $\sqrt{3}$ **31.** $5i$ **33.** $-1 + 7i$ **35.** 0 **37.** $7 + 3i$ **39.** -2 **41.** $1 + 13i$ **43.** $6 + 6i$ **45.** $4 + 2i$ **46.** -5 **47.** -81 **49.** -16 **51.** $-10 - 30i$ **53.** $-10 + 6i$ **55.** $10 - 5i$ **57.** $1 - 17i$ **59.** $-9 + 40i$ **61.** 53 **63. (a)** $a - bi$ **(b)** $a^2; b^2$ **64.** C **65.** $1 + i$ **67.** $-1 + 2i$ **69.** $2 + 2i$ **71.** $-\dfrac{5}{13} - \dfrac{12}{13}i$ **73.** $-1 - 3i$ **75.** $-5 + 2i$ **77.** -1 **79.** i **81.** 1 **83.** $-i$ **85.** $-i$ **87.** 1 **89.** $\dfrac{1}{2} + \dfrac{1}{2}i$

91. Substitute $1 + 5i$ for x in the equation. A true statement results—that is, $(1 + 5i)^2 - 2(1 + 5i) + 26$ will simplify to 0 when the operations are applied. Thus, $1 + 5i$ is a solution. **92.** Substituting $1 - 5i$ for x in the equation results in a true statement, indicating that $1 - 5i$ is a solution. **93.** They are complex conjugates. **94.** Substituting $3 + 2i$ for x in the equation results in a true statement, indicating that $3 + 2i$ is a solution. **95.** $3 - 2i$; Substituting $3 - 2i$ for x in the equation results in a true statement, indicating that $3 - 2i$ is a solution.

Chapter 10 REVIEW EXERCISES

1. 12 **2.** -17 **3.** not a real number **4.** 6 **5.** -2 **6.** $|x|$ **7.** x **8.** $|x|^5$ (or $|x^5|$)

9.

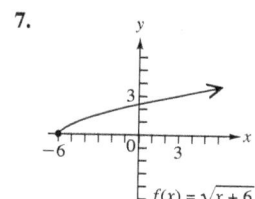

domain: $[1, \infty)$;
range: $[0, \infty)$

10.

domain: $(-\infty, \infty)$;
range: $(-\infty, \infty)$

11. 6.325 **12.** 8.775 **13.** 17.607 **14.** n must be even, and a must be negative. **15.** 1.9 sec **16.** 66 in.² **17.** 7 **18.** -2 **19.** not a real number **20.** 32 **21.** -4 **22.** $\dfrac{216}{125}$ **23.** -32 **24.** $\dfrac{1000}{27}$ **25.** 3^9 **26.** 7^3, or 343 **27.** $\sqrt[15]{y^8}$ **28.** $\sqrt[12]{y^5}$ **29.** 25 **30.** 96 **31.** $a^{2/3}$ **32.** $\dfrac{1}{y^{1/2}}$ **33.** $\dfrac{z^{1/2} x^{8/5}}{4}$ **34.** $r^{1/2} + r$ **35.** $s^{1/2}$ **36.** $r^{3/2}$ **37.** $p^{1/2}$ **38.** $k^{9/4}$ **39.** $m^{13/3}$ **40.** $z^{1/12}$ **41.** $\sqrt{66}$ **42.** $\sqrt{5r}$ **43.** $\sqrt[3]{30}$ **44.** $\sqrt[4]{21}$ **45.** $2\sqrt{5}$ **46.** $-5\sqrt{5}$ **47.** $-3x\sqrt[3]{4xy}$ **48.** $4pq^2\sqrt[3]{p}$ **49.** $\dfrac{7}{9}$ **50.** $\dfrac{y\sqrt{y}}{12}$ **51.** $\dfrac{m^5}{3}$ **52.** $\dfrac{\sqrt[3]{r^2}}{2}$ **53.** $\sqrt[12]{2}$ **54.** $\sqrt[10]{x^3}$ **55.** $\sqrt[4]{200}$ **56.** $\sqrt[6]{1125}$ **57.** $\sqrt{130}$ **58.** $\sqrt{53}$ **59.** $-11\sqrt{2}$ **60.** $23\sqrt{5}$ **61.** $7\sqrt{3y}$ **62.** $26m\sqrt{6m}$ **63.** $19\sqrt[3]{2}$ **64.** $-8\sqrt[4]{2}$ **65.** $-3\sqrt{5}$ **66.** $1 - \sqrt{3}$ **67.** 2 **68.** $9 - 7\sqrt{2}$ **69.** $17 - 4\sqrt{13}$ **70.** $12 + 2\sqrt{35}$ **71.** $\dfrac{\sqrt{30}}{5}$ **72.** $-3\sqrt{6}$ **73.** $-\dfrac{\sqrt[3]{45}}{5}$ **74.** $\dfrac{3m\sqrt[3]{4n}}{n^2}$ **75.** $\dfrac{\sqrt{2} - \sqrt{7}}{-5}$ **76.** $\dfrac{5(\sqrt{6} + 3)}{3}$ **77.** $\dfrac{1 - \sqrt{5}}{4}$ **78.** $\dfrac{-6 + \sqrt{3}}{2}$ **79.** $\{2\}$ **80.** $\{6\}$ **81.** $\varnothing$ **82.** $\{0, 5\}$ **83.** $\{9\}$ **84.** $\{3\}$ **85.** $\{7\}$ **86.** $\left\{-\dfrac{1}{2}\right\}$ **87.** $\{6\}$ **88.** $5i$ **89.** $10i\sqrt{2}$ **90.** $4i\sqrt{10}$ **91.** $10 - 2i$ **92.** $14 + 7i$ **93.** $-\sqrt{35}$ **94.** -45 **95.** 3 **96.** $5 + i$ **97.** $32 - 24i$ **98.** $1 - i$ **99.** $-i$ **100.** 1 **101.** $-i$ **102.** -1

Chapter 10 MIXED REVIEW EXERCISES

1. $-13ab^2$ **2.** $\dfrac{1}{100}$ **3.** $\dfrac{1}{y^{1/2}}$ **4.** $\dfrac{x^{3/4}}{z^{3/4}}$ **5.** k^6 **6.** $3z^3t^2\sqrt[3]{2t^2}$ **7.** $35 + 15i$ **8.** $\sqrt[12]{2000}$ **9.** $49a - 70\sqrt{a} + 25$ **10.** $57\sqrt{2}$ **11.** $6x\sqrt[3]{y^2}$ **12.** $\sqrt{35} + \sqrt{15} - \sqrt{21} - 3$ **13.** $-\dfrac{\sqrt{3}}{6}$ **14.** $\dfrac{\sqrt[3]{60}}{5}$ **15.** $\dfrac{2\sqrt{z}(\sqrt{z} + 2)}{z - 4}$ **16.** $7i$ **17.** $3 - 7i$ **18.** $-5i$ **19.** $\{5\}$ **20.** $\left\{\dfrac{3}{2}\right\}$ **21. (a)** $H = \sqrt{L^2 - W^2}$ **(b)** 7.9 ft **22.** $\left(12\sqrt{3} + 5\sqrt{2}\right)$ ft

Chapter 10 TEST

1. -29 **2.** -8 **3.** 5 **4.** C **5.** 21.863 **6.** -9.405
7.

$f(x) = \sqrt{x + 6}$

domain: $[-6, \infty)$;
range: $[0, \infty)$

8. $\sqrt{145}$ **9.** $\dfrac{1}{256}$ **10.** $\dfrac{125}{64}$ **11.** $7^{1/2}$, or $\sqrt{7}$ **12.** $x^{4/3} y^6$ **13.** $\dfrac{9y^{3/10}}{x^2}$ **14.** $3x^2 y^3\sqrt{6x}$ **15.** $2ab^3\sqrt[4]{2a^3b}$ **16.** $\sqrt[6]{200}$ **17.** $40\sqrt{3}$ **18.** $26\sqrt{5}$ **19.** $66 + \sqrt{5}$ **20.** $23 - 4\sqrt{15}$ **21.** $\dfrac{-\sqrt{10}}{4}$ **22.** $\dfrac{2\sqrt[3]{25}}{5}$ **23.** $-2\left(\sqrt{7} - \sqrt{5}\right)$ **24.** $3 + \sqrt{6}$ **25.** $\sqrt{26}$ **26.** $\{-1\}$ **27.** $\{6\}$ **28.** $\{-3\}$ **29. (a)** 59.8 **(b)** $T = \dfrac{V_0^2 - V^2}{-V^2 k}$, or $T = \dfrac{V^2 - V_0^2}{V^2 k}$ **30.** $-5 - 8i$ **31.** $-10 + 10i$ **32.** $3 + 4i$ **33.** $-i$ **34. (a)** true **(b)** true **(c)** false **(d)** true

Chapters R–10 CUMULATIVE REVIEW EXERCISES

1. $\left\{\dfrac{4}{5}\right\}$ **2.** $\{-12\}$ **3.** $\left\{\dfrac{11}{10},\dfrac{7}{2}\right\}$ **4.** $(-6,\infty)$ **5.** $(1,3)$ **6.** $(-2,1)$

7. $12x+11y=18$ **8.** C **9.** x-intercept: $(2,0)$; y-intercept: $(0,6)$

10. -3

11.

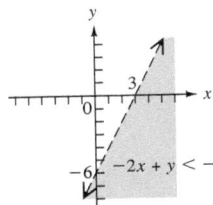

12. Both angles measure $80°$.
13. $\{(7,-2)\}$ **14.** $\varnothing$
15. $\{(x,y,z)\mid 2x+y-z=5\}$
16. 2-oz letter: 0.65; 3-oz letter: 0.85
17. $-k^3-3k^2-8k-9$
18. $8x^2+17x-21$ **19.** $z-2+\dfrac{3}{z}$

20. $3y^3-3y^2+4y+1+\dfrac{-10}{2y+1}$ **21.** $(2p-3q)(p-q)$

22. $(3k^2+4)(6k^2-5)$ **23.** $(x+8)(x^2-8x+64)$ **24.** $\dfrac{y}{y+5}$

25. $\dfrac{4x+2y}{(x+y)(x-y)}$ **26.** $\dfrac{x-6}{x-2}$ **27.** $-\dfrac{9}{4}$ **28.** $-\dfrac{1}{a+b}$ **29.** $\dfrac{3}{2r^2s^2}$

30. $\dfrac{1}{243}$ **31.** $x^{1/12}$ **32.** $8\sqrt5$ **33.** $\dfrac{-9\sqrt5}{20}$ **34.** $4\left(\sqrt6+\sqrt5\right)$

35. $6\sqrt[3]{4}$ **36.** $\sqrt{29}$ **37.** $\left\{-3,-\dfrac{5}{2}\right\}$ **38.** $\left\{-\dfrac{2}{5},1\right\}$ **39.** $\left\{\dfrac{7}{2}\right\}$

40. $\{6\}$ **41.** 15 mph **42.** $\dfrac{80}{39}$ L, or $2\dfrac{2}{39}$ L

43. dimes: 17; quarters: 12 **44.** Brenda: 8 mph; Chuck: 4 mph

CHAPTER 11 Quadratic Equations, Inequalities, and Functions

SECTION 11.1

1. B, C **2.** B **3.** C **4.** A **5.** D **6.** B **7.** According to the square root property, -9 is also a solution, so her answer was not completely correct. The solution set is $\{-9,9\}$, or $\{\pm9\}$. **8.** The fractions cannot be simplified because 2 is *not* a common factor in the numerator. The correct solution set is $\left\{\dfrac{3+2\sqrt5}{2},\dfrac{3-2\sqrt5}{2}\right\}$. **9.** $\{-7,8\}$

11. $\{3,5\}$ **13.** $\{-11,11\}$ **15.** $\left\{-\dfrac{5}{3},6\right\}$ **17.** $\{-9,9\}$

19. $\left\{-\sqrt{14},\sqrt{14}\right\}$ **21.** $\left\{-4\sqrt3,4\sqrt3\right\}$ **23.** $\left\{-\dfrac{5}{2},\dfrac{5}{2}\right\}$

25. $\{-0.5,0.5\}$ **27.** $\{-8,8\}$ **29.** $\left\{-\sqrt3,\sqrt3\right\}$ **31.** $\left\{-3\sqrt2,3\sqrt2\right\}$

33. $\left\{-3\sqrt3,3\sqrt3\right\}$ **35.** $\left\{-2\sqrt6,2\sqrt6\right\}$ **37.** $\left\{-\dfrac{2\sqrt7}{7},\dfrac{2\sqrt7}{7}\right\}$

39. $\left\{-\dfrac{2\sqrt5}{5},\dfrac{2\sqrt5}{5}\right\}$ **41.** $\{-2,8\}$ **43.** $\{-1,13\}$

45. $\left\{4+\sqrt3,4-\sqrt3\right\}$ **47.** $\left\{8+3\sqrt3,8-3\sqrt3\right\}$

49. $\left\{-3,\dfrac{5}{3}\right\}$ **51.** $\left\{0,\dfrac{3}{2}\right\}$ **53.** $\left\{\dfrac{5+\sqrt{30}}{2},\dfrac{5-\sqrt{30}}{2}\right\}$

55. $\left\{\dfrac{-1+3\sqrt2}{3},\dfrac{-1-3\sqrt2}{3}\right\}$ **57.** $\left\{\dfrac{1+4\sqrt3}{4},\dfrac{1-4\sqrt3}{4}\right\}$

59. $\{10i,-10i\}$ **61.** $\left\{2i\sqrt3,-2i\sqrt3\right\}$ **63.** $\{-3+2i,-3-2i\}$

65. $\left\{5+i\sqrt3,5-i\sqrt3\right\}$ **67.** $\left\{\dfrac{1}{6}+\dfrac{\sqrt2}{3}i,\dfrac{1}{6}-\dfrac{\sqrt2}{3}i\right\}$

69. 5.6 sec **71.** $\dfrac{1}{2}$ sec **73.** 9 in.

SECTION 11.2

1. square root property for $(2x+1)^2=5$; completing the square for $x^2+4x=12$ **2.** Divide each side by 2. **3.** 9; $(x+3)^2$
4. 49; $(x+7)^2$ **5.** 36; $(p-6)^2$ **6.** 100; $(x-10)^2$
7. $\dfrac{81}{4}$; $\left(q+\dfrac{9}{2}\right)^2$ **8.** $\dfrac{9}{4}$; $\left(t+\dfrac{3}{2}\right)^2$ **9.** $\{-3,-2\}$ **11.** $\{1,3\}$
13. $\left\{-1+\sqrt6,-1-\sqrt6\right\}$ **15.** $\left\{-5+\sqrt7,-5-\sqrt7\right\}$
17. $\left\{4+2\sqrt3,4-2\sqrt3\right\}$ **19.** $\left\{\dfrac{-1+\sqrt5}{2},\dfrac{-1-\sqrt5}{2}\right\}$
21. $\left\{\dfrac{3+\sqrt{17}}{2},\dfrac{3-\sqrt{17}}{2}\right\}$ **23.** $\left\{-\dfrac{8}{3},3\right\}$ **25.** $\left\{-\dfrac{3}{2},\dfrac{1}{2}\right\}$
27. $\left\{\dfrac{-5+\sqrt{41}}{4},\dfrac{-5-\sqrt{41}}{4}\right\}$ **29.** $\left\{\dfrac{-7+\sqrt{97}}{6},\dfrac{-7-\sqrt{97}}{6}\right\}$
31. $\left\{\dfrac{5+\sqrt{15}}{5},\dfrac{5-\sqrt{15}}{5}\right\}$ **33.** $\left\{\dfrac{2+\sqrt{10}}{2},\dfrac{2-\sqrt{10}}{2}\right\}$
35. $\{-4,2\}$ **37.** $\left\{4+\sqrt3,4-\sqrt3\right\}$ **39.** $\left\{\dfrac{3+\sqrt{13}}{2},\dfrac{3-\sqrt{13}}{2}\right\}$
41. $\{-2+3i,-2-3i\}$ **43.** $\left\{-3+i\sqrt3,-3-i\sqrt3\right\}$
45. $\left\{-\dfrac{5}{2}+\dfrac{\sqrt{15}}{2}i,-\dfrac{5}{2}-\dfrac{\sqrt{15}}{2}i\right\}$ **47.** $\left\{-\dfrac{2}{3}+\dfrac{2\sqrt2}{3}i,-\dfrac{2}{3}-\dfrac{2\sqrt2}{3}i\right\}$
49. x^2 **50.** x^2+8x **51.** $x^2+8x+16$
52. It occurred when we added the 16 squares.

SECTION 11.3

1. No. The fraction bar should extend under the term $-b$. The correct formula is $x=\dfrac{-b\pm\sqrt{b^2-4ac}}{2a}$. **2.** No. The patron forgot the $\pm$ symbol in the numerator. (See the correct formula in the **Exercise 1** answer.) **3.** The last step is wrong. Because 5 is not a common factor of the terms in the numerator, the fraction cannot be simplified further. The solution set is $\left\{\dfrac{5+\sqrt5}{10},\dfrac{5-\sqrt5}{10}\right\}$. **4.** The quadratic formula can be used to solve *any* quadratic equation. The equation can be written as $2x^2+0x-5=0$, so it follows that $a=2$, $b=0$, and $c=-5$. The solution set is $\left\{\dfrac{\sqrt{10}}{2},-\dfrac{\sqrt{10}}{2}\right\}$. **5.** $\{3,5\}$ **7.** $\left\{-\dfrac{5}{2},\dfrac{2}{3}\right\}$ **9.** $\left\{-\dfrac{3}{2}\right\}$ **11.** $\left\{\dfrac{1}{6}\right\}$

13. $\left\{\dfrac{-2+\sqrt2}{2},\dfrac{-2-\sqrt2}{2}\right\}$ **15.** $\left\{\dfrac{1+\sqrt3}{2},\dfrac{1-\sqrt3}{2}\right\}$

17. $\left\{5+\sqrt7,5-\sqrt7\right\}$ **19.** $\left\{\dfrac{-1+\sqrt2}{2},\dfrac{-1-\sqrt2}{2}\right\}$

21. $\left\{\dfrac{-1+\sqrt7}{3},\dfrac{-1-\sqrt7}{3}\right\}$ **23.** $\left\{1+\sqrt5,1-\sqrt5\right\}$

25. $\left\{\dfrac{-2+\sqrt{10}}{2},\dfrac{-2-\sqrt{10}}{2}\right\}$ **27.** $\left\{-1+3\sqrt2,-1-3\sqrt2\right\}$

29. $\left\{3+i\sqrt5,3-i\sqrt5\right\}$ **31.** $\left\{\dfrac{3}{2}+\dfrac{\sqrt{59}}{2}i,\dfrac{3}{2}-\dfrac{\sqrt{59}}{2}i\right\}$

33. $\left\{\frac{1}{2} + \frac{\sqrt{6}}{2}i, \frac{1}{2} - \frac{\sqrt{6}}{2}i\right\}$ **35.** $\left\{-\frac{2}{3} + \frac{\sqrt{2}}{3}i, -\frac{2}{3} - \frac{\sqrt{2}}{3}i\right\}$

37. $\left\{\frac{1}{2} + \frac{1}{4}i, \frac{1}{2} - \frac{1}{4}i\right\}$ **39.** 0; C; zero-factor property

41. 8; B; quadratic formula **43.** 49; A; zero-factor property

45. -80; D; quadratic formula **47.** $\left\{-\frac{7}{5}\right\}$

49. $\left\{-2 + \sqrt{2}, -2 - \sqrt{2}\right\}$

SECTION 11.4

1. Multiply by the LCD, x. **2.** Isolate the radical term on one side.
3. Substitute a variable for $r^2 + r$. **4.** Square each side.
5. The proposed solution -1 does not check. The solution set is $\{4\}$.
6. The solutions given are for u. Each must be set equal to $m - 1$ and
solved for m. The solution set is $\left\{\frac{3}{2}, 2\right\}$. **7.** $\{-4, 7\}$ **9.** $\left\{-\frac{2}{3}, 1\right\}$

11. $\left\{-\frac{14}{17}, 5\right\}$ **13.** $\left\{-\frac{11}{7}, 0\right\}$ **15.** $\left\{\frac{-1 + \sqrt{13}}{2}, \frac{-1 - \sqrt{13}}{2}\right\}$

17. $\left\{\frac{2 + \sqrt{22}}{3}, \frac{2 - \sqrt{22}}{3}\right\}$ **19. (a)** $(20 - t)$ mph **(b)** $(20 + t)$ mph

20. (a) $\frac{1}{m}$ job per hr **(b)** $\frac{2}{m}$ job **21.** table entries: (third column)
$x + 15$; (fourth column) $\frac{4}{x - 15}, \frac{16}{x + 15}$; 25 mph **23.** 80 km per hr

25. table entries: (second column) $\frac{1}{x + 1}$; (fourth column) $\frac{2}{x}, \frac{2}{x + 1}$; 3.6 hr

27. Rusty: 25.0 hr; Nancy: 23.0 hr **29.** 9 min **31.** $\{1, 4\}$ **33.** $\{3\}$

35. $\left\{\frac{8}{9}\right\}$ **37.** $\{9\}$ **39.** $\left\{\frac{2}{5}\right\}$ **41.** $\{-2\}$ **43.** $\{-5, -2, 2, 5\}$

45. $\{-3, 3\}$ **47.** $\left\{-\frac{3}{2}, -1, 1, \frac{3}{2}\right\}$ **49.** $\left\{-2\sqrt{3}, -2, 2, 2\sqrt{3}\right\}$

51. $\left\{\frac{\sqrt{9 + \sqrt{65}}}{2}, -\frac{\sqrt{9 + \sqrt{65}}}{2}, \frac{\sqrt{9 - \sqrt{65}}}{2}, -\frac{\sqrt{9 - \sqrt{65}}}{2}\right\}$

53. $\{-6, -5\}$ **55.** $\left\{-\frac{16}{3}, -2\right\}$ **57.** $\left\{-\frac{1}{3}, \frac{1}{6}\right\}$ **59.** $\{-8, 1\}$

61. $\{-64, 27\}$ **63.** $\left\{-\frac{27}{8}, -1, 1, \frac{27}{8}\right\}$

SUMMARY EXERCISES Applying Methods for Solving Quadratic Equations

1. square root property **2.** zero-factor property **3.** quadratic formula
4. quadratic formula **5.** zero-factor property **6.** square root property
7. $\left\{\sqrt{7}, -\sqrt{7}\right\}$ **8.** $\left\{-\frac{3}{2}, \frac{5}{3}\right\}$ **9.** $\left\{-4 + \sqrt{10}, -4 - \sqrt{10}\right\}$

10. $\{-3, 11\}$ **11.** $\left\{-\frac{1}{2}, 5\right\}$ **12.** $\left\{-3, \frac{1}{3}\right\}$

13. $\left\{\frac{9 + \sqrt{33}}{6}, \frac{9 - \sqrt{33}}{6}\right\}$ **14.** $\left\{2i\sqrt{3}, -2i\sqrt{3}\right\}$ **15.** $\left\{\frac{1}{2}, 2\right\}$

16. $\left\{-\frac{\sqrt{6}}{3}, -\frac{1}{2}, \frac{1}{2}, \frac{\sqrt{6}}{3}\right\}$ **17.** $\left\{\frac{-5 + 2\sqrt{3}}{2}, \frac{-5 - 2\sqrt{3}}{2}\right\}$

18. $\left\{\frac{4}{5}, 3\right\}$ **19.** $\left\{-\sqrt{7}, -\sqrt{2}, \sqrt{2}, \sqrt{7}\right\}$

20. $\left\{\frac{-2 + \sqrt{14}}{2}, \frac{-2 - \sqrt{14}}{2}\right\}$ **21.** $\left\{-\frac{1}{2} + \frac{\sqrt{7}}{2}i, -\frac{1}{2} - \frac{\sqrt{7}}{2}i\right\}$

22. $\left\{\sqrt{4 + \sqrt{15}}, -\sqrt{4 + \sqrt{15}}, \sqrt{4 - \sqrt{15}}, -\sqrt{4 - \sqrt{15}}\right\}$

23. $\left\{\frac{3}{2}\right\}$ **24.** $\left\{\frac{2}{3}\right\}$ **25.** $\left\{6\sqrt{2}, -6\sqrt{2}\right\}$ **26.** $\left\{-\frac{2}{3}, 2\right\}$

27. $\{-4, 9\}$ **28.** $\{13, -13\}$ **29.** $\left\{1 + \frac{\sqrt{3}}{3}i, 1 - \frac{\sqrt{3}}{3}i\right\}$

30. $\{3\}$ **31.** $\left\{-\frac{1}{3}, \frac{1}{6}\right\}$ **32.** $\left\{\frac{1}{6} + \frac{\sqrt{47}}{6}i, \frac{1}{6} - \frac{\sqrt{47}}{6}i\right\}$

33. $\{3\}$ **34.** $\left\{-\frac{8}{3}, -1\right\}$ **35.** $\left\{-i, i, -\frac{1}{2}i, \frac{1}{2}i\right\}$ **36.** $\{-2, 7\}$

SECTION 11.5

1. Solve for w^2 by dividing each side by g. **2.** Write it in standard form
(with 0 on one side, in descending powers of w). **3.** $m = \sqrt{p^2 - n^2}$

5. $t = \frac{\pm \sqrt{dk}}{k}$ **7.** $d = \frac{\pm \sqrt{skw}}{kw}$ **9.** $d = \frac{\pm \sqrt{skI}}{I}$ **11.** $v = \frac{\pm \sqrt{kAF}}{F}$

13. $r = \frac{\pm \sqrt{V\pi h}}{\pi h}$ **15.** $t = \frac{-B \pm \sqrt{B^2 - 4AC}}{2A}$ **17.** $h = \frac{D^2}{k}$

19. $\ell = \frac{p^2 g}{k}$ **21.** 2.3, 5.3, 5.8 **23.** eastbound ship: 80 mi; southbound
ship: 150 mi **25.** 8 in., 15 in., 17 in. **27.** length: 24 ft; width: 10 ft
29. 2 ft **31.** length: 26 m; width: 16 m **33.** 20 in. by 12 in.
35. 1 sec and 8 sec **37.** 9.2 sec **39.** It reaches its *maximum* height at
5 sec because this is the only time it reaches 400 ft. **40.** Because the
discriminant is negative, the ball never reaches a height of 425 ft.
41. $1.50 **43. (a)** $560 billion **(b)** $560 billion **(c)** They are the same.
45. 2008 **47.** 5.5 m per sec **49.** 5 or 14 **51.** isosceles triangle;
right triangle **52.** no; The formula for the Pythagorean theorem involves
the *squares* of the sides, not the square roots.

53.

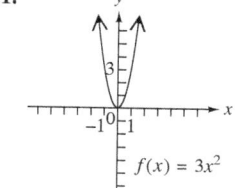

$\sqrt{9} + \sqrt{9} = 3 + 3 = 6$;
$\sqrt{4} = 2$;
$6 \neq 2$

54. The sum of the squares of the two shorter sides (legs) of a right
triangle is equal to the square of the longest side (hypotenuse).

SECTION 11.6

1. (a) B **(b)** C **(c)** A **(d)** D **2. (a)** D **(b)** C **(c)** B **(d)** A
3. (a) I **(b)** IV **(c)** II **(d)** III **(e)** up **(f)** down **(g)** narrower
(h) wider **4. (a)** D **(b)** B **(c)** F **(d)** C **(e)** A **(f)** E **5.** $(0, 0)$
7. $(0, 4)$ **9.** $(1, 0)$ **11.** $(-3, -4)$ **13.** $(5, 6)$ **15.** down; wider
17. up; narrower **19.** down; narrower

21.

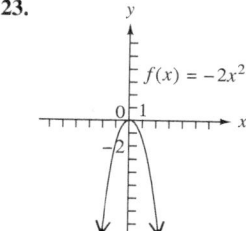

$f(x) = 3x^2$

23.

$f(x) = -2x^2$

vertex: $(0, 0)$; axis: $x = 0$;
domain: $(-\infty, \infty)$; range: $[0, \infty)$

vertex: $(0, 0)$; axis: $x = 0$;
domain: $(-\infty, \infty)$; range: $(-\infty, 0]$

ANSWERS

25.

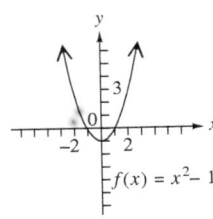

vertex: $(0, -1)$; axis: $x = 0$;
domain: $(-\infty, \infty)$; range: $[-1, \infty)$

27.

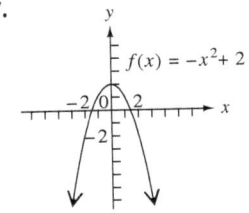

vertex: $(0, 2)$; axis: $x = 0$;
domain: $(-\infty, \infty)$; range: $(-\infty, 2]$

29.

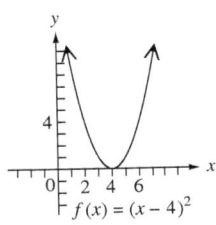

vertex: $(4, 0)$; axis: $x = 4$;
domain: $(-\infty, \infty)$; range: $[0, \infty)$

31.

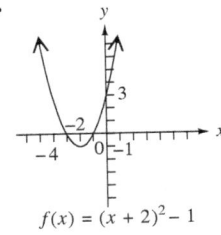

vertex: $(-2, -1)$; axis: $x = -2$;
domain: $(-\infty, \infty)$; range: $[-1, \infty)$

33.

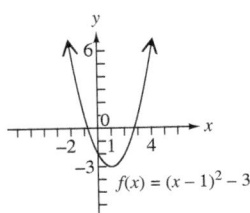

vertex: $(1, -3)$; axis: $x = 1$;
domain: $(-\infty, \infty)$; range: $[-3, \infty)$

35.

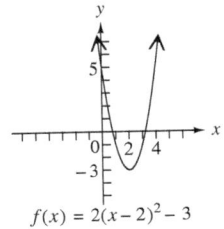

vertex: $(2, -3)$; axis: $x = 2$;
domain: $(-\infty, \infty)$; range: $[-3, \infty)$

37.

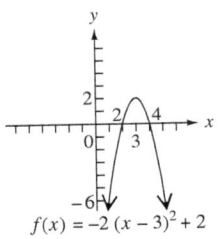

vertex: $(3, 2)$; axis: $x = 3$;
domain: $(-\infty, \infty)$; range: $(-\infty, 2]$

39.

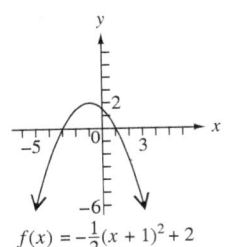

vertex: $(-1, 2)$; axis: $x = -1$;
domain: $(-\infty, \infty)$; range: $(-\infty, 2]$

41. linear function; positive   **43.** quadratic function; positive
45. quadratic function; negative

47. (a)

FEDERAL STUDENT LOANS

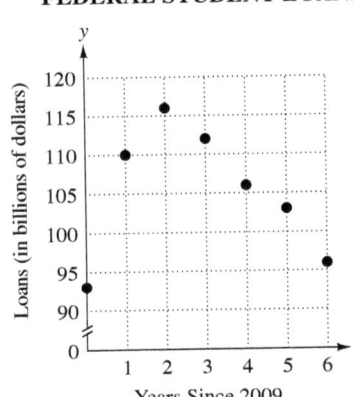

Years Since 2009

(b) quadratic function
(c) negative
(d) $y = -4.125x^2 + 19.75x + 93$
(e) 2012: $115 billion; 2014: $89 billion; The model approximates the data for 2012 fairly well, but it gives a low approximation for 2014.

SECTION 11.7

1. If x is squared, it has a vertical axis. If y is squared, it has a horizontal axis.   **2.** A parabola with a horizontal axis of symmetry fails the conditions of the vertical line test.   **3.** $(-4, -6)$ **5.** $(1, -3)$

7. $\left(-\dfrac{1}{2}, -\dfrac{29}{4}\right)$ **9.** $(-1, 3)$; up; narrower; no x-intercepts

11. $\left(\dfrac{5}{2}, \dfrac{37}{4}\right)$; down; same shape; two x-intercepts   **13.** $(-3, -9)$; to the right; wider   **15.** F   **16.** A   **17.** C   **18.** B   **19.** D   **20.** E

21.

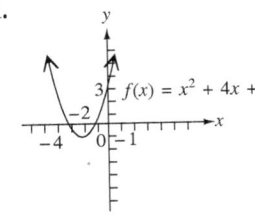

vertex: $(-2, -1)$; axis: $x = -2$;
domain: $(-\infty, \infty)$; range: $[-1, \infty)$

23.

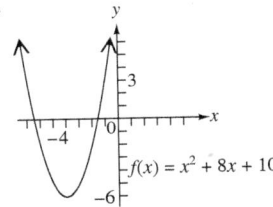

vertex: $(-4, -6)$; axis: $x = -4$;
domain: $(-\infty, \infty)$; range: $[-6, \infty)$

25.

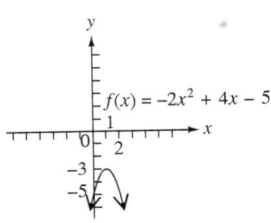

vertex: $(1, -3)$; axis: $x = 1$;
domain: $(-\infty, \infty)$; range: $(-\infty, -3]$

27.

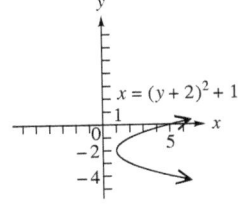

vertex: $(1, -2)$; axis: $y = -2$;
domain: $[1, \infty)$; range: $(-\infty, \infty)$

29.

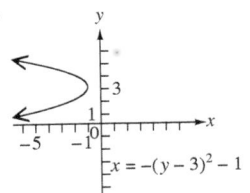

vertex: $(-1, 3)$; axis: $y = 3$;
domain: $(-\infty, -1]$; range: $(-\infty, \infty)$

31.

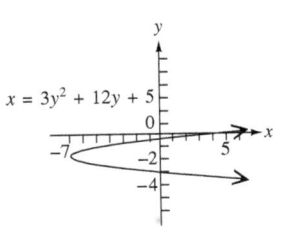

vertex: $(1, 5)$; axis: $y = 5$;
domain: $(-\infty, 1]$; range: $(-\infty, \infty)$

33.

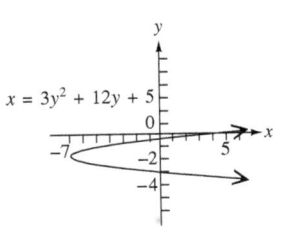

vertex: $(-7, -2)$; axis: $y = -2$;
domain: $[-7, \infty)$; range: $(-\infty, \infty)$

35. one   **36.** none   **37.** 30 and 30
39. 140 ft by 70 ft; 9800 ft²
41. 20 units; $210
43. 16 ft; 2 sec
45. (a) minimum   **(b)** 1967; 5.4%
47. $(18.45, 3860)$; In 2018 Social Security assets will reach their maximum value of $3860 billion.

48. The coefficient of x^2 is negative because a parabola that models the data must open down.   **49. (a)** $R(x) = 20{,}000 + 200x - 4x^2$
(b) 25   **(c)** $22,500

SECTION 11.8

1. Include the endpoints if the symbol is ≥ or ≤. Exclude the endpoints if the symbol is > or <.   **2.** $(-\infty, -4] \cup [3, \infty)$

3. (a) $\{1, 3\}$ **(b)** $(-\infty, 1) \cup (3, \infty)$ **(c)** $(1, 3)$

5. (a) $\left\{-3, \dfrac{5}{2}\right\}$ **(b)** $\left[-3, \dfrac{5}{2}\right]$ **(c)** $\left(-\infty, -3\right] \cup \left[\dfrac{5}{2}, \infty\right)$

7. $(-\infty, -1) \cup (5, \infty)$

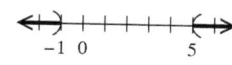

9. $(-4, 6)$

11. $(-\infty, 1] \cup [3, \infty)$

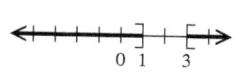

13. $\left(-\infty, -\dfrac{3}{2}\right] \cup \left[\dfrac{3}{5}, \infty\right)$

15. $\left(-\dfrac{2}{3}, \dfrac{1}{3}\right)$

17. $\left(-\infty, -\dfrac{1}{2}\right] \cup \left[\dfrac{1}{3}, \infty\right)$

19. $\left[-\dfrac{3}{2}, \dfrac{3}{2}\right]$

21. $(-\infty, 0) \cup (4, \infty)$

23. $\left(-\infty, 3 - \sqrt{3}\right] \cup \left[3 + \sqrt{3}, \infty\right)$ **25.** $(-\infty, \infty)$ **27.** $\varnothing$
29. $\varnothing$ **31.** $(-\infty, \infty)$

33. $(-\infty, 1) \cup (2, 4)$

35. $\left[-\dfrac{3}{2}, \dfrac{1}{3}\right] \cup [4, \infty)$

37. $(-\infty, 1) \cup (4, \infty)$

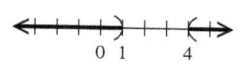

39. $\left[-\dfrac{3}{2}, 5\right)$

41. $(2, 6]$

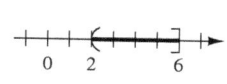

43. $\left(-\infty, \dfrac{1}{2}\right) \cup \left(\dfrac{5}{4}, \infty\right)$

45. $[-4, -2)$

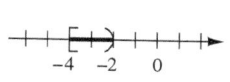

47. $\left(0, \dfrac{1}{2}\right) \cup \left(\dfrac{5}{2}, \infty\right)$

49. $[-7, -2)$

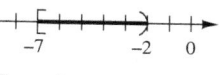

51. $(-\infty, 2] \cup (4, \infty)$

53. $\left[\dfrac{3}{2}, \infty\right)$

55. 3 sec and 13 sec   **56.** between 3 sec and 13 sec   **57.** at 0 sec (the time when it is initially projected) and at 16 sec (the time when it hits the ground)   **58.** between 0 and 3 sec and between 13 and 16 sec

Chapter 11 REVIEW EXERCISES

1. $\{-5, 2\}$ **2.** $\left\{-\dfrac{2}{3}, -\dfrac{1}{2}\right\}$ **3.** $\left\{-\dfrac{1}{4}, 3\right\}$ **4.** $\left\{\dfrac{3}{2}, 5\right\}$ **5.** $\{11, -11\}$

6. $\{\sqrt{3}, -\sqrt{3}\}$ **7.** $\left\{-\dfrac{15}{2}, \dfrac{5}{2}\right\}$ **8.** $\left\{\dfrac{2}{3} + \dfrac{5}{3}i, \dfrac{2}{3} - \dfrac{5}{3}i\right\}$

9. $\{-2 + \sqrt{19}, -2 - \sqrt{19}\}$ **10.** $\left\{\dfrac{1}{2}, 1\right\}$ **11.** By the square root property, the first step should be $x = \sqrt{12}$ or $x = -\sqrt{12}$. The solution set is $\{2\sqrt{3}, -2\sqrt{3}\}$.   **12.** 5.9 sec   **13.** $\left\{-\dfrac{7}{2}, 3\right\}$

14. $\left\{\dfrac{-5 + \sqrt{53}}{2}, \dfrac{-5 - \sqrt{53}}{2}\right\}$ **15.** $\left\{\dfrac{1 + \sqrt{41}}{2}, \dfrac{1 - \sqrt{41}}{2}\right\}$

16. $\left\{-\dfrac{3}{4} + \dfrac{\sqrt{23}}{4}i, -\dfrac{3}{4} - \dfrac{\sqrt{23}}{4}i\right\}$ **17.** $\left\{\dfrac{2}{3} + \dfrac{\sqrt{2}}{3}i, \dfrac{2}{3} - \dfrac{\sqrt{2}}{3}i\right\}$

18. $\left\{\dfrac{-7 + \sqrt{37}}{2}, \dfrac{-7 - \sqrt{37}}{2}\right\}$ **19.** 17; B; quadratic formula

20. 64; A; zero-factor property   **21.** 0; C; zero-factor property

22. −92; D; quadratic formula   **23.** $\left\{-\dfrac{5}{2}, 3\right\}$ **24.** $\left\{-\dfrac{1}{2}, 1\right\}$

25. $\{-4\}$ **26.** $\left\{-\dfrac{11}{6}, -\dfrac{19}{12}\right\}$ **27.** $\left\{-\dfrac{343}{8}, 64\right\}$ **28.** $\{-2, -1, 1, 2\}$

29. 40 mph   **30.** 4.6 hr   **31.** $v = \dfrac{\pm\sqrt{rFkw}}{kw}$

32. $t = \dfrac{3m \pm \sqrt{9m^2 + 24m}}{2m}$ **33.** 9 ft, 12 ft, 15 ft   **34.** 12 cm by 20 cm

35. 1 in.   **36.** 5.2 sec   **37.** $(1, 0)$ **38.** $(3, 7)$ **39.** $\left(\dfrac{2}{3}, -\dfrac{2}{3}\right)$

40. $(-4, 3)$

41.

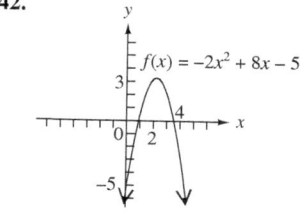

$y = 2(x - 2)^2 - 3$

vertex: $(2, -3)$; axis: $x = 2$; domain: $(-\infty, \infty)$; range: $[-3, \infty)$

42.

$f(x) = -2x^2 + 8x - 5$

vertex: $(2, 3)$; axis: $x = 2$; domain: $(-\infty, \infty)$; range: $(-\infty, 3]$

43.

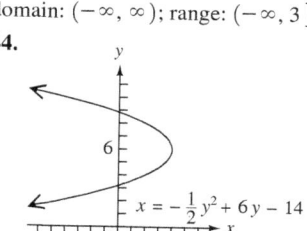

$x = 2(y + 3)^2 - 4$

vertex: $(-4, -3)$; axis: $y = -3$; domain: $[-4, \infty)$; range: $(-\infty, \infty)$

44.

$x = -\dfrac{1}{2}y^2 + 6y - 14$

vertex: $(4, 6)$; axis: $y = 6$; domain: $(-\infty, 4]$; range: $(-\infty, \infty)$

45. 5 sec; 400 ft   **46.** length: 50 m; width: 50 m; maximum area: 2500 m²

47. $\left(-\infty, -\dfrac{3}{2}\right) \cup (4, \infty)$ **48.** $[-4, 3]$

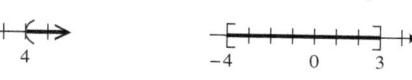

49. $(-\infty, -5] \cup [-2, 3]$

50. $\varnothing$

51. $\left(-\infty, \dfrac{1}{2}\right) \cup (2, \infty)$

52. $[-3, 2)$

Chapter 11 MIXED REVIEW EXERCISES

1. $R = \dfrac{\pm \sqrt{Vh - r^2 h}}{h}$ **2.** $\left\{1 + \dfrac{\sqrt{3}}{3}i, \, 1 - \dfrac{\sqrt{3}}{3}i\right\}$

3. $\left\{\dfrac{-11 + \sqrt{7}}{3}, \dfrac{-11 - \sqrt{7}}{3}\right\}$ **4.** $d = \dfrac{\pm \sqrt{SkI}}{I}$ **5.** $\{4\}$

6. $\left\{-\dfrac{5}{3}, -\dfrac{3}{2}\right\}$ **7.** $\left(-5, -\dfrac{23}{5}\right]$ **8.** $(-\infty, \infty)$ **9.** $\left\{\dfrac{1}{5}\right\}$

10. $\{-2, -1, 3, 4\}$ **11.** $(-\infty, -6) \cup \left(-\dfrac{3}{2}, 1\right)$

12. (a) F (b) B (c) C (d) A (e) E (f) D   **13.** 10 mph

14. length: 2 cm; width: 1.5 cm

Chapter 11 TEST

1. $\left\{-3, \dfrac{2}{5}\right\}$ **2.** $\{3\sqrt{6}, -3\sqrt{6}\}$ **3.** $\left\{-\dfrac{8}{7}, \dfrac{2}{7}\right\}$

4. $\{-1 + \sqrt{2}, -1 - \sqrt{2}\}$ **5.** $\left\{\dfrac{3 + \sqrt{17}}{4}, \dfrac{3 - \sqrt{17}}{4}\right\}$

6. $\left\{\dfrac{2}{3} + \dfrac{\sqrt{11}}{3}i, \dfrac{2}{3} - \dfrac{\sqrt{11}}{3}i\right\}$ **7.** $\left\{\dfrac{2}{3}\right\}$ **8.** 88; two irrational solutions

9. $\left\{-\dfrac{2}{3}, 6\right\}$ **10.** $\left\{\dfrac{-7 + \sqrt{97}}{8}, \dfrac{-7 - \sqrt{97}}{8}\right\}$ **11.** $\left\{-2, -\dfrac{1}{3}, \dfrac{1}{3}, 2\right\}$

12. $\left\{-\dfrac{5}{2}, 1\right\}$ **13.** $r = \dfrac{\pm \sqrt{\pi S}}{2\pi}$ **14.** Andrew: 11.1 hr; Kent: 9.1 hr

15. 7 mph   **16.** 2 ft   **17.** 16 m   **18.** (a) 10 hr (b) 180 students

19. 160 ft by 320 ft; 51,200 ft^2 **20.** A

21.

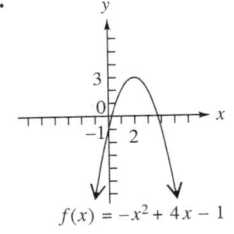

vertex: $(0, -2)$; axis: $x = 0$;
domain: $(-\infty, \infty)$; range: $[-2, \infty)$

22.

vertex: $(2, 3)$; axis: $x = 2$;
domain: $(-\infty, \infty)$; range: $(-\infty, 3]$

23.

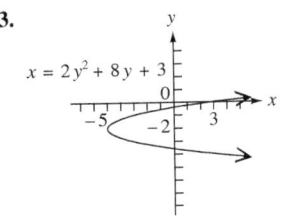

vertex: $(-5, -2)$; axis: $y = -2$;
domain: $[-5, \infty)$; range: $(-\infty, \infty)$

24. $(-\infty, -5) \cup \left(\dfrac{3}{2}, \infty\right)$

25. $(-\infty, 4) \cup [9, \infty)$

Chapters R–11 CUMULATIVE REVIEW EXERCISES

1. (a) $-2, 0, 7$ (b) $-\dfrac{7}{3}, -2, 0, 0.7, 7, \dfrac{32}{3}$ (c) All are real except $\sqrt{-8}$.

(d) All are complex numbers.   **2.** $\{1\}$ **3.** $[1, \infty)$

4. $\left[2, \dfrac{8}{3}\right]$ **5.** $\left\{\dfrac{11}{10}, \dfrac{7}{2}\right\}$ **6.** $\left\{\dfrac{2 + \sqrt{10}}{2}, \dfrac{2 - \sqrt{10}}{2}\right\}$ **7.** $\{-3, 5\}$

8. $\varnothing$ **9.** $\{-3, -1, 1, 3\}$ **10.** $\left\{\dfrac{2}{3}\right\}$ **11.** slope: $\dfrac{1}{2}$;

y-intercept: $\left(0, -\dfrac{7}{4}\right)$ **12.** $x + 3y = -1$

13.

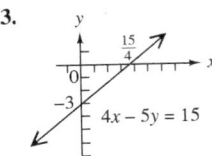

function; domain: $(-\infty, \infty)$;
range: $(-\infty, \infty)$

14.

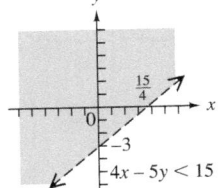

not a function

15.

function; domain: $(-\infty, \infty)$;
range: $(-\infty, 3]$

16. $\{(1, -2)\}$

17. $\{(x, y) \mid x - y = 5\}$

18. $\{(3, -4, 2)\}$

19. $\dfrac{x^8}{y^4}$ **20.** $\dfrac{4}{xy^2}$

21. $4t^2 + 36t + 81$

22. $4x^2 - 6x + 11 + \dfrac{4}{x + 2}$

23. $x(4 + x)(4 - x)$

24. $(4m - 3)(6m + 5)$

25. $(3x - 5y)^2$ **26.** $-\dfrac{5}{18}$ **27.** $-\dfrac{8}{k}$ **28.** $\dfrac{r - s}{r}$ **29.** $\dfrac{3\sqrt[3]{4}}{4}$

30. $\sqrt{7} + \sqrt{5}$ **31.** 44 mg   **32.** southbound car: 57 mi;

eastbound car: 76 mi

CHAPTER 12 Inverse, Exponential, and Logarithmic Functions

SECTION 12.1

1. B   **2.** D   **3.** A   **4.** C   **5.** The student multiplied the functions
instead of composing them. The correct answer is $(f \circ g)(x) = 2x^2 - 8$.

6. In general, $(f \circ g)(x) \neq (g \circ f)(x)$. The correct answer is
$(g \circ f)(x) = 2x + 8$.   **7.** 16   **9.** 83   **11.** 13   **13.** $2x + 13$

15. $x^2 + 10x + 29$ **17.** $2x + 8$ **19.** $\dfrac{137}{4}$ **21.** 8   **23.** 1   **24.** 9

25. 9   **26.** 12   **27.** 1   **28.** 12   **29.** $(f \circ g)(x) = 63{,}360x$; It computes

the number of inches in x miles.   **31.** (a) $s = \dfrac{x}{4}$ (b) $y = \dfrac{x^2}{16}$ (c) 2.25

33. $(\mathcal{A} \circ r)(t) = 4\pi t^2$; This is the area of the circular layer as a function
of time.

SECTION 12.2

1. A   **2.** The function $f(x) = x^2 - 1$ is not one-to-one and therefore
does not have an inverse function.   **3.** It is not one-to-one. France and
the United States are paired with the same trans fat percentage, 11.

4. It is one-to-one. Each year corresponds to only one concentration, and each concentration corresponds to only one year. **5.** This function is not one-to-one because two sodas in the list have 41 mg of caffeine. **6.** Yes. Adding 1 to 1058 would make two distances the same. The function would not then be one-to-one. **7.** A **8.** D **9.** $\{(6, 3), (10, 2), (12, 5)\}$
11. not one-to-one **13.** $\{(4.5, 0), (8.6, 2), (12.7, 4)\}$

15. $f^{-1}(x) = x - 3$ **17.** $f^{-1}(x) = \dfrac{x - 4}{2}$, or $f^{-1}(x) = \dfrac{1}{2}x - 2$

19. $g^{-1}(x) = \dfrac{-x + 3}{4}$, or $g^{-1}(x) = -\dfrac{1}{4}x + \dfrac{3}{4}$

21. $g^{-1}(x) = x^2 + 3$, $x \geq 0$ **23.** $f^{-1}(x) = x^2 - 6$, $x \geq 0$
25. not one-to-one **27.** $g^{-1}(x) = \sqrt[3]{x} - 1$ **29.** $f^{-1}(x) = \sqrt[3]{x + 4}$
31. not one-to-one **33. (a)** 8 **(b)** 3 **35. (a)** 1 **(b)** 0
37. (a) one-to-one **39. (a)** not one-to-one
(b)

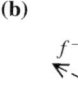 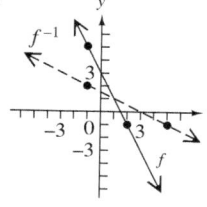

41. (a) one-to-one **43.**
(b)

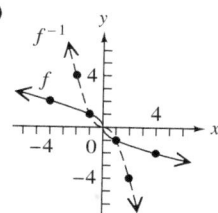 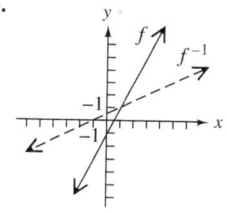

45. **47.** 0, 1, 2

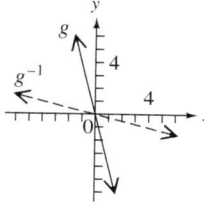 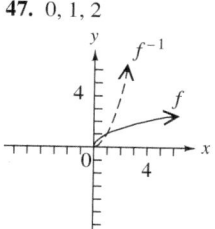

49. $-3, -2, -1, 6$ **51.** $f^{-1}(x) = \dfrac{x + 5}{4}$, or $f^{-1}(x) = \dfrac{1}{4}x + \dfrac{5}{4}$

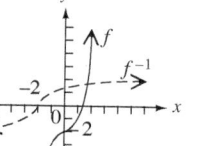

52. MY CALCULATOR IS THE GREATEST THING SINCE SLICED BREAD. **53.** If the function were not one-to-one, there would be ambiguity in some of the characters because they could represent more than one letter.

54. Answers will vary. For example, Jane Doe is
1004   5   2748   129   68   3379   129.

SECTION 12.3

1. C **2.** A **3.** C **4.** B
5. **7.**

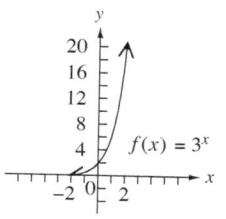 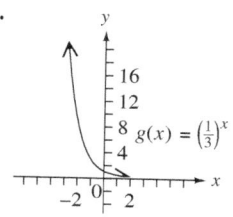

9. **11.**

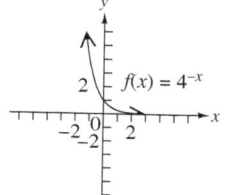 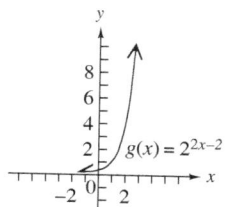

13. The division in the second step does not lead to x on the left side. By expressing each side using the same base, $2^x = 2^5$, we obtain the correct solution set, $\{5\}$. **14.** Subtracting 3 from each side in the second step does not help to obtain x. By expressing each side using the same base, $3^x = 3^4$, we obtain the correct solution set, $\{4\}$. **15.** $\{2\}$ **17.** $\left\{\dfrac{3}{2}\right\}$ **19.** $\left\{\dfrac{3}{2}\right\}$

21. $\{-1\}$ **23.** $\{7\}$ **25.** $\{-3\}$ **27.** $\left\{-\dfrac{3}{2}\right\}$ **29.** $\{-1\}$ **31.** $\{-3\}$
33. $\{-2\}$ **35. (a)** 0.6°C **(b)** 0.3°C **37. (a)** 1.4°C **(b)** 0.5°C
39. 100 g **41.** 0.30 g

SECTION 12.4

1. (a) C **(b)** F **(c)** B **(d)** A **(e)** E **(f)** D **2. (a)** B **(b)** E
(c) D **(d)** F **(e)** A **(f)** C **3.** $\log_4 1024 = 5$ **5.** $\log_{1/2} 8 = -3$

7. $\log_{10} 0.001 = -3$ **9.** $\log_{625} 5 = \dfrac{1}{4}$ **11.** $\log_8 \dfrac{1}{4} = -\dfrac{2}{3}$ **13.** $\log_5 1 = 0$

15. $4^3 = 64$ **17.** $12^1 = 12$ **19.** $6^0 = 1$ **21.** $9^{1/2} = 3$ **23.** $\left(\dfrac{1}{4}\right)^{1/2} = \dfrac{1}{2}$

25. $5^{-1} = 5^{-1}$ **27. (a)** C **(b)** B **(c)** B **(d)** C **28.** By using the word "radically," the teacher meant for him to consider roots. Because 3 is the square (2nd) root of 9, $\log_9 3 = \dfrac{1}{2}$. **29.** $\left\{\dfrac{1}{3}\right\}$ **31.** $\left\{\dfrac{1}{125}\right\}$

33. $\{81\}$ **35.** $\left\{\dfrac{1}{5}\right\}$ **37.** $\{1\}$ **39.** $\{x \mid x > 0, x \neq 1\}$ **41.** $\{5\}$

43. $\left\{\dfrac{5}{3}\right\}$ **45.** $\{4\}$ **47.** $\left\{\dfrac{3}{2}\right\}$ **49.** $\{30\}$ **51.** $\left\{\dfrac{37}{9}\right\}$

53. **55.**

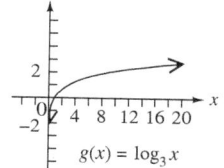 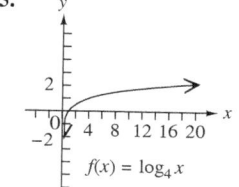

57.

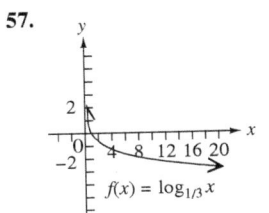

$f(x) = \log_{1/3} x$

59.

$g(x) = \log_{1/4} x$

61. 8   **62.** 16   **63.** 24   **64.** $f(0) = 8$; $f(10) = 16$; $f(60) = 24$; The points $(0, 8)$, $(10, 16)$, and $(60, 24)$ all lie on the graph of f.
65. Because every real number power of 1 equals 1, if $y = \log_1 x$, then $x = 1^y$ and so $x = 1$ for every y. This contradicts the definition of a function.
66. If the base is a negative number, say -2, then $y = \log_{-2} x$. For a y-value of $\frac{1}{2}$, x is not a real number. Also, for any odd y-value, such as 3, x is a negative number, which is outside the domain restriction for logarithmic functions.   **67.** $x = \log_a 1$ is equivalent to $a^x = 1$. The only value of x that makes $a^x = 1$ is 0. (Recall that $a \neq 1$.)   **68.** Because $a^1 = a$ for any positive real number a, the equivalent logarithmic statement $\log_a a = 1$ must also be true.   **69. (a)** 130 thousand units   **(b)** 160 thousand units   **(c)** 190 thousand units   **71.** 5

73. $\frac{1}{100}, \frac{1}{10}, 1, 10, 100$

$y = 10^x$

74. $-2, -1, 0, 1, 2$

$y = \log_{10} x$

domain: $(-\infty, \infty)$; range: $(0, \infty)$ domain: $(0, \infty)$; range: $(-\infty, \infty)$
75. The graphs have symmetry across the line $y = x$.   **76.** They are inverses.

SECTION 12.5

1. $\log_{10} 7 + \log_{10} 8$ **2.** $\log_{10} 7 - \log_{10} 8$ **3.** 4   **4.** $6 \log_{10} 3$
5. false; $\log_b x + \log_b y = \log_b xy$ **6.** true   **7.** true   **8.** false; $b^{\log_b r} = r$
9. true   **10.** false; $\log_b x^r = r \log_b x$ **11.** $\log_7 4 + \log_7 5$
13. $\log_5 8 - \log_5 3$ **15.** $2 \log_4 6$ **17.** $\frac{1}{3} \log_3 4 - 2 \log_3 x - \log_3 y$
19. $\frac{1}{2} \log_3 x + \frac{1}{2} \log_3 y - \frac{1}{2} \log_3 5$ **21.** $\frac{1}{3} \log_2 x + \frac{1}{5} \log_2 y - 2 \log_2 r$
23. In the notation $\log_a (x + y)$, the parentheses do not indicate multiplication. They indicate that $x + y$ is the result of raising a to some power.   **24.** We cannot apply the product rule because $\log_b xy = \log_b x + \log_b y$ only if x and y are positive numbers.   **25.** $\log_b xy$ **27.** $\log_a \frac{m^3}{n}$ **29.** $\log_a \frac{rt^3}{s}$
31. $\log_a \frac{125}{81}$ **33.** $\log_{10} (x^2 - 9)$ **35.** $\log_p \frac{x^3 y^{1/2}}{z^{3/2} a^3}$ **37.** false   **39.** true
41. true   **43.** false   **45.** 4   **46.** It is the exponent to which 3 must be raised in order to obtain 81.   **47.** 81   **48.** It is the exponent to which 2 must be raised in order to obtain 19.   **49.** 19   **50.** m

SECTION 12.6

1. C   **2.** A   **3.** D   **4.** C   **5.** 19.2   **6.** $\sqrt{2}$ **7.** $\sqrt{3}$ **8.** 75.2
9. 2.5164   **11.** -1.4868 **13.** 9.6776   **15.** 2.0592   **17.** -2.8896
19. 2.3026   **21.** poor fen   **23.** bog   **25.** rich fen   **27.** 11.6   **29.** 8.4
31. 4.3   **33.** 1.0×10^{-2} **35.** 4.0×10^{-8} **37.** 2.5×10^{-5}
39. (a) 35.0 yr   **(b)** 14.2 yr   **41. (a)** 142 dB   **(b)** 126 dB   **(c)** 120 dB
43. (a) 55%   **(b)** 90%

SECTION 12.7

1. common logarithms   **2.** common logarithms   **3.** natural logarithms
4. natural logarithms   **5.** $\{0.827\}$ **7.** $\{1.201\}$ **9.** $\{0.833\}$
11. $\{2.269\}$ **13.** $\{15.967\}$ **15.** $\{-6.067\}$ **17.** $\{261.291\}$
19. $\{-10.718\}$ **21.** $\{3\}$ **23.** $\{5.879\}$ **25.** $\{-1.571\}$ **27.** $\{1\}$
29. $\left\{\frac{2}{3}\right\}$ **31.** $\left\{\frac{33}{2}\right\}$ **33.** $\{-1 + \sqrt[3]{49}\}$ **35.** $\{4 + \sqrt[5]{216}\}$
37. 2 cannot be a solution because $\log (2 - 3) = \log (-1)$, and -1 is not in the domain of $\log x$.   **38.** -4 is a solution because it leads to a *positive* value of $3 - x$: $3 - (-4) = 7$. The number -4 is in the domain of $\log (3 - x)$.
39. $\left\{\frac{1}{3}\right\}$ **41.** $\{2\}$ **43.** $\varnothing$ **45.** $\{8\}$ **47.** $\left\{\frac{4}{3}\right\}$ **49.** $\{8\}$
51. (a) $\$2539.47$ **(b)** 10.19 yr   **53.** $\$4934.71$ **55.** 27.73 yr
57. (a) 179.73 g   **(b)** 21.66 yr   **59.** 1.4315   **61.** 3.3030   **63.** -0.0947
65. -2.3219 **67.** $\log 5^x = \log 125$ **68.** $x \log 5 = \log 125$
69. $x = \frac{\log 125}{\log 5}$ **70.** $\frac{\log 125}{\log 5} = 3$; $\{3\}$

Chapter 12 REVIEW EXERCISES

1. (a) 167   **(b)** 1495   **2. (a)** 20   **(b)** 42   **3. (a)** $75x^2 + 220x + 160$
(b) $15x^2 + 10x + 2$ **4.** No, composition of functions is not a commutative operation. For example, the results of **Exercise 3** show that $(f \circ g)(x) \neq (g \circ f)(x)$ in this case.   **5.** not one-to-one
6. one-to-one   **7.** not one-to-one   **8.** not one-to-one
9. $\{(-8, -2), (-1, -1), (0, 0), (1, 1), (8, 2)\}$ **10.** $f^{-1}(x) = \frac{x - 7}{-3}$,
or $f^{-1}(x) = -\frac{1}{3}x + \frac{7}{3}$ **11.** $f^{-1}(x) = \frac{x^3 + 4}{6}$ **12.** not one-to-one

13.

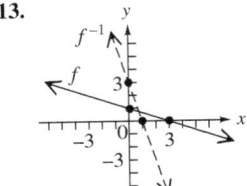

14.

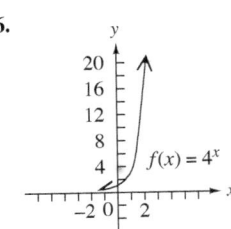

15.

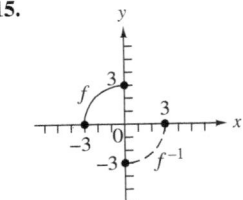

16.

$f(x) = 4^x$

17.

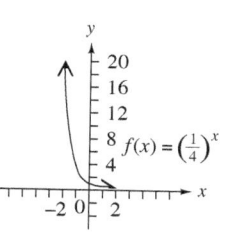

18.

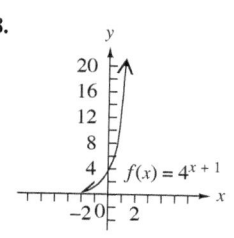

19. $\{4\}$ **20.** $\left\{\dfrac{3}{7}\right\}$ **21.** $\{0\}$ **22.** $\{-3\}$ **23. (a)** 55.8 million

(b) 81.0 million **24. (a)** $5^4 = 625$ **(b)** $\log_5 0.04 = -2$ **25.** 5; 2; fifth; 32

26.

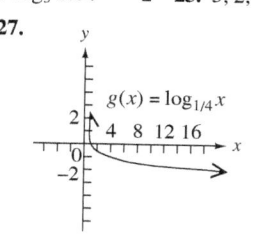

27.

28.

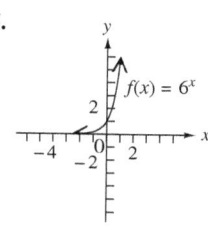

29. $\{2\}$ **30.** $\{-2\}$ **31.** $\{8\}$

32. $\{b \mid b > 0, b \neq 1\}$

33. $\log_4 3 + 2\log_4 x$

34. $3\log_5 a + 2\log_5 b - 4\log_5 c$

35. $\dfrac{1}{2}\log_4 x + 2\log_4 w - \log_4 z$

36. $2\log_2 p + \log_2 r - \dfrac{1}{2}\log_2 z$ **37.** $\log_a \dfrac{49}{16}$ **38.** $\log_a 250$ **39.** $\log_b \dfrac{3x}{y^2}$

40. $\log_3 \dfrac{x+7}{4x+6}$ **41.** 1.4609 **42.** -0.5901 **43.** 3.3638 **44.** -1.3587

45. 6.4 **46.** 8.4 **47.** 6.3×10^{-3} **48.** $\{2.042\}$ **49.** $\{4.907\}$

50. $\{18.310\}$ **51.** $\left\{\dfrac{1}{9}\right\}$ **52.** $\{-6 + \sqrt[3]{25}\}$ **53.** $\{2\}$ **54.** $\left\{\dfrac{3}{8}\right\}$

55. $\{4\}$ **56.** $\{1\}$ **57.** $\$7112.11$ **58.** Plan A, the better plan, would pay $\$2.92$ more. **59.** 0.9251 **60.** 1.7925 **61.** 1.4315 **62.** -2.0437

Chapter 12 MIXED REVIEW EXERCISES

1. 7 **2.** 0 **3.** -3 **4.** 36 **5.** 4 **6.** e **7.** -5 **8.** 5.4 **9.** 2.5855

10. -0.3857 **11.** 4.6439 **12.** -2.4022 **13.** $\{72\}$ **14.** $\{5\}$

15. $\left\{\dfrac{1}{9}\right\}$ **16.** $\left\{\dfrac{4}{3}\right\}$ **17.** $\{3\}$ **18.** $\left\{\dfrac{1}{8}\right\}$ **19.** $\left\{\dfrac{11}{3}\right\}$ **20.** $\{0\}$

21. $\left\{\dfrac{2}{63}\right\}$ **22.** $\{-2, -1\}$ **23.** $\$4267$ **24.** 11% **25.** 0.325

26. 0.673

Chapter 12 TEST

1. (a) 23 **(b)** $3x^2 + 11$ **(c)** $9x^2 + 30x + 27$ **2. (a)** not one-to-one

(b) one-to-one **3.** $f^{-1}(x) = x^3 - 7$

4.

5.

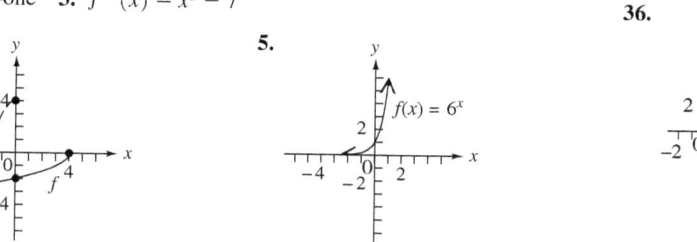

6.

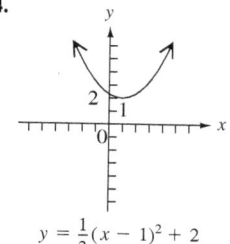

7. Interchange the x- and y-values of the ordered pairs, because the functions are inverses. **8.** $\{-4\}$

9. $\left\{-\dfrac{13}{3}\right\}$ **10. (a)** 775 millibars

(b) 265 millibars

11. $\log_4 0.0625 = -2$ **12.** $7^2 = 49$ **13.** $\{32\}$ **14.** $\left\{\dfrac{1}{2}\right\}$ **15.** $\{2\}$

16. $2\log_3 x + \log_3 y$ **17.** $\dfrac{1}{2}\log_5 x - \log_5 y - \log_5 z$ **18.** $\log_b \dfrac{s^3}{t}$

19. $\log_b \dfrac{r^{1/4}s^2}{t^{2/3}}$ **20. (a)** 1.3284 **(b)** -0.8440 **(c)** 2.1245

21. $\{3.9656\}$ **22.** $\{3\}$ **23. (a)** $\$11,903.40$ **(b)** 19.9 yr

24. (a) $\$17,427.51$ **(b)** 23.1 yr **25. (a)** $\dfrac{\log 19}{\log 3}$ **(b)** $\dfrac{\ln 19}{\ln 3}$

(c) 2.6801

Chapters R–12 CUMULATIVE REVIEW EXERCISES

1. $-2, 0, 6, \dfrac{30}{3}$ (or 10) **2.** $-\dfrac{9}{4}, -2, 0, 0.6, 6, \dfrac{30}{3}$ (or 10)

3. $-\sqrt{2}, \sqrt{11}$ **4.** $\left\{-\dfrac{2}{3}\right\}$ **5.** $[1, \infty)$ **6.** $\{-2, 7\}$

7. $(-\infty, -3) \cup (2, \infty)$ **8. (a)** yes **(b)** 1.955; The number of travelers shows an increase of an average of 1.955 million per year during the period 2000–2020. **9.** $\{(4, 2)\}$ **10.** $\{(1, -1, 4)\}$ **11.** $6p^2 + 7p - 3$

12. $16k^2 - 24k + 9$ **13.** $-5m^3 + 2m^2 - 7m + 4$ **14.** $2t^3 + 5t^2 - 3t + 4$

15. $z(5z + 1)(z - 4)$ **16.** $(4a + 5b^2)(4a - 5b^2)$

17. $(2c + d)(4c^2 - 2cd + d^2)$ **18.** $-\dfrac{1875p^{13}}{8}$ **19.** $\dfrac{x + 5}{x + 4}$

20. $\dfrac{-3k - 19}{(k + 3)(k - 2)}$ **21.** $12\sqrt{2}$ **22.** $-\dfrac{1}{4}$ **23.** $-27\sqrt{2}$ **24.** 41

25. $-i$ **26.** $\{0, 4\}$ **27.** $\left\{\dfrac{1 + \sqrt{13}}{6}, \dfrac{1 - \sqrt{13}}{6}\right\}$

28. $(-\infty, -4) \cup (2, \infty)$ **29.** $\{-2, -1, 1, 2\}$ **30.** $\{-1\}$ **31.** $\{1\}$

32. $5^3 = 125$ **33.** $3\log x + \dfrac{1}{2}\log y - \log z$

34.

$y = \dfrac{1}{3}(x - 1)^2 + 2$

35.

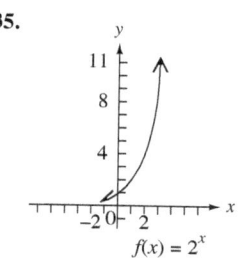

$f(x) = 2^x$

36.

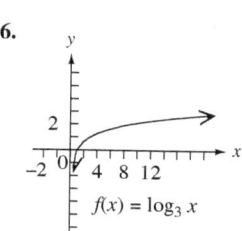

$f(x) = \log_3 x$

CHAPTER 13 Nonlinear Functions, Conic Sections, and Nonlinear Systems

SECTION 13.1

1. E; 0; 0   **2.** D; $(-\infty, \infty)$; $[0, \infty)$
3. A; $(-\infty, \infty)$; $\{\ldots, -2, -1, 0, 1, 2, \ldots\}$ **4.** C; $[0, \infty)$; $[0, \infty)$
5. B; It does not satisfy the conditions of the vertical line test.
6. F; asymptotes

7.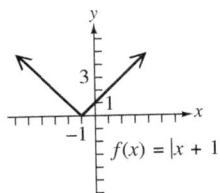
domain: $(-\infty, \infty)$;
range: $[0, \infty)$

9.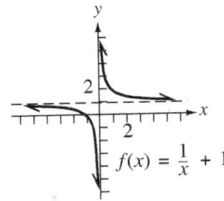
domain: $(-\infty, 0) \cup (0, \infty)$;
range: $(-\infty, 1) \cup (1, \infty)$

11.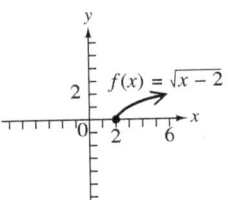
domain: $[2, \infty)$;
range: $[0, \infty)$

13.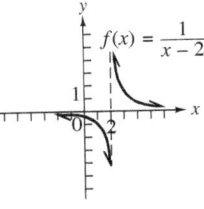
domain: $(-\infty, 2) \cup (2, \infty)$;
range: $(-\infty, 0) \cup (0, \infty)$

15.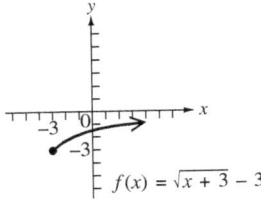
domain: $[-3, \infty)$;
range: $[-3, \infty)$

17.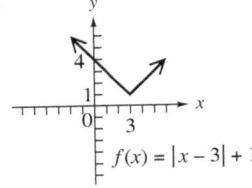
domain: $(-\infty, \infty)$;
range: $[1, \infty)$

19. B   **20.** C   **21.** A   **22.** D   **23.** Shift the graph of $g(x) = \frac{1}{x}$ to the right 3 units and up 2 units.   **24.** Shift the graph of $g(x) = \frac{1}{x}$ to the left 5 units and down 3 units.   **25.** 3   **27.** 4   **29.** 0   **31.** 2   **33.** -14
35. -11

37.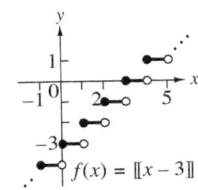
$f(x) = [\![x - 3]\!]$

39.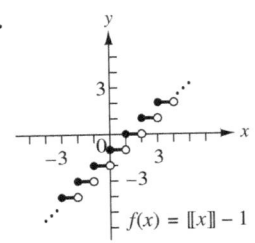
$f(x) = [\![x]\!] - 1$

41.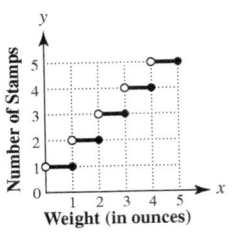

43. $2.75

SECTION 13.2

1. B   **2.** C   **3.** D   **4.** A
5. (a) $(0, 0)$ **(b)** 5
(c)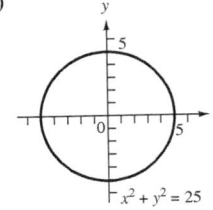

6. There will always be domain values that yield more than one range value. A circle fails to meet the conditions of the vertical line test.
7. $x^2 + y^2 = 1$ **9.** $x^2 + y^2 = 3$
11. $(x + 4)^2 + (y - 3)^2 = 4$
13. $(x - 1)^2 + y^2 = 9$
15. $x^2 + (y - 4)^2 = 36$
17. $(x + 8)^2 + (y + 5)^2 = 5$ **19.** $(-2, -3)$; $r = 2$
21. $(-5, 7)$; $r = 9$ **23.** $(2, 4)$; $r = 4$

25.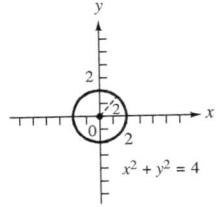
center: $(0, 0)$; radius: 2

27.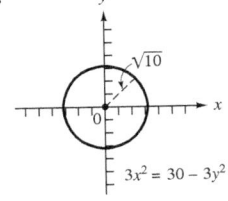
center: $(0, 0)$; radius: $\sqrt{10}$

29.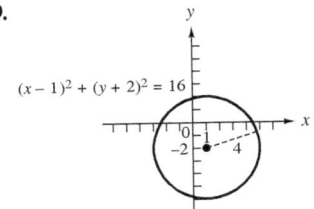
center: $(1, -2)$; radius: 4

31.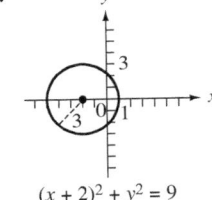
center: $(-2, 0)$; radius: 3

33.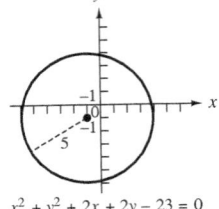
center: $(-1, -1)$; radius: 5

35.
center: $(-3, 3)$; radius: 3

37. The thumbtack acts as the center, and the length of string acts as the radius. This satisfies the definition of a circle.   **38.** The two thumbtacks act as foci, and the length of string is constant. This satisfies the definition of an ellipse.

39.

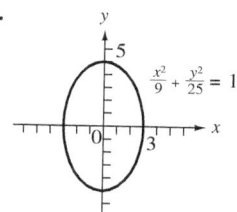

$\frac{x^2}{9} + \frac{y^2}{25} = 1$

41.

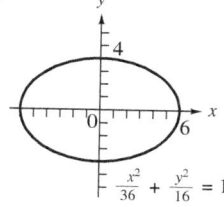

$\frac{x^2}{36} + \frac{y^2}{16} = 1$

43.

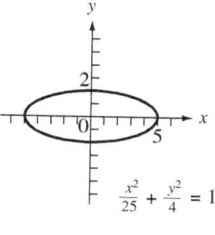

$\frac{x^2}{25} + \frac{y^2}{4} = 1$

45.

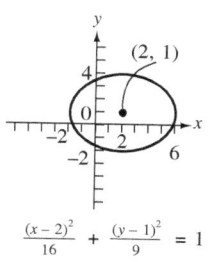

$\frac{(x-2)^2}{16} + \frac{(y-1)^2}{9} = 1$

47.

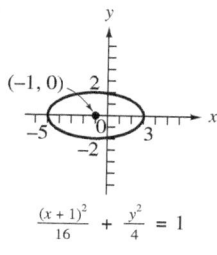

$\frac{(x+1)^2}{16} + \frac{y^2}{4} = 1$

49.

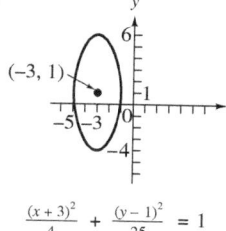

$\frac{(x+3)^2}{4} + \frac{(y-1)^2}{25} = 1$

51. (a) 10 m **(b)** 36 m   **53.** $3\sqrt{3}$ units

SECTION 13.3

1. C **2.** B **3.** D **4.** A **5.** Because the coefficient of the x^2-term is positive, this is a horizontal hyperbola with x-intercepts $(-3, 0)$ and $(3, 0)$.
6. Because the function represents the principal square root, $f(x)$ must be nonnegative. This restricts the graph to the upper half of the circle centered at the origin with radius 7.

7.

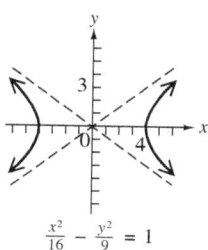

$\frac{x^2}{16} - \frac{y^2}{9} = 1$

9.

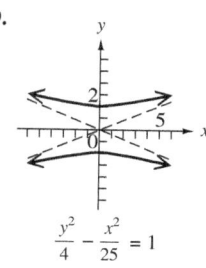

$\frac{y^2}{4} - \frac{x^2}{25} = 1$

11.

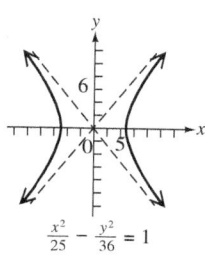

$\frac{x^2}{25} - \frac{y^2}{36} = 1$

13.

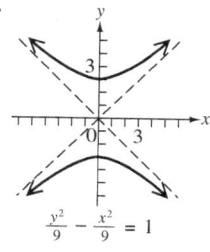

$\frac{y^2}{9} - \frac{x^2}{9} = 1$

15. hyperbola

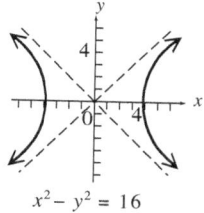

$x^2 - y^2 = 16$

19. circle

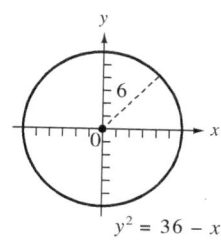

$y^2 = 36 - x^2$

23.

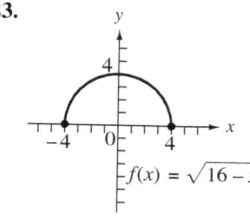

$f(x) = \sqrt{16 - x^2}$

domain: $[-4, 4]$;
range: $[0, 4]$

27.

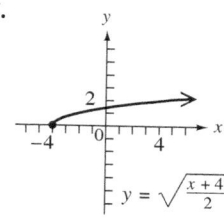

$y = \sqrt{\frac{x+4}{2}}$

domain: $[-4, \infty)$;
range: $[0, \infty)$

31. (a) 50 m **(b)** 69.3 m

33.

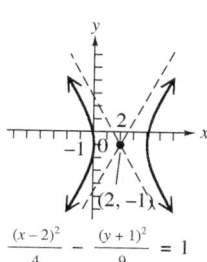

$\frac{(x-2)^2}{4} - \frac{(y+1)^2}{9} = 1$

35.

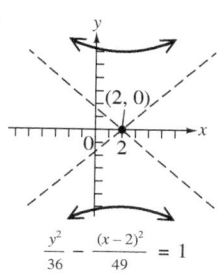

$\frac{y^2}{36} - \frac{(x-2)^2}{49} = 1$

17. ellipse

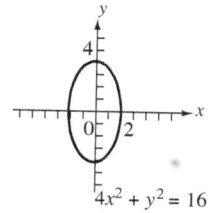

$4x^2 + y^2 = 16$

21. ellipse

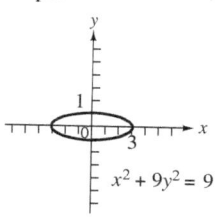

$x^2 + 9y^2 = 9$

25.

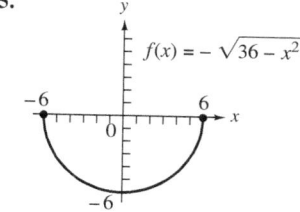

$f(x) = -\sqrt{36 - x^2}$

domain: $[-6, 6]$;
range: $[-6, 0]$

29.

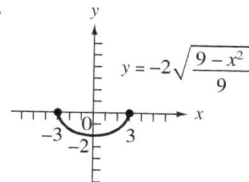

$y = -2\sqrt{\frac{9 - x^2}{9}}$

domain: $[-3, 3]$;
range: $[-2, 0]$

34.

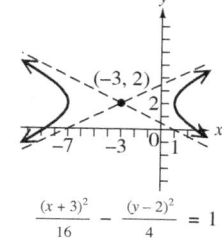

$\frac{(x+3)^2}{16} - \frac{(y-2)^2}{4} = 1$

36.

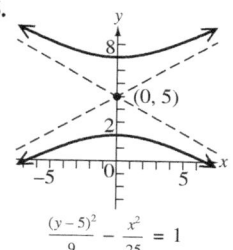

$\frac{(y-5)^2}{9} - \frac{x^2}{25} = 1$

SECTION 13.4

1. one   **2.** two   **3.** none   **4.** four

In Exercises 5–12, answers may vary.

5.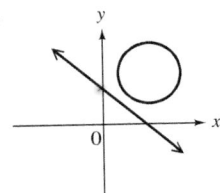

6.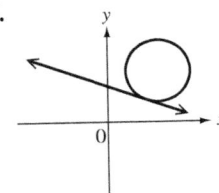

7.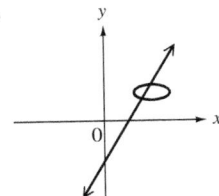

8.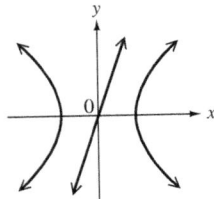

9.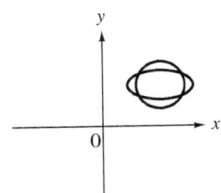

10.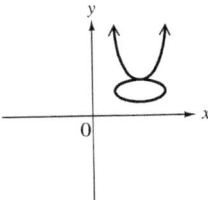

11.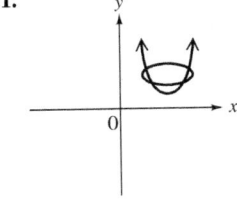

12.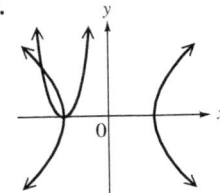

7.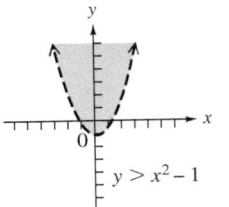
$y > x^2 - 1$

9.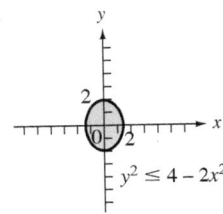
$y^2 \le 4 - 2x^2$

11.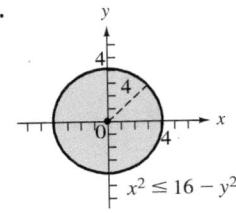
$x^2 \le 16 - y^2$

13.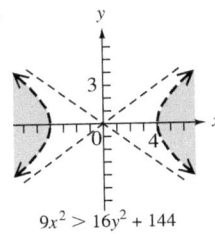
$9x^2 > 16y^2 + 144$

15.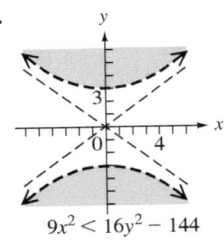
$9x^2 < 16y^2 - 144$

17.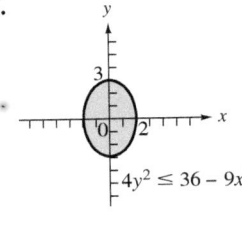
$4y^2 \le 36 - 9x^2$

19.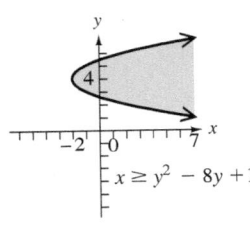
$x \ge y^2 - 8y + 14$

21.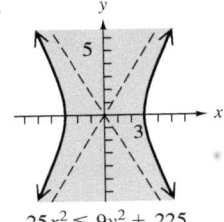
$25x^2 \le 9y^2 + 225$

23.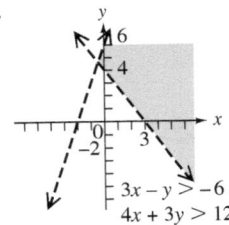
$3x - y > -6$
$4x + 3y > 12$

25.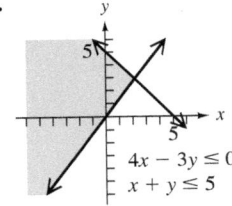
$4x - 3y \le 0$
$x + y \le 5$

27.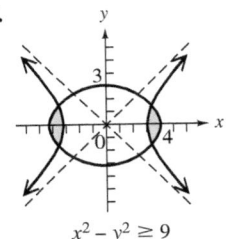
$x^2 - y^2 \ge 9$
$\frac{x^2}{16} + \frac{y^2}{9} \le 1$

29.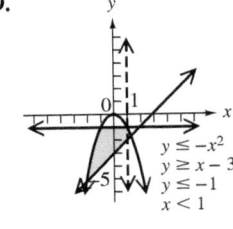
$y \le -x^2$
$y \ge x - 3$
$y \le -1$
$x < 1$

13. $\left\{ (0,0), \left(\dfrac{1}{2}, \dfrac{1}{2} \right) \right\}$ **15.** $\{(-6, 9), (-1, 4)\}$

17. $\left\{ \left(-\dfrac{1}{5}, \dfrac{7}{5} \right), (1, -1) \right\}$ **19.** $\left\{ (-2, -2), \left(-\dfrac{4}{3}, -3 \right) \right\}$

21. $\{(-3, 1), (1, -3)\}$ **23.** $\left\{ \left(-\dfrac{3}{2}, -\dfrac{9}{4} \right), (-2, 0) \right\}$

25. $\left\{ (-\sqrt{3}, 0), (\sqrt{3}, 0), (-\sqrt{5}, 2), (\sqrt{5}, 2) \right\}$

27. $\{(-2, 0), (2, 0)\}$ **29.** $\left\{ (\sqrt{3}, 0), (-\sqrt{3}, 0) \right\}$

31. $\left\{ (-2\sqrt{3}, -2), (-2\sqrt{3}, 2), (2\sqrt{3}, -2), (2\sqrt{3}, 2) \right\}$

33. $\left\{ (i\sqrt{2}, -3i\sqrt{2}), (-i\sqrt{2}, 3i\sqrt{2}), (-\sqrt{6}, -\sqrt{6}), (\sqrt{6}, \sqrt{6}) \right\}$

35. $\left\{ (-2i\sqrt{2}, -2\sqrt{3}), (-2i\sqrt{2}, 2\sqrt{3}), (2i\sqrt{2}, -2\sqrt{3}), (2i\sqrt{2}, 2\sqrt{3}) \right\}$ **37.** $\left\{ (-\sqrt{5}, -\sqrt{5}), (\sqrt{5}, \sqrt{5}) \right\}$

39. $\{(-3, -1), (3, 1), (-i, 3i), (i, -3i)\}$ **41.** length: 12 ft; width: 7 ft

SECTION 13.5

1. C   **2.** above; outside; below   **3.** B   **4.** D   **5.** A   **6.** C

Chapter 13 REVIEW EXERCISES

1.
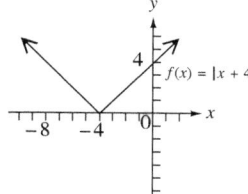
$f(x) = |x + 4|$
domain: $(-\infty, \infty)$;
range: $[0, \infty)$

2.
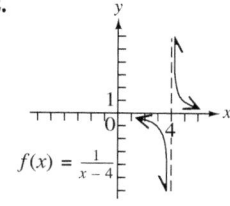
$f(x) = \dfrac{1}{x - 4}$
domain: $(-\infty, 4) \cup (4, \infty)$;
range: $(-\infty, 0) \cup (0, \infty)$

3.
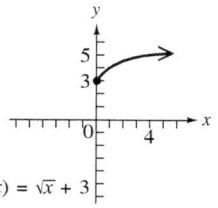
$f(x) = \sqrt{x} + 3$
domain: $[0, \infty)$;
range: $[3, \infty)$

4.
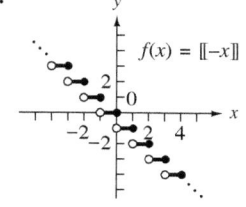
$f(x) = [\![-x]\!]$
domain: $(-\infty, \infty)$;
range: $\{\ldots, -2, -1, 0, 1, 2, \ldots\}$

5. 12 **6.** 2 **7.** -21 **8.** -5 **9.** $x^2 + y^2 = 49$
10. $(x + 2)^2 + (y - 4)^2 = 9$ **11.** $(x + 1)^2 + (y + 3)^2 = 25$
12. $(x - 4)^2 + (y - 2)^2 = 36$ **13.** $(-3, 2); r = 4$
14. $(4, 1); r = 2$ **15.** $(-1, -5); r = 3$ **16.** $(3, -2); r = 5$

17.
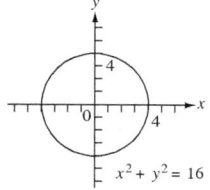
$x^2 + y^2 = 16$

18.
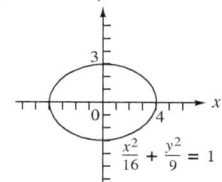
$\dfrac{x^2}{16} + \dfrac{y^2}{9} = 1$

19.
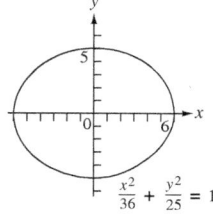
$\dfrac{x^2}{36} + \dfrac{y^2}{25} = 1$

20.
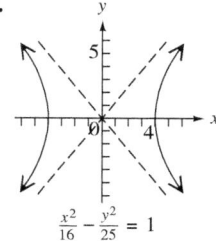
$\dfrac{x^2}{16} - \dfrac{y^2}{25} = 1$

21.
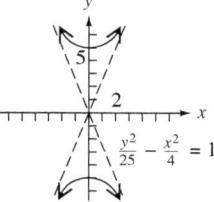
$\dfrac{y^2}{25} - \dfrac{x^2}{4} = 1$

22.
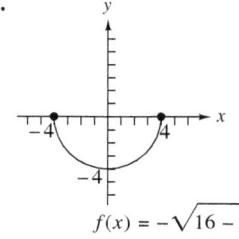
$f(x) = -\sqrt{16 - x^2}$

23. circle **24.** parabola **25.** hyperbola **26.** ellipse **27.** parabola
28. hyperbola **29.** $\{(6, -9), (-2, -5)\}$ **30.** $\{(1, 2), (-5, 14)\}$
31. $\{(4, 2), (-1, -3)\}$ **32.** $\{(-2, -4), (8, 1)\}$
33. $\{(-\sqrt{2}, 2), (-\sqrt{2}, -2), (\sqrt{2}, -2), (\sqrt{2}, 2)\}$

34. $\{(-\sqrt{6}, -\sqrt{3}), (-\sqrt{6}, \sqrt{3}), (\sqrt{6}, -\sqrt{3}), (\sqrt{6}, \sqrt{3})\}$
35. 0, 1, or 2 **36.** 0, 1, 2, 3, or 4

37.
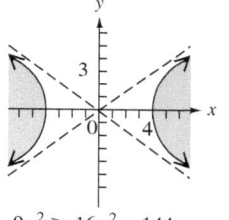
$9x^2 \geq 16y^2 + 144$

38.
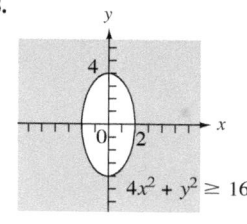
$4x^2 + y^2 \geq 16$

39.
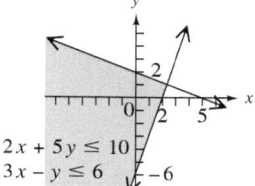
$2x + 5y \leq 10$
$3x - y \leq 6$

40.
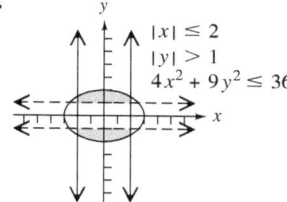
$|x| \leq 2$
$|y| > 1$
$4x^2 + 9y^2 \leq 36$

Chapter 13 MIXED REVIEW EXERCISES

1. center: $(-2, 5)$; radius: 6

2.
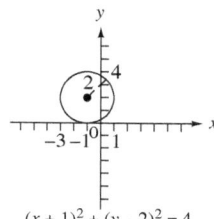
$(x + 1)^2 + (y - 2)^2 = 4$

3.
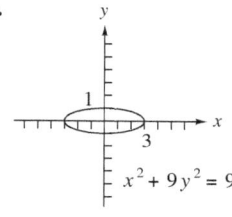
$x^2 + 9y^2 = 9$

4.
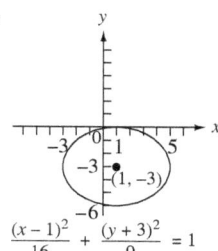
$\dfrac{(x - 1)^2}{16} + \dfrac{(y + 3)^2}{9} = 1$

5.
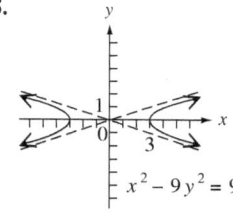
$x^2 - 9y^2 = 9$

6.
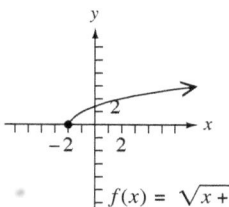
$f(x) = \sqrt{x + 2}$

7.
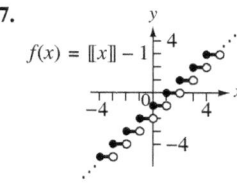
$f(x) = [\![x]\!] - 1$

8.
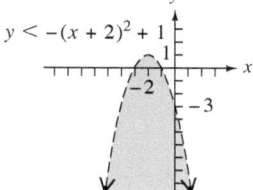
$y < -(x + 2)^2 + 1$

9.
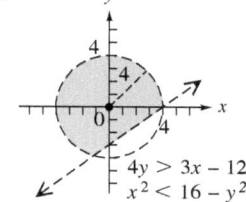
$4y > 3x - 12$
$x^2 < 16 - y^2$

10.

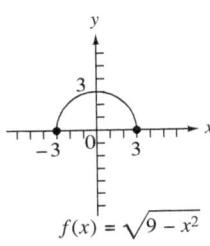

$$9x^2 \le 4y^2 + 36$$
$$x^2 + y^2 \le 16$$

11. $\{(-7, -35), (12, 60)\}$

12. $\{(-1, -2), (1, 2), (-2i, i), (2i, -i)\}$

Chapter 13 TEST

1. 0 **2.** $[0, \infty)$ **3.** $\{\dots, -2, -1, 0, 1, 2, \dots\}$

4. (a) C **(b)** A **(c)** D **(d)** B

5.

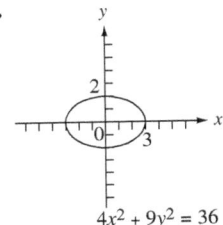

$f(x) = |x - 3| + 4$

domain: $(-\infty, \infty)$;
range: $[4, \infty)$

6.

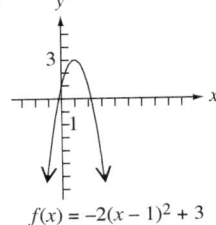

$$(x - 2)^2 + (y + 3)^2 = 16$$

center: $(2, -3)$; radius: 4

7. D **8.** $(0, 0)$; 1 **9.** center: $(-4, 1)$; radius: 5

10.

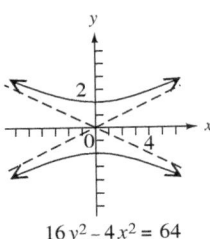

$f(x) = \sqrt{9 - x^2}$

11.

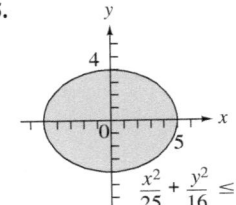

$$4x^2 + 9y^2 = 36$$

12.

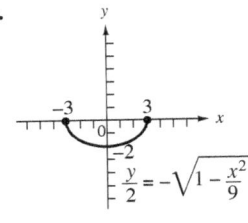

$$16y^2 - 4x^2 = 64$$

13.

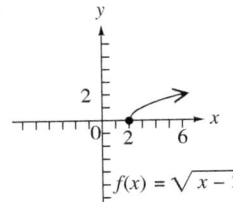

$$\frac{y}{2} = -\sqrt{1 - \frac{x^2}{9}}$$

14. ellipse **15.** hyperbola **16.** parabola **17.** circle

18. $\left\{\left(-\frac{1}{2}, -10\right), (5, 1)\right\}$ **19.** $\left\{(-2, -2), \left(\frac{14}{5}, -\frac{2}{5}\right)\right\}$

20. $\{(-\sqrt{22}, -\sqrt{3}), (-\sqrt{22}, \sqrt{3}), (\sqrt{22}, -\sqrt{3}), (\sqrt{22}, \sqrt{3})\}$

21.

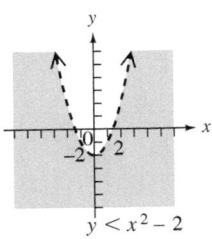

$$y < x^2 - 2$$

22.

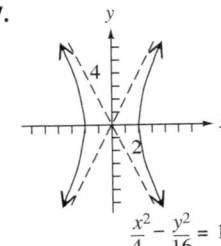

$$x^2 + 25y^2 \le 25$$
$$x^2 + y^2 \le 9$$

Chapters R–13 CUMULATIVE REVIEW EXERCISES

1. $\left\{\frac{2}{3}\right\}$ **2.** $\left(-\infty, \frac{3}{5}\right]$ **3.** $\{-4, 4\}$ **4.** $\frac{2}{3}$ **5.** $3x + 2y = -13$

6. $\{(3, -3)\}$ **7.** $\{(4, 1, -2)\}$ **8.** $\left\{(-1, 5), \left(\frac{5}{2}, -2\right)\right\}$

9. $\frac{a^5}{4}$ **10.** $2\sqrt[3]{2}$ **11.** $\frac{3\sqrt{10}}{2}$ **12.** -2.76×10^{-4} **13.** $25y^2 - 30y + 9$

14. $4x^3 - 4x^2 + 3x + 5 + \frac{3}{2x + 1}$ **15.** $\frac{7}{5} + \frac{11}{5}i$ **16.** $\frac{y - 1}{y(y - 3)}$

17. $\frac{3c + 5}{(c + 5)(c + 3)}$ **18.** $\frac{1}{p}$ **19.** $(3x + 2)(4x - 5)$

20. $(z^2 + 1)(z + 1)(z - 1)$ **21.** $(a - 3b)(a^2 + 3ab + 9b^2)$

22. $1\frac{1}{5}$ hr **23.** $\varnothing$ **24.** $\left\{\frac{1}{5}, -\frac{3}{2}\right\}$ **25.** $\left\{\frac{3 + \sqrt{33}}{6}, \frac{3 - \sqrt{33}}{6}\right\}$

26. $\left\{-\frac{\sqrt{6}}{2}, \frac{\sqrt{6}}{2}, -\sqrt{7}, \sqrt{7}\right\}$ **27.** $\{3\}$ **28.** $v = \frac{\pm\sqrt{rFkw}}{kw}$

29. (a) -1 **(b)** $9x^2 + 18x + 4$ **30.** $f^{-1}(x) = \sqrt[3]{x - 4}$

31. (a) 4 **(b)** 7 **32.** $\log\frac{(3x + 7)^2}{4}$

33.

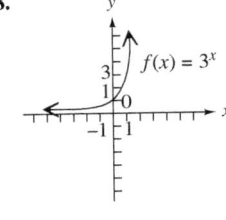

$f(x) = -3x + 5$

34.

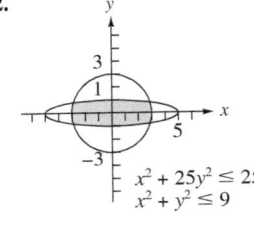

$f(x) = -2(x - 1)^2 + 3$

35.

$$\frac{x^2}{25} + \frac{y^2}{16} \le 1$$

36.

$f(x) = \sqrt{x - 2}$

37.

$$\frac{x^2}{4} - \frac{y^2}{16} = 1$$

38.

$f(x) = 3^x$

APPENDIX A   Review of Exponents, Polynomials, and Factoring

1. $\dfrac{1}{a^2b}$ **3.** $\dfrac{100y^{10}}{x^2}$ **5.** 0   **7.** $\dfrac{x^{10}}{2w^{13}y^5}$ **9.** $\dfrac{a^{15}}{-64b^{15}}$ **11.** $\dfrac{x^{16}z^{10}}{y^6}$

13. $-6a^4 + 11a^3 - 20a^2 + 26a - 15$ **15.** $8x^3 - 18x^2 + 6x - 16$

17. $x^2y - xy^2 + 6y^3$ **19.** $-3x^2 - 62x + 32$ **21.** $10x^3 - 4x^2 + 9x - 4$

23. $6x^2 - 19x - 7$ **25.** $4x^2 - 9x + 2$ **27.** $16t^2 - 9$ **29.** $4y^4 - 16$

31. $16x^2 - 24x + 9$ **33.** $36r^2 + 60ry + 25y^2$ **35.** $c^3 + 8d^3$

37. $64x^3 - 1$ **39.** $14t^3 + 45st^2 + 18s^2t - 5s^3$ **41.** F   **42.** G   **43.** A

44. B   **45.** D   **46.** A   **47.** C   **48.** E   **49.** H   **50.** D

51. $8a(5b - 2)$ **53.** $4xy^3(2x^2y + 3x + 9y)$ **55.** $(x + 3)(x - 5)$

57. $(2x + 3)(x - 6)$ **59.** $4(x - 5)(x - 2)$ **61.** $(6t + 5)(6t - 5)$

63. $(4t + 3)^2$ **65.** $p(2m - 3n)^2$ **67.** $(x + 1)(x^2 - x + 1)$

69. $(2t + 5)(4t^2 - 10t + 25)$ **71.** $(t^2 - 5)(t^4 + 5t^2 + 25)$

73. $(4 + m)(5 + 3n)$ **75.** $(5x + 2y)(t + 3r)$

77. $(6r - 5s)(a + 2b)$ **79.** $(t^2 + 1)(t + 1)(t - 1)$

APPENDIX B   Synthetic Division

1. C   **2.** C   **3.** $x - 5$ **5.** $4m - 1$ **7.** $2a + 4 + \dfrac{5}{a + 2}$

9. $p - 4 + \dfrac{9}{p + 1}$ **11.** $4a^2 + a + 3$

13. $x^4 + 2x^3 + 2x^2 + 7x + 10 + \dfrac{18}{x - 2}$

15. $-4r^5 - 7r^4 - 10r^3 - 5r^2 - 11r - 8 + \dfrac{-8}{r - 1}$

17. $-3y^4 + 8y^3 - 21y^2 + 36y - 72 + \dfrac{143}{y + 2}$ **19.** $y^2 + y + 1 + \dfrac{2}{y - 1}$

21. 7   **23.** -2 **25.** 0   **27.** yes   **29.** no   **31.** yes   **33.** no

35. $(2x - 3)(x + 4)$ **36.** $\left\{ -4, \dfrac{3}{2} \right\}$ **37.** 0   **38.** 0   **39.** a

40. Yes, $x - 3$ is a factor; $Q(x) = (x - 3)(3x - 1)(x + 2)$

APPENDIX C   Solving Systems of Linear Equations by Matrix Methods

1. (a) $0, 5, -3$ **(b)** $1, -3, 8$ **(c)** yes; The number of rows is the same as the number of columns (three).   **(d)** $\begin{bmatrix} 1 & 4 & 8 \\ 0 & 5 & -3 \\ -2 & 3 & 1 \end{bmatrix}$

(e) $\begin{bmatrix} 1 & -\dfrac{3}{2} & -\dfrac{1}{2} \\ 0 & 5 & -3 \\ 1 & 4 & 8 \end{bmatrix}$ **(f)** $\begin{bmatrix} 1 & 15 & 25 \\ 0 & 5 & -3 \\ 1 & 4 & 8 \end{bmatrix}$

2. (a) 3×2 **(b)** 2×3 **(c)** 4×2

3. $\left[\begin{array}{cc|c} 1 & 2 & 11 \\ 2 & -1 & -3 \end{array} \right]$; $\left[\begin{array}{cc|c} 1 & 2 & 11 \\ 0 & -5 & -25 \end{array} \right]$; $\left[\begin{array}{cc|c} 1 & 2 & 11 \\ 0 & 1 & 5 \end{array} \right]$; $x + 2y = 11$;

$y = 5$; $\{(1, 5)\}$ **5.** $\{(4, 1)\}$ **7.** $\{(1, 1)\}$ **9.** $\{(-1, 4)\}$ **11.** $\varnothing$

13. $\{(x, y) \mid 2x + y = 4\}$ **15.** $\{(0, 0)\}$

17. $\left[\begin{array}{ccc|c} 1 & 1 & -1 & -3 \\ 0 & -1 & 3 & 10 \\ 0 & -6 & 7 & 38 \end{array} \right]$; $\left[\begin{array}{ccc|c} 1 & 1 & -1 & -3 \\ 0 & 1 & -3 & -10 \\ 0 & -6 & 7 & 38 \end{array} \right]$;

$\left[\begin{array}{ccc|c} 1 & 1 & -1 & -3 \\ 0 & 1 & -3 & -10 \\ 0 & 0 & -11 & -22 \end{array} \right]$; $\left[\begin{array}{ccc|c} 1 & 1 & -1 & -3 \\ 0 & 1 & -3 & -10 \\ 0 & 0 & 1 & 2 \end{array} \right]$; $x + y - z = -3$;

$y - 3z = -10$; $z = 2$; $\{(3, -4, 2)\}$ **19.** $\{(4, 0, 1)\}$

21. $\{(-1, 23, 16)\}$ **23.** $\{(3, 2, -4)\}$ **25.** $\varnothing$

27. $\{(x, y, z) \mid x - 2y + z = 4\}$ **29.** $\{(0, 0, 0)\}$

Photo Credits

Index

A

Absolute value
  adding numbers with different signs, 58–59
  adding numbers with same sign, 57
  evaluating, 52
  explanation of, 52, 106
  simplifying roots using, 732
Absolute value equations
  explanation of, 614–615, 662
  solving, 615–619, 665
Absolute value functions, 968, 1007
Absolute value inequalities
  explanation of, 614–615, 662
  solving, 615–619, 665
Addends, 57–58, 106
Addition
  applications of, 60
  associative property of, 88–89, 93, 98, 109
  with brackets, 59–60
  commutative property of, 88–89, 93, 98, 109
  of complex numbers, 791, 800
  of decimals, 18
  of exponential expressions, 360
  of fractions, 6–8
  identity element for, 90, 107
  identity property of, 89–90, 93, 109
  inverse property of, 90–91, 93, 109
  of like terms, 385–386
  with number line, 57–58
  phrases that indicate, 60
  of polynomial functions, 698–699, 719
  of polynomials, 385–386, 388–390, 422, 1018
  of radical expressions, 762–764, 799
  of rational expressions, 530–533, 578
  of real numbers, 57–60, 108
  of signed numbers, 57–59
  word phrases for, 60
Addition property
  of equality, 118–122, 202, 591–592
  of inequality, 187–188, 597
Additive identity element, 90, 107
Additive inverse
  explanation of, 51, 90–91, 106
  quotient of opposites rule, 513
Agreement on domain, 684
Algebraic expressions
  distinguishing between equations and, 42
  evaluating, 39–40
  examples of, 590
  explanation of, 39, 106
  simplifying, 98–101, 109
  translating word phrases into, 40–41, 60, 67, 80–81, 101, 140
Algebraic fractions. See Rational expressions
Alternative forms of logarithms, 936–937
Angles
  complementary, 153–154, 201
  measure of, 153–154, 164
  right, 153, 201
  straight, 153, 164, 201
  supplementary, 153–154, 201
  vertical, 164, 201
Apogee, 710

Applications
  for addition, 60
  of exponents, 377–380, 421
  of fractions, 10–11
  from geometry, 161–166
  of inequalities, 192–195
  of linear equations, 147–154, 203, 234–235, 274
  of linear systems, 330–335, 349
  with mixed numbers, 10–11
  of negative numbers, 48
  of percents, 24, 177–178, 332–333
  of proportions, 177
  of Pythagorean theorem, 485–486
  of quadratic equations, 482–488, 497
  of rational expressions, 564–570, 580
  for scientific notation, 380
  steps to solve, 147–154, 482, 564
  for subtraction, 68
Applied problems
  methods to solve, 848, 870–871
  modeled by quadratic functions, 849–850
  Pythagorean theorem to solve, 847
(is) Approximately equal to, 797
Approximations, for roots, 733
Area
  of circles, 168
  explanation of, 161, 201
  of rectangles, 161, 417
  of trapezoids, 161, 167
  of triangles, 163, 167
Area formula
  explanation of, 161, 363
  use of, 417, 482–483
Area of triangle, 738
Associative property
  of addition, 88–89, 93, 98, 109
  distinguishing between commutative property and, 89
  of multiplication, 88–89, 93, 109
  use of, 88–89, 98
Asymptotes
  explanation of, 1006
  of hyperbola, 985–986, 1006
  of reciprocal function, 968
Augmented matrix, 1031–1032
Average (mean), 85
Average rate of change, 250–251
Axes of a coordinate system, 218, 289
Axis
  of parabola, 856, 859, 889
  transverse, 985, 1006
  x-, 218, 233, 289, 628, 662
  y-, 218, 233, 289, 628, 662

B

Barometers, 943
Base
  explanation of, 30, 106, 177–178, 358
  of exponents, 358
  of percentage, 177–178
Binomials
  explanation of, 387, 420

Binomials *(continued)*
   factoring, 468–469
   factoring out as the greatest common factor, 436
   finding greater powers of, 405
   multiplication of, 397–398, 422, 767–768
   square of, 402–403, 422, 781
Body mass index (BMI), 711
Boundary lines
   explanation of, 282, 289
   graphs of linear inequalities with vertical, 285
Braces, 31
Brackets, 31, 32–33, 59–60, 66
Breaching, 114
Break-even quantity, 338

C

Calculator tips
   for logarithms, 940, 943
   for roots, 733
Cartesian coordinate system. *See* Rectangular coordinate system
Celsius-Fahrenheit conversions, 198, 278
Center
   of circle, 975–978, 1006
   of ellipse, 978
Center-radius form of circle, 976
Change-of-base rule, 951
Characteristic impedance, 783
Circle(s)
   center of, 975–978, 1006
   center-radius form of, 976
   circumference of, 168, 706
   equation of, 975–977, 1008
   explanation of, 1006
   formulas for, 168
   graphs of, 975–978, 987
   radius of, 706, 975–978, 1006
Circle graphs, 11–12
Circumference of circles, 168, 706
Classifying polynomials, 387
Closed intervals, 596
Coefficients
   identifying, 385
   numerical, 98–99, 107, 385
   of polynomials, 385
Columns, of matrix, 1031
Combined variation, 711, 717
Combining like terms, 99–101, 122, 385–386
Common denominators, 6–7, 90. *See also* Least common
   denominator (LCD)
Common factors
   explanation of, 3, 432
   factoring out binomial, 436
   factoring out negative, 435
   factoring trinomials with, 450, 456
   greatest. *See* Greatest common factor (GCF)
   looking for, 446
   quadratic equations with, 475
Common logarithms
   applications of, 940–942
   evaluating, 940
   explanation of, 940, 955, 957
Commutative property
   of addition, 88–89, 93, 98, 109
   distinguishing between associative property and, 89
   of multiplication, 88–89, 93, 109
   use of, 88–89, 98
Complementary angles
   explanation of, 153, 201
   solving problems involving, 153–154

Completing the square
   explanation of, 817, 890
   to find vertex, 866–867
   to graph horizontal parabolas, 872
   simplifying before, 822
   solving quadratic equations by, 817–821, 844
Complex conjugates, 792, 797
Complex fractions
   explanation of, 540, 576
   simplifying, 540–545, 579
Complex numbers
   addition of, 791, 800
   conjugates of, 792
   division of, 792–793, 800
   explanation of, 790, 797, 800
   imaginary part of, 790
   multiplication of, 791–792, 800
   nonreal, 790, 797
   powers of i and, 793
   real part of, 790, 797
   simplifying, 788–789
   standard form of, 790, 797
   subsets of, 790
   subtraction of, 791, 800
Components, of ordered pair, 628, 662
Composite functions, 902–904, 955, 956
Composite numbers, 2
Compound inequalities
   explanation of, 605–607, 662
   solving, 664
   solving with *and,* 605–607
   solving with *or,* 608–609
Compound interest formulas, 949–950
Compound interest problems, 949–950
Conditional equations, 137–138, 201, 594–595, 662
Conic sections
   examples of, 975
   explanation of, 975, 1006
   summary of, 987
Conjugates, 404, 420, 771, 792, 797
Consecutive integers
   even, 152, 201, 483
   explanation of, 201
   odd, 152, 201, 483
   solving problems involving, 151–152, 483–485
Consistent system, 305, 347, 641, 663
Constant, explanation of, 39, 106
Constant functions, 692, 717
Constant of variation, 576, 706, 717
Consumer Price Index (CPI), 182, 849
Continuously compounded interest, 950
Contradiction equation, 137–138, 201, 594–595, 662
Coordinates
   of a point, 48, 106, 218, 289, 628, 662
   of a vertex, 871
Coordinate system, rectangular. *See* Rectangular coordinate
   system
Cost-benefit equation, 945
Cost per unit, 174–175
Costs
   fixed, 267
   solving problems about, 331–332
   variable, 267
Counting numbers, 1, 47, 106
Cross products
   explanation of, 175, 201
   solving equations using, 176–177
Cube root function, 731
Cube roots, 729–731, 797

Cubes
  difference of, 463–464, 468
  factoring difference of, 463–464
  factoring sum of, 464
  of numbers, 30
  perfect, 463, 729, 797
  sum of, 464, 468
Cubing function, 701, 702, 717, 719

D

Data, equations of lines that describe, 274
dB (decibel), 942
Decimal(s)
  addition of, 18
  converting percents to, 22
  converting to percents, 22
  division of, 18–20
  explanation of, 17
  linear equations with, 128
  multiplication of, 18–19, 20
  place value in, 17
  repeating, 21
  rounding of, 20, 21
  solving equations with, 128, 139–140, 594
  solving linear systems with, 317
  subtraction of, 18
  terminating, 21
  writing as fractions, 17–18
  writing as percents, 21–22
  writing fractions as, 21
  writing percents as, 21–22
Decimal places, 18
Degree
  of polynomials, 387, 420
  symbol for, 153
  of a term, 387, 420, 697
Denominators
  adding fractions with different, 8
  adding fractions with same, 6–7
  common, 6–7, 90
  of complex fractions, 543–545
  explanation of, 1
  least common. See Least common denominator (LCD)
  quotient of opposites rule, 513
  rationalizing, 769–772, 799
  writing rational expressions with given, 526–527
Dependent equations
  explanation of, 305, 347, 641, 663
  solving a linear system with, 315
  solving system of, 645
  in three variables, 653
Dependent variable, 680, 717
Depreciation, 240, 962
Descartes, René, 217, 628
Descending powers, 386, 420
Difference
  of cubes, 463–464, 468
  of squares, 459–460, 468, 496
Difference (in subtraction), 9, 41, 64, 106
Direct variation, 576, 580, 706–708, 717, 719
Discriminant
  explanation of, 829, 869, 889, 890
  use of, 829–830, 869
Disjoint intervals, 596
Distance, rate, and time problems, 167, 334–335, 565–568, 580
Distance formula, 754–755, 799
Distributive property
  explanation of, 91–93, 109
  to simplify terms in equations, 122

to solve linear equations, 592–593
  to solve linear inequalities, 599
  use of, 98–99, 130, 385, 514
Diversity, index of, 962
Dividend, 19, 106, 1025
Division
  of complex numbers, 792–793, 800
  of decimals, 18–20
  definition of, 75–78
  of fractions, 5–6, 11
  of polynomial functions, 700, 719
  of polynomials, 409–410, 413–417, 422, 1025–1027
  by powers of ten, 20
  of radical expressions, 767–773, 799
  of rational expressions, 519–521, 577
  of real numbers, 75–78, 109
  with scientific notation, 379–380
  of signed numbers, 75–78
  synthetic, 1025–1028
  word phrases for, 80–81
  by zero, 77
Divisor
  explanation of, 19, 107, 1025
  greatest common, 432
Domain
  agreement on, 684
  explanation of, 681, 717, 718
  of functions, 681–682, 718
  of relations, 681–682, 718
Double negative rule, 51
Doubling time of money, 945, 949

E

e, 942
Earthquake intensities, 384
Elements
  of a matrix, 1031
  of a set, 47, 106
Elimination method
  explanation of, 320
  to solve linear systems, 320–324, 349, 643–645, 650–652, 666–667
  to solve nonlinear systems, 994–995
Elimination number, 173
Ellipse(s)
  center of, 978
  equation of, 978, 1008
  explanation of, 975, 978, 1006
  foci of, 978
  graphs of, 978–980, 987, 989
  intercepts of, 978
Empty set, 137
Equality
  addition property of, 118–122, 202, 591–592
  multiplication property of, 126–130, 202, 591–592
  symbols for, 33–34, 41–42, 550
Equation(s)
  absolute value, 614–619, 662, 665
  of circle, 975–977, 1008
  conditional, 137–138, 201, 594–595, 662
  contradiction, 137–138, 201, 594–595, 662
  cost-benefit, 945
  dependent, 305, 315, 347, 641, 645, 653, 663
  distinguishing between expressions and, 42, 81, 550–551
  of ellipse, 978, 1008
  equivalent, 118, 126, 201, 590, 662
  explanation of, 41, 106
  exponential. See Exponential equations
  factoring to solve, 844

I-4   Index

Equation(s) *(continued)*
  first-degree, 630, 662
  graphs of, 630–632, 662, 988
  of horizontal lines, 273, 632–633
  of hyperbola, 985, 1008
  identifying functions from, 684–685
  identity, 137–138, 201, 594–595, 662
  independent, 305, 347, 641, 663
  with infinitely many solutions, 137–138
  of inverse function, 909–910
  linear in one variable. *See* Linear equations in one variable
  linear in two variables. *See* Linear equations in two variables
  linear systems of, 640, 649, 663
  of lines, 246–247
  logarithmic. *See* Logarithmic equations
  mathematical models as, 45, 220, 234–235, 274, 487–488
  nonlinear, 590, 993, 1006
  nonlinear systems of, 993–997, 1006, 1009
  with no solutions, 137
  ordered pairs satisfying, 629
  of parallel lines, 272–273
  of perpendicular lines, 272–273
  power rule for, 779–782
  quadratic. *See* Quadratic equations
  radical, 779–782, 797
  second-degree, 810, 889, 987, 994–995
  simplifying terms in, 122, 129–130
  solution of, 41, 106, 118, 590, 662
  solving literal, 165
  solving using cross products, 176–177
  solving with decimals, 139–140
  solving with fractions, 138–139
  solving with rational expressions, 550–557, 562–563, 579
  square root property of, 810–813, 890
  system of, 302–307, 312–317, 320–324, 347
  systems of. *See* Systems of equations
  translating word sentences to, 42, 81
  variation, 706–711
  of vertical lines, 273, 632–633
  working, 650
Equilibrium demand, 311
Equilibrium supply, 311
Equivalent equations, 118, 126, 201, 590, 662
Equivalent forms for positive numbers, 78
Equivalent forms of rational expressions, 513–514
Equivalent inequalities, 597, 662
Euler, Leonhard, 942
Even consecutive integers, 152, 201, 483
Even index, 729
Exponent(s)
  applications of, 377–380, 421
  base of, 358
  explanation of, 30, 106, 358
  integer, 366–372, 421
  negative, 367–369, 421, 546
  negative-to-positive rules, 1017
  positive, 369
  power rules for, 360–363, 421, 1017
  product rule for, 358–360, 362–363, 421, 1017
  quotient rule for, 369–370, 421, 1017
  rational, 739–744, 798
  rules for, 371, 1017
  scientific notation and, 377–380
  zero, 366, 421, 1017
Exponential equations
  explanation of, 918, 955
  growth and decay problems, 950–951
  properties of, 946
  solving, 918–920, 946–947, 958

Exponential expressions
  addition vs. multiplication of, 360
  explanation of, 30, 106, 358, 420
Exponential form to logarithmic form, 924
Exponential functions
  applications of, 920–921
  explanation of, 916, 956
  graphs of, 916–918, 956
Exponential growth and decay problems, 920–921, 927, 950–951
Expressions
  algebraic. *See* Algebraic expressions
  distinguishing between equations and, 42, 81, 550–551
  evaluating, 79, 108
  exponential. *See* Exponential expressions
  radical. *See* Radical expressions
  rational. *See* Rational expressions
  simplifying, 90, 98–101, 109
Extraneous solutions (values), 553, 576, 779, 797
Extremes of a proportion, 175, 201

F

Factored form
  explanation of, 432, 494
  prime, 2–3, 432–433
Factoring
  binomials, 468–469
  difference of cubes, 463–464, 468
  difference of squares, 459–460, 468, 496
  explanation of, 432, 494
  by grouping, 436–438, 449–450, 495
  perfect square trinomials, 461–462, 469, 496
  polynomials, 434–438, 442–446, 449–450, 453–456, 459–462, 468–470, 1020–1021
  rational expressions, 510–513
  to solve equations, 844
  to solve quadratic equations, 473–478, 496
  sum of cubes, 464, 468
  trinomials, 442–446, 449–450, 453–456, 469, 494–496
Factors
  distinguishing between terms and, 99
  explanation of, 2, 432, 494
  greatest common. *See* Greatest common factor (GCF)
  of numbers, 2, 432
Factor tree, 2
Fahrenheit-Celsius conversions, 198, 278
First-degree equations. *See* Linear equations; Linear equations in one variable; Linear equations in two variables
Fixed cost, 267
Foci *(sing: Focus)*
  of ellipse, 978
  of hyperbola, 985
Focus variable, 650
FOIL method
  explanation of, 397, 420, 422
  factoring trinomials using, 442, 453–456, 496
  inner product of, 397, 420
  multiplying binomials by, 397–398, 422, 767
  multiplying complex numbers, 792
  outer product of, 397, 420
  squaring by, 402
Formula(s)
  for body mass index, 711
  for circumference of circle, 706
  compound interest, 949–950
  continuous compound interest, 950
  distance, 754–755, 799
  to evaluate variables, 161
  explanation of, 201
  Galileo's, 812

from geometry, 161–166
involving squares and square roots, 847–848
for Pythagorean theorem, 753–754, 799, 847
for the Pythagorean theorem, 485–486, 496
quadratic, 825–829, 889, 890
rotational rate of space station, 787
slope, 242–245, 633
solving for specified variables in, 165–166, 203, 556–557
vertex, 867
Fourth root, 729–730
Fraction bar, 1, 31, 32–33
Fractions
addition of, 6–8
applications of, 10–11
complex, 540–545, 576, 579
division of, 5–6, 11
explanation of, 1
improper, 1, 4
linear equations with, 127–128, 593
lowest terms of, 3, 90
multiplication of, 4–5
proper, 1
reciprocals of, 5
simplifying, 3
solving equations with, 138–139
solving linear systems with, 316–317
subtraction of, 9–10
writing as decimals, 21
writing as percents, 23
writing decimals as, 17–18
writing percents as, 23
Froude, William, 855
Froude number, 855
Function(s)
absolute value, 968, 1007
composite, 902–904, 955, 956
concept of, 394
constant, 692, 717
cube root, 731
cubing, 701, 702, 717, 719
defined by radical expressions, 730–731, 798
domain of, 681–682, 718
equation of the inverse, 909–910
evaluating, 689–690
explanation of, 481, 679, 717, 718
exponential, 916–921, 956
exponential decay, 920–921
exponential growth, 920–921
greatest integer, 970–971, 1006
identifying from equations, 684–685
identifying from graphs, 682–683
identity, 701, 717, 719
inverse. *See* Inverse functions
linear, 692, 701, 717, 718
logarithmic, 926–927, 957
one-to-one, 907–910, 955, 956
polynomial. *See* Polynomial functions
quadratic. *See* Quadratic functions
range of, 681–682, 718
reciprocal, 968, 1007
relations as, 679–680
square root, 730, 968, 988–989, 1008
squaring, 701, 702, 717, 719
step, 971, 1006
translation of, 968–970
variations in definition of, 685
vertical line test for, 682–683
Function notation
explanation of, 717, 718

symbol for, 717
use of, 689–691
Fundamental property of rational expressions, 510, 577
Fundamental rectangle of hyperbola, 985–986, 1006
$f(x)$ notation. *See* Function notation

G
Galilei, Galileo, 473, 481, 812
Galileo's formula, 812
GCF. *See* Greatest common factor (GCF)
Geometry
formulas and applications from, 161–166
solving problems in, 655–656
of systems of linear equations, 649–650
Googol, 382
Graph(s)
of absolute value function, 968
circle, 11–12
of circles, 975–978, 987
of cube root functions, 731
of elementary functions, 968–970
of ellipses, 978–980, 987, 989
of equations, 630–632, 662, 988
explanation of, 228, 289
of exponential functions, 916–918, 956
of greatest integer functions, 971, 1007
of horizontal lines, 632–633
of hyperbolas, 985–986
identifying functions from, 682–683
of inequalities, 186–187
interpretation of, 214–215
of intervals on number lines, 186–187
of inverse functions, 911
line, 628
of linear equations, 228–235, 258–260, 291, 640–641
of linear inequalities, 186–187, 282–285, 342–344, 596
of linear systems, 302–307, 640–641
of lines, 214–215, 232–233, 259–262, 289
of logarithmic functions, 926–927
of numbers, 48–49
of ordered pairs, 220, 628
of parabolas, 701, 857–860, 871–873, 892, 987
pie charts, 11–12
of polynomial functions, 701–702, 719
of quadratic functions, 856–861, 868, 891
of radical functions, 730–731
of rational numbers, 49
of reciprocal functions, 968
of relations, 682–683
of second-degree inequalities, 1000–1001
of semicircles, 989
to solve quadratic inequalities, 878–879
of square root functions, 730, 968, 988–989, 1007
of systems of inequalities, 1001–1003, 1009
using slope-intercept form, 259–260
of vertical lines, 632–633
(is) Greater than, 33–34, 186
(is) Greater than or equal to, 33–34, 186
Greatest common divisor, 432
Greatest common factor (GCF)
explanation of, 432, 494
factoring out, 434–436, 446
for numbers, 432–433
steps to find, 433, 495
of variable terms, 433–434
Greatest integer functions
explanation of, 1006
graphs of, 971, 1007
method for applying, 970–971

Grouping
  factoring by, 436–438, 495
  factoring trinomials by, 449–450
  with negative signs, 438
Grouping symbols
  addition with, 59–60
  explanation of, 31–33
  subtraction with, 66
Growth and decay applications, 919–921, 927, 950–951

H

Half-life, 951
Half-open interval, 596
Heron's formula, 738
Horizontal lines
  equations of, 233, 273, 632–633
  graphs of, 233, 261–262, 632–633
  slope of, 245–246, 291, 635, 666
Horizontal line test, 909, 956
Horizontal parabolas, 871–873, 892
Horizontal shift
  of ellipse, 980
  explanation of, 857–858
  method for applying, 969–970
  of parabola, 857–859
Hyperbola(s)
  asymptotes of, 985–986, 1006
  equations of, 985, 1008
  explanation of, 975, 1006
  foci of, 985
  fundamental rectangle of, 985–986, 1006
  graphs of, 985–986
  intercepts of, 985
Hypotenuse of a right triangle, 485–486, 494, 753

I

i, 788, 793, 797
Identity element
  for addition, 90, 107
  for multiplication, 90, 107
Identity equation, 137–138, 201, 594–595, 662
Identity function, 701, 717, 719
Identity properties
  of addition, 89–90, 93, 109
  of multiplication, 89–90, 93, 109
Imaginary numbers, 790, 797
Imaginary part, 790, 797
Imaginary unit, 788, 793, 797
Impedance, characteristic, 783
Improper fractions, 1, 4
Incidence rate, 517
Inconsistent system
  explanation of, 305, 347, 641, 663, 1035
  solving, 646, 654
  substitution method to solve, 314–316
Independent equations, 305, 347, 641, 663
Independent variable, 680, 717
Index of a radical, 729, 753, 762, 783, 797
Index of diversity, 962
Inequality(ies)
  absolute value, 614–619, 662, 665
  addition property of, 187–188, 597
  compound, 605–607, 605–609, 662, 664
  equivalent, 597, 662
  explanation of, 106, 201, 596, 662
  graphs of, 186–187
  interval notation for, 596
  linear in one variable. *See* Linear inequalities in one variable
  linear in two variables. *See* Linear inequalities in two variables

  multiplication property of, 189–190, 598
  polynomial, 882
  quadratic, 878–881, 889, 892
  rational, 882–884, 889, 892
  second-degree, 1000–1001, 1006, 1009
  solutions to, 190–195
  symbols of, 33–34, 186, 282
  systems of, 1001–1003, 1009
  three-part, 193–195, 201, 600
Infinite intervals, 596
Infinity symbol, 186, 663
Inner product, 397, 420
Input-output (function) machine, 680
Integers
  consecutive, 151–152, 201, 483–485
  explanation of, 47, 106
  as exponents, 366–372, 421
Intensities, 384
Intercepts
  of ellipse, 978
  of hyperbola, 985
  of a line, 230–231
  method for finding, 230
  x-, 230–232, 289, 630–632, 662, 665
  y-, 230–232, 258–259, 289, 630–632, 662, 665
Interest, compound, 949–950
Interest formula, 168
Intersection of sets, 605, 609, 662
Interval notation, 186, 201, 596, 662
Intervals
  explanation of, 186, 201
  graphing, 186–187
  on number line, 596, 662
  types of, 596
Inverse functions
  equations of, 909–910
  explanation of, 907–908, 955, 956
  graphs of, 911
  horizontal line test and, 909
  notation for, 955
Inverse properties, 90–91, 93, 109
Inverse variation, 576, 580, 708–710, 717, 719
Irrational numbers, 49, 106, 728, 797
Irrational square roots, 728

J

Joint variation, 710–711, 717, 719

L

Least common denominator (LCD)
  in equations, 138–139
  explanation of, 7, 524, 576
  to simplify complex fractions, 543–545
  to solve equations with rational expressions, 551–556
  steps to find, 524–525, 578
Legs of a right triangle, 485–486, 494, 753
Leonardo da Pisa, 726
(is) Less than
  interpretation of, 67, 283
  symbol for, 33–34, 186
(is) Less than or equal to, 33–34, 186
Light-year, 427
Like terms
  combining, 99–101, 122, 385–386
  explanation of, 99, 107, 420
Linear equations in one variable
  applications of, 147–154, 203
  with decimals, 128, 594
  explanation of, 118, 201, 590, 662

with fractions, 128, 593
identifying, 590
simplifying terms in, 129–130
solution of, 664
solution set of, 590
solving, 133–140, 203, 590–595
types of, 594–595
Linear equations in three variables, 649–657
Linear equations in two variables
applications of, 234–235, 274
explanation of, 215, 273, 289, 630, 662
graphs of, 228–235, 259–260, 291
intercepts of, 230–231, 630
point-slope form of, 270–274
real data described by, 262–263
slope-intercept form of, 258–262
slope of, 242–249, 291
standard form of, 215, 273, 274, 630
systems of, 640–645
Linear functions, 692, 701, 717, 718
Linear inequalities in one variable
addition property to solve, 597
explanation of, 186, 201, 596, 662
graphs of, 186–187, 596
multiplication property to solve, 598
solution of, 664
solving, 190, 204
steps to solve, 599
with three parts, 600
Linear inequalities in two variables
boundary line of, 282, 285
explanation of, 282, 289
graphs of, 282–285
system of, 342–344
Linear systems. *See* Systems of linear equations
Linear systems of equations, 640, 649, 663. *See also* Systems of
linear equations; Systems of linear equations in three variables;
Systems of linear equations in two variables
Line graphs
explanation of, 232–233, 289
interpreting, 214–215
using slope and point on the line, 259–260
Lines. *See also* Number lines
boundary, 282, 289
equations of, 246–247
graphs of, 214–215, 232–233, 259–262, 289
horizontal. *See* Horizontal lines
parallel, 248–249, 272–273, 289, 291
perpendicular, 248–249, 272–273, 289, 291
slopes of, 242–249, 291, 633–635
vertical. *See* Vertical lines
Literal equations, 165
Lithotripter, 984
Logarithmic equations
explanation of, 924, 955
properties of, 946
solving, 925–926, 947–948, 958
Logarithmic form to exponential form, 924
Logarithmic functions
applications of, 927
with base *a*, 926–927
explanation of, 926, 957
graphs of, 926–927, 957
Logarithms
alternative forms of, 936–937
on calculators, 940, 943
change-of-base rule for, 951
common, 940–942, 955, 957
explanation of, 924, 955

natural, 942–943, 955, 957
power rules for, 934–936, 957
product rule for, 932–933, 936, 957
properties of, 926, 932–937, 957
quotient rule for, 933, 936, 957
Loudness of sound, 942
Lowest terms
explanation of, 510, 576
of fractions, 3, 90
of rational expressions, 510–513, 577, 773

M

Magic number, 173
Mathematical expressions. *See* Algebraic expressions
Mathematical models
explanation of, 45, 220
with linear equations, 220, 234–235, 274
quadratic, 487–488
Matrices
augmented, 1031–1032
on calculators, 1031
columns of, 1031
elements of, 1031
explanation of, 1031
row echelon form of, 1032
row operations on, 1032–1035
rows of, 1031
square, 1031
Matrix method for solving systems, 1031–1035
Maximum value problems, 870–871
Mean (average), 85
Means of a proportion, 175, 201
Minimum value problems, 870–871
Minuend, 64, 106
Mixed numbers
applications with, 10–11
converting between improper fractions
and, 4
explanation of, 4
Mixture problems, 332–333
Models. *See* Mathematical models
Money, doubling time of, 945, 949
Monomials
dividing polynomials by, 409–410, 422
explanation of, 387, 420
multiplying polynomials and, 395
Motion problems, 334–335, 565–568, 833–834
Multiplication
associative property of, 88–89, 93, 109
of binomials, 397–398, 422, 767–768
commutative property of, 88–89, 93, 109
of complex numbers, 791–792, 800
of decimals, 18–19, 20
of exponential expressions, 360
FOIL method of, 397–398, 422
of fractions, 4–5
identity element for, 90, 107
identity property of, 89–90, 93, 109
inverse property of, 90–91, 93, 109
of polynomial functions, 700, 719
of polynomials, 395–398, 422, 1019
by powers of ten, 20
properties of, 74
of radical expressions, 767–773, 799
of rational expressions, 518–519, 521, 577
of real numbers, 74–75, 109
with scientific notation, 379–380
of signed numbers, 74–75
word phrases for, 80

Multiplication property
    of equality, 126–130, 202, 591–592
    of inequality, 189–190, 598
    of zero, 74
Multiplicative identity element, 90, 107
Multiplicative inverses. *See also* Reciprocals
    explanation of, 75, 90–91, 107
    of rational expressions, 519
Multivariable polynomials, 390

N

Natural logarithms
    applications of, 943
    evaluating, 942–943
    explanation of, 942, 955, 957
Natural numbers, 1, 47, 106
Negative exponents
    changing to positive exponents, 369
    explanation of, 367–368, 421, 1017
    simplifying rational expressions with, 546
Negative infinity symbol, 186, 663
Negative numbers
    addition with, 57–58
    applications of, 48
    explanation of, 47, 106
    multiplication with, 74–75
    square roots of, 788–789
Negative slope, 245, 636
Negative square roots, 726–728
Negative-to-positive rules, 421
Noncollinear points, 661
Nonlinear equations, 590, 993, 1006
Nonlinear systems of equations
    explanation of, 993, 1006
    solving, 993–997, 1009
Nonreal complex number, 790, 797
Notation
    function, 689–691, 717, 718
    interval, 186, 201, 596, 662
    set-builder, 667
    subscript, 663
(is) Not equal, 33–34
nth root, 729–730, 732, 739, 797
Null set, 137
Number(s)
    absolute value of, 52, 107
    complex, 788–793, 797, 800
    composite, 2
    counting, 47, 106
    factored form of, 432–433
    factors of, 2
    fraction. *See* Fractions
    Froude, 855
    graphs of, 48–49
    greatest common factor of, 432–433
    imaginary, 797
    integer. *See* Integers
    irrational. *See* Irrational numbers
    mixed, 4, 10–11
    natural, 1, 47, 106
    negative. *See* Negative numbers
    nonreal complex, 790, 797
    opposite of, 47, 51
    ordering of, 50, 108
    positive. *See* Positive numbers
    prime, 2–3
    prime factored form of, 2–3
    rational, 48–49, 106, 508
    real. *See* Real numbers

signed. *See* Signed numbers
    whole, 1, 47, 106, 413–414
Number lines
    addition with, 57–58
    explanation of, 47, 106
    graphing intervals on, 186–187
    inequalities on, 596
    intervals on, 662
    irrational numbers on, 49
    linear inequalities on, 186–195
    ordering real numbers on, 50, 108
    subtraction with, 64
Numerators
    of complex fractions, 543–545
    explanation of, 1
Numerical coefficients, 98–99, 107, 385

O

Odd consecutive integers, 152, 201, 483
Ohm's law, 796
One-to-one functions
    explanation of, 907–908, 955, 956
    horizontal line test for, 909
    inverse of, 907–910
Open intervals, 596
Operations
    order of, 31–33, 78, 108
    on polynomial functions, 698–700, 719
    set, 605, 607, 609
    with signed numbers, 57–60, 64–66, 74–78
Opposite
    explanation of, 47, 90, 106
    of a number, 47, 51
    quotient of opposites rule, 513
    of real numbers, 51, 90
Order
    of operations, 31–33, 78, 108
    of radicals, 729, 797
    of real numbers, 50, 108
Ordered pair
    completing, 216
    components of, 628, 662
    explanation of, 215, 289, 291, 628–629, 662
    graphs of, 220
    plotting, 218–220, 228–230, 289, 628, 662
    satisfying a given equation, 629
    solutions as, 215–216, 302–303
    symbol for, 663
Ordered triple, 649, 663
Order of radical. *See* Index of a radical
Origin
    explanation of, 218, 289, 628, 662
    graphing inequalities with boundary lines through, 285
    graphing line through, 232, 632
Outer product, 397, 420

P

Pair, ordered. *See* Ordered pair
Parabola(s)
    applications of, 870–871
    axis of, 856, 859, 889
    explanation of, 701, 856, 889
    graphs of, 701, 857–860, 871–873, 892, 987
    horizontal, 871–873, 892
    horizontal shift of, 857–859
    symmetry of, 856
    vertex of, 856, 859, 866–867, 869, 889
    vertical, 866–867, 869, 873

vertical shift of, 857–859
  x-intercepts, number of, 869
Parallel lines
  equations of, 272–273
  explanation of, 289
  slopes of, 248–249, 291
Parentheses, 93, 533, 628
Percents and percentages
  applications of, 24, 178, 332–333
  base of, 177
  converting decimals to, 22
  converting to decimals, 22
  explanation of, 177
  solutions to, 204
  writing as decimals, 21–22
  writing as fractions, 23
  writing decimals as, 21–22
  writing fractions as, 23
Perfect cubes, 463, 729, 797
Perfect fourth powers, 729
Perfect squares, 461–462, 728, 797
Perfect square trinomials, factoring, 461–462, 469, 494, 496
Perigee, 710
Perimeter
  explanation of, 15, 162, 201
  formulas for, 161, 167
Perpendicular lines
  equations of, 272–273
  explanation of, 289
  slopes of, 248–249, 291
pH, 940–941
Pi (π), 49
Pie chart, 11–12
Place value in decimals, 17
Plane, 218, 289, 628
Plotting ordered pairs, 218–220, 228–230, 289, 628, 662
Point-slope form, 270–274, 292
Polynomial(s)
  addition of, 385–386, 388–390, 422, 1018
  binomial, 387
  classifying, 387
  coefficients of, 385
  degree of, 387, 420
  descending powers of, 386, 420
  divided by monomials, 409–410, 422
  divided by polynomials, 413–417, 422
  division of, 409–410, 413–417, 422, 1025–1027
  evaluating, 388
  explanation of, 420
  factoring, 434–438, 442–446, 449–450, 453–456, 459–462, 468–470, 1020–1021
  monomial, 387
  multiplication of, 395–398, 422, 1019
  multivariable, 390
  prime, 445, 494
  subtraction of, 385–386, 389–390, 422, 1018
  terms of, 416
  trinomial, 387
  vocabulary for, 386–387
  in x, 386
Polynomial functions
  addition of, 698–699, 719
  of degree n, 697, 717
  division of, 700, 719
  evaluating, 697
  graphs of, 701–702
  multiplication of, 700, 719
  subtraction of, 698–699, 719
Polynomial inequalities, 882

Positive exponents, 369
Positive numbers
  equivalent forms for, 78
  explanation of, 47, 106
  subtracting, 64
  writing in scientific notation, 377–378
Positive or negative (plus or minus) symbol, 797
Positive slope, 245, 636
Positive square root, 726–728
Power(s). See also Exponent(s)
  descending, 386, 420
  explanation of, 30, 106, 358
  of i, 793
Power rules
  for exponents, 360–363, 421
  for logarithms, 934–936, 957
  for radical equations, 779–782
Powers of ten
  division by, 20
  explanation of, 17
  multiplication by, 20
Price problems, 656–657
Prime factored form, 2–3, 432–433
Prime numbers, 2–3
Prime polynomials, 445, 494
Principal nth roots, 797
Principal square root, 726–728, 797
Problem-solving strategies for applied problems, 147–154, 482, 656
Product
  explanation of, 2, 74, 106
  factored form as, 440
  of sum and difference of two terms, 403–405
Product rule
  for exponents, 358–360, 362–363, 421, 1017
  for logarithms, 932–933, 936, 957
  for radicals, 749, 788, 798
Proper fractions, 1
Properties of one, 3
Proportions
  applications of, 177
  cross products of, 175–177, 201
  explanation of, 175–176, 201
  extremes of, 175, 201
  finding unknown in, 176
  means of, 175, 201
  solutions of, 177, 204
  terms of, 175, 201
Proposed solution, 552–556, 562–563, 576, 779, 797
Pure imaginary numbers, 790, 797
Pyramids, 168
Pythagoras, 485
Pythagorean theorem, 485–486, 496, 753–754, 799, 847

Q

Quadrants, 218, 289, 628, 662
Quadratic equations
  applications of, 482–488, 497, 833–836
  with common factor, 475
  completing the square to solve, 817–821, 844, 890
  discriminant of, 829–830, 869, 889, 890
  explanation of, 473, 494, 810, 889
  factoring to solve, 473–478, 496
  methods for solving, 844
  nonreal complex solutions of, 813
  quadratic formula to solve, 825–829
  solving equation that leads to, 833
  solving using zero-factor property, 473–478, 810
  square root property to solve, 810–813, 812–813, 890
  standard form of, 473, 494, 810

Quadratic formula
  derivation of, 825–826
  explanation of, 889, 890
  solving quadratic equations using, 825–829, 844
  use of discriminant and, 829–830
Quadratic functions
  applied problems modeled by, 849–850
  discriminant of, 869
  explanation of, 856, 889
  graphs of, 856–861, 868, 891
Quadratic inequalities
  explanation of, 878, 889
  solving by graphing, 878–879
  special cases of, 881
  steps to solve, 880
  using test values to solve, 879–880
Quotient
  explanation of, 5, 76, 106, 1025
  translating in words and phrases, 80–81
  writing in lowest terms, 773
Quotient rule
  for exponents, 369–370, 421, 1017
  of opposites, 513
  or logarithms, 933, 936, 957
  or radicals, 750, 798

R
Radical equations
  explanation of, 797
  power rules for, 779–782
Radical expressions
  addition of, 762–764, 799
  division of, 767–773, 799
  explanation of, 726, 730, 797, 798
  functions defined by, 730–731, 798
  multiplication of, 767–773, 799
  simplifying, 749–755, 762–764, 798–799
  squaring, 727
  subtraction of, 762–764, 799
Radicals
  converting between rational exponents and, 742
  explanation of, 726, 797
  index of, 729, 753, 762, 783, 797
  order of, 729
  product rule for, 749, 788, 798
  quotient rule for, 750, 798
  simplifying, 750–753, 798
  solving equations with, 779–782, 800, 836–837
Radical symbol, 726, 797
Radicand, 726, 729, 797
Radius, 706, 975–978, 1006
Range
  explanation of, 681, 717, 718
  of functions, 681–682, 718
  of relations, 681–682, 718
Rate of work problems, 568–570, 580
Rates of change, 250–251
Rational exponents
  converting between radicals and, 742
  evaluating, 739–741
  explanation of, 798
  negative, 740
  rules for, 743–744
Rational expressions
  addition of, 530–533, 578
  applications of, 564–570, 580
  distinguished from equations, 550–551
  division of, 519–521, 577
  equivalent forms of, 513–514

evaluating, 508
explanation of, 508, 576
factoring, 510–513
fundamental property of, 508–514, 577
lowest terms of, 510–513, 577, 773
multiplication of, 518–519, 521, 577
multiplicative inverses of, 519
numerical values of, 508
quotient of opposites rule, 513
reciprocals of, 519
simplifying with negative exponents, 546
solving equations with, 550–557, 562–563, 579
subtraction of, 533–535, 578
tips when working with, 563
undefined, 509
written with given denominators, 526–527
Rational inequalities
  explanation of, 882, 889
  solving, 882–884, 892
Rationalizing the denominator
  with binomials involving radicals, 771–772
  explanation of, 799
  with one radical term, 769–771, 799
Rational numbers, 48–49, 106, 508
Ratios
  explanation of, 174–175, 201
  writing, 174, 204
Real numbers. See also Number(s)
  addition of, 57–60, 108
  division of, 75–78, 109
  explanation of, 49, 106
  multiplication of, 74–75, 109
  opposite of, 51, 90
  ordering of, 50, 108
  properties of, 88–93, 109
  reciprocals of, 75–78, 90
  set of, 663
  subtraction of, 64–68, 109
Real part, 790, 797
Reciprocal function, 968, 1007
Reciprocals
  to apply definition of division, 75–78
  explanation of, 5, 75, 107
  of fractions, 5
  negative exponents and, 367–368
  of rational expressions, 519
  of real numbers, 75–78, 90
Rectangles
  area of, 161, 417
  length of, 162
  perimeter of, 167
  width of, 162
Rectangular coordinate system
  explanation of, 218, 289–291, 628, 662
  graphing lines in, 630–636
  ordered pairs in, 628
Relation(s)
  domain of, 681–682, 718
  explanation of, 678–682, 717, 718
  as functions, 679–680
  graphs of, 682–683
  range of, 681–682, 718
Relative error (tolerance), 620
Remainder theorem, 1027
Repeating decimals, 21
Resonant frequency, 733, 737
Richter scale, 384
Right angles, 153, 201

Right triangle
   hypotenuse of, 485–486, 494, 753
   legs of, 485–486, 494, 753
Rise
   comparing run to, 242–244
   explanation of, 242, 289, 663
   in slope formula, 633
Root(s)
   approximations for, 733
   on calculators, 733
   cube, 729–731, 797
   fourth, 729–730
   nth, 729–730, 732, 739, 797
   simplifying, 751
   square, 788–789
Rotational rate of space station formula, 787
Rounding, of decimals, 20, 21
Row echelon form of matrix, 1032
Row operations on matrix, 1032–1035
Rows, of matrix, 1031
Run
   comparing rise to, 242–244
   explanation of, 242, 289, 663
   in slope formula, 633

S

Scatter diagrams, 220, 289
Scientific notation
   applications for, 380
   calculations using, 379–380
   explanation of, 377, 420
   use of, 377–380, 421
   writing positive numbers in, 377–378
Scrap value, 962
Second-degree equations. *See* Quadratic equations
Second-degree inequalities
   explanation of, 1000, 1006
   graphs of, 1000–1001, 1009
Semicircles, 989
Semiperimeter, 738
Set(s)
   elements of, 47, 106
   empty, 137
   explanation of, 106
   intersection of, 605, 609, 662
   null, 137
   of numbers, 790
   of real numbers, 596, 663
   solution. *See* Solution sets
   union of, 605, 607, 609, 662, 663
Set-builder notation, 48, 106, 305, 667
Set operations, 605, 607, 609
Signed numbers
   addition of, 57–59
   division of, 75–78
   explanation of, 47, 106
   multiplication of, 74–75
   subtraction of, 64–65
Similar triangles, 181, 855
Simple interest formula, 168
Simplifying a fraction, 3
Slope(s)
   from an equation, 246–247
   as average rate of change, 250–251
   from equations of lines, 635
   explanation of, 242–244, 289, 633, 663, 666
   formula for, 242–245, 633
   of horizontal lines, 245–246, 291, 635
   of a line, 242–249, 291

   of lines, 633–635
   negative, 245, 636
   of parallel lines, 248–249, 291
   of perpendicular lines, 248–249, 291
   positive, 245, 636
   symbol for, 663
   undefined, 636
   of vertical lines, 246, 291, 635
   zero, 636
Slope-intercept form
   explanation of, 258, 273, 292
   graphing lines using, 259–260
   of a linear equation, 258–262
   use of, 304
Solution(s)
   of equations, 41, 106, 118, 590, 662, 1028
   explanation of, 41, 106, 118
   extraneous, 553, 576, 779, 797
   proposed, 552–556, 562–563, 576, 779, 797
Solution sets
   explanation of, 118, 201, 347, 590, 662
   of linear equations, 302, 596
   of system of equations, 640, 663
   of system of inequalities, 1001–1003
Sound, loudness of, 942
Spheres, volume of, 168
Square brackets, 31, 32–33, 59–60, 66
Square matrix, explanation of, 1031
Square root functions
   explanation of, 730, 988, 1008
   graphs of, 730, 968, 988–989, 1007
Square root property, 810–813, 844, 890
Square roots
   explanation of, 726, 797
   finding, 726–727
   irrational, 728
   negative, 726–728
   of negative numbers, 788–789
   positive, 726–728
   principal, 726–728, 797
   simplifying, 732, 788
   solving for variables involving, 847–848
Squares
   of binomials, 402–403, 422, 781
   completing, 890
   difference of, 468
   factoring difference of, 459–460, 496
   of numbers, 30
   perfect, 461–462, 728, 797
   solving for variables involving, 847–848, 891
Squaring function, 701, 702, 717, 719
Standard form
   of complex numbers, 790, 797
   of a linear equation, 215, 274, 292
   of linear equations, 273, 630
   of a quadratic equation, 473–475, 494, 810
   of quadratic equations, 810
Standard notation, 379, 420
Step functions, 971, 1006
Straight angles, 153, 164, 201
Study skills
   analyzing test results, 227
   completing your homework, 73
   managing time, 125
   preparing for math final exam, 281
   reading your math text, 46
   reviewing a chapter, 105
   taking lecture notes, 38
   taking math tests, 200

Study skills *(continued)*
   using study cards, 56, 145
   using your math text, 28
Subscript notation, 243, 289, 663
Substitution method
   explanation of, 312
   for linear systems, 641–643, 666
   to solve equation quadratic in form, 837–840, 891
   to solve nonlinear systems, 993–994
   solving linear systems with, 312–317
Subtraction
   application of, 68
   of complex numbers, 791, 800
   of decimals, 18
   definition of, 64
   of fractions, 9–10
   with grouping symbols, 66
   interpreting expressions involving, 67
   of like terms, 385–386
   with number line, 64
   phrases that indicate, 67
   of polynomial functions, 698–699, 719
   of polynomials, 385–386, 389–390, 422, 1018
   of radical expressions, 762–764, 799
   of rational expressions, 533–535, 578
   of real numbers, 64–68, 109
   of signed numbers, 64–66
   of variable terms, 120–121
   word phrases for, 67
Subtrahend, 64, 106
Sum (in addition), 6, 40, 106
Sum and difference of two terms, 403–405, 422
Sum of cubes, 464, 468
Supplementary angles
   explanation of, 153, 201
   solving problems involving, 153–154
Supply and demand, 311
Symbol(s)
   for (is) approximately equal to, 797
   for degree, 153
   for equality and inequality, 33–34, 41–42, 186, 282, 550
   for grouping, 31–33, 59–60, 66
   for infinity, 186, 663
   for negative infinity, 186, 663
   for positive or negative, 811
   for radicals, 726, 797
   for subtraction, 66
   word phrases converted to, 34
Symmetry, of parabola, 856
Synthetic division
   to determine solutions of equations, 1028
   to divide by polynomial, 1025–1027
   to evaluate polynomials, 1027
   explanation of, 1026
Systems of equations. *See also* Systems of linear equations
   consistent, 641, 663
   explanation of, 640, 663
   inconsistent, 641, 663
   nonlinear, 1006
   solution set of, 663
   special cases of, 645–646, 1035
Systems of inequalities
   explanation of, 1001
   graphs of, 1001–1003, 1009
   solution set of, 1001–1003
Systems of linear equations
   applications of, 330–335, 349, 655–657, 667
   consistent, 305, 347

   with decimals, 317
   elimination method to solve, 320–324, 349
   explanation of, 302, 347
   with fractions, 316–317
   graphing method to solve, 302–307
   inconsistent, 305, 314–315, 347
   with infinitely many solutions, 305
   matrix method to solve, 1031–1035
   methods to solve, 328, 348–349
   with no solution, 305
   solution set of, 302
   substitution method to solve, 312–317
Systems of linear equations in three variables
   elimination method to solve, 650–652, 667
   explanation of, 649
   geometry of, 649–650
   graphs of, 649–650
   inconsistent, 654
   matrix method to solve, 1031–1035
   with missing terms, 652–653
   special cases of, 653–654
Systems of linear equations in two variables
   consistent, 641
   elimination method to solve, 643–645, 666
   graphs of, 640–641
   inconsistent, 641
   matrix method to solve, 1031–1035
   special cases of, 645–646
   steps to solve, 642, 644, 666
   substitution method to solve, 641–643, 666
Systems of linear inequalities
   explanation of, 347
   graphing to solve, 342–344
   solutions of, 342–344, 347, 349
Systems of nonlinear equations, 993–997, 1006

T

Table of values, 217–218, 289
Temperature conversion, 198, 278
Terminating decimals, 21
Terms
   combining, 99–101
   degree of, 387, 420, 697
   distinguishing between factors and, 99
   explanation of, 98, 107, 201, 420
   identifying, 385
   like, 99–101, 107, 385–386, 420
   lowest. *See* Lowest terms
   numerical coefficient of, 98–99, 107, 385
   of polynomials, 416
   product of sum and difference of, 403–405, 422
   of proportions, 175
   unlike, 99
Three-dimensional objects, 168
Three-part inequalities, 193–195, 201, 600
Threshold sound, 942
Threshold weight, 737
Tolerance (relative error), 620
Translating sentences into equations, 42, 81
Translating word phrases into expressions, 40–41, 60, 67, 80–81, 101, 140
Translations of functions, 968–970
Translations of parabola, 857
Transverse axis, 985, 1006
Trapezoids, 161, 167
Triangle(s)
   area formula for, 163, 167
   area of, 738

perimeter of, 162–163, 167
right, 485–486, 494
similar, 181, 855
Trinomials
explanation of, 387, 420
factoring, 442–446, 449–450, 453–456, 469, 494–496
perfect square, 461–462, 469, 494
Triple, ordered, 649, 663

U

Undefined rational expressions, 509
Undefined slope, 636
Union of sets, 605, 607, 609, 662, 663
Unit pricing, 174–175
Unlike terms, 99

V

Value(s)
absolute, 52, 57–59, 106
extraneous, 553, 576, 779, 797
table of, 217–218, 289
Variable(s)
dependent, 680, 717
evaluating expressions with, 39–40, 79, 108
explanation of, 39, 106
focus, 650
formulas to evaluate, 161
greatest common factor for, 433–434
independent, 680, 717
simplifying radicals involving, 752
solving for specified, 165–166, 203, 556–557
solving for squared, 847–848, 891
Variable cost, 267
Variation
combined, 711, 717
constant of, 576, 706, 717
direct, 576, 580, 706–708, 717, 719
inverse, 576, 580, 708–710, 717, 719
joint, 710–711, 719
Variation equations, 706–711
Vertex
coordinates of, 856, 871
explanation of, 856, 859, 889
formula, 867
of parabolas, 856, 859, 866–867, 869, 889
Vertical angles, 164, 201
Vertical lines
equations of, 233, 273, 632–633
graphs of, 233, 261–262, 632–633
slope of, 246, 291, 635, 666
Vertical line test, 682–683
Vertical parabolas
explanation of, 873
vertex of, 866–867, 869
x-intercepts of, 869

Vertical shift
of ellipse, 980
explanation of, 857
method for applying, 969–970
of parabola, 857–859
Volume
explanation of, 168
formulas for, 168

W

Whole numbers
division of, 413–414
explanation of, 1, 47, 106
Windchill factor, 748
Word phrases
for addition, 60
converted to symbols, 34
for division, 80–81
for multiplication, 80
as ratios, 174
for subtraction, 67
translating to algebraic expressions, 40–41, 60, 67, 80–81, 101, 140
Working equation, 650
Work rate problems, 568–570, 580, 835–836

X

x, polynomial in, 386
x-axis, 218, 233, 289, 628, 662
x-intercepts
explanation of, 230, 289, 630, 662
finding, 630–632, 665
graphing equations with, 231–232
of parabola, number of, 869

Y

y-axis, 218, 233, 289, 628, 662
y-intercepts
explanation of, 230, 258–260, 289, 630, 662
finding, 630–632, 665
graphing equations with, 231–232

Z

Zero
division by, 77
multiplication property of, 74
Zero exponents, 366, 421, 1017
Zero-factor property
explanation of, 473, 496, 810
solving quadratic equations using, 473–478, 844
use of, 473–478, 810
Zero slope, 636

Triangles and Angles

Right Triangle
Triangle has one 90° (right) angle.

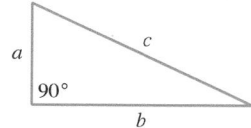

Pythagorean Theorem (for right triangles)

$a^2 + b^2 = c^2$

Right Angle
Measure is 90°.

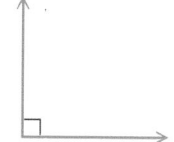

Isosceles Triangle
Two sides are equal.

$AB = BC$

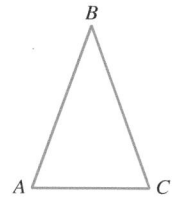

Straight Angle
Measure is 180°.

Equilateral Triangle
All sides are equal.

$AB = BC = CA$

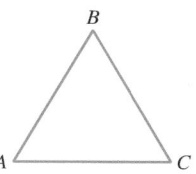

Complementary Angles
The sum of the measures of two complementary angles is 90°.

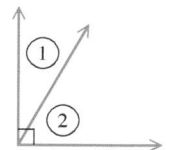

Angles ① and ② are complementary.

Sum of the Angles of Any Triangle

$A + B + C = 180°$

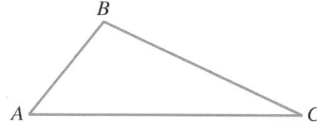

Supplementary Angles
The sum of the measures of two supplementary angles is 180°.

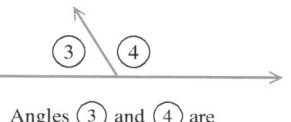

Angles ③ and ④ are supplementary.

Similar Triangles
Corresponding angles are equal. Corresponding sides are proportional.

$A = D, B = E, C = F$

$\dfrac{AB}{DE} = \dfrac{AC}{DF} = \dfrac{BC}{EF}$

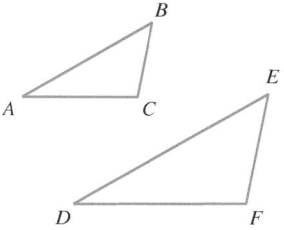

Vertical Angles
Vertical angles have equal measures.

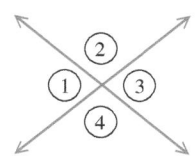

Angle ① = Angle ③

Angle ② = Angle ④

Geometry Formulas

Square
Perimeter: $P = 4s$
Area: $\mathcal{A} = s^2$

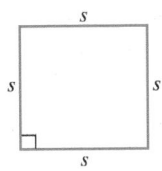

Rectangular Solid
Volume: $V = LWH$
Surface area: $\mathcal{A} = 2HW + 2LW + 2LH$

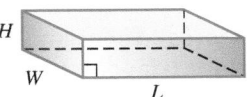

Rectangle
Perimeter: $P = 2L + 2W$
Area: $\mathcal{A} = LW$

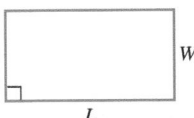

Cube
Volume: $V = e^3$
Surface area: $S = 6e^2$

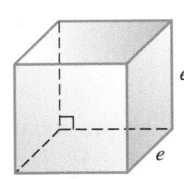

Triangle
Perimeter: $P = a + b + c$
Area: $\mathcal{A} = \dfrac{1}{2}bh$

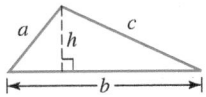

Right Circular Cylinder
Volume: $V = \pi r^2 h$
Surface area: $S = 2\pi rh + 2\pi r^2$
(Includes both circular bases)

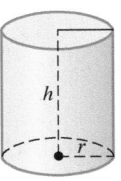

Parallelogram
Perimeter: $P = 2a + 2b$
Area: $\mathcal{A} = bh$

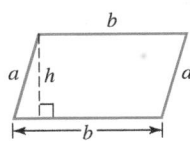

Cone
Volume: $V = \dfrac{1}{3}\pi r^2 h$
Surface area: $S = \pi r \sqrt{r^2 + h^2} + \pi r^2$
(Includes circular base)

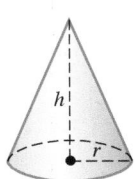

Trapezoid
Perimeter: $P = a + b + c + B$
Area: $\mathcal{A} = \dfrac{1}{2}h(b + B)$

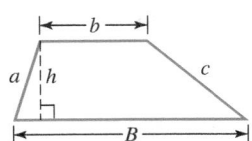

Right Pyramid
Volume: $V = \dfrac{1}{3}Bh$
B = area of the base

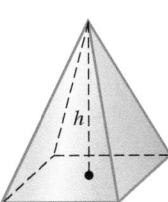

Circle
Diameter: $d = 2r$
Circumference: $C = 2\pi r$
$C = \pi d$
Area: $\mathcal{A} = \pi r^2$

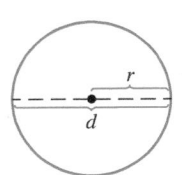

Sphere
Volume: $V = \dfrac{4}{3}\pi r^3$
Surface area: $S = 4\pi r^2$

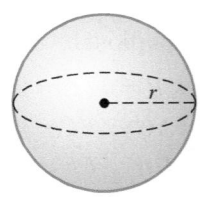